Oxfor
Learn
Thes

a dictionary of synonyms

Chief Editor Diana Lea

Editors Jennifer Bradbery
Richard Poole
Helen Warren

OXFORD
UNIVERSITY PRESS

Great Clarendon Street, Oxford, OX2 6DP, United Kingdom

Oxford University Press is a department of the University of Oxford. It furthers the University's objective of excellence in research, scholarship, and education by publishing worldwide. Oxford is a registered trade mark of Oxford University Press in the UK and in certain other countries

First published in 2008
This edition 2022

2026 2025 2024 2023 2022

12

No unauthorized photocopying

The British National Corpus is a collaborative project involving Oxford University Press, Longman, Chambers, the Universities of Oxford and Lancaster and the British Library

ISBN: 978 0 19 484081 1 (book and app pack)

ISBN: 978 0 19 475201 5 (book in pack)
ISBN: 978 0 19 484082 8 (app in pack)

ACKNOWLEDGEMENTS

Advisory Board: Dr Keith Brown; Prof. Guy Cook; Dr Alan Cruse; Ruth Gairns; Moira Runcie; Prof. Gabriele Stein; Dr Norman Whitney; Prof. Henry Widdowson

Designed by: Peter Burgess
Study pages designed by: Pauline Hall
Cover design by: Julian Littlewood

Back cover photograph: Oxford University Press building/ David Fisher.

We would like to thank the following for their permission to reproduce photographs and illustrations: comstock 892 (reading from scripts); *Corbis* 890 (visitor to hospital), 890 (ill in bed, girl with doctor); *Corel* 446 (light fitting); *David Eaton/OUP* 444 (bottle with cork, bottles), 534 (jars, yogurt and cream, ketchup), 538 (baking tins), 425 (honey); *Digital Vues* 890 (paramedics); *Digital vision* 898 (presentation), 900 (reporter); *Eyewire* 898 (businessmen meeting); *Getty Images* 247 (envelopes); *Hardlines* 78 (pin); *Hemera Technologies Inc.* 44 (sports trophy, trophy, medals, medal with ribbon), 85 (american single-decker bus, articulated lorry, coach with flame design, hatchback car, jeep, lorry, muddy van, old-fashioned double-decker bus, pickup truck), 92 (armchair, bench, child's car seat, deckchair, highchair, pew, sofa, stool, straight backed chair, throne, wheelchair), 423 (carving knife, dagger, flick knife, knife with black handle, machete, meat cleaver, penknife, scalpel), 446 (chinese lantern, clip light fixture, desk lamp, lantern, table lamp), 247 (A4 files, cardboard folder, card folder with tab, clipboard, plastic folder with elastic, ring binder), 755 (girl with backpack, holdall, leather handbag, metal trunk, rucksack, suitcase, suitcase with wheels), 896 (protest); *Ian McCaughrean/OUP* 301 (man with wrinkles), 301 (folded paper), 301 (creased shirt); *Image Source* 896 (people shouting); *Karen Hiscock/OUP* 417 (road junctions); *Mark Dunn/OUP* 196 (charts x3); *Martin Shovel/OUP* 48 (leg in plaster), 56 (crouching, kneeling, man bending, squatting), 149 (sneezing, sore throat), 170 (cartoon of cafe); *Michael Woods/ OUP* 78 (buckle, Velcro, button, zip, shoe lace), 666 (wire); *OUP* 47 (barbecue, chef, frying, grill, roasting in oven, toast), 56 (ducking), 78 (chain, drawstring, safety pin, trunk with metal corners), 164 (curved line, crescent, arches, circle segments, loop of rope, parabola), 196 (wavelength, line graph), 425 (suitcase with stickers, beanie), 441 (books), 444 (bin, highlighter, marker pen, pan lid and chocolate box lid), 531 (oven, microwave), 534 (can of cola, cartons, cookies, pack of cigarettes and gum, tins, tubs, toothpaste), 538 (pots and pans), 666 (dressing gown, rope, needle and thread, ball of string), 699 (handsaw, rocks, scissors, steak knife), 755 (plastic bag), 842 (wallet, purse), 898 (interview), 900 (watching tv); *Photodisc/Getty* 888 (maths test, school, students in a library, girl winning prize), 892 (children playing, painting a canvas), 894 (beach at sunset, flags, supreme court, baby), 898 (newspaper, scales), 896 (Arlington National Cemetery, karate), 892 (football, hammock), 900 (sale advert, news reader, rack of newspapers); *Shutterstock* cover (prism and foil patterns); *Stockbyte/Getty* 888 (bored boy); *Tech graphics/OUP* 441 (three seater sofa, set of drawers)

Text capture, processing and typesetting by Oxford University Press

Printed in China

CONTENTS

PREFACE

'More help with synonyms' has been one of the most frequent requests from students and teachers to us as lexicographers at Oxford University Press. To give genuine help with synonyms we need to do more than just list them; we need to explain exactly when one word can substitute for another and when it cannot. We therefore conceived of a dictionary – or a *learner's thesaurus* – that would do exactly that, and which would be aimed at refining and expanding the active vocabulary of learners at upper-intermediate level and above. For an account of the principles and methodology behind the selection and presentation of synonyms in this thesaurus, please see the introduction that follows.

The *Oxford Learner's Thesaurus – a dictionary of synonyms* is the result of many years of research, experiment and concentrated work by a large number of people. I would first like to thank the small but dedicated team of editors who worked with me on the project: Jennifer Bradbery, Richard Poole and Helen Warren. I am also grateful to Frank Keenan and his team for managing the technical side of things. And I should like to acknowledge Moira Runcie, whose brainchild the *Oxford Learner's Thesaurus* was, and who has been a support and an inspiration throughout.

Penny Stock created the framework for assigning words to areas of meaning and drawing up the synonym groups. The following lexicographers worked on compiling the entries: Andrew Delahunty, Penny Hands, Tim McLeish, Julie Moore, Stella O'Shea and Daryl Tayar. Daniel Barron, Lisa Isenman, Karen Stern and Ashley Wagner were American English consultants.

Finally, thanks are due to the many students and teachers in different countries who have assisted with piloting and research through all stages of the project. It is the input from learners and dictionary users that has enabled us, I believe, to produce the thesaurus that best meets learners' needs.

Diana Lea
December 2007

INTRODUCTION

What is a learner's thesaurus?

According to the *Oxford Dictionary of English* a thesaurus is 'a book that lists words in groups of synonyms and related concepts'. It is typically used by someone who is writing and cannot quite think of the right word to use. The person looks up a word with nearly the right meaning and is offered a list of other words to choose from.

Language learners need synonyms too. They need to be able to express themselves in more precise and interesting ways. They need to choose language of an appropriate register for the context. But the needs of learners when consulting a thesaurus are actually much more complex than those of native or expert speakers of the language. Native speakers have a large bank of language stored in their brains; the thesaurus, for them, is simply a means of accessing this information. It reminds them of words that they already know but cannot bring to mind. Their chief requirement from a thesaurus is that it should offer as wide a choice as possible. The *New Oxford Thesaurus of English* gives 37 different words for *fast* as an adjective, but that is all it gives: no definitions, minimal usage information and no way of distinguishing between the words on offer.

Language learners, on the other hand, need not only range but depth. They need to learn new words; and they also need to be able to choose more effectively between words that they have met before, where their knowledge of the exact meaning and usage of the words was previously incomplete. They need a thesaurus that will not only enable them to access information, but will also teach them things.

It is often said that there are no absolute synonyms in English: that there is always some difference of nuance, register or collocation, that makes one word choice better, or at least different, from another. These differences may be very slight; they may not matter in every context. But it is a frustrating experience for learners at any level to be prevented from saying exactly what they mean by lack of the appropriate vocabulary. And as learners progress with their English it becomes increasingly important for them to be aware of the nuances of words, to be sure that the meaning conveyed to the reader or listener is the one that was intended.

Therefore we designed a new kind of thesaurus: a *learner's* thesaurus. It does not just offer lists of synonyms, but is a true dictionary of synonyms. Words of similar meaning are grouped together, as in a thesaurus, but they are also given definitions and example sentences, and grammar and usage information, as in a learner's dictionary. Words within each group are compared and contrasted, in terms of their meanings, use and collocations, in special notes that pinpoint the exact differences between them. There are over 17,000 synonyms and opposites explained in these pages, which is a large number of words and expressions for anyone's active vocabulary. (It has been estimated that English native-speaking university graduates know around 20,000 word families, but that includes both active and passive vocabulary.) However, the entry structure of this thesaurus has been carefully designed to enable learners to find the precise information they want as quickly and easily as possible.

How are synonyms presented in the Oxford Learner's Thesaurus?

In the course of researching and compiling the *Oxford Learner's Thesaurus* we established a number of principles governing the information that should be included and how it should be presented. This thesaurus is intended to help learners at upper-intermediate level and above with their writing and speaking in English. This means that all the words and expressions included are such as might reasonably form part of a learner's active vocabulary. How did we decide whether or not a word qualified for inclusion? Synonym groups were based around key words, mostly drawn from a 3,000-word core vocabulary for learners. As many synonyms as possible were gathered for each key word. The words in each group were then ordered according to frequency across a range of corpora. (A *corpus*, in this context, is a database of millions of words of running English text, from which it is possible call up, view and count all occurrences of any given word, in context. This makes it possible to establish the overall frequency of any word within the corpus.

In the case of words with more than one meaning, we of course counted the frequency only of the relevant meaning in each case. We used corpora of written and spoken British and American English, plus a corpus of business English.) Less frequent words were rejected. The aim was to present learners with manageable groups of between three and ten synonyms. In a few cases the upper limit was extended to twelve; a few entries present just a pair of synonyms, when there simply was not a third synonym to add to the number.

The frequency ranking was also used to order the synonyms within the entries. The idea was that learners still at upper-intermediate level could focus on the more frequent and general words near the top of the entry; more advanced learners could skip straight to the less well-known expressions near the bottom. Consultation with teachers and practical research with students showed how important it was for learners to be able to find what they want quickly, without always having to read through the whole entry. The list of synonyms at the top of each entry serves as a menu. Within the body of the entry, each synonym is treated separately. The main definition for each word is kept as short as possible. Examples are carefully chosen to show the most typical and distinctive usage patterns. Essential grammar and usage information precedes each definition, in the form of short codes and labels. These will already be familiar to users of the *Oxford Advanced Learner's Dictionary*, but they are explained on the pages 1006–7 just inside the back cover of this book. Irregular plurals are given, but irregular forms of verbs are listed in the table on pages 1004–5. The aim was to keep the entries as far as possible uncluttered by information on form, in order to enable learners to focus more easily on meaning, register and collocation.

The definitions in the entries have to work hard, conveying as much meaning as possible, clearly, in as few words as possible. When two close synonyms have definitions that are nearly the same, but not quite, this is not an accident.

The difference in wording means something: it signals a slight but distinct difference in meaning or use, which will usually be reflected in the choice of example sentences. The definitions and examples for *gift* and *present* in the entry for *gift* are a good example of this. It was not our intention, however, to make learners puzzle over the differences between two very similar definitions. With very close synonyms the individual definitions and examples are backed up by a note in a tinted box, which explicitly compares and contrasts two or more synonyms in terms of meaning, register, collocation and whatever else may distinguish them. Again, there is a typical example on 'Gift or present?' in the entry for *gift*. Notes preceded by an ❶ symbol, on the other hand, give extra information about one particular word or expression.

For a more detailed survey of all the elements in an entry, see the Guide to the Entries inside the front cover, and the Thesaurus Trainer, which also includes lots of practical examples and exercises.

How to use the Oxford Learner's Thesaurus

The *Oxford Learner's Thesaurus* can be used in a number of different ways. It is expected that the most frequent uses will be to find a synonym for a particular word, and to check on the exact differences between two particular words. Entries are ordered alphabetically by headword, the headword being the most frequent word in each synonym group. To find any word or expression in any entry (whether it is the headword or not), use the alphabetical index at the back of the book. The first two pages of the

Thesaurus Trainer give detailed instructions on how to use the index.

It is also possible to search the thesaurus by topic, if, for example, you are interested in building vocabulary in a particular topic area. The Topic Index lists entries under 30 different topics. Further help with building and using topic vocabulary is provided by the Topic Maps, with accompanying exercises. The Study Pages offer practice in a variety of topic areas through a number of different tasks, aimed especially at students preparing for exams.

THESAURUS TRAINER

These pages explain how the *Oxford Learner's Thesaurus* works. They will show you how to find the right entry, and then how to find your way around that entry so that you can find exactly the information you need.

There are exercises on each page to practise looking up words and extracting information from entries. The key to these exercises starts on page 913. See also the quick **Guide to Thesaurus Entries** inside the front cover.

Finding the Right Entry

The *Oxford Learner's Thesaurus* contains over 17,000 words and expressions in over 2,000 entries. In order to find a particular word you first need to know which entry it is in. All the words and expressions are listed in the **alphabetical index** on pages 921-1003.

Here, for example, you can see that **accuse** *verb* is in the entry at **accuse**. This means that it is the most important and frequent word in its synonym group and is the headword of the entry:

accurate *adj.*   ▸ EXACT
accusation *noun*   ▸ CHARGE
accuse *verb*   ▸ ACCUSE
accustomed to *adj.*   ▸ USED TO STH
ache *noun*   ▸ PAIN

accuse *verb*

accuse · charge · prosecute · indict · impeach · cite
These words all mean to say that sb has done sth wrong or committed a crime and must appear in court.

Accusation, on the other hand, is one of the synonyms in the entry at **charge** *noun*:

charge *noun*

charge · accusation · indictment · impeachment · recrimination
These are all words for a claim that sb has done sth wrong or is guilty of sth.

A Look up the following words in the index. In which entries will you find them?

1 become *verb* _____

2 calendar *noun* _____

3 daring *noun* _____

4 daring *adj.* _____

More than One Meaning

Accurate, **accusation** and **accuse** each have just one meaning and appear in just one entry. Some words, however, such as **act** *noun*, have more than one meaning, and each meaning has a different set of synonyms. **Act** appears in four different entries, with a different meaning in each entry.

The index entry for **act** shows the four entries that it appears in (**action**, **performance**, **pretence** and **rule**). It also gives a short example to show which meaning of **act** is treated in each entry.

act *noun*   ▸ ACTION (an act of kindness)   ▸ PERFORMANCE (a circus act)   ▸ PRETENCE (put on an act)   ▸ RULE (the Higher Education Act)

B Look up the index entry for **fix** *verb*. In which entry will you find synonyms of **fix** in the meaning used in each of the following sentences?

1 Can I **fix** you a sandwich?

_____

2 We need to **fix** a time when we can meet.

_____

3 The chairs were all **fixed** to the floor.

_____

4 This should **fix** it. Let me know if you have any more problems.

_____

Very Frequent Words

Some very frequent words, such as **get**, **give**, **go** and **good**, not only have more than one meaning, each with a different set of synonyms, but are the most important word

in each of two or more groups. Thus, the entry for **get** begins with a brief menu that shows the five different meanings of **get** that are treated in this entry with their synonyms:

---

get *verb*
1 get tickets/a job/some sleep
2 get a letter/shock
3 Go and get help.
4 We got there at 9.
5 get the bus

---

1 See also the entry for GAIN 1
get · obtain · acquire · take · pick sth up · take sth out · get hold of sth
These words all mean to do sth in order to make sure you have sth.

In the index, numbers are used to show which synonym group is meant in entries that have more than one.

receive *verb*
▸ GET2 (receive a letter)
▸ GREET (be received as an honoured guest)
▸ HAVE3 (receive attention)
▸ LET SB IN (be received into the Church)
▸ RESPOND (well received by critics)

Different meanings of **receive** are treated in the second synonym group in the entry for **get**, and the third synonym group in the entry for **have**, as well as in the entries for **greet**, **let sb in** and **respond**.

Phrasal Verbs and Idioms

Phrasal verbs are often very important as synonyms and are given equal status with all other verbs. They are listed in the index, in alphabetical order with all the other synonyms.

goal *noun*
▸ TARGET
go along with *phrasal verb*
▸ AGREE2
go around *phrasal verb*
▸ SPIN
go away *phrasal verb*
▸ GO AWAY
go back *phrasal verb*
▸ RETURN1
go back on *phrasal verb*
▸ BREAK4
go-between *noun*
▸ NEGOTIATOR

D Look up these phrasal verbs in the index. In which entries will you find them?

  1 Give it some more thought. I'm sure you'll **come up with** something.

  _____

  2 Can we **go over** the procedure one more time?

  _____

  3 If you're not sure what it means, **look** it **up** in the dictionary.

  _____

  4 It's not fair. I'm always getting **told off**.

  _____

C Find the entry and synonym group that includes the **bold** words in each of the following sentences. You will need to look for the base form of the word (for example **bring** not 'brought', **man** not 'men'). There is a table of irregular verbs on pages 1004-1005.

  1 This fruit has a **sharp** flavour.

  entry _____ number _____

  2 Are you sure the branch will **hold** your weight?

  entry _____ number _____

  3 Jo **led** the way and we all followed.

  entry _____ number _____

  4 Do you **play** any musical instruments?

  entry _____ number _____

Idioms and phrases are listed under the main words in the idiom or phrase, so that **pay attention** is listed at **pay** *verb* and **attention** *noun*, and **think twice** is listed at **think** and **twice**:

think *verb*
▸ THINK (I think it looks good.)
▸ CONSIDER (I'll think about it.)
▸ EXPECT (It took longer than we thought.)
▸ IMAGINE (Just think how nice it would be.)
▸ **think twice** HESITATE

twice *adv.*
▸ **think twice** HESITATE

E Look up these phrases and idioms in the index. In which entries will you find them?

  1 It's a pleasant way to **earn a living**.

  _____

  2 We can all **play a part** in protecting the environment.

  _____

  3 That noise is **driving me mad**.

  _____

  4 He suddenly **lost his temper** with them all.

The Synonym Groups

All the words and expressions within entries are listed in order according to **how frequent they are** in English.

At the top of each entry you will see a list of synonyms. The first word in each entry is the one that is used most frequently overall across a range of contexts (in written and spoken English; in British and American English; in general and business English). All the other synonyms in the group are then also given in order of frequency.

This means that you will find the most frequent and important words and expressions near the top of the entry. Lower down the entry you will find less frequent and less familiar words and expressions. However, one of these may be the best word to use *in particular contexts*.

A Look up the entry for **fabric** and find three synonyms. Which is the most frequent? Which is the least frequent?

B Look at this group of synonyms. Can you guess the frequency order? Put them in a list according to how frequent you think they are.

1 _____	bright
2 _____	brilliant
3 _____	intelligent
4 _____	clever
5 _____	smart

Now look up the entry for **intelligent** and see if you were right.

The General Definition

Synonyms are grouped together into one entry because they all share the same general meaning. For example the **intelligent** synonyms all describe people who are good at learning. This meaning is given straight after the list of synonyms. You can use this definition to check that you have looked up the right entry: is this the general meaning that you want to express?

C Match each general definition with the right group of synonyms – **i**, **ii** or **iii**.

1 These are all words for a piece of work that sb has to do.

2 These are all words for a position doing work for which you receive regular payment.

3 These are all words for the extra effort or work involved in doing sth, especially sth that is hard to do.

i **job, position, post, vacancy, opening, appointment**

ii **difficulty, trouble, job, hassle, bother**

iii **task, work, duty, mission, job, business, housework, chore**

Synonym Scales

Some synonyms in a group express an idea or feeling more strongly than others. This is shown in entries by a **synonym scale**. The 'weakest' synonyms in the group are shown on the left, and the arrow points through the 'medium-strength' synonyms towards the 'strongest' synonyms on the right:

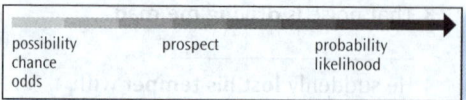

| possibility chance odds | prospect | probability likelihood |

D Put the following synonyms into the table below, depending on how strongly you think they express the idea of liking sth.

| like | love | be fond of sth |
| be keen on sth | | adore | go for sth |

| you like sth |
| you like sth very much |
| you like sth very much indeed |

Now look at the synonym scale at the entry for **like** and see if you were right.

Patterns and Collocations

Words that have the same general meaning sometimes also combine with other words in a similar way. They may be followed by the same preposition or the same grammatical structure: these are the **patterns** they take. Or they may combine with the same adjectives, nouns, verbs and adverbs: these are their **collocations**.

Consider, for example, the following synonyms:

plan   programme   policy

You can say:

* a plan/programme/policy *for* sth
  (= followed by the same preposition)

* a plan/programme/policy *to do sth*
  (= followed by the same grammatical structure)

* an *economic* plan/programme/policy
  (= adjective + noun collocation)

* to *develop* a plan/programme/policy
  (= verb + noun collocation)

Sometimes, however, words have the same general meaning, but they have different patterns and collocations. For example:

* a policy *on* sth (NOT plan/programme)

* a *political* programme (NOT plan/policy)

You can find all this information in the PATTERNS AND COLLOCATIONS in each entry.

A Look at the prepositions and structures in the PATTERNS AND COLLOCATIONS section from the entry for **choose**. Correct any errors in the sentences below. Some sentences do not have any errors, and sometimes more than one answer is possible.

> **PATTERNS AND COLLOCATIONS**
> ▶ to choose / select / pick / single out A **from** B
> ▶ to choose / select / pick / decide **between** A and / or B
> ▶ to choose/select/pick/opt for/go for/single out/adopt sb/sth **as** sb / sth
> ▶ to choose/select/pick/single out sb/sth **for** sb / sth
> ▶ to choose/select/pick/opt for/go for/single out/adopt **sb/sth to do sth**
> ▶ to choose / decide / opt **to do sth**
> ▶ to pick / single sb / sth **out**

1 Students can **choose** from a wide range of courses.

2 They had to **opt** between two different candidates for the job.

3 He was **picked** out as the best player.

4 Some workers **selected** to take a pay cut rather than lose their jobs.

B Look at the adjective and verb collocations in the PATTERNS AND COLLOCATIONS section from the entry for **luck**.

> **PATTERNS AND COLLOCATIONS**
> ▶ **by** ...luck / chance / coincidence / accident
> ▶ It's no coincidence / accident **that...**
> ▶ **pure / sheer** luck / chance / coincidence / accident
> ▶ **good / bad / ill** luck / fortune
> ▶ a / an **happy / unfortunate / strange** chance / coincidence / accident
> ▶ to **bring sb** good / bad luck / fortune
> ▶ to **have the ...** luck / fortune **to do sth**
> ▶ to **leave sth to** chance / fate / providence
> ▶ to **believe in** luck / coincidences / fate / destiny / providence
> ▶ to **tempt** fate / providence

Correct any errors in the sentences below. Some sentences do not have any errors, and sometimes more than one answer is possible.

1 It was pure **fortune** that we met like that.

2 What a strange **coincidence**!

3 Do you believe in **fate**?

4 It would be tempting **luck** not to take an umbrella.

C For each of the sentences below, delete any synonyms that do not fit the pattern or collocation that is being used. Use the PATTERNS AND COLLOCATIONS sections from the entries in SMALL CAPS to help you.

1 We have a hectic *schedule/agenda/ programme* this afternoon.
   SCHEDULE *noun*

2 You may find it hard to change your *habits/ways/rules*. HABIT

3 She *got/obtained/acquired* a reputation for being lazy. GET 1

4 Taking photographs is strictly *banned/ prohibited/forbidden*. BAN *verb*

5 He sat back, a *satisfied/content/ contented* smile on his face. HAPPY

6 It really *hurts/aches/stings* when you do that. HURT 2

The Individual Synonyms

The entry now takes each individual synonym, *in order of frequency*, and gives each a mini-entry of its own, including all the information that you need about meaning, grammar, register and use. Mini-entries include example sentences, and sometimes special collocations are highlighted in **bold**.

Meaning

Look at the entry for **discussion** on page 209 and read the mini-entries for **discussion** and **conversation**.

A Which of these two words, **discussion** or **conversation**, is more frequent?

B What is the difference in *meaning* between the two words?

C Choose the best word, **discussion** or **conversation**, for each of these sentences:

1 A chance *discussion/conversation* led to a brilliant new career for the young scientist.

2 She could hear him over the buzz of *discussion/conversation* and laughter.

3 The company has been in *discussion/conversation* with companies in Italy and Greece.

4 The two governments are to hold *discussions/conversations* on the border issue.

Grammar

Grammar information is given in square brackets before the definition. For example, verbs can be labelled [I] (intransitive – takes no object), [T] (transitive – takes an object) or both: [T, I] or [I, T].

> **refuse** [I, T] to say that you will not do sth that sb has asked you to do, or that you do not want sth that has been offered to you; to decide not to accept or consider sth; to say that you will not give sb sth that they want or need: *Go on, ask her. She can hardly refuse.* ◇ *She refused to accept that there was a problem.* ◇ *He flatly refused to discuss the matter.* ◇ *We invited her to the wedding but she refused.* ◇ *The job offer was simply too good to refuse.* ◇ *The government has refused all demands for a public enquiry.* ◇ *They refused him a visa.* ◇ *She would never refuse her kids anything.* **OPP** agree → AGREE 2, **accept** → TAKE 5, See also **refusal** → REFUSAL

> **reject** [T] to decide or say that you will not accept or consider sth; to decide not to accept sb for a job or position: *He urged the committee to reject the plans.* ◇ *The proposal was rejected as too costly.* ◇ *I've been rejected by all the colleges I applied to.* **OPP** approve → AGREE 2, **accept** → LET SB IN

D Which of these two verbs, **refuse** or **reject**, *cannot* be used without an object?

The object of a verb can be a noun, a noun phrase or a clause; some verbs can take both a direct and an indirect object; some can combine with a particular preposition. For example:

- *to reject a **plan***
- *to refuse sth **as** too costly*
- *to refuse **to accept** sth*
- *to reject sth **in favour of** sth else*
- *to refuse **sb** permission*

The grammatical structures and prepositions are shown in **bold**, either in the PATTERNS AND COLLOCATIONS section, or within the example sentences for that verb.

E Choose the correct word, **refuse** or **reject**, for each of these sentences:

1 All our suggestions were *refused/rejected* as 'useless'.

2 Gerard flatly *refused/rejected* to cooperate.

3 She offered to help and it seemed churlish to *refuse/reject*.

4 You surely wouldn't *refuse/reject* me this simple favour?

For a full list of grammar labels for nouns, verbs and adjectives, and what they mean, see page 1007.

Register

Sometimes words can be close in meaning, but different in register: that is, one of the words is more formal or informal than the other. Often it is important to choose a word of the right level of formality for the context, for example academic writing or everyday conversation. A synonym may have a register label before its definition. If there is no label, the word is neither formal nor informal and can usually be used in a wide range of situations.

F Look up the entry for **popular** and complete this table with the synonyms in the entry:

slang (= very informal)	informal	rather informal	neither formal nor informal	rather formal	formal
			popular		

G For each of the sentences below, choose the synonym that best matches the register of the sentence. Look at the entries in SMALL CAPS to help you.

1 Yuk! What *an odour/a stink*! ODOUR
2 You might be entitled to *get/receive* compensation. GET 2
3 This is a *desirable/hot* property in an exclusive residential district. POPULAR
4 All that sugary stuff is really *damaging/ bad* for you. HARMFUL
5 Don't buy stuff from the street traders – you'll get *defrauded/ripped off*. DEFRAUD

Register labels can also show whether a word is used only or especially in spoken or written English. In general, informal words are used more in speech, and formal words more in writing, but this is not always the case. For example, some words are used mainly in writing (especially in stories) without actually being formal:

*Her face was white with **fury**.*

And some expressions are used mainly in formal speech:

*I **beg your pardon**. I must have the wrong room.*

For a full list of register labels and what they mean, see page 1006.

Use

Some words are used only or especially in British or American English. Some are used mainly in a particular field of study or activity, for example business or journalism. Some words show a particular attitude, either of approval or disapproval. All these restrictions on use are shown by labels before the definition.

H The following words are British or especially British. What words could you use in American English? Look up the entries in SMALL CAPS to help you.

1 **pip** *noun* GRAIN
2 **burgle** *verb* ROB
3 **scruffy** *adj.* SCRUFFY
4 **packet** *noun* PACKET

I In which particular subject areas or fields of activity might you hear or use the following words?

1 **impact** *verb* AFFECT
2 **estate** *noun* LEGACY
3 **rupture** *verb* EXPLODE
4 **mass** *noun* WEIGHT

J Are the following words approving or disapproving? For each one find another word that has the same basic meaning but shows a more negative/positive attitude.

1 **cramped** *adj.* CRAMPED
2 **innocence** *noun* IGNORANCE
3 **cultured** *adj.* INTELLECTUAL 2
4 **solitude** *noun* PRIVACY

For a full list of style and usage labels and what they mean, see page 1006.

Examples

Every synonym has one or more example sentences, which show how the word is most commonly used. In particular a synonym's examples show the patterns and contexts where this is the only or best word to use, and none of the other synonyms in the group will do as well. Collocations that are unique to this word are highlighted in **bold**.

A Look at the entry for **action** on pages 5-6 and read the example sentences for **measure**, **step**, **act** and **move**. Then choose the best word to complete each of the sentences. Use each word once.

1 In a/an _____ of sheer desperation, she turned to face her pursuers.

2 Neither of them wanted to be the one to make the first _____.

3 This arrangement is simply a temporary _____ until we appoint a new director.

4 These talks are a first _____ towards a global agreement on carbon trading.

B Some of these sentences are correct, but some contain a wrong choice of word. Use information from the example sentences in the entries in SMALL CAPS to help you correct the sentences that are wrong.

1 There wasn't a **speck** of dust to be seen anywhere. MARK *noun*

2 Let's take the scenic **way**. WAY 3

3 I was never very good at playing the trumpet for the **simple** reason that I never practised. PLAIN *adj.* 2

4 The United Nations imposed an arms **boycott** on both countries. BAN *noun*

5 The **bargain** fell through when they could not agree a price. AGREEMENT 1

6 I **get** the message – you'd rather not be involved. UNDERSTAND 1

7 I don't know, but I'm willing to **venture** a guess. DARE

8 I was so tired I felt ready to **collapse**. COLLAPSE 2

Notes

Entries contain two different kinds of note. Notes marked ❶ give you extra information about a particular word or expression. This extra information can be about anything to do with a word's meaning or use.

> **countryside** [U] land outside towns and cities, with fields, woods and farms: *a little village in the French countryside* ◇ *You can walk through miles and miles of unspoilt countryside.* ❶ **Countryside** is usually used when you are talking about the beauty or peacefulness of a country area. See also **nature** → NATURE 2

> **terrain** /təˈreɪn/ [U, C] (*written*) land: *Make sure you have equipment that is suitable for the terrain.* ◇ *There were several miles of **difficult terrain** to be covered.* ❶ **Terrain** is used when you are describing the natural features of an area, for example if it is rough, flat, etc.

A Which is the best word to use in these sentences, **countryside** or **terrain**?

1 The surrounding *countryside/terrain* is magnificent.

2 The truck bumped its way over the rough *countryside/terrain*.

3 The cottage backs directly onto glorious open *countryside/terrain*.

4 They walked for miles across steep and inhospitable *countryside/terrain*.

Notes marked **NOTE** compare and contrast two or more very close synonyms to help you understand the differences between them.

> **NOTE** GIFT OR PRESENT? **Gift** is more formal than **present** and is used especially in business contexts: a store will advertise its *Christmas gift ideas*; the people who buy them will talk about the *Christmas presents* they have bought for family and friends. A **present** is usually given by and to an individual; a **gift** may be given by a company (*a corporate gift*) and/or to an organization. A **present** is usually an object, but a **gift** may be a sum of money, or sth such as *the gift of love/life: funded by a present of £50 000* ◇ *She gave me the present of love.* Especially in American English, however, **gift** is not always so formal and is sometimes used in personal contexts instead of **present**: *The watch was a gift/present from my mother.*

B Which is the best word to use in these sentences, **gift** or **present**?

1 Our catalogue contains hundreds of fabulous *gift/present* ideas.

2 The charity has received a *gift/present* of £100,000 from an anonymous donor.

3 Life is the greatest *gift/present* you can give anyone.

4 What can I get Stephen for a birthday *gift/present*?

C Some of these sentences are correct, but some contain a wrong choice of word. Use information from the notes in the entries in SMALL CAPS to help you correct the sentences that are wrong.

1 I had a terrible **fright** of failure. FEAR

2 Badly fed children suffer a lot of minor **illnesses**. DISEASE

3 A mile further on we saw our first **flock** of antelope. HERD

4 I've **checked** the calculations and they are all quite correct. CHECK 1

5 As a **seasoned** traveller I knew what to expect. EXPERIENCED

6 They were trying to navigate with a hopelessly **incorrect** map. WRONG 1

7 The chairman refused to **remark** on the allegations made against him. COMMENT

8 They had a **pool** in their garden with goldfish and water lilies. LAKE

Opposites

If a word or expression has a direct **opposite** (or **antonym**), this is shown after an **OPP** symbol. If the opposite has synonyms of its own there will be a cross-reference to the entry where you can find more information about the opposite and its synonyms.

> **horizontal** /ˌhɒrɪˈzɒntl; AmE ˌhɔːrəˈzɑːntl; ˌhɑːr-/ going across and parallel to the ground rather than going up and down: *Draw a grid of horizontal and vertical lines.* **OPP vertical → UPRIGHT**

This tells you that the opposite of **horizontal** is **vertical**, and you can find more information about **vertical** in the entry for **upright**.

If the opposite has no synonyms of its own, or is not used very frequently, there will be an ❶ note to explain what it means and/or how it is used:

> **forbidding** seeming unfriendly and frightening and likely to cause harm or danger: *a forbidding appearance/ atmosphere/manner* ◇ *The house looked dark and forbidding.* **OPP welcoming ❶** A welcoming place is attractive and looks comfortable to be in: *the welcoming atmosphere of the club*

A Match up the words on the left with their opposites on the right.

accelerate	approve
condemn	clear
criticize	condone
hasten	delay
reject	exact
rough	praise
turn sb/sth down	retard
vague	take sth up

You can check your answers in the entries for ACCELERATE, BLAME, REFUSE and VAGUE.

B Choose the correct opposite of the word in **bold** in these sentences. Look up the entry given in SMALL CAPS as a starting point; you may also need to follow the cross-references to the entries for the opposites and their synonyms.

1 He was dressed in a white shirt and a **formal** jacket. (*casual/informal*) FORMAL

2 **Adult** crime statistics have fallen in recent years. (*childish/juvenile*) ADULT

3 My sister and I are very **different** in some respects. (*the same/similar*) DIFFERENT

4 She politely **refused** the dinner invitation. (*accepted/agreed*) REFUSE

Derivatives

Many words belong to **word families**. A word family contains words with related meanings that have different parts of speech. For example:

> **happy** *adjective*
> happiness *noun*, happily *adverb*
>   (= derivatives)
> **question** *noun*
> question *verb* (= derivative)

Derivatives that are closely related in meaning are often shown at the end of a mini-entry, as **happily** is here:

> **happy** feeling, showing or giving pleasure; pleased enough with sth or not worried about it: *I looked around at all the happy faces.* ◇ *a happy marriage/memory/childhood* ◇ *Those were the happiest days of my life.* ◇ *The story has a* **happy ending**. ◇ *Happy birthday!* ◇ *If there's anything you're not* **happy about**, *come and ask.* ◇ *I said I'd go, just to* **keep him happy**. **OPP** sad, unhappy → UNHAPPY 1, **unhappy** → UNHAPPY 2, See also **happiness** → SATISFACTION
> ▸ **happily** *adv.*: *children playing happily on the beach* ◇ *They had been happily married for ten years.*

However, if the derivative is a frequent word with different synonyms of its own, as **happiness** is, there will be a cross-reference to the entry where you can find more information about it. This cross-reference tells you that you can find more information about **happiness** and its synonyms in the entry for **satisfaction**.

Sometimes it is possible to express the same idea using different parts of speech from the same word family. Where this is possible, the examples at the derivative will show you:

> **snort** [I, T] to make a loud sound by breathing air out noisily through your nose, especially to show that you are angry or amused; to say sth using this sound: *He snorted with laughter at the idea.* ◇ *'You!' he snorted contemptuously.*
> ▸ **snort** *noun* [C]: *She gave a snort of disgust.*

This shows that you can *snort with* a feeling or *give a snort of* a feeling.

Rewrite these sentences, using a form of the word in (brackets) instead of the **bold** word. Look up the word in the entry given in SMALL CAPS to help you.

1 Take **care** not to disturb nesting birds. (careful *adj.*) CARE

2 Police **arrested** several people. (arrest *noun*) ARREST

3 You have brought **disgrace** on the whole school. (disgrace *verb*) DISGRACE 2

4 You should **apologize** to her for what you did. (apology *noun*) APOLOGIZE

5 The situation is constantly being **reviewed**. (review *noun*) EXAMINE

6 He ran onto the train, hotly **pursued** by three police officers. (pursuit *noun*) FOLLOW 1

Related Entries

Sometimes two or more whole groups of synonyms are fairly close in meaning. For example, the entry for **excellent** offers six different synonyms that are all very close in meaning; in addition, the entries at **good 1**, **great 1** and **wonderful** provide a total of twenty more words with a similar meaning to choose from. Cross-references at the top of entries will direct you to other groups of synonyms with a similar meaning:

> **excellent** *adj.* See also the entries for GOOD 1, GREAT 1 and WONDERFUL
>
> **excellent · outstanding · perfect · superb · classic · first-rate**
> These words all describe sth that is extremely good.

You can also explore entries related to a particular topic by using the **Topic Index** on pages 903-912. This lists entries under topics from 'The arts' through to 'Work and business'. **Excellent**, for example, can be found on page 905 listed under *Describing things*. The Topic Index is a good starting point when you are interested in general vocabulary building around a particular topic, rather than looking for a synonym of a particular word. A full list of the topics is given on page 903.

For more work on topic vocabulary, see the **Study Pages** and **Topic Maps** on pages 871-902.

A a

abandon verb

abandon · desert · vacate · evacuate
These words all mean to go away from a building or place, leaving it empty.

PATTERNS AND COLLOCATIONS
▸ to abandon/desert/vacate/evacuate a **building/house/home**
▸ to vacate/evacuate the **office/premises**
▸ to abandon/vacate/evacuate sth **immediately**

abandon /ə'bændən/ [T] (*rather formal*) to leave a thing or place, especially because it is impossible or dangerous to stay: *Snow forced many drivers to abandon their vehicles.* ◇ *They had to **abandon** their lands and property to the invading forces.* ◇ *He gave the order to **abandon ship** (= to leave the ship because it was sinking).* See also **abandon** → LEAVE 5, **abandoned** → DESERTED

desert /dɪ'zɜːt; AmE dɪ'zɜːrt/ [T, often passive] to go away from a place and leave it empty: *The villages had been deserted.* ◇ *The owl seems to have deserted its nest.* ❶ People are more likely to **desert** their homes because there is no longer work or food for them in the area, rather than because of danger. **Desert** is most often used in the past participle form, and is mainly used to talk about places where people have lived at some time in the past: *The house/croft/encampment/village/settlement had been deserted.* See also **deserted** → DESERTED

vacate /və'keɪt; veɪ'k-; AmE also 'veɪkeɪt/ [T] (*formal*) to leave a building, room or seat, especially so that sb else can use it: *Guests are requested to vacate their rooms by noon on the day of departure.*

evacuate /ɪ'vækjueɪt/ [T, I] (*rather formal*) to move out of a place because of danger, and leave the place empty: *Employees were urged to evacuate their offices immediately.* ◇ *Locals were told to evacuate.*
▸ **evacuation** noun [U]: *the emergency evacuation of the building*

ability noun

ability · capability · capacity · power
These are all words for the fact that sb is able to do sth, or the qualities necessary to do sth.

PATTERNS AND COLLOCATIONS
▸ a capability/capacity **for** sth
▸ the ability/capability/capacity/power **to do sth**
▸ **beyond/within** your ability/capability/capacity/power
▸ (a/an) **great/remarkable/extraordinary/amazing** ability/capacity/powers
▸ **natural/physical/intellectual/mental/limited** ability/capability/capacity/powers
▸ to **have/develop/acquire/lack/lose** the ability/capability/capacity/power
▸ to **demonstrate/show** your ability/capability/capacity/power
▸ to **restrict** sb's ability/capability/capacity/power

ability [sing., U] the fact that sb/sth is able to do sth: *The system has the ability to run more than one program at the same time.* ◇ *Everyone has the right to good medical care regardless of their ability to pay.* ◇ *I try to do the job **to the best of my ability** (= as well as I can).* **OPP** **inability** ❶ **Inability** [sing., U] is the fact of not being able to do sth: *the government's inability to provide basic services* ◇ *Some families go without medical treatment because of their inability to pay.*

▸ **able** *adj.*: *You must be able to speak French for this job.* ◇ *A viral illness left her barely able to walk.* **OPP** **unable to do sth** ❶ *not able* is also used: *He lay there, unable to move.* ◇ *Unfortunately they weren't able to come.*

capability /ˌkeɪpə'bɪləti/ [U, C] (*rather formal*) the ability or qualities necessary to do sth: *Animals in the zoo have lost the **capability of** catching food for themselves.* ◇ *Age affects the range of a person's capabilities.* ❶ **Capability** is often used to talk about how able a company or country is to produce sth: *a company/country's manufacturing/production/processing/defence/weapons/nuclear capability*
▸ **capable** *adj.*: *You are capable of better work than this.* ◇ *I'm perfectly capable of doing it myself, thank you.*

capacity /kə'pæsəti/ [C, usually sing.] (*rather formal*) the ability to understand or do sth: *She has an enormous capacity for hard work.* ◇ *A habit becomes an addiction when it reduces your capacity to enjoy life.* ❶ **Capacity** is often used to talk about social, educational and work-related life skills: *a capacity for hard work/humour/enjoying life/learning languages/love/reflective thinking*

power [U] (also **powers** [pl.]) a particular ability of the body or mind; all the abilities of your body or mind: *He had lost the power of speech.* ◇ *The drug may affect your powers of concentration.* ◇ *At 26, he is **at the height of his powers** and ranked fourth in the world.* ❶ Sb's **power** [U] is also their ability or opportunity to do sth, used especially in the phrases *(not) within sb's power, beyond sb's power* and *do everything within your power*: *It is not within my power (= I am unable) to help you.* ◇ *I will **do everything in my power** to help you.*

abnormal adj.

abnormal · rogue · deviant · anomalous · non-standard
These words all describe things or people that are different from what is usual or expected or considered normal by most people.

PATTERNS AND COLLOCATIONS
▸ abnormal/deviant/anomalous **behaviour/patterns**
▸ abnormal/anomalous **results**
▸ an abnormal/a non-standard **size**
▸ abnormal/rogue **cells**
▸ **highly** abnormal/deviant/anomalous

abnormal /æb'nɔːml; AmE -'nɔːrml/ different from what is usual or expected, especially in a way that is worrying, harmful or not wanted: *There was nothing abnormal about her behaviour.* ◇ *The test detects abnormal cells that could become cancerous.* **OPP** **normal** → NORMAL, **normal** → SANE
▸ **abnormality** /-nɔː'ræm-/ noun [C, U]: *abnormalities of the heart* ◇ *congenital/foetal abnormality*
▸ **abnormally** *adv.*: *abnormally low weight*

rogue /rəʊg; AmE roʊg/ [only before noun] (*often disapproving*) behaving in a different way from other similar people or things, often causing damage: *My suitcase was destroyed by a rogue conveyor belt at the airport.* ◇ *Rogue cells may survive in the body to form a tumour.*

deviant /'di:viənt/ (*disapproving*) (of people or their behaviour) different from what most people consider to be normal and acceptable: *Not all deviant behaviour is criminal.*
▶ **deviance** *noun* [U]: *a study of social deviance and crime*

anomalous /ə'nɒmələs; *AmE* -'nɑːm-/ (*formal*) (especially of facts or situations) different from what is normal or expected: *We need to look again at any apparently anomalous cases.* ◇ *They could find no explanation for the seemingly anomalous data.* See also **anomaly** → EXCEPTION

non-'standard not the usual type or size of sth; (of language) not considered correct by most educated people: *The documents are stored in files that are of non-standard size.* ◇ *Standard English and non-standard dialects have much in common.* **OPP** **standard** → USUAL

abolish *verb* See also the entries for CUT 1 and REMOVE 1

abolish · cancel · scrap · dismiss · do away with sth · axe · call sth off
These words all mean to change plans so that sth no longer happens.

PATTERNS AND COLLOCATIONS
▶ to abolish / cancel / scrap / axe a **service**
▶ to abolish / scrap a **system / plan / scheme / tax**
▶ to cancel / call off a / an **game / match / engagement**
▶ to scrap / axe **jobs**
▶ to abolish / scrap sth **completely**
▶ to cancel / scrap sth **altogether**

abolish /ə'bɒlɪʃ; *AmE* ə'bɑːl-/ [T, often passive] to officially end a law, system or institution: *Slavery was abolished in the US in 1865.* ◇ *Over the past six years we have abolished a whole range of direct taxes.*
▶ **abolition** /ˌæbə'lɪʃn/ *noun* [U]: *the abolition of slavery/ apartheid/the death penalty*

cancel (-ll-, *AmE* -l-) [T, often passive] to decide that sth that has been arranged will not now take place: *All flights have been cancelled because of bad weather.* ◇ *Don't forget to cancel the newspaper* (= arrange for it not to be delivered) *before going away.* See also **postpone** → DELAY
▶ **cancellation** (*AmE* also **cancelation**) *noun* [U, C]: *We need at least 24 hours' notice of cancellation.* ◇ *Cancellations must be made in writing.*

scrap (-pp-) [T, often passive] (*rather informal, especially journalism*) to cancel sth, especially plans, that are no longer practical or useful: *The government has been forced to scrap plans for a proposed tax reform.*

dismiss [T] (*law*) to say that a trial or legal case should not continue, usually because there is not enough evidence: *Judges have to state their reasons for dismissing a case.* ◇ *'Case dismissed!'*

do a'way with sth *phrasal verb* (*rather informal, especially spoken, often approving*) to abolish sth, especially when you think this is a good thing: *He thinks it's time we did away with the monarchy.*

axe (*BrE*) (*AmE* **ax**) [T, often passive] (*rather informal, journalism*) to get rid of sth such as a service or system, or to reduce the money spent on it by a large amount: *Other less profitable services are to be axed later this year.* ◇ *The series was axed after only six episodes.*

call sth 'off *phrasal verb* to cancel sth, especially a plan involving lots of people; to decide that sth will not happen: *Union leaders last night called off strike action planned for today.* ◇ *They have called off their engagement* (= decided not to get married).

accelerate *verb*

accelerate · speed (sth) up · speed · hasten · quicken
These words all mean to go faster or make sth happen faster.

PATTERNS AND COLLOCATIONS
▶ to accelerate / speed up / speed / hasten / quicken the **pace / progress** (of sth)
▶ to accelerate / speed up / speed / hasten the **development** (of sth)
▶ to accelerate / speed / hasten the **death** of sb / sth
▶ to **greatly** accelerate / speed up / speed / hasten sth

accelerate /ək'seləreɪt/ [I, T] (of a vehicle or person) to start to go faster; to happen or make sth happen faster or sooner than expected: *The car accelerated to overtake me.* ◇ *Inflation continues to accelerate.* ◇ *Exposure to the sun can accelerate the ageing process.* **OPP** **retard** → HOLD SB/ STH UP, **decelerate ⓘ** Decelerate is more formal than **accelerate**, used mostly in writing: (*formal, written*) *Economic growth decelerated sharply in January.*
▶ **acceleration** /əkˌselə'reɪʃn/ *noun* [U, sing.]: *a car with good acceleration* ◇ *an acceleration in the rate of growth*

speed 'up, speed sth 'up *phrasal verb* (*rather informal*) to move or happen faster; to make sth move or happen faster: *The train soon speeded up.* ◇ *Can you try and speed things up a bit?* ◇ *They have speeded up production of the new car.* **OPP** **slow down ⓘ** The opposite is **slow down**: *Slow down! I can't keep up with you.*

speed [T] (*written*) to make sth happen sooner or faster, especially sb/sth's recovery or the development of sth: *The drugs will speed her recovery.* ◇ *More is needed to speed the development of a safe and effective vaccine.* See also **speedy** → QUICK

NOTE SPEED STH UP OR SPEED? Speed is more formal than **speed sth up** and it is used to talk about making things happen faster but NOT vehicles moving faster: ~~The train soon speeded.~~ See also **speed** → FLY 2

hasten /'heɪsn/ [T] (*written*) to make sth happen sooner or faster, especially the death, destruction or end of sb/sth: *The treatment she received may, in fact, have hastened her death.* ◇ *News of the scandal certainly hastened his departure from office.* **OPP** **delay** → DELAY

quicken [I, T] (*written*) to become faster; to make sth faster: *She felt her heartbeat quicken as he approached.* ◇ *He quickened his pace to catch up with them.* **ⓘ** Quicken is often used to talk about sth that is connected with living and the body, such as sb's *heartbeat, pulse, breathing* or *pace*. **OPP** **slacken ⓘ** The opposite is **slacken**: *She slackened her pace a little* (= walked more slowly).

accept *verb*

accept · face · come to terms with sth · live with sth · face up to sth · make the best of sth · resign yourself to sth · reconcile
These words all mean to recognize that a difficult situation exists and cannot be changed, and that you must continue or deal with it.

PATTERNS AND COLLOCATIONS
▶ to accept / face / come to terms with / live with / face up to / resign yourself to / reconcile yourself to **the fact that…**
▶ to accept / face / come to terms with / make the best of a **situation**
▶ to accept / face / come to terms with / face up to **the truth / the reality of sth**
▶ to accept / face / come to terms with / live with **the consequences**
▶ to accept / face / face up to **the facts / your responsibilities**
▶ **finally** accept / face / come to terms with / resign yourself to sth

accept [T] to be willing to continue in a difficult situation without complaining, because you realize that it cannot be changed: *They accept the risks as part of the job.* ◇ *He refused to accept that his father was no longer there.* ◇ *Most people had come to accept that war was inevitable.*

face [T] to accept that a difficult or unpleasant situation exists, although you would prefer not to: *She had to face the fact that her life had changed forever.* ◇ *Face facts – she isn't coming back.* ◇ *Let's face it, we're not going to win.*

come to 'terms with sth *idiom* to accept sth unpleasant by learning to deal with it: *She is still coming to terms with her son's death.*

'live with sth *phrasal verb* to accept sth unpleasant and continue without complaining: *You get used to jet lag in the sense that you learn to live with it.*

face 'up to sth *phrasal verb* to accept and deal with sth difficult or unpleasant, especially after ignoring it: *You have to face up to your responsibilities.*

make the best of sth *idiom* (*rather informal*) to accept a bad situation and do as well as you can: *She was a pragmatic woman who always **made the best of things**.* ◇ *Conditions were harsh, but we **made the best of it**.*

re'sign yourself to sth *phrasal verb* to accept sth unpleasant that cannot be changed or avoided: *She resigned herself to her fate.* ◇ *We have to resign ourselves to making a loss on the sale.* See also **resignation** → PATIENCE
▸ **resigned** *adj.*: *He was **resigned to** never seeing his birthplace again.*

reconcile /ˈrekənsaɪl/ [T] (*rather formal*) to make sb/ yourself accept an unpleasant situation that cannot be changed: *He could not **reconcile himself to** the prospect of losing her.*

access *noun*

access · entry · admission · entrance
These are all words for a way of entering a place or the right or opportunity to enter a place or join a group.

▸ access / entry / admission / entrance **to** sth
▸ access / entry **for** sb
▸ **free** access / entry / admission / entrance
▸ **unlimited** access / entry
▸ to **refuse** / **deny** (sb) access / entry / admission / entrance
▸ to **gain** access / entry / admission / entrance
▸ an entry / admission / entrance **charge** / **fee**

access [U] a way of entering or reaching a place; the right or opportunity to use sth or see sb/sth: *Double doors **give access to** the terrace.* ◇ *There is easy access by road.* ◇ *There is **wheelchair access** to most of the facilities.* ◇ *Students must **have access** to good resources.* ◇ *You need a password to **get access** to the computer system.* ◇ *Journalists were denied access to the President.*
▸ **access** *verb* [T]: (*formal*) *The loft can be accessed by a ladder.*

entry [U] the right or opportunity to enter a place, take part in sth or become a member of a group; the fact of taking part in sth or becoming a member of a group: *A sign said: No Entry.* ◇ *Entry to the museum is free.* ◇ *How did the thieves gain entry into the building?* ◇ *That was before the American entry into the war.* See also **enter** → ENTER

admission /ədˈmɪʃn/ [U, C] the act of allowing sb to enter a place or join an organization; the right to enter a place or join an organization: ***Last admission** 30 minutes before closing time.* ◇ *Hospital admissions for asthma attacks have doubled.* ◇ *Admission is by ticket only.* ◇ *The country has applied for admission to the European Union.* See also **admit** → LET SB IN

entrance [U] the right or opportunity to enter a building or place; permission to join an organization: *They were refused entrance to the club.* ◇ *The police were unable to gain entrance to the house.* ◇ *What are the entrance requirements for this course?*

accident *noun*

accident · crash · collision · wreck · mishap · pile-up
These are all words for an unpleasant event, especially in a vehicle, that happens unexpectedly and causes injury or damage.

▸ **in** an accident / a crash / a collision / a wreck / a pile-up
▸ a **serious** accident / crash / collision / wreck / mishap
▸ a **major** accident / crash / collision / wreck / pile-up
▸ a **minor** accident / collision
▸ a **slight** / **little** accident / mishap
▸ a **car** / **train** accident / crash / wreck
▸ a **plane** crash / wreck
▸ a **head-on** crash / collision
▸ to **have** an accident / a collision / a mishap
▸ to **cause** an accident / a crash / a collision / a wreck / a pile-up
▸ an accident / a crash / a collision / a wreck / a mishap / a pile-up **happens** / **occurs**

accident [C] an unpleasant event, especially in a vehicle, that happens unexpectedly and causes injury or damage: *a road/traffic accident* ◇ *a climbing/riding accident* ◇ *It's Dad. He's had an accident at work.* ◇ *I didn't mean to break it – it was an accident.* ◇ *It is the first fatal accident* (= in which sb is killed) *to have occurred at the factory.*
▸ **accidental** *adj.*: *a verdict of accidental death* **OPP** **deliberate** → DELIBERATE
▸ **accidentally** *adv.*: *As I turned around, I accidentally hit him in the face.* **OPP** **deliberately** → DELIBERATE

crash [C] an accident in which a vehicle hits sth, for example another vehicle, usually causing damage and often injuring or killing the passengers: *A girl was killed in a crash involving a stolen car.* See also **crash** → CRASH *verb*

collision /kəˈlɪʒn/ [C] an accident in which two vehicles or people crash into each other: *Stewart was injured in a collision with another player.* ◇ *His car was **in collision with** a motorbike.* See also **collide** → CRASH *verb*

wreck [C] (*AmE*) a crash: *The wreck occurred at milepost 534, just west of Greenup, Kentucky.* See also **wreck** → CRASH *verb*

mishap /ˈmɪshæp/ [C, U] (*rather formal*) a small accident or piece of bad luck that does not have serious results: *I'm afraid your son had a slight mishap in the playground.* ◇ *I managed to get home without further mishap.*

'pile-up [C] (*rather informal, especially journalism*) a road accident involving several vehicles crashing into each other: *Three people died in a multiple pile-up in freezing fog.*

accommodate *verb*

accommodate · house · take sb in · billet · put sb up
These words all mean to provide a place for sb to live, sleep or sit.

▸ to accommodate / house / take in **refugees**
▸ to accommodate / take in / put up **guests**
▸ to accommodate / take in **students**

accommodate /əˈkɒmədeɪt; *AmE* əˈkɑːm-/ [T] (*rather formal*) to provide sb with a room or place to sleep, live or sit: *The hotel can accommodate up to 500 guests.* ◇ *The aircraft is capable of accommodating 23 passengers.* See also **accommodation** → HOUSING

house /haʊz/ [T] (*rather formal*) to provide a place for sb to live or work: *The government is committed to housing the refugees.* ◇ *The new offices will house 600 administration staff.* ❶ **House** is often used in texts relating to business, economics and politics. See also **housing** → HOUSING

take sb 'in *phrasal verb* to allow sb to live in your home: *He was homeless, so we took him in.* ◇ *She took in lodgers in order to pay the bills.* See also **adopt** → BRING SB UP

billet /ˈbɪlɪt/ [T, usually passive] (always used with an adverb or preposition) (*BrE*) to send soldiers to live somewhere temporarily, especially in private houses during a war: *The troops were billeted in the town with local families.*

put sb 'up *phrasal verb* (*rather informal*) to allow sb to stay in your home, usually for a short time: *We can put you up for the night.*

accompany *verb* See also the entry for TAKE 2

accompany · go with sb · tag along · keep sb company
These words all mean to be with sb when they are doing sth, especially when they are going somewhere.

PATTERNS AND COLLOCATIONS
▸ to accompany / go with sb **to…**
▸ to accompany sb / go with sb **everywhere**
▸ to accompany sb / go with sb / keep sb company **on a trip / journey**

accompany [T] (*formal*) to travel or go somewhere with sb: *I must ask you to accompany me to the police station.* ◇ *The groups are always accompanied by an experienced mountain guide.*

go with sb *phrasal verb* to move or travel with sb to a particular place or in order to be present at an event: *He was looking for someone to go with him to the award ceremony.*

,tag a'long *phrasal verb* (-**gg**-) (*rather informal, sometimes disapproving*) to go somewhere with sb, especially when you have not been invited: *Do you mind if I tag along with you tonight?* ◇ *She walked in with the little boy **tagging along behind.***

keep sb 'company *idiom* to stay with sb so that they are not alone: *I'll **stay and keep you company** if you like.*

accomplice *noun* See also the entry for ASSISTANT

accomplice · conspirator · accessory · plotter
These are all words for a person who helps to commit a crime.

PATTERNS AND COLLOCATIONS
▸ an accomplice / accessory **to** a crime
▸ an **alleged** accomplice / conspirator / plotter
▸ a / an **willing / unwilling / unwitting** accomplice / accessory
▸ a **fellow** conspirator / plotter

accomplice /ə'kʌmplɪs; *AmE* ə'kɑːm-/ [C] (*rather formal*) a person who helps sb else to commit a crime or to do sth wrong: *The police suspect that he had an accomplice.*

conspirator /kən'spɪrətə(r)/ [C] (*rather formal*) a person who is involved in a conspiracy (= a secret plan by a group of people to do sth illegal or harmful): *The emperor pardoned five of the conspirators.* ❶ **Conspirator** is often used in writing about history, about plans to kill or remove rulers or governments. See also **conspiracy** → CONSPIRACY, **conspire** → PLOT *verb*

accessory /ək'sesəri/ [C] (*law*) a person who helps sb to commit a crime or who knows about it and protects the person from the police: *She was charged with being an accessory to murder.*

plotter [C] a person who makes a secret plan to harm sb: *He alleged that the plotters had intended to assassinate him.* ❶ **Plotter** is often used to talk about sb who plans a *coup* (= a sudden, illegal and often violent change of government): *a coup plotter* See also **plot** → PLOT *verb*

accuse *verb*

accuse · charge · prosecute · indict · impeach · cite
These words all mean to say that sb has done sth wrong or committed a crime and must appear in court.

PATTERNS AND COLLOCATIONS
▸ to prosecute / indict / impeach / cite sb **for** sth
▸ to charge / indict sb **with** sth
▸ to be prosecuted / indicted / impeached / cited **on charges / on a charge** of sth

accuse [T] to say that sb has done sth wrong or committed a crime: *She **accused** him **of** lying.* ◇ *The government was accused of incompetence.* ◇ (*formal*) *They **stand accused** of crimes against humanity.* See also **accusation** → CHARGE *noun*

charge [T, usually passive] to accuse sb formally of a crime so that there can be a trial in court: *He was charged with murder.* ◇ *Several people were arrested but nobody was charged.* ❶ In formal language **charge** can also mean 'to accuse sb formally in public of doing sth wrong': *Opposition MPs charged the minister with neglecting her duty.* See also **charge** → CHARGE *noun*

prosecute /'prɒsɪkjuːt; *AmE* 'prɑːs-/ [T, I] to put sb on trial for a crime in court: *The company was prosecuted for breaching the Health and Safety Act.* ◇ *The police decided not to prosecute.* See also **prosecution** → CASE

indict /ɪn'daɪt/ [T, usually passive] (*law*) (in the US) to officially charge sb with a crime: *The senator was indicted for murder.* ◇ *They were indicted on a number of corruption charges.* See also **indictment** → CHARGE *noun*

> NOTE **CHARGE** OR **INDICT?** In Britain the Crown Prosecution Service decides whether to **charge** sb with a crime. In the US **charge** is used when this is done by a prosecutor (= a public official) and **indict** when this is done by a Grand Jury (= a group of 23 people).

impeach [T] (especially in the US) to charge an important public figure with a serious crime in connection with their job: *The President was impeached by Congress for lying.* See also **impeachment** → CHARGE *noun*

cite /saɪt/ [T, usually passive] (*law*) to order sb to appear in court; to name sb officially in a legal case: *He was cited for contempt of court.* ◇ *She was cited in the divorce proceedings.*

achieve *verb*

achieve · manage · succeed · reach · accomplish · effect · arrive at sth · pull sth off · attain · get there · fulfil
These words all mean to succeed in doing sth or making sth happen.

PATTERNS AND COLLOCATIONS
▸ to achieve / succeed in / reach / accomplish / attain / fulfil a / an **goal / objective**
▸ to achieve / reach / attain / fulfil a **target**
▸ to achieve / succeed in / accomplish / attain / fulfil a / an **aim**
▸ to achieve / accomplish / attain a / an **purpose / end**
▸ to achieve / succeed in / accomplish / fulfil a **task**
▸ to achieve / accomplish / fulfil an **ambition**
▸ to achieve / attain / fulfil an **ideal**
▸ to achieve / reach / arrive at a / an **agreement / result**
▸ to achieve / accomplish / effect a **change / transformation**
▸ to reach / pull off / attain a **deal**
▸ to achieve / reach / attain a **balance**
▸ to achieve / manage / accomplish / pull off a **feat**
▸ to achieve / pull off a **coup / victory**
▸ to **actually** achieve / manage / succeed in / reach / accomplish / arrive at / pull off / attain / fulfil sth
▸ to **finally** achieve / manage / succeed in / reach / accomplish / arrive at / attain / fulfil sth

achieve [T] to be successful in reaching a particular goal, status or standard, especially by making an effort for a long time; to be successful in doing sth or making sth happen: *He had finally achieved success.* ◇ *I haven't achieved very much today.* ◇ *All you've achieved is to upset my parents.* See also **achieve** → SUCCEED
> ▸ **achievement** *noun* [U]: *Even a small success gives you a sense of achievement* (= a feeling of pride). See also **achievement** → WORK 3

manage [T, I] to be successful in doing sth, especially sth difficult: *In spite of his disappointment, he managed a weak smile.* ◇ *I don't know exactly how we'll **manage it**, but we will, somehow.* ◇ *We **managed to** get to the airport in time.* ◇ *How did you manage to persuade him?* ◇ *We couldn't have managed without you.* ◇ *'Need any help?' 'No, thanks. I can manage.'*

succeed [T] to achieve sth that you have been trying to do or get; to have the result or effect that was intended: *He **succeeded in** getting a place at art school.* ◇ *I tried to*

discuss it with her but **only succeeded** in making her angry (= I failed and did the opposite of what I intended). ◇ *Our plan succeeded.* **OPP** fail → FAIL 2, See also **succeed** → SUCCEED, **successful** → SUCCESSFUL 1
▸ **success** [U]: *I didn't have much **success in** finding a job.* ◇ *commercial/economic/electoral success* **OPP** **failure** → FAILURE

reach [T] to succeed in deciding, agreeing or finding sth, especially after discussion and thought; to succeed in achieving a particular goal: *The jury took two days to reach a verdict.* ◇ *Greater efforts are needed to reach the goal of universal education.*

accomplish /əˈkʌmplɪʃ; AmE əˈkɑːm-/ [T] (*rather formal*) to succeed in doing or completing sth: *The first part of the plan has been safely accomplished.* ◇ *That's it.* **Mission accomplished** (= we have done what we aimed to do). ❶ **Accomplish** is most often used to talk about succeeding in a *task, mission, plan, job* or your *work*. See also **accomplishment** → WORK 3

effect [T] (*formal*) to succeed in making sth happen: *These drugs can sometimes effect miraculous cures.*

ar'rive at sth *phrasal verb* to succeed in deciding on or finding sth, especially after discussion and thought: *We need to make sure we have all the facts before arriving at a decision.* ❶ **Arrive at sth** is a slightly more informal way of saying **reach**. However, it cannot be used to mean 'achieve a goal': *to reach a goal/a target/an objective* ◇ ~~to arrive at a goal/a target/an objective~~

,pull sth 'off *phrasal verb* (*informal, spoken*) to succeed in doing sth difficult: *We pulled off the deal.* ◇ *I never thought you'd pull it off.*

attain /əˈteɪn/ [T] (*formal*) to succeed in getting sth, usually after a lot of effort: *Most of our students attained five 'A' grades in their exams.* ❶ **Attain** is usually used to talk about levels of achievement: *attain (a) degree/standard/level/proficiency/mastery*, as well as *objectives* and *status*.
▸ **attainment** *noun* [U]: *schools with high levels of academic attainment*

'get there *idiom* (*informal, spoken*) to achieve your aim or complete a task: *I'm sure you'll get there in the end.* ◇ *It's not perfect but we're getting there* (= making progress).

NOTE PULL STH OFF OR **GET THERE?** **Get there** suggests a long and hard struggle to achieve an aim; **pull sth off** places more emphasis on the success at the end.

fulfil (*BrE*) (*AmE* **fulfill**) /fʊlˈfɪl/ (-ll-) [T] to do or achieve what was hoped for or expected: *Fulfil your dreams with a new career.* ◇ *Turkey is a market that has never quite fulfilled its potential.*

acquit *verb*

acquit · clear · exonerate · vindicate · absolve
These words all mean to state that sb is not guilty of doing sth wrong or illegal.

PATTERNS AND COLLOCATIONS
▸ to acquit / clear / exonerate / absolve sb **of** sth
▸ a **defendant** is acquitted / cleared / exonerated

acquit /əˈkwɪt/ (-tt-) [T] (*rather formal, especially written*) to decide and state officially in court that sb is not guilty of a crime: *The jury acquitted him of murder.* ◇ *She was acquitted on all charges.* **OPP** **convict** ❶ To **convict** sb is to decide and state officially in court that sb is guilty of a crime: *He was convicted of fraud.* ◇ *a convicted murderer*
▸ **acquittal** /əˈkwɪtl/ *noun* [C, U]: (*rather formal, especially written*) *The case resulted in an acquittal.* ◇ *The jury voted for acquittal.*

clear [T] to prove officially that sb is not guilty of a crime: *She was cleared of all charges against her.* ◇ *Throughout his years in prison, he fought to **clear his name**.* See also **in the clear** → INNOCENT

NOTE ACQUIT OR **CLEAR?** When you are talking about the result of a trial in court you can use either word, although **acquit** is more formal: *He was acquitted/*

cleared *of murder.* **Clear** can also be used when sb has been convicted (= found guilty) of a crime, but successfully campaigns to have the conviction overturned (= cancelled): *After spending more than ten years on death row, the two men were finally cleared of a crime they did not commit.*

exonerate /ɪgˈzɒnəreɪt; AmE -ˈzɑːn-/ [T] (*formal*) to state officially that sb is not responsible for a crime or dishonest act that they have been blamed for: *The king cannot be **exonerated from** responsibility for the massacre.*

vindicate /ˈvɪndɪkeɪt/ [T] (*formal*) to prove that sb is not guilty of a crime or dishonest act that they have been accused of: *New evidence emerged, vindicating him completely.*

NOTE EXONERATE OR **VINDICATE?** You can be **exonerated** by a person or report that states officially that you are not guilty; you are **vindicated** by evidence that proves you are not guilty.

absolve /əbˈzɒlv; AmE əbˈzɑːlv/ [T] (*rather formal, especially written*) to state officially that sb is not guilty or responsible for sth: *The court absolved him of all responsibility for the accident.*

act *verb*

act · do something · take action · take steps · move · make a, your, etc. move
These words all mean to deal with a situation in a particular way.

PATTERNS AND COLLOCATIONS
▸ to act / take action / take steps / move / make your move **against** sb / sth
▸ to act / do something / take action / take steps / move **to do sth**
▸ to act / do something / take action / take steps / move / make your move **immediately**
▸ to act / do something / take action / move **quickly**

act [I] to do sth for a particular purpose or in order to deal with a situation: *It is vital that we act to stop the destruction of the rainforests.* ◇ *The girl's life was saved because the doctors acted so promptly.* ◇ *He claims he acted in self-defence.* ❶ **Act** in this meaning is often followed by an adverb relating to speed or urgency: *They acted at once/immediately/promptly/quickly/swiftly.* **Act** is also often used when people are talking about whether sb should be blamed for doing sth that has had a negative effect: *He acted in self-defence/in good faith.*

'do something *phrase* (*rather informal, especially spoken*) to act with a particular purpose or in order to deal with a situation: *The company ought to **do something about** the poor service.* ◇ *Don't just stand there – do something.*

,take 'action *phrase* (*especially journalism*) to act with a particular purpose or in order to deal with a situation: *Firefighters took action immediately to stop the blaze from spreading.*

,take 'steps *phrase* (*especially written*) to do a series of things in order to achieve sth: *We are taking steps to prevent pollution.* ❶ Unlike other verbs in this group, **take steps** does not necessarily suggest that sth is very urgent.

move [I] (*especially journalism*) to act with a particular purpose or in order to deal with a situation: *The police moved quickly to dispel the rumours.* ❶ **Move** is usually followed by an adverb relating to speed or urgency such as *swiftly* or *quickly*.

make a, your, etc. 'move *phrase* (*especially written*) to do the action that you intend to do or need to do in order to achieve sth: *The rebels waited until nightfall before they made their move.*

action *noun* See also the entry for PROCESS

action · measure · step · act · move · gesture · deed · stunt · doing
These are all words for a thing that sb does.

PATTERNS AND COLLOCATIONS
▸ an action / a measure / a step / an act / a move / a gesture / a deed / a stunt **by** sb
▸ a step / move / gesture **towards** sth
▸ a **heroic / brave / daring** action / step / act / move / gesture / deed
▸ a **kind / charitable / generous** action / act / gesture / deed
▸ a / an **evil / terrible** act / deed
▸ to **take** actions / measures / steps
▸ to **do** an action / an act / a deed / a stunt
▸ to **perform** an action / an act / a deed / a stunt
▸ to **make** a step / move / gesture

action [C, U] a thing that sb does; the process of doing sth in order to make sth happen or to deal with a situation: *Her quick action saved the child's life.* ◇ *Each of us must take responsibility for our own actions.* ◇ *Only the priest can perform these actions.* ◇ *We shall take whatever actions are necessary.* ◇ *Firefighters **took action** immediately to stop the blaze from spreading.* ◇ *What is the best **course of action** in the circumstances?* ◇ *She began to explain her **plan of action** to the group.*

measure [C] an official action that is done in order to achieve a particular aim: *Special measures are being taken to protect the local water supplies.* ◇ *Tougher **measures against** racism are needed.* ◇ *This is just a temporary measure, while the emergency exists.* ◇ *The government introduced emergency measures to stave off an economic crisis.*

step [C] one of a series of things that you do in order to achieve sth: *This was a first step towards a united Europe.* ◇ *We are taking steps to prevent pollution.* ◇ *This won't solve the problem but it's **a step in the right direction**.* ◇ *The new drug is a major **step forward** in the treatment of the disease.*

act [C] a thing that sb does: *an act of kindness / generosity / love / aggression / desperation* ◇ *You have committed a serious criminal act.* ◇ *The very act of writing out your plan clarifies what you need to do.* ◇ *He was **caught in the act** of stealing (= caught stealing).*

NOTE ACTION OR ACT? These two words have the same meaning but are used in different patterns. An **act** is usually followed by *of* and / or used with an adjective. **Action** is not usually used with *of* but is often used with *his, her, etc.*: *a heroic act of bravery* ◇ *a heroic action of bravery* ◇ *his heroic actions / acts during the war.* **Action** often combines with **take** but **act** does not: *We shall take whatever acts are necessary.*

move [C] (*especially journalism*) an action that you do or need to do to achieve sth: *This latest move by the government has aroused fierce opposition.* ◇ *The management has made no move to settle the strike.* ◇ *If he wants to see me, he should **make the first move**.* ◇ *Getting a job in marketing was a good **career move**.*

gesture /'dʒestʃə(r)/ [C] a thing that you do or say to show a particular feeling or intention: *It was a **nice gesture** (= it was kind) to invite his wife too.* ◇ *Words and empty gestures are not enough – we demand action!* ◇ *We do not accept responsibility but we will refund the money as a **gesture of goodwill / a goodwill gesture**.*

deed [C] (*formal or literary*) a thing that sb does that is usually very good or very bad: *It's a stirring tale of heroic deeds.* ◇ *These were evil deeds perpetrated by wicked people.* ◇ (*rather informal, especially spoken*) *I took Sarah's children to school so I've done **my good deed for the day**.*

stunt [C] a dangerous and difficult action that sb does to entertain people, especially as part of a film: *He did all his own stunts in the movie.* ◇ *a stunt pilot / rider / team* ◇ *a stuntman / stuntwoman* ❶ **Stunt** is also used, sometimes in a disapproving way, for sth that is done in order to attract people's attention: *They jumped off London Bridge as a publicity stunt.*

doing [C, usually pl., U] a thing done or caused by sb: *I've been hearing a lot about your doings recently.*

active *adj.*

active · in operation · in force · in action · up and running · operational
These words all describe sb/sth being able to do, or doing, the activity or work that is typical for them.

active doing sth regularly; functioning; having or causing a chemical effect: *These animals are active only at night.* ◇ *Numbers of sexually active teenagers have continued to rise.* ◇ *The virus is still active in the blood.* ◇ *What is the active ingredient in aspirin?* **OPP** **inactive** ❶ **Inactive** describes sb/sth that is not doing anything, is not in use or not working or has no effect: *Some animals are inactive during the daytime.* ◇ *an inactive drug / disease*

in ope'ration *phrase* (*rather formal*) (of a system) working, being used or having an effect: *The system needs to be in operation for six months before it can be assessed.* ◇ *Temporary traffic controls are in operation on New Road.* ❶ When a system **comes into operation** it starts working or having an effect: *The new rules come into operation from next week.* When you **put sth into operation** you start using it or make it start working: *It's time to put our plan into operation.* See also **operate** → ORGANIZE, **operate** → WORK *verb* 3

in 'force *phrase* (of a law or rule) being used: *The new regulations are now in force.* ❶ When a law or rule **comes / enters into force** it starts being used: *When do the new regulations come into force?* When you **bring sth into force** you make a law or rule start being used: *They are hoping to bring the new legislation into force by the end of the year.*

in 'action *phrase* (of a person or thing) doing the activity or work that is typical for them: *I've yet to see all the players in action.*

‚up and 'running *idiom* (of a system, for example a computer system) working; being used: *By that time the new system should be up and running.* ❶ **Up and running** is usually used to talk about sth starting to work or be used after a period of development. See also **run** → WORK *verb* 3

operational [not usually before noun] (*rather formal*) ready to be used; in use: *The new airport should be fully operational by the end of the year.* ❶ **Operational** is very often used in the phrase *fully operational*. See also **operate** → WORK *verb* 3

activist *noun* See also the entry for ADVOCATE

activist · campaigner · reformer · crusader · fighter
These are all words for a person who does things or makes significant things happen.

PATTERNS AND COLLOCATIONS
▸ an activist / a campaigner / a crusader **for** sth
▸ a **leading / great** activist / campaigner / reformer / crusader
▸ a **political** activist / campaigner / reformer

activist [C] a person who works to achieve political or social change, especially as a member of an organization with particular aims: *Gay activists marched in London today to protest against the new law.*

campaigner /kæm'peɪnə(r)/ [C] a person who works to achieve political or social change, either as a member of an organization or as an individual: *She's a leading human rights campaigner.* ◇ *In his youth he was a **campaigner on** environmental issues.* ◇ *She has been a tireless **campaigner against** education cuts.* ◇ (*especially AmE*) *Bush campaigners* (= people working for Bush in a campaign) *were out in force.* See also **campaign** → CAMPAIGN *noun*, **campaign** → CAMPAIGN *verb*

NOTE ACTIVIST OR CAMPAIGNER? In many cases you can use either word: *a / an peace / human rights / animal rights / anti-war / anti-nuclear / pro-democracy / environmental activist / campaigner.* An **activist** is likely to belong to an organization with particular aims, often representing a particular group of people: *student /*

disabled/union/party activists. Some activists use extreme methods, including *direct action* (= the use of protests and strikes instead of discussion) and even violence. A **campaigner** may belong to an organization or may work as an individual, sometimes for a quite specific aim: *He has long been a campaigner for better communication between doctors and patients.* **Campaigners** are more likely to use discussion and legal means to achieve their aims.

reformer [C] (especially in the past) a person who works to achieve political or social change: *Many social reformers have been regarded as criminals and law-breakers in the past.* See also **reform** → IMPROVE 1

crusader /kruːˈseɪdə(r)/ [C] (*especially written*) a person who takes part in a crusade: *She was a moral crusader who campaigned on a range of issues.* ❶ A **crusade** is a determined effort over a period of time to achieve sth that you believe to be right or to stop sth that you believe to be wrong. See also **crusade** → CAMPAIGN

fighter [C] (*rather informal, approving*) a person who does not give up hope or admit that they are defeated: *She's a fighter — if anyone's going to finish the course, she will.*

activity noun

activity · action · rush · bustle
These are all words for a situation in which a lot of things are being done.

PATTERNS AND COLLOCATIONS
▸ (a) **great** activity / action / rush / bustle
▸ (a) **frantic** activity / action / rush
▸ **increased** / **intense** activity / action
▸ to **be involved in** / **stop** the activity / action

activity [U] a situation in which sth is happening or a lot of things are being done: *The streets were noisy and full of activity.* ◇ *Economic activity has taken a downturn this year.* ◇ *Muscles contract and relax during physical activity.* **OPP** inactivity ❶ The opposite is **inactivity**: *periods of enforced inactivity and boredom*

action [U] (*rather informal*) exciting events: *I like films with plenty of action.* ◇ *New York is where the action is.*

rush [sing.] a situation in which people are very busy and there is a lot of activity: *Book now and avoid the last-minute rush.* ◇ *The evening rush was just starting.* ❶ **Rush** is usually used after an adjective for a particular time when there is a lot of activity.

bustle /ˈbʌsl/ [U] busy and noisy activity of a lot of people in one place: *Do you enjoy the hustle and bustle of city life?* See also **bustling** → CROWDED

actor noun

actor · actress · performer · artist · comedian · entertainer · movie/film star · artiste
These are all words for a person whose job is to entertain an audience.

PATTERNS AND COLLOCATIONS
▸ a **young** actor / actress / performer / artist / comedian / entertainer / artiste
▸ a **famous** actor / actress / performer / artist / comedian / entertainer / movie star
▸ a / an **talented** / **aspiring** actor / actress / performer / artist / comedian / entertainer

actor [C] a person who performs on the stage, on television or in films, especially as a profession: *She is one of the country's leading actors.* See also **act** → PLAY *verb 2*

actress /ˈæktrəs/ [C] a female actor: *In 1940 he married actress Jane Wyman.*

> **NOTE** ACTOR OR ACTRESS? An **actor** can be a man or a woman. Using **actor** for a woman emphasizes professional acting abilities. Using **actress** emphasizes that the actor is a woman.

performer [C] a person who performs for an audience, for example in a show or concert: *By the age of 15, Allan had become an experienced circus performer.* See also **perform** → PLAY *verb 2*

artist [C] a performer, especially a musician or actor: *After the band broke up, Joe relaunched his career as a solo artist.* ◇ *A mime artist's movements must be clear to the audience.*

comedian /kəˈmiːdiən/ [C] a person whose job is making people laugh by telling jokes or funny stories: *Peter was in his thirties when he decided to be a stand-up comedian.* ❶ **Stand-up comedy** consists of one person standing in front of an audience and telling jokes.

entertainer [C] a person whose job is amusing people, for example, by singing, telling jokes or dancing: *Covent Garden is famous for its street entertainers.* See also **entertain** → ENTERTAIN

ˈmovie star (*especially AmE*) (*BrE usually* **ˈfilm star**) [C] a male or female actor who is famous for being in films: *I always wanted to be a movie star, even when I was a child.*

artiste /ɑːˈtiːst; *AmE* ɑːrˈtiːst/ [C] (*especially BrE, sometimes ironic*) a skilled entertainer, especially a singer, dancer or actor: *He was a true artiste: sensitive, dramatic and tragic.*

addictive adj. See also the entry for REGULAR

addictive · obsessive · compulsive · obsessional · consuming
These words all describe behaviour that is difficult or impossible to stop or control.

PATTERNS AND COLLOCATIONS
▸ obsessive / compulsive / obsessional **about** sth
▸ the **addictive** / obsessive / compulsive **nature** of sth
▸ addictive / obsessive / compulsive / obsessional **behaviour**
▸ an obsessive / a compulsive / a consuming **need** / **desire**
▸ **almost** obsessive / compulsive / obsessional

addictive /əˈdɪktɪv/ (of a drug or activity) making you want or enjoy it more and more and therefore difficult to give up: *Tobacco is highly addictive.* ◇ *The game is very addictive.* ◇ *Some people have an addictive personality* (= they easily get addicted to things). See also **addict** → FAN

obsessive /əbˈsesɪv/ (*disapproving*) thinking too much about one particular person or thing; showing this: *An obsessive fan was making the singer's life a misery.* ◇ *He's becoming more and more obsessive about punctuality.* ◇ *The play is about obsessive jealousy.*
▸ **obsessively** *adv.*: *She was obsessively tidy.*

compulsive /kəmˈpʌlsɪv/ (of behaviour) difficult to stop or control: *His family had been unaware of his compulsive gambling.*
▸ **compulsively** *adv.*: *He was compulsively generous.*

obsessional /əbˈseʃənl/ (*formal or medical*) obsessive: *She is obsessional about cleanliness.* ◇ *They were receiving medical treatment for obsessional symptoms.*

> **NOTE** OBSESSIVE OR OBSESSIONAL? Both these words can describe people or behaviour but **obsessional** is more usual in medical contexts.

consuming /kənˈsjuːmɪŋ; *AmE* -ˈsuː-/ [only before noun] (of a feeling or interest) so strong or important that it takes up all your time and energy: *They both had a consuming interest in cricket.* ◇ *Theatre was his consuming passion.*

adequate adj. See also the entries for DECENT, FINE and GOOD 2

adequate · not bad · reasonable · all right · acceptable
These words all describe sth that is good enough, but not very good.

PATTERNS AND COLLOCATIONS
▸ to be adequate / not bad / reasonable / all right / acceptable **for** sb / sth
▸ an adequate / a reasonable / an acceptable **level** / **degree** / **standard** of sth

▸ adequate / reasonable / acceptable **provision** for sb / sth
▸ **just (about)** adequate / all right / acceptable
▸ **barely / scarcely** adequate / acceptable

adequate /ˈædɪkwət/ enough in quantity or good enough in quality for a particular purpose or need: *They'll need an adequate supply of hot water.* ◇ *The room was small but adequate.* ◇ *The space available is not adequate for our needs.* ◇ *The training given should be adequate to meet the future needs of the industry.* **OPP** inadequate → INADEQUATE
▸ **adequately** adv.: *Are you adequately insured?*

not 'bad (*informal*, *spoken*) fairly good; better than you expected: *'How are you?' 'Not too bad.'* ◇ *That wasn't bad for a first attempt.*

reasonable fairly good, but not very good: *Most people here have a reasonable standard of living.* ◇ *The hotel was reasonable, I suppose.* See also **reasonably** → QUITE 1

all 'right [not before noun] only just good enough: *Your work is all right, but you could do better.*

acceptable not very good, but good enough: *The food was acceptable, but no more.*

adjust *verb* See also the entry for CHANGE *verb* 1

adjust · modify · amend · revise · qualify
These words all mean to change sth, often slightly, in order to make it better suited to a situation.

PATTERNS AND COLLOCATIONS
▸ to adjust / modify / revise your **ideas**
▸ to modify / amend / revise a **text** / **constitution**
▸ to modify / amend / qualify a **statement**
▸ to adjust / modify / amend / revise sth **slightly**
▸ to modify / amend / revise / qualify sth **heavily**
▸ to adjust / modify / revise sth **constantly**

adjust [T] to change sth slightly to make it more suitable for a new set of conditions or to make it work better: *This button is for adjusting the volume.* ◇ *Adjust your language to the age of your audience.* ◇ *The brakes need to be adjusted.* See also **adjustment** → CHANGE *noun* 2, **adjustable** → FLEXIBLE 1

modify /ˈmɒdɪfaɪ; AmE ˈmɑːd-/ [T] (*rather formal*) to change sth slightly, especially in order to make it more suitable for a particular purpose: *Patients are taught how to modify their diet.* ◇ *We found it cheaper to modify existing equipment rather than buy new.* See also **adapt** → CHANGE *verb* 1, **modification** → CHANGE *noun* 2

NOTE ADJUST OR MODIFY? **Adjust** is used especially to talk about changing the setting on a piece of equipment: *to adjust the setting/dial/volume/speed/angle/level/tension/clock/sails/straps.* It is often a continuous process, in response to changing conditions: *to adjust sth continually/constantly/accordingly.* **Modify** is used especially to talk about making a more permanent change to a piece of equipment in order to make it perform a new function. You can also either **adjust** or **modify** your *behaviour* or *language* according to the situation you find yourself in.

amend /əˈmend/ [T] (*rather formal*) to change a law, document or statement slightly in order to correct a mistake or to improve it: *He asked to see the amended version.* ◇ *The law has been amended to read as follows:...* See also **amendment** → CHANGE *noun* 2

revise [T] to change your opinions or plans, for example because of sth you have learned: *I can see I will have to revise my opinions of his abilities now.* ◇ *The government may need to revise its policy in the light of this report.* ❶ You can **revise** your *opinion*, *ideas* or a *decision*, as well as *plans* or *arrangements*. An official body may **revise** the *constitution*, a *policy*, a *law* or *guidelines*. In business a person may need to **revise** a *draft*, an *estimate*, *figures* or a *proposal.* See also **revise** → REVISE, **revision** → CHANGE *noun* 2

qualify [T] (*rather formal*) to add sth to a previous statement to make the meaning less strong or less general: *I want to qualify what I said earlier — I didn't mean he couldn't do the job, only that he would need supervision.* See also **qualification** → CONDITION

admiration *noun*

admiration · respect · awe · recognition · esteem · appreciation
These are all words for the good feeling you have towards sb/sth because you are impressed by their/its good qualities or achievements.

respect   admiration   awe
recognition
esteem
appreciation

PATTERNS AND COLLOCATIONS
▸ admiration / respect / recognition **for** sb
▸ to do sth **in** admiration / awe / recognition / appreciation
▸ **great** admiration / respect / awe / esteem / appreciation
▸ **deep** / **genuine** admiration / respect / appreciation
▸ **mutual** admiration / respect / esteem / appreciation
▸ **grudging** admiration / respect / recognition
▸ to **have** a lot of, no, etc. admiration / respect / appreciation (for sb / sth)
▸ to **show** your admiration / respect / appreciation (for sb / sth)
▸ to **win** / **gain** / **deserve** admiration / respect / recognition
▸ to **earn** respect / recognition / esteem
▸ to **inspire** admiration / respect / awe

admiration [U] a feeling of liking sb/sth and being impressed by their/its good qualities or achievements: *I have great admiration for her as a writer.* ◇ *We watched in admiration as the gymnasts practised their routines.* See also **admire** → RESPECT *verb*, **admiring** → GOOD 6

respect [U, sing.] the high opinion you have of sb/sth because of their good qualities or achievements: *I have the greatest respect for your brother.* ◇ *A two-minute silence was held as a mark of respect.* See also **respect** → RESPECT *verb*

NOTE ADMIRATION OR RESPECT? **Admiration** suggests that you like sb and would like to be like them: *He was full of admiration for the way she never lost her patience.* You can have **respect** for sb even though you do not like them very much: *She had a lot of respect for him as an actor, but didn't like the way he treated other members of the cast.* **Admiration** is only concerned with the feeling you have; **respect** can refer to the polite way you behave towards sb because of your feelings: *I have nothing but admiration/respect for the winning team.* ◇ *He always treated me with respect.* ◇ ~~He always treated me with admiration.~~

awe /ɔː/ [U] a feeling of great respect and slight fear because you are very impressed by sb/sth: *They gazed in awe at the beauty of the scene.* ◇ *While Diana was in awe of* (= she admired and was slightly afraid of) *her grandfather, she adored her grandmother.* See also **be/ stand in awe of sb** → RESPECT *verb*

recognition [U] public praise and respect for sb's work or actions: *She gained only minimal recognition for her work.* ◇ *He received the award in recognition of his success over the past year.*

esteem /ɪˈstiːm/ [U] (*formal*) a feeling of respect and admiration for sb: *She is held in high esteem by her colleagues.* See also **esteem** → RESPECT *verb*, **self-esteem** → DIGNITY

appreciation /əˌpriːʃiˈeɪʃn/ [U] the good feeling that you have when you recognize and enjoy the good qualities of sb/sth: *She shows little appreciation of good music.* ◇ *The crowd murmured in appreciation.* See also **appreciate** → APPRECIATE

admit verb
1 Admit it! You were terrified!
2 She admitted to the theft.

1 admit · acknowledge · recognize · concede · confess · grant
These words all mean to agree, often unwillingly, that sth is true.

▸ to admit / confess **to sth**
▸ to admit / concede / confess sth **to sb**
▸ to admit / acknowledge / recognize / concede / confess / grant **that...**
▸ It is / was (generally) admitted / acknowledged / recognized / conceded / granted **that...**
▸ to admit / acknowledge / recognize **the truth**
▸ to admit / confess your **mistakes / ignorance**
▸ you **must** admit / acknowledge / recognize / concede / confess / grant sth
▸ to admit / acknowledge / concede / confess / grant sth **freely / readily**
▸ to admit / acknowledge / concede / confess sth **grudgingly / privately / reluctantly**

admit (-tt-) [I, T] to agree, often unwillingly, that sth is true: *She admits to being strict with her children. ◇ It was a stupid thing to do, I admit. ◇ Admit it! You were terrified! ◇ Why don't you just **admit defeat** (= recognize that you cannot do sth and let sb else try)? ◇ You must admit that it all sounds very strange. ◇ The appointment is now generally admitted to have been a mistake.* ❶ This pattern is only used in the passive.
acknowledge /ək'nɒlɪdʒ; *AmE* ək'nɑːl-/ [T] (*rather formal*) to accept that sth exists, is true or has happened: *She refuses to acknowledge the need for reform. ◇ He did not acknowledge that he had done anything wrong. ◇ It is generally acknowledged to be true.*
recognize (*BrE also* **-ise**) [T] to admit or be aware that sth exists or is true: *They recognized the need to take the problem seriously. ◇ Drugs were not **recognized as** a problem then. ◇ Nobody recognized how urgent the situation was.*
▸ **recognition** *noun* [sing., U]: *a growing recognition that older people have potential too ◇ There is general recognition of the urgent need for reform.*
concede /kən'siːd/ [T] (*rather formal*) to admit, often unwillingly, that sth is true or logical: *He was forced to concede (that) there might be difficulties. ◇ He reluctantly conceded the point to me.*

> **NOTE** **ADMIT** OR **CONCEDE?** When sb **admits** sth, they are usually agreeing that sth which is generally considered bad or wrong is true or has happened, especially when it relates to their own actions. When sb **concedes** sth, they are usually accepting, unwillingly, that any particular fact or statement is true or logical.

confess [T, I] (*rather formal*) to admit sth that you feel ashamed or embarrassed about: *She was reluctant to confess her ignorance. ◇ I must confess to knowing nothing about computers.*
grant [T] to admit that a statement or claim is true, usually while denying that a greater claim is also true: *She's a smart woman, I grant you, but she's no genius. ◇ Granted, he is a beginner, but he should know the basic rules.* ❶ **Grant** is most commonly used in the expressions *I/I'll grant you (that)... and Granted...* (at the beginning of a sentence). You often use *but* in the second part of a sentence containing **grant**.

2 admit · confess · own up
These words all mean to say that you have done sth wrong or illegal.

▸ to admit / confess / own up **to sth**
▸ to admit / confess / own up **that...**

admit (-tt-) [I, T] to say that you have done sth wrong or illegal, especially when sb asks you: *She refused to admit to the other charges. ◇ He freely admitted that he had taken bribes. ◇ He refused to **admit his guilt**. ◇ (BrE) She admitted theft. ◇ (especially AmE) She admitted to the theft.* **OPP** **deny** → DENY
▸ **admission** /əd'mɪʃn/ *noun* [C]: *an admission of guilt ◇ He is a thief **by his own admission** (= he has admitted it).*
confess /kən'fes/ [I, T] to admit, especially formally or to the police, that you have done sth wrong or illegal: *He confessed that he had stolen the money. ◇ We persuaded her to confess her crime. ◇ After hours of questioning, the suspect confessed.*
▸ **confession** /kən'feʃn/ *noun* [C, U]: *I have a confession to make – I lied about my age. ◇ His confession was extracted under torture.*
,own 'up *phrasal verb* (*rather informal*) to admit that you are responsible for sth bad or wrong, especially sth that is not very serious: *I'm still waiting for someone to own up to the breakages.*

adult adj.

adult · mature · grown · grown-up
These words all describe a person or animal that is fully developed physically or mentally.

▸ to be mature / grown-up **about** sth
▸ an adult / a mature / a grown **man / woman**
▸ a mature / grown-up **child / boy / girl**
▸ **fully** mature / grown

adult fully grown or developed; behaving in an intelligent and responsible way; typical of what is expected of an adult: *adult monkeys ◇ the adult population ◇ preparing young people for adult life ◇ When my parents split up, it was all very adult and open.* **OPP** **juvenile** → YOUNG, **childish** → CHILDISH
▸ **adult** *noun* [C]: *Children must be accompanied by an adult. ◇ The fish return to the river as adults in order to breed. ◇ Why can't you two act like civilized adults?* **OPP** **child, minor** → CHILD
mature (of a child or young person) behaving in a sensible way, like an adult; (of a person, tree, bird or animal) fully grown and developed: *Jane is very mature for her age. ◇ He shows a mature and sensible attitude. ◇ a mature oak/eagle/elephant* **OPP** **immature** → CHILDISH, See also **mature** → OLD 2, **sensible** → WISE
▸ **maturity** *noun* [U]: *He has maturity beyond his years.* **OPP** **immaturity**

> **NOTE** **ADULT** OR **MATURE?** **Adult** most often refers to physical development; **mature** most often refers to mental development: *an adult male ◇ adult education* (= for adults, not children) *◇ a mature conversation/ attitude* (= sensible, not childish). **Adult** is also, but less often, used to describe mental development, and **mature** to describe physical development: *She dealt with it in a very adult way* (= in a sensible way, as an adult should). *◇ a mature fish* (= fully grown).

grown [only before noun] (of a person) mentally and physically an adult: *It's pathetic that grown men have to resort to violence like this. ◇ The little girl she remembered was now a grown woman.*
,grown-'up (of a person) mentally and physically an adult; suitable for or typical of an adult: *What do you want to be when you're grown-up? ◇ She has a grown-up son.*
▸ **'grown-up** *noun* [C]: *If you're good you can eat with the grown-ups.* **OPP** **child** → CHILD ❶ The word **grown-up** is often used by and to children: *Wow, look at you! You look so grown-up! ◇ Ask a grown-up to help you cut this shape out.*

advertise *verb* See the Topic Map for THE MEDIA on p.900

advertise · market · promote · push · merchandise · hype · plug

These words all mean to do sth to encourage people to buy or use a product or service, or to accept a new idea.

PATTERNS AND COLLOCATIONS
► to advertise/market/promote/push/merchandise/hype/plug sth **as** sth
► to advertise/market/promote/merchandise sth **through** sth
► to advertise/market sth **to** sb
► to advertise/market/promote/push/merchandise/hype/plug a **product**
► to advertise/market/promote/hype/plug a/an **book**/**film**/ **movie**/**CD**/**album**
► to advertise/market/promote a **service**
► to market/promote/push an **idea**
► to advertise/market/promote/hype sth **heavily**

advertise [I, T] to tell the public about a product or service in order to encourage people to buy or use it: *If you want to attract more customers, try advertising in the local paper.* ◊ *The cruise was advertised as the 'journey of a lifetime'.* See also **advertise** → PUBLISH 1
► **advertising** *noun* [U]: *She's hoping to make a career in advertising.*

market [T] to advertise and offer a product for sale; to present a product, service or idea in a particular way and make people want to buy, use or accept it: *It is marketed as a low-alcohol wine.* ◊ *School meals need to be marketed to children in the same way as other food.*
► **marketing** *noun* [U]: *He works in* **sales and market-ing.**

promote [T] to help sell a product or service, or make an idea more popular, by advertising it or offering it at a special price: *The band has gone on tour to promote their new album.* ◊ *The area is being promoted as a tourist destination.*

push [T] (*rather informal*) to try hard to persuade people to accept a new idea or buy a new product: *She didn't want to push the point any further at that moment.* ◊ *Sales promotion is designed to push certain products.*

merchandise /'mɜːtʃəndaɪs; -daɪz; *AmE* 'mɜːrtʃ-/ [T] (*business*) to advertise and offer a product for sale, often a product connected with a popular film, person or event: *She works with companies that want to make or merchandise products related to the company's films.*

hype /haɪp/ [T] (*informal, disapproving*) to advertise sth a lot and exaggerate its good qualities, in order to get a lot of public attention for it: *This week his much hyped new movie opens in London.*

plug (-gg-) [T] (*informal*) to give praise or attention to a new book, film, CD, etc. in order to encourage people to buy it or see it: *She came on the show to plug her latest album.*

advertisement *noun* See the Topic Map for THE MEDIA on p.900

advertisement · publicity · ad · commercial · promotion · advert · trailer · blurb · plug

These are all words for a notice, picture or film telling people about a product, job or service.

PATTERNS AND COLLOCATIONS
► an advertisement/publicity/an ad/a commercial/a promotion/an advert/a trailer/a blurb/a plug **for** sth
► (a) **TV**/**television**/**radio**/**cinema** advertisement/ad/ commercial/promotion/advert
► to **run**/**show** an advertisement/an ad/a commercial/an advert/a trailer
► to **put**/**place**/**take out** an advertisement/ad/advert
► the advertisement/ad/commercial/advert/blurb **says**/**states**/ **claims**...
► the advertisement/ad/commercial/advert/trailer **appears**/ **shows** sth/**features** sb/sth

advertisement [C, U] a notice, picture or film telling people about a product, job or service; an example of sth that shows its good qualities; the act of advertising sth and making it public: *Put an advertisement in the local paper to sell your car.* ◊ *Dirty streets and homelessness are no advertisement for a prosperous society.* ◊ *We are employing an assistant to help with the advertisement of the group's activities.*

publicity [U] the business of attracting the attention of the public to sb/sth such as a company, book, film, film star or product; the things that are done to attract attention: *She works in publicity.* ◊ *There has been a lot of advance publicity for her new film.* ◊ *publicity material* ◊ *a publicity campaign* ◊ *The band dressed up as the Beatles as a* **publicity stunt.**

ad [C] (*informal*) a notice, picture or film telling people about a product, job or service: *We put an ad in the local paper.* ◊ *They've produced an ad for a new chocolate bar.*

commercial [C] an advertisement on television or the radio: *The company has made commercials for leading sportswear manufacturers.* ◊ *a commercial break* (= a time during or between shows when advertisements are broadcast)

promotion /prə'məʊʃn; *AmE* -'moʊʃn/ [C, U] a set of advertisements for a particular product or service; activities done in order to increase the sales of a product or service: *We are doing a special promotion of Chilean wines.* ◊ *Her job is mainly concerned with sales and promotion.*

advert [C] (*BrE, informal*) an advertisement: *I never watch the adverts on TV.*

trailer [C] (*especially BrE*) a series of short scenes from a film or television programme, shown in advance to advertise it: *The review said that if you've seen the trailer, you needn't bother watching this film.*

blurb [C] a short description of a book, film, etc., written by the people who have produced it, that is intended to attract your attention and make you want to buy it: *The blurb says that this is Tarantino's greatest movie.* ❶ The **blurb** is usually written on the cover or case of the book, DVD, or other product that it describes.

plug [C] (*informal*) praise or attention that sb gives to a new book, film, etc. in order to encourage people to buy or see it: *He managed to get in a plug for his new book.*

advice *noun*

advice · counselling · tip · guidance

These are all words for an opinion or suggestion about what sb should do in a particular situation.

PATTERNS AND COLLOCATIONS
► advice/counselling/tips/guidance **on** sth
► advice/counselling/tips **for** sb/sth
► advice/guidance **about** sth
► **helpful**/**practical**/**useful**/**valuable**/**general** advice/tips/ guidance
► **professional** advice/counselling/tips/guidance
► **spiritual** advice/counselling/guidance
► to **give** sb advice/counselling/a tip/guidance
► to **offer**/**provide**/**seek** advice/counselling/guidance

advice [U] an opinion about what sb should do in a particular situation: *Can you give me some advice on where to buy good maps?* ◊ *We were advised to seek* **legal advice.** ◊ *Let me give you a* **piece of advice.** ◊ *Take my advice — don't get married.* ◊ *I chose it* **on his advice.** ◊ *Permission was given* **against the advice** *of the planning officers.* ❶ **Advice** is usually given by sb who has greater experience or authority than the person they are advising. If you say *take my advice* to sb who is older or more experienced than you, they may be offended. See also **advise** → RECOMMEND 1, **recommendation** → EN-DORSEMENT

counselling (*BrE*) (*AmE* **counseling**) /ˈkaʊnsəlɪŋ/ [U] professional advice about what sb should do to deal with a personal or emotional problem: *Many of the victims of the tragedy still need counselling.*

tip [C] (*rather informal*) a small piece of practical advice; a secret or expert piece of advice about what the result of sth, such as a horse race, is likely to be: *There are lots of useful tips on how to save money.* ◇ *He said he'd been given a **hot tip** for that afternoon's race.*

guidance /ˈgaɪdns/ [U] help or advice about how to do sth or about how to deal with problems, especially given by sb older or with more experience: *Activities take place **under the guidance of** an experienced tutor.* ◇ *The handbook gives helpful guidance on writing articles.*

adviser *noun*

adviser · consultant · counsellor · mentor · guide
These are all words for a person who gives advice or help to sb either personally or because it is their job.

PATTERNS AND COLLOCATIONS
▸ an adviser / a consultant / a mentor **to** sb
▸ an adviser / a consultant **on** sth
▸ a **political** adviser / consultant / mentor
▸ a **spiritual** adviser / counsellor / mentor / guide
▸ to **act as** an adviser / a consultant / a mentor / a guide

adviser (also *less frequent* **advisor**) [C] a person who gives advice, especially sb who knows a lot about a particular subject: *He works as an adviser on environmental issues.* ◇ *As your legal adviser, it is my duty to warn you against it.* See also **aide** → ASSISTANT

consultant /kənˈsʌltənt/ [C] a person who knows a lot about a particular subject and is paid by a company to give advice about it: *The professor also acted as a consultant to the Department of Education.* ◇ *Management consultants were brought in to sort out the mess.*

> **NOTE** ADVISER OR CONSULTANT? An **adviser** may be employed permanently by a company, government, politician, etc. or may be an independent person who is brought in to give advice on a particular issue or project. **Consultants** give advice in a particular area to businesses, politicians, etc. and are not usually employed permanently by the person or company they give advice to but often work for a **consultancy** firm.

counsellor (*especially BrE*) (*AmE usually* **counselor**) [C] a person who has been trained to help people deal with problems, especially personal problems: *The centre is staffed by specially trained counsellors.* ◇ (*BrE*) *Have you thought of talking to a **marriage guidance counsellor**?* ◇ (*AmE*) *a **marriage counselor***

mentor /ˈmentɔː(r)/ [C] an experienced person who advises and helps sb with less experience over a period of time: *The agent was a friend and mentor to many young artists.* See also **guru** → EXPERT, **mentoring** → EDUCATION

guide [C] a person who advises you on how to live and behave: *His sister had been his guide, counsellor and friend.*

advocate *noun* See also the entries for ACTIVIST and SUPPORTER

advocate · proponent · lobbyist · champion · exponent · promoter
These are all words for a person who supports an idea and tries to persuade others that it is good or important.

PATTERNS AND COLLOCATIONS
▸ an advocate / a lobbyist / a champion **for** sth
▸ a **leading** / **great** advocate / proponent / champion / exponent / promoter
▸ a / the **principal** / **main** advocate / proponent / exponent / promoter
▸ an **enthusiastic** advocate / proponent / exponent
▸ an **outspoken** advocate / proponent / champion
▸ a **powerful** advocate / exponent / promoter

▸ a / the **chief** advocate / proponent / exponent / promoter
▸ a **prominent** advocate / lobbyist / champion
▸ advocates / proponents / lobbyists **argue** sth

advocate /ˈædvəkət/ [C] a person who supports or speaks in favour of sb or of a public plan or action: *He is one of the leading advocates for a more modern style of worship.* ◇ *She became a **firm advocate** of overseas ventures.*

proponent /prəˈpəʊnənt; *AmE* -ˈpoʊ-/ [C] (*rather formal*) a person who supports and speaks in favour of an idea or course of action: *She is among the most outspoken proponents of the plan.* **OPP** **opponent** → PROTESTER

lobbyist /ˈlɒbiɪst; *AmE* ˈlɑːbi-/ [C] a person who tries to influence politicians or the government and persuade them to support an idea or course of action: *The plan has caused uproar among environmental lobbyists.*

champion [C] a person who fights for, or speaks in support of, a group of people or a belief: *She was a champion of the poor all her life.*

exponent /ɪkˈspəʊnənt; *AmE* -ˈspoʊ-/ [C] (*rather formal*) a person who supports an idea, belief or theory and tries to explain it to others and persuade them that it is good: *Huxley was an exponent of Darwin's theory of evolution.*

promoter /prəˈməʊtə(r); *AmE* -ˈmoʊ-/ [C] a person who tries to persuade others about the value or importance of sth: *She is a leading promoter of European integration.*

affect *verb* See also the entry for INFLUENCE

affect · involve · concern · influence · work · impact · take (a) hold · leave a mark · act · colour
These words all mean to have an effect on sb/sth.

PATTERNS AND COLLOCATIONS
▸ to impact / act / leave a mark **on** sth
▸ to be involved / concerned **in** sth
▸ to affect / influence **what** happens
▸ to affect / influence **how** / **why** / **when** / **where** sth happens
▸ to affect / influence / colour sb's **judgement** / **attitude**
▸ to **directly** / **indirectly** affect / involve / concern / influence / impact on / act on sb / sth
▸ to **adversely** / **inevitably** affect / influence / impact on sth

affect [T, *often passive*] to have an effect on sb/sth: *How will these changes affect us?* ◇ *Your opinions will not affect my decision.* ◇ *The south of the country was worst affected by the drought.* ◇ *The type of audience will affect what you say and how you say it.* See also **effect** → EFFECT *noun*, **bias** → INFLUENCE *verb*

involve [T] to be a situation, event or activity that sb takes part in or is affected by: *There was a serious incident involving a group of youths.* ◇ *How many vehicles were involved in the crash?*

concern [T, *often passive*] (*rather formal*) (of an issue, situation or event) to involve sb because they have a particular reason to be interested in it or a particular part to play in it: *Don't interfere in what doesn't concern you.* ◇ *The meetings were often embarrassing for **all concerned**.* ◇ *The individuals concerned will have some explaining to do.*

> **NOTE** INVOLVE OR CONCERN? **Involve** suggests a greater degree of physical activity, when sb is actually doing sth or sth happens to them: ~~an incident concerning a group of youths~~ ◇ ~~the vehicles concerned in the crash~~. **Concern** suggests a greater degree of interest or responsibility, when an issue particularly affects sb, or a situation is caused by sb.

influence [T] to have an effect on a particular situation and the way it develops: *A number of social factors influence life expectancy.* ◇ *The local climate is influenced by the Gulf Stream.* ◇ *At college she met the two people who most influenced her career.* See also **influence** → INFLUENCE *verb*, **influence** → EFFECT *noun*

work [I] (*always used with an adverb or preposition*) to have a particular effect on sb/sth, especially either a positive or negative effect: *Your age can **work against** you in this job.* ◇ *Speaking Italian should **work in his favour**.*

impact /'ɪmpækt/ [I, T] (*especially journalism or business*) to have an effect on sth, especially a bad one: *The border dispute could impact on the work of aid agencies.* ◇ *The company's performance was impacted by the high value of the pound.* See also **impact** → EFFECT *noun*

take (a) 'hold *idiom* to begin to have a strong effect on sth or have complete control over sb/sth; to become very strong: *Panic took hold of him and he couldn't move.* ◇ *It was in the sixties that the cult of the teenager first took hold.*

leave your/its/a 'mark *idiom* to have an effect on sb/sth, especially a bad one, that lasts for a long time: *Such a traumatic experience is bound to leave its mark.*

act [I] (especially of a drug, chemical or physical force) to have a physical effect on sth: *Alcohol acts quickly on the brain.* ◇ *It took a few minutes for the drug to act.* See also **action** → EFFECT *noun*

colour (*BrE*) (*AmE* **color**) [T] to have an effect on sth, especially sb's opinion or attitude, often in a negative way: *The experience moulded and coloured her whole life.* ◇ *Don't let your judgement be coloured by personal feelings.*

afraid *adj.* See also the entry for WORRIED

---

afraid · frightened · scared · terrified · alarmed · fearful · paranoid · intimidated · startled · petrified
These words all describe feeling or showing fear.

---

alarmed	afraid	terrified	petrified
intimidated	frightened		
startled	scared		
	fearful		
	paranoid		

PATTERNS AND COLLOCATIONS
▸ frightened / scared / fearful / paranoid **about** sth
▸ afraid / frightened / scared / terrified / fearful / petrified **of** sb/sth
▸ terrified / alarmed / intimidated / startled **by** sb/sth
▸ afraid / frightened **for** sb
▸ afraid / frightened / scared / terrified / fearful / petrified **that**…
▸ afraid / frightened / scared **to do** sth
▶ **Don't be** afraid / frightened / scared / alarmed / intimidated.
▶ **There's no need to be** afraid / frightened / scared / alarmed / paranoid / intimidated.
▸ to **feel** afraid / frightened / scared / alarmed / paranoid / terrified / petrified
▸ to **look** afraid / frightened / scared / terrified / alarmed / startled / petrified
▸ to **sound** afraid / frightened / scared / terrified / alarmed
▸ to **get** frightened / scared / paranoid
▸ frightened / scared / terrified **out of your wits**
▸ frightened / scared **to death**

afraid [not before noun] feeling fear; worried that sth bad might happen: *There's nothing to be afraid of.* ◇ *Aren't you afraid (that) you'll fall?* ◇ *Don't be afraid to ask if you don't understand.* **OPP** **unafraid** ❶ Unafraid is rather formal and only used in written English; it is much more frequent to say **not afraid**: *I'm not afraid of you!* ◇ (*rather formal, written*) *He felt calm and unafraid.*

frightened feeling fear; worried that sth bad might happen: *a frightened child* ◇ *She was frightened that the glass would break.* ◇ *I'm frightened for him* (= for example, that he will be hurt). See also **frighten** → FRIGHTEN, **frightening** → FRIGHTENING, **fright** → FEAR *noun*

scared (*rather informal*) feeling fear; worried that sth bad might happen: *The thieves got scared and ran away.* ◇ *a very scared face/expression* See also **scare** → FRIGHTEN, **scary** → FRIGHTENING

NOTE **AFRAID, FRIGHTENED** OR **SCARED**? **Scared** is more informal, more common in speech, and often describes small fears. **Afraid** cannot come before a noun: ~~an afraid child~~ It can only take the preposition *of*, not *about*. If you are *afraid/frightened/scared of sb/sth/ doing sth* or *afraid/frightened/scared to do sth,*

you think you are in danger of being hurt or suffering in some way. If you are *frightened/scared about sth/doing sth*, it is less a fear for your personal safety and more a worry that sth unpleasant might happen: *frightened about the exam tomorrow* ◇ ~~frightened of the exam tomorrow~~.

terrified /'terɪfaɪd/ very frightened: *I was terrified (that) she wouldn't come.* ◇ *She looked at him with wide, terrified eyes.* See also **terror** → FEAR *noun*, **terrify** → FRIGHTEN, **terrifying** → FRIGHTENING

alarmed [not before noun] afraid that sth dangerous or unpleasant might happen: *She was alarmed at the prospect of travelling alone.* See also **alarm** → FEAR *noun*, **alarm** → FRIGHTEN *verb*

fearful (*formal*) afraid and nervous: *Fearful of an attack, the government declared a state of emergency.* ◇ *Parents are ever fearful for their children.* **OPP** **fearless** → BRAVE, See also **fear** → FEAR *noun*
▶ **fearfully** *adv.*: *We watched fearfully.*

paranoid (*rather informal*) afraid or suspicious of other people and believing that they are trying to harm you, in a way that is not reasonable: *She's getting really paranoid about what other people say about her.* ◇ *You're just being paranoid.* See also **paranoia** → FEAR *noun*

intimidated [not before noun] (*rather formal*) feeling frightened and not confident in a particular situation: *We try to make sure children don't feel intimidated on their first day at school.* See also **intimidate** → THREATEN 1

startled suddenly frightened or surprised: *She looked at him with startled eyes.* ◇ *He seemed startled to see me.* See also **startle** → SURPRISE *verb*

petrified /'petrɪfaɪd/ extremely frightened, especially so that you cannot move or do anything: *I'm petrified of snakes.* ◇ *They were petrified with fear.*

be against sb/sth See the Topic Map for CONFLICT on p.896

---

against · hostile · opposed · resistant · antagonistic
These are all words that can be used when sb disagrees with sth and wants to stop or prevent it.

PATTERNS AND COLLOCATIONS
▸ hostile / opposed / resistant / antagonistic **to** sb / sth
▸ hostile / antagonistic **towards** sb / sth
▸ against / hostile to / opposed to / resistant to **the idea** of sth
▸ **strongly** against / hostile / opposed to sth
▸ **openly** / **bitterly** / **fiercely** hostile / opposed / antagonistic

be against sb/sth *phrase* [not before noun] opposing or disagreeing with sb/sth: *I'm strongly against animal testing.* ◇ *Are you for or against the death penalty?* ◇ *If you are not with us, you are against us.* **OPP** **for**

hostile /'hɒstaɪl; *AmE* 'hɑːstl; -taɪl/ *adj.* showing or feeling strong dislike for or opposition to sb/sth: *Many of the employees were hostile to the idea of change.* ◇ *The proposals have provoked a hostile response from opposition parties.* See also **hostility** → OPPOSITION

opposed *adj.* [not usually before noun] disagreeing strongly with sth and trying to stop or prevent it: *They are totally opposed to abortion.* **OPP** **in favour of sth** → IN FAVOUR, See also **opposition** → OPPOSITION

resistant /rɪ'zɪstənt/ *adj.* not liking sth and trying to stop it from affecting you: *Elderly people are not always resistant to change.* See also **resistance** → OPPOSITION

antagonistic /æn,tægə'nɪstɪk/ *adj.* (*formal*) showing or feeling strong dislike for or opposition to sb/sth, especially a whole class of people or set of ideas: *Marx saw these issues in terms of antagonistic class relationships.*

age *noun*

---

age · generation · age group · peer group
These are all words for the number of years that a person has lived, or a group of people who have lived for about the same number of years.

▸ the **younger** / **older** generation / age group
▸ people **of your own** age / generation
▸ people **of all** ages / generations / age groups

age [C, U] the number of years that a person has lived or a thing has existed; a particular period of a person's life: *He left school **at the age of** 18.* ◇ *children from 5–10 **years of age*** ◇ *When I was your age I was already married.* ◇ *He started playing the piano **at an early age**.* ◇ *She was beginning to **feel her age** (= feel that she was getting old).* ◇ *ways of calculating the age of the earth* ◇ *15 is an awkward age.* ◇ *It was only now, in **middle age**, that she was beginning to enjoy life.* ◇ *He died of **old age**.*

generation [C+sing./pl. *v.*, U] all the people who were born at about the same time; a single stage in the history of a family; a group of people of similar age involved in a particular activity: *The older generation tends to have more traditional views.* ◇ *My generation has grown up without the experience of a world war.* ◇ *I often wonder what **future generations** will make of our efforts.* ◇ *These stories were passed down from generation to generation.* ◇ *a first-/second-generation American (= a person whose family has lived in America for one/two generations)* ◇ *She has inspired a whole generation of fashion school graduates.* See also **generation** → PERIOD

'age group [C] people of a similar age or within a particular range of ages: *men in the older age group* ◇ *education for the 16–18 age group*

'peer group [C] a group of people of the same age or social status: *She gets on well with her peer group.* ◇ *He started smoking because of **peer-group pressure**.* See also **peer** → PEER

> **NOTE** GENERATION, AGE GROUP OR PEER GROUP? Your **generation** is people who are nearer your age than your parents' or your children's ages. Your **age group** may be a much narrower range of ages: **age group** is often used in official forms and figures, and the exact range of ages may be stated: ~~the 16–18 generation/peer group.~~ Your **peer group** includes the people of your own age that you actually know and are influenced by: ~~She gets on well with her generation/age group.~~

agent *noun*

agent · spy · mole · double agent
These are all words for a person who tries to get secret information about another country, organization or person.

▸ an agent / a spy / a double agent **for** sb
▸ a / an **enemy** / **foreign** / **government** agent / spy
▸ to **work** / **act** / **recruit** sb as an agent / a spy / a double agent

agent /'eɪdʒənt/ [C] a person who is used by a government to find out secret information about other countries or governments: *He would have made a good **secret agent** – a James Bond type.* ◇ *She was operating as an undercover agent in London.* ❶ When **agent** is used alone, without an adjective, the context must show that you are talking about sb who secretly gathers information: *He was convicted of acting as an agent for the Soviet Union.* If it is not clear from the context, an adjective such as *secret, undercover, intelligence, government, British* or *CIA* is necessary.

spy [C] a person who tries to get secret information about another country, organization, or person, especially sb who is employed by a government or the police: *He became a government spy during the war.* ◇ *Video spy cameras are being used in public places.*

> **NOTE** SPY OR AGENT? Spy covers a wider range of uses than **agent** or **secret agent**, as it can be used to talk about sb who is employed to get information about a person or organization, not just a country or government. **Spy** is also often used before another noun to

describe things that are used to spy on people *a spy satellite/camera/system/plane*. A *spy story/novel/thriller* is a book or a film about **spies**.

mole [C] (*especially journalism*) a person who works within an organization and secretly passes important information to another organization or country: *A police mole working inside the company had supplied them with the details.*

double 'agent [C] a person who is a spy for a particular country, and also for another country which is an enemy of the first one: *They couldn't prove it, but he was almost certainly a double agent.*

aggressive *adj.*

1 aggressive behaviour
2 an aggressive marketing campaign

---

1 See the Topic Map for CONFLICT on p.896
aggressive · hostile · militant · warlike
These words all describe sb/sth who is ready to fight or attack sb.

▸ aggressive / hostile **towards** sb / sth
▸ an aggressive / a hostile / a militant / a warlike **attitude**
▸ an aggressive / a hostile / a militant **person**
▸ a hostile / warlike **nation**
▸ aggressive / hostile **behaviour** / **feelings**
▸ **very** aggressive / hostile / militant / warlike

aggressive angry, and behaving in a threatening way; ready to attack: *He warned that his dog could be aggressive towards strangers.* ◇ *It is important at all times to discourage aggressive behaviour in young children.* See also **aggression** → TENSION
▸ **aggressively** *adv.*: *'What do you want?' she demanded aggressively.*

hostile /'hɒstaɪl; *AmE* 'hɑːstl; -taɪl/ unfriendly and ready to argue or fight: *The speaker got a very hostile reception from the audience.* ◇ *She was openly hostile towards her parents.* **OPP friendly** → FRIENDLY 2, See also **hostility** → TENSION

militant (*rather formal*) /'mɪlɪtənt/ using, or willing to use, force or strong pressure to achieve your aims, especially to achieve social or political change: *Militant groups have been blamed for a series of attacks in the region.*

warlike (*rather formal*) wanting to start wars or fight in them: *It is the most warlike nation on earth, and perhaps in all of history.* **OPP peace-loving** ❶ Peace-loving people prefer to live in peace and to avoid arguments and fighting: *peace-loving citizens*

---

2 aggressive · ambitious · competitive · assertive · pushy · forceful
These words all describe a person who behaves in a determined, confident way, trying hard to succeed or to express their opinions.

▸ aggressive / ambitious / competitive / assertive **in** sth
▸ aggressive / assertive / forceful **in doing** sth
▸ an aggressive / a competitive / an assertive / a forceful **approach** / **attitude** / **manner**
▸ an aggressive / a competitive / a pushy / a forceful **style**
▸ aggressive / competitive / assertive **behaviour**
▸ an aggressive / an ambitious / a competitive / an assertive / a forceful **person**
▸ ambitious / pushy / forceful **parents**

aggressive (*sometimes disapproving*) behaving in a very determined way in order to succeed or to get what you want: *I was put off by his aggressive sales pitch.* ◇ *We need to be more aggressive in our strategy.*
▸ **aggressively** *adv.*: *The products were aggressively promoted.*

ambitious /æmˈbɪʃəs/ determined to be successful, rich, powerful, etc: *She's a great student — dedicated, hard-working and ambitious.* ◇ *They became fiercely ambitious for the boy.* **OPP** **unambitious** ❶ Unambitious people are not interested in becoming successful, rich or powerful. See also **ambition** → AMBITION

competitive /kəmˈpetətɪv/ trying very hard to be better than others: *He has a strong competitive streak.*

assertive /əˈsɜːtɪv; AmE əˈsɜːrtɪv/ (*often approving*) expressing opinions or desires strongly and with confidence, so that people take notice: *Learn to be assertive and stand up for your rights.* ◇ *There was a new assertive foreign policy in the White House.* **OPP** **submissive** → PASSIVE, See also **assertiveness** → CONFIDENCE, **confident** → CONFIDENT
▸ **assertively** *adv*.: *You are taught to handle tricky situations assertively.*

pushy (*informal, disapproving*) trying hard to get what you want, especially in a way that seems rude: *What's the best way to get rid of a pushy salesman?*

forceful expressing opinions firmly or clearly in a way that persuades other people to believe them: *His mother was a forceful character and had a big influence on him.*
▸ **forcefully** *adv*.: *He argued his case forcefully.*

NOTE AGGRESSIVE, ASSERTIVE, PUSHY OR FORCEFUL? These words all describe a person's behaviour and attitude in trying to get what they want or to express their opinions. **Aggressive** and **pushy** are usually disapproving and often describe sb who is trying too hard and may appear rude. **Assertive** and **forceful** are more approving and describe sb who is strong and confident, but in a more respectful and appropriate way.

agree *verb*
1 'That's true,' she agreed.
2 agree to a proposal
3 agree a price

1 agree · concur
These words both mean to have the same opinion as sb, or to say that you do.

PATTERNS AND COLLOCATIONS
▸ to agree / concur **with** sb / sth
▸ to agree / concur **that**...
▸ to agree / concur **entirely / fully / strongly / wholeheartedly**
▸ to agree / concur with sb's **assessment / conclusion / idea / view**

agree [I] to have the same opinion as sb; to say that you have the same opinion: *I agree absolutely.* ◇ *They said she didn't look well and I had to agree.* ◇ *'That's true,' she agreed.* ◇ *He agreed with them about the need for change.* ◇ *I agree with that analysis of the situation.* ◇ *They all agree (that) the research is hard work.* ◇ *The two sides failed to agree on any of the proposals.* ❶ Agree can also be used in the form **be agreed**: [T] *Are we all agreed on this* (= do we all agree on this)*?* ◇ *It was agreed (that)* (= everyone agreed) *we should hold another meeting.* **OPP** **disagree** → DISAGREE

concur /kənˈkɜː(r)/ (-**rr**-) [I] (*formal*) to agree with sb's opinion; to say that you agree: *I therefore concur with the decision of the other judges.* ◇ *Historians have concurred in this view.* ❶ Concur is only used in formal debate or when reporting a formal debate. It is not used to express agreement about everyday matters: ~~They said she didn't look well and I had to concur.~~

2 agree · accept · approve · go along with sb/sth · consent · take sth on board · acquiesce
These words all mean to say that you will do what sb wants or that you will allow sth to happen.

PATTERNS AND COLLOCATIONS
▸ to agree / consent / acquiesce **to** sth
▸ to agree / consent **to do sth**
▸ to agree to / accept / approve / go along with / consent to a **plan / scheme / proposal**
▸ to agree to / accept / approve / go along with / acquiesce in a **decision**
▸ to agree to / accept / approve / consent to a **change**
▸ to agree to / accept / approve / take on board a **suggestion**
▸ to agree to / accept / approve a **request**
▸ to **meekly** accept / go along with sth / acquiesce

agree [I, T] to say that you will do what sb wants or that you will allow sth to happen; to officially accept a plan or request: *I asked for a pay rise and she agreed.* ◇ *Do you think he'll agree to their proposal?* ◇ *She agreed (that) we could finish early.* ◇ *He agreed to let me go early.* ◇ *Next year's budget has been agreed.* **OPP** **refuse** → REFUSE, See also **agreement** → APPROVAL

accept [T] to be satisfied with sth that has been done, decided or suggested: *They accepted the court's decision.* ◇ *He accepted all the changes we proposed.* ◇ *She won't accept advice from anyone.* See also **acceptance** → APPROVAL

approve [T] to officially agree to a plan, suggestion or request: *The committee unanimously approved the plan.* ◇ *His appointment has not been formally approved yet.* **OPP** **reject** → REFUSE, See also **approval** → APPROVAL

,go aˈlong with sb/sth *phrasal verb* (*rather informal*) to agree to sth that sb else has decided; to agree with sb else's ideas: *She just goes along with everything he suggests.* ◇ *I don't go along with her views on abortion.*

consent /kənˈsent/ [I] (*rather formal*) to agree to sth or give your permission for sth: *When she told them what she intended they readily consented.* ◇ *He reluctantly consented to his daughter's marriage.* See also **consent** → PERMISSION

take sth on ˈboard *idiom* (*rather informal*) to understand and accept an idea or suggestion: *I told him what I thought, but he didn't take my advice on board.*

acquiesce /ˌækwiˈes/ [I] (*formal*) to accept sth without arguing, even if you do not really agree with it: *Senior government figures must have acquiesced in the cover-up.* ◇ *She explained her plan and reluctantly he acquiesced.* See also **acquiescence** → APPROVAL

3 agree · negotiate · conclude · settle · hammer sth out · thrash sth out · broker · understand
These words all mean to arrange the final details of a plan or agreement.

PATTERNS AND COLLOCATIONS
▸ to agree / negotiate / conclude / settle / hammer out / thrash out / broker sth **with** sb
▸ to agree sth / negotiate sth / conclude sth / settle sth / hammer sth out / broker sth / be understood **between** A and B
▸ to agree / be understood **that**...
▸ to agree / negotiate / conclude / settle / hammer out / broker a **deal**
▸ to negotiate / conclude / hammer out / thrash out / broker an **agreement**
▸ to agree / negotiate / hammer out / thrash out / broker a **plan**
▸ to agree / negotiate / hammer out / broker a **compromise**
▸ to agree / negotiate / settle / hammer out / thrash out **the details of** sth
▸ to agree / negotiate / settle / thrash out **terms**
▸ to agree / negotiate / conclude / broker a **settlement / ceasefire**
▸ to agree / negotiate / conclude a **contract / truce / pact**

agree [T, I] to decide with sb else to do sth or have sth: *Have you agreed on a date?* ◇ *Can we agree a price?* ◇ *We agreed to meet on Thursday.* ◇ *We couldn't agree what to do.* ◇ *They left at ten, as agreed.*

negotiate /nɪˈɡəʊʃieɪt; AmE ˈɡoʊ-/ [T] to arrange or agree the details of sth by formal discussion: *Rents are individually negotiated between landlord and tenant.* ◇ *We successfully negotiated the release of the hostages.*

conclude /kənˈkluːd/ [T] (*rather formal*) to formally arrange the final details of an agreement with sb: *They concluded a treaty with Turkey.* ◇ *A trade agreement was concluded between the two countries.*

settle [T] to finally arrange the details of a plan or some business: *It's all settled — we're leaving on the nine o'clock plane.* ◇ *He had to settle his affairs* (= arrange all his personal business) *in Paris before he could return home.*

,hammer sth 'out *phrasal verb* (*rather informal*) to discuss a plan or idea until everyone agrees or a decision is made: *He failed to hammer out a deal with the team boss.*

,thrash sth 'out *phrasal verb* (*rather informal*) to discuss a situation or problem thoroughly until everyone agrees or a solution is found: *The details have not been thrashed out yet.*

broker [T] (*rather formal*) to arrange the details of an agreement, especially between different countries: *A peace plan was brokered by the UN.*

understand [T, usually passive] to agree sth with sb without it needing to be said: *I thought it was understood that my expenses would be paid.*

agreement *noun*

1 sign an agreement with sb
2 be in agreement with sb

---

1 See also the entry for CONTRACT

agreement · deal · settlement · arrangement · pact · bargain · understanding
These are all words for sth which two or more people or groups agree or promise.

PATTERNS AND COLLOCATIONS
▸ an agreement/a deal/a settlement/an arrangement/a pact/a bargain/an understanding **with** sb
▸ an agreement/a deal/an arrangement/a pact/a bargain/an understanding **between** sb and sb
▸ an agreement/a deal/a settlement/an arrangement/a pact/an understanding **on** sth
▸ an agreement/a deal/a settlement/an arrangement/an understanding **over** sth
▸ **under** an agreement/a deal/an arrangement/a pact
▸ an agreement/an arrangement/a pact/an understanding **that...**
▸ an agreement/an arrangement/a pact **to do sth**
▸ an **informal** agreement/arrangement/understanding
▸ a **political** agreement/deal/settlement/arrangement/pact/bargain
▸ a **financial** agreement/deal/settlement/arrangement/bargain
▸ to **have** an agreement/an arrangement/a pact/an understanding
▸ to **enter into** an agreement/a deal/an arrangement/a pact
▸ to **negotiate** an agreement/a deal/a settlement/an arrangement/a pact
▸ to **reach** an agreement/a deal/a settlement/an arrangement/an understanding
▸ to **make**/**sign** an agreement/a deal/a pact
▸ to **conclude** an agreement/a deal/a settlement/a pact

agreement [C] something that two or more people or groups agree should happen or be done: *An agreement was finally reached between management and employees.* ◇ *We are working towards a formal ceasefire agreement.* ◇ *The agreement will be legally binding.* ◇ *They had made a verbal agreement to sell.* ◇ *They had an agreement never to talk about work at home.*

deal [C] an agreement, especially in business, on particular conditions for doing or buying sth: *The unions were ready to **do a deal** over pay.* ◇ *The company expects to **close the deal** (= finish making it) in the first quarter of next year.* ◇ *The **deal fell through** (= no agreement was reached).* ◇ *I got **a good deal** on the car (= a good price).* ◇ (*spoken*) *It's a deal! (= I agree to your terms).* ◇ *This is **the deal** (= this is what we have agreed and are going to do).* See also **do a deal** → NEGOTIATE

settlement [C] an official agreement that ends an argument between two people or groups; the conditions, or a legal document stating the conditions, on which money or property is given to sb: *There have been efforts to broker a peace settlement with the militia groups.* ◇ *Lawyers are seeking an **out-of-court settlement**.* ◇ *The house was put on the market as part of a **divorce settlement**.* See also **settle** → RESOLVE

arrangement [C, U] an agreement that you make with sb that you can both accept, especially concerning the practical details of sth: *The company has a special arrangement with the bank.* ◇ *We can come to an arrangement over the price.* ◇ *Viewing of the property is only possible **by arrangement** with the owner.* ◇ *You can cash cheques here **by prior arrangement** with the bank.* See also **arrange** → ORGANIZE

pact [C] a formal agreement between two or more people, groups or countries, especially one in which they agree to help each other: *He helped to negotiate a non-aggression pact between the two countries.* ◇ *The two parties agreed on an electoral pact.* ◇ *She died with her lover in a **suicide pact** (= an agreement by two or more people to kill themselves at the same time).*

bargain /ˈbɑːgən; *AmE* ˈbɑːrgən/ [C] an agreement between two or more people or groups to do sth for each other: *Finally the two sides **struck a bargain**.* ◇ *I've done what I promised and I expect you to keep your side of the bargain.* See also **bargain** → NEGOTIATE *verb*

NOTE **PACT** OR **BARGAIN?** People make a **pact** when they both want the same thing and agree to help each other achieve it. People make a **bargain** when they want different things, but each agrees to do what the other wants in exchange for the other doing what they want: ~~a non-aggression/suicide bargain~~ ◇ ~~I expect you to keep your side of the pact.~~

understanding [C, usually sing.] an informal agreement between two people or groups: *We finally came to an **understanding about** what hours we would work.* ◇ *I thought you gave me the book **on the understanding** that I could keep it.*

---

2 **agreement · unity · consensus · solidarity · harmony · consent · in accord · identity · unanimity**
These are all words for a situation in which people share opinions or feelings.

PATTERNS AND COLLOCATIONS
▸ **by** agreement/consensus/consent
▸ **in** agreement/unity/harmony/accord
▸ **in** agreement/unity/solidarity/harmony/accord **with** sb/sth
▸ agreement/unity/consensus/solidarity/harmony/identity/unanimity **among** people
▸ agreement/unity/consensus/solidarity/harmony/identity **between** people
▸ agreement/consensus/solidarity/unanimity **over** sth
▸ agreement/consensus/unanimity **about**/**on** sth
▸ agreement/consensus/unanimity **that...**
▸ **apparent** agreement/unity/consensus/solidarity/harmony/consent/unanimity
▸ **complete** agreement/unity/consensus/harmony/accord/identity/unanimity
▸ **common**/**general**/**unspoken** agreement/consensus/consent
▸ **political**/**social** agreement/unity/consensus/solidarity/harmony

agreement [U] the state of sharing the same opinion or feeling: *Are we in agreement about the price?* ◇ *He nodded in agreement.* ◇ *The two sides failed to reach agreement.* ◇ *There was broad agreement on what was needed.* **OPP** **disagreement** → DEBATE

unity /ˈjuːnəti/ [U, sing.] the state of being in agreement and working together: *Complete political unity is impossible to achieve.* ◇ *The dispute has destroyed unity among the workers.* **OPP** **disunity** → DIVISION 2

consensus /kənˈsensəs/ [sing., U] an opinion that all members of a group agree with: *There is a general consensus among teachers about the need for greater security in schools.* ◇ *There is a growing consensus of opinion on this issue.* ◇ *She is skilled at achieving consensus on sensitive issues.*

solidarity /ˌsɒlɪˈdærəti; *AmE* ˌsɑːl-/ [U] support by one person or group for another because they share feelings, opinions or aims: *Demonstrations were held as a gesture of solidarity with* the hunger strikers. ❶ **Solidarity** is a term used especially in the context of strikes and industrial relations.

harmony [U] a state of peaceful existence and agreement: *These communities lived in greater harmony with the environment than modern urban societies.* ◇ *The measures are designed to promote **racial harmony** (= the peaceful coexistence of people of different races).*

consent /kən'sent/ [U] a situation in which a decision is made or an opinion is held by two or more people: *The marriage ended **by mutual consent** (= with the agreement of both husband and wife).* ◇ *The museum bought the collection for $2 million, **by common consent** (= everyone thinks it is) a very good price.*

in accord *phrase* (*formal*) in agreement: *This action would not be in accord with our policy.* ◇ *Botanists are not in complete accord about how many species exist.*

identity [U] (*rather formal*) the state of feeling or being very similar to and able to understand sb/sth: *The two companies started working together as a result of a clear identity of interest.* ◇ *The close identity between the fans and the team has been eroded.*

unanimity /ˌjuːnə'nɪməti/ (*rather formal, written*) complete agreement about sth among a group of people: *We won't all agree, but we need to achieve a degree of unanimity.*
▸ **unanimous** /ju'næniməs/ *adj.*: *a unanimous vote/decision/verdict*
▸ **unanimously** *adv.*: *The motion was passed unanimously.*

aid *noun*

aid · help · welfare · relief · charity · social security · handout
These are all words for help, money, food and other supplies that are given to people who are poor, sick or in need in some way.

PATTERNS AND COLLOCATIONS
▸ aid / help / welfare / relief / charity / social security / handouts **for** sb
▸ to be **on** welfare / social security
▸ **emergency** aid / help / relief
▸ **government / state** aid / help / welfare / relief / handouts
▸ **direct / immediate / financial / medical** aid / help / relief
▸ to **get/receive** aid / help / welfare / relief / charity / social security / handouts
▸ to **accept** aid / help / charity
▸ to **give** (sb) aid / help / relief / charity / handouts
▸ to **provide / send / promise** aid / help / relief
▸ to **ask for** aid / help / welfare / relief / charity
▸ to **rely / depend on** help / welfare / charity / social security / handouts
▸ to **live on** welfare / charity / social security

aid [U] money, food, medicine and other supplies that are sent to help countries in difficult situations: *An extra £10 million in foreign aid has been promised.* ◇ *Much of the funding has come from international **aid agencies** (= organizations that provide help).*

help [U] advice or money that is given to sb in order to solve their problems: *I decided to seek legal help.* ◇ *The organization offers practical help in dealing with paperwork.* See also **help → HELP** *verb* 2

welfare /'welfeə(r)*; AmE* -fer/ [U] practical or financial help that is provided, often by the government, for people or animals that need it: *The state is still the main provider of welfare.* ◇ *Animal welfare groups want this practice banned altogether.* ❶ In American English **welfare** is also money that the government pays regularly to people who are poor, unemployed or sick. In British English this is called **social security**: *They would rather work than live on welfare.* See also **on welfare → UNEMPLOYED**

relief [U] money, food, medicine and other supplies that are sent to help people in countries where there has been a war or natural disaster: *We raised £5 000 for famine relief.* See also **relieve → EASE**

> **NOTE** **AID** OR **RELIEF**? **Aid** is often used to talk about money given to countries in financial trouble, often over a period of time. **Relief** is used more often to talk about money, medicine, food, etc. given to people in places where there has been a war or natural disaster, usually as an immediate response to a sudden emergency.

charity [U] the aim of giving money, food and help to people who are in need: *Most of the runners in the London Marathon are **raising money for charity**.* ◇ *He refused to **live off charity** (= to live on money which other people give you because you are poor).*

,**social se'curity** [U] (*BrE*) money that the government pays regularly to people who are poor, unemployed or sick: *He's been living on social security for the past two months.*

handout /'hændaʊt/ [C] (*sometimes disapproving*) food, money or clothes that are given to a person who is poor: *I don't want to be dependent on handouts.* See also **handout → GIFT, hand sth out → DISTRIBUTE**

aim *verb*

aim · focus · point · direct · turn
These words all mean to point or send sth in the direction of sb/sth.

PATTERNS AND COLLOCATIONS
▸ to aim / point / direct (sth) **at** sb / sth
▸ to focus / turn (sth) **on** sb / sth
▸ to aim / focus / point a **camera**
▸ to aim / focus / direct (a) **light**
▸ to aim / point / turn a **gun** at / on sb
▸ to aim / focus / point sth **directly**

aim [I, T] to point or send sth such as a weapon, shot, hit or kick at a particular person or place that you want to hit: ***Aim for** the middle of the target.* ◇ *The gun was aimed at her head.*
▸ **aim** *noun* [U]: *The gunman **took aim** (= pointed his weapon) and fired.*

focus /'fəʊkəs; AmE 'foʊ-/ [I, T] (of your eyes or a camera) to adapt or be adjusted so that things can be seen clearly; to adjust your eyes, etc. so that you can see things clearly; to aim rays of light onto a particular point using a lens (= a curved piece of glass): *It took a few moments for her eyes to focus in the dark.* ◇ *I quickly focused the camera on the children.* ◇ *She used her glasses to focus the sun's rays on the twigs and spark a fire.*
▸ **focus** *noun* [U]: *The children's faces are badly **out of focus** (= not clearly shown) in the photograph.* ◇ *The binoculars were not **in focus** (= were not showing things clearly).*

point [T] to aim sth at sb/sth, especially by holding it up in front of you: *He pointed the gun at her head.* ◇ *A hundred camera lenses were being pointed at her.*

direct [T] to aim a weapon or light in a particular direction or at a particular person or thing: *The machine directs a powerful beam at the affected part of the body.* See also **direction → WAY** 3

turn [T, I] to suddenly aim, and usually fire, a weapon at sb: *Police turned water cannon on the rioters.* ◇ *He turned the gun on himself.*

air *noun*

air · sky · atmosphere · airspace · the heavens
These words all mean the space above or around you.

PATTERNS AND COLLOCATIONS
▸ **in / into** the air / sky / atmosphere / sb's airspace / the heavens
▸ **through** the air / sky / atmosphere / sb's airspace

air (usually **the air**) [U] the space above the ground or that is around things: *I kicked the ball high into the air.* ◇ *Spicy smells wafted through the air.* ◇ *Music filled the night air.* ❶ **Air** is also the space above the earth where planes fly: *It only takes three hours by air* (= in a plane). ◇ *air travel/traffic/fares* ◇ *The temple was clearly visible from the air.*

sky [C, U] the space above the earth that you can see when you look up, where clouds and the sun, moon and stars appear: *What's that in the sky?* ◇ *Stars began to twinkle in the night sky.* ◇ *I had blue skies and sunshine nearly every day I was there.* ❶ You usually say **the sky**. When **sky** is used with an adjective, use **a … sky**: *We made our way home under a cloudless sky.* You can also use the plural form **skies**, especially when you are thinking about the great extent of the sky: *The skies above London were ablaze with a spectacular firework display.*

atmosphere (usually **the atmosphere**) [C, usually sing.] the layer of air that surrounds the earth; the mixture of gases that surrounds a large object in space such as a planet or star: *Pollution of the atmosphere is a global problem.* ◇ *The outermost part of the sun's atmosphere is called the corona.*

▶ **atmospheric** /ˌætməsˈferɪk/ *adj.*: *atmospheric pollution*

airspace /ˈeəspeɪs; *AmE* ˈers-/ [U] the part of the sky where planes fly, usually the part above a particular country that is legally controlled by that country: *The jet entered Chinese airspace without permission.*

the heavens [pl.] (*literary*) the sky above, as seen from the ground: *Four tall trees stretched up to the heavens.*

alarm *noun*

alarm · siren · horn
These are all words for a device that makes a noise to warn people or attract their attention.

PATTERNS AND COLLOCATIONS
▸ to **hear** an alarm / a siren / a horn
▸ an alarm / a siren / a horn **sounds**

alarm [C] a device that makes a noise to warn people of a particular danger: *All new houses must be fitted with a smoke alarm.* ◇ *The earthquake set off burglar alarms throughout the city.* ◇ *A car alarm went off in the middle of the night.* See also **alarm** → WARNING

siren /ˈsaɪrən/ [C] a device that makes a long, very loud noise as a warning or signal: *Air-raid sirens sounded to warn everyone in the city that an attack was coming.* ◇ *A police car raced past with its siren wailing.*

horn [C] a device in a vehicle for making a loud noise as a warning or signal: *She flashed her lights and honked her horn at the car in front.* ◇ *Behind him, a horn blared.*

alive *adj.*

alive · living · live · animate
These words all describe sb/sth that has life.

PATTERNS AND COLLOCATIONS
▸ a living / live **animal / plant / bird**
▸ a living / live **organism / creature**
▸ still alive / living

alive [not before noun] having life; not dead: *We don't know whether he's alive or dead.* ◇ *She had to steal food just to stay alive.* ◇ *Doctors fought to keep the baby alive.* ◇ *I was glad to hear you're alive and well.* ◇ *He was buried alive in the earthquake.*

living (*rather formal*) alive now: *She taught us to show respect for all living things.* ◇ *Many people say he is the finest living pianist.* **OPP dead** → DEAD

NOTE ALIVE OR LIVING? **Alive** is never used before a noun: *all alive things*. **Living** can be used after *be* but is not usually used after other linking verbs: *She stole just to stay living.* ◇ *Doctors fought to keep the baby living.*

live /laɪv/ [usually before noun] living: *We saw a real live rattlesnake!* ◇ *the number of live births* (= babies born alive) **OPP dead** → DEAD

NOTE LIVING OR LIVE? **Living** is usually used to talk about people/animals in a wide context: *The elephant is the biggest living land animal* (= elephants in general, not one particular elephant). ◇ *The elephant is the biggest live land animal.* ◇ *the finest living pianist* (= out of all pianists alive today) ◇ *the finest live pianist.* **Live** is usually used to talk about a person or animals in a particular situation, especially when it is important to be reacting to the situation: *I need to talk to a live person* (= not a recorded message). ◇ *I need to talk to a living person.* ◇ *Customs officials seized 400 live snakes packed in crates.* ◇ *Customs officials seized 400 living snakes.*

animate /ˈænɪmət/ (*formal*) having life; moving or able to move by itself: *Children quickly learn to distinguish between animate and inanimate motion.* **OPP inanimate** ❶ Things that are **inanimate** are not alive in the way that people, animals and plants are: *A rock is an inanimate object.*

allocate *verb*

allocate · set · assign · allot
These words all mean to give sth officially to sb/sth for a particular purpose.

PATTERNS AND COLLOCATIONS
▸ to allocate / set / assign / allot sth **for** sth
▸ to allocate / assign / allot sth **to** sb
▸ to allocate / assign / allot (a) **room / space / seats / resources / time / day / task**
▸ to allocate / assign a **duty / responsibility**
▸ to allocate / allot **money / funds**
▸ to allocate / set / assign **work**
▸ to set / assign **homework**
▸ to allocate / assign sth **randomly**

allocate /ˈæləkeɪt/ [T] (*rather formal*) to give sb part of sth (such as an amount of time, space or money), as a share of what is available; to decide that sth should be used for a particular purpose: *They intend to allocate more places to mature students this year.* ◇ *The project is being allocated more resources.* See also **allocation** → SHARE *noun*

set [T] to give sb a task or test: *She's set herself a difficult task.* ◇ *Who will be setting* (= writing the questions for) *the French exam?*

assign /əˈsaɪn/ [T] (*rather formal*) to give sb sth that they can use, or a task or responsibility: *We have been assigned the two large classrooms.* ◇ *The teacher assigned a different task to each of the children.*

allot /əˈlɒt; *AmE* əˈlɑːt/ (-tt-) [T] to allocate sth: *I managed to complete the test within the time allotted.* ◇ *How much money has been allotted to us?*

NOTE ALLOCATE OR ALLOT? **Allocate** is used far more than **allot** in business-related contexts. Companies and managers **allocate** *money, funds, resources, time* or *a percentage of the budget* to projects; *space, classrooms, tasks* and *seats* are **allotted** to people in more general, everyday situations.

allow *verb* See the Topic Map for THE INDIVIDUAL AND SOCIETY on p.894

allow · let · grant · permit · entitle · authorize · license · qualify · OK · sanction · empower · clear
These words all mean to decide or say that sb may do sth or receive sth, or that sth may happen.

PATTERNS AND COLLOCATIONS
▸ to allow / permit / entitle / authorize / license / empower / clear **sb to do sth**
▸ to let **sb do sth**
▸ to allow / let / permit **yourself** sth / (to) do sth

▶ to allow / be entitled to / authorize / sanction **payment**
▶ to be **legally** allowed / permitted / entitled / authorized / sanctioned / empowered
▶ to be **officially** allowed / permitted / entitled / authorized / sanctioned
▶ to be **(not) normally** allowed / granted / permitted / entitled
▶ to **automatically** grant sth / entitle sb to sth / qualify sb for sth

allow [T] to decide or say that sb may do or have sth, or that sth may happen or be done: *His parents won't allow him to stay out late.* ◇ *He is not allowed to stay out late.* ◇ *Smoking is not allowed in here.* ◇ *No dogs allowed* (= you cannot bring them in). ◇ *The prisoners are allowed out of their cells for two hours a day.* ◇ *You're allowed half an hour to complete the test.* ◇ *I sometimes allow myself the luxury of a cigar.* ◇ *He allowed his mind to wander.* **OPP** forbid → BAN

let [T] to allow sb to do sth or allow sth to happen without trying to stop it: *They never let the children play outside.* ◇ *I wanted to drive but she wouldn't let me.* ◇ *Don't let it upset you.* ◇ *Let me help you with your luggage.* ❶ When it means 'allow' **let** is not used in the passive: ~~The children are never let play outside.~~ However, **let** can also mean 'to open a door so that sb can go in or out' and in this meaning it can be active or passive: *I'll give you a key so you can let yourself in.* ◇ *The cat wants to be let out.* Note the difference between *let sb out* (= open the door for them) and *allow sb out* (= give them permission to go out).

grant [T, often passive] (*rather formal*) to agree to give sb what they ask for, especially formal or legal permission to do sth: *Planning permission for the development was granted last week.* ◇ *The government granted an amnesty to all political prisoners.* ◇ *She was granted a divorce.* ◇ *Her wish was granted.* See also **award** → GIVE 1

permit /pə'mɪt; *AmE* pər'm-/ (-tt-) [T] (*formal*) to allow sb to do sth; to allow sth to happen: *The banks were not permitted to invest overseas.* ◇ *The rules of the club do not permit it.* ◇ *Radios are not permitted in the library.* ◇ *Permit me to make a suggestion.* **OPP** ban, forbid, prohibit → BAN, See also **permission** → PERMISSION, **permit** → LICENCE *noun*

entitle /ɪn'taɪtl/ [T, often passive] to give sb the right to have or do sth: *Passengers will be entitled to a full refund of the cost of the ticket.* ◇ *Of course, he's entitled to his opinion but I think he's wrong.* See also **entitlement** → RIGHT *noun*

authorize (*BrE also* -ise) /'ɔːθəraɪz/ [T] to give official permission for sth, or for sb to do sth: *I can authorize payments up to £5 000.* ◇ *I have authorized him to act for me while I am away.* **OPP** prohibit → BAN, See also **authorization** → PERMISSION, **authorization** → LICENCE *noun*

license (*BrE also, less frequent* **licence**) /'laɪsns/ [T] to give sb official permission to do, own or use sth; to give official permission for sth to be done: *The drug is not licensed for long-term use.* ◇ *The hotel is licensed to sell alcohol.* ◇ *The company plans to license the technology to others.* See also **licence** → LICENCE *noun*

qualify [I, T] to have the right to do or receive sth; to give sb this right: *You have to be over 60 to qualify.* ◇ *She didn't qualify for a full pension.* ◇ *Membership of the scheme qualifies you for the discount.*

OK (*also* **okay**) [T] (*informal*) to officially agree to sth or allow it to happen: *The chairman OK'd the request.* ◇ *The property has to be valued before a mortgage loan is OK'd.*

sanction /'sæŋkʃn/ [T] (*formal*) to give permission for sth to happen: *The military refused to sanction a transfer of power to a civilian government.*

empower /ɪm'paʊə(r)/ [T, often passive] (*formal*) to give sb the power or authority to do sth: *The courts were empowered to impose the death sentence for certain crimes.*

clear [T] to give or get official approval for sth to be done; to give official permission for a person, ship, plane or goods to leave or enter a place, or for a person to be given special work or see special papers: *I'll have to clear it*

with *the manager before I can refund your money.* ◇ *The plane had been cleared for take-off.* ◇ *She hasn't been cleared by security.* See also **clearance** → PERMISSION

almost *adv.*

almost · nearly · virtually · more or less · not quite · practically · about · pretty much/well
These words are all used to mean to a great degree but not completely.

PATTERNS AND COLLOCATIONS
▶ almost / nearly / virtually / more or less / not quite / practically / pretty much **all / every**
▶ almost / virtually / more or less / practically / pretty much **any / anything**
▶ almost / nearly / virtually / more or less / practically **always**
▶ almost / nearly / virtually / more or less / not quite / practically **empty**
▶ almost / virtually / more or less / practically **impossible**
▶ almost / nearly / virtually / more or less / not quite / practically **finished**

almost to a great degree but not completely: *I like almost all of them.* ◇ *It's a mistake they almost always make.* ◇ *The story is almost certainly false.* ◇ *Dinner's almost ready.* ◇ *Their house is almost opposite ours.* ◇ *He slipped and almost fell.*

nearly almost: *I've worked here for nearly two years.* ◇ *The bottle's nearly empty.* ◇ *It's nearly time to leave.* ◇ *He's nearly as tall as you are.* ◇ (*especially BrE*) *She very nearly died.*

NOTE **ALMOST OR NEARLY?** In many cases you can use either word: *I've got almost/nearly every CD they've made.* ◇ *She almost/nearly missed her train.* You can also use them in negative sentences, but it is much more common to make a positive sentence with **only just**: *We only just got there in time.* (or: *We almost/nearly didn't get there in time.*) **Nearly** is more common with numbers: *There were nearly 200 people at the meeting.* **Almost**, but NOT **nearly** can be used before words like *any, anybody* and *anything*: *They'll eat almost anything.* ◇ ~~They'll eat nearly anything.~~ You can also use **almost** before *no, nobody* and *never*, but it is much more common to use **hardly** or **scarcely** with *any, anybody* or *ever*: *She's hardly ever in.* (or: *She's almost never in.*) **Almost** can be used when you are saying that one thing looks like another: *The boat looked almost like a toy.* In British English you can use *very* and *so* before **nearly**: (*BrE*) *He was very nearly caught.*

virtually very nearly, so that any slight difference is not important: *He virtually admitted he was guilty.* ◇ *This year's results are virtually the same as last year's.* ◇ *The red squirrel has become virtually extinct in most of the country.*

,more or 'less *phrase* almost, especially when any difference is not very important: *The story is more or less true.* ◇ *His estimate has turned out to be more or less correct.* ◇ *The two houses were more or less identical.* ◇ *I've more or less finished the book.* ❶ **More or less** is not as nearly as **virtually**, but is used in cases where it is not so important that sth should be completely correct, the same, finished, etc.

not quite not completely, but almost: *The theatre was not quite full.* ◇ *That's not quite the same thing, is it?* ◇ *The room was full of old furniture that didn't quite match.* ◇ *He didn't feel quite ready for marriage.* ❶ **Not quite** is a less positive expression than the other words and phrases in this group: it often emphasizes the small degree to which sth is NOT complete or satisfactory, rather than the large degree to which it *is*.

practically (*especially spoken*) virtually: *She practically accused me of starting the fire!* ◇ *With that crack in it, the vase is worth practically nothing.* ◇ *There's practically no difference between the two options.*

NOTE VIRTUALLY OR PRACTICALLY? In many cases you can use either word: *This drug was virtually/practically unknown in Britain.* You can also use both these words in negative sentences, although you can also use **hardly** or **scarcely** with *any, anything, ever,* etc.: *There's virtually/practically no money left.* ◇ *There's hardly any money left.* **Practically** is slightly more informal than **virtually** and is used especially in spoken English.

about (*especially spoken*) nearly; very close to: *I'm just about ready.* ◇ *This is about the best we can hope for.*

pretty 'much/'well (*spoken*) almost; almost completely: *One sheep looks pretty much like another to me.* ◇ *He goes out pretty well every night.* ◇ *The first stage is pretty much finished.*

alone *adj., adv.*

alone · on your own · by yourself/yourselves · single-handed/single-handedly · solitary · solo · unattended · lonely · sole · unaccompanied · unaided
These words all describe sb/sth that is not with other people or things.

PATTERNS AND COLLOCATIONS
▸ to **do sth** alone / on your own / by yourself / single-handed / unaided
▸ to **live** alone / on your own / by yourself
▸ **people are** alone / on their own / by themselves / unaided / unaccompanied
▸ a solitary / lonely **existence / life / walk**
▸ solo / unaccompanied **singing / violin**
▸ unattended / unaccompanied **baggage / luggage**
▸ **all** alone / on your own / by yourself

alone [not before noun] without any other people; without help: *I don't like going out alone at night.* ◇ *She was sitting all alone in the hall.* ◇ *Finally the two of us were alone together.* ◇ *You are not alone in finding him hard to work with.* ◇ *The assassin said he had acted alone.* ◇ *The press photographers just won't leave her alone* (= stop annoying her). ◇ *He decided to go it alone* (= to do sth without help from anyone) *and start his own business.*

on your 'own *idiom* (*rather informal*) without any other people; without help: *I'm all on my own today.* ◇ *She lives on her own.* ◇ *He did it on his own.*

by your'self/your'selves *idiom* (*rather informal*) without any other people; without help: *How long were you by yourself in the house?* ◇ *Are you sure you did this exercise all by yourself?*

NOTE ON YOUR OWN OR BY YOURSELF? There is very little difference in meaning or use between these expressions. **On your own** is often used when sb manages to do or achieve sth without help, because there is no help available: *to manage/cope/survive/act/achieve sth/make it/set up on your own* ◇ *This is not something that you can achieve on your own.* but you can also use **by yourself** in these cases. **By yourself** is often used when sb has chosen to be or do sth without anyone else: *to sit/play/walk/go off by yourself* ◇ *She loved to walk by herself on the wild lonely moors.* However, you can also use **on your own** in these cases.

,single-'handed, ,single-'handedly (*often approving*) on your own, with nobody helping you to do sth difficult: *Her ambition is to sail around the world single-handed.* ◇ *He single-handedly saved the town from disaster.*

solitary /'sɒlətri; *AmE* 'sɑːləteri/ *adj.* [usually before noun] (of life or an activity) done alone; without other people: *She enjoys long solitary walks.* ◇ *He led a solitary life.* See also **solitude** → PRIVACY

solo /'səʊləʊ; *AmE* 'soʊloʊ/ [only before noun] done by one person on their own, without anyone helping or doing it with them: *His first solo flight was in 1954.* ◇ *She went on to record a solo album after the band split up.* ◇ *She wanted to fly solo across the Atlantic.* ◇ *After three years with the*

band he decided to go solo. ❶ **Solo** is used especially to talk about performing music or flying: *a solo instrument/piano/voice/performance/act/piece/album/record/artist/career/flight/pilot.* It can also be used to talk about other sorts of artistic or sporting performances or achievements: *a solo exhibition/show/climb/goal*

unattended /,ʌnə'tendɪd/ *adj.* without the owner present; not being watched or cared for: *The insurance policy covers loss of money or valuables from an unattended vehicle.* ◇ *She was reprimanded for leaving the children unattended.*

lonely *adj.* [usually before noun] (of a situation or period of time) sad and spent alone: *He thought back to all those lonely nights at home watching TV.*

sole *adj.* [only before noun] (*rather formal*) belonging to one person or group; not shared: *She has **sole responsibility** for the project.* ◇ *We may have the opportunity to take over **sole ownership** of the company.*

unaccompanied /,ʌnə'kʌmpənid/ (*formal*) without a person going together with sb/sth; (of music) performed without anyone else playing or singing at the same time: *No unaccompanied children allowed.* ◇ *She played a sonata for unaccompanied violin.* ◇ *Unaccompanied baggage* (= travelling separately from its owner) *must be hand-checked by security staff.*

unaided /ʌn'eɪdɪd/ (*rather formal*) without help from anyone or anything: *He can now walk unaided.* ◇ *Photographs can show things invisible to the unaided eye.*

amazing *adj.* See also the entries for REMARKABLE and SURPRISING

amazing · astonishing · awesome · staggering · breathtaking · miraculous · stunning · sensational
These words all describe things that are very surprising, often because they are greater than usual or normal.

PATTERNS AND COLLOCATIONS
▸ to be amazing / astonishing / staggering / miraculous **that…**
▸ to be amazing / astonishing / staggering **how…**
▸ an amazing / an astonishing / an awesome / a staggering **achievement**
▸ an amazing / astonishing / awesome **feat**
▸ an amazing / an astonishing / a miraculous / a stunning / an astounding **success**
▸ an amazing / an astonishing / a stunning **victory / result**
▸ amazing / astonishing / breathtaking / stunning **news**
▸ an amazing / an astonishing / an awesome / a breathtaking / a stunning **sight**
▸ astonishing / awesome / breathtaking / stunning **beauty**
▸ **quite** amazing / astonishing / awesome / staggering / breathtaking / miraculous / stunning / sensational
▸ **truly** amazing / astonishing / awesome / staggering / breathtaking / sensational
▸ **absolutely** amazing / astonishing / staggering / breathtaking / stunning
▸ **pretty** amazing / awesome / sensational

amazing very surprising, often in a way that makes you feel pleasure or admiration: *I made an amazing discovery today.* ◇ *The virus spread at amazing speed.* ◇ *It's amazing what you can do if you have to.* ◇ *It's amazing the difference a few polite words make.* ◇ *The amazing thing is, he really believes he'll get away with it.* See also **amaze** → SURPRISE
  ▸ **amazingly** *adv.*: *Amazingly, they won.* ◇ *The meal was amazingly cheap.*

astonishing /ə'stɒnɪʃɪŋ; *AmE* ə'stɑːn-/ very surprising; difficult to believe: *The painting was sold at auction for an astonishing $30 million.* ◇ *Then he had an astonishing piece of luck.* ◇ *During this period London grew at an astonishing rate.* See also **astonish** → SURPRISE
  ▸ **astonishingly** *adv.*: *He took the news astonishingly well.*

awesome /'ɔːsəm/ very impressive or very difficult and perhaps rather frightening: *It is a region of awesome gorges and spectacular peaks.* ◇ *After the war the country faced the awesome task of reconstruction.*

staggering (*rather informal*) so great, shocking or surprising that it is difficult to believe: *The attention to detail is staggering.* ◇ *The paintings on the wall were evidence of a staggering lack of talent.* See also **stagger** → SURPRISE

▸ **staggeringly** *adj.*: *The painting sold for a staggeringly high figure.*

breathtaking /'breθteɪkɪŋ/ very exciting or impressive (usually in a pleasant way); very surprising: *The scene was breathtaking in its beauty.* ◇ *He spoke with breathtaking arrogance.* See also **spectacular** → MAGNIFICENT, **take sb's breath away** → IMPRESS

▸ **breathtakingly** *adv.*: *breathtakingly beautiful*

miraculous /mɪ'rækjələs/ completely unexpected and very lucky; like a miracle: *The child had a miraculous escape when the firework exploded in her hand.* ◇ *Doctors feared she would die but she's made a miraculous recovery.* See also **miracle** → MIRACLE

▸ **miraculously** *adv.*: *Miraculously, no one was hurt.*

stunning (*rather informal*) extremely surprising or shocking: *The election result was a stunning blow for the party.* ◇ *The team is celebrating a stunning victory.* See also **stun** → SURPRISE

sensational /sen'seɪʃənl/ causing great surprise, excitement or interest: *Police have uncovered sensational new evidence.* ◇ *It was the most sensational 24 hours of the jockey's career.*

▸ **sensationally** *adv.*: *The trial ended sensationally.*

ambition *noun*

ambition · drive
These are both words for the desire to be successful and to achieve things.

PATTERNS AND COLLOCATIONS
▸ the ambition / drive **to do** / **be** sth
▸ **personal** ambition / drive
▸ to **have** / **lack** ambition / drive

ambition [U] the desire or determination to be successful, rich or powerful: *He was a young man with the ambition to succeed in his chosen career.* ◇ *She's a woman of driving ambition.* See also **ambition** → HOPE *noun* 2, **ambitious** → AGGRESSIVE 2

drive [U] (*approving*) the strong desire to do things and to achieve sth; great energy: *He'll do very well — he has tremendous drive.* ◇ *He lacks the competitive drive he needs to succeed.* See also **drive** → DRIVE *verb* 2

analyst *noun* See the Topic Map for THE MEDIA on p.900

analyst · critic · observer · commentator · watcher
These are all words for a person who watches and considers events and situations, usually in order to give an opinion about them on television or radio or in a newspaper.

PATTERNS AND COLLOCATIONS
▸ an analyst / a critic / a commentator **for** sb / sth
▸ an **astute** / **independent** analyst / critic / observer / commentator
▸ a **keen** analyst / critic / observer
▸ a **social** analyst / critic / commentator / observer
▸ a / an **media** / **industry** analyst / observer / commentator / watcher
▸ a **political** / **military** analyst / observer / commentator
▸ to **surprise** analysts / critics / commentators / observers / watchers
▸ to **strike** critics / observers / watchers

analyst [C] a person whose job is to watch and consider events and situations in a particular area such as finance or politics so that they can give their opinion on them: *City analysts forecast pre-tax profits of £40 billion this year.*

critic [C] a person whose job is to express their opinions about the good and bad qualities of things such as books, films, music, changes in society, etc: *He's a restaurant critic for 'The Times'.* ◇ *The critics loved the movie.*

observer /əb'zɜːvə(r); *AmE* -'zɜːrv-/ [C] a person who watches and studies particular events and situations as they happen: *Observers noted an absence of the violence which had been a feature of previous elections.*

commentator /'kɒmənteɪtə(r); *AmE* 'kɑːm-/ [C] a person whose job is to watch and consider events and situations in a particular area, such as politics or society and talk or write about them on television or radio, or in a newspaper: *She's a political commentator for the BBC.* ◇ *He is best known as a commentator on culture and the arts.*

watcher [C] (*often in compounds*) (*rather informal, especially journalism*) a person who watches and considers particular people or a particular subject and talks or writes about them in books, on television or radio, or in a newspaper: *There are now several books on the princess by various royal watchers.*

NOTE WHICH WORD? Analysts, critics and **commentators** do a job and they are usually employed by or do work for a company or organization. **Observers** and **watchers** are informed people who may write books and articles or be paid to give advice, but are not usually employed on a regular basis.: ~~She's a political observer / watcher for the BBC.~~ A **commentator** has the job of explaining a subject and giving opinions on it for the general public, on television or radio or in the newspapers. An **analyst** has the job of explaining a subject and giving opinions and advice to other professional people.

anger *noun*

anger · rage · fury · outrage · indignation
These are all words for the strong feelings you have when you are angry or very angry about sth.

anger	outrage	rage
indignation		fury

PATTERNS AND COLLOCATIONS
▸ to do sth **in** anger / rage / fury / outrage / indignation
▸ **public** / **widespread** anger / outrage / indignation
▸ to **provoke** anger / fury / outrage / indignation
▸ to **arouse** sb's anger / fury / indignation
▸ to **be filled** / **shake** / **tremble** / **seethe** with anger / rage / fury / outrage / indignation
▸ to **express** anger / rage / fury / outrage / indignation
▸ to **vent** your anger / rage / fury
▸ to **fly into** a rage / fury

anger [U] the strong feeling that you have when sth has happened that you think is bad and unfair: *Jan slammed the door in anger.* ◇ *I am acutely aware of the growing anger and frustration of young unemployed people.*

rage [U, sing.] a feeling of violent anger that is difficult to control: *She was speechless with rage.* ◇ *She stormed out of the room in a rage.* See also **rage** → TEMPER, **enraged** → FURIOUS

fury /'fjʊri/ [U, sing.] (*written*) a feeling of violent anger: *Her face was white with fury.* ◇ *In a cold fury my uncle hurled his son from the room.* See also **furious** → FURIOUS

NOTE RAGE OR FURY? Both **rage** and **fury** may result in violent behaviour, but **fury** is usually a more controlled feeling than **rage**. **Rage** may be *hot* or *cold*, *red* or *white*: *His face was red/white with rage.* **Fury** is only *cold* and *white*.

outrage /'aʊtreɪdʒ/ [U] a strong feeling of anger and shock: *The judge's remarks caused public outrage.* ◇ *She was filled with an overwhelming sense of moral outrage.* See also **outraged** → FURIOUS, **outrageous** → OUTRAGEOUS

indignation /ˌɪndɪg'neɪʃən/ [U] a feeling of anger and shock caused by sth that you think is unfair or unreasonable: *Some benefits apply only to men, much to* *the indignation of* working women. ◇ *She was full of righteous indignation* (= the belief that you are right to be angry even though other people do not agree).

> **NOTE** **OUTRAGE** OR **INDIGNATION?** Both words include a feeling of surprise as well as anger, but **outrage** is stronger. **Indignation** often suggests that you feel that you have been treated unfairly; **outrage** may be less personal and involves a more general sense of anger.

anger *verb* See also the entry for ANNOY

anger · infuriate · antagonize · drive sb mad/crazy · outrage · enrage · rankle · rile · incense · (*taboo*) **piss sb off**
These verbs all mean to make sb angry or very angry.

rankle	anger	drive sb mad	infuriate
rile	antagonize	outrage	enrage
	piss sb off		incense

PATTERNS AND COLLOCATIONS
▸ What really angers/infuriates/enrages/riles/incenses me is…
▸ What pisses us off/drives us mad/crazy is…
▸ It infuriated/enraged/riled/incensed him that…

anger [T] to make sb angry: *The question clearly angered him.* ◇ *They stayed silent but were angered by the decision.* ❶ It is also common to say **make sb angry**, especially in more informal or spoken English: (*spoken*) *It really makes me angry the way they keep changing the rules.*
infuriate /ɪn'fjʊərieɪt; *AmE* -'fjʊr-/ [T] to make sb extremely angry: *Her silence infuriated him even more.* See also **infuriating** → ANNOYING
antagonize (*BrE* also **-ise**) [T] to do sth to make sb angry with you: *Not wishing to antagonize her further, he said no more.* See also **antagonism** → TENSION
drive sb mad/crazy *idiom* (*informal*) to make sb very angry or crazy: *That noise is driving me mad!* ◇ *He drove me crazy with his constant questions.*
outrage /'aʊtreɪdʒ/ [T] to make sb very shocked and angry: *The killings have outraged the entire community.* See also **outraged** → FURIOUS, **outrageous** → OUTRAGEOUS
enrage /ɪn'reɪdʒ/ [T] (*rather formal, written*) to make sb extremely angry: *The newspaper article enraged him.* See also **enraged** → FURIOUS
rankle [I] (of sth such as a remark or event) to make sb feel angry or upset for a long time: *Her comments still rankled.* ◇ *His decision to sell the land rankled with her.*
rile [T] to annoy sb or make them angry: *Nothing ever seemed to rile him.* ◇ *She regretted at once that she had let herself become riled.*
incense /ɪn'sens/ [T] to make sb extremely angry, especially for moral reasons: *The decision incensed the entire workforce.* See also **incensed** → FURIOUS

> **NOTE** **INFURIATE, ENRAGE** OR **INCENSE?** Infuriate usually emphasizes how you feel about sb else's behaviour that you think is unreasonable; **enrage** can suggest that it is the angry person whose behaviour is unreasonable; **incense** is often used when you think people are right to be angry.

,piss sb 'off *phrasal verb* (*taboo, slang*) to make sb angry or annoyed: *Her attitude really pisses me off.*

angle *noun*

angle · slope · gradient · grade
These are all words for the position of sth that is not in a vertical or horizontal line.

PATTERNS AND COLLOCATIONS
▸ at an angle/a slope/a gradient
▸ a **slight/steep/gentle** angle/slope/gradient

angle [C] the direction that sth is leaning or pointing in when it is not in a vertical or horizontal line: *The tower of Pisa leans at an angle.* ◇ *The plane was coming in at a steep angle.* ◇ (*BrE*) *His hair was sticking up at all angles.* See also **angle** → LEAN *verb* 1
slope [sing., U] the amount by which a surface is higher at one end than at the other: *The land rises in a gentle slope from the sea to the foot of the mountains.* ◇ *The angle of slope must be determined before construction can begin.* See also **slope** → SLOPE *verb*, **slope** → LEAN 1
gradient /'greɪdiənt/ [C] (*especially BrE*) the degree to which the ground slopes, especially on a road, path or railway: *The line here is on a steep gradient climbing towards Merstham Tunnel.* ◇ *The hill has a gradient of 1 in 4 (or 25%).*
grade [C] (*especially AmE*) a gradient: *The hill has a grade of 25%.* ❶ In American English **grade** can also mean a slope or hill: *We hiked up a short steep grade.*

angry *adj.* See also the entries for ANNOYED and FURIOUS

angry · mad · indignant · cross · irate · (*taboo*) **pissed off**
These words all describe people feeling and/or showing anger.

cross	angry	irate
	mad	
	indignant	
	pissed off	

PATTERNS AND COLLOCATIONS
▸ angry/mad/indignant/cross/pissed off **about/at** sth
▸ angry/indignant **over** sth
▸ angry/cross/pissed off **with** sb **for** sth
▸ to be angry/mad/indignant/cross/pissed off **that**…
▸ to **get** angry/mad/cross/pissed off
▸ to **make sb** angry/mad/cross

angry feeling or showing anger: *Please don't be angry with me.* ◇ *I was very angry with myself for making such a stupid mistake.* ◇ *Thousands of angry demonstrators filled the square.* ◇ *an angry voice/letter/response*
▸ **angrily** *adv.*: *Some senators reacted angrily to the President's remarks.* ◇ *He swore angrily.*
mad [not before noun] (*especially AmE, informal*) angry: *He got mad and walked out.* ◇ *She's mad at me for being late.* ◇ *That noise is driving me mad.* ❶ Mad is the usual word for 'angry' in informal American English. When used in British English, especially in the phrase go mad, it can mean 'very angry': *Dad'll go mad when he sees what you've done.* 'Go mad' can also mean 'go crazy' or 'get very excited'. See also **mad** → MAD, **maddening** → ANNOYING
indignant feeling or showing anger and surprise because you think that you or sb else has been treated unfairly: *an indignant look/letter* ◇ *She was very indignant at the way she had been treated.*
▸ **indignantly** *adv.*: *'I'm certainly not asking him!' she retorted indignantly.*
cross (*especially BrE, rather informal*) quite angry or annoyed: *If you don't do as you're told I shall get very cross.* ❶ Cross is often used by or to children.
▸ **crossly** *adv.*: *'Well what did you expect?' she said crossly.*

> **NOTE** **ANGRY** OR **CROSS?** A *cross man* is always cross because it is part of his character. An *angry man* may be always angry or may just be angry on a particular occasion.

irate /aɪ'reɪt/ very angry: *irate customers/callers* ◇ *an irate letter/phone call* ❶ Irate is not usually followed by a preposition: *She was irate with me/about it.*
,pissed 'off (*AmE* also **pissed**) (*taboo, slang*) angry, bored or unhappy, especially with a situation that has continued for too long: *I'm pissed off with the way they've treated me.* ◇ *a very pissed off taxi driver*

animal *noun*

animal · creature · being · beast · organism · thing
These are all words for sth which is alive but which is not a human or a plant.

PATTERNS AND COLLOCATIONS
▸ a **living** animal / creature / being / organism / thing
▸ a **strange** animal / creature / being / beast
▸ a **wild** animal / creature / beast / thing
▸ a / an **savage** / **exotic** animal / creature / beast
▸ a / an **marine** / **aquatic** animal / creature / organism
▸ a **social** animal / creature / being
▸ a **mythical** creature / beast

animal [C] something that is alive but is not a plant or a human: *These birds perform a ritual which is unique in the* **animal kingdom**. ◇ *This product has not been tested on animals.* ◇ **Animal rights** *groups are staging a protest against the fur trade this Saturday.* ❶ Humans are not usually considered to be animals, but in technical contexts they can be: *Humans are the only animals to have developed speech.* In other, non-technical contexts, **animal** is used as a less formal synonym of **mammal**, to mean any creature that is not a bird, fish, reptile, insect or human being: *the animals and birds of South America*

creature [C] a real or imaginary animal, especially if it is considered unusual in some way: *The dormouse is a shy, nocturnal creature.* ◇ *Goblins and other dangerous creatures lurked inside the cave.*

being [C] a living creature, especially when considered in the context of science or philosophy: *Human beings learned to control fire around 100 000 years ago.* ◇ *Dolphins are highly intelligent beings.*

beast [C] (*old-fashioned or formal*) an animal, especially one that is large or dangerous, or one that is unusual: *He was ripped apart by wild beasts in the forest.* ◇ *mythical beasts such as unicorns and dragons*

organism /ˈɔːɡənɪzəm; *AmE* ˈɔːrɡ-/ [C] (*formal or biology*) something that is alive, especially sth that is extremely small: *Even the simplest, single-celled organisms show examples of this behaviour.*

thing [C] a living creature: *All living things are composed of cells.* ◇ *He ran down the hill, screaming like a wild thing.* ❶ In this meaning **thing** is used especially in the collocation *living thing*.

annoy *verb* See also the entry for ANGER

annoy · frustrate · irritate · get on sb's nerves · wind sb up · bug · displease · exasperate
These words all mean to make sb slightly angry or impatient.

displease	annoy	exasperate
bug	frustrate	
	irritate	
	get on sb's nerves	
	wind sb up	

PATTERNS AND COLLOCATIONS
▸ It annoys me / irritates me / gets on my nerves / bugs me **that** / **when**...
▸ **What** annoys me / frustrates me / irritates me / gets on my nerves / bugs me **is the way** / **the fact that**...
▸ to **really** annoy sb / irritate sb / get on sb's nerves / wind sb up / bug sb

annoy [T] to make sb slightly angry: *His constant joking was beginning to annoy her.* ◇ *It really annoys me when people don't say thank you.* ◇ *It annoys me to see him getting ahead of me.* See also **annoyance** → FRUSTRATION

frustrate /frʌˈstreɪt; *AmE* ˈfrʌstreɪt/ [T] to make sb feel annoyed or impatient because they cannot do or achieve what they want: *What frustrates him is that there's too little money to spend on the project.* See also **frustration** → FRUSTRATION, **frustrated** → UNHAPPY 2

irritate [T] to annoy sb, especially by sth that you continuously do or by sth that continuously happens: *The way she puts on that accent really irritates me.* ◇ *She was irritated by his continued refusal to believe her.* See also **irritable** → IRRITABLE, **irritation** → FRUSTRATION

get on sb's 'nerves *idiom* (*informal*) to annoy sb: *That music is getting on my nerves.* ◇ *It didn't take long before we started getting on each other's nerves.* See also **nerves** → NERVOUS

,wind sb 'up *phrasal verb* (*BrE, informal*) to deliberately say or do sth in order to annoy sb: *Calm down! Can't you see he's only winding you up?* ◇ *That can't be true! You're winding me up!*

bug (**-gg-**) [T] (*informal*) to slightly annoy or worry sb: *What's the matter? Is there something bugging you?*

displease [T] (*formal*) to make sb feel upset, annoyed or not satisfied: *The tone of the letter displeased her.* **OPP please** → PLEASE, See also **displeasure** → FRUSTRATION

exasperate /ɪɡˈzæspəreɪt; *BrE* also -ˈzɑːsp-/ [T] to annoy sb very much: *Her moods exasperated him.* ◇ *She was clearly exasperated by all my questions.* See also **exasperation** → FRUSTRATION

annoyed *adj.* See also the entry for ANGRY

annoyed · irritated · exasperated · put out
These words all describe sb feeling slightly angry about sth.

PATTERNS AND COLLOCATIONS
▸ annoyed / irritated / put out **at** sth
▸ irritated / exasperated **by** sb / sth
▸ annoyed / put out **about** sth
▸ annoyed / irritated / exasperated **with** sb
▸ annoyed / irritated / put out **that**...
▸ annoyed / irritated / put out **to find** / **see**...
▸ to **feel** annoyed / irritated / exasperated / put out
▸ a **bit** / **slightly** / **quite** / **rather** annoyed / irritated / put out

annoyed slightly angry: *I was* **annoyed with myself** *for giving in so easily.* ◇ *I bet she was annoyed at having to write it out again.* ◇ *He tried to ignore the annoyed looks from the other customers.* See also **annoyance** → FRUSTRATION

irritated slightly angry: *She was getting more and more irritated by his comments.* See also **irritable** → IRRITABLE, **irritation** → FRUSTRATION

NOTE ANNOYED OR IRRITATED? In many cases you can use either word, although **annoyed** is more frequent, especially in spoken English. You are usually **irritated** by things that other people do or say. You can be **annoyed** with yourself or at things that you have to do.

exasperated /ɪɡˈzæspəreɪtɪd; *BrE* also -ˈzɑːsp-/ extremely annoyed, especially if you cannot do anything to improve the situation: *She was becoming exasperated with all the questions they were asking.* ◇ *'Why not?' he asked in an exasperated voice.* See also **exasperation** → FRUSTRATION

,put 'out [not before noun] (*rather informal, especially spoken*) annoyed, offended or upset by sth that sb has said or done: *She looked really put out when I said I didn't agree.*

annoying *adj.*

annoying · irritating · frustrating · tiresome · infuriating · maddening · galling · trying · pesky
These words all describe sb / sth that makes you feel angry or annoyed.

▶ to **send** an answer / a reply / an acknowledgement
▶ to **make no** answer / reply / response

PATTERNS AND COLLOCATIONS

▶ annoying / irritating / frustrating / tiresome / infuriating / galling / trying **for** sb
▶ an annoying / an irritating / a tiresome / an infuriating / a pesky **man**
▶ an annoying / an irritating / a tiresome / an infuriating / a maddening **habit**
▶ to **find sb / sth** annoying / irritating / frustrating / tiresome / infuriating / galling
▶ **very** annoying / irritating / frustrating / tiresome / galling / trying
▶ **absolutely** infuriating / maddening

annoying making you feel slightly angry or annoyed: *I find her very annoying.* ◇ *The annoying thing was that I only had myself to blame.* See also **annoyance** → FRUSTRATION
▶ **annoyingly** *adv.*: *Annoyingly, I'd left my wallet at home.*
irritating annoying: *The way she stares at me is extremely irritating.* ◇ *His most irritating habit was eating with his mouth open.* See also **irritable** → IRRITABLE, **irritation** → FRUSTRATION
▶ **irritatingly** *adv.*: *He was irritatingly quiet all day.*

NOTE ANNOYING OR IRRITATING? You can usually use either word, although **annoying** is more frequent, especially in spoken English. It is usually other people or their habits that are **irritating**; **annoying** can also describe facts and situations that make you feel annoyed.

frustrating making you feel annoyed and impatient because you cannot do or achieve what you want: *It's frustrating to have to wait so long.* ◇ *The frustrating thing is, they probably won't even be in when we get there.*
❶ Facts and situations are **frustrating**, but NOT people or their habits: a frustrating man/habit See also **frustrated** → UNHAPPY 2, **frustration** → FRUSTRATION
▶ **frustratingly** *adv.*: *Progress was frustratingly slow.*
tiresome (*especially written*) making you feel annoyed or bored: *The children were being very tiresome.* ◇ *Buying a house can be a tiresome business.*
infuriating /ɪnˈfjʊəriːeɪtɪŋ; *AmE* -ˈfjʊr-/ making you feel very angry: *an infuriating child/delay* ◇ *It is infuriating trying to talk to someone who just looks out of the window.* See also **infuriate** → ANGER *verb*
▶ **infuriatingly** *adv.*: *He just smiled infuriatingly.* ◇ *Infuriatingly, the shop had just closed.*
maddening making you very angry or crazy: *He found her behaviour maddening.* See also **mad** → ANGRY *adj.*
▶ **maddeningly** *adv.*: *Progress is maddeningly slow.*
galling /ˈɡɔːlɪŋ/ making you angry because it is unfair: *It was galling to have to do it all over again.*
trying annoying or difficult to deal with: *She can be very trying.* ◇ *These are **trying times** for all of us.*
pesky [only before noun] (*especially AmE, informal*) annoying: *those pesky insects/kids* ◇ *I can't go out tonight – I've got that pesky interview tomorrow.*

answer *noun*

answer · reply · response · acknowledgement · retort
These are all words for sth that you say, write or do to react to a question or situation.

PATTERNS AND COLLOCATIONS

▶ an answer / a reply / a response / a retort **to** sb / sth
▶ an answer / a reply / a response / an acknowledgement **from** sb
▶ **in** answer / reply / response **to** sb / sth
▶ a / an **quick / immediate / appropriate / suitable** answer / reply / response / retort
▶ a **written** answer / reply / response / acknowledgement
▶ a / an **sharp / angry / curt** reply / response / retort
▶ a **formal** reply / response / acknowledgement
▶ to **get / receive** an answer / a reply / a response / an acknowledgement
▶ to **give / write / elicit / produce / wait for** an answer / a reply / a response

answer [C] something that you say, write or do to react to a question, request or situation: *Have you had an answer to your letter?* ◇ *As if in answer to our prayers, she offered to lend us the money.* ◇ *I rang the bell, but there was no answer.* ◇ *I expect a **straight answer** to a straight question.*
reply [C, U] (*especially written*) a spoken or written answer to a question, request, invitation, advertisement, etc: *We had over 110 replies to our advertisement.* ◇ *I haven't received a reply from him yet.* ◇ *What did they say **in reply**?* ◇ *I asked her what her name was but she made no reply.*
response [C, U] (*rather formal*) a spoken or written answer to a question, request or suggestion: *95% of customers can expect a response to their enquiries within 10 days.* ◇ *I knocked on the door but there was no response.*

NOTE ANSWER, RESPONSE OR REPLY? **Reply** is slightly more formal than **answer** and is used especially in written English. It is often used when reporting a conversation or to refer to a written answer to an advertisement or invitation. **Response** is more formal than **reply** and is often used in business contexts.

acknowledgement (also **acknowledgment**) /ək-ˈnɒlɪdʒmənt; *AmE* ək'nɑːl-/ [C] (*rather formal*) a letter saying that sth has been received: *I didn't receive an acknowledgement of my application.*
retort /rɪˈtɔːt; *AmE* rɪˈtɔːrt/ [C] (*rather formal, written*) a quick, angry or humorous reply to sth, especially to sth sb says: *He opened his mouth to **make a** caustic **retort**.* ◇ *She bit back* (= stopped herself from making) *a sharp retort.*

answer *verb*

answer · reply · respond · retort · acknowledge · write back · get back to sb
These words all mean to say, write or do sth as a reaction to a question or situation.

PATTERNS AND COLLOCATIONS

▶ to reply / respond / get back / write back **to** sb / sth
▶ to answer / reply / respond / retort / acknowledge sth / get back to sb **with** sth
▶ to answer / reply / respond / retort / write back **that…**
▶ to answer / reply to / respond to / acknowledge a / an **question / letter / email**
▶ to answer / reply to / respond to **mail / correspondence**
▶ to answer / reply to / respond to an **ad / advert / advertisement / accusation**
▶ to answer / reply to / acknowledge a **claim**
▶ to answer / reply to / acknowledge a / an **query / enquiry / charge**
▶ to answer / reply / respond / acknowledge sth **quickly**
▶ to answer / reply / respond **directly / promptly / personally**
▶ to answer / reply / respond / retort **coldly / curtly / sharply / stiffly / angrily / bitterly / indignantly / sarcastically / bluntly**
▶ to answer / reply / respond **honestly / politely / truthfully / vaguely / cautiously / calmly / quietly / slowly**

answer [I, T] to say, write or do sth as a reaction to a question or situation: *I repeated the question, but she didn't answer.* ◇ *You haven't answered my question.* ◇ *Come on, answer me! Where were you?* ◇ *Could somebody **answer the phone*** (= pick up the phone when it rings)? ◇ *They never bother to **answer the door*** (= open the door when sb knocks/rings). ◇ *My prayers have been answered* (= I have got what I wanted). ◇ *'I'd prefer to walk,' she answered.*
reply [I, T] (*especially written*) to say, write or do sth as an answer to sb/sth: *He never replied to any of my letters.* ◇ *She only replied with a smile.* ◇ *The senator replied that he was not in a position to comment.*
respond [I, T] (*rather formal, especially business*) to say or write sth as an answer to sb/sth: *I asked him his name, but he didn't respond.* ◇ *More than fifty people responded to the advertisement.* ◇ *'I'm not sure,' she responded.*

You can *answer sb/sth* or just *answer*, but NOT 'answer to sb/sth'; you can *reply/respond to sb/sth* or just *reply/respond*, but NOT 'reply/respond sb/sth'. **Reply** is slightly more formal than **answer** and is used especially in written English; **respond** is more formal than **reply** and is also used especially in business contexts. The three words share many uses but you can only *answer the phone/the door/ sb's prayers*, NOT: ~~reply/respond to the phone/the door/ sb's prayers~~; you can *answer/respond to a call* but NOT: ~~reply to a call~~.

retort /rɪˈtɔːt; AmE rɪˈtɔːrt/ [T] (*rather formal, written*) to reply quickly to a comment in an angry, offended or humorous way: *'Don't be ridiculous!' Pat retorted angrily.*

acknowledge /əkˈnɒlɪdʒ; AmE əkˈnɑːl-/ [T] (*rather formal*) to tell sb that you have received sth that they sent to you; to show that you have heard and understood a question or comment: *All applications will be acknowledged.* ◇ *Please acknowledge receipt of this letter.*

,write 'back *phrasal verb* to write sb a letter replying to their letter: *I'm afraid I never wrote back to him.* ◇ *She wrote back saying that she couldn't come.*

,get 'back to sb *phrasal verb* (*informal*) to speak or write to sb again later, especially in order to give a reply: *I'll find out and get back to you.*

anticipate *verb*

anticipate · pre-empt · forestall · beat sb to sth
These words all mean to prevent or prepare for sth that you think will happen in the future, or to do sth before sb else does it.

PATTERNS AND COLLOCATIONS
▸ to anticipate / pre-empt **what**…
▸ to anticipate / pre-empt / forestall a **problem** / **question** / **possibility** / **plan**
▸ to pre-empt / forestall **criticism** / **discussion**
▸ to anticipate / forestall **possible** / **potential** problems, etc.

anticipate /ænˈtɪsɪpeɪt/ [T] to see what might happen in the future and take action to prepare for it; to do sth before sb else does it: *We need someone who can anticipate and respond to changes in the fashion industry.* ◇ *Try and anticipate what the interviewer will ask.* See also **anticipation** → EXPECTATION

pre-empt /priˈempt/ [T] (*rather formal, especially written*) to prevent sth from happening by taking action to stop it; to do or say sth before sb else does it: *The government announced it had pre-empted a coup attempt.* ◇ *I do not want to pre-empt anything that the treasurer is going to say.*

forestall /fɔːˈstɔːl; AmE fɔːr-/ [T] (*rather formal, especially written*) to pre-empt sth: *Any plans for a peaceful settlement were forestalled by the intervention of the army.*

NOTE PRE-EMPT OR FORESTALL? In most cases you can use either word: *to pre-empt/forestall problems/questions/ criticism/discussion/plans* ◇ *He opened his mouth to speak but Richard pre-empted/forestalled him.* However, although you can either **pre-empt** or **forestall** sth bad that is going to happen, you can also **pre-empt** sth good, such as good *news*, that sb has to say: *I would not want to pre-empt any hopeful news that he might tell us tonight.* ◇ ~~to forestall any hopeful news~~

'beat sb to sth, ,beat sb 'to it *phrasal verb* (*rather informal*) to get somewhere or do sth before sb else does: *She beat me to the top of the hill.* ◇ *I was about to take the last cake, but he beat me to it.*

apologize (*BrE also* -ise) *verb*

apologize · regret · beg sb's pardon
These words all mean to say sorry for sth.

PATTERNS AND COLLOCATIONS
▸ to apologize / beg sb's pardon **for** sth
▸ to apologize / regret **that** …
▸ to apologize / beg sb's pardon **if** …

apologize (*BrE also* -**ise**) [I] to say that you are sorry for doing sth wrong or causing a problem: *Why should I apologize?* ◇ *Go and **apologize to** her.* ◇ *We apologize for the late departure of this flight.* See also **apologetic** → SORRY
▸ **apology** *noun* [C, U]: *to offer/make/demand/accept an apology* ◇ *You **owe him an apology** for what you said.* ◇ *a letter of apology*

regret (-**tt**-) [T, I] (*formal, especially written*) used to say in a polite or formal way that you are sorry or sad about a situation: *The airline regrets any inconvenience.* ◇ *I regret that I am unable to accept your kind invitation.* See also **regret** → GUILT *noun*

beg sb's 'pardon *idiom* (-**gg**-) (*especially BrE, formal, spoken*) used to apologize to sb in a polite or formal way for sth that you have done or said: *I beg your pardon. I must have the wrong room.*

NOTE REGRET OR BEG SB'S PARDON? **Regret** is used in writing and in formal announcements, especially on behalf of a company or organization; **beg sb's pardon** is also formal but it is more personal, used by an individual speaking to another individual.

apparent *adj.*

apparent · outward · purported · seeming · superficial · ostensible
These words all describe things that appear to be real or true but may not be.

PATTERNS AND COLLOCATIONS
▸ apparent / outward **calm**
▸ an apparent / a purported **attack**
▸ an apparent / a seeming **contradiction** / **failure** / **inability** / **indifference** / **reluctance**
▸ an apparent / a superficial **similarity**
▸ an outward / a superficial **appearance**
▸ the apparent / ostensible **purpose** / **reason**

apparent /əˈpærənt/ [usually before noun] that appears to be real or true but may not be: *My parents were concerned at my apparent lack of enthusiasm for school.* ◇ *Their affluence is more apparent than real* (= they are not as rich as they seem to be). See also **apparent** → CLEAR *adj.* 1, **appear** → SEEM
▸ **apparently** *adv.*: *I thought she had retired, but apparently* (= in fact) *she hasn't.* ◇ *He paused, apparently lost in thought.*

outward [only before noun] connected with the way people or things appear to be rather than with what is actually true: *Mark showed no outward signs of distress.* ◇ *To all outward appearances* (= as far as it was possible to judge from the outside) *they were perfectly happy.* ❶ **Outward** collocates especially with words for different kinds of form or sign: *form, appearance, display, expression, indication* and *sign*. **OPP** **inward** ❶ **Inward** describes things that are inside your mind and not shown to other people: *Her calm expression hid her inward panic.*
▸ **outwardly** *adv.*: *Though badly frightened, she remained outwardly composed.* ◇ *Outwardly, the couple seemed perfectly happy.* **OPP** **inwardly**

purported /pəˈpɔːtɪd; AmE pərˈpɔːrt-/ [only before noun] (*formal*) that has been stated to have happened or be true, when this might not be the case: *He was seen at the scene of the purported crime.*
▸ **purportedly** *adv.*: *a letter purportedly written by Mozart*

seeming [only before noun] (*formal*) apparent: *We discussed the seeming contradiction of his arguments.* See also **seem** → SEEM
▸ **seemingly** *adv.*: *a seemingly endless journey* ◇ *a*

seemingly impossible task ◇ *Seemingly, he borrowed the money from the bank.*

superficial /ˌsuːpəˈfɪʃl; ˌsjuː-; *AmE* ˌsuːpərˈf-/ appearing to be true, real or important until you look at it more carefully: *Superficial similarities can be deceptive.* ◇ *When you first meet her, she gives a superficial impression of warmth and friendliness.* ❶ Typical collocates of **superficial** in this meaning are *impression, appearance* and words relating to how things look the same, such as *likeness, resemblance* and *similarity*.

ostensible /ɒˈstensəbl; *AmE* ɑːˈst-/ [only before noun] (*formal*) appearing or stated to be real or true, when this is perhaps not the case: *The ostensible reason for his absence was illness.* ❶ **Ostensible** is used especially to talk about sb's *reason* for doing sth or the *purpose* of doing sth.

▸ **ostensibly** *adv.*: *Troops were sent in, ostensibly to protect the civilian population.*

appear *verb*

appear · emerge · show · loom · pop · manifest itself · form · come out
These words all mean to start to be seen in a place.

▸ to appear / emerge **from** sth
▸ to appear / pop **into view / up**
▸ to appear / emerge / loom / pop **out of** sth
▸ to **suddenly** appear / emerge / show / loom / pop / come out
▸ to **gradually** appear / emerge / manifest itself / form
▸ to **eventually** appear / emerge / show
▸ to **finally** appear / emerge / loom

appear [I] (usually used with an adverb or preposition) to start to be seen: *She suddenly appeared in the doorway.* ◇ *If a rash appears, call a doctor immediately.* ◇ *Posters for the gig appeared all over town.* ◇ *New shoots are just appearing at the base of the plant.* ◇ *Her dead mother appeared to her in a dream.* **OPP disappear** → DISAPPEAR

emerge /iˈmɜːdʒ; *AmE* iˈmɜːrdʒ/ [I] (usually used with an adverb or preposition) to leave a dark, confined or hidden place and be seen: *The swimmer emerged from the lake.* ◇ *They suddenly emerged into brilliant sunshine.* ◇ *The crabs emerge at low tide to look for food.*

show [I, T] to be visible; to allow sth to be seen: *The cloth was folded so that the stain didn't show.* ◇ *His hands were clenched, the whites of the knuckles showing.* ◇ *She had a warm woollen hat on that left only her eyes and nose showing.* ◇ *A white carpet will show every mark.* ◇ *Come out and show yourselves* (= let us see you)*!*

loom /luːm/ [I] (usually used with an adverb or preposition) (*written*) to start to appear as a large shape that is not clear, especially in a frightening or threatening way: *Something huge and black loomed out of the mist.* ◇ *The city walls loomed up ahead of them.*

pop (-**pp**-) [I] (always used with an adverb or preposition) to suddenly appear, especially when not expected: *The window opened and a head popped out.* ◇ *When you send a fax, a dialog box pops up on the screen.* ◇ *An idea suddenly popped into his head.*

manifest itself /ˈmænɪfest/ [T] (*formal*) to become visible or noticeable: *Heatstroke sometimes manifests itself as red spots on the skin.* ◇ *A new trend seems to have manifested itself.*

form [I] (*rather formal*) (especially of natural things) to begin to exist and gradually develop into a particular shape: *Flowers appeared, but fruits failed to form.* ◇ *Storm clouds are forming on the horizon.*

ˌcome ˈout *phrasal verb* (of the sun, moon or stars) to become visible: *The rain stopped and the sun came out.*

appearance *noun*

appearance · look · manner · air · looks
These are all words for the way that sb/sth looks, behaves or seems to be.

▸ (a) **striking / distinctive** appearance / look / looks
▸ sb's **general** appearance / manner / air
▸ a **confident** appearance / manner / air
▸ to **have** a … appearance / look / manner / air
▸ to **lose** your / its … appearance / air / looks
▸ to **improve** sb / sth's appearance / look / looks
▸ to **like** sb / sth's appearance / look / manner / looks
▸ to **give sb** the appearance / look / air of sth

appearance [C] the way that sb/sth looks on the outside; what sb/sth seems to be: *The dog was similar in general appearance to a spaniel.* ◇ *She had never been greatly concerned about her appearance.* ◇ ***To all appearances*** (= as far as people could tell) *he was dead.* ◇ *He **gave every appearance of*** (= seemed very much to be) *enjoying himself.* ◇ *When she lost all her money, she was determined to **keep up appearances*** (= hide the true situation and pretend that everything was going well). See also **appear** → SEEM

look [C, usually sing.] the way that sb/sth looks; the appearance of sb/sth: *It's going to rain today **by the look of it*** (= judging by appearances). ◇ *I don't like the look of that guy* (= I don't trust him, judging by his appearance). ◇ *Looks can be deceptive.* See also **look** → SEEM

> **NOTE APPEARANCE OR LOOK? Appearance** is often used in talking about how sb/sth seems in contrast to how they really are. Typical collocates are *outward* and *external* and the phrase *keep up appearances*. **Appearance** is also commonly used to talk about how people make themselves look attractive: *She was always very particular about her appearance.* **Look** is used more in spoken English and is used especially in the phrases *by the look of it/him/her, etc.* and *(not) like the look of sb.*

manner [sing.] the way that sb behaves and speaks towards other people: *She has a friendly, relaxed manner.* ◇ *His manner was polite but cool.*

air [sing.] the particular feeling or impression that is given by sb/sth; the way sb does sth: *The room had an air of luxury.* ◇ *There was an air of complete confidence about her.* See also **aura** → ATMOSPHERE

looks [pl.] a person's appearance, especially when the person is attractive: *She has her father's good looks.* ◇ *He lost his looks* (= became less attractive) *in later life.* See also **good-looking** → BEAUTIFUL 1

appetite *noun*

1 Don't spoil your appetite by eating between meals.
2 an appetite for scandal

1 appetite · hunger · palate
These are all words for the desire to eat food.

▸ to **satisfy** sb's appetite / hunger

appetite /ˈæpɪtaɪt/ [U, C, usually sing.] a physical desire for food: *He suffered from headaches, insomnia and **loss of appetite**.* ◇ *She's always had a **healthy appetite*** (= likes to eat a lot, but in a healthy way). ◇ *Let's go for a walk to **work up an appetite**.* ◇ *Don't **spoil your appetite** by eating between meals.*

hunger [U] the feeling caused by a need to eat: *The meal had not satisfied his hunger.* ◇ *The walkers were weak from hunger.* See also **hungry** → HUNGRY

> **NOTE APPETITE OR HUNGER? Appetite** is a positive, healthy desire for food; **hunger** is a less pleasant feeling.

palate /ˈpælət/ [C, usually sing.] (*rather formal*) the ability to recognize and/or enjoy good food and drink: *The restaurant offers a menu to tempt even the most **jaded palate*** (= even people who are really bored with the food and drink that is usually on offer). ◊ *Children do not usually have the sophisticated palate necessary to enjoy such delicate flavours.*

2 appetite · longing · yearning · craving · hunger
These are all words for a strong desire for sth.

PATTERNS AND COLLOCATIONS
▶ an appetite/a longing/a yearning/a craving/a hunger **for** sth
▶ a longing/yearning/craving **to do** sth
▶ a **great** appetite/longing/yearning/hunger
▶ a **desperate** longing/yearning/craving
▶ sb's **sexual** appetite/longings/hunger
▶ to **have** an appetite/a longing/a yearning/a craving/a hunger
▶ to **feel** a longing/yearning/craving/hunger
▶ to **satisfy** your appetite/longing/yearnings/craving/hunger

appetite /'æpɪtaɪt/ [C] a strong desire for sth, especially more of sth that you have already had: *The public has an insatiable appetite for scandal.* ◊ *The preview was intended to whet your appetite* (= make you want more). ❶ People typically have an *enormous, healthy, huge* or *insatiable* **appetite**. They may have an appetite for *information, knowledge, life, more, power, recognition, sex* or *work*.

longing [C, U] a strong and emotional desire, especially for sb/sth that you have not got or cannot have: *Her diary entries reflect a longing for home.* ◊ *He was filled with romantic longings.* ◊ *His voice was husky with longing* (= sexual desire). ❶ **Longing** is mainly used to talk about wanting people or things that you feel emotionally attached to. See also **long** → LONG *verb*

yearning /'jɜːnɪŋ; AmE 'jɜːrnɪŋ/ [C, U] (*written*) a longing: *He repressed his yearnings for a quiet life.* ◊ *She had no great yearning to go back.* See also **yearn** → LONG *verb*

NOTE LONGING OR YEARNING? In many cases you can use either word. **Yearning** is more literary than **longing** and is not used to talk about physical or sexual desires.

craving [C] a strong desire for sth that you cannot get enough of: *I have this terrible craving for chocolate.* ◊ *She felt a desperate craving to be loved.* ❶ A **craving** is nearly always for sweet or fatty foods, cigarettes or love. See also **crave** → LONG *verb*

NOTE APPETITE OR CRAVING? People have an **appetite** for things that they enjoy; they have **cravings** for things that they feel ill without. A **craving** is an unpleasant feeling, but an **appetite** may be seen as quite healthy.

hunger [sing.] (*rather formal, written*) a strong desire for sth: *She has an incredible hunger for success.* ◊ *Nothing seemed to satisfy their hunger for truth.* ❶ People typically have a **hunger** for *success, truth, information* or *knowledge*. See also **hungry** → EAGER

apply *verb*
1 apply sanction/common sense
2 special conditions apply

1 See also the entry for USE 1
apply · impose · enforce · put sth into effect · put sth into practice
These words all mean to cause sth such as a law, or knowledge or skills to be used.

PATTERNS AND COLLOCATIONS
▶ to apply/impose/enforce/put into effect/put into practice **measures**
▶ to apply/impose/enforce/put into practice a **law**
▶ to apply/impose/enforce a **rule/regulation/restriction/penalty/punishment/regime/sanction/standard**
▶ to apply/impose/enforce **guidelines/discipline**
▶ to enforce/put into effect/put into practice **recommendations**
▶ to apply/impose/put into practice a **principle**
▶ to apply/impose/put into effect/put into practice **ideas**

apply [T] (*rather formal*) to use a law or punishment, or knowledge or skills, or make sth work in a particular situation: *Political pressure has been applied to the colony's government in an attempt to win the contract.* ◊ *The new technology was applied to farming.* ◊ *Now is the time to apply the insights you have gained from your studies.* See also **application** → USE *noun*

impose [T] (*rather formal*) to introduce a new law, rule or tax; to order that a particular rule or punishment be used; to force sb/sth to have to deal with sth that is difficult or unpleasant: *A new tax was imposed on fuel.* ◊ *A prison sentence of 25 years was imposed on each of the defendants.* ◊ *The time limits are imposed on us by factors outside our control.*

enforce [T] (*rather formal*) to make sure that people obey a particular law or rule: *The legislation will be difficult to enforce.* ◊ *United Nations troops enforced a ceasefire in the area.*

ˌput sth into efˈfect *phrase* to cause sth such as a rule or recommendation to come into use: *The recommendations will soon be put into effect.*

ˌput sth into ˈpractice *phrase* to cause ideas or knowledge to come into use: *She's determined to put her new ideas into practice.* See also **practice** → USE *noun*

2 apply · relate to sb/sth · be about sth · have/be to do with sth · concern · refer to sb/sth · deal with sth · treat
These words all mean to be relevant to or connected with sb/sth, or to have sb/sth as a subject.

PATTERNS AND COLLOCATIONS
▶ a **rule/law** applies to/relates to/concerns/refers to/deals with sth
▶ a **chapter/poem** is about/is concerned with/refers to/deals with sth
▶ a **book/film** is about/is concerned with/deals with sth
▶ to **specifically/directly** apply to/relate to/be about/have to do with/be concerned with/refer to/deal with sth

apply [I, T] (not used in the progressive tenses) to be relevant to or connected with sb/sth: *Special conditions apply if you are under 18.* ◊ *What I am saying applies only to some of you.* ◊ *The word 'unexciting' could never be applied to her novels.*

relate to sb/sth *phrasal verb* (not used in the progressive tenses) to be connected with sb/sth; to refer to sb/sth: *We shall discuss the problem as it relates to our specific case.* ◊ *The second paragraph relates to the situation in Scotland.*

be about sth *phrase* (not used in the progressive tenses) to have sb/sth as a subject; to be the purpose of sth: *What's his new book about?* ◊ *Movies are all about making money these days* (= they make movies for the purpose of making money). ◊ *What was all that about* (= what was the reason for what has just happened)? See also **cover** → INCLUDE 1

have/be to do with sth *phrase* (not used in the progressive tenses) to be connected with sth; to be the reason for sth: *Her job has something to do with computers.* ◊ *'What do you want to see me about?' 'It's to do with that letter you sent me.'* ◊ *Hard work has a lot to do with* (= is an important reason for) *her success.* ❶ You can also use **have/be to do with** to talk about people, especially in negative sentences and questions. In these cases it means to be involved with sb, or to be of interest to sb for a good reason: *I'd have nothing to do with him, if I were you.* ◊ *Mind your own business – this is nothing to do with you.*

concern (also **be concerned with sth**) [T] (not used in the progressive tenses) (*rather formal*) to have sb/sth as a subject: *The story concerns the prince's efforts to rescue Pamina.* ◊ *The book is primarily concerned with Soviet-American relations during the Cold War.* ◊ *This chapter concerns itself with the historical background.*

reˈfer to sb/sth *phrasal verb* (-rr-) to describe or be connected to sb/sth: *The term 'Arts' usually refers to humanities and social sciences.* ◊ *This paragraph refers to the events of last year.*

'deal with sth *phrasal verb* (not used in the progressive tenses) to have sth as a subject: *Her poems often deal with the subject of death.* ◇ *The second half of the book deals exclusively with public relations.*

> **NOTE** BE ABOUT STH, CONCERN OR DEAL WITH STH? **Be about sth** is the most general of these expressions; **concern** and **deal with sth** both suggest a formal, serious or thorough discussion of a subject.

treat [T] to deal with or discuss a subject in a particular way: *The question is treated in more detail in the next chapter.*
  ▶ **treatment** *noun* [U, C]: *Shakespeare's treatment of madness in 'King Lear'*

appoint *verb* See also the entry for EMPLOY

appoint · elect · name · nominate · designate · co-opt · commission · vote sb in · vote sb into/onto sth
These verbs all mean to officially or formally choose sb for a job, especially an important one, or for a position of responsibility.

PATTERNS AND COLLOCATIONS
▶ to appoint sb / name sb / nominate sb / designate sb / commission sb / vote sb in **as** sth
▶ to appoint / elect / name / nominate sb **to** sth
▶ to appoint / elect / name / nominate / designate / co-opt sb **to do** sth
▶ to **officially / formally** appoint / name / nominate / designate sb

appoint [T] to choose sb for a job, especially an important one, or for a position of responsibility: *They have appointed a new principal at my son's school.* ◇ *She has recently been appointed to the committee.* ◇ *They appointed him (as) captain of the national team.* ◇ *A lawyer was appointed to represent the child.* **OPP** dismiss → FIRE *verb*
  ▶ **appointment** *noun* [C, U]: *Following her recent appointment to the post...* ◇ *the appointment of a new captain for the England team* See also **appointment** → JOB
elect [T] to choose sb to do a particular job by voting for them: *an elected assembly/leader/representative* ◇ *the newly elected government* ◇ *She became the first black woman to be elected to the Senate.* ◇ *What changes will he make if he gets elected?* ❶ **Elect** is most often used in political contexts to refer to choosing governments, leaders and representatives, who are chosen by a formal, written vote. See also **election** → CHOICE 1, **election** → ELECTION
  ▶ **electoral** *adj.*: *electoral systems/reforms*
name [T] to choose sb for a job or position: *I had no hesitation in naming him (as) captain.* ◇ *Mr Shah has been named to run the new research unit.*
nominate /'nɒmɪneɪt; AmE 'nɑːm-/ [T] (*rather formal*) to choose sb to do a particular job or task: *I have been nominated to the committee.* ◇ *She was nominated to speak on our behalf.* See also **nomination** → CHOICE 1
designate /'dezɪgneɪt/ [T] (*formal*) to choose sb for a particular job or position: *The director is allowed to designate his/her successor.*

> **NOTE** NAME, NOMINATE OR DESIGNATE? **Name** is much more frequent, especially in written language. It is often used in business contexts to talk about appointing a new boss, committee member, etc. However, **nominate** is used when you are talking about a particular task, not a job or position that continues for a period of time: ~~She was named to speak on our behalf.~~ **Designate** is a formal way of saying **name**.

co-'opt [T] to make sb a member of a group or committee by the agreement of all the other members: *She was co-opted onto the board.*
commission /kə'mɪʃn/ [T, usually passive] to choose sb as an officer in one of the armed forces: *He has just been commissioned (as a) pilot officer.*

vote sb 'in, vote sb 'into/'onto sth *phrasal verb* to choose sb for a position by voting for them: *He was voted in as treasurer.* ◇ *She was voted onto the board of governors.* **OPP** vote sb out, vote sb out of/off sth, See also **vote** → ELECTION

appreciate *verb*

appreciate · value · admire · treasure · cherish · prize
These words all mean to think that sb/sth is important or special.

PATTERNS AND COLLOCATIONS
▶ to value / prize sb / sth **as / for** sth
▶ to value / treasure / prize sb's **friendship**
▶ to treasure / cherish a **memory**
▶ to **really** appreciate / value / treasure / cherish sb / sth
▶ to value / prize sth **highly**

appreciate [T] (not used in the progressive tenses) to recognize the good qualities of sb/sth: *You can't really appreciate foreign literature in translation.* ◇ *His talents are not fully appreciated in that company.* ◇ *Her family doesn't appreciate her.* See also **appreciation** → ADMIRATION, **appreciative** → GOOD 6
value [T] (not used in the progressive tenses) to think that sb/sth is important: *I really value him as a friend.* ◇ *They don't seem to value honesty very highly.* See also **value** → VALUE *noun* 1, **valuable** → VALUABLE 2

> **NOTE** APPRECIATE OR VALUE? If you **value** sb/sth, they are/it is important to you, for example you value *your friends, your health, your freedom* or *sb's opinion*. If you **appreciate** sb/sth, you recognize the value of sb/sth, although they/it may not be important to you personally. It is often used in negative sentences to mean that the good qualities of sb/sth are not recognized when they should be.

admire [T] to look at sth and think that it is attractive and/or impressive: *He stood back to admire his handiwork.* ◇ *Let's just sit and admire the view.* ◇ *I've just been admiring your new car.*
treasure /'treʒə(r)/ [T] (not used in the progressive tenses) to have or keep sth that you love and that is very valuable to you: *I shall always treasure the memory of our time together.* See also **treasured** → DEAR
cherish /'tʃerɪʃ/ [T] (not used in the progressive tenses) (*formal*) to love sb/sth very much and want to protect them/it; to keep a memory or pleasant feeling in your mind for a long time: *Children need to be cherished.* ◇ *Cherish the memory of those days in Paris.* See also **cherished** → DEAR
prize [T, usually passive] to value sth highly: *an era when honesty was prized above all other virtues* ◇ *Oil of cedarwood is highly prized for its use in medicine and perfumery.* See also **prized** → DEAR

approach *verb*

approach · touch · approximate · border on sth · verge on sth · be getting on for sth
These words all mean to come close to, or just reach, sth in amount, level or quality.

PATTERNS AND COLLOCATIONS
▶ to border on / verge on **paranoia / hysteria / fanaticism / contempt / arrogance**
▶ to border on / verge on the **insane / obsessive**
▶ to approach / be getting on for **midnight / three o'clock / tea time / lunchtime, etc.**

approach [T] (*rather formal*) to come close to sth in amount, level or quality: *They have just announced profits approaching $30 million.* ◇ *Few writers approach his richness of language.*
touch [T] to just reach a particular level: *The speedometer was touching 90.*

approximate /ə'prɒksɪmeɪt; AmE ə'prɑːk-/ [T, I] (*formal*) to come close to sth in nature, amount, level or quality: *The animals were reared in conditions which approximated the wild as closely as possible.* ◇ *His story* **approximates to** *the facts that we already know.*

'**border on sth** *phrasal verb* to come very close to being sth, especially an extreme or unpleasant quality or emotion: *His devotion bordered on the obsessive.* ◇ *She felt an anxiety bordering on hysteria.*

'**verge on sth** *phrasal verb* to border on sth: *Some of his suggestions verged on the outrageous.* ◇ *She felt a dislike for him verging on contempt.*

NOTE **BORDER ON STH** OR **VERGE ON STH?** There is no real difference in meaning between these two words. **Border on sth** is about twice as frequent as **verge on sth**, which is slightly more literary.

be getting on for sth *phrase* (*especially BrE, rather informal*) to be nearly a particular time, age or number, especially a late time or old age: *It must be getting on for midnight.* ◇ *He's getting on for eighty.*

approval *noun* See also the entry for PERMISSION

approval · acceptance · agreement · favour · assent · blessing · thumbs up · acquiescence
These are all words for allowing sth to happen, usually because you think it is a good thing.

acquiescence	acceptance	approval	blessing
	agreement	favour	thumbs up
	assent		

PATTERNS AND COLLOCATIONS
▸ approval / acceptance / agreement / assent / thumbs up **for** sth
▸ **with** the approval / agreement / assent / blessing / acquiescence **of** sb
▸ **full** approval / acceptance / agreement / blessing
▸ **widespread / total / tacit / prior** approval / acceptance / agreement
▸ (the) **official** approval / acceptance / blessing
▸ to **give** your approval / your agreement / your assent / your blessing / the thumbs up **to** sth
▸ to **get** sb's approval / sb's acceptance / sb's agreement / sb's assent / sb's blessing / the thumbs up
▸ to **secure** approval / acceptance / agreement / assent / acquiescence
▸ to **receive** approval / acceptance / sb's assent / sb's blessing
▸ to **gain** approval / acceptance / agreement / assent
▸ to **nod** approval / agreement / your assent

approval [U] official permission for sth, especially a plan or request, that is given because the plan or request is considered good or good enough: *The treaty still required approval by the Senate.* ◇ *The plan will be submitted for approval next month.* ◇ *The offer is* **subject to approval** *by the shareholders* (= they need to agree to it). ◇ *The project needs the bank's* **seal of approval** (= official approval). See also **approve** → AGREE 2

acceptance [U] approval of sth by the members of a group or people in general: *A new theory emerged that quickly gained wide acceptance.* ◇ *The Assembly voted against acceptance of constitutional reform.* **OPP** **refusal, rejection** → REFUSAL, See also **accept** → AGREE 2

agreement [U] approval of a request, especially by an individual or group of individuals who have special rights in the matter: *No images may be reproduced without the artist's agreement.* ◇ *The museum secured the* **agreement** *of the owners* **to** *the loan of the statue.* ❶ **Agreement** is less official than **approval**: it is usually a matter for individuals, or all the members of a group acting as individuals, not as an official body. **OPP** **refusal** → REFUSAL, See also **agree** → AGREE 2

favour (*BrE*) (*AmE* **favor**) [U] support or approval for sb/ sth, either from a particular group of people, or from a person or group in authority: *The suggestion to close the road has* **found favour with** (= been supported by) *local people.* ◇ *The show has* **lost favour** *with viewers recently.* ◇ *It seems Tim is* **back in favour** *with the boss* (= the boss likes him again).

assent /ə'sent/ [U] (*formal*) the expression of approval or agreement; official approval of sth: *There was a general murmur of assent.* ◇ *She gave her assent to publication.* **OPP** **dissent** → DEBATE

blessing [sing.] approval of sth, especially when it is seen as a good thing and the person or group giving their approval wants it to succeed: *This arrangement received the full blessing of the committee.*

thumbs 'up *idiom* (*rather informal*) an expression of satisfaction with sth that sb has done, or approval of sth that they plan to do: *The programme is getting a big thumbs up from our target audience.* ◇ *The government is likely to give the thumbs up to the merger.* ❶ **Thumbs up** is nearly always used with the verbs *get* or *give*. **OPP** **thumbs down** ❶ If you give sth the **thumbs down** it means you are not satisfied with it or do not approve of it: *The proposals were given the thumbs down.*

acquiescence /ˌækwi'esns/ [U] (*formal*) the fact of doing what sb wants or accepting their opinions, even if you do not really want to or are not sure that they are right: *The best one can hope for is grudging acquiescence from the majority in the party.* See also **acquiesce** → AGREE 2

approve *verb*

approve · confirm · recognize · uphold · ratify · sustain · validate · certify
These words all mean to officially accept and approve of sth.

PATTERNS AND COLLOCATIONS
▸ to approve / confirm / recognize / uphold / ratify / validate / certify sth **as** sth
▸ to approve / recognize / validate a **course**
▸ to approve / uphold / ratify a **treaty**
▸ to confirm / uphold / ratify a / an **decision / agreement**
▸ to be approved / confirmed / recognized / upheld / sustained by the **court**
▸ to **officially** approve / confirm / recognize / ratify sth

approve [T, often passive] to say that sth is good enough to be used, or is correct: *The course is approved by the Department for Education.* ◇ *The auditors approved the company's accounts.*

confirm /kən'fɜːm; AmE -'fɜːrm/ [T] to make sth such as a position or agreement more definite or official: *After a six-month probationary period, her position was confirmed.* ◇ *He was confirmed as captain for the rest of the season.*
▸ **confirmation** *noun* [U, C]: *You will receive written confirmation of our decision in the next few days.*

recognize (*BrE* also **-ise**) [T, often passive] to accept and approve of sb/sth officially: *The qualifications are internationally recognized.* ◇ *The UK has refused to recognize the new regime.*

uphold /ʌp'həʊld; AmE -'hoʊld/ [T] (especially of a court) to agree that a previous decision was correct or that a request is reasonable: *The conviction was upheld by the Court of Appeal.* ◇ *The Press Council refused to uphold the complaint.*

ratify /'rætɪfaɪ/ [T] to make an agreement officially valid by voting for or signing it: *The treaty was ratified by all the member states.*
▸ **ratification** *noun* [U]: *The agreement is subject to ratification by the Senate.*

sustain /sə'steɪn/ [T] (*law*) (especially in court) to decide that a claim or objection is valid: *The court sustained his claim that the contract was illegal.* ◇ *Objection sustained!* (= said by a judge when a lawyer makes an objection in court)

validate /'vælɪdeɪt/ [T] (*formal*) to state officially that sth is useful and of an acceptable standard: *Check that their courses have been validated by a reputable organization.*

certify /'sɜːtɪfaɪ; *AmE* 'sɜːrt-/ [T, usually passive] (*rather formal*) to give sb an official document proving that they are qualified to work in a particular profession: *I was certified as a teacher in 1989.*

area *noun*

1 rural/urban areas
2 areas of study/policy/growth

---

1 area · region · part · zone · neighbourhood · district · belt · climate · quarter

These are all words for an area of land or part of a town.

PATTERNS AND COLLOCATIONS

▸ (a / an) **eastern / northern / southern / western** area / region / parts / zone / district / quarter
▸ the **central** area / region / part / zone / district
▸ the **whole / entire** area / region / zone / neighbourhood / district
▸ the **surrounding** area / region / neighbourhood / district
▸ a **remote** area / region / part
▸ a **border / coastal / geographical** area / region / zone / district
▸ an **industrial** area / region / zone / district / belt / quarter
▸ a **residential** area / zone / neighbourhood / district / quarter
▸ (a) **rural** area / region / parts / zone / district
▸ an **urban** area / region / zone / neighbourhood / district
▸ a **military** area / region / zone / district

area [C] a part of a place, town, country or the world, usually without exact limits or borders: *mountainous/ desert areas* ◇ *She knows the local area very well.* ◇ *The farm and surrounding area was flooded.* ◇ *There is heavy traffic in the downtown area tonight.* ◇ *Wreckage from the plane was scattered over a **wide area**.* ◇ *John is the London area manager.*

region [C] a large area of land, usually without exact limits or borders: *This is one of the most densely populated regions of North America.* ◇ *Soil erosion is particularly serious in dry tropical regions.* See also **region** → COUNTY

> **NOTE** **AREA** OR **REGION**? **Area** has a wider range of meaning than **region**. A **region** is always a fairly large area of a country or continent, especially when it is considered in terms of its geographical features, or its economic or political importance. An **area** can be part of a country or continent, or part of a city or town (or even a building or room or sth even smaller). See also **area** → PLACE *noun* 1

part [C] (usually followed by *of*) an area or region of the world, a country or a town: *Apples grow in many parts of the world.* ◇ *The northern part of the country is richer than the south.* ◇ *Which part of London do you come from?*

zone [C] an area or region with a particular feature or use; one of the five parts that the earth's surface is divided into by imaginary lines that are parallel to the equator: *Medical teams are on standby to fly out to the **war zone**.* ◇ *Aid workers were advised to leave the **danger zone**.* ◇ *This species is found widely distributed throughout the northern **temperate zone**.* ❶ A **time zone** is one of the 24 areas that the world is divided into, each with its own time that is one hour earlier than that of the time zone immediately to the east. See also **zone** → COUNTY

neighbourhood (*BrE*) (*AmE* **neighborhood**) /'neɪbəhʊd; *AmE* 'neɪbər-/ [C] a district or area of a town; the people who live there: *We grew up in the same neighbourhood.* ◇ *He shouted so loudly that the whole neighbourhood could hear him.* See also **neighbourhood** → PROXIMITY

district [C] an area of a country or town, especially one that has particular features: *The financial district of London is usually referred to as 'the City'.* ◇ *The house was like all the others in this exclusive residential district.* See also **district** → COUNTY

belt [C] (used with an adjective) an area with particular characteristics or where a particular group of people live: *Towns in the country's industrial belt were particularly affected by the recession.* ◇ *the US **corn belt*** ◇ (*BrE*) *We live in the **commuter belt**.* ◇ *Buffalo is an American **rust belt** city* (= in an area that used to have a lot of heavy industry) *that was home to several steel mills.*

climate [C] an area with particular weather conditions: *They wanted to move to a warmer climate.* See also **climate** → WEATHER

quarter [C, usually sing.] a district or part of a town: *The historic quarter of the city is full of grand buildings.*

---

2 area · sector · field · domain · subject · discipline · sphere · specialty · realm · branch · specialism

These are all words for divisions of activity, knowledge or interest.

PATTERNS AND COLLOCATIONS

▸ **within / outside** the area / sector / field / domain / discipline / sphere / realm of sth
▸ **beyond** the domain / sphere / realm of sth
▸ the **public / private / domestic** sector / domain / sphere / realm
▸ the **cultural** sector / field / domain / sphere / realm
▸ the **social** sector / field / sphere / realm
▸ the **economic / military** sector / field / sphere
▸ (the) **financial** area / sector / sphere
▸ the **political** field / domain / sphere / realm
▸ (the) **scientific** field / subjects / disciplines / sphere
▸ to **open up** a (new) area / field / realm of sth
▸ to **work in** the area / sector / field / domain of sth
▸ to **fall within / move into** the area / sector / domain / realm of sth

area [C] a particular aspect or division of business, knowledge, politics or other activity: *The report covers several areas of social policy.* ◇ *Don't ask me about finance – that's Mark's area.* ◇ *The big growth area of recent years has been in health clubs.*

sector [C] a part of an area of activity, especially of a country's economy: *Public sector institutions have much to learn from private sector companies.* ◇ *the manufacturing/ service sector*

field [C] an area of work or study that sb works in or is interested in: *He was equally famous in the fields of politics and of science.* ◇ *All of them are experts in their **chosen field**.* ◇ *This discovery has opened up a whole new field of research.* ◇ *'How big was the bomb if it did all that damage?' 'I don't know. It's not my field* (= that is not one of the subjects I know about).'

domain /də'meɪn; dəʊ-; *AmE* doʊ-/ [C] an area of activity or knowledge, especially one that sb is responsible for: *Physics used to be very much a male domain.* ◇ *Sensitive information should not be released into the public domain.*

subject [C] an area of knowledge studied in a school, college or university: *My favourite subject is biology.* ◇ *The core subjects are English, maths and science.* See also **subject** → SUBJECT

discipline [C] (*formal*) an area of knowledge; a subject that people study or are taught, especially at university: *Scholars from various disciplines have been working on these problems.*

sphere /sfɪə(r); *AmE* sfɪr/ [C] an area of activity, influence or interest; a particular section of society: *Debate should be confined to the sphere of economics rather than politics.* ◇ *This area was formerly within the **sphere of influence** of the US.* ◇ *He and I moved in totally different social spheres.*

specialty /'speʃəlti/ [C] (*especially AmE*) an area of work or study that sb gives most of their attention to and knows a lot about; sth that sb is good at: *He is a lawyer with a specialty in international tax.* ◇ *Telling jokes is my specialty!*

realm /relm/ [C] an area of activity, interest or knowledge: *Questions of consciousness lie outside the realm of physics.* ◇ *At the end of the speech he seemed to be moving **into the realms of** fantasy.* ❶ The word **realm** is often used to draw attention to the boundaries between one area of interest and another: things are *within/outside/ beyond the realms of sth* or people *enter/move into the realms of sth*.

branch [C] a division of a subject: *The aim is to bring together researchers from different branches of geography.*

specialism /ˈspeʃəlɪzəm/ [C, U] an area of study or work that sb officially gives most of their attention to, especially in the context of a course of study or a particular company: *He's doing a business degree with a specialism in computing.* ◇ *Dr Crane's specialism is tropical diseases.*

argue *verb* See the Topic Map for CONFLICT on p.896

argue · quarrel · bicker · fight · clash · squabble · row · fall out

These words all mean to have an angry discussion with sb because you do not agree about sth.

PATTERNS AND COLLOCATIONS
▸ to argue / quarrel / bicker / fight / clash / squabble / row / fall out **with** sb
▸ to argue / quarrel / bicker / fight / clash / squabble / row / fall out **over** sth
▸ to argue / quarrel / bicker / fight / squabble / row / fall out **about** sth

argue [I] to speak angrily to sb because you disagree with them: *You two are always arguing.* ◇ *We're always arguing with each other about money.* ◇ *I don't want to argue with you – just do it!*

quarrel (-ll-, AmE -l-) [I] to have an angry disagreement with sb, usually about a personal matter: *My sister and I used to quarrel all the time.* ◇ *She quarrelled with her brother over their father's will.*

bicker [I] to quarrel about things that are not important: *The children are always bickering about something or other.* ◇ *I'm fed up with their constant bickering.*

fight [I] (*AmE*) to argue with sb you know well, such as a family member, friend or romantic partner: *It's a trivial matter and not worth fighting about.* ◇ *I remember lying in bed listening to my parents fighting.*

clash [I] (*especially journalism*) to argue or disagree seriously with sb about sth, and to show this in public: *The leaders **clashed** with party members **on** the issue.* ◇ *The Prime Minister and his old rival clashed over European policy.*

squabble /ˈskwɒbl; AmE ˈskwɑːbl/ [I] to quarrel noisily about sth that is not important: *My sisters were squabbling over what to watch on TV.* ◇ *Will you two stop squabbling!*

NOTE BICKER OR SQUABBLE? **Squabbling** usually refers to noisy but small arguments, and happens especially between family members, close friends or children. **Bickering** can suggest that you think the arguing is childish. It is often used to describe arguments between couples in a romantic relationship.

row /raʊ/ [I] (*BrE, informal*) to have a noisy argument: *Mike and Sue are always rowing.* ◇ *She rowed with her parents about her new boyfriend.*

fall 'out *phrasal verb* to quarrel with sb, especially a friend or family member, so that you are no longer friendly with them: *He had fallen out with his family.*

argument *noun*

1 have an argument with sb
2 arguments for and against sth

1 See the Topic Map for CONFLICT on p.896, See also the entry for DEBATE

argument · row · fight · quarrel · squabble · tiff · shouting match

These are all words for a situation in which people disagree and speak angrily to each other.

PATTERNS AND COLLOCATIONS
▸ an argument / a row / a fight / a quarrel / a squabble / a tiff / a shouting match **with** sb
▸ an argument / a row / a fight / a quarrel / a squabble / a tiff / a shouting match **between** two people
▸ an argument / a row / a fight / a quarrel / a squabble **about/ over** sth
▸ a **bitter / fierce / violent** argument / row / quarrel
▸ a **big** argument / row / fight
▸ to **become / get involved in** an argument / a row / a fight / a quarrel
▸ to **have** an argument / a row / a fight / a tiff
▸ to **get into / start** an argument / a fight
▸ to **pick** a fight / a quarrel
▸ to **win / lose** an argument / a fight
▸ an argument / a row / a fight / a quarrel **breaks out**

argument [C, U] a conversation or discussion in which two or more people disagree, often angrily: *She got into an argument with the teacher.* ◇ *After some heated argument a decision was finally made.*

row /raʊ/ [C] (*BrE, informal*) a noisy argument between two or more people, especially about a personal matter: *She left him after a **blazing row**.* ◇ *He'd had a row with his son.* ❶ In journalism, **row** is also used to talk about a public disagreement between people or organizations. See also **row → CONFRONTATION**

fight [C] (*especially AmE*) an argument between people who know each other, such as family members, friends or romantic partners: *Did you two have a fight?* ◇ *We had a fight over money.*

quarrel /ˈkwɒrəl; AmE ˈkwɔːr-; ˈkwɑːr-/ [C] (*especially written*) an angry disagreement between people, often about a personal matter: *I don't want to pick a quarrel with her.* ❶ **Quarrel** [U] is also a reason for complaining about sb/sth or for disagreeing with sb/sth: *We have no quarrel with his methods.*

NOTE ARGUMENT, ROW, FIGHT OR QUARREL? A **row**, **fight** or **quarrel** is usually about a personal matter between people who know each other: *We had an argument with the waiter about the bill.* ◇ ~~*We had a row/fight/quarrel with the waiter about the bill.*~~ **Row** is only really used in British English; **fight** is mostly used in American English. A **quarrel** is usually less violent than a **row** or **fight**, but it can be a disagreement that continues over a period of time; an **argument** can be violent or it can be a serious discussion that involves defending an opinion or position.

squabble /ˈskwɒbl; AmE ˈskwɑːbl/ [C] (*rather informal*) a noisy argument, especially about sth that is not very important: *There were endless squabbles over who should sit where.*

tiff [C] (*informal*) a small argument between close friends or lovers: *She was upset because she'd had a tiff with her boyfriend.* ◇ *It's just a lovers' tiff.*

'shouting match [C] an argument in which people shout loudly at each other: *The meeting had turned into a shouting match between the tenants and the landlord.*

2 See also the entry for REASON

argument · case · defence · plea

These are all words for a reason or set of reasons that sb uses to show that sth is true or correct.

PATTERNS AND COLLOCATIONS
▸ an argument / a case / a defence **for / against** sth
▸ a **strong / robust / legal** argument / case / defence
▸ to **put forward / strengthen / weaken** an argument / a case / a defence
▸ to **support** an argument / a case

argument [C] a reason or set of reasons that sb uses to show that sth is true or correct: *There are strong arguments for and against childhood vaccinations.* ◇ *His argument was that public spending must be reduced.* ◇ *He was able to see both sides of the argument.* See also **argue → CLAIM** *verb*

case [C, usually sing.] a set of facts or arguments that support one side in a trial or discussion: *Our lawyer didn't think we had a case* (= had enough good arguments to win in court). ◇ *The report **makes out** a strong **case*** (= gives good arguments) *for spending more money on hospitals.* ◇ *the case for the defence/prosecution* ◇ *the case for/against private education*

defence (*BrE*) (*AmE* **defense**) [C] what is said in court to prove that a person did not commit a crime; the act of presenting this argument in court: *Her defence was that she was somewhere completely different at the time of the crime.* ◇ *He wanted to conduct his own defence.*
▸ **defend** *verb* [T, I]: *He has announced that he will defend himself in the case.* ◇ *Who's defending?*

plea /pliː/ [C] (always followed by *of*) (*law*) a reason given to a court for doing or not doing sth: *He was charged with murder, but got off on a plea of insanity.*
▸ **plead** *verb* [T]: *They hired a top lawyer to plead their case.*

aristocratic *adj.* See the Topic Map for THE INDIVIDUAL AND SOCIETY on p.894

aristocratic · noble · posh · upper-class
These words all describe people or things which belong to or are typical of a high social class.

PATTERNS AND COLLOCATIONS
▸ an aristocratic/ a noble/ an upper-class **family**
▸ an aristocratic/ a noble **name**/ **landowner**
▸ aristocratic/ noble **origins**/ **blood**/ **connections**
▸ an aristocratic/ upper-class **background**
▸ aristocratic/ upper-class **society**/ **culture**
▸ an aristocratic/ a posh/ an upper-class **voice**
▸ a posh/ an upper-class **person**/ **accent**

aristocratic /ˌærɪstəˈkrætɪk; *AmE* əˌrɪstə-/ belonging to or typical of the aristocracy (= people born in the highest social class who have special titles): *The memoir provided a revealing glimpse of aristocratic society.* ◇ *They were impressed by his accent and aristocratic manner.* See also **aristocracy** → ELITE, **aristocrat** → LORD

noble [usually before noun] (*rather formal*) belonging to the nobility (= people born in the highest social class who have special titles): *He was a young man **of noble birth**.* See also **nobility** → ELITE, **noble**, **nobleman** → LORD

> **NOTE** **ARISTOCRATIC** OR **NOBLE**? In this meaning **noble** is only used to talk about the family that sb was born into. **Aristocratic** can also be used to talk about families but more often it is used in a wider sense to talk about the society, culture, manners and appearance of people from such families; you can talk about *aristocratic society/culture* or sb's *aristocratic manner/voice/face/nose* but not: ~~noble society/culture~~ or sb's: ~~noble manner/voice/face/nose~~

posh (*BrE, rather informal, sometimes disapproving*) typical of or used by people who belong to a high social class: *Her parents are very posh.* ◇ *They pay for their children to go to a posh school.* **OPP** **common** → WORKING CLASS
▸ **posh** *adv.*: *She was trying to talk posh.*

ˌupper-ˈclass belonging to or typical of a high social class: *Her family is very upper-class.* ◇ *He was irritated by Blanche's upper-class accent.* See also **middle-class** → MIDDLE-CLASS, **working-class** → WORKING-CLASS, **the upper class** → ELITE

army *noun* See the Topic Map for CONFLICT on p.896

army · force · unit · contingent · legion
These are all words for an organized group of soldiers.

PATTERNS AND COLLOCATIONS
▸ (a/ the) **British**/ **French, etc.** army/ forces/ unit
▸ (a/ an) **enemy**/ **rebel** army/ forces/ units
▸ (a) **military** forces/ unit/ contingent

▸ to **deploy** an army/ a force/ a unit/ a contingent
▸ to **command**/ **be in command of** an army/ a force/ a unit/ a contingent
▸ an army/ a force/ a legion **invades** a place
▸ an army/ a force/ a unit/ a legion **advances**/ **retreats**
▸ an army/ a force/ a unit/ a contingent/ a legion **withdraws**/ **is withdrawn**

army [C+sing./pl. *v.*] a large organized group of soldiers who are trained to fight on land: *The two opposing armies faced each other across the battlefield.* ❶ **The army** [sing.+ sing./pl. *v.*] is the part of a country's armed forces that fights on land: *Her husband is **in the army**.* ◇ *After leaving school, Mike **went into the army**.* ◇ *He's an army officer.*

force [C+sing./pl. *v.*] a group of people who have been trained to protect or attack other people, usually by using weapons: *A peace-keeping force was deployed to the area.* ◇ *The country now has its own army, **air force** and navy.* ◇ *A UN-led **task force** of 28 000 troops was sent to the area.* ❶ **Forces** [pl.] are the weapons and soldiers that an army has, considered as things that may be used: *The government is negotiating cuts to nuclear forces.* **The armed forces** [pl.] (or just **the forces** in British English) are the army, navy and air force.

unit [C] a group of people who work or live together, especially a group of soldiers who form a part of an army: *The army is collaborating with guerrilla units in the border region.* ◇ *Medical units were operating in the disaster area.* See also **unit** → DEPARTMENT, **detachment** → TEAM 1

contingent /kənˈtɪndʒənt/ [C+sing./pl. *v.*] a group of soldiers that are part of a larger force: *The French contingent in the UN peacekeeping force withdrew.*

legion /ˈliːdʒən/ [C, sing.+ sing./pl. *v.*] a large group of soldiers that forms part of an army, especially the one that existed in ancient Rome: *A Roman Legion consisted of 6 000 men.*

arrange *verb*

arrange · manage · organize · set sth out · lay sth out · sort sth out · align · line sb/sth up
These words all mean to put sth in a particular order, to make it look neat or to make it work efficiently.

PATTERNS AND COLLOCATIONS
▸ to arrange/ manage/ organize/ set out/ lay out/ align/ line up sth **in** a particular way
▸ to arrange/ manage/ organize/ set out/ lay out/ sort out (your) **things**
▸ to arrange/ organize/ set out/ sort out your **thoughts**/ **ideas**
▸ to arrange/ manage/ organize/ set out **information**/ **data**
▸ to arrange/ manage/ organize/ sort out your **affairs**
▸ to organize/ set out/ lay out your **work**
▸ to arrange/ manage/ organize/ set out/ lay out/ align sth **carefully**
▸ to arrange/ organize/ set out/ lay out sth **neatly**
▸ to arrange/ manage/ organize/ set out/ lay out sth **well**/ **systematically**

arrange [T] to put sth in a particular order or position; to make sth neat or attractive: *The books are arranged alphabetically by author.* ◇ *I must arrange my financial affairs and make a will.* ◇ *She arranged the flowers in a vase.* See also **arrangement** → DESIGN *noun*

manage [T] to use or arrange resources such as money, time or information in a sensible way: *Don't tell me how to manage my affairs.* ◇ *It's a computer program that helps you to manage data efficiently.*

organize (*BrE* also **-ise**) [T] to arrange sth or the parts of sth into a particular order or structure: *Modern computers can organize large amounts of data very quickly.* ◇ *You should try and organize your time better.*

ˌset sth ˈout *phrasal verb* to arrange or display things such as furniture, ideas or information: *We'll need to set out some chairs for the meeting.* ◇ *Her work is always very well set out.*

,lay sth 'out *phrasal verb* [often passive] to plan how sth should look and arrange it in this way: *The gardens were laid out with lawns, flower beds and fountains.* ◇ *This is a very well laid out magazine.* See also **layout** → DESIGN *noun*

NOTE SET STH OUT OR LAY STH OUT? **Set out** is used more to talk about how individual things are arranged; **lay out** is used more to talk about how houses, gardens, shops, etc. are planned. When talking about text on a page, **set out** usually refers to the order of ideas or information, and **lay out** refers to how the page actually looks.

,sort sth 'out *phrasal verb* (*informal*) to organize a collection of things or the contents of sth; to organize your thoughts: *Have you sorted out all those things on the floor in the hall?* ◇ *The closet needs sorting out.* ◇ *She wanted to be alone to sort out her muddled thoughts.*

align /ə'laɪn/ [T, I] (*rather formal*) to arrange sth in the correct position; to be in the correct position, in relation to sth else, especially in a straight line: *Make sure the shelf is **aligned with** the top of the window.* ◇ *The top and bottom line of each column on the page should align.*

,line sb/sth 'up *phrasal verb* to arrange people or things in a straight line or row: *The suspects were lined up against the wall.* ◇ *He lined the bottles up along the shelf.*

arrest *verb*

arrest · catch · capture · take · apprehend · bust
These words all mean to stop sb and prevent them from escaping.

PATTERNS AND COLLOCATIONS
▸ to arrest / take / apprehend / bust sb **for** sth

arrest [T, often passive] (of the police) to formally stop and question sb about a crime that they might have committed: *A man has been arrested in connection with the robbery.* ◇ *You could **get arrested** for doing that.* ❶ A person who has been arrested will often be taken to a police station, where they can be questioned further so that the police can decide if they should be released or charged (= formally accused of a crime).
▸ **arrest** *noun* [C, U]: *The police made several arrests.* ◇ *She was put **under arrest**.*

catch [T] to stop sb and prevent them from escaping: *The police say they are doing all they can to catch the culprits.*

capture [T] to catch a person and keep them as a prisoner: *Allied troops captured over 300 enemy soldiers.*
▸ **capture** *noun* [U]: *He evaded capture for three days.*

take [T] to get control of sb and prevent them from escaping by using force or the threat of force, especially in a war: *The rebels **took him prisoner**.* ◇ *The bank robbers **took** several employees **hostage**.*

apprehend /,æprɪ'hend/ [T] (*formal*) (of the police) to catch sb and arrest them: *The police apprehended an armed suspect near the scene of the crime.*

bust [T] (*informal*) to arrest sb for a crime; (of the police) to suddenly enter a place and search it or arrest sb: *He was busted for drunk driving.* ◇ *The cops busted the place frequently.* ❶ Saying that sb has been **busted** for a crime often means that they have been arrested, charged *and* found guilty of the crime in court. **Bust** is not often used in this way to talk about very serious crimes such as murder. It is often used to talk about crimes involving drugs or alcohol.

arrival *noun*

1 the arrival of the train
2 new arrivals

1 arrival · appearance · coming · advent · approach · entrance
These are all words for an act of reaching a place or for sth new beginning.

PATTERNS AND COLLOCATIONS
▸ sb's / sth's arrival / appearance **at / in** sth
▸ a **sudden** arrival / appearance / entrance
▸ sb / sth's **imminent** arrival / appearance / approach
▸ a **dramatic** arrival / appearance / entrance
▸ to **signal** sb / sth's arrival / coming / advent / approach / entrance
▸ to **announce** sb / sth's arrival / coming / advent / approach
▸ to **await** sb / sth's arrival / appearance / coming / approach
▸ the arrival / coming / advent / approach of **spring**
▸ the arrival / coming / advent of **television** / **the railways**

arrival [C, usually sing., U] an act of reaching a place; the time when new technology is introduced: *Her arrival was a complete surprise.* ◇ *A rainstorm greeted our arrival.* ◇ *We apologize for the late arrival of the Paris train.* ◇ *There are 30 **arrivals and departures** at the ferry terminal daily.* ◇ *Tea will be served **on arrival** at the hotel.* ◇ *the arrival of pay TV* **OPP** **departure** → DEPARTURE 1

appearance [C, usually sing.] the arrival of sb/sth which is seen by other people, especially when it is not expected; the moment at which sth begins to exist or starts to be seen or used: *They were startled by the young man's sudden appearance.* ◇ *I suppose I'd **put in an appearance** at the party* (= go there for a short time). ◇ *Gas lighting made its first appearance in 1802.* **OPP** **disappearance** → DISAPPEAR

coming [C, usually sing.] an act of arriving; the time when sth new begins: *Her coming meant that the department could complete the project on time.* ◇ *From her window she could watch the **comings and goings** of visitors.* ◇ *Many jobs were lost with **the coming of** modern technology.* **OPP** **going** → DEPARTURE 1, See also **come** → COME 1

advent /'ædvent/ [sing.] (*formal, written*) the arrival of an important event, person or invention: *The fighting continued until the advent of winter.* ◇ *Before the advent of the railways, communications were slow and difficult.*

approach [sing.] movement nearer to sb/sth in distance or time: *She hadn't heard his approach.* ◇ *They felt apprehensive about the approach of war.* See also **approach** → COME 1

entrance [C, usually sing.] the act of entering a room, building or place, especially in a way that people notice: *A fanfare signalled the entrance of the king.* ◇ *After so many years in show business he knew how to **make an entrance**.* ◇ *The hero **makes his entrance** (= comes onto the stage) in scene two.* **OPP** **exit** → DEPARTURE 1, See also **enter** → ENTER

2 arrival · newcomer · entrant · latecomer
These are all words for a person who arrives at a place.

PATTERNS AND COLLOCATIONS
▸ an arrival / a newcomer **at / in** sth
▸ a newcomer / an entrant / a latecomer **to** sth
▸ **late** / **new** / **recent** arrivals / entrants

arrival [C] a person who comes to a place: *The first arrivals are going through immigration control now.* ◇ *We're expecting a **new arrival** (= a baby) in the family.* ❶ In this meaning **arrival** is usually used with an adjective such as *late, new* or *recent*.

newcomer /'njuːkʌmə(r); AmE 'nuː-/ [C] a person who has only recently arrived in a place or started an activity: *The villagers were hostile to the newcomers.* ◇ *The singer received an award for most promising newcomer.*

entrant /'entrənt/ [C] (*rather formal*) a person who has recently joined a profession or started at a college or university: *There are now more women entrants to the profession.* ◇ *The book is a useful guide for university entrants.*

latecomer /'leɪtkʌmə(r)/ [C] a person who arrives late: *Latecomers will not be admitted until the interval.*

arrive *verb* See also the entry for GET 4

---

arrive · come · get here/there · turn up · get in · come in · land · show up · appear · roll in · show
These words all mean to get to a place.

PATTERNS AND COLLOCATIONS
▸ to arrive/ turn up/ land/ show up/ appear **at/ in/ on** a place
▸ to arrive/ come **for** sb
▸ to arrive/ come/ turn up/ land/ show up/ appear **here/ there**
▸ to **have just** arrived/ come/ got here/ turned up/ got in/ come in/ landed/ appeared
▸ to **be the first/ last to** arrive/ come/ get here/ turn up/ get in/ come in/ land/ show up/ roll in/ appear
▸ to arrive/ come/ get here/ turn up/ get in/ come in **late**
▸ to arrive/ come/ get here/ turn up/ get in/ come in **early**
▸ to arrive/ get here/ turn up/ get in/ come in/ land **on time**
▸ to arrive/ come/ get here/ turn up/ show up/ appear **soon**
▸ to arrive/ get here/ land **safely**
▸ to **finally** arrive/ come/ get here/ turn up/ get in/ come in/ show up/ appear/ show
▸ to **eventually** arrive/ get here/ get in/ come in/ show up/ appear/ roll in

arrive [I] (of people) to get to a place, especially at the end of a journey; (of things) to be brought or sent to sb: *What time did they arrive?* ◇ *We were the first to arrive.* ◇ *She'll arrive in New York at around noon.* ◇ *We didn't* **arrive back** *at the hotel till very late.* ◇ *Ambulances quickly* **arrived at the scene.** ◇ *A package arrived for you this morning.* ◇ *Your application should arrive by 29 June.* **OPP** **leave, depart** → LEAVE 1

come [I] to arrive at or reach a place; to arrive somewhere in order to do or get sth: *They continued until they* **came to** *a river.* ◇ *Your breakfast is coming soon!* ◇ *Have any letters come for me?* ◇ *Help came at last.* ◇ *I've* **come for** *my book.* ◇ *I've* **come to** *get my book.* ◇ *I've* **come about** *my book.* ◇ *He came looking for me.*

'get here/there *phrase* (*rather informal, especially spoken*) to arrive somewhere: *Email me when you get there.* ◇ *Why did it take you so long to get here?* ◇ *By the time I got there, I was very cold and hungry.*

,turn 'up *phrasal verb* (*rather informal, especially spoken*) to arrive at a place or event, especially when you are not expected: *She was surprised when they turned up on her doorstep.* ◇ *After two days the child* **turned up safe and well.** ◇ *She hadn't turned up for work that morning.*

,get 'in, ,get 'into sth *phrasal verb* (*rather informal, especially spoken*) to arrive at a place, especially your home, work or the place where a journey ends: *What time did you get in (= arrive home) last night?* ◇ *I got in (= at work) late that morning.* ◇ *I'll ask him as soon as he gets in.* ◇ *His train gets into Glasgow at 12.22.*

,come 'in *phrasal verb* to arrive at a place where a journey ends; to be received: *A few minutes later our train came in.* ◇ *Come in (= enter) and make yourself at home.* ◇ *News is coming in of a serious accident.*

land [I] (usually used with an adverb or preposition) (of people) to arrive somewhere in a plane or boat; (of things) to arrive somewhere and cause difficulties that have to be dealt with: *Troops landed on the island.* ◇ *We were due to land at Gatwick.* ◇ *Who were the first men to land on the moon?* ◇ *Why do complaints always* **land on my desk** *(= why do I always have to deal with them)?*

,show 'up *phrasal verb* (*informal*) to arrive at a place, especially when you are expected: *When she* **failed to show up** *by eight we got worried.*

appear [I] (usually used with an adverb or preposition) to arrive at a place and be seen there: *By ten o'clock Lee still hadn't appeared.* ◇ *A man appeared at the door and asked to see her.* ◇ *The file appeared on my desk yesterday.*

,roll 'in *phrasal verb* (*informal*) to arrive somewhere without worrying about the time: *Steve eventually rolled in around lunchtime.*

show [I] (often used in negative sentences) (*informal*) to arrive somewhere, especially at a place where sb is waiting for you: *I waited till ten o'clock but she didn't show.* ◇ *What if nobody shows?*

---

article *noun* See also the entry for PAPER

---

article · editorial · piece · column · feature
These words all mean a piece of writing in a newspaper or magazine.

PATTERNS AND COLLOCATIONS
▸ an article/ an editorial/ a piece/ a column/ a feature **in/ on/ about** sth
▸ a **recent** article/ editorial/ piece/ column/ feature
▸ a **newspaper** article/ editorial/ column/ feature
▸ a **magazine** article/ piece/ column/ feature
▸ to **write/ read/ run/ publish** an article/ an editorial/ a piece/ a column/ a feature

article [C] a piece of writing about a particular subject in a newspaper or magazine: *Have you seen that article about skyscrapers?*

editorial /ˌedɪˈtɔːriəl/ [C] an article in a newspaper that expresses the editor's opinion on a subject of particular interest at the present time: *In a scathing editorial, the paper called on the director to resign.* ❶ In the US an **editorial** can also be part of a radio or television broadcast that expresses the opinion of the station or its owner.

piece [C] an article in a newspaper or magazine or a broadcast on television or radio: *Did you see her piece about the Internet in the paper today?* See also **piece** → WORK *noun* 4

column [C] a part of a newspaper or magazine that appears regularly and is always by a particular writer or always about a particular subject: *He writes a* **gossip column** *(= a column about social events and famous people) for the local paper.* ◇ *The website runs an online advice column for teenagers.* See also **columnist** → REPORTER

feature [C] a special article in a newspaper or magazine, or a part of a television or radio broadcast, that deals with a particular subject: *In today's programme we have a special feature on education.*

---

articulate *adj.*

---

articulate · fluent · eloquent · coherent
These words all describe the clever or effective expression of ideas or feelings in words.

PATTERNS AND COLLOCATIONS
▸ an articulate/ an eloquent/ a coherent **answer/ response**
▸ articulate/ fluent/ eloquent/ coherent **speech**
▸ an articulate/ a fluent/ an eloquent **speaker**
▸ articulate/ fluent/ eloquent **language**
▸ **very/ perfectly/ remarkably** articulate/ fluent/ eloquent/ coherent
▸ **highly/ extremely** articulate/ fluent/ eloquent

articulate /ɑːˈtɪkjələt; *AmE* ɑːrˈt-/ (*rather formal*) (of a person) good at expressing ideas or feelings clearly in words; (of speech) clearly expressed or pronounced: *He was unusually articulate for a ten-year-old.* ◇ *All we could hear were loud sobs, but no articulate words.* **OPP** **inarticulate** → SILENT

fluent /ˈfluːənt/ able to speak, read or write a language, especially a foreign language, easily and well; (of a language, especially a foreign language) expressed easily and well: *She's fluent in Polish.* ◇ *She's a fluent reader of Arabic.* ◇ *He speaks fluent Italian.*
▸ **fluently** *adv.*: *She speaks Russian fluently.* ◇ *a child just beginning to read fluently*

eloquent /ˈeləkwənt/ (*rather formal*) (of a person) able to use language and express your opinions well, especially when you are speaking in public; (of a speech) expressed well: *She was an eloquent speaker, with a beautiful voice.* ◇ *It was an eloquent and well-informed speech.*
▶ **eloquently** *adv.*: *She spoke eloquently on the subject for about an hour.*

coherent /kəˈhɪərənt; AmE koʊˈhɪr-/ (*rather formal*) (of a person) able to talk and express yourself clearly: *She only became coherent again two hours after the attack.* **OPP in-coherent →** HYSTERICAL
▶ **coherently** *adv.*: *Try to express yourself more coherently.*

artificial *adj.*

1 artificial light
2 an artificial situation

1 artificial · synthetic · false · man-made · fake · imitation

These words all describe things that are not real, or not naturally produced or grown.

PATTERNS AND COLLOCATIONS
▶ artificial / synthetic / man-made **fabrics / fibres / materials / products**
▶ artificial / synthetic / fake / imitation **fur / leather**
▶ artificial / synthetic / false / fake / imitation **diamonds / pearls**

artificial made or produced to copy sth natural; not real: *The patient was kept alive by the artificial heart for nearly two months.* ◇ *All food served in the restaurant is completely free from any artificial colours and flavours.* ◇ *I don't like having to do detailed work in artificial light.* **OPP natural ❶** Natural things exist in nature and are not made or caused by human beings: *the natural world* (= of trees, rivers, animals and birds) ◇ *a country's natural resources* (= its coal, oil, forests, etc.) ◇ *My hair soon grew back to its natural colour* (= after being dyed).
▶ **artificially** *adv.*: *artificially created lakes*

synthetic made by combining chemical substances rather than being produced naturally by plants or animals: *synthetic drugs/dyes* ◇ *shoes with synthetic soles* **OPP natural**
▶ **synthetically** *adv.*: *synthetically produced drugs*

false not natural; artificial: *false teeth/eyelashes* ◇ *a false beard and moustache* See also **false →** SO-CALLED

man-ˈmade made by people; not natural: *man-made fibres such as nylon and polyester* ◇ *Europe's largest man-made lake* **OPP natural**

fake made to look like sth else; not real: *a fake fur jacket* ◇ *We sprayed fake snow over the trees to make it look like winter.* **OPP genuine →** REAL, See also **fake →** SO-CALLED *adj.*, **fake →** FAKE *noun*

imitation [only before noun] made to look like sth else; not real: *She would never wear imitation pearls.* ◇ *He threatened them with an imitation gun.* **OPP genuine →** REAL, See also **imitation →** FAKE *noun*

2 artificial · forced · laboured · contrived · strained

These words all describe an action, emotion or situation which is not natural or not what it appears to be.

PATTERNS AND COLLOCATIONS
▶ a forced / strained **smile**
▶ an artificial / a contrived **situation / example**
▶ to **sound** forced / laboured / contrived / strained
▶ **rather** artificial / forced / laboured
▶ **somewhat** artificial / laboured / strained

artificial created by people; not happening naturally: *A job interview is a very artificial situation.*

forced (*disapproving*) not sincere; not the result of genuine emotions but produced by a deliberate effort: *'Good,' he said with forced cheerfulness.* **OPP genuine →** DEEP 1

laboured (*BrE*) (*AmE* **labored**) (*disapproving*) (of speech, writing, etc.) not natural and seeming to take a lot of effort: *She knew better than to interrupt one of her father's rather laboured jokes.*

contrived /kənˈtraɪvd/ (*disapproving*) planned in advance and not natural or genuine; written or arranged in a way that is not natural or realistic: *The letter was full of contrived excuses.* ◇ *The book's ending seemed contrived.*

strained (*often disapproving*) not the result of genuine emotions; produced by a deliberate effort: *She gave a strained laugh.* **❶ Strained** is not always as disapproving as **forced**: sometimes it can show or invite sympathy for a person under stress: *I put on my strained smile for the next patiently waiting customer.*

artist *noun*

artist · painter · sculptor

These words all mean a person who creates works of art.

PATTERNS AND COLLOCATIONS
▶ a **contemporary / talented / famous** artist / painter / sculptor
▶ a / an **abstract / impressionist / portrait / landscape** artist / painter
▶ an artist / a painter **paints** sb / sth

artist [C] a person who creates works of art, especially paintings or drawings: *an exhibition of work by contemporary British artists* ◇ *a graphic artist* ◇ *a make-up artist* ◇ *Police have issued an artist's impression of her attacker.*

painter [C] an artist who paints pictures: *Chardin was a gifted still-life painter.* See also **paint →** DRAW *verb*

sculptor /ˈskʌlptə(r)/ [C] an artist who makes sculptures (= works of art that are solid figures or objects made of wood, stone, clay, metal, etc.): *Many sculptors work in clay, but I can get greater detail and flexibility from wax.* See also **sculpt →** SHAPE *verb*

ask *verb*

1 ask a question
2 ask for sth

1 ask · enquire · demand · pose · consult

These words all mean to say or write sth in the form of a question, in order to get information.

PATTERNS AND COLLOCATIONS
▶ to ask / enquire **about / after** sb / sth
▶ to ask / enquire / demand sth **of** sb
▶ to ask / enquire / demand **what / who / how…**, etc.
▶ to ask / enquire **politely**
▶ to ask / demand **fiercely / aggressively**

ask [T, I] to say or write sth in the form of a question, in order to get information: *'Where are you going?' she asked.* ◇ *The interviewer asked me about my future plans.* ◇ *Did you ask the price?* ◇ *She asked the students their names.* ◇ *I often get asked that!* ◇ *She asked where I lived.* ◇ *I was asked if/whether I could drive.* ◇ *Can I ask a question?* ◇ *How old are you, if you don't mind me/my asking?* ◇ *He asked about her family.* **❶** You cannot say 'ask to sb': *I asked to my friend what had happened.*

enquire (also **inquire** especially in *AmE*) [I, T] (*rather formal*) to ask sb for information: *I called the station to enquire about train times.* ◇ *She enquired after my father.* ◇ *She enquired as to your whereabouts.* ◇ *Might I enquire why you never mentioned this before?* ◇ *He enquired her name.* See also **enquiry →** QUESTION *noun*

demand [T] to ask a question very firmly: *'And where have you been?' he demanded angrily.* ◇ *'What's your name?' she demanded of the girl.*

pose [T] (always used with *question*) (*formal*) to ask a question, especially one that needs serious thought: *The new play poses some challenging questions.*

consult [T] to go to sb for information or advice: *If the pain continues, consult your doctor.* See also **consult →** REFER TO STH, **consultation →** INTERVIEW 1

2 See also the entry for DEMAND

ask · seek · call for sth · request · apply · invite · appeal · claim · petition

These words all mean to tell sb that you would like them to do sth or give you sth, or that you would like sth to happen.

PATTERNS AND COLLOCATIONS

▶ to ask / call / apply / appeal / petition **for** sth
▶ to ask for / seek / call for / request / invite / appeal for / claim sth **from** sb
▶ to ask / request sth **of** sb
▶ to ask / call for / request / invite / appeal for / petition **sb to do sth**
▶ to ask / apply **to do sth**
▶ to ask / request **that…**
▶ to **formally** ask for / seek / call for / request / apply for / invite sb to do / claim / petition for sth
▶ to **repeatedly** ask for / call for / request / apply for / appeal for sth
▶ to **explicitly** ask for / call for / request / invite sth

ask [I, T] to tell sb that you would like them to do or give you sth, or that you would like sth to happen; to say that you would like permission to do sth: *If you want anything, just ask.* ◇ *I went up to the bar and asked for a beer.* ◇ *He asked me for a job yesterday.* ◇ *Why don't you ask David's advice?* ◇ *Can I ask a favour of you?* ◇ *I asked to see the manager.* ◇ *All the students were asked to complete a form.* ◇ *I'll ask if it's all right to park here.*

seek [T] (*formal*) to ask sb for sth: *I think it's time we sought legal advice.* ◇ *She managed to calm him down and seek help from a neighbour.* See also **seek** → LOOK *verb* 2, **seek** → TRY *verb* 1

'call for sth *phrasal verb* (*especially journalism*) to ask publicly for sth to happen: *The group called for the immediate release of the hostages.* ◇ *The opposition is calling for the prime minister to resign.* See also **call** → REQUEST *noun*

request [T] (*formal*) to ask for sth or ask sb to do sth in a polite or formal way: *She requested permission to film at the White House.* ◇ *You are politely requested not to smoke in this restaurant.* See also **request** → REQUEST *noun*, **request** → WISH *noun*

apply [I] to make a formal request, usually in writing, for sth such as a job or a place at a college or university: *to apply for a job/passport/grant* ◇ *I decided to apply to Manchester University.* ◇ *You can apply by letter or on-line.* ◇ *He's applied to join the army.* See also **applicant** → CANDIDATE, **application** → REQUEST *noun*

invite [T] (*formal*) to ask sb formally to go somewhere or do sth: *Successful candidates will be invited for interview next week.* ◇ *He invited questions from the audience.*

appeal [I] to make a serious and urgent request for sth: *Nationalist leaders have appealed for calm.* ◇ *Organizers appealed to the crowd not to panic.* ◇ *I am appealing on behalf of the famine victims* (= asking for money). See also **appeal** → REQUEST *noun*

claim [T, I] to ask for money from the government or a company because you have a right to it: *He's not entitled to claim unemployment benefit.* ◇ *She claimed damages from the company for the injury she had suffered.* ◇ *You can claim on your insurance for that coat you left on the train.* See also **claim** → REQUEST *noun*

petition /pə'tɪʃn/ [I, T] to make a formal request to sb in authority, especially by sending them a petition (= a written request signed by a large number of people); to formally ask for sth in court: *Local residents have successfully petitioned against the proposals.* ◇ *The group intends to petition the governor for reform of the law.* ◇ *His wife petitioned for divorce in 1997.* See also **petition** → REQUEST *noun*

aspect *noun* See also the entry for ELEMENT 1

aspect · side · respect · dimension · strand · end

These are all words for a particular part or feature of a situation, idea or sb's character, or a way of looking or thinking about sth.

PATTERNS AND COLLOCATIONS

▶ an aspect / a side / a dimension / a strand **to** sth
▶ an **important** aspect / respect / dimension / strand
▶ a **crucial** aspect / respect / dimension
▶ a / an **political / economic / social / cultural / historical / religious / spiritual / moral / human** aspect / side / dimension
▶ to **consider** an aspect / a side / a dimension of sth
▶ to **deal with / look at** an aspect / a side of sth

aspect [C] a particular part or feature of a situation, idea, problem or person's character; a way of looking or thinking about sth: *The book aims to cover all aspects of city life.* ◇ *This was one aspect of her character he hadn't seen before.* ◇ *She felt she had looked at the problem from every aspect.*

side [C] a particular aspect of sth, especially a situation or a person's character: *Her novels deal with the darker side of human nature.* ◇ *It's good you can* **see the funny side** *of the situation.* ◇ *I'll take care of that* **side of things**. ❶ In this meaning, **side** is often, though not always, rather informal, used especially in spoken English in the phrases *see the funny side* and *that/the business/the political, etc. side of things.*

respect [C] a particular aspect or detail of sth: *In this* **respect** *we are very fortunate.* ◇ *He takes after his father* **in some respects***, but he's very different in other ways.* ◇ *There was one respect, however, in which they differed.* ❶ **Respect** is used especially to draw attention to one particular aspect of sth, in order to contrast it with other aspects. It is used very often in the phrases *in some/ many/all respects* and *in one/every respect* but it is NOT followed by *of sth* and you should use *one* before it instead of *a*: *an important aspect of the problem* ◇ ~~an important respect of the problem~~. ◇ *They differed in one respect.* ◇ ~~They differed in a respect.~~

dimension /daɪ'menʃn; dɪ-/ [C] a feature of sth; a way of looking at or thinking about sth: *Her job added a new dimension to her life.* ◇ *We should also consider the social dimension of unemployment.* ❶ **Dimension** is used especially to talk about issues in society and history; common collocates include *social, economic, political, ideological, cultural, linguistic, historical, geographical, environmental, regional, national, international, human, personal, moral, ethical, religious* and *spiritual.*

strand [C] one of the different parts of sth, especially an idea, plan or story: *There are three main strands to the policy.* ◇ *The author draws the different strands of the plot together in the final chapter.*

end [C, usually *sing.*] a part of an activity with which sb is concerned, especially in business: *We need someone to handle the marketing end of the business.* ◇ *Are there any problems at your end?* ◇ *I have kept my end of the bargain.*

assembly *noun*

assembly · council · parliament · congress · senate · house · chamber · legislature

These are all words for a group of people who are elected to make decisions or make laws for a country or region.

PATTERNS AND COLLOCATIONS

▶ an **elected** assembly / council / parliament / senate / house / chamber / legislature
▶ the **federal / national** assembly / parliament / council / legislature
▶ a **local / regional** assembly / council / parliament
▶ the **upper / lower** house / chamber (**of** the parliament / legislature, etc)
▶ to **elect** an assembly / a council / a parliament
▶ to **elect sb to** an assembly / a council / parliament / the senate
▶ to **convene** parliament / congress / the legislature
▶ to **dissolve** the assembly / parliament / congress / the legislature
▶ the assembly / council / parliament / congress / senate / house / chamber / legislature **votes** (for / on sth)
▶ the assembly / council / parliament / congress / senate / house / legislature **passes** a resolution / bill / law, etc.

▶ a **member** of the assembly / council / parliament / congress / senate / legislature
▶ a **session** of the assembly / council / parliament / congress / senate / legislature

assembly (also **Assembly**) [C+sing./pl. v.] a group of people who are elected to make decisions or laws for a region or country: *Power has been handed over to provincial and regional assemblies.* ◇ *The party has only 3 seats in the 51-seat National Assembly.*

council (also **Council**) [C+sing./pl. v.] a group of people who are elected to make decisions for an area such as a city or county: *She's **on the** local **council** (= is a member of the council).* ◇ *He's the former leader of Liverpool City Council.*

parliament [C+sing./pl. v., usually sing.] the group of people who are elected to make the laws of a country: *She was elected as a member of the Dutch parliament in 1996.* ◇ *Riot police yesterday surrounded the Georgian **parliament building**.* ❶ In many countries, the **parliament** is made up of two parts called **houses** or **chambers**. See also **parliament →** GOVERNMENT 1

congress (also **Congress**) [C+sing./pl. v., usually sing., U] the group of people who are elected to make the laws of a country, especially a republic (= a country governed by an elected president, not a king or queen): *Congress will vote on the proposals tomorrow.* ❶ In the US, **Congress** is the name of the parliament and consists of the **Senate** which is the upper house, and the **House of Representatives**, which is the lower house.

NOTE **PARLIAMENT** OR **CONGRESS?** A **congress** is slightly different from a **parliament** because its role is just that of making laws (= it is the *legislature*). The laws are put into effect by the *executive*, which is a separate group of people and not part of the **congress**. In a *parliamentary system* the **parliament** is the *legislature*, and the *executive* is made up of a smaller group of people from within the **parliament**.

senate (*usually* **the Senate**) [C+sing./pl. v., usually sing.] one of the two groups of people who are elected to make laws in some countries, for example in the US, France and Australia: *The bill was passed by the Senate last month.* ❶ The **Senate** is the smaller of the two groups that make up a *parliament* or *congress* in some countries, but higher in rank. Many state parliaments in the US also have a **Senate**.

house (also **House**) [C+sing./pl. v.] a group of people who make the laws of a country, usually one of two groups which make up the parliament of the country: *Legislation requires approval by both houses of parliament.*

chamber /ˈtʃeɪmbə(r)/ [C+sing./pl. v.] a group of people who make the laws of a country, usually one of two groups who make up the parliament of the country: *They are seeking to overturn the Liberal majority in the **second chamber** (= the upper part of the parliament).*

legislature /ˈledʒɪsleɪtʃə(r)/ [C+sing./pl. v., usually sing.] (*formal*) a group of people who make the laws of a country: *She is the youngest woman to be elected to the **national legislature**.* ❶ The **legislature** is the part of a country's government that makes laws. It contrasts with the **executive**, which is responsible for putting laws into effect, and the **judiciary**, the judges who apply the laws. See also **executive →** GOVERNMENT 1

assessment *noun* See the Topic Map for EDUCATION on p.888

---

assessment · evaluation · review · appraisal · commentary · critique · criticism · estimation
These are all words for an opinion or judgement of sb/sth, especially in a piece of writing.

PATTERNS AND COLLOCATIONS
▶ **in** an assessment / an evaluation / a review / an appraisal / a commentary / a critique / sb's estimation

▶ a **detailed** / **general** assessment / evaluation / appraisal / commentary / critique
▶ a **critical** assessment / evaluation / review / appraisal / commentary
▶ a/an **thorough** / **subjective** / **effective** assessment / evaluation / appraisal / critique
▶ a / an **objective** / **careful** assessment / evaluation / appraisal / criticism
▶ a **searching** assessment / appraisal / critique / criticism
▶ a **written** assessment / appraisal / commentary / critique
▶ to **give** an assessment / a review / an appraisal / a critique
▶ to **write** an assessment / a review / a commentary / a critique
▶ to **carry out** / **make** an assessment / evaluation / appraisal

assessment /əˈsesmənt/ [C, U] (*rather formal*) an opinion or judgement about sb/sth that has been thought about carefully; the act of forming this kind of judgement or opinion: *What is your assessment of the situation?* ◇ *We need to make a detailed assessment of the risks involved.* ◇ *written and oral exams and other forms of assessment* ◇ *We are developing new methods of **risk assessment** for chemicals.* ❶ An **assessment** is usually about the quality of sth, such as a student's work or ability, or about the problems, risks or needs involved in a situation. See also the entry for TEST *noun* 2, See also **assess →** JUDGE *verb* 1, **assess →** TEST *verb* 2

evaluation /ɪˌvæljuˈeɪʃn/ [C, U] (*rather formal*) an assessment of the amount, value or quality of sth; the process of forming this assessment: *We've still got to carry out an evaluation of the results.* ◇ *The new programme is still under evaluation.* See also **evaluate →** JUDGE *verb* 2

review [C, U] a report in a newspaper or magazine in which sb gives their opinion of a book, play, film, etc.; the act of writing this kind of report: *The book received **mixed reviews** (= some people liked it, some did not).* ◇ *The new musical opened to **glowing reviews**.* ◇ *He submitted his latest novel for review.* ❶ In American English, **review** is also the term for a meeting in which an employee discusses with their manager how well they have been doing their job, and for the system of holding such meetings: (*AmE*) *I have my **performance review** tomorrow.* ◇ *A formal performance review system was introduced five years ago.* In British English this is called an **appraisal**. See also **reviewer →** REPORTER
▶ **review** *verb* [T]: *The play was reviewed in the national newspapers.*

appraisal /əˈpreɪzl/ [C, U] (*rather formal*) an assessment of the quality, performance or nature of sb/sth; the act of making this kind of assessment: *She had read many detailed critical appraisals of his work.* ◇ *She made a quick appraisal of the other guests.* ❶ **Appraisal** is also the usual term in British English for an employee's performance review (see above): (*especially BrE*) *I've got my appraisal tomorrow.* ◇ *A formal system of **performance appraisal** was introduced five years ago.* In American English this is usually called a **review**, although **appraisal** is also used.
▶ **appraise** [T]: (*formal*) *She stepped back to appraise her workmanship.*

commentary /ˈkɒməntri; AmE ˈkɑːmənteri/ [C, U] a written explanation or discussion of sth such as a book or play; a discussion or sign of sth, especially of its good and bad qualities: *He wrote a **commentary on** Paul's letters to the Romans.* ◇ *The film is part love story and part **social commentary**.* ❶ You can *write* a **commentary** on a book, play or film; or a book, play or film can *be* a commentary on social, political or other issues.

critique /krɪˈtiːk/ [C] a piece of writing discussing the good and bad qualities of sth such as a set of ideas or a work of art: *She wrote a feminist critique of Freud's theories.*
▶ **critique** *verb* [T]: *Her job involves critiquing designs by fashion students.*

criticism [U] the work or activity of making fair, careful judgements about the good and bad qualities of sb/sth, especially books, music, etc: *She has written several works of **literary criticism**.* ◇ *art criticism*

▶ **criticize** (*BrE* also **-ise**) *verb* [T]: (*BrE*) *We were taught how to criticize poems.*

estimation /ˌestɪˈmeɪʃn/ [sing.] (*rather formal*) a judgement or opinion about the value or quality of sb/sth, especially a personal opinion: *Who is the best candidate **in your estimation**? ◇ Since he left his wife, he's certainly **gone down in my estimation** (= I have less respect for him). ◇ She **went up in my estimation** (= I have more respect for her) when I discovered how much charity work she does.*

assignment *noun* See the Topic Map for EDUCATION on p.888, See also the entries for PAPER and TASK

assignment · project · homework · exercise
These are all words for a task or piece of work that sb has to do, especially as part of their studies.

PATTERNS AND COLLOCATIONS

▶ a project / homework / an exercise **on** sth
▶ a / an **easy / difficult** assignment / exercise
▶ (a) **geography / history / biology, etc.** project / homework
▶ to **do** an assignment / a project / your homework / an exercise
▶ to **have** an assignment / some homework **to do**
▶ to **get on with** an assignment / a project / your homework
▶ to **finish** an assignment / a project / your homework
▶ to **give sb / set (sb)** an assignment / their homework / some exercises

assignment /əˈsaɪnmənt/ [C] a task that sb is given to do, usually as part of their job or studies: *You will be expected to complete three written assignments. ◇ I'd set myself a tough assignment. ◇ She's **on assignment** in Greece at the moment.*

project [C] a piece of work involving careful study of a subject over a period of time, done by school or college students: *My class is doing a project on medieval towns. ◇ The final term will be devoted to **project work**.*

homework [U] work that is given by teachers for students to do at home: *I still haven't done my geography homework. ◇ How much homework do you get? ◇ I have to write up the notes **for homework**.*

exercise [C] a set of questions in a book that tests your knowledge or practises a skill: *grammar exercises ◇ Do one exercise for homework.*

assistant *noun* See also the entry for ACCOMPLICE

assistant · aide · helper · henchman · sidekick · right-hand man
These are all words for a person who helps sb else, especially in their job.

PATTERNS AND COLLOCATIONS

▶ an assistant / an aide / a sidekick / a right-hand man **to** sb
▶ a **trusted** assistant / aide / henchman / sidekick
▶ a **chief** assistant / aide / henchman
▶ a **senior / personal / junior** assistant / aide
▶ sb's **loyal** assistant / sidekick
▶ to **work as** an assistant / aide

assistant [C] a person who helps sb do their job, often by doing some of the less difficult or important tasks for them: *He worked as an assistant to the Sales Director. ◇ She works as a **care assistant** in a nursing home. ◇ a research/ teaching assistant*

aide /eɪd/ [C] a person who helps an important person, especially a politician, in their job: *A statement was read to reporters by a White House aide.* See also **adviser** → ADVISER

helper [C] a person who helps sb to do sth, especially without being paid for it: *She's a regular helper at the youth club. ◇ He recruited a band of willing helpers.*

henchman /ˈhentʃmən/ (pl. **-men**) [C] a faithful supporter of a powerful person, for example a political leader or criminal, who is prepared to use violence or become involved in illegal activities to help that person: *He sent one of his henchmen with orders to seize the pictures.*

sidekick /ˈsaɪdkɪk/ [C] (*informal*) a person who helps another more important or intelligent person: *The show is about a detective and his trusty sidekick.*

right-hand ˈman [sing.] a person who helps sb a lot and whom they rely on, especially in an important job: *He agreed to the deal after consulting his lawyer and right-hand man, Charles Alton.*

association *noun*

association · connotation · overtone · nuance · undercurrent
These are all words for an idea or feeling which is not expressed directly but is suggested or felt.

PATTERNS AND COLLOCATIONS

▶ associations / connotations / overtones / a nuance / an undercurrent **of** sth
▶ (a) **strong** associations / connotations / overtones / undercurrent
▶ **negative / unpleasant / pejorative** associations / connotations / overtones
▶ (a) **racial** connotation / overtones / undercurrent
▶ (a) **social** connotation / overtones / nuance / undercurrent
▶ (a) **political** connotation / overtones / undercurrent
▶ to **have** associations / connotations / overtones
▶ to **take on** associations / connotations / overtones

association [C, usually pl.] an idea, feeling or memory that is suggested by sb/sth; a mental connection between ideas: *The seaside had all sorts of pleasant **associations with** my childhood. ◇ Tourists visit the city for its historical associations. ◇ The cat soon made the **association between** human beings and food.* See also **associate** → RELATE

connotation /ˌkɒnəˈteɪʃn; *AmE* ˌkɑːn-/ [C] (*rather formal*) an idea or attitude suggested by a word in addition to its main meaning: *The word 'professional' has connotations of skill and excellence.*

overtone /ˈəʊvətəʊn; *AmE* ˈoʊvərtoʊn/ [C, usually pl.] an attitude or feeling that is suggested but is not expressed in a direct way: *There were political **overtones to** the point he was making.*

nuance /ˈnjuːɑːns; *AmE* ˈnuː-/ [C, U] a very slight difference in meaning, sound, colour or sb's feelings that is not usually very obvious: *He watched her face intently to catch every nuance of expression. ◇ You need to be able to convey the **subtle nuances** of meaning of each word. ◇ Her singing has both warmth of sound and delicacy of nuance.*

undercurrent /ˈʌndəkʌrənt; *AmE* -dərkɜːr-/ [C] a feeling, especially a negative one such as anger, fear or sadness, that is hidden but whose effects are felt: *I sensed an undercurrent of resentment among the other girls.*

> **NOTE** CONNOTATION, OVERTONE OR UNDERCURRENT?
> **Connotation** and **overtone** often refer to an idea, attitude or feeling which sb intends when they say or write sth, but which they do not express directly. The idea or attitude may be expressed by carefully choosing the words which are used. An **undercurrent** is usually a feeling or attitude which is felt very strongly and so can be sensed even when sb tries to hide it.

atmosphere *noun*

atmosphere · climate · mood · tone · spirit · aura · feeling · feel · flavour
These are all words for the general sense or feeling that you have in a particular place or situation.

PATTERNS AND COLLOCATIONS

▶ the **general** atmosphere / climate / mood / tone / spirit / feeling / feel / flavour
▶ an **international** atmosphere / climate / feel / flavour

▸ (a) **hostile** atmosphere / climate / tone
▸ a **festive** atmosphere / mood / spirit / feel
▸ a **welcoming** atmosphere / aura / feel
▸ the **political** atmosphere / climate / mood / tone / flavour
▸ to **create** an atmosphere / a climate / a mood / a spirit / an aura / a feeling / a feel
▸ to **reflect** the atmosphere / climate / mood / tone / spirit / feeling (of sth)
▸ to **capture** the atmosphere / mood / tone / spirit / feeling / flavour of sth
▸ to **evoke** an atmosphere / a mood / a spirit / a feeling
▸ to **take on** an atmosphere / a tone / an aura / a feel / a flavour
▸ to **convey** an atmosphere / a mood / a spirit / a feeling / a flavour

atmosphere [C, U] the way that a particular place or situation feels to you; a feeling between two people or in a group of people: *The hotel offers a friendly atmosphere and personal service.* ◇ *The children grew up in an atmosphere of violence and insecurity.* ◇ *The old house is full of atmosphere* (= it is very interesting). ◇ *There was an atmosphere of mutual respect between them.*

climate [C] the general attitude or feeling among people at a particular time; a set of conditions which exist in a particular place: *The new policies have created a climate of fear.* ◇ *There's been a change in the **climate of opinion*** (= what people generally are thinking about a particular issue). ◇ *He admitted that the economic climate has rarely been worse.* ❶ **Climate of** is often used with negative words such as *fear, suspicion, distrust, despair* and *hostility.*

mood [sing.] the way a group of people feel about sth; the atmosphere among a group of people: *The mood of the meeting was distinctly pessimistic.* ◇ *We need a leader who can gauge the **popular mood**.* ◇ *The movie captures the mood of the interwar years perfectly.*

NOTE **ATMOSPHERE OR MOOD?** An **atmosphere** belongs especially to a place, and may stay the same over a period of time; a **mood** belongs to a group of people at a particular time and may change as time passes: ~~The hotel offers a friendly mood.~~ ◇ ~~The children grew up in a mood of violence.~~ ◇ ~~a leader who can gauge the popular atmosphere~~

tone [sing.] the general character and attitude of sth such as a piece of writing or the atmosphere of an event: *The overall tone of the book is gently nostalgic.* ◇ *The article was moderate **in tone** and presented both sides of the case.* ◇ *She **set the tone for** the meeting with a firm statement of company policy.* ◇ *Trust you to **lower the tone** of the conversation!*

spirit [sing.] the typical or most important quality or mood of sth: *The exhibition captures the spirit of the Swinging Sixties.* ◇ *His poetry summed up **the spirit of the age**.* ❶ **Spirit** is used especially to talk about how people are feeling, their attitudes and their behaviour at a particular period in time: *the spirit of the 70s / the age / the times / the Enlightenment*

aura /ˈɔːrə/ [C] a quality or feeling that is very noticeable and seems to surround a person or place: *There was a faint aura of mystery about him.* ◇ *The mountains have a magical aura.* See also **air →** APPEARANCE

feeling [sing.] the atmosphere or character of a place or situation and the effect it has on how people feel: *They have managed to recreate the feeling of the original theatre.* ◇ *There was a general feeling of change in the air.* See also **feel →** SEEM

feel [sing.] the impression or atmosphere that is created by a place or situation: *It's a big city but it has the feel of a small town.* ◇ *There is an international **feel to** the restaurant.*

flavour (*BrE*) (*AmE* **flavor**) [sing.] a particular quality or atmosphere that sth has that reminds you of sth else: *The children experience a flavour of medieval life.* ◇ *The music festival has taken on a distinctly German flavour.*

attach *verb*

attach · tie · fix · put · stick · secure · strap · glue · tape · fasten
These words all mean to place sth in, on or with sth else using sth that makes it stay there.

PATTERNS AND COLLOCATIONS
▸ to attach / tie / fix / stick / secure / strap / glue / tape / fasten sth **to** sth
▸ to tie / fix / put / stick / strap / glue / tape / fasten sth **on** sth
▸ to tie / fix / stick / fasten sth **into** sth
▸ to tie / fix / stick / strap / glue / tape / fasten sth **together**
▸ to tie / fix / stick / strap / glue sth **down**
▸ to tie / fix / fasten sth **back**
▸ to tie / glue / tape sth **up**
▸ to attach / tie / fix / stick / secure sth **firmly**
▸ to attach / tie / fix / tape / fasten sth **securely**

attach [T] to put sth together with sth else so that it stays there: *He attached the rope securely to a tree.* ◇ *I attach a copy of the contract for your records.* ◇ *I am attaching the image as a PDF file* (= sending it with an email). ❶ **Attach** is often used when writing business letters. **OPP detach** → UNDO

tie [T] (usually used with an adverb or preposition) to attach or hold two or more things together using string, rope, etc.; to attach sth to sth else in this way or put sth around sth else: *Her hands had been tied together.* ◇ *The label was tied on with string.* ◇ *She tied back her hair with a ribbon.* **OPP untie** → UNDO

fix [T] (*especially BrE*) to put sth firmly in a particular place so that it will not move: *Start by fixing a post in the ground.* ◇ *He fixed the shelf to the wall.*

put [T] (always used with an adverb or preposition) to attach or fix sth to sth else: *We're not allowed to put posters on the walls.* ◇ *We had to put new locks on all the doors.*

stick [T, I] (usually used with an adverb or preposition) to attach sth to sth else, usually with a sticky substance; to become attached in this way: *I forgot to stick a stamp on the envelope.* ◇ *Her wet hair was sticking to her head.* ◇ *This glue's useless – the pieces just won't stick.*
▸ **sticky** *adj.*: *sticky tape*

secure [T] (usually used with an adverb or preposition) (*rather formal*) to attach sth firmly to sth else: *She secured the rope to the back of the car with a firm knot.* ◇ *Wrap a bandage around the arm and secure it with tape or a pin.*

strap (-**pp**-) [T] (always used with an adverb or preposition) to make sb / sth stay in place using a strap or straps: *He strapped the knife to his leg.* ◇ *Make sure your passengers are strapped in* (= wearing their seat belts).

glue [T] (usually used with an adverb or preposition) to join two things together or make sth stay in place using glue: *She glued the label onto the box.* ◇ *Glue the pieces of wood together.* ◇ *Make sure the edges are glued down.*

tape [T] (usually used with an adverb or preposition) to keep sth in place by sticking it with tape; to attach sth to sth else using sticky tape: *Put it in a box and tape it up securely.* ◇ *Someone had taped a message onto the door.*

fasten [T] (usually used with an adverb or preposition) to use sth to fix or place sth in a particular position so that it will not move, or in order to attach it to sth else: *She opened the window and fastened back the shutters.* ◇ *He fastened the papers together with a paper clip.*

attack *noun*

1 a bomb attack
2 a vicious knife attack
3 an attack of flu / nerves

1 See the Topic Map for CONFLICT on p.896

attack · strike · invasion · raid · assault · offensive · aggression · incursion
These are all words for military acts against an enemy.

attack → attack

PATTERNS AND COLLOCATIONS

▸ an attack/a strike/a raid/an assault/an offensive/aggression **against** sb/sth
▸ an attack/a strike/an assault/an offensive/an incursion **on** sb/sth
▸ **in** an attack/a strike/an invasion/a raid/an assault/an offensive/an incursion
▸ (a) **military** attack/strike/invasion/raid/assault/offensive/aggression/incursion
▸ a **full-scale** attack/strike/invasion/assault/offensive
▸ a **successful** attack/strike/invasion/raid/assault/offensive
▸ an **all-out** attack/assault/offensive
▸ an **air** attack/strike/raid/assault/offensive
▸ to **plan**/**launch** an attack/a strike/an invasion/a raid/an assault/an offensive
▸ to **mount** an attack/an assault/an offensive
▸ to **make** an attack/a raid/an assault/an incursion
▸ to **resist** (an) attack/an invasion/an assault/(an) aggression

attack [C, U] (in a war) an aggressive attempt to hurt or defeat the enemy using weapons and violence: *He ordered his men to mount an attack on the city.* ◇ *The patrol came under attack from all sides.*

strike [C] a rapid, powerful military attack, especially by aircraft: *The effects of the air strikes had been devastating.* ◇ *They launched a **pre-emptive strike** (= before the enemy could attack).*

invasion /ɪnˈveɪʒn/ [C, U] the act of an army entering another country by force in order to take control of it: *She left Czechoslovakia after the Russian invasion in 1968.* ◇ *The invasion force comprised 3 000–5 000 heavily armed troops.* See also **invade** → INVADE

raid [C] a short surprise attack on the enemy by soldiers, ships or aircraft: *Hundreds of civilians were killed in the air raids.*

assault /əˈsɔːlt/ [C] an attack on a place in order to take control of it: *An assault on the capital was launched in the early hours of the morning.*

offensive [C] a planned series of military attacks which sometimes take place over a long period of time: *The final offensive was launched in the spring.*

aggression [U] a violent attack or threats by one country against another: *Each country agreed to halt all **acts of aggression** against the other's territory.*

incursion /ɪnˈkɜːʃn; AmE ɪnˈkɜːrʒn/ [C] (*formal*) a sudden, temporary entry into a place controlled by the enemy, especially across a border: *Border patrols were increased to deter further incursions by foreign forces.*

2 attack · rape · assault · attempt

These are all words for an act of using violence to try to hurt or kill sb.

PATTERNS AND COLLOCATIONS

▸ an attack/a rape/an assault **by** sb
▸ an attack/assault **on**/**against** sb
▸ a/an **violent**/**brutal**/**savage**/**vicious**/**alleged** attack/rape/assault
▸ a/an **serious**/**unprovoked**/**racial**/**sexual**/**physical** attack/assault
▸ an **attempted** rape/assault
▸ to **carry out** an attack/assault

attack [C] an act of using violence to try to hurt or kill sb: *Police have reported a series of racist attacks.* ◇ *A child is recovering in hospital after a serious attack by a stray dog.*

rape [U, C] the crime of forcing sb to have sex with you, especially using violence: *He was charged with rape.* ◇ *There has been an increase in the number of reported rapes.* See also **rape** → RAPE *verb*

assault /əˈsɔːlt/ [U, C] (*rather formal*) the crime of attacking sb physically: *Both men were charged with assault.* ◇ *A significant number of **indecent assaults** on women go unreported.* See also **assault** → RAPE *verb*

attempt [C] an act of trying to kill sb: *Someone has **made an attempt on** the President's life.*

3 See the Topic Map for HEALTH on p.890

attack · burst · bout · flurry · outburst · fit · spurt

These are all words for a short and often sudden period of a particular activity, an illness or an emotion.

PATTERNS AND COLLOCATIONS

▸ an attack/a burst/a bout/a flurry/an outburst/a fit/a spurt **of** sth
▸ a **sudden** attack/burst/bout/flurry/outburst/fit/spurt
▸ an **occasional** attack/burst/bout/flurry/outburst
▸ a **brief** burst/bout/flurry/spurt
▸ a **violent** bout/outburst/fit
▸ a burst/an outburst/a fit of **laughter**
▸ a burst/flurry/spurt of **activity**
▸ a burst/a bout/an outburst/a fit/a spurt of **anger**
▸ a burst/an outburst/a fit of **temper**
▸ to **suffer** (**from**)/**have** an attack/a bout/a fit (of sth)
▸ to **bring on** an attack/a bout/a fit (of sth)
▸ to **trigger** an attack/an outburst/a fit (of sth)
▸ to **cause** an attack/a flurry/a fit (of sth)

attack [C] a sudden, short period of illness, usually severe, especially an illness that you have often; a sudden period of feeling an emotion such as fear: *He died after suffering an asthma attack.* ◇ *He is recovering in hospital after an acute attack of food poisoning.* ◇ *An attack of nerves took hold of her.* ◇ *Not everyone who has problems with stress and anxiety will have **panic attacks**.* ❶ Attack is always used to describe negative things. A **heart attack** is a sudden serious medical condition in which the heart stops working normally, sometimes causing death.

burst [C] a short period of a particular activity or strong emotion that often starts suddenly: *I had a sudden burst of energy and cleaned the house from top to bottom.* ◇ *I tend to work **in bursts**.* ◇ *Her breath was coming **in short bursts**.* ◇ *There was a spontaneous burst of applause.* ❶ Burst is usually used to talk about short periods of positive things such as *energy, enthusiasm, laughter* and *applause*, but it is also possible to talk about a **burst** of negative feelings such as *pain, jealousy, irritation, impatience* and *frustration*.

bout /baʊt/ [C] a short period of great activity; a short period during which there is a lot of a particular thing, usually sth unpleasant; an attack or period of illness: *They had been fighting after a **drinking bout**.* ◇ *Regular exercise is better than occasional bouts of strenuous activity.* ◇ *He's just recovering from a severe bout of flu.*

NOTE ATTACK OR BOUT? Both **attack** and **bout** can be used to talk about a period of illness. **Attack**, however, can give an impression of a shorter and more sudden period of illness.

flurry /ˈflʌri; AmE ˈflɜːri/ [C, usually sing.] an occasion when there is a lot of activity, interest or excitement within a short period of time: *Her arrival caused a flurry of excitement.* ◇ *A flurry of shots rang out in the darkness.* ❶ You **have** an **attack/burst/bout** of sth; a **flurry** of sth is sth that *there is/was*, or that is caused or happens in some way.

outburst /ˈaʊtbɜːst; AmE -bɜːrst/ [C] a sudden strong expression of an emotion, especially anger; a sudden increase in a particular activity or attitude: *He was alarmed by her violent outburst.* ◇ *This outburst of racism manifested itself most in the suburbs.* ❶ Outburst is used most frequently to talk about negative feelings such as *anger, violence, hatred, annoyance* and *rage*. It is also used to describe sudden increases in political or social behaviour: *an outburst of militancy/nationalism/patriotism/racism*

fit [C] a sudden short period of coughing or laughter, that you cannot control; a sudden strong expression of an emotion: *Laughing brought on a terrible fit of coughing.* ◇ *He had us all **in fits (of laughter)** with his jokes.* ◇ *The defendant claimed to have acted in a fit of anger.*

spurt /spɜːt; AmE spɜːrt/ [C] a sudden increase in speed, effort, activity or emotion for a short period of time: *You'd better put on a spurt* (= hurry up) *if you want to finish that work today.* ◇ *Babies get very hungry during* **growth spurts**. ◇ *I felt a little spurt of pleasure at the prospect.*

attack verb

1 attack sb with a knife
2 attack a city

1 See the Topic Map for CONFLICT on p.896
attack · assault · beat sb up · mug · strike
These words all mean to use violence to try to hurt, kill or rob sb.

PATTERNS AND COLLOCATIONS
▸ to attack / assault / beat up sb **with** sth
▸ to **get** beaten up / mugged
▸ to **violently** attack sb / assault sb / beat sb up

attack [T, I] to use violence to try to hurt or kill sb: *The man attacked him with a knife.* ◇ *Most dogs will not attack unless provoked.*
assault /əˈsɔːlt/ [T] (*rather formal*) to attack sb violently, especially when this is considered as a crime: *He has been charged with assaulting a police officer.* ◇ *He admitted* **indecently assaulting** *the child.*
beat sb ˈup *phrasal verb* to hit or kick sb hard, many times: *He was badly beaten up by a gang of thugs.*
mug (-gg-) [T, often passive] to attack sb violently in order to steal their money, especially in a public place: *She was mugged in the street in broad daylight.*
  ▸ **mugging** *noun* [U, C]: *Mugging is on the increase in the area, especially after dark.* ◇ *Murders, kidnaps and muggings are reported daily in the newspapers.*
strike [I] to attack sb/sth, especially suddenly: *Police fear that the killer may strike again.* ◇ *The lion crouched ready to strike.*

2 See the Topic Map for CONFLICT on p.896, See also the entry for INVADE
attack · strike · storm · charge · raid
These words all mean to make an aggressive movement against your enemy in a war.

PATTERNS AND COLLOCATIONS
▸ to strike / charge **at** sb / sth
▸ to attack / strike / charge **the enemy**
▸ to attack / strike / charge **a target**
▸ to attack / storm a / an **house / building / embassy**
▸ **soldiers / troops / police** attack / storm / charge / raid sth
▸ **aircraft** attack / strike / raid sth

attack [T, I] to use weapons, such as guns and bombs against an enemy in a war or battle: *At dawn the army attacked the town.* ◇ *The guerrillas usually attack at night.*
strike [I, T] to attack sb/sth, especially suddenly: *The guerrillas struck with deadly force.* ◇ *Warplanes struck several targets in the city.*
storm [T, I] to suddenly attack a place, especially in order to capture it: *Police stormed the building and captured the gunman.* ◇ *Soldiers stormed into the city at dawn.*
charge [I, T] to rush forward and attack sb/sth: *We charged at the enemy.* ◇ *The bull put its head down and charged.* ◇ *He ordered his troops to charge the enemy lines.*
raid [T] to attack a place without warning and then leave: *Villages along the border are regularly raided.* ◇ *a raiding party* (= a group of soldiers, etc. that attack a place)

attempt noun

attempt · effort · try · go · shot · stab
These are all words for an act of trying to do sth, especially sth difficult.

PATTERNS AND COLLOCATIONS
▸ an attempt / a try / a go / a shot / a stab **at** sth
▸ an attempt / effort **to do** sth
▸ **in** an attempt / effort **to do** sth
▸ a **first / last / good** attempt / effort / try / go / shot / stab
▸ a **serious** attempt / effort / go / shot
▸ a / an **valiant / brave / feeble / unsuccessful** attempt / effort / stab
▸ to **have** a try / go / shot / stab
▸ to **make** an attempt / an effort / a stab
▸ to **give** sth a try / go / shot
▸ to **take** a shot / stab at sth
▸ to **be worth** a try / go / shot / stab

attempt [C, U] an act of trying to do sth, especially sth difficult, often with no success; an act of trying to do better than sth, such as a good performance in sport: *Two factories were closed in an attempt to cut costs.* ◇ *The couple made several attempts at a compromise.* ◇ *They* **made no attempt to** *escape.* ◇ *I passed my driving test at the first attempt.* ◇ *The previous* **attempt on** *the world record was abandoned last year due to bad weather.* See also **attempt** → TRY *verb* 1
effort [C] an act of trying to do sth, especially sth difficult that needs energy or determination: *I'll make a special effort to finish on time this week.* ◇ *I didn't really feel like going out, but I'm glad I* **made the effort**. ◇ *The local clubs are* **making every effort** *to interest more young people.* ◇ *Despite* **our best efforts**, *we didn't manage to win the game.*

> **NOTE** **ATTEMPT** OR **EFFORT**? In many cases you can use either word: *They met once more in an attempt/effort to find a solution.* **Attempt** often emphasizes the event or action involved in trying to do or achieve sth: *a coup/ assassination/suicide attempt* ◇ *a coup/assassination/ suicide effort.* **Effort** especially emphasizes the work or energy that sb puts into trying to do sth: *a great/ enormous/strenuous effort* ◇ *a great/enormous/strenuous attempt*

try [C, usually sing.] (*rather informal*) an act of trying to do sth, especially sth which you think may not be successful: *I don't think I'll be any good at tennis, but I'll give it a try.* ◇ *I doubt they'll be able to help, but it's worth a try* (= worth asking them). ◇ *Never mind — it was a good try.* ◇ (*AmE*) *The US negotiators decided to* **make** *another* **try at** *reaching a settlement.* See also **try** → TRY *verb* 1
go [C] (*BrE, rather informal*) a try: *You should have a go at answering all the questions.* ◇ *It took three goes to get it right.*
shot [C, usually sing.] (*informal*) an attempt to do or achieve sth: *The team are looking good for a shot at the title.* ◇ *Just* **give it your best shot** (= try as hard as you can) *and you'll be fine.*
stab [C, usually sing.] (*informal*) an attempt to do sth, especially sth that you are not very experienced or skilled at doing: *I've always enjoyed acting, but I'd like to have a stab at directing one day.*

attend verb See also the entry for GET 4

attend · come · go · come along
These words all mean to be present at an event.

PATTERNS AND COLLOCATIONS
▸ to come / go / come along **to** sth
▸ to attend / come / go / come along **with** sb
▸ to attend / come to / go to / come along to a **meeting / wedding**
▸ to attend / come to / go to a **conference**
▸ to attend / come to / go to a **party**

attend [T, I] (*rather formal*) to be present at an organized event such as a meeting or wedding: *Over 600 people attended the conference.* ◇ *The lecture was attended by most of the faculty.* ◇ *Several members were unable to attend.*
  ▸ **attendance** /əˈtendəns/ *noun* [U, C]: *Attendance at these lectures is not compulsory.*

come [I] to travel to a place in order to be present at an event: *Please come to my party on September 10th.* ◇ *Thanks for coming!* ◇ *I'm sorry, I won't be able to come.* ◇ *Why don't you come skating with us tonight?*

go [I] to travel to a place in order to be present at an event: *He was going to a concert that evening and invited her to go with him.* ◇ *Who else is going?*

NOTE COME OR GO? Come expresses the point of view of a person who arranges an event or attends it. Go is used when the speaker is talking about other people.

,come a'long *phrasal verb* to go to an event with sb: *Come along to a meeting and see what you think.*

attention *noun* See also the entry for CARE

attention · interest · notice · concentration · regard
These are all words for the act of listening to, looking at or thinking about sth carefully because you think it is important.

PATTERNS AND COLLOCATIONS
▸ close / media / personal / special attention / interest
▸ deep / growing / great / intense interest / concentration
▸ full / total / undivided attention / concentration
▸ careful / public attention / notice
▸ to catch / get / grab / lose sb's attention / interest
▸ to lose interest / concentration
▸ to hold / focus sb's attention / interest / concentration
▸ to attract / bring sth to / come to / escape sb's attention / notice
▸ to turn your attention / interest / concentration to sth
▸ to pay (no) attention / regard to sth

attention [U] the act of listening to, looking at or thinking about sb/sth carefully: *He wanted to call/draw attention to the problem.* ◇ *Now, please sit up and pay attention* (= listen carefully) *to what I am going to say.* ◇ *Don't pay any attention to what they say* (= don't think that it is important or be upset by it). ◇ *She tried to attract the waiter's attention.* ◇ *Films with the big stars always attract great attention.* ◇ *Small children have a very short attention span* (= become easily bored). ◇ *(formal, spoken) Can I have your attention please?* ◇ *The child was used to being the centre of attention.*

interest [sing., U] the feeling that you have when you want to know or learn more about sb/sth: *I told him about it but he showed no interest.* ◇ *Several people expressed an interest in learning the game.* ◇ *Does she take an interest in your research?* ◇ *As a matter of interest* (= I would like to know) *what time did the party finish?* ◇ *Just out of interest,* (= I would like to know but it is not important) *how much did it cost?*

notice [U] the fact of sb paying attention to sb/sth or knowing about sth: *Don't take any notice of what you read in the papers.* ◇ *Take no notice of what he says.* ◇ *(formal) It was Susan who brought the problem to my notice* (= told me about it). ◇ *(formal) It will not have escaped your notice that there have been some changes in the company.* See also notice → NOTICE verb

concentration [U] the ability to direct all your effort and attention on one thing, without thinking of other things; the process of people directing effort and attention on a particular thing: *Tiredness affects your powers of concentration.* ◇ *The noise had disturbed his concentration.* ◇ *He stressed the need for greater concentration on environmental issues.*
▸ concentrate *verb* [I, T]: *I can't concentrate with all that noise going on.* ◇ *I decided to concentrate all my efforts on finding somewhere to live.*

regard [U] *(formal)* attention to or thought and care for sb/sth: *They show scant regard for other people's property.* ◇ *He was driving without regard to speed limits.* ◇ *Social services should pay proper regard to the needs of inner-city areas.*

attitude *noun* See the Topic Map for FACT AND OPINION on p.898, See also the entry for VIEW 1

attitude · view · perspective · point of view · stance · position · outlook · level · line · angle · side · stand
These are all words for the particular way you think or feel about sb/sth.

PATTERNS AND COLLOCATIONS
▸ sb's view / a perspective / a stance / a position / an outlook / a line / an angle / a stand **on** sth
▸ a stance / stand **against** sb / sth
▸ **from** the perspective / point of view / position / angle of sb / sth
▸ **different / various** attitudes / views / perspectives / points of view / stances / positions / outlooks / levels / angles / sides
▸ an **alternative** view / perspective / point of view / position / angle
▸ a **personal** attitude / view / perspective / point of view / stance / position / level / angle / stand
▸ the **general** attitude / view / perspective / point of view / position / outlook
▸ a **popular** attitude / view / perspective
▸ a **positive / negative** attitude / view / perspective / point of view / stance / outlook / angle
▸ a **sympathetic** attitude / view / point of view / angle
▸ a **critical** attitude / view / perspective / point of view / stance
▸ a **practical** attitude / view / perspective / point of view / outlook
▸ to **take** an attitude / a view / a perspective / a point of view / a stance / a position / a line / a side / a stand
▸ to **adopt** an attitude / a view / a perspective / a point of view / a stance / a position / an outlook / a line
▸ to **have** an attitude / a view / a perspective / a point of view / an outlook / a line / an angle
▸ to **change** an attitude / your view / your perspective / your point of view / your stance / your position / your outlook / sides
▸ to **challenge** an attitude / a view / a perspective

attitude [C] the way that you think and feel about sb/sth; the way that you behave towards sb/sth that shows how you think and feel: *Her attitude to her parents has always been somewhat negative.* ◇ *What is your attitude towards the job as a whole?* ◇ *I tend to take the attitude that it's best to leave well alone.* ◇ *If you want to pass your exams you'd better change your attitude.*

view [C, usually sing.] a way of understanding or thinking about sth: *He has a pretty optimistic view of life.* ◇ *The traditional view was that marriage was for life.*

perspective /pə'spektɪv; AmE pər's-/ [C, usually sing.] a particular attitude towards an issue or problem; a particular way of thinking about sth: *Try to approach the problem from a different perspective.* ◇ *We need to take a global perspective on the environment.*

,point of 'view [C] a particular way of considering or judging a situation: *These statistics are important from an economic point of view.* ◇ *The book is written from a child's point of view.*

stance /stæns; BrE also stɑːns/ [C] the opinion that sb has on a particular issue that they express publicly: *What's the newspaper's stance on the war?* ◇ *He's known for his anti-immigration stance.*

position [C] an attitude that sb has towards a particular subject that influences how they act: *Our party's position on education is very clear.* ◇ *The official position was that of refusing to talk to terrorists.*

NOTE STANCE OR POSITION? A stance can be more temporary and/or more personal than a position, in reaction to a new issue in current affairs, when it is considered necessary for public figures and newspapers to make their opinions known. A position is often more long-term and/or official and is concerned with how people or organizations act on a particular issue, rather than what they say.

outlook /'aʊtlʊk/ [C] the attitude to life and the world of a particular person or group: *He has a very practical outlook on life.* ◇ *Most western societies are liberal in outlook.*

level [C] a particular way of looking at, reacting to or understanding sth: *On a more personal level, I would like to thank Jean for all the help she has given me.* ◊ *Fables can be understood on various levels.*

line [C, usually sing.] an attitude or belief, especially one that is officially supported by a government, political party or politician: *The government took a **hard line** on the strike.* ◊ *The MP supported the **official line** on education.* ◊ *He was expelled from the party for refusing to **toe the party line** (= follow the party's official opinions and policies).*

angle [C] a particular way of thinking about or presenting a situation, problem or subject: *We're looking for a new angle for our next advertising campaign.* ◊ *The article concentrates on the human angle (= the part that concerns people's emotions) of the story.*

side [C] one of the opinions, attitudes or positions taken by sb in an argument or agreement: *You need to listen to both sides of the argument.* ◊ *The other side maintains that the project will not be affordable.* ◊ *Will you keep your side of the bargain?*

stand [C, usually sing.] an attitude that you take publicly, usually against sth that you disapprove of: *We need to take a tough stand on tax avoidance.*

be **attracted to sb** *verb*

be attracted to sb · want · fancy · have a crush on sb · go for sb · be into sb
These words and phrases all mean to find sb attractive, so that you want to have a sexual or romantic relationship with them.

PATTERNS AND COLLOCATIONS
▸ to want / fancy sb **a lot / very much**
▸ to **really** want / fancy sb / to be **really** into sb
▸ A and B are attracted to / want / fancy **each other**

be at'tracted to sb *phrase* (not used in the progressive tenses) to like sb in a romantic or sexual way: *It was obvious that they were physically attracted to each other.* See also **attraction** → LOVE *noun* 1

want [T] (not used in the progressive tenses) to feel a sexual or romantic desire for sb: *'I want you so much,' she whispered in his ear.* ❶ **Want** can refer to a more general feeling of wanting sb as a romantic partner. The context should make this clear: *Alice, please don't leave me. I want you. I need you. I can't live without you.*

fancy [T] (not used in the progressive tenses) (*BrE, informal*) to be sexually attracted to sb: *I think she fancies me.*

have a 'crush on sb *idiom* (not used in the progressive tenses) to have a strong feeling of love for sb, that usually does not last very long: *I had a huge crush on her when I was younger.* ❶ **Have a crush on sb** is usually used about a young person's feelings for sb older or for sb that they know they cannot have a relationship with. See also **crush** → LOVE *noun* 1

'go for sb *phrasal verb* (not used in the progressive tenses) (*rather informal*) to find a particular type of person attractive: *She generally goes for tall, slim men.* ❶ **Go for sb** refers to preferring types of people in general. You cannot use it to refer to a particular person: *I always go for dark-haired girls.* ◊ I really go for that dark-haired girl.

be 'into sb *phrase* (not used in the progressive tenses) (*AmE, informal*) to be attracted to sb: *You know Ed? I'm really into him.*

audience *noun* See the Topic Map for THE MEDIA on p.900, See also the entry for WITNESS

audience · viewer · spectator · listener
These are all words for people who watch or listen to a performance, show or sports game.

PATTERNS AND COLLOCATIONS
▸ **before / in front of** an audience / spectators

▸ a **television / TV / cinema** audience / viewer
▸ to **attract** the audience / viewers / spectators / listeners
▸ to **draw** an audience / spectators
▸ to **pull in** an audience / viewers
▸ to **entertain / be a hit with / shock** the audience / viewers / listeners
▸ an audience / a viewer / a spectator **sees / watches** sb / sth
▸ an audience / a listener **hears / listens to** sb / sth
▸ an audience / a spectator **cheers / applauds / boos**

audience [C+sing./pl. *v.*] a group of people who have gathered to watch or listen to sth such as a play or concert; the number of people who watch or listen to the same thing on television, the radio or in the cinema: *The debate was televised in front of a **live audience**.* ◊ *An audience of millions watched the wedding on TV.* See also **audience** → MARKET 1

viewer [C] a person watching television; a person who looks at sth: *The show attracted millions of viewers.* ◊ *Some of her art is intended to shock the viewer.*

spectator /spek'teɪtə(r)/ [C] a person who is watching an event, especially a sports event: *The new football stadium will hold 75 000 spectators.* ◊ *I think soccer is the best **spectator sport** (= a sport that many people watch or that is interesting to watch) there is.*

listener [C] a person listening to a radio programme: *Regular listeners will know this is the Year of Czech Music.*

authoritarian *adj.* See the Topic Map for THE INDIVIDUAL AND SOCIETY on p.894, See also the entry for REPRESSIVE

authoritarian · authoritative · autocratic · bossy · overbearing
These words all describe people who try to control other people or expect to be obeyed, especially without considering the others' wishes, feelings or opinions.

PATTERNS AND COLLOCATIONS
▸ an authoritarian / an authoritative / an autocratic / an overbearing **manner**
▸ an authoritarian / an authoritative / a bossy **attitude**
▸ **very** authoritarian / authoritative / bossy
▸ **rather** authoritarian / bossy / overbearing

authoritarian /ɔː'θɒrɪ'teəriən; *AmE* ə'θɔːrə'ter-; ə'θɑːr-/ (of a person or system) expecting that people should obey authority and rules, even when these are unfair and even if it means that they lose their personal freedom: *Many have accused him of an authoritarian style of leadership.* ◊ *The school was very authoritarian and exam-orientated.*

authoritative /ɔː'θɒrətətɪv; *AmE* ə'θɔːrəteɪtɪv; ə'θɑːr-/ (*often approving*) (of a person's behaviour) showing that you expect people to obey and respect you: *His tone was clear and authoritative.*

autocratic /ˌɔːtə'krætɪk/ (*disapproving*) (of a person or system) expecting to be obeyed by other people without considering their wishes, feelings or opinions: *Critics have accused him of being autocratic and intolerant of dissent.* ◊ *She introduced a less autocratic approach to management.*

> **NOTE** AUTHORITARIAN, AUTHORITATIVE OR AUTOCRATIC?
> **Autocratic** always shows disapproval; **authoritative** often shows approval that sb is strong and in control of a situation; **authoritarian** can show disapproval but is usually simply a descriptive term, neither approving nor disapproving.

bossy (*rather informal, disapproving*) (of a person) always telling people what to do: *We were told to move by a bossy woman in a green uniform.*

overbearing /ˌəʊvə'beərɪŋ; *AmE* ˌoʊvər'ber-/ (*disapproving*) (of a person) trying to control other people, without considering their wishes, feelings and opinions: *She found him rude and overbearing.*

the **authorities** *noun* See the Topic Map for THE INDIVIDUAL AND SOCIETY on p.894

the authorities · bureaucracy · the establishment · the system · the top brass · officialdom
These words all refer to the people who have power to make decisions in an organization, country or area of activity, or the system they are part of, especially when the system seems unfair because you cannot change or influence it.

PATTERNS AND COLLOCATIONS
▸ **within** the bureaucracy / establishment / system
▸ the **military** authorities / bureaucracy / establishment / top brass
▸ the **medical / political** authorities / bureaucracy / establishment
▸ the **local / federal / government / state** authorities / bureaucracy
▸ **to rebel against / fight** the establishment / system

the authorities [pl.] the people who have the power to make decisions or who have a particular area of responsibility in a country or region: *The health authorities are investigating the problem.* ◇ *Someone reported him* **to the immigration authorities**.
bureaucracy /bjʊəˈrɒkrəsi; *AmE* bjʊˈrɑːk-/ [U, C] a system of government in which there are a large number of state officials who are not elected; a country with this system: *Many people believed that the state bureaucracy was corrupt.* ◇ *We are living in a modern bureaucracy.* See also **bureaucracy** → BUREAUCRACY, **bureaucrat** → OFFICIAL *noun*
the establishment (also **the Establishment**) [sing.+ sing./pl. v.] (*often disapproving*) the people in a society or profession who have influence and who do not usually support change: *As a young designer she soon became known for kicking* **against the Establishment**. ◇ *His ideas have not been widely accepted within the academic establishment.*
the system the rules or people that control a country or organization, especially when they seem unfair because you cannot change them: *You should know you can't beat* **the system** (= you must accept the way things are done). ◇ *Graham knew how to* **work the system** (= make it work to his own advantage).
the ˌtop ˈbrass (*BrE*) (*AmE* **the brass**) [sing.+ sing./pl. v.] (*informal*) the people who are in the most important positions in an organization or area of activity: *There will be a meeting of the sport's top brass in Paris this week.*
officialdom /əˈfɪʃldəm/ [U] (*disapproving*) state officials, or people who are in important positions in large organizations, when they seem to be more interested in following rules than being helpful: *The report is critical of attempts by officialdom to deal with the problem of homelessness.*

available *adj.*

available · for sale · on the market · on sale
These words all describe sth that can be bought, obtained or found.

PATTERNS AND COLLOCATIONS
▸ available / on sale **from** sb / sth
▸ **to go** on the market / on sale
▸ **now / still** available / for sale / on the market / on sale

available (*rather formal*) that you can get, buy or find: *This was the only room available.* ◇ *When will the information be made available?* ◇ *We have used all available resources.*
  ▸ **availability** *noun* [U]: *the availability of cheap flights* ◇ *This offer is* **subject to availability**.
for ˈsale *phrase* available for sb to buy, especially from the owner: *I'm sorry, it's not for sale.* ◇ *They've* **put their house up for sale**. ◇ *There has been an increase in the number of stolen vehicles being* **offered for sale**.

on the ˈmarket *phrase* available for people to buy: *There are hundreds of different brands on the market.* ◇ *Don't put your house on the market until spring.* ◇ *The house came on the market last year.*
on ˈsale *phrase* available for people to buy, especially in a shop: *Tickets are on sale from the booking office.* ◇ *The new model goes on sale next month.*

average *adj.*

average · simple · ordinary · plain · unremarkable
These words all describe things or people that are not special because they are not unusual, interesting or clever.

PATTERNS AND COLLOCATIONS
▸ an average / ordinary **sort of** person / thing
▸ an average / a simple / an ordinary / an unremarkable **person**
▸ average / ordinary **players**
▸ simple / plain **ignorance / common sense**
▸ **pretty** average / ordinary / unremarkable
▸ **very** average / simple / ordinary

average (*often disapproving*) not special in any way; not better than most others: *He was quite an average sort of student, nothing out of the ordinary.* ◇ *The quality has been pretty average.* See also **average** → NORMAL
simple [usually before noun] (*often approving*) (of a person) not grand, rich, clever or hard to understand; (of a thing or quality) not special or complicated: *They were simple country people.* ◇ *In some cases his argument is based on simple ignorance.* ❶ When used to describe a person or a good quality **simple** is usually approving; when it is used to describe a bad quality it is usually disapproving.
ordinary (*disapproving*) having no unusual or interesting features: *The meal was very ordinary.* ◇ *I lead a very ordinary life.* ❶ In this meaning **ordinary** very often follows *very*, which emphasizes that **ordinary** is being used in a disapproving way. See also **ordinary** → NORMAL
OPP extraordinary → REMARKABLE
plain [only before noun] (*often approving*) (of a quality) not special or complicated; (of a person) not trying to appear more important or intelligent than they are: *It doesn't require special skills, just plain common sense.* ◇ *He prided himself on being a plain, honest man with no nonsense about him.* See also **plain** → PLAIN *adj.* 2

NOTE SIMPLE OR PLAIN? Both these words can describe people or qualities, but **simple** is used more about people and **plain** is used more about qualities. When used to describe people, **simple** tells you how other people see sb (= not grand, rich or clever, but in a good way); **plain** tells you more about how sb sees himself/ herself (= not pretending to be grand, rich or clever).

unremarkable not special in any way so that people do not take notice of it: *It was a pleasant but unremarkable town.*
OPP remarkable → REMARKABLE

avoid *verb*

avoid · stay away · boycott · shun · steer clear · keep your distance
These words all mean to try not to go near a particular person or place, or to try not to do sth.

PATTERNS AND COLLOCATIONS
▸ to avoid / shun **publicity / the limelight**
▸ to **deliberately** avoid / stay away from / steer clear of sb / sth

avoid [T] to not go near a particular person, place, event or situation: *He's been avoiding me all week.* ◇ *She kept avoiding my eyes* (= would not look at me). ◇ *I left early to avoid the rush hour.*
ˌstay aˈway *phrasal verb* to not go near a particular person or place: *I want you to* **stay away from** *my daughter.*

boycott /ˈbɔɪkɒt; AmE -kɑːt/ [T] to refuse to buy, use or take part in sth as a way of protesting: *We are asking people to boycott goods from companies that use child labour.* See also **boycott** → BAN *noun*

shun (**-nn-**) [T] (*written*) to permanently avoid, ignore or reject sb/sth, because you do not like them or are afraid of them: *She was shunned by her family when she remarried.* ◇ *He is an actor who shuns publicity.*

steer clear *idiom* to avoid a person, place, event or situation because it may cause problems: *Steer clear of the centre of town at this time of the evening.* ◇ *It is prudent to steer well clear of political subjects.*

keep your ˈdistance *idiom* to make sure you are not too near sb/sth; to avoid getting too friendly or involved with a person or group: *The lighthouse warns ships to keep their distance.* ◇ *She was warned to keep her distance from Charles if she didn't want to get hurt.* ❶ **Keep your distance** is usually used to talk about avoiding sb/sth that may be dangerous.

award *noun*

award · prize · reward · title · medal · trophy · honour · cup · championship
These are all words for sth that you are given for winning or achieving sth, or the position of winning sth.

PATTERNS AND COLLOCATIONS
▸ an award / a prize / a reward / a medal / a trophy / a cup **for** sth
▸ a **major** award / prize / title / trophy / honour / championship
▸ a **coveted** / **prestigious** award / prize / title / trophy
▸ a / an **special** award / prize / reward / honour
▸ a / an **top** / **academic** award / prize / honour
▸ the **supreme** award / prize / title
▸ a **European** / **world** title / trophy / cup / championship
▸ a **championship** title / medal / trophy
▸ to **win** an award / a prize / a reward / a title / a medal / a trophy / an honour / a cup / the championship
▸ to **take** an award / a prize / a reward / a title / a medal / the trophy / the championship
▸ to **earn** an award / a prize / a reward / a title / a medal
▸ to **receive** an award / a prize / a reward / a medal / a trophy / an honour
▸ to **accept** an award / a prize / a reward / a title / an honour
▸ to **lose** a title / medal / the cup / the championship
▸ to **defend** / **retain** a title / a trophy / the championship
▸ an award / a prize / a title / a medal / a trophy / an honour / a cup / the championship **goes to** sb

award [C] something, such as money or a special title, given to sb for sth they have done or achieved: *He was nominated for the best actor award.* ◇ *Stephen's quick thinking has earned him a bravery award.* ◇ *The association is presenting its annual awards this week.* ◇ *Helen received her prize at an **awards ceremony** in New York.* See also **award** → GIVE *verb* 1

prize [C] something, such as money, given to sb who wins a competition or race or who does very good work; sth very important or valuable that is difficult to achieve or obtain: *She was awarded the Nobel Prize for Literature.* ◇ *He took **first prize** in the woodwind section.* ◇ *I won £500 in **prize money**.* ◇ *Win a car in our grand **prize draw**!* ◇ *World peace is the greatest prize of all.* See also **prizewinner** → WINNER

reward [C, U] something that you are given because you have done sth good or worked hard; an amount of money that is offered to sb for helping the police to find a criminal or for finding sth that is lost: *You deserve a reward for being so helpful.* ◇ *The company is now **reaping the rewards** of their investments.* ◇ *Winning the match was **just reward** for the effort the team made.* ◇ *The look on her face when I told her was **reward enough**.* ◇ *A $100 reward has been **offered** for the return of the necklace.* ◇ *The company has **put up** a reward of £25 000 for information.* **OPP** **punishment**, **penalty** → PUNISHMENT
▸ **reward** *verb* [T, often passive]: *Se was rewarded for her*

efforts with a cash bonus. ◇ *Our patience was finally rewarded.*

title [C] the position of being the winner of a competition, especially a sports competition: *She has three world titles.* ◇ *She'll be defending her title at this week's French Open.*

medal [C] a flat piece of metal, usually shaped like a coin, that is given to the winner of a competition or to sb who

award

medals

cup

trophies

has been brave, for example in a war: *He received a medal for his service in the war.* ◇ *Anyone who does that job deserves a medal!* ◇ *She won the **gold medal** at the World Championships.* See also **medallist** → WINNER

trophy /ˈtrəʊfi; AmE ˈtroʊfi/ [C] an object, such as a silver cup, that is given as a prize for winning a competition: *He picked up a trophy for best news editor.* ◇ *The team paraded their League Championship trophy.*

honour (*BrE*) (*AmE* **honor**) [C] an award or official title given to sb as a reward for sth they have done: *It was the British who scooped the honours at last night's Oscars.* ◇ *He was buried **with full military honours** (= with a special military service as a sign of respect).*

cup [C] a gold or silver cup on a stem, often with two handles, that is given as a prize in a competition: *She has won several cups for skating.*

championship /ˈtʃæmpiənʃɪp/ [C] the position of winning a competition to become champion: *They've held the championship for the past two years.* See also **champion** → WINNER

aware *adj.*

aware · conscious · mindful · alert to sth
These words all mean knowing about or realizing sth.

PATTERNS AND COLLOCATIONS
▸ aware / conscious / mindful **of** sth
▸ aware / conscious / mindful **that**...
▸ **very** aware / conscious / mindful / alert
▸ **keenly** aware / conscious / alert

aware [not before noun] knowing or realizing sth; noticing that sth is present or that sth is happening: *He was **well aware** of the problem.* ◇ *Were you aware that something was wrong?* ◇ *As far as **I'm aware** no one has done anything about it.* ◇ *Helen slipped out without him being aware of it.* **OPP** **unaware** → UNAWARE

conscious [not before noun] (*rather formal*) aware of sth, especially in a way that makes you feel responsibility or anxiety: *He was painfully conscious of his mother's embarrassment.* ◊ *I was vaguely conscious that I was being watched.*

mindful [not before noun] (*formal*) aware of sb/sth and considering them when you do sth: *Mindful of his advice, I decided to return to my hotel.*

alert to sth [not before noun] aware of sth, especially a problem or danger: *Soldiers must be alert to danger but not constantly frightened.* See also **alert** → WATCH *noun*

awareness *noun*

awareness · knowledge · consciousness · realization · perception

These are all words for the fact of knowing, recognizing or understanding sth or the ability to do this.

PATTERNS AND COLLOCATIONS

▶ an awareness/the knowledge/a consciousness/the realization/ a perception **of** sth
▶ an awareness/the knowledge/a consciousness/the realization/ a perception **that**...
▶ a **sudden** awareness/realization/perception
▶ a/the **growing/increasing/greater** awareness/knowledge/ consciousness/realization/perception
▶ **full** awareness/knowledge/consciousness/realization
▶ a **heightened** awareness/consciousness/perception
▶ (a/the) **public** awareness/knowledge/consciousness/ perception
▶ to **raise** awareness/consciousness
▶ to **develop/increase** sb's awareness/knowledge/perception

▶ to **heighten** sb's awareness/perception
▶ a **lack** of awareness/knowledge/consciousness/perception

awareness [U, sing.] the fact of knowing about or understanding sth: *There is growing awareness of the link between diet and health.* ◊ *I seemed to have a heightened awareness of my surroundings.* ◊ *It's the start of Breast Cancer Awareness week.*

knowledge [U] the state of knowing about a particular fact or situation: *She sent the letter **without my knowledge**.* ◊ *The documentary was made **with** the singer's full **knowledge** and permission.* ◊ *They could relax, **safe/ secure in the knowledge** that the money would be available.* ◊ *He **denied all knowledge** of the affair.* ◊ *Their relationship is **common/public knowledge** (=* everyone knows about it). **OPP** **ignorance** → IGNORANCE, See also **know** → KNOW 1

consciousness [U, sing.] the state of being aware of sth; the ideas and opinions of a person or group: *We need to raise people's consciousness of environmental issues.* ◊ *The memory remained deep in his consciousness.*

realization (*BrE* also **-isation**) [U, sing.] the process of becoming aware of sth: *The realization of what she had done suddenly hit her.* ◊ *the gradual realization that they were losing the war* See also **realize** → KNOW 1

perception /pə'sepʃn; *AmE* pər's-/ [U, sing.] (*formal or technical*) the way that you notice things, especially with the senses; the opinion or idea that you have of sth as a result of the way in which you understand it: *Everyone's perception of reality is slightly different.* ◊ *There's a general perception that standards of health care are falling.* See also **perceive** → NOTICE

B b

background

background noun See also the entry for FAMILY 3

background · record · past · history · upbringing · track record · life history
These are all words for the things that sb has done or the things that have happened to sb before now.

PATTERNS AND COLLOCATIONS
▸ sb has a background / record / history / track record **of** sth
▸ sb has a background / record / track record **in** sth
▸ a/an **proven/impressive/excellent/poor** record/track record
▸ a **religious / working class/ middle class** background / upbringing
▸ a **colourful / chequered** history / past
▸ sb's **criminal** background / record / past / history
▸ sb's **medical** record / history
▸ your background / upbringing **prepares you for/ gives you** sth

background [C] the details of a person's life before now, especially concerning their family, education and experience: *sb's family/social/cultural/educational/class background* ◇ *The classes are designed for students with a background in history or theology.* ◇ *The job would suit someone with a* **business background**. ◇ *We are from very* **different backgrounds** *but we get on very well.* ❶ You can also talk about the **background** to an event or situation. See also **background** → CONTEXT

record [sing.] the facts that are known about sb/sth's past behaviour, character or achievements: *The report criticizes the government's* **record on** *housing.* ◇ *The airline has a good* **safety record**. ◇ *He has an impressive* **record of achievement**.

past [C, usually sing.] a person's life or career before now: *We don't know anything about his past.* ◇ *She didn't tell them about her boyfriend's criminal past.* ❶ **Past** can also be used to talk about an aspect of a place before now: *The country still suffers as a result of its colonial past.*

history [sing.] a record of sth happening frequently in the past of a person, family or place; the set of facts that are known about sb's past: *He has a history of violent crime.* ◇ *There is a history of heart disease in my family.* ◇ *The area has a history of subsidence problems.*

upbringing /ˈʌpbrɪŋɪŋ/ [sing., U] the way in which a child is cared for and taught how to behave while it is growing up: *She had had a very sheltered upbringing.* ◇ *He was a Catholic by upbringing.*

track record [sing.] all the past achievements, successes or failures of a person or organization: *As a company we have a proven track record in catering.* ◇ *Britain has a poor track record in foreign language teaching.*

life history [C] all the events that happen in the life of a person, animal or plant: *He sat at the bar and told me his whole life history.* ◇ *The aim of the project is to study the life histories of insects.*

bad

bad adj. See also the entry for TERRIBLE 1

bad · nasty · unpleasant · grim · lousy · wretched · ghastly
These words all describe sth that is full of problems and/or makes you feel upset, uncomfortable, disappointed or depressed.

bad	nasty	wretched
unpleasant	grim	ghastly
	lousy	

PATTERNS AND COLLOCATIONS
▸ a bad / a nasty/ an unpleasant / a grim / a ghastly **situation**
▸ a bad / a nasty/ an unpleasant / a ghastly **experience / feeling**
▸ bad / nasty / unpleasant / grim / lousy / wretched / ghastly **weather**
▸ a bad / a nasty / an unpleasant / a grim **mood**
▸ a bad / a nasty / an unpleasant **taste / smell**
▸ bad / grim / ghastly **news**
▸ a bad / a grim / a lousy / a wretched **day / night / time**
▸ a nasty/ an unpleasant / a grim / a wretched / a ghastly **thought**
▸ the nasty / unpleasant / grim **truth / reality / facts**
▸ to **find sth** unpleasant / grim
▸ **very** bad / nasty / unpleasant / grim / wretched
▸ **really** bad / nasty / unpleasant / grim / lousy / wretched / ghastly
▸ **pretty** bad / nasty / unpleasant / grim / lousy / ghastly
▸ **rather** bad / nasty / unpleasant / grim / ghastly
▸ **particularly** bad / nasty / unpleasant / grim / ghastly

bad full of problems; not what you hope for or want: *I'm having a really bad day.* ◇ *It was the worst experience of her life.* ◇ *Smoking gives you bad breath.* ◇ *Things are bad enough without our own guns shelling us.* **OPP** good → NICE 1

nasty very bad or serious; making you feel upset, uncomfortable or disgusted: *He had a nasty accident.* ◇ *The news gave me a nasty shock.* ◇ *He had a nasty moment when he thought he'd lost his passport.* ◇ *This coffee tastes nasty.* ◇ *Don't buy that coat – it looks* **cheap and nasty**. **OPP** nice → NICE 1

unpleasant (*rather formal*) not pleasant or comfortable: *There was an unpleasant atmosphere in the room.* ◇ *The minerals in the water made it unpleasant to drink.* ◇ *He may make life unpleasant for the rest of us.* ❶ **Unpleasant** is usually less strong than **nasty** and is not used to mean 'serious': *He had an unpleasant accident.* However, it is sometimes used in a rather polite or formal way to describe sth that really is nasty, when you don't want to say exactly how nasty it is: *Things started to get unpleasant when the neighbours called in the police.* **OPP** pleasant → NICE 1

grim unpleasant and depressing: *The accident serves as a grim reminder of what drinking and driving can do.* ◇ *The outlook is pretty grim.* ◇ *Things are looking grim for workers in the building industry.* ❶ **Grim** is used especially to talk about things that have just happened and things that are likely to happen in the future. Collocates include *news, reminder, discovery, reality, picture, legacy, fate, future, prospect, forecast, outlook* and *warning*.

lousy /ˈlaʊzi/ (*informal*) very bad or disappointing: *What lousy weather!* ◇ *I've had a lousy day.* ❶ **Lousy** is used especially to talk about things or people that you are disappointed with. Collocates include *day, food, husband, lover, summer* and *weather*.

wretched /ˈretʃɪd/ (*written*) extremely bad or unpleasant: *She had a wretched time of it at school.* ◇ *The animals are kept in the most wretched conditions.* ❶ **Wretched** is used especially to talk about extreme situations that affect other people (or animals) and that you sympathize with.

ghastly /ˈɡɑːstli; AmE ˈɡæstli/ (*informal*) extremely bad or unpleasant: *The weather was ghastly.* ◇ *It's all been a ghastly mistake.* ❶ **Ghastly** is used especially to talk about extreme situations that affect your senses or emotions.

ways of cooking

bake

fry

roast

grill (*BrE*) / broil (*AmE*)

toast

barbecue

bake *verb* See also the entry for COOK

bake · fry · roast · grill · broil · toast · barbecue
These are all words for ways of cooking food.

PATTERNS AND COLLOCATIONS
▸ to fry / roast / grill / broil / barbecue **chicken**
▸ to fry / grill / barbecue a **steak**
▸ to fry / grill / barbecue **sausages**
▸ to bake / fry / grill / broil **fish**
▸ to fry / grill **bacon**
▸ to bake / fry / roast **potatoes**
▸ to bake / fry / toast **bread**
▸ to roast / toast **nuts**

bake [T, I] to cook food, especially bread, cakes and potatoes, in an oven without extra fat or liquid; to be cooked in this way: *baked potatoes* ◇ *I'm **baking** a birthday **cake** for Alex.* ◇ *I'm baking Alex a cake.* ❶ Bake is not used about cooking meat; use **roast** instead. See also **baking** → COOKING

fry [T, I] to cook sth in hot fat or oil; to be cooked in this way: *fried fish/eggs* ◇ *I woke up to the smell of bacon frying.*

roast [T, I] to cook meat without liquid in an oven or over a fire; to cook vegetables in oil or fat in an oven; to cook nuts or beans in order to dry them and turn them brown; to be cooked in any of these ways: *You should boil the potatoes for a little before you roast them.* ◇ *The smell of roasting meat came from the kitchen.* ❶ The past participle of **roast** is usually **roasted**, except when it is used before a noun, when **roast** is usually used: *roast beef/chicken/ potatoes/parsnips* ◇ ~~roasted beef/chicken/potatoes/parsnips~~ However, **roasted** is used to describe nuts and beans: *roasted chestnuts/coffee beans/peanuts*

grill [T] to cook food under or over a very strong heat: *Grill the sausages for ten minutes, turning occasionally.* ◇ *At night we used to grill steaks over charcoal in the open air.* ❶ Food can be **grilled** in an oven under the **grill** (*BrE*) or **broiler** (*AmE*), or outdoors over a fire; however, it is even more frequent to talk about **barbecuing** food that is cooked outdoors.

broil [T] (*AmE*) to cook meat or fish under direct heat: *We ate broiled chicken with vegetables.* ❶ In British English use **grill** for this.

toast [T, I] to make sth, especially bread, turn brown by heating it in a toaster or close to heat; to turn brown in this way: *a toasted sandwich* ◇ *Place under a hot grill until the nuts have toasted.*

barbecue /ˈbɑːbɪkjuː; *AmE* ˈbɑːrb-/ [T] to cook food on a barbecue (= a metal frame on or over an open fire outdoors): *barbecued chicken*

ban *noun*

ban · sanction · boycott · embargo · prohibition · moratorium · veto · taboo
These are all words for a rule, order or custom which does not allow people to do sth or for the act of stopping sth from being done.

PATTERNS AND COLLOCATIONS
▸ a ban/sanctions/a boycott/an embargo/a prohibition/a veto/ a moratorium / a taboo **on** sb / sth
▸ a ban/sanctions/a boycott/an embargo/a prohibition/a veto/ a taboo **against** sb / sth
▸ a **total** ban / boycott / embargo / prohibition / moratorium
▸ (an) **international** ban / sanctions / boycott / embargo / moratorium
▸ (a) **trade** ban / sanctions / boycott / embargo
▸ (an) **economic** sanctions / boycott / embargo
▸ to **impose** a ban / sanctions / a boycott / an embargo / a prohibition / a veto
▸ to **call for / introduce** a ban / sanctions / a boycott / a prohibition / a moratorium
▸ to **enforce / tighten / ease** a ban / sanctions / an embargo
▸ to **comply with** a ban / sanctions / a prohibition
▸ to **break** a ban / sanctions / an embargo / a taboo
▸ to **lift** a ban/sanctions/a boycott/an embargo/a prohibition/a veto
▸ a ban / sanctions / an embargo **come / comes into force**

ban [C] an official rule that says that sth is not allowed; the fact of sb being officially stopped from doing sth for a period of time as a punishment: *There is to be a total ban on smoking in the office.* ◇ *The students took to the streets, defying a ban on political gatherings.* ◇ *The sprinter received a lengthy **ban for** failing a drugs test.* ◇ *He faces a possible life **ban from** international football.*

sanction /ˈsæŋkʃn/ [C, usually pl.] an official order that limits trade or contact with a particular country, in order to make it do sth, such as obeying international law: *Trade sanctions were imposed against any country that refused to sign the agreement.*

boycott /ˈbɔɪkɒt; *AmE* -kɑːt/ [C] the act of refusing to buy, use or take part in sth as a way of protesting: *Opposition groups declared a boycott of the elections.* ◇ *The group is calling for a **consumer boycott** of the company's products.* See also **boycott** → AVOID *verb*

embargo /ɪmˈbɑːɡəʊ; *AmE* ɪmˈbɑːrɡoʊ/ [C] an official order that forbids trade with another country, sometimes of a particular type of goods: *There is a strict embargo on oil imports.* ◇ *We knew the **arms embargo** was being broken.*

prohibition /ˌprəʊɪˈbɪʃn; *AmE* ˌproʊə'b-/ [U, C] the act of stopping sth being done or used, especially by law; a law or rule that says that sth is not allowed: *The RSPB has called for the prohibition of all imports of wild birds.*

moratorium /ˌmɒrəˈtɔːriəm; *AmE* ˌmɔːr-/ (pl. **moratoriums** or **moratoria**) [C] an official agreement that an activity must stop for a period of time: *The convention called for a two-year moratorium on commercial whaling.*

veto /ˈviːtəʊ; *AmE* -toʊ/ (pl. **-oes**) [C] an occasion when sb uses their right to refuse to allow sth to be done: *For months there was a veto on employing new staff.* See also **veto** → REFUSAL *noun*, **veto** → REFUSE *verb*

taboo /təˈbuː/ [C] a cultural or religious custom that does not allow people to do, use or talk about a particular thing as people find it offensive or embarrassing; a general agreement not to do or talk about sth: *Death is one of the great taboos in our culture.* ◇ *There is still a taboo on the subject in our family.* See also **taboo** → FORBIDDEN *adj.*

ban *verb* See also the entry for EXCLUDE 2

ban · prohibit · bar · forbid · outlaw
These words all mean to order sb to stop doing sth or to stop sth being done, especially officially or by law.

PATTERNS AND COLLOCATIONS
▶ to ban/ prohibit/ bar sb **from** sth
▶ to ban/ prohibit/ bar/ forbid sb **from doing sth**
▶ to ban/ prohibit/ forbid/ outlaw the **practice/ use/ sale of** sth
▶ to ban/ prohibit/ forbid the **import/ export of** sth
▶ to be **effectively** banned/ prohibited/ barred/ forbidden/ outlawed
▶ to be **officially** banned/ prohibited
▶ to be **strictly** prohibited/ forbidden

ban (-nn-) [T] to officially stop sth from being done or used; to order sb not to do sth, go somewhere, etc: *There are plans to ban smoking in public places.* ◇ *He claimed that the government had tried to ban the book.* ◇ *He was banned from the meeting.* ◇ *The sprinter has been banned for life after failing a drugs test.* **OPP** permit → ALLOW, See also **banned** → FORBIDDEN
prohibit /prəˈhɪbɪt; *AmE* also prooˈh-/ [T, often passive] (*formal*) to stop sth from being done, especially by law: *The convention strictly prohibits the dumping of waste at sea.* ◇ *The import of these products is prohibited by law.* **OPP** permit, authorize → ALLOW, See also **prohibited** → FORBIDDEN
bar (-rr-) [T] (*rather formal*) (of a rule or law) to ban or prevent sb from doing sth: *The curfew has effectively barred migrant workers from their jobs.* ◇ *Certain activities are still barred to women.*
forbid /fəˈbɪd; *AmE* fərˈb-/ [T] (*rather formal*) to order sb not to do sth; to order that sth must not be done: *You are all forbidden to leave.* ◇ *Her father forbade the marriage.* ◇ *Smoking is strictly forbidden.* **OPP** allow, permit → ALLOW, See also **forbidden** → FORBIDDEN
outlaw /ˈaʊtlɔː/ [T] to forbid sth by law: *There are plans to outlaw the carrying of knives.* ◇ *He was found to be a member of the outlawed rebel movement.*

bandage *noun*

bandage · plaster · Band-Aid™ · dressing
These words all refer to material which is put on wounds or injuries.

PATTERNS AND COLLOCATIONS
▶ to **apply** a bandage/ dressing
▶ to **put on/ take off** a bandage/ plaster/ Band-Aid

bandage /ˈbændɪdʒ/ [C, U] a strip of fabric used to wrap or cover a part of the body that has been hurt, in order to protect it or apply pressure; the fabric used for this: *Make sure the bandage isn't too tight.* ◇ *He had a strip of bandage tied around his head.*
▶ **bandage** *verb* [T]: *Don't bandage the wound too tightly.* ◇ *They bandaged up my leg and told me to rest.*
plaster /ˈplɑːstə(r); *AmE* ˈplæs-/ [C, U] (*BrE*) a small piece of fabric or plastic which can be stuck to the skin to protect a small wound or cut; the material used for this: *Have you got any plasters? I've cut my finger.* ◇ *Cut off a small piece of plaster.*
¹Band-Aid™ [C] (*especially AmE*) a plaster: *Do you have a Band-Aid? I've cut my finger.*
dressing [C] a piece of soft fabric placed over a wound to absorb blood and prevent infection: *Place the dressing directly onto the wound and hold it in place.*
▶ **dress** *verb* [T]: *The nurse will dress that cut for you.*

bandage

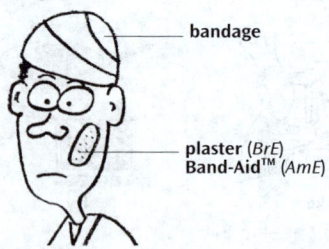

bandage

plaster (*BrE*)
Band-Aid™ (*AmE*)

bang *noun*

bang · thud · crash · thump · snap · clang · crack
These are all words for a sudden loud sound.

PATTERNS AND COLLOCATIONS
▶ **with** a bang/ thud/ crash/ thump/ snap/ clang/ crack
▶ a **loud** bang/ thud/ crash/ thump/ snap/ clang/ crack
▶ a **muffled** bang/ thud/ thump
▶ a **dull** thud/ thump
▶ a **sharp** snap/ crack
▶ to **hear** a bang/ thud/ crash/ thump/ snap/ clang/ crack
▶ **There was** a bang/ thud/ crash/ thump/ snap/ clang/ crack
▶ a **crash/ crack of thunder**

bang [C] a sudden very loud noise: *The door swung shut with a bang.* ◇ *Suddenly there was a loud bang and a puff of smoke.*
thud [C] a dull sound like the one that is made when a heavy object hits sth else: *His head hit the floor with a dull thud.* ◇ *She could hear the thud of her own heartbeat sounding heavily in her ears.*
crash [C, usually sing.] a sudden loud noise made, for example, by sth falling or breaking: *The tree fell with a great crash.* ◇ *She heard the crash of shattering glass as the vehicles collided.* ◇ *The first distant crash of thunder shook the air.*
thump [C] a thud: *There was a thump as the truck hit the bank.* ◇ *As I got closer, I heard the thump of dance music coming from the second floor.*

NOTE THUD OR THUMP? There is no real difference in meaning or use between these words, in this sense. A **thump** can also be an act of hitting sb/sth. See also **thump** → HIT 2

snap [C] a sudden sharp sound, especially one made by sth closing or breaking: *She closed her purse with a snap.* ◇ *He heard the snap of a twig behind him.*
clang [C] a loud ringing noise like the noise of metal being hit: *There was a clang as the heavy metal door was slammed shut.* See also **clang** → RING *verb*
crack [C] a sudden loud sharp sound: *She heard the sharp crack of a rifle shot.*

bang *verb*

1 The door banged shut.
2 bang your head

1 bang · crash · pop · crack · explode · clash
These words all mean to make a short, sudden sound.

PATTERNS AND COLLOCATIONS
▶ a **door** bangs/ crashes
▶ **thunder** crashes/ cracks/ explodes
▶ **cymbals** crash/ clash
▶ to bang/ crash/ pop/ crack/ explode **loudly**

bang [T, I] to make a sudden loud noise, especially the noise made by a door or window closing: *Don't bang the door when you go out!* ◇ *A window was banging somewhere* (= opening and closing noisily). ◇ *The door banged shut behind her.* See also **bang** → HIT 1

crash [I] to make a sudden loud noise, especially the noise made by waves or thunder: *The waves crashed deafeningly.* ◇ *Thunder crashed overhead.*

pop (-pp-) [I, T] to make a short explosive sound; to cause sth to make this sound: *Flashbulbs were popping all around them.* ◇ *He popped the cork on the champagne bottle.*

crack [I, T, no passive] to make a sudden loud sharp sound; to cause sth to make this sound: *A shot cracked across the ridge.* ◇ *He cracked his whip and galloped away.*

explode [I] to make a sudden very loud noise: *Thunder exploded overhead.*

clash [I, T] to hit together and make a harsh ringing noise; to make two metal objects do this: *The long blades clashed together.* ◇ *She clashed the cymbals.*

2 bang · knock · hit · crack · bump

These words all mean to accidentally hit sth, especially a part of the body, against sth.

▸ to bang/ knock/ hit/ crack/ bump your head/ knee, etc. **on**/ **against** sth
▸ to bang/ knock/ hit/ crack/ bump your **head**/ **forehead**
▸ to bang/ knock/ hit/ bump your **arm**/ **knee**/ **elbow**

bang [T] to accidentally hit a part of your body against sth, especially when this is painful: *He banged his head as he tried to stand up.* ◇ *She tripped and banged her knee on the desk.* See also **bang** → HIT 1

knock [T, I] to accidentally hit sth, especially a part of the body, against sth: *The door's very low – mind you don't knock your head!* ◇ *Her hand knocked against the glass.* See also **knock** → HIT 1

hit [T] to accidentally knock a part of your body against sth: *He fell, hitting his head on the hard stone floor.* See also **hit** → HIT 1, **hit** → HIT 2

crack [T] to accidentally hit a part of your body, especially your head, against sth in a painful way: *He stood up suddenly, cracking his head on the low ceiling.*

bump [T] to accidentally hit a part of your body against sth: *Toddlers are always falling over and bumping their heads.* See also **bump** → HIT 1

NOTE WHICH WORD? These words are all used in very similar ways. **Bang** is the most frequent word used when talking about hitting a part of the body, especially when this is painful. **Knock** and **hit** are more general and can be used for a hard, painful hit, or a gentle one. **Crack** is used especially when you hit your head. **Bump** is used especially without a preposition; **bang** can also be used in this way but the other words cannot.: *Toddlers are always falling over and knocking/hitting/cracking their heads.*

bankrupt *adj.* See also the entry for POOR 1

bankrupt · bust · insolvent · broke
These words all describe a person or business that has little or no money and therefore cannot pay what they owe.

▸ to **go** bankrupt/ bust/ broke
▸ to **declare sb** bankrupt/ insolvent
▸ **virtually** bankrupt/ bust/ insolvent

bankrupt not having enough money to pay what you owe: *The firm went bankrupt in 2003 and all its assets were sold off.*
▸ **bankrupt** *verb* [T]: *The company was almost bankrupted by legal costs.*
▸ **bankruptcy** /'bæŋkrʌptsi/ *noun* [U, C]: *The company filed for bankruptcy* (= asked to be officially bankrupt) *in 2006.* ◇ *There could be further bankruptcies among small farmers.*

bust [not usually before noun] (*informal*) bankrupt: *We lost our money when the travel company went bust.*

insolvent /ɪnˈsɒlvənt; *AmE* -ˈsɑːl-/ (*finance*) bankrupt: *The company has been declared insolvent.* **OPP** **solvent** ❶ If a person or company is **solvent** they have enough money to pay their debts: *The company managed to remain solvent during the recession.*
▸ **insolvency** *noun* [U, C]: *The company is close to insolvency.*

broke [not before noun] (*rather informal*) having no money: *I'm always broke by the end of the month.*

bar *noun*

bar · pub · inn · tavern · public house · saloon · local
These words all mean a building or a part of a building where people can go to drink alcohol and other drinks.

▸ **in** a bar/ pub/ tavern/ public house/ saloon
▸ **at** the pub/ the tavern/ your local
▸ a/ the **local** bar/ pub/ inn/ tavern/ public house/ saloon
▸ to **go to** a bar/ the pub/ an inn/ a tavern/ a public house/ the saloon
▸ to **run** a bar/ a pub/ an inn/ a tavern/ a public house/ saloon
▸ to **keep** an inn/ a tavern/ a public house

bar [C] a place where you can buy and drink alcoholic and/or other drinks; (in compounds) a place that sells a particular thing or that is for particular people: *We could meet at the theatre and have a drink in the bar.* ◇ *It's the island's only **licensed bar*** (= one that is allowed to sell alcoholic drinks). ◇ *a wine/cocktail bar* ◇ (*BrE*) *I found David in the bar of the Red Lion* (= a room in a pub where drinks are served). ❶ **Bar** is often used in compounds for a place where a particular kind of food or drink is the main thing that is served: *a sandwich/snack/coffee bar*

pub [C] (*BrE*) a building where people go to drink and meet their friends. Pubs serve alcoholic and other drinks, and often also food: *We stopped on the way for a pub lunch.* ◇ *He's the landlord of the local pub.* ◇ (*informal*) *He's gone **down the pub** for a pint.* ◇ (*informal*) *to go on a **pub crawl*** (= a visit to several pubs, going straight from one to the next and drinking at each of them)

inn [C] (*BrE*) an old pub in the country, especially one where people can or could stay the night: *The building was a 16th-century **coaching inn*** (= where in the past coaches stopped to rest or change the horses). ❶ **Inn** is now an old-fashioned term, unless you are talking about the past; however, it is still used in the names of many pubs, hotels and restaurants: *We stopped on the way at a good inn.* ◇ *the Holiday Inn*

tavern /'tævən; *AmE* -vərn/ [C] (*old-fashioned or literary*) (in the past) a pub in a town or city; sometimes used today in the names of pubs: *It is said he was killed in a tavern brawl.* ◇ *the Bell Tavern*

public 'house [C] (*BrE, formal*) a pub: *The company owns over 300 public houses.*

saloon /səˈluːn/ [C] (in the past) a bar in the western US and Canada: *The cowboy died in a fight in a saloon.*

local [C] (*BrE, informal*) a pub near where you live, especially one you often go to: *We met for a pie and a pint at his local.*

bare *adj.*

bare · exposed · desolate · windswept · bleak
These words all describe places and natural features that are not covered with anything, usually because plants cannot grow there.

▸ bare/ desolate/ bleak **countryside**/ **landscape**/ **mountains**
▸ an exposed/ a desolate/ a windswept/ a bleak **coast**/ **hillside**
▸ an exposed/ a desolate/ a windswept/ a bleak **area**
▸ desolate/ windswept/ bleak **country**/ **moors**

▸ **rather** bare / exposed / desolate / bleak
▸ **very** bare / exposed / bleak

bare (of trees or countryside) not covered with leaves; without plants or trees: *The winter sun filtered through the bare branches of the trees.* ◇ *The windows looked out onto a bare field.*

exposed (*especially written*) (of a place) not protected from the weather by trees, buildings or high ground: *The plant is suitable for both sheltered and exposed sites.* ◇ *The house is rather* **exposed to the weather.** See also **exposed** → VULNERABLE

desolate /ˈdesələt; *AmE* / (*written*) (of a place) empty and without people, making you feel sad or frightened: *They looked out on a bleak and desolate landscape.*

windswept /ˈwɪndswept/ (*especially written*) (of a place) having strong winds and little protection from them: *the windswept Atlantic coast*

bleak /bliːk/ (*especially written*) (of a place) exposed, empty or with no pleasant features: *There is just a bleak expanse of concrete.* ◇ *It was a small bleak town near the main highway.*

barrel *noun*

barrel · tank · drum · cylinder · vat · canister · tub
These are all words for a large container that can be used for holding liquid.

PATTERNS AND COLLOCATIONS
▸ a barrel / tank / drum / cylinder / vat / canister / tub **of** sth
▸ **in** a barrel / tank / drum / cylinder / vat / canister / tub
▸ a **5-gallon, 20-litre, etc.** barrel / tank / drum / canister
▸ a **gas** tank / cylinder / canister
▸ an **oil** barrel / tank / drum
▸ to **fill** a barrel / tank / drum / cylinder / vat / tub

barrel /ˈbærəl/ [C] a tall, round container made of wood, metal or plastic, with a flat top and bottom; the amount contained in a barrel: *They got through two barrels of beer.* ❶ Traditional wooden barrels have curved sides that make them wider in the middle than at the ends. Modern metal and plastic barrels often have straight sides. In the oil industry the **barrel** is a unit of measurement equal to 42 U.S. gallons (about 159 litres): *Crude oil prices hit record highs of more than $70 a barrel.*

tank [C] a container for holding liquid or gas that is often connected to sth else with a pipe or tube; the amount contained in a tank: *Water from the boiler is pumped into the hot water tank.* ◇ *a fuel/petrol/fish tank* ◇ *We drove there and back on one tank of petrol.* ❶ **Tanks** are often large containers that are made to stay in one place. However, **tank** can also mean a container that you carry that has air or other gases in it that you can breathe, for example underwater: *Firefighters sometimes need to use air tanks and special breathing masks.*

drum [C] a large round container with long straight sides used for storing or transporting oil or chemicals: *Hazardous waste is stored in drums until it can be disposed of.*

cylinder /ˈsɪlɪndə(r)/ [C] a container made of thick metal with round ends and long straight sides that is used for holding or transporting gases: *All our aircraft carry at least one oxygen cylinder for emergency use on board.*

vat [C] a large container for holding liquids, especially in industrial processes: *The grape juice is then transferred to a fermentation vat.* ◇ *a vat of whisky*

canister /ˈkænɪstə(r)/ [C] a strong metal container containing gas or a chemical substance, especially one that bursts when it is fired from a gun or thrown: *Police fired tear-gas canisters at the demonstrators.*

tub [C] a large round container without a lid, used for washing clothes or growing plants in: *There were tubs of flowers on the balcony.*

barrier *noun*

barrier · barricade · obstacle · roadblock · obstruction · hurdle
These are all words for an object that blocks a road, path, entrance, etc. and stops people from getting past.

PATTERNS AND COLLOCATIONS
▸ **behind** a barrier / barricade
▸ **over** a barricade / hurdle
▸ **at / through** a barrier / roadblock
▸ a **physical** barrier / obstacle / obstruction
▸ a **police** barrier / barricade / roadblock
▸ to **erect / set up** a barrier / barricade / roadblock
▸ sth **forms** a barrier / a barricade / an obstacle
▸ to **clear** a barricade / an obstacle / an obstruction / a hurdle
▸ to **hit** a barrier / an obstacle / an obstruction / a hurdle
▸ to **remove** a barricade / a roadblock / an obstruction

barrier [C] an object like a fence across a path or entrance that stops people from getting past: *The crowd had to stand behind barriers.* ◇ *Show your ticket at the barrier.* ◇ *Crash barriers* were erected along the roads to be used for the race. See also **bar** → BLOCK *verb* 3

barricade /ˌbærɪˈkeɪd/ [C] a line of objects placed across a road, path, etc. to stop people from getting past, especially as part of a protest: *The police stormed the barricades the demonstrators had put up.* ◇ *The protesters formed a human barricade.* See also **barricade** → BLOCK *verb* 3

obstacle /ˈɒbstəkl; *AmE* ˈɑːb-/ [C] an object that is in your way and makes it difficult for you to get past; a fence for a horse to jump over in showjumping: *The area was full of streams and bogs and other natural obstacles.* ◇ *This huge open ditch forms the biggest obstacle on the course.*

roadblock /ˈrəʊdblɒk; *AmE* ˈroʊdblɑːk/ [C] a barrier put across a road by the police or army so that they can stop and search vehicles: *They were stopped at an army roadblock leaving the city.*

obstruction /əbˈstrʌkʃn/ [C] (*written*) something that blocks a road, an entrance, etc: *The train driver receives a warning if there's an obstruction on the line ahead.* See also **obstruct** → BLOCK *verb* 3

hurdle [C] each of a series of upright frames that a person or horse jumps over in a race: *She cleared the first hurdle* (= jumped over it without hitting it) *in the lead.* See also **hurdle** → JUMP 1

base *verb*

base · locate · be situated · site
These words all mean to build or put sth in a particular place.

PATTERNS AND COLLOCATIONS
▸ to be based / located / situated / sited **in / at / close to** sth
▸ to be based / located / situated / sited **between** A and B
▸ **conveniently** based / located / situated / sited
▸ **strategically** located / situated / sited
▸ **centrally** located / situated

base, be based [T, often passive] to use a particular city, country or region as the main place for sth such as a business; to stay in a particular place in order to be able to do sth in the local area, such as working or taking a holiday: *She works for a company based in Chicago.* ◇ *a Chicago-based company* ◇ *We're going to base ourselves in Tokyo and make trips from there.*
▸ **base** *noun* [C]: *The town is an ideal base for touring the area.*

locate, be located [T, often passive] (always used with an adverb or preposition) (*rather formal, especially written*) to put or build sth in a particular place; to exist or have been built in a particular place: *They located their headquarters in Paris.* ◇ *The offices are conveniently located just a few minutes from the main station.* ❶ Especially in American English, **locate** [I] also means to move a business to a particular place: *There are tax breaks for businesses that locate in rural areas.* See also **location** → PLACE *noun* 1, **relocate** → LEAVE *verb* 2

be situated [T] (always used with an adverb or preposition) (*formal*) to exist or have been built in a particular place or position: *My bedroom was situated on the top floor of the house.*

site, be sited [T, often passive] (*rather formal*) (always used with an adverb or preposition) to build sth in a particular place or position: *There was a meeting to discuss the siting of the new school.* ◇ *The castle is magnificently sited high up on a cliff.* See also **site** → PLACE *noun* 1

> **NOTE** LOCATED, SITUATED OR SITED? **Located** and **situated** can both be used to talk about where sth is, including sth such as a natural feature that has always been there or has not been placed there by people. **Sited** is normally only used to describe sth that people have built or placed in a particular position, especially a particular type of building such as a factory, school or hospital: *Goose Island is located/situated in the Chicago River.* ◇ *Goose Island is sited in the Chicago River.*

basement *noun*

basement · cellar · bunker · crypt
These words all mean a room that is below the level of the ground.

PATTERNS AND COLLOCATIONS
▸ **in** a basement / cellar / bunker / crypt
▸ the basement / cellar **door / stairs / steps**

basement [C] a part of a building consisting of rooms that are partly or completely below the level of the ground: *Kitchen goods are sold in the basement.*

cellar /ˈselə(r)/ [C] a room under the ground floor of a building, usually used for storing things: *We looked all over the house, even down in the coal cellar.*

> **NOTE** BASEMENT OR CELLAR? **Basement** is usually to talk about an underground level in a large or modern building. **Cellar** is usually used to describe an underground space for storing things, especially in an older building, that is not usually suitable for living in.

bunker /ˈbʌŋkə(r)/ [C] a strongly built shelter for soldiers or guns, usually underground: *In preparation for the worst, huge underground bunkers were built.*

crypt /krɪpt/ [C] a large room or series of rooms under the floor of a church, used especially in the past as a place for burying people: *Nelson's final resting place was in the crypt of St Paul's Cathedral.*

basics *noun*

basics · fundamentals · introduction · essentials · practicalities
These are all words for the most important things, facts or knowledge that people need in a particular situation.

PATTERNS AND COLLOCATIONS
▸ the / a **basic** fundamentals / introduction / essentials
▸ to **teach / grasp** the basics / fundamentals / essentials
▸ to **learn / master** the basics / fundamentals
▸ to **understand / know / cover / concentrate on** the basics / essentials

basics [pl.] the most important and necessary facts, skills or ideas from which other things develop: *I need to learn the basics of computer programming.* ◇ *Managers should get back to basics and examine the kind of products people really want.* See also **basic** → FUNDAMENTAL

fundamentals [pl.] (*rather formal, especially written*) the most important rules or principles of an area of knowledge; the most important parts of sth: *He wrote 'The Fundamentals of Modern Physics'.* ◇ *She taught me the fundamentals of the job.* See also **fundamental** → FUNDAMENTAL

introduction [C] a book or programme of study for people beginning to study a subject: *'An Introduction to Astronomy'* ◇ *It's a useful introduction to an extremely complex subject.* See also **introductory** → FIRST

essentials [pl.] the most important facts or principles in an area of knowledge: *We will concentrate on the essentials of English grammar.* See also **essential** → FUNDAMENTAL

> **NOTE** BASICS, FUNDAMENTALS OR ESSENTIALS? In many cases you can use any of these words. However, **basics** are usually the most practical, concerned with how to do things that you need to do, or how things work in practice: *the basics of dinghy sailing/good nutrition/how to set it up and operate it.* **Essentials** are often slightly more theoretical, concerned with how things work in theory and practice: *the essentials of arithmetic/design/ how we communicate using language.* **Fundamentals** are the most theoretical, concerned with the ideas and principles on which systems, knowledge and beliefs are based: *the fundamentals of Christian belief/microbiology/the western concept of law.*

practicalities [pl.] the real facts and circumstances rather than ideas or theories: *It sounds like a good idea; let's look at the practicalities and work out the costs.* ❶ People usually *consider, look at* or *discuss* the **practicalities** of a situation. See also **practical** → REALISTIC 1

basis *noun*

basis · foundation · base
These are all words for the ideas or facts that sth is based on.

PATTERNS AND COLLOCATIONS
▸ a / the basis / foundation / base **of / for** sth
▸ a / an **excellent / firm / good / secure / solid / sound / strong / weak** basis / foundation / base
▸ a / an **ideological / intellectual / philosophical / theoretical / economic** basis / foundation / base
▸ to **have sth as / establish / use sth as** a / the basis / foundation / base for / of sth
▸ to **form** the basis / foundation / base of sth
▸ to **give sb / provide (sb with)** a / the basis / foundation / base
▸ to **have no** basis / foundation **in fact**
▸ to **be without** basis / foundation

basis [C, usually sing.] a principle, idea or fact that supports sth and that it can develop from: *The basis of a good marriage is trust.* ◇ *This article will form the basis for our discussion.* ◇ *This theory seems to have no basis in fact.*

foundation [C, usually sing.] a principle, idea or fact that supports sth and that it develops from: *Respect and friendship provide a solid foundation for marriage.* ◇ *The rumour is totally without foundation* (= is not based on any facts).

> **NOTE** BASIS OR FOUNDATION? **Foundation** is often used to talk about larger or more important things than **basis**: *He laid the foundation of Japan's modern economy.* ◇ *Worship is the foundation of all the Church's activities.* ◇ *These figures formed the basis of their pay claim.* ◇ *The research will provide a basis for nature conservation.*

base [C, usually sing.] an idea, fact or situation from which sth is developed: *She used her family's history as a base for her novel.* ◇ *His arguments have a sound economic base.*

bath *noun*

bath · shower · wash · cleaning · rinse · clean
These are all words for an act or process of making sb/sth clean.

PATTERNS AND COLLOCATIONS
▸ **in** the bath / shower / wash
▸ a **quick** bath / shower / wash / rinse
▸ a **hot / cold** bath / shower
▸ to **need** a bath / shower / wash / rinse / clean
▸ to **have** a bath / shower / wash
▸ to **take** a bath / shower
▸ to **give** sb / sth a bath / wash / rinse / clean

bath [C] an act of washing your whole body by sitting or lying in water: (*BrE*) *I think I'll have a bath and go to bed.* ◇ (*especially AmE*) *to take a bath* ◇ *She took the baby upstairs to give him a bath.* See also **bath, bathe** → WASH *verb*

shower [C] an act of washing yourself under a shower: (*BrE*) *I think I'll have a shower.* ◇ (*especially AmE*) *to take a shower* ◇ *He's in the shower at the moment – can you call back later?* See also **shower** → WASH *verb*

wash [C, usually sing.] an act of cleaning sth using water and usually soap: *Your blue shirt's in the wash* (= being washed or waiting to be washed). ◇ *My sweater shrank in the wash.* ◇ *That blouse shouldn't look like that after only two washes.* ❶ In British English **wash** is also used to talk about people washing themselves: (*BrE*) *I'll just have a quick wash before dinner.* See also **wash** → CLEAN *verb*, **wash** → WASH *verb*

cleaning [U] the work of making the inside of a building or vehicle clean: *They pay someone to **do the cleaning**.* ◇ *The shop on the corner sells cheap cleaning products.* See also **clean** → CLEAN *verb*

rinse /rɪns/ [C, usually sing.] an act of washing sth with clean water only, not using soap: *That glass doesn't look very clean – I'd better give it a rinse.* See also **rinse** → CLEAN *verb*

clean [sing.] (*BrE*) an act of cleaning sth: *Why don't you give the carpet a clean?* See also **clean** → CLEAN *verb*

be *linking verb*

be · total · equal · add up to sth · amount to sth · number · run to sth
These words all mean to reach a particular number or amount when all numbers/amounts have been added together.

PATTERNS AND COLLOCATIONS
▸ to **be** / total / equal / add up to / amount to / number / run to 50 / 2 million, etc.
▸ to **be** / total / equal / add up to / amount to / run to $250 / 75%
▸ to **be** / total / add up to / amount to / run to **about / around / approximately** sth
▸ to **be** / total / add up to / amount to / number / run to **nearly / almost / over / more than / at least** sth
▸ to **be** / total / add up to / amount to / number **fewer than / no more than** sth
▸ to **be** / total / add up to / amount to **less than** sth
▸ to total / amount to / number / run to **some** 50, 300, pages, pieces, etc.
▸ **profits / scores** total / add up to / amount to sth
▸ **income** totals / adds up to / amounts to sth
▸ a / an **group / crowd / army** totals / numbers 25, 1000, etc.

be to be the same in size, quantity, value, etc. as sth else: *Three and three is six.* ◇ *How much is a thousand pounds in euros?* ◇ *Let x be the sum of a and b.*

total (-ll-, *AmE* -l-) (*especially business*) to reach a particular number or amount when added together: *Imports totalled $1.5 billion last year.* ◇ *In 2005–6, college enrolments totalled some 5400.* See also **total** → WHOLE *adj.*

equal (-ll-, *AmE* -l-) to be the same in size, quantity, value, etc. as sth else: *2x plus y equals 7 (2x+y=7)* ◇ *A metre equals 39.38 inches.* See also **equal** → EQUAL *adj.*

NOTE **BE OR EQUAL?** In some cases you can use either word: *Three and three is/equals six.* ◇ *Let x be/equal the sum of a and b.* However, **equal** is not usually used in questions: *How much does a thousand pounds equal in Euros?* It is slightly more formal than **be** and is usually only used in exact sums: *A metre is about/around/ approximately 40 inches.* ◇ *A metre equals about/ around/approximately 40 inches.*

add 'up to sth *phrasal verb* to make a total amount or number of sth: *The numbers add up to exactly 100.* ◇ *Their earnings were £250, £300 and £420, adding up to a total of £970.*

a'mount to sth *phrasal verb* to reach a particular number or amount when added together: *His earnings are said to amount to £300 000 per annum.*

number to make a particular number when added together: *The crowd numbered more than a thousand.* ◇ *We numbered 20* (= there were 20 of us in the group).

NOTE **TOTAL, ADD UP TO STH, AMOUNT TO STH OR NUMBER?** **Add up to** and **number** can be used to emphasize the process of calculating a total through mathematics or counting; **total** and **amount to sth** focus more on the number/amount rather than the process of arriving at the result. **Total** and **amount to sth** are used especially in business writing when describing the performance of a company or industry. **Number** usually has people as the subject of the sentence; **total** is the only other verb that can be used like this: *The crew totalled/numbered sixteen.* ◇ *The crew added up to/amounted to sixteen.*

'run to sth *phrasal verb* to be of a particular size or amount, especially when this is surprisingly large: *The book runs to nearly 800 pages.* ◇ *The cost of repairing damaged roads alone will run to £1 million.*

beat *verb*

1 beat a drum/child
2 a heart/drum beating

1 See also the entry for HIT 2
beat · batter · pound · lash · hammer · dash · pummel
These words all mean to hit sb/sth many times, especially hard.

PATTERNS AND COLLOCATIONS
▸ to **beat** / batter / pound / lash / hammer / pummel sb/sth **with** sth
▸ to **beat** / batter / pound / lash / hammer / pummel sb/sth **at** sb / sth
▸ to **beat** / batter / pound / lash / hammer / dash sb/sth **against** sth
▸ to **beat** / batter / pound / hammer **on** sth
▸ to **beat** / batter / hammer sth **down**
▸ to **beat** / batter / pound / lash / hammer / dash sb **to death**
▸ to **beat** / batter sb **about / around the head**
▸ the **rain / wind / sea** beats / batters / pounds / lashes / dashes (at) sth
▸ **waves** beat / batter / pound / lash / dash (at) sth
▸ **storms** beat / batter / pound / lash (at) sth

beat [I, T] to hit sb/sth a lot of times, especially very hard: *Someone was beating at the door.* ◇ *Hailstones beat against the window.* ◇ *Someone was beating a drum.* ◇ *A young man was found beaten to death at his home last night.*

batter [I, T] to hit sb/sth hard a lot of times, especially in a way that causes serious damage: *She battered at the door with her fists.* ◇ *Severe winds have been battering the north coast.* ◇ *The police had to batter the door down.*

pound [I, T] to hit sb/sth hard a lot of times, especially in a way that makes a lot of noise: *The machines pounded away day and night.* ◇ *She pounded him with her fists.*

lash [I, T] to hit sb/sth with a lot of force: *The rain lashed at the window.* ◇ *Great waves lashed the shore.* ❶ The subject of **lash** is often *rain, wind, hail, sea* or *waves*.

hammer [I, T] to hit sb/sth hard a lot of times, in a way that is noisy or violent: (*figurative*) *I was so scared my heart was hammering* (= beating very fast) *in my chest.* ◇ *He hammered the door with his fists.*

NOTE **POUND OR HAMMER?** There is not much difference in meaning between these two, but to **pound** is sometimes a steadier action.: *The machines hammered away day and night.* To **hammer** can be more violent and it is often used figuratively.

dash [T, I] (always used with an adverb or preposition) to throw or make sth fall violently onto a hard surface; to beat against a surface: *The boat was dashed repeatedly against the rocks.* ◇ *The waves were dashing against the harbour wall.*

pummel /ˈpʌml/ (-ll-, AmE -l-) [I, T] to hit sb/sth a lot of times, especially with your fists (= tightly closed hands): *Her fists pummelled at his chest.* ◇ *He pummelled the pillow with his fists.*

2 beat · pulse · throb · pound · flutter
These words all mean to make a regular repeated movement or sound.

PATTERNS AND COLLOCATIONS
▶ to beat / pulse / throb / pound / flutter **with** excitement, fear, emotion, etc.
▶ sb's **heart** beats / pulses / throbs / pounds / flutters
▶ sb's **blood** beats / pulses / throbs / pounds
▶ sb's **pulse** beats / throbs / pounds / flutters
▶ **music** pulses / throbs / pounds
▶ pulsing / throbbing / pounding **rhythms**
▶ to beat / pulse / flutter **wildly**
▶ to beat / pulse / throb **rhythmically**

beat [I] (of sb's heart or blood or of drums) to make a regular repeated sound or movement: *Her heart began to beat a little faster.* ◇ *I could detect a pulse beating very faintly.* ◇ *We could hear the drums beating in the distance.*

pulse [I] to beat or flow with a strong regular rhythm: *A vein pulsed in his temple.* ◇ *The pulsing rhythm of the music could be heard throughout the valley.*

throb (-bb-) [I] to beat with a strong regular rhythm: *The ship's engines throbbed quietly.* ◇ *The blood was throbbing in my veins.* ◇ *I could feel a dull throbbing pain in my side.*

NOTE BEAT, PULSE OR THROB? Pulse and throb are stronger than beat but are NOT used to talk about drums. *Music* and *pain* can pulse or throb. *Machines* throb but don't pulse.

pound [I] to beat quickly, strongly and often loudly: *Her heart was pounding with fear.* ◇ *The blood was pounding in his ears.* ◇ *Her head began to pound.*

flutter (*written*) (of the heart, etc.) to beat very quickly and not regularly: *I could feel a fluttering pulse.* ◇ *Her heart fluttered every time she looked at him.*

beautiful *adj.*
1 a beautiful woman
2 a beautiful place

1 beautiful · pretty · handsome · attractive · lovely · cute · good-looking · gorgeous · stunning · striking
These words all describe people who are pleasant to look at.

pretty	beautiful	gorgeous
handsome	lovely	stunning
attractive		
cute		
good-looking		
striking		

PATTERNS AND COLLOCATIONS
▶ a beautiful / a pretty / a handsome / an attractive / a lovely / a cute / a good-looking / a gorgeous / a stunning / a striking **girl / woman**
▶ a beautiful / a pretty / a handsome / an attractive / a lovely / a cute / a good-looking / a gorgeous **boy**
▶ a beautiful / a handsome / an attractive / a cute / a good-looking / a gorgeous **man**
▶ a beautiful / a pretty / a handsome / an attractive / a lovely / a cute / a good-looking **child**
▶ a beautiful / a pretty / a handsome / an attractive / a lovely / a cute / a good-looking / a striking **face**

▶ a beautiful / a handsome / an attractive / a lovely / a cute / a gorgeous **body**
▶ **really / quite** beautiful / pretty / handsome / attractive / lovely / cute / good-looking / gorgeous / stunning / striking
▶ **very / rather** beautiful / pretty / handsome / attractive / lovely / cute / good-looking / gorgeous / striking
▶ **strikingly** beautiful / pretty / handsome / attractive / lovely / good-looking
▶ **almost** beautiful / pretty / handsome / attractive / good-looking

beautiful (especially of a woman or girl) very pleasant to look at: *What a beautiful baby!* ◇ *She looked stunningly beautiful that night.* ◇ *She had a classically beautiful face.* **OPP** ugly → UGLY
▶ **beauty** *noun* [U]: *She was a woman of great beauty.*

pretty (especially of a girl or woman) pleasant to look at: *She's got a very pretty face.* ◇ *A pretty little girl was standing in the doorway.* ◇ *You look so pretty in that dress!* ❶ Pretty is used most often to talk about girls. When it is used to talk about a woman, it usually suggests that she is like a girl, with small, delicate features. **OPP** plain → UGLY

handsome /ˈhænsəm/ (of a man) pleasant to look at; (of a woman) pleasant to look at, with large strong features rather than small delicate ones: *He was aptly described as 'tall, dark, and handsome'.* ◇ *She was a tall, handsome woman.* ◇ *The bride and groom made a handsome couple.*

attractive pleasant to look at, especially in a sexual way: *She's a very attractive woman.* ◇ *I like John as a person, but I don't **find him attractive** physically.* **OPP** unattractive → UGLY

lovely (*especially BrE*) beautiful; very attractive: *You've got lovely eyes.* ◇ *She looked particularly lovely that night.* ❶ When you describe sb as lovely, you are usually showing that you also have a strong feeling of affection for them.

cute (*especially AmE, informal*) sexually attractive: *Check out those cute guys over there!*

good-looking pleasant to look at, often in a sexual way: *She arrived with a very good-looking man.* See also **looks** → APPEARANCE

NOTE ATTRACTIVE OR GOOD-LOOKING? If you describe sb as **attractive** you often also mean that they have a pleasant personality as well as being pleasant to look at; **good-looking** just describes sb's physical appearance.

gorgeous /ˈɡɔːdʒəs; AmE ˈɡɔːrdʒəs/ (*informal*) extremely attractive, especially in a sexual way: *He's got gorgeous eyes.* ◇ *You look gorgeous!*

stunning (*informal*) extremely beautiful or attractive: *You look absolutely stunning!*

striking attractive, often in an unusual way: *He was a young man with dark hair and striking good looks.* See also **striking** → MARKED

2 See also the entry for MAGNIFICENT
beautiful · lovely · attractive · pretty · charming · scenic · exquisite · picturesque
These words all describe things and places that are pleasant to look at.

attractive	charming	beautiful
pretty		lovely
scenic		exquisite
picturesque		

PATTERNS AND COLLOCATIONS
▶ a beautiful / a lovely / an attractive / a pretty / a charming / a picturesque **place / town / village**
▶ a beautiful / a lovely / an attractive / a charming / a scenic / an exquisite / a picturesque **setting / view**
▶ a beautiful / a lovely / pretty / scenic / picturesque **spot**
▶ beautiful / lovely / attractive / picturesque **countryside / scenery / surroundings**
▶ a beautiful / a lovely / an attractive / a pretty / an exquisite **design**
▶ a beautiful / a lovely / an attractive / a pretty / a charming / an exquisite **voice**

▸ a beautiful / a lovely / an attractive / a charming **smile**
▸ **very** beautiful / lovely / attractive / pretty / charming / scenic / picturesque
▸ **quite** beautiful / lovely / attractive / pretty / charming / exquisite
▸ **rather** beautiful / lovely / attractive / pretty / charming
▸ **absolutely** beautiful / lovely / charming / exquisite

beautiful pleasing to the eyes, to the other senses or to the mind: *'They're just beautiful,'* breathed Jo, when she saw the earrings. ◇ *We sat and listened to the beautiful music.* ◇ *What a beautiful thing to say!* **OPP** **ugly** → UGLY
▸ **beautifully** adv.: *She sings beautifully.* ◇ *a beautifully decorated house*
▸ **beauty** noun [U]: *The woods were designated an area of outstanding natural beauty.*

lovely (*especially BrE*) beautiful; pleasant to look at, listen to or experience: *We travelled through some lovely countryside.* ◇ *It was a lovely evening – calm and still.* ◇ *He has a lovely voice.*

> **NOTE** BEAUTIFUL OR LOVELY? **Lovely** is slightly more informal than **beautiful**, used more in spoken English than in written English. Something that is **lovely** always has a warm quality that appeals not only to the eyes but also to the heart: **lovely** does not just describe physical appearance. **Beautiful** things often have this quality too, but they can appeal to the eyes and mind rather than the heart: *The designs were pure, austere and coldly beautiful.* ◇ ~~The designs were pure, austere and coldly lovely.~~

attractive pleasant to look at: *This is a big house with an attractive garden.* ◇ *Antique furniture is used to make an attractive contrast with a modern setting.* ❶ **Attractive** is often used when the speaker or writer does not want to give the impression of being influenced by strong personal feelings or emotion. **OPP** **unattractive** → UGLY
▸ **attractively** adv.: *The room is arranged very attractively.*

pretty attractive and pleasant to look at or to listen to without being large, beautiful or impressive: *That's a pretty flower – what's it called?* ◇ *Lydia – what a pretty name!* ❶ **Pretty** is often used to describe things that women and girls might be likely to find attractive. It is also used in a humorous way in some negative expressions: *You should have seen him in his swimming trunks – not a pretty sight!*

charming (*especially written*) very pleasant or attractive, especially in a way that is slightly old-fashioned: *The cottage is tiny, but charming.* ◇ *What a charming name.* ❶ **Charming** is often used to describe places, but not countryside. See also **charm** → INTEREST noun 1

scenic /'si:nɪk/ [usually before noun] having beautiful natural scenery: *Loch Lomond is an area of scenic beauty.* ◇ *We took the scenic route* (=using country roads, not the motorway) *back to the hotel.*

exquisite /ɪk'skwɪzɪt/ 'ekskwɪzɪt/ (*rather formal*) extremely beautiful or carefully made: *Look at the exquisite craftsmanship in this vase.* ❶ **Exquisite** describes things that are beautiful in a fine, delicate way, rather than a grand, impressive way.

picturesque /ˌpɪktʃə'resk/ (of a place) pretty, especially in a way that looks old-fashioned: *This picturesque setting is perfect for a relaxing holiday.*

become *linking verb*

become · get · go · grow · come · turn
These verbs all mean to start to be sth or to change from one state or condition to another.

PATTERNS AND COLLOCATIONS
▸ to get / grow / come **to know / like** sb / sth
▸ to become / get / grow / turn **cold / warm / chilly**
▸ to become / get / grow **fat / old**
▸ to become / get / grow **angry / hungry / tired**
▸ to become / get **annoyed / confused / involved / worried**
▸ to become / get / grow **used / accustomed to sth**
▸ to become / get **engaged / pregnant**

▸ to become / go / turn **red / white / blue**, etc.
▸ to become / go **blind / crazy / mad**
▸ to become / come **loose**
▸ to go / turn **bad / sour**

become to start to be sth: *She was becoming confused.* ◇ *It was becoming more and more difficult to live on his salary.* ◇ *She became queen in 1952.* ◇ *The bill will become law next year.*

get to reach, or make sb/sth/yourself reach, a particular state or condition; to reach the point at which you feel, know, are, etc. sth: *We ought to go; it's getting late.* ◇ *to get dressed/ undressed* (= to put your clothes on/take your clothes off) ◇ *They plan to get married in the summer.* ◇ *She's upstairs getting ready.* ◇ *Don't get your dress dirty!* ◇ *She soon got the children ready for school.* ◇ *You'll like her once you get to know her.* ◇ *She's getting to be an old lady now.*

> **NOTE** BECOME OR GET? Both these verbs can describe changes in sb's state or condition: *to become/get tired/ cold/angry/scared/pregnant/thin/old/better.* In general, **become** is more formal than **get**, and **get** is more frequent in spoken language. However, there are some cases when you can only use one of these words: *I became/got hungry/upset* (= verb + adjective). ◇ *She became Queen/a teacher/a member of the club* (= verb + noun) ◇ ~~She got Queen, etc.~~ ◇ *Don't get your dress dirty!* (= verb + noun + adjective)! ◇ ~~Don't become your dress dirty!~~ ◇ *It took me a long time to get to know her properly* (= verb + to + infinitive). ◇ ~~to become to know her.~~ Use **get** for changes that are the result of deliberate actions by you or sb else: *to get dressed/married/ divorced/killed/mugged/fired* ◇ ~~to become dressed/married, etc.~~. There are also some adjectives that you can only use with **become** (not *get*). These include adjectives connected with ability (*able/unable/proficient/skilled*), knowledge (*aware, certain, convinced*), availability (*available, common, extinct, useful*) and clarity (*clear, obvious, evident, apparent*).

go to become different in a particular way, especially a bad way; to reach a particular state or condition: *Her hair is going grey.* ◇ *This milk has gone sour.* ◇ *The children went wild with excitement.* ◇ *She went to sleep.* ◇ *That colour has gone out of fashion.* ❶ **Go** is often used to talk about changes in colour (*to go red/white/grey*) and other, especially negative, changes (*to go mad/bad/bald/crazy/ wrong/bankrupt*).

grow to begin to have a particular quality or feeling over a period of time; to gradually begin to do sth: *The skies grew dark and it began to rain.* ◇ *As time went on he grew more and more impatient.* ◇ *I'm sure you'll grow to like her in time.* ❶ **Grow** is used to talk about changes that happen over a period of time rather than suddenly. It is often used with comparative adjectives to show this gradual change: ~~She suddenly grew angry.~~ ◇ *She grew braver with time.*.

come to become; to reach a point where you realize, understand or believe sth: *The buttons had come undone.* ◇ *Everything will come right in the end.* ◇ *I've come to expect this kind of behaviour from him.*

> **NOTE** GROW AND COME In this meaning, these two verbs are either followed by an adjective (*come loose/grow calm*), or by 'to' + infinitive (*I came/grew to realize, understand, believe, etc.*).

turn to change into a particular state or condition; to make sth do this: *The leaves were turning brown.* ◇ *He turned nasty when we refused to give him the money.* ◇ *She turned a deathly shade of white when she heard the news.* ◇ *He's a lawyer turned politician* (= he used to be a lawyer but is now a politician). ❶ **Turn** is used to talk about colours: *to turn blue/red/white*; about changes in the weather: *to turn cold/warm/chilly* and negative changes: *to turn nasty/mean/sour/bad.*

beg verb

beg · plead · implore
These words all mean to ask for sth in a serious or anxious way because you want or need it very much.

PATTERNS AND COLLOCATIONS
▸ to beg / plead **for** sth
▸ to beg / implore **sb to do sth**
▸ to **almost / practically** beg / plead with sb
▸ I beg / implore **you!**

beg (-**gg**-) [T, I] to ask sb for sth, especially in an anxious way, because you want or need it very much: *They begged him for help.* ◇ *I managed to beg a ride from a passing motorist.* ◇ *He wants to see them beg for mercy.* ◇ *She begged him not to go.* ◇ *'Give me one more chance,' he begged.*

plead /pliːd/ [I] to ask sb for sth in a very strong and serious way: *She pleaded with him not to go.* ◇ *I was forced to plead for my child's life.* ◇ *He pleaded to be allowed to see his mother one more time.* See also **plea** → REQUEST

NOTE BEG OR PLEAD? **Plead** can suggest a stronger, more urgent or more emotional request, especially one that affects your personal happiness or the safety of those you love. **Beg** is often used by the person making the request, to emphasize how important it is, but **plead** is not used in this way: *Please don't do this, I'm begging you!* ◇ *Please, I'm pleading with you!*

implore /ɪmˈplɔː(r)/ [T, I] (*formal or literary*) to beg sb: *She implored him to stay.*

begin verb See also the entries for ESTABLISH, INTRODUCE 1 and START

begin · start · open · embark on/upon sth · take sth up · set about sth · go about sth · commence
These words all mean to do the first part of sth, or to do sth or make sth happen or exist for the first time.

PATTERNS AND COLLOCATIONS
▸ to begin / start / take up / set about / go about / commence **doing** sth
▸ to begin / start **to do sth**
▸ to begin / start sth **by doing / with** sth
▸ to begin / start / open / embark on a / an **campaign / enquiry**
▸ to begin / start / open a **discussion / conversation**
▸ to begin / start / embark on a **war / scheme**
▸ to begin a / start a / commence **battle**
▸ to begin / start / take up / commence **work**
▸ to begin / start / open a **story / letter / sentence**
▸ to begin / start / open a **day / year / meeting**
▸ to begin / start / embark on / take up / commence a **career / life**
▸ to begin / start / embark on a **journey / search / relationship**
▸ to begin / start / take up a / your **employment / duties / hobby**
▸ to begin / start / commence **production**
▸ to **immediately** begin / start / embark on / set about / commence / launch into sth
▸ to have **just** begun / started / opened / embarked on / taken up / launched into sth

begin [I, T] to do the first part of sth; to do sth that you were not doing just before: *She began by thanking us all for coming.* ◇ *We began work on the project in May.* ◇ *I began* (= started reading) *this novel last month and I still haven't finished it.* ◇ *She began to cry.* ◇ *I was beginning to think you'd never come.* ◇ *Everyone began talking at once.* **OPP end** → END, See also **beginning** → START *noun*, **begin** → START *verb*

start [T, I] to begin doing sth; to make sth begin to happen: *I start work at nine.* ◇ *The kids start school next week.* ◇ *We need to start* (= begin using) *a new jar of coffee.* ◇ *It started to rain.* ◇ *Mistakes were starting to creep in.* ◇ *She started laughing.* ◇ *Let's start by reviewing what we did last week.* ◇ *It's time you started on your*

homework. ◇ *Who started the fire?* ◇ *Do you start the day with a good breakfast?* **OPP finish**, **stop** → END, **finish** → FINISH, **stop** → STOP 3, See also **start** → START *noun*, **start** → START *verb*

NOTE BEGIN OR START? There is not much difference in meaning between these words. **Start** is more frequent in spoken English and in business contexts; **begin** is more frequent in written English. **Start**, but NOT **begin**, can also mean 'to make sth start happening' or 'to make a machine start working': *Who began the fire?* ◇ *I can't begin the car.*

open [T] to make an activity or event begin; to make a story, piece of writing or period of time begin in a particular way: *Who is going to open the conference?* ◇ *The police have opened an investigation into the death.* ◇ *They will open the new season with a performance of 'Carmen'.* ◇ *I opened the story with Viola because I wanted the reader to 'meet' everybody through her eyes.* **OPP close** → END, See also **open** → START *verb*, **opening** → LAUNCH *noun*, **opening** → START *noun*, **opening** → FIRST *det. adj.*

em'bark on/upon sth *phrasal verb* (*rather formal*) to begin doing sth new or difficult: *She is about to embark on a diplomatic career.* ◇ *Remember these basic rules before embarking upon major home improvements.*

,take sth 'up *phrasal verb* [no passive] to begin sth such as a job or hobby: *He takes up his duties next week.* ◇ *She has taken up* (= started to learn to play) *the oboe.* **OPP give sth up** → STOP 1

'set about sth *phrasal verb* [no passive] to begin doing sth: *She set about the business of cleaning the house.* ◇ *We need to set about finding a solution.*

'go about sth *phrasal verb* [no passive] (often used in negative statements and questions with *how*) to begin working on sth, especially in a particular way: *You're not going about the job in the right way.* ◇ *How should I go about finding a job?*

commence /kəˈmens/ [T] (*formal*) to begin sth: *The company commenced operations in April.* See also **commence** → START *verb*

beginner noun See also the entry for RECRUIT

beginner · novice · rookie
These are words for sb who is new to sth and has little knowledge or experience.

PATTERNS AND COLLOCATIONS
▸ a beginner / novice **in** sth
▸ a / an **absolute / complete** beginner / novice

beginner [C] a person who is starting to learn sth and cannot do it very well yet: *She's in the beginners' class.* ◇ *Italian for beginners*

novice /ˈnɒvɪs; *AmE* ˈnɑːv-/ [C] a person who has just started a job or activity and has very little experience: *I'm a complete novice at diving.* ◇ *Some ski resorts are ideal for novices.*

rookie /ˈrʊki/ [C] (*especially AmE, informal*) a novice: *The transition from rookie to fighter pilot starts with selection day.* ❶ **Rookie** is often used to talk about soldiers, police officers or sportsmen and women: *Derek Jeter was voted American League Rookie of the Year in 1996.* ◇ *a rookie quarterback*

behave verb

behave · treat · do · act · conduct yourself
These words all mean to do things in a particular way.

PATTERNS AND COLLOCATIONS
▸ to behave / treat sb / act / conduct yourself **as if / though** sth were the case
▸ to behave / treat sb / act / conduct yourself **like** sb / sth
▸ to behave / treat sb / act / conduct yourself **with** sth
▸ to behave / act in a particular way **towards** sb
▸ to behave / treat sb / act / conduct yourself **properly**

▶ to behave / treat sb / conduct yourself **well**
▶ to behave / treat sb / act **appropriately / reasonably / accordingly / differently / with dignity**
▶ to behave / treat sb / sth **badly / abominably**
▶ to behave / act **sensibly / stupidly / normally / strangely / suspiciously / aggressively**
▶ to treat sb / act **fairly / unfairly / unjustly / wrongly**

behave [I] (always used with an adverb or preposition) to do things in a particular way: *They behaved very badly towards their guests.* ◇ *He behaved like a true gentleman.* ◇ *She behaved with great dignity.* ◇ *He behaved as if nothing had happened.* ❶ In spoken English people often use *like* instead of *as if* or *as though*, especially in American English: *He behaved like nothing had happened.* This is considered incorrect in written British English.
▶ **behaviour** (*BrE*) (*AmE* **behavior**) *noun* [U]: *good/bad behaviour* ◇ *His behaviour towards her was becoming more and more aggressive.*

treat [T] (always used with an adverb or preposition) to behave in a particular way towards sb/sth: *You should treat people with more respect.* ◇ *Treat your keyboard with care and it should last for years.* ◇ *My parents still treat me like a child.*
▶ **treatment** *noun* [U]: *the brutal treatment of political prisoners* ◇ *Certain city areas have been singled out for special treatment.*

do [I] (always used with an adverb or preposition) to behave in the way mentioned: *Do as you're told!* ◇ *They are free to do as they please.* ◇ *Just do what they tell you to do.* ◇ *Do whatever you like.* ❶ In this meaning **do** is usually followed by *as*, but can also be followed by *what* or *whatever*.

act [I] (always used with an adverb or preposition) to behave in a particular way: *John's been acting very strangely lately.* ◇ *Stop acting like spoilt children!* ◇ *She was acting as if she'd seen a ghost.* ◇ *You acted very wisely in coming to me.* ❶ See the note about *like, as if* and *as though* at **behave**.

> **NOTE** BEHAVE OR ACT? Behave is usually used to talk about sb's general behaviour, NOT a particular action: ~~You behaved very wisely in coming to me.~~ Behave is used to talk about how well, how sensibly or how normally sb has behaved, but NOT how fairly or legally: *to behave well/impeccably/sensibly/suspiciously* ◇ ~~to behave unfairly/illegally/unlawfully/wrongly~~. Act is used to talk about how sensibly, how normally, how fairly or how legally sb has behaved, but NOT how well: *to act wisely/out of character/fairly/unlawfully* ◇ ~~to act well/impeccably/badly/abominably~~

con'duct yourself [T] (*formal*) (always used with an adverb or preposition) to behave in a particular way: *He conducted himself far better than expected.* ◇ *The report challenges them to examine how they conduct themselves in the workplace.*
▶ **conduct** /'kɒndʌkt; *AmE* 'kɑːn-/ *noun* [U]: (*formal*) *We need to improve standards of training and professional conduct.* ◇ *The sport has a strict code of conduct.*

bend *verb*

bend · kneel · crouch · bow · squat · stoop · duck · hunch · hunker down · curtsy
These words all mean to move your body into a position near the ground and/or with your head downwards.

PATTERNS AND COLLOCATIONS
▶ to bend / kneel / crouch / bow / squat / stoop / duck / hunch / hunker **down**
▶ to bend / bow / duck your **head**

bend [I, T] (especially of sb's body or head) to lean in a particular direction; to make your body, head, arm, leg, etc. lean or move in a particular direction: *He bent and kissed her.* ◇ *She bent forward to pick up the newspaper.* ◇ *She was bent over her desk writing a letter.* ◇ *Bend your knees, keeping your back straight.*

kneel [I] to be in or move into a position where your body is supported on your knees, with the lower legs bent back: *We knelt down on the ground to examine the tracks.* ◇ *He knelt and prayed for guidance.*

crouch [I] (usually used with an adverb or preposition) to lower your body close to the ground by bending your legs under you: *He crouched down beside her.* ◇ *Doyle crouched behind a hedge.*
▶ **crouch** *noun* [sing.]: *She dropped to a crouch.*

bow /baʊ/ [I, T] to move your head or the top half of your body forwards and downwards as a sign of respect or as a greeting; to move your head forwards and downwards: *He bowed low to the assembled crowd.* ◇ *She bowed her head in shame.*
▶ **bow** *noun* [C]: *He gave her a deep bow.*

squat /skwɒt; *AmE* skwɑːt/ (-**tt**-) [I] to sit on your heels with your knees bent up close to your body: *Children were squatting on the floor.*

stoop [I] to bend your body forwards and downwards; to stand or walk with your head and shoulders bent forwards: *She stooped down to pick up the child.* ◇ *He tends to stoop because he's so tall.*
▶ **stoop** *noun* [sing.]: *He walks with a slight stoop.*

duck [I, T] to move your head or body downwards quickly in order to avoid being hit or seen: *He had to duck as he came through the door.* ◇ *She just managed to **duck out of sight**.* ◇ *He ducked the first few blows, then started to fight back.*

hunch [I, T] (always used with an adverb or preposition) to bend the top part of your body forwards and raise your shoulders and back: *She leaned forward, hunching over the desk.* ◇ *He **hunched his shoulders** and thrust his hands deep into his pockets.*

hunker 'down *phrasal verb* (*especially AmE, rather informal*) to squat: *He hunkered down beside her.*

curtsy (also **curtsey**) [I] to bend your knees with one foot in front of the other, done by a woman or girl as a sign of respect to sb very important, or as part of a dance: *She curtsied to the Queen.*
▶ **curtsy** (also **curtsey**) *noun* [C]: *to make/drop/bob a curtsy*

bend

bend

crouch

kneel

squat
hunker down (*esp AmE*)

duck

benefit *noun*

1 the benefit of a good education
2 pay and benefits

1 benefit · advantage · strength · merit · good · virtue · asset · plus · good point

These are all words for a good or useful effect or quality that sth has.

PATTERNS AND COLLOCATIONS

▸ some / any / no benefit / advantage / virtue **in** sth
▸ a benefit / an advantage / an asset **for** sb / sth
▸ to be **to** sb's benefit / advantage
▸ to do sth **for** sb's benefit / good
▸ to be **with** / **without the** benefit / advantage **of** sth
▸ to **be of** great / major / real, etc. benefit / advantage / merit
▸ **considerable** / **great** / **real** benefits / advantages / strengths / merits / good / virtues / assets
▸ **maximum** / **additional** benefit / advantage
▸ **relative** benefits / advantages / strengths / merits / virtues
▸ to **have** the benefit / advantage / merit / virtue
▸ to **see** the benefit / advantage / merit / good / virtue

benefit [U, C] a good or useful effect of sth: *She had the benefit of a good education.* ◇ *The new regulations will be of benefit to everyone.* ◇ *For maximum benefit, take the tablets before meals.* ◇ *It was good to see her finally* **reaping the benefits** (= getting the results) *of all her hard work.* See also **beneficial** → VALUABLE 2

advantage [C, U] a thing that helps you to be better or more successful than other people; a quality that sth has that makes it better or more useful than other things: *Having a degree is a huge advantage when it comes to getting a job.* ◇ *You will be* **at an advantage** (= have an advantage) *if you have thought about the interview questions in advance.* ◇ *Is there any advantage in getting there early?* ◇ *A small car has the added advantage of being cheaper to run.* ◇ *Each of these systems has its* **advantages and disadvantages.** **OPP disadvantage** → DISADVANTAGE

strength [C] a quality or ability that sb / sth has that gives them an advantage: *The ability to keep calm is one of her many strengths.* ◇ *Consider all the* **strengths and weaknesses** *of the argument.* **OPP weakness** → WEAKNESS 1, **weakness** → WEAKNESS 2

merit /ˈmerɪt/ [C, usually pl.] a good quality that sb / sth has: *We will consider each case* **on its (own) merits** (= without considering any other issues, feelings, etc.). ◇ *They weighed up the relative merits of the four candidates.*

good [U] something that helps or is useful to sb / sth: *Cuts have been made for* **the good of** *the company.* ◇ *I'm telling you this* **for your own good.** ◇ *What's the good of earning all that money if you've no time to enjoy it?* ◇ *What good would it do to tell her about it after all this time?*

virtue /ˈvɜːtʃuː; AmE ˈvɜːrtʃuː/ [C, U] (*rather formal*) an attractive or useful quality that sth has: *The plan has the virtue of simplicity.* ◇ *They could see no virtue in discussing it further.*

> **NOTE BENEFIT, ADVANTAGE, MERIT** OR **VIRTUE?** A **benefit** is sth that you get or that comes from sth that you do. An **advantage**, **merit** or **virtue** is sth that a person, thing, plan or action has as a quality, which may be of use or benefit to you or to sb else. An **advantage** makes the person, thing, etc. better than sb / sth else. With **merit** and **virtue** there is no explicit comparison, although you can talk about the *relative advantages / merits / virtues of sb / sth*. **Merits** is usually used in the plural to talk about all sb / sth's good qualities taken together. **Virtue** may be singular, plural or uncountable and can be used to talk about a particular quality that is good because it is attractive and / or useful.

asset /ˈæset/ [C] a person or thing that is valuable or useful, especially because they help you to be successful: *She'll be a great* **asset to** *any company she works for.* ◇ *I'm not sure if his forcefulness is an asset or a liability.* **OPP liability** ❶ A **liability** is a person or thing that causes you a lot of problems: *Since his injury, Jones has become more of a liability than an asset to the team.*

plus [C] (*rather informal*) an advantage or benefit: *Being able to speak French is* **a definite plus** *when you're travelling in North Africa.* ◇ *You should carefully consider* **the pluses and minuses** (= good and bad points) *of going to live in the country.* **OPP minus**

good point [C] a good or positive feature that sb / sth has: *One of the good points about the system is that it treats everyone equally.* ◇ *His one good point is that he knows how to fix cars.* ❶ A **good point** is similar to an **advantage**, **merit** or **virtue**, but it is less an essential quality of sth, and more an additional feature.

2 benefit · bonus · perk

These are all words for extra things or money that you are given by your employer in addition to the money you regularly earn.

PATTERNS AND COLLOCATIONS

▸ **annual** / **taxable** benefits / bonuses
▸ **tax-free** benefits / bonuses / perks
▸ to **receive** / **enjoy** benefits / a bonus / perks

benefit [C, usually pl.] something that you are given by your employer in addition to the money that they pay you; money from an insurance company: *Benefits include a company pension and free health insurance.* ◇ *We offer a generous* **benefits package** (= several additional benefits). ◇ *The insurance plan will provide substantial cash benefits to your family in case of your death.*

bonus /ˈbəʊnəs; AmE ˈboʊ-/ money that you get from your employer in addition to the money that you regularly earn, especially for doing your job well; extra money that is paid on an insurance policy, in addition to the amount that is guaranteed (= promised): *Everyone in the company gets a 10%* **Christmas bonus.** ◇ *a* **productivity / performance bonus** (= as a reward for producing a lot or getting good results) ◇ *What is actually paid will depend on the bonus payments made at the end of the policy.*

perk [C] (*rather informal*) something that you are given by your employer in addition to the money that they pay you: *Perks offered by the company include a car and subsidized accommodation.*

benefit *verb*

benefit · gain · profit · cash in

These words all mean to obtain an advantage or benefit from sth.

PATTERNS AND COLLOCATIONS

▸ to benefit / gain / profit **from** sth
▸ the **company** / **industry** / **farmer** benefits / gains / profits / cashes in
▸ the **customer** / **consumer** / **individual** benefits / gains
▸ to **expect** / **hope to** benefit / gain / profit / cash in
▸ to **stand to** benefit / gain / profit

benefit [I] (*rather formal*) to get an advantage or benefit from sth: *Most crime victims benefit greatly by talking about their experiences.*

gain [T, I] to get an advantage or benefit from sth: *There is nothing to be gained from delaying the decision.* ◇ *Who stands to gain from the deal?*

> **NOTE BENEFIT** OR **GAIN?** In many cases you can use either word: *Who stands to benefit / gain from these changes?* However, **gain** is used more often to talk about financial advantages, or having an advantage over other people; **benefit** is used more often to talk about sb being in a better position than before, for example because they are happier, healthier or better educated. **Benefit** is slightly more formal than **gain** and cannot be used with an object: ~~There is nothing to be benefited from delaying.~~

profit [I, T] (*formal*) to get an advantage from a situation, especially in business; (of a situation) to give sb an advantage: *Farmers are profiting from the new legislation.* ◇ *Many local people believe the development will profit them.* ❶ **Profit** is more formal than **benefit** or **gain** and is mostly used to talk about financial gain. See also **profit** → MAKE 3

,**cash 'in** *phrasal verb* (*rather informal, disapproving*) to gain an advantage for yourself from a situation, especially in a way that other people think is wrong or immoral: *The film studio is being accused of **cashing in on** the singer's death.*

bent *adj.*

bent · twisted · deformed · crooked · gnarled
These words all describe sth that is not straight or normal in shape.

PATTERNS AND COLLOCATIONS
▸ gnarled / twisted **roots / branches**
▸ deformed / gnarled **hands**
▸ a twisted / crooked **smile**
▸ to **become** bent / twisted / deformed
▸ to **get** bent / twisted
▸ **slightly** bent / twisted / deformed / crooked
▸ **badly** twisted / deformed

bent not straight; (of a person) not able to stand up straight, usually because of old age or disease: *He tried to pick the lock with a piece of bent wire.* ◇ *Do this exercise with your knees bent (= not with your legs straight).* ◇ *She whirled around to see a small, bent old woman leaning on a cane.* ◇ *He was **bent double** with laughter.* See also **bend** → TWIST *verb*

twisted turned or bent so that the original shape is lost: *After the crash the car was a mass of twisted metal.* ◇ *She gave a small twisted smile.* See also **twist** → TWIST *verb*

deformed /dɪˈfɔːmd; *AmE* -ˈfɔːrmd/ (of a person or part of the body) having a shape that is not normal because it has grown wrongly: *She was born with deformed hands.* See also **deform** → TWIST *verb*
▸ **deformity** /dɪˈfɔːməti; *AmE* -ˈfɔːrm-/ *noun* [C, U]: *Drugs taken during pregnancy may cause physical deformity in babies.*

crooked /ˈkrʊkɪd/ not in a straight line; bent or twisted: *She had prim lips and, above them, a slightly crooked nose.* ◇ *The old part of the city is a maze of crooked streets and small alleys.* ◇ *Your glasses are on crooked.*
▸ **crookedly** *adv.*: *He grinned crookedly.*

gnarled /nɑːld; *AmE* nɑːrld/ (of trees) twisted and rough; covered with hard lumps; (of a person or part of the body) bent and twisted because of age or illness: *I stood against the oak, gazing up at its gnarled branches.* ◇ *His hands were gnarled with age and arthritis.*

best *adj.* See also the entries for FAVOURITE and IDEAL

best · wise · desirable · sensible · advisable
These are all words for describing the most appropriate thing to do in a particular situation.

PATTERNS AND COLLOCATIONS
▸ to be best / wise / desirable / sensible / advisable **to do sth**
▸ the best / a wise / a sensible **choice / thing to do / use of sth**
▸ the best / a wise / a sensible **course (of action) / investment**
▸ it is / it might be best / wise / desirable / sensible / advisable (to do sth)

best most suitable or appropriate: *What's the best way to cook steak?* ◇ *The best thing to do would be to apologize.* ◇ *He's the best man for the job.* ◇ *I'm not in the best position to advise you.* ◇ *It's best if you go now.* **OPP worst** ❶ **Worst** describes the thing, person, course of action, etc. that is least suitable or appropriate: *Going back now is just about the worst thing you could do.*

wise based on or showing good judgement: *Locking your car doors is always a wise precaution.* ◇ *The wisest course of action is just to say nothing.* ◇ *It was very wise of you to leave when you did.* **OPP unwise** → RECKLESS
▸ **wisely** *adv.*: *He wisely decided to tell the truth.*

desirable /dɪˈzaɪərəbl/ (*formal*) that you would like to happen or be done: *It is **desirable that** interest rates be reduced.* ◇ *It is no longer **desirable for** adult children to live with their parents.* ◇ *An end to the hostilities remains a highly desirable objective.* **OPP undesirable** → UNWANTED

sensible (*especially spoken*) based on good judgement and reason rather than feelings; practical and likely to be a good thing to do or a good way of doing sth: *That wasn't a very sensible thing to do!* ◇ *The sensible thing would be to take a taxi home.* ◇ *I think it's a very sensible idea.* ◇ *Choose a sensible diet and stick to it.* **OPP stupid** → CRAZY
▸ **sensibly** *adv.*: *Try to drive carefully, courteously and sensibly.*

advisable /ədˈvaɪzəbl/ [not usually before noun] (*rather formal*) a good idea in order to achieve sth: *Early booking is advisable.* ◇ *It is advisable to practise each exercise individually at first.* **OPP inadvisable** ❶ **Inadvisable** describes a course of action that is not sensible and you would advise against: *It is inadvisable to bring children on this trip.*

bet *verb*

bet · gamble
These words both mean to risk money on a sport, game, etc.

PATTERNS AND COLLOCATIONS
▸ to bet / gamble (sth) **on** sth
▸ to bet / gamble **money / £50**

bet [I, T] to risk money on a race or event by trying to predict the result: *I wouldn't bet on them winning the next election.* ◇ *Not many people are **betting against** France retaining their title.* ◇ *She bet me £20 that I wouldn't do it.* ◇ *You have to be over 16 to bet in the UK.*
▸ **bet** *noun* [C]: *to win / lose a bet* ◇ *We've got a **bet on** who's going to arrive first.* ◇ *I did it **for a bet** (= because sb had agreed to pay me money if I did).*

gamble [I, T] to risk money on a game or sport, such as a card game or horse race: *He doesn't drink or gamble any more.* ◇ *He had **gambled** all their money **away** (= lost all their money by gambling).*

betrayal *noun*

betrayal · treason · infidelity · bad faith · disloyalty
These are all words for the act of betraying sb/sth.

PATTERNS AND COLLOCATIONS
▸ infidelity / disloyalty **to** sb
▸ to **regard / see / view** sth as (a) betrayal / treason
▸ to **be guilty of / accuse sb of** treason / infidelity / bad faith / disloyalty

betrayal /bɪˈtreɪəl/ [U, C] (*rather formal*) the act of giving information to an enemy, hurting sb who trusts you, or ignoring your principles or beliefs in order to get an advantage for yourself; the fact of being betrayed in any of these ways: *The incident left me with a **sense of betrayal**.* ◇ *I saw her actions as a **betrayal of my trust**.* ◇ *This is a betrayal of their election promises.* See also **betray** → CHEAT *verb*, **betray** → TELL 2

treason /ˈtriːzn/ (also ,**high 'treason**) [U] the crime of doing sth that could cause danger to your country, such as helping its enemies during a war: *They were charged with treason and sentenced to death.*

infidelity /ˌɪnfɪˈdeləti/ [U, C] (*rather formal*) the act of not being faithful to your wife, husband or partner, by having sex with sb else: *His reputation has been damaged by allegations of marital infidelity.* ◇ *She could not forgive his* infidelities. **OPP** **fidelity** ❶ **Fidelity** is the quality of being faithful to your wife, husband or partner: *marital/sexual fidelity*

bad 'faith [U] (*formal or law*) the intention of deceiving sb, especially of not keeping a promise, even at the time that you make the promise: *He accused the local authority of acting in bad faith, in making promises that it knew it would not be able to keep.* **OPP** **good faith** → TRUTH

disloyalty [U] (*rather formal*) behaviour that involves not being loyal or faithful to your friends, family or country: *She felt guilty of disloyalty to her dead husband.* **OPP** **loyalty** → RELIABLE 1, See also **disloyal** → TREACHEROUS

better *adj.* See also the entry for GOOD 1

better · superior · preferable
These words all describe sb/sth that is better than sb/sth else.

PATTERNS AND COLLOCATIONS
▸ superior / preferable **to** sb / sth
▸ better than / superior to / preferable to **the rest**
▸ **far / greatly / vastly / infinitely** better / superior / preferable
▸ **slightly** better / superior

better (comparative of **good**) of a higher standard or less poor quality; not as bad as sb/sth else: *The weather should get better towards the end of the week.* ◇ *Her new movie is **much better** than her last one.* ◇ *Your work is **getting better all the time**.* ◇ *Her work is getting **better and better**.* ◇ *There's **nothing better than** a long soak in a hot bath.* ◇ *If you only exercise once a week, that's **better than nothing** (= better than no exercise at all).* **OPP** **worse** ❶ Things that are **worse** are of a lower standard or less high quality: *The weather **got worse** during the day.* ◇ *The interview was **much worse than** he had expected.*

superior /suːˈpɪəriə(r); sjuː-; *AmE* suːˈpɪr-/ (*rather formal*) better in quality than sb/sth else; greater than sb/sth else: *This model is far superior to its competitors.* ◇ *Her superior intellect makes her the ideal candidate for the position.* ◇ *This computer is technically superior to the others, but it's not as user-friendly.* ◇ *They won the battle because of their superior numbers.* **OPP** **inferior** → POOR 2

preferable /ˈprefrəbl/ more attractive or more suitable than sb/sth else; preferred to sb/sth else: *Anything was preferable to the tense atmosphere at home.* ◇ *It would be preferable to employ two people rather than one.*
▸ **preferably** *adv.*: *We're looking for a new house, preferably near the school.*

biased *adj.* See the Topic Map for FACT AND OPINION on p.898

biased · prejudiced · partisan · discriminatory · intolerant · one-sided · unbalanced
These words all describe sb/sth that unreasonably dislikes or favours sb/sth more than sb/sth else, usually with the result that one is treated unfairly.

PATTERNS AND COLLOCATIONS
▸ biased / prejudiced / discriminatory **against** sb / sth
▸ biased / prejudiced **in favour of** sb / sth
▸ a partisan / a prejudiced / a discriminatory / an intolerant **attitude**
▸ a biased / a prejudiced / a partisan / a one-sided / an unbalanced **view**
▸ a biased / prejudiced / partisan **opinion**
▸ a biased / partisan / one-sided **account**
▸ biased / partisan / one-sided **coverage**
▸ **somewhat / rather** biased / prejudiced / partisan / one-sided / unbalanced

biased /ˈbaɪəst/ (*disapproving*) unfairly supporting or showing favour towards one person, group or set of ideas rather than another: *They admit that they're **biased towards** the Republican Party.* ◇ *The article was heavily biased against the current regime.* ◇ *There is little doubt*

that most media coverage is biased. ◇ *She gave a somewhat biased account of the proceedings.* **OPP** **unbiased** → OBJECTIVE, See also **bias** → DISCRIMINATION, **bias** → INFLUENCE *verb*

prejudiced /ˈpredʒədɪst/ (*disapproving*) disliking or approving of sb/sth in particular, especially when this is unreasonable or unfair, often based on sb's race, religion, sex, age, etc: *Few people will admit to being racially prejudiced.* ◇ *They are strongly prejudiced against older candidates.* See also **prejudice** → DISCRIMINATION *noun*, **prejudice** → INFLUENCE *verb*

partisan /ˌpɑːtɪˈzæn; ˈpɑːtɪzæn; *AmE* ˈpɑːrtəzn/ (*usually disapproving*) strongly supporting one particular person, group or set of ideas, especially without considering it carefully: *Most newspapers are politically partisan.* ◇ *The speakers were encouraged by a large partisan crowd.* **OPP** **non-partisan** → OBJECTIVE

discriminatory /dɪˈskrɪmɪnətəri; *AmE* dɪˈskrɪmɪnətɔːri/ (*formal, disapproving*) unfairly treating one group of people, or member of a group, worse than others: *Women's groups claim that the laws are discriminatory.* ◇ *Companies were urged to tackle sexually and racially discriminatory recruitment practices.* See also **discrimination** → DISCRIMINATION

intolerant /ɪnˈtɒlərənt; *AmE* -ˈtɑːl-/ (*rather formal, disapproving*) not willing to accept ideas or ways of behaving that are different from your own: *He was deeply intolerant of all opposition.* **OPP** **tolerant** → TOLERANT, See also **intolerance** → DISCRIMINATION

one-'sided (*disapproving*) (of an argument, view or account of sth) giving only one point of view and not considering any facts or arguments that might suggest that this is wrong: *The debate was very one-sided, and lacking in any serious thinking.*

unbalanced [usually before noun] (*usually disapproving*) giving too much or too little importance towards one part or aspect of sth: *The media often presents a somewhat unbalanced picture of scientific progress.* **OPP** **balanced** ❶ A **balanced** view or treatment of a subject looks at or treats it fairly, giving the right level of importance to all aspects of it: (*approving*) *The programme presented a balanced view of the two sides of the conflict.*

bill *noun*

bill · account · invoice · check · tab
These are all words for a record of how much you owe for goods or services that you have bought or used.

PATTERNS AND COLLOCATIONS
▸ the bill / invoice / tab / check **for** sth
▸ to **pay / settle** a bill / an account / an invoice / a check
▸ to **pick up** the bill / check / tab
▸ to **put sth on** the bill / (sb's) account / the tab
▸ to **send / submit** a bill / an invoice to a customer
▸ to **ask for / get** the bill / check

bill [C] a list of goods that you have bought or services that you have used, showing how much you owe; the price or cost of sth: *the telephone/electricity/gas bill* ◇ *We **ran up** a massive hotel bill.* ◇ *Is the company going to **foot the bill** (= pay) for the repairs?* ◇ *I'll be sending you the bill (= I will expect you to pay) for the dry-cleaning!* ◇ (*especially BrE*) *The waiter brought the bill to their table.* See also **bill** → CHARGE *verb*

account [C] an arrangement with a shop or business to pay bills for goods or services at a later time, for example in regular amounts every month; the money owed in such an arrangement: *Put it **on my account** please.* ◇ *We have accounts with most of our suppliers.* ◇ *She bought the furniture she wanted **on account** (= she would pay for it later).*

invoice [C] (*rather formal*) a bill for goods that sb has bought or work that has been done for sb: *The timber merchants sent an invoice for £250.* See also **invoice** → CHARGE *verb*

NOTE BILL OR **INVOICE?** You would get a **bill** in a restaurant, bar or hotel; from a company that supplies you with gas, electricity, etc.; or from sb whose property you have damaged. An **invoice** is for goods supplied or work done as agreed between a customer and supplier, and is usually sent after the goods have been delivered or the work finished.

check [C] (*AmE*) a piece of paper that shows how much you have to pay for the food and drinks that you have had in a restaurant: *Can I have the check, please?* ❶ In British English the usual word for this is **bill**.

tab [C] (*rather informal*) a bill for goods you receive but pay for later, especially for food or drinks in a restaurant or bar; the price or cost of sth: *a bar tab* ◇ *Can I put it on my tab?* ◇ *He walked out of the restaurant and left me to pick up the tab* (= pay) *for the whole meal.*

birthday noun

birthday · anniversary · commemoration · jubilee
These are all words for a time when you remember sth that happened a year or a number of years ago.

PATTERNS AND COLLOCATIONS
▶ a **first** / **second** / **fiftieth** birthday / anniversary
▶ a **silver** / **golden** / **diamond** anniversary / jubilee
▶ it is sb's / sth's birthday / anniversary / jubilee
▶ to **have** a birthday / an anniversary
▶ to **celebrate** / **mark** a birthday / an anniversary / a jubilee
▶ to **forget** / **remember** sb's birthday / anniversary
▶ a birthday / anniversary **party** / **present** / **card**
▶ **Happy** Birthday / Anniversary!

birthday [C] the day in each year which is the same date as the one on which you were born: *My birthday is in August.* ◇ *It's Sam's birthday tomorrow. He'll be seven.* ◇ *Would you like a piece of **birthday cake**?*
anniversary [C] a date that is an exact number of years after the date of an important or special event: *Today is the anniversary of his wife's death.* ◇ *It's our **wedding anniversary** tomorrow.* ◇ *She's organizing the theatre's 25th anniversary celebrations* (= it is 25 years since it began).
commemoration /kə,meməˈreɪʃn/ [U, C] (*rather formal*) an event, ceremony, etc. that makes people remember and show respect for an important person or event in the past; the action of remembering sb/sth in this way: *a commemoration service/service of commemoration in the cathedral* ◇ *a statue **in commemoration of** the founder of the nation/of the soldiers' sacrifice*
jubilee /ˈdʒuːbɪliː/ [C] a special anniversary of an event, especially one that took place 25, 50 or 60 years ago; the celebrations connected with this: *Queen Victoria had been on the throne for 60 years and her diamond jubilee was being celebrated.* ◇ *The school's silver jubilee will be marked in style.*

NOTE ANNIVERSARY AND JUBILEE A *silver wedding anniversary/wedding/anniversary/jubilee* marks 25 years, *golden* 50 years and *diamond* 60 years. In British English it is more usual to say *silver/golden/diamond wedding*; in American English it is more usual to say *silver/golden/diamond anniversary*.

bit noun See also the entries for FRAGMENT and PIECE

bit · piece · scrap · grain · particle · morsel · speck
These are all words for a small amount of sth.

PATTERNS AND COLLOCATIONS
▶ a bit / piece / scrap / grain / particle / morsel / speck **of** sth
▶ a **small** / **tiny** bit / piece / scrap / grain / particle / morsel / speck
▶ a **little** bit / piece / scrap / speck
▶ a **large** bit / piece / particle
▶ **odd** bits / pieces / scraps
▶ a grain / particle / speck **of dust**

▶ a bit / piece / scrap **of information** / **news**
▶ a bit / piece / scrap **of paper**
▶ to **smash** sth **to** bits / pieces
▶ to **pick up** the bits / pieces of sth

bit [C] (*especially BrE, rather informal*) a small amount or part of sth: *Do you want a bit of pizza?* ◇ *Can you save me a bit?* ◇ *You've got bits of grass in your hair.* ◇ *A big bit of plaster just fell down from the ceiling.* ◇ *I've got a bit of shopping to do.* ◇ *With a bit of luck, we'll be there by 12.*
piece [C] one of the bits or parts that sth breaks into; a single example or an amount of sth: *There were tiny pieces of glass all over the road.* ◇ *The vase lay **in pieces** on the floor.* ◇ *It was an interesting piece of research.* ❶ A piece of can be used with many different uncountable nouns, including *advice, bread, chewing gum, equipment, furniture, information, luck, luggage, news, paper* and *research.* See also the entry for PIECE
scrap [C] a small piece of sth, especially paper, fabric or information: *She scribbled his phone number on a scrap of paper.* ◇ *We need to check every scrap of information that might give us a clue as to what happened.*
grain [C] a small hard piece of a particular substance: *She sprinkled a few more **grains of rice** into the pan.* ◇ *I got a grain of sand caught in my eye.* ❶ **Grain** is used especially in the following collocations: *a grain of rice/wheat/salt/sugar/sand*
particle /ˈpɑːtɪkl; AmE ˈpɑːrt-/ [C] a very small piece of sth: *He watched the particles of dust floating in the light.* ◇ *There was **not a particle of evidence*** (= no evidence at all) *to prove his case.*
morsel /ˈmɔːsl; AmE ˈmɔːrsl/ [C] (*rather formal*) a small amount or piece of sth, especially food: *They put out some **tasty morsels** for the hedgehogs.*
speck [C] a small piece of sth, especially dirt or dust: *There wasn't a speck of dirt anywhere.* ◇ *He brushed a few specks of dust from his sleeve.*

bite verb

bite · chew · munch · nibble · gnaw · crunch
These words all mean to use your teeth in a particular way, especially to eat food.

PATTERNS AND COLLOCATIONS
▶ to bite / chew / munch / gnaw / crunch **through** sth
▶ to bite / chew / munch / nibble / gnaw **at** sth
▶ to bite / chew / munch / nibble / crunch **on** sth
▶ to chew / munch / nibble / gnaw **away at** sth
▶ to bite / munch / nibble / crunch an **apple**
▶ to chew on / gnaw / crunch a **bone**
▶ to bite / chew **your lip** / **nails**
▶ to chew / munch / nibble / gnaw / crunch **your way through** sth

bite [I, T] to use your teeth to cut into or through sth: *She **bit into** a ripe juicy pear.* ◇ *Does your dog bite?* ◇ *She was bitten by the dog.* ◇ *He **bit off** a large chunk of bread.* ◇ *Stop biting your nails.*
▶ **bite** noun [C]: *She took a huge bite out of the chocolate bar.* ◇ *The dog gave me a playful bite.*
chew [T, I] to bite food into small pieces in your mouth with your teeth to make it easier to swallow; to bite sth continuously, for example because you are nervous or to taste it: *Chew your food up well before you swallow it.* ◇ *He is always chewing gum.* ◇ *After the operation you may find it difficult to chew and swallow.* ◇ *The dog was chewing on a bone.* ◇ *Rosa chewed on her lip and stared at the floor.* ❶ If you put sth in your mouth in order to eat it, you *chew it* or *chew it up.* If you bite sth continuously without eating it, for example your lip, you *chew on it.*
munch [I, T] to eat sth steadily and often noisily, especially sth crisp: *She munched on an apple.* ◇ *He sat in a chair munching his toast.* ◇ *I munched my way through a huge bowl of cereal.*
nibble [T, I] to take small bites of sth, especially food: *We sat drinking wine and nibbling olives.* ◇ *She took some cake from the tray and nibbled at it.*

gnaw /nɔː/ [T, I] to keep biting sth or chewing it hard, so that it gradually disappears: *The dog was gnawing a bone.* ◊ *Rats had gnawed through the cable.*

crunch [T, I] to crush sth noisily between your teeth when you are eating: *She crunched her apple noisily.* ◊ *He was crunching on a piece of toast.*

bitter *adj.*

1 a bitter taste
2 bitter feelings

---

1 bitter · pungent · sour · acrid · sharp · acid
These words all describe a strong, unpleasant taste or smell.

▸ a bitter/ a pungent/ an acrid/ a sharp/ an acid **taste**/ **flavour**
▸ a bitter/ a pungent/ a sour/ an acrid/ a sharp/ an acid **smell**/ **odour**
▸ a bitter/ a pungent/ an acrid/ a sharp **scent**
▸ a bitter/ a sour/ a sharp/ an acid **fruit**
▸ a pungent/ sharp **cheese**
▸ pungent/ acrid **smoke**
▸ to **taste** bitter/ sour/ sharp
▸ to **smell** bitter/ sharp

bitter (of a taste or smell) strong and usually unpleasant; (of food or drink) having a bitter taste: *bitter coffee/ chocolate* ◊ *The drink tasted bitter.* ◊ *This plant is ignored by livestock because of the bitter taste.*

pungent /ˈpʌndʒənt/ (of a smell or taste) strong and usually unpleasant; (of food or smoke) having a pungent smell or taste: *the pungent smell of burning rubber* ◊ *The air was pungent with the smell of spices.*

sour (of a taste) bitter like the taste of a lemon or of fruit that is not ripe; (of food or drink) having a sour taste: *Too much pulp produces a sour wine.* **OPP sweet ❶ Sweet** food contains sugar or tastes of sugar: *I need a cup of hot sweet tea.* ◊ *This wine is too sweet for me.* See also **sour** → ROTTEN

acrid /ˈækrɪd/ (of a smell or taste) strong and unpleasant; (of smoke) having an acrid smell: *The fog was yellow and acrid and bit at the back of the throat.*

sharp (of a taste or smell) strong and slightly bitter; (of food or drink) having a sharp taste: *The cheese has a distinctively sharp taste.*

acid (of a taste or smell) bitter, like the taste of a lemon or of fruit that is not ripe; (of food or drink) having an acid taste: *It's a very juicy fruit with a slightly acid flavour.*

NOTE WHICH WORD? Bitter, sour, sharp and **acid** are all used more for tastes. **Pungent** and **acrid** are used more for smells. A **bitter** taste is usually unpleasant, but some people enjoy the bitter flavour of coffee or chocolate. You cannot use any other word to describe this flavour: *pungent/sour/acrid/sharp/acid coffee/chocolate.* **Sour** and **acid** both describe the taste of a lemon or fruit that is not ripe. **Sour** is usually a negative term; acid can be negative or simply descriptive. A **sharp** or **pungent** flavour is more strong than unpleasant, especially when describing cheese: *bitter/sour/acrid/acid cheese.* A **pungent** smell is usually unpleasant, but some people enjoy the pungent smell of rich, spicy food. An **acrid** smell is always unpleasant; **acrid** is not used for the smell of food.

---

2 bitter · sour · resentful · acrimonious · embittered
These words all describe people feeling angry and unhappy after a bad experience.

▸ bitter/ resentful **about** sth
▸ bitter/ resentful **towards** sb
▸ a bitter/ a sour/ an embittered **man**
▸ a sour/ resentful **expression**
▸ a bitter/ an acrimonious **debate**/ **dispute**/ **divorce**

bitter (of people) feeling very angry and unhappy because you feel that you have been treated unfairly; (of situations) full of angry feelings and words: *He is very bitter about losing his job.* ◊ *She bit her lip hard to stop the rush of bitter words.* ◊ *They are locked in a bitter custody battle over their three children.* See also **bitterness** → RESENTMENT
▸ **bitterly** *adv.*: *They complained bitterly.*

sour feeling or expressing bitterness or disappointment: *She was a sour and disillusioned old woman.* ◊ *The meeting ended on a sour note with several people walking out.* ◊ *As time went by the marriage turned sour.* ❶ **Sour** is not usually followed by a preposition: *She was sour about it.* See also **sour** → INFLUENCE *verb*
▸ **sourly** *adv.*: *'Who asked you?' he said sourly.*

resentful /rɪˈzentfl/ (*especially written*) feeling bitter or angry about sth that you think is unfair: *She was resentful at having been left out of the team.* ◊ *They seemed to be resentful of our presence there.* See also **resent** → RESENT, **resentment** → RESENTMENT
▸ **resentfully** *adv.*: *He looked at me resentfully.*

NOTE BITTER, SOUR OR **RESENTFUL? Bitter** feelings are the strongest and most openly expressed: *feeling extremely/ intensely/very bitter* ◊ *a bitter laugh/smile.* If you feel **sour** or **resentful** it may be less obvious: *vaguely/ silently resentful* ◊ *resentful eyes* ◊ *a sour face.* **Sour** especially describes relationships which may *go/turn sour.*

acrimonious /ˌækrɪˈməʊniəs; *AmE* -ˈmoʊ-/ (*rather formal*) (of a situation) angry and full of strong bitter feelings and words: *His parents went through an acrimonious divorce.* See also **acrimony** → RESENTMENT
▸ **acrimoniously** *adv.*: *The relationship ended acrimoniously.*

embittered (*rather formal, especially written*) feeling angry and unhappy about sth over a long period of time: *He died an embittered man.*

black *adj.*

---

black · African American · of colour · coloured · mixed race · non-white
These words all describe people who have dark skin.

▸ black/ African American/ coloured/ mixed-race/ non-white **people**
▸ **people** of colour/ mixed race
▸ black/ African American **culture**

black (*especially BrE*) belonging to a race of people who have dark skin and are originally from Africa; connected with black people: *a black girl* ◊ *black culture* ❶ **Black** is the word most widely used and generally accepted in Britain. The currently accepted term for a black person from the US is **African American**. **Black** can also be a noun, but it is generally only used in the plural: *equality for blacks and whites* It can sound offensive in the singular; instead you can use the adjective: *a black man/ woman*

African American belonging to a race of people who have dark skin, originally from Africa but now American: *the first African American president*
▸ **African American** *noun* [C]: *African Americans in Hollywood* ◊ *a young African American*

of colour (*BrE*) (*AmE* **of color**) (*especially AmE*) belonging to a race of people who do not have white skin: *They say that prejudice against people of color persists.* ❶ **Of color** is also widely used in the US; it includes not only Americans of African origin, but also people of many different origins, for example Asian. See also **colour** → COLOUR 2

coloured (*BrE*) (*AmE* **colored**) (*old-fashioned or offensive*) not having white skin, because one or both parents have dark skin ❶ This term is now considered offensive except in South Africa, where **Coloured** is used to describe people who have parents of different races. In Britain and the US, use **black**, **African American** or **of color**.

mixed 'race having parents of different races; belonging to different races: *people of mixed race* ◇ *mixed-race children/couples* ❶ Mixed race can refer to people of any race, for example white, African, Asian, etc.

non-'white (*rather formal*) belonging to any race that does not have white skin: *the non-white population* ❶ Non-white can refer to people of many different origins, for example Indian and Chinese as well as African. It is used to talk about people in general, but not usually about individual people: ~~I got talking to a non-white girl about her studies.~~

▶ **non-white** *noun* [C, usually pl.]: *the ratio of whites to non-whites*

blame *verb* See also SCOLD

blame · criticize · condemn · attack · denounce · censure
These words all mean to say that you disapprove of sb/sth because you think they have done sth bad.

PATTERNS AND COLLOCATIONS
▶ to blame/criticize/condemn/attack/denounce/censure sb/sth **for** sth
▶ to blame/criticize/condemn/attack/denounce/censure the **government/president**
▶ to criticize/condemn/attack/denounce/censure a **decision**
▶ to criticize/condemn/attack/denounce sb/sth **strongly**
▶ to blame/criticize/condemn/attack/denounce/censure sb/sth **publicly**
▶ to blame/criticize/attack sb/sth **unfairly**
▶ to be **widely** blamed/criticized/condemned/attacked/denounced
▶ to be **roundly** criticized/condemned/attacked

blame [T] to say or think that sb/sth is responsible for sth bad: *She blamed the government for failing to respond to the crisis.* ◇ *A dropped cigarette is being blamed for the fire.* ◇ *Police are **blaming** the accident **on** dangerous driving.* ◇ *If you lose your job you'll **only have yourself to blame** (= it will be your fault).* ◇ *(spoken)'I just slammed down the phone when he said that.' 'I don't blame you! (= I think that was reasonable and the right thing to do)'* ◇ *Call her if you like but **don't blame me** (= because I have advised you not to do it) if she's angry.* See also **blame** → FAULT, **to blame** → GUILTY

criticize (*BrE* also **-ise**) [T, I] to say that you disapprove of sb/sth; to say what you do not like or think is wrong about sb/sth: *The decision was criticized by environmental groups.* ◇ *The government has been criticized for not taking the problem seriously.* ◇ *All you ever do is criticize!* **OPP praise** → PRAISE, See also **critical** → CRITICAL, **criticism** → CRITICISM
▶ **critic** *noun* [C]: *She is one of the ruling party's most outspoken critics.* ◇ *She is looking for a chance to prove her critics wrong.*

condemn /kən'dem/ [T] (*rather formal*) to express very strong disapproval of sb/sth, usually for moral reasons: *The government issued a statement condemning the killings.* **OPP condone** → FORGIVE, See also **condemnation** → CRITICISM

attack [T] (*rather informal*) to criticize sb/sth strongly, especially in order to make people stop respecting them: *The studio audience repeatedly attacked the minister for her stance.* ◇ *He attacked the idea that the company's practices were bad for the environment.* See also **attack** → CRITICISM *noun*

denounce /dɪ'naʊns/ [T] (*rather formal*) to criticize sb/sth strongly, usually in public: *The project was denounced as a scandalous waste of public money.* ❶ You **denounce** things because you think they are wrong, not just because you do not like them. See also **denunciation** → CRITICISM

censure /'senʃə(r)/ [T] (*formal*) to criticize sb strongly, and often officially, because of sth they have done: *He was censured by the council for leaking information to the press.* See also **censure** → CRITICISM

blank *adj.*

blank · expressionless · impassive · flat · inscrutable · glazed · bland · unreadable · unemotional
These words all describe a person, their expression or voice which doesn't show any emotion.

PATTERNS AND COLLOCATIONS
▶ a blank/an impassive/an inscrutable/a glazed/a bland/an unreadable **expression**
▶ a blank/an expressionless/an impassive/an inscrutable/a bland/an unreadable **face**
▶ blank/expressionless/inscrutable/glazed/unreadable **eyes**
▶ an expressionless/a flat/a bland **tone**
▶ a flat/a dry/an unemotional **voice**
▶ a blank/inscrutable/a glazed **look**

blank not showing any feeling, understanding or interest: *Her explanation was met with blank looks.* ◇ *Steve looked **blank** and said he had no idea what I was talking about.* ◇ *Suddenly **my mind went blank** (= I could not remember anything).*
▶ **blankly** *adv.*: *She stared blankly into space.*

expressionless not showing feelings or thoughts: *His expressionless gaze followed her every move.* **OPP expressive** ❶ Something that is **expressive** shows sb's feelings and thoughts clearly: *She has wonderfully expressive eyes.* ◇ *the expressive power of his music*

impassive /ɪm'pæsɪv/ not showing any feeling or emotion: *The two men remained impassive throughout the trial.* **OPP animated** → LIVELY
▶ **impassively** *adv.*: *The accused listened impassively as the judge sentenced him.*

flat (of a voice) not showing much emotion; not changing much in tone: *Her voice was flat and expressionless.* ◇ *He spoke in a flat Midlands accent.*

inscrutable /ɪn'skru:təbl/ if a person or their expression is **inscrutable**, it is hard to know what they are thinking or feeling, because they do not show any emotion: *He was wearing that inscrutable look again.*

glazed (especially of the eyes) showing no real emotion or awareness: *With glazed eyes he was staring into the middle distance.*

bland showing no strong emotions or excitement; not saying anything very interesting: *He stared back at her with a bland expression.* ◇ *After the meeting, a bland statement was issued.*

unreadable if sb's face or expression is **unreadable**, it is hard to know what they are thinking or feeling: *His eyes were unreadable as he led her into the office.*

unemotional not showing your feelings: *She seemed very cool and unemotional.* **OPP emotional** → INTENSE

block *verb*

1 block plans
2 block the drain
3 block sb's exit

1 See also the entries for DISRUPT and HOLD SB/STH UP
block · interfere with sth · handicap · inhibit · hamper · hinder · obstruct · hold sb/sth back
These words all mean to prevent sth from happening, developing or making progress.

PATTERNS AND COLLOCATIONS
▶ to hamper sb/hinder sb/hold sb back **from (doing)** sth
▶ to block/interfere with/inhibit/hamper/hinder/obstruct/hold back **progress**
▶ to block/interfere with/handicap/inhibit/hamper/hinder/hold back **growth**

- ▶ to block/ interfere with/ inhibit/ hamper/ hinder/ obstruct **development**
- ▶ to block/ interfere with/ inhibit/ hinder/ obstruct a **process**
- ▶ to interfere with/ inhibit/ hamper/ hinder/ obstruct sb's **work**
- ▶ to block/interfere with/inhibit/hamper/hinder sb's **ability** (to do sth)
- ▶ to inhibit/ hamper/ hinder/ hold back the **recovery** of sb/ sth
- ▶ to block/ hamper/ hinder/ obstruct an **investigation**
- ▶ to block/ hamper/ hinder sb's **efforts**
- ▶ to **seriously** interfere with/ handicap/ inhibit/ hamper/ hinder sb/ sth
- ▶ to **deliberately** block/ hinder/ obstruct sth
- ▶ to **greatly / significantly / severely** handicap / hamper / hinder

block [T] to prevent sth from happening, developing or making progress, especially by using official rules or procedures: *The proposed merger has been blocked by the government.* ◇ *The new rules would effectively block protesters' attempts to assert their rights.*

inter'fere with sth *phrasal verb* to prevent sth from succeeding or happening as planned: *She never allows her personal feelings to interfere with her work.* ◇ *Poor language skills can seriously interfere with communication.*
▶ **interference** *noun* [U]: *We will not allow any interference with the normal democratic processes.*

> **NOTE** **BLOCK OR INTERFERE WITH STH?** People usually **block** things such as *plans* or *efforts* deliberately. Things usually **interfere with sth** without anyone particularly intending them to.

handicap /'hændikæp/ (**-pp-**) [T, usually passive] to be a disadvantage which makes it more difficult for sb to do or achieve sth: *British exports have been handicapped by the strong pound.* ◇ *The team was handicapped by the loss of their key striker early in the game.* See also **handicap** → OBSTACLE

inhibit /ɪn'hɪbɪt/ [T] (*formal*) to prevent sth from happening or developing as quickly or as much as it would normally do: *A lack of oxygen may inhibit brain development in the unborn child.* ◇ *Alcohol significantly inhibits the action of the drug.*

hamper [T] to make it more difficult for sb to do sth or achieve sth: *High winds hampered the rescue attempt.* ◇ *Our efforts were severely hampered by a lack of money.* **OPP** **help** → HELP 2

hinder [T] to make it more difficult for sb to do sth or achieve sth, often by delaying progress: *These killings have seriously hindered progress towards peace.* ◇ *Some teachers felt hindered by a lack of resources.* **OPP** **help** → HELP 2, See also **hindrance** → OBSTACLE

> **NOTE** **HANDICAP, HAMPER OR HINDER?** If a person, project or process is **handicapped**, it is difficult for them to make progress or to achieve sth because of a weakness or disadvantage, such as lack of money or equipment, rules and regulations, etc. If sb is **hindered** or **hampered** in doing sth, making progress may also be difficult because of a weakness or disadvantage, or there might be some outside person or factor which actively makes progress difficult, for example bad weather or people who do not cooperate with them.

obstruct /əb'strʌkt/ [T] (*rather formal*) to deliberately prevent sb from doing sth or from making progress: *They were charged with obstructing the police in the course of their duty.* ◇ *He accused terrorists of attempting to obstruct the peace process.*

hold sb/sth back *phrasal verb* to prevent or slow down the progress or development of sb/sth: *Do you think that mixed ability classes hold back better students?* ◇ *They are determined that nothing should hold back the negotiations.* **OPP** **encourage** → ENCOURAGE 3

2 block · seal · clog · stop · dam · plug · choke · block sth up

These words all mean to stop sth from moving or flowing through a road, pipe or hole by putting sth in or across it.

- ▶ to block/ seal / clog/ stop/ dam / plug/ choke sth **up**
- ▶ to block/ seal / clog/ stop/ choke sth **with** sth
- ▶ to block/ seal / plug/ block up a **hole**
- ▶ to block/ seal / plug a **gap**
- ▶ a **road** is blocked / clogged / choked (with sth)
- ▶ to **completely** block/ seal / clog sth

block [T] to stop sth from moving or flowing through a pipe, passage, road, etc. by putting sth in it or across it: *After today's heavy snow, many roads are still blocked.* ◇ *The exit was blocked with beer crates.* ◇ *Fat that is poured down the sink will block the drain.* **OPP** **unblock** ❶ To **unblock** a *pipe* or *drain* is to clean it by removing sth that is blocking it. A *road* or *exit* can be **cleared**. See also **clear** → CLEAR *verb*

seal [T, often passive] to close a container tightly or fill a crack or hole, especially so that air or liquid cannot get in or out: *The containers must be carefully sealed so that no air can get in.* ◇ *The windows and doors had been sealed up with bricks.* ◇ *The samples are kept in sealed plastic bags.*

clog (**-gg-**) [T, I, often passive] to block sth or to become blocked, especially by a number of objects or a substance gradually collecting in one place: *The narrow streets were clogged with traffic.* ◇ *The wheels got clogged up with mud.* ◇ *Within a few years the pipes began to clog up.*

stop (**-pp-**) [T] to deliberately block, close or fill a hole or opening: *Stop up the other end of the hose, will you?* ◇ *I stopped my ears but still heard her cry out.*

dam (**-mm-**) [T] to build a dam across a river, especially to make a reservoir (= a lake to store water): *Locals strongly opposed plans to dam the river.*

plug (**-gg-**) [T] to fill a hole with a substance or object that fits tightly into it, especially to stop liquid from coming out: *He plugged the hole in the pipe with an old rag.* ◇ *Divers succeeded in plugging the leaks from the tanker.*

choke [T, often passive] to block or fill a passage or space so that it is difficult for anything to move through it: *The pond was choked with rotten leaves.*

block sth 'up *phrasal verb* [often passive] to completely fill a hole or opening and stop anything from passing through it: *One door had been blocked up.* ◇ *My nose is really blocked up.*

3 block · be/get in sb's/the way · obstruct · barricade · cut sth off · block sth off · seal · bar

These words all mean to stop sb from going somewhere by standing in front of them or putting sth in across their path.

- ▶ to block/ obstruct/ bar an **entrance**
- ▶ to block/ obstruct/ bar sb's **path / way**
- ▶ to block/ cut off/ bar sb's **retreat**
- ▶ to block/ barricade/ block off a **road**
- ▶ to block/ bar sb's **progress/ exit**
- ▶ to block/ cut off sb's **escape**
- ▶ to block/ obstruct sb's **view**
- ▶ to **deliberately** block/ obstruct sb/ sth

block [T] to stop sb from getting past or seeing sth by standing in front of them or in their path: *She had her back to the door, blocking his exit.* ◇ *An ugly new building blocked the view from the window.*

be/get in sb's/the way *idiom* to stop sb from moving or doing sth by standing in front of them or in their path: *You'll have to move — you're in my way.* ◇ *Do you want me to move my bike — is it getting in your way?* **OPP** **get out of sb's/the way**

obstruct /əb'strʌkt/ [T] (*formal*) to block a road, entrance, passage, etc. so that sb/sth cannot get through or see past: *You can't park here, you're obstructing my driveway.* ◇ *First check that the accident victim doesn't have an obstructed airway.*

barricade /ˌbærɪ'keɪd/ [T] to place a line of objects across a road or door to stop people from getting past: *They barricaded all the doors and windows.* ◇ *He had barricaded himself inside his room.* See also **barricade** → BARRIER

,cut sth 'off *phrasal verb* to stop sb from getting somewhere by standing or moving in front of them or in their path: *They cut off the enemy's retreat.* ◇ *The only other escape route was cut off by the rising tide.*

> **NOTE** BLOCK, CUT STH OFF OR BE/GET IN SB'S/THE WAY? You usually **block** sb's way deliberately by standing still in one place; you can deliberately **cut off** sb's *escape* or *route* by moving between them and the way they want to go; you usually **get in sb's way** by accident by being in the wrong place at the wrong time.

,block sth 'off *phrasal verb* to close a road or an opening by placing a barrier at one end or in front of it: *The main roads out of the city have been blocked off.*

seal [T] (of the police or army) to stop people from passing through a place, especially a border: *Troops have sealed the border between the countries.*

bar (-rr-) [T] to be standing or placed in sb's way on a road or path or in an entrance so they cannot get past: *Two police officers were barring her exit.* ◇ *We found our way barred by rocks.* See also **barrier** → BARRIER

blow *noun*

---

blow · setback · hitch · hiccup · knock
These are all words for a problem or other event which has a damaging effect on sth or which delays it.

PATTERNS AND COLLOCATIONS
▸ a blow / setback **to / for** sb / sth
▸ a setback / hitch / hiccup **in** sth
▸ a **serious** blow / setback / hiccup
▸ a **slight / minor** setback / hitch / hiccup
▸ to **suffer** a blow / setback / knock

blow [C] a sudden problem or event which has a damaging effect on sb/sth, causing sadness or disappointment: *It was a shattering blow to her pride.* ◇ *Losing his job came as a terrible blow to him.* ◇ *Can you stay with Cathy tonight? She's had a bit of a blow.*

setback /'setbæk/ [C] a difficulty or problem which delays or prevents sth or makes a situation worse: *These closures are a further setback for the coal industry.* ◇ *The team suffered a major setback when their best player was injured.* See also **set sb/sth back** → HOLD SB/STH UP

hitch [C] a problem or difficulty that causes a short delay: *The ceremony went off without a hitch.* ◇ *There are always a few last-minute hitches at the dress rehearsals.* ◇ *There was a slight technical hitch which delayed the plane's take-off.*

hiccup (also **hiccough**) /'hɪkʌp/ [C] (*rather informal*) a small problem or sth that causes a short delay: *Apart from the occasional hiccup, things ran pretty well.*

knock [C, usually sing.] an experience or event that makes sb/sth less confident or successful: *Industry in the area has taken a knock with the closure of two factories.* ◇ *Her confidence took a knock when she lost her job.* ❶ In this meaning **knock** is always used with the verb *take*.

blow *verb*

---

1 The leaves were blown everywhere.
2 blow out smoke from your cigarette
3 blow a whistle

---

1 blow · flutter · fly · flap · waft
These words all mean to move or make sth move in the air.

PATTERNS AND COLLOCATIONS
▸ a flag flutters / flies / flaps
▸ to blow / flutter / flap / waft **gently**
▸ to blow / flutter / fly / flap **in the wind / breeze**

blow [I, T] (always used with an adverb or preposition) to be moved by the wind, sb's breath or a movement of air; to move sth in this way: *My hat blew away in the wind.* ◇ *The door blew open.* ◇ *I was almost blown over by the force of the blast.* ◇ *She blew the dust off the book.*

flutter [I, T] to move lightly and quickly, for example in the air; to make sth move in this way: *Flags fluttered in the breeze.* ◇ *Her eyelids fluttered but did not open.* ◇ *She fluttered her eyelashes at him* (= tried to attract him).

fly [T, I] to display a flag, especially on a long pole; (of a flag) to be displayed in this way; (of sth light and flowing) to move around freely in the air: *Flags were flown at half mast* (= half way down the pole, as a mark of respect to sb who has died) *on all public buildings.* ◇ *The Japanese flag flew outside the embassy.* ◇ *Her hair was flying in the breeze.*

flap (-pp-) [I, T] to move up and down or from side to side in the air, often making a noise; to make sth move in this way: *The sails flapped in the breeze.* ◇ *Her wet skirt flapped around her knees.* ◇ *The man was flapping a large white sheet.* ❶ **Flap** is used about sth, especially sth wide and flat, that is fixed or held at one edge. See also **flap** → SHAKE 1

waft /wɒft; *AmE* wɑːft; wæft/ [I, T] (always used with an adverb or preposition) (of a smell or sound) to move gently through the air; to make a smell or sound move gently through the air: *The sound of their voices wafted across the lake.* ◇ *The scent of the flowers was wafted through the window by the breeze.*

---

2 blow · pant · gasp · snore · wheeze · sniff · puff
These words are all ways of breathing.

PATTERNS AND COLLOCATIONS
▸ to pant / gasp **with** excitement, exhaustion, etc.
▸ to blow / pant / sniff / puff **hard**
▸ to pant / snore / sniff **loudly / noisily**
▸ to blow / snore **softly / gently**
▸ to pant / wheeze **slightly**
▸ to pant / gasp **breathlessly**
▸ to pant / gasp **for breath**

blow [I, T] (always used with an adverb or preposition) to send out air from the mouth: *You're not blowing hard enough!* ◇ *He drew on his cigarette and blew out a stream of smoke.*

pant [I, T] to breathe quickly with short breaths, usually with your mouth open, because you have been doing some physical exercise, or because it is very hot: *Eventually he arrived at the gate, puffing and panting.* ◇ *'Keep going, we'll get there in time!' she panted.*

gasp /ɡɑːsp; *AmE* ɡæsp/ [I, T] to have difficulty breathing or speaking: *He came to the surface of the water gasping for air.* ◇ *She managed to gasp out her name.* See also **gasp** → BREATH *noun*

snore [I] to breathe noisily through your nose and mouth while you are asleep: *I could hear Paul snoring in the next room.*

wheeze /wiːz/ [I, T] to breathe noisily and with difficulty: *He was coughing and wheezing all night.* ◇ *'I have a chest infection,' she wheezed.*

sniff [I] to breathe air in through your nose in a way that makes a sound, especially when you are crying or have a cold: *She sniffed and wiped her nose with a tissue.* See also **sniff** → BREATH *noun*

puff [I] (*rather informal*) to breathe loudly and quickly, especially after you have been running: *He hurried down the street, huffing and puffing.*

---

3 blow · blare · sound · honk · blast
These words all mean to make a sound like the sound made by a car horn.

PATTERNS AND COLLOCATIONS
▸ to blow / blare / sound / honk / blast a **horn**
▸ a **horn** blows / blares / sounds / honks / blasts
▸ to blow / sound a **whistle**
▸ a **whistle** blows / sounds
▸ **music** blares / blasts

blow [T, I] to make a sound with a whistle, car horn or musical instrument such as a horn or trumpet; (of a whistle, car horn, etc.) to make this sound: *The referee blew his whistle.* ◊ *The sound of trumpets blowing grew louder.*

blare [I, T] to make a loud unpleasant noise, especially the noise made by car horns or electrical equipment such as radios and televisions: *Police cars sped past with their lights flashing and sirens blaring.* ◊ *The radio was blaring out rock music.*
▶ **blare** *noun* [sing.]: *She was woken by the blare of car horns from outside the window.*

sound [T] to make a sound with a car horn, whistle or musical instrument, especially as a warning or signal: *Passing motorists sounded their horns in support.* See also **sound** → RING *verb*

honk [I, T] to make a loud noise with a car horn; (of a car horn) to make a loud noise: *She rushed from the room at the sound of the taxi honking.* ◊ *Why did he honk at me?* ◊ *People honked their horns as they drove past.*

blast [I, T] to make a loud unpleasant noise, especially the noise made by loud music or a car horn: *Music suddenly blasted out from the speakers.* ◊ *The radio blasted out rock music at full volume.*

boast *verb*

boast · show off · pride yourself on sth · brag · gloat · congratulate yourself
These words all mean to talk proudly about sth, especially too proudly, or to feel proud about sth.

PATTERNS AND COLLOCATIONS
▶ to boast / show off / brag / gloat **about** sth
▶ to show off / brag / crow **to** sb
▶ to boast / brag **of** sth
▶ to boast / brag / congratulate yourself **that** ...

boast [I] (*usually disapproving*) to talk too proudly about your abilities, achievements or possessions in order to impress other people: *I don't want to boast, but I can actually speak six languages.* ◊ *She is always boasting about how wonderful her children are.* ◊ *He openly boasted of his skill as a burglar.* See also **boastful** → PROUD 2
▶ **boast** *noun* [C]: *It was her proud boast that she had never missed a day's work because of illness.*

show 'off *phrasal verb* (*rather informal, disapproving*) to try to impress others by talking about your abilities or possessions, or by showing what you can do: *He's just showing off because that girl he likes is here.* ◊ *They drive around in their new cars, showing off to their friends.*
▶ **'show-off** *noun* [C]: *She's always been a real show-off.*

'pride yourself on sth *phrasal verb* to be proud of sth, such as an ability or quality: *The school prides itself on its academic record.* See also **pride** → SATISFACTION, **proud** → GLAD

brag (-gg-) [I] (*disapproving*) to talk too proudly and in an annoying way about sth you have done or sth you own: *I'm not bragging but I think I did very well in the interview.*

gloat [I] (*disapproving*) to feel or show pleasure in your own success or good luck or sb else's failure or bad luck, in an unpleasant way: *She was still gloating over her rival's disappointment.*

congratulate yourself [T] to feel pleased and proud because you have achieved sth: *You can congratulate yourself on having done an excellent job.*

boat *noun*

boat · ship · vessel · yacht · ferry · submarine · barge · raft · cruiser · canoe · dinghy · craft
These are all words for vehicles that travel on or in water.

PATTERNS AND COLLOCATIONS
▶ **by** boat / ship / ferry / barge / canoe
▶ a boat / ship / ferry **from / to / for / bound for**...

▶ **on / onto / off** a boat / ship / vessel / yacht / ferry / submarine / barge / raft / cruiser / craft
▶ **in / into / out of** a boat / submarine / barge / raft / canoe / dinghy / craft
▶ **aboard / on board** a boat / ship / vessel / yacht / ferry / submarine / barge / cruiser / craft
▶ to **travel / go / come by** boat / ship / ferry / barge / canoe
▶ to **sail** a boat / ship / vessel / yacht / dinghy / craft
▶ to **row** a boat / vessel / raft / dinghy / craft
▶ to **paddle** a raft / canoe / dinghy / craft
▶ to **anchor** a boat / ship / vessel / cruiser
▶ to **tie up** a boat / yacht / barge / raft / dinghy
▶ to **moor** a boat / ship / vessel / barge / yacht
▶ a boat / ship / vessel / yacht / ferry / cruiser / dinghy / craft **sails / sets sail**
▶ a boat / ship / vessel / ferry / cruiser / craft **docks**
▶ a boat / ship / vessel / yacht / ferry / submarine / barge / raft / cruiser / canoe / dinghy / craft **floats / capsizes / sinks / goes down**
▶ a boat / ship / vessel / ferry / submarine / barge / raft / cruiser / craft **carries** sb / sth

boat [C] any vehicle that travels on water, moved by oars, sails or a motor: *They spent the day on the boat.* ◊ *They crossed the island to catch a boat for islands south of Skye.* ◊ *You can take a boat trip along the coast.* ❶ **Boat** is used in many one-word and two-word compounds: *a lifeboat / rowboat / speedboat / motorboat / houseboat* ◊ *a rowing / sailing / fishing / canal boat* ◊ *a rescue / patrol / pleasure / passenger boat*
▶ **boating** *noun* [U]: *to go boating* ◊ *Local activities include walking, boating and golf.*

ship [C] a large boat that travels by sea, carrying people or goods: *They boarded a ship bound for India.* ◊ *Raw materials and labour come by ship, rail or road.* ◊ *There are two restaurants on board ship.* ❶ **Ship** is also used in many compounds: *a cargo ship* ◊ *a container ship* ◊ *a sailing ship*

> **NOTE** **BOAT OR SHIP?** A **boat** can travel on the sea or on a river or lake, but a **ship** only travels by sea. Smaller vehicles are **boats**, not ships. Very large ones are usually called **ships**. You can use **boat**, but NOT **ship**, as a general term to describe any vehicle that travels on water.

vessel /'vesl/ [C] (*formal*) a large ship or boat, especially one that travels by sea: *ocean-going vessels* ◊ *The vessel was registered in Bermuda.*

yacht /jɒt; *AmE* jɑːt/ [C] a large sailing boat, often also with an engine and a place to sleep on board, used for pleasure trips and racing: *a yacht club / race* ◊ *a motor yacht* ◊ *a luxury yacht* ❶ In American English, this is also called a **sailboat**.
▶ **yachting** *noun* [U]: *to go yachting* ◊ *a yachting holiday*

ferry [C] a boat that carries people, vehicles and goods across a river or across a narrow part of the sea: *the cross-channel ferry service* ◊ *We caught the ferry at Ostend.* ◊ *the Dover–Calais ferry crossing* ◊ *the Staten Island ferry*

submarine /ˌsʌbməˈriːn; ˈsʌbməriːn/ (*also informal* **sub**) [C] a ship that can travel underwater: *a nuclear submarine* ◊ *a submarine base*

barge [C] a large boat with a flat bottom, used for carrying goods and people on canals and rivers: *I travelled by barge.* ◊ *cruising the canals of France in a barge*

raft /rɑːft; *AmE* ræft/ [C] a small boat made of rubber or plastic that is filled with air; a flat structure made of pieces of wood tied together and used as a boat or floating platform: *an inflatable raft* ◊ *a life raft* (= used for rescuing people from sinking ships or planes) ◊ *They built a raft of logs.*
▶ **rafting** *noun* [U]: *We went white-water rafting on the Colorado River.*

cruiser /'kruːzə(r)/ [C] a large fast ship used in war; a boat with a motor and room for people to sleep, used for pleasure trips: *He served on a merchant cruiser.* ◊ *a luxury 20-foot cabin cruiser* ❶ A ship used for going on pleasure trips can be called a **cruise ship**.

canoe /kə'nuː/ [C] a light narrow boat which you sit in and move along in the water with a paddle: *We crossed the lake by canoe.*
▶ **canoeing** noun [U]: *to go canoeing*
dinghy /'dɪŋi; 'dɪŋgi/ [C] a small open boat that you sail or row; a small boat made of rubber or plastic that is filled with air to make it float: *She sailed the dinghy across the bay.* ◇ *The crew were taken to shore in an inflatable dinghy.*
craft (pl. **craft**) [C] (*formal*) a boat or ship: *Hundreds of small craft bobbed around the ship as it steamed into the harbour.* ◇ *a landing/pleasure craft*

body noun

1 Her whole body trembled.
2 a dead body

1 body · skeleton · figure · physique · build · anatomy
These are all words for the physical structure or shape of a person or animal.

PATTERNS AND COLLOCATIONS
▶ the **human** body / skeleton / figure / anatomy
▶ a / the **female** / **male** body / skeleton / figure / anatomy
▶ a **good** body / figure / physique
▶ a **powerful** body / physique / build
▶ a **slim** body / figure / build
▶ to **have** a good, large, slim, etc. body / figure / physique / build
▶ a **part** of the body / anatomy

body [C] the whole physical structure of a human being or animal: *Her whole body was trembling.* ◇ *He pulled the sheet up over his naked body.* ◇ *The heart pumps blood around the body.* ◇ *body weight/size/temperature/heat* ◇ *body fat/tissues*
skeleton /'skelɪtn/ [C] the structure of bones that supports the body of a person or animal; a model of this structure: *The human skeleton consists of 206 bones.* ◇ *a dinosaur skeleton*
figure [C] the shape of a person's body, especially a woman's body that is attractive: *She's always had a good figure.* ◇ *I'm watching my figure* (= trying not to get fat). See also **figure** → SHAPE noun
physique /fɪ'ziːk/ [C, U] (*often approving*) the size and shape of a person's body: *He has the physique of a rugby player.* ◇ *She doesn't have the physique to be a dancer.*
build [U, C, usually sing.] the size and shape of a person's body: *He was described as a man of average build.* ◇ *He's heavier in build than his brother.*

> **NOTE** PHYSIQUE OR BUILD? A person's **physique** is often described in approving terms: *his magnificent/muscular physique* ◇ *the physique of an athlete/a bodybuilder.* **Build** is simply a descriptive term, neither approving or disapproving, and is mostly concerned with a person's size: *to be of average/medium/slight/slim/heavy/strong build*

anatomy /ə'nætəmi/ [C, U] the structure of an animal or plant: *the anatomy of the horse* ◇ *human anatomy* ❶ In humorous language sb's **anatomy** is their body: (*humorous*) *Various parts of his anatomy were clearly visible.*

2 body · corpse · carcass · remains
These are all words for the body of a dead person or animal.

PATTERNS AND COLLOCATIONS
▶ to **identify** / **bury** a body / a corpse / remains

body [C] the body of a dead person or animal: *a dead body* ◇ *The family of the missing girl has been called in by the police to identify the body.* ◇ *His body is being brought back to his home town for burial.*
corpse /kɔːps; AmE kɔːrps/ [C] a dead body, especially of a human being: *The corpse was barely recognizable.* ◇ *The ground was littered with the corpses of enemy soldiers.*

> **NOTE** BODY OR CORPSE? **Body** is a gentler word to use than **corpse**. It reminds you that this was once a person who was alive, possibly sb that you knew. **Corpse** is a more direct and unpleasant word; it is used especially when you do not know or do not care who the dead person was, or when you want to make the reality of death more shocking.

carcass (*BrE* also, *less frequent* **carcase**) /'kɑːkəs; AmE 'kɑːrkəs/ [C] the dead body of an animal, especially of a large one or of one that is ready for cutting up as meat: *There were vultures scavenging for carcasses on the road.* ◇ *She boiled up the chicken carcass* (= the bones of a cooked chicken) *to make soup.*
remains [pl.] (*rather formal*) the body of a dead person or animal, especially sb/sth that has been dead for a long time: *human remains* ◇ *The remains have been identified as those of a Mr Thomas, who lived in Richmond.*

bold adj. See also the entry for BRAVE

bold · adventurous · daring
These words all describe sb/sth that is not afraid to do sth dangerous or take risks.

PATTERNS AND COLLOCATIONS
▶ a bold / an adventurous **design** / **spirit**
▶ a bold / a daring **plan** / **move**
▶ adventurous / daring **exploits**

bold /bəʊld; AmE boʊld/ (of people or behaviour) brave and confident; not afraid to say what you feel or to take risks: *It was a bold move on their part to open a branch of the business in France.* ◇ *The wine made him bold enough to approach her and introduce himself.* ◇ *The slaughter of his family turned him into a bold and fearless warrior.* **OPP meek** → PASSIVE, **timid** → SHY
▶ **boldly** adv.: *He stepped forward boldly to speak.*
adventurous /əd'ventʃərəs/ (of a person) willing to try new things or enjoying being in exciting new situations; (of a thing) new and exciting or unusual and sometimes dangerous: *For the more adventurous tourists, there are trips into the mountains with a local guide.* ◇ *Many teachers would like to be more adventurous and creative.* ◇ *The menu contained traditional favourites as well as more adventurous dishes.* **OPP unadventurous** ❶ Unadventurous people are not willing to take risks or try new and exciting things.
daring /'deərɪŋ; AmE 'der-/ (of a person) brave and willing to do dangerous or unusual things; (of a thing) involving danger and taking risks: *'Should you be drinking so much?' she asked, greatly daring.* ◇ *There are plenty of activities at the resort for the less daring.* ◇ *She wore a daring strapless dress in black silk.* See also **daring** → COURAGE, **dare** → DARE verb
▶ **daringly** adv.: *This house would have looked daringly modern when it was built.*

bomb noun

bomb · missile · explosive · grenade · device · mine · rocket
These are all words for weapons that explode.

PATTERNS AND COLLOCATIONS
▶ an **unexploded** bomb / missile / grenade / device / mine / rocket
▶ a **home-made** bomb / explosive / grenade / device / rocket
▶ to **carry** bombs / missiles / explosives / grenades / rockets
▶ to **plant** / **set off** a bomb / explosives / a device / a mine
▶ to **place** / **put** / **defuse** a bomb / explosives / a device
▶ to **fire** / **launch** / **intercept** / **shoot down** missiles / rockets
▶ a bomb / missile / grenade / rocket **hits** / **misses** sb / sth
▶ a bomb / an explosive / a grenade / a device / a mine **goes off** / **detonates**
▶ a bomb / missile / grenade / device / mine / rocket **explodes**
▶ a bomb / a missile / an explosive / a grenade / a device / a mine / a rocket **kills** sb

▸ a bomb/a missile/an explosive/a device/a rocket **destroys** sth
▸ a bomb/a missile/an explosive/a grenade/a device **blows sth up**
▸ a bomb/missile/rocket **attack**

bomb [C] a weapon designed to explode at a particular time or when it is dropped or thrown: *Police suspect terrorists planted the bomb.* ◇ *Hundreds of bombs were dropped on the city.* ◇ *There was no warning of the bomb blast which ripped through the packed station.* ◇ *The building was evacuated after* **a bomb scare**.

missile /ˈmɪsaɪl; *AmE* ˈmɪsl/ [C] a weapon that is sent through the air and that explodes when it hits the thing it is aimed at: *All of the missiles missed their target.*

explosive [C, U] a substance that is able or likely to cause an explosion: *They planted explosives in the tunnel.* ◇ *The bomb was packed with several pounds of* **high explosive**.

grenade /ɡrəˈneɪd/ [C] a small bomb that can be thrown by hand or fired from a gun: *The hijackers were carrying* **hand grenades**. ◇ *His vehicle was damaged by a rocket-propelled grenade.*

device [C] a bomb or weapon that will explode: *A powerful device exploded outside the station.* ◇ *It was the world's first atomic device.*

mine [C] a type of bomb that is hidden under the ground or in the sea and that explodes when sb/sth touches it: *He was killed when his jeep ran over a* **land mine**.

rocket [C] a weapon that travels through the air, carries a bomb and is driven by a stream of burning gases: *A rocket smashed into the side of the building.* ❶ Unlike a **missile**, a **rocket** cannot be controlled while it is in the air.

bomb *verb*

bomb · blow sth up · shell · strafe · bombard
These words all mean to attack sb/sth with explosives.

▸ to bomb/blow up/strafe a **building**
▸ to bomb/shell/strafe/bombard **a village/town**
▸ to bomb/shell/bombard a/an **city/area**
▸ to bomb/shell sb's **positions**
▸ **aircraft** bomb/strafe/bombard sth
▸ **artillery/warships** shell/bombard sth
▸ **terrorists** bomb/blow sth up
▸ to bomb/shell/bombard/ sth **heavily**

bomb [T, I] to attack sb/sth by leaving a bomb in a place or by dropping bombs from a plane: *Terrorists bombed several army barracks.* ◇ *Coventry was heavily bombed during the last war.*

blow sth 'up *phrasal verb* to destroy sth by an explosion: *The police station was blown up by terrorists.*

shell [T, I] to fire shells (= metal cases filled with explosives) at sth from large guns: *They shelled the city all night.* ◇ *Just as they were leaving the rebels started shelling.*

strafe /strɑːf; *AmE* streɪf/ [T] to attack a place with bullets fired from automatic weapons, especially from an aircraft flying low: *Military aircraft strafed the village.*

bombard /bɒmˈbɑːd; *AmE* bɑːmˈbɑːrd/ [T] to attack a place by firing large guns at it or dropping bombs on it continuously: *Madrid was heavily bombarded for several months.*

bond *noun* See also the entry for RELATIONSHIP 1

bond · rapport · empathy · affinity
These are all words for a close connection, friendship or understanding between people or groups.

▸ a bond/a rapport/empathy/an affinity **between** A and B
▸ a rapport/empathy/an affinity **with** sb/sth
▸ empathy/an affinity **for/towards** sb/sth
▸ a **close** bond/rapport/affinity
▸ (a) **great** rapport/empathy/affinity
▸ (a) **real** bond/rapport/empathy/affinity

▸ (a) **natural** bond/empathy/affinity
▸ a **special** bond/rapport/affinity
▸ to **feel/have** a bond/a rapport/empathy/an affinity
▸ to **develop** a bond/a rapport/empathy

bond [C] something that forms a connection between people or groups, such as a feeling of friendship or shared ideas and experiences: *A bond of friendship had been forged between them.* ◇ *The agreement strengthened the bonds between the two countries.* ◇ *the special bond between mother and child*
▸ **bond** *verb* [I]: *Mothers who are depressed sometimes fail to bond with their children.*

rapport /ræˈpɔː(r)/ [sing., U] a friendly relationship in which people like and understand each other: *Honesty is essential if there is to be a* **good rapport** *between patient and therapist.* ◇ *There was little rapport between the two women.*

> **NOTE** BOND OR RAPPORT? Rapport is more commonly used to describe a personal relationship between individuals; **bond** is more general and describes relationships between countries and groups as well. A **rapport** is based on understanding and liking each other; a **bond** can exist because of many different things, for example a shared interest, a family relationship, or financial reasons. If people or groups share a **bond**, they have a connection that is difficult to break and that affects the way they behave. It is stronger and more important than a **rapport**. A bond may be *forged* over a period of time; a **rapport** may need to be *established* but you can also have an *instant rapport* with sb, that just happens without effort.

empathy /ˈempəθi/ [U, sing.] the ability to understand another person's feelings or experience: *the writer's imaginative empathy with his subject* ◇ *She shows a lack of empathy for other people's situations.* ❶ You feel **empathy** for sb because you are able to imagine what it is like to be that person and to share their feelings. It is sometimes confused with **sympathy**: *Both authors have the skill to make you feel empathy with their heroines* (= you understand and share their feelings). ◇ *I have great sympathy for the flood victims* (= I feel very sorry for them). See also **sympathy** → SYMPATHY See also **empathize** → UNDERSTAND 2

affinity /əˈfɪnəti/ [sing.] (*formal*) a strong feeling that you understand and like sb/sth: *Sam was born in the country and had a deep affinity with nature.* ◇ *Humans have a special affinity for dolphins.*

book *noun*

book · publication · novel · guide · title · manual · textbook · text · volume
These are all words for a set of printed pages that are fastened together inside a cover.

▸ a book/publication/novel/guide/manual/textbook/text/volume **about** sb/sth
▸ a book/publication/guide/title/manual/textbook/text/volume **on** sb/sth
▸ a book/publication/novel/title/text/volume **by** sb
▸ a **reference** book/publication/guide/title/manual
▸ a **best-selling** book/novel/guide/title/textbook
▸ a **paperback** book/publication/novel/title/volume
▸ a **children's** book/novel/guide/title
▸ to **read** a book/publication/novel/guide/manual/textbook/text/volume
▸ to **publish** a book/a novel/a guide/titles/manuals/textbooks/a volume
▸ to **write** a book/publication/novel/guide/manual/textbook/text/volume

book [C] a set of printed pages that are fastened together inside a cover so that you can turn them and read them; a written work published in printed or electronic form: *His desk was covered with piles of books.* ◇ *The book has received some terrible reviews.* ◇ *a library/hardback book*

publication /ˌpʌblɪˈkeɪʃn/ [C] (*rather formal*) a book, magazine, newspaper or document in which information or stories are published: *Her work has appeared in a wide variety of mainstream publications.*

novel [C] a printed story long enough to fill a complete book, in which the characters and events are usually imaginary: *detective/historical/romantic novels* ◇ *His first novel was published in 1934.* See also **novelist** → WRITER

guide [C] a book or magazine that gives you information, help or instructions about sth: *a Guide to Family Health* ◇ *Let's have a look at the TV guide and see what's on.* ❶ A **guide** or **guidebook** is also a book that gives information about places for travellers or tourists: *He has written a number of travel guides.* ◇ *a guidebook to Peru*

title [C] a book or magazine, especially one that is being published or sold by sb/sth: *The company publishes twenty new titles a year.*

manual /ˈmænjuəl/ [C] a book that tells you how to do sth, or operate sth such as a machine: *Why do you never read the instruction manual?*

textbook /ˈtekstbʊk/ (*AmE* also **text**) [C] a book that teaches a particular subject and that is used especially in schools and colleges: *a school/medical/history textbook* ◇ *I would not recommend it as a classroom textbook.* See also **text** → LITERATURE, **text** → SCRIPT

text [C] a book, play or piece of writing, especially one that you study as part of a programme of study: *It is one of the most difficult literary texts of all time.* ◇ *(BrE)'Macbeth' is a set text for the exam.* ❶ A **text** can also mean a **textbook**, especially in American English: *Students are requested not to buy texts prior to the first class.*

volume [C] (*formal*) a book: *She published her first book, a slim volume of poetry, at the age of sixteen.* ❶ **Volume** can be used in formal contexts when you are considering the size of a book or the number of books: *a slim/thick volume* ◇ *a library of over 50 000 volumes* It is not used in more general contexts: *His desk was covered with piles of volumes.* ◇ *The volume has received some terrible reviews.* See also **volume** → CHAPTER

border noun

border · boundary · line · frontier
These are all words for a line that marks the edge of sth and separates it from other areas or things.

PATTERNS AND COLLOCATIONS
▸ **across/along/on/over** a/the border/boundary/line/frontier
▸ **inside/within/beyond/outside** the borders/boundaries/frontiers
▸ **at** the boundary/frontier
▸ the border/boundary/line/frontier **between** one place and another
▸ the border/boundary/frontier **with** a place
▸ **north/south/east/west/one side/both sides** of the border/boundary/line/frontier
▸ the **northern/southern/eastern/western** border/boundary/frontier
▸ a **national/common** border/boundary/frontier
▸ to **form/mark/cross** a/the border/boundary/line/frontier
▸ to **arrive at/reach/stop at** a/the border/boundary/frontier
▸ to **share** a border/boundary/frontier

border [C] the line that separates two countries or areas; the land near this line: *They spent a week in a national park on the border between Kenya and Tanzania.* ◇ *The treaty fixed Denmark's new border with Germany.* ◇ *I live in a small town in the US, near the Canadian border.* ◇ *Thousands of illegal immigrants cross the border every day.*

boundary /ˈbaʊndri/ [C] a line that marks the edges of an area of land and separates it from other areas: *After the war the national boundaries were redrawn.* ◇ *Three settlers were killed in a boundary dispute last week.* ◇ *The fence marked the boundary between my property and hers.*

line [C] a long thin mark on the ground to show the limit or border of sth, especially of a playing area in some sports; an imaginary boundary between one area of land and another; a line on a map that shows this: *The ball went over the line.* ◇ *(BrE) The two horses crossed the finishing line together.* ◇ *(AmE) the finish line* ◇ *He was convicted of illegally importing weapons across state lines.* ◇ *Lines of longitude and latitude are marked on the map.*

frontier /ˈfrʌntɪə(r); AmE frʌnˈtɪr/ [C] (*BrE*) the line that separates two countries or areas; the land near this line: *The river formed the frontier between the land of the Saxons and that of the Danes.* ◇ *There were very few border controls on the south-western frontier.* ❶ **The frontier** [sing.] is used in both British and American English to talk about the edge of land where people live and have built towns, beyond which the country is wild and unknown, especially in the Western US in the 19th century: *a remote frontier settlement* ◇ *(figurative) Is space the final frontier?*

> **NOTE** WHICH WORD? The point where you cross from one country to another is usually called the **border**. In British English it can also be called the **frontier**, but this is often in a context of wildness, danger and uncertainty: *The rebels control the frontier and the surrounding area.* The line on a map that shows the border of a country can be called the **boundary** but 'boundary' is NOT used when you cross from one country to another: *After the war the national boundaries were redrawn.* ◇ *Thousands of immigrants cross the boundary every day.* **Boundary** is used for the borders between counties in Britain, both on the map and on the ground: *We crossed the county boundary into Devon.* States and counties in the US are separated by **lines** but 'line' is NOT used for national borders: *crossing state/county lines* ◇ *national lines.* **Boundary** can also be a physical line between two places, for example between property belonging to two different people, marked by a fence or wall: *the boundary fence/wall between the properties*

bored adj. See also the entry for UNHAPPY 2

bored · fed up · sick of sth
These words all describe a person who feels tired and impatient because of a situation that has continued for too long.

PATTERNS AND COLLOCATIONS
▸ bored/fed up/sick **of** sth
▸ bored/fed up **with** sth
▸ to **get** bored/fed up/sick of sth
▸ **really** bored/fed up/sick of sth
▸ bored/sick **to death** (of sb/sth)

bored feeling tired and impatient because you have lost interest in sb/sth or because you have nothing to do: *The children quickly got bored with staying indoors.* ◇ *There was a bored expression on her face.* ◇ *You must be bored stiff stuck at home all day.* OPP **interested** → INTERESTED
▸ **bore** verb [T]: *I'm not boring you, am I?* ◇ *He was a restless child and easily bored.*
▸ **boredom** noun [U]: *I started to eat too much out of sheer boredom.*

fed 'up [not before noun] (*rather informal, especially spoken*) bored or not happy, especially with a situation that has continued for too long: *You look fed up. What's the matter?* ◇ *In the end, I just got fed up with his constant complaining.* ◇ *He still sounds pretty fed up about everything.*

sick of sth [not before noun] (*informal*) bored with or annoyed about sth that has continued for too long: *You get sick of the same old routine day after day.* ◇ *I'm sick and tired of your moaning.*

boring *adj.*

boring · dull · tedious · repetitive · monotonous · uninteresting · dry
These words all describe a subject, activity, person or place that is not interesting or exciting.

PATTERNS AND COLLOCATIONS
▸ to be boring / dull / tedious / uninteresting **for** sb
▸ boring / dull / tedious / dry **subjects / books**
▸ boring / dull / tedious / repetitive / monotonous **jobs / work**
▸ boring / dull / tedious **games / lectures / details**
▸ a boring / dull / tedious **evening**
▸ a boring / a dull / an uninteresting **place**
▸ a boring / dull **man / woman / person**
▸ **rather** boring / dull / tedious / repetitive / monotonous / uninteresting / dry
▸ **very** boring / dull / tedious / repetitive / uninteresting / dry
▸ **pretty** boring / dull / tedious / uninteresting

boring (*disapproving*) not interesting; making you feel tired and impatient: *He's such a boring man!* ◇ *Try not to make the diet boring.* ◇ (*BrE, informal, spoken*) *That film was dead boring.* **OPP** **interesting** → INTERESTING
▸ **boredom** *noun* [U]: *Television helps to relieve the boredom of the long winter evenings.*
dull (*disapproving*) not interesting or exciting: *Life in a small town could be deadly dull.* ◇ *The work gets a bit dull at times.* ◇ *There's never a dull moment when John's around.* **OPP** **interesting** → INTERESTING
tedious /'ti:diəs/ (*disapproving*) lasting or taking too long and not interesting, so that you feel bored and impatient: *The journey soon became tedious.* ◇ *It was tedious, repetitive work.* ◇ *We had to listen to all the tedious details of his operation.*
▸ **tedium** /'ti:diəm/ *noun* [U]: (*written*) *She longed for something to relieve the tedium of everyday life.*
repetitive /rɪ'petətɪv/ (*often disapproving*) saying or doing the same thing many times, so that it becomes boring: *Machines can now perform many repetitive tasks in the home.*
monotonous /mə'nɒtənəs; *AmE* mə'nɑ:t-/ (*disapproving*) never changing and therefore boring: *a monotonous voice / diet / routine* ◇ *New secretaries came and went with monotonous regularity.*
▸ **monotonously** *adv.*: *As the clock ticked monotonously on the wall Mr Simons slowly and methodically cut up and ate his food.*
▸ **monotony** /mə'nɒtəni; *AmE* mə'nɑ:t-/ *noun* [U]: *She watches television to relieve the monotony of everyday life.*
uninteresting (*disapproving*) not attracting your interest or attention: *The food was dull and uninteresting.* **OPP** **interesting** → INTERESTING, See also **uninterested** → INDIFFERENT
dry (*disapproving*) boring because it lacks human interest: *Government reports tend to make dry reading.*

borrow *verb*

borrow · beg · scrounge
These words all mean to get sb to lend or give you sth that belongs to them.

PATTERNS AND COLLOCATIONS
▸ to borrow / beg / scrounge (sth) **from** sb
▸ to borrow / scrounge sth **off** sb
▸ to beg / scrounge **for** sth
▸ to borrow / beg for **money**

borrow [T, I] to take and use sth that belongs to sb else, and return it to them at a later time; to take money from a person or bank and agree to pay it back to them at a later time: *Can I borrow your pen?* ◇ *You can borrow the book from the local library.* ◇ *How much did you have to borrow to pay for this?* ◇ *I don't like to borrow from friends.* **OPP** **lend** → LEND
beg (-**gg**-) [I, T] to ask sb for money, food, etc., especially in the street when you have nothing: *There were homeless people begging in the streets.* ◇ *He gets thousands of begging letters* (= letters asking for money). ◇ *We managed to beg a meal from the cafe owner.* See also **beggar** → TRAMP
scrounge /skraʊndʒ/ [T, I] (*informal, disapproving*) to get sth from sb by asking them to give it to you because you do not want to pay for it: *Can I scrounge a cigarette off you?* ◇ *I don't want to spend my life scrounging from other people.* See also **scrounger** → TRAMP

bottle *noun* See also the entry for PACKET

bottle · pot · jug · pitcher · flask · vial · decanter
These words all mean a container for holding or serving liquids and drinks.

PATTERNS AND COLLOCATIONS
▸ a bottle / a pot / a jug / a pitcher / a flask / a vial / a decanter **of** sth
▸ **in** a bottle / a pot / a jug / a pitcher / a flask / a vial / a decanter
▸ **a four-pint / two-litre, etc.** bottle / pot / jug / pitcher / flask / decanter
▸ a **glass** bottle / pot / jug / pitcher / vial / decanter
▸ a **wine** bottle / jug / pitcher / flask / decanter
▸ a **water** bottle / jug / pitcher / flask
▸ a **milk** bottle / jug / pitcher
▸ to **fill** a bottle / pot / jug / pitcher / flask / vial / decanter

bottle [C] a glass or plastic container, usually round with straight sides and a narrow neck, used especially for storing liquids: *a wine / beer / milk bottle* ◇ *Put the top back on the bottle.* ◇ *We drank a whole bottle of wine.*
pot [C] (especially in compounds) a container of various kinds, made for a particular purpose; a bowl or other round object that is made by a potter (= a person who makes clay pots by hand): *a teapot* ◇ *a coffee pot* ◇ *a flower pot* (= a round container for growing plants in) ◇ *Is there any more tea in the pot?* ◇ *She made a pot of strong coffee.* ◇ *The newly made pots are glazed when they are completely dry.* ❶ **Pot** has a very wide range and can describe many different kinds of container. Pots are usually round, and many kinds of pot are made of clay.
jug [C] (*especially BrE*) a container for holding and serving liquids which has a handle and a lip (= a shaped opening on the side at the top) for pouring: *Pour the milk into a measuring jug.* ◇ *She spilled a jug of water.* ❶ The usual American English word for **jug** in this meaning is **pitcher**. In American English a **jug** is also a large plastic bottle used to hold milk or fruit juice; in British English this is a *plastic milk bottle / container.* A smaller container for milk or juice made of cardboard is called a **carton** in both British and American English. See also **carton** → PACKET
pitcher /'pɪtʃə(r)/ [C] (*AmE*) a jug: *Pour the ingredients into a pitcher, add ice and stir.*
flask [C] a bottle with a narrow top, used in scientific work for mixing or storing chemicals; a small flat bottle, usually made of metal, that fits in your pocket and is used for carrying alcohol: *Heat the solution gently in a conical flask.* ◇ *He reached into a pocket of his greatcoat and brought out a flat silver flask.*
vial /'vaɪəl/ (*BrE* also **phial** /'faɪəl/) [C] a small glass container, especially one that is used for chemicals, medicine or perfume: *a vial of pills / perfume / toilet water*
decanter /dɪ'kæntə(r)/ [C] a glass bottle, often decorated, that wine and other alcoholic drinks are poured into from an ordinary bottle before serving: *a crystal port decanter* See also **decant** → POUR

bottom *noun*

bottom · base · foundation · foot
These are all words for the lowest part of sth.

▸ **at / near / towards** the bottom / base / foot of sth
▸ **on** the bottom / base of sth
▸ (a) **firm / solid / strong** base / foundations
▸ to **have** a bottom / a base / foundations

bottom [C, usually sing.] the lowest part of sth: *Footnotes are given at the bottom of each page.* ◇ *The wind blew through gaps at the top and bottom of the door.* ◇ *I waited for them at the bottom of the hill.* ◇ *The book I want is right at the bottom* (= of the pile). **OPP top** → TOP

base [C, usually sing.] the lowest part of sth, especially the part or surface on which it rests or stands: *The lamp has a heavy base.* ◇ *He felt a sharp pain at the base of his spine.* ◇ *Four bronze lions stand at the base of the column.*

foundation [C, usually pl.] a layer of bricks, concrete, etc. that forms the solid underground base of a building: *The builders are now beginning to* **lay the foundations** *of the new school.* ◇ *The explosion shook the foundations of the houses nearby.*

foot [sing.] the lowest part of sth: *At the foot of the stairs she turned to face him.*

NOTE **BOTTOM** OR **FOOT?** **Foot** is used to talk about a limited number of things: it is used most often with *tree, hill, mountain, steps, stairs* and *page.* **Bottom** can be used to talk about a much wider range of things. **Foot** is generally used in more literary contexts.

box *noun*

box · basket · case · crate · container · tin · hamper · carton
These are all words for containers for holding or transporting solid things.

▸ a box / basket / case / crate / tin / hamper / carton **of** sth
▸ **in** a box / basket / case / crate / container / tin / hamper / carton
▸ a **jewellery** box / case
▸ a **picnic / laundry** basket / hamper
▸ to **fill** a box / basket / case / crate / tin
▸ to **carry** a box / basket / crate

box [C] (especially in compounds) a container with a flat base and sides and often a lid, usually made of a stiff material like wood, cardboard or metal, and used especially for holding solid things; a box and its contents, or the amount of sth that the box can hold: *Everything we owned was neatly packed in cardboard boxes.* ◇ *a money box* ◇ *a toolbox* ◇ *The device is about the size of a matchbox.* ◇ *He produced a box of matches from his pocket.* ◇ *a box of chocolates*

basket [C] a container for holding or carrying things made of thin strips of material that bends and twists easily, for example plastic, wood or wire; a basket and its contents, or the amount of sth that the basket can hold: *The logs were in a wicker basket next to the fireplace.* ◇ *a shopping basket* ◇ *a cat basket* (= in which a cat sleeps or is carried around) ◇ *She found a basket of fruit waiting for her in the hotel room.*

case [C] (especially in compounds) a container or covering used to protect or store things; a case and its contents, or the amount of sth that the case can hold: *The museum was full of stuffed animals in glass cases.* ◇ *a pencil case* ◇ *a packing case* (= a large wooden box for packing things in) ◇ *The winner will receive a case of champagne* (= 12 bottles).

crate [C] a large wooden container for transporting goods; a container made of plastic, wood or metal divided into small sections, for transporting or storing bottles; a crate and its contents, or the amount of sth that the crate can hold: *The spider was found hiding in a crate of bananas.* ◇ *An old man was sitting on an upturned beer crate.* ◇ *They drank two crates of beer.*

container [C] a large box of a standard size, usually made of metal, in which goods are packed so that they can easily be lifted onto a ship, train or lorry to be transported: *It's a thirty thousand tonne* **container ship** (= a ship designed to transport containers).

tin [C] a metal container with a lid, used for keeping food in: *a cake/biscuit/cookie tin* ◇ *This cake will keep moist for several days if stored in an airtight tin.*

hamper [C] a large basket with a lid, especially one used to carry food in: *a picnic hamper* ❶ Especially in British English a **hamper** can also be a box or parcel containing food, sent as a gift: *The lucky winner will receive a luxury hamper crammed full of local produce.* In American English a **hamper** is also a large container, often a basket, used for keeping dirty clothes in while they are waiting to be washed: *a laundry/clothes hamper.* In British English this is called a *laundry basket.*

carton [C] (*especially AmE*) a large container in which goods are packed in smaller containers; a carton and its contents, or the amount of sth that the carton can hold: *A carton of cigarettes contains 10 packets.*

brand *noun*

brand · model · make · label
These are all words for a type of product made by a particular company, or a company that makes a particular type of product.

▸ a brand / model / make **of** car
▸ a **popular / leading / major / famous / well-known** brand / model / make / label

brand [C] a type of product made by a particular company, especially a food or drink product that you might buy in a supermarket: *Which brand of toothpaste do you use?* ◇ (*BrE*) *You pay less for the supermarket's* **own brand.** ◇ (*AmE*) *You pay less for the* **store brand.** ◇ *Our main aim is to encourage* **brand loyalty** (= the tendency of customers to continue buying the same brand). ◇ *Champagne houses owe their success to* **brand image.**

model [C] a particular design or type of product, especially a vehicle or machine, that is made by a particular company: *The latest models will be on display at the motor show.*

make [C] the name of the company that makes a particular product, especially a vehicle or machine: *What make of car does he drive?*

NOTE **MODEL** OR **MAKE?** All cars made by one company are the same **make.** For each make there will be a range of different **models** (= designs): *We need to know the make, model and year of your car.*

label [C] a company that produces and sells CDs: *the Virgin record label* ◇ *It's his first release for a major label.*

brave *adj.* See also the entry for BOLD

brave · courageous · heroic · gallant · fearless · gutsy
These words all describe sb who is willing to do difficult or dangerous things.

▸ a brave / courageous / heroic / gallant **attempt / effort / action / resistance / struggle**
▸ a brave / courageous **decision**
▸ brave / heroic **deeds**
▸ a brave / courageous / gallant / fearless **soldier**
▸ a brave / fearless **warrior**

brave (of a person) willing to do things which are difficult, dangerous or painful; (of an action) showing no fear of doing sth difficult, dangerous or painful: *Be brave!* ◇ *I wasn't brave enough to tell her what I thought of her.* ◇ *She died after a brave fight against cancer.* ◇ *I had to* **put on a brave face** *and try to show him that I wasn't worried.* **OPP cowardly** → COWARD, See also **bravery** → COURAGE

▸ **bravely** adv.: Though they fought bravely, they were no match for the trained mercenaries.

courageous /kə'reɪdʒəs/ willing to face danger, pain or opposition, especially when doing sth that you believe to be right: I think he made a very courageous decision to resign. ◇ I hope people will be courageous enough to speak out against this injustice. See also **courage** → COURAGE

heroic /hə'rəʊɪk; AmE -'roʊ-/ showing extreme courage and admired by many people: She is a heroic figure we can all look up to. ◇ Rescuers made heroic efforts to save the crew. See also **heroism** → COURAGE
▸ **heroically** adv.

gallant /'gælənt/ (old-fashioned or literary) brave, especially in war or a very difficult situation: Our gallant soldiers have had to endure many hardships in the field. ◇ She made a gallant attempt to hide her tears.
▸ **gallantly** adv.

fearless (written) not afraid, in a way that people admire: He was known as a powerful king and a fearless warrior. ◇ She was fearless and full of energy. **OPP** **fearful** → AFRAID

gutsy /'gʌtsi/ (informal) showing strength, courage and determination: Her gutsy performance in the game impressed everyone, even her teammates. See also **guts** → COURAGE

break verb

1 break a window/leg
2 a machine breaks
3 break the law
4 break a promise

1 See also the entry for SMASH

break · crack · fracture · snap
These words all refer to sth being damaged as a result of force, usually so that it separates into two or more parts.

PATTERNS AND COLLOCATIONS
▸ to break / crack / fracture **a bone / rib**
▸ to break / fracture **your hip / jaw / wrist**
▸ to crack / fracture **your skull**
▸ to break / crack a / an **cup / egg / mirror**
▸ a **branch / cable / rope** breaks / snaps
▸ a broken / cracked / fractured **pipe**

break [I, T] to damage sth or be damaged so that it separates into two or more parts, as a result of force: She dropped the plate and it **broke into pieces**. ◇ She fell off a ladder and broke her arm. ◇ I didn't mean to break the window. ◇ He **broke** the chocolate **in two** and gave me half. ◇ How did this dish **get broken**?
▸ **breakage** /'breɪkɪdʒ/ noun [C, U]: The last time we moved house there were very few breakages. ◇ Wrap it up carefully to protect against breakage.

crack [I, T] (of sth hard) to break so that lines appear in it, but without dividing into separate parts; to break sth in this way: The ice cracked as I stepped on it. ◇ The leather / mud / paint / plaster had cracked. ◇ He has cracked a bone in his arm. ◇ Her lips were dry and cracked. ❶ Less frequently, to **crack** can involve breaking into separate parts, if it is used with a preposition: She cracked an egg into the pan. See also **crack** → CRACK noun

fracture /'fræktʃə(r)/ [I, T] (rather formal) to break or crack; to make sth break or crack: Cast iron is not only heavy, but likely to fracture. ◇ A gas escape from a fractured pipe was the likely cause of the explosion. ◇ He fell and fractured his skull.
▸ **fracture** noun [C, U]: She sustained two **fractures to her leg**. ◇ Ground movements could cause fracture of the pipe.

NOTE BREAK, CRACK OR FRACTURE? Any of these verbs can be used for bones; **break** or **fracture** but NOT **crack** can be used for joints: ~~He cracked his hip/jaw/wrist.~~; only **break** can be used for arms and legs: ~~She cracked/ fractured her arm/leg.~~ **Fracture** is the usual verb for talking about skulls (= the bone structure in the head); you can also use **crack**, but NOT **break**: ~~He fell and broke his skull.~~

snap (-pp-) [I, T] to break suddenly into two pieces with a sharp noise; to break sth in this way: Suddenly the rope snapped. ◇ The wind had snapped the tree in two.

2 break · fail · break down · go wrong · crash · go down
These are all words that can be used when a machine stops working because of a fault.

PATTERNS AND COLLOCATIONS
▸ a **video / watch** breaks / goes wrong
▸ a **washing machine** breaks down / goes wrong
▸ an **engine** fails / breaks down
▸ a **computer** goes wrong / crashes
▸ a **system** fails / crashes / goes down

break [I, T] (of a device or small machine) to stop working as a result of being damaged; to damage a device or small machine and stop it from working: My watch has broken. ◇ I think I've broken the video.

fail [I] (of a system, part of a machine or system, or part of the body) to stop working: The air-conditioning system failed on the hottest day of the year. ◇ The brakes on my bike failed halfway down the hill.
▸ **failure** noun [U, C]: patients suffering from heart / kidney failure ◇ A **power failure** plunged everything into darkness.

break 'down phrasal verb (of a machine or vehicle) to stop working because of a fault: The washing machine has broken down again. ◇ We (= our car) broke down on the motorway.
▸ **breakdown** /'breɪkdaʊn/ noun: a breakdown on the motorway

go 'wrong phrase to stop working correctly: My watch keeps going wrong. ◇ The new television set will contain fewer components to go wrong. ❶ Machines, devices and parts inside machines and vehicles can **go wrong**; whole vehicles cannot: ~~The car has gone wrong again.~~ If sth **goes wrong**, it may not stop working completely, as it does if it **breaks** or **breaks down**.

crash [I, T] (of a computer or computer system) to stop working suddenly; to make a computer or computer system stop working suddenly: Files can be lost if the system suddenly crashes.
▸ **crash** noun [C]: A systems crash in the morning and a bomb scare in the afternoon provided enough excitement.

go 'down phrasal verb [I] (of a computer system) to stop working temporarily: The system is going down in ten minutes.

NOTE CRASH OR GO DOWN? Individual computers or whole systems can **crash** and this is always sudden and unexpected; when a system **goes down**, it may have been turned off deliberately to prevent people from using it while work is carried out on it.

3 break · breach · infringe · violate
These words all mean to do sth that is against the law, an agreement or a principle.

PATTERNS AND COLLOCATIONS
▸ to break / breach / infringe a **regulation**
▸ to break / breach / violate a **rule / law / treaty**
▸ to break / infringe / violate a **code**
▸ to break / violate a **ceasefire / truce**
▸ to breach / infringe / violate **copyright**
▸ to breach / infringe / violate **Article** 12 of the treaty

break [T] to do sth that is against the law or a rule or agreement: to break an agreement/a contract ◇ Would you be willing to break the law to achieve your goal? ◇ They insist that they have not broken any rules. ◇ He was breaking the speed limit (= driving faster than the law allows). **OPP** **obey** → FOLLOW 3

breach [T] (formal) to not keep an agreement; to not obey a rule or law: The government is accused of breaching the terms of the treaty. **OPP** **comply** → FOLLOW 3

▶ **breach** noun [C, U]: *a breach of contract/copyright/warranty* ◇ *This action is* **in breach of** *Article 119 of the Constitution.*

NOTE BREAK OR BREACH? Breach is more formal. You can **breach** a particular rule, but you would **break** 'the law' in general.: *areas where EU limits were breached* ◇ ~~They are breaching the law and could be in serious trouble.~~ People *break laws.* Either people or actions can *breach rules.*

infringe /ɪnˈfrɪndʒ/ [T, I] (*formal*) (of an action or plan) to break a law; to limit sb's legal rights: *The material can be copied without infringing copyright.* ◇ *They said that compulsory identity cards would infringe civil liberties.* ◇ *She refused to answer questions that* **infringed on** *her private affairs.*
▶ **infringement** noun [U, C]: *copyright infringement* ◇ *an infringement of his personal liberty*

violate /ˈvaɪəleɪt/ [T] (*formal*) to refuse to obey or keep a law, principle or agreement; to disturb or not respect sb's peace or privacy: *The directive violates fundamental human rights.* ◇ *She accused press photographers of violating her privacy.* **OPP** respect → FOLLOW 3, See also **invade** → INTERFERE
▶ **violation** noun [C, U]: *gross violations of human rights* ◇ *They were* **in** *open* **violation** *of the treaty.*

NOTE INFRINGE OR VIOLATE Violate often describes actions that are not just illegal, but morally wrong. **Infringe** can be about sb's personal rights, but it is not as strong as **violate**, which is more about universal human rights.

4 break · withdraw · do a U-turn · retract · recant · take sth back · backtrack · go back on sth
These words all mean to change an earlier statement, opinion or promise.

PATTERNS AND COLLOCATIONS
▶ to break/ withdraw/ go back on a **promise**
▶ to break/ go back on **your word**/ **an agreement**
▶ to withdraw/ retract a/ an **claim**/ **allegation**/ **confession**

break [T] to not keep a promise or agreement: *I've never broken my word; why should I do it now?* ◇ *She has already broken three appointments* (= not gone to them). **OPP** keep → KEEP 5

withdraw /wɪðˈdrɔː; wɪθˈd-/ [T] (*formal*) to say that you no longer believe that sth you previously said is true: *The newspaper withdrew the allegations the next day.*

do a 'U-turn (*informal, especially journalism*) to make a complete change in policy or behaviour, usually one that is embarrassing: *The Prime Minister may be forced to do another humiliating U-turn on Europe.* ❶ **Do a U-turn** is most often found in contexts relating to politics and business. Because **doing a U-turn** is seen as being an embarrassing experience, it usually used with verbs such as **have to** and **be forced to.** See also **U-turn** → REVOLUTION 2

retract /rɪˈtrækt/ [T] (*formal*) to say that sth you said earlier is not true or correct or that you did not mean it: *He made a false confession which he later retracted.* See also **retraction** → DENIAL

NOTE WITHDRAW OR RETRACT? In many cases you can use either word: *to withdraw/retract a claim/an allegation/ a confession.* However, **retract** is used more often when sb has been forced to say sth (like a *false confession*) that they did not really mean and wish to give their true opinion; **withdraw** is used more often when sb has made a claim or accusation against sb that they cannot prove, and is forced to admit that it is not true.

recant /rɪˈkænt/ [T, I] (*formal*) (especially in the past) to say publicly that you no longer have the same belief or opinion: *In 1633 he was forced to recant his assertion that the earth orbited the sun.*

take sth 'back *phrasal verb* (*rather informal, especially spoken*) to admit that sth you said was wrong or that you should not have said it: *OK, I take it all back!* ❶ **Take sth back** is most often used in spoken expressions such as *Would you like to take that back?* (said to sb who has just offended the speaker), *Can I take that back?* or *I take it (all) back.*

backtrack /ˈbæktræk/ [I] (*especially business or politics*) to change an earlier statement, opinion or promise because of pressure from sb/sth: *The trade unions have had to* **backtrack on** *their main demand.*

go 'back on sth *phrasal verb* (*rather informal*) to fail to keep a promise; to change your mind about sth: *They have no intention of going back on any of their commitments.*

break out *phrasal verb* See the Topic Map for CONFLICT on p.896

break out · erupt · develop · blow up
These words are all used when sth unpleasant starts suddenly or becomes serious.

PATTERNS AND COLLOCATIONS
▶ to erupt/ develop **into** sth
▶ (a) **crisis**/ **row**/ **storm**/ **trouble** breaks out/ erupts/ develops/ blows up
▶ a/ an **argument**/ **controversy**/ **dispute** breaks out/ erupts/ develops
▶ (a) **fight**/ **fighting**/ **riot**/ **violence**/ **war** breaks out/ erupts
▶ to break out/ erupt/ develop/ blow up **suddenly**

break 'out *phrasal verb* (of war, fighting, arguments, diseases or disasters) to start happening suddenly: *They had escaped to America shortly before war broke out.* ◇ *A fierce controversy has broken out over the issue.* ◇ *An epidemic of cholera broke out and over 7 000 people died.* ◇ *Fire broke out during the night.* See also **outbreak** → WAVE 3

erupt /ɪˈrʌpt/ [I] (of war, fighting or arguments) to start happening, suddenly and with force; to get suddenly larger, more serious and more violent: *Violence erupted outside the embassy gates.* ◇ *The unrest erupted into revolution.*

NOTE BREAK OUT OR ERUPT? Erupt suggests a greater degree of violence than **break out**; it is NOT used to talk about diseases or disasters: ~~An epidemic of cholera erupted.~~ ◇ ~~Fire erupted during the night.~~ **Erupt**, but NOT **break out** can be used when an argument or violence suddenly becomes worse: ~~The unrest broke out into revolution.~~

develop [I] to start happening and then become more serious or important: *A crisis was rapidly developing in the Gulf.* See also **development** → EVENT 1

blow 'up *phrasal verb* (*rather informal, especially journalism*) (of a storm, argument or serious situation) to start suddenly and with force: *A storm was blowing up.* ◇ *A crisis has blown up over the President's latest speech.* ❶ The main collocates of **blow up** in this meaning are *storm, trouble, crisis* and *row.*

breath noun

breath · gasp · gulp · sniff
These are all words for an amount of air which enters the lungs at one time.

PATTERNS AND COLLOCATIONS
▶ a **great**/ **big** breath/ gasp/ gulp
▶ a **deep** breath/ gulp/ sniff
▶ a **loud** gasp/ gulp/ sniff

▸ to **take** a breath / gulp / sniff
▸ to **let out** a breath / gasp / sniff
▸ to **give** a gasp / gulp / sniff

breath [C] an amount of air that enters the lungs at one time: *I opened the window and took a deep breath.* ◇ *He recited the whole poem in one breath.* ❶ **Breath** is [U] is the air that you take into your lungs and send out again: *His breath smelt of garlic.* ◇ *We had to stop for breath before we got to the top.*

gasp /gɑːsp; AmE gæsp/ [C] a quick deep breath, usually caused by a strong emotion: *She opened the newspaper and gave a gasp of shock.* ◇ *His breath came in short gasps.* See also **gasp** → BLOW *verb* 2

gulp [C] an act of breathing in or swallowing sth: *She gave an audible gulp.* ◇ *He drank his glass of whisky in one gulp.*

sniff [C] an act or the sound of **sniffing** (= breathing air in noisily through your nose): *She held the bottle to her nose and took a good sniff.* ◇ *My mother gave a sniff of disapproval.* See also **sniff** → BLOW *verb* 2

bribe *noun* See also the entry for INCENTIVE

bribe · bait · pay-off · kickback
These are all words for sth which is used to persuade sb to do sth you want them to.

PATTERNS AND COLLOCATIONS
▸ bait / a pay-off / a kickback **for** sb
▸ a £1 000 / $500, etc. bribe / pay-off
▸ to **offer (sb)** a bribe / a pay-off
▸ to **offer sth as** a bribe / bait
▸ to **pay sb** a bribe / kickback
▸ to **take** bribes / the bait / kickbacks

bribe [C] a sum of money or sth valuable that you give or offer to sb to persuade them to do sth, especially to help you by doing sth dishonest: *She had been offered a $50 000 bribe to drop the charges.* ◇ *It was alleged that he had taken bribes while in office.* ◇ *The tax cut was described as a pre-election bribe.* See also **bribery** → CORRUPTION
▸ **bribe** *verb* [T]: *They bribed the guards with cigarettes.* ◇ *She was bribed into handing over secret information.*

bait [U, C] a person or thing that is used to attract, trick or catch sb, especially to make them do what you want: *The police used him as bait to trap the killers.* ◇ *She covered her face and began to sob, but he wouldn't rise to the bait (= react as she wanted him to).*

pay-off [C] (*informal, usually disapproving*) a sum of money paid to sb so that they will not cause you any trouble, to make them keep a secret, or to persuade them to leave their job: *The government are investigating pay-offs to high-ranking officials.* ◇ *The Chief Executive left a year early with a £1.5 million pay-off.*
▸ **pay sb 'off** *phrasal verb*: *All the witnesses had been paid off.*

kickback /ˈkɪkbæk/ [C] (*especially AmE, rather informal*) a sum of money paid illegally to sb in return for work or help, especially to politicians or officials as part of a business deal: *They were accused of paying kickbacks to politicians to obtain public contracts.*

bright *adj.* See also the entry for STRONG 3

bright · brilliant · vivid · vibrant · bold
These words all describe things that are shining or full of light, or colours that are strong and easy to see.

PATTERNS AND COLLOCATIONS
▸ bright / brilliant / vivid / vibrant / bold **colours**
▸ bright / brilliant **light / sunlight / sunshine / eyes**

bright full of light; shining strongly; (of colours) strong and easy to see: *a bright room* ◇ *a bright morning* (= with the sun shining) ◇ *Her eyes were bright with tears.* ◇ *a bright yellow dress* ◇ *a bright tie* **OPP** dim, faint → DIM 1, **dim, gloomy** → DIM 2, **grey, dull** → CLOUDY, **dull** → PALE 1
▸ **brightly** *adv.*: *a brightly lit room*

brilliant very bright: *brilliant blue eyes* ◇ *The sky was a brilliant blue.*
▸ **brilliantly** *adv.*: *It was brilliantly sunny.*

vivid /ˈvɪvɪd/ (*approving*) (of colours) bright and strong: *His eyes were a vivid green.*

vibrant /ˈvaɪbrənt/ (*approving*) (of colours) bright and strong: *The room was decorated in vibrant blues and greens.*

NOTE VIVID OR VIBRANT? **Vivid** emphasizes how bright a colour is; **vibrant** suggests a more lively and exciting colour or combination of colours.

bold /bəʊld; AmE boʊld/ (of colours) strong, clear and easy to see: *a bold black and yellow sign* ◇ *The furniture was painted in bold, primary colours.*
▸ **boldly** *adv.*: *boldly patterned / coloured*

NOTE BRIGHT OR BOLD? **Bold** emphasizes how easy to see a colour is, especially in contrast to what is around it. It can be used with a wider range of colours than **bright**, which is used with light colours.

bring sb up *phrasal verb*

bring sb up · adopt · raise · rear · foster · be born and bred
These words all refer to how a child grows up and is cared for.

PATTERNS AND COLLOCATIONS
▸ to be brought up / raised / reared / born and bred **in** a place
▸ to be brought up / raised / reared / born and bred **as** sth
▸ to be brought up / raised / reared / born and bred (**as**) a **Catholic / Protestant / Muslim / Jew**, etc.
▸ to bring up / adopt / raise / rear / foster a **child**
▸ to bring up / adopt / raise / rear a **daughter / son / family**
▸ to bring up / adopt / raise / foster a **baby**
▸ to raise / rear **young / animals / sheep / chickens / poultry**

bring sb 'up *phrasal verb* [often passive] to care for a child, teaching him/her how to behave, until he/she is grown up: *She brought up five children.* ◇ *He was brought up by his aunt.* ◇ *What a well brought up child!* ◇ *They were brought up (= taught as children) to respect authority.*

adopt [I, T] to take sb else's child into your family and become its legal parent(s): *He led a campaign to encourage childless couples to adopt.* ◇ *She was forced to have her baby adopted.* See also **take sb in** → ACCOMMODATE
▸ **adoption** /əˈdɒpʃn; AmE əˈdɑːpʃn/ *noun* [U, C]: *She put the baby up for adoption.*

raise [T, often passive] (*especially AmE*) to care for a child or young animal until it is grown up: *They were both raised in the South.* ◇ *These kids have been raised on a diet of hamburgers.* ◇ *I was born and raised a city boy.* See also **raise** → KEEP 4

NOTE BRING SB UP OR RAISE? When it is used in British English to talk about caring for a child, **raise** is slightly more formal than **bring sb up**.

rear /rɪə(r); AmE rɪr/ [T, often passive] (*rather formal*) to care for young animals or children until they are grown up: *She reared a family of five on her own.* ◇ *Lions usually manage to rear about half the number of cubs born to them.* See also **rear** → KEEP 4

NOTE RAISE OR REAR? **Raise** is more often used to talk about children; **rear** is more often used to talk about animals.

foster [T, I] (*especially BrE*) to take sb else's child into your family for a period of time, without becoming his or her legal parent(s): *They have fostered over 60 children during the past ten years.* ◇ *We couldn't adopt a child, so we decided to foster.*
▸ **foster** *adj.* [only before noun]: *a foster mother / father / family / child / home* ◇ *foster parents* ◇ *foster care*

be ‚born and 'bred *idiom* to have been born and to have grown up in a particular place with a particular background and education: *He was born and bred in Boston.* ◇ *I'm a Londoner, born and bred.*

brood *verb*

brood · pout · sulk · mope
These words all mean to behave in way that shows that you are angry or upset.

PATTERNS AND COLLOCATIONS
▸ to brood / sulk / mope **about** sth
▸ to brood / sulk **over** sth

brood /bruːd/ [I] (*sometimes disapproving*) to think a lot about sth that makes you annoyed, anxious or upset: *You're not still brooding over what he said, are you?* ◇ *He sits in his armchair* **brooding on** *how life has let him down.*
pout /paʊt/ [I, T] (*often disapproving*) to push out your lips, to show that you are annoyed or unhappy about sth; (of sb's lips) to be pushed out in this way: *She pouted angrily.* ◇ *The young clerk* **pouted his lips** *as if he was going to object.* ❶ You can also **pout** to look sexually attractive: *Her* **lips pouted** *invitingly.*
▸ **pout** *noun* [sing.]: *Her lips were set in a pout of annoyance.*
sulk [I] (*disapproving*) to look angry and refuse to speak or smile because you want people to know that you are upset about sth: *He went off to sulk in his room.* See also **sulk → TEMPER** *noun*, **sulky → IRRITABLE**
mope [I] (*disapproving*) to spend your time doing nothing and feeling sorry for yourself: *Instead of* **moping around** *the house all day, you should be out there looking for a job.*

brush *verb* See also the entries for CLEAN and WIPE

brush · scrub · sweep · dust · comb · groom
These words all mean to make sth clean or neat by using a brush, cloth or comb.

PATTERNS AND COLLOCATIONS
▸ to brush / sweep / dust sth **off** / **from** sth
▸ to brush / sweep sth **away**
▸ to brush / comb your **hair**
▸ to scrub / sweep the **floor**
▸ to scrub / dust the **table** / **surfaces**
▸ to brush / scrub / sweep sth **clean**

brush [T] to clean, polish or make sth smooth with a brush; to remove sth from a surface with a brush or your hand: *to brush your hair/teeth/shoes* ◇ *The non-slip surface is easy to brush clean.* ◇ *He brushed the dirt off his jacket.* ◇ *She brushed the fly away.*
▸ **brush** *noun* [sing.]: *to give your hair/teeth a good brush*
scrub (-**bb**-) [T, I] to clean sth by rubbing it hard, often with a brush and usually with soap and water: *She scrubbed the counters down with bleach.* ◇ *The woman* **scrubbed at** *her face with a tissue.*
▸ **scrub** *noun* [sing.]: *I've given the floor a good scrub.*
sweep [T] to clean a room or surface using a broom (= a type of brush with a long handle); to remove sth from a surface with a brush or your hand: *to sweep the floor/ street/stairs* ◇ *She swept the crumbs into the wastebasket.* ◇ *He* **swept** *the leaves* **up** *into a pile.*
dust [I, T] to clean furniture or a room by removing dust from surfaces with a cloth; to remove dirt from a surface with your hands or a brush: *I broke the vase while I was dusting.* ◇ *Could you dust the sitting room?* ◇ *She dusted some ash from her sleeve.*
comb /kəʊm; *AmE* koʊm/ [T] to pull a comb through your hair in order to make it neat: *Don't forget to comb your hair.*
▸ **comb** *noun* [sing.]: *Your hair needs a good comb.*
groom /gruːm/ [T] to clean or brush an animal: *to groom a horse/dog/cat*
▸ **grooming** *noun* [U]: *Grooming is a vital part of caring for your dog.*

build *verb*

build · construct · assemble · erect · set sth up · put sth up
These words all mean to make sth, especially by putting different parts together.

PATTERNS AND COLLOCATIONS
▸ to build / construct sth **from** / **out of** / **of** sth
▸ to build / construct / assemble a **machine** / **engine**
▸ to build / construct / erect / set up / put up a **barrier**
▸ to build / construct / erect / put up a **house** / **shelter** / **wall** / **fence**
▸ to build / construct / erect / put up some **shelves**
▸ to build / construct / erect a **bridge**
▸ to build / construct a **road** / **railway** / **railroad** / **tunnel** / **nest**
▸ to erect / put up a **tent** / **statue** / **monument**

build [T, I] to make sth, especially a building, by putting parts together: *Robins build nests almost anywhere.* ◇ *a house built of stone* ◇ *apartment blocks* **built in** *brick and concrete* ◇ *They had a house built for them.* ◇ *David built us a shed in the backyard.* ◇ *They're going to build on the site of the old power station.* **OPP** **demolish → DEMOLISH**, See also **builder → MAKER**, **building → PRODUCTION**
construct [T, often passive] (*rather formal*) to build sth such as a road, building or machine: *When was the bridge constructed?* ◇ *They constructed a shelter out of fallen branches.* **OPP** **demolish → DEMOLISH**, See also **construction → PRODUCTION**, **construction → STRUCTURE**
assemble /əˈsembl/ [T] (*rather formal*) to fit together all the separate parts of sth such as a piece of furniture or a machine: *The shelves are easy to assemble.* ◇ *The company assembles vehicles for Renault and Toyota.* See also **assembly → PRODUCTION**
erect /ɪˈrekt/ [T] (*formal*) to build sth; to put sth in position and make it stand upright: *The church was erected in 1582.* ◇ *Police had to erect barriers to keep crowds back.*
‚**set sth 'up** *phrasal verb* to build sth or place sth somewhere: *The police set up roadblocks on routes out of the city.* ◇ *We decided to* **set up camp** *for the night.*
‚**put sth 'up** *phrasal verb* to build sth or place sth somewhere: *They're putting up new hotels to boost tourism in the area.* ◇ *Do you know how to put this tent up?*

NOTE SET STH UP OR PUT STH UP? **Set sth up** is not used for permanent buildings: ~~They're setting up new hotels.~~ You *set up camp* but *put up a tent.* For other temporary structures you can use either word: *to set up/put up a fence/barrier/shelter*

building *noun*

building · property · premises · complex · structure · block
These are all words for a structure such as a house, office block or factory that has a roof and four walls.

PATTERNS AND COLLOCATIONS
▸ (a) **commercial** / **residential** building / property / premises / complex / block
▸ a / an **factory** / **hospital** / **office** building / premises / complex / block
▸ a / an **prison** / **apartment** building / complex / block
▸ a / an **imposing** / **magnificent** building / structure
▸ a **brick** / **stone** building / structure
▸ to **build** a property / a complex / a structure / a block
▸ to **erect** a building / complex / structure / block
▸ to **put up** a building / structure / block
▸ to **demolish** a building / property / complex / structure / block
▸ to **pull down** a building / a structure / a block
▸ to **restore** / **renovate** a building / property

building [C] a structure such as a house, office block or factory that has a roof and four walls: *a tall/high-rise/ten-storey building* ◇ *The Blue Mosque at Isfahan is the most beautiful building I have ever seen.*

property [C, U] a building or buildings and the surrounding land; land and buildings: *We have a potential buyer who would like to view the property.* ◇ *The price of property has risen enormously.* ◇ *a property developer* ❶ **Property** is often used when talking about buying/ selling houses or other buildings and land.

premises [pl.] the building or buildings and surrounding land that a business owns or uses: *The company is looking for larger premises.* ◇ *No alcohol may be consumed **on the premises**.* ◇ *Police were called to escort her **off the premises**.*

complex [C] a group of buildings of a similar type together in one place: *a leisure/sports/shopping complex*

structure [C] a thing that is made of several parts, especially a building: *The pier is a wooden structure and was built in 1867.*

block [C] (*especially BrE*) a tall building that contains flats or offices; a building that forms part of a school, hospital, etc. and is used for a particular purpose: (*BrE*) *a block of flats* ◇ (*BrE*) *a tower block* ◇ *the school's science block* ◇ (*especially AmE*) *an apartment block*

build up *phrasal verb*

build up · accumulate · pile up · accrue · multiply · mount up
These words all mean to increase in number or amount over a period of time.

PATTERNS AND COLLOCATIONS
▸ to build up/ multiply/ mount up **to** sth **a large number/ amount, 50 000, etc.**
▸ **debts** build up/ accumulate/ pile up/ mount up
▸ **problems** build up/ accumulate/ multiply
▸ to build up/accumulate/pile up/mount up **slowly/gradually/ steadily**
▸ to build up/ accumulate/ multiply **rapidly**
▸ to build up/ pile up/ multiply/ mount up **quickly**

,build 'up *phrasal verb* to become greater, more powerful or larger in number: *All the pressure built up and he was off work for weeks with stress.* ◇ *The music builds up to a rousing climax.*
▸ **'build-up** *noun* [U]: *a steady build-up of traffic in the evenings* ◇ *carbon dioxide build-up in the atmosphere*

accumulate /ə'kju:mjəleɪt/ [I] to gradually increase in number or amount over a period of time: *Debts began to accumulate.* ◇ *Dust and dirt soon accumulate if a house is not cleaned regularly.* ❶ **Accumulate** can be used to talk about money in the form of *interest*, *benefits* or *debts*. It can also be used to talk about material or substances that build up in a place, the environment or the atmosphere over a long period of time. **Accumulate** can also be used with an object.
▸ **accumulation** *noun* [U, C]: *the accumulation of wealth* ◇ *an accumulation of toxic chemicals*

,pile 'up *phrasal verb* (*rather informal*) (of sth unwanted, especially work or debts) to increase in amount, so that there is too much of it to deal with: *Work always piles up at the end of the year.*

accrue [I] (*formal*) to increase in amount over a period of time: *Interest will accrue if you keep your money in a savings account.* ◇ *There are economic benefits accruing to the country from tourism.* ❶ **Accrue** is often used when talking about money, and the increase is usually a good thing: *Interest/benefits/profits will accrue.*

multiply [I, T] to increase or make sth increase very much in number, amount or level: *Our problems have multiplied since last year.* ◇ *Cigarette smoking multiplies the risk of cancer.*

,mount 'up *phrasal verb* (of sth unwanted, especially costs or debts) to increase gradually in size or amount: *Meanwhile, the bills were mounting up.* ◇ *It's surprising how the cost of all those little extras can mount up.*

bullet *noun*

bullet · ammunition · shell · shot · gunshot · round · cartridge
These are all words for an object that is fired from a gun.

PATTERNS AND COLLOCATIONS
▸ **live** bullets/ ammunition/ rounds/ cartridges
▸ **blank** ammunition/ rounds/ cartridges
▸ a **stray** bullet/ shell/ round
▸ **machine-gun** bullets/ ammunition/ rounds
▸ to **fire** bullets/ ammunition/ shells/ rounds/ cartridges
▸ to **shoot** a bullet/ round
▸ to **put** a bullet/ round **into** sb/ sth
▸ to **be riddled with** bullets/ shot
▸ a bullet/ shell/ round **hits/ strikes/ misses sb/ sth**
▸ a bullet/ shot/ round **enters/ lodges in/ is lodged in** sb/ sth
▸ a bullet/ shell/ shot/ round/ pellet **kills** sb
▸ a bullet/ a shell/ shot **whistles**

bullet [C] a small object that is fired from a gun: *The second bullet hit her in the back.* ◇ *There were bullet holes in the door.* ◇ *He was found to have a single bullet wound in his chest.*

ammunition /ˌæmjuˈnɪʃn/ [U] a supply of bullets, etc. to be fired from guns: *A few of the men had run out of ammunition.*

shell [C] a metal case filled with explosive, that is fired from a large gun: *A shell burst only yards away from us.* ◇ *They braved heavy shell fire to rescue the wounded.* ❶ In American English **shell** is also another word for **cartridge**.

shot [U] a large number of small metal balls that are fired together from a shotgun: *Conservationists have called on the government to ban the use of **lead shot** in shotgun cartridges.* ◇ *Round shot whistled over our heads.* ❶ A **shot** [C] is the act of firing a gun or the sound this makes: *Someone **took a shot at** the car.* ◇ *We heard some shots in the distance.*

gunshot /'ɡʌnʃɒt; AmE -ʃɑːt/ [U] the bullets that are fired from a gun ❶ In this meaning **gunshot** is only used in the phrase *gunshot wound/wounds*: *He died of a single gunshot wound to the chest.* A **gunshot** can also be the sound of a gun being fired: *I heard the sound of gunshots out in the street.*

round [C] a single shot from a gun; a bullet for one shot: *They fired several rounds at the crowd.* ◇ *We only have three **rounds of ammunition** left.*

cartridge [C] a tube or case containing explosive and a bullet or shot for firing from a gun: *He was armed with a replica pistol, capable of firing blank cartridges.*

bully *verb*

bully · terrorize · victimize · pick on sb
These are all words that can be used when a person, especially sb strong or powerful, frightens sb or makes them suffer unfairly.

PATTERNS AND COLLOCATIONS
▸ to bully/ terrorize sb **into doing sth**
▸ to **get** bullied/ picked on

bully /'bʊli/ [T] to frighten or hurt a weaker person; to use your strength or power to make sb do sth: *My son is being bullied at school.* ◇ *I won't be bullied into signing anything.*
▸ **bully** *noun* [C]: *Leave him alone, you **big bully**!* ◇ *school/playground bullies*
▸ **bullying** *noun* [U]: *Bullying is a problem in many schools.* ◇ *He refused to give in to bullying and threats.*

terrorize (*BrE* also **-ise**) /'terəraɪz/ [T] to make people very frightened so that they will not oppose sth, or in order to make them do sth: *Drug dealers have been terrorizing the neighbourhood.* ◇ *Thousands of people were terrorized into leaving their homes.*

victimize (*BrE* also **-ise**) /'vɪktɪmaɪz/ [T, often passive] to make sb suffer unfairly because you do not like them, their opinions, or sth that they have done: *For years the family had been victimized by racist neighbours.*

'pick on sb *phrasal verb* (*rather informal*) to treat sb unfairly by blaming, criticizing or punishing them: *She was picked on by the other girls because of her size.* ◇ *Why is everybody picking on me?* ◇ *He should **pick on someone his own size** (= not attack sb who is smaller or weaker).*

bureaucracy *noun*

bureaucracy · paperwork · red tape · rules and regulations
These are all words for official rules or ways of doing things, such as filling in forms, especially when these seem too complicated and waste time.

PATTERNS AND COLLOCATIONS
▸ **unnecessary/too much/endless** bureaucracy/paperwork/red tape
▸ **government** bureaucracy/red tape/rules and regulations
▸ to **involve** bureaucracy/paperwork/red tape
▸ to **reduce/cut** bureaucracy/paperwork/red tape
▸ to **deal with** bureaucracy/paperwork

bureaucracy /bjʊəˈrɒkrəsi; *AmE* bjʊˈrɑːk-/ [U] (*often disapproving*) official rules and ways of doing things, created by a government or organization, especially when these seem too complicated: *She is initiating a project to eliminate unnecessary bureaucracy.* See also **bureaucracy →** AUTHORITIES, **bureaucrat →** OFFICIAL *noun*

paperwork /'peɪpəwɜːrk/ [U] the written work that is part of a job or is necessary to do sth, such as filling in forms or writing letters and reports: *She spent the day catching up on the vast mound of paperwork that had built up.* ❶ **Paperwork** is not always as disapproving as **bureaucracy** or **red tape**. It often refers to written work which people accept is necessary, even if they do not like dealing with it and would rather spend their time doing other things. It can also refer to the documents that you need for sth. See also **paperwork →** DOCUMENT

,red 'tape [U] (*disapproving, journalism*) official rules that seem too complicated and prevent things from being done quickly: *Plans may take longer and involve more red tape than you expect.*

,rules and regu'lations *phrase* official rules and ways in which things should be done: *They seem to be more concerned with enforcing petty rules and regulations than really improving employee safety.*

burn *verb*

1 a fire/house is burning
2 burn paper/toast/buildings

1 burn · be on fire · smoulder · go up · blaze
These words all mean to produce heat and often flames, and turn into smoke.

PATTERNS AND COLLOCATIONS
▸ a **fire/bonfire/log** burns/smoulders/blazes
▸ a **building/house** burns/is on fire/goes up
▸ to **burn/blaze fiercely**

burn [I] (usually used in the progressive tenses) (of a fire, thing or place) to produce flames and heat: *A welcoming fire was burning in the fireplace.* ◇ *By night the whole city was burning.* ◇ *Two children were rescued from the burning car.*

be on 'fire *phrase* (of a thing or place) to be burning: *The car was now on fire.* ◇ *They doused the car in petrol and **set it on fire**.* ❶ **Be on fire** is used especially about things or places that are not supposed to be burning. See also **set fire to sth/set sth on fire →** LIGHT *verb* 1

smoulder (*BrE*) (*AmE* **smolder**) /'sməʊldə(r); *AmE* 'smoʊl-/ to burn slowly without a flame: *The bonfire was still smouldering the next day.*

,go 'up *phrasal verb* to be destroyed by fire or an explosion: *The whole building **went up in flames**.* ◇ *He watched his hard work **going up in smoke**.* ◇ *They managed to get out before the whole place went up.*

blaze [I] (usually used in the progressive tenses) to burn brightly and strongly: *A huge fire was blazing in the fireplace.* ◇ *Within minutes the whole building was blazing.* See also **blaze →** FIRE *noun* 1

2 burn · char · scald · cremate · incinerate · scorch · singe · sear
These words all mean to damage, injure, destroy or kill sb/sth with heat or fire.

PATTERNS AND COLLOCATIONS
▸ to burn/scald **yourself/your hand**
▸ to burn/scorch/singe your **hair/clothes**
▸ burned out/charred **remains/ruins/buildings**

burn [T, I] to damage, injure, destroy or kill sb/sth with fire, heat or acid; to be damaged, etc. by fire, heat or acid: *She burned all his letters.* ◇ *The cigarette burned a hole in the carpet.* ◇ *His greatest fear is of being **burnt alive**.* ◇ *The house was **burnt to the ground** (= completely destroyed) by protesters.* ◇ *The car was found abandoned in a wood, completely **burnt out**.* ◇ *Sorry — I burned the toast.* ◇ *The soup's hot. Don't burn your mouth.* ◇ *The house **burned down** in 1995.* ◇ *Ten people **burned to death** in the hotel fire.* ◇ *I can smell something burning in the kitchen.*

char (**-rr-**) [T, usually passive, I] to make sth black by burning it; to become black by burning: *The bodies were charred beyond recognition.* ◇ *The flame licked through the paper, which charred and crinkled.* ◇ *Nearby were the charred remains of a burnt-out car.*

scald /skɔːld/ [T] to burn yourself or part of your body with very hot liquid or steam: *Be careful not to scald yourself with the steam.*

cremate /krəˈmeɪt/ [T, often passive] to burn a dead body, especially as part of a funeral ceremony: *When she dies she wants to be cremated, not buried.*
▸ **cremation** *noun* [U, C]: *More people are choosing cremation rather than burial.*

incinerate /ɪnˈsɪnəreɪt/ [T, often passive] (*rather formal*) to burn sth until it is completely destroyed: *Most of the waste is incinerated.*

scorch [T] to burn and slightly damage a surface by making it too hot: *I scorched my dress when I was ironing it.* ◇ *The buildings around us were scorched by the fire.* ❶ In American English **scorch** is also used, especially in journalism, when large areas of land are destroyed by fire: (*AmE, journalism*) *Wildfires have scorched over two million acres of forest.*

singe [T, I] to burn the surface of sth slightly, usually by mistake; to be burnt in this way: *He singed his hair as he tried to light his cigarette.* ◇ *the smell of singeing fur*

NOTE SCORCH OR SINGE? Things are **scorched** by heat or fire. Things can only be **singed** by fire or a flame.

sear [T] to burn the surface of sth in a way that is sudden and powerful: *The heat of the sun seared their faces.* ◇ *Sear the meat first* (= cook the outside of it quickly at a high temperature) *to retain its juices.*

business *noun*

1 none of your business
2 Thank you for your business.

1 business · concern · preserve · affair
These are all words for sth that concerns a particular person, group or organization.

PATTERNS AND COLLOCATIONS
▸ (a) **private/personal** business/concern/affair
▸ sth is sb's **own** business/concern/affair
▸ to be **none of sb's** business/concern
▸ sth is **no** business/concern **of** sb's

business [sing.] something that is a particular person's or organization's responsibility or that they have a right to know about: *It is the business of the police to protect the community.* ◊ *My private life is none of your business* (= you do not have a right to know about it). ◊ *It's no business of yours who I invite to the party.* ◊ *I shall make it my business to find out who is responsible.*

concern [C, usually sing.] (*formal*) sb/sth's business: *This matter is their concern.* ◊ *How much money I make is none of your concern.*

> **NOTE** BUSINESS OR CONCERN? There is no real difference in meaning between these words, but **concern** is more formal, used mostly in written English. Both are used in the phrase *sth is sb's business/concern* but only **business** is used in the phrase *sth is the business of sth*: ~~It is the concern of the police to protect the community.~~ You can *make it your business to do sth*, meaning that you decide that you have a right to do or know sth, and will do it or find out about it; **concern** is not used in this way: ~~I shall make it my concern to find out who is responsible.~~

preserve [sing.] an activity, job or interest that is thought to be suitable for one particular person or group of people: *Higher education is no longer the preserve of the wealthy.* ◊ *I began my career in the days when nursing was a female preserve.*

affair [sing.] (*rather formal*) sb/sth's business: *How I spend my money is my affair.* ◊ *The details of your relationship should be a private affair.* ❶ **Affair** can be used in the same way as **business** and **concern** in the phrase *That's my business/concern/affair*. However, you cannot say that sth is: ~~none of sb's affair~~ or: ~~no affair of sb's~~. However, it is quite common to say that sth is, or should be *a private/ personal affair*.

2 See also the entries for COMPANY, INDUSTRY, TASK and TRADE

business · custom
These are both words for the fact of a person or people buying goods or services at a shop or business.

PATTERNS AND COLLOCATIONS
- to **lose / get / compete for / keep / retain / want** (sb's) business/ custom
- **Thank you for your** business / custom.

business [U] the fact of a person or people buying goods or services at a shop or business: *We're losing business to our main rivals.* See also **do business** → SELL 2

custom [U] (*BrE, formal*) business: *Thank you for your custom. Please call again.* See also **customer** → CUSTOMER

> **NOTE** BUSINESS OR CUSTOM? In British English **custom** is the term often used by shops and businesses when talking to their customers; when talking about the amount of trade done by a shop or business, **business** is often preferred. In American English **business** is always used whether talking to or about customers.

busy *adj.*
1 a busy woman
2 a busy weekend

1 busy · active · engaged · involved · occupied · hard-pressed · at work
These words all describe people doing a lot or having a lot to do.

PATTERNS AND COLLOCATIONS
- busy / involved / occupied **with** sth
- active / engaged / involved / occupied **in** sth
- engaged / at work **on** sth
- to **keep sb** busy / active / involved / occupied
- **very / particularly / quite** busy / active / involved
- **currently** busy / active / engaged / involved / occupied / at work
- **constantly** busy / engaged / involved / occupied / at work
- **actively** engaged / involved in sth

busy having a lot to do; not free to do sth else because you are working on sth; spending a lot of time on sth: *Are you busy tonight?* ◊ *I'm afraid the doctor is busy at the moment. Can he call you back?* ◊ *The principal is a very busy woman.* ◊ *She was always too busy to listen.* ◊ *James is busy practising for the school concert.*

> **busily** *adv.*: *He was busily engaged in repairing his bike.*

active (*rather formal*) giving a lot of time or attention to sth; making a determined effort and not leaving sth to happen by itself: *They were both politically active.* ◊ *She takes an active part in school life.* ◊ *The parents were active in campaigning against cuts to the education budget.* ◊ *They took active steps to prevent the spread of the disease.*
OPP **inactive, passive** ❶ The opposite of **active** in this meaning is **inactive** or **passive**: *The area has a large, but politically inactive population.* ◊ *He played a passive role in the relationship.* See also **passive** → PASSIVE See also **active** → ENERGETIC

> **actively** *adv.*: *She was actively looking for a job.*

engaged [not before noun] (*formal*) giving a lot of time or attention to sb/sth; not free to do sth: *They were engaged in conversation.* ◊ *He is now engaged on his second novel.* ◊ *I can't come to dinner on Tuesday — I'm otherwise engaged* (= I have already arranged to do sth else). See also **engagement** → MEETING 2

involved [not usually before noun] giving a lot of time or attention to sb/sth: *She was deeply involved with the local hospital.* ◊ *I was so involved in my book I didn't hear you knock.* ◊ *He's a very involved father* (= he spends a lot of time with his children). See also **involvement** → INVOLVEMENT

occupied [not before noun] (*rather formal*) giving a lot of time or attention to sb/sth: *He's fully occupied looking after three small children.* ◊ *Only half her time is occupied with politics.* ◊ *The most important thing is to keep yourself occupied.*

> **NOTE** INVOLVED OR OCCUPIED? **Involved** usually suggests that sb has a personal or emotional connection with the person or thing mentioned; **occupied** simply suggests that sb has a lot to do.

hard-'pressed having a lot of problems, especially too much work, and too little time or money: *Hard-pressed junior doctors want shorter working hours.*
at 'work [not before noun] busy doing sth: *He is still at work on the painting.* ◊ *Danger — men at work.*

2 busy · hectic · full · eventful · lively
These words all describe a period of time that is full of work or activity.

PATTERNS AND COLLOCATIONS
- a busy / a hectic / a full / an eventful **day / weekend / week**
- a busy / hectic / full / lively **programme**
- a busy / hectic / full **schedule / timetable**
- a busy / a hectic / a full / an eventful **life**
- **very** busy / hectic / full / eventful / lively

busy full of work and activity: *Have you had a busy day?* ◊ *This is one of the busiest times of the year for the department.* **OPP** **quiet** → QUIET 1

hectic very full of work and activity; too busy: *I don't want to lead such a hectic life any more.* ◊ *We were involved in the hectic last-minute preparations.*

full (*often approving*) busy; involving a lot of activities: *He'd had a very full life.* ◊ *Her life was too full to find time for hobbies.*

> **NOTE** BUSY, HECTIC OR FULL? **Busy** is the most general of these words. **Full** often describes a period of time, especially sb's life, that is busy in a good way. **Hectic** usually describes a period of time or an activity that is too busy.

eventful full of things that happen, especially exciting, important or dangerous things: *It had been a long and eventful journey.* **OPP** **uneventful** → PREDICTABLE 2

lively (*especially BrE*) busy and active: *They do a lively trade in souvenirs and gifts.* ❶ In this meaning, **lively** is mainly used to describe *trading, business, bidding* and *the market* (= the activity of buying and selling things).

button *noun*

1 Press the red button.
2 a jacket with gold buttons

---

1 button · switch · control · wheel · key · handle · lever · knob · dial

These are all words for the part of a machine, vehicle or piece of equipment that you press, turn or move to make it work.

PATTERNS AND COLLOCATIONS
▸ a button / switch / key / handle / lever / knob / dial **on** sth
▸ the **on** / **off** / **on-off** button / switch
▸ a **control** button / switch / key / level / knob
▸ a **door** handle / knob
▸ a **volume control** button / switch / knob / dial
▸ to **be at** / **take** the controls / wheel
▸ to **press** a button / switch / key / lever
▸ to **push** a button / switch / handle / lever
▸ to **pull** a switch / handle / lever
▸ to **turn** a wheel / handle / knob / dial
▸ to **hit** a button / switch / key
▸ to **adjust** the controls / lever / knob / dial
▸ a button / switch / handle / lever / knob / dial **controls** sth
▸ a / the button / switch / controls / wheel / handle / lever **operates** sth
▸ a / the button / switch / controls / lever / knob / dial **adjusts** sth

button [C] a small part of a machine that you press to make it work: *the play/stop/rewind button* ◇ *Adam pressed a button and waited for the doors to open.* ◇ *Choose 'printer' from the menu and click with the right **mouse button**.* ◇ *The windows slide down **at the touch of a button**.*

switch [C] a small device that you press or move up and down in order to turn a light or piece of electrical equipment on and off: *a light switch* ◇ *That was in the days before electricity was available **at the flick of a switch**.* ◇ *Which switch do I press to turn it off?* ◇ *to throw a switch* (= to move a large switch) See also **switch (sth) off** → TURN STH OFF, **switch sth on** → TURN STH ON

control [C, usually pl.] the switches and buttons, etc. that you use to operate a machine or vehicle, for example a plane: *the controls of an aircraft* ◇ *the control panel* ◇ *the volume control of a CD player* ◇ *The co-pilot was at the controls when the plane landed.* See also **control** → OPERATE

wheel [C, usually sing.] the round object used to steer a car, bus, etc. or ship: *He drummed his fingers on the **steering wheel** and waited.* ◇ *This is the first time I've sat **behind the wheel** since the accident.* ◇ *A car swept past with Laura at the wheel.* ◇ *Do you want to take the wheel* (= drive/steer) *now?*

key [C] any of the buttons that you press to operate a computer or typewriter; any of the wooden or metal parts that you press to play a piano and some other musical instruments: *Press the return key to enter the information.* ◇ *His hands flew over the piano keys and beautiful sounds filled the theatre.*
▸ **key** *verb* [T]: *Key (in) your password.*

handle [C] the part of a door, drawer, window, etc. that you use to open it: *She turned the handle and opened the door.* ◇ *He tried the handle but the window was locked.*

lever [C] a handle used to operate a vehicle or piece of machinery: *Pull the lever towards you to adjust the speed.*

knob /nɒb/ *AmE* nɑːb/ [C] a round switch on a machine such as a radio that you use to turn it on and off, etc.; a round handle on a door or drawer: *the volume control knob* ◇ *I've tried twiddling the knobs, but nothing seems to happen.* ◇ *She turned the heavy brass door knob.*

dial /'daɪəl/ [C] the round control on a radio, cooker, etc. that you turn in order to adjust sth, for example to choose a particular station or temperature: *You can tune into our station at 1460 on the radio dial.* ◇ *Set the dial for the number of copies requested.*

---

2 button · pin · buckle · zip · zipper · fastener · clasp · catch · Velcro™ · lace/shoelace · drawstring

These are all words for objects or devices that are used to close or fasten clothes or other objects.

PATTERNS AND COLLOCATIONS
▸ to **do up** / **undo** a / your button / buckle / zip / zipper / clasp / catch / laces / shoelaces
▸ to **fasten** / **unfasten** a / your button / buckle / zip / zipper / clasp
▸ a / your button / buckle / zip / zipper / clasp / catch / laces / shoelaces **is** / **are** / **comes** / **come undone**
▸ a zip / zipper / fastener / fastening / clasp / catch **is** / **gets stuck**

button [C] a small round piece of metal, plastic, etc. that is sewn onto a piece of clothing and used for fastening two parts together: (*BrE*) *to do up/undo your buttons* ◇ (*AmE*) *to button/unbutton your buttons* ◇ *The top button of his shirt was undone.* ◇ *My coat has lost a button.* ◇ *I need to sew this button back on.* See also **button** → TIE *verb*, **unbutton** → UNDO *verb*

pin [C] a short thin piece of stiff wire with a sharp point at one end and a round head at the other, used especially for fastening together pieces of fabric when sewing: *Use pins to keep the patch in place while you sew it on.* ◇ *The*

fasteners

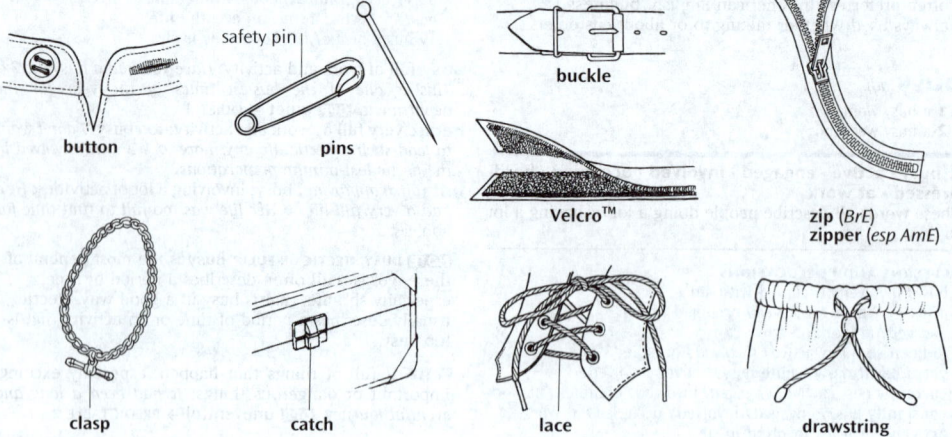

button   safety pin   buckle
                           pins
                                        Velcro™
                                                           zip (*BrE*)
                                                           zipper (*esp AmE*)
clasp   catch   lace   drawstring

map had a lot of little pins stuck into it. ◇ *Fasten the baby's nappy with a **safety pin** (= a pin with a point bent back towards the head, that is covered when closed so that it cannot hurt you).*

▸ **pin** *verb* [T]: *She pinned the badge onto her jacket.* ◇ *Pin all the pieces of material together.*

buckle [C] a piece of metal or plastic used for joining the ends of a belt or for fastening a part of a bag, shoe, etc: *He adjusted his belt buckle.*

▸ **buckle** *verb* [T, I]: *She buckled her belt.* ◇ *These shoes buckle at the side.* **OPP** **unbuckle**

zip (*BrE*) [C] a thing that you use to fasten clothes, bags, etc. It consists of two rows of metal or plastic teeth that you can pull together to close sth or pull apart to open it: *My zip's stuck.* ◇ *a bag with a zip* See also **zip** → TIE, **unzip** → UNDO

zipper (*especially AmE*) [C] a zip: *My zipper's stuck.*

fastener (also **fastening**) [C] a device, such as a button, buckle or zip, used to close a piece of clothing; a device used to close a window, suitcase, etc. tightly: *buttons, zippers and other fasteners* ◇ *She fumbled with the unfamiliar fastening of the seatbelt.* See also **fasten** → TIE, **unfasten** → UNDO

clasp /klɑːsp; *AmE* klæsp/ [C] a device that fastens sth, such as a bag or the ends of a belt or a piece of jewellery: *the clasp of a necklace/handbag* ◇ *He tried to undo the clasp on the briefcase, but it was stuck.*

catch [C] a device used for fastening sth, for example a door, window or box: *a catch on the door* ◇ *safety catches for the windows* ◇ *I can't open the catch on this bracelet.*

Velcro™ /'velkrəʊ; *AmE* -kroʊ/ [U] a material for fastening clothes, etc. with two different surfaces, one rough and one smooth, that stick to each other when they are pressed together: *He did up the Velcro straps on his shoes.*

lace (also **shoelace** /'ʃuːleɪs/) [C, usually pl.] a long thin piece of material like string that goes through the holes on a shoe and is used to fasten it: *to tie/untie your laces/shoelaces* ◇ *a pair of shoelaces* ◇ *My shoelaces came undone and I nearly tripped.*

▸ ˌlace 'up, ˌlace sth 'up *phrasal verb*: *a dress that laces up at the side* ◇ *He was sitting on the bed lacing up his shoes.*

drawstring /'drɔːstrɪŋ/ [C] a piece of string sewn inside the material at the top of a bag, pair of trousers/pants, etc. that can be pulled tighter in order to make the opening smaller: *They fasten with a drawstring.* ◇ *a drawstring waist*

buy *verb*

buy · get · purchase · acquire · shop · take · pick sth up · snap sth up
These words all mean to obtain sth by paying money for it.

PATTERNS AND COLLOCATIONS
▸ to buy sth / get sth / purchase sth / acquire sth / shop / pick sth up / snap sth up **for £10, $2 million, etc.**
▸ to buy sth / get sth / go shopping **for sb**
▸ to buy / get / purchase / acquire sth **from** sb / a particular shop
▸ to buy / get / purchase / acquire / pick up / snap up **shares**
▸ to buy / get / purchase / acquire / snap up (a) **property / company / house**
▸ to buy / get / purchase / acquire / take **goods / a lease**
▸ to buy / get / purchase / acquire **land / premises / a site / tickets**
▸ to buy / get / purchase / take a **newspaper / magazine**
▸ to get / pick up / snap up **a bargain**
▸ to buy sth / purchase sth / acquire sth / pick up **cheaply**

buy [T, I] to obtain sth by paying money for it; (of money) to be enough to pay for sth: *I bought this from a friend for £10.* ◇ *He bought me a new coat.* ◇ *If you're thinking of getting a new car, now is a good time to buy.* ◇ *Five pounds doesn't buy much nowadays.* ◇ *He gave his children the best education that money can buy.* See also **buyer** → CUSTOMER

get [T, no passive] (*rather informal, especially spoken*) to obtain sth by paying money for it; to buy sth, for example a newspaper or magazine, regularly: *Did you get a present for your mother?* ◇ *Did you get your mother a present?* ◇ *You can get the basic model for $100.* ◇ *Which newspaper do you get?* ❶ **Get** also has the wider meaning of 'obtain sth', whether you pay money for it or not. Compare: *'Where did you get that skirt?' ' I bought it.'* ◇ *'Where did you buy/get that skirt?' ' Top Shop.'* **Get** is frequently used to mean 'buy', especially in spoken English and when talking about less expensive items, but if you need to make it clear that sb paid money for sth, use **buy**. See also **get** → GET 1

purchase /'pɜːtʃəs; *AmE* 'pɜːrtʃəs/ [T] (*formal*) to buy sth: *The equipment can be purchased from your local supplier.* ◇ *Please ensure that you purchase your ticket in advance.* See also **purchaser** → CUSTOMER

acquire /ə'kwaɪə(r)/ [T] (*formal, especially business*) to obtain sth by buying it: *The company has just acquired new premises.* ◇ *How did the gallery come to acquire so many Picassos?*

> **NOTE** **PURCHASE** OR **ACQUIRE**? **Acquire** is used especially with words relating to business: *company, firm, franchise, land, lease, premises, site, stake, subsidiary.* **Purchase** is simply a formal alternative to **buy**, and can be used with a far wider range of nouns. **Acquire** can also mean 'obtain sth by being given it'; if you need to make it clear that sb paid money for sth, use **buy** or **purchase**. See also **acquire** → GET 1

shop (-**pp**-) [I] to buy things in shops: *We tend to go into Edinburgh to **shop** for clothes.* ◇ *He likes to shop at the local market.* ❶ To **go shopping** is to spend time going to shops and looking for things to buy: *There should be plenty of time to go shopping before we leave New York.* See also **shopper** → CUSTOMER

take [T] to choose to buy sth: *I'll take the grey jacket.* ❶ In this meaning **take** is only used when it is clear that you are choosing sth, especially in the phrase *I'll take…* In the sentence *She took the grey jacket*, for example, *took* could be misunderstood to mean *stole*. **Take** can also be used as a more formal way of saying **get**, when it means 'to buy a newspaper or magazine regularly': (*formal*) *We take the 'Express'.*

ˌpick sth 'up *phrasal verb* (*informal*) to buy sth, especially cheaply or by chance: *We managed to pick up a few bargains at the auction.*

ˌsnap sth 'up *phrasal verb* (-**pp**-) (*informal*) to buy or obtain sth quickly because it is cheap or you want it very much: *All the best bargains were snapped up within hours.*

buzz *verb*

buzz · whirr · whistle · hum · hiss · drone · whine
These words all mean to make a long or continuous sound.

PATTERNS AND COLLOCATIONS
▸ **bees** buzz / hum / drone
▸ a **helicopter** buzzes / whirrs
▸ a **machine** whirrs / hums / whines
▸ an **engine** hums / drones / whines
▸ a **bullet** whistles / whines
▸ to whirr / hiss / whine **softly**
▸ to buzz / hiss **loudly**
▸ to buzz / whirr / whistle / drone **overhead**

buzz [I] to make a continuous low sound, especially the sound made by flying insects or aircraft: *Bees buzzed lazily among the flowers.* ◇ *A large helicopter buzzed overhead.* ❶ Various different insects can **buzz**, including flies, wasps and mosquitoes.

▸ **buzz** *noun* [C, usually sing.]: *The air was alive with the buzz of bees and dragonflies.*

whirr (*especially BrE*) (*AmE* usually **whir**) /wɜː(r)/ [I] to make a continuous low sound like the sound made by parts of a machine turning round and round very quickly: *The clock began to whirr before striking the hour.* ◇ *Three large fans whirred overhead in the afternoon heat.*
▶ **whirr** *noun* [C, usually sing.]: *The men heard the distant whirr of a helicopter's rotor blades.*

whistle [I] (of a machine) to make a long high sound; (of the wind or a small object) to move quickly, making a long high sound: *The kettle began to whistle.* ◇ *The train whistled and shot into the tunnel.* ◇ *The wind whistled down the chimney.* ◇ *A bullet whistled past his ear.*

hum (-**mm**-) [I] (especially of a machine) to make a continuous low smooth sound: *The computers were humming away.* ◇ *The overhead wires hummed with power.*

hiss [I] to make a sound like a long 's': *The steam escaped with a loud hissing noise.* ◇ *The snake lifted its head and hissed.*
▶ **hiss** *noun* [C, usually sing.]: *The hiss of air brakes announced the arrival of the tour bus.*

drone /drəʊn; *AmE* droʊn/ [I] to make a continuous low dull sound, especially the sound made by voices and light aircraft: *A small plane was droning in the distance.* ◇ *I fell asleep to the sound of their voices droning through the warm afternoon.*

whine /waɪn/ [I] (of a machine) to make a long high unpleasant sound: *The jet engines whined as the plane accelerated down the runway.*

C c

calculate
calculate *verb* See also the entries for COUNT and ESTIMATE

calculate · work sth out · compute · quantify · figure sth out · figure · put a figure on sth
These words all mean to use numbers to find or express a total.

PATTERNS AND COLLOCATIONS
▸ to calculate / compute / figure sth **at** 400, $1 000, 25%, etc.
▸ to calculate / work out / compute / quantify / figure out / figure / put a figure on **how much / how many …**
▸ to calculate / work out / figure out / figure **that …**
▸ to calculate / work out / compute / quantify / figure out / figure / put a figure on the **cost / number / amount** (of sth)
▸ to calculate / work out / compute **a total**
▸ to calculate sth / work sth out / quantify sth / figure sth out **exactly**

calculate [T, I] (*rather formal*) to use numbers to find out a total number, amount, size, distance or level: *Use the formula to calculate the volume of the container.* ◇ *The sum involved was calculated at $82 million.* ◇ **It has been calculated that** *at least 47 000 jobs were lost last year.* See also **calculate** → ESTIMATE *verb*, **calculation** → ESTIMATE *noun*

work sth 'out *phrasal verb* (*rather informal, especially spoken*) to calculate sth: *I just need a minute to work out the answer.* ◇ *I can't work this out — have you got a calculator?* ◇ *You'll need to work out how much time the assignment will take.*

compute /kəm'pjuːt/ [T] (*formal*) to calculate sth: *The losses were computed at £5 million.*

> **NOTE** CALCULATE, WORK STH OUT OR COMPUTE? **Calculate** is the most frequent of these words in written English, but **work sth out** is the most frequent in spoken English. It is used especially to describe small, quick calculations done by people. **Compute** is used in formal, written English, especially to describe calculations done by a machine.

quantify /'kwɒntɪfaɪ; *AmE* 'kwɑːn-/ [T] (*rather formal*) to describe or express sth as an amount or number: *The risks to health are impossible to quantify.*

figure sth 'out *phrasal verb* (*informal*) to calculate an amount or the cost of sth: *Have you figured out how much the trip will cost?*

figure [T] (*AmE*) to calculate an amount or the cost of sth: *We figured the attendance at 150 000.* See also **figure** → ESTIMATE *verb*

> **NOTE** FIGURE STH OUT OR FIGURE? **Figure** is only used in American English; **figure sth out** is used in both British and American English. However, it cannot be used with *at* to give a total: ~~We figured out the attendence at 150 000~~

put a figure on sth *phrase* (usually used in questions and negative statements) to say the exact price or number of sth: *It's impossible to put a figure on the number of homeless people in the country.*

call
call *verb*

1 We called the baby Mia.
2 call the office/the police/a taxi
3 hear a voice calling

1 call · name · term · entitle · label · designate · dub · brand · nickname · address · christen
These verbs all mean to give sb/sth a name or title.

PATTERNS AND COLLOCATIONS
▸ to label / designate / brand / address sb / sth **as** sth
▸ to call / address sb **by** their full name, their first name, etc.
▸ to call / name / dub / nickname / christen sb **Mary, Ali** etc.
▸ to call / dub / nickname sb **captain, the wizard, etc.**
▸ **officially** called / named / termed / entitled / labelled / designated / dubbed / christened
▸ **aptly** called / named / termed / entitled / nicknamed
▸ **commonly** called / termed / labelled

call [T] to give sb/sth a particular name; to use a particular name or title when you are talking to sb: *They decided to call the baby Mark.* ◇ *His name's Hiroshi but everyone calls him Hiro.* ◇ *What do they call that new fabric?* ◇ *They called their first daughter after her grandmother.* ◇ *We call each other by our first names here.*

name [T] to officially give a name to sb/sth: *They named their son John.* ◇ *He was **named after** his father* (= given his father's first name). ◇ (*especially AmE*) *The planet Mars is named for the Roman god of war.* ❶ You can also **rename** sb/sth by giving them/it a new name: *Leningrad was renamed St Petersburg.* ◇ *to rename a file* (= on a computer) See also **name** → NAME *noun*

term [T, usually passive] (*formal*) to use a particular name or word to describe sb/sth, especially in scientific and technical contexts: *At his age, he can hardly be termed a young man.* ◇ *REM sleep is termed 'active' sleep.* See also **term** → WORD

entitle [T, usually passive] to give a title to a book, play, film, painting, etc: *The company launched a huge marketing campaign entitled 'Buy Blue'.* ◇ *He read a poem entitled 'Salt'.* See also **title** → NAME *noun*

label (-ll-, *AmE* -l-) [T, often passive] (*sometimes disapproving*) to describe sb/sth in a particular way, especially in a negative way and often unfairly: *He was labelled (as) a traitor by his former colleagues.* ◇ *It is unfair to label a small baby as naughty.* See also **label** → NAME *noun*

designate /'dezɪgneɪt/ [T, usually passive] (*rather formal*) to say officially that sth has a particular character or name; to describe sth in a particular way: *This area has been designated (as) a National Park.* ◇ *designated seats for the elderly*

dub (-bb-) [T, often passive] to give sb/sth an unofficial name, especially in the media, sometimes in a humorous or critical way: *The media dubbed anorexia 'the slimming disease'.*

brand [T] (*sometimes disapproving*) to describe sb as being bad or unpleasant, especially unfairly: *They were branded as liars and cheats.* ◇ *The newspapers branded her a hypocrite.*

nickname /'nɪkneɪm/ [T, often passive] to give sb/sth an informal, often humorous, name that is used instead of or in addition to their/its real name: *She was nicknamed 'The Ice Queen'.* ❶ When you **nickname** sb/sth, you usually choose a new name that is connected with their real name, their personality, appearance or qualities, or with sth they have done or can do: *Michael Jackson, nicknamed 'Jacko'* ◇ *He was nicknamed 'Stretch' because he was so tall.* See also **nickname** → NICKNAME *verb*

address [T] to use a particular name or title for sb when you speak or write to them: *The judge should be addressed as 'Your Honour'.* ◇ *How should I address her?* ◇ *Please address my client by his full name, Mr Babic.*

christen /'krɪsn/ [T, often passive] to give a name to a baby at a religious ceremony to welcome him or her into the Christian Church; to give a name to sb/sth: *The child was christened Mary.* ◊ *Did you have your children christened?* ◊ *They christened the boat 'Oceania'.*
  ▸ **christening** *noun* [C]: *my nephew's christening* (= the ceremony in which a baby is christened)

2 call · ring · phone · dial · telephone · reach · call sb up
These words all mean to make a telephone call to sb.

PATTERNS AND COLLOCATIONS
▸ to call sb/ring sb/phone sb/telephone sb/call sb up **about** sth
▸ to call/ring/phone/telephone **from** somewhere
▸ to call/ring/phone/telephone **to do** sth
▸ to call/ring/phone/dial/telephone **a number/a hotline/the switchboard/reception**
▸ to call/ring/phone/dial/telephone **New York/India, etc.**
▸ to call/ring/phone/telephone the **doctor/fire brigade/police/hospital**
▸ to call/ring/phone/telephone **home**
▸ to call/ring/phone/dial/telephone **direct**
▸ to call/ring/phone (sb) **up/back**

call [T, I] to make a telephone call to sb; to ask sb/sth to come quickly to a particular place by telephoning: *My brother called me from Germany last night.* ◊ *I called the office to tell them I'd be late.* ◊ *Has anyone called the police?* ◊ *I'll call you a taxi.* ◊ *I'll call back later.*
  ▸ **call** *noun* [C]: *to get/have/receive a call from sb* ◊ *to give sb/to make a call* ◊ *Were there any calls for me while I was out?* ◊ *I'll take* (= answer) *the call upstairs.*

ring [T, I] (*BrE, rather informal, especially spoken*) to make a telephone call to sb: *I'll ring you later.* ◊ *When is the best time to ring New York?* ◊ *David rang up while you were out.* ◊ *He said he was ringing from London.* ◊ *Could you ring for a cab?* ◊ *She rang to say she'd be late.*

phone [I, T] (*BrE, rather informal, especially spoken*) to make a telephone call to sb: *Could you phone back later?* ◊ *I'm phoning about your ad in the paper.* ◊ *For reservations, phone 0207 281 3964.*
  ▸ **phone** *noun* [C, U]: *The phone rang and Pat answered it.* ◊ *They like to do business by phone/over the phone.* *He's been on the phone* (= using the phone) *to Kate for more than an hour.*

> NOTE **CALL, RING OR PHONE?** Call is the only one of these three words used in American English. **Ring** and **phone** are the most frequent words in this group in spoken British English, but **call** is usually preferred, even in British English, when there is an emergency: *call the police/fire brigade* is much more frequent than 'ring/phone the police/fire brigade'. You **call/ring/phone** a person, place or institution; you **call** *a cab/a taxi/an ambulance*: *I'll ring/phone you a cab.*

dial /'daɪəl/ (-ll-, *AmE* -l-) [T, I] to use a telephone by pushing the buttons or turning the dial (= the round part on some older telephones with holes for the fingers) to call a number: *He dialled the number and waited.* ◊ *Dial 0033 for France.* ◊ *She picked up the receiver, paused a moment, and then dialled.*

telephone [I, T] (*especially BrE, formal*) to make a telephone call to sb: *Please write or telephone for details.* ◊ *You can telephone your order 24 hours a day.* ◊ *I was about to telephone the police.*
  ▸ **telephone** *noun* [C, U]: *The telephone rang and Pat answered it.* ◊ *You're wanted* (= sb wants to speak to you) *on the telephone.*

reach [T] to communicate with sb, especially by telephone: *Do you know where I can reach him?* ◊ *You can reach me at this number.*

‚call sb'up *phrasal verb* (*especially AmE, rather informal*) to make a telephone call to sb: *I called him up and asked him how he was doing.*

3 See also the entry for SHOUT
call · cry out (sth) · exclaim · blurt · burst out
These words all mean to shout or say sth loudly or suddenly.

PATTERNS AND COLLOCATIONS
▸ to call/cry out/exclaim/blurt out (sth) **to** sb
▸ to call/cry out **for** sb/sth
▸ to cry out/exclaim/blurt out/burst out **in/with** sth
▸ to call/cry out/exclaim/blurt out/burst out **suddenly**
▸ to call/cry out/exclaim/burst out **loudly**

call [I, T] to shout or say sth loudly to attract sb's attention: *I thought I heard someone calling.* ◊ *Did somebody call my name?* ◊ *He called out a warning to her.* ◊ *'Don't forget what I said!' she called after him.* ◊ *I started to leave but they called me back again.*

‚cry 'out, ‚cry 'out sth *phrasal verb* to shout sth loudly, especially when you need help or are in trouble: *She cried out for help.* ◊ *I cried out his name.* ◊ *'Thank God you're here!' she cried out.* See also **cry out → SCREAM**
  ▸ **cry** *noun* [C]: *With a cry of 'Stop thief!' he ran after the boy.*

exclaim /ɪk'skleɪm/ [T, I] (*written*) to say sth suddenly and loudly, especially because of a strong emotion: *'It isn't fair!' he exclaimed angrily.* ◊ *The visitors were led through the gardens, all of them exclaiming with delight.*
  ▸ **exclamation** /ˌekskləˈmeɪʃn/ *noun* [C]: *He gave an exclamation of surprise.*

blurt /blɜːt; *AmE* blɜːrt/ [T] to say sth suddenly and without thinking carefully enough: *He blurted out the question without thinking.* ◊ *'I know what you're thinking,' she blurted.*

‚burst 'out *phrasal verb* to say sth suddenly and loudly, especially with a lot of emotion: *'He's just a bully!' the little boy burst out.*

calm *verb*

calm · soothe · appease · placate · pacify · calm sb down
These verbs all mean to make sb feel more relaxed and less anxious, excited, angry or upset.

PATTERNS AND COLLOCATIONS
▸ to calm sb/soothe sb/appease sb/placate sb/pacify sb/calm sb down **with** sth
▸ to calm/soothe **your nerves**
▸ to soothe/appease **your conscience**

calm [T] to make sb/sth become quiet and more relaxed, especially after strong emotion or excitement: *Have some brandy; it'll calm your nerves.*
  ▸ **calming** *adj.*: *His presence had a calming influence.*

soothe /suːð/ [T] to make sb who is anxious, upset or nervous feel calmer and more relaxed: *The music soothed her for a while.* ◊ *He soothed my worries by promising that we could visit whenever we wanted.*
  ▸ **soothing** *adj.*: *He placed an arm around her shoulder, and spoke in a soothing voice.*
  ▸ **soothingly** *adv.*: *'There's no need to worry,' he said soothingly.*

appease /ə'piːz/ [T] (*formal, usually disapproving*) to make sb calmer or less angry by giving them what they want: *The move was widely seen as an attempt to appease critics of the regime.* ◊ *Even dismissing them had not appeased his anger.*

placate /plə'keɪt; *AmE* 'pleɪkeɪt/ [T] to make sb feel calmer and less angry about sth: *The concessions did little to placate the students.*
  ▸ **placatory** /plə'keɪtəri; *AmE* 'pleɪkətɔːri/ *adj.*: (*formal*) *a placatory remark/smile/gesture*

pacify /'pæsɪfaɪ/ [T] to make sb who is angry or upset become calm and quiet: *The baby could not be pacified.* ◊ *The announcement was designed to pacify the irate crowd.*

Both these verbs suggest that you bring peace to a person or situation, but **pacify** can emphasize a person's angry *behaviour*, while **placate** emphasizes their angry *feelings*.

,calm sb 'down *phrasal verb* to make sb become calm: *I put my arm around her and tried to calm her down.* ◇ *He took a few deep breaths to calm himself down.*

calm *adj.* See also the entry for CASUAL

calm · patient · cool · relaxed · controlled · easy-going · placid · laid-back · unperturbed · unfazed · composed
These words all describe sb who controls their emotions and is not excited, anxious or angry.

PATTERNS AND COLLOCATIONS
▶ calm / patient / cool / easy-going / laid-back **about** sth
▶ unperturbed / unfazed **by** sth
▶ a calm / a cool / a relaxed / a controlled / an easy-going / a laid-back **manner**
▶ a calm / cool / relaxed / controlled / placid **voice**
▶ a calm / a cool / a relaxed / a controlled / an easy-going **way**
▶ a calm / cool / placid **exterior**
▶ a relaxed / an easy-going / a laid-back **atmosphere**

calm not excited, anxious or upset: *Strangely, she felt quite calm about it.* ◇ *It is important to keep calm in an emergency.* ◇ *She handled the situation with calm assurance.* **OPP** agitated → RESTLESS, **excitable** → MOODY, See also **calm** → COMPOSURE *noun*
▶ **calmly** *adv.*: *'I'll call the doctor,' he said calmly.*

patient able to wait for a long time or accept annoying behaviour without becoming angry: *You'll just have to be patient and wait till I'm finished.* ◇ *She's very patient with the children.* **OPP** impatient → RESTLESS, See also **patience** → PATIENCE
▶ **patiently** *adv.*: *to listen/sit/wait patiently*

cool not excited, angry or emotional: *Keep cool. We'll sort this out.* ◇ *She tried to remain cool, calm and collected.* ◇ *He has a cool head* (= he stays calm in an emergency). See also **cool** → COMPOSURE *noun*

relaxed not anxious or worried: *I had to learn to be more relaxed about things.* ◇ *She appeared relaxed and confident before the match.* **OPP** nervous → NERVOUS, **nervous** → WORRIED

NOTE CALM, COOL OR RELAXED? **Relaxed** describes how you feel about sth: you are genuinely not anxious or worried about it. **Cool** is used more to describe how sb behaves: whether or not they feel angry or emotional, they don't let it affect their behaviour but continue to think clearly and act sensibly. **Calm** can describe feelings or behaviour.

controlled remaining calm and not getting angry or upset, especially by making a special effort to do so: *He spoke in a controlled, even voice.*

,easy-'going relaxed and happy to accept things without worrying or getting angry: *His friends described him as an easy-going person.* ❶ **Easy-going** is used especially to describe sb's personality and the way they behave usually, rather than in a particular situation or on a particular occasion. **OPP** uptight → TENSE, See also **tolerant** → TOLERANT

placid /'plæsɪd/ (of a person or animal) not easily excited or irritated: *The cattle are placid, so easy to work with.* ◇ *My second child was a placid baby.* **OPP** high-spirited ❶ **High-spirited** animals, especially horses, are lively and difficult to control.
▶ **placidly** *adv.*: *'Of course,' said Helen placidly.*

,laid-'back (*rather informal*) calm and relaxed; seeming not to worry about anything: *Steve was very laid-back about it all.* ◇ *He loved the laid-back Caribbean lifestyle.*

unperturbed /ˌʌnpə'tɜːbd; AmE ˌʌnpər'tɜːrbd/ [not usually before noun] not worried or anxious, especially when sth surprising or unpleasant happens: *She seemed unperturbed by the news.*

unfazed /ʌn'feɪzd/ [not usually before noun] (*rather informal*) not worried or surprised by sth unexpected that happens: *The President seems unfazed by the ongoing crises around the world.*

composed /kəm'pəʊzd; AmE -'poʊzd/ [not usually before noun] calm and in control of your emotions: *She sat with a book on her lap, apparently quite composed.* **OPP** flustered → RESTLESS, See also **composure** → COMPOSURE

campaign *noun* See the Topic Map for THE MEDIA on p.900

campaign · battle · struggle · drive · war · fight · crusade
These are all words for an effort made to achieve or prevent sth.

PATTERNS AND COLLOCATIONS
▶ a campaign / battle / struggle / drive / fight / crusade **for** sth
▶ a campaign / battle / struggle / drive / war / fight / crusade **against** sth
▶ a battle / struggle / war / fight **between** people
▶ a **big / major** campaign / battle / struggle / drive
▶ a **successful** campaign / battle / struggle / drive / fight
▶ a / an **national / international** campaign / battle / struggle / drive / crusade
▶ a **personal / one-man / one-woman** campaign / battle / struggle / war / crusade
▶ a **bitter** campaign / battle / struggle / fight
▶ a **brave / desperate** battle / struggle / fight
▶ a **political** campaign / battle / struggle
▶ to **launch / embark on** a campaign / battle / drive / crusade
▶ to **lead / continue** the campaign / battle / struggle / drive / war / fight / crusade
▶ to **win / lose** the battle / struggle / war / fight
▶ to **give up** the battle / struggle / fight
▶ The campaign / battle / war / fight **is on**.

campaign /kæm'peɪn/ [C] a series of planned activities that are intended to achieve a particular social, commercial or political aim: *She led the campaign for parliamentary reform.* ◇ *We're launching an anti-smoking campaign in the New Year.* ◇ *The advertising campaign was responsible for the massive rise in sales.* See also **campaigner** → ACTIVIST

battle [C] a competition or argument between people or groups of people trying to win power or control: *She finally won the legal battle for compensation.* ◇ *Looking after a two-year-old needn't be a constant battle of wills* (= when each side is very determined to win). ◇ *He had been conducting a personal battle of wits* (= when each side uses their ability to think quickly to try and win) *with the sales manager since his first day at work.*

struggle [C] a competition or argument between people or groups of people trying to win power or control: *He was a major player in the struggle for independence.* ◇ *It is an epic tale of the struggle between good and evil.* ◇ *She will not give up her children without a struggle.* See also **struggle** → RESIST *verb*

NOTE BATTLE OR STRUGGLE? In many cases you can use either word, but a **struggle** is always about things that seem absolutely necessary, such as life and death or freedom. A **battle** can also be about things that are not absolutely necessary, just desirable, or about the pleasure of winning: *the battle/struggle between good and evil/man and nature* ◇ *a legal struggle for compensation* ◇ *a struggle of wills/wits*

drive [C] an organized effort by a group of people to achieve sth: *He played a crucial role in the drive for greater efficiency.* ◇ *She is leading the recruitment drive.*

NOTE CAMPAIGN OR DRIVE? A **campaign** is usually aimed at getting other people to do sth; a **drive** may be an attempt by people to get themselves to do sth: *From today, we're going on an economy drive* (= we must spend less). ◇ *an economy campaign.* A **campaign** may be larger, more formal and more organized than a **drive**.

war [U, sing.] an effort over a long period of time to get rid of or stop sth bad: *The government has declared war on drug dealers.* ◇ *We seem to be winning the war against crime.*

fight [sing.] the work of trying to stop or prevent sth bad or achieve sth good; an act of competing, especially in a sport: *Workers won their fight to stop compulsory redundancies.* ◇ *The team put up a good fight* (= they played well) *but were finally beaten.*

crusade /kruːˈseɪd/ [C] a long and determined effort to achieve sth that you believe to be right or to stop sth that you believe to be wrong: *We must continue the crusade against crime.* ◇ *Her moral crusade began in 1963.* ◇ *He led a crusade to give terminally ill people the right to die.* See also **crusader → ACTIVIST**

NOTE WAR, FIGHT OR CRUSADE? A **war** is about stopping things, like drugs and crime, that everyone agrees are bad. A **fight** can be about achieving justice for yourself. A **crusade** is often about persuading other people to share your beliefs about what is right and wrong.

campaign *verb*

campaign · fight · lobby · work · agitate
These words all mean to try hard to achieve sth, by asking or trying to persuade or influence people in power.

PATTERNS AND COLLOCATIONS
▸ to campaign / fight / lobby / work / agitate **for** sth
▸ to campaign / lobby / agitate **against** sth
▸ to campaign / fight / lobby **on behalf of** sb
▸ to campaign / fight / lobby / work / agitate **to do sth**
▸ to campaign / fight / lobby for **changes**
▸ to campaign / fight / agitate for **reform**
▸ a **group** campaigns / fights / lobbies / works
▸ to campaign / fight / lobby / work **hard**
▸ to campaign / lobby / work **actively** / **vigorously**
▸ to **successfully** campaign / fight / lobby for sth

campaign [I] to carry out a series of planned activities over a period of time in order to try to achieve sth, especially a political or social aim: *We have campaigned against whaling for the last 15 years.* ◇ *The group campaigns on environmental issues.* ◇ *They are campaigning to save the area from building development.* See also **campaigner → ACTIVIST**

fight [I, T] to try very hard to get or achieve sth: *He's still fighting for compensation after the accident.* ◇ *Campaigners fought to save the hospital from closure.* ◇ *She gradually fought her way to the top of the company.*

NOTE CAMPAIGN OR FIGHT? **Campaigning** often involves such activities as making speeches, putting advertisements in newspapers and writing to members of the government. The aim is often to persuade people that a political or social change is needed or a practice needs to be stopped. You can **fight** for social or political change too, but this word is also used to talk about achieving justice for yourself, for example gaining the right to do sth. The emphasis with **fight** is on the determination sb shows to achieve sth.

lobby [I, T] to try to influence a politician or the government and, for example, persuade them to support or oppose a change in the law: *Teachers have lobbied hard against education cuts.* ◇ *Farmers will lobby Congress for higher subsidies.* See also **lobby → PARTY noun 1**

work [I] to try hard to achieve sth, especially over a period of time and in a way that involves acting together with other people: *She dedicated her life to working for peace.* ◇ *The police and public need to work together to combat crime.*

agitate /ˈædʒɪteɪt/ [I] (*rather formal*) to argue strongly for sth that you want, especially changes in the law or social conditions: *Some militant groups have been agitating for autonomy for the region.* See also **agitation → TROUBLE 1**

cancel *verb*

cancel · lift · revoke · repeal · invalidate · annul
These words all mean to officially end a law or agreement or to say that a document or policy is no longer valid.

PATTERNS AND COLLOCATIONS
▸ to cancel / revoke an **agreement**
▸ to cancel / revoke / invalidate a **will**
▸ to cancel / invalidate a **contract**
▸ to lift / revoke / repeal a **ban**
▸ to revoke / repeal / annul a **law**
▸ to revoke / invalidate the **constitution**
▸ to revoke / invalidate a **licence** / **permit**
▸ to invalidate / annul a **marriage**

cancel (-ll-, *AmE* -l-) [T, I] to say that you no longer want to continue with an agreement, especially one that has been legally arranged: *to cancel a policy/subscription* ◇ *Is it too late to cancel my order?* ◇ *The US has agreed to cancel debts* (= say that they no longer need to be paid) *totalling $10 million.* ◇ *No charge will be made if you cancel within 10 days.*
▸ **cancellation** noun [U, C]: *the cancellation of a contract* ◇ *Cancellations must be made in writing.*

lift [T] to remove or end restrictions: *to lift a ban/curfew/blockade* ◇ *Martial law has now been lifted.*

revoke /rɪˈvəʊk; *AmE* -ˈvoʊk/ [T] (*formal*) (of a group or person in authority) to officially cancel a document, decision or agreement, so that it is no longer legally or officially valid: *Your licence may be revoked at any time.*

repeal /rɪˈpiːl/ [T] (*rather formal*) (of a government or group in authority) to officially make a law no longer valid: *The committee does not have the power to repeal the ban.*

invalidate /ɪnˈvælɪdeɪt/ [T] (*rather formal*) to have the effect of making a document or contract no longer legally or officially valid: *Misuse of the mattress will invalidate the guarantee.* ❶ Things are usually **invalidated** as a result of sth that happens or that sb does, but not because sb intends or decides to invalidate them. **OPP** **validate** ❶ To **validate** sth is to make it legally valid: *An official stamp was used to validate the voting papers.*

annul /əˈnʌl/ (-ll-) [T] (*formal*) to state officially that a marriage, law or election result is no longer legally valid, usually because the rules or correct procedure were not followed: *Their marriage was annulled after just six months.*

candidate *noun* See also the entry for PARTICIPANT

candidate · nominee · applicant · entrant
These are all words for sb who is applying for sth such as a job or position.

PATTERNS AND COLLOCATIONS
▸ a candidate / a nominee / an applicant / an entrant **for** sth
▸ a candidate / an entrant **in** sth
▸ a nominee / an applicant / an entrant **to** sth
▸ the **successful** candidate / applicant
▸ a **potential** / **prospective** candidate / applicant / entrant
▸ a / an **good** / **ideal** / **suitable** candidate / applicant
▸ a **Democratic** / **Republican** / **presidential** candidate / nominee
▸ to **attract** candidates / applicants / entrants
▸ to **interview** / **choose** / **select** / **shortlist** / **reject** a candidate / an applicant
▸ to **appoint** a candidate / a nominee / an applicant

vehicles

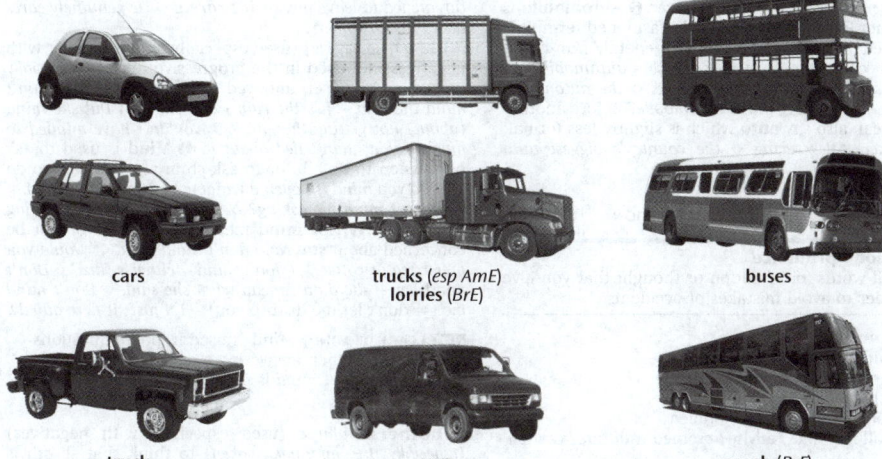

cars

trucks (esp AmE)
lorries (BrE)

buses

truck

van

coach (BrE)
bus (esp AmE)

candidate [C] a person who is trying to be elected or is applying for a job: *The committee will select the best candidate for the job.* ◇ *Prospective **parliamentary candidates** met party leaders last week.* ◇ *The party intends to **field** a candidate in the next general election.* ◇ (*BrE*) *He **stood as** a candidate in the local elections.* ❶ In British English a **candidate** can also be a person who is taking an exam: (*BrE*) *Candidates are allowed to use dictionaries in this examination.*

nominee /ˌnɒmɪˈniː; *AmE* ˌnɑːmˈniː/ [C] a person who has been formally suggested for a job or prize or to take part in an election: *And here are the nominees for Best Director.* ◇ *The President will present his nominee for Supreme Court Justice to Congress for approval.* ◇ *He was chosen as the party's presidential nominee.* See also **nominate** → REC-OMMEND 2

NOTE CANDIDATE OR NOMINEE? In some political elections, especially for a president in the US, several people are *nominated* (= suggested) to represent a political party: they are *nominees*. The party then chooses, often through a vote, one of the **nominees** who they want to become the party's **candidate** to take part in the election against candidates from other parties. In other situations where a person is being chosen for sth such as a job or a prize, **candidate** is a general word which can refer either to people who applied for the job or prize themselves, or who were suggested for it by other people. A **nominee** is always sb who was suggested for sth by other people.

applicant /ˈæplɪkənt/ [C] a person who is applying for sth, especially a job or a place at a college or university: *There were over 500 applicants for the job.* ◇ *What can be done about the falling number of applicants to medical schools?* ◇ *The factory was accused of turning away **job applicants** who belong to a union.* See also **apply** → ASK 2

entrant /ˈentrənt/ [C] a person or animal that enters a race or competition: *You will automatically be registered as an entrant in the Prize Draw.* ◇ *The **winning entrant** received tickets to the theatre.* ❶ In British English an **entrant** can also be a person who enters an exam: *The average score for all A-level entrants was 5.4.* See also **enter** → PLAY *verb* 1

car *noun*

car · bus · vehicle · truck · van · lorry · coach · automobile
These are all words for different types of motor vehicle.

PATTERNS AND COLLOCATIONS
▸ **by** car / bus / truck / van / lorry / coach
▸ **in** a car / vehicle / truck / van / lorry
▸ **on** a bus / coach
▸ a **heavy** vehicle / truck / lorry
▸ to **drive** a car / bus / vehicle / truck / van / lorry / coach
▸ to **get into / out of** a car / vehicle / truck / van
▸ to **get on / off** a bus / coach
▸ a car / bus / truck / van / lorry / coach **driver**
▸ (**in**) **the back / front of** a car / bus / vehicle / van

car [C] a road vehicle with an engine and four wheels that can carry a small number of passengers: *'How did you come?' 'By car.'* ◇ *Are we going in the car?* ◇ *They parked the car and walked the rest of the way.*

bus [C] a large road vehicle that carries passengers, especially one that travels along a fixed route and stops regularly to let people get on and off: *Shall we walk or go by bus?* ◇ *It's a short bus ride from here.* ◇ *I was waiting at the **bus stop**.* ❶ Especially in American English a **bus** is also a large road vehicle that carries passengers over long distances; in British English, this is usually called a **coach**.

vehicle /ˈviːəkl; *AmE* also ˈviːhɪkl/ [C] (*rather formal*) a thing that is used for transporting people or goods, such as a car, bus or truck: *Are you the driver of this vehicle, Madam?* ◇ *The paths will separate cycles from motor vehicles.*

truck [C] (*especially AmE*) a large vehicle used for carrying heavy goods by road: *The bus crashed into a truck loaded with timber.* ◇ *A tanker truck filled with gas exploded on the highway.* ❶ In British English the usual word for a large goods vehicle is **lorry**. However, a lorry usually has more than four wheels and is closed at the back. A smaller vehicle of this type is called a **van** if it is closed at the back, and a **truck** if it is open: *The soldiers were travelling in the back of the truck.* All these vehicles can be called a **truck** in American English.

van [C] a covered vehicle with no side windows in the back half, usually smaller than a truck, used for carrying goods or people: *A delivery van was almost blocking the narrow street.* ❶ In American English a **van** can also be a vehicle with side windows that can carry about 12 passengers. In British English this is called a **minibus**.

lorry [C] (*BrE*) a large vehicle with more than four wheels, used for carrying heavy goods by road: *The lorry rumbled over the bridge.* ◇ *150 **lorry loads** of steel were used.*

coach [C] (*BrE*) a comfortable bus for carrying passengers over long distances: *They went to Italy on a **coach tour**.* ◇ *They travelled by coach from London to Berlin.* ❶ In American English this is called a **bus**.

automobile /ˈɔːtəməbiːl/ [C] (*AmE, becoming old-fashioned, rather formal or humorous*) a car ❶ **Automobile** is now a rather formal and slightly old-fashioned term; it is mostly used to talk about cars in general, NOT about individual cars: *the influence of the automobile on American society* ◇ *automobile exports* ◇ *the automobile industry* ◇ *Are we going in the automobile?* Before another noun you can also say **auto** which is slightly less formal: *auto workers/sales/racing* ◇ *the country's biggest auto insurance company*

care *noun* See also the entry for ATTENTION

care · caution · prudence
These are all words for attention or thought that you give to sth in order to avoid mistakes or accidents.

PATTERNS AND COLLOCATIONS
▸ to do sth **with** care / caution / prudence
▸ **great** / **extreme** care / caution / prudence
▸ **due** / **the utmost** care / caution
▸ to **use** / **exercise** care / caution / prudence
▸ to **need** / **call for** / **urge** / **advise** / **proceed with** care / caution

care [U] attention or thought that you give to sth that you are doing so that you will do it well and avoid mistakes or damage: *She chose her words with care.* ◇ *Extreme **care** should be **taken to** ensure that the equipment is clean.* ◇ *He takes excessive **care of** his appearance.* ◇ *Fragile — **handle with care** (= written on a container holding sth which is easily broken or damaged).* **OPP** carelessness → CARELESS
▸ **careful** *adj.* [not before noun]: *Be careful!* ◇ *Be careful not to wake the baby.* ◇ *Please be **careful with** my glasses (= Don't break them).* ◇ *Be careful you don't bump your head.* See also **careful** → DETAILED
▸ **carefully** *adv.*: *Please listen carefully.* ◇ *She put the glass down carefully.* ◇ *Drive carefully.*
caution /ˈkɔːʃn/ [U] care that you take in order to avoid danger or mistakes; not taking any risks: *These statistics should be treated with some caution.* ◇ *We urge caution in the use of this medication.* ◇ *It is better to **err on the side of caution** (= to be too cautious rather than not cautious enough)* **OPP** recklessness → RECKLESS
▸ **cautious** *adj.*: *He was very cautious about committing himself to anything.* ◇ *They've taken a very **cautious approach**.* ◇ *They expressed cautious optimism about a solution to the crisis.*
▸ **cautiously** *adv.*: *She looked cautiously around and then walked away from the house.*
prudence /ˈpruːdns/ [U] (*formal*) being sensible and careful when you make judgements and decisions; avoiding unnecessary risks: *As a matter of prudence, agreement on these issues should be reached at an early stage in the partnership.* ◇ *Maybe you'll exercise a little more financial prudence next time.* ❶ **Prudence** is used especially in financial conexts. See also **prudent** → WISE

care *verb*

care · mind · be bothered
These words all mean to have strong feelings about sth because you think it is important.

PATTERNS AND COLLOCATIONS
▸ to care / mind / be bothered **about** sth
▸ to care / mind / be bothered **that...**
▸ to **not** care / mind / be bothered **what people think**
▸ to **not seem to** care / mind / be bothered
▸ to care / mind **very much**
▸ to **not** care / mind **very much / at all**
▸ to **not really** care / mind
▸ to **not** be **really / at all** bothered

care [I] (not used in the progressive tenses) to feel that sth is important and worth worrying about; to worry about what happens to sb because you like or love them: *She cares passionately about environmental issues.* ◇ *I don't*

care (= I will not be upset) *if I never see him again!* ◇ *He threatened to leave me, **as if I cared!*** ◇ *He genuinely cares about his customers.*
mind [T, I, no passive] (used especially in questions or with negatives; not used in the progressive tenses) (*especially spoken*) to be upset, annoyed or worried by sth: *I don't mind the cold — it's the rain I don't like.* ◇ *Did she mind (about) not getting the job?* ◇ *I wouldn't have minded so much if you hadn't lied about it.* ❶ **Mind** is used to ask permission to do sth, or to ask sb in a polite way to do sth: *Do you mind if I open a window?* ◇ *How old are you, if you don't mind me asking?* ◇ *Would you mind explaining that again?* ❶ **Not mind** means to not care or not be concerned about sth: *No, I don't mind a bit.* ◇ *'Would you prefer tea or coffee?' 'I don't mind — either's fine.'* ◇ *Don't mind her — she didn't mean what she said.* ◇ *Don't mind me (= don't let me disturb you) — I'll just sit here quietly.*

NOTE CARE OR MIND? **Mind** is used in polite questions and answers. When answering a question about what you prefer *I don't mind* is polite; *I don't care* is very rude.

be bothered *phrase* (used especially with negatives) (*especially BrE, informal, spoken*) to think that sb/sth is important: *'Where shall we have lunch?' 'Anywhere, I'm not bothered.'* ◇ *I'm not all that bothered about the delay.*

careless *adj.*

careless · negligent · forgetful · absent-minded
These words all describe people not giving enough attention and thought to what they are doing so that they forget things or make mistakes.

PATTERNS AND COLLOCATIONS
▸ **very** careless / negligent / forgetful
▸ **extremely** careless / negligent
▸ **a bit** careless / forgetful

careless not giving enough attention and thought to what you are doing, so that you make mistakes: *It was **careless of me** to leave the door open.* ◇ *Don't be so **careless about** spelling.* ◇ *He's very **careless with** money.*
▸ **carelessly** *adv.*: *Someone had carelessly left a window open.*
▸ **carelessness** *noun* [U]: *a moment of carelessness* **OPP** care → CARE
negligent /ˈneɡlɪdʒənt/ (*formal or law, especially written*) failing to give sb/sth enough care or attention, especially when this has serious results: *The school had been **negligent in** not informing the child's parents about the incident.*
▸ **negligence** *noun* [U]: *The accident was caused by negligence on the part of the driver.*
▸ **negligently** *adv.*: *The defendant drove negligently and hit a lamp post.*
forgetful often forgetting things: *She has become very forgetful in recent years.*
absent-'minded tending to forget things, perhaps because you are not thinking about what is around you, but about sth else: *Grandpa's becoming quite absent-minded.* ❶ Very clever people who don't think a lot about practical things are often described as **absent-minded**: *an absent-minded professor/scientist*
▸ **absent-mindedly** *adv.*: *She absent-mindedly twisted a strand of hair around her fingers.*

cargo *noun* See also the entry for LOT

cargo · goods · load · freight · burden
These are all words for things that are carried by road, rail, sea or air.

PATTERNS AND COLLOCATIONS
▸ a cargo / load **of** sth
▸ (a) **heavy** cargo / goods / load / freight / burden
▸ (a) **bulk** cargo / goods / freight

▶ to **carry** a cargo / goods / a load / freight / a burden
▶ to **handle** cargo / goods / freight
▶ to **transport** / **deliver** goods / freight
▶ a goods / freight **train**
▶ goods / freight **traffic**

cargo (pl. **-oes**, *AmE* also **-os**) [C, U] things that are transported by ship or plane: *The tanker began to spill its cargo of oil.* ◇ *a cargo ship/jet*

goods [pl.] (*BrE*) things that are transported by road or rail: *The road was closed both to passengers and goods.* ◇ *You need a special licence to drive a **heavy goods vehicle**.* ❶ **Heavy goods vehicle** is often abbreviated to **HGV**: *Do you have an HGV licence?*

load [C] something that is being carried, usually in large amounts, by a vehicle, person or animal: *They struggled down the hill with their loads of firewood.* ◇ *A truck had **shed its load** (= accidentally dropped its load) on the way to the depot.*

freight /freɪt/ [U] (*rather formal or business*) goods that are transported by road, rail, sea or air: *The trains were designed specifically to haul (= carry) freight.* ◇ *A freight train pulled into the station.* See also **freight** → CARGO

burden [C] (*formal*) a heavy load that is difficult to carry: *She shifted her burden from one arm to the other.* ◇ *The donkey was the traditional **beast of burden** (= animal used for carrying things).*

carriage *noun*

1 a railway carriage
2 a horse-drawn carriage

1 carriage · car · truck · wagon · compartment · coach · freight car · van

These are all words for a separate section of a train.

PATTERNS AND COLLOCATIONS
▶ a **railway** carriage / truck / wagon / compartment / coach
▶ a **railroad** car
▶ an **empty** carriage / car / truck / wagon / compartment / coach
▶ a **first-class** / **second-class, etc.** carriage / compartment / coach
▶ a **non-smoking** / **smoking** carriage / car / compartment
▶ a **sleeping** car / compartment / coach
▶ a **passenger** carriage / car / compartment / coach

carriage [C] (*BrE*) a separate section of a train for carrying passengers: *Several people got into the carriage.*

car [C] (*AmE*) a train carriage of any kind: *Several cars went off the rails.* ◇ *She was sitting in the smoking car.* ❶ **Car** is used in British English in compounds to mean a railway carriage of a particular type: *a buffet car* (= where you can buy food and drinks) ◇ *a sleeping/dining car*

truck [C] (*BrE*) an open railway vehicle for carrying goods or animals: *a cattle/coal truck*

wagon /ˈwæɡən/ [C] (*BrE*) a railway truck for carrying goods: *He tried to hide in a container wagon.*

compartment /kəmˈpɑːtmənt; *AmE* -ˈpɑːrt-/ [C] a separate section of a railway carriage: *He found an empty first-class compartment.*

coach [C] (*BrE*) a railway carriage: *When the train finally came into the platform it only had two coaches.*

NOTE CARRIAGE OR COACH? Carriage is used especially to talk about individual carriages and is used more in everyday speech: *We had to go right to the end of the carriage to find a seat.* **Coach** is used to talk about the number of coaches a train is pulling, or to say that a train is pulling passenger coaches rather than goods wagons. **Coach** is the word used in official language by train companies and on train tickets and reservations: *Our seats are in Coach D.*

'freight car /freɪt/ [C] (*especially AmE*) a railroad truck for carrying goods: *Most of the freight cars had been left unlocked overnight.*

van [C] (*BrE*) a closed railway vehicle for carrying bags, cases or mail: *a mail/luggage van*

2 carriage · cart · wagon · stagecoach

These are all words for a vehicle with wheels that is pulled by a horse or horses.

PATTERNS AND COLLOCATIONS
▶ **in** a carriage / wagon / stagecoach
▶ **on** a cart / wagon
▶ a **horse-drawn** carriage / cart / wagon
▶ to **drive** a carriage / cart / wagon
▶ to **climb** / **get into** a carriage / wagon
▶ to **climb** / **get onto** a cart / wagon
▶ a **horse and** carriage / cart

carriage [C] a road vehicle, usually with four wheels, that is pulled by one or more horses and was used in the past to carry people: *A horse and carriage awaited the happy couple.*

cart [C] a simple open vehicle with two or four wheels that is pulled by a horse or other animal and used for carrying loads: *The bundles were slung onto the back of a cart.* ◇ *An ox cart (= pulled by an ox) made its way through the village.*

wagon (*BrE* also **waggon**) /ˈwæɡən/ [C] a vehicle with four wheels, pulled by horses or oxen and used in the past for carrying heavy loads: *They travelled from Tennessee in a **covered wagon**.*

stagecoach /ˈsteɪdʒkəʊtʃ; *AmE* -koʊtʃ/ [C] a large vehicle pulled by horses, that was used in the past for carrying passengers, and often mail, along a regular route: *Travel by stagecoach was uncomfortable and often hazardous.*

carry *verb*

1 carry a bag/child
2 Pipes carry the water away.

1 carry · bear · lug · cart · tote

These words all mean to support the weight of sb/sth in your hands or arms and take them/it somewhere.

PATTERNS AND COLLOCATIONS
▶ to carry / bear / lug / cart / tote sth **to** / **from** / **up** / **along** sth
▶ to carry / lug / cart / tote sth **around**
▶ to carry / bear sth **on your back**

carry [T] to support the weight of sb/sth in your hands or arms and take them/it from one place to another: *He was carrying a battered suitcase.* ◇ *She **carried** a tiny baby **in her arms**.* ◇ *How are we going to get this home? It's too heavy to carry.*

bear [T] (*old-fashioned or formal*) to carry sb/sth, especially while moving: *Her two sons helped bear the coffin.* ◇ *Guests started arriving, mostly bearing gifts.*

lug (**-gg-**) [T] (always used with an adverb or preposition) (*informal*) to carry or drag sth heavy with a lot of effort: *I had to lug his stuff all the way to the top floor.*

cart [T] (always used with an adverb or preposition) (*informal*) to carry sth that is large, heavy or awkward: *They carted the logs back up to the house.*

tote [T] (*especially AmE, informal*) to carry sth, especially sth heavy: *They finally arrived, toting their bags and cases.*

2 carry · convey · transmit · conduct

These words all mean to take sth, especially sth that flows such as water or electricity, from one place to another

PATTERNS AND COLLOCATIONS
▶ to carry / convey / transmit sth **to** / **from** sth
▶ to carry / transmit sth **through** sth
▶ to transmit / conduct **heat**

carry [T] to contain and direct a flow of liquid, gas or electricity: *The pipelines carry oil across Siberia.* ◇ *Blood vessels carry blood to every part of the body.*

convey /kənˈveɪ/ [T] (*formal*) to take or transport sth from one place to another: *Pipes convey hot water to the radiators.* ◇ *The stone was conveyed by river to the site.*

transmit (-tt-) [T] (*physics*) (of a substance) to allow heat, light, sound or another form of energy to pass through: *Steam only transmits heat when it condenses.* ◇ *This chapter explains how sounds are transmitted through the air.*

conduct /kən'dʌkt/ [T] (*physics*) (of a substance) to allow heat or electricity to pass through: *Copper conducts electricity better than other materials do.*

case *noun*

case · trial · hearing · appeal · action · suit · lawsuit · proceeding · prosecution · litigation · court martial
These are all words for a formal legal dispute between people that is decided in court.

PATTERNS AND COLLOCATIONS
▸ (a) **legal** case / hearing / appeal / action / proceedings
▸ (a) **criminal** case / hearing / appeal / action / proceedings / prosecution / litigation
▸ (a) **civil** case / hearing / appeal / action / suit / lawsuit / proceedings / litigation
▸ a **murder / rape / fraud** case / trial
▸ (a) **libel** case / trial / hearing / action / suit / proceedings
▸ to **bring** a case / an action / a suit / a lawsuit / proceedings / a prosecution (**against** sb / sth)
▸ to **take** action / proceedings (**against** sb / sth)
▸ to **file** an appeal / a suit / a lawsuit
▸ to **face** trial / a hearing / an action / a suit / a lawsuit / proceedings / prosecution / litigation / court martial
▸ to **hear** a case / an appeal
▸ to **win / lose** a case / an appeal / an action / a suit / a lawsuit

case [C] a question to be decided in court; the facts and evidence that are used to accuse or defend sb/sth in court: *The case will be heard next week.* ◇ *The new evidence weakened the **case for** the defence.* ◇ *Our lawyer didn't think we **had a case** (= had good enough arguments to win in court).*

trial [U, C] a formal examination of evidence in court by a judge and often a jury, to decide if sb accused of a crime is guilty or not: *He's **on trial** for murder.* ◇ *She will **stand trial** for fraud.* ◇ *The men were arrested but not **brought to trial**.* ◇ *The case never **came to trial**.* ◇ *He did not receive a fair trial.*

hearing [C] an official meeting at which the facts about a crime, complaint, etc. are presented to the person or group of people who will have to decide what action to take: *a court/disciplinary hearing* ◇ *At a preliminary hearing the judge announced that the trial would begin on March 21.* ◇ *She was granted a divorce in a five-minute hearing.*

appeal [C, U] a formal request to a court or to sb in authority for a judgement or decision to be changed: (*BrE*) *to lodge an appeal* ◇ (*AmE*) *to file an appeal* ◇ (*BrE*) *an appeal court/judge* ◇ (*AmE*) *an appeals court/judge* ◇ *He lost his **appeal against** the 3-match ban.*

action [C, U] (*rather formal*) a legal process to settle a dispute or deal with a complaint: *A libel action is being brought against the magazine that published the article.* ◇ *He is considering taking legal action against the hospital.*

suit [C] (*rather formal*) a claim or complaint against sb that a person or organization can make in court: *His former business associate filed a suit against him claiming £5 million damages.* ◇ *Their arguments grew worse and worse and ended with a divorce suit.*

lawsuit /'lɔːsuːt; -sjuːt/ [C] (*rather formal*) a suit: *The opening of the factory was delayed because of a lawsuit brought by an environmental group.*

proceeding /prə'siːdɪŋ/ [C, usually pl.] (*rather formal*) the process of using a court to settle a dispute or to deal with a complaint: *The company has started legal proceedings against its competitor.*

prosecution /ˌprɒsɪ'kjuːʃn; *AmE* ˌprɑːs-/ [U, C] the process of trying to prove in court that sb is guilty of a crime; the process of being officially charged with a crime in court: *Prosecution for a first minor offence rarely leads to imprisonment.* ◇ *He threatened to bring a private prosecution against the doctor.* See also **prosecute → ACCUSE**

litigation /ˌlɪtɪ'geɪʃn/ [U] (*rather formal*) the process of making or defending a claim in court: *The company has been in litigation with its auditors for a full year.*

ˌcourt 'martial /'mɑːʃl; *AmE* 'mɑːrʃl/ (pl. **courts martial**) [C, U] a military court that deals with members of the armed forces who break military law; a trial at such a court: *He was convicted at a court martial.* ◇ *All the soldiers now face court martial.*

cash *verb*

cash · exchange · cash sth in · change · clear
These words all mean to exchange money in one form for the same value of money in a different form.

PATTERNS AND COLLOCATIONS
▸ to cash / change **traveller's cheques**
▸ to cash / clear a **cheque**
▸ to exchange / change your **currency / pounds / dollars for / into** pounds / dollars / the local currency

cash [T] to exchange a cheque for the amount of money that it is worth: *The company cashed my cheque but then failed to send the goods I'd ordered.* See also **cash → MONEY** *noun* 2

exchange [T] to give an amount of money and get back the same value in the money of another country: *You can exchange your currency for dollars in the hotel.*

ˌcash sth 'in *phrasal verb* to exchange sth, such as an insurance policy, for the amount of money which it is then worth, before the date on which you would normally receive the full amount of money: *It's not a good idea to cash in your bonds before the five years are up.*

change [T] (*especially spoken*) to exchange money into the money of another country; to exchange money for the same amount in different coins or notes: *Where can I change my traveller's cheques?* ◇ *Can you change a £20 note?* See also **change → MONEY** *noun* 2

clear [I, T] if a cheque that you pay into your bank account **clears**, or a bank **clears** it, the money is available for you to use: *Cheques usually take three working days to clear.*

castle *noun*

castle · tower · fort · fortress · stronghold · garrison
These are all words for a place that protects people or an area from attack.

PATTERNS AND COLLOCATIONS
▸ an **old / ancient** castle / tower / fort / fortress / stronghold
▸ a **medieval** castle / tower / fortress / stronghold
▸ a **Roman** fort / fortress / garrison
▸ a **ruined** castle / tower / fort / fortress
▸ a **mountain** fortress / stronghold
▸ to **build** a castle / tower / fort / fortress / stronghold / garrison

castle [C] a large strong building with thick high walls, built in the past in order to defend an area from attack: *The ruins of an ancient castle stand to the west of the town.*

tower [C] a tall narrow building or part of a building, especially of a castle or church: *The castle is rectangular in shape, with a tower at each corner.*

fort [C] a building or buildings built in order to defend an area against attack: *Evidently a medieval castle had been built on the site of an Iron Age fort.*

fortress /'fɔːtrəs; *AmE* 'fɔːrt-/ [C] a building or place that has been strengthened and protected against attack, especially a large, permanent military structure that often includes a town: *The medieval fortress town is enclosed by four miles of ramparts.* ◇ *Fear of terrorist attack has turned the conference centre into a fortress.*

stronghold /'strɒŋhəʊld; *AmE* 'strɔːŋhoʊld/ [C] a castle or place that is strongly built and difficult to attack: *The castle was an important royal stronghold for hundreds of years.*

garrison [C] buildings in a town or fort that a group of soldiers live in, in order to defend the town or area: *A number of Roman garrisons are still standing today.*

casual *adj.* See also the entries for CALM and INDIFFERENT

casual · offhand · blasé · relaxed
These words all describe a person who behaves in a calm and relaxed way or who seems not to be interested in sb/sth.

PATTERNS AND COLLOCATIONS
▸ casual / offhand / blasé / relaxed **about** sth
▸ a casual / an offhand **tone / voice / manner**
▸ a casual / blasé / relaxed **attitude**
▸ **almost** casual / offhand / blasé

casual /ˈkæʒuəl/ [usually before noun] (*sometimes disapproving*) not showing much care or thought; seeming not to be worried; not wanting to show that sth is important to you: *She seemed just too casual about the whole thing.* ◇ *At a casual glance, everything seemed normal.* ◇ *He tried to sound casual, but I knew he was worried.*
▸ **casually** *adv.*: *'What did he say about me?' she asked, as casually as she could.*

offhand /ˌɒfˈhænd; *AmE* ˌɔːf-; ˌɑːf-/ (*disapproving*) not showing much interest in sb/sth: *He was surprisingly offhand with me.* ◇ *She seemed offhand about the danger involved.*

blasé /ˈblɑːzeɪ; *AmE* blɑːˈzeɪ/ [not usually before noun] (*usually disapproving*) not impressed, excited or worried about sth, because you have seen or experienced it many times before: *She was becoming quite blasé about the dangers of travel in the region.*

relaxed not caring too much about discipline or making people follow rules: *I take a fairly relaxed attitude towards what the kids wear to school.*

catch *verb*

catch · trap · capture
These words all mean to get hold of an animal that tries or would try to escape.

PATTERNS AND COLLOCATIONS
▸ to catch / trap sth **in** sth
▸ to catch / trap a / an **bird / animal**

catch [T] to get hold of an animal that tries or would try to escape: *Our cat is hopeless at catching mice.* ◇ *How many fish did you catch?*

trap (**-pp-**) [T] to catch an animal in a trap: *Raccoons used to be trapped for their fur.*

capture [T] to catch an animal and keep it in an enclosed space: *The animals are captured in nets and sold to local zoos.*

category *noun* See also the entry for KIND

category · class · heading · league · bracket · classification
These are all words for a group of people or things that all share particular features.

PATTERNS AND COLLOCATIONS
▸ to be **under** a category / heading / classification
▸ to be **in / within** a category / class / league / bracket / classification
▸ the **same** category / class / heading / league / bracket / classification
▸ a **different** category / class / heading / league / classification
▸ a / the **main / broad / general / separate** category / class / heading / classification
▸ a **subject** category / heading / classification
▸ to **fall / come under** a category / heading
▸ to **fall into** a category / bracket
▸ to **belong to** a category / class / league

▸ to **divide sb / sth into** categories / classes / headings
▸ to **group sb / sth under** categories / headings
▸ to **put sth in / into** a category / bracket

category /ˈkætəɡəri; *AmE* -ɡɔːri/ [C] a group of people or things that are considered to share particular features; a definition of such a group used for official or academic purposes: *We have created a special category for part-time workers.* ◇ *Patients fell into two broad categories.* ◇ *There are two main categories of homicide according to the law.* See also **categorize** → CLASSIFY

class [C] a group of people or things that have similar characteristics, especially when they are of a similar standard or quality: *It was pretty cheap for this class of hotel.* ◇ *There are several distinct classes of drugs.* ◇ *Dickens was in a different class from* (= much better than) *most of his contemporaries.* ◇ *As a jazz singer she's in a class of her own* (= there is no one as good as her). See also **class** → CLASSIFY *verb*

heading [C] a general category in which you can consider a number of things together as a group; the subject of each section of a speech or piece of writing: *Sex education often comes under the general heading of 'Biology' or 'Health'.* ◇ *We can examine these issues under four headings.*

league /liːɡ/ [C] (*rather informal*) a level of quality or ability, especially one that separates sb/sth from other people or things of the same type but not the same level: *As a painter, he is in a league of his own* (= there is no one as good as him). ◇ *They're in a different league from us.* ◇ *When it comes to cooking, I'm not in her league.* ◇ *A house like that is out of our league* (= too expensive for us).

bracket [C] (*rather formal, especially written*) a category relating especially to sb/sth's price, income, financial status or age: *This model remains firmly in the upper price bracket.* ◇ *Most respondents were in the 45–60 age bracket.* ❶ Collocates of **bracket** in this meaning include *price, income, earnings, tax* and *age.* See also **bracket** → CLASSIFY *verb*

classification /ˌklæsɪfɪˈkeɪʃn/ [C] a group or class into which sth is put according to the features it shares with other things: *The material was put into the highest security classification.* ◇ *The classification 'science' covers a great many different subjects.* See also **classify** → CLASSIFY

cause *verb* See also the entries for ENCOURAGE 3, PROMPT and STIMULATE

cause · result in sth · lead (sth) to sth · produce · bring sth about · give rise to sth · create · make · induce
These words all mean to make sth happen.

PATTERNS AND COLLOCATIONS
▸ to cause / result in / lead to / produce / bring about / give rise to a / an **change / shift / increase**
▸ to cause / result in / lead to / produce / bring about a **reduction** in sth
▸ to cause / result in / lead to / produce / give rise to / create **problems / difficulties**
▸ to cause / result in / lead to / produce **damage / friction**
▸ to cause / result in / lead to / bring about the **collapse / destruction / demise** of sth
▸ to cause / lead to / produce / give rise to / create **speculation / uncertainty**
▸ to cause / lead to / give rise to / create **discontent / dissatisfaction / resentment**
▸ to result in / lead to / produce **improvements / success**
▸ to **inevitably** cause / result in / lead to / produce / bring about / give rise to / create sth

cause [T] to make sth happen, especially sth bad or unpleasant: *Do they know what caused the fire?* ◇ *Are you causing trouble again?* ◇ *Doctors say her condition is causing some concern.* ◇ *The project is still causing him a lot of problems.* ◇ *The poor harvest caused prices to rise sharply.* See also **cause** → SOURCE *noun*

re'sult in sth *phrasal verb* to cause a particular situation, especially the loss or increase of sth; to have sth as a result: *Closure of the plant could result in the loss of thousands of jobs .* ◇ *In 1965 their work resulted in a Nobel Prize.* ◇ *These policies resulted in many elderly and disabled people suffering hardship.* See also **result** → RESULT *noun*, **resulting**, **resultant** → RELATED

lead to sth, **lead sth to sth** *phrasal verb* to be the reason why sth happens; to have sth as a result: *The scandal ultimately led to his resignation.* ◇ *A reward was offered for information leading to an arrest.* ◇ *These policies could lead the country to environmental catastrophe.* ❶ **Lead to sth** is often used as part of a process of explaining or understanding sth.

produce [T] to cause a particular result or reaction: *A phone call to the manager produced the result she wanted.* ◇ *The prime minister's speech produced an angry response from opposition parties.* ◇ *The drug produces a feeling of great happiness and excitement.*

,bring sth a'bout *phrasal verb* to make sth happen, especially to cause sth to change over a period of time or in a number of stages: *What brought about the change in his attitude?* ◇ *It was this scandal that finally brought about her downfall.*

give 'rise to sth *idiom* (*formal*) to make or allow sth to happen or come into existence: *The novel's success gave rise to a number of sequels.* ◇ *The ocean gave rise to the first life on Earth.*

create [T] to produce a particular feeling or impression: *The company is trying to create a young energetic image.* ◇ *The announcement only succeeded in creating confusion.*

make [T] to cause sth to appear as a result of breaking, tearing, hitting or removing material: *The rock made a dent in the roof of the car.* ◇ *The holes in the cloth were made by moths.*

induce /ɪnˈdjuːs; *AmE* -ˈduːs/ [T] (*formal*) to cause sth or make sth more likely to happen: *A glass of warm milk at bedtime may help to induce sleep.* ◇ *Doctors will begin bringing him out of a drug-induced coma on Sunday.* ❶ **Induce** is often used to talk about the effects that sth such as medicine, disease or injury has on the body: *Hearing loss is often induced by exposure to loud noise.*

ceremony *noun*

ceremony · ritual · rite · service · liturgy · sacrament · prayers
These are all words for a series of actions that form part of religious worship or a formal occasion.

PATTERNS AND COLLOCATIONS
▸ **at** a ceremony / a ritual / a rite / a service / prayers
▸ a **religious** ceremony / ritual / rite / service
▸ a/an **ancient/primitive/traditional/pagan** ceremony/ritual/rite
▸ an **initiation** ceremony / ritual / rite
▸ a **funeral** ceremony / rite / service
▸ (a) **Christian** ceremony / ritual / liturgy
▸ to **perform** a ceremony / ritual / rite
▸ to **attend** a ceremony / service / prayers
▸ to **hold** a ceremony / service

ceremony [C] a public or religious occasion that includes a series of formal or traditional actions: *They were married in a simple ceremony.* ◇ *an awards ceremony* ◇ *the opening ceremony of the Olympic games* ◇ *the Japanese tea ceremony*
▸ **ceremonial** /ˌserɪˈməʊniəl; *AmE* -ˈmoʊ-/ *adj.*: *a ceremonial occasion/sword*

ritual /ˈrɪtʃuəl/ [C, U] a series of actions that are always carried out in the same way, especially as part of a religious ceremony: *Many folk dances have their origins in ancient pagan rituals.* ◇ *She objects to the ritual of organized religion.* See also → HABIT
▸ **ritual** *adj.*: *ritual chanting/practices*
▸ **ritually** *adv.*: *The goat was ritually slaughtered.*

rite [C] a ritual: *He received the last rites from a Roman Catholic priest and died an hour later.* ◇ *New members of the cult have to undergo a secret initiation rite.*

NOTE RITUAL OR RITE? Both these words are connected with ancient religious practices, especially ones that mark the important events in sb's life or in the cycle of life and death: *religious/ancient/primitive/traditional/ pagan rituals/rites* ◇ *initiation/fertility rituals/rites.* In many cases you can use either word. However, there can be a slight difference of emphasis: **ritual** often emphasizes the complicated form of the ceremony more than its meaning and you can talk about an *elaborate ritual* or an *empty ritual* that has lost its meaning altogether. A **rite** is often simpler and more serious, especially when it is connected with death: **ritual** is not used in these cases: ~~He received the last rituals from a Roman Cathloc priest.~~ ◇ ~~funeral rituals~~

service [C] a religious ceremony, either as part of the regular worship of a particular church or community, or to mark a particular occasion: *He always attends morning service.* ◇ *A special service of praise and thanksgiving was held in the cathedral.*

liturgy /ˈlɪtədʒi; *AmE* ˈlɪtərdʒi/ [C, U] a fixed form of public worship used in churches: *Henry VIII ordered that the English Prayer Book was to replace the old Latin liturgy in church services.* ◇ *He has written several books on theology and liturgy.*

sacrament /ˈsækrəmənt/ [C] (*rather formal*) an important Christian ceremony such as marriage, baptism or communion: *to receive the sacrament of Christian baptism*

prayers [pl.] a religious meeting that takes place regularly, in which people say prayers to give thanks to God or ask him for help: *He reads the Koran, attends daily prayers and has made a pilgrimage to Mecca.*

certain *adj.* See also the entry for CONCLUSIVE

certain · bound · sure · definite · destined · guaranteed · assured
These words all describe sth that will definitely happen or is definitely true.

PATTERNS AND COLLOCATIONS
▸ certain / sure / assured **of** sth
▸ certain / bound / sure / destined / guaranteed **to do** sth
▸ certain / definite **that…**
▸ I **couldn't say for** certain / sure / definite.
▸ to **seem** certain / bound to… / sure / definite / destined / guaranteed / assured
▸ to **look** certain / sure / definite / destined / guaranteed / assured
▸ **by no means** certain / sure / definite / guaranteed / assured
▸ **fairly / quite / absolutely** certain / sure / definite

certain that you can rely on to happen or be true: *It's certain that they will agree.* ◇ *She looks certain to win an Oscar.* ◇ *If you want to be certain of getting into the concert, buy your ticket now.* ◇ *The climbers face certain death if the rescue attempt is unsuccessful.* **OPP uncertain** → UNCERTAIN
▸ **certainly** *adv.*: *This will certainly make them think again.* ◇ *She was certainly attractive but you couldn't call her beautiful.*

bound /baʊnd/ [not before noun] certain to happen, or to do or be sth: *There are bound to be changes when the new system is introduced.* ◇ *You've done so much work — you're bound to pass the exam.* ◇ *It was bound to happen sooner or later* (= we should have expected it). ❶ **Bound** is only used in the phrase *bound to do/be*, etc.

sure certain to happen or be true; that can be trusted or relied on: *She's sure to be picked for the team.* ◇ *There's only one sure way of knowing.* ◇ *It's a sure sign of economic recovery.* ◇ (*rather informal*) *He's a sure bet for the presidential nomination* (= he is certain to get it).

definite (*especially spoken*) certain to happen; that is not going to change: *Is it definite that he's leaving?* ◇ *I've heard rumours, but nothing definite.* ◇ *Can you give me a definite answer by tomorrow?* ◇ *Have they made you a definite offer of a job?*
▸ **definitely** *adv.*: *I definitely remember sending the letter.* ◇ *'Do you plan to have children?' 'Definitely not!'* ◇ *The date of the move has not been definitely decided yet* (= it may change). ◇ *Please say definitely whether you will be coming or not.*

destined /'destɪnd/ (*formal*) having a future which has been decided or planned at an earlier time, especially by fate: *He was destined for a military career, like his father before him.* ◇ *We seem destined never to meet.* See also **destiny** → LUCK

guaranteed /ˌɡærən'tiːd/ certain to have a particular result: *If we try to keep it a secret, she's guaranteed to find out.* ◇ *That kind of behaviour is guaranteed to make him angry.*

assured /ə'ʃʊəd; ə'ʃɔːd; AmE ə'ʃʊrd/ (*written*) certain to happen; certain to get sth: *Victory seemed assured.* ◇ *The French team are now assured of a place in the final.*

certainty *noun*

certainty · inevitability · necessity · a foregone conclusion · a sure thing
These are all words for sth that you believe will definitely happen.

PATTERNS AND COLLOCATIONS
▸ a certainty / an inevitability **about** sth
▸ an **absolute** certainty / necessity
▸ the **one** / **only** certainty / necessity

certainty [C] an event that will definitely happen; a fact or situation that is not doubted by anybody: *Her return to the team now seems a certainty.* ◇ *The end of the Cold War marked the collapse of many old political certainties.* **OPP** **uncertainty** → DOUBT 2

inevitability /ɪnˌevɪtə'bɪləti/ [U, C, usually sing.] the fact that sth will definitely happen and cannot be avoided or prevented, especially sth bad or unpleasant; an event that will definitely happen: *We must all, sooner or later, confront the inevitability of death.* ◇ *World war has ceased to be an inevitability.* See also **inevitable** → INEVITABLE

necessity /nə'sesəti/ [C, usually sing.] a situation that must happen and that cannot be avoided, especially in order to do or achieve sth else: *Living in London he felt, was an unfortunate necessity.*

a ˌforegone con'clusion *idiom* a result that is certain to happen: *The outcome of the vote is a foregone conclusion.*

a ˌsure 'thing *idiom* (*especially AmE, rather informal, especially business*) something that is certain to happen: *An increase in crude oil prices now looks like a sure thing.*

certificate *noun* See also the entry for LICENCE

certificate · documentation · papers · ID · credentials
These are all words for an official document that gives proof of sth.

PATTERNS AND COLLOCATIONS
▸ **on** a certificate / the documentation
▸ **in** the documentation / papers
▸ (a/an) **official** / **necessary** certificate / documentation / papers
▸ to **have** (a/an) certificate / documentation / papers / ID / credentials
▸ to **get** / **obtain** (a) certificate / documentation / papers / credentials
▸ to **issue** / **give** (sb) (a) certificate / documentation / papers
▸ to **see** / **check** sb's certificate / documentation / papers / ID / credentials
▸ to **examine** sb's documentation / papers / ID / credentials
▸ to **show** / **present** your certificate / documentation / papers / ID / credentials

certificate /sə'tɪfɪkət; AmE sər't-/ [C] an official document that may be used to prove that the facts it states are true: *This certificate is an important document. Keep it in a safe place.* ◇ *a birth/marriage/death certificate* ◇ *She showed her certificate of insurance.*

documentation /ˌdɒkjumen'teɪʃn; AmE ˌdɑːk-/ [U] the documents that are required for sth or that give proof of sth: *I couldn't enter the country because I didn't have all the necessary documentation.* ◇ *We send comprehensive travel documentation, including tickets, hotel vouchers and a detailed itinerary.* ◇ *If the technical documentation is inadequate, your system is not a quality product.* See also **document** → DOCUMENT

papers [pl.] official documents that prove your identity or give you permission to do sth: *We had to show our papers at the border.* ◇ *Do you have your identification papers with you?* ◇ *He hasn't received his divorce papers yet.* See also **papers** → DOCUMENT

NOTE **DOCUMENTATION** OR **PAPERS**? Either word may be used for documents that prove your identity, especially when these are needed to travel between countries. *Travel documentation*, however, usually refers to tickets. **Documentation** can also be detailed printed technical information about a product such as a machine or computer system. **Papers** can also be legal documents that give you permission to do sth.

ID /ˌaɪ 'diː/ [U, C] (*rather informal*) an official way of showing who you are, for example a document with your name, date of birth, and often a photograph on it (abbreviation for 'identity' or 'identification'): *Do you have any ID?* ◇ *You must carry ID at all times.* ◇ *The police checked IDs at the gate.* ◇ *You will need some form of photo ID.*

credentials /krə'denʃlz/ [pl.] documents such as letters that prove you are who you claim to be and can therefore be trusted: *The ambassador presented his diplomatic credentials.* ◇ *Check the credentials of any unknown caller.*

chair *noun*

chair · seat · couch · sofa · bench · stool · armchair · pew · throne
These are all words for a piece of furniture that you sit on or a place where you can sit.

PATTERNS AND COLLOCATIONS
▸ **in** / **into** / **out of** a chair / a seat / an armchair / a pew
▸ **on** / **onto** / **off** a chair / a seat / a couch / a bench / a stool / an armchair / a settee / a pew / a throne
▸ a **wooden** chair / seat / bench / stool / pew
▸ a **leather** chair / seat / couch / sofa / armchair
▸ an **upholstered** chair / seat / couch / sofa / stool / armchair
▸ a **comfortable** chair / seat / couch / sofa / armchair
▸ an **empty** chair / seat / bench / pew
▸ to **sit (down) on** / **in** a chair / a seat / a couch / a sofa / a bench / a stool / an armchair / a pew / a throne
▸ to **perch on** a chair / a seat / a bench / a stool
▸ to **sprawl** / **lounge** / **slump in** / **on** a chair / a seat / a couch / a sofa / a bench / an armchair
▸ to **collapse** / **settle** / **flop** / **sink into** / **onto** a chair / a seat / a couch / a sofa / an armchair
▸ the **arm** / **back** / **leg** of a chair / a couch / a sofa / a bench / an armchair

chair [C] a piece of furniture for one person to sit on, with a back, four legs and a space to put your bottom on: *a table and chairs* ◇ *Sit on your chair!* ◇ *a set of dining/kitchen chairs* ◇ *She dropped her bags and flopped down into the nearest chair.* ❶ **Chair** is often used in compounds to describe different types of chair: *a wheelchair* ◇ *a deckchair* (= a folding chair with a seat made from a long strip of material on a wooden or metal frame, used for example on a beach) ◇ *a high chair* (= a chair with long legs and a little seat and table, for a baby or small child to

chair

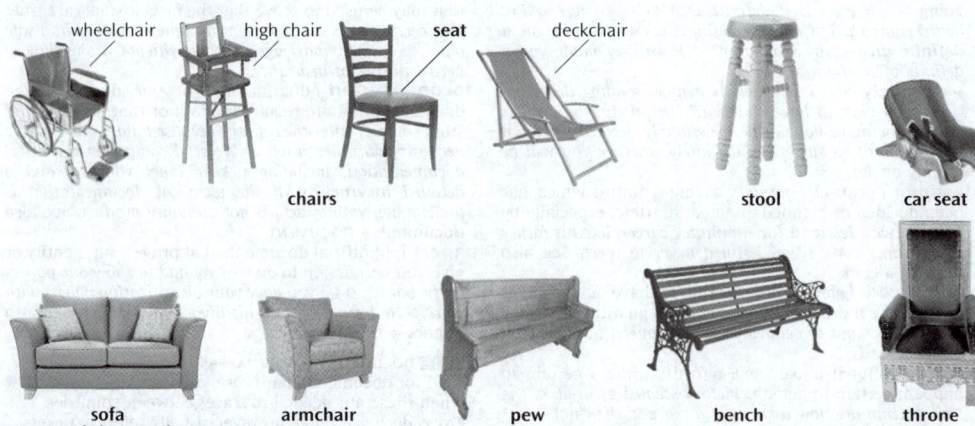

wheelchair   high chair   seat   deckchair   stool   car seat

chairs

sofa   armchair   pew   bench   throne
couch (*esp AmE*)

sit in when eating) ◊ *a rocking chair* (= a chair with two curved pieces of wood under it that make it move backwards and forwards)

seat [C] a place where you can sit, for example a chair; the part of a chair, etc. on which you actually sit: *Is this seat taken?* (= Is somebody already sitting here?) ◊ *She sat back in her seat.* ◊ *He put his shopping on the seat behind him.* ◊ *We all filed back to our seats in silence.* ◊ *Please take a seat* (= sit down). ◊ *a window/corner seat* (= one near a window/in a corner) ◊ *a car seat* (= for a child in a car) ◊ *a steel chair with a plastic seat* See also **take a seat → SIT**

NOTE CHAIR OR SEAT? A **chair** is a piece of furniture designed for sitting on, which you can buy in a shop or have in your home, office, etc. A **seat** may be other things/places that you can use as a seat, or places to sit that do not look like a traditional chair with a back, four legs, etc.: *a dining table and six matching chairs.* ◊ ~~a dining table and six matching seats~~ ◊ *We used the branch of an old tree as a seat.* ◊ ~~We used the branch of an old tree as a chair.~~ **Seat** can also be more figurative: *Ladies and gentlemen, please take your seats* (= sit down). ◊ ~~take your chairs~~ **Seat** is used for the place where you can sit in a vehicle: *the passenger seat/back seat/driver's seat* (= in a car) ◊ *an aisle/a window seat* (= on a plane/bus/train) ◊ ~~the passenger chair/back chair/driver's chair~~ ◊ ~~an aisle/a window chair~~

couch /kaʊtʃ/ [C] (*especially AmE*) a long comfortable seat with a back and arms, for two or more people to sit on: *They sat down on the wide couch.* ◊ *We didn't have any spare beds so he slept on the couch.* ❶ In informal language, the disapproving expression *couch potato* is used to describe sb who spends a lot of time sitting and watching television: (*informal, disapproving*) *He's turned into a real couch potato since he subscribed to the sports channel.*

sofa /ˈsəʊfə; *AmE* ˈsoʊfə/ [C] a couch: *I spent the evening sprawled on the sofa, watching TV.* ◊ *a sofa bed* (= a sofa that can be folded out to form a bed)

NOTE SOFA OR COUCH? In British English the usual word is **sofa**. In American English both are possible, although **couch** is more frequent.

bench [C] a long seat for two or more people, usually made of wood: *a park bench*

stool [C] (often in compounds) a seat with legs but with nothing to support your back or arms: *a bar stool* ◊ *a piano stool*

armchair /ˈɑːmtʃeə(r); ɑːmˈtʃeə(r); *AmE* ˈɑːrmtʃer; ɑːrmˈtʃer/ [C] a comfortable chair with sides on which you can rest your arms, like a sofa for one person: *He eased himself into the big armchair.*

pew /pjuː/ [C] a long wooden seat in a church: *The first two rows of pews were occupied by the families of the bride and groom.* ❶ In informal spoken British English, you can invite sb in a humorous way to sit down by saying 'take a pew': (*BrE, informal, spoken, humorous*) *Come in and take a pew. Can I get you a cup of tea?*

throne [C] a special chair used by a king or queen to sit on at ceremonies: *He sat very upright in his chair, as if he were a king on his throne.*

challenge *verb* See the Topic Map for CONFLICT on p.896

challenge · dare · throw down the gauntlet
These words all mean to invite sb to fight or compete with you, or do sth that you think they may be afraid to do.

PATTERNS AND COLLOCATIONS
▸ to challenge / dare sb **to do sth**

challenge /ˈtʃælɪndʒ/ [T] to invite sb to enter a competition or fight; to suggest strongly that sb should do sth, especially when you think that they might be unwilling to do it: *Mike challenged me to a game of chess.* ◊ *The opposition leader challenged the prime minister to call an election.* See also **challenger → PARTICIPANT**
▸ **challenge** *noun* [C]: *She took up his challenge.*

dare [T] to try to persuade sb to do sth dangerous, difficult or embarrassing so that they can show that they are not afraid: *Go on! Take it! I dare you.* ◊ *Some of the older boys had dared him to do it.*
▸ **dare** *noun* [C, usually sing.]: (*BrE*) *He climbed onto the roof for a dare.* ◊ (*AmE*) *She learned to fly on a dare.*

throw down the ˈgauntlet *idiom* to invite sb to fight or compete with you: *She has thrown down the gauntlet to the newspaper by accusing it of libel.* **OPP take up the gauntlet** ❶ To **take up the gauntlet** is to accept sb's invitation to fight or compete: *His Republican rival may be expected to take up the gauntlet.*

change *noun*

1 a change in the weather
2 make changes to sth

1 change · shift · variation · swing · fluctuation · variability · alternation
These are all words for the act of becoming different, especially frequently.

PATTERNS AND COLLOCATIONS

- a **change** / a **shift** / a **variation** / a **swing** / a **fluctuation** / **variability** / an **alternation** **in** sth
- a **shift** / a **variation** / a **fluctuation** / an **alternation** **between** A and B
- a **shift** / **swing** **towards** sth
- (a) **considerable** change / shift / variation / fluctuation / variability
- a **big** / **dramatic** / **massive** change / shift / variation / swing
- (a) **small** change / shift / variation / swing / fluctuations
- (a) **rapid** change / shift / fluctuation / alternation
- (a) **random** change / variation / fluctuation / alternation
- (a) **seasonal** change / variation / fluctuation
- to **cause** a change / a shift / a variation / a swing / fluctuations / variability
- to **produce** a change / a shift / a variation / swing / fluctuations
- to **show** a change / a shift / a variation / a swing / fluctuation / an alternation / variability
- a change / a shift / a variation / a swing / fluctuation **occurs**

change [C, U] the result of sth becoming different: *We're hoping for a change in the weather.* ◊ *There was **no change** in the patient's condition overnight.* ◊ *She is someone who hates change.* ◊ *How far does war bring about social change?* ❶ **a change** [sing.] is the fact of a situation, place or experience being different from what is usual and therefore likely to be interesting or enjoyable: *Let's stay in tonight **for a change**.* ◊ *It **makes a change** to read some good news for once.*

shift [C] (*especially journalism*) a change in position or direction: *These results mark a dramatic shift in public opinion.* ◊ *There was a gradual **shift** in the population **away from** the countryside to the towns.* ◊ *I detected a subtle shift towards our point of view.* ◊ *These climate shifts occurred over less than a decade.*

variation [C, U] frequent change in the amount, quality or level of sth: *The dial records very slight variations in pressure.* ◊ *Currency exchange rates are always subject to variation.* ◊ *We need to take seasonal variation into account* (= depending on the time of year). See also **variation** → DIFFERENCE

swing [C] a change from one opinion or situation to another; the amount by which sth changes: *He is liable to abrupt **mood swings*** (= for example from being very happy to being very sad). ◊ *Voting showed a 10% swing to Labour.* ◊ *There are indications of a swing towards nuclear power.* ❶ **Swing** is used especially to talk about political, social and cultural changes, as well as *mood swings* or *swings of mood*.

fluctuation /ˌflʌktʃuˈeɪʃn/ [C, U] (*rather formal*) frequent change in the size, amount, level or quality of sth, especially from one extreme to another: *The situation led to wild fluctuations in interest rates.* ◊ *Recent ice-cap surveys reveal climatic fluctuation.*

variability /ˌveəriəˈbɪləti; *AmE* ˌver-; ˌvær-/ [U] (*written*) the fact of sth being likely to vary: *The changes were attributed to natural climatic variability.* ◊ *There is always a degree of variability in the exchange rate.* See also **variable** → VARIABLE

alternation /ˌɔːltəˈneɪʃn; *AmE* -tər'n-/ [U, C] (*rather formal*) a repeated change between different situations, feelings, types of behaviour or ideas: *the alternation of day and night* ◊ *Such rapid alternations of mood are a feature of her writing.* ❶ **Alternations** involve changing from one situation to another, and then back to the first situation again.

---

2 change · amendment · transition · adjustment · conversion · modification · switch · alteration · revision · adaptation

These are all words for the act or result of making sth different.

PATTERNS AND COLLOCATIONS

- a change / an amendment / a transition / an adjustment / a conversion / a modification / a switch / an alteration / a revision / an adaptation **to** sth
- a change / an adjustment / a modification / a switch / an alteration **in** sth
- (a) **major** change / amendment / transition / adjustment / modification / alteration / revision / adaptation
- (an) **important** change / amendment / transition / adjustment / modification / switch / alteration / revision
- (a) **radical** change / adjustment / alteration / revision / adaptation
- (a) **slight** change / amendment / adjustment / modification / alteration / revision
- (a) **constant** change / adjustment / modification / alteration / revision / adaptation
- to **propose** / **suggest** a change / an amendment / a modification / an alteration / a revision / an adaptation
- to **make** a change / an amendment / the transition / an adjustment / a modification / a switch / an alteration / a revision / an adaptation
- to **carry out** / **undertake** a conversion / modification / an alteration / revision
- to **need** / **require** amendment / adjustment / modification / alteration / revision
- to **undergo** a transition / modification / alteration / revision

change [C, U] the act or result of making sth different: *I made a couple of minor changes to the opening paragraph.* ◊ *He made a rapid gear change as he approached the bend.* ◊ *He called for a change of mood in Scottish politics.* ◊ *Train times are subject to change without notice.* See also **change over** → SWITCH *verb*

amendment /əˈmendmənt/ [C, U] (*rather formal*) a small change or improvement that is made to a law or document; the process of changing a law or document: *A major amendment was introduced into the legislation.* ◊ *Parliament passed the bill without further amendment.* See also **amend** → ADJUST

transition /trænˈzɪʃn; -ˈsɪʃn/ [U, C] (*rather formal*) the process or a period of changing from one state or condition to another: *The company was slow to make the transition from paper to computer.* ◊ *He will remain head of state during the **period of transition** to democracy.* ◊ *This class is useful for students who are **in transition*** (= in the process of changing) *from one training programme to another.* ◊ *We need to ensure a smooth **transition between** the old system and the new one.*

▸ **transitional** *adj.*: *a transitional period* ◊ *a transitional government*

adjustment /əˈdʒʌstmənt/ [C, U] (*rather formal*) a small change that is made to sth in order to correct or improve it; a change in the way a person behaves or thinks: *I've made a few adjustments to the design.* ◊ *Some adjustment of the lens may be necessary.* ◊ *She went through a period of emotional adjustment after her marriage broke up.* ❶ **Adjustment** is usually used to talk about small changes made to objects, rather than documents. See also **adjust** → ADJUST

conversion /kənˈvɜːʃn; *AmE* -ˈvɜːrʒn; -ʃn/ [U, C] the act or process of changing sth from one form, use or system to another: *Their main business is the **conversion** of farm buildings **into** family homes.* ◊ *Conversion to gas central heating will save you a lot of money.* ◊ *The firm specializes in house conversions* (= turning large houses into several smaller flats or apartments). See also **convert** → TURN 2, **conversion** → SWITCH *verb*

modification /ˌmɒdɪfɪˈkeɪʃn; *AmE* ˌmɑːd-/ [U, C] (*rather formal*) the act or process of changing sth in order to correct or improve it or make it more acceptable; a change that is made: *Considerable modification of the existing system is needed.* ◊ *It might be necessary to make a few slight modifications to the design.* See also **modify** → ADJUST

switch [C] (*rather informal, especially journalism*) a change from one thing to another, especially when this is sudden and complete: *She made the switch from full-time to part-time work when her first child was born.* ◊ *He has vehemently opposed the policy switch.* See also **switch** → SWITCH *verb*

alteration /ˌɔːltəˈreɪʃn/ [C, U] a change to sth that makes it different; the act of making a change to sth: *They are making some major alterations to the house.* ◇ *The dress will not need much alteration.*

NOTE ADJUSTMENT, MODIFICATION OR ALTERATION? **Adjustments** are usually small changes that are made to designs or equipment. **Modification** can be used to talk about a wider variety of changes, but it is often used to describe larger changes made to systems or vehicles. **Alteration** is often used to talk about changes people make to buildings, especially their houses.

revision /rɪˈvɪʒn/ [U, C] (*rather formal*) the act of changing sth, or of examining sth with the intention of changing it; a change or set of changes made: *The system is in need of revision.* ◇ *He made some minor revisions to the report before printing it out.* ❶ **Revisions** are usually made to correct sth that is wrong, or to bring sth up to date. See also **revise** → ADJUST, **revise** → REVISE

adaptation /ˌædæpˈteɪʃn/ [U] (*rather formal*) the process of changing sth, for example your behaviour, to suit a new situation: *We've been studying the adaptation of species to hot conditions.*

change verb

1 change your habits
2 changing attitudes towards education

1 See also the entry for ADJUST
change · alter · adapt · shift · tailor · vary
These words all mean to make sb/sth different.

PATTERNS AND COLLOCATIONS
▸ to change / alter / adapt / tailor sth **for** sb / sth
▸ to change / alter / adapt a **plan / story**
▸ to change / alter / shift / vary the **emphasis**
▸ to change / alter / shift the **balance / perspective**
▸ to change / alter / adapt your **behaviour**
▸ to change / alter / vary your **routine**
▸ to change / alter / shift your / sb's **attitude / opinion**
▸ to change / alter / adapt / tailor sth **accordingly**
▸ to change / adapt / tailor sth **specially / carefully**

change [T] to make sb/sth different: *Information technology has changed the way people work.* ◇ *This incident changed the whole course of events.* ◇ *What made you* **change your mind** (= change your opinion)? ◇ *The fruit* **changes colour** *as it ripens.* ◇ *Don't keep* **changing the subject***.*
alter /ˈɔːltə(r)/ [T] to make sb/sth different: *This development will alter the character of the town.* ◇ *Nothing can alter the fact that we are to blame.*

NOTE CHANGE OR ALTER? Sometimes you can use either word: *Fame hasn't really changed/altered him.* However, **change** often suggests a complete change, whereas **alter** can suggest a smaller change: *This law needs to be altered* (= changed slightly in order to improve it). ◇ *This law needs to be changed* (= changed completely or got rid of). **Alter** is often used when sth does NOT change: *It doesn't alter the way I feel.* or to talk about making changes to particular aspects of sth: *They can alter the programme until success is achieved.* **Change** can also be used in all of these cases, but its range of uses is much wider, including particular collocations such as *change your mind, change your name, change colour, change tack* and *change the subject*.

adapt [T] to change sth in order to make it suitable for a new use or situation: *Most of these tools have been specially adapted for use by disabled people.* ◇ *These styles can be adapted to suit individual tastes.* See also **modify** → ADJUST, **adaptable** → FLEXIBLE 1
shift [T] to change the way that people think about sth: *They are trying to shift public attitudes about the nature of old age.* ◇ *We need to shift the focus of this debate.* ❶ Typical collocates of **shift** are *attitudes, opinions, balance, emphasis, focus* and *perspective*.

tailor /ˈteɪlə(r)/ [T] to make or adapt sth for a particular purpose or person: *Special programmes of study are* **tailored to** *the needs of specific groups.* ◇ *Most travel agents are prepared to tailor travel arrangements to meet individual requirements.*
vary [T] to make changes to sth to make it slightly different: *The job enables me to vary the hours I work.* ◇ *The aerobics instructor varies the routine each week.* ❶ **Vary** is used especially to talk about making slight changes to a *routine* of sth that you do regularly.

2 change · vary · shift · fluctuate · swing · alter · alternate
These words all mean to become different.

PATTERNS AND COLLOCATIONS
▸ to change / shift / swing **from** sth **to** sth
▸ to vary / fluctuate / swing / alternate **between** A and B
▸ to change / vary / fluctuate **according to** sth
▸ to change / vary / fluctuate / swing **wildly**
▸ to change / vary / shift / fluctuate / swing / alter **dramatically / sharply**
▸ to change / vary / shift / fluctuate / alter **significantly**
▸ to change / vary / shift / fluctuate **constantly / continually**
▸ to change / shift / fluctuate / swing **rapidly**
▸ to change / shift / swing **suddenly**
▸ to change / vary / alter **little / slightly / somewhat**
▸ to **hardly / never** change / vary / alter

change [I] to become different: *Rick hasn't changed. He looks exactly the same as he did at school.* ◇ *We examined changing attitudes towards education.* ◇ *The language is changing all the time.* ◇ *Leeds changed from a small market town into a busy city.* ◇ *Her life changed completely when she won the lottery.*
vary [I] to change frequently or be different according to the situation: *The menu* **varies with** *the season.* ◇ *Prices vary according to the type of room you require.* ◇ *Class numbers vary between 25 and 30.* ◇ *Pulse rates vary slightly from person to person.* ◇ *'What time do you start work?' 'It* **varies***.'*
shift [I] (*especially journalism*) (of a situation or opinion) to change from one state or position to another: *The balance of power shifted away from workers towards employers.* ◇ *Public attitudes towards marriage have shifted over the past 50 years.*
fluctuate /ˈflʌktʃueɪt/ [I] (*rather formal or written*) to change frequently in size, amount, level or quality, especially from one extreme to another: *During the crisis, oil prices fluctuated between $30 and $50 a barrel.* ◇ *Temperatures can* **fluctuate by** *as much as 10 degrees.* ◇ *My weight fluctuated wildly depending on how much I ate.*
swing [I] (*especially journalism*) to change from one opinion, mood or situation to another, especially from one extreme to another: *The state has swung from Republican to Democrat.* ◇ *His emotions swung between fear and curiosity.* ◇ *The game could swing either way* (= either side could win it).
alter /ˈɔːltə(r)/ [I] to become different: *Property prices did not significantly alter during 2007.* ◇ *He had not altered greatly in the last ten years.*

NOTE CHANGE OR ALTER? Sometimes you can use either word: *Rick hasn't changed/altered much.* However, **change** is much more frequent and has a much wider range than **alter**: it often suggests a complete change to sth important: *Her life changed completely when she won the lottery.* ◇ *Her life altered completely.* It can also be used to talk about things that are in the process of changing: *changing attitudes to education* ◇ *altering attitudes to education.* **Alter** is often used when sth has changed only slightly or not at all: *The party's policies have hardly altered, but public opinion has.*

alternate /ˈɔːltəneɪt; *AmE* -tərn-/ [I] (always followed by *between*) to keep changing from one thing to another and back again: *Her mood alternated between happiness and despair.*

channel *noun*

channel · station · network · frequency
These are all words for television and radio companies, the shows they broadcast, or the radio waves used for broadcasting them.

PATTERNS AND COLLOCATIONS
▶ a **television** channel / station / network
▶ a **radio** station / network / frequency
▶ to **tune to** a channel / station / frequency
▶ to **watch** a channel / station
▶ to **change / switch** channels / stations

channel [C] a television company and the shows it broadcasts; a band of radio waves used for broadcasting television or radio shows: *What's on Channel 4 tonight?* ◇ *a movie/sports channel* ◇ *terrestrial/satellite/cable/digital channels*

station [C] (often in compounds) a radio or television company and the shows it broadcasts: *a local radio/TV station* ◇ *He tuned to another station.*

network [C] a group of radio or television stations in different places that are connected and that broadcast the same shows at the same time: *the four big US television networks*

frequency /ˈfriːkwənsi/ [C, U] (*technical*) the number of radio waves for every second of a radio signal: *There are only a limited number of broadcasting frequencies.* ◇ *a frequency band*

chaos *noun* See also the entry for MESS 2

chaos · confusion · mess · commotion · mayhem · havoc · shambles · pandemonium · uproar
These are all words for a state of confusion and lack of order.

PATTERNS AND COLLOCATIONS
▶ **in** chaos / (the) confusion / a mess / the commotion / the mayhem / a shambles / pandemonium / (an) uproar
▶ (a) **complete / total** chaos / confusion / mess / mayhem / shambles / pandemonium
▶ **general** chaos / confusion / commotion / mayhem / pandemonium
▶ (a) **great** confusion / commotion / uproar
▶ to **cause** chaos / confusion / a mess / a commotion / mayhem / havoc / pandemonium / (an) uproar
▶ to **create** chaos / confusion / a mess / mayhem / havoc
▶ to **bring** chaos / mayhem / havoc
▶ to **sort out** the chaos / mess / shambles
▶ chaos / a commotion / mayhem / pandemonium / uproar **breaks out**
▶ chaos / confusion / pandemonium **reigns**
▶ **There is / was** chaos / confusion / a commotion / mayhem / pandemonium / uproar.
▶ **It is/was** chaos / a mess / mayhem / a shambles / pandemonium.

chaos /ˈkeɪɒs; *AmE* ˈkeɪɑːs/ [U] a situation in which things are happening in a confused way and there is no order or control at all: *Heavy flooding is causing total chaos across the country.* ◇ *The house was in chaos after the party.* ◇ *People started shouting and the meeting descended into chaos.* **OPP** order → EFFICIENCY
▶ **chaotic** /keɪˈɒtɪk; *AmE* -ˈɑːtɪk/ *adj.*: *It's a bit chaotic around here at the moment.* ◇ *Amid chaotic scenes in court, the long-awaited verdict was announced.*

confusion [U] a situation in which a lot of things are happening at the same time and people do not know what action to take: *The protesters set off smoke bombs to create confusion and panic.* ◇ *The local council has been thrown into total confusion by her resignation.*

NOTE **CHAOS** OR **CONFUSION?** Chaos generally describes a total lack of order in a system or situation; **confusion** is mainly used about a group of people who suddenly don't know what to do.

mess [C, usually sing.] (*rather informal*) a situation that is full of problems because of a lack of organization or because people have made mistakes: *The economy is in a mess.* ◇ *The whole situation is a mess.* ◇ *I feel I've made a terrible mess of things.* ◇ *A new managing director has been appointed to clear up the financial mess.* ◇ *Who got us into this mess in the first place?*
▶ **messy** *adj.*: *The divorce was painful and messy.*

commotion /kəˈməʊʃn; *AmE* -ˈmoʊ-/ [C, usually sing., U] sudden noisy confusion or excitement: *I heard a commotion upstairs and went to see what was happening.* ◇ *She waited until the commotion died down.*

mayhem /ˈmeɪhem/ [U] (*rather formal*) confusion and fear, sometimes involving violence or injury, usually caused by some sudden shocking event: *The gales caused mayhem across much of the country.* ◇ *The terrorists brought mayhem to the crowded shopping area.*

havoc /ˈhævək/ [U] a situation in which there are a lot of problems and confusion because of the bad effect of sth: *This new virus has created havoc for computer users.* ◇ *The fog is playing havoc with flight schedules.* ◇ *Continuing strikes are beginning to wreak havoc on the economy.*

shambles [sing.] (*rather informal*) a situation that is completely unsuccessful because of a lack of organization or because people have made mistakes: *The economy was in a shambles last year.* ◇ *Our defending was a complete shambles.* ◇ *What a shambles!*

NOTE **MESS** OR **SHAMBLES?** Shambles is a stronger word than **mess** and suggests a situation in which organization has broken down completely.

pandemonium /ˌpændəˈməʊniəm; *AmE* -ˈmoʊ-/ [U] (*rather formal*) a situation in which there is a lot of noise, activity and confusion, especially because people are feeling angry or frightened: *Pandemonium broke out when the news was announced.* ◇ *It was absolute pandemonium in there.*

uproar [U, sing.] a situation in which people shout and make a lot of noise because they are angry or upset about sth: *The trial ended in uproar.* ◇ *Her comments provoked an uproar from the audience.*

chapter *noun*

chapter · issue · part · episode · unit · edition · volume · contents · instalment
These are all words for part of a book or story, or one of a number of books, newspapers, magazines, stories, or TV or radio programmes that are published or broadcast.

PATTERNS AND COLLOCATIONS
▶ a / the **first / second / next** chapter / issue / part / episode / unit / edition / volume / instalment
▶ the **final / last** chapter / part / episode / unit / volume / instalment
▶ the **January / February / March, etc.** issue / edition of sth
▶ **Monday's / Tuesday's / Wednesday's, etc.** issue / edition / episode / instalment of sth
▶ to **produce** an issue / a part / an edition / an episode / a volume / an instalment
▶ to **publish** an issue / a part / an edition / a volume / an instalment
▶ to **bring out** an issue / an edition / a volume
▶ to **show / broadcast / see / watch / miss** a part / an episode / an edition / an instalment of sth
▶ to **read** a chapter / an issue / a part / a unit / an edition / a volume / an instalment
▶ an issue / a part / an edition **appears / is out / comes out**

chapter [C] a separate section of a book, usually with a number or title: *I've just finished Chapter 3.* ◇ *Have you read the chapter on the legal system?*

issue [C] one of a regular series of magazines or newspapers: *I'm after the July issue of 'What Car?'.*

part [C] a section of a book, television series, etc., especially one that is published or broadcast separately: *an encyclopedia published in 25 weekly parts* ◊ *Henry IV, Part II* ◊ *The final part will be shown next Sunday evening.*

episode /ˈepɪsəʊd; *AmE* -soʊd/ [C] one part of a story that is broadcast on television or radio in several parts: *The soap opera is ending after 175 episodes.*

unit [C] one of the parts into which a textbook or series of lessons is divided: *The present perfect is covered in Unit 8.*

edition /ɪˈdɪʃn/ [C] a particular newspaper or magazine, or radio or television programme, especially one in a regular series: *Tonight's edition of 'Panorama' looks at unemployment.* ◊ *The story was in Tuesday's edition of 'The New York Times'.*

volume [C] a book, especially one that is part of a series of books: *The encyclopedia is a huge work, running to 20 volumes.*

NOTE ISSUE, EDITION OR VOLUME? **Issue** is usually used to talk about magazines and journals; **edition** is usually used to talk about newspapers. Academic journals usually publish several **issues** each year; all the issues for one year are considered to belong to one **volume** of the journal. See also **volume** → BOOK

contents [pl.] the different sections that are contained in a book: *a table of contents* (= the list at the front of the book) ◊ *a contents page*

instalment (*especially BrE*) (*AmE* usually **installment**) /ɪnˈstɔːlmənt/ [C] one of the parts of a story that appears regularly over a period of time in a newspaper, on television, etc: *Dickens completed the last instalment of Martin Chuzzlewit in June of that year.* (Dickens originally wrote his stories in instalments for newspapers).

NOTE EPISODE OR INSTALMENT? An **episode** is a programme that forms part of a series on TV or radio; an **instalment** is used more often to talk about the parts of a story that appear in a magazine. When **instalment** is used to talk about TV or radio programmes, it often refers to one part of a very short series: *Now for the second instalment of our exclusive three-part series.*

character noun

character · role · part
These are all words for a person who appears in a story.

PATTERNS AND COLLOCATIONS
▸ the character / role / part **of** sb
▸ a part / role **in** sth
▸ a **major** / **minor** character / role / part
▸ to **play** a character / role / part

character [C] a person, animal or other creature that appears as a figure in a story: *The minor characters in the novel provide a lot of the humour.* ◊ *cartoon characters* ◊ *a character actor* (= an actor who always plays interesting secondary characters in films)

role [C] a character that an actor plays in a play or film: *It is one of the greatest roles she has played.* ◊ *Who is in the leading role* (= the most important one)?

part [C] a character that an actor plays in a play or film; the words spoken by an actor in a particular role: *She was very good in the part.* ◊ *Have you learned your part yet?* ◊ (*figurative*) *He's always playing a part* (= pretending to be sth that he is not).

charge noun

charge · accusation · indictment · impeachment · recrimination
These are all words for a claim that sb has done sth wrong or is guilty of sth.

PATTERNS AND COLLOCATIONS
▸ a charge / an accusation / an indictment / recriminations **against** sb
▸ a charge / an accusation **of** sth
▸ a charge / an accusation **that**...
▸ a **formal** / **serious** charge / accusation / indictment
▸ **bitter** accusations / recriminations
▸ to **face** a charge / an accusation / an indictment / impeachment
▸ to **make** / **deny** a charge / an accusation
▸ to **issue** / **bring** / **drop** a charge / an indictment

charge [C] an official claim made by the police that sb has committed a crime; a statement accusing sb of doing sth wrong or bad: *The investigation resulted in criminal charges against three police officers.* ◊ *After being questioned by the police, she was released without charge.* ◊ *She rejected the charge that the story was untrue.* See also **charge** → ACCUSE *verb*

accusation /ˌækjuˈzeɪʃn/ [C, U] a statement saying that you think a person is guilty of doing sth wrong or bad, especially of committing a crime; the fact of accusing sb: *No one believed her wild accusations against her husband.* ◊ *There was a hint of accusation in her voice.* See also **accuse** → ACCUSE

indictment /ɪnˈdaɪtmənt/ [C, U] (*especially AmE*) a written statement accusing sb of a crime; the act of officially accusing sb of a crime: *There is sufficient evidence against him to support an indictment for murder.* ◊ *This led to his indictment on allegations of conspiracy.* See also **indict** → ACCUSE

impeachment [C, U] the act of a court or other official body charging an important public figure with a serious crime, especially in the US: *If Congress should rule that the President's actions were unconstitutional, it would be a big step towards his impeachment.* See also **impeach** → ACCUSE

recrimination /rɪˌkrɪmɪˈneɪʃn/ [C, usually pl., U] an angry statement that sb makes accusing sb else of sth, especially in response to a similar statement from them: *There were bitter recriminations within the party about who was to blame for the disastrous election results.* ◊ *We spent the rest of the evening in mutual recrimination.*

charge verb

charge · fine · ask · levy · bill · invoice
These words all mean to ask sb for money for goods or a service, or as a payment of a tax.

PATTERNS AND COLLOCATIONS
▸ to charge (sb) / levy sth **on** sth
▸ to charge (sb) / fine sb / ask sth / bill sb / invoice sb **for** sth
▸ to be charged / levied **at** one per cent / 17%
▸ to charge / bill sth **to** sb's account
▸ to charge / ask a high / low **price** / **fee** / **commission** / **rent**

charge [T, I] to ask for an amount of money for goods or a service, or as payment of a tax: *What did the builders charge for the repairs?* ◊ *Calls are charged at 36p per minute.* ◊ *Your broker will charge you a 6% commission on the transaction.* See also **charge** → RATE *noun* 2

fine [T, often passive] to make sb pay money as an official punishment: *She was fined for speeding.* ◊ *The company was fined £20 000 for breaching safety regulations.* See also **fine** → RATE *noun* 2

ask [T] (usually used in the progressive tenses) to request a particular amount of money for sth that you are selling: *He's asking £2 000 for the car.*

levy /ˈlevi/ [T] (*formal or law*) to use official authority to demand and collect a payment or tax: *It was a local tax levied by the council on the occupiers of land and buildings.* ◊ *A $30 million fine was levied against the company.*

bill [T] (*rather formal*) to send sb a bill for a service that you have provided or goods that you have supplied: *You will be billed monthly for the service.* ◊ *The cost will be billed to your account.* See also **bill** → BILL *noun*

invoice [T] (*rather formal*) to send sb a bill for goods that you have supplied or work that you have done for them: *You will be invoiced for these items at the end of the month.* See also **invoice** → BILL *noun*

> **NOTE** BILL OR **INVOICE?** A company that supplies a service such as telephone, gas or electricity, **bills** its customers, usually monthly or quarterly (= every three months). A company or person that has supplied goods or done work will usually **invoice** its customers or employer, although **bill** can also be used for this. Both these words are rather formal; less formally you can say *send sb a bill/an invoice.*

charity *noun*

charity · cause · foundation · trust
These are all words for an organization for helping people in need.

PATTERNS AND COLLOCATIONS
▸ a charity / foundation / trust **for** sth
▸ a **local** charity / cause / foundation / trust
▸ a **deserving / worthwhile / worthy** charity / cause
▸ a **charitable** foundation / trust
▸ a/an **national / private / independent / family / educational / medical / conservation / housing** charity / foundation / trust
▸ to **help / support** a charity / cause / foundation / trust
▸ to **give / donate to** a charity / cause / foundation
▸ to **set up** a charity / foundation / trust
▸ to **establish / create** a foundation / trust

charity [C] an organization for helping people in need: *Many charities sent money to help the victims of the famine.* ◇ *The concert will raise money for local charities.*
▸ **charitable** *adj.*: *a charitable institution/foundation/ trust* ◇ *a charitable donation/gift*
cause [C] an organization or idea that people support or fight for: *Animal welfare campaigners raised £70 000 for their cause last year.* ◇ *Oh well, it's all for a good cause* (= an organization that does good work, such as a charity). ◇ *He dedicated his life to fighting for the Republican cause.*
foundation /faʊnˈdeɪʃn/ [C] an organization that is established to invest money and use the profits for a particular purpose, for example for scientific research or charity: *The money will go to the San Francisco AIDS Foundation.* ◇ *Many of the hospitals were originally established by religious foundations.* See also the entry for ORGANIZATION
trust [C] (*law*) an organization or group of people that holds money or property that it has been given or lent, and uses the profits to help a charity: *She's hoping a charitable trust will soon pay for her operation.*

> **NOTE** FOUNDATION OR **TRUST?** A **trust** is defined in law: it is an organization in which two or more individuals (the *trustees*) hold money, land or other property for charitable purposes. A **foundation** is defined more by its purpose than by its legal structure: it may be a trust or a company of some kind.

charm *noun*

charm · personality · character · charisma · presence
These are all words for the qualities sb has that make them attractive, interesting or impressive.

PATTERNS AND COLLOCATIONS
▸ **great** charm / character / charisma / presence
▸ **natural** charm / charisma
▸ **personal** charm / charisma / presence
▸ to **lack** charm / personality / character / charisma
▸ to **have** charm / charisma / presence

charm [U] (*often approving*) the power of pleasing and attracting other people and making them like you: *He was a man of great charm.* ◇ *He oozes charm, but I wouldn't trust him.* See also **charm** → DELIGHT *verb*, **charming** → NICE 2
personality [U] (*approving*) the qualities of a person's character that make them interesting and attractive to other people: *We need someone with lots of personality to head the project.*
character [U] (*approving*) strong personal qualities such as the ability to deal with difficult or dangerous situations: *He showed great character returning to the sport after his accident.* ◇ *Everyone admires her **strength of character** and determination.*
charisma /kəˈrɪzmə/ [U] (*approving*) the powerful personal quality that some people have to attract, impress and influence other people: *The President has great personal charisma.* See also **charismatic** → NICE 2
presence [U, sing.] (*approving*) the quality of making a strong impression on other people by the way you look, talk or behave: *She has a strong voice but absolutely no **stage presence**.* ◇ *He had a commanding presence in meetings.*

chat *verb* See also the entry for TALK

chat · gossip · chatter
These words all mean to talk in a friendly informal way to sb.

PATTERNS AND COLLOCATIONS
▸ to chat / gossip / chatter **about** sth
▸ to chat / gossip / chatter **to / with** sb
▸ to chat / gossip / chatter **away**

chat (-**tt**-) [I] (*rather informal*) to talk in a friendly informal way to sb: *What were you chatting about?* ◇ *My kids spend hours chatting on the phone to their friends.* See also **chat** → DISCUSSION *noun*
gossip [I] (*sometimes disapproving*) to talk about other people's private lives, sometimes in an unkind way; to talk about things that are not very important: *She's been gossiping about you.* ◇ *I can't stand here gossiping all day.* See also **gossip** → DISCUSSION *noun*, **gossip** → REPORT *noun* 4, **gossip** → SPEAKER *noun* 1
chatter [I] to talk quickly and continuously, especially about things that are not important: *They chattered away happily for a while.* See also **chatter** → DISCUSSION *noun*

cheap *adj.*

cheap · competitive · budget · affordable · reasonable · inexpensive · economical · half-price
These words all describe a product or service that costs little money or less money than you expected.

competitive	cheap	half-price
affordable	budget	
reasonable	economical	
inexpensive		

PATTERNS AND COLLOCATIONS
▸ cheap / competitive / budget / affordable / reasonable / economical **prices / rates / fares**
▸ cheap / competitive / budget / affordable / inexpensive / economical **products / services**
▸ cheap / competitive / affordable / inexpensive **goods**
▸ **very / quite** cheap / competitive / affordable / reasonable / inexpensive / economical
▸ **highly** competitive / economical
▸ **relatively** cheap / competitive / affordable / inexpensive

cheap costing little money or less money than you expected; charging low prices: *A good education is not cheap.* ◇ *A quality pair of Italian shoes **doesn't come cheap**.* ◇ *They've got brand new CD players **going cheap**.* ◇ *Her school managed to get a couple of computers **on the**

cheap. ◇ *The town is full of immigrant workers, used as a source of **cheap labour** (= workers who are paid very little, especially unfairly). ◇ (BrE) We found a **cheap and cheerful** cafe (= one that is simple and charges low prices but is pleasant).* ❶ **Cheap** can also be used in a disapproving way to suggest that sth is poor quality as well as low in price: *It was just a bottle of cheap perfume.* ◇ *(BrE) a **cheap and nasty** bottle of wine* See also **cheap** → POOR 2, OPP **expensive** → EXPENSIVE
▶ **cheaply** *adv.*: *I'm sure I could buy this more cheaply somewhere else.* ◇ *You can live very cheaply in Greece.*

competitive /kəm'petətɪv/ (*especially business*) (of prices, goods or services) as cheap as or cheaper than those offered by other companies; able to offer goods or services at competitive prices: *We aim to provide a first-rate competitive service.* ◇ *We need to work harder to remain **competitive with** other companies.* ◇ *They had gained a **competitive advantage** over rival companies.* OPP **uncompetitive** ❶ **Uncompetitive** goods and services are not cheaper or better than others and therefore not able to compete equally: *an uncompetitive industry* ◇ *uncompetitive prices*
▶ **competitively** *adv.*: *competitively priced goods*

budget [only before noun] (used especially in advertising) cheap because it offers only a basic level of service: *Save pounds on budget flights to the sun.* ◇ *a budget airline/hotel*

affordable cheap enough for most people to afford: *We offer the best at affordable prices.* ◇ *There is less and less affordable housing in this town.*

reasonable (of prices) not too expensive: *We sell good quality food at reasonable prices.* OPP **unreasonable** → HIGH 1
▶ **reasonably** *adv.*: *The apartments are reasonably priced.*

inexpensive (*rather formal*) cheap: *Can you recommend an inexpensive hotel?* ❶ **Inexpensive** is often used to mean that sth is good value for its price. It is used instead of **cheap**, because **cheap** can suggest that sth is poor quality. OPP **expensive** → EXPENSIVE

economical /ˌiːkə'nɒmɪkl; 'ekə-; AmE -nɑːm-/ providing good value or service in relation to the cost: *These cars are very economical to run* (= they do not use too much fuel). ◇ *It would be more economical to buy the bigger size.* OPP **uneconomical** ❶ Something that is **uneconomical** uses too much money or time, or too many materials, and is therefore not likely to make a profit: *It soon proved to be uneconomical to stay open 24 hours a day.*
▶ **economically** *adv.*: *I'll do the job as economically as possible.*

half-'price costing half the usual price: *We waited in line and managed to get two half-price tickets.* OPP **full-price**
▶ **'half-'price** *adv.*: *Children aged under four go half-price.*
▶ **'half price** *noun* [U]: *We have many items at half price or less.*

cheat *noun*

cheat · cheater · con man · hustler · swindler
These are all words for a person who deceives or tricks people.

cheat [C] (*disapproving*) a person who cheats, especially in a game: *You little cheat!* ◇ *(informal, journalism) The government has announced a plan to crack down on tax cheats.* ❶ In American English **cheat** is mainly used in written language; in spoken American English use **cheater**.

cheater [C] (*AmE, disapproving*) a cheat: *You cheater — I saw you looking at my cards!*

'con man [C] (*informal*) a man who tricks sb into giving him money: *The screenplay focuses on the friendship between a dim-witted stud and a petty con man.*

hustler /'hʌslə(r)/ [C] (*informal, especially AmE*) a person who tries to make money by selling things in the street in an aggressive, dishonest or illegal way; a person who tries to win money from less experienced players in a gambling game: *a street hustler selling fake designer T-shirts* ◇ *Johnny was a small-time pool room hustler.*

swindler [C] (*written, disapproving, especially journalism*) a person who tricks sb into giving them money: *A swindler who tricked banks out of £2.2 million was jailed for four years yesterday.*

cheat *verb* See also the entry for DEFRAUD

cheat · fool · deceive · betray · take sb in · trick · con · dupe
These words all mean to make sb believe sth that is not true, especially in order to get what you want.

PATTERNS AND COLLOCATIONS
▶ to cheat / trick / con / dupe sb **out of** sth
▶ to cheat / fool / deceive / trick / con / dupe sb **into doing sth**
▶ to cheat / fool / deceive / trick / con / dupe sb into **believing** sth
▶ to cheat / trick / con **your way** into sth
▶ to fool / deceive **yourself**
▶ to **feel** cheated / deceived / betrayed / tricked
▶ to **easily** cheat / fool / deceive / take in / trick / con / dupe sb
▶ to **completely** cheat / fool / deceive / take in / trick sb

cheat [T] (*disapproving*) to make sb believe sth that is not true, in order to get money or sth else from them: *She is accused of attempting to cheat the taxman.* ◇ *He cheated his way into the job.* ❶ **Cheat** also means to act in a dishonest way in order to gain an advantage, especially in a game, competition or exam: *He cheats at cards.* ◇ *You're not allowed to look at the answers — that's cheating.* ◇ *Anyone caught cheating will automatically be disqualified from the examination.*

fool [T] (*sometimes disapproving*) to make sb believe sth that is not true, especially in order to laugh at them or to get what you want: *Ha! Fooled you! You really thought I was going to jump, didn't you?* ◇ *You can't/don't fool me!* ◇ *She certainly had me fooled — I really believed her!*

deceive [T] (*disapproving*) to make sb believe sth that is not true, especially sb who trusts you, in order to get what you want: *Her husband had been deceiving her for years.* ◇ *She deceived him into handing over all his savings.* See also **deception** → FRAUD 1

betray [T] (*disapproving*) to hurt sb who trusts you, especially by deceiving them or not being loyal to them: *She felt betrayed when she found out the truth about him.* ◇ *She **betrayed his trust** over and over again.* ◇ *I have never known him to **betray a confidence*** (= tell other people sth that should be kept secret). See also **betray** → TELL 2, **betrayal** → BETRAYAL

take sb 'in *phrasal verb* [often passive] (*disapproving*) to deceive sb, usually in order to get what you want: *I was completely taken in by her story.* ◇ *Don't be taken in by his charm — he's ruthless.*

trick [T] (*sometimes disapproving*) to deceive sb, especially in a clever way, in order to get what you want: *I realized that I'd been tricked and then I felt so stupid.* ◇ *He managed to trick his way past the security guards.* See also **trick** → TRICK *noun*

con (-nn-) [T] (*rather informal*) to deceive sb, especially in order to get money from them or get them to do sth for you: *I was conned into buying a useless car.* ◇ *They had been conned out of £100 000.* See also **con** → FRAUD *noun* 2

dupe /djuːp; AmE duːp/ [T, often passive] (*disapproving*) to deceive sb, in order to get sth from them, especially in a way that makes them look stupid: *They soon realized they had been duped.* ◇ *He was duped into giving them his credit card.*

check verb

1 check for mistakes/damage
2 Go and check that I've locked the windows.

---

1 check · look at sth · examine · inspect · audit · visit · go over sth · look sb/sth over · check over sb/sth · view · check through sth
These words all mean to look at sb/sth closely to make sure that everything is correct, in good condition or acceptable.

PATTERNS AND COLLOCATIONS
▶ to check/examine/inspect/check over/check through (sth) **for** sth
▶ to check/look at/examine/inspect sth **to see if/whether...**
▶ to check/look at/examine/inspect/go over/look over/check over/check through sth **carefully**
▶ to check/examine/inspect/go over sth **thoroughly**
▶ to check/look at/examine/inspect sth **closely**
▶ to check/examine/inspect/visit sth **regularly/daily**

check [T] to look at sb/sth closely to make sure that everything is correct, in good condition, safe or satisfactory: *Check your work before handing it in.* ◇ *Check the container for cracks or leaks.* See also **check** → INSPECTION

'look at sth phrasal verb to take a close look at sth, especially in order to see if there is anything wrong or to find out information about sth: *Your ankle's swollen – I think a doctor ought to look at it.* ◇ *I haven't had time to look at (= read) the papers yet.* See also **look** → LOOK noun

examine [T] to look at sb/sth closely to see if there is anything wrong or to find the cause of a problem: *The goods were examined for damage on arrival.* ◇ *The doctor examined her but could find nothing wrong.* See also **examination** → INSPECTION, **examiner** → INSPECTOR

inspect [T] to look at sb/sth closely to make sure that everything is satisfactory; to officially visit a school, factory, etc. in order to check that rules are being obeyed and that standards are acceptable: *The teacher walked around the classroom inspecting the children's work.* ◇ *The Tourist Board inspects all recommended hotels at least once a year.* See also **inspection** → INSPECTION, **inspector** → INSPECTOR

NOTE CHECK, EXAMINE OR INSPECT? These words can all be used when you are looking for possible problems, but only **check** is used about looking for mistakes: Examine/Inspect your work before handing it in. Only **examine** is used when looking for the cause of a problem: The doctor checked/inspected her but could find nothing wrong. **Examine** is used more often about a professional person: *The surveyor examined the walls for signs of damp.* **Inspect** is used more often about an official: *Public health officials were called in to inspect the restaurant.*

audit /'ɔːdɪt/ [T] (business) to officially examine the financial accounts of a company to see that they are true and correct: *The National Audit office is responsible for auditing the accounts of a wide range of bodies.* See also **audit** → INSPECTION noun

visit [T] to make an official visit somewhere, for example to carry out checks or give advice: *Government inspectors are visiting all schools in the area next month.*

,go 'over sth phrasal verb to check sth carefully for mistakes, damage or anything dangerous: *Go over your work for spelling mistakes before you hand it in.* ◇ *The Health and Safety Officer went over the whole school, checking every fire door.*

,look sb/sth 'over phrasal verb to look at sb/sth closely to see if it is satisfactory: *We looked over the house again before we decided to rent it.* ◇ *The sergeant looked him over and told him to polish his shoes.*

,check 'over sb/sth phrasal verb to check sb/sth carefully to make sure that everything is correct, in good condition, or satisfactory: *We checked over the house, looking for damp or rot.* ◇ *The doctor checked him over and said he was fit and healthy.*

view [T] (rather formal) to visit a house, etc. and examine it so that you can decide whether to buy or rent it: *The property can only be viewed by appointment.*

,check 'through sth phrasal verb to examine all parts of sth closely to make sure that everything is correct or satisfactory or in order to find sth: *We checked through the photographs to make sure there were none missing.*

---

2 check · make sure · verify · assure yourself
These words all mean to find out if sth is true.

PATTERNS AND COLLOCATIONS
▶ to check/verify sth **with** sb
▶ to check/make sure/verify/assure yourself **that...**
▶ to check/verify **what/whether...**
▶ to check/verify the **accuracy/authenticity/results** (of sth)
▶ to **go and** check/make sure
▶ to **always** check/make sure/verify sth

check [I, T] to find out if sth is correct or true or if sth is how you think it is: *Go and check that I've locked the windows.* ◇ *'Is Mary in the office?' 'Just a moment. I'll go and check.'* ◇ *You'd better check with Jane what time she's expecting us.*

make 'sure phrase to check that sth is true or has been done: *She looked around to make sure that she was alone.* ◇ *I think the door's locked, but I'll just go and make sure.*

verify /'verɪfaɪ/ [T, I] (formal) to check that sth is true or accurate: *We have no way of verifying his story.* ◇ *Please verify that your password was entered correctly.* See also **verifiable** → RELIABLE 2

assure yourself (formal) to make yourself certain about sth; to tell yourself that sth is certain: *He assured himself of her safety.* ◇ *She assured herself that the letter was still in the drawer.*

cheerful adj.

cheerful · bright · cheery · jolly · in a good mood
These words all describe people who feel happy and show this in their behaviour.

PATTERNS AND COLLOCATIONS
▶ a cheerful/bright/cheery/jolly **face**
▶ a cheerful/cheery/jolly **person/manner**
▶ **in a** cheerful/cheery/jolly/good **mood**
▶ **bright and** cheerful/cheery/jolly

cheerful happy and showing it in your behaviour or expression: *She tried to sound cheerful and unconcerned.* ◇ *You're not your usual cheerful self today.* ◇ *She wrote him a chatty, cheerful letter.* **OPP** **gloomy** → DEPRESSED, **miserable** → UNHAPPY 1
▶ **cheerfully** adv.: *He waved cheerfully at them and hurried on.* ◇ *She cheerfully admitted that she had no experience at all (= she wasn't afraid to admit it).*

bright (of a person or their expression) cheerful and lively: *He felt bright and cheerful and full of energy.* ◇ *His face was bright with excitement.*
▶ **brightly** adv.: *'Hi!' she called brightly.*

NOTE CHEERFUL OR BRIGHT? When describing people, **bright** is used in the phrase *bright and cheerful* or after the verbs to be or to feel: *I was not feeling very bright that morning.* You can say a *cheerful boy/girl* but a *bright boy/girl* is intelligent, not cheerful. See also **bright** → INTELLIGENT

cheery (informal, especially spoken) (of a person or their manner) cheerful: *He left with a cheery 'See you again soon.'*

jolly (rather informal) (of a person or their manner) cheerful: *The manager was fat and jolly.* ◇ *He had a round, jolly face.*

in a ,good 'mood idiom (of a person) feeling happy so that you behave well to other people, usually because sth good has happened to you: *He was not in a good mood with her.* ◇ *This announcement put the fans in a good mood.*

child *noun* See also the entries for GIRL and SON

---

child · boy · girl · baby · kid · infant · youngster · toddler · minor · brat · junior
These are all words for a young person who is not yet an adult.

PATTERNS AND COLLOCATIONS
▸ a **young** child / boy / girl / baby / kid / infant
▸ a **little** child / boy / girl / baby / kid / brat
▸ a **small** / **good** / **naughty** child / boy / girl / baby / kid
▸ a **healthy** / **normal** child / boy / girl / baby / kid / infant
▸ a **bright** / **local** child / boy / girl / kid / youngster
▸ a **difficult** child / boy / baby / toddler
▸ a **spoilt** / **spoiled** child / kid / brat
▸ to **look after** / **take care of** a child / baby / kid
▸ a child / boy / girl / baby / kid / infant / youngster / toddler **learns** sth
▸ a child / boy / girl / baby / kid / youngster / toddler / junior **plays**
▸ a child / boy / girl / baby / kid / youngster **grows (up)**

child (pl. **children**) [C] a young person who is not yet an adult: *a child of three/a three-year-old child* ◇ *men, women and children* ◇ *I lived in London as a child.* ◇ *The group campaigns for the rights of the unborn child.* ◇ *She was a **child star** but never made it as an adult.* **OPP** **adult**, **grown-up** → ADULT *adj.*, See also **child** → SON
boy [C] a male child: *The older boys at school used to tease him.* ◇ *Be a good boy and get me my coat.* **OPP** **girl**, See also **boy** → SON
girl [C] a female child: *She's a bright little girl.* **OPP** **boy**, See also **girl** → GIRL, **girl** → SON
baby [C] a very young child, especially from birth until it starts to walk: *The baby's crying!* ◇ *He just broke down and cried like a baby.* ◇ *The illness is common in **newborn babies** and is easily treated.* See also **baby** → SON
kid [C] (*informal, especially spoken*) a child: *He's only a kid. You can't expect him to understand what's going on.* ◇ *A bunch of kids were hanging around outside.* See also **kid** → SON

NOTE **CHILD** OR **KID?** Kid is much more frequent than **child** in informal and spoken American English. A **kid** can also be older than a **child**: you can talk about *a kid of 15* but people generally stop being called *children* at around the age of 12. Above that age you can call them *kids, teenagers, young people, girls, youths* or *lads*.

infant /ˈɪnfənt/ [C] (*formal or technical*) a baby or very young child: *We studied newborn infants up to two months old.* ◇ *The country has an appallingly high **infant mortality rate**.* ❶ In the British and Australian education systems **infant** is also the word for a child at school between the ages of four and seven: *The majority of infant teachers are women.* ◇ *I've known her since we were in the infants* (= at infant school).
youngster [C] (*informal*) a child or young person: *The camp is for youngsters aged 8 to 14.*
toddler [C] a young child who has only recently learnt to walk: *She was left at home with a toddler and a four-month-old baby to care for.*
minor [C] (*law*) a young person who is under the age at which you legally become an adult and are responsible for your actions: *It is an offence to serve alcohol to minors.* ◇ *He was jailed for having sex with a minor.* **OPP** **adult** → ADULT
brat [C] (*informal, disapproving*) a person, especially a child, who behaves badly: *He's a spoilt little brat!*
junior [C] (*BrE*) (in sport) a young person below a particular age, rather than an adult; a child at school in Britain between the ages of 7 and 11: *At 16, he's still eligible to play for the juniors.* ◇ *Sam is going to be a junior next year.* ◇ *a junior school*

---

childhood *noun*

---

childhood · youth · adolescence · teens · infancy · puberty
These are all words for the period of sb's life when they are a child or young person.

infancy   childhood   youth
                                                         adolescence
                                                         teens
                                                         puberty

PATTERNS AND COLLOCATIONS
▸ **in** (sb's) childhood / youth / adolescence / teens / infancy
▸ **during** (sb's) childhood / youth / adolescence / teens / infancy / puberty
▸ **from** (sb's) childhood / youth / infancy
▸ **since** / **throughout** (sb's) childhood / youth / adolescence / teens / infancy
▸ (sb's) **early** childhood / youth / adolescence / teens / infancy
▸ (sb's) **late** childhood / adolescence / teens
▸ a / an **happy** / **unhappy** childhood / youth
▸ to **reach** adolescence / your teens / puberty
▸ to **spend** your childhood / youth / adolescence / teens...

childhood [U, C] the period of sb's life when they are a child: *From her earliest childhood she'd had a love of dancing.* ◇ *She had a very happy childhood.* ◇ *childhood memories/experiences*
youth [U, sing.] the period of sb's life when they are young, especially the time before a child becomes an adult; the quality or state of being young: *He had been a talented musician in his youth.* ◇ *His lack of qualification was taken as a sign of **a misspent youth*** (= having wasted his time when he was young). ◇ *She brings to the job a rare combination of youth and experience.* ❶ A **youth** can also be a young person. See also **youth** → GIRL
adolescence /ˌædəˈlesns/ [U] (*rather formal*) the time in sb's life when they develop from a child into an adult: *Adolescence brings about major changes in a young person's body.* ◇ *She developed the problem in early adolescence.* ❶ **Adolescence** is often used when talking about the problems that young people have when they are becoming adults. See also **adolescent** → GIRL
teens [pl.] the years of a person's life when they are between 13 and 19 years old: *She began writing poetry in her teens.* ◇ *An eyewitness described a boy in his mid to late teens wearing a dark jacket.* **Teens** is always used after *my, his, her, etc.*: ~~I met him in teens.~~ See also **teen** → GIRL
infancy [U] the time when a child is a baby or very young: *Tragically, she died in infancy.* ◇ *The vaccination is given in early infancy.* ❶ **Infancy** is often used to talk about babies being ill or dying: *to survive infancy* ◇ *deaths during infancy.*
puberty /ˈpjuːbəti; *AmE* -bərti/ [U] the period in sb's life when their sexual organs develop and their body changes from a child's to an adult's body: *He reached puberty at the age of fourteen.* ◇ *The body undergoes many changes during puberty.* ❶ **Puberty** is used more in medical or scientific contexts than in personal accounts of childhood.

---

childish *adj.*

---

childish · immature · youthful · boyish · childlike · girlish
These words all describe a person or animal that is young and not fully developed, or that has the qualities that are typical of a young person or animal.

PATTERNS AND COLLOCATIONS
▸ childish / immature / childlike **behaviour**
▸ youthful / boyish **charm** / **energy** / **enthusiasm** / **(good) looks**
▸ a youthful / boyish / girlish **figure**
▸ **very** childish / immature / youthful
▸ **almost** childish / childlike / girlish

childish connected with or typical of a child: *At the front of the book I found her name, in childish handwriting.* ❶ **Childish** can also be used in a disapproving way to describe an adult or older child who is behaving in a stupid or silly way: *(disapproving) Don't be so childish!* **OPP** **adult** → ADULT
▸ **childishly** *adv.*: *to behave childishly*

immature /ˌɪməˈtjʊə(r); *AmE* -ˈtʃʊr; -ˈtʊr/ *(disapproving)* behaving in a way that is not sensible and is typical of people who are much younger: *Oh, don't be so immature.* ◊ *Although she was older than her husband, she was emotionally quite immature.* ❶ **Immature** can also describe animals or plants that are not fully grown or developed: *The immature birds have shorter tails and brown, speckled plumage.* **OPP** **mature** → ADULT
▸ **immaturity** *noun* [U]: *I'm fed up with his selfishness and immaturity.* **OPP** **maturity**

youthful typical of young people: *She brought a tremendous youthful enthusiasm to the job.*

boyish *(usually approving)* looking or behaving like a boy, in a way that is attractive: *She had a slim, almost boyish figure.* ◊ *Jane fell for his boyish charm.*

childlike *(usually approving)* having the qualities that children usually have, especially innocence: *She responded with childlike simplicity.* See also **innocent** → NAIVE

girlish looking or behaving like a girl: *His face was delicate, almost girlish.* ◊ *She gave a girlish giggle.*

choice *noun*

1 make a choice
2 the obvious/first choice

---

1 **choice · selection · nomination · election · pick**
These are all words for the act of choosing between two or more people, things or possibilities.

PATTERNS AND COLLOCATIONS
▸ sb's **selection** / **nomination** / **election as** sth
▸ sb's **selection** / **nomination for** sth
▸ a / an **careful** / **initial** / **final** choice / selection
▸ to **make** a choice / selection / nomination
▸ to **have** a choice / your pick
▸ to **take your** choice / pick
▸ to **get first** choice / pick
▸ to **secure** selection / the nomination / election
▸ to **win** selection / the nomination

choice [C] an act of choosing between two or more possibilities: *Many women are forced to make a choice between family and career.* ◊ *We aim to help students make more informed career choices.* ◊ *We are faced with a difficult choice.* See also **choice** → OPTION

selection [U] *(rather formal)* the process of choosing sb/sth, usually according to a system, from a group of people or things: *The final team selection will be made tomorrow.* ◊ *The game is based on the random selection of numbers.* ◊ *What are their selection criteria?*

nomination /ˌnɒmɪˈneɪʃn; *AmE* ˌnɑː-/ [U, C] the act of suggesting or choosing sb as a candidate in an election, or for a job or award; the fact of being suggested for this: *Membership of the club is by nomination only.* ◊ *They opposed her nomination to the post of Deputy Director.* ◊ *How many Oscar nominations has she had in her career?* See also **nominate** → APPOINT, **nominate** → RECOMMEND 2

election [U] the fact of having been chosen in an election: *We welcome his election as president.* See also **elect** → APPOINT

pick [sing.] *(rather informal)* an act of choosing sb/sth: *Red or green? Take your pick* (= choose). ◊ *The winner gets first pick of the prizes.* ◊ *She had her pick of the young single men at the party.* ❶ **Pick** is nearly always used in the phrases shown in these examples.

---

2 **choice · favourite · preference · selection · pick**
These are all words for a person or thing that is chosen, or that is liked more than others.

PATTERNS AND COLLOCATIONS
▸ sb's **choice** / **favourite** / **pick for** sth
▸ sb's **choice** / **favourite** / **pick as** sth
▸ an **obvious** choice / favourite / selection
▸ a / an **excellent** / **good** / **popular** / **fine** choice / selection

choice [C] a person or thing that is chosen: *She's the obvious choice for the job.* ◊ *This colour wasn't my first choice.* ◊ *I don't like his choice of friends* (= the people he chooses as his friends). See also **choice** → OPTION, **of choice** → FAVOURITE *adj.*

favourite *(BrE)* *(AmE* **favorite***)* [C] a person or thing that you like more than the others of the same type: *This song is a particular favourite of mine.* ◊ *These cakes are great favourites with the children.* ◊ *The show has become a firm favourite with young people.* See also **favourite** → FAVOURITE *adj.*

preference /ˈprefrəns/ [C] a thing that is liked better or best: *They are undertaking a study of consumer preferences.* ◊ *Tastes and preferences vary from individual to individual.* See also **preference** → TASTE 1, **prefer** → PREFER, **preferred** → FAVOURITE *adj.*

NOTE **FAVOURITE** OR **PREFERENCE**? Your **favourites** are the things you like best, and that you have, do, listen to, etc. often; your **preferences** are the things that you would rather have or do if you can choose.

selection [C] a number of people or things that have been chosen from a larger group: *A selection of readers' comments are published below.* ◊ *The orchestra played selections from Hollywood musicals.*

pick [sing.] *(especially AmE, rather informal)* a person or thing that is chosen: *She was his pick for best actress.*

choose *verb*

---

choose · select · pick · decide · opt · go for sth · single sb/sth out · adopt
These words all mean to make a decision about which thing or person you want out of the ones that are available.

PATTERNS AND COLLOCATIONS
▸ to **choose** / **select** / **pick** / **single out** A **from** B
▸ to **choose** / **select** / **pick** / **decide between** A **and** / **or** B
▸ to **choose** / **select** / **pick** / **opt for** / **go for** / **single out** / **adopt** sb / sth **as** sb / sth
▸ to **choose** / **select** / **pick** / **single out** sb / sth **for** sth
▸ to **choose** / **select** / **pick** / **opt for** / **go for** / **single out** / **adopt** sb / sth **to do** sth
▸ to **choose** / **decide** / **opt to do** sth
▸ to **pick** / **single** sb / sth **out**
▸ to **choose** / **select** / **pick** sb / sth **carefully** / **at random**
▸ **randomly** chosen / selected / picked
▸ **well** chosen / selected

choose [I, T] to make a decision about which thing or person you want out of the ones that are available: *You choose — I can't decide.* ◊ *There are plenty of restaurants to choose from.* ◊ *She had to choose between giving up her job or hiring a nanny.* ◊ *You have to take any job you can get — you can't pick and choose.* ◊ *He chose banking as a career.* ◊ *You'll have to choose whether to buy it or not.* ◊ *We chose Paul Stubbs to be chairperson.* See also **choice** → OPTION, **choice** → RANGE 1

select [T, often passive] *(rather formal)* to choose sb/sth, usually according to a system, from a group of people or things: *He hasn't been selected for the team.* ◊ *All our hotels have been carefully selected for the excellent value they provide.* ◊ *a randomly selected sample of 23 schools* ◊ *selected poems of T.S. Eliot* ◊ *Select 'New Mail' from the 'Send' menu.* See also **selection** → RANGE 1

pick [T] *(rather informal)* to choose sb/sth from a group of people or things: *Pick a number from one to twenty.* ◊ *Names were picked at random out of a hat.* ◊ *He was picked out as the best player.*

> **NOTE** **CHOOSE, SELECT** OR **PICK? Choose** is the most general of these words and the only one that can be used without an object: ~~You select/pick — I can't decide.~~ When you **select** sth, you choose it carefully, unless you actually say that it is selected randomly/at random. **Pick** is a more informal word and often a less careful action, used especially when the choice being made is not very important: ~~Select a number from one to twenty.~~

decide [I] to choose between two or more possibilities: *It was difficult to decide between the two candidates.* ◇ *We're still trying to **decide on** a venue.* ◇ *You choose — I can't decide.* See also **decide** → DECIDE

opt [I] to choose to take or not to take a particular course of action: *After graduating she **opted for** a career in music.* ◇ *After a lot of thought, I **opted against** buying a motorbike.* ◇ *Many workers opted to leave their jobs rather than take a pay cut.* ◇ *Employees may **opt out of** the company's pension plan.* See also **option** → OPTION

'go for sth phrasal verb (*rather informal*) to choose sth: *I think I'll go for the fruit salad.*

single sb/sth 'out phrasal verb to choose sb/sth from a group for special attention: *She was singled out for criticism.* ◇ *He was singled out as the outstanding performer of the games.*

adopt [T] to choose a new name, country, etc. and begin to use it as your own: *The royal family adopted the name of Windsor early in the last century.*

church noun

church · temple · mosque · shrine · cathedral · chapel · synagogue · abbey · sanctuary · place of worship
These are all words for religious buildings.

PATTERNS AND COLLOCATIONS
▸ to **go to** church / temple / chapel / synagogue

church [C, U] a building where Christians go to worship; a service or services in a church: *The procession moved into the church.* ◇ *a church tower* ◇ *church services* ◇ *How often do you go to church?* ◇ (*BrE*) *They're **at church** (= attending a church service).* ◇ (*AmE*) *They're **in church**.* ◇ *Church is at 9 o'clock.* See also **church** → RELIGION

temple [C] a building used for the worship of a god or gods, especially in religions other than Christianity: *a Buddhist/Hindu/Sikh temple* ◇ *the Temple of Diana at Ephesus* ◇ (*AmE*) *to go to temple (= to a service in a synagogue, where Jews worship)*

mosque /mɒsk; *AmE* mɑːsk/ [C] a building where Muslims go to worship: *We were woken by the call to prayer from a nearby mosque.*

shrine [C] a place where people come to worship because it is connected with a holy person or event: *a shrine to the Virgin Mary* ◇ *to visit the shrine of Mecca*

cathedral /kə'θiːdrəl/ [C] the main church of a district, under the care of a bishop (= a priest of high rank): *St Paul's Cathedral* ◇ (*BrE*) *a cathedral city*

chapel /'tʃæpl/ [C] a small building or room used for Christian worship in a school, prison or large private house; a separate part of a church or cathedral with its own altar, used for some services and private prayer; a small church; a small building or room used for funeral services, especially at a cemetery or crematorium: *the school/college chapel* ◇ *Evening prayer will be held in the Lady Chapel.* ◇ *a tiny chapel in the mountains* ◇ *a chapel of rest* ❶ In British English **chapel** [C, U] is also the word used for a church in some Christian denominations, for example Nonconformists: *a Methodist/Mormon chapel* ◇ *She always went to chapel on Sundays.*

synagogue /'sɪnəgɒg; *AmE* -gɑːg/ [C] a building where Jews go to worship: *They went to synagogue every Saturday.*

abbey [C] a large church together with a group of buildings in which monks or nuns live or lived in the past: *Westminster Abbey* ◇ *a ruined abbey*

sanctuary /'sæŋktʃuəri; *AmE* -ueri/ [C] a holy building or the part of it that is considered most holy: *Women were excluded from entering the sanctuary where the priest stood at the altar.*

place of worship (pl. **places of worship**) [C] (*rather formal*) a building where people of a particular religion go to worship, such as a church, temple, mosque or synagogue: *The statistics show the number of people who regularly attend a place of worship.* ❶ **Place of worship** is used especially in official contexts, when collecting information about the people who live in a country, city or area.

circle noun

circle · ring · disc · hoop
These are all words for a round flat shape or object.

PATTERNS AND COLLOCATIONS
▸ **in** a circle / ring
▸ **through** a circle / ring / hoop
▸ **concentric** circles / rings

circle [C] a completely round flat shape; the line that encloses a round shape; a thing or a group of people or things shaped like a circle: *Cut out two circles of paper.* ◇ *Draw a circle.* ◇ *She walked the horse round in a circle.* ◇ *The children ran around the circle of chairs until the music stopped.*

ring [C] a flat circular object with a large hole in the middle; a circular mark or shape: *a key ring* ◇ *Onion rings should be thin and crispy.* ◇ *She had dark rings around her eyes from lack of sleep.*

disc (also **disk** especially in *AmE*) [C] a thin flat circular object or shape: *He wears an identity disc around his neck.* ◇ *In a total eclipse, the moon completely covers the disc of the sun.*

hoop /huːp/ [C] a large ring made of plastic, wood or metal; a small arch made of metal or plastic, put into the ground: *The barrel was bound with three iron hoops.* ◇ *She was wearing a pair of hoop earrings (= in the shape of a hoop).* ◇ *Grow lettuce under plastic stretched over wire hoops.*

citizen noun See the Topic Map for THE INDIVIDUAL AND SOCIETY on p.894

citizen · voter · taxpayer · native · national · subject
These are all words for a person who belongs to a particular country and has legal rights there.

PATTERNS AND COLLOCATIONS
▸ a citizen / native / national **of** a country
▸ a **British** citizen / voter / taxpayer / national / subject
▸ a **US / Australian, etc.** citizen / voter / taxpayer / national
▸ an **ordinary / average** citizen / voter / taxpayer
▸ a **foreign / fellow** citizen / national

citizen [C] a person who has the legal right to belong to a particular country: *She's Italian by birth, but is now an Australian citizen.* See also **citizen** → RESIDENT
▸ **citizenship** noun [U]: *You can apply for citizenship after five years' residency.*

voter [C] a person who votes or has the right to vote, especially in a political election: *Only 60% of eligible voters actually used their vote.*

taxpayer /'tækspeɪə(r)/ [C] a person who pays tax to the government, especially on the money that they earn: *The changes make an average taxpayer £2.50 a week better off.* ◇ *Hundreds of thousands of pounds of **taxpayers' money** have been spent on the project.* ❶ **The taxpayer** is often used to refer to the ordinary people of a country as a group, when talking about government spending: *What is the cost to the taxpayer of hosting the Olympics?* ◇ *Should politicians be able to travel first class **at the taxpayer's expense**?* ◇ *It was estimated to have cost **the US taxpayer** $35 billion.*

native [C] a person who was born in a particular country or area: *She was not a native of the island, but had lived there for many years.* See also **native** → RESIDENT *noun*, **native** → CULTURAL *adj.*

national [C] (*rather formal*) a person who belongs to a particular country: *The government has advised British nationals to leave the area.* ❶ **Nationals** is used especially when talking about people of a particular nationality who are abroad, for example living and working in a foreign country.

▸ **nationality** /ˌnæʃəˈnæləti/ *noun* [U, C]: *She has dual nationality* (= is a citizen of two countries). ◊ *The college attracts students of all nationalities.*

subject [C] (*rather formal*) a person who has the right to belong to a particular country, especially one with a king or queen: *British subjects and Commonwealth citizens do not need visas.* ◊ *The prince had to tax his subjects heavily to raise money for the war.*

city *noun*

city · town · village · borough · municipality · metropolis · conurbation
These words all mean a place with streets and buildings where people live and work.

PATTERNS AND COLLOCATIONS
▸ in a **city** / **town** / **village** / **borough** / **municipality** / **metropolis** / **conurbation**
▸ a **small** city / town / village / borough / municipality
▸ a **major** city / town / metropolis / conurbation
▸ a **big** city / town / village / metropolis
▸ a **large** city / town / village / conurbation
▸ a **great** city / metropolis
▸ a **provincial** city / town
▸ the **local** borough / municipality
▸ the city / town / village / borough **council**

city [C] a place with many streets and buildings where many people live and work: *The city of Boston is one of America's most historic cities.* ◊ *Ely is a cathedral city in East Cambridgeshire.*

town [C] a place where people live and work that is larger than a village but smaller than a city: *The nearest town is ten miles away.* ◊ *Sackville is a small university town in eastern Canada.* ❶ Especially in American English, **town** [U] is also used to mean the particular town where sb lives and works or one that has just been referred to: *I'll be in town next week if you want to go out for a drink.* ◊ *He married a girl from out of town.* ◊ *They live in a rough part of town.* ◊ *This restaurant serves the best steaks in town.* **The town** [sing.] can also be used to talk about the idea of life in towns or cities in general, as opposed to life in the country: *Do you prefer the town to the country?* See also **hometown** → HOME 2

> **NOTE** CITY OR TOWN? A **city** is usually bigger than a **town**, but not always. Official city status is given by the king or queen (in Britain) or state governments in the US. As time went by towns and cities changed in size, so that these days it is possible to find some cities that are smaller than many towns. In American English **town** can also describe a smaller place than in British English, as the term **village** is not used so much in American English.

village [C] a very small town situated in a country area: *Appledore is a fishing village on the north coast of Devon.* ◊ (*especially BrE*) *Most basic items are available from the village shop.* ◊ *Her books are about village life.* ❶ Do not use **village** to talk about small towns in the US. In American English **village** is used for a small place in another country that seems more old-fashioned than a town in the US.

borough /ˈbʌrə; AmE ˈbɜːroʊ/ [C] a town or part of a city that has its own local government: *She served as a local councillor in the London Borough of Westminster.*

municipality /mjuːˌnɪsɪˈpæləti/ [C] (*formal*) a political unit, such as a city, town, village or district, that has its own local government; the group of officials who govern it: *The municipality provides services such as electricity, water and rubbish collection.*

▸ **municipal** *adj.* [usually before noun]: *municipal elections*

metropolis /məˈtrɒpəlɪs; AmE məˈtrɑːp-/ [C] a large important city, often the capital city of a country or region: *Barcelona has all the amenities you would expect to find in a great metropolis.*

▸ **metropolitan** /ˌmetrəˈpɒlɪtən; AmE -ˈpɑːl-/ *adj.* [only before noun]: *the New York metropolitan area*

conurbation /ˌkɒnɜːˈbeɪʃn; AmE ˌkɑːnɜːrˈb-/ [C] (*formal*) a large area where towns have grown and joined together, often around a city: *The region has several medium-sized towns and cities, but no major conurbations.*

claim *noun* See the Topic Map for FACT AND OPINION on p.898

claim · allegation · assertion · contention
These are all words for a statement that sth is true, although it has not been proved.

PATTERNS AND COLLOCATIONS
▸ a claim / an allegation / an assertion / a contention **that...**
▸ a claim / an allegation / an assertion **about** / **of** sth
▸ **false** / **unfounded** / **unsubstantiated** claims / allegations / assertions
▸ to **make** / **deny** a claim / an allegation / an assertion
▸ to **support** a claim / an allegation / an assertion / a contention
▸ to **investigate** / **withdraw** a claim / an allegation
▸ to **reject** a claim / an assertion / a contention
▸ to **question** a claim / an assertion
▸ to **dispute** a claim / contention

claim [C] a statement that sth is true, although it has not been proved: *There are conflicting claims about the cause of the fire.* ◊ *The report examines claims of corrupt links between politicians.* **OPP** **denial** → DENIAL

allegation /ˌæləˈɡeɪʃn/ [C] (*rather formal*) a public statement that is made without giving proof, accusing sb of doing sth that is wrong or illegal: *He has made serious allegations against the company.* ◊ *He has resigned amid corruption allegations.*

assertion /əˈsɜːʃn; AmE əˈsɜːrʃn/ [C] (*rather formal*) a statement of sth that you strongly believe to be true, although it has not been proved: *She made sweeping assertions about the role of women in society.* ◊ *He was correct in his assertion that the minister had been lying.*

> **NOTE** CLAIM OR ASSERTION? When the point in doubt is a matter of opinion, not fact, use **assertion**: ~~She made sweeping claims about the role of women in society.~~ When you are talking about a matter of fact you can use either word; an **assertion** may be slightly stronger than a **claim** and it is a more formal word.

contention /kənˈtenʃn/ [C] (*formal*) a belief or opinion that you express, especially in an argument: *It is our client's contention that the fire was an accident.*

claim *verb* See the Topic Map for FACT AND OPINION on p.898

claim · argue · insist · allege · contend · maintain · assert · protest · affirm
These words all mean to say that sth is true.

PATTERNS AND COLLOCATIONS
▸ to claim / argue / insist / allege / contend / maintain / assert / protest / affirm **that...**
▸ It is claimed / argued / alleged / contended / maintained / asserted / affirmed **that...**
▸ to insist on / maintain / assert / protest **your innocence**
▸ to argue / insist / protest / assert sth **strongly**

claim [T] to state sth as a fact, but without giving proof: *He claims (that) he was not given a fair hearing.* ◇ *I don't claim to be an expert.* ◇ *Scientists are claiming a major breakthrough in the fight against cancer.* ◇ *It was claimed that some doctors were working 80 hours a week.*

argue [I, T] to give reasons why you think that sth is right or wrong, true or not true, especially to persuade people that you are right: *They argued for the right to strike.* ◇ *He was too tired to* **argue the point** (= discuss the matter). ◇ *She argued that they needed more time to finish the project.* See also **argument** → ARGUMENT 2

insist /ɪn'sɪst/ [I, T] to say very firmly and often repeatedly that sth is true, especially when other people do not believe you: *He insisted on his innocence.* ◇ *He insisted (that) he was innocent.*

▸ **insistence** noun [U]: *No one was convinced by her insistence that she was not to blame.*

allege /ə'ledʒ/ [T, often passive] (*formal*) to claim sth, especially in the context of a legal dispute: *It is alleged that he mistreated the prisoners.* ◇ *He is alleged to have mistreated the prisoners.* ◇ *This procedure should be followed in cases where dishonesty has been alleged.* See also **alleged** → SUPPOSED

contend /kən'tend/ [T] (*formal*) to say that sth is true, especially in an argument: *I would contend that the prime minister's thinking is flawed on this point.*

maintain /meɪn'teɪn/ [T] (*rather formal*) to continue to say that sth is true, even though other people do not agree or do not believe it: *The men maintained (that) they were out of the country when the crime was committed.* ◇ *She has always maintained her innocence.*

assert /ə'sɜːt; AmE ə'sɜːrt/ [T] (*formal*) to state clearly and firmly that sth is true: *She continued to assert her innocence.* ◇ *She continued to assert that she was innocent.*

protest [T] to say firmly that sth is true, especially when you have been accused of sth or when other people do not believe you: *She has always protested her innocence.* ◇ *He protested that the journey was too far by car.* ◇ *'That's not what you said earlier!' Jane protested.*

affirm /ə'fɜːm; AmE ə'fɜːrm/ [T] (*formal*) to state firmly or publicly that sth is true or that you support sth strongly: *I can affirm that no one will lose their job.* ◇ *Both sides affirmed their commitment to the ceasefire.*

NOTE ASSERT OR AFFIRM? You **assert** sth when you want other people to believe and support you. You **affirm** sth in order to reassure people that it is true.

class *noun*

1 Which classes are you taking?
2 work hard in class
3 the youngest in the class
4 all classes of society

1 See the Topic Map for EDUCATION on p.888
class · course · programme · curriculum · syllabus
These are all words for a series of subjects or skills that are taught or studied for the purposes of education or training.

PATTERNS AND COLLOCATIONS
▸ a / the course / programme / curriculum / syllabus **for** sb / sth
▸ **in** a / the class / course / programme / curriculum / syllabus
▸ **on** a / the course / programme / curriculum / syllabus
▸ a **narrow / wide / broad** curriculum / syllabus
▸ a **core** programme / curriculum / syllabus
▸ a **day / evening** class / course / programme
▸ a / an **English / history / mathematics, etc.** class / course / programme / curriculum / syllabus
▸ to **design / plan** a class / course / programme / curriculum / syllabus
▸ to **follow / teach / offer** a / the course / programme / curriculum / syllabus
▸ to **run / take / do / enrol on / sign up for** a class / course / programme
▸ to **complete** a class / course / programme / syllabus
▸ a / the class / course / programme / curriculum / syllabus **covers** sth

class [C] (also **classes** [pl.]) a series of lessons on a particular subject or in a particular skill: *I'm taking a management class this semester.* ◇ *The college runs specialist language classes.* ◇ (*BrE*) *Are you still doing your French evening class?* ◇ (*AmE*) *I'm taking* **night classes** *in art appreciation.*

course [C] (*BrE or formal, AmE*) a series of classes or lectures on a particular subject: *She's taking a* **course in** *Art and Design.* ◇ *I've signed up for an evening* **course on** *media techniques.* ◇ (*BrE*) *Over 50 students have enrolled* **on the course**. ❶ In American English this meaning of **course** is only used in formal or official language: *Registration for courses begins tomorrow.* In everyday conversation, use **class**: *What classes did you register for?* In British English **course** can be used in both formal, written English and everyday spoken English. In British English a **course** is also a period of study at a college or university that leads to an exam or qualification; in American English this is called a **program**: *It's a four-year course.* ◇ *She had taught on a range of undergraduate courses.*

programme (*BrE*) (also **program** especially in *AmE*) [C] a course of study or training, especially at a college or university: *Take a look at our new history and language programs.* ◇ *We especially encourage those from minorities to apply for our* **degree programs**. ◇ *We urge as many people as possible to enrol on our management training programme.* ❶ In American English, **program** is the usual word for a course or period of time studying in a college or university; in this context it is short for *degree program*. A degree program is made up of a number of classes or courses. It is also becoming more common for British universities to talk about their *undergraduate programmes*.

curriculum /kə'rɪkjələm/ (pl. **curricula** /-lə/ or **curriculums**) [C, usually sing.] the subjects that are included in a course of study or taught in a school, college or university: *The school curriculum should be as broad as possible.* ◇ *These subjects are not part of the core curriculum* (= consisting of the most basic and important subjects). ◇ (*BrE*) *They all have to study French because it's* **on the curriculum**. ◇ (*AmE*) *Nutrition education is now* **in the curriculum**.

NOTE ON OR IN? Note that in British English it is usual to talk about students being *on* a **course** or **programme** or subjects being *on* the **curriculum** or **syllabus**; in American English students enrol *in* a program, and subjects are *in* the curriculum or syllabus.

syllabus /'sɪləbəs/ [C, usually sing.] (*BrE*) a list of the topics and books that students should study in a particular subject at school or college: *A group of experienced teachers were asked to design a new English syllabus.* ◇ *The courses do not follow any particular exam syllabus.* ❶ In American English a **syllabus** is a summary of the main points of course: *a teacher might give a copy of the syllabus to the students on the first day of a class, so that they will know what they will be studying during the semester.*

2 See the Topic Map for EDUCATION on p.888
class · session · lesson · seminar · workshop · tutorial · period
These are all words for a period of time that is spent learning sth.

PATTERNS AND COLLOCATIONS
▸ a class / session / lesson / seminar / workshop / tutorial **on** sth
▸ **in / during** a class / session / lesson / seminar / workshop / tutorial / period
▸ **at** a class / session / lesson / seminar / workshop / tutorial
▸ to **go to / attend** a class / session / lesson / seminar / workshop / tutorial
▸ to **miss** a class / session / lesson / seminar / workshop / tutorial / period

▸ to **have** a class / lesson / seminar / workshop / tutorial
▸ to **give** / **conduct** a class / session / lesson / seminar / workshop / tutorial
▸ to **teach** a class / session / lesson / seminar
▸ to **hold** / **run** a class / session / seminar / workshop
▸ a class / session / lesson / seminar / workshop / tutorial **takes place**

class [C, U] an occasion when a group of students meet to be taught: *I have an English class at 11.* ◊ *Please see me after class.* ◊ *She works hard **in class*** (= during lessons)

session [C] a period of time that is spent doing a particular activity: *a photo/recording/training session* ◊ *Your presentation will be part of the morning session.* ◊ *The programme is made up of 12 two-hour sessions.*

lesson [C] a period of time in which sb is taught sth: *New students get **lessons in** how to use the library.* ◊ *piano/driving lessons* ◊ *I've decided to **take** golf **lessons**.* ◊ *She made a living giving private lessons in English.* ◊ (*especially BrE*) *What did we do last lesson?*

> **NOTE** **CLASS** OR **LESSON?** A **class** is always for a group of people being taught together; a **lesson** can be for a group of people or for just one person.

seminar /'semnɑː(r)/ [C] a class at a college or university when a group of students and a teacher discuss or study a particular topic; a meeting of people for training or discussion: *Teaching is by lectures and seminars.* ◊ *a seminar room/group* ◊ *The company organizes management seminars.*

workshop /'wɜːkʃɒp; *AmE* 'wɜːrkʃɑːp/ [C] a period of discussion and practical work on a particular subject, in which a group of people share ideas, knowledge or experience: *a drama/poetry workshop* ◊ *There are two management development workshops per year.*

tutorial /tjuː'tɔːriəl; *AmE* tuː-/ [C] a period of teaching in a college or university that involves discussion between an individual student or a very small group of students and a teacher: *Students have to write an essay for each weekly tutorial.* See also **tutor** → TEACHER

period [C] any of the parts that a day is divided into at a school or college for study: *We've got French next period.* ◊ *I have two **free/study periods*** (= for private study) *on Tuesday afternoons.*

3 See the Topic Map for EDUCATION on p.888
class · grade · year · stream · track · set
These are all words for groups in which students are taught together.

PATTERNS AND COLLOCATIONS
▸ **in** a class / grade / year / stream / set

class [C+sing./pl. *v.*] a group of students who are taught together: *We were in the same class at school.* ◊ *He finished **top of the class*** (= got better results than all the others). ◊ *The whole class was told to stay behind after school.* ◊ (*especially AmE*) the **class of** *2008* (= group of students who finished their studies at school or college in 2008) ◊ (*AmE*) *the freshman/sophomore/junior/senior class*

grade [C] (in the US school system) one of the levels in a school with children of similar age: *He is in (the) second grade.*
▸ **grader** *noun* [C]: *The play is open to all seventh and eighth graders.*

year [C] (*especially BrE*) (at a school or university) a level that you stay in for one year; a student at a particular level: *We didn't start Latin until year nine.* ◊ *The language students go abroad in their third year.* ◊ *The project is the work of a group of year-seven pupils.* ◊ *First and second years usually live in college.*

stream [C] (*especially BrE*) a group in which students of the same age and level of ability are placed in some schools: *He was put into the top stream.*
▸ **stream** *verb* [T, usually passive]: (*especially BrE*) *Pupils are streamed for English and Maths.*

track [C] (*AmE*) a group in which students of the same age and level or ability, or studying the same group of subjects, are placed in some schools and colleges: *Students pursue one of three tracks: professional writing, film/television/video or new media.*
▸ **track** *verb* [I, T, usually passive]: *a comparison of schools that track and don't track in math*

set [C] (*BrE*) a group of school students of the same age and similar ability in a particular subject who are taught together in that subject although they are normally taught in a different group: *She is in the top set for French.*

---

4 See the Topic Map for THE INDIVIDUAL AND SOCIETY on p.894
class · level · position · rank · status · rating · standing · ranking · grade
These are all words for a group in society or within an organization that sb belongs to, based on how much importance or authority they have, or for a measure of how good or important sb/sth is compared with sb/sth else.

PATTERNS AND COLLOCATIONS
▸ sb's class / level / position / rank / status / standing / ranking **in** / **within** sth
▸ a / the **high** / **higher** level / position / rank / status / rating / standing / ranking / grade
▸ a / the **low** / **lower** class / level / position / rank / status / rating / standing / ranking / grade
▸ the **top** level / rank / rating / ranking / grade
▸ the **upper** class / level / rank
▸ the **middle** class / level / rank / ranking / grade
▸ a / the **senior** level / position / rank / grade
▸ sb's **social** class / position / rank / status / standing / ranking
▸ a / sb's **professional** class / status / standing
▸ to **improve** your position / status / standing / ranking
▸ to **have** a ... rank / rating / status / standing
▸ to **give** (**sb** / **sth**) a status / rating / ranking
▸ to **achieve** a rank / status / rating
▸ sb's class / position / rank / status / standing **in society**
▸ a / the class / level / ranks **of society**

class [C+sing./pl. *v.*, U] one of the groups of people in a society that are thought of as being at the same social or economic level; the way that people are divided into different social or economic groups: *His ideas had an appeal among the wealthy, professional classes.* ◊ *Do you consider yourself to be middle class?* ◊ *A lot of British comedy is based on class differences.* ◊ *The old **class system** is not appropriate in a modern age.* See also **the upper class** → ELITE, **the middle class** → MIDDLE CLASS *noun*, **the working class** → GENERAL PUBLIC

level [C] one of a number of positions in a scale of importance, for example in society or within an organization: *He promised reforms at all levels of government.* ◊ *She reached a very high level at a very young age.* ◊ *The decision is being made at top level.*

position [C, U] the level of importance of a person or organization when compared with others: *We need to improve the position of women and girls in these societies.* ◊ *The company has a dominant position in the world market.* ◊ *Wealth and position are not important to her.*

rank [C, U] a position, especially an important position, that sb has in a particular organization or society; the position that sb has in one of the armed forces or the police: *She **rose through the ranks** to become managing director* (= she started in a low position). ◊ *She was not used to mixing with people of high social rank.* ◊ *He was promoted to the rank of major.* ◊ *I gave them only my name, rank and serial number.*

status /'steɪtəs; *AmE* also 'stætəs/ [U, C, usually sing.] the social or professional position of sb/sth in relation to others, based on the amount of respect they get from other people: *The only jobs on offer were of low status and badly paid.* ◊ *How do people perceive the status of the full-time mother?*

rating [C] a measurement of how good, important, popular, etc. sb/sth is, especially in relation to other people or things: *It was a very good rating for an amateur* performance. ◇ *The poll gave an* **approval rating** *of 39% for the president.* See also **rate** → RANK *verb*, **rate** → JUDGE *verb 1*

standing [U] the position or reputation of sb/sth within a group of people or in an organization: *The prime minister needs to improve his* **standing** *with the public.* ◇ *Their standing as a profession has declined in recent years.*

ranking [C] the position of sb/sth on a scale that shows how good or important they are compared with other people or things, especially in sport: *She has retained her No. 1* **world ranking.** ◇ *The product has consistently been given a high ranking by consumer groups.* See also **rank** → RANK *verb*

grade [C] a rank or level that sb has within an organization, often related to how much they are paid for doing their job: *She's still only on a secretarial grade.* ◇ *The higher grades within the organization usually get bigger pay rises.*

classify *verb*

classify · file · sort · categorize · class · group · bracket
These words all mean to arrange people or things into groups because they are similar.

▸ to classify / sort / categorize / group sb / sth **according to** sth
▸ to classify / file / categorize / class / group / bracket sb / sth **as** sth
▸ to classify / file / sort / categorize / class / group sb / sth **under** sth
▸ to classify / categorize / class / group / bracket sb / sth **with** sth
▸ to classify / sort / categorize / group sb / sth **into** sth
▸ to classify / sort / categorize / group sb / sth **by** sth
▸ to classify / file / class sth **alongside** sth
▸ to classify / file / class / group / bracket sb / sth **together**

classify /ˈklæsɪfaɪ/ [T] to arrange things in groups according to features that they have in common; to decide which group sb/sth belongs to: *The books in the library are classified according to subject.* ◇ *Soils can be classified under two main headings.* ◇ *The study recorded and classified accidents over a period of a year.* ◇ *Eleven accidents were classified as major.* See also **classification** → CATEGORY

file [T] to put and keep things such as documents in a particular place and in a particular order so that you can find them easily; to put a document into a file: *The forms should be filed alphabetically.* ◇ *Wynne-Jones should be filed under 'W'.* ◇ *The report was* **filed away** *in the archives.* See also **file** → DOCUMENT, **file** → ENVELOPE

sort [T] to arrange things in groups or in a particular order according to their type; to separate things according to their type: *The mail is sorted automatically.* ◇ *The documents were sorted by age and type.* ◇ *Waste is sorted for recycling.* See also **sort** → KIND *noun*

categorize /ˈkætəɡəraɪz/ (also BrE **-ise**) [T] to decide what type people or things are and put them in a group with others of the same type: *Her latest work cannot be categorized as either a novel or an autobiography.* ◇ *Some types of investment risk are difficult to categorize.* See also **category** → CATEGORY

class [T, often passive] to think or decide that sb/sth is a particular type of person or thing: *Prisoners classed as illiterate were given a basic education.* ◇ *I wouldn't have classed you as a Shakespeare fan.* See also **class** → CATEGORY *noun*

group [T] to arrange people or things into groups according to features that they share, to make it easier to deal with them: *Topics for the second year can be grouped under three headings.*

bracket [T, often passive] to consider people or things to be similar or connected in some way: *The two writers are often bracketed together by critics.* See also **bracket** → CATEGORY *noun*

clean *verb* See also the entry for BRUSH

clean · wash · rinse · cleanse · hose · shampoo · dry-clean · bathe
These words all mean to remove dirt from sth, especially by using water and/or soap.

▸ to clean / wash / rinse / cleanse / bathe sth **in / with** sth
▸ to clean / wash / rinse sth **from** sth
▸ to clean / wash / rinse sth **out**
▸ to clean / wash / hose sth **down**
▸ to clean / wash / cleanse / bathe a **wound**
▸ to clean / wash / rinse the **glasses**
▸ to clean / wash / hose (down) the **car**
▸ to clean / wash the **windows / floor**
▸ to wash / rinse / shampoo your **hair**
▸ to **have** sth cleaned / washed / shampooed / dry-cleaned

clean [T, I] to remove dirt or dust from sth, especially by using water or chemicals; to become clean: *The villa is cleaned twice a week.* ◇ *This product cleans baths very effectively.* ◇ *Have you cleaned your teeth?* ◇ *This coat is filthy. I'll have it cleaned* (= dry-cleaned) ◇ *I must clean the fish tank out.* ◇ *I spent all day cooking and cleaning.* ◇ *This oven cleans easily* (= is easy to clean). See also **clean (sth) up** → TIDY, **clean, cleaning** → BATH

wash [T, I] to remove dirt from sth using water and usually soap; (of clothes or fabric) to be able to be washed without losing colour or being damaged: *He quickly washed his hands and face.* ◇ *Wash the fruit thoroughly before eating.* ◇ *These jeans need washing.* ◇ *She washed the blood from his face.* ◇ *The beach had been washed clean by the tide.* ◇ *Wash down the walls before painting them.* ◇ *This sweater washes well.* See also **wash** → BATH *noun*, **wash, wash up** → WASH *verb*

rinse [T] to remove dirt from sth using clean water only, not soap; to remove the soap from sth with clean water after washing it: *Rinse the dishes in warm water.* ◇ *Rinse the cup out before use.* ◇ *Make sure you rinse all the soap out.* ◇ *I wanted to rinse the taste out of my mouth.* See also **rinse** → BATH

cleanse /klenz/ [T] to clean your skin or a wound: *a lotion to cleanse the face/skin* ◇ *This is a treatment to* **cleanse** *the body* **of** *toxins.*

hose /həʊz; AmE hoʊz/ [T] to wash or pour water on sth using a hose (= a long rubber tube): *I'll just hose down the car.* ◇ *Firemen hosed the burning car.*

shampoo /ʃæmˈpuː/ [T] to wash or clean hair, carpets or furniture covers with shampoo (= a type of liquid soap): *She showered and shampooed her hair.* ◇ *If you can afford it, have the carpet shampooed professionally.*

dry-ˈclean [T, often passive] to clean clothes using chemicals instead of water: *I took the coat in to be dry-cleaned.*

bathe /beɪð/ [T] to wash sth with water, especially a wound or a part of the body: *Bathe the wound and apply a clean dressing.*

clean *adj.*

clean · pure · sterile · hygienic · spotless
These words all describe sth which is not dirty.

▸ clean / pure / sterile (**drinking**) **water**
▸ clean / pure **air**
▸ clean / sterile / hygienic **conditions**
▸ (a) clean / sterile **equipment / dressing / needle**
▸ to **keep** sth clean / pure / sterile / spotless
▸ **very** clean / pure / hygienic
▸ **completely** clean / sterile

clean not dirty; having an appearance and surroundings that are not dirty; free from harmful or unpleasant substances: *Are your hands clean?* ◇ *He wiped his plate clean with a piece of bread.* ◇ *(BrE) It is your responsibility to keep the room* **clean and tidy.** ◇ *(AmE) Keep your room* neat and clean. ◇ I can't find a clean shirt (= one that I haven't worn since it was washed). ◇ Cats are very clean animals. ◇ Thousands were left without food or clean drinking water. **OPP** dirty → DIRTY

pure (especially of air or water) clean and not containing any harmful substances: *Much of the population still does not have access to pure drinking water.* ◇ *The mountain air was sweet and pure.*

sterile /'steraɪl; AmE 'sterəl/ completely clean and free from bacteria and therefore unable to spread disease: *All the equipment used is new and sterile.*

hygienic /haɪ'dʒiːnɪk; AmE usually -'dʒen-/ clean and free from bacteria and therefore unlikely to spread disease: *Food must be prepared in hygienic conditions.* ◇ *The kitchen didn't look very hygienic.* **OPP** unhygienic → UNHEALTHY
▸ **hygienically** adv.: *Medical supplies are disposed of hygienically.*

spotless perfectly clean: *She keeps the house absolutely spotless.* ◇ *He wore a smart jacket and a spotless white shirt.*
▸ **spotlessly** adv.: *The room was poorly furnished but spotlessly clean.*

clear verb

clear · empty · drain · unload · unpack
These words all mean to remove things from somewhere or take things out of sth.

PATTERNS AND COLLOCATIONS
▸ to clear / empty / drain sth **of** sth
▸ to empty / drain / unload the **contents** of sth
▸ to empty / unpack a **suitcase / bag**
▸ to unload / unpack **a car / the shopping**
▸ to empty / drain **water** from sth
▸ to empty / drain **your glass**

clear [T] to remove sth that is not wanted or needed from a place: *Clear all those papers off the desk.* ◇ *It's your turn to **clear the table** (= to take away the dirty plates and other things after a meal).* ◇ *She **cleared a space** on the sofa for him to sit down.* ◇ *It was several hours before the road was cleared after the accident.* ◇ *It's time your toys were **cleared away**.* ❶ **Clear away** can also be used without an object: *He cleared away and made coffee.* See also **block** → BLOCK 2

empty [T] to remove everything that is in a container; to take out the contents of sth and put them somewhere else: *I **emptied out** my pockets but could not find my keys.* ◇ *She emptied the water out of the vase.* ◇ *He emptied the ashtrays, washed the glasses and went to bed.* ◇ *The room had been emptied of all furniture.* ◇ *She emptied the contents of her bag onto the table.* **OPP** fill → FILL, See also **empty** → DRAIN verb, **empty** → EMPTY

drain [T] to make sth empty or dry by removing all the liquid from it: *Drain and rinse the pasta.* ◇ *The marshes have been drained.* ◇ *You will need to turn off the water and drain the tank.*

unload [T, I] to remove things from a vehicle or ship after it has taken them somewhere; to remove the contents of sth after you have finished using it, especially the bullets from a gun or the film from a camera: *Everyone helped to unload the luggage from the car.* ◇ *This isn't a suitable place to unload the van.* ◇ *The truck driver was waiting to unload.* ◇ *Each time a gun is laid down it must first be broken and unloaded.* **OPP** load → FILL

unpack /ˌʌn'pæk/ [T, I] to take things out of a suitcase, bag, etc. when you arrive somewhere after a journey: *I unpacked my bags as soon as I arrived.* ◇ *She unpacked all the clothes she needed and left the rest in the case.* ◇ *She went to her room to unpack.* **OPP** pack → FILL

clear adj. See also the entry for VISIBLE
1 It is clear to me that...
2 clear instructions
3 clear blue water

1 See also the entries for MARKED and OPEN

clear · obvious · apparent · evident · plain · self-evident
These words all describe a fact, quality or situation that is easy to see or understand and leaves no doubts.

PATTERNS AND COLLOCATIONS
▸ clear / obvious / apparent / evident / plain / self-evident **to** sb/sth
▸ clear / obvious / apparent / evident / plain / self-evident **from / in** sb/sth
▸ clear / obvious / apparent / evident / self-evident **what... / that...**
▸ clear / obvious / apparent / evident / plain **who / how / where / why...**
▸ to **seem** clear / obvious / apparent / evident / plain / self-evident
▸ to **become / make sth** clear / obvious / apparent / evident / plain
▸ **very / quite / perfectly** clear / obvious / apparent / evident / plain
▸ **all too** clear / obvious / apparent / evident / plain
▸ **fairly** clear / obvious / evident / plain / self-evident
▸ **far from** clear / obvious / evident / self-evident
▸ **by no means** clear / obvious / self-evident

clear easy to see or understand and leaving no doubts: *It was quite clear to me that she was lying.* ◇ *It is not clear what they want us to do.* ◇ *It is clear from the graph that sales have dropped sharply.* ◇ *This is a clear case of fraud.* ◇ *She won the election by a **clear majority**.* **OPP** unclear → UNCLEAR
▸ **clearly** adv.: *Clearly, this will cost a lot more than we realized.*

obvious easy to see or understand: *It's obvious from what she said that something is wrong.* ◇ *I know you don't like her but try not to make it so obvious.* ◇ *He put his book down with obvious annoyance.* ◇ ***For obvious reasons**, I'd prefer not to give my name.*
▸ **obviously** adv.: *He was obviously drunk.* ◇ *'I didn't realize it was a formal occasion.' 'Obviously!'* (= I can see by the way you are dressed)

apparent /ə'pærənt/ [not usually before noun] (rather formal) easy to see or understand: *His devotion to her was increasingly apparent.* ◇ *It soon became apparent to everyone that he couldn't sing.* ◇ *Then, **for no apparent reason**, the train suddenly stopped.*

evident (rather formal) easy to see or understand: *The growing interest in history is clearly evident in the number of people visiting museums.* ◇ *The orchestra played with evident enjoyment.*
▸ **evidently** adv.: *She walked slowly down the road, evidently in pain.* ◇ *'I'm afraid I couldn't finish the work last night.' 'Evidently too.'*

plain easy to see or understand: *He **made it** very **plain** that he wanted us to leave.* ◇ *She made her annoyance plain.* ◇ *The facts were **plain to see**.*
▸ **plainly** adv.: *She had no right to interfere in what was plainly a family matter.* ◇ *Plainly something was wrong.*

NOTE WHICH WORD? These words all have almost exactly the same meaning. There are slight differences in register and patterns of use. If you *make sth clear/plain*, you do so deliberately because you want people to understand sth; if you *make sth obvious*, you usually do it without meaning to: *I hope I make myself clear/plain.* ◇ *I hope I make myself obvious.* ◇ *Try not to make your dislike so obvious.* ◇ *Try not to make it so clear/plain.* In the expressions *clear majority*, *for obvious reasons*, *for no apparent reason* and *plain to see*, none of the other words can be used instead. **Apparent** and **evident** are both rather formal. They can always be replaced by **obvious**. **Obvious** and **evident** can be used before a noun for an emotion, meaning that the emotion is easy to see with your eyes: *Jane took the letter and read it out with obvious/evident reluctance.* In *apparent reluctance*, **apparent** has the meaning of 'seeming'. See also **apparent** → APPARENT

self-'evident so obvious that it needs no further proof or explanation: *The dangers of such action are self-evident.* ◇ *a self-evident truth*

2 clear · explicit · plain · express · accessible · unambiguous · intelligible · comprehensible · lucid
These words all describe speech or writing that is easy to understand and does not cause any confusion.

PATTERNS AND COLLOCATIONS
▶ clear / explicit / unambiguous **about** sth
▶ clear / plain / accessible / intelligible / comprehensible **to** sb
▶ clear / explicit / express **instructions / directions**
▶ a clear / an accessible / a lucid **style**
▶ clear / plain / intelligible / comprehensible **language / English**
▶ to **make** sth clear / explicit / plain / accessible / intelligible / comprehensible (to sb)
▶ to **make yourself** clear / explicit / plain
▶ to **make it** clear / explicit / plain that...
▶ **quite** clear / explicit / plain / accessible / unambiguous / intelligible / comprehensible
▶ **perfectly** clear / plain / intelligible / comprehensible

clear easy to understand and not causing any confusion: *She gave me clear and precise directions.* ◇ *Your meaning needs to be* **crystal clear.** ◇ *You'll do as you're told. Is that clear?* ◇ *This behaviour must stop! Do I make myself clear?* (= used when you are angrily telling sb what they should do). **OPP unclear** → UNCLEAR, **confusing** → CONFUSING
▶ **clearly** *adv.*: *She explained everything very clearly.*
explicit /ɪkˈsplɪsɪt/ (*rather formal*) saying sth clearly in a way that is easy to understand; said, shown or drawn in an open or direct way, so that there is no doubt: *The author is quite explicit about her political bias.* ◇ *The reasons for the decisions should be made explicit.* ◇ *She made some very explicit references to my personal life.* ❶ **Explicit** is also used to talk about books, films, language and pictures that describe or show sex in a clear and detailed way: *sexually explicit films/material/languge.* *Explicit language* always refers to sex, even if the word 'sexually' is not used. If you want to talk about language that is clear and easy to understand, use **clear**, **plain** or **unambiguous**.
▶ **explicitly** *adv.*: *He made this point much more explicitly in his next speech.*
plain easy to understand: *He made it plain that we should leave.* ◇ *Her intentions were plain enough.* ◇ *Teachers should encourage students to write in plain English.* See also **plain** → PLAIN *adj.* 2
▶ **plainly** *adv.*: *The agreement plainly states that all damage must be paid for.*
express (*formal*) (of a wish or aim) clearly and openly stated: *It was his* **express wish** *that you should have his gold watch after he died.* ◇ *I came here with the* **express purpose** *of speaking with the manager.*
▶ **expressly** *adv.*: *She was expressly forbidden to touch my papers.*
accessible /əkˈsesəbl/ (*especially written*) easy for most people to understand: *Her poetry is always very accessible.* ◇ *The programme tries to make science more accessible to young people.*
unambiguous /ˌʌnæmˈbɪɡjuəs/ clear in meaning, especially because it can only be understood in only one way: *The message was clear and unambiguous: get out of town.* **OPP ambiguous** → MISLEADING
▶ **unambiguously** *adv.*: *The essential information should be displayed clearly and unambiguously.*
intelligible /ɪnˈtelɪdʒəbl/ (*rather formal*) that can be understood: *The child's speech was barely intelligible.* **OPP unintelligible** → CONFUSING
▶ **intelligibly** *adv.*: *You need to be able to write clearly and intelligibly.*
comprehensible /ˌkɒmprɪˈhensəbl/ (*rather formal*) that can be understood: *The novel is easily comprehensible to the average reader.* **OPP incomprehensible** → CONFUSING

NOTE INTELLIGIBLE OR **COMPREHENSIBLE?** These words are very similar and in most cases you can use either. **Intelligible** is used slightly more to talk about sb's speech or language; **comprehensible** is used slightly more for ideas, actions and processes.

lucid /ˈluːsɪd/ (*especially written*) (especially of sb's writing) clearly expressed and easy to understand: *She writes in a very lucid style.* ◇ *It was a lucid account of the main facts of the case.*

3 clear · transparent · translucent · colourless · see-through
These words all describe sth which you can see through.

PATTERNS AND COLLOCATIONS
▶ clear / transparent / translucent **glass**
▶ clear / transparent / see-through **plastic**
▶ clear / transparent / colourless **varnish**
▶ a clear / colourless **liquid**
▶ clear / translucent **skin**
▶ **almost** transparent / translucent / colourless

clear that you can see through: *Items must be carried in a clear plastic bag.* ◇ *The water was so clear we could see the bottom of the lake.* ◇ *The water comes out of the spring* **crystal clear** (= completely clear) *and totally pure.* **OPP cloudy** ❶ **Cloudy** liquid is not very clear because it contains lots of small bits of dust or another substance: *The water looked cloudy and not fit to drink.*
transparent that you can see through: *The insect's wings are almost transparent.* ◇ *I've covered the photographs with transparent plastic sheets.* **OPP opaque** ❶ **Opaque** glass or liquid is not clear enough to see through or allow light through: *If you add water to the glass the liquid will go milky and opaque.*

NOTE CLEAR OR **TRANSPARENT? Clear** is the word used most often to describe water. When it is used to describe things other than water it usually comes before the noun: *clear blue water* ◇ ~~*The water was blue and clear.*~~ ◇ *a clear plastic bag* ◇ ~~*The plastic bag was clear.*~~ **Transparent** is usually used to describe solid things or material, not liquids (except *varnish*).

translucent /trænsˈluːsnt; trænz-/ (*written*) allowing light to pass through but not transparent: *The sky was a pale translucent blue.* ◇ *His skin was translucent with age.*
colourless (*BrE*) (*AmE* **colorless**) without colour or very pale: *Water is a colourless compound of hydrogen and oxygen.* ◇ *Her illness had left her face deathly white and her lips colourless.*
'see-through [usually before noun] (of clothes or fabric) very thin so that you can see through it: *She was wearing a see-through blouse.*

climb *verb*

climb · go up (sth) · scramble · clamber · mount · ascend · scale
These words all mean to move up towards the top of sth.

PATTERNS AND COLLOCATIONS
▶ to climb / go / scramble / clamber **up** sth
▶ to climb / scramble / clamber **over** sth
▶ to climb / go up / mount / ascend a **hill**
▶ to climb / go up / ascend / scale a **mountain**
▶ to climb / ascend / scale a **peak**
▶ to climb / go up / scramble up / clamber up / ascend / scale a **ladder**
▶ to climb / go up / mount / ascend the **stairs / steps**
▶ to climb / scramble over / clamber over / scale a **wall**
▶ to climb / clamber over / scale a **fence**

climb [T, I] to move up sth towards the top, especially when this takes some effort; to move somewhere, especially with difficulty or effort: *I loved climbing trees when I was a kid.* ◇ *The car slowly climbed the hill.* ◇ *As they climber higher, the air became cooler.* ◇ *I climbed through the window.* ◇ *Can you climb down?* ❶ To **go climbing** is to climb mountains or rocks as a hobby or sport: *He goes climbing most weekends.*
▶ **climb** *noun* [C]: *It's an hour's climb to the summit.*

,go 'up sth, ,go 'up *phrasal verb* to move up sth towards the top: *She went up the stairs to bed.* ◇ *It gets colder as you go up (by 0.5°C with each 100 m rise).* **OPP** **go down (sth), come down (sth)** → FALL 2

> **NOTE CLIMB OR GO UP?** To **climb** sth usually takes more effort than to just **go up** it. You can *climb/go up a hill/ mountain*, but **climb** places more emphasis on the effort involved. You can *climb a wall/fence/tree* but NOT: *go up a wall/fence/tree.* You *climb the stairs* when you are feeling tired or the stairs are very steep; at other times you just *go up the stairs.*

scramble [I] (always used with an adverb or preposition) to climb or move somewhere quickly, especially with difficulty, using your hands to help you: *She managed to scramble over the wall.* ◇ *He **scrambled to his feet** as we came in.*
> ▸ **scramble** *noun* [sing.]: *It was a stiff two-hour walk, followed by a difficult scramble over slimy rock faces.*
clamber [I] (always used with an adverb or preposition) to climb or move with difficulty or a lot of effort, using your hands to help you: *The children clambered up the steep bank.*

> **NOTE SCRAMBLE OR CLAMBER?** Scramble places more emphasis on speed; **clamber** emphasizes the difficulty or effort involved.

mount [T] (*formal*) to go up sth, or up on to sth that is raised: *She slowly mounted the steps.* ◇ *He mounted the platform and addressed the crowd.*
ascend /ə'send/ [I, T] (*formal*) to go up sth: *The air became colder as we ascended.* ◇ *Her heart was thumping as she ascended the stairs.* **OPP** **descend** → FALL 2
> ▸ **ascent** *noun* [C, usually sing.]: *the first ascent of Mount Everest*
scale [T] (*written*) to climb to the top of sth very high and steep: *He somehow managed to scale the sheer outside wall of the tower.*

clink *verb* See also the entry for RING

clink · beep · tinkle · jingle · ping
These words all mean to make a high, sharp ringing sound.

PATTERNS AND COLLOCATIONS
> ▸ **coins** clink/ jingle
> ▸ **a bell** tinkles/ jingles/ pings

clink [I, T] to make a sharp ringing sound, like the sound made by glasses being hit against each other; to make sth produce this sound: *The coins clinked into the slot in the machine.* ◇ *They clinked glasses and drank each other's health.*
> ▸ **clink** *noun* [C, sing.]: *She heard the sound of voices and the clink of glasses.* ◇ *He placed the glass in front of her with a clink.*
beep [I] to make a short high electronic sound: *The microwave beeps to let you know when it has finished.*
> ▸ **beep** *noun* [C]: *You should hear a beep when you switch it on.*
tinkle [I, T] to make a series of light high ringing sounds; to make sth produce this sound: *Water tinkled in the fountains.* ◇ *Outside, we could hear the tinkling laughter of children.* ◇ *He tinkled the ice in his glass and took a sip.*
> ▸ **tinkle** *noun* [usually sing.]: *She heard the tinkle of breaking glass from downstairs.*
jingle [I, T] to make the pleasant ringing sound that is made when small metal objects are shaken together; to make sth produce this sound: *A bell jingled as he entered the shop.* ◇ *She jingled the coins in her pocket.*
> ▸ **jingle** *noun* [sing.]: *He heard a jingle of keys at the door.*
ping [I, T] to make a short, high ringing sound, especially the sound made when a small object hits sth hard at speed; to make sth produce this sound: *He threw himself to the ground as bullets pinged off the metal behind him.* ◇ *You have to ping the bell on the desk to get someone to come and attend to you.*
> ▸ **ping** *noun* [C]: *The bell went ping and the doors of the lift opened.*

close /kləʊz; AmE kloʊz/ *verb*

1 close a door/your eyes/a book
2 a factory closes/close a factory

1 close · shut · lock · slam · draw · bolt
These words all mean to put sth such as a door into a position so that it covers an opening, or to move the parts of sth together so that it is no longer open.

PATTERNS AND COLLOCATIONS
> ▸ to close/ shut/ lock/ slam/ bolt a **door**/ **gate**
> ▸ to close/ shut/ lock a **window**/ **drawer**/ **case**/ **suitcase**
> ▸ to close/ shut/ slam a **shutter**
> ▸ to close/ shut/ bolt a **hatch**
> ▸ to close/ shut a/ an/ your **box**/ **lid**/ **eyes**/ **mouth**/ **flap**/ **valve**/ **book**/ **umbrella**
> ▸ to close/ draw the **curtains**/ **blinds**
> ▸ a **door**/ **gate** closes/ shuts/ slams
> ▸ sb's **eyes** close/ shut
> ▸ to **hear** sth close/ shut/ slam
> ▸ to close/ shut/ lock/ slam/ bolt sth **behind** you
> ▸ to close/ shut/ lock/ bolt sth **firmly**
> ▸ to close/ shut sth **tightly**
> ▸ to **half**/ **partly** close/ shut/ draw sth

close [T, I] to put sth such as a door, window or lid into a position so that it covers an opening; to get into this position; to move the parts of sth together so that it is no longer open: *She closed the gate behind her.* ◇ *She closed her eyes and fell asleep immediately.* ◇ *The doors open and close automatically.* **OPP** **open** ❶ The opposite is **open**: *She opened her bag and took out her passport.* ◇ *The door opened and Alan walked in.*
shut [T, I] to make sth close; to become closed: *I can't shut my suitcase — it's too full.* ◇ *I shut my eyes against the bright light.* ◇ *He shut his book and looked up.* ◇ *The window won't shut.* **OPP** **open**

> **NOTE CLOSE OR SHUT?** You can use **close** and **shut** with the same range of nouns, but **shut** is used more often for containers such as *boxes* and *suitcases*. **Shut** is often used to talk about sudden actions, and can suggest more noise. **Close** often suggests doing things more slowly or gently: *Close your eyes and go to sleep.* ◇ *She quietly closed the window and crept out of the room.*

lock [T, I] to close sth firmly so that it will not open, using a lock; to be able to be closed firmly in this way; to put sth in a safe place and lock it: *The gates are locked at 6 o'clock.* ◇ *This suitcase doesn't lock.* ◇ *She locked her passport and money in the safe.* ❶ A **lock** is a device that keeps a door, window, lid, etc. shut, usually needing a key to open it. **OPP** **unlock** ❶ To **unlock** sth is to undo the lock of a door, window, etc. using a key.
slam (-mm-) [I, T] to shut, or to make sth shut, with a lot of force, making a loud noise: *I heard the door slam behind him.* ◇ *He stormed out of the house, slamming the door as he left.* See also **slam** → CRASH
> ▸ **slam** *noun* [C, usually sing.]: *The front door closed with a slam.* ◇ *She gave the door a good hard slam.*
draw [T] to close or open curtains or blinds: *Draw the curtains — it's dark outside.* ◇ *She drew back the curtains and let the sunlight in.*
bolt [T, I] to lock a door or window by sliding a bolt across; to be able to be locked in this way: *Don't forget to bolt the door.* ◇ *The gate bolts on the inside.* ❶ A **bolt** is a long, narrow piece of metal that you slide across the inside of a door or window in order to lock it.

2 close · cease trading · fail · close (sth) down · collapse · go bust · crash · go bankrupt · fold · flop
These are all words that can be used when a business stops operating, often because it does not have enough money to pay the bills and cannot borrow any more.

PATTERNS AND COLLOCATIONS
- a **firm** / **company** closes / ceases trading / fails / closes down / collapses / goes bust / crashes / goes bankrupt / folds
- a **business** closes / ceases trading / fails / closes down / collapses / goes bust / crashes / folds
- an **industry** closes down / collapses
- a **person** goes bust / goes bankrupt
- a / an **factory** / **newspaper** / **operation** / **shop** closes / closes down
- **shares** / **prices** / **markets** collapse / crash
- a **show** / **play** closes / folds / flops
- to **suddenly** close / close down / collapse / fold

close [I, T] (of a business, service or show) to stop operating; to cause a business, service or show to stop operating: *The hospital closed at the end of last year.* ◇ *The play closed after just three nights.* ◇ *The club was closed by the police.* ◇ *They are closing their Liverpool factory.* **OPP** **open** ❶ When a business, service or show **opens** it starts business or starts playing to the public for the first time: *The show opened to great reviews.* ◇ *The company* **opened its doors** *for business a month ago.*
- **closure** /ˈkləʊʒə(r); AmE ˈkloʊ-/ noun [C, U]: *factory closures* ◇ *The hospital has been threatened with closure.*

ˌcease ˈtrading phrase (*formal, business*) (of a business) to stop operating: *A leading travel firm has ceased trading with the loss of a number of jobs.*

fail [I] (of a business) to be unable to continue operating: *More banks failed as people rushed to withdraw their money.*
- **failure** noun [C, U]: *There has been an alarming increase in business failures.*

ˌclose ˈdown, ˌclose sth ˈdown phrasal verb (of a business or service) to stop operating; to cause a business or service to stop operating: *Companies were closing down or reducing their workforce.* ◇ *Banks are closing down their smaller branches.* **OPP** **open (sth) up** ❶ When a business or service **opens up** it starts operating; to **open sth up** is to start a new business or service: *There's a new Thai restaurant opening up in town.*

NOTE CLOSE OR CLOSE DOWN? There is not much difference in meaning between these words. Both can be used to talk about either a business or service; **close** but NOT **close down** can also be used to talk about a play or show: ~~The play closed down after just three nights.~~

collapse [I] (of a business, prices, a market or an economy) to lose all or most of its value: *Share prices collapsed after news of poor trading figures.* ◇ *The region's economy has virtually collapsed.*
- **collapse** noun [C, usually sing.]: *the collapse of share prices / the dollar / the market*

go ˈbust idiom (*informal*) (of a business or the person running it) to be unable to continue operating because there is no money: *We lost our deposit when the travel company went bust.*

crash [I] (*rather informal*) (of a business, market or prices) to lose all or most of its value suddenly: *Share prices crashed to an all-time low yesterday.*
- **crash** noun [C]: *the 1929 stock market crash*

NOTE COLLAPSE OR CRASH? There is not much difference in meaning between these words. An *economy* can **collapse** but NOT **crash**. **Crash** is slightly more informal and suggests an even more sudden event.

go ˈbankrupt phrase (of a person or company) to stop running a business because you do not have enough money to pay what you owe; (of a person) to ask a judge in court to officially say that you cannot pay your debts and are not allowed to borrow money: *Unfortunately the firm went bankrupt before the work was completed.* ◇ *I have thousands of pounds of debt which I can't afford to pay back and am thinking of going bankrupt.*

fold [I] (*rather informal*) (of a business, organization or show) to close because it is no longer successful: *His business folded and his wife left him.* ◇ *The musical folded after 16 performances.* ◇ *Her fan club has folded.*

flop (-pp-) [I] (*rather informal*) (of a film, show, product or project) to be a failure, especially because it is not popular: *The play flopped on Broadway.* ◇ *Many of his ambitious schemes have flopped in the past.* See also **flop** → DISASTER *noun*

close /kləʊs; AmE kloʊs/ adj.

close · even · near · narrow · level · marginal · hard-fought · neck and neck
These words all describe a race or contest in which two people or teams are equal, or a situation in which sth nearly happens or does not happen.

close	even
near	level
narrow	neck and neck
marginal	
hard-fought	

PATTERNS AND COLLOCATIONS
- level / neck and neck **with** sb
- a close / an even / a hard-fought **contest**
- a close / hard-fought **battle** / **finish**
- a narrow / hard-fought **win** / **victory**
- a narrow / marginal **lead**
- a close / narrow **vote**
- **desperately** close / hard-fought

close (of a race or contest) won by only a small amount or distance; used to describe sth that nearly happens, usually a dangerous or unpleasant situation: *It's a desperately close race – I can't quite see who is ahead.* ◇ *The California election looks* **too close to call** (= it is impossible to predict the result) *as voters go to the polls.* ◇ *The invasion never happened but it was* **a close run thing** (= it almost did). ◇ *Phew! That was close – the motorbike nearly hit us.*

even (of an amount) equal or the same for each person, team, place, etc.; (of two people or teams) equally balanced or of an equal standard: *The scores were even at 2–2.* ◇ *The political goal was a more even distribution of wealth.* ◇ *The two players were pretty even.* ◇ *This seems to be a more even contest.* **OPP** **uneven** ❶ An **uneven** contest is one in which one group, team or player is much better than the other.

near [only before noun] (no comparative or superlative) being almost sth or almost happening: *The election proved to be a* **near disaster** *for the party.* ◇ *We won in the end but it was a* **near thing**. ◇ *The climbers had already had one* **near miss** (= almost had an accident) *on the summit.*

narrow [usually before noun] only just achieved or avoided: *He blamed the goalkeeper for the* **narrow defeat** *against Ireland.* ◇ *She lost the race by the narrowest of margins.* ◇ *She was elected by a* **narrow majority**. ◇ *He had a* **narrow escape** (= nearly had a bad accident) *when his car skidded on the ice.*

level [not before noun] (*especially BrE*) (in sport) having the same score as sb: *A good second round brought him* **level with** *the tournament leader.* ◇ *The clubs are* **level on** *points.* ◇ *The score was level at 5 points each.* ◇ *France took an early lead but Wales soon* **drew level** (= scored the same number of points).

marginal /ˈmɑːdʒɪnl; AmE ˈmɑːrdʒ-/ [usually before noun] (*especially BrE*) (in politics) won or lost by a very small number of votes in the last election and therefore very important or interesting politically: *Their campaign targeted* **marginal constituencies**. ◇ *They risk losing key* **marginal seats** *at the next election.* **OPP** **safe** ❶ In British politics a **safe seat** is a constituency where a particular party has a lot of support and is unlikely to be defeated in an election.

hard-'fought (of a contest or competition) that involves both sides fighting very hard to win: *It was a lively and hard-fought match.* ◊ *It was a hard-fought game.*

neck and 'neck *idiom* level with sb in a race or competition: *The cyclists were neck and neck as they approached the final lap.* ◊ *He was running **neck and neck** with his Democrat rival.*

clothes *noun*

clothes · clothing · garment · dress · costume · apparel · wear · wardrobe · gear
These are all words for the things that you wear, such as shirts, jackets, dresses and trousers.

PATTERNS AND COLLOCATIONS
▶ **casual** clothes / clothing / dress / apparel / wear / gear
▶ **evening / formal** clothes / dress / wear
▶ (sb's) **summer / winter** clothes / clothing / apparel / wear / wardrobe
▶ **designer / sports** clothes / clothing / apparel / wear / gear
▶ **children's / men's / women's** clothes / clothing / garments / apparel / wear
▶ (sb's) **new** clothes / garments / wardrobe / gear
▶ (sb's) **old** clothes / garments / gear
▶ **warm** clothes / clothing / garments
▶ to **have / buy** ... clothes / apparel / wardrobe / gear
▶ to **have on / be in** ...clothes / garments / dress / gear
▶ to **wear** ... clothes / garments / dress / costume / gear
▶ to **be dressed in** ... clothes / garments / costume / gear

clothes [pl.] the things that you wear, such as shirts, jackets, dresses and trousers: *I bought some new clothes for the trip.* ◊ *I quickly threw on some clothes and ran downstairs.* ◊ *Bring a **change of clothes** with you.* ❶ You can *change/put on/remove/take off your clothes,* but these verbs do not collocate with the other words in this group, and it is even more common to say *get changed/dressed/undressed.*

clothing [U] (*rather formal*) clothes, especially a particular type of clothes: *Please make sure you bring warm clothing.* ◊ *What was the last item of clothing you bought?*

> **NOTE** CLOTHES OR CLOTHING? **Clothing** is more formal than **clothes** and is used especially to mean 'a particular type of clothes'. There is no singular form of **clothes** or **clothing**: *a piece/an item/an article of clothing* is used to talk about one thing that you wear such as a dress or shirt.

garment /'gɑːmənt; *AmE* 'gɑːrm-/ [C] (*formal*) a piece of clothing: *He was wearing a strange shapeless garment.* ❶ **Garment** should only be used in formal or literary contexts; in everyday contexts use *a piece of clothing.*

dress [U] clothes, especially when worn in a particular style or for a particular occasion: *All the guests were in evening dress.* ◊ *He has no **dress sense** (= no idea of how to dress well).* ◊ *The company has a strict **dress code** – all male employees are expected to wear suits.*

costume [C, U] the clothes worn by people from a particular place or during a particular historical period: *Some of the singers wore the Welsh **national costume**.* ◊ *The film is a **costume drama** based on a 19th-century novel.* See also **costume** → COSTUME

apparel /ə'pærəl/ [U] (*AmE*) clothing, when it is being sold in stores: *The store sells women's and children's apparel.*

wear [U] (usually in compounds) clothes for a particular purpose or occasion, especially when it is being sold in shops: *We headed straight for the children's wear department.* ◊ *They manufacture designer sportswear.*

wardrobe [C, usually sing.] (*rather formal*) the clothes that a person has: *We have everything you need for your summer wardrobe.*

gear /gɪə(r); *AmE* gɪr/ [U] (*informal*) clothes: *Her friends were all wearing the latest gear* (= fashionable clothes). See also **gear** → EQUIPMENT

cloud *noun*

1 The sun went behind a cloud.
2 a cloud of dust

1 cloud · fog · mist · haze
These are all words for a mass of very small drops of water in the air.

PATTERNS AND COLLOCATIONS
▶ **in / through** (a) cloud / fog / mist / haze
▶ (a) **thick / heavy** cloud / fog / mist
▶ **dense / grey / swirling** cloud / fog / mist
▶ **thin / light** cloud / mist
▶ a **sea** fog / mist
▶ to **be shrouded in** cloud / fog / mist
▶ cloud / mist **hangs** in the air / over a place

cloud [C, U] a grey or white mass made of very small drops of water, that floats high in the sky: *The sun went behind a cloud.* ◊ *It was scorching and there wasn't a cloud in the sky.* ◊ *Above the mountains **storm clouds** were gathering.* ◊ *Thick cloud hung over the moor.*

fog [U, C] a thick cloud of very small drops of water in the air close to the land or sea, that is very difficult to see through: ***Freezing fog** will make driving conditions very treacherous.* ◊ *We get heavy fogs on this coast in winter.* See also **smog** → SMOKE

mist [U, C] a mass of very small drops of water in the air close to the land or sea, that make it difficult to see, usually thinner than fog: *The hills were shrouded in mist.* ◊ (*figurative*) *She gazed at him through a mist of tears.*

haze [C, U] (*written*) air that is difficult to see through because it contains very small drops of water, especially caused by hot weather: *A **heat haze** shimmered above the fields.* ◊ *The plain stretched for miles until it became lost in blue haze.*

2 cloud · plume · haze
These are all words for a large mass of dust or smoke in the air.

PATTERNS AND COLLOCATIONS
▶ a cloud / plume / haze **of** sth
▶ a cloud / plume / haze of **smoke / dust / steam**
▶ **in / through** a cloud / haze
▶ a **black** cloud / plume

cloud [C, U] a large mass of sth in the air, for example dust or smoke, or a number of insects flying all together: *They watched the car disappearing in a cloud of dust.* ◊ *The sky turned dark as a great cloud of locusts blocked out the sun.*

plume /pluːm/ [C] (*written*) a cloud of sth that rises and curves upwards in the air: *A great plume of dust and ash rose from the volcano.*

haze [sing.] (*written*) air containing sth that makes it difficult to see through, such as smoke or dust: *Meetings were always conducted in a haze of cigarette smoke.*

cloudy *adj.*

cloudy · misty · grey · foggy · hazy · overcast · dull · murky
These words all describe the weather when there are lots of clouds in the sky.

PATTERNS AND COLLOCATIONS
▶ cloudy / grey / foggy / dull **weather**
▶ misty / foggy / overcast **conditions**
▶ a cloudy / misty / grey / overcast / dull **day**
▶ a cloudy / misty / foggy / murky **night**
▶ a dull / grey / misty **morning**

▶ a dull / grey **afternoon**
▶ (a) cloudy / grey / dull / overcast **sky / skies**
▶ misty / grey / hazy / dull / murky **light**

cloudy (of the sky or weather) with a lot of clouds: *It was a dark, cloudy night.* OPP **clear, sunny** → SUNNY, See also **cloud** → DARKEN

misty with a lot of mist: *It was a beautiful misty morning.* OPP **clear** → SUNNY

grey (*especially BrE*) (*AmE usually* **gray**) (*usually disapproving*) (of the sky or weather) without bright sunshine; full of clouds: *I hate these grey days.* OPP **bright** → BRIGHT

foggy not clear because of fog: *He was driving much too fast for the foggy conditions.* OPP **clear** → SUNNY

hazy /ˈheɪzi/ not clear because of haze: *There will be a dry start to the day with some **hazy sunshine** in the east.* ◊ *The mountains were hazy in the distance.*

NOTE **MISTY, FOGGY** OR **HAZY?** Misty and **foggy** weather both happen especially when it is cold, but if it is **hazy**, it is usually hot. If the weather is **foggy**, it is more difficult to see than if it is **misty**.

overcast /ˌəʊvəˈkɑːst; *AmE* ˌoʊvərˈkæst/ (of the sky or weather) without bright sunshine; full of clouds: *The sky was overcast and we needed to use artificial light.*

dull (*sometimes disapproving, especially written*) (of the sky or weather) without bright sunshine; full of clouds: *The town seemed deserted in the dull afternoon light.* OPP **bright** → BRIGHT

NOTE **CLOUDY, GREY, OVERCAST** OR **DULL?** Grey, **overcast** and **dull** all suggest that the whole sky is covered with clouds, so that you cannot see the blue sky behind. If it is **cloudy**, there may be a lot of clouds while the rest of the sky is blue. **Grey** and **dull** often suggest that the speaker is unhappy about the weather. **Overcast** is a more neutral word for describing the sky when none of it is blue. **Dull** is less frequent than the other words, used especially in literary or descriptive writing.

murky /ˈmɜːki/; *AmE* /ˈmɜːrki/ (*often disapproving*) (of air, the sky or light) dark and unpleasant, especially because of smoke or fog; difficult to see through: *The light was murky and it was difficult to see ahead.*

coach noun See the Topic Map for EDUCATION on p.888, See also the entry for TEACHER

coach · trainer · instructor
These are all words for a person who trains a team or person in a practical skill or a sport.

PATTERNS AND COLLOCATIONS
▶ the / an **chief / assistant** coach / trainer / instructor
▶ a / an **qualified / experienced** coach / trainer / instructor
▶ to **work as** a coach / a trainer / an instructor

coach [C] a person who trains a team or person in a sport: *a football/basketball/tennis coach* ◊ *Who's the team coach?* ◊ *The Giants coach had this to say last night:...* ❶ In American English especially, **coach** is used to talk to or about a coach: *See you tomorrow, Coach.* ◊ *Coach Bob Shapiro* See also **coach** → TRAIN *verb* 1, **coaching** → EDUCATION

trainer [C] a person who trains sb in a particular job, skill or sport; a person who trains an animal: *Her trainer was on hand to give some advice.* ◊ *There was a shortage of teacher trainers* (= people who train teachers). ◊ *Only rich people can afford a personal trainer* (= sb who helps an individual to exercise and get fit). ◊ *a dog/racehorse trainer* See also **train** → TRAIN *verb* 1, **training** → EDUCATION

instructor [C] a person who trains sb in a practical skill or sport: *a swimming/diving/fitness/flying/riding/ski instructor* ◊ *I once worked as a driving instructor.* See also **instruct** → TRAIN *verb* 1, **instruction** → EDUCATION

coarse *adj.*

coarse · rough · spiky · leathery · scratchy · scaly · spiny · prickly · bristly
These words all describe things that are not soft to touch.

PATTERNS AND COLLOCATIONS
▶ coarse / rough / leathery / scaly / spiny **skin**
▶ a rough / leathery / scaly **hand**
▶ coarse / rough / scratchy **cloth / fabric / material**
▶ coarse / spiky / bristly **hair**
▶ a spiky / spiny / prickly **leaf / bush**

coarse /kɔːs; *AmE* kɔːrs/ (*rather formal or literary*) (of skin or fabric) having a surface that is not even or regular; (of hair, sand, etc.) consisting of relatively thick or large pieces: *The monks wore coarse linen habits.* ◊ *The coarse sand produces soils which are very free-draining.* OPP **soft, fine** ❶ Soft skin, hair, fur or fabric is smooth and pleasant to touch: *a dress made from the finest, softest silk* A **fine** powder is made of very small grains: *fine sand/flour.*

rough (of skin or fabric) having a surface that is not even or regular: *The skin on her hands was hard and rough.* OPP **soft**

NOTE **COARSE** OR **ROUGH?** When talking about skin or fabric, **coarse** is a more literary word than **rough**; **coarse** but NOT **rough** also describes *hair* with thick strands (= individual hairs) or *sand, salt* or *gravel* with relatively large grains or stones.

spiky (of plants) having sharp points; (of hair) sticking straight up from the head: *It has spiky leaves, tinged with a delicate pink around the edges.* ◊ *He had spiky hair, strong opinions and a wacky sense of humour.* See also **spike** → TIP

leathery that looks or feels hard and tough like leather: *He was a slim man, with leathery skin and clear blue eyes.*

scratchy (of clothes or fabric) rough and unpleasant to the touch: *This sweater is too scratchy.*

scaly /ˈskeɪli/ (of skin) dry, rough and tending to break into small, thin pieces; covered with scales like the skin of a fish or reptile: *Typical symptoms are redness, acne, dry scaly skin and rashes.*

spiny /ˈspaɪni/ (*rather formal or technical*) (of animals or plants) having sharp points like needles: *Beware spiny sea urchins on the sea bed.*

prickly covered with prickles (= small sharp points): *The hedgehog curled up in a prickly ball.*

NOTE **SPIKY, SPINY** OR **PRICKLY?** Spiky is used more in everyday language or literary contexts to talk about sth that is covered in, or is shaped like sharp points. **Spiny** is used in more scientific texts describing plants and animals covered in points that look like needles: *a spiny anteater/lobster/mouse/mollusc/sea urchin* **Prickly** is often used to describe how you imagine it would feel if you touched it. *Prickles* are usually shorter than the points on **spiky** or **spiny** things.

bristly /ˈbrɪsli/ like or full of bristles (= short stiff hairs): *He stroked his bristly chin.*

coast noun See also the entry for SEA

coast · beach · seaside · coastline · waterfront · shoreline · sand · lakeside · seaboard · seashore
These are all words for the land beside or near to the sea, a river or a lake.

PATTERNS AND COLLOCATIONS
▶ along the coast / beach / coastline / waterfront / shoreline / sand / seaboard / seashore
▶ on the coast / beach / coastline / waterfront / shoreline / sands / lakeside / seaboard / seashore
▶ at the coast / beach / seaside / waterfront / seashore
▶ by the coast / seaside / waterfront / seashore / lakeside
▶ a long / beautiful / rocky coast / beach / coastline / shoreline
▶ a / an spectacular / unspoilt coast / beach / coastline

▶ a **rugged** coast / coastline / shoreline
▶ the **north / northern / south / southern**, etc. coast / coastline / seaboard
▶ to **go to** the coast / beach / seaside / seashore
▶ to **follow** the coast / coastline / shoreline
▶ the coast / beach / coastline / sand **stretches** for miles

coast [C, usually sing., U] the land beside or near to the sea or ocean: *We live in a town on the south coast of England.* ◊ *Have you visited any of the islands off the west coast of Ireland?* ◊ *We walked along the coast for five miles.* ◊ *The coast road is closed due to bad weather.* ❶ It is nearly always **the coast**, except when it is uncountable or in the British English expression *a sea coast*: *That's a pretty stretch of coast.* ◊ (*BrE*) *The next scene is famously set on 'a sea coast in Bohemia'.*

beach [C] an area of sand, or small stones, beside the sea or a lake: *We could see tourists sunbathing on the beach.* ◊ *There are miles of beautiful sandy beaches.*

seaside /'si:saɪd/ [sing.] (*especially BrE*) an area that is by the sea, especially one where people go for a day or a holiday: *The children would love a day at the seaside.* ❶ It is always **the seaside**, except when it is used before a noun: *a seaside resort/hotel/villa.* **The seaside** is British English; in American English **seaside** is only used before a noun.

coastline /'kəʊstlaɪn; *AmE* 'koʊst-/ [C, usually sing., U] the land along a coast, especially when you are thinking of its shape or appearance: *The highway gives stunning views of California's rugged coastline.* ◊ *Here are long stretches of unspoilt coastline.*

waterfront /'wɔːtəfrʌnt; *AmE* 'wɔːtərf-; 'wɑːt-/ (often **the waterfront**) [C, usually sing.] a part of a town or an area that is next to water, for example in a harbour: *We stayed in a beautiful apartment on the waterfront.*

shoreline /'ʃɔːlaɪn; *AmE* 'ʃɔːrl-/ (often **the shoreline**) [C] the edge of the sea, the ocean or a lake: *We walked along the rocky shoreline.*

NOTE COASTLINE OR SHORELINE? A **coastline** is always the edge of the sea or ocean, not a lake; **coastline** is usually used to talk about an area that is longer than a **shoreline**: *the British/Mediterranean/Saudi/Turkish coastline* ◊ *the Dublin shoreline.* **The shoreline** can also be used like **the seashore** to talk about the area next to the sea: *She ran along the shoreline.*

sand [U, C, usually pl.] a large area of sand on a beach: *We went for a walk along the sand.* ◊ *With its miles of golden sands, this resort is heaven on earth.*

lakeside /'leɪksaɪd/ [sing.] (usually **the lakeside**) the area around the edge of a lake: *We went for a walk by the lakeside.*

seaboard /'si:bɔːd; *AmE* -bɔːrd/ [C, usually sing.] the part of a country that is along its coast: *The whales have been sighted along the north-eastern seaboard, from Maine to New Jersey.* ❶ **Seaboard** is used most often in the phrases *eastern/western/Atlantic seaboard*, especially when referring to the United States, although it is also used to talk about other countries.

seashore /'si:ʃɔː(r)/ (usually **the seashore**) [C, usually sing.] the land along the edge of the sea or ocean, usually where there is sand and rocks: *He liked to look for shells on the seashore.*

NOTE BEACH OR SEASHORE? **Beach** is usually used to talk about a sandy area next to the sea where people lie in the sun or play, for example when they are on holiday. **Seashore** is used more to talk about the area by the sea in terms of things such as waves, sea shells, rocks, etc., especially where people walk for pleasure.

coat noun

coat · jacket · cloak · shawl · cape · waistcoat · vest · tuxedo/tux · blazer · anorak · mac · tails
These are all words for a piece of clothing that you wear over other clothes to keep you warm and dry outdoors or to look smart on formal occasions.

PATTERNS AND COLLOCATIONS
▶ a **long** coat / jacket / cloak / cape / mac
▶ a **short** coat / jacket / cape / mac
▶ a **heavy** coat / jacket / cloak / shawl
▶ a **light** coat / jacket / shawl
▶ to **wear / put on / take off / remove** a coat / a jacket / a cloak / a shawl / a cape / a waistcoat / a vest / a tuxedo / a blazer / an anorak / a mac / tails
▶ to **do up / undo** a coat / a jacket / a waistcoat / a vest / a blazer / an anorak / a mac
▶ to **button (up) / unbutton** a coat / jacket / waistcoat / vest / blazer / mac
▶ to **zip up / unzip** a coat / a jacket / an anorak / a mac
▶ a coat / jacket / waistcoat / vest **pocket**

coat [C] a piece of outdoor clothing with sleeves that is worn over other clothes to keep warm or dry: *a fur coat* ◊ *a long winter coat* ◊ *Why don't you take off your coat if you're hot?* ❶ **Coat** is often used in one-word and two-word compounds to describe different types of coat: *overcoat* (= a long warm coat worn in cold weather) ◊ *raincoat* (= a long light coat that keeps you dry in the rain) ◊ *trench coat* (= a long loose coat with a belt, worn especially to keep off rain) ◊ *duffel coat* (= a heavy coat made of wool, that usually has a hood and is fastened with toggles). In American English, a **coat** can also be a jacket that is worn as part of a suit. This use is old-fashioned in British English.

jacket [C] a piece of clothing worn on the top half of the body over a shirt, etc. that usually has sleeves and fastens down the front; a short, light coat: *a linen/suede/tweed jacket* ◊ *He pulled his passport from his inside jacket pocket.* ◊ *I have to wear a jacket and tie to work.* ❶ Common compounds are: *dinner jacket* (= a black or white jacket worn with a bow tie at formal occasions in the evening) ◊ *sports jacket* (= a man's jacket for informal occasions) ◊ *ski jacket* ◊ *bomber jacket* (= a short jacket that fits tightly around the waist and fastens with a zip)

NOTE COAT OR JACKET? A **jacket** might be worn outside in warmer weather, and it is often worn inside, for example as part of a suit. A **coat** is usually worn outside, especially in order to keep you warm and dry. When it is worn inside, it is a protective garment worn over clothes: *doctors in their white coats* ◊ *a lab coat* (= worn in a laboratory). A **jacket** usually comes down to the waist or hips, but not below; a **coat** is usually hip-length or longer. A **coat** has sleeves; a **jacket** may not: *a padded sleeveless jacket* ◊ *a sleeveless coat.*

cloak [C] a type of coat that has no sleeves, fastens at the neck and hangs loosely from the shoulders, worn especially in the past: *She threw a heavy woollen cloak over her shoulders.*

shawl [C] a large piece of cloth worn by a woman around the shoulders or head, or wrapped around a baby: *Ruth draped a shawl over her shoulders.*

cape [C] a loose outer piece of clothing that has no sleeves, fastens at the neck and hangs from the shoulders, like a cloak but shorter: *a bullfighter's cape* ◊ *Superman's cape*

waistcoat /'weɪskəʊt; *AmE* usually 'weskət; *AmE* also 'weɪskoʊt/ [C] (*BrE*) a short piece of clothing with buttons down the front but no sleeves, usually worn over a shirt and under a jacket, often forming part of a man's suit: *He always wore a brightly-coloured waistcoat under his dark grey suit.*

vest [C] (*AmE*) a waistcoat: *He is smartly dressed in a suit complete with vest, tie and polished Gucci loafers.*

tuxedo /tʌkˈsiːdəʊ; AmE -doʊ/ (also informal **tux**) [C] (especially AmE) a black or white jacket, worn with a bow tie at formal occasions, especially in the evening: He went to pick up his girlfriend, dressed in a tuxedo and carrying a red rose. ◇ I had to rent a tux for the ceremony. ❶ Tuxedo can also refer to a whole suit, including both jacket and trousers/pants. In British English the terms **dinner jacket** and **dinner suit** are usually used.

blazer /ˈbleɪzə(r)/ [C] a jacket, not worn with matching trousers, worn by schoolchildren or sports players and showing the colours or badge of a school, club, team, etc.; a formal jacket: a school blazer ◇ He was smartly dressed in a blazer and slacks (= trousers).

anorak /ˈænəræk/ [C] (BrE) a short coat with a hood that is worn as protection against rain, wind and cold: hikers in anoraks and walking boots

mac [C] (BrE, informal) a coat made of material that keeps you dry in the rain: He was standing in the pouring rain with his mac on. ❶ Mac is a short form of the more old-fashioned word **mackintosh**. In American English this is just called a **raincoat**.

tails [pl.] a long jacket divided at the back below the waist into two pieces that become narrower at the bottom, worn by men at very formal events: The men all wore top hat and tails.

cold adj.
1 cold water/weather/hands
2 a cold look of disapproval

1 cold · cool · chilly · chill · lukewarm · tepid · crisp
These words all describe sb/sth that has a low temperature.

lukewarm	cool	chilly	cold
tepid		chill	
		crisp	

PATTERNS AND COLLOCATIONS
▶ a cold / cool / chilly / chill / crisp **day / morning**
▶ a cold / cool / chilly **night / afternoon / evening**
▶ cold / cool / chilly / chill / crisp **air**
▶ a cold / cool / chilly / chill **wind**
▶ cold / cool / chilly **weather**
▶ cold / cool / lukewarm / tepid **water**
▶ a cold / cool / lukewarm / tepid **shower**
▶ a cold / lukewarm / tepid **bath**
▶ a cold / cool **temperature**
▶ cold / lukewarm / tepid **tea / coffee / food**
▶ a cold / cool **climate / drink**
▶ to **feel** cold / cool / chilly
▶ to **get** cold / cool / chilly
▶ It's cold / chilly outside.

cold having a temperature that is lower than usual or lower than the human body; (of food or drink) not heated; cooked after being cooked: I'm cold. Turn the heating up. ◇ It's freezing cold! ◇ The stream was icy cold. ◇ A cold wind blew. ◇ It was the coldest winter on record. ◇ Every room has hot and cold water. ◇ It's cold chicken for lunch. **OPP** hot, warm → HOT, mild → SUNNY
▶ **cold** noun [U]: He shivered with cold. ◇ Don't stand outside **in the cold**. ◇ She doesn't seem to **feel the cold**.
▶ **coldness** noun [U]: the icy coldness of the water

cool (usually approving) fairly cold, especially in a pleasant way: a long cool drink ◇ Store medicines in a cool dry place. ◇ A cool breeze played in the trees. ◇ Cooler weather is forecast for the weekend. ◇ The water was blissfully cool. ◇ Let's sit in the shade and keep cool. **OPP** warm → HOT, See also **cool** → COOL verb

chilly (rather informal) too cold to be comfortable: Bring a coat. It might turn chilly later. ◇ She was beginning to feel chilly. ◇ The room was uncomfortably chilly.

chill (rather formal) (especially of the weather, wind or air) unpleasantly cold: the chill grey dawn ◇ Their breath steamed in the chill air. ◇ It was a chill day in February.
▶ **chill** noun [sing.]: There's a chill in the air this morning.

> **NOTE** CHILLY OR CHILL? Chilly is more informal than chill. People can feel chilly but they do NOT usually 'feel chill'. It is more usual to say: It's quite chilly outside. but: A chill wind was blowing.

lukewarm /ˌluːkˈwɔːm; AmE -ˈwɔːrm/ (not used in comparative forms) (often disapproving) slightly warm, sometimes in an unpleasant way: The food was barely lukewarm. ◇ Add half a cup of lukewarm water to the mixture.

tepid /ˈtepɪd/ (not used in comparative forms) (often disapproving) lukewarm: The tea was weak and tepid. ◇ She stood under the tepid shower.

> **NOTE** LUKEWARM OR TEPID? There is really no difference in meaning or use between these words.

crisp (approving) (of the air or weather) pleasantly dry and cold: It was a crisp winter morning. ◇ The air was crisp and clear and the sky was blue.

2 cold · impersonal · unfriendly · cool · aloof · frosty · remote · distant
These words all describe a person or place that is not friendly or lacks feeling.

impersonal	cold	frosty
cool	unfriendly	
	aloof	
	remote	
	distant	

PATTERNS AND COLLOCATIONS
▶ unfriendly / cool **towards** sb
▶ a cold / an unfriendly / a cool / a frosty **look**
▶ a cold / an impersonal / an unfriendly / a cool / an aloof / a frosty **manner**
▶ a cold / an unfriendly / a cool **voice**
▶ a cold / cool / frosty **stare**
▶ a cold / an unfriendly / a cool **glance**
▶ a cool / frosty **reception**
▶ an impersonal / an unfriendly / a cool **attitude**

cold (disapproving) without emotion; not friendly: Her manner was cold and distant. ◇ He was portrayed as a cold, calculating terrorist. ◇ He was staring at her with cold eyes. **OPP** warm → FRIENDLY 1
▶ **coldly** adv.: to stare/smile/reply coldly
▶ **coldness** noun [U]: She was hurt by the coldness in his voice.

impersonal (usually disapproving) lacking friendly human feelings or atmosphere; making you feel unimportant: Business letters do not always need to be impersonal and formal. ◇ The hotel room looked bare and impersonal. **OPP** personal ❶ A **personal** service or action is done for a particular person rather than for a large group of people or people in general; the term is used to suggest a warm and friendly service: We offer a **personal service** to all our customers.

unfriendly not kind or pleasant to sb: The report said that the Church can appear **unfriendly to** outsiders. ◇ The atmosphere in the room was distinctly unfriendly. **OPP** friendly → FRIENDLY 1

cool not friendly, interested or enthusiastic: She was decidedly **cool about** the proposal. ◇ He has been cool towards me ever since we had the argument. **OPP** warm → FRIENDLY 1
▶ **coolly** adv.: He received my suggestion coolly.

aloof /əˈluːf/ [not usually before noun] (written) not friendly or interested in other people: She had always **kept herself aloof from** her colleagues.

frosty not friendly, in a way that suggests that sb does not approve of sth: *He received a frosty reception from the US media.*
▶ **frostily** *adv.*: *'No thank you,' she said frostily.*

remote [not usually before noun] not friendly; not letting other people get to know you: *He somehow remains a remote figure.*
▶ **remoteness** *noun* [U]: *His remoteness made her feel unloved.*

distant remote: *He seemed distant and distracted.* See also **distance** → DIVISION 2

collapse *verb*

1 the roof collapses
2 collapse from fatigue

1 collapse · crumble · give way · disintegrate · cave (sth) in

These are all words that can be used when sth falls down or breaks apart.

PATTERNS AND COLLOCATIONS
▶ the **ceiling / roof / tunnel** collapses / caves in
▶ the **walls** collapse / cave in
▶ the **pillars / supports** collapse / give way
▶ the **door / floor / ground** gives way / caves in
▶ a building collapses / caves **in on itself**
▶ to collapse / give way / cave in **under the weight of sth**

collapse [I] (of a building or structure) to fall down or fall in suddenly: *Timber buildings may simply rot and collapse.* ◇ *The roof collapsed under the weight of snow.*
crumble [I, T] to break, or break sth, into very small pieces: *Rice flour makes the cake less likely to crumble.* ◇ *crumbling stonework* ◇ *She crumbled the dry earth into fine powdery dust.* ❶ If a building or a piece of land **is crumbling**, parts of it are breaking off: *The cliff is gradually crumbling away.*
,**give 'way** *idiom* to fall down or inwards under pressure; to stop supporting sb/sth: *The pillars gave way and a section of the roof collapsed.* ◇ *Her legs gave way beneath her.*
disintegrate /dɪsˈɪntɪɡreɪt/ [I] to break into small parts or pieces and be destroyed: *The plane disintegrated as it fell into the sea.* ◇ *The raw cotton disintegrated between her fingers.*
,**cave 'in**, ,**cave sth 'in** *phrasal verb* (of a roof, wall, door or the ground) to fall down or fall in suddenly; to make a roof, wall door or the ground do this: *The ceiling suddenly caved in on top of them.* ◇ *Part of the wall was caved in.*

NOTE COLLAPSE, GIVE WAY OR CAVE IN? Whole buildings **collapse**; roofs and walls may **collapse** or **cave in**; supports may **collapse** or **give way**; a door or the ground may **give way** or **cave in.**

2 collapse · faint · drop · pass out

These words all mean to fall down and/or become unconscious because you are very ill or tired or have had a shock.

PATTERNS AND COLLOCATIONS
▶ to collapse / faint / drop / pass out **from** exhaustion / hunger / loss of blood / the heat, etc.

collapse [I] to fall down, and usually become unconscious, especially because you are very ill: *He collapsed in the street and died two hours later.* ◇ *They finally arrived, collapsing from fatigue.*
▶ **collapse** *noun* [U, C, usually sing.]: *She was taken to hospital after her collapse at work.*
faint [I] to become unconscious when not enough blood is going to your brain, usually because of the heat, a shock, etc: *She thought she would faint from sheer happiness.* ◇ (*informal, especially spoken*) *I almost fainted (= I was very surprised) when she told me.*
▶ **faint** *noun* [sing.]: *He fell to the ground in a dead faint.*

drop (-**pp**-) [I] (*informal, especially spoken*) to fall down or be no longer able to stand because you are extremely tired: *I feel **ready to drop**.* ◇ *She expects everyone to work till they drop.*
,**pass 'out** *phrasal verb* (*rather formal*) to become unconscious: *I think I must have passed out after that, because I don't remember anything more.*

NOTE FAINT OR PASS OUT? People **faint** because not enough blood is going to the brain; people can **pass out** for this reason, or because they have been hit on the head or because they are drunk.

collect *verb*

collect · gather · accumulate · rack up sth · run sth up · amass · accrue

These words all mean to get more of sth over a period of time, or to increase in quantity over a period of time.

PATTERNS AND COLLOCATIONS
▶ to collect / gather / accumulate / amass **data / evidence / information**
▶ to accumulate / rack up / run up / amass / accrue **debts**
▶ to accumulate / rack up / run up / accrue **losses**
▶ to accumulate / rack up **profit**
▶ to accumulate / amass a **fortune**
▶ to accumulate / accrue **interest**
▶ **debts** accumulate / accrue
▶ **dirt / dust / debris** collects / accumulates
▶ to **gradually / slowly / steadily** collect / gather / accumulate (sth)

collect [T, I] to bring things or information together from different people or places; to gradually increase in amount in a place: *We've been collecting data from various sources.* ◇ *Samples were collected from over 200 patients.* ◇ *We seem to have collected an enormous number of boxes (= without intending to).* ◇ *Dirt had collected in the corners of the room.* ❶ People sometimes **collect** things of a particular type as a hobby: *to collect stamps/postcards/fossils*
gather [T] to bring things together that have been spread around; to collect information from different sources: *I waited while he **gathered up** his papers.* ◇ *She **gathered** her things **together** and got to her feet.* ◇ *Detectives have spent months gathering evidence.*

NOTE COLLECT OR GATHER? Both **collect** and **gather** can be used in the same way to talk about bringing together data, information or evidence. When talking about things, **gather** is used with words like *things*, *belongings* or *papers* when the things are spread around within a short distance. **Collect** is used to talk about getting examples of sth from different people or places that are physically separated.

accumulate /əˈkjuːmjəleɪt/ [T, I] (*rather formal*) to gradually get more and more of sth over a period of time; to gradually increase in number or amount over a period of time: *I seem to have accumulated a lot of books.* ◇ *By investing wisely she accumulated a fortune.* ◇ *Debts began to accumulate.* ◇ *Dust and dirt soon accumulate if a house is not cleaned regularly.*
▶ **accumulation** *noun* [U, C]: *the accumulation of wealth* ◇ *an accumulation of toxic chemicals*

NOTE COLLECT OR ACCUMULATE? Dust and dirt or some other material can **collect** or **accumulate** in a place if it gradually increases in amount over a period of time. **Collect** is used especially when a small amount of dust or dirt gets stuck in places that are hard to clean: *Food debris collects in holes in the teeth.* **Accumulate** is used especially about a larger amount of material that increases very gradually over a very long period of time: *The sediment accumulates over millions of years.*

‚rack 'up sth phrasal verb (rather informal, business or journalism) to collect sth, such as profits or losses in a business, or points in a competition: *The company racked up $200 million in losses in two years.* ◊ *In ten years of boxing he racked up a record 176 wins.*

‚run sth 'up phrasal verb (rather informal) to allow a bill, debt or loss to reach a large total: *She had run up a huge phone bill during the course of the relationship.* ❶ **Run up** is nearly always used with *bill, debt* or *loss.*

amass /ə'mæs/ [T] (especially written) to collect sth in large amounts, especially money, debts or information: *He amassed a fortune from silver mining.* ◊ *They amassed enough evidence to convict her.*

accrue /ə'kruː/ [T] (formal) to allow a sum of money or debts to grow over a period of time: *The money was placed in a special account to accrue interest.* ◊ *The firm had accrued debts of over $6m.*

colour (BrE) (AmE color) noun

1 the colour of the sky
2 people of colour

1 colour · shade · hue · tint · tinge

These words all describe the appearance of things, resulting from the way in which they reflect light.

PATTERNS AND COLLOCATIONS
▸ a **shade** / **tinge** of blue, green, etc.
▸ a **bluish** / **greenish**, etc. colour / shade / hue / tint / tinge
▸ a **warm** / **rich** colour / shade / hue / tint
▸ a **bright** / **vivid** / **vibrant** / **dark** / **deep** colour / shade / hue
▸ a **pale** / **pastel** / **soft** / **subtle** colour / shade / hue
▸ a **light** / **strong** / **neutral** / **natural** colour / shade
▸ to **have** a colour / shade / hue / tint / tinge

colour (AmE **color**) [C, U] the appearance that things have, resulting from the way in which they reflect light. Red, green and blue are colours: *What's your favourite colour?* ◊ *The paint is available in 12 different colours.* ◊ *the colour of the sky* ◊ *Her hair is a reddish-brown colour.* ◊ *These flowers certainly give the room a bit of colour.* ❶ **Colour** also means the use of all the colours, not only black and white: *a colour TV in every room* ◊ *colour photography/printing* ◊ *a full-colour brochure* ◊ *Do you dream in colour?* **OPP** **black and white**

shade [C] a particular form of a colour, especially when describing how light or dark it is. Sky blue is a shade of blue: *Her eyes were a delicate shade of green.* ◊ *Use different shades of the same colour, rather than lots of different colours.*

hue /hjuː/ [C] (literary or technical) a colour; a particular shade of a colour: *Her paintings capture the subtle hues of the countryside in autumn.* ◊ *His face took on an unhealthy, whitish hue.*

tint [C] a shade or small amount of a particular colour; a faint colour covering a surface: *leaves with red and gold autumn tints* ◊ *the brownish tint of an old photo* See also **tint** → PAINT verb

tinge /tɪndʒ/ [C, usually sing.] a small amount of a colour: *There was a pink tinge to the sky.* See also **tinge** → ELEMENT 2

> **NOTE** TINT OR TINGE? You can say: *a reddish tint/tinge* or: *a tinge of red* but NOT: *a tint of red.* **Tint** is often used in the plural, and **tinge** is almost always singular: *reddish tints* ◊ *a reddish tinge*

2 colour · colouring · pigment · complexion · coloration

These are all words for the colour in the appearance of plants, animals or people.

PATTERNS AND COLLOCATIONS
▸ a **dark** colouring / pigment / complexion / coloration
▸ a **fair** colouring / complexion
▸ to **have** a dark / fair, etc. colouring / pigment / complexion / coloration

colour (BrE) (AmE **color**) [U, C] the colour of a person's skin, when it shows the race they belong to: *Discrimination on the grounds of race, religion or colour was outlawed.* ◊ *(especially AmE) a person/man/woman of colour* (= who is not white) See also **of colour** → BLACK adj.

colouring (BrE) (AmE **coloring**) [U] the colour of a person's skin, eyes and hair; the colours that exist in sth: *Their colouring was identical: white skin, black hair and very dark eyes.* ◊ *monarch butterflies, with their spectacular black, brown and orange colouring*

pigment [C, U] a substance that exists naturally in people, animals and plants and gives their skin, leaves, etc. a particular colour: *Melanin is the dark pigment responsible for brown eyes and dark hair.*

complexion /kəm'plekʃn/ [C] the natural colour and condition of the skin on a person's face: *a dark/pale/healthy complexion* ◊ *Her auburn hair and blue eyes, together with a fine complexion, made her extremely attractive.*

> **NOTE** COLOURING OR COMPLEXION? **Complexion** describes only a person's skin; **colouring** describes their skin, hair and eyes.

coloration (BrE also **colouration**) /ˌkʌlə'reɪʃn/ [U] (technical) the natural colours and patterns on a plant or animal: *Many insects have bright coloration, which has evolved as a protection against predators.*

coloured (BrE) (AmE colored) adj.

coloured · colourful · flamboyant · lurid · gaudy · garish · loud

These words all describe things that are a bright colour or that have a lot of different colours.

PATTERNS AND COLLOCATIONS
▸ a **lurid** / **gaudy** / **garish** / **loud** colour
▸ a **gaudy** / **garish** / **loud** pattern / green / pink / red, etc.
▸ **colourful** / **flamboyant** / **gaudy** / **loud** clothes
▸ **colourful** / **flamboyant** / **loud** designs

coloured (BrE) (AmE **colored**) (often used in compounds) having a particular colour or different colours: *The street was ablaze with coloured lights.* ◊ **brightly coloured** *balloons* ◊ *She was wearing a cream-coloured suit.*

colourful (BrE) (AmE **colorful**) (often approving) full of bright colours; having a lot of different colours: *The male birds are more colourful than the females.* ◊ *a small but colourful garden* **OPP** **colourless** → DRAB

> **NOTE** COLOURED OR COLOURFUL? On its own, **coloured** describes things which have a particular colour when they are normally white or clear: *coloured glass/lights/paper.* Otherwise it is used in compounds: *brightly coloured* ◊ *cream-coloured.* **Colourful** is always used on its own.

flamboyant /flæm'bɔɪənt/ (often approving) bright, colourful and noticeable: *a flamboyant silk tie*

lurid /'lʊərɪd; 'ljʊər-; AmE 'lʊr-/ (disapproving) too bright in colour, in an unpleasant way: *She was wearing a lurid orange and green blouse.*

gaudy /'ɡɔːdi/ (disapproving) too brightly coloured in a way that lacks taste: *She wore gaudy colours and lots of gold jewellery.*

garish /'ɡeərɪʃ; AmE 'ɡerɪʃ/ (disapproving) very brightly coloured in an unpleasant way: *I can't stand those garish Christmas lights.*

loud (sometimes disapproving) very brightly coloured in a way that lacks taste: *He wore a loud checked jacket and a green tie.*

> **NOTE** LURID, GAUDY, GARISH OR LOUD? **Gaudy** is used to describe bright colours when you want to suggest that they have been chosen by sb lacking good taste (= the ability to choose things that are attractive and of good

quality). **Garish** is used more to describe bright colours that are ugly. **Loud** mainly describes clothes with bright, ugly patterns and suggests less disapproval and more humour. **Lurid** is the most unpleasant of all, used especially to describe for lighter colours that reflect light, such as yellow, orange, green and pink.

combination noun See also the entries for MIXTURE and RANGE 1

combination · mixture · mix · blend · composite
These are all words for things that are made up of two or more different things.

▶ a combination / a mixture / a mix / a blend / a composite **of** sth
▶ a / an **interesting / good / wonderful / unusual / strange** combination / mixture / mix / blend

combination [C] two or more things that are put together to form a single unit: *His treatment was a combination of surgery, radiation and drugs.* ◇ *What an unusual combination of flavours!* ◇ *Technology and good management:* **a winning combination** (= one that will certainly be successful).
mixture [C, U] two or more different things that come together in the same place or situation: *The city is a mixture of old and new buildings.* ◇ *We listened to the news with a mixture of surprise and horror.* See also **mixture** → MIXTURE, **mix** → MIX *verb*

> **NOTE** COMBINATION OR MIXTURE? A **combination** of things has usually been put together deliberately, because they work well together, or sb wants them to be together; a **mixture** of things usually just happens.

mix [C, usually sing.] (*rather informal, often approving*) a mixture of different people or things: *It's a school with a good social and ethnic mix of children.* ◇ *The town offers a fascinating mix of old and new.* See also **mix** → MIX *verb*

> **NOTE** MIXTURE OR MIX? **Mix** is slightly more informal than **mixture** and is often used in an approving way to emphasize the good or interesting variety of people or things that are there.

blend [C, usually sing.] a pleasant or useful combination of different things: *a blend of youth and experience* ◇ *This charming hotel is a delightful blend of the old and the new.* See also **blend** → MIX *verb*
composite /ˈkɒmpəzɪt; *AmE* kəmˈpɑːzət/ [C, usually sing.] something made by putting together different parts or materials: *The document was a composite of information from various sources.*

combine verb See also the entry for MIX

combine · integrate · merge · consolidate · unify · unite · fuse
These words all mean to to come together to form a single thing or group, or to join two or more things or groups together to form a single one.

▶ to combine / integrate / merge / consolidate / unify / unite / fuse (sth) **with** sth
▶ to combine / integrate / merge / consolidate / fuse (sth) **into** sth
▶ to combine / integrate / merge / fuse (sth) **together**
▶ to combine / merge / unite / fuse **to form** sth
▶ to combine / integrate / consolidate / unify **knowledge**
▶ to combine / integrate / consolidate **resources / skills**
▶ to combine / integrate / fuse **elements**
▶ to unify / unite a / an **country / area**
▶ to **successfully** combine / integrate / merge / consolidate / unite / fuse sth
▶ to **fully** integrate / consolidate / unify sth

combine [I, T] to come together to form a single thing or group; to join or put together two or more things, groups,

features or qualities; to do two things at the same time: *Hydrogen combines with oxygen to form water.* ◇ *Several factors had combined to ruin our plans.* ◇ *Combine all the ingredients in a bowl.* ◇ *The German team scored a* **combined total** *of 652 points.* ◇ *The hotel combines comfort with convenience.* ◇ *The other room was a kitchen and dining room combined.* ◇ *The trip will* **combine business with pleasure.**
integrate /ˈɪntɪgreɪt/ [T, I] (*rather formal*) to combine two or more things so that they work together; to combine with sth else in this way: *The department has successfully integrated new ideas into the traditional course structure.* ◇ *These programs will integrate with your existing software.* **OPP** segregate → ISOLATE
▶ **integration** noun [U]: *The aim is to promote closer economic integration.*
merge [I, T] (of two or more groups) to combine to form a single larger group; (of qualities) to combine in a way that makes them hard to separate; to combine groups or qualities in these ways: *The banks are set to merge next year.* ◇ *His department will merge with mine.* ◇ *Fact and fiction merge together in his latest thriller.* ◇ *The company was formed by merging three smaller firms.* ❶ **Merge** is used especially in business and political contexts to talk about groups or organizations that join together.
▶ **merger** noun [C]: *a merger between the two banks*
consolidate /kənˈsɒlɪdeɪt; *AmE* -ˈsɑːl-/ [T, I] (*business or technical*) to join things together into one; to be joined into one: *All the debts have been consolidated.* ◇ *The two companies consolidated for greater efficiency.*
▶ **consolidation** noun [U]: *the consolidation of Japan's banking industry*
unify /ˈjuːnɪfaɪ/ [T] to join the parts of a country, region or system so that they form a single unit or work together well; to join the people of a country, region or organization together so that they have the same aims and work together well: *What we need is a unified transport system.* ◇ *The new leader hopes to unify the party.*
▶ **unification** noun [U]: *the unification of Germany in the 19th century*
unite /juˈnaɪt/ [T, I] to join the parts of a country so that they form a single unit; to join people so that they have the same aims; to combine different qualities to form sth new and complete; (of the parts of a country) to join together: *His aim was to unite Italy.* ◇ *A special bond unites our two countries.* ◇ *She unites keen business skills with a charming personality.* ◇ *The two countries united in 1887.* **OPP** divide → ISOLATE

> **NOTE** UNIFY OR UNITE? Both of these words can be used to talk about a group or area into which individuals are brought together: *to unify/unite the country/the party/ Europe.* **Unite** but NOT **unify** can be used to talk about the individuals who are brought together: *to unite two political parties/the two Germanies/the people* ◇ ~~to unify two political parties/the two Germanies/the people~~. **Unify** but NOT **unite** can be used to talk about joining together the parts of a system: *to unify the tax/transport system* ◇ ~~to unite the tax/transport system~~

fuse /fjuːz/ [I, T] (*formal or technical*) (of substances, groups, ideas or qualities) to join together, especially to form sth new; to make things join together in this way: *As they heal, the bones will fuse together.* ◇ *Our different ideas fused into a plan.* ◇ *Atoms of hydrogen are fused to make helium.*
▶ **fusion** /ˈfjuːʒn/ noun [U, sing.]: *the fusion of copper and zinc to produce brass* ◇ *The movie displayed a perfect fusion of image and sound.*

come verb
1 come here
2 when the time comes

1 come · approach · draw · come along · near · close in · converge
These words all mean to move to or towards a person or place.

PATTERNS AND COLLOCATIONS
▸ to come / draw **in** / **into** sth
▸ to come / draw **up** / **up to** sb / sth
▸ to close **in** / converge **on** sb / sth
▸ to come / draw **close** / **near** / **closer** / **nearer**
▸ to **slowly** come / approach / draw / close in on sb

come [I] (usually used with an adverb or preposition) to go towards a particular place or to a particular event; to go towards sb/sth in a particular way or from a particular distance: *He came into the room and shut the door.* ◇ *She came to work wearing a very smart suit.* ◇ *Come here!* ◇ **Come and** *see us soon!* ◇ (*AmE*) *Come see us soon!* ◇ **Here comes** *Jo* (= Jo is coming)! ◇ *He's come all the way from Tokyo.* ◇ *Why don't you come with us?* ◇ *It's looks as if there's a storm coming.* ◇ *The kids* **came running** *into the room.* ❶ **Come** is usually used from the point of view of the person or place that sb is moving to or towards. **OPP go →** GO 1 See also **coming →** ARRIVAL 1

approach [I, T] (*rather formal*) to come near or towards sb/sth: *We could hear the train approaching.* ◇ *Police said the suspect should not be approached.* ◇ *She approached the crossroads cautiously.* See also **approach →** ARRIVAL 1

draw [I] (*written*) (always used with an adverb or preposition) to move in the direction mentioned, usually towards sb/sth: *The train drew into the station.* ◇ *Their car* **drew alongside** *ours.* ◇ *She waved to me as I drew up* (= arrived in a car and stopped). ◇ *As he drew near, I could see that he was limping.*

,**come a'long** *phrasal verb* to come closer and then arrive at a place: *We'll get the next bus that comes along.* ◇ *I'd hate someone to come along and see me like this.*

near [I, T] (*formal*) to come nearer to sb/sth: *As the bus neared we could see someone waving.* ◇ *We were obviously nearing the airport.*

,**close 'in** *phrasal verb* to move nearer to sb/sth, especially in order to attack or capture them: *They knew the police were closing in.* ◇ *It was a shark* **closing in for the kill.** ◇ *Rebel troops were closing in on the city.*

converge /kən'vɜːdʒ; *AmE* -'vɜːrdʒ/ [I] (usually used with an adverb or preposition, especially *on*) (of people or vehicles) to move towards a place from different directions and form a crowd there: *Thousands of supporters converged on Washington for the rally.*

2 come · arrive · approach · near · draw near
These words all relate to a time or event that comes or happens, especially one that you have been waiting for.

PATTERNS AND COLLOCATIONS
▸ **spring** / **summer** / **autumn** / **fall** / **winter** comes / arrives / approaches / draws near
▸ the **day** / **time** comes / arrives / approaches / draws near
▸ to come / arrive **early** / **late**
▸ to **finally** come / arrive

come [I] (of a particular time) to be now: *When the moment actually came, I began to feel a little nervous.* ◇ *Business improved as Christmas came nearer.* ◇ *The deadline* **came and went,** *but there was no reply from them.*

arrive [I] (*written*) (of a time or event) to come or happen, especially after you have been waiting for it: *The day of the wedding finally arrived.* ◇ *The age of industrialization had arrived.*

approach [I, T] to come closer in time: *The deadline was* **fast approaching.** ◇ *He was approaching a turning point in his life.*

near [I, T] (*rather formal*) to come close in time: *It was nearing midnight.* ◇ *The project is nearing completion.* ◇ *Many of the teachers were nearing retirement.*

draw near [I] (*rather formal*) to come close in time: *The time for her departure was drawing near.*

come up with sth *phrasal verb* See also the entry for INVENT

come up with sth · devise · conceive · work sth out · hatch · hit on/upon sth · think sth up · dream sth up
These words all mean to think of an idea, plan or solution.

PATTERNS AND COLLOCATIONS
▸ to come up with / devise / conceive / work out / hatch / hit on / think up / dream up a **plan** / **scheme**
▸ to come up with / conceive / hatch / hit on / think up / dream up an **idea** / **the idea of doing sth**
▸ to come up with / devise / conceive / work out / think up / dream up a **system** / **theory**
▸ to come up with / devise / conceive / work out a **strategy**
▸ to come up with / devise / work out / hit on / think up a **way of doing sth**
▸ to come up with / devise / work out / hit on a **method** / **formula** / **means**
▸ to come up with / devise / work out a **solution**
▸ to come up with / work out an **answer**
▸ to come up with / think up / dream up an **excuse**

,**come 'up with sth** *phrasal verb* [no passive] (*rather informal*) to think of or produce an idea, plan or solution: *He's come up with a really good design for a solar-powered car.* ◇ *She believed she had come up with one of the greatest innovations of modern times.*

devise /dɪ'vaɪz/ [T] to invent sth new or a new way of doing sth: *Scientists have devised a method of recycling the contaminated oil.* ◇ *All the recipes in this book have been devised by our team of experts.*

conceive (also **conceive of sth**) [T] (*formal*) to form an idea or plan in your mind: *He conceived of the idea of transforming the old power station into an arts centre.* ◇ *They conceived of a theory and stuck to it.*

,**work sth 'out** *phrasal verb* to think of a plan, a solution or a way of doing sth: *I've worked out a new way of doing it.*

hatch [T] (*rather informal*) to think of a plan or idea, especially in secret: *Rebel MPs are hatching a secret plot to oust the prime minister.* ◇ *Have you been* **hatching up** *a deal with her?*

'**hit on/upon sth** *phrasal verb* [no passive] (*rather informal*) to think of a good idea suddenly or by chance: *She hit on the perfect title for her new novel.*

,**think sth 'up** *phrasal verb* (*rather informal*) to think of an idea, plan or excuse (= a reason to explain your behaviour): *Can't you think up a better excuse than that?*

,**dream sth 'up** *phrasal verb* (*rather informal*) to think of an idea, especially a very unusual or silly one: *Trust you to dream up a crazy idea like this!*

comfort *noun*

comfort · ease
These are both words for the state of being relaxed and free from pain or worry.

PATTERNS AND COLLOCATIONS
▸ **comparative** / **relative** comfort / ease
▸ a **life of** comfort / ease

comfort [U] the state of being physically relaxed and free from pain; the state of having a pleasant life, with everything that you need: *These tennis shoes are designed* **for comfort** *and performance.* ◇ *With DVD, you can watch the latest movies* **in the comfort of** *your own home.* ◇ *The hotel offers a high standard of comfort and service.* ◇ *They had enough money to live* **in comfort** *in their old age.*

ease [U] (*rather formal, especially written*) the state of feeling relaxed or comfortable without worries, problems or pain: *In his retirement he lived a life of ease.*

comfortable *adj.*

comfortable · cosy · snug · homely · comfy · homey
These words all describe an indoor place or a thing that makes you feel relaxed or warm.

PATTERNS AND COLLOCATIONS
▶ a comfortable / cosy / homely / homey **atmosphere**
▶ a comfortable / cosy / snug / homely **room**
▶ a comfortable / cosy / snug **house**
▶ a comfortable / cosy / snug / comfy **bed**
▶ a comfortable / cosy / comfy **armchair**
▶ a comfortable / cosy / snug / homely / homey **little** place
▶ to **feel** comfortable / cosy / snug / homely / comfy / homey
▶ **very / quite** comfortable / cosy / snug / homely / comfy / homey
▶ **nice and** comfortable / cosy / snug / homely / comfy
▶ **warm and** comfortable / cosy / homely / comfy / homey
▶ comfortable / cosy / snug **and warm**

comfortable *(approving)* (of clothes, furniture or a place) making you feel physically relaxed; pleasant to wear, sit on or be in; (of a person) feeling pleasantly physically relaxed; warm enough and without pain: *It is advisable to wear loose, comfortable clothing.* ◇ *Let me slip into something more comfortable* (= change into more comfortable clothing). ◇ *It's an elegant, comfortable house with good views from the windows.* ◇ *She shifted into a more comfortable position on the chair.* ◇ *Please **make yourself comfortable** while I get some coffee.* ◇ *The patient is comfortable* (= not in pain) *after his operation.*
OPP **uncomfortable** ❶ **Uncomfortable** clothes, furniture, etc. do not let you feel physically comfortable: *I couldn't sleep because the bed was so uncomfortable.* If you are **uncomfortable** you do not feel physically relaxed, warm enough, etc.: *She still finds it uncomfortable to stand without support.*
▶ **comfortably** *adv.*: *All the rooms were comfortably furnished.* ◇ *If you're all sitting comfortably, then I'll begin.*
cosy *(BrE)* *(AmE* **cozy***)* /ˈkəʊzi; *AmE* ˈkoʊzi/ *(approving)* warm, comfortable and safe, especially because of being small or enclosed: *We stopped in a cosy little cafe for a cup of tea.* ◇ *I felt warm and cosy sitting by the fire.*
▶ **cosily** *adv.* *(BrE)* *(AmE* **cozily***)*: *We were sitting cosily by the fire.*
▶ **cosiness** *(BrE)* *(AmE* **coziness***) noun* [U]: *I wished I was back in the cosiness and warmth of the kitchen.*
snug *(approving)* warm, comfortable and protected, especially from the cold: *I spent the afternoon snug and warm in bed.* ◇ *It had rained during the night but our tents were snug and dry.*
▶ **snugly** *adv.*: *I left the children tucked up snugly in bed.*

NOTE **COSY OR SNUG?** Both of these words can be used to talk about a place or a person, but it is slightly more common to use **snug** to talk about a person and **cosy** to talk about a place.

homely *(BrE, approving)* (of a place) making you feel comfortable, as if you were in your own home: *The hotel has a lovely homely feel to it.*
comfy /ˈkʌmfi/ *(informal, approving)* comfortable: *These slippers aren't as comfy as my old ones.* ◇ *Put some pillows behind you so you're nice and comfy.*
homey (also **homy**) /ˈhəʊmi; *AmE* ˈhoʊmi/ *(especially AmE, informal, approving)* homely: *The lamp in the window made the room feel homey and welcoming.*

comment *verb* See the Topic Map for FACT AND OPINION on p.898

comment · note · remark · observe
These words all mean to say or write a fact or opinion.

PATTERNS AND COLLOCATIONS
▶ to comment / remark **on** sth
▶ to comment / remark / observe **to** sb
▶ to comment / note / remark / observe **that**...
▶ to comment on / note / remark / observe **how**...
▶ to comment / note / remark / observe **drily / wryly**
▶ to comment / remark / observe **coolly / acidly / casually**

comment [I, T] to express an opinion or give facts about sth: *He refused to comment until after the trial.* ◇ *We were just commenting on how well you look.* ◇ *'Not his best performance,' she commented to the woman sitting next to her.* See also **comment** → STATEMENT *noun*
note [T] *(rather formal)* to mention sth because it is important or interesting: *It is worth noting that the most successful companies had the lowest prices.* ❶ **Note** is often used to draw sb's attention to an important or interesting fact: *Visitors should note that the tower is not open to the public.* ◇ *There are two other points to note from this graph.*
remark [I, T] to say or write what you have noticed about a situation: *The judges remarked on the high standard of entries for the competition.* ◇ *Critics remarked that the play was not original.* See also **remark** → STATEMENT *noun*
observe /əbˈzɜːv; *AmE* əbˈzɜːrv/ [T] (not usually used in the progressive tenses) *(formal)* to say or write what you have noticed about a situation: *She observed that it was getting late.* See also **observation** → STATEMENT *noun*

NOTE **COMMENT, REMARK OR OBSERVE?** If you **comment** on sth you say sth about it; if you **remark on** sth or **observe** sth, you say sth about it that you have noticed: there is often not much difference between them. However, while you can *refuse to comment,* you cannot 'refuse to remark' or 'refuse to observe': *He refused to remark/observe until after the trial.*

committee *noun*

committee · council · commission · board · jury · panel · delegation · body · task force · mission
These are all words for a group of people who make decisions, give advice, deal with problems, etc., especially on a particular subject.

PATTERNS AND COLLOCATIONS
▶ a committee / commission / panel / task force **on** sth
▶ a committee/council/commission/board/delegation/body **for** sth
▶ to be **on** a committee / council / commission / board / jury / panel / body
▶ a **special** committee / commission / task force / mission
▶ a/an **joint / independent** committee / council / commission / board / delegation / body / task force / mission
▶ a **government/parliamentary** committee/commission/board/ delegation / body
▶ a **congressional** committee / commission / delegation / body
▶ an **official** committee / commission / delegation / body
▶ a **governing** committee / council / commission / board / body
▶ a / an **executive / management** committee / council / board / body
▶ a / an **advisory / consultative** committee / council / board / panel / body
▶ a **research** committee / council / commission / board / body
▶ to **choose / select** a committee / jury / panel
▶ to **head** a committee/council/commission/board/delegation/ task force / mission
▶ to **chair** a committee/council/commission/board/panel/body
▶ to **lead** a commission / delegation / task force / mission
▶ to **serve on/sit on** a committee / council / commission / board / jury / panel / body
▶ to **send** a delegation / task force / mission

committee [C+sing./pl. *v.*] a group of people who are chosen, usually by a larger group, to make decisions or to deal with a particular subject: *They have set up a committee on the safety of medicines.* ◇ *She's on the management committee.*
council (also **Council**) [C+sing./pl. *v.*] a group of people chosen to give advice, make rules, do research, provide money, etc. in a particular area of activity: *In Britain, the Arts Council gives grants to theatres.* ◇ *There are plans to establish a funding council for higher education.*

commission [C+sing./pl. v.] an official group of people chosen to control sth or find out about sth, usually for a government: *Sweden's Environment Commission has ruled against the dam project.* ◇ *The commission is expected to report its findings next month.*

> **NOTE** COMMITTEE, COUNCIL OR COMMISSION? These words can all refer to very similar groups of people with similar functions. The title they are given is often just the choice of the organization which sets up the group. **Committee** is the most general word and can refer to a group which is part of a government, a company, or an organization such as a trade union, political party or university. It can be at a high level or just at a local level making routine decisions, but it usually works within a larger organization. A **council** is more often an independent group of experts whose role is to promote the arts, sport, academic research, etc: *the Medical Research Council.* A **commission** is usually a group of important politicians or experts set up by a government or other political organization with responsibility for a particular area, such as trade or agriculture or to investigate a particular issue, such as a serious accident or a social problem: *the Atomic Energy Commission – the United Nations High Commission for Refugees (UNHCR).*

board [C+sing./pl. v.] a group of people who have power to make decisions and control a company or other organization: *The project will have to go to the board for consideration.* ◇ *There have been discussions about the issue at board level.* ◇ *She has a seat on the board of directors.*

jury /ˈdʒʊəri; AmE ˈdʒʊri/ [C+sing./pl. v.] a group of members of the public who listen to the facts of a case in court and decide whether or not sb is guilty of a crime; a group of people who decide who is the winner of a competition: *Everyone should have the right to trial by jury.* ◇ *The jury was sworn in.* ◇ *The jury has retired to consider its verdict.* ◇ *(BrE) It was the second time he had been called up for jury service* (= to be a member of a jury). ◇ *(AmE) jury duty* ◇ *He was on the jury for this year's Booker Prize.*

panel /ˈpænl/ [C+sing./pl. v.] a group of specialists who give their advice or opinion about sth, or who discuss topics of interest on television or radio: *The designs will be judged by a panel of experts.* ◇ *A distinguished panel of speakers considered the role of global corporations.* ◇ *The decision of the judging panel is final.*

delegation /ˌdelɪˈɡeɪʃn/ [C+sing./pl. v.] a group of people who represent the views of an organization or country and who speak for them: *The prime minister met with an all-party delegation from the city council.* ◇ *The Canadian delegation walked out of the talks in protest.*

body [C+sing./pl. v.] a group of people who work together, often for an official purpose: *The government is consulting trade unions and other professional bodies.* ❶ **Body** can be a general word to describe any group of people working together, especially an official group which controls sth, makes decisions, etc. For example, we often refer to a *sport's governing body*, but the actual title of the group may be an *association*, as in the *Football Association (FA)*, a *federation*, as in the *International Association of Athletics Federations (IAAF)* or a *committee*, as in the *International Olympic Committee (IOC)*.

'task force [C] a group of people who are chosen to deal with a particular problem, usually by a government: *She is expected to lead a task force on health care reform.*

mission /ˈmɪʃn/ [C+sing./pl. v.] a group of people doing an important official job, especially when they are sent to another country; the place where they work: *She led a recent trade mission to China.* ◇ *He will be part of a four-member UN fact-finding mission to the disputed region.*

common *adj.*

common · public · joint · collective · popular · communal · cooperative
These words all describe sth that is shared by or involves a number of people.

> **PATTERNS AND COLLOCATIONS**
> ▸ common / public / joint / collective / communal **property**
> ▸ common / public / communal **land**
> ▸ common / joint / collective / communal **ownership / responsibility**
> ▸ a common / joint / collective / communal / cooperative **enterprise**
> ▸ a joint / collective / communal / cooperative **effort**
> ▸ joint / collective / communal / cooperative **action**
> ▸ a joint / collective / communal **decision**
> ▸ common / collective / popular **opinion**

common [usually before noun] shared by or belonging to two or more people or by the people in a group: *They share a common interest in photography.* ◇ *This decision was taken for the common good* (= the advantage of everyone). ◇ *It is, by common consent, Scotland's prettiest coast* (= everyone agrees that it is). ◇ *Some basic features are common to all human languages.*

public [only before noun] provided, especially by the government, for the use of people in general: *(BrE) There is a desperate need to improve public transport in the city.* ◇ *(AmE) public transportation* ◇ *The information is available in any public library.* ◇ *He was charged with destroying public property.* **OPP** private → OWN

joint [only before noun] involving or shared by two or more people together: *They were joint owners of the house.* ◇ *We opened a joint account when we got married.* ◇ *They divorced two years ago, but he has joint custody of the children* (= he shares care of the children with his ex-wife). ◇ *They finished in joint first place.* **OPP** separate → PARTICULAR

> ▸ **jointly** *adv.*: *The event was organized jointly by students and staff.*

collective /kəˈlektɪv/ [usually before noun] done or shared by all members of a group of people; involving a whole group or society; used to refer to all members of a group: *MPs heaved a collective sigh of relief when the news was announced last night.* ◇ *The austerities of wartime Europe were still fresh in the collective memory* (= memories shared by the whole of society). ◇ *The collective name for mast, boom and sails on a boat is the 'rig'.* **OPP** individual → PARTICULAR

> ▸ **collectively** *adv.*: *We have had a successful year, both collectively and individually.*

popular [only before noun] (of ideas, beliefs and opinions) shared by a large number of people: *By popular demand, the tour has been extended by two weeks.* ◇ *Contrary to popular belief, women cause fewer road accidents than men.*

> ▸ **popularly** *adv.*: *a popularly held belief*

communal /kəˈmjuːnl; ˈkɒmjənl; AmE ˈkɑːm-/ shared by, or for the use of, a number of people, especially people who live together: *As a student I tried communal living for a few years.* ◇ *He led me down the corridor to the communal kitchen.* **OPP** individual → OWN, separate → PARTICULAR

> ▸ **communally** *adv.*: *The property was owned communally.*

cooperative (BrE also **co-operative**) /kəʊˈɒpərətɪv; AmE koʊˈɑːp-/ [usually before noun] involving people or groups doing sth together or working together towards a shared aim: *Cooperative activity is essential to effective community work.* ◇ *This is a cooperative venture with the University of Copenhagen.*

communication *noun*

communication · contact · dealings · correspondence
These are all words for the activity of communicating with sb.

PATTERNS AND COLLOCATIONS
▸ communication / contact / dealings / correspondence **with** sb
▸ communication / contact / dealings / correspondence **between** people
▸ **regular** communication / contact / dealings / correspondence
▸ **business** communication / dealings / correspondence
▸ **to be in** communication / contact / correspondence (with sb)
▸ **to have** contact / dealings with sb

communication [U] the activity or process of expressing ideas and feelings or of giving people information: *Speech is the fastest method of communication between people.* ◇ *All* **channels of communication** *need to be kept open.* ◇ *Doctors do not always have good* **communication skills**. ◇ *non-verbal communication such as gestures or facial expressions* See also **communication** → LETTER, **communicate** → CONVEY, **communicate** → TALK

contact [U] the act of communicating with sb, especially regularly: *Have you* **kept in contact** *with any of your friends from college* (= do you still see them or speak or write to them)? ◇ *She's* **lost contact with** (= no longer sees or writes to) *her son.* ◇ *I finally* **made contact with** (= succeeded in speaking to or meeting) *her in Paris.* ◇ *In her job she often* **comes into contact with** (= meets) *lawyers.* ◇ *The organization* **put me in contact with** *other people in a similar position* (= gave me their addresses or phone numbers). ◇ *He carefully avoided* **eye contact** (= looking directly at sb else's eyes).
▸ **contact** *verb* [T]: *I've been trying to contact you all day.*

dealings [pl.] (*rather formal*) business activities; the relations that you have with sb in business: *Have you had any previous dealings with this company?* ◇ *I knew nothing of his business dealings.* See also **deal with sb** → NEGOTIATE

correspondence /ˌkɒrəˈspɒndəns; *AmE* ˌkɔːrəˈspɑːn-; ˌkɑː-/ [U, C] (*formal*) the activity of writing letters: *I refused to* **enter into** *any* **correspondence** (= to exchange letters) *with him about it.* ◇ *We kept up a correspondence for many years.* See also **correspondence** → LETTER
▸ **correspond** *verb* [I]: *I have corresponded with him in the past.*

community *noun* See the Topic Map for THE INDIVIDUAL AND SOCIETY on p.894

community · society · population · the public · the country · the nation
These are all words for all the people who live in a country or area.

PATTERNS AND COLLOCATIONS
▸ the community / society / the population / the public / the country / the nation **at large**
▸ the community / society / the population / the public / the country / the nation **as a whole**
▸ the **entire** community / population / country / nation
▸ the **general** community / population / public
▸ the **wider** community / society / population / public
▸ to **shock** the community / public / country / nation
▸ the **rest of** the community / society / the population / the country / the nation
▸ a **section / cross-section of** the community / society / the population / the public
▸ a **member of** the community / society / the population / the public

community [sing.] all the people who live in a particular local area when talked about as a group: *The local community was shocked by the murders.* ◇ *There needs to be more support for the elderly in the community* (= in the local area). ◇ *He urged* **the international community** (= the countries of the world as a group) *to take decisive action on debt relief.*

society [U] people in general, living together in communities: *They carried out research into the roles of men and women in today's society.* ◇ *Racism exists at all* **levels of society**.

population [C+sing./pl. *v.*, U] all the people who live in a particular area, city or country; the total number of people who live somewhere: *One third of the world's population consumes two thirds of the world's resources.* ◇ *Muslims make up 55% of the population.* ◇ *Japan has a very high* **population density**.

the public [sing.+ sing./pl. *v.*] the ordinary people in a country, especially when compared with politicians or famous people: *The public has the right to know what is contained in the report.* ◇ *The palace is now* **open to the public**. See also **the general public** → GENERAL PUBLIC

the country [sing.] all the people of a country: *It was the rich, rather than the country as a whole, that benefited from the reforms.* ◇ *The issue of the single currency has divided the country.*

the nation [sing.] all the people of a country: *The entire nation, it seemed, was watching TV.* ◇ *The savage murder shocked the nation.*

NOTE THE COUNTRY OR THE NATION? In many cases you can use either word. **The country** is used slightly more when talking about political and economic issues; **the nation** is used slightly more when talking about cultural issues.

company *noun* See also the entries for BUSINESS 2 and GROUP 3

company · firm · business · operation · corporation · enterprise · practice · house
These are all words for an organization that makes money by producing or selling goods or services.

PATTERNS AND COLLOCATIONS
▸ a **multinational** company / firm / business / operation / corporation / enterprise
▸ a **state-owned** company / firm / business / corporation / enterprise
▸ a **private** company / firm / business / operation / corporation / enterprise / practice / … house
▸ a **family** company / firm / business / operation / enterprise / practice / … house
▸ a **commercial** company / firm / business / operation / corporation / enterprise / … house
▸ a **business** company / firm / operation / corporation / enterprise
▸ to **manage / run / have / own** a company / a firm / a business / an operation / a corporation / an enterprise / a … house
▸ to **buy / acquire / take over** a company / firm / business / an operation / an enterprise
▸ to **set up** a company / firm / business / an operation / a corporation / an enterprise / a practice / a … house
▸ to **found** a company / firm / business / practice / … house
▸ to **work for / join / leave / resign from** a company / firm / business / corporation / practice / … house
▸ a company / a firm / a business / a corporation / an enterprise / a … house **fails**

company [C+sing./pl. *v.*] a business organization that makes money by producing or selling goods or services: *During the 1980s it was one of the largest computer companies in the world.* ◇ *Mike gets a company car with his new job.*

firm [C] a company: *He got a job with a London engineering firm.* ◇ *the city's oldest and most prestigious law firm* ◇ *I'm working for a* **firm of** *accountants.*

NOTE COMPANY OR FIRM? **Firm** is often used to talk about a small, fairly specialized organization, especially one that sells professional advice or services: *a/an engineering/law/consulting/insurance/security firm* ◇ *a* firm *of accountants/consultants/lawyers/solicitors*. **Firm** is also often used to talk about companies run by members of a family: *a/the family firm* ◇ *his father's firm* or companies that have been operating for a long time: *a/an old/long-established/old-fashioned/reputable/renowned firm*. **Company** is much wider in range, and can be used to talk about any type of organization that makes money by producing or selling goods or services.

business [C] a commercial organization such as a company, shop or factory: *I've decided to start my own business.* ◇ *They've got a small catering business.* ◇ *This legislation will hurt small businesses.* ❶ **Business** is a general term for commercial organizations or any type or size: *Almost all businesses will be closed on Christmas Day* (= shops, factories, offices, etc.). It is also used especially to talk about small organizations, including those run by a single person or family, without any employees. (A **company** or **firm** always has employees.) **Business** is often used when people *start up* or *set up* in business for the first time. You can also have a *big business* but **big business** is used even more often as an uncountable noun to mean 'large companies as a group'. See also **business →** INDUSTRY, **business →** TRADE

operation [C] a company or business involving many parts; one part of a large company or business: *It's a huge multinational operation.* ◇ *Network Computing Inc. plans to open a UK operation in Britain next year.*

corporation(*abbr.* **Corp.**) [C] a large business company: *They provide banking facilities to multinational corporations.* ❶ **Corporation** is often used to talk about very large American business companies.

enterprise /'entəpraɪz; *AmE* -tərp-/ [C] (*business, journalism*) a company or business: *They plan to privatize over 100 state-owned enterprises.* ❶ **Enterprise** is often used in government texts and business journalism.

practice [C] a business or place that offers professional advice or treatment, especially in law and medicine: *She runs a successful law practice.* See also **practice →** WORK 2, **surgery →** SURGERY

house [C] (used in compounds) a company involved in a particular type of business: *The publishing house made its name by encouraging first-time writers.* ❶ **House** is used in compounds such as *a/an fashion/publishing/software/investment/auction house.*

compare *verb*

1 We compared the two reports carefully.
2 Our results compare favourably with theirs.

---

1 compare · contrast · juxtapose · balance sth against sth · match sth against sth
These words all mean to examine people or things to see how they are similar and/or how they are different.

PATTERNS AND COLLOCATIONS
▸ to compare / contrast / juxtapose A **and** / **with** B
▸ to compare / contrast sth **favourably** / **unfavourably** with sth

compare [T] to examine people or things in order to see how they are similar and how they are different: *It is interesting to compare their situation and ours.* ◇ *We compared the two reports carefully.* ◇ *My own problems seem insignificant compared with other people's.* ◇ *Standards in health care have improved enormously compared to 40 years ago.* ❶ Some people prefer only to use *with*, NOT *to* with **compare** in this meaning; however, both *with* and *to* are in fact very frequently used. *Compare sth to sth* is always used when the meaning is 'to show or suggest that two people or things are similar': *The critics compared his work to that of Hemingway.*

contrast [T] (*rather formal*) to compare two things in order to show the differences between them: *It is interesting to contrast the British legal system with the American one.* ◇ *The poem contrasts youth and age.* ◇

Compare and contrast the two main characters in the play. See also **contrast →** DIFFERENCE, **contrast →** OPPOSITE *noun*

juxtapose /ˌdʒʌkstə'pəʊz; *AmE* -'poʊz/ [T, usually passive] (*formal*) to put people or things together, especially in order to show a difference or a new relationship between them: *In the exhibition, abstract paintings are juxtaposed with shocking photographs.* ❶ **Juxtapose** is often used with adverbs such as *crudely, sharply, starkly* and *dramatically,* and with phrases like *to good/great/maximum effect.*

balance sth against sth *phrasal verb* (*rather formal*) to compare the relative importance of two contrasting things: *The cost of obtaining legal advice needs to be balanced against its benefits.*

'**match sth against sth** *phrasal verb* to compare things in order to find two that are the same or similar: *New information is matched against existing data in the computer.* ❶ **Match sth against sth** is often used to talk about comparing items of information such as words with a large collection or *database* of information on a computer or in the mind.

2 compare · match · rival · equal · be on a par with sb/sth
These words all mean to be as good as sb/sth else.

PATTERNS AND COLLOCATIONS
▸ to match / rival / equal sth **in** / **for** sth
▸ to compare with / match / rival / be on a par with sth **in terms of** sth
▸ to compare with / match / equal sb's **achievements**
▸ to match / rival / equal the **performance** of sth
▸ to match / equal a **feat** / **record**
▸ to be matched / rivalled / equalled **only by** sth

compare [I] to be as good as sb/sth else; to be similar to sb/sth else, either better or worse: *Few trees can compare with our native rowan for ease of cultivation.* ◇ *How do these results compare with last year's* (= are they better or worse)? ◇ *This Roman gold doesn't compare to* (is not as good as) *a recent find by a local farmer, which is worth millions.* ◇ *This government's record compares favourably with* (= is better than) *that of our predecessors.* ◇ *The profit of £23 million compares* (= contrasts) *with a £32 million loss in the previous financial year.* See also **comparable →** EQUIVALENT

match [T] to be as good, interesting or successful as sb/sth else; to make sth the same or better than sth else: *The teams were evenly matched* (= of a similar standard). ◇ *The two firms are quite closely matched in terms of size and profitability.* ◇ *The firm was unable to match the salaries offered by their rivals.* See also **match →** PEER *noun*

rival (-ll-, *AmE* -l-) [T] to be as good or impressive as sb/sth else: *You will find scenery to rival anything you can see in the Alps.* ◇ *Golf cannot rival football for excitement.*

equal (-ll-, *AmE* -l-) [T] to be as good as sth else; to do sth to the same standard as sb else: *Half-year profits equalled the best expectations.* ◇ *With his last jump he equalled the world record.* See also **equal →** PEER *noun*

be on a par with sb/sth *idiom* (*rather informal*) to be as good, bad, important, etc. as sb/sth else: *Profits should be on a par with last year.* ◇ *It's quite impressive, but it's not on a par with the stadiums we have back home.*

comparison *noun* See also the entry for SIMILARITY

comparison · analogy
These are both words for the process of comparing two or more people or things.

PATTERNS AND COLLOCATIONS
▸ a comparison / an analogy **between** A and B
▸ a comparison / an analogy **with** sth
▸ **by** comparison / analogy
▸ a/an **simple** / **close** / **interesting** / **striking** comparison / analogy

▶ a/an **direct/useful/appropriate/apt/obvious/good/clear** comparison/analogy
▶ to **draw/make/suggest** a comparison/an analogy

comparison [U, C] the process of comparing two or more people or things; an occasion when two or more people or things are compared: *I enclose the two plans* **for comparison.** ◇ *The tallest buildings in London are small* **in comparison with** *New York's skyscrapers.* ◇ *His problems seemed trivial by comparison.* ◇ *The education system* **bears no comparison** *with that in many Central European countries* (= it is not as good). ◇ *a comparison of the rail systems in Britain and France* ◇ *You can draw comparisons with the situation in Australia* (= say how the two situations are similar). See also **comparable** → EQUIVALENT *adj.*

analogy /əˈnælədʒi/ [C, U] (*rather formal*) a comparison of one thing with another thing that has similar features, especially in order to explain it; a similar feature: *The teacher drew an analogy between the human heart and a pump.* ◇ *They promote learning by analogy.* ◇ *There are no analogies with any previous legal cases.* See also **analogous** → EQUIVALENT *adj.*

compensate *verb*

compensate · offset · counter · cancel (sth) out · make up for sth · counteract · balance
These words all mean to reduce or remove the effect of sth else.

PATTERNS AND COLLOCATIONS
▶ to compensate/counter/counteract sth **with** sth
▶ to compensate/make up **for** sth
▶ to compensate for/offset/counter/cancel out/counteract the **effect** of sth
▶ to compensate for/offset/counter/counteract a **problem**
▶ to counter/counteract sb's **efforts**
▶ to counter/counteract/balance the **tendency** to do sth
▶ to **partly/partially** compensate for/offset/make up for/counteract sth
▶ to **more than** compensate for/offset/make up for/balance sth

compensate /ˈkɒmpenseɪt; *AmE* ˈkɑːm-/ [I, T] (*usually approving*) to provide or do sth good to balance or reduce the bad effects of sth: *Nothing can compensate for the death of a loved one.* ◇ *She was so ashamed of her treatment of him that she felt she should compensate him in some way.*
▶ **compensation** *noun* [C, usually pl.]: *I wish I were young again, but getting older has its compensations.*

offset /ˈɒfset; *AmE* ˈɔːf-; ˈɑːf-/ [T] (*rather formal, especially business*) to use one cost, payment or situation to reduce or remove the effect of another: *Fuel prices have risen to offset the increased costs of crude oil.* ◇ *The company's losses in the US were more than offset by gains everywhere else.* ◇ **Offset against** *this return will be all the costs involved in developing the product.*

counter [T] to do sth to reduce or prevent the bad effects of sth: *Businesses would like to see more laws to counter late payments of debts.* ◇ *It's often necessary to counter negative images with positive images.*

cancel sth 'out, cancel 'out *phrasal verb* (-ll-, *AmE* -l-) (*sometimes disapproving*) to have an equal but opposite effect to sth, so that the situation does not change; (of two things) to have an equal but opposite effect to each other: *Recent losses have cancelled out any profits made at the start of the year.* ◇ *The advantages and disadvantages would appear to* **cancel each other out.** ◇ *Small variations in the electron count will cancel out over the course of the experiment.*

make 'up for sth *phrasal verb* (*rather informal, usually approving*) to provide or do sth good that makes a bad situation better: *He made up for the missed penalty by scoring two magnificent goals.* ◇ *After all the delays we were anxious to* **make up for lost time.** ◇ *What they* **lacked in** *talent they* **made up for in** *enthusiasm.*

NOTE **COMPENSATE** OR **MAKE UP FOR STH**? **Compensate** is more formal than **make up for sth** but can be used in a wider range of structures, with or without *for: You should be able to eat more on this diet without having to compensate by going hungry.* ◇ ~~You should be able to eat more on this diet without having to make up by going hungry~~.

counteract /ˌkaʊntərˈækt/ [T] to do sth to reduce or prevent the effects of sth, especially the bad effects of sth: *These exercises aim to counteract the effects of stress and tension.* ◇ *The thrust of the rocket engines counteracts gravity.*

NOTE **COUNTER** OR **COUNTERACT**? There is very little difference in meaning between these two words. **Counteract** is used especially to talk about reducing physical effects or feelings: collocates include *feelings* and *symptoms*.

balance [T, I] (*usually approving*) to be equal in value, amount or strength to sth else that has the opposite effect: *His lack of experience was balanced by a willingness to learn.* ◇ *The good and bad effects of any decision will usually balance* **out.**

compensation *noun*

compensation · refund · rebate · award · restitution · reimbursement
These are all words for sth, especially money, that sb gives you because they have hurt you, caused you to lose or spend money, or damaged sth that you own.

PATTERNS AND COLLOCATIONS
▶ compensation/a refund/a rebate/an award/restitution/reimbursement **from** sb **to** sb
▶ compensation/a refund/a rebate/an award/restitution/reimbursement **for** sth
▶ a refund/rebate **on** sth
▶ to pay/receive, etc. money **as/in** compensation/restitution
▶ (a) **full** compensation/refund/rebate/restitution/reimbursement
▶ to **receive** compensation/a refund/a rebate/an award/restitution/reimbursement
▶ to **get** compensation/a refund/a rebate/an award/restitution
▶ to **pay** compensation/a refund/a rebate/restitution/reimbursement
▶ to **make** compensation/a refund/an award/restitution/reimbursement
▶ to **offer** (sb) compensation/a refund/a rebate/restitution/reimbursement
▶ to **be entitled to** compensation/a refund/a rebate/restitution/reimbursement
▶ to **seek** compensation/a refund/restitution/reimbursement
▶ to **claim** compensation/a refund/a rebate/restitution/reimbursement
▶ to **demand** compensation/a refund/restitution/reimbursement

compensation [U, C] something, especially money, that sb gives you because they have hurt you, caused you to lose money or damaged sth that you own; the act of giving this to sb: *The employer has a duty to pay full compensation for injuries received at work.* ◇ *She received a cash sum by way of compensation.* See also **compensate** → REPAY

refund /ˈriːfʌnd/ an amount of money that is paid back to you, especially because you paid too much or because you returned goods to a shop: *If there is a delay of 12 hours or more, you will receive a full refund of the price of your trip.* See also **refund** → REPAY *verb*

rebate /ˈriːbeɪt/ an amount of money that is paid back to you because you have paid too much: *You may be entitled to a rebate on your car insurance.*

NOTE **REFUND** OR **REBATE**? **Refund** is more general than **rebate** which only applies when you have paid too much, especially in tax or insurance money. You can get a **refund** when you take goods back to a shop or when the goods or service that you bought were not of the quality or standard that you had a right to expect.

award [C, U] the amount of money that a court decides should be given to sb who has won a case; the decision to give this money: *an award of £600 000 libel damages* ◇ *The court must specify the different elements in its award of compensation.* See also **award** → GIVE *verb* 1

restitution /ˌrestɪˈtjuːʃn; *AmE* -ˈtuː-/ [U] (*formal or law*) the act of giving back sth that was lost or stolen to its owner; payment that sb gives you because they have hurt you, caused you to lose money or damaged sth that you own: *The family's lawyer is demanding the restitution of all family property seized under the previous regime.* ◇ *The company has a legal duty to make restitution to passengers for any inconvenience caused.*

reimbursement /ˌriːɪmˈbɜːsmənt; *AmE* -ˈbɜːrs-/ [U] (*rather formal*) the act of paying back money to sb which they have had to spend or have lost, when it is not their fault: *You will receive reimbursement for any additional costs incurred while on company business.* See also **reimburse** → REPAY

compete *verb*

compete · fight · battle · take sb on · struggle · contest · vie · pit sb/sth against sb/sth
These words all mean to try to be more successful or better than sb else who is trying to do the same as you, for example in a competition, contest or election.

PATTERNS AND COLLOCATIONS
▸ to compete / fight / battle / struggle / vie **for** sth
▸ to compete / battle / struggle / vie **with** sb
▸ to compete / battle / vie **to do sth**
▸ to compete for / battle for / contest / vie for a (first / second, etc.) **place**
▸ to compete / fight / struggle / vie **for power**
▸ to fight / battle / struggle / vie **for control**
▸ to compete / fight / vie **for a share of sth**
▸ to compete / fight / battle / struggle **hard**
▸ to **successfully** compete for / fight (for) / contest sth

compete [I] to try to be more successful or better than sb else who is trying to do the same as you: *Small bookshops can't compete with the large stores.* ◇ *Several projects are competing against each other for scarce resources.* ◇ *Travel firms are competing fiercely on price.* ◇ *Colleges will have to compete to attract the best students.* See also **competitor, the competition** → ENEMY

fight [I, T] to take part in a contest, especially when you compete very hard: *She's fighting for a place in the national team.* ◇ *Collins fought back to level the match at 2 sets all.* ◇ (*especially BrE*) *There are twelve parties fighting the election.*

battle [I] (*especially journalism*) to try very hard to be more successful than an opponent in a contest or argument or to achieve sth difficult: *Unions are battling with the company over the job losses.* ◇ *The players have battled hard.* ◇ *The two sides will battle it out in the final next week.* ❶ Battle can also mean 'to deal with sth unpleasant or dangerous': *She's still battling with a knee injury.* In this meaning it is also used with an object in American English: *He battled cancer for four years.* See also **fight** → OPPOSE

take sb 'on *phrasal verb* [no passive] to accept sb as an opponent: *He'll take on the former Olympic champion in the 5 000 metres.* ◇ *Why don't you take him on at chess?*

struggle [I] to compete or argue with sb, especially in order to get sth: *The two men struggled for control of the party.* ◇ *The firms are struggling for market share.*

contest [T] to take part in a competition or election: *Three candidates contested the leadership.* ◇ *It turned out to be another hotly contested tournament.*

vie /vaɪ/ [I] (*rather formal*) to compete strongly against sb in order to get sth: *The boys would vie with each other to impress her.* ◇ *They are all vying for a place in the team.*

'pit sb/sth against sb/sth *phrasal verb* (-**tt**-) to test sb or their strength, intelligence or determination in a contest against sb/sth else: *The issue of water supply pitted farmers against environmentalists.* ◇ *They pit their wits against each other in the weekly sports quiz.*

competition *noun*

1 a drawing/dancing competition
2 competition between businesses

1 See also the entry for RACE
competition · contest · quiz
These are all words for events in which people compete against each other to win a prize or to find out who is the best at sth.

PATTERNS AND COLLOCATIONS
▸ a competition / contest **between** sb
▸ a competition / contest **for** sth
▸ **in** a competition / contest / quiz
▸ a / an **international / national / sporting** competition / contest
▸ to **enter / take part in / win / have / hold** a competition / contest / quiz

competition [C] an event in which people compete with each other to win a prize or to find out who is the best at sth: *I won a car in a competition.* ◇ *We're going to have a competition to see who can swim the furthest.* ◇ *The competition is open to all readers of the magazine.* See also **competitor** → PARTICIPANT

contest [C] a competition: *They won the doubles contest against the Williams sisters.* ◇ *Jackson has injured his knee and is now out of the contest.* ◇ *She's the favourite for this year's Eurovision Song Contest.* ◇ *a beauty/talent contest* ❶ If you say that sth **is no contest** you mean that one side in a competition is so much stronger or better than the other that it is sure to win easily.

NOTE COMPETITION OR CONTEST? Both of these words can refer to events in which people compete in sports or games, or to show their talent or knowledge, for example in performing, art or writing. **Competition** is a slightly more general word and can involve teams, groups or individuals competing. A **contest** is more often between a small number of individuals who are competing against each other to win a prize. In British English, **competition**, but NOT **contest** can describe an event that a large number of people enter by post or telephone, including events in which sb wins more by luck than by talent or skill, for example by being the first person to have their name picked out of a hat: *Competition: to win an Oxford Mini car, customers must guess how many copies of the Oxford Minidictionary will fit into the car.* However, in American English, **contest** can also be used in this way: *To enter the contest, simply send an email to this address...* See also **contestant** → PARTICIPANT

quiz (pl. **quizzes**) [C] a competition or game in which people try to answer questions to test their knowledge: *I'm useless at general knowledge quizzes.* ◇ *He's the host of a popular TV quiz show.* ◇ *The club has weekly quiz nights.*

2 **competition · race · contest · rivalry · competitiveness**
These are all words for a situation in which people or organizations compete with each other for sth that not everyone can have.

PATTERNS AND COLLOCATIONS
▸ competition / a race / a contest / rivalry **for** sth
▸ competition / a race / a contest / rivalry / competitiveness **between** people
▸ **in** competition / a race / a contest / rivalry **with** sb / sth
▸ competition / a race **to do sth**
▸ (a) **fierce** competition / contest / rivalry / competitiveness
▸ (an) **open** competition / race / contest

▶ **international** competition / rivalry / competitiveness
▶ to **enter** / **win** / **lose** the race / contest

competition [U] a situation in which people or organizations compete with each other for sth that not everyone can have: *There is now intense competition between schools to attract students.* ◇ *We are in competition with four other companies.* ◇ *We face strong competition from other countries.* ◇ *They won the order against fierce international competition.* ◇ *The company is having to lay off workers in the face of stiff competition.* See also **competitor** → PARTICIPANT

race [sing.] (*especially journalism*) a competition between a number of people, groups or organizations, especially for political power, economic advantage or to achieve sth first: *Polls give him the edge over his Democratic rival in the race for the presidency.* ◇ *Two right-wing candidates lead the presidential race.* ◇ *The rival TV companies are in a race to bring out the first film drama of her life.* ◇ *The race is on* (= has begun) *to find a cure for this disease.*

contest [C] (*especially journalism*) a competition between candidates for political power or between businesses for economic advantage: *During the election contest newspapers are not allowed to publish opinion polls.* ◇ *The other bidders for the contract complained that it had not been a fair contest.*

> **NOTE** RACE OR CONTEST? Both these words are used about political elections and in many cases you can use either word. However, **contest** usually refers to the election itself and sometimes the two or three weeks of campaigning just before it; **race** covers the whole period of campaigning for an election which can last months, especially in the case of US presidential elections. You can say that sb *wins/loses a race/contest* and that sb *leads/is ahead in the race for sth* but NOT usually that sb '*leads/is ahead in the contest for sth*'. **Race**, but NOT **contest** can also be used to talk about the drive to achieve sth, especially before anyone else has achieved it.

rivalry /ˈraɪvlri/ [C, U] a situation in which two people, teams, groups or companies, are competing for the same thing: *Bitter ethnic rivalries within the region have grown.* ◇ *There is a certain amount of friendly rivalry between the teams.* ◇ *Her parents had been very aware of the problems of sibling rivalry* (= between brothers and sisters) *before the younger child was born.*

> **NOTE** COMPETITION OR RIVALRY? In this meaning **competition** is used most often in the context of business; **rivalry** is used more in the contexts of politics, sport and personal relationships.

competitiveness /kəmˈpetətɪvnəs/ [sing., U] the feeling of being in competition with sb/sth for sb/sth; how well sb/sth competes: *Jenny brings a fierce competitiveness to the team.* ◇ *The move is an attempt to improve the competitiveness of British industry.*
▶ **competitive** *adj.*: *It's a fiercely competitive market.*

complain *verb*

complain · protest · object · grumble · moan · whine · carp
These words all mean to say that you are annoyed, unhappy or not satisfied about sb/sth.

PATTERNS AND COLLOCATIONS
▶ to complain / protest / grumble / moan / whine / carp **about** sth
▶ to grumble / moan / carp **on** about sth
▶ to complain / protest / grumble / moan **at** sth
▶ to grumble / moan / whine **at** sb
▶ to complain / protest / object / grumble / moan / whine **to** sb
▶ to complain / protest / object / grumble / moan / whine **that...**
▶ to complain / protest / grumble **loudly**

complain [I, T] to say that you are annoyed, unhappy or not satisfied about sb/sth: *She never complains, but she's obviously exhausted.* ◇ *I'm going to complain to the*
manager about this. ◇ *'It's not fair,' she complained.* ◇ (*rather formal*) *The defendant complained of intimidation during the investigation.*

protest [I, T] to say or do sth to show that you disagree with or disapprove of sth, especially publicly; to give sth as a reason for protesting: *Students took to the streets to protest against the decision.* ◇ *It's no use protesting, I won't change my mind.* ◇ *She protested that she could not receive a fair trial.* ❶ In American English **protest** can also take a noun as object.: (*AmE*) *They fully intend to protest the decision.* See also **protest** → OPPOSITION, **protest** → DEMONSTRATION, **protester** → PROTESTER

object [I, T] to say that you disagree with or disapprove of sth; to give sth as a reason for objecting: *If nobody objects, we'll postpone the meeting till next week.* ◇ *I really object to being charged for parking.* ◇ *He objected that the police had arrested him without sufficient evidence.* See also **objection** → OPPOSITION

grumble [I, T] (*rather informal, disapproving*) to complain about sb/sth in a bad-tempered way: *She's always grumbling to me about how badly she's treated at work.*

moan [I, T] (*rather informal, disapproving*) to complain about sb/sth in an annoying way: *They're always moaning and groaning about how much they have to do.* ◇ (*BrE*) *What are you moaning on about now?* See also **moan** → WHISPER

whine /waɪn/ [I, T] (*rather informal, disapproving*) to complain in an annoying, crying voice: *Stop whining!* ◇ *'I want to go home,' whined Toby.* ❶ **Whine** is often used to talk about the way that young children complain.

carp [I] (*rather informal, disapproving*) to repeatedly complain about sth in a way that criticizes other people and is annoying: *I've had enough of him constantly carping and criticizing.* ◇ *Lord, how you carp on, Lucy!* ❶ **Carp** is often followed by *on*, which emphasizes the repeated nature of this sort of complaining.

complaint *noun*

complaint · grievance · gripe
These are all words for sth which you are not happy or satisfied about and that you complain or protest about.

PATTERNS AND COLLOCATIONS
▶ a complaint / grievance / gripe **about** sb / sth
▶ a complaint / grievance **over** sth
▶ a complaint / grievance **against** sb / sth
▶ a complaint / gripe **from** sb
▶ to **have** a complaint / grievance / gripe
▶ to **register / voice / deal with / handle / investigate / hear / resolve** a complaint / grievance

complaint [C, U] a reason why sb is not satisfied; a statement that sb makes saying that they are not satisfied; the act of complaining: *I'd like to make a complaint about the noise.* ◇ (*formal*) *The couple have lodged an official complaint against the hospital.* ◇ *I can see no grounds for complaint.* ◇ *I'm planning to write a formal letter of complaint.*

grievance /ˈɡriːvəns/ [C, U] (*rather formal*) something that you think is unfair and that you complain or protest about; a sense of being unfairly treated: *Parents were invited to air their grievances* (= express them). ◇ *He had been nursing a grievance against his boss for months.* ◇ *Does the company have a formal grievance procedure?* ◇ *The offer did nothing to take away her sense of grievance.* See also **aggrieved** → UNHAPPY 2

> **NOTE** COMPLAINT OR GRIEVANCE? **Complaint** is a general word and can refer to serious or minor problems, practical problems or personal unhappiness about sth. A **complaint** can be informal, and *made* to a friend, a colleague, etc. or it can be *filed* or *lodged* more formally, often in writing, to a company or organization. A **grievance** is a strong feeling that sth is unfair or that you have been treated unfairly. It is often a feeling which has developed over a period of time. We often

say that a person *harbours* or *nurses* a **grievance**: they develop strong negative feelings about sth over a period of time.

gripe [C] (*informal*) something that you complain about because you are not satisfied, especially sth small or not very important: *My only gripe about the hotel was the food.*

complete *adj.* See also the entry for PURE 2

complete · total · real · absolute · outright · utter · perfect · positive · downright
These words are all used to emphasize how great sth is in degree.

PATTERNS AND COLLOCATIONS
▸ a complete / a total / a real / an absolute / an utter **disaster**
▸ a complete / a total / a real / an absolute **mess**
▸ a complete / a total / a real **idiot**
▸ a complete / a total / an absolute / an utter **fool**
▸ complete / total / absolute / utter **rubbish / nonsense / darkness**
▸ complete / total / absolute / utter / perfect **silence**
▸ a complete / a total / perfect **stranger**
▸ a complete / a real / an absolute **beginner**
▸ a complete / a total / an absolute / an outright **ban**

complete [usually before noun] used when you are emphasizing sth, to mean 'to the greatest degree possible': *We were in complete agreement.* ◇ *It came as a complete surprise.* ◇ *The whole thing has been a complete waste of time.* See also **completely** → QUITE 2
total [only before noun] complete: *The room was in total darkness.* ◇ *I always expect total honesty from my employees.* ◇ *Six years of total war had left no citizen untouched.* See also **total** → WHOLE, **totally** → QUITE 2

NOTE COMPLETE OR TOTAL? In nearly all cases you can use either of these words: *complete/total agreement/ honesty/darkness* ◇ *a complete/total surprise/idiot/waste of time/lack of understanding.* Total war is a fixed collocation that cannot be changed: ~~Six years of complete war...~~. **Total** is only used before a noun; **complete** can also be used after a linking verb, although this is not frequent and rather formal: (*rather formal*) *Her misery was made complete when she was separated from her children.* ◇ ~~Her misery was made total...~~

real [only before noun] (*rather informal, especially spoken*) complete: *He looks like a real idiot.* ◇ *This accident could have produced a real tragedy.* ◇ *Her next play was a real contrast.* ❶ **Real** is used in rather informal language to emphasize the degree to which sth is bad or different. See also **really** → VERY *adv.*
absolute [usually before noun] (*especially spoken*) complete: *He must earn an absolute fortune.* ◇ *'You're wrong,' she said with absolute certainty.* ❶ **Absolute** is used especially in spoken English to emphasize how bad or how large sth is. In slightly more formal and written English it is also used to describe a feeling or quality; it is usually used before a noun, but in literary contexts it can also be used after a linking verb: (*literary*) *Around them the darkness was absolute, the silence oppressive.* See also **absolutely** → QUITE 2
outright /ˈaʊtraɪt/ [only before noun] complete: *She was the outright winner.* ◇ *No one party is expected to gain an outright majority.* ◇ *They may introduce tougher restrictions or even an outright ban.* ❶ Collocates of **outright** in this meaning include *win, victory, winner, majority, ban, rejection, refusal* and *lie.*
▸ **outright** *adv.*: *Neither candidate won outright.*
utter [only before noun] complete: *That's complete and utter nonsense!* ◇ *To my utter amazement she agreed.* ❶ **Utter** is used especially to describe feelings and qualities, especially of surprise, disgust, despair, confusion, belief and peace. Collocates include *surprise, disgust, despair, failure, confusion, chaos, conviction, delight, silence* and *stillness.* See also **utterly** → QUITE 2

perfect [only before noun] complete: *I don't know her — she's a perfect stranger.* ◇ *I have a **perfect right** to ask you — and you have the right not to answer.* ❶ Collocates of **perfect** in this meaning include *stranger, gentleman, right, accuracy, freedom, harmony* and *happiness.* See also **perfectly** → QUITE 2
positive [only before noun] (*rather informal*) complete: *He has a positive genius for upsetting people.* ◇ *It was a positive miracle that we survived.*
downright /ˈdaʊnraɪt/ [only before noun] (*rather informal, usually disapproving*) used to emphasize sth negative or unpleasant: *It's a downright disgrace that they still haven't paid you.*
▸ **downright** *adv.*: *It's not just stupid — it's downright dangerous.*

complex *adj.*

complex · complicated · elaborate · intricate · tortuous · involved · convoluted · tangled
These words all describe sth that has many parts or details and is difficult to understand.

PATTERNS AND COLLOCATIONS
▸ a complex / a complicated / an elaborate / an intricate **system**
▸ a complex / a complicated / an elaborate / an intricate / a convoluted **story / plot**
▸ a complex / a complicated / an elaborate / an intricate **design / structure / network**
▸ a complex / a complicated / an intricate / a tangled **web / relationship**
▸ complex / complicated / elaborate **machinery**
▸ a complex / complicated / tortuous **process**
▸ **extremely** complex / complicated / elaborate / intricate / involved
▸ **highly** complex / complicated / elaborate / intricate

complex made of many different things or parts that are connected; difficult to understand: *This is a highly complex matter.* ◇ *The mechanism involves a complex arrangement of rods and cogs.* ◇ *She managed to put over a fairly complex argument in a brilliantly simple way.* OPP **simple** → EASY 1
complicated /ˈkɒmplɪkeɪtɪd; AmE ˈkɑːm-/ complex: *The instructions look very complicated.* ◇ *This is where the story gets complicated.* ◇ *It's all very complicated — but I'll try and explain.* OPP **uncomplicated, straightforward** → EASY 1, See also **complication** → PROBLEM

NOTE COMPLEX OR COMPLICATED? In many cases you can use either word: *a complex/complicated problem* ◇ *complex/complicated instructions.* **Complicated** is used slightly more in conversation and to describe everyday situations: *I'll send you map of how to get here. It's a bit too complicated to describe.* **Complex** is used slightly more in written English to describe serious, academic, scientific or technical issues: *a complex mathematical equation/formula.* Both words can describe sth that is difficult to understand because of its nature or design. **Complicated** is often used to describe a situation that has become less simple, more messy and more difficult to understand or deal with over time because of events, changes or problems.

elaborate /ɪˈlæbərət/ [usually before noun] having a lot of different parts and small details; carefully prepared and organized: *The ceiling was tiled in an elaborate pattern.* ◇ *She had prepared a very elaborate meal.* ◇ *This elaborate deception fooled his family for ages.* OPP **simple** → EASY 1
intricate /ˈɪntrɪkət/ having a lot of different parts and small details that fit together: *The building has intricate geometric designs on several of the walls.* ◇ *It is difficult to describe the intricate network of loyalties and relationships.*
▸ **intricately** *adv.*: *intricately carved/decorated/patterned*
tortuous /ˈtɔːtʃuəs; AmE ˈtɔːrtʃ-/ [usually before noun] (*written, usually disapproving*) not simple and direct; long, complicated and difficult to understand: *the long, tortuous process of negotiating peace in the region*

involved having a lot of different parts or stages and difficult to understand or follow: *Avoid long, involved debates which could be just delaying tactics.* **OPP** straightforward → EASY 1

convoluted /ˈkɒnvəluːtɪd; *AmE* ˈkɑːn-/ (*written, usually disapproving*) extremely complicated and difficult to follow, especially more complicated than necessary: *The book has a rather convoluted plot.*

tangled complicated and difficult to understand: *The series involves the tangled relationships of two London families.* ◇ *He spent the next few days wrestling with very tangled emotions.* ❶ Something which was originally quite simple or straightforward often becomes **tangled** over time because of changes or problems which together make it more complicated and difficult to understand.

complicate verb

complicate · blur · confuse · cloud
These words all mean to make sth less clear or more difficult to understand.

PATTERNS AND COLLOCATIONS
▸ to complicate / confuse / cloud **the issue**
▸ to complicate / confuse **matters / things / the situation**
▸ to **further** complicate sth / confuse sth / cloud the issue, etc.

complicate [T] to make a situation or problem more difficult to deal with: ***To complicate matters*** *further, there will be no transport available till 8 o'clock.* ◇ *The issue* ***is complicated by the fact that*** *a vital document is missing.*

blur /blɜː(r)/ (-rr-) [T, I] to make the difference between two things become less clear; (of the difference between two things) to become less clear: *His work has* ***blurred the boundaries between*** *children's and adults' fiction.* ◇ *The* ***line between*** *make-believe and reality became increasingly* ***blurred***. ◇ *She tends to* ***blur the distinction between*** *her friends and her colleagues.*

confuse [T] to make a situation or problem more difficult to understand or deal with: *His latest comments only serve to confuse the issue further.*

NOTE **COMPLICATE** OR **CONFUSE**? Something **complicates** a situation that is already difficult by being an additional problem that makes it even less straightforward. With **confuse** the emphasis is more on the fact that it is difficult to recognize or understand what needs to be done.

cloud [T] to make sth you are discussing or considering less clear or more difficult to understand, especially by introducing subjects that are not connected with it: *Cost factors should not be allowed to cloud the issue.*

composure noun See also the entry for RESTRAINT

composure · poise · calm · cool
These are all words for the state of being in control of your feelings or behaviour, especially in difficult situations.

PATTERNS AND COLLOCATIONS
▸ **with** composure / poise / calm
▸ to **lose** your composure / poise / cool
▸ to **keep** your composure / cool
▸ to **recover** your composure / poise

composure /kəmˈpəʊʒə(r); *AmE* -ˈpoʊ-/ [U] (*rather formal, especially written*) the state of being in control of your feelings or behaviour, and having a quiet and relaxed manner: *She answered with perfect composure.* ◇ *He maintained his composure despite a desperate desire to laugh.* See also **composed** → CALM *adj.*

poise /pɔɪz/ [U] a calm and confident manner with control of your feelings and behaviour: *She seemed embarrassed for a moment but quickly recovered her poise.*

calm [U] a quiet and relaxed manner, in control of your feelings and behaviour: *Alex spoke with studied calm.* ◇ *Her previous calm gave way to terror.* See also **calm** → CALM *adj.*

cool [U] (always used in the phrases *keep/lose your cool*) (*informal*) the state of being calm and in control of your feelings or behaviour, especially in difficult situations: *He kept his cool on the convention floor when he was heckled by a young Republican.* ◇ *I lost my cool and shouted at them.* See also **cool** → CALM *adj.*

compromise noun

compromise · concession · trade-off · middle ground · sop · give and take
These words all refer to a balance between the needs and wishes of two people or groups, or between two opposing things, especially in order reach an agreement or solve a problem.

PATTERNS AND COLLOCATIONS
▸ a compromise / a trade-off / middle ground / give and take **between** sb / sth and sb / sth
▸ a compromise / concession **on / over** sth
▸ a concession / a sop **to** sb
▸ **as** a compromise / concession / trade-off / sop
▸ a **necessary** compromise / concession / trade-off
▸ a / an **possible / obvious** compromise / concession / trade-off
▸ to **make** a compromise / a concession / a trade-off
▸ to **look for / seek / offer / reject** a compromise / concession

compromise /ˈkɒmprəmaɪz; *AmE* ˈkɑːm-/ [C, U] an agreement between two people or groups in which each side gives up some of the things they want so that both sides are happy in the end; a solution to a problem in which two things that are opposed to each are balanced; the act of reaching such a position: *They came to a compromise over the exact amount to be paid.* ◇ *In any relationship, you have to make compromises.* ◇ *This model represents the best compromise between price and quality.* ◇ *Compromise is an inevitable part of life.*
▸ **compromise** *verb* [I, T]: *Neither side is prepared to compromise.* ◇ *We are not prepared to* ***compromise on*** *safety standards.* ◇ *I refuse to compromise my principles.*

concession /kənˈseʃn/ [C, U] something that you agree to or allow sb to do in order to end an argument or to make a situation less difficult; the act of agreeing to sth like this: *The management will be forced to make concessions to the union.* ◇ *The pressure group has* ***won*** *a number of concessions on environmental policy.* ◇ *Military support was offered in return for the* ***concession of*** *territory.* See also **concede** → GIVE STH UP

'trade-off [C] the act of balancing two things that you need or want but which are opposed to each other: *There is a trade-off between the benefits of the drug and the risk of side effects.*

'middle ground [U] a set of opinions, ideas or decisions that opposing groups can agree on; a position that is not extreme: *Negotiations have failed to establish any middle ground.* ◇ *The ballet now* ***occupies the middle ground between*** *classical ballet and modern dance.*

sop [C, usually sing.] (*especially written*) a small, not very important thing that is offered to sb who is angry or disappointed in order to make them feel better: *The move was seen as another sop to the moderates in the party.*

ˌgive and 'take *idiom* willingness in a relationship to accept what sb else wants and give up some of what you want: *We must accept a certain amount of give and take.*

concern noun

concern · worry · anxiety · apprehension · unease · angst · agitation
These are all words for the state of worrying about something, or for things that cause you to worry.

unease anxiety concern
apprehension worry
angst
agitation

PATTERNS AND COLLOCATIONS

▶ concern / worry / anxiety / apprehension / unease / angst **over / about** sth
▶ concern / worry / anxiety / apprehension / unease **that...**
▶ **great / considerable / growing** concern / worry / anxiety / apprehension / unease / agitation
▶ **deep** concern / anxiety / unease
▶ to **express** concern / your worries / anxiety / apprehension / unease
▶ to **voice** your concern / unease
▶ to **share** your concerns / worries
▶ to **cause** concern / anxiety / apprehension / unease

concern [U, C] (*rather formal*) a feeling of worry, especially one that is shared by many people; sth that worries people: *She hasn't been seen for four days and there is concern for her safety.* ◇ *The report expressed concern over continuing high unemployment.* See also **concern** → WORRY *verb 2*, **concerned** → WORRIED

worry [U, C] the state of worrying about sth; sth that worries you: *He claims the illness was caused by stress and worry.* ◇ *He was sick with worry.* ◇ *financial/family worries* See also **worried** → WORRIED

anxiety /æŋˈzaɪəti/ [U, C] the state of feeling nervous or worried; a worry or fear about sth: *Some hospital patients experience high levels of anxiety.* ◇ *She felt a nagging anxiety that could not be relieved.* See also **anxious** → WORRIED

NOTE CONCERN, WORRY OR ANXIETY? Worry is a more informal word than **concern** and **anxiety**, although in informal English it is more common to use the expression *be worried* than any of these nouns. **Worry** and **anxiety** are especially used to refer to personal matters; a **concern** often affects many people.

apprehension [U, C] (*rather formal*) worry or fear that sth unpleasant may happen: *There is growing apprehension that fighting will begin again.* ◇ *She felt some apprehension at seeing him again.* See also **apprehensive** → WORRIED

unease /ʌnˈiːz/ [U, sing.] the feeling of being slightly worried or unhappy about sth: *He was unable to hide his unease at the way the situation was developing.* See also **uneasy** → WORRIED

angst /æŋst/ [U] a feeling of anxiety and worry about a situation, or about your life: *songs full of teenage angst*

agitation [U] worry and anxiety that you show by behaving in a nervous way: *Dot arrived in a state of great agitation.* ◇ *He started to pace up and down the room in agitation.* See also **agitate** → SHAKE 4, **agitated** → RESTLESS

concert *noun*

concert · gig · show · recital
These words all mean a performance of music in front of an audience.

PATTERNS AND COLLOCATIONS

▶ **at** a concert / gig / show / recital
▶ a **solo** concert / gig / show / recital
▶ a **rock / charity / live** concert / gig / show
▶ a **pop** concert / gig
▶ a / an **piano / organ / classical** concert / recital
▶ to **give / play / do** a concert / gig / show / recital
▶ to **put on** a concert / gig / show / recital

concert [C] a performance of music in front of an audience: *They performed a concert of music by Rachmaninoff and Prokofiev.* ◇ *We saw Muse in concert at Reading Festival.* ◇ *a concert hall/pianist*

gig [C] (*especially BrE*) a concert of pop music or jazz, especially a small one held in a pub, club or theatre: *The guide lists live music events in the area, including pub gigs.*

show [C] (*AmE, informal*) a concert, especially of rock music: *My first full-scale rock show was Fleetwood Mac, Madison Square Gardens, back in 1977.* See also **show** → PERFORMANCE, **show** → PROGRAMME

recital /rɪˈsaɪtl/ [C] a performance of music or poetry in front of an audience, usually given by one person or a small group of people: *They put on a song recital in honour of Mozart's 250th birthday.*

conclude *verb*

conclude · understand · figure · infer · deduce · gather · reason · read sth into sth
These words all mean to decide or believe sth according to the evidence or information that you have.

PATTERNS AND COLLOCATIONS

▶ to conclude / understand / figure / infer / deduce / gather / reason **from** sth
▶ to conclude / understand / figure / infer / deduce / gather sth **about** sth
▶ to conclude / understand / figure / infer / deduce / gather / reason **that...**
▶ to figure / deduce **what / how / who / why...**
▶ It is concluded / understood / inferred / deduced / reasoned that...
▶ It can be concluded / inferred / deduced that...

conclude [T] (not used in the progressive tenses) to decide or believe sth on the basis of the information that you have: *What do you conclude from that?* ◇ *The report concluded that the cheapest option was to close the laboratory.*

understand [T] (not used in the progressive tenses) (*rather formal*) to think or believe that sth is true because you have been told that it is: *Am I to understand that you refuse?* ◇ *The prime minister is understood to have been extremely angry about the report.* See also **understanding** → DEFINITION

figure [T] (not used in the progressive tenses) (*rather informal*) to think or decide that sth will happen or is true: *I figured (that) if I took the night train, I could be in Scotland by morning.* ◇ *There was only one thing to do, he figured.*

infer /ɪnˈfɜː(r)/ (-rr-) [T] (not usually used in the progressive tenses) to form an opinion or decide that sth is true using evidence and reasoning, not statements of fact: *Much of the meaning can be inferred from the context.* ◇ *It is reasonable to infer that the government knew all about this.*

deduce /dɪˈdjuːs; AmE dɪˈduːs/ [T] (not used in the progressive tenses) to find out a fact or the answer to a question using evidence and reasoning: *We can deduce a lot from what people spend their money on.*

NOTE INFER OR DEDUCE? In many cases, you can use either of these words, but there can be a slight difference in meaning: sth that you **infer** is probably true, considering the evidence available; sth that you **deduce** logically has to be true, considering the facts.

gather [T] (not used in the progressive tenses) (*rather informal, especially spoken*) to think or believe that sth is true because you have been told that it is: *I gather you wanted to see me.* ◇ *'There's been a delay.' 'So I gather.'* ◇ *As far as I can gather, he got involved in a fight.* ◇ *From what they could gather, there had been some kind of problem back at the base.*

NOTE UNDERSTAND OR GATHER? Both of these words are often used in spoken English, but **understand** is more formal than **gather**. **Gather** can suggest greater activity than **understand**: what you **understand** is what you have been told, usually without asking; what you **gather** is either what you have been told, or what you have found out by asking people. **Gather**, but NOT **understand**, is often used with *can/could*: *As far as I can understand...* ◊ *From what they could understand...*

reason [T, I] to form a judgement about sth by considering the facts and using your power to think in a logical way: *They reasoned, correctly, that the enemy would not attempt an attack at night.* See also **reason** → REASON *noun*, **reasoned** → RATIONAL, **reasoning** → REASONING

read sth 'into sth *phrasal verb* to conclude that sth has a particular meaning, especially when you think it means more than it really does: *Yes, he's going over to talk to her, but don't read too much into it.*

conclusion *noun* See also the entry for SPECULATION

conclusion · finding · judgment · ruling · verdict · inference · deduction
These are all words for sth that you decide or know is true after considering all the facts of a situation.

PATTERNS AND COLLOCATIONS
▸ a conclusion / findings / a judgment / a ruling / an inference / a deduction **about** sth
▸ a judgment / ruling / verdict **against** / **in favour of** / **on** sb / sth
▸ the conclusion / finding / judgment / ruling / verdict / inference / deduction **that...**
▸ a / the **general** conclusion / finding / verdict / inference / deduction
▸ a / the **correct** / **wrong** conclusion / verdict / inference
▸ a **logical** / **reasonable** / **valid** conclusion / inference / deduction
▸ the **final** conclusion / judgment / ruling / verdict
▸ **reach** a conclusion / judgment / verdict
▸ **make** a judgment / a finding / a ruling / an inference / a deduction
▸ to **give** judgment / a ruling / a verdict
▸ to **challenge** sb's findings / a ruling / a verdict
▸ to **base** your conclusion / findings / judgment / ruling / verdict **on** sth

conclusion /kən'kluːʒn/ [C] something that you decide is true after you have considered all the facts relating to a particular situation: *We can safely draw some conclusions from our discussion.* ◊ *I've* **come to the conclusion** *that he's not the right person for the job.* ◊ *Don't* **jump to conclusions** (= do not decide that sth is true without knowing the facts).

finding [C, usually pl.] information that is discovered as the result of research into sth: *These findings suggest that there is no direct link between unemployment and crime.* ◊ *The findings are based on interviews with more than 2 000 people.* ❶ In formal or legal English a **finding** is also a decision made by the judge or jury in court: *The facts of this case do not justify a finding of negligence.* See also **find** → FIND 1

judgment (also **judgement**) [C, U] the decision of a court or judge: *They are hoping for a judgment in their favour from the European Court of Justice.* ◊ *The court has yet to* **pass judgment** (= to say what its decision is) *in this case.* ❶ The usual spelling of this word in most of its meanings is **judgement** in British English and **judgment** in American English. However, in legal contexts **judgment** is preferred in both British and American English. See also **judge** → JUDGE *verb* 2

ruling [C] an official decision made by sb in a position of authority, especially a judge: *The court will make its ruling on the case next week.* See also **rule** → RULE *verb* 2

verdict [C] a decision that is made by a jury in court, stating if sb is considered guilty of a crime or not; a decision that you make or an opinion that you give about sth, after you have tested it or considered it carefully: *The jury* **returned a verdict** (= gave a verdict) *of not guilty.* ◊ *The coroner* **recorded a verdict** *of accidental death.* ◊ *The panel will give their verdict on the latest video releases.*

NOTE FINDING, JUDGMENT, RULING OR VERDICT? These are all words that can be used for a decision made in court. **Finding** is the most formal and is usually used in the

phrase *a finding of negligence/murder/unfair dismissal,* etc., when a court has decided the nature of a crime or offence that has been committed; **finding** is much more frequent in its non-legal sense of *research findings.* **Judgment** and **ruling** are more general words, used especially to talk about decisions made when a complaint or dispute has been taken to court for a decision. **Judgment** emphasizes that the decision is made by a court, whether by a judge or jury; **ruling** emphasizes that the decision is made by a person in authority, often (but not always) a judge, but NOT by a jury: *The judgment of the jury cannot be overturned.* ◊ *the ruling of the jury.* A **verdict** is the decision made by a jury in criminal cases about whether the person accused of the crime is guilty or not guilty. **Verdict** is also used to talk about the decision of a coroner at an inquest (= an official investigation to find out the cause of sb's death).

inference /'ɪnfərəns/ [C, U] something that you can find out indirectly from what you already know; the act or process of forming an opinion based on what you already know: *What inferences can we draw from this data?* ◊ *If he is guilty then,* **by inference**, *so is his partner* (= it is logical to think so, from the same evidence).

deduction /dɪ'dʌkʃn/ [U, C] the process of using the information that you have in order to understand a particular situation or to find the answer to a problem: *He arrived at the solution by a simple process of deduction.* ◊ *If my deductions are correct, I can tell you who the murderer is.*

NOTE INFERENCE OR DEDUCTION? An **inference** is slightly more uncertain than a **deduction**: it is sth that is probably true, given what you already know. A **deduction** is sth that, logically, has to be true, if the facts you have are correct. Making an **inference** is usually more complicated than making a **deduction**: *He arrived at the solution by a simple process of inference.*

conclusive *adj.* See also the entries for CERTAIN and UNDOUBTED

conclusive · undeniable · indisputable · unquestionable
These words all describe sth that is definitely true and allows no doubt or uncertainty.

PATTERNS AND COLLOCATIONS
▸ conclusive / undeniable / indisputable / unquestionable **that...**
▸ conclusive / undeniable / indisputable / unquestionable **evidence**
▸ conclusive / undeniable / indisputable **proof**
▸ an undeniable / indisputable / unquestionable **fact** / **truth**

conclusive /kən'kluːsɪv/ proving sth and allowing no doubt or uncertainty: *The results of the test were not conclusive* (= they did not prove anything). ◊ *It's difficult to get conclusive evidence of the existence of black holes in space.* **OPP** inconclusive ❶ Something that is **inconclusive** does not lead to a definite decision or result: *inconclusive evidence/results/tests* ◊ *inconclusive talks/discussions*
▸ **conclusively** *adv.*: *He was able to prove conclusively that the virus could be passed to humans.*

undeniable /ˌʌndɪ'naɪəbl/ that definitely exists or is true: *Her charm is undeniable.* ◊ *It's an undeniable fact that drug-related crime is increasing.*
▸ **undeniably** *adv.*: *He was an undeniably attractive young man.*

indisputable /ˌɪndɪ'spjuːtəbl/ (*rather formal*) that definitely exists or is true: *It is indisputable that the crime rate has been rising.* ◊ *The report should distinguish clearly between indisputable fact, firm opinion and mere speculation.* See also **undisputed** → UNDOUBTED, **dispute** → DOUBT *verb*

▶ **indisputably** *adv.*: *The painting is indisputably one of his finest works.*

unquestionable /ʌnˈkwestʃənəbl/ that cannot be doubted: *He is a man of unquestionable honesty and integrity.* **OPP** **questionable** → SUSPICIOUS 2, See also **unquestioned** → UNDOUBTED, **question** → DOUBT *verb*

NOTE **WHICH WORD?** These words are very similar in meaning but there are slight differences in emphasis and register. They can all describe facts or evidence, but **unquestionable** is more often used to describe qualities, **undeniable** is frequently used for both facts and qualities and **indisputable** can also be used for qualities; **conclusive** cannot: ~~conclusive charm/honesty~~. **Undeniable** and **indisputable** both describe facts that are so clearly true that nobody would try to deny them. **Conclusive** describes facts that can be proved and is quite often used in negative statements, when there is *no conclusive proof/evidence.*

condition *noun*

condition · requirement · terms · provision · qualification · prerequisite · proviso · the small print
These are all words for sth that must happen or be agreed to before an agreement can be reached or before sth else can happen.

PATTERNS AND COLLOCATIONS
▶ a condition/requirement/terms/a provision/a prerequisite **for** sth
▶ **under** the conditions/ terms/ provisions **of** sth
▶ **with** the qualification/ proviso **that**…
▶ an **important** condition/ requirement/ provision/ qualification/ prerequisite/ proviso
▶ **strict** conditions/ requirements/ terms/ provisions
▶ the **basic** condition/ requirements/ terms/ provision/ prerequisite
▶ a/an **absolute/essential/necessary** condition/ requirement/ prerequisite
▶ **special** conditions/ requirements/ terms/ provisions
▶ a **legal** requirement/ provision/ prerequisite
▶ to **lay down** conditions/ requirements/ terms/ provisions
▶ to **add** a provision/ proviso/ qualification
▶ to **contain** a requirement/ terms/ provisions/ qualifications/ a proviso
▶ to **accept/observe/comply with** the conditions/requirements/ terms/ provisions
▶ to **satisfy/ fulfil** the conditions/ requirements/ terms

condition [C] a rule or decision that you must agree to, sometimes as part of a contract or official agreement; a situation that must exist in order for sth else to happen: *They agreed to lend us the car* **on condition that** (= only if) *we returned it before the weekend.* ◇ *They will give us the money* **on one condition** *– that we pay it back within six months.* ◇ *(AmE) They agreed* **under the condition that** *the matter be dealt with promptly.* ◇ *Congress can impose strict conditions on the bank.* ◇ *They have agreed to a ceasefire provided their conditions are met.* ◇ *Stable political leadership is a necessary condition for economic growth.*

requirement [C] *(rather formal, especially written)* something that you must have, or a standard that you must meet, in order to be able or allowed to do sth: *What is the minimum entrance requirement for this programme?* ◇ *Be sure to check passport and visa requirements with your travel agent.* See also **require** → DEMAND *verb*

terms [pl.] the conditions that people offer, demand or accept when they make an agreement or contract: *Under the terms of the agreement, their funding of the project will continue until 2009.* ◇ *You should check your* **terms and conditions** *of employment.* See also **terms** → RATE 2

provision [C] *(rather formal, especially written)* a condition or arrangement in a legal document: *The Act contains detailed provisions for appeal against the court's decision.*

qualification [C, U] something that you add to a statement to limit the effect it has or the way it is applied: *I accept his theories, but not without certain qualifications.* ◇ *The plan was approved* **without qualification.** See also **qualify** → ADJUST

prerequisite /ˌpriːˈrekwəzɪt/ [C, usually sing.] *(formal)* something that must exist or happen before sth else can happen or be done: *Flexibility of approach is an important* **prerequisite to** *successful learning.*

proviso /prəˈvaɪzəʊ; AmE -zoʊ/ (pl. **-os**) [C] *(rather formal)* a condition that must be agreed to before an agreement can be made: *He agreed to their visit with the proviso that they should stay no longer than one week.*

the ˌsmall ˈprint *(BrE) (AmE* **the ˌfine ˈprint**) [U] the important details of an agreement or legal document that are usually printed in small type and are therefore easy to miss: *Make sure you* **read the small print** *before signing.*

confidence *noun*

confidence · self-confidence · assertiveness · aplomb · assurance
These are all words for a belief in yourself and your abilities.

PATTERNS AND COLLOCATIONS
▶ **with** confidence/ self-confidence/ aplomb/ assurance
▶ **great** confidence/ self-confidence/ aplomb/ assurance
▶ **growing** confidence/ self-confidence/ assurance
▶ **total** aplomb/ assurance
▶ **quiet/ calm/ easy** confidence/ assurance
▶ sb's **usual** confidence/ aplomb
▶ to **have/ show** confidence/ self-confidence/ assurance
▶ to **lose/ be lacking in/ lack** confidence/ self-confidence
▶ an **air of** confidence/ self-confidence/ assurance

confidence [U] a belief in your own ability to do things and be successful: *He answered the questions with confidence.* ◇ *She has very little* **confidence in** *her own abilities.* ◇ *He* **gained confidence** *when he went to college.* ◇ *Winning the competition really* **boosted** *her* **confidence.**

ˌself-ˈconfidence [U] a belief in yourself and your abilities: *He constantly tried to undermine her self-confidence.* ◇ *A few months living away from home have given him renewed self-confidence.*

NOTE **CONFIDENCE OR SELF-CONFIDENCE?** In many cases you can use either word: *to have/exude/lack/gain/give sb confidence/self-confidence* ◇ *to boost/dent/shake/ undermine sb's confidence/self-confidence*. However, **confidence** can be a belief in your abilities generally, or in your ability to do a particular thing; **self-confidence** can only be a belief in your abilities generally and you cannot 'have self-confidence in sth': *She had no confidence in her ability to persuade anyone.* ◇ ~~She had no self-confidence in her ability to persuade anyone.~~

assertiveness /əˈsɜːtɪvnəs; AmE əˈsɜːrtɪv-/ [U] *(rather formal)* the confidence to express opinions and desires strongly, so that people take notice: *an assertiveness training programme for women managers* ❶ **Assertiveness** is talked about especially in work contexts See also **assertive** → AGGRESSIVE 2

aplomb /əˈplɒm; AmE əˈplɑːm/ [U] *(rather formal, approving)* a confident manner that enables you to succeed in managing difficult situations: *He delivered the speech with his usual aplomb.*

assurance /əˈʃʊərəns; -ˈʃɔːr-; AmE əˈʃʊr-/ [U] a confident manner that shows a belief in your own abilities and strengths: *There was an air of easy assurance and calm about him.*

NOTE **CONFIDENCE OR ASSURANCE?** **Confidence** or **self-confidence** is what you feel when you believe in yourself; **assurance** is the manner and behaviour that shows this feeling.

confident adj.

confident · independent · brash · self-confident
These words all describe sb who is sure about their own ability to do things and be successful.

PATTERNS AND COLLOCATIONS
▸ **very** confident / independent / self-confident

confident feeling sure about your own ability to do things and be successful; showing this: *She was in a relaxed, confident mood.* ◇ *They gave a very confident performance of the piece.* **OPP insecure** → SHY, **nervous** → WORRIED, See also **assertive** → AGGRESSIVE 2
independent confident and free to do things without needing help from other people: *Going away to college has made me much more independent.* ◇ *Students should aim to become more **independent of** their teachers.* See also **independence** → FREEDOM
brash (*disapproving*) confident in an aggressive way: *Beneath his brash exterior, he's still a little boy inside.*
self-'confident [U] having confidence in yourself and your abilities: *a self-confident child*

> **NOTE CONFIDENT** OR **SELF-CONFIDENT Confident** can describe a person or what they do; **self-confident** only describes a person: *a self-confident performance*

confine sb/sth to sth phrasal verb See also
the entry for LIMIT

confine sb/sth to sth · limit · constrain · restrict
These words all mean to keep sb/sth within particular limits.

PATTERNS AND COLLOCATIONS
▸ to confine / limit / restrict sb / sth **to** sth
▸ to confine / limit / restrict **yourself to** sth
▸ to confine / limit / restrict **a discussion / your attention** to sth
▸ **severely** constrained / restricted

confine sb/sth to sth *phrasal verb* [often passive] to keep sb/sth inside the limits of a particular activity, subject or area, especially by making a deliberate decision to do this: *The work will not be confined to the Glasgow area.* ◇ *I will confine myself to looking at the period from 1900 to 1916.* See also **confines** → LIMIT *noun* 2
limit [T, often passive] to control the amount of sth that you or sb can have or use; to make sth exist or happen only in a particular place or within a particular group: *Families are limited to four free tickets each.* ◇ *I've limited myself to 1 000 calories a day to try and lose weight.* ◇ *Violent crime is not limited to big cities.* See also **limit** → LIMIT *noun* 1
constrain /kən'streɪn/ [T, often passive] (*formal*) to force sb/sth to be kept within a particular limit or not to develop properly: *Research has been constrained by a lack of funds.* ◇ *She felt constrained from continuing by the threat of losing her job.* See also **constraint** → LIMIT *noun* 1
restrict [T] to control sth with rules or laws, especially ones that allow only a particular group to do or have sth; to allow yourself or sb to have only a limited amount of sth or to do only a particular kind of activity: *Access to the club is restricted to members only.* ◇ *I restrict myself to one cup of coffee a day.* See also **restriction** → LIMIT *noun* 1

confirm verb

1 His guilty expression confirmed my suspicions.
2 Can you confirm what happened?
3 The walk in the mountains confirmed his fear of heights.

1 confirm · support · bear witness · substantiate · validate · evidence · corroborate · authenticate · testify to sth
These words all mean to provide evidence to help prove that sth is true.

PATTERNS AND COLLOCATIONS
▸ to confirm / validate / authenticate sth **as** sth
▸ to bear witness / testify to sth
▸ to confirm / support / substantiate / corroborate **what...**
▸ to confirm / support / substantiate / validate / corroborate / authenticate a **claim**
▸ to confirm / support / substantiate / validate / corroborate a **theory**
▸ to confirm / support / substantiate / validate an **argument**
▸ to confirm / support / substantiate / corroborate a **story**
▸ to confirm / support / substantiate a **point**
▸ to confirm / support / corroborate a **statement**

confirm [T] to show that a guess or theory is definitely true or correct: *His guilty expression confirmed my suspicions.* ◇ *The results confirm the findings of our earlier research.* **OPP disprove, refute** → DISPROVE
support [T] to help to show that a claim or theory is true or correct: *The witness's story was not supported by the evidence.* See also **support** → EVIDENCE *noun*
bear 'witness *idiom* (*rather formal, written*) to provide evidence of the existence or truth of a feeling, quality or situation: *The crowd of mourners at his funeral bore witness to the great affection in which he was held.*
substantiate /səb'stænʃieɪt/ [T] (*formal*) to provide evidence to prove that a claim or theory is true: *They made accusations which could not be substantiated.*
validate /'vælɪdeɪt/ [T] (*formal*) to prove that a claim or theory is true: *The research findings do not validate the claims made by the manufacturer.*

> **NOTE SUBSTANTIATE** OR **VALIDATE? Substantiate** emphasizes the *substance* (= evidence) behind the claims; **validate** emphasizes the *validity* (= truth or rightness) of the claim. **Validate** is used especially about matters of reason or logic, with words like *theory, argument* and *claim* (especially when it is sb's claim to have a right to sth). **Substantiate** can also be used in this way, but it can also be used about matters of fact, with words like *story* and *claim*, when it is a claim about a fact.

evidence [T, usually passive] (*formal*) to be evidence of sth, especially of a general fact about sth, or a trend (= a general direction in which a situation is changing or developing): *The legal profession is still a largely male world, **as evidenced by** the small number of women judges.* See also **evidence** → EVIDENCE *noun*
corroborate /kə'rɒbəreɪt; AmE -'rɑːb-/ [T, often passive] (*formal*) to provide evidence that supports a claim or theory, especially when sb has been accused of doing sth wrong: *Complaints will be investigated only if there is some corroborating evidence.*
authenticate /ɔː'θentɪkeɪt/ [T] (*rather formal*) to prove that sth such as a document is genuine, real or true: *Experts have authenticated the writing as that of Byron himself.*
'testify to sth *phrasal verb* (*formal*) to be considered as strong evidence that sth is true: *The film testifies to the courage of ordinary people during the war.*

2 confirm · verify · back sb/sth up · certify · bear sb/sth out · testify · vouch for sb/sth
These words all mean to say that you think sth is true because you have evidence for it.

PATTERNS AND COLLOCATIONS
▸ to confirm / verify / certify sth **as** sth
▸ to confirm / verify / certify / bear out / testify **that...**
▸ **It was** confirmed / verified / certified **that...**
▸ to confirm / verify / certify / bear out **what...**
▸ to confirm / verify **whether...**
▸ to confirm / verify / back up / bear out a **claim / statement / theory / story / point**
▸ to **officially** confirm / certify sth

confirm [T] to say that sth is definitely true or correct: *The doctor confirmed my suspicions and prescribed an antibiotic.* ◇ *Rumours of job losses were later confirmed.* ◇

Please write to confirm your reservation (= say that it is definite). ◇ *Has everyone confirmed that they're coming?* ◇ *Can you confirm what happened?* **OPP deny** → DENY
▸ **confirmation** *noun* [U, C]: *I'm still waiting for confirmation of the test results.*

verify /ˈverɪfaɪ/ [T] (*formal*) to say that sth is true or accurate: *Her version of events was verified by neighbours.*

> **NOTE CONFIRM OR VERIFY? Verify** can be close in meaning to **confirm**: *Several witnesses confirmed/ verified his story.* However, **verify** is generally used in more formal and or technical contexts: *Data that would aptly verify or refute this are not available.*

,**back sb/sth 'up** *phrasal verb* (*rather informal*) to say that what sb has said is true; to say or do sth in order to support an opinion, claim or argument: *I'll back you up if they don't believe you.* ◇ *The writer doesn't back up his opinions with examples.*

certify /ˈsɜːtɪfaɪ; *AmE* ˈsɜːrt-/ [I, T] (*formal*) to state officially, especially in writing, that sth is true: *This* (= this document) *is to certify that...* ◇ *He was certified dead on arrival.* ◇ *The accounts were certified as correct by the finance department.*

,**bear sb/sth 'out** *phrasal verb* (*especially BrE, rather formal*) to say or show that sb is right or that sth is true: *The other witnesses will bear me out.* ◇ *The other witnesses will bear out what I say.*

testify /ˈtestɪfaɪ/ [I] (*rather formal*) to say that you believe sth is true because you have evidence of it: *Too many young people are unable to write or spell well, as employers will testify.*

'**vouch for sb/sth** *phrasal verb* (*rather formal*) to say that you believe that sb will behave well and that you will be responsible for their actions; to say that you believe that sth is true or good because you have evidence for it: *Are you willing to vouch for him?* ◇ *I was in bed with the flu. My wife can vouch for that.*

---

3 confirm · settle · decide · clinch
These words all mean to make sb feel or believe sth even more strongly, or make a final decision about sth.

PATTERNS AND COLLOCATIONS
▸ to confirm / settle / clinch an **argument**
▸ to **finally** confirm / settle / decide / clinch sth
▸ That settles / clinches **it**.

confirm [T] to make sb feel or believe sth even more strongly: *The walk in the mountains confirmed his fear of heights.* ◇ *Both teams played badly, which confirms the impression left by earlier games.*

settle [T, often passive] to make a final decision about sth: *Good, that's settled, then.* ◇ (*spoken*) *Bob will be there? That settles it. I'm not coming.*

decide [T] to be the reason why sb does sth: *They offered me free accommodation for a year, and that decided me.* ◇ *That **decided it for** me: I wasn't carrying my bike back up those stairs.*

clinch [T] (*rather informal*) to provide the answer to sth; to settle sth that was not certain: *'I'll pay your air fare.' 'Okay, that clinches it – I'll come with you.'*

conflict *noun*

conflict · contradiction · clash · collision · opposition
These are all words for a situation in which two things are very different from each other and cannot easily exist together.

PATTERNS AND COLLOCATIONS
▸ **in** conflict / contradiction / opposition
▸ a conflict / clash / collision **with** sb / sth
▸ **in** contradiction / opposition **to** sb / sth
▸ conflict / a contradiction / a clash / a collision / an opposition **between** sb / sth
▸ (a / an) **fundamental / apparent** conflict / contradiction / opposition

▸ **in direct** conflict / contradiction / opposition
▸ to **see / create** a conflict / contradiction
▸ to **avoid** a conflict / clash / collision
▸ to **resolve** a conflict / contradiction / clash

conflict [C, U] a situation in which there are opposing ideas, opinions, feelings or wishes: *The story tells of a classic conflict between love and duty.* ◇ *There is often a **conflict of interests** between farmers and conservationists.* ◇ *Many of these ideas appear to be in conflict with each other.*

contradiction [C, U] a situation in which two facts or statements are so different from each other that they cannot both be accepted together as true: *A healthy suntan is a **contradiction in terms**.* ◇ *His public speeches are in direct contradiction to his personal lifestyle.* See also **contradictory** → INCONSISTENT

clash [C] the effect of trying to combine two things that are very different from each other and cannot easily exist together: *Simply put, the conflict comes down to a clash of cultures.* ◇ *Personality clashes led to the break-up of the band.*

collision /kəˈlɪʒn/ [C, U] (*written*) a strong disagreement between two people or between opposing ideas or opinions; the meeting of two things that are very different: *The problem comes from a collision between two opposing points of view.* ◇ *In his work we see the collision of two different traditions.*

> **NOTE CLASH OR COLLISION? A collision** is the meeting of two different things, a **clash** is the negative effect this meeting can have. The effects of a **collision** are sometimes good or interesting: *Australian food is an exciting collision of native, Asian and European cuisines.*

opposition [U, C] (*formal*) the state of being as different as possible; two things that are as different as possible: *Many fairy stories are based on the opposition between good and evil.* ◇ *His poetry is full of oppositions and contrasts.*

conflict *verb* See the Topic Map for CONFLICT on p.896

conflict · contrast · contradict · be at odds · clash · go against sth
These are all words and expressions that can be used when two very different ideas, feelings or personalities come together.

PATTERNS AND COLLOCATIONS
▸ to conflict / contrast / be at odds / clash **with** sth
▸ to be at odds / clash **over** sth
▸ **stories / versions** conflict / contradict each other / are at odds
▸ conflicting / contrasting **opinions / personalities / emotions**

conflict /kənˈflɪkt/ [I] (of two ideas, beliefs, stories, feelings or personalities) to be so different from each other that they cannot easily exist together or both be true: *These results conflict with earlier findings.* ◇ *Reports conflicted on how much of the aid was reaching the famine victims.* ◇ *He was torn between conflicting loyalties to family and work.*

contrast /kənˈtrɑːst; *AmE* -ˈtræst/ [I] (of two things) to show a clear difference when close together or when compared: *Her actions contrasted sharply with her promises.* ◇ *Her actions and her promises contrasted sharply.* See also **contrast** → DIFFERENCE, **contrast** → OPPOSITE *noun*, **contrasting** → DIFFERENT

contradict /ˌkɒntrəˈdɪkt; *AmE* ˌkɑːn-/ [T] (of statements or pieces of evidence) to be so different from each other that they cannot both be true: *The two stories contradict each other.* ◇ *This version of events was contradicted by eyewitness reports.* See also **contradictory** → INCONSISTENT

be at 'odds *idiom* to be very different from sth, when it should be the same: *Her story was at odds with the police report.* See also **at odds** → INCONSISTENT

clash [I] (*rather informal, especially journalism*) (of two ideas, beliefs or personalities) to be so different from each other that they cannot easily exist together and often cause arguments: *He clashed with his father over politics.* ◇ *His views and his father's clashed.*

> **NOTE** CONFLICT OR CLASH? **Conflict** has a wider range and is often used to talk about stories, beliefs and emotions that are very different from each other. **Clash** is more often used to talk about the angry disagreement caused by people having very different opinions. People or their opinions can **clash** but people cannot **conflict**: *He conflicted with his father over politics.*

go a'gainst sth *phrasal verb* (of an idea, belief or action) to not fit or agree with another idea or belief: *Paying for hospital treatment goes against her principles.* ◇ *His thinking goes against all logic.*

confront *verb* See also the entries for FACE and TACKLE

confront · tackle · challenge
These words all mean to face or speak to sb in a difficult or dangerous situation, especially when you show courage or authority.

PATTERNS AND COLLOCATIONS
▶ to confront / tackle / challenge sb **directly**

confront [T] to face sb so that they cannot avoid seeing and hearing you, especially in an unfriendly or dangerous situation: *This was the first time he had confronted an armed robber.*
tackle [T] to speak to sb about a problem or difficult situation, especially when you need them to do sth and you know that it might be hard to persuade them: *I tackled him about the money he owed me.*
challenge [T] to order sb to stop and say who they are or what they are doing: *We were challenged by police at the border.*

confrontation *noun*

confrontation · row · showdown · clash
These are all words for an unfriendly disagreement between two people or groups of people.

PATTERNS AND COLLOCATIONS
▶ a confrontation / row / showdown / clash **with / between** sb / sth
▶ a confrontation / row / showdown / clash **over** sb / sth
▶ a **major** confrontation / row / clash
▶ a **bitter** confrontation / row / clash
▶ to **cause** a confrontation / row
▶ to **avoid** a confrontation / row / showdown / clash
▶ to **face** a row / showdown

confrontation [U, C] a situation in which there is an angry disagreement between people or groups who have different opinions: *Confrontation between employers and unions has resulted in strike action.* ◇ *She wanted to avoid another confrontation with her father.*
row /raʊ/ [C] (*especially BrE, informal, journalism*) a serious disagreement about sth between people or groups of people: *A row has broken out over education.* ❶ A **row** can also be a noisy argument between two people about a personal matter. See also **row** → ARGUMENT 1
showdown /'ʃəʊdaʊn; *AmE* 'ʃoʊ-/ [usually sing.] an argument, fight or test that will settle a disagreement that has lasted for a long time: *Management are facing a showdown with union members today.* ◇ *Fans gathered outside the stadium for the final showdown* (= the game that will decide the winner of the competition).
clash [C] an argument between two people or groups of people who have different beliefs or values: *There has been a head-on clash between the two candidates over education policy.* See also **clash** → CONFLICT *verb*

> **NOTE** ROW OR CLASH? Both of these words are used in journalism. A **row** is a situation that can continue over a long period of time. A **clash** is an event that happens when people with different opinions argue with each other, and is likely to be about sth like policy or principle.

confuse *verb*

confuse · puzzle · bewilder · baffle · mystify · perplex · defeat · stump · beat
These are all words that can be used when you cannot understand or explain sth.

PATTERNS AND COLLOCATIONS
▶ It puzzles / baffles / beats **me how / why...**
▶ It puzzles / baffles **me that...**
▶ What puzzles / baffles / mystifies / beats **me is...**

confuse [T] to make sb feel that they do not understand sth and so cannot think clearly about it: *These instructions confused everyone.* ◇ *Doctors love to confuse us with obscure Latin names and terms.*
puzzle [T] (of a question or strange fact or behaviour) to be too difficult or strange for sb to answer or understand: *This question has puzzled scientists for decades.* ◇ *What puzzles me is why he left without telling anyone.*
bewilder /bɪ'wɪldə(r)/ [T, usually passive] (*rather formal*) to confuse and worry sb because they do not know what is happening or do not know what to do: *His complete lack of interest in money bewilders his family.*
baffle [T] to puzzle you very much: *Scientists are baffled as to why so many young people are affected.*
mystify /'mɪstɪfaɪ/ [T] (*rather formal*) to puzzle you very much: *The popularity of the programme mystifies me.*
perplex /pə'pleks; *AmE* pər'p-/ [T, usually passive] (*rather formal*) to puzzle you very much, especially in a way that makes you feel slightly worried: *That is a question which has perplexed philosophers.*

> **NOTE** CONFUSE, PUZZLE, BEWILDER, BAFFLE, MYSTIFY OR PERPLEX? When sth **confuses** you, it is difficult for you to think clearly and you are not sure what to say or do. With **bewilder** or **perplex** there is a sense of being upset or worried as well as being unable to understand. Something **puzzles** you when you don't know why it has happened or don't know what the answer is. **Baffle** and **mystify** are stronger words than **puzzle**; they suggest that you can't explain or understand sth at all.

defeat [T] (*rather formal*) to be too difficult for sb to understand or answer: *The instruction manual completely defeated me.* ◇ *Question 6 defeated us.*
stump [T, usually passive] (*informal*) to ask sb a question that is too difficult for them to answer or give them a problem that they cannot solve: *At first I was stumped by the question.* ◇ *I'm stumped. I don't know how they got here before us.*
beat [T] (*informal, spoken*) to be sth that you cannot understand or explain or do not know: *It beats me* (= I don't know) *why he did it.* ◇ *'Where's she gone?' 'Beats me.'*

confused *adj.*

1 feel confused about sth
2 a confused account of sth

1 confused · puzzled · at a loss · bewildered · dazed · bemused · perplexed · muddled · disoriented · disorientated
These words all describe the feeling that you cannot understand sth or do not know what is happening.

PATTERNS AND COLLOCATIONS
▶ to be confused / puzzled / perplexed / muddled **about** sth
▶ to be puzzled / bewildered / bemused / perplexed **at** sth

▶ to be confused / puzzled / at a loss / perplexed **as to** how… / why…

▶ a confused / puzzled / bewildered / dazed / bemused / perplexed **expression / look**

▶ puzzled / bewildered / dazed **eyes**

▶ **slightly** confused / puzzled / at a loss / bewildered / dazed / bemused / perplexed / muddled

▶ **rather** confused / puzzled / at a loss / bewildered / bemused

▶ **a little** confused / puzzled / bewildered / dazed / bemused

▶ **totally** confused / bewildered / bemused / disoriented / disorientated

▶ **completely** confused / at a loss / bewildered / disoriented / disorientated

confused feeling that you do not understand sth and so cannot think clearly about it: *People are confused about all the different labels on food these days.* ◊ *I'm confused — say all that again.* ◊ *She was beginning to get rather confused.* ◊ *He was depressed and in a confused state of mind.* See also **confusion** → DOUBT *noun* 1

puzzled unable to understand sth or the reason for sth: *He looked puzzled so I repeated the question.* ◊ *She had a puzzled expression on her face.*

at a 'loss *idiom* not knowing what to say or do: *I'm **at a loss** to explain what happened.* ◊ *Ruth was completely at a loss.* ◊ *His comments left me **at a loss for words.***

bewildered /bɪˈwɪldəd; bɪˈwɪldərd/ (*rather formal*) confused and worried because you do not know what is happening or do not know what to do: *She was totally bewildered by the whole affair.*

dazed /deɪzd/ unable to think clearly, especially because of a shock or because you have been hit on the head: *Survivors waited for the rescue boats, dazed and frightened.*

bemused /bɪˈmjuːzd/ looking as if you are confused and do not know what is happening: *Her bizarre performance left the audience looking bemused.*

perplexed /pəˈplekst; AmE pərˈp-/ (*rather formal*) very puzzled, especially in a way that makes you feel slightly worried: *We are all perplexed as to how this happened.*

muddled (*especially BrE*) not clear in your mind about which thing is which: *There were so many names that she became hopelessly muddled.* ◊ *This is the result of **muddled thinking.***

disoriented /dɪsˈɔːrientɪd/ (*rather formal*) feeling confused and not able to understand what is happening around you: *The patient appeared disoriented.*

disorientated /dɪsˈɔːrienteɪtɪd/ (*BrE, rather formal*) disoriented: *She felt shocked and totally disorientated.* ❶ In British English **disorientated** is more frequent than **disoriented**, although both forms are used. In American English only **disoriented** is used.

---

2 confused · discursive · disjointed · rambling · incoherent · woolly · jumbled

These words all describe thought, speech or writing that does not have a clear structure.

PATTERNS AND COLLOCATIONS

▶ confused / disjointed / rambling / incoherent / jumbled **thoughts**

▶ disjointed / incoherent / jumbled **words**

▶ rambling / incoherent **speech**

▶ a confused / rambling **account** of sth

confused (of thoughts, a description or a situation) not clear or easy to understand: *The children gave a confused account of the events of the previous day.* ◊ *A confused situation followed the military coup.*

discursive /dɪsˈkɜːsɪv; AmE -ˈkɜːrs-/ (*formal*) (of a style of writing or speaking) moving from one point to another without any strict structure: *Poetry is closer to music than to the more extended and discursive literary forms.*

disjointed (of different things or the parts of sth) not having a clear or logical connection with each other: *Disjointed words and phrases jumped out at her.*

rambling (*disapproving*) (of speech or writing) very long and confused: *The letter was long and rambling.*

incoherent /ˌɪnkəʊˈhɪərənt; AmE ˌɪnkoʊˈhɪr-/ (*often disapproving*) (of ideas or systems) not logical or well organized: *The theory was outdated and incoherent.* **OPP** **coherent** → RATIONAL

woolly (*AmE also* **wooly**) /ˈwʊli/ (of people or their ideas or statements) not thinking clearly; not clearly defined or expressed: *The Government have been woolly about the exact meaning of their proposals.* ◊ *You should challenge any vague and woolly replies.*

jumbled /ˈdʒʌmbld/ (of words or thoughts) not in the correct order; confused: *She tried to rearrange her jumbled thoughts.*

confusing *adj.*

confusing · incomprehensible · puzzling · bewildering · inexplicable · unintelligible · baffling
These words all describe things or experiences that are difficult to understand.

PATTERNS AND COLLOCATIONS

▶ confusing / incomprehensible / puzzling / bewildering / inexplicable / baffling **to** sb

▶ confusing / puzzling / bewildering / baffling **for** sb

▶ confusing / incomprehensible / puzzling / bewildering / inexplicable / baffling **that** …

▶ a confusing / bewildering **experience / variety**

▶ incomprehensible / unintelligible **language**

▶ a puzzling / baffling **problem**

▶ **for some** incomprehensible / inexplicable **reason**

▶ **totally** confusing / incomprehensible / bewildering / inexplicable / unintelligible

▶ **quite** confusing / incomprehensible / puzzling / bewildering / baffling

▶ **rather / somewhat** confusing / puzzling / bewildering / baffling

confusing (of information or experience) difficult to understand: *The news bulletins were confusing, giving different versions of what was happening.* ◊ *It was all very confusing.* ◊ *The signposts are confusing for people who don't know the area.* ◊ *She experienced a confusing mixture of emotions.* **OPP** **clear** → CLEAR 2, See also **confusion** → DOUBT *noun* 1

▶ **confusingly** *adv.*: *The biology lectures were in a big hall, confusingly called the Physics Theatre.*

incomprehensible /ɪnˌkɒmprɪˈhensəbl; AmE -ˌkɑːm-/ impossible to understand: *Their dialect is incomprehensible to most speakers of Standard English.* ◊ *From a child's point of view, adult behaviour is often just as incomprehensible.* **OPP** **comprehensible** → CLEAR 2

puzzling (of language or behaviour) difficult to understand or explain: *I had noticed something puzzling.* ◊ *Marlowe was a puzzling character.* ❶ **Puzzling** is used especially to describe problems or a particular feature of a situation. Collocates include *problem, question, aspect,* and *feature.* See also **puzzle** → MYSTERY

bewildering /bɪˈwɪldərɪŋ/ making you feel confused because there is too much choice or because sth is difficult to understand: *Voters have a bewildering array of 116 parties to choose from.* ◊ *The complexity of these 'simplest' forms of life is bewildering.* ❶ **Bewildering** is used especially about the *number, range* or *speed* of sth. Collocates also include *array, choice, variety, rapidity* and *complexity.*

inexplicable /ˌɪnɪkˈsplɪkəbl/ (of events, behaviour or feelings) impossible to explain or understand: *He was shocked at the sudden, inexplicable sense of loss he felt.* ◊ *For some inexplicable reason her mind went completely blank.*

▶ **inexplicably** *adv.*: *The switch had inexplicably turned itself on.*

unintelligible /ˌʌnɪnˈtelɪdʒəbl/ (of sounds, speech or writing) impossible to understand: *She murmured something unintelligible.* ◊ *Dolphin sounds are unintelligible to humans.* **OPP** **intelligible** → CLEAR 2

baffling (of a fact or event) confusing because it is too strange or difficult to understand or explain: *He is still the chief suspect in this baffling case.*

connection noun

connection · junction · seam · joint · join · link
These words all mean the point or line where two things are joined together.

PATTERNS AND COLLOCATIONS
▸ a connection / junction / seam / joint / join **between** sth and sth
▸ a **loose** connection / joint

connection [C] a point, especially in an electrical, telephone or computer system, where two parts connect: *A faulty connection caused the machine to stop.* ◇ *Sorry, could you repeat that? This is a very bad connection.*
▸ **connect** verb [T]: *First connect the printer to the computer.* ◇ *We're waiting for the telephone to be connected.* **OPP disconnect** → TURN STH OFF

junction /'dʒʌŋkʃn/ [C] a place where two or more cables, etc. meet or are joined: *The telephone junction box was opened and the phone line was disconnected.* ◇ *The disease affects the junction between nerves and muscles.*

seam [C] a line where two things are joined together, especially a line of sewing joining two pieces of fabric or leather: *Finish the edges before sewing the shoulder seam.*

joint [C] a place where two or more parts of an object are joined together, especially to form a corner: *The joint was sealed with waterproof tape.*

join [C] a place where two things are fixed together: *The two pieces were stuck together so well that you could hardly see the join.* See also **join** → LINK verb 2

NOTE JOINT OR JOIN? A **joint** is part of the structure of sth; it is usually carefully made in a particular way and the two parts often meet at an angle to form a corner. A **join** is usually made from necessity, not design, for example because sth has broken, or in order to put two pieces of sth together to make a larger piece; the two parts often meet in a straight line.

link [C] one of the rings of a chain: *The chain was too long so I removed a few of the links.*

conscientious adj.

conscientious · hard-working · meticulous · painstaking · diligent · thorough · industrious
These words all describe people showing care and effort in their work or duties.

PATTERNS AND COLLOCATIONS
▸ conscientious / meticulous **about** sth
▸ meticulous / thorough **in** sth
▸ a conscientious / a hard-working / a diligent / an industrious **person**
▸ a conscientious / hard-working / diligent **student**
▸ a conscientious / meticulous / diligent **worker**
▸ a hard-working / diligent **member** (of staff, a team, etc.)
▸ conscientious / meticulous / painstaking / diligent **work**
▸ meticulous / painstaking **research** / **attention**
▸ **very** conscientious / hard-working / diligent / thorough / industrious

conscientious /ˌkɒnʃi'enʃəs; AmE ˌkɑːn-/ taking care to do things carefully and correctly: *She was a popular and conscientious teacher.* ◇ *He was thorough and conscientious, rather than brilliant.*
▸ **conscientiously** adv.: *She performed all her duties conscientiously.*

hard-'working putting a lot of effort into your work and doing it well: *I want to stand up for all the decent, hard-working families in this country.*

meticulous /mə'tɪkjələs/ (rather formal) paying careful attention to every detail: *He's always meticulous in keeping the records up to date.* ◇ *The room had been prepared with meticulous care.*
▸ **meticulously** adv.: *a meticulously planned schedule*

painstaking /'peɪnzteɪkɪŋ/ [usually before noun] needing or giving a lot of care, effort and attention to detail: *The event had been planned with painstaking attention to detail.*

diligent /'dɪlɪdʒənt/ (formal) working hard and showing care in your work or duties: *After a diligent search, the police found the missing child.*
▸ **diligently** adv.: *They worked diligently on the task they had been given.*

thorough [not usually before noun] doing things very carefully and with great attention to detail: *He was determined to be thorough in his research.* See also **thorough** → DETAILED

industrious /ɪn'dʌstriəs/ (rather formal) working hard; busy: *She was surrounded by energetic, industrious people.*
▸ **industriously** adv.: *The three of them worked industriously, cutting, stitching and shaping the leather.*

conservative adj. See also the entry for TRADITIONAL

conservative · conventional · traditionalist · conformist
These words all describe people whose behaviour is not different from that of most other people and who may therefore be considered boring.

PATTERNS AND COLLOCATIONS
▸ conservative / conventional / traditionalist **thinkers** / **views** / **values**
▸ conventional / conformist **behaviour**
▸ **very** / **highly** conservative / conventional

conservative /kən'sɜːvətɪv; AmE -'sɜːrv-/ opposed to great or sudden social change; showing that you prefer traditional styles and values: *They were conservative in their political outlook.* ◇ *Popular taste in art remained conservative.* **OPP radical, progressive** → RADICAL
▸ **conservatively** adv.: *He was conservatively dressed in a dark suit.*

conventional (often disapproving) tending to follow what is done or considered acceptable by society in general and therefore not interesting or original: *The imagery in the poem is somewhat conventional.* ◇ *They rejected what they saw as the hypocrisy of conventional society.* **OPP unconventional** → UNUSUAL
▸ **conventionally** adv.: *She was not a conventionally beautiful girl.*

traditionalist (rather formal) believing that customs and tradition are more important than modern ideas: *The proposals appeal to traditionalist teachers.*

conformist (often disapproving) behaving and seeming to think in the same way as most other people; not wanting to be different: *Don't forget how conformist and resistant to change many people are.*

consider verb

consider · think · look at sth · wonder · reflect · ponder · contemplate · take · deliberate · mull sth over · meditate
These words all mean to use your mind in order to try to understand sth, make a decision, solve a problem, etc.

PATTERNS AND COLLOCATIONS
▸ to think / reflect / ponder / deliberate / meditate **on** sth
▸ to think / ponder / deliberate / mull / meditate **over** sth
▸ to think / wonder / ponder / contemplate **about** sth
▸ to consider / think / look at / wonder / reflect / ponder / contemplate / deliberate **how / what / whether…**
▸ to consider / think / reflect **that…**
▸ to consider / think / look at sth / reflect / ponder **carefully / briefly**
▸ to consider / think / look at sth / reflect / contemplate **seriously**
▸ to think / look at sth / reflect / ponder / deliberate **long and hard**

consider [T, I] to think carefully about sth, especially in order to make a decision: *She considered her options.* ◇ *Let us consider the facts.* ◇ *It was a carefully considered decision.* ◇ *We're considering buying a new car.* ◇ *He was considering what to do next.* ◇ *I'd like some time to consider.* See also **consider → REGARD**

think [I] to use your mind to form connected ideas, to make a decision or to try to solve problems: *Are animals able to think?* ◇ *Let me think* (= Give me time before I answer). ◇ *I can't tell you now – I'll have to **think about it**.* ◇ *She had thought very deeply about this problem.* ◇ *All he ever thinks about is money.* ◇ *I'm sorry, I wasn't thinking* (= said when you have upset or offended sb accidentally). ◇ *He was trying to think what to do.* ❶ **Think** is also used, especially in the progressive tenses, when you have ideas, words or images in your mind: *You're very quiet. What are you thinking?* ◇ *I was just thinking what a long way it is.* ◇ *'I must be crazy,' she thought.*

'look at sth *phrasal verb* to consider, think about or study sth, especially in order to learn sth useful or important: *The implications of the new law will need to be looked at.* ◇ *I suggest the government looks long and hard at this new report.* ◇ *In this chapter we will be looking at three different theories.* See also **look at sth → REGARD**

wonder [I, T] to think about sth and try to decide what is true, what will happen or what you should do: *I wonder who she is.* ◇ *'Why do you want to know?' 'No particular reason. I was just wondering.'* ◇ *We were wondering about next April for the wedding.*

reflect [I, T] (*rather formal*) to think carefully about sth, in order to make a decision, understand sth or realize sth: *Before I decide, I need time to reflect.* ◇ *She was left to reflect on the implications of her decision.* ◇ *I paused to reflect how I would answer that question.* ❶ **Reflect** cannot be used with a noun phrase as object. Instead you must use *on*, *upon*, *that* or *how*.: ~~She reflected the implications.~~ See also **reflection → REASONING**

ponder [I, T] (*especially written*) to think carefully about sth, especially in order to understand it: *She pondered over his words.* ◇ *The senator pondered the question for a moment.*

contemplate /'kɒntəmpleɪt; AmE 'kɑːn-/ [T, I] to think about sth that is a possibility; to think deeply about sth for a long time: *He's only 55, but he's already contemplating retirement* (= thinking about whether he should retire). ◇ *The thought of war is too awful to contemplate* (= to think about and accept as a possibility). ◇ *She lay in bed, contemplating.*

take [T] (used especially in instructions) to consider sb/sth as an example: *Lots of couples have problems in the first year of marriage. Take Ann and Paul.*

deliberate /dɪ'lɪbəreɪt/ [I] (*rather formal*) to think about or discuss sth carefully, usually before making a decision: *The jury deliberated for five days before finding him guilty.* ❶ **Deliberate** is mainly used when a group of people, such as a jury in court, think about and discuss sth together because they have to make a decision.

,mull sth 'over *phrasal verb* to spend time thinking carefully about sth such as a plan or proposal: *I need some time to mull it over before making a decision.*

meditate /'medɪteɪt/ [I] to think deeply, usually in silence, especially for religious reasons or in order to make your mind calm: *She meditates for half an hour every evening to help herself relax after work.* ❶ **Meditate** can also be used with an object to mean 'to consider doing sth or plan sth in your mind'. This meaning is more formal, used mainly in written English: *They were meditating revenge.*

consideration noun

consideration · thought · look · deliberation ·
reflection · meditation · contemplation
These are all words for the act of thinking carefully about sth.

▶ **after** (some, etc.) consideration / thought / deliberation / reflection / contemplation
▶ **on** consideration / reflection
▶ to be **for** (sb's) consideration / deliberation / contemplation
▶ (a) **serious** consideration / thought / look / deliberation / reflection / contemplation
▶ (a) **careful** consideration / thought / look / deliberation / reflection
▶ **quiet** consideration / thought / deliberation / reflection / meditation / contemplation
▶ **deep** consideration / thought / reflection / meditation / contemplation
▶ to **give sth** some consideration / some thought / a look
▶ to be **deep / lost in** thought / meditation / contemplation
▶ a **moment's** consideration / thought / reflection

consideration /kən,sɪdə'reɪʃn/ [U, C, usually sing.] (*rather formal*) an act of thinking carefully about sth, especially in order to make a decision about it: *Careful consideration should be given to matters of health and safety.* ◇ *Don't forget to **take** the cost of insurance **into consideration**.* ◇ *The plan is currently **under consideration*** (= being considered). ◇ *There needs to be a consideration of the legal issues involved.*

thought [U] the power or process of thinking; the act of thinking seriously and carefully about sth: *A good teacher always encourages independent thought.* ◇ *She was lost in thought* (=thinking very hard about sth and not paying attention to anything else). ◇ *I've been giving the matter careful thought.* ◇ *Not enough thought has gone into this assignment.*

look [C, usually sing.] an act of considering sth: *We'll be taking a close look at the proposals.* ◇ *We need to take a long hard look at all the facts.*

deliberation /dɪ,lɪbə'reɪʃn/ [U, C, usually pl.] (*formal*) the process of carefully considering or discussing sth in order to make a decision about it: *After much deliberation, we have decided to award the title to Springfield College.* ◇ *The jury's deliberations lasted over five days.*

reflection [U] (*rather formal*) careful thought about sth, sometimes over a long period of time: *She decided, on reflection, not to take the job.* ◇ *A period of calm reflection is now needed.*

meditation /,medɪ'teɪʃn/ [U] (*rather formal*) the practice of thinking deeply in silence, especially for religious reasons or in order to make your mind calm: *He was deep in meditation and didn't see me come.* ◇ *More and more people **practise meditation** on a regular basis.*

contemplation /,kɒntəm'pleɪʃn; AmE ,kɑːn-/ [U] (*rather formal*) the act of thinking deeply and quietly about sth: *He sat by the window, deep in contemplation.* ◇ *The monks dedicate themselves to a life of prayer and contemplation.*

consist of sb/sth *phrasal verb*

consist of sb/sth · comprise · make up sth · constitute ·
be composed of sb/sth · have
These words all mean to be formed from the things or people mentioned, or to be the parts that form sth.

▶ **The group** consists of / comprises / is made up of / is composed of / has **ten people**.
▶ **Ten people** make up / constitute / comprise **the group**.

con'sist of sb/sth *phrasal verb* [no passive] (not used in the progressive tenses) to be formed from the things, people or activities mentioned: *Their diet consists largely of vegetables.* ◇ *Most of the fieldwork consisted of making tape recordings.*

comprise /kəm'praɪz/ [T, no passive] (not used in the progressive tenses) (*rather formal*) to be formed from the things or people mentioned: *The collection comprises 327 paintings.* ❶ **Comprise** can also be used to refer to the parts or members of sth: *Older people comprise a large proportion of those living in poverty. However, this use is less frequent.*

,make 'up sth *phrasal verb* (not used in the progressive tenses) (*rather informal*) to be the parts or people that form sth: *Women make up 56% of the student numbers.* ◇ *She wore a necklace made up of hundreds of glass beads.* See also **make-up** → STRUCTURE

constitute /'kɒnstɪtjuːt; *AmE* 'kɑːnstətuːt/ [T] (not used in the progressive tenses) to be the parts or people that form sth: *People under the age of 40 constitute the majority of the labour force.*

be com'posed of sb/sth *phrasal verb* (not used in the progressive tenses) (*rather formal*) to be formed from the things or people mentioned: *Our inspection teams are composed of the most qualified and experienced experts available.* ◇ *Around 15% of our diet is composed of protein.* See also **composition** → STRUCTURE

have (also **have got**) [T] (not used in the progressive tenses) to be formed from the people or things mentioned: *In 2006 the party had 10 000 members.*

> **NOTE** **WHICH WORD? Consist of sb/sth** is the most general of these words and the only one that can be used for activities with the *-ing* form of a verb: *My life at that time just consisted of feeding the baby and washing nappies.* The other main difference is between those verbs that take the whole as the subject and the parts as the object: *The group consists of/comprises/is made up of/is composed of/has ten people.* and those that take the parts as the subject and the whole as the object: *Ten people make up/constitute/comprise the group.* It is NOT correct to use 'comprises of' or 'is composed by/from'.

conspiracy *noun*

conspiracy · scheme · plot · intrigue · collusion · sting
These are all words for a secret plan to do sth illegal or harmful, or to deceive sb.

PATTERNS AND COLLOCATIONS
▸ a conspiracy / a plot / intrigue **against** sb
▸ a conspiracy / collusion **between** people / groups
▸ a conspiracy / scheme / plot **to do sth**
▸ (an) **alleged** conspiracy / scheme / plot / intrigue / collusion
▸ (a) **political** / **international** conspiracy / plot / intrigue
▸ to **be involved in** a conspiracy / a scheme / a plot / intrigue / collusion / a sting
▸ to **engage in** a conspiracy / a scheme / a plot / intrigue
▸ to **uncover** a conspiracy / scheme / plot

conspiracy /kən'spɪrəsi/ [C, U] a secret plan by a group of people to do sth illegal or harmful: *He claimed there had been a conspiracy to overthrow the government.* ◇ *They were charged with conspiracy to murder.* ◇ *A lot of people subscribe to the **conspiracy theory** (= believe that a conspiracy is responsible for a particular event).* See also **conspirator** → ACCOMPLICE, **conspire** → PLOT *verb*

scheme /skiːm/ [C] a plan for getting money or some other advantage for yourself, especially one that involves deceiving other people: *Police uncovered a scheme to steal paintings worth more than $250 000.* See also **scheme** → PLOT *verb*, **ploy** → TACTIC

plot [C] a secret plan by a group of people to do sth illegal or harmful: *The military had foiled an assassination plot against the president.* See also **plot** → PLOT *verb*

> **NOTE** **CONSPIRACY OR PLOT?** Both of these words are used about secret plans to remove sb from a position of power, although a **plot** may be more likely to involve murder and violence. (You can talk about *an assassination plot* but NOT: ~~an assassination conspiracy~~.) **Conspiracy**, but NOT **plot**, is also used to talk about plans by people in power to keep sth secret.

intrigue /'ɪntriːg; ɪn'triːg/ [U, C] (*especially written*) the activity of making secret plans in order to achieve an aim, often by deceiving people; a secret plan or relationship, especially one which involves sb else being deceived: *The young heroine steps into a web of intrigue in the academic world.* ◇ *Sexual intrigues were almost part of the culture of high politics.*

collusion /kə'luːʒn/ [U] (*formal*) a secret agreement, especially in order to do sth dishonest or to deceive people: *The police were operating **in collusion with** the drug dealers.* See also **colllude** → PLOT *verb*

sting [C] (*especially AmE*) a clever secret plan by the police to catch criminals; a clever plan by criminals to cheat people out of a lot of money: *The FBI conducted a sting operation to catch heroin dealers in Detroit.*

contempt *noun*

contempt · scorn · disdain · mockery · ridicule · disrespect · derision
These are all words for a feeling that sb/sth does not deserve respect or comments which make fun of sb/sth.

PATTERNS AND COLLOCATIONS
▸ contempt / scorn / disdain / disrespect **for** sb / sth
▸ scorn / mockery / derision **from** sb
▸ **with** contempt / scorn / disdain / mockery / ridicule / disrespect / derision
▸ **in** scorn / disdain / mockery / derision
▸ **gentle** mockery / ridicule / derision
▸ to **risk / invite** (sb's) contempt / scorn / ridicule / derision
▸ to **show** contempt / scorn / disdain / disrespect
▸ to **treat sb / sth with** contempt / disdain / ridicule / disrespect
▸ to **feel** contempt / scorn / disdain
▸ an **object of** scorn / ridicule / derision

contempt /kən'tempt/ [U, sing.] a strong feeling of dislike that you have for sb/sth because you think they are without value and deserve no respect at all: *She looked at him with barely disguised contempt.* ◇ *I shall treat that remark with the contempt it deserves.* ◇ *Politicians seem to be generally **held in contempt** by the police.* ◇ *His treatment of his children is **beneath contempt** (= so unacceptable that it is not even worth feeling contempt for).* ◇ *They had shown a contempt for the values she thought important.* OPP **respect** → RESPECT, See also **contemptible** → DESPICABLE

scorn [U] a strong feeling that sb/sth is stupid or not good enough and deserves no respect, usually shown by the way you speak: *Opposition politicians **poured scorn** on the proposals.* ◇ *She was unable to hide the scorn in her voice.*

disdain /dɪs'deɪn/ [U, sing.] (*rather formal*) a feeling that sth is not good enough for you and does not deserve respect or attention: *She turned her head away in disdain.* ◇ *Imitation jewellery is regarded with disdain.*
▸ **disdain** *verb* [T]: *He disdained his offer of help.*

mockery [U] unkind comments, laughter or actions that are intended to make sb/sth look stupid or ridiculous: *They left themselves open to mockery from the left-wing press.* ◇ *There was a **hint of mockery** in his voice.* See also **mock** → LAUGH AT SB/STH

ridicule /'rɪdɪkjuːl/ [U] unkind comments that are intended to make people laugh at sb: *She might find herself exposed to **public ridicule**.* ◇ *She soon became an object of ridicule.* See also **ridicule** → LAUGH AT SB/STH *phrasal verb*, **ridiculous** → RIDICULOUS

disrespect [U, sing.] (*rather formal*) a lack of respect for sb/sth: *They have shown a total disrespect for the law.* ◇ *I mean no **disrespect to** the team, but their performance was poor.* OPP **respect** → RESPECT, See also **disrespectful** → RUDE

derision /dɪ'rɪʒn/ [U] (*rather formal*) unkind laughter or comments that show you think sth is ridiculous and not worth considering seriously: *He snorted in derision.* ◇ *The statement was met with **hoots of derision**.*

> **NOTE** **WHICH WORD? Contempt, scorn** and **disdain** put the emphasis on showing that you have no respect for sb/sth rather than laughing at them. **Contempt** suggests a strong feeling of dislike. **Disdain** and **scorn** involve rejecting sth because it is not good enough. **Disdain** suggests a sense of your own superiority; a

person's **scorn** for sth is often shown by the things they say. **Mockery**, **ridicule** and **derision** put the emphasis on making sb/sth look silly. **Mockery** and **ridicule** invite other people to laugh at sb/sth. **Derision** is a more formal word and emphasizes that sth is being greeted with laughter because it is not worth taking seriously.

contemptuous *adj.*

contemptuous · scathing · mocking · scornful · withering · derisive · disdainful
These words all describe sb who feels or shows that sb/sth is not good enough to deserve their respect or attention.

PATTERNS AND COLLOCATIONS
▸ contemptuous/ scathing/ scornful/ disdainful **of** sb/ sth
▸ a contemptuous/ scathing/ mocking/ scornful/ withering/ disdainful **look/ glance**
▸ a contemptuous/ mocking/ derisive/ disdainful **smile**
▸ a contemptuous/ mocking/ scornful/ derisive **laugh**
▸ a contemptuous/ scathing/ mocking/ scornful **tone**
▸ a contemptuous/ derisive/ disdainful **attitude**
▸ a scathing/ withering/ derisive **remark**

contemptuous /kən'temptʃuəs/ (*especially written*) feeling or showing that you have no respect for sb/sth: *You're contemptuous of everything I do.* ◇ *The company has shown a contemptuous disregard for Henry's complaints.*
▸ **contemptuously** *adv.*: *She laughed contemptuously.*
scathing /'skeɪðɪŋ/ criticizing sb/sth very severely: *He was scathing about the government's performance.* ◇ *She launched a **scathing attack** on the new management.*
▸ **scathingly** *adv.*: *'Oh, she's just a kid,' he said scathingly.*
mocking (of sb's behaviour or expression) showing that you think sb/sth is ridiculous: *Her voice was faintly mocking.* ◇ *The sound of **mocking laughter** followed her as she left the room.* See also **mock** → LAUGH AT SB/STH
scornful feeling or showing that you think sb/sth is stupid or not good enough to deserve your respect or attention: *He was scornful of such 'female' activities as cooking.* ◇ *'Oh — them,' Oliver sounded scornful.*
▸ **scornfully** *adv.*: *She laughed scornfully.*
withering /'wɪðərɪŋ/ [usually before noun] (*written*) (of a look, remark or attitude) intended to make sb feel silly or ashamed: *He treated the club directors with withering contempt.* ◇ *She gave him a withering look.*
derisive /dɪ'raɪsɪv/ unkind and showing that you think sb/sth is ridiculous: *She gave a short, derisive laugh.*
disdainful /dɪs'deɪnfl/ feeling or showing that you think sb/sth is not good enough to deserve your respect or attention: *She's always been disdainful of people who haven't been to college.*

context *noun*

context · background · backdrop · setting · milieu
These are all words for the situation in which sth exists or happens.

PATTERNS AND COLLOCATIONS
▸ **in** (a) context/ a setting/ a milieu
▸ **against** a background/ backdrop
▸ **cultural/ historical/ economic/ political** context/ background/ setting/ milieu
▸ to **provide (sb with)** a context/ background/ backdrop/ setting
▸ to **describe** the context/ background/ setting

context [C, U] the situation in which sth exists, happens or is placed, especially when it helps you to understand it: *This speech needs to be set **in the context of** Britain in the 1960s.* ◇ *His decision can only be understood **in context**.* ◇ *Such databases are being used in a wide range of contexts.*
▸ **contextualize** (*BrE* also **-ise**) /kən'tekstʃuəlaɪz/ *verb* [T]: (*formal*) *As important as the photograph is a caption to contextualize the image.*

background [C, usually sing., U] the situation that existed before a particular event happened, which helps to explain why it happened; information about this situation: *The book explains the complex historical background to the war.* ◇ *The elections are taking place against a background of violence.* ◇ *Encyclopedias are a good source of **background information**.* ◇ *Can you give me more background on the company's financial position?* See also **background** → BACKGROUND
backdrop [C] (*written*) the general situation in which a particular event happens, which sometimes helps to explain this event: *It was against this backdrop of racial tension that the civil war began.*

NOTE BACKGROUND OR BACKDROP? **Background** has a much wider range than **backdrop**, which is used especially in more literary texts and in the phrase *against a backdrop of sth*: ~~backdrop information~~ ◇ ~~Can you give me more backdrop?~~

setting [C] the place and time at which the action of sth such as a play, novel or film happens; the situation in which sth exists or happens: *It is the first story she has written with a contemporary setting.* ◇ *The writer fails to place the events in their wider political setting.*
▸ **set** *verb* [T, usually passive]: *The movie is set in Los Angeles in the year 2019.*
milieu /miː'ljɜː/ (pl. **milieux**) or (pl. **milieus** /-'ljɜːz/) [C, usually sing.] (from *French*, *formal*) the social environment that you live or work in: *The findings of the report refer to a particular social and cultural milieu.* See also the entry for ENVIRONMENT

continue *verb*

1 The rain continued all day.
2 continue fighting
3 the story continues

1 continue · take · last · go on · carry on · keep on · drag on
These words all mean to still be happening over a period of time.

PATTERNS AND COLLOCATIONS
▸ to continue/last/go on/carry on/keep on/drag on **for** hours/a week/ two years, etc.
▸ to continue/ last/ go on / carry on/ keep on/ drag on **until** morning/ next year, etc.
▸ to continue/ last **into** the night/ next week, etc.
▸ to take/ last **a few minutes/ an hour/ all day/ years, etc.**

continue [I] (*rather formal, especially written*) to keep existing or happening without stopping: *The exhibition continues until 25 July.* ◇ *The rain will continue into the evening.* ◇ *The rain **continued to** fall all afternoon.* ◇ *The rain continued falling all afternoon.* **OPP** suspend → STOP 3
take [T, I] to need a particular amount of time: *The journey to the airport takes about half an hour.* ◇ *It takes about half an hour to get to the airport.* ◇ *It took her three hours to repair her bike.* ◇ *It'll **take time** (= take a long time) for her to recover from the illness.* ◇ *I need a shower — I **won't take long**.*
last [T, I] (not used in the progressive tenses) to continue for a particular period of time: *Each game lasts (for) about an hour.* ◇ *The trial is expected to last until the end of the week.* ◇ *The celebrations lasted well into the next week.* ◇ *How long does the play last?*
go 'on *phrasal verb* (*especially spoken*) (of a situation) to continue without changing, especially when you feel that it needs to change: *This cannot be allowed to go on.* ◇ *How much longer will this hot weather go on for?* ◇ *We **can't go on like this** — we seem to be always arguing.*
carry 'on *phrasal verb* (*especially BrE, especially spoken*) to continue moving: *Carry on until you get to the junction, then turn left.*

,keep 'on *phrasal verb* (*especially spoken*) to continue: *The rain kept on all day.* ◇ *Keep on until you get to the church.* ❶ **Keep on** sometimes suggests that sb/sth continues for a long time in a very determined and/or annoying way.

,drag 'on *phrasal verb* (**-gg-**) (*disapproving*) to go on for too long: *The dispute has dragged on for months.*

---

2 continue · keep · go on with sth/go on doing sth · proceed · pursue · carry (sth) on · keep sth up/keep up with sth · press ahead/on · stick with sb/sth
These words all mean to do sth without stopping over a period of time.

PATTERNS AND COLLOCATIONS
▸ to continue/keep on/go on/proceed/carry on/keep up/press ahead/stick **with** sth
▸ to continue/keep/go on/carry on/press ahead with **doing sth**
▸ to continue/go on/proceed/pursue/carry on/keep up/press ahead (with) the/your **work**
▸ to continue/go on with/pursue/carry on/keep up a **conversation**
▸ to continue/proceed/pursue/carry on/press ahead (with) **plans**
▸ to continue/proceed/pursue/carry on/press ahead/stick (with) a **policy**
▸ to proceed/pursue/press ahead (with) **legislation**
▸ to continue/proceed/pursue/carry on (with) an **investigation**
▸ to continue/pursue/carry on/keep up a **relationship/tradition**
▸ to continue/keep/go on/carry on **fighting/working/talking/improving sth/believing/building sth**
▸ to continue/go on/carry on **regardless**

continue [T, I] (*rather formal*) to not stop doing sth: *She wanted to continue working after the baby was born.* ◇ *He continued to ignore everything I was saying.* ◇ *The board of enquiry is continuing its investigations.* ◇ *Are you going to continue with the project?*

keep [T, I] (*especially spoken*) to continue doing sth; to do sth repeatedly: *Keep smiling!* ◇ *I wish you wouldn't keep on interrupting me!* ◇ *I want to keep on with part-time work for as long as possible.* ❶ In spoken English *keep doing sth* is much more frequent than *continue doing sth*, which sounds rather formal. In this meaning **keep** is always followed by a verb in the *-ing* form; by *on* + a verb in the *-ing* form, or by *on with sth*.

,go 'on with sth, go on doing sth *phrasal verb* to continue an activity without stopping: *She shrugged and went on with her writing.* ◇ *Neil nodded and went on eating.*

proceed /prə'si:d; *AmE* prou-/ [I] (*rather formal*) to continue doing sth that has already been started; to continue being done: *We're not sure whether we still want to proceed with the sale.* ◇ *Work is proceeding slowly.* ❶ You might **proceed with** work, plans, reforms, a *transaction* or an *investigation*; or a *conversation, meeting, sale, transaction* or *trial* might **proceed** (in a particular way).

pursue /pə'sju:; *AmE* pər'su:/ [T] (*formal*) to continue to discuss, find out about or be involved in sth: *We have no option but to pursue legal action.* ◇ *We have decided not to pursue the matter.* ❶ Typical collocates of **pursue** are *enquiry, investigation, lawsuit, line, matter, policy, quest* and *strategy*.

,carry 'on, ,carry sth 'on *phrasal verb* (*especially spoken*) to continue doing sth: *Carry on with your work while I'm away.* ◇ *After he left I just tried to carry on as normal* (= do the things I usually do). ◇ *He carried on peeling the potatoes.*

,keep sth 'up, ,keep 'up with sth *phrasal verb* to continue sth at the same, usually high, level; to continue to pay or do sth regularly: *The enemy kept up the bombardment day and night.* ◇ *Well done! Keep up the good work/Keep it up.* ◇ *If you do not keep up with the payments you could lose your home.*

,press a'head/'on *phrasal verb* to continue with an activity or journey in a determined way: *The company is pressing ahead with its plans for a new warehouse.* ◇ *'Shall we stay here for the night?' 'No, let's press on.'*

'stick with sb/sth *phrasal verb* [no passive] (*informal*) to continue with sth; to continue doing sth: *They decided to stick with their original plan.* ◇ *Even if you find it hard at first, stick with it* – *it will get easier with practice.* ❶ **Stick with sb/sth** is often used to talk about not changing or moving away from what you already know: *to stick with the old system/the original plan/what you know/what you already have/the status quo*

---

3 continue · go on · resume · return to sth · renew · reopen · restart · take sth up
These words all mean to start sth again after stopping for a time.

PATTERNS AND COLLOCATIONS
▸ to continue/go on **with** sth
▸ to continue/go on/resume **doing sth**
▸ to continue/resume/return to/renew/reopen/restart **talks**
▸ to continue/resume/return to/reopen a **discussion**
▸ to continue/resume/return to/take up a **conversation**
▸ to return to/reopen/take up a/an **case/issue**
▸ to continue/renew/take up the **campaign**
▸ to continue/resume/return to/renew/take up the **attack**
▸ to continue/resume/restart **production**
▸ to continue/resume/return to your **duties**
▸ **work** continues/goes on/restarts

continue [I, T] (*especially written*) to start or start sth again after stopping for a time; to start speaking again after stopping: *The story continues in our next issue.* ◇ *The story will be continued in our next issue.* ◇ *Please continue with the work you were doing before.* ◇ *Please continue* – *I didn't mean to interrupt.* ◇ *'In fact,' he continued, 'I'd like to congratulate you.'* ❶ The written abbreviation of **continue** is *cont*. This is often found at the bottom of the page: *cont. p.161*; or at the top of a page: *cont. from p.159*
▸ **continuation** *noun* [C]: *The new book is a continuation of her autobiography.*

,go 'on *phrasal verb* (*rather informal, especially spoken*) to continue an activity, especially after a pause or break; to start speaking again, after a short pause: *That's enough for now* – *let's go on with it tomorrow.* ◇ *She hesitated for a moment and then went on.* ◇ *'You know,' he went on, 'I think my brother could help you.'*

resume /rɪ'zu:m; *BrE* also -'zju:-/ [T, I] (*formal*) to start or start sth again after stopping for a time; to go back to the seat or place that you had before: *She resumed her career after an interval of six years.* ◇ *There is no sign of the peace talks resuming.* ◇ *He resumed his seat opposite her.*
▸ **resumption** /rɪ'zʌmpʃn/ *noun* [sing., U]: *We are hoping for an early resumption of the peace talks.*

return to sth *phrasal verb* (*rather formal, especially written*) to start discussing a subject that you were discussing earlier, or doing an activity that you were doing earlier: *He returns to this topic later in the report.* ◇ *She looked up briefly, then returned to her sewing.* ◇ *The doctor may allow her to return to work next week.*
▸ **a return to sth** *noun* [sing.]: *his return to public life*

renew /rɪ'nju:; *AmE* -'nu:/ [T] (*especially journalism*) to start sth again after stopping for a time: *The army renewed its assault on the capital.* ◇ *We have to renew our efforts to attract young players.* ◇ *The annual dinner is a chance to renew acquaintance with old friends.* ❶ **Renew** is often used to talk about people, countries or governments trying again either to attack or form a relationship with another person, country or government: *to renew efforts/a bid/calls/demands/threats/an assault/an attack* ◇ *to renew a friendship/an acquaintance*
▸ **renewal** *noun* [C, U]: *a renewal of interest in traditional teaching methods*

reopen /,ri:'əupən; *AmE* -'ou-/ [T, I] (*especially written*) to deal with or start sth again after a period of time; to start again after a period of time: *The police have decided to* reopen the file on the missing girl. ◇ The trial reopened on 6 March. ❶ People typically **reopen** sth such as a *debate*, a *discussion*, an *issue*, a *controversy*, an *argument*, a *case*, a *file*, *negotiations* or *talks*.

restart /ˌriːˈstɑːt; AmE -ˈstɑːrt/ [I, T] to make an activity or process start again; to make a machine or sb's heart start working again; (of an activity or process) to start again; (of a machine) to start working again: *The umpire tried to restart the game after 35 minutes.* ◇ *The doctors struggled to restart his heart.* ◇ *The engine did not restart and the plane dived to the ground.*

take sth 'up *phrasal verb* (*especially spoken*) to continue sth that sb else has not finished, or that has not been mentioned for some time: *She took up the story where Tim had left off.* ◇ *I'd like to take up the point you raised earlier.* ❶ In this meaning, **take sth up** is mainly used to talk about going back to talk about what sb said earlier, or starting a story again after stopping for a time.

continuous *adj.* See also the entry for ENDLESS

continuous · relentless · continual · persistent · round-the-clock · unbroken · uninterrupted · incessant · non-stop
These words all describe things that continue for a long time without interruption.

PATTERNS AND COLLOCATIONS
▶ the continuous/relentless/uninterrupted/incessant **flow** of sth
▶ continuous/continual/relentless **struggle**
▶ continuous/continual/persistent **change/conflict**
▶ continuous/relentless/persistent **pressure**
▶ continuous/relentless/persistent/incessant **rain**
▶ continuous/continual/incessant **noise**
▶ unbroken/uninterrupted **peace**
▶ a continuous/an unbroken/an uninterrupted **succession/series/sequence/period**
▶ **almost** continuous/continual/unbroken/uninterrupted/incessant/non-stop

continuous happening or existing for a period of time without interruption: *It was a week of almost continuous sunshine.* ◇ *Do the exercise in one continuous flowing motion.* ◇ *You need to have been in continuous employment for at least two years.* ◇ *Awards are based on continuous assessment of course work as well as a final examination.* OPP intermittent → OCCASIONAL
▶ **continuously** *adv.*: *The radio station now transmits continuously.*

relentless /rɪˈlentləs/ not stopping or getting less strong: *The wind was relentless.* ◇ *His relentless energy made him come alive in every role he played.* ◇ *The relentless pursuit of increased profit at any cost is questionable.*
▶ **relentlessly** *adv.*: *The sun beat down relentlessly.*

continual [only before noun] continuing without interruption: *They live in continual fear.* ◇ *The body is in a continual state of chemical activity.* ◇ *He was in a continual process of rewriting his material.*
▶ **continually** *adv.*: *All living organisms are continually in competition with other species.*

NOTE **CONTINUAL** OR **CONTINUOUS?** In many cases you can use either word: *a continuous/continual process/movement/struggle* ◇ *continuous/continual change/conflict/noise.* However, **continuous** is more frequent and has a wider range of uses. **Continual** is used especially to describe states of mind or body that continue for a long time; collocates include *state, fear, pain, delight, threat* and *reminder*. Both words can also mean 'repeated very often'. See also the entry for FREQUENT

persistent /pəˈsɪstənt; AmE pərˈs-/ continuing for a long period of time without interruption, especially in a way that is annoying and cannot be stopped: *Persistent heavy rain held up work on the bridge for more than a week.* ◇ *Persistent pressure from the water authority forced the company to comply with the rules.*
▶ **persistently** *adv.*: *persistently high interest rates*

round-the-'clock (also a round-the-'clock) [only before noun] lasting or happening all day and night: *His family kept a round-the-clock vigil at his bedside.* ◇ *Round-the-clock police surveillance was necessary.*
▶ **around/round the 'clock** *idiom*: *Emergency teams were working round the clock to make the homes secure.*

unbroken not disturbed in any way; continuous: *It was the first unbroken night of sleep I had had for months.* ◇ *She retired from the company after 45 years of unbroken service.*

uninterrupted /ˌʌnˌɪntəˈrʌptɪd/ not stopped by anything; continuous: *We had two weeks of uninterrupted warm sunshine.* ◇ *You need to find a place where you can do uninterrupted work.*

incessant /ɪnˈsesnt/ (*rather formal*, *disapproving*) never stopping: *She raised her voice above the incessant beat of the music.*
▶ **incessantly** *adv.*: *The dogs barked incessantly.*

non-'stop (*rather informal*) (especially of an activity) without any pauses or stops: *It will be a real fun day out for everyone. Seven hours of non-stop entertainment.*
▶ **non-'stop** *adv.*: *They talked non-stop about the play.*

contract *noun* See the Topic Map for CONFLICT on p.896, See also the entry for AGREEMENT 1

contract · treaty · accord · convention
These are all words for an official agreement between people, organizations or countries.

PATTERNS AND COLLOCATIONS
▶ a contract/a treaty/an accord/a convention **between** sb and sb
▶ a contract/a treaty/an accord **with** sb
▶ a treaty/an accord/a convention **on** sth
▶ a contract/a treaty/an accord **to do** sth
▶ **under** (a) contract/a treaty/an accord/a convention
▶ a **draft** contract/treaty/accord/convention
▶ an **international** contract/treaty/accord/convention
▶ to **sign** a contract/a treaty/an accord/a convention
▶ to **comply with** a contract/a treaty/an accord/a convention
▶ to **approve** a contract/a treaty/an accord/a convention
▶ to **ratify** a treaty/an accord/a convention
▶ to **accept/draw up/negotiate/conclude/violate** a contract/a treaty/an accord

contract [C] a formal written agreement between individuals, companies or organizations: *These clauses form part of the contract between buyer and seller.* ◇ *They won a **contract for** the delivery of five fighter planes.* ◇ *I was on a three-year fixed-term **contract** that expired last week.* ◇ *She is **under contract to** (= has a contract to work for) a major US computer firm.* ◇ *All employees have a written **contract of employment**.* ◇ *The offer has been accepted, **subject to contract** (= the agreement is not legally binding before contracts are signed).* ◇ *They were sued for **breach of contract** (= not keeping to a contract).* See also contract → EMPLOY *verb*

treaty [C] a formal agreement between two or more countries: *The government concluded a **peace treaty** with the rebels.* ◇ *The new law may be in breach of the Treaty of Rome.*

accord /əˈkɔːd; AmE əˈkɔːrd/ [C] a formal agreement between two organizations or countries: *The countries drew up accords on economic and technical cooperation.*

convention [C] a formal agreement between countries or leaders: *This is forbidden under the European Convention on Human Rights.* ◇ *Over 60 countries have yet to ratify the climate convention.*

NOTE **TREATY, ACCORD** OR **CONVENTION?** A **treaty** and an **accord** are both official agreements between countries, for example concerned with restoring peace after a conflict, or trade, military or economic cooperation. Both are used in the names of particular agreements, often using the name of the place in which they were signed: *the Treaty of Rome* ◇ *the Algiers Accord*. An **accord** can also be an official agreement between organizations, such as between a government and a trade union. A **convention** is an international agreement between several countries. It usually contains rules about a particular activity, for example the sale of weapons, the treatment of refugees or controlling pollution. **Conventions** usually try to control a problem which affects many countries, and by signing the convention a country agrees to apply the rules or standards within it.

control noun See the Topic Map for THE INDIVIDUAL AND SOCIETY on p.894

control · power · rule · authority · jurisdiction · discipline · command · hold · grasp · force
These are all words for the ability that a person or group has to control sb/sth else.

PATTERNS AND COLLOCATIONS
▶ control / power / rule / authority / jurisdiction / command / a hold **over** sb / sth
▶ a hold / grasp **on** sb / sth
▶ to be **in** control / power / authority / command / force
▶ to be **under** sb's control / rule / authority / jurisdiction / command
▶ to be **beyond** / **outside** the control / power / authority / jurisdiction **of** sb
▶ the power / authority / jurisdiction **to do sth**
▶ **absolute** / **complete** control / power / authority / command
▶ **direct** control / rule / authority / command
▶ to **have** control / power / authority / jurisdiction / command / a hold over sb / force
▶ to **exercise** control / power / authority / jurisdiction
▶ to **take** control / power / command
▶ to **assume** control / power / authority / command
▶ to **give** sb control / power / authority / jurisdiction / command / a hold over sb
▶ to **delegate** power / authority / command (to sb)
▶ to **lose** control / power / authority / command / your hold on sth
▶ to **relinquish** control / power / command / your hold on sth

control [U] the power to make decisions about how a country, an area, an organization or sb's life is run; the ability to make sb/sth do what you want: *The party is expecting to* **gain control of** *the council in the next election.* ◇ *The aim is to give people more control over their own lives.* ◇ *The city is* **under enemy control**. ◇ *The teacher had no control over the children.* ◇ *She struggled to* **keep control of** *her voice.* ◇ *She lost control of her car on the ice.* ◇ *Owing to* **circumstances beyond our control** *the flight to Rome has been cancelled.* See also **self-control** → RESTRAINT, **controlled** → DISCIPLINED

power [U] the ability to control people or things; political control of a country or area: *He has the power to make life very difficult for us.* ◇ *The Emperor had absolute power over all his subjects.* ◇ *She was determined to go through with her plan, now that she* **had him in her power** (= was able to do what she liked with him). ◇ *The party* **came to power** *at the last election.* ◇ *He* **seized power** *in a military coup.* ◇ *It was the beginning of a* **power struggle** *between rival factions within the party.* ◇ *The war brought about a shift in the* **balance of power**. See also **office** → ROLE

rule [U] the government of a country or area by a particular person, group or political system: *There was a gradual process of returning the country to civilian rule.* ◇ *The country remained under direct rule by the occupying powers.* ❶ **Rule** often refers to control by an outside country or group, by a political system which allows little freedom, or sth which contrasts with this: *colonial/ British/Ottoman rule* ◇ *Communist/military rule* ◇ *a return to civilian/democratic/majority rule* See also **rule** → RULE *verb* 1

authority [U] the power to give orders to people: *She now has authority over the people who used to be her bosses.* ◇ *Nothing will be done because no one in authority* (= who has the power to do sth) *takes the matter seriously.*

jurisdiction /ˌdʒʊərɪsˈdɪkʃn; AmE ˌdʒʊr-/ [U, C] (*formal*) the power that an official organization has to make legal decisions about sb/sth: *These matters do not* **fall within** *our* **jurisdiction**. ◇ *The agreement doesn't come under the jurisdiction of the EU courts.*

discipline [U] the practice of training people to obey rules and orders and punishing them if they do not; the controlled behaviour or situation that results from this training: *The school has a reputation for high standards of discipline.* ◇ *Strict discipline is imposed on army recruits.* ◇ *She keeps good discipline in class.* See also **discipline** → PUNISH *verb*, **disciplined** → DISCIPLINED, **self-discipline** → RESTRAINT

command [U] the power to give orders to a group of people, especially in the armed forces or police: *He has 1 200 men under his command.* ◇ *Who's in command here?* ◇ *The police arrived and took command of the situation.* See also **command** → ORDER *verb*, **command** → RUN 2

hold [sing.] influence or control over a person or situation: *What she knew about his past gave her a hold over him.* ◇ *Enemy forces have consolidated their hold on the northern province.*

grasp [sing.] (*rather informal*) control over a situation, especially when it is hard to hold on to: *The company continues to maintain its grasp on the business computer market.* ◇ *Don't let the situation escape from your grasp.*

> **NOTE HOLD OR GRASP?** In this meaning, a **hold** is stronger than a **grasp**. You *have*, *strengthen* or *consolidate* a **hold**. A **grasp** has to be *maintained* or things may *slip* or *escape from* it.

force [U] the authority of a law or rule: *These guidelines do not have* **the force of law**. ◇ *The court ruled that these standards have force in British law.*

control verb

control · handle · manage
These words all mean to have power over sb/sth so that you are able to decide what a person must do or how sth will work.

PATTERNS AND COLLOCATIONS
▶ to control / manage a **child**
▶ to be **easy** / **difficult to** control / handle / manage
▶ to control / handle / manage sb / sth **properly**
▶ to control / manage sb / sth **effectively**

control [T] to have power over a person so that you are able to make them do or behave as you say: *Can't you control your children?* ◇ *Time out is an effective way of* **controlling** *aggressive* **behaviour**. ◇ *Mounted police had been called to* **control the crowds**. See also **uncontrollable** → UNCONTROLLABLE

handle [T] to control a vehicle, animal, tool or machine, so that it does what you want it to: *I wasn't sure if I could handle such a powerful car.* ◇ *She's a difficult horse to handle.*

manage [T] to keep sb/sth under control, so that it doesn't cause you problems: *It's like trying to manage an unruly child.* ◇ *I really liked the chapter about how to manage stress.* ◇ *They have learnt to successfully manage their diabetes.* See also **unmanageable** → UNCONTROLLABLE

controversial adj. See the Topic Maps for CONFLICT on p.896 and FACT AND OPINION on p.898

controversial · questionable · debatable · dubious · contentious · arguable
These words all describe sth that people disagree about.

PATTERNS AND COLLOCATIONS
▸ It is questionable / debatable / dubious / arguable **whether**...
▸ a controversial / questionable / dubious / contentious **decision**
▸ a controversial / a debatable / a contentious / an arguable **point**
▸ a controversial / debatable / contentious **issue** / **subject** / **question**
▸ a controversial / contentious **matter** / **view** / **opinion**
▸ **highly** / **very** / **extremely** / **rather** / **somewhat** controversial / questionable / debatable / dubious / contentious

controversial /ˌkɒntrə'vɜːʃl; AmE ˌkɑːntrə'vɜːrʃl/ causing a lot of angry public discussion and disagreement: *Her controversial new play sparked a riot outside the theatre.* ◇ *Winston Churchill and Richard Nixon were both controversial figures.* **OPP** **uncontroversial** ❶ Something that is **uncontroversial** does not cause, or is not likely to cause, any disagreement: *an uncontroversial policy/opinion* See also **controversy → DEBATE** *noun*
▸ **controversially** *adv.*: *Punishments for prisoners include loss of privileges and, more controversially, the stopping of visits.*

questionable /'kwestʃənəbl/ that you have doubts about because you think it is not accurate or correct: *The conclusions that they come to are highly questionable.* ◇ *It is questionable whether this is a good way of solving the problem.*

debatable /dɪ'beɪtəbl/ not certain because people can have different ideas and opinions about the thing being discussed: *Whether or not that's a good thing remains a debatable point.* ◇ *It is highly debatable whether conditions have improved for low-income families.*

dubious /'djuːbiəs; AmE 'duː-/ that you cannot be sure about; that is probably not good: *They consider the plan to be of dubious benefit to most families.* ◇ (*ironic*) *She had the dubious honour of being the last woman to be hanged in England* (= it was not an honour at all).

contentious /kən'tenʃəs/ (*formal*) likely to cause disagreement between people: *Both views are highly contentious.* ◇ *Try to avoid any contentious wording.* **OPP** **uncontentious** ❶ Something that is **uncontentious** is not likely to cause disagreement between people: *The proposal is relatively uncontentious.*

> **NOTE** **CONTROVERSIAL** OR **CONTENTIOUS**? These words are very close in meaning but **controversial** has a wider range and can describe people and things as well as issues and opinions: *a controversial figure/book/film/play/plan/building* ◇ ~~a contentious figure/book/film/play/plan/building~~

arguable /'ɑːgjuəbl; AmE 'ɑːrg-/ (*formal*) not certain; that you do not accept without question: *It is arguable whether the case should have ever gone to trial* (= perhaps it should not have).

convey *verb* See also the entry for TELL 1

convey · send · communicate · relay · repeat · impart · get sth across · pass sth on · break
These words all mean to make sure sb receives and understands information, ideas or feelings about sth.

PATTERNS AND COLLOCATIONS
▸ to convey / send / communicate / relay / repeat / impart / get across / pass on / break sth **to sb**
▸ to convey / communicate / relay / repeat / break it to sb **that**...
▸ to convey / communicate / relay / repeat to sb **what**...
▸ to convey / send / communicate / relay / repeat / impart / get across / pass on a **message**
▸ to convey / communicate / get across your **ideas**
▸ to convey / pass on / break **the news**
▸ to convey sth / communicate sth / get sth across **clearly** / **effectively**

convey /kən'veɪ/ [T] (*rather formal*) to make information, ideas or feelings known to sb: *He tried desperately to convey how urgent the situation was.* ◇ *Colours like red convey a sense of energy and strength.* ◇ (*formal, spoken*) *Please convey my apologies to your wife.*

send [T] to tell sb sth in a message: *My parents **send their love**.* ◇ *What sort of message is the irresponsible behaviour of these celebrities sending to young people?* ◇ (*formal or literary*) *She **sent word** that she could not come.*

communicate [T, I] (*rather formal*) to make information, ideas or feelings known to other people: *He was eager to communicate his ideas to the group.* ◇ *Her nervousness was communicating itself to the children.* ◇ *Candidates must be able to communicate effectively.* See also **communication → COMMUNICATION**, **communication → LETTER**, **communicator → SPEAKER 1**

> **NOTE** **CONVEY** OR **COMMUNICATE**? You can **convey** information, an idea or a feeling to one other person, a group of people or people in general. You can **communicate** sth to a group of people or people in general, but not usually to one other person: ~~Please communicate my apologies to your wife.~~ **Convey** must take an object, which must be different from the subject: ~~Her nervousness was conveying itself to the children.~~ ◇ ~~Candidates must be able to convey effectively.~~

relay /'riːleɪ; rɪ'leɪ/ [T] (*rather formal*) to give information to sb else after receiving it yourself: *He relayed the message to his boss.* ◇ *Instructions were relayed to her by phone.*

repeat [T] to tell sb sth that you have heard or been told by sb else: *I don't want you to repeat a word of this to anyone.* ◇ *The rumour has been widely repeated in the press.* ◇ *Why did you go and repeat what I said to Ian?* See also **repeat → REPEAT 1**

impart /ɪm'pɑːt; AmE ɪm'pɑːrt/ [T] (*formal*) to pass information or knowledge to other people: *Her aim was not merely to impart knowledge, but rather to help students learn for themselves.*

get sth a'cross *phrasal verb* (*rather informal*) to succeed in communicating sth: *He's not very good at getting his ideas across.*

pass sth 'on *phrasal verb* (*rather informal*) to give information to sb else after receiving it yourself: *I passed your message on to my mother.* ❶ You can also **pass on** things other than information. See also **pass sth on → PASS STH ON**

break [T, I] to be the first to tell sb some bad news, especially in a kind way; (of news) to become known: *I don't know how to **break it to him**.* ◇ *Just break the news to her gently.* ◇ *There was a public outcry when the scandal broke.*

convince *verb* See also the entry for PERSUADE

convince · satisfy · persuade
These words all mean to make sb believe that sth is true.

PATTERNS AND COLLOCATIONS
▸ to convince / satisfy / persuade sb **of** sth
▸ to convince / satisfy / persuade sb **that**...
▸ to convince / satisfy / persuade **yourself**

convince [T] (not used in the progressive tenses) to make sb firmly believe that sth is true: *He was like a politician who wants to convince you of his sincerity.* ◇ *I had convinced myself (that) I was right.* ◇ *The events in Paris convinced him that Europe was on the brink of revolution.* ◇ *I wasn't convinced by her arguments.* See also **convince sb to do sth → PERSUADE**, **convinced → SURE** *adj.*

satisfy [T] (not used in the progressive tenses) (*rather formal*) to show or prove to sb that sth is true: *Her explanation didn't satisfy the teacher.* ◇ *First people need to be satisfied of the need for a new system.* See also **satisfied → SURE** *adj.*

persuade [T] to make sb believe that sth is true, especially by what you say: *No one was persuaded by his argument.* ◇ *It has been difficult to persuade people that we have no political objectives.*

convincing *adj.*

convincing · compelling · persuasive · strong · forceful · cogent
These words all describe an argument, opinion or evidence that is expressed firmly and clearly so that sb believes it is true.

persuasive   convincing   compelling
strong
forceful
cogent

PATTERNS AND COLLOCATIONS
▶ a convincing / compelling / persuasive / strong / forceful / cogent **argument**
▶ convincing / compelling / persuasive / strong / cogent **evidence**
▶ a convincing / compelling / persuasive / strong / cogent **reason / case**
▶ a convincing / compelling / cogent **explanation**
▶ **very** convincing / compelling / persuasive / strong / forceful / cogent
▶ **extremely** convincing / compelling / persuasive / strong

convincing /kən'vɪnsɪŋ/ (of an argument, a reason or evidence) that makes sb believe that sth is true: *This explanation is not entirely convincing.* ◇ *She sounded very convincing to me* (= I believed what she said). **OPP un-convincing** → UNLIKELY 2
▶ **convincingly** *adv.*: *Her case was convincingly argued.*

compelling [usually before noun] (*especially written*) very convincing: *The new studies provide compelling evidence in support of these concepts.*

NOTE CONVINCING OR COMPELLING? Compelling is slightly stronger than **convincing**. Things can *seem/ sound/look convincing*, with just a slight suggestion that things may not be exactly as they seem. **Compelling** is usually used before a noun and leaves no room for any doubt that sth is true.

persuasive /pə'sweɪsɪv; *AmE* pər's-/ (of an argument, reason, etc. or a person) able to persuade sb to believe or do sth: *Advertising relies heavily on the persuasive power of imagery.* ◇ *He can be very persuasive.*
▶ **persuasively** *adv.*: *They argue persuasively in favour of a total ban on handguns.*

strong (of an argument, a reason or evidence) difficult to attack or criticize: *You have a strong case for getting your job back.* ◇ *There is strong evidence of a link between exercise and a healthy heart.* **OPP weak** → UNLIKELY 2

forceful (of opinions or arguments) expressed firmly and clearly in a way that makes other people believe them: *The minister launched a forceful defence of the policy.*

cogent /'kəʊdʒənt; *AmE* 'koʊ-/ (*formal*) (of an argument, a reason or evidence) expressed firmly and clearly in a way that influences what people believe: *His criticisms still seem cogent today as they did twenty years ago.*

cook *verb* See also the entry for BAKE

cook · make · prepare · get · brew · fix
These words all mean to make food or drink ready to be eaten.

PATTERNS AND COLLOCATIONS
▶ to make / prepare / brew sth **from sth**
▶ to cook / make / get / fix sth **for** sb
▶ to cook / make / get / fix **sb / yourself** sth
▶ to cook / make / prepare / fix a **meal**
▶ to cook / make / prepare / get / fix **breakfast / lunch / dinner**

▶ to cook / make / prepare a **dish**
▶ to make / prepare / fix a **sandwich**
▶ to make / prepare a **salad**
▶ to make / brew **tea / coffee / beer**
▶ to make / get / fix (sb / yourself) **something to eat / drink**

cook [T, I] to make food ready to be eaten by heating it, for example by boiling, baking or frying it; (of food) to be made ready to be eaten in this way: *What's the best way to cook trout?* ◇ *Add the onion and cook for three minutes.* ◇ *Where did you learn to cook?* ◇ *While the pasta is cooking, prepare the sauce.*

make [T] to create a meal or sth to eat or drink by combining and/or cooking different things: *How do you make that dish with the peppers and olives in it?* ◇ *She made coffee for us all.* ◇ *She made us all coffee.*

prepare [T] (*especially written*) to make food ready to be eaten; to make a medicine by mixing different things: *The women were busy preparing the wedding feast.* ◇ *The remedies are all prepared from wild flowers.*

get [T] (*spoken*) to prepare a meal; to provide food or drink for sb: *Can I get you anything to eat or drink?* ◇ *You sit down and relax. I'll get supper.*

brew [T] to make beer; to make a hot drink of tea or coffee: *The beer is brewed in the Czech Republic.* ◇ *I love the smell of freshly brewed coffee.*

fix (*especially AmE, spoken*) to provide or prepare sth, especially food or drink: *Go right on through. I'm just fixing the drinks.* ◇ *I'm just going to fix myself some breakfast.*

cooking *noun*

cooking · cuisine · cookery · baking
These are all words for the process of preparing food.

PATTERNS AND COLLOCATIONS
▶ **vegetarian** cooking / cuisine / cookery
▶ **French / Chinese, etc.** cooking / cuisine / cookery
▶ **excellent / superb / traditional / local** cooking / cuisine
▶ **home** cooking / baking
▶ to **offer / serve** a particular kind of cooking / cuisine

cooking [U] the process of preparing food; food that has been prepared in a particular way: *My husband does all the cooking.* ◇ *The restaurant offers traditional home cooking* (= food similar to that cooked at home).

cuisine /kwɪ'ziːn/ [U, C] (from *French*, *rather formal*) a style of cooking; the food served in a restaurant (usually an expensive one): *You must sample the local cuisine.* ◇ *The hotel restaurant is noted for its excellent cuisine.*

cookery [U] (*BrE*) the art or activity of preparing and cooking food: *Before he leaves home he'll have to learn some basic cookery.* ◇ *I'm going on a cookery course.* ◇ *I've bought a new cookery book.* ❶ In both British and American English this can also be called a **cookbook**.

baking [U] the process of cooking using dry heat in an oven: *A warm smell of baking came from the kitchen.* ◇ *Arrange the mushrooms in a greased baking tray.* ❶ **Baking** is used especially about making bread and cakes. See also **bake** → BAKE

cool *verb*

cool · chill · cool (sb/sth) down · freeze · refrigerate
These words all mean to become or make sth become cold or less warm.

PATTERNS AND COLLOCATIONS
▶ chilled / frozen **food**
▶ to **leave sth to / allow sth to / let sth** cool / cool down
▶ to **keep sth** frozen / refrigerated

cool [I, T] to become cool or cooler; to make sth cool or cooler: *Glass contracts as it cools.* ◇ *The cylinder is cooled by a jet of water.* See also **cool** → COLD *adj.* 1

chill [T, I] to make sb very cold; to make food or drink very cold without turning it to ice; (of food or drink) to become very cold without turning to ice: *They were chilled by the icy wind.* ◇ *This wine is best **served chilled**.* ◇ *Let the pudding chill for an hour until set.*

‚**cool ˈdown**, ‚**cool sb/sth ˈdown** *phrasal verb* (*rather informal*) to become cool or cooler; to make sb/sth cool or cooler: *Let the charger cool down before using it again.* ◇ *Drink plenty of cold water to cool yourself down.* ◇ *Blow on it to cool it down or you'll burn your mouth.* ❶ It is also possible, but less common, to use **cool off**, especially without an object: *We cooled off with a swim in the lake.*

> **NOTE** **COOL** OR **COOL (SB/STH) DOWN?** Cool down is slightly more informal than **cool**, and is used more in spoken English. **Cool down** is used more often than **cool** with *myself, yourself, himself*, etc.: *How about a swim to cool ourselves down?* Use **cool** in technical language or when talking about a process or system: ~~The cylinder is cooled down by a jet of water.~~

freeze [I, T] to be very cold or so cold that you die; to keep food at a very low temperature in order to preserve it; (of food) to be able to be preserved in this way: *Every time she opens the window we all freeze.* ◇ *Two men **froze to death** on the mountain.* ◇ *These meals are ideal for home freezing.* ◇ *Some fruits freeze better than others.* **OPP** melt, thaw, defrost → MELT, See also **freezing, frozen** → FREEZING

refrigerate /rɪˈfrɪdʒəreɪt/ [T, often passive] (*formal*) to keep sth, especially food, cold in order to keep it fresh: *Once opened, this product should be kept refrigerated.*

cool *adj.*

cool · brazen · shameless · presumptuous · unabashed · unashamed
These words describe sb who is very confident or feels no embarrassment, often in a way that does not show respect or that other people find shocking.

PATTERNS AND COLLOCATIONS
▶ brazen / presumptuous **of** sb
▶ a brazen / shameless **display**
▶ in a shameless / presumptuous **way**
▶ unabashed / unashamed **luxury**

cool (*rather informal*) calm and confident in a way that lacks respect for other people, but makes people admire you as well as disapprove: (*BrE*) *She just took his keys and walked out with them, cool as you please.*

brazen /ˈbreɪzn/ (*disapproving*) open and not feeling ashamed, usually about sth that people find shocking: *She's known for her own brand of brazen sexuality.* ◇ *I can't believe anyone would be so **brazen about** something like that.*
▶ **brazenly** *adv.*: *She brazenly admitted cheating.*

shameless (*disapproving*) feeling or showing no shame about sth, although other people feel you should: *It was a shameless display of greed.* **OPP** ashamed → SORRY, See also **shame** → GUILT

presumptuous /prɪˈzʌmptʃuəs/ [not usually before noun] (*disapproving*) too confident, in a way that shows a lack of respect for other people: *Isn't it rather presumptuous of you to decide what he needs?* ❶ Someone is **presumptuous** if they think that they know what sb else feels, thinks, wants or needs when they really have no reason or right to do so. See also **presume** → DARE

unabashed /ˌʌnəˈbæʃt/ (*written*) not ashamed, embarrassed or affected by people's disapproval, when other people would be: *I rather liked her unabashed frankness.* ◇ *The ruling classes live in unabashed luxury.* **OPP** ashamed → SORRY

unashamed not ashamed or embarrassed about sth, especially when other people would be: *She would have been quite unashamed if anyone had caught her.* **OPP** ashamed → SORRY, See also **shame** → GUILT

> **NOTE** **SHAMELESS, UNABASHED** OR **UNASHAMED?** Shameless is the most disapproving of these words; unashamed is usually neither approving nor disapproving; unabashed is sometimes even admiring.

cope *verb*

cope · manage · get by · get on · muddle through
These words all mean to deal successfully with a situation, often in spite of difficulties.

PATTERNS AND COLLOCATIONS
▶ to cope / manage / get by / muddle through **without** sth
▶ to manage / get by **on** sth
▶ to cope / manage / get by / muddle through **somehow**
▶ to cope / manage / get on **on your own**
▶ to cope / manage **well**
▶ to **just** cope / manage / muddle through

cope [I] to deal successfully with the difficulties of a particular situation: *He wasn't able to **cope with** the stresses and strains of the job.* ◇ *She copes very well under pressure.* ◇ *I got to the stage where I just **couldn't cope** any more.* ◇ *In heavy rain the system can't cope and it floods.* ◇ *Desert plants are adapted to cope with extreme heat.*

manage [I] to be able to solve your problems or deal with a difficult situation: *How do you manage without a car?* ◇ *Many find it difficult to manage on their weekly income.* ◇ *It won't be easy, but I'm sure we'll manage somehow.*

> **NOTE** **COPE** OR **MANAGE?** The subject of **manage** in this meaning is always a person; the subject of **cope** may be a person, thing or system: ~~In heavy rain the system can't manage.~~ People or systems often have to **cope** with a particular difficulty such as *stress, pressure, problems, demands*, a *workload*, a *challenge*, a *situation* or an *emergency*. People often have to **manage** in a particular situation, *without* a particular thing that they need or usually have, or *on* a limited amount of money.

‚**get ˈby** *phrasal verb* (*rather informal*) to manage to live or do a particular thing using the money, knowledge or equipment that you have, especially when it is limited or less than normal: *How does she get by on such a small salary?* ◇ *I can just about **get by in** German* (= I can speak basic German). ◇ *You don't need specialist clothing – you can **get by with** shorts and a T-shirt.*

get on *phrasal verb* (*rather informal*) to manage to live or do sth, especially with little help: *This is a chance to see how you get on on your own.* ◇ *We can get on perfectly well without her.*

‚**muddle ˈthrough** *phrasal verb* (*especially BrE, rather informal*) to deal successfully with sth even though you do not know exactly what you are doing and/or do not have the correct equipment: *He'd got used to muddling through without any formal training.*

copy *noun*

1 a copy of a report
2 a copy of a painting

1 copy · transcript · printout · photocopy · hard copy
These are all words for a written or printed copy of text or images.

PATTERNS AND COLLOCATIONS
▶ to **make** a copy / transcript / photocopy
▶ to **send** a copy / printout / transcript / photocopy / hard copy
▶ to **attach** / **enclose** a copy / printout / photocopy / hard copy
▶ to **keep** a copy / printout / transcript / photocopy

copy [C] a printed or photographic copy of a document: *I will send you a copy of the report.* ◇ *Could I have ten copies of this page, please?*

transcript /ˈtrænskrɪpt/ [C] a written or printed copy of words that have been spoken: *They are going to publish a transcript of the interview.* See also **transcribe** → WRITE 1

printout /ˈprɪntaʊt/ [C, U] a page or set of pages containing information in printed form from a computer: *a printout of text downloaded from the Internet* ◇ *There were a few pages of computer printout on her desk.*

photocopy [C] a photographic copy of a document: *Make as many photocopies as you need.*

> **NOTE COPY** OR **PHOTOCOPY?** A **copy** can be any kind of printed reproduction of a document; a **photocopy** is one made on a **photocopier** (= a photographic copying machine). However, a **photocopy** is often referred to simply as a **copy**, especially when it is already clear what kind of copy you are talking about.

hard 'copy [U] (*computing*) information from a computer that has been printed on paper: *Most of our material is online, but this course is still only available in hard copy.*

> **NOTE HARD COPY** OR **PRINTOUT?** **Hard copy** is used to talk about printed material in contrast to electronic material. People talk about having **hard copy** as well as, or instead of, electronic files. A **printout** is the printed piece of paper itself.

2 copy · model · replica · reproduction · facsimile · duplicate · reconstruction · mock-up
These are all words for a thing that is made to look like sth else.

PATTERNS AND COLLOCATIONS
▸ in replica / facsimile / duplicate
▸ a/ an **good** / **accurate** copy / model / reproduction / facsimile / reconstruction
▸ an **exact** copy / replica / reproduction / facsimile / duplicate / reconstruction
▸ a **faithful** copy / model / reproduction
▸ a **crude** copy / model
▸ a **full-scale** / **life-size** model / replica / reconstruction
▸ a **working** model / replica / reconstruction
▸ to **make** a copy / a model / a replica / a reproduction / a facsimile / a duplicate / a reconstruction
▸ to **keep** a copy / duplicate

copy [C] a thing that is made to look like sth else, especially a work of art, a document or a disk: *The thieves replaced the original painting with a copy.* ◇ *It must be certified as a true copy of the original document.* ◇ *You should make a copy of the disk as a back-up.*

model [C] a copy of sth, usually smaller than the original object: *They have a working model* (= one in which the parts move) *of a water mill.* ◇ *I used to build model aeroplanes.* ◇ *The architect had produced a scale model of the proposed shopping complex* (= in which all the parts are the correct size in relation to each other.)

replica /ˈreplɪkə/ [C] a very good or exact copy of sth, especially an object: *There is even a scaled-down replica of the Eiffel Tower there.* ◇ *The weapon used in the raid was a replica.* ◇ *replica guns*

reproduction [C] a copy of sth, especially a work of art or piece of furniture: *They have a catalogue with colour reproductions of the paintings for sale.* ◇ *reproduction furniture* (= furniture made as a copy of an earlier style) ❶ **Reproductions** are usually copies that are legal and official, rather than ones that are made in order to deceive people. See also FAKE *noun*

facsimile /fækˈsɪməli/ [C] an exact copy of sth, especially a book or document: *A facsimile of the document is available in the British Library.* ◇ *a facsimile edition* ❶ **Facsimile** is used especially to talk about a printed photographic copy of a very old book or document.

duplicate /ˈdjuːplɪkət; *AmE* ˈduː-/ [C] one of two or more things that are the same in every detail: *Is this a duplicate or the original?* ◇ *The contract is prepared in duplicate* (= two copies are made)*, so that both parties can keep a copy.* ❶ **Duplicate** is usually used to talk about a document, a disk, a CD or a key.

reconstruction /ˌriːkənˈstrʌkʃn/ [C] a copy of sth that no longer exists: *The doorway is a 19th century reconstruction of Norman work.* See also **reconstruct → REBUILD**

'mock-up [C] a model or a copy of sth, often the same size as it, that is used for testing, or for showing people what the real thing will look like: *He was looking at a mock-up of the following day's front page.* ❶ **Mock-up** is often used by designers or about their work.

copy *verb*

copy · reproduce · photocopy · duplicate
These words all mean to make sth that is exactly like sth else.

PATTERNS AND COLLOCATIONS
▸ to copy / reproduce sth **from** sth
▸ to copy / reproduce / photocopy / duplicate a **letter** / **document**
▸ to copy / photocopy / duplicate a **form**
▸ to copy / reproduce a **painting**
▸ to copy / duplicate a **disk** / **CD**
▸ to copy / reproduce / duplicate sth **exactly**
▸ to copy / reproduce sth **accurately** / **faithfully**
▸ to **merely** / **simply** copy / reproduce sth

copy [T] to make sth that is exactly like sth else; to make a photocopy of sth: *They copied the designs from those on Greek vases.* ◇ *Data can be copied from the computer onto a memory stick.* ◇ *Finally, the notes can be copied and distributed to the audience.*

reproduce [T] (*rather formal*) to make a copy of a picture or piece of text or information: *All illustrations are reproduced by kind permission of the Mercury Gallery.* ◇ *The results are reproduced in Table 2.* ❶ **Reproduce** is used especially to talk about copying the text and pictures in books, or a painting, photograph or some other piece of art.

photocopy [T, I] to make a photographic copy of a document using a special machine (= a photocopier): *The photocopied letter had been sent to all the houses in the street.* ◇ *I seem to have spent most of the day photocopying.* ❶ People often simply say **copy** when it is clear that they are talking about **photocopying**: *Can you get these copied / photocopied for me by 5 o'clock?*

duplicate /ˈdjuːplɪkeɪt; *AmE* ˈduː-/ [T, often passive] to make an exact copy of sth: *Please keep the duplicated form and send us the original.* ❶ **Duplicate** is mainly used to talk about making one or more photocopies of a document, letter or form, but it can also be used to talk about making a copy of a computer disk or CD.
▸ **duplicate** /ˈdjuːplɪkət; *AmE* ˈduː-/ *adj.*: *a duplicate invoice*

corner *noun*

corner · turn · bend · zigzag · hairpin bend · twist
These are all words for a curve where a road or a river changes direction.

PATTERNS AND COLLOCATIONS
▸ **around** / **round** / **at** / **on** a corner / bend / hairpin bend
▸ a **left-hand** / **right-hand** corner / turn / bend
▸ a **left** / **right** corner / turn
▸ a **sharp** corner / turn / bend / twist
▸ a **tight** corner / turn / bend
▸ a **blind** / **dangerous** corner / bend
▸ to **negotiate** a corner / turn / bend / hairpin bend
▸ to **round** / **take** a corner / bend / hairpin bend
▸ to **come around** / **round** a corner / bend / hairpin bend

corner [C] a place where two streets join; a sharp curve in a road: *There was a large group of youths standing on the street corner.* ◇ *Turn right at the corner of Avalon Road and Radnor Street.* ◇ *The wind hit him as he **turned the corner.***

turn [C] a change in direction in a vehicle; a curve or corner in a road: *Make a right turn into West street.* ◊ *The narrow lane was full of twists and turns.* See also **turn** → CURVE *verb*

bend [C] a curve or turn, especially in a road or river: *The two vehicles collided on a sharp bend in the road.* ◊ *You took that bend very fast!* See also **bend** → CURVE *verb*, **curve** → CURVE *noun*

zigzag /ˈzɪɡzæɡ/ [C] a line or pattern that looks like a series of letter W's as it bends to the left and then to the right again: *The path descended the hill in a series of zigzags.* See also **zigzag** → CURVE *noun*

hairpin 'bend (*BrE*) (*AmE* ˌhairpin 'curve, ˌhairpin 'turn) (also **hairpin** *BrE*, *AmE*) [C] a very sharp bend in a road, especially a mountain road: *The road winds uphill in a series of hairpin bends.*

twist [C] a sharp bend in a road or river that makes it difficult or dangerous to travel on: *The car followed the twists and turns of the mountain road.* See also **twist** → CURVE *verb*

correct *verb*

correct · fix · put sth right · set sb/sth straight · remedy · rectify · redress · cure
These words all mean to make sth right or accurate, or free of mistakes or problems.

PATTERNS AND COLLOCATIONS
▸ to correct / fix / put right / remedy / rectify / redress / cure **what...**
▸ to correct / fix / put right / remedy / rectify / redress / cure a **problem**
▸ to correct / put right / remedy / rectify / redress a **situation**
▸ to correct / fix / put right / remedy / rectify a / an **mistake / error / fault**
▸ to correct / remedy / cure a **defect / deficiency**
▸ to put right / rectify / redress a **wrong**
▸ to **easily** correct sth / fix sth / put sth right / remedy sth / rectify sth / cure sth

correct [T] to make sth right or accurate, for example by changing it or removing mistakes: *Read through your work and correct any mistakes that you find.* ◊ *Minor problems with eyesight can now be corrected in a few seconds.* ◊ *They issued a statement correcting what they had said earlier.*
▸ **correction** *noun* [C, U]: *I've made a few small corrections to your report.* ◊ *There are some programming errors that need correction.*

fix [T] (*rather informal*) to correct a problem or mistake or make a situation better: *The company had a bad image that needed fixing.* ◊ *Don't imagine that the law can fix everything.* See also **fix** → SOLUTION *noun*

put sth 'right *phrase* (*especially BrE, rather informal*) to fix sth: *If you find a mistake, let your bank know and they will put it right.* ◊ *It's not too late to put things right.*

NOTE FIX OR PUT STH RIGHT? These are both rather informal expressions. **Fix** is often used in business contexts. **Put sth right** is used especially in spoken English and more in British English than American English.

set sb/sth 'straight *idiom* (*informal*) to correct sb's mistake; to make sure that people know the correct facts when they have had the wrong idea or impression: *I just want to set the record straight – everything I did was perfectly legal.* ◊ *Let me just set you straight on one or two points.* ❶ In British English this expression is nearly always used in the phrases *set sb straight* and *set the record straight*; in American English you can also use *set the story straight* or *set things straight*.

remedy /ˈremədi/ [T] (*rather formal*) to correct or improve a problem or situation: *I tried my best to remedy the situation.* ◊ *The 1997 law was intended to remedy the deficiencies in the previous law.* See also **remedy** → SOLUTION *noun*

rectify /ˈrektɪfaɪ/ [T] (*formal*) to correct sth that is wrong: *There were some errors in the report, but these were easy to rectify.* ◊ *It's not too late to rectify matters.*

redress /rɪˈdres/ [T] (*formal*) to correct sth that is unfair or wrong: *Attempts were made to redress some of the injustices of the previous regime.* ◊ *For years poorer children have had to put up with a lower quality education, and now is the time to redress the balance* (= make the situation more fair).

cure [T] to deal with a problem successfully: *Charities alone can't cure basic social injustices.* ◊ *I finally managed to cure the rattling noise in my car.*
▸ **cure** *noun* [C]: *a cure for poverty*

corridor *noun* See also the entry for HALL 2

corridor · hall · hallway · aisle · passage · passageway · walkway · catwalk
These words all mean a long, narrow enclosed area that you can walk along in order to get from one place to another.

PATTERNS AND COLLOCATIONS
▸ **in** the corridor / hall / hallway / aisle / passage / passageway / walkway
▸ **along / down** the corridor / hall / hallway / aisle / passage / passageway / walkway / catwalk
▸ **through** the corridor / hall / hallway / passage / passageway
▸ a **narrow** corridor / hall / hallway / aisle / passage / passageway / walkway / catwalk
▸ a **long** corridor / hall / hallway / aisle / passage / passageway / walkway
▸ an **underground** passage / passageway / walkway
▸ to **stand** in the corridor / hall / hallway / aisle
▸ at / to **the end of** the corridor / hall / hallway / aisle / passage / passageway / walkway / catwalk

corridor /ˈkɒrɪdɔː(r); *AmE* ˈkɔːr-; ˈkɑːr-/ [C] (*especially BrE*) a long narrow area with walls on either side that connects different rooms or parts of a building, especially in a large building such as a hospital, school or office building: *Go along the corridor, turn left, and you'll see his office in front of you.* ❶ On a train, a **corridor** is a long, narrow enclosed area that people use to walk from one compartment (= room) in a railway carriage to another.

hall [C] a long narrow area with walls on either side that connects different rooms or parts of a building: *Her office is just down the hall.* See also **hall** → HALL 2

hallway /ˈhɔːlweɪ/ [C] (*especially AmE*) a hall: *As I walked along the hallway, I passed several open doors.* See also **hallway** → HALL 2

NOTE CORRIDOR, HALLWAY OR HALL? These words are very close in meaning. A **corridor** is usually long and straight, and is normally used when talking about large public buildings. **Hall** and **hallway** can be used to talk about a connecting space in both public buildings and large private houses. **Corridor** is mainly used in British English, and is much the most frequent of these words in British English; **hall** is used in both British and American English, and is the most frequent of these words in American English; **hallway** is used especially in American English.

aisle /aɪl/ [C] a passage between rows of seats, especially down the middle of sth such as a church, theatre or train; the space or passage between rows of shelves in a supermarket: *She looked radiant as she walked down the aisle on her father's arm* (= when getting married in a church). ◊ *She managed to get an aisle seat* (= in a plane). ◊ *Coffee and tea are in the next aisle.*

passage [C] a long narrow area with walls on either side that connects one room or place with another: *It is said that the two houses were connected by a secret underground passage.* ◊ *A dark, narrow passage led to the main hall.* ❶ A **passage** is usually narrower and often longer and darker than a **corridor** or **hallway**. See also **alley** → ROAD

passageway /'pæsɪdʒweɪ/ [C] (*especially AmE*) a passage: *They followed him through a narrow passageway into the old town.*

walkway /'wɔːkweɪ/ [C] a passage or path for walking along, often outside and raised above the ground: *A covered walkway joins the two buildings.*

catwalk /'kætwɔːk/ [C] a narrow platform high above the ground for people to walk on, for example along the side of a bridge or above a theatre stage: *The lights were mounted on a catwalk above the stage.* ❶ Especially in British English, a **catwalk** is also the long stage that models walk on during a fashion show: the usual American English word for this is **runway**: *He presented his latest collection at a catwalk show during Paris fashion week.*

corrupt *adj.*

corrupt · fraudulent · unscrupulous · dirty · rotten · crooked · unprincipled · amoral
These words all describe people who are willing to do dishonest or illegal things for their own advantage.

PATTERNS AND COLLOCATIONS
▶ corrupt / fraudulent / unscrupulous / unprincipled / amoral **behaviour**
▶ corrupt / fraudulent / unscrupulous / dirty **dealings**
▶ corrupt / fraudulent / unscrupulous **practices**
▶ a corrupt / rotten / crooked **system**
▶ a corrupt / an unscrupulous / a crooked **businessman / lawyer / politician**
▶ **thoroughly / totally** corrupt / unscrupulous / amoral

corrupt /kə'rʌpt/ (*disapproving*) (of people) willing to use their power to do dishonest or illegal things in return for money or to get an advantage; (of behaviour) dishonest or immoral: *It was seen as the only way to overthrow a corrupt regime.*

fraudulent /'frɔːdjələnt; AmE -dʒə-/ (*formal*) intended to deceive sb, usually in order to make money illegally: *Steps are being taken to crack down on fraudulent advertising.* ◇ *The number of fraudulent insurance claims has risen.* ❶ **Fraudulent** is used more often to talk about things or actions, rather than a person. It is a more neutral, descriptive term than most of the other words in the group, which are disapproving. Typical collocates are *claim, statement, use* and *trading.* See also **fraud** → FRAUD 1
▶ **fraudulently** *adv.*: *She was charged with fraudulently obtaining a bank loan.*

unscrupulous /ʌn'skruːpjələs/ (*rather formal, disapproving*) (of people) willing to do dishonest or illegal things in return for money or to get an advantage; (of behaviour) dishonest or immoral: *The new law will give unscrupulous landlords an easy way of getting rid of people.* **OPP** scrupulous → GOOD 5, See also **scruple** → DOUBT *noun* 2

NOTE CORRUPT OR UNSCRUPULOUS? **Corrupt** is often used to talk about the authorities or a system and people who work for them. Typical collocates are *regime, system* and *official.* Common collocations of **unscrupulous** are mainly connected with people and their work, especially those who manage their own businesses: *dealer, employer, landlord, lender, operator, people, politician, dealings* and *practices.*

dirty [usually before noun] (*informal, disapproving*) unpleasant or dishonest: *You dirty liar!* ◇ *She's a dirty player.* ◇ *He always gets someone else to* **do the dirty work** *for him* (= tasks which are unpleasant because they involve being dishonest or unkind to people). ❶ Collocates of **dirty** in this meaning include *play, player, work* and *job.*
▶ **dirty** *adv.*: *We would have won if the other team hadn't* **played dirty** (= cheated).

rotten [not usually before noun] (*informal, disapproving*) (of systems and organizations) corrupt: *The organization is* **rotten to the core.**

crooked /'krʊkɪd/ (*rather informal, especially journalism, disapproving*) (especially of people doing business) dishonest: *The president has vowed to jail crooked executives.*

unprincipled (*rather formal, especially written, disapproving*) without moral principles; not caring about right and wrong: *She saw him as an unprincipled opportunist.* **OPP** principled → GOOD 5, See also **principle** → PRINCIPLE 1

amoral /ˌeɪ'mɒrəl; AmE -'mɔːr-; -'mɑːr-/ (*rather formal, especially written, sometimes disapproving*) showing that you do not care about right and wrong: *She had led them to believe that she shared their amoral values.* **OPP** moral → GOOD 5, See also **morals** → PRINCIPLE 1

NOTE UNPRINCIPLED OR AMORAL? **Unprincipled** is mostly used to describe people: *an unprincipled charlatan/creature/opportunist/scoundrel.* **Amoral** is used more to describe people's attitudes and behaviour. Typical collocates are *behaviour, society, attitude* and *values.*

corruption *noun*

corruption · bribery · extortion · blackmail
These are all words for dishonest or illegal behaviour, especially of people in authority.

PATTERNS AND COLLOCATIONS
▶ **alleged** corruption / bribery / extortion
▶ **attempted** bribery / extortion / blackmail
▶ **political** corruption / bribery / blackmail
▶ to **be involved in** corruption / bribery / extortion
▶ to **resort to** bribery / blackmail
▶ to **accuse sb of / charge sb with** corruption / bribery / extortion
▶ a corruption / bribery **scandal**
▶ **allegations of** corruption / bribery

corruption [U] dishonest or illegal behaviour, especially of people in authority: *There were allegations of* **bribery and corruption.** ◇ *The new district attorney has promised to fight police corruption.*

bribery /'braɪbəri/ [U] the act of giving or taking bribes (= money or sth valuable that you give or offer to sb to persuade them to help you, especially by doing sth dishonest): *She was arrested on bribery charges.* See also **bribe** → BRIBE

NOTE CORRUPTION OR BRIBERY? **Corruption** covers a wider range of activities than **bribery. Bribery** is a form of **corruption.**

extortion /ɪk'stɔːʃn; AmE ɪk'stɔːrʃn/ [U, C] (*rather formal*) the crime of making sb give you sth by threatening them, especially by threatening to use violence: *He was arrested and charged with extortion.*
▶ **extort** *verb* [T]: *The gang extorted money from over 30 local businesses.*

blackmail /'blækmeɪl/ [U] the crime of demanding money from a person by threatening to tell sb else a secret about them; the act of putting pressure on a person to do sth they do not want to do, for example by making threats or by making them feel guilty: *He was convicted of blackmail at Bristol Crown Court last month.* ◇ *We can't let them practise this emotional blackmail on us.*
▶ **blackmail** *verb* [T]: *She blackmailed him for years by threatening to tell the newspapers about their affair.*

cost *verb*

cost · be · sell · trade · go · retail · set sb back sth
These are all words that can be used when sth costs a particular amount of money and you need to pay that amount in order to buy, make or do it.

PATTERNS AND COLLOCATIONS
▶ **How much** does this cost / is this?
▶ That costs / will set you back **a lot of money**.

▸ sth sells / trades / retails **at** £9.95
▸ sth sells / goes / retails **for** £9.95

cost [T] If sth **costs** a particular amount of money, you need to pay that amount in order to buy, make or do it: *I didn't get it because it cost too much.* ◇ *Calls to the helpline cost 38p per minute.* ◇ *All these reforms will **cost money** (*= be expensive).* ◇ *Good food need not **cost a fortune** (*= be very expensive).* See also **cost** → PRICE *noun*

be *linking verb* (*especially spoken*) to cost: *'How much is that dress?' 'Eighty dollars.'*

sell [I] to be sold at a particular price: *The painting sold for $70 000 at auction.*

trade [I, T] (*business*) to be bought and sold, or to buy and sell sth, on a stock exchange (= a place where shares in companies are bought and sold): *Shares were trading at under half their usual value.* ◇ *The futures contract is traded at a clean price and does not include accrued interest payments.*

go [I] (*rather informal*) to be sold, especially for a particular price on a particular occasion: *We won't let the house go for less than £200 000.* ◇ *There was usually some bread **going cheap** (*= being sold cheaply) at the end of the day.*

retail /'riːteɪl/ [I] (*business*) to be sold in a shop at a particular price: *The book retails for $14.95.*

> **NOTE** SELL, GO OR RETAIL? Sell is a more general word than **retail**, which is used mostly in Business English, and only for goods that are sold to the public through shops: *The book retails/sells at £14.95.* ◇ ~~The painting retailed for $70 000 at auction.~~ Go in this meaning is more informal than **sell**. In British English it is used especially in the phrase *going cheap* and about particular items being sold on particular occasions: *The painting went for $70 000 at auction.* In informal American English you can also use **go** to talk about the usual price of sth in a shop: *These boots usually go for around $30 a pair.*

,set sb 'back sth *phrasal verb* [no passive] (*informal*) to cost sb a particular amount of money: *The repairs could set you back over £200.* ❶ **Set sb back sth** is used especially about things that are considered expensive.

costs *noun*

costs · spending · expenditure · expenses · overheads · outlay
These are all words for money spent by a government, organization or person.

▸ spending / expenditure / outlay **on** sth
▸ **total** costs / spending / expenditure / expenses / overheads / outlay
▸ **considerable / low** costs / spending / expenditure / expenses / overheads / outlay
▸ **high** costs / spending / expenditure / expenses / overheads
▸ **capital** costs / spending / expenditure / expenses / outlay
▸ **government / public / education / health / defence / military / household** costs / spending / expenditure / expenses
▸ to **increase / reduce** costs / spending / expenditure / expenses / overheads / the outlay
▸ to **control / cover** costs / spending / expenditure / expenses / overheads
▸ to **cut** costs / spending / expenditure / expenses / overheads
▸ to **meet** costs / expenditure / expenses / overheads
▸ to **incur** costs / expenditure / expenses

costs [pl.] the total amount of money that needs to be spent by a business: *labour/operating/production/running/transport costs* ◇ *These factories use cheap labour to keep costs down.* ◇ *The money they're making is barely enough to cover their costs.*

spending [U] the amount of money that is spent, especially by a government or organization: *This government wants to keep a tight rein on public spending.* ◇ *More spending on health was promised.* See also **spend** → SPEND 1

expenditure /ɪk'spendɪtʃə(r)/ [U, C] (*rather formal*) an amount of money spent by a government, organization or person: *There are plans to increase expenditure on education.* ◇ *The budget provided for a total expenditure of £27 billion.*

expenses [pl.] money that has to be spent by a person or organization; money that you spend while you are working which your employer will pay back to you later: *living/medical/legal expenses* ◇ *Can I give you something towards expenses?* ◇ *You can claim back your travel expenses.* ◇ *The company sent her on a two-day **all-expenses-paid** course in London.* ◇ *Just put the cost of the train fare **on your expense account**.* See also **expense** → PRICE *noun*

overheads /'əʊvəhedz; AmE 'oʊvərh-/ [pl.] (*especially BrE*) (*especially AmE* **overhead**) [U]) the regular costs of running a business or organization, such as rent, electricity and wages: *High overheads mean small profit margins.*

outlay /'aʊtleɪ/ [C, U] the money that you have to spend in order to start a new business or project, or in order to save yourself money or time later: *The business quickly repaid the initial outlay on advertising.*

costume *noun*

costume · disguise · fancy dress · camouflage
These are all words for sth that you wear to make you look different from the way you usually look.

▸ **in** costume / disguise / fancy dress / camouflage
▸ to **wear** a costume / a disguise / fancy dress / camouflage
▸ to **put on** a costume / disguise

costume [C, U] the clothes worn by actors in a play or film, or worn by sb to make them look like sb/sth else: *I can't believe you didn't notice that guy in the giant chicken costume.* ◇ *The actors were still in costume and make-up.* ◇ *a costume designer* See also **costume** → CLOTHES

disguise /dɪs'ɡaɪz/ [C, U] a thing that you wear or use to change your appearance so that people do not recognize you; the art of changing your appearance in this way: *She wore glasses and a wig as a disguise.* ◇ *The girl in the park turned out to be a policewoman in disguise.*
▸ **disguise** *verb* [T]: *She disguised herself as a boy.* See also **disguise** → HIDE *verb* 1

> **NOTE** COSTUME OR DISGUISE? You wear a **costume** for fun, or to take part in a performance; you wear a **disguise** in order to trick people so that they do not recognize you.

,fancy 'dress [U] (*BrE*) clothes that you wear, especially at parties, to make you appear to be a different character: *I went to a fancy dress party as a pirate.*

camouflage /'kæməflɑːʒ/ [U] a way of hiding soldiers and military equipment, using clothes, paint, leaves or nets, so that they look like part of their surroundings: *a camouflage jacket* (= covered with green and brown marks and worn by soldiers) ◇ *A dozen men walked by, dressed in army camouflage and holding automatic weapons.* See also **camouflage** → HIDE 1

cough *verb* See the Topic Map for HEALTH on p.890

cough · sneeze · choke · clear your throat
These are all words for what you do when sth is blocking the passage of air to your lungs, or when air is forced suddenly out of your throat or nose.

▸ to **make sb** cough / sneeze / choke
▸ to cough / clear your throat **loudly / nervously**

cough [I] to force out air suddenly and noisily through your throat, for example when you have a cold: *I couldn't stop coughing.* ◇ *She coughed nervously and looked at me.*

▸ **cough** *noun* [C]: *She gave a little cough to attract my attention.*

sneeze [I] to have air come suddenly and noisily out through your nose and mouth in a way that you cannot control, for example because you have a cold: *I've been sneezing all morning.*
▸ **sneeze** *noun* [C]: *He gave a violent sneeze.*

choke [I, T] to be unable to breathe because the passage to your lungs is blocked or you cannot get enough air; to make sb unable to breathe: *He was choking on a piece of toast.* ◇ *She almost choked to death in the thick fumes.* ◇ *The device contains small parts which could easily choke a child.*

clear your 'throat *idiom* to cough so that you can speak clearly: *She cleared her throat. 'I hope I'm not interrupting,' she said.*

cough

cough   sneeze

count *verb* See also the entries for CALCULATE and ESTIMATE

count · add · tally · tot sth up · total
These words all mean to calculate a total number or amount.

PATTERNS AND COLLOCATIONS
▸ to count / add / tally / tot / total **up how much / many...**
▸ to count / add / tally / tot up **the number of sth**
▸ to add up / tot up **the amount / the cost of sth**
▸ to count / add up / tally / tot up / total sb's **points / score**

count [T, I] to calculate the total number of people or things in a particular group: *The diet is based on counting calories.* ◇ *She began to count up how many guests they had to invite.* ◇ *There are 12 weeks to go, counting from today.* See also **count** → ESTIMATE *noun*

add [T] to put numbers or amounts together to get a total: *Add 9 to the total.* ◇ *If you add all these amounts together you get a huge figure.* OPP **take, subtract** → DISCOUNT
▸ **addition** *noun* [U]: *children learning addition and subtraction* OPP **subtraction** → DISCOUNT

NOTE COUNT OR ADD? Adding involves at least two numbers or amounts (you **add** sth to sth else), **counting** involves just one step (you **count** sth). You **add** numbers or amounts, but you cannot **count** amounts: *to add up / count the number of people* ◇ *to add up the amount of rainfall* ◇ *to count the amount of rainfall.* This is because you can only count countable nouns, not uncountable ones. You can also **count**, but not **add**, people and objects: *to count tickets / people / votes* ◇ *to add up people / tickets / votes*

tally [T] (*rather informal, especially business*) to calculate the total number or amount of sth: *When we tallied up the cost of moving, we decided against it.* ❶ **Tally** is often used in business, when referring to things such as sales figures, costs or other economic results. See also **tally** → ESTIMATE *noun*

‚tot sth 'up *phrasal verb* (-tt-) (*BrE, informal*) to add together several numbers or amounts in order to get a total: *Let's tot up everybody's points and see who's won.* ◇ *The trip isn't really that cheap when you tot everything up.*

total (-ll-, *AmE* -l-) [T, usually passive] to add up the numbers of sb / sth and get a total, especially a total score: *Each student's points were totalled and entered in a list.* See also **total** → WHOLE *adj.*

country *noun*
1 a foreign country
2 country life

1 country · nation · state · land · superpower · power
These are all words for an area of land that has its own government and laws.

PATTERNS AND COLLOCATIONS
▸ a **foreign** country / nation / state / land / power
▸ a / an **great / major / leading / industrial / colonial** country / nation / state / power
▸ a / an **independent / free / powerful / Third World / Communist / democratic** country / nation / state
▸ an **allied / enemy** country / nation / power
▸ a **sovereign** nation / state / power
▸ to **rule** a country / nation / state / land
▸ to **govern** a country / nation / state
▸ to **lead** a country / nation
▸ to **serve** your country / nation

country [C] an area of land that has or used to have its own government and laws: *They are holding special events all over the country.* ◇ *This is just one of 30 sites around the country.* ◇ *It's good to meet people from different parts of the country.* ◇ *'It's a free country!' he shouted. 'I can do what I like.'* ◇ *Sugar is only produced in tropical countries.* ◇ *She represented her country at the Olympics.*

nation [C] a country considered as a group of people with the same language, culture and history, who live in a particular area under one government: *This is an important moment in our nation's history.* ◇ *They are a nation of food lovers.* ◇ *Leaders of the G8 leading industrial nations backed the plan.* See also **national** → NATIONAL, **national** → CULTURAL

state (also **State**) [C] a country considered as an organized political community controlled by one government: *It has not yet been recognized as an independent sovereign state.* ◇ *The action was opposed by several UN member states.* ◇ *Many Third World countries are one-party states of one type or another.* ◇ *After the collapse of the Soviet Union, many new nation states were created.* See also **state** → PUBLIC

NOTE COUNTRY, NATION OR STATE? To refer to a country as a political unit or to its government, you can use **country, nation** or **state**: *relations between the two countries / nations / states* ◇ *a newly independent country / nation / state.* **Country** and **nation** can also refer to an area where people live, its economy, culture, etc.: *a rich / wealthy country / nation* ◇ *an oil-producing country / nation.* **Country** is the only word which can be used to refer to a country as a geographical area: *a hot / cold / tropical country*

land [C] (*literary*) used to refer to a country or region in an emotional or imaginative way: *She longed to return to her native land.* ◇ *America was seen as the land of freedom and opportunity.*

superpower /ˈsuːpəpaʊə(r); ˈsjuː-; *AmE* ˈsuːpərp-/ [C] one of the countries in the world with very great military or economic power and a lot of influence: *The United States was left as the only global superpower.* ◇ *Japan's status as an economic superpower*

power [C] a country with a lot of influence in world affairs, or the affairs of a region, or with great military strength: *Major European powers, such as France and Germany, are against the plan.* ◇ *He transformed a backward country into a world power.*

2 country · landscape · countryside · terrain · land · scenery · topography
These are all words for areas away from towns and cities, with fields, woods and farms.

PATTERNS AND COLLOCATIONS
▸ **the surrounding** country / landscape / countryside / terrain / land / scenery

▸ **mountain / mountainous / wild / rugged** country / landscape / countryside / terrain / scenery
▸ **beautiful / glorious / stunning / dramatic / magnificent / spectacular** country / landscape / countryside / scenery
▸ **open** country / landscape / countryside / terrain / land
▸ **rolling** country / landscape / countryside
▸ to **protect** the landscape / countryside / land

country [U] (often **the country**) an area that is away from towns and cities, especially one with particular natural features: *She lives in the country.* ◇ *We came to an area of wooded country.* ◇ *a little country town* ◇ *I don't really enjoy country life.* ◇ *There have often been disagreements between town and country.*

landscape [C, usually sing.] everything that you can see when you look across a large area of land, especially in the country: *This pattern of woods and fields is typical of the English landscape.* ◇ *The mountains dominate the landscape.* ◇ *The power station is a **blot on the landscape** (= completely spoils the landscape).*

countryside [U] land outside towns and cities, with fields, woods and farms: *a little village in the French countryside* ◇ *You can walk through miles and miles of unspoilt countryside.* ❶ **Countryside** is usually used when you are talking about the beauty or peacefulness of a country area. See also **nature** → NATURE 2

terrain /təˈreɪn/ [U, C] (*written*) land: *Make sure you have equipment that is suitable for the terrain.* ◇ *There were several miles of **difficult terrain** to be covered.* ❶ **Terrain** is used when you are describing the natural features of an area, for example if it is rough, flat, etc.

land [U] (usually **the land**) the countryside; the way people live in the country as opposed to in towns and cities: *Many younger people are leaving the land to find work in the cities.* ◇ *Almost a third of the population **live off the land** (= grew or produced their own food).* ◇ *Her family had **farmed the land** for generations.* See also **land** → LAND *noun* 1

scenery [U] the natural features of an area, such as mountains, valleys, rivers and forests, especially when these are attractive to look at: *Alpine scenery* ◇ *We stopped on the mountain pass to admire the scenery.* ◇ (*especially AmE*) *They went abroad for **a change of scenery** (= to see and experience new surroundings).* ❶ In British English it is more usual to say **a change of scene**. See also **scene** → VIEW 2, **nature** → NATURE 2

topography /təˈpɒɡrəfi; *AmE* təˈpɑːɡ-/ [U] (*technical*) the natural features of an area, especially the positions of its rivers, mountains, etc.; the study of these features: *a map showing the topography of the island*

county *noun*

county • state • district • province • region • zone
These are all words for an area that forms part of a country and has its own official boundaries (= borders).

PATTERNS AND COLLOCATIONS
▸ **in** a county / state / district / province / region / zone
▸ a **border / coastal** county / state / district / province / region / zone
▸ the **northern, southern, etc.** counties / states / districts / provinces / region / zone

county [C] an area, especially in Britain, Ireland and the US, that has its own official boundaries and local government: *The US state of California is divided into 58 counties.* ◇ *Originally, county boundaries often followed the course of a river.*

state (also **State**) [C] a large area, especially in the US and Australia, that has its own official boundaries and government: *The hurricane swept across the southern states of the US.*

district [C] an area of a country, town or state that has official boundaries for administrative purposes: *Delivery is free within the London postal district.* ◇ *The district council granted planning permission for ten new houses.* See also **district** → AREA 1

province /ˈprɒvɪns; *AmE* ˈprɑːv-/ [C] a large area in countries such as Canada and South Africa that has its own official boundaries and government: *Canada is divided into ten provinces and three territories.*
▸ **provincial** /prəˈvɪnʃl/ *adj.*: *the provincial assembly*

NOTE COUNTY, STATE OR PROVINCE? These words are used differently for different parts of the world, depending on a country's traditions and how it is organized. Britain and Ireland are both divided into **counties**, but in Ireland these counties are organized into four large **provinces**. There are no provinces in Britain. The US is divided into **states**, and nearly all these states are divided into counties. Canada is divided into provinces, but only some of these provinces are divided into counties. **State** and **province** usually describe an area that is larger than a **county**.

region [C] one of the areas that a country is divided into, that has its own customs and/or its own government: *Bilbao is the largest city in the Basque region in northern Spain.* See also **region** → AREA 1
▸ **regional** *adj.*: *the regional council*

zone [C] one of the areas that a larger area is divided into for the purposes of organization: *The ticket may be used on any bus in zone 2.* ◇ *All countries in zones 1 and 2 have free incoming calls.* See also **zone** → AREA 1

courage *noun*

courage • bravery • nerve • guts • heroism • valour • audacity • daring
These are all words for the willingness to do things even though they are dangerous or difficult.

PATTERNS AND COLLOCATIONS
▸ **great** courage / bravery / nerve / heroism / valour / audacity / daring
▸ **true** courage / bravery / heroism
▸ to **have** the courage / bravery / nerve / guts / audacity
▸ to **show** courage / bravery
▸ doing sth **takes** courage / bravery / nerve / guts
▸ an **act of** courage / bravery / heroism / valour

courage [U] a willingness to face danger, pain or opposition, especially when doing sth that you believe to be right: *She displayed remarkable **courage in the face of** danger.* ◇ *I haven't yet **plucked up the courage** to ask her.* ◇ *Unfortunately, they lack the **moral courage** to speak out against what is happening.* ◇ *You need to have the **courage of your convictions** (= be brave enough to do what you believe to be right).* **OPP** **cowardice** → COWARD, See also **courageous** → BRAVE

bravery /ˈbreɪvəri/ [U] a willingness to face danger, pain or difficulty, especially without showing fear: *My great grandfather received the medal as an award for outstanding bravery in World War I.* See also **brave** → BRAVE

NOTE COURAGE OR BRAVERY? **Courage** is very often about facing opposition, for moral reasons, although this may involve the threat of physical punishment, as well as threats to your career or reputation; **bravery** is more often a willingness to face physical danger or pain: *They lack the moral bravery to speak out.* ◇ *He received the medal as an award for courage.*

nerve [U] the ability to control your emotions in order to do sth difficult or dangerous: *It took a lot of nerve to take the company to court.* ◇ *I was going to have a go at parachuting but **lost my nerve** at the last minute.* ◇ *She **kept her nerve** to win the final set 6–4.*

guts [pl.] (*informal*) the courage and determination that it takes to do sth difficult or unpleasant: *He doesn't have the guts to walk away from a well-paid job.* See also **gutsy** → BRAVE

heroism /'herəʊɪzəm; AmE -roʊ-/ [U] very great courage, especially when you have done sth dangerous that is admired by other people: *He showed great heroism in going back into the burning building.* See also **heroic** → BRAVE

valour (BrE) (AmE **valor**) /'vælə(r)/ [U] (*literary*) great courage, especially the courage shown by soldiers in a war: *The purpose of the award is to recognize acts of valour by members of the armed services.*

audacity /ɔː'dæsəti/ [U] brave but rude or shocking behaviour: *The sheer audacity of the plan amazed everyone.*

daring /'deərɪŋ; AmE 'der-/ [U] willingness to take risks: *He was saved by the skill and daring of the mountain rescue team.* See also **daring** → BOLD, **dare** → DARE *verb*

court noun

court · tribunal · courtroom · court of law · court of appeal · courthouse · law court
These are all words for a place where trials and other legal cases are held and judged.

PATTERNS AND COLLOCATIONS
▸ **in** a court / tribunal / courtroom / court of law / courthouse / law court
▸ **before** a court / tribunal / court of law / court of appeal
▸ **at** a court / tribunal / law court
▸ a **local** court / tribunal / courthouse / law court
▸ to **take sb to / come before / set up / apply to** a court / tribunal / court of appeal
▸ to **go to / refer sth to / appear before / attend / tell / preside over** a court / tribunal
▸ a court / tribunal / court of appeal **hears / dismisses / upholds** sth
▸ a court / tribunal **orders / rules sth**

court [C, U] a place where legal trials take place and are judged: *She will appear in court tomorrow.* ◇ *They took their landlord to court for breaking the contract.* ◇ *The case took five years to* **come to court.** ◇ *There wasn't enough evidence to* **bring the case to court.** ◇ *The case was* **settled out of court** (= a decision was reached without a trial). ◇ *He won the* **court case** *and was awarded damages.* ❶ **The court** [sing.] is the people in a court, especially those who make decisions, such as a judge and jury: *The case is now before the court.* ◇ *Please tell the court what happened.*

tribunal /traɪ'bjuːnl/ [sing.+ sing./pl. v.] a type of court with the authority to deal with a particular problem or disagreement: *A war crimes tribunal was set up to prosecute those charged with atrocities.* ◇ *The fee for the player will be decided* **by tribunal.** ◇ (BrE) *He lost his appeal against the decision at an* **industrial tribunal** (= a court that can decide on disputes between employees and employers).

courtroom /'kɔːtruːm; -rʊm; AmE 'kɔːrt-/ [C] a room in which trials or other legal cases are held: *The judge came back into the packed courtroom.* ◇ *She could face a bitter* **courtroom battle.**

court of 'law (pl. **courts of law**) [C] (*formal*) a place where legal cases are held: *There was nothing that could be proved in a court of law.*

court of ap'peal (also **appeal court**) (pl. **courts of appeal, appeal courts**) [C] a court that people can go to in order to try and change legal decisions that have been made in a lower court: *There is a* **right of appeal** *to the court of appeal.* ❶ In Britain, the **Court of Appeal** is the highest court apart from the House of Lords and can change legal decisions made by a lower court. In the US, the highest court is the Supreme Court. Below this, there are a number of **Courts of Appeals**, which can change legal decisions made by a lower court.

courthouse /'kɔːthaʊs; AmE 'kɔːrt-/ (AmE) a building containing courts of law: *The prison is opposite the courthouse.*

'law court [C] (BrE) a court of law; a building containing courts of law: *He has a job as an interpreter in the law courts.*

> **NOTE** COURT, COURTROOM, COURT OF LAW, COURTHOUSE OR LAW COURT? **Court** is the most general of these words, and is used to talk about both the room or building where trials take place and the process of holding, attending and judging legal cases: *to go / take sb / bring a case to court.* **Court of law** is a more formal way of saying **court**, used especially when talking about the place or building, rather than the process of going to court. A **courtroom** is the actual room where a trial takes place, used especially to suggest all the people crowded into the room, or facing each other across the room. **Law courts** (in British English) is more often used to refer to the building where the courts are; **courthouse** is used for this in American English.

courtyard noun

courtyard · yard · square · compound · cloister · quadrangle · precinct · quad
These words all mean an open space that is surrounded by a wall or buildings.

PATTERNS AND COLLOCATIONS
▸ **in** the courtyard / yard / square / compound / cloister / quadrangle / … precincts / quad
▸ **across** the courtyard / yard / square / compound / quadrangle / quad
▸ the **central / main** courtyard / yard / square / quadrangle
▸ a **cobbled** courtyard / yard / square
▸ a **walled** courtyard / yard / compound

courtyard /'kɔːtjɑːd; AmE 'kɔːrtjɑːrd/ [C] an open space that is partly or completely surrounded by buildings and is usually part of a building such as a large house or castle: *The entrance leads through an arch and into a cobbled inner courtyard.*

yard /jɑːd; AmE jɑːrd/ [C] (BrE) an area outside a building, usually with a hard surface and a surrounding wall: *The children were playing in the yard at the front of the school.* ◇ *They rode out of the stable yard.*

square [C] an open area in a town, usually with four sides, surrounded by buildings: *The next day, a large crowd gathered in the market square.*

compound /'kɒmpaʊnd; AmE 'kɑːm-/ [C] an area surrounded by a fence or wall in which a factory or other group of buildings stands: *Angry crowds stormed the presidential palace compound.*

cloister /'klɔɪstə(r)/ [C, usually pl.] a covered stone passage with arches around a square garden that sometimes forms part of a religious building such as a cathedral or monastery: *The 12th century church and cloisters remain surprisingly intact.*

quadrangle /'kwɒdræŋgl; AmE 'kwɑːd-/ [C] (*formal*) an open square area that has buildings all around it, especially in a school or college: *It has a large central quadrangle entered from the south side.*

precinct /'priːsɪŋkt/ [C, usually pl.] (*formal*) the area around a place or building, sometimes enclosed by a wall: *The school uses many of the splendid medieval buildings in the cathedral precincts.*

quad /kwɒd; AmE kwɑːd/ [C] (*rather informal*) a word for quadrangle: *Her office window overlooks the quad.*

cover noun

cover · wrapper · casing · wrapping · sheath · tarpaulin · tarp · covering · wrap
These are all words for sth that covers or is wrapped around an object.

PATTERNS AND COLLOCATIONS
▸ **under** a cover / tarpaulin / tarp / covering

▶ a **protective** cover / wrapper / casing / wrapping / sheath / covering
▶ (a) **plastic** cover / wrapper / casing / wrapping / sheath / tarpaulin / tarp / covering / wrap
▶ (a) **paper** cover / wrapper / wrapping / covering
▶ to **take off** / **remove** the cover / wrapper / wrapping / covering / wrap
▶ to **take sth out of** its wrapper / casing / wrapping / sheath

cover [C] a thing that is put over or around another thing, usually to protect it or make it look attractive: *The buggy had a plastic waterproof cover.* ◇ *The plants provide a protective cover for the soil.* ◇ *It's a good idea to put a dust cover over your computer at night* (= to protect it from dust). ◇ *Brighten up your room with some colourful cushion covers.* See also **cover → HIDE** verb 1

wrapper [C] a piece of paper, plastic, etc. that is wrapped around sth in order to protect it. Food that you buy will often have a wrapper on it in order to protect it and keep it clean: *Each meal is packed in a sealed wrapper.* ◇ *He eagerly tore the wrapper off.* ◇ (*BrE*) *The floor was covered with sweet wrappers.* ◇ (*AmE*) **candy wrappers**

casing /'keɪsɪŋ/ [C] a cover that protects sth, especially one made of a hard substance such as wood or hard plastic: *The printer has an attractive black casing.*

wrapping [U] (also **wrappings**) [pl.] paper, plastic, etc. that is used for wrapping sth in, in order to protect it: *She tore the cellophane wrapping off the box.* ◇ *The dress still hung in its plastic wrappings.* ◇ *I bought several rolls of* **wrapping paper**.

sheath /ʃiːθ/ (pl. **sheaths** /ʃiːðz/) [C] a cover that fits closely around sth to protect it, especially sth such as a knife or other weapon or tool: *He put the dagger back in its sheath.* ◇ *The cable is protected by a strong plastic sheath.*

tarpaulin /tɑːˈpɔːlɪn; *AmE* tɑːrˈpɔːl-/ [C] a large sheet made of a heavy waterproof material, used to cover things to keep rain or water off: *The car was covered with a black tarpaulin.*

tarp [C] (*AmE*, *informal*) a tarpaulin: *The men huddled under the tarp.*

covering [U, C] a material that is used to cover sth, especially sth such as floors or walls in order to protect them or make them look attractive: *The cell had bare walls and no floor covering.*

wrap [U] (usually in compounds) paper, plastic, etc. that is used for wrapping sth in, in order to protect it or make it look attractive: *We stock a wide range of cards and* **gift wrap**. ◇ *Use* **bubble wrap** (= a sheet of plastic full of small bubbles of air) *to pack things which might get broken.* ◇ (*AmE*) *Just cover the plate of sandwiches with* **plastic wrap** (= a thin transparent plastic material that sticks to a surface and to itself). ❶ The British English word for **plastic wrap** is **cling film**.

cover verb

cover · coat · spread · rub · smear · daub · cake
These words all mean to put a liquid or a soft substance onto sth.

PATTERNS AND COLLOCATIONS
▶ to cover / coat / spread / rub / smear / daub / cake sth **with** sth
▶ to cover / coat / cake sth **in** sth
▶ to spread / rub / smear / daub sth **on** sth
▶ to spread / smear sth **over** sth
▶ to cover sth with / coat sth with / spread a **layer** of sth
▶ to rub / smear **oil** into / onto sth
▶ to be covered / coated / caked in / with **dust**
▶ to be covered / caked in / with **dirt**
▶ to be covered / smeared / caked in / with **mud**
▶ to be covered / coated / smeared in / with **grease** / **oil**
▶ to be covered / coated / smeared / daubed with **paint**
▶ to be covered / smeared / daubed / caked in / with **blood**
▶ to be covered / coated / spread with **chocolate**
▶ **liberally** covered / coated / spread / smeared
▶ **thickly** / **thinly** covered / coated / spread

cover [T, often passive] (usually used with an adverb or preposition) to put a layer of sth, especially sth liquid, soft or dirty, on sb/sth: *The players were soon covered in mud.* ◇ *The wind blew in from the desert and covered everything with sand.*

coat [T, often passive] to cover sth with a layer of a substance: *The cookies were thickly coated with chocolate.* ◇ *A film of dust coated the table.*

> **NOTE** **COVER OR COAT?** Cover is a more general word than **coat**. **Coat** is used especially when sth is deliberately covered with a fixed layer for decoration or protection: *The flakes are coated with sugar* (= the sugar is fixed onto them). ◇ *The flakes are covered with sugar* (= the sugar is not fixed onto them). When sth gets **coated** in dust or grease, it suggests that the dust or grease may be quite thick and hard to remove: *More than 400 birds were coated with oil when 50 tonnes of crude oil spilled into the sea.*

spread [T, I] (usually used with an adverb or preposition) to deliberately put a layer of a substance onto the surface of sth; to be able to be put onto a surface: *She spread butter on a piece of toast.* ◇ *Spread the cake with cream and then sprinkle flakes of chocolate on top.* ◇ *If the paint is too thick, it will not spread easily.* ❶ **Spread** is used about substances that you spread deliberately; it is not used about dirt or grease that gets onto sth by accident.

rub (-**bb**-) [T] (always used with an adverb or preposition) to spread a liquid or other substance over a surface while pressing firmly: *She* **rubbed** *moisturizer* **into** *her skin.* ◇ *Rub some salt on the fish before cooking.*

smear /smɪə(r); *AmE* smɪr/ [T] to spread a soft substance over a surface in a rough or careless way: *The children had smeared mud on the walls.* ◇ *His face was smeared with blood.* See also **smear → MARK** noun

daub /dɔːb/ [T, often passive] (always used with an adverb or preposition) to spread a substance such as paint or mud on to sth thickly and/or carelessly: *The walls of the building were daubed with red paint.*

> **NOTE** **SMEAR OR DAUB?** Daub is often passive; **smear** is often active or passive. **Daub** always needs an adverb or preposition; **smear** can be used without: *She had smeared her make-up.* ◇ ~~*She had daubed her make-up.*~~ **Daub** is often used when talking about words which are written on sth; **smear** is not usually used in this way: *They found a message daubed onto the wall of the cell.* ◇ ~~*They found a message smeared onto the wall of the cell.*~~

cake [T, usually passive] to cover sth with a thick layer of sth soft that becomes hard when it dries: *Her shoes were caked with mud.*

coward noun

coward · wimp · sissy · nervous wreck · chicken · wuss
These are all words for a person who is not brave, strong or confident.

PATTERNS AND COLLOCATIONS
▶ **You're such a** / **Don't be a** coward / wimp / sissy / chicken / wuss!
▶ **You** coward / wimp / sissy / chicken / wuss!

coward /'kaʊəd; *AmE* -ərd-/ [C] (*disapproving*) a person who is not brave or who does not have the courage to do things that other people do not think are especially difficult: *I'm a real coward when it comes to going to the dentist.*
▶ **cowardice** /'kaʊədɪs/ noun [U]: *The lieutenant had displayed cowardice in the face of the enemy.* **OPP courage** → COURAGE
▶ **cowardly** adj.: *a weak, cowardly man* ◇ *your cowardly refusal to tell the truth* **OPP brave** → BRAVE

wimp [C] (*informal*, *disapproving*) a person who is not strong, brave or confident: *He won't go on his own – he's a complete wimp!*

sissy (*BrE* also **cissy**) [C] (*informal, disapproving*) a boy that other men or boys laugh at because they think he is weak or frightened, or only interested in the sort of things girls like: *The other boys kept calling him a sissy.*

,nervous 'wreck [C] (*informal*) a person who is worried or is suffering from stress: *The interview reduced him to a nervous wreck.*

chicken [C] (*informal, disapproving*) a person who is not brave enough to do sth: *He called me a chicken because I wouldn't swim in the river.*
► **chicken** *adj.* [not before noun]: *They were too chicken to follow us.*

wuss /wʊs/ [C] (*spoken, disapproving*) a person who is not brave or strong: *Don't be such a wuss! She won't hurt you!*

crack *noun*

crack · fissure · crevice · cleft · chink · fault
These are all words for a long, narrow opening in sth hard.

► a **crack** / fissure / crevice / cleft / chink / fault **in** sth
► a **narrow** crack / fissure / crevice / cleft / chink
► a **long** crack / fissure / cleft
► a crack / fissure **opens**

crack [C] a line on the surface of sth hard where it has broken but not split into separate parts; a narrow space or opening: *This cup has a crack in it.* ◇ *Cracks began to appear in the walls.* ◇ *She peeped through a crack in the curtains.* ◇ *The door opened a crack* (= a small amount). See also **crack** → BREAK *verb* 1

fissure [C] (*technical*) a long deep crack in sth, especially in rock or in the earth: *fissures in the ocean floor*
► **fissured** *adj.*: *fissured rock/terrain*

crevice [C] a narrow crack in a rock or wall: *Most of the year the insects are hidden in rock crevices.*

cleft [C] a natural opening or crack, for example in the ground or in rock, or in part of the body: *a cleft in the rocks/hills* ◇ *the cleft in his chin*

chink [C] a narrow opening in sth, especially one that lets light through: *a chink in the curtains* ◇ *I noticed a chink of light under the door* (= a small area of light shining through a narrow opening).

> **NOTE** CRACK OR CHINK? Crack is a more general word than **chink**. You can say: *a crack/chink in the curtains* and: *The door opened a crack.* but NOT: *The door opened a chink.* You can have *a chink of light* but NOT: *a crack of light.*

fault [C] a place where there is a break that is longer than usual in the layers of rock in the earth's crust: *the San Andreas fault* ◇ *a fault line*

cramped *adj.*

cramped · compact · tight · confined
These words all describe a place that only has limited space.

► a cramped / compact / confined **place**
► a cramped / compact **room**
► a cramped / tight / confined **space**
► a cramped / confined **area**
► cramped / confined **conditions**

cramped /kræmpt/ (*disapproving*) (of a room or space) without enough space for the people in it: *It's difficult working in such cramped conditions.* ◇ *He lived for six months in a cold, cramped attic room.* ❶ You describe a place as **cramped** when you think it is uncomfortable because it is too small. **OPP** spacious → SPACIOUS

compact /kəmˈpækt; ˈkɒmpækt; *AmE* ˈkɑːm/ (*approving*) (of a room or place) using only a small amount of space: *The kitchen was compact but well equipped.* ◇ *Edinburgh is a compact city.* ❶ You describe a place as **compact** when you think this is a good thing, because the available space has been used as effectively as possible.

tight [usually before noun] with things or people packed closely together, leaving little space between them: *There was a tight group of people around the speaker.* ◇ *With six of us in the car it was a tight squeeze.*

confined /kənˈfaɪnd/ [usually before noun] (of a space or area) small and enclosed by walls or sides: *It is cruel to keep animals in confined spaces.*

crash *verb*

crash · slam · collide · smash · plough into sth · bang into sth · wreck · write sth off · total
These are all words that can be used when sth, especially a vehicle, hits sth else very hard.

► to crash / slam / smash / plough / bang **into** sth
► to crash / slam / smash **sth into** sth
► **two vehicles** crash / collide
► **two vehicles** crash / slam / smash / bang **into each other**
► to crash / smash / wreck / write off / total a **car / truck / vehicle**
► to crash / collide **head-on**

crash [I, T] (*rather informal*) to hit an object or another vehicle, causing damage; to make a vehicle do this: *I was terrified that the plane would crash.* ◇ *Look out! We're* (= our car is) *going to crash!* ◇ *He crashed the car into a tree.* See also **crash** → ACCIDENT *noun*

slam *phrasal verb* (**-mm-**) [I, T] (always used with *into* or *against*) to crash into sth with a lot of force; to make sth do this: *The car skidded and slammed into a tree.* ◇ *The force of the explosion slammed me against the wall.* See also **slam** → CLOSE *verb* 1

collide /kəˈlaɪd/ [I] (*rather formal*) (of two vehicles or people) to crash into each other; (of a vehicle or person) to crash into sb/sth else: *The car and the van collided head-on in thick fog.* ◇ *As he fell, his head collided with the table.* See also **collision** → ACCIDENT

smash [I, T] (*rather informal*) to crash into sth with a lot of force; to make sth do this; to crash a car: *A bullet smashed into the wall behind them.* ◇ *Ram-raiders smashed a stolen car through the shop window.*

> **NOTE** CRASH, SLAM OR SMASH? Crash is used especially to talk about vehicles and can be used without a preposition: *We're going to crash, aren't we?* In this meaning **slam** and **smash** always take a preposition: *We're going to slam/smash, aren't we?* They are used for talking about a much wider range of things than just vehicles. **Crash** can also be used to talk about other things, if used with a preposition: *He crashed down the telephone receiver.*

'plough into sth *phrasal verb* (*BrE*) (*AmE* **plow into sth**) (especially of a vehicle or its driver) to crash into sth with a lot of force, especially because you are driving too fast or not paying enough attention: *A truck ploughed into the back of the bus.*

,bang 'into sth *phrasal verb* (*rather informal*) to crash into or hit sth by mistake: *I banged into a chair and hurt my leg.*

wreck /rek/ [T] to crash a vehicle and damage it so badly that it is not worth repairing: *The road was littered with wrecked cars.* See also **wreck** → VANDALIZE *verb*, **wreck** → ACCIDENT, **wreck** → REMAINS 1

,write sth 'off *phrasal verb* (*BrE, rather informal*) to crash a vehicle and damage it so badly that it is not worth repairing: *He's written off two cars this year.*
► 'write-off *noun* [C]: *She survived the crash with minor injuries, but the car was a write-off.*

total [T] (**-ll-**, *AmE* **-l-**) (*especially AmE, informal, spoken*) to damage sth, especially a vehicle, so badly that it is not worth repairing: *She never forgave him for totaling her car.*

NOTE WRECK, WRITE STH OFF OR TOTAL? Vehicles are **written off** or **totalled** by accident. They can be **wrecked** by accident or deliberately, especially for fun: *youths who steal and wreck fast cars*

crazy *adj.* See also the entry for RECKLESS

crazy · stupid · silly · foolish · dumb · mad · insane · idiotic
These words all describe sb not showing good sense or judgement.

stupid	crazy	insane
silly	mad	
foolish	idiotic	
dumb		

PATTERNS AND COLLOCATIONS
▸ crazy/stupid/silly/foolish/dumb/mad/insane/idiotic **to do sth**
▸ crazy/stupid/silly/foolish/dumb/mad/insane/idiotic **of sb** to do sth
▸ a crazy/a stupid/a silly/a foolish/a dumb/a mad/an insane/ an idiotic **idea**
▸ a crazy/a stupid/a silly/a foolish/a dumb/a mad/an insane/ an idiotic **thing to do**
▸ a crazy/a stupid/a silly/a foolish/a dumb/an idiotic **question**
▸ a stupid/a silly/a foolish/a dumb/an idiotic **mistake**
▸ to **seem/look/sound** crazy/stupid/silly/foolish/dumb/ insane/idiotic
▸ to **act** crazy/stupid/dumb
▸ to **feel** stupid/silly/foolish/dumb
▸ **Are you** crazy/stupid/dumb/mad/insane?
▸ Sb **must be** crazy/stupid/mad/insane!
▸ **really/plain/a bit/a little/quite** crazy/stupid/silly/foolish/ dumb/mad/insane
▸ **completely/totally** crazy/stupid/dumb/mad/insane
▸ **pretty/rather** crazy/stupid/silly/foolish/dumb/mad

crazy (*especially AmE, informal, usually disapproving*) showing a lack of good sense or judgement: *Are you crazy? We could get killed doing that.* ◇ *She must be crazy to lend him money.* ◇ *I know it sounds crazy, but it just might work. What a crazy idea!* ❶ In this meaning, **crazy** is used more to talk about people than actions.
stupid (*often disapproving*) showing a lack of thought, good sense or judgement: *I've made a stupid mistake.* ◇ *I was stupid enough to believe him.* ◇ *It was stupid of you to get involved.* ❶ It is considered offensive to tell sb that they are **stupid**. **OPP** sensible → BEST, **sensible** → WISE
▸ **stupidity** /stjuːˈpɪdəti; *AmE* stuː-/ *noun* [U, C, usually pl.]: *I couldn't believe my own stupidity.* ◇ *the errors and stupidities of youth*
▸ **stupidly** *adv.*: *I stupidly agreed to lend him the money.*
silly (*rather informal, especially spoken, usually disapproving*) stupid: *No, actually that's a silly idea.* ◇ *'I can walk home.' 'Don't be silly — it's much too far!'* ◇ *You silly boy!* ◇ *How silly of me to expect them to help!*
foolish (*rather formal, especially written*) stupid: *She's just a vain, foolish woman.* ◇ *How could she have been so foolish as to fall in love with him?* ◇ *It was a very foolish thing to do.* **OPP** wise → WISE, See also **unwise** → RECKLESS, **fool** → FOOL
dumb /dʌm/ (*especially AmE, informal, usually disapproving*) stupid: *That was a pretty dumb thing to do.* ◇ *That's the dumbest idea I ever heard.*

NOTE CRAZY, STUPID, SILLY, FOOLISH OR DUMB? Crazy usually describes a person; if it describes an action, it is usually a deliberate action, but one that is dangerous or could harm sb in some way: *That was a crazy thing to do! Are you trying to get us killed?* **Stupid**, **silly**, **foolish** and **dumb** describe people or their actions. These may be deliberate actions or they can be careless actions caused by sb not thinking: *a stupid/silly/foolish/dumb*

mistake ◇ *a crazy mistake*. It is often considered offensive to tell sb that they are **stupid**; **dumb** is slightly less offensive, and can be used between friends in a way that shows affection; **silly** is a kinder word, especially when used to a child, but can still be offensive if used to an adult. **Foolish** is a rather formal word, used especially in writing.

mad (*especially BrE, informal, sometimes disapproving*) very stupid; not at all sensible: *You must be mad to risk it.* ◇ *'I'm going to buy some new clothes.' 'Well, don't go mad* (= spend more than is sensible).*'* ❶ The normal American English word for this is **crazy**. In this meaning, **mad** is used more to talk about people than actions.
▸ **madness** *noun* [U]: *In a moment of madness she had agreed to go out with him.*
insane /ɪnˈseɪn/ (*informal, usually disapproving*) extremely stupid or dangerous: *I must have been insane to agree to the idea.* ◇ *It was an insane risk to take.*
▸ **insanity** /ɪnˈsænəti/ *noun* [U]: *It would be sheer insanity to attempt the trip in such bad weather.*
idiotic /ˌɪdiˈɒtɪk; *AmE* -ˈɑːtɪk/ (*disapproving*) very stupid: *What an idiotic question.* ◇ *Don't be so idiotic!* ❶ Idiotic is often used by people who are angry. See also **idiot** → FOOL

creak *verb*

creak · scrape · groan · squeak · scratch · rasp
These words all mean to make a long sound like the sound made when two objects rub against each other.

PATTERNS AND COLLOCATIONS
▸ to scrape/scratch/rasp **against** sth
▸ to creak/groan/squeak **open**
▸ a **door/bed/floorboard** creaks/groans
▸ a **pen** scrapes/scratches
▸ a **voice** squeaks/rasps

creak /kriːk/ [I] to make a long low sound like the sound that is sometimes made when you open a door or step on a wooden stair or floor: *The stairs creaked as she went up them.* ◇ *The door creaked open.*
▸ **creak** *noun* [C]: *Distant creaks and groans echoed eerily along the dark corridors.*
scrape /skreɪp/ [I, T] (*usually used with an adverb or preposition*) to make an unpleasant rough sound like the sound made by rubbing or dragging a hard object across a surface; to make sth produce this sound: *I could hear his pen scraping across the paper.* ◇ *Bushes scraped against the car windows.*
groan [I] to make a long deep sound like the sound sb makes when they are unhappy or in pain: *The trees creaked and groaned in the wind.* See also **groan** → WHISPER

NOTE CREAK OR GROAN? Groan is often used when sth **creaks** loudly, especially when the sound is caused by sth big or heavy being moved with a lot of effort.

squeak /skwiːk/ [I] to make a short high sound that is not very loud: *My new shoes squeak.* ◇ *The mouse ran away, squeaking with fear.*
▸ **squeak** *noun* [C]: *Shirley gave a little squeak of surprise.*
scratch [I] (*usually used with an adverb or preposition*) to make an unpleasant rough sound like the sound made by rubbing or dragging a sharp object across a surface: *His pen scratched away on the paper.*

NOTE SCRAPE OR SCRATCH? Scrape is often used to describe the sound made by sth that does not have a sharp point: *Don't scrape your chairs on the floor.* ◇ *Don't scratch your chairs on the floor.* **Scratch** is often used when an object with a sharp point is making the sound, like the nails on an animal's foot: *The dog kept scratching at the door to go out.* ◇ *The dog kept scraping at the door to go out.*

rasp /rɑːsp; AmE ræsp/ [I] to make a harsh unpleasant sound, especially a sound made by speaking or breathing: *He struggled to the top of the hill, his breath rasping loudly.*

creative *adj.* See the Topic Map for SPORT AND LEISURE on p.892

creative · artistic · innovative · original · imaginative · ingenious · inventive
These words all describe sb/sth having or showing skill or imagination to create sth new and interesting.

PATTERNS AND COLLOCATIONS
▸ a creative / an artistic / an innovative / an original / an imaginative / an ingenious / an inventive **mind**
▸ creative / artistic **ability / achievement / skill / talent**
▸ a creative / an innovative / an original / an imaginative / an ingenious / an inventive **idea / design / solution**
▸ creative / innovative / original / imaginative **thinking**
▸ a creative / an innovative / an original **thinker**
▸ **highly** creative / innovative / original / imaginative / ingenious / inventive

creative /kriˈeɪtɪv/ involving the use of skill and the imagination to produce sth new or a work of art; having or showing an ability to do this: *classes on **creative writing*** (= writing stories, plays and poems) ◇ *the company's creative team* ◇ *She's very creative – she writes poetry and paints.* See also **create** → MAKE 1, **creation** → DEVELOPMENT, **creativity** → INSPIRATION
artistic showing a natural skill in or enjoyment of art, especially being able to paint or draw well; done with skill and imagination: *He comes from a very artistic family.* ◇ *The decor inside the house was very artistic.*
innovative /ˈɪnəveɪtɪv; ˈɪnəvətɪv/ (*approving*) introducing or using new ideas or ways of doing sth: *their innovative use of existing technology* See also **innovation** → DEVELOPMENT, **innovator** → LEADER 2
original (*usually approving*) having or showing new, different and interesting ideas: *The film is challenging and highly original.* ◇ *This work is the product of a highly original mind.* See also **originality** → INSPIRATION, **novel** → NEW 1
imaginative /ɪˈmædʒɪnətɪv/ (*usually approving*) having or showing new, different and interesting ideas: *an imaginative child* ◇ *recipes that make imaginative use of seasonal vegetables* OPP **unimaginative** → LACKLUSTRE, See also **imagination** → IMAGINATION, **imagination** → INSPIRATION
▸ **imaginatively** *adv.*: *The stables have been imaginatively converted into offices.*
ingenious /ɪnˈdʒiːniəs/ having or showing clever new ideas; good at inventing things: *an ingenious device / invention / experiment* ◇ *She's very ingenious when it comes to finding excuses.* See also **ingenuity** → INSPIRATION
▸ **ingeniously** *adv.*: *ingeniously designed*
inventive (*often approving*) having or showing new, different and interesting ideas; good at inventing things: *She is one of the most inventive of modern writers.* ◇ *This is a courageous and inventive piece of film-making.* See also **invent** → DESIGN *verb* 1, **invention** → DEVELOPMENT, **inventiveness** → INSPIRATION

NOTE INNOVATIVE, ORIGINAL, IMAGINATIVE, INGENIOUS OR INVENTIVE? **Innovative** is often used in practical and business contexts and is as much about using new ideas as having them; **original**, **imaginative** and **inventive** are often used in more artistic contexts. *Original / imaginative ideas* are interesting whether they work in practice or not; things that are **ingenious** are clever and must work, or they are not ingenious; however, they may not be as big or important as things that are **innovative** or **original**.

crime *noun*
1 the fight against crime
2 commit a crime

1 crime · wrongdoing · misconduct · delinquency · vice
These are all words for activities that involve breaking the law or breaking rules.

PATTERNS AND COLLOCATIONS
▸ **serious** crime / wrongdoing / misconduct / delinquency
▸ **sexual** crime / misconduct / vice
▸ **male / female** crime / delinquency / vice
▸ **juvenile** crime / delinquency
▸ **cause / tackle / control / prevent** crime / delinquency
▸ to **be driven / turn** to crime / vice
▸ to **deny** wrongdoing / misconduct

crime [U] activities that involve breaking the law: *This month's figures show an increase in **violent crime**.* ◇ *More needs to be done to help the **victims of crime**.* ◇ *These youngsters are often involved in **petty crime** such as shoplifting and casual theft.* ◇ *There is a strong link between drugs and **organized crime**.* ◇ *The **crime rate** is rising.* ◇ *She writes crime novels* (= stories about crime). See also **criminal** → ILLEGAL *adj.*
wrongdoing /ˈrɒnduːɪŋ; AmE ˈrɔːŋ-/ [U, C] (*formal*) illegal or dishonest behaviour: *The company denies any wrongdoing.* ❶ **Wrongdoing** is often used when people claim to be, or are found to be, innocent of doing sth wrong.
misconduct /ˌmɪsˈkɒndʌkt; AmE -ˈkɑːn-/ [U] (*formal*) unacceptable behaviour, especially by a professional person: *The doctor was accused of **gross misconduct*** (= very serious misconduct).
delinquency /dɪˈlɪŋkwənsi/ [U, C] (*rather formal*) bad or criminal behaviour, usually by young people: *There has been an increase in juvenile delinquency.* ◇ *The boys drift into minor delinquencies while hanging around the streets.* See also **delinquent** → ILLEGAL *adj.*
vice [U] criminal activities that involve sex or drugs: *At the door were two plain-clothes detectives from the vice squad.*

2 crime · offence · sin · felony · misdemeanour · atrocity · wrong · outrage
These are all words for an illegal, wrong or unacceptable act.

PATTERNS AND COLLOCATIONS
▸ a crime / an offence / a sin / an atrocity / an outrage **against** sb / sth
▸ a **serious** crime / offence / felony / misdemeanour / wrong
▸ a **terrible** crime / sin / wrong
▸ a **capital** crime / offence / felony
▸ a **minor / petty** crime / offence / misdemeanour
▸ a **sexual** crime / offence / sin / misdemeanour
▸ a **terrorist** crime / offence / atrocity / outrage
▸ to **commit** a crime / an offence / a sin / a felony / a misdemeanour / an atrocity / an outrage
▸ to **forgive** a crime / an offence / a sin / a misdemeanour / a wrong / an outrage

crime [C] an illegal act or activity that can be punished by law: *The massacre was a crime against humanity.* ◇ *Many crimes are never reported to the police.* ◇ *No weapon was found at the **scene of the crime**.*
offence (*BrE*) (*AmE* **offense**) [C] (*rather formal*) an illegal act or activity that can be punished by law: *It is a criminal offence to inflict cruelty on any wild animal.* ◇ *He was given a warning since it was a **first offence*** (= the first time that he had been found guilty of a crime). ◇ *The rebels could face charges of treason, a **capital offence*** (= one for which sb may be punished by death).
▸ **offend** *verb* [I]: (*formal*) *He started offending at the age of 16.*

NOTE CRIME OR OFFENCE? In everyday language, **crime** is used more often than **offence** to talk about more serious illegal acts, such as murder or rape. **Offence** is used more frequently to talk about illegal activities such as driving too fast: (*BrE*) *a driving/motoring offence* ◊ (*AmE*) *a traffic offense*; carrying a gun: (*BrE*) *a firearms offence*; and using drugs: (*BrE*) *a drugs offence* ◊ (*AmE*) *a drug offense*. However, in legal contexts, **offence** is the preferred technical term for all illegal acts and activities.

sin [C] an offence against God or against a religious or moral law: *Confess your sins to God and he will forgive you.*
▶ **sin** *verb* [I]: *Forgive me, Lord, for I have sinned.*

felony /'feləni/ [C, U] (*AmE or old-fashioned, law*) a serious crime such as murder or rape: *He was indicted on three felony charges of lying to the grand jury.*

misdemeanour (*BrE*) (*AmE* **misdemeanor**) /ˌmɪsdɪ-'miːnə(r)/ [C] (*especially AmE, law*) a crime that is less serious than a felony: *He pleaded guilty to the misdemeanor of domestic violence.* ❶ In formal language, in both British and American English, a **misdemeanour** can also be any action that is bad or unacceptable, but not very serious: *He thought about his own youthful misdemeanours.*

atrocity /ə'trɒsəti; *AmE* ə'trɑːs-/ [C, usually pl., U] (*rather formal*) a terrible, cruel and violent act, especially in a war: *They have accepted responsibility for the atrocities committed during the war.*

wrong [C] (*formal*) an act that is not legal, honest or morally acceptable: *It is time to forgive past wrongs if progress is to be made.* ◊ *It's the job of the newspapers to expose the wrongs suffered by such people.* ❶ **Wrong** places emphasis on the victim (= the person who has been badly treated): *to suffer a wrong*. It is often used when talking about trying to correct sth bad that sb has done: *to redress/right/forgive a wrong*

outrage /'aʊtreɪdʒ/ [C] a terrible, cruel and violent act that shocks people or makes them very angry: *No one has yet claimed responsibility for this latest bomb outrage.*

NOTE ATROCITY OR OUTRAGE? **Outrage** is most often used to talk about terrorist acts; **atrocity** refers to both wartime and terrorist acts.

criminal *noun*

criminal · offender · culprit · sinner · felon · crook · delinquent
These are all words for a person who does sth that is wrong, dishonest or against the law.

PATTERNS AND COLLOCATIONS
▶ a **convicted** / **habitual** criminal / offender / felon
▶ to **catch** a criminal / an offender / the culprit / a crook
▶ to **identify** / **apprehend** a criminal / an offender / a culprit
▶ to **convict** / **sentence** a criminal / an offender
▶ to **punish** criminals / offenders / the culprit / sinners / felons

criminal [C] a person who commits a crime: *Society does not know how to deal with hardened criminals* (= people who regularly commit crimes and are not sorry for what they do). ◊ *I was treated just like a common criminal.* ◊ (*BrE*) *Sending these youngsters to prison simply trains them to become professional criminals.* ◊ (*AmE*) *career criminals*

offender [C] (*rather formal*) a person who commits a crime; a person or thing that does sth wrong: *He spent some time in a young offender institution.* ◊ *First offenders* (= people who had never committed a crime before this one) *were treated more leniently.* ◊ *He favours tougher punishments for repeat offenders* (= people who commit the same crime more than once). ◊ *Child protection groups are calling for a national register of sex offenders* (= people found guilty of illegal sexual acts). ◊ *When it comes to pollution, the chemical industry is a major offender.*

NOTE CRIMINAL OR OFFENDER? **Criminal** suggests that not only has sb committed a crime, but that they have a tendency to commit crimes. **Offender** simply means than sb has broken the law at least once. For example, a

driver who has broken the speed limit is an **offender**, but you would not call them a **criminal**. **Offender** is the word that is preferred by people whose job involves dealing with people who break the law.

culprit /'kʌlprɪt/ [C] a person who has done sth wrong or against the law; a person or thing responsible for causing a problem: *The police quickly identified the real culprits.* ◊ *The main culprit in the current crisis seems to be modern farming techniques.*

NOTE OFFENDER OR CULPRIT? **Culprit** is nearly always used after *the*, because it is used to talk about the person, people or thing responsible for a particular thing that has happened. The most common adjectives used for describing a **culprit** are *biggest, main, major, prime, real* and *worst*. **Offender** can also be used in this way, although it is a little more formal that **culprit**.

sinner [C] (*formal*) a person who has committed a sin or sins (= broken God's law): *God forgives all sinners who repent.*

felon /'felən/ [C] (*especially AmE, law*) a person who has committed a felony (= a serious crime such as murder or rape): *The law requires convicted felons entering the state to register their address with the police.*

crook /krʊk/ [C] (*informal*) a dishonest person, especially one who steals money: *That salesman is a real crook.* ◊ *The film portrays a world of small-time crooks, petty crime and drinking clubs.*

delinquent /dɪ'lɪŋkwənt/ [C] (*rather formal*) a person, especially a young person, who shows a tendency to commit crime: *What can be done to help these juvenile delinquents turn away from crime?*

crisis *noun*

crisis · emergency · disaster · tragedy · catastrophe · calamity
These are all words for an unexpected situation or event that creates difficulties for sb/sth, kills a lot of people or causes a lot of damage.

crisis	calamity	disaster
emergency		tragedy
		catastrophe

PATTERNS AND COLLOCATIONS
▶ a crisis / disaster / tragedy / catastrophe / calamity **for** sb
▶ **in** a crisis / an emergency
▶ a **major** crisis / emergency / disaster / tragedy / catastrophe / calamity
▶ a **great** crisis / disaster / tragedy / catastrophe / calamity
▶ a/an **awful** / **dreadful** / **terrible** disaster / tragedy / catastrophe / calamity
▶ a **potential** crisis / disaster / tragedy / catastrophe
▶ a **national** crisis / emergency / disaster / tragedy / catastrophe / calamity
▶ an **environmental** crisis / emergency / disaster / tragedy / catastrophe
▶ a/an **ecological** / **personal** crisis / disaster / tragedy / catastrophe
▶ a / an **economic** / **financial** crisis / disaster / catastrophe
▶ a **nuclear** disaster / catastrophe
▶ to **cause** a crisis / an accident / a disaster / a tragedy / a catastrophe
▶ to **bring** disaster / tragedy / catastrophe / calamity
▶ to **deal with** / **cope with** a crisis / an emergency / a disaster
▶ to **avert** a crisis / disaster / tragedy / catastrophe / calamity
▶ a disaster / tragedy / catastrophe / calamity **happens** / **occurs**
▶ disaster / tragedy / catastrophe **strikes**

crisis /'kraɪsɪs/ (pl. **crises** /-siːz/) [C, U] a time of great danger, difficulty or uncertainty when problems must be solved or important decisions must be made: *It is hoped that his resignation will end the latest political crisis in the country.* ◊ *The Communist Party was facing an identity crisis.* ◊ *The party was suffering a crisis of confidence among its supporters* (= they did not trust it any longer).

◇ *The business is still in **crisis** but it has survived the worst of the recession.* ◇ *In **times of crisis** I know which friends I can turn to.*

emergency [C, U] a sudden serious and dangerous event or situation which needs immediate action to deal with it: *This door should only be used in an emergency.* ◇ *I always have some extra cash with me **for emergencies**.* ◇ *The government has declared a **state of emergency** following the earthquake.* ◇ *There is an emergency exit (= to be used in an emergency) on each side of the aeroplane.*

disaster [C, U] an unexpected event such as a very bad accident, a flood or a fire that kills a lot of people or causes a lot of damage: *Thousands died in the disaster.* ◇ *They were involved in the 2001 ferry disaster.* ◇ *They will not insure you against a natural disaster (= one that is caused by nature).* ◇ *Although there was always the possibility of flooding, the Nile seldom brought disaster to Egypt.* See also **disaster** → DISASTER, **disastrous** → DISASTROUS

tragedy /'trædʒədi/ [C, U] a very sad event or situation, especially one that involves death: ***It's a tragedy that** she died so young.* ◇ *Tragedy struck the family when their three-year-old son was hit by a car and killed.* ◇ *The whole affair **ended in tragedy**.* See also **tragic** → SAD

catastrophe /kə'tæstrəfi/ [C] a sudden disaster that causes many people to suffer: *Early warnings of rising water levels prevented another major catastrophe.* See also **catastrophe** → DISASTER, **catastrophic** → DISASTROUS

> **NOTE** DISASTER OR CATASTROPHE? Either **disaster** or **catastrophe** can be used with such words as *nuclear, environmental, ecological* and *economic*, but **disaster** is preferred when you are talking about a famous event in which people were killed: *the Chernobyl/Lockerbie/Challenger disaster*

calamity /kə'læməti/ [C, U] an event that causes great harm, especially to the political or financial affairs of a country or organization, or to sb's personal life: *Sudan suffered a series of calamities during the 1980s.* ◇ *His financial help saved the magazine from total calamity.* ❶ A **calamity** is less serious than a **disaster** or **catastrophe** and is not usually used for an event in which people die.

criterion *noun*

criterion · standard · test · measure · benchmark · guide · guideline · gauge · yardstick · norm
These are all words for amounts, or levels of quality, that are used to help you estimate or judge sb/sth.

PATTERNS AND COLLOCATIONS
▸ a criterion / measure / benchmark / yardstick / norm **for** sth
▸ **by** any criteria / standard / measure / yardstick
▸ **against** the criteria / standard / benchmark / yardstick / norm
▸ a **useful** criterion / test / measure / benchmark / guide / gauge / guideline / yardstick
▸ (an) **objective** criterion / standards / test / measure / guide
▸ (a) **general** standards / measure / guide / guideline
▸ (a) **reliable** test / measure / guide / gauge / guidelines
▸ to **serve as** a criterion / measure / guide / gauge / guideline / yardstick
▸ to **provide** a criterion / standard / measure / benchmark / guide / yardstick
▸ to **set / establish** criteria / a standard / the benchmark / norms

criterion /kraɪ'tɪəriən; AmE -'tɪr-/ (pl. **criteria** /-iə/) [C] a principle or level of quality by which sth is judged or by the help of which a decision is made: *The **sole criterion** is the market price of the land.* ◇ *What are the criteria used in evaluating student performance?* ◇ *The listing in the guide is proof that the restaurant **meets** certain **criteria**.*

standard [C, usually pl.] a level of quality that is normal or acceptable for a particular person or in a particular situation: *No matter how hard I tried I could never **reach their standards**.* ◇ *You'd better **lower your standards** if you want to find somewhere cheap to live.* ◇ *I don't know if*

it's **up to your standards**. ◇ *It was a simple meal, by Eddie's standards.* ◇ *The equipment was slow and heavy **by modern standards**.*

test [C] a situation or event that shows how good, strong, etc. sb/sth is: *The local elections will be a good test of the government's popularity.* ◇ *The game against Dundee will be a real **test of character** for us.* ◇ *The latest pay dispute has really **put** her management skills **to the test**.*

measure [C] a way of judging or measuring sth; a sign of the size or strength of sth: *Exam results are only one **measure of** a school's success.* ◇ *Is this test a good measure of reading comprehension?* ◇ *Her hand trembled slightly, a measure of her anxiety.*

benchmark /'bentʃmɑːk; AmE -mɑːrk/ [C] something that can be measured and used as a standard that other things can be compared with: *The German recycling system is seen as a benchmark for schemes throughout Europe.* ◇ *The central bank has cut its benchmark interest rate four times.*

guide [C, usually sing.] something that gives you enough information to be able to make a decision about sth or form an opinion: *As a general guide, large dogs need more exercise than small ones.* ◇ *These figures should be taken as a **rough guide**.*

guideline /'ɡaɪdlaɪn/ [C] something that can be used to help you make a decision or form an opinion: *These prices are a guideline only.* ◇ *It may help to have a few guidelines to follow.*

> **NOTE** GUIDE OR GUIDELINE? There is very little difference in meaning between these two words. **Guide** is often used in situations where being exact is less important; **guideline** is often used in business situations, where it is impossible to be exact, but still important to be as nearly right as possible. **Guide** is NOT usually used in the plural: ~~It may help to have a few guides to follow.~~

gauge (AmE also **gage**) /ɡeɪdʒ/ [C, usually sing.] (written, especially business) a thing, event or fact that can be used to estimate or judge sth: *The company was regarded as a gauge of Britain's industrial well-being.* See also **gauge** → ESTIMATE, **gauge** → JUDGE *verb* 1

yardstick /'jɑːdstɪk; AmE 'jɑːrd-/ [C] something that can be measured and used as a standard that other things can be compared with: *Exam results are not the only yardstick of a school's performance.* ◇ *Rates of progress are difficult to compare without a common yardstick.*

> **NOTE** BENCHMARK OR YARDSTICK? A **benchmark** is usually the particular standard that is used or recommended for measuring a particular thing; a **yardstick** is more often one of several possible standards that can be used.

norm [C] a required or agreed standard, level or amount: *The level of background radioactivity is well below international norms.*

critical *adj.*

critical · disapproving · judgemental · damning
These words all describe your reaction to sb/sth when you think that they are bad or wrong.

PATTERNS AND COLLOCATIONS
▸ critical / disapproving **of** sb / sth
▸ a critical / disapproving **glance / look / voice**
▸ a critical / disapproving / judgemental **tone / attitude**
▸ critical / disapproving / judgemental / damning **comments**
▸ a critical / judgemental **person**
▸ to **cast** a critical / disapproving **eye** at sb / sth
▸ **very** critical / disapproving / judgemental
▸ **mildly** critical / disapproving

critical expressing what you think is bad or wrong about sb/sth: *They issued a critical report on the government's handling of the crisis.* ◇ *Tom's parents were highly critical of the school.* **OPP uncritical** ❶ **Uncritical** is usually used

in a disapproving way: *Her uncritical acceptance of everything I said began to irritate me.* See also **criticize**
→ BLAME
▸ **critically** adv.: *He spoke critically of the government.*
disapproving showing that you feel that sb/sth is bad or wrong: *She gave him a disapproving glance.* ◊ *She sounded disapproving as we discussed my plans.* **OPP** **approving** → GOOD 6, See also **disapprove** → DISAPPROVE
▸ **disapprovingly** adv.: *He shook his head disapprovingly.*
judgemental (*BrE*) (also **judgmental**, especially in *AmE*) /dʒʌdʒˈmentl/ (*disapproving*) judging sb/sth and criticizing them too quickly: *Stop being so judgemental!* See also **judge** → JUDGE *verb* 1
damning /ˈdæmɪŋ/ very critical of sb/sth; producing evidence to suggest that sb is guilty: *damning criticism/ evidence* ◊ *a damning conclusion/report* ◊ *Her report is expected to deliver a damning indictment of education standards.* **OPP** **glowing** → GOOD 6

criticism *noun*

criticism · attack · disapproval · condemnation · denunciation · censure · assault · rap · quibble · flak
These are all words for the act of expressing a negative opinion about sb/sth.

PATTERNS AND COLLOCATIONS
▸ criticism/disapproval/condemnation/a denunciation/censure **of** sb/sth
▸ an attack/assault **on** sb/sth
▸ criticism/an attack/condemnation/flak **from** sb/sth
▸ (a) **strong** criticism/attack/disapproval/condemnation
▸ a **fierce/severe** criticism/attack/denunciation/censure
▸ (a) **public** criticism/attack/disapproval/condemnation/ denunciation/censure
▸ to **launch** a criticism/an attack/an assault
▸ to **make** a criticism/an attack/a denunciation/an assault
▸ to **express** criticism/disapproval/condemnation
▸ to **bring/draw** criticism/condemnation from sb/sth
▸ to **come under** criticism/attack/censure/assault
▸ to **take** criticism/flak

criticism [U, C] the act of expressing a negative opinion about sb/sth because you think they have faults: *The plan has **attracted criticism** from consumer groups.* ◊ *People in public life must always be **open to criticism** (= willing to accept being criticized).* ◊ *Ben is very sensitive, he just can't take criticism.* ◊ *I didn't mean it as a criticism.* ◊ *My only criticism of the house is that it is on a busy main road.* See also **criticize** → BLAME
attack [C, U] (*especially journalism*) strong, aggressive criticism of sb/sth in speech or writing: *She launched a scathing attack on the government's policies.* ◊ *The school has come under attack for failing to encourage bright students.* See also **attack** → BLAME *verb*
disapproval [U] a feeling that you do not like an idea, an action or sb's behaviour because you think it is bad, not suitable or going to have a bad effect on sb else: *He shook his head **in disapproval**.* ◊ *She looked at my clothes **with disapproval**.* **OPP** **approval** → PRAISE, See also **disapprove** → DISAPPROVE
condemnation /ˌkɒndemˈneɪʃn; *AmE* ˌkɑːn-/ [U, C] (*rather formal*) strong criticism of sb/sth, especially for moral reasons: *There was widespread condemnation of the invasion.* ◊ *The report will be seen by many as a strong condemnation of the prison system.* See also **condemn** → BLAME
denunciation /dɪˌnʌnsiˈeɪʃn/ [C, U] (*formal*) an act of criticizing sb/sth strongly in public: *The bishop made an angry denunciation of the government's policies.* ◊ *All parties joined in bitter denunciation of the terrorists.* See also **denounce** → BLAME
censure /ˈsenʃə(r)/ [U] (*formal*) strong criticism, especially from a court, parliament or other official body: *Her dishonest behaviour came under severe censure.* See also **censure** → BLAME *verb*

assault /əˈsɔːlt/ [C] strong, aggressive criticism of sb/sth in speech or in writing, especially in order to cause damage: *The paper's assault on the president was totally unjustified.*

NOTE ATTACK OR ASSAULT? **Attack** is used more frequently than **assault** as a way of describing a criticism of sb/sth. **Assault** can be more severe and suggests a serious, deliberate attempt to hurt sb's reputation or damage a policy.

rap [C] (*AmE, informal*) an unfair judgement on sb/sth: *He denounced the criticisms as 'just one bum rap after another'.* ◊ *Wolves **get a bad rap**, says a woman who owns three.*
quibble /ˈkwɪbl/ [C] a small complaint or criticism, especially one that is not important: *The only quibble about this book is the lack of colour illustrations.*
flak [U] (*informal*) severe criticism intended to damage or destroy sb/sth that comes from several different sources: *He's taken a lot of flak for his left-wing views.* ◊ *She **came in for a lot of flak** from the press.*

cross *verb*

cross · cut across sth · cut through sth · take · negotiate
These words all mean to go across a road, river or other boundary, or across, over, or around an area of land.

PATTERNS AND COLLOCATIONS
▸ to cross/cut through the **hills/mountains**
▸ to cross/negotiate a **road/bridge**
▸ to cross/cut across a **field**
▸ to cut across/cut through a **park**
▸ to take/negotiate a **bend/corner**
▸ to cross/negotiate sth **successfully/safely**

cross [I, T] to go from one side of sth to the other: *The ferry crosses from Portsmouth to Santander.* ◊ *He **crossed over** from the other side of the road.* ◊ *A bridge crosses the river a few miles upstream.* ◊ *It was the first time she had crossed the Atlantic.* ◊ *They were arrested as they tried to **cross the border**.* See also **crossing** → CRUISE
ˌcut aˈcross sth *phrasal verb* to cross an area instead of going around it, especially because it is quicker than the usual route: *We'll go round past the stables and cut across the fields.*
ˌcut ˈthrough sth *phrasal verb* to cut across sth: *They cut through the woods towards the farm.* ◊ *He cut through the station to get to his office.*

NOTE CUT ACROSS STH OR CUT THROUGH STH? People generally **cut across** an open area such as *fields* or a *park*, but **cut through** a place that is more enclosed or presents a barrier such as *woods, mountains* or a *forest*.

take [T] to go over a barrier or around a bend: *The horse took the jump (= jumped over the barrier) safely but then stumbled.* ◊ *He took the bend (= drove the car around it) much too fast.*
negotiate /nɪˈɡəʊʃieɪt; *AmE* ˈɡoʊ-/ [T] (*rather formal*) to successfully get over or past a difficult part on a path or route: *We then had to negotiate a steep rock face.* ◊ *She **negotiated her way** past the hot ovens.*

crowd *noun*

crowd · mob · horde · throng · drove · crush · rabble
These are all words for a lot of people together.

PATTERNS AND COLLOCATIONS
▸ a crowd/hordes/a throng/droves/a crush **of people**
▸ a crowd/mob/horde/rabble **of youths**
▸ a crowd/throng **of journalists/photographers**
▸ people do sth **in** hordes/droves
▸ a/an **angry/unruly/hostile** crowd/mob
▸ a **disorderly** crowd/rabble

▶ to **push** / **fight** / **force your way through** the crowd / mob / hordes / throng / crush
▶ to **break up** / **disperse** a crowd / mob
▶ to **join** the crowd / throng
▶ a crowd / mob / throng **gathers**

crowd [C+sing./pl. v.] a large number of people gathered together in a public place, for example in the streets or at a sports game: *A small crowd had gathered outside the church.* ◇ *Crowds of people poured into the street.* ◇ *I want to get there early to avoid the crowds.* ◇ *The game attracted a* **capacity crowd** *of 80 000.* ◇ *Nearly 300 marshals will be involved in* **crowd control**. ◇ *A whole crowd of us* (= a lot of us) *are going to the ball.*

mob [C+sing./pl. v.] (*often disapproving*) a large crowd of people, especially one that may become violent or cause trouble: *An angry mob of demonstrators came charging around the corner.* ◇ **mob rule** (= a situation in which a mob has control, rather than people in authority) ◇ *a* **lynch mob** (= a group of people who capture and kill sb illegally because they consider them guilty of a crime)

horde /hɔːd; *AmE* hɔːrd/ [C] (*sometimes disapproving*) a large crowd of people: *There are always hordes of tourists here in the summer.* ◇ *Football fans turned up in hordes.*

throng [C] (*written*) a crowd of people: *We pushed our way through the throng.* ◇ *He was met by a throng of journalists and photographers.*

> **NOTE** **CROWD** OR **THRONG**? Crowd is a much more frequent and general word than **throng**. Throng is used especially in descriptive writing to suggest lots of people crowding together in a busy or excited way. A **throng** attracts people who want to join in or find out what is going on. You might want to *avoid/get away from the crowds* but you would not usually 'avoid/get away from the throng'. At a sports game you talk about the **crowd**, NOT the **throng**.

drove /drəʊv; *AmE* droʊv/ [C, usually pl.] a large number of people or animals, often moving or doing sth as a group: *People are leaving the countryside* **in droves** *to look for work in the cities.*

crush [C, usually sing.] (*sometimes disapproving*) a crowd of people pressed close together in a small space: *There's always a big crush in the bar during the interval.*

rabble [sing., pl.] (*disapproving*) a large group of noisy people who are or may become violent: *As he arrived he was met by a rabble of noisy youths.*

crowd verb See also the entry for PACK

crowd · cluster · flock · huddle · throng · herd
These words are all used to talk about people standing or moving together in a group.

PATTERNS AND COLLOCATIONS
▶ to crowd / cluster / flock / huddle / throng / herd **together**
▶ to crowd / cluster / flock / huddle / throng **into** somewhere
▶ to crowd / cluster / flock / huddle / throng **round** / **around** somewhere
▶ to flock / throng **to** somewhere
▶ to flock / throng **to do sth**
▶ to crowd / throng the **streets**
▶ **people** crowd / cluster / flock / huddle / throng somewhere

crowd [I, T] to form a group of people that fills a place so there is little room to move: *We all crowded into her office to sing 'Happy Birthday'.* ◇ *Photographers were crowding around outside.* ◇ *Thousands of people crowded the narrow streets.* ❶ When there is no object, **crowd** is always used with an adverb or preposition.

cluster [I] (usually used with an adverb or preposition) to come together in a small group or groups: *Guests clustered at tables scattered around the hotel's bar.* See also **cluster** → GROUP *noun* 1

flock [I] (used with an adverb, preposition or *to* infinitive) (of people or birds) to go or gather together somewhere in large numbers: *Thousands of people flocked to the beach this weekend.* ◇ *People flocked to hear him speak.* See also **flock** → HERD *noun*

huddle [I] (usually used with an adverb or preposition) (of people or animals) to gather closely together, usually because of cold or fear: *People* **huddled up** *close to each other.*

throng [I, T] (*rather formal, written*) to go somewhere or be present somewhere in large numbers: *The children thronged into the hall.* ◇ *Crowds thronged the stores.* ❶ When there is no object, **throng** is always used with an adverb or preposition.

herd [I, T] (always used with an adverb or preposition) to move or make sb/sth move in a particular direction in a group: *We all herded on to the bus.* ◇ *They were herded together into trucks and driven away.* See also **herd** → HERD *noun*

crowded adj. See also the entry for FULL

crowded · busy · lively · bustling · vibrant
These words all describe places that have a lot of people in them.

PATTERNS AND COLLOCATIONS
▶ crowded / busy / bustling **with** people
▶ a crowded / busy / lively / bustling / vibrant **city**
▶ crowded / busy / lively / bustling **streets**
▶ a crowded / busy / lively / bustling **place** / **town** / **resort** / **port** / **harbour** / **market** / **bar**
▶ a crowded / busy / lively **pub**
▶ crowded / busy / bustling **shops**

crowded (*sometimes disapproving*) having a lot of people or too many people: *We made our way through the crowded streets.* ◇ *In the spring the place is crowded with skiers.* ◇ *London was very crowded.*

busy full of people, vehicles and activity: *We have to cross a busy main road to get to school.* ◇ *Victoria is one of London's busiest stations.*

lively (*approving*) full of life and excitement, with a lot of people enjoying themselves: *'Les vignes' is a lively bar just off the main street.* ◇ *Younger people may prefer a livelier resort such as Malia.*

bustling /ˈbʌslɪŋ/ (*written, approving*) full of people moving about in a busy way: *Naples is a bustling city located in a beautiful natural setting.* See also **bustle** → ACTIVITY

vibrant /ˈvaɪbrənt/ (*written, approving*) full of life and excitement: *Thailand is at its most vibrant during the New Year celebrations.* ❶ Vibrant is often used in tourism literature to describe busy cities where there are many different types of people and commercial activities. It also suggests that there is a lot of activity at night, with bright lights and an exciting atmosphere.

cruel adj. See also the entry for RUTHLESS

cruel · brutal · savage · vicious · sadistic · barbaric · inhuman · inhumane
These words all describe people deliberately causing pain and suffering.

PATTERNS AND COLLOCATIONS
▶ cruel / brutal / savage / vicious / sadistic / barbaric / inhuman / inhumane **treatment**
▶ cruel / brutal / savage / vicious / sadistic / barbaric / inhuman **acts**
▶ cruel / brutal / sadistic **torture**
▶ a cruel / an inhuman / inhumane **punishment**
▶ a cruel / brutal / vicious **man**
▶ cruel / savage / sadistic / inhuman **eyes**
▶ brutal / vicious / barbaric **crimes**
▶ brutal / savage / sadistic **violence**

▸ a brutal / savage / vicious / barbaric **murder**
▸ a brutal / savage / vicious **attack** / **assault**
▸ a brutal / savage **killing** / **beating**
▸ a brutal / vicious / sadistic **killer** / **murderer**

cruel deliberately causing pain and suffering; showing a desire to cause pain and suffering: *He was known to be a cruel dictator.* ◇ *I can't stand people who are **cruel to** animals.* ◇ *Her eyes were cruel and hard.* **OPP** **kind** → KIND, **humane** → SENSITIVE 1
▸ **cruelly** *adv.*: *The dog had been cruelly treated.*

brutal /ˈbruːtl/ deliberately causing physical pain and suffering: *We did not want to hear the details of the brutal attack.* ◇ *He had escaped from a **brutal** and repressive regime.* See also **brutal** → RUTHLESS
▸ **brutally** *adv.*: *He had been brutally assaulted.*

NOTE **CRUEL** OR **BRUTAL?** Brutal is usually used to talk about murders or attacks, or the people or regimes that carry these out. **Cruel** is used to talk about physical attacks too, but it is also commonly used to describe acts which cause mental pain and suffering. **Cruel** can often give the impression that the person carrying out the violence is enjoying the experience; it can be used with words describing how people look: *a cruel mouth/ grin/look*. **Cruel** can vary in strength: it can mean 'deliberately causing extreme pain' or it can just mean 'rather unkind'; **brutal** is always much stronger than 'unkind'. See also **unkind** → MEAN *adj.* 1

savage /ˈsævɪdʒ/ (*especially journalism*) fierce and violent; causing great harm: *She had been badly hurt in what police described as 'a savage attack'.*

vicious /ˈvɪʃəs/ violent and cruel: *He was set upon by vicious thugs.* ◇ *She has a **vicious temper**.* ❶ Vicious is often also used, sometimes with *attack*, to talk about things that people say or write. See also **vicious** → VICIOUS

sadistic /səˈdɪstɪk/ getting pleasure, especially sexual pleasure, from hurting other people: *He took sadistic pleasure in taunting the boy.*

barbaric /bɑːˈbærɪk; *AmE* bɑːrˈb-/ cruel and violent, and not as expected from people who are educated and respect each other: *It was described as a particularly barbaric act.* ◇ *The way these animals are killed is barbaric.*

inhuman (*rather formal*) completely lacking the qualities of kindness and pity: *We regard their treatment of the prisoners as inhuman.* ◇ *The photos showed inhuman and degrading conditions.*
▸ **inhumanity** *noun* [U]: *man's inhumanity to man* **OPP** **humanity** → SYMPATHY

inhumane (*rather formal*) not caring about the suffering of other people or animals, especially in the way they are treated or punished: *They protested about the inhumane treatment of the prisoners.* **OPP** **humane** → SENSITIVE 1

cruise *noun*

cruise · voyage · crossing · passage · sail
These are all words for a journey on water.

PATTERNS AND COLLOCATIONS
▸ a cruise / voyage / crossing / passage / sail **from** / **to** sth
▸ a cruise / voyage / passage / sail **across** sth
▸ a cruise / voyage / passage **around** sth
▸ a **long** cruise / voyage / crossing / passage
▸ a **sea** voyage / crossing / passage
▸ to **take** a cruise / voyage / crossing / passage
▸ to **go for** a cruise / sail

cruise /kruːz/ [C] a journey in a ship visiting different places, especially for pleasure: *They are going on a Mediterranean cruise.* ◇ *You can take a leisurely cruise on the lake.* ◇ *Modern cruise liners* (= ships) *have every conceivable luxury on board.*

voyage /ˈvɔɪɪdʒ/ [C] (*especially written*) a long journey, especially by sea or in space: *The spacecraft began its voyage to Jupiter.* ◇ *The Titanic sank on its **maiden voyage*** (= its first voyage).

crossing [C] a journey across a sea or wide river: *The ship held the record for the fastest Atlantic crossing.* ◇ *The ferry crossing will take three hours.* See also **cross** → CROSS *verb*

passage [sing.] (*written*) a journey from one place to another by ship: *The canal route was shorter than the sea passage around the northern coast.* ◇ *My grandfather had **worked his passage*** (= worked on a ship to pay for the journey) *to America.*

sail [sing.] a trip in a sailing boat; a sea journey of a particular length: *He took us for a sail up the river.* ◇ *The island is a five-hour sail from the mainland.*

crumple *verb*

crumple · rumple · ruffle · crease
These words all mean to make sth, especially fabric, paper or hair, no longer smooth or neat.

PATTERNS AND COLLOCATIONS
▸ to crumple / ruffle sth **up**
▸ to rumple / ruffle sb's **hair**
▸ a **bed** is crumpled / rumpled
▸ **sheets** / **bedclothes** are crumpled / rumpled
▸ **clothes** are crumpled / creased
▸ **fabric** / **material** crumples / creases

crumple [T, I] to crush paper or fabric so that it becomes covered in untidy lines or folds; to become crushed in this way: *She **crumpled** the letter **up into a ball** and threw it on the fire.* ◇ *He wore a crumpled linen suit.* ◇ *This material crumples very easily.*

rumple [T, usually passive] to make sth, especially hair or fabric, no longer smooth and neat: *She rumpled his hair playfully.* ◇ *The bed was rumpled where he had slept.*

ruffle [T] to make sth, especially hair or water, no longer smooth: *She ruffled his hair affectionately.* ◇ *A light breeze ruffled the water.*

crease [T, I] to make lines on fabric or paper by folding or crushing it; to develop lines in this way: *Pack your suit carefully so that you don't crease it.* ◇ *His clothes had got badly creased.* ◇ *This fabric creases very easily.* See also **crease** → FOLD

cry *verb*

cry · sob · be in tears · weep · whimper · snivel · whine
These words all mean to produce tears from your eyes and/ or make a particular sound, usually because you are unhappy or hurt.

PATTERNS AND COLLOCATIONS
▸ to cry / be in tears / whimper / snivel / whine **about** sth
▸ to cry / sob / weep / whimper **with** an emotion
▸ to cry / sob / weep / whimper **softly** / **quietly**
▸ to cry / sob / weep **a little** / **silently** / **bitterly** / **loudly** / **uncontrollably** / **hysterically**

cry [I] to produce tears from your eyes because you are unhappy or hurt: *It's all right. Don't cry.* ◇ *There's nothing to cry about.* ◇ *The baby was **crying for*** (= because it wanted) *its mother.* ◇ *I found him **crying his eyes out*** (= crying very much). ◇ *That night she **cried herself to sleep**.*
▸ **cry** *noun* [sing.]: *I felt a lot better after a good long cry.*

sob (-bb-) [I, T] to cry noisily, taking sudden, sharp breaths; to say sth while you are crying: *I heard a child sobbing loudly.* ◇ *'I hate him,' she sobbed.* ◇ *She flung herself at his chest and **sobbed her heart out**.*
▸ **sob** *noun* [C]: *Her body was racked* (= shaken) *with sobs.*

be in ˈtears *phrase* to be crying: *As she left the room I could see that she was in tears .*

NOTE **CRY** OR **BE IN TEARS?** Be in tears is slightly more formal than **cry**. It is often used to talk about adults crying; **cry** is used more to describe children crying or to tell them not to cry.

weep [I, T] (*formal or literary*) to cry, usually because you are sad: *She started to weep uncontrollably.* ◇ *He wept for joy.* ◇ *I could have wept thinking about what I'd missed.* ◇ *She wept bitter tears of disappointment.*

whimper /ˈwɪmpə(r)/ [I, T] to make low, weak crying noises; to speak in this way: *The child was lost and began to whimper.* ◇ *'Don't leave me alone,' he whimpered.*
▸ **whimper** *noun* [C]: *The puppy gave a little whimper of fear.*

snivel /ˈsnɪvl/ (-ll- (*AmE* -l-) [I] (*disapproving*) to cry and complain in a way that people think is annoying: *Stop snivelling! I can't stand it.* ◇ *What a snivelling little brat!*

whine /waɪn/ [I] to make a long high unpleasant sound because you are in pain or unhappy: *The dog whined and scratched at the door.*

cultural *adj.* See the Topic Map for THE INDIVIDUAL AND SOCIETY on p.894

cultural · national · ethnic · native · racial · tribal · indigenous · folk
These words all describe sth connected with a particular country, culture or group of people.

PATTERNS AND COLLOCATIONS
▸ native / indigenous **to** somewhere
▸ a cultural / a national / an ethnic / a racial / a tribal / an indigenous **group**
▸ a cultural / an ethnic / a native / a tribal / an indigenous **community**
▸ native / tribal / indigenous **population / peoples / leaders**
▸ cultural / national / tribal / indigenous / folk **traditions**
▸ a national / an ethnic / a native / a tribal / an indigenous **language**
▸ national / ethnic / native / tribal / folk **dress / costume**
▸ ethnic / native / indigenous / folk **art / music**
▸ sb's cultural / national / ethnic / racial **identity / origin**
▸ a cultural / national / racial **stereotype**
▸ cultural / ethnic / racial / tribal **divisions**
▸ cultural / ethnic / racial **differences / factors / background / diversity / minorities**
▸ native / indigenous **species / plants**

cultural [usually before noun] connected with the culture of a particular society or group, its customs and beliefs: *Teachers need to be aware of cultural differences.* ◇ *The custom is deeply rooted in the religious and cultural heritage of the region.*
▸ **culturally** *adv.*: *a culturally diverse society*

national [usually before noun] connected with or typical of a particular country; shared by all the people of a country: *During your visit, you should take the opportunity to sample the national dish.* ◇ *This is not just a sporting event; for many it is a matter of national pride.* See also **nation** → COUNTRY 1

ethnic [usually before noun] connected with or belonging to a nation, race or tribe that shares a cultural tradition; happening or existing between people of different races or tribes; typical of a country or culture that is very different from modern western culture and therefore interesting for people in western cultures: *This region of Bulgaria has a large ethnic Turkish population.* ◇ *The conference strongly condemned the practice of ethnic cleansing* (= mass killing of one ethnic group by another). ◇ *The country is divided along ethnic lines.* ◇ *There was a stall selling ethnic jewellery from Afghanistan.*
❶ **Ethnic** has become a more popular word in recent years to describe a person's background or origins, or the group they belong to, in phrases such as *ethnic group/ origin/minority*. It is considered more general and less offensive than words such as **race** or **tribe**. It can describe not just the racial background of a group of people, but also their religion, customs and culture. See also **ethnic group** → PEOPLE 2
▸ **ethnically** *adv.*: *an ethnically divided region*

native [only before noun] connected with the place where you were born and lived for the first years of your life, the place where you have always lived or a place where you

have lived for a long time: *It's a long time since he visited his native Poland.* ◇ *Her native language is German.* ◇ *His work is barely known in his native country of Sweden.* ◇ *Are you a native Berliner* (= a person who has always lived in Berlin)? ❶ **Native** can also mean 'connected with the people who originally lived in a country before other people, especially white people, came there': *The native peoples depend on the forest for their livelihoods.* Some people find this use of the word offensive and prefer the term **indigenous**; however, *Native American* is still the preferred term for members of the races of people who were the original people living in America. As with many words to describe race, the most acceptable terms often change over time. ❶ **Native** can also describe animals or plants that exist naturally in a place. In this meaning it can be used before a noun or in the phrase *native to a place*: *Introduced species are often a threat to native plants.* ◇ *There are about 17 hedgehog species native to Europe, Asia and Africa.* **OPP** **foreign, alien** → FOREIGN, See also **native** → CITIZEN *noun*, **native** → RESIDENT *noun*

racial /ˈreɪʃl/ [usually before noun] happening or existing between people of different races; connected with a person's race: *The killings came at the end of a week of racial violence.* ◇ *He struggled to overcome racial prejudice.* See also **race** → PEOPLE 2
▸ **racially** *adv.*: *The attacks were not racially motivated.* ◇ *racially mixed schools*

tribal /ˈtraɪbl/ [usually before noun] connected with a tribe or tribes; happening or existing between people of different tribes: *In rural areas, family and tribal loyalties remain important.* ◇ *The area had been ravaged by tribal warfare.* See also **tribe** → PEOPLE 2

indigenous /ɪnˈdɪdʒənəs/ (*formal*) (of people or their culture, animals or plants) belonging to a particular place rather than coming to it from somewhere else: *Antarctica has no indigenous population.* ◇ *The reserve supports a wide range of indigenous species.* ◇ *The kangaroo is indigenous to Australia.*

folk /fəʊk; *AmE* foʊk/ [only before noun] (of art or culture) traditional and typical of the ordinary people of a country or community; based on the beliefs of ordinary people: *Scottish folk dancing* ◇ *a Russian folk song* ◇ *Garlic is widely used in Chinese folk medicine.*

culture *noun* See the Topic Map for THE INDIVIDUAL AND SOCIETY on p.894

culture · society · community · world · civilization · race
These are all words for groups of people who share the same customs, beliefs and way of life.

PATTERNS AND COLLOCATIONS
▸ (the) **Western** culture / society / world / civilization
▸ (the) **Arab / Islamic** culture / society / community / world
▸ **European / American / African, etc.** culture / society / civilization
▸ an / the **English-speaking** culture / community / world
▸ (a / an / the) **ancient / modern / contemporary** culture / society / world / civilization
▸ (an) **industrial** culture / society / community / civilization
▸ a **primitive** culture / society / community / race
▸ (a) **traditional / mainstream** culture / society / community
▸ a / the **secular** culture / society / world
▸ to **create** a culture / society / civilization

culture [U, C] the customs and beliefs, art, way of life and social organization of a particular country or group; a country or group with its own customs, beliefs, etc: *These ideas have always been central to Western culture.* ◇ *As young people started to have more money, a significant youth culture developed.* ◇ *The children are taught to respect different cultures.*

society [C, U] a country or group of people who share the same customs and laws: *Can Britain ever be a classless society?* ◇ *Singapore has a delicately balanced multi-cultural society.* ◇ *They were discussing the problems of Western society.*

community [C+sing./pl. v.] a group of people who share the same race, religion, job or interests, especially when they live in the same place: *Representatives of the city's Asian community had a meeting with the mayor.* ◇ *He grew up in a **close-knit** fishing **community**.*

world [C, usually sing.] a particular part of the earth; a particular group of countries or people; a particular period of history and the people of that period: *Heads of state from all over the Arab world gathered for the conference.* ◇ *The motto was inscribed on buildings throughout the Roman world.*

civilization (*BrE* also **-isation**) /ˌsɪvəlaɪˈzeɪʃn; *AmE* -ləˈz-/ [U, C] a society and its culture during a particular period of time or in a particular part of the world: *These diseases are common in Western civilization.* ◇ *The Minoan civilization of Crete used two forms of script.* ❶ **Civilization** is used especially to describe a society which is considered to have a highly developed social structure, art and beliefs. *Ancient civilizations* include the Greeks, the Romans, the Egyptians, the Chinese and the Sumerians.

race [C] a group of people who share the same language, history and culture: *Evidence suggests they were a race of nomadic hunters.* ◇ *He admired Canadians as a hardy and determined race.* See also **race** → PEOPLE 2

cunning *adj.*

cunning · crafty · sly · sneaky · wily · sharp · calculating · scheming
These words all describe people behaving in a dishonest or indirect way in order to get sth.

PATTERNS AND COLLOCATIONS
▸ a cunning / sly / sneaky **trick**
▸ a cunning / calculating / scheming **mind**
▸ a cunning / crafty / sly / sneaky / scheming **bastard**
▸ a cunning / crafty / sneaky / calculating / scheming **bitch**
▸ a crafty / sly / sneaky **devil** / **thing**
▸ a cunning / crafty / sly / sneaky / scheming **little...**
▸ a cunning / crafty / sly / sneaky / wily **old...**

cunning (*sometimes disapproving*) having or showing skill at getting what you want, especially by indirect or dishonest methods: *That cunning old rogue is up to something, I'm sure.* ◇ *It's just a cunning ploy by the marketing people to get us to buy more cornflakes.* See also **devious** → DISHONEST
▸ **cunning** *noun* [U]: *It took energy and cunning just to survive.*

crafty cunning: *He's a crafty old devil.* ◇ *She's one of the party's craftiest political strategists.*

> **NOTE** CUNNING OR CRAFTY? **Cunning** can describe a person or a plan. **Crafty** usually describes a person; it can also describe a single action, but not a whole plan: *That was a crafty move/touch.* ◇ *a crafty ploy by the marketing people.* When used to describe people, both **cunning** and **crafty** can suggest admiration for sb's cleverness as much as disapproval of their dishonesty.

sly (*disapproving*) behaving or done in a secret and usually dishonest way: *That was a sly political move.* ◇ *She's a sly one – never lets on what she's thinking.* ❶ If you do sth **on the sly**, you do it secretly, not wanting other people to discover what you are doing: *He has to visit them on the sly.*

sneaky (*informal, sometimes disapproving*) behaving or done in a secret and sometimes dishonest or unpleasant way: *I took a sneaky glance at my watch.* ◇ *That was a sneaky trick to play!*

> **NOTE** SLY OR SNEAKY? **Sneaky** is a less formal word than **sly** and shows less serious disapproval.

wily /ˈwaɪli/ (of a person) clever at getting what you want, and willing to trick people: *He was outwitted by his wily opponent.*

sharp (*disapproving*) (of a person or their way of doing business) clever but possibly dishonest: *His lawyer's **sharp operator**.* ◇ *The firm had to face some **sharp practice** from competing companies.* ❶ *Operator* and *practice* are by far the most frequent collocates of **sharp** in this meaning.

calculating (*disapproving*) (of a person) good at planning things so that they have an advantage, without caring about other people: *The judge called him 'a cold and calculating killer'.*

scheming /ˈskiːmɪŋ/ (*rather formal, disapproving*) (of a person) often planning secretly to do sth for their own advantage, especially by deceiving other people: *She plays the role of a scheming wife in a doomed marriage.*

cupboard *noun*

cupboard · closet · wardrobe · cabinet · locker · chest of drawers · dresser · unit · bureau · pantry
These are all words for a piece of furniture or a space with doors which is used for storing or displaying things.

PATTERNS AND COLLOCATIONS
▸ a **kitchen** cupboard / closet / cabinet / unit / dresser
▸ a **bathroom** cupboard / closet / cabinet
▸ a **medicine** cupboard / cabinet
▸ a **wall** / **storage** cupboard / closet / cabinet / unit
▸ a **walk-in** cupboard / closet / wardrobe / pantry
▸ a **fitted** cupboard / wardrobe / unit
▸ a **built-in** cupboard / closet / wardrobe
▸ to **open** / **close** a cupboard / closet / wardrobe / cabinet / locker / bureau

cupboard [C] a piece of furniture with doors and shelves used for storing things such as dishes, food or clothes: *The kitchen has built-in cupboards and shelves.* ❶ In British English a **cupboard** can also be built into a wall, not a separate piece of furniture; in American English this is called a **closet**: *The tool kit is in the cupboard under the stairs.*

closet [C] (*especially AmE*) a small room or a space in a wall with a door that reaches the floor, used for storing things: *She has a walk-in closet for all her clothes.*

wardrobe /ˈwɔːdrəʊb; *AmE* ˈwɔːrdroʊb/ [C] a large cupboard for hanging clothes in: *The master bedroom has fitted wardrobes and en suite bathroom facilities.* ❶ In British English a **wardrobe** can either be a piece of furniture or it can be built into the wall. In American English a **wardrobe** is always a piece of furniture; if it is built into the wall it is called a **closet**.

cabinet /ˈkæbɪnət/ [C] a piece of furniture with doors, drawers and/or shelves, that is used for storing or showing things: *There's a medicine cabinet in the bathroom.* ◇ *The china was displayed in a glass cabinet.* ❶ A **filing cabinet** (*BrE*) / **file cabinet** (*AmE*) is a piece of office furniture with deep drawers for storing files.

locker [C] a small cupboard that can be locked, where you can leave your clothes and bags while you play a sport or go somewhere: *I left my things in my locker.*

chest of ˈdrawers (pl. **chests of drawers**) [C] a piece of furniture with drawers for keeping clothes in: *She rose from the bed and crossed to the chest of drawers.* ❶ In American English a **chest of drawers** is also called a **dresser** or a **bureau**.

dresser [C] (*AmE*) a chest of drawers ❶ **Dresser** is the most frequent word for this piece of furniture in American English, although **chest of drawers** and **bureau** are also used. In British English a **dresser** is a large piece of wooden furniture with shelves in the top part and cupboards below, used for displaying and storing items such as cups and plates: *I put the kettle on and took two cups and saucers down from the dresser.*

unit [C, usually pl.] a piece of furniture, especially a cupboard, that fits with and matches others of the same type: *We offer a wide choice of kitchen units in traditional* *and modern styles.* ❶ **Unit** is used especially in shops and advertising by companies that make and sell this kind of furniture.

bureau /ˈbjʊərəʊ; *AmE* ˈbjʊroʊ/ (pl. **bureaux** or **bureaus** /-rəʊz; *AmE* -roʊz/) [C] (*AmE*) a chest of drawers: *There was just enough space for a fold-up bed, washstand and bureau.*

pantry /ˈpæntri/ [C] a cupboard or small room in a house, used for storing food, especially in the past: *There's bread and cheese in the pantry.*

---

cure *verb* See the Topic Map for HEALTH on p.890

---

cure · heal · resuscitate · rehabilitate · make sb better
These words all mean to make sb healthy again.

PATTERNS AND COLLOCATIONS
▸ to cure sb/heal sb/rehabilitate sb/make sb better **by** doing sth
▸ to cure/heal sb **of** sth

cure [T] to make a person or animal healthy again after an illness; to make an illness go away: *She was **miraculously cured**.* ◊ *They will try to cure her of her alcoholism.* ◊ *It is better to prevent rather than cure diseases.* See also **cure** → DRUG 2, **cure** → TREATMENT

heal [T] to cure sb, especially without medicine; to make sb feel happy again: *He told stories of Jesus **healing the sick**.* ◊ *The children were healed by a local witch doctor.* ◊ *I felt healed by his love.* ❶ **Heal** is often used to talk about people being cured through faith (= religious belief) or magic. See also **healing** → TREATMENT

resuscitate /rɪˈsʌsɪteɪt/ [T] to make sb start breathing again or become conscious again after they have almost died: *He had a heart attack and all attempts to resuscitate him failed.*
▸ **resuscitation** *noun* [U]: *mouth-to-mouth resuscitation* (= breathing air into the mouth of an unconscious person to make them start breathing again)

rehabilitate /ˌriːəˈbɪlɪteɪt/ [T] (*rather formal or written*) to help sb have a normal, useful life again after they have been very ill or in prison for a long time: *He was sent to a unit for rehabilitating drug addicts.* ❶ **Rehabilitate** is used more often in a figurative sense: *He played a major role in rehabilitating Magritte as an artist* (= causing people to again think highly of Magritte as an artist).
▸ **rehabilitation** *noun* [U]: *a drug rehabilitation centre*

ˌmake sb ˈbetter *phrase* (*rather informal, especially spoken*) to cure sb: *Here, take this medicine, it'll make you better.*

---

curious *adj.*

---

curious · intrigued · inquisitive · nosy
These words all describe sb who wants to know or learn more about sth.

PATTERNS AND COLLOCATIONS
▸ curious/inquisitive **about** sth
▸ curious/intrigued **as to** sth
▸ curious/intrigued **to do** sth
▸ **rather** curious/intrigued/nosy
▸ **highly** intrigued/inquisitive
▸ **naturally** curious/inquisitive

curious having or showing a strong desire to know more about sth: *They were curious about the people who lived upstairs.* ◊ *He is such a curious boy, always asking questions.* See also **curious** → STRANGE 1
▸ **curiosity** /ˌkjʊəriˈɒsəti; *AmE* ˌkjʊriˈɑːs-/ *noun* [U, sing.]: *The letter wasn't addressed to me but I opened it **out of curiosity**.* ◊ *I felt a certain curiosity to see what would happen next.*
▸ **curiously** *adv.*: *'Are you really an artist?' Sara asked curiously.*

intrigued /ɪnˈtriːɡd/ [not usually before noun] very interested in sth and wanting to know more about it, especially because it seems unexpected or difficult to explain: *He was intrigued by her story.* ◊ *I'm intrigued to know what you thought of the movie.*

inquisitive /ɪnˈkwɪzətɪv/ enjoying learning about many different things: *Children are naturally inquisitive.* ◊ *The young man possessed a sharp and inquisitive mind.* ❶ **Inquisitive** can also be used in a disapproving way to describe sb who asks too many questions, trying to find out about what other people are doing: (*disapproving*) *Don't be so inquisitive! It's none of your business.* However, this use is less frequent.

nosy (also **nosey**) /ˈnəʊzi; *AmE* ˈnoʊzi/ (*informal, disapproving*) (of a person) too interested in things that do not concern him or her, especially other people's affairs: *Don't be so nosy — it's none of your business.* ◊ *I'm surrounded by nosy neighbours.*

---

current *noun*

---

current · flow · circulation · passage
These are all words for the movement of sth, such as a liquid, a gas or electricity.

PATTERNS AND COLLOCATIONS
▸ **against/with** the current/flow
▸ a current/the flow/the circulation/the passage of **water/air**
▸ a current/the flow/the passage of **electricity**
▸ the flow/circulation of **blood**
▸ **air** currents/circulation
▸ a **constant** current/flow/circulation
▸ a **steady** current/flow
▸ a **free** flow/passage

current [C] an amount of water or air that moves continuously in one direction, especially through a larger amount of water or air in which there is less movement; the movement of electricity in one direction, for example through a wire: *He swam to the shore against a **strong current**.* ◊ *Changes in **ocean currents** can have drastic effects on marine life.* ◊ *Birds use warm air currents to help their flight.* ◊ *He leaped as though a powerful **electric current** had passed through him.* ◊ *Measure the current flowing through the wire.*

flow [U, C, usually sing.] the steady and continuous movement of liquid, air or electricity in one direction: *She tried to stop the flow of blood from the wound.* ◊ *The whole operation depends on a steady flow of electricity.* See also **flow** → FLOW *verb*

circulation /ˌsɜːkjəˈleɪʃn; *AmE* ˌsɜːrk-/ [U, C] the movement of blood around the body; the movement of air, gas or water around an area or inside sth such as a system or machine: *People with poor circulation are more likely to suffer from the condition.* ◊ *The design of the shoe allows for a greater circulation of air around the foot, keeping it cool.* See also **circulate** → FLOW *verb*

passage [U] (*formal*) the action of light, liquid, gas or electricity going across, through or past sth: *Large trees may obstruct the passage of light.* ◊ *The operation will allow free passage of fluid in and out of the organ.*

---

curse *verb*

---

curse · swear · damn · blaspheme
These words all mean to say or think rude things about sb/sth.

PATTERNS AND COLLOCATIONS
▸ to curse/swear **loudly/quietly/softly/silently/under your breath**

curse [I, T] to use rude or offensive language; to say rude things to sb or think rude things about sb/sth: *He hit his head as he stood up and cursed under his breath.* ◊ *She cursed her bad luck.* ◊ *He **cursed** himself **for** his stupidity.*
▸ **curse** *noun* [C]: *He muttered a curse at the other driver.*

swear [I] to use rude or offensive language, usually because you are angry: *She fell over and swore really loudly.* ◊ *Why did you let him **swear at** you like that?*

NOTE **CURSE** OR **SWEAR**? You can **curse** a person or thing, but **swear** never takes an object in this meaning. **Swear** is used much more often than **curse** in spoken English.

damn /dæm/ (*informal, spoken*) used when swearing at sb/sth to show that you are angry: *Damn you! I'm not going to let you bully me.* ◊ *Damn this machine! Why won't it work?*

blaspheme /blæsˈfiːm/ [I, T] (*rather formal*) to speak about God or the holy things of a particular religion in an offensive way; to swear using the names of God or holy things: *How dare you blaspheme in front of your own father?* ◊ *He was accused of blaspheming the prophet.*
▶ **blasphemy** /ˈblæsfəmi/ *noun* [U, C]: *He was accused of blasphemy.*

curtain *noun*

curtain · blind · drape · screen · shade · hanging
These are all words for window coverings.

PATTERNS AND COLLOCATIONS
▶ to **draw / close** the curtains / blinds / drapes / shades
▶ to **pull** the curtains / drapes
▶ to **open** the curtains / blinds / drapes / shades
▶ to **draw / draw back / pull back** the curtains / drapes
▶ to **pull up / down** the blinds / shades

curtain [C] a piece of fabric that is hung to cover a window; a piece of fabric that is hung up as a screen in a room or around a bed, for example; a piece of thick, heavy fabric that hangs in front of the stage in the theatre: *It was ten in the morning but the curtains were still drawn* (= closed). ◊ *a pair of curtains* ◊ *a shower curtain* ◊ *The audience was waiting for the curtain to rise* (= for the play to begin). ◊ *There was tremendous applause when the curtain came down* (= when the play ended). ◊ *We left just before the final curtain.* ❶ In American English **curtain** is used especially to describe a very thin piece of fabric that you hang at a window and that stops people outside from being able to see inside; in British English these are called **net curtains**.

blind [C] a covering for a window, especially one made of a roll of fabric that is fixed at the top of the window and can be pulled up and down: *Pull up the blinds and let some light in.* ❶ A **venetian blind** is a blind that has flat horizontal plastic or metal strips going across it that you can turn to let in as much light as you want.

drape (*especially AmE*) (*AmE also* **drapery** /ˈdreɪpəri/) [C, usually pl.] a long thick curtain: *blue velvet drapes*

screen [C] (*especially AmE*) a wire or plastic net that is held in a frame and fastened on a window, or a door, to let in air but keep out insects: *Do you have screens on your windows?* ◊ *screen windows/doors*

shade (also ˈ**window shade**) (both *AmE*) a blind: *The sun peered through the shades in the hotel room.*

hanging [C, usually pl.] a large piece of fabric that is hung on a wall for decoration: *wall hangings* See also **hang** → DECORATE

curve *noun*

curve · arc · loop · curvature · crescent · arch · semicircle · parabola
These are all words for a line or shape that is not straight but bends.

PATTERNS AND COLLOCATIONS
▶ **in** a curve / an arc / a loop / a crescent / an arch / a semicircle / a parabola
▶ (a / an) **downward / upward** curve / arc / curvature
▶ (a) **slight** curve / arc / curvature
▶ (a) **graceful** curve / arc / curvature
▶ a **gentle / smooth** curve / arc
▶ a **tight** curve / loop
▶ a **delicate** curve / arch
▶ to **form** a curve / an arc / a loop / an arch / a semicircle
▶ to **draw** a curve / an arc / a semicircle / a parabola

curve [C] a line or surface that bends gradually; a smooth bend: *The pattern was made up of straight lines and curves.* ◊ *The program automatically plots the curve on a graph.* ◊ (*especially AmE*) *The park is located on a curve in the road just past a large church on your left.* See also **bend** → CORNER

arc [C] part of a circle or curved line; a curved shape: *The arc of the rainbow reached out across the valley.* ◊ *The beach swept around in an arc.* ◊ (*geometry*) *Set the point of the compasses at one end of the line and draw an arc.*

loop /luːp/ [C] a shape like a curve or circle made by a line curving right round so that it crosses itself or nearly crosses itself: *The road went in a huge loop around the lake.* ◊ *Duclair is a small town on a loop of the River Seine.*

curvature /ˈkɜːvətʃə(r)/ *AmE* ˈkɜːrv-/ [U] (*technical*) the state of being curved; the amount that sth is curved: *From 60 miles up, the curvature of the earth is clearly visible.*

crescent /ˈkresnt; *BrE* also ˈkreznt/ [C] a curved shape that is wide in the middle and pointed at each end: *The crescent moon was shining dimly in a cloudless sky.*

arch [C] anything that forms a curved shape at the top: *He studied the delicate arch of her eyebrows and the smooth curve of her jaw.*
▶ **arch** *verb* [T, I]: *The cat arched its back and hissed.* ◊ *Tall trees arched over the path.*

semicircle /ˈsemisɜːkl; *AmE* -sɜːrkl/ [C] one half of a circle; a thing, or a group of people or things, shaped like one half of a circle: *At the front of the stage was a semicircle of chairs for the prize winners.* ◊ *We sat in a semicircle around the fire.*
▶ **semicircular** *adj.*: *The main building has four large columns and a semicircular driveway.*

parabola /pəˈræbələ/ [C] (*geometry*) a curve like the path of an object thrown into the air and falling back to earth: *A ball thrown over a long distance travels in a parabola.*

curve

curve/arc

loop

crescent

arch

semicircle

parabola

curve *verb*

curve · turn · wind · snake · bend · twist · arc · zigzag
These words all mean to have a shape or move in a direction that is not straight.

PATTERNS AND COLLOCATIONS
▶ to curve / snake / wind / bend / twist **around / round** sth
▶ to curve / snake / wind / twist / arc / zigzag **through / across** sth
▶ to curve / turn / snake / wind / arc **away** (from sth)
▶ to curve / turn / wind / arc **toward / towards** sth
▶ to curve / turn / bend (**to the**) **left / right / north / south**, etc.
▶ the **road / path** curves / turns / snakes / winds / bends / twists / zigzags
▶ the **river** curves / turns / snakes / winds / bends
▶ to curve / turn / wind / bend / twist **sharply / slightly**

curve [I, T] (usually used with an adverb or preposition) to move or make sth move in a long smooth bend; to have this shape: *The ball curved through the air.* ◇ *The road curved around the bay.* ◇ *His lips curved in a smile.* ◇ *A smile curved his lips.*

turn [I] (usually used with an adverb or preposition) (of a road or river) to curve in a particular direction: *The road turns to the left after the church.* See also **turn** → CORNER

wind /waɪnd/ [I, T] (always used with an adverb or preposition) (of a road, river or path) to have many bends and twists: *The path wound down to the beach.* ◇ *The river winds its way between two meadows.* ◇ *The walk follows a winding path through the forest.*

snake [T, I] (*written*) (usually used with an adverb or preposition) to move like a snake, in long twisting curves; to go in a particular direction in long twisting curves: *The procession snaked its way through narrow streets.* ◇ *The road snaked away into the distance.*

bend [I, T] to change direction suddenly to form a curve or angle; to make sth change direction in this way: *The road bent sharply to the right.* ◇ *Glass and water both bend light.* See also **bend** → CORNER

twist [I] (of a road or river) to bend and change direction often, especially in a way that makes it dangerous or difficult to travel: *The road **twists and turns** along the coast.* ◇ *From the cellar a twisting staircase leads down to the dungeon.* See also **twist** → CORNER

arc [I] (usually used with an adverb or preposition) (*technical*) to move in a long curved shape, especially through the air: *For a few seconds a perfect rainbow arced across the city.*

zigzag /ˈzɪɡzæɡ/ (-gg-) [I] (usually used with an adverb or preposition) to move forward by making sharp sudden turns first to the left and then to the right: *The narrow path zigzags up the cliff.* See also **zigzag** → CORNER

curved *adj.*

curved · round · rounded · vaulted · domed · convex · concave · arched
These words all describe a shape that is not straight and bends continuously.

PATTERNS AND COLLOCATIONS

▶ a curved / rounded / convex / concave **surface**
▶ a curved / a vaulted / a domed / an arched **ceiling / roof**
▶ curved / convex / concave **mirror / lens**
▶ gently curved / rounded / arched

curved having a shape that bends continuously and has no straight parts: *A ball follows a curved path as it travels through the air.* ◇ *The knife has a curved blade.* ◇ *She had a curved smile.* **OPP** **straight** ❶ Something that is **straight** has no bends or curves: *The shortest distance between two points is a straight line.*

round having a full, curved shape: *Most of the county is undulating land, with low round hills and shallow valleys.* ◇ *Put both the surname and publication date in round brackets.* ◇ *She had a small mouth and round pink cheeks.*

rounded /ˈraʊndɪd/ [usually before noun] having a curved shape, especially at the ends, sides or edges of sth: *Furniture with rounded edges and corners is safer for children.* ◇ *His head sagged between his rounded shoulders.*

vaulted /ˈvɔːltɪd/ (*architecture*) (especially of a roof or ceiling) made in the shape of an arch or a series of arches: *The vaulted ceiling is supported by twelve columns.*

domed /dəʊmd; AmE doʊmd/ [usually before noun] (especially of a roof or ceiling) having a dome or shaped like a dome (= a shape like half a ball): *The domed ceiling of the temple is painted to resemble the sky.* ◇ *He had the high, domed forehead of a scholar and thinker.*

convex /ˈkɒnveks; AmE ˈkɑːn-/ (of an outline or surface) curved outwards: *A convex lens is thicker at its centre than at its edges.*

concave /kɒnˈkeɪv; AmE kɑːnˈk-; ˈkɑːn-/ (of an outline or surface) curved inwards: *The inside of a shiny spoon is a common example of a concave mirror.* **OPP** **convex**

arched /ɑːtʃt; AmE ɑːrtʃt/ (especially of a bridge, door or window) having an arch; shaped like an arch: *The entrance to the church is through an arched door.*

customer *noun*

customer · client · consumer · buyer · purchaser · shopper · patron · punter · regular · end-user
These are all words for a person or organization that buys sth from a shop or business.

PATTERNS AND COLLOCATIONS

▶ to **have** / **deal with** / **get** / **lose** a customer / client / buyer
▶ to **attract** customers / clients / consumers / buyers / shoppers / punters
▶ to **encourage** customers / clients / consumers / buyers / shoppers
▶ to **entice** / **persuade** customers / clients / consumers / buyers
▶ to **tempt** customers / buyers / shoppers
▶ customers / clients / consumers / buyers / purchasers / shoppers **buy** / **spend** sth

customer [C] a person or organization that buys sth from a shop or business or who uses a bank: *He comes in twice a week and is one of our best customers.* ◇ *Schools are among the biggest customers for this service.* ◇ *I'd like to speak to someone in the customer service department, please.* See also **custom** → BUSINESS 2

client /ˈklaɪənt/ [C] a person who uses the services or advice of a professional person or organization: *She's a well-known lawyer with many famous clients.* ◇ *It is our job to act on behalf of the client.* See also **clientele** → MARKET 1

consumer /kənˈsjuːmə(r); AmE -ˈsuː-/ [C] a person who buys goods or uses services: *Health-conscious consumers want more information about the food they buy.* ◇ *The big stores are, of course, responding to consumer demand.* ◇ *We live in a **consumer society** (= one in which buying and selling is considered to be very important)* ❶ **Consumer** is usually used to talk about the habits and behaviour of people who buy things in general, rather than about any person in particular. **Consumer** is often used like an adjective before words such as *demand, boycott, boom, confidence,* and *spending.*

buyer [C] a person who buys sth, especially sth expensive: *Have you found a buyer for your house?* ❶ **Buyer** is most often used to talk about a person buying a house or car, or a large amount of goods for a company. See also **buy** → BUY

purchaser /ˈpɜːtʃəsə(r); AmE ˈpɜːrtʃ-/ [C] (*formal, especially written*) a person who buys sth, especially sth expensive: *The purchaser reserves the right to change his or her mind.* ❶ **Purchaser** is most often used in formal written English to talk about a person buying a house or car, a business or shares in a business. See also **purchase** → BUY

shopper [C] a person who buys goods from a shop: *Crowds of shoppers had to be evacuated from the store after the bomb threat.* ◇ *Competition between stores can result in big savings for shoppers.* ❶ **Shopper** is most often used in the plural, after words relating to large numbers such as *hundreds / thousands / crowds* of or words relating to times when large numbers of people buy things in shops: *Christmas / Saturday-morning shoppers.* See also **shop** → BUY

patron /ˈpeɪtrən/ [C] (*formal*) a person who uses a particular shop, restaurant, theatre, etc: *Patrons are requested not to smoke.*

punter [C] (*BrE, informal*) a person who buys or uses a particular product or service: *It's important to keep the punters happy.* ◇ *Your average punter won't notice the difference.*

regular [C] a customer who often goes to a particular shop, bar, restaurant, etc: *He's one of our regulars.*

end-'user [C] a person who actually uses a product rather than one who makes or sells it, especially a person who uses a product connected with computers: *Programs are tailored to meet the needs of end-users.*

cut *verb*

1 cut taxes
2 cut the bread
3 have your hair cut
4 cut your finger

1 See also the entries for ABOLISH, REDUCE and SAVE 2
cut · slash · cut sth back · cut sth down · scale sth back · rationalize · downsize · scale sth down
These words all mean to reduce the amount or size of sth, especially of an amount of money or a business.

PATTERNS AND COLLOCATIONS
▸ to cut sth / cut sth back / cut sth down / downsize sth / scale sth down **from** $50 000 **to** $40 000
▸ to cut sth / cut sth back / cut sth down / scale sth down **by** $5 000 / 30%
▸ to cut back / cut down **on** sth
▸ to cut / slash / cut back on / cut down on / scale back / rationalize **spending / production**
▸ to cut / slash / cut back on **jobs**
▸ to cut / slash / downsize **the workforce**
▸ to cut / slash / rationalize **the cost** of sth
▸ to cut sth / slash sth / cut sth back / cut sth down / scale sth down **drastically**
▸ to cut sth / cut sth back / cut sth down **considerably**

cut [T] to reduce sth, especially an amount of money that is demanded, spent, earned, etc. or the size of a business: *The President has promised to cut taxes significantly.* ◇ *Could you cut your essay from 5 000 to 3 000 words?* See also **cut → REDUCTION** *noun*

slash [T, often passive] (*rather informal, journalism*) to reduce sth by a large amount: *The workforce has been slashed by half.* ◇ *A slump in the retail trade has forced the company to slash prices.*

cut sth 'back, cut 'back on sth *phrasal verb* to reduce sth, especially an amount of money or business: *If we don't sell more we'll have to cut back production.* ◇ *The local authority is trying to cut back significantly on spending this year.* See also **cutback → REDUCTION**

cut sth 'down, cut 'down on sth *phrasal verb* to reduce the size, amount or number of sth: *The doctor told him to cut down on his drinking.* ◇ *I won't have a cigarette, thanks – I'm trying to cut down* (= smoke fewer).

scale sth 'back *phrasal verb* (*especially AmE or business*) to reduce sth, especially an amount of money or business: *The IMF has scaled back its growth forecasts for the next decade.*

rationalize (*BrE also* **-ise**) [T, I] (*BrE, business*) to make changes to a business or system, in order to make it more efficient, especially by spending less money: *Twenty workers lost their jobs when the department was rationalized.*
▸ **rationalization** (*BrE also* **-isation**) *noun* [U, C]: *a need for rationalization of the industry*

downsize /'daʊnsaɪz/ [I, T] (*business*) to make a company or organization smaller by reducing the number of jobs in it, in order to reduce costs: *The worsening situation forced the company to downsize from 39 employees to 7.* ◇ *The larger companies are all planning to downsize their US operations.* ❶ **Downsize** is often used by people who want to avoid saying more obvious words like 'fire', 'dismiss', 'lay sb off' or 'make sb redundant' because they sound too negative.

scale sth 'down *phrasal verb* to reduce the number, size or extent of sth: *We are thinking of scaling down our training programmes next year.* ◇ *He was using scaled-down versions of his father's tools.*

> **NOTE** CUT, CUT STH BACK, CUT STH DOWN, SCALE STH BACK OR SCALE STH DOWN? **Cut** is the most general of these words. **Cut sth back** and **scale sth back** are both used especially to talk about money or business. **Cut sth down** and **scale sth down** are both more general, but are used more for talking about things other than money or business.

2 cut · chop · slice · carve · dice
These words all mean to make smaller pieces of sth by using sth sharp such as a knife.

PATTERNS AND COLLOCATIONS
▸ to cut / chop / slice / carve sth **into** sth
▸ to cut / chop / slice sth **off** sth
▸ to cut / slice sth **in half / two**
▸ to cut / chop / slice sth **up**
▸ to cut / chop / slice / carve / dice **meat**
▸ to cut / slice **bread / cake**
▸ to chop / slice an **onion**
▸ to cut / chop / slice / dice sth **finely**
▸ to cut / slice sth **thinly**

cut [T] to remove sth or a part of sth, or divide sth into two or more pieces with a knife, etc.; to make or form sth by removing material with a knife, etc: *He cut four slices from the loaf.* ◇ *He cut the loaf into thick slices.* ◇ *Shall I cut you a piece of cake?* ◇ *Don't cut the string; untie the knot.* ◇ *The climbers cut steps in the ice.*

chop (**-pp-**) [T] to make smaller pieces of sth using sth sharp such as a knife: *He was chopping logs for firewood.* ◇ *Roughly chop the herbs.*

slice [T, I] to cut sth into slices; to cut sth easily with or as if with a sharp blade: *Slice the cucumber thinly.* ◇ *a sliced loaf* ◇ *a loaf of sliced bread* ◇ *He accidentally **sliced through** his finger.* See also **slice → PIECE**

carve [T, I] to cut a large piece of cooked meat into smaller pieces for eating: *She taught me how to carve a leg of lamb.* ◇ *Lunch is ready. Who's going to carve?*

dice [T] to cut meat, vegetables, etc. into small square pieces: *diced carrots / lamb*

3 cut · trim · shave · mow · lop · shear · snip · crop · clip
These words all mean to make sth shorter or neater by removing part of it with a sharp tool.

PATTERNS AND COLLOCATIONS
▸ to cut / trim / shave / lop / snip / clip sth **off** sth
▸ to cut / trim / shave / lop / shear / snip / clip sth **off**
▸ to cut / shave / lop / shear / snip / clip sth **from** sth
▸ to cut / trim / shave / shear / snip / crop / clip **hair**
▸ to cut / trim / clip a **hedge**
▸ to cut / clip your / sb's **nails**
▸ to cut / mow the **grass / lawn**
▸ to cut / trim / clip sth **neatly**

cut [T] to make sth shorter by cutting; to remove sth from sth larger by cutting: *I'm going to **get / have my hair cut** really short.* ◇ *He had his finger cut off in an accident at work.*
▸ **cut** *noun* [C]: *Using sharp scissors, make a small cut in the material.* ◇ *to have a haircut*

trim (**-mm-**) [T] to make sth neater, smaller or better by cutting parts from it; to cut away unnecessary parts from sth: *Trim the edges with a sharp knife.* ◇ *His beard was neatly trimmed.* ◇ *Trim some of the fat off the meat.*
▸ **trim** *noun* [C, usually sing.]: *The hedge needs a trim.*

shave [T, I] to cut hair from the skin, especially the face, using a razor (= a special instrument that cuts close to the skin): *He has completely shaved his head.* ◇ *I cut myself* (= made myself bleed) *when I was shaving.*
▸ **shave** *noun* [C, usually sing.]: *I need a shave.*

mow /məʊ; *AmE* moʊ/ [T] to cut grass, etc. using a machine or tool that has a special blade or blades: *The lawn needs mowing every week in summer.*

lop (**-pp-**) [T] to remove part of sth by cutting it, especially to remove branches from a tree: *The men began lopping branches from a row of beech trees.*

shear /ʃɪə(r); *AmE* ʃɪr/ [T] to cut the wool off a sheep; to cut off sb's hair: *It was time for the sheep to be shorn.* ◇ (*formal*) *The prisoners' hair was shorn.*

snip (**-pp-**) [T] to cut sth with scissors using short, quick strokes: *Snip a tiny hole in the paper.* ◇ *She **snipped at** the stitching.* ◇ *Snip off the end of the tube.*

▸ **snip** *noun* [C]: *Make a series of snips along the edge of the fabric.*

crop (-**pp**-) [T] to cut sb's hair very short: *His hair was closely cropped.*

clip (-**pp**-) [T] to cut sth with scissors, etc. in order to make it shorter or neater; to remove sth by cutting it off: *The trees had been clipped into formal shapes.* ◇ *He clipped off a piece of wire with the pliers.*

---

4 See the Topic Map for HEALTH on p.890

cut ⋅ slash ⋅ slit ⋅ split ⋅ nick ⋅ gash

These words all mean to make an opening or wound in sth with sth sharp.

PATTERNS AND COLLOCATIONS
▸ to cut / slash / slit sb's throat / your wrists
▸ to cut / split your **head** / **lip**
▸ to cut / nick **yourself**
▸ to cut / slit / split sth **open**

cut [T] to make an opening or a wound in sth, especially with a sharp tool such as a knife or scissors: *She cut her finger on a piece of glass.* ◇ *He cut himself* (= his face) *shaving.* ◇ *Workmen cut a hole in the pipe.* ◇ *You need a powerful saw to cut through metal.* See also **cut** → INJURY

slash [T] to make a long cut with a sharp object, especially in a violent way: *Someone had slashed the tyres on my car.* ◇ *She tried to kill herself by slashing her wrists.* ◇ *We had to slash our way through the undergrowth with sticks.* ◇ *He slashed at his opponent with his sword.*

slit [T] to make a long narrow cut or opening in sth: *Slit the roll with a sharp knife.* ◇ *The victim's throat had been slit.* ◇ *He slit open the envelope and took out the letter.*

split [T] to accidentally cut your skin and make it bleed: *She fell downstairs and split her head open.* ◇ *How did you split your lip?*

nick [T] to make a small cut in the surface or edge of sth, especially sb's skin: *He nicked himself while shaving.* ◇ *I nicked my finger opening the tin.*

gash [T] to make a long deep cut in sth, especially sb's skin: *He gashed his hand on a sharp piece of rock.* See also **gash** → INJURY

D d

daily *adj.* See also the entry for MUNDANE

daily · everyday · day-to-day
These words all describe things that happen regularly or every day.

PATTERNS AND COLLOCATIONS
▶ daily / everyday / day-to-day **life / existence / experience / activities / business / work / tasks / use / problems / needs**
▶ everyday / day-to-day **affairs / matters / situations / things**
▶ the everyday / day-to-day **world**

daily [only before noun] happening, done or produced every day: *Keep a daily record of your progress.* ◇ *The daily routine is the same for all prisoners.* ◇ *There was increased state interference in all spheres of daily life.* ◇ *The equipment is used* **on a daily basis**.
▶ **daily** *adv.*: *The temperature was recorded daily.*
everyday /ˈevrideɪ/ [only before noun] used or happening every day or regularly and therefore not special: *The invention was explained in non-technical everyday language.* ◇ *Using* **everyday objects**, *basic scientific principles can be explained to young children.*
day-to-'day [only before noun] involving the usual events or tasks of each day: *Most of the training was not relevant to their day-to-day work.* ◇ *Neither of the owners is involved in the day-to-day running of the business.* ❶ **Day-to-day** can also mean 'planning for only one day at a time': *I have organized the cleaning* **on a day-to-day basis**, *until our usual cleaner returns.* This has a different meaning from *on a daily basis* (= every day).

damage *noun*

damage · harm · detriment
These are all words for the bad effects on sb/sth of an accident, crime, disease or other unfortunate event.

PATTERNS AND COLLOCATIONS
▶ damage / harm / detriment **to** sth
▶ damage / harm **from** sth
▶ **great / serious / severe / lasting / long-term / environmental** damage / harm / detriment
▶ **real / irreparable / permanent / physical / bodily / personal / emotional / psychological** damage / harm
▶ to **cause / do / inflict / suffer / escape / prevent** damage / harm
▶ damage / harm **results from** sth

damage [U] the fact of sth being broken or spoiled, or the pain or suffering felt by sb, as a result of an accident, crime, disease or other unfortunate event: *The earthquake caused damage to property estimated at $60 million.* ◇ *We assessed the storm damage.* ◇ *He was hit by a car and suffered severe* **brain damage**. ◇ *I insist on paying for the damage.* ◇ *I'm going — I've done enough damage here already.* See also **damaging** → HARMFUL
harm [U] damage or suffering caused to sb/sth: *The accident could have been worse; luckily* **no harm was done**. ◇ *The treatment they gave him did him* **more harm than good**. ◇ *Hard work* **never did anyone any harm**. ◇ *He may look fierce, but he* **means no harm**. ◇ *Don't worry, we'll see that the children* **come to no harm**. ◇ *I prefer the children to play in the garden where they're* **out of harm's way**. See also **harmful** → HARMFUL

> **NOTE** DAMAGE OR HARM? Use **damage** to talk about the effects of storms, floods, fire, etc. on buildings and other objects: *storm/flood/fire/smoke/bomb/structural damage*. Use **damage** to talk about the physical state of unhealthy organs in the body: *liver/kidney/lung/brain damage*. Use **damage** or **harm** to talk about mental or emotional suffering: *emotional/psychological/social damage/harm*. Use **harm** in a number of fixed phrases (see above) to express opinions about what or who may cause harm, or whether harm has been caused.

detriment /ˈdetrɪmənt/ [U, C, usually sing.] (*formal*) the act of causing harm or damage; sth that causes harm or damage: *Wood accounts for 90% of energy production in some countries, with consequent environmental detriment.* ◇ *He was engrossed in the job* **to the detriment of** *his health.* ◇ *The tax cannot be introduced* **without detriment to** *people's living standards.* See also **detrimental** → HARMFUL

damage *verb*

damage · hurt · harm · impair · compromise
These words all mean to have a bad effect on sb/sth.

PATTERNS AND COLLOCATIONS
▶ to damage / hurt / harm / impair / compromise sb's **chances**
▶ to damage / hurt / harm / compromise sb's **reputation**
▶ to damage / hurt / harm sb's **interests / image**
▶ to damage / harm / impair / compromise sb's **health**
▶ to **seriously** damage / hurt / harm / impair / compromise sb / sth
▶ to **greatly** damage / hurt / harm / impair sb / sth
▶ to **severely / badly** damage / hurt / impair sb / sth

damage [T] to cause physical harm to sth, making it less attractive, useful or valuable; to have a bad effect on sb/sth's life, health, happiness or chances of success: *Several vehicles were damaged in the crash.* ◇ *Smoking seriously damages your health.* ◇ *The allegations are likely to damage his political career.* ◇ *He works with emotionally damaged children.* See also **damaging** → HARMFUL
hurt [T] (*rather informal*) to have a bad effect on sb/sth's life, health, happiness or chances of success: *Many people on low incomes will be hurt by the government's plans.* ◇ *Hard work never hurt anyone.* ◇ *High interest rates are hurting the local economy.*
harm [T] to hurt sb/sth: *Pollution can harm marine life.* ◇ *These revelations will harm her chances of winning the election.* See also **harmful** → HARMFUL

> **NOTE** DAMAGE, HURT OR HARM? **Hurt** is slightly less formal than **damage** or **harm**, especially when it is used in negative statements: *It won't hurt him to have to wait a bit.* ◇ *These prices won't hurt your wallet.* ◇ ~~It won't damage/harm him to have to wait a bit.~~ ◇ ~~These prices won't damage/harm your wallet.~~ **Harm** is also often used to talk about ways in which things in the natural world such as *birds, animals, wildlife* and the *environment* are affected by human activity; people also talk about how an action may **harm** an *unborn child/baby* or a *foetus*.

impair /ɪmˈpeə(r); AmE ɪmˈper/ [T] (*rather formal*) to damage sb's health, abilities or chances: *There are a number of factors which can directly impair memory.* ◇ *Even one drink can impair driving performance.* **OPP** im-prove → IMPROVE 1
▶ **impaired** *adj.* (used in compounds): *the problems faced by people who are* **visually/hearing impaired**
compromise /ˈkɒmprəmaɪz; AmE ˈkɑːm-/ [T] to bring sb/sth/yourself into danger or under suspicion, especially by acting in a way that is not very sensible: *She has*

already **compromised herself** *by accepting his invitation.* ◇ *Defeat at this stage would compromise their chances of reaching the finals of the competition.*

dangerous *adj.*

dangerous · hazardous · risky · unsafe · high-risk · treacherous
These words all describe sth that is a risk or danger to sb/sth.

PATTERNS AND COLLOCATIONS
▸ dangerous/ hazardous/ risky/ unsafe **for** sb (to do sth)
▸ dangerous/ hazardous **to** sb/ sth
▸ dangerous/ hazardous/ risky/ unsafe **to do sth**
▸ a dangerous/ a hazardous/ a risky **business/ situation**
▸ a dangerous/ hazardous/ high-risk **occupation/ operation**
▸ **very** dangerous/ hazardous/ risky/ unsafe/ treacherous
▸ **highly** dangerous/ hazardous/ risky

dangerous likely to injure or harm sb, or to damage or destroy sth: *Flu can be a dangerous illness for some people, including the very young.* ◇ *He received a conviction for **dangerous driving**.* ◇ *It would be dangerous for you to stay here.* ◇ *The prisoners who escaped are violent and dangerous.* ◇ *We'd be **on dangerous ground** if we asked about race or religion (= it might make people angry).* **OPP** safe, harmless → SAFE 2, See also **danger** → RISK 1, **danger** → THREAT
 ▸ **dangerously** *adv.*: *She was standing dangerously close to the fire.* ◇ *His father is dangerously ill (= so ill that he might die).*
hazardous /ˈhæzədəs; *AmE* -ərdəs/ (*rather formal*) involving risk or danger, especially to sb's health or safety: *Britain produces almost five million tonnes of hazardous waste each year.* ◇ *They endured a hazardous journey through thickening fog.* ◇ *They attached a list of products that are potentially hazardous to health.* See also **hazard** → THREAT *noun*
risky involving the possibility of sth bad happening, especially in business: *Predicting the weather is a risky business for farmers.* ◇ *Even a very good company can be a risky investment if it is overvalued.* ◇ *It's far too risky to generalize from one set of results.* See also **risk** → RISK *noun* 1 2
unsafe (*rather formal*) (especially of a place, action or activity) not safe: *The roof was **declared unsafe**.* ◇ *It was considered unsafe to release the prisoners.* ◇ ***Unsafe sex** (= for example, sex without a condom) carries a high risk of spreading HIV.* **OPP** safe → SAFE 2
high-risk [usually before noun] involving a lot of danger and the risk of loss, damage, injury or death; (of people) very likely to get a particular illness: *It's a high-risk venture that will require a lot of capital.* ◇ *Ideally the technique should be limited to high-risk patients.* ❶ **High-risk** is used especially in the contexts of business and medicine. Collocates include *investment, strategy, venture* and *project*, and *patients, subjects, children, category* and *group*. **OPP** low-risk ❶ **Low-risk** activities involve only a small amount of danger and little risk or loss, damage or injury; **low-risk** patients are very unlikely to get a particular illness.
treacherous /ˈtretʃərəs/ dangerous, especially when seeming safe: *The ice on the roads made driving conditions treacherous.* ❶ **Treacherous** is used especially in the context of bad weather conditions.

dare *verb*

dare · risk · go so/as far as to… · venture · hazard · stick your neck out · pluck up (the) courage · presume · chance
These words all mean to be brave enough to try to do sth that may not succeed.

PATTERNS AND COLLOCATIONS
▸ to dare/go so far as/venture/pluck up courage/presume **to do sth**
▸ to risk/ chance **doing sth**
▸ to venture/ hazard an **opinion**
▸ to risk/ chance a **look** (at sth)
▸ to risk/ chance **it**

dare [I] (not usually used in the progressive tenses) to be brave enough to do sth difficult or dangerous; to be rude enough to do sth that you have no right to do: *She said it as loudly as she dared.* ◇ *He didn't dare (to) say what he thought.* ◇ *Dare to be different!* ◇ (*BrE*) *They daren't ask for any more money.* ◇ (*spoken*)*I'll tell her about it.' **'Don't you dare!'*** ◇ *How dare you talk to me like that!* See also **daring** → BOLD *adj.*, **daring** → COURAGE *noun*
risk [T] to do sth that may mean that you get into a situation which is unpleasant for you; to do sth that you know is not really a good idea or may not be successful: *There was no choice. If they stayed there, they risked death.* ◇ *They knew they risked being arrested.* ◇ *He risked a glance at her furious face.* ◇ *It was a difficult decision but we decided to risk it.* See also **risk** → RISK *noun* 1, **risk** → RISK *noun* 2
go so/as 'far as to… *phrase* to go to extreme or surprising limits in dealing with sth: *In June 2006 he went so far as to offer his resignation.* ◇ *I wouldn't go as far as to say that he's a liar (= but I think he may be slightly dishonest).*
venture /ˈventʃə(r)/ [T] (*formal*) to say or do sth in a careful way, especially because it might upset or offend sb: *She hardly dared to venture an opinion.* ◇ *I ventured to suggest that she might have made a mistake.*
hazard /ˈhæzəd; *AmE* -ərd/ [T, I] (*formal*) to make a suggestion or guess that you know may be wrong: *Would you like to **hazard a guess**?* ◇ *'Is it Tom you're going with?' she hazarded.*
stick your 'neck out *idiom* (*informal*) to do or say sth when there is a risk that you may be wrong: *I'll stick my neck out and say that Bill is the best candidate for the job.*
pluck up (the) 'courage *idiom* (*usually approving*) to make yourself do sth even though you are afraid to do it: *I finally plucked up the courage to ask her for a date.*
presume /prɪˈzjuːm; *AmE* -ˈzuːm/ [I] (*formal, usually disapproving*) to behave in a way that shows a lack of respect by doing sth that you have no right to do: *I wouldn't presume to tell you how to run your own business.* See also **presumptuous** → COOL *adj.*
chance [T] (*informal*) to risk sth, although you know the result may not be successful: *'Take an umbrella.' 'No, I'll chance it (= take the risk that it may rain).'* ◇ (*especially BrE*) *She was **chancing her luck** driving without a licence.*

dark *adj.*

1 a dark night
2 a dark colour

---

1 dark · black · shady · shadowy · unlit
These words all describe a place where there is little or no light.

PATTERNS AND COLLOCATIONS
▸ a dark/ shady/ shadowy **place/ corner**
▸ a dark/ shadowy/ unlit **room**
▸ a dark/ unlit **road**
▸ a dark/ black **night**
▸ black/ shadowy **darkness**
▸ to go dark/ black
▸ **pitch** dark/ black
▸ **cool and** dark/ shady

dark with no or very little light, especially because it is night: *What time does it **get dark** in summer?* ◇ *It was dark outside and I couldn't see much.* ◇ *He stumbled along through the dark forest.* **OPP** light → LIGHT *noun* 1

black without light; completely dark: *Through the black night came the sound of thunder.* ◇ *It's pitch black* (= very dark) *outside.* ◇ *My head banged on a rock and everything went black.*

shady protected from direct sunlight by sth, for example trees or buildings: *We went to find somewhere cool and shady to have a drink.* ◇ *This is a nice shady spot for a picnic.* **OPP** **sunny** → SUNNY

shadowy [usually before noun] dark and full of shadows: *Someone was hiding in the shadowy doorway.* ◇ *The lights went out, plunging the room into a shadowy darkness.*

unlit dark because there are no lights or the lights are not switched on: *The room was unlit and they could hardly see the man in the gloom.* ◇ *Avoid walking through parks or down quiet, unlit roads.* **OPP** **lighted** → LIGHT *verb* 2

2 dark · rich · deep · warm · mellow
These words all describe strong and/or pleasant colours.

PATTERNS AND COLLOCATIONS
▸ a dark / rich / deep / warm **colour / tone / shade**
▸ (a) dark / rich / deep / warm **red / orange**
▸ (a) dark / rich / deep **blue / green / purple**
▸ **very** dark / deep

dark (of colours) not light; closer in shade to black than white: *Darker colours are more practical and don't show stains.* ◇ *Mahogany is a dark-coloured wood.* ◇ *He was dressed in a dark suit and a plain white shirt.* ◇ *The dark clouds in the sky meant that a storm was coming.* **OPP** **pale, light** → PALE 2

rich [usually before noun] (of colours) strong and dark, in a way that is beautiful or pleasing: *The colour of the flower is a rich deep red.* ◇ *the rich tones of autumn*

deep [usually before noun] (of colours) strong and dark, especially in an attractive way: *He had a pale face with deep blue eyes.* ◇ *The colour is deeper when the grapes are dried.* **OPP** **pale** → PALE 2

warm [usually before noun] (of colours) creating a pleasant, comfortable and relaxed feeling or atmosphere: *The house is decorated in warm shades of red and orange.* **OPP** **cool** → PALE 2

mellow (of colours) soft, rich and pleasant: *The floor was of mellow golden stone.*

darken *verb*

darken · dim · cloud
These words all mean to become or make sth become dark or darker.

PATTERNS AND COLLOCATIONS
▸ the **sky** darkens / clouds (over)

darken [I, T] (*especially written*) to become dark; to make sth dark: *The sky began to darken as the storm approached.* ◇ *We walked quickly through the darkened streets.* ◇ *a darkened room*

dim (-mm-) [I, T] (of a light) to become less bright; to make a light less bright: *The lights in the theatre dimmed as the curtain rose.* ◇ *Dim the lights to create some atmosphere.* See also **dim** → DIM *adj.* 1 2

cloud [I] (of the sky) to fill with clouds: *It was beginning to cloud over.* ◇ *The sky clouded over and it started to rain.* **OPP** **clear** → DISAPPEAR, See also **cloudy** → CLOUDY

darkness *noun*

darkness · the dark · shadow · shade · gloom · blackness
These are all words for the state of not being light or bright.

PATTERNS AND COLLOCATIONS
▸ **in / into / out of** the darkness / dark / shadows / shade / gloom / blackness
▸ **through** the darkness / dark / shadows / gloom / blackness
▸ **deep** darkness / shadow / shade / gloom

▸ the **gathering** darkness / dark / shadows / gloom
▸ **pitch** darkness / dark / blackness
▸ to **peer into** the darkness / dark / shadows / gloom / blackness
▸ to **adjust to** the darkness / dark / gloom
▸ your **eyes become accustomed to** the darkness / dark / gloom
▸ to be **shrouded in / plunged into** darkness / shadow / gloom
▸ **light and** darkness / dark / shadow / shade

darkness [U] the state of being dark, without any light; the quality or state of being dark in colour: *After a few minutes our eyes got used to the darkness.* ◇ *In the west the sun went down and darkness fell* (= it became night). ◇ *They managed to escape under cover of darkness.* ◇ *It depends on the darkness of your skin.* **OPP** **light** → LIGHT 1

the dark [sing.] the lack of light in a place, especially because it is night: *All the lights went out and we were left in the dark.* ◇ *Are the children afraid of the dark?* ◇ *They say that eating carrots helps you see in the dark.* ❶ **Before/after dark** means 'before/after the sun goes down and it is night': *She won't go out alone after dark.* ❶ **Dark** [U] is an amount of sth that is dark in colour: *We examined the patterns of light and dark in the painting.* **OPP** **light** → LIGHT 1

shadow [U] (*also* **shadows** [pl.]) darkness in a place or on sth, especially so that you cannot easily see who or what is there: *His face was deep in shadow, turned away from her.* ◇ *I thought I saw a figure standing in the shadows.* See also **shadow** → SHAPE *noun*

shade [U] an area that is dark and cool under or behind sth, for example under a tree or building, because the sun's light does not get to it; the dark areas in a picture, especially the use of these to produce variety: *We sat down in the shade of the tree.* ◇ *The temperature can reach 40°C in the shade.* ◇ *The trees provide shade for the animals in the summer.* ◇ *The painting needs more light and shade.* **OPP** **sun** → SUN, **light** → LIGHT 1

gloom /gluːm/ [U] (*literary*) almost total darkness: *We watched the boats come back in the gathering gloom.* **OPP** **brightness** → LIGHT 1, See also **gloomy** → DIM 2

blackness [U] the state or quality of being dark or black: *She peered out into the inky blackness of the night.* ◇ *His bright silk tie contrasted with the blackness of his hair.*

darkness

shade

shadow

darling *noun*

darling · honey · love · baby · sweetheart · dear · sweetie · loved one · babe · beloved
These are all words for addressing or describing sb that you like or care about very much.

PATTERNS AND COLLOCATIONS
▸ **thank you, hello, yes, etc.** darling / honey / love / baby / sweetheart / dear / sweetie / babe
▸ **my** darling / love / baby / sweetheart / dear / beloved

darling [C] (*especially BrE, informal, spoken*) a way of addressing sb that you love: *What's the matter, darling?* ◇ *I love you too, my darling.* See also **darling** → DEAR *adj.*

honey /ˈhʌni/ [C] (*especially AmE, informal, spoken*) a way of addressing sb that you love or like very much: *Have you seen my keys, honey?*

love [C] a person that you love: *Take care, my love.* ◇ *He was the love of my life* (= the person I loved most).

baby [C] (*especially AmE, informal, spoken*) a way of addressing sb that you love, especially in a romantic way: *Come on baby, let's dance!* ❶ Baby can be offensive if used by a man to a woman that he does not know.

sweetheart /'swi:thɑ:t; *AmE* -hɑ:rt/ [sing.] (*informal, spoken*) a way of addressing sb that you love or like very much: *Do you want a drink, sweetheart?* ❶ Sweetheart is used especially by a man to a woman or by a woman to a child.

dear [C] (*becoming old-fashioned, informal, spoken*) a way of addressing sb that you like or love: *Come here, my dear.* ❶ Dear is used especially by older people. See also **dear** → DEAR *adj.*

sweetie [sing.] (*especially AmE, informal, spoken*) a way of addressing sb that you love or like very much: *Oh, sweetie. Don't cry.* ◇ *If you ask me, sweetie, you're making a big mistake.* ❶ In British English **sweetie** is mostly used by a woman to a child; in American English it is also used between female friends.

loved one (*rather informal, especially written*) a person you care about very much, especially a member of your family: *He longed to be at home with his loved ones.* ❶ Loved one is the only term in this group that cannot be used as a way of addressing sb: ~~Are you all right, loved one?~~

babe [C] (*informal, spoken*) a way of addressing a close friend or sb that you love: *Hi, babe, how are you doing?* ❶ Babe is used especially by young people. It can be offensive if used by a man to a woman he does not know. The word **babes** is also used, but this is less frequent.

beloved /bɪˈlʌvɪd/ (*old use or literary*) a person who is loved very much by sb, especially in a romantic way: *It was a gift from her beloved.* See also **beloved** → DEAR *adj.*

dawn *noun*

dawn · sunrise · first thing · first light · daybreak
These are all words for the time of day when light first appears.

PATTERNS AND COLLOCATIONS
▸ at / before / since / by / until / till dawn / sunrise / first light / daybreak

dawn [U, C] the time of day when light first appears: *They start work at dawn.* ◇ *It's almost dawn.* ◇ *We arrived in Sydney as dawn broke* (= as the first light could be seen). ◇ *She's always up at the crack of dawn* (= when dawn begins). ◇ *She awoke to another glorious dawn.* **OPP** dusk → NIGHT 2
▸ **dawn** *verb* [I]: (*written*) *The following morning dawned bright and warm.*

sunrise /'sʌnraɪz/ [U, C, usually sing.] dawn; the colours in the part of the sky where the sun first appears in the morning: *It was an exceptionally beautiful sunrise.* **OPP** sunset → NIGHT 2

first thing *adv.* the first moment of the day; before anything else that you do that day: *He's always grumpy first thing in the morning.* ◇ *I'll call him first thing tomorrow.* **OPP** last thing ❶ Last thing means 'late in the evening, after everything else that you do that day': *I took the dog for a walk last thing before going to bed.*

first light [U] (*written or literary*) dawn: *At first light the soldiers were on the move again.* ◇ *We sailed at the first light of dawn.*

daybreak /'deɪbreɪk/ [U] (*written or literary*) dawn: *He was woken shortly before daybreak.* **OPP** nightfall → NIGHT 2

> **NOTE** DAWN, SUNRISE, FIRST LIGHT OR DAYBREAK? Dawn emphasizes the time of day when the sun comes up; sunrise emphasizes what you see in the sky at this time. First light and daybreak are less common and are used mostly in written or descriptive language.

day *noun*

day · morning · afternoon · noon · midday · daytime
These are all words for times of the day when it is not dark.

PATTERNS AND COLLOCATIONS
▸ in / during the day / morning / afternoon / daytime
▸ at / around noon / midday
▸ (on) Monday / Tuesday, etc. morning / afternoon
▸ this / tomorrow / yesterday morning / afternoon
▸ noon / midday tomorrow / yesterday
▸ all / every / each / day / morning / afternoon
▸ a beautiful / hot / nice / warm / cold day / morning / afternoon
▸ Good morning / afternoon!
▸ to spend the day / morning / afternoon doing sth

day [U, C] the time between when it becomes light in the morning and when it gets dark in the evening; the time when you are awake, working, etc: *I could sit and watch the river all day long.* ◇ *Nocturnal animals sleep by day and hunt by night.* ◇ *The short winter days prevented them from finishing all the work.* ◇ *What a beautiful day!* ◇ *It's been a long day* (= I've been very busy). ◇ *Did you have a good day?* ◇ *She didn't do a full day's work.* ◇ (*BrE*) *a seven-hour working day* **OPP** night → NIGHT 1

morning [U, C] the early part of the day from the time when people wake up until 12 midday or before lunch: *They left early in the morning.* ◇ *He's been in a meeting all morning.* ◇ *Our group meets on Friday mornings.* ◇ *It was a beautiful morning, with not a cloud in the sky.* **OPP** afternoon, evening, night → NIGHT 2

afternoon [U, C] the part of the day from 12 midday until about 6 o'clock: *In the afternoon they went shopping.* ◇ *Come over on Sunday afternoon.* ◇ *She studies art two afternoons a week.* ◇ *We spent a long lazy afternoon by the river.* **OPP** morning

noon [U] 12 o'clock in the middle of the day: *The conference opens at 12 noon on Saturday.* ◇ *I'm leaving on the noon train.*

midday [U] noon; the period around noon: *The rain will continue until around midday tomorrow.* ◇ *Most people here eat their midday meal in the canteen.* ◇ *They rode on through the heat of the midday sun.* **OPP** midnight → NIGHT 1

daytime /'deɪtaɪm/ [U] the time between when it becomes light in the morning and when it gets dark in the evening; the time during the day when a lot of people usually work: *You don't often see this bird in the daytime.* ◇ *Daytime temperatures never fell below 80°F.* ◇ *Please give your name, address and daytime phone number.* **OPP** night-time → NIGHT 1

> **NOTE** DAY OR DAYTIME? A day can either be seen as a completed whole, or as a period of time that is continuing; daytime is a period of time that is continuing, never a completed whole: *during the day / daytime* ◇ *I've been busy all day.* ◇ ~~I've been busy all daytime.~~ ◇ *Did you have a good day?* ◇ ~~Did you have a good daytime?~~ Daytime is used especially in compounds: *daytime phone number / television / temperatures* ◇ ~~day phone number / television / temperatures~~

dead *adj.*

dead · late · deceased · lifeless · at peace
These words all describe people, animals or plants that are no longer alive.

PATTERNS AND COLLOCATIONS
▸ to lie dead / lifeless / at peace
▸ a dead / late / deceased wife / husband / mother / father / brother / sister / relative
▸ a / sb's dead / lifeless body
▸ almost / nearly / apparently / seemingly dead / lifeless

dead no longer alive: *a dead person/animal/tree* ◇ *dead leaves/wood/skin* ◇ *My mother's dead; she died in 1997.* ◇ *He was shot dead by a gunman outside his home.* ◇ (*informal*) *He **dropped dead** (= died suddenly) last week.* **OPP** **alive, living, live** → ALIVE, See also **die** → DIE
▸ **the dead** *noun* [pl.]: *The dead and wounded in that one attack amounted to 6 000.*
▸ **death** *noun* [C, U]: *a sudden/violent/peaceful death* ◇ *the anniversary of his wife's death* ◇ *Two children were burnt **to death** in the fire* (= they died as a result of the fire). ◇ *Police are still trying to establish the cause of death.* **OPP** **life** → LIFE 1

late [only before noun] (*rather formal*) (of a person) no longer alive: *She spoke of her late husband with passion.* ◇ *The event was organized in memory of the late Christopher Reeve.* ❶ **Late** in this meaning is usually used in the phrases *sb's late husband/wife/father/mother*, etc. or the *late John Smith/Mary Brown*, etc. to talk about sb who has died quite recently.

deceased /dɪˈsiːst/ (*law or formal*) dead: *She took over her deceased parents' business.*
▸ **the deceased** *noun* [C]: *The funeral was attended by only the male relations of the deceased.* ❶ **The deceased** is used especially about sb who has died recently.

lifeless (*formal*) dead or appearing to be dead: *He knelt beside her lifeless body.* ❶ **Lifeless** is usually used to talk about bodies or parts of the body: *his/her lifeless body/ form/eyes/hand*

at ˈpeace *idiom* dead, and therefore having no more worries: *Her illness would develop, and soon she would be at peace.*

dealer *noun*

dealer · trader · supplier · seller · merchant · retailer · vendor · distributor · wholesaler · shopkeeper
These are all words for a person or company whose business is buying and selling things.

PATTERNS AND COLLOCATIONS
▸ to buy/ sell sth **through** a dealer / distributor / wholesaler
▸ a **small** dealer / trader / supplier / merchant / retailer / vendor / distributor / wholesaler / shopkeeper
▸ a **large** dealer / trader / supplier / merchant / retailer / vendor / distributor / wholesaler
▸ a **local** dealer / trader / supplier / merchant / retailer / vendor / distributor / wholesaler / shopkeeper
▸ an **international** dealer / trader / supplier / merchant / distributor / wholesaler
▸ a **foreign** dealer / trader / supplier / seller / merchant / vendor
▸ a **street** trader / seller / vendor
▸ an **independent** dealer / trader / supplier / retailer / vendor / distributor / wholesaler
▸ a **licensed** dealer / trader / seller / retailer / vendor / distributor
▸ a **leading** dealer / supplier / merchant / retailer / distributor / wholesaler
▸ a/an **food / clothing / electrical** supplier / retailer / distributor / wholesaler
▸ a dealer / trader / supplier / seller / merchant / retailer / vendor / distributor / wholesaler / shopkeeper **sells** sth
▸ a dealer / trader / merchant / retailer / distributor / wholesaler **buys** sth

dealer [C] a person whose business is buying and selling a particular product: *She set up in business as an antiques dealer.* ◇ *He's a **dealer in** second-hand cars.* ❶ **Dealer** is most frequently used to talk about people who buy and sell art, antiques, cars or arms. The phrase *your dealer* is often used in contexts in which advice is being given to a person who has recently bought sth: *Contact your dealer for more information.* ◇ *Return the unit to your dealer for repair.* In this case, **dealer** can refer to any type of business or shop that sells things. ❶ In British English a **dealer** is also a person who buys and sells currencies, company shares, etc. on the stock exchange: (*BrE*) *She's a dealer in the financial futures market.* The usual American English word for this is **trader**. See also **dealing** → TRADE

trader [C] a person whose business is buying and selling things: (*especially BrE*) *Many of the small local traders have been forced to close.* ◇ (*especially BrE*) *Being a **sole trader** (= a person who runs a business on their own) is a risky venture.* ◇ (*especially AmE*) *Numerous risks are taken every day by currency traders.* ❶ In British English **trader** can be used in a variety of contexts. A *small/local/independent trader* is usually a person who owns a shop in a town. A *market/street trader* is sb who sells food or other everyday items on the street or in a marketplace. Especially in American English a *currency/bond/commodity trader* buys and sells currencies, company shares, etc. on the stock exchange. The usual British English word for this is **dealer**. See also **trade, trading** → TRADE

supplier /səˈplaɪə(r)/ [C] a person or company that supplies goods to businesses or shops: *They are a leading supplier of computers in the UK.* ◇ *You will need to be able to deal with both customers and suppliers.*

seller [C] a person who sells sth: *The law is intended to protect the buyer and the seller.* ◇ *She stopped to buy a bunch of violets from a flower seller in the market square.*

merchant [C] a person who buys and sells goods in large quantities, especially one who imports and exports goods: *Venice was once a city of rich merchants.* ◇ *He was the eldest son of a wealthy wine merchant.*

retailer /ˈriːteɪlə(r)/ [C] (*especially written*) a person or business that sells goods to the public: *They are one of the country's largest food retailers.*

vendor /ˈvendə(r)/ [C] a person who sells things, for example food or newspapers, usually outside on the street: *Jewellery, leather and clothes are offered by street vendors at every corner.* ❶ In legal English the **vendor** is a person who is selling a house or other property: *The cost to the vendor of selling land by auction is normally higher than by private treaty.* In American English **vendor** can also be used like **supplier**: *Get a list of vendors who deliver frozen food.*

distributor /dɪˈstrɪbjətə(r)/ [C] a person or company that supplies goods to shops: *They are Japan's largest software distributor.*

NOTE **SUPPLIER** OR **DISTRIBUTOR**? Supplier has a wider range of uses than **distributor**. **Supplier** can be used to talk about any company that sells goods to businesses and shops. A **supplier** might be the company that makes the goods – the manufacturer – or the company that sells raw materials to the manufacturer. A **distributor** works with a manufacturer, buying the goods they have made and selling them to shops. A company can be both a **supplier** and a **distributor**, depending on your point of view: the manufacturer whose goods they sell will see them as the **distributor** of their goods; the business that buys from them will see them as the **supplier** of their materials or equipment.

wholesaler /ˈhəʊlseɪlə(r); *AmE* ˈhoʊl-/ [C] a person involved in the business of buying and selling goods in large quantities, especially so they can be sold again to make a profit: *The majority of stock is bought through wholesalers, before being repackaged for retailing to the public.*

shopkeeper /ˈʃɒpkiːpə(r)/ [C] a person who owns or manages a shop, usually a small one: *the village shopkeeper*

deal with sb/sth *phrasal verb* See also the entry for TACKLE

deal with sb/sth · handle · take care of sth · look after sth · contend with sb/sth · see to sth
These words all mean to manage or control a situation or area of work.

PATTERNS AND COLLOCATIONS
▸ to deal with / handle sth **with** ease, assurance, etc.
▸ to deal with/handle/take care of/look after/see to **the matter**

▶ to deal with / handle / take care of / look after / contend with a **problem**
▶ to deal with / handle / take care of / look after the **correspondence / paperwork / customers**
▶ to **have sth to** deal with / contend with / attend to
▶ to deal with / handle / look after sb / sth **properly**
▶ to deal with / handle / take care of sth **easily**

'deal with sb/sth *phrasal verb* to solve a problem, or manage or control a situation, an area of work, a person or a strong emotion: *There are various possible ways of dealing with this problem.* ◇ *My job is to deal with enquiries from the public.* ◇ *She smiled the same smile she used when dealing with difficult customers.* ◇ *He's good at dealing with pressure.*

handle [T] to deal with sb/sth: *We can handle up to 500 calls an hour at our new offices.* ◇ *She's very good at handling patients.* ◇ *We all have to learn to handle stress.* ◇ *The matter has been handled very badly.* ◇ *(informal)'Any problems?' 'Nothing I can't handle.'*
▶ **handling** *noun* [U]: *I was impressed by his handling of the situation.* ◇ *This horse needs firm handling.*

NOTE DEAL WITH STH OR HANDLE? **Handle** often suggests control and calmness. It is often used to talk about whether people are *capable of handling* or *can handle* a situation. **Deal with sth** is usually used in more businesslike situations. It is often used to discuss *ways*, *methods* and *means* of **dealing with** problems.

take care of sth *phrase* to be responsible for or to deal with a situation or task: *Don't worry about the travel arrangements. They're all being taken care of.* ◇ *Celia takes care of the marketing side of things.*

‚look 'after sth *phrasal verb* (*especially BrE, rather formal*) to be responsible for sth and for making sure it is done correctly: *I'm looking after his affairs while he's in hospital.* ◇ *She also looks after quality control.* ❶ **Look after sth** is used especially to talk about sb's personal finances or a particular area of a business.

con'tend with sb/sth *phrasal verb* to have to deal with a problem or difficult situation: *Nurses often have to contend with violent or drunken patients.* ◇ *He had troubles enough of his own to contend with.* ❶ People **have to contend with** sth or **have sth to contend with**, because of the situation that they are in: people never choose or offer to contend with sth: *Don't worry — I'll contend with it.*

'see to sth *phrasal verb* (*spoken*) to deal with sth: *Will you see to the arrangements for the next meeting?* ◇ *Don't worry — I'll see to it.* ◇ (*BrE*) *We'll have to get that door seen to* (= repaired).

dear *adj.*

dear · beloved · precious · prized · cherished · darling · treasured · much loved
These words all describe things or people that are very important or special to sb.

PATTERNS AND COLLOCATIONS
▶ beloved / prized / cherished / treasured / much loved **by** sb
▶ dear / precious **to** sb
▶ a / sb's dear / beloved / cherished / darling / much loved **friend**
▶ a / sb's dear / beloved / darling / much loved **daughter / son**
▶ a prized / cherished / treasured / much loved **possession**
▶ a precious / cherished / treasured **memory**
▶ dear / darling **Henry / Sarah, etc.**
▶ **very** dear / precious
▶ **much** beloved / prized / cherished / treasured / loved

dear (*written or becoming old-fashioned*) loved by or important to sb: *He's one of my dearest friends.* ◇ *They lost everything that was dear to them.* ❶ **Dear** can sound rather old-fashioned when used in spoken language, and can be rather literary in written language. In more everyday language, say *one of my closest/best friends* or *everything that is important/special to me.* See also **dear** → DARLING *noun*

beloved /bɪˈlʌvɪd/ (*formal*) loved very much by sb; very popular with sb: *in memory of our dearly beloved son, John* ◇ *They were glad to be back in their beloved Ireland.* ◇ *the deep purple flowers so beloved by artists* See also **beloved** → DARLING *noun*

precious /ˈpreʃəs/ loved or valued very much by sb: *My family is the most precious thing I have in my life.* ◇ *They managed to salvage a few precious possessions from the fire.*

prized [only before noun] very valuable or important to sb: *I lost some of my most prized possessions in the fire.* ❶ **Prized** is only used about things, NOT people: *my prized daughter* See also **prize** → APPRECIATE

cherished /ˈtʃerɪʃd/ loved very much and looked after by sb: *her most cherished possession* See also **cherish** → APPRECIATE

darling [only before noun] (*informal*) loved very much; very special or attractive: *my darling daughter* ◇ *'Darling Henry,' the letter began.* ❶ **Darling** is only used about people, NOT things: *darling possessions/memories* See also **darling** → DARLING *noun*

treasured /ˈtreʒəd; AmE ˈtreʒərd/ very valuable or important to sb: *This ring is my most treasured possession.* ❶ **Treasured** is only used about things, NOT people: *my treasured daughter* See also **treasure** → APPRECIATE

much loved very special to sb: *the boys' much loved grandfather, James* ◇ *She is much loved in this town.*

debate *noun* See the Topic Map for CONFLICT on p.896, See also the entry for ARGUMENT 1

debate · conflict · dispute · controversy · disagreement · difference · war · dissent · contention
These are all words for an argument between people, groups or countries.

PATTERNS AND COLLOCATIONS
▶ a debate / conflict / a dispute / controversy / disagreement / differences / a war / contention **about / over / between** sb / sth
▶ to be **in** debate / conflict / dispute **with** sb / sth
▶ (a) **serious** debate / conflict / dispute / controversy / disagreement / differences / dissent / contention
▶ (a) **growing** debate / conflict / controversy / differences / dissent
▶ (an) **unresolved** debate / conflict / dispute / differences
▶ a **bitter** debate / conflict / dispute / controversy / disagreement / war
▶ (an) **internal** debate / conflict / dispute / controversy / disagreement / differences / dissent
▶ **open** debate / conflict / disagreement / dissent
▶ (a) **political** debate / conflict / dispute / controversy / disagreement / differences / war / dissent / contention
▶ to **cause** debate / conflict / a dispute / controversy / dissent
▶ to **lead to / avoid** debate / conflict / controversy / a war
▶ to **resolve** a debate / conflict / a dispute / a controversy / a disagreement / sb's differences
▶ a debate / conflict / dispute / controversy / disagreement / difference **arises**
▶ a conflict / dispute / controversy / war **breaks out**
▶ a debate / conflict / dispute / controversy **continues**

debate [C, U] (*usually approving*) an argument or discussion expressing different opinions, especially when this is seen as a good or necessary thing: *This accident has sparked off an intense debate.* ◇ *the current debate about tax* ◇ *There has been much debate on the issue of childcare.* ◇ *Whether he deserved what happened to him is open to debate/a matter for debate* (= cannot be certain or decided yet).

conflict [C, U] (*rather formal, usually disapproving*) a situation in which people, groups or countries are involved in a serious disagreement or argument: *The violence was the result of political and ethnic conflicts.* ◇ *John often comes into conflict with his boss.*

dispute [C, U] (*rather formal*) an argument or disagreement between two people, groups or countries; discussion about a subject where there is disagreement: *His job is to settle pay disputes.* ◇ *The cause of the accident was still in dispute* (= being argued about). ◇ *The matter was* settled **beyond dispute** by the court judgment (= it could no longer be argued about). ◇ *His theories are* **open to dispute** (= can be disagreed with). See also **dispute** → DISAGREE *verb*

NOTE CONFLICT OR DISPUTE? A **conflict** is generally more serious than a **dispute**. A **dispute** is often about a particular issue, such as who owns sth, or how much money sb should earn. A **conflict** often lasts a long time, and may be connected with wider issues such as power and religion.

controversy /ˈkɒntrəvɜːsi; *BrE* also kənˈtrɒvəsi; *AmE* ˈkɑːntrəvɜːrsi/ [U, C] (*rather formal*) public discussion and argument about sth that many people strongly disagree about, disapprove of, or are shocked by: *The President resigned amid continuing controversy.* ◇ *A fierce controversy has broken out over the issue.* See also **controversial** → CONTROVERSIAL

disagreement [U, C] a situation in which people disagree about sth and often argue: *Disagreement arose about exactly how to plan the show.* ◇ *They have had several disagreements with their neighbours.* **OPP** **agreement** → AGREEMENT 2, See also **disagree** → DISAGREE *verb*

difference [C] (*rather formal*) a disagreement between people: *We* **have our differences***, but she's still my sister.* ◇ *There was a* **difference of opinion** *over who had won.* See also **differ** → DISAGREE *verb* ❶ **Difference** is used especially when people try to avoid getting angry or having a noisy argument, but still continue to disagree. It is also used when sb wants to suggest that there was no noisy argument, even if there was: *There was a difference of opinion… can be a polite way of saying 'There was an argument/a fight…'*

war [C, U] (used in compounds) a situation in which there is aggressive competition between groups, companies or countries: *The US threatened a trade war with Europe after the breakdown of the talks.* ◇ *The country seemed at times to be close to class war.*

dissent /dɪˈsent/ [U] (*formal*) the fact of having or expressing opinions that are different from those that are officially accepted: *The authorities continue their suppression of political dissent.* **OPP** **assent** → APPROVAL

contention /kənˈtenʃn/ [U] (*formal*) angry or bad-tempered disagreement between people: *One area of contention is the availability of nursery places.* ❶ A **bone/point of contention** is a subject that causes arguments or disagreement between people: *Privatization of the health service remains a point of contention.*

debt *noun*

debt · loss · liability · arrears · debit
These are all words for the situation of owing or losing money or the amount of money you owe or have lost.

PATTERNS AND COLLOCATIONS
▸ **in** debt / arrears / debit
▸ **heavy / massive** debts / losses
▸ **mortgage / tax / outstanding** debts / liabilities / arrears
▸ to **fall / get into** debt / arrears
▸ to **have** debts / liabilities
▸ to **run up** debts / losses
▸ to **pay off** debts / arrears

debt [C, U] a sum of money that sb owes; the situation of owing money, especially when you cannot pay: *She had run up credit card debts of thousands of dollars.* ◇ *He died* **heavily in debt***.* ◇ *It's hard to* **stay out of debt** *when you are a student.*

loss [C] money that has been lost by a business or organization: *The company has announced net losses of $1.5 million.* ◇ *We* **made a loss on** (= lost money on) *the deal.* ◇ *We are now operating* **at a loss***.* **OPP** **profit** → PROFIT, See also **gain** → INCREASE *noun*, **loss-making** → LOSS-MAKING

liability /ˌlaɪəˈbɪləti/ [C, usually pl.] (*finance*) the amount of money that a person or company owes: *The company is reported to have liabilities of nearly $90 000.* ◇ *Our financial advisers will concentrate on minimizing your tax liabilities and maximizing your income.* **OPP** **asset** → THING 3

arrears /əˈrɪəz; *AmE* əˈrɪrz/ [pl.] (*formal or finance*) money that sb owes that they have not paid at the right time: *Unions are demanding the settlement of pay arrears.* ❶ If you *are* **in arrears** or *get/fall* **into arrears**, you are late in paying money that you owe: *Our tenants have fallen into arrears with their rent.* If money or a person is paid for work *in* **arrears**, the money is paid after the work has been done: *You will be paid monthly in arrears.*

debit /ˈdebɪt/ [C] (*finance*) a written note in a bank account or other financial record of a sum of money owed or spent; a sum of money taken from a bank account: *This expenditure should all be shown on the debit side of the account.* ◇ *If the debits exceed the credits you're in trouble.* **OPP** **credit** ❶ A **credit** is a sum of money paid into a bank account or a record of this payment. See also **credit** → LOAN, **debit** → DISCOUNT *verb*

debut *noun*

debut · initiation · inauguration · introduction · induction
These are all words for the process of introducing sb to a new job, skill, organization, etc., or a ceremony at which this takes place.

PATTERNS AND COLLOCATIONS
▸ an initiation / induction **into** sth
▸ a **formal** inauguration / induction
▸ an initiation / inauguration **ceremony**

debut (also **début**) /ˈdeɪbjuː; ˈdebjuː; *AmE* deɪˈbjuː/ [C] the first public appearance of a performer or sports player: *He will* **make his debut** *for the first team this week.* ◇ *The group's debut album was released last week.* ◇ *She's making her New York debut at Carnegie Hall.*

initiation /ɪˌnɪʃiˈeɪʃn/ [U] (*rather formal*) the process of introducing a new member to a group, often with a special ceremony; the process of introducing sb to an activity or skill: *There was an established initiation ceremony for new boys.* ◇ *Her initiation into the world of marketing has not been straightforward.* ❶ An **initiation** ceremony is an occasion which is often set up unofficially by the members of a group, and can sometimes involve unpleasant actions that the new member is forced to do. ▸ **initiate** *verb* [T]: *Many of them had been* **initiated into** *drug use at an early age.* ◇ *Hundreds are initiated into the sect each year.*

inauguration /ɪˌnɔːɡjəˈreɪʃn/ [U, C] (*rather formal*) the process of introducing a new public official or leader at a special ceremony: *Eight months after Hoover's inauguration came the Wall Street Crash.* ◇ *an inauguration speech* ▸ **inaugurate** *verb* [T, often passive]: *She will be inaugurated (as) president in January.*

introduction [sing.] (*especially written*) a person's first experience of sth: *This album was my first introduction to modern jazz.* ▸ **introduce** *verb* [T]: *She has developed her love of archery since being* **introduced to** *the sport by a workmate.*

induction /ɪnˈdʌkʃn/ [U, C] (*rather formal*) the process of introducing sb to a new job, skill or organization; a ceremony at which this takes place: *The induction of new students will take place in the main hall.* ❶ **Induction** is often used to talk about people being introduced to their job or course in education. There is often an official *induction period* when you start a new job or course.

decent *adj.* See also the entry for ADEQUATE

decent · solid · respectable · sound
These words all describe sth that is of a good enough standard or quality.

▸ a decent/ solid/ respectable/ sound **performance**
▸ a decent/ solid/ respectable **result**
▸ **pretty** decent/ solid/ sound
▸ **perfectly** decent/ respectable/ sound
▸ decent/ respectable/ sound **enough**

decent /ˈdiːsnt/ (*rather informal, especially spoken*) of a good enough standard or quality: *He looks as if he could do with a decent meal.* ◇ *I need a decent night's sleep.* ◇ *This place looks decent enough — let's stay here.*
▸ **decently** *adv.*: *The car is decently sized and cheap to run.*

solid [usually before noun] (*especially business*) good and steady, but not always excellent or special: *2006 was a year of solid achievement.* ◇ *He's a good, solid player.* ◇ *Trade remained solid throughout the year.* ❶ **Solid** is used especially to talk about how a person or company performs or achieves over a period of time.

respectable fairly good; not giving you any reason to feel ashamed: *It was a perfectly respectable result.* ◇ *Economic growth has averaged at a respectable 2.5 per cent.* ❶ **Respectable** is used especially to talk about sb/sth's performance in a game, competition or entertainment, or in business.
▸ **respectably** *adv.*: *The candidate did respectably rather than brilliantly.*

sound good and accurate, but not excellent: *This was another sound performance by the team.*

decide *verb*

decide · choose · determine · make up your mind · elect · resolve
These words all mean to think carefully about what to do and make a choice from the possibilities that are available to you.

▸ to decide/ determine/ resolve **on** sth
▸ to decide/ choose/ determine/ make up your mind/ elect/ resolve **to do** sth
▸ to decide/ determine/ resolve **that...**
▸ to decide/ choose/ make up your mind **whether/ what/ how...**
▸ to **be free to** decide/ choose/ determine
▸ to **be difficult to** decide/ make your mind up
▸ to **eventually/ consciously** decide/ choose/ resolve
▸ to **finally** decide/ make up your mind/ resolve

decide [I, T] to think carefully about the different possibilities that are available to you and then make a choice or judgement about what to do: *It's up to you to decide.* ◇ *They **decided against** taking legal action.* ◇ *We've decided not to go away after all.* ◇ *I can't decide what to do.* ◇ *I can't tell you what to do — you'll have to **decide for yourself**.* ◇ *It **was decided (that)** the school should purchase new software.* ◇ *We might be hiring new people but nothing has been decided yet.* See also **decide** → CHOOSE, **undecided** → UNSURE
▸ **decision** *noun* [C, U]: *to **make a decision** (= to decide)* ◇ (*BrE*) *to **take a decision** ◇ We need a **decision on** this by next week.* ◇ *We finally **reached a decision** (= decided after some difficulty).* ◇ *a **big** (= important) decision* ◇ *The moment of decision had arrived.*

choose [I] to prefer or decide to do sth or behave in a particular way, after thinking about the different possibilities that are available: *Employees can retire at 60 if they choose.* ◇ *Many people choose not to marry.* See also **choice** → OPTION

determine [T, I] (*formal*) to officially decide and/or arrange sth; to make a firm decision to do sth: *A date for the meeting has yet to be determined.* ◇ *As she walked home, she determined to speak to her boss the next day.* ◇ *The government determined on a change of policy.* See also **determined** → DETERMINED 1

make up your 'mind (also **make your 'mind up**) to make a firm decision about sth, especially after a period of thinking carefully about it: *I couldn't **make up my**

mind about the new job.* ◇ *He had clearly made up his mind to leave.* ◇ *You'll never persuade him to stay — his mind's made up.*

elect [T] (usually used in the phrase *elect to do sth*) (*formal*) to choose to do sth, especially rather than being told or forced to do it: *Increasing numbers of people elect to work from home nowadays.*

resolve [I] (*rather formal, written*) to make a firm decision to do sth; to reach a decision in a meeting, etc. by means of a formal vote: *We had resolved on making an early start.* ◇ *She resolved that she would never see him again.* ◇ *The Supreme Council resolved to resume control over the press.*
▸ **resolution** *noun* [C]: *She **made a resolution** to visit her relatives more often.* ◇ *The UN Security Council unanimously adopted a resolution calling for a halt to hostilities.*

declare *verb* See the Topic Map for FACT AND OPINION on p.898, See also the entry for SAY 2

declare · state · indicate · announce · proclaim · pronounce
These words all mean to say sth, usually firmly and clearly and often in public.

▸ to declare/ state/ indicate/ announce/ proclaim/ pronounce sth **to** sb
▸ to declare/ state/ indicate/ announce/ proclaim/ pronounce **that...**
▸ **It was** declared/ stated/ indicated/ announced/ proclaimed **that...**
▸ to declare/ state/ proclaim/ pronounce sb/ sth **to be** sth
▸ to declare/ state/ indicate/ announce/ proclaim your **intention** to do sth
▸ to declare/ state/ indicate/ announce your **support**
▸ to declare/ state/ announce/ proclaim/ pronounce sth **formally/ officially**
▸ to declare/ state/ announce/ proclaim sth **publicly/ proudly/ boldly**
▸ to declare/ state/ announce/ pronounce sth **confidently/ firmly**

declare /dɪˈkleə(r); *AmE* dɪˈkler/ [T] (*rather formal*) to say sth officially or publicly; to say sth firmly and clearly: *Germany **declared war** on France on 3 August 1914.* ◇ *The president declared a state of emergency.* ◇ *The court declared that strike action was illegal.* ◇ *The painting was declared to be a forgery.* ◇ *The area has been declared a national park.* ◇ *I declare this bridge open.* See also **declaration** → STATEMENT

state [T] (*rather formal*) to formally write or say sth, especially in a careful and clear way: *The facts are clearly stated in the report.* ◇ *There is no need to **state the obvious** (= to say sth that everyone already knows).* ◇ *State clearly how many tickets you require.* See also **statement** → STATEMENT

indicate [T] (*rather formal, especially spoken or journalism*) to state sth, sometimes in a way that is slightly indirect: *As I've already indicated to you, what we do next depends on a number of factors.* ◇ *During our meeting, he indicated his willingness to cooperate.* See also **indication** → SIGN 1, **indicate** → SHOW 1, **indicate** → SUGGEST

announce [T] to tell people officially about a decision or plans; to give information about sth in a public place, especially through a loudspeaker; to say sth in a loud and/or serious way: *They haven't formally announced their engagement yet.* ◇ *Has our flight been announced yet?* ◇ *'I've given up smoking,' she announced.* See also **announcement** → STATEMENT

NOTE DECLARE OR ANNOUNCE? **Declare** is used more often for giving judgements; **announce** is used more often for giving facts: ~~The painting was announced to be a forgery.~~ ◇ ~~They haven't formally declared their engagement yet.~~

proclaim /prəˈkleɪm/ [T] (*rather formal*) to publicly and officially tell people about sth important: *The charter proclaimed that all states would have their own govern-*

ment. ◇ *He proclaimed himself emperor.* **❶ Proclaim** is often used to talk about a statement made by sb in authority about a situation that affects everyone. A situation that is **proclaimed** is usually being presented as a positive one.

pronounce [T] (*formal*) to say sth formally, officially or publicly: *The judge will **pronounce sentence** today.* ◇ *I now pronounce you man and wife* (= in a marriage ceremony). ◇ *She was pronounced dead on arrival at the hospital.*

decorate *verb*

decorate · adorn · garnish · illustrate · edge · hang · festoon · deck · ornament · trim
These words all mean to make sth look more attractive by putting things on it.

PATTERNS AND COLLOCATIONS
▸ to decorate / adorn / garnish / illustrate / edge / hang / festoon / deck / ornament / trim sth **with** sth
▸ to decorate / festoon / deck sth **in** sth
▸ **richly** decorated / adorned / ornamented

decorate [T] to make sth look more attractive by putting things on it; to be placed on sth in order to make it look more attractive: *They decorated the room with flowers and balloons.* ◇ *The cake was decorated to look like a car.* ◇ *Photographs of actors decorated the walls of the restaurant.* See also **decoration** → ORNAMENT

adorn [T, often passive] (*formal*) to make sb/sth look more attractive by decorating it or them with sth: *The walls were adorned with paintings.*

garnish [T] to decorate a dish of food with a small amount of another food: *Garnish the chicken with almonds.* ◇ *soup garnished with croutons*

illustrate [T, usually passive] to use pictures, photographs, diagrams, etc. in a book, etc: *a beautifully illustrated book* ◇ *His lecture was illustrated with slides taken during the expedition.* See also **illustration** → DIAGRAM

edge [T, usually passive] to put sth around the edge of sth, especially as a decoration: *The handkerchief was edged with lace.*

hang [T, usually passive] (always used with *with*) to decorate a place by placing paintings, etc. on a wall: *The room was hung with tapestries.* See also **hanging** → CURTAIN

festoon /fe'stu:n/ [T, usually passive] (*literary*) to decorate sb/sth with flowers, lights or coloured paper, often as part of a celebration: *The streets were festooned with banners and lights.*

deck [T, usually passive] to decorate sb/sth with sth, especially colourful clothes, fabric, flowers or plants: *The Conservative candidate and his supporters were decked in blue rosettes.* ◇ *The room was **decked out** in flowers and balloons.* **❶** In everyday language, **deck** is only used in the phrase *decked (out) in/with sth*. It is only used in the active in literary or poetic contexts: *Deck the halls with boughs of holly!*

ornament /'ɔːnəmənt; *AmE* 'ɔːrn-/ [T, usually passive] (*formal*) to add decoration to sth: *The room was richly ornamented with carving.* See also **ornament** → ORNAMENT *noun*

trim (-mm-) [T, usually passive] to decorate sth, especially a piece of clothing, especially around its edges: *She wore gloves trimmed with fur.*
▸ **trimming** *noun* [U, C, usually pl.]: *a white blouse with navy-blue trimming*

decoration *noun*

decoration · accessory · ornament · frills · finery · garnish
These are all words for sth that is added to sth to make it look more attractive.

PATTERNS AND COLLOCATIONS
▸ **without** decoration / frills
▸ **little** / **no** decoration / ornament
▸ **few** / **no** accessories / frills
▸ **personal** decoration / ornament / finery

decoration [C, U] a pattern or design that is added to sth and that stops it from being plain; the style in which sth is decorated: *We admired the elaborate decorations on the carved wooden door.* ◇ *They chose a Chinese theme in the interior decoration.* See also **pattern**, **design** → PATTERN 2, **decoration** → ORNAMENT

accessory /ək'sesəri/ [C, usually pl.] an extra piece of equipment that is useful but not essential or that can be added to sth else as a decoration; a thing that you can wear or carry that matches your clothes, for example a belt or bag: *We stock a large range of bicycle accessories.* ◇ *Why not invest in some **fashion accessories** to dress up your wardrobe?*

ornament /'ɔːnəmənt; *AmE* 'ɔːrn-/ [U] (*formal*) the use of objects or designs as decoration: *The clock is simply for ornament — it doesn't work any more.* See also **ornament** → ORNAMENT

frills [pl.] (always used in negative sentences) things that are not necessary but are added to make sth more attractive or interesting: *It was a simple meal, with no frills.*

finery /'faɪnəri/ [U] (*written*) colourful and elegant clothes and jewellery, especially those that are worn for a special occasion: *The mayor was dressed in all his finery.*

garnish [C, U] a small amount of food that is used to decorate a larger dish of food: *Add a garnish of tomato.* ◇ *Keep some olives to one side for garnish.*

decorative *adj.*

decorative · fancy · ornamental
These words all describe things that are highly decorated.

PATTERNS AND COLLOCATIONS
▸ a decorative / a fancy / an ornamental **design**
▸ decorative / fancy **packaging**
▸ a decorative / an ornamental **fountain** / **plant** / **tree**
▸ **very** decorative / fancy
▸ **highly** / **purely** / **merely** decorative / ornamental

decorative /'dekərətɪv; *AmE* 'dekəreɪtɪv/ (of an object or building) decorated in a way that makes it attractive; intended to look attractive or pretty: *The mirror is functional yet decorative.* ◇ *These are purely decorative arches.*

fancy [usually before noun] unusually complicated, often in an unnecessary way; (especially of small things) with a lot of decorations or bright colours: *The kitchen was full of fancy gadgets.* ◇ *They added a lot of fancy footwork to the dance.* ◇ *We sell a wide range of **fancy goods** (= things sold as ornaments or gifts).* **OPP** plain, simple → PLAIN 1

ornamental /ˌɔːnə'mentl; *AmE* ˌɔːrn-/ used as decoration rather than for a practical purpose: *There was an ornamental fountain in the middle of the garden.* See also **ornament** → ORNAMENT

NOTE DECORATIVE OR ORNAMENTAL? Both these words can describe sth that is used as a decoration rather than for practical purposes, but **decorative** is also used to describe anything that is highly decorated. It has a very wide range of collocates. **Ornamental** is used especially to describe features of a building or garden; collocates include *garden, fountain, lake, pond, pool, plant, tree* and *shrub.*

deep adj.

1 deep sympathy
2 a deep voice/sound

---

1 deep · sincere · real · genuine · heartfelt · from the heart · wholehearted
These words all describe an emotion or belief that you feel or believe strongly.

PATTERNS AND COLLOCATIONS
- sincere / genuine **about** sth
- deep / sincere / real / genuine / heartfelt **sympathy / concern**
- deep / sincere / real / genuine **affection / respect / regret**
- a deep / real / genuine **sense** of sth
- sincere / heartfelt **thanks / apologies**
- a sincere / genuine **attempt** (to do sth)
- a sincere / genuine **person**
- **very** deep / real / sincere / genuine
- **really / completely** sincere / genuine

deep (of feelings or beliefs) strongly felt; showing what you really think or feel: *He expressed deep concern over the government's handling of the incident.* ◇ *I felt a deep sense of loss when I heard of her death.*
- **deeply** *adv.*: *They were deeply disturbed by the accident.*

sincere (of feelings, beliefs or intentions) showing what you really think or feel: *Please accept our sincere apologies.* ◇ *I would like to express my sincere gratitude for your care and concern during this past week.* **OPP insincere** → FALSE, See also **sincerity** → TRUTH
- **sincerely** *adv.*: *I sincerely believe that this is the right decision.*

real (of feelings or behaviour) strong and sincere: *I had no real interest in politics.* ◇ *He was making a real effort to be nice to her.*

genuine (of people, their feelings or intentions) sincere and honest; that can be trusted: *She always showed genuine concern for others.* ◇ *He came across as a very genuine person.* **OPP forced** → ARTIFICIAL 2
- **genuinely** *adv.*: *He seemed genuinely sorry for what had happened.*

NOTE SINCERE OR GENUINE? In many cases you can use either word. However, **sincere** is more likely to be used by sb about their own feelings and intentions; **genuine** is more likely to be used to express a judgement on sb else's feelings and intentions: *She insisted that they were making a sincere attempt to resolve the problem.* ◇ *He made a genuine attempt to improve conditions.* ◇ *Please accept our genuine apologies.*

heartfelt /'hɑːtfelt; *AmE* 'hɑːrt-/ [usually before noun] showing strong feelings that are sincere: *She made a heartfelt plea for her son to give himself up.* ◇ *Christina breathed a heartfelt sigh of relief.*

from the (bottom of your) 'heart *idiom* in a way that is sincere: *I beg you, from the bottom of my heart, to spare his life.* ◇ *It was clearly an offer that came from the heart.*

wholehearted /ˌhəʊl'hɑːtɪd; *AmE* ˌhoʊl'hɑːrtəd/ (*approving*) complete and enthusiastic: *The plan was given wholehearted support.*
- **wholeheartedly** *adv.*: *I wholeheartedly agree with you.*

---

2 deep · low · rich · bass · sonorous · full · resounding
These words all describe voices or sounds that are near the bottom of a musical scale and/or loud, and not high or soft.

PATTERNS AND COLLOCATIONS
- a deep / low / rich / bass / sonorous / full **voice**
- a deep / low / rich / bass / full / resounding **sound**
- a deep / low **groan / roar / rumble**
- a deep / resounding **thud / thump / thwack**

deep (of a voice) like a man's, not high like a woman's; (of a sound) near the bottom of the musical scale: *I heard his deep warm voice filling the room.* ◇ *We heard a deep roar in the distance.* **OPP high** → HIGH 3

low (of a sound) near the bottom of the musical scale; (of a voice) quiet and often deep, like a man's: *The cello is lower than the violin.* ◇ *They were speaking in low voices.* **OPP high** → HIGH 3

NOTE DEEP OR LOW? A **low** voice or sound is a quiet one, but you would not use **low** to describe a quiet, high voice. It is only when you are talking about musical notes that a **low** sound can be either loud or quiet. A **deep** voice or sound can be loud or quiet. Musical notes that are **deep** are very low.

rich (*approving*) (of sounds, especially singing and music) strong and deep in a pleasant way: *Her rich contralto voice filled the concert hall.* ❶ A **rich** voice is usually a singing voice, not a speaking voice.

bass /beɪs/ [only before noun] (*music*) (of a voice, instrument or music) low in tone: *He was musically talented, with a fine bass voice.* ◇ *a bass drum* ❶ **Bass** is a more technical word for a voice than **low** or **deep**, used in singing. **OPP treble** → HIGH 3

sonorous /'sɒnərəs; *AmE* 'sɑːn-; sə'nɔːrəs/ (*formal, approving*) (of a voice or sound) strong, deep and ringing, in a pleasant way: *Her clear, sonorous voice is perfect for opera.*
- **sonorously** *adv.*

full (*approving*) (of sounds, especially music) deep, strong and rich: *He draws a unique full sound from the instrument.*

resounding /rɪ'zaʊndɪŋ/ [only before noun] (*written*) (of a sound) very loud and continuing for a long time: *The boulder hit the ground with a resounding thud.*

---

deep-seated adj.

deep-seated · deep-rooted · entrenched · rigid · set · ingrained · inflexible · fixed
These words all describe an idea or behaviour that is difficult to change.

PATTERNS AND COLLOCATIONS
- deep-seated / deep-rooted / entrenched / ingrained **prejudices**
- deep-seated / entrenched / rigid / ingrained / fixed **beliefs**
- deep-seated / entrenched / ingrained / inflexible **attitudes**
- entrenched / rigid / ingrained / fixed **habits**
- deep-seated / deep-rooted / entrenched **problems**
- a deep-seated / deep-rooted **fear / hatred** (of sb / sth)
- entrenched / rigid / set / fixed **views / ideas**
- **deeply / firmly** entrenched / set / ingrained

deep-'seated [usually before noun] (of feelings, beliefs and problems) very fixed and strong; difficult to change, destroy or solve: *Jealousy usually stems from a deep-seated fear of being rejected.* ◇ *She had a deep-seated desire to be different from everybody else.*

deep-'rooted [usually before noun] deep-seated: *Discrimination is a deep-rooted problem in our society.* ◇ *The country's political divisions are deep-rooted.*

NOTE DEEP-SEATED OR DEEP-ROOTED? These words are very close in meaning and range. **Deep-seated** is often used to describe negative feelings or beliefs that may be difficult to examine because they are held so deeply: *They have a deep-seated hatred of the modern world.* **Deep-rooted** is slightly more positive and is often used for describing principles or practices that have become established in some way over time: *The custom of sending a greeting in a card had become a deep-rooted tradition.*

entrenched /ɪn'trentʃt/ (of attitudes or habits) established very firmly so that they are very difficult to change: *The challenge of combating and changing deeply entrenched attitudes is enormous.*

rigid /'rɪdʒɪd/ (*disapproving*) (of attitudes or habits) that sb is not willing to change, especially when this is unreasonable: *Her rigid ideas and stern manner had frightened the children.*

set (of attitudes or habits) not likely to change: *He had very set ideas of what he wanted.* ◇ *As people get older, they get set in their ways.*

ingrained /ɪnˈɡreɪnd/ (of attitudes or habits) that sb has had for a long time and that are therefore difficult to change: *I have reached that age where I have started to question some of my ingrained prejudices.* ◇ *The belief that we should do our duty is deeply ingrained in most of us.*

> **NOTE** **ENTRENCHED OR INGRAINED? Entrenched** is used more to talk about the attitudes of a society or whole class of people; **ingrained** is used more to talk about the attitudes or habits of an individual person.

inflexible /ɪnˈfleksəbl/ (*disapproving*) (of attitudes or systems) that cannot be changed or made more suitable for a particular situation: *The government has shown an increasingly inflexible attitude to dealing with the problem.* ◇ *The rules are too inflexible to allow for human error.* **OPP** **flexible** → FLEXIBLE 1

fixed (of ideas and wishes) held very firmly; not easily changed: *My parents had fixed ideas about what I should become.*

defeat *verb* See also the entry for WIN

defeat · beat · overcome · vanquish · get the better of sb · rout · trounce · best · prevail · thrash
These words all mean to win against sb in sport or in a contest or conflict.

get the better of sb	defeat	vanquish
best	beat	rout
prevail	overcome	trounce
		thrash

PATTERNS AND COLLOCATIONS
> to defeat / beat / rout / trounce / thrash sb **by** 10 points / 4 goals, etc.
> to defeat / beat / overcome / vanquish / get the better of / rout / trounce / thrash an **opponent**
> to defeat / beat / overcome / vanquish / trounce a **rival**
> to defeat / beat / overcome / vanquish / rout an **enemy**
> to defeat / beat / vanquish a **foe**
> to **finally** defeat / beat / overcome / get the better of / rout sb
> to **totally** defeat / overwhelm / thrash sb
> to **easily** defeat / beat / overcome sb

defeat [T] (*especially written*) to win against sb in a war, competition, sport or vote: *The English were **heavily** defeated here by the Scots in 1314.* ◇ *He defeated the champion in three sets.* ◇ *The government was defeated by 200 votes to 83.*
> **defeat** *noun* [C, U]: *The battle ended in humiliating defeat.* ◇ *He was gracious **in defeat**, acknowledging his opponent's greater skill.* ◇ *The Prime Minister **conceded defeat** and resigned.* ◇ *They finally had to **admit defeat** (= stop trying to be successful).* **OPP** **victory** → VICTORY, See also **defeat** → VICTORY

beat [T] (*especially spoken*) to win against sb in sport, a game, an election or a war: *He beat me at chess.* ◇ *He was beaten into second place by the American.* ◇ *She **beat him hands down** (= easily).* ◇ *Their recent wins have proved that they're still **the ones to beat** (= the most difficult team to beat).*

> **NOTE** **DEFEAT OR BEAT? Defeat** is more often used when talking about winning against one opponent in a particular contest or battle and finishing as the winner: *He defeated the incumbent president.* **Beat** can be used to talk about winning against one opponent or several opponents in a game, competition or race: *She won the 100 metres, beating a number of top Europeans.* **Beat** is more common in everyday spoken language and **defeat** is used more in written language.

overcome /ˌəʊvəˈkʌm; AmE ˌoʊvərˈkʌm/ [T] (*written*) to defeat sb, especially when it is difficult: *She overcame*

strong opposition to take the title. ◇ *In the final, Sweden easily overcame France.*

vanquish /ˈvæŋkwɪʃ/ [T] (*literary*) to defeat sb completely in a war or competition: *Government forces vanquished the rebels.*

get the better of sb *idiom* [I] to defeat sb or gain an advantage over them in a fight, argument or contest: *No one can get the better of her in an argument.*

rout /raʊt/ [T] to defeat sb completely in a battle or contest: *The Royalist forces were routed.*
> **rout** *noun* [sing.]: *The offensive into rebel-held territory had ended in a rout.*

trounce /traʊns/ [T] (*written*) to defeat sb completely, especially in a sport: *Brazil trounced Italy 5–1 in the final.*

best [T, usually passive] (*formal*) to defeat or be more successful than sb: *A great colonial power was nearly bested by a few farmers.*

prevail /prɪˈveɪl/ [I] (*formal*) to defeat sb, especially after a long struggle: *Ultimately, Rome **prevailed over** her neighbours.* ◇ *In a one-sided final, Spain **prevailed against** title-holder Croatia 40–34.* See also **prevail** → WIN

thrash [T] (*especially BrE, informal*) to defeat sb very easily in a sport or game: *They were thrashed 5–0 in the League.*

defect *noun*

defect · fault · flaw · virus · bug · glitch · imperfection
These are all words for sth that is wrong with sth or in the way it has been made, which means it is not perfect or does not work properly.

PATTERNS AND COLLOCATIONS
> a defect / a fault / a flaw / a virus / a bug / a glitch / an imperfection **in** sth
> a **small / minor** defect / fault / flaw / bug / glitch / imperfection
> a **major / serious** defect / fault / flaw
> a **temporary** fault / flaw / glitch
> a **technical / mechanical** defect / fault / flaw / glitch
> a **structural / design** defect / fault / flaw
> a **computer / software** fault / virus / bug / glitch
> to **have** a defect / a fault / a flaw / a virus / a bug / a glitch / an imperfection
> to **detect** a defect / fault / flaw / virus
> to **look for / discover** a defect / fault / flaw / bug
> to **identify / correct** a defect / fault / flaw

defect /ˈdiːfekt; dɪˈfekt/ [C] something that is wrong with a machine, system or part of the body, which means that it is not perfect or unable to work properly: *The manufacturer is responsible for any defects that may cause damage.* ◇ *Vulnerable people are going short of money because of defects in the payment system.* ◇ *The drug is widely known to cause **birth defects**.* See also **defective** → WRONG 2

fault [C] something that is wrong with sth that has been made or created such as a machine or system, which means that it is not perfect or unable to work properly: *The book's virtues far outweigh its faults.* ◇ *There seemed to be some **fault with** the cooling system.* ◇ *The healthcare system, **for all its faults**, is far better than ever before.* ◇ *The fire was caused by an electrical fault.* ◇ *If a fault develops in the equipment, you can call us 24 hours a day.* See also **faulty** → WRONG 2

> **NOTE** **DEFECT OR FAULT?** In many cases you can use either word: *a technical / mechanical / structural / design defect / fault.* A **fault** can only exist in sth that has been made or created by people, but it can be permanent or temporary, can be present from the beginning or develop later. A **defect** can exist in part of the body, although it is always present from birth: *birth / congenital / genetic defects* ◇ ~~*birth / congenital / genetic faults*~~. A **defect** of any kind exists from the beginning and cannot develop later. It might be repaired, but will not just go away, and cannot be called 'temporary': ~~*If a defect develops in the equipment...*~~ ◇ ~~*We're hoping this is just a temporary defect.*~~

flaw [C] a fault in sth that means that it is not correct or does not work properly: *There are some very basic flaws in his argument.* ◊ *Engineers have detected serious design flaws.*
▸ **flawed** *adj.*: *a flawed argument*

virus /'vaɪrəs/ [C] instructions that are deliberately hidden in a computer program and are designed to cause problems or destroy data in a computer system: *Most viruses can only spread if you open an email attachment.* ◊ *My computer has **caught** some kind of **virus**, and it won't let me log on to the Internet.* ◊ **anti-virus** software (= software that finds and destroys viruses in a computer system)

bug [C] (*rather informal*) a fault in a machine, especially in a computer program or system: *The latest software is full of bugs.* ◊ *My computer's really slow at the moment — it must be some kind of bug.*

glitch [C] (*informal*) a small problem or fault that stops sth from working properly, especially for just a short time: *It was only a temporary glitch but it could have put people's lives in danger.*

imperfection /ˌɪmpəˈfekʃn; *AmE* -pərˈf-/ [C, U] a small fault in sth, especially in the appearance of sth, that spoils it slightly and makes it less beautiful or perfect: *The only slight imperfection in the painting is a scratch in the corner.* ◊ *Nature is full of imperfection.* See also **blemish** → MARK
▸ **imperfect** *adj.*: *All our sale items are slightly imperfect.*

definition *noun*

definition · interpretation · understanding · reading
These are all words for the particular way in which sth is understood or explained.

PATTERNS AND COLLOCATIONS
▸ (a) **careful** definition / interpretation / understanding / reading
▸ a **clear / precise / narrow / broad / wide / conventional** definition / interpretation / understanding
▸ a **literal** interpretation / understanding / reading
▸ **different** definitions / interpretations / understandings / readings
▸ to **give / provide / offer** a definition / an interpretation

definition /ˌdefɪˈnɪʃn/ [C, U] an explanation of the meaning of a word or phrase, especially in a dictionary; what an idea means to a particular person or group: *The dictionary provides clear, simple definitions.* ◊ *The term 'partner' requires careful definition.* ◊ *Neighbours **by definition** live close by* (= this is what being a neighbour means). ◊ *What's your definition of happiness?* See also **define** → EXPLAIN 1, **define** → LIST *verb*

interpretation /ɪnˌtɜːprɪˈteɪʃn; *AmE* -ˌtɜːrp-/ [C, U] (*rather formal*) the particular way in which sb understands or explains sth: *Her evidence suggests a different interpretation of the events leading to his death.* ◊ *Dreams are **open to interpretation*** (= they can be explained in different ways).
▸ **interpret** /ɪnˈtɜːprɪt; *AmE* -ˈtɜːrp-/ *verb* [T]: *I didn't know whether to interpret her silence as acceptance or refusal.* ◊ *The data can be interpreted in many different ways.* See also **interpret** → EXPLAIN 1, **interpretative** → DESCRIPTIVE

understanding [U, C] the particular way in which sb understands sth: *My understanding of the situation is...* ◊ *Students will gain an active understanding of the workings of Parliament.* See also **understand** → CONCLUDE

reading [C] (*rather formal, especially written*) the particular way in which sb understands a book, situation, etc: *Those conclusions are based on a literal reading of the text.* ◊ *My own reading of events is less optimistic.*
▸ **read** *verb* [T]: *How do you read the present situation?*

NOTE INTERPRETATION, UNDERSTANDING OR READING? In some cases you can use any of these words: *a different interpretation / understanding / reading of the situation / history.* However, **interpretation** is used especially when you are talking about understanding what

happened or what sth means: *interpretation of data / information / results / findings / events / the law / sb's theory / dreams.* **Understanding** is used especially when you are talking about understanding how sth works or what problems are involved: *an understanding of a process / a relationship / sb's role / the workings of sth / the principles of sth / a problem / an issue.* **Reading** is used especially when you are talking about understanding a written text: *my reading of the text / poem / novel / story.*

defraud *verb* See also the entry for CHEAT

defraud · rip sb off · swindle · fleece · bilk · screw · short-change
These words all mean to get money or sth else from sb in a dishonest, illegal or unfair way.

PATTERNS AND COLLOCATIONS
▸ to **defraud / swindle / fleece / bilk / screw** sb **out of** sth
▸ to **defraud / rip off / fleece / bilk / short-change customers**
▸ to **defraud / swindle / bilk investors**
▸ to **defraud / rip off / bilk a company**
▸ to **defraud / swindle / bilk the government**
▸ to **rip off / fleece tourists**

defraud /dɪˈfrɔːd/ [T, I] (*rather formal, disapproving*) to get money illegally from a person or organization by deceiving them: *They were accused of **defrauding** the company **of** $14 000.* ◊ (*law*) *All three men were charged with conspiracy to defraud.* See also **fraud** → FRAUD 1, **fraud** → FRAUD 2

ˌrip sb ˈoff *phrasal verb* (**-pp-**) [often passive] (*informal, disapproving*) to cheat sb by making them pay too much or by selling them sth of poor quality: *Tourists complain of being ripped off by local cab drivers.*
▸ **ˈrip-off** [C, usually sing.]: *$70 for a T-shirt! What a rip-off!*

swindle [T] (*disapproving*) to get money illegally from a person or organization by deceiving them: *They swindled him out of thousands of dollars.*
▸ **swindle** *noun* [C, usually sing.]: *We think she was mixed up in an insurance swindle.*

NOTE DEFRAUD OR SWINDLE? Defraud is more formal than swindle, especially when it is used without an object. Swindle cannot be used without an object.

fleece [T] (*informal, disapproving*) to take a lot of money from sb by making them pay too much for sth: *Some local shops have been fleecing tourists.*

bilk [T] (*especially AmE, informal, disapproving*) to swindle sb: *He was a con man who bilked investors out of millions of dollars.*

screw [T] (*slang, disapproving*) to cheat sb, especially by making them pay too much money for sth: *We've been screwed.* ◊ *How much did they **screw you for*** (= how much did you have to pay)?

ˌshort-ˈchange [T, often passive] (*disapproving*) to give back less than the correct amount of money to sb who has paid with more than the exact price for sth: *I think I've been short-changed at the bar.*

delay *verb*

delay · postpone · adjourn · wait · put sth off · defer · suspend · shelve · reschedule
These words all mean to not do sth until a later time or to make sth happen at a later time.

PATTERNS AND COLLOCATIONS
▸ to **delay** sth / **postpone** sth / **adjourn** sth / **wait** / **put** sth **off** / **defer** sth / **suspend** sth / **shelve** sth **for** a few days / the time being, etc.
▸ to **wait / reschedule** sth **for** later in the year, etc.
▸ to **delay** sth / **postpone** sth / **adjourn** sth / **wait** / **put** sth **off** / **defer** sth **until** sth
▸ to **postpone / defer** sth **to** sth
▸ to **delay / postpone / put off / defer doing** sth

▶ to delay / postpone / adjourn / reschedule a **meeting**
▶ to delay / postpone / adjourn a **case / trial**
▶ to delay / postpone / put off your **departure / return**
▶ to delay / postpone / put off / reschedule a **visit**
▶ to delay / postpone a **flight**
▶ to suspend **visits / flights**
▶ to delay / postpone / put off / defer a **decision**
▶ to delay / postpone / suspend **plans**
▶ to delay / postpone/adjourn / put off/defer/suspend/shelve sth **indefinitely**

delay [T] (*rather formal*) to not do sth until a later time; to make sth happen at a later time: *The judge will delay his verdict until he receives medical reports on the offender.* ◇ *He delayed telling her the news, waiting for the right moment.* ◇ *These drugs can significantly delay the onset of the disease.* ◇ *She's suffering a **delayed reaction** (= a reaction that did not happen immediately.)* **OPP hasten** → ACCELERATE, See also **delay** → HOLD SB/STH UP, **delay** → TAKE YOUR TIME

postpone /pə'spəʊn; *AmE* poʊ'spoʊn/ [T, often passive] (*rather formal*) to arrange for an event or action to take place at a later time or date: *The game has already been postponed three times.* ◇ *They have agreed to postpone repayment of the loan to a future unspecified date.* See also **cancel** → ABOLISH
▶ **postponement** *noun* [U, C]: *Riots led to the postponement of local elections.*

adjourn /ə'dʒɜːn; *AmE* ə'dʒɜːrn/ [I, T, often passive] (*formal*) to stop a meeting or official process for a period of time, especially in court: *The court adjourned for lunch.* ◇ *The trial has been adjourned until next week.*
▶ **adjournment** *noun* [C, U]: *The judge granted us a short adjournment.*

wait [I] (*rather informal*) to be left to be dealt with at a later time because it is not urgent: *I've got some calls to make but they can wait until tomorrow.* ◇ *I'm afraid this can't wait. It's very important.* ❶ Note that with **wait**, the thing that is left until a later time is the subject of the sentence, not the object: ~~I can wait those calls.~~

put sth 'off *phrasal verb* (*rather informal*) to arrange for an event to take place at a later time or date; to not do sth until a later time: *We've had to put off our wedding until September.* ◇ *He keeps putting off going to the dentist.*

defer /dɪ'fɜː(r)/ (-**rr**-) [T] (*formal*) to delay a decision or action until a later time: *The department deferred the decision for six months.* ◇ *She had applied for deferred admission to college.*

suspend /sə'spend/ [T] (*rather formal*) to officially delay carrying out a plan or making a judgement; to stop a system from operating until a later date: *The jury was asked to suspend judgement (= delay forming or expressing an opinion).* ◇ *Aid flights have been suspended for a week after fighting near the city's airport.* ❶ **Suspend** can mean to delay starting sth, or to stop sth that has already been started: things that might be **suspended** include plans, work, aid, flights, visit and payments.
▶ **suspension** /sə'spenʃn/ *noun* [U, sing.]: *These events led to the suspension of talks.*

shelve /ʃelv/ [T] (*rather formal*) to decide not to continue with a plan, either for a short time or permanently: *The government has shelved the idea until at least next year.* ◇ *Plans to expand the company have been quietly shelved.*

reschedule /ˌriː'ʃedjuːl; *AmE* ˌriː'skedʒuːl/ [T, often passive] (*rather formal*) to change the time at which sth has been arranged to happen, especially so that it takes place later: *The meeting has been rescheduled for next week.*

NOTE POSTPONE OR RESCHEDULE? Postpone often has negative associations, giving a sense of disappointment. It is often used with verbs like *have to*, *be forced to* and *be obliged to*. **Reschedule** has more a positive feel, and is often followed by *for* + a date or time: *The event has been rescheduled for 5 June/Sunday/the spring.*

delete *verb*

delete · erase · cut · cross sth out · wipe · strike sth out · rub sth out · cross sb/sth off
These words all mean to take away a piece of information, especially written information.

PATTERNS AND COLLOCATIONS
▶ to delete / erase / cut / wipe sth **from** sth
▶ to delete / erase / cross out / strike out / rub out a **word**
▶ to delete / cut / cross out / strike out a **sentence**
▶ to delete / cut / cross out / strike out a **paragraph**
▶ to delete sth **from** / cross sb / sth off a **list**
▶ to delete / erase / wipe a **file** (on a computer)
▶ to delete / erase / wipe sth **accidentally**
▶ to erase / wipe sth **completely**

delete /dɪ'liːt/ [T] (*rather formal or computing*) to remove sth that has been written or printed, or that has been stored on a computer: *Your name has been deleted from the list.* ◇ *This command deletes files from the directory.* ◇ *I deleted your last email by mistake — could you send it again?*
▶ **deletion** /dɪ'liːʃn/ *noun* [C, U]: *He made several deletions to the manuscript.*

erase /ɪ'reɪz; *AmE* ɪ'reɪs/ [T] to remove sth completely from your mind; to make a mark or sth you have written disappear, for example by rubbing it, especially in order to correct it; to remove a recording from a tape or information from a computer's memory: *She tried to erase the memory of that evening.* ◇ *All doubts were suddenly erased from his mind.* ◇ *All the phone numbers had been erased.* ◇ *Parts of the recording have been erased.*

cut [T, I] to remove part of a piece of writing, a sound recording or film; to delete part of a text on a computer screen in order to place it somewhere else: *This scene was cut from the final version of the movie.* ◇ *You can cut out this whole paragraph without losing any of the impact.* ◇ *You can cut and paste between different programs.*
▶ **cut** *noun* [C]: *The director objected to the cuts ordered by the film censor.*

cross sth 'out *phrasal verb* to draw a line through a word, usually because it is wrong: *She crossed out 'Miss' and wrote 'Ms'.* ◇ *He's crossing the days out on the calendar until the start of the World Cup.*

wipe [T] to remove information, sound or images from a computer, tape or video: *You must have **wiped off** that show I recorded.* ◇ *Somebody had wiped all the tapes.* See also **wipe** → FORGET

strike sth 'out *phrasal verb* to remove sth by drawing a line through it: *The editor struck out the whole paragraph.*

rub sth 'out *phrasal verb* (-**bb**-) (*BrE*) to remove the marks made by sth, for example a pencil or chalk: *She reached up and rubbed out the words on the board.* ◇ *Use a pencil so you can rub it out if you make a mistake.* ❶ In American English use **erase**.

cross sb/sth 'off, cross sb/sth 'off sth *phrasal verb* to draw a line through a person's name or an item on a list because they are/it is no longer required or involved: *We can cross his name off the list — he's not coming.*

deliberate *adj.*

deliberate · intended · conscious · intentional · wilful · calculated · premeditated · purposeful
These words all describe an action which is done on purpose, is planned in advance or aims to achieve sth.

PATTERNS AND COLLOCATIONS
▶ a deliberate / a conscious / an intentional/a wilful/a calculated/ a premeditated / a purposeful **act**
▶ a deliberate / an intended / a conscious / an intentional / a calculated / a purposeful **action**
▶ deliberate / conscious / wilful **neglect**
▶ deliberate / intentional / wilful **cruelty**
▶ deliberate / conscious / calculated **attempts / manipulation**

deliberate done on purpose rather than by accident: *The speech was a deliberate attempt to embarrass the government.* ◇ *The emphasis on Europe was quite deliberate.* **OPP** **accidental** → ACCIDENT
▸ **deliberately** *adv.*: *She was accused of deliberately misleading Parliament.* ◇ *Her tone was deliberately insulting.* **OPP** **accidentally** → ACCIDENT

intended [only before noun] that you are trying to achieve or reach: *The bullet missed its intended target.* ◇ *The intended victims were selected because they seemed vulnerable.* **OPP** **unintended** → UNCONSCIOUS, See also **intend** → INTEND

conscious (of actions or feelings) deliberate or controlled, with the person doing it being fully aware of what they are doing: *She made a conscious decision to spend more time with her family.* ◇ *I made a conscious effort to get there on time.* **OPP** **unconscious, subconscious** → UNCONSCIOUS
▸ **consciously** *adv.*: *I never really consciously set out to be a war photographer.* ◇ *Whether consciously or unconsciously, you made a choice.* **OPP** **unconsciously** → UNCONSCIOUS

intentional (*rather formal*) deliberate: *I'm sorry I left you off the list – it wasn't intentional.* ◇ *She felt she was a victim of intentional discrimination.* **OPP** **unintentional** → UNCONSCIOUS
▸ **intentionally** *adv.*: *He'd never intentionally hurt anyone.* ◇ *Intentionally or not, police procedures may be biased.* **OPP** **unintentionally** → UNCONSCIOUS

NOTE **DELIBERATE** OR **INTENTIONAL?** There is no real difference in meaning between these words, but **intentional** is less frequent and more formal and has a narrower range of collocates.

wilful (*especially BrE*) (*AmE usually* **willful**) [usually before noun] (*formal, disapproving or law*) (of a bad or harmful action) done on purpose, even though the person doing it knows that it is wrong: *He was charged with wilful damage to property.*
▸ **wilfully** *adv.*: *They were charged with wilfully neglecting their children.*

calculated [usually before noun] carefully planned to get what you want: *It was either a ridiculous mistake or a calculated insult.* ◇ *He took a* **calculated risk** (= a risk that you decide is worth taking even though you know it might have bad results). ❶ **Calculated** is often used to talk about sth a person does that deliberately causes harm to others.

premeditated /ˌpriːˈmedɪteɪtɪd/ (*often disapproving*) (of a crime or bad action) planned in advance: *The killing had not been premeditated.* ◇ *This was a callous, premeditated attack on a defenceless young man.* **OPP** **unpremeditated** ❶ **Unpremeditated** crimes are not planned in advance.

purposeful acting with a clear aim and with determination: *She looked purposeful and determined.* ◇ *He approached each task in the same purposeful manner.*
▸ **purposefully** *adv.*: *Edward strode purposefully towards the door.*

delicious *adj.*

delicious · tasty · appetizing · mouth-watering · yummy
These words all describe food or drink that tastes nice.

| tasty | yummy | delicious |
| appetizing | | mouth-watering |

PATTERNS AND COLLOCATIONS
▸ delicious / tasty / appetizing **food**
▸ a delicious / tasty **meal**
▸ a delicious / an appetizing **smell**
▸ a delicious / tasty **lunch**
▸ delicious / tasty / mouth-watering **dishes**
▸ to **look** delicious / tasty / appetizing / mouth-watering

▸ **really** delicious / tasty / yummy
▸ **not very** tasty / appetizing

delicious having a very pleasant taste or smell: *Who cooked this? It's absolutely delicious.* ◇ *What's that? It smells delicious.* ◇ *Lentils cooked with garlic make a delicious accompaniment to sausages or red meat.*
▸ **deliciously** *adv.*: *deliciously creamy soup*

tasty having a strong and pleasant taste: *The food is wholesome, tasty and well-presented.* ◇ *There is a range of tasty snacks available at the bar.*

appetizing (*BrE also* **-ising**) /ˈæpɪtaɪzɪŋ/ (of food) that smells or looks attractive, making you want to eat it: *The appetizing aroma of sizzling bacon was coming from the kitchen.* ◇ *The meals he cooked were always nourishing but never particularly appetizing.* ❶ **Appetizing** is not usually used with the verb *to be* unless the sentence is negative: *The food wasn't very appetizing.* ◇ ~~The food was very appetizing.~~ **OPP** **unappetizing** → UNATTRACTIVE

'mouth-watering [usually before noun] that looks or smells so good that you want to eat it immediately: *They looked through the window at the mouth-watering display of cakes.*

yummy /ˈjʌmi/ (*informal, spoken*) very good to eat; delicious: *These biscuits are yummy.* ◇ *Chocolate cake? Yummy!* ❶ **Yummy** is used especially by or to children. **OPP** **yucky** ❶ **Yucky** is an informal way of describing food that is disgusting or very unpleasant; it is used especially by children.

delight *verb* See also the entries for INTEREST and PLEASE

delight · charm · captivate · entrance · enthral · enchant · bewitch
These are all words that can be used when sb/sth gives you great pleasure or makes you want it/them very much.

delight	captivate
charm	entrance
	enthral
	enchant
	bewitch

PATTERNS AND COLLOCATIONS
▸ to **be** delighted / charmed / captivated / enthralled / enchanted / bewitched **by** sb / sth

delight [T, I] to give sb great pleasure: *This news will delight his fans all over the world.* ◇ (*written*) *She had a limitless capacity to astonish and delight.* See also **delight** → JOY, **delight** → PLEASURE

charm [T, I] to please or attract sb in a way that makes them like you or be willing to do what you want: *He charmed his mother into letting him have his own way.* ◇ *Her words had lost their power to charm.* See also **charm** → CHARM *noun*, **charming** → NICE 2

captivate [T, often passive] (*especially written*) to get and keep sb's close attention by being extremely interesting or attractive: *The children were captivated by her stories.* ◇ *Men were captivated by her charm.*

entrance /ɪnˈtrɑːns; *AmE* -ˈtræs/ [T, usually passive] (*written*) to get and keep sb's close attention by making them feel great pleasure or admiration: *He listened to her, entranced.* ◇ *I was entranced by the bird's beauty.*

enthral (*BrE*) (*AmE* **enthrall**) /ɪnˈθrɔːl/ (-ll-) [T, often passive] (*especially written*) to get and keep sb's close attention by being extremely interesting or attractive: *This book will enthral readers of all ages.* ◇ *The child watched, enthralled by the bright moving images.*

NOTE **CAPTIVATE, ENTRANCE** OR **ENTHRAL?** You can be **captivated** by another person – their looks, charm or what they say or do. You can be **entranced** by a person or by sth that appeals to your senses, such as music, art or beauty. You can be **enthralled** by sth that you see or sth that appeals to your imagination, such as a story.

enchant /ɪnˈtʃɑːnt; AmE -ˈtʃænt/ [T, I] (especially written) to attract sb strongly and make them feel great pleasure or interest: The happy family scene had enchanted him.

bewitch /bɪˈwɪtʃ/ [T, often passive, I] (written) to attract or impress sb so much that they cannot think in a sensible way: He was completely bewitched by her beauty.

delivery noun

delivery · distribution · freight · transport · transit · shipment · shipping · haulage · handling
These are all words for the act or business of carrying or sending goods from one place to another.

▸ **for** delivery / distribution / freight / transport / shipment / shipping / haulage
▸ delivery / distribution / freight / transport / transit / shipping / haulage / handling **costs**
▸ a / the delivery / freight / handling **charge**
▸ a delivery / distribution / freight / transport / shipping / haulage **company / business**
▸ the freight / transport / transit / shipping / haulage **industry**

delivery /dɪˈlɪvəri/ [U, C] the act of taking goods or letters to the people they have been sent to: We offer free delivery on orders over $200. ◇ Allow 28 days for delivery. ◇ Please pay for goods **on delivery** (= when they are delivered). ◇ (formal) When will you be able to **take delivery of** the car? ◇ At the moment there are two deliveries a day (= of mail). ◇ She had **made a delivery** to the address earlier that day. See also **deliver** → TAKE 1

distribution /ˌdɪstrɪˈbjuːʃn/ [U] (business) the act of making goods available to customers by supplying them to shops; the system of transporting and delivering goods to shops or customers: They have systems in place for sales, distribution and marketing. ◇ He worked in the milk distribution business. See also **distribute** → DISTRIBUTE

freight /freɪt/ [U] the system of carrying goods from one place to another by road, air or rail: We tend to use air freight for lighter goods. See also **freight** → CARGO

transport (especially BrE) (also **transportation**, especially in AmE) [U] the activity or business of carrying goods from one place to another, especially by road or rail: We need stricter controls on the transport of nuclear waste. ◇ Transportation costs have virtually crippled our business. See also **transport** → TAKE 1

transit /ˈtrænzɪt; -sɪt/ [U] the process of being moved or carried from one place to another: The total cost includes transit. ◇ Your insurance should cover transit by air, sea or rail. ◇ We will pay for any goods lost or damaged **in transit**.

shipment [U] the process of sending goods from one place to another, especially from one country to another, but not necessarily by ship: The goods are ready for shipment. ◇ The illegal shipment of weapons continues to be a multimillion dollar industry. See also **ship** → TAKE 1

shipping [U] the activity of carrying people or goods from one place to another by ship: She arranged for the shipping of her furniture to England. ◇ She married a **shipping magnate** (= sb who has made a lot of money from shipping) in 1997. ❶ In American English **shipping** is also another word for **shipment**, especially of goods being sold to the public: (AmE) We offer free shipping on orders over $50. See also **ship** → TAKE 1

haulage /ˈhɔːlɪdʒ/ [U] (BrE) the business or cost of transporting goods by road or rail: There have been protests from the road haulage industry. ◇ How much will haulage be (= how much will it cost)?

handling [U] (formal) the act or cost of packing an object or material and sending it to a customer: There is a $5 handling charge for each order. ◇ (AmE) You pay only $29.99 plus **shipping and handling**. ❶ In British English this is called postage and packing.

demand noun

demand · market · a run on sth · (no) call for sth
These are all words for the number of people who want to buy goods or services.

▸ demand / a market / (no) call **for** sth
▸ (a) **big / buoyant / huge / growing / steady / changing / current / potential / total / falling** demand / market
▸ (the) **consumer / domestic / local / export / foreign / worldwide** demand / market
▸ to **create** demand / a market
▸ to **stimulate / boost / increase** demand / the market

demand [U, sing.] (especially business) the number of people who want to buy goods or services: We are struggling to **meet the demand** for the product. ◇ Demand is exceeding supply. ◇ There's an increased demand for organic produce these days.

market [sing.] (business) the number of people who want to buy goods or services: The second-hand car market is declining. ◇ There's not much of a market for black and white televisions nowadays. See also **market** → MARKET 1

> **NOTE** DEMAND OR MARKET? These words have the same basic meaning, but **demand** is a more general term, and **market** is a more specialist business term. They have different grammar and collocation patterns: people talk about the housing/labour market and different product markets, but demand for housing/labour/a product. You can create demand/a market, but you meet/satisfy/increase demand and supply/expand the market. You influence/forecast demand but find/identify a market. People talk about a fall/a decline/an increase/growth in demand but a slump/recovery in the market. When a business has trouble producing enough goods because so many people want them, people talk about **demand** rather than the **market**: We're struggling to meet the market. ◇ The market exceeds supply.

a run on sth phrase (business) a sudden demand for sth by a lot of people: There's been a run on the dollar. ◇ When the new currency measures were announced there was **a run on the bank** (= a lot of people suddenly took their money out of the bank). ❶ **Run** is often found in financial contexts, but a shop or business might experience a run on anything, for example sun cream, petrol or red roses, especially when sth happens, such as a change in the weather, to create a sudden demand.

(no) call for sth phrase [sing.] (rather informal) the desire or need of customers for goods or services: There isn't a lot of call for small specialist shops nowadays.

demand verb See also the entry for ASK 2

demand · require · expect · insist · press (sb) for sth · ask · stipulate · clamour · hold out for sth · exact
These words all mean to say that sb should do or have sth.

▸ to demand / require / expect / ask / exact sth **from** sb
▸ to demand / require / expect / ask sth **of** sb
▸ to ask / press / push / clamour / hold out **for** sth
▸ to demand / require / expect / insist / ask / stipulate **that…**
▸ to require / expect / ask **sb to do sth**
▸ to demand / require / expect / insist on **high standards**
▸ to demand / require / expect / ask **a lot / too much / a great deal**
▸ to **be too much to** expect / ask

demand [T] to ask for sth very firmly; to say very firmly that sb should have or do sth: She demanded an immediate explanation. ◇ The group demands a high level of loyalty from its members. ◇ The UN has demanded that all troops be withdrawn. ◇ They **demanded to** see the ambassador. See also **demand** → REQUEST noun

require [T, often passive] (not usually used in the progressive tenses) (*rather formal*) to make sb do or have sth, especially because it is necessary according to a law or set of rules or standards: *The wearing of seat belts is required by law.* ◇ *Several students failed to reach the required standard.* ◇ *'Hamlet' is required reading (= must be read) for the class.* See also **requirement** → CONDITION

expect [T] to demand that sb should do, have or be sth, especially because it is their duty or responsibility: *Are you clear about what is expected of you?* ◇ *Don't expect too much from him.* ◇ *They expected all their children to be high achievers.* ◇ *I expect to be paid promptly for the work.*
▶ **expectation** *noun* [C, usually pl.]: *Some parents have unrealistic expectations of their children.* ◇ *Unfortunately the new software has failed to meet expectations.*

insist /ɪn'sɪst/ [I, T] to demand that sth happens or that sb agrees to do sth: *I didn't want to go but he insisted.* ◇ *We insist on the highest standards at all times.* ◇ (*spoken*) *Stay and have lunch. I insist!* ◇ *'Please come with us.' 'All right, if you insist.'* ◇ *The company insisted that the money be paid immediately.* ❶ The phrasal verb **insist on/upon sth** also means 'to demand sth and refuse to accept anything else': *We insisted on a refund of the full amount.*
▶ **insistence** *noun* [U]: *their insistence on strict standards of behaviour* ◇ *At her insistence, the matter was dropped.*

'press for sth, **'press sb for sth** *phrasal verb* to keep asking for sth in a determined way: *They are pressing for a change in the law.* ◇ *The bank is pressing us for repayment of the loan.* See also **press** → PRESS 2

ask [T] to expect or demand sth: *I know I'm asking a great deal.* ◇ *You're asking too much of him.* ◇ *It's asking a lot to expect them to win again.*

NOTE DEMAND, EXPECT OR ASK? **Ask** is not as strong as **demand** or **expect**, both of which can be more like a command.

stipulate [T] (*formal*) to state firmly and clearly that sth must be done, or how it must be done: *A delivery date is stipulated in the contract.* ◇ *The job advertisement stipulates that the applicant must have teaching experience.*

clamour (*BrE*) (*AmE* **clamor**) /'klæmə(r)/ [I] (*rather formal, written*) to demand sth loudly: *People began to clamour for his resignation.* ◇ *Everyone was clamouring to know how much they would get.*

'hold 'out for sth *phrasal verb* [no passive] to refuse to accept less than what you are asking for, especially when this causes a delay in reaching an agreement: *They are holding out for a 10% raise.*

exact [T] (*formal*) to demand and get sth from sb: *She was determined to exact a promise from him.*

demolish *verb*

demolish · tear sth down · knock sth down · raze · cut sth down · fell · level · flatten · bulldoze
These are all words that can be used to talk about destroying buildings or trees.

PATTERNS AND COLLOCATIONS
▶ to demolish/tear down/knock down/level/flatten a **building/ house**
▶ to demolish/ tear down/ knock down a **factory / wall**
▶ to raze / level / flatten / bulldoze an **area**
▶ to raze / level / flatten a **village / town / city**
▶ to raze / cut down / fell / bulldoze a **forest**
▶ to cut down / fell / bulldoze **trees**

demolish /dɪ'mɒlɪʃ; *AmE* -'mɑːl-/ [T] (*rather formal*) to destroy a building or part of a building by breaking its walls, usually deliberately: *The old slums are being demolished to make way for a new housing project.* ❶ Buildings are usually **demolished** deliberately, because they are not safe or are no longer needed, or the land is needed for sth else. In informal usage, especially in American English, buildings, vehicles and other objects can be **demolished** by accident: (*especially AmE, informal*) *Tornadoes demolished trailers and blew roofs off houses.* **OPP** **build, construct** → BUILD
▶ **demolition** /ˌdemə'lɪʃn/ *noun* [U, C]: *The whole row of houses is scheduled for demolition.* **OPP** **construction, building** → PRODUCTION

'tear sth 'down *phrasal verb* (*sometimes disapproving*) to deliberately destroy a building, wall or barrier; to pull down pictures, curtains, etc: *They're tearing down these old houses to build a new office block.* ◇ *Demonstrators tore down posters of the president.*

'knock sth 'down *phrasal verb* to deliberately destroy a building, wall or fence; to make a door fall inwards: *You could knock this wall down and make one large room.* ◇ *They didn't need to knock the door down!*

NOTE DEMOLISH, TEAR STH DOWN OR KNOCK STH DOWN? **Tear sth down** can suggest that unnecessary violence was used, or that the speaker has negative feelings about what was done. **Demolish** and **knock sth down** are both neutral terms (= neither positive nor negative).

raze [T, usually passive] to completely destroy a building, town, forest, etc. so that nothing is left: *The village was razed to the ground.* ❶ **Razing** a place involves the most complete destruction of all. It often involves large areas of land; it is usually done deliberately, often as an act of war; it is done or finished off by burning the area.

'cut sth 'down *phrasal verb* to make a tree fall down, by cutting it at the base: *Some care must be taken before deciding to cut down large trees.*

fell [T] (*rather formal*) to cut down a tree: *Trees were felled and floated downstream.* ◇ *illegally felled timber*

NOTE CUT STH DOWN OR FELL? **Fell** is a more formal word and is used in more commercial contexts and where large numbers of trees or whole forests are involved.

level (-ll-, *AmE* -l-) [T] to destroy a building, town or group of trees completely, so that no part of it is left standing: *Bulldozers are now waiting to level their home.* ◇ *The blast levelled several buildings in the area.*

flatten [T] to destroy a building, town, tree, garden, etc. completely, so that no part of it is left standing: *The hurricane flattened thousands of homes.* ◇ *Most of the factory was flattened by the explosion.*

NOTE LEVEL OR FLATTEN? Places are often **levelled** deliberately, so that the land can be used again, or when bombed by terrorists. Places are more often **flattened** by accident, by natural forces or by explosions.

bulldoze /'bʊldəʊz; *AmE* -doʊz/ [T] (*sometimes disapproving*) to destroy buildings, trees, etc. with a bulldozer (= a powerful motor vehicle with a broad steel blade in front): *The trees are being bulldozed to make way for a new superstore.* ❶ **Bulldoze** can suggest that unnecessary force was used, or that the speaker has negative feelings about what was done. **Knock sth down** or **cut sth down** would be a more neutral choice.

demonstration *noun*

demonstration · protest · march · demo
These are all words for a public meeting, which may involve walking along the streets, at which people show that they are protesting against or supporting sb/sth.

PATTERNS AND COLLOCATIONS
▶ a demonstration / protest / march / demo **against** sth
▶ a **big / mass** demonstration / protest / march / demo
▶ a / an **anti-war / pro-democracy / anti-government** demonstration / protest / march / demo
▶ a **peaceful** demonstration / protest / march
▶ a **violent** demonstration / protest

▶ to **hold** / **organize** / **stage** a demonstration / protest / march / demo

▶ to **go on** / **join** / **participate in** / **take part in** a demonstration / protest / march / demo

▶ to **ban** / **suppress** a demonstration / protest / march

demonstration /ˌdemən'streɪʃn/ [C] an organized public meeting, usually outdoors, at which people show that they are protesting against or supporting sb/sth: *There were mass demonstrations in support of the exiled leader.* ◇ *(BrE) Protesters go on demonstrations, armed with flowers to give to the police.*

▸ **demonstrate** verb [I]: *students demonstrating against the war*

protest [C] an organized meeting, usually outdoors, where people show strong disagreement with or opposition to sth: *The workers staged a protest against the proposed changes in their contracts* ◇ *The riot began as a peaceful protest.*

▸ **protest** verb [I]: *Students took to the streets to protest against the decision.* See also **protest** → COMPLAIN

NOTE DEMONSTRATION OR PROTEST? A **demonstration** can be against sb/sth or in support of sb/sth; a **protest** is always against sb/sth. A **demonstration** is usually about a public issue that affects a whole country, region or city; a **protest** can be about a more private matter, for example by workers against their employers. Either can involve a march, but both may simply consist of a number of people standing together holding up signs or shouting a message. **Demonstration** can suggest a larger number of people than **protest**, which can involve a large or small number of people. **Protest** is a slightly more informal word and is often used by journalists.

march [C] an organized walk by a large group of people from one place to another, in order to protest about sth, or to express their opinions: *Thousands of people from all over the country attended the march.*

▸ **march** verb [I]: *Hundreds of people marched in support of the teachers' pay claim.*

demo /'deməʊ; AmE -moʊ/ [C] (BrE, informal, especially spoken) a demonstration: *We all went on the demo.* ❶ **Demo** is most often used in spoken language, but it also appears in headlines in popular newspapers when journalists want to use the shortest words possible.

denial noun

denial · disclaimer · rebuttal · refutation · retraction
These are all words for a statement that says that sth is not true or that you are not responsible for sth.

PATTERNS AND COLLOCATIONS
▶ a denial / rebuttal **from** sb
▶ a denial / disclaimer **that...**
▶ a **firm** denial / rebuttal / refutation
▶ to **issue** a denial / disclaimer / rebuttal / retraction
▶ to **publish** a denial / rebuttal / retraction
▶ to **offer** a denial / rebuttal / refutation

denial /dɪ'naɪəl/ [C, U] a statement that says that sth is not true or does not exist: *The terrorists issued a denial of responsibility for the attack.* ◇ *There was an official denial that there would be an election before the end of the year.* **OPP** claim → CLAIM

disclaimer [C] (formal) a statement in which sb says that they are not connected with or responsible for sth, or that they do not have any knowledge of it: *There was a disclaimer of liability in the surveyor's report.*

rebuttal /rɪ'bʌtl/ [C, U] (formal) a statement that says or proves that a statement or criticism is false; the act of making this kind of statement: *The accusations met with a firm rebuttal.* ◇ *These assumptions require careful and express rebuttal.* See also **rebut** → DISPROVE

refutation /ˌrefju'teɪʃn/ [C, U] (formal) a statement that says or proves that sth is not true; the act of making this kind of statement: *These comments are not offered as a refutation of the theory.* See also **refute** → DISPROVE

NOTE REBUTTAL OR REFUTATION? A **rebuttal** is often more personal than a **refutation**: it is usually a response to an accusation or criticism of some kind. A **refutation** is usually more academic, a response to a theory or argument.

retraction /rɪ'trækʃn/ [C] (formal) a statement saying that sth you previously said or wrote is not true: *He demanded a full retraction of the allegations against him.* See also **retract** → BREAK verb 4

deny verb

deny · contradict · repudiate · refute · disclaim
These words all mean to say that a report or claim is not true.

PATTERNS AND COLLOCATIONS
▶ to deny / contradict / repudiate / refute a **report** / **suggestion**
▶ to deny / repudiate / refute a **claim**
▶ to deny / repudiate an **accusation** / **allegation**
▶ to deny / disclaim **knowledge** / **responsibility**
▶ to **flatly** deny / contradict sth
▶ to **strongly** / **publicly** deny / repudiate / refute sth

deny /dɪ'naɪ/ [T] to say that a report or claim is not true; to refuse to admit or accept knowledge of or responsibility for sth: *He denied accusations of corruption and mismanagement.* ◇ *There's no denying the fact that quicker action could have saved them.* ◇ *He denies attempting to murder his wife.* ◇ *She **denied that** there had been any cover-up.* ◇ *It can't be denied that we need to devote more resources to this problem.* ◇ *She denied all knowledge of the incident.* **OPP** admit → ADMIT 2, confirm → CONFIRM 2

contradict /ˌkɒntrə'dɪkt; AmE ˌkɑːn-/ [T] to say that what sb has said is not true, and that the opposite is true: *All evening her husband contradicted everything she said.* ◇ *You've just **contradicted yourself** (= said the opposite of what you said before).*

repudiate /rɪ'pjuːdieɪt/ [T] (formal) to say officially and/or publicly that a report or claim is not true: *A spokeswoman repudiated the article, calling it unbalanced and inaccurate.*

refute /rɪ'fjuːt/ [T] (especially journalism) to say that a report or claim is not true or fair: *She strongly refutes any suggestion that she behaved unprofessionally.* ❶ The original meaning of **refute** is 'to prove a statement or theory to be wrong'; however, in modern usage **refute** is often used as a synonym of **deny**, when no evidence or argument is given to prove that sth is untrue. Some people object to this usage but it is now widely accepted in standard English, and used especially in journalism. See also **refute** → DISPROVE

disclaim [T] (formal) to state publicly that you have no knowledge of sth, or that you are not responsible for sth: *The rebels disclaimed all responsibility for the explosion.*

department noun

department · division · branch · unit · arm · wing
These are all words for a part of an organization.

PATTERNS AND COLLOCATIONS
▶ an **administrative** department / division / branch / arm
▶ a **research** department / division / unit / arm
▶ the **finance** / **marketing** department / division / arm
▶ a **political** department / unit / arm / wing
▶ a **military** unit / arm / wing
▶ a **regional** department / division / branch / unit

department [C] a part of a large organization, especially a business, shop, university, government or hospital, that deals with one particular activity: *I work in the sales* department. ◇ *The children's department sells a wide range of good quality clothes.* ◇ *Several professors from the history department will also speak at the event.* ◇ *The Department of Trade and Industry refused to comment on the allegations.*

division [C] a large and important part of an organization, especially a military one or a business: *The commander of the fourth infantry division defied orders.* ◇ *The company's sales division is going to be restructured.*

branch [C] a local office or shop belonging to a large company or organization: *The bank has branches all over the country.* ◇ *Our New York branch is dealing with the matter.* ❶ Some departments of a government or other organization may have a name which includes the word **branch**: *Scotland Yard's anti-terrorist branch swung into action.*

unit [C] a department, especially in a hospital, that provides a particular kind of care or treatment; a part of a military organization: *She was taken to the **intensive care unit**.* ◇ *The hospital's **maternity unit** is to be closed.* ◇ *Enemy units have infiltrated the territory.* See also **unit** → ARMY

arm [C, usually sing.] (used especially in compounds) a department of an organization: *The report was published by the research arm of the Department of Transport.* ◇ *The bank plans to sell part of its US finance arm.*

wing [C] one section of an organization, especially a political or military one, which has a particular function or whose members share the same opinions: *The radical wing of the party was dissatisfied with the policies.*

departure noun

1 his sudden departure
2 a radical departure from tradition

1 departure · exit · going

These are all words for the act of leaving a place.

PATTERNS AND COLLOCATIONS
▶ departure / exit **from** sth
▶ sb's **sudden / unexpected / abrupt** departure / exit
▶ a **hasty / speedy** departure / exit
▶ to **hasten** sb's departure / exit
▶ to **make** a departure / an exit

departure [C, U] the act of leaving a place or organization: *His sudden departure threw the office into chaos.* ◇ *She had made arrangements for their immediate **departure for Canada**.* ◇ *She postponed her **departure to Scotland**.* ◇ *The company has announced the departure of its chief executive.* ◇ *Flights should be confirmed 24 hours before departure.* ◇ *Departure for London will be at 18.45.* **OPP arrival** → ARRIVAL 1, See also **depart** → LEAVE 1

exit [C, usually sing.] an act of leaving a room, building, stage, country or competition: *He made a quick exit to avoid talking to her.* ◇ *The dancers made their exits and entrances with perfect timing.* ◇ *They were disappointed by the team's early exit from the Cup.* ◇ *an **exit visa** (= an official stamp in your passport giving you permission to leave)* **OPP entrance** → ARRIVAL 1, See also **exit** → LEAVE 1

going [C, usually sing.] (*formal*) an act of leaving a place: *A silence followed their going.* ◇ *What was the reason for his going?* ◇ *There had been lots of **comings and goings** at the house.* **OPP coming** → ARRIVAL 1, See also **go** → LEAVE 1

2 departure · deviation · diversion · digression · parenthesis

These are all words for an action that is different from what is usual or expected.

PATTERNS AND COLLOCATIONS
▶ a departure / deviation / diversion / digression **from** sth
▶ a **welcome** departure / diversion

departure [C] (*rather formal*) an action that is different from what is usual or expected: *It was a radical departure from tradition.* ◇ *Their latest single represents a new departure for the band.* ❶ A **departure** is usually sth that is regarded as a big change (*dramatic, fundamental, major, radical, revolutionary, significant*) or a pleasant change (*fresh, new, welcome*).

▶ **de'part from sth** phrasal verb: *Departing from her usual routine, she took the bus to work.*

deviation /ˌdiːviˈeɪʃn/ [U, C] the act of moving away from what is normal or acceptable; a difference from what is expected or acceptable: *Modern examples of this type of weaving showed little deviation from traditional patterns.* ◇ *sexual deviation*

▶ **deviate** /ˈdiːvieɪt/ verb [I]: *He never deviated from his original plan.*

diversion /daɪˈvɜːʃn; AmE -ˈvɜːrʒn/ [C] (*rather formal*) something that takes your attention away from sb/sth while sth else is happening: *For the government, the war was a welcome diversion from the country's economic problems.* ◇ *A smoke bomb **created a diversion** while the robbery took place.*

▶ **divert** verb [T]: *The war diverted people's attention away from the economic situation.*

digression /daɪˈɡreʃn/ [C, U] (*rather formal*) the act of starting to talk about sth that is not connected with the main point of what you are saying: *After several digressions, he finally got to the point.* ❶ A **digression** may be seen as interesting or entertaining, or it may be seen as long, boring and annoying.

▶ **digress** verb [I]: (*formal, especially spoken*) *Anyway, I digress. Back to the story.*

parenthesis /pəˈrenθəsɪs/ (pl. **parentheses** /-əsiːz/) [C] (*formal*) a word, phrase or sentence that is added to a speech or piece of writing, especially in order to give extra information: *I should say, **in parenthesis**, that these figures cannot always be trusted.* ❶ In writing, a **parenthesis** is separated from the rest of the text using brackets, commas or dashes. People often talk about sth being said *in parenthesis*. People also sometimes use the plural **parentheses** to talk about the brackets themselves, so they may say that a piece of information is *in parentheses*.

depend on/upon sth phrasal verb

depend on/upon sth · rest on sth · hinge on/upon sth · hang on sth
These words all mean to be affected or decided by sth.

PATTERNS AND COLLOCATIONS
▶ It depends (on) / rests on / hinges on **what / how / who / where / whether…**
▶ a **case** depends on / rests on / hinges on sth
▶ to **entirely / solely / largely / mainly / partly / ultimately** depend on / rest on sth
▶ It **all** depends on / hinges on sth.

de'pend on/upon sth phrasal verb (not used in the progressive tenses) to be affected or decided by sth: *Does the quality of teaching depend on class size?* ◇ *It would depend on the circumstances.* ◇ *We might need more food, depending on how many people turn up.* ❶ In informal English, it is quite common to say **depend** rather than **depend on** before words like *what, how* or *whether*: *It depends what you mean by 'hostile'.* In formal written English, **depend** should always be followed by **on** or **upon**: *It depends on how you define the term 'hostile'.* Upon is more formal and less frequent than **on**. In spoken English you can also say **that depends** or **it (all) depends** when you are not certain about sth because other things have to be considered: (*spoken*) '*Is he coming?*' '*That depends. He may not have the time.*' ◇ *I don't know if we can help — it all depends.*

'rest on sth phrasal verb (especially written) (especially of a decision, argument or what happens in the future) to be based on sth; to depend on sth: *The whole argument rests on a false assumption.* ◊ *The case rests on who owned the knife.* ◊ *Europe's political future rests on its economic strength.* ❶ **Rest on sth** is used especially to talk about the reasons for a decision or judgement and whether it is based on true facts: *The argument/case/decision/evidence/theory rests on sth.* You can also say that sb/sth's *fame*, *future* or *hopes* **rest on sth**.

'hinge on/upon sth phrasal verb (especially written, especially journalism) (of an action or result) to depend on sth: *Everything hinges on the outcome of these talks.* ◊ *His success hinged on how well he did at the interview.* ❶ **Hinge on/upon sth** is often used when people are talking about results, for example of *talks*, an *election*, a *debate*, a *case* or a *match*.

'hang on sth phrasal verb (rather informal) to depend on sth: *A lot hangs on this decision.* ❶ **Hang on sth** is usually used in the third person, and in the present tense. Typical subjects are *everything*, *it all*, *a lot* and sb's *reputation*.

depressed *adj.* See also the entry for UNHAPPY 1

depressed · gloomy · demoralized · glum · despondent · dejected · down
These words all describe sb who feels unhappy and without hope.

PATTERNS AND COLLOCATIONS
▶ depressed / gloomy / glum / despondent **about** sth
▶ a depressed / gloomy / glum **silence / mood**
▶ to **feel** depressed / gloomy / demoralized / despondent / dejected / down
▶ to **look** depressed / gloomy / glum
▶ to **get** depressed / gloomy / demoralized
▶ **increasingly** depressed / gloomy / despondent

depressed unhappy and without hope: *She felt very depressed about the future.* ◊ *He was really depressed at the thought of going into the office.* ◊ *You mustn't let yourself get depressed.* See also **depress** → DISCOURAGE 2, **depressing** → NEGATIVE, **depression** → GLOOM

gloomy unhappy and without hope, especially when you show this in your expression and behaviour: *Don't look so gloomy. Things aren't that bad.* ◊ *He mopes around all the time with that gloomy expression on his face.* **OPP** **cheerful** → CHEERFUL. See also **gloom** → GLOOM
▶ **gloomily** adv.: *He stared gloomily at the phone.*

demoralized (BrE also -ised) /dɪˈmɒrəlaɪzd; AmE -ˈmɔːr-; -ˈmɑːr-/ without confidence or hope any longer, especially after a period of being unsuccessful or making little progress: *The workers here seem very demoralized.* ◊ *What can we do to revitalize a demoralized sales force?* ❶ **Demoralized** is used especially to describe the feeling among a group of people, such as a team, army or workforce, when their situation has become worse over a period of time and **morale** (= confidence and enthusiasm) has become low. See also **morale** → MOOD

glum unhappy, quiet and without hope, especially when you show this in your expression: *The couple looked distinctly glum.* ◊ *Her tone was flat and glum.*
▶ **glumly** adv.: *We sat glumly looking out to sea.*

despondent /dɪˈspɒndənt; AmE -ˈspɑːn-/ (rather formal, especially written) unhappy and without much hope: *She was becoming increasingly despondent about the way things were going.* See also **despondency** → GLOOM

dejected /dɪˈdʒektɪd/ (rather formal, especially written) unhappy and disappointed: *She looked so dejected when she lost the game.*

down [not before noun] (rather informal) unhappy or depressed: *I feel a bit down today.* ◊ *Don't let the weather get you down.*

describe *verb* See also the entry for PRESENT 2

describe · report · tell · unfold · recount · relate · weave · chronicle · cover · narrate
These words all mean to say what sb/sth is like or give an account of events.

PATTERNS AND COLLOCATIONS
▶ to describe / report / tell / recount / relate **what / how...**
▶ to report / recount / relate **that...**
▶ to describe / report / recount / relate / chronicle / cover / narrate **events / a series of events**
▶ to describe / report / recount / relate your **adventures**
▶ to tell / unfold / recount / relate / weave / cover / narrate a **story**
▶ to tell / unfold / recount / relate / weave / narrate a **tale**
▶ to report / recount **details**
▶ to describe / report sth **accurately / clearly**
▶ to describe / tell / recount sth **vividly**

describe [T] to say what sb/sth is like: *Can you describe him to me?* ◊ *The current political situation in Vietnam is described in chapter 8.* ◊ *Describe how you did it.* ◊ *Several people described seeing strange lights in the sky.* See also **describe** → REGARD

report [T, I] to present a written or spoken account of an event in a newspaper, on television, etc: *The stabbing was reported in the local press.* ◊ *It was reported that several people had been arrested.* ◊ *She reports on royal stories for the BBC.* See also **report** → REPORT noun 2, **report** → REPORT noun 3, **reporter** → REPORTER, **reporting** → MEDIA

tell [T] to give a spoken account of sth; to express sth in words: *They told stories and jokes while sitting around the camp fire.* ◊ *Are you telling the truth?* ◊ *She is always telling lies.* ◊ *Did anyone tell you what happened?* ◊ *I can't tell you how happy I am.* See also **tell** → TELL 1

unfold /ʌnˈfəʊld; AmE ʌnˈfoʊld/ [I, T] (literary) to be gradually made known; to gradually make sth known to other people: *The audience watched the story unfold before their eyes.* ◊ *Dramatic events were about to unfold.* ◊ *She unfolded her tale to us.*

recount /rɪˈkaʊnt/ [T] (formal) to give an account of sth that has happened, especially sth that has happened to you: *She was asked to recount the details of the incident to the court.*

relate [T] (formal) to give an account of sth that has happened: *She relates her childhood experiences in the first chapters.* ◊ *He related the whole conversation to the police.*

NOTE **TELL, RECOUNT** OR **RELATE?** Recount and relate are more formal than **tell**. Recount is used more often than **relate** to talk about telling an informal and sometimes entertaining story about events that you have experienced: *Brian and I recounted the awful story.* Relate is often used to talk about more formal, neutral accounts: *An audio-visual presentation relates the story of the Battle of Hastings.*

weave [T] (literary) to put facts, events and details together to make a story or a closely connected whole: *The author weaves the narrative around the detailed eyewitness accounts.*

chronicle /ˈkrɒnɪkl; AmE ˈkrɑːn-/ [T] (formal) to record events in the order in which they happened: *Her achievements are chronicled in a new biography.* See also **chronicle** → STORY 2

cover [T] to report on an event for television, etc.; to show an event on television: *She's covering the party's annual conference.* ◊ *The BBC will cover all the major games of the tournament.* See also **coverage** → MEDIA

narrate /nəˈreɪt; AmE also ˈnæreɪt/ [T] (formal) to tell a story: *She entertained them by narrating her adventures in Africa.* ◊ *The story is narrated in flashback.* See also **narrative** → STORY 1

description *noun* See also the entry for REPORT 2

description · picture · representation · profile · portrayal · portrait · depiction · evocation
These are all words for sth such as a piece of writing or a picture that describes or shows sb/sth.

PATTERNS AND COLLOCATIONS
▸ a/an description / picture / representation / profile / portrayal / portrait / depiction / evocation **of** sb / sth
▸ an **accurate** description / picture / representation / profile / portrayal / portrait / depiction / evocation
▸ a **true/realistic** description / picture / representation / portrayal / depiction
▸ a **detailed** description / picture / representation / profile / depiction / evocation
▸ a **vivid** description / picture / representation / portrayal / depiction / evocation
▸ to **give** a description / picture / representation
▸ to **draw / paint** a picture / a portrait
▸ to **build up** a picture / profile

description [C, U] a piece of writing or speech that says what sb/sth is like; the act of writing or saying in words what sb/sth is like: *Police have issued a description of the gunman.* ◇ *'Scared stiff' is an apt description of how I felt at that moment.* ◇ *There was no mention of any cleaning in my* **job description**. ◇ *I experienced a personal pain that goes* **beyond description** (= is too great to express in words).

picture [C, usually sing.] a description that gives you an idea in your mind of what sth is like: *The writer paints a gloomy picture of the economy.* ◇ *From newspaper reports a picture emerges of a country barely under control.* See also **picture** → IMAGINE *verb*

representation /ˌreprɪzenˈteɪʃn/ [C, U] (*rather formal*) something that shows or describes sth; the act of presenting sb/sth in a particular way: *The snake swallowing its tail is a representation of infinity.* ◇ *the negative representation of single mothers in the media* See also **represent** → PRESENT *verb* 2, **represent** → REPRESENT *verb* 2

profile /ˈprəʊfaɪl; *AmE* ˈproʊ-/ [C] a description of sb/sth that gives useful information: *We first build up a detailed profile of our customers and their requirements.* ◇ *His psychological profile is revealing.*

portrayal /pɔːˈtreɪəl; *AmE* pɔːrˈt-/ [U, C] (*rather formal*) the act of showing or describing sb/sth, especially a person or group of people, in a picture, book, film, etc; a particular way in which this is done: *The article examines the portrayal of gay men in the media.* ◇ *He is best known for his chilling portrayal of Hannibal Lecter.* See also **portray** → PRESENT *verb* 2

portrait /ˈpɔːtreɪt; -trət; *AmE* ˈpɔːrtrət/ [C] a detailed description or dramatic presentation of sb/sth in a book, film, etc: *Her first film was a stunning portrait of life in the sugar plantations of her native Martinique.*

NOTE **PORTRAYAL** OR **PORTRAIT**? The **portrayal** of sb/sth is the way sb/sth is shown in words or pictures. A **portrait** is the description, play or film itself. See also **portrait** → PICTURE

depiction [C, U] (*formal*) a picture of sth; a description or dramatic presentation of sb/sth in newspapers, films, etc: *The latest addition to the gallery is a depiction of Amsterdam.* ◇ *They object to the movie's depiction of black people.* See also **depict** → PRESENT *verb* 2

NOTE **REPRESENTATION, PORTRAYAL** OR **DEPICTION**? **Representation** is the most general of these words and it can be a written description, a picture or work of art, but NOT usually a film or anything that moves or changes; a **representation** can be of a person, group, place or thing. A **portrayal** can be a description or performance but is NOT usually a picture; a **portrayal** is usually of a person or group of people and is often used about an actor's performance as a real or imaginary character. **Depiction** is often used as a formal word for a picture, especially of a place, when this is a work of art; a **depiction** can also be a description or dramatic presentation of a person or group of people.

evocation /ˌiːvəʊˈkeɪʃn; *AmE* ˌiːvoʊ-/ [C, U] (*written*) a description, film or work of art that brings a feeling, memory or image into your mind: *The film is a brilliant evocation of childhood in the 1940s.* ◇ *The artist's work has been praised for its richness of evocation.* See also **evoke** → REMIND SB OF SB/STH

descriptive *adj.*

descriptive · explanatory · interpretative · illustrative
These words all describe sth that describes or explains sth.

PATTERNS AND COLLOCATIONS
▸ for descriptive / explanatory / interpretative / illustrative **purposes**
▸ descriptive / explanatory / interpretative **notes**
▸ a descriptive / explanatory / interpretative **statement / passage**
▸ descriptive / explanatory / illustrative **material**

descriptive /dɪˈskrɪptɪv/ saying what sth is like; describing sth: *She read out some of the descriptive passages in the novel.* ◇ *The term I used was meant to be purely descriptive* (= not judging).

explanatory /ɪkˈsplænətri; *AmE* -tɔːri/ [usually before noun] (*rather formal*) giving the reasons for sth; intended to describe how sth works or to make sth easier to understand: *There are explanatory notes at the back of the book.* ❶ Something that is **self-explanatory** is easy to understand and does not need any more explanation: *I think the title is self-explanatory.* See also **explain** → EXPLAIN 1

interpretative /ɪnˈtɜːprɪtətɪv; *AmE* ɪnˈtɜːrprəteɪtɪv/ (also **interpretive** especially in *AmE*) /ɪnˈtɜːprɪtɪv; *AmE* -ˈtɜːrp-/) [usually before noun] (*formal*) connected with the particular way in which sth is understood, explained or performed; providing an interpretation: *The interpretative problems arise from concepts that may be understood in different ways by different people.* See also **interpret** → EXPLAIN 1, **interpretation** → DEFINITION

illustrative /ˈɪləstrətɪv; *AmE* ɪˈlʌs-/ (*formal*) helping to explain sth or show it more clearly: *Be sure to include plenty of illustrative examples.* See also **illustrate** → EXPLAIN 1, **illustration** → EXAMPLE 1

NOTE **EXPLANATORY** OR **ILLUSTRATIVE**? **Explanatory** notes explain sth in a direct way; **illustrative** materials show sth by giving examples.

desert *noun*

desert · wilderness · bush · wasteland · the wilds · no-man's land · the outback · dust bowl · wastes
These words all mean a large area of land where very few people live or can survive.

PATTERNS AND COLLOCATIONS
▸ **in / into** the desert / the wilderness / the bush / the wilds / no-man's land / the outback
▸ **across** the desert / no-man's land / the outback
▸ **arid / barren / arctic / frozen** desert / wilderness / wasteland / wastes
▸ the **Australian** desert / wilderness / bush / outback
▸ the **African** desert / wilderness / bush
▸ a **cultural** desert / wasteland
▸ to **become** a desert / wasteland

desert [C, U] a large area of land that has very little water and very few plants growing on it. Many deserts are covered by sand: *the Sahara Desert* ◇ *Somalia is mostly desert.* ◇ *They travelled many miles across burning desert sands.*

wilderness /'wɪldənəs; *AmE* -dərn-/ [C, usually sing.] a large area of land that has never been developed or used for growing crops because it is difficult to live there; a place that people do not take care of or control: *The Antarctic is the world's last great wilderness.* ◊ (*AmE*) *The US Department of Agriculture designated the land a* **wilderness area** (= where it is not permitted to build houses or roads) *in 1978.* ◊ *That part of the city is a wilderness of run-down houses and derelict factories.*

bush (*often* **the bush**) [U] an area of wild land that has not been cleared, especially in Africa and Australia: *Children are taught from an early age how to survive in the bush.*

wasteland /'weɪstlænd/ [C, U] an area of land that cannot be used or that is no longer used for building or growing things on: *City life could be improved by turning urban wastelands into parks.* ◊ *The film was shot in the desert wasteland of southern California.*

the wilds [pl.] areas of a country far from towns or cities, where few people live: *It's a true tale of survival in the wilds of Alaska.* ◊ (*humorous*) *They live on a farm somewhere out* **in the wilds.**

'no-man's land [U, sing.] an area of land between the borders of two countries or between two armies, that is not controlled by either: *He led his platoon across no-man's land.*

the outback [C, sing.] the area of Australia that is a long way from the coast and the towns, where few people live: *They live an isolated life in the outback of New South Wales.*

'dust bowl [C, usually sing.] an area of land that has recently been turned into desert by lack of rain or too much farming: *Many families struggled to survive in the Oklahoma Dust Bowl of the 1930s.*

wastes [pl.] (*formal*) a large area of land where there are very few people, animals or plants: *Millions of people were exiled to the frozen wastes of Siberia.*

deserted *adj.*

deserted · abandoned · disused · unoccupied · uninhabited
These words all describe a place where there are no longer any people, or a person or thing that people have left behind.

PATTERNS AND COLLOCATIONS
▸ a deserted / an abandoned / an unoccupied / an uninhabited **area**
▸ a deserted / an abandoned / a disused / an unoccupied **building**
▸ a deserted / an abandoned / an unoccupied **house**
▸ an abandoned / a disused **mine / railway / railroad**
▸ a deserted / an abandoned **village**
▸ a deserted / an uninhabited **island**
▸ largely / completely / totally deserted / abandoned / uninhabited

deserted /dɪ'zɜːtɪd; *AmE* -'zɜːrt-/ (of a place) with no people in it; (of a place, person or thing) left by a person or people who do not intend to return: *The office was completely deserted.* ◊ *A large proportion of the remaining community was made up of widows and* **deserted wives.** See also **desert** → ABANDON

abandoned /ə'bændənd/ (of a person, place or thing) left and no longer wanted, used or needed: *The charity's work involves finding foster homes for abandoned children.* ◊ *Police found several guns in an abandoned car.* See also **abandon** → ABANDON

disused /ˌdɪs'juːzd/ [usually before noun] no longer used: *The party was held in a disused warehouse.* ❶ **Disused** should not be confused with **unused**, which means 'not being used at the moment or never having been used'.

unoccupied empty, with nobody living there or using it: *The building appeared to be unoccupied.* ◊ *Children must sit on a parent's lap unless an unoccupied seat is available.* **OPP** **occupied** ❶ A building, room, seat, etc. that is **occupied** is being used by sb: *Only half the rooms are occupied at the moment.* See also **vacant** → EMPTY

uninhabited /ˌʌnɪn'hæbɪtɪd/ with no people living there: *They landed on an uninhabited island off the Newfoundland coast.* ◊ *The area is largely uninhabited.* ❶ A more common name for an uninhabited tropical island is a **desert island.**

deserve *verb*

deserve · earn · merit
These words are all used when it is right that sb/sth should have sth, because of the way they have behaved or because of what they are.

PATTERNS AND COLLOCATIONS
▸ to deserve / earn a **rest / drink**
▸ to deserve / merit a **mention**
▸ to deserve / merit **attention / consideration / recognition**
▸ to **really / certainly** deserve / earn / merit sth
▸ to **hardly** deserve / merit sth

deserve [T] (not used in the progressive tenses) if sb/sth **deserves** sth, it is right that they should have it, because of the way they have behaved or because of what they are: *You deserve a rest after all that hard work.* ◊ *The report deserves careful consideration.* ◊ *What have I done to deserve this* (= this bad treatment)? ◊ *They didn't deserve to win* (= they did not play well enough). ◊ *He deserves to be locked up for ever for what he did.* See **undeserved** → UNJUSTIFIED

▸ **sb's deserts** *phrase*: *The family of the victim said that the killer had* **got his just deserts** *when he was jailed for life.* ❶ Sb's **(just) deserts** are usually sth unpleasant that they deserve because of sth bad that they have done.

earn [T] (used especially in the perfect tenses) to deserve sth pleasant because of sth good that you have done: *I need a drink. I think I've earned it, don't you?* ◊ *She's having a well-earned rest this week.*

NOTE DESERVE OR EARN? **Deserve** can be used to talk about either sth pleasant sb should have for doing sth good, or a punishment sb should have for doing sth bad. **Earn** is only used to talk about sth pleasant you should have for doing sth good. Note that you say that sb **deserves** sth, but that they *have* **earned** it.

merit /'merɪt/ [T] (not used in the progressive tenses) (*formal*) to deserve praise or attention: *He claims that their success was not merited.* ◊ *The case does not merit further investigation.* ❶ **Merit** is often used to talk about things (rather than people) that deserve attention. See also **merit** → VALUE *noun* 1

design *noun*

design · format · layout · configuration · arrangement · geography
These are all words for the way in which the different parts of sth are arranged.

PATTERNS AND COLLOCATIONS
▸ a design / format / layout / configuration **for** sth
▸ **in** a / the (…) design / format / layout / configuration / arrangement / geography **of** sth
▸ **in** design / format / layout
▸ a / the **basic / simple** design / format / layout / arrangement
▸ a **complex** design / format / layout / arrangement
▸ a **new** design / format / layout / configuration / arrangement
▸ the **original** design / format / layout
▸ a **similar / different** design / format / layout / arrangement
▸ the **same** design / format / layout / arrangement
▸ the **standard** design / format / layout / configuration / arrangement
▸ a **traditional** design / format / layout / arrangement
▸ to **use** a design / format / layout / configuration
▸ to **follow** a design / format / layout
▸ to **change** the format / layout / configuration

design [U, C] the general arrangement of the different parts of sth that is made, such as a building, book or machine: *The machine's unique design prevents it from overheating.* ◊ *The equipment is quite complex in design.* ◊ *Our house was built to a traditional design.* ◊ *There was a basic design fault in the new computer.* ◊ *What new design features does the TV have?* See also **design** → DEVELOPMENT

format /ˈfɔːmæt/ *AmE* ˈfɔːrmæt/ [C] the general arrangement or plan of an event or activity; the shape and size of a book or magazine: *The format of the new quiz show has proved very popular.* ◊ *We will follow the same format as last year.* ◊ *Books are available in a larger format.*

layout /ˈleɪaʊt/ [C, usually sing., U] the way in which the parts of sth such as the page of a book, a garden or building are arranged: *You'll soon get used to the layout of the building.* ◊ *Editing and layout is now usually done on computer.* See also **lay sth out** → ARRANGE

configuration /kənˌfɪɡəˈreɪʃn; *AmE* -ˌfɪɡjəˈr-/ [C] (*formal or technical*) an arrangement of the parts of sth or a group of things; the form or shape that this arrangement produces: *The design is based on four configurations of squares.* ◊ *The stars seemed to appear in a different configuration.*

arrangement [C, U] a group of things that are organized or placed in a particular order or position; the act of placing things in a particular order: *Has the seating arrangement been worked out yet?* ◊ *She's taking a class in flower arrangement.* See also **arrange** → ARRANGE

geography [sing.] the way in which the physical features of a place are arranged: *She knew the geography of the building well.* ◊ *The island's geography is very simple.*

design verb

1 design a kitchen/poster
2 instruments designed for use in cold conditions

1 design · invent · engineer

These words all mean to produce sth new by deciding or working out how it will look or work.

design [T] to decide how sth will look or work, especially by drawing plans or making models: *to design a dress/an office* ◊ *a badly designed kitchen* ◊ *He designed and built his own house.* ◊ *They asked me to design a poster for the campaign.* See also **design** → DEVELOPMENT *noun*

invent [T] to produce or design sth that has not existed before: *I wish television had never been invented!* ◊ *Louis Braille invented an alphabet to help blind people.* See also **invention** → DEVELOPMENT, **inventive** → CREATIVE

engineer [T, usually passive] to design and build a vehicle, machine or structure: *The car is beautifully engineered and a pleasure to drive.* ◊ *the men who engineered the tunnel*

> **NOTE** DESIGN, INVENT OR ENGINEER? When you **invent** sth, it is completely new and nothing of that kind has existed before: *Who invented the motor car?* ◊ ~~*Who designed/engineered the motor car?*~~ You can **design** or **engineer** a new version of sth that already exists: *They've designed/engineered a new car.* You would not use **invent** in this context, unless the car really is very new and different: *They've invented/designed/engineered a revolutionary new car.* ◊ *They've invented/designed/engineered a whole new type of car.*

2 design · be aimed at sth · be intended for/as/to be sth · mean

These verbs all mean to make or plan sb/sth for a particular purpose, aim or role.

design [T, usually passive] (not used in the progressive tenses) to make, plan or intend sth for a particular purpose: *The method is specifically designed for use with small groups.* ◊ *These classes are primarily designed as an introduction to the subject.* ◊ *The programme is designed to help people who have been out of work for a long time.*

be aimed at sth *phrase* to have sth as an aim: *These measures are aimed at preventing violent crime.*

be intended for/as/to be sth *phrase* to be planned or designed for a particular purpose or group of people: *The book is intended for children.* ◊ *The notes are intended as an introduction to the classes.* ◊ *The programme was intended to encourage more local involvement in education.*

mean [T, usually passive] (not used in the progressive tenses) to plan, intend or expect sb/sth to be sth or to do sth particular: *The house was clearly meant to be a family home.* ◊ (*especially BrE*) *His father meant him to be an engineer.* ◊ *I was never meant for the army* (= did not have the qualities needed to become a soldier). ◊ *Philip and Kim were meant for each other* (= are very suitable as partners).

designer *noun* See also the entry for MAKER

designer · engineer · architect · developer · creator · inventor · planner
These are all words for people who design or create new things or products.

designer [C] a person whose job is to decide how things such as clothes, furniture or tools will look by making drawings, plans or patterns: *a fashion/graphic/industrial/theatre designer* ◊ *They brought in an interior designer to suggest colour schemes for the house.*

engineer [C] a person whose job involves designing and building engines, machines, roads, bridges, etc: *a chemical/civil/electrical/mechanical engineer* ◊ *You need the advice of a qualified engineer.*

architect /ˈɑːkɪtekt; *AmE* ˈɑːrk-/ [C] a person whose job is designing buildings; a person who created or planned an idea, event or situation: *The tower was designed by architect Daniel Libeskind.* ◊ *He was one of the principal architects of the revolution.*

developer [C] a person or company that designs and creates new products: *Canada has emerged as the world's leading developer of hit board games.* ❶ **Developer** is most often used in business contexts and includes not only the act of designing a product but also the process of making it, usually to be sold. See also **develop** → DEVELOP 2

creator [C] a person who has made or invented a particular thing: *Walt Disney, the creator of Mickey Mouse* See also **create** → MAKE 1

inventor [C] a person who has invented sth or whose job is inventing things: *Trevor Bayliss, inventor of the clockwork radio* ◊ *He made a career as an inventor of quick-selling gadgets.*

NOTE CREATOR OR INVENTOR? **Creator** is used more for ideas and **inventor** is used more for physical objects, but in many cases you can use either word: *Tim Berners-Lee, creator/inventor of the World Wide Web*. A **creator** is always the creator *of* a particular thing: it is not a job or career.

planner [C] a person whose job is to plan the growth and development of a town: *town/city/urban planners* ◇ *A meeting was held with the architects and planners to finalize plans for the new shopping complex.*

desire noun See also the entry for HOPE 2

desire · need · wish · temptation · urge · impulse · inclination · whim · want · compulsion
These are all words for a feeling, especially a strong one, that you would like to have or do sth.

PATTERNS AND COLLOCATIONS
▸ a desire / a need / a wish / an urge / an inclination **for** sth
▸ the desire/need/wish/temptation/urge/impulse/inclination/compulsion **to do sth**
▸ a **strong** desire / need / wish / temptation / urge / impulse / inclination
▸ an **overwhelming** desire / need / temptation / urge / impulse
▸ an **irresistible** desire / temptation / urge / impulse
▸ a **natural** desire/wish/temptation/urge/impulse/inclination
▸ a **sudden** desire / need / urge / impulse / inclination / whim
▸ **sexual** desires / needs / urges / impulses / inclinations
▸ to **have** a desire / a need / a wish / a temptation / an urge / an impulse / an inclination / wants / a compulsion
▸ to **feel** a desire / a need / a temptation / an urge / an impulse / an inclination / a compulsion
▸ to **express / make known** a desire / need / wish
▸ to **satisfy** a desire / a need / an urge / impulse / sb's whims / sb's wants
▸ to **pander to** sb's wishes / whims / wants
▸ to **resist / fight** a desire / a temptation / an urge / an impulse

desire [C, U] (*rather formal, especially written*) a feeling that you want to have or do sth: *Most children have an insatiable desire for knowledge.* ◇ *She felt an overwhelming desire to return home.* ◇ *He now had enough money to satisfy all his desires.* ◇ (*formal*) *I have no desire (= I do not want) to discuss the matter further.* See also **desire** → WANT *verb*

need [C, U] a strong feeling that you want or must have or do sth: *She felt the need to talk to someone.* ◇ *I'm in need of some fresh air.* ◇ *It can be difficult to express our needs and desires.* See also **need** → NEED *noun*, **need** → NEED *verb*

NOTE DESIRE OR NEED? A **need** is usually stronger than a **desire**: it is usually sth which you feel you must have, not just sth that you would like; when it is used in negative sentences, however, it can mean sth that you don't want: *She had no more need of me (= did not want me any more).*

wish [C] (*especially written*) a feeling that you want to have or do sth: *I can understand her wish for secrecy.* ◇ *He had no wish to start a fight.* ◇ *His dearest wish (= what he wants most of all) is to see his grandchildren again.* ◇ *It was her dying wish that I should have it.* See also **wish** → WANT *verb*, **wish** → WISH *noun*

NOTE DESIRE OR WISH? When it is used alone, **desire** only suggests a slightly stronger feeling than **wish**. However, **desire** is often used with adjectives such as *deep, great, urgent, burning, insatiable* and *overwhelming*, expressing a much stronger feeling; **wish** is not often used with these adjectives.

temptation /temp'teɪʃn/ [C, U] the desire to do or have sth that you know is bad or wrong: *The temptation of easy profits was too much for them.* ◇ *Don't give in to temptation.* ◇ *I couldn't resist the temptation to open the letter.* See also **tempt** → TEMPT *verb*

urge [C] a strong feeling that you must do sth, especially one that is hard to control or hard to understand: *I had a sudden urge to hit him.* ◇ *Freud claimed that this behaviour was caused by the repression of sexual urges.* See also **urgent** → URGENT

NOTE NEED OR URGE? Both these words often describe feelings that seem to come from the body rather than the mind: *a/an biological/instinctive/primitive need/urge* ◇ *sexual needs/urges*. However, **needs** are usually feelings that are shared by a lot of people and are easy to understand and accept; an **urge** may be less easy to understand and sth that you try to prevent yourself from doing or expressing: *She felt a violent urge to laugh, but suppressed it, with difficulty.*

impulse /'ɪmpʌls/ [C, usually sing., U] a sudden strong desire to do sth, without stopping to think about the results: *He had a sudden impulse to stand up and sing.* ◇ *Her first impulse was to run away.* ◇ *The door was open and on an impulse she went inside.* ◇ *He tends to act on impulse.* See also **impulsive** → SPONTANEOUS

inclination /ˌɪnklɪ'neɪʃn/ [U, C] (*rather formal*) a feeling that makes you want to do sth: *He did not show the slightest inclination to leave.* ◇ *He was a loner by nature and by inclination.* ◇ *You must follow your own inclinations when choosing a career.* ❶ An **inclination** may not be a very strong feeling: people act according to their inclinations when there is no stronger force to work against them. When people lack any inclination to do sth, it shows that they do not want to do it at all. See also **inclined** → PRONE TO

whim /wɪm/ [C] (*often disapproving*) a sudden desire to do or have sth, especially when it is sth unusual or unnecessary: *He was forced to pander to her every whim.* ◇ *We bought the house on a whim.* ◇ *She hires and fires people at whim (= as and when she wants to, without good reason).*

want [C, usually pl.] something that you want: *She spent her life pandering to the wants of her children.* ❶ In this meaning, **wants** is usually used in a possessive phrase such as *my/your/his/her/our/their/the customers' wants* or *the wants of sb*. See also **want** → NEED *noun*, **want** → WANT *verb*

compulsion /kəm'pʌlʃn/ (*rather formal, written*) a strong desire to do sth that you cannot easily control, especially sth that is wrong, silly or dangerous: *He felt a great compulsion to drive too fast.* ◇ *Obsessions and compulsions often develop in people who live stressful lives.* See also **compelling** → URGENT

despair noun

despair · desperation · hopelessness · desolation
These are all words for a feeling of having no hope.

PATTERNS AND COLLOCATIONS
▸ despair / desperation **at** sth
▸ **in** despair / desperation
▸ **utter** despair / desperation / hopelessness
▸ to **drive sb to / feel** despair / hopelessness / desolation
▸ a **feeling / sense of** despair / hopelessness / desolation

despair /dɪ'speə(r); AmE dɪ'sper/ [U] the feeling of having lost all hope because a situation is so bad and you feel you can do nothing to improve it: *He gave up the struggle in despair.* ◇ *She was close to despair.* ◇ *Eventually, driven to despair, he threw himself under a train.* ◇ *One harsh word would send her into the depths of despair.* **OPP** hope → HOPE 1

desperation /ˌdespə'reɪʃn/ [U] the feeling of being in such a bad situation that you are ready to try anything to improve it without worrying about danger to yourself or others: *In desperation, she called Louise and asked for help.* ◇ *There was a note of desperation in her voice.* ◇ *The robbery was an act of sheer desperation.*

hopelessness [U] a feeling of having no hope about the future: *This way of thinking can lead to feelings of hopelessness and despair.* **OPP** hope → HOPE 1

desolation /ˌdesəˈleɪʃn/ [U] (*written*) a feeling of being very lonely and without hope: *Her death left him with a terrible sense of desolation.* See also **desolate** → LONELY

despair *verb*

despair · give up hope · lose hope · lose heart
These words all mean to stop believing that sth you want will happen.

PATTERNS AND COLLOCATIONS
▸ to despair / give up hope / lose hope **of** sth
▸ to despair / give up hope **that**...
▸ to **almost** despair / give up hope / lose hope
▸ to **never** give up hope / lose hope / lose heart
▸ to give up / lose **all** hope
▸ **Don't** despair / give up hope.

despair /dɪˈspeə(r); *AmE* dɪˈsper/ [I] to stop believing that there is any possibility that a bad situation will change or improve: *Don't despair! We'll think of a way out of this.* ◇ *They'd almost despaired of ever having children.* ◇ *I despair of him; he can't keep a job for more than six months.*

give up 'hope *phrase* to stop believing that sth you want will happen: *Don't give up hope yet.* ◇ *They have given up hope of finding any more survivors.* See also **hope** → HOPE *noun* 1

lose 'hope *phrase* to stop believing that sth you want will happen: *We have lost all hope of a negotiated settlement.* ◇ *I never lost hope, even when I was told I would never walk again.* See also **hope** → HOPE *noun* 1

> **NOTE** GIVE UP HOPE OR LOSE HOPE? You often **lose hope** gradually as a situation gets worse or the chances of sth happening seem to get less. You **give up hope** when you realize at a particular point that sth is not going to happen as you want.

lose 'heart *idiom* to stop hoping for sth or trying to do sth because you have not been successful so far and you no longer feel confident: *We mustn't lose heart just because of a temporary setback.* **OPP** take heart ❶ If you **take heart**, you start to feel more positive about sth: *The government can take heart from the latest opinion polls.*

desperate *adj.*

desperate · in despair · despairing · suicidal · hopeless
These words all describe sb who feels or shows little or no hope.

PATTERNS AND COLLOCATIONS
▸ desperate / in despair / despairing **about** sth
▸ a desperate / despairing **cry / look**
▸ to **feel** desperate / suicidal / hopeless
▸ **almost** desperate / in despair / despairing / suicidal

desperate /ˈdespərət/ (of a person) feeling that you have little hope and are ready to do anything without worrying about danger to yourself or others; (of an action) giving little hope of success; tried when everything else has failed: *I was starting to get desperate.* ◇ *Somewhere out there was a desperate man, cold, hungry, hunted.* ◇ *I heard sounds of a desperate struggle.* ◇ *He made a desperate bid for freedom.* ◇ *She clung to the edge in a desperate attempt to save herself.*
▸ **desperately** *adv.*: *He took a deep breath, desperately trying to keep calm.* ◇ *She looked desperately around for a weapon.*

in de'spair *phrase* feeling that you have lost all hope: *Ruth shook her head in despair.* ◇ *Eventually, he gave up in despair.*

despairing (*written*) feeling or showing that you have lost all hope: *With every day that passed he became ever more despairing.* ◇ *With a despairing cry, she flung herself onto the sofa.*
▸ **despairingly** *adv.*: *She looked despairingly at the mess.*

suicidal /ˌsuːɪˈsaɪdl; *BrE* also ˌsjuːɪ-/ people who are **suicidal** feel that they want to kill themselves: *On bad days I felt almost suicidal.* ◇ *Some sufferers admit to suicidal tendencies.* See also **suicide** → MURDER

hopeless feeling or showing no hope: *She felt lonely and hopeless.* ◇ *With a hopeless shrug of resignation, he turned back.* **OPP** hopeful → OPTIMISTIC

> **NOTE** IN DESPAIR, DESPAIRING OR HOPELESS? If you are **in despair** or **despairing**, you often feel frustrated that sth is not going to happen or change after waiting or trying for a long time. This feeling is often shown as anger, crying or shouting. If you are **hopeless**, you are sad and depressed because you feel that nothing good can happen. This feeling is often shown as sadness or being quiet.

despicable *adj.*

despicable · cheap · dishonourable · worthless · feckless · contemptible
These words all describe people or actions that deserve hatred or no respect.

PATTERNS AND COLLOCATIONS
▸ despicable / dishonourable **of** sb
▸ despicable / dishonourable **conduct**
▸ a despicable / worthless / feckless / contemptible **man / woman**
▸ a worthless / feckless **husband / wife / father / mother / parent**
▸ **absolutely** despicable / worthless

despicable /dɪˈspɪkəbl/ (*formal, disapproving*) deserving hatred and condemnation (= the expression of very strong disapproval): *That was a despicable act.* ◇ *I hate you! You're despicable.* See also **despise** → HATE

cheap (*disapproving*) (of a person) having a low status and therefore not deserving respect; (of an action) unpleasant or unkind and rather obvious: *His treatment of her made her feel cheap* (= ashamed, because she had lost her respect for herself). ◇ *I was tired of her cheap jokes at my expense.* ❶ When **cheap** is used to describe a person, it nearly always refers in an offensive and disapproving way to a woman who likes to attract men and have sex: *a cheap floozy/tart/whore.* When used to describe an action, **cheap** usually collocates with *joke, laugh, trick* or *jibe*.

dishonourable (*BrE*) (*AmE* **dishonorable**) /dɪsˈɒnərəbl; *AmE* -ˈɑːn-/ (*rather formal, disapproving*) not deserving any respect; immoral or unacceptable: *It would have been dishonourable of her not to keep her promise.* ◇ *He was given a dishonourable discharge* (= an order to leave the army for unacceptable behaviour). **OPP** honourable → RESPECTABLE, honourable → WORTHY, See also **dishonour** → DISGRACE *noun* 2
▸ **dishonourably** *adv.*: *She acted dishonourably in accepting money for information.*

worthless (*disapproving*) (of a person) having no good qualities or useful skills: *He's just a worthless individual.* ◇ *Constant rejections made her feel worthless.* See also **worth** → VALUE *noun* 1

feckless (*rather formal, written, disapproving*) (of a person) having a weak character; not behaving in a responsible way: *Her husband was a charming, but lazy and feckless man.*

contemptible /kənˈtemptəbl/ (*formal, disapproving*) not deserving any respect at all: *I will not tolerate this mean and contemptible behaviour.* See also **contempt** → CONTEMPT

destroy *verb* See also the entry for ERADICATE

destroy · wipe sb/sth out · devastate · ravage · decimate · annihilate · exterminate · zap
These words all mean to damage, remove or kill sb/sth so that they no longer exist.

PATTERNS AND COLLOCATIONS
▸ to destroy / wipe out / devastate / ravage / decimate a **village / town / city**
▸ a **bomb / blast** destroys / devastates **buildings**
▸ to destroy / wipe out / decimate / annihilate / exterminate / zap **the enemy**
▸ to destroy / wipe out **profits / savings**
▸ a/an **earthquake / flood / fire** destroys / devastates / ravages sth

destroy [T] to damage sth so badly that it no longer exists or works; to kill sb: *The building was completely destroyed by fire.* ◇ *They've destroyed all the evidence.* ◇ *Heat gradually destroys vitamin C.* ◇ (*figurative*) *Failure was slowly destroying him* (= making him less confident and happy).
▸ **destruction** *noun* [U]: *a tidal wave bringing **death and destruction** in its wake* ◇ ***weapons of mass destruction***
,**wipe sb/sth 'out** *phrasal verb* to destroy or remove sb/sth completely: *Whole villages were wiped out by the earthquake.* ◇ *a campaign to wipe out malaria* ◇ *Their life savings were wiped out.*
devastate /'devəsteɪt/ [T] to completely destroy a place, area or building: *The bomb devastated much of the old part of the city.* See also **devastating** → DISASTROUS
▸ **devastation** *noun* [U]: *The bomb caused widespread devastation.*

NOTE DESTROY OR DEVASTATE? Devastate is stronger than **destroy**, but is only used about places or buildings, not substances or objects. When used about people it has a different meaning.

ravage /'rævɪdʒ/ [T, usually passive] (*rather formal*) to damage a place or business very badly: *The countryside has been ravaged by pollution.* ◇ *the flood-/quake-/ tornado-/war-ravaged country* ◇ *a recession that has ravaged the textile industry*
▸ **ravages** *noun* [pl.]: *the ravages of inflation/poverty/ war* ◇ *Her looks had not survived **the ravages of time**.*
decimate /'desɪmeɪt/ [T, usually passive] to kill large numbers of animals, plants or people in a particular area; to make an industry or service much weaker: *The rabbit population was decimated by the disease.* ◇ *Rural transport provision has been decimated.*
▸ **decimation** *noun* [U]: *the decimation of the rainforests*
annihilate /ə'naɪəleɪt/ [T] to destroy or defeat sb completely: *The human race has enough weapons to annihilate itself.*
▸ **annihilation** *noun* [U]: *the annihilation of the whole human race*
exterminate /ɪk'stɜːmɪneɪt; AmE -'stɜːrm-/ [T] to deliberately kill all the members of a group of people or animals: *They use poison to exterminate moles.* See also **extermination** → MASSACRE

NOTE DECIMATE OR EXTERMINATE? People, animals or plants are usually **decimated** by accident, especially as a result of a disease in which most (but not all) of them die. If people **exterminate** animals or people, they deliberately kill all of them.

zap (**-pp-**) [T] (*informal*) to destroy, kill or hit sb/sth suddenly and with force: *The monster got **zapped** by a flying saucer* (= in a computer game). ◇ *He jumped like a man who'd been **zapped with** 1000 volts.*

detailed *adj.*

detailed · comprehensive · careful · thorough · close · rigorous · minute · in-depth · exhaustive · full-scale
These words all describe an act of considering, studying or testing sth in a way that pays great attention to detail and/ or includes everything that might be considered.

PATTERNS AND COLLOCATIONS
▸ a detailed / a comprehensive / a careful / a thorough / a close / a rigorous / a minute / an in-depth / an exhaustive **analysis**
▸ a detailed / a comprehensive / a careful / a thorough / a close / a rigorous / an in-depth / an exhaustive / a full-scale **study / investigation**
▸ a detailed / a comprehensive / a careful / a thorough / a close / a rigorous / a minute / an exhaustive **examination** of sth
▸ a detailed / a comprehensive / a careful / a thorough / a close / an in-depth **look** at sth
▸ a detailed / a careful / a thorough / a rigorous / an exhaustive / a full-scale **search**
▸ detailed / comprehensive / careful / thorough / rigorous / in-depth / exhaustive **research**
▸ detailed / comprehensive / thorough / rigorous / exhaustive **tests**
▸ a detailed / a comprehensive / a thorough / an in-depth / an exhaustive **survey**
▸ detailed / comprehensive / thorough / in-depth / exhaustive **coverage**
▸ detailed / comprehensive / careful / minute **instructions**
▸ a detailed / a comprehensive / a thorough / an in-depth / an exhaustive **discussion**
▸ detailed / comprehensive / thorough / in-depth / exhaustive **knowledge**
▸ detailed / careful / thorough / close **consideration**
▸ detailed / careful / close / rigorous / minute **attention**

detailed giving many details and a lot of information; paying great attention to details: *She was able to give a detailed description of her attacker.* ◇ *He gave detailed instructions on what to do in an emergency.* See also **detail** → INFORMATION
comprehensive /,kɒmprɪ'hensɪv; AmE ,kɑːm-/ including all, or almost all, the items, details, facts or information that may be concerned: *a comprehensive list of addresses* ◇ *You are advised to take out comprehensive insurance* (= covering all risks).
▸ **comprehensively** *adv.*: *The matter has been comprehensively discussed.*
careful giving a lot of attention to details when considering, studying or explaining sth: *This is a very careful piece of work.* ◇ *After careful consideration we have decided to offer you the job.* **OPP** careless → LAX, See also **care** → CARE *noun*
▸ **carefully** *adv.*: *Read the contract carefully before signing it.* ◇ *He chose his words carefully.*
thorough including everything and with great attention to detail: *You will need a thorough understanding of the subject.* ◇ *The police carried out a thorough investigation.* See also **thorough** → CONSCIENTIOUS ❶ Thorough is used especially to describe sb's *knowledge* or *understanding* or the way they carry out a task.
▸ **thoroughly** *adv.*: *Wash the fruit thoroughly before use.* ◇ *The work had not been done very thoroughly.*
close [only before noun] giving careful attention to detail when looking at or considering sth: *Take a close look at this photograph.* ◇ *On closer examination the painting proved to be a fake.*
▸ **closely** *adv.*: *I sat and watched everyone very closely.*
rigorous /'rɪgərəs/ very thorough, especially when study-ing or testing sth or dealing with a problem: *Few people have gone into the topic in such rigorous detail.* ◇ *The second team adopted a much more rigorous approach to the problem.*
▸ **rigorously** *adv.*: *Each product is rigorously tested before being put on sale.*
▸ **rigour** (*BrE*) (*AmE* **rigor**) /'rɪgə(r)/: *academic/intellec-tual/scientific rigour*
minute /maɪ'njuːt; AmE also -'nuːt/ giving very detailed attention to sth: *A minute inspection of the vase revealed tiny cracks in the glaze.* ◇ *She remembered everything in minute detail/in the minutest detail(s).*
▸ **minutely** *adv.*: *The agreement has been examined minutely.*
,**in-'depth** [usually before noun] knowing or considering a subject in a lot of detail: *We will be providing in-depth coverage of the election as the results come in.* ◇ *Tonight's*

programme is an in-depth look at the long-term effects of unemployment.

exhaustive /ɪɡˈzɔːstɪv/ very complete, especially when discussing, studying or testing sth: *Exhaustive research has been carried out into the effects of the drug.* ◇ *The information in this leaflet is not intended to be exhaustive, but it does tell you the basic facts.*

▸ **exhaustively** *adv.*: *Every product is exhaustively tested before being sold.*

full-scale [only before noun] (of an organized activity) that is as complete as possible: *Rebel troops launched a full-scale attack on the city.* ◇ *The police made a full-scale search of the area.* See also **scale** → LEVEL

NOTE WHICH WORD? In most cases there are several different words from this group that you could use. Some of these words focus more on *depth*, that is the quality of understanding or providing a lot of details about sth: these include **detailed**, **close**, **minute** and **in-depth**. Some of these words focus more on *range*, that is the quality of including everything about a subject from every possible point of view: these include **comprehensive**, **exhaustive** and **full-scale**. **Thorough** and **rigorous** focus on both depth and range.

determination *noun*

determination · persistence · resolve · spirit · purpose · tenacity · perseverance
These are all words for personal qualities that help you to continue doing sth that is difficult or unpleasant.

PATTERNS AND COLLOCATIONS
▸ determination / resolve **to do sth**
▸ **great** determination / persistence / resolve / spirit / purpose / tenacity / perseverance
▸ **sheer** / **dogged** determination / persistence / perseverance
▸ to **show** (your) determination / persistence / resolve / spirit / tenacity
▸ to **have** determination / persistence / spirit / purpose / tenacity / perseverance

determination [U] (*often approving*) the quality that makes you continue trying to do sth even when this is difficult: *The key to his success was his dogged determination to see things through.* ◇ *She fought the illness with courage and determination.*
persistence /pəˈsɪstəns; *AmE* pərˈs-/ [U] the fact of continuing to try to do sth in spite of difficulties, especially when other people are against you and think that you are being annoying or unreasonable: *His persistence was finally rewarded when the insurance company agreed to pay for the damage.* ◇ *It was her sheer persistence that wore them down in the end.* See also **persist** → PERSIST
resolve /rɪˈzɒlv; *AmE* rɪˈzɑːlv/ [U] (*formal, often approving*) strong determination to do sth that you believe to be right: *The difficulties in her way merely strengthened her resolve.* ◇ *He did not weaken in his resolve.*
spirit [U] (*approving*) a personal quality that is a combination of courage, determination and energy: *Show a little **fighting spirit**.* ◇ *Although the team lost, they played with tremendous spirit.* ◇ *They took away his freedom and **broke his spirit**.* See also **spirited** → LIVELY
purpose [U] (*rather formal*) the ability to plan sth and work successfully to achieve it: *He has enormous confidence and **strength of purpose**.*
tenacity /təˈnæsəti/ [U] (*rather formal, written*) the determination to continue trying to do sth: *They competed with skill and tenacity.*

NOTE DETERMINATION OR TENACITY? Determination has a wider range of meaning than **tenacity**. People often show **determination** in the face of difficulty, danger or suffering; it is often spoken of in the phrase *courage and*

determination. People show **tenacity** in less important or serious situations, that do not need courage, but do require people to keep trying if they are to succeed.

perseverance /ˌpɜːsɪˈvɪərəns; *AmE* ˌpɜːrsəˈvɪr-/ [U] (*rather formal, approving*) the fact of continuing to try to achieve a particular aim in spite of failure or difficulties: *They showed great perseverance in the face of difficulty.* See also **persevere** → PERSIST

NOTE PERSISTENCE OR PERSEVERANCE? People show **perseverance** in the face of difficult circumstances, usually created by situations outside anyone's control, such as illness, bad economic conditions, or just bad luck. **Persistence** is necessary when other people create difficulties, either by refusing to help or by actively trying to stop you.

determine *verb*

determine · shape · govern · dictate · form · decide · rule
These words all mean to control or to influence the way that sth happens or that sb/sth develops.

shape	govern	determine
form	rule	dictate
		decide

PATTERNS AND COLLOCATIONS
▸ to determine / shape / govern / dictate / decide **how…**
▸ to determine / govern / dictate / decide **what** / **when** / **why…**
▸ to determine / dictate **that** …
▸ to determine / shape / dictate / decide the **outcome** / **result** (of sth)
▸ to determine / shape / dictate the **course** / **direction** / **future** (of sth)
▸ to determine / shape / form the **character** of sb / sth
▸ to determine / shape / govern **behaviour**
▸ a **factor** determines / shapes / governs / decides sth
▸ a **force** determines / shapes / governs sth
▸ to be **largely** determined / governed / dictated by sth

determine [T, often passive] (*formal*) to make sth happen in a particular way or be of a particular type: *Female employment was determined by economic and social factors.* ◇ *The physical capabilities of a plant determine where it can and cannot live.* ◇ *Upbringing plays an important part in determining a person's character.*
shape [T] to have an important influence on the way sb/sth develops: *Historical events helped to shape the town.* ◇ *She had a leading role in shaping party policy.* ◇ *Religion had long been losing its power to shape and control behaviour.*
govern [T, often passive] (*rather formal*) to control or influence how sth happens or works or how sb behaves: *Prices are very much governed by market demand.* ◇ *We need changes in the **law governing** school attendance.* ◇ *All his decisions had been entirely governed by self-interest.*
dictate [T, I] (of particular circumstances) to control what happens or the way that sth happens: *It's generally your job that dictates where you live now.* ◇ *Circumstances dictated that I had to wait nearly two years.* ◇ *This is clearly the best choice, unless financial considerations **dictate otherwise**.* ◇ *She had to remain indoors for 30 days before the wedding, as **custom dictates**.*
form [T] to have an important influence on the way sb's character or ideas develop: *Positive and negative experiences form a child's character.* ◇ *No other work of fiction has had such an influence in forming public attitudes.*

NOTE SHAPE OR FORM? Both these words can be used to talk about the influences on a person's character or ideas: *to shape/form sb's character/ideas/attitude/opinions*. **Shape**, but not **form** can also be used to talk about influencing sb's behaviour or a course of events: *Historical events helped to form the town.* ◇ *the power of religion to form behaviour*

decide [T, I] to determine the result of sth: *A mixture of skill and good luck decided the outcome of the game.* ◇ *In the end, price was the deciding factor.*

rule [T, often passive] (*often disapproving*) to be the main thing that influences and controls sb's life or choices, especially in a way that restricts them: *The pursuit of money **ruled his life**.* ◇ *We live in a society where we are ruled by the clock.*

determined *adj.*
1 determined to succeed
2 determined opposition

1 determined · resolved · intent on/upon sth · bent on sth · insistent
These words all describe people who have made a firm decision to do sth and will not let anyone change their mind.

PATTERNS AND COLLOCATIONS
▸ intent / bent / insistent **on** sth
▸ intent / insistent **upon** (doing) sth
▸ determined / resolved / insistent **that...**
▸ determined / resolved **to do** sth

determined [not before noun] having made a firm decision to do or not do sth, make sth happen or prevent sth from happening, and not willing to let anyone prevent you: *I'm determined to succeed.* ◇ *They were quite determined that he wasn't going to do it.* See also **determine** → DECIDE

resolved /rɪ'zɒlvd; AmE rɪ'zɑːlvd/ [not before noun] (*formal*) determined: *I was resolved not to see him.*

in'tent on/upon sth [not before noun] (*formal*) determined to do sth, especially sth that will harm other people: *They were intent on murder.* ◇ *Are you intent upon destroying my reputation?*

'bent on sth determined to do sth even though the results may be bad: *She seems bent on making life difficult for me.*

insistent /ɪn'sɪstənt/ [not usually before noun] (*rather formal*) demanding sth firmly and refusing to accept any opposition or excuses: *Why are you so insistent that we leave tonight?* ◇ *She didn't want to go but her brother was insistent.* ❶ Someone who is **insistent** repeats over and over again what they want or what they think should be done. See also **insist** → DEMAND *verb*

2 determined · persistent · heroic · resolute · single-minded · dogged · tenacious
These words all describe people and actions having a clear and definite purpose, and continuing to do sth even when it is difficult.

PATTERNS AND COLLOCATIONS
▸ determined / persistent / resolute / single-minded / tenacious **in** sth
▸ determined / resolute / single-minded **about** sth
▸ determined / persistent / heroic / resolute **opposition** to sth
▸ a determined / persistent / heroic **struggle / effort / attempt**
▸ determined / persistent / resolute **action**
▸ a determined / heroic / resolute **stand**
▸ determined / heroic / dogged **resistance**
▸ heroic / resolute / single-minded / dogged **determination**
▸ a heroic / resolute / dogged / tenacious **defence** of sth
▸ a determined / persistent / resolute / tenacious **man / woman**

determined showing that you want to do sth very much and trying hard not to let anyone or any difficulties stop you: *The proposal had perished in the face of determined opposition.* ◇ *She's a very determined young woman.*

persistent /pə'sɪstənt; AmE pər's-/ (*rather formal*) continuing to do sth in spite of difficulties, especially when other people are against you and think that you are being annoying or unreasonable: *She can be very persistent*

when she wants something. ◇ *He introduced a plan for dealing with **persistent offenders** (= people who continue to commit crimes after they have been caught and punished).* See also **persist** → PERSIST

▸ **persistently** *adv.*: *They have persistently denied claims of illegal dealing.*

heroic /hə'rəʊɪk; AmE -'roʊ-/ (*approving*) showing great determination to succeed or to achieve sth, especially sth difficult: *We watched our team's heroic struggle to win back the cup.*

resolute /'rezəluːt/ (*rather formal*) having or showing great determination to keep to a plan or decision that you have made: *She became even more resolute in her opposition to the plan.* ◇ *Her voice sounded calm and resolute.* **OPP** **irresolute** ❶ Someone who is **irresolute** is unable to decide what to do.

▸ **resolutely** *adv.*: *They remain resolutely opposed to the idea.*

single-'minded (*sometimes disapproving*) only thinking about one particular aim or goal because you are determined to achieve sth: *She is very single-minded about her career.* ◇ *He spent his life in the single-minded pursuit of wealth and power.* ❶ **Single-minded** can suggest that the person does not care about what other people think.

▸ **single-mindedly** *adv.*: *They devoted themselves single-mindedly to making money.*

dogged /'dɒgɪd; AmE 'dɔːg-/ [usually before noun] (*usually approving*) showing determination; not giving up easily: *His success is down to sheer dogged persistence.* ◇ *Despite their dogged defence of the city, the enemy was too strong for them.* ❶ **Dogged** is usually used to describe positive qualities in people, especially *determination*, *persistence* and *perseverance*.

▸ **doggedly** *adv.*: *Although the men fought doggedly on, a sense of hopeless despair engulfed them.*

tenacious /tə'neɪʃəs/ (*rather formal, written*) that does not stop holding sth or give sth up easily: *He paused, without releasing his tenacious grip.* ◇ *The party has kept its tenacious hold on power for more than twenty years.* ❶ Collocates of **tenacious** include *grip* and *hold* in both literal and figurative meanings, and *defence*.

▸ **tenaciously** *adv.*: *Though seriously ill, he still clings tenaciously to life.*

develop *verb*
1 develop from a small village into a thriving resort
2 develop new software

1 See also the entry for IMPROVE 2
develop · move · evolve · progress · gain ground · advance · shape up · come on/along · mature
These words all mean to gradually become bigger, better, stronger or more advanced.

PATTERNS AND COLLOCATIONS
▸ to develop / move / evolve / progress / mature **from** sth
▸ to develop / move / evolve / progress **to** sth
▸ to develop / evolve / mature **into** sth
▸ to develop / move / evolve / progress / advance **towards** sth
▸ to develop / move / evolve / progress / advance **beyond** sth
▸ an **idea** develops / evolves / gains ground
▸ a **style / theory** develops / evolves
▸ a **war / campaign** develops / progresses
▸ to develop / move / evolve / progress / gain ground / advance / mature **rapidly / slowly**
▸ to develop / move / evolve / progress / gain ground / advance **steadily**
▸ to develop / move / evolve / progress / advance **further**
▸ to be developing / progressing / shaping up / coming on **well**

develop [I] to gradually become bigger, better, stronger or more advanced; to start to have a skill or quality that becomes better and stronger: *The child is developing normally.* ◇ *The place has rapidly developed from a small fishing community into a thriving tourist resort.* ◇ *Their relationship has developed over a number of years.* See also **development** → PROGRESS

move [I] (always used with an adverb or preposition) (*rather informal*) to make progress in the way or direction mentioned: *Time is **moving on**.* ◊ *Share prices **moved ahead** today.* ◊ *Things are not moving as fast as we hoped.* ❶ **Move** is usually followed by an adverb of direction such as *on, ahead* or *up*, or an adverb indicating speed such as *fast, slowly, quickly, rapidly,* or *steadily*.

evolve /i'vɒlv; *AmE* i'vɑːlv/ [I] (*rather formal*) to develop gradually, especially from a simple to a more complicated form: *The idea evolved from a drawing I discovered in the attic.* ◊ *The company has evolved into a major chemical manufacturer.* See also **evolve** → TURN 2
▸ **evolution** /ˌiːvə'luːʃn; ˌev-/ *noun* [U]: *In politics Britain has preferred evolution to revolution* (= gradual development to sudden violent change).

progress /prə'gres/ [I] to improve or develop over a period of time; to make progress: *The course allows students to progress at their own speed.* ◊ *Work on the new road is progressing slowly.* ❶ In this meaning **progress** is used to talk about a person such as a student who is learning over a period of time, or a piece of work or a project. See also **progress, progression** → PROGRESS *noun*

gain 'ground *idiom* to become more powerful or successful: *Sterling continues to gain ground against the dollar.* ◊ *These ideas slowly gained ground over the next ten years.* ❶ **Gain ground** is most often used to talk about a *system*, a *party* or *movement*, or sb's *views* or *ideas*.

advance [I] (of knowledge or technology) to develop and improve: *Our knowledge of the disease has advanced considerably in recent years.* ◊ *As medical science advances, treatments are becoming more and more expensive.* See also **advance, advancement** → PROGRESS *noun*

shape 'up *phrasal verb* (often used in the progressive tenses) (*rather informal, especially journalism*) to develop in a particular way, especially in a satisfactory way: *Our plans are shaping up nicely* (= showing signs that they will be successful). ◊ *It's shaping up to be an exciting climax to the championships.*

come 'on/along *phrasal verb* (usually used in the progressive tenses) (*spoken*) to improve or develop in the way you want: *'How's the project going?' 'Oh, it's coming on.'* ◊ *It was spring, and the garden was coming along nicely.*

mature /mə'tʃʊə(r); -'tjʊə(r); *AmE* -'tʃʊr; -'tʊr/ [I] (*rather formal*) to fully develop a particular skill or quality: *She has matured into one of the country's finest actresses.*

2 See also the entry for MAKE 1
develop · pioneer · evolve
These words all mean to think of or produce a new idea or product and make it successful.

PATTERNS AND COLLOCATIONS
▸ to develop/ pioneer/ evolve a/ an **idea/ technique/ method/ strategy** / system / way / style / design / policy / plan
▸ to develop/ pioneer a/ an **concept/ model/ approach/ scheme** / project / service / technology
▸ to develop/ evolve a **theory/ framework/ programme**
▸ a/ an **scientist/ team/ group/ institute/ company/ authority** develops/ pioneers sth

develop [T] to think of or produce a new idea or product and make it successful: *The company develops and markets new software.* ◊ *A new type of painkilling drug has recently been developed.* See also **developer** → DESIGNER

pioneer /ˌpaɪə'nɪə(r); *AmE* -'nɪr/ [T, often passive] (*especially written*) to be one of the first people to do, discover or use sth new: *This is a new technique, pioneered by surgeons in a London hospital.* ❶ **Pioneer** is often used in scientific contexts. People typically **pioneer** a *treatment, new approach* or *technique*. It is often used in the passive, to talk about where a treatment or technique was first developed. See also **pioneer** → LEADER *noun* 2

evolve /i'vɒlv; *AmE* i'vɑːlv/ [T] (*rather formal, written, especially business*) to develop sth gradually, especially from a simple to a more complicated form: *Each school*

must evolve its own way of working. ❶ People in organizations typically **evolve** a *method, system, policy, style* or *technique*.

development *noun*

development · design · creation · innovation · invention
These are all words for the process or act of creating sth new, or for the thing created.

PATTERNS AND COLLOCATIONS
▸ sb's **new/ latest** design/ creation/ innovation/ invention
▸ a **brilliant** design/ innovation/ invention
▸ a/ an **ingenious/ wonderful** design/ invention
▸ **product** development/ design/ innovation
▸ the development/ design **process**

development [U, C] the process of producing or creating sth new or more advanced; a new or advanced product: *the development of vaccines against tropical diseases* ◊ *A more powerful version of this engine is currently **in development*** (= being developed). ◊ *developments in aviation technology*

design [U, C] the art or process of deciding how sth will look, work, etc. by drawing plans, making models, etc; a drawing or plan from which sth may be made: *the design and development of new products* ◊ *a course in **art and design*** ◊ *designs for aircraft* ◊ *I made this one **to my very own design**.* See also **design** → DESIGN *noun*, **design** → DESIGN *verb*

creation [U, C] the act or process of making sth new, or of causing sth to exist that did not exist before; a thing that sb has made, especially sth artistic or imaginative: *Job creation needs to be the top priority.* ◊ *The committee recommended the creation of a new government agency to be responsible for the environment.* ◊ *a literary creation* See also **create** → MAKE 1, **creative** → CREATIVE

innovation /ˌɪnə'veɪʃn/ [U, C] the introduction of new things, ideas or ways of doing sth; a new idea or way of doing sth: *an age of technological innovation* ◊ *recent innovations in steel-making technology* See also **innovative** → CREATIVE, **innovator** → LEADER 2
▸ **innovate** *verb* [I]: *We must constantly adapt and innovate to ensure success in a growing market.*

invention [C, U] a thing or idea that has been invented; the act of inventing sth: *Fax machines were a wonderful invention at the time.* ◊ *Such changes have not been seen since the invention of the printing press.* See also **invent** → DESIGN *verb* 1, **inventive** → CREATIVE

devote *verb*

devote · dedicate · commit · give sth over to sth
These words all mean to give a lot of your time and effort to a particular activity or purpose because you think it is important

PATTERNS AND COLLOCATIONS
▸ to devote sth/ dedicate sth/ commit sth/ give sth over **to** sb/ sth
▸ to devote/ dedicate **yourself** to sb/ sth
▸ to devote/ dedicate/ commit/ give over your **life/ time** to sb/ sth
▸ to devote/ dedicate/ commit (your) **resources/ funds** to sb/ sth
▸ to devote/ dedicate/ give over (a) **space/ page/ chapter/ section**
▸ to devote/ dedicate your **effort/ energy**
▸ to devote/ give over your **attention/ thoughts**
▸ to **entirely/ mainly** devote/ dedicate sth/ yourself to sb/ sth
▸ to **exclusively/solely/specifically** devote sth/yourself/dedicate sth/ yourself/ give sth over to sb/ sth

devote [T] (*rather formal*) to give a lot of your time, effort, attention or resources to a particular activity or purpose because you think it is important: *I could only devote two hours a day to work on the project.* ◊ *He devoted all his attention to his mother.* ◊ *Most companies devote resources to quality control and product testing.* See also **devotee** → FAN

▸ **devotion** /dɪˈvəʊʃn; AmE -ˈvoʊ-/ noun [U, sing.]: (approving) Her devotion to the job left her with very little free time. ◇ The judge praised the firefighters for their courage and devotion to duty. See also **devotion** → LOVE noun 2

dedicate /ˈdedɪkeɪt/ [T] (rather formal, usually approving) to give a lot of your time, effort or resources to a particular activity or purpose because you think it is important: She dedicates herself to her work. ◇ He dedicated his life to helping the poor. See also **dedicated** → RELIABLE 1

▸ **dedication** noun [U]: (approving) I really admire Gina for her dedication to her family. ◇ The job requires total dedication.

> **NOTE** DEVOTE OR DEDICATE? There is little difference in meaning between these words. **Dedicate** is usually used in an approving way; **devote** can be either approving or neutral (= neither approving nor disapproving), although the nouns **devotion** and **dedication** are both approving. **Devote** can be used with a slightly larger range of nouns, including thoughts and attention: He dedicated all his attention to his mother. By far the most frequent collocates of **dedicate** are yourself and your life.

commit (-tt-) [T] (rather formal) to spend money or time on sb/sth: The council has committed large amounts of money to housing projects. See also **committed** → RELIABLE 1

▸ **commitment** noun [U]: (approving) He was best known for his lifelong commitment to the socialist cause. ◇ I was saddened to see their lack of commitment.

give sth 'over to sth phrasal verb [usually passive] to use sth for one particular purpose: This gallery is given over to British art.

diagrams and charts

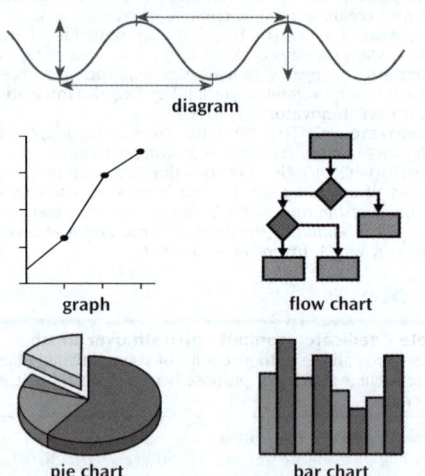

diagram

graph

flow chart

pie chart

bar chart

diagram noun

diagram · figure · chart · illustration · graph · pie chart · bar chart · grid · flow chart
These are all words for ways in which information is presented without using words, for example using lines or drawings.

PATTERNS AND COLLOCATIONS
▸ **in** a diagram / a figure / a chart / an illustration / a graph / a pie chart / a bar chart / a flow chart
▸ **on** a diagram / chart / graph
▸ a **simple** diagram / chart / graph / pie chart / bar chart / grid / flow chart

▸ to **draw** a diagram / chart / graph / pie chart / bar chart / grid / flow chart
▸ to **show** sth in / on a diagram / a chart / an illustration / a graph / a pie chart
▸ to **show / present** sth as a pie chart / bar chart
▸ to **produce** a diagram / chart / graph / pie chart / bar chart
▸ **See** the diagram / figure / chart / illustration / graph / pie chart / bar chart / flow chart...
▸ a diagram / a figure / a chart / an illustration / a graph / a pie chart / a bar chart / a flow chart **shows** sth
▸ a diagram / figure / chart / graph **illustrates / indicates** sth

diagram [C] a simple drawing using lines to explain where sth is, how sth works or what sth is like: She drew a diagram of an electrical circuit on the board. ◇ The whole process can be shown in a simple diagram.

figure (abbr. **fig.**) [C] (written) a picture or diagram in a book that is referred to by a number: Food passes down the oesophagus to the stomach (see fig. 4). ◇ Figure 4 represents the process of soil erosion. ❶ Figure or fig. is usually used in technical or educational books

chart [C] a page or sheet of information in the form of diagrams or lists of figures: A chart on the wall showed sales figures for the previous year. ◇ The Greek astronomer Hipparchus drew the first accurate star chart. See also **table** → LIST

illustration /ˌɪləˈstreɪʃn/ [C] a drawing or picture in a book or magazine, especially one that explains sth: The book has 50 full-colour illustrations. ◇ The illustration on page 10 shows the layout of the area. See also **illustrate** → DECORATE, **illustrate** → EXPLAIN 1, **picture** → PICTURE

graph /ɡræf; BrE also ɡrɑːf/ [C] a planned drawing, consisting of a line or lines, showing how two or more sets of numbers or measurements are related to each other: Draw a graph showing how wages increased in the 18th century. ◇ Plot the information on a graph.

'pie chart [C] a diagram consisting of a circle that is divided into sections to show the size of particular amounts in relation to the whole: Produce a pie chart of each week's figures.

'bar chart (AmE also **'bar graph**) [C] a diagram that uses narrow bands of different heights to show different amounts, so that they can be compared: The bar chart shows what the average American consumes in a year compared with other nationalities.

grid [C] a pattern of squares on a map that are marked with letters or numbers to help you find the exact position of a place: Each of the grid squares on the map is equal to one square kilometre. ◇ The **grid reference** is C8.

'flow chart (also **'flow diagram**) [C] a diagram that shows the connections between the different stages of a process or parts of a system: The flow chart below shows what happens to the product between manufacture and final delivery.

dictate to sb phrasal verb

dictate to sb · push sb around/about · tyrannize · order sb around/about · lay down the law
These words all mean to tell sb what to do in a rude or forceful way.

| push sb about/ around | dictate to sb | tyrannize |
| order sb about/ around | lay down the law | |

PATTERNS AND COLLOCATIONS
▸ sb **will not be** dictated to / pushed around / tyrannized (by sb)
▸ to **allow yourself to be** dictated to / pushed around
▸ sb **thinks they can** push sb around / order sb around

dic'tate to sb phrasal verb [often passive] to give orders to sb, often in a rude and aggressive way: She refused to be dictated to by anyone.

,**push sb a'round/a'bout** phrasal verb (*rather informal*) to keep telling sb what to do in a rude and aggressive way: *She's wrong if she thinks she can push me around.*

tyrannize (*BrE* also **-ise**) /'tɪrənaɪz/ [T, I] (*rather formal, written*) to use your power to give orders to sb and treat them in a cruel and unfair way: *After years of obeying her own husband's mother, she felt that she was now entitled to tyrannize her daughter-in-law.* ◇ *Since he took power five years ago, he has **tyrannized over** the people of this small nation.*

,**order sb a'round/'a'bout** phrasal verb (*rather informal*) to keep telling sb what to do in a rude or annoying way: *How dare he order her around like that?*

> **NOTE DICTATE TO SB, PUSH SB AROUND** OR **ORDER SB AROUND?** If sb **dictates to** sb else, they say what they should do, without listening to them or taking their opinions into account, especially because they believe they are in a strong position to do so. If sb **pushes sb about/around** they tell them what to do, often using threats or violence, especially over a period of time. The person who is being pushed around is often in a weaker position and cannot say no. If sb **orders sb around/about**, they give them orders because they believe that they are more important or powerful. The person who is being ordered around may or may not do what they are told.

lay down the 'law idiom to tell sb what they should and should not do, in a forceful way: *My dad started laying down the law about what time I should come home.*

dictator noun

dictator · tyrant · despot · autocrat

These are all words for a ruler who has complete power over a country, especially one who uses it in a cruel way, or a person who behaves as if they have complete power over others.

> **PATTERNS AND COLLOCATIONS**
> ▸ a / an **cruel / brutal / evil / ruthless** dictator / tyrant / despot
> ▸ a **benevolent** dictator / despot
> ▸ a dictator / tyrant / despot **rules** a country

dictator [C] (*disapproving*) a ruler who has complete power, especially one who has gained it using military force; a person who behaves as if they have complete power over people, and tells them what to do: *The country suffered at the hands of a series of **military dictators**.* ◇ *He was seen by many as a benevolent dictator* (= one who tries to use his power in a good way). ◇ *Her father was a dictator and the whole family was afraid of him.* See also **dictatorship** → REPRESSION, **dictatorial** → REPRESSIVE

tyrant /'taɪrənt/ [C] (*disapproving*) a ruler who has complete power, or a person who has complete power over other people, especially when they use their power in a cruel way: *The country was ruled by a succession of tyrants.* ◇ *Many of the naval officers were no more than **petty tyrants**.* See also **tyranny** → REPRESSION, **tyrannical** → REPRESSIVE

despot /'despɒt; *AmE* 'despɑːt/ [C] (*disapproving, rather formal*) a ruler who has complete power, especially one who uses it in a cruel way: *It is the story of a military coup which brings a brutal despot to power.* ◇ *He was seen by many as **an enlightened despot*** (= one who tries to use his power in a good way).

autocrat /'ɔːtəkræt/ [C] (*often disapproving, rather formal, written*) a ruler who has complete power; a person who behaves as if they have complete power over people, and tells them what to do: *He governed as an autocrat.* ◇ *The article painted her as an autocrat, angry with her husband and out of touch with her family.* See also **autocratic** → REPRESSIVE

> **NOTE WHICH WORD?** A **tyrant** is always cruel, whether they are the ruler of a country or a manager or teacher who just has authority over a few other people. A **dictator** or **despot** has complete power and is usually cruel, but it is possible to talk about *a benevolent dictator/despot* or an *enlightened despot* who tries to use their power in a good way. When used about the ruler of a country **autocrat** is not necessarily disapproving – it can be just a descriptive term for a ruler with complete power; however, **autocrat** is more often used, in a disapproving way, to describe a person in a position of power within a household or organization who always expects to be obeyed without question.

die verb

die · perish · pass away

These words all mean to stop living.

> **PATTERNS AND COLLOCATIONS**
> ▸ to die / perish **of** / **from** sth
> ▸ to die / perish **in** an accident, a fire, etc.
> ▸ to die / pass away **peacefully**

die [I, T] to stop living: *Her father died of cancer.* ◇ *He died for his beliefs.* ◇ *That plant's died.* ◇ *She died young.* ◇ *He died a poor man.* ◇ *I'll never forget it **to my dying day*** (= until I die). ◇ *She died a natural death.* See also **dead** → DEAD

perish /'perɪʃ/ [I] (*formal or literary*) to die, especially in a sudden violent way: *A family of four perished in the fire.* ◇ *Thousands perished at the hands of the invading forces.* ❶ **Perish** is usually used in texts describing the results of war and accidents.

,**pass a'way** phrasal verb to die: *His mother passed away last year.* ❶ People say **pass away** to avoid saying 'die'.

diet noun See the Topic Map for HEALTH on p.890

diet · fast · regime · regimen

These words all describe the process of controlling what you eat, usually for health reasons.

> **PATTERNS AND COLLOCATIONS**
> ▸ **on** a diet / regime / regimen
> ▸ a **strict** diet / regime / regimen
> ▸ to **go on** / **be on** / **follow** / **keep to** / **stick to** a diet / regime

diet /'daɪət/ [C] a limited variety or amount of food that you eat for medical reasons or because you want to lose weight; a time when you only eat this limited variety or amount: *The doctor recommended a low-fat, salt-free diet.* ◇ *I decided to go on a diet.* See also **diet** → FOOD
> ▸ **diet** verb [I]: *She's always dieting but she never seems to lose weight.*

fast [C] a period during which you do not eat food, especially for religious or health reasons: *He observes the fast of Ramadan.* ◇ *In Cyprus this soup is served on Easter morning to break the long Lenten fast.*
> ▸ **fast** verb [I]: *During Ramadan they fast from sunrise to sunset.*

regime /reɪ'ʒiːm/ [C] a regimen: *I'm going swimming every day as part of my new fitness regime.*

regimen /'redʒɪmən/ [C] (*medical or formal*) a set of rules about food and exercise or medical treatment that you follow in order to stay healthy or to improve your health: *We used a combined regimen of injection treatment and radiation therapy.*

> **NOTE REGIME** OR **REGIMEN?** **Regimen** is a formal word, used especially in medical contexts; a patient may be *put on a regimen* by their doctor. **Regime** is less formal and is used just as often by people who decide to put themselves on a new programme of diet and exercise.

differ verb

differ · range · vary · diverge
These words all mean to be different from sb/sth else.

PATTERNS AND COLLOCATIONS
▶ to differ / range / vary / diverge **in** size, shape, etc.
▶ to differ / diverge **from** sth
▶ to range / vary **from** sth **to** sth
▶ to differ / range / vary **between** things / A and B
▶ to differ / vary **according to** sth
▶ to differ / range / vary / diverge **widely**
▶ to differ / range / vary **enormously**
▶ to differ / vary / diverge **considerably / markedly / significantly**

differ [I] (*rather formal*) to be different from sb/sth; (of two things) to be different from each other: *French differs from English in this respect.* ◇ *French and English differ in this respect.* ◇ *They hold differing views.* ◇ *Ideas on childcare may differ considerably between the parents.*

range [I] (always used with an adverb or preposition) (of a group of similar things) to include a variety of amounts, levels, sizes or points of view, between two particular amounts, levels, etc.; to include a variety of different things in addition to those mentioned: *The disease ranges widely in severity.* ◇ *Estimates of the damage range between $1 million and $5 million.* ◇ *The opinions they expressed* **ranged** *right* **across** *the political spectrum.* ◇ *She has had a number of different jobs, ranging from chef to swimming instructor.* ◇ *The conversation ranged widely* (= covered a lot of different topics). See also **range** → RANGE *noun* 1

vary [I] (of a group of similar things) to be different from each other in size, shape, amount, level or quality: *The students' work varies considerably in quality.* ◇ *The quality of the students' work varies considerably.* ◇ *New techniques were introduced with* **varying degrees of** *success.* See also **varied** → DIVERSE, **variable** → VARIABLE, **variety** → RANGE *noun* 1

diverge /daɪ'vɜːdʒ; *AmE* -'vɜːrdʒ/ [I] (*formal*) (of opinions) to be different from each other: *Opinions diverge greatly on this issue.*

difference noun

difference · contrast · distinction · variation · imbalance · variance · disparity · divergence
These are all words for the way in which people or things are not like each other.

PATTERNS AND COLLOCATIONS
▶ a difference / a contrast / a distinction / a variation / an imbalance / a variance / a disparity / a divergence **between** A and B
▶ a difference / a contrast / a variation / an imbalance / a variance / a disparity / a divergence **in** sth
▶ a **huge** difference / contrast / variation / imbalance / disparity
▶ a **considerable** difference / contrast / variation / imbalance / variance / disparity / divergence
▶ a **major / fundamental** difference / contrast / distinction / variation / imbalance
▶ a **clear** difference / contrast / distinction / variation / disparity
▶ a **slight** difference / variation / variance / divergence
▶ a **regional / gender** difference / variation / imbalance
▶ to **show** a difference / a contrast / a distinction / a variation / an imbalance / a variance / a disparity / a divergence
▶ to **see / be aware of / look at** a difference / contrast / distinction / variation
▶ to **highlight** a difference / contrast / distinction / variation / disparity
▶ to **explain** a difference / a distinction / a variation / an imbalance / a variance / a disparity / a divergence
▶ to **cause** a difference / a variation / an imbalance / a divergence
▶ to **make** a difference / contrast / distinction

difference [C, U] the way in which two people or things are not like each other; the way in which sb/sth has changed: *There are no significant differences between the education systems of the two countries.* ◇ *She noticed a marked difference in the children on her second visit.* ◇ **What a difference!** *You look great with your hair like that* ◇ *I can never* **tell the difference** (= distinguish) *between the twins.* **OPP** **similarity** → SIMILARITY

contrast [C, U] a difference between two or more people or things that you can see clearly when they are compared or put close together; the fact of comparing two or more things in order to show the differences between them: *There is an obvious contrast between the cultures of East and West.* ◇ *A wool jacket with silk trousers provides an interesting contrast in texture.* ◇ *The company lost $7 million this quarter* **in contrast to** *a profit of $6.2 million a year earlier.* ◇ *The poverty of her childhood* **stands in** *total* **contrast to** *her life in Hollywood.* ◇ *When you look at their new system, ours seems very old-fashioned* **by contrast.** See also **contrast** → COMPARE 1, **contrast** → CONFLICT *verb*

distinction [C] (*rather formal*) a clear difference between two or more people or things that are similar or related: *Philosophers did not make a distinction between arts and science.* ◇ *She tends to* **blur the distinctions** *between family and friends.* ❶ In this meaning, **distinction** is often used in the phrase *make/draw a distinction between A and B,* to talk about a difference that people see when they carefully examine things that might at first seem very similar: *We need to* **draw a distinction** *between democratic socialism and social democracy.* See also **distinguish** → DISTINGUISH 1, **distinguish** → DISTINGUISH 2

variation [C, U] the way in which people or things are not like each other: *There may be striking variations within a species.* ◇ *regional variations in voting patterns* ◇ *There is considerable variation in tastes across the country.* ◇ *There is little variation by sex or social class in these attitudes.* ❶ **Variation** is usually used to talk about differences that are apparent between groups of people or things, especially in different places, regions and cultures: *local/regional/geographical/environmental/climatic/cultural/ethnic variation* See also **variation** → CHANGE *noun* 1

imbalance /ɪm'bæləns/ [C, U] (*rather formal or technical*) a situation in which two or more things are not the same size or are treated differently, in a way that is unfair or causes problems: *a global imbalance of/in power* ◇ *Attempts are being made to redress* (= put right) *the imbalance between our import and export figures.* ◇ *Postnatal depression is usually due to hormonal imbalance.* **OPP** **balance** ❶ A **balance** is a situation in which different things exist in equal, correct or good amounts: *Try to keep a balance between work and relaxation.* ◇ *This newspaper maintains a good balance in its presentation of different opinions.*

variance /'veəriəns; *AmE* 'ver-; 'vær-/ [U, C] (*formal*) the amount by which sth changes or is different from sth else: *There is considerable variance in pay across the company.* ◇ *a note with subtle variances of pitch*

disparity /dɪ'spærəti/ [U, C] (*formal*) a difference, especially one connected with an unfair situation or unfair treatment: *The wide disparity between rich and poor was highlighted.* ◇ *There are growing regional disparities in economic prosperity.*

divergence /daɪ'vɜːdʒəns; *AmE* -'vɜːrdʒ-/ [C, U] (*formal*) the amount by which sth is different from sth else: *There is a wide divergence of opinion within the group.*

> **NOTE** VARIANCE OR DIVERGENCE? **Variance** is used especially in technical contexts, for example when analysing figures; **divergence** is used especially to talk about the *opinions* or *views* of groups of people: ~~considerable divergence in pay~~ ◇ ~~a wide variance of opinion~~

different adj. See also the entry for DIVERSE

different · unlike · contrasting · disparate · dissimilar · unequal
These words all describe sb/sth that is not the same as sb/sth else.

PATTERNS AND COLLOCATIONS
▸ different / dissimilar **from** sth
▸ different / contrasting / disparate **views / ways**
▸ to **look** different / unlike sth / dissimilar
▸ **very** different / unlike / disparate / dissimilar / unequal
▸ **quite / totally** different / unlike / disparate / dissimilar
▸ **not altogether / not entirely** different / unlike / dissimilar

different not the same as sb/sth; not like sb/sth else: *The room looks different without the furniture.* ◇ *People often give very different accounts of the same event.* ◇ *American English is significantly different from British English.* ◇ *(AmE) He saw he was no different than anybody else.* ◇ *(BrE, spoken) It's very different to what I'm used to.* **❶** *Different to sb/sth is considered incorrect in written English; use different from sb/sth instead.* **OPP** the same → EQUAL, **similar** → LIKE
▸ **differently** adv.: *Boys and girls behave differently.* ◇ *The male bird has a differently shaped head.*

unlike prep., adj. [not before noun] different from a particular person or thing; (of two people or things) different from each other: *Music is quite unlike any other art form.* ◇ *(written) The sound was not unlike that of birds singing.* ◇ *They are both teachers. Otherwise they are quite unlike.* **❶** *Unlike is most often used with the adverbs quite, most, so and very or after not. If you describe sth as not unlike sth, you mean that it is fairly similar to that thing.* **OPP** like → LIKE

contrasting [usually before noun] very different in style, colour or attitude: *Choose bright, contrasting colours for a child's room.* ◇ *The book explores contrasting views of the poet's early work.* See also **contrast** → CONFLICT verb, **contrast** → OPPOSITE noun

disparate /'dɪspərət/ (formal) (of two or more things) so different from each other that they cannot be compared or cannot work together: *It's an ambitious book that tries to cover such disparate forms as Anglo-Saxon poetry and the modern novel.* ◇ *The machine can keep the disparate parts of the system coordinated.*

dissimilar /dɪ'sɪmɪlə(r)/ (often used in negative sentences) (formal) not the same: *These wines are not dissimilar (= are similar).* ◇ *They had spent their childhoods in highly dissimilar circumstances.* **OPP** similar → LIKE

unequal different in size, quantity, value, etc: *The sleeves are unequal in length.* ◇ *The rooms upstairs are of unequal size.* **OPP** equal → EQUAL

difficult adj.

1 a difficult task
2 make life difficult for sb

1 difficult · hard · challenging · demanding · taxing · testing
These words all describe sth that is not easy and requires a lot of effort or skill to do.

PATTERNS AND COLLOCATIONS
▸ difficult / hard / challenging / demanding / taxing **for** sb
▸ difficult / hard **to do** sth
▸ difficult / hard **to believe / see / tell / say**
▸ a difficult / hard / challenging / demanding / taxing / testing **time / week / year**
▸ difficult / hard / challenging / demanding / taxing **work**
▸ a difficult / hard / challenging / demanding / taxing **job**
▸ a difficult / hard / challenging / demanding **task / target**
▸ a difficult / hard / challenging / taxing / testing **question**
▸ **very / quite** difficult / hard / challenging / demanding / taxing / testing
▸ **physically** difficult / hard / challenging / demanding / taxing

▸ **emotionally** difficult / challenging / demanding / taxing
▸ **technically** difficult / challenging / demanding
▸ **mentally / intellectually** challenging / demanding / taxing

difficult not easy; needing effort or skill to do or understand: *It's really difficult to read your writing.* ◇ *It can be difficult for young people to find jobs around here.* ◇ *We didn't realize how difficult it was going to be.* ◇ *Senior lawyers handle the most difficult cases.* **OPP** easy, simple → EASY 1, See also **difficulty** → PROBLEM

hard difficult: *I always found languages quite hard at school.* ◇ *It was one of the hardest things I ever did.* ◇ *It must be hard for her, bringing up four children on her own.* ◇ *It's hard to believe she's only nine years old.* ◇ *'When will the job be finished?' 'It's hard to say.'* ◇ *I find his attitude quite hard to take (= difficult to accept).* **OPP** easy → EASY 1

NOTE DIFFICULT OR HARD? **Hard** is slightly less formal than **difficult**. It is used particularly in the structure *hard to believe/say/find/take/come by, etc.*, although **difficult** can also be used in any of these examples.

challenging (approving) difficult in an interesting way that tests your ability: *I have had a challenging and rewarding career as a teacher.* ◇ *We have changed the programme to make it more academically challenging.* See also **challenge** → PROBLEM

demanding difficult to do or deal with and needing a lot of effort, skill or patience: *It is a technically demanding piece of music to play.* ◇ *This event is considered one of the most demanding in the sporting calendar.* **OPP** undemanding → EASY 1

taxing (often used in negative statements) difficult to do and needing a lot of mental or physical effort: *This shouldn't be too taxing for you.* ◇ *There was nothing intellectually taxing about the exercise.*

testing difficult to deal with and needing particular strength or abilities: *This has been a testing time for us all.*

NOTE DEMANDING, TAXING OR TESTING? **Demanding** is the strongest of these words and describes tasks and experiences. It is often used with *more* or *most* or an adverb such as *physically, mentally* or *emotionally* that says in what way the activity is difficult. **Taxing** is used especially in negative statements and to talk about problems or tasks that need (or do not need) mental effort. **Testing** describes experiences but NOT tasks and is used particularly with *time, week* or *year*.

2 difficult · tough · bad · hard · adverse · rough · unfavourable · disadvantageous
These words all describe sth that is full of problems or causes a lot of problems.

PATTERNS AND COLLOCATIONS
▸ difficult / tough / bad / hard / unfavourable / disadvantageous **for** sb
▸ tough / hard / rough **on** sb
▸ unfavourable / disadvantageous **to** sb
▸ a difficult / a bad / a hard / an adverse / an unfavourable / a disadvantageous **position**
▸ a difficult / a tough / a bad / a hard / a rough / an unfavourable **situation**
▸ difficult / tough / bad / hard / adverse / rough / unfavourable **conditions**
▸ difficult / tough / adverse / unfavourable **circumstances**
▸ a difficult / tough / bad / hard / rough **time / day / week / year**
▸ a difficult / tough / hard / rough **life / childhood**
▸ a bad / an adverse / an unfavourable / a disadvantageous **effect**

difficult involving or causing a lot of problems: *The next few months were quite difficult.* ◇ *My boss is making life very difficult for me.* ◇ *What's the most difficult personal situation you've ever been in?* ◇ *There was a great deal of difficult terrain to be covered.* See also **difficulty** → PROBLEM

tough /tʌf/ involving or causing a lot of problems, especially personal problems: *She's been having a tough time of it.* ◇ *This will be the toughest test of his leadership* *yet.* ◇ *It's tough out there in the real world.* ❶ **Tough** is a less general word than **difficult** and is used to talk about personal problems, NOT physical conditions: ~~tough terrain/weather conditions~~

bad full of problems; likely to cause problems in a particular situation: *Things were bad enough without her interfering.* ◇ *The situation couldn't get any worse.* ◇ *It was the worst time of my life.* ◇ *I think it was probably a bad time to ask him.* ◇ *He realized it had been a bad decision.*

hard full of problems, especially because of bad conditions or a lack of money: *My grandmother had a hard life.* ◇ *Times were hard at the end of the war.* ◇ *Conditions were extremely hard in the camps.* See also **hardship** → TROUBLE 2

adverse /ˈædvɜːs; ədˈvɜːs; AmE -vɜːrs/ [usually before noun] (*rather formal*) negative and unpleasant; having a negative effect on what you are trying to do: *Lack of money will have an adverse effect on the research programme.* ◇ *Adverse weather conditions meant the rescue had to be abandoned.* ◇ *They have attracted strong adverse criticism.*
  ▸ **adversely** *adv.*: *This move could adversely affect the UK's position in the market.*

rough difficult and unpleasant: *He's had a really rough time recently.* ◇ *Life was rough on the streets.* ◇ *They set sail in rough conditions.* ❶ Life or times can be **rough** if they are full of personal problems or violence; conditions are **rough** if they are physically difficult.

unfavourable (*BrE*) (*AmE* **unfavorable**) /ʌnˈfeɪvərəbl/ (*formal*) (of conditions or situations) not good and likely to cause problems or make sth more difficult: *The conditions were unfavourable for increased crop production.* ◇ *The country's geographical position is **highly** unfavourable.* **OPP** favourable → VALUABLE 2

disadvantageous /ˌdɪsædvænˈteɪdʒəs/ (*formal*) causing sb to be in a worse situation than other people; likely to cause problems: *The deal would not be disadvantageous to your company.* ◇ *Growing conditions here are disadvantageous.* **OPP** advantageous → VALUABLE 2, See also **disadvantage** → DISADVANTAGE

difficulty noun

difficulty · trouble · job · hassle · bother
These are all words for the extra effort or work involved in doing sth, especially sth that is hard to do.

PATTERNS AND COLLOCATIONS
▸ difficulty / trouble / hassle / bother **with** sth
▸ trouble / hassle / bother **over** sth
▸ hassle / bother **about** sth
▸ the trouble / hassle / bother **of doing sth**
▸ **without** (any) difficulty / trouble / hassle / bother
▸ **considerable / enormous / great / little** difficulty / trouble
▸ to **have** difficulty / trouble / a job
▸ to **cause** (sb) difficulty / trouble / hassle / bother
▸ to **be worth / save sb** the trouble / hassle / bother
▸ to **put sb to / go to** a lot of / all that trouble / bother

difficulty [U] the state or quality of being hard to do or to understand; the effort that sth involves: *I had considerable **difficulty in** persuading her to leave.* ◇ *I had no difficulty making myself understood.* ◇ *We found the house without difficulty.* ◇ *They discussed the **difficulty of** studying abroad.* **OPP** ease → EASY 1, See also **difficulty** → PROBLEM

trouble [U] extra effort or work: *I hope the children weren't too much trouble.* ◇ *Nothing is ever **too much trouble** for her* (= she's always ready to help). ◇ *I can call back later — it's no trouble at all* (= I don't mind). ◇ (*BrE*) *I don't want to put you to a lot of trouble.* ◇ *He went to a lot of trouble to find the book for me.* ◇ *Making your own yogurt is **more trouble than it's worth**.* ◇ *The children didn't **give** me any **trouble** at all.*

job [sing.] (*BrE, rather informal*) the difficulty or effort involved in doing sth: *You'll **have a job** convincing them you're right.* ◇ *She had a **hard job** to make herself heard above the noise.* ❶ In this meaning **job** is always used with the verb **have**.

hassle /ˈhæsl/ [U, C] (*informal*) a situation that is annoying because it involves doing sth difficult or complicated that involves a lot of work: *She got the computer set up with no hassle at all.* ◇ *Send them an email — it's a lot less hassle than phoning.* ◇ *It saves you a lot of hassle if you buy tickets in advance.* ◇ *It's a hassle having to travel with so many bags.*

bother [U] (*especially BrE, rather informal, especially spoken*) trouble or difficulty: *You seem to have got yourself into a **spot of bother**.* ◇ *I don't mind looking after the children; they aren't any bother.* ◇ *'Thanks for your help!' 'It was no bother.'*

> **NOTE** TROUBLE OR BOTHER? The main difference between these words is register: **bother** is more informal and used more in spoken English than in written English. It is also used more in British English.

dignity noun

dignity · ego · pride · self-esteem · feelings · self-respect · self-image · sensibilities
These are all words for your sense of yourself, your own importance and value.

PATTERNS AND COLLOCATIONS
▸ **injured** dignity / pride / self-esteem / feelings
▸ **wounded** ego / pride / self-esteem / feelings
▸ **personal** dignity / pride / self-esteem / feelings
▸ **professional** dignity / pride / self-respect
▸ to **damage** sb's dignity / ego / pride / self-esteem / self-respect
▸ to **hurt** sb's pride / feelings
▸ to **bolster** sb's ego / pride / self-esteem / self-image
▸ to **boost** sb's ego / self-esteem / self-respect / self-image
▸ to **restore** sb's dignity / pride / self-esteem / self-respect
▸ to **lose / keep** sb's dignity / pride / self-respect
▸ a **loss of** dignity / pride / self-esteem
▸ a **lack of** dignity / ego / self-esteem

dignity /ˈdɪɡnəti/ [U] the sense you have of your own importance and value and of other people's respect for you: *It's difficult to preserve your dignity when you have no job and no home.* ◇ *He needed a way to retreat with his dignity intact.* See also **dignified** → PROUD 1

ego /ˈiːɡəʊ; ˈeɡəʊ; AmE ˈiːɡoʊ/ (pl. **-os**) [C, U] (*sometimes disapproving*) the opinion that you have of your own importance and value: *He has the **biggest ego** of anyone I've ever met.* ◇ *Winning the prize really boosted her ego* (= made her feel more confident). ◇ *It was a huge blow to his ego to find out he was so unpopular.* See also **egoism** → PRIDE

pride [U] a feeling of respecting yourself and wanting other people to respect you too: *She refused their help **out of pride**.* ◇ *Pride would not allow him to accept the money.* ◇ *It's time to **swallow your pride*** (= hide your feelings of pride) *and ask for help.* See also **proud** → PROUD 1

self-esteem /ˌself ɪˈstiːm/ [U] a feeling of being happy with and confident about your own character and abilities; the way you feel about yourself: *Some children suffer from **low self-esteem** and expect to do badly.* ◇ *You need to build your self-esteem.* See also **esteem** → ADMIRATION

feelings [pl.] a person's emotional state, especially the extent to which they are offended, upset or embarrassed by sth: *I didn't mean to hurt your feelings.* ◇ *I kept off the subject of divorce so as to **spare her feelings**.*

self-respect /ˌself rɪˈspekt/ [U] a feeling of respect for yourself and that what you do and say is right and valuable: *Despite poverty and appalling conditions, these people still manage to keep their dignity and self-respect.* See also **self-respecting** → PROUD 1

self-image /ˌself ˈɪmɪdʒ/ [C, usually sing., U] the opinion or idea that you have of yourself, especially of your appearance or abilities: *It's very easy to get a **negative self-image** and lose confidence.*

sensibilities /ˌsensəˈbɪlətiz/ [pl.] (*rather formal, written*) a person's feelings about what is important to them, especially when they are easily offended or influenced: *The article offended her religious sensibilities.*

dim adj.
1 a dim light/shape
2 a dim room

---

1 dim · faint · weak · soft · thin
These words all describe light which is not very strong.

PATTERNS AND COLLOCATIONS
▸ dim / faint / weak / soft / thin **light**
▸ a dim / faint / soft **glow**
▸ a dim / soft **lamp**
▸ dim / soft **lighting**
▸ faint / thin **moonlight**
▸ a dim / faint **outline**

dim (of light) not easy to see by; (of an object) not easily seen because there is not much light: *It was hard to see in the dim glow of the streetlights.* ◇ *The light is too dim to read by.* ◇ *I could see a dim shape in the doorway.* **OPP** bright → BRIGHT, See also **dim** → DARKEN *verb*
▸ **dimly** *adv.*: *a dimly lit room*
▸ **dimness** *noun* [U]: *It took a while for his eyes to adjust to the dimness.*

faint (of light or an object) not easily seen: *There was a faint glimmer of light from her window.* ◇ *We saw the faint outline of the mountain through the mist.* **OPP** bright → BRIGHT
▸ **faintly** *adv.*: *A streetlight glowed faintly through the frosted glass.*

weak (of light) not very bright or warm: *The weak winter sunlight spread across the lake.* **OPP** strong → STRONG 2
▸ **weakly** *adv.*: *The sun was shining weakly.*

NOTE DIM, FAINT OR WEAK? **Dim** is used to describe the light in the sky or in a room or place when it is not bright and makes it hard to see things clearly. **Faint** more often describes a particular point of light such as a *glimmer* or *glow*, when it is the light itself that is hard to see. **Weak** is used especially to describe the light in the sky when the sun is shining, but is not particularly bright or warm; you can see things clearly but the light does not make them shine.

soft [usually before noun] (of light) not too bright, in a way that is pleasant and relaxing to the eyes: *The kitchen was filled with the soft cosy glow of candlelight.* **OPP** dazzling, harsh → STRONG 2
▸ **softly** *adv.*: *The room was softly lit by a lamp.*

thin [usually before noun] (*literary*) (of light) not very bright or warm: *the thin grey light of dawn*

---

2 dim · gloomy · dreary · dingy
These words all describe a place or situation where there is not much light, especially in a way that makes you feel sad.

PATTERNS AND COLLOCATIONS
▸ a dim / gloomy / dreary / dingy **room**
▸ a dim / gloomy **corridor / interior / street**
▸ a gloomy / dingy **house**
▸ a dim / gloomy / dreary **place / day**
▸ a gloomy / dreary **morning**
▸ **rather** dim / gloomy / dreary / dingy
▸ a gloomy / dreary / dingy **little** sth

dim where you cannot see well because there is not much light: *They stepped into the dim and cluttered little shop.* **OPP** bright → BRIGHT, See also **dim** → DARKEN *verb*
gloomy nearly dark, or badly lit in a way that makes you feel sad: *The gloomy weather showed little sign of lifting.* ◇ *The house is very grand, but rather gloomy when you're alone.* **OPP** bright → BRIGHT, See also **gloom** → DARKNESS
dreary /'drɪəri/ *AmE* 'drɪri/ without much light or colour and making you feel sad: *We left at seven o'clock on a dark and dreary February morning.*
▸ **dreariness** *noun* [U]: *She hated the dreariness of her everyday life.*
dingy /'dɪndʒi/ (of place) dark and dirty, and often small: *The kitchen was rather dark and dingy.*

dine verb See also the entry for EAT

---

dine · eat · lunch · feast · snack · breakfast
These words all mean to eat food at a meal.

PATTERNS AND COLLOCATIONS
▸ to dine / eat / lunch / breakfast **at** a place
▸ to dine / lunch / feast / snack / breakfast **on** a particular food
▸ to dine / eat / lunch / breakfast **with** sb
▸ to dine / eat **out**
▸ to dine / eat / breakfast **early / late**
▸ to dine / eat **well**

dine [I, T] (*formal*) to have dinner, especially at a restaurant or formal dinner party: *The guests dined on lobster.* ◇ *He dined out every night* (= had dinner in a restaurant or in sb else's home). ◇ *His boss took him out to be **wined and dined*** (= given expensive meals in a restaurant). **❶** Dine, **lunch** and **breakfast** are formal verbs; in less formal contexts it is more usual to say *have dinner/lunch/breakfast*.
eat [I] to have a meal: *We ate at a pizzeria in town.* ◇ *I can't be bothered to cook. Shall we eat out tonight* (= have a meal in a restaurant)? ◇ *You can eat really well* (= eat delicious and/or healthy meals) *without spending a fortune.* See also **eat** → EAT
lunch [I] (*formal*) to have lunch, especially at a restaurant: *He lunched with a client at the Ritz.*
feast [I] (*written*) to eat a large amount of food, with great enjoyment: *They feasted on eggs, bacon, toast and coffee.* ◇ *Flies were feasting on the rotting flesh.* See also **feast** → MEAL *noun*
snack [I] to eat snacks (= small amounts of food) between or instead of main meals: *I usually have a light lunch and then snack on fruit and nuts during the afternoon.* ◇ *If you snack between meals, try to avoid sugary foods like chocolate.* See also **snack** → SNACK *noun*
breakfast [I] (*formal*) to have breakfast: *They breakfasted on coffee and hot rolls.*

dinner noun See also the entry for MEAL

---

dinner · lunch · breakfast · tea · supper · luncheon
These are all words for meals.

PATTERNS AND COLLOCATIONS
▸ **for / over** dinner / lunch / breakfast / tea / supper / luncheon
▸ a / an **early / late** dinner / lunch / breakfast / supper
▸ a **hot / cold** dinner / lunch / supper
▸ a **business** dinner / lunch / breakfast / luncheon
▸ a / an **annual / awards / gala** dinner / luncheon
▸ to **have / eat / serve** dinner / lunch / breakfast / tea / supper / luncheon
▸ to **have / eat your** dinner / lunch / breakfast / tea / supper
▸ to **invite sb for / to** dinner / lunch / breakfast / tea / supper / luncheon
▸ to **have sth for** dinner/lunch/breakfast/tea/supper/luncheon
▸ to **go out for** dinner / lunch / breakfast
▸ to **come / go to / for** dinner / lunch / breakfast / tea / supper
▸ to **sit down to** dinner / lunch / breakfast / tea / supper
▸ to **get** dinner / lunch / breakfast / tea / supper
▸ a dinner / lunch / tea / supper / luncheon **party**
▸ dinner / lunch / breakfast / tea / supper **things**

dinner [U, C] the main meal of the day, eaten either in the middle of the day or in the evening: *It's time for dinner.* ◇ *Have you had dinner yet?* ◇ *What time do you serve dinner?* ◇ *Let's invite them to dinner.* ◇ *What shall we have for dinner tonight?* ◇ *It's your turn to get dinner.* ◇ *I never eat a big dinner.* **❶** Dinner also refers to an event at which dinner is eaten: *The club's **annual dinner** will be held on the 4th of June.*
lunch [U, C] a meal eaten in the middle of the day: *She's gone to lunch.* ◇ *I'm ready for some lunch.* ◇ *Let's **do lunch*** (= have lunch together). ◇ *We took a **packed lunch*** (= a

meal, often of sandwiches, which you can carry with you). ◇ *We serve hot and cold lunches.* ◇ *I have a one-hour* **lunch break**.

breakfast [U, C] the first meal of the day: *They were having breakfast when I arrived.* ◇ *I'm going to have a nice leisurely breakfast tomorrow.* ◇ *(especially BrE) I always have a* **cooked breakfast**. ❶ An **English breakfast** is a large breakfast, usually including cooked bacon and eggs. A **continental breakfast** is a light breakfast, usually consisting of coffee and bread rolls with butter and jam. These terms are used especially in hotels: *The price per person includes a* **full English breakfast**.

tea [U, C] *(BrE)* a light meal eaten in the afternoon or early evening, usually with sandwiches and/or biscuits and cakes and with tea to drink; a cooked meal eaten in the evening, especially when it is eaten early in the evening: *Would you like to come to tea on Sunday?* ◇ *You can have your tea as soon as you come home from school.* ❶ A cooked tea that is eaten instead of a later, larger meal, is sometimes called **high tea**.

supper [U, C] the last meal of the day, either a main meal, usually smaller and less formal than dinner, or a snack (= a small meal) eaten before you go to bed: *I'll do my homework after supper.* ◇ *Let's talk about it over supper.* ◇ *We'll have an early supper tonight.*

> **NOTE DINNER, LUNCH, TEA OR SUPPER?** People use these words in different ways depending on which English-speaking country they come from. In Britain it may also depend on which part of the country or which social class a person comes from. A meal eaten in the middle of the day is usually called **lunch**. If it is the main meal of the day it may also be called **dinner** in British English, especially in the north of the country. A main meal eaten in the evening is usually called **dinner**, especially if it is a formal meal. **Supper** is also an evening meal, but more informal than **dinner** and usually eaten at home. It can also be a late meal or something to eat and drink before going to bed. In British English **tea** is a light meal in the afternoon with sandwiches, cake and a cup of tea. It can also be a main meal eaten early in the evening, especially by children.

luncheon /ˈlʌntʃən/ [C, U] *(formal)* a formal lunch or a formal word for lunch: *They organized a charity luncheon.* ◇ *Luncheon will be served at one, Madam.*

direction *noun*

direction · path · course · road · route
These are all words for the general way in which sb/sth develops or sb achieves sth, over a period of time.

PATTERNS AND COLLOCATIONS
▸ a / the path / road / route **to** sth
▸ **on** a / the path / course / road / route
▸ the **right** / **wrong** direction / path / course / road / route
▸ a **new** direction / path / course / road / route
▸ a **different** direction / path / course / road / route
▸ the **future** direction / path / course (of sth)
▸ a **clear** direction / path / course / road / route
▸ to **take** a / the ... direction / path / course / road / route
▸ to **follow** / **pursue** a / the ... direction / path / course / route
▸ to **go down** a / the ... path / road / route
▸ to **change** (a / the) direction / course

> **NOTE PATH, COURSE, ROAD AND ROUTE** These words all have literal meanings relating to the way you travel to get somewhere. Many of the collocations used with the literal meanings are shared by the meanings in this group, for example *follow this path, change course, go down that road* and *take that route*.

direction [C, U] the general way in which a person, thing, organization or sb's ideas or actions is/are developing or changing: *The exhibition provides evidence of several new directions in her work.* ◇ *They are debating the future direction of the party.* ◇ *I am very unhappy with the*

direction the club is taking. ◇ *It's only a small improvement but at least it's a* **step in the right direction**. ◇ *It seems that things are at last* **moving in** *the right* **direction**.

path [C] a plan of action or the series of actions sb takes to achieve sth: *There is no clear* **career path** *in this field.* ◇ *The party seemed to be on the path to assured victory.* ◇ *Power sharing is a difficult path to tread.* ◇ *Everyone has to find their own path in life.*

course [C, usually sing.] the general direction in which sb's ideas or actions, or a series of events, develop: *Her career followed a similar course to her sister's.* ◇ *This was an event that changed the whole course of his thinking.* ◇ *We'll just have to let things take their natural course.* ◇ *They were obliged to* **steer a course** *between the interests of the two groups.*

> **NOTE DIRECTION OR COURSE?** The **direction** of a person or thing is usually the way they are developing now or the way they are likely to develop in the future; **direction** is not usually used if you are looking back at the way things developed in the past: *Her career followed a similar direction to her sister's.* The **course** of a person or thing is usually the way they developed over a period of time or have been developing until now; **course** is not usually used if you are looking forward to the way things are likely to develop in the future: *They are debating the future course of the party.* **Course** also has the closely related meaning of 'a way of acting in or dealing with a particular situation'.

road [C] a series of events or course of action that will lead to a particular result: *The economy is well on the road to recovery.* ◇ *We would prefer not to go down that particular road.* ◇ *She set out on the road to stardom too early in life.* ◇ *They seem to be* **on the road to ruin**.

route [C] the way in which sb achieves sth or tries to achieve sth: *The biography charts her route to fame from humble beginnings.* ◇ *Education was the traditional route out of poverty.* ◇ *Some young people see marriage as a kind of* **escape route** (= a way of getting out of a situation they do not like).

> **NOTE PATH, ROAD OR ROUTE?** **Path** is often more personal than **road**. People talk about *your/his/her career path/ path in life* (= the one that sb in particular follows) but *the road to stardom/ruin* (= the one that everyone follows if they become a star/are ruined). **Route** may be used to talk about a particular person or people in general: *her route to fame* ◇ *the traditional route out of poverty.* However, it is usually used when reporting things in a more factual, less emotional way. You can talk about sth being *a difficult path to tread* or *a difficult road to travel* (note the different verbs, according to the different literal meanings of **path** and **road**) but such terms are not usually used to describe **route** in this meaning.

dirt *noun*

dirt · dust · pollution · soot · grime
These are all words for substances that make sth dirty.

PATTERNS AND COLLOCATIONS
▸ to be **covered in** / **with** dirt / dust / soot / grime
▸ to be **streaked with** dirt / soot
▸ to **remove** dirt / dust / soot / grime
▸ to **wash** the dirt / dust / grime **off** / **from** sth
▸ to **clean** the dirt / dust **off** / **from** sth
▸ to **brush** the dirt / dust **off** / **from** sth
▸ a **layer of** dirt / dust / grime
▸ a **speck of** dirt / dust

dirt [U] any substance that makes sth dirty, for example soil or mud: *First remove any dirt from the surface.* ◇ *The problem with white is that it soon shows the dirt.*

dust [U] the fine powder of dirt that forms in buildings, on furniture, floors and other surfaces: *There wasn't a speck of dust anywhere.* ◇ *She is allergic to house dust.*

pollution /pəˈluːʃn/ [U] any substance that makes air, water, soil or other natural things dirty: *The new buses emit no more pollution than the average car.* ◇ *Pollution on British beaches is a serious problem.*
▸ **pollute** *verb* [T]: *the exhaust fumes that are polluting our cities*

soot /sʊt/ [U] black powder that is produced when sth such as wood or coal is burnt: *The fireplace was blackened with soot.*

grime [U] dirt that forms a layer on the surface of sth: *The window sills were covered in dust and grime.*

dirty *adj.*

dirty · dusty · filthy · muddy · soiled · grubby · stained · messy · unwashed · grimy
These words all describe sb/sth that is not clean.

PATTERNS AND COLLOCATIONS
▸ dirty / dusty / filthy / muddy / soiled / grubby / stained / unwashed **clothes**
▸ dirty / dusty / filthy / grubby / unwashed / grimy **hands**
▸ dirty / dusty / filthy / grubby / grimy **windows**
▸ a dirty / dusty / filthy **room**
▸ a dirty / filthy / messy **job**
▸ to **look** dirty / dusty / grubby / messy / grimy
▸ to **get** dirty / dusty / filthy / muddy / stained / messy
▸ **rather** dirty / dusty / muddy / grubby / messy / grimy
▸ **a bit** dirty / dusty / muddy / grubby / messy
▸ **slightly** dirty / dusty / grubby / soiled / stained
▸ **really** dirty / dusty / filthy / messy / grimy
▸ **very / extremely** dirty / dusty / muddy / filthy

dirty not clean; covered with dust, soil, mud, oil, etc: *If your hands are dirty, go and wash them.* ◇ *My thumb had left a dirty mark on the paper.* ◇ *Try not to get too dirty!* ◇ *The soot had made everything dirty.* ◇ *I always get given the dirty jobs* (= jobs that make you become dirty). **OPP clean** → CLEAN

dusty full of dust; covered with dust: *The room was dark and dusty.* ◇ *We tramped for miles down the dusty road.* ◇ *There were shelves full of faded dusty books.*

filthy /ˈfɪlθi/ very dirty and unpleasant: *Why are the streets so filthy in this part of the city?* ◇ *It's absolutely filthy in here.* ◇ *There were two beggars dressed in filthy rags.*

muddy full of or covered in mud: *Don't you come in here with those muddy boots on!* ◇ *We drove along the muddy track.* ◇ *Look, you've made the floor all muddy.* See also **mud** → SOIL

soiled (*rather formal*) dirty, especially with waste from the body: *She changed the soiled bedding.*

grubby (*rather informal*) rather dirty, usually because it has not been washed: *My hands are a bit grubby.* ◇ *He hoped she wouldn't notice his grubby shirt cuffs.*

stained (often in compounds) covered with stains; marked with a stain (= a dirty mark that is difficult to remove): *The sheets were old and stained.* ◇ *The shirt was heavily stained with blood.* ◇ *She was wearing a pair of paint-stained jeans.* See also **stain** → MARK *noun*

messy (*rather informal*) dirty, especially with sth wet or sticky; that makes sb/sth dirty in this way: *The children got really messy painting and gluing.* ◇ *Painting can be a messy job.* ❶ A *messy house/room/desk* is often untidy rather than dirty. See also **messy** → SCRUFFY, **messy** → UNTIDY, **mess** → MESS *noun* 1

unwashed (*especially written*) that needs to be washed: *The sink was full of unwashed dishes.* ◇ *Their clothes were dirty and their hair unwashed.*

grimy /ˈɡraɪmi/ dirty, especially with a layer of dust, soil, mud or oil on the surface: *Her hands were grimy from changing the car wheel.*

disability *noun*

disability · handicap · impairment
These are all words for a condition that means that you cannot use a part of your body completely or easily.

PATTERNS AND COLLOCATIONS
▸ a **severe** disability / handicap / impairment
▸ **permanent** disability / impairment
▸ to **have / be born with / suffer from** a disability / a handicap / an impairment
▸ to **cope with** a disability / handicap

disability [C, U] a permanent physical or mental condition that means that you cannot use a part of your body completely or easily, or that you cannot learn easily: *He has a permanent disability which prevents him from working as a labourer.* ◇ *She works in a school for children with **learning disabilities**.* ◇ *He qualifies for help on the grounds of disability.*

handicap [C, U] (*old-fashioned, sometimes offensive*) a physical or mental condition that means that you cannot use a part of your body completely or easily or that you cannot learn easily: *The knee injury turned out to be a considerable handicap to Paul.* ◇ *Despite her handicap, Jane is able to hold down a full-time job.* ❶ The word **handicap** to mean a permanent physical or mental disability is now rather old-fashioned, can be offensive, and should be avoided. Instead of 'mental disability/handicap' use *learning disability*. **Handicap** can still be used to talk about a temporary injury that prevents sb from using a part of their body for a time; **disability** cannot be used in this way: *The knee injury turned out to be a considerable disability.* See also **handicap** → OBSTACLE

impairment /ɪmˈpeəmənt; *AmE* -ˈperm-/ [U, C] (*technical*) a physical or mental condition that means that a part of your body or brain does not work correctly: *The doctor noted impairment of the functions of the kidney.* ◇ *A new day-care centre will be opened for people with a **visual impairment**.*
▸ **impaired** *adj.*: (*rather formal*) *He has impaired hearing as a result of long-term exposure to noise pollution.* ◇ *the problems faced by people who are **visually/hearing impaired***

disable *verb*

disable · paralyse · cripple · incapacitate · immobilize · put sb/sth out of action
These words all mean to injure or damage sb/sth so that they cannot move or work.

PATTERNS AND COLLOCATIONS
▸ He was disabled / paralysed / crippled **in a car accident**.
▸ people who are disabled / crippled / incapacitated **by illness**
▸ a disabling / crippling **accident / condition / disease / illness / injury**
▸ The **country** has been paralysed / crippled / immobilized **by a general strike**.

disable /dɪsˈeɪbl/ [T] to damage sb's body so that, for example, they cannot walk or cannot use a part of their body; to prevent sth from working correctly: *The gunfire could kill or disable the pilot.* ◇ *The burglars gained entry to the building after disabling the alarm.*

paralyse (*BrE*) (*AmE* **paralyze**) /ˈpærəlaɪz/ [T, often passive] to make sb unable to feel or move all or part of their body; to prevent sth from functioning normally: *The accident left him **paralysed from the waist down**.* ◇ *The airport is still paralysed by the strike.* ◇ (*figurative*) *She stood there, **paralysed with fear**.*
▸ **paralysis** /pəˈræləsɪs/ *noun* [U]: *paralysis of both legs* ◇ *The strike caused total paralysis in the city.*

cripple [T, usually passive] to damage sb's body so that they are no longer able to walk or move normally; to seriously damage or harm sb/sth so that it/they cannot work or live normally: *He was crippled by polio as a child.* ◇ *to be **crippled with** arthritis* ◇ *Sugar producers have been crippled by plummeting prices.* ◇ *The pilot tried to land his crippled plane.*
▸ **crippling** *adj.*: *a crippling disease* ◇ *crippling debts*

incapacitate /ˌɪnkəˈpæsɪteɪt/ [T, usually passive] (*formal*) to make sb unable to live or work normally: *He was incapacitated by old age and sickness.* ◇ *mentally incapacitated people*

immobilize (*BrE* also **-ise**) /ɪˈməʊbəlaɪz; *AmE* ɪˈmoʊ-/ [T] to prevent sth from moving or working normally: *a device to immobilize the car engine in case of theft* ◊ *The firm has been immobilized by a series of strikes.* ◊ *Always immobilize a broken leg immediately.*

‚put sb/sth out of 'action *idiom* to make sb/sth unable to work or be used because of injury or damage: *Jon has been put out of action for weeks by a broken leg.*
▶ **out of 'action**: *The photocopier is out of action today.*

disabled *adj.*

disabled · handicapped · lame
These words all refer to sb who cannot use a part of their body completely or easily.

PATTERNS AND COLLOCATIONS
▶ a disabled / handicapped **person / child**
▶ to **be born** disabled / handicapped
▶ to **leave sb** disabled / handicapped / lame
▶ **badly / profoundly / seriously / severely / permanently / mentally / physically** disabled / handicapped

disabled unable to use a part of your body completely or easily because of a physical condition, illness or injury; unable to learn easily: *My son is disabled and needs extra support at school.* ◊ *The museum has special facilities for disabled people.* ◊ *Does the theatre have disabled access?* **OPP** **able-bodied** ❶ Able-bodied describes sb who is physically healthy and strong, in contrast to sb who is weak or disabled: *Military service is compulsory for every able-bodied male between 18 and 27.*
▶ **the disabled** noun [pl.]: *She spends a lot of her free time caring for the disabled.* ❶ The expressions *disabled people* or *people with disabilities* are often preferred to *the disabled* because they sound more personal.

handicapped (*old-fashioned, sometimes offensive*) disabled: *The accident left him physically handicapped.*

> **NOTE** DISABLED OR HANDICAPPED? The word **handicapped** to mean permanently physically or mentally disabled is now rather old-fashioned, can be offensive, and should be avoided. Instead of saying that sb is *mentally disabled/handicapped*, say that they *have a learning disability*.

lame (of people or animals) unable to walk well because of an injury to the leg or foot: *The accident left her slightly lame.* ◊ *His horse had gone lame.* ❶ When talking about people, **lame** usually refers to a long-term disability. If you have hurt your leg or foot temporarily, you can say that you *limp* or *walk with a limp*. However, when a horse *goes lame*, this can be only a temporary injury.

disadvantage *noun*

disadvantage · drawback · pitfall · snag · downside · catch
These are all words for a problem or difficulty with sth or a less positive aspect of sth.

PATTERNS AND COLLOCATIONS
▶ a / the disadvantage / drawback / snag / downside / catch **to** sth
▶ a / the disadvantage / drawback / pitfall / snag / downside **for** sb
▶ a disadvantage / pitfall / snag **in** sth
▶ the disadvantages / drawbacks / pitfalls **associated with** sth
▶ The disadvantage / drawback / snag / downside / catch **is that…**
▶ a **possible** disadvantage / drawback / pitfall / snag / downside
▶ the **only** disadvantage / drawback / pitfall / snag / catch
▶ a / an **major / obvious / potential** disadvantage / drawback / pitfall / snag
▶ a / the **big / main / minor / slight** disadvantage / drawback / snag
▶ to **have** a disadvantage / drawback / snag / downside
▶ to **overcome** a disadvantage / drawback / snag / pitfall

disadvantage [C, U] something that causes problems and tends to stop sb/sth from succeeding or making progress: *There are disadvantages to the plan.* ◊ *The fact that he*

didn't speak a foreign language put him at a distinct disadvantage. ◊ *I hope my lack of experience won't be to my disadvantage.* ◊ *The advantages of the plan far outweigh the disadvantages.* ◊ *Many children in the class suffered severe social and economic disadvantage.* **OPP** **advantage** → BENEFIT 1, **advantage** → LEAD 2, See also **disadvantageous** → DIFFICULT 2
▶ **disadvantage** verb [T]: *Some pension plans may disadvantage women.*

drawback /ˈdrɔːbæk/ [C] a problem or less positive aspect of sth that makes it a less attractive idea: *The main drawback to it is the cost.* ◊ *This strategy has its drawbacks.*

pitfall /ˈpɪtfɔːl/ [C] a danger or difficulty, especially one that is hidden or not obvious at first: *We need to be alert to potential pitfalls.* ◊ *Buying property holds many pitfalls for the unwary.*

snag [C] (*rather informal*) a problem or difficulty, especially one that is small, hidden or unexpected: *The only snag with the course is that it's quite short.* ◊ *There is just one small snag – where is the money coming from?* ◊ *We've hit a technical snag: the printer isn't compatible with my PC.*

downside /ˈdaʊnsaɪd/ [sing.] (*rather informal, especially journalism*) the disadvantages or less positive aspects of sth that is generally good: *The downside of all this success is that I don't get to spend much time with my family.* ◊ *On the downside, such improvements in efficiency often mean job losses.* **OPP** **The upside** is the more positive aspects of sth that is generally bad: *The upside is that I do get to spend more time with my family.*

catch [C, usually sing.] (*rather informal*) a hidden difficulty or disadvantage: *It sounds too good. There must be a catch.* ◊ *All that money for two hours' work – what's the catch?*
▶ **‚catch sb 'out** *phrasal verb*: *Many investors were caught out by the fall in share prices.*

disagree *verb* See the Topic Map for CONFLICT on p.896

disagree · differ · dispute · be at odds · take issue with sb · not see eye to eye with sb
These are all words and expressions that can be used when people have different opinions about sth.

PATTERNS AND COLLOCATIONS
▶ to disagree / differ / dispute / be at odds / take issue / not see eye to eye **with** sb / sth
▶ to disagree / differ / be at odds / take issue / not see eye to eye **on** sth
▶ to disagree / differ / be at odds / take issue **over** sth
▶ to disagree / differ / take issue **about** sth
▶ to disagree / differ **as to** sth
▶ to **agree to** disagree / differ

disagree [I] to have a different opinion about sth: *Even friends disagree sometimes.* ◊ *He disagreed with his parents on most things.* ◊ *Some people disagree with this argument.* ◊ *No, I disagree. I don't think it would be the right thing to do.* ◊ *She disagreed that building more roads was the only way to handle traffic congestion.* **OPP** **agree** → AGREE 1, See also **disagreement** → DEBATE

differ [I] (*rather formal*) to have a different opinion on sth from sb else: *I have to differ with you on that.* ◊ *Medical opinion differs as to how to treat the disease.* ◊ *I think you're wrong. Let's just agree to differ.* See also **difference** → DEBATE

> **NOTE** DISAGREE OR DIFFER? If you **disagree** with sb you will probably tell them why and try to persuade them you are right. **Differ** is a more formal word and is used more to state the fact of disagreeing than the reasons for it. Only people can **disagree**; people or their opinions can **differ**: *Medical opinion disagrees as to how to treat the disease.*

dispute /dɪˈspjuːt; ˈdɪspjuːt/ [T, I] to argue or disagree strongly with sb about sth, especially about who owns sth: *The ownership of this land has been disputed for centuries.* ◊ *The United Nations recognizes the area as a disputed territory.* ◊ *The issue remains hotly disputed.* See also **dispute** → DEBATE *noun*

be at 'odds idiom to disagree strongly with sb about sth: *He's always at odds with his father over politics.*
take 'issue with sb idiom (*formal*) to start disagreeing or arguing about sth with sb: *I must take issue with you on that point.*
not see eye to 'eye with sb idiom to not share the same opinions as sb about sth: *The two of them have never seen eye to eye on politics.*

disappear verb

disappear · vanish · fade · die out · dissolve · clear · melt
These words all mean to stop existing or being in a place.

PATTERNS AND COLLOCATIONS
▸ to disappear / vanish / fade / dissolve / melt **into** sth
▸ to fade / melt **away**
▸ **anger / hope** disappears / vanishes / fades / melts
▸ **a smile** disappears / vanishes / fades
▸ **cloud / smoke / mist** disappears / clears
▸ **a species** disappears / vanishes / dies out
▸ **a tradition / custom** disappears / dies out
▸ disappear / vanish / fade / die out / dissolve / clear **completely**
▸ disappear / fade / die out / dissolve / clear **gradually**
▸ to disappear / vanish / fade **from view / sight**
▸ to disappear / vanish / melt **into thin air**

disappear [I] to become impossible to see; to stop existing; to be lost or impossible to find: *The plane disappeared behind a cloud.* ◇ *The problem won't just disappear.* ◇ *Our countryside is disappearing at an alarming rate.* ◇ *The child **disappeared from** his home some time after four.* **OPP** **appear** → APPEAR
▸ **disappearance** noun [U, C]: *Police are investigating the disappearance of a young woman.* **OPP** **appearance** → ARRIVAL 1
vanish /'vænɪʃ/ [I] to disappear suddenly and/or in a way that you cannot explain; to stop existing: *The magician vanished in a puff of smoke.* ◇ *My glasses seem to have vanished.* ◇ *The boys vanished without trace during a snowstorm.* ◇ *All hopes of a peaceful settlement had now vanished.*
fade [I] to disappear gradually: *Her smile faded.* ◇ *The laughter faded away.* ◇ *His voice **faded to** a whisper (= gradually became quieter).* ◇ *All other issues **fade into insignificance** compared with the struggle for survival.*
die 'out phrasal verb (of types of animal or plant; of customs and traditions) to stop existing: *The report estimates that up to 40 000 species will have died out by the end of the century.* ◇ *Most of these traditions died out during the 19th century.*
dissolve /dɪ'zɒlv; AmE -'zɑːlv/ [I, T] (*rather formal or literary*) to disappear; to make sth disappear: *When the ambulance had gone, the crowd dissolved.* ◇ *His calm response dissolved her confusion.*
clear [I] (of the sky or weather) to become brighter and free of cloud or rain; (of smoke or fog) to disappear so that it is easier to see things: *The sky cleared after the storm.* ◇ *The rain is clearing slowly.* ◇ *As the smoke cleared, two fighter planes came into view.* **OPP** **cloud** → DARKEN
melt [I] (usually used with an adverb or preposition) (of people or feelings) to disappear gradually: *At the first sign of trouble, his supporters melted away.* ◇ *All her anger and hurt melted away in his embrace.*

disappoint verb

disappoint · let sb down · fail · leave sb in the lurch
These words all mean to not help or support sb or to not do sth as sb hoped or expected.

disappoint   let sb down   leave sb in the lurch
                  fail

PATTERNS AND COLLOCATIONS
▸ to disappoint / let down / fail your **fans / children / family / colleagues / friends**
▸ to be **sorry to** disappoint sb / let sb down / leave sb in the lurch
▸ sb **won't** disappoint sb / let sb down / fail sb / leave sb in the lurch

disappoint [T, I] to make sb feel sad because sth that they hope for or expect to happen does not happen or is not as good as they hoped: *Her decision to cancel the concert is bound to disappoint her fans.* ◇ *I hate to disappoint you, but I'm just not interested.* ◇ *The movie had disappointed her (= it wasn't as good as she had expected).* ◇ *His latest novel does not disappoint.*
let sb 'down phrasal verb (*disapproving*) to not help or support sb as they had hoped or expected: *I'm afraid she let us down badly.* ◇ *This machine won't let you down.* ◇ *He trudged home feeling lonely and let down.*
fail [T] (*rather formal*) to not help or support sb as they had hoped, or had a right to expect: *When he lost his job, he felt he had failed his family.* ◇ *She tried to be brave, but her courage failed her.* ◇ (*figurative*) *Words fail me* (= I cannot express how I feel). **❶** People can **fail** other people, especially those who depend on them, such as their *family, children, friends* or *colleagues*; or your *courage, nerve* or *heart* (= meaning 'courage') can **fail** you.
leave sb in the 'lurch idiom (*informal, disapproving*) to fail to help sb when they are relying on you to do so: *I'm sorry to leave you in the lurch but I can't do the presentation with you this afternoon.* ◇ *She felt she had been left in the lurch by all her colleagues.* **❶** To **leave sb in the lurch** is like **letting sb down** very badly: it does not just disappoint sb, but puts them in a very difficult position.

disappointed adj. See also the entry for UNHAPPY 2

disappointed · disillusioned · disenchanted
These words all describe sb who is unhappy or upset because sb/sth is not as good as they expected or believed.

PATTERNS AND COLLOCATIONS
▸ disappointed / disillusioned / disenchanted **by / with** sb / sth
▸ disappointed / disillusioned **about** sth
▸ to **feel** disappointed / disillusioned
▸ to **become / grow** disillusioned / disenchanted
▸ **rather** disappointed / disillusioned / disenchanted
▸ **very / extremely / sadly** disappointed / disillusioned

disappointed upset or unhappy because sth that you hoped for has not happened or has not been as good or successful as you expected: *They were bitterly **disappointed at** the result of the game.* ◇ *I'm **disappointed in** you — I really thought I could trust you!* ◇ *He was **disappointed to see** she wasn't at the party.* ◇ *I'm **disappointed (that)** it was sold out.* ◇ *Disappointed applicants will be placed on a waiting list in case of cancellations.* **OPP** **pleased** → GLAD
disillusioned /ˌdɪsɪ'luːʒnd/ disappointed because the person you admired or the idea you believed to be good and true now seems without value: *I soon became disillusioned with the job.* ◇ *Her book is the testimony of a disillusioned woman.* See also **illusion** → ILLUSION
▸ **disillusionment** noun [U]: (*rather formal*) *There is widespread disillusionment with the current government.*
disenchanted /ˌdɪsɪn'tʃɑːntɪd; AmE -'tʃænt-/ (*rather formal*) no longer feeling enthusiasm for sb/sth; no longer believing that sth is good or worth doing: *Many in the party had become disenchanted with the reforms.*
▸ **disenchantment** noun [U]: *a growing sense/feeling of disenchantment*

disappointing adj.

disappointing · unsatisfactory · wanting · discouraging
These words all describe sth that is not as good as you hoped or expected.

PATTERNS AND COLLOCATIONS
▸ disappointing/ unsatisfactory/ discouraging **that...**
▸ a disappointing/ an unsatisfactory/ a discouraging **result**/ **experience**
▸ a disappointing/ an unsatisfactory **outcome**/ **performance**
▸ to **find** sth disappointing/ unsatisfactory/ wanting/ discouraging

disappointing not as good, successful or enjoyable as you had hoped; making you feel disappointed: *They gave a very disappointing performance.* ◇ *The outcome of the court case was disappointing for the family involved.*
unsatisfactory (*rather formal*) not good enough: *The results were considered to be thoroughly unsatisfactory.* ◇ *He reflected on the unsatisfactory nature of his relationship with the school principal.* **OPP satisfactory** → FINE, See also the entry for INADEQUATE
wanting [not before noun] (*formal*) not good enough: *This explanation is wanting in many respects.* ◇ *The new system was tried and found wanting.*
discouraging /dɪsˈkʌrɪdʒɪŋ; AmE -ˈkɜːr-/ making you feel less confident or enthusiastic about doing sth: *The response to our appeal has been rather discouraging.* **OPP encouraging** → PROMISING, See also **discourage** → DISCOURAGE 2

disappointment noun See also the entry for DISASTER

disappointment · let-down · anticlimax
These are all words for sth that is disappointing.

PATTERNS AND COLLOCATIONS
▸ a disappointment/ let-down **for** sb
▸ a **real** disappointment/ let-down
▸ a **big** disappointment/ let-down
▸ **something**/ **a bit of** a disappointment/ a let-down/ an anticlimax

disappointment [C] something that is disappointing: *It was a great disappointment to us when she left.* ◇ *That new restaurant was a big disappointment.* ◇ *This news has come as a disappointment to business leaders.* ◇ *He's suffered a whole string of disappointments this week.* See also **disappoint** → THWART
'let-down [C, usually sing., U] (*rather informal*) something that is disappointing because it is not as good as you expected it to be: *The London exhibition was a bit of a let-down.* ◇ *Afterwards there was just a feeling of let-down.*
anticlimax /ˌæntiˈklaɪmæks/ [C, U] something that is disappointing because it is the end of sth that was much more exciting, or because it is not as exciting as you expected it to be: *Travelling in Europe was something of an anticlimax after the years he'd spent in Africa.* ◇ *There was no hiding the sense of anticlimax, if not downright disappointment.* **OPP climax** → PEAK

disapprove verb

disapprove · deplore · frown on/upon sth
These words all mean to think that sb/sth is not good, suitable or acceptable.

frown on/upon sth   disapprove   deplore

PATTERNS AND COLLOCATIONS
▸ to disapprove of/ deplore/ frown on a/ an **practice**/ **action**
▸ to disapprove of/ deplore/ frown on **the use of** sth
▸ to disapprove of/ deplore **the way** sb does sth
▸ to **strongly** disapprove of/ deplore sth

disapprove [I] to think that sb/sth is not good, suitable or acceptable: *She wants to be an actor but her parents disapprove.* ◇ *He strongly disapproved of the changes that had been made.* **OPP approve** → IN FAVOUR, See also **disapproval** → CRITICISM, **disapproving** → CRITICAL
deplore /dɪˈplɔː(r)/ [T] (*rather formal*) to strongly disapprove of sth and criticize it, especially publicly: *Like everyone else, I deplore and condemn this killing.* ◇ *He deplored the fact that these criminals were treated by many as heroes.* See also **deplorable** → OUTRAGEOUS
'frown on/upon sth phrasal verb (*rather formal*) to disapprove of sth, but usually without doing much to prevent it other than express your disapproval: *In her family, any expression of feeling was frowned upon.* ◇ *According to the Home Office, this practice is frowned upon, but it is not illegal.*

disaster noun See also the entry for DISAPPOINTMENT

disaster · failure · catastrophe · fiasco · debacle · flop · washout
These are all words for sth that is very unsuccessful, causes a lot of problems or is disappointing.

PATTERNS AND COLLOCATIONS
▸ a disaster/ failure/ catastrophe **for** sb
▸ a fiasco/ debacle **over** sth
▸ a **total** disaster/ failure/ catastrophe/ fiasco/ flop/ washout
▸ a **complete** disaster/ failure/ catastrophe/ fiasco/ flop
▸ a **financial** disaster/ failure/ fiasco/ debacle
▸ an **economic** disaster/ failure/ catastrophe
▸ to **prove** a disaster/ failure/ fiasco/ flop

disaster [C, U] a very bad situation that causes problems; sth that is very unsuccessful: *Losing your job doesn't have to be such a disaster.* ◇ *Disaster struck when the wheel came off.* ◇ *Letting her organize the party is a recipe for disaster* (= sth that is likely to go badly wrong). ◇ *The play's first night was a total disaster.* See also **disaster** → CRISIS
failure [C] something that is not successful: *The whole thing was a complete failure.* ◇ *A team learns from experience, both successes and failures.* ◇ *The venture proved to be a costly failure.* **OPP success** → SUCCESS, See also **failure** → FAILURE
catastrophe /kəˈtæstrəfi/ [C] an event that causes sb suffering or that causes problems: *The attempt to expand the business was a catastrophe for the firm.* ◇ *We've had a few catastrophes with the food for the party.* See also **catastrophe** → CRISIS
fiasco /fiˈæskəʊ; AmE fiˈæskoʊ/ [C] (*rather informal*) something that is a complete failure especially because it is badly planned or organized, often in a way that causes embarrassment: *What a fiasco!* ◇ *After the fiasco over the brochures, I decided to take charge of the marketing.*
debacle /deɪˈbɑːkl; dɪˈb-/ [C] something that is a complete failure, especially because of disagreements between those involved, in a way that causes embarrassment: *He should take responsibility for the debacle and resign.*
flop [C] (*informal*) something such as a film, party or product, that is not successful, especially because it is not popular or is not bought by many people: *The film has been labelled the year's biggest box-office flop.* ◇ *The share sale has been a flop with investors.* **OPP hit** → SUCCESS, See also **flop** → CLOSE1 verb 2
washout /ˈwɒʃaʊt; AmE ˈwɑːʃ-; ˈwɔːʃ-/ [C, usually sing.] (*informal*) an event that is a complete failure, especially because of rain: *They feared that the wedding was going to be a washout after torrential rain.*

disastrous adj.

disastrous · devastating · catastrophic
These are all words to describe events and situations that cause great suffering or damage.

PATTERNS AND COLLOCATIONS
▶ disastrous / devastating / catastrophic **for** sb / sth
▶ a disastrous / devastating / catastrophic **effect / impact / failure / defeat / fire / storm / flood**
▶ disastrous / devastating / catastrophic **consequences / results / events**
▶ **potentially** disastrous / devastating / catastrophic
▶ **particularly / quite / absolutely / utterly** disastrous / devastating

disastrous /dɪˈzɑːstrəs; AmE -ˈzæs-/ (rather informal) very bad, harmful or unsuccessful: *Lowering interest rates could have disastrous consequences for the economy.* ◇ *The church was rebuilt after a disastrous fire in 1824.* ◇ *It was a disastrous start to the season for the team.* See also **disaster** → CRISIS
▶ **disastrously** adv.: *How could everything go so disastrously wrong?*

devastating /ˈdevəsteɪtɪŋ/ causing a lot of damage and destruction; extremely shocking to sb: *She was injured in a devastating explosion.* ◇ *It will be a devastating blow to the local community if the factory closes.* ◇ *It was then that she heard the devastating news that her father was dead.* See also **devastate** → DESTROY, **devastated** → UPSET

catastrophic /ˌkætəˈstrɒfɪk; AmE -ˈstrɑː-/ causing great damage or suffering: *Catastrophic floods inundated the region in 1636.* ◇ *Increased tourism has been catastrophic for the local ecology.* ◇ *He may come to be blamed for the party's catastrophic defeat at the polls.* See also **catastrophe** → CRISIS
▶ **catastrophically** adv.: *The system has failed catastrophically.*

NOTE **DEVASTATING** OR **CATASTROPHIC?** Both these words are used to describe the harmful effects of events such as war, fires and floods on the economy, the environment or people's lives. **Devastating** also describes events and news that deeply affect sb emotionally. **Catastrophic** also describes defeats and failures in politics.

disciplined adj.

disciplined · sober · moderate · controlled · restrained
These words all describe people showing calm control in the way they behave.

PATTERNS AND COLLOCATIONS
▶ a disciplined / moderate / controlled / restrained **approach**
▶ a disciplined / controlled / restrained **manner**
▶ **very** disciplined / sober / moderate / controlled / restrained
▶ **strictly** disciplined / controlled

disciplined /ˈdɪsəplɪnd/ showing control in the way you behave, and making yourself do things that you believe you should do: *This was a well-led and disciplined army.* ◇ *He needs a more disciplined approach to work.* **OPP** **undisciplined** ❶ Undisciplined people or behaviour lack control and organization: *This was an undisciplined performance from his team.* See also **discipline** → CONTROL noun

sober /ˈsəʊbə(r); AmE ˈsoʊ-/ [not usually before noun] not affected by alcohol: *I promised him that I'd stay sober tonight.* **OPP** **drunk** → DRUNK

moderate /ˈmɒdərət; AmE ˈmɑːd-/ staying within limits that are considered to be reasonable by most people: *I class myself as a moderate drinker.* ◇ *Their wage demands were generally considered to be moderate.* **OPP** **extreme** → RADICAL
▶ **moderately** adv.: *He only drinks moderately.*

controlled (of a person) remaining calm and not showing emotion; (of an emotion, especially anger) felt but carefully not expressed in a loud or violent way: *She remained quiet and controlled.* ◇ *He spoke with a hint of tightly controlled anger.* **OPP** **uncontrolled** ❶ Uncontrolled describes emotions or behaviour that sb cannot control or stop: *uncontrolled anger/fear* See also **control** → CONTROL noun

restrained showing calm control rather than emotion: *She smiled a restrained smile.* **OPP** **unrestrained** ❶ Unrestrained emotions are not controlled: *unrestrained aggression/delight* See also **restraint** → RESTRAINT noun

NOTE **CONTROLLED** OR **RESTRAINED?** Controlled is usually used to describe a person or their behaviour when they are able to stop themselves from panicking or getting angry (or showing their anger): *controlled panic/aggression/anger/fury.* Restrained is used more to talk about people being polite, and not shouting or getting too excited about things. Restrained is used mostly to describe actions and behaviour rather than the people themselves: *a restrained approach/attitude* ◇ *restrained optimism/passion*

discount verb

discount · deduct · take · subtract · knock sth off (sth) · take sth out of sth · take sth off sth · debit · dock
These words all mean to take a number or amount away from another number or amount.

PATTERNS AND COLLOCATIONS
▶ to deduct / take / subtract / debit / dock sth **from** sth
▶ to discount / deduct / take / subtract / knock sth off / debit an **amount** (from sth)
▶ to take / subtract one **number** from another
▶ to discount / knock sth off / take sth off **prices**
▶ to deduct / knock off / take off / dock **points / marks**
▶ to deduct sth from / take sth out of / dock sb's **pay / wages**

discount /dɪsˈkaʊnt; AmE also ˈdɪskaʊnt/ [T, usually passive] (especially business) to sell sth at less than the usual price in order to encourage people to buy it: *We're offering discounted prices throughout March.* ◇ *You can find discounted flights on the Internet.* ◇ *Most of our stock has been discounted by up to 40%.* ❶ Things that might **be discounted** include *prices, rates, fees, fares, tickets, books* and *subscriptions.*
▶ **discount** /ˈdɪskaʊnt/ noun [C, U]: *The store manager gave us a 10% discount on the drum set.* ◇ *They were selling everything at a discount.* ◇ *Do you give any discount?*

deduct /dɪˈdʌkt/ [T, often passive] (rather formal) to remove an amount of money or a number of points or marks in order to reduce the total: *The cost of your uniform will be deducted from your wages.* ◇ *Ten points will be deducted for a wrong answer.* ❶ In financial contexts, **deduct** is most often used to talk about taking money away from an amount such as a payment in order to pay tax: *Tax is deducted at source* (= before you actually receive the payment). In other contexts, **deduct** is mainly used to talk about taking away points or stars that have previously been awarded in a competition or rating system, for example.
▶ **deduction** /dɪˈdʌkʃn/ noun [C, U]: *deductions from your pay for tax and pension contributions*

take [T] (not used in the progressive tenses) to reduce one number by the value of another: *Take 5 from 12 and you're left with 7.* ◇ *(informal, spoken) 28 take away 5 is 23.* **OPP** **add** → COUNT

subtract /səbˈtrækt/ [T] (rather formal) to reduce one number by the value of another: *6 subtracted from 9 is 3* (9−6 = 3). ◇ *If you subtract 6 from 9, you get 3.* **OPP** **add** → COUNT
▶ **subtraction** noun [U]: *children learning addition and subtraction* **OPP** **addition** → COUNT verb

knock sth ˈoff, knock sth ˈoff sth phrasal verb (rather informal) to remove an amount of money or a number of points or marks in order to reduce the total: *They knocked off $60 because of a scratch.* ◇ *The news knocked 13% off the company's shares.*

take sth ˈout of sth phrasal verb to remove an amount of money from a larger amount, especially as a payment: *The fine will be taken out of your wages.* ❶ Take sth out of sth is usually followed by *wages* or *pay.*

,**take sth 'off sth** *phrasal verb* to remove an amount of money or a number of points or marks in order to reduce the total: *The manager took $10 off the bill.* ◇ *(rather informal) That experience took ten years off my life (=* made me feel ten years older). ◇ *That new hairstyle takes years off you (= makes you look several years younger)!*

debit /'debɪt/ [T] *(rather formal, finance)* (of a bank) to take money from an account: *The money will be debited from your account each month.* ◇ *The bank will debit your account with any withdrawals made using your payment card.* **OPP credit ❶** A bank can **credit** an account with money, or **credit** money to an account, when it adds money to the account: *Your account has been credited with $50 000.* ◇ *$50 000 has been credited to your account.* See also **debit** → DEBIT *noun*

dock [T] to take away part of sb's pay, especially as a punishment: *If you're late, your wages will be docked.* ◇ *They've docked 15% off my pay for this week.* **❶** Your employer might **dock** your *pay* or *wages*, or *money* from your pay.

discourage *verb*

1 a campaign to discourage smoking among teenagers
2 Don't be discouraged by failure.

---

1 discourage · dissuade · talk sb out of sth · warn sb off (sth)
These words all mean to try to persuade sb not to do sth.

PATTERNS AND COLLOCATIONS
▶ to discourage / dissuade sb **from** doing sth
▶ to talk sb out of / warn sb off **doing sth**
▶ to **try to** discourage / dissuade / talk sb out of / warn sb off sth
▶ to **manage to** dissuade sb / talk sb out of sth

discourage /dɪs'kʌrɪdʒ; AmE -'kɜːr-/ [T] to try to prevent sb from doing sth, especially by making it difficult to do or by showing that you do not approve of it: *They are launching a new campaign to discourage smoking among teenagers.* ◇ *I leave a light on when I'm out to discourage burglars.* ◇ *His parents tried to discourage him from being an actor.* **OPP encourage** → ENCOURAGE 2
▶ **discouragement** *noun* [U, C]: *the government's discouragement of political protest*

dissuade /dɪ'sweɪd/ [T] *(rather formal, especially written)* to persuade sb not to do sth: *I tried to dissuade him from resigning.* ◇ *They were going to set off in the fog but were dissuaded.* **OPP persuade** → PERSUADE

,**talk sb 'out of sth** *phrasal verb (rather informal)* to persuade sb not to do sth: *I tried to talk him out of giving up his job.* **OPP talk sb into sth** → PERSUADE

NOTE DISSUADE OR TALK SB OUT OF STH? Dissuade is mainly used in writing or in more formal spoken contexts. **Talk sb out of sth** is used especially in more informal contexts, such as in conversation. It is also very common, in all contexts, to use **persuade sb not to do sth**: *I tried to persuade him not to resign/give up his job.*

,**warn sb 'off**, ,**warn sb 'off sth** *phrasal verb (rather informal)* to advise sb not to do sth or to stop doing sth: *We were warned off buying the house.* ◇ *She wanted to ask him about it but the look in his eyes warned her off.*

2 discourage · demoralize · depress · daunt · crush · get sb down · oppress
These words all mean to make sb feel less confident, less enthusiastic or unhappy.

PATTERNS AND COLLOCATIONS
▶ a **thought** depresses / daunts / oppresses sb

discourage /dɪs'kʌrɪdʒ; AmE -'kɜːr-/ [T, often passive] to make sb feel less confident or enthusiastic about doing sth: *Don't be discouraged by the first failure – try again!* ◇ *The weather discouraged most people from attending.* ◇

High interest rates will discourage investment. **OPP encourage** → ENCOURAGE 1, See also **discouraging** → DISAPPOINTING
▶ **discouragement** *noun* [U, C]: *an atmosphere of discouragement and despair* ◇ *Despite all these discouragements, she refused to give up.* **OPP encouragement** → ENCOURAGE 1

demoralize *(BrE also* -**ise***)* /dɪ'mɒrəlaɪz; AmE -'mɔːr-; -'mɑːr-/ [T, often passive] to make sb lose confidence and hope, especially by creating a negative feeling among a group of people: *Constant criticism is enough to demoralize anybody.* ◇ *Many members were demoralized by the leadership's failure to implement reforms.* See also **morale** → MOOD
▶ **demoralizing** *(BrE also* -**ising***) adj.: the demoralizing effects of unemployment*

depress /dɪ'pres/ [T] to make sb feel sad and without hope or enthusiasm: *Wet weather always depresses me.* ◇ *It depresses me to see so many young girls smoking.* See also **depressed** → DEPRESSED, **depressing** → NEGATIVE, **depression** → GLOOM

daunt /dɔːnt/ [T, often passive] to make sb feel nervous and less confident about doing sth, because it seems difficult or frightening: *She was a brave woman but she felt daunted by the task ahead.* See also **daunting** → FRIGHTENING

crush [T] *(especially written)* to destroy sb's confidence or happiness: *She felt completely crushed by the teacher's criticism.* ◇ *Their new self-confidence could not be crushed.*
▶ **crushing** *adj.: a crushing defeat in the election*

,**get sb 'down** *phrasal verb (rather informal, especially spoken)* to make sb feel sad or depressed: *Don't let it get you down too much.* ◇ *The lack of sleep is getting me down.* **OPP cheer sb up** → ENCOURAGE 1

oppress /ə'pres/ [T] *(rather formal, written)* to make sb only able to think about sad or worrying things: *The gloomy atmosphere in the office oppressed her.*

discredit *verb*

discredit · libel · slander · defame · vilify · malign · smear
These words all mean to say, write or do things that damage sb/sth's reputation.

PATTERNS AND COLLOCATIONS
▶ to be discredited / vilified / maligned **for** / **as** sth
▶ to discredit / smear the **government**

discredit /dɪs'kredɪt/ [T] to cause people to stop respecting sb/sth: *The photos were deliberately taken to discredit the President.* See also **discredit** → DISGRACE *noun* 2

libel /'laɪbl/ [T] to publish a printed statement about sb/ sth that is not true and is likely to damage their reputation; to commit the legal offence of making this kind of statement: *He claimed he had been libelled in an article the magazine had published.*
▶ **libel** *noun* [U, C]: *He sued the newspaper for libel.* ◇ *In a libel action a newspaper must prove that any comments it printed are true.*
▶ **libellous** /'laɪbələs/ *adj.: There have been several libellous statements posted on a website in the UK.*

slander /'slɑːndə(r); AmE 'slæn-/ [T] to make a spoken statement about sb/sth that is not true and is likely to damage their reputation; to commit the legal offence of making this kind of statement: *He angrily accused the investigators of slandering both him and his family.*
▶ **slander** *noun* [C, U]: *She regarded his comments as a vicious slander on her reputation.* ◇ *He's suing them for slander.*
▶ **slanderous** /-dərəs/ *adj.: You have no right to make such slanderous, evil accusations.*

defame /dɪ'feɪm/ [T] *(formal)* to libel or slander sb: *The newspaper denies any intention to defame the senator's reputation.*
▶ **defamation** /ˌdefə'meɪʃn/ *noun* [U, C]: *He brought a*

legal action against the magazine for **defamation of character**.

▶ **defamatory** /dɪˈfæmətri; AmE -ˌtɔːri/ adj.: He claims that defamatory comments were made about him.

vilify /ˈvɪlɪfaɪ/ [T] (formal) to say or write things that show hatred for sb/sth and make them seem evil: They were vilified by the press as 'international terrorists'. ❶ A person or thing is usually **vilified** by a group of people over a period of time.

▶ **vilification** /ˌvɪlɪfɪˈkeɪʃn/ noun [U]: the vilification of single parents by right-wing politicians

malign /məˈlaɪn/ [T] (written) to say or write things about sb/sth that are unfair and damage their reputation: She feels she has been **much maligned** by the press.

smear /smɪə(r); AmE smɪr/ [T] (rather informal) to make claims about sb/sth that are intended to damage their reputation, especially in politics: The story was an attempt to smear the party leader.

▶ **smear** noun [C]: The Prime Minister has called for an end to smears and personal attacks in the run-up to the election. ◇ He was a victim of a **smear campaign**.

discrimination noun See also the entry for
RACISM

---

discrimination · prejudice · bias · apartheid · affirmative action · intolerance · favouritism
These are all words for the unfair treatment of a particular group in society, for example because of their race, sex or religion.

PATTERNS AND COLLOCATIONS
▶ discrimination / prejudice / bias / intolerance / favouritism **towards / toward** sb / sth
▶ discrimination / prejudice / bias **in favour of / against** sb / sth
▶ **sexual** discrimination / prejudice / bias / apartheid
▶ **racial / religious** discrimination / prejudice / bias / intolerance
▶ **race / class / age / political** discrimination / prejudice / bias
▶ **blatant / clear** discrimination / prejudice / bias
▶ to **have** a prejudice / bias
▶ to **show** discrimination / prejudice / a bias / intolerance / favouritism
▶ to **fight** discrimination / prejudice / apartheid
▶ to **reduce / eliminate** discrimination / prejudice / bias

---

discrimination /dɪˌskrɪmɪˈneɪʃn/ [U] (disapproving) unfair treatment of a particular person or group in society, for example because of their race, sex or religion: This is blatant discrimination against people with disabilities. ◇ Our policy forbids **discrimination on the grounds of** a person's race, sex or sexuality. ◇ (BrE, approving) Some colleges feel there is a real need for **positive discrimination** in favour of applicants from poorer backgrounds (= more favourable treatment for that group). ❶ In American English this is usually called **affirmative action** (see below). **Reverse discrimination**, in both British and American English, is the same policy when it is considered to be a bad thing: (disapproving) The court heard arguments that programs to reserve some public works contracts for minorities cause reverse discrimination. See also **segregation** → DIVISION 1, **discriminatory** → BIASED

▶ **discriminate** verb [I]: practices that discriminate against women ◇ It is illegal to discriminate on grounds of race, sex or religion.

prejudice /ˈpredʒudɪs/ [U, C] (disapproving) an unreasonable dislike or negative attitude towards a particular person or group of people, especially when it is based on their race, religion, sex, etc: Prejudice towards new immigrants meant that many were unable to find work. ◇ He was just talking out of **blind prejudice**. ◇ I'm afraid all the debate did was confirm my own prejudices. ❶ You can also have a **prejudice** in favour of a particular person or group, but this is less common than its negative meaning: I must admit to a prejudice in favour of British universities. See also **prejudiced** → BIASED

bias /ˈbaɪəs/ [U, C, usually sing.] (disapproving) a strong feeling in favour of or against a particular group or side in an argument, often not based on a fair judgement: There is plenty of evidence of gender bias in the classroom. ◇ Employers must consider all candidates without bias. ◇ There is a systematic bias in favour of employers in this country. See also **biased** → BIASED

apartheid /əˈpɑːtaɪt; -eɪt; AmE əˈpɑːrtaɪt; -eɪt/ [U] the former political system in South Africa in which only white people had full political and social rights and other people, especially black people, were forced to live away from white people, go to separate schools, etc: **Under apartheid**, white people were not allowed to marry non-white people. ◇ He was jailed for advocating the violent overthrow of the **apartheid system**. ❶ Although the apartheid system no longer exists in South Africa, the word **apartheid** is sometimes used about other situations in which one group of people is treated much worse than a more powerful group: (disapproving) It was a system of educational apartheid in which children were divided, at the age of eleven, into 'achievers' and 'non-achievers'. See also **segregation** → DIVISION 1

af.firmative 'action /əˈfɜːmətɪv; AmE əˈfɜːrm-/ [U] (usually approving) (in the US) the policy of giving special treatment or preference to members of groups likely to suffer discrimination, especially on the grounds of race: The City Council implemented the affirmative action hiring plan in response to critics' charges that the police department did not reflect the city's racial makeup.

intolerance /ɪnˈtɒlərəns; AmE -ˈtɑːl-/ [U] (rather formal, disapproving) the refusal to accept ideas or ways of behaving that are different from your own: Refugees are people whose lives have been shattered by intolerance, persecution, torture and fear of death. **OPP tolerance** → PATIENCE. See also **intolerant** → BIASED

favouritism (BrE) (AmE **favoritism**) /ˈfeɪvərɪtɪzəm/ [U] (disapproving) a situation in which sb, especially sb in authority, treats one person better than others; the act of doing this: She tries not to show any favouritism towards her own children.

discussion noun See the Topic Map for FACT AND
OPINION on p.898

---

discussion · conversation · dialogue · talk · debate · consultation · chat · gossip · chatter · exchange
These are all words for an occasion when people talk about sth.

PATTERNS AND COLLOCATIONS
▶ a discussion / a conversation / a dialogue / a talk / a debate / a consultation / a chat / a gossip / chatter / an exchange **about** sth
▶ a discussion / conversation / dialogue / debate / consultation **on** sth
▶ a discussion / a conversation / a dialogue / a talk / a debate / a consultation / a chat / a gossip / an exchange **with** sb
▶ a discussion / a conversation / a dialogue / a debate / a consultation / an exchange **between** two people / groups
▶ **in (close)** discussion / conversation / dialogue / debate / consultation **with** sb
▶ to **have** a discussion / a conversation / a dialogue / a talk / a debate / a consultation / a chat / a gossip / an exchange
▶ to **hold** a discussion / conversation / debate / consultation
▶ to **be involved in / join in / participate in / take part in / engage in** (a) discussion / conversation / dialogue / debate
▶ to **get into** (a) discussion / conversation with sb
▶ to **conclude / end / continue** a discussion / conversation / debate
▶ to **break off** a discussion / conversation

---

discussion [C, U] an occasion when people talk in detail about sth that is considered to be important; the process of talking with sb about sth important: Discussions are still taking place between the two leaders. ◇ We will choose a different topic for discussion each week. ◇ After considerable discussion, they decided to accept our offer. ◇ The plans have been **under discussion** (= being talked about) *for a year now.* ◇ *We can use the draft document as a basis for discussion.* See also **discuss** → TALK

conversation [C, U] an occasion when two people or a small group talk about sth, especially in a private or informal way; the activity of talking in this way: *a telephone conversation* ◇ *He struggled to keep the conversation going.* ◇ *The conversation turned to gardening.* ◇ *The main topic of conversation was the likely outcome of the election.* ◇ *Don was deep in conversation with the girl on his right.* ◇ *I tried to make polite conversation* (= to speak in order to appear polite). ◇ *(BrE) I got into conversation with a man on the bus.* ◇ *(AmE) I got into a conversation with a man on the bus.*

dialogue (*AmE* also **dialog**) /ˈdaɪəlɒɡ; *AmE* -lɔːɡ; -lɑːɡ/ [U, C] conversations in a book, play or film; a formal discussion between two groups, especially when they are trying to solve a problem or end a dispute: *The novel has long descriptions and not much dialogue.* ◇ *Learners are asked to listen to three short dialogues.* ◇ *The President told waiting reporters there had been a constructive dialogue.*

talk [C] a conversation or discussion, often one about a problem or sth important for the people involved: *I had a long talk with my boss about my career prospects.* ◇ *She looked worried so we had a talk.* See also **talk** → TALK *verb*

debate [C, U] a formal discussion of an issue at a public meeting or in a parliament. In a **debate** two or more speakers express opposing views and then there is often a vote on the issue: *a debate on prison reform* ◇ *The prime minister opened the debate* (= was the first to speak). ◇ *After a long debate, Congress approved the proposal.* ◇ *The motion under debate* (= being discussed) *was put to a vote.* See also **debate** → TALK *verb*

consultation /ˌkɒnslˈteɪʃn; *AmE* -kɑːn-/ [C, U] a formal discussion between groups of people before a decision is made about sth; the act of discussing sth in this way: *There have been extensive consultations between the two countries.* ◇ *The decision was taken after close consultation with local residents.* ◇ *A consultation period will be required.* See also **consult** → TALK *verb*

chat [U, C] informal talking; a friendly informal conversation: *(especially BrE) I just called in for a chat about the kids.* ◇ *That's enough chat from me — on with the music!* ❶ The countable use of **chat** is especially British English. See also **chat** → CHAT *verb*

gossip [C, usually sing.] a conversation about other people and their private lives: *We had a good gossip about the boss.* See also **gossip** → CHAT *verb*, **gossip** → SPEAKER *noun* 1

chatter [U] continuous rapid informal talk about things that are not important: *Jane's constant chatter was beginning to annoy him.* See also **chatter** → CHAT *verb*

exchange [C] a short conversation or an angry argument: *There was only time for a brief exchange.* ◇ *There was a heated exchange between the parents and the school managers.* See also **exchange** → REPLACE *verb* 2

disease *noun* See the Topic Map for HEALTH on p.890, See also the entry for ILLNESS

disease · illness · disorder · infection · condition · ailment · bug · complaint · virus · sickness
These are all words for a medical problem.

PATTERNS AND COLLOCATIONS
▸ a **serious / chronic** disease / illness / disorder / infection / condition / ailment
▸ a **minor** disease / illness / disorder / infection / ailment
▸ a **common / rare** disease/illness/disorder/infection/condition/ailment / virus
▸ an **infectious** disease / illness / condition / virus
▸ a **childhood** disease / illness / disorder / infection / ailment
▸ to **have / suffer from** a disease / an illness / a disorder / an infection/a condition/an ailment/a bug/a complaint/a virus/ sickness
▸ to **cause** a disease / an illness / a disorder / an infection / a condition / an ailment / sickness

▸ to **catch / contract / get / pick up** a disease / an illness / an infection / a bug / a virus
▸ to **diagnose / treat** a disease / an illness / a disorder / an infection / a condition / an ailment / a virus
▸ to **cure** a disease / an illness / a disorder / an infection / a condition / an ailment
▸ to **recover from** a disease/an illness/a disorder/an infection/ a bug/a virus/ a sickness
▸ to **die from / of** a disease/an illness/a disorder/an infection/ a condition / a bug / a virus
▸ a disease/an illness/an infection/a virus/a sickness **spreads**

disease [C, U] a medical problem affecting humans, animals or plants, often caused by infection: *He suffers from a rare blood disease.* ◇ *The problem was finally diagnosed as heart disease.* ◇ *Measures have been taken to prevent the spread of disease.*

illness [C] a medical problem, or a period of suffering from one: *Have you suffered from any serious illnesses in the past six months?* ◇ *He died after a long illness.* See also **ill** → SICK 1

NOTE DISEASE OR ILLNESS? **Disease** is used to talk about more severe physical medical problems, especially those that affect the organs. **Illness** is used to talk about both more severe and more minor medical problems, and those that affect mental health: *heart/kidney/liver disease* ◇ ~~*heart/kidney/liver illness*~~ ◇ *mental illness* ◇ ~~*mental disease*~~ **Disease** is NOT used about a period of illness: ~~*He died after a long disease.*~~ **Illness** also means 'the state of being ill'. See also the entry for ILLNESS

disorder [C, U] (*rather formal*) an illness that causes a part of the body to stop functioning correctly: *This is a rare disorder of the liver.* ◇ *Most people with acute mental disorder can be treated at home.* ❶ A **disorder** is usually not infectious. **Disorder** is used most frequently with words relating to mental problems: *a/an psychiatric/ personality/mental/depressive/eating disorder.* When it is used to talk about physical problems, it is used most often with *blood, bowel* and *kidney*, and these are commonly *serious, severe* or *rare.*

infection [C] an illness that is caused by bacteria or a virus and that affects one part of the body: *He's been off work with a throat infection.* ◇ *Sneezing is the most common way of spreading an infection.* See also **infect** → PASS STH ON

condition [C] (*rather formal*) a medical problem that you have for a long time because it is not possible to cure it: *Does your child have any kind of medical condition that we should know about?* ◇ *He suffers from a serious heart condition.*

ailment [C] (*rather formal*) an illness that is not very serious: *Below is a list of common childhood ailments.*

bug [C] (*informal*) an infectious illness that is usually fairly mild: *There's a stomach bug going round* (= people are catching it from each other).

complaint [C] (*rather formal*) an illness, especially one that is not serious, and often one that affects a particular part of the body: *He suffers from a skin complaint called 'rosacea'.*

virus /ˈvaɪrəs/ [C] (*informal*) a disease caused by a virus (= a living thing, too small to be seen without a microscope, that causes infectious disease): *There's a virus going around the office.* ❶ A more formal way of talking about a **virus** in this meaning is **viral infection**.

sickness [U, C, usually sing.] (in compounds) a particular type of illness or disease: *Do you need any travel sickness tablets?* ❶ Words that form compounds with **sickness** include *altitude, morning, mountain, radiation* and *travel*.

disgrace *noun*
1 *It's a national disgrace.*
2 *bring disgrace on your family*

1 disgrace · crime · evil · abomination · iniquity
These are all words for a bad or immoral person, thing or action.

PATTERNS AND COLLOCATIONS
▸ It's a disgrace / crime.
▸ It's a disgrace / crime **to do sth**.

disgrace /dɪsˈɡreɪs/ [sing.] a person, thing or act that is so bad that the people connected with them/it should feel ashamed: *The state of our roads is a national disgrace.* ◇ *That sort of behaviour is **a disgrace to** the legal profession.* ◇ *It's **a disgrace that** (= it is very wrong that) they are paid so little.* See also **disgraceful** → OUTRAGEOUS

crime [sing.] (*informal*) an act that you strongly disapprove of: *It's a crime to waste so much money.* ❶ In this meaning, **crime** is always used in the expression *It's a crime....* See also **criminal** → OUTRAGEOUS

evil [C, usually pl.] (*formal*) a wicked or harmful thing; the bad effect of sth: *We were warned against the evils of drugs.* ◇ *They hardly mentioned such social evils as racism and sexism.* ❶ **Evils** is most often used in the patterns *the evils of...* and *social evils*.

abomination /əˌbɒmɪˈneɪʃn; AmE əˌbɑːm-/ [C] (*formal*) a thing or act that strongly offends people's sense of morality, religion or good taste: *A strict Puritan, he regarded all theatres and play acting as an abomination.* ◇ *The building was described as 'a concrete abomination masquerading as a hotel'.*

iniquity /ɪˈnɪkwəti/ [U, C] (*formal*) the fact of being very unfair or wrong; sth that is very unfair or wrong: *the iniquity of racial prejudice* ◇ *the iniquities of the criminal justice system*

2 disgrace · disrepute · shame · dishonour · discredit
These are all words for the loss of other people's respect and approval.

PATTERNS AND COLLOCATIONS
▸ **in** disgrace / disrepute
▸ to **bring** disgrace / shame / dishonour / discredit **on** sb / sth
▸ to **fall into** disgrace / disrepute
▸ **There is no** disgrace / shame / dishonour **in** sth.

disgrace /dɪsˈɡreɪs/ [U] the loss of other people's respect caused by doing sth immoral or unacceptable: *Her behaviour has brought disgrace on her family.* ◇ *The swimmer was **sent home** from the Olympics **in disgrace**.* ◇ *Sam was in disgrace with his parents.* See also **disgraceful** → OUTRAGEOUS
▸ **disgrace** *verb* [T]: *I **disgraced myself** by drinking far too much.* ◇ *He had disgraced the family name.*

disrepute /ˌdɪsrɪˈpjuːt/ [U] (*rather formal, especially written*) the loss of public respect for an activity or idea: *The players' behaviour on the field is likely to **bring** the game **into disrepute**.* ❶ People can bring an activity into disrepute, especially a game such as football, by their bad behaviour, for example by cheating or fighting. A theory, system or law can be *in disrepute* or *fall into disrepute*, if it is no longer thought to be true or useful.

shame [U] public disgrace: *There is no shame in wanting to be successful.* ◇ *(formal) She felt that her failure would bring shame on her family.* See also **shame** → EMBARRASS *verb*, **shameful** → OUTRAGEOUS

dishonour (*BrE*) (*AmE* **dishonor**) /dɪsˈɒnə(r); AmE -ˈɑːn-/ [U] (*formal*) public disgrace: *Her actions have brought shame and dishonour on the profession.* ◇ *There is no dishonour in such a defeat.* **OPP** **honour** → INTEGRITY, **honour** → REPUTATION, See also **dishonourable** → DESPICABLE
▸ **dishonour** *verb* (*BrE*) (*AmE* **dishonor**): [T] *You have dishonoured the name of the school.*

discredit /dɪsˈkredɪt/ [U] (*formal*) public disgrace, especially for a group or organization: *Britain, **to its discredit**, did not speak out against these atrocities.* ◇ *My brother's behaviour did great **discredit to** the family.* See also **discredit** → DISCREDIT *verb*

NOTE **DISGRACE, SHAME, DISHONOUR** OR **DISCREDIT?** In some cases you can use any of these words: *Her behaviour has brought disgrace/shame/dishonour/discredit on her family.* **Disgrace** is the most frequent of these words and has the widest range of collocates: ~~The swimmer was sent home in shame/dishonour/discredit.~~ ~~Sam was in shame/dishonour/discredit with his parents.~~ **Disgrace** can be a public loss of respect or the loss of respect of people you are close to. **Shame, dishonour** and **discredit** are all used to talk about a public loss of respect. **Shame** and **dishonour** are both used especially in the phrases *bring shame/dishonour on sb/sth* and *There is no shame/dishonour in (doing) sth*. There is no real difference in meaning, but **dishonour** is more formal. **Discredit** is used especially to talk about the loss of respect for a family, group, organization or country, caused by the behaviour of its members or representatives; it is used especially in the phrases *to sb/sth's discredit* and *do discredit to sb/sth*.

disgusting *adj.*

1 smell/taste disgusting
2 a disgusting thing to say

1 See also the entry for TERRIBLE 1

disgusting · foul · revolting · repulsive · offensive · gross · nauseating
These words all describe sth, especially a smell, taste or habit, that is extremely unpleasant and often makes you feel slightly ill.

PATTERNS AND COLLOCATIONS
▸ disgusting / repulsive / offensive **to** sb
▸ a disgusting / a foul / a revolting / an offensive / a gross / a nauseating **smell**
▸ a disgusting / foul / gross / nauseating **taste**
▸ a disgusting / revolting / gross / nauseating **habit**
▸ disgusting / offensive / gross **behaviour**
▸ a disgusting / revolting / repulsive **man / woman / person**
▸ to **find sb / sth** disgusting / revolting / repulsive / offensive / nauseating
▸ to **smell / taste** disgusting / foul / gross
▸ **really** disgusting / foul / revolting / offensive / gross / nauseating
▸ **quite** disgusting / revolting / offensive / gross
▸ **absolutely** disgusting / foul / revolting

disgusting (*especially spoken*) extremely unpleasant and making you feel slightly ill: *The kitchen was in a disgusting state.* ◇ *What a disgusting smell!* ◇ *The sink was full of a disgusting black slime.* ◇ *This tastes absolutely disgusting.* ◇ *Picking your nose is a disgusting habit.* See also **disgust** → SHOCK *verb*
▸ **disgust** *noun* [U]: *She wrinkled her nose **in disgust** at the smell of urine.*
▸ **disgustingly** *adv.*: *The kitchen was disgustingly dirty.*

foul /faʊl/ dirty, and tasting or smelling bad: *This tastes foul!* ◇ *The air in the cell was foul.* ◇ *She could smell his foul breath.* ◇ *Foul drinking water was blamed for the epidemic.*

revolting disgusting: *The stew looked revolting.* ◇ *He's an absolutely revolting man.*
▸ **revoltingly** *adv.*: *a revoltingly sentimental story*

NOTE **DISGUSTING** OR **REVOLTING?** Both of these words are used to describe things that smell and taste unpleasant, unpleasant personal habits and people who have them. There is no real difference in meaning, but **disgusting** is more frequent, especially in spoken English.

repulsive /rɪˈpʌlsɪv/ (*rather formal*) extremely unpleasant in a way that offends you or makes you feel slightly ill: *What a repulsive person!* ◇ *He found her habits quite repulsive.* ❶ **Repulsive** usually describes people, their behaviour or habits, which you may find offensive for physical or moral reasons. See also **repel** → SHOCK *verb*

offensive (*formal*) (especially of smells) extremely unpleasant: *The problem is how to eliminate offensive smells from the processing plant.*

gross /grəʊs; *AmE* groʊs/ (*informal, spoken*) (of a smell, taste or personal habit) extremely unpleasant: *'He ate it with mustard.' 'Oh, gross!'*

nauseating /'nɔːzieɪtɪŋ; 'nɔːsieɪtɪŋ/ making you feel that you want to vomit: *He woke to the nauseating smell of burning flesh.* See also **nauseous** → SICK 2

---

2 disgusting · distasteful · sickening · hateful · repugnant · abominable
These words all describe sth that you think is unacceptable and shocking.

disgusting	sickening	hateful
distasteful		repugnant
		abominable

PATTERNS AND COLLOCATIONS
▸ disgusting / distasteful / hateful / repugnant / abominable **to** sb
▸ disgusting / distasteful / sickening / hateful / repugnant / abominable **that**…
▸ a disgusting / an abominable **practice**
▸ a sickening / an abominable **crime**
▸ to **find sth** disgusting / distasteful / repugnant
▸ **absolutely** / **quite** disgusting / sickening / hateful / repugnant

disgusting (*rather informal, especially spoken*) shocking and unacceptable, especially for moral reasons: *I think it's disgusting that they're closing the hospital.* ◇ *That's a disgusting thing to say.* ❶ **Disgusting** is commonly used in spoken English to describe things you disapprove of for moral reasons, but they are usually not such absolutely evil things as some of the other words describe: ~~a cruel and disgusting regime which tortures its opponents~~ See also **disgust** → SHOCK *verb*
▸ **disgust** *noun* [U]: *Much **to my disgust** they refused to help.* ◇ *He walked away **in disgust**.*

distasteful (*rather formal*) unpleasant, especially because it deals with subjects such as death, sex or crime in a shocking or offensive way: *Parts of this story may be distasteful, even shocking.* ◇ *Some viewers might find the pictures distasteful.*
▸ **distaste** *noun* [U, sing.]: *He looked around the filthy room in distaste.* ◇ *She felt a **distaste for** anything to do with bodily functions.*

sickening extremely shocking, especially because it involves sb being physically hurt: *She was the victim of a sickening attack.* ◇ *His head hit the ground with a sickening thud.* ❶ **Sickening** is often used to describe a sound that makes you think sb has been hurt or sth has been badly damaged.

hateful (*rather formal*) extremely unpleasant or cruel, or morally unacceptable: *I tried to ignore her hateful words.* ◇ *The idea of fighting their own people was hateful to them.*

repugnant /rɪ'pʌɡnənt/ (*formal*) completely unacceptable, especially because it goes against your beliefs about what is morally right: *We found his suggestion quite repugnant.* ◇ *The idea of eating meat was repugnant to her.*

> **NOTE** HATEFUL OR REPUGNANT? **Hateful** usually describes ideas that most people would find unacceptable. **Repugnant** can also describe ideas that are unacceptable to a particular person, but not to some other people: *We found his suggestion quite repugnant.* ◇ ~~We found his suggestion quite hateful.~~

abominable /ə'bɒmɪnəbl/ (*rather formal*) extremely cruel and shocking: *The judge described the attack as an abominable crime.* ❶ **Abominable** is sometimes used in slightly more informal language in an exaggerated way, to describe behaviour that is not physically cruel but shows no thought for other people's feelings or wishes: *I think you are utterly selfish and your behaviour has been abominable.*

---

dishonest *adj.*

dishonest · devious · hypocritical · deceitful · underhand · lying · two-faced
These words all describe people not being honest and intending to deceive people.

PATTERNS AND COLLOCATIONS
▸ to be dishonest / devious / hypocritical **of** sb to do sth
▸ a dishonest / a devious / a hypocritical / a deceitful / an underhand **manner** / **way**
▸ dishonest / devious / deceitful / underhand **tactics** / **means**
▸ a dishonest / devious / underhand **method**
▸ dishonest / underhand **dealings**
▸ a lying / two-faced **hypocrite**
▸ to do **something** / **nothing** dishonest / underhand

dishonest (*rather formal*) not honest; intending to deceive people: *Beware of dishonest traders in the tourist areas.* ◇ *I don't like him, and it would be dishonest of me to pretend otherwise.* **OPP** **honest** → HONEST, See also **dishonesty** → FRAUD 1
▸ **dishonestly** *adv.*: *He was accused of dishonestly obtaining property.*

devious /'diːviəs/ behaving in a dishonest or indirect way in order to get sth: *He's as devious as a politician needs to be.* ◇ *They got rich by devious means.* ❶ **Devious** is used to describe people, their *minds, plans* and *schemes*, and the *ways, means, methods* and *tactics* that they use. See also the entry for CUNNING

hypocritical /,hɪpə'krɪtɪkl/ (*rather formal*) pretending to have moral standards or opinions that you do not actually have: *It would be hypocritical of me to have a church wedding when I don't believe in God.*
▸ **hypocrisy** /hɪ'pɒkrəsi; *AmE* hɪ'pɑːk-/ *noun* [U, C]: (*rather formal*) *It's hypocrisy for them to pretend they were shocked at the news.* ◇ *She refused to conform to the usual practices and hypocrisies of high society.*
▸ **hypocrite** /'hɪpəkrɪt/ *noun* [C]: *Charles was a liar and a hypocrite who married her for her money.*

deceitful /dɪ'siːtfl/ (*formal*) behaving in a dishonest way by telling lies and making people believe things that are not true: *The government was accused of being hypocritical and deceitful.* See also **deceit** → FRAUD 1

> **NOTE** DISHONEST OR DECEITFUL? People talk about *dishonest dealings/practices/conduct* in business, in which people are tricked, as well as *dishonest workmen* (= people who do building work and repairs in your home who trick you). **Deceitful** is used especially to describe sb who has told you a lie.

underhand /,ʌndə'hænd; *AmE* -dər'h-/ (*rather formal*) (of behaviour) secret and dishonest: *I would never have expected her to behave in such an underhand way.* ◇ *I promise you there's nothing underhand about this agreement.* ❶ **Underhand** is used to talk about the *ways, methods, means* and *tactics* that people use to get what they want.

lying (*informal, especially spoken*) saying or writing sth that you know is not true: *You lying little toad!*

two-'faced (*informal*) not sincere; not acting in a way that supports what you say that you believe; saying different things to different people about a particular subject: *He accused her of being a two-faced liar.*

---

dismiss *verb*

dismiss · brush sb/sth aside · shrug sth off/aside · discount · banish · set sth aside · laugh sth off
These words all mean to refuse to accept, talk about or think about sb/sth, especially because you think it is not important.

PATTERNS AND COLLOCATIONS
▶ to dismiss/ brush sb/sth aside/ shrug sth off/ discount sth/ set sth aside **as** irrelevant, unimportant, etc.
▶ to dismiss/ brush aside/ shrug off/ discount/ laugh off a **suggestion**
▶ to dismiss/ brush aside/ shrug off **criticism**
▶ to dismiss/ brush aside/ discount/ banish/ laugh off a **fear**
▶ to dismiss/ brush aside/ discount/ shrug off/ banish a **thought**
▶ to dismiss/ brush aside/ discount/ banish a/ an **idea**
▶ to dismiss/ brush aside/ banish a/ an **memory**
▶ to dismiss/ shrug off/ banish a **feeling**
▶ to dismiss/ discount/ banish sth **quickly**
▶ to dismiss/ banish sth **easily**

dismiss [T] (*rather formal*) to treat sth as if it is not important and not worth thinking or talking about; to put thoughts or feelings out of your mind: *I think we can safely dismiss their objections.* ◇ *He dismissed the opinion polls as worthless.* ◇ *The suggestion should not be dismissed out of hand* (= without thinking about it). ◇ *Dismissing her fears, she climbed higher.* ◇ *He dismissed her from his mind.*
▶ **dismissal** noun [U]: *Her casual dismissal of the threats seemed irresponsible.*

,**brush sb/sth a'side** *phrasal verb* to ignore sb/sth; to treat sb's feelings, suggestions or protests as if they are not important: *I tried to protest, but he brushed me aside.* ◇ *She brushed aside my fears.*

,**shrug sth 'off/a'side** *phrasal verb* (-**gg**-) to treat sth as if it is not important: *Shrugging off her injury, she played on.* ◇ *He shrugged aside suggestions that he resign.*

NOTE BRUSH STH ASIDE OR SHRUG STH OFF? You brush aside concerns or fears that are important to sb else, you **shrug off** sth about yourself that other people expect you to be upset about.

discount /dɪsˈkaʊnt; AmE also ˈdɪskaʊnt/ [T] (*formal*) to think or say that sth is not important or not true: *We cannot discount the possibility of further strikes.* ◇ *The news reports were being discounted as propaganda.*

banish /ˈbænɪʃ/ [T] (*written*) to make a thought or feeling go away: *The sight of food banished all other thoughts from my mind.* ◇ *He was determined to banish all feelings of guilt.*

,**set sth a'side** *phrasal verb* to not consider sth, because other things are more important: *Let's set aside my personal feelings for now.*

,**laugh sth 'off** *phrasal verb* (*informal*) to try to make people think that sth is not serious or important, especially by making a joke about it: *He laughed off suggestions that he was going to resign.*

disperse verb

disperse · break (sth) up · separate · scatter · part
These words all refer to people or things moving apart in different directions.

PATTERNS AND COLLOCATIONS
▶ a **crowd** disperses/ scatters/ parts
▶ **clouds** disperse/ part
▶ **police** disperse sb/ break sth up

disperse /dɪˈspɜːs; AmE dɪˈspɜːrs/ [I, T] (*rather formal, written*) to move apart and go away in different directions; to make sb/sth do this: *The fog began to disperse.* ◇ *The crowd dispersed quickly.* ◇ *Police dispersed the protesters with tear gas.* ◇ *They dispersed the chemicals with a sheet of water.* ◇ *The community was dispersed by the war.* ❶ **Disperse** can be used to talk about groups of people, *clouds* or substances in the air.

,**break 'up**, ,**break sth 'up** *phrasal verb* [I] (of a meeting) to finish, with the people going away in different directions; to make people leave a meeting or stop fighting, especially by using force: *The meeting broke up at eleven o' clock.* ◇ *Police broke up the demonstration.* ◇ *A woman was hurt as she tried to* **break up a fight.**

NOTE DISPERSE OR BREAK UP? A *meeting* **breaks up** but the *people, group* or *crowd* at the meeting **disperse(s)**: *The meeting dispersed at eleven o'clock.* ◇ *The crowd broke up quickly.* You can **break up** a *demonstration* or a *fight*, but police **disperse** the *crowds* or *protesters* at the demonstration: *Police dispersed the demonstration.* ◇ *Police broke up the protesters with tear gas.*

separate /ˈsepəreɪt/ [I, T] to stop being a group or one whole thing and move apart in different directions; to make people move apart: *We separated into several different search parties.* ◇ *Two men separated from the others and walked towards me.* ◇ *South America and Africa separated 200 million years ago.* ◇ *The war separated many families.* See also **isolate** → ISOLATE, **separate** → SEPARATE 1, **separation** → DIVISION 1

scatter [I, T] (of a group of people, animals or things) to move apart very quickly in different directions; to make people or animals do this: *At the first gunshot, the crowd scattered.* ◇ *He banged his fist on the table and the chess pieces scattered over the floor.* ◇ *The explosion scattered a flock of birds roosting in the trees.*

part [I, T] (*rather formal, written*) (of two things or two parts of sth) to move apart; to make two things or two parts of sth move apart: *The crowds parted in front of them.* ◇ *The elevator doors parted and out stepped the President.* ◇ *Her lips were slightly parted.* ◇ *She parted the curtains a little and looked out.*

disprove verb

disprove · refute · discredit · rebut · confound · debunk · invalidate · explode · demolish
These words all mean to show that sth is wrong or false.

PATTERNS AND COLLOCATIONS
▶ to disprove/ refute/ discredit/ debunk/ invalidate/ explode/ demolish a **theory**
▶ to disprove/ refute/ debunk/ invalidate/ explode/ demolish a **myth**
▶ to disprove/ refute/ discredit/ rebut/ confound/ invalidate/ demolish an **argument**
▶ to disprove/ refute/ discredit/ rebut/ invalidate/ explode/ demolish **claims**
▶ to disprove/ refute/ confound/ invalidate a **thesis**
▶ to disprove/ refute/ rebut an **allegation**
▶ **evidence** disproves/ refutes/ discredits/ rebuts sth
▶ to **successfully** refute/ confound/ debunk/ demolish sth
▶ to be **easily** disproved/ refuted/ discredited/ rebutted/ demolished

disprove /ˌdɪsˈpruːv/ [T] to show that a theory or claim is wrong or false by using evidence: *It is difficult to confirm or disprove the existence of such a group.* ◇ *It cannot be disproved that a meeting took place.* **OPP** **prove** → SHOW 1, **confirm** → CONFIRM 1

refute /rɪˈfjuːt/ [T] (*formal*) to show that an argument, theory or claim is wrong by using arguments or evidence: *She tried to understand how to refute the argument on moral grounds.* ◇ *This study cannot provide data to confirm or refute this hypothesis.* **OPP** **confirm** → CONFIRM 1, See also **refute** → DENY, **refutation** → DENIAL

discredit /dɪsˈkredɪt/ [T] to make people stop believing that sth is true; to make sth appear unlikely to be true: *These theories are now largely discredited among linguists.* ◇ *This new evidence discredits earlier findings.*

rebut /rɪˈbʌt/ (-**tt**-) [T] (*formal*) to say or show that a claim or accusation is wrong or false: *An attempt was made to publicly rebut rumours of a divorce.* ◇ *The defendants were unable to rebut the charges of negligence.* See also **rebuttal** → DENIAL

NOTE DISPROVE, REFUTE OR REBUT? In some cases you can use any of these words: *to disprove/refute/rebut a claim/an allegation/an argument.* **Disprove** is the most frequent and is less formal than the other two. It is used especially to talk about matters of scientific or historical fact. **Refute** is used more often to talk about arguments or accusations; **rebut** is used especially to talk about accusations. People can **rebut** a claim just by denying it, without producing evidence. To **refute** a claim originally meant to disprove it with evidence; however, in modern usage, **refute** is also often used to mean 'deny'. See also **refute** → DENY

confound /kən'faʊnd/ [T] (*formal*) to show that sb/sth is wrong, especially by doing sth that people did not expect or predict: *She confounded her critics and proved she could do the job.* ◇ *The rise in share prices confounded expectations.*

debunk /ˌdiː'bʌŋk/ [T] (*rather informal*) to show that an idea or belief is false, especially one that has existed for a long time; to show that sth is not as good as people think it is: *Let's start by debunking a few myths.* ◇ *She attempts to debunk unrealistic expectations about marriage.*

invalidate /ɪn'vælɪdeɪt/ [T] to prove that an idea, story or argument is wrong, especially by showing it has mistakes in it: *This new piece of evidence invalidates his version of events.* ◇ *Flawed research methods may invalidate the study's conclusions.* ❶ An idea, story, etc. is **invalidated** by evidence or circumstances, not by a person trying to disprove it: *She tried to think how to invalidate the argument on moral grounds.*

explode [T] to show that an idea or belief, especially sth that many people think or believe, is false: *Here, at last, is a women's magazine to explode the myth that thin equals beautiful.*

demolish /dɪ'mɒlɪʃ; AmE -'maːl-/ [T] (*rather informal*) to show that an idea or theory is completely wrong: *A recent book has demolished this theory.*

disrupt *verb* See also the entry for BLOCK 1

disrupt · interrupt · upset
These words all mean to make it difficult for sth to continue in the normal or planned way.

PATTERNS AND COLLOCATIONS
▸ to disrupt / interrupt **services** / **work**
▸ to disrupt / interrupt a **meeting**
▸ to disrupt / upset **plans**
▸ to **threaten to** disrupt / upset sth
▸ to **badly** / **completely** / **totally** disrupt / upset sth

disrupt /dɪs'rʌpt/ [T] to make it difficult for sth to continue in the normal way or in the way that was planned: *Public transport services are likely to be severely disrupted tomorrow.* ◇ *The award ceremony was completely disrupted by a technicians' strike.* See also **disruptive** → WILD 1

interrupt [T] to stop the continuous progress of sth for a short time: *The game was interrupted several times by rain.* ◇ *We interrupt this programme to bring you an important news bulletin.* ◇ *Sorry to interrupt your dinner.* See also **interruption** → PAUSE *noun*

upset [T] to make a plan, event or situation go wrong: *He arrived an hour late and upset all our arrangements.* ◇ *The disagreement further upset relations between the two countries.*

disruption *noun*

disruption · turmoil · upheaval · disturbance · turbulence · disarray
These are all words you can use when sth prevents a situation from continuing in the normal way or when there is confusion.

PATTERNS AND COLLOCATIONS
▸ disruption / disturbance **to** sth
▸ an upheaval / a disturbance **in** sth
▸ **in** (a) turmoil / disarray / disorder
▸ (a) **great** disruption / turmoil / upheaval / disturbance / turbulence
▸ **considerable** disruption / turmoil / upheaval / disturbance / turbulence
▸ (a) **major** disruption / upheaval / disturbance

▸ **economic** disruption / turmoil / upheaval / turbulence
▸ **social** disruption / upheaval / turbulence
▸ **emotional** turmoil / upheaval / turbulence
▸ to **cause** disruption / turmoil / an upheaval / (a) disturbance
▸ to **throw sth into** turmoil / disarray
▸ a **period of** disruption / turmoil / upheaval / turbulence
▸ a **state of** turmoil / turbulence / disarray

disruption /dɪs'rʌpʃn/ [U, C] a situation in which sth is prevented from continuing or working in the normal way, because of the problems caused by a particular course of action: *The strike caused serious disruption for three days.* ◇ *To avoid disruption most of the work will be done at night.* ◇ *There could be disruptions to rail services.* See also **disruptive** → WILD 1

turmoil /'tɜːmɔɪl; AmE 'tɜːrm-/ [U, sing.] a state of great anxiety and confusion: *His mind was in (a) turmoil.* ◇ *I walked away in a state of mental turmoil.* ◇ *The country was hurled into the turmoil of another general election.*

upheaval /ʌp'hiːvl/ [C, U] a big change that causes a lot of confusion, worry and problems: *The country has undergone a major political upheaval.* ◇ *I can't face the upheaval of moving house again.*

disturbance [U, C, usually sing.] a situation in which people have to interrupt what they are doing, or in which the normal state of sth is upset: *The repairs have been carried out with minimal disturbance to local residents.* ◇ *Their arrival had caused a disturbance in the usual pattern of events.* See also **disturb** → INTERRUPT

> **NOTE** DISRUPTION OR DISTURBANCE? These words are often used when people are being told or promised that sth that is being done will not cause many problems. They are often used with words such as *avoid, prevent, minimize, little, minimal* and *minimum*. A **disruption** usually affects a thing such as *work*, a *service* or sb's *life*; a **disturbance** more often affects people or animals, although it can also affect sb's life or the normal way in which things happen.

turbulence /'tɜːbjələns; AmE 'tɜːrb-/ [U] (*rather formal, especially written*) a situation in which there is a lot of sudden change, confusion, strong feelings and sometimes violence: *Europe was in a state of turbulence.* ◇ *The country is facing a summer of political turbulence.*

disarray /ˌdɪsə'reɪ/ [U] (*especially written*) a state of confusion and lack of organization in a situation: *The peace talks broke up in disarray.* ◇ *Our plans were thrown into disarray by her arrival.* ◇ *The party's election campaign is in total disarray.* ❶ In this meaning **disarray** is always used in the phrase *in/into (a state of) disarray.*

distinguish *verb*

1 distinguish between right and wrong
2 The power of speech distinguishes humans from animals.

1 distinguish · differentiate · tell
These words all mean to recognize the difference between two people or things.

PATTERNS AND COLLOCATIONS
▸ to distinguish / differentiate / tell A **from** B
▸ to distinguish / differentiate **between** A **and** B
▸ to **easily** distinguish / differentiate / tell sb / sth
▸ to **clearly** / **sharply** / **carefully** distinguish / differentiate sb / sth

distinguish [I, T] (not used in the progressive tenses) (*rather formal*) to recognize or show the difference between people or things: *At what age are children able to distinguish between right and wrong?* ◇ *Sometimes reality and fantasy are hard to distinguish.* See also **distinction** → DIFFERENCE, **discern** → IDENTIFY

differentiate /ˌdɪfə'renʃieɪt/ [I, T] (not used in the progressive tenses) (*rather formal, especially written*) to distinguish between people or things: *She can just differentiate between light and dark.* ◇ *Birds are able to differentiate colours.*

NOTE DISTINGUISH OR DIFFERENTIATE? There is very little difference in meaning or use between these words. **Distinguish** is more frequent and more general; **differentiate** is slightly more formal, used more in scientific matters than in matters of human judgement: *differentiate between right and wrong* ◇ *Sometimes reality and fantasy are hard to differentiate.*

tell [T, no passive] (not used in the progressive tenses) to recognize the difference between two people or things: *It was hard to **tell the difference** between the two versions.* ◇ *I can't tell one twin from the other.* ◇ *It's difficult to **tell them apart.*** ◇ *The kittens looked exactly alike – how could you **tell which was which?*** ❶ You say *tell the difference between A and B* (two things) or *tell A and B apart*, NOT 'tell between A and B': *It's difficult to tell between them.*

2 distinguish · set sb/sth apart · differentiate
These words all mean to be the characteristic that makes two people, animals or things different.

PATTERNS AND COLLOCATIONS
▸ to distinguish / set apart / differentiate A from B
▸ a **feature** distinguishes / sets apart / differentiates A from B
▸ a **factor** distinguishes / differentiates A from B

distinguish [T] (not used in the progressive tenses) (*rather formal, especially written*) to be a characteristic that makes two people, animals or things different: *What was it that distinguished her from her classmates?* ◇ *Does your cat have any distinguishing marks?* ◇ *The power of speech distinguishes human beings from animals.* See also **distinction → DIFFERENCE**

,set sb/sth a'part *phrasal verb* (not used in the progressive tenses) to be a characteristic that makes sb/sth different from or better than others: *Her clear and elegant writing sets her apart from other journalists.*

differentiate /ˌdɪfəˈrenʃieɪt/ [T] (not used in the progressive tenses) (*rather formal, especially written*) to be a characteristic that makes two people, animals or things different: *The male's yellow beak differentiates it from the female.*

NOTE DISTINGUISH OR DIFFERENTIATE? There is little difference in meaning between these words. **Distinguish** is more frequent and has a wider range; it is often used about differences that make sb/sth better or more interesting than sb/sth else; **differentiate** is more often used about scientific matters, without any suggestion of a value judgement being made: *What was it that differentiated her from her classmates?* ◇ *The power of speech differentiates human beings from animals.*

distort *verb* See the Topic Map for FACT AND OPINION on p.898

distort · falsify · rig · misrepresent · fix · fiddle · misquote
These words all mean to make changes to information or to arrange the result of sth so that it is no longer correct or true.

PATTERNS AND COLLOCATIONS
▸ to distort / falsify / rig / fix / fiddle the **results**
▸ to distort / misrepresent the **truth** / **facts**
▸ to rig / fix an **election**
▸ to **deliberately** / **easily** distort / falsify / misrepresent sth
▸ to **grossly** / **seriously** / **completely** distort / misrepresent sth

distort /dɪˈstɔːt; *AmE* dɪˈstɔːrt/ [T] (*rather formal*) to change facts or ideas so that they are no longer correct or true: *Newspapers are often guilty of distorting the truth.* ◇ *The article gave a distorted picture of his childhood.* ❶ **Distort** is often used to talk about the way in which the media or people in authority such as the government change facts and ideas in this way.

falsify /ˈfɔːlsɪfaɪ/ [T] (*formal*) to change a written record or information so that it is no longer correct: *She was arrested for falsifying information and obstructing the course of justice.*

rig (-**gg**-) [T, usually passive] (*especially journalism*) to arrange the result of sth in a way that is not honest or fair: *He said the election had been rigged.* ◇ *It was a deliberate attempt to rig the market* (= to cause an artificial rise or fall in prices) *against the consumer.*

misrepresent /ˌmɪsˌreprɪˈzent/ [T, often passive] (*formal*) to give information about sb/sth that is not true or complete so that other people have the wrong impression about them/it: *He felt that the book misrepresented his opinions.* ◇ *In the article she was **misrepresented as** an uncaring mother.*

fix [T, often passive] (*informal, especially journalism*) to arrange the result of sth in a way that is not honest or fair: *I'm sure the match was fixed.*

NOTE RIG OR FIX? These words are very similar in meaning and sometimes you can use either: *to rig/fix an election.* Both are used especially in journalism, but **rig** is used especially in political and business contexts, and **fix** for talking about sport: the most frequent collocates of **fix** in this meaning are *match* and *race*.

fiddle [T] (*BrE, informal*) to change the details or figures of sth in order to try to get money dishonestly, or gain an advantage: *Are you saying you've never even been tempted to **fiddle your expenses?***

misquote /ˌmɪsˈkwəʊt; *AmE* -ˈkwoʊt/ [T] (*rather formal*) to repeat what sb has said or written in a way that is not correct: *The senator claims to have been misquoted in the article.*

distress *noun*

distress · pain · suffering · anguish · torture · agony · hurt · misery
These are all words for a feeling of great unhappiness that you get when you are hurt emotionally by sth that happens or what sb does or says.

distress	anguish	torture
pain	misery	agony
suffering		
hurt		

PATTERNS AND COLLOCATIONS
▸ distress / pain / anguish / hurt / misery **at** sth
▸ **in** distress / pain / anguish / agony / misery
▸ **great** distress / pain / suffering / anguish / agony / hurt / misery
▸ **real** distress / pain / suffering / anguish / torture / hurt / misery
▸ **sheer** / **absolute** torture / agony / misery
▸ **physical** / **emotional** distress / pain / suffering / anguish / torture / agony / hurt
▸ **mental** distress / pain / suffering / anguish / torture / agony
▸ **personal** distress / pain / suffering / anguish / agony / hurt / misery
▸ to **endure** the distress / pain / suffering / torture / agony / misery
▸ to **bear** the pain / suffering / anguish / torture / misery
▸ to **go through** pain / suffering / anguish / torture / agony / misery
▸ to **suffer** distress / pain / anguish / torture / agony / hurt / misery
▸ to **inflict** pain / suffering / anguish / torture / agony / hurt / misery
▸ to **cause (sb)** distress / pain / suffering / anguish / agony / hurt / misery
▸ to **spare sb** the distress / pain / anguish / torture / agony / misery
▸ to **ease** sb's distress / pain / suffering / anguish / agony / misery

distress [U] a feeling of great unhappiness or worry caused by sth unpleasant that has happened to you or that you think might happen: *He was obviously in distress after the attack.* ◇ *The newspaper article caused the actor considerable distress.* See also **distress → HURT** *verb* 1, **distressed → UPSET**, **distressing → PAINFUL** 2

pain [U] a feeling of great unhappiness caused by sth unpleasant that has happened to you or that sb has done or said: *The pain of separation remained intense.* ◇ *She had* *never meant to cause him any pain.* ❶ **Pain** can also be a physical feeling. See also **pain** → PAIN **OPP** **pleasure** → FUN, **pleasure** → PLEASURE, See also **pain** → HURT *verb* 1, **painful** → PAINFUL 2

suffering [U] a feeling of great unhappiness caused by sth unpleasant that has happened to you, sometimes involving being without a home, money, food or safety: *The taunts of her schoolmates caused her intense mental suffering.* ◇ *This war has caused widespread human suffering.* ❶ **Suffering** can also be a physical feeling. See also **suffering** → PAIN

NOTE DISTRESS, PAIN OR SUFFERING? These are all words for a feeling of great unhappiness. **Distress** can also be a feeling of worry: *I was in such distress, wondering what had happened to them.* ◇ ~~I was in such pain/suffering, wondering what had happened to them.~~ Both **pain** and **suffering** can also be physical and sometimes they can be both physcial and emotional at the same time: *It was a life full of pain and suffering.* **Pain** is used especially when the hurt is more individual and the cause more personal, such as the death of a loved one or sth unkind that sb has said or done to you. **Suffering** is used especially when the hurt affects a large number of people and is caused by sth on a larger scale such as a war or natural disaster.

anguish /ˈæŋgwɪʃ/ [U] (*rather formal*) great suffering, especially emotional suffering: *Tears of anguish filled her eyes.* ◇ *He groaned in anguish.* See also **anguished** → UPSET

torture /ˈtɔːtʃə(r); *AmE* ˈtɔːrtʃ-/ [U] (*informal*) extreme suffering, especially emotional suffering; sth that causes this: *Falling in love with a man she could never have was exquisite torture.* ◇ *The interview was sheer torture from start to finish.* ❶ **Torture** is the only word in this group that cannot be used after 'in': ~~He cried out in torture.~~

agony /ˈægəni/ [U, C] extreme emotional suffering; sth that causes this: *It was agony not knowing where the children were.* ◇ *She waited in an agony of suspense.* ◇ *The worst agonies of the war were now beginning.* ❶ **Agony** can also be physical pain. See also **agony** → PAIN

hurt [U, sing.] (*rather informal*) a feeling of unhappiness because sb has been unkind or unfair to you: *There was hurt and real anger in her voice.* ◇ *It was a hurt that would take a long time to heal.* See also **hurt** → HURT *verb* 1, **hurt** → UPSET *adj.*, **hurtful** → MEAN *adj.* 1

misery /ˈmɪzəri/ [U, C] great suffering, especially emotional suffering, that lasts a long time; a very unpleasant experience or situation in which people suffer very much: *Fame brought her nothing but misery.* ◇ *The bad news had plunged him into abject misery.* ◇ (*BrE*) *My old boss used to* **make my life a misery.** ❶ In American English say **make my life miserable.** See also **miserable** → NEGATIVE, **miserable** → UNHAPPY 1

NOTE ANGUISH, TORTURE, AGONY OR MISERY? The main differences between these words are the degree of suffering and the level of formality. **Agony** suggests the most suffering. **Torture** also suggests extreme suffering, but it is used in informal spoken Enlgish in an exaggerated way: the situations that cause the torture may not in fact be very serious. **Anguish** is a rather formal word and is slightly less extreme than **agony** and **torture**. **Misery** may be less intense suffering but it may last a much longer time.

distribute *verb*

distribute · hand sth out · give sth out · dispense · dole sth out · pass sth out · dish sth out · deal
These words all mean to give sth to a number of people.

PATTERNS AND COLLOCATIONS
▸ to distribute / hand out / give out / dispense / dish out **food**
▸ to distribute / hand out / give out / dispense / dole out **money**
▸ to distribute / hand out / dispense **cash**
▸ to distribute / hand out / give out / pass out **copies**
▸ to distribute / hand out / give out / pass out / dole out / dish out **leaflets**
▸ to distribute / hand out / give out / dish out **awards / prizes**
▸ to hand out / give out / dole out / dish out **punishments**

distribute /dɪˈstrɪbjuːt; ˈdɪstrɪbjuːt/ [T] (*rather formal*) to give sth to each person in a group, especially when this is a large number of people; to share sth between a number of people; to send goods to shops and businesses so that they can be sold: *The organization distributed food and blankets to the earthquake victims.* ◇ *The newspaper is distributed free.* ◇ *The money was* **distributed among** *schools in the area.* ◇ *'Plastika' distributes our products in the UK.*
▸ **distribution** /ˌdɪstrɪˈbjuːʃn/ *noun* [U]: *the distribution of food and medicine to the flood victims* See also **distribution** → DELIVERY

hand sth 'out *phrasal verb* to give sth to each person in a group: *Could you hand these books out, please?* ◇ *She handed out medals and certificates to the winners.* See also **handout** → AID, **handout** → GIFT, **handout** → LEAFLET

give sth 'out *phrasal verb* (*especially spoken*) to give sth to each person in a group: *The teacher gave out the exam papers.*

NOTE HAND STH OUT OR GIVE STH OUT? There is no real difference in meaning between these words. **Give sth out** is used more often in spoken English than in written English; **hand sth out** is used fairly equally in both.

dispense /dɪˈspens/ [T] (*rather formal*) to give sth out to people, especially food, drink or money from a machine: *The machine dispenses a range of drinks and snacks.*

dole sth 'out *phrasal verb* (*informal*) to give out an amount of food or money to each person in a group: *Dad began to dole out the porridge from the saucepan.*

pass sth 'out *phrasal verb* (*especially AmE*) to give sth to each person in a group: *Information sheets were passed out before the talk.*

dish sth 'out *phrasal verb* (*informal*) to give sth, often to a lot of people or in large amounts: *Students dished out leaflets to passers-by.* ◇ *She's always dishing out advice, even when you don't want it.*

deal [I, T] to give cards to each player in a game of cards: *Whose turn is it to deal?* ◇ *Start by* **dealing out** *ten cards to each player.* ◇ *He dealt me two aces.*

ditch *noun*

ditch · trench · channel · gully · moat · furrow
These are all words for a passage in the ground which water can flow through.

PATTERNS AND COLLOCATIONS
▸ an **open** ditch / trench / channel / gully
▸ a **deep** ditch / trench / channel / gully / moat / furrow
▸ a **shallow** ditch / trench / channel / gully / furrow
▸ a **wide** ditch / trench / channel / gully / moat
▸ a **narrow** trench / channel / gully
▸ to **dig** a ditch / trench / channel / moat
▸ a ditch / trench / channel / gully **runs** down / along sth

ditch [C] a long hole dug along the side of a field or road, to hold or take away water: *The car went out of control and plunged into a ditch.* ◇ *Farm drainage ditches ensure that water runs directly into streams.*

trench [C] a long deep hole dug in the ground, for example for carrying away water: *They are digging a trench to hold a water pipe which will divert water from the river.* ❶ A **trench** is also a long deep hole dug in the ground in which soldiers can be protected from enemy attacks (for example in northern France and Belgium in the First World War): *He spoke movingly of his time in the* **trenches** *during the First World War.* ◇ *They had not been prepared for the horrors of* **trench warfare.**

channel [C] a passage that water can flow along, especially in the ground or on the bottom of a river: *A channel is being dug to divert the river.*

gully (also **gulley**) [C] a small, narrow passage which water flows along, usually formed by a stream or by rain; a deep ditch: *The slope was still awash with water spilling down deep gullies.*

moat [C] a deep wide channel that was dug around a castle and filled with water to make it more difficult for enemies to attack: *The castle was ringed by a moat spanned by a wooden drawbridge.*

furrow /ˈfʌrəʊ; *AmE* ˈfɜːroʊ/ [C] a long narrow cut in the ground, especially one made by a plough for planting seeds in: *Water lay in the furrows of the ploughed fields.* ◇ *Truck wheels had dug furrows in the tracks.*

diverse *adj.* See also the entries for DIFFERENT and WIDE 1

diverse · varied · mixed · assorted · miscellaneous · heterogeneous · eclectic · motley
These words all describe things that are very different from each other and of various kinds.

PATTERNS AND COLLOCATIONS
▸ a diverse / a varied / a mixed / an assorted / a miscellaneous / a heterogeneous / a motley **group**
▸ a diverse / varied / mixed / miscellaneous / heterogeneous / motley **collection**
▸ a diverse / varied / mixed / heterogeneous / motley **array**
▸ a diverse / varied / mixed / motley **assortment**
▸ diverse / assorted / miscellaneous **items**
▸ very diverse / varied / mixed / heterogeneous / eclectic
▸ rather diverse / mixed / heterogeneous
▸ racially / ethnically / culturally / socially diverse / varied / mixed

diverse /daɪˈvɜːs; *AmE* -ˈvɜːrs/ (*rather formal*) very different from each other and of various kinds; consisting of people or things that are very different from each other: *People from diverse cultures were invited to the event.* ◇ *My interests are very diverse.* ◇ *The US is a vast and diverse country.* See also **diversity** → RANGE 1

varied /ˈveərid; *AmE* ˈverid; ˈvær-/ (*often approving*) of many different kinds; consisting of things of many different kinds: *The opportunities the job offers are **many and varied.*** ◇ *They stock a wide and varied selection of cheeses.* See also **vary** → DIFFER, **variety** → RANGE 1

mixed [only before noun] consisting of different kinds of people, for example people from different races and cultures, or people of different abilities: *She was born to parents of **mixed race**.* ◇ *a **mixed marriage*** (= between two people of different races or religions) ◇ *Do you have experience of teaching **mixed-ability** classes?* ❶ In this meaning **mixed** is used especially in these fixed collocations.

assorted /əˈsɔːtɪd; *AmE* əˈsɔːrtəd/ [only before noun] (*rather formal*) of various different kinds: *The meat is served with salad or assorted vegetables.* ◇ *The sweater comes in assorted colours.* ◇ *a box of assorted chocolates* ❶ **Assorted** is used especially by restaurants, shops or companies producing goods to describe what they have to offer or sell. See also **assortment** → RANGE 1

miscellaneous /ˌmɪsəˈleɪniəs/ [usually before noun] (*rather formal*) consisting of many different kinds of things that are not connected and do not easily form a group: *The museum houses a miscellaneous collection of iron age artefacts.* ◇ *She gave me some money to cover any miscellaneous expenses.*

heterogeneous /ˌhetərəˈdʒiːniəs/ (*formal*) consisting of many different kinds of people or things: *She cited the heterogeneous population of the United States to support her argument.* **OPP** **homogeneous** → EQUAL *adj.*

eclectic /ɪˈklektɪk/ (*formal*) not following one style or set of ideas but choosing from or using a wide variety: *She has very eclectic tastes in literature.* ◇ *His house is an eclectic mixture of the antique and the modern.*

motley [only before noun] (*especially written*, *often disapproving*) consisting of many different types of people or things that do not seem to belong together: *The room was filled with a motley collection of furniture and paintings.* ◇ *The audience was a **motley crew** of students and tourists.* ❶ **Motley** usually collocates with **bunch, collection, crew** and **group**. It is often used to suggest that the people or things described are disorganized and untidy, or that they look strange or funny together.

divide *verb*

1 cells divide/divide sth up into sections
2 The issue has divided the government.

1 divide · break (sth) up · split · cut sth up · subdivide · split (sb) up · separate (sth) out
These words all mean to become, or to make sth become, two or more parts instead of one whole thing.

PATTERNS AND COLLOCATIONS
▸ to divide / break / split / cut sth **up**
▸ to divide (sth) / break sth up / split sth / subdivide sth **into parts**
▸ to divide (sth) / break sth up / split sth **into sections**
▸ to divide (sth) / split sth / cut sth up **into pieces**
▸ to divide (sb) / split sb / subdivide sth / split (sb) up **into groups**
▸ to divide / split (sth) **in two / in half**

divide [I, T] to become, or to make sth become, two or more parts or groups instead of one whole thing: *The cells began to divide rapidly.* ◇ *We reached the point where the river divides in two.* ◇ *This report is divided broadly into two parts.* ◇ *A sentence can be divided up into meaningful segments.*

break ˈup, **break sth ˈup** *phrasal verb* to divide, or to make sth divide, into several smaller parts: *The grey clouds had begun to break up.* ◇ *Much has changed since the Soviet Union broke up.* ◇ *Break up the chocolate and place it in a bowl.* ◇ *The ship was broken up for scrap metal.* ◇ *Sentences can be broken up into clauses.*

split [I, T] to divide, or to make sth divide, into two or more parts or groups: *The results split neatly into two groups.* ◇ *Slate splits easily into thin sheets.* ◇ *Which scientist first **split the atom**?* ◇ *She split the class into groups of four.* ◇ *The day was split up into six one-hour sessions.*

> **NOTE** DIVIDE, BREAK UP OR SPLIT? **Divide** is slightly more formal than **break up** or **split**. **Break up** often suggests a degree of force: things **break up** because people or circumstances have forced them to and they cannot hold together any more. When sth has broken up, or been broken up, it can no longer be considered part of a whole thing: *The empire was broken up into different parts* (= it was no longer an empire). ◇ *The empire was divided/split into different parts* (= it was still an empire but contained separate areas). Things usually **divide** or **split** because it is natural for them to do so, although this is not always the case with particular collocations: *cells divide* naturally, but *atoms* can only be *split* using a great deal of force.

cut sth ˈup *phrasal verb* to divide sth into small pieces, especially by using a knife or scissors: *He cut up the meat on his plate.* ◇ *I cut the paper up into small segments.*

subdivide /ˈsʌbdɪvaɪd; ˌsʌbdɪˈvaɪd/ [T, often passive] (*rather formal*) to divide sth into smaller parts, especially when it has already been divided once and each part is being divided again: *Each of the chapters is subdivided into several double-page spreads.*

split ˈup, **split sb ˈup** *phrasal verb* (of a group of people) to separate from each other, either as individuals or in smaller groups; to divide a group of people into smaller groups; to separate two or more people from each other: *Let's split up now and meet again at lunchtime.* ◇ *We were split up into groups to discuss the question.* ◇ *You two are talking too much. I'm going to have to split you up.*

,separate 'out, ,separate sth 'out *phrasal verb* (of the different parts of sth) to move apart and become separate; to make the different parts of sth do this; to see the difference between things which are different but together: *Particles will separate out as the smoke disperses.* ◇ *More and more households are separating out recyclable waste.* ◇ *We need to separate out fact from speculation.* ❶ **Separate out** is used to emphasize that each part can be considered a complete thing in itself: *The particles separate out* (= they move away from each other). ◇ *The particles will divide* (= each particle will become two or more separate parts).

2 See the Topic Map for THE INDIVIDUAL AND SOCIETY on p.894
divide · split · alienate · separate · be/become estranged · come between sb and sb
These words all mean to make people disagree or become emotionally distant from each other.

▸ to be **divided** / **split over** sth
▸ to be **alienated** / **estranged from** sb
▸ to be **increasingly** divided / split / alienated / separated / estranged
▸ to be **deeply** divided / split
▸ to be **totally** alienated / separated
▸ to be **completely** separated / estranged

divide [T] (of an issue) to make two or more people disagree: *The issue has bitterly divided the community.* ◇ *The government is divided on the question of tax cuts.*

split [I, T] to divide into smaller groups that have very different opinions; (of an issue) to make a group of people do this: *The committee split over government subsidies.* ◇ *The debate has split the country down the middle.*

NOTE DIVIDE OR SPLIT? **Divide** suggests that the disagreement may be temporary; if two or more people **split**, the disagreement may be permanent. **Divide** is not usually used in this meaning without an object.

alienate /'eɪliəneɪt/ [T] (*rather formal*) to make sb feel that they do not belong in a particular group: *Very talented children may feel alienated from the others in their class.* ◇ *It is important that the new policies do not alienate our core supporters.*

separate [T] to make sb/sth different in some way from sb/sth else: *Politics is the only thing that separates us* (= that we disagree about). ◇ *Her lack of religious faith separated her from the rest of her family.* ◇ *Only four points separate the top three teams.*

be/become estranged [I] (*rather formal*) to no longer be, or to stop being, friendly, loyal or in contact with sb, especially sb in your family: *He became estranged from his family after the argument.*

,come be'tween sb and sb *phrasal verb* [no passive] to damage a relationship between two people: *I'd hate anything to come between us.* ◇ *Must she always come between us?* ❶ The subject of **come between sb and sb** can be a person, a problem, a feeling, a belief, an argument, a situation or almost anything.

division *noun*

1 a clear division between things
2 a political division between people

1 division · separation · isolation · segregation · quarantine · split · partition · dissolution
These are all words for the act or result of dividing things or people.

▸ division / separation / isolation / segregation **from** sb / sth
▸ (a) division / separation / segregation / split **between** sth and sth else
▸ (a) division / separation / segregation / split **into** parts
▸ (a) division / isolation / segregation **within** sth
▸ **strict** division / separation / isolation / segregation / quarantine
▸ (a) **clear** division / separation / split
▸ **complete** separation / isolation / segregation

division [U, sing.] the act or result of dividing, or of dividing sth into separate parts: *The organism begins as a single cell and grows by cell division.* ◇ *We need to ensure a fair division of time and resources.* ◇ *In many traditional societies, the division of labour between the sexes is strict.* See also **divide** → SHARE *verb*

separation [U, sing.] the act of separating people or things; the state of being separate: *Many years passed before the state's eventual separation from the federation.* ◇ *He argued for the need for a clear separation between Church and State.* See also **separate** → SEPARATE *verb* 1, **separate** → SEPARATE *verb* 2, **separate** → DISPERSE

isolation /,aɪsə'leɪʃn/ [U] complete separation from other people, groups or things: *The country has been threatened with complete isolation from the international community unless the atrocities stop.* ◇ *He lives in splendid isolation* (= far from, or in a superior position to, everyone else). See also **isolate** → ISOLATE

NOTE SEPARATION OR ISOLATION? **Separation** is the more general of these words. **Isolation** is used when discussing a country or its politics: collocates include *diplomatic, geographical, political* and *international*. This kind of **isolation** is usually seen as a bad thing; **separation** (for example *between Church and State* or *between the executive and the judiciary* in government) is often seen as a good thing. **Isolation** is also used in the context of preventing the spread of infectious diseases: *an isolation hospital/ward*

segregation /,segrɪ'geɪʃn/ [U] the act or policy of separating people of different races, religions or sexes and treating them differently: *The social structure was based on the policy of racial segregation.* ◇ *Segregation by sex and age is relatively common in these societies.* ❶ In formal language **segregation** can also be the act of separating people or things from a larger group: *the segregation of smokers and non-smokers in restaurants* See also **segregate** → ISOLATE, **discrimination**, **apartheid** → DISCRIMINATION

quarantine /'kwɒrəntiːn; AmE 'kwɔːr-; 'kwɑːr-/ [U] a period of time when an animal or person that has or may have a disease is kept away from others in order to prevent the disease from spreading: *The dog was kept in quarantine for six months.* ◇ *Quarantine regulations have been introduced.* See also **quarantine** → ISOLATE

split [sing.] (*rather informal*) a division between two or more things; one of the parts that sth is divided into: *He demanded a 50–50 split in the profits.* See also **split** → SHARE *verb*

partition /pɑː'tɪʃn; AmE pɑːr't-/ [U] the division of one country into two or more countries: *The effects of the partition of Germany can still be seen today.* See also **partition** → SEPARATE *verb* 2

dissolution /,dɪsə'luːʃn/ [U] (*rather formal*) the act of breaking up an organization, institution or other group: *The company was set up following the dissolution of the Soviet Union.*

2 See the Topic Map for THE INDIVIDUAL AND SOCIETY on p.894
division · split · rift · alienation · schism · distance · disunity · estrangement
These are all words for disagreements or differences between people or groups of people.

PATTERNS AND COLLOCATIONS

▸ division / a split / a rift / a schism / distance / disunity / estrangement **between** people or groups
▸ division / disunity **among** people or groups
▸ division / a split / a rift / a schism / disunity **within** a group
▸ a split / rift **with** sb
▸ a split / alienation / distance / estrangement **from** sb
▸ (a / an) **deep / serious / internal / ideological** division / split / rift
▸ (a) **growing** division / split / rift / alienation / distance / estrangement
▸ (a) **political** division / split / rift / alienation / disunity
▸ to **cause / lead to** divisions / a split / a rift / alienation / a schism
▸ to **create** divisions / a rift / a distance
▸ to **heal** divisions / a split / a rift

division [C, U] a disagreement or difference in opinion or way of life, especially between members of a society or organization: *We need to work together to heal the divisions within society.* ◇ *The party was weakened by division between various factions.*

split [C] (*rather informal*) a disagreement that divides a group of people or makes sb separate from sb else, usually permanently: *A damaging split within the party leadership has occurred.* ◇ *He found it difficult to cope in the years following his bitter split with his wife.*

rift [C] a disagreement that divides people or makes sb separate from sb else, not always permanently: *The rift within the party deepens.* ◇ *Efforts to heal the rift between the two countries have failed.*

> **NOTE** SPLIT OR RIFT? A **rift** is a serious disagreement that often leads to a **split**, when two people or groups, or the members of a group actually separate. A **rift** is more likely to be *healed* than a **split**.

alienation /ˌeɪliəˈneɪʃn/ [U] a situation in which sb becomes less friendly or sympathetic towards you; a situation in which sb feels that they do not belong in a particular group: *The new policy resulted in the alienation of many voters.* ◇ *Many immigrants suffer from a feeling of alienation.*

schism /ˈskɪzəm; ˈsɪzəm/ [C, U] (*formal*) a split within an organization, especially a religious one, that makes its members divide into separate groups: *The disagreement eventually led to a schism within the Church.* ◇ *By 1914 the party was dangerously close to schism.*

distance [U, C] a situation in which there is a lack of friendly feelings or of a close relationship between two people or groups of people: *He worried about the increasing distance between his children and himself.* ◇ *The coldness and distance in her voice took me by surprise.* See also **distant** → COLD 2

disunity /dɪsˈjuːnəti/ [U] (*formal*) a lack of agreement between people: *Disunity among opposition groups will prevent real change from happening.* **OPP** **unity** → AGREEMENT 2

estrangement /ɪˈstreɪndʒmənt/ [U, C] (*formal*) the situation of being estranged (= no longer living with, friendly with or involved with sb/sth that used to be important to you): *A period of estrangement from his wife had left him feeling isolated and alone.* ◇ *The misunderstanding had caused a seven-year estrangement between them.* See also **estranged** → SINGLE

divorce verb

divorce · break (sth) up · split up · disband · separate · split · get divorced

These words all refer to people ending a relationship, especially a romantic one.

PATTERNS AND COLLOCATIONS

▸ to break up / split up / split **with** sb
▸ to split up / separate / split **from** sb
▸ a **couple** divorces / breaks up / splits up / separates / splits / gets divorced
▸ a **group** breaks up / splits up / disbands / splits
▸ a **partnership** breaks up / splits up
▸ to have **recently** divorced / split up / (been) disbanded

divorce [T, I] to legally end your marriage to sb: *She's divorcing her husband.* ◇ *I'd heard they're divorcing.* See also **divorced** → SINGLE

▸ **divorce** noun [U, C]: *The marriage ended in divorce.* ◇ *They have agreed to get a divorce.*

break 'up, **break sth 'up** phrasal verb (of a relationship) to come to an end; to end a relationship or business company: *Their marriage has broken up.* ◇ *My brother has broken up with his girlfriend.* ◇ *They decided to break up the partnership* (= in business).

▸ **'break-up** noun [C]: *family break-ups* ◇ *the break-up of the company*

split 'up phrasal verb (*rather informal*) to end a relationship with sb: *My parents split up last year.* ◇ *She's split up with her boyfriend.*

> **NOTE** BREAK UP OR SPLIT UP? People or a *marriage* or *relationship* can **break up** and it can refer to a personal or a business relationship. Only people can **split up** and it usually refers to a personal relationship.

disband /dɪsˈbænd/ [T, I] (*rather formal*) to stop sb/sth from operating as a group; to separate or no longer operate as a group: *They set about disbanding the terrorist groups.* ◇ *The committee formally disbanded last year.*

separate /ˈsepəreɪt/ [I] to stop living as a couple with your husband, wife or partner: *He separated from his wife after 20 years of marriage.* ◇ *They separated last year.* See also **separated** → SINGLE

▸ **separation** noun [C, U]: *a legal separation* ◇ *She would not consider separation or divorce.*

split [I] (*rather informal, especially journalism*) to leave sb and stop having a relationship with them: *The singer split with his wife last June.* ◇ *She intends to split from the band at the end of the tour.* ❶ **Split** is used especially in newspapers and can refer to personal or business relationships, especially when one person takes the decision to leave.

get di'vorced phrase to legally end your marriage to sb: *They're getting divorced.* ◇ *People get divorced nowadays more than they used to.* See also **divorced** → SINGLE

> **NOTE** DIVORCE OR GET DIVORCED? One person can **divorce** another person, but **get divorced** usually refers to an action by two people: *She divorced her husband last year.* ◇ *They got divorced last year.* You can, however, use **be divorced from** sb: *She is divorced from the boy's father.* When there is no object either **divorce** or **get divorced** may be used, but **get divorced** is more common in spoken English.

dizzy adj. See the Topic Map for HEALTH on p.890

dizzy · faint · light-headed

These words all describe sb feeling as though they might fall over.

PATTERNS AND COLLOCATIONS

▸ dizzy / faint / light-headed **from / with** sth
▸ to **feel** dizzy / faint / light-headed
▸ **a bit / a little / slightly / quite** dizzy / faint / light-headed
▸ **very** dizzy / light-headed

dizzy feeling as if everything is spinning around you and that you are not able to balance: *Climbing so high made me feel dizzy.* ◇ *I suffer from **dizzy spells*** (=short periods when I am dizzy).

faint [not before noun] feeling weak and tired and likely to lose consciousness: *She suddenly felt faint.* ◇ *The walkers were faint from hunger.*

light-'headed [not before noun] not completely in control of your thoughts or movements; slightly faint: *After four glasses of wine he began to feel light-headed.* ◇ *She felt hollow and light-headed with happiness.*

> **NOTE** FAINT OR LIGHT-HEADED? People usually feel **faint** from weakness, pain or fear; they feel **light-headed** from weakness, alcohol or happiness.

do verb

1 do the washing/some research
2 do well at school

---

1 do · carry sth out · conduct · undertake · perform · implement · commit · practise · go through sth
These words all mean to work at an activity or task.

PATTERNS AND COLLOCATIONS
▸ to do / carry out / conduct / undertake / perform the **work**
▸ to do / carry out / conduct / undertake / perform a / an **activity / analysis / investigation / review / assessment / evaluation**
▸ to do / carry out / conduct / undertake **business**
▸ to do / carry out / conduct / perform / go through a **test**
▸ to do / carry out / undertake / perform a **task / job**
▸ to do / carry out / perform / go through a **manoeuvre**
▸ to do / carry out / perform / practise **surgery**
▸ to do / carry out / implement a **plan / policy / strategy**
▸ to do / carry out / conduct / undertake / perform / implement sth **effectively / efficiently / properly / successfully**
▸ to do / conduct / perform / implement sth **well / poorly**

do [T] to work at an activity, task or job: *I do aerobics once a week.* ◇ *I'm doing some research on the subject.* ◇ *I have a number of things to do today.* ◇ **What do you do** (= what is your job)? ◇ *What did she do for a living?* **❶ Do** is often used to refer to actions that you do not mention by name or do not know about: *What are you doing this evening?* ◇ *There's* **nothing to do** (= no means of passing the time in an enjoyable way) *in this place.* ◇ *The company ought to* **do something** *about the poor service.* ◇ *There's* **nothing we can do** *about it* (= we can't change the situation). ◇ *What can I do for you* (= how can I help)? **❶ Do** is often used with nouns for activities or tasks such as shopping or cleaning: (*BrE*) *I like listening to the radio when I'm doing the ironing.* ◇ *She did a lot of acting when she was at college.* ◇ *You could help me by doing* (= washing) *the dishes.* ◇ *I like the way you've done your hair.*
‚carry sth 'out phrasal verb (*rather formal*) to do and complete a task or action: *We carry out routine maintenance of the equipment.* ◇ *The company has just carried out a major cost-cutting exercise.* ◇ *The pilot has to carry out a series of complex manoeuvres.* ◇ *The massacre was carried out by enemy troops.* **❶ Carry out** is used to talk about work, tasks or crimes; but even in the case of crimes, they are often crimes that have been carefully planned or ordered.
conduct /kən'dʌkt/ [T] (*formal*) to organize and/or do a particular activity: *We conducted the experiment under controlled circumstances.* ◇ *The negotiations have been conducted in a positive manner.* ◇ *The interrogation was conducted by senior police officers.* **❶ Conduct** is often used with words like *enquiry, inquest, interview, interrogation, investigation, survey* and *study*, in which people are trying to get answers to questions.
undertake /ˌʌndə'teɪk/ [T] (*formal*) to make yourself responsible for sth and start doing it: *The directors of the company refused to undertake such a risky venture.* ◇ *A group of enthusiasts has undertaken the reconstruction of a steam locomotive.* **❶ Undertake** is usually used to talk about an important job that a person or group of people takes responsibility for. See also **undertaking → PROJECT**
perform [T] (*rather formal, especially written*) to do sth, such as a piece of work, task or duty: *A computer can perform many tasks at once.* ◇ *She performs an important role in our organization.* ◇ *He performed miracles to get everything ready in time.*

> **NOTE** CARRY OUT OR PERFORM? **Carry out** places emphasis on the amount of work, especially when this lasts a period of time and is done according to a plan. **Perform** often emphasizes the skill involved: ~~carry out miracles/an important role~~ ◇ ~~perform inquiries/a cost-cutting exercise~~. **Carry out**, but NOT **perform**, can be used to talk about negative actions such as *attack, abuse, assault, assassination* and *killing*.

implement /'ɪmplɪmənt/ [T] (*rather formal*) to make sth that has been officially decided start to happen or be used: *We have not yet begun to implement the changes.* ◇ *We are implementing a new system of stock control.*
commit (-tt-) [T] to do sth wrong or illegal: *What leads someone to commit murder?* ◇ *We heard of some of the appalling crimes committed against innocent children.* **❶ Commit** collocates with *crime, offence, atrocity, outrage* and *sin* and some words for different crimes and sins, including *murder, assault, robbery, adultery* and *blasphemy*. To *commit suicide* is to kill yourself deliberately.
practise (*BrE*) (*AmE* **practice**) [T] (*rather formal*) to do sth regularly as part of your normal behaviour: *A lot of couples now practise safe sex.* ◇ *Do you still practise your religion?* ◇ *Train yourself to practise self-restraint.* See also **practice → USE noun**
go through sth phrasal verb to perform a series of actions; to follow a method or procedure: *Certain formalities have to be gone through before you can emigrate.* ◇ *We go through the same old routine every morning.*

---

2 do · go · perform · fare · get on/along
These verbs are all used to talk or ask about the success or progress of sb/sth.

PATTERNS AND COLLOCATIONS
▸ to do / go / perform / fare / get on / get along **well**
▸ to do / go / perform **brilliantly / excellently / badly**
▸ to do / perform / fare **poorly**

do [I] (always used with an adverb or preposition) (*especially spoken*) used to talk or ask about the success or progress of sb/sth: *How is the business doing?* ◇ *She did well out of* (= made a big profit from) *the deal.* ◇ *He's doing very well at school* (= his work is good). ◇ *Both mother and baby are doing well* (= after the birth of the baby). ◇ (*informal*) *How are you doing* (= how are you)?
go [I] (*especially spoken*) used to talk or ask about the success or progress of sth: '*How did your interview go?' 'It went very well, thank you.'* ◇ *Did everything go smoothly?* ◇ *How's it going* (= is your life enjoyable, successful, etc. at the moment)? ◇ *The way things are going the company will be bankrupt by the end of the year.*

> **NOTE** DO OR GO? **Do** can be used to talk about the progress or success of either a person or a thing; **go** can only be used to talk about a thing. When you use **do** to talk about a thing, you are interested in how popular or profitable it is, so **do** is generally used to talk about the success of sth such as a business or other enterprise. **Go** is more general, used to describe sth that you experience, such as an event, an *interview*, a *test*, or *things* or *life* in general.

perform [I] (*rather formal*) used to talk or ask about the success or progress of sb/sth, especially in business, sport or a test: *The company has been performing poorly over the past year.* ◇ *If Rooney performs* (= performs well) *then I believe England can win.* ◇ *She performed less well in the second test.*
▸ **performance** noun [U, C]: *the country's economic performance* ◇ *It was an impressive performance by the French team.*
fare [I] (*especially written*) used to talk or ask about the success or progress of sb/sth: *The party fared very badly in the last election.* ◇ *The North, by and large, has fared better than most regions in avoiding high unemployment figures.*

> **NOTE** PERFORM OR FARE? **Perform** is more active than **fare**: a person or company that *performs well* is successful because of what they do; a person or group that *fares well* is successful, or just lucky, because good things happen to them or the conditions are right for them. Both these words are used to talk about people, groups or organizations, but NOT events: ~~The interview performed/fared well.~~

,get 'on/a'long *phrasal verb* (*especially BrE, rather informal*) used to talk or ask about the success or progress of sb: *He's getting on very well at school.* ◇ *I went to see how they were getting along.* ❶ When **get on/along** is used with an adverb, it is usually *well*; it is not common to talk about sb *getting on/along badly.* The subject of **get on/along** is usually a person or small group of people in an informal context; it is NOT used to talk about businesses, organizations or events.

doctor *noun* See the Topic Map for HEALTH on p.890

doctor · nurse · surgeon · GP · physician · medic · paramedic · internist
These are all words for a person who has been trained to treat or take care of sick or injured people.

▶ to **see** a doctor/ a nurse/ the surgeon/ your GP/ a physician/ a medic/ your internist
▶ to **consult** a doctor/ a surgeon/ your GP/ a physician/ your internist
▶ to **call** a doctor/your GP/a physician/a medic/the paramedics
▶ a doctor/ surgeon/ GP/ physician **examines** sb
▶ a doctor/ surgeon/ GP/ physician/ paramedic **treats** sb
▶ a doctor/ GP/ physician **diagnoses/ prescribes** sth

doctor (*abbr.* **Dr**) [C] a person who has been trained in medical science, whose job is to treat sick or injured people: *You'd better see a doctor about that cough.* ◇ *Why won't he go to the doctor?* ◇ *Dr Staples* (= as a title/form of address) ◇ *a hospital doctor* ◇ *a family doctor* (= who works in the local community, not in a hospital) See also **doctor's** → SURGERY
nurse [C] a person whose job is to take care of sick or injured people: *a qualified/registered nurse* ◇ *student nurses* ◇ *a male nurse* ◇ *a dental nurse* (= one who helps a dentist) ◇ *a psychiatric nurse* (= one who works in a hospital for people with mental illnesses) ◇ *Nurse Bennett* ◇ *Nurse, come quickly!* See also **nursing** → TREATMENT
surgeon /'sɜːdʒən; *AmE* 'sɜːrdʒən/ [C] a doctor who is trained to perform medical operations in a hospital: *a brain/heart surgeon* See also **specialist** → EXPERT
GP /,dʒiː 'piː/ [C] (*BrE*) a doctor who is trained in general medicine and who works in the local community, not in a hospital (abbreviation for 'general practitioner'): *Go and see your GP as soon as possible.* ◇ *There are four GPs in our local practice.* ❶ In American English a **GP** is usually called a **family doctor**.
physician /fɪ'zɪʃn/ [C] (*especially AmE, formal*) a doctor, especially one who is a specialist in general medicine, not a surgeon: *Please consult your physician before beginning any new exercise program.* ❶ This word is now old-fashioned in British English. Use **doctor** or **GP** instead.
medic /'medɪk/ [C] (*especially AmE, informal*) a doctor: *Somebody call a medic!* ❶ In informal British English, a **medic** is a medical student. In American English a **medic** is also a person in the armed forces who can give medical treatment.
paramedic /,pærə'medɪk/ [C] a person whose job is to help people who are sick or injured, but who is not a doctor or nurse: *Paramedics treated the injured at the roadside before taking them to the hospital.*
internist [C] (*AmE, rather formal*) a doctor who is a specialist in the treatment of diseases of organs inside the body and who does not usually do medical operations: *Consult an internist if you are experiencing any of the following symptoms:...*

document *noun*

document · file · papers · archive · deed · paperwork · dossier
These are all types of written paper containing information or records.

▶ a document / a file/ the paperwork / a dossier **on** sb/ sth
▶ **in** a document / a file/ the archives/ the paperwork/ a dossier
▶ the **relevant** document/ file/ papers/ paperwork
▶ the **necessary** documents/ papers/ paperwork
▶ (an) **important** document/ papers/ archive
▶ **confidential** documents/ files/ papers
▶ (a) **personal / secret** documents/ file/ papers/ archive/ dossier
▶ (a / an) **official / government / state** document/ file/ paper/ archive
▶ to **prepare** a document/ a file/ the paperwork/ a dossier
▶ to **draw up** a document/ papers/ the paperwork
▶ to **release** a document/ a file/ papers
▶ to **keep** a document/a file/papers/an archive/the deeds/the paperwork/ a dossier
▶ to **leak** a document/ a file/ papers
▶ to **read (through)** a document / a file/ the papers/ the paperwork/ a dossier
▶ to **study** a document/ papers/ a dossier

document [C] an official paper or book that gives information about sth or that gives evidence or proof of sth; a computer file that contains text and that has a name that identifies it: *Keep all your travel documents in a safe place.* ◇ *This is an important legal document.* ◇ *They have produced a new* **policy document**. ◇ *The committee presented a* **discussion document** (= to be discussed) *at yesterday's meeting.* ◇ *Save the document before closing.* See also **documentation** → CERTIFICATE
file [C] a collection of documents and the information they contain, for example about a particular person or subject; a collection of information stored together in a computer, under a particular name: *The police were accused of keeping secret files on political activists.* ◇ *Please add this document to your files.* ◇ *Exactly what information is kept in these files?* ◇ *Your application will be* **kept on file**. ◇ *Every file on the same disk must have a different name.* See also **file** → ENVELOPE, **file** → CLASSIFY
papers [pl.] pieces of paper with writing on them such as letters, pieces of work or private documents: *His desk was covered with books and papers.* ◇ *I was sorting through his papers when I came upon a letter from my mother.* ❶ **Papers** can also be official documents that give you permission to do sth or prove your identity. See also **papers** → CERTIFICATE
archive /'ɑːkaɪv; *AmE* 'ɑːrk-/ [C] (also **archives** [pl.]) a collection of historical documents or records of a government, family, place or organization: *These papers are an important part of the national archive.* ◇ *The data is now held in the company archives.* ◇ *The recording is preserved in the BBC's* **sound archive**. ◇ *It is one of the most important* **film archives** *in the world.*
deed [C] (often plural in British English) a legal document that you sign, especially one that proves that you own a house, a building or land: *The* **deeds to** *the property are with my lawyer.* ◇ *Who currently keeps the* **title deed** (= a deed showing who owns sth)?
paperwork /'peɪpəwɜːk; *AmE* 'peɪpərwɜːrk/ [U] all the documents that you need for sth, for example a court case or buying a house: *We can get the necessary paperwork signed tomorrow.* See also **paperwork** → BUREAUCRACY
dossier /'dɒsieɪ; *AmE* 'dɔːs-; 'dɑːs-/ [C] (*formal*) a collection of documents that contain information about a person, event or subject: *They kept dossiers on all trade union members.* ◇ *The group* **compiled a dossier** *of patients' complaints.*

door *noun*

door · gate · entrance · doorway · hatch · exit · mouth · gateway · way · turnstile
These are all words for the opening where you go into or out of a building, room or place, or the barrier that covers that opening.

PATTERNS AND COLLOCATIONS
▸ **at** the door / gate / entrance / exit / mouth / turnstile
▸ **in** the doorway / entrance / gateway
▸ **through** the door / gate / doorway / hatch / gateway / turnstile
▸ the **front / back / side** door / gate / entrance / exit / way
▸ the **main** door / gate / entrance / hatch / exit
▸ the **rear** door / entrance / exit
▸ to **open / shut / close / slam** the door / gate / hatch
▸ to **lock / bolt** the door / gate

door [C] a piece of wood, glass, etc. that is opened and closed so that people can get in and out of a room, building, car, etc.; a similar thing in a cupboard; the space when a door is open; the area close to the entrance of a building: *Shut the door!* ◇ *The door closed behind him.* ◇ *There was a knock on the door.* ◇ *Go and answer the door* (= go and open it because sb has knocked on it or rung the bell). ◇ *the bedroom/wardrobe door* ◇ *the door frame* ◇ *a four-door saloon car* ◇ *Mark appeared through a door at the far end of the room.* ◇ *There's somebody at the door* (= at the front door of a house).

gate [C] a barrier like a door that is used to close an opening in a fence or wall outside a building; an opening that can be closed by a gate or gates; a way out of an airport through which passengers go to get on their plane: *He pushed open the garden gate.* ◇ *A crowd gathered at the factory gates.* ◇ *We drove through the palace gates.* ◇ *BA flight 726 to Paris is now boarding at gate 16.*

entrance [C] a door, gate or passage that is used for entering a room, building or place: *I'll meet you at the main entrance.* ◇ *A lighthouse marks the **entrance to** the harbour.* **OPP** **exit**, See also the entry for HALL 2

doorway /ˈdɔːweɪ; AmE ˈdɔːrweɪ/ [C] an opening into a building or room, where the door is: *She stood in the doorway for a moment before going in.*

hatch [C] an opening or door in a floor, ceiling or wall, through which things can be passed or people can climb: *She returned her tray to the serving hatch.* ◇ *Karen climbed through the hatch and disappeared from view.* ◇ *an escape hatch* ◇ *There's a hatch to the attic.* ❶ **Hatch** is used especially to talk about an opening in the deck of a ship or the bottom of an aircraft, through which goods can be lowered; or about an opening in a wall between a kitchen and dining room, for passing food through; or about any door in an aircraft or spacecraft.

exit /ˈeksɪt; ˈegzɪt/ [C] (*rather formal*) a way out of a public building or vehicle: *Where's the exit?* ◇ *There is a **fire exit** on each floor of the building.* ◇ *The **emergency exit** is at the back of the bus.* **OPP** **entrance**

mouth [C] the entrance or opening of a cave, tunnel, hole, etc: *They drew nearer to the mouth of the cave.* ◇ (*BrE*) *Up ahead was the tunnel mouth.*

gateway /ˈgeɪtweɪ/ [C] an opening in a wall or fence that can be closed by a gate: *They turned through the gateway on the left.*

way [C, usually sing.] a means of going into or leaving a place, such as a door or gate: *Is this **the way in/out**?* ◇ *They escaped out the back way.*

turnstile /ˈtɜːnstaɪl; AmE ˈtɜːrn-/ [C] a gate at the entrance to a public building or stadium that turns in a circle when pushed, allowing one person to go through at a time: *Fans were already lining up at the turnstiles.*

doubt *noun*

1 a feeling of doubt
2 raise/express doubts about sth

1 doubt · question · uncertainty · confusion · a question mark over sth · indecision

These are all words for a feeling that you are not sure about sb/sth.

PATTERNS AND COLLOCATIONS
▸ doubt / uncertainty / confusion / a question mark / indecision **over** sth
▸ doubt / uncertainty / confusion / indecision **about / as to** sth
▸ **in** doubt / question / uncertainty
▸ **beyond / without** doubt / question
▸ **considerable** doubt / uncertainty / confusion
▸ **serious** doubt / confusion
▸ **slight** uncertainty / confusion
▸ to **come into / be open to** doubt / question
▸ to **express** doubt / uncertainty
▸ to **clear up / dispel** doubt / uncertainty / confusion

doubt [U] the state of not being sure about sth or not believing sth: *There is some doubt about the best way to do it.* ◇ *There is no doubt at all that we did the right thing.* ◇ *New evidence has **cast doubt on** the guilt of the man jailed for the crime.* ◇ *The success of the system is not in doubt.* ◇ *If in doubt, wear black.* ◇ *He's made some great movies. There's **no doubt about it**.* ◇ (*law*) *The prosecution was able to establish **beyond reasonable doubt** that the woman had been lying.* See also **doubtful** → UNLIKELY 1, **doubtful** → UNSURE

question [U] a lack of certainty about sth that is shared with other people: *Her honesty is beyond question.* ◇ *His suitability for the job is open to question.* ◇ *Her version of events was accepted without question.* ◇ *The incident brought into question the safety of travellers in the region.*

uncertainty [U] (*rather formal*) the state of not being sure about sth: *There is considerable uncertainty about the company's future.* ◇ *He had an air of uncertainty about him.* **OPP** **certainty** → FAITH, See also **uncertain** → UNSURE

> **NOTE** **DOUBT** OR **UNCERTAINTY**? **Doubt** often refers to an active state of mind that questions sb/sth: *Religious doubt is an integral element of faith.* **Uncertainty** is less forceful and means a more passive lack of certainty about sth: ~~Religious uncertainty is an integral element of faith.~~

confusion [U, C] a state of uncertainty about what is happening, what you should do or what sth means: *There is some confusion about what the correct procedure should be.* ◇ *There was a confusion as to what to do next.* See also **confused** → CONFUSED 1, **confusing** → CONFUSING

a 'question mark over sth *idiom* (*rather informal*) used to say that sth is not certain, especially what will happen to sth in the future: *There's still a big question mark hanging over his future with the team.*

indecision /ˌɪndɪˈsɪʒn/ [U] the state of being unable to decide on sth: *After a moment's indecision, he said yes.* ◇ *She went through a period of terrible uncertainty and indecision.*

▸ **indecisive** /ˌɪndɪˈsaɪsɪv/ *adj.*: *a weak and indecisive man*

2 doubt · suspicion · uncertainty · misgiving · second thoughts · qualm · scruple · compunction

These are all words for a feeling that you may not be doing the right thing.

PATTERNS AND COLLOCATIONS
▸ doubts / suspicions / uncertainties / misgivings / second thoughts / qualms / scruples / compunction **about** sth
▸ **without** a doubt / misgivings / a qualm / scruples / compunction
▸ **considerable / great / grave / deep / serious** doubts / suspicion / misgivings
▸ to **have** doubts / suspicions / misgivings / second thoughts / qualms / scruples
▸ to **have no** doubts / suspicions / misgivings / qualms / scruples / compunction
▸ to **feel (no)** doubt / qualms / compunction
▸ to **express** doubts / suspicions / misgivings
▸ to **raise / arouse / voice** doubts / suspicions

doubt [C] a feeling of not being sure about sth or not believing sth: *His failure to appear raises serious **doubts as to** his reliability.* ◇ *Doubts have arisen **over** the viability of the schedule.* ◇ *They say they'll be here on time but I **have my doubts** about that.* ◇ *I had been aware of a **nagging doubt** growing in my mind.* See also **doubt** → SUSPECT *verb*

suspicion [U, C] a feeling that sb has done sth wrong, illegal or dishonest, even though you have no proof: *He was arrested on suspicion of murder.* ◇ *They drove away slowly to avoid arousing suspicion.* ◇ *I have a sneaking suspicion that she's not telling the truth.* ◇ *She was reluctant to voice her suspicions.* See also **suspicion** → SCEPTICISM, **suspect** → SUPPOSE, **suspicious** → SUSPICIOUS 1, **suspicious** → SUSPICIOUS 2

uncertainty [C] something that you cannot be sure about; a situation that causes you to feel uncertain: *All of us are a bit afraid of life's uncertainties and unexpected problems.* ◇ *She tried to get on with her life amidst the uncertainties of war.* **OPP certainty** → CERTAINTY, See also **uncertain** → UNCLEAR

misgiving /ˌmɪsˈgɪvɪŋ/ [C, usually pl., U] (*rather formal*) feelings of doubt or anxiety about what might happen, or about whether or not sth is the right thing to do: *I had grave misgivings about making the trip.* ◇ *I read the letter with a sense of misgiving.*

second thoughts *phrase* a change in your opinion after thinking about sth again: *You're not having second thoughts about it, are you?* ◇ (*BrE*) *I'll wait here. No, on second thoughts, I'll come with you.* ◇ (*AmE*) *On second thought, I'll come with you.* ❶ **Second thoughts** is used in the two idioms **have ˌsecond ˈthoughts** and **on ˈsecond thoughts** (**on ˈsecond thought** in American English).

qualm /kwɑːm; kwɔːm/ [C, usually pl.] an uncomfortable feeling of doubt or worry about whether what you are doing is right: *He had been working very hard so he had no qualms about taking a few days off.*

scruple /ˈskruːpl/ [C, usually pl., U] a feeling that makes you reluctant to do sth that you think may be morally wrong: *I overcame my moral scruples.* ◇ *He had no scruples about spying on her.* ◇ *She is totally without scruple.* See also **scrupulous** → GOOD *adj.* 5, **unscrupulous** → CORRUPT

compunction /kəmˈpʌŋkʃn/ [U] (*formal*) a slight feeling of guilt for sth you have done or might do: *She felt no compunction about leaving her job.* ❶ In American English **compunction** can also be countable: (*AmE*) *She has no compunctions about rejecting the plan.*

doubt *verb*

doubt · **question** · **challenge** · **dispute** · **contest** · **query**
These words all mean to have or express uncertainty about sb/sth.

PATTERNS AND COLLOCATIONS
▸ to doubt / question / challenge / dispute / query **whether**...
▸ to doubt / dispute **that**...
▸ to doubt / question / challenge / dispute / contest the **validity** of sth
▸ to doubt / question / challenge the **wisdom** of sb / sth
▸ to doubt / question / challenge a **story**
▸ to doubt / question sb's **integrity** / **motives**
▸ to question / challenge / dispute / contest / query a **decision**
▸ to **seriously** doubt / question / challenge / dispute / contest sth

doubt [T] to feel uncertain about sth; to feel that sth is not true or will probably not happen: *There seems no reason to doubt her story.* ◇ *'Do you think England will win?' – 'I doubt it.'* ◇ *I never doubted (that) she would come.* ◇ *I doubt if the new one will be any better.* See also **doubtful** → UNLIKELY 1, **doubtful** → UNSURE, **undoubted** → UNDOUBTED

question [T] to have or express doubts or suspicions about sth: *I just accepted what he told me. I never thought to question it.* ◇ *No one has ever questioned her judgement.* ◇ *He questioned whether the accident was solely the truck driver's fault.* See also **unquestioned** → UNDOUBTED, **unquestionable** → CONCLUSIVE

challenge /ˈtʃælɪndʒ/ [T] to express or cause doubts about whether sth is true or legal; to refuse to accept sth: *The story was completely untrue and was successfully challenged in court.* ◇ *This discovery challenges traditional beliefs.* ◇ *She does not like anyone challenging her authority.* See also **unchallenged** → UNDOUBTED

dispute /dɪˈspjuːt/ [T] to express doubts about whether sth is true and valid: *These figures have been disputed.* ◇ *The players disputed the referee's decision.* ◇ *No one is disputing that there is a problem.* See also **undisputed** → UNDOUBTED, **indisputable** → CONCLUSIVE

contest /kənˈtest/ [T] to formally oppose a decision or statement and try to have it changed: *Her son contested the will, stating that she was not of sound mind when she signed it.* ◇ *The divorce was not contested.* See also **uncontested** → UNDOUBTED

query /ˈkwɪəri; AmE ˈkwɪri/ [T] to express doubts about whether sth is correct or not: *We queried the bill as it seemed far too high.*

> **NOTE** QUESTION OR QUERY? These words are very close in meaning, although **question** is more frequent. **Query** is often used to express doubts about the details of sth, such as a bill, a report or an expenses claim. **Question** expresses stronger doubt, including the doubt that sth exists at all: *I question the existence of life on other planets.* ◇ ~~I query the existence of life on other planets.~~

do well *verb*

do well · **flourish** · **thrive** · **prosper** · **boom** · **blossom** · **bloom** · **be going places**
These words all mean to be successful, or to grow or develop quickly or successfully.

PATTERNS AND COLLOCATIONS
▸ to flourish / thrive / prosper **on** / **under** sth
▸ to do well / prosper / blossom **as** sth
▸ to blossom / bloom **into** sth
▸ a **business** does well / flourishes / thrives / prospers / is booming / blossoms
▸ an **industry** does well / flourishes / thrives / prospers
▸ **tourism** / **trade** / **a market** flourishes / thrives / prospers / is booming
▸ the **economy** does well / flourishes / prospers / is booming
▸ a **plant** / **town** does well / flourishes / thrives
▸ to **really** flourish / thrive / blossom
▸ to do **really** well / be **really** going places

do ˈwell [I] (*especially spoken*) to be successful or make good progress: *Jack is doing very well at school.* ◇ *Her last play had done well.* ◇ *The company is doing well now after a difficult start.* ◇ *This shrub will do well even in a small city garden.* ❶ **Do well** can be used to talk about people, places, businesses and plants.

flourish /ˈflʌrɪʃ; AmE ˈflɜːrɪʃ/ [I] (*especially written*) to develop quickly and be successful; to grow well and be strong, healthy and happy: *His international career has flourished under captain James Murray.* ◇ *The arts began to flourish at that time.* ◇ *There was a flourishing black market.* ❶ **Flourish** can be used to talk about people, their careers and relationships, places, traditions, businesses and plants. It is used especially to talk about art and culture, especially in a historical context.

thrive /θraɪv/ [I] to develop quickly and be successful; to grow well and be strong, healthy and happy: *He's clearly thriving in his new job.* ◇ *New businesses thrive in this area.* ◇ *These animals rarely thrive in captivity.* ◇ *She seems to thrive on stress* (= enjoy it). ❶ **Thrive** can be used to talk about people, businesses, places, plants or animals. It is used especially to talk about the conditions in which a person, animal or plant can become strong, healthy or happy. See also **thriving** → SUCCESSFUL 2

prosper [I] (*especially written*) (of a person, business or economy) to develop in a successful way; to be successful, especially financially: *The economy prospered under his administration.* ◇ *The railway prospered from the new mining traffic.* See also **prosperity** → MONEY 3, **prosperous** → RICH

boom [I] (used especially in the progressive tenses) (*rather informal, especially journalism*) (of a business or economy) to have a period of rapid growth; to become bigger or more successful: *The club scene was booming.* ◇ *Business is booming!* ◇ *Tourist numbers have boomed in recent years.*

▸ **boom** *noun* [C]: *a boom in car sales* ◇ *a property/ housing boom* ◇ *a boom year for exports* **OPP** **slump** → RECESSION

blossom *verb* [I] (of people) to become more healthy, confident and successful; (of a relationship, career or talent) to develop into sth better or quickly become successful: *She has visibly blossomed over the last few months.* ◇ *The friendship blossomed into love.*

bloom [I] (especially of people) to become or be healthy or become confident and successful: *She was blooming with good health.*

be ˈgoing places *idiom* (*rather informal*) (of a person) to be getting more and more successful in your life or career: *He's a young architect who's really going places.*

drab *adj.*

drab · grey · featureless · nondescript · colourless
These words all describe things or people that are not interesting or unusual so that you do not notice or remember them.

PATTERNS AND COLLOCATIONS
▸ a drab / grey / featureless / colourless **world**
▸ a drab / grey / featureless **landscape**
▸ a drab / featureless / nondescript **building**
▸ a drab / featureless **room**
▸ drab / featureless **corridors / walls**
▸ a grey / nondescript / colourless **man**
▸ **rather** drab / grey / featureless / nondescript / colourless

drab (especially of a place) without interest or bright colour: *She longed to be out of the cold, drab little office.*

grey (*especially BrE*) (*AmE usually* **gray**) (of a person or life) not interesting, unusual or attractive in any way: *Ours is a company that isn't run by grey men in suits.* ◇ *It is thought of as a city of grey bureaucracy.*

featureless (especially of a place) without any noticeable features or qualities: *It is a barren and featureless wasteland.*

nondescript /ˈnɒndɪskrɪpt; *AmE* ˈnɑːn-/ (of a person or place) without any interesting or unusual features or qualities: *He wore a shabby suit and looked thoroughly nondescript.* ◇ *It was a bare landscape occasionally interrupted by nondescript villages.*

colourless (*BrE*) (*AmE* **colorless**) without any interesting features or qualities; showing, or making people feel, no emotion: *He was a small, colourless man who worked as a clerk.* ◇ *'I suppose so,' she said in a colourless voice.* ◇ *Too many passive verbs make for flabby, colourless prose.* ❶ **Colourless** is used especially to describe sb's personality or voice, or a piece of writing. **OPP** **colourful** → COLOURED

drag *verb*

drag · rush · haul · hustle · bundle · pack sb off
These words all mean to take or send sb somewhere, especially quickly, roughly, or to somewhere they do not want to go.

PATTERNS AND COLLOCATIONS
▸ to drag / haul / hustle / bundle sb **off / away** (from sth)
▸ to drag / rush / haul / hustle / bundle sb **out of** sth
▸ to rush / haul / hustle / bundle sb **into** sth
▸ to drag / haul **yourself** somewhere

drag (-gg-) [T] (always used with an adverb or preposition) to make sb/yourself go somewhere that they/you do not really want to go to; to move yourself slowly and with a lot of effort: *I'm sorry to drag you all this way in the heat.* ◇ *It's time you dragged yourself away from that computer!* ◇ *I dragged myself out of bed and got a glass of water.*

rush [T] (always used with an adverb or preposition) to take or send sb somewhere in a great hurry: *Ambulances rushed the injured to hospital.*

haul /hɔːl/ [T] (always used with an adverb or preposition) to force sb to go somewhere they do not want to go, especially by pulling them; to move yourself somewhere slowly and with a lot of effort: *A number of suspects have been hauled in for questioning.* ◇ *She hauled him back onto the dance floor.* ◇ *Laura hauled herself up from the sofa.* ◇ *The creature began to haul itself out of the water.*

NOTE DRAG OR HAUL? There is more of a sense of physical force being used with **haul** than with **drag**. You usually *haul yourself* somewhere when an upward movement is involved; it is used especially with *up* and *out.*

hustle [T] (always used with an adverb or preposition) to make sb move forward quickly by pushing them in a rough or aggressive way: *He grabbed her arm and hustled her out of the room.* ◇ *I was hustled into a waiting car.*

bundle [T] (always used with an adverb or preposition) to push or send sb somewhere quickly and roughly: *Bodyguards quickly bundled the President into the car.* ◇ *They bundled her off on the next train.*

NOTE HUSTLE OR BUNDLE? There is often more aggression and force shown with **hustle** than with **bundle**. A person might be **bundled** somewhere in order to protect or hide them.

ˌpack sbˈoff *phrasal verb* (*informal*) to send sb somewhere, especially because you do not want them with you: *He was packed off to a boarding school at the age of seven.*

drain *noun*

drain · sewer · gutter
These are all words for a pipe or channel that waste water can flow through.

PATTERNS AND COLLOCATIONS
▸ an **open** drain / sewer
▸ a drain / gutter is **blocked**
▸ a drain / sewer / gutter **runs** down / along sth

drain [C] a pipe that carries away dirty water or other liquid waste: *We had to call in a plumber to unblock the drain.* ◇ *The drains* (= the system of pipes) *date from the beginning of the last century.* See also **drain** → PUMP *verb*

sewer /ˈsuːə(r); *BrE* also ˈsjuː-/ [C] an underground pipe that is used to carry sewage (= used water and waste substances that are produced by human bodies) away from houses and other buildings: *Drainage in the village was very poor, with open sewers* (= not underground) *and gutters.*

gutter [C] a long piece of curved metal or plastic that is fixed under the edge of a roof to carry away the water when it rains; the area between the main part of a road and a pavement where water collects and is carried to drains: *A leaking gutter can be repaired quickly and at minimal cost.* ◇ *I stepped off the pavement and walked in the gutter.*

drain *verb*

drain · empty
These words both mean to make sth empty or dry.

PATTERNS AND COLLOCATIONS
▸ to drain / empty **out**
▸ to drain / empty **of / into** sth
▸ to drain / empty **slowly / completely**

drain [I] to become empty or dry by having all the liquid removed; (of a liquid) to leave sth dry: *The swimming pool drains very slowly.* ◇ *Leave the dishes to drain.* ◇ *She pulled out the plug and the water **drained away**.* See also **drain** → PUMP *verb*

empty [I] to become empty: *The tank empties out in five minutes.* ◇ *The streets soon emptied when the rain started.* ◇ *She watched as the beach gradually emptied of people.* See also **empty** → CLEAR *verb*, **empty** → EMPTY *adj.*

drama *noun*

drama · theatre · stage · acting · show business · the performing arts · showbiz
These words are all used to talk about the activity or profession of performing plays.

PATTERNS AND COLLOCATIONS
▸ **improvisational / serious** drama / theatre / acting
▸ **classical / Elizabethan / modern** drama / theatre
▸ to **study** drama / theatre / acting
▸ a drama / theatre / stage / acting / performing arts **school**
▸ a drama / theatre / acting / performing arts **student**
▸ a drama / theatre **critic**

drama /ˈdrɑːmə/ [U] the performing of plays, especially when considered as a form of literature: *Television drama is a powerful cultural medium.* See also **drama** → PLAY *noun*
▸ **dramatic** *adj.* [usually before noun]: *Students will study various plays and dramatic texts.*
theatre (*BrE*) (*AmE* **theater**) [U] the performing of plays, especially when considered as a form of entertainment: (*BrE*) *I like music, theatre and cinema.* ◇ *The play challenges current ideas about what makes good theatre* (= what makes good entertainment when performed).
▸ **theatrical** *adj.* [only before noun]: *a theatrical career*
stage (often **the stage**) [sing.] the theatre and the performing of plays as a profession or a form of entertainment: *His parents didn't want him to go on the stage* (= to be an actor). ◇ *She was a popular star of stage and screen* (= theatre and cinema). See also **stage** → PLAY *verb* 2
acting [U] the activity or profession of performing in plays, films, etc: *She started her acting career while still at school.* See also **act** → PLAY *verb* 2
'show business [U] the business of providing public entertainment, for example in the theatre, films or television: *The whole family is in show business.*
the per'forming 'arts [C, pl.] (*rather formal*) arts such as music, dance and drama which are performed for an audience: *The book examines recent trends in the performing arts.*
showbiz /ˈʃəʊbɪz; *AmE* ˈʃoʊ-/ [U] (*informal*) show business: *The club is a favourite haunt of showbiz stars and celebrities.* ◇ *That's showbiz!*

draw *noun*

draw · tie · dead heat
These are all words for a situation in which two or more people or groups have the same score in a game or competition.

PATTERNS AND COLLOCATIONS
▸ a draw / tie / dead heat **with / between** sb
▸ a draw / tie **against** sb
▸ to **end in** a draw / tie / dead heat
▸ to **finish in** a tie / dead heat
▸ to **declare** a draw / dead heat

draw [C] (*especially BrE*) a game in which both teams or players finish with the same score: *It was a disappointing one–all draw against France.* ◇ *They could only manage a goalless draw at Upton Park.* ◇ *He managed to hold Smith to a draw* (= to stop him from winning when he seemed likely to do so).
▸ **draw** *verb* [I, T]: *England and France drew 3–3.* ◇ *England drew with/against France.* ◇ *England drew their game against France.*

tie [C] a situation in a game or competition when two or more players have the same score: *There was a tie for first place.* ◇ *The chair has the casting vote in the event of a tie.* See also **tie** → GAME *noun* 1
▸ **tie** *verb* [I, T]: *They tied for second place.* ◇ *The scores are tied at 3–3.*

NOTE **DRAW** OR **TIE?** In sport a **draw** is always between two teams or players and is the final result of the game. A **tie** can be between more than two players and can be used to describe the situation at any stage of a game or competition, as well as the final result.

dead 'heat [C] (*especially BrE*) a result in a race when two competitors finish at exactly the same time: *The race was declared a dead heat.* ❶ In American English **dead heat** also means a situation during a race or competition when two or more people are at the same level: (*AmE*) *The two candidates are in a dead heat in the polls.*

draw *verb*

draw · paint · sketch · colour
These words all mean to make a picture of sb/sth.

PATTERNS AND COLLOCATIONS
▸ to draw / paint / sketch / colour a **picture**
▸ to draw / paint / sketch a **landscape / portrait**
▸ to draw / sketch a **diagram / graph**

draw [T, I] to make a picture or design using a pencil, pen or chalk (but NOT paint): *She drew a house* (= a picture of a house). ◇ *He drew a circle in the sand with a stick.* ◇ *You draw beautifully.*
▸ **drawing** *noun* [U]: *I'm not very good at drawing.* ◇ *technical drawing* See also **drawing** → PICTURE
paint [T, I] to make a picture or design using paints: *A friend painted the children for me* (= a picture of the children). ◇ *She paints in oils.* ◇ *My mother paints quite well.* See also **paint** → PAINT *verb*, **painter** → ARTIST
▸ **painting** *noun* [U]: *Her hobbies include music and painting.* See also **painting** → PICTURE
sketch [T, I] to draw a quick picture of sb/sth using a pen or pencil: *He quickly sketched the view from the window.* ◇ *He enjoyed sketching, writing poetry and playing music.* See also **sketch** → PICTURE *noun*
colour (*BrE*) (*AmE* **color**) [I, T] to put colour on sth using coloured pens, pencils, etc: *The children love drawing and colouring.* ◇ *I'll draw a tree and you can colour it in* (= put colour inside the lines). ◇ *a colouring book* (= with pictures that you can colour in) See also **colour** → PAINT *verb*

dream *noun*

dream · vision · illusion · nightmare · hallucination
These are all words for sth that seems to happen or exist, but in fact only happens/exists in your mind.

PATTERNS AND COLLOCATIONS
▸ a dream / nightmare **about** sth
▸ to **have** a dream / a vision / an illusion / a nightmare / hallucinations
▸ to **experience** dreams / visions / nightmares / hallucinations
▸ to **cause** an illusion / nightmares / hallucinations
▸ a dream / a vision / an illusion **fades**

dream [C] a series of images, events and feelings that happen in your mind while you are asleep: *I had a vivid dream about my old school.* ◇ *I thought someone came into the bedroom, but it was just a dream.* ◇ *She was like a child frightened by a bad dream.* ◇ *'Good night. Sweet dreams.'*
▸ **dream** *verb* [I, T]: *Did I talk in my sleep? I must have been dreaming.* ◇ *I dreamed about you last night.* ◇ *Did it really happen or did I just dream it?* ◇ *I dreamed (that) I got the job.*
▸ **dreamlike** *adj.*: *The place has an almost dreamlike quality.*

vision [C] (*especially written*) a dream or similar experience, especially of a religious kind: *The idea came to her in a vision.* ◊ *A young girl in the village experienced a prophetic vision.*
▸ **visionary** *adj.* [only before noun]: *visionary experiences*

illusion /ɪˈluːʒn/ [C] (*rather formal*) something that seems to exist but in fact does not, or seems to be sth that it is not: *Mirrors in a room often give an illusion of space.* ◊ *The idea of absolute personal freedom is an illusion.* ❶ An **optical illusion** is sth that tricks your eyes and makes you think that you can see sth that is not there: *The road ahead looks wet, but in fact this is an optical illusion.*
▸ **illusory** /ɪˈluːsəri/ *adj.*: (*formal*) *Any power he may seem to have is purely illusory.*

nightmare /ˈnaɪtmeə(r)/; *AmE* -mer/ [C] a dream that is very frightening or unpleasant: *He still has nightmares about the accident.* ◊ *Horror films always give me nightmares.*
▸ **nightmarish** *adj.*: *The party began to take on an unreal, almost nightmarish quality.*

hallucination /həˌluːsɪˈneɪʃn/ [C, U] the fact of seeming to see or hear sb/sth that is not really there, especially because of illness or drugs; something that is seen or heard when it is not really there: *She was admitted to hospital suffering from hallucinations.* ◊ *High temperatures can cause hallucination.* ◊ *Was the figure real or just a hallucination?*
▸ **hallucinatory** /həˈluːsɪnətri; həˌluːsɪˈneɪtəri; *AmE* həˈluːsənətɔːri/ *adj.* [only before noun]: *hallucinatory experiences/drugs*

drink *noun*

1 a drink of water
2 alcoholic drinks

1 **drink · beverage · soft drink**
These are all words for liquid that you drink.

PATTERNS AND COLLOCATIONS
▸ a / an **hot** / **cold** / **alcoholic** / **non-alcoholic** drink / beverage

drink [C, U] liquid for drinking: *Can I have a drink?* ◊ *I felt better after having a drink of water.* ◊ (*BrE*) *There are crisps and fizzy drinks* (= drinks with bubbles of gas in them) *in the kitchen.* ◊ *Food and drinks will be available.*

beverage /ˈbevərɪdʒ/ [C] (*formal*) any type of drink except water: *Studies on the consumption of various alcoholic beverages have been conducted.*

soft ˈdrink [C] a cold drink that does not contain alcohol: *Snacks, soft drinks, tea and coffee will be served during the interval.* ❶ In American English **soft drink** usually only refers to a fizzy drink.

2 **drink · alcohol · liquor · spirit · booze**
These are all words for drinks which contain alcohol and can make you drunk.

PATTERNS AND COLLOCATIONS
▸ **alcoholic** drinks / liquor
▸ **strong** drink / liquor
▸ to **drink** alcohol / liquor / spirits / booze
▸ to **consume** alcohol / liquor
▸ to **turn to** / **keep off** / **stay off** (the) drink / alcohol / booze
▸ a drink / an alcohol / a booze **problem**

drink [C, U] alcohol or an alcoholic drink; sth that you drink on a social occasion: *Let's go for a drink.* ◊ *He downed his drink.* ◊ *I need a stiff drink* (= a strong drink). ◊ *She bought another round of drinks.* ◊ *The drinks are on me* (= I'll pay for them). ◊ (*BrE*) *Jim's got a drink problem.* ◊ (*AmE*) *a drinking problem* See also **drunk → DRUNK**

alcohol [U] drinks such as beer, wine and whisky, that can make people drunk: *He never touches alcohol.* ◊ *The level of alcohol in his blood was over the legal limit.*

liquor /ˈlɪkə(r)/ [U] (*especially AmE*) strong alcoholic drink: *They were standing outside the liquor store.* ◊ *She drinks beer and wine but no hard liquor.* ❶ In technical British English **liquor** means any alcoholic drink: *The sale of liquor to persons under 18 is prohibited.*

spirit [C, usually pl.] (*especially BrE*) a strong alcoholic drink: *I don't drink whisky or brandy or any other spirits.* ◊ *A standard measure of spirits is 25ml.*

booze [U] (*informal*) alcoholic drink: *The party was great but we had run out of booze by midnight.*

drink *verb*

drink · sip · suck · drain · booze · swig
These words all mean to take liquid into the body through the mouth.

PATTERNS AND COLLOCATIONS
▸ to sip / suck / swig **at** sth
▸ to drink / sip / swig **from** a bottle / glass of sth
▸ to drink / suck sth **up**
▸ to drink / sip / drain your **drink** / **pint**
▸ to drink / sip / swig **beer** / **wine**
▸ to drink / sip **tea** / **coffee** / **water**

drink [T, I] to take liquid into the mouth and swallow it; to drink alcohol, especially regularly: *What would you like to drink?* ◊ *I don't drink coffee.* ◊ *He was drinking straight from the bottle.* ◊ *He doesn't drink* (= doesn't drink alcohol). ◊ *Don't drink and drive* (= drive a car after drinking alcohol). ◊ *She's been drinking heavily since she lost her job.* ◊ *I drank far too much last night.* See also **drink → SIP noun, drunk → DRUNK**

sip (-**pp**-) [T, I] to drink sth, taking a very small amount each time: *He slowly sipped his wine.* ◊ (*BrE*) *She sat there, sipping at her tea.* See also **sip → SIP noun**

suck [T, I] to take liquid or air into your mouth by using the muscles of your lips; to keep sth in your mouth and pull on it with your lips and tongue: *She was noisily sucking up milk through a straw.* ◊ *He sucked a mint.* ◊ *He sucked on a mint.*

drain [T] to empty a cup or glass by drinking everything in it: *In one gulp, he drained the glass.* ◊ *She quickly drained the last of her drink.*

booze [I] (usually used in the progressive tenses) (*informal*) to drink alcohol, especially in large quantities: *He's out boozing with his mates.*

swig (-**gg**-) [T] (*informal*) to take a quick drink of sth, especially alcohol: *They sat around swigging beer from bottles.* See also **swig → SIP noun**

drive *verb*

1 drive a car
2 drive yourself too hard

1 **drive · fly · steer · manoeuvre · handle · pilot · navigate · sail**
These words all mean to operate a vehicle such as a car, plane or boat.

PATTERNS AND COLLOCATIONS
▸ to drive / fly / steer / manoeuvre / navigate / sail sth **into** / **out of** sth
▸ to drive / fly / steer / navigate / sail sth **across** / **through** sth
▸ to drive / steer / manoeuvre / handle / navigate a **car**
▸ to fly / steer / manoeuvre / handle / pilot / navigate a **plane**
▸ to steer / manoeuvre / handle / pilot / navigate / sail a **boat** / **ship**
▸ to **learn to** drive / fly / navigate / sail
▸ to drive / fly / steer / manoeuvre / pilot / navigate sth **skilfully**
▸ a driving / flying / sailing **lesson** / **instructor** / **course** / **school**

drive [I, T] to control a vehicle with wheels such as a car or truck: *Can you drive?* ◊ *Don't drive so fast!* ◊ *He drives a taxi* (= as his job). ◊ *You need a special licence to drive a heavy goods vehicle.* See also **drive → GO verb 2, drive → FLIGHT noun**

fly [I, T] to control an aircraft in the air: *Where did you learn to fly?* ◇ *She's trained to fly passenger planes, not military jets.* ◇ *They deliberately flew the plane into enemy airspace.* ◇ *I've never flown one of these before.* See also **fly** → GO 2

steer [T, I] to control the direction in which a boat, car or other vehicle moves: *The captain steered the boat into the narrow harbour.* ◇ *Pilots need to learn to steer on the ground as well as in the air.*

manoeuvre (*BrE*) (*AmE* **maneuver**) /mə'nu:və(r)/ [T, I] to move or turn a vehicle skilfully or carefully: *She manoeuvred the car carefully into the garage.* ◇ *There was very little room to manoeuvre.*

handle [T] to control a vehicle: *I wasn't sure if I could handle such a powerful car.* ❶ A vehicle that *handles well/badly* is easy/difficult to drive or control: [I] *This type of car handles well in all weather conditions.*

pilot [T] to fly an aircraft or guide a boat: *The plane was piloted by the instructor.* ◇ *The captain piloted the boat into a mooring.*

navigate /'nævɪgeɪt/ [I, T] to find the position of a car, boat or plane that you are travelling in and the direction you need to go in, for example by using a map: *I'll drive and you can navigate.* ◇ *Ships used to be navigated by the stars* (= using the position of the stars to find out the position of the ship).

sail [T, I] to control a boat or ship with a sail: *She sails her own yacht.* ◇ *He managed to sail the boat between the rocks.* ◇ *I learned to sail as a child.*

2 drive · push · overwork · work

These words all mean to make sb/yourself work very hard.

▶ to drive / push / work sb **hard**
▶ to drive / push sb **too far / to the limit**
▶ to drive / work sb **into the ground**

drive [T] (*sometimes disapproving*) to make sb/yourself work very hard: *You're driving yourself too hard.* ❶ In this meaning **drive** is usually used with a reflexive pronoun such as *yourself, himself, herself,* etc. See also **drive** → AMBITION *noun*

push [T] (*usually approving*) to make sb/yourself work hard: *The music teacher really pushes her pupils.* ◇ *Lucy should push herself a little harder.*

overwork /ˌəʊvər'wɜːrk/ [I, T] (*disapproving*) to make sb/yourself work too hard: *You look tired. Have you been overworking?* ◇ *The staff are grossly overworked.*
▶ **overwork** *noun* [U]: *His illness was brought on by money worries and overwork.*

work [T] to make sb/yourself work, especially hard: *She works herself too hard.* ◇ *He says they're working him hard.* ❶ In this meaning **work** is usually used with *hard* or *too hard.*

driver *noun*

driver · motorist · chauffeur

These are all words for sb who drives a vehicle.

▶ **speeding** drivers / motorists
▶ to **be sb's** driver / chauffeur

driver [C] a person who drives a vehicle: *a bus/train/taxi/truck/lorry driver* ◇ *She's a good driver.* ◇ *The ambassador and his driver were both killed in the explosion.* ◇ *Many accidents involve* **drunk drivers**. ◇ (*AmE*) *Can I see your* **driver's license** *please?* ◇ *a racing driver* ◇ (*BrE*) *a learner driver* ◇ (*AmE*) *a student driver* ❶ A **driver's license** (*AmE*) is usually called a **driving licence** in British English.

motorist [C] (*especially journalism*) a person who drives a car: *The accident was reported by a* **passing motorist**. ◇ *Motorists face being hit even harder by rising taxes.* ◇ *Police had to rescue stranded motorists.*

NOTE **DRIVER** OR **MOTORIST**? **Motorists** only drive cars: ~~a bus/train/taxi/truck/lorry motorist~~ and they only drive their own cars, not other people's as a job: ~~the ambassador and his motorist~~. **Motorist** is usually used in journalism or in the plural to talk about car drivers as a group in society. **Motorists** are sometimes contrasted with other groups such as **pedestrians** (= people walking in the street, not travelling in a vehicle) and **cyclists** (= people riding bicycles).

chauffeur /'ʃəʊfə(r); *AmE* ʃoʊ'fɜːr/ [C] a person whose job is to drive a car, usually for sb rich or important: *They were met at the airport by a chauffeur in uniform.*
▶ **chauffeur** *verb* [T]: *He was chauffeured to all his meetings.*

drop *noun*

drop · bead · splash · globule · blob · drip

These are all words for a small amount of a liquid.

▶ a drop / bead / splash of **blood**
▶ a drop / bead of **moisture / perspiration / sweat**
▶ a drop / splash of **water**
▶ a splash / blob of **paint**

drop [C] a very small amount of liquid that forms a round shape: *A few* **drops of rain** *fell.* ◇ *Mix a few drops of milk into the cake mixture.* ◇ *He drained the last few drops from his glass.* See also **drip** → TRICKLE *verb*

bead /biːd/ [C] (*always followed by of*) a small drop of a liquid, especially sweat: *There were beads of sweat on his forehead.*

splash [C] a small amount of liquid that falls onto sth; the mark that this makes: *There were dark splashes of mud on her skirt.* See also **splash** → SPRAY *verb*

globule /'glɒbjuːl; *AmE* 'glɑːb-/ [C] a small drop or ball of a liquid or of a solid that has been melted: *The milk's small* **fat globules** *make it easy to digest.*

blob [C] (*informal*) a small amount or drop of liquid, especially a liquid which is stiff or sticky: *A blob of ketchup was rolling down his chin.*

drip a small drop of liquid that falls from sth: *We put a bucket under the hole in the roof to catch the drips.* See also **drip** → LEAK *verb*, **drip** → TRICKLE *verb*

NOTE **SPLASH** OR **DRIP**? A **splash** is bigger than a **drip** and falls once or a few times by accident; **drips** fall regularly or continuously, especially because of a leak (= hole or crack) in sth. With **splash** the emphasis is on what the splashes fall *on*; with **drip** the emphasis is on where the drips fall *from*.

drug *noun*

1 take illegal drugs
2 prescribe drugs for a medical condition

1 drug · dope · narcotic · stimulant

These are all words for substances, especially illegal substances, that people take and that affect the mind in some way.

▶ to **use** drugs / dope / narcotics / stimulants
▶ to **take** drugs / narcotics / stimulants
▶ to **abuse** drugs / narcotics
▶ to **deal** drugs / dope
▶ a drug / dope **test**
▶ a drug / dope / narcotics **dealer**
▶ drug / narcotics **trafficking / traffickers**
▶ the drug / narcotics **trade**

drug [C] a substance that some people smoke, drink, inject, etc. to give them pleasant or exciting feelings, especially an illegal substance of this kind: *He does not smoke or take drugs.* ◇ *I found out Tim was* **on drugs** (=

regularly used drugs). ◇ (*informal*) *I don't* **do drugs** (= use them). ◇ **hard drugs** (= very harmful drugs, such as heroin) ◇ **soft drugs** (= drugs that are not considered so harmful) ◇ *drug and alcohol abuse* ◇ *a drug addict/dealer* ◇ *Drugs have been seized with a street value of 2 million dollars.*

dope [U] (*informal*) a drug that is taken illegally for pleasure, especially cannabis or, in the US, heroin; a drug that is taken by a person or given to an animal to affect their performance in a race or sport: *He has admitted smoking dope as a teenager.* ◇ *The athlete had failed a dope test* (= a medical test showed that he had taken such drugs). See also **dope** → POISON *verb*

narcotic /nɑːˈkɒtɪk; *AmE* nɑːrˈkɑː-/ [C] (*rather formal*) a powerful illegal drug that affects the mind in a harmful way, for example heroin or cocaine: *Narcotics trafficking represents 30 to 50 per cent of organized crime's take.* ◇ *a narcotics agent* (= a police officer investigating the illegal trade in drugs) ❶ **Narcotic** is used especially to talk about the illegal trade in drugs and attempts by the police to stop it.

stimulant /ˈstɪmjələnt/ [C] a drug or substance that makes you feel more awake and gives you more energy: *Coffee and tea are mild stimulants.*

---

2 See the Topic Map for HEALTH on p.890
drug · medicine · prescription · medication · cure · remedy · placebo · antidote
These are all words for treatments for people who are ill.

PATTERNS AND COLLOCATIONS
▸ a drug/ medicine/ a prescription/ medication/ a cure/ a remedy/ an antidote **for** sth
▸ (an) **effective** drug/ medicine/ medication/ cure/ remedy
▸ a **herbal** medicine/ cure/ remedy
▸ to **take** your medicine/your medication/a remedy/a placebo/ the antidote
▸ to **prescribe** drugs/ medicine/ medication/ a cure/ a remedy
▸ to **find** a cure/ a remedy/ an antidote

drug [C] a substance which is used to cure or fight an illness or its symptoms (= signs of illness): *The doctor put me on a course of pain-killing drugs.* ◇ **Drug companies** *are always developing new products.* ❶ Do not say *take drugs* if you are talking about legal, medical drugs: ~~Are you taking any drugs for your headaches?~~ ◇ *Are you taking anything for your headaches?*

medicine [U, C] a substance, especially a liquid, that you drink or swallow in order to cure an illness: *She gave me a dose of cough medicine.* ◇ *Food and medicines are being airlifted to the flood-hit area.* See also **medicine** → TREATMENT

prescription /prɪˈskrɪpʃn/ [C] an official piece of paper on which a doctor writes the type of medicine you should have, and which enables you to get it from a pharmacist (= a person who has been trained to prepare medicines); the medicine that your doctor has ordered for you: *The doctor gave me a prescription for antibiotics.* ◇ *Antibiotics are only available* **on prescription**. ◇ *The pharmacist will make up your prescription.*
▸ **prescribe** *verb* [T]: *The doctor may be able to prescribe something for that cough.*

medication /ˌmedrˈkeɪʃn/ [U, C] (*rather formal*) a medical drug; a course of medical drugs taken to treat or prevent an illness: *Are you currently taking any medication?* ◇ *My grandmother has been* **on medication** *for years.* ◇ *Many flu medications are available without a prescription.*

NOTE DRUG, MEDICINE OR MEDICATION? **Drug** emphasizes what the substance is made of; it is used especially when talking about the chemicals industry that makes these substances. **Medicine** and **medication** emphasize what the substance is used for. **Medicine** is used especially when talking about treating illnesses in general. **Medication** is used especially when talking about treating a particular illness or person; it is often used to talk about the treatment of more serious medical conditions.

cure [C] a medicine or medical treatment that cures an illness: *Although there is no cure for this illness, it can be treated to reduce the pain.* ◇ *The only real cure is rest.* See also **cure** → CURE *verb*, **cure** → TREATMENT *noun*

remedy /ˈremədi/ [C] a medicine or treatment for an illness that is not very serious: *I prefer to use herbal remedies when I have a cold.* ◇ *The best* **home remedy** *for a sore throat is honey and lemon.*

placebo /pləˈsiːbəʊ; *AmE* -boʊ/ (pl. **-os**) [C] a substance that has no physical effects, given to patients who do not need medicine but think they do, or used when testing new drugs: *Half of the people taking part in the experiment were given a placebo.*

antidote /ˈæntidəʊt; *AmE* -doʊt/ [C] a substance that controls the effect of a particular poison: *There is no known* **antidote to** *the poison produced by this fish.*

---

drunk *adj.*

drunk · drunken · (*taboo*) pissed · wasted · tipsy · under the influence · intoxicated
These words all describe people who have drunk so much alcohol that they cannot think or speak clearly.

PATTERNS AND COLLOCATIONS
▸ drunk/ pissed/ tipsy **on** sth
▸ to **get** drunk/ pissed/ wasted/ tipsy
▸ **completely** pissed/ wasted/ intoxicated

drunk [not usually before noun] having drunk so much alcohol that it is impossible to think or speak clearly: *She was too drunk to remember anything about the party.* ◇ *His only way of dealing with his problems was to go out and get drunk.* ◇ *They got drunk on vodka.* **OPP** **sober** → DISCIPLINED, See also **drink** → DRINK *noun* 2, **drink** → DRINK *verb*

drunken [only before noun] drunk or often getting drunk; showing the effects of too much alcohol; involving people who are drunk: *She was often beaten by her drunken husband.* ◇ *He came home to find her in a drunken stupor.* ◇ *a drunken brawl* ◇ *drunken laughter/singing*
▸ **drunkenly** *adv.*: *He staggered drunkenly to his feet.*

pissed [not before noun] (*BrE*, *taboo*, *slang*) drunk: *They would pretend to get pissed and start a fight.*

wasted /ˈweɪstɪd/ [not usually before noun] (*slang*) very drunk: *They both came home completely wasted.*

tipsy [not usually before noun] (*rather informal*) slightly drunk: *He was by now tired, angry and a little tipsy.*

under the ˈinfluence *idiom* (*rather formal*) having had too much alcohol to drink: *She was charged with* **driving under the influence**.

intoxicated (*formal*) under the influence of alcohol or drugs: (*AmE*) *He was arrested for DWI* (= driving while intoxicated). ❶ In the US, **DWI** and **DUI** (= driving under the influence) are often used in news reports to refer to the criminal offence of driving while drunk. It is more frequently called **drunk driving**, which is also the term used in British English.

E e

eager *adj.* See the Topic Map for SPORT AND LEISURE on p.892

eager · enthusiastic · keen · anxious · hungry · avid · mad · zealous · impatient
These words all describe people who want to do sth, or want sth to happen, very much.

eager very interested and excited by sth that is going to happen or about sth that you want to do: *Eager crowds waited outside the stadium.* ◇ *She is eager for* (= wants very much to get) *her parents' approval.* ◇ *Everyone in the class seemed eager to learn.* ◇ *They're **eager to please*** (= they want to be helpful). **OPP reluctant** → RELUCTANT
▸ **eagerly** *adv.*: *the band's eagerly awaited new CD*
▸ **eagerness** *noun* [U, sing.]: *I couldn't hide my eagerness to get back home.*
enthusiastic feeling or showing a lot of excitement about and/or interest in sb/sth: *I love playing to such an enthusiastic audience.* ◇ *They gave her an enthusiastic welcome.* ◇ *You don't sound very enthusiastic about the idea.* **OPP lukewarm** → INDIFFERENT, See also **enthusiast** → FAN
▸ **enthusiastically** *adv.*: *They responded enthusiastically to the plan.*
▸ **enthusiasm** *noun* [U, sing.]: *I can't say I share your enthusiasm for the idea.*

> **NOTE** EAGER OR ENTHUSIASTIC? Being **enthusiastic** can be a more generous feeling than being **eager**. People are often **eager** about things that they want for themselves: *The low prices still pull in crowds of eager buyers.* People are often **enthusiastic** about other people and their ideas and achievements: *an enthusiastic welcome/reception/response* ◇ *enthusiastic support/applause/praise*

keen [not usually before noun] (*especially BrE, rather informal*) wanting to do sth or wanting sth to happen very much: *John was very keen to help.* ◇ *We are keen that Britain should get involved too.* ◇ *I wasn't too keen on going to the party.* ❶ **Keen** can also be used, especially before a noun, to describe sb who is very enthusiastic about an activity or idea: *He's a keen sportsman and enjoys football, fishing and rugby.* ◇ *She takes a keen interest in politics.* A person who is enthusiastic about an activity might be *a keen collector/fisherman/footballer/gardener/golfer/ photographer/sailor/sportsman/swimmer/traveller.* A person who is enthusiastic about an idea has a *keen interest* in sth, or is a *keen supporter* of sth. **Keen** is not used much in American English, except in the phrase *keen interest*; instead it is more usual to say *eager to help* or *avid sportsman/collector/photographer, etc.* See also **be keen on sth** → LIKE *verb*

anxious [not usually before noun] wanting sth very much: *He was anxious to finish school and get a job.* ◇ *I'm anxious for her to do as little as possible.* ◇ *She was anxious that he should meet her father.* ❶ **Anxious**, in this meaning, is often used when sb wants things to return to a normal condition: *He seemed anxious to return to more familiar ground.* ◇ *She was anxious to put the past behind her/set the record straight/get the whole thing over with.*
▸ **anxiety** *noun* [U]: *A couple of photographers fell over themselves in their anxiety to get a shot of her.*
hungry having or showing a strong desire for sth, especially to achieve sth: *Both parties are hungry for power.* ◇ *We like to use small agencies that are hungry for our business.* ❶ People are typically **hungry** for *change, company, excitement, information, knowledge, news, power, success* and *victory.* See also **hunger** → APPETITE 2
avid /ˈævɪd/ [usually before noun] showing great enthusiasm for sth such as a hobby: *I have always been an avid reader.* ❶ If you are *avid for sth* you want to get it very much: *She was avid for more information.* In British English **avid** is rather a formal word and it is more usual to use **keen** in less formal contexts; in American English **avid** is the usual word.
▸ **avidly** *adv.*: *She reads avidly.*
mad [not usually before noun] (*informal*) liking sb/sth very much; very interested in sth: *She's mad on tennis.* ◇ *He's always been mad about kids.* ◇ *football-mad boys* ◇ *She's completely power-mad.*
zealous /ˈzeləs/ (*rather formal, written*) showing great energy and enthusiasm in doing sth, especially because of strong moral or religious beliefs: *He was a zealous reformer, utterly devoted to rooting out corruption.*
▸ **zeal** *noun* [U, sing.]: *her missionary/reforming/religious/political zeal*
impatient [not usually before noun] wanting to do sth soon; wanting sth to happen soon: *She was clearly impatient to leave.* ◇ *We are impatient for change.* ❶ People are often *impatient for success/change*, or *impatient to leave/get away/escape/go home/get on.*
▸ **impatience** *noun* [U]: *She was bursting with impatience to tell me the news.*

early *adj.*

early · on time · punctual · prompt · on the dot
These words all describe sb/sth that arrives or happens before or at the usual or arranged time.

early arriving or happening before the usual or arranged time: *You're early! I wasn't expecting you till seven.* ◇ *The bus was ten minutes early.* ◇ *We had an early breakfast.* ◇ *Let's **make an early start** tomorrow.* ◇ *She's an **early riser*** (= she gets up early in the morning). ◇ *He learned to play the piano at an **early age**.* **OPP late** → LATE
▸ **early** *adv.*: *I arrived a few minutes early for my interview.* ◇ *The baby arrived earlier than expected.*
on ˈtime *phrase* arriving at the arranged or correct time; not late: *Please try to be on time in future.* ◇ *The train arrived **right on time**.* **OPP late** → LATE
punctual /ˈpʌŋktʃuəl/ (*rather formal*) arriving or happening at the arranged or correct time; not late: *Always be punctual for an interview.* ◇ *Punctual attendance at all classes is required.* **OPP late** → LATE

▸ **punctuality** /ˌpʌŋktʃuˈæləti/ *noun* [U]: *He insists on regular attendance and punctuality.*

▸ **punctually** *adv.*: *They always pay punctually.*

prompt [not before noun] arriving at the right time; acting without delay: *Please be prompt when attending these meetings.* ◇ (*BrE*) *He's* **prompt to** *criticize but not so ready to do any work himself.*

▸ **prompt** *adv.*: *The meeting will begin at ten o'clock prompt.*

▸ **promptly** *adv.*: *They arrived promptly at two o'clock.* ◇ *She deals with all the correspondence promptly and efficiently.*

on the ˈdot *idiom* (*informal*) exactly on time; at the exact time mentioned: *The taxi showed up on the dot.* ◇ (*AmE*) *Breakfast is served at 8* **right on the dot.** ◇ (*BrE*) *Please tell him I'll call him* **on the dot of** *twelve.*

ease *verb*

ease · relieve · alleviate · soften · allay · cushion · soothe · lighten
These words all mean to become or make sth less unpleasant or severe.

PATTERNS AND COLLOCATIONS
▸ to ease / relieve / alleviate / soothe the **pain**
▸ to ease / relieve / alleviate / allay / soothe sb's **fear / anxiety**
▸ to ease / relieve / alleviate / soothe sb's **problems / suffering**
▸ to ease / relieve / alleviate / soften / allay / soothe / lighten a **feeling**
▸ to ease / relieve / alleviate **pressure / stress / poverty**
▸ to ease / relieve / alleviate / lighten the **burden**
▸ to ease / relieve / lighten the **load**
▸ to ease / alleviate / soften / cushion the **impact** of sth
▸ to **do little / nothing to** ease / relieve / alleviate / soften / allay / soothe / lighten sth

ease [T, I] to make sth less painful, severe or strong; to become less painful, severe or strong: *The plan should ease traffic congestion in the town.* ◇ *It would* **ease my mind** (= make me less worried) *to know that she was happy.* ◇ *The pain gradually eased a little.* ◇ *The snow was* **easing up** *and people were leaving their houses.*

relieve /rɪˈliːv/ [T] to remove or reduce an unpleasant feeling or pain; to make a problem less serious: *Take painkillers and hot drinks to relieve the symptoms.* ◇ *Don't resort to alcohol to relieve stress.* ◇ *Being able to tell the truth at last seemed to relieve her.* ◇ *Aid workers called for further effort from governments to relieve the famine.* See also **relief → RELIEF, relief → AID**

alleviate /əˈliːvieɪt/ [T] (*rather formal*) to make a feeling or problem less severe or strong: *Her words did little to alleviate his fears.* ◇ *A number of measures were taken to alleviate the problem.* **OPP aggravate, exacerbate → WEAKEN**

soften /ˈsɒfn; *AmE* ˈsɔːfn/ [T] to reduce the force or the unpleasant effects of sth: *Airbags are designed to soften the impact of a car crash.* ◇ *The government may try to* **soften the blow** (= make things seem less unpleasant and easier to accept) *with a cut in interest rates.*

allay /əˈleɪ/ [T] (*formal*) to make an unpleasant feeling less strong: *The government is keen to allay the public's fears.* ◇ *The inquiry has done little to allay suspicion.*

cushion /ˈkʊʃn/ [T] to protect sb/sth from harm or the unpleasant effects of sth: *The south of the country has been* **cushioned from** *the worst effects of the recession.* ◇ *He broke the news of my brother's death to me, making no effort to* **cushion the blow** (= make the news less shocking).

NOTE SOFTEN OR **CUSHION?** In many cases you can use either word. However, when **cushion** is used in the passive, the focus is on who or what benefits from the situation, rather than what has been reduced or eased: *Homeowners will be cushioned from any tax rises.* ◇ *All grief is softened with time.*

soothe /suːð/ [T] to reduce an unpleasant feeling or pain: *Only when Maisie came to hold him and soothe his fears did he feel safe.* ◇ *Take a warm bath to soothe tense, tired muscles.*

NOTE RELIEVE OR **SOOTHE?** You can **relieve** or **soothe** pain or painful feelings; you can **soothe**, but NOT **relieve** a painful part of the body: ~~Take a warm bath to relieve tense, tired muscles.~~ You can **relieve**, but NOT **soothe** the cause of the pain or feelings: ~~Don't resort to alcohol to soothe stress.~~

lighten [T] to reduce the amount of work, debt, worry or other problem that sb has: *This equipment is designed to lighten the load of domestic work.* ◇ *The measures will lighten the tax burden on small businesses.* ❶ In this meaning **lighten** is nearly always followed by the nouns *load* or *burden*.

easy *adj.*

1 Is it easy to make?
2 anything for an easy life

1 easy · simple · straightforward · effortless · uncomplicated · undemanding · painless · cushy · plain sailing
These words all describe sth that is not difficult and that can therefore be done, obtained or understood without a lot of effort or problems.

PATTERNS AND COLLOCATIONS
▸ to be easy / simple / straightforward / plain sailing **for** sb
▸ to be easy / simple / straightforward / painless / plain sailing **to do** sth
▸ an easy / a simple / a straightforward / an undemanding / a cushy **job**
▸ an easy / a simple / a straightforward / an undemanding **task**
▸ an easy / a simple / a straightforward / a painless **method**
▸ an easy / a simple / a straightforward **matter / decision / test / question**
▸ There's no easy / simple / straightforward **answer**.
▸ **relatively** easy / simple / straightforward / uncomplicated / undemanding / painless
▸ **apparently** easy / simple / straightforward / effortless

easy done or obtained without a lot of effort or problems: *It was a really easy exam.* ◇ *This encyclopedia is designed for quick and easy reference.* ◇ *Their house isn't the easiest place to get to.* ◇ *It can't be easy for her, on her own with the children.* ◇ *Several schools are* **within easy reach** (= not far away). **OPP difficult, hard → DIFFICULT 1**

▸ **ease** *noun* [U]: *He passed the exam with ease.* ◇ *The computer is popular for its good design and* **ease of use.** **OPP difficulty → DIFFICULTY**

▸ **easily** *adv.*: *The museum is easily accessible by car.* ◇ *Learning languages doesn't come easily to him.*

simple easy to understand or do because it contains very few, very basic parts or actions: *I used a very simple method to obtain the answer.* ◇ *This machine is simple to use.* ◇ *Give the necessary information but* **keep it simple.** ◇ (*especially spoken*) *We lost because we played badly. It's* **as simple as that.** **OPP complex, elaborate → COMPLEX, difficult → DIFFICULT 1**

▸ **simplicity** /sɪmˈplɪsəti/ *noun* [U]: *the relative simplicity of the new PC* ◇ **For the sake of simplicity,** *let's divide the discussion into two parts.*

▸ **simply** *adv.*: *Anyway,* **to put it simply,** *we still owe them £2 000.*

NOTE EASY OR **SIMPLE? Easy** means 'not difficult': an *easy test / task* is one that causes you no problems because you have the ability and understanding to do it; some people might find it easy, but some might not, depending on their abilities. **Simple** means 'not complicated': a *simple test / task* is one that only needs very few, very basic actions and does not really depend on people's abilities. **Easily** means 'without having any difficulty': *I can easily finish it tonight.* **Simply** means 'without causing any difficulty of understanding': *The book explains grammar simply and clearly.*

straightforward easy to do or understand because it contains nothing unexpected: *It's a relatively straightforward process.* ◊ *It's quite straightforward to get here from your house.* **OPP** complicated, involved → COMPLEX

NOTE SIMPLE OR STRAIGHTFORWARD? These two words are very similar in meaning and use. Collocates of both words include *question, answer, case, matter, method, procedure* and *exercise*. Something that is **straightforward** may not be quite as basic as sth that is **simple** but it causes no problems because there is nothing unusual or unexpected about it.

effortless seeming to need little or no effort: *She dances with effortless grace.* ◊ *He made playing the guitar look effortless.*
▶ **effortlessly** *adv.*: *Your presentation must move effortlessly from one point to the next.*

uncomplicated [U] (*rather formal*) without any difficulty or confusion: *It's an uncomplicated computer interface that is truly easy to use.* ◊ *It came as a relief to hold a light, uncomplicated conversation with an ordinary guy.* ❶ **Uncomplicated** is used especially to talk about life, relationships and emotions. It can describe people who have uncomplicated relationships and emotions: *He was an easygoing, uncomplicated young man.* It is also used in medical contexts to mean 'without medical complications': *an uncomplicated pregnancy/birth* **OPP** complicated → COMPLEX

undemanding (*written*) not needing a lot of effort or thought: *I wanted an undemanding job which would leave me free to pursue my hobbies.* **OPP** demanding → DIFFICULT 1

painless (*written*) not unpleasant or difficult to do: *The interview turned out to be relatively painless.*

cushy /ˈkʊʃi/ (*informal, often disapproving*) very easy and pleasant; needing little or no effort: *His father found him a cushy job in the office.*

plain 'sailing *idiom* simple and free from trouble: *If you get the measurements right, the rest of the job should be plain sailing.*

2 See the Topic Map for SPORT AND LEISURE on p.892, See also the entry for SLOW

easy · leisurely · languid · unhurried · at leisure · lazy
These words all describe people or activities that are comfortable and relaxed.

PATTERNS AND COLLOCATIONS
▶ an easy/ a leisurely/ a languid/ an unhurried **manner**
▶ a leisurely/ an unhurried/ a lazy **way**
▶ an easy/ a leisurely/ a lazy **day** / **morning**/ **afternoon**/ **time**
▶ an easy/ a leisurely/ an unhurried **pace**
▶ an easy/ a leisurely **trip**/ **stroll**/ **ride**/ **drive**

easy comfortable, relaxed and not worried: *I'll agree to anything for an easy life.* ◊ *His easy charm soon won her over.* ◊ *I don't feel easy about letting the kids go out alone.* ❶ **Easy** can be used to describe a person, their behaviour or their way of life. See also **uneasy** → WORRIED

leisurely /ˈleʒəli; AmE ˈliːʒərli/ [usually before noun] relaxed; done without hurrying: *We went for a leisurely stroll after dinner.* ◊ *They set off at a leisurely pace.* ❶ **Leisurely** is most often used to talk about travelling without hurrying: *a leisurely trip/stroll/ride/pace/drive.* It is also used to talk about a relaxed meal that is eaten without hurrying: *a leisurely breakfast/lunch/dinner*

languid /ˈlæŋgwɪd/ (*written*) moving or speaking slowly in a graceful manner, without using too much energy: *She gave a languid wave of the hand.* ◊ *'Ah, my dear,' said the languid voice.* ❶ People's movements are often **languid** when it is too hot to be energetic.

unhurried /ʌnˈhʌrid; AmE -ˈhɜːr-/ (*written*) relaxed; done without hurrying: *His conversation was relaxed and unhurried.* ◊ *It's a quiet resort where life is taken at an easy, unhurried pace.* **OPP** hurried → QUICK

at 'leisure with no particular activities; free; without hurrying: *Spend the afternoon at leisure in the city.* ◊ *Let's have lunch so we can talk at leisure.* ◊ *I suggest you take the forms away and read them at your leisure.* ❶ **At leisure** is used especially with verbs relating to discussing sth, or deciding whether you like sth or whether it is good enough in a relaxed way, without anyone hurrying you for an answer: *to discuss sth/talk/study sth/examine sth/ look round/browse/try sth on at leisure.* In British English, travel brochures often use **at leisure** to talk about periods when you are free to spend time as you want, when there are no activities planned.

lazy not involving much energy or activity; slow and relaxed: *We spent a lazy day on the beach.* ◊ *She smiled a lazy smile.*

eat *verb* See also the entry for DINE

eat · have · swallow · consume · finish · ingest · devour · taste · wolf · stuff · tuck in/tuck into sth
These words all mean to put food or drink into your stomach through your mouth.

PATTERNS AND COLLOCATIONS
▶ to eat/ finish sth **up**
▶ to eat/ swallow/ consume/ devour/ wolf down/ stuff yourself with/ tuck into your **food**
▶ to eat/ have/ finish/ devour/ tuck into a **meal**
▶ to eat/ have/ finish/ wolf/ tuck into your **lunch**/ **dinner**
▶ to eat/ have/ consume/ taste some **meat**/ **fruit**

eat [I, T] to put food into your mouth, chew it, and make it go down your throat into your stomach: *I was too nervous to eat.* ◊ *She doesn't eat sensibly* (= eat food that is good for her). ◊ *Eat up!* (= Eat all your food.) ◊ *I don't eat meat.* ◊ *Would you like something to eat?* ◊ *I couldn't eat another thing* (= I have had enough food). See also **eat** → DINE

have [T] to eat or drink sth: *Have you had breakfast yet?* ◊ *I just had a sandwich for lunch.* ◊ *I'll have the salmon* (= in a restaurant).

swallow [T, I] to make sth, especially food, drink or medicine, go down your throat into your stomach: *Always chew food well before swallowing it.* ◊ *The pills should be swallowed whole* (= in one piece). ◊ *I had a sore throat and it hurt to swallow.*

consume /kənˈsjuːm; AmE -ˈsuːm/ [T] (*formal*) to eat or drink sth: *Red meat should be consumed in moderation.* ◊ *Before he died he had consumed a large quantity of alcohol.* See also **consume** → USE *verb* 2
▶ **consumption** /kənˈsʌmpʃn/ *noun* [U]: *The meat was declared unfit for human consumption.* ◊ *She was advised to reduce her alcohol consumption.*

finish [T] to eat, drink or use what remains of sth: *He finished off his drink with one large gulp.* ◊ *We might as well finish up the cake – there isn't much left.* ◊ *We'll go out after you've finished your dinner.*

ingest /ɪnˈdʒest/ [T] (*technical*) to take sth into your body, usually by swallowing: *Food is the major source of ingested bacteria.*

devour /dɪˈvaʊə(r)/ [T] (*formal*) to eat all of sth quickly, especially because you are very hungry: *He devoured half of his burger in one bite.*

taste [T] to eat or drink sth, especially sth which you do not usually eat or drink: *I've never tasted anything like it.* ◊ *I haven't tasted meat since I started the journey.*

wolf /wʊlf/ [T] (*rather informal*) to eat food very quickly, especially by putting a lot of it in your mouth at once: *He wolfed down his breakfast and left the house in a hurry.*

stuff [T] (*informal*) to eat a lot of food or too much food; to give sb a lot or too much to eat: *He sat at the table stuffing himself.* ◊ *We stuffed our faces at the party.* ◊ *Don't stuff the kids with chocolate before their dinner.*

,tuck 'in, ,tuck 'into sth *phrasal verb* (*BrE, especially spoken*) to eat a lot of food, especially when it is done quickly and with enthusiasm: *Come on everyone, tuck in!* ◊ *He was tucking into a huge plateful of pasta.*

echo *verb*

echo · ring · ring out · reverberate · resound · resonate
These words all mean to make a sound that is still heard after the sound is no longer being made.

PATTERNS AND COLLOCATIONS
▸ to echo / ring / ring out / reverberate / resound / resonate **through / around** a place
▸ to echo / ring / ring out / reverberate / resound / resonate **with** sth
▸ to echo / ring / reverberate / resound **to** sth
▸ a **voice** echoes / rings / rings out / reverberates / resounds / resonates
▸ **laughter** echoes / rings / rings out / reverberates / resounds
▸ to echo / ring / ring out / resonate **loudly**

echo /'ekəʊ; *AmE* 'ekoʊ/ [I, T] (of a sound) to be reflected off a wall or other surface so that the sound is heard again; (of a place) to send back and repeat a sound; to be full of sound: *Her footsteps echoed in the empty room.* ◊ *The whole house echoed.* ◊ *The street echoed with the cries of children.* ◊ *The valley echoed back his voice.* See also **echo** → REPEAT *verb* 1
▸ **echo** *noun* [C]: *The hills sent back a faint echo.* ◊ *There was an echo on the line and I couldn't hear clearly.*

ring [I] (*literary*) (of a place) to be full of a particular sound; to fill a place with sound: *The house rang with children's laughter.* ◊ *Applause rang through the hall.*

,ring 'out *phrasal verb* to be heard loudly and clearly, especially outdoors or in a large open space: *A number of shots rang out.* ◊ *His deep voice rang out for all to hear.*

reverberate /rɪ'vɜːbəreɪt; *AmE* -'vɜːrb-/ [I] (of a sound) to be repeated several times as it is reflected off different surfaces; (of a place) to seem to shake because of a loud, deep noise: *Her voice reverberated around the hall.* ◊ *The hall reverberated with the sound of music and dancing.*

> **NOTE** ECHO OR REVERBERATE? Echo is much more frequent and has a wider range than **reverberate**. Echo is often used for sounds that are made outdoors or in a large open space. **Reverberate** is often used for sounds that are made in smaller enclosed spaces, particularly when the sound is very loud: *Birdcalls echoed across the lake.* ◊ ~~Birdcalls reverberated across the lake.~~

resound /rɪ'zaʊnd/ [I] (*rather formal, written*) (of a place) to be full of a particular sound; to fill a place with sound: *The street resounded to the thud of marching feet.* ◊ *Laughter resounded through the house.*

> **NOTE** RING OR RESOUND? There is no real difference in meaning between these words. **Ring** is more frequent and is used especially in stories and literature; **resound** is used in rather formal written language, including literature.

resonate /'rezəneɪt/ [I] (*formal*) to make a deep, clear sound that continues for a long time, especially the sound made by a voice or musical instrument; (of a place) to be filled with sound or make a sound continue longer: *Her voice resonated through the theatre.* ◊ *The body of the violin acts as a resonating chamber and makes the sound louder.*

economic *adj.*

economic · financial · commercial · monetary · budgetary
These words all describe activities or situations that are connected with the use of money, especially by a business or country.

PATTERNS AND COLLOCATIONS
▸ economic / financial / commercial / monetary / budgetary **policy / arrangements / systems / problems**
▸ economic / financial / commercial / monetary **gain / loss / value**
▸ economic / financial / commercial / monetary **affairs / consequences**
▸ economic / financial / commercial / budgetary **data / decisions**
▸ the economic / financial / commercial / budgetary **climate**
▸ economic / financial / commercial **advantage / interest**
▸ economic / financial / commercial **markets / centres**
▸ the economic / financial / commercial **side / status** of sth
▸ economic / financial / monetary / budgetary **control / restrictions**
▸ an economic / a financial / a monetary / a budgetary **crisis**
▸ economic / financial / budgetary **planning**

economic [only before noun] connected with the trade, industry and development of wealth of a country, area or society: *This book deals with the social, economic and political issues of the period.* ◊ **Economic growth** *was fastest in Japan.* ◊ *She's a lecturer in economic history.* See also **economics** → FINANCE
▸ **economically** *adv.*: *The factory is no longer economically viable.*

financial [usually before noun] connected with money and finance (= money used to run a business or country or the activity of managing it): *He is an independent financial adviser.* ◊ *She had got into financial difficulties.* ◊ *banks and other financial institutions* ◊ (*BrE*) *The firm made a loss in the first quarter of the current* **financial year**. ❶ In American English the term **fiscal year** is used. See also **finance** → FINANCE
▸ **financially** *adv.*: *She is still financially dependent on her parents.*

commercial [usually before noun] connected with the buying and selling of goods and services: *They have offices in the commercial heart of the city.* ◊ *She is developing the commercial side of the organization.* See also **commerce** → TRADE *noun*
▸ **commercially** *adv.*: *The product is not yet commercially available.*

monetary /'mʌnɪtri; *AmE* -teri/ [only before noun] (*formal or finance*) connected with money, especially all the money in a country: *The sculptures were of little monetary value.* ◊ *closer European political, monetary and economic union*

budgetary [only before noun] (*finance*) connected with a budget (= the money available or a plan of how it will be spent): *The new accounting procedures will improve budgetary control.* See also **budget** → FUND *noun*

edge *noun*

edge · end · side · perimeter · limit · fringe · periphery · margin
These are all words for the part of sth that is furthest away from the centre.

PATTERNS AND COLLOCATIONS
▸ **at** the edge / end / side / perimeter / limits / fringe / periphery / margins
▸ **on** the edge / end / side / perimeter / fringe / periphery / margins
▸ **beyond** the edge / end / perimeter / limits / fringe / margins
▸ **along / around** the edge / sides / perimeter / fringe / periphery / margins
▸ the **outer** edge / end / perimeter / limit / fringe / periphery / margins of sth
▸ the **inner** edge / end / perimeter of sth
▸ the **northern / eastern / southern / western** edge / end / side / limit / fringe / periphery / margins of sth
▸ the **very** edge / end / limit / fringe of sth
▸ to **reach** the edge / end / perimeter / limit / fringe / periphery
▸ to **remain on / stand on** the edge / end / fringe

edge [C] the outside limit of an object, area or surface; the part furthest from the centre: *He stood on the edge of the cliff.* ◊ *They live right on the edge of town.* ◊ *I sat down at* the water's edge. ◇ Stand the coin on its edge and spin it. ◇ She tore the page out roughly, leaving a ragged edge in the book. **OPP** **the middle** → MIDDLE

end [C] the part of an object or place that is the furthest from its centre, front or from where you are: *Turn right at the end of the road.* ◇ *That's his wife sitting at the far end of the table.* ◇ *Go to the end of the line!* ◇ *You've got something on the end of your nose.* ◇ *Tie the ends of the string together.* ◇ *These two products are from opposite ends of the price range.* ◇ *We walked along the whole promenade from end to end.* ◇ *They arranged the tables end to end.* ◇ *Stand the box on end.* ◇ *They live in the end house.* **OPP** **the middle** → MIDDLE

side [C] a part of an object or place near the edge and away from the middle: *She sat on the side of the bed.* ◇ *A van was parked at the side of the road.* ◇ *the south side of the lake* **OPP** **the middle** → MIDDLE

NOTE EDGE, END OR SIDE? The **edge** of an object or area goes all the way around it; the two **ends** of an object or area are points on the edge that are opposite each other with the longest distance between them; the **sides** of an object or area are the parts of the edge that are opposite each other but do not have the longest distance between them.

perimeter /pəˈrɪmɪtə(r)/ [C] (*rather formal*) the furthest edge of an enclosed area of land: *Guards patrol the perimeter of the estate.* ◇ *There is a 15-foot perimeter fence.*

limit [C] the furthest edge of an area or place: *We were reaching the limits of civilization.* ◇ *The houses lie outside the city limits* (= the official boundary of the city).

fringe [C] a narrow strip of trees or buildings along the edge of sth: *West of the river there was a fringe of woodland along its bank.* ◇ *Along the coast, an industrial fringe had already developed.* ❶ In British English a **fringe** can also be the furthest edge of an area or group: *The factories are located on the northern fringes of the city.*

periphery /pəˈrɪfəri/ [C, usually sing.] (*formal*) the furthest edge of an area; the less important part of an activity or political or social group: *There is a lot of industrial development on the periphery of the town.* ◇ *It is a minor party on the periphery of American politics.* See also **peripheral** → MINOR

margin /ˈmɑːdʒɪn; AmE ˈmɑːrdʒən/ [C] (*formal*) the furthest edge of an area, especially an area of water; the less important part of an activity or political or social group: *The island is on the eastern margin of the Indian Ocean.* ◇ *These are desperate people, often homeless, living on the margins of society.*

edge *verb*

edge · inch · crawl · thread · creep
These words all mean to move or move sth slowly and carefully in a particular direction.

PATTERNS AND COLLOCATIONS
▸ to edge / inch / crawl / creep **along**
▸ to edge / crawl / thread / creep **through** sth
▸ to edge / inch / crawl / creep **forwards / towards** sth
▸ to edge / inch / crawl / creep **slowly** along / through / down, etc.
▸ to edge / inch / crawl / creep **closer / nearer**
▸ to edge / inch / thread **your way**

edge [I, T] (always used with an adverb or preposition) to move or make sth move slowly and carefully in a particular direction, making small movements: *She edged a little closer to me.* ◇ *I edged nervously past the dog.* ◇ *Emily edged her chair forward.*

inch [I, T] (always used with an adverb or preposition) to move or make sth move slowly and carefully, usually in a forward direction, making small movements: *She inched cautiously towards the edge of the cliff.* ◇ *I inched the car forward.* ◇ *He inched his way through the narrow passage.*

NOTE EDGE OR INCH? When you **inch** somewhere you tend to be moving forwards or towards sth. You can use **edge** when you are moving forwards, sideways or back, towards or away from sth.

crawl [I] (usually used with an adverb or preposition) (of a vehicle or its driver) to move forwards much more slowly than usual: *She was forced to crawl along through the thickening mist.* ◇ *The taxi crawled to a halt.*

thread /θred/ [I, T] (always used with an adverb or preposition) to move or make sth move through a narrow space, carefully going around things that are in the way: *The waiters threaded between the crowded tables.* ◇ *It took me a long time to thread my way through the crowd.*

creep [I] (always used with an adverb or preposition) (of a vehicle) to move forwards much more slowly than usual; (of sb's hand or arm) to move somewhere in a slow and uncertain manner, as if it is likely to be pushed away: *Trucks are creeping along Interstate 70 in convoys.* ◇ *Her arms crept around his neck.*

education *noun* See the Topic Map for EDUCATION on p.888

education · training · study · teaching · learning · instruction · tuition · schooling · mentoring · coaching · tutoring
These are all words for the process of learning or being taught.

PATTERNS AND COLLOCATIONS
▸ education / training / teaching / instruction / tuition / schooling / coaching / tutoring **in** sth
▸ education / training / study / teaching / tuition / coaching **for** sth
▸ education / teaching / learning / instruction **about** sth
▸ **(a) good** education / training / teaching / instruction / schooling / mentoring
▸ **formal** education / training / study / teaching / learning / instruction / tuition / schooling / coaching
▸ **(a) basic** education / training / teaching / instruction / tuition / schooling / coaching
▸ **compulsory** education / training / study / schooling
▸ **private** education / teaching / study / tuition / schooling / coaching / tutoring
▸ **public / state** education / schooling
▸ **individual / one-to-one** education / training / teaching / learning / instruction / tuition / mentoring / coaching / tutoring
▸ **college / university** education / teaching / study / tuition
▸ to **have** an education / training / instruction / tuition / schooling / coaching / tutoring
▸ to **get / receive** an education / training / instruction / tuition / coaching / tutoring
▸ to **provide** an education / training / instruction / tuition / schooling / mentoring / coaching / tutoring
▸ to **give sb** an education / training / instruction / tuition / coaching / tutoring
▸ to **continue / complete / finish** your education / training / studies / schooling

education [U, sing.] the process of teaching and learning, especially in schools or colleges, in order to improve knowledge or develop skills; a particular type of teaching or training: *He had little formal education* (= education in school, college, etc.). ◇ *It is only through education that prejudice can be overcome.* ◇ *Will she go on to higher education* (= university or college)? ◇ *Sex education in schools needs to be improved.* ◇ *(BrE) In those days it was very difficult for poorer people to get a university education.* ◇ *(AmE) a college education* See also **educate** → TEACH, **educate** → TRAIN *verb* 1, **educator** → TEACHER

training [U] the process of learning the skills that you need to do a job: *Few candidates had any training in management.* ◇ *No one is allowed to operate the machinery without proper training.* ◇ *Vocational training should not be seen as less important than an academic education.* ◇ *She's an accountant by training.* See also **train** → TRAIN *verb* 1, **trainer** → COACH *noun*

study [U] the activity of learning or gaining knowledge, either from books or by examining things: *Physiology is the study of how living things work.* ◇ *There's a quiet room set aside for private study.* ◇ *It's important to develop good study skills.* ◇ *Students in the same field of study may have very different skill levels.* ❶ **Studies** [pl.] (*formal*) are a particular person's learning activities, for example at a college or university: *Many undertake further studies after passing their exams.* See also **study** → LEARN *verb*

teaching [U] the work of a teacher: *What made you go into teaching?* ◇ *The system should reward good classroom teaching.* ◇ *She retired at the end of a 40-year teaching career.* See also **teach** → TEACH, **teacher** → TEACHER

learning [U] the process of learning sth: *Effective teaching inevitably leads to effective learning.* ◇ *They run special classes for students with **learning difficulties.*** ◇ *You may get extra help if your child has a **learning disability.*** ◇ *They're new to the job and will be on a steep **learning curve** (= will have to learn a lot in a short time).* See also **learn** → LEARN

instruction [U] (*formal*) the act of teaching sth to sb: *She had no formal instruction in music.* ◇ *Religious instruction is banned in all state schools in the country.* ◇ *The medium of instruction in these classes is English.* See also **instruct** → TRAIN *verb* 1, **instructor** → COACH *noun*

tuition /tjuˈɪʃn; *AmE* tu-/ [U] (*rather formal*) the act of teaching sth to sb, especially to one person or to people in small groups: *The price includes two weeks' horse riding plus expert tuition.* ◇ *One-to-one tuition can be arranged in certain languages.*

schooling [U] (*formal*) the education you receive at school: *He received very little formal schooling.*

mentoring /ˈmentɔːrɪŋ/ [U] individual help with learning a particular job, given by an experienced person to sb younger and less experienced: *The company provides mentoring programmes as well as specialized training for its new employees.* See also **mentor** → ADVISER

coaching [U] (*BrE*) the process of giving a student extra teaching in a particular subject: *Extra coaching is available for students who might need a little more help.* ❶ In American English **coaching** is usually only used for talking about extra teaching in activities such as sports and acting. See also **coach** → COACH *noun*, **coach** → TRAIN *verb* 1

tutoring /ˈtjuːtərɪŋ; *AmE* ˈtuː-/ (*especially AmE*) coaching: *Volunteer tutoring programs help children who are having trouble reading.* See also **tutor** → TEACH *verb*, **tutor** → TEACHER *noun*

educational *adj.* See the Topic Map for EDUCATION on p.888

educational · academic · scholarly · informational · instructional · pedagogic · didactic
These words all mean connected with education or providing education or information.

▶ an educational/ an academic/ an informational/ an instructional/ a pedagogic **programme**
▶ educational/academic/scholarly/informational/instructional/ pedagogic **value/ use**
▶ educational/ academic/ scholarly/ pedagogic **practice/ methods**
▶ an educational/ an academic/ a scholarly **career**
▶ educational/ academic/ scholarly **standards/ excellence**
▶ educational/ academic/ informational/ pedagogic **needs**
▶ an academic/ a scholarly/ an instructional/ a pedagogic/ a didactic **work**

educational connected with education; providing education: *The two women were from similar social and educational backgrounds.* ◇ *Many of the kids here have **special educational needs** (= they need extra help that is not given to all children).* ◇ *Sometimes television can be highly educational.*

▶ **educationally** *adv.*: *Children living in inner-city areas may be educationally disadvantaged.*

academic [usually before noun] connected with education and learning, especially studying in schools and colleges: *academic research* ◇ *He retired from **academic life** and went into politics.* ◇ *The **academic year** usually starts in September.* See also **academic** → SCHOLAR

▶ **academically** *adv.*: *She was always regarded as academically gifted.*

scholarly /ˈskɒləli; *AmE* ˈskɑːlərli/ (*often approving*) connected with or involving serious academic study: *The issue has given rise to much scholarly debate.* ◇ *They have produced a detailed and scholarly study of the composer's works.* See also **scholar** → SCHOLAR, **scholarship** → KNOWLEDGE

informational [usually before noun] (*rather formal, written*) providing or containing information about sth: *The materials do not have much real informational content.*

instructional [usually before noun] (*rather formal, written*) designed or used to teach sth: *The activities are intended to be both interesting and instructional.*

pedagogic /ˌpedəˈɡɒdʒɪk; *AmE* -ˈɡɑːdʒ-/ (*also* **pedagogical**) (*formal, written*) connected with teaching methods: *Most teachers have excellent pedagogic skills.*

didactic /daɪˈdæktɪk/ (*formal, written*) designed to teach people sth, especially a moral lesson: *This form of didactic literature was popular in Victorian times.*

effect *noun* See also the entry for RESULT

effect · impact · influence · power · force · impression · action
These are all words for the changes in sb/sth that are caused by sb/sth else.

▶ an effect/ impact/ influence/ impression **on/ upon** sb/ sth
▶ **under** the effect/ impact/ influence **of** sth/ sb
▶ (a) **considerable/tremendous/great** effect/impact/influence/ power/ force/ impression
▶ a **profound/ significant/ strong/ big/ positive/ lasting** effect/ impact/ influence/ impression
▶ a/ an **cultural/ economic/ political/ social** effect/ impact/ influence
▶ to **have** an effect/ impact/ influence
▶ to **make** an impact/ impression
▶ to **feel** the effect/ impact of sth

effect [C, U] a change in sb/sth that is caused by sb/sth else: *Despite her ordeal, she seems to have suffered no **ill effects.*** ◇ *Her criticisms **had the effect of** discouraging him completely.* ◇ *It's not always easy to distinguish between **cause and effect.*** ◇ *The management changes had **little or no effect** on output.* See also **affect** → AFFECT *verb*

impact /ˈɪmpækt/ [C, usually sing., U] the powerful effect that sth has on sb/sth: *Her speech made a profound impact on everyone.* ◇ *The programme examined the environmental impact of power generation.* ◇ *We are trying to **minimize the impact** of price rises on customers.* See also **impact** → AFFECT *verb*

influence [U, C] the effect that sb/sth has on the way a person thinks or behaves, or on the way that sth works or develops: *Children around the age of eight are especially vulnerable to the influence of television.* ◇ *The artists **exerted** a strong **influence** on a younger generation.* ◇ *They said she was a **bad influence** on the other children.* See also **influence** → AFFECT *verb*

power [U] the influence of a particular thing or group within society: *He talked about the enormous power of the mass media.* ◇ *The government promised greater opportunities for **parent power.***

force [U] the strong effect of sb's arguments or personality: *She spoke **with force** and deliberation.* ◇ *He felt the full force of her criticism.* ◇ *He controlled himself by **sheer force of will.***

impression [C, usually sing.] the effect that an experience or person has on sb/sth, especially on the way that sb thinks or behaves in the future: *The stillness and silence leave a deep impression on visitors.* ◇ *You'll have to play better than that if you really want to **make an impression*** (= to make people admire and remember you). ◇ *My words **made no impression** on her.* See also **impress** → IMPRESS, **impressive** → IMPRESSIVE

action [U] (always followed by *of*) the effect that one substance or chemical has on another: *Vitamin D can be made in the body by the action of sunlight on the skin.* See also **act** → AFFECT *verb*

efficiency *noun*

efficiency · order · coherence · organization · structure · method
These are all words for the quality of being organized and working well.

▸ efficiency / coherence / method **in** sth
▸ **great** efficiency / coherence
▸ to **bring** / **give** order / coherence / structure **to** sth
▸ to **have** order / coherence / organization / structure
▸ to **impose** order / coherence / structure **on** sth
▸ to **achieve** efficiency / coherence
▸ to **create** order / coherence
▸ to **lack** order / coherence / organization / structure
▸ a **lack of** order / coherence / organization / structure

efficiency /ɪˈfɪʃnsi/ [U] the quality of doing sth well with no waste of time or money: *The new computer system will cut costs and increase efficiency.* ◇ *New standards of **energy efficiency*** (= not wasting energy) *are being introduced.* **OPP** **inefficiency** → INEFFECTIVE

order [U] the state of being well organized or neatly arranged: *Get your ideas into some sort of order before you begin to write.* ◇ *She always liked creating order out of chaos.* ◇ *The house had been kept **in good order**.* ◇ *I felt it was time to **put my life in order.*** **OPP** **disorder** → MESS 1, **chaos** → CHAOS, See also **ordered, orderly** → NEAT

coherence /kəʊˈhɪərəns; AmE koʊˈhɪr-/ [U] (*formal*) the situation in which all the parts of sth fit or work well together: *Some of the points you make are good, but the essay as a whole lacks coherence.* ◇ *The party tried to find some kind of ideological coherence.* See also **coherent** → RATIONAL

organization (*BrE* also **-isation**) [U] the quality of being arranged in a neat, careful or logical way: *She's highly intelligent but her work lacks organization.* ◇ *As a manager he's obsessed with organization.*

> **NOTE** ORDER OR ORGANIZATION? Order is a state that can be *created* or that sth can be *put into*; organization is a quality that sth either *has* or *lacks*: *Get your ideas into some sort of organization.* ◇ *creating organization out of chaos*

structure [U, C] the state of being well organized or planned with all the parts linked together: *In terms of structure the novel has several flaws.* ◇ *Children need structure in their lives.* See also **structure** → STRUCTURE *noun*

method [U] the quality of being well planned and well organized: *We have to apply some method to this investigation.* **❶** Method is used especially to talk about a way of doing a task or solving a problem.

efficient *adj.*

efficient · systematic · orderly · tidy · businesslike · methodical · organized · neat
These words all describe sb/sth that is able to do or does sth well, thoroughly or according to a system.

▸ efficient / systematic / businesslike / methodical / organized **in** sth

▸ **in** a systematic / an orderly / a businesslike / a methodical / an organized **fashion**
▸ **an** efficient / a systematic / an orderly / a businesslike / a methodical / an organized **approach** / **way**
▸ **relatively** efficient / systematic / orderly / organized
▸ **fairly** efficient / systematic / orderly / tidy
▸ **quite** efficient / businesslike / methodical
▸ **extremely** efficient / organized / neat
▸ **highly** efficient / systematic / organized

efficient doing sth well and thoroughly with no waste of time, money or energy: *It's an incredibly efficient system.* ◇ *The more efficient firms have lower costs.* ◇ *More efficient use of energy resources is vital.* ◇ *Our bodies become less efficient at burning off calories.* ◇ *She was helpful, quietly efficient and tactful.* ◇ *Which software is the most efficient at processing the data?* **OPP** **inefficient** → INEFFECTIVE
▸ **efficiently** *adv.*: *They began to work harder and more efficiently.* **OPP** **inefficiently** → INEFFECTIVE

systematic /ˌsɪstəˈmætɪk/ done according to a system or plan, in a thorough, efficient or determined way: *No systematic analysis has ever been carried out in this area.* ◇ *This was a systematic attempt to infiltrate a democratic organization.* **OPP** **unsystematic** → RANDOM, See also **system** → WAY 2
▸ **systematically** /-kli/ *adv.*: *The topic has never been systematically studied.*

orderly doing things in a careful and logical way: *She had led a calm and orderly life.* ◇ *Public policy changes can be made in an orderly and rational manner.* ◇ *It was a civilized and orderly society.* **OPP** **disorderly** → WILD 1

tidy (*especially BrE*) keeping things ordered and arranged in the right place, or liking to keep things like this: *I'm not a very tidy person.* ◇ *Even young children can be taught tidy habits.* ◇ *He is obsessively tidy.* **OPP** **untidy** → RANDOM, See also **tidy** → NEAT

businesslike /ˈbɪznəslaɪk/ (of a person) working in an efficient way, not wasting time or thinking about personal matters: *Wearing the suit made him feel more businesslike.* ◇ *She adopted a brisk, businesslike tone.*

methodical /məˈθɒdɪkl; AmE -ˈθɑːd-/ doing things or done in a careful and logical way: *He was slow, methodical and reliable.* ◇ *Police carried out a methodical search of the premises.*
▸ **methodically** /-kli/ *adv.*: *The investigation was proceeding slowly but methodically.*

organized (*BrE* also **-ised**) (of a person) able to plan your life and work well and in an efficient way: *The chairman is one of the most organized people I know.* ◇ *Isn't it time you started to get organized?* **OPP** **disorganized** → RANDOM

neat (of a person) liking to keep things in order; careful about your appearance: *She was a very efficient, neat woman.* ◇ *The children are always **neat and tidy**.* ◇ *By nature he was **clean and neat**.* **❶** In American English neat can also be used for things and places: (*AmE*) *Each resident is expected to keep their room neat.* See also **neat** → NEAT

effort *noun*

effort · hard work · struggle · endeavour · energy · exertion
These are all words for the physical or mental energy that you need to do sth, or sth that takes a lot of energy.

▸ (a) **great** effort / struggle / endeavour / exertion
▸ (a) **physical** effort / struggle / exertion
▸ (a) **mental** effort / struggle / exertion
▸ (a) **creative** effort / endeavour / energies
▸ to **need** effort / hard work / your energies / exertion
▸ to **take** / **demand** effort / hard work
▸ to **put** effort / hard work / your energies **into** sth
▸ to **expend** effort / your energies

effort [U, C] the physical or mental energy that you need to do sth; sth that takes a lot of energy: *It's a long climb to the top, but well worth the effort.* ◇ *A lot of **effort has gone into** making this event a success.* ◇ *Getting up this morning was quite an effort* (= it was difficult).

,hard 'work [U] the use of physical strength or mental effort over a period of time in order to do or achieve sth: *She earned her grades through sheer hard work.* ◇ *They put in a lot of hard work to achieve this result.* ◇ *It's hard work trying to get him to do anything for himself.*

struggle [sing.] something that is difficult for you to do or achieve: *It was a real **struggle to** be ready on time.* ◇ *They face an **uphill struggle** to get to the finals of the competition.* See also **struggle** → TRY *verb* 1

endeavour (*BrE*) (*AmE* **endeavor**) /ɪnˈdevə(r)/ [U] (*formal*) the act of trying to do sth, especially sth new or difficult: *There have been great advances in the field of scientific endeavour.* See also **endeavour** → TRY *verb* 1

energy [U] (also **energies** [pl.]) the physical and mental effort that you use to do sth: *She put all her energy into her work.* ◇ *Provide a means of channelling your child's creative energies.* ❶ **Energy** or **energies** is usually used after a possessive pronoun, that is *his, her, my, your, our* or *their*. Verb collocates include *concentrate, devote, direct, focus* and *channel*.

exertion /ɪɡˈzɜːʃn; *AmE* -ˈzɜːrʃ-/ [U] (also **exertions** [pl.]) (*rather formal*) physical or mental effort; the act of making an effort: *She was hot and breathless from the exertion of cycling uphill.* ◇ *He needed to relax after the exertions of a busy day at work.*

NOTE **EFFORT** OR **EXERTION**? **Exertion** is usually used to talk about the act of using energy to carry out an activity, or the result of doing this: *His voice was breathless from exertion.* **Effort** tends to be used to talk about the work people do to achieve sth: *A lot of effort has gone into achieving this result.*

election *noun*

election · vote · poll · referendum · ballot · exit poll · straw poll · show of hands
These are all words for an event in which people choose a representative or decide sth by voting.

PATTERNS AND COLLOCATIONS
▸ an election/ a vote/ a poll/ a referendum/ a ballot **on** sth
▸ a **democratic/ free** election/ vote/ poll/ ballot
▸ a **secret** election/ vote/ ballot
▸ a **national / local** election/ poll/ referendum/ ballot
▸ a **state** election/ poll/ referendum
▸ to **conduct** an election/ a vote/ a poll/ a referendum/ a ballot/ an exit poll
▸ to **have** an election/ a vote/ a poll/ a referendum/ a ballot/ a show of hands
▸ to **hold** an election/ a vote/ a poll/ a referendum/ a ballot
▸ to **call/ lose/ win** an election/ a vote/ a referendum/ a ballot
▸ an election/ a vote/ a poll/ a referendum/ a ballot **takes place**
▸ the **outcome/ result of** an election/ a vote/ a poll/ a referendum/ a ballot

election [C, U] an occasion on which people officially choose a political representative or government by voting: *Who did you vote for in the last election?* ◇ *The first election results will be coming in very soon.* ◇ (*BrE*) *Labour won a landslide victory in the 1945 **general election*** (= a national election for a new government). ◇ (*BrE*) *He first **stood for election** when he was 21.* ◇ *She's yet to say whether she will be **running for election**.* See also **elect** → APPOINT

vote [C] an occasion on which a group of people vote for sb/sth: *They **took a vote** on who should be their new leader.* ◇ *I think it's time to **put this issue to the vote**.* ◇ *The vote was unanimous* (= everyone voted the same way). ◇ (*BrE*) *Let me propose a **vote of thanks*** (= a vote to formally thank sb). See also **vote sb in** → APPOINT

poll /pəʊl; *AmE* poʊl/ [C] (also **the polls** [pl.]) (*especially journalism*) the process of voting in an election: *The final result of the poll will be known tomorrow.* ◇ *They suffered a resounding defeat **at the polls**.* ◇ *The **polls close*** (= voting ends) *at 10 pm.* ◇ *Thursday is traditionally the day when Britain **goes to the polls*** (= votes in an election).

referendum [C] an occasion on which all the adults in a country can vote on a particular issue: *The president called a referendum on the new divorce laws.* ◇ *The issue will be decided **by referendum**.*

ballot /ˈbælət/ [U, C] the system of voting by marking an election paper, especially in secret; an occasion on which a vote is held: *The leader will be chosen by secret ballot.* ◇ *The union cannot call a strike unless it holds a ballot amongst its members.* ❶ **Ballot** is usually used about a vote within an organization rather than an occasion on which the public vote. See also **ballot** → SURVEY *verb*

'exit poll [C] an occasion on which people who have just voted are asked how they voted. This is used to try to predict the final result before the votes have been officially counted: *Exit polls show that the Republicans are slightly ahead.*

,straw 'poll [C] an occasion on which a number of people are asked in an informal way to give their opinion about sth: *I took a quick straw poll among my colleagues to see how many agreed.*

show of 'hands *idiom* an occasion on which a group of people vote on sth by raising their hands: *OK, let's have a show of hands. Who's in favour of the proposal?*

electronic *adj.*

electronic · digital · automatic · automated · computerized · mechanical · robotic
These words all describe machines that work without needing a person to supply power or movement.

PATTERNS AND COLLOCATIONS
▸ an electronic/ a digital/ an automatic/ an automated/ a computerized/ a mechanical/ a robotic **system**
▸ an electronic/ an automatic/ an automated/ a computerized/ a robotic **machine**
▸ an electronic/ an automatic/ a mechanical/ a robotic **device**
▸ an electronic/ a digital/ a computerized **database**
▸ **fully** electronic/ digital/ automatic/ automated/ computerized/ mechanical

electronic [usually before noun] (of a device) having or using many small parts, such as microchips, that control and direct a small electric current: *Sophisticated electronic calculators could give some students an unfair advantage.* ◇ *This dictionary is available in electronic form.* ❶ **Electronic** is often used to talk about services available through computers and the Internet: *electronic communication/ information/ mail/ banking/ payment/ publishing* ◇ *an electronic book/ edition/ text*
▸ **electronically** *adv.*: *The data is all processed electronically* (= using a computer) *these days.*

digital /ˈdɪdʒɪtl/ using a system of receiving and sending data as a series of the numbers one and zero, showing that an electronic signal is there or not there: *a digital camera* ◇ *Get the very latest advice and information on digital TV services.* **OPP** **analogue** ❶ **Analogue** (*BrE*) (*AmE* **analog**) processes use a continuously changing range of physical quantities to measure or store data: *an analogue circuit/ signal*
▸ **digitally** *adv.*: *digitally remastered tapes*

automatic (of a machine or device) having controls that work without needing a person to operate them: *The automatic doors opened as she approached.* ◇ *The line will operate with fully automatic driverless trains.* **OPP** **manual** ❶ **Manual** devices are operated by hand: *a car with a manual gearbox* ◇ *My camera has manual and automatic functions.*
▸ **automatically** *adv.*: *The heating switches off automatically.*

automated /'ɔːtəmeɪtɪd/ using machines and computers instead of people to do a job or task: *The factory is now fully automated.*

> **NOTE** AUTOMATIC OR **AUTOMATED**? **Automatic** is usually used to describe the machines themselves; **automated** is more often used to describe a process or a place such as factory where machines are used to do a job.

computerized (*BrE* also **-ised**) /kəm'pjuːtəraɪzd/ having a computer or computers to do the work of sth: *The factory is fully computerized.*

> **NOTE** AUTOMATED OR **COMPUTERIZED**? **Automated** emphasizes the fact that a machine, rather than a person performs a task or provides a service; **computerized** places greater emphasis on the high-level technology used.

mechanical /mə'kænɪkl/ operated by power from an engine or by machinery with moving parts: *All the vehicle's mechanical parts seem in very good order.* ◇ *The accuracy of all early mechanical clocks was low.*
> ▸ **mechanically** *adv.*: *a mechanically powered vehicle*

robotic /rəʊ'bɒtɪk; *AmE* roʊ'bɑːtɪk/ connected with robots (= machines that can do some tasks that humans can do and that work automatically or are controlled by computers): *A new robotic arm could be used by disabled people to perform everyday tasks.*

elegant *adj.* See also the entry for FASHIONABLE

elegant · smart · stylish · graceful · classic · well dressed
These words all describe the look of people and things that are attractive and have a good style.

PATTERNS AND COLLOCATIONS
> ▸ an elegant / a smart / a stylish / a graceful / a well-dressed **woman**
> ▸ an elegant / a smart / a well-dressed **man**
> ▸ smart / stylish / well-dressed **people**
> ▸ an elegant / a smart / a stylish / a classic **suit / dress**
> ▸ an elegant / a stylish / a classic **cut / design**
> ▸ an elegant / a smart / a classic **style**
> ▸ an elegant / a smart / a stylish **restaurant**
> ▸ an elegant / a graceful **movement**
> ▸ elegant / graceful / classic **lines**

elegant (*approving*) (of people) attractive and showing a good sense of style; (of clothes, places and things) attractive and designed well: *She was tall, slim and elegant.* ◇ *She was looking for something cool and elegant to wear.* ◇ *Guests can dine and relax in comfortable elegant surroundings.* See also **elegance → STYLE**
> ▸ **elegantly** *adv.*: *elegantly dressed women*

smart (*especially BrE, approving*) (of people) looking clean and neat; wearing fashionable and/or formal clothes; (of clothes, etc.) clean, neat and looking new and attractive: *You look very smart in that suit.* ◇ *They wear smart blue uniforms.* **OPP** scruffy → SCRUFFY
> ▸ **smartly** *adv.*: *smartly dressed*

stylish (*approving*) fashionable, elegant and attractive: *His pale grey suit was stylish.* ◇ *It was a stylish performance by both artists.* See also **style → STYLE, style → FASHION**
> ▸ **stylishly** *adv.*: *stylishly cut hair*

graceful moving in a controlled, attractive way; having a smooth, attractive form: *He gave a graceful bow to the audience.* ◇ *The flowers have graceful, arching stems.* See also **grace → STYLE**
> ▸ **gracefully** *adv.*: *He bowed gracefully.*

classic (*especially written*) elegant, but simple and traditional in style or design; not affected by changes in fashion: *She was wearing a classic little black dress.* ◇ *The shop specializes in classic English style.* See also **class → STYLE**
> ▸ **classically** *adv.*: *classically beautiful*

well 'dressed (*especially written*) wearing attractive clothes that look good on you, especially clothes that are fashionable and expensive: *It's what today's well-dressed man is wearing.* ◇ *She was always well dressed.*

element *noun*
1 have all the elements of a soap opera
2 an element of risk

1 See also the entry for ASPECT

element · component · module · unit · part · piece · ingredient · section
These are all words for sth which belongs to, but can be considered separately from, sth larger.

PATTERNS AND COLLOCATIONS
> ▸ an element / a component / an ingredient **in** sth
> ▸ an **individual** element / component / module / unit / part / piece / ingredient
> ▸ a **basic** element / component / module / unit / part / ingredient
> ▸ a **core** element / component / module / unit
> ▸ a / an **major / important / fundamental** element / component / unit / ingredient
> ▸ a / an **necessary / essential** element / component / part / ingredient
> ▸ the **main / principal** element / component / ingredient
> ▸ **component / constituent** elements / modules / parts

element /'elɪmənt/ [C] a necessary or typical part or aspect of sth: *Cost was a key element in our decision.* ◇ *The story has all the elements of a soap opera.*

component /kəm'pəʊnənt; *AmE* -'poʊ-/ [C] (*rather formal*) one of several parts which combine to form the whole: *Car components are manufactured in the other factory.* ◇ *Trust is a vital component in any relationship.*
> ▸ **component** *adj.* [only before noun]: *This concept can be broken down into its component parts.*

module /'mɒdjuːl; *AmE* 'mɑːdʒul/ [C] one of several courses that can combine to form a programme of study, especially at a college or university in Britain; one of a set of separate parts that can be joined together to make a machine or structure: *The course consists of ten core modules and five optional modules.* ◇ *Each student takes five modules.* ◇ *Ships are now built in modules rather than built in a whole from the base up.* ❶ In computing, a **module** is a part of a computer system or program that has a particular function: *New software modules include a virtual memory tool.* A **module** is also a part of a spacecraft that can function independently of the main part: *Photographs were taken from a lunar module.*

unit [C] a single thing, person or group that is complete by itself but can also form part of sth larger: *The cell is the unit of which all living organisms are composed.* ◇ *The basic unit of society is the family.*

part [C] a piece of a machine or structure: *Where can I get spare parts for my motorbike?* ◇ *Although it is no longer a working watermill, several of the working parts remain.*

piece [C] one of the parts from which sth is made: *He took the clock to pieces.* ◇ (*AmE*) *He broke the clock down into pieces.* ◇ *The bridge was taken down piece by piece.* ◇ *She's been doing a 500-piece jigsaw.* ◇ *There had to be some missing piece of the story.*

ingredient /ɪn'griːdiənt/ [C] one of the things from which sth is made, especially one of the foods that are used together to make a particular dish; one of the things or qualities that are necessary to make sth successful: *Coconut is a basic ingredient in many curries.* ◇ *Our skin cream contains only natural ingredients.* ◇ *The only active ingredient in this medicine is aspirin.* ◇ *Determination is one of the essential ingredients for success.* ◇ *It has all the ingredients of a good mystery story.* ◇ *The magic / secret ingredient is love.*

section [C] a separate part of a structure from which the whole can be put together: *The shed comes in sections that you assemble yourself.*

2 element · touch · trace · hint · spot · tinge · pinch · dash
These are all words for a small amount of sth.

▸ a **slight** element / touch / trace / hint / tinge of sth
▸ a **faint** touch / trace / hint / tinge
▸ the **slightest** touch / trace / hint of sth
▸ to **detect** an element / a touch / a trace / a hint / a tinge of sth
▸ to **contain** elements / traces / a hint of sth
▸ to **add** an element / a touch / a hint / a pinch / a dash of sth
▸ a touch / trace / hint of **humour** / **irony** / **sarcasm**
▸ a touch / hint / tinge / dash of **colour**
▸ a trace / hint of a / an **smile** / **accent**
▸ a touch / hint of **impatience** / **irritation**
▸ a trace / hint of **amusement** / **bitterness**
▸ a hint / tinge of **sadness** / **regret** / **envy**

element /ˈelɪmənt/ [C, usually sing.] (always followed by *of*) a small amount of a quality: *We need to preserve the **element of surprise**. ◇ There appears to be an **element of truth** in his story. ◇ All outdoor activities carry an **element of risk**.* ❶ **Element** is used especially to talk about a small amount of *truth* and also of qualities that suggest uncertainty, including *luck, chance, risk, danger, surprise, mystery, choice, uncertainty* and *doubt*.

touch [C, usually sing.] (always followed by *of*) a very small amount of sth, especially a quality: *There was a **touch** of sarcasm in her voice. ◇ Give your garden a **touch of class** with a sundial as a focal point. ◇ There could be a **touch of frost** tonight.* ❶ **Touch** is used especially to talk about small amounts of special or expensive qualities including *class, elegance, glamour, luxury, genius* and *colour*; also small amounts of humorous and/or negative qualities, including *humour, irony, sarcasm, impatience* and *irritation*.

trace [C] (always followed by *of*) a very small amount of a substance, feeling or quality: *The police found traces of blood in the bathroom. ◇ She spoke **without a trace** of bitterness. ◇ He spoke in English with only the trace of an accent.* ❶ Collocates of **trace** include *blood, gold, emotion, amusement, anxiety, bitterness, cynicism, sarcasm, irony* and *humour*. It is often used in a more negative way than **touch**: *Her speech brought a welcome touch of humour to the evening. ◇ There was no trace of humour in his expression.*

hint [C, usually sing.] (always followed by *of*) a very small amount of a feeling, quality, colour or taste: *There was more than a hint of sadness in his voice. ◇ He vowed that no hint of scandal would ever be attached to him. ◇ The walls were painted with a hint of peach.* ❶ You can talk about a **hint** of both positive and negative feelings and qualities, including *amusement, humour, laughter, triumph, anger, bitterness, impatience, irritation, sadness, desperation, malice, mischief, mockery, jealousy, suspicion* and *scandal*.

spot [C, usually sing.] (always followed by *of*) (*BrE, informal*) a small amount of sth: *There was a **spot of rain** in the afternoon, but otherwise the weather has been perfect. ◇ We got into a **spot of bother** with the police.*

tinge /tɪndʒ/ [C] a small amount of a colour or feeling: *There was a faint pink **tinge** to the sky. ◇ He felt a tinge of sadness as the train began to pull away.* See also **tinge** → COLOUR *noun* 1

> **NOTE** HINT OR TINGE? **Hint** is more frequent than **tinge** and can be used to describe a wider range of feelings; however, both words can be used to describe *sadness, regret* and *envy*. With colours, you can say *a pink tinge to sth* or *a hint of pink* but NOT: *a tinge of pink* or: *a pink hint*.

pinch [C, usually sing.] (always followed by *of*) the amount of salt or a spice that you can hold between your finger and thumb: *Add a **pinch of salt** to the mixture and stir well. ◇ a pinch of cayenne pepper/cinnamon/curry powder/ground ginger/nutmeg/paprika/snuff*

dash [C, usually sing.] (always followed by *of*) a small amount of sth that is added to sth else: *Add a **dash of** lemon juice. ◇ The rug adds a **dash of colour** to the room.* ❶ **Dash** is used especially to describe a small amount of a liquid which is added to food or drink.

elite *noun* See the Topic Map for THE INDIVIDUAL AND SOCIETY on p.894

elite · society · the nobility · the aristocracy · the gentry · the upper class
These are all words for the group of people in a society who belong to a high social class and/or have a lot of power, money or influence.

▸ **among** the elite / nobility / aristocracy / gentry / upper class
▸ the **local** elite / nobility / aristocracy / gentry
▸ the **British** / **French, etc.** elite / nobility / aristocracy / gentry / upper class
▸ the **landed** / **landowning** / **minor** / **lesser** nobility / aristocracy / gentry
▸ to **belong to** an elite / the nobility / the aristocracy / the gentry / the upper classes

elite /erˈliːt; rˈliːt/ [C+sing./pl. v.] a group of people in a society or area of activity who are powerful and have a lot of influence, because they are rich and/or educated: *In these countries, only the elite can afford an education for their children. ◇ He came from the country's **intellectual elite**.* See also **elite** → TOP *adj.*, **elitist** → EXCLUSIVE

society [U] a group of people in a country or area who are fashionable, rich and powerful: *She was a poor Irish girl who married into New York society. ◇ She moved in **high society** and had many literary friends. ◇ The revelations have outraged **polite society**. ◇ He was a popular photographer for **society weddings**.*

the nobility [sing.+ sing./pl. v.] (in some countries) people of the highest social class, who have special titles such as Duke or Duchess: *She had some influential supporters, including members of the nobility.* See also **noble** → LORD *noun*, **noble** → ARISTOCRATIC *adj.*

the aristocracy /ˌærɪˈstɒkrəsi; AmE -ˈstɑːk-/ [C+sing./pl. v.] (in some countries) people of the highest social class, who have special titles such as Duke or Duchess: *He claimed to be a member of the minor aristocracy (= with a lower title).* See also **aristocrat** → LORD, **aristocratic** → ARISTOCRATIC

the gentry [pl.] (used to talk about the past) people belonging to a high social class: *The influence of the Church and the landed gentry (= those owning a lot of land) at that time cannot be overemphasized.*

> **NOTE** NOBILITY, ARISTOCRACY OR GENTRY? **The nobility** or **the aristocracy** are the group of people in some countries, especially in the past, who were born in the highest social class, below royalty. They have special titles such as Duke, Duchess, Count or Earl. They are usually rich and powerful, and often own land. In the past, **the gentry** were people with a high social class, just below the nobility in rank, who were usually rich and owned land, but did not always have special titles, and were usually powerful at a local level rather than at a national level.

the ˌupper ˈclass [sing.+ sing./pl. v.] (*especially AmE*) (also **the ˌupper ˈclasses** [pl.]) the group of people in a society that are considered to have the highest social status and that have more money and/or power than other people: *They produced luxury furniture for the middle and upper classes.* ❶ **The upper class** is sometimes used to refer just to the aristocracy, but is often used with a wider meaning, including the gentry and sometimes also business and professional people with enough money to buy the property, education and culture needed to enable them to mix socially with other members of the upper class: *Wealthy industrialists joined the upper class by virtue* *of their newly acquired spending power.* See also **class** → CLASS 4, **the middle class** → MIDDLE CLASS, **the working class** → GENERAL PUBLIC, **upper-class** → ARISTOCRATIC

embarrass *verb*

embarrass · humiliate · shame · mortify
These words all mean to make sb feel awkward or ashamed.

embarrass → humiliate → mortify
shame

PATTERNS AND COLLOCATIONS
▸ to embarrass / humiliate sb **in front of** sb
▸ to be embarrassed / mortified **at** sth
▸ to embarrass / humiliate / shame sb **by doing** sth
▸ to be embarrassed / humiliated / mortified **to do** sth
▸ to embarrass / humiliate / shame **yourself**
▸ to **publicly / deeply / utterly** embarrass / humiliate / shame sb

embarrass [T] to make sb feel shy, awkward or ashamed, especially in a social situation; to cause problems or difficulties for sb: *Her questions about my private life embarrassed me.* ◊ *It embarrassed her to meet strange men in the corridor at night.* ◊ *The speech was deliberately designed to embarrass the prime minister.*
▸ **embarrassing** *adj.*: *an embarrassing mistake/question/situation* ◊ *It was so embarrassing having to sing in public.*
▸ **embarrassment** *noun* [U, C]: *Much to her embarrassment she realized that everybody in the room had heard her.* ◊ *His resignation will be a severe embarrassment to the party.*

humiliate /hjuːˈmɪlieɪt/ [T] to make sb feel ashamed or stupid and lose the respect of other people: *I didn't want to humiliate her in front of her colleagues.* ◊ *The party was humiliated in the recent elections.*
▸ **humiliating** *adj.*: *a humiliating defeat*
▸ **humiliation** *noun* [U, C]: *She suffered the humiliation of being criticized in public.*

shame [T] (*written or formal*) to make sb feel ashamed; to make sb feel that they have lost honour or respect: *His generosity shamed them all.* ◊ *She shamed her father into promising to help* (= persuaded him to do it by making him feel ashamed not to do it). ◊ *The companies that pollute our rivers should be named and shamed.* See also **shame** → GUILT *noun*, **shame** → DISGRACE *noun* 2

mortify /ˈmɔːtɪfaɪ; *AmE* ˈmɔːrt-/ [T, usually passive] to make sb feel extremely ashamed or embarrassed: *She was mortified to realize he had heard every word she said.* ❶ Mortify is sometimes used in an exaggerated way in spoken English, when it means 'slightly embarrassed', not 'extremely embarrassed': *I was mortified when I realized I had forgotten our lunch date.*
▸ **mortification** *noun* [U]: *Imagine my mortification when I found out.*
▸ **mortifying** *adj.*: *How mortifying to have to apologize to him!*

embarrassed *adj.*

embarrassed · uncomfortable · awkward · self-conscious · sheepish
These words all describe a person who feels anxious, ashamed or unable to relax, or sth which makes sb feel like this.

PATTERNS AND COLLOCATIONS
▸ embarrassed / uncomfortable / awkward / self-conscious / sheepish **about** sth
▸ an embarrassed / uncomfortable / awkward **silence**
▸ an embarrassed / a self-conscious / a sheepish **smile**
▸ to **feel / look** embarrassed / uncomfortable / awkward / self-conscious / sheepish
▸ **a little / a bit** embarrassed / uncomfortable / self-conscious / sheepish

▸ **slightly / somewhat / acutely / highly** embarrassed / uncomfortable / self-conscious

embarrassed shy, ashamed or unable to relax, especially in a social situation: *She's embarrassed about her height.* ◊ *He felt embarrassed at being the centre of attention.* ◊ *Some women are too embarrassed to consult their doctor about the problem.* ◊ *Her remark was followed by an embarrassed silence.*

uncomfortable anxious or embarrassed and unable to relax; making you feel like this: *He looked distinctly uncomfortable when the subject was mentioned.* ◊ *It was an uncomfortable situation for everyone.* **OPP** **comfortable** ❶ If you are **comfortable** in a situation you are confident and not worried or afraid: *I never feel very comfortable in her presence.*
▸ **uncomfortably** *adv.*: *I became uncomfortably aware that no one else was laughing.* ◊ *Her comment was uncomfortably close to the truth.*

awkward embarrassed or anxious and unable to relax and behave naturally; making you feel like this: *She is awkward with people when they ask about his wife.* ◊ *There was an awkward moment when they asked about his wife.*
▸ **awkwardly** *adv.*: *'I'm sorry,' he said awkwardly.*

NOTE EMBARRASSED, UNCOMFORTABLE OR AWKWARD?
Embarrassed is used especially to describe how sb feels, especially when they think everyone is looking at them, laughing at them or knows sth too personal about them. **Uncomfortable** is often used to describe a situation in which people are unsure how to behave, especially because there is a subject that people do not want to mention but do not know how to avoid. **Awkward** is often used to describe sb's personality or usual behaviour, not just their feelings on a particular occasion. However, in many cases any of these words can be used: *He felt embarrassed/uncomfortable/awkward about being the centre of attention.* ◊ *an embarrassed/uncomfortable/awkward silence*

self-conscious nervous or embarrassed about your appearance or what other people think of you: *He's always been self-conscious about being so short.* ◊ *She was a shy, self-conscious girl.* **OPP** **unselfconscious** ❶ If you are **unselfconscious** you are not worried about or not aware of what other people think of you.
▸ **self-consciously** *adv.*: *She was self-consciously aware of his stare.*

sheepish looking or feeling embarrassed because you have done sth silly or wrong: *He came into the room looking distinctly sheepish.* ◊ *Mary gave a sheepish grin.*

emerge *verb* See also the entry for HAPPEN

emerge · come up · surface · present itself
These words all mean to begin to exist or suddenly appear.

PATTERNS AND COLLOCATIONS
▸ to emerge / surface **as / from** sth
▸ a **problem** emerges / comes up / surfaces / presents itself
▸ a / an **situation / opportunity** emerges / comes up / presents itself
▸ a **chance** comes up / presents itself

emerge /iˈmɜːdʒ; *AmE* iˈmɜːrdʒ/ [I] to begin to exist; to appear or become known: *After the elections opposition groups began to emerge.* ◊ *He rapidly emerged as a key figure in the campaign.* ◊ *the emerging markets of South Asia* ❶ In this meaning **emerge** is used especially to talk about changes in politics, economics, technology and society, with new situations and events, and people and groups playing new roles.
▸ **emergence** *noun* [U]: *the emergence of new technologies*

,come 'up *phrasal verb* (of a subject) to be mentioned or discussed; (of an opportunity) to become available: *The subject came up in conversation.* ◇ *The question is bound to come up at the meeting.* ◇ *When the chance came up to go to Paris, she jumped at it.*

surface [I] to suddenly appear or become obvious after having been hidden for a while: *Doubts began to surface.* ◇ *No further information has surfaced yet.* ◇ *She surfaced again years later in London.* ❶ In this meaning **surface** can be used to talk about feelings, facts or people.

present itself *phrase* (of a problem, solution or opportunity) to suddenly happen or become available: *Thankfully, a solution presented itself to him surprisingly soon.* ◇ *As soon as the opportunity presented itself, she would get another job.*

emotion *noun*

emotion · feeling · passion · fervour · heat · sentiment
These are all words for sth which sb feels strongly, such as love, fear or anger.

⟶

emotion	heat	passion
feeling		fervour
sentiment		

PATTERNS AND COLLOCATIONS
▸ **with** emotion / feeling / passion / fervour / heat
▸ **intense / considerable / profound / strong / violent** emotion / feelings / passion
▸ **great** emotion / passion / fervour
▸ **human** emotion / feelings / passion
▸ **personal** emotion / feeling / sentiment
▸ to **arouse** emotion / feelings / passion / fervour
▸ to **stir up** emotion / feelings / fervour
▸ to **be full of** emotion / passion / fervour
▸ emotions / feelings / passions **are running high**

emotion [U, C] something which sb feels strongly such as love, fear or anger; the part of a person's character that consists of what they feel: *She spoke with deep emotion.* ◇ *She showed no emotion at the verdict.* ◇ *He lost control of his emotions.* See also **emotional** → INTENSE

feeling [C, usually pl., U] a person's emotions rather than their thoughts or ideas; strong emotion: *He hates talking about his feelings.* ◇ *The debate aroused strong feelings on both sides.* ◇ *He still harboured feelings of resentment.* ◇ *She spoke with feeling about the plight of the homeless.* See also **feel** → FEEL *verb*, **feeling** → SENSE *noun*

passion [C, U] a very strong feeling of love, hatred, anger, enthusiasm, etc: *He's a man of violent passions.* ◇ *She argued her case with considerable passion.* ◇ *She killed her husband's lover in a crime of passion.* See also **passionate** → INTENSE

fervour (*BrE*) (*AmE* **fervor**) /ˈfɜːvə(r); *AmE* ˈfɜːrv-/ [U] (*written*) very strong feelings about sth, especially sth you believe in strongly: *She kissed him with unusual fervour.* ◇ *They were fired by religious fervour.* See also **fervent** → INTENSE

heat [U] strong feelings, especially of anger or excitement: *'No, I won't,' he said with heat in his voice.* ◇ *The chairman tried to take the heat out of the situation* (= to make people calmer). ◇ *In the heat of the moment she forgot what she wanted to say* (= because she was so angry or excited). See also **heated** → INTENSE

sentiment [U] (*rather formal, sometimes disapproving*) feelings of pity, romantic love or sadness which may be too strong or not appropriate: *There is no room for sentiment in business.* ◇ *There was no fatherly affection, no display of sentiment.*
▸ **sentimental** *adj.*: *She kept the letters for sentimental reasons.* ◇ *The ring wasn't worth much but it had great sentimental value.* ◇ (*disapproving*) *a slushy, sentimental love story* ◇ *He's not the sort of man who gets sentimental about old friendships.*

emotional *adj.*

emotional · spiritual · inner
These words all describe sth connected with your feelings and emotions rather than physical or practical things.

PATTERNS AND COLLOCATIONS
▸ emotional / spiritual / inner **development / needs / strength / turmoil**
▸ sb's emotional / spiritual / inner **self / state**
▸ emotional / spiritual **growth / support / welfare / well-being**

emotional [usually before noun] connected with people's feelings and emotions: *Victims require emotional support and reassurance.* ◇ *Physical and emotional well-being are inextricably linked.* ◇ *An enduring emotional attachment between mother and baby develops in the first year.*
▸ **emotionally** *adv.*: *emotionally disturbed children* ◇ *I try not to become emotionally involved.*

spiritual [usually before noun] connected with the human spirit, rather than the body or physical things: *Many Eastern cultures put spiritual values before material values.* ◇ *He was committed to the welfare, both spiritual and physical, of the men under his command.* **OPP material** ❶ **Material** things are connected with money and possessions rather than with the needs of the mind or spirit: *material comforts* ◇ *changes in your material circumstances*
▸ **spiritually** *adv.*: *a spiritually uplifting book*

inner [only before noun] (of thoughts or feelings) private and secret; not expressed or shown to other people: *She doesn't reveal much of her inner self.* ◇ *An inner voice told him that what he was doing was wrong.*

employ *verb* See also the entry for APPOINT

employ · hire · recruit · sign · contract · engage · retain · take sb on
These words all mean to give sb a job to do for payment.

PATTERNS AND COLLOCATIONS
▸ to employ / hire / recruit / sign / engage / retain / take on sb **as** sth
▸ to employ / hire / recruit / sign / contract / engage / retain / take on sb **to do sth**
▸ to hire / recruit / sign sb **from** a place / company / group
▸ to employ / hire / recruit / contract / take on **workers / staff**
▸ to employ / hire / recruit a **manager**
▸ to employ / hire / engage / retain a **lawyer**
▸ to sign / contract a **player**
▸ to engage / retain sb's **services**

employ [T] to have sb working for you for payment; to give sb a job: *How many people does the company employ?* ◇ *A number of people have been employed to deal with the backlog of work.* See also **be employed** → WORK *verb* 2, **employer** → MANAGER, **employment** → WORK *noun* 2

hire [T, I] (*especially AmE*) to give sb a job; to find new people to work for a company or organization: *She was hired three years ago.* ◇ *He does the hiring and firing in our company.* ◇ *We're not hiring right now.* ❶ In both British and American English **hire** also means 'to employ sb for a short time to do a particular job': *They hired a firm of consultants to design the new system.* **OPP fire** → FIRE

recruit /rɪˈkruːt/ [T, I] (*rather formal*) to find new people to join a company, an organization or the armed forces: *The police are trying to recruit more officers from ethnic minorities.* ◇ *They recruited several new members to the club.* ◇ *He is responsible for recruiting at all levels.* See also **recruit** → RECRUIT *noun*

sign [T, I] to arrange for sb, especially a musician or sports player, to sign a contract agreeing to work for your company or team; to sign a contract agreeing to work for a company or team: *The team has just signed a new goalkeeper.* ◇ (*BrE*) *He signed for United yesterday.* ◇ (*especially AmE*) *He signed with the San Francisco 49ers.* ◇ *The band signed with Virgin Records.*

contract /kən'trækt/ [T, usually passive] (*rather formal*) to make a legal agreement with sb for them to work for you or provide you with a service, especially for a limited period of time: *The player is contracted to play until August.* ◇ *Several computer engineers have been contracted to the finance department.* ❶ In this meaning **contract** is usually followed by *to*. In American English it is sometimes followed by *with*: *He can't work for them because he is contracted with another company.* See also **contract** → CONTRACT *noun*

engage /ɪn'geɪdʒ/ [T] (*formal, especially BrE*) to employ sb to do a particular job: *He is currently engaged as a consultant.* ◇ *We will have to engage the services of a translator.*

retain /rɪ'teɪn/ [T] (*law*) to pay money regularly or in advance to a professional person such as a lawyer, so that they will do work for you when you need them to: *You will need to retain the services of a lawyer.* ◇ *You will be paid a retaining fee.* ❶ A lawyer, etc. can be **retained** by a member of the public as well as by a company; sb who is **retained** may do work for other people or companies as well.

take sb 'on *phrasal verb* to give sb a job: *We're not taking on any new staff at present.* **OPP lay sb off** → FIRE

empty *adj.*

empty · vacant · bare · free
These words all describe sth with no people or things inside.

PATTERNS AND COLLOCATIONS
▶ empty / bare / free **of** sth
▶ an empty / a vacant / a bare **room**
▶ an empty / a vacant / a free **seat**
▶ an empty / a vacant **house**
▶ an empty / a bare **cupboard**

empty not containing any things or people: *an empty box/ glass* ◇ *an empty house/room/bus* ◇ *The theatre was half empty.* ◇ *empty hands* (= not holding anything) ◇ *an empty plate* (= with no food on it) ◇ *The house had been standing empty* (= without people living in it) *for some time.* ◇ *It's not good to drink alcohol on an empty stomach* (= without having eaten sth). ◇ (*formal*) *The room was empty of furniture.* **OPP full** → FULL, See also **empty** → CLEAR *verb*, **empty** → DRAIN *verb*

vacant /'veɪkənt/ (*rather formal*) (of a seat, a hotel room, a house or land) empty and not being used: *There are very few vacant properties available in the area.* ◇ *The seat next to him was vacant.* ◇ (*especially AmE*) *a vacant lot* (= a piece of land in a town that is not being used) ◇ *There is a room vacant, as it happens.* See also **unoccupied** → DESERTED

bare (especially of a room or cupboard) empty and lacking its usual contents: *At many stores bare shelves greeted shoppers.* ◇ *The room was bare of furniture.*

free (especially of sth that you need to use) empty and ready to be used: *Is this seat free?* ◇ *The device allows you to talk on the phone with both hands free.*

enable *verb*

enable · allow · permit
These words all mean to make sth possible.

PATTERNS AND COLLOCATIONS
▶ to enable / allow / permit sb **to do** sth
▶ to enable / allow / permit **access**
▶ to enable / allow / permit the **creation** / **development** / **expansion** of sth

enable [T] (*rather formal*) to make it possible for sb to do sth; to make it possible for sth to happen or exist by creating the necessary conditions: *This new programme will enable older people to study at college.* ◇ *Insulin enables the body to use and store sugar.*

allow [T] (*rather formal, especially written*) to enable sth: *Wear clothing that allows easy movement.* ◇ *The schedule is designed to allow maximum flexibility.*

permit /pə'mɪt; *AmE* pər'm-/ (-**tt**-) [I, T] (*formal*) to enable sth: *We hope to visit the cathedral, if time permits.* ◇ *I'll come tomorrow, weather permitting* (= if the weather is fine).

NOTE **ENABLE, ALLOW** OR **PERMIT**? These words all have the same meaning, but there are some differences in their use. **Enable** is used especially with a person as object, in the phrase *enable sb to do sth.* **Allow** and **permit** can also be used in this structure, but usually with the meaning 'give sb permission to do sth'; in this meaning they are more often used with a thing as object, including in the phrase *allow/permit sth to happen/be done.* **Permit** is more formal than **allow** and is used especially in the fixed phrases *if time permits* and *weather permitting.*

encourage *verb*

1 be encouraged by the news
2 encourage people to cycle
3 encourage violent behaviour/debate

1 See also the entry for REASSURE
encourage · cheer sb up · cheer · uplift · lift/raise sb's spirits
These words all mean to give sb a feeling of encouragement, hope or confidence.

PATTERNS AND COLLOCATIONS
▶ to be **greatly** encouraged / cheered

encourage [T] to give sb support, courage or hope: *My parents have always encouraged me in my choice of career.* ◇ *We were greatly encouraged by the positive response of the public.* ◇ *'Good girl, you're doing fine,' he encouraged her.* **OPP discourage** → DISCOURAGE 2
▶ **encouragement** *noun* [U]: *He needs all the support and encouragement he can get.* **OPP discouragement** → DISCOURAGE 2

cheer sb 'up *phrasal verb* to make sb feel more cheerful: *I asked her out to lunch to cheer her up.* ◇ *Give John a call — he needs cheering up.* **OPP get sb down** → DISCOURAGE 2

cheer [T, usually passive] to give sb hope, comfort or encouragement: *She was cheered by the news from home.*

NOTE **ENCOURAGE** OR **CHEER**? People or events can **encourage** you; you can be **cheered** by events or things. **Cheer** is more about comfort; **encourage** is more about confidence.

uplift /,ʌp'lɪft/ [T, usually passive] (*formal*) to make sb feel happier or more hopeful: *Although it is an emotional play you leave the theatre feeling strangely uplifted.* See also **uplifting** → MOVING

lift/raise sb's 'spirits *idiom* to make sb feel more cheerful or brave: *The sunny weather raised my spirits a little.*

2 **encourage · urge · spur · galvanize · exhort · put sb up to sth · egg sb on**
These words all mean to try hard to persuade sb to do sth, especially by making them excited or by making them believe it is the right thing to do.

PATTERNS AND COLLOCATIONS
▶ to spur sb on / galvanize sb / exhort sb **to** sth
▶ to encourage sb / urge sb / spur sb / galvanize sb / exhort sb / egg sb on **to do** sth
▶ to encourage / urge / exhort sb **not to do** sth
▶ to **constantly** / **repeatedly** encourage / urge / exhort sb to do sth
▶ to **strongly** encourage / urge sb to do sth
▶ to spur / galvanize sb **into action**

encourage [T] to persuade sb to do sth by making it easier for them and making them believe it is a good thing to do: *Banks actively encourage people to borrow money.* ◇ *We're looking at ways to encourage recycling.* ◇ *The new measures are designed to encourage more people to cycle.* **OPP** **discourage** → DISCOURAGE 1

urge /ɜːdʒ; *AmE* ɜːrdʒ/ [T] to strongly advise or try hard to persuade sb to do sth: *She urged him to stay.* ◇ *Police are urging anyone who saw the accident to contact them immediately.* ◇ *The report **urged that** all children be taught to swim.* ◇ *'Please come!' he urged.*

spur /spɜː(r)/ (-rr-) [T] (of a person or event) to encourage sb to do sth or to try harder to achieve sth: *Her difficult childhood **spurred her on** to succeed.* ◇ *The band has been spurred on by the success of their last single.*

galvanize (*BrE* also **-ise**) /ˈɡælvənaɪz/ [T] (*especially written*) (of a person or event) to make sb take action or try harder by shocking them or making them excited: *The win galvanized the whole team.* ◇ *The industry was **galvanized into doing** something about the problem.*

exhort /ɪɡˈzɔːt; *AmE* ɪɡˈzɔːrt/ [T] (*formal*) to try hard to persuade sb to do sth, especially by speaking with strong feeling: *The party leader exhorted his members to start preparing for government.*

put sb 'up to sth *phrasal verb* (*informal*) to encourage or persuade sb to do sth wrong or stupid: *Some of the older boys must have put him up to it.*

egg sb 'on *phrasal verb* (*rather informal*) to encourage sb to do sth, especially sth they should not do or would normally be afraid to do: *He hit the girl again and again as his friends egged him on.*

---

3 See also the entries for CAUSE and STIMULATE

encourage · fuel · incite · stir sth up · stoke · whip sb/sth up

These words all mean to make sth happen or develop, especially by making people feel a strong emotion or take part in an activity, often one that is violent, illegal or unpleasant.

PATTERNS AND COLLOCATIONS
▸ to encourage / incite sb **to do sth**
▸ to encourage / fuel / stir up / stoke / whip up **interest**
▸ to encourage / incite / stir up / whip up **opposition**
▸ to fuel / stir up / stoke **anger / fears**
▸ to incite / whip up a / an **crowd / audience**
▸ to **deliberately** encourage / incite / stir up / whip up sth

encourage [T] to make sth more likely to happen or develop; to make sth increase: *They claim that some computer games encourage violent behaviour in children.* ◇ *The questions are designed to encourage debate.* ◇ *Music and special lighting are used to encourage shoppers to spend more.* ❶ **Encourage** is used about both good and bad things. **OPP** **hold sb/sth back** → BLOCK 1

fuel (-ll-, *AmE* -l-) [T] (*especially journalism, especially business*) to increase sth or make it stronger, especially sth that may cause damage: *Higher oil prices helped to fuel inflation.* ◇ *Yesterday's meeting is likely to fuel further speculation about a takeover.*

incite /ɪnˈsaɪt/ [T] (*rather formal, disapproving*) to encourage sb to do sth, usually sth violent, illegal or unpleasant, especially by making them angry or excited: *There is legislation to ban material that incites racial hatred.* ◇ *They were accused of inciting the crowd to violence.*
▸ **incitement** /ɪnˈsaɪtmənt/ *noun* [U, C]: *incitement to murder*

stir sth 'up *phrasal verb* (-rr-) to make people feel strong emotions, especially unpleasant ones; to try to cause arguments or problems: *The memory stirred up feelings of guilt.* ◇ *Whenever he's around, he always manages to stir up trouble.* ◇ (*informal*) *We've got enough problems without you trying to stir things up.*

stoke [T] (*especially journalism or business*) to make people feel sth more strongly; to make sth increase, sometimes dangerously: *His departure has stoked fears that the company is planning job cuts.* ◇ *Increased borrowing was stoking up a consumer boom.*

whip sb/sth 'up *phrasal verb* (-pp-) to deliberately try to make people excited or feel strongly about sth: *He was a speaker who could really whip up a crowd.* ◇ *The advertisements were designed to whip up public opinion.*

---

end *noun*

end · close · conclusion · finish · ending · termination · finale · cessation

These are all words for the final part of a period of time, an event, activity or story.

PATTERNS AND COLLOCATIONS
▸ a / an (...) end / finish / ending / finale **to** sth
▸ **at** the end / close / conclusion / finish / finale
▸ an **abrupt** end / conclusion / finish / ending / termination
▸ a **dramatic** end / conclusion / finish / ending / finale
▸ a **fitting** end / conclusion / finale
▸ to **have** a / an (...) end / conclusion / ending / finale
▸ to **provide** a / an (...) conclusion / finish / ending / finale
▸ to **bring sth to** an end / a close / a conclusion
▸ to **come / draw to** an end / a close
▸ to **reach** the end / finale

end [C] the final part of a period of time, an event, activity or story; a situation in which sth does not exist any more: *I hope to finish this by the end of the week.* ◇ *They finally get named at the end of the book.* ◇ *There'll be a chance to ask questions at the end.* ◇ *We had to hear about the whole journey **from beginning to end**.* ◇ *It's the end of an era.* ◇ *It was the end of all his dreams.* ◇ *The war was finally **at an end**.* ◇ *Let's **put an end to** (= stop) these rumours once and for all.* **OPP** **beginning** → START

close /kləʊz; *AmE* kloʊz/ [sing.] (*formal, especially business*) the final part of a period of time, an event or activity: *Can we bring this meeting to a close?* ◇ *By the close of London trading, Wall Street was up 9.78 points.* ❶ **Close** is most often used in business contexts or in sport, especially cricket or baseball: *At the **close of play**, the scores were almost level.*

conclusion /kənˈkluːʒn/ [C, usually sing.] (*rather formal*) the final part of sth such as a speech or piece of writing: *The conclusion of the book was disappointing.* ◇ *If we took this argument to its **logical conclusion**...* ◇ *In conclusion,* (= finally) *I would like to thank...*

finish [C, usually sing.] the final part of sth, especially a race: *It was a **close finish**, as they had predicted.* ◇ *He led the race **from start to finish**.* ◇ *I want to see the job right through to the finish.* ❶ **Finish** is mainly used to talk about sports events, especially races, or other activities where the time that sb takes is considered to be important. **OPP** **start** → START

ending [C] the last part of a story, film, etc.; the act of finishing sth; the final part of sth: *His stories usually have a **happy ending**.* ◇ *Today is the anniversary of the ending of the Pacific War.* ◇ *It was the perfect ending to the perfect day.* **OPP** **opening, beginning** → START

termination /ˌtɜːmɪˈneɪʃn; *AmE* ˌtɜːrm-/ [U] (*formal, especially business*) the act of ending sth; the end of sth: *Failure to comply with these conditions will result in termination of the contract.*

finale /fɪˈnɑːli; *AmE* fɪˈnæli/ [C] the last part of a show or piece of music: *the rousing finale of Beethoven's Ninth Symphony* ◇ *The festival ended with a **grand finale** of fireworks and music.* ❶ **Finale** can also be used after an adjective to mean 'an ending to sth of the type mentioned': *It was a fitting finale to the day's events.*

cessation /seˈseɪʃn/ [sing.] (*formal, especially journalism*) the stopping of sth; a pause in sth: *Mexico called for an immediate cessation of hostilities.*

end *verb* See also the entry for FINISH

---

end · finish · stop · terminate · conclude · close · wind (sth) up
These words all mean to come to an end or to bring sth to an end.

PATTERNS AND COLLOCATIONS
▸ to end / finish / conclude **by / with** sth
▸ to end / finish / conclude / close / wind up a **meeting**
▸ to end / finish / conclude / wind up a **speech**
▸ a **play / show / film** ends / finishes / concludes
▸ a **concert** ends / finishes
▸ a **story / letter / note** ends / concludes
▸ to **almost / nearly / effectively** end / finish / stop / terminate / conclude
▸ to **virtually / all but / never** end / finish / stop / terminate / conclude
▸ to end / finish / stop / terminate / conclude **at last / eventually / finally**
▸ to end / stop / terminate **suddenly / abruptly / automatically**

end [I, T] to come to an end; to bring sth to an end: *The road ends here.* ◇ *How does the story end?* ◇ *The speaker ended by suggesting some topics for discussion.* ◇ *They decided to end their relationship.* ◇ *They ended the play with a song.* OPP **begin** → BEGIN, **begin** → START

finish [I, T] to come to an end; to bring sth to an end, especially in an appropriate way: *The play finished at 10.30.* ◇ *The symphony finishes with a flourish.* ◇ *A cup of coffee finished the meal perfectly.* ◇ *They finished off the show with one of their most famous songs.* OPP **start** → BEGIN

stop (-pp-) [I, T] to end; to make sth end: *When is this fighting going to stop?* ◇ *The bus service stops at midnight.* ◇ *Has it stopped raining yet?* ◇ *Doctors couldn't stop the bleeding.* ◇ *The referee was forced to stop the game because of snow.* OPP **start** → BEGIN

terminate /ˈtɜːmɪneɪt; *AmE* ˈtɜːrm-/ [I, T] (*formal*) (of an arrangement or agreement) to end; to make an arrangement, agreement or pregnancy end: *Your contract of employment terminates in December.* ◇ *to terminate a pregnancy* (= to have an abortion)

conclude /kənˈkluːd/ [I, T] (*formal*) to finish: *Let me make just a few concluding remarks.* ◇ *The commission concluded its investigation last month.*

NOTE **END, STOP, FINISH** OR **CONCLUDE**? **End** can be used for things that end in space as well as things that end in time: *The road ends here.* **End**, **finish** and **conclude** are used especially about things that you do not expect to start again after they have ended: *The war ended in 1945, after almost six years of fighting.* ◇ *The concert should finish by 10 o'clock.* ◇ *She concluded her speech with a quotation from Shakespeare.* **Finish** and **conclude**, in particular, suggest that sth has come to an end because it has been completed. **Finish** is used more to talk about *when* sth ends; **conclude** is used more to talk about *how* sth ends. **Stop** is used about things that may or will start again, or that cannot ever be 'completed': *The rain stopped just long enough for us to have a quick walk in the park.*

close [T, I] to bring sth such as a meeting or investigation to an end; (of a meeting or offer) to come to an end: *Mr Hunt then closed the debate for the government.* ◇ *A police spokesman said that the case was now closed.* ◇ *The offer closes at the end of the week.* ❶ If a *case, investigation* or *subject* is **closed**, no further investigation or discussion takes place; however, it does not necessarily mean that the case or problem under investigation or discussion has been solved: it may simply have been decided to stop trying to solve it. OPP **open** → BEGIN, **open** → START

wind 'up, **wind sth 'up** *phrasal verb* to bring sth such as a speech or meeting to an end: *The speaker was just winding up when the door was flung open.* ◇ *If we all agree, let's wind up the discussion.* OPP **kick off** → START

---

endless *adj.* See also the entry for CONTINUOUS

---

endless · perpetual · never-ending · interminable
These words all describe things that continue for a long time and seem to have no end.

PATTERNS AND COLLOCATIONS
▸ the endless / never-ending **flow** of sth
▸ an endless / a never-ending **stream / process**
▸ an endless / a never-ending **succession / series**
▸ an endless / a perpetual / a never-ending **struggle / battle**
▸ endless / interminable **discussions / meetings**
▸ to **seem** endless / never-ending / interminable
▸ **seemingly** endless / never-ending / interminable

endless that continues for a long time and seems to have no end: *The journey home seemed endless.* ◇ *She was getting bored with the endless round of parties.*
▸ **endlessly** *adv.*: *They talked endlessly about the war.*

perpetual /pəˈpetʃuəl; *AmE* pərˈp-/ [usually before noun] that never ends or changes: *They exist in a state of perpetual fear.* ◇ *The country seems to be in a perpetual state of chaos.* ◇ *His travel schedule keeps him in perpetual motion.*
▸ **perpetually** /-tʃuəli/ *adv.*: *The mountain is almost perpetually in thick cloud.*

never-'ending seeming to last for ever; impossible to finish: *The monkeys have a never-ending supply of food at their disposal.* ◇ *Updating the catalogue is a never-ending task.*

interminable /ɪnˈtɜːmɪnəbl; *AmE* -ˈtɜːrm-/ lasting a very long time and therefore boring or annoying: *There were the usual interminable speeches.*
▸ **interminably** /-əbli/ *adv.*: *The discussion dragged on interminably.*

---

endorsement *noun*

---

endorsement · recommendation · reference · testimonial
These are all words for a statement saying that you support sb/sth or that sb would be suitable for a particular job.

PATTERNS AND COLLOCATIONS
▸ an endorsement / a recommendation / a reference / a testimonial **from** sb
▸ an endorsement / a reference **for** sb / sth
▸ a **glowing** endorsement / recommendation / reference / testimonial
▸ a **written** reference / testimonial
▸ a **personal** endorsement / recommendation
▸ to **give / get / receive** an endorsement / recommendation
▸ a **letter of** endorsement / recommendation / reference

endorsement /ɪnˈdɔːsmənt; *AmE* -ˈdɔːrs-/ [C, U] a public statement or action showing that you support sb/sth; a statement made in an advertisement, usually by sb famous or important, saying that they use and like a particular product: *The election victory is a clear endorsement of their policies.* ◇ *We are happy to give the product our full endorsement.* See also **endorse** → RECOMMEND 2

recommendation /ˌrekəmenˈdeɪʃn/ [U, C] the act of telling sb that sth is good or useful or that sb would be suitable for a particular job, etc.; a formal letter or statement that sb would be suitable for a particular job: *We chose the hotel on their recommendation.* ◇ *It's best to find a builder through personal recommendation.* ◇ *The new housekeeper came on the highest recommendation.* ◇ *The company gave her a glowing recommendation.* See also **recommend** → RECOMMEND 2, **advice** → ADVICE

reference [C] a letter written by sb who knows you about your character and abilities, especially to a new employer: *You should supply a reference from your current employer.* ◇ (*BrE*) *We will take up references after the interview.*

NOTE RECOMMENDATION OR REFERENCE? **Reference** is the usual word for a letter written by sb to say that another person is suitable for sth, such as a new job. It can be from a former employer or from another person who knows the person well, such as a former teacher or other respected person. A **recommendation** is usually from a former employer and can be a letter or a statement. In American English students may be given a *recommendation letter*: *a recommendation letter for an internship/a scholarship/college*

testimonial /ˌtestɪˈməʊniəl; *AmE* -ˈmoʊ-/ [C] a formal statement about sb's abilities, qualities and character; a formal statement about the quality of sth: *Other testimonials to his character proved hard to come by.* ◊ *The catalogue is full of testimonials from satisfied customers.*

enemy noun See the Topic Map for CONFLICT on p.896

enemy · competitor · rival · opponent · the opposition · the competition · foe · adversary
These are all words for a person, group or country that fights, opposes or competes with sb/sth.

PATTERNS AND COLLOCATIONS
▸ a competitor / rival **for** sth
▸ **against** an enemy / a competitor / a rival / an opponent / the opposition / the competition / a foe / an adversary
▸ the **main** enemy / competitor / rival / opponent / opposition / competition / adversary
▸ a **formidable** / **worthy** enemy / competitor / rival / opponent / foe / adversary
▸ an **old** enemy / rival / opponent / foe / adversary
▸ a **dangerous** enemy / rival / opponent / foe / adversary
▸ **bitter** enemies / rivals / opponents / foes
▸ to **have** an enemy / a competitor / a rival / an opponent / a foe
▸ to **face** an enemy / an opponent / the opposition / the competition / a foe
▸ to **fight** an enemy / an opponent / the opposition / a foe
▸ to **defeat** an enemy / a rival / the opposition / a foe / an adversary

enemy [C] a person who hates sb or who acts or speaks against sb/sth: *After just one day, she had already* **made an enemy of** *her manager.* ◊ *They used to be friends but now they are* **sworn enemies.** ◊ *Birds are the natural enemies of many insect pests.* ❶ **The enemy** [sing.+ sing./pl. v.] is a country that you are fighting a war against or the armed forces of this country: *The enemy was forced to retreat.* In this meaning **enemy** is also often used before another noun: *enemy aircraft* ◊ *to go* **behind enemy lines** **OPP** ally → PARTNER 1, friend ❶ A person who has the same interests and opinions as yourself, and who will help and support you is your **friend**: *You're among friends here – you can speak freely.*

competitor /kəmˈpetɪtə(r)/ [C] a company or organization that competes against others, especially in business: *The company has no serious competitors.* See also **compete** → COMPETE

rival /ˈraɪvl/ [C] a person, company or thing that competes with others for the same thing or in the same area: *They were* **rivals in** *love.* ◊ *Grand it may be, but this cathedral is no* **rival to** *the great cathedral of Amiens.* ◊ *The Japanese are our biggest economic rivals.*
▸ **rival** adj. [only before noun]: *a rival bid/claim/offer* ◊ *He was shot by a member of a rival gang.*

opponent [C] a person who disagrees strongly with sb else and tries to argue against them; a person who fights or competes with sb in politics, business or sport: *As a man he was greatly respected, even by his political opponents.* ◊ *He drew his sword and turned to face his opponent.* See also **oppose** → OPPOSE

the opposition [sing.+ sing./pl. v.] the people you are competing against in business, a competition or a game, etc: *He's gone to work for the opposition.*

the competition [sing.+ sing./pl. v.] the people who are competing against sb in business or sport: *We'll be able to*

assess the competition at the conference. See also **compete** → COMPETE

foe /fəʊ; *AmE* foʊ/ [C] (*old-fashioned or formal*) an enemy: *He knew that Burton could be an implacable foe.* ◊ *She was unsure yet whether he was* **friend or foe.** **OPP** friend

adversary /ˈædvəsəri; *AmE* -verseri/ [C] (*formal*) a person that sb is opposed to and competing with in an argument or fighting against in a battle: *The two of them were old adversaries.*

energetic adj. See the Topic Map for SPORT AND LEISURE on p.892, See also the entry for LIVELY

energetic · vigorous · active · dynamic · mobile
These words all describe people or activities that have or show a lot of energy.

PATTERNS AND COLLOCATIONS
▸ an energetic / an active / a dynamic **person** / **man** / **woman**
▸ an energetic / active **member** of sth
▸ a vigorous / an active **supporter** / **opponent** of sb / sth
▸ an energetic / a vigorous / an active / a dynamic **campaign**
▸ a vigorous / an active **interest** in sth
▸ energetic / vigorous **exercise**

energetic /ˌenəˈdʒetɪk; *AmE* ˌenərˈdʒ-/ (of a person or activity) having or needing a lot of energy: *He knew I was energetic and would get things done.* ◊ *The heart responds well to energetic exercise.* ◊ *For the more energetic* (= people who prefer physical activities) *we offer wind-surfing and diving.*
▸ **energetically** adv.: *He strode out energetically towards the gate.*

vigorous /ˈvɪɡərəs/ (of a person or activity) showing great energy and determination: *They conducted a vigorous campaign against tax fraud.* ◊ (*BrE*) *Take vigorous exercise for several hours a week.* **OPP** gentle → GENTLE
▸ **vigorously** adv.: *She shook her head vigorously.* ◊ *The accusation was vigorously denied.*

NOTE ENERGETIC OR VIGOROUS? In some cases you can use either word: *energetic/vigorous exercise.* **Energetic** tends to refer more to physical energy and activities; **vigorous** often refers to business or political activities. A *vigorous man/woman* is really a strong and healthy person. In this meaning **vigorous** more often describes people engaged in business or political activity: *a vigorous opponent/supporter/campaigner*

active always busy doing things, especially physical activities: *Although he's nearly 80, he is still very active.* ◊ *Before our modern age, people had a more physical and active lifestyle.* ❶ **Active** is used especially to describe older people who are always busy. It is also commonly used with *life* and *lifestyle*. It can also describe people who give a lot of their time and attention to sth. See also **active** → BUSY 1

dynamic /daɪˈnæmɪk/ (*approving*) (of a person) having a positive attitude and a lot of energy and new ideas: *She has a dynamic personality.* ◊ *He was a dynamic young advertising executive.*

mobile /ˈməʊbaɪl; *AmE* ˈmoʊbl/ [not usually before noun] (of a person) able to move or travel around easily: *The kitchen is specially designed for the elderly or people who are less mobile.* ◊ *You really need to be mobile* (= have a car) *if you live in the country.*
▸ **mobility** /məʊˈbɪləti; *AmE* moʊ-/ noun [U]: *An electric wheelchair has given her greater mobility.*

energy noun
1 *nuclear/solar energy*
2 *She's always full of energy.*

1 energy · power
These are both words for the fuel, strength of the sun or wind, etc. that is used to drive machines, make electricity, provide heat, etc.

PATTERNS AND COLLOCATIONS
▶ **electrical / nuclear / atomic / solar / wind / tidal** energy / power
▶ to **generate / produce / provide / supply / use / harness** energy / power
▶ an energy / a power **supply**
▶ a **source of** energy / power

energy [U] a source of power such as fuel, used for driving machines, providing heat, etc: *the change from fossil fuel to renewable energy* ◇ *The nuclear plant provides a fifth of the nation's energy.* ◇ *It is important to conserve energy.* ◇ *Energy-saving features can reduce energy bills by 50%.* ◇ *The country could face an energy crisis* (= when fuel is not freely available) *if demand continues to rise.* ❶ In physics **energy** is the ability of matter or radiation to work because of its mass, movement, electric charge, etc.: *kinetic/potential energy*

power [U] energy that can be collected and used to operate a machine, to make electricity, etc.; the public supply of electricity: *Wind power was used to drive the machinery.* ◇ *This wheel provides the power to the cutting machine.* ◇ *To go higher the pilot increases the engine power.* ◇ *They've switched off the power.* ◇ *There seems to have been a power failure.*

NOTE ENERGY OR POWER? **Energy** is the source of power: the fuel, the light and heat from the sun or a nuclear reaction, the strength of the wind, water or waves. **Power** is energy that has been collected and used to produce electricity, operate machinery, etc. In practice you can often use either word: *electrical/nuclear/ atomic/solar/wind/tidal energy/power* ◇ *to generate/ produce/provide/supply/use/harness energy/power.* However, although you can say *generate/produce energy,* **energy** is often seen as sth that cannot be created (and in a scientific sense this is true): you can *store, conserve* or *save* energy, or you can *waste* it. **Power** is less frequently seen in this way: you *generate/produce power* and then *use* it to *drive* sth, but it is less usual to talk about storing or saving it. The *energy supply* is all the energy that has not yet been used up; the *power supply* is the continuous flow of power to where it is being used: *The world's energy supply is heading for crisis.* ◇ ~~*The world's power supply is heading for crisis.*~~ ◇ *interruptions in the power supply* ◇ ~~*interruptions in the energy supply*~~

2 See the Topic Map for SPORT AND LEISURE on p.892
energy · life · vigour · vitality · fire · dynamism · spark · gusto · zest
These are all words for the ability or quality of putting effort and enthusiasm into sth.

PATTERNS AND COLLOCATIONS
▶ to do sth **with** energy / vigour / vitality / dynamism / gusto / zest
▶ **great** energy / vigour / vitality / gusto / zest
▶ **tremendous** energy / vigour / vitality / dynamism / gusto
▶ **new** energy / life / vigour / vitality / zest
▶ sb's **old** energy / fire / spark
▶ **renewed / youthful** energy / vigour / vitality / zest
▶ to **have** energy / vigour / vitality / dynamism / spark / zest
▶ to **lack** energy / vigour / vitality / dynamism / spark
▶ to **lose** energy / vigour / vitality / fire / spark / zest
▶ to **add** energy / life / zest (to sth)
▶ to **be full of** energy / life / vigour / vitality / fire / dynamism / zest

energy [U] (in a person) the ability to put effort and enthusiasm into sth you do: *I admire her boundless energy.* ◇ *It's a waste of time and energy.* ◇ *Bringing up twins requires a great deal of energy.* See also **strength → FORCE** *noun*

life [U] (in a person, place or situation) the quality of being active, lively and exciting: *We need to inject some new life into this project.* ◇ *The city only comes to life at night.* See also **lively → LIVELY**

vigour (*BrE*) (*AmE* **vigor**) /'vɪɡə(r)/ [U] (in a person) energy, force and determination: *He worked with renewed vigour and enthusiasm.* ◇ *She attacked both political parties with equal vigour.*

vitality /vaɪ'tæləti/ [U] (in a person, place or work of art) energy and enthusiasm: *She is bursting with vitality and new ideas.* ◇ *The music has a wonderful freshness and vitality.* ◇ *The project will provide jobs and help to restore economic vitality to the region.*

fire [U] (in a person) very strong emotion, especially anger or enthusiasm that drives you to do sth: *The fire seemed to die in him when his wife died.* ◇ *Something of the old fire had returned to their rivalry.*

dynamism /'daɪnəmɪzəm/ [U] (in a person, project or idea) energy and enthusiasm to make new things happen or to make things succeed: *The freshness and dynamism of her approach was welcomed by all her students.* ◇ *The campaign lacked dynamism.*

spark [U, sing.] (in a person) a special quality of energy, intelligence or enthusiasm that makes sb very imaginative or amusing: *As a writer he seemed to lack creative spark.* ◇ *She had a certain spark — that something extra that made her a star.*

gusto /'ɡʌstəʊ; AmE -toʊ/ [U] (in a person) enthusiasm and energy in doing sth, especially sth you enjoy: *They sang with gusto.* ◇ *She attacked the huge slice of chocolate cake with great gusto.*

zest [U, sing.] (in a person) enjoyment and enthusiasm: *Last month's victory has given him renewed **zest for** the game.* ◇ *He had a great **zest for** life.*

enjoy *verb* See the Topic Map for SPORT AND LEISURE on p.892

enjoy · relish · savour · revel in sth · delight in sth · bask in sth · wallow in sth · glory in sth
These words all mean to get pleasure from an activity or experience.

PATTERNS AND COLLOCATIONS
▶ to enjoy / relish / revel in / delight in **doing sth**
▶ to enjoy / relish / savour / revel in / bask in **the moment**
▶ to enjoy / relish / bask in **your moment of** glory / triumph / victory / power
▶ to enjoy / relish / revel in / bask in in the **attention**
▶ to enjoy / relish / revel in your **freedom**
▶ to enjoy / relish a **challenge**
▶ to enjoy / delight in **sb's company**
▶ to **really** enjoy / relish / revel in / delight in sth

enjoy [T] to get enjoyment from an activity, event or experience: *We thoroughly enjoyed our time in New York.* ◇ *Thanks for a great evening. I really **enjoyed** it.* ◇ *I hope you enjoy your trip.* ◇ *I enjoy playing tennis and squash.* ❶ In informal spoken English, **enjoy** can also be used without an object to say that you hope sb gets enjoyment from sth that you are giving them or recommending to them: *Here's that book I promised you. Enjoy!* In all other situations **enjoy** must have an object: ~~*Thanks for a great evening. I really enjoyed.*~~ ◇ ~~*I hope you enjoy.*~~ See also **enjoyment → FUN**

relish /'relɪʃ/ [T] to get great pleasure from an activity or experience or the thought of doing sth: *I always relish a good debate.* ◇ *I **don't relish the prospect** of getting up early tomorrow.*

savour (*BrE*) (*AmE* **savor**) /'seɪvə(r)/ [T] (*especially written*) to enjoy the full taste or flavour of sth, especially by eating or drinking it slowly; to get great pleasure from an experience or feeling: *He ate his meal slowly, savouring every mouthful.* ◇ *I wanted to savour every moment.*

'revel in sth *phrasal verb* (-**ll**-, *AmE* -**l**-) [no passive] to enjoy an activity or experience very much: *He revelled in the freedom he was allowed.*

de'light in sth *phrasal verb* [no passive] (*especially written*) to get great pleasure from sth; to enjoy doing sth very much, especially sth that makes other people feel embarrassed or uncomfortable: *He was tall, handsome* and amiable and she delighted in his company. ◇ He delighted in playing tricks on colleagues. See also **delight** → JOY noun

'bask in sth phrasal verb [no passive] to enjoy the good feelings that you have when other people praise or admire you, or when they give you a lot of attention: I never minded **basking in** my wife's **reflected glory** (= enjoying the praise and attention that she got).

'wallow in sth phrasal verb [no passive] (often disapproving) to enjoy a feeling or activity that gives you pleasure, especially one that is considered bad or self-indulgent: He seemed to wallow in his self-pity. ◇ She wallowed in the luxury of the hotel.

'glory in sth phrasal verb [no passive] (especially written) to get great pleasure or enjoyment from a feeling or achievement: She gloried in her new-found independence. ◇ They were wonderful horsemen and gloried in their skills.

ensure verb

ensure · make sure · guarantee · assure · see to it that...
These words all mean to make sth certain to happen.

PATTERNS AND COLLOCATIONS
▶ to ensure / make sure / guarantee / see to it **that...**
▶ to ensure / guarantee / assure the **success / survival / quality** of sth
▶ to **absolutely** ensure / guarantee / assure sth
▶ to make **absolutely** sure
▶ to **virtually** ensure / guarantee / assure sth

ensure (also **insure** especially in AmE) /ɪnˈʃʊə(r); -ˈʃɔː(r); AmE ɪnˈʃʊr/ [T, I] (rather formal) to make sth certain to happen; to check that sth is done: The book ensured his success. ◇ Please ensure that all lights are switched off.

make 'sure phrase to do sth in order to be certain that sth else happens: Make sure (that) no one else finds out about this. ◇ They scored another goal and **made sure of** victory.

guarantee /ˌɡærənˈtiː/ [T] to make sth certain to happen: Tonight's victory guarantees the team's place in the final. ◇ These days getting a degree doesn't guarantee you a job.

assure /əˈʃʊə(r); -ˈʃɔː(r); AmE əˈʃʊr/ [T] to make sth certain to happen: Victory would assure a place in the finals. ◇ This achievement has assured her a place in the history books.

> **NOTE** ENSURE, GUARANTEE OR ASSURE? Ensure is often used in orders or instructions: *Please guarantee/assure that all lights are switched off.* Assure and **guarantee** can suggest that feelings of worry or doubt about sth are removed; **guarantee**, but NOT **assure** is often used in negative statements to show that feelings of worry or doubt are not removed: *Getting a degree doesn't assure you a job.*

'see to it that... phrase to give your attention to sth in order to make sure that it is done: Can you see to it that the fax goes this afternoon?

enter verb

enter · go in · come in · set foot in/on sth
These words all mean to move into a place.

PATTERNS AND COLLOCATIONS
▶ to enter / go in / come in **by / through** sth
▶ to enter / go into / come into / set foot in a **room / building / country / town**

enter [I, T] (not usually used in the passive) (formal) to move into a place: I knocked and a bored voice said, 'Enter'. ◇ Enter Hamlet and three of the players (= used in the text of a play to say who should go onto the stage). ◇ He was refused permission to enter the country. ◇ Where did the bullet enter the body? **OPP** exit, leave → LEAVE 1, See also **entrance** → ARRIVAL 1, **entry** → ACCESS

,go 'in, ,go 'into sth phrasal verb to enter a place, especially a building or room: It's getting cold. Let's go in. ◇ They went into the kitchen. ◇ Don't go in there – it could be dangerous. ◇ Troops went in (= to a city or region) to restore order.

,come 'in, ,come 'into sth phrasal verb to enter a place, especially a building or room: Tell her to come in. ◇ I knocked at the door and he shouted, 'Come in!' ◇ Two more customers came into the shop. See also **come** → GO 2

> **NOTE** GO IN OR COME IN? Go in is used from the point of view of the person who is moving; **come in** is used from the point of view of sb who is already in the place that the person is moving to.

set 'foot in/on sth idiom to enter or visit a place: I vowed never to set foot in the place again. ◇ He was the first person to set foot on the moon.

entertain verb See the Topic Map for SPORT AND LEISURE on p.892

entertain · amuse
These words both mean to keep sb interested and happy by telling them things, performing for them or doing an activity with them.

PATTERNS AND COLLOCATIONS
▶ to entertain / amuse sb **with** sth
▶ to **keep sb** entertained / amused

entertain [T, I] to interest sb and make them enjoy themselves by telling them things or performing for them: He entertained us for hours with his stories and jokes. ◇ The aim of the series is both to entertain and inform. See also **entertainer** → ACTOR, **entertaining** → FUNNY

amuse [T] to make time pass pleasantly for sb/yourself by doing an activity: Playing with water can keep children amused for hours. ◇ The visitors **amused themselves** with sightseeing, painting and picnics. See also **amusing** → FUNNY

entertainment noun See the Topic Map for SPORT AND LEISURE on p.892

entertainment · fun · recreation · relaxation · play · pleasure · amusement
These are all words for things or activities used to entertain people when they are not working.

PATTERNS AND COLLOCATIONS
▶ to do sth **for** entertainment / fun / recreation / relaxation / pleasure / amusement
▶ to do sth **for sb's** entertainment / amusement
▶ **pure** entertainment / fun / pleasure
▶ to **provide** entertainment / fun / recreation / relaxation / amusement
▶ a **form of** entertainment / recreation / relaxation / amusement

entertainment [U] films, television, music, etc. used to entertain people: There are three bars, with **live entertainment** seven nights a week. ◇ There was no TV or radio so we had to make our own entertainment (for example by playing games). ◇ The stories will be judged purely on their **entertainment value**.

fun [U] (rather informal) behaviour or activities that are not serious but come from a sense of enjoyment: She's very lively and **full of fun**. ◇ It wasn't serious – it was all done **in fun**. ◇ Teaching isn't all **fun and games**, you know. ❶ Fun is often used in fixed phrases when sb is trying to defend an activity that other people might think is dangerous or silly: The lottery provides **harmless fun** for millions. ◇ (BrE) We didn't mean to hurt him. It was just **a bit of fun**. See also **have fun** → PLAY verb 1

recreation /ˌrekriˈeɪʃn/ [U] (*rather formal*) things people do for enjoyment when they are not working: *She cycles for recreation.* ◇ *His only form of recreation is playing cards.*

▸ **recreational** *adj.*: *recreational activities/facilities*

relaxation /ˌriːlækˈseɪʃn/ [U] (*rather formal*) things people do to rest and enjoy themselves when they are not working; the ability to relax: *I go hillwalking for relaxation.* ◇ *a chance for* **relaxation from** *work* ◇ *It's a good idea to learn some relaxation techniques.* See also **relax** → REST *verb*

> **NOTE** RECREATION OR RELAXATION? Both these words can be used for a wide range of activities, physical and mental, but **relaxation** is sometimes used for gentler activities than **recreation**: *I play the flute in a wind band for recreation.* ◇ *I listen to music for relaxation.* **Relaxation** is a skill as well as a pleasure, but **recreation** is not: ~~recreation techniques~~

play [U] things that people, especially children, do for enjoyment rather than as work: *the happy sounds of children at play* ◇ *the importance of learning through play* See also **play** → PLAY *verb* 1

pleasure [U] the activity of enjoying yourself, especially in contrast to working: *Are you in Paris* **on business or pleasure**? ◇ *I never* **mix business with pleasure**. **OPP** **business** → TASK

amusement [U] (*rather formal*) the fact of being entertained by sth: *What do you do for amusement around here?* ◇ *I write purely* **for my own amusement**. *I don't expect to make money out of it.*

envelope *noun*

envelope · file · folder · binder · clipboard · portfolio
These words all mean a flat container or cover for holding sheets of paper.

PATTERNS AND COLLOCATIONS
▸ **in** an envelope / a file / a folder / a binder / a portfolio
▸ a **plastic** envelope / folder / binder / clipboard / portfolio
▸ to **open** an envelope / a file / a folder / a binder
▸ an envelope / a file / a folder / a binder / a portfolio **containing** sth

envelope [C] a flat paper container used for sending letters in; a flat container made of plastic for keeping papers in: *The envelope was addressed in my mother's round handwriting.* ◇ *Each item was tagged and sealed in a plastic envelope.*

file [C] a box or folded piece of card, often with a wire or metal rod, used to store papers, letters and other documents in an ordered way, especially in an office: *A*

stack of files awaited me on my desk. ◇ (*BrE*) *a lever arch/ box file* ◇ (*AmE*) *a file folder* See also **file** → DOCUMENT *noun*, **file** → CLASSIFY *verb*

folder /ˈfəʊldə(r)/; *AmE* ˈfoʊld-/ [C] a cover for holding loose papers together, especially one made out of a piece of plastic or cardboard that is folded around the paper: *There were two new buff folders on my desk.*

binder /ˈbaɪndə(r)/ [C] a hard cover that keeps sheets of paper or magazines together by holding them along one edge: *Subscribe today and get a free binder with your first issue.* ◇ *a ring binder*

> **NOTE** FOLDER OR BINDER? **Folder** has a wider range of meaning than **binder**. A binder usually holds pieces of paper together as if they were pages in a book. Some kinds of folder can also be called binders, especially if they have a way of holding paper in place.

clipboard /ˈklɪpbɔːd; *AmE* -bɔːrd/ [C] a small board with a clip at the top for holding papers, used by sb who wants to write while standing or moving around: *Add your name to the list on the clipboard.*

portfolio /pɔːtˈfəʊliəʊ; *AmE* pɔːrtˈfoʊlioʊ/ (pl. **-os**) [C] a large thin flat case used for carrying and protecting drawings, photographs or documents: *Under his arm he carried a large portfolio of drawings.*

environment *noun*

environment · setting · surroundings · background · backdrop
These are all words for the type of place in which sb/sth exists or is situated.

PATTERNS AND COLLOCATIONS
▸ **in** an environment / a setting / surroundings
▸ **against** a / the background / backdrop (of sth)
▸ (a/an) **attractive/perfect** environment/setting/surroundings/ background / backdrop
▸ (a / an) **pleasant / idyllic** environment / setting / surroundings
▸ (a) **beautiful** setting / surroundings / backdrop
▸ a **dramatic** setting / background / backdrop
▸ (a) **peaceful** environment / setting / surroundings
▸ (a / an) **new / unfamiliar** environment / setting / surroundings
▸ sb / sth's **immediate** environment / surroundings
▸ (a) **rural** environment / setting / surroundings / backdrop
▸ the / sb's / sth's **natural** environment / setting / surroundings / backdrop
▸ to **provide / create** an environment / a setting / surroundings / a background / a backdrop
▸ to **adapt to / blend in with** your / the environment / surroundings

envelope

envelope   files   folders

clipboard   portfolio   binder

environment [C] the conditions in a place that affect the behaviour and development of sb/sth: *For many, school seemed to be a hostile environment.* ◇ *An unhappy **home environment** can affect children's behaviour.* ◇ *We aim to provide a pleasant **working environment**.* See also **milieu** → CONTEXT

setting [C] a place or situation of a particular type, in which sth happens or exists: *It was the perfect setting for a wonderful celebration.* ◇ *People behave differently in different social settings.*

surroundings [pl.] everything that is around or near sb/sth: *His paintings try to capture the beauty of the surroundings.* ◇ *She was not aware of her surroundings for a while.*

background [C, usually sing.] the things or area behind or around the main objects or people in a place or picture: *The mountains in the background were capped with snow.* ◇ *The areas of water stand out against the dark background.* **OPP the foreground** → LEAD 1

backdrop [C, usually sing.] (*written*) the scenery surrounding an event; the things or area behind the main objects in a place: *The events took place against the dramatic backdrop of the Atlas mountains.* ◇ *White walls provide the perfect backdrop for wooden furniture.*

equal *adj.*

equal · the same · identical · uniform · synonymous · homogeneous · indistinguishable · tantamount to sth · interchangeable
These words all describe things that are the same in size, quantity and value.

PATTERNS AND COLLOCATIONS
▸ equal / identical / tantamount **to** sth
▸ identical / synonymous / interchangeable **with** sth
▸ to **become** equal / synonymous / homogeneous / indistinguishable / interchangeable
▸ **exactly** equal / the same / identical / synonymous
▸ **almost** equal / the same / identical / uniform / synonymous / indistinguishable / interchangeable
▸ **apparently** the same / identical / uniform / homogeneous
▸ **roughly** equal / the same / synonymous

equal the same in size, quantity, value, etc. as sth else: *There is an equal number of boys and girls in the class.* ◇ *Take two pieces of wood of equal length.* ◇ *Cut it into four equal parts.* ◇ *One unit of alcohol is equal to half a pint of beer.* ◇ *The two books are more or less **equal in** length.* **OPP unequal** → DIFFERENT. See also **equal** → BE *linking verb*, **equal** → PEER *noun*
▸ **equally** *adv.*: *The money was divided equally among her four children.* ◇ *They share the housework equally.*

the same exactly like the one or ones referred to or mentioned: *I bought the same car as yours* (= another car of that type). ◇ *She was wearing the same dress that I had on.* ◇ *The same thing happened to me last week.* **OPP different** → DIFFERENT

identical /aɪˈdentɪkl/ similar in every detail: *I came to a row of identical houses.* ◇ *The two pictures are similar, although not identical.* ◇ *The number on the card should be identical with the one on the cheque book.*
▸ **identically** *adv.*: *The children were dressed identically.*

uniform the same in all parts: *The walls were a uniform grey.* ◇ *Growth has not been uniform across the country.* See also **uniformity** → SIMILARITY
▸ **uniformly** *adv.*: *The principles were applied uniformly across all the departments.* ◇ *The quality is uniformly high.*

synonymous /sɪˈnɒnɪməs; *AmE* -ˈnɑːn-/ (*rather formal*) (of words or expressions) having the same, or nearly the same, meaning; so closely connected with sth that the two things appear to be the same: *Few words are truly synonymous.* ◇ *Wealth is not necessarily synonymous with happiness.*

homogeneous /ˌhɒməˈdʒiːniəs; *AmE* ˌhoʊm-/ (*formal*) consisting of things or people that are all the same or all of the same type: *Old people are not a homogeneous group,*

as some people seem to think. ◇ *We no longer live in a culturally homogeneous society.* **OPP heterogeneous** → DIVERSE

indistinguishable /ˌɪndɪˈstɪŋɡwɪʃəbl/ (*rather formal*) if two things are **indistinguishable**, or one is **indistinguishable from** the other, it is impossible to see any differences between them: *The male of the species is almost **indistinguishable from** the female.* ◇ *The two parties' policies are almost indistinguishable.* **OPP distinguishable** → RECOGNIZABLE

ˈtantamount to sth *phrase* (*written*) having the same bad effect as sth else: *If he resigned it would be tantamount to admitting that he was guilty.* ❶ **Tantamount** typically combines with nouns such as *a crime, a declaration of war, cruelty, killing, stealing, treachery* and *treason*.

interchangeable /ˌɪntəˈtʃeɪndʒəbl; *AmE* -tərˈtʃ-/ (*rather formal*) that can be exchanged, especially without affecting the way in which sth works: *The two words are virtually interchangeable* (= have almost the same meaning). ◇ *The V8 engines are all interchangeable with each other.*
▸ **interchangeably** *adv.*: *These terms are used interchangeably.*

equip *verb*

1 equip yourself with a map
2 equip students for a career in nursing

1 equip · arm · stock · outfit · fit sb/sth out · provision · kit sb/sth out
These words all mean to provide sb/sth/yourself with the things that are needed for a particular purpose or activity.

PATTERNS AND COLLOCATIONS
▸ to equip sb/sth/arm sb/stock sth/fit sb/sth out/provision sth/ kit sb out **with** sth
▸ to equip / arm **yourself**
▸ to equip / outfit / fit out / provision a **ship**
▸ to equip / arm **soldiers**
▸ to equip / provision an **army**
▸ to be **well** equipped / armed / stocked / provisioned
▸ to be **fully** / **properly** / **poorly** equipped / armed / stocked

equip /ɪˈkwɪp/ (**-pp-**) [T] (*rather formal*) to provide sb/sth/ yourself with the things that are needed for a particular purpose or activity: *She got a bank loan to rent and equip a small workshop.* ◇ *He equipped himself with a street plan.* ◇ *We travelled in a specially equipped medical jeep.* ◇ *The centre is well **equipped for** canoeing and mountaineering.*

arm [T, I] to provide weapons for sb/yourself in order to fight a battle or war: *The crowd armed themselves with sticks and stones.* ◇ *The country was arming against the enemy.* See also **arms** → WEAPON

stock [T, often passive] to fill sth with food, books, plants, fish, etc: *The pond was well stocked with fish.* ◇ *The college has a well-stocked library.* ❶ **Stocked** and **well stocked** are typically used to describe a garden or pond, a shop or library, or a place in the home where food is kept, such as a fridge. See also **stock** → SUPPLY *noun*

outfit /ˈaʊtfɪt/ (**-tt-**) [T, often passive] (*especially AmE*) to supply sb/sth with equipment or clothes for a special purpose: *The ship was outfitted with a 12-bed hospital.* ◇ *They had enough swords and suits of armour to outfit an army.* ❶ **Outfit** is often used to talk about providing equipment for a ship, or for soldiers or sportspeople.

ˌfit sb/sth ˈout *phrasal verb* (**-tt-**) [often passive] (*BrE*) to supply sb/sth with all the equipment they need: *It was their job to fit out ships before long voyages.* ◇ *The room has been fitted out with a stove and a sink.* ❶ People usually **fit out** *rooms, houses* and *vehicles.*

provision /prəˈvɪʒn/ [T, often passive] (*formal*) to supply sb/sth with enough of sth, especially food, to last for a particular period of time: *The main business of the port is to provision passing ocean liners.* ❶ **Provision** is usually used to talk about supplying food for ships, but it can also be used to talk about supplying food to a city, an army or some other group of people. See also **provisions** → SUP-PLIES *noun*

,kit sb/sth 'out *phrasal verb* (-tt-) [usually passive] (*BrE, rather informal*) to give sb/sth the correct clothes and/or equipment for a particular activity: *They were all kitted out in brand new ski outfits. ◇ The London studio is lavishly kitted out with six cameras.* ❶ You **kit sb/sth out** *with* equipment, and you **kit sb out** *in* particular clothes.

2 See the Topic Map for EDUCATION on p.888

equip · fit · qualify
These words all mean to make sb/sth suitable for a particular job or role.

PATTERNS AND COLLOCATIONS
▸ to equip / fit / qualify sb **for** sth
▸ to be equipped / fitted / qualified **to do** sth
▸ to be **well** / **perfectly** equipped / fitted / qualified for sth
▸ to be **suitably** equipped / qualified for sth

equip (-pp-) [T] (*rather formal, especially business*) to prepare sb for an activity or task, especially by teaching them what they need to know: *The programme is designed to equip students for a career in nursing. ◇ Here he received the education that would equip him to take his place in society.* ❶ *Skills, professional training* and *education* are typical things that **equip** people for sth or to do sth.

fit (-tt-) [T, often passive] (*BrE*) to make sb/sth suitable for a particular job, role or purpose: *His experience fitted him perfectly for the job. ◇ She was well fitted to the role of tragic heroine. ◇ Natural selection will see to it that animals are well fitted to survive in their environment.* ❶ Things which typically **fit** sb for a particular job are *expertise, personality, background, experience, skills, life, education, manners* and *appearance*. In the context of jobs, American English would use **equip**; sb might be *suited to* a particular role; animals might be *well adapted to survive* in an environment. These words can all be used in British English as well.

qualify [T] (*rather formal*) to provide sb with the skills and knowledge they need to do sth: *The training should qualify you for a better job. ◇ The test qualifies you to drive heavy vehicles. ◇ Are you qualified to administer drugs?* ❶ **Qualify** is usually used to talk about the result of a particular *course, programme* or course of *training*, or a *test* or *examination*. Students usually receive a certificate to show that they are qualified to do a particular job.

equipment *noun* See also the entry for THING 3

equipment · material · gear · kit · apparatus · hardware · tackle
These are all words for the things that you need for a particular purpose or activity.

PATTERNS AND COLLOCATIONS
▸ **basic** equipment / materials / kit / apparatus / hardware
▸ **state-of-the-art** / **up-to-date** / **the latest** equipment / gear / kit / hardware
▸ **electronic** / **electrical** equipment / gear / apparatus / hardware
▸ **laboratory** equipment / apparatus / hardware
▸ to **have** the right equipment / materials / gear / kit / apparatus / hardware
▸ to **use** the equipment / materials / gear / kit / apparatus / hardware
▸ a **piece of** equipment / apparatus

equipment [U] the things that are needed for a particular purpose or activity: *We loaded the camping equipment into the car. ◇ The plane uses state-of-the-art navigation equipment.*

material [C, usually pl., U] things that are needed for a particular activity: *You have to buy your own art materials. ◇ Many household cleaning materials are highly toxic. ◇ We usually produce our own teaching material.*

NOTE **EQUIPMENT OR MATERIAL? Equipment** is usually solid things, especially large ones. **Materials** may be liquids, powders or books or tapes containing information, as well as small solid items.

gear /gɪə(r); *AmE* gɪr/ [U] the equipment or clothes needed for a particular activity: *Skiing gear can be expensive.* See also **gear** → CLOTHES

kit [C, U] a set of tools or equipment that you use for a particular purpose: *a first-aid kit ◇ a tool kit ◇ a wine-making kit ◇ They left most of their kit at the camp.* ❶ In British English, **kit** can also be the clothes that you wear for a particular activity.

apparatus /ˌæpəˈreɪtəs/ [U] the tools or other pieces of equipment that are needed for a particular activity or task: *The firefighters had to use breathing apparatus. ◇ Science departments say they are lacking basic apparatus.* ❶ **Apparatus** is used especially for scientific, medical or technical purposes.

hardware /ˈhɑːdweə(r); *AmE* ˈhɑːrdwer/ [U] tools and equipment that are used in the house and garden: *a hardware store* ❶ **Hardware** in this meaning is usually used in relation to shops that buy and sell such equipment. In technical language **hardware** is also weapons and other military equipment and vehicles: (*technical*) *The cargo consisted entirely of military hardware – rifles, machine guns, hand grenades and rockets.*

tackle [U] the equipment used to do a particular sport or activity, especially fishing: *You can hire bait and fishing tackle from the outdoor centre.*

equivalent *noun*

equivalent · counterpart · parallel · your opposite number
These are all words for a person or thing that is the same or similar, or that has the same function, as sb/sth else in a different place or situation.

PATTERNS AND COLLOCATIONS
▸ an equivalent / a counterpart / a parallel **to** sb / sth
▸ the / your **American** / **British** / **Chinese**, etc. equivalent / counterpart / opposite number
▸ a **modern** / **direct** equivalent / counterpart / parallel
▸ to **have** an equivalent / a counterpart / a parallel / an opposite number
▸ to **meet** your counterpart / opposite number

equivalent /ɪˈkwɪvələnt/ [C] a thing, amount, word, etc. that is equal in value, amount, meaning or importance to sth else: *Send $20 or the equivalent in your own currency. ◇ The 'Gymnasium' is the closest equivalent to the grammar school in England. ◇ Is there a French word that is the exact equivalent of the English word 'home'?* See also **equivalence** → SIMILARITY

counterpart /ˈkaʊntəpɑːt; *AmE* -tərpɑːrt/ [C] (*rather formal*) a person or thing that has the same position or function as sb/sth else in a different place or situation: *The Foreign Minister held talks with his Chinese counterpart. ◇ The women's shoe, like its male counterpart, is specifically designed for the serious tennis player.* ❶ **Counterpart** is less formal in American English.

parallel [C, U] (*especially written*) a person, situation, event, etc. that is very similar to another, especially one in a different place or time: *These ideas have parallels in Freud's thought too. ◇ This is an achievement without parallel in modern times. ◇ This tradition has no parallel in our culture.* See also **parallel** → SIMILARITY
▸ **parallel** *adj.*: *Two poisonings have been reported recently in London and now there has been a parallel case in the Netherlands.*

your ,opposite 'number *idiom* (*rather informal, especially BrE*) a person who does the same job as you in another organization: *The Foreign Secretary is currently having talks with his opposite number in the White House.* ❶ In more formal situations, use **counterpart** to talk about this person.

equivalent *adj.* See also the entry for RELATIVE

equivalent · comparable · corresponding · matching · analogous
These words all describe things being equal in value, amount, meaning, importance, etc.

PATTERNS AND COLLOCATIONS
▸ equivalent / comparable / corresponding / analogous **to** sth
▸ comparable / analogous **with** sth
▸ equivalent / comparable **in** size, amount, etc.
▸ an equivalent / a comparable / a corresponding **increase**
▸ an equivalent / a comparable **size / amount / proportion**
▸ **broadly / roughly / directly** equivalent / comparable / analogous
▸ **exactly** equivalent / comparable / matching / analogous
▸ **closely** equivalent / comparable / analogous

equivalent /ɪˈkwɪvələnt/ (*rather formal*) equal in value, amount, meaning or importance: *Eight kilometres is roughly equivalent to five miles.* ◊ *You'll need 250 grams or an equivalent amount in ounces.* ◊ *The new regulation was seen as equivalent to censorship.* See also **equivalence** → SIMILARITY

comparable /ˈkɒmpərəbl; *AmE* ˈkɑːm-/ (*rather formal*) similar to another thing, situation or person and able to be compared with it/them: *A comparable house in the south of the city would cost twice as much.* ◊ *Inflation is now at a rate comparable with that in other European countries.* ◊ *The situation in the US is not directly comparable to that in the UK.* ❶ **Comparable** is less formal in American English. See also **compare** → COMPARE 2, **comparison** → COMPARISON

corresponding (*rather formal*) equal to or connected with sth that you have just mentioned: *A change in the money supply brings a corresponding change in expenditure.* ◊ *Profits have risen by 15 per cent compared with the corresponding period last year.* ◊ *Give each picture a number corresponding to its position on the page.* See also **correspond** → MATCH *verb* 1, **correspondence** → SIMILARITY

▸ **correspondingly** *adv.*: *a period of high demand and correspondingly high prices*

matching [only before noun] (of clothes, fabric or objects) having the same colour, pattern or style and therefore looking attractive together: *We got a pine table with four matching chairs for only £240.* See also **match** → MATCH *verb* 2

analogous /əˈnæləgəs/ (*formal*) similar to another thing or situation in some way and able to be compared to it: *Sleep has often been thought of as being in some way analogous to death.* See also **analogy** → COMPARISON

NOTE COMPARABLE OR ANALOGOUS? Things that are **comparable** can be compared because they are the same type of thing: you compare them to see how they are similar and how they are different. Things that are **analogous** are usually different types of thing that are similar in one particular way: you compare one to the other to suggest a way in which they are similar.

eradicate *verb* See also the entries for DESTROY and REMOVE 1

eradicate · stamp sth out · weed sb/sth out · root sb/sth out
These words all mean to destroy or get rid of sb/sth bad.

PATTERNS AND COLLOCATIONS
▸ to eradicate / weed out sth **from** sth
▸ to eradicate / stamp out / root out **corruption / drug abuse**
▸ to eradicate / stamp out a **disease**
▸ to eradicate / root out **inefficiency**

eradicate /ɪˈrædɪkeɪt/ [T] (*rather formal*) to destroy or get rid of sth completely, especially sth bad: *Polio has been virtually eradicated in Brazil.* ◊ *We are determined to eradicate racism from our sport.*

,stamp sth 'out *phrasal verb* to get rid of sth that is bad, unpleasant or dangerous, especially by using force or a lot of effort: *We've got to stamp out this nonsense before it goes any further.* ◊ *The harder the police try to stamp out drug abuse the more it grows.*

,weed sb/sth 'out *phrasal verb* to remove or get rid of people or things from a group because they are not wanted or are less good than the rest: *Most candidates get weeded out before reaching the interview stage.* ◊ *It's my job to weed out the false claims from the genuine ones.*

,root sb/sth 'out *phrasal verb* to find the person or thing that is causing a problem and remove or get rid of them: *The secret agency was charged with rooting out subversives.* ◊ *They have vowed to root out corruption within the police force.*

escape *verb*

escape · get away · elude · evade · lose
These words all mean to get away from sb who is chasing you or a dangerous situation that threatens you.

PATTERNS AND COLLOCATIONS
▸ to escape / get away **from** sb / sth
▸ to escape / evade **being** captured, hit, killed, etc.
▸ to escape / get away from / elude / evade / lose your **pursuers**
▸ to escape / elude / evade **capture / detection / the police**
▸ to escape / evade **arrest**
▸ to **manage to** escape sb / get away from sb / elude sb / evade sb

escape [I, T, no passive] to get away from or avoid an unpleasant or dangerous situation or event; to suffer no harm or less harm than you would expect: *She managed to escape from the burning car.* ◊ (*figurative*) *As a child he would often **escape into** a dream world of his own.* ◊ ***There was no escaping** the fact that he was overweight.* ◊ *The police will not escape criticism in this affair.* ◊ *She managed to escape the fate of the other rebels.* ◊ *The pilot **escaped death** by seconds.* ◊ *He **narrowly escaped** being killed.* ◊ *She only just **escaped with** her life.* ◊ *Both drivers **escaped unhurt**.* ❶ You can **escape** being caught or punished: *to escape detection/capture/arrest/justice/prosecution/conviction/punishment/prison.* Note that to *escape prison* means to avoid being sent to prison; to get out of prison once you have been sent there is to *escape from prison.* You can also **escape** being killed or injured: *to escape death/assassination/the massacre/drowning/injury/being hit/the fighting.* You can **escape** being blamed for sth: *to escape blame/censure/criticism/sb's wrath* or you can *escape your fate* or *destiny* or other serious problems such as *bankruptcy* or a *recession.* People are often *lucky* to escape sth, especially if they *only just* or *narrowly* escape.

▸ **escape** *noun* [C, U]: *I had a **narrow escape** (= I was lucky to have escaped).* ◊ *There was no hope of escape from her disastrous marriage.* ◊ *As soon as he turned his back, she would **make her escape**.*

,get a'way *phrasal verb* to escape from a person, place or situation: *He felt that he had to get away from home, away from his parents and their efforts to rule his life.* ◊ *You'd better get away — the soldiers are coming.*

▸ **getaway** *noun* [C, usually sing.]: *We'll have to **make a quick getaway**.* ◊ *a getaway car*

elude /iˈluːd/ [T] (*rather formal*) to avoid or escape from sb/sth, especially in a clever way: *The two men managed to elude the police for six weeks.* ◊ *How did the killer elude detection for so long?*

evade /ɪˈveɪd/ [T] (*rather formal*) to avoid or escape from sb/sth: *For two weeks they evaded the press.* ◊ *He managed to evade capture.*

NOTE ELUDE OR EVADE? In many cases you can use either word: *to elude/evade detection/capture/the police/your pursuers.* **Elude** emphasizes the skill or cleverness required to avoid being caught; **evade** simply emphasizes the fact of not being caught.

lose [T] to escape from sb/sth who is following or chasing you: *We managed to lose our pursuers in the darkness.*

essential *adj.* See also the entries for IMPORTANT and NECESSARY

essential · vital · crucial · critical · decisive · indispensable · imperative · pivotal · of the essence
These words all describe sb/sth that is extremely important and completely necessary because a particular situation or activity depends on them.

PATTERNS AND COLLOCATIONS
▸ essential / vital / crucial / critical / decisive / indispensable / imperative / of the essence **for** sth
▸ essential / vital / crucial / critical / indispensable / pivotal **to** sth
▸ to be essential / vital / crucial / critical / imperative **that...**
▸ to be essential / vital / crucial / critical / imperative **to do** sth
▸ an essential / a vital / a crucial / a critical / a decisive / an indispensable / a pivotal **part / factor**
▸ an essential / a vital / a crucial / a critical / an indispensable **ingredient / tool**
▸ an essential / a vital / a crucial / a critical **component**
▸ essential / vital / crucial **services**
▸ the crucial / critical / decisive / pivotal **moment**
▸ to **play** an essential / a vital / a crucial / a critical / a decisive / a pivotal **part / role** in sth
▸ of vital / crucial / critical / decisive **importance**
▸ **absolutely** essential / vital / crucial / critical / decisive / indispensable / imperative / pivotal
▸ **quite** essential / vital / crucial / critical / decisive / indispensable

essential extremely important and completely necessary, because without it sth cannot exist, be made or be successful: *Experience is essential for this job.* ◇ *Money is not essential to happiness.* ◇ *It is essential that you have some experience.* ◇ *It is essential to keep the two groups separate.* ◇ *The museum is closed while essential repairs are being carried out.* **OPP inessential** ❶ **Inessential** things are not necessary: *inessential luxuries* See also **essential** → NEED *noun*

vital /'vaɪtl/ essential: *Bean sprouts contain many of the vitamins that are vital for health.* ◇ *Good financial accounts are vital to the success of any enterprise.* ◇ *It is vital that you keep accurate records when you are self-employed.* ◇ *The police play a vital role in our society.*
▸ **vitally** *adv.*: *Education is **vitally important** for the country's future.*

NOTE ESSENTIAL OR **VITAL?** There is no real difference in meaning between these words and they can be used with the same range of nouns and structures. However, there can be a slight difference in tone. **Essential** is used to state a fact or opinion with authority. **Vital** is often used when there is some anxiety felt about sth, or a need to persuade sb that a fact or opinion is true, right or important. **Vital** is less often used in negative statements: *It was vital to show that he was not afraid.* ◇ *Money is not vital to happiness.*

crucial /'kruːʃl/ extremely important because a particular situation or activity depends on it: *Winning this contract is absolutely crucial to our long term success.* ◇ *It is crucial that we get this right.* ◇ *He wasn't there at the crucial moment* (= when he was needed most).
▸ **crucially** *adv.*: *These things are all crucially important.*
critical /'krɪtɪkl/ crucial: *Price and availability are the critical factors that will determine product success.* ◇ *If the temperature drops those critical two degrees, the engine will stop functioning.*
▸ **critically** *adv.*: *The next few days will be critically important to the President's election chances.*

NOTE CRUCIAL OR **CRITICAL?** There is no real difference in meaning between these words and they can be used with the same range of nouns and structures. However, there is sometimes a slight difference in context.

Critical is often used in technical matters of business or science; **crucial** is often used to talk about matters that may cause anxiety or other emotions.

decisive /dɪ'saɪsɪv/ of the greatest importance in affecting the final result of a particular situation: *Gettysburg was the decisive battle of the Civil War.* ◇ *Signing the treaty was a decisive step* (= an important action that will change a situation) *towards a cleaner environment.* ❶ **Decisive** is NOT used simply to mean 'extremely important': *Reducing levels of carbon dioxide in the atmosphere is of decisive importance.* It is used when you are making a judgement that sb/sth was or will be the most important fact affecting the result of a particular past or future situation: *Morrison scored the decisive goal in the 75th minute of the game.*
▸ **decisively** *adv.*: *The governing party is expected to win decisively in the elections.*
indispensable /ˌɪndɪ'spensəbl/ essential; too important to be without: *Cars have become an indispensable part of our lives.* ◇ *She made herself virtually indispensable to the department.* **OPP dispensable** ❶ **Dispensable** things are not necessary and can be got rid of: *They looked on music and art lessons as dispensable.*
imperative /ɪm'perətɪv/ [not usually before noun] (*formal*) extremely important and needing immediate attention or action: *It is absolutely imperative that we finish by next week.*
pivotal /'pɪvətl/ (*rather formal, especially written*) extremely important because a particular situation or activity depends on it: *The Foreign Secretary has played a pivotal role in European affairs.* ◇ *Accountancy, law and economics are pivotal to a successful career in any financial services area.* ❶ **Pivotal** is used especially to describe the part that sb/sth plays in a particular situation; it is NOT used to describe items or actions that are just extremely important: *pivotal services/supplies/repairs* ◇ *It is pivotal that we get this right.*
of the 'essence *phrase* (*rather informal*) essential: *In this situation time is of the essence* (= we must do things as quickly as possible). ◇ *Speed is of the essence when transporting casualties to hospital.*

establish *verb* See also the entry for BEGIN

establish · set sth up · form · found
These words all mean to start or create an organization or system.

PATTERNS AND COLLOCATIONS
▸ to establish / set up / form / found a / an **group / society / club / party / company / institute / movement / colony / republic**
▸ to establish / set up / form a / an **relationship / partnership / alliance / government / committee / team / network / database**
▸ to establish / set up / found a **business / firm / programme**
▸ to establish / set up a / an **fund / initiative / project / scheme / procedure / monopoly / regime / monarchy**
▸ to establish / found a / an **dynasty / empire / church**

establish [T] (*rather formal, especially written*) to start or create sth, such as an organization or system, that is meant to last for a long time; to start having a relationship, especially a formal one, with another person, group or country: *The new treaty establishes a free trade zone.* ◇ *Let's establish some ground rules.* ◇ *The school has established a successful relationship with the local community.* See also **establishment** → INTRODUCTION 1
ˌset sth 'up *phrasal verb* to start or create sth, such as an organization or system: *I'm planning to set up my own business.* ◇ *A fund will be set up for the dead men's families.* ◇ *The company has set up its European headquarters in the UK.* ❶ **Set sth up** is often used in business contexts, to talk about starting a business or making financial arrangements: *to set up a business/a company/a firm/a fund/a project/a scheme/a venture/an initiative/a monopoly/a headquarters/a base*

form [T, I] to start or create sth such as an organization or system; to come together in a group of this kind: *They hope to form the new government.* ◇ *We are a newly-formed political party.* ◇ *The band formed in 2005.* ❶ **Form** is often used in political contexts: *to form a government/an administration/a cabinet/a coalition/a committee/a council/an assembly/a party/a league/an alliance/a trade union/a syndicate.* **Form** is also the most common verb used to talk about starting a band (= a group of musicians). See also **formation** → INTRODUCTION 1

found [T] (*especially written*) to start or create sth such as an organization or institution, especially by providing money; to be the first to start building and living in a town or country: *He founded the company 20 years ago.* ◇ *Her family founded the college in 1895.* ◇ *The town was founded by English settlers in 1790.* ❶ Collocates of **found** include *institute, society, company, firm, town, city, church, monastery* and *convent.* See also **foundation** → INTRODUCTION 1

estate *noun*

estate · development · project
These words all mean a group of houses or factories built together in a planned way.

PATTERNS AND COLLOCATIONS
▶ a **housing** estate / development / project
▶ a / an **industrial** / **commercial** estate / development

estate /ɪˈsteɪt/ [C] (*BrE*) an area of land with a lot of houses or factories of the same type on it: *We're planning to move the business to an industrial estate on the outskirts of the town.* ◇ *There are around six million people living on council estates* (= an area owned by the local council with cheaply rented houses or flats) *in Britain.* ❶ In American English **estate** refers to the grounds and buildings of a large country home. Use **development**.

development [C] a piece of land with new buildings on it: *The protesters oppose plans to build a commercial development on the site.* ❶ In American English, **development** is not just used to talk about new buildings; it is used in the same way as **estate** in British English: *a luxury residential development* ◇ *We live in a new housing development.*

project (also **'housing project**) [C] (*AmE*) a group of apartments built for poor families, usually with government money: *She lives in a housing project on the edge of town.* ◇ *Going into the projects* (= a poor district with high-rise apartments) *alone can be dangerous.*

estimate *noun*

estimate · count · calculation · tally · reckoning
These are all words for ways of using numbers to guess or find out an amount or total.

PATTERNS AND COLLOCATIONS
▶ a / an **accurate** / **precise** estimate / count / calculation
▶ a **rough** / **quick** / **approximate** estimate / count / calculation
▶ to **make** an estimate / a calculation
▶ to **do** a count / calculation
▶ to **keep** a count / tally **of** sth
▶ **By** my / his, etc. estimate / calculations / reckoning...

estimate [C] a judgement that you make about the size, amount, cost, etc. of sth, without having the exact details or figures: *I can give you a rough estimate of the amount of wood you will need.* ◇ *a ballpark estimate* (= an approximate estimate) ◇ *These are the official government estimates of traffic growth over the next decade.* ◇ *At least 5 000 people were killed, and that's a conservative estimate* (= the real figure will be higher).

count [C, usually sing.] an act of counting to find the total number of sth; the total number that you find; an act of saying numbers in order beginning with 1: *If the election result is close, there will be a second count.* ◇ (*BrE*) *At the last count she had 43 cats!* ◇ (*AmE*) *At last count she had 43 cats!* ◇ *The body count* (= the total number of people who have died) *stands at 24.* ◇ *I've lost count of the* (= forgotten how many) *times I've heard that joke.* ◇ *On the count of three, take one step forward.* See also **count** → COUNT *verb*

calculation [C, U] the act or process of using numbers to find out an amount: *She made a rough calculation in her head.* ◇ *By my calculations, we made a profit of £20 000 last year.* ◇ *Our guess was confirmed by calculation.* See also **calculate** → CALCULATE

> **NOTE** **COUNT** OR **CALCULATION?** **Count** refers to adding numbers together; **calculation** often refers to other mathematical functions such as multiplying and dividing numbers.

tally [C] a record of the number or amount of sth, especially one that you can keep adding to: *Keep a tally of how much you spend while you're away.* ◇ *She scored four more points, taking her tally to 15.* See also **tally** → COUNT *verb*

reckoning [U, C] the act of using numbers to find out an amount, especially in a way that is not very exact: *By my reckoning you still owe me £5.*

estimate *verb* See also the entries for CALCULATE and COUNT

estimate · guess · judge · reckon · calculate · gauge · figure · extrapolate
These words all mean to form an idea of the cost, size, value, etc. of sth but without calculating it exactly.

PATTERNS AND COLLOCATIONS
▶ to estimate / guess / judge / reckon / calculate / gauge / extrapolate sth **from** sth
▶ to estimate / reckon / calculate sth **at** sth
▶ to estimate / guess / judge / reckon / calculate / figure / extrapolate **that...**
▶ to estimate / guess / judge / figure / calculate / gauge **how much** / **how many** / **how far**, etc.
▶ to estimate / guess / judge / reckon / calculate / gauge / figure sth **to be sth**
▶ to estimate / guess / judge / calculate / gauge the **amount** / **value** / **size** / **distance**
▶ to estimate / guess / calculate sb / sth's **age**
▶ to estimate / judge / gauge the **depth**

estimate [T, often passive] (*rather formal*) to form an idea of the likely cost, size, value, etc. of sth, but without calculating it exactly: *Police estimated the size of the crowd at 50 000.* ◇ *Estimate the time it will take to complete each section.* ◇ *The satellite will cost an estimated $500m.* ◇ *It is estimated that the project will last about four years.* See also **estimate** → VALUATION *noun*

guess [T] to find the right answer to a question or the truth about sth without knowing all the facts: *She guessed the answer straight away.* ◇ *I guessed, rightly, that the keys would be under the doormat.* ◇ *You'll never guess where they've gone.* See also **guess** → SPECULATION *noun*

judge [T] to estimate the size, amount, etc. of sth without measuring it exactly: *Young children are unable to judge the speed of traffic.* ◇ *I judged him to be about 50.*

> **NOTE** **ESTIMATE** OR **JUDGE?** **Estimate** is used especially to talk about things such as *costs*, which you would have to calculate to know exactly. **Judge** is used more for things such as *distances, depths* and *speeds*, which you would have to measure to know exactly. People often use **estimate** future costs and lengths of time which cannot be calculated exactly, by thinking carefully about what is likely, given the information that they have. People often have to **judge** distances and speeds quickly, not by thinking carefully about all the available information, but by using their past experience as a guide.

reckon [T, often passive] to estimate an amount or time approximately: *The age of the earth is reckoned to be about 4 600 million years.* ◇ *They reckon (that) their profits were* down by 30%. ◇ *The trip was reckoned to take over two days.* ❶ An amount or time that is **reckoned** may be more approximate than one that has been **estimated**.

calculate [T] to guess sth or form an opinion by using all the information available: *It's impossible to calculate the extent of his influence on her.* ◇ *Environmentalists calculate that hundreds of plant species may be affected.* See also **calculate** → CALCULATE

gauge (*AmE* also **gage**) /geɪdʒ/ [T] (*rather formal*) to estimate the level or amount of sth approximately: *We were able to gauge the strength of the wind from the movement of the trees.* See also **gauge** → CRITERION *noun*

figure [T] (*especially AmE, rather informal*) to estimate the amount, cost or age of sb/sth, especially approximately: *If we can figure roughly how much it will cost, we can decide what to do.* ❶ In American English **figure** can also be used to talk about calculating sth exactly. See also **figure** → CALCULATE

extrapolate /ɪkˈstræpəleɪt/ [I, T] (*formal*) to estimate sth or form an opinion about sth, using the facts that you have now and that are valid for one situation and supposing that they will be valid for the new one: *The figures were obtained by extrapolating from past trends.* ◇ *These results cannot be **extrapolated to** other patient groups.*
▸ **extrapolation** *noun* [U, C]: *Their age can be determined by extrapolation from their growth rate.*

evacuate *verb* See also the entries for EXCLUDE 2 and EXPEL

evacuate · throw sb out · evict · clear · eject · kick sb out · chuck sb out · move sb on
These words all mean to force sb to leave a place.

PATTERNS AND COLLOCATIONS
▸ to evacuate / evict / eject sb **from** a place
▸ to throw / kick / chuck sb **out of** a place
▸ to evacuate / evict / eject a **person**
▸ to evacuate / clear a **place** / **building**
▸ to evacuate / throw sb out of / evict sb from a **house**
▸ the **police** evacuate / evict sb from / clear / eject sb from / move sb on from a place
▸ a **landlord** throws sb out / evicts sb / ejects sb / kicks sb out / chucks sb out

evacuate /ɪˈvækjueɪt/ [T] (*rather formal*) to move people from a place of danger to a safer place: *Children were evacuated from London to escape the bombing.* ◇ *Police evacuated nearby buildings.* ❶ Note that you can **evacuate** people (children, families, refugees, civilians, troops or forces) or a place (a building, an area, a school). See also **evacuee** → REFUGEE
▸ **evacuation** *noun* [U, C]: *the emergency evacuation of thousands of people after the earthquake*

throw sb ˈout *phrasal verb* (*rather informal*) to force sb to leave a place or organization, especially so they cannot come back: *She threw him out and had the locks changed.* ◇ *He's been thrown out of every art college in London.*

evict /ɪˈvɪkt/ [T] to force sb to leave a house or land, especially when you have the legal right to do so: *A number of tenants have been evicted for not paying the rent.* ◇ *Police had to evict demonstrators from the building.*
▸ **eviction** *noun* [U, C]: *to face eviction from your home*

clear [T] to make a place empty of people: *Police were still clearing the streets when the bomb went off.*

eject /iˈdʒekt/ [T] (*formal*) to force sb to leave a place: *Angry supporters were forcibly ejected from the premises.*

kick sb ˈout *phrasal verb* (*informal*) to throw sb out: *The Football League should have kicked him out of the club.*

chuck sb ˈout *phrasal verb* (*especially BrE, informal*) to throw sb out: *You can't just chuck him out — he's got nowhere to go.*

NOTE KICK SB OUT OR CHUCK SB OUT? There is very little difference in meaning or use between these words. **Kick sb out** can sometimes suggest that you think the person deserves it; **chuck sb out** is more often used when you feel some sympathy for the person.

move sb ˈon *phrasal verb* (*especially BrE*) (of the police or sb in authority) to order sb to move away from a place, for example the scene of an accident; to order sb to move away from somewhere because they do not have the legal right to be there: *The policeman waved his hand and moved us on.* ◇ *Travellers are going to court to challenge the council's right to move them on.*

evade *verb*

evade · get out of sth · dodge · duck · sidestep · wriggle out of sth · fudge · fend sb/sth off · skirt
These words all mean to try to avoid doing sth that you do not want to do.

PATTERNS AND COLLOCATIONS
▸ to get / duck / wriggle **out of** sth
▸ to evade / get out of / dodge / wriggle out of **doing sth**
▸ to evade / dodge / duck / wriggle out of your **responsibilities**
▸ to evade / dodge / duck / sidestep / fudge / skirt the **issue**
▸ to evade / dodge / duck / sidestep / fend off / skirt round a **question**
▸ to evade / dodge **taxes**

evade /ɪˈveɪd/ [T] (*rather formal*) to avoid doing sth, especially sth that legally or morally you should do; to avoid dealing with or talking about a subject: *She is trying to evade all responsibility for her actions.* ◇ *There is no point in evading the issue any longer.* ❶ The most frequent collocates of **evade** are *taxes, responsibility/responsibilities* and *the issue.*
▸ **evasion** /ɪˈveɪʒn/ *noun* [U, C]: *She's been charged with tax evasion.* ◇ *His speech was full of evasions and half-truths.*

get ˈout of sth *phrasal verb* (*rather informal*) to avoid a difficult or unpleasant duty or responsibility: *We promised we'd go — we can't get out of it now.* ◇ *I wish I could get out of going to that meeting.* See also **shirk** → MISS 1

dodge [T] (*rather informal, disapproving, journalism*) to avoid paying taxes or doing military service, especially in a dishonest way; to avoid dealing with or talking about a subject: *She tried to dodge paying her taxes.* ◇ *Claims that he **dodged the draft** for the Vietnam War could damage his election chances.*

duck [I, T] (*rather informal, disapproving*) to avoid a difficult or unpleasant duty or responsibility: *It's his turn to cook dinner, but I bet he'll try to duck out of it.* ◇ *The government is ducking the issue.*

NOTE GET OUT OF STH OR DUCK? **Duck** is more disapproving than **get out of sth**: you might admit to wanting to **get out of sth** yourself; you would accuse sb else of trying to **duck** sth.

sidestep /ˈsaɪdstep/ (**-pp-**) [T] to avoid answering a question or dealing with a problem: *Did you notice how she neatly sidestepped the question?*

wriggle out of sth *phrasal verb* (*informal, disapproving*) to avoid doing sth that you should do or admitting responsibility for sth, especially by thinking of clever excuses: *She tried to wriggle out of it by saying that she had an appointment elsewhere.* ◇ *He tried desperately to wriggle out of responsibility for the crash.*

fudge [T] (*disapproving*) to avoid giving clear and accurate information, or a clear answer: *I asked how long he was staying, but he fudged the answer.* ◇ *Politicians are often very clever at fudging the issue.*

fend sb/sth ˈoff *phrasal verb* to protect yourself from difficult questions or criticisms, especially by avoiding them: *The Prime Minister fended off three challenges to her leadership.*

skirt [T] to avoid talking about a subject, especially because it is difficult or embarrassing: *He carefully skirted the issue of where they would live.* ◊ *She tactfully **skirted around** the subject of money.* ❶ **Skirt** is used to talk about careful behaviour, intended to avoid embarrassment, rather than behaviour that is dishonest or immoral.

event *noun*

1 a sequence of events
2 a social event

---

1 event · affair · incident · experience · phenomenon · episode · business · development · occurrence · proceedings · eventuality
These are all words for sth which happens.

PATTERNS AND COLLOCATIONS

▸ the **whole** event / affair / incident / experience / phenomenon / episode / business / proceedings
▸ (a) **strange** event / affair / incident / experience / phenomenon / development / occurrence
▸ (a) **terrible** event / affair / incident / experience / business
▸ (a) **dramatic** event / incident / experience / episode / development
▸ an **enjoyable** event / affair / experience
▸ (an) **everyday** event / affair / incident / experience / occurrence
▸ an **isolated** event / incident / experience / phenomenon / episode / occurrence
▸ a **rare / common** event / experience / phenomenon / occurrence
▸ to **witness** an event / an incident / a phenomenon / an episode
▸ an event / an incident / an experience / a phenomenon / an episode **occurs**
▸ an event / an incident / an experience / a phenomenon / an episode / proceedings **takes place / take place**

event [C] a thing that happens, especially sth important: *The election was the main event of 2005.* ◊ *In the light of later events the decision was proved to be right.* ◊ *The decisions we take now may influence the **course of events** (= the way things happen) in the future.* ◊ *Everyone was frightened by the strange **sequence of events**.*
affair [C, usually sing.] an event that people are talking about or describing in a particular way: *I ended up disillusioned and bitter about the whole affair.* ◊ *The debate was a pretty disappointing affair.* ◊ *She wanted the celebration to be a simple family affair.* ❶ **Affairs** [pl.] are events of public interest or political importance: *world / international / business affairs* ◊ *He's an expert on **foreign affairs**.* ◊ *He believed in a strict separation of the **affairs of state** and those of the church.* ◊ *The talk ranged over a variety of topics, from sport to **current affairs** (= events of political or social importance that are happening now).*
incident /ˈɪnsɪdənt/ [C, U] (*rather formal*) something that happens, especially sth unusual or unpleasant; a serious or violent event, such as a crime, accident or attack: *His bad behaviour was just an isolated incident.* ◊ *There was a shooting incident near here last night.* ◊ *The demonstration passed off **without incident**.*
experience [C] an event or activity that affects you in some way: *It was her first experience of living alone.* ◊ *Living in Africa was very different from home and **quite an experience** (= unusual for us).* ◊ *I had a bad experience with fireworks once.* ◊ *He seems to have had some sort of religious experience.* See also **experience** → KNOWLEDGE *noun*, **experience** → LIFE *noun* 3, **experience** → HAVE *verb* 3
phenomenon /fəˈnɒmɪnən; *AmE* fəˈnɑːm-/ (pl. **phenomena**) [C] a fact or event in nature or society, especially one that is not fully understood: *natural / cultural / social phenomena* ◊ *This kind of crime is a phenomenon of the modern age .*
episode /ˈepɪsəʊd; *AmE* -soʊd/ [C] an event, situation or period of time in sb's life or a story that is important or interesting in some way: *I'd like to try and forget the whole episode.* ◊ *It turned out to be one of the funniest episodes in the novel.*

business (usually used with an adjective) [sing.] (*rather informal, especially spoken*) a matter, event or situation: *I found the whole business very depressing.* ◊ *That plane crash was a terrible business.* ◊ *The business of the missing tickets hasn't been sorted out.*
development [C] a new event or stage that is likely to affect what happens in a continuing situation: *the latest developments in the war* ◊ *Are there any further developments in the investigation?* See also **develop** → BREAK OUT
occurrence /əˈkʌrəns; *AmE* əˈkɜːr-/ [C] (*formal*) something that happens or exists: *Vandalism has become a regular occurrence in recent times.* ◊ *The program counts the number of occurrences of any word or group of words, within the text.* See also **occur** → HAPPEN
proceedings /prəˈsiːdɪŋz/ [pl.] an event or series of actions: *The Mayor will **open the proceedings** at the City Hall tomorrow.* ◊ *We watched the proceedings from the balcony.*
eventuality /ɪˌventʃuˈæləti/ [C] (*formal*) something that may possibly happen, especially sth unpleasant: *We were prepared for every eventuality.* ◊ *This strategy will allow us to cope with all eventualities which may arise.*

---

2 See the Topic Map for SPORT AND LEISURE on p.892, See also PARTY 2

event · celebration · occasion · function · reception · reunion · festivities · get-together
These are all words for a public or social situation where people are invited to a place for a particular reason.

PATTERNS AND COLLOCATIONS

▸ (a) **special** event / celebration / occasion / reception / reunion / festivities
▸ (a) **family** event / celebration / occasion / reunion / festivities / get-together
▸ a **social** event / occasion / function
▸ a **school** event / function / reunion
▸ (a) **wedding** celebrations / reception
▸ **Christmas** celebrations / festivities
▸ an **annual** event / celebration / reunion / get-together
▸ an event / celebrations / a function / a reception / a reunion / festivities **is / are held**
▸ an event / celebrations / a reception / a reunion / festivities **takes place / take place**

event [C] a time when lots of people are invited to a particular place in order to spend time together having fun or taking part in an activity: *Details of meetings and social events are sent out to all club members.* ◊ *The hospital is planning a major fund-raising event for June.*
celebration [C, usually pl.] a special event that people organize in order to celebrate sth: *They are already preparing for his 80th birthday celebrations in October.* ◊ *The celebrations continued with a cabaret dinner.* See also **celebrate, celebration** → PLAY *verb* 1
▸ **celebrate** *verb* [I, T]: *Jake's passed his exams. We're going out to celebrate.* ◊ *How do people celebrate New Year in your country?*
occasion [C] a special event, ceremony or celebration: *Turn every meal into a special occasion.* ◊ *Their wedding turned out to be quite an occasion.* ◊ *They **marked the occasion** (= celebrated it) with an open-air concert.* ◊ *He was presented with the watch **on the occasion of** his retirement.*
function [C] (*rather formal*) a social event or official ceremony: *The hall provided a venue for weddings and other functions.* ◊ *He and his wife were guests of honour at a function held by the society last weekend.*
reception [C] a formal social occasion to welcome sb or celebrate sth: *They held a reception for 100 guests at the golf club.* ◊ *The hall is a popular venue for wedding receptions.*
reunion /riːˈjuːniən/ [C] a social occasion or party attended by a group of people who have not seen each other for a long time: *The seventh annual reunion will take place in March.* ◊ *a school reunion*

festivities /fe'stɪvətiz/ [pl.] (*rather formal*) the activities that are organized to celebrate a special event: *Bonfires and fireworks will form part of the festivities.*

'**get-together** [C] (*informal*) an informal meeting; a party: *I'm going back for the usual family get-together at Thanksgiving.* See also **get together** → MEET 1

evidence *noun*

evidence · proof · support · testimony · demonstration
These are all words for the facts, signs or objects that make you believe that sth is true.

▸ evidence / support **for** sth
▸ evidence / proof / testimony / a demonstration **that...**
▸ (a) **clear / convincing** evidence / proof / support / testimony / demonstration
▸ (a) **conclusive** evidence / proof / support / demonstration
▸ (an) **ample / adequate** evidence / proof / testimony / demonstration
▸ **sufficient / good / direct** evidence / proof / testimony
▸ **to provide / give** evidence / proof / support / testimony / a demonstration
▸ **to find** evidence / proof / support

evidence [U] the facts, signs or objects that make you believe that sth is true; the information that is used in court to try to prove sth: *Have you any evidence to support this allegation?* ◇ *There is **not a shred of evidence** that the meeting actually took place.* ◇ *A **body of evidence** emerged suggesting that smoking tobacco caused serious diseases.* ◇ ***On the evidence** of their recent games, it is unlikely the Spanish team will win the cup.* ◇ *I was asked to **give evidence** (= to say what I knew, describe what I had seen, etc.) at the trial.* ◇ *The jury **heard evidence** from 38 witnesses.* See also **evidence** → CONFIRM *verb* 1

proof [U, C] facts or documents that show that sth is true: *There is no proof that the knife belonged to her.* ◇ *Can you provide any **proof of identity**?* ◇ *Keep the receipt as **proof of purchase**.* ◇ *These results are a further proof of his outstanding ability.* See also **prove** → SHOW 1

NOTE **EVIDENCE** OR **PROOF**? **Evidence** is what makes you believe that sth is true; **proof** shows that sth is true in a way that no one can argue against.

support [U] evidence that helps to show that a theory or idea is true or correct: *The statistics offer further support for our theory.* See also **support** → CONFIRM *verb* 1

testimony /'testɪməni/ *AmE* -mouni/ [U, sing.] (*formal*) a thing that shows that sth else exists or is true: *The pyramids are an eloquent **testimony to** the ancient Egyptians' engineering skills.* ◇ *This increase in imports **bears testimony to** the successes of industry.*

demonstration [C, U] an act of giving proof or evidence of sth: *This is a clear demonstration of how something that seems simple can turn out to be very complicated.* See also **demonstrate** → SHOW 1

evil *noun*

evil · sin · wrong · wickedness · immorality · vice
These are all words for morally bad behaviour, or a force that causes bad things to happen.

▸ to **do** evil / wrong
▸ to **turn (away) from** evil / sin / wickedness
▸ a **life of** evil / sin / wickedness / vice

evil [U] a force that causes bad things to happen; morally bad behaviour: *The film is about the eternal struggle between good and evil.* ◇ *He believed he could rid the world of the forces of evil.* ◇ *Humans have the capacity to do more evil than any other species on earth.* **OPP** **good** → MORALITY

sin [U] (*rather formal*) behaviour that involves breaking a religious or moral law: *Believers are called on to turn away from sin and embrace a life of prayer.*

wrong [U] behaviour that is not honest or morally acceptable: *Children must be taught the difference between right and wrong.* ◇ *Her son can do no wrong in her eyes.* ◇ *I see no wrong in taking a little time off.* ❶ In this meaning, **wrong** is nearly always used in the phrases *do/see no wrong* and *right and wrong.* **OPP** **right** → MORALITY, See also **wrong** → WRONG *adj.* 4

wickedness [U] morally bad behaviour, especially when it has no reason except sb's pleasure in being bad: *They started to beat me for no reason except sheer wickedness.*

immorality /,ɪmə'ræləti/ [U, C] (*rather formal*) behaviour, especially sexual behaviour, that does not follow accepted standards: *For him, the besetting sins of the age were greed and sexual immorality.* **OPP** **morality** → MORALITY, See also **immoral** → WRONG *adj.* 4

vice [U] (*especially journalism*) evil or immoral behaviour: *The film ended most satisfactorily: vice punished and virtue rewarded.* ❶ In journalism and other more informal contexts **vice** usually refers to activities such as sex, taking drugs, drinking alcohol and gambling (= playing games of chance for money). **OPP** **virtue** → MORALITY

evil *adj.*

evil · wicked · bad · dark · satanic · base · demonic · sinful
These words all describe cruel or morally bad people or behaviour.

▸ an evil / a wicked / a bad / a sinful **man / woman / person / life / act / thought**
▸ an evil / a wicked / a base / a sinful **creature**
▸ an evil / a wicked **demon**
▸ a wicked / bad **child**
▸ an evil / a wicked / a bad / a dark / a sinful **deed**
▸ an evil / a wicked **crime**
▸ an evil / a bad / a satanic **influence**
▸ an evil / a bad **omen**
▸ evil / dark / demonic **forces / powers**

evil (of people or actions) very bad; showing great enjoyment in hurting or killing others; connected with the Devil: *He gave an evil laugh.* ◇ *In his speech he described the evil effects of racism.* ◇ *It was an ancient charm to ward off evil spirits.* **OPP** **good** → GOOD 5

wicked (of people or actions) very bad; showing great enjoyment in being bad and hurting others: *She despised herself for being selfish, even wicked.* ◇ *That was a wicked thing to do!* ◇ *The wicked witch casts a spell on the princess.* **OPP** **good** → GOOD 5

NOTE **EVIL** OR **WICKED**? These are both very strong words to describe people and actions that are very bad: they should be used with great care. **Evil** is stronger than **wicked**. **Wickedness** is bad behaviour, caused by sb's pleasure in being bad, and it is basically a human characteristic. **Evil** is a force outside a person that makes them do bad things, and is often connected with the Devil. A **wicked** person enjoys being bad and hurting other people's feelings. An **evil** person enjoys hurting people physically and does not even consider their feelings. *Children, witches* and *stepmothers* are **wicked**, especially in children's stories. *Spirits, forces, monsters, killers* and *masterminds* are **evil**, especially in stories for adults and popular news reports.

bad criminal or morally unacceptable: *The hero gets to shoot all the bad guys.* ◇ *He said I must have done something bad to deserve it.* **OPP** **good** → GOOD 5

dark evil or frightening: *There was a darker side to his nature.* ◇ *There are dark forces at work here.*

satanic (also **Satanic**) /sə'tænɪk; *AmE* also seɪ't-/ connected with the worship of the Devil: *There was no evidence of satanic rituals.*

base (*formal*) not having moral principles or rules: *He acted from base motives.*

demonic /dɪ'mɒnɪk; *AmE* -'mɑːn-/ connected with, or like, an evil spirit: *This was a society in which demonic possession was greatly feared.*

sinful (*formal*) morally wrong; against the rules of a religion: *He tried to keep his sinful thoughts to himself.*

exact *adj.*

exact · precise · accurate · specific
These words all describe sth that gives all the details of sth correctly.

PATTERNS AND COLLOCATIONS
▶ precise / accurate / specific **about** sb / sth
▶ exact / precise / accurate / specific **instructions / details**
▶ exact / precise / accurate **measurements**
▶ an exact / a precise / an accurate **answer / description**
▶ a precise / an accurate **account**
▶ an exact / an accurate **picture / copy**
▶ the exact / precise **time**
▶ quite exact / precise / accurate / specific

exact [usually before noun] giving all the details correctly: *She gave an exact description of the attacker.* ◇ *What were his exact words?* ◇ *She's in her mid-thirties — 36, to be exact.* **OPP** **approximate, rough** → VAGUE, See also **exact** → VERY *adj.*
▶ **exactly** *adv.*: *Do exactly as I tell you.* ◇ *It happened almost exactly a year ago.*

precise /prɪ'saɪs/ giving all the details clearly and correctly; based on correct and careful measurement or judgement: *Please give precise details about your previous experience.* ◇ *She was reasonably precise about the time of the incident.* ◇ *It measures 3.4 metres, to be precise.* **OPP** **imprecise** → VAGUE, See also **precise** → VERY *adj.*
▶ **precisely** *adv.*: *That's precisely what I meant.*
▶ **precision** /prɪ'sɪʒn/ *noun* [U]: *Her writing is imaginative but lacks precision.*

accurate correct in every detail: *Accurate records must be kept at all times.* ◇ *The test results are accurate in 99% of cases.* ◇ *The novel wasn't intended to be historically accurate.* **OPP** **inaccurate** → WRONG 1, See also the entry for RELIABLE 2
▶ **accuracy** /'ækjərəsi/ *noun* [U]: *They questioned the accuracy of the information in the file.*
▶ **accurately** *adv.*: *The report accurately reflects the current state of the industry.*

NOTE **EXACT, PRECISE** OR **ACCURATE?** Accurate can often be used before a noun in the same way as **exact** and **precise**: *exact/precise/accurate records.* When the words are used after a linking verb, there is a slightly different emphasis, especially in negative statements. A description that is *not very exact/precise* lacks details; a description that is *not very accurate* gives details, but the details are wrong. **Precise** includes the idea of being clear and certain as well as correct and can be used to talk about people in the phrase *be precise about sth.* **Exact** is NOT usually used in this way: ~~She was reasonably exact about the time of the incident.~~ If you are *reasonably accurate about sth* you are reasonably correct about it, NOT reasonably clear and certain.

specific giving all the details clearly and carefully: *I gave you specific instructions.* ◇ *'I'd like your help tomorrow.' 'Can you be more specific* (= tell me exactly what you want)*?'* ❶ **Specific** is often used in the same way as **precise**; it is frequently used in order to ask sb to be more precise, to complain that sb has not been precise, or to insist that you have been precise (for example, when sb has ignored your instructions).

exaggerate *verb*

exaggerate · overstate · dramatize · embellish · inflate
These words all mean to make sth seem more interesting or important than it really is.

PATTERNS AND COLLOCATIONS
▶ to exaggerate / overstate / inflate the **importance / significance** of sth
▶ to exaggerate / overstate the **extent** of sth
▶ to exaggerate / dramatize / embellish a **story**
▶ to **greatly / grossly / vastly / wildly / somewhat** exaggerate / overstate / inflate sth

exaggerate [I, T] to make sth seem longer, better, worse or more important than it really is: *The hotel was really filthy and I'm not exaggerating.* ◇ *Demand for satellite television has been greatly exaggerated.*
▶ **exaggerated** *adj.*: *He made some wildly exaggerated claims about what they had achieved.*
▶ **exaggeration** *noun* [C, usually sing., U]: *That's a slight exaggeration!* ◇ *He told his story simply and without exaggeration.*

overstate /ˌəʊvə'steɪt; *AmE* ˌoʊvər's-/ [T] (*rather formal*) to say sth in a way that makes it seem greater or more important than it really is: *He tends to overstate the case when talking politics.* ◇ *The seriousness of the crime cannot be overstated.* ❶ Typical collocates of **overstate** are *importance, significance, seriousness* and *the case.* **OPP** **understate** → UNDERSTATE
▶ **overstatement** *noun* [C, U]: *It is not an overstatement to say a crisis is imminent.* ◇ *He was well known for his fondness for overstatement.*

dramatize (*BrE* also **-ise**) /'dræmətaɪz/ [T, I] (*rather formal*) to make a problem seem more serious or an event or situation more exciting than it really is: *Don't worry too much about what she said — she tends to dramatize things.*

embellish /ɪm'belɪʃ/ [T] (*rather formal*) to make a story more interesting by adding details that are not always true: *His account of his travels was embellished with details of famous people he met.*

inflate /ɪn'fleɪt/ [T] (*especially journalism*) to make sth seem more important or impressive than it really is: *The media have grossly inflated the significance of this meeting.* ❶ Typical collocates of **inflate** in this meaning are *importance, significance* and *value.*
▶ **inflated** *adj.*: *She has an inflated sense of her own importance.*

examine *verb* See the Topic Map for FACT AND OPINION on p.898

examine · analyse · review · study · discuss · go into sth · take stock · survey
These words all mean to think about, study or describe sb/sth carefully, especially in order to understand them, form an opinion of them or make a decision about them.

PATTERNS AND COLLOCATIONS
▶ to examine / analyse / review / study / discuss / go into / take stock of / survey **what / how / whether...**
▶ to examine / analyse / review / study / discuss / take stock of / survey the **situation**
▶ to examine / analyse / review / study / discuss the **possibility** of sth
▶ to examine / analyse / review / study / discuss a / an **proposal / idea**
▶ to examine / analyse / review / study / discuss / survey the **evidence / sb's work**
▶ to examine / analyse / review / study / discuss / go into sth **in depth / in detail**
▶ to examine / analyse / review / study / discuss sth **in the light of** sth
▶ to examine / analyse / review / study / discuss / survey sth **carefully / critically / systematically / briefly**

examine [T] to think about, study or describe an idea, subject or piece of work very carefully: *These ideas will be examined in more detail in Chapter 10.* ◇ *It is necessary to examine how the proposals can be carried out.* See also **examination** → RESEARCH *noun*

analyse (*BrE*) (*AmE* **analyze**) [T] to examine the nature or structure of sth, especially by separating it into its parts, in order to understand or explain it: *The job involves gathering and analysing data.* ◇ *He tried to analyse his feelings.* ◇ *We need to analyse what went wrong.* See also **analysis** → RESEARCH *noun*

review [T] to examine sth again, especially so that you can decide if it is necessary to make changes: *Staff performance is reviewed annually.* ◇ *The decision may need to be reviewed in the light of new evidence.* ◇ *Safety procedures are being urgently reviewed after a chemical leak at the factory.*

▸ **review** *noun* [U, C]: *The case is subject to judicial review.* ◇ *The terms of the contract are under review.* ◇ *a pay/salary review* See also **review** → REPORT *noun* 1

study [T] to examine sb/sth in order to understand them: *We will study the report carefully before making a decision.* ◇ *The group will study how the region coped with the loss of thousands of jobs.* See also **study** → RESEARCH *noun*, **study** → REPORT *noun* 1

NOTE EXAMINE OR STUDY? You **examine** sth in order to understand it or to help other people understand it, for example by describing it in a book; you **study** sth in order to understand it yourself.

discuss [T] to write or talk about sth in detail, showing the different ideas and opinions about it: *This topic will be discussed at greater length in the next chapter.* See also **discussion** → RESEARCH

go 'into sth *phrasal verb* (*rather informal, especially spoken*) to examine a subject or question carefully, especially for practical reasons: *We need to go into the question of costs.*

take 'stock *idiom* to think carefully about the way in which a particular situation is developing in order to decide what to do next: *It was time to stand back and take stock of his career.*

survey /sə'veɪ; *AmE* sər'veɪ/ [T] to examine and give a general description of sth: *This chapter briefly surveys the current state of European politics.* See also **survey** → REPORT *noun* 1

example *noun*

1 give an example of sth
2 Her courage is an example to us all.

1 example · case · instance · specimen · illustration

These are all words for a thing or situation that is typical of a particular group or set, and is sometimes used to support an argument.

PATTERNS AND COLLOCATIONS

▸ **in** a particular case / instance
▸ **for** example / instance
▸ a **typical** example / case / instance / specimen / illustration
▸ a **classic** example / case / instance / illustration
▸ a **famous** / **well-known** example / case / instance
▸ a **prime** example / case / specimen
▸ a / an **good** / **fine** / **excellent** / **perfect** example / specimen / illustration
▸ to **give sb** / **provide** an example / an instance / a specimen / an illustration
▸ to **cite** / **take** / **highlight** an example / a case / an instance
▸ an example / a case / an illustration **shows** sth

example [C] something such as an object, fact or situation that shows, explains or supports what you say; a thing that is typical of or represents a particular group or set: *Can you give me an example of what you mean?* ◇ *It is important to cite examples to support your argument.* ◇ *It is a classic example of how not to design a new town.*

case [C] a particular situation or a situation of a particular type; a situation that relates to a particular person or thing: *In some cases people have had to wait several weeks for an appointment.* ◇ *Many professions feel they deserve higher pay, and nurses are a case in point.* ◇ *In this case, we are prepared to be lenient.*

instance /'ɪnstəns/ [C] (*rather formal*) a particular situation or a situation of a particular type: *The report highlights a number of instances of injustice.* ◇ *What would you do, for instance, if you found an employee stealing?*

specimen /'spesɪmən/ an example of sth, especially an animal or plant: *The aquarium has some interesting specimens of unusual tropical fish.* ◇ *Redwood trees can live for a long time; one specimen is 4 000 years old.*

illustration /ˌɪlə'streɪʃn/ [C, U] (*rather formal, especially written*) a story, event or example that clearly shows the truth about sth: *The statistics are a clear illustration of the point I am trying to make.* ◇ *Let me, by way of illustration, quote from one of her poems.* See also **illustrate** → EXPLAIN 1, **illustrate** → SHOW 1, **illustrative** → DESCRIPTIVE

NOTE EXAMPLE OR ILLUSTRATION? An **illustration** is often used to show that sth is true. An **example** is used to help to explain sth.

2 example · model · ideal · role model · embodiment · epitome · inspiration · archetype

These are all words for a person or thing that is considered to be a good example of sth.

PATTERNS AND COLLOCATIONS

▸ an example / a model / the embodiment / the epitome / the archetype **of** sth
▸ an example / inspiration **to** sb

example [C] (*approving*) a person or their behaviour that is thought to be good for others to copy: *Her courage is an example to us all.* ◇ *She is a shining example of what people with disabilities can achieve.* ◇ *He is a captain who leads by example.* See also **example** → INFLUENCE *noun*, **exemplify** → REPRESENT 2

model [C] (*approving*) a person or thing that is considered an excellent example of sth: *Her essay was a model of clarity.* ◇ *He's a model student.* ❶ **Model** is always used in the phrase *a model of sb/sth* or like an adjective before another noun: *a model farm* (= one that has been specially designed to work well) See also **model** → MODEL *noun*

ideal /aɪ'diːəl/ [C, usually sing.] a person or thing that you think is perfect: *It's my ideal of what a family home should be.* ❶ **Ideal** is often used with possessive pronouns such as *my*, *his* or *her*.

'role model [C] a person that you admire and try to copy: *We need positive role models for young men to aspire to.*

embodiment /ɪm'bɒdimənt; *AmE* -'bɑːd-/ [C, usually sing.] (*formal*) a person or thing that represents or is a typical example of an idea or quality: *He is the embodiment of the young successful businessman.* ❶ **Embodiment** can be used to talk about a positive or a negative idea. See also **embody** → REPRESENT 2

epitome /ɪ'pɪtəmi/ [sing.] (*formal, especially written*) a perfect example of a person or quality: *Her clothes are the epitome of good taste.* ❶ **Epitome** is almost always used in the phrase *the epitome of sb/sth*. It is often used to talk about how people look or behave. Although many examples of **epitome** show good qualities, this is not always the case: a common phrase is *the epitome of evil*. See also **epitomize** → REPRESENT 2

inspiration /ˌɪnspə'reɪʃn/ [C, usually sing.] a person or thing that makes you want to be better or more successful: *Her charity work is an inspiration to us all.* See also **inspire** → INSPIRE

archetype /'ɑːkitaɪp/ [sing.] (*rather formal, written*) the most typical or perfect example of a particular kind of person or thing: *She is the archetype of an American movie star.* ❶ **Archetype** is not usually used with words that describe qualities, like *kindness* or *style*: it is more often used with concrete nouns to talk about how people and things match what we expect from a person or thing of a particular class, profession or type.

excellent *adj.* See also the entries for GOOD 1, GREAT 1 and WONDERFUL

excellent · outstanding · perfect · superb · classic · first-rate
These words all describe sth that is extremely good.

PATTERNS AND COLLOCATIONS
▸ an excellent / an outstanding / a perfect / a superb / a first-rate **performance / job**
▸ an excellent / an outstanding / a perfect / a superb / a first-rate **service**
▸ an excellent / an outstanding / a superb **achievement**
▸ **really** excellent / outstanding / perfect / superb / first-rate
▸ **absolutely** excellent / outstanding / perfect / superb / classic
▸ **quite** excellent / outstanding / perfect / superb

excellent extremely good: *The rooms are excellent value at $20 a night.* ◇ *The meals here are generally excellent* (= usually excellent). ◇ *She made one factual error in her otherwise excellent article.* ◇ *He speaks excellent English.* ❶ **Excellent** is used especially about standards of service or of sth that sb has worked to produce **OPP** **mediocre** → MEDIOCRE, See also **excellence** → VALUE 1
outstanding extremely good: *She's one of their most outstanding young players.* ◇ *The valley has been designated an Area of Outstanding Natural Beauty.* ❶ **Outstanding** is used especially about how well sb does sth or how good sb is at sth.
▸ **outstandingly** *adv.*: *The team has been outstandingly successful.* ◇ *He performed well but not outstandingly.*
perfect extremely good: *The weather was perfect.* ◇ *Conditions were perfect for walking.* ❶ **Perfect** is used especially about conditions or how suitable sth is for a purpose.
superb /suːˈpɜːb; sjuː-; *AmE* suːˈpɜːrb/ (*informal, especially spoken*) extremely good or impressive: *The car's in superb condition.* ◇ *It was a superb goal, scored just seconds before half-time.*
▸ **superbly** *adv.*: *a superbly illustrated book*
classic [usually before noun] accepted or deserving to be accepted as one of the best or most important of its kind: *This classic novel was first published in 1938.*
▸ **classic** *noun* [C]: *The second goal was an absolute classic.*
first-rate extremely good; of the highest quality: *They did a first-rate job.* ◇ *We aim to provide a first-rate service.* **OPP** **second-rate** → POOR 2

exception *noun*

exception · anomaly · aberration · freak · vagaries · oddity
These are all words for a person or thing that is different from what is considered normal or usual.

PATTERNS AND COLLOCATIONS
▸ an exception / an anomaly / an aberration / vagaries / an oddity **in** sth
▸ **a bit of** an exception / an anomaly / a freak / an oddity
▸ a / an **curious** / **apparent** exception / anomaly

exception /ɪkˈsepʃn/ [C] a person or thing that is not included in a general statement or does not follow a general rule: *With a few exceptions the children can speak good French by the time they leave.* ◇ *Most families were poor and mine was no exception.* ◇ *Unfortunately, considerate motorists are the exception rather than the rule* (= they are unusual). ◇ *Children are not normally allowed in but I'm prepared to make an exception in this case.* ◇ *All students without exception must take the English examination.* See also **exceptional** → SPECIAL

anomaly /əˈnɒməli; *AmE* əˈnɑːm-/ [C] (*rather formal*) a thing or situation that is different from what is normal or expected, often one that therefore needs to be changed: *The existing law is full of loopholes and anomalies.* ◇ *He argued that Parliament should remove the anomaly that no member could be imprisoned for debt.* See also **anomalous** → ABNORMAL
aberration /ˌæbəˈreɪʃn/ [C, U] (*formal*) an act, fact or situation that is different from what is usual or normal and that may be unacceptable: *It was nothing more than a* **mental aberration** *on my part.* ◇ *They claimed he was a caring parent who had used violence in a moment of aberration.*
freak /friːk/ [C] (*sometimes offensive*) a person, animal, plant or thing that is not physically normal: *This butterfly is a* **freak of nature**, *black and white instead of blue.* ◇ *I wish people wouldn't stare, as if I were some kind of freak.*
vagaries /ˈveɪɡəriz/ [pl.] (*rather formal*) changes that are difficult to predict or control: *All farmers are exposed to the vagaries of the weather.*
oddity /ˈɒdəti; *AmE* ˈɑːd-/ [C] a person or thing that is strange or unusual: *She was regarded as a bit of an oddity, but likeable.* ◇ *The book deals with some of the oddities of grammar and spelling.* See also **odd** → STRANGE 1

excess *adj.*

excess · spare · surplus · superfluous · leftover
These words all describe an amount or number that is more than you want or need.

PATTERNS AND COLLOCATIONS
▸ an excess / a surplus **amount**
▸ excess / surplus **demand** / **supply**
▸ excess / spare / surplus **cash** / **capacity** / **energy**
▸ excess / surplus / leftover **food**

excess /ˈekses/ [only before noun] more than is necessary, usual or legal: *Excess food is stored as fat.* ◇ *Driving with excess alcohol in the blood is a serious offence.*
▸ **excess** *noun* [U, sing.]: *The drug can be harmful if taken* **in excess**. ◇ *He started drinking* **to excess** *after losing his job.* ◇ *The increase will not be* **in excess of** (= more than) *two per cent.* ◇ *Are you suffering from an excess of stress in your life?*
spare [usually before noun] that is not being used or is not needed at the present time; kept in case you need to replace the one you usually use: *We've got a spare bedroom, if you'd like to stay.* ◇ *I'm afraid I haven't got any spare cash.* ◇ *Take some spare clothes in case you get wet.*
surplus /ˈsɜːpləs; *AmE* ˈsɜːrp-/ more than is needed or used: *Surplus grain is being sold for export.* ◇ *These items are* **surplus to requirements** (= not needed).
▸ **surplus** *noun* [C, U]: (*rather formal*) *Agricultural surpluses lead to the disposal of thousands of tonnes of food every year.* ◇ *After meeting domestic needs any surplus will be exported.* **OPP** **deficit**, **shortage** → LACK

NOTE **EXCESS, SPARE OR SURPLUS?** Spare is the most informal of these words, and is the one that is most likely to be used in spoken language and everyday contexts. **Surplus** is often used in business contexts to refer to extra goods or money: *surplus stock/material/ products, surplus capital/funds/income/profits.* To talk about an extra amount that is seen as a bad thing, **excess** is often used: *excess body fat/carbon dioxide/ baggage*

superfluous /suːˈpɜːfluəs; sjuː-; *AmE* suːˈpɜːrf-/ [not usually before noun] (*rather formal*) more than you need or want: *She gave him a look that made words superfluous.*
leftover /ˈleftəʊvə(r); *AmE* -oʊv-/ [only before noun] still remaining after you have eaten, drunk or used what you want or need: *Use any leftover meat to make a curry.* ❶ **Leftover** is used especially to talk about food, but it can also be used to talk about a supply of other things: *leftover vegetables/porridge* ◇ *leftover paper/paint/wool* See also **leftover** → REMAINS *noun* 2

excessive *adj.* See also the entry for HIGH 1

---

excessive · undue · over the top · disproportionate · inordinate · a bit much

These words all describe sb's behaviour or an amount of sth that you think is more than is necessary, reasonable or appropriate.

PATTERNS AND COLLOCATIONS
- an excessive / an undue / a disproportionate / an inordinate **amount** of sth
- an excessive / a disproportionate / an inordinate **number** of sth
- an excessive / an undue / a disproportionate / an inordinate **burden**
- an excessive / an undue / a disproportionate **influence**
- excessive / undue / inordinate **delays / emphasis**
- to **seem** excessive / over the top / disproportionate / a bit much
- **a bit / a little / slightly / rather** excessive / over the top
- **grossly** excessive / disproportionate
- **totally** over the top / disproportionate

excessive /ɪkˈsesɪv/ greater than what is or seems reasonable or appropriate: *The amounts she borrowed were not excessive.* ◇ *Excessive drinking can lead to stomach disorders.* ◇ *He claimed that the police had used excessive force.*
- **excessively** *adv.*: *excessively high prices*

undue [only before noun] (*rather formal*) more than you think is reasonable or necessary: *They are taking undue advantage of the situation.* ◇ *We did not want to put any undue pressure on them.*

NOTE EXCESSIVE OR UNDUE? **Excessive** is often used to talk about matters of fact, when there is too much of sth, but a smaller amount might not be a problem: *excessive use/growth/heat/drinking.* **Undue** is more often used to talk about matters of opinion, when you think sth is unreasonable: *undue delay/hardship/alarm.* **Undue** is often used in negative phrases: *without/no undue pressure* and is usually followed by an uncountable noun.

over the 'top *idiom* (*especially BrE, informal*) done to an exaggerated degree and with too much effort: *His performance in the movie is completely over the top.* ◇ *OK, you've already thanked me, there's no need to go over the top!*

disproportionate /ˌdɪsprəˈpɔːʃənət; AmE -ˈpɔːrʃ-/ (*rather formal*) too great in size, number, amount or degree when compared with sth else: *The area contains a disproportionate number of young unemployed people.* ◇ *The punishment was grossly disproportionate to the crime.*
OPP proportionate → RELATIVE
- **disproportionately** *adv.*: *The lower-paid spend a disproportionately large amount of their earnings on food.*

inordinate /ɪnˈɔːdɪnət; AmE -ˈɔːrd-/ (*formal*) far more than is usual or expected: *They spent an inordinate amount of time and money on the production.* ◇ *The strike has led to inordinate delays.*
- **inordinately** *adv.*: *inordinately high prices*

a bit 'much (*informal, disapproving*) (especially of sb's actions) not fair or reasonable, in a way that annoys you: *I think it's a bit much calling me at three in the morning, don't you?* ◇ *The noise from next door is getting a bit much.*

---

exchange *noun*

---

exchange · replacement · substitution · swap · barter · reversal

These are all words for the act of giving sth to sb or doing sth for sb and receiving sth in return.

PATTERNS AND COLLOCATIONS
- an exchange / a swap / a reversal **between** A and B
- a **direct** exchange / replacement / substitution
- a **straight** exchange / swap
- a **complete / total** replacement / reversal

- to **result in** an exchange / the replacement / the substitution of sth

exchange [C, U] an act of giving sth to sb or doing sth for sb and receiving sth in return; the process of changing an amount of one currency (= the money used in one country) for an equal value of another: *There was a brief exchange of glances.* ◇ *Woollen cloth and timber were sent to Egypt in exchange for linen.* ◇ *I'll type your report if you'll babysit in exchange.* ◇ *I get you out of the country and you keep your mouth shut. Is that a fair exchange?* ◇ *We have currency exchange facilities.* ◇ *Where can I find the best exchange rate/rate of exchange?* See also **exchange** → REPLACE *verb* 2

replacement [U] the act of replacing one thing with another, especially sth that is newer or better: *Complete replacement of the roof tiles would be very expensive.* ◇ *The original furnishings are now in need of replacement.* See also **replace** → REPLACE 2, **replacement** → REPLACEMENT

substitution /ˌsʌbstɪˈtjuːʃn; AmE -ˈtuː-/ [U, C] (*rather formal*) the act of using sb/sth instead of sb/sth else: *the substitution of low-fat spreads for butter* ◇ *Two substitutions were made during the game* (= two players were taken off and two others sent on in their place). See also **substitute** → REPLACEMENT, **substitute** → REPLACE *verb* 1, **substitute** → REPLACE *verb* 2

swap (also **swop**) /swɒp; AmE swɑːp/ [C, usually sing.] (*especially BrE, rather informal, spoken or journalism*) an act of exchanging one thing or person for another: *Let's do a swap. You work Friday night and I'll do Saturday.* ◇ *Why not arrange a job swap with someone in another city or state?* ❶ **Swap** is often used by journalists as a short and rather informal way of saying **exchange**. However, it is not used in the wide variety of ways that **exchange** is used. You can *do/make a swap*, or be involved in a *job/spy swap.* See also **swap** → REPLACE *verb* 2, **swap** → SWITCH *verb*

barter [U] the act of exchanging goods or services for other goods, etc. without using money: *The islanders use a system of barter instead of money.* See also **barter** → REPLACE 2

reversal [C, U] an exchange of positions or functions between two or more people: *It's a complete role reversal/reversal of roles* (= for example when a husband cares for the house and children while the wife works). ❶ In this meaning, **reversal** is almost always used in the phrases *role reversal* or *reversal of roles.* See also **reverse** → REPLACE 2

---

excited *adj.* See also the entry for HAPPY

---

excited · ecstatic · elated · euphoric · rapturous · exhilarated

These words all describe sb feeling or showing happiness and enthusiasm.

PATTERNS AND COLLOCATIONS
- excited / ecstatic / elated / euphoric **at** sth
- excited / ecstatic / elated **about** sth
- excited / elated / exhilarated **by** sth
- ecstatic / elated / exhilarated **with** sth
- ecstatic / rapturous **applause / praise**
- an ecstatic / a rapturous **welcome**
- to **feel** excited / elated / euphoric / exhilarated

excited feeling or showing happiness and enthusiasm: *The kids seem pretty excited about the trip.* ◇ *He was really excited to be asked to play for Wales.* ◇ *The buzz of excited chatter was quite deafening.*
- **excitedly** *adv.*: *She waved excitedly as the car approached.*

ecstatic /ɪkˈstætɪk/ very happy, excited and enthusiastic; showing this enthusiasm: *Sally was ecstatic about her new job.* ◇ *He gave an ecstatic sigh of happiness.* ❶ **Ecstatic** is sometimes connected with religion, sex or death: *an ecstatic vision of God* ◇ *their brief but ecstatic honeymoon* ◇ *a strange kind of ecstatic death by drowning* See also **ecstasy** → JOY

▶ **ecstatically** *adv.*: *He sighed ecstatically.* ◊ *For a time, we were ecstatically happy.*

elated /iˈleɪtɪd/ happy and excited because of sth good that has happened or will happen: *I was elated by the prospect of the new job ahead.* ◊ *I was elated with the thrill of success.*

euphoric /juːˈfɒrɪk; *AmE* -ˈfɔːr-/ very happy and excited, but usually only for a short time: *My euphoric mood could not last.* ❶ **Euphoric** is quite often used in the negative for an ironic effect: *His parents were less than euphoric at the news of his engagement.* See also **euphoria** → JOY

rapturous /ˈræptʃərəs/ [usually before noun] expressing extreme pleasure or enthusiasm: *He was greeted with rapturous applause.*

exhilarated /ɪgˈzɪləreɪtɪd/ happy and excited, especially after physical activity: *She felt exhilarated with the speed and the rush of air.*

excitement *noun* See the Topic Map for SPORT AND LEISURE on p.892

excitement · thrill · buzz · charge · exhilaration · high · kick

These are all words for the feeling that you get when you are doing or expecting sth exciting.

PATTERNS AND COLLOCATIONS
▶ (a) **real** excitement / thrill / buzz / charge / high / kick
▶ a **big** thrill / high / kick
▶ to **give sb** a thrill / buzz / high / kick
▶ to **get** a thrill / buzz / charge / kick **out of** sth

excitement [U, C] the pleasant and lively feeling that you get when sth exciting happens or is going to happen; sth that you find exciting: *The news caused great excitement among her friends.* ◊ *In her excitement she dropped her glass.* ◊ *A shiver of excitement ran through her.* ◊ *The new job was not without its excitements.*

thrill [C] a strong feeling of excitement or pleasure; an experience that gives you this feeling: *It gave me a big thrill to meet my favourite author in person.* ◊ *They were just in search of cheap thrills (= excitement that has no real value).*

buzz [sing.] (*informal*) a strong feeling of pleasure, excitement or achievement: *Flying gives me a real buzz.* ◊ *There was a buzz of excitement all around the room.* ◊ *You can sense the creative buzz in the city.*

charge [sing.] (*rather informal*) a strong feeling of pleasure, excitement or achievement; the power to cause this feeling: *I get a real charge out of working hard and seeing good results.* ◊ *a film in which every scene carries an emotional charge*

exhilaration /ɪgˌzɪləˈreɪʃn/ [U] a strong feeling of excitement and happiness especially one that you get from physical activity: *the exhilaration of galloping over miles of open country*

high [C] (*informal*) the strong feeling of pleasure and excitement that you get from doing sth enjoyable or being successful at sth: *He was on a real high after winning the competition.* ◊ *the highs and lows of her acting career* ❶ A **high** is also the strong feeling of pleasure and excitement that sb gets after taking some types of drugs: *The high lasted all night.*

kick [C] (*informal*) a strong feeling of pleasure and excitement, especially one that you get from doing sth slightly dangerous: *I get a kick out of driving fast cars.* ◊ *He gets his kicks from skiing.* ◊ *What do you do for kicks?*

exciting *adj.* See the Topic Map for SPORT AND LEISURE on p.892, See also the entry for MOVING

exciting · dramatic · heady · thrilling · exhilarating · stirring

These words all describe an event, experience or feeling that causes excitement.

exciting   thrilling   exhilarating
dramatic
heady
stirring

PATTERNS AND COLLOCATIONS
▶ exciting / dramatic / heady / thrilling / exhilarating / stirring **stuff**
▶ an exciting / a dramatic / a heady / a thrilling / an exhilarating **experience / moment**
▶ an exciting / a dramatic / a heady **atmosphere**
▶ an exciting / a dramatic / a thrilling / an exhilarating / a stirring **performance**
▶ an exciting / a dramatic / a thrilling / a stirring **finish / finale / victory / win**
▶ an exciting / a dramatic / a stirring **tale**

exciting causing great interest or excitement: *They waited and waited for something exciting to happen.* ◊ *This is one of the most exciting developments in biology in recent years.* ◊ *I still find the job exciting.* OPP **unexciting** → PREDICTABLE 2

dramatic (of events or scenes) exciting and impressive: *They watched dramatic pictures of the police raid on TV.* ◊ *The village is set against the dramatic backcloth of Mont Blanc.*
▶ **dramatically** *adv.*: *The mountains rose dramatically behind them.*

heady [usually before noun] having a strong effect on your senses; making you feel excited and hopeful: *the heady scent of hot spices* ◊ *a heady mixture of desire and fear* ◊ *Profits grew last year by a heady 35%.*

thrilling exciting and enjoyable: *Don't miss next week's thrilling episode!* ◊ *The game had a thrilling finale, with three goals scored in the last five minutes.*

exhilarating /ɪgˈzɪləreɪtɪŋ/ very exciting and enjoyable: *My first parachute jump was an exhilarating experience.*

NOTE **EXCITING, THRILLING** OR **EXHILARATING**? Exhilarating is the strongest of these words and exciting the least strong. **Exciting** is the most general and can be used to talk about any activity, experience, feeling or event that excites you. **Thrilling** is used particularly to talk about contests and stories where the ending is uncertain. **Exhilarating** is used particularly to talk about physical activities that involve speed and/or danger.

stirring [usually before noun] causing strong feelings, especially feelings of excitement: *a stirring performance of Beethoven's Fifth Symphony* ◊ *stirring memories of past victories*

exclude *verb*

1 exclude sugar from your diet
2 exclude sb from a club

1 exclude · eliminate · rule sb/sth out

These words all mean to deliberately not include sth or decide sth is not possible.

PATTERNS AND COLLOCATIONS
▶ to exclude / eliminate / rule out sth **as** sth
▶ to exclude / eliminate sth **from** sth
▶ to be excluded / eliminated / ruled out **by** sb / sth
▶ to exclude / eliminate / rule out a / an **possibility / explanation**
▶ to eliminate / rule out sb **as a suspect**
▶ to exclude / rule out **the idea of** sth
▶ to **completely / entirely / totally / effectively** exclude / eliminate / rule out sth

exclude [T] to deliberately not include sth in what you are doing or considering; to decide that sth is not possible or cannot be true: *The cost of borrowing has been excluded from the inflation figures.* ◊ *Try to exclude sugar and fat from your diet.* ◊ *Buses run every hour, Sundays excluded.* ◊ *We should not exclude the possibility of negotiation.* ◊ *The police have excluded theft as a motive for the murder.* OPP **include** → INCLUDE 1

▶ **excluding** *adj.*: *Lunch costs £10 per person, excluding drinks.* **OPP** **including** → INCLUDE *verb* 1
▶ **exclusion** /ɪkˈskluːʒn/ *noun* [U, C]: *Memories of the past filled her mind* **to the exclusion of** *all else.* **OPP** **inclusion** → INCLUDE *verb* 1

eliminate /ɪˈlɪmɪneɪt/ [T] (*rather formal*) to decide that sth cannot be true: *The police have eliminated two suspects from their investigation.* ◇ *Malaria was eliminated as a cause of death.* ◇ *We can only be certain once we have eliminated every other possible explanation.*
▶ **elimination** *noun* [U]: *You can crack the code by a process of elimination.*

,**rule sb/sth 'out** *phrasal verb* to decide or state that sth is not possible or that sb/sth is not suitable: *The proposed solution was ruled out as too expensive.* ◇ *We aren't ruling anything out at this stage.* ◇ *He has not explicitly ruled out increasing taxes.*

2 See the Topic Map for THE INDIVIDUAL AND SOCIETY on p.894, See also the entries for BAN, EVACUATE and EXPEL

exclude · expel · keep sb/sth out · drop · shut sb/sth out · ostracize · blacklist · excommunicate
These words all mean to prevent sb/sth from taking part in sth or entering a place, or to make sb leave a place.

PATTERNS AND COLLOCATIONS
▶ to exclude / expel / drop / excommunicate sb **from** sth
▶ to exclude / expel / drop / ostracize / blacklist / excommunicate sb **for** sth
▶ to exclude / expel a **pupil** / **student** / **child**
▶ to **feel** excluded / ostracized

exclude [T, often passive] to prevent sb/sth from entering a place or taking part in sth: *Women are still excluded from some golf clubs.* ◇ *Large multinationals can make bids which effectively exclude local firms.* ◇ *Many local people feel excluded from decisions that affect their own community.* ❶ In British English, **exclude** can also mean to forbid a student to attend school for a time because of bad behaviour: (*BrE*) *Concern is growing over the number of children excluded from school.* In American English use **expel**. **OPP** **admit** → LET SB IN, **involve** → INCLUDE 1
▶ **exclusion** /ɪkˈskluːʒn/ *noun* [U, C]: (*rather formal*) *the causes of social exclusion* ◇ (*BrE*) *Two exclusions from one school in the same week is unusual.*

expel /ɪkˈspel/ (-**ll**-) [T] to officially make sb leave a school or an organization, usually because they have broken the rules or done sth wrong: *She was expelled from school at 15.* ◇ *A number of Olympic athletes were expelled for drug-taking.* ◇ *They were forcibly expelled from their farm by the occupying authorities.*
▶ **expulsion** /ɪkˈspʌlʃn/ *noun* [U, C]: *The principal threatened the three girls with expulsion.*

,**keep sb/sth 'out** *phrasal verb* to prevent sb/sth from entering a place: *Keep that dog out of my study!* ◇ *They took security precautions to keep intruders out.* ◇ *The house has extra insulation to keep out the cold.* **OPP** **let sb in** → LET SB IN

drop (-**pp**-) [T] to no longer include sb in a team or group: *She's been dropped from the team because of injury.*

,**shut sb/sth 'out** *phrasal verb* to prevent sb/sth from entering a place: *Mum, Ben keeps shutting me out of the bedroom!* ◇ *They make sunglasses which shut out 99% of the sun's harmful rays.* ◇ *He carefully locked the door behind him, shutting out the world.*

NOTE EXCLUDE, KEEP SB/STH OUT OR SHUT SB/STH OUT?
Exclude is slightly more formal and usually refers to a rule or policy which stops sb from entering a place, such as a building or event. **Keep sb/sth out** and **shut sb/sth out** are slightly more informal and usually refer to sth which physically stops sb from entering a place. **Shut sb/sth out** emphasizes the idea of a physical barrier, such as a door.

ostracize (*BrE* also -**ise**) /ˈɒstrəsaɪz; *AmE* ˈɑːs-/ [T] (*formal*) (of a group of people) to refuse to let sb be a member of a social group; to refuse to meet or talk to sb: *He was ostracized by his colleagues for refusing to support the strike.* ◇ *The regime risks being ostracized by the international community.*

blacklist /ˈblæklɪst/ [T] to put the name of sb/sth on a list of people, products or countries that an organization or government considers unacceptable or that must be avoided: *She was blacklisted by all the major Hollywood studios because of her political views.* ◇ *At present, anything except specifically blacklisted substances can be dumped at sea.* ❶ The list of people, products or countries is called a **blacklist**: *a blacklist of countries where illegal copying of software is thought to be widespread*

excommunicate /ˌekskəˈmjuːnɪkeɪt/ [T] to punish sb by officially stating that they can no longer be a member of a Christian Church, especially the Roman Catholic Church: *The Vatican upheld its decision to excommunicate seven women who were ordained as priests last year.*
▶ **excommunication** *noun* [U, C]: *They were threatened with excommunication.*

exclusive *adj.* See the Topic Map for THE INDIVIDUAL AND SOCIETY on p.894

exclusive · elitist · select
These words all describe a group, society, place, etc. which is only available to a small group of people, especially those with money or a high social position.

PATTERNS AND COLLOCATIONS
▶ an exclusive / a select **group** / **clientele**
▶ an exclusive / elitist **image**
▶ **very** exclusive / select

exclusive /ɪkˈskluːsɪv/ (of a group or society) not willing to allow new people to become members, especially if they are from a lower social class; (of a product or service) of a high quality and expensive and therefore not often bought or used by most people: *She had been sent to one of London's most exclusive girls' schools.* ◇ *His clientele was exclusive and wealthy.* ◇ *an exclusive hotel* ◇ *exclusive designer shops/clothes* **OPP** **inclusive** ❶ **Inclusive** describes sth that includes a wide range or people, things or ideas: *The party must adopt more inclusive strategies and a broader vision.*

elitist /eɪˈliːtɪst; ɪl-/ (especially of a system or society) organized in such a way that only a few people have power or influence: *Teachers deny that the system is elitist.* ◇ *Sailing is seen as an elitist sport.* See also **elite** → ELITE *noun*, **elite** → TOP *adj.*
▶ **elitism** /eɪˈliːtɪzəm; ɪl-/ *noun* [U]: *Many people believe that private education encourages elitism.*

select (of a society, club or place) used only by people who have a lot of money and/or a high social position: *They live in a very select area.* ◇ *It is a select restaurant with fine Italian food.*

execution *noun*

execution · the death penalty · capital punishment · hanging · firing squad · the electric chair · the chair · gallows · scaffold
These are all words for the act of killing a person as a legal punishment, or of ways of doing this.

PATTERNS AND COLLOCATIONS
▶ a **public** / **mass** execution / hanging
▶ to **attend** / **watch** / **witness** an execution / a hanging
▶ to **face** execution / the death penalty / the firing squad / the electric chair / the chair
▶ to **send sb to** the electric chair / gallows / scaffold
▶ to **abolish** / **bring back** the death penalty / capital punishment / hanging / the electric chair

execution [U, C] the act of killing sb, especially as a legal punishment: *She faced execution by hanging for murder.* ◇ *Over 200 executions were carried out last year.* See also **execute** → KILL

the death penalty /'deθ penəlti/ [sing.] the punishment of being killed that is used in some countries for very serious crimes: *She spent many years campaigning for the abolition of the death penalty.* ◇ *This is a crime which carries the death penalty.*

capital 'punishment [U] punishment by death: *Public opinion was in favour of bringing back capital punishment.*

> **NOTE** THE DEATH PENALTY OR CAPITAL PUNISHMENT? Both these terms can be used when you are talking about the existence of this type of punishment in a country's legal system. If you are talking about a particular instance of punishment by death, you should use **the death penalty**: *He faces the death penalty for his crimes.* ◇ *He faces capital punishment for his crimes.*

hanging [U, C] the practice of killing sb as a punishment by putting a rope around their neck and hanging them from a high place; an occasion when this happens: *She was sentenced to death by hanging.* ◇ *Attending public hangings was a popular pastime.*

firing squad /'faɪərɪŋ skwɒd; *AmE* skwɑːd/ [C+sing./pl. v., U] a group of soldiers who are ordered to shoot and kill sb who is found guilty of a crime: *She was executed by (a) firing squad.*

the e,lectric 'chair [sing.] (especially in the US) a chair in which criminals are killed by passing a powerful electric current through their bodies; the method of execution which uses this chair: *He was sent to the electric chair.* ◇ *They face death by the electric chair.*

the chair [sing.] (*AmE, informal*) the electric chair: *I can't sit here and see an innocent man get the chair.*

gallows /'gæləʊz; *AmE* -loʊz/ [C] a structure on which criminals are killed by hanging: *It was common to send a man to the gallows* (= to send him to his death by hanging) *for such crimes.*

scaffold /'skæfəʊld; *AmE* -foʊld/ [C] a platform used when executing criminals by cutting off their heads or hanging them from a rope: *He knew he was destined to die on the scaffold.*

executive *noun*

executive · businessman/businesswoman/business person · entrepreneur · industrialist · magnate · tycoon
These are all words for a person who has an important job as a manager of a company or organization.

PATTERNS AND COLLOCATIONS
▸ a **local** executive / businessman / businesswoman / entrepreneur / industrialist / magnate
▸ a **leading** executive / businessman / businesswoman / entrepreneur / industrialist / magnate
▸ a **successful / wealthy** businessman / businesswoman / entrepreneur / industrialist
▸ an **ambitious** executive / businessman / businesswoman / entrepreneur
▸ a **business** executive / entrepreneur / magnate / tycoon
▸ a **media / property** executive / entrepreneur / magnate / tycoon
▸ a / an **newspaper / publishing / oil** executive / magnate / tycoon

executive /ɪg'zekjətɪv/ [C] a person who has an important job as a manager of a company or organization: *He's a senior executive in a computer firm.* See also **executive** → MANAGEMENT

businessman, businesswoman, business person [C] a person who works in business, especially at a high level: *For many years he was a successful businessman, running his own small business.* ◇ *She's a brilliant and highly successful businesswoman.* ◇ *a hotel that caters to business people* ❶ **Businessman** or **businesswoman** is often used to describe sb who works for himself or herself rather than for an employer. It is also used to describe sb who is skilful in business and financial matters: *I should have got a better price for the car, but I'm not much of a businessman.* **Business people** is often used in the plural to talk about businessmen and women as a group; when

you are talking about an individual person it is more usual to use **businessman** or **businesswoman**: *She's a highly successful business person.*

entrepreneur /ˌɒntrəprə'nɜː(r); *AmE* ˌɑːn-/ [C] a person who makes money by starting or running businesses, especially when this involves taking financial risks: *A creative entrepreneur, he was continually dreaming up new projects.*

industrialist /ɪn'dʌstriəlɪst/ [C] a person who owns or runs a large factory or industrial company: *He was the son of a wealthy industrialist.*

magnate /'mægneɪt/ [C] a person who is successful, especially in business or industry, and has become rich and powerful: *The company was owned by shipping magnate Fred Olsen.*

tycoon /taɪ'kuːn/ [C] (*sometimes disapproving*) a person who is successful in business or industry and has become rich and powerful: *Tapie, business tycoon and football club owner, was appointed Minister for Cities.*

> **NOTE** MAGNATE OR TYCOON? **Magnate** tends to have more positive associations of strength and power; **tycoon** sometimes suggests a dishonest type of person who is likely to lose people's respect at some point: *the disgraced/fallen/discredited media tycoon*

exempt *verb*

exempt · spare · pardon · excuse · get (sb) off the hook · let sb off the hook · let sb off
These words all mean to not punish sb for sth they have done wrong, or to give them only a light punishment.

PATTERNS AND COLLOCATIONS
▸ to exempt / spare / excuse sb **from** sth

exempt /ɪg'zempt/ [T] (*formal*) to give or get sb official permission not to do sth or not to pay sth they would normally have to do or pay: *In 1983, charities were exempted from paying the tax.* ◇ *His bad eyesight exempted him from military service.*
▸ **exemption** noun [U, C]: *He applied for exemption from military service.* ◇ *The owner was granted an exemption from the law and the painting was exported.*

spare [T, usually passive] (not usually used in the progressive tenses) (*literary*) to allow sb/sth to escape harm, damage or death, especially when others do not escape it: *They killed the men but spared the children.* ◇ *She begged them to spare her life.* ◇ *During the bombing only one house was spared* (= was not hit by a bomb).

pardon [T] (not usually used in the progressive tenses) to officially allow sb who has been found guilty of a crime to leave prison and/or avoid punishment: *She was pardoned after serving ten years of a life sentence.*
▸ **pardon** noun [C]: *They were released from prison yesterday as a result of a presidential pardon.*

excuse [T, usually passive] to give sb permission not to do sth that they would normally have to do: *She was excused from giving evidence because of her age.*

> **NOTE** EXEMPT OR EXCUSE? **Exempt** is used especially when a whole group of people or organizations is given permission not to do sth, if they fall into a particular category; **excuse** is used especially when an individual asks for and is given permission not to do sth, because of their particular situation. However, **exempt** is used about individual people when the subject of the verb is not the person or law that gives permission, but the reason why it is given: *His bad eyesight exempted him from military service.*

get (sb) off the 'hook, let sb off the 'hook *idiom* to free yourself or sb else from a difficult situation or a punishment: *Perhaps he could get off the hook by saying it was an accident?* ◇ *Why should I let you off the hook? You stole from my shop!* ❶ When you **get sb off the hook**, you arrange things so that they are not punished. When you

get off the hook, especially in British English, you manage to avoid punishment yourself. When you **let sb off the hook**, you decide not to punish them.

let sb 'off *phrasal verb* to not punish sb for sth they have done wrong, or to give them only a light punishment: *They let us off lightly.* ◇ *She was **let off with** a warning.* ❶ If you **let sb off**, you do not punish them. If you *let sb off lightly/with a warning/with a caution*, you only give them a light punishment.

exhibition *noun*

exhibition · show · display · exhibit · fair · trade show/ trade fair
These are all words for a collection of things that are shown to the public.

▸ to be **on** exhibition / show / display / exhibit
▸ a **big** exhibition / show / display / exhibit / fair
▸ a **major** exhibition / show / display / exhibit
▸ an **international** exhibition / show / exhibit / trade show / trade fair
▸ a **public** exhibition / show / display / exhibit
▸ a **permanent / temporary** exhibition / display / exhibit
▸ an **annual** show / fair / trade show / trade fair
▸ a **travelling / touring** exhibition / show / display / exhibit
▸ to **see** an exhibition / a show / a display / an exhibit
▸ to **attend/go to/visit** an exhibition/a show/an exhibit/a fair/a trade show / a trade fair
▸ to **have/hold/host** an exhibition/a show/an exhibit/a fair/a trade show / a trade fair
▸ to **mount/present/put on** an exhibition/a display/an exhibit
▸ The exhibition / show / exhibit / fair / trade show / trade fair **opens/ closes/ ends** on a particular date.

exhibition /ˌeksɪˈbɪʃn/ [C] (*especially BrE*) a collection of things, for example works of art, that are shown to the public; the act of showing things to the public: *They are putting on an exhibition of old photographs.* ◇ *The Mappa Mundi is now on permanent exhibition at Hereford Cathedral.* ❶ The usual American English word for an **exhibition** [C] is **exhibit**.

show [C, U] an occasion when a collection of things are brought together for people to look at; the fact of being brought together for people to look at: *They hold an agricultural show once a year.* ◇ *The first couple of days at the Paris fashion shows are always a thrill.* ◇ *The latest technology will be on show at the trade fair.* See also **show** → PRESENT *verb* 1

NOTE EXHIBITION OR SHOW? A **show** is usually temporary. An **exhibition** is often temporary, but can be permanent; if it is temporary, it may last for several months and/or travel to museums in different cities or countries. An **exhibition** usually contains works of art or items of special cultural or scientific interest. **Show** is a more general word, and suggests an event that might appeal to a wider range of people.

display [C] an arrangement of things in a public place to inform or entertain people or advertise sth for sale: *The window display changes once a month.* ◇ *The medals can be seen in a display cabinet on the first floor.* See also **show** → PRESENT *verb* 1

exhibit /ɪgˈzɪbɪt/ [C] (*AmE*) an exhibition: *a Matisse exhibit at the National Gallery*

fair [C] (*AmE*) a type of entertainment in a field or park, especially one at which farm animals and products are shown and take part in competitions: *We all went south for the state fair.* ❶ In British English this is called *an agricultural show*. In both British and American English *an art/craft fair* is an event at which artists show and sell their work; *a jobs/careers fair* is an event at which people who are looking for jobs can get information about companies that might employ them.

trade show, **trade fair** [C] an event at which many different companies show and sell their products: *Opening on June 11, the trade show will feature a wide range of goods.*

exist *verb*

exist · find · occur · prevail · live
These words all mean to be present in a place or situation.

▸ to exist / be found / occur / prevail **in / among** sth
▸ to **still** exist / be found / occur / prevail
▸ to **never** exist / be found / occur

exist [I] (not used in the progressive tenses) to be real; to be present in a place or situation: *Does life exist on other planets?* ◇ *The problem only exists in your head, Ben.* See also **existence** → LIFE 1

find [T] (not used in the progressive tenses) used to say that sth exists and is noticeable in a particular place: *These flowers are found only in Africa.* ◇ *You'll find this style of architecture all over the town.*

occur /əˈkɜː(r)/ (**-rr-**) [I] (not used in the progressive tenses, used with an adverb or preposition) (*rather formal*) to exist in a place or be present as a part of sth: *Lemurs occur in the wild only in Madagascar.* ◇ *Sugar occurs naturally in fruit.*
▸ **occurrence** /əˈkʌrəns; *AmE* əˈkɜːr-/ *noun* [U]: *The document addresses the occurrence of arsenic in drinking water.*

prevail /prɪˈveɪl/ [I] (not used in the progressive tenses) (*formal*) to exist or be very common at a particular time or in a particular place: *We were horrified at the conditions prevailing in local prisons.* See also **prevalent** → GENERAL *adj.* 1

live [I] (not usually used in the progressive tenses) to be alive, especially at a particular time: *He's the greatest player who ever lived.* ◇ *When did Handel live?* See also **life** → LIFE 1, **life** → LIFE 2

expand *verb*

1 Student numbers are expanding.
2 expand a business

1 expand · widen · extend · enlarge · broaden · lengthen · stretch
These words all mean to become or make sth larger.

▸ to expand / widen / extend / enlarge / lengthen / stretch **to a** particular amount
▸ to expand / widen / extend / enlarge / lengthen **by a** particular amount
▸ to expand/widen/extend/enlarge/broaden sth's **scope/range**
▸ to expand / widen / extend / broaden your **knowledge**
▸ to widen / broaden / extend your **experience**
▸ to expand / extend / enlarge your **vocabulary**
▸ sth is **considerably / slightly** expanded / widened / extended / enlarged / broadened
▸ sth is **greatly** expanded / widened / extended / enlarged

expand [I, T] to become or make sth greater in size, number or importance: *Metals expand when they are heated.* ◇ *Student numbers are expanding rapidly.* ◇ *The waist expands to fit all sizes.* ◇ *The new system expanded the role of family doctors.* ◇ *There are no plans to expand the local airport.* **OPP** **contract** → SHRINK, See also **grow** → RISE
▸ **expansion** /ɪkˈspænʃn/ *noun* [U, C]: *The expansion of higher education will continue.* ◇ *The book is an expansion of a series of lectures given last year.*

widen [I, T] to become or make sth wider; to become or make sth larger in degree or range: *Her eyes widened in surprise.* ◇ *Here the stream widens into a river.* ◇ *They may* have to widen the road to cope with the increase in traffic. ◇ *The legislation will be widened to include all firearms.* **OPP narrow** → SHRINK

extend /ɪkˈstend/ [T] to make sth longer or larger; to make an idea, influence or business cover more areas or operate in more places: *You can add value to your house by extending or renovating it.* ◇ *There are plans to extend the road network in the north of the country.* ◇ *The school is extending the range of subjects taught.* ◇ *The company plans to extend its operations into Europe.*

▸ **extension** /ɪkˈstenʃn/ noun [C, U]: *the gradual extension of the powers of central government* ◇ *(especially BrE) a planned extension to the hospital*

enlarge [T, I] to make sth bigger; to become bigger: *There are plans to enlarge the recreation area.* ◇ *Reading will enlarge your vocabulary.* ◇ *The little blisters enlarge and eventually burst to form ulcers.* ❶ **Enlarge** is used especially in the passive to mean 'to make a bigger copy of a photograph or document': *We're going to have this picture enlarged.*

NOTE EXTEND OR ENLARGE? Things that you **extend** are usually on a larger scale than things that you **enlarge**: you might **extend** a *house* or other *building*; you might **enlarge** a *picture*, or an *area* within a room, place or building.

broaden [I, T] to become wider; to affect or make sth affect more people or things: *Her smile broadened.* ◇ *The party needs to broaden its appeal to voters.* **OPP narrow** → SHRINK

lengthen [I, T] to become or make sth longer: *The afternoon shadows lengthened.* ◇ *I need to lengthen this skirt.* ◇ *He lengthened his stride to catch up with them.* **OPP shorten** → SHRINK

stretch [I, T] to become or make sth longer, wider or looser by pulling it; to become longer, etc. when you pull it: *This sweater has stretched.* ◇ *Stop stretching your sleeves like that!* ❶ Fabric that **stretches** becomes bigger or longer when you pull it and returns to its original shape when you stop: *The jeans stretch to provide a perfect fit.*

2 expand · move on · diversify · branch out · broaden
These words all mean to start doing sth new, either to increase your experience or to be more successful, for example in business.

PATTERNS AND COLLOCATIONS
▸ to expand / diversify / branch out **into** sth
▸ to expand / diversify the **business / economy**
▸ to expand / broaden your **horizons**
▸ a / an **company / firm / economy** expands / diversifies
▸ to expand / move on / diversify / broaden **further**
▸ to expand / move on / diversify **quickly / rapidly**

expand [I, T] *(especially business)* to make a business bigger by opening new branches and making more money; (of a business) to become bigger in this way: *We've expanded the business by opening two more stores.* ◇ *It's a country with an expanding economy (= with more businesses starting and growing).*

▸ **expansion** /ɪkˈspænʃn/ noun [U]: *a period of rapid economic expansion*

move 'on *phrasal verb (especially spoken)* to start doing or discussing sth new: *I've been in this job long enough – it's time I moved on.* ◇ *Can we move on to the next item on the agenda?*

diversify /daɪˈvɜːsɪfaɪ; AmE -ˈvɜːrs-/ [I, T] *(rather formal, especially business)* to develop a wider range of products, interests, skills, etc. in order to be more successful or reduce risk; to make a business do this: *Farmers are being encouraged to diversify into new crops.* ◇ *The company has been trying to diversify its business.*

branch 'out *phrasal verb* to start to do an activity that you have not done before, especially in your work or business: *The company has now branched out into selling insurance.* ◇ *I decided to branch out on my own (= for example, set up my own business).*

broaden [T] to increase your experience or knowledge: *Few would disagree that travel broadens the mind (= helps you to understand other people's beliefs, customs, etc.).* ◇ *Spending a year working in the city helped to broaden his horizons.* ❶ Typical collocates of **broaden** are *horizons, mind, outlook, understanding, knowledge* and *interests.*

expect *verb* See also the entries for HOPE and WAIT

expect · think · anticipate · await · look forward to sth · look for sth · look ahead · watch for sb/sth · bargain for/on sth
These words all mean to believe that sth will happen or to wait for it to happen.

PATTERNS AND COLLOCATIONS
▸ to expect / think / anticipate **that...**
▸ **It is** expected / thought / anticipated that...
▸ to anticipate / look forward to / bargain on **doing sth**
▸ to expect / anticipate / await / look forward to / look for **results**
▸ to expect / anticipate / await / look forward to a **reply**
▸ to expect / anticipate / await / look forward to the **arrival** of sb / sth
▸ to await / look for / watch for **signs** of sth
▸ to expect / anticipate / watch for **trouble**
▸ to **eagerly** anticipate / await / look forward to / look for / watch for sth
▸ to **confidently** expect / anticipate / await / look forward to sth
▸ to **anxiously** expect / await / watch for sth

expect [T] to believe that sth will happen or that sb will do sth; to be waiting for sb/sth to arrive, as this has been arranged: *You can't expect to learn a foreign language in a few months.* ◇ *I looked back, half expecting to see someone following me.* ◇ *It is expected that the report will suggest some major reforms.* ◇ *Don't expect sympathy from me!* ◇ *Are you expecting visitors?* ◇ *I'm expecting an important call.* See also **to be expected** → PREDICTABLE 1

think [T] to expect that sth will happen or that sb will do sth: *I never thought (that) I'd see her again.* ◇ *The job took longer than we thought.* ◇ *You'd think she'd have been grateful for my help (= but she wasn't).* ◇ *Who would have thought (= I didn't expect) to find you here?* ❶ **Think** is only used to mean 'expect' when your expectations prove to be false: ~~It is thought that the report will suggest some major reforms.~~ It is usually followed by a 'that' clause (even if the word 'that' is missed out), and cannot take a noun phrase as object: ~~Don't think sympathy from me.~~

anticipate [T] *(rather formal)* to believe that sth will happen or that sb will do sth; to think with pleasure and excitement about sth that is going to happen: *We don't anticipate any major problems.* ◇ *They anticipate moving to bigger premises by the end of the year.* ◇ *We anticipate that sales will rise next year.* ◇ *The band today announced details of their widely anticipated third album.*

NOTE EXPECT OR ANTICIPATE? Expect is used in both formal and informal speech and writing, including everyday conversation. **Anticipate** is mostly used in slightly more formal spoken or written contexts, especially in business or official statements.

await /əˈweɪt/ [T] *(formal)* to wait for sb/sth, especially sth that you expect to happen or arrive: *He is in custody awaiting trial.* ◇ *Her latest novel is eagerly awaited.* See also **wait** → WAIT *verb*

look' forward to sth *phrasal verb* (often used in the progressive tenses) to be thinking with pleasure and excitement about sth that is going to happen, because you expect to enjoy it: *We're really looking forward to seeing you again.* ◇ *Customers can look forward to a 5% cut in their bills.* ◇ *It will give her something to look forward to.* ❶ The progressive tense *I'm looking forward to...* is often used to talk about sth that you expect to enjoy. The present tense *I/We look forward to...* is often used as a polite formula at the end of formal or business communication: *I look forward to hearing from you (= please* reply). ◇ *We look forward to working with you again in the future.* Do not use **expect** at the end of a letter: *I expect your reply.* **OPP** dread → FEAR

ˈlook for sth *phrasal verb* (*rather formal*) to hope for sth; to expect sth to happen: *We are a peaceful people and we are not looking for revenge.* ◇ *We shall be looking for an improvement in your work this term.*

ˌlook aˈhead *phrasal verb* to think about what is going to happen in the future: *They have to learn to look ahead to the possible consequences of their actions.* ◇ *Looking ahead, nuclear power may have the best growth prospects.*

ˈwatch for sb/sth *phrasal verb* to look and wait for sb/sth to appear or for sth to happen: *Watch for the early signs of stress.* ◇ *The cat was on the wall watching for birds.*

ˈbargain for/on sth *phrasal verb* (usually used in negative sentences) (*rather informal*) to expect sth to happen and be prepared for it: *He obviously hadn't bargained on finding you there already.* ◇ *When he agreed to answer a few questions, he got more than he bargained for.*

expectation *noun*

expectation · forecast · prediction · projection · anticipation · prophecy · foresight
These are all words for a statement or belief about what will happen in the future, or the ability to make such a statement.

PATTERNS AND COLLOCATIONS
▶ expectations/a forecast/a prediction/a projection/a prophecy **about** sth
▶ expectations / a forecast / predictions / projections **for** sth
▶ **contrary to/ against** expectation/ predictions
▶ **in** expectation/ anticipation **of** sth
▶ (a/ an) **current/ optimistic** expectations/ forecast/ prediction/ projection
▶ **future** expectations/ predictions/ projections
▶ an **official** forecast/ prediction/ projection
▶ an **accurate** forecast/ prediction/ prophecy
▶ to **make** a forecast/ prediction/ projection/ prophecy
▶ to **revise** expectations/ a forecast/ predictions / projections
▶ sth **is based on** an expectation/ a forecast/ a projection
▶ an expectation/ a forecast/ a prediction/ a projection **is based on** sth

expectation [C, U] a belief that sth will happen because it is likely: *We are confident in our expectation of a full recovery.* ◇ *The expectation is that property prices will rise.* ◇ *Against all expectations, she was enjoying herself.* ◇ *I applied for the job more in hope than expectation.* See also **expectation** → HOPE *noun* 2

forecast /ˈfɔːkɑːst; *AmE* ˈfɔːrkæst/ [C] a statement about what will happen in the future, based on information that is available now: *It is too early to make firm forecasts about demand.* ◇ *The sales forecasts are encouraging.* ◇ *The weather forecast wasn't too bad.* See also **forecast** → PREDICT

prediction [C, U] a statement of what you think will happen in the future; the act of making such a statement: *Not many people agree with the government's prediction that the economy will improve.* ◇ *Our prediction turned out to be correct.* ◇ *Skilled readers make use of context and prediction.* See also **predict** → PREDICT

projection [C] an estimate of what figures, amounts or events will be in the future, based on what is happening now: *Sales have exceeded our projections.* ◇ *On current projections, there will be more than 12 million people aged 65 and over in 2020.* ◇ *Calculations are based on a projection of existing trends.* See also **project** → PREDICT

anticipation [U] the fact of seeing that sth might happen in the future and perhaps preparing for it or doing sth to prevent it now: *People are buying extra groceries in anticipation of heavy snowstorms.* See also **anticipate** → ANTICIPATE, **anticipate** → EXPECT

prophecy /ˈprɒfəsi; *AmE* ˈprɑːf-/ [C, U] a statement that sth will happen in the future, especially one made by sb with magic or religious powers; the power of being able to say what will happen in the future: *Macbeth believed the witches' prophecy about his future.* ◇ *Low expectations can become a self-fulfilling prophecy.* ◇ (*formal*) *She was believed to have the gift of prophecy.* See also **prophesy** → PREDICT

foresight /ˈfɔːsaɪt; *AmE* ˈfɔːrs-/ [U] (*approving*) the ability to predict what is likely to happen and to use this to prepare for the future: *She had had the foresight to prepare herself financially in case of an accident.* ◇ *The government's policies show a remarkable lack of foresight.* **OPP** hindsight ❶ Hindsight is the understanding that you have of a situation only after it has happened and that means you would have done things differently: *With hindsight it is easy to say that they should not have released him.* ◇ *What looks obvious in hindsight was not at all obvious at the time.* See also **foresee** → PREDICT

expel *verb* See also the entries for EVACUATE and EXCLUDE 2

expel · deport · exile · banish · extradite · repatriate · displace
These words all mean to force sb to go to another country.

PATTERNS AND COLLOCATIONS
▶ to expel/deport/exile/banish/extradite/repatriate sb **to/from** a country
▶ to expel/ deport/ repatriate/ displace **refugees**
▶ to expel/ deport/ repatriate **immigrants**
▶ to **forcibly** expel/ deport/ repatriate sb

expel /ɪkˈspel/ (-ll-) [T] to force sb to leave a country: *Foreign journalists are being expelled.*
▶ **expulsion** /ɪkˈspʌlʃn/ *noun* [U, C]: *These events led to the expulsion of senior diplomats from the country.*

deport /dɪˈpɔːt; *AmE* dɪˈpɔːrt/ [T] to force sb to leave a country, usually because they have broken the law or because they have no legal right to be there: *He was convicted of drug offences and deported.*
▶ **deportation** /ˌdiːpɔːˈteɪʃn; *AmE* -pɔːrˈt-/ *noun* [U, C]: *Several of the asylum seekers now face deportation.*

exile /ˈeksaɪl; ˈegzaɪl/ [T, usually passive] to force sb to leave their country, especially for political reasons or as a punishment: *Exiled opposition leaders have made an appeal to the international community.*
▶ **exile** *noun* [U]: *to be/live in exile* ◇ *to go/be forced/be sent into exile* ◇ *a place of exile* ◇ *He returned after 40 years of exile.* See also **exile** → REFUGEE

banish /ˈbænɪʃ/ [T, usually passive] to order sb to leave a place, especially a country, as a punishment: *He was banished to Australia, where he died five years later.* ◇ *The servants were banished from the upstairs rooms.* ❶ Banish is often used about events in the past. It is not often used in a modern or legal context.
▶ **banishment** *noun* [U]: *Lady Montague dies of grief at Romeo's banishment.*

extradite /ˈekstrədaɪt/ [T] to officially send back sb who has been accused or found guilty of a crime to the country where the crime was committed: *The courts have refused to extradite the suspects from Spain.*
▶ **extradition** /ˌekstrəˈdɪʃn/ *noun* [U]: *The extradition of terrorist suspects will cause controversy.* ◇ *an extradition treaty* ◇ *to start extradition proceedings*

repatriate /ˌriːˈpætrieɪt; *AmE* -ˈpeɪt-/ [T] to send or bring sb back to their own country: *The refugees were forcibly repatriated.* ◇ *Tourists who are injured or fall sick are repatriated.*
▶ **repatriation** *noun* [U, C]: *Several refugees took part in the voluntary repatriation programme.*

displace /dɪsˈpleɪs/ [T, often passive] (*rather formal*) to force people to move away from their home to another place: *An estimated 50 000 people have been displaced from their homes by the conflict.*

▸ **displacement** *noun* [U]: (*formal*) *the largest displacement of civilian population since World War II*

expensive *adj.* See also the entry for HIGH 1

expensive · costly · overpriced · pricey
These words all describe sth that costs a lot of money.

▸ expensive / costly / pricey **for** sb / sth
▸ expensive / costly **to do sth**
▸ **very / too / fairly / quite / pretty** expensive / costly / pricey

expensive costing a lot of money; charging high prices: *Art books are enormously expensive to produce.* ◇ *Making the wrong decision could prove to be expensive.* ◇ *That dress was an expensive mistake.* ◇ *an expensive restaurant* **OPP cheap, inexpensive** → CHEAP, See also **expense** → PRICE *noun*
▸ **expensively** *adv.*: *expensively dressed/furnished*
costly (*rather formal*) costing a lot of money, especially more than you want to pay: *You want to avoid costly legal proceedings if you can.*
overpriced /ˌəʊvəˈpraɪst; *AmE* ˌoʊvərˈp-/ too expensive; costing more than it is worth: *ridiculously overpriced designer clothes* ◇ *The commission is set to investigate claims that CDs are overpriced.*
pricey (*informal*) expensive: *Houses in the village are now too pricey for local people to afford.*

experienced *adj.*

experienced · veteran · seasoned · practised · long-serving
These words all describe people who have a lot of experience of a particular activity.

▸ to be experienced / practised **in** sth
▸ an experienced / a veteran / a seasoned **campaigner**
▸ an experienced / a veteran **actor / diplomat / politician / soldier**
▸ an experienced / a seasoned **observer**
▸ an experienced / a practised **eye / hand**
▸ **well** seasoned / practised

experienced having knowledge or skill in a particular job or activity through having done it a lot or for a long time: *She's a very experienced teacher.* ◇ *He's very experienced in looking after animals.* See also **experience** → KNOWLEDGE, **experienced** → SOPHISTICATED
veteran /ˈvetərən/ [only before noun] (*especially journalism*) having a lot of experience in a particular job or activity: *The speech was given by the veteran British actor and producer, Sir Richard Attenborough.* ❶ **Veteran** is used especially to talk about actors, sportspeople, soldiers and politicians. It is usually used to talk about people who are quite old and have achieved a lot in their careers.
seasoned [usually before noun] (*especially written*) having a lot of experience in a particular activity: *Mitchell is a seasoned campaigner for peace.* ❶ Typical collocates of **seasoned** are *traveller, campaigner, performer* and *observer.*
practised (*BrE*) (*AmE* **practiced**) (*especially written*) good at doing sth because you have been doing it regularly: *It takes a practised eye to spot the difference.* ◇ *He has good ideas but he isn't practised in the art of marketing.* ❶ **Practised** is often used to talk about people's physical abilities: (*a*) *practised eye/hand/skill.* People also sometimes say that sb does sth with *practised ease.* See also **practise** → PRACTISE
long-serving [only before noun] having had the job or position mentioned for a long time: *Several long-serving employees are due to retire this year.* ❶ **Long-serving** is typically used to talk about *employees, a member of staff/a committee/the Cabinet, a councillor, minister, senator* or *representative.*

experimental *adj.* See also the entry for MODERN

experimental · modern · modernist · futuristic · avant-garde · postmodernist
These words all describe sth that is based on new and unusual ideas, forms or methods that are intended to be different from traditional ones and that may be surprising or shocking.

▸ an experimental / a modern / a modernist **approach**
▸ experimental / modern / modernist / avant-garde / postmodernist **art / writing / works**
▸ experimental / modern / modernist / postmodernist **fiction / novels**
▸ experimental / modern / avant-garde **music / theatre**
▸ a modern / a modernist / a futuristic / an avant-garde **style**
▸ a modern / modernist / futuristic **building**

experimental based on new ideas, forms or methods that are used to find out what effect they have: *The equipment is still at the experimental stage.* ◇ *Doctors stress that this kind of treatment is still experimental.*
▸ **experimentally** *adv.*: *The new drug is being used experimentally on some patients.*
modern (of ways of behaving or thinking) new and intended to be different from traditional ways, and therefore not always accepted by most members of society: *She has very modern ideas about educating her children.* **OPP old-fashioned** → OLD-FASHIONED, **traditional** → TRADITIONAL, See also **modern** → MODERN
modernist [only before noun] following the ideas of modernism ❶ **Modernism** was a style and movement in art, architecture and literature popular in the middle of the 20th century in which modern ideas, methods and materials were used rather than traditional ones: *The museum devotes a large gallery to modernist art.*
futuristic /ˌfjuːtʃəˈrɪstɪk/ (of architecture or design) extremely modern and unusual in appearance, as if belonging to a future time: *The cover of the novel shows a futuristic city on the moon.*
avant-garde /ˌævɒ̃ ˈɡɑːd; *AmE* ˌævɑ̃ː ˈɡɑːrd/ (of art, music or literature) based on very new and unusual ideas, and therefore sometimes surprising or shocking: *The theatre shows a lot of avant-garde work.*
postmodernist /ˌpəʊstˈmɒdənɪst; *AmE* ˌpoʊstˈmɑːdərn-/ [only before noun] following the ideas of postmodernism ❶ **Postmodernism** is a style and movement in art, architecture and literature in the late 20th century that reacts against modern styles, for example by mixing features from traditional and modern styles: *an analysis of postmodernist cultural forms*

expert *noun*

expert · specialist · authority · guru · pundit · buff · connoisseur · aficionado
These are all words for a person who has a lot of knowledge about a particular subject.

▸ an expert / a specialist / an authority **in / on** sth
▸ an expert / a specialist / an authority **in the field** (of sth)
▸ a **great** expert / authority / connoisseur
▸ a **leading** expert / specialist / authority / pundit
▸ a **recognized** expert / specialist / authority
▸ an **independent / outside** expert / specialist / authority
▸ a **financial / technical** expert / specialist / guru
▸ a **media** expert / specialist / guru / pundit
▸ a **computer** expert / specialist / guru / buff
▸ a **wine / food** expert / guru / buff / connoisseur
▸ a **film / cinema / movie** pundit / buff / connoisseur

expert [C] a person with special knowledge, skill or training in sth: *She's a leading expert in child psychology.* ◇ *He's an expert at getting his own way.* ◇ *I'm no expert, but I think you should get that cut seen to.* See also **expert** → IMPRESSIVE *adj.*, **expertise** → SKILL 2

specialist [C] a person who is an expert in a particular area of work or study; a doctor who is an expert in a particular area of medicine: *He's a noted specialist in his field.* ◇ *I was sent to see a specialist at the local hospital.* ◇ *a/an cancer/ear/eye/heart specialist* See also the entry for DOCTOR

▸ **specialist** *adj.*: *You need some specialist advice.*
▸ **specialize** (*BrE* also **-ise**) *verb* [I]: *He specialized in criminal law.* ◇ *Many students prefer not to specialize too soon.*

authority [C] a person with special knowledge of a subject: *She is an authority on early musical instruments.* See also **authoritative** → RELIABLE 2

> **NOTE EXPERT OR AUTHORITY?** An **expert** is usually sb who is very skilled at sth, and/or is able to give useful advice or training to sb else. An **authority** is usually sb who knows a lot about an academic subject, which may be very interesting, but may not be necessary or useful for other people to know or be advised about.

guru /'guːruː/ (*informal, especially journalism*) a person who is well-known as an expert on a particular subject, especially in the areas of business, politics and fashion: *Most management gurus base their appeal on one big theme.* ❶ Common collocates of **guru** include *business, management, leadership, investment, marketing, fashion, design* and *style.* See also **mentor** → ADVISER

pundit [C] a person who knows a lot about a particular subject and often talks about it in public, especially on television: *Football pundit Ron Atkinson has resigned from his TV job.* ◇ *Political pundits agree that the government has scored a major victory.*

buff [C] (used in compounds) a person who is very interested in a particular subject or activity and knows a lot about it: *Opera buffs should enjoy the summer season this year.* See also **enthusiast** → FAN

connoisseur /ˌkɒnə'sɜː(r); *AmE* ˌkɑːnə'sɜːr; -'sʊr/ [C] an expert who is skilled at judging the quality of such as food, art or music: *She's a respected connoisseur and collector of modern sculpture.*

aficionado /əˌfɪʃə'nɑːdəʊ; *AmE* -doʊ/ [C] a person who is very interested in a particular subject or activity and knows a lot about it: *He's an aficionado of the history of the game.* ◇ *Jazz aficionados gathered at the Hollywood Bowl last night for a tribute concert.*

> **NOTE BUFF OR AFICIONADO? Buff** is always used in compounds after another noun: its most frequent collocates are *opera, wine, film, movie, cinema, theatre, computer* and *cricket.* **Aficionado** can also be used in this way, with a wider range of different nouns, or in the phrase *an aficionado of sth.*

explain *verb*

1 explain how sth works
2 explain your behaviour

1 explain · illustrate · define · clarify · shed/cast/ throw light on sth · spell sth out · interpret · expound
These words all mean to tell sb about sth in a way that makes them able to understand it.

PATTERNS AND COLLOCATIONS
▸ to explain / clarify / spell sth out / expound sth **to** sb
▸ to explain / spell sth out **that**…
▸ to explain / illustrate / clarify / shed light on / spell out **how/ what**… / **why**…
▸ to explain / clarify / shed light on a / an **situation** / **issue**
▸ to explain / illustrate / clarify / expound an **idea**
▸ to explain / illustrate / clarify a **point**
▸ to explain/illustrate/define/clarify the **position** / **role** / **nature** / **meaning** of sth
▸ to explain / illustrate / expound a **theory**
▸ to **clearly** explain / illustrate / define / spell out / expound sth

explain [T, I] to tell sb about sth in a way that makes it easy or easier for them to understand: *First, let me explain the rules of the game.* ◇ *I tried to explain the problem to the technician.* ◇ *She explained to them what to do in the event of an emergency.* ◇ *'It was like this,' she explained.* ◇ *There's no need to explain. We understand.* ❶ You cannot say 'explain me/him/her, etc.': *Can you explain the situation to me?* ◇ ~~Can you explain me the situation?~~ See also **explanatory** → DESCRIPTIVE

▸ **explanation** [C]: *For a full explanation of how the machine works, turn to page 5.*

illustrate [T] to make the meaning of sth clearer by using examples, pictures, diagrams, etc: *To illustrate my point, let me tell you a little story.* ◇ *Last year's sales figures are illustrated in Figure 2.* See also **illustrate** → SHOW 1, **illustration** → DIAGRAM, **illustration** → EXAMPLE 1, **illustrative** → DESCRIPTIVE

define [T] to say or explain what the meaning of a word or phrase is: *The term 'mental illness' is difficult to define.* ◇ *Life imprisonment is defined as 60 years under state law.* See also **definition** → DEFINITION

clarify /'klærəfaɪ/ [T] (*rather formal*) to make sth clearer or easier for sb to understand: *Let me clarify my position on this matter.* ◇ *There are one or two issues that need to be clarified.* ◇ *I hope I managed to clarify things a little.*

▸ **clarification** *noun* [U, C]: *I am seeking clarification of the regulations.*

shed/cast/throw 'light on sth *idiom* to make sth easier to understand by explaining parts of it: *Recent research has thrown some new light on the causes of the disease.* ◇ *The report casts no light on* (= does not explain) *why some children are still failing to achieve at school.* ❶ A person, sth they say or write, or a new discovery can **shed/cast/ throw light on sth.**

spell sth 'out *phrasal verb* to explain sth in a very clear, simple way: *You know what I mean – I'm sure I don't need to spell it out.*

interpret [T] to explain the meaning of sth such as a text or work of art, especially when it is possible to understand or explain it in several different ways: *The students were asked to interpret the poem.* See also **interpretation** → DEFINITION, **interpretative** → DESCRIPTIVE

expound [T, I] (*formal*) to explain sth by talking about it in detail: *She expounded her theory further in the course of her talk.* ◇ *He was there to expound on the government's latest policy initiative.*

2 explain · justify · account for sth · defend · stand up for sb/sth · stick up for sb/sth
These words all mean to support sb/sth that is being criticized or attacked or to give an explanation for sth.

PATTERNS AND COLLOCATIONS
▸ to explain / justify / account for / defend sth **to** sb
▸ to explain / justify / account for **what** / **why** / **how**…
▸ to explain / justify / defend / stand up for / stick up for **yourself**
▸ to explain / justify / account for / defend a **decision**
▸ to explain / justify / account for / defend your / sb's **behaviour**
▸ to defend / stand up for / stick up for sb's **rights**

explain [I, T] to give a reason for sth; to be a reason for sth: *She tried to explain but he wouldn't listen.* ◇ *Ed explained that his car had broken down.* ◇ *The government now has to explain its decision to the public.* ◇ *Well, that doesn't explain why you didn't call me.* ◇ (*spoken*) *Oh well then, that explains it* (I understand now why sth happened). See also **explanation** → REASON

justify [T] to show that sb/sth is right or reasonable; to give an explanation or excuse for sth or for doing sth, especially sth that other people think is wrong or unreasonable: *How can they justify paying such huge salaries?* ◇ *Her success had justified the faith her teachers had put in her.* ◇ *You don't need to justify yourself to me.* See also **justification** → REASON, **unjustified** → UNJUSTIFIED

ac'count for sth *phrasal verb* (*rather formal*) to be the explanation or cause of sth; to give an explanation of sth: *The poor weather may have accounted for the small crowd.* ◇ *How do you account for the show's success?*

defend [T] to say or write sth in support of sb/sth that has been criticized, or to give an explanation for sth: *Politicians are skilled at **defending** themselves **against** their critics.* ◇ *How can you defend such behaviour?* See also **defence** → SECURITY

,**stand 'up for sb/sth** *phrasal verb* [no passive] to strongly support or defend sb/sth that has been criticized: *Always stand up for your friends.* ◇ *You must stand up for your rights.* ◇ *She had learnt to stand up for herself.*

,**stick 'up for sb/sth** *phrasal verb* [no passive] (*rather informal*) to support or defend sb/sth that has been criticized: *Stick up for what you believe.* ◇ *She taught her children to stick up for themselves at school.* ❶ **Stick up for sb/sth** is used especially to talk about sb defending another person or themselves when no one else will.

explode *verb*

explode · blow (sth) up · go off · burst · erupt · detonate · rupture
These are all words that can be used when sth bursts apart violently, causing damage or injury.

PATTERNS AND COLLOCATIONS
▶ a **bomb** explodes / blows up / goes off / bursts / detonates
▶ a **car / plane / vehicle** explodes / blows up
▶ a **firework / rocket** explodes / goes off
▶ a **shell** explodes / bursts
▶ a **volcano** explodes / erupts
▶ a **pipe / tank** bursts / ruptures
▶ to **burst** / rupture a **pipe / tank**
▶ a **burst** / ruptured **appendix / artery**

explode [I, T] to burst loudly and violently, causing damage; to make sth burst in this way: *The jet smashed into a hillside and exploded.* ◇ *Bomb disposal experts exploded the device under controlled conditions.*

,**blow 'up** , **blow sth 'up** *phrasal verb* to be destroyed by an explosion; to destroy sth by an explosion: *A police officer was killed when his car blew up.* ◇ *They were trying to blow up the bridge.*

,**go 'off** *phrasal verb* (of a bomb) to explode; (of a gun) to be fired: *The bomb went off in a crowded street.* ❶ When used about guns, the choice of **go off** (NOT 'be fired') can suggest that the gun was fired by accident, or that the person who fired it was not really responsible: *A police gun went off during the search of his home.*

burst [I, T] to break open or apart, especially because of pressure from inside; to make sth break in this way: *The dam burst under the weight of water.* ◇ *Shells were bursting all around us.* ◇ *Don't burst that balloon!* ◇ *He burst a blood vessel during a fit of coughing.*

erupt /ɪˈrʌpt/ [I, T] (of a volcano) to throw out burning rocks and smoke; (of burning rocks and smoke) to be thrown out of a volcano: *The volcano could erupt at any time.* ◇ *Ash began to erupt from the crater.* ◇ *Lava erupted close to the summit.*

detonate /ˈdetənet/ [I, T] (*rather formal*) (of a bomb) to explode; to make a bomb explode: *Two other bombs failed to detonate.* ◇ *The bomb was detonated by remote control.*

rupture /ˈrʌptʃə(r)/ [I, T] (*formal or medical*) to burst or break apart a pipe, container or organ inside the body; to be burst or broken apart: *A pipe ruptured, leaking water all over the house.* ◇ *The impact ruptured both fuel tanks.* ◇ *Barnes played his first game since rupturing an Achilles tendon five months ago.*

exploit *verb*

exploit · abuse · use · misuse
These words all mean to treat sb/sth in a bad way, especially in order to gain an advantage for yourself.

PATTERNS AND COLLOCATIONS
▶ to exploit / abuse your **position**
▶ to abuse / misuse your **power / authority**
▶ to abuse / misuse **drugs / alcohol / solvents**
▶ to exploit / use sb / sth **for your own ends**

exploit /ɪkˈsplɔɪt/ [T] (*usually disapproving*) to treat a person or situation as an opportunity to gain an advantage for yourself; to treat sb unfairly by making them work and not giving them much in return: *He exploited his father's name to get himself a job.* ◇ *She realized that her youth and inexperience were being exploited.* ◇ *What is being done to stop employers from exploiting immigrants?*
▶ **exploitation** /ˌeksplɔɪˈteɪʃn/ *noun* [U]: *his exploitation of the situation for his own purposes* ◇ *the exploitation of children*

abuse /əˈbjuːz/ [T] (*disapproving*) to treat sth, especially power or knowledge, as an opportunity to gain an advantage for yourself; to drink or take so much of sth that it harms your health; to treat a person or animal in a cruel or violent way: *He felt they had **abused his trust** by talking about him to the press* (= deceived him, although he had trusted them). ◇ *People who abuse alcohol over a long period will develop health problems.* ◇ *He systematically abused his body with heroin and cocaine.* ◇ *All the children had been physically and emotionally abused.* See also **abuse** → RAPE *verb*
▶ **abuse** /əˈbjuːs/ *noun* [U, sing.]: *The system of paying cash bonuses is **open to abuse*** (= might be used in the wrong way). ◇ *alcohol/drug/solvent abuse* ◇ *child abuse*

use [T] (*disapproving*) to be kind or friendly to sb with the intention of gaining an advantage for yourself from them: *Can't you see he's just using you for his own ends?* ◇ *I felt used.*

misuse /ˌmɪsˈjuːz/ [T] (*formal*) to use sth in the wrong way or for the wrong purpose: *The apostrophe is often misused, even by native English speakers.* ◇ *Several cabinet ministers were found guilty of misusing public funds.*
▶ **misuse** /ˌmɪsˈjuːs/ *noun* [U, C, usually sing.]: *the misuse of power/authority* ◇ *a misuse of public funds*

explorer *noun* See also the entry for TOURIST

explorer · pioneer · adventurer · discoverer
These are all words for a person who travels to unknown or unusual places.

PATTERNS AND COLLOCATIONS
▶ a **great** explorer / pioneer / adventurer / discoverer
▶ an **early** explorer / pioneer / adventurer
▶ a **polar** explorer / adventurer
▶ a **band of** explorers / pioneers / adventurers

explorer /ɪkˈsplɔːrə(r)/ [C] a person who travels to unknown places in order to find out more about them: *Early explorers traded directly with Native Americans for furs.* See also **explore** → TOUR

pioneer /ˌpaɪəˈnɪə(r); AmE -ˈnɪr/ [C] one of the first people to go to a particular area in order to live and work there: *Early pioneers settled on both sides of the Maple River.*

adventurer /ədˈventʃərə(r)/ [C] a person who enjoys exciting new experiences, especially going to unusual places: *He's a born adventurer.*

discoverer /dɪˈskʌvərə(r)/ [C] the first person to find that a particular place exists: *There is a statue of Sir John Franklin, the discoverer of the North-West Passage.* See also **discover** → FIND 2

explosion *noun*

explosion · blast · eruption
These are all words for a sudden violent bursting and loud noise when sth explodes.

PATTERNS AND COLLOCATIONS
▶ a **massive** explosion / blast / eruption
▶ a **loud / deafening / powerful / huge** explosion / blast

► a **bomb** / **gas** / **chemical** / **nuclear** explosion / blast
► to **cause** an explosion / a blast / an eruption
► an explosion / a blast **rips through** / **rocks** sth

explosion [C] the sudden violent bursting and loud noise of sth such as a bomb exploding; the act of deliberately causing sth to explode: *There were two loud explosions and then the building burst into flames.* ◇ *Bomb Squad officers carried out a controlled explosion of the device.*

blast [C] (*rather informal, journalism*) an explosion or a powerful movement of air caused by an explosion: *Bomb blast kills 50* (= in a newspaper headline). ◇ *The blast ripped through the building.*

eruption /ɪˈrʌpʃn/ [C] an explosion from a volcano: *The eruption of Krakatoa was heard 3 000 miles away.*

expose *verb*

expose · subject sb/sth to sth · put sb through sth · lay sb open to sth
These words all mean to make sb experience sth unpleasant or to put them in a situation where they might experience sth unpleasant.

expose	subject sb/sth to sth
lay sb open to sth	put sb through sth

PATTERNS AND COLLOCATIONS
► to expose / subject / lay sb open **to** sth
► to expose / subject **yourself** to sth
► to put **yourself** through sth
► to lay **yourself** open to sth
► to expose sb to / subject sb to / lay sb open to **criticism** / **ridicule** / **abuse** / **attack**
► to expose sb / lay sb open to **charges** / **risk**
► to subject sb to / put sb through an **ordeal**

expose [T] to put sb/sth in a place or situation where they are not protected from sth harmful or unpleasant: *You could be exposing yourself to unnecessary risks.* ◇ *Do not expose babies to strong sunlight.* See also **exposed** → VULNERABLE
► **exposure** /ɪkˈspəʊʒə(r)/; *AmE* -ˈspoʊ-/ *noun* [U]: *prolonged exposure to harmful radiation*

subˈject sb/sth to sth *phrasal verb* [often passive] (*rather formal*) to make sb/sth experience, suffer or be affected by sth, usually sth unpleasant: *Referees are often subjected to verbal abuse.* ◇ *The city was subjected to heavy bombing.*

ˌput sb ˈthrough sth *phrasal verb* (*rather informal*) to make sb experience sth very difficult or unpleasant: *You have put your family through a lot recently.* ◇ *Why am I putting myself through all this?*

ˌlay sb ˈopen to sth *idiom* to put sb in a situation where they are likely to suffer criticism or embarrassment: *He has laid himself wide open to political attack.* See also **open to sth** → VULNERABLE

expression *noun*

1 expressions of sympathy
2 a worried expression on her face

1 expression · display · show · demonstration · exhibition
These are all words for actions that show feelings or qualities or express opinions or ideas.

PATTERNS AND COLLOCATIONS
► an expression / a display / a show / a demonstration of **support** / **affection**
► an expression / a display / a show of **concern** / **emotion**
► an expression / a display of **sympathy**
► an expression / a show of **gratitude**
► a display / show / demonstration of **strength**
► a display / show of **unity** / **force**
► a display / demonstration of **skill**
► a **public** expression / display / show / demonstration of sth

► an **open** expression / display of sth
► an **impressive** display / show / demonstration of sth
► a **great** display / show of sth

expression [C, U] (*rather formal*) things that people say, write or do in order to show their feelings, opinions and ideas: *The riots are the most serious expression of anti-government feeling yet.* ◇ *Freedom of expression* (= freedom to say what you think) *is a basic human right.* ◇ (*formal*) *Only in his dreams does he give expression to his fears.* ◇ *The poet's anger finds expression in* (= is shown in) *the last verse of the poem.* See also **express** → SAY 2

display [C] an act of showing a feeling, quality or skill: *My family has never gone in for open displays of affection.* ◇ *an ostentatious display of wealth* ◇ *a magnificent display of goalkeeping* See also **display** → SHOW *verb* 2

show [C] an act of showing a feeling, quality or skill: *He was completely unmoved by her little show of temper.* ◇ *She made a great show of wanting to leave, but I knew she didn't mean it.* See also **show** → SHOW *verb* 2

demonstration [C] (*rather formal*) an act of showing a feeling, quality or skill: *She was given to quite embarrassing public demonstrations of emotion.* ◇ *The performance was a remarkable demonstration of his abilities.* See also **demonstrate** → SHOW *verb* 3

NOTE DISPLAY, SHOW OR DEMONSTRATION? A **display** or **show** may be insincere, exaggerated, intended to impress, or not really intended at all (*a display/show of temper*). A **demonstration** is usually more sincere.

exhibition /ˌeksɪˈbɪʃn/ [C] (*especially BrE, rather formal*) an act of showing a skill or kind of behaviour: *We were treated to an exhibition of the footballer's speed and skill.* ◇ *It was an appalling exhibition of bad manners.*

2 expression · look · face
These are all words for the way your thoughts and feelings show in your face

PATTERNS AND COLLOCATIONS
► an expression / a look of **amazement** / **disbelief** / **horror**, etc.
► an expression / a look **on** sb's face
► an expression / a look **in** sb's eyes
► a/an **happy** / **sad** / **worried** / **anxious** / **troubled** / **angry** / **furious** / **stern** / **grim** / **serious** expression / look / face
► a/an **curious** / **odd** / **thoughtful** / **doubtful** / **pained** / **vacant** / **smug** expression / look

expression [C] the way your thoughts and feelings show in your face: *There was a worried expression on her face.* ◇ *His expression changed from surprise to one of amusement.* ◇ *facial expressions*

look [C] an expression in your eyes or face: *He didn't like the look in her eyes.* ◇ *We got a number of curious looks from passers-by.*

NOTE EXPRESSION OR LOOK? Your **expression** is usually a reflection of what you happen to be thinking or feeling at any particular moment; if you deliberately *put on* an expression, this is usually an attempt to hide your true thoughts or feelings: *She carefully put on her most innocent expression* (= she was not actually as innocent as she pretended). A **look** can be the expression that happens to be in your eyes, or it can be a way of deliberately communicating a thought or feeling to a particular person: you can *give* or *throw* sb a look or *exchange* looks with sb: *She threw him a dirty look.* ◇ *They exchanged meaningful looks.*

face [C] the expression on sb's face: *The news for the company isn't good, judging from the long faces* (= sad/worried faces) *in the boardroom.* ◇ *Her face lit up* (= showed happiness) *when she spoke of the past.* ◇ *His face fell* (= showed disappointment, sadness, etc.) *when he read the headlines.* ◇ *She pulled a face and gave a snorting kind of laugh.* ❶ In this meaning **face** is used especially in particular collocations, to show that sb is happy (*sb's face lights up*) or sad or disappointed *long faces; sb's face falls; sb pulls a face.*

extravagant *adj.*

extravagant · wasteful · lavish
These words all describe sb/sth that costs or uses too much money.

PATTERNS AND COLLOCATIONS
▸ extravagant / lavish **with** sth
▸ extravagant / wasteful / lavish **expenditure**
▸ the extravagant / wasteful / lavish **use** of sth
▸ extravagant / wasteful **consumption**
▸ an extravagant / a lavish **gift** / **present** / **lifestyle**

extravagant /ɪkˈstrævəgənt/ (*sometimes disapproving*) spending a lot more money or using a lot more of sth than you can afford or than is necessary; costing a lot more money than you can afford or is necessary: *I felt very extravagant spending £500 on a dress.* ◇ *She has very extravagant tastes.* ◇ *He bought us all these extravagant presents he couldn't really afford.*
▸ **extravagance** *noun* [U, C]: *Such extravagance is shameful when there are people starving in the world.* ◇ *Going to the theatre is our only extravagance.*

wasteful (*disapproving*) using more of sth than is necessary; not saving or keeping sth that could be used: *The whole process is wasteful and inefficient.* ◇ *This system is **wasteful of** time and energy.* See also **waste** → WASTE *verb*

lavish /ˈlævɪʃ/ large in amount, or impressive, and usually costing a lot of money: *He willingly accepted their lavish hospitality.* ◇ *a lavish dining room*

F f

fabric noun

fabric · cloth · material · textile
These are all words for woven or knitted cotton, silk, wool, etc., used for making things such as clothes and curtains, and for covering furniture.

PATTERNS AND COLLOCATIONS
- **fine / quality** fabric / cloth / material / textiles
- **beautiful / rich / coarse / soft / thick / thin** fabric / cloth / material
- **woven / cotton / woollen** fabric / cloth / material / textiles
- **synthetic** fabric / material / textiles
- **printed** fabric / cloth / textiles
- **furnishing / curtain / dress** fabric / material
- to **make / produce / weave / dye** fabric / cloth / textiles
- a **length / piece / strip / roll / scrap** of fabric / cloth / material

fabric [U, C] woven or knitted cotton, silk, wool, etc., used for making things such as clothes and curtains, and for covering furniture: *They sell a wide variety of printed cotton fabric.* ◇ *We manufacture quality furnishing fabrics.* **❶ Fabric** is often fairly strong material, and is often used when talking about covering furniture or making curtains.

cloth [U] fabric made by weaving or knitting cotton, wool, silk, etc: *They used to export cotton cloth.* ◇ *His bandages had been made from strips of cloth.* **❶ Cloth** is often fairly light material, especially in a form that has not been printed, treated, or prepared for use in any way: ~~dress / curtain / furnishing cloth~~. **Cloth** is frequently used in talking about buying and selling woven material.

material [U, C] fabric used for making clothes, curtains, etc: *You'll need a piece of material about 20 cm square.* ◇ *'What material is this dress made of?' 'Cotton.'* **❶ Material** is a more general word than **fabric** or **cloth** as it has the related meaning of 'a substance that things can be made from'. It is not used when it might not be clear which type of material is meant: ~~furnishing material~~ ◇ ~~the material industry / trade~~ ◇ ~~a material merchant / mill / manufacturer~~

textile [C, usually pl.] any type of fabric made by weaving or knitting: *He owns a factory producing a range of textiles.* ◇ *They're advertising for a textile designer.* **❶ Textile** is used mostly when talking about the business of making woven materials. The industry of making textiles is called **textiles**: *He got a job in textiles.*

face verb See also the entries for CONFRONT and TACKLE

face · confront · brave
These words all mean to have to deal with a problem or difficult situation.

PATTERNS AND COLLOCATIONS
- to be faced / confronted **with** sth
- to face / confront a **problem / dilemma / challenge / difficulty / crisis / situation**
- a **problem / dilemma / challenge / difficulty / situation** faces / confronts sb

face [T] to have to deal with a particular situation, especially a difficult one; (of problems or a difficult situation) to appear and need to be dealt with by sb: *We could all face higher fuel bills this winter.* ◇ *On their journey across the desert they faced danger of all sorts.* ◇ *I just can't face* (= am not willing to deal with) *work today.* ◇ *She is faced with a difficult situation.*

confront /kən'frʌnt/ [T] (of problems or a difficult situation) to appear and need to be dealt with by sb; to deal with a problem or difficult situation, especially one that you need to stop avoiding: *The government found itself confronted by massive opposition.* ◇ *She knew that she had to confront her fears.*

NOTE FACE OR CONFRONT? If you **confront** a problem or a situation, you usually actively decide to do sth to deal with it, rather than trying to ignore it. If you **face** sth, the problem or situation exists and you have no choice but to deal with it.

brave [T] (*written*) to show that you are willing to deal with sth difficult or unpleasant in order to achieve sth: *He did not feel up to braving the journalists at the airport.* ◇ *Over a thousand people braved the elements* (= went out in bad weather) *to attend the march.*

facilities noun

facilities · service · utility · resource · amenity
These are all words for things which are provided in a place for people to use.

PATTERNS AND COLLOCATIONS
- **public / basic / local** facilities / services / utilities / resources / amenities
- **essential / limited / adequate** facilities / services / resources
- **recreational / leisure** facilities / services / resources / amenities
- the facilities / services / resources / amenities **available**
- to **provide / lack** facilities / services / resources / amenities
- to **have access to** facilities / services / resources

facilities [pl.] things that are provided for a particular purpose, especially buildings or equipment: *Each apartment has basic cooking facilities and a small bathroom.* ◇ *All rooms have private facilities* (= a private bathroom). ◇ *The hotel has special facilities for welcoming disabled people.*

service [C] a system that provides sth that the public needs, organized by the government or a private company: *A free bus service to and from the venue is available.* ◇ *The postal service here is rather unreliable.* ◇ *The government aims to improve public services, especially education.* ◇ *Essential services* (= the supply of water, gas and electricity) *will be maintained.* ◇ *(BrE) A massive operation was launched by the emergency services* (= the police, fire and ambulance services). **❶** In American English these are usually referred to together as the **first responders**.

utility /juː'tɪləti/ [C] (*especially AmE*) a service provided for the public, for example a water, gas or electricity supply: *Public utilities such as water, gas and electricity come under the control of the government.* ◇ *Legislation will be introduced to regulate the privatized utilities.*

resource /rɪ'sɔːs; -'zɔːs; AmE 'riːsɔːrs; rɪ'sɔːrs/ [C] something that can be used to help achieve an aim, especially a book or piece of equipment that provides information for teachers and students: *The database could be used as a teaching resource in colleges.* ◇ *Time is your most valuable resource, especially in exams.*

amenity /ə'miːnəti; AmE ə'menəti/ [C, usually pl., U] (*rather formal*) a feature that makes a place pleasant, comfortable or easy to live in: *Many of the houses lacked even basic amenities* (= for example baths, showers or hot water). ◇ *(especially BrE) The area now has a far higher standard of amenity.*

fact *noun* See the Topic Map for FACT AND OPINION on p.898

fact · the truth · reality · so · the real world · real life
These words are all used to refer to a situation that you believe is true and not invented.

PATTERNS AND COLLOCATIONS
▶ in fact / reality / the real world / real life
▶ the fact / truth (of the matter) **is that…**
▶ to **face / accept / ignore** the fact / the truth / reality
▶ to be **based on** fact / the truth

fact [sing., U] used to refer to a particular situation that exists; things that are true rather than things that have been invented: *I could no longer ignore the fact that he was deeply unhappy.* ◊ **Despite the fact that** *she was wearing a seat belt, she was thrown sharply forward.* ◊ **The fact remains** *that we are still two teachers short.* ◊ *I thought the work would be difficult.* **In actual fact**, *it's very easy.* ◊ *The story is based on fact.* ◊ *It's important to distinguish fact from fiction.* **OPP** **fiction** → LIE, See also **fact** → INFORMATION, **factual** → RELIABLE 2, **the case** → SITUATION
the truth [sing.] the true facts about sth, rather than things that have been invented or guessed: *Do you think she's* **telling the truth?** ◊ *We are determined to get at (=* discover*) the truth.* ◊ *I don't think you are telling me the* **whole truth** *about what happened.* ◊ *The sad truth is that, at 72, he is past his prime.* See also **true** → TRUE
reality [U] the true situation and the problems that actually exist in life, in contrast to how you would like life to be: *You're out of touch with reality.* ◊ *Outwardly she seemed confident but in reality she felt extremely nervous.* **OPP** **fantasy** → IMAGINATION
so *adv.* (*especially spoken*) used to refer back to sth that has already been mentioned as being true: *I hear that you're a writer –* **is that so** (= is that true)? ◊ *He thinks I dislike him but that just* **isn't so.** ◊ *I might be away next week.* **If so,** *I won't be able to see you.* ❶ The adverb **so** can be used in the phrases *is that so?* and *that isn't so* to ask if or deny that sth is true, or in the phrase *if so,* when you are not sure if sth is true or a fact, and sth else depends on it.
the ˌreal ˈworld *idiom* the situations that people have to deal with in their lives, rather than artificial or imagined situations: *Politicians seem to be out of touch with the real world.* ❶ The expression **the real world** is sometimes used to refer to being outside a particular institution, such as a school or place of employment, where people are protected from some of life's difficulties: *The purpose of school is to prepare students to go out into the real world.*
ˌreal ˈlife *idiom* what happens in genuine situations rather than in an imaginary situation such as a story or film: *In the movies guns kill people instantly, but it's not like that in real life.*

factor *noun*

factor · point · consideration
These are all words for sth that is important or has an effect in a situation.

PATTERNS AND COLLOCATIONS
▶ a factor / consideration **in** sth
▶ a / an / the **additional / main / major / important / key / vital / chief / crucial / essential / prime** factor / point / consideration
▶ **political / practical** factors / points / considerations
▶ **economic / environmental** factors / considerations
▶ factors / points / considerations **to be taken into account**

factor [C] one of several things that cause or influence sth: *The closure of the mine was the single most important factor in the town's decline.* ◊ *Money proved to be the* **deciding factor.** ◊ *Studies have established that smoking is a* **risk factor** *for cancer.*
point [C] a fact that sb puts forward as part of an argument: *She* **made** *several interesting* **points** *in the article.* ◊ *How long it will last is a* **moot point** (= sth

which is uncertain or not agreed). ❶ Sb's **point** can be their opinion or argument, rather than a simple fact. See also **point** → VIEW 1
consideration /kənˌsɪdəˈreɪʃn/ [C] something that must be thought about when you are planning or deciding sth: *Financial considerations will obviously play a big part.* See also **concern** → ISSUE

factory *noun*

factory · plant · mill · works · yard · workshop · foundry
These are all words for buildings or places where things are made or where industrial processes take place.

PATTERNS AND COLLOCATIONS
▶ a **car / chemical / munitions** factory / plant
▶ an **engineering** plant / works
▶ to **manage / run** a factory / plant / mill / works / yard / workshop / foundry
▶ to **work in / at** a factory / plant / mill / yard / workshop / foundry
▶ a factory / plant / mill / works / workshop / foundry **makes / manufactures / produces** sth
▶ factory / mill / foundry **owners / managers / workers**

factory [C] a building or group of buildings where goods are made: *a chocolate/cigarette/clothing/soap factory* ◊ *The factory closed down ten years ago.*
plant [C] a factory or place where power is produced or an industrial process takes place: *a nuclear power plant* ◊ *a/ an assembly/manufacturing/production plant* ◊ *a sewage (treatment) plant* (= a place where chemicals are used to clean sewage)
mill [C] (often in compounds) a factory that produces a particular type of material: *a cotton/paper/textile/woollen mill*
works [C+sing./pl. v.] (often in compounds) a place where things are made or an industrial process takes place: *a steelworks* ◊ *Raw materials were carried to the works by barge.*
yard [C] (usually in compounds) an area of land used for building or growing sth: *a shipyard* ◊ *a construction yard* ◊ *a vineyard* (= for growing grapes to make wine)
workshop [C] a room or building where things are made or repaired using tools or machinery: *a car repair workshop* ◊ *The craftsmen worked in a freezing cold workshop.* See also **workroom** → OFFICE 2
foundry [C] a factory where metal or glass is melted and made into different shapes or objects: *an iron foundry*

fail *verb*
1 fail to keep an appointment
2 fail in your attempt
3 fail an exam

1 fail · forget · neglect · omit
These words all mean to not do sth that you should do.

PATTERNS AND COLLOCATIONS
▶ to **fail / forget / neglect / omit to do** sth
▶ to **completely / totally / almost / never / conveniently** fail / forget **to do** sth

fail [T, I] (*rather formal*) to not do sth: *He failed to keep the appointment.* ◊ *She never fails to email every week.* ◊ *I* **fail to see** (= I don't understand) *why you won't even give it a try.* ◊ *He felt he would be failing in his duty if he did not report it.*
▶ **failure** *noun* [U, C]: *Failure to comply with the regulations will result in prosecution.* ◊ *His confession followed repeated failures to appear in court.*
forget [I, T] to not remember to do sth that you ought to do: *'Why weren't you at the meeting?' 'Sorry – I forgot.'* ◊ *Take care, and don't forget to write.* ◊ (*spoken*) **Aren't you forgetting something?** (= I think you have forgotten to do sth). **OPP** **remember** → REMEMBER, See also **forget** → LEAVE 4

neglect /nɪˈglekt/ [I] (*formal*) to fail or forget to do sth that you ought to do: *You neglected to mention the name of your previous employer.*

omit /əˈmɪt/ (-**tt**-) [I] (*especially BrE, formal*) to fail to do sth: *She omitted to mention that they were staying the night.*

NOTE **NEGLECT** OR **OMIT**? **Neglect** can suggest that you think the person simply forgot or did not bother to carry out the necessary action; **omit** can suggest that not doing or saying sth was deliberate. **Omit** is used most often with speech-related verbs such as *ask, disclose, inform, mention, say* and *tell.*

2 **fail · go wrong · collapse · break down · get/go nowhere · backfire · founder · fall through · come to nothing**
These words all mean to be unsuccessful, especially after a period of time trying to do sth.

PATTERNS AND COLLOCATIONS
▸ a **plan** fails/ goes wrong/ backfires/ founders/ falls through/ comes to nothing
▸ a **relationship** / **marriage** fails/ goes wrong/ collapses/ breaks down
▸ **talks** fail/ collapse/ break down/ founder/ fall through
▸ a **project** fails/ collapses/ founders/ falls through
▸ a **deal** goes wrong/ collapses/ falls through
▸ to **fail** / backfire **badly**
▸ to **completely** fail/ break down
▸ to go **badly** / **completely** wrong

fail [I, T] (of a person or thing) to not be successful in achieving sth: *They had tried and they had failed.* ◊ *I **failed in** my attempt to persuade her.* ◊ *I tried to cheer her up, but **failed miserably**.* ◊ *She **failed** to get into art college.* **OPP** **succeed** → ACHIEVE, **succeed** → SUCCEED, See also **failure** → LOSER 2

go' wrong *idiom* (*rather informal*) (of a thing) to experience problems or difficulties; (of a person) to make a mistake: *The relationship started to go wrong when they moved abroad.* ◊ *What would you do if something **went wrong**?* ◊ *He was badly injured when the joke **went horribly wrong**.* ◊ *Where did we go wrong with those kids* (= what mistakes did we make for them to behave so badly)? ◊ *If you do what she tells you, you **won't go far wrong**.*

collapse /kəˈlæps/ [I] (of a thing or group of people) to fail suddenly and completely: *Talks between management and unions have collapsed.* ◊ *All opposition to the plan has collapsed.* ◊ *The home side collapsed spectacularly in the second half.*

,break 'down *phrasal verb* (of talks or a relationship) to fail after a period of time, especially because of a problem or difficulty: *The agreement broke down almost immediately.* ◊ ***Communication** between the two sides has **broken down**.* ◊ *They were divorced on the grounds that their marriage had **broken down irretrievably**.*

get/go 'nowhere, get sb 'nowhere *idiom* (*rather informal*) (usually of a person) to make no progress or have no success; to allow sb to do this: *We discussed it all morning but got nowhere.* ◊ *Do you ever get the feeling your job is going nowhere?* ◊ *Talking to him will get you nowhere.* **OPP** **get somewhere** ❶ To be **getting somewhere** is to be making progress in what you are doing: *At last I feel we're getting somewhere.*

backfire /ˌbækˈfaɪə(r)/ [I] (of a plan) to have the opposite effect to the one intended, with bad or dangerous results: *Unfortunately the plan backfired.* ◊ *The surprise I had planned **backfired on** me.*

founder [I] (*rather formal, written*) (of a plan or attempt to do sth) to fail because of a particular problem or difficulty: *The peace talks **foundered on** a basic lack of trust.* ◊ *The project foundered after problems with the funding.*

,fall 'through *phrasal verb* (of a plan) to not be completed, or not happen: *The deal fell through when the author received a more attractive offer.*

come to 'nothing, not 'come to anything *idiom* (*rather informal*) (of a plan or attempt to do sth) to be unsuccessful; to have no successful result: *How sad that all his hard work should come to nothing.* ◊ *Her plans didn't come to anything.*

3 See the Topic Map for EDUCATION on p.888
fail · flunk
These words both mean to not pass a test or exam, or to decide that sb has not passed a test or exam.

PATTERNS AND COLLOCATIONS
▸ to **fail** / flunk a / an **exam** / **examination** / **test** / **course**

fail [I, T] to not pass a test, exam or course; to decide that sb/sth has not passed a test, exam or course: *Once a student has **failed on** a few tasks, they lose motivation.* ◊ *What will you do if you fail?* ◊ *He failed his driving test.* ◊ *She was disqualified after failing a drugs test.* ◊ *My car failed its MOT.* ◊ *The examiners failed over half the candidates.* **OPP** **pass** → GRADUATE

flunk [I, T] (*especially AmE, informal*) (of a person) to fail a test, exam or course; to make sb fail a test, exam or course by giving them a low grade: *I flunked math in second grade.* ◊ *She's flunked 13 of the 18 students.* ◊ *He **flunked out of** college after four semesters* (= had to leave because his grades were not good enough). **OPP** **pass** → GRADUATE

failure *noun*

failure · collapse · breakdown
These are all words for a situation in which sth fails.

PATTERNS AND COLLOCATIONS
▸ a **failure** / collapse / breakdown **in** sth
▸ a / an **complete** / **total** / **general** / **apparent** failure / collapse / breakdown
▸ (an) **economic** failure / collapse / breakdown
▸ to **contribute to** / **lead to** / **result in** / **cause** / **avoid** the failure / collapse / breakdown (of sth)
▸ to **end in** failure / the breakdown (of sth)

failure [U] a lack of success in doing or achieving sth: *The success or failure of the plan depends on you.* ◊ *All my efforts ended in failure.* ◊ *There is a high failure rate with this treatment.* **OPP** **success** → ACHIEVE, See also **failure** → DISASTER

collapse /kəˈlæps/ [C, usually sing., U] a situation in which sth, such as an institution, a business or an attempt to do sth, fails suddenly: *The war has led to the collapse of agriculture in the area.* ◊ *He charted the villagers' **collapse into** poverty.* ◊ *The peace talks were **on the verge of** collapse.*

breakdown /ˈbreɪkdaʊn/ [C, U] the failure of a relationship, discussion or system: *A growing proportion of children are affected by family breakdown.* ◊ *The breakdown of negotiations was not expected.* ◊ *There seems to be a complete breakdown in law and order.*

faith *noun*

faith · belief · trust · confidence · certainty · conviction
These are all words for the feeling that you have when you are sure about sb/sth's abilities or good qualities.

PATTERNS AND COLLOCATIONS
▸ faith / belief / trust / confidence **in** sb / sth
▸ **great** / **absolute** faith / belief / trust / confidence / certainty / conviction
▸ **public** faith / belief / trust / confidence
▸ to **have** / **show** faith / trust / confidence
▸ to **lack** faith / belief / confidence / conviction
▸ to **lose** faith / sb's trust / confidence

▶ to **undermine** faith / belief / trust / confidence / certainty
▶ to **shake** sb's faith / belief / confidence / conviction
▶ to **destroy** sb's faith / belief / trust / confidence
▶ to **put** / **place** your faith / trust **in** sb / sth
▶ a **lack of** faith / belief / trust / confidence / certainty / conviction

faith [U, sing.] the feeling of being sure about sb's ability or good qualities; the feeling of being sure that sb/sth will do what they promise: *I have great faith in you − I know you'll do well.* ◇ *Her friend's kindness restored her faith in human nature.* ❶ If you have **blind faith** in sb/sth, you believe in them without question, often in a way that seems unreasonable to others. See also **faith** → RELIGION, **faithful** → RELIABLE 1

belief [U] a strong feeling that sb/sth exists or is true; faith that sb/sth is good or right: *I admire his passionate belief in what he is doing.* ◇ *Belief in God is more than a matter of logic.* See also **believe in sth** → IN FAVOUR, **believe in sb** → TRUST *verb*

▶ **believe** *verb* [T, I] (not used in the progressive tenses): *I don't believe you!* ◇ *People used to believe that the earth was flat.* ◇ *The god appears only to those who believe.* **OPP disbelieve** → SUSPECT

trust [U] the feeling that you can rely on sb/sth because they are good, sincere and honest and will not try to harm or deceive you: *It has taken years to earn their trust.* ◇ *She will not betray your trust* (= do sth that you have asked her not to do). ◇ *Many people feel it is a breach of trust to give out information about their loved one.* See also **trust** → TRUST *verb*, **trusted** → RELIABLE 1, **trusting** → NAIVE

confidence [U] the feeling that you can be sure about the abilities or good qualities of sb/sth: *A fall in unemployment will help to restore consumer confidence.* ◇ *She has every confidence in her students' abilities.* See also **confident** → SURE, **have confidence in sb/sth** → TRUST *verb*

> **NOTE FAITH** OR **CONFIDENCE?** **Faith** is used especially in the context of human relationships; **confidence** is used especially in business contexts.

certainty [U] the state of having no doubt that sth is true or correct: *There is no certainty that the president's removal would end the civil war.* ◇ *I can't say with any certainty where I'll be next week.* **OPP uncertainty** → DOUBT 1, See also **certain** → SURE

conviction /kən'vɪkʃn/ [U] the feeling or appearance of believing sth strongly and of being sure about it: *'Not true!' she said with conviction.* ◇ *The leader's speech in defence of the policy didn't carry much conviction.*

fake *noun* See also the entry for COPY 2

─────────────────────────────

fake · imitation · forgery · dummy
These are all words for an object that is not genuine but has been made to look as if it is.

PATTERNS AND COLLOCATIONS
▶ a **good** fake / imitation / forgery
▶ a **cheap** fake / imitation
▶ a **poor** / **crude** imitation / forgery

fake [C] an object such as a work of art, a coin or a piece of jewellery that is not genuine but has been made to look as if it is: *All the paintings proved to be fakes.* ◇ *She had long ago sold the diamonds and replaced them with fakes.* See also **fake** → ARTIFICIAL *adj.* 1, **fake** → SO-CALLED *adj.*

imitation /ˌɪmɪ'teɪʃn/ [C] a copy of a type of product, material or production, especially sth expensive or well known: *Many tourists cannot tell the difference between authentic Indian craftwork and imported imitations.* ◇ *The remake is a pale imitation of the original 1966 film* (= it is not nearly as good). ❶ People often use **imitation** to suggest that the copy is not nearly as good as the real thing: *a poor/cheap/pale/second-rate imitation.* It can also be used like an adjective to talk about materials from which things are made: *imitation fur/gold/leather/*

marble/silk/pearls or about copies of weapons: *an imitation sword/firearm/gun/bomb* See also **imitation** → ARTIFICIAL 1

forgery /'fɔːdʒəri; *AmE* 'fɔːrdʒ-/ [C] something, for example a document, a piece of paper money or a painting, that has been copied in order to deceive people: *Experts are dismissing claims that the painting is a forgery.* ◇ *If the signature on the deed is a forgery, the whole legal position changes.*

▶ **forge** *verb* [T]: *She was getting good at forging her mother's signature.*

> **NOTE FAKE** OR **FORGERY?** **Forgery** is mostly used to talk about things that can be written, drawn, printed or painted, where this is done in order to deceive people. **Fake** can refer to any object that is made or produced, as well as artificial copies of natural objects (for example, jewels); **fakes** may or may not be used to deceive people.

dummy [C] a thing that seems to be real but is only a copy of the real thing: *The bottles of whisky on display are all dummies.* ❶ A **dummy** is often sth that has been made to look real so that people can use it for practising a possibly dangerous skill such as driving or shooting, or for a film or play. See also **dummy** → SO-CALLED *adj.*

fall *verb*

1 the temperature falls
2 fall into the river
3 slip and fall on the ice

─────────────────────────────

1 See also the entry for SLUMP

fall · decline · drop · diminish · decrease · sink · come down
These are all words that can be used when the amount, level or number of sth goes down.

PATTERNS AND COLLOCATIONS
▶ to fall / decline / drop / diminish / decrease / sink / come down **by** 100, 25%, a half, etc.
▶ to fall / decline / drop / decrease / sink / come down **from** 15 000 **to** 1 000
▶ to decline / diminish / decrease / come down **in** number, level, size, etc.
▶ to decline / diminish / decrease **with** age, time, experience, etc.
▶ **numbers** fall / decline / drop / diminish / decrease / come down
▶ **levels** fall / decline / drop / decrease
▶ **prices** / **rates** fall / decline / drop / decrease / sink / come down
▶ **profits** / **sales** fall / decline / drop / decrease / sink
▶ the **temperature** falls / drops
▶ sb's **voice** falls / drops / sinks
▶ to fall / decline / drop / diminish / decrease / sink **sharply** / **rapidly**
▶ to fall / decline / drop / decrease **dramatically** / **suddenly**
▶ to fall / decline / drop / diminish / decrease **slightly** / **slowly** / **gradually** / **steadily**

fall [I, T] to become lower or less in level, number or strength: *Their profits have fallen by 30 per cent.* ◇ *The temperature fell sharply in the night.* ◇ *Falling birth rates could have an impact on future economic growth.* ◇ (written) *Her voice fell to a whisper.* ◇ *Share prices fell 30p.* **OPP rise** → RISE, See also **fall** → REDUCTION *noun*

decline /dɪ'klaɪn/ [I] (*rather formal, especially written*) to become lower or less in level, number, size, strength or importance: *The number of tourists visiting the resort declined by 10% last year.* ◇ *Manufacturing industry has slowly declined in importance.* **OPP increase** → RISE, See also **decline** → REDUCTION *noun*

drop (**-pp-**) [I] (not used in the progressive tenses) to become lower or less in level, number or strength: *The Dutch team have dropped to fifth place.* ◇ *At last the wind dropped.* **OPP rise**, **climb** → RISE, See also **drop** → REDUCTION *noun*

> **NOTE FALL, DECLINE** OR **DROP?** In many cases you can use any of these words: *Sales have fallen/declined/dropped by 20%.* They can all be used to talk about numbers,

levels, rates, prices, profits and sales. To talk about a loss of economic strength in a particular place or industry, use **decline**: *The area/city/industry/market/ sector has declined (in importance).* You can also use **decline** to talk about support for or interest in sth, or a person's health. A person's *voice* can **fall** or **drop**. *Temperatures* **fall** or **drop**. The *wind* can only **drop**. Things can **fall** or **decline** over a period of time, but **drop** cannot be used in the progressive tenses: *Sales have been falling/declining.* ◇ *falling/declining sales* ◇ ~~Sales have been dropping.~~ ◇ ~~dropping sales~~

diminish /dɪˈmɪnɪʃ/ [I] (*rather formal, especially written*) to become lower or less in number, amount or strength: *The world's resources are rapidly diminishing.* ◇ *His influence has diminished with time.* ◇ *Our efforts were producing diminishing returns* (= we achieved less although we spent more time or money). ❶ *Numbers* and *amounts* of sth can **diminish**, but figures, rates, levels, profits and sales cannot. **OPP** **enhance** → IMPROVE 1

decrease [I] (*rather formal*) to fall in number or level: *The number of new students decreased from 210 to 160 this year.* ◇ *The number of quarrels among children decreases with age* (= the older they are, the fewer quarrels they have). **OPP** **increase** → RISE, See also **decrease** → REDUCTION noun

sink [I] (*especially business*) to fall in value or strength: *The pound has sunk to its lowest recorded level against the dollar.* ◇ *His voice sank almost to a whisper.* **OPP** **rise** → RISE

come 'down *phrasal verb* (especially of prices) to fall in level: *The price of gas is coming down.* ◇ *Gas is coming down in price.* **OPP** **go up** → RISE

---

2 fall · go down (sth) · come down (sth) · descend · drop · sink · crash · tumble · topple · plunge
These words all mean to move downwards, especially suddenly and/or by accident.

PATTERNS AND COLLOCATIONS
▶ to fall / go / come / drop / sink / crash / tumble **down**
▶ to go down / come down / descend the **stairs / steps**
▶ to go down / come down / descend a **ladder**
▶ to fall / plunge **to your death**

fall [I] (usually used with an adverb or preposition) to go from a higher place to a lower place, especially suddenly and/or by accident: *Several of the books had fallen onto the floor.* ◇ *One of the kids fell into the river.* ◇ *September had come and the leaves were starting to fall.* ◇ *He fell 23 metres onto the rocks below.*
▶ **fall** *noun* [C]: *She was killed in a fall from a horse.*

go 'down sth, **go 'down** *phrasal verb* to move from a higher place to a lower place; to fall to the ground: *I've been going up and down the stairs all day.* ◇ *The sun went down below the horizon.* ◇ *She tripped and went down with a bump.* **OPP** **go up (sth)** → CLIMB

come 'down sth, **come 'down** *phrasal verb* to move from a higher place to a lower place; to break and fall to the ground: *She came down the steps two at a time.* ◇ *The ceiling came down with a terrific crash.* **OPP** **go up (sth)** → CLIMB

NOTE GO DOWN OR COME DOWN? Go is usually used from the point of view of the person who is moving somewhere. Come is usually used from the point of view of the person or place that sb/sth is moving to or towards.

descend /dɪˈsend/ [I, T] (*formal*) to go down from a higher place to a lower place: *The plane began to descend.* ◇ *She descended the stairs slowly.* **OPP** **ascend** → CLIMB
▶ **descent** *noun* [C, usually sing.]: *The plane began its descent to Heathrow.*

drop (-pp-) [I] to fall by accident; to fall or sit down, especially because you are no longer able to stand: *The climber slipped and dropped to his death.* ◇ *He staggered in and dropped into a chair.*

sink [I] (usually used with an adverb or preposition) (of a person) to move downwards, especially by falling or sitting down; (of an object) to move slowly downwards: *She sank back into her seat.* ◇ *The old man had sunk to his knees.* ◇ *The foundations of the building are starting to sink.*

crash [I] (usually used with an adverb or preposition) to hit sth hard while moving, causing noise and/or damage: *A brick crashed through the window.* ◇ *With a sweep of his hand he sent the glasses crashing to the floor.* ◇ *The door crashed open.*

tumble [I] to fall suddenly and in a dramatic way: *The scaffolding came tumbling down.*
▶ **tumble** *noun* [C, usually sing.]: *The jockey took a nasty tumble at the third fence.*

topple [I] (always used with an adverb or preposition) to become unsteady and fall down: *The pile of books toppled over.*

plunge [I] (always used with an adverb or preposition) to move suddenly forwards and/or downwards: *She lost her balance and plunged 100 feet to her death.*

---

3 fall · fall over · stumble · trip · fall down
These words all mean to stop standing suddenly.

PATTERNS AND COLLOCATIONS
▶ to stumble / trip **over** sth

fall (usually used with an adverb or preposition) [I] (*especially written*) to suddenly stop standing: *She slipped and fell on the ice.*

fall 'over *phrasal verb* (*especially spoken*) to suddenly stop standing: *I fell over and cut my knee.*

stumble [I] to hit your foot against sth while you are walking or running and fall or almost fall: *The child stumbled and fell.* ◇ *I stumbled over a rock.*

trip (-pp-) [I] (usually used with an adverb or preposition) to catch your foot on sth and fall or almost fall: *Someone will trip over that cable.* ◇ *Be careful you don't trip up on the step.*

fall 'down *phrasal verb* to suddenly stop standing: *The house looked as if it was about to fall down.*

NOTE FALL, FALL OVER OR FALL DOWN? Fall and fall over are only used to talk about people in this meaning; fall down can be used to talk about people, buildings, or other structures that can *stand* and then suddenly stop standing. Fall is used more in writing. In British English fall over is used more in speech. In American English fall down is used more in speech.

---

fall asleep *verb*

fall asleep · go to sleep · get to sleep · drift off · crash · nod off
These words all mean to start to sleep.

PATTERNS AND COLLOCATIONS
▶ to fall asleep / go to sleep / nod off **during/in the middle of** sth
▶ sb **must have** fallen asleep / gone to sleep / drifted off / nodded off
▶ to drift off / nod off **to sleep**
▶ to **finally** fall asleep / go to sleep / get to sleep / drift off

fall a'sleep *phrase* to start to sleep, sometimes when you do not intend to or in a situation that is not appropriate: *When she finally fell asleep, she began to dream.* ◇ *Half of the audience was falling asleep.* **OPP** **wake, wake up** → WAKE UP

go to 'sleep *phrase* to start to sleep, especially when you intend to: *Go to sleep — it's late.* ◇ *The baby just wouldn't go to sleep.* ◇ *He woke for a moment and then went to sleep again.* **OPP** **wake, wake up** → WAKE UP

get to 'sleep *phrase* to start sleeping, especially after a long time or when this is difficult: *When I finally got to sleep, I had the strangest dream.*

,drift 'off *phrasal verb* (*especially BrE*) to fall asleep, especially gradually: *I must have drifted off, because when I woke we were nearly home.* ◇ *The thought came back to me just before I drifted off to sleep.*

crash [I] (*informal*) to fall asleep; to sleep somewhere where you do not usually sleep: *I was so tired I **crashed out** on the sofa.* ◇ *Can I crash at your place tonight?*

,nod 'off *phrasal verb* (-dd-) (*especially BrE*, *informal*) to fall asleep for a short time, especially when you are sitting down and when you are not supposed to be sleeping: *I was practically nodding off in that meeting.*

false *adj.*

false · hollow · insincere
These words all describe people saying or doing things that they do not really mean or believe.

PATTERNS AND COLLOCATIONS
▸ false / hollow / insincere **words**
▸ a false / a hollow / an insincere **smile**
▸ a false / hollow **promise**
▸ to **look / sound / ring** false / hollow
▸ **completely / totally** false / insincere

false saying or doing sth that you do not really mean or believe: *Come on – this is no time for **false modesty**.* ◇ *She gave a tinkly little laugh, which sounded horribly false even to her own ears.* ❶ **False** is often used to describe people trying to appear more interesting, pleasant or important than they really are.

hollow [*usually before noun*] false: *He gave a hollow laugh.* ◇ *Their appeal for an end to the violence **had a hollow ring** (= quality) **to it**.* ❶ A **hollow** *laugh* or *voice* sounds sad or angry rather than happy or sincere. **Hollow** *promises*, *threats* or *words* are about things that will not really happen. Something that *has a hollow ring to it*, or that *rings hollow*, does not seem sincere or real.

insincere (*rather formal*) false: *She gave him one of her insincere smiles.* ❶ **Insincere** is often used to describe people trying to appear kinder or more moral or religious than they really are, especially in order to help their careers, for example in politics or television. **OPP** sincere → DEEP 1, sincere → HONEST

fame *noun* See the Topic Map for THE MEDIA on p.900

fame · publicity · prominence · celebrity · stardom
These are all words for the state of being well known to the public because of what you do or who you are.

PATTERNS AND COLLOCATIONS
▸ fame / prominence / celebrity **as** sth
▸ **international** fame / publicity / prominence / celebrity / stardom
▸ to **achieve / shoot to** fame / prominence / stardom

fame [U] the state of being known and talked about by many people: *She **found fame** on the stage.* ◇ *Tennis brought him **fame and fortune**, but it didn't bring happiness.* ◇ *He disappeared in 1934, **at the height of his fame**.* ◇ *The town's only **claim to fame** is that it is the birthplace of Einstein.* **OPP** obscurity ❶ **Obscurity** is the state of not being well known or of being forgotten: *The actress was only 17 when she was plucked from obscurity and made a star.* See also **famous**, **famed** → FAMOUS

publicity [U] the attention that is given to sb/sth by newspapers, television, etc: *Taking part in the event will be good publicity for our school.* ◇ *There has been a great deal of publicity surrounding his disappearance.*

prominence /'prɒmɪnəns; *AmE* 'prɑːm-/ [U, sing.] (*written*) the state of being important, well known or noticeable: *She **came to prominence** as an artist in the 1960s.* ◇ *The issue was given great prominence in the press.* See also **prominent** → FAMOUS

celebrity /sə'lebrəti/ [U] the state of being a famous person, especially in the media: *Does she find her new celebrity intruding on her private life?* ◇ *He briefly achieved*

celebrity *as a radical politician.* See also **celebrity** → STAR 1, **celebrated** → FAMOUS

NOTE FAME OR CELEBRITY? **Fame** is a general word for the state of being known by many people. It can refer to people, groups, events or places and can last over a short or a long period of time. **Celebrity** usually refers to individual people and is used about sb who is well known at a particular time, especially an actor, singer, sportsperson, etc. who is often seen or discussed in the media.

stardom [U] the state of being very famous as an actor, singer or musician: *The group is being **tipped for stardom** (= people say they will be very famous).* ◇ *He achieved almost instant stardom.* See also **star** → STAR *noun* 1

family *noun*

1 a family of four
2 the support of family and friends
3 The painting has been in our family for generations.

1 family · household · home · house
These are all words for the people who live together in the same building.

PATTERNS AND COLLOCATIONS
▸ a **low-income / poor / high-income / wealthy / rich** family / household / home
▸ a **middle-class / working-class** family / household / home
▸ a **one-parent / single-parent** family / household / home
▸ a **large / big / small** family / household
▸ a **friendly / happy** family / home / house
▸ an / the **average** family / household / home
▸ to **come from** a …family / home
▸ to **be one of the** family / household
▸ family / household **income**
▸ sb's family / home **life / background / situation**
▸ a / the **member / head** of the family / household

family [C+sing./pl. v.] a group consisting of one or two parents and their children: *a family of four* ◇ *families with young children* ◇ *the other members of my family* ◇ *All my family enjoy skiing.* ◇ *Almost every family in the country owns a television.* ◇ *He's a friend of the family (= he is known and liked by the parents and the children).* ◇ *Not everybody lives in the conventional **nuclear family** (= a family that consists of father, mother and children).* ◇ *a family business/car*

household [C] all the people living together in a house, especially when considered as an economic unit: *Most households now own at least one car.* ◇ *House prices are rising, driven by the big increase in the number of **single-person households**.* ◇ *The average household pays 27p a day in water rates.* ◇ *household bills/chores/goods*

NOTE FAMILY OR HOUSEHOLD? Members of a **family** are related to each other, but a member of a **household** could be sb who rents a room in the house, or sb who lives with the family and works for them, for example. **Family** emphasizes the individuals involved and is used to talk about who they are, what activities they like, how good the relationship is, etc. **Household** is often used in news reports and business writing, emphasizing the group as a unit, especially when referring to their position in society, the money they spend or earn, etc.

home [C] a family living together, and the way it behaves: *They wanted to give the boy a secure and loving home.* ◇ *She comes from a **broken home** (= a family in which the parents are divorced or separated).* ◇ *She had never had a stable home life.*

house [sing.] all the people in a house: *Be quiet or you'll wake the whole house!*

2 family · relative · relation · kin · connections
These are all words for a person who is related to sb else, or a group of people who are related to each other.

PATTERNS AND COLLOCATIONS
▶ a relative / relation **of mine, yours, his, etc.**
▶ (a) **close / near / distant** relative / relation / kin
▶ the / sb's **immediate** family / relatives / relations
▶ (a) **female / male** relative / relation / kin
▶ a **living / surviving** relative / relation
▶ to **have** family / relatives / relations (in Australia, abroad, in the car trade, etc.)
▶ to **stay with / visit** family / relatives / relations
▶ **friends and** family / relatives / relations

family [C+sing./pl. v., U] a group consisting of one or two parents, their children and other people who are related to them, for example grandparents, wives and husbands: *All our family came to Grandad's eightieth birthday party.* ◇ *The support of family and friends is vital.* ◇ *I always think of you as one of the family.* ◇ (*informal*) *She's family* (= she is related to us). ◇ *She grew up surrounded by a large **extended family*** (= a family group that includes not only parents and children but also uncles, aunts, grandparents, etc.).

relative [C] a person who is in the same family as sb else; a thing that belongs to the same group as sth else: *I have close relatives.* ◇ *She's looking after an elderly relative.* ◇ *The ibex is a distant relative of the mountain goat.*
▶ **related** *adj.*: *We're distantly related.* ◇ *The llama is related to the camel.*

relation [C] a person who is in the same family as sb else: *She's a distant relation of mine.* ◇ *He's called Brady too, but we're **no relation*** (= not related). ◇ *Is he any **relation to** you?*

> **NOTE** **RELATIVE** OR **RELATION?** Sometimes you can use either word: *She's a distant relative/relation of mine.* **Relative** is often used when the exact relationship between the people is not known or does not matter: *On his death, the house will pass to the nearest surviving relative* (= whichever relative that happens to be). **Relation** is used especially when you are stating or asking the degree of relationship between people: *We're no relation.* ◇ *What relation is Rita to you?* It is also used, both literally and figuratively, in the phrase *poor relation*: *Our branch of the family was always regarded as the **poor relations**.* ◇ (*figurative*) *He believes that interior design is the **poor relation** of* (= inferior to) *architecture.*

kin [pl.] (*old-fashioned or formal*) your family or your relatives: *Marriage between close kin is prohibited.* ◇ *I'm her **next of kin*** (= her closest living relative). ❶ **Kin** is most often used in the expression **next of kin**.

connections [pl.] people who are your relatives, but not members of your close family: *She is British but also has German connections.* ◇ *He has a whole network of family connections in Italy.*

3 See also the entry for BACKGROUND
family · origin · dynasty · lineage · blood · descent · ancestry · birth · pedigree · roots · parentage
These are words for all the people who are related to each other, including those who are dead.

PATTERNS AND COLLOCATIONS
▶ **by** origin / descent / birth
▶ to be **of** noble, Scottish, etc. origin / lineage / blood / descent / ancestry / birth / pedigree / parentage
▶ **ethnic / racial / social / cultural** origin / descent / ancestry / pedigree / roots
▶ **African, Scottish, Italian, etc.** family / origin / lineage / blood / descent / ancestry / roots / parentage
▶ (of) **humble / lowly** family / origins / birth / roots
▶ (of) **noble** family / origins / lineage / blood / descent / ancestry / birth
▶ (of) **unknown** origin / descent / parentage
▶ **middle-class / working-class / peasant** family / origins / roots
▶ to **trace** your family / origin / lineage / ancestry / pedigree / roots

family [C+sing./pl. v.] all the people who are related to each other, including those who are now dead: *Some families have farmed in this area for hundreds of years.* ◇ *This painting has **been in our family** for generations.* ◇ *How far back can you trace your **family tree*** (= a diagram that shows the relationship between members of a family over a long period of time)? ◇ *Heart disease **runs in the family**.*

origin [C, U] (also **origins** [pl.]) a person's social and family background: *children of various ethnic origins* ◇ *people of German origin* ◇ *a person's country of origin* (= where they were born) ◇ *She has risen from humble origins to immense wealth.* See also **origin** → SOURCE

dynasty /'dɪnəsti; *AmE* 'daɪ-/ [C] a series of rulers of a country who all belong to the same family; a period of years during which members of a particular family rule a country: *the Nehru-Gandhi dynasty* ◇ *a Ming dynasty vase* ◇ *Eventually the dynasty was overthrown, and the country became a Republic.*
▶ **dynastic** /dɪ'næstɪk; *AmE* daɪ-/ *adj.* [usually before noun]: *dynastic history*

lineage /'lɪniɪdʒ/ [U, C] (*formal*) the series of families that sb is descended from, especially when these are families of high social position that go back a long way in history: *a French nobleman of ancient lineage* See also **line** → SERIES

blood [U] (*rather formal*) family origins: *She is of noble blood.* ◇ *There is some Polish blood on his father's side.*

descent /dɪ'sent/ [U] (*rather formal*) family origins: *people of West Indian descent* ◇ *He traces his **line of descent** from the Stuart kings.*

ancestry /'ænsestri/ [C, usually sing., U] (*rather formal*) family origins: *His eyes owed their startling blueness to his Irish ancestry.* ◇ *He was able to trace his ancestry back over 1000 years.*
▶ **ancestor** *noun* [C]: *His ancestors had come to America from Ireland.* ◇ *a reptile that was the common ancestor of lizards and turtles* **OPP** **descendant** → SON

> **NOTE** **BLOOD, DESCENT** OR **ANCESTRY?** These are all rather formal ways of talking about sb's family origins. You *trace your descent from* sb, starting in the past and coming forward to the present; you *trace your ancestry back to* sb, starting with yourself and working back. **Blood** is used especially to emphasize either the high social position of sb's family, or the fact that sb is descended from a number of different families in different places: *of noble blood* ◇ *of mixed Chinese and Portuguese blood* ◇ *some Polish blood on his father's side*

birth [U] a person's origin or the social position of their family, especially when this is different from their current situation, or when they are of high social position: *Anne was French by birth but lived most of her life in Italy.* ◇ *a woman of noble birth*

pedigree /'pedɪgriː/ [C, U] a person's family history or the background of sth, especially when this is impressive: *She was proud of her long pedigree.* ◇ *The product has a pedigree going back to the last century.*

roots [pl.] the feelings or connections that you have with a place because you have lived there or your family came from there: *I'm proud of my African roots.* ◇ *After 20 years in America, I still feel my roots are in Ireland.* See also **root** → SOURCE

parentage /'peərəntɪdʒ; *AmE* 'per-/ [U] the origin of a person's parents and who they are: *a young American of German parentage* ◇ *Nothing is known about her parentage and background.*

famous *adj.* See the Topic Map for THE MEDIA on p.900

famous · historic · well known · prominent · public · legendary · renowned · famed · glorious · celebrated
These words all describe people, places or things that are known about and often liked or admired by many people.

PATTERNS AND COLLOCATIONS
▸ famous/well known/prominent/renowned/famed/celebrated **as** sb
▸ famous/well known/legendary/renowned/famed/celebrated **for** sth
▸ a famous/historic/well-known/prominent/legendary/glorious/celebrated **name**
▸ a famous/historic/well-known/prominent/public/legendary/renowned **figure**
▸ a famous/well-known/prominent/renowned/celebrated **writer/author/actor/architect/artist/collection**
▸ a famous/well-known/prominent **politician/personality**
▸ a famous/well-known/renowned **brand**
▸ **very** famous/well known/prominent/celebrated
▸ **justly** famous/renowned/famed/celebrated
▸ **internationally** famous/renowned/celebrated

famous known about by a lot of people: *He became a world-famous conductor.* ◇ *Loch Ness is probably the most famous lake in Scotland.* ◇ *One day, I'll be rich and famous.* ◇ *So this is the famous dress!* (= the one we have heard a lot about but have not seen) See also **fame** → FAME

▸ **famously** *adv.*: *the words he famously uttered on his deathbed*

historic important in history; likely to be thought of as important at some time in the future: *a historic building/monument* ◇ *The area is of special historic interest.* ◇ *The party has won a historic victory at the polls.* See also **ancient** → OLD 1

well 'known known about by a lot of people: *She's married to a well-known actor, whose name I've forgotten.* ◇ *His books are not well known.* ❶ Remember to use a hyphen when **well known** comes before the noun.

prominent /'prɒmɪnənt; *AmE* 'prɑːm-/ (*rather formal, especially written*) important or well known: *A number of prominent politicians made public statements supporting the change.* ◇ *He played a prominent part in the campaign.* ◇ *She was prominent in the fashion industry.* ❶ **Prominent** is often used to talk about people in politics and business. See also **prominence** → FAME, See also the entries for GREAT 2 and TOP *adj.*

public known to people in general: *She entered public life* (= started a job in which she became known to the public) *at the age of 23.* ◇ *Details of the government report have not yet been made public.* **OPP** **private** → SECRET 1, See also **public figure** → STAR 1

legendary /'ledʒəndri; *AmE* -deri/ very famous and talked about a lot by people, especially in a way that shows admiration: *We once received a visit from the legendary Orson Welles.* ◇ *Her patience and tact are legendary.* ❶ **Legendary** is often used to talk about people who are dead or old, but who are still talked about and admired. See also **legend** → STAR 1

renowned /rɪ'naʊnd/ (*especially written*) famous and respected: *We asked for advice from the renowned legal expert, Sam Pincher.* ◇ *It is renowned as one of the region's best restaurants.* ◇ *She is renowned for her patience.* ❶ A person who is **renowned** is respected because they do their job very well, or because they have a special skill or ability. A place that is **renowned** is respected because it provides a service of a very high standard.

famed (*written*) (of a person or place) known about by many people, especially for a special quality that they have: *As a player she was famed for her grace and artistry, as well as her success.* ◇ *The movie was filmed in the famed Blue Ridge Mountains, possibly the last forested wilderness in the United States.* See also **fame** → FAME

glorious [usually before noun] (*formal*) deserving or bringing great fame and success: *We congratulate you on this glorious victory.* ◇ *This is a glorious chapter in our country's history.* ❶ **Glorious** is used especially in historical or political literature. See also **glory** → STATUS

celebrated /'selɪbreɪtɪd/ [usually before noun] (*written*) famous for having good qualities: *He is one of France's most celebrated painters.* ◇ *'The Kiss' is one of Rodin's most celebrated works.* ❶ **Celebrated** is often used to talk about

people who are successful in the arts, as well as their works: *a celebrated artist/painter/sculptor/poet/novelist/actor/actress/painting/work/poem/novel* See also **celebrity** → FAME

fan *noun* See the Topic Map for SPORT AND LEISURE on p.892

fan · enthusiast · supporter · lover · admirer · fanatic · devotee · groupie · follower · addict · freak
These are all words for a person who likes a particular thing, activity or person very much.

PATTERNS AND COLLOCATIONS
▸ a **great** fan/enthusiast/lover/admirer
▸ a **true** fan/enthusiast/admirer
▸ a **keen** fan/enthusiast/supporter/admirer/follower
▸ a **real** fan/enthusiast/fanatic/freak
▸ a **big** fan/supporter/admirer
▸ a **music/art/jazz** fan/enthusiast/lover/fanatic/devotee
▸ a **sports/football/boxing/cricket**, etc. fan/enthusiast/fanatic/devotee
▸ a **fitness/health** enthusiast/fanatic/freak

fan [C] a person who admires sb/sth or enjoys watching or listening to sb/sth very much: *Movie fans will be familiar with his work already.* ◇ *Crowds of football fans filled the streets.* ◇ *He's always been a big fan of Pavarotti.* ◇ *She received bags of fan mail* (= letters from her fans). ◇ (*AmE*) *He's a big Yankees fan.*

enthusiast /ɪn'θjuːziæst; *AmE* -'θuː-/ [C] a person who is very interested in sth and spends a lot of time doing it: *Railway enthusiasts were given the chance to ride on the old steam train during the weekend.* ◇ *She was a lifelong enthusiast of dancing, running and waterskiing.* See also **enthusiastic** → EAGER

NOTE **FAN** OR **ENTHUSIAST?** Both words can be used about an activity or subject, but only **fan** can be used about a person: *jazz/fishing/DIY fans/enthusiasts* ◇ *fans of the pop star Madonna* ◇ ~~enthusiasts of the pop star Madonna~~. An **enthusiast** is often more actively involved in sth than a **fan**: **enthusiast** emphasizes the fact that sb spends a lot of their free time doing sth; **fan** emphasizes the enjoyment of sth. See also **buff** → EXPERT

supporter [C] (*BrE*) a person who supports a particular sports team, especially a football team: *They are both keen Arsenal supporters.* ❶ To **support** a sports team means to watch their games, follow their progress, etc. In American English use *fan* instead.

lover [C] (often in compounds) a person who likes or enjoys a particular thing very much: *He was a devoted animal lover, and had a large number of pets at home.* ◇ *She was a great lover of the arts, and of Greek architecture in particular.* ◇ *an art-lover/a nature-lover* See also **love** → LIKE *verb*

admirer [C] (*rather formal*) a person who admires sb/sth, especially a well-known person or thing: *He is a great admirer of Picasso's early paintings.* See also **admire** → RESPECT *verb*

fanatic /fə'nætɪk/ [C] (*rather informal, sometimes disapproving*) a person who is very enthusiastic about sth, especially in a way that other people think is extreme: *He's a non-smoking, non-drinking, fitness fanatic.*
▸ **fanatical** *adj.*: *a fanatical interest in football* ◇ *She's fanatical about healthy eating.*

devotee /ˌdevə'tiː/ [C] a person who admires and is very enthusiastic about sb/sth: *He's been a golf devotee for 23 years.* ◇ *a devotee of science fiction* ❶ **Devotee** emphasizes the fact that sb is willing to put a lot of time and effort into sth. See also **devote** → DEVOTE

groupie [C] (*rather informal, sometimes disapproving*) a person, especially a young woman, who follows pop musicians around and tries to meet them: *The groupies were waiting around at the exit, hoping for a glimpse of the band.*

follower [C] a person who is very interested in a particular activity and follows all the recent news about it: *He is a keen follower of both football and cricket.* ◇ *a follower of fashion* See also **follow** → FOLLOW 4

addict /ˈædɪkt/ [C] (*often disapproving*) a person who spends a lot of their free time doing sth because they are so interested in it that they cannot stop: *I used to be a video game addict — I literally spent all my free time playing games.* See also **addictive** → ADDICTIVE

freak /friːk/ (usually in compounds) [C] (*informal, often disapproving*) a person who is very interested in a particular subject, especially when other people think they are a little strange for liking it so much: *He's a real fitness freak — he goes to the gym every single day.*

farm *noun*

farm · ranch · plantation · orchard · vineyard · grove · homestead
These words all mean an area of land that is used for growing crops or keeping animals.

PATTERNS AND COLLOCATIONS
▸ **on** a farm / ranch / plantation / vineyard / homestead
▸ **at** a farm / ranch / plantation / vineyard
▸ **in** a plantation / an orchard / a vineyard / a grove
▸ a **5-hectare, 100-acre, etc.** farm / ranch / plantation / orchard / vineyard
▸ a **cattle / sheep** farm / ranch
▸ a **fruit** farm / plantation / orchard

farm [C] an area of land, and the buildings on it, used for growing crops and/or keeping animals; the main house on a farm, where the farmer lives: *It's a dairy farm producing speciality cheeses.* ◇ *Many farm workers face low wages and poor working conditions.* ❶ **Farm** is also used in compounds to mean a place where particular fish or animals are bred: *a fish/trout/mink/pig farm*

ranch /rɑːntʃ; *AmE* ræntʃ/ [C] a large farm, especially in North America or Australia, where large animals such as cows, horses or sheep are bred: *She grew up on a cattle ranch in Wyoming.* ◇ *We hired three new ranch hands* (= the people who work on a ranch).

plantation /plɑːnˈteɪʃn; *AmE* plæn-/ [C] a large area of land, especially in a hot country, where crops such as coffee, sugar and rubber are grown: *a banana/coffee plantation*

orchard /ˈɔːtʃəd; *AmE* ˈɔːrtʃərd/ [C] a piece of land, normally enclosed, in which fruit trees are grown: *an apple/a cherry orchard.*

vineyard /ˈvɪnjəd; *AmE* -jərd/ [C] a piece of land where grapes are grown in order to produce wine: *Dutch settlers planted the first vineyard when they arrived in 1652.*

grove /ɡrəʊv; *AmE* ɡroʊv/ [C] a small area of land with fruit trees of a particular type on it: *olive/lemon groves*

NOTE ORCHARD OR GROVE? An **orchard** is usually enclosed and is usually for growing fruit such as apples, pears, plums and cherries that grow well in cooler countries; **groves** are usually open and are usually for growing fruit such as olives, oranges and lemons that grow well in warmer countries.

homestead /ˈhəʊmsted; *AmE* ˈhoʊm-/ [C] (*especially AmE*) a house where a family lives and the land and buildings around it, especially a small farm; (in the US in the past) a piece of land given to sb by the government on condition that they lived on it and grew crops on it: *What began as a small family homestead is now a 5 000-acre ranch.*

farm *verb*

farm · grow · plough · cultivate · plant · work
These words all mean to use or prepare ground for growing crops.

PATTERNS AND COLLOCATIONS
▸ to **farm** / **plough** / **cultivate** / **plant** / **work the land**
▸ to **grow** / **cultivate** / **plant crops**
▸ to **plough** / **plant** / **work a field**
▸ to be **organically** / **intensively** farmed / grown / cultivated

farm [I, T] to use land for growing crops and/or keeping animals: *The family has farmed in Kent for over two hundred years.* ◇ *They farm dairy cattle.* ◇ *He farmed 200 acres of prime arable land.*
▸ **farming** *noun* [U]: *sheep/dairy/organic farming*

grow [T] to put seeds or plants in the ground and take care of them, usually in order to use or sell the plants later: *I didn't know they grew rice in Spain.* ◇ *I grew all these flowers from one packet of seeds.*

plough (*BrE*) (*AmE* **plow**) /plaʊ/ [T, I] to turn over and break up the ground in a field or other area of land by using a plough (= a large piece of farming equipment), especially in order to prepare the ground for growing crops: *The land was divided into large ploughed fields.*

cultivate /ˈkʌltɪveɪt/ [T] (*formal or written*) to prepare and use land for growing plants or crops; to grow plants or crops: *The land around here has never been cultivated.* ◇ *The people cultivate mainly rice and beans.*
▸ **cultivation** *noun* [U]: *fertile land that is under cultivation* ◇ *rice cultivation*

plant [T] to cover an area of land such as a garden or field with plants: *The field had been ploughed and planted with corn.*

work [T] to do the hard physical work that is needed to grow crops on an area of land: *Boys who didn't go to school worked the land with their fathers.*

fashion *noun* See also the entry for STYLE

fashion · style · vogue · fad · trend · look · craze
These are all words for particular things being very popular for a limited period of time.

PATTERNS AND COLLOCATIONS
▸ a fashion / vogue / fad / trend / craze **for** sth
▸ a fashion / style / trend **in** sth
▸ a fashion / trend / craze **among** people
▸ **in** fashion / style / vogue / trend
▸ a **new** fashion / style / vogue / fad / trend / look / craze
▸ the **latest** fashion / style / fad / trend / look / craze
▸ the **current** fashion / vogue / fad / trend
▸ a **passing** fashion / fad / craze
▸ to **come (back) into** / **(be / go) out of** fashion / vogue
▸ to **set** a fashion / style / trend
▸ to **create** a style / vogue / trend / look
▸ to **follow** fashion / a style / a trend

fashion [U, C] clothes, ways of wearing your hair, ways of behaving, activities, etc. that are popular at a particular time or place; the business of making or selling clothes in new and different styles: *Long skirts have come into fashion again.* ◇ *The stores are full of the spring fashions.* ◇ *Fashions in art and literature come and go.* ◇ *a fashion designer/magazine/show* ◇ *the fashion industry* ◇ *the world of fashion*

style [C, U] a particular design of sth, especially clothes or hair; the quality of looking fashionable: *We stock a wide variety of styles and sizes.* ◇ *Why not have your hair cut in a shorter style?* ◇ *hot tips for style-conscious teenagers* ◇ *Short skirts are back in style.* See also **stylish** → ELEGANT

vogue /vəʊɡ; *AmE* voʊɡ/ [C, usually sing.] (*rather formal, written*) a fashion for sth: *the vogue for child-centred education* ◇ *Black is in vogue again this winter.*

fad [C] (*disapproving*) something that people are interested in for only a short period of time: *It's just a fad. It won't last.* ◇ *Fads for vitamin supplements have been overtaken by a vogue for minerals and trace elements.*

trend [C] a general direction in the way fashion changes: *You seem to have set* (= started) *a new trend.* ◇ *fashion trends in sunglasses* ◇ (*BrE, rather informal*) *Their new knitwear is very on trend* (= in the latest fashion). See also **trend** → TREND

look [sing.] a particular type of appearance: *The punk look is in again.* ◇ *She said she was aiming for a more sophisticated look.*

craze [C] an enthusiastic interest in sth that is shared by many people but that usually does not last very long; a thing that people have a craze for: *I don't understand this craze for collecting labels.* ◇ *Pet pigs are the latest craze.*

fashionable *adj.* See also the entry for ELEGANT

fashionable · glamorous · trendy · classy · smart · hip
These words all describe things that many people admire or want at a particular time.

PATTERNS AND COLLOCATIONS
▸ fashionable / glamorous / trendy / classy / smart **people**
▸ fashionable / glamorous / smart **women**
▸ fashionable / smart **men**
▸ fashionable / glamorous / trendy / smart **clothes**
▸ a fashionable / trendy / classy / smart **hotel / restaurant**
▸ a fashionable / trendy / smart **audience / shop**
▸ very fashionable / glamorous / trendy / classy
▸ quite fashionable / glamorous / trendy / classy / smart
▸ rather fashionable / glamorous / classy / smart

fashionable following a style that is popular at a particular time; used or visited by people who know what is the current fashion: *Everything Italian suddenly became fashionable.* ◇ *The play is a satire on **fashionable society** (= the upper classes) in Victorian times.* ◇ *Such thinking is **fashionable among** right-wing politicians at the moment.* ◇ *It's a very fashionable part of London.* **OPP** **unfashionable** ❶ Unfashionable things, places, ideas or people are not popular or fashionable at a particular time: *an unfashionable part of the city* ◇ *unfashionable ideas/attitudes*
▸ **fashionably** *adv.*: *fashionably dressed*

glamorous /ˈɡlæmərəs/ especially attractive and exciting, and different from ordinary things or people: *glamorous movie stars* ◇ *a glamorous lifestyle* See also **glamour** → INTEREST *noun* 1, **glamour** → STYLE
▸ **glamorously** *adv.*: *glamorously dressed*

trendy (*informal, sometimes disapproving*) following what is fashionable, especially in design and ideas: *She wasn't a trendy sort of person.* ◇ *People are buying them just to be trendy.*

classy (*informal, approving*) of high quality; expensive and/or fashionable: *United play some classy football.* ◇ *The car was a classy German make.* See also **class** → STYLE

smart (*especially BrE*) connected with rich fashionable people: *The restaurant has a smart new decor.* ◇ *The reception would be very grand and smart.*

hip (*informal, approving*) following what is fashionable, especially in clothes and music: *He said it was the hip place to hang out.* ◇ *It's hard to be hip and forty.*

fast *adj.* See also the entry for QUICK

fast · quick · high-speed · brisk · supersonic · express
These words all describe things and people moving or doing things with speed.

fast	high-speed	supersonic
quick	express	
brisk		

PATTERNS AND COLLOCATIONS
▸ to be fast / quick **at** doing sth
▸ a fast / supersonic **speed**
▸ a fast / quick / brisk **movement / pace / walk / run**
▸ quick / brisk **footsteps**
▸ a fast / quick **reader / worker / learner / rhythm**
▸ a fast / a high-speed / an express **train / link**
▸ a fast / high-speed **computer / modem**
▸ a fast / an express **bus / coach / lane**
▸ very / quite / fairly fast / quick / brisk

fast moving or able to move with speed; able to do sth with speed; producing or allowing fast movement: *She loves driving fast cars.* ◇ *Are you a fast reader with the ability to retain the key points?* ◇ *These are complex programs needing very large and fast computers.* ◇ *It's a very fast road and people do not realize what speed they are doing.* **OPP** **slow** → SLOW
▸ **fast** *adv.*: *Don't drive so fast!* ◇ *I can't go any faster.*

quick moving or doing sth fast: *He's a very quick worker.* ◇ *The kids were **quick to** learn.* ◇ *She was quick (= too quick) to point out the mistakes I'd made.* ◇ *Her quick hands suddenly stopped moving.* ◇ *Try to **be quick**! We're late already.* **OPP** **slow** → SLOW
▸ **quickly** *adv.*: *She walked away quickly.*

NOTE **FAST OR QUICK?** **Fast** is the usual word when you are talking about travelling, especially in a vehicle: *a quick car/road* ◇ *Don't drive so quickly!* A person who is able to do sth with speed may be **fast** or **quick**: *a fast/quick reader/worker/runner/thinker/learner/brain.* However, **fast** is NOT used in other expressions when sb does sth in a short time: *The kids were fast to learn.* ◇ *Try to be fast! We're late already.* See also the entry for QUICK

high-'speed [usually before noun] that travels, works or happens very fast: *We are talking about a network of modern highways, high-speed trains, airports and air routes.* ◇ *There should be a large market for cheap high-speed modems.* ◇ *A police officer was injured during a high-speed chase across two counties.*

brisk moving fast, especially on foot: *We went for a brisk walk before lunch.* ◇ *They set off at a brisk pace.*
▸ **briskly** *adv.*: *He walked briskly down the street.*

supersonic /ˌsuːpəˈsɒnɪk/ *AmE* /ˌsuːpərˈsɑːnɪk/ faster than the speed of sound: *Until then, no aircraft was capable of supersonic flight.*

express [only before noun] travelling very fast; sent or done very quickly: *An express coach runs once an hour from the airport.* ◇ *We provide express delivery services seven days a week.* ❶ **Express** is used to talk about transport and other services.

fat *noun*

fat · butter · oil · margarine · lard · grease · blubber · spread
These are all words for soft solid or liquid substances from animals or vegetables which are used for cooking or spreading on bread.

PATTERNS AND COLLOCATIONS
▸ **low fat** margarine / spread
▸ **vegetable** fat / oil / margarine
▸ to **spread** butter / margarine **on** sth
▸ to **fry / cook sth in** fat / butter / oil / margarine / lard
▸ to **heat** the fat / butter / oil
▸ **bread and** butter / margarine

fat [U, C] a white or yellow substance in the bodies of animals and humans, stored under the skin; a solid or liquid substance from animals or plants, treated so that it becomes pure for use in cooking; these fats, when you are thinking of them as a part of what sb eats: *Aerobic exercise will help you burn off excess body fat.* ◇ *Cook the meat in shallow fat.* ◇ *Stick to foods which are **low in fat**.* ◇ *You should cut down on fats and carbohydrates.* ❶ **Fat** is a general word which can be used instead of **butter, oil, margarine, lard** or **grease** but you only use it when you do not know or it is not important which kind of fat you are talking about.

butter [U] a soft yellow food made from cream or milk, used in cooking and for spreading on bread: *Fry the onions in butter.* ◇ *If you're still hungry, have some bread and butter.*
▸ **butter** *verb* [T]: *She buttered four thick slices of bread.*

oil [U, C] a smooth thick liquid that is made from plants and is used in cooking: *Heat a little olive oil in a non-stick frying pan.*

margarine /ˌmɑːdʒəˈriːn; AmE ˈmɑːrdʒərən/ [U] a yellow substance like butter made from vegetable fat, used in cooking or spread on bread: *She took some margarine and spread it on the bread.*

lard [U] a firm white substance made from the melted fat of pigs, that is used in cooking: *Use sunflower oil instead of lard.*

grease /griːs/ [U] (*disapproving*) animal fat that has been softened by cooking or heating: *He collected the plates, which were covered with grease.* ❶ **Grease** is unwanted fat that comes out of food; it is not used to talk about fat used for cooking in: *Heat a little grease in the pan.*
▸ **greasy** *adj.*: *The hotel smelt of stale smoke and greasy food.*

blubber [U] the fat of some sea animals such as whales: *A thick layer of blubber helps insulate seals against the cold.*

spread [C, U] a soft food, like margarine, that you put on bread: *Use a low-fat spread instead of butter.* ◇ *They offered me some crackers with cheese spread.*

fat *adj.*

---

fat · overweight · plump · obese · chubby · stout
These words all describe people who have too much flesh on their body and weigh too much.

> **NOTE** Although people talk a lot about their own size or weight, it is generally not considered polite to refer to a person's large size or their weight when you talk to them.

---

plump   stout   fat   obese
chubby   overweight

PATTERNS AND COLLOCATIONS
▸ a fat / an overweight / a plump / an obese / a chubby / a stout **man / woman**
▸ a fat / an overweight / a plump / an obese / a chubby **child**
▸ a fat / an overweight / a plump / a chubby **baby**
▸ a fat / plump / chubby **boy / girl**
▸ a fat / plump / chubby / stout **body**
▸ a fat / plump / chubby **face**
▸ fat / plump / chubby **arms / cheeks / fingers / legs / hands**

fat (of a person or part of the body) having too much flesh and weighing too much: *A big fat man walked into the room.* ◇ *You'll get fat if you eat so much chocolate.* ◇ *I was ashamed of my fat flabby legs.* ❶ **Fat** is the most common and direct word, but it is not polite to say to sb that they are fat. **Fat** is used more frequently in spoken English than in written English. **OPP** thin → THIN
▸ **fatness** *noun* [U]: *Fatness tends to run in families.*

overweight (of a person) too heavy and fat; weighing more than you should to be perfectly healthy: *She was only a few pounds overweight.* ◇ *A number of medical conditions are due to being overweight.* ❶ It is less offensive to talk about sb being **overweight** than to talk about them being **fat**, but it is still not polite to say to sb that they are **overweight**. **OPP** underweight → THIN

plump (of a person or part of the body) having a soft, round body; slightly fat: *Our new teacher was a short, plump woman.* ◇ *His plump face was pink with embarrassment.* ❶ **Plump** suggests that a person is slightly fat in an attractive way. **OPP** slim → THIN

obese /əʊˈbiːs; AmE oʊ-/ (*rather formal or medical*) (of a person) very fat, in a way that is not healthy: *Obese patients are given dietary advice.* ❶ **Obese** is used by doctors to describe people who are so fat that they are unhealthy. It is also used in a general way to mean 'very fat'.
▸ **obesity** *noun* [U]: *Obesity can increase the risk of heart disease.*

chubby (*often approving*) (of a person or part of the body) slightly fat in a way that people usually find attractive: *Aah, look at his chubby little hands!* ◇ *She was eleven years old and pretty in a chubby sort of way.* ❶ **Chubby** is used mainly to describe babies and children. **OPP** skinny → THIN

stout /staʊt/ (*especially BrE, rather formal*) (of a man or woman) rather fat: *He was a stout man with a red face.*
▸ **stoutly** *adv.*: *He was tall and stoutly built.*

fatal *adj.* See the Topic Map for HEALTH on p.890

---

fatal · deadly · lethal · malignant · terminal · incurable · inoperable
These words all describe things that cause or can cause death.

PATTERNS AND COLLOCATIONS
▸ fatal / deadly / lethal **to** sb / sth
▸ fatal / lethal **for** sb / sth
▸ a fatal / a deadly / a lethal / a malignant / a terminal / an incurable **disease**
▸ a fatal / a terminal / an incurable **illness / condition**
▸ a deadly / lethal **cocktail / poison / venom / weapon**
▸ potentially fatal / deadly / lethal / malignant

fatal /ˈfeɪtl/ causing or ending in death: *They were involved in a fatal accident.* ◇ *He suffered fatal injuries when he was struck by a car.* ❶ **Fatal** is used to talk about *accidents, injuries, illnesses* or *attacks* on people. It is NOT used to talk about *poisons* or *weapons*. See also *fatality* → VICTIM 1
▸ **fatally** *adv.*: *fatally injured/wounded*

deadly causing or likely to cause death: *The cobra is one of the world's deadliest snakes.* ◇ *The terrorists have chosen to play a deadly game with the civilian population.* ❶ **Deadly** is used to talk about *poisons* and poisonous animals, *weapons* and *attacks*. It is NOT used about accidents or injuries. It collocates with *disease* and *virus* but NOT *illness*.

lethal /ˈliːθl/ causing or likely to cause death: *She had been given a lethal dose of poison.* ◇ *He has been sentenced to death by lethal injection.* ❶ **Lethal** is most commonly used with *dose, cocktail, mixture, injection* and *weapon*. It is NOT used to talk about accidents, injuries or attacks.

malignant /məˈlɪɡnənt/ (*medical*) (of a disease or tumour) that cannot be controlled and is likely to cause death: *The tests found some malignant cells.* ❶ **Malignant** is most often used with the words *disease* and *tumour*. A *tumour* is a mass of cells growing in or on a part of the body where they should not be. Other words that are used frequently with **malignant** are more technical medical words describing these types of cells, such as *carcinoma* and *melanoma*.

terminal (*rather formal*) (of an illness or disease) that cannot be cured and will lead to death, often slowly; (of a person) suffering from a terminal illness: *He has terminal lung cancer.* ◇ *Many terminal patients would prefer to end their days at home.*
▸ **terminally** *adv.*: *terminally ill patients*

incurable /ɪnˈkjʊərəbl; AmE -ˈkjʊr-/ (of an illness or disease) that cannot be cured: *He's suffering from an incurable disease.* **OPP** curable ❶ A **curable** illness or disease can be cured: *Most skin cancers are curable if treated early.*
▸ **incurably** *adv.*: *incurably ill*

> **NOTE** TERMINAL OR INCURABLE? Both **terminal** and **incurable** collocate with *disease, condition* and *illness*. **Terminal** is more formal and is used in more technical medical contexts; **incurable** is more likely to be used in everyday English. **Terminal** is the preferred term for talking about *cancer*.

---

inoperable /ɪnˈɒpərəbl; AmE ɪnˈɑːp-/ (of a disease or tumour) that cannot be cured by a medical operation: *He was diagnosed with an inoperable brain tumour.* **OPP** operable ❶ An **operable** disease or tumour can be treated by a medical operation.

fault noun

fault · responsibility · blame · guilt
These are all words for the fact of being responsible for sth wrong or bad that has happened.

PATTERNS AND COLLOCATIONS
▸ the responsibility/ blame/ guilt **for** sth
▸ (not) **without** fault/ responsibility/ blame/ guilt
▸ to **admit** your fault/ responsibility/ your guilt
▸ to **bear** the responsibility/ blame/ guilt for sth
▸ to **accept/ share/ absolve sb from/ shift** the responsibility/ blame/ guilt
▸ to **take/ shoulder/ carry/ lay/ place/ put/ attribute** the responsibility/ blame
▸ to **deny** responsibility/ your guilt
▸ the fault/ responsibility/ blame/ guilt **lies with sb**
▸ the fault/ responsibility/ blame **rests with sb**

fault [U] (*especially spoken*) the fact of being responsible for sth wrong or bad that has happened: *Why should I say sorry when it's not **my fault**?* ◇ *It's nobody's fault.* ◇ *It was his **fault that** we were late.* ◇ *It's **your own fault** for being careless.* ◇ *Many people live in poverty **through no fault of their own**.* ◇ *I think the owners are **at fault** (=* responsible*) for not warning us.* See also **at fault** → GUILTY
responsibility [U] (*rather formal*) the fact of being responsible for sth wrong or bad that has happened: *The bank refuses to accept responsibility for the mistake.* ◇ *Nobody has **claimed** responsibility for the bombing.* ◇ *We must all bear some responsibility for what happened.* See also **responsible** → GUILTY

NOTE **FAULT** OR **RESPONSIBILITY**? These words have the same basic meaning but the patterns and collocations are different. **Fault** is usually used in the phrases *my/ your/his/her/our/their/sb's (own) fault* or *sb is at fault*: It was his responsibility that we were late. ◇ I think the owners are at responsibility. People typically *accept/ share/admit/claim/deny responsibility for sth*: The bank refuses to accept fault for the mistake. ◇ *The bank refuses to accept that it is at fault for the mistake.* ◇ *He refused to accept that the mistake was his fault.*

blame [U] responsibility for sth wrong or bad that has happened; saying that sb is responsible for sth, even if they are not: *She put the blame on me.* ◇ *The government will have to take the blame for the riots.* ◇ *Why do I always **get the blame** for everything that goes wrong?* ❶ A person often *gets/takes/accepts/bears the blame for sth*, even if they are not really the person who did it. Somebody can *lay/pin/place/put the blame on sb for sth* by saying that they did it, even if they did not. OPP **credit** → PRAISE, See also **blame** → BLAME *verb*, **to blame** → GUILTY, **blameless** → INNOCENT
guilt [U] (*rather formal, especially written*) the fact that sb has done sth illegal; blame or responsibility for sth wrong or bad that has happened: *His **guilt was proved** beyond all doubt by the prosecution.* ◇ *Do you think this statement amounts to an admission of guilt?* ❶ People typically *admit* their own **guilt**, or *establish* or *prove* sb else's **guilt**. OPP **innocence** → INNOCENT, See also **guilty** → GUILTY

favourite (*BrE*) (*AmE* **favorite**) *adj.* See also the entries for BEST and IDEAL

favourite · preferred · favoured · of choice · pet · best-loved
These words all describe the person, thing or place that is liked more than others of the same kind.

PATTERNS AND COLLOCATIONS
▸ sb's **least** favourite/ preferred / favoured sth
▸ sb's favourite/ preferred/ favoured **food / activity / method / way/ type**
▸ sb's **method** of choice
▸ sb's favourite/ preferred **choice**
▸ sb's favourite/ **pet subject/ topic**

▸ sb's preferred/ favoured **option/ approach/ strategy/ version/ location/ candidate/ school**

favourite (*BrE*) (*AmE* **favorite**) liked more than others of the same kind: *It's one of my favourite movies.* ◇ *Who is your favourite writer?* See also **favourite** → CHOICE *noun* 2, **favour** → PREFER *verb*
preferred [only before noun] (*especially business*) that most people think is the best: *The company has not yet identified a preferred candidate for the job.* ◇ *Watching TV was high on the children's list of preferred activities.* See also **prefer** → PREFER, **preference** → CHOICE 2, **preference** → TASTE 1
favoured (*BrE*) (*AmE* **favored**) (*rather formal, especially written*) preferred by most people: *David Prince is widely viewed as the favoured candidate to replace Mr Wallace.* See also **favour** → PREFER *verb*

NOTE **PREFERRED** OR **FAVOURED**? There is little difference in meaning between these two words. In spoken English, **preferred** is much more common than **favoured**.

of 'choice *idiom* [after noun] that is chosen by a particular group of people or for a particular purpose: *It's the software of choice for business use.* ◇ *Cheap handguns are the weapon of choice for young criminals.* See also **choice** → CHOICE *noun* 2
pet [only before noun] that you are very interested in: *One of the council's pet projects is to reduce traffic speeds in residential areas.* ❶ In British English, sth that you particularly dislike is your *pet hate*. In American English, it is called your *pet peeve*: *According to our survey, your number one pet peeve is junk email.*
best-'loved loved the most or by the most people: *It remains one of the best-known and best-loved movies of all time.* ❶ *Best-loved* is often used about films, books, pieces of music, etc. and the people who created them (writers, actors, musicians, etc.). It can be used about people or things that are popular in general: *This play has become the best-loved of all his works.* but is often used about a particular country: *one of Britain's best-loved comedians* or a particular time: *one of the best-loved authors of the last century.*

fear noun

fear · terror · panic · alarm · fright · hysteria · dread · paranoia · phobia
These are all words for the bad feeling you have when you are afraid.

alarm	fear	panic	terror
	fright	paranoia	hysteria
		dread	
		phobia	

PATTERNS AND COLLOCATIONS
▸ a fear/ terror/ dread **of** sth
▸ panic/ alarm/ paranoia/ a phobia **about** sth
▸ **in** fear/ terror/ panic/ alarm/ fright/ dread
▸ fear/ terror/ panic/ alarm/ dread **that...**
▸ **absolute/ pure/ sheer** terror/ panic/ hysteria/ dread
▸ to be **filled with** fear/ terror/ panic/ alarm/ dread
▸ to **have** a fear/ panic/ fright/ dread/ phobia
▸ a **feeling of** fear/ terror/ panic/ alarm/ hysteria/ dread/ paranoia

fear [U, C] the bad feeling that you have when you are in danger, when sth bad might happen, or when a particular thing frightens you: *(a) fear of the dark/spiders/flying* ◇ *Her eyes showed no fear.* ◇ *The child was shaking with fear.* ◇ *We lived in constant fear of losing our jobs.* ◇ *He spoke of his **fears for** the future.* ◇ *The doctor's report confirmed our worst fears.* OPP **hope** → HOPE 2, See also **fearful** → AFRAID
▸ **fear** *verb* [T]: (*written*) *to fear death/danger/persecution* ◇ *Hundreds of people are feared dead.* ◇ *We **feared for** their*

safety. ◇ *Don't worry, you have **nothing to fear from** us.* ❶ Although there are a number of ways to use the verb **fear**, it is more common and usually more natural to use the expression *be afraid/frightened/scared of sb/sth/doing sth.* See also the entry for AFRAID

terror [U, sing.] a feeling of extreme fear: *Her eyes were wild with terror.* ◇ *People fled from the explosion in terror.* ◇ *Some women have a terror of losing control in the birth process.* See also **terrified** → AFRAID

panic [U, C, usually sing.] a sudden feeling of great fear that cannot be controlled and prevents you from thinking clearly: *I had a sudden moment of panic.* ◇ *There's no point getting into a panic about the exams.* See also **panic** → PANIC *verb,* **panicky, panic-stricken** → HYSTERICAL

alarm [U] a sudden or continuing feeling of worry that sth dangerous might happen or might have already happened: *'What have you done?' Ellie cried in alarm.* ◇ *The doctor said there was **no cause for alarm**.* See also **alarm** → FRIGHTEN *verb,* **alarmed** → AFRAID

fright [U, C] a feeling of fear, usually sudden: *She cried out in fright.* ◇ *He suffered from **stage fright** (= nervous feelings felt by performers before they appear in front of an audience).* ❶ A **fright** can also be an experience or an event that makes you feel fear. See also **fright** → SHOCK *noun 2,* **frighten** → FRIGHTEN, **frigntened** → AFRAID

NOTE FEAR OR FRIGHT? Fright is a reaction to sth that has just happened or is happening now. Use **fear,** NOT **fright,** to talk about things that always frighten you and things that may happen in the future: *I have a fright of spiders.* ◇ *his fright of what might happen*

hysteria /hɪˈstɪəriə; AmE -ˈstɪr-/ [U] a state of extreme excitement, fear or anger in which a person or a group of people loses control of their emotions and starts to cry, laugh, etc: *A note of hysteria crept into her voice.* ◇ *Fear infected people with mass hysteria.* See also **hysterical** → HYSTERICAL

dread [U, C, usually sing.] (*rather informal*) a feeling of great fear about sth that might or will happen in the future; a thing that causes this fear: *The prospect of growing old alone fills me with dread.* ◇ *She has an irrational dread of hospitals.*
▸ **dread** *verb* [T]: *This was the moment he had been dreading.* ◇ *She dreads her husband finding out.* ◇ *I dread to think what would happen if there really was a fire.*
OPP look forward to sth → EXPECT

paranoia /ˌpærəˈnɔɪə/ [U] (*informal*) fear or suspicion of other people, especially when there is no reason for this: *his paranoia that people might find out* See also **paranoid** → AFRAID

phobia /ˈfəʊbiə; AmE ˈfoʊ-/ [C] (*rather formal*) a strong unreasonable fear or hatred of sth: *He has a phobia about flying* ◇ *One of the symptoms of the disease is water phobia.* ❶ **Phobia** is also used in compounds to make the names of particular phobias: *arachnophobia* (= fear of spiders) ◇ *claustrophobia* (= fear of enclosed spaces) ◇ *xenophobia* (= fear or hatred of people from other countries)

feature *noun*

feature · characteristic · quality · property · attribute · trait · point
These are all words for sth which is typical of sb/sth, especially making them different from others.

PATTERNS AND COLLOCATIONS
▸ a/an **essential/ desirable/ individual** feature/ characteristic/ quality/ property/ attribute/ trait
▸ a **distinctive** feature/ characteristic/ quality/ attribute/ trait
▸ a/ an **important/ natural/ special/ useful** feature/ characteristic/ quality/ property/ attribute
▸ a **unique** feature/ characteristic/ quality/ property
▸ a **common** feature/ characteristic/ property/ attribute/ trait
▸ a **positive/ negative** feature/ characteristic/ quality/ attribute/ trait

▸ a **human/ physical** feature/ characteristic/ quality/ attribute/ trait
▸ a **psychological/ mental** characteristic/ quality/ attribute/ trait
▸ a **biological** feature/ characteristic/ property/ trait
▸ to **possess/display/share** a feature/ a characteristic/ a quality/ a property/ an attribute/ a trait/ ...points
▸ to **show** a feature/ a characteristic/ a quality/ an attribute/ a trait/ ...points
▸ to **exhibit** a feature/ characteristic/ quality/ property/ trait

feature [C] something important, interesting or typical of a place or thing: *An interesting feature of the city is the old market.* ◇ *Teamwork is a key feature of the training programme.* ◇ *The one **redeeming feature** of the plan was its low cost to the council.* ◇ *The design has many new built-in **safety features**.* ❶ A **feature** tends to be sth noticeable, and is usually sth desirable.

characteristic [C] a part of a person's character, appearance or behaviour; something typical of a place or thing: *The need to communicate is a key characteristic of human society.* ◇ *His melodies have distinguishing characteristics which make them instantly identifiable.* ◇ *Personal characteristics, such as age, sex and marital status are taken into account.* ❶ A **characteristic** is usually sth that helps to make sb/sth clearly different from others.

quality [C, U] a part of a person's character, especially a good one such as the ability to do sth or a good way of behaving; a feature of a thing, especially one that is good and makes it different from sth else: *personal qualities such as honesty and generosity* ◇ *It's hard to find people with the right qualities for the job.* ◇ *He showed great energy and **leadership qualities**.* ◇ *The ancient city of Assisi has a wonderful magical quality.*

property [C, usually pl.] (*formal or technical*) a feature of a substance or material, especially of its physical form or behaviour: *Compare the physical and chemical properties of the two substances.* ◇ *The plant is thought to have medicinal properties.*

attribute /ˈætrɪbjuːt/ [C] (*rather formal*) a quality or feature of sb/sth, especially one that people think is good: *Patience is an essential attribute for a teacher.* ◇ *The most basic attribute of all animals is consciousness.*

trait /treɪt/ [C] a particular quality in a person's character that is noticeable and makes them behave in a particular way: *personality/character traits* ◇ *Awareness of class is a typically British trait.*

point [C, usually pl.] a particular quality or feature that sb/sth has: *Tact is not one of her **strong points**.* ◇ *Living in Scotland **has its good points** but the weather is not one of them.* ◇ *One of the hotel's **plus points** is that it is very central.* ❶ **Points** is often used when you are considering the good and bad qualities of sth.

feature *verb*

feature · star · figure · appear
These words all mean to have an important part in sth, or to include sb/sth as an important part.

PATTERNS AND COLLOCATIONS
▸ to feature/ star/ figure/ appear **in** sth
▸ to feature/ star/ figure/ appear **as** sb/ sth
▸ a **film/ movie** features/ stars sb
▸ to feature/ star/ appear in a **film/ movie**
▸ to feature/ figure/ appear **prominently** in sth

feature [T, I] to include a particular person or thing as a special part; to have an important part in sth: *The film features Anne Hathaway as Jane Austen.* ◇ *The latest model features alloy wheels and an electronic alarm.* ◇ *Many of the hotels featured in the brochure offer special deals for weekend breaks.* ◇ *Olive oil and garlic feature prominently in his recipes.*

star (**-rr-**) [I, T, no passive] to have one of the main parts in a film, play or show; (of a film, play or show) to have a particular person in one of the main parts: *She starred opposite Johnny Depp in 'Pirates of the Caribbean'.* ◇ *No* one has yet been chosen for the **starring role** (= the main part). ◇ *The movie stars Aishwarya Rai.* See also **star** → STAR *noun* 2

figure [I] (usually used with an adverb or preposition) to be part of a process or situation, especially an important part: *The question of the peace settlement is likely to figure prominently in the talks.* ◇ *It did not figure high on her list of priorities.* ◇ *Do I still figure in your plans?*

appear [I] (usually used with an adverb or preposition) to take part in a film, play or show; to be written or mentioned somewhere: *He has appeared in over 60 movies.* ◇ *She regularly appears on TV.* ◇ *Your name will appear at the front of the book.*

feel *verb*

feel · know · sense · experience · taste
These words all mean to have and be aware of a particular emotion or physical feeling.

PATTERNS AND COLLOCATIONS
▸ to feel / know / experience / taste **joy**
▸ to feel / know / experience **pain / satisfaction / shame**
▸ to feel / sense / experience **a need**
▸ to feel / experience a / an **sense / sensation / emotion / urge / pang / surge / rush / stab**
▸ to know / experience **poverty / hardship / difficulties**
▸ to experience / taste **success / life**
▸ to **have never** felt / known / experienced / tasted sth
▸ to **actually** feel / know / sense / experience sth
▸ to feel / experience sth **suddenly / sometimes / often**
▸ to know / experience sth **directly / first-hand**

feel [I, T] to have and be aware of a particular feeling or emotion; to notice or be aware of sth because it is touching you or having a physical effect on you; to become aware of sth even though you cannot see, hear, touch, smell or taste it: *The heat made him feel faint.* ◇ *She sounded more confident than she felt.* ◇ *How are you feeling today?* ◇ *I know exactly how you feel* (= I feel sympathy for you). ◇ *He felt no remorse at all.* ◇ *I could feel the warm sun on my back.* ◇ *She could not feel her legs.* ◇ *He felt a hand on his shoulder.* ◇ *Can you feel the tension in this room?* ❶ When **feel** is used to talk about becoming aware of things outside yourself, it is not usually used in the progressive tenses: *I was feeling guilty.* ◇ ~~I was feeling the sun on my back.~~ ◇ ~~Are you feeling the tension in this room?~~ See also **feeling** → EMOTION, **feeling** → SENSE *noun*

know [T] (not used in the progressive tenses) to have personal experience of an emotion or situation: *She thought she would never know the joy of seeing a child grow up in her care.* ◇ *She may be successful now, but she has known what it is like to be poor.*

sense [T] (not used in the progressive tenses) to become aware of sth outside yourself, even though you cannot see, hear, touch, smell or taste it: *Sensing danger, they started to run.* ◇ *I sensed a note of tension in his voice.* ◇ *Lisa sensed that he did not believe her.* See also **sense** → SENSE *noun*

NOTE FEEL OR SENSE? You usually **feel** your own feelings and emotions, but **sense** other people's: *He felt a terrible pain in his chest.* ◇ ~~She sensed a terrible pain in his chest.~~ ◇ *She sensed the terrible pain he was feeling* (= she was aware of it). ◇ *I feel your pain* (= I know how you are suffering and it makes me suffer too).

experience [T] (*rather formal*) to have and be aware of a particular emotion or physical feeling: *I have never experienced such pain before.* ◇ *I experienced a moment of panic as I boarded the plane.*

taste [T] (*especially written*) to have a short experience of sth, especially sth that you want more of: *He had tasted freedom only to lose it again.* ❶ People typically **taste** *victory, success* and *freedom*.

fend sb/sth off *verb*

fend sb/sth off · block · deflect · repel · ward sb/sth off · parry
These words all mean to defend or protect yourself from an attack or from sth that hits you.

PATTERNS AND COLLOCATIONS
▸ to fend off / block / deflect / repel / ward off / parry an **attack**
▸ to fend off / block / deflect / ward off / parry a **blow**
▸ to block / deflect / parry a **shot / ball**
▸ to fend off / repel an **assault**

fend sb/sth 'off *phrasal verb* to defend or protect yourself from sb/sth that is attacking you: *The police officer fended off the blows with his riot shield.* ◇ *She used a chair to fend off her attacker.*

block [T] to stop a ball or blow from reaching somewhere or hitting sb/sth by moving part of your body in front of it: *Terry's shot was blocked by the goalie.* ◇ *We learned some basic punching and blocking techniques.*

deflect /dɪˈflekt/ [T] to make sth, such as a ball or a blow, change the direction it is moving in, by moving in front of it or hitting it: *He raised his arm to try to deflect the blow.* ◇ *The defender nearly deflected the ball into his own net.*

repel /rɪˈpel/ (-ll-) [T] (*formal*) to fight sb who is attacking you and drive them away: *Troops repelled an attempt to invade the south island.* ◇ *He had a great army which repelled all invaders.*

ward sb/sth 'off *phrasal verb* to protect or defend yourself against danger, illness or attack: *She put up her hands to ward him off.* ◇ *The charms are meant to ward off evil spirits.*

parry [T, I] to defend yourself against sb who is attacking you by pushing their hand, arm, weapon, etc. to one side: *He parried a blow to his head.* ◇ *He watched the boxers jab and parry.*

fibre (*BrE*) (*AmE* fiber) *noun*

fibre · hair · strand · thread
These are all words for a long, very thin piece of sth.

PATTERNS AND COLLOCATIONS
▸ a **long / single** fibre / hair / strand / thread
▸ a **fine** hair / strand / thread
▸ **delicate** fibres / threads
▸ a **loose** strand / thread
▸ **cotton** fibres / threads

fibre (*BrE*) (*AmE* **fiber**) /ˈfaɪbə(r)/ [C] one of the many long, very thin strings which form body tissue, such as muscle, and natural materials, such as wood and cotton: *The function of nerve fibres is to transmit coded information from one place to another.* ◇ *Wood fibres or synthetic fibres may be used in the manufacturing process.*

hair [C] one of the long thin fibres which grow on the body of people, especially on the head, and on some animals: *There's a hair in my soup.* ◇ *The rug was covered with cat hairs.* See also **hairy** → HAIRY

strand [C] a single long thin piece of sth such as thread, wire or hair; several hairs on sb's head that hang together in one long piece: *Thin strands of copper wire can be bent easily.* ◇ *She tucked a strand of hair behind her ear.*

thread [C] a single strand of cotton, wool, silk or other material used for sewing or making fabric: *Have you got a* **needle and thread**? ◇ *The threads of a spider's web are delicate and will break easily.*

fictional *adj.*

fictional · virtual · non-existent · fictitious · imaginary · pretend
These words all describe things that are not real but only exist in stories or in people's minds.

▸ a fictional / a fictitious / an imaginary **story** / **character**
▸ a fictional / a virtual / an imaginary **world**
▸ **purely** / **wholly** fictional / fictitious / imaginary
▸ **totally** non-existent / fictitious

fictional invented by sb for a story; connected with fiction: *a fictional account of life on a desert island* ◇ *the fictional world of J.K. Rowling* ◇ *fictional techniques* ❶ **Fiction** is a type of literature that describes people and events that are not real. **OPP** **real-life** → RELIABLE 2

virtual /ˈvɜːtʃuəl; *AmE* ˈvɜːrtʃ-/ [only before noun] made to appear to exist by the use of computer software: *The technology has enabled development of an online virtual library.* ◇ *Immersion in a **virtual world** of monsters and aliens helped alleviate pain in children with severe burns.*

,**non-e'xistent** not existing; not real: *They would waste their time worrying about non-existent dangers.* ◇ *Hospital beds were scarce and medicines were practically non-existent.* ❶ **Non-existent** is often used to talk about people or things that sb claims exist: *She was claiming welfare for two non-existent children.*

fictitious /fɪkˈtɪʃəs/ invented by sb for a story; invented by sb in order to trick people: *All the places and characters in my novel are fictitious* (= they do not exist in real life). ◇ *The account he gives of his childhood is fictitious.* **OPP** **factual** → RELIABLE 2

NOTE FICTIONAL OR FICTITIOUS? Both these words can be used to talk about characters, places and events that are invented by sb for a story. **Fictional**, but NOT **fictitious** can also describe the process of writing fiction: ~~fictitious techniques~~. **Fictitious**, but NOT **fictional**, is used especially when sb has invented sth in order to trick people and tries to pretend it is true: *Police said the name John Haydon was fictitious, but the address given was genuine.* ◇ ~~The name John Haydon was fictional.~~

imaginary /ɪˈmædʒɪnəri; *AmE* -neri/ existing only in your mind or imagination: *I had an imaginary friend when I was a child.* ◇ *Children experience a lot of imaginary fears at this age.* ◇ *The equator is an imaginary line around the middle of the earth.* **OPP** **real** → REAL

pretend [usually before noun] (*informal*) (often used by children) not real; imaginary: *The children gave out their pretend cakes on little plastic plates.* **OPP** **real** → REAL

field *noun*

field · meadow · pasture · paddock · grazing
These words all mean an area of land in the country where crops are grown or animals are kept.

▸ **in** a field / a meadow / (a) pasture / a paddock
▸ **open** fields / meadows / pasture / grazing
▸ **green** / **lush** fields / meadows / pastures

field [C] an area of land in the country used for growing crops or keeping animals in, usually surrounded by a fence, wall or hedge: *Golden fields of wheat stretched as far as the eye could see.* ◇ *We camped in a field near the village.*

meadow /ˈmedəʊ; *AmE* -doʊ/ [C] a field with grass and often wild flowers in it, especially a field that is used for producing hay for animals to eat: *Traditional hay meadows are important wildlife areas.* ◇ *Water meadows* (= fields next to a river that can be flooded) *were constructed along the river valleys.*

pasture /ˈpɑːstʃə(r); *AmE* ˈpæs-/ [U, C] land covered with grass that is used for feeding animals on; grass or similar plants that are suitable for animals to eat: *The cattle were put **out to pasture**.* ◇ *Almost all the land is covered with rough pasture of low nutritional value.*

paddock /ˈpædək/ [C] a small field where animals, especially horses, are kept: *There was an orchard and a paddock for the horses behind the house.*

grazing /ˈɡreɪzɪŋ/ [U] land with grass or similar plants that are suitable for animals to eat: *There is poor grazing in the hills.*
▸ **graze** verb [I, T]: *There were cows grazing beside the river.* ◇ *The field had been grazed by sheep.*

fight *noun* See the Topic Map for CONFLICT on p.896

fight · clash · brawl · struggle · scuffle · tussle
These are all words for a situation in which people try to defeat each other using physical force.

▸ a fight / clash / brawl / struggle / scuffle / tussle **with** sb
▸ a fight / clash / brawl / struggle / scuffle / tussle **between** people
▸ a fight / clash / brawl / struggle / scuffle / tussle **over** sth
▸ **in** a fight / clash / brawl / struggle / scuffle / tussle
▸ a **violent** fight / clash / struggle
▸ to **be in** / **get into** / **be involved in** a fight / clash / brawl / scuffle / tussle
▸ to **have** a fight / brawl / scuffle
▸ to **break up** a fight / brawl
▸ a fight / clash / brawl / scuffle **breaks out**

fight [C] a situation in which two or more people try to defeat each other using physical force: *He got into a fight with a man in the bar.* ◇ *A fight broke out between rival groups of fans.* ◇ *They got tickets to watch the world title fight* (= fighting as a sport).

clash [C] (*journalism*) a short fight between two groups of people: *Eight people were wounded in a clash with border guards.*

brawl [C] a noisy and violent fight involving a group of people, usually in a public place: *a street/pub/tavern/nightclub/bar-room brawl*

struggle [C] a fight between two people or groups of people, especially when one of them is trying to escape, or to get sth from the other: *There were no signs of a struggle at the murder scene.*

scuffle [C] a short and not very violent fight or struggle: *He was involved in a scuffle with a photographer.*

tussle [C] a short struggle, fight or argument, especially in order to get sth: *He was injured during a **tussle** for the ball.*

fight *verb*

1 He fought in the war.
2 My little brothers are always fighting.

1 See the Topic Map for CONFLICT on p.896
fight · wage · engage · skirmish · take up arms
These all mean to take part in a war or battle against an enemy.

▸ to fight / engage / skirmish **with** sb / sth
▸ to fight / take up arms **against** sb / sth
▸ to fight / wage (a) **war** / **battle** / **campaign**
▸ to fight / engage / take up arms against **the enemy**

fight [I, T] to take part in a war or battle against an enemy: *The soldiers were trained to fight in the jungle.* ◇ *The country fought several wars against its neighbours.* ◇ *They gathered soldiers to fight the invading army.* See also **fighting** → WAR

wage [T] to begin and continue a war, battle or campaign: *The rebels have waged a guerrilla war since 1995.* ◇ *He alleged that a press campaign was being waged against him.*

engage /ɪnˈɡeɪdʒ/ [T, I] (*formal*) to begin fighting a battle with sb: *He ordered his men to engage (with) the enemy.*

skirmish /ˈskɜːmɪʃ; *AmE* ˈskɜːrmɪʃ/ [I] to take part in a short fight between small groups of soldiers, especially one that is not planned: *The patrol skirmished with the enemy for several hours.* See also **skirmish** → WAR

take up 'arms idiom (*rather formal*) to prepare to fight a war: *He encouraged his supporters to take up arms against the state.*

2 See the Topic Map for CONFLICT on p.896

fight · struggle · wrestle · clash · brawl · grapple · box · scuffle

These are all words that can be used when two or more people use physical force against each other.

PATTERNS AND COLLOCATIONS
▸ to fight/struggle/wrestle/clash/brawl/grapple/scuffle **with** sb
▸ to fight/ struggle/ box **against** sb
▸ to fight/ struggle **fiercely/ furiously**
▸ to struggle/ clash **violently**

fight [I, T] to use physical force to try to defeat another person; to take part in a boxing match: *My little brothers are always fighting.* ◇ *She fought her attacker, eventually forcing him to flee.* ◇ *Doctors fear he may never fight again following his injury in last night's match.*

struggle [I] to fight sb or try to get away from them: *Ben and Jack struggled together on the grass.* ◇ *I struggled and screamed for help.* ◇ *How did she manage to struggle free?*

wrestle /'resl/ [I, T] to fight sb by holding them and trying to throw or force them to the ground, sometimes as a sport: *As a boy he had boxed and wrestled.* ◇ *Armed guards wrestled with the intruder.* ◇ *Shoppers wrestled the raider to the ground.*

clash [I] (*especially journalism*) to come together and fight or compete in a contest: *The two teams clash in tomorrow's final.* ◇ *Demonstrators clashed violently with police.*

brawl /brɔːl/ [I] to take part in a noisy and violent fight, usually in a public place: *They were arrested for brawling in the street.*

grapple [I, T] to take a firm hold of sb/sth and struggle with them: *Passers-by grappled with the man after the attack.* ◇ *They managed to grapple him to the ground.*

box [I, T] to fight sb in the sport of boxing, wearing very large thick gloves: *He boxed for Ireland in the Olympics.* ◇ *The newcomer boxed the champion for the full twelve rounds.*

scuffle [I] (of two or more people) to fight or struggle with each other for a short time, in a way that is not very serious: *She scuffled with photographers as she left her hotel.*

fight back *phrasal verb*

fight back · retaliate · get back at sb · avenge · hit back · get even · strike back · settle a score

These words all mean to harm or punish sb in return for sth that they have done to you.

PATTERNS AND COLLOCATIONS
▸ to retaliate/ get back at sb **for** sth
▸ to fight back/ retaliate/ strike back/ settle a score **against** sb
▸ to fight back/ hit back/ strike back **at** sb
▸ to retaliate/ hit back/ strike back **with** sth
▸ to fight back/ retaliate/ hit back **by doing** sth

‚fight 'back *phrasal verb* to resist strongly or attack sb who has attacked you: *Don't let them bully you. Fight back!* ◇ *It is time to fight back against street crime.* ◇ *The team fought back from 3–0 down to get a 3–3 draw.*

retaliate /rɪ'tælieɪt/ [I] to do sth that harms sb because they have harmed you first: *The police were pelted with stones and retaliated with tear gas.* ◇ *The boy hit his sister, who retaliated by kicking him.* See also **retaliation → REVENGE**

‚get 'back at sb *phrasal verb* (*informal, especially spoken*) to do sth that harms or punishes sb because they have harmed you first: *I'll find a way of getting back at him!*

avenge /ə'vendʒ/ [T] (*formal or literary*) to punish or hurt sb in return for sth bad or wrong they have done to you, your family or friends: *He promised to avenge his father's murder.* ◇ *She was determined to avenge herself on the man who had betrayed her.* See also **vengeance → REVENGE**

‚hit' back *phrasal verb* (*rather informal*) to reply angrily to criticism: *In a TV interview she hit back at her critics.* ◇ *The chairman has hit back at claims in a national newspaper.*

get 'even *idiom* (*informal*) to cause sb the same amount of trouble or harm as they have caused you: *I'll get even with you for this, just you wait.*

‚strike 'back *phrasal verb* to retaliate: *He urged his people to strike back if they were attacked.*

> **NOTE** RETALIATE OR STRIKE BACK? **Strike back** can be a more emotional term than **retaliate**. People talk about their own desire to **strike back** at sb who has hurt them; when you are talking about a situation that you are not involved in yourself, you might use the word **retaliate**: *She was filled with a desire to strike back at him.* ◇ *Kay was sent off for retaliating against Walsh.*

settle a 'score *idiom* to hurt or punish sb who has harmed or cheated you in the past: *It was a chance to **settle a few scores with** their neighbours.* ◇ *'Who would do such a thing?' 'Maybe someone with an old score to settle.'*

figure *noun* See also the entries for INFORMATION and NUMBER 2

figure · number · statistics · fraction · stats

These are all words for a word or symbol that represents a particular quantity.

PATTERNS AND COLLOCATIONS
▸ a **high/ low/ round** figure/ number
▸ **exact** figures/ numbers/ statistics
▸ **approximate** figures/ numbers
▸ **accurate/ reliable/ alarming** figures/ statistics
▸ to **add/ multiply/ subtract/ divide** figures/ numbers/ fractions
▸ to **publish** figures/ statistics

figure [C] a number that represents a particular amount or quantity, especially one given in official information: *Viewing figures for the series have dropped dramatically.* ◇ *Figures for April show a slight improvement on previous months.* ◇ *By 2004, this figure had risen to 14 million.*

number [C] a word or symbol that represents an amount or quantity: *Think of a number and multiply it by two* ◇ *The houses on this side of the road are all **even numbers** (= 2, 4, 6, etc.).* ◇ *Pick out all the **odd numbers** (= 1, 3, 5, etc.).* ◇ *'So you owe me 28 dollars?' 'Make it 30, that's a good round number.'*

statistics /stə'tɪstɪks/ [pl.] (*rather formal*) a collection of information shown in numbers: *According to official statistics the disease kills 10 000 people a year.* ❶ A **statistic** [C] is a piece of information shown in numbers: *An important statistic is that 94 per cent of crime relates to property.* ◇ *I felt I was no longer being treated as a person but as a statistic.*
▸ **statistical** /stə'tɪstɪkl/ *adj.*: *statistical analysis/methods/data*
▸ **statistically** *adv.*: *The difference between the two samples was not statistically significant.*

> **NOTE** FIGURES OR STATISTICS? In many cases either of these words can be used: *official/government/crime/unemployment figures/statistics.* **Statistics** can suggest a greater level of science and calculation (for example, working out percentages and changes over time, not just adding up numbers). **Statistics** can also be used in a more general way than **figures**: *Statistics show that far more people are able to ride a bicycle than can drive a car.* With **figures** it is usually necessary to say which figures: *Government/Inflation figures show that...* ◇ ~~Figures show that...~~

fraction [C] a division of a number, for example ⅝ or 0.625: *How do you express 25% as a fraction?*

stats [pl.] (*informal*) statistics: *The match stats show that there were 16 instances of players being offside.* ❶ **Stats** is often used to talk about the results or an analysis of a sports game.

fill verb

fill · pack · load · fill (sth) up · refill · replenish · top sb/sth up · restock
These words all mean to put a quantity of sth into a container until it is full.

PATTERNS AND COLLOCATIONS
▸ to fill / pack / load / fill up / refill / replenish / top up / restock sth **with** sth
▸ to fill / pack / load sth **in / into** sth
▸ to fill / fill up / refill / replenish / top up sb's **glass**

fill [T, I] to make sth full of sth; to become full of sth: *She filled the kettle from the tap. ◇ Smoke filled the room. ◇ The school is filled to capacity* (= completely full). *◇ The room was filling quickly* (= with people). *◇ (figurative) Her eyes suddenly filled with tears.* **OPP empty** → CLEAR

pack [I, T] to put clothes and other possessions into a bag in preparation for a trip or journey; to put sth into a container so that it can be stored, transported or sold: *I haven't packed yet. ◇ He packed a bag with a few things and was off. ◇ He packed a few things into a bag. ◇ He found a part-time job packing eggs.* **OPP unpack** → CLEAR

load [T, I] to put a large quantity of sth onto or into sth: *We loaded the car in ten minutes. ◇ Can you help me load the dishwasher? ◇ Men were loading up a truck with timber. ◇ Sacks were being loaded onto the truck. ◇ We finished loading and set off.* **OPP unload** → CLEAR, See also **load** → LOT *noun*

fill 'up, **fill sth 'up** *phrasal verb* to become completely full; to make sth completely full: *The ditches had filled up with mud and debris. ◇ First we need to fill up the tank with water. ◇ We can't be out of petrol! I filled up* (= put petrol in the car) *yesterday.*

refill /ˌriːˈfɪl/ [T] to fill sth again: *She refilled the kettle with fresh water.*
▸ **refill** /ˈriːfɪl/ *noun* [C]: *Would you like a refill* (= another drink of the same type)?

replenish /rɪˈplenɪʃ/ [T] (*formal*) to make sth full again by replacing what has been used: *Sailors used the islands to replenish their food and water supplies.*

NOTE REFILL OR REPLENISH? You usually **refill** a container, but **replenish** a supply of sth. With a drinking glass you can use either word, although **replenish** is much more formal.

top sb/sth 'up *phrasal verb* (**-pp-**) (*especially BrE, rather informal*) to fill a container that already has some liquid in it with more liquid: *I want to top up the oil in the car before we set off. ◇ (informal) Can I top you up* (= give you some more to drink)?
▸ **'top-up** *noun* [C]: (*BrE, rather informal*) *Can I give anybody a top-up* (= some more to drink)?

restock /ˌriːˈstɒk; AmE -ˈstɑːk/ [T, I] to fill sth with new or different things to replace those that have been used, sold or taken away; to get a new supply of sth: *Environmentalists are planning to restock the river with fish.*

film noun

1 see a film
2 study film and photography

1 See the Topic Map for THE MEDIA on p.900
film · movie · video · DVD
These are all words for a series of moving pictures that is shown in a cinema or on television.

PATTERNS AND COLLOCATIONS
▸ **in** a film / movie / video
▸ **on** video / DVD
▸ a **low-budget** film / movie / video
▸ a **horror / silent** film / movie
▸ a **home** movie / video
▸ to **make** a film / movie / video
▸ to **see / watch** a film / movie / video / DVD
▸ to **produce / direct** a film / movie / video

▸ a film / movie **director / producer / star / audience**

film [C] (*especially BrE*) a series of moving pictures, usually shown in a cinema or on television and often telling a story: *Let's go to the cinema – there's a good film on this week. ◇ The film was shot on location in France. ◇ an international film festival* See also **film** → RECORD *verb* 2

movie [C] (*especially AmE*) a film: *Have you seen the latest Tarantino movie? ◇ a home movie* (= a film that you make yourself, especially one of family or holiday activities)

NOTE FILM OR MOVIE? **Film** is used especially in British English; **movie** is used especially in American English. **Movie** can also emphasize that a film is being talked about as a piece of entertainment, rather than as an artistic product. In American English **film** is used especially to emphasize that a film is not just entertainment, but has artistic value: *an art film ◇ a film festival ◇ an art movie ◇ a movie festival*

video [U, C] a type of magnetic tape for recording television pictures and sound; a film or programme that is recorded on videotape: *The movie will be released on video in June. ◇ You can view and share video clips on this website. ◇ The school made a short promotional video.* See also **video** → RECORD *verb* 2

DVD /ˌdiː viː ˈdiː/ [C] a disk on which large amounts of information, especially films or photographs, can be stored, for use on a DVD-player or computer; a film that is stored on a DVD: *Is it available on DVD yet? ◇ Let's just stay in and watch a DVD.*

2 See the Topic Map for THE MEDIA on p.900
film · cinema · movies
These are all words for the art or business of making films.

PATTERNS AND COLLOCATIONS
▸ **British / French / classic / avant-garde** film / cinema
▸ to **work** in film / cinema / movies
▸ the film / cinema / movie **industry**

film [U] the art or business of making films: *She wants to study film and photography. ◇ the minister responsible for film and the theatre*

cinema [U, sing.] (*especially BrE*) the art or business of making films: *one of the great successes of British cinema*

movies [pl.] (*especially AmE*) the art or business of making films: *I've always wanted to work in movies.*

NOTE WHICH WORD? There is very little difference in meaning between these words. **Movies** is used more frequently in American English. In British English, **cinema** often emphasizes the business side of making films; **film** emphasizes the artistic side.

filter verb

filter · purify · refine · strain · sieve · sift
These words all mean to separate sth from sth else, especially a solid from a liquid or larger solids from smaller solids.

PATTERNS AND COLLOCATIONS
▸ to filter / strain / sieve / sift sth **into** sth
▸ to filter / strain / sieve sth **through** sth
▸ to filter / purify **air / water**
▸ to refine / sieve / sift **sugar**
▸ to sieve / sift **flour**
▸ to be **finely** sieved / sifted

filter [T] to pass a substance or light through a special device, especially to remove sth that is not wanted: *All drinking water must be filtered. ◇ Use a sunblock that filters UVA effectively. ◇ The air was improving as the recyclers filtered out the smoke.*

purify /ˈpjʊərɪfaɪ; AmE ˈpjʊr-/ [T] to make sth pure by removing substances that are dirty, harmful or not wanted: *One tablet will purify a litre of water in 10 minutes. ◇ House plants can help to purify the air.*

▸ **purification** /ˌpjʊərɪfɪˈkeɪʃn; AmE ˌpjʊr-/ noun [U]: *a water purification plant*

refine /rɪˈfaɪn/ [T] to make a substance pure by taking other substances out of it, especially as part of an industrial process: *The process of refining oil produces several useful chemicals.*

strain [T] to pour food or another substance through sth with very small holes in it, for example a sieve, in order to separate the solid part from the liquid part: *Use a colander to strain the vegetables.* ◇ **Strain off** *any excess liquid.*

sieve /sɪv/ [T] to put sth through a sieve: *Liquidize or sieve half the soup and return it to the pot.* ❶ A **sieve** is a tool for separating solids from liquids or larger solids from smaller solids, made of a wire or plastic net attached to a ring. The liquid or small pieces pass through the net but the larger pieces do not.

sift [T] to put flour, sugar or some other fine substance through a sieve or sifter: *Sift the flour, baking powder and salt into a bowl.* ❶ In American English a **sifter** is a small sieve used especially for sifting flour.

final *adj.*

final · firm · concrete · proven · definitive · hard · absolute · positive · categorical
These words all describe information or a decision that is certain and cannot be changed.

PATTERNS AND COLLOCATIONS
▸ firm / concrete / definitive / hard / absolute / positive **evidence**
▸ final / firm / concrete / definitive / absolute / positive **proof**
▸ a final / firm / definitive **decision / conclusion / diagnosis / agreement / answer**
▸ a final / firm **offer**
▸ concrete / proven / hard **facts**
▸ a final / definitive **judgement / ruling**

final that cannot be argued with or changed: *The judge's decision is final.* ◇ *Who has* **the final say** *around here?* ◇ *I'll give you $500 for it, and that's my final offer!* ◇ *(spoken) I'm not coming,* **and that's final!** *(= I will not change my mind)*
▸ **finally** *adv.*: *The matter was not finally settled until much later.*

firm not likely to change: *At the age of 87 he is still a firm believer in socialism.* ◇ *No firm date has yet been set for the launch.* ◇ *She is a* **firm favourite** *with the children.* ◇ *They remained* **firm friends.**
▸ **firmly** *adv.*: *It is now firmly established as one of the leading brands in the country.*

concrete /ˈkɒŋkriːt; AmE ˈkɑːŋ-/ based on facts, not on ideas or guesses: *By the end of the meeting some fairly concrete proposals had been put forward.* ◇ *'It's only a suspicion,' she said, 'nothing concrete.'* **OPP** abstract → IN-TELLECTUAL 1

proven /ˈpruːvn; ˈprəʊvn; AmE ˈproʊ-/ [only before noun] *(rather formal)* tested and shown to be true: *The award will be presented to a student of proven ability.* ◇ *The candidate should have a proven track record of handling large projects.* **OPP** **unproven** ❶ Something that is **unproven** has not been proved or not been tested: *unproven theories* See also **prove** → SHOW *verb* 1

definitive /dɪˈfɪnətɪv/ *(rather formal)* final; that cannot or need not be changed or added to: *The definitive version of the text is ready to be published.*
▸ **definitively** *adv.*: *The question has never been definitively resolved.*

hard [only before noun] definitely true and based on information that can be proved: *Is there any hard evidence either way?* ◇ *The newspaper story is based on hard facts.*

absolute /ˈæbsəluːt/ definitely true or existing and not dependent on anything else: *There was no absolute proof.* ◇ *He taught us that the laws of physics were absolute.* ◇ *The divorce became absolute last week.*

positive giving clear and definite proof or information: *We have no positive evidence that she was involved.*

▸ **positively** *adv.*: *Her attacker has now been positively identified by police.*

categorical /ˌkætəˈɡɒrɪkl; AmE -ˈɡɔːr-/ [usually before noun] *(formal)* expressed clearly and in a way that shows that you are very sure about what you are saying: *The government has yet to make a categorical statement on the issue.*
▸ **categorically** /-kli/ *adv.*: *He categorically rejected our offer.*

finance *noun*

finance · economics · banking
These words all refer to the way in which large amounts of money are managed or organized, especially by a government, company or bank.

finance [U] the activity of managing money, especially by a government or company: *the Minister of Finance* ◇ *Please send all invoices to the finance department.* ◇ *The bank offers advice and guidance on personal finance.* ◇ *He's a big wheel in the world of* **high finance** *(= finance involving large companies or countries).* See also **finance** → MONEY 1, **financial** → ECONOMIC

economics [U, pl.] how a society organizes its money, trade and industry; how money influences, or is organized within, an area of business or society: *He studied politics and economics at Yale.* ◇ *Keynesian/Marxist economics* ◇ *The economics of the project are very encouraging.* See also **economic** → ECONOMIC

NOTE FINANCE OR ECONOMICS? **Finance** is the practical process of managing money. **Economics** is the theory of how money works.

banking [U] the business activity of banks: *She's thinking about a career in banking.*

find *verb*

1 find that sth is true
2 Look what I've found!
3 find a cure for cancer
4 I can't find my keys.

1 find · find out (sth) · hear · discover · learn
These words all mean to become aware of sth or get some information about sb/sth.

PATTERNS AND COLLOCATIONS
▸ to find out / hear / learn **about** sth
▸ to hear / learn **of** sth
▸ to find / find out / hear / discover / learn **that...**
▸ It was found / discovered **that...**
▸ to find out / hear / discover / learn **how / what / why...**
▸ to find / discover **sb / sth to be / have,** etc. sth
▸ to find out / discover / learn the **facts / truth / secret / identity**
▸ to **be surprised / saddened / shocked / delighted / pleased / interested to** find / hear / discover / learn sth
▸ to **quickly / eventually** find / discover / learn sth

find [T] to become aware that sth is true after you have tried it, tested it or experienced it: *I find (that) it pays to be honest.* ◇ *The report found that 30% of the firms studied had failed within a year.* ◇ *We found the beds very comfortable.* ◇ *Her blood was found to contain poison.* See also **finding** → CONCLUSION

find ˈout, find ˈout sth *phrasal verb* to get some information about sb/sth by asking, reading, researching or being told: *She'd been seeing the boy for a while, but didn't want her parents to find out.* ◇ *Did your sister ever find out about it?* ◇ *I haven't found anything out about him yet.* ◇ *Can you find out what time the meeting starts?* ◇ *We found out later that we had been at the same school.* ◇ *She was determined to find out the truth.*

hear (not usually used in progressive tenses) [I, T] *(especially spoken)* to become aware of sth, especially news about a person, because sb tells you about it:

Haven't you heard? She's resigned. ◇ *'He's being promoted.'* ***'So I've heard.'*** ◇ *I was sorry to hear about your accident.* ◇ *We had heard nothing for weeks.* ◇ *I was delighted to hear your good news.*

discover [T] (not usually used in progressive tenses) to find out about sth or to find some information about sth, often sth surprising or shocking: *It was a shock to discover that he couldn't read.* ◇ *We never did discover why she gave up her job.* ◇ *He was later discovered to be seriously ill.* ◇ *It was later discovered that the diaries were a fraud.*

▶ **discovery** *noun* [C, U]: *He was shocked by the discovery that she had been unfaithful.*

learn [I, T] (not usually used in progressive tenses) (*rather formal*) to become aware of sth by hearing about it from sb else or by reading about it; to gradually change your attitudes about sth so that you behave in a different way: *I learned of her arrival from a close friend.* ◇ *We were very surprised to learn that she had got married again.* ◇ *I'm sure she'll learn from her mistakes.* ◇ *I soon learned not to ask too many questions.*

---

2 find · discover · come across sb/sth · catch · turn sth up · unearth · come upon sb/sth · stumble on/upon/across sb/sth

These words all mean to become aware of the existence or location of sb/sth by chance.

PATTERNS AND COLLOCATIONS

▸ to find / discover / come across / catch sb **doing sth**
▸ to find / discover / unearth the **remains** (of sth)
▸ to find / discover a **fault** / **wreck**
▸ to find / discover / stumble upon a **body**
▸ to **happen to** find / discover / come across sth
▸ to find / discover / stumble upon sth **by accident**

---

find [T] to become aware of the existence or location of sb/sth unexpectedly or by chance: *Look what I've found!* ◇ *We've found a great new restaurant near the office.* ◇ *A whale was found washed up on the shore.* ◇ *I didn't expect to come home and find him gone.*

▶ **find** *noun* [C]: *This is an important archaeological find.*

discover [T] to be the first person to become aware that a particular thing or place exists; to find sb/sth that was hidden or that you did not expect to find: *Cook is credited with discovering Hawaii.* ◇ *Police discovered a large stash of drugs while searching the house.* ◇ *He was discovered hiding in the shed.* ◇ *She was discovered dead at her home in Leeds.* See also **discoverer** → EXPLORER

▶ **discovery** *noun* [C, U]: *All these were chance discoveries made by scientists engaged in other investigations.* ◇ *The discovery of a child's body in the river has shocked the community.*

come a'cross sb/sth *phrasal verb* [no passive] to meet or find sb/sth by chance, especially while you are looking for or doing sth else: *I came across children sleeping under bridges.* ◇ *She came across some old photographs in a drawer.* See also **encounter** → MEET 2

catch [T] to find or discover sb doing sth, especially sth wrong: *I caught her smoking in the bathroom.* ◇ *He was* ***caught with*** *bomb-making equipment in his home.* ◇ *Mark walked in and* ***caught them at it*** *(= in the act of doing sth wrong).* ◇ *You've caught me at a bad time (= at a time when I am busy).*

turn sth 'up *phrasal verb* to find sth after spending time searching: *Our efforts to trace him turned up nothing.* ◇ *If I turn anything up, I'll let you know* ❶ You often **turn sth up** as part of a general search when you do not know in advance exactly what you might find.

unearth /ʌnˈɜːθ; *AmE* ʌnˈɜːrθ/ [T] to find sth in the ground by digging; to find or discover sth by chance or after searching for it, especially sth that has been hidden for a long time: *Police have unearthed a human skeleton.* ◇ *I unearthed my old diaries when we moved house.* ◇ *The newspaper has unearthed some disturbing facts.*

come upon sb/sth *phrasal verb* [no passive] (*rather formal*) to meet or find sb/sth by chance: *Jamie came upon her unawares.* ◇ *He was on vacation in Italy when he came upon the engravings in a local market.*

stumble on/upon/across sb/sth *phrasal verb* to find or meet sb/sth by chance, especially when this has surprising or serious consequences: *He was killed after he stumbled on a cocaine factory.*

---

3 find · establish · identify · determine · ascertain · discover

These words mean to become aware of sth by searching, studying or thinking carefully.

PATTERNS AND COLLOCATIONS

▸ to establish / identify / determine / ascertain **what** / **how** / **when** / **where** / **why** / **whether**...
▸ to establish / ascertain **that**...
▸ It was established / ascertained **that**...
▸ to find / establish / identify / determine / ascertain / discover the **cause**
▸ to find / establish / identify / determine / discover the **correlation**
▸ to find / establish / identify / discover a **connection**
▸ to find / identify / discover a **solution**
▸ to find / discover the **answer**
▸ to find / discover a **cure**
▸ to establish / ascertain the **facts**

---

find [T] to become aware of sb/sth by searching, studying or thinking carefully: *Scientists are still trying to find a cure for cancer.* ◇ *I'm having trouble finding anything new to say on this subject.* ◇ *Have they found anyone to replace her?* ◇ *Can you find me a hotel?*

establish [T] (*rather formal*) to find or prove the facts of a situation: *Police are still trying to establish the cause of death.* ◇ *They have established that his injuries were caused by a fall.* ◇ *We need to establish where she was at the time of the shooting.*

identify [T] (*rather formal*) to find a connection, cause or solution to a problem by studying the matter carefully: *Scientists have identified a link between diet and cancer.* ◇ *As yet they have not identified a buyer for the company.* ◇ *They are trying to identify what is wrong with the present system.* ❶ You usually **identify** sth by first thinking of a possible connection, cause, etc. and then looking for evidence to prove or disprove it. See also **identify** → IDENTIFY

determine [T] (*formal*) to find the facts about sth; to calculate sth exactly: *An enquiry was set up to determine the cause of the accident.* ◇ *Computer models help to determine whether a particular area is likely to flood.*

ascertain /ˌæsəˈteɪn; *AmE* ˌæsərˈt-/ [T] (*formal*) to establish the facts of a situation: *It should be ascertained that the plans comply with the law.*

> **NOTE** ESTABLISH OR ASCERTAIN? Ascertain is an even more formal way of saying **establish**. However, **establish** is usually only used in the context of official or scientific investigations; **ascertain** can also be used when you are trying to find out about sb's personal intentions and feelings, although it is still very formal: *Could you ascertain whether she will be coming to the meeting?* ◇ ~~Could you establish whether she will be coming to the meeting.~~

discover [T] to be the first person to become aware that a particular thing or place exists by searching, studying or thinking: *Scientists around the world are working to discover a cure for AIDS.*

▶ **discovery** *noun* [C, U]: *Researchers have* ***made*** *some important new* ***discoveries***. ◇ *the discovery of antibiotics in the 20th century*

---

4 find · locate · trace · track sb/sth down · search sb/sth out · sniff sb/sth out

These words all mean to discover where sb/sth is, or get sb/sth back after looking for them/it.

PATTERNS AND COLLOCATIONS

▸ to find sth / locate sth / track sth down / search sth out **for** sb/sth
▸ to find / trace / track down the **killer** / **location**
▸ to locate / trace / track down / sniff out sb's **whereabouts**

▶ to find / locate / trace / track down the **missing** …
▶ to **finally** / **eventually** find / locate / trace / track down sb / sth

find [T] to get back sb/sth that was lost or missing after looking for them/it: *I can't find my keys.* ◊ *Can you find my bag for me?* ◊ *The child was eventually found safe and well.* ◊ *He went through the drawers but found nothing.* ◊ *I wanted to talk to him but he was* **nowhere to be found**.

locate /ləʊˈkeɪt; *AmE* ˈloʊkeɪt/ [T] (*rather formal*) to find the exact position of sb/sth: *The mechanic located the fault immediately.* ◊ *Rescue planes are trying to locate the missing sailors.* See also **location** → PLACE *noun* 1

trace [T] to find or discover sb/sth that has disappeared by looking carefully for them/it, often by looking for evidence of places where the person or thing has previously been: *We finally* **traced** *him* **to** *an address in Chicago.* ◊ *We have not been able to trace the original letter.* See also **trace** → SIGN *noun* 1

track sb/sth 'down *phrasal verb* to find sb/sth after spending time searching in several places: *The police have so far failed to track down the attacker.* ◊ *I finally tracked the reference down in a book of quotations.*

search sb/sth 'out *phrasal verb* to look for sb/sth until you find them/it: *Fighter pilots searched out and attacked enemy aircraft.*

sniff sb/sth 'out *phrasal verb* (*rather informal*) to find sb/sth by using your sense of smell; to find sb/sth by looking or asking questions: *The dogs are trained to sniff out drugs.* ◊ *Journalists are good at sniffing out a scandal.*

fine *adj.* See also the entries for ADEQUATE and GOOD 2

fine · all right · fair · OK · acceptable · satisfactory · reasonable · in order · right
These words all describe sth that is good enough for you to accept.

PATTERNS AND COLLOCATIONS
▶ to be fine / all right / fair / OK / acceptable / satisfactory / reasonable / in order **to do sth**
▶ to be fine / all right / fair / OK / acceptable / satisfactory / reasonable / in order **that...**
▶ a fair / an acceptable / a satisfactory / a reasonable **solution**
▶ a fair / an acceptable / a reasonable **wage / price**
▶ a fair / reasonable **question**
▶ That's fine / all right / OK **by me**.
▶ **perfectly** fine / all right / fair / OK / acceptable / satisfactory / reasonable / in order
▶ **(not) entirely** fair / acceptable / satisfactory / reasonable

fine (often used as an exclamation) (*spoken*) used to tell sb that you are satisfied with an action, suggestion, decision or situation: *'I'll leave this here, OK?' 'Fine.'* ◊ *'Bob wants to know if he can come too.' 'That's fine by me.'* ◊ *Your speech was* **absolutely fine**. ◊ *'Can I get you another drink?' 'No thanks. I'm fine.'*

all 'right [not before noun] (*informal, especially spoken*) good enough; that can be allowed: *Is the coffee all right?* ◊ *Is it all right for me to leave early?* ◊ *Is it all right if I leave early?* ◊ *'I'm afraid I have to go now.' 'That's all right.'*
▶ **all right** *adv.*: *Are you getting along all right in your new job?*

fair good enough or appropriate in a particular situation: *Scoring twenty points was a fair achievement.* ◊ *It wasn't really fair to ask him to do all the work.* ◊ *It seems only fair that they should give us something in return.* ◊ **It's fair to say that** *they're very pleased with the offer.* ◊ **To be fair**, *she behaved better than we expected.* See also **fair** → REASONABLE

OK (also **okay**) [not usually before noun] (*informal, spoken*) all right; good enough: *Is it OK if I leave now?* ◊ *Is it OK for me to come too?* ◊ *She looks OK to me.* ◊ *We had an okay time on the trip – not great.*
▶ **OK** *adv.*: *I think I did OK in the exam.*

NOTE ALL RIGHT OR OK? **OK** is only used in spoken English; **all right** can be written, although it is informal.

---

acceptable that sb agrees is good enough or should be allowed: *We want a solution that is acceptable to all parties.* ◊ *To get on this course, a pass in English at grade B is acceptable.* ◊ *Air pollution in the city has reached four times the acceptable level.* **OPP** **unacceptable** → UNACCEPTABLE

satisfactory good enough for a particular purpose: *Their work is satisfactory but not outstanding.* ◊ *You haven't yet given us a satisfactory explanation.* **OPP** **unsatisfactory** → DISAPPOINTING
▶ **satisfactorily** /-tərəli/ *adv.*: *Our complaint was dealt with satisfactorily.*

reasonable acceptable and appropriate in a particular situation: *The furniture is in reasonable condition.* ◊ *You must submit your claim within a reasonable time.* ◊ *If the price is reasonable, we'll buy it.* See also **reasonable** → REASONABLE
▶ **reasonably** *adv.*: *The instructions are reasonably straightforward.*

NOTE FAIR OR REASONABLE? In many cases you can use either of these words, but **fair** is used in a lot of spoken expressions, where **reasonable** is not usually used. **Fair** does not collocate with *time*: ~~You must submit your claim within a fair time.~~

in 'order *idiom* (*formal*) as it should be: *Is everything in order, sir?* ◊ *We need to check that all your papers are in order.*

right [not before noun] (used especially in negative statements) in a normal or satisfactory condition: *That sausage doesn't smell right.* ◊ *Things aren't right between her parents.* ◊ *If only I could have helped* **put** *matters* **right**. **OPP** **wrong** → WRONG 2
▶ **right** *adv.*: *Nothing's going right for me today.*

finish *verb* See also the entry for END

finish · be done · complete · finalize · wrap sth up · follow (sth) through · round sth off · round sth out
These words all mean to make sth whole or perfect.

PATTERNS AND COLLOCATIONS
▶ to finish sth / be done / follow through / round sth off / round sth out **with** sth
▶ to finish sth / complete sth / follow through / round sth off / round sth out **by** doing sth
▶ to finish / complete / finalize the **preparations / arrangements**
▶ to finish / complete / wrap up / round off / round out a / an **discussion / evening / meal**
▶ to finish / complete / wrap up the **championship / game / series**
▶ to finish / complete / round off / round out the **day / season**
▶ to finish / complete / round off / round out a / an **tour / interview / campaign**
▶ to complete / finalize / wrap up a **deal**
▶ to **finally** finish sth / be done / complete sth / round sth off / round sth out

finish [T, I] (*especially spoken*) to stop doing sth or making sth because it is complete: *Haven't you finished your homework yet?* ◊ *I'll just finish the chapter, then I'll come.* ◊ *She finished law school last year.* ◊ *Be quiet! He hasn't finished speaking.* ◊ *She* **put the finishing touches** *to her painting* (= did the things that made it complete). ◊ *I thought you'd never finish!* **OPP** **start** → BEGIN, See also **unfinished** → PARTIAL

be 'done *phrase* (*especially AmE, especially spoken*) to have finished doing sth: *Aren't you done with your homework yet?* ◊ *No, I'll be done in a minute.* ◊ *Be quiet – he's not done yet.* ◊ (*rather informal*) *I thought you'd never* **get done**.

complete [T, often passive] (*rather formal, especially written*) to finish sth: *She's just completed a master's degree in Law.* ◊ *The project should be completed within a year.* ❶ In this meaning **complete** is often used to talk about work or study: *to complete a project/an assignment/a degree/a thesis/a deal/an apprenticeship.* **Complete** can also mean 'to make sth whole or perfect': *I only need one more card* *to complete the set.* Collocates of this meaning include *set, collection, scene, picture, series, sequence* and *transformation.*

▶ **completion** /kəmˈpliːʃn/ *noun* [U]: *The project is due for completion in the spring.* ◇ *The road is nearing completion* (= it is nearly finished).

NOTE FINISH, BE DONE OR COMPLETE? **Finish** is more frequent in spoken English; **complete** is more frequent in written English. Note that you can *finish doing sth* but you CANNOT *complete doing sth: He hasn't completed speaking.* In spoken American English **be done** is more frequent than **finish**, although **finish** is also used.

finalize (*BrE* **-ise**) /ˈfaɪnəlaɪz/ [T] (*especially business*) to complete the last part of a plan or agreement: *We need to finalize our plans.* ◇ *They met to finalize the terms of the treaty.* ❶ **Finalize** is often used to talk about business agreements, arrangements and plans. It is also used in business to talk about finishing the act of agreeing on a sale: *to finalize a deal/transaction/sale*

,**wrap sth 'up** *phrasal verb* (**-pp-**) (*informal, especially business or sport*) to complete sth such as an agreement, meeting or sports competition in a satisfactory way: *That just about wraps it up for today.* ◇ *He is the one driver who could have beaten the Brazilian and wrapped up the world championship.*

,**follow 'through**, ,**follow sth 'through** *phrasal verb* (*rather informal, especially spoken*) to complete sth that you have started: *The key to success is having the motivation to follow through with your ideas.* ◇ *The project only has any value if you follow it through.*

,**round sth 'off** *phrasal verb* (*BrE*) to finish an activity or complete sth in a good or suitable way: *She rounded off the tour with a concert at Carnegie Hall.* ❶ You can **round off** a *day*, an *evening* or a *campaign* with *sports, dancing* or a *party*; you could **round off** a *meal* with *coffee* or *cheese*; or a sports team might *round off the season with a win.*

,**round sth 'out** *phrasal verb* (*AmE*) to round sth off: *The book is rounded out with a new cover and introduction.* ❶ You can also **round out** a list or group of people or things: *Julia Roberts and Gwyneth Paltrow round out the cast.*

fire *noun*

1 destroyed by fire
2 Get warm by the fire.

---

1 fire · flames · blaze · combustion · inferno

These are all words for the flames, light and heat that are produced when sth burns, especially when they are out of control.

PATTERNS AND COLLOCATIONS
▶ (a) **raging** fire / flames / inferno
▶ to **start** a fire / blaze
▶ to **fight/tackle/contain/control/put out/extinguish** a fire / the flames / a blaze
▶ to **bring** a fire / blaze **under control**
▶ to **douse** a fire / the flames
▶ to **escape (from)** a fire / the flames / a blaze / an inferno
▶ to **fan** the fire / the flames
▶ a fire / flames / an inferno **rages / rage**
▶ a fire / flames / a blaze **spreads / spread**
▶ a fire / blaze **breaks out / starts**
▶ a fire / flames **roars / roar**

fire [U, C] the flames, light and heat, and often smoke, that are produced when sth burns; fire that is out of control and destroys buildings, trees or other things: *Most animals are afraid of fire.* ◇ *The car was now on fire.* ◇ *Several youths had set fire to the police car* (= had made it start burning). ◇ *These thatched roofs frequently catch fire* (= start to burn). ◇ *It took several days to bring the forest fires under control.*

flames [pl.] the hot bright streams of burning gas that come from sth that is on fire: *The flames were leaping higher and higher.* ◇ *The building was in flames* (= was

burning). ◇ *The plane burst into flames* (= suddenly began burning). ◇ *Everything went up in flames* (= was destroyed by fire).

blaze [C, usually sing.] (*especially journalism*) a very large fire, especially a dangerous one: *Five people died in the blaze.* ◇ *Firefighters were called in to tackle the blaze.* ❶ **Blaze** is a dramatic word which is often used in newspapers, especially in headlines, to catch the attention of the reader: *Two die in pub blaze.* See also **blaze** → BURN *verb* 1

combustion /kəmˈbʌstʃən/ [U] (*technical*) the process of burning; a chemical process in which substances combine with the oxygen in the air to produce heat and light: *Poisonous gases are produced during fossil fuel combustion.*

inferno /ɪnˈfɜːnəʊ; *AmE* ɪnˈfɜːrnoʊ/ (pl. **-os**) [C, usually sing.] (*written, especially journalism*) a very large dangerous fire that is out of control: *The flames quickly turned the house into a raging inferno.* ❶ **Inferno** is a dramatic word that is often used to make literary texts or newspaper stories seem more powerful.

---

2 fire · bonfire · campfire

These are all words for a pile of burning fuel such as wood or coal.

PATTERNS AND COLLOCATIONS
▶ a **blazing** fire / bonfire / campfire
▶ to **build / make / light** a fire / bonfire / campfire
▶ to **throw / put sth on** a fire / bonfire / campfire
▶ to **put out** a fire / bonfire / campfire
▶ to **sit / gather round / around** a fire / bonfire / campfire
▶ a fire / bonfire / campfire **burns**

fire [C] a pile of burning fuel, such as wood or coal, used for cooking food or heating a room: *Come and get warm by the fire.* ◇ *We sat in front of a roaring fire.* ❶ A *roaring/blazing fire* is a large fire that sb has lit in a room in order to make the room warm and comfortable. A *raging fire* is a fire that has started by accident and is out of control.

bonfire /ˈbɒnfaɪə(r); *AmE* ˈbɑːn-/ [C] a large outdoor fire for burning waste or as part of a celebration: *There will be a bonfire and a firework display.* ◇ *What are you doing for Bonfire Night* (= a festival in Britain on 5 November)?

campfire /ˈkæmpfaɪə(r)/ [C] an outdoor fire made by people who are sleeping outside or living in a tent: *We sat around the campfire telling stories and singing.*

---

fire *verb*

fire · lay sb off · dismiss · sack · axe · make sb redundant · let sb go · discharge · give sb/get the sack

These words all mean to officially remove sb from their job.

PATTERNS AND COLLOCATIONS
▶ to **fire** sb / **lay** sb **off** / **dismiss** sb / **sack** sb / **make** sb **redundant** / **discharge** sb / **get the sack from** a job
▶ to **fire** sb / **dismiss** sb / **sack** sb / **give** sb **the sack for** sth
▶ to **fire / lay off / dismiss / sack / axe staff / workers / employees**
▶ to **make staff / workers / employees redundant**
▶ to **let staff / employees go**
▶ to **make jobs / posts / positions redundant**
▶ to **axe jobs / posts / positions**
▶ to **get fired / laid off / dismissed / sacked / made redundant**
▶ to **be unfairly / summarily fired / dismissed / sacked**
▶ to **be wrongfully fired / dismissed**

fire [T, often passive] (*AmE or rather informal, BrE*) to officially remove sb from their job: *We had to fire him for dishonesty.* ◇ *She got fired from her first job.* ◇ *He was responsible for hiring and firing employees.* **OPP** hire → EMPLOY

,**lay sb 'off** *phrasal verb* [often passive] to stop employing sb, often for a temporary period, because there is not enough work for them to do: *200 workers at the factory have been laid off.* **OPP** take sb on → EMPLOY. See also **lay-off** → UNEMPLOYMENT

dismiss [T, usually passive] (*rather formal*) to officially remove sb from their job: *She claims she was unfairly dismissed from her position.* **❶ Dismiss** is the preferred term used in legal contexts, especially in the phrase *unfairly/wrongfully dismissed.* **OPP appoint** → APPOINT, See also **dismissal** → UNEMPLOYMENT

sack [T, often passive] (*especially BrE, informal*) to dismiss sb from a job, usually because they have done sth wrong: *She was sacked for refusing to work on Sundays.* See also **sacking** → UNEMPLOYMENT

axe (*BrE*) (*AmE* **ax**) [T, usually passive] (*journalism*) to remove sb from their job: *300 jobs are to be axed at a local chemical works.* ◇ *Jones has been axed from the team.* **❶ Axe** is used especially in journalism when a large number of people are made redundant at the same time; it is more usual to talk about the *jobs* being axed, rather than the people.

make sb re'dundant *phrase* [usually passive] (*BrE*) to remove sb from their job because there is no more work available for them: *She was made redundant from her job.* ◇ *A further five senior posts are to be made redundant.* **❶** Officially, it is *jobs* or *posts* that become **redundant**, not the people who hold them; in practice it is more common to talk about people being made redundant. See also **redundant** → UNEMPLOYED, **redundancy** → UNEMPLOYMENT

let sb 'go *idiom* to make sb have to leave their job: *They're having to let 100 employees go because of falling profits.* **❶ Let sb go** is used as a gentler way of saying *fire, sack* or *make sb redundant.*

discharge /dɪs'tʃɑːdʒ; *AmE* -'tʃɑːrdʒ/ [T, usually passive] (*rather formal*) to give sb official permission to leave a job or a position in the army; to make sb leave a job or a position in the army: *He was discharged from the army following his injury.* ◇ *She was discharged from the police force for bad conduct.* See also **discharge** → UNEMPLOYMENT *noun*

give sb the 'sack, **get the 'sack** *phrase* (*especially BrE, informal*) to sack sb; to be sacked: *I've never had to give anyone the sack.* ◇ *He got the sack from his last job.*

> **NOTE SACK** OR **GIVE SB THE SACK?** Sack can sound more sudden or dramatic than **give sb the sack**, and is used more by journalists. **Give sb the sack** is more frequent in everyday spoken English.

firm *adj.*

firm · secure · steady · stable
These words all describe sth that is strongly fixed in place and not likely to move.

PATTERNS AND COLLOCATIONS
▸ a firm / secure / steady / stable **foundation**
▸ a firm / secure / stable **base**

firm strongly fixed in place, especially on sth heavy or strong that is not likely to move or change: *Stand the fish tank on a firm base.* ◇ *No building can stand without firm foundations, and neither can a marriage.* See also **firm** → SOLID, **firm** → TIGHT
▸ **firmly** *adv.*: *Make sure the cover is firmly fixed in place.*

secure /sɪ'kjʊə(r); *AmE* sə'kjʊr/ fixed firmly and correctly and therefore not likely to move, fall or break: *The aerial doesn't look very secure to me.* ◇ *It was difficult to maintain a secure foothold on the ice.*

steady firmly fixed, supported or balanced; not shaking or likely to fall: *He held the boat steady as she got in.* ◇ *Such fine work requires a good eye and a steady hand.* ◇ *She's not very steady on her feet these days.* **OPP unsteady ❶ Unsteady** describes a person who is not completely in control of their movements and might fall, or a part of the body that is shaking or moving in a way that is not controlled: *She is still a little unsteady on her feet after the operation.* ◇ *With unsteady hands he opened the door and peered out.* See also **steady** → LEAN *verb 2*, **steady** → STEADY *adj.*

stable /'steɪbl/ not likely to fall over: *This ladder doesn't seem very stable.* **OPP unstable**, See also **stable** → STEADY

first *det., adj.*

first · initial · original · preliminary · opening · earliest · primary · introductory · preparatory
These words all describe sth that happens or exists at the beginning.

PATTERNS AND COLLOCATIONS
▸ preliminary / preparatory **to** sth
▸ the first / initial / preliminary / opening / earliest / primary / introductory / preparatory **stage**
▸ first / initial / original / preliminary / opening / introductory **remarks**
▸ a first / an initial / an original / a preliminary **estimate / draft / version**
▸ the first / initial / preliminary / introductory / preparatory **meeting**
▸ a first / an initial / a preliminary **step / appointment / visit**
▸ the first / opening / introductory **chapter / paragraph**
▸ the initial / the original / a preliminary / a preparatory **study**
▸ the initial / original / preliminary **findings**

first *det.* (of a person or thing) happening or coming before all other similar things or people; 1st: *his first wife* ◇ *King Richard I* (= said as 'King Richard the First') ◇ *It was the first time they had ever met.* ◇ *She resolved to do it at the first opportunity.* ◇ *First impressions can be misleading.* ◇ *You can have **first choice** of all the rooms.* ◇ *We're having chicken for the **first course.*** **OPP last** → LAST 1, **last** → LAST 2
▸ **first** *adv.*: *First I had to decide what to wear.* ◇ *Who came first in the race* (= who won)?
▸ **at first** *phrase*: *At first I thought she was joking but then I realized she meant it.* ◇ *I didn't like the job much at first.*

initial /ɪ'nɪʃl/ [only before noun] happening at the beginning; first: *My initial reaction was to decline the offer.* ◇ *It is the initial preparation that takes the time.* ◇ *There is an initial payment of £60 followed by ten instalments of £25.* **❶ Initial** is used especially to talk about a reaction or feeling that does not last very long: *By 1960 the initial optimism had evaporated.* ◇ *sb's initial response/impression/instinct/shock/surprise/enthusiasm/euphoria/excitement/scepticism/reluctance;* about a stage in a process: *the initial stage/phase/step/planning/preparation;* or about paying or spending money: *the initial investment/payment/outlay* **OPP final** → LAST 1
▸ **initially** *adv.*: *My contract is initially for three years.* ◇ *Initially, the system worked well.*

original [only before noun] existing at the beginning of a particular period, process or activity, especially before being changed into sth else: *The room still has many of its original features.* ◇ *I think you should go back to your original plan.*
▸ **originally** *adv.*: *The school was originally very small.* ◇ *He comes originally from Peru.*

preliminary /prɪ'lɪmɪnəri; *AmE* -neri/ happening before a more important action or event, especially by introducing or preparing for it: *After a few preliminary remarks he announced the winners.* ◇ *This is just a pilot study preliminary to a full-scale study.*

opening [only before noun] (especially of sth that sb says or writes, or a piece of music, etc.) happening at the beginning: *She was humming the opening bars of a song she had heard on the radio.* ◇ *United scored in the opening minutes of the game.* **OPP closing** → LAST 1, See also **opening** → START *noun*, **open** → BEGIN *verb*

earliest the nearest to the beginning of an event or period of time: *The earliest description of this species dates from 1816.* ◇ *The earliest possible date I can make is the third.*

primary /'praɪməri; *AmE* -meri/ [usually before noun] (*formal or technical*) developing or happening first; earliest: *The disease is still in its primary stage.* ◇ *It is not self-evident what the primary causes of this phenomenon are.* See also **primary** → MAIN

introductory /ˌɪntrəˈdʌktəri/ written or said at the beginning of sth as an introduction to what follows; intended as an introduction to a subject or activity for people who have never done it before: *The booklist at the end of the chapter contains some introductory reading on the subject.* ◇ *I took an introductory class in psychology during my first year at college.* See also **introduction** → BASICS, **introduction** → INTRODUCTION 2

preparatory /prɪˈpærətri; *AmE* -tɔːri/ [only before noun] (*especially BrE, formal*) done in order to prepare for sth: *After a few preparatory drawings, she completed the portrait in one session.* ◇ *Security checks had been carried out preparatory to* (= to prepare for) *the President's visit.* See also **preparation** → PLANNING, **prepare** → PREPARE 1, **prepare** → PREPARE 2

flash *verb*

flash · flicker · catch
These words all mean to shine or burn for a moment.

PATTERNS AND COLLOCATIONS
▸ a **light** / **lightning** / a **bulb** / a **screen** flashes / flickers
▸ sb's **eyes** flash / flicker
▸ to flash / flicker **on and off** / **briefly** / **momentarily**

flash [I, T] to shine or make sth shine very brightly for a short time; to use a light to give sb a signal: *Lightning flashed in the distance.* ◇ *A neon sign flashed on and off above the door.* ◇ *The guide flashed a light into the cave.* ◇ *Red lights flashed a warning at them.* ◇ *Why is that driver flashing his lights at us?*
▸ **flash** *noun* [C]: *a flash of lightning* ◇ *There was a blinding flash and the whole building shuddered.*

flicker [I] (of a light or flame) to keep going on and off as it shines or burns: *Black and white images were flickering on the screen.* ◇ *The candle flickered and went out.*

catch [T] if sth **catches** the light or the light **catches** it, the light shines on it and makes it shine too: *The knife gleamed as it caught the light.* ◇ *A colourful glow appears as the light catches the glass.*

flashy *adj.*

flashy · grandiose · pretentious · showy · ostentatious · snazzy · glitzy
These words all describe people or things that are expensive or noticeable in a way that is intended to impress people.

PATTERNS AND COLLOCATIONS
▸ flashy / showy **technique** / **footwork**

flashy (*informal, usually disapproving*) (of things) attracting attention by being bright, expensive, large, etc.; (of people) attracting attention by wearing expensive clothes, etc.; (of actions) intended to impress by looking very skilful: *I just want a good reliable car, nothing flashy.* ◇ *He was one of those flashy guys with too much money to throw around.* ◇ *She threw in a lot of flashy footwork to impress the judges.*

grandiose /ˈɡrændiəʊs; *AmE* -oʊs/ (*disapproving*) seeming very impressive but too large, complicated or expensive to be practical or possible: *The grandiose scheme for a journey across the desert came to nothing.* ◇ *The city is home to a new, and particularly grandiose opera house.* ❶ **Grandiose** is used especially to talk about *claims, ideas, objectives, plans, projects, proposals* and *schemes*, as well as buildings.

pretentious /prɪˈtenʃəs/ (*disapproving*) trying to appear important or intelligent in order to impress other people; trying to be sth that you are not, in order to impress: *That's a pretentious name for a cat!* ◇ *It was just an ordinary house – nothing pretentious.* ◇ *He's so pretentious!* **OPP unpretentious** → MODEST, See also **pretension** → PRETENSION

showy (*often disapproving*) so bright, colourful, large or exaggerated that it attracts a lot of attention: *These showy flowers make wonderful patio plants.* ◇ *She wore a lot of showy jewellery.*

ostentatious /ˌɒstenˈteɪʃəs; *AmE* ˌɑːs-/ (*rather formal, usually disapproving*) (of a thing) expensive or noticeable in a way that is intended to impress people; (of a person) behaving in a way that is meant to impress people by showing how rich or important they are; (of an action) done in a very obvious way so that people will notice it: *She was dripping with ostentatious gold jewellery.* ◇ *As her fame and fortune grew, she never became ostentatious.* ◇ *He gave an ostentatious yawn.*

snazzy (*informal, often approving*) (of clothes, cars, etc.) fashionable, bright and modern, and attracting your attention: *He'd booked us a table in a snazzy restaurant.* ◇ *They've designed some snazzy graphics for the new version of the game.*

NOTE FLASHY OR SNAZZY? **Flashy** is usually used in a disapproving way; **snazzy** is usually approving.

glitzy (*sometimes disapproving*) appearing very attractive, exciting and impressive, in a way that is not always genuine: *This was a glitzy, Hollywood-style occasion.*
▸ **glitz** *noun* [U]: *the glitz and glamour of the music scene*

flat *noun* See also the entry for HOUSE

flat · apartment · suite · penthouse · condominium · condo
These are all words for a set of rooms for living in.

PATTERNS AND COLLOCATIONS
▸ **in** a flat / an apartment / a suite / a penthouse / a condominium / a condo
▸ **at** sb's flat / apartment
▸ a **luxury** flat / apartment / suite / penthouse / condominium / condo
▸ a **penthouse** flat / apartment / suite
▸ a **one-** / **two-** / **three-bedroom** flat / apartment / condominium / condo
▸ to **live in** a flat / an apartment / a suite / a penthouse / a condominium / condo
▸ to **stay in** a flat / an apartment / a suite / a penthouse
▸ to **rent** a flat / an apartment / a suite

flat [C] (*BrE*) a set of rooms for living in, including a kitchen, usually on one floor of a building: *Do you live in a flat or a house?* ◇ *Children from the flats* (= the block of flats) *across the street were playing outside.*

apartment [C] (*especially AmE*) a set of rooms rented for living in, usually on one floor of a building: *Finding an apartment in any city can be a difficult task.* ◇ *an apartment building* ❶ **Apartment** is also used in British English, especially when it means a set of rooms rented for a holiday: *Our self-catering apartments are located just a minute's walk from the beach.*

NOTE FLAT OR APARTMENT **Apartment** and **flat** are both used in British English, although **flat** is the more usual word. Some people use **apartment** to mean accommodation that is larger, finer or more expensive than an ordinary **flat**. **Apartments** are usually part of a large building. **Flats** may be part of a large building, but may also be part of an ordinary house.

suite /swiːt/ [C] a set of rooms, especially in a hotel: *She booked a hotel suite overlooking Central Park.* ◇ *The science centre is located in a suite of offices on the third floor.*

penthouse /ˈpenthaʊs/ [C] an expensive and comfortable flat or set of rooms at the top of a tall building: *The hotel has 54 fully appointed rooms plus a luxury penthouse suite.*

condominium /ˌkɒndəˈmɪniəm; *AmE* ˌkɑːn-/ [C] (*especially AmE*) an apartment building in which each apartment is owned by the person living in it but the building and shared areas are owned by everyone together; an apartment in such a building: *There are town house and condominium developments going up in town.*

condo [C] (*AmE, informal*) a condominium: *He bought an ocean-front condo in his native Florida.*

flat *adj.*

flat · smooth · level · horizontal

These words all describe things that have a surface that is not curved, sloping or rough.

PATTERNS AND COLLOCATIONS
▸ a flat / smooth / level / horizontal **surface**
▸ a flat / smooth / level **road** / **floor**
▸ a flat / smooth **rock** / **stone**
▸ flat / level **ground** / **land**
▸ **completely** flat / smooth / level / horizontal

flat having a surface that is not curved or sloping; (of land) without any slopes or hills; (of surfaces) very even, without lumps or holes: *The town consisted mainly of low buildings with flat roofs.* ◇ *People used to think the earth was flat.* ◇ *The road stretched ahead across the flat landscape.* ◇ *I need a flat surface to write on.*

smooth (*often approving*) completely flat and even, without any lumps, holes or rough areas: *The water was as smooth as glass.* ◇ *Use a paint that gives a smooth, silky finish.* ◇ *Over the years, the stone steps had worn smooth.* **OPP** **rough** → ROUGH 1

level having a flat surface that does not slope: *Pitch the tent on level ground.* ◇ *Add a level tablespoon of flour (= enough to fill the spoon but not so much that there is a round heap on the spoon).*

NOTE FLAT OR LEVEL? Level is used most often with the words *ground* and *floor*, especially when this feature is a positive or desired one. **Flat** is used more to talk about surfaces that are not rounded: *a flat screen/base/ bottom/sheet/stomach/surface* (an exception is *a flat roof* which is a roof that does not slope), or landscapes that do not have any hills: *a flat field/landscape/ plateau/plain/region/beach.* **Flat** landscapes are often considered to be plain and boring; **level** ground is considered a good thing, since it is possible to build on it or walk easily on it.

horizontal /ˌhɒrɪˈzɒntl; *AmE* ˌhɔːrəˈzɑːntl; ˌhɑːr-/ going across and parallel to the ground rather than going up and down: *Draw a grid of horizontal and vertical lines.* **OPP** **vertical** → UPRIGHT

flatter *verb* See also the entry for PRAISE *verb*

flatter · grovel · fawn · ingratiate yourself

These words all mean to say nice things to sb or be nice to them, so that they will like you or so that you will get what you want.

flatter [T] to say nice things about sb, often in a way that is not sincere, because you want them to do sth for you or you want to please them: *Are you trying to flatter me?* ◇ *He was flattered by her attention.* ◇ *She was flattered to hear that he had been asking about her.* See also **flattery** → PRAISE *noun*, **flattering** → GOOD 6

grovel /ˈɡrɒvl; *AmE* ˈɡrɑːvl/ (-ll-, *AmE* -l-) [I] (*disapproving*) to behave in a very humble way towards sb who you want to forgive you, or who can give you sth that you want: *He went grovelling to her for forgiveness.* ◇ *a grovelling letter of apology*

fawn [I] (*disapproving*) to try to please sb by praising them or paying them too much attention: *Why is everybody fawning over him as if he's a national hero?* ◇ *He seemed unaware of the girl's fawning admiration.*

ingratiate yourself [T, no passive] (*disapproving*) to do things in order to make sb like you, especially sb who will be useful to you: *The first part of his plan was to ingratiate himself with the members of the committee.* See also **ingratiating** → SERVILE

flee *verb*

flee · run away · run off · take off · make off · bolt · run for it

These words all mean to leave a place very quickly, especially in order to escape from sb/sth.

PATTERNS AND COLLOCATIONS
▸ to flee / run away / bolt **from** sb / sth
▸ to flee / run away / run off / bolt **to** sth
▸ to run / take / make / bolt **off**
▸ to flee / run away / run off / take off / make off / bolt **down** / **into** sth
▸ to run away / run off / take off / make off **with** sb / sth
▸ to **turn and** flee / run away / run off

flee [I, T] (*especially written*) to leave a place very quickly, especially because you are in danger: *Refugees fled from the city.* ◇ *People fled in terror as the bomb exploded.* ◇ *Hundreds of people were forced to flee their homes.* ◇ *They fled the country in 1987.* ◇ *The man looked at me in horror, and then turned and fled.*

run aˈway *phrasal verb* (*especially spoken*) to leave a person or place quickly or suddenly, especially in order to get away from danger or trouble: *'Don't run away', the stranger said, 'We're here to help.'* ◇ *I tried to run away from home several times when I was a kid.*

run ˈoff *phrasal verb* (*especially BrE*) to leave a person or place quickly by running, often in order to escape from sb/sth: *The dog ran off across the park, barking loudly.* ◇ *She ran off when I tried to talk to her.*

NOTE RUN AWAY OR RUN OFF? In British English, if you **run off**, you physically run away from a person or danger that is right where you are; **run away** can also be used in this way, but it can also mean to make a sudden journey to get away from a more general trouble or problem in your life: *Why don't we run away to Paris?* ◇ *Why don't we run off to Paris?* When people physically **run away**, it is usually because they are frightened; they may **run off** through fear or just because they want to get away. In American English **run away** is used for both meanings.

take ˈoff *phrasal verb* (*informal*) to leave a place, especially in a hurry: *When he saw me coming he took off in the opposite direction.*

make ˈoff *phrasal verb* to hurry away from a place, especially after committing a crime or doing sth wrong: *The robbers made off before the police arrived.* ❶ **Make off with sth** means 'to steal sth and hurry away with it': *The raiders made off with £20 000 worth of jewellery.*

bolt [I] (of an animal, especially a horse) to run away suddenly, especially because it is frightened; (of a person) to run away, especially in order to escape: *The plane swooped down low and the horses bolted.* ◇ *For a moment I thought about bolting, but there was no escape.*

ˈrun for it *idiom* (often used in orders) to run in order to escape from sb/sth: *'Run for it!' Billy yelled.*

fleet *noun*

fleet · convoy · procession · parade · motorcade · caravan

These are all words for a group of vehicles that are travelling together.

PATTERNS AND COLLOCATIONS
▸ a fleet / convoy / procession of **cars**
▸ a fleet / convoy of **buses** / **lorries** / **trucks** / **vehicles**
▸ a **large** fleet / convoy / procession
▸ a **great** fleet / procession / parade
▸ to **join** a fleet / convoy / procession
▸ to **ride in** convoy / procession / the parade

fleet [C] a group of buses, taxis, planes, etc. travelling together or all owned by the same organization: *The injured were taken to hospital in a fleet of ambulances.* ◇ *The airline is doubling the size of its fleet.*

convoy /'kɒnvɔɪ; *AmE* 'kɑːn-/ [C] a group of vehicles or ships travelling together, especially one that is protected by soldiers or other vehicles or ships: *The UN aid convoy finally got through with supplies of food.* ◇ *They drove in convoy* (= as a group) *in case one of the cars broke down.*

procession [C] a line of people or vehicles that moves along slowly, especially as part of a ceremony: *Eight cars led the funeral procession.* ◇ *Protesters marched in procession to the town hall.*

parade /pə'reɪd/ [C] a public celebration of a special day or event, usually involving bands in the streets and decorated vehicles: *the St Patrick's Day parade in New York*

motorcade /'məʊtəkeɪd; *AmE* 'moʊtərk-/ [C] a line of vehicles travelling together, including one that a famous or important person is travelling in: *There was an attack on the presidential motorcade.*

caravan [C] a group of people with vehicles or animals who are travelling together, especially across the desert: *They travelled by horse and camel caravan.*

flexible *adj.*

1 flexible working hours
2 flexible materials

1 flexible · versatile · adjustable · convertible · adaptable · multi-purpose · all-purpose

These words all describe people or things that can change to suit new conditions or situations.

flexible /'fleksəbl/ (*approving*) that can change or be changed to suit new conditions or situations: *What is needed is a more flexible design.* ◇ *We can offer you flexible working hours.* ◇ *Can you be flexible about when you take your leave?* **OPP** inflexible → DEEP-SEATED

▸ **flexibility** *noun* [U]: *Computers offer a much greater degree of flexibility in the way work is organized.*
▸ **flexibly** *adv.*: *Managers must respond flexibly to new developments in business practice.*

versatile /'vɜːsətaɪl; *AmE* 'vɜːrsətl/ (*approving*) (of a person) able to do many different things; (of a thing) having many different uses: *He's a versatile actor who has played a wide variety of parts.* ◇ *Eggs are easy to cook and are an extremely versatile food.*

adjustable that can be moved to different positions or changed in shape or size: *The golf buggy comes equipped with fully adjustable seat belts.* ◇ *The height of the bicycle seat is adjustable.* See also **adjust** → ADJUST

convertible that can be changed to a different form or use: *a convertible sofa* (= one that can be used as a bed) ◇ *The bonds are convertible into ordinary shares.* ❶ **Convertible** is most often used in the context of sofas or finance: *convertible bonds/currencies/debt/shares/stocks/securities* See also **convert** → TURN *verb* 2

adaptable (*approving*) that can change or be changed in order to deal successfully with new situations: *Older workers can be as adaptable and quick to learn as anyone else.* ◇ *Successful businesses are highly adaptable to economic change.* See also **adapt** → CHANGE *verb* 1

NOTE FLEXIBLE OR ADAPTABLE? **Flexible** is used especially to talk about working situations in which people and systems need to be able to change frequently to suit conditions such as customers' requirements or financial restrictions. **Adaptable** is used more to talk about how easily people or animals manage when conditions change in the longer term, for example, if the climate becomes much colder or warmer, if particular types of food are no longer available, or if the economy fails.

,multi-'purpose [only before noun] that can be used for several different purposes: *Just one multi-purpose cleaner should be enough for the whole house.* ◇ *The concert hall is actually a multi-purpose building that doubles as a theatre, exhibition hall and community centre.*

,all-'purpose [only before noun] that can be used for several different purposes: *Cheddar is an all-purpose cheese for cooking and eating.* ◇ *Each child had one pair of all-purpose shoes.*

NOTE MULTI-PURPOSE OR ALL-PURPOSE? **Multi-purpose** is a more positive word than **all-purpose** and emphasizes how useful and versatile a thing is. An **all-purpose** thing is more likely to be sth quite ordinary that you just use for everything because you cannot afford or cannot be bothered to make or get sth different for each purpose. **All-purpose** is used more in American English.

2 flexible · springy · elastic · supple

These words all describe sth that can bend easily.

flexible /'fleksəbl/ (especially of materials) that can bend easily without breaking: *You'll need 2 metres of flexible plastic tubing.* **OPP** rigid → SOLID

springy /'sprɪŋi/ returning quickly to its original shape after being pushed, pulled or stretched: *We walked across the springy grass.* ❶ **Springy** is used mainly to talk about things such as *hair, grass, moss* and *heather.*

elastic (especially of materials) able to stretch and return to its original size and shape: *An elastic material is usually placed around the upper arm.*

supple soft and able to bend easily without cracking: *Moisturizing cream helps to keep your skin soft and supple.* ❶ **Supple** is used most often with words relating to the body: *skin, fingers, spine* and *movement.*

flight *noun*

flight · ride · drive · lift

These are all words for a journey in a vehicle such as a plane, car or train.

flight [C] a journey made by air, especially in a plane: *Enjoy your flight.* ◇ *All international and domestic flights were suspended.* ◇ *He began to feel ill during the return flight.* ◇ *Flight 420 to Oslo is now boarding at Gate 23.* ◇ *Hurry or you'll miss your flight.* ◇ *UN relief flights were bringing food into the area.* ◇ *We were offered a flight in a hot-air balloon.* See also **fly** → FLY *verb* 1

ride [C] a short journey in a vehicle or on a bicycle, motorcycle or horse: *It's a ten-minute bus ride into town.* ◇ *John took me for a ride in his new car.* ◇ *I was taking my usual morning ride* (= on a horse) *along the beach .* ◇ *(AmE) She hitched a ride* (= stopped a passing car and travelled in it) *to the nearest town.* ❶ In British English say *hitch a lift.* See also **ride** → GO *verb* 2

drive [C] a journey in a car or other vehicle: *We went for a drive along the coast.* ◇ *He was tired after the long drive home.* ◇ *The beach is a 20-minute drive away.* ◇ *I took the car for a test drive* (= a drive to try out a car that you might buy). See also **drive** → DRIVE *verb* 1, **drive** → GO *verb* 2

lift [C] (*BrE*) a free ride in a vehicle or on a motorcycle to a place you want to get to: *She offered me a lift home.* ◇ *His car broke down and he hitched a lift* (= stopped a passing car and travelled in it) *into town.* ❶ In American English use **ride**.

flirt *verb*

flirt · chat sb up · tease · come on to sb · make a pass at sb
These verbs all mean to try to attract sb sexually by talking or behaving in a particular way.

flirt [I] to behave towards sb as if you find them sexually attractive, without seriously wanting to have a relationship with them: *He **flirts** outrageously **with** his female clients.*
▶ **flirt** *noun* [C, usually sing.]: *She's a real flirt.*
▶ **flirtatious** /flɜː'teɪʃəs; *AmE* flɜːr't-/ *adj.*: *a flirtatious young woman* ◇ *a flirtatious giggle*
,chat sb 'up *phrasal verb* (-tt-) (*BrE, informal*) to talk in a friendly way to sb you are sexually attracted to: *She went straight over and tried to chat him up.*
▶ 'chat-up *noun* [C, U]: *Is that your best chat-up line?*

NOTE FLIRT OR CHAT SB UP? Chat sb up only refers to the actual words spoken by a person; **flirt** refers to sb's behaviour as well. If sb **chats** you **up**, it usually means that they want to have a relationship with you, but this is not always the case if they **flirt** with you.

tease /tiːz/ [I, T] (*disapproving*) to make sb sexually excited, especially when you do not intend to have sex with them: *She teased the men with an expression that was both innocent and knowing.* See also **lead sb on** → MISLEAD
▶ **tease** *noun* [C, usually sing.]: *She's a wicked little tease.*
,come 'on to sb *phrasal verb* (*informal*) to behave in a way that shows sb that you want to have a sexual relationship with them: *When he started coming on to me, I assumed he wasn't married.*
▶ 'come-on *noun* [C, usually sing.]: (*informal*) *She tried to ignore his come-ons.*
make a 'pass at sb *idiom* (*informal*) to try to start a sexual relationship with sb: *Are you making a pass at me?*

float *verb*

float · hang · drift · hover
These words all mean to move slowly or remain still on water or in the air.

PATTERNS AND COLLOCATIONS
▶ to float / hang / drift / hover **over** sth
▶ to float / hang / hover **above / overhead / in the air / in the sky**
▶ a **boat** floats / drifts
▶ **clouds** float / hang / drift / hover
▶ a **smell** floats / hangs / drifts
▶ **smoke** hangs / drifts
▶ to float / drift **slowly / gently**

float [I] to move slowly on water or in the air; to stay on or near the surface of a liquid and not sink: *A group of swans floated by.* ◇ *We tried to make a raft but it wouldn't float.* ❶ When it means 'to move on water or in the air', **float** is always used with an adverb or preposition. **OPP** sink ❶ To **sink** is to to go below the surface or towards the bottom of a liquid or soft substance, especially when this is an accident: *The Titanic sank about 400 miles south of Newfoundland in 1912.*
hang [I] (always used with an adverb or preposition) to stay in the air, especially for a long time: *Smoke hung in the air above the city.* ◇ *The smell of burning plastic hung in the air.* ◇ *The question seemed to hang in the space between them.* ❶ You usually use **hang** when you are talking about clouds, mist, smoke, dust and smells. You can also use **hang** to describe the *moon, sun* or *stars*.

drift [I] (usually used with an adverb or preposition) to move along smoothly and slowly in water or air: *The boat drifted out to sea.* ◇ *White clouds drifted across the sky.*

NOTE FLOAT OR DRIFT? In many cases you can use either word. **Float** places slightly more emphasis on the idea of sth being supported on the surface of the water or in the air. **Drift** places more emphasis on the fact that sth is moving slowly in a particular direction, often without any control.

hover /'hɒvə(r); *AmE* 'hʌvər/ [I] (usually used with an adverb or preposition) to stay in the air in one place: *The hawk hovered in the air and then plunged to the ground.* ◇ *A police helicopter hovered overhead.* ❶ Birds, insects and helicopters **hover**, but NOT planes.

flood *noun*

1 The rain caused floods.
2 a flood of calls/refugees/tears

1 **flood · torrent · flash flood · tidal wave · deluge · tsunami**
These are all words for a very large amount of water moving quickly or in a place which is usually dry.

PATTERNS AND COLLOCATIONS
▶ a **great** flood / torrent
▶ to **cause** a flood / flash flood / tidal wave / tsunami
▶ floods / flash floods / a tidal wave / a tsunami **hit / hits** sth
▶ a flood / tidal wave / tsunami **destroys** sth
▶ a torrent / deluge **of rain**

flood [C, U] a large amount of water covering an area that is usually dry: *The heavy rain has caused floods in many parts of the country.* ◇ *The building was evacuated as flood water filled the basement.* ◇ (*especially BrE*) *The river is in flood* (= has more water in it than normal and has caused a flood). See also **SOAK** *verb*
torrent /'tɒrənt; *AmE* 'tɔːr-; 'tɑːr-/ [C] a large amount of water moving very quickly: *After the winter rains, the stream becomes a raging torrent.* ◇ *The rain was coming down in torrents.*
▶ **torrential** /tə'renʃl/ *adj.*: *torrential rain*
'flash flood [C] a sudden flood of water caused by heavy rain: *More than 80 people were feared dead last night after flash floods, the worst in 34 years.*
,tidal 'wave /'taɪdl/ [C] a very large ocean wave, especially one caused by an earthquake or a volcano erupting: *According to one account, the explosion caused a tidal wave 65 feet high.* See also **wave** → WAVE *noun* 1
deluge /'deljuːdʒ/ [C, usually sing.] (*especially written*) a sudden very heavy fall of rain: *The earlier deluge had given way to more normal rain.*
tsunami /tsuː'nɑːmi/ [C] a very large ocean wave caused, for example, by an earthquake or a volcano erupting: *The tsunami caused immeasurable damage.*

NOTE TIDAL WAVE OR TSUNAMI? The correct scientific term for a very large ocean wave cause by an earthquake is **tsunami** or **seismic sea wave**. Technically, a **tidal wave** is caused by the pull of the moon and the sun that causes the tides. However, in popular, non-technical language, **tidal wave** is usually used to mean **tsunami**.

2 **flood · stream · barrage · shower · battery · torrent · hail · outpouring · volley**
These are all words for the movement of a large amount of sth, or a large number of things or people that arrive or happen at the same time.

PATTERNS AND COLLOCATIONS
▶ a flood / stream / torrent of **words**
▶ a flood / stream of **calls**
▶ a flood / barrage of **complaints**
▶ a stream / barrage / torrent of **abuse**

▸ a barrage / torrent / hail of **criticism**
▸ a barrage / battery / volley of **questions**
▸ **floods** / a torrent of **tears**
▸ a torrent / an outpouring of **emotion**
▸ a shower / hail / volley of **arrows** / **bullets** / **stones**
▸ a hail / volley of **shots** / **fire**
▸ a **constant** / **continuous** stream / barrage of sth
▸ to **unleash** a flood / barrage / torrent / volley of sth

flood [C] (usually followed by *of*) a very large amount of sth or number of things or people that appear at the same time: *They took on temporary workers in anticipation of a flood of calls.* ◇ *Authorities are struggling to cope with the flood of refugees.* ◇ *The child was in floods of tears (= crying a lot).* See also **flood** → OVERWHELM *verb*, **flood** → SURGE *verb*

stream [C] (always followed by *of*) a large amount of sth or number of things that happen one after the other: *She had to deal with a constant stream of enquiries.* ◇ *He let loose a stream of insults and obscenities.* ◇ *The agency provided me with a steady stream of work.* ❶ A **stream** can also be a continuous flow of people or vehicles. See also **stream** → FLOW *verb*

barrage /ˈbærɑːʒ; *AmE* bəˈrɑːʒ/ [sing.] (usually followed by *of*) a large number or amount of sth, for example questions or comments, that are directed at sb very quickly, one after the other, often in an aggressive way: *She had not been prepared to face this barrage of questions.*

shower [C, usually sing.] (usually followed by *of*) (*written*) a large number or amount of sth that falls together: *A log in the fire broke and fell, sending out a shower of sparks.* See also **shower** → SCATTER *verb*

battery [C, usually sing.] (always followed by *of*) a large number of things of the same type: *A whole battery of measures was tried in an attempt to get them to give up cigarettes.* ❶ Collocates of **battery** in this meaning include *questions, tests* and *measures*.

torrent /ˈtɒrənt; *AmE* ˈtɔːr-; ˈtɑːr-/ [C] (usually followed by *of*) a large number or amount of words or emotion that comes suddenly and violently: *A torrent of words poured out as thoughts raced around in his head.* ◇ *She was subjected to a torrent of abuse.*

hail [sing.] (always followed by *of*) (*written*) a lot of bullets, stones or arrows that fall somewhere at the same time; a lot of criticism that is directed at sb/sth: *A passer-by was caught in the hail of bullets.* ◇ *The attempt to bring in new legislation was met by a hail of criticism.*

outpouring /ˈaʊtpɔːrɪŋ/ [C] (*written*) a strong and sudden expression of feeling; a large amount of sth produced in a short time: *Her death prompted huge outpourings of grief.* ◇ *His early career was characterized by a remarkable outpouring of new ideas.*

volley [C, usually sing.] a lot of bullets, stones or arrows that are fired or thrown at the same time; a lot of questions, comments or insults that are directed at sb quickly one after the other: *A volley of shots rang out.* ◇ *Police fired a volley over the heads of the crowd.* ◇ *She faced a volley of angry questions from her mother.*

> **NOTE** HAIL OR VOLLEY? A **hail** of *bullets, arrows, stones, shots* or *fire* is usually considered from the point of view of the person or people it falls on: sb might be *caught, killed* or *die in* a hail of bullets. A **volley** is usually considered from the point of view of the people who *fire* it.

flood *verb*

flood · overflow · spill over (sth) · burst its banks
These words all refer to rivers or containers which are so full that the contents go over the sides.

PATTERNS AND COLLOCATIONS
▸ a **river** floods / overflows / bursts its banks
▸ a river overflows / bursts **its banks**
▸ **tears** overflow / spill over

flood [I] to become filled or covered with water; (of a river) to become so full that it spreads out onto the land around it: *The cellar floods whenever it rains heavily.* ◇ *When the Ganges floods, it causes considerable damage.* See also **flood** → SOAK *verb*

overflow /ˌəʊvəˈfləʊ; *AmE* ˌoʊvərˈfloʊ/ [I, T] (of a container or river) to be so full that the contents go over the sides: *The bath is overflowing!* ◇ (*figurative*) *Her heart overflowed with love.* ◇ *If it keeps raining the river could overflow its banks.*

spill 'over, spill 'over sth *phrasal verb* to go over the sides, edge or surface of sth, especially a container: *The bag was so full of presents that it was spilling over.* ◇ *The tears spilled over and trickled down her cheeks.* ◇ *A few drops of wine spilled over the edge of her glass.* ◇ *She lay with her back spilling over the pillow.*

burst its 'banks *idiom* (of a river) to flood suddenly or dramatically: *Many sheep were swept to their deaths when the river burst its banks after rising eight feet overnight.*

floor *noun*

1 sit on the floor
2 the first floor of a building

1 floor · ground · land · earth · soil
These are all words for the surface that you walk on.

PATTERNS AND COLLOCATIONS
▸ **on** / **under** the floor / ground / earth
▸ **bare** floor / ground / earth
▸ to **drop** / **fall to** the floor / the ground / (the) earth
▸ to **hit** the floor / ground
▸ to **reach** the floor / the ground / land

floor [C, usually sing.] the surface of a room that you walk on: *She was sitting on the floor watching TV.* ◇ *to clean/wash/sweep the floor* ◇ *There's not really enough floor space in here.* ◇ *There were wooden panels from floor to ceiling.* OPP **ceiling** ❶ The **ceiling** is the top inside surface of a room: *It was a large room with a high ceiling.*

ground (often **the ground**) [U] the solid surface of the earth that you walk on: *I found her lying on the ground.* ◇ *The ground fell away to the left of the road.* ◇ *It was buried three metres below ground.* ◇ *The plant grows to about two feet above ground.* ◇ *Most of the animals' food is found at ground level.* ◇ *The rocket crashed a few seconds after it left the ground.* See also **ground** → SOIL

land [U] the surface of the earth that is not sea: *At last we sighted land (= saw land from the sea).* ◇ *It was good to be back on dry land again.* ◇ *They fought both at sea and on land.* ◇ *We travelled mainly by land.* ◇ *a land mass that covers over a quarter of the earth's surface* OPP **sea** → SEA, See also **land** → LAND *noun* 1, **land** → LAND *noun* 2, **land** → SOIL

earth (often **the earth**) [U, sing.] the solid surface of the world that is made of rock, soil, etc: *It was good to feel the earth beneath our feet again.* ◇ *The earth was dry and scorched.* ◇ *You could feel the earth shake as the truck came closer.* See also **earth** → SOIL

> **NOTE** GROUND, LAND OR EARTH? **Ground** is the normal word for the solid surface that you walk on when you are not in a building or vehicle. You can use **earth** if you want to draw attention to the rock, soil etc. that the ground is made of, but **ground** can also be used in any of the examples for **earth**. **Land** is only used when you want to contrast it with the sea: ~~the land beneath our feet~~ ◇ ~~feel the land shake~~ ◇ ~~sight ground/earth~~ ◇ ~~travel by ground/earth~~

soil [U] (*literary*) a country; an area of land: *It was the first time I had set foot on American soil.* ❶ This meaning of **soil** is almost always used in the phrase *on African/British, etc soil*, meaning 'in Africa/Britain, etc.' See also **soil** → SOIL

2 floor · storey · level · deck · tier

These are all words for the different levels or layers of a building, place, ship or bus.

▸ **on** the top, etc. floor / storey / level / deck / tier
▸ the **upper** / **lower** floors / storeys / levels / decks / tiers
▸ the **top** floor / storey / level / deck / tier
▸ the **main** floor / deck

floor /; *AmE* / [C] all the rooms that are on the same level of a building: *Her office is on the second floor.* ◇ *the Irish guy who lives two floors above* ◇ *Their house is on three floors* (= it has three floors). ❶ In British English the floor of a building at street level is the **ground floor**, the one above it is the **first floor** and the one below it is the **basement**, or **lower ground floor** if it is in a public building. In American English the floor at street level is usually called the **first floor**, the one above it is the **second floor** and the one below it is the **basement**. In public buildings the floor at street level can also be called the **ground floor**.

storey (*especially BrE*) (*AmE usually* **story**) [C] a floor of a building: *a single-storey/two-storey/three-storey building*

> **NOTE** **FLOOR** OR **STOREY?** **Floor** is used especially to talk about which particular level in a building sb lives on, goes to, etc.: *His office is on the fifth floor.* **Storey** is used especially to talk about the number of floors a building has: *a five-storey house* ◇ *The office building is five storeys high.*

level [C] a floor of a building; a layer of ground: *The library is all on one level.* ◇ *Archaeologists found pottery in the lowest level of the site.* ◇ *a multi-level parking lot* ❶ The **levels** of a building or site are not necessarily one above the other; **level** is often used when the different areas of a building or site are at different heights. You can talk about the *upper/lower levels* of a place; it is less usual for the levels in a building to be numbered, except in the case of large multi-storey car parks/parking garages: *His office is on the fifth level.* ◇ *Remember that we parked on level 5.*

deck [C] one of the floors of a ship or bus: *My cabin is on deck C.* ◇ *We sat on the top deck of the bus.*

tier /tɪə(r); *AmE* tɪr/ [C] a row or layer of sth that has several rows or layers placed one above the other: *a wedding cake with three tiers* ◇ *The seating is arranged in tiers.*

flow noun

flow · stream · tide · trickle

These are all words for the movement of people or things in one direction.

▸ a flow / stream (of sb / sth) **into** / **through** sth
▸ a **steady** / **constant** flow / stream / trickle
▸ a **continuous** / **endless** flow / stream
▸ to **halt** / **control** the flow / tide
▸ to **go** / **swim against** the flow / tide

flow [C, usually sing., U] a steady and continuous movement of people or things in one direction: *There was a continuous flow of refugees across the border.* ◇ *We need further measures to increase* **traffic flow** (= make it move faster).

stream [C] a long series or line of sth, especially people or vehicles, moving in a continuous flow: *I've had a steady stream of visitors.* ◇ *Cars filed past in an endless stream.* ❶ A **stream** can also be a large amount of sth or number of things that arrive or happen one after another. See also **stream** → FLOOD *noun* 2, **stream** → SURGE *verb*

> **NOTE** **FLOW** OR **STREAM?** The **flow** of people or vehicles is the fact of them moving; a **stream** of people or vehicles is a long series or line of them, coming one after another. In many cases you can use either word, but in some only **flow** can be used: *a continuous flow/stream of people* ◇ ~~to increase traffic stream~~

tide [C, usually sing.] a large amount or number of sth that is increasing or moving in one direction and may be difficult to control: *There is anxiety about the* **rising tide** *of crime.* ◇ *Measures have been taken to* **stem the tide** (= stop it from getting worse) *of pornography.* ◇ *The 1830s saw a tide of emigrants leave Europe for Australia.*

trickle [C, usually sing.] a small amount or number of sth coming or going slowly: *As a result of the civil war, the steady trickle of immigration became a flood of refugees.*

flow verb See also the entry for TRICKLE

flow · run · pour · stream · circulate · spew · pump · cascade · spurt · gush

These words can all be used when a liquid or gas moves from one place to another, especially in large quantities.

▸ to flow / pour / stream / spew / pump / cascade / spurt / gush **out**
▸ to flow / run / pour / stream / spew / pump / spurt / gush **out of** sth
▸ to flow / run / pour / stream / spew / pump / cascade / spurt / gush **from** sth
▸ to flow / run / pour / stream / cascade / spurt / gush **into** sth
▸ to flow / run / pour / stream / circulate / pump / cascade / spurt / gush **through** sth
▸ to flow / run / pour / stream / cascade / gush **down** (sth)
▸ to flow / circulate / pump (sth) **around** / **round** sth
▸ to be flowing / running / streaming / gushing **with** sth
▸ **water** flows / runs / pours / streams / circulates / cascades / spurts / gushes
▸ **blood** flows / runs / pours / streams / circulates / pumps / cascades / spurts / gushes
▸ **tears** flow / run / pour / stream / gush
▸ **adrenalin** flows / pours / pumps
▸ a **waterfall** pours / cascades / gushes
▸ **light** flows / pours / streams / cascades
▸ **smoke** pours / streams / spews
▸ to flow / run / circulate **freely** / **slowly**

flow [I] (usually used with an adverb or preposition) (of liquid, gas or electricity) to move steadily and continuously in one direction: *It's here that the river flows down into the ocean.* ◇ *This can prevent air from flowing freely to the lungs.* ◇ *The current flowing in a circuit is measured by connecting an ammeter.* See also **flow** → CURRENT *noun*

run [I] (of a liquid) to flow; to send out a liquid: *The tears ran down her cheeks.* ◇ *Who left the tap running?* ◇ *Your nose is running.* ◇ *The smoke makes my eyes run.* ❶ If sth *is running with sth*, it is covered with liquid: *His face was running with sweat.*

pour [I] (always used with an adverb or preposition) (of liquid, smoke or light) to flow quickly in large amounts: *Blood was pouring from the wound.* ◇ *Thick black smoke was pouring out of the roof.* ◇ *The kitchen door opened and light poured into the hallway.*

stream [I, T] (when there is no object an adverb or preposition is used) (of liquid, gas, smoke or light) to flow quickly and continuously; to make a liquid or gas do this: *Sunlight streamed through the windows.* ◇ *Her head was streaming with blood.* ◇ *The exhaust streamed black smoke.*

circulate /ˈsɜːkjəleɪt; *AmE* ˈsɜːrk-/ [I, T] (of a liquid or gas) to move continuously around a place or system; to make a liquid or gas do this: *The condition prevents blood from circulating freely.* ◇ *Cooled air is circulated throughout the building.* See also **circulation** → CURRENT *noun*

spew /spjuː/ [I, T] (always used with an adverb or preposition) (especially of smoke or flames) to flow out quickly in large amounts; to make smoke or flames do this: *Flames spewed from the aircraft's engine.* ◇ *Massive chimneys were spewing out smoke and flames.*

pump [I] (always used with an adverb or preposition) (of a liquid) to flow in a particular direction as if it is being forced by a pump: *Blood was pumping out of the wound on his shoulder.*

cascade /kæˈskeɪd/ [I] (*written*) (of liquid) to flow downwards in large amounts: *Water cascaded down the mountainside.*

spurt [I, T] (when there is no object an adverb or preposition is used) (of liquid, gas or flames) to burst or pour out suddenly in a fast stream; to produce a sudden fast stream of liquid, gas or flames: *Blood was spurting from her nose.* ◇ *The volcano spurted clouds of steam and ash high into the air.*
▶ **spurt** noun [C]: *a spurt of blood*

gush /ɡʌʃ/ [I, T] (when there is no object an adverb or preposition is used) (of a liquid) to flow out suddenly and quickly in large amounts; (of a container or vehicle) to suddenly let out large amounts of a liquid: *Water gushed out of the pipe.* ◇ *The tanker was gushing oil.*

flush *verb*

flush · blush · glow · colour · burn
These words all mean to become red in the face, especially because of embarrassment or another emotion.

colour	flush	burn
	blush	
	glow	

PATTERNS AND COLLOCATIONS
▶ to flush / blush / glow / colour / burn **with** sth
▶ sb's **cheeks** flush / glow / colour / burn
▶ sb's **face** flushes / glows / colours / burns
▶ to flush / blush **scarlet**

flush [I] (of a person or their face) to become red, especially because you are embarrassed, excited, angry or hot: *He flushed with anger at her reply.* ◇ *She felt her cheeks flush red and she looked away in embarrassment.* ◇ *A patient with a fever may be very hot and flushed.*
▶ **flush** noun [C, usually sing.]: *There was an unhealthy flush across his thin face.*

blush [I] to become red in the face because you are embarrassed or ashamed: *She felt herself blushing scarlet at the thought.* ◇ *I blush to think* (= feel embarrassed or ashamed to think) *of how I behaved the last time we met.*
▶ **blush** noun [C]: *She felt a warm blush rise to her cheeks.*

> **NOTE** BLUSH OR FLUSH? **Blush** is only used when sb feels embarrassment or shame; **flush** can be used in other situations. The subject of **blush** must be a person: *Her cheeks/face blushed.*

glow [I] to look or feel warm or pink, especially after exercise or because of excitement or embarrassment: *Her cheeks were glowing.* ❶ **Glow** is often used to describe a positive reaction to sth: *She glowed with pleasure at the compliment.*
▶ **glow** noun [sing.]: *The fresh air had brought a healthy glow to her cheeks.*

colour (*BrE*) (*AmE* **color**) [I] (not usually used in the progressive tenses) to become red in the face because of embarrassment, shame or anger: *Everyone in the room stared at Gerry, and he coloured slightly.* ◇ *He grinned at Mary, who coloured up instantly.*
▶ **colour** (*BrE*) (*AmE* **color**) noun [U]: *Colour flooded her face when she thought of what had happened.* ◇ *His face was drained of colour* (= he looked pale and ill).

burn [I] to be very red and feel very hot because of embarrassment or shame: *Her cheeks burned with embarrassment.*

fly *verb*

1 a bird/plane flies
2 A stone came flying through the window.

1 fly · flutter · glide · soar
These words all mean to move through the air, for example in a plane or using wings.

PATTERNS AND COLLOCATIONS
▶ to fly / flutter / glide / soar **away**
▶ to fly / glide / soar **off / above / over / overhead / up**
▶ to fly / glide **through the air**
▶ to fly / soar **into the air / sky / clouds**
▶ to fly / soar **high / higher**

fly [I] to move through the air or through space: *A wasp had flown in through the window.* ◇ *It was autumn, and the birds were flying south.* ◇ *Helicopters flew to and fro overhead.* See also **fly** → GO 2
▶ **flight** noun [U]: *the age of supersonic flight* ◇ *The bird is easily recognized in flight* (= when it is flying). See also **flight** → FLIGHT

flutter [I] (always used with an adverb or preposition) (of a bird or insect) to fly somewhere, moving the wings quickly and lightly: *A butterfly fluttered from flower to flower.* ◇ *The birds fluttered nervously in their cage.*

glide [I] (usually used with an adverb or preposition) (of birds and aircraft) to fly using air currents, not moving the wings or using engine power: *The swan spread its wings and glided gently downward.* ◇ *He cut the engines and glided silently into the clearing.*

soar /sɔː(r)/ [I] (*written*) to fly very high in the air; to fly very quickly up into the air: *An eagle was soaring high above the cliffs.* ◇ *The plane was soon soaring up into the sky.*

2 See also the entry for RUN 1
fly · shoot · speed · hurtle · whizz · zoom · career · flash · streak
These words all mean to go or move very fast.

PATTERNS AND COLLOCATIONS
▶ to fly / shoot / speed / hurtle / whizz / zoom / career / flash / streak **down / across** (sth)
▶ to fly / shoot / speed / hurtle / whizz / zoom / flash / streak **past** (sb / sth)
▶ to fly / shoot / speed / hurtle / whizz / career / streak **through** sth
▶ to fly / shoot / speed / hurtle / whizz / zoom **along** (sth)
▶ to fly / shoot / speed / hurtle / career **into** sth
▶ to fly / speed / hurtle / whizz / zoom / flash / streak **by**
▶ to fly / shoot / speed / hurtle / zoom / career **off**

fly [I] (usually used with an adverb or preposition) to move suddenly and with force in a particular direction: *A large stone came flying in through the window.* ◇ *David gave the door a kick and it flew open.* ◇ *The other player was sent flying by the tackle.* ◇ *She flew at him with clenched fists.* ◇ *He flew into her arms.*

shoot [I, T] (always used with an adverb or preposition) to move suddenly and quickly in a particular direction; to make sb/sth do this: *Flames were shooting up through the roof.* ◇ *A cat shot out into the road in front of him.* ◇ *He shot an arm out to stop her.*

speed (*especially written*) to move along very fast, especially in a vehicle: *The car sped along the road towards the village.* ◇ *Jock sped away on his bike.* See also **speed** → ACCELERATE

hurtle /ˈhɜːtl; *AmE* ˈhɜːrtl/ [I] (always used with an adverb or preposition) to move forward very fast, especially in an uncontrolled way: *A train came hurtling through the station.*

whizz (*especially BrE*) (also **whiz**, especially in *AmE*) /wɪz/ [I] (always used with an adverb or preposition) (*rather informal*) to move or go somewhere very fast, making a high continuous sound: *A bullet whizzed past my ear.* ◇ *He whizzed down the road on his motorbike.*

zoom [I] (always used with an adverb or preposition) (*rather informal*) to move or go somewhere very fast, often with a loud noise: *Traffic zoomed past us.* ◇ *He jumped into his car and zoomed off.*

career /kəˈrɪə(r); AmE kəˈrɪr/ [I] (*especially BrE*) (always used with an adverb or preposition) (*rather formal*) to move very fast in a particular direction, especially in an uncontrolled way: *The vehicle careered off the road and hit a pedestrian.*

flash [I] (always used with an adverb or preposition) to move past or across sb/sth very quickly, so that you only see it for a moment: *The countryside flashed past as we sped along.* ◇ *A look of terror flashed across his face.*

streak /striːk/ [I] (always used with an adverb or preposition) to move so fast that it is difficult for you to see it clearly: *Some kind of animal leaped out of the grass and streaked across the meadow.*

foam *noun*

foam · surf · lather · froth · suds
These are all words for the mass of little bubbles that forms on the surface of a liquid.

PATTERNS AND COLLOCATIONS
▸ a **head** of foam / froth

foam [U] a mass of very small air bubbles on the surface of a liquid; a chemical substance that forms or produces a soft mass of very small bubbles, used for washing, shaving or putting out fires, for example: *She poured each of us a glass of beer with a good head of foam.* ◇ *The breaking waves left the beach covered with foam.* ◇ *The fire extinguisher directs foam onto the fire.*
　▸ **foam** *verb* [I]: *He brought out a tray of foaming ice-cold beer.* ◇ *The dog started foaming at the mouth* (= producing a lot of liquid in its mouth, especially because it is ill or angry).

surf /sɜːf; AmE sɜːrf/ [U] large waves in the sea or ocean, and the white foam that they produce as they fall on the shore or on rocks: *They listened to the **surf** as it **broke** on the beach.*

lather /ˈlɑːðə(r); AmE ˈlæð-/ [U, sing.] a white mass of small bubbles that is produced by mixing soap with water: *She tipped in a little shampoo and began to work up a lather.*

froth [U] a mass of small bubbles, especially on the surface of a liquid: *He wiped the froth from his lips with a handkerchief.*
　▸ **froth** *verb* [I]: *The waiter brought us two cups of frothing coffee.*

suds [pl.] a mass of small bubbles that forms on top of water that has soap in it: *She was up to her elbows in suds.*

focus *noun* See the Topic Map for FACT AND OPINION on p.898

focus · centre · heart · hub · focal point
These are all words for the central and most important part of a particular place or activity.

PATTERNS AND COLLOCATIONS
▸ an **important** focus / hub / focal point
▸ the **central** focus / hub
▸ the **commercial** centre / heart / hub of sth
▸ to **act** / **serve as** a focus / centre / focal point
▸ to **give sth** / **provide** a focus / focal point
▸ the focus / centre **of attention**

focus /ˈfəʊkəs; AmE ˈfoʊ-/ [U, C, usually sing.] the thing or person that people are most interested in; the act of paying special attention to sth and making people interested in it: *His comments provided a **focus** for debate.* ◇ *We shall maintain our **focus on** the needs of the customer.* ◇ *The incident brought the problem of violence in schools **into** sharp **focus**.* ◇ *What we need now is a **change of focus*** (= to look at things in a different way).

centre (*BrE*) (*AmE* **center**) [C, usually sing.] the point towards which people direct their attention: *Children like to be the centre of attention.* ◇ *He could never doubt that he*

was the centre of her world. ◇ *The prime minister is **at the centre of** a political row over leaked Cabinet documents.* ❶ Notice that you can say that sb/sth *is the centre of attention* or *the centre of sb's world/universe*, but you say that sb is *at the centre of things/the action/a discussion*. You can also say that sb is *at the centre of sb's world/ universe*.

heart [C, usually sing.] the central part of a place: *'Hillsdown' is a quiet hotel in the very heart of the city.* ❶ In this meaning **heart** is mainly used to talk about the central part of a city, country or region. It is often used in advertising trying to attract people to a place. See also **heart** → POINT *noun*

hub [C, usually sing.] the central and most important part of a particular place or activity: *The bank is situated in the commercial hub of the city.* ◇ *The kitchen was the hub of family life.* ◇ *a hub airport* (= a large important one where people often change from one plane to another)

> **NOTE** **HEART** OR **HUB?** In some cases you can use either word: *the commercial heart/hub of the city.* However, *the heart of the village/the town/the city/England* usually suggests an attractive, historic place; *the hub of the city/ operations/business activity* suggests a busy place where a lot of business is done.

'focal point /ˈfəʊkl; AmE ˈfoʊkl/ [C, usually sing.] a thing or person that is the centre of interest or activity: *In rural areas, the school is often the focal point for the local community.* ◇ *The focal point of the policy developed by the government was the construction of a rail network.* ❶ **Focal point** is often used to talk about a place in a community which brings people together, for example a school, shop, church or play area. It can also be used to describe the central point of a discussion, lecture, or of sb's political activities; or the main part of a design or arrangement; or the main event in a series of planned events.

focus *verb*

focus · target · direct · be aimed at sb · turn · address · orient · pitch
These words all mean to give attention or a message to one particular person or group of people rather than another.

PATTERNS AND COLLOCATIONS
▸ to focus / target / turn sth **on** sb / sth
▸ to target sth / direct sth / be aimed / pitch sth **at** sb / sth
▸ to target / direct / orient sth **towards** sb / sth
▸ to turn / address / orient sth **to** sb / sth
▸ **efforts** / **resources** / **campaigns** are focused on / targeted at / directed at sb / sth
▸ **attention** is focused on / directed at / turned to sb / sth
▸ **research** is focused on / directed at / oriented towards sth
▸ sth is focused on / targeted at a / directed at / an **group** / **area**
▸ **primarily** focused on / targeted at / directed at / aimed at / addressed to / oriented towards / pitched at sb / sth
▸ **particularly** focused on / targeted at / directed at / aimed at / oriented towards / pitched at sb / sth
▸ **specifically** focused on / targeted at / directed at / aimed at / addressed to / oriented towards sb / sth
▸ **principally** targeted at / directed at / aimed at / addressed to / oriented towards sb / sth
▸ **directly** focused on / targeted at / aimed at / addressed to / pitched at sb / sth
▸ **mainly** / **clearly** focused on / targeted at / directed at / aimed at sb / sth

focus [I, T] to give attention, effort, time etc. to one particular person, thing or situation rather than another: *The discussion focused on three main issues.* ◇ *Schools should not focus exclusively on exam results.* ◇ *I was finding it hard to focus my mind properly.* ◇ *The visit helped to **focus** world attention **on** the plight of the refugees.* ◇ *Much recent concern has been **focused upon** sea level rises.* ◇ *Where do you really wish to focus your time and energy?*

target [T, often passive] to try to help or influence a particular group of people, especially by offering a product or service designed for them: *The booklet is targeted at people approaching retirement.* ◇ *We target our services towards specific groups of people.* ◇ *This hospital is targeted for additional funding.*

direct [T] (always used with a preposition) to say or do sth that is intended to influence, affect or deal with a particular person, group, situation or issue: *Was that remark directed at me?* ◇ *Most of his anger was directed against himself.* ◇ *There are three main issues we need to direct our attention to.*

be aimed at sb *phrase* (of a product, service or remark) to be directed at a particular person or group of people: *The book is aimed at very young children.* ◇ *My criticism wasn't aimed at you.*

turn [T, I] to give attention to a particular person, subject or situation, especially after attention has been on sb/sth else: *She looked at him, then turned her attention back to me.* ◇ *Don't turn your anger on the children.* ◇ *His thoughts turned to his dead wife.*

address [T] (*formal*) to say or write sth directly to a particular person: *I was surprised when he addressed me in English.* ◇ *Any questions should be addressed to your teacher.* ◇ *The book is addressed to the general reader.*

orient /ˈɔːrient/ (*BrE* also **orientate** /ˈɔːriənteɪt/) [T, usually passive] to make sb/sth give more interest, attention or effort towards a particular subject, person or situation; to make or adapt sb/sth for a particular purpose: *Our students are oriented towards science subjects.* ◇ *We run a commercially oriented operation.*

pitch [T, often passive] (*rather informal, especially business*) to aim a product or a service at a particular group of people: *The new software is being pitched at banks.* ◇ *Orange juice is being pitched as an athlete's drink.*

fold *noun*

fold · wrinkle · line · crease
These are all words for a line on fabric or on sb's skin.

fold [C] a part of sth, especially fabric, that is folded or hangs as if it had been folded; a mark or line made by folding sth, or showing where sth should be folded: *The child hid his face in the folds of his mother's skirt.* ◇ *the loose folds of flesh under her chin* ◇ *Why is the place I want to find always on the fold of the map?*

wrinkle /ˈrɪŋkl/ [C, usually pl.] a line or small fold in your skin, especially on your face, that forms as you get older; a small fold that you do not want in a piece of fabric or paper: *There were fine wrinkles around her eyes.* ◇ *Is there anything you can do to prevent wrinkles?*
▸ **wrinkled** *adj.*: *She kissed his wrinkled face.*

NOTE FOLD OR WRINKLE? Fold is more frequently used about fabric; **wrinkle** is more frequently used about skin. **Folds** in fabric are tidy or are made deliberately; **wrinkles** are usually unwanted, and appear because you have not ironed, folded or hung fabric properly or tidily: *I arranged the cloth so that it hung in neat folds.* ◇ *While she was waiting, she anxiously smoothed out the wrinkles in her skirt.* **Wrinkles** in the skin are thin lines; **folds** in sb's skin or flesh are fatter and occur because the person has loose skin, or because they are overweight.

line [C, usually pl.] a mark like a line on sb's skin that people usually get as they grow older: *He has fine lines around his eyes.* ◇ *laughter / frown / worry lines* ❶ A **line** in sb's skin may be thinner or less deep than a **wrinkle**, but in many cases you can use either word.
▸ **lined** *adj.*: *a deeply lined face*

crease /kriːs/ [C] a line that is made in fabric or paper when you press, crush or fold it; a line in the skin, especially on the face: *She smoothed the creases out of her skirt.* ◇ *trousers with a sharp crease in the legs* ◇ *She had lots of deep creases at the corners of her eyes.* ❶ **Crease** is more often used about fabric or paper than about skin. It can be an untidy line, that appears when you press or crush fabric or paper, or it can be a neat line that you make in sth, for example when you fold it: *He ironed out the creases in his shirt.* ◇ *My mother always irons creases into my trousers.* See also **crease** → CRUMPLE *verb*
▸ **crease** *verb* [T, I]: *A frown creased her forehead.* ◇ *Her face creased into a smile.*
▸ **creased** *adj.*: *I can't wear this blouse. It's creased.*

fold

fold   wrinkles/lines   creases

fold *verb*

fold · tuck · roll · gather
These words all mean to arrange sth such as clothing, fabric or paper or by bending or pulling it.

fold [T, I] to bend sth, especially paper or fabric, so that one part lies on top of another part; to bend sth so that it becomes smaller or flatter and can be stored or carried more easily; to bend or be able to bend in this way: *He folded the map up and put it in his pocket.* ◇ *First, fold the paper in half.* ◇ *The blankets had been folded down.* ◇ *The bird folded its wings.* ◇ *The bed can be folded away during the day.* ◇ *The table folds up when not in use.* **OPP** **unfold** → SPREAD

tuck [T] (always used with an adverb or preposition) to push, fold or turn the ends or edges of fabric, clothes or paper so that they are held in place or look neat: *She tucked up her skirt and waded into the river.* ◇ *Tuck your shirt in* (= into your trousers). ◇ *Tuck the flap of the envelope in.*

roll [T] (always used with an adverb or preposition) to fold the edge of a piece of clothing or fabric over and over on itself to make it shorter: *Roll up your sleeves.* ◇ *She rolled her jeans to her knees.*

gather [T] (always used with an adverb or preposition) to pull a piece of clothing tighter to your body: *She gathered up her skirts and ran.*

follow *verb*

1 You lead, I'll follow.
2 A news report will follow shortly.
3 follow instructions / sb's advice / the rules
4 follow the fashions / sb's example

1 follow · chase · hunt · pursue · stalk · tail · trail · track
These words all mean to go after a person or animal because you have a particular reason to do so.

PATTERNS AND COLLOCATIONS
▶ to follow / chase / pursue sb / sth **into** sth
▶ to follow / chase / pursue / stalk / tail / trail / track a **person**
▶ to follow / chase / hunt / pursue / stalk / trail / track an **animal**
▶ to chase / hunt / pursue / stalk (its) **prey**
▶ to chase / hunt / pursue a **criminal**
▶ the **police** follow / chase / hunt / pursue / tail sb
▶ to follow / pursue sb / sth **closely**

follow [T, I] to come or go after or behind sb/sth: *Follow me, please. I'll show you the way.* ◇ *I think we're being followed.* ◇ *She walked in and we all followed.* **OPP** lead → TAKE 2

chase [T, I] to run, drive, etc. fast after sb/sth in order to catch them: *My dog likes chasing rabbits.* ◇ *The boys were chasing each other around the yard.* ◇ *They chased after the burglar but didn't catch him.*
▶ **chase** [C]: *a high-speed car chase* ◇ *We lost him in the narrow streets and had to give up the chase.*

hunt [I, T] to chase wild animals or birds in order to catch or kill them for food, sport or to make money: *Lions sometimes hunt alone.* ◇ *The animals are hunted for their fur.* ◇ (*BrE*) *They hunt* (= chase and kill foxes as a sport, riding horses and using dogs) *when they stay with friends in Ireland.*
▶ **hunt** [C] (often in compounds): *a tiger/seal hunt*
▶ **hunting** noun [U]: *traditional country pursuits like hunting, shooting and fishing*

pursue (*formal or written*) to follow sb/sth, because you want to catch them: *She drove away, hotly pursued by the photographers.* ◇ *Police pursued the car at high speed.*
▶ **pursuit** /pə'sju:t; *AmE* pər'su:t/ noun [U]: *We drove away with two police cars in pursuit* (= following).

stalk /stɔ:k/ [T, I] to move slowly and quietly towards an animal or person in order to kill, catch or harm it/them; to illegally follow and watch sb over a long period of time, in a way that is annoying or frightening: *The lion was stalking a zebra.* ◇ *He stalked his victim as she walked home, and then attacked her.* ◇ *He was arrested and accused of stalking the actor over a period of three years.*
▶ **stalking** noun [U]: *the deer stalking season* ◇ *An undercover detective said 'Stalking has become a problem that we must take seriously.'*

tail [T] to follow sb closely and secretly, especially in order to see where they go and what they do: *A private detective had been tailing them for several weeks.*

trail [T] to follow sb/sth by looking for signs that show you where they have been: *The police trailed Dale for years.* ◇ *Sharks were trailing the ship.* See also **trail** → TRAIL noun

track [T, I] to find sb/sth by following the marks, signs or information that they have left behind them: *The men earned their living tracking and shooting bears.* See also **track** → TRAIL noun

---

2 follow · result · arise · stem from sth · ensue
These words all mean to come after sb/sth else in time or order.

PATTERNS AND COLLOCATIONS
▶ to follow / result / arise / stem / ensue **from** sth
▶ to follow / result / arise **out of** sth
▶ sth follows / results / arises / stems **from the fact that…**

follow [T, I] (not used in the progressive tenses) to come after sb/sth else in time or order; to happen as a result of sth else: *The first two classes are followed by a break of ten minutes.* ◇ *A period of unrest followed the president's resignation.* ◇ *A detailed news report will follow shortly.* ◇ *There followed a short silence.* ◇ *Our opening hours are as follows…* ◇ *A new proposal followed on from the discussions.*

result [I] (not used in the progressive tenses) to happen because of sth else that happened first: *job losses resulting from changes in production* ◇ *When water levels rise, flooding results.* See also **resulting, resultant** → RELATED

arise /ə'raɪz/ [I] (not used in the progressive tenses) (*rather formal*) (especially of a problem, question or difficulty) to happen as a result of a particular situation: *The current debate arose out of the concerns of parents.* ◇ *Are there any matters arising from the minutes of the last meeting?*

'stem from sth phrasal verb (-**mm**-) (not used in the progressive tenses) (especially of a problem or difficulty) to be the result of sth: *Most people's insecurities stem from something that happened in their childhood.*

ensue /ɪn'sju:; *AmE* -'su:/ [I] (not used in the progressive tenses) (*rather formal, written*) (especially of a fight, struggle or confused situation) to happen after or as a result of another event: *The riot police swooped in and chaos ensued.* See also **ensuing** → RELATED

---

3 follow · comply · obey · act on/upon sth · adhere to sth · abide by sth · observe · carry sth out · respect
These words all mean to accept advice, instructions or rules and do what you have been told or shown to do.

PATTERNS AND COLLOCATIONS
▶ to follow / comply with / obey / adhere to / abide by / observe / respect the **conventions / rules / regulations / law**
▶ to follow / comply with / obey / abide by / respect sb's **will / wishes**
▶ to follow / comply with / adhere to / abide by / carry out a **policy**
▶ to follow / obey / act on / carry out **instructions / orders**
▶ to follow / act on / carry out a **recommendation**
▶ to comply with / carry out / respect an **obligation**
▶ to follow / obey / adhere to / observe / carry out sth **faithfully**
▶ to comply with / adhere to / observe / carry out / respect sth **fully**
▶ to follow / comply with / adhere to / abide by / observe sth **strictly**

follow [T] to accept advice or instructions and do what you have been told or shown to do: *I didn't really follow the recipe.* ◇ *He has trouble following simple instructions.*
❶ Follow is often used to talk about acting according to written instructions such as a *recipe, timetable* or *syllabus,* as well as *orders* or *commands.*

comply /kəm'plaɪ/ [I] (*rather formal*) to act according to a rule or the law: *They refused to comply with the UN resolution.* ◇ *What sanctions can they take against us if we fail to comply?* **❶ Comply** is usually used in contexts relating to law and diplomatic situations. **OPP** breach → BREAK 3, See also **compliant** → PASSIVE
▶ **compliance** /kəm'plaɪəns/ noun [U]: *to ensure full compliance with the law*

obey [T, I] to do what you are told or expected to do: *He consistently refuses to obey rules.* ◇ *He had always obeyed his parents without question.* ◇ *'Sit down!' Meekly, she obeyed.* **❶** The object of **obey** can be a person (for example a *parent*) or a thing (for example *rules*). Using **obey** often emphasizes the relationship of power between people. **OPP** disobey → OPPOSE, break → BREAK 3, See also **obedient** → GOOD 7

'act on/upon sth phrasal verb to take action as a result of advice, information or a feeling: *Acting on information from a member of the public, the police raided the club.* ◇ *Why didn't you act on her suggestion?* ◇ *Acting on impulse, he picked up the phone and dialled her number.*

ad'here to sth phrasal verb (*formal*) to act according to a law, rule or set of instructions; to follow a particular set of beliefs or a fixed way of doing sth: *For ten months he adhered to a strict no-fat low-salt diet.* ◇ *She adheres to teaching methods she learned over 30 years ago.*
▶ **adherence** noun [U]: *strict adherence to the rules*

a'bide by sth phrasal verb (*formal*) to accept and act according to a law, agreement or decision: *You'll have to abide by the rules of the club.* ◇ *We will abide by their decision.*

observe /əb'zɜ:v; *AmE* əb'zɜ:rv/ [T] (*formal*) to act according to a law, agreement or custom: *Will the rebels observe the ceasefire?* ◇ *We observed a two-minute silence for the victims of the bombing.*

,**carry sth 'out** *phrasal verb* to do sth that you have been asked to do: *He made it clear that they must carry out orders immediately.* See also **carry sth out** → KEEP 5

respect [T] to not break a law or principle: *The new leader has promised to respect the constitution.* ❶ **Respect** is often used to talk about people who have the power to break the rules without being punished, but choose or are encouraged not to do so as a matter of principle. **OPP** **violate** → BREAK 3, See also **respect** → RESPECT *noun*

4 follow · imitate · emulate · follow suit · mimic · copy · follow in sb's footsteps · model yourself/sth on sb/sth
These words all mean to behave or do sth in the same way as sb else.

PATTERNS AND COLLOCATIONS
▶ to follow / imitate / emulate / copy a **style**
▶ to imitate / mimic / copy sb / sth's **movements**
▶ to imitate / mimic sb / sth's **appearance**
▶ to follow / mimic / copy sb / sth **exactly**
▶ to follow / copy sb / sth **faithfully / slavishly**
▶ to imitate / mimic sb / sth **accurately**
▶ to mimic / model sth / yourself on sb / sth **closely**

follow [T, I] to accept sb/sth as a guide, leader or example; to behave or do sth in the same way as sb else: *They followed the teachings of Buddha.* ◇ *He always followed the latest fashions* (= dressed in fashionable clothes). ◇ *I don't want you to* **follow my example** *and rush into marriage.* ◇ *The movie follows the book faithfully.* ◇ *It wasn't in his nature to follow blindly.* See also **follower** → FAN, **follower** → SUPPORTER

imitate /ˈɪmɪteɪt/ [T] (*rather formal*) to behave or do sth in the same way as sb else: *Her style of painting has been imitated by other artists.* ◇ *Teachers provide a model for children to imitate.* ◇ *No computer can imitate the complex functions of the human brain.* ❶ Typical collocates of **imitate** are *crime, movements, sound, model, style* and *behaviour.*
▶ **imitation** *noun* [U]: *A child learns to talk by imitation.* ◇ *Many corporate methods have been adopted by American managers* **in imitation of** *Japanese practice.*

emulate /ˈemjuleɪt/ [T] (*formal*) to try to do sth as well as sb else because you admire them: *She hopes to emulate her sister's sporting achievements.*

follow 'suit *idiom* (*especially business or journalism*) to behave or do sth in the way that sb else has just done: *The Bank of England has announced a 0.5% rise in interest rates, and other banks are expected to follow suit.*

mimic /ˈmɪmɪk/ (-**ck**-) [T] (*rather formal or technical*) to look or behave like sth else: *The robot was programmed to mimic a series of human movements.* ◇ *Scientists have created a vaccine that mimics the virus.*
▶ **mimicry** /ˈmɪmɪkri/ *noun* [U]: *Parrots specialize in vocal mimicry.*

copy [T] to behave or do sth in the same way as sb else: *She copies everything her sister does.* ◇ *Their tactics have been copied by other terrorist organizations.* ❶ Typical collocates of **copy** are *work, style, behaviour, ideas, actions* and *movements.*

follow in sb's 'footsteps *idiom* to do the same job or have the same style of life as sb else, especially sb in your family: *She works in television, following in her father's footsteps.*

'model yourself/sth on sb/sth *phrasal verb* (-**ll**-, *AmE* -**l**-) (*written*) to copy the behaviour or style of sb you like and respect in order to be like them; to make sth so that it looks or works like sth else: *As a politician, he modelled himself on Churchill.* ◇ *The country's parliament is modelled on the British system.* See also **model** → MODEL *noun*

food *noun*

food · meal · diet · foodstuff · refreshment · fare · nourishment
These are all words for things that people eat.

PATTERNS AND COLLOCATIONS
▶ (a) **delicious** food / meal / fare
▶ (a) **staple** food / diet / foodstuff / fare
▶ (a) **simple / traditional / vegetarian** food / meal / diet / fare
▶ (a / an) **English / Chinese, etc.** food / meal / diet / fare
▶ (an) **adequate** food / meal / diet / nourishment
▶ (a) **healthy / nourishing** food / meal / diet
▶ to **provide** food / a meal / a … diet / refreshment / nourishment
▶ to **serve** food / a meal / … fare
▶ to **eat** food / a meal / a… diet / …fare
▶ to **obtain** food / a meal / nourishment

food [U, C] things that people or animals eat; a particular type of food: *He obviously enjoys good food.* ◇ *Gina had prepared* **food and drink** *for the work party.* ◇ *Do you like Italian food?* ◇ *Could you buy a can of* **dog food***?* ◇ *This street is full of* **fast food** *restaurants.* ◇ *You shouldn't eat so much* **junk food***.* ◇ *The store specializes in* **frozen foods***.*

meal [C] the food that is eaten when people sit down to eat: *Enjoy your meal.* ◇ *They gave us a three-course meal.* See also **meal** → MEAL

diet [C, U] the food that you eat regularly: *It is important to have a healthy, balanced diet.* ◇ *I loved the Japanese diet of rice, vegetables and fish.* ◇ *For general advice on diet, see pages 26–27.* See also **diet** → DIET *noun*

foodstuff [C, usually pl.] (*formal or technical*) any substance that is used as food: *Rationing of basic foodstuffs was introduced.*

refreshment [U] (*formal*) food and drink: *In York we had a short stop for refreshment.*

fare [U] (*written, especially journalism*) food that is offered as a meal, especially in a restaurant, hotel or bar: *The restaurant serves good traditional fare.* ❶ **Fare** sounds old-fashioned if used in everyday speech; however, it is still frequently used in journalism or advertising to talk about the food offered in a restaurant, especially when this is *simple, plain, traditional, staple, English, Scottish* or *local.*

nourishment /ˈnʌrɪʃmənt; *AmE* ˈnɜːr-/ [U] (*formal or technical*) the goodness in food that is needed to stay alive, grow and stay healthy: *Can plants obtain adequate nourishment from such poor soil?* ◇ *You need natural, fresh food with lots of nourishment.* See also **nourish** → SERVE 1

fool *noun*

fool · idiot · jerk · moron · bimbo · prat · dork
These are all words for a person who you think is stupid.

NOTE All these words can be offensive, especially if you tell sb directly that they are a **fool**, an **idiot**, a **jerk**, etc. **Jerk**, **moron** and **bimbo** are the most offensive; the other words can sometimes be used in an affectionate way between friends.

PATTERNS AND COLLOCATIONS
▶ like a / an fool / idiot / jerk / bimbo / prat
▶ **What a / an** fool / idiot / jerk / moron / prat / dork!
▶ **You** fool / idiot / jerk / moron / prat / dork!
▶ a **complete** fool / idiot / jerk / moron / prat / dork
▶ an **absolute** fool / idiot / moron / prat / dork
▶ a / an **stupid / utter** fool / idiot / jerk / prat
▶ to **feel/look like** a fool / an idiot / a jerk / a moron / a prat / a dork
▶ to **act like** a fool / an idiot / a jerk / a moron / a prat
▶ to **call sb** sb a fool / an idiot / a jerk
▶ to **make** a fool / an idiot / a prat / a dork **of yourself**

fool [C] (*disapproving, sometimes offensive*) a person who behaves or speaks in a way that shows a lack of intelligence or good judgement: *Don't be such a fool!* ◇ *I felt like such a fool when I realized my mistake.* ◇ *He told me he was an actor and I* **was fool enough to** *believe him.* See also **foolish** → CRAZY, **foolish** → RIDICULOUS

idiot /ˈɪdiət/ [C] (*rather informal, disapproving, sometimes offensive*) a person who behaves or speaks in a very stupid or annoying way: *I just stood there like an idiot with my mouth open.* ◇ *Not that switch, you idiot!* ◇ *What stupid idiot left their shoes on the stairs?* See also **idiotic** → CRAZY

jerk (*especially AmE, informal, disapproving, offensive*) a person, especially a man or boy, who is stupid, rude or annoying: *He was acting like a complete jerk.* ◇ *He silently swore at himself for being such a jerk.*

moron /ˈmɔːrɒn; AmE -rɑːn/ [C] (*rather informal, disapproving, offensive*) a stupid person who deserves no respect: *Shut up, you moron!* ◇ *The people responsible for this are mindless morons.*

bimbo (pl. **-os**) [C] (*informal, disapproving, offensive*) a young person, usually a woman, who is sexually attractive but not very intelligent: *He's going out with an empty-headed bimbo half his age.*

prat [C] (*BrE, informal, disapproving, sometimes offensive*) a person who behaves or speaks in a very stupid or embarrassing way: *You look a right prat in that outfit.* ◇ *He got drunk and made a complete prat of himself.*

dork [C] (*especially AmE, informal, disapproving, sometimes offensive*) a person who you think is boring and stupid, sometimes because they behave in a strange way and wear unfashionable clothes: *He's such a dork!* ◇ *Oh no, what a dork I am!*

forbidden *adj.*

forbidden · banned · prohibited · taboo
These words all describe things that are not allowed.

PATTERNS AND COLLOCATIONS
▸ forbidden / banned / prohibited / taboo **areas**
▸ forbidden / banned / prohibited **books**
▸ banned / prohibited **substances / weapons**
▸ forbidden / prohibited **foods / places**
▸ a forbidden / taboo **subject**
▸ **officially / specifically** forbidden / banned / prohibited
▸ **strictly** forbidden / taboo
▸ forbidden / banned / prohibited **by law**

forbidden not allowed: *Smoking is strictly forbidden in the museum.* ◇ *Entry to the room was **forbidden to** the children.* ◇ *It is not forbidden to dream of a better world.* See also **forbid** → BAN *verb*

banned officially not allowed; prevented from doing sth or taking part in a competition, etc. as a punishment for past behaviour: *He belongs to one of the banned opposition parties.* ◇ *Traces of a banned pesticide were found in chocolate.* ◇ *The group included several athletes banned for using illegal substances.* See also **ban** → BAN *verb*

prohibited /prəˈhɪbɪtɪd; AmE also proʊˈh-/ (*formal*) not allowed, especially by law: *The police searched the vehicle for stolen or prohibited articles.* ◇ *He was the leader of a prohibited right-wing organization.* See also **prohibit** → BAN *verb*

taboo /təˈbuː/ not done, talked about or used because religion or social custom forbids it: *The subject is still taboo in many families.* ◇ *The guide includes a list of swear words and taboo words.* See also **taboo** → BAN *noun*

force *noun*

force · strength · power · might
These are all words for the quality of being physically strong, or the use of physical strength.

PATTERNS AND COLLOCATIONS
▸ **physical** force / strength / power
▸ **brute** force / strength
▸ to **use** force / your strength / your power / your might

force [U] physical strength used in violent action; violent physical action to obtain or achieve sth: *We had to resort to force to get the door open.* ◇ *The police were accused of using excessive force.* ◇ *The rioters were taken* away **by force**. ◇ (*disapproving*) *We achieve much more by persuasion than by brute force.* See also **force** → PUSH *verb* 1

strength [U] muscle power; the health and fitness needed to do physical work or actions: *His superior physical strength won him the title.* ◇ *It may take a few weeks for you to build up your strength again.* ◇ *She didn't have the strength to walk any further.* See also **strong** → STRONG 1, **strong** → WELL, **strengthen** → STRENGTHEN, **energy** → ENERGY 2

power [U] physical strength used in action; physical strength that sb possesses and might use: *He hit the ball with as much power as he could.* ◇ *the sheer physical power of the man* See also **powerful** → STRONG 1

might (*formal or literary*) great strength, energy or power: *America's military might* ◇ *He pushed against the rock with all his might.*

force *verb*

force · make · oblige · compel · drive · impel
These words all mean to put sb in a situation where they have to do sth, especially sth that they do not want to do.

PATTERNS AND COLLOCATIONS
▸ to drive / impel sb **to** sth
▸ to force sb / be made / be obliged / compel sb / drive sb / impel sb **to do** sth
▸ to **feel** obliged / compelled / impelled to do sth

force [T, often passive] to put sb in a situation in which they have to do sth that they do not want to do: *Ill health forced him into early retirement.* ◇ *I was forced to take a taxi because the last bus had left.* ◇ *She forced herself to be polite to them.* ◇ *Public pressure managed to force a change in the government's position.* ◇ *He didn't force me — I wanted to go.* See also **force** → PRESSURE *noun* 2

make [T] to put sb in a situation in which they have to do sth whether they want to or not: *They made me repeat the whole story.* ◇ *His snoring was so bad, she made him sleep on the sofa downstairs.* ◇ *We were made to work very hard.*

> **NOTE** FORCE OR MAKE? Make is slightly more informal and is used especially in conversation. It is usually a person who makes sb else do sth, especially by ordering or telling them in a firm way: *Mum makes us eat lots of vegetables*. Force often suggests strong persuasion or threats from sb, or describes a situation in which there is no choice about what to do: *The hijackers forced the passengers to lie on the ground.* ◇ *The plane was forced to make an emergency landing because of bad weather.* In the passive both verbs are followed by the infinitive with *to*: *to be forced / made **to do sth*** but note the difference between the two verbs in the active: *to force sb **to do sth*** ◇ *to make sb **do sth***.

oblige /əˈblaɪdʒ/ [T, usually passive] (always followed by *to* + infinitive) (*rather formal*) to force sb to do sth, for example by law or because it is a duty: *Parents are **obliged by law** to send their children to school.* ◇ *Suppliers aren't **legally obliged to** provide a warranty.* ❶ Oblige is used especially in official contexts to describe sth that sb is required to do by law or because it is their responsibility: *The landlord is obliged to give tenants 24 hours' notice of a visit.* It can also be used to describe a moral or social **obligation**, but in this context it is formal: *We felt obliged to sit with them.* See also **obligation** → RESPONSIBILITY

compel /kəmˈpel/ (-ll-) [T] (*formal*) to use your authority to force sb to do sth; to make sth necessary: *The law can compel fathers to make regular payments for their children.* ◇ *Last year ill health compelled his retirement.* See also **compulsion** → PRESSURE *noun* 2

drive [T] to force sb to act in a particular way, often an extreme way: *The urge to survive **drove them on**.* ◇ *It's the story of a teenager **driven to despair** by the hypocrisy of the adult world.*

impel /ɪmˈpel/ (-ll-) [T, often passive] (*formal*) to be forced to do sth by a feeling or idea, especially one that seems to be beyond your control: *He felt impelled to investigate further.* ◇ *There are various reasons that impel me to that conclusion.*

foreign *adj.*

foreign · overseas · external · alien
These words all describe things that are connected with other countries.

PATTERNS AND COLLOCATIONS
▸ a foreign / an overseas / an alien **country**
▸ foreign / an overseas / alien **territory**
▸ foreign / overseas / external **trade / markets / debt / policy**
▸ a foreign / an overseas **bank / firm / holiday / tour / trip**
▸ foreign / overseas **demand / visitors / buyers / investors**
▸ foreign / external **affairs / interference / relations**
▸ a foreign / an alien **culture / language / species / system**

foreign in or from a country that is not your own; dealing with or involving other countries: *What foreign languages do you speak?* ◇ *Tourism is the country's biggest foreign currency earner.* ◇ *You could tell she was foreign by the way she dressed.* ◇ *She was working as a foreign correspondent* (= one who reports on foreign countries in the media). **OPP** native → CULTURAL, **domestic, home** → NATIONAL

overseas /ˌəʊvəˈsiːz; *AmE* ˌoʊvərˈs-/ [only before noun] (*especially business*) connected with foreign countries, especially those separated from your country by the sea or ocean; (of a person) from or living in a foreign country: *The overseas aid budget has been cut.* ◇ *The hotel is popular with overseas visitors to London.* **OPP** domestic, **home** → NATIONAL
▸ **overseas** *adv.*: *He was working overseas for an oil company.*

external [only before noun] (*business or politics*) connected with foreign countries: *External trade increased last year.* ◇ *The country was* **OPP** internal → NATIONAL *promised military aid in the case of external threat.*
▸ **externally** *adv.*: *Externally borrowed funds were used to stimulate economic growth.*

alien /ˈeɪliən/ (*often disapproving*) from another country or society; foreign: *His last years were spent alone and insecure in an alien land.* ◇ *Native woodland was destroyed and alien conifers were planted.* **OPP** native → CULTURAL

> **NOTE** WHICH WORD? **Foreign** is by far the most frequent of these words and has the widest range. When describing groups of people such as *visitors, investors* or *buyers*, **overseas** is often preferred, especially when the group includes people who are not foreign but are living in a foreign country: *In this constituency only 65 overseas voters registered in time to vote.* 'Foreign voters' would be people living in your own country who are from a foreign country. Both **overseas** and **external** are used especially in the contexts of business and politics: they are factual, businesslike words and contain no suggestion of 'difference' or 'strangeness', which **foreign** sometimes does. **Alien** is a more literary word and often carries a stronger sense of difference or strangeness, often in a negative or disapproving way. It is also used to describe plants and animals from a foreign country.

forest *noun*

forest · wood · jungle · woodland · rainforest · plantation
These words all mean an area of land that is covered with trees.

PATTERNS AND COLLOCATIONS
▸ **in** a forest / a wood / the jungle / woodland / the rainforest / a plantation
▸ (a) **dense** forest / wood / jungle / woodland

▸ **tropical** forest / jungle / rainforest

forest [C, U] a large area of land that is thickly covered with trees: *The species is found in both coniferous and deciduous forests.* ◇ *One careless match can start a forest fire.* ◇ *Thousands of hectares of forest are destroyed each year.*

wood [C] (also **woods** [pl.]) an area of trees that is smaller than a forest, and often with more space between the trees than in a forest: *We descended through an oak wood to the village below.* ◇ *She went for a walk in the woods.* ❶ In American English **woods** [pl.] is usually used, except in literature.

jungle [C, U] an area of tropical forest where trees and plants grow very thickly: *The plant originates from the jungles of South-East Asia.* ◇ *We trekked for miles through dense jungle.*

woodland [U, C] (also **woodlands** [pl.]) an area of land that is covered with trees: *The house is fringed by fields and woodland.* ◇ *These ancient woodlands are under threat from new road developments.*

rainforest /ˈreɪnfɒrɪst; *AmE* -fɔːr-; -fɑːr-/ [C, U] a thick forest in parts of the world that have a lot of rain, especially in tropical countries: *The Amazon rainforest is home to 30% of all known plant and animal species.*

> **NOTE** JUNGLE OR RAINFOREST? A **rainforest** is an environment that has taken millions of years to reach its present state, so that the sizes and types of plants in it do not change any more. Not all **rainforests** are in tropical parts of the world. A **jungle** can be any tropical place where plants grow so much that is difficult to move through.

plantation /plɑːnˈteɪʃn; *AmE* plæn-/ [C] a large area of land that is planted with trees to produce wood: *Most of these conifer plantations will be felled over the next 10 years.*

forget *verb*

forget · shut sb/sth out · blot sth out · wipe
These words all mean to deliberately try not to think about sb/sth.

PATTERNS AND COLLOCATIONS
▸ to shut / blot sth out **of** sth
▸ to shut sth out of / blot sth out of / wipe sth from your **mind**
▸ to shut / blot / wipe out a **memory**

forget [I, T] to deliberately stop thinking about sb/sth: *Try to forget about what happened.* ◇ *Forget him!* ◇ *Let's forget our differences and be friends.* ◇ *Forget I said anything!* **OPP** remember → REMEMBER

shut sb/sth 'out *phrasal verb* to not allow a person to share or be part of your thoughts or feelings; to stop yourself from having particular feelings: *I wanted to shut John out of my life forever.* ◇ *If you shut me out, how can I help you?* ◇ *She learned to shut out her angry feelings.*

blot sth 'out *phrasal verb* (-tt-) to deliberately try to forget an unpleasant memory or thought: *He tried to blot out the image of Helen's sad face.* ◇ *I wish I could just blot it out – pretend the last few months never happened.*

wipe [T] to deliberately forget an experience because it was unpleasant or embarrassing: *I tried to wipe the whole episode from my mind.* ◇ *You can never wipe out the past.* See also **wipe** → DELETE

forgive *verb*

forgive · pardon · condone · excuse
These words all mean to accept sb's mistake or bad behaviour, or to stop being angry with sb who has made a mistake or behaved badly.

PATTERNS AND COLLOCATIONS
▸ to forgive / pardon / condone / excuse sb **for** sth
▸ to forgive / condone / excuse sb's **behaviour**

▸ Forgive / Pardon / Excuse **my ignorance**.

forgive [T] (*especially spoken*) to stop feeling angry with sb who has done sth to harm, annoy or upset you; to stop feeling angry with yourself: *I'll never forgive her for what she did.* ◇ *I can't forgive that type of behaviour.* ◇ *She'd forgive him anything.* ◇ *I'd never **forgive myself** if she heard the truth from someone else.* ◇ *I know what he did was wrong but don't you think it's time to **forgive and forget*** (= stop being angry with him about it and behave as if it had not happened). ❶ In formal spoken English **forgive** can be used to say in a polite way that you are sorry if what you are doing or saying seems rude or silly: *Forgive my ignorance, but what exactly does the company do?* ◇ *Forgive me, but I don't see that any of this concerns me.* See also **forgiveness** → MERCY, **forgiving** → LENIENT

pardon [T] (*rather formal, spoken*) used to say in a polite way that you are sorry if what you are doing or saying seems rude or silly: *Pardon my ignorance, but what is a 'duplex'?* ◇ *The place was, **if you'll pardon the expression**, a dump.* ◇ *Pardon me for interrupting you.* See also **pardon** → MERCY *noun*

condone /kən'dəʊn; *AmE* -'doʊn/ [T] (often used in negative sentences) (*rather formal*) to accept behaviour that is morally wrong or to treat it as if it were not serious: *Terrorism can never be condoned.* ◇ *The college cannot condone any behaviour that involves illicit drugs.* ❶ Note that you cannot **condone** a person; you can only **condone** (of refuse to condone) behaviour. **OPP** condemn → BLAME

excuse [T] (*especially AmE, especially spoken*) used to ask sb not to be angry with sb, for example for not being polite or making a small mistake: *Please excuse the mess.* ◇ *I hope you'll excuse me for being so late.* ◇ *You'll have to excuse my father — he's not always that rude.* See also **excuse** → REASON *noun*

form *noun*

1 The disease can take several different forms.
2 an application form

1 form · shape · guise
These are all words for the way in which sth appears or is presented.

PATTERNS AND COLLOCATIONS
▸ **in** the form / shape / guise **of** sb / sth
▸ to **take** a form / shape

form [C, U] the particular way sth is, seems, looks or is presented: *The disease can take several different forms.* ◇ *Help in the form of money will be very welcome.* ◇ *Most political questions involve morality **in some form or other**.* ◇ *We need to come to **some form of** agreement.* ◇ *This dictionary is also available in electronic form.* See also **form** → KIND *noun*, **form** → SHAPE *noun*

shape [U] the particular qualities or characteristics of sth: *Will new technology change the shape of broadcasting?* ◇ *A new song began to take shape in her mind.* ◇ *Prices vary according to the **size and shape** of each project.* ◇ (*informal*) *I don't approve of violence **in any way, shape or form**.* ◇ *Are solar-powered cars **the shape of things to come*** (= the way things are likely to develop in the future)?

guise /gaɪz/ [C] a way in which sb/sth appears, often in a way that is different from usual or that hides the truth about them/it: *His speech presented racist ideas **under the guise of** nationalism.* ◇ *The story appears in different guises in different cultures.* ◇ *She had been invited to the conference in her guise as a professional counsellor.*

2 form · questionnaire · coupon
These are all words for a document containing questions and spaces for answers.

PATTERNS AND COLLOCATIONS
▸ an entry form / coupon

▸ to **design** / **draw up** / **prepare** / **send out** / **receive** a form / questionnaire
▸ to **complete** / **fill in** / **fill out** / **return** a form / questionnaire / coupon

form [C] an official document containing questions and spaces for answers: (*especially BrE*) *Please fill in the application form in black ink.* ◇ (*especially AmE*) *There are a lot of official forms to fill out.* ◇ *This is a standard form sent to all applicants.*

questionnaire /ˌkwestʃə'neə(r); *AmE* -'ner/ [C] a written list of questions that are answered by a number of people so that information can be collected from the answers: *Students completed a **questionnaire about** their social attitudes.* ◇ *Companies were sent a **questionnaire on** their environmental practices.*

coupon /'kuːpɒn; *AmE* -paːn; 'kjuː-/ [C] a printed form, often cut out from a newspaper or magazine, that is used to enter a competition or order goods: *Contestants were invited to complete an entry coupon.*

formal *adj.*

formal · staid · stuffy · stiff
These words all describe a person who behaves in a very serious way and is often boring or old-fashioned, not friendly or relaxed.

PATTERNS AND COLLOCATIONS
▸ formal / stuffy **about** sth
▸ a formal / stiff **manner**
▸ **rather** formal / staid / stuffy / stiff
▸ a staid / stuffy / stiff **old** sb

formal very correct and serious; suitable for official or important occasions: *She has a very formal manner, which can seem unfriendly.* ◇ *He insisted on formal dress for dinner.* ◇ *He kept the tone of the letter formal and businesslike.* **OPP** informal, casual → INFORMAL. See also **formality** → RESPECT *noun*
▸ **formally** *adv.*: *'How do you do?' she said formally.*

staid (*disapproving*) not amusing or interesting; boring and old-fashioned: *The museum is trying to get rid of its staid image.*

stuffy (*rather informal, disapproving*) very serious, formal, boring or old-fashioned: *He reminded her of a stuffy old headmaster she once had.*

stiff (*usually disapproving*) not friendly or relaxed: *The speech he made to welcome them was stiff and formal.* **OPP** relaxed → INFORMAL

former *adj.*

former · old · then · ex-
These words all describe sb/sth that used to have a particular position or status in the past.

PATTERNS AND COLLOCATIONS
▸ sb's former / old / then / ex-**partner** / boyfriend / girlfriend
▸ sb's former / then / ex-**husband** / wife
▸ sb's former / old / then **boss**
▸ a former / an old / an ex-**lover** / colleague / member
▸ a former / an old **friend** / ally / enemy
▸ the former / then / ex-**president** / ambassador
▸ a former / an old / an ex-**student**
▸ a former / an ex-**communist** / king / patient / smoker
▸ a former / an old / an ex-**colony**

former [only before noun] (*rather formal*) that used to have a particular position or status in the past: *She's the former world champion.* **OPP** current → RECENT, future → NEXT

old [only before noun] used to refer to sth that has been replaced by sth else: *We had more room in our old house.* ◇ *I met up with some old school friends.* **OPP** new ❶ A **new** person or thing is one that you have not met, had or experienced before: *He's made a lot of new friends.* ◇ *When do you start your new job?* ◇ *This is a new experience for me.* ◇ *Our system is probably new to you.*

then [only before noun] used to refer to sb who had a particular title or position at the time in the past that is being discussed: *That decision was taken more than ten years ago by the then president.* **OPP** current → RECENT

ex- *combining form* former: *My ex-wife and I are not on speaking terms.* **OPP** current → RECENT, **future** → NEXT

> **NOTE** FORMER OR EX-? **Former** has a wider range of collocates than **ex-**: *sb's ex-boss/friend/ally/enemy.* When **ex-** can be used it is less formal than **former** and is preferred in spoken English.

forum *noun*

forum · arena · stage · platform
These words all mean a place or area of activity where people can exchange opinions.

PATTERNS AND COLLOCATIONS
▸ a forum / an arena / a stage / a platform **for** sth
▸ **in** a forum / an arena
▸ a / an **international** / **political** / **global** forum / arena / stage / platform
▸ to **provide** a forum / an arena / a platform

forum /'fɔːrəm/ [C] a place where people can exchange opinions and ideas on a particular issue; a meeting organized for this purpose: *Television is now an important forum for political debate.* ◇ *The city is to host an international forum on global climate change.*

arena /ə'riːnə/ [C] (*written*) an area of activity that concerns the public, especially one where there is a lot of opposition between different groups or countries: *Space became an arena for global competition between the United States and the Soviet Union.*

stage [C, sing.] an area of activity where important things happen, especially in politics: *Germany is playing a leading role on the world stage.*

platform [C, usually sing.] an opportunity or place for sb to express their opinions publicly or make progress in a particular area: *She used the newspaper column as a platform for her feminist views.*

fragile *adj.*

fragile · delicate · brittle
These words all describe things that break easily.

PATTERNS AND COLLOCATIONS
▸ fragile / delicate / brittle **bones** / **glass**
▸ fragile / delicate **china**
▸ a fragile / delicate **thread**
▸ the fragile / delicate **ecology**

fragile /'frædʒaɪl; *AmE* -dʒl/ easily broken or damaged: *Be careful not to drop it, it's very fragile.* ◇ *fragile habitats threatened by pollution*

delicate /'delɪkət/ easily broken or damaged: *The eye is one of the most delicate organs of the body.* ◇ *the delicate ecological balance of the rainforest*

> **NOTE** FRAGILE OR DELICATE? **Delicate** fabrics, like wool and silk, need special care: *a cool wash for delicate fabrics.* **Fragile** fabrics need even more care, usually because they are very old: *What sort of cleaning method will avoid damaging these fragile old fabrics?*

brittle with a hard texture or surface, but easily broken: *Bones become more brittle with age.* ◇ *She had thin, brittle, permed hair.* ❶ **Brittle** is used to describe *bones, nails, hair, glass* and other hard materials. Bones that break easily because of age or disease are **brittle** or **fragile**; bones that break easily because they are small and light are **delicate** or **fragile**.

fragment *noun* See also the entries for BIT and PIECE

fragment · flake · shard · splinter · chip · sliver · crumb · shred · shavings · filings
These are all words for a small piece of sth broken or cut from sth larger.

PATTERNS AND COLLOCATIONS
▸ **in** fragments / flakes / shards / slivers / shreds
▸ (a) **small** fragments / flakes / shards / splinters / chip / sliver
▸ (a) **tiny** fragments / flakes / shard / sliver / shreds
▸ (a) **thin** flakes / splinters / sliver / shreds
▸ **flying** fragments / shards
▸ **glass** / **metal** fragments / shards / splinters
▸ **wood** chips / shavings
▸ a fragment / shard / splinter / sliver of **glass**
▸ a fragment / shard of **pottery**

fragment [C] a small piece of glass, stone, metal or pottery that was part of sth larger that has broken: *Police found fragments of glass near the scene.* ◇ *The shattered vase lay in fragments on the floor.*

flake [C] a small, very thin, flat piece of a substance or material, especially one that has broken off from sth larger: *Large flakes of paint were peeling off the walls.* ◇ *As they neared home the first flakes of snow fell.*

shard /ʃɑːd; *AmE* ʃɑːrd/ (also **sherd** /ʃɜːd; *AmE* ʃɜːrd/) [C] (*rather formal, written*) a sharp piece of broken glass, metal, plastic or pottery: *The brickwork exploded in dust and flying shards of clay.*

splinter [C] a small, thin, sharp piece of wood, glass, metal, bone or ice that has broken off a larger piece, especially when it has become stuck in sb's flesh: *I've got a splinter in my finger* (= a small piece of wood). ◇ *A small splinter of metal had lodged in his thumb.* ❶ Unless otherwise stated, a **splinter** is a splinter of wood. If it is of some other material, it is a *splinter of sth* or a *glass/metal, etc. splinter.*

chip [C] a small piece of glass, china, wood or tooth that has broken off an object or tooth: *She had a slight chip off her front tooth.* ◇ *The gutted raw fish are smoked slowly over wood chips.* ❶ **Chip** is more frequently used to mean the place from which this piece has broken off: *This mug has a chip in it.*

sliver /'slɪvə(r)/ [C] a small or thin piece of sth, especially glass, ice, wood or food, that is cut or broken off from a larger piece: *Slivers of glass crackled and crunched beneath her feet.* ◇ *Top each canapé with a sliver of cheese.*

> **NOTE** FRAGMENT OR SLIVER? A **fragment** is usually part of sth that has broken into lots of pieces. A **sliver** may have been cut off sth that is still whole except for this one piece.

crumb [C] a very small piece of food, especially of bread or cake, that has fallen off a larger piece: *She stood up and brushed the crumbs from her sweater.*

shred [C, usually pl.] a small thin piece of fabric or paper that has been torn or cut from sth: *His jacket had been torn to shreds by the barbed wire.* See also **shred** → TEAR *verb*

shavings [pl.] thin pieces cut from a piece of wood, using a sharp tool: *His study smelled of dust, ink and pencil shavings.*

filings /'faɪlɪŋz/ [pl.] very small pieces of metal, made when a larger piece of metal is filed (= rubbed with a metal tool): *copper/iron filings*

frame *noun*

frame · hull · body · fuselage · chassis · shell · bodywork
These are all words for the basic structure of a vehicle or building, which supports the rest of it.

PATTERNS AND COLLOCATIONS
▸ the frame / body / chassis / shell / bodywork of a **car**
▸ the frame / body / fuselage of a / an **aircraft** / **plane**

▶ the frame / hull of a **ship**
▶ (a) **metal / steel** frame / hull / body / chassis / shell / bodywork
▶ a **wooden** frame / hull / body
▶ a **concrete** frame / shell

frame [C] the supporting structure of a piece of furniture, a building or a vehicle that gives it its shape: *a bicycle frame ◇ The bed frame is made of pine.*

hull [C] the main, bottom part of a ship, which goes in the water: *They climbed onto the upturned hull and waited to be rescued.*

body [C, sing.] the main part of sth, especially a vehicle: *The new car body weighed 9.55 tonnes. ◇ Although parts were scattered over the surrounding fields, the main body of the plane had landed in one piece.*

fuselage /ˈfjuːzəlɑːʒ; AmE ˈfjuːs-/ [C] (*formal or technical*) the main part of an aircraft in which passengers and goods are carried: *Repairs to the fuselage are almost complete.*

chassis /ˈʃæsi/ (pl. **chassis** /-siz/) [C] the frame that a vehicle is built on: *The company makes chassis for motorhomes, ambulances and other large vehicles.* ❶ A **chassis** can also be the outside structure of a piece of computer equipment: *a computer/printer chassis*

shell [C] the walls or outer structure of sth, for example an empty building after a fire or a bomb attack; any structure that forms a hard outer frame: *The fire reduced the school to a hollow shell. ◇ the body shell of a car*

bodywork [U] the main outside structure of a vehicle, usually made of painted metal: *The car had damaged bodywork but a very good engine.*

fraud noun

1 obtain sth by fraud
2 a $1 million fraud

1 fraud · deception · dishonesty · deceit
These are all words for the act of deceiving sb.

PATTERNS AND COLLOCATIONS
▶ to **be guilty of / accuse sb of** fraud / deception / dishonesty / deceit
▶ to **practise / obtain sth by** fraud / deception / deceit
▶ to **use / admit / confess to / deny** fraud / deception

fraud /frɔːd/ [U] the crime of deceiving sb in order to get money or goods illegally: *She was charged with credit card fraud.* See also **defraud** → DEFRAUD, **fraudulent** → CORRUPT

deception /dɪˈsepʃn/ [U] (*rather formal or law*) behaviour that involves deliberately making sb believe sth that is not true: *It's a drama full of lies and deception.* See also **deceive** → CHEAT *verb*

dishonesty [U] (*rather formal*) behaviour that involves doing things that are not honest, for example lying, stealing or cheating: *Five civil servants were dismissed for dishonesty and misconduct.* **OPP** honesty → INTEGRITY, See also **dishonest** → DISHONEST

deceit /dɪˈsiːt/ (*rather formal, especially written*) behaviour that involves deliberately making sb believe sth that is not true: *He did not want to get drawn into this web of deceit.* See also **deceitful** → DISHONEST

NOTE DECEPTION OR DECEIT? **Deception** is often used in legal contexts: *She admitted two charges of deception. ◇ She admitted two charges of deceit.* **Deceit** is used more in fiction and literary writing, although **deception** can also be used in these contexts. They are used especially to describe behaviour that involves making sb believe sth that is not true, without actually telling lies.

2 fraud · game · scam · racket · con
These are all words for a dishonest plan.

PATTERNS AND COLLOCATIONS
▶ a **$1 million** fraud / scam / racket
▶ a / an **insurance / financial** fraud / scam

▶ to **operate / run / be involved in** a fraud / scam / racket
▶ to **control** a fraud / racket

fraud /frɔːd/ [C] an act of committing fraud (= the crime of deceiving sb in order to get money or goods illegally): *He helped prevent a $100 million fraud.* See also **defraud** → DEFRAUD

game [C] (*informal*) a secret and clever plan or trick: *So that's his little game* (= now I know what he has been planning).

scam [C] (*informal*) a clever plan for getting money illegally by deceiving people: *She got involved in an insurance scam.*

racket [C] (*informal*) an organized way of getting money illegally: *They believe that he was the victim of a protection racket.*

NOTE SCAM OR RACKET? A **racket** usually involves exchanging money for illegal activities such as buying and selling drugs, or forcing people to pay money by threatening them: *an extortion/protection racket.* A **scam** usually involves getting money by cheating the system in some way: *a gambling/insurance/credit card/ VAT scam.*

con [sing.] (*informal*) an act of cheating sb: *The so-called bargain was just a con! ◇ (BrE) It was all one big con trick. ◇ (AmE) a con game ◇ He's a real con artist* (= a person who regularly cheats others). ❶ **Con** is a short form of the term **confidence trick** (*BrE*) or **confidence game** (*AmE*). See also **con** → CHEAT *verb*

free verb

1 free the passengers from the wreckage
2 free the body of tension

1 free · let (sb/sth) go · cut · release · disengage · disentangle
These words all mean to stop holding sb/sth or to move them out of a place or position in which they have been trapped or held.

PATTERNS AND COLLOCATIONS
▶ to free / cut / release / disengage / disentangle sb / sth **from** sth
▶ to free / release / disengage / disentangle **yourself** from sth
▶ to free / release a **passenger**
▶ to free / let go of / release / disengage / disentangle your / sb's **arm / hand**
▶ to let go of / release a **strap**

free [T] to manage to move sb/sth that is trapped or fixed somewhere: *Three people were freed from the wreckage. ◇ He managed to free his arms from their bonds. ◇ A good kick finally freed the door. ◇ (figurative) Counselling may help you to free yourself from the past.* See also **free** → RELEASE *verb*

let 'go, let sb/sth 'go *phrase* (often used in orders) (*especially spoken*) to stop holding sb/sth and allow them to fall or move freely: *Don't let go of the rope. ◇ Let go! You're hurting me! ◇ Let me go!* See also **let sb go** → RELEASE *verb*

cut [T] to free sb from somewhere by cutting the rope, object, etc. that is holding them: *The injured driver had to be cut from the wreckage. ◇ Two survivors were cut free after being trapped for twenty minutes.*

release [T] (*rather formal*) to manage to move sb/sth that is trapped somewhere; to stop holding sth or stop it from being held so that it can move, fly or fall freely: *Firefighters took two hours to release the driver from the wreckage. ◇ He refused to release her arm. ◇ 10 000 balloons were released at the ceremony. ◇ (figurative) Death released him from his suffering.* See also **release** → RELEASE *verb*

disengage /ˌdɪsɪnˈɡeɪdʒ/ [T, I] (*formal*) to free sb/sth from the person or thing that is holding them/it; to become free: *She gently disengaged herself from her sleeping son. ◇ We saw the booster rockets disengage and fall into the sea. ◇*

(*figurative*) *They wished to disengage themselves from these policies.* ❶ People often **disengage** themselves *gently* from a situation, without a lot of noise or activity.

disentangle /ˌdɪsɪnˈtæŋgl/ [T] to free sb/sth from sth that has become wrapped or twisted around them: *He tried to disentangle his fingers from her hair.*

2 free · rid · purge

These words all mean to remove sb/sth that is unpleasant, annoying or causing a problem.

PATTERNS AND COLLOCATIONS
▸ to free / rid / purge sb / sth / yourself **of** sb / sth
▸ to free / rid / purge sb / sth **from** sth
▸ to free / rid / purge **yourself** of sb / sth
▸ to free / rid yourself of a **burden**
▸ to rid / purge yourself of **guilt**

free [T] (always used with *of* or *from*) to remove sth that is unpleasant or not wanted from sb/sth: *These exercises help free the body of tension.* ◇ *We aim to free young people from dependency on drugs.* ❶ You can *free A of/from B*: they both mean to remove B from A. Compare **purge**, below.
▸ **free from/of sth** *adj.*: *free from difficulty/doubt/fear* ◇ *free from artificial colours and flavourings* ◇ *It was several weeks before he was completely free of pain.*
▸ **freedom** *noun* [U]: *freedom from fear/hunger/pain*

rid [T] (always used with *of*) (*formal*) to free sb/sth from sth: *Further measures will be taken to rid our streets of crime.* ◇ *He wanted to rid himself of the burden of the secret.*

> **NOTE** **FREE OR RID?** **Free** emphasizes the good feeling which follows when you remove sth unpleasant. **Rid** emphasizes how bad or unpleasant that thing was.

purge [T] (usually used with *of* or *from*) (*rather formal*) to remove people from an organization, often violently, because their opinions or activities are unacceptable to the people in power; to make yourself/sb/sth pure, healthy or clean by getting rid of bad thoughts or feelings: *He purged the party of extremists.* ◇ *He purged extremists from the party.* ◇ *We need to purge our sport of racism.* ◇ *Nothing could purge the guilt from her mind.* ❶ To *purge A of B* means to remove B from A. If you use *from* it is the other way round: to *purge B from A* means to remove B from A. Compare **free**, above.

free *adj.*

1 a free man
2 free tickets
3 Are you free for lunch?

1 See the Topic Map for THE INDIVIDUAL AND SOCIETY on p.894
free · loose · at large
These words all describe a person or an animal that is able to move around without control.

PATTERNS AND COLLOCATIONS
▸ to **set** sb / sth free / loose
▸ to **break** / **get** / **run** free / loose
▸ to **remain** free / loose / at large

free (of a person) not a prisoner or slave; (of an animal) not tied up or in a cage: *He walked out of jail a free man.* ◇ *The protesters set the animals free.* ◇ *He subdues one of the wild horses and then allows it to go free.* See also **free** → RELEASE *verb*
▸ **freedom** *noun* [U]: *He finally won his freedom after twenty years in jail.*

loose [not usually before noun] free to move around without control; not tied up or shut in somewhere: *The sheep had got out and were loose on the road.* ◇ *The horse had broken loose* (= escaped) *from its tether.* ◇ *During the night, somebody had cut the boat loose from its moorings.* See also **let sb/sth loose** → RELEASE *verb*

at 'large *idiom* (of a dangerous person or animal) not captured; free: *Her killer is still at large.*

2 free · free of charge · complimentary · for nothing · on the house

These words all describe sth that is given or obtained without payment.

PATTERNS AND COLLOCATIONS
▸ a free / complimentary **ticket** / **sample** / **copy** / **subscription**
▸ to **get** sth free / free of charge / for nothing

free costing nothing: *Admission is free.* ◇ *We're offering a fabulous free gift with each copy you buy.* ◇ *There's a new website that offers free legal advice to homeowners.* ◇ *You can't expect people to work for free* (= without payment).
free of 'charge *phrase* (especially in business) given or obtained without payment, especially when payment would normally be expected: *Delivery is free of charge.*
complimentary /ˌkɒmplɪˈmentri; *AmE* ˌkɑːm-/ (*rather formal*) (especially in business) given free, especially as part of selling other goods or services: *The hotel offers a complimentary breakfast and evening cocktails.*
for 'nothing *idiom* (*informal*) given or obtained without the need for payment, work or effort: *We could have got in for nothing — nobody was collecting tickets.* ◇ *Don't expect somebody to give you a big salary for nothing!*
on the 'house *idiom* (*rather informal*) (especially drinks or food) given free by a business, especially a bar or restaurant: *Have a drink on the house.*

3 free · available · spare

These words all describe people not having particular plans or arrangements or not being busy.

PATTERNS AND COLLOCATIONS
▸ free / available **for** sth
▸ free / available **to do sth**
▸ free / available / spare **time**
▸ a free / spare **afternoon** / **morning** / **weekend** / **moment**

free (of a person or time) without particular plans or arrangements; not busy: *If Sarah is free for lunch I'll take her out.* ◇ *Keep Friday night free for my party.* See also **free time** → LEISURE
available (*rather formal*) (of a person) free to see or talk to people: *The director was not available for comment.*
spare (of time) available to do what you want with rather than work: *I haven't had a spare moment this morning.* See also **spare time** → LEISURE

freedom *noun* See the Topic Map for THE INDIVIDUAL AND SOCIETY on p.894

freedom · independence · autonomy · liberty · leeway
These are all words for the right or ability of sb to do things or make decisions without being controlled by sb else or without needing help from sb else.

PATTERNS AND COLLOCATIONS
▸ freedom / liberty / leeway **to do sth**
▸ **greater** freedom / independence / autonomy / liberty / leeway
▸ **complete** / **individual** / **personal** freedom / independence / autonomy / liberty
▸ to **have** freedom / independence / autonomy / liberty / leeway
▸ to **enjoy** / **lose** freedom / independence / autonomy / liberty
▸ to **encourage** / **promote** freedom / independence / autonomy
▸ to **undermine** sb's freedom / independence / autonomy

freedom [U, C] the right or ability to do or say what you want without anyone or anything stopping you: *Branch managers have considerable freedom in running their offices.* ◇ *This case is about protecting our freedom of speech.* ◇ *The new syllabus allows students greater freedom of choice.* ◇ *The constitution contains guarantees of democratic rights and freedoms.* ❶ In this meaning **freedom** is often used in the expression *the freedom of sth: freedom of speech/thought/expression/worship/*

choice/action/movement. Freedom of information is the right to see secret information that a government has about people and organizations; freedom of association is the right to meet and talk to whoever you like, even in large groups. People also often talk about press/academic freedom or the freedom of the press, which is the right to write and publish anything, so long as it is true.

▶ **free** adj.: I have no ambitions other than to have a happy life and be free. ◇ Students have a **free choice** of classes in their final year. ◇ You are **free to** come and go as you please. ◇ A true democracy complete with **free speech** and a free press was called for.

independence [U] the freedom to make decisions, organize your life, do your job, etc. without needing help from other people or being controlled by other people: Some people have questioned the independence of the inspectors. ◇ Her work gave her a degree of financial independence. ◇ The car became a symbol of independence. **OPP** **dependence** ❶ Dependence is the state of needing the help and support of sb/sth in order to survive or be successful: his **dependence on** his parents ◇ financial/economic dependence See also **independence** → INDEPENDENCE

▶ **independent** adj.: It was important to me to be financially independent. See also **independent** → CONFIDENT

autonomy /ɔːˈtɒnəmi; AmE ɔːˈtɑːn-/ [U] (formal) the freedom to make decisions and do things without being controlled by anyone else: Schools have gained greater **autonomy from** government control. ◇ One of the aims of modern nursing is to encourage patient autonomy. ❶ Autonomy is a more formal way of saying independence. It is used especially about organizations or classes of people being free from official control; it is used less about individual people: ~~She doesn't want to lose her hard-won autonomy.~~ See also **autonomy** → INDEPENDENCE

▶ **autonomous** /ɔːˈtɒnəməs; AmE ɔːˈtɑːn-/ adj.: Teachers help children to become autonomous learners.

liberty [U] the freedom to live as you choose without too many restrictions from government or authority: The system allows us complete liberty to do the task as we like. ◇ The concept of individual liberty is enshrined in the constitution.

leeway /ˈliːweɪ/ [U] the amount of freedom that you have to change sth or to do sth in the way you want to: How much leeway should parents give their children?

freezing adj.

freezing · icy · snowy · wintry · frozen · bitter · frosty
These words all describe sb/sth that is extremely cold.

PATTERNS AND COLLOCATIONS
▶ freezing/ icy/ snowy/ wintry/ bitter/ frosty **weather**
▶ freezing/ icy/ snowy/ wintry/ frozen/ frosty **conditions**
▶ a freezing/ an icy/ a wintry/ a bitter **wind**
▶ freezing/ icy/ wintry/ frosty **air**
▶ a freezing/ an icy/ a snowy/ a wintry/ a frosty **day**/ **night**/ **morning**
▶ freezing/ icy/ bitter **cold**
▶ a freezing/ an icy/ a bitter **winter**
▶ freezing/ icy **water**
▶ an icy/ a snowy/ a wintry/ a frozen **landscape**
▶ I'm freezing/ frozen.
▶ It's freezing/ bitter outside.

freezing extremely cold; having a temperature below 0° Celsius: It's absolutely freezing outside. ◇ I'm freezing! Close the window! ◇ Expect icy roads and freezing fog tonight. **OPP** **boiling** → HOT, See also **freeze** → COOL verb

▶ **freezing** adv.: It was a freezing cold morning.

icy /ˈaɪsi/ (especially written) (of weather, air and landscapes) extremely cold; covered with ice: An icy blast (= of wind) hit them. ◇ the icy wastes of the Russian Steppes ◇ The car skidded on the icy road.

▶ **icy** adv.: The water was icy cold.

snowy covered with snow; when a lot of snow falls: snowy fields/peaks ◇ a snowy weekend ◇ The weather in January is often cold and snowy.

wintry (of weather, air and landscapes) very cold and typical of winter: The weather will turn wintry over the next few days. ◇ There will still be one or two wintry showers (= with snow or sleet) around. ◇ She gazed out at the wintry landscape (= with frost and snow).

NOTE **ICY** OR **WINTRY**? Icy just means 'extremely cold' and is used especially about wind, especially in literary writing. Wintry suggests snow and frost as well as cold; it is used in literary writing and also in spoken weather forecasts on televsion or the radio.

frozen /ˈfrəʊzn; AmE ˈfroʊzn/ (of people or parts of the body) extremely cold; (of rivers, lakes or landscape) with a layer of ice on the surface: My hands are frozen. ◇ The surface of the lake is permanently frozen. ◇ You look **frozen stiff**. See also **freeze** → COOL verb

bitter (disapproving) (of weather) extremely cold and unpleasant: They had no protection against the bitter cold. ◇ It's really bitter out today.

frosty (of weather) cold with frost (= when a thin white layer of ice forms on the ground); covered with frost: It was a bright, frosty day. ◇ I looked out over the frosty fields.

▶ **frost** noun [U, C]: It will be a clear night with some **ground frost**. ◇ a sharp/hard/severe frost

frequent adj.

frequent · constant · regular · persistent · perpetual · continual · continuous · habitual
These words all describe things that happen or are done very often.

frequent	persistent	constant
regular		perpetual
habitual		continual
		continuous

PATTERNS AND COLLOCATIONS
▶ frequent/ constant/ regular/ persistent/ continual/ continuous/ habitual **use**
▶ frequent/ constant/ regular/ persistent/ continual/ continuous **attacks**
▶ frequent/ constant/ regular/ continual/ continuous **changes**
▶ a frequent/ constant/ persistent/ perpetual/ continual/ continuous **problem**
▶ frequent/ constant/ perpetual **interruptions**
▶ a frequent/ constant/ regular **visitor**
▶ a frequent/ constant/ perpetual/ continual/ continuous **source** of sth
▶ frequent/ constant/ regular/ persistent **reports**/ **complaints**

frequent happening often; doing sth often: There is a frequent bus service into town. ◇ Power failures are frequent occurrences in the city. ◇ His calls became less frequent. ◇ The case was reviewed **at frequent intervals**. ◇ He was a frequent guest at the palace. **OPP** **infrequent** → RARE, **occasional** → OCCASIONAL, See also **frequently** → OFTEN

constant /ˈkɒnstənt; AmE ˈkɑːn-/ [usually before noun] happening or doing sth all the time or very often: He is very ill and needs constant attention. ◇ Her constant chatter was beginning to annoy him. ◇ Her daughter is a constant source of worry to her.

▶ **constantly** adv.: How can finish if I am constantly interrupted?

regular done or happening often; doing sth often: In the 1950s he made regular appearances on Broadway. ◇ Eat a healthy diet and take regular exercise. ◇ He became a regular visitor to Hamilton Road. **OPP** **irregular** → VARIABLE, **occasional** → OCCASIONAL, See also **regular** → STEADY

▸ **regularly** /ˈreɡjələli; AmE -lərli/ adv.: *She regularly wins prizes for her designs.*

NOTE FREQUENT OR REGULAR? **Frequent** is the more common of these words in this meaning; however, **regular** is used more often in more active examples, when you are talking about people doing things, rather than things that happen: *Take frequent exercise.* **Regular** also means 'happening at fixed intervals' and sometimes it may not be clear which meaning is intended: *a regular bus service* may mean frequent buses and/or buses at the same time every day or hour. See also the entry for REGULAR

persistent /pəˈsɪstənt; AmE pərˈs-/ repeated often, in a way that is annoying and cannot be stopped: *The most common symptom is a persistent cough.* ◇ *He resigned over persistent rumours of his part in the scandal.*
▸ **persistently** adv.: *a prison for juveniles who persistently reoffend*

perpetual /pəˈpetʃuəl; AmE pərˈp-/ [usually before noun] (*especially written*) repeated very often, in a way that is annoying: *The perpetual interruptions made conversation difficult.* ◇ *Lack of time is a perpetual problem for nurses on the ward.*

continual [only before noun] repeated very often, especially in a way that is annoying: *There were continual arguments because he felt he was being treated unfairly.* ◇ *He seemed to need continual reassurance.*
▸ **continually** adv.: *People were continually tripping over the cable.*

continuous continual: *The soldiers suffered continuous attacks for four days.* ◇ *The company said the reasons for closure were poor margins and continuous losses.*

NOTE PERSISTENT, PERPETUAL, CONTINUAL OR CONTINUOUS? In some cases you can use any of these words: *a persistent/perpetual/continual/continuous problem.* **Persistent** is used more in factual writing and reporting, to talk about medical problems or problems in society. **Perpetual** is used more in personal and imaginative writing and to talk about annoying personal habits or problems. **Continual** and **continuous** are generally less frequent in this meaning, but are often preferred in spoken English and less formal contexts. All these words also have the meaning 'continuing for a long time without stopping'; **continuous** is more frequent in that meaning, and some people think it should not be used to mean 'repeated many times', but in fact it often is. See also the entry for CONTINUOUS

habitual /həˈbɪtʃuəl/ (of an action) done often, especially in a way that is annoying or difficult to stop: *The mechanic had been dismissed for habitual lateness.* See also **habit** → HABIT, **habitually** → OFTEN

fresh adj.

fresh · raw · uncooked
These words all describe food that has not been prepared.

PATTERNS AND COLLOCATIONS
▸ fresh / raw / uncooked **food / meat / fish / eggs / vegetables**

fresh (of food) recently produced or picked and not frozen, dried or preserved in tins or cans: *Eat plenty of fresh fruit and vegetables.* ◇ *Put the milk in the fridge to* **keep it fresh.** ◇ *These vegetables are* **fresh** *from the garden.*

raw (of food) not cooked: *These fish are often eaten raw.* ◇ *Choose dishes based on raw vegetables, such as crudités or tomato salad.*

uncooked (of food) not cooked: *Don't be tempted by uncooked cake mixture — it contains raw eggs.* ◇ *The steak was uncooked in the middle.*

NOTE RAW OR UNCOOKED? **Raw** describes fresh food that is usually eaten cooked, such as meat, fish, eggs or vegetables, but NOT fruit, which is considered to be usually eaten without being cooked. **Uncooked** can be used in the same way as **raw**, but more frequently it

describes food that has been prepared in some way but not cooked, such as *pastry, dough* or *ham* or food that should have been cooked or has not been cooked properly.

friend noun See also the entry for PARTNER 1

friend · companion · mate · buddy · pal · acquaintance · the girls · confidant · the boys · crony
These are all words for sb that you know well and enjoy spending time with.

PATTERNS AND COLLOCATIONS
▸ a friend / mate / buddy / pal **of mine / yours / his / hers / ours / theirs / my mother's / Diana's, etc.**
▸ an **old** friend / mate / buddy / pal / acquaintance
▸ a / sb's **close** friend / companion / pal / acquaintance
▸ a / sb's **good** friend / companion / mate / buddy / pal
▸ a / sb's **loyal** friend / companion / mate / pal
▸ sb's **best** friend / mate / buddy / pal
▸ a **real** / **true** friend / mate / pal
▸ a **drinking** companion / buddy / pal
▸ to **become** friends / mates / buddies / pals
▸ to **have** friends / mates / buddies / pals / acquaintances
▸ a **night out with** the girls / boys
▸ sb's **friend and** companion / confidant

friend [C] a person you know well and like, and who is not usually a member of your family: *This is my friend Tom.* ◇ *Is he a friend of yours?* ◇ *She's an old friend (= I have known her a long time).* ◇ *He's one of my best friends.* ◇ *I heard about it through* **a friend of a friend.** ◇ *She has a wide* **circle of friends.** ◇ *He finds it difficult to* **make friends.** ◇ *a childhood/family/lifelong friend* See also **friendship** → FRIENDSHIP

companion /kəmˈpæniən/ [C] a person who has similar tastes and interests to your own and whose company you enjoy; a person or animal that travels with you or spends a lot of time with you: *His younger brother is not much of a companion for him.* ◇ *He was an entertaining travelling companion.* ◇ *Jeff was my companion on the journey.* See also **companionship** → FRIENDSHIP

mate [C] (*BrE, informal*) a friend: *They've been best mates ever since they were at school together.* ◇ *I was with a mate.*

buddy [C] (*informal, AmE*) a friend: *I'd like you to meet an old college buddy of mine.* ◇ *Howard and Mick were drinking buddies (= they went out drinking together).*

pal [C] (*informal, old-fashioned*) a friend: *We've been pals for years.* ◇ *Thanks — you're a real pal.*

NOTE MATE, BUDDY OR PAL? **Mate** is used in informal British English and **buddy** in informal American English. They are both also used by men as an informal friendly way of addressing another man: *Sorry mate, you'll have to wait.* ◇ *'Where to, buddy?' the driver asked.* **Pal** is both British and American English but is now old-fashioned except when used as a form of address; however, when **pal** is used in this way, it is unfriendly: *If I were you, pal, I'd stay away from her!*

acquaintance /əˈkweɪntəns/ [C] a person that you know but who is not a close friend: *Claire has a wide circle of friends and acquaintances.* ◇ *I don't know him socially, he's just a business acquaintance.* ◇ *I bumped into an old acquaintance on the train.* See also **acquaintance** → FRIENDSHIP, **make sb's acquaintance** → MEET 3

the girls [pl.] a woman's female friends: *I'm having a night out with the girls.*

confidant /ˈkɒnfɪdænt; ˌkɒnfɪˈdɑːnt; AmE ˈkɑːnfɪdænt/ [C] a person that you trust and who you talk to about private or secret things: *He was a trusted confidant of the President.* ❶ A **confidant** can be male or female. If a **confidant** is female you can also spell it **confidante**. Both words are used and pronounced in the same way.

the boys [pl.] (*informal*) a group of male friends who often go out together: *Are you free tomorrow? How about a night out with the boys?*

crony /'krəʊni; *AmE* 'kroʊni/ [C, usually pl.] (*often disapproving*) a person that sb spends a lot of time with: *He was playing cards with his cronies.* ❶ **Crony** is used to talk in a disapproving or humorous way about other people's friends, not your own.

friendly *adj.*

1 a friendly person/smile
2 a friendly atmosphere/relationship

1 See also the entry for NICE 2
friendly · warm · pleasant · welcoming · amiable · good-natured · genial · hospitable · approachable
These words all describe sb who behaves in a kind and pleasant way to other people.

▸ friendly / pleasant / welcoming / hospitable **to** sb
▸ a friendly / a warm / a pleasant / an amiable / a good-natured / a genial / a hospitable / an approachable **person**
▸ a welcoming / genial / hospitable **host / hostess**
▸ a friendly / a warm / a pleasant / a welcoming / an amiable / a genial / a hospitable **manner**
▸ a friendly / warm / pleasant / welcoming / good-natured / genial **smile**
▸ a friendly / a pleasant / an amiable / a genial **tone**
▸ a friendly / an amiable / a genial **mood**

friendly behaving in a kind and pleasant way because you like sb or want to help them; showing this: *Everyone was exceptionally friendly towards me.* ◊ *John gave me a friendly smile.* **OPP** **unfriendly** → COLD 2
warm showing affection and/or enthusiasm: *Please send her my warmest congratulations.* ◊ *His comments were greeted with warm applause.* **OPP** **cold, cool** → COLD 2
▸ **warmly** *adv.*: *He kissed her warmly on both cheeks.*
▸ **warmth** *noun* [U]: *Her warmth and kindness made her universally liked.*
pleasant (*rather formal*) friendly and polite: *He seemed a very pleasant young man.* ◊ *Please try to be pleasant to our guests.* **OPP** **unpleasant** → MEAN 1
▸ **pleasantly** *adv.*: *'Can I help you?' he asked pleasantly.*
welcoming pleased to welcome guests; generous and friendly to visitors: *He found the locals extremely welcoming.* **OPP** **unwelcoming** ❶ A person who is **unwelcoming** is not friendly towards sb who is visiting or arriving: *The locals were distinctly unwelcoming.* See also **welcome** → GREET, **welcome** → GREETING
amiable /'eɪmiəbl/ (*rather formal, written*) friendly and easy to like: *Her parents seemed very amiable.* ◊ *He uses an amiable tone of voice to soothe stressed clients.*
good-'natured kind, friendly and patient when dealing with people: *Anthony is so good-natured – he finds it difficult to hate anyone.* ◊ *The discussion was good-natured and positive.*
genial /'dʒiːniəl/ (*written*) friendly and cheerful: *Graham was a genial and modest host.*
hospitable /hɒ'spɪtəbl; 'hɒspɪtəbl; *AmE* hɑː's-; 'hɑːs-/ (*rather formal*) welcoming: *The local people are very hospitable to strangers.* ❶ **Hospitable** is less frequent and more formal than **welcoming**. See also **hospitality** → GREETING
approachable friendly and easy to talk to; easy to understand: *Despite being a big star, she's very approachable.* ◊ *It's quite an approachable piece of music.* **OPP** **unapproachable** ❶ A person who is **unapproachable** is unfriendly and not easy to talk to: *Librarians have a reputation for being difficult and unapproachable.*

2 **friendly · cordial · amicable · easy**
These words all describe a relationship or atmosphere that is pleasant and polite, not aggressive or full of arguments.

▸ a friendly / a cordial / an amicable / an easy **relationship**
▸ friendly / cordial / amicable / easy **relations**
▸ a friendly / a cordial / an amicable **meeting**

▸ a friendly / cordial **atmosphere**
▸ to be **on** friendly / cordial / amicable / easy **terms** (with sb)

friendly treating sb as a friend; (especially of the relationship between countries) not treating sb/sth as an enemy: *The boss had a friendly chat with me about the problem after work.* ◊ *We soon became friendly with the couple next door.* ◊ *We were not on the friendliest of terms* (= we were not friendly at all). ◊ *The government has maintained friendly relations with the Japanese.* **OPP** **hostile** → AGGRESSIVE 1
cordial /'kɔːdiəl; *AmE* 'kɔːrdʒəl/ (*formal*) (of a relationship, meeting or atmosphere) friendly in a formal way: *The talks took place in a cordial atmosphere.*
amicable /'æmɪkəbl/ (of a relationship or the way an agreement is reached) polite and fairly friendly, without any quarrelling or aggression: *The government and the union managed to reach an amicable settlement of the dispute.* ◊ *It was an amicable divorce.*
easy [only before noun] (of sb's manner or a relationship) pleasant and friendly; not awkward: *He had a very easy manner.* ◊ *Their success at the game did not make for an easy relationship off court.*

friendship *noun*

friendship · intimacy · acquaintance · companionship · camaraderie · fellowship · closeness · togetherness · comradeship
These are all words for the feeling or state of being friends with sb.

acquaintance	friendship	intimacy
	companionship	closeness
	camaraderie	
	fellowship	
	togetherness	
	comradeship	

▸ friendship / intimacy / acquaintance / companionship / camaraderie / fellowship / closeness / comradeship **with** sb
▸ **the** friendship / intimacy / companionship / camaraderie / fellowship / closeness / comradeship **between** A and B
▸ **close** friendship / intimacy / companionship / camaraderie / fellowship
▸ **great** friendship / intimacy / companionship / camaraderie
▸ **real** friendship / intimacy / togetherness / comradeship
▸ **true** friendship / intimacy / camaraderie / fellowship
▸ to **make** a friendship / sb's acquaintance
▸ to **develop** a friendship / an intimacy / a camaraderie / a closeness
▸ to **offer** friendship / companionship / fellowship / closeness
▸ friendship / intimacy / camaraderie / closeness / comradeship **develops**
▸ a **feeling of** friendship / intimacy / companionship / camaraderie / togetherness / comradeship

friendship [C, U] a relationship between friends; the feeling or relationship that friends have; the state of being friends: *Theirs was a lifelong friendship.* ◊ *He had already struck up* (= begun) *a friendship with Jo.* ◊ *Your friendship is very important to me.* ◊ *a conference to promote international friendship* See also **friend** → FRIEND
intimacy /'ɪntɪməsi/ [U, sing.] the state of having a close personal relationship with sb: *The old intimacy between them had gone for ever.* ◊ *I sensed a close intimacy between them.*
▸ **intimate** *adj.*: *intimate friends* ◊ *We're not on intimate terms with our neighbours.*

NOTE FRIENDSHIP OR INTIMACY? **Friendship** is by far the most frequent and general word in this group. **Intimacy** has a stronger meaning, and is used to describe the relationship between very good friends, or between people who are connected romantically, for example boyfriend and girlfriend or husband and wife.

acquaintance /əˈkweɪntəns/ [U, C] (*formal*) the fact of knowing sb slightly; slight friendship: *I'm delighted to make your acquaintance, Mrs Baker.* ◊ *No one else of my acquaintance was as rich and successful.* ◊ *He hoped their acquaintance would develop further.* See also **acquaintance** → FRIEND, **make sb's acquaintance** → MEET 3

companionship [U] (*rather formal*) the pleasant feeling that you have when you have a friendly relationship with sb and are not alone: *They meet at the club for companionship and advice.* ◊ *She has only her cat for companionship.* See also **companion** → FRIEND

camaraderie /ˌkæməˈrɑːdəri; AmE ˌkɑːməˈrɑːdəri/ [U] (*especially written*) a feeling of friendship and trust among people who work or spend a lot of time together: *the wartime spirit of camaraderie*

fellowship [U] (*rather formal*) a feeling of friendship between people who do things together or share an interest: *The sessions offer students counselling and fellowship.*

closeness [U] the feeling of knowing sb very well and liking them very much: *She couldn't help feeling jealous of the closeness between him and Dylan.*
▶ **close** *adj.*: *Jo is a very close friend.* ◊ *She and her father are very close.*

togetherness [U] the happy feeling that you have when you are with people you like, especially family and friends: *By the end of the week, there was a tremendous feeling of togetherness in the group.*

comradeship /ˈkɒmreɪdʃɪp; AmE ˈkɑːmræd-/ [U] a feeling of friendship, especially between people who work together or who fight together during a war: *After a few weeks together, there was a real sense of comradeship between them.*

frighten *verb*

frighten · scare · alarm · terrify · traumatize · spook
These words all mean to make sb afraid.

alarm | frighten | terrify
 | scare | traumatize
 | spook

PATTERNS AND COLLOCATIONS
▶ to frighten / scare sb / sth **away / off**
▶ to frighten / scare / terrify sb **into** doing sth
▶ It frightens / scares / alarms / terrifies me **that...**
▶ It frightens / scares / alarms / terrifies me **to** think, see, etc.

frighten [T] to make sb feel afraid, often suddenly: *Stop it! You're frightening me!* ◊ *Oh sorry. I didn't mean to frighten you.* ◊ *He brought out a gun and frightened them off.* See also **frightened** → AFRAID, **fright** → FEAR *noun*, **intimidate** → THREATEN 1

scare [T] (*rather informal*) to frighten sb: *It scared me to think I was alone in the building.* ◊ *They managed to scare the bears away.* ◊ (*informal*) *The very thought of flying scares him silly/stiff.* See also **scared** → AFRAID

NOTE **FRIGHTEN** OR **SCARE**? Scare is slightly more informal than **frighten**, so it is used more in spoken than in written English. Both verbs can also be used without an object: *He doesn't frighten/scare easily,* but this is not very frequent. It is more natural to say: *Nothing frightens/scares him,* or: *He doesn't get frightened/scared easily.*

alarm [T] (not usually used in the progressive tenses) to make sb anxious or afraid: *It alarms me that nobody takes this problem seriously.* ◊ *The captain knew there was a problem but didn't want to alarm the passengers.* ❶ **Alarm** is used when sb has a feeling that sth unpleasant or dangerous might happen in the future; the feeling is often more one of worry than actual fear. See also **alarm** → FEAR *noun*, **alarmed** → AFRAID, **startle** → SURPRISE *verb*

terrify [T] to make sb feel extremely afraid: *Flying terrified her.* ◊ *He terrified employees at the bank into handing over cash.* See also **terrified** → AFRAID

traumatize (*BrE* also **-ise**) /ˈtrɔːmətaɪz; AmE ˈtraʊm-/ [T, usually passive] to make sb feel very upset, afraid or shocked, often making them unable to think or work normally: *We were traumatized by what we saw.* ◊ *He was traumatized for life.* See also **trauma** → NIGHTMARE, **traumatic** → PAINFUL 2

spook [T] (*informal*) to frighten a person or animal: *We were spooked by the strange noises and lights.*

frightening *adj.* See also the entry for WORRYING

frightening · terrifying · scary · alarming · daunting · chilling · eerie · intimidating · spooky · creepy · hair-raising
These words all describe people, things, events, etc. that make you feel afraid.

alarming | frightening | terrifying
daunting | scary | chilling
intimidating | eerie | hair-raising
 | spooky
 | creepy

PATTERNS AND COLLOCATIONS
▶ frightening / terrifying / scary / alarming / daunting / intimidating **for** sb
▶ It's frightening / terrifying / scary / daunting **to think...**
▶ a frightening / a terrifying / a scary / an alarming / a daunting / a chilling **experience / thought / prospect**
▶ a frightening / a terrifying / a scary / an eerie / an intimidating / a spooky / a creepy **place**
▶ a scary / an intimidating / a creepy **woman**
▶ an eerie / a terrifying / a spooky / a creepy **atmosphere**
▶ an eerie / a spooky / a creepy **feeling**
▶ to **find sth** frightening / terrifying / scary / daunting / chilling / intimidating / creepy
▶ **rather / pretty** frightening / terrifying / scary / alarming / daunting / chilling / eerie / intimidating / spooky
▶ **very** frightening / scary / alarming / daunting / intimidating / spooky
▶ **a bit** frightening / scary / daunting / spooky / creepy

frightening making you feel afraid: *It's frightening to think it could happen again.* ◊ *The noise was frightening.* ❶ **Frightening** is rather formal in American English. See also **frightened** → AFRAID

terrifying making you feel extremely afraid: *The sudden silence was terrifying.* See also **terrified** → AFRAID

scary (*informal*) making you feel afraid: *a scary movie* ◊ *This is the scariest thing I've ever done in my life.* ◊ *a scary-looking guy* See also **scared** → AFRAID

alarming making you feel worried or afraid: *an alarming increase in the number of cases of skin cancer* ◊ *The rainforest is disappearing at an alarming rate.* ❶ **Alarming** is rather formal in American English. **OPP** **reassuring** → REASSURE
▶ **alarmingly** *adv.*: *Prices have risen alarmingly.*

NOTE **FRIGHTENING**, **SCARY** OR **ALARMING**? If a situation is **alarming**, it is usually a warning that sth unpleasant will happen in the future, especially sth that means a loss of comfort or pleasant conditions. **Frightening** and **scary** can describe people as well as situations and refer to a fear about now or in the future; and this may be a fear about personal safety, not just loss of comfort.

daunting /ˈdɔːntɪŋ/ making you feel nervous and not confident about doing sth: *Starting a new school can be very daunting.* ◊ *She has the daunting task of cooking for 20 people every day.* See also **daunt** → DISCOURAGE 2

chilling very frightening, usually because it is connected with sth violent or cruel: *a chilling tale of murder and revenge* ◊ *The film evokes chilling reminders of the war.*

eerie /ˈɪəri; AmE ˈɪri/ strange and frightening: *an eerie green light* ◇ *He had an eerie feeling that he was not alone.*
▶ **eerily** adv.: *It was eerily quiet.*

intimidating (*rather formal*) frightening in a way that makes you feel less confident in a particular situation: *He had a very intimidating manner.* ◇ *The atmosphere was less intimidating than I had imagined.*

> **NOTE** DAUNTING OR **INTIMIDATING**? **Daunting** describes sth you do or are going to do: *a daunting experience* ◇ *a daunting thought/prospect/task/challenge.* **Intimidating** describes a person or place.

spooky /ˈspuːki/ (*informal*) strange and frightening: *a spooky old house* ◇ *I was just thinking about her when she phoned, which was a bit spooky.*

creepy (*informal*) strange, frightening and unpleasant: *It's kind of creepy down in the cellar!* ◇ *What a creepy coincidence.* ◇ *a creepy little man with a nervous tic*

> **NOTE** EERIE, SPOOKY OR **CREEPY**? These words are all used especially to describe a feeling that sth strange or unnatural is happening or is near you. **Spooky** and **creepy** are both used to describe things that happen that cannot be explained scientifically. **Creepy** can describe people as well as places, events and situations, and suggests sth unpleasant as well as strange. **Eerie** is less informal than the other two.

ˈ**hair-raising** very frightening but often exciting too: *a hair-raising adventure/journey*

frown verb

frown · scowl · grimace
These words all mean to show what you feel on your face, especially when you are angry or worried.

frown	grimace	scowl

PATTERNS AND COLLOCATIONS
▸ to frown / scowl / grimace **at** sb / sth
▸ to frown / grimace **in** concentration, anxiety, etc.
▸ to frown / grimace **slightly**
▸ to frown / scowl **darkly / heavily**

frown [I, T] to make a serious, angry or worried expression by bringing your eyebrows closer together so that lines appear above them: *She studied the map, frowning thoughtfully.* ◇ *By then the customer was frowning impatiently.* ◇ *'I see,' he frowned.* **OPP** smile → SMILE
▶ **frown** noun [C]: *She looked up with a puzzled frown on her face.* ◇ *a slight frown of disapproval/concentration*

scowl /skaʊl/ [I] (*disapproving*) to look at sb with an angry or annoyed look on your face: *She scowled fiercely at them.* **OPP** grin → SMILE
▶ **scowl** noun [C]: *He looked up at me with a scowl.*

grimace /ɡrɪˈmeɪs; ˈɡrɪməs/ [I] to make an ugly expression that shows pain, disgust or regret: *He grimaced at the bitter taste of the medicine.* ◇ *She grimaced as the needle went in.*
▶ **grimace** noun [C]: *to make/give a grimace of pain*

frustration noun

frustration · irritation · annoyance · exasperation · displeasure · chagrin · pique
These are all words for the feeling of being slightly angry.

PATTERNS AND COLLOCATIONS
▸ frustration / irritation / annoyance / exasperation / displeasure **at** sth
▸ irritation / annoyance / exasperation / displeasure **with** sb / sth
▸ to do sth **in** frustration / irritation / annoyance / exasperation
▸ to do sth **with** irritation / annoyance / exasperation / displeasure / chagrin
▸ **to my / his / her, etc.** irritation / annoyance / chagrin

▸ **great / considerable** frustration / irritation / annoyance / displeasure
▸ **intense** frustration / irritation / annoyance
▸ **deep** frustration / displeasure
▸ to **hide** your frustration / irritation / annoyance / exasperation / displeasure / chagrin
▸ to **show** your frustration / irritation / annoyance / displeasure
▸ to **cause** frustration / irritation / annoyance / displeasure

frustration [U, C, usually pl.] the feeling of being slightly angry and impatient because you cannot do or achieve what you want; something that causes you to feel this way: *Dave thumped the table in frustration.* ◇ *She couldn't stand the frustration of not being able to help.* ◇ *Every job has its difficulties and frustrations.* ◇ *Inevitably she took out her frustrations on the children.* See also **frustrate** → ANNOY, **frustrated** → UNHAPPY 2, **frustrating** → ANNOYING

irritation [U, C] the feeling of being slightly angry; something that makes you slightly angry: *He noted, with some irritation, that the letter had not been sent.* ◇ *He could hear the irritation in her voice.* ◇ *the minor irritation of having to wait* See also **irritable** → IRRITABLE, **irritate** → ANNOY, **irritated** → ANNOYED, **irritating** → ANNOYING

annoyance [U, C] irritation: *He could not conceal his annoyance at being interrupted.* ◇ *Much to our annoyance, they decided not to come after all.* ◇ *petty annoyances and irritations* See also **annoy** → ANNOY, **annoyed** → ANNOYED, **annoying** → ANNOYING

> **NOTE** IRRITATION OR **ANNOYANCE**? There is almost no difference in the way these two words are used.

exasperation /ɪɡˌzæspəˈreɪʃn; AmE ˌzɑːspˈ-/ [U] extreme annoyance or impatience, especially when you cannot change the situation: *He shook his head in exasperation.* ◇ *a groan/look/sigh of exasperation* See also **exasperate** → ANNOY, **exasperated** → ANNOYED

displeasure [U] (*formal*) the feeling of being upset and annoyed: *She made no attempt to hide her displeasure at the prospect.* ◇ *The incident has heightened public displeasure with the authorities.* **OPP** pleasure → FUN, See also **displease** → ANNOY

chagrin /ˈʃæɡrɪn/ [U] (*formal*) a feeling of being annoyed or disappointed: *To her chagrin, neither of her sons became doctors.*

pique /piːk/ [U] (*formal*) annoyed or bitter feelings that you have, usually because your pride has been hurt: *When he realized nobody was listening to him, he left in a fit of pique.* ◇ *She'd lied about it out of pique.*

full adj. See also the entry for CROWDED

full · packed · crammed · overcrowded · congested · stuffed
These words all describe sth that contains a lot of sth.

PATTERNS AND COLLOCATIONS
▸ full / packed / crammed / overcrowded / congested **with** sb / sth
▸ packed / crammed **full** of sb / sth
▸ overcrowded / congested **cities / roads**

full containing or holding as much or as many of sth as possible, having no empty space; having or containing a large number or amount of a thing, feeling or quality: *a full bottle of wine* ◇ *She could only nod, because her mouth was full.* ◇ *There were cardboard boxes **stuffed full of** clothes.* ◇ *The sky was **full of** brightly coloured fireworks.* ◇ *She was full of admiration for the care she had received.* ❶ In British English **full up** is also used to describe sth that has no empty space in it, but NOT sth that has a large amount of sth: *Sorry, the hotel is full up tonight.* ◇ ~~Life is full up of coincidences.~~ **Full** (or **full up** in British English) can also be used when sb has had enough to eat: *The kids still weren't full, so I gave them an ice cream each.* ◇ *You shouldn't swim **on a full stomach**.* ◇ (*BrE*) *No more for me, thanks – I'm full up.* **OPP** empty → EMPTY

packed (of a room or building) very full of people; containing a lot of a particular thing: *The restaurant was packed.* ◊ *The show played to **packed houses*** (= large audiences). ◊ *The book is packed with information.* ◊ (*informal*) *The train was absolutely **jam-packed**.* See also **pack** → PACK *verb*

crammed [not before noun] (always followed by *with sb/sth* or *full of sb/sth*) completely full of people or things: *The room was **crammed full** of people.* ◊ *All the shelves were crammed with books.* ◊ *The article was crammed full of ideas.* See also **cram** → PACK *verb*

> **NOTE** **PACKED** OR **CRAMMED**? A place or thing that is **crammed** contains even more than one that is **packed**, so that it is often uncomfortable (if full of people) or untidy (if full of things). A theatre, cinema, etc. where every seat is occupied because the show is so popular is **packed**, NOT **crammed**: *The theatre was packed every night.* ◊ *The theatre was crammed every night.*

overcrowded /ˌəʊvəˈkraʊdɪd; *AmE* ˌoʊvərˈk-/ (*disapproving*) (of a place) with too many people or things in it: *Drugs and violence are rife in our filthy, overcrowded prisons.* ◊ *Too many poor people are living in overcrowded conditions.*

congested /kənˈdʒestɪd/ (*usually disapproving*) so full of traffic that vehicles cannot move easily: *Traffic engineers believe that the new road could free up congested city streets.* ◊ *Many of Europe's airports are heavily congested.* See also **congestion** → TRAFFIC

stuffed [not before noun] (*informal*) having eaten so much that you cannot eat anything else: *I couldn't eat another thing. I'm absolutely stuffed.*

fumble *verb*

fumble · grope · rummage · scrabble · fish · feel · poke around/about
These words all mean to look for sth, often with difficulty, using your hands.

fumble [I, T] (usually used with an adverb or preposition) to use your hands in an awkward way when you are doing sth or looking for sth: *She was fumbling around in the dark looking for the light switch.* ◊ *He **fumbled with** the buttons on his shirt.* ◊ *He fumbled the key into the ignition.*

grope [I, T] (always used with an adverb or preposition) to try and find sth that you cannot see, by feeling with your hands; to try and reach a place by feeling with your hands because you cannot see clearly: *I groped for the light switch.* ◊ *He groped his way up the staircase in the dark.*

rummage /ˈrʌmɪdʒ/ [I] (always used with an adverb or preposition) to search for sth by moving things or turning things over: *I rummaged through the contents of the box until I found the book I wanted.*
▸ **rummage** *noun* [sing.]: *Have a rummage around in the drawer and see if you can find a pen.*

scrabble [I] (always used with an adverb or preposition) (*especially BrE*) to try to find or to do sth in a hurry or with difficulty, often by moving your hands or feet about quickly, without much control: *He was scrabbling for a foothold on the steep slope.*

fish [I] (always used with an adverb or preposition) to search for sth, using your hands: *She fished around in her bag for her keys.* ❶ You usually *fish around/about (for sth)* in a pocket, box, bag, etc.

feel [I] (always used with an adverb or preposition) to search for sth with your hands, feet, or other parts of the body: *He felt in his pockets for some money.*

> **NOTE** **GROPE** OR **FEEL**? You can **feel** or **grope** around in the dark. When you **feel** around, you are likely to do it in an easier, more controlled way than if you **grope** around.

poke aˈround/aˈbout *phrasal verb* (*informal*) to look for sth, especially sth that is hidden among other things that you have to move: *The police spent the day poking around in his office but found nothing.* ◊ (*figurative*) *We've had journalists poking around and asking a lot of questions.*

fun *noun*

fun · pleasure · good time · enjoyment · great time · blast
These are all words for the feeling of enjoying yourself, or activities or time that you enjoy.

fun [U] (*rather informal, especially spoken*) the feeling of enjoying yourself; activities that you enjoy: *We had a lot of fun at Sarah's party.* ◊ (*especially BrE*) *Sailing is good fun.* ◊ *I decided to learn Spanish just for fun.* ◊ *I didn't do all that work just **for the fun of it**.* ◊ *It's not much fun going to a party on your own.* ◊ (*spoken*) ***Have fun!*** (= Enjoy yourself!) See **have fun** → PLAY *verb* 1

pleasure [U] (*rather formal*) the feeling of enjoying yourself or being satisfied: *Reading for pleasure and reading for study are not the same.* ◊ *He **takes no pleasure** in his work.* ◊ (*formal, spoken*) *It gives me great pleasure to introduce our guest speaker.* ◊ (*formal, written*) *We request the pleasure of your company at the marriage of our daughter Lisa.* **OPP** **displeasure** → FRUSTRATION, **pain** → DISTRESS

good ˈtime [C] (*rather informal*) a time that you spend enjoying yourself: *Did you have a good time in Spain?* ◊ *Mike and I shared some really good times.*

enjoyment [U] (*rather formal*) the feeling of enjoying yourself: *I get a lot of enjoyment from gardening.* See also **enjoy** → ENJOY, **enjoy yourself** → PLAY *verb* 1

> **NOTE** **PLEASURE** OR **ENJOYMENT**? **Enjoyment** usually comes from an activity that you do; **pleasure** can come from sth that you do or sth that happens.: *He beamed with pleasure at seeing her.* ◊ *He beamed with enjoyment at seeing her.*

great ˈtime [C] (*rather informal*) a time that you spend enjoying yourself very much: *We had a really great time together.*

blast [sing.] (*AmE, informal, spoken*) a very enjoyable experience that is a lot of fun: *The party was a blast.* ◊ *We had a blast at the party.*

function *noun*

function · use · purpose
These are all words for a special activity of sb/sth, or the way or reason sth is used.

function [C, U] a special activity of a person or thing: *The committee* **performs** *a useful* **function** *despite not having executive powers.* ◇ *The function of the heart is to pump blood through the body.* ◇ *bodily functions* (= for example eating, sex, using the toilet) ◇ *This design aims for harmony of form and function.*

use [C, U] a reason for which sth is used; a way in which sth is or can be used: *I'm sure you'll think of a* **use for** *it.* ◇ *This chemical has a wide range of industrial uses.* ◇ *Don't throw that box away – I'm sure I could* **put it to some use.** See also **use → USE** *noun*

purpose [C] the reason why sth is done or made; what is needed in a situation for a particular reason: *The experiments* **serve no useful purpose.** ◇ *The building is used for religious purposes.* ❶ For...purposes is used when you are talking about what is needed in a particular situation: *These gifts count as income for tax purposes.* ◇ **For the purposes of** *this study, the three groups have been combined.*

fund *noun*

fund · budget · account · savings · reserve · pocket · purse · stash
These are all words for money that has been saved or is available for a particular purpose.

PATTERNS AND COLLOCATIONS
▸ to pay sth **from / out of** a fund / a budget / an account / your savings / your reserves / your own pocket / the purse
▸ to have sth **in** a fund / a budget / an account
▸ (a) **small** fund / budget / reserves / stash
▸ (a) **large** fund / budget / reserves
▸ sb's **private** fund / budget / account / savings / purse
▸ sb's **family** fund / budget / savings / purse
▸ sb's **personal** budget / account / savings / stash
▸ a / the **public** fund / budget / purse
▸ to **have** a fund / a budget / an account / savings / reserves / a stash
▸ to **dip into** a fund / a budget / your savings / your reserves / your pocket / your purse
▸ to **build up** a fund / savings / reserves
▸ to **spend** a fund / a budget / your savings / your reserves
▸ to **manage** a fund / a budget / an account / your savings / your reserves

fund [C] money that has been saved or has been made available for a particular purpose: *She made a donation to the local cancer relief fund.* ◇ *He's been paying into the firm's pension fund for thirty years.* See also **funds → MONEY 1**

budget [C, U] the money that is available to an organization, government or person and a plan of how it will be spent over a period of time; an official government statement of this: *The government is planning to double the education budget.* ◇ *It's one of those big-budget Hollywood movies.* ◇ *We decorated the house* **on a tight budget** (= without much money to spend). ◇ *Every year the school has a struggle to* **balance its budget** (= not spend more than it has). ◇ *The work was finished on time and* **within budget** (= did not cost more money than was planned). ◇ *The company must not go* **over budget** (= spend too much money). See also **budget → SAVE** *verb* 2, **budgetary → ECONOMIC**

account [C] an arrangement with a bank to keep your money there and to allow you to take it out when you need to: *I don't have a* **bank account.** ◇ *to open/close an account* ◇ *(BrE) I paid the cheque into my current account.* ◇ *(AmE) She deposited the check in her account.*

savings [pl.] money that you have saved, especially in a bank, etc: *Your savings will grow if you invest them wisely.* ◇ *He put all his savings into buying a boat.* See also **save → SAVE** *verb* 2, **save → SAVE** *verb* 3

reserve [C, usually pl.] *(finance)* money that is available to be used when it is needed: *The company has substantial reserves of capital to fall back on if necessary.*

pocket [C] *(rather informal)* the money that is available to a person to spend: *We have a range of gifts to suit every pocket.* ◇ *He had no intention of paying for the meal* **out of his own pocket.** ◇ *(especially BrE) That one mistake left him thousands of pounds* **out of pocket** (= having lost thousands of pounds). See also **pocket → MAKE** *verb* 3

purse [sing.] *(rather formal)* the money that is available to a person, organization or government to spend: *Should spending on the arts be met out of the public purse* (= from government money)?

NOTE **POCKET** OR **PURSE?** **Pocket** is more informal than **purse**; it is used more to talk about a person's own money; **purse** is used more to talk about public money.

stash [C, usually sing.] *(informal)* an amount of sth that is kept secretly: *Luckily the thieves never found my small stash of ten pound notes.* See also **stash → KEEP** *verb* 1

fund *verb*

fund · support · finance · sponsor · guarantee · subsidize · underwrite · endow · bankroll
These words all mean to provide money for sb/sth in order to help them function or be successful.

PATTERNS AND COLLOCATIONS
▸ to fund / support / finance / sponsor / subsidize / underwrite / bankroll a **project / programme**
▸ to fund / support / finance / sponsor / underwrite / bankroll a **campaign**
▸ to fund / support / finance / sponsor / subsidize **research**
▸ sth is **fully / properly** funded / financed / guaranteed / underwritten
▸ sth is **generously** funded / supported / sponsored / endowed
▸ sth is **poorly** funded / supported / financed / endowed
▸ sth is **privately** funded / financed / sponsored / endowed
▸ sth is **publicly** funded / financed / sponsored / subsidized

fund [T] to provide money for sth, often sth official that continues over a long period: *There is an annual dance festival funded by the Arts Council.* ◇ *She used the stolen money to fund her extravagant lifestyle.* See also **funding → INVESTMENT, funds → MONEY 1**

support [T] to provide money for sth in order to help it to be successful: *Several major companies are supporting this project.*
▸ **support** *noun* [U]: *Local businesses have provided financial support.*

finance [T] to provide money for sth: *The building project will be financed by the government and by public donations.* ◇ *He took a job to finance his stay in Germany.* See also **finance → MONEY 1**

NOTE **FUND** OR **FINANCE?** These two words are very similar, but **fund** is used more than **finance** for programmes or projects that continue or are repeated year after year.

sponsor /ˈspɒnsə(r); AmE ˈspɑːn-/ [T] (of a company, etc.) to pay the costs of a particular event or programme as a way of advertising; to support sb by paying for their training or education: *Many sports events on TV used to be sponsored by the tobacco industry.* ◇ *She found a company to sponsor her through college.* See also **sponsor → SPONSOR** *noun*, **sponsorship → INVESTMENT**

guarantee /ˌgærənˈtiː/ [T] *(finance)* to agree to be legally responsible for repaying an amount of money if the person who owes it fails to repay it: *His father agreed to guarantee the bank loan.*

subsidize (BrE also **-ise**) [T] to give part of the money that a person or organization needs in order to reduce their costs or prices: *The housing projects are subsidized by the government.* ◇ *She's not prepared to subsidize his gambling any longer.* See also **subsidy → INVESTMENT**

underwrite /ˌʌndəˈraɪt; AmE -dərˈr-/ [T] *(finance)* to accept financial responsibility for a project or event so that you will pay for special costs or for losses it may make: *The British government ended up underwriting the entire project.* ◇ *The record company may underwrite the costs of a band's first tour.*

endow /ɪnˈdaʊ/ [T] to give a large amount of money to a school, college or other institution to provide it with an income, often to be used for a particular purpose: *In her will, she endowed a scholarship in the physics department.* See also **endowment** → INVESTMENT

bankroll /ˈbæŋkrəʊl; *AmE* -roʊl/ [T] (*especially AmE, rather informal*) to support sb/sth financially: *They claimed his campaign had been bankrolled with drug money.*

fundamental *adj.*

fundamental · underlying · radical · basic · essential · elementary · ultimate · rudimentary
These words all describe things such as problems and ideas that concern the most basic and important parts of sth.

PATTERNS AND COLLOCATIONS
▸ fundamental / basic **to** sth
▸ a fundamental / an underlying / a radical / a basic / an essential **difference / distinction**
▸ a fundamental / an underlying / a radical / a basic **change / improvement**
▸ a fundamental / radical / basic **approach**
▸ a fundamental / an underlying / a basic / an essential / an elementary **rule / principle**
▸ a fundamental / an underlying / a basic / an essential / the ultimate **truth**
▸ a fundamental / an underlying / a basic / an essential / the ultimate **cause / reason**
▸ a fundamental / an underlying / a basic / an essential **assumption / aim / problem / cause / reason / need / weakness**
▸ a fundamental / a basic / an elementary / a rudimentary **skill / understanding / knowledge / level**
▸ a fundamental / a basic / an elementary **error / mistake**

fundamental /ˌfʌndəˈmentl/ (*rather formal, especially written*) serious and very important; concerning the most central and important parts of sth; forming the necessary basis of sth: *There is a fundamental difference between the two points of view.* ◇ *A fundamental change in the organization of health services was required.* ◇ *Hard work is fundamental to success.* See also **fundamentals** → BASICS
▸ **fundamentally** *adv.*: *The two approaches are fundamentally different.* ◇ *By the 1960s the situation had changed fundamentally.*

underlying /ˌʌndəˈlaɪɪŋ; *AmE* -dərˈl-/ [only before noun] (*rather formal, especially written*) important in a situation but not always easily noticed or stated clearly: *The underlying assumption is that the amount of money available is limited.* ◇ *Unemployment may be an underlying cause of the rising crime rate.* ❶ Typical collocates of **underlying** include *cause, assumption, reason, motive, trend, theme, problem, reality* and *aim*.

radical [usually before noun] (*rather formal, especially written*) (of changes or differences) concerning the most central and important parts of sth; thorough and complete: *There have been demands for radical reform of the law.* ◇ *This document marks a radical departure from earlier recommendations.* See also **radical** → RADICAL *adj.*
▸ **radically** *adv.*: *The new methods are radically different from the old.* ◇ *Attitudes have changed radically.*

NOTE FUNDAMENTAL OR RADICAL? A **fundamental** change or difference is one that involves the whole structure of a system or the principles on which sth is based. A **radical** change is an important change which has wide-ranging effects.

basic concerning the most central and important parts of sth from which other things develop: *They haven't even given us the most basic information we need.* ◇ *During the first term, we will concentrate on the basic principles of law.* ◇ *Drums are basic to African music.* ❶ **Basic** can also be used before a noun to mean 'necessary and important to

all people': *Aren't food and shelter basic human rights?* ◇ *The report sets out the cost of basic foods in several European countries.* See also **basics** → BASICS
▸ **basically** *adv.*: *Yes, that's basically correct.* ◇ *There have been some problems but basically it's a good system.*

essential [only before noun] connected with the most important aspect or basic nature of sb/sth: *The essential difference between Sara and me is our attitude to money.* ◇ *The essential character of the town has been destroyed by the new road.* See also **essence** → NATURE 1, **essentials** → BASICS
▸ **essentially** *adv.*: *There are three essentially different ways of tackling the problem.* ◇ *The pattern is essentially the same in all cases.*

NOTE BASIC OR ESSENTIAL? **Basic** looks at things from a practical point of view, concentrating on what is important in order to do or understand sth. **Essential** looks at things from a more philosophical point of view, considering the very nature of things and what makes them different from or similar to other things.

elementary /ˌelɪˈmentri/ (*rather formal*) concerning the most central and important matters or ideas: *How could you make such an elementary mistake?* ◇ *It's an elementary law of economics: the scarcer the commodity, the higher the price.* ❶ When it is used to talk about education or learning, **elementary** usually describes a *level* or a stage in learning a subject: *I'm taking classes in elementary Italian.*

ultimate [only before noun] from which sth originally comes: *the ultimate truths of philosophy and science* ◇ *We could not trace the ultimate source of the rumours.*
▸ **ultimately** *adv.*: *All life depends ultimately on oxygen.*

rudimentary /ˌruːdɪˈmentri/ (*formal*) concerning only the most basic matters or ideas: *His understanding of the language is very rudimentary.* ◇ *They were given only rudimentary training in the job.* ❶ **Rudimentary** most often describes *knowledge, understanding, skill* or *training.*

funny *adj.*

funny · amusing · entertaining · witty · humorous · comic · hilarious · light-hearted
These words all describe sb/sth that makes you laugh or smile.

humorous	funny	hilarious
light-hearted	amusing	
	entertaining	
	witty	
	comic	

PATTERNS AND COLLOCATIONS
▸ a funny / an amusing / an entertaining / a witty / a humorous / a comic / a light-hearted **story**
▸ a funny / an amusing / an entertaining / a witty / a humorous / a light-hearted **speech**
▸ a funny / an entertaining / a witty / a humorous / a comic **writer**
▸ a funny / an entertaining / a witty / a humorous **speaker**
▸ a funny / an amusing / a witty **guy / man / woman**
▸ a funny / an amusing / a humorous / a hilarious **incident**
▸ a funny / an amusing / a hilarious **joke**
▸ to **find** sth funny / amusing / entertaining / witty / humorous / hilarious

funny that makes you laugh: *That's the funniest thing I've ever heard.* ◇ *It's not funny! Someone could have been hurt.* ◇ *I was really embarrassed, but then I saw the funny side of it.* ◇ *'What's so funny?' she demanded.*

amusing funny and enjoyable: *This can be a very amusing game to play.* ◇ *He writes very amusing letters.*
▸ **amuse** *verb* [T]: *My funny drawings amused the kids.* ◇ *This will amuse you.* See also **amuse** → ENTERTAIN
▸ **amusement** *noun* [U]: *She could not hide her amuse-*

ment at the way he was dancing. ◇ *Much* **to their** **amusement** *I couldn't get the door open.*

entertaining (*rather formal*) amusing and interesting: *It was a very entertaining evening.* ◇ *She found him a charming and entertaining companion.* See also **entertain** → ENTERTAIN

witty clever and amusing; able to say or write clever and amusing things: *Somebody made a witty remark about needing a forklift truck.* ◇ *He was much in demand as a witty public speaker.* See also **wit** → HUMOUR

humorous funny and entertaining; showing a sense of humour: *It's a humorous look at the world of fashion.* ◇ *She had not intended to be humorous.* See also **humour** → HUMOUR

comic /'kɒmɪk; *AmE* 'kɑːmɪk/ that makes you laugh: *Many of the scenes in the book are richly comic.* ◇ *She can always be relied on to provide* **comic relief** (= sth to make you relax and laugh) *at a boring party.* ❶ **Comic** also means 'connected with comedy' (= entertainment that is funny and makes people laugh); in this meaning it is only used before a noun: *a comic opera* ◇ *a very fine comic actor.* See also **comedy** → HUMOUR

NOTE FUNNY, AMUSING, HUMOROUS OR COMIC? **Amusing** is the most general of these words because it includes the idea of being enjoyable as well as making people laugh and can be used to describe events, activities and occasions: *an amusing party/game/evening* ◇ *a funny/ humorous/comic party/game/evening.* **Humorous** is not quite as strong as **funny** or **comic** and is more about showing that you see the humour in a situation, than actually making people laugh out loud. **Comic** is used especially to talk about writing and drama or things that are funny in a deliberate and theatrical way. It is not used to describe people (except for *comic writers*). **Funny** can describe people, jokes and stories, things that happen, or anything that makes people laugh.

hilarious /hɪ'leəriəs/ extremely funny: *Lynn found the whole situation absolutely hilarious.* ◇ *Do you know Pete? He's hilarious.*

ˌlight-ˈhearted intended to be amusing or easily enjoyable rather than too serious: *She gave a light-hearted speech that was just right for the occasion.* **OPP** **serious** → SERIOUS 2

furious *adj.* See also the entry for ANGRY

furious · outraged · enraged · incensed · fuming · seething
These words all mean very or extremely angry.

PATTERNS AND COLLOCATIONS
▶ furious/ outraged/ incensed/ fuming/ seething **about/ at/ over** sth
▶ furious/ outraged/ incensed **that…**
▶ a furious/ an outraged **expression**
▶ **absolutely** furious/ outraged/ incensed/ fuming

furious /'fjʊəriəs; *AmE* 'fjʊr-/ extremely angry: *I was furious at the way we'd been treated.* ◇ *She was* **furious with** *me when she found out.* ◇ *He was* **furious with** **himself** *for letting things get so out of control.* See also **fury** → ANGER *noun*
▶ **furiously** *adv.*: *furiously angry* ◇ *He banged the door furiously.*

outraged /'aʊtreɪdʒd/ very shocked and angry, especially about sth that you think is unfair or morally wrong: *I was outraged when I heard of the decision.* ◇ *a group of outraged customers/residents/passengers* ◇ *She wrote an outraged letter to the newspaper.* See also **outrage** → ANGER *noun*, **outrage** → ANGER *verb*, **outrageous** → OUTRAGEOUS

enraged (*written*) extremely angry, especially when this makes you lose control or be violent: *She was enraged at his stupidity.* ◇ *an enraged mob* See also **rage** → ANGER *noun*, **enrage** → ANGER *verb*

incensed /ɪn'senst/ extremely angry, especially because you think you have been treated or judged unfairly: *Workers were incensed by the decision to lengthen working hours.* See also **incense** → ANGER *verb*

NOTE OUTRAGED OR INCENSED? In many cases you can use either word; however, **outraged** suggests a stronger feeling that sth is morally wrong; **incensed** suggests a stronger feeling that you have personally been badly treated.

fuming [not before noun] extremely angry, especially when you have no effective way of expressing your anger or doing anything about the cause of your anger: *She sat in the car, silently fuming at the traffic jam.*

seething [not before noun] extremely angry but trying not to show other people how angry you are: *Inwardly seething, she did as she was told.*

fuss *noun*

fuss · storm · outcry · furore · uproar · scene
These are all words for a situation in which people express strong feelings about sth, especially in public.

PATTERNS AND COLLOCATIONS
▶ a fuss/ an outcry/ a furore/ an uproar **about** sth
▶ a fuss/ a storm/ an outcry/ a furore/ an uproar **over** sth
▶ **amid** a/ the fuss/ storm/ furore/ uproar
▶ a **great** fuss/ outcry/ uproar/ scene
▶ a **public** fuss/ outcry/ furore/ uproar
▶ a **political** storm/ outcry/ furore/ uproar
▶ to **cause** a fuss/ a storm/ an outcry/ a furore/ an uproar/ a scene
▶ to **create** a fuss/ a storm/ a furore/ an uproar/ a scene
▶ to **make** a fuss/ scene
▶ to **provoke** a storm/ an outcry/ an uproar

fuss /fʌs/ [U, sing.] unnecessary excitement, worry or activity; anger or complaints about sth, especially sth that is not important: *He does what he's told without any fuss.* ◇ *It's a very ordinary movie – I don't know* **what all the fuss** **is about** (= why other people think it is so good). ◇ *It was all* **a fuss about nothing.** ◇ *Steve* **kicks up a fuss** *every time I even suggest seeing you.*

storm [C] (*rather informal, especially journalism*) a situation in which people suddenly express strong feelings about sth, especially public anger or criticism in reaction to sth: *His comments created a* **storm** *of protest in the media.* ◇ *The government is determined to* **ride out the** *political* **storm** *sparked by its new immigration policy.*

outcry /'aʊtkraɪ/ [C, U] a reaction of anger or strong protest shown by people in public: *There was a massive public* **outcry against** *the harsh prison sentence.* ◇ *There was* **outcry at** *the judge's statement.*

furore /fjuˈrɔːri; 'fjʊərɔːri/ *AmE* 'fjʊr-/ (*BrE*) (also **furor** /'fjʊərɔːr/; *AmE* 'fjʊr-/ especially in *AmE*) [sing.] great anger or excitement expressed by people, especially in reaction to a public event: *His resignation passed almost unnoticed amid the furore of the elections.*

uproar /'ʌprɔːr(r)/ [sing., U] a situation in which people suddenly express strong feelings about sth, especially angry argument or criticism in reaction to sth: (*BrE*) *There was a great uproar over plans to pull down the old library.* ◇ *Financial markets were* **in uproar** *after the crash of the rouble.* ❶ In American English say *in an uproar.*

NOTE STORM, OUTCRY OR UPROAR? These are all words for a public expression of anger, criticism or protest by a large number of people. **Storm** and **uproar** both suggest a noisy, confused situation with a lot of people complaining or protesting at once. **Storm** is used especially in journalism to talk about politics. **Outcry** can suggest a more united protest from a particular group of people who are angry at a particular bad or unfair thing.

scene [C, usually sing.] a loud, angry argument, especially one that happens in public and which is embarrassing because it draws people's attention: *There have been a couple of ugly scenes between him and the manager.* ◇ *She had made a scene in the middle of the party.*

future noun

---

future · fate · destiny · fortune · lot · doom
These are all words for the things that happen or will happen to a person, family, country, etc. and cannot be avoided.

PATTERNS AND COLLOCATIONS
▸ a **grim** future/ fate/ destiny/ lot
▸ a/ sb's **tragic** fate/ destiny/ lot/ doom
▸ sb's **certain/ inevitable/ ultimate** fate/ destiny/ doom
▸ to **meet** your fate/ destiny/ doom
▸ to **accept** your fate/ destiny/ lot
▸ to **avoid/ escape** your fate/ destiny

future [C, U] what will happen to sb/sth at a later time; the possibility of being successful at a later time: *His future is uncertain.* ◇ *This deal could safeguard the futures of 2 000 employees.* ◇ *She has a great future ahead of her.* ◇ *I can't see any future in this relationship.*

fate [C, usually sing.] the things, especially unpleasant things, that will happen or have happened to sb/sth: *The fate of the ship's captain is unknown.* ◇ *He had no idea what fate was in store for him.* ◇ *Each of the managers suffered the same fate.* ◇ *The government had abandoned the refugees to their fate.* ◇ *From the moment the hijackers took over the plane, their fate was sealed (= their future was certain).*

▸ **fated** *adj.* [not usually before noun]: *We were fated never to meet again.*

destiny /'destəni/ [C, usually sing.] the things that will happen to sb/sth, especially an important thing that cannot be avoided: *The destinies of five nations were decided at the peace conference.* ◇ *She set up her own business because she wanted to be in control of her own destiny.* ◇ *He was convinced that sooner or later he would fulfil his destiny.*

▸ **destined** *adj.* [not before noun]: *He was destined for a military career, like his father before him.* ◇ *We seemed destined never to meet.*

fortune [C, usually pl., U] the good and bad things that happen to sb/sth; what will happen to a person in the future: *The share price tends to follow the changing fortunes of the film industry.* ◇ *Her family business suffered a reversal of fortune when public taste changed.* ◇ *The fortune teller said she could tell my fortune by looking at the lines on my hand.*

lot [sing.] (*especially BrE*) a person's luck or situation in life: *She was feeling very dissatisfied with her lot.* ◇ (*formal*) *It fell to her lot (= became her responsibility) to organize the Christmas party.* ◇ *He threw in his lot with the pirates (= decided to join them and share their successes and problems).*

doom [U] (*literary*) death or destruction; any terrible event that you cannot avoid: *The ordinary soldiers went to meet their doom with great bravery.* ◇ *She had a sense of impending doom (= felt that sth very bad was going to happen soon).* ◇ *Fuel shortages spelt doom (= meant the end) for such huge gas-guzzling cars.*

▸ **doomed** *adj.* [not before noun]: *The plan was doomed to failure.* ◇ *The marriage was doomed from the start.*

G g

gain *verb*

1 gain entry/your independence
2 gain confidence/weight

---

1 See also GET 1

gain · win · secure · earn · land · procure · net
These words all mean to obtain sth through skill, good qualities or effort.

▸ to gain / win / secure / earn / procure sth **by** (doing) sth
▸ to gain / win / secure / earn / procure sth **for** sb
▸ to gain / win / secure / earn **support / approval**
▸ to gain / win / earn **respect / admiration**
▸ to gain / earn a **reputation**
▸ to win / secure / land a **contract**
▸ to gain / win / secure **access / entry**
▸ to gain / win / secure / earn / land **yourself** sth

gain [T] (*rather formal*) to obtain sth, especially sth that you need or want: *The country gained its independence ten years ago.* ◇ *The party gained over 50% of the vote.* ◇ *Her unusual talent gained her worldwide recognition.* ❶ **Gain** is used especially to talk about obtaining freedom (*access, entry, independence*), recognition by others (*recognition, reputation*) and knowledge (*insight, experience, knowledge, understanding*).

win [T] to achieve or get sth that you want, especially through hard work or ability or because of the good qualities you have: *She won the admiration of many people in her battle against cancer.* ◇ *He won a scholarship to study at Stanford.* ❶ In this meaning **win** is used especially to talk about getting people's *admiration, support* and *respect*, as well as agreements to provide money (a *scholarship*) or work (a *contract*).

secure [T] (*formal*) to obtain or achieve sth, especially through hard work or ability: *He's just secured a $5 million contract.* ◇ *She secured 2 000 votes.* ◇ *He secured himself a place at law school.* ❶ **Secure** is often used in legal, financial or other business contexts.

earn [T] to get sth that you deserve, usually because of sth good you have done or the good qualities you have: *He earned a reputation as an expert on tax law.* ◇ *Her outstanding ability earned her a place on the team.*

land [T] to succeed in getting a job or other opportunity, especially one that a lot of other people want: *He's just landed a starring role in Spielberg's next movie.* ◇ *She's just landed herself a company directorship.*

procure /prə'kjʊə(r); *AmE* -'kjʊr/ [T] (*formal*) to obtain sth, especially with difficulty: *She managed to procure a ticket for the concert.* ◇ *They procured us a copy of the report.*

net (-tt-) [T] (*written, especially journalism*) to catch sb or obtain sth in a skilful way: *A swoop by customs officers netted a large quantity of drugs.* ❶ People might also **net** such things as *business*, a *contract* or *clients*.

---

2 **gain · increase in sth · put sth on**
These words all mean to gradually get more of sth.

▸ to gain / increase in / put on **weight**
▸ to gain / increase in **strength**

gain [T] to gradually get more of sth: *She has gained confidence since the World Championships.* ◇ *His ideas gradually gained acceptance.* ◇ *I've gained weight recently.* See also **gain** → INCREASE *noun*

increase in sth *phrasal verb* to become greater in amount, number, value or strength: *Oil has increased in price.* ◇ *As the storm increased in strength huge waves crashed over the decks.* See also **increase** → INCREASE *noun*

put sth 'on *phrasal verb* to become heavier, especially by the amount mentioned: *She looks like she's put on weight.* ◇ *He must have put on several pounds.*

---

game *noun*

1 a game of football/chess/cards.
2 ball/party games

---

1 See the Topic Map for SPORT AND LEISURE on p.892

game · match · final · test · tie · fixture · play-off · fight · round · replay · bout
These are all words for sports events where people or teams compete against each other.

▸ a game / match / final / test / tie / fixture / play-off / fight / replay / bout **against / between / with** sb
▸ an **exciting** game / match / final / tie / fight
▸ a **tough** game / match / tie / fixture / fight / bout
▸ a **big** game / match
▸ a **home** game / match / test / tie / fixture
▸ an **away** game / match / tie / fixture
▸ a / an **international / friendly** game / match / fixture
▸ a **football** game / match / final / fixture
▸ a **tennis** game / match / final
▸ a **rugby** game / match / test
▸ a **cricket** match / test
▸ to **win / lose** a game / match / final / test / tie / play-off / fight / replay / bout
▸ to **play** a game / a match / in a final / a test / a tie / a fixture / a round
▸ to **go to / see / watch** a game / match / final / test / tie / play-off / fight / replay

game [C] a sports event or other activity in which people or teams compete against each other: *a game of chess* ◇ *Will he be available for Saturday's game against the Bears?*

match [C] (*especially BrE*) a sports event in which people or teams compete against each other: *They're playing an important match against Chelsea on Saturday.* ◇ *I'll probably watch the match on TV.*

NOTE **GAME OR MATCH?** **Game** has a wider range of uses than **match**: it is used to talk about team sports, or activities in which individuals play against each other: *a game of football/chess/cards* However, it is not used so often in this meaning to talk about individual sports such as tennis: *a* **game** in tennis has a more particular meaning, as one part of a *tennis match*. In British English **match** is used to talk about individual or team sports but NOT other activities: *a chess/cards match*. In American English **match** is used for individual sports, but **game** is preferred for team sports: (*BrE*) *a football match* ◇ (*BrE, AmE*) *a football game*. You can say *a game of football* or *a football game/match* but NOT: *a match of football*. *Chess game* is less frequent than *a game of chess*; in British English *a card game* is a type of card game, such as bridge or poker, not an occasion when people play cards, but in American English it can be either.

final [C] the last in a series of games or competitions in which the winner is decided: *She reached the final of the 100m hurdles.* ◇ *The players met in last year's final.* ◇ *The country will stage next year's World Cup finals* (= the last few games in the competition).

test (also **Test**) (also **'test match**) [C] (*BrE*) (in cricket or rugby) a match played between the teams of two different countries, usually as part of a series of matches on a tour: *They played well in the first test against South Africa.*

tie [C] (*BrE*) (in sport, especially football) a match that is part of a larger competition: *It was the first leg of the Cup tie between Leeds and Roma.* See also **tie** → DRAW *noun*

fixture /ˈfɪkstʃə(r)/ [C] (*BrE*) a sports event that has been arranged to take place on a particular date and at a particular place: *There are plans to make the race an annual fixture.* ◇ *It will be difficult to fit the match into an already crowded fixture list* (= list of planned matches to be played).

'play-off (*BrE*) (*AmE* **playoff**) [C] (in sport) a match or series of matches between two teams or players with equal points or positions to decide the winner: *Britain now face a play-off for the bronze medal against South Korea.* ❶ In many US sports **the playoffs** are the part of the season, after the regular sports season is over, when the best teams play each other for the title: *It looks like the Red Sox and the Yankees will meet in the playoffs again this year.*

fight [C] a match between two people in a sport in which people fight with their hands or bodies, such as boxing or wrestling: *He is unbeaten in 34 fights.* ◇ *He has lined up a world title fight against Lewis.*

round [C] a complete game of golf; a complete way around a course in some other sports, such as showjumping (= riding a horse and jumping over a set of fences): *We played a round of golf.* ◇ *It was the first horse to jump a clear round.*

replay /ˈriːpleɪ/ [C] (*BrE*) a match that is played again because neither side won in the previous match: *They scored a late goal to force a replay.*

bout /baʊt/ [C] a match between two people in a fighting sport such as boxing or wrestling: *It was hailed as one of the best heavyweight bouts of recent times.*

2 See the Topic Map for SPORT AND LEISURE on p.892
game · sport
These are both words for an activity with rules in which people or teams compete against each other.

▸ to **play / take part in** a game / sport
▸ **team** games / sports

game [C] an activity or sport with rules in which people or teams compete against each other: *ball / card / board / computer / video games* ◇ *competitive games in which there is always a winner and a loser* ◇ *children's party games like Musical Chairs* ◇ *This is a good game for getting people to mix.* ◇ *Chess is a game of skill.* ❶ **Games** [pl.] is used for a large organized sports event: *the Olympic Games* See also **game** → INTEREST *noun* 2

sport [C] an activity that you do for pleasure or to keep fit and that needs physical effort or skill, usually done in a special playing area and according to fixed rules: *skiing, skating and other winter sports* ◇ *Which is the country's most popular spectator sport* (= which sport do the most people watch)? ◇ *I need to take up a sport to get fit.* ◇ (*AmE*) *Did you play any sports in high school?* ❶ In British English use *do* and the uncountable **sport**: (*BrE*) *Did you do any sport at school?* See also **sport** → SPORT

gap *noun*

gap · margin · gulf
These are all words for the difference between people or groups in the way they think or live or in how successful they are in a contest.

margin   gap   gulf

PATTERNS AND COLLOCATIONS
▸ the gap / margin / gulf **between** A and B
▸ to **bridge** the gap / gulf between A and B
▸ a gap / gulf **separates** A and B

gap [C] a difference between people or groups in the way that they think, live or feel; a difference between two sets of ideas or actions or between ideas and reality: *The gap between rich and poor gets wider every year.* ◇ *the gap between theory and practice* ◇ *a movie that is sure to bridge the generation gap* (= the difference in attitude or behaviour between younger and older people that causes a lack of understanding)

margin /ˈmɑːdʒɪn; *AmE* ˈmɑːrdʒən/ [C, usually sing.] the amount of time, or number of votes or points, by which sb wins sth: *He won by a narrow margin.* ◇ *She beat the other runners by a margin of ten seconds.*

gulf [C, usually sing.] a large gap between people or groups in the way that they think, live or feel: *There appeared to be a growing gulf between the prosperous south and the declining towns of the north.* ◇ *It felt as if a gulf had opened up between his life and mine.*

garden *noun*

1 a back garden
2 a rose garden

1 garden · yard · grounds · backyard · park · parkland
These are all words for a piece of land that belongs to a house.

PATTERNS AND COLLOCATIONS
▸ **in** the garden / the yard / the grounds / the backyard / the park / parkland
▸ (a) **beautiful / landscaped** garden / yard / grounds / backyard / park / parkland
▸ (an) **extensive** garden / grounds / park / parkland
▸ the **front / back** garden / yard

garden [C] (*BrE*) a piece of land next to or around a house, usually with a lawn (= an area of grass) and often with trees, bushes and flower beds: *They sat in the garden and enjoyed the sunshine.* ◇ *Ease of cultivation makes it one of the best garden plants.* See also **gardens** → PARK

yard [C] (*AmE*) a garden: *I had to cut the grass in the yard.* ◇ *They have a gorgeous old oak tree in their front yard.* ❶ In British English a **yard** is an area outside a building with a hard surface and no grass. See also **yard** → COURTYARD

grounds [pl.] the land or gardens around a large building that belong to it: *They scrambled over the wall and into the embassy grounds.* ◇ *Concerts are often held in the grounds of the castle.*

backyard (also **back yard**) [C] (*AmE*) a garden behind a house: *The kids were out playing in the backyard.* ❶ In British English, a **backyard** is an area with a hard surface (and no grass) behind a house, often surrounded by a wall: (*BrE*) *They lived in a little terraced house with a backyard behind it and a tiny garden in front.*

park [C] (*BrE*) an enclosed area of land, usually with fields and trees, attached to a large country house: *The cottage is set within the park of a country house.* See also **park** → PARK

parkland [U] (*BrE*) open land with grass and trees, for example around a large house in the country: *The house stands in 500 acres of rolling parkland.*

2 garden · bed · allotment · border · patch · kitchen garden
These are all words for a small piece of land where you can grow things such as flowers, fruit and vegetables.

PATTERNS AND COLLOCATIONS
▸ **in** a garden / a bed / an allotment / a border / a patch / a kitchen garden

▶ a **flower** / **rose** garden / bed
▶ a **vegetable** garden / patch

garden [C] (*especially AmE*) a part of the piece of land next to or around your house where you can grow things such as flowers, fruit and vegetables: *They planted a garden of woodland plants that were native to the area.* ❶ This is the usual meaning of **garden** in American English; in British English, **garden** is only used in this meaning in compounds: (*BrE, AmE*) *a flower/rose/vegetable garden*

bed [C] an area of ground in a garden or park for growing plants, especially flowers: *Raised flower beds are ideal for people in wheelchairs.*

allotment /ə'lɒtmənt; AmE ə'lɑːt-/ [C] (*especially BrE*) a small area of land in a town which a person can rent in order to grow vegetables or other plants on it: *She grew beautiful flowers on her allotment.*

border [C] a strip of soil along the edge of an area of grass in a garden, which is planted with flowers or other plants: *The back garden is mostly lawn with herbaceous borders.*

patch [C] (in compounds) a small piece of land, especially one used for growing vegetables or fruit that grows on or near the ground: *We had a strawberry patch beside the greenhouse.* See also **plot** → LAND *noun* 2

kitchen 'garden [C] a part of a garden where you grow vegetables and fruit for your own use: *Herbs and seasonal vegetables are picked fresh from our own kitchen garden.*

general *adj.*

1 a general problem
2 in general terms

---

1 See also the entry for WIDE 1
general · common · widespread · universal · prevalent · commonplace · ubiquitous · rife
These words all describe things that are often or almost always found, done, thought or felt.

PATTERNS AND COLLOCATIONS
▶ the **disease** is common / widespread / prevalent / rife
▶ **violence** is common / widespread / commonplace / rife
▶ in general / common / widespread / universal **use**
▶ the general / common / widespread / universal / prevalent **view**
▶ a general / common / widespread / universal / prevalent **problem**
▶ a general / common / widespread / universal **feeling**
▶ general / widespread / universal **acclaim**

general affecting all or most people, places or things: *The general opinion is that a new bridge is needed.* ◇ *As a foreigner and a teacher, I was the object of general interest.* ◇ *The unions threatened a further general strike* (= one that affects all workers in an industry or country). ◇ *The bad weather has been fairly general* (= has affected most areas). See also **general** → USUAL
▶ **generally** *adv.*: *The software will be generally available from January.*

common happening often; existing in large numbers or in many places: *Jones and Davies are common Welsh names.* ◇ *The fungus is a common sight in woodlands at this time of year.* ◇ *It's a common enough situation, I know.* **OPP** **rare**, **uncommon** → RARE, See also **commonly** → USUALLY

widespread /'waɪdspred/ existing or happening over a large area or among many people: *The storm caused widespread damage.* ◇ *The decision met with widespread approval.* ◇ *The use of steroids was widespread in many sports.*

universal /ˌjuːnɪ'vɜːsl; AmE -'vɜːrsl/ done by or involving all the people in the world or in a particular group: *A representative assembly is a near universal feature of modern democracies.* ◇ *Agreement on this issue is almost universal.* ◇ *The party wanted to introduce a universal health care system.*
▶ **universally** *adv.*: *The document is now universally acknowledged as a forgery.*

prevalent /'prevələnt/ (*formal*) that exists or is very common at a particular time or in a particular place: *Temporary working is most prevalent among people in service occupations.* ◇ *Our diet contributes to the high levels of heart disease prevalent in this country.* See also **prevail** → EXIST

commonplace /'kɒmənpleɪs; AmE 'kɑːm-/ done very often, or existing in many places, and therefore not unusual or surprising: *It is commonplace for soldiers to get very little sleep.* ◇ *Violent incidents of this kind have become commonplace.*

ubiquitous /juː'bɪkwɪtəs/ [usually before noun] (*formal or humorous*) seeming to be everywhere or in several places at the same time: *The ubiquitous portraits of the president usually showed him in military uniform.*

rife /raɪf/ [not before noun] (of sth bad) very common in a particular place: *Rumours have been rife in media circles all summer.* ◇ *Speculation is rife that the company is about to be sold.*

---

2 See also the entry for OVERALL
general · broad · sweeping
These words all describe sth such as an opinion, a statement or a description that is not exact or detailed.

PATTERNS AND COLLOCATIONS
▶ a general / broad / sweeping **assertion** / **conclusion** / **statement**
▶ the general / broad **context**
▶ in general / broad **terms**
▶ a broad / sweeping **generalization**

general not exact or detailed but including the most important aspects of sth; approximately, but not exactly, the direction or area mentioned: *I check the bookings to get a general idea of what activities to plan.* ◇ *I know how it works in general terms.* ◇ *They fired in the general direction of the enemy.* See also **general** → USUAL

broad [only before noun] not exact or detailed but including the most important aspects of sth: *Computer viruses fall into three broad categories.* ◇ *She's a feminist, in the broadest sense of the word.* See also **broad** → WIDE 1

NOTE **GENERAL** OR **BROAD**? In many cases you can use either word. However, **general** is used slightly more when you are talking about trends: *a general trend/ tendency/direction*; **broad** is used slightly more when you are talking about categories, meanings and aims: *a broad category/area* ◇ *a broad definition/sense/outline* ◇ *a broad aim/objective*

sweeping /'swiːpɪŋ/ [usually before noun] (*disapproving*) not exact or detailed and failing to think about or understand particular examples: *To make such sweeping generalizations about a whole race of people is foolish.*

the **general public** *noun* See the Topic Map for
THE INDIVIDUAL AND SOCIETY on p.894

---

the general public · the masses · the working class · the proletariat · the populace · the crowd · riff-raff
These are all words for the ordinary people in a society or country.

PATTERNS AND COLLOCATIONS
▶ the **French** / **Russian**, etc. masses / working class / proletariat / populace
▶ the **rural** / **urban** masses / working class / proletariat

the ˌgeneral 'public [sing.+ sing./pl. *v.*] ordinary people, especially when contrasted with members of a particular group or organization who have greater knowledge of or involvement in a particular situation: *At that time, the general public was not aware of the health risks.* ◇ *The exhibition is not open to the general public.* See also **the public** → COMMUNITY

the masses [pl.] (*rather formal*) ordinary people in society who are not leaders or who are not considered to be very well educated: *The railways provided cheap transport for the masses.* ◇ *This is yet another bid to introduce opera to the masses.*

the ˌworking ˈclass [sing.+ sing./pl. v.] (also **the working classes** [pl.]) the social class of people who do not have much money or power and are usually employed to do manual work (= physical work with their hands): *His films were the first to address the real issues of the working class.* ◇ *Boxing was seen as a sport for the working classes.* See also **the middle class** → MIDDLE CLASS *noun*, **the upper class** → ELITE *noun*, **working-class** → WORKING-CLASS *adj.*, **class** → CLASS *noun* 4

the proletariat /ˌprəʊləˈteəriət; *AmE* ˌproʊləˈter-/ [sing.+ sing./pl. v.] (*technical*) (used especially when talking about the past) ordinary people who earn money by working, especially those who do not own any property: *Marx wrote of the class struggle between the bourgeoisie and the proletariat.* ◇ *There was a rapid growth of the industrial proletariat.* **OPP** **the bourgeoisie** → MIDDLE CLASS, See also **proletarian** → WORKING-CLASS

the populace /ˈpɒpjələs; *AmE* ˈpɑːp-/ [sing.+ sing./pl. v.] (*formal*) all the ordinary people of a particular area or country: *He recorded the effects of the war on the local populace.*

the crowd [sing.] (*sometimes disapproving*) ordinary people who are not special or unusual in any way: *We all like to think we **stand out from the crowd** (= are different from other people).* ◇ *He prefers to be **one of the crowd** (= not noticed as different or unusual).* ◇ *She's quite happy to **follow the crowd** (= to do the same as other people).*

ˈriff-raff [U+sing./pl. v.] (*disapproving, often humorous*) an insulting way of referring to people of low social class or people who are not considered socially acceptable: *We don't want to let all the riff-raff in.*

generous *adj.*

generous · liberal · free with sth
These words all describe sb being willing to give freely, or sth that is given freely or in large amounts.

PATTERNS AND COLLOCATIONS
▸ to be generous/ liberal/ free **with** sth
▸ a generous/ liberal **amount** of sth
▸ liberal/ free with your **advice**/ **criticism**

generous (*approving*) (of a person) giving or willing to give freely; (of a gift) given freely or in large amounts; (of an amount of sth) more than is necessary: *He's a kind and generous man.* ◇ *They were very generous with their time.* ◇ *It was very generous of her to offer to pay.* ◇ *That's a very generous offer.* ◇ *He took a generous helping of pasta.* **OPP** **mean** → MEAN 2
▸ **generosity** /ˌdʒenəˈrɒsəti; *AmE* -ˈrɑːs-/ *noun* [U, sing.]: *He treated them with great generosity.*
▸ **generously** *adv.*: *Please give generously.*

liberal /ˈlɪbərəl/ (*rather formal, written, sometimes disapproving*) generous; given in large amounts: *She is very liberal with her money.* ◇ *I think Sam is too liberal with his criticism (= he criticizes people too much).* ◇ *We ate cake with liberal amounts of whipped cream.*

> **NOTE** **GENEROUS OR LIBERAL?** In this meaning **liberal** is only used in the patterns *liberal with sth* or *liberal amounts of sth*. People can be liberal with their *money, cash, criticism* or *advice*, often in a way that other people do not approve of. People are more likely to be **generous** with their *time* or *help*, and this is sth that other people do approve of. If sb is generous with their money, you can just say that they are **generous** (without stating 'with their money').

ˈfree with sth *phrase* (*written, often disapproving*) ready to give sth, especially when it is not wanted: *He's too free with his opinions.*

genius *noun*

genius · prodigy · mastermind · brain
These are all words for a person who is very intelligent or one who is very skilled at music, art, science, etc.

PATTERNS AND COLLOCATIONS
▸ the genius/ mastermind/ brains **behind** sth
▸ a **great** genius/ brain
▸ a **true** genius/ prodigy
▸ an **evil** genius/ mastermind
▸ a **child** genius/ prodigy
▸ a **musical** genius/ prodigy/ mastermind
▸ a **scientific** genius/ brain

genius /ˈdʒiːniəs/ [C] a person who is unusually intelligent or artistic or has a particularly high level of skill, especially in one area: *He was undoubtedly the greatest comic genius of his age.* ◇ *She's a genius at getting things organized.* ◇ *You don't have to be a genius to see that this plan is not going to work.* ❶ **Genius** is sometimes used informally when sb has just had a very good idea or done sth particularly well: *You're an absolute genius!*

prodigy /ˈprɒdədʒi; *AmE* ˈprɑːd-/ [C] a young person who is unusually intelligent or skilful for their age: *The 12-year-old prodigy will play America's reigning chess champion next week.*

mastermind /ˈmɑːstəmaɪnd; *AmE* ˈmæstərm-/ [C] an intelligent person who plans and directs a complicated project or activity, often a criminal one: *There's a criminal mastermind behind all this.*

brain [C, usually pl.] a very intelligent person: *We have the best scientific brains in the country working on this.* ❶ **The brains** [sing.] is the most intelligent person in a particular group or the person who is responsible for thinking of and organizing sth: *She's always been the brains of the family.* ◇ *The band's drummer is the brains behind their latest venture.*

gentle *adj.*

gentle · light · mild
These words all describe things that are not strong or extreme and do not hurt or harm you too much.

PATTERNS AND COLLOCATIONS
▸ a gentle/ light **breeze**/ **wind**/ **rain**
▸ gentle/ light **work**/ **exercise**
▸ a light/ mild **punishment**

gentle not strong or extreme; not making you tired or hurting you: *the gentle swell of the sea* ◇ *Cook over a gentle heat.* ◇ *We went for a gentle stroll.* ◇ *This soap is very gentle on the hands.* **OPP** **vigorous** → ENERGETIC

light not strong or extreme; not making you tired or punishing you too much: *The forecast is for light showers.* ◇ *light traffic* ◇ *After his accident he was moved to lighter work.* ◇ *He was convicted of assaulting a police officer but he got off with a **light sentence**.* **OPP** **heavy** ❶ **Heavy** conditions, activity or punishments are greater or worse than usual: *heavy traffic* ◇ *heavy frost/rain/snow* ◇ *heavy drinking/fighting* ◇ *The penalty for speeding can be a heavy fine.*

mild not strong or extreme; not harming, hurting or punishing you too much: *a mild form of the disease* ◇ *It's safe to take a mild sedative.* ◇ *It was a very mild criticism but he took it very badly.* **OPP** **severe** → SERIOUS 1

> **NOTE** **GENTLE, LIGHT OR MILD?** **Gentle** is used especially to describe weather, temperature, work and exercise. **Light** is used especially to describe weather, work, exercise and punishments. **Mild** is used especially to describe diseases, drugs, criticism and punishment. It can also describe weather. See also **mild** → SUNNY

get verb

1 get tickets/a job/some sleep
2 get a letter/shock
3 Go and get help.
4 We got there at 9.
5 get the bus

1 See also the entry for GAIN 1

get · obtain · acquire · take · pick sth up · take sth out · get hold of sth
These words all mean to do sth in order to make sure you have sth.

PATTERNS AND COLLOCATIONS
▶ to get/ obtain/ acquire/ take/ pick up sth **from** sb/ sth
▶ to get/ obtain/ acquire/ pick up/ get hold of a **ticket**
▶ to get/ obtain/ take out a **loan/ mortgage/ patent**
▶ to get/ obtain/ take out **insurance/ cover**
▶ to get/ obtain/ take **water/ oil/ minerals** (from sth)
▶ to get/ obtain/ acquire/ take/ get hold of **information**
▶ to get/ obtain/ take a/ an **extract/ example/ sample**
▶ to get/ obtain/ acquire a **licence/ permit**
▶ to get/ obtain **permission/ approval/ advice**
▶ to get/ acquire a **reputation/ taste** for sth

get [T, no passive] (not usually used in the progressive tenses) (*rather informal, especially spoken*) to do sth in order to make sure you have sth: *Did you manage to get tickets for the concert?* ◇ *Try to get some sleep.* ◇ *He has just got a new job.* ◇ *Did you get a present for your mother?* ◇ *Did you get your mother a present?* See also **get → BUY**

obtain [T] (*rather formal, especially written*) to get sth, especially by making an effort: *I finally managed to obtain a copy of the report.* ◇ *Further details can be obtained by writing to the above address.* See also **extract → PUMP**

acquire /ə'kwaɪə(r)/ [T] (*rather formal*) to get sth by your own efforts, ability or behaviour; to get sth by being given it: *She has acquired a good knowledge of English.* ◇ *He has acquired a reputation for dishonesty.* ◇ *I have recently acquired a taste for olives.* ◇ *How did the gallery come to acquire so many Picassos?* ❶ **Acquire** is often used to talk about the way sb starts to look or behave, or when sb starts to like sth: *to acquire a reputation/bad name/ criminal record/tan/look/appearance* ◇ *to acquire a love of/taste for sth.* It can also be used when sb learns a new skill. See also **acquire → BUY, acquire → LEARN**

take [T] to get sth from a particular source: *The scientists are taking water samples from the river.* ◇ *Part of her article is taken straight (= copied) out of my book.* ◇ *The machine takes its name from its inventor.* ❶ In this meaning **take** is often used to talk about people such as scientists or engineers getting *samples, specimens, water, cells, minerals,* etc. from a particular source. It is also used to talk about getting *information,* a *story,* an *extract* or an *example* from a larger written text.

pick sth 'up *phrasal verb* (*rather informal*) to get sth: *I picked up a few leaflets when I was out today.* ◇ *I picked up £30 in tips today.* ◇ *I seem to have picked up a terrible cold from somewhere.* ❶ **Pick sth up** is often used to talk about getting sth when you are out somewhere. It is also used to talk about getting money that you have earned or won, and about getting an illness or injury. See also the entry for SUFFER FROM STH for other ways of talking about getting illnesses.

take sth 'out *phrasal verb* to obtain an official document or service: *We had to take out a loan to pay for the car.* ◇ *How much does it cost to take out an ad in a newspaper?* ❶ People typically **take out** *insurance,* a *pension,* a *subscription,* a *loan,* a *mortgage,* or an *advertisement.*

get 'hold of sth *phrase* to find sth that you want or need: *It's almost impossible to get hold of tickets for the final.* ◇ *How did the press get hold of the story?*

2 **get · receive · accept · derive sth from sth · reap · collect**
These words all mean to obtain sth by being given or sent it.

PATTERNS AND COLLOCATIONS
▶ to get/ receive/ accept/ derive/ reap/ collect sth **from** sb/ sth
▶ to get/ receive/ accept/ collect a/ an **medal/ award/ prize**
▶ to get/ receive/ accept/ collect (your) **winnings/ compensation**
▶ to get/ receive/ accept **treatment/ payment/ help**
▶ to get/ receive/ accept a/ an **call/ message/ complaint/ invitation/ request/ answer**
▶ to get/ receive/ derive/ reap (a/ the) **benefit**
▶ to get/ receive/ reap the **dividends/ profits/ rewards**
▶ to get/ receive a/ an **reply/ letter/ impression/ shock/ prison sentence**
▶ to get/ derive **amusement/ enjoyment/ pleasure/ satisfaction/ comfort** from sth

get [T, no passive] (*rather informal, especially spoken*) to obtain sth by being given or sent it: *I got a letter from Dave this morning.* ◇ *He gets (= earns) about $40 000 a year.* ◇ *This room gets very little sunshine.* ◇ *I get the impression that he is bored with his job.* ◇ *I got a shock when I saw the bill.* ◇ *She got great satisfaction from seeing his embarrassment.*

receive [T] (*rather formal, especially written*) to obtain sth by being given or sent it: *I've just received this letter from an old friend.* ◇ *Please let me know as soon as you receive payment.* ◇ *He received an award for bravery from the police service.*

NOTE GET OR RECEIVE? The main difference between these words is register. **Receive** is rather formal, used especially in written English; **get** is the more usual word in spoken English. You can **get** or **receive** a sudden feeling such as a *shock* or an *impression*; but feelings that you experience over a period of time such as *enjoyment, pleasure* and *satisfaction* you usually **get,** NOT **receive.**

accept [T] (*rather formal*) to receive sth as suitable or good enough: *My article has been accepted for publication.* ◇ *This machine only accepts coins.* ◇ *Will you accept a cheque?*

de'rive sth from sth *phrasal verb* (*formal*) to get a good feeling or result from doing sth: *He derived great pleasure from painting.* ❶ People typically **derive** *amusement, benefit, comfort, enjoyment, fulfilment, inspiration, pleasure* or *satisfaction* from sth.

reap [T] (*especially written*) to obtain sth, especially sth good, as a direct result of sth that you have done: *They are now reaping the fruits of all their hard work.* ❶ People typically **reap** *dividends, fruits, profits* or *rewards* from their work. When people obtain sth bad as a result of sth bad they have done, you can say that they *reap the consequences* of their actions.

collect [T] to win or receive a prize, or money in compensation for an injury or damage that you have suffered: *We were invited to London to collect our prize.* ◇ *She collected £25 000 in compensation.*

3 See also the entry for TAKE 1

get · pick sb/sth up · fetch · collect
These words all mean to go to a place where sb/sth is and bring them/it back.

PATTERNS AND COLLOCATIONS
▶ to get/ pick up/ fetch/ collect sb/ sth **from** sth/ somewhere
▶ to get/ pick up/ fetch/ collect sth **for** sb
▶ to get/ fetch **sb sth**
▶ to **go/ come to** get/ pick up/ fetch/ collect sb/ sth
▶ to **go/ come and** get/ fetch sth
▶ to get/ fetch **help/ a doctor**

get [T] (*rather informal, especially spoken*) to go to a place where sb/sth is and bring them/it back: *Could you go upstairs and get my wallet for me, please?* ◇ *Somebody get a doctor!* ◇ *I have to go and get my mother from the airport.* ◇ *Get a drink for John.* ◇ *Get John a drink.*

pick sb/sth 'up *phrasal verb* (*rather informal, especially spoken*) to go to a place where sb is waiting or sth is ready or has been left for you, and bring them/it back or take them/it somewhere: *Call me from the station and I'll come and pick you up.* ◇ *We can pick our bags up on the way back.* ❶ You might be on foot or in a car when you **pick sth up** but you always **pick sb up** in a car.

fetch [T] (*BrE, rather informal, especially spoken*) to go to a place where sb/sth is and bring them/it back: *He ran to fetch help.* ◇ *They have to walk over a mile to fetch water.* ◇ *She's gone to fetch the kids from school.*

> **NOTE** GET OR FETCH? **Get** has a wider range of meaning than **fetch**: you usually **fetch** people or things that are in a place and just need to be collected; you can **get** things that need to be prepared or obtained: ~~Fetch John a drink.~~ **Fetch** is not usually used in American English.

collect [T] (*rather formal*) to pick sb/sth up: *They usually collect the rubbish/garbage on a Thursday.* ◇ *Your package is ready to be collected.* ◇ (*BrE*) *What time do you have to collect the children from school?* ❶ When you are talking about people, **collect** is used in British English; in American English it is more usual to say **pick sb up**. When you are talking about rubbish/garbage **collect** is the usual word for the regular collection of waste from your house by dustmen/garbage men; **pick up** can also be used for this in American English, but to *pick up rubbish/garbage* more often means to bend down and pick up a piece of rubbish/garbage from the ground.
> ▸ **collection** *noun* [U]: *rubbish/garbage collection*

4 See also the entries for ARRIVE and ATTEND

get · reach · make · make it · hit · catch up
These words all mean to arrive at a particular place after travelling there.

PATTERNS AND COLLOCATIONS
▸ to get / make it **to** a place
▸ to get / reach / make it **here / home / there**
▸ to get to / reach / make / make it to your **destination**
▸ to get to / reach / make it to / hit the **summit**
▸ to get to / reach / make it to / hit the **border**

get [I] (*always used with an adverb or preposition*) (*especially spoken*) to arrive at a particular place after travelling: *We're aiming to get to the party at about nine.* ◇ *I got back an hour ago.* ◇ *They got in very late last night.* ◇ *We only got as far as the next town.* See also **get** → GO 1

reach [T] (*especially written*) to arrive at the place you have been travelling to; to come to sb's attention: *It took them three hours to reach the opposite shore.* ◇ *The beach can only be reached by boat.* ◇ *I hope this letter reaches you.* ◇ *The rumours eventually reached the President.*

> **NOTE** GET OR REACH? The main difference between these words is register. **Reach** is used especially in written English; **get** is the usual word in spoken English. **Get** takes no object, but always takes an adverb or adverbial phrase, often one that is not specific, when the listener is expected to understand the place that is meant by *there*, *in* or *back*. **Reach** always takes an object and is usually more specific about the place that is arrived at.

make [T, no passive] (*rather informal*) to succeed in arriving at a particular event, place or position: *I'm sorry I didn't make the party last night.* ◇ *He'll never make (= get a place in) the team.* ◇ *The story made (= appeared on) the front pages of the national newspapers.*

make it *phrase* (*rather informal*) to succeed in arriving at an event or place, or arriving there in time, especially when this is difficult: *I don't think I'll be able to make it to the meeting.* ◇ *Even if we take a taxi I don't think we'll make it in time.* ◇ *The flight leaves in twenty minutes — we'll never make it.*

hit [T] (*informal*) to arrive at a place or road: *Traffic was heavy when they hit the main road.* ◇ *The president hits town (= is visiting the town) tomorrow.*

catch 'up (*BrE also* **catch sb 'up**) to join sb who is ahead of you by going faster: *We stopped for a few minutes to let the others catch up.* ◇ *On lap 45 Hunt's car was catching up fast.* ◇ *You go on ahead. I'll catch up with you.* ◇ (*BrE*) *She hurried to catch him up.*

5 **get · take · catch · go by sth**
These words all mean to travel using a particular form of transport.

PATTERNS AND COLLOCATIONS
▸ to get / take / catch / go by sth **from / to** sth
▸ to get the / take the / catch the / go by **bus / train / plane / boat**
▸ to get / catch a **flight**
▸ to get a / take a / go by **taxi**

get [T, no passive] to travel somewhere using a particular form of public transport; to be in time for a bus, train, etc. that you intend to travel on: *Where do I get the bus for the airport?* ◇ *I'll try and get a flight home tomorrow.* ◇ *I ran all the way to the station and just managed to get my train.*

take [T, no passive] (*rather formal, especially written*) to travel somewhere using a particular form of public transport: *They took the night train to Vienna.* ❶ **Take** is more formal than **get** in this meaning, used especially in written English. It CANNOT be used, like **get**, to mean 'to be in time for a bus, train, etc. that you intend to travel on': ~~I only just managed to take my train.~~

catch [T, no passive] to be in time for a train, bus, plane, etc. and travel on it: *They caught the 12.15 from Kings Cross.* ◇ *I must go — I have a train to catch.* **OPP** miss → MISS 1

go by sth *phrasal verb* to travel somewhere using a particular form of transport: *If it's not raining, I'll go by bike.* ◇ *It'll probably be cheaper to go by air.* ❶ You can **go by** any form of transport; the other words in this group are only used about public transport. You can also *go by air/rail/road/sea*.

get in *phrasal verb*

get in · board · get on · embark · mount
These words all mean to go inside or onto a form of transport.

PATTERNS AND COLLOCATIONS
▸ to get in / board / get on a **bus / train**
▸ to get on / board a **plane / ship**
▸ to get on / mount a **horse / bike / bicycle / motorcycle**

get 'in/get into sth *phrasal verb* to go inside a vehicle such as a car or into a small boat: *'Get in,' she said, opening the passenger door.* ◇ *The two of us got in the back.* ◇ *She checked the tyres and got back into the van.* **OPP** get out → GET OUT

board [T, I] (*rather formal*) to go onto a ship, plane, train or bus: *The ship was boarded by customs officials.* ◇ *Passengers were waiting to board.* ❶ If a plane or ship is **boarding**, it is ready for passengers to get on: *BA Flight 943 for Istanbul is now boarding at Gate 14.*

get 'on *phrasal verb* to go inside a form of transport that carries a lot of people, such as a plane, bus, train or boat; to climb onto a bicycle, motorcycle or horse: *I think the men got on at the last stop.* ◇ *Let's just go to the airport and get on a plane.* ◇ *She got back on the horse and rode off.* **OPP** get off → GET OUT

embark /ɪmˈbɑːk; *AmE* ɪmˈbɑːrk/ [I] (*formal*) to go onto a ship at the start of a journey; to put sb onto a ship: *The invasion force was ready to embark.* ◇ *The team embarked for (= started their journey to) Italy.* **OPP** disembark → GET OUT

mount [T, I] (*rather formal*) to climb on a horse, bicycle or motorcycle in order to ride it: *Carla mounted her bike and pedalled off.* ◇ *He mounted and galloped off.* ❶ When **mount** is used without an object it usually means to get on a horse. *Mount a bicycle/motorcycle* is more formal than *mount a horse*; it is more usual to say *get on a bicycle/bike/motorcycle/motorbike*. **OPP** dismount → GET OUT

get out *phrasal verb*

get out · get off · disembark · alight · dismount
These words all mean to leave a form of transport.

PATTERNS AND COLLOCATIONS
▶ to disembark/ alight/ dismount **from** sth
▶ to get out/ get off/ alight **here**

‚get 'out, **‚get 'out of sth** *phrasal verb* to leave a vehicle such as a car, train or small boat: *She stopped the car and told him to get out.* ◇ *He got out of the taxi and paid the driver.* **OPP** **get in** → GET IN

‚get 'off *phrasal verb* to leave a form of transport that carries a lot of people such as a plane, bus, train or boat; to get down from a bicycle, motorcycle or horse: *Get off at the next stop.* ◇ *I had to get off the bike and push it up the hill.* **OPP** **get on** → GET IN

disembark /ˌdɪsɪm'bɑːk; *AmE* -'bɑːrk/ [I] (*formal*) to leave a vehicle, especially a ship or plane, at the end of a journey: *We will be disembarking at midday.* ◇ *They had just disembarked from their tour bus after a 12-hour journey.* **OPP** **embark** → GET IN

alight /ə'laɪt/ (*formal or literary*) [I] to leave a bus, train or other form of public transport: *Alight here for the National Conference Centre.*

dismount /dɪs'maʊnt/ [I] (*rather formal*) to get off a horse, bicycle or motorcycle: *He dismounted and tied the reins to a tree.* **OPP** **mount** → GET IN

ghost *noun*

ghost · spirit · apparition
These are all words for an image of a person who is dead, especially one that a living person believes they can see or hear.

PATTERNS AND COLLOCATIONS
▶ to **see** a ghost/ a spirit/ an apparition
▶ a ghost/ a spirit/ an apparition **haunts** sth
▶ a ghost/ spirit **appears**

ghost /gəʊst; *AmE* goʊst/ [C] an image of a dead person that a living person believes they can see or hear: *Do you believe in ghosts* (= believe that they exist)*?* ◇ *It was the ghost of her father that had come back to haunt her.* ◇ *He looked as if he had seen a ghost* (= looked very frightened)*.* ◇ *We used to sit around the campfire telling **ghost stories**.*

spirit [C] the soul thought of as separate from the body and believed to live on after death: *He is dead, but his spirit lives on.* ◇ *It was believed that people could be possessed by **evil spirits**.* See also **spirit** → MIND *noun*

apparition /ˌæpə'rɪʃn/ [C] (*rather formal, especially written*) a ghost or image of a dead person that appears to sb: *Apparitions of a woman in white robes have been reported.*

gift *noun*

gift · present · donation · contribution · tip · gratuity · handout
These are all words for a thing that you give to sb, for example on a special occasion, to help them, or to say thank you.

PATTERNS AND COLLOCATIONS
▶ a gift/ present/ donation/ contribution/ tip/ gratuity/ handout **for/ from** sb
▶ a gift/ present/ donation/ contribution **to** sb/ sth
▶ £50 000, $10, etc. **in** gifts/ donations/ contributions/ tips/ handouts
▶ a **small** gift/ present/ donation/ contribution/ tip/ gratuity
▶ a **large/ generous** gift/ present/ donation/ contribution/ tip
▶ a/an **birthday/wedding/anniversary/Christmas** gift/ present
▶ a **cash** gift/ donation/ handout
▶ a **free** gift/ handout
▶ to **get** a gift/ present/ donation/ contribution/ tip/ handout
▶ to **receive** a gift/ present/ donation/ contribution/ gratuity
▶ to **send** (sb) a gift/ present/ donation/ contribution
▶ to **leave** (sb) a gift/ present/ donation/ tip/ gratuity
▶ to **give** (sb) a gift/ present/ donation/ tip
▶ to **make** a donation/ contribution

gift [C] (*rather formal, especially written*) a thing or a sum of money that you give to sb: *There's a free gift for every reader.* ◇ *The gift of love is the greatest gift a person can give or receive.* ◇ *The party was originally funded by a gift of £50 000 from a top motor manufacturer.* ◇ (*BrE*) *All such posts are **in the gift of** the managing director* (= only given by the managing director)*.* See also **give** → GIVE 5

present [C] a thing that you give to sb, especially on a special occasion or to say thank you: *What can I get him for a birthday present?*

NOTE GIFT OR PRESENT? Gift is more formal than **present** and is used especially in business contexts: a store will advertise its *Christmas gift ideas*; the people who buy them will talk about the *Christmas presents* they have bought for family and friends. A **present** is usually given by and to an individual; a **gift** may be given by a company (*a corporate gift*) and/or to an organization. A **present** is usually an object, but a **gift** may be a sum of money, or sth such as *the gift of love/life:* ~~*funded by a present of £50 000*~~ ◇ ~~*She gave me the present of love.*~~ Especially in American English, however, **gift** is not always so formal and is sometimes used in personal contexts instead of **present**: *The watch was a gift/ present from my mother.*

donation /dəʊ'neɪʃn; *AmE* doʊ-/ [C] something that is given to a person or organization such as a charity, in order to help them; the act of giving sth in this way: *I made a £200 donation to charity.* ◇ *The work of the charity is funded by voluntary donations.* ◇ *Organ donation* (= allowing doctors to use organs from your body after your death in order to save a sick person's life) *has not kept pace with the demand for transplants.* See also **donate** → GIVE 5

contribution /ˌkɒntrɪ'bjuːʃn; *AmE* ˌkɑːn-/ [C, U] a sum of money or sth that is given to a person or organization in order to help pay for sth or raise money for sth; the act of giving sth in this way: *He has made several valuable **contributions towards** the upkeep of the cathedral.* ◇ *Contributions of cakes and other items for the cake sale can be left in the school office.* ◇ *We rely entirely on voluntary contribution.* See also **contribute** → GIVE 5

NOTE DONATION OR CONTRIBUTION? Contribution places more emphasis on the money or thing given being part of a whole, to be added to other amounts or things that other people have given. **Contributions** are often expected or asked for; **donations** are seen more as voluntary gifts.

tip [C] a small amount of extra money that you give to sb who has provided a service for you, for example in a restaurant: *Are we supposed to leave a tip?* ◇ *He gave the waiter a generous tip.*
▶ **tip** *verb* (**-pp-**) [T, I]: *Did you remember to tip the waiter?* ◇ *Americans were always welcome because they tended to tip heavily.*

gratuity /grə'tjuːəti; *AmE* -'tuː-/ [C] (*formal*) a tip: *Our employees may not accept gratuities.*

handout /'hændaʊt/ [C] (*often disapproving*) money that is given to a person or organization by the government, for example to encourage commercial activity: *The company is currently thriving thanks to a £70 000 government handout.* ❶ **Handouts** can also be given to people who are poor. See also **handout** → AID *noun*, **hand sth out** → DISTRIBUTE

girl, youth *nouns* See also the entry for CHILD

girl · youth · lad · teenager · teen · adolescent · juvenile
These are all words for young people who are not yet adults.

PATTERNS AND COLLOCATIONS
▶ a **young** girl/ lad/ teenager/ adolescent
▶ an **older** girl/ youth/ teenager
▶ a **local** girl/ youth/ lad/ teenager

▶ an **awkward** teenager / teen / adolescent
▶ youth / juvenile **crime** / **unemployment**

girl [C] (*sometimes offensive*) a young woman: *Alex is not interested in girls yet.* ◊ *One of the girls at work told me about it.* ◊ *He married the girl next door.* ❶ **Girl** is often used to refer to a young woman in informal or friendly contexts. However, some young women find it offensive and lacking in respect when sb refers to them as a **girl** in a more formal or professional context. **OPP guy** → MAN 1, See also **girl** → CHILD, **girl** → SON

youth [C] (*often disapproving*) a young man, especially one who is behaving badly or doing sth illegal: *The fight was started by a gang of youths.* ❶ **Youth** or **the youth** [pl.] are used in phrases to mean 'young people considered as a group': *The Royal Family is facing an uncertain future, according to **the nation's youth**.* ◊ *Many people think **the youth of today** are not taught proper standards of behaviour.* ◊ *youth politics/culture* ◊ *an increase in youth unemployment* In this meaning **(the) youth** is always used as part of a longer phrase, not on its own: ~~The youth are not taught proper standards of behaviour.~~ See also **youth** → CHILDHOOD

lad [C] (*especially BrE, informal*) a boy or young man: *He's a nice lad.* ◊ *Things have changed since I was a lad.*

teenager [C] a person who is between 13 and 19 years old: *a magazine aimed at teenagers* ◊ *Many teenagers are embarrassed by their parents.* See also **teenage** → YOUNG

NOTE YOUTH, LAD OR TEENAGER? A **teenager** can be a boy or a girl but must be aged between 13 and 19; **youth** is less specific and can describe sb up until their early twenties; **lad** is also less specific but is not usually used about sb older than 19. When it refers to a young person, **youth** is more negative than **lad** or **teenager**, and collocates are often (but not always) negative: *angry/drunken/masked youths*. The collocates of **lad** are mostly positive: *a handsome/decent/fine/good/great/lovely/nice/smashing/bright/sensible lad*. To talk about young people in general, **youth** is more common than **teenagers**, especially in newspapers or more formal English: *unemployed/modern/educated youth* ◊ *youth crime/employment*

teen [C] (*informal, especially AmE*) a teenager: *Two plain-looking teens were sitting on the couch watching TV.* See also **teen** → YOUNG *adj.*, **teens** → CHILDHOOD

adolescent /ˌædəˈlesnt/ [C] (*rather formal*) a young person who is developing from a child into an adult: *adolescents between the ages of 13 and 18, and the problems they face* ◊ *Stop acting like an adolescent!* See also **adolescence** → CHILDHOOD, **adolescent** → YOUNG *adj.*

juvenile /ˈdʒuːvənaɪl; AmE -vənl/ [C] (*formal or law*) a young person who is not yet an adult, especially one that has done sth illegal or is accused of doing sth illegal: *Most of the suspects were juveniles under the age of 17.* See also **juvenile** → YOUNG *adj.*

give *verb*

1 give sb a present
2 Give your mother the letter.
3 give sb drugs/advice/a punishment
4 give sb a headache/an air of mystery
5 give money to charity/give blood

1 give · award · present · confer · transfer · accord · bestow · lavish sth on/upon sb/sth

These words all mean to allow sb to have sth.

PATTERNS AND COLLOCATIONS
▶ to give / award / present / transfer / accord sth **to** sb
▶ to confer / bestow / lavish sth **on** sb
▶ to give / award / accord **sb sth**
▶ to give / present / bestow **gifts**
▶ to lavish **gifts** on / upon sb / sth
▶ to give / present / bestow an **award**
▶ to give / award / present a **prize**
▶ to give / confer / accord / bestow (a / an) **honour** / **title** / **status**

▶ to confer / bestow a **favour**
▶ to give / accord / bestow an **accolade**

give [T, I] hand sth to sb as a present; to allow sb to have sth as a present: *What are you giving your father for his birthday?* ◊ *Did you give the waiter a tip?* ◊ *We don't usually give presents to people at work.* ◊ *They say it's better to give than to receive.*

award [T] to make an official decision to give sth to sb as a payment or prize: *He was awarded damages of £50 000.* ◊ *The judges awarded equal points to both finalists.* ❶ Typical collocates of **award** are *points, prize, trophy* and *compensation* and *damages*. See also **award** → AWARD *noun*, **award** → COMPENSATION *noun*, **grant** → ALLOW

present [T] to give sth to sb, especially formally at a ceremony: *The local MP will start the race and present the prizes.* ◊ *The sword was presented by the family to the museum.* ◊ *On his retirement, colleagues **presented him with** a set of golf clubs.* ❶ Note that you can *present sth*, you can *present sb with sth*, or you can *present sth to sb*.

confer /kənˈfɜː(r)/ (**-rr-**) [T] (*formal*) to give sb an award, a university degree or a particular honour or right: *An honorary degree was conferred on him by Oxford University in 2005.*

transfer /trænsˈfɜː(r)/ (**-rr-**) [T] to officially arrange for sth to belong to sb else or for sb else to control sth: *He transferred the property to his son.*

accord [T] (*formal*) to give sb/sth authority, status or a particular type of treatment: *Our society accords the family great importance.* ◊ *There were complaints about the special treatment accorded to some minority groups.* ❶ **Accord** is often used to talk about the status and recognition that people give particular groups such as a particular profession or religion in society.

bestow /bɪˈstəʊ; AmE bɪˈstoʊ/ [T] (*formal*) to give sth to sb, especially to show how much they are respected: *It was a title bestowed upon him by the king.* ❶ **Bestow** is most often used to talk about giving *rights, respect, honours* and *titles* to people, but it can also be used to talk about special gifts given to people to show how much they are respected.

'lavish sth on/upon sb/sth *phrasal verb* (*written*) to give a lot of sth, often too much, to sb/sth: *She lavishes most of her attention on her youngest son.* ❶ Typical collocates of **lavish sth on/upon sb/sth** are *gifts, praise* and *attention*.

2 give · hand · hand sb/sth over · pass

These words all mean to put sth into sb's hand or hands, or in a place where they can easily reach it.

PATTERNS AND COLLOCATIONS
▶ to give / hand / hand sb / sth over / pass sth **to** sb
▶ to **just** give / hand / hand over / pass sth
▶ to give / hand / hand over / pass sth **immediately** / **promptly**

give [T] to put sth into sb's hand or hands so that they can look at it, use it or keep it for a time: *They were all given a box to carry.* ◊ *She gave her ticket to the woman at the check-in desk.*

hand [T] to put sth into sb's hand: *She handed the letter to me.* ◊ *She handed me the letter.*

,hand sb/sth 'over *phrasal verb* to give sb/sth officially or formally to another person: *He handed over a cheque for $20 000.* ◊ *I knew I should have handed you over to the police!*

pass [T] to give sth to sb by putting it into their hands or in a place where they can easily reach it: *Pass the salt, please.* ◊ *Could you pass me that book?* ❶ **Pass** is often used in spoken English when one person is asking another to pick up sth that they can't reach themselves, and give it to them.

NOTE GIVE, HAND OR PASS? **Hand** is used more in written (especially literary) English than in spoken English; **give** is used frequently in both written and spoken English, but especially frequently in spoken English. **Pass** is often used in spoken requests, but is also used in written, literary English.

3 give · administer · dispense · hand sth out

These words all mean to give drugs, treatment, advice or a punishment to sb.

PATTERNS AND COLLOCATIONS
▶ to give/ administer/ dispense/ hand out sth **to** sb
▶ to give/ administer/ hand out **punishment/ treatment**
▶ to give/ administer/ dispense **justice**
▶ to give/ hand out a **prison/ jail sentence**
▶ to give/ administer/ dispense **medicine/ drugs/ medication**
▶ to give/ administer a/ an **dose/ sedative/ remedy/ injection**
▶ to give/ administer **first aid/ oxygen**
▶ to administer/ dispense a **prescription**
▶ to give/ dispense/ hand out **advice**

give [T] to make sb suffer a particular punishment or treatment; to give drugs, medicine or advice to sb: *The judge gave him a nine-month suspended sentence.* ◊ *She gave me some medicine that sent me off to sleep.* ◊ *Let me give you a word of advice.*

administer /əd'mɪnɪstə(r)/ [T] (*formal*) to give sth such as a punishment, especially in a formal way; to give drugs, medicine or treatment to sb: *The teacher has the authority to administer punishment.* ◊ *The priest was called to administer the last rites.* ◊ *A taxi driver administered first aid to the victims.*

dispense /dɪ'spens/ [T] (*rather formal*) to give sb help, advice or justice: *His role is to dispense advice and control the budget.* ❶ In British English **dispense** also means 'to prepare medicine and give it to people, as a job': (*BrE*) *A pharmacist will never dispense a prescription unless he or she knows it is genuine.* In American English a pharmacist *fills* a prescription.

hand sth 'out *phrasal verb* (*rather informal*) to give advice, a punishment or a particular type of treatment: *He's always handing out advice to people.*

4 give · add · lend · impart

These words all mean to produce a particular feeling in sb or a particular quality in sth.

PATTERNS AND COLLOCATIONS
▶ to give/ add/ lend/ impart sth **to** sth
▶ to give/ add/ lend/ impart a/ an **sense/ feeling/ air of** sth
▶ to give/ add/ lend a **touch of** sth
▶ to give/ add/ lend (a) **flavour/ colour** to sth
▶ to give/ add/ lend (a) **new dimension/ credibility/ distinction** (to sth)
▶ to add/ lend **glamour/ elegance** (to sth)

give [T] to produce a particular feeling in sb or a particular quality in sth: *All that driving has given me a headache.* ◊ *This shampoo will give your hair a nice healthy sheen.* ◊ *The dark glasses gave him an air of mystery.*

add [T] to give a particular quality to a person, place, event or situation: *The suite will add a touch of class to your bedroom.* ◊ *The Easter Festival added a new dimension to Salzburg's musical life.* ❶ **Add** is typically used to talk about producing an effect of impressive style to places or situations: *to add a touch/sense/feeling of glamour/ elegance/luxury/opulence/distinction/class*

lend [T] (*written*) to give a particular atmosphere to an event or situation; to give support to a claim or theory and make it seem more likely to be true or genuine: *The setting sun lent an air of melancholy to the scene.* ◊ *Her presence lent the occasion a certain dignity.* ◊ *This latest evidence lends support to her theory.* ❶ Something might also **lend** *weight* or *credence* to a claim or theory.

impart /ɪm'pɑːt; *AmE* ɪm'pɑːrt/ [T] (*rather formal, written*) to give a particular quality to sth, especially a flavour or smell: *The spice imparts an Eastern flavour to the dish.*

5 give · contribute · donate · chip in

These words all mean to give sth, especially money or goods, to help sb/sth.

PATTERNS AND COLLOCATIONS
▶ to give/ contribute/ donate (sth) **to** sth
▶ to give/ contribute/ donate/ chip in **£10/ $100 000,** etc.
▶ to give/ contribute/ donate **cash/ a sum**
▶ to give/ chip in with a **donation**
▶ to give/ donate **blood**
▶ to give/ contribute/ donate **generously**

give [T, I] to pay money to a charity, or let them have food and clothes to help people; to have blood taken from you so that it can be used in the medical treatment of other people: *We need your help – please give generously.* ◊ *They both gave regularly to charity.* ◊ *I gave a small donation.* See also **gift** → GIFT

contribute /kən'trɪbjuːt; *BrE* also 'kɒntrɪbjuːt/ [T, I] (*rather formal*) to give sth, especially money or goods, to help sb/sth: *The writer personally contributed £5 000 to the earthquake fund.* ◊ *Would you like to contribute to our collection?* ◊ *Do you wish to contribute?* See also **contribution** → GIFT, **contributor** → SPONSOR

donate /dəʊ'neɪt; *AmE* 'doʊneɪt/ [T] (*rather formal*) to give money or goods to help sb/sth, especially a charity; to allow doctors to remove blood or a body organ in order to help sb who needs it: *I would like to thank our sponsors, The Woodworks, for donating the prizes for this competition.* ◊ *All donated blood is tested for HIV and other infections.* See also **donation** → GIFT, **donor** → SPONSOR

> **NOTE** CONTRIBUTE OR DONATE? **Contribute** suggests that a number of people are all giving money, food, clothes, etc. to a charity or a fund. **Donate** places the emphasis on an individual person or company that has given sth. If **contribute** is used about an individual, it is usually sb who has given a large amount.

chip in, **chip in sth** *phrasal verb* (**-pp-**) (*informal*) to give some money so that a group of people can buy sth together: *If everyone chips in we'll be able to buy her a really nice present.* ◊ *We each chipped in (with) £5.*

give sth up *phrasal verb*

give sth up · concede · sacrifice · surrender · relinquish · waive · forfeit · cede · renounce · abdicate
These words all mean to let sb else have sth or to not do or demand sth.

PATTERNS AND COLLOCATIONS
▶ to give up/ concede/ surrender/ relinquish/ cede/ abdicate sth **to** sb
▶ to give up/ concede/ sacrifice/ surrender/ relinquish/ waive/ forfeit/ renounce a **right/ claim**
▶ to give up/ concede/ sacrifice/ surrender/ relinquish/ cede/ renounce **sovereignty**
▶ to give up/ concede/ sacrifice/ surrender/ forfeit your **independence**
▶ to give up/ concede/ surrender/ relinquish/ cede/ renounce **authority/ power**
▶ to give up/ concede/ surrender/ relinquish/ cede **control/ territory**
▶ to give up/ renounce/ abdicate **the throne**
▶ to give up/ renounce your **citizenship/ nationality**
▶ to give up/ surrender your **passport/ weapons**

give sth 'up *phrasal verb* to hand sth over to sb else; to let sb else have sth; to no longer claim sth as yours: *He gave up his claim to the throne.*

concede /kən'siːd/ [T] to give away power, a right or an advantage, especially unwillingly; to allow sb to have sth: *The president was obliged to concede power to the army.* ◊ *England conceded a goal immediately after half-time.* ◊ *Women were only conceded full voting rights in the 1920s.* See also **concession** → COMPROMISE *noun*

sacrifice /'sækrɪfaɪs/ [T] to give up sth that is important or valuable to you in order to get or do sth that seems more important for yourself or for another person: *She sacrificed everything for her children.* ◊ *The designers have sacrificed speed for fuel economy.*

▶ **sacrifice** *noun* [C, U]: *Her parents made sacrifices so that she could have a good education.* ◊ *The makers assured us that there had been no sacrifice of quality.*

surrender /səˈrendə(r)/ [T] (*formal*) to give sb/sth up when you are forced to: *He agreed to surrender all claims to the property.* ◇ *They surrendered their guns to the police.*
▸ **surrender** *noun* [U, C]: *They insisted on the immediate surrender of all weapons.*

relinquish /rɪˈlɪŋkwɪʃ/ [T] (*formal*) to give sb/sth up, especially unwillingly: *He was forced to relinquish control of the company.* ◇ *They had relinquished all hope that she was alive.*

> **NOTE** SURRENDER OR RELINQUISH? There is very little difference in meaning between these words; **surrender** can suggest an even stronger element of force, and is the word to choose when sb is forced to physically hand sth over, such as *guns*, *weapons* or a *passport*. The strongest collocate of **relinquish** is *control*.

waive /weɪv/ [T] (*rather formal*) to choose not to demand sth in a particular case, even though you have a legal or official right to do so: *She waived her right to appeal against the verdict.* ◇ *We have decided to waive the tuition fees in your case.*

forfeit /ˈfɔːfɪt; *AmE* ˈfɔːrfət/ [T] (*rather formal*) to lose sth or have sth taken away from you because you have done sth wrong: *If you cancel your flight, you will forfeit your deposit.* ◇ *He has forfeited his right to be taken seriously.*

cede /siːd/ [T] (*formal*) to give up land or rights, especially to another country after a war: *Cuba was ceded by Spain to the US in 1898.*

renounce /rɪˈnaʊns/ [T] (*formal*) to state officially that you are no longer going to keep or claim a title or position: *The Prince has refused to renounce his right to the throne.* ◇ *She even threatened to renounce her citizenship.*

abdicate /ˈæbdɪkeɪt/ [I, T] (*rather formal*) to give up the position of being king or queen: *He abdicated in favour of his son.* ◇ *She was forced to abdicate the throne of Spain.*
▸ **abdication** *noun* [U, C]: *the forced abdication of the king*

give way *verb*

give way · give in · submit · bow to sth · back down · relent · yield
These words all mean to stop resisting pressure or demands from sb/sth.

PATTERNS AND COLLOCATIONS
▸ to give way / give in / submit / bow / yield **to** sb / sth
▸ to give way / give in / back down / relent **on** sth
▸ to give way / give in / submit / bow / yield to sb's **demands**
▸ to give way / give in / submit / bow / yield to **pressure**
▸ to give in / submit to **authority**
▸ to give in / yield to **temptation**
▸ to **be forced to** give way / give in / submit / bow to sth / back down / yield
▸ to **refuse to** give in / submit / bow to sth / back down / yield

give ˈway *idiom* (*especially BrE*) to stop resisting pressure or demands from sb, often by agreeing to do sth that you do not really want to do; to stop resisting an emotion: *He refused to give way on any of the points.* ◇ *In the end she always gave way to him because she could not bear his moods.* ◇ *She never gave way to anger.*

give ˈin *phrasal verb* to give way to sb/sth: *The authorities have shown no signs of giving in to the kidnappers' demands.* ◇ *He reluctantly gave in to the pressure.* ◇ *In the end, they were forced to give in.* **OPP** resist → RESIST

> **NOTE** GIVE WAY OR GIVE IN? In many cases you can use either word. **Give way** is used more often than **give in** when you are talking about giving way to a person, rather than to sb's demands or pressure; you can also **give way** but NOT **give in** to an emotion: ~~She never gave in to anger~~

submit /səbˈmɪt/ (-tt-) [I, T] (*rather formal*) to accept the authority, control or greater strength of sb/sth; to agree to sth because of this: *She refused to submit to threats.* ◇ *He submitted himself to a search by the guards.* **OPP** resist → RESIST, See also **submissive** → PASSIVE

ˈ**bow to sth** /baʊ/ *phrasal verb* to agree unwillingly to do sth because other people want you to: *He felt he had to bow to her wishes.* ◇ *She bowed to the inevitable* (= accepted a situation in which she had no choice) *and resigned.*

ˌ**back ˈdown** *phrasal verb* to take back a demand or opinion that other people are strongly opposed to: *She refused to back down on a point of principle.* ◇ *We cannot back down from the decision, which we believe is right and just.* See also **retreat** → WITHDRAW 2

relent /rɪˈlent/ [I] (*rather formal*) to finally agree to sth after refusing: *'Well, just for a little while then,' she said, finally relenting.*

yield /jiːld/ [I] (*rather formal, written*) to stop resisting pressure or demands from sb/sth; to stop resisting your own desires: *After a long siege, the town was forced to yield.* ◇ *I yielded to temptation and had a chocolate bar.*

glad *adj.* See also the entry for GRATEFUL

glad · happy · pleased · delighted · proud · relieved · thrilled · overjoyed
These words all describe people feeling happy about sth that has happened or is going to happen.

relieved	glad	delighted	thrilled
	happy		overjoyed
	pleased		
	proud		

PATTERNS AND COLLOCATIONS
▸ glad / happy / pleased / delighted / relieved / thrilled / overjoyed **about** sth
▸ pleased / delighted / relieved / thrilled / overjoyed **at** sth
▸ pleased / delighted / thrilled / overjoyed **with** / **by** sth
▸ glad / happy / pleased / delighted / thrilled / overjoyed **for** sb
▸ glad / happy / pleased / delighted / proud / relieved / thrilled / overjoyed **that...**
▸ glad / happy / pleased / delighted / proud / relieved / thrilled / overjoyed **to see** / **hear** / **find** / **know...**
▸ glad / happy / pleased / delighted / proud **to say (that...)**
▸ a happy / delighted **smile** / **laugh**
▸ **very** glad / happy / pleased / proud / relieved
▸ **absolutely** delighted / thrilled

glad [not usually before noun] happy about sth or grateful for it: *'He doesn't need the pills any more.' 'I'm glad about that.'* ◇ *He was glad he'd come.* ◇ *She's absolutely fine, I'm glad to say.* ◇ *She was glad when the meeting was over.* **OPP** sorry → UPSET

happy pleased about sth nice that you have to do or sth that has happened to sb: *We are happy to announce the engagement of our daughter.* ◇ *'We're getting married!' 'I'm so happy for you both!'* **OPP** sorry → UPSET

pleased [not before noun] happy about sth that has happened or sth that you have to do: *She was very pleased with her exam results.* ◇ *I was pleased to hear you've been promoted.* ◇ (*especially BrE, formal, spoken*) *Pleased to meet you* (= said when you are introduced to sb). **OPP** displeased → UNHAPPY 2, disappointed → DISAPPOINTED, See also **please** → PLEASE *verb*

> **NOTE** GLAD, HAPPY OR PLEASED? Feeling **pleased** can suggest that you have judged sb/sth and approve of them. The opposite, **displeased**, involves judgement and disapproval. Feeling **pleased** can also mean that sth has happened that is particularly good for you: the opposite of this meaning is **disappointed**. Feeling **glad** can be more about feeling grateful for sth, either for yourself or sb else. The opposite, **sorry**, involves sympathy, not judgement. **Happy** can mean glad or pleased or satisfied. See also the entry for HAPPY

delighted very pleased about sth; very happy to do sth; showing your delight: *I'm delighted by your news.* ❶ **Delighted** is often used to accept an invitation: *'Can you stay for dinner?' 'I'd be delighted (to).'*
▸ **delightedly** *adv.*: *She laughed delightedly.*

proud pleased and satisfied about sth that you own or have done, or are connected with: *proud parents* ◇ *the* **proud owner** *of a new car* ◇ *He was* **proud of** *himself for not giving up.* ◇ *Your achievements are* **something to be proud of.** ◇ *I feel very proud to be a part of the team.* See also **pride** → SATISFACTION, **pride yourself on sth** → BOAST
▸ **proudly** *adv.*: *She proudly displayed her prize.*

relieved feeling happy because sth unpleasant has stopped or has not happened; showing this: *You'll be relieved to know your jobs are safe.* ◇ *I'm just relieved that nobody was hurt.* ◇ *They exchanged relieved glances.* See also **relief** → RELIEF, **thankful** → GRATEFUL

thrilled [not before noun] (*rather informal*) extremely pleased and excited about sth: *I was thrilled to be invited.*

overjoyed [not before noun] extremely happy about sth: *She was overjoyed at the birth of her daughter.*

> **NOTE** DELIGHTED, THRILLED OR OVERJOYED? Overjoyed or **thrilled** may express a stronger feeling than **delighted**, but **delighted** can be made stronger with *absolutely*, *more than* or *only too*: *I was* **more than delighted** *at the great success he had achieved.* **Overjoyed** and **thrilled** can be made negative and ironic with *not exactly* or *less than*: *She was* **not exactly overjoyed** *at the prospect of looking after her niece.* ◇ *He's* **less than thrilled** *at the prospect of working for his old rival.*

glance *verb* See also the entries for LOOK 1 and STARE

glance · peek · peep
These words all mean to look at sb/sth quickly.

PATTERNS AND COLLOCATIONS
▸ to glance / peek / peep **through** / **at** / **into** / **out of** / **over** sth
▸ to glance / peep **cautiously**

glance /glɑːns; *AmE* glæns/ [I] (always used with an adverb or preposition) to look quickly at sb/sth; to read sth quickly and not thoroughly: *She glanced at her watch.* ◇ *She glanced through the report on the way to the meeting.* See also **glance** → LOOK *noun*

peek [I] to look at sb/sth quickly and secretly, especially through a small opening, usually because you should not be looking at it: *No peeking!* ◇ *She peeked at the audience from behind the curtain.*
▸ **peek** *noun* [sing.]: *I took a quick peek inside.*

peep [I] to look at sb/sth quickly and secretly, especially through a small opening: *We caught her peeping through the keyhole.* ◇ *Could I just peep inside?*
▸ **peep** *noun* [sing.]: *I took a quick peep at the last page.*

> **NOTE** PEEK OR PEEP? These words are almost exactly the same in meaning. With **peek** there is sometimes a slightly stronger sense that you are looking at sth that you should not be looking at.

gloom *noun* See also the entry for GRIEF

gloom · depression · the blues · despondency
These are all words for a feeling of being sad and without hope.

PATTERNS AND COLLOCATIONS
▸ gloom / despondency **about** sth
▸ **deep** / **deepening** gloom / depression / despondency
▸ to **fill sb with** / **sink into** / **plunge into** gloom / depression
▸ the gloom / depression **deepens** / **lifts**
▸ a **feeling of** gloom / depression / despondency
▸ a **fit of** gloom / depression / the blues

gloom /gluːm/ [U, sing.] a feeling of being sad and without hope, especially among a group of people: *There is general gloom about the farming industry.* ◇ *The gloom deepened as the election results came in.* ◇ *An air of* **gloom and despondency** *settled over the household.* See also **gloomy** → DEPRESSED, **gloomy** → NEGATIVE

depression /dɪˈpreʃn/ [U] a feeling of being very sad, worried and without hope, often because you do not feel you can overcome your difficulties: *These results should not be a cause for depression.* ◇ *Her mood swung from the* **depths of depression** *to coping well.* See also **depress** → DISCOURAGE 2, **depressed** → DEPRESSED, **depressing** → NEGATIVE

the blues [pl.] (*rather informal*) feelings of sadness or unhappiness: *Everyone has had the feeling of the Monday morning blues.* ◇ *I'm planning a break in the sun as a way to* **beat the blues**.

despondency /dɪˈspɒndənsi; *AmE* -ˈspɑːn-/ [U] (*rather formal*) a feeling of being sad and without much hope, especially because sth you are doing is not successful or not going well: *Their earlier enthusiasm has been replaced by a mood of despondency.* See also **despondent** → DEPRESSED

go *verb*

1 go into the kitchen
2 go to China

1 go · get · head · pass · move · travel · make your way · make for sth · advance · proceed · run
These words all mean to move from one place to another.

PATTERNS AND COLLOCATIONS
▸ to go / get / pass / move / travel / make your way / advance / proceed / run **from... to...**
▸ to go / get / head / move / travel / make your way / advance / proceed **to** sb / sth
▸ to go / head / move / travel / make your way / advance / proceed / run **towards** sb / sth
▸ to head / make **for** sb / sth
▸ to go / get somewhere / make your way **by** bus / train / car, etc.
▸ to go / get / head / make your way / make for **home**

go [I] (always used with an adverb or preposition) to move from one place to another; to move somewhere in order to get to a particular place; to move in a particular way: *She went into her room and shut the door behind her.* ◇ *She's gone to see her sister.* ◇ *Could you* **go and** *get me a towel?* ◇ (*AmE*) *Go get me a towel.* ◇ *Slow down — you're going too fast.* ◇ *The car went skidding off the road.* ❶ **Been**, not **gone**, is used as the past participle when sb has gone to a place and come back: *She's gone to town* (= and is there now or on her way there). ◇ *I've just been to town* (= I went to town and have now returned) ❶ **Go** is usually used from the point of view of the person who is moving somewhere. **OPP** **come** → COME 1 See also **go** → LEAVE 1

get [I, T] (always used with an adverb or preposition) to go to or from a particular place or in a particular direction, sometimes with difficulty; to make sb/sth do this: *How can we get to the other side of town?* ◇ *I don't know how he managed to get down from the roof.* ◇ *She got back into bed.* ◇ *Where have they got to* (= where are they)? ◇ *We'd better call a taxi and get you home.* See also **get** → GET 4

head [I] (always used with an adverb or preposition) (*rather informal*) to move in a particular direction; to start going to a particular place: *Where are we heading?* ◇ *She headed for the door.* ◇ *The boat was heading out to sea.*

pass [I] (*rather formal*) (always used with an adverb or preposition) to go along or through a place or past a particular point: *The procession passed slowly along the street.* ◇ *Bomber planes were passing overhead all night.*

move [I] (always used with an adverb or preposition) to go in a particular direction, especially a short distance: *Phil moved towards the window.* ◊ *We moved a little nearer.* ◊ *The traffic moved slowly along the highway.*

travel (-ll-, *AmE* -l-) [I] to go or move at a particular speed, in a particular direction or over a particular distance: *The truck was travelling at 90 mph when it veered off the road.* ◊ *Messages travel from the nerve endings to the brain.* ◊ *News travels fast these days.*

make your 'way *phrase* (always used with an adverb or preposition) to go somewhere, especially slowly or when this is difficult to do: *Will you be able to **make your own way** to the airport* (= get there without help or a ride)*?* ◊ *She turned and made her way home.*

'make for sth *phrasal verb* to move towards sth, especially when you are in a hurry or feel the need to get somewhere or get out of somewhere: *People were making for the exits.* ◊ *He advised us to get out of the city and make for the coast.*

advance [I] (*rather formal*) to move forwards or towards sb/sth, often in a threatening way or in order to attack: *Troops were given the order to advance.* ◊ *They had advanced 20 miles by nightfall.* ◊ *The mob **advanced on us**, shouting angrily.* **OPP** retreat → WITHDRAW 1
▶ **advance** *noun* [C]: *Their **advance on** the city seemed unstoppable.*

proceed /prə'siːd; *AmE* proʊ-/ [I] (always used with an adverb or preposition) (*formal*) to move or travel in a particular direction, especially to continue a journey: *The marchers proceeded slowly along the street.* ◊ *Passengers for Frankfurt should proceed to Gate 14.*

run [I] (always used with an adverb or preposition) to move over a surface, especially quickly, in a particular direction: *The car ran off the road into a ditch.* ◊ *A shiver ran down my spine.* ◊ *The sledge ran smoothly over the snow.* ◊ *The old tramlines are still there but no trams run on them now.*

---

2 go · fly · travel · come · do · drive · ride · run · cover
These words all mean to move between different places, especially over a long distance.

PATTERNS AND COLLOCATIONS
▶ to go / fly / travel / come / drive / ride / run **from / to** sth
▶ to go / fly / travel / come / drive / ride **with** sb
▶ to go / fly / travel / come / do / drive / ride / cover **50 miles / 1 000 km**
▶ to go / travel / come **by air / sea / boat / ship / train / car**
▶ to go / travel / come / do sth / cover sth **on foot**
▶ to go / fly / travel / come / drive **east / north / south / west**
▶ to go / travel / come / drive **overland**
▶ to travel / come / drive **a long distance**

go [I] to make a journey from one place to another; to do so over a particular distance: *I usually go to work by bus.* ◊ *She's gone to Brazil on vacation.* ◊ *I have to go to Rome on business.* ◊ *Here's a list of things to remember before you go.* ◊ *We had gone many miles without seeing another car.* ❶ **Been**, not **gone**, is used as the past participle when sb has gone to a place and come back: *She has gone to China* (= she is now in China or is on her way there). ◊ *She's been to China* (= she went to China and has now returned). See also **go** → LEAVE 1

fly [I, T] to go on a journey in an aircraft: *When are you flying to Bangkok?* ◊ *It was the first time I'd ever flown.* ◊ *She always flies business class.* ◊ *Who was the first person to fly the Atlantic* (= travel over it in an aircraft)*?* See also **fly** → DRIVE 1, **fly** → FLY 1

travel (-ll-, *AmE* -l-) [I, T] to go from one place to another, especially over a long distance: *I spent a year travelling around Africa.* ◊ *Here are some tips on how to keep healthy while you're travelling.* ◊ *He **went travelling*** (= spent time visiting different places) *for six months.* ◊ *We **travelled the length and breadth of*** (= all over) *the country.* ◊ *Children under five **travel free**.* See also **travel** → TRAVEL *noun*, **traveller** → PASSENGER

come [I, T] to make a journey to a place; to make a journey of a particular length, in a particular type of vehicle, etc: *People came from all over the world to settle here.* ◊ *How far have you come?* ◊ *He came to England by ship.* See also **come in** → ENTER

NOTE **GO** OR **COME?** **Go** is used when speaking from the point of view of sb who is at the place where the journey starts. **Come** expresses the point of view of sb who is at the place where the journey ends: *We're going to Australia to visit our daughter.* ◊ *I hope you can come to Australia to visit us.*

do [T] to travel a particular distance or go at a particular speed; to complete a journey: *How many miles did you do yesterday?* ◊ *My car does 40 miles to the gallon* (= uses one gallon of petrol to travel 40 miles). ◊ *The car was doing 90 miles an hour.* ◊ *We did the round trip* (= went there and back) *in under three hours.*

drive [I, T] to make a journey by road, especially in a car: *Shall we drive or go by train?* ◊ *We must have driven over 600 kilometres today.* ◊ *We drove the rest of the way in silence.* See also **drive** → DRIVE *verb* 1, **drive** → FLIGHT *noun*

ride [I, T] (usually used with an adverb or preposition) (*especially AmE*) to travel in a vehicle, especially as a passenger: *The men loaded my stuff onto the pick-up and I rode with them in the cab.* ◊ *You could ride right along the coast by tram.* ◊ *(AmE) He rides the subway every day.* See also **ride** → FLIGHT *noun*

run [I] (of a bus, train, etc.) to travel on a particular route: *The buses run every thirty minutes.* ◊ *He claimed that 95 per cent of trains **run on time**.* ◊ *The train was **running late*** (= was not going to arrive on time). ❶ **Run** is usually used to talk about how often or at what times there are buses, trains, etc.

cover [T] to travel the distance mentioned: *We must have covered over 20 miles.* ◊ *I **covered a lot of ground** rapidly and soon caught up with them.*

---

go away *phrasal verb*

go away · get out of here · get away · go off · decamp · be/go on your way · clear out
These words all mean to leave a place.

NOTE **GO AWAY** OR **LEAVE?** The words in the **leave** entry emphasize the act or time of leaving sb/sth; the words in the **go away** entry emphasize the need or desire of the speaker to be somewhere else or for sb else to be somewhere else. See also the entry for LEAVE 1

PATTERNS AND COLLOCATIONS
▶ to go away / get away / decamp **from** sb / sth
▶ to go off / decamp **to** sth
▶ to go off / decamp / clear out **with** sth
▶ to go away / get out of here / get away **now / soon**

,go a'way *phrasal verb* (used especially in orders) to leave a person or place: *Just go away and leave me alone!* ◊ *Go away and think about it.* ◊ *It's been over seven years since he went away.* **OPP** come back → RETURN 1

,get 'out of here *phrase* (used especially in orders) (*especially AmE, informal*) to leave a person or place: *I'm bored — let's get out of here.* ◊ *Hey you two, you'd better get out of here before the teacher catches you!* ❶ In very informal spoken American English you can say *I'm/We're outta here!* meaning 'I'm/We're leaving', often, though not always, because you are feeling angry or bored: *(AmE, slang) I wasn't going to listen to her yell at me anymore so I just said, 'Bye — I'm outta here.'*

,get a'way *phrasal verb* to succeed in leaving a place: *I won't be able to get away from the office before seven.*

,go 'off *phrasal verb* to leave a person or place, especially in order to do sth: *'Where did David go?' 'He went off to find his dad.'* ◊ *She went off to college last year and I haven't seen her since.* ◊ *Matt went off in search of a flashlight.* See also **retire** → WITHDRAW 1

decamp /dɪˈkæmp/ [I] (*especially BrE, written*) to leave a place, often suddenly or secretly: *The first person to take up the job decamped after a few days.* ◇ *The firm's production unit has decamped to California.*

be/go on your 'way idiom (*especially BrE*) to leave a person or place: *It's time we were on our way* (= we should leave). ◇ *He went on his way and I never saw him again.*

,clear 'out phrasal verb (*especially BrE, informal*) to leave a place quickly, especially taking all your things with you: *He cleared out with the money and left her with the kids.* ◇ *You'd better clear out of here before they find you.* ❶ In American English **clear out** is only used about a whole group of people leaving a place, not an individual person: *Homeless people in the camp have been given 72 hours to pack up and clear out.*

go by *phrasal verb*

go by · pass · elapse · wear on · progress · tick away
These are all words that can be used when an hour, day, year, etc. moves forward in time.

▸ **hours / days** go by / pass / elapse
▸ a **season / a year / time** goes by / passes / elapses
▸ the **day / night / season / year / time** wears on / progresses
▸ the **minutes / seconds** go by / pass / elapse / tick away
▸ **time** ticks away
▸ time goes by / passes / wears on / ticks away **slowly**
▸ time goes by / passes **quickly**

,go 'by phrasal verb (of time) to move forward: *Things will get easier as time goes by.* ◇ *The weeks went slowly by.*
pass [I] (of time) to go by: *Six months passed and we still had no news of them.* ◇ *We grew more anxious with every passing day.*
elapse /ɪˈlæps/ [I] (not usually used in the progressive tenses) (*formal, written*) (of time) to go by: *Many years elapsed before they met again.*

> **NOTE** GO BY, PASS OR ELAPSE? The main difference between these words is in register: **go by** is the least formal and the most frequently used in spoken English; **elapse** is the most formal and is only really used in written English.

,wear 'on phrasal verb (*especially written*) (of a period of time) to go by, especially in a way that seems slow: *As the evening wore slowly on, she became more and more tired.*
progress [I] (*written*) to go forward in time: *The weather became colder as the day progressed.*

> **NOTE** WEAR ON AND PROGRESS These words are both used especially to say that sth developed during a particular period of time or during a particular event or activity: *The situation worsened as the year wore on.* ◇ *The visiting team's confidence increased as the game progressed.* They are not usually used with a noun in the plural: *Many years progressed/wore on before they met again.*

,tick a'way phrasal verb (of minutes, seconds or time) to pass steadily, especially when you do not have much time to do what you need to do: *I had to get to the airport by two, and the minutes were ticking away.*

good *adj.*

1 in good condition/Good work!
2 Now is a good time to...
3 a good idea/reason/question/point
4 a good actor; good at languages; good with your hands
5 a good person/deed/life
6 a good impression/opinion/reputation
7 a good boy/girl/dog

1 See also the entries for BETTER, EXCELLENT, GREAT 1 and WONDERFUL
good · fine · quality · high quality · sterling · prime · superior
These words all describe sth that is of a good quality.

▸ (of) good / fine / sterling / prime / superior **quality**
▸ a good / fine / quality / high quality / sterling / superior **performance / service**
▸ a good / fine / quality / high quality / superior **product**

good of a high quality or an acceptable standard: *I think that make of car's pretty good.* ◇ *The old piano was in good condition.* ◇ *Your work is just not good enough.* ◇ *This is as good a place as any to spend the night.* ❶ **Good** is used especially about everyday things and places and work that people do. **OPP** bad → POOR 2
fine [usually before noun] of a high quality: *It's a particularly fine example of Saxon architecture.* ◇ *They enjoy good food and fine wines.* ◇ *people who enjoy the finer things in life* (= for example, art, good food etc.) ◇ *It was his finest hour* (= most successful period) *as manager of the England team.* ❶ **Fine** is used especially about art, culture and food. **OPP** poor → POOR 2
quality [only before noun] (*rather informal*) of a high quality: *We specialize in quality furniture.* ◇ *We offer a quality service to all customers.* ❶ **Quality** is used especially in advertising and selling. See also **quality** → VALUE *noun* 1
high quality [only before noun] of a good quality: *We always use the highest quality ingredients.* ◇ *High quality TV shows are getting rarer all the time.*

> **NOTE** QUALITY OR HIGH QUALITY? These words have the same meaning but **quality** is more informal than **high quality** and is only used by people trying to advertise or sell sth.

sterling [usually before noun] (*especially BrE, formal*) of very good quality: *He's done some sterling work.* ◇ *Thanks to all your sterling efforts, we've raised over £12 000.* ◇ *She has some sterling qualities.*
prime [only before noun] of the best quality: *Use only prime cuts* (= pieces) *of beef.* ◇ *a prime location in the centre of town*
superior /suːˈpɪəriə(r); sjuː-; *AmE* suːˈpɪr-/ [usually before noun] of a very good quality; better than other, similar things: *The hotel offers superior accommodation and leisure facilities.* ❶ **Superior** is used especially in advertisements. **OPP** inferior → POOR 2

2 See also the entries for ADEQUATE, FINE
good · appropriate · suitable · right · convenient · fitting · apt · cut out for/to be sth · fit
These words all describe sb/sth that will work well for a particular purpose or situation.

▸ good / appropriate / suitable / right / convenient / fitting / apt / cut out / fit **for** sb / sth
▸ good / appropriate / suitable **as** sb / sth
▸ good / appropriate / suitable / right / convenient / fitting / apt / fit **that...**
▸ good / appropriate / suitable / right / convenient / fitting / fit **to do sth**
▸ a good / an appropriate / a suitable / the right / a convenient **time** to do sth / **place** for sth
▸ a good / an appropriate / a suitable / the right / a fitting **thing** to do / say
▸ a good / an appropriate / a suitable / the right **person** for sth

good suitable or convenient for a particular purpose or person: *Now is a good time to buy a house.* ◇ *Do you think she would be good for the job?* ◇ *Can we change the time of the meeting? Monday is no good for me.* **OPP** bad → WRONG 3

appropriate acceptable or correct for a particular situation or person: *Jeans are not appropriate for a formal interview.* ◇ *Would it be appropriate to take him a small gift?* ◇ *We must make sure that appropriate action is taken.* **OPP inappropriate** → WRONG 3
▸ **appropriately** *adv.*: *Make sure you dress appropriately for the meeting.*

suitable (*BrE or formal, AmE*) acceptable or correct for a particular purpose, person or situation: *The exercise-with-answer-key format makes the book suitable for self-study.* ◇ *I don't think he's a suitable partner for her.* ◇ *Do you think he's suitable as a babysitter for such young kids?* ❶ In American English **suitable** is only used in formal or official language; in everyday spoken or written American English use **appropriate** or **right**. **OPP unsuitable** → WRONG 3
▸ **suitably** *adv.*: *suitably qualified candidates*

right correct for a particular situation, purpose, thing or person: *He's definitely the right man for the job.* ◇ *I don't think she was right for you* (= for you to have a relationship with). ◇ *Next time we'll get it right.* ◇ *You're not holding it the right way up.* ◇ (*BrE*) *Are you sure that sweater's on the right way round?* ◇ (*AmE*) *Are you sure that sweater's on the right way (around)?* **OPP wrong** → WRONG 3

NOTE GOOD, APPROPRIATE, SUITABLE OR RIGHT? How **appropriate** or **suitable** sb/sth is, is a matter of judgement and it depends on what is acceptable to other people. How **good** sb/sth depends more on what you like yourself or what is convenient. How **right** sb/sth is is more a matter of fact: *Do you think she would be a/an good/appropriate/suitable person to ask?* ◇ *a right person to ask* ◇ *She's definitely the good/appropriate/suitable person to ask.* ◇ *She's definitely the right person to ask.* **Good**, **suitable** and **right** can all be used when sth is correct for a particular purpose, but **appropriate** is only used about people or situations.

convenient (especially about times and arrangements) not causing any problems: *I can't see them now. It's not convenient.* ◇ *We'll arrange a mutually convenient meeting place.* **OPP inconvenient** → WRONG 3

fitting (*formal*) suitable or right for an occasion: *The award was a fitting tribute to her years of devoted work.* ◇ *It was a fitting end to a glamorous career.*

apt suitable for a particular situation: *That question seemed quite apt in the circumstances.* ◇ *'Love at first sight' is an apt description of how I felt when I first saw her.*
▸ **aptly** *adv.*: *the aptly named Grand Hotel*

cut 'out for sth, **cut 'out to be sth** *idiom* (*rather informal*) to have the qualities and abilities that are suitable for a particular job or activity: *He's not cut out for teaching.* ◇ *He's not cut out to be a teacher.*

fit suitable; having the right qualities or skills for sth: *The food was not fit for human consumption.* ◇ *It was a meal fit for a king* (= of very good quality). ◇ (*BrE*) *He's in no fit state to see anyone.* ❶ In American English **fit** is not needed here: (*AmE*) *He's in no state to see anyone.* **OPP unfit** → WRONG 3

3 See also the entry for RATIONAL

good · solid · sound · valid · legitimate · well founded
These words all describe sth that has a sensible, logical basis and that there are good reasons for.

▸ a good / solid / sound / valid / legitimate **reason / basis**
▸ good / solid / sound / valid **evidence**
▸ good / solid / sound **advice**
▸ a good / sound / valid / legitimate **argument**
▸ a good / sound / valid **conclusion**
▸ to have good / sound **judgement**
▸ a good / valid / legitimate **question / point / excuse**
▸ **perfectly** good / sound / valid / legitimate

good sensible, logical and very appropriate to what is being discussed or considered: *'They won't be able to find the way without a map.' 'Good point.'* ◇ *You'll have to think of a better excuse than that!* ◇ *That's a really good idea.* ◇ *Students are not allowed to miss classes without good reason.* ◇ *I have good reason to be suspicious.* ❶ **Good** is used especially about sb's ideas, statements, questions and reasons for doing sth. **OPP bad** → WRONG 3

solid sensible and logical; having a strong basis in fact or reality: *Her advice is always solid and practical.* ◇ *There's solid evidence to show he wasn't there when the crime took place.* ◇ *Their friendship provided a solid foundation for their future together.* **OPP flimsy** ❶ A *flimsy excuse* or *flimsy evidence* is difficult to believe: *He keeps calling on the flimsiest of pretexts.*
▸ **solidly** *adv.*: *Their argument was solidly based on fact.*

sound that you can rely on and that will probably give good results: *He's a person of very sound judgement.* ◇ *The proposal makes sound commercial sense.* ◇ *Their policies are environmentally sound.* **OPP unsound** ❶ A method that is **unsound** contains mistakes and cannot be relied on to give good results; an idea or practice that is **unsound** is not acceptable, especially for moral or political reasons: *The use of disposable products is considered ecologically unsound.*

valid based on what is logical or true, in a way that supports the decision or claim being made: *The point you make is perfectly valid.* ◇ *Accepting valid criticism is an important part of the learning process.* **OPP invalid** ❶ An **invalid** point, criticism, argument, etc. is not based on all the facts, and therefore not correct.
▸ **validity** /vəˈlɪdəti/ *noun* [U]: *Of course we recognize the validity of that argument.*

legitimate /lɪˈdʒɪtɪmət/ (*rather formal*) based on a fair and acceptable reason: *All legitimate grievances should be raised with your line manager.* ◇ *The court ruled that celebrities' children were not a legitimate target for press intrusion.*

,well 'founded (*rather formal*) having good reasons or evidence to cause or support it: *His fears proved to be well founded.*

---

4 See also the entry for IMPRESSIVE

good · skilled · great · able · competent · talented · capable · gifted · skilful · proficient · accomplished · professional
These words all describe sb who does sth with skill.

▸ good / skilled / great / competent / gifted / skilful / proficient / accomplished **at** sth
▸ good / skilled / great / competent / gifted **with** sb / sth
▸ skilled / competent / gifted / proficient / professional **in** sth
▸ a good / a skilled / a great / an able / a competent / a talented / a capable / a gifted / a skilful **teacher**
▸ a good / a skilled / a great / a talented / a capable / a skilful / an accomplished **performer**
▸ a good / a skilled / a great / a competent / a talented / a gifted / a skilful / an accomplished **player**
▸ a good / a great / a competent / a talented / a gifted / an accomplished **actor / musician / singer / artist / painter / writer**
▸ a good / great / competent / capable **manager**
▸ sb's competent / skilful / professional **handling** of sth
▸ **very** good / skilled / able / competent / talented / capable / gifted / skilful / proficient / accomplished / professional
▸ **extremely** good / skilled / able / competent / talented / capable / gifted / skilful / accomplished / professional
▸ **highly** skilled / able / competent / capable / gifted / skilful / proficient / accomplished / professional
▸ **perfectly** able / competent / capable
▸ **naturally** good at sth / talented / gifted
▸ **technically** skilled / able / competent / proficient / accomplished

good able to do, use sth or deal with people well: *She's a really good actor.* ◇ *I'm not really a very good cook.* ◇ *Are you any good at languages?* ◇ *Nick has always been good at finding cheap deals.* ◇ *Jo's very **good with** her **hands*** (= able to make things, etc.). **OPP** **bad**, **poor** → INCOMPETENT

skilled (of a person) having enough ability, experience and knowledge to be able to do a particular job or activity well; (of a job) needing special abilities or training: *We need more skilled engineers.* ◇ *Skilled workers can expect to earn pretty high wages after a few years.* ◇ *There's a shortage of **skilled labour*** (= workers who are able to do jobs that need particular skills). ◇ *Furniture-making is very skilled work.* **OPP** **unskilled ❶** Unskilled people have no special skills; **unskilled** work needs no special skills: *unskilled manual workers* See also **skill** → SKILL 1, **skill** → SKILL 2

great (*informal*, *especially spoken*) extremely good at sth: *She's great at chess.* ◇ *You're a great cook – this is delicious!* ◇ *He's great with the kids.* **OPP** **rotten** → INCOMPETENT

able (*rather formal*) good at tasks and activities that require intelligence or academic ability: *He was a very able man in business matters.* ◇ *We aim to help the less able in society to lead an independent life.* See also **ability** → SKILL 1

▶ **ably** *adv.*: *We were ably assisted by a team of volunteers.*

competent /ˈkɒmpɪtənt; *AmE* ˈkɑːm-/ having enough skill or knowledge to do sth well or to the necessary standard: *Make sure the builders are **competent to** carry out the work.* **❶** Competent can either mean that sb can do sth well, or that they can do it just well enough: *He's very competent in all his work.* ◇ *Ron was a competent player – more than that, he was good!* **OPP** **incompetent** → IN-COMPETENT, See also **competence** → SKILL 2

▶ **competently** *adv.*: *You must be able to perform competently and efficiently the following task:…*

talented /ˈtæləntɪd/ having a natural ability to do sth well, especially sth connected with art, music, literature, drama or sport: *We're looking for talented young designers to join our team.* ◇ *The kids at this school are all exceptionally talented in some way.* See also **talent** → SKILL 1

capable having the ability to manage things well: *She's an extremely capable teacher.* ◇ *I'll leave things in your **capable hands*** (= leave you to deal with sth because I know you will deal with it well).

gifted having a lot of natural ability or intelligence: *She goes to a school for gifted children.* ◇ *He's an extremely gifted young player.* ◇ *She's especially gifted at art.* See also **gift** → SKILL 1

NOTE **TALENTED** OR **GIFTED?** People who are **talented** are usually good at a particular thing such as music or sport. People who are **gifted** may be good at a particular thing or just very intelligent. You can be *academically gifted* but NOT: ~~academically talented~~. **Gifted** is often used about children or young people because you do not need to have a lot of experience in sth to be gifted at it.

skilful (*BrE*) (*AmE* **skillful**) (of a person) good at doing sth, especially sth that needs a particular ability or special training; (of an action) done with skill: *As Foreign Secretary he proved to be a skilful diplomat.* ◇ *Everyone admired her skilful handling of the affair.* See also **skill** → SKILL 1, **skill** → SKILL 2

proficient /prəˈfɪʃnt/ (*rather formal*) able to do sth well because of training and practice: *She's proficient in several languages.* ◇ *With practice, you should become proficient within six months.* See also **proficiency** → SKILL 2

accomplished /əˈkʌmplɪʃt; *AmE* əˈkɑːm-/ (*rather formal*) having become very good at a particular thing through training or experience; having learned a lot of skills: *He was an accomplished linguist, fluent in French and German.* ◇ *She was an elegant and accomplished woman.*

professional showing that sb is well trained and extremely skilled: *He dealt with the problem in a highly professional way.* **❶** In this meaning **professional** is often used with *very* or *highly*; it is NOT used with the names of

jobs: *a professional teacher/actor/singer, etc.* is a person who teaches/acts/sings as a job. **OPP** **amateurish ❶** An **amateurish** attempt at sth is not done well or with skill: *Detectives described the burglary as 'crude and amateurish'.*

5 good · ethical · moral · principled · virtuous · scrupulous
These words all describe behaviour, actions and ideas that are morally right, or a person whose behaviour is morally right.

PATTERNS AND COLLOCATIONS
▶ a good / moral / principled / virtuous / scrupulous **person**
▶ a good / principled / virtuous / scrupulous **man / woman**
▶ a good / moral / virtuous **life**
▶ good / ethical / moral **behaviour / practices / principles**
▶ an ethical / a moral / a principled **stand / stance / position**
▶ **very** good / ethical / moral / virtuous / scrupulous
▶ **highly** moral / principled

good morally right; behaving in a way that is morally right: *Giving her that money was a good thing to do.* ◇ *He prayed that God would make him a better person.* **OPP** **bad**, **evil**, **wicked** → EVIL, See also **good** → KIND *adj.*, **good**, **goodness** → MORALITY *noun*

ethical /ˈeθɪkl/ morally right or acceptable: *Is it ethical to promote cigarettes through advertising?* ◇ *There needs to be a greater emphasis on **ethical investment*** (= investing money in businesses that are considered to be morally acceptable). **❶** Ethical is not used to describe a person, but it can describe a person's behaviour. It is often used to talk about the actions and activities of businesses. **OPP** **unethical** → WRONG 4, See also **ethical** → MORAL *adj.*, **ethics** → PRINCIPLE 1

▶ **ethically** *adv.*: *Most people find the commercial exploitation of children ethically unacceptable.*

moral following the standards of behaviour considered acceptable and right by most people: *He led a very moral life.* ◇ *We try to teach our students to be conscientious, moral young people.* **OPP** **immoral** → WRONG 4, See also **amoral** → CORRUPT *adj.*, **moral** → MORAL *adj.*, **morals**, **morality** → PRINCIPLE 1

▶ **morally** *adv.*: *They try to live a life that is morally pure.*

principled /ˈprɪnsəpld/ having strong beliefs about what is right and wrong; based on strong beliefs: *The new biography presents her as a deeply principled woman.* ◇ *We need to take a principled stand against the government's actions.* **OPP** **unprincipled** → CORRUPT

virtuous /ˈvɜːtʃuəs; *AmE* ˈvɜːrtʃ-/ (*rather formal*) behaving in a very good and moral way: *Unmarried women were expected to live modest, virtuous lives.* See also **virtue** → MORALITY

scrupulous /ˈskruːpjələs/ very careful to be honest and to do what is morally right: *She has a reputation for scrupulous honesty.* ◇ *He is **scrupulous in** all his business dealings.* **OPP** **unscrupulous** → CORRUPT, See also **scruple** → DOUBT *noun* 2

▶ **scrupulously** *adv.*: *All court proceedings need to be scrupulously fair to each side.*

6 good · positive · favourable · glowing · admiring · complimentary · appreciative · flattering · approving
These words all describe sb/sth that shows approval of sb/sth.

PATTERNS AND COLLOCATIONS
▶ positive / complimentary **about** sb / sth
▶ favourable / complimentary **to** sb / sth
▶ admiring / appreciative / approving **of** sb / sth
▶ a good / a positive / a favourable / a complimentary / an appreciative / a flattering / an approving **comment**
▶ a good / a positive / a complimentary / an appreciative / a flattering / an approving **remark**
▶ a good / positive / favourable **response**
▶ a good / positive / favourable / glowing **report**
▶ a good / positive / favourable **opinion / impression / reaction / response**

▶ to **show** sb / sth in a good / positive / favourable **light**
▶ **very** good / positive / favourable / complimentary / appreciative / flattering / approving
▶ **highly** positive / favourable / complimentary

good showing or getting approval or respect: *The school has an extremely good reputation.* ◇ *Initial reactions to the proposal have been good so far.* ◇ *Her school report was much better this year.*

positive expressing agreement, approval or support for sb/sth: *Most of his remarks were positive, but there were a few criticisms.* ◇ *You should try to be a bit more positive about your students.* **OPP** negative → NEGATIVE
▶ **positively** adv.: *She was portrayed very positively in the movie.*

favourable (*BrE*) (*AmE* **favorable**) /ˈfeɪvərəbl/ (*rather formal*) showing or getting approval of sb/sth: *The performance drew a lot of favourable comments from reviewers.* ◇ *The report was very favourable to the existing government.* **OPP** unfavourable ❶ An **unfavourable** comment or attitude shows disapproval of sb/sth: *The documentary presents him in a very unfavourable light.*
▶ **favourably** adv.: *He speaks very favourably of your work.*

NOTE GOOD OR FAVOURABLE? Favourable is a more formal way of saying **good**. It is used with some structures and collocations where you cannot use **good** in this meaning: *a favourable comment* is a comment showing approval, but *a good comment* is a clever comment; if sth is *favourable to sb* it shows approval, but to be *good to sb* is to be kind to them.

glowing /ˈɡləʊɪŋ; *AmE* ˈɡloʊɪŋ/ [usually before noun] giving enthusiastic praise: *He described her performance in glowing terms.* **OPP** damning → CRITICAL

admiring showing strong approval and admiration of sb/sth: *She was used to receiving admiring glances from men.* ❶ Common collocates of this word are *glance, look, gaze, smile* and *audience/crowd*.
▶ **admiringly** adv.: *'That's very clever,' he said admiringly.* See also **admire** → RESPECT *verb*, **admiration** → ADMIRATION

complimentary /ˌkɒmplɪˈmentri; *AmE* ˌkɑːm-/ expressing admiration, praise or strong approval: *She was extremely complimentary about his work.* See also **compliment** → PRAISE *verb*, **compliment** → TRIBUTE *noun*

appreciative /əˈpriːʃətɪv/ showing pleasure in or enjoyment of sb/sth: *The audience was highly appreciative.* ◇ *She watched them with an appreciative smile.* See also **appreciate** → APPRECIATE

flattering saying nice things about sb/sth: *He made several flattering remarks.* See also **flatter** → FLATTER

approving showing that you think sb/sth is good or acceptable: *He gave me an approving nod.* **OPP** disapproving → CRITICAL
▶ **approvingly** adv.: *'Your work's very good,' she said approvingly.*

7 good · obedient · dutiful · well behaved
These words all describe a person, especially a child, who behaves well.

PATTERNS AND COLLOCATIONS
▶ a good / an obedient / a dutiful / a well-behaved **child**
▶ a good / an obedient / a dutiful **daughter / son / wife / servant**
▶ a good / an obedient / a well-behaved **boy / girl**
▶ a good / an obedient **dog**

good (especially of a child) behaving well by doing what they are told or expected to do: *You can stay up late if you're good.* ◇ *Get dressed now, there's a good boy.* ◇ *'That's a good dog,' I said, patting its head.* ❶ **Good** in this meaning usually describes children or dogs, but it can also be used to describe a loyal wife or servant, especially in societies where wives and servants are expected to do as they are told. A *good husband* is also loyal and takes care of his wife, but is not usually expected to obey her. **OPP** bad, naughty → NAUGHTY

obedient /əˈbiːdiənt/ (of a person or animal) doing what they are told to do: *He was always **obedient to** his father's wishes.* ◇ *Did he really expect her to trot right after him, like an obedient dog?* **OPP** disobedient → NAUGHTY, See also **obey** → FOLLOW 3
▶ **obedience** noun [U]: *blind/unquestioning obedience* ◇ *He has acted in obedience to the law.* **OPP** disobedience → NAUGHTY
▶ **obediently** adv.: *He ate up his dinner obediently, like a child.*

dutiful /ˈdjuːtɪfl; *AmE* ˈduː-/ (*rather formal, written*) (especially of sb's son, daughter or wife) doing everything that they are expected to do; (of actions) showing how dutiful sb is: *It's about time she helped out like a dutiful daughter.* ◇ *He paid a dutiful visit to his grandmother.*

,well be'haved (especially of a child) behaving in a way that other people think is polite and correct: *All her children were cheerful and well behaved.* ◇ *On the whole, the crowd was pretty well behaved.*

good thing *noun*

good thing · bonus · help · blessing · boon · godsend
These are all words for sth that helps sb or is useful to them, or sth that improves a situation.

PATTERNS AND COLLOCATIONS
▶ a good thing / bonus / blessing / boon / godsend **for** sb
▶ a bonus / help / blessing / boon / godsend **to** sb
▶ a good thing / bonus / help / blessing **that...**
▶ a **real / great** bonus / help / blessing / boon

'good thing [C] something that you are pleased about because it makes a situation good or better: *It's a good thing (that) I remembered the camera.* ◇ *Think about all the good things in your life.* ◇ *The good thing about living in the city is the number of good restaurants there are.* **OPP** bad thing ❶ The opposite is **bad thing**: *If you ask me, a little uncertainty is no bad thing – you can make mistakes if you're overconfident.*

bonus /ˈbəʊnəs; *AmE* ˈboʊ-/ [C] something extra that is more or better than you were expecting: *The fact that I can walk to work in the morning is an **added bonus**.* ◇ *It came as an unexpected bonus when Jim said he'd lend us his car.*

help [sing.] a person or thing that helps sb: *Your advice was a great help to me.* ◇ *He was more of a hindrance than a help* (= caused more problems than he helped with). ◇ (*ironic*) *You're a great help, I must say!* (= you are no help at all). **OPP** hindrance → OBSTACLE

blessing [C] something that makes a situation good or better: *It's a blessing that no one was in the house when the fire started.* ◇ *You should stop complaining and count your blessings* (= think of the good things you have). ◇ *Not getting that job proved to be a blessing in disguise* (= it seemed to be a bad thing at first, but in fact was a good thing). ◇ *Being famous can be a mixed blessing* (= sth that has advantages and disadvantages). **OPP** curse ❶ The opposite is **curse**: *Noise is the curse of modern life.* ◇ *Her looks turned out to be more of a curse than a blessing.*

NOTE GOOD THING OR BLESSING? A **blessing** is sth important, that is good from any point of view (such as not getting burnt to death). A **good thing** can be important, but it is also used for less important things that you just happen to be pleased about (such as remembering your camera).

boon [sing.] something that is very helpful or useful to you: *The new software will be an enormous boon to home computer users.*

godsend [sing.] something good that happens unexpectedly and helps sb/sth when they need help: *Her new job was a godsend – now she could finally be independent.*

go on to sth *phrasal verb*

go on to (do) sth · follow sth up · proceed to do sth · follow sth with sth
These words all mean to do sth after finishing sth else.

PATTERNS AND COLLOCATIONS
▶ to go on / proceed to **discuss / explain / discuss / state** sth

,go 'on to sth, go on to do sth *phrasal verb* to move to the next thing in a series; to do sth after finishing sth else: *Let's go on to the next item on the agenda.* ◇ *I hope eventually to go on to postgraduate work.* ◇ *The book goes on to describe his experiences in the army.* ❶ **Go on to sth** is often followed by a verb relating to a formal discussion or presentation of a subject: *to go on to describe/explain/discuss/state/argue/suggest sth.* It is also often used to talk about how people's lives or careers develop: *She went on to become a doctor/perform the role of Juliet/do well.* And it is used in sports journalism to describe a team's or sportsperson's successes: *The team went on to defeat sb/win sth/prove themselves/score.*

,follow sth 'up *phrasal verb* (*especially written*) to add to sth that you have just done by doing sth else: *You should follow up your phone call with an email or a letter.* ◇ *The initial order for four machines was followed up by an order for five more.* ❶ People might typically **follow up** a *phone call, a sale, a discussion or a conversation.*

proceed to do sth [T] (*rather formal, especially written*) to do sth next, having done sth else first: *He outlined his plans and then proceeded to explain them in more detail.* ◇ (*humorous*) *Having said she wasn't hungry, she then proceeded to order a three-course meal.* ❶ **Proceed to** is often followed by a verb relating to people explaining or describing sth as part of a formal presentation: *to proceed to tell sb/state/show/demonstrate/outline/explain/describe/discuss/examine/consider sth*

follow sth with sth *phrasal verb* [T] to do sth after doing sth else: *Follow your treatment with plenty of rest.*

go out *phrasal verb*

go out · see · date · be together · court · woo
These words all mean to have a romantic relationship with sb.

go 'out *phrasal verb* (used especially in the progressive tenses) (especially of young people) to spend time with sb and have a romantic or sexual relationship with them: *Tom has been **going out with** Lucy for six weeks.* ◇ *How long have Tom and Lucy been going out?*

see [T] (used especially in the progressive tenses) to spend time with sb and have a romantic or sexual relationship with them: ***Are you seeing anyone** at the moment?*

date [T, I] (used especially in the progressive tenses) (*especially AmE*) to spend time with sb and have a romantic or sexual relationship with them: *She's been dating Ron for several months.* ◇ *How long have you two been dating?* See also **date** → MEETING *noun* 2, **date** → PARTNER *noun* 2

NOTE **GO OUT WITH, SEE** OR **DATE?** These expressions are all commonly used in the progressive tenses with time expressions such as *how long, for three months,* etc. This suggests a temporary relationship that may or may not lead to sth more serious or permanent. **Date** is not used much in British English and is just beginning to sound old-fashioned in American English. Both **go out** and **date** place an emphasis on going out to different places and doing things with your partner, but **see** does not.

be together *phrase* (*rather informal, especially spoken*) to have a romantic or sexual relationship with sb, especially one that has continued for a period of time: *We've been together seven years – that's practically married, isn't it?*

court [I, T] (*old-fashioned*) to have a romantic relationship with sb, especially sb that you would like to marry in the future: *At that time they had been courting for several*

months. ◇ *He courted Jane for two years before she finally agreed to marry him.* ❶ **Court** is now quite an old-fashioned term, but it is still used to talk about people in the past. Older people may also use it to talk about their relationship before they were married: *Your grandfather and I were still courting at the time* (= we spent time together as a couple, but were not married yet). See also **courtship** → RELATIONSHIP 2

woo [T] (*old-fashioned or literary*) (of a man) to try to persuade a woman to love him and marry him: *He wooed her with flowers, poetry and compliments.*

government *noun*

1 the British government
2 strong government

1 government · administration · regime · cabinet · reign · parliament · the executive
These are all words for a group of people who govern a country or the period for which they govern.

PATTERNS AND COLLOCATIONS
▶ **under** a government / an administration / a regime / sb's reign
▶ **the former / previous / current** government / administration / regime
▶ **the central / local / national** government / administration
▶ a **left-wing / right-wing / communist / fascist** government / administration / regime
▶ a / an **authoritarian / totalitarian / repressive / military / revolutionary** government / regime
▶ to **elect** a government / an administration
▶ to **form** a government / an administration / a cabinet
▶ to **bring down / overthrow** a government / an administration / a regime
▶ a government / an administration / a regime **comes to power**
▶ a government / an administration **takes office / is in office**

government [C+sing./pl. v.] (*often* **the government** [sing.]) the group of people who are responsible for controlling a country or state: *The government has been considering further tax cuts.* ◇ *She has resigned from the government.* ◇ *The interests of the state should not be confused with the interests of **the government of the day** (= the people in government at a particular time).* See also **govern** → RULE *verb* 1

administration [C+sing./pl. v.] the government of a country; the period for which it governs: *The current administration will remain in office until elections in November.* ◇ *He was Secretary of Education in Bush's first administration* (= first period as president).

NOTE **GOVERNMENT** OR **ADMINISTRATION?** Administration is used especially about a government that is led by a president, and especially the US government. It usually refers to the government of a particular president or the period for which this lasts: *during/under the Reagan/Clinton/Bush Administration* ◇ *during/under the Reagan/Clinton/Bush government.* It is not usually used to refer to the institution or process of government which remains the same while presidents and administrations change: *Approximately 2.7 million people are employed by the federal government.* ◇ *employed by the federal administration.* In countries where the government is led by a prime minister, with more limited powers than a president – especially the United Kingdom – the word **government** is usually preferred: *the Thatcher/Major/Blair/Brown government* ◇ *government employees.* To use the word **administration** after the name of the prime minister can sometimes suggest disapproval of the prime minister for trying to act like a president.

regime /reɪˈʒiːm/ [C] the government of a country, especially one that has not been elected in a fair way: *She was imprisoned because of her opposition to the regime.* ◇ *They are investigating human rights abuses under the previous military regime.* See also **leadership** → MANAGEMENT

cabinet (also **Cabinet**) /'kæbɪnət/ [C+sing./pl. v.] a group of the most important government ministers, or advisers to a president, responsible for advising and deciding on government policy: *Several **cabinet ministers** have been implicated in the scandal.* ◇ *The issue was discussed at yesterday's **cabinet meeting**.* ◇ *She lost her position as Health Minister in a recent **cabinet reshuffle** (= change).* ◇ *He is a member of the **Shadow Cabinet** (= senior politicians of the party not in government).*

reign /reɪn/ [C] the period during which a king, queen, emperor, etc. rules: *The house was built during the reign of Henry VIII.* ◇ *By the end of his **reign**, the vast empire was in decline.* See also **reign** → RULE *verb* 1

parliament [C, U] a period during which a parliament is working; parliament as it exists between one general election and the next: *We are now into the second half of the parliament.* ◇ *The prime minister unexpectedly **dissolved parliament** (= formally ended its activities) and called a general election.* ◇ *The legislation is expected to be introduced early in the next **session of parliament**.* See also **parliament** → ASSEMBLY

the executive the part of a government responsible for putting laws into effect: *The constitution calls for a separation of the powers of the executive, the legislature and the judiciary.* See also **legislature** → ASSEMBLY

---

2 government · management · leadership · regulation · administration · supervision · direction
These are all words for the activity of running or controlling a business or organization, or of governing a country.

PATTERNS AND COLLOCATIONS
▸ leadership / supervision / direction **from** sb
▸ regulation / supervision **by** sb
▸ **under** the management / leadership / administration / supervision / direction **of** sb
▸ (to be / work, etc.) **in** government / management / administration
▸ **good** government / management / leadership / administration
▸ **firm / strong** government / management / leadership / direction
▸ **effective** government / management / leadership / regulation / administration / supervision / direction
▸ **weak** government / management / leadership
▸ **poor** management / leadership / regulation / administration / supervision
▸ **day-to-day** government / management / administration / supervision
▸ **general** management / regulation / administration / supervision
▸ **government** regulation / administration / supervision / direction
▸ to **be responsible for** the management / regulation / administration / supervision **of** sth
▸ to **take over** the management / leadership / administration

government [U] the activity of controlling a country; the way in which a country is controlled: *The Nationalists had been in government for most of the 1980s.* ◇ *Democratic government has now replaced military rule.* See also **govern** → RULE *verb* 1

management [U] the activity of running and controlling a business or other organization; the way in which it is run: *She studied hotel management in Munich.* ◇ *The report blames bad management.* ◇ *The company's top-down management style made decision-making slow.* See also **management** → MANAGEMENT, **manage** → RUN 2, **manager** → MANAGER

leadership [U] the activity or position of being a leader; the abilities or qualities needed to be a leader: *The party thrived under her leadership.* ◇ *In the crisis he showed real leadership.* See also **lead** → LEAD *verb* 2, **leader** → LEADER 1

regulation /ˌreɡjuˈleɪʃn/ the practice of controlling sth by means of rules: *There are calls for **tighter regulation** of the industry.* ◇ *Theatre, cinema and broadcasting are all subject to regulation by local authorities.* See also **regulation** → RULE *noun*, **regulate** → REGULATE

administration [U] the activities that are done in order to plan, organize and run a business or other organization: *A large part of his job involves routine administration.*

◇ *Administration costs are passed on to the customer.*
❶ Although **administration** refers to all the activities needed to organize and run a company which are not the actual business of the company (such as producing or selling a product), it is often used especially to refer to the paperwork necessary, such as filling in forms, writing letters or emails and filing. See also **administer** → RUN 2, **administrator** → ORGANIZER

supervision /ˌsuːpəˈvɪʒn; ˌsjuː-; AmE ˌsuːpərˈv-/ [U] the activity of being in charge of sb/sth and making sure that everything is done correctly or safely: *New employees are trained to work without **direct supervision**.* ◇ *There was inadequate supervision of children in the swimming pool.* See also **supervise** → REGULATE, **supervisor** → MANAGER

direction [U] (*rather formal*) the activity of managing or guiding sb/sth: *All the work was produced by the students under the direction of John Williams.* ◇ *The teacher provided **clear direction**, but allowed children some autonomy.* See also **direct** → RUN 2, **director** → MANAGER

go without, go without sth *phrasal verb*

go without (sth) · forgo · give sth up · do without (sb/sth)
These words all mean to not have or do sth that you usually have or do.

PATTERNS AND COLLOCATIONS
▸ to go without / forgo / do without **food / sleep**
▸ to go without / forgo / give up / do without your **holiday**
▸ to forgo / give up your **break**

go with'out, go with'out sth *phrasal verb* to not have sth that you usually have or need: *There wasn't time for breakfast, so I had to go without.* ◇ *She went without eating for three days.*

forgo (also **forego**) /fɔːˈɡəʊ; AmE fɔːrˈɡoʊ/ [T] (*formal*) to decide not to have or do sth that you would like to have or do: *No one was prepared to forgo their lunch hour to attend the meeting.*

give sth 'up *phrasal verb* to decide not to spend time in the way you usually do, in order to do a particular task: *I gave up my weekend to help him paint his apartment.*

do with'out, do with'out sb/sth *phrasal verb* to manage without sb/sth: *She **can't do without** a secretary.* ◇ *If they can't get it to us in time, we'll just have to do without.*

> **NOTE** GO WITHOUT OR DO WITHOUT? **Do without** usually comes after *can, can't* or *have to*, and can be used to talk about not having a person as well as a thing. **Go without** is only used to talk about a thing. **Do without** suggests that sb manages to do sth successfully despite not having sb/sth; **go without** suggests more that sb tolerates a situation where sth is missing.

graduate *verb* See the Topic Map for EDUCATION on p.888

graduate · pass · qualify · get through (sth) · sail through (sth)
These words all mean to successfully complete a course of study or to be successful in an exam or test.

PATTERNS AND COLLOCATIONS
▸ to graduate / qualify **as** sth
▸ to graduate / pass **with** sth
▸ to pass / get through / sail through a / an **course / exam / test**
▸ **students** graduate / pass / qualify / sail through

graduate /'ɡrædʒueɪt/ [I] to get a degree, especially your first degree, from a university or college; (in the US) to complete a course in education, especially at high school: *Only thirty students **graduated in** Chinese last year.* ◇ *She taught in France after graduating.* ◇ *Martha **graduated***

from high school two years ago. ❶ In American English the 'from' can be left out: (*AmE*) *Martha graduated high school two years ago.*

▸ **graduate** /'grædʒuət/ *noun* [C]: *a science graduate* ◇ *high school graduates*

pass [I, T] to achieve the required standard in an exam or test: *I'm not really expecting to pass first time.* ◇ *I passed my driving test.* OPP **fail, flunk** → FAIL 3

▸ **pass** *noun* [C] (*especially BrE*): *She got a pass in French.* ◇ *12 passes and 3 fails*

qualify [I] (*especially BrE*) to reach the standard of ability or knowledge needed to do a particular job, for example by completing a course of study or passing exams: *How long does it take to qualify?* ◇ *She qualified as a doctor last year.*

▸ **qualification** *noun* [U, C, usually pl.]: *Nurses in training should be given a guarantee of employment following qualification.* ◇ (*BrE*) *He left school with no formal qualifications.*

get 'through sth, get 'through *phrasal verb* (*BrE, rather informal*) to be successful in an exam or test especially when this is difficult: *I got through the final exam by avoiding questions that required factual knowledge.*

sail' through sth, sail 'through *phrasal verb* (*rather informal*) to pass an exam or test or successfully complete a course of study without any difficulty: *She's very bright and sailed through college.*

grain *noun*

grain · seed · nut · pip · stone · pit · kernel
These are all words for the part of a food plant from which a new plant can grow

▸ to **produce / grow / sow** grain / seeds
▸ to **remove** seeds / pips / stones / pits

grain [U, C] the small hard parts produced by food plants such as wheat or rice from which a new plant can grow, and which may be used to make flour or bread; one of these parts: *The government intends to import only five per cent of the country's grain.* ◇ *There were just a few grains of corn left.* ❶ You can talk about *grains of wheat, rice* or *corn.*

seed [C, U] the small hard part produced by a plant, from which a new plant can grow: *I bought some seeds to plant in the garden.* ◇ *Those vegetables can be grown from seed.* ❶ You can talk about *flower, grass, herb* or *wildflower seeds.* The seeds of some spice plants, vegetables or flowers are used in cooking to give flavour or texture to food: *coriander/cumin/mustard/poppy/pumpkin/sesame/sunflower seeds.* In American English **seed** is also the usual word for **pip**: (*AmE*) *apple/orange seeds*

nut [C] a small hard fruit with a very hard shell that grows on some trees: *I cracked a nut* (= opened it) *and ate it.* ◇ *She is allergic to nuts.* ❶ **Nut** is often used in compounds, such as *walnut, hazelnut, chestnut, peanut* and *Brazil nut.*

pip [C] (*especially BrE*) one of the small hard seeds that are found in some types of fruit: *Cut the apples into quarters and remove the pips.* ◇ *orange pips* ❶ The usual American English word for this is **seed.**

stone [C] (*especially BrE*) a hard shell in the middle of some types of fruit which contains the nut or seed: *cherry/peach stones*

pit [C] (*especially AmE*) a fruit stone: *cherry/peach pits*

kernel /'kɜːnl; *AmE* 'kɜːrnl/ [C] the inner part of a nut, which you can eat; the part inside the stone/pit of a fruit: *pine/apricot kernels*

grass *noun*

grass · lawn · turf · green · common
These are all words for an area of ground covered with grass.

▸ **on** the grass / lawn / turf / green / common
▸ to **sit on / cut / mow** the grass / lawn

grass [sing., U] (*usually* **the grass**) an area of ground covered with grass: *We all sat down on the grass.* ◇ *Keep off the grass.*

lawn [C] an area of ground covered in short grass in a garden or park, or used for playing a game: *They served afternoon tea on the lawn.* ◇ *The hotel boasts two tennis courts and a croquet lawn.*

turf /tɜːf; *AmE* tɜːrf/ [U] short grass and the surface layer of soil that is held together by its roots: *Try not to walk on newly laid turf until it has rooted down into the soil.*

green [C] (*BrE*) an area of grass, especially in the middle of a town or village: *Children were playing on the village green.* ❶ In golf (in both British and American English) a **green** is an area of grass cut short around a hole in a golf course: *the 18th green* ◇ *Did the ball land on the green?*

common [C] an area of open land in a town or village that anyone may use: *We went for a walk on the common.* ◇ *Wimbledon Common covers an area of 1 200 acres.*

grateful *adj.* See also the entry for GLAD

grateful · thankful · glad · indebted · appreciative
These words all describe people feeling or showing thanks because sb has done sth kind for them or has done as they asked.

▸ grateful / thankful **for** sth
▸ grateful / indebted **to** sb
▸ grateful / thankful **that…**
▸ grateful / thankful **to be / have, etc.…**
▸ a grateful / an appreciative **smile**
▸ to **feel** grateful / thankful / glad / indebted
▸ **deeply** grateful / thankful / indebted / appreciative
▸ **very** grateful / thankful / glad / appreciative

grateful feeling or showing thanks because sb has done sth kind for you or has done as you asked: *I am extremely grateful to all the teachers for their help.* ◇ *Kate gave him a grateful look.* ❶ **Grateful** is often used when making a request, especially in a letter or a formal situation: (*formal*) *I would be grateful if you could send the completed form back as soon as possible.* See also **gratitude** → THANKS

▸ **gratefully** *adv.*: *All donations will be gratefully received.*

thankful [not usually before noun] pleased about sth good that has happened, or sth bad that has not happened: *I was thankful to see they'd all arrived safely.* ◇ *He wasn't badly hurt − that's something to be thankful for.* See also **thanks** → THANKS, **relieved** → GLAD

▸ **thankfully** *adv.*: *There was a fire in the building, but thankfully no one was hurt.*

glad (always followed by *of* or *if*) grateful for sth: *She was very glad of her warm coat in the biting wind.* ◇ *I'd be glad if you could help me.*

indebted /ɪn'detɪd/ [not usually before noun] (*formal*) grateful to sb for helping you: *I am deeply indebted to my family for all their help.*

appreciative /ə'priːʃətɪv/ (*rather formal*) feeling or showing thanks because sb has done sth kind for you: *The company was very appreciative of my efforts.* ❶ People are typically *appreciative of* sb's *work, efforts, support* or *loyalty.* See also **appreciation** → THANKS

great *adj.*

1 It's great to see you.
2 a great man/achievement

1 See also the entries for EXCELLENT and GOOD 1
great · cool · fantastic · fabulous · terrific · brilliant · tremendous · awesome · wicked
These are all informal words that describe sb/sth that is very good, pleasant or enjoyable.

▶ a great/a cool/a fantastic/a fabulous/a terrific/a brilliant/an awesome/a wicked **place**
▶ to **have** a great/a cool/a fantastic/a fabulous/a terrific/a brilliant/a tremendous/an awesome **time**
▶ a great/cool/fantastic/fabulous/terrific/brilliant **guy/girl**
▶ a great/a fantastic/a terrific/a brilliant/a tremendous/an awesome **achievement**
▶ a great/cool/fantastic/fabulous/terrific/brilliant **goal**
▶ to **look/sound** great/cool/fantastic/fabulous/terrific/brilliant/awesome
▶ **really** great/cool/fantastic/fabulous/terrific/brilliant/tremendous/awesome/wicked
▶ **absolutely** great/fantastic/fabulous/terrific/brilliant/tremendous/awesome
▶ **That's** great/cool/fantastic/fabulous/terrific/brilliant/tremendous/awesome/wicked.

great (*informal*) very good; giving a lot of pleasure or satisfaction: *That was a great goal!* ◇ *It's great to see you again.* ◇ *We had a great time in Madrid.* ◇ *'I'll pick you up at seven.' 'That'd be great, thanks.'* ◇ (*ironic*) *Oh, great! They left without us!* ◇ (*ironic*) *You've been a great help, I must say* (= no help at all). **OPP** awful → TERRIBLE 3

cool (*informal, spoken*) used to show that you admire or approve of sth, often because it is fashionable, attractive or different: *His new car's pretty cool.* ◇ *'What's his new girlfriend like?' 'She's cool.'* ❶ People say **Cool!** or **That's cool!** to show that they approve of sb/sth or that they agree to a suggestion: *'We're meeting Jake later.' 'Cool!'* **OPP** uncool ❶ Things that are **uncool** are not considered acceptable by fashionable young people: *My mum is so uncool it's funny.*

fantastic (*informal*) extremely good; causing a lot of pleasure or admiration: *We found a fantastic beach about a mile away.* ◇ *You look fantastic!* ◇ *'How was your trip?' 'Fantastic!'* ◇ *'You've got the job?' 'Fantastic!'*

fabulous /ˈfæbjələs/ (*informal*) extremely good: *Jane's a fabulous cook.* ◇ *Enter our fabulous free draw now!* ❶ **Fabulous** is slightly more old-fashioned than the other words in this group.

terrific /təˈrɪfɪk/ (*informal*) extremely good: *She's doing a terrific job.* ◇ *'How do you feel today?' 'Terrific!'* ◇ *To win one of our terrific prizes, answer these three questions.*

brilliant (*BrE, informal, spoken*) extremely good: *'How was the show?' 'Brilliant!'* ◇ *Thanks. You've been brilliant* (= very kind or helpful).

tremendous /trəˈmendəs/ (*informal*) extremely good: *It was a tremendous experience.* ◇ *The support they gave us was tremendous.*

awesome /ˈɔːsəm/ (*especially AmE, informal, spoken*) very good, impressive, or enjoyable: *The show was just awesome.* ◇ *Hey, come look at this! It's awesome!*

wicked (*slang*) used to show that you admire or approve of sb/sth: *'What do you think of her?' 'She's wicked!'* ◇ *'OK, we can all go to the beach now.' 'Wicked!'* ◇ *Jo just bought a wicked new computer game.* ❶ **Wicked** is used especially by young people.

2 great · prestigious · distinguished · eminent · exalted

These are all words for people or things that are extremely good in ability or quality and therefore admired by many people.

▶ a great/a distinguished/an eminent **scientist/painter/poet/writer/architect/historian/philosopher/scholar/professor**
▶ a great/prestigious/distinguished **collection**
▶ a great/prestigious/distinguished **university/award**
▶ a great/distinguished **achievement/career/tradition**
▶ a prestigious/a distinguished/an exalted **position**
▶ **very** prestigious/distinguished/eminent
▶ **highly** prestigious/distinguished

great extremely good in ability or quality and therefore admired by many people: *He has been described as the world's greatest violinist.* ◇ *Sherlock Holmes, the great detective* ◇ *Great art has the power to change lives.* See also **great** → STAR *noun* 1

prestigious /preˈstɪdʒəs/ [usually before noun] respected and admired as very important or of very high quality: *The Gold Cup is one of the most prestigious events in the racing calendar.* ◇ *It's the city's most prestigious and exclusive hotel.* See also **prestige** → STATUS

distinguished /dɪˈstɪŋgwɪʃt/ (*especially written*) successful and respected, especially in a particular profession: *His eldest brother was the distinguished mathematician and geologist John Playfair.* ◇ *He has had a long and distinguished career in medicine.* ◇ *Wales has a long and distinguished tradition of choral singing.* **OPP** undistinguished → MEDIOCRE

eminent /ˈemɪnənt/ [usually before noun] (*especially written*) (of a person) famous and respected, especially in a particular profession: *The house was designed by the eminent architect, Robert Adam.*

NOTE DISTINGUISHED OR EMINENT? You can use either word to describe a person in terms of their profession: *a distinguished/an eminent scientist/artist/painter/poet/writer/architect/historian/philosopher/scholar/professor.* **Distinguished** can also describe sb's *career, achievement, record* or *position*, or the *record* or *tradition* of an organization or group; **eminent** cannot be used in this way: *a long and eminent career in medicine/ tradition of choral singing* See also **prominent** → FAMOUS

exalted /ɪɡˈzɔːltɪd/ (*formal or humorous, written*) of high rank or position or great importance: *She was the only woman to rise to such an exalted position.* ◇ *You're moving in very exalted circles!*

greedy *adj.*

greedy · insatiable · materialistic · voracious · mercenary · acquisitive · grasping

These words all describe people who want more money, power, food or possessions than they need.

▶ an insatiable/a voracious **appetite**
▶ a materialistic/mercenary **attitude**
▶ a materialistic/an acquisitive **society**

greedy (*disapproving*) wanting more money, power, possessions or food than you really need: *The shareholders are greedy for profit.* ◇ *You greedy pig! You've already had two helpings!*
▶ **greed** *noun* [U]: *Nothing would satisfy her greed for power.*
▶ **greedily** *adv.*: *He ate noisily and greedily.*

insatiable /ɪnˈseɪʃəbl/ (*rather formal*) always wanting more of sth; not able to be satisfied: *The public seems to have an insatiable appetite for celebrity news.* ◇ *There seems to be an insatiable demand for more powerful computers.* ❶ **Insatiable** is typically used to talk about sb's *appetite, curiosity, demand, desire* or *hunger.* You can also talk about a person being **insatiable**, although this is not very common.

materialistic /məˌtɪəriəˈlɪstɪk; AmE -ˌtɪr-/ (*disapproving*) caring more about money and possessions than anything else: *Children today are so materialistic.* ❶ People often talk about *materialistic attitudes/views*, as well as about *society, culture* and the *world* being **materialistic**.
▶ **materialism** *noun* [U]: *He had had enough of the greed and materialism of modern society.*

voracious /vəˈreɪʃəs/ (*rather formal*) eating or wanting large amounts of food: *A dragonfly and its larva are both voracious eaters of their fellow creatures.*

mercenary /'mɜːsənəri; AmE 'mɜːrsəneri/ (disapproving) only interested in making or getting money: *She's interested in him for purely mercenary reasons.* ❶ Someone who is **mercenary** does not usually care about hurting other people's feelings in order to get more money.

acquisitive /ə'kwɪzətɪv/ (formal, often disapproving) wanting very much to buy or get new possessions: *We examine the role of the consumer in the post-war acquisitive society.* ◊ *It is an acquisitive company looking for ways to expand.*

grasping (disapproving) always trying to get money, possessions or power for yourself: *The owners were regarded as grasping landlords.*

greet verb

greet · accept · welcome · entertain · meet · receive
These words all mean to say 'hello' to sb when they arrive and/or to make them feel welcome somewhere.

PATTERNS AND COLLOCATIONS
▸ to greet / welcome / meet / receive sb **with** a smile, etc.
▸ to accept / receive sb **as** sth
▸ to accept / receive sb **into** sth
▸ to greet / welcome / entertain / meet / receive a **guest** / **visitor**
▸ to **be there to** greet / welcome / entertain / meet / receive sb
▸ to greet / accept / welcome sb **formally**
▸ to greet / welcome / receive sb **enthusiastically** / **warmly** / **with open arms**

greet [T] to say hello to sb or to be there for them when they arrive somewhere: *He greeted all the guests warmly as they arrived.* ◊ *She greeted us with a smile.* ◊ *The winning team was greeted by cheering crowds.*

accept [T] (not usually used in the progressive tenses) to make sb feel welcome and part of a group: *She had never been accepted into what was essentially a man's world.* **OPP** **reject** → REJECT, See also **accept** → LET SB IN

welcome [T, I] to greet sb in a friendly way or to be there for them when they arrive somewhere: *They were at the door to welcome us.* ◊ *It is a pleasure to welcome you to our home.* See also **welcome** → LET SB IN, **welcoming** → FRIENDLY 1

NOTE GREET OR WELCOME? You **greet** sb when when you say hello to them, usually, but not always, in a friendly way. You might greet sb in the street or when they come to visit you. You **welcome** sb when they come to visit you or when they return home after being away for a long time. You make a special effort to show them that you are happy that they are with you, and to make them feel happy to be with you, or to be home.

entertain [I, T] to invite people to eat or drink with you as your guests, especially in your home: *The job involves a lot of entertaining.* ◊ *Barbecues are a favourite way of entertaining friends.*

meet [T] to go to a place and wait there for a particular person to arrive: *Will you meet me at the airport?* ◊ *The hotel bus meets all incoming flights.*

receive [T, often passive] (formal) to welcome or entertain a guest, especially formally: *He was received as an honoured guest at the White House.* See also **receive** → LET SB IN

greeting noun

greeting · welcome · hospitality · reception
These are all words for sth that you say or do when sb arrives or joins a group.

PATTERNS AND COLLOCATIONS
▸ a greeting / a welcome / hospitality / a reception **from** sb
▸ to do sth **in** greeting / welcome
▸ (a) **warm** / **friendly** greeting / welcome / hospitality / reception
▸ (a) **great** welcome / hospitality / reception
▸ a / an **rapturous** / **rousing** / **enthusiastic** welcome / reception
▸ to **receive** / **expect** / **give** sb a ... welcome / reception
▸ to **get** / **have** / **meet** (**with**) a ... welcome / reception

greeting [C, U] (especially written) something that you say or do when sb arrives or when you meet them: *She waved a friendly greeting.* ◊ *They exchanged greetings and sat down to lunch.* ◊ *He raised his hand in greeting.*

welcome [C, U] a greeting that is given to sb when they arrive, especially a friendly one: *Thank you for your warm welcome.* ◊ *Ellen received a hero's welcome on returning to her home town.* ◊ *Her wrinkled face broke into a smile of welcome.* See also **welcoming** → FRIENDLY 1

NOTE GREETING OR WELCOME? A **welcome** is a particularly friendly type of greeting that you give sb when they have come to visit you, or when they have come home after being away for a long time. A **greeting** usually means a few words or a simple action such as a smile or a wave from one person; a **welcome** often comes from a group of people and may involve sth more, such as a party or a meal.

hospitality /ˌhɒspɪ'tæləti; AmE ˌhɑːs-/ [U] (rather formal) friendly and generous behaviour towards guests: *Thank you for your kind hospitality.* See also **hospitable** → FRIENDLY 1

reception /rɪ'sepʃn/ [sing., U] the type of welcome that is given to sb; the act of receiving or welcoming people, especially people who need help: *Delegates at the conference gave him a warm reception.* ◊ *The locals provided facilities for the reception of children from the war zone.*

grief noun See also the entry for GLOOM

grief · sadness · regret · unhappiness · sorrow · melancholy · heartache · heartbreak
These are all words for the feeling of being sad.

PATTERNS AND COLLOCATIONS
▸ grief / sadness / regret / unhappiness / sorrow / melancholy / heartache / heartbreak **at** / **about** / **over** sth
▸ grief / sadness / regret / sorrow **for** sth
▸ **to** your grief / regret / sorrow
▸ **with** sadness / regret / sorrow
▸ **deep** / **great** / **real** / **personal** / **private** grief / sadness / regret / unhappiness / sorrow / melancholy / heartache / heartbreak
▸ to be **filled with** / **full of** / **overcome with** grief / sadness / regret / unhappiness / sorrow / melancholy / heartache / heartbreak
▸ to **feel** / **experience** grief / sadness / regret / unhappiness / sorrow / melancholy / heartache / heartbreak
▸ to **bring** / **cause** (sb) grief / sadness / regret / unhappiness / sorrow / heartache / heartbreak
▸ to **cope with** / **deal with** grief / sadness / regret / unhappiness / sorrow / heartache / heartbreak
▸ to **express** / **show** / **hide** your grief / sadness / regret / unhappiness / sorrow

grief /griːf/ [U, C] the feeling of being very sad, especially when sb dies: *She was stricken with grief when her husband died.* ◊ *Children can feel real grief at the loss of a pet.* ◊ *They were able to share their common joys and griefs.* **OPP** joy → JOY, joy → PLEASURE, See also **grieve** → MOURN

sadness [U, sing.] (rather formal) the feeling of being sad, especially for other people or because a happy time has come to an end: *His memories of that time were tinged with sadness.* ◊ *I felt a deep sadness for them all.* ❶ Although **sadness** is a more general word than **grief** it is less frequent and is usually rather formal. It is less formal and more common to use the adjective **sad**: *I felt very sad when I heard that she had died.* **OPP** happiness → SATISFACTION, See also **sad** → SAD, **sad** → UNHAPPY 1

regret [U, C] a feeling of sadness or disappointment because of sth that has happened or sth that you have done or not done: *He gave up teaching in 2007, much to the regret of his students.* ◊ *What is your greatest regret* (= the thing that you are most sorry about doing or not doing)? ◊ *I have no regrets about leaving Newcastle* (= I do not feel sorry about it). ❶ You can also use **regret**

when you are sorry about sth bad that you have done. **OPP** **satisfaction** → SATISFACTION, See also **regret** → GUILT *noun*

▶ **regret** *verb* -tt- [T] (: *If you don't do it now, you'll only regret it.* ◇ *He **bitterly regretted** ever having mentioned it.*

unhappiness [U] the feeling of being unhappy, especially because life is difficult or unpleasant for you: *A marriage break-up can cause a lot of unhappiness.* **OPP** **happiness** → SATISFACTION, See also **unhappy** → UNHAPPY 1

sorrow [U, C] (*rather formal*) a feeling of great sadness because sth bad has happened; a sad event or situation: *He found to his sorrow that his childhood home was no longer there.* ◇ *His death was a great **sorrow to** everyone who knew him.* ◇ *It was an opportunity to share the **joys and sorrows** of the past few months.* **OPP** **joy** → PLEASURE

melancholy /'melənkəli; -kɒli; AmE -kɑːli/ [U] (*literary*) a feeling of sadness that lasts for a long time and often cannot be explained: *A mood of melancholy descended on us that evening.* See also **melancholy** → UNHAPPY *adj.* 1

heartache /'hɑːteɪk; AmE 'hɑːrt-/ [U, C] (*rather informal*) a feeling of great sadness and worry: *The relationship caused her a great deal of heartache.* ◇ *I remember the heartaches of being a parent.*

heartbreak /'hɑːtbreɪk; AmE 'hɑːrt-/ [U, C] (*rather informal*) a feeling of great sadness because sth bad has happened to you: *They suffered the heartbreak of losing a child through cancer.* See also **heartbreaking** → SAD, **heartbroken** → UNHAPPY 1

group *noun*

1 a group of people/houses
2 a peer/support/drama group
3 a newspaper/an investment group

1 group · set · cluster · collection · bunch · clump

These are all words for a number of things or people that are together in the same place.

PATTERNS AND COLLOCATIONS
▶ a group / set / cluster / collection / bunch / clump **of** sth
▶ **in** a group / set / cluster / bunch / clump
▶ **as** a group / set
▶ a **large** / **small** / **little** group / set / cluster / collection / bunch / clump
▶ a **big** group / set / bunch / clump
▶ to **form** a group / set / cluster / clump
▶ to **divide** sth **into** groups / sets / clusters

group [C+sing./pl. *v.*] a number of people or things of the same type that are together in the same place: *On the hillside was a little group of houses.* ◇ *A group of us are going to the theatre this evening.* ◇ *Students were sitting around in groups on the grass.* ◇ *Classes will involve both individual and group activities.*

set [C] a group of similar things that belong together in some way: *a set of six matching chairs.* ◇ *She had a complete set of the author's novels.* ◇ *You can borrow my keys – I have a spare set.*

cluster [C] a group of things of the same type that grow or appear close together; a group of people, animals or things that are close together: *The plants have clusters of white flowers in early June.* ◇ *The telescope is focused on a dense cluster of stars at the edge of the galaxy.* ◇ *A woman had emerged from the cluster of buildings.* See also **cluster** → CROWD *verb*

collection [C] a group of objects or people that are close together, especially objects or people of different types: *There was a collection of books and shoes on the floor.* ◇ *They appeared to be a **motley collection** (= a rather strange group of people) of college students.*

bunch [C] a number of things of the same type that are growing or fastened together: *a bunch of keys* ◇ *a bunch of flowers/grapes/bananas* ❶ In this meaning **bunch** is used about *keys, grapes, bananas* and different types of *flowers* and *herbs*.

clump [C] a small group of things or people very close together, especially trees or plants; a bunch of sth such as grass or hair: *They planted trees in clumps around the park.* ◇ *He tore out a clump of her hair.*

2 See also the entries for PARTY 3 and TEAM 1

group · circle · bunch · crowd · gang · set · clique

These are all words for a number of people who have sth in common and often spend time together.

PATTERNS AND COLLOCATIONS
▶ a group / circle / bunch / crowd / gang / clique **of** sth
▶ a group / circle / bunch / crowd / gang / set of **friends**
▶ **in** a group / circle / set / clique
▶ a **small** group / circle / clique
▶ a **mixed** / **motley** group / bunch / crowd
▶ a **social** group / circle / set / clique
▶ to **belong to** a group / set / clique
▶ to **join** a group / circle / set
▶ **part of** a group / circle / crowd / gang / clique
▶ a **member of** a group / circle / clique

group [C+sing./pl. *v.*] a number of people who are connected in some way, for example because they share interests, problems or experiences, or because they spend time together: *She worked with groups of college students who had literacy problems.* ◇ *The college has a small but active women's group.* ◇ *People in the younger **age groups** tended to vote less.* ◇ *Members of some **ethnic groups** say that the law is discriminatory.* ◇ ***Minority groups** are entitled to equal protection under the law.*

circle [C] a group of people who are connected because they have the same interests or jobs, or they spend time together socially: *He has a **wide circle** of friends.* ◇ *Talk of religion was forbidden in the **family circle**.* ◇ *He maintained influence in the **inner circle** of the president's political advisers.* ◇ *Her ideas have caused controversy in scientific circles in recent years.* ◇ *My brother and I **move in** completely different **circles** (= we have very different friends).*

bunch [sing.] (*informal*) a group of people, especially people who are friends or have the same interests or job: *The people that I work with are a great bunch.* ◇ *He's been hanging out with a bunch of yobs and hooligans.*

crowd [C+sing./pl. *v.*] (*informal*) a group of people, especially people who are friends or have the same interests or job: *Do you ever see any of the **old crowd** (= people who used to be friends) from college?* ◇ *Bob introduced him to some of **the usual crowd** (= people who often meet each other).* ◇ *He got in with the **wrong crowd** (= people you disapprove of).*

> **NOTE** **BUNCH** OR **CROWD**? In many cases you can use either word: *They are a great bunch/crowd of people to work with.* ◇ *They were a bit of a motley bunch/crowd (= a strange mix of types of people).* However, **crowd** can suggest a larger group of people, and/or one that is slightly less united: you might talk about *one/some of the usual crowd* but not: ~~one/some of the usual bunch~~: a **bunch** is more likely to be seen as a whole, single unit.

gang [C+sing./pl. *v.*] (*informal*) a group of friends who meet regularly: *There was a **whole gang** of us who went out together at weekends.* ◇ *Her friends made me feel welcome and treated me like **one of the gang**.*

set [C+sing./pl. *v.*] (*sometimes disapproving*) a group of people who have the same interests and spend a lot of time together socially: *It's a favourite meeting place for Berlin's **smart set** (= rich, fashionable people).* ◇ *Several members of Dublin's literary set turned up for her funeral.* ❶ A **set** is often a group of people who are rich or educated. It is often connected with ideas about social class and is sometimes disapproving because the group is seen as privileged and separate from ordinary people.

clique /kliːk/ [C+sing./pl. *v.*] (*often disapproving*) a small group of people who have the same interests and spend time together, but do not like to include others: *The club is dominated by a small clique of intellectuals.*

3 See also the entry for COMPANY
group · partnership · conglomerate · consortium · outfit · syndicate · cooperative
These are all words for a number of people or companies working together in business.

PATTERNS AND COLLOCATIONS
▶ a **large** group / partnership / conglomerate / consortium / outfit / syndicate
▶ an **international** group / partnership / conglomerate / consortium / syndicate
▶ a **multinational** group / conglomerate / consortium
▶ a **small** group / partnership / outfit / syndicate / cooperative
▶ a **local** partnership / consortium / outfit / cooperative
▶ a **business / financial** group / partnership / conglomerate / consortium
▶ a **media** group / partnership / conglomerate / consortium / outfit
▶ to **form** a group / a partnership / a conglomerate / a consortium / an outfit / a syndicate / a cooperative
▶ to **set up** a partnership / a consortium / an outfit / a syndicate / a cooperative
▶ to **join** a group / a partnership / a consortium / an outfit / a syndicate / a cooperative
▶ to **run** a group / a conglomerate / a consortium / an outfit / a syndicate / a cooperative

group [C+sing./pl. v.] (*business*) a number of companies that are owned by the same person or organization: *This acquisition will make them the largest newspaper group in the world.* ◇ *Our group sales director attended the conference in Munich this year.*
partnership [C] a business owned by two or more people who share the profits: *a junior member of the partnership* See also **partner** → PARTNER noun 1
conglomerate /kən'ɡlɒmərət; AmE -'ɡlɑːm-/ [C] (*business*) a large company formed by joining together different firms: *He turned the business into a huge media conglomerate.*

NOTE **GROUP** OR **CONGLOMERATE?** **Conglomerate** gives an impression of extremely large size. Typical collocations relate to industrial areas of business: *a/an chemical/industrial/engineering/mining conglomerate.* Other common collocates are *financial, media* and *publishing,* as well as words relating to size and reach: *a/an huge/vast/international/multinational conglomerate.* **Group** has a wider range of meaning and can describe any collection of companies working together.

consortium /kən'sɔːtiəm; AmE -'sɔːrt-/ (pl. **consortia** or **consortiums**) [C] (*business*) a group of people, countries or companies who are working together on a particular project: *He led the Anglo-French consortium that built the Channel Tunnel.* ❶ A **consortium** is usually a temporary arrangement with a particular aim. See also the entry for UNION
outfit [C+sing./pl. v.] (*informal*) a group of people working together as an organization, business or team: *A London-based market research outfit has been appointed for the job.* ◇ *This was the fourth album by the top rock outfit.* ❶ **Outfit** is used most often to talk about a sports team, rock band or business organization, especially a small independent one.
syndicate /'sɪndɪkət/ [C] a group of people or companies who work together and help each other in order to achieve a particular aim: *It is the home of the largest crime syndicate in Japan.* ❶ **Syndicate** is used most often to talk about a group of criminals: *a drug(s)/crime syndicate,* a group of people who try to win money: *a lottery syndicate* or a group of financial companies working together: *a/an banking/insurance/investment syndicate* See also the entry for UNION
cooperative (BrE also **co-operative**) /kəʊ'ɒpərətɪv; AmE koʊ'ɑːp-/ [C] a business or other organization owned and run by the people involved, with the profits shared by them: *The 'Daily Worker' was run as a cooperative.* ❶ **Cooperative** businesses are often local or community-based, and often connected with producing or selling food: *a/an local/community/farming/agricultural/food/dairy cooperative*

grunt verb

grunt · snort · croak · rasp · squawk
These words all mean to say sth or make a sound in a way that shows how you are feeling.

PATTERNS AND COLLOCATIONS
▶ to grunt / snort / croak / squawk **at** sb / sth
▶ to grunt / snort / croak / squawk **in / with** surprise, pain, etc.
▶ a **voice** croaks / rasps
▶ to grunt / squawk **loudly**
▶ to grunt / snort **softly**
▶ to croak / rasp **hoarsely**

grunt [I, T] to make a short low sound in your throat, especially to show that you are in pain, annoyed or not interested; to say sth using this sound: *He pulled harder on the rope,* **grunting and groaning** *with the effort.* ◇ *When I told her what had happened she just grunted and turned back to her book.* ◇ *He grunted something about being late and rushed out.*
▶ **grunt** noun [C]: *With a grunt of effort he lifted the cases.*
snort [I, T] to make a loud sound by breathing air out noisily through your nose, especially to show that you are angry or amused; to say sth using this sound: *He snorted with laughter at the idea.* ◇ *'You!' he snorted contemptuously.*
▶ **snort** noun [C]: *She gave a snort of disgust.*
croak [I, T] to speak or say sth with a low harsh voice: *I had a sore throat and could only croak.* ◇ *He managed to croak a greeting.*
▶ **croak** noun [C]: *Her voice came out in a croak.*
rasp /rɑːsp; AmE ræsp/ [I, T] to say sth in an unpleasant harsh voice: *He rasped out some instructions.* ◇ *'Where have you been?' she rasped.*
▶ **rasp** noun [sing.]: *There was a rasp of impatience in his voice.*
squawk [T, I] to speak or make a noise in a loud, sharp voice because you are angry or surprised: *'You did what?!' she squawked.*
▶ **squawk** noun [C]: *The man gave a little squawk of indignation.*

guard noun

guard · bodyguard · sentry · garrison · minder · bouncer · lookout
These are all words for a person whose job is to protect sb/sth.

PATTERNS AND COLLOCATIONS
▶ a / an **armed / uniformed** guard / bodyguard
▶ to **stand** guard / sentry
▶ to **post** a guard / sentry / lookout
▶ guard / sentry / garrison **duty**

guard [C] a person, such as a soldier or police officer, who protects a place or people: *The* **border guard** *checked our papers before waving us through.* ◇ *She saw the* **security guards** *wrestle him to the ground.* ❶ **Guard** [C+sing./pl. v.] can also mean 'a group of guards': *The President always travels with an armed guard* (= a group of armed guards). ◇ *A group of tourists was watching* **the changing of the guard** *outside the palace* (= when one group of guards replaces another). See also **guard** → WATCH noun, **guard** → PROTECT verb
bodyguard /'bɒdɪɡɑːd; AmE 'bɑːdɪɡɑːrd/ [C+sing./pl. v.] a person or group of people whose job is to protect sb, especially sb who is in danger of being attacked by other people: *A personal bodyguard was assigned to her and is with her day and night.*
sentry /'sentri/ [C] a soldier whose job is to guard a place, often by standing at its entrance: *People approaching the gate were challenged by the sentry.*

garrison [C+sing./pl. *v.*] a group of soldiers living in a town or fort in order to defend or control it: *The Romans maintained a garrison of 5 000 soldiers in the city.* ❶ A **fort** is a building or group of buildings built to defend an area against attack.

minder [C] (*especially BrE, rather informal*) a person whose job is to protect sb, often a famous person, from danger or public attention: *Her minders hurried her past the journalists and into a waiting car.*

bouncer [C] a person employed to stand at the entrance to a club or bar to stop people who are not wanted from going in, and to throw people out if they cause trouble inside: *The bouncers threw him out when he became aggressive.*

lookout /ˈlʊkaʊt/ [C] a person who has the responsibility of watching for sth, especially danger: *One of the men stood at the door to act as a lookout.*

guerrilla (also guerilla) noun See the Topic Map for CONFLICT on p.896, See also the entry for SOLDIER

guerrilla · rebel · terrorist · insurgent · revolutionary · partisan · bomber · paramilitary
These are all words for a person who uses violence against a government or other authority.

PATTERNS AND COLLOCATIONS
▸ **armed** guerrillas/rebels/terrorists/insurgents/revolutionaries
▸ to **support** the guerrillas/rebels/terrorists/insurgents/partisans/paramilitaries
▸ to **join** the guerrillas/rebels/insurgents/partisans
▸ to **lead** the guerrillas/rebels/rebels
▸ guerrillas/rebels/terrorists/insurgents/partisans/bombers **attack**/**kill** sb/sth
▸ a guerrilla/rebel/a terrorist/an insurgent/a revolutionary/a paramilitary **group**
▸ guerrilla/rebel/terrorist/insurgent/revolutionary/paramilitary **activity**
▸ a guerrilla/a rebel/a terrorist/an insurgent/a paramilitary **attack**

guerrilla (also **guerilla**) /ɡəˈrɪlə/ [C] a person who fights with weapons against the government of a country, as a member of an organized military force that is not an official army: *Seven soldiers and two guerrillas were killed after an attack on a border post.* ◊ *The peace talks have put an end to the 17-year guerrilla war.*

rebel /ˈrebl/ [C] a person who fights against the government of their own country: *A group of armed rebels seized control of the national radio headquarters.* ◊ *Rebel forces clashed with government troops.* See also **rebel** → REBEL *verb*, **rebellion** → REVOLUTION 1

terrorist /ˈterərɪst/ [C] (*disapproving*) a person who uses violent action in order to achieve political aims or to force a government to act: *International terrorists are threatening to blow up the plane.* ◊ *Three suspected terrorists have been arrested.*
▸ **terrorism** *noun* [U]: *an act of terrorism*

insurgent /ɪnˈsɜːdʒənt; AmE -ˈsɜːrdʒ-/ [C, usually pl.] (*formal*) a person who fights against the government or armed forces of their own country: *Government forces continue to face deadly attacks by armed insurgents.* See also **insurgency** → REVOLUTION 1

> **NOTE** REBEL OR INSURGENT? People talk about insurgents in the early stages of a fight against a government or authority. **Rebel** is the less formal and more frequent of the two words, and can be used in the early or later stages of a conflict.

revolutionary [C] a person who starts or supports a revolution, especially a political one: *The revolutionaries tried to encourage soldiers to mutiny or desert.* See also **revolution** → REVOLUTION 1, **revolutionary** → RADICAL *adj.*

partisan [C] a member of an armed group that is fighting secretly against enemy soldiers who have taken control of its country: *By the end of 1944 German forces had driven the Italian partisans out of the region.* ❶ **Partisan** is usually used to refer to a person involved in a war or conflict in history, especially the Second World War, rather than in the present.

bomber [C] a person who puts a bomb somewhere illegally: *The suicide bomber blew himself up in a crowded restaurant, killing twelve people.*

paramilitary /ˌpærəˈmɪlətri; AmE -teri/ [C, usually pl.] a member of an armed group that is organized like an army but is not official, and may be opposed to the government: *The army has blamed paramilitaries for heavy civilian casualties in the area.*

guess verb

guess · surmise · conjecture
These words all mean to form an idea of what is happening or what is true when you do not have many facts to base this on.

PATTERNS AND COLLOCATIONS
▸ to guess/surmise/conjecture **that…**
▸ to guess/surmise/conjecture sth **from** sth
▸ to guess/surmise/conjecture **what/how/why…**
▸ to guess/surmise sth **correctly**

guess [I, T] to try to give an answer or make a judgement about sth without being sure of all the facts: *I don't really know. I'm just guessing.* ◊ *We can only guess at her reasons for leaving.* ◊ *He guessed right/wrong.* ◊ *How old do you think I am? Go on, guess!* ◊ *I guessed from John's expression that something was badly wrong.* ◊ *Guess who's here!* ◊ *We can't begin to guess his reasons.* ◊ *What did you get her for Christmas?* **Let me guess** (= used when you think you probably know). See also **guess** → SPECULATION *noun*

surmise /səˈmaɪz; AmE sərˈm-/ [T] (*formal*) to guess or suppose sth using the evidence that you have, without definitely knowing: *I surmised that they had been having an argument.* ◊ *What he had done with the money can only be surmised.*
▸ **surmise** /ˈsɜːmaɪz; AmE ˈsɜːrm-/ *noun* [U, C, usually sing.]: *This is pure surmise on my part.* ◊ *He was glad to have his surmise confirmed.*

conjecture /kənˈdʒektʃə(r)/ [T, I] (*formal*) to form an opinion about sth even though you do not have much information about it: *He conjectured that the population might double in ten years.* ◊ *We can only conjecture about what was in the killer's mind.* See also **conjecture** → SPECULATION *noun*

guilt noun

guilt · shame · regret · remorse · repentance
These are all words for the state of feeling sorry, stupid or sad because of sth that you have done or not done.

PATTERNS AND COLLOCATIONS
▸ guilt/shame/regret/remorse **at** sth
▸ guilt/regret/remorse **over** sth
▸ guilt/regret **about** sth
▸ regret/remorse/repentance **for** sth
▸ to do sth **without** guilt/shame/regret/remorse/repentance
▸ **deep** shame/regret/remorse
▸ **genuine** regret/remorse/repentance
▸ to **feel** (no) guilt/shame/regret/remorse
▸ to **have** no shame/regret/remorse
▸ to **show** regret/remorse/repentance
▸ a **pang/stab of** guilt/regret/remorse

guilt [U] the unhappy feelings caused by knowing or thinking that you have done sth wrong: *She had feelings of guilt about leaving her children and going to work.* ◊ *Many survivors were left with a sense of guilt.* See also **guilty** → SORRY

shame [U] the feelings of guilt, sadness and embarrassment that you have because of sth wrong or stupid that you have done: *His face burned with shame.* ◊ *She hung her head in shame.* ◊ *I would die of shame if she ever found out.* ◊ *To my shame* (= I feel shame that) *I refused to listen to her side of the story.* ❶ In formal language **shame** can also be the ability to feel shame at sth you have done; this meaning is only used in questions and negative

sentences: *Have you no shame?* OPP **pride** → SATISFAC-
TION, See also **shame** → EMBARRASS *verb*, **ashamed** → SOR-
RY, **shameless, unashamed** → COOL *adj.*

NOTE **GUILT** OR **SHAME**? You feel **guilt** when you have
done sth that you believe to be wrong, and it does not
matter whether other people know about it or not; you
usually only feel **shame** when other people know that
you have done sth wrong or stupid and you feel that
you have lost their respect: *He could not live with the
guilt of knowing it was all his fault.* ◇ *He could not live
with the shame of other people knowing the truth.*

regret /rɪˈgret/ [U, C] a feeling of being sorry about sth
that you have done or not done: *The police offered no
expression of regret at his wrongful arrest.* ❶ You can also
use **regret** when you are sad or disappointed about sth
that you have done or not done or chances that you have
missed. See also **regret** → GRIEF *noun*, **regret** → APOLO-
GIZE *verb*

remorse /rɪˈmɔːs; *AmE* rɪˈmɔːrs/ [U] (*rather formal,
especially written*) the feeling of being extremely sorry
because of sth wrong or bad that you have done: *I felt
guilty and full of remorse.* ◇ *He was filled with remorse for
not believing her.* ❶ If sb *shows no remorse* for a crime
they have committed, they are likely to receive a stronger
punishment in court.

repentance /rɪˈpentəns/ [U] (*formal, especially religion*)
the fact of showing that you are sorry for sth wrong that
you have done: *He shows no sign of repentance.* ◇ *Sins are
wiped out by sincere repentance.*

▶ **repent** *verb* [I, T]: *She had **repented of** what she had
done.* ◇ *He came to repent his hasty decision.*

guilty *adj.*

guilty · responsible · to blame · at fault · in the wrong
These words all describe sb who has done sth wrong or
illegal.

PATTERNS AND COLLOCATIONS
▸ responsible / to blame / at fault **for** sth
▸ to **feel** guilty / responsible / to blame
▸ to **consider / hold sb** guilty / responsible / to blame / at fault
▸ **clearly** guilty / responsible / to blame / at fault
▸ **entirely / partly / partially** responsible / to blame / at fault

guilty proved in court to have done sth illegal; having
done sth wrong: *The jury found the defendant **not guilty**.*
◇ *My lawyer urged me to **plead guilty*** (= say in court that
I was guilty of a crime). ◇ *Under the UK judiciary system,
everyone is **innocent until proved guilty**.* ◇ *Who was the
guilty party* (= the person who was mainly responsible)
in the affair? ◇ *We've all been **guilty of** selfishness at some
time in our lives.* OPP **innocent, not guilty** → INNOCENT,
See also **guilt** → FAULT *noun*

responsible [not before noun] having done sth wrong;
having caused a bad situation: *Who's responsible for all
this mess?* ◇ *Everything will be done to bring those
responsible to justice.* ◇ *Smoking is responsible for over
90% of deaths from lung cancer.* See also **responsibility**
→ FAULT *noun*

to ˈblame *phrase* responsible for a bad situation: *For once,
the government was not to blame.* ◇ *If anyone's to blame,
it's me.* ◇ *Modern intensive farming methods are largely to
blame for this loss of habitat.* ❶ **To blame** is used
especially in negative statements and questions, and
when deciding how to share out the blame for a situation
between a number of people or things. See also **blame**
→ FAULT *noun*, **blame** → BLAME *verb*

,at ˈfault *phrase* responsible for a bad situation; wrong in a
particular thing that you have done: *I think it's the law
that's at fault.* ◇ *The manager was **at fault in** refusing to
listen to her initial concerns.* See also **fault** → FAULT *noun*

in the ˈwrong *phrase* responsible for an accident or
mistake; arguing against sb who is right about sth, while
you are wrong: *The motorcyclist was clearly in the wrong.*
◇ *You're just trying to **put me in the wrong*** (= prove
that I am to blame), *aren't you?* ◇ *Why do you keep on
arguing when you must know you are in the wrong?*

❶ Responsibility, blame or fault can be shared: sb/sth can
be *partly responsible / to blame / at fault*. You cannot be:
~~*partly in the wrong*.~~ **In the wrong** is used in situations
where one person is wrong and the other is right. OPP **in
the right**

gun *noun*

**gun · rifle · pistol · shotgun · artillery · cannon ·
firearm · handgun · mortar · revolver · machine gun**
These are all words for weapons that fire bullets, bombs or
shells.

PATTERNS AND COLLOCATIONS
▸ **heavy** guns / artillery / cannon / mortars / machine guns
▸ to **be armed with** a gun / a rifle / a pistol / a shotgun / cannon / a
  handgun / mortars / a revolver / a machine gun
▸ to **carry** a gun / a rifle / a pistol / a shotgun / firearms / a
  handgun / a revolver
▸ to **draw** a gun / pistol / revolver
▸ to **load** a gun / rifle / pistol / shotgun / cannon / handgun / revolver
▸ to **fire** a gun / rifle / pistol / shotgun / cannon / handgun / mortar /
  revolver / machine gun
▸ to **shoot sb / sth with** a gun / rifle / pistol / shotgun / handgun /
  revolver / machine gun

gun [C] a weapon that is used for firing bullets or shells (=
metal cases filled with explosives): *He walked into the
bank and pointed his gun at the cashier.* ◇ *He was injured
in a gun battle between rival gangs.* ◇ *Anti-aircraft guns
opened fire* (= started to shoot) *as the bombers flew
overhead.*

rifle [C] a long gun that can be fired from the shoulder
and is designed to be accurate at long distances: *a
hunting rifle* ◇ *an assault rifle* ❶ An **air rifle** (or **air gun**)
is a gun that uses air pressure to fire pellets (= small
metal balls).

pistol [C] a small gun that can be held and fired with one
hand: *The assassin shot the two men with a 9mm
automatic pistol.* ◇ *The official fired a starting pistol to
begin the race.* ❶ A **water pistol** (*BrE*) or **water gun**
(*AmE*) is a toy gun that shoots water.

shotgun /ˈʃɒtɡʌn; *AmE* ˈʃɑːt-/ [C] a long gun that fires a lot
of small metal bullets (called **shot**) and is used especially
for shooting birds or animals: *The farmer kept a shotgun
for killing crows and foxes.* ◇ (*BrE*) *The raiders were armed
with **sawn-off shotguns**.* ◇ (*AmE*) **sawed-off shotguns**

artillery /ɑːˈtɪləri; *AmE* ɑːrˈt-/ [U] large, heavy guns which
are often moved on wheels: *The town is under heavy
artillery fire.* ◇ *A stray artillery shell struck the hospital.*

cannon (pl. **cannon**) [C] an old type of large heavy gun,
usually on wheels, that fires solid metal or stone balls; a
gun fitted in an aircraft that fires small explosive shells:
Three cannon opened fire. ◇ *The helicopter directed a burst
of cannon fire at the target.*

firearm /ˈfaɪərɑːm; *AmE* -ɑːrm/ [C, usually pl.] (*formal*) a
gun that fires bullets and that can be carried with one or
both hands: *The police were issued with firearms.*

handgun [C] a small gun that can be held and fired with
one hand: *A man carrying a handgun ordered bank
employees to fill a large plastic bag with cash.*

mortar /ˈmɔːtə(r)/ [C] a heavy gun that fires bombs high
into the air; the bombs that are fired by this gun: *Two
soldiers were killed when their patrol came under mortar
fire.*

revolver [C] a small gun that has a container for bullets
that turns around so that shots can be fired quickly
without having to stop to put more bullets in: *The man
stood over him, aiming the revolver at his head.*

NOTE **PISTOL, HANDGUN** OR **REVOLVER**? A **revolver** and a
pistol are both types of **handgun** that fire the bullets in
different ways. However, in non-technical use the words
are often used in the same way.

maˈchine gun [C] a gun that automatically fires many
bullets one after the other very quickly: *Suddenly there
was a long burst of machine-gun fire.* ❶ A **sub-machine
gun** is a short, light machine gun that can be held in the
hands to fire.

H h

habit noun

habit · practice · policy · ways · ritual · rule
These are all words for things that you do often or for your usual behaviour.

PATTERNS AND COLLOCATIONS
▶ to **be** sb's habit / practice / policy **to do sth**
▶ **as is** sb's habit / practice
▶ the / sb's **usual** habit / practice / policy / ritual
▶ sb's **personal** habits / practice / ritual
▶ **bad** habits / practices / policy / ways
▶ to **make** a habit / practice **of** doing sth
▶ to **make it** a habit / practice / policy / rule **to do sth**
▶ to **become** a habit / practice / ritual
▶ to **have** a habit / policy / ritual / rule
▶ to **follow** a policy / ritual / rule
▶ to **change** a / your habit / practice / policy / ways

habit [C, U] a thing that you do often and almost without thinking, especially sth that is hard to stop doing; usual behaviour: *You need to change your eating habits* (= what and how you eat). ◇ *It's all right to borrow money occasionally, but don't* **let it become a habit**. ◇ *I'm not* **in the habit** *of letting strangers into my apartment.* ◇ *I* **got into the habit** *of going there every night for dinner.* ◇ *I do it* **out of habit**. ◇ *When it comes to clothes, men are* **creatures of habit** (= have fixed and regular ways of doing things). See also **habitual** → FREQUENT, **habitual** → REGULAR, **habitual** → USUAL

practice [C] (*rather formal*) a thing that is done regularly, either for a good reason, or out of habit: *I like the German practice of giving workers a say in how their company is run.* ◇ *Established practices can be difficult to modify.*

policy [C, U] (*formal*) a principle that influences how you behave; a way in which you usually behave: *It is my policy not to say anything to the press.* ◇ *As the old saying goes, honesty is the best policy.*

ways [pl.] your usual behaviour: *It's unlikely that your boss will change his ways.* ◇ *They seem to have seen* **the error of their ways**. ◇ *You're going to have to* **mend your ways** (= stop behaving badly). ◇ *She had become* **set in her ways** (= did not want to or was not able to change her habits and opinions).

ritual /'rɪtʃuəl/ [C] a thing that is done regularly and always in the same way: *She had been following this daily ritual for several months.* ◇ *It was all part of the ritual of returning home.* ◇ ❶ *A* **ritual** *is often a series of small actions that are done at a particular time or in particular circumstances, for no obvious reason except that they have been done in that way on those occasions for a long time and people like to continue doing them.* See also **ritual** → CEREMONY

rule [C, usually sing.] a thing that you usually do because you think it is wise: *I make it a rule never to mix business with pleasure.* ◇ *He occasionally allowed himself to break his own rule.* See also **rule** → PRINCIPLE 1, **as a rule** → USUALLY

habitat noun

habitat · territory · home · haunt
These words all mean a place where sb/sth usually is or can be found.

PATTERNS AND COLLOCATIONS
▶ a habitat / home / haunt **for** sb / sth
▶ a **breeding** habitat / territory
▶ a **native** habitat / home

habitat /'hæbɪtæt/ [C, U] the kind of place where a particular type of animal or plant is normally found: *The panda's natural habitat is the bamboo forest.* ◇ *Population growth is causing destruction of wildlife habitat throughout the world.*

territory /'terətri; AmE -tɔːri/ [C, U] an area that a person, group or animal considers as their own and defends against others who try to enter it: *Mating blackbirds will defend their territory against intruders.* ◇ *She seems to regard that end of the office as her territory.*

home [sing., U] the place where sth such as a plant or animal usually lives; the place where sb/sth can be found: *The Rockies are* **home to** *bears and mountain lions.* ◇ *Beverly Hills is the home of the stars.*

haunt /hɔːnt/ [C] a place that sb visits often or where they spend a lot of time: *Is this one of your usual haunts?* ◇ *The pub is a favourite haunt of artists.*

hairy adj.

hairy · bearded · furry · unshaven · shaggy · bushy
These words are all used to describe a person or animal with a lot of hair or fur, or to describe hair or fur that is very thick.

PATTERNS AND COLLOCATIONS
▶ a hairy / a bearded / an unshaven **man / face**
▶ a hairy / furry **creature / monster / body**
▶ a hairy / furry / shaggy **coat**
▶ a furry / bushy **tail**
▶ hairy / unshaven **armpits**
▶ a bearded / an unshaven **chin**
▶ shaggy / bushy **hair / brows / eyebrows**
▶ a shaggy / bushy **beard**

hairy covered with a lot of hair: *His shirt was unbuttoned, revealing a hairy chest.* ◇ *The plant's rough, hairy stems can grow up to 6 feet tall.* See also **hair** → FIBRE

bearded /'bɪədɪd; AmE bɪrd-/ (*especially written*) having a beard: *His bearded face peered around the door.* ◇ *He was a huge bearded man with a shock of dark hair.*

furry /'fɜːri/ covered with fur; soft, like fur: *small furry animals* ◇ *The moss was soft and furry to the touch.*

unshaven /ˌʌn'ʃeɪvn/ not having shaved or been shaved recently: *He looked pale and unshaven.*

shaggy (of hair or fur) long and untidy; having long untidy hair or fur: *He was a solid man with a shaggy mane of hair.* ❶ *Typical collocates of* **shaggy** *are beard, coat, eyebrows and mane.*

bushy /'bʊʃi/ (of hair or fur) growing thickly; (of plants) growing thickly, with a lot of leaves: *He was short and stocky, with thick bushy eyebrows.* ◇ *It grows into a bushy plant, with soft leaves.* ❶ **Bushy** *is usually used to talk about a man's, rather than a woman's, hair, eyebrows, etc. Typical collocates are moustache, eyebrows and beard, and for an animal, tail.*

hall noun

1 a concert hall
2 the entrance hall

---

1 hall · theatre · auditorium · chamber · ballroom · amphitheatre
These are all words for a large room that can hold a lot of people and is used for public and social events.

▸ a **500-seat** hall / theatre / auditorium / chamber / amphitheatre
▸ a **crowded** / **packed** hall / theatre / auditorium
▸ a **huge** hall / auditorium
▸ an **open-air** theatre / auditorium / amphitheatre
▸ a **conference** hall / chamber

hall [C] a building or large room that is used for events such as public meetings, meals and concerts: *It's important for a **concert hall** to have good acoustics.* ◇ *There are three **dining halls** on campus.* ◇ *They will be performing at The Royal Albert Hall.* ❶ In British English a **hall** is also a large room in a school used for assemblies (= meetings of all the teachers and students in the school) and performances; in American English this is called the **auditorium**.

theatre (*BrE*) (*AmE* **theater**) [C] a building where plays and similar types of entertainment are performed: *She left the theatre a few minutes after the curtain fell.* ◇ *How often do you **go to the theatre**?*

auditorium /ˌɔːdɪˈtɔːriəm/ (pl. **auditoriums** or **auditoria**) [C] the part of a theatre or concert hall in which the audience sits; a large building or room in which events such as public meetings and concerts are held: *He stood at the back of the packed auditorium.* ◇ *The new building will include an exhibition hall, auditorium, bookshop and restaurant.* ❶ In American English an **auditorium** is also a large room in a school used for assemblies (= meetings of all the teachers and students in the school) and performances; in British English this is called the school **hall**.

chamber /ˈtʃeɪmbə(r)/ [C] a hall in a public building that is used for formal meetings: *The members left the council chamber.* ◇ *He had to answer some tricky questions from the floor of the **debating chamber**.*

ballroom [C] a very large room used for dancing on formal occasions: *He entered the palatial ballroom and took in his surroundings.*

amphitheatre (*BrE*) (*AmE* **amphitheater**) /ˈæmfɪθɪətə(r)/; *AmE* -θiːətər/ [C] a circular building without a roof and with rows of seats that rise in steps around an open space, used especially in ancient Greece and Rome for public entertainments; a circular or semi-circular room, hall or theatre with rows of seats that rise in steps: *The Roman amphitheatre stands just outside the fortress walls.* ◇ *Here in a vast amphitheatre you can dance the night away.* See also **arena** → PITCH

---

2 See also the entry for CORRIDOR
hall · lobby · reception · foyer · hallway · entry · entryway
These are all words for a room or area that you go through when you enter a building.

▸ **in** the the hall / the lobby / reception / the foyer / the hallway / the entry / the entryway
▸ **at** reception / the entry / the entryway
▸ an **entrance** hall / lobby / foyer
▸ the **main** lobby / foyer / entry / entryway
▸ (a) **hotel** lobby / reception / foyer

hall [C] the room just inside the main entrance of a house, apartment or other building which leads to other rooms and usually to the stairs: *She ran into the hall and up the stairs.* See also **hall** → CORRIDOR, **entrance** → DOOR

lobby /ˈlɒbi; *AmE* ˈlɑːbi/ [C] a large area inside the entrance of a public building where people can meet or wait: *Long-distance calls can only be made from the lobby of the hotel.*

reception /rɪˈsepʃn/ [U] (*especially BrE*) the area inside the entrance of a building such as a hospital, hotel or office building where visitors or guests go first when they arrive: *We arranged to meet in reception at 6.30.* ◇ *You can leave a message with reception.* ❶ In this meaning **reception** is used mostly in British English, but the term *reception desk* is used in both British and American English: (*BrE, AmE*) *For more information, please contact the reception desk.*

foyer /ˈfɔɪeɪ; *AmE* ˈfɔɪər/ [C] (*rather formal*) a large area inside the entrance of a theatre or hotel where people can meet or wait: *I'll meet you in the foyer at 7 o'clock.* ❶ In American English a **foyer** can also be an entrance hall in a private house or apartment: *An elegant foyer leads directly to the living room.*

hallway /ˈhɔːlweɪ/ [C] (*especially BrE*) a space or passage inside the entrance or front door of a building: *He walked down the tiled hallway and into the kitchen.* See also **hallway** → CORRIDOR

> **NOTE** **HALL** OR **HALLWAY?** There is very little difference in the meaning of these words. **Hall** is more frequent and has a broader range. **Hallway** is used especially to describe a hall that is long and narrow.

entry [C] (*AmE*) a door, gate or passage where you enter a building: *You can leave your umbrella in the entry.*

entryway /ˈentriweɪ/ [C] (*AmE*) the area just inside or outside that leads to the main entrance of a building: *The glass-enclosed entryway gives access to the lobby.*

hang verb

hang · suspend · put sth up
These all mean to attach sth to a high place, so that the lower part is free or loose, or so that lots of people can see it.

▸ to hang / suspend sth **from** / **by** sth
▸ to hang / put up a **picture**

hang [T, I] (always used with an adverb or preposition) to attach sth, or to be attached, at the top so that the lower part is free or loose; to attach sth, especially a picture, to a hook on a wall; to be attached in this way: *Hang your coat **up** on the hook.* ◇ *There were several expensive suits hanging in the wardrobe.* ◇ *We hung her portrait above the fireplace.* ◇ *Several of his paintings hang in the Museum of Modern Art.*

suspend /səˈspend; *AmE* / [T] (*rather formal*) (usually used with an adverb or preposition) to hang sth from sth else: *A lamp was suspended from the ceiling.* ◇ *Her body was found suspended by a rope.*

put sth 'up *phrasal verb* to fix sth in a place where it will be seen: *Put up a notice about it on the board.* ◇ *They've been putting up posters all over town.* See also **display** → PRESENT *verb* 1

> **NOTE** **HANG** OR **PUT STH UP?** You **hang** a *painting* in a frame, that hangs on a hook; you **put up** a *notice* or *poster* that has no frame and is just stuck to the wall.

happen verb See also the entry for EMERGE

happen · occur · take place · arise · come up · come about · turn out · materialize · crop up
These are all verbs that can be used when an event takes place or a situation starts to exist.

▸ a **change** happens / occurs / takes place / arises / comes about
▸ a **situation** happens / occurs / arises / comes about
▸ an **event** / **accident** happens / occurs / takes place

▸ a **problem** occurs / arises / comes up / crops up
▸ to **be likely to** happen / occur / take place / arise / come up / come about / materialize / crop up
▸ to happen / occur / take place / arise / come up **in the future**

happen [I] (of an event or situation) to take place or start to exist, especially without being planned; to take place or start to exist as a result of sth: *Let's see what happens next week.* ◇ *What happens if nobody comes to the party?* ◇ *I don't know how this happened.* ◇ *Is this really happening or is it a dream?* ◇ *I'll be there* **whatever happens.** ◇ *She pressed the button but nothing happened.*

occur /əˈkɜː(r)/ (-**rr**-) [I] (*formal*) (especially of an unexpected event such as a crime or accident) to happen: *When exactly did the incident occur?* ◇ *Something unexpected occurred.* See also **occurrence** → EVENT 1

take ˈplace *idiom* to happen, often after previously being arranged or planned: *The film festival takes place in October.* ◇ *When did this conversation take place?*

arise /əˈraɪz/ [I] (*formal*) (especially of a problem, argument or difficult situation) to start to exist: *We keep them informed of any changes as they arise.* ◇ *Children should be disciplined* **when the need arises** (= when it is necessary.) ◇ *A storm arose during the night.*

ˌcome ˈup *phrasal verb* (of a problem or opportunity) to happen suddenly; (of an event or time) to be going to happen very soon: *I'm afraid something urgent has come up.* ◇ *We'll let you know if any vacancies come up.* ◇ *Her birthday is coming up soon.*

ˌcome aˈbout *phrasal verb* to happen, especially as the result of sth: *How did this dramatic transformation come about?* ◇ *How has* **it come about that** *such a small group has been able to achieve such influence?* ❶ **Come about** is used especially to explain how sth happened, or to ask how sth has happened or been allowed to happen, especially sth that you disapprove of.

ˌturn ˈout *phrasal verb* (used with an adverb or adjective, or in questions with *how*) to happen in a particular way; to develop or end in a particular way: *Despite our worries everything turned out well.* ◇ *You never know how your children will turn out!* ◇ *If the day turns out wet, we may have to change our plans.*

materialize (*BrE* also **-ise**) /məˈtɪəriəlaɪz; *AmE* -ˈtɪr-/ [I] (usually used in negative sentences) to take place or start to exist as expected or planned: *The promotion he had been promised failed to materialize.* ◇ *The hoped-for boom never materialized.*

ˌcrop ˈup *phrasal verb* (-**pp**-) (*rather informal*) to appear or happen, especially occasionally or when it is not expected: *It's the kind of problem that crops up from time to time.* ◇ *I'll be late — something's cropped up at the office.*

happy *adj.* See also the entries for EXCITED and GLAD

happy · satisfied · content · contented · joyful · blissful
These words all describe feeling, showing or giving pleasure or satisfaction.

satisfied	happy	joyful
	content	blissful
	contented	

PATTERNS AND COLLOCATIONS
▸ happy / satisfied / content / contented **with** sth
▸ a happy / satisfied / contented / blissful **smile**
▸ a happy / contented / joyful **mood**
▸ a happy / joyful **occasion / celebration**
▸ happy / blissful **days / weeks / years**
▸ to **feel** happy / satisfied / content / contented / joyful
▸ **very / perfectly / quite** happy / satisfied / content / contented

happy feeling, showing or giving pleasure; pleased enough with sth or not worried about it: *I looked around at all the happy faces.* ◇ *a happy marriage / memory / childhood* ◇ *Those were the happiest days of my life.* ◇ *The*

story has a **happy ending.** ◇ *Happy birthday!* ◇ *If there's anything you're not* **happy about**, *come and ask.* ◇ *I said I'd go, just to* **keep him happy.** OPP **sad, unhappy** → UNHAPPY 1, **unhappy** → UNHAPPY 2, See also **happiness** → SATISFACTION

▸ **happily** *adv.*: *children playing happily on the beach* ◇ *They had been happily married for ten years.*

satisfied pleased because you have achieved sth or because sth has happened as you wanted it to; showing this satisfaction: *She's never satisfied with what she's got.* ◇ *Keep all letters from* **satisfied customers.** ◇ *Sarah watched, a satisfied expression on her face.* OPP **dissatisfied** → UNHAPPY 2, See also **satisfaction** → SATISFACTION, **satisfy** → PLEASE

content /kənˈtent/ [not before noun] happy and satisfied with what you have: *I'm perfectly* **content just to** *lie in the sun.* ◇ *Not content with* stealing my boyfriend (= not thinking that this was enough) *she has turned all my friends against me.* See also **contentment** → SATISFACTION

contented happy and comfortable with what you have; showing this: *a contented baby / workforce / cat* ◇ *I felt warm and cosy and contented.* ◇ *He gave a long contented sigh.* OPP **discontented** → UNHAPPY 2, See also **contentment** → SATISFACTION

▸ **contentedly** *adv.*: *She smiled contentedly.*

> **NOTE** CONTENT OR CONTENTED? Being **contented** depends more on having a comfortable life; being **content** can depend more on your attitude to your life: you can **have to be content** or **learn to be content**: *He had to be content with third place.* ◇ *I really should try to be like her, she is so content.* People or animals can be **contented** but only people can be **content**.

joyful (*formal*) very happy; making people very happy: *Easter is a time to be joyful.* See also **joy** → JOY

blissful making people very happy; showing this happiness: *We spent three blissful weeks away from work.* ❶ **Blissful ignorance** is when you don't know sth that you would much rather not know: *We preferred to remain in blissful ignorance of what was going on.* See also **bliss** → JOY

▸ **blissfully** *adv.*: *blissfully happy* ◇ *blissfully ignorant / unaware*

> **NOTE** JOYFUL OR BLISSFUL? **Joy** is a livelier feeling; **bliss** is more peaceful.

harass *verb* See also the entry for THREATEN 1

harass · nag · pester · hound · harry · hector · persecute · go on
These words all mean to annoy sb by repeatedly asking them sth or complaining about sth.

PATTERNS AND COLLOCATIONS
▸ to harass / nag / pester / hector / go on at sb **about** sth
▸ to hound / pester sb **for** sth
▸ to harass / pester / harry sb **with** sth
▸ to nag / go on **at** sb
▸ to harass / nag / harry / hector sb **into doing sth**
▸ to nag / pester / go on at sb **to do sth**
▸ to **stop** harassing / nagging / pestering / hounding / persecuting / going on at sb
▸ to **keep** nagging / pestering sb
▸ to be **always** nagging / pestering / going on at sb

harass /ˈhærəs; həˈræs/ [T, often passive] (*disapproving*) to annoy or worry sb by putting pressure on them, or by saying or doing unpleasant things to them, especially repeatedly over a period of time: *He has complained of being harassed by the police.* ◇ *The man harassed a neighbour with racist abuse.* ◇ *There were claims that he* **sexually harassed** *female employees.*

▸ **harassment** *noun* [U]: *racial / sexual / police harassment*

nag (-**gg**-) [T, I] (used especially in the progressive tenses) (*rather informal, disapproving*) to keep complaining to sb about their behaviour or keep asking them to do sth, in an annoying way: *She had been nagging him to mend the gate.* ◇ *Stop nagging — I'll do it as soon as I can.* ◇ *He's always nagging at her for wearing too much make-up.*

pester [T, I] (*rather informal, disapproving*) to annoy sb, especially by repeatedly asking them questions or asking them to do sth: *Journalists pestered neighbours for information.* ◇ *The kids kept pestering me to buy them ice creams.* ◇ *Stop pestering!*

hound [T] (*written, disapproving*) to keep following or contacting sb in order to get sth from them or ask them questions: *They were hounded day and night by the press.*

harry [T] (*rather formal, written, often disapproving*) to repeatedly ask sb questions or ask them to do sth, especially in a way that annoys or upsets them: *She has been harried by the press all week.* ◇ *The superintendent sent him to harry the forensic lab over the blood tests.*

hector /ˈhektə(r)/ [T] (*written, disapproving*) to try to make sb do sth by talking to them in an aggressive way: *Unlike most environmentalists, she doesn't hector us about giving things up.*

▸ **hectoring** *adj.*: *a hectoring tone of voice*

persecute /ˈpɜːsɪkjuːt; *AmE* ˈpɜːrs-/ [T] (*disapproving*) to deliberately annoy sb all the time and make their life very unpleasant: *Why are the media persecuting him like this?*

go ˈon *phrasal verb* (*especially BrE, rather informal, disapproving*) to repeatedly complain to sb about their behaviour, work etc: *She goes on at him continually.* ◇ *Stop going on about it!*

hard *adj.*

hard · strenuous · arduous · gruelling · punishing
These words all describe things that need a lot of physical strength or effort.

PATTERNS AND COLLOCATIONS
▸ hard / strenuous / arduous / gruelling **work**
▸ a hard / a strenuous / an arduous **climb**
▸ a hard / an arduous / a gruelling **journey**
▸ a hard / gruelling / punishing **schedule**
▸ a hard / gruelling **day**

hard needing a lot of physical strength or mental effort, especially over a period of time: *It's hard work shovelling snow.* ◇ *I've had a long hard day.*
▸ **hard** *adv.*: *They work hard at school.* ◇ *I trained as hard as I could.* ◇ *You must try harder.* ◇ *She tried her hardest not to show her disappointment.*

strenuous needing a lot of physical effort and energy; showing great energy and determination: *Avoid tasks which require strenuous physical activity.* ◇ *The ship went down although strenuous efforts were made to save it.*
▸ **strenuously** *adv.*: *He still works out strenuously every morning.* ◇ *The government strenuously denies the allegations.*

arduous /ˈɑːdjuəs; -dʒu-; *AmE* ˈɑːrdʒuəs/ involving a lot of physical or mental effort and energy, especially over a period of time: *She was now faced with an arduous trek across the mountains.* ◇ *an arduous task/process*

NOTE STRENUOUS OR ARDUOUS? Strenuous activity may require more effort than **arduous** work, but it may take less time: *The exercise need not take long, but it should be fairly strenuous.*

gruelling (*especially BrE*) (*AmE* usually **grueling**) very difficult and tiring, needing great physical or mental effort over a period of time: *a gruelling work schedule* ◇ *a sporting event that represents a gruelling test of endurance*

punishing (of planned activities) gruelling: *a punishing exercise regime* ◇ *The president has a punishing schedule for the next six months.*

NOTE PUNISHING OR GRUELLING? Punishing is only used for planned activities and collocates only with *schedule, programme* and *regime*.

harmful *adj.*

harmful · destructive · negative · damaging · bad · ill · detrimental · pernicious
These are all words for things that are likely to cause harm or damage to sth.

PATTERNS AND COLLOCATIONS
▸ harmful / destructive / damaging / detrimental **to** sb / sth
▸ harmful / damaging / bad **for** sb
▸ a harmful / destructive / negative / damaging / bad / detrimental / pernicious **effect**
▸ **ill effects**
▸ a harmful / destructive / negative / damaging / bad / pernicious **influence**
▸ harmful / destructive / negative / damaging / detrimental / pernicious **consequences**
▸ harmful / negative / damaging / bad **publicity**
▸ **very / extremely** harmful / destructive / negative / damaging / bad / detrimental
▸ **potentially** harmful / destructive / damaging / detrimental
▸ **positively** harmful / damaging / detrimental
▸ **highly** destructive / damaging / detrimental
▸ **environmentally / socially** harmful / destructive / damaging / detrimental

harmful (*rather formal*) causing damage or injury to sb/ sth, especially to a person's health or to the environment: *The harmful effects of alcohol are well established.* ◇ *Keep food chilled to prevent the spread of harmful bacteria.* ◇ *pesticides that are harmful to the environment* **OPP** **harmless** → SAFE 2, See also **harm** → DAMAGE *noun*, **harm** → DAMAGE *verb*

destructive (*rather formal*) causing physical destruction, or physical or emotional damage: *The war demonstrated the destructive power of modern weapons.* ◇ *People have to learn how to handle destructive emotions like anger.*

negative causing damage to a relationship, to a business or a country's economy, or to a person's health or happiness: *The crisis had a negative effect on trade.* ◇ *The whole experience was definitely more positive than negative.*
❶ **Negative** is used especially to describe the *effect, impact, influence, consequences* or *side effects* of sth. **OPP** **positive** → VALUABLE 2, See also **negative** → NEGATIVE

damaging causing damage to sb's health, happiness or reputation, or to the environment: *A strike would hit public services and be politically damaging for the government.* ◇ *Lead is potentially damaging to children's health.* See also **damage** → DAMAGE *noun*, **damage** → DAMAGE *verb*

NOTE HARMFUL OR DAMAGING? Things that are **harmful** hurt the environment or people's health. Things that are **damaging** can also hurt the environment or health, but more often they hurt people's social or economic welfare (= how much money they have and how comfortable their position in society is), or sb/sth's reputation (= the opinion people have of them).

bad (*rather informal, especially spoken*) causing or likely to cause damage to sb's health, business, character or reputation: *Sugary drinks are bad for your teeth.* ◇ *Weather like this is bad for business.* ◇ *That girl's a bad influence on Tom.* ◇ *Sunbeds have received a lot of bad publicity in recent years. Are they safe?* ❶ In this meaning **bad** is used in the phrase *bad for sb/sth* and with the collocates *influence, publicity* and *effect.* **OPP** **good** → VALUABLE 2

ill [only before noun] (*rather formal*) causing or meaning to cause damage to sb's health, comfort or reputation: *He resigned because of ill health.* ◇ *She suffered no ill effects from the experience.* ◇ (*formal*) *I bear you no ill will* (=

do not wish any harm to come to you), *but I am simply not in a position to help you.* ❶ In this meaning **ill** is used especially with the collocates *health, effects, treatment, will* and *repute.*

detrimental /ˌdetrɪˈmentl/ (*formal*) causing damage to the environment, or sb's health or welfare; blocking people's attempts to do sth good: *Emissions from the factory are widely suspected of having a detrimental effect on health.* ◇ *The policy will be detrimental to the peace process.* ❶ **Detrimental** is nearly always used in the phrases *detrimental effect/effects* or *detrimental to sb/sth.* **OPP** **beneficial** → VALUABLE 2, See also **detriment** → DAMAGE *noun*

pernicious /pəˈnɪʃəs; AmE pərˈn-/ (*formal*) having a very harmful effect on society or morals, especially in a way that is gradual and not easily noticed: *They discussed the pernicious influence of TV violence on children.* ◇ *Ageism is just as offensive and pernicious as sexism.*

harsh *adj.*

harsh · severe · hard · bleak
These words all describe weather conditions which are not pleasant or are difficult to live in.

PATTERNS AND COLLOCATIONS
▸ a harsh / severe / hard / bleak **winter**
▸ harsh / severe **weather / conditions**
▸ a harsh / severe **climate**
▸ a severe / hard **frost**

harsh (of weather or living conditions) very difficult and unpleasant to live in: *These plants will not grow in this harsh climate.* ◇ *He stood outside, blinking in the harsh sunlight.* ◇ *Life expectancy is extremely low due to the harsh conditions.* **OPP** **mild** → SUNNY

severe (of weather) very unpleasant and/or dangerous: *Severe weather conditions can lead to an increase in the demand for electricity.* ◇ *A severe storm blew the ship off course.*

hard [usually before noun] (of weather) very cold and severe: *There was a hard frost that night.*

bleak /bliːk/ (of weather) very cold and unpleasant: *She left on a bleak November day.*

> **NOTE** WHICH WORD? **Harsh** weather or conditions make living physically difficult; **harsh** is used especially when these conditions exist all the time in a place or last for a long time. **Severe** weather may last only a short time, but can cause immediate danger, not just difficulty over a longer period. **Hard** typically describes a *winter* (= harsh) or a *frost* (= making the ground very hard). **Bleak** describes a time, such as a *day* or a *winter*, that makes you feel depressed, whether or not life is physically difficult.

harvest *verb*

harvest · pick · gather
These words all mean to take and collect plants for food.

PATTERNS AND COLLOCATIONS
▸ to harvest / pick / gather **fruit**
▸ to harvest / gather a **crop**

harvest /ˈhɑːvɪst; AmE ˈhɑːrv-/ [I, T] to cut and collect a crop; to catch and collect a large number of animals to eat: *Winter wheat is harvested in late July and early August.* ◇ *In the US, more than 130 000 tons of live oysters are harvested each year.*
▸ **harvest** *noun* [C, U]: *the grain harvest* ◇ *at harvest time*

pick [T] to take and collect part of a plant such as the flowers or fruit: *They picked some flowers and arranged them into a beautiful bouquet.* ◇ *to pick grapes/strawberries/cotton*

gather [T] (*rather formal or literary*) to pick or cut and collect crops to be stored; to collect wild plants or fruit

from a wide area: *It was late August and the harvest had been safely gathered in.* ◇ *They lived in the forest, gathering mushrooms and berries to eat.*

hat *noun*

hat · helmet · cap · crown · hood · beret · headscarf · turban · headdress · bonnet · headgear · bandanna
These are all words for things that you wear on your head.

PATTERNS AND COLLOCATIONS
▸ to **have on / wear** (a) hat / helmet / cap / crown / beret / headscarf / turban / headdress / bonnet / headgear / bandanna
▸ to **put on / take off / remove** a, your, etc. hat / helmet / cap / crown / beret / headscarf / turban / headdress / bonnet / headgear / bandanna
▸ to **tie** a headscarf / turban / bandanna

hat [C] a covering made to fit the head, often with a brim (= a flat edge that sticks out) and worn out of doors: *He placed a battered straw hat on his head.* ◇ *The doorman tipped his hat* (= touched it lightly as a mark of respect) *as we entered.* ❶ **Hat** is often used in compounds: *a fur/straw/woolly hat* ◇ *a sun hat* ◇ *a cowboy hat* ◇ *a riding hat* ◇ *a hard hat* (= that building workers, etc. wear to protect their heads) ◇ *a top hat* (= a man's tall black or grey hat, worn with formal clothes on very formal occasions)

helmet [C] a type of hard hat that protects the head, worn, for example, by a police officer, a soldier or a person playing some sports: *It is illegal to ride a motorcycle without a **crash helmet**.* ◇ *A protective helmet should be worn at all times.*

cap [C] a type of soft flat hat with a peak (= a hard curved part sticking out in front); (usually in compounds) a soft hat that fits closely and is worn for a particular purpose: *a baseball cap* ◇ *a cloth cap* ◇ *a shower cap* ❶ A **cap** is often worn as part of a uniform: *a school cap* ◇ *a soldier's/nurse's/chauffeur's cap*, or it is worn in order to protect or cover your hair: *a swimming cap* ◇ *a skullcap* (= a small round cap worn especially by Jewish men and Catholic bishops)

crown [C] an object in the shape of a circle, usually made of gold and precious stones, that a king or queen wears on his or her head on official occasions: *the emperor's jewel-encrusted crown*

hood /hʊd/ [C] a part of a coat, jacket, etc. that you can pull up to cover the back and top of your head: *a jacket with a detachable hood* ◇ *You can always **put your hood up** if it rains.* ❶ A **hood** is also a piece of fabric put over sb's face and head so that they cannot be recognized, or so that they cannot see: *The victim was sitting tied to a chair with a black hood over her head.*
▸ **hooded** *adj.*: *a hooded jacket* ◇ *A hooded figure was waiting in the doorway.*

beret /ˈbereɪ; AmE bəˈreɪ/ [C] a round flat cap made out of soft cloth and with a tight band around the head: *a soldier wearing the light blue beret of the United Nations*

headscarf /ˈhedskɑːf; AmE -skɑːrf/ (pl. -scarves) [C] a square piece of cloth worn by women and girls as a covering for the head, usually fastened or tied under the chin: *The number of women choosing to wear the Islamic headscarf is on the rise in this country.* ❶ **Headscarf** is often used as a general word to describe a head covering worn by a Muslim woman: *Muslim women wearing headscarves, known in Arabic as hijabs*

turban /ˈtɜːbən; AmE ˈtɜːrbən/ [C] a long piece of cloth wound tightly around the head, worn, for example, by Muslim or Sikh men; a woman's hat that looks like a turban: *He was dressed all in white except for his red turban.*

headdress /ˈhedres/ [C] a covering worn on the head on special occasions, for example a religious ceremony or a carnival: *An elaborate feathered headdress completed her costume.* ❶ **Headdress** is also often used to describe the traditional head covering worn, for example by men living in hot, desert countries. It consists of a square of cloth that is folded and wrapped around the head to protect it from strong sun. If necessary it can also be drawn up over the chin and face to protect it from heat, sand, etc.: *He was wearing traditional Arab robes and headdress.*

bonnet [C] a hat tied with strings under the chin, worn by babies and, especially in the past, by women: *a baby's bonnet* ◇ *an Easter bonnet*

headgear /'hedgɪə(r)/; *AmE* -gɪr/ [U] (*rather formal*) anything worn on the head, for example a hat or helmet: *Protective headgear must be worn at all times.*

bandanna (also **bandana**) /bæn'dænə/ [C] a square or triangle-shaped piece of cloth worn around the head and tied with a knot at the back: *He was wearing dark glasses and a red bandanna.* ❶ **Bandannas** are usually brightly coloured and often patterned. They can also be worn around the neck.

hate *verb*

hate · dislike · can't stand · despise · can't bear · loathe · detest · abhor
These words all mean to have a strong feeling of dislike for sb/sth.

dislike	hate	can't bear	loathe
despise	can't stand		detest
			abhor

PATTERNS AND COLLOCATIONS
▸ to hate / dislike / despise / loathe / detest sb / sth **for** sth
▸ to hate / dislike / despise / loathe / detest sth **about** sb / sth
▸ I hate / dislike / can't stand / can't bear / loathe / detest **doing** sth
▸ I hate / can't bear **to do** sth
▸ I hate / dislike / can't stand / can't bear **it when…**
▸ to hate / despise / loathe **yourself**
▸ they hate / dislike / can't stand / despise / loathe / detest **each other**
▸ I **really** hate / dislike / can't stand / despise / can't bear / detest sb / sth
▸ I **absolutely** hate / can't stand / loathe / detest / abhor sb / sth

hate [T, I] (not used in the progressive tenses) to have a strong feeling of dislike for sb/sth: *He hates violence in any form.* ◇ *I've always hated cabbage.* ◇ *Sometimes I really hate her.* ◇ *I hated myself for feeling jealous.* ◇ *She hates making mistakes.* ◇ *I would hate him to think he wasn't welcome here.* ◇ *I hate to think what would have happened if you hadn't been there.* ◇ *She hated it in France* (= did not like the life there). ◇ *When children are taught to hate, the whole future of society is in danger.* ❶ Although **hate** is generally a very strong verb, it is also commonly used in spoken or informal English to talk about people or things that you dislike in a less important way, for example a particular type of food. **OPP** love → LOVE, **love** → LIKE

dislike [T] (not used in the progressive tenses) (*rather formal*) to not like sb/sth: *Why do you dislike him so much?* ◇ *Not only would she rather not go swimming, she actively dislikes it.* ◇ *The new regime is universally disliked.* ◇ *Much as she disliked asking for help, she knew she had to.* ❶ **Dislike** is a rather formal word; it is less formal, and more usual to say that you *don't like* sb/sth, especially in spoken English: *I don't like it when you phone me so late at night.* **OPP** like → LIKE, **like** → LOVE

stand [T, no passive] (not used in the progressive tenses) (*rather informal, especially spoken*) used in negative statements and questions to emphasize that you really do not like sb/sth: *I can't stand his brother.* ◇ *She can't stand the sight of blood.* ◇ *I can't stand it when you do that.* ◇ *How could she have stood such treatment for so long?*

despise /dɪ'spaɪz/ [T] (not used in the progressive tenses) to dislike and have no respect for sb/sth: *She despised gossip in any form.* ◇ *He despised himself for being so cowardly.* See also **despicable** → DESPICABLE

bear [T] (not used in the progressive tenses) used in negative statements and questions to say that you dislike sth so much that you cannot accept or deal with it: *How can you bear to eat that stuff?* ◇ *I just can't bear it any more!* ◇ *The pain was almost more than he could bear.* ◇ *She couldn't bear the thought of losing him.*

NOTE CAN'T STAND OR CAN'T BEAR? In many cases you can use either word, but **can't bear** is slightly stronger and slightly more formal than **can't stand**. Bear, but NOT stand, has the closely related meaning of 'to accept and deal with sth unpleasant', used in positive statements: *She bore it all with her usual patience.* ◇ *She stood it all with her usual patience.* See also the entry for STAND 2

loathe /ləʊð; *AmE* loʊð/ [T] (not used in the progressive tenses) to hate sb/sth very much: *They loathe each other.* ◇ *Many of the people fear and loathe the new government.* ◇ *He loathed hypocrisy.* ❶ **Loathe** is generally an even stronger verb than **hate**, but it can also be used more informally to talk about less important things, meaning 'really don't like': *Whether you love or loathe their music, you can't deny their talent.* **OPP** love, adore → LOVE, **adore** → LIKE

detest /dɪ'test/ [T] (not used in the progressive tenses) (*rather formal*) to hate sb/sth very much: *They absolutely detest each other.* ◇ *I detest being treated like a child.* **OPP** love → LOVE

abhor /əb'hɔː(r)/ (not used in the progressive tenses) (*formal*) to hate sth very much, for example a way of behaving or thinking, especially for moral reasons: *Most decent people abhor corruption in government.*

hatred *noun*

hatred · dislike · hate · aversion · loathing
These are all words for a strong feeling of not liking sb/sth.

dislike	hatred	loathing
aversion	hate	

PATTERNS AND COLLOCATIONS
▸ hatred / dislike / hate / loathing **for / of** sb / sth
▸ **deep** hatred / dislike / aversion / loathing
▸ **absolute** hatred / hate / loathing
▸ to **be filled with** hatred / hate / loathing
▸ to **develop** a hatred / an aversion / a loathing
▸ **fear and** hatred / hate / loathing

hatred [U, C] a very strong feeling of not liking sb/sth: *She felt nothing but hatred for her attacker.* ◇ *He was accused of stirring up racial hatred.* ◇ *The debate simply revived old hatreds.* **OPP** love → LOVE

dislike [U, C] a feeling of not liking sb/sth; a thing that you do not like: *He did not try to hide his dislike of his boss.* ◇ *She took an instant dislike to the house and the neighbourhood.* ◇ *I've told you all my likes and dislikes.* **OPP** liking → LOVE 2, **likes** ❶ Your **likes** are the things that you like, but the word is only really used in the phrase *sb's likes and dislikes.*

hate [U] a very strong feeling of dislike for sb, that makes you want to harm them: *His eyes were flashing with hate and anger.* ◇ *He had received racist hate mail.* **OPP** love → LOVE 2

NOTE HATRED OR HATE? **Hatred** is more frequent, slightly more formal and used especially in writing. Although it can be used to refer to the abstract concept, it is more often used to describe a very strong feeling of dislike for a particular person or thing: *Her deep hatred of her sister was obvious.* ◇ *a cat's hatred of water.* You are more likely to use **hate** when you are talking about this feeling in a general way: *a look of pure hate* ◇ *people* filled with hate. **Hate** is more often used in informal or spoken contexts. It can also be used before another noun, as in *a hate campaign* or *a hate figure*.

aversion /ə'vɜːʃn; *AmE* ə'vɜːrʒn/ [C, U] a strong feeling of not liking sb/sth, that makes you want to avoid them/it: *He had an **aversion to** getting up early.* ◊ *She has a deep-rooted aversion to dogs, almost amounting to a phobia.*

loathing /'ləʊðɪŋ; *AmE* 'loʊð-/ [sing., U] (*formal*) a very strong feeling of hatred and disgust for sb/sth: *Many soldiers returned with a deep loathing of war.* ◊ *She looked at her attacker with fear and loathing.*

have *verb*

1 have a new car/coat/job
2 have an ability/two children
3 have an accident
4 have a meeting/party/conversation

1 have · have got · own · hold · possess
These words all mean to have sth that belongs to you.

▸ to have / have got / own / possess a **car** / **house**
▸ to have / have got / own a **company**
▸ to have / have got / hold a **driving licence** / **passport**
▸ to have / have got **money**
▸ to own / hold sth **legally** / **jointly**

have [T, no passive] (not used in the progressive tenses) to have sth as a possession; to have sth that belongs to you: *He had a new car and a boat.* ◊ *I don't have that much money on me.* ◊ *She has a BA in English.*
▸ **the haves** *noun* [pl.]: *the division between **the haves and the have-nots** (= between the people who have enough money and possessions and those who don't)

have got [T, no passive] (*especially BrE*) (not used in the progressive tenses) to have sth: *He's got a new job.* ◊ *We haven't got much time, I'm afraid.* ◊ *Have you got a belt I could borrow?*

> **NOTE** HAVE OR HAVE GOT? There is no difference in meaning between these two verbs, but **have got** is not often used in American English. It is common in British English, especially in spoken and informal written language and especially in the present tense. In the past tense, a form of **have** is used more often than the forms *had got* and *hadn't got*: *He had a house by the sea.* ◊ ~~*He had got a house by the sea.*~~ ◊ *Did you have this toy when you were a child?* ◊ *We didn't have enough bedrooms.* ◊ (*less frequent*) *I hadn't got a car at the time.*

own [T] (not used in the progressive tenses) to have sth that legally belongs to you, especially because you have bought it: *Do you own your house or do you rent it?* ◊ *I don't own anything of any value.* ◊ *Most of the apartments are privately owned.* ◊ *an American-owned company* ◊ *Don't tell me what to do – you don't own me!*

hold [T] (not used in the progressive tenses) (*rather formal*) to have or own sth, especially money, shares or official documents: *Employees hold 30% of the shares.* ◊ *The company has held the advertising contract since 2005.* ◊ *Applicants must hold a full driving licence.* ❶ You can also **hold** an *opinion, views, a job, position or office* or a *record* or *title*: *He holds strange views on education.* ◊ *How long has he held office?* ◊ *She held the title of world champion for three years.*

possess [T] (not used in the progressive tenses) (*formal*) to have or own sth, especially sth special or valuable: *He was charged with possessing a shotgun without a licence.* ◊ *I'm afraid this is the only suitcase I possess.* ◊ *The gallery possesses a number of the artist's early works.* See also **possession** → THING 3

2 have · have got · enjoy · possess · boast · be endowed with sth · be blessed with sb/sth
These words and expressions all mean to show a particular quality or feature.

▸ to have / have got / possess / be blessed with **charm** / **talent** / **charisma**
▸ to have / have got / possess / be endowed with **intelligence**
▸ to have / have got / possess **beauty**
▸ to have / have got / enjoy / possess / be endowed with / be blessed with an / the **ability to do sth**
▸ to have / have got / possess / be endowed with / be blessed with a **talent** (for sth)
▸ to have / have got / be blessed with a **child**

have [T, no passive] (not used in the progressive tenses) to show a quality or feature; used to show a particular relationship: *The ham had a smoky flavour.* ◊ *The car has four-wheel drive.* ◊ *They have a lot of courage.* ◊ *Do you have a client named Peters?*

have got [T, no passive] (*especially BrE*) (not used in the progressive tenses) to have sth: *He's got a front tooth missing.* ◊ *Has the house got a garden?* ◊ *I've got three children and two cats!*

> **NOTE** HAVE OR HAVE GOT? There is no difference in meaning between these two verbs, but **have got** is not often used in American English. It is common in British English, especially in spoken and informal written language and especially in the present tense. In the past tense, a form of **have** is used more often than the forms *had got* and *hadn't got*: *He had a special talent.* ◊ *You had blond hair as a child.* ◊ *The hotel didn't have a swimming pool.* ◊ (*less frequent*) *I hadn't got a clue what they were talking about.*

enjoy [T] (not used in the progressive tenses) (*formal*) to have sth good that is an advantage to you, especially because it is sth that other people do not have: *People in this country enjoy a high standard of living.* ◊ *He has always enjoyed good health.*

possess [T] (not used in the progressive tenses) (*formal*) (especially of people) to have a particular quality or feature: *I'm afraid he doesn't possess a sense of humour.* ◊ *He credited her with a maturity she did not possess.*

boast [T] (not used in the progressive tenses or the passive) (*especially written*) to have sth that is impressive and that you can be proud of: *The hotel boasts two swimming pools and a golf course.* ◊ *Rhodes boasts 300 days of sunshine a year.* ◊ *This is a region which proudly boasts its own distinct culture.* ❶ **Boast** is often used to advertise places, for example in information for tourists on a hotel, city, etc.

be en'dowed with sth *phrase* (*rather formal*) to naturally have a particular positive ability or quality: *She was endowed with intelligence and wit.* ◊ *The stones are believed to be endowed with magical powers.*

be 'blessed with sb/sth *phrase* (*rather formal*) to have sth good that brings you great happiness or pleasure: *She's blessed with excellent health.* ◊ *We're blessed with five lovely grandchildren.* ❶ Using this expression suggests that you feel that you or sb else is lucky to have sth, as if it was given to you by God or some other higher power.

3 have · suffer · experience · receive · feel · undergo · go through sth · take · encounter · run into sth · meet
These words all mean to have a particular situation affect you or happen to you.

▸ to have / experience / encounter / run into / meet **problems**
▸ to have / experience / encounter / run into **difficulties** / **trouble**
▸ to experience / encounter / run into / meet **resistance**
▸ to receive / encounter / run into / meet **opposition**
▸ to have / suffer / experience / receive / encounter a **setback**
▸ to have / suffer / experience / receive / feel a / the **shock**
▸ to suffer / experience / undergo / go through an **ordeal**
▸ to have / experience / receive / undergo **treatment**
▸ to have / suffer / experience / receive / encounter sth **directly**

have [T] to have a particular situation affect you or happen to you: *I went to a few parties and had a good time.*

◇ *I was having difficulty in staying awake.* ◇ *She'll have an accident one day.* ❶ People typically **have** *problems* and *difficulties*, a *shock*, a *fright*, an *accident* and a *good* or *bad time.*

suffer [T] (*rather formal*) to have sth unpleasant happen to you, such as injury, defeat or loss: *He suffered a massive heart attack.* ◇ *The party suffered a humiliating defeat in the general election.* ◇ *The company suffered huge losses in the last financial year.*

experience [T] (*rather formal*) to have a particular situation affect you or happen to you: *The country experienced a foreign currency shortage for several months.* ◇ *He had not directly experienced the fighting in the city.* See also **experience** → EVENT *noun* 1 **experience** → LIFE *noun* 3

receive [T] (*rather formal*) to get an injury or be given a particular type of treatment: *Several of the passengers received severe injuries.* ◇ *Emergency cases will receive professional attention immediately.* ◇ *We received a warm welcome from our hosts.*

NOTE SUFFER OR RECEIVE? You can **suffer** or **receive** an *injury*. **Receive** suggests less emotional attachment to the situation; **suffer** places more emphasis on the bad effect or pain experienced by the person.

feel [T] to experience the effects or results of physical conditions or an event, often strongly: *He feels the cold a lot.* ◇ *She felt her mother's death very deeply.* ◇ *The effects of the recession are being felt everywhere.* ◇ *We all felt the force of his arguments.*

undergo /ˌʌndəˈɡəʊ; AmE ˌʌndərˈɡoʊ/ [T] (*rather formal, especially written*) to have sth happen to you, especially a change or sth unpleasant: *Some children undergo a complete transformation when they become teenagers.* ◇ *My mother underwent major surgery last year.* ◇ *The drug is currently undergoing trials in America.* ❶ People and things typically **undergo** *tests* and *trials*, medical procedures such as *operations* and *examinations*, and *changes*, *transformation* or *metamorphosis*.

go through sth *phrasal verb* (*rather informal*) to suffer an unpleasant experience or difficult period of time: *She's been going through a bad patch recently.* ◇ *He's amazingly cheerful considering all he's had to go through.* ◇ *I went through hell in my first year at the school.* ❶ **Go through sth** is often used to talk about a difficult period of time such as a *phase*, a *patch*, a *period* or a *stage*. It is also used with words like *hell*, *agony* and *ordeal* to talk about people experiencing extremely unpleasant situations.

take [T] (not usually used in the progressive tenses) to have sth happen to you, especially sth that involves you being hit or hurt: *She's taken a nasty fall and has her leg in plaster.* ◇ *The team took a terrible beating.* ◇ *The school took the full force of the explosion.*

encounter [T] (*rather formal, especially written*) to experience sth, especially sth unpleasant or difficult, while you are trying to do sth else: *We encountered a number of difficulties in the first week.* ◇ *I had never encountered such resistance before.*

'run into sth *phrasal verb* (*rather informal*) to have difficulties: *Be careful not to run into debt.* ◇ *We were worried that she may have run into trouble.* ❶ Apart from *debt* and *bad weather*, people typically run into *problems*, *difficulties* or *trouble*.

meet [T] to experience sth, often sth unpleasant: *Others have met similar problems.* ◇ *How she met her death will probably never be known.* ❶ People typically **meet** *problems*, *resistance* or their *death* or *fate*.

---

4 have · hold · host · call · give · convene · throw
These words all mean to arrange for people to be together for a particular purpose.

PATTERNS AND COLLOCATIONS
▸ to have / hold / host / call / give / convene a **conference**
▸ to have / hold / call / convene a **meeting**
▸ to have / hold / host / give / throw a **party**
▸ to have / hold / host / give a **dinner**
▸ to have / hold / call an **election**
▸ to have / hold / host a **competition / contest**
▸ to have / hold a **conversation / debate / discussion**

have [T] to organize an event; to organize or take part in a discussion or conversation: *Let's have a party to celebrate.* ◇ *We had a very interesting discussion about climate change.*

hold [T, often passive] (*rather formal*) to organize or have an event or discussion: *The next conference will be held in Ohio.* ◇ *It's impossible to hold a conversation with all this noise.*

host [T] to organize an event to which others are invited and make all the arrangements for them: *The President hosted a banquet in her honour.* ◇ *Germany hosted the World Cup finals.*
▸ **host** *noun* [C]: *Ian, our host, introduced us to the other guests.* ◇ *The college is **playing host to** a group of visiting Russian scientists.*

call [T] to order sth to happen; to announce that sth will happen: *The principal called a staff meeting to discuss the changes.* ◇ *The drivers were going to call a strike.*

give [T] to organize an event and invite people to it; to perform sth in public: *The Chancellor will be giving a press conference later today.* ◇ *She gave a reading from her latest novel.*

convene /kənˈviːn/ [T] (*formal*) to arrange for people to come together for a formal meeting or meetings: *A Board of Enquiry was convened immediately after the accident.*

throw [T] (*rather informal*) to organize a party and invite people to it: *They threw a party for him on his birthday.* ◇ (*informal*) *He always throws a big bash on Oscar night.* ❶ In this meaning **throw** always collocates with *party* or *bash*.

---

health *noun* See the Topic Map for HEALTH on p.890

health · condition · fitness · well-being · shape · constitution
These are all words for sb's physical state and whether they are healthy or unhealthy.

PATTERNS AND COLLOCATIONS
▸ sb's **general / physical** health / condition / fitness / well-being
▸ sb's **personal** health / fitness / well-being
▸ **full** health / fitness
▸ sb's health / condition / fitness **deteriorates / improves**
▸ to **maintain / regain** your health / fitness
▸ to **be in good** health / shape

health [U] sb's good or bad physical or mental state; the state of being physically and mentally healthy: *Exhaust fumes are **bad for your health**.* ◇ *Smoking can seriously **damage your health**.* ◇ *She was forced to resign because of **ill health**.* ◇ *He has been **in poor health** for some time now.* ◇ *She has always enjoyed **the best of health**.* ◇ *Her **mental health** began to deteriorate.* ◇ *He was nursed back to health by his wife.* See also **healthy** → WELL *adj.*

condition [U, sing.] (*rather formal*) the state of sb's body, especially after they have become ill or injured: *You are **in no condition** (= too ill or injured) to go anywhere.* ◇ *The cyclist was in a **critical condition** in hospital last night.* ◇ *Her **condition is** said to be **stable**.* ◇ *She shouldn't be drinking so much **in her condition** (= because she is pregnant).*

fitness [U] the state of being physically healthy and strong: *She has a good level of physical fitness.* ◇ *a fitness instructor* See also **fit** → WELL *adj.*

'well-being [U] general health and happiness: *Being with my family gives me a wonderful **sense of well-being**.*

shape [usually before noun] (always used with *in* or *into*) (*rather informal*) the state of being fit and healthy: *He's in good shape for a man of his age.* ◇ *I need to **get myself into shape** for the race on Saturday.* ◇ *She always manages to **stay in shape**.*

constitution /ˌkɒnstɪˈtjuːʃn; *AmE* ˌkɑːnstəˈtuːʃn/ [U] the ability of sb's body to stay healthy: *I have a **strong constitution** and my stomach can handle anything.*

healthy *adj.*

healthy · nutritional · good · nutritious · nourishing
These words all describe things, especially food, which are good for your health.

healthy [usually before noun] good for your health: *More public awareness of **healthy eating** has made us think more about our diet.* ◇ *Many people today are adopting a **healthy lifestyle**.* OPP **unhealthy** → UNHEALTHY
▸ **healthily** *adv.*: *Try to eat healthily.*

nutritional /njuˈtrɪʃənl; *AmE* nu-/ connected with nutrition (= the process by which living things receive the food necessary for them to grow and be healthy): *Parents may be unaware of the **nutritional value** of certain foods.* ◇ *Check the nutritional information on the side of the packet before you eat it.*
▸ **nutritionally** *adv.*: *a nutritionally balanced menu*

good having a good effect on your health: *Too much sun isn't good for you.* ◇ *He doesn't seem to have a very good diet.* ◇ *Citrus fruits are a good source of vitamin C.* OPP **bad** → UNHEALTHY

nutritious /njuˈtrɪʃəs; *AmE* nu-/ (of food) good for your health, because it contains many of the substances which help the body to grow and stay healthy: *Lentil soup is **highly nutritious** and easy to prepare.*

nourishing /ˈnʌrɪʃɪŋ; *AmE* ˈnɜːrɪʃ/ (of food) nutritious; providing the conditions to allow sth to develop or grow stronger: *Vegetarian food can be both **nourishing** and cheap.* ◇ *The environment was **nourishing to** the young girl's developing personality.*

hear *verb*

hear · listen · pay attention · heed · catch · tune in/ tune in to sb/sth
These words all mean to be aware of the sound made by sb/sth, or the meaning of sb's words.

hear [I, T] (not used in the progressive tenses) to be aware of sounds with your ears; to give your attention to the sound produced by sb/sth: *I can't hear very well.* ◇ *I couldn't hear anything.* ◇ *He could hear a dog barking.* ◇ *Did you hear him go out?* ◇ *Didn't you hear what I said?* ◇ *Did you hear that play on the radio last night?* ◇ *Don't decide until you've heard both sides of the argument.*

listen [I] to give your attention to the sound produced by sb/sth; to take notice of what sb says to you so that you follow their advice or believe them: *'What were you doing?' 'Just listening to the radio.'* ◇ *Listen! What's that noise?* ◇ *Sorry, I wasn't really listening.* ◇ *He had been listening at the door.* ◇ *Can you **listen out for** the doorbell?* ◇ *None of this would have happened if you'd listened to me.* ◇ *Why won't you **listen to reason**?* ◇ *(spoken)* Listen, there's something I have to tell you.* ◇ *(especially AmE)* OK everyone, **listen up**! ❶ *You cannot 'listen sb/sth' (without 'to'):* I'm fond of listening to classical music.* ◇ ~~I'm fond of listening classical music.~~

HEAR OR LISTEN? Hear usually describes what happens when a sound comes to your ears, whether you are giving the sound your attention or not. **Listen** means that you are deliberately trying to hear a sound: *She heard them talking to each other* (= she became aware of their conversation). ◇ *She listened to them talking to each other* (= she was trying to hear what they were saying). Sometimes **hear** can have the same meaning as **listen**: *Don't decide until you've heard/ listened to both sides of the argument.* However, **hear** is NOT used in the progressive tenses and is used to talk about a complete action, not an activity; you can *hear a radio programme/broadcast/lecture/argument/debate*, but if you *hear music/the radio* you hear it by accident, not because you are deliberately listening: *I could hear music playing/the radio blaring out in the next room.* ◇ ~~He enjoys hearing music.~~ ◇ ~~'What were you doing?' 'Just hearing the radio.'~~

pay atˈtention *phrase* to listen to sb/sth carefully: *Can you all pay attention please?* ◇ *Don't pay any attention to what they say* (= don't think that it is important). OPP **ignore** → IGNORE

heed [T] *(formal)* to listen to and act on a warning or piece of advice: *They failed to heed the lessons of history.* ◇ *Calls for more legislation to protect tenants were not heeded.*

catch [T] to manage to hear or understand sth: *Sorry, I didn't quite catch what you said.* ◇ *Did you catch that show on the radio?* ❶ **Catch** is used especially in negative sentences to say that sb did not hear or understand sth.

tune ˈin *phrasal verb* to listen to a radio show or watch a television show: *More than five million listeners tuned in to his afternoon radio show.* ❶ In slightly more informal language, **tune in to sb/sth** can mean 'to become aware of other people's thoughts and feelings': *(rather informal) She can understand what babies need by listening to their cries and tuning in to their body language.*

heat *noun*
1 the heat of the sun
2 the heat in the factory

1 heat · warmth
These are both words for the state or quality of being hot or warm.

heat [U, sing.] the state or quality of being hot: *He could feel the heat of the sun on his back.* ◇ *Heat rises.* ◇ *The fire gave out a **fierce heat**.*

warmth [U] the state or quality of being warm, rather than hot or cold: *She felt the warmth of his arms around her.* ◇ *The animals huddled together **for warmth**.*

2 heat · drought · heatwave
These are all words for hot weather or hot conditions in an enclosed space.

heat [U] hot weather; hot conditions in an enclosed space: *We avoided going out in **the heat of the day** (= at the hottest time).* ◇ *The air shimmered in the midday heat.* ◇ *The heat in the factory was unbearable.* ◇ *Products which may be damaged by heat are stored in a separate area.*

drought /draʊt/ [C, U] a long period of time when there is little or no rain: *The country suffered from one of the worst droughts on record.* ◇ *Farmers are facing ruin after two years of severe drought.* See also **dry** → SUNNY

heatwave /'hi:tweɪv/ [C] a period of unusually hot weather: *They said on the news the heatwave is going to continue for weeks.*

heat *verb*

heat · warm · warm (sth) up · heat (sth) up · reheat
These words all mean to become or make sth become warmer or hotter.

PATTERNS AND COLLOCATIONS
▸ to heat / warm sth **through**
▸ to heat / warm up / heat up / reheat **soup**
▸ to heat / warm / warm up a **room / house**
▸ to heat / warm / reheat sth **gently**
▸ to heat sth / warm sth / warm sth up / heat sth up / reheat sth **in the oven / microwave**

heat [T] to make sth hot or warm: *Heat the oil and add the onions.* ◇ *The system produced enough energy to heat several thousand homes.* ◇ *Metals expand when heated.* ◇ *Check the lasagne is heated through* (= that all parts of it are hot) *before serving.* See also **heated** → HOT

warm [T, I] to make sb/sth warm or warmer; to become warm or warmer: *Come in and warm yourself by the fire.* ◇ *The alcohol warmed and relaxed him.* ◇ *As the climate warms the ice caps will melt.* See also **warm** → HOT

warm sth 'up, **warm 'up** *phrasal verb* (*rather informal, especially spoken*) to make sb/sth warm or warmer; to become warm or warmer: *I'll warm up some milk.* ◇ *Come in and get warmed up.* ◇ *When spring comes the weather begins to warm up.*

NOTE WARM OR WARM (STH) UP? Warm (sth) up is slightly more informal than **warm** and is used more in spoken English. **Warm** is used more often in literary or formal writing.

heat sth 'up, **heat 'up** *phrasal verb* to make sth hot or warm; to become hot or warm: *I'll just heat up some soup.* ◇ *The oven takes a while to heat up.*

NOTE HEAT OR HEAT (STH) UP? Heat (sth) up is slightly more informal than **heat** and is used more in spoken English. **Heat** is not usually used without an object: *The oven is heating up.* ◇ *The oven is heating.* Use **heat** in technical language or when talking about a system or process, for example a system which heats buildings: *The system produced enough energy to heat up several thousand homes.*

reheat /ˌriːˈhiːt/ [T] to heat cooked food again after it has been left to go cold: *Reheat the sauce carefully without boiling it.*

heating *noun*

heating · heat · boiler · furnace · heater · radiator · central heating · fire · stove
These are all words for a piece of equipment or a system that makes a place warmer.

PATTERNS AND COLLOCATIONS
▸ (a) **gas** heating / heat / boiler / furnace / heater / central heating / fire / stove
▸ (an) **electric** heating / boiler / furnace / heater / fire
▸ to **put / turn / leave on** the heating / the heat / a boiler / a furnace / a heater / a radiator / the central heating / a fire
▸ to **turn up / down / off** the heating / the heat / a boiler / a furnace / a heater / a radiator / the central heating / a fire
▸ to **switch on / off** the heating / the heat / a boiler / a furnace / a heater / the central heating / a fire
▸ to **install** heating / a boiler / a furnace / a heater / a radiator / central heating / a (gas) fire

▸ the heating / the heat / a boiler / a furnace / a heater / a radiator / the central heating / a fire **is on / off**
▸ the heating / the heat / a boiler / a furnace / a heater / a radiator / the central heating **works**
▸ the heating / the heat / a boiler / a furnace / the central heating **breaks down**
▸ a heating / boiler / furnace / central heating **system**

heating [U] (*especially BrE*) the process of supplying heat to a room or building; a system used to do this: *If you insulate your house properly you'll end up spending less on heating bills.* ◇ *Who turned the heating off?* ◇ *What type of heating do you have?*

heat [U] (*especially AmE*) heating: *The heat wasn't on and the house was freezing.*

boiler [C] a container in which water is heated to provide hot water and heating in a building or to produce steam in an engine: *There was a gas boiler mounted on the far wall.* ◇ *She took the clothes to the boiler room to hang them up.*

furnace /'fɜːnɪs; AmE 'fɜːrnɪs/ [C] (*AmE*) a container in which heat is produced to provide hot water and heating in a building: *You'll be able to turn the furnace down which means a lower heating bill.* ❶ A **furnace** does the same job as a **boiler**, but the heat is produced using air, not hot water or steam.

heater [C] a machine used for making air or water warmer: *It is thought that the fire was caused by a gas leak from a water heater.* ◇ *a fan heater* (= that heats a place by blowing hot air out) ◇ (*AmE*) *a space heater* (= that heats a small room or area)

radiator /'reɪdieɪtə(r)/ [C] a hollow metal device for heating rooms. Radiators are usually connected by pipes through which hot water is pumped: *The radiator in the kitchen isn't working.*

central 'heating [U] (*BrE*) a system for heating a building from one source which then pumps the hot water or hot air through pipes all around the building: *There is a central heating system with a radiator in each room.* ◇ *Gas-fired central heating has been installed.*

fire [C] (*BrE*) a piece of equipment for heating a room: *There's a small gas fire under the mantelpiece.* ◇ *Shall I put the fire on?*

stove /stəʊv; AmE stoʊv/ [C] a piece of equipment that can burn various fuels and is used for heating rooms: *There is no heating in the house apart from a small wood-burning stove.* See also **stove** → OVEN

heavy *adj.*

heavy · bulky · massive · dense
These words all describe things that weigh a lot, are large and solid or are difficult to move.

PATTERNS AND COLLOCATIONS
▸ a heavy / bulky **item / object**

heavy weighing a lot; large and solid or powerful: *The suitcase was too heavy for me to carry.* ◇ *How heavy is it* (= how much does it weigh)*?* ◇ *My brother is much heavier than me.* ◇ *He was tall and strong with heavy features.* ◇ *big, dark rooms full of heavy furniture* ◇ *a wide range of engines and heavy machinery* ◇ *heavy goods vehicles* **OPP light** ❶ Things that are **light** do not weigh much and are easy to lift or move: *Modern video cameras are light and easy to carry.* ◇ *The little girl was as light as a feather.*

bulky large and difficult to carry; large and heavy: *She laid two bulky files on the table.* ◇ *The bulky figure of Inspector Jones appeared at the door.*

massive very large, heavy and solid: *She could see the whole massive bulk of the cathedral.* ◇ *massive rock formations* See also **massive** → HUGE

dense (*physics*) heavy in relation to its size: *All that is left of the star is a small, dense core.*

help noun

help · assistance · support · aid · service · cooperation · backup
These are all words for the act of helping sb.

help [U] the act of helping sb to do sth or of giving them sth they need; the fact of being useful: *None of this would have been possible without her help.* ◊ *The passengers were screaming for help.* ◊ *Quick, run and get help!* ◊ *The place was difficult to find and the map **wasn't much help**.* See also **helpful** → VALUABLE 2

assistance [U] (*formal*) help: *technical/economic/military assistance* ◊ *financial assistance for people on low incomes* ◊ *The other passengers went to her assistance.* ◊ *Good afternoon Sir, **can I be of any assistance**?*

support [U] sympathy and help that you give to sb who is in an unhappy or difficult situation: *We'll need to give her lots of support when she comes out of hospital.* ◊ *He needed constant emotional support.* ◊ *Friends came to the lecture to give me **moral support*** (= encouragement).
▸ **supportive** adj.: *My sister was very supportive when my baby was ill.* ◊ *a supportive family*

aid [U] (*formal*) help that you need to perform a particular task; help that is given to sb in a difficult or dangerous situation: *The job would be impossible without the aid of a computer.* ◊ *Two other swimmers came to his aid.*

service [C, usually pl.] (*rather formal*) the particular skills or help that a person is able to offer: *I think you are going to need the services of a good lawyer.* ◊ *I offered my services as a babysitter for the evening.*

cooperation (*BrE* also **co-operation**) /kəʊˌɒpəˈreɪʃn; *AmE* koʊˌɑːp-/ [U] (*rather formal*) willingness to help and do what sb asks you to do: *We would be grateful for your cooperation in leaving as quietly as possible.*

backup /ˈbækʌp/ [U, C] extra help or support that you can get if you need it: *The police called for backup from the army.* ◊ *We can use him as a backup if one of the team can't play.* ◊ *The hospital has a backup power supply.*

help verb

1 I was only trying to help.
2 This should help reduce the pain.

1 help · assist · support · cooperate · help (sb) out · aid · aid and abet · lend (sb) a hand · be of service
These words all mean to make it easier or possible for sb to do sth by doing sth for them or by giving them sth that they need.

help [I, T] to make it easier or possible for sb to do sth by doing sth for them or by giving them sth that they need: *Help, I'm stuck.* ◊ *I was only trying to help.* ◊ *He always helps with the housework.* ◊ *I need contacts that could help in finding a job.* ◊ *We must all try and help each other.* ◊ *Jo will help us with some of the organization.* ◊ *She helped (to) organize the party.*

assist [T, I] (*rather formal, especially written*) to make it easier or possible for sb to do sth by doing sth for them: *We'll do all we can to assist you.* ◊ *The play was directed by Mike Johnson, assisted by Sharon Gale.* ◊ *Anyone willing to assist can contact this number.*

support [T] to give or be ready to give help to sb if they need it, especially by being kind to them in a difficult or unhappy situation: *She **supported** her husband **through** many difficult times.* ◊ *The organization supports people with AIDS.*

cooperate (*BrE* also **co-operate**) /kəʊˈɒpəreɪt; *AmE* koʊˈɑːp-/ [I] to work together with sb else in order to achieve sth; to be helpful by doing what sb asks you to do: *The two groups agreed to **cooperate with** each other.* ◊ *They had cooperated closely in the planning of the project.* ◊ *Their captors told them they would be killed unless they cooperated.*

ˌhelp ˈout, **ˌhelp sb ˈout** *phrasal verb* to help sb, especially in a difficult or busy situation: *He's always willing to help out.* ◊ *When I bought the house, my sister helped me out with a loan.*

aid [T] (*rather formal, written*) to help sb to do sth, especially by making it easier: *Each group is aided by a tutor or consultant.* ◊ *They were accused of aiding him in his escape.*

ˌaid and aˈbet *idiom* (-**tt**-) (*law or humorous*) to help sb to do sth illegal or wrong: *He stands accused of aiding and abetting the bombing.* ◊ *His black mood receded, aided and abetted by two glasses of wine.*

lend (sb) a ˈhand *idiom* (*rather informal*) to help sb to do sth, often by doing practical things for them: *I went over to see if I could lend a hand.* ◊ *I'll be there to lend him a hand with anything if required.* ◊ *She's always ready to lend a helping hand.*

be of ˈservice *idiom* (*formal, spoken*) to be useful or helpful: *Can I be of service to anyone?* ◊ *Glad to be of service.*

2 help · facilitate · benefit · assist · aid · clear the way · ease · open the way
These words all mean to make it easier for sth to happen or to improve sth.

help [I, T] to improve a situation; to make it easier for sth to happen: *The money raised **helped towards** the cost of organizing the event.* ◊ *Iron **helps in** the formation of red blood cells.* ◊ *This should **help (to)** reduce the pain.* ◊ *The exhibition helped her establish herself as an artist.* ◊ *It certainly **helped** being able to talk about it.* **OPP** hinder, hamper → BLOCK 1, See also **help** → AID *noun*, **helpful** → VALUABLE 2

facilitate /fəˈsɪlɪteɪt/ [T] (*formal*) to make an action or process possible or easier: *The new trade agreement should facilitate more rapid economic growth.* ◊ *Structured teaching facilitates learning.*

benefit (-t- *or* -tt-) [T] to be useful or bring an advantage to sb, especially a particular group of people, or improve their life in some way: *We should spend the money on something that will benefit everyone.* ◇ *The new tax laws will clearly benefit those on low wages.* **OPP** **disadvantage** ❶ To **disadvantage** sb or a group of people is to bring them a disadvantage [T, usually passive]: *In the past women have been disadvantaged by the narrow range of occupations open to them.* See also **beneficial** → VALUABLE 2

assist [I, T] (*rather formal, especially written*) to make it easier for sth to happen: *Two approaches might assist in tackling the problem.* ◇ *These activities will assist the decision-making process.*

aid [T, I] (*formal*) to make it easier for sth to happen: *New drugs are now available to aid recovery.* ◇ *Aided by strong winds, the fire quickly spread.* ◇ *Computers can be used to aid in management decision-making.*

NOTE FACILITATE, ASSIST OR AID? In some cases you can use any of these words: *to facilitate/assist/aid a process/ transition* ◇ *to facilitate/assist/aid the development of sth.* **Facilitate** and **assist** have a wider range of collocates than **aid**, including many nouns that describe a process such as *passage, flow, transition, transfer, introduction* and *removal*. **Assist** is often followed by *in*: *assist in the development of sth.* **Aid** can also be used in this way, but NOT **facilitate**: *facilitate in the development of sth.* **Facilitate** and **assist** are nearly always used to describe making helpful processes easier; **aid** can also be used to talk about unhelpful processes: *Facilitated/ assisted by fire and strong winds, the fire quickly spread.*

clear the way *idiom* to remove things that are stopping the progress or movement of sth: *The ruling could clear the way for extradition proceedings.*

ease [T] to make sth easier, especially by removing or changing sth that has been making it difficult: *Ramps have been built to ease access for the disabled.*

open the way *idiom* to make it possible for sb to do sth or for sth to happen, especially sth which was not possible before: *The agreement could open the way for the country to pay off its debts.*

helpful *adj.*

helpful · cooperative · willing · obliging · accommodating · neighbourly
These words all describe sb who is friendly and willing to help other people.

PATTERNS AND COLLOCATIONS
▸ helpful / obliging / accommodating **to** sb
▸ to **find sb** helpful / cooperative / willing
▸ **friendly and** helpful / cooperative / obliging / accommodating

helpful willing to help sb: *I called the police but they weren't very helpful.* ◇ *The staff couldn't have been more helpful.* ◇ *She's one of the most helpful people I know.* **OPP** **unhelpful** → PERVERSE
▸ **helpfully** *adv.*: *She helpfully suggested that I try the local library.*

cooperative (*BrE also* **co-operative**) /kəʊˈɒpərətɪv; *AmE* koʊˈɑːp-/ helpful by doing what you are asked to do: *Employees will generally be more cooperative if their views are taken seriously.* **OPP** **uncooperative** → PERVERSE

willing [usually before noun] ready or pleased to help and not needing to be persuaded; done or given in an enthusiastic way: *willing helpers/volunteers* ◇ *willing support/consent* ◇ *She's very willing.* **OPP** **unwilling** → RELUCTANT
▸ **willingly** *adv.*: *People would willingly pay more for better services.*

obliging /əˈblaɪdʒɪŋ/ (*formal*) very willing to do sth for sb: *They were very obliging and offered to wait for us.*
▸ **obligingly** *adv.*: *'I'll go for you,' she said, obligingly.*

accommodating /əˈkɒmədeɪtɪŋ; *AmE* əˈkɑːm-/ (*rather formal*) willing to change your plans in order to do things for other people: *They are very accommodating to people with special needs.*

neighbourly (*BrE*) (*AmE* **neighborly**) /ˈneɪbəli; *AmE* -bərli/ friendly and helpful: *It was a neighbourly gesture of theirs.*

herd *noun*

herd · flock · pack · swarm
These are all words for a group of animals of a particular kind.

PATTERNS AND COLLOCATIONS
▸ a herd / flock / pack / swarm **of** sth
▸ to do sth **in** herds / flocks / packs / swarms
▸ a herd / flock **of** sheep
▸ the herd / pack **instinct**

herd [C+sing./pl. *v.*] a group of animals of the same type that live and feed together: *a herd of cows/deer/elephants* ◇ *a beef/dairy herd* (= cows kept on a farm for meat/ milk) ◇ *Zebras live in herds with a dominant stallion as the herd leader.* ❶ **Herd** is used especially to talk about animals that live in very large groups and eat grass, including *cows, sheep, deer, zebras, antelope, buffalo* and *wildebeest*. See also **herd** → CROWD *verb*

flock [C+sing./pl. *v.*] a group of sheep, goats or birds of the same type: *A flock of birds passed overhead.* ◇ *He looks after a flock of 500 sheep.* See also **flock** → CROWD *verb*

pack [C+sing./pl. *v.*] a group of animals, especially dogs or wolves, that hunt together or are kept for hunting: *Packs of savage dogs roamed the hills.* ◇ *Killer whales hunt in packs, as do wolves.*

swarm /swɔːm; *AmE* swɔːrm/ [C] a large group of insects, especially bees, moving together in the same direction: *a swarm of bees/flies/locusts* ◇ *A typical locust swarm can destroy around 20 000 tons of vegetation.* See also **swarm** → SURGE *verb*

hero *noun* See also the entry for STAR 1

hero · icon · idol · heroine
These are all words for a person that you admire very much.

PATTERNS AND COLLOCATIONS
▸ a hero / an idol / a heroine **of mine, his,** etc.
▸ a hero / heroine **to** sb
▸ **sb is my, his,** etc. hero / idol / heroine
▸ a **sporting / cultural / national** hero / icon / heroine
▸ a **film / pop / sports** hero / icon / idol
▸ to **become / make sb** a hero / an icon / an idol / a heroine

hero /ˈhɪərəʊ; *AmE* ˈhɪroʊ; ˈhiː-/ (*pl.* **-oes**) [C] a person, especially a man, who is admired by many people for doing sth brave or good, or that you admire because of a particular quality or skill that they have: *He was a war hero* (= sb who was very brave during a war), *but he never talked about it.* ◇ *The Olympic team were given a hero's welcome on their return home.* ◇ *James Dean was a childhood hero of mine.*

icon /ˈaɪkɒn; *AmE* -kɑːn/ [C] a famous person or thing that people admire and see as a symbol of a particular idea or way of life: *Madonna and other pop icons of the 1980s* ◇ *Sandra has become a style icon, for the fashion world particularly.*

NOTE HERO OR ICON? You can use **hero** to talk about sb that you admire yourself: *a personal hero* ◇ *my hero* ◇ *my icon* ◇ *an icon of mine.* Use **icon** to talk about sb who is special to a particular group of people (a group that you may or may not belong to yourself): *a feminist/gay icon* (= sb that feminists/gay people admire) ◇ *a feminist/gay hero*

idol /'aɪdl/ [C] a person that is loved and admired very much: *As a young man, he was a teen idol.* ◇ *She has been my idol since I was a child.* ❶ **Idol** is often used about young people's attitude to sb famous, for example pop stars, film actors, etc. Common collocates are *pop*, *teen* and *screen.* See also **idolize** → LOVE *verb*

heroine /'herəʊɪn; *AmE* -roʊ-/ [C] a woman who is admired by many people for doing sth brave or good, or that you admire because of a particular quality or skill that she has: *She is widely regarded as one of the heroines of the revolution.* ◇ *Madonna was her teenage heroine.*

hesitant *adj.*

hesitant · faltering · uncertain · tentative · halting
These words all describe a way of doing sth that is not confident or certain.

PATTERNS AND COLLOCATIONS
▸ hesitant / faltering / uncertain / tentative / halting **steps**
▸ a hesitant / a faltering / an uncertain / a halting **voice**
▸ hesitant / halting **speech**
▸ a hesitant / an uncertain / a tentative **smile**

hesitant /'hezɪtənt/ [only before noun] showing that you are slow to speak or act because you feel uncertain, embarrassed or unwilling: *It was a few seconds before she heard a hesitant reply.* ◇ *Holding his hand, she managed to take her first few hesitant steps.* See also **hesitate** → PAUSE *verb*, **hesitant** → UNSURE
▸ **hesitantly** *adv.*: *He smiled hesitantly.*

faltering /'fɔːltərɪŋ/ moving, speaking or progressing in a way that is not steady or confident: *She was only 10 months old when she took those first faltering steps.* ◇ *Both sides have been asked to give the faltering peace talks another chance.*
▸ **falter** *verb* [I]: *His voice faltered as he began his speech.* ◇ *He never faltered in his commitment to the party.*

uncertain showing a lack of confidence or decision: *The baby took its first uncertain steps.* ◇ *She had been dismissed and in no uncertain manner.*
▸ **uncertainly** *adv.*: *They smiled uncertainly at one another.*

tentative /'tentətɪv/ (*written*) showing a lack of confidence: *He acknowledged me with a tentative nod.* ◇ *Her English is correct but tentative.*
▸ **tentatively** *adv.*: *She smiled tentatively.*

halting /'hɔːltɪŋ; *BrE* also 'hɒlt-/ [usually before noun] (especially of speech or movement) stopping and starting often, especially because you are not certain or are not very confident: *We carried on a halting conversation.* ◇ *The crisis is threatening the country's halting progress towards democracy.*
▸ **haltingly** *adv.*: *'Well...', she began haltingly.*

hesitate *verb*

hesitate · shy away from sth · shrink from sth · hold back · think twice · baulk · recoil
These words all mean to avoid doing sth because you are worried that it might be difficult or unpleasant.

PATTERNS AND COLLOCATIONS
▸ to shy away / shrink / hold back / recoil **from** sth
▸ to baulk / recoil **at** sth
▸ to shy away from / shrink from / think twice about / baulk at **doing sth**
▸ to shy away from / shrink from / recoil from a / an **idea / thought / prospect**
▸ to shy away from / shrink from the **truth**
▸ to **make sb** hesitate / hold back / think twice / baulk / recoil
▸ to hesitate / hold back **(for) a moment**
▸ to hesitate / hold back / recoil **a little**

hesitate [I] (*rather formal*) to be worried about doing sth, especially because you are not sure that it is right or appropriate: *Please do not hesitate to contact me if you have any queries.* See also **hesitate** → PAUSE *verb*

▸ **hesitation** *noun* [U]: *She agreed without the slightest hesitation.* ◇ *I have no hesitation in recommending her for the job.*

shy a'way from sth *phrasal verb* to avoid doing sth because you are nervous, afraid or shy: *Hugh never shied away from his responsibilities.* ◇ *The newspapers have shied away from investigating the story.* ❶ Typical collocates of **shy away from sth** are *question, subject, idea, prospect, commitment, truth, publicity* and *scandal.*

'shrink from sth *phrasal verb* (*written*) to be unwilling to do sth that is difficult or unpleasant: *We made it clear to them that we would not shrink from confrontation.* ◇ *They did not shrink from doing what was right.*

hold 'back *phrasal verb* to hesitate to act or speak: *He wanted to tell her about it, but held back for fear of upsetting her again.* ◇ *She held back from saying what she really thought about it.*

> NOTE HESITATE OR HOLD BACK? People **hesitate** when they are not sure what to do and are worried about doing the wrong thing; people **hold back** when they feel that what they really want to do may not actually be the best thing or what other people want.

think 'twice *idiom* to think carefully before deciding to do sth: *You should think twice about employing someone you've never met.*

baulk (*BrE*) (*AmE* usually **balk**) /bɔːk/ [I] (*rather formal*) to be unwilling to do sth or become involved in sth because it is difficult, dangerous or expensive: *Many parents may baulk at the idea of paying $100 for a pair of shoes.* ❶ **Baulk** suggests sb stopping suddenly when you are told sth such as a price or a new idea. There is a stronger sense of protest suggested in **baulk** compared with **shy away from sth** or **shrink from sth.**

recoil /rɪ'kɔɪl/ [I] (*written*) to react to an idea or situation with strong dislike or fear: *She recoiled from the idea of betraying her own brother.*

> NOTE SHRINK FROM STH OR RECOIL? **Recoil** suggests a reaction of shock or horror; **shrink from sth** suggests a strong feeling of not wanting to do sth, but the feeling is less strong than with **recoil.**

hide *verb*

1 hide your papers/your feelings/the truth
2 Quick, hide!

1 hide · conceal · cover · disguise · mask · bury · camouflage
These words all mean to put or keep sb/sth in a place where they/it cannot be seen or found, or to keep the truth or your feelings secret.

PATTERNS AND COLLOCATIONS
▸ to hide / conceal / disguise / mask / camouflage sth **behind** sth
▸ to hide / conceal / bury sth **under** sth
▸ to hide / conceal sth **from** sb
▸ to hide / conceal / disguise / mask the **the truth / the fact that...**
▸ to hide / conceal / disguise / mask / bury your **feelings**
▸ to hide / conceal / cover / disguise / mask your **disappointment / surprise**
▸ to hide / conceal / disguise your **emotion / shock**
▸ to hide / conceal / cover your **embarrassment**
▸ to hide / conceal / mask your **anger**
▸ to **completely / partly** hide / conceal / cover / disguise / mask / bury sth
▸ to **carefully** hide / conceal / cover / disguise / camouflage sth
▸ to **cleverly** hide / conceal / disguise sth
▸ to **barely / scarcely** hide / conceal / cover / disguise sth

hide [T] to put or keep sb/sth in a place where they/it cannot be seen or found; to keep sth secret, especially your feelings: *He hid the letter in a drawer.* ◇ *I keep my private papers hidden.* ◇ *They hid me from the police in their attic.* ◇ *She struggled to hide her disappointment.* ◇

They claim that they **have nothing to hide** (= there was nothing wrong or illegal about what they did). ◇ *His brusque manner hides a shy and sensitive nature.*

conceal /kən'siːl/ [T] (*formal*) to hide sb/sth; to keep sth secret: *The paintings were concealed beneath a thick layer of plaster.* ◇ *For a long time his death was concealed from her.* ◇ *She sat down to conceal the fact that she was trembling.* ❶ When it is being used to talk about emotions, **conceal** is often used in negative statements: *He could not conceal his joy/disappointment.* ◇ *She could barely/ scarcely/hardly conceal her delight.*

cover [T] to place sth over or in front of sth in order to hide it; to hide a particular feeling from people: *She covered her face with her hands.* ◇ *He laughed to cover (= hide) his embarrassment.* See also **cover** → COVER *noun*

disguise /dɪs'gaɪz/ [T] to hide or change the nature of sth, so that it cannot be recognized: *He tried to disguise his accent.* ◇ *She made no attempt to disguise her surprise.* ◇ *It was a thinly disguised attack on the President.* See also **disguise** → COSTUME *noun*

mask /mɑːsk; *AmE* mæsk/ [T] to hide a feeling, smell, fact, etc. so that it cannot be easily seen or noticed: *She masked her anger with a smile.* ◇ *Spices were used to mask the unpleasant taste of the meat.*

bury [T] to hide sth in the ground; to ignore or hide a feeling, mistake, etc: *We used to dig for hours, looking for buried treasure.* ◇ *She had learnt to bury her feelings.*

camouflage /'kæməflɑːʒ/ [T] to hide sb/sth by making them/it look like the things around, or like sth else: *The soldiers camouflaged themselves with leaves and twigs.* See also **camouflage** → COSTUME *noun*

---

2 hide · lurk · lie low · hole up/be holed up
These words all mean to go or be somewhere where you hope you will not be found.

PATTERNS AND COLLOCATIONS
▸ to hide / lurk / lie low / hole up **in a place**
▸ a **place to** hide / lie low / hole up

hide [I, T] to go or be somewhere where you hope you will not be seen or found: *Quick, hide!* ◇ *I hid under the bed.* ◇ *They're hiding from the police.* ◇ *She hides herself away in her office all day.*

lurk [I] (usually used with an adverb or preposition) to wait somewhere secretly, especially because you are going to do sth bad or illegal: *Why are you lurking around outside my house?* ◇ *A crocodile was lurking just below the surface.*

lie 'low *idiom* (*rather informal*) to try not to attract attention to yourself, especially for quite a long time: *Maybe we should lie low for a few days.*

hole 'up, be holed 'up *phrasal verb* (*informal*) to hide in a place: *We've got to find out where he holes up at night.* ◇ *We believe the gang are holed up in the mountains.*

---

high *adj.*

1 a high price/speed/demand
2 a high mountain
3 a high voice/sound

---

1 See also the entries for EXCESSIVE and EXPENSIVE
high · inflated · steep · prohibitive · unreasonable · exorbitant · astronomical · extortionate
These words all describe a level, especially the price or cost of sth, that is more than normal or too much.

high	unreasonable	prohibitive
inflated		exorbitant
steep		astronomical
		extortionate

PATTERNS AND COLLOCATIONS
▸ high / inflated / steep / prohibitive / unreasonable / exorbitant / astronomical / extortionate **prices**
▸ high / steep / prohibitive / exorbitant / astronomical / extortionate **costs**
▸ high / exorbitant / astronomical / extortionate **rates**
▸ high / exorbitant / extortionate **charges / taxes / fees / rents**
▸ a high / an unreasonable / an astronomical **level**
▸ a high / an inflated / an astronomical **figure**

high greater than normal in level or degree: *They charge very high prices for a pretty average service.* ◇ *a high level of pollution* ◇ *a high standard of craftsmanship* ◇ *A high degree of accuracy is needed.* ◇ *Demand is high at this time of the year.* ◇ *The cost in terms of human life was high.* ◇ *We had high hopes for the business* (= we believed it would be successful). **OPP** low → POOR 2

inflated (of an amount or level) higher than is reasonable or acceptable: *company directors with inflated salaries* ◇ *Consumers are paying inflated prices for food.*

steep (*informal*) (of a price or demand) too much: *£2 for a cup of coffee seems a little steep to me.*

prohibitive /prə'hɪbətɪv; *AmE* also proʊ'h-/ (of a price or cost) so high that it prevents people from buying sth or doing sth: *a prohibitive tax on imported cars* ◇ *The price of property in the city is prohibitive.*

▸ **prohibitively** *adv.*: *Car insurance can be prohibitively expensive for young drivers.*

unreasonable (often used in negative sentences) (of a price or level) too high in a way that is unfair or not realistic: *The fees they charge are not unreasonable.* **OPP** reasonable → CHEAP

▸ **unreasonably** *adv.*: *The bank was found to be charging unreasonably high prices for its services.*

exorbitant /ɪg'zɔːbɪtənt; *AmE* -'zɔːrb-/ (*rather formal*, *disapproving*) (of prices) much higher than is reasonable: *The lawyer charged us an exorbitant fee for two days' work.*

astronomical /ˌæstrə'nɒmɪkl/ (*informal*) (of a price or amount) extremely high or large: *the astronomical costs of land for building* ◇ *The figures are astronomical.*

▸ **astronomically** *adv.*: *Interest rates are astronomically high.*

extortionate /ɪk'stɔːʃənət; *AmE* -'stɔːrʃ-/ (*rather informal*, *disapproving*) (of prices) much higher than is reasonable: *They are offering loans at extortionate rates of interest.*

NOTE EXORBITANT OR **EXTORTIONATE**? Exorbitant is more frequent and more formal than **extortionate** but there is no real difference in meaning.

---

2 high · tall · towering · high-rise · lofty
These words all describe sth which measures a long distance from the bottom to the top, or is at a level which is far away from the ground or sea.

PATTERNS AND COLLOCATIONS
▸ a high / tall / towering / lofty **mountain / cliff**
▸ a high / tall / high-rise / lofty **tower / building**
▸ high / tall / towering **walls**
▸ high / tall **trees / grass**
▸ a high / tall / lofty **peak**
▸ a high / lofty **ceiling**
▸ towering / lofty **heights**

high measuring a long distance from the bottom to the top; at a level which is a long way above the ground or sea: *What's the highest mountain in the US?* ◇ *Her shoes were black, with high heels.* ◇ *He has a round face with a high forehead.* ◇ *They were flying at high altitude.* ◇ *I can't reach the top shelf – it's too high.* ❶ High is also used to talk about or ask about the distance that sth measures from the bottom to the top: *How high is Everest?* ◇ *It's only a low wall – about a metre high.* ◇ *The grass was waist-high.* **OPP** low ❶ In this meaning low has no synonyms of its own: *a low wall/building/table* ◇ *a low range of hills* ◇ *flying at low altitude* ◇ *The sun was low in the sky.* See also **height** → LENGTH

tall having a greater than average height; measuring a long distance from the bottom to the top: *What's the tallest building in the world?* ◊ *Pollutants are dispersed through* **tall** *chimneys.* ◊ *a* **tall** *glass* of iced tea

> **NOTE** HIGH OR TALL? In many cases, where the meaning is 'measuring a long distance from the bottom to the top', either word can be used. However, they are most common in these collocations: *a* **high** *mountain/cliff/peak/wall* ◊ *(a)* **tall** *building/tower/tree/grass.* **Tall** is not used to talk about sth which is at a level a long way above the ground, it only refers to the distance between the top and the bottom of sth: *The room has* **tall** *windows* (= the windows stretch from the bottom of the wall to the top). ◊ *The room has* **high** *windows* (= they are at the top of the wall, near the ceiling).

towering [only before noun] extremely tall or high and therefore impressive: *The coastline consists of wild, towering cliffs.* ◊ *The building erupted in a* **towering** *inferno* (= a very tall fire).

'high-rise [only before noun] (of a building) very tall and having lots of floors: *These* **high-rise apartment blocks** *were built in the 1960s.*

lofty [usually before noun] (*formal or literary*) very high and impressive: *From the lofty heights of his apartment you could see right across New York.*

---

3 high · shrill · high-pitched · sharp · treble · piercing
These words all describe voices or sounds that are at or near the top of a musical scale, and not deep or low.

PATTERNS AND COLLOCATIONS
> a high / shrill / high-pitched / sharp / treble / piercing **voice**
> a high / shrill / high-pitched / sharp / piercing **sound**
> a high / shrill / sharp **note**
> a shrill / high-pitched / sharp / piercing **scream / whistle**
> a shrill / high-pitched / piercing **shriek**
> a shrill / high-pitched **laugh**
> in shrill / sharp / piercing **tones**

high (of a voice or sound) at or near the top of a musical scale: *She has a high voice.* ◊ *That note is definitely too high for me.* **OPP** **low, deep** → DEEP 2

shrill (*disapproving*) (of a voice or sound) very high and loud, in an unpleasant way: *The PE teacher's shrill voice rang out across the school fields.* ◊ *A shrill scream rent the air.*
> **shrilly** *adv.*: *She laughed shrilly.*

high-'pitched (*sometimes disapproving*) (of sounds) high, sometimes in an unpleasant way: *She had a high-pitched giggle which irritated me intensely.* **OPP** **low-pitched** ❶ The opposite of **high-pitched** is **low-pitched**, but this is not very frequent and it is more usual just to use **low**: there is no unpleasantness associated with low sounds as there is with some high-pitched ones.

> **NOTE** HIGH OR HIGH-PITCHED? This meaning of **high** combines with a few very frequent nouns for sounds: *a high voice/note/key.* **High-pitched** is used for most other sounds: *a high-pitched noise/scream/whistle/tone.* Both words can be used with *sound*: *a high/high-pitched sound.* **High-pitched** can sometimes suggest a rather unpleasant sound.

sharp [usually before noun] (of a voice or sound) loud, sudden and often high in tone: *She read out the list in sharp, clipped tones.* ◊ *There was a sharp knock on the door.* **OPP** **soft** → QUIET 2
> **sharply** *adv.*: *He rapped sharply on the window.* ❶ In musical terminology a note that is **sharp** is above the correct pitch (= how high or low a note sounds). The opposite is **flat**. This meaning of **sharp** can also be used as an adverb: *That note was slightly sharp.* ◊ *You played that note sharp.*

treble /'trebl/ [only before noun] (*music*) (of a voice or musical note) high in tone: *He sang in a high, clear treble voice.* **OPP** **bass** → DEEP 2

> **NOTE** HIGH OR TREBLE? **Treble** is a more technical word than **high**, used in singing.

piercing /'pɪəsɪŋ; *AmE* 'pɪrsɪŋ/ [usually before noun] (*disapproving*) (of a voice or sound) very high, loud and unpleasant: *She gave a piercing scream.* ◊ *She has such a piercing voice.*

> **NOTE** SHRILL OR PIERCING? A **piercing** sound or voice is loud and even higher and more unpleasant than a **shrill** sound or voice.

highway *noun*

highway · motorway · freeway · interstate · turnpike · dual carriageway · divided highway · ring road · beltway · bypass
These are all words for major roads.

PATTERNS AND COLLOCATIONS
> **on** a highway / a motorway / a freeway / an interstate / a turnpike / a dual carriageway / a divided highway / a ring road / a beltway / a bypass
> **along / down / up** the highway / motorway / freeway / interstate / turnpike / dual carriageway / divided highway
> a highway / a motorway / a freeway / an interstate **from… to…**
> a **busy** highway / motorway / freeway / interstate / ring road / beltway / bypass
> to **get on / get off** the highway / freeway / interstate
> to **join / leave** the motorway
> highway / motorway / freeway **traffic**
> a highway / a motorway / an interstate **system**
> a **stretch of** highway / motorway / freeway / dual carriageway / divided highway

highway [C, U] (*especially AmE*) a main road for travelling long distances, especially one connecting and going through large towns: *There's a 55 mph speed limit on most highways.* ◊ *The hotel is located off Highway 21.* ❶ In the US individual highways are often given numbers: *Highway 85.* In American English, the abbreviation **Hwy** is often used to talk about a particular highway: *Hwy 1.* ❶ In British English, **highway** is usually used in official or legal contexts, where it can mean any public road: *All citizens have the right to use the* **public highway**.

motorway /'məʊtəweɪ; *AmE* 'moʊtərweɪ/ [C, U] (in Britain) a wide road, with at least two lanes in each direction, where traffic can travel fast for long distances between large towns. You can only enter and leave motorways at special junctions: *I left the motorway at the next exit.* ◊ *He doesn't like motorway driving.* ❶ **Motorways** in the UK are given a number and referred to by the abbreviation **M**: *Take the M4 as far as Swindon.*

freeway /'friːweɪ/ [C, U] (in the US) a wide road, similar to a motorway in Britain: *They were called to an accident on the freeway at 2:46.* ◊ *It's one of the busiest stretches of freeway in the county.*

interstate /'ɪntəsteɪt; *AmE* -tərs-/ (also **,interstate 'highway**) [C] (in the US) a highway between different states: *There has been an increase in traffic deaths on rural interstates.* ❶ Individual **interstates** are given the capital letter I and a number: *I-40* (= said 'eye forty').

turnpike /'tɜːnpaɪk; *AmE* 'tɜːrn-/ [C] (in the US) a highway that people have to pay a toll (= an amount of money) to use: *Turnpike tolls are going up next month.* ❶ In the names of individual roads, **turnpike** is given a capital letter: *the New Jersey Turnpike.* In informal spoken English you can also say **pike**: *I was going north on the Jersey Pike.*

> **NOTE** HIGHWAY, FREEWAY, INTERSTATE OR TURNPIKE? **Highway** is the most general of these terms and can mean any main road connecting and going through cities. An **interstate** is a highway with two or more lanes of traffic in each direction; you can only enter or leave the interstate at particular points (called *exits* in American English, not 'junctions'). In the western US interstates are usually called **freeways**: this was originally to distinguish them from the **turnpikes** of the

east, which you have to pay to travel on. The same road may be referred to in different ways in different parts of the country. For example, Interstate 90 goes from east to west across the whole country; in Massachussetts in the east it is called a **turnpike** because you pay to travel on the part that runs through Massachussetts. In the west it is called the **freeway**. In the places in between it may be referred to as a **highway** or by its letter and number (I-90).

,dual 'carriageway [C, U] (*BrE*) a road with a strip of land in the middle that divides the lines of traffic moving in opposite directions: *He was caught driving the wrong way down the dual carriageway. ◇ The road is being converted to dual carriageway.*

di,vided 'highway [C, U] (*AmE*) a dual carriageway: *Continue on through the light, staying on the divided highway 6 East.*

'ring road [C] (*BrE*) a road that is built around a city or town to reduce traffic in the centre: *Her house is just off the inner ring road.*

beltway /'beltweɪ/ [C] (*AmE*) a ring road: *Traffic was snarled as a two-mile stretch of the beltway was closed for four hours.* ❶ The only road regularly referred to as **the beltway** is the one around Washington D.C. Most people would refer to a particular beltway by its three-digit number: *I was going south on 495, and I saw a huge accident in the northbound lane.*

bypass /'baɪpɑːs/ [C] a road that passes around a town or city rather than through its centre: *There were protests against the building of the bypass.*

hill *noun*

hill · mountain · moor · summit · ridge · peak · mound · moorland · fell · highlands · foothills
These are all words for areas of land that are higher than the land around them.

mound	hill	mountain
	moor	summit
	moorland	ridge
	fell	peak
	foothills	highlands

PATTERNS AND COLLOCATIONS
▸ **on** a hill / a mountain / the moors / the summit / a ridge / a peak / a mound / the fells
▸ **in** the hills / mountains / fells / highlands / foothills
▸ a **steep** hill / mountain / ridge / mound
▸ a **grassy** hill / mound
▸ **open** hills / moors / moorland / fells
▸ to **climb** a hill / mountain / ridge / peak / fell

hill [C] an area of land that is higher than the land around it, but not as high as a mountain; a slope on a road: *a region of gently rolling hills ◇ a hill farm / town / fort ◇ I love walking in the hills* (= in the area where there are hills). *◇ Always take care when driving down steep hills.* **OPP** valley → VALLEY
▸ **hilly** *adj.*: *a hilly area / region*
mountain [C] a very high hill, often with rocks near the top: *a chain / range of mountains ◇ We stopped to enjoy the mountain scenery. ◇ mountain roads / streams / villages ◇ a mountain rescue team*
▸ **mountainous** /'maʊntənəs/ *adj.*: *mountainous regions*
moor /mɔː(r); mʊə(r); *AmE* mʊr/ [C, usually pl., U] (*especially BrE*) a high open area of land that is not used for farming, especially an area covered with rough grass: *the North York Moors ◇ We went for a walk on the moors. ◇ moor and rough grassland*
summit /'sʌmɪt/ [C] the highest point of sth, especially the top of a mountain: *We reached the summit at noon.*

ridge [C] a narrow area of high land along the top of a line of hills; a high pointed area near the top of a mountain: *walking along the ridge ◇ the north-east ridge of Mount Everest*

peak [C] the pointed top of a mountain; a mountain with a pointed top: *a mountain peak ◇ snow-capped / jagged peaks ◇ The climbers made camp halfway up the peak.*

NOTE SUMMIT OR PEAK? A mountain can have more than one **peak**; only the highest peak of the mountain is the **summit**. A whole mountain can be called a **peak**; only the top is called the **summit**.

mound /maʊnd/ [C] a large pile of earth or stones; a small hill: *a Bronze age burial mound ◇ The castle was built on top of a natural grassy mound.*
moorland /'mɔːlənd; 'mʊə-; *AmE* 'mʊrlənd/ [U, C, usually pl.] (*especially BrE*) land that consists of moors: *walking across open moorland*
fell [C] a hill or area of hills in northern England: *The long green line of the fells rose before me.*
highlands /'haɪləndz/ [pl.] an area of land with hills or mountains: *Peru's Andean highlands* ❶ The Highlands usually refers to the high mountain region of Scotland. **OPP** lowland → PLAIN
foothills /'fʊthɪlz/ [pl.] hills or low mountains at the base of a higher mountain or range of mountains: *the foothills of the Himalayas*

hit *verb*

1 hit by a car
2 hit sb over the head
3 be badly hit by the recession

1 **hit · knock · bang · strike · bump · bash**
These words all mean to come against sth with a lot of force.

PATTERNS AND COLLOCATIONS
▸ to hit / knock / bang / bump / bash **against** sb / sth
▸ to knock / bang / bump / bash **into** sb / sth
▸ to hit / strike the **ground / floor / wall**

hit [T, I] to come against sth with force, especially causing damage or injury; to bring a bat, etc. against a ball and push it away with force: *The boy was hit by a speeding car. ◇ The grenade will explode as soon as it hits the ground. ◇ The boat hit against an object under the surface of the water. ◇ She hit the ball too hard and it went out of the court.* **OPP** miss ❶ To **miss** sb / sth is to fail to hit them: *The bullet missed her by about six inches. ◇ She threw a plate at him and **narrowly missed** hitting him.* See also hit → BANG *verb* 2
▸ **hit** *noun* [C]: *The bomber scored a **direct hit** on the bridge. ◇ We finished the first round with a score of two hits and six misses.*

knock [T] to hit sth so that it moves or breaks; to put sb / sth into a particular state or position by hitting them / it: *Someone had knocked a hole in the wall. ◇ The two rooms had been knocked into one. ◇ They had to **knock** the door **down** to get into the apartment. ◇ I accidentally **knocked over** his drink. ◇ The blow knocked him senseless* (= he became unconscious). See also knock → KNOCK *verb*, knock → BANG *verb* 2
▸ **knock** *noun* [C]: *Knocks and scratches will lower the value of antique furniture.*
bang [T, I] to hit sth in a way that makes a loud noise: *The baby was banging the table with his spoon. ◇ She banged on the door angrily. ◇ A branch banged against the window.* See also bang → BANG *verb* 1, bang → BANG *verb* 2
strike [T] (*formal*) to hit sb / sth hard: *The ship struck a rock. ◇ The stone struck him on the forehead. ◇ The old tree had been **struck by lightning**.*

bump [I, T] to hit sb/sth accidentally: *In the darkness I bumped into a chair.* ◇ *The car bumped against the kerb.* ◇ *Their boat came up alongside, bumping the side of ours.* See also **bump** → BANG *verb* 2
▶ **bump** *noun* [C]: *He fell to the ground with a bump.*

bash [I, T] (*informal*) to hit against sth very hard: *I braked too late, bashing into the car in front.* ◇ *He stood up, bashing his head on the low ceiling.*

---

2 See the Topic Map for CONFLICT on p.896, See also the entry for BEAT 1

hit · punch · slap · strike · smack · spank · thump · whack · swat · sock

These words all mean to bring your hand, or sth that you are holding in your hand, onto or against sb/sth very hard.

▶ to hit / strike / whack / swat sb / sth **with** sth
▶ to hit / strike / thump / whack sb **over the head**
▶ to hit / punch / strike / thump sb **in the stomach / chest**
▶ to hit / punch sb **on the nose**
▶ to hit / punch / slap / strike / smack / spank / thump / whack / sock sb **hard**
▶ to hit / punch / strike sb **repeatedly**

hit [T] to bring your hand, or an object that you are holding, against sb/sth quickly and with force: *I felt like hitting him.* ◇ *She hit him hard in the stomach.* ◇ *He hit the nail squarely on the head with the hammer.* See also **hit** → BANG *verb* 2
▶ **hit** *noun* [C]: *Give it a good hit.*

punch [T] to hit sb/sth with your fist (= tightly closed hand), especially as hard as you can: *They repeatedly kicked and punched the man as he lay on the ground.* ◇ *He was punching the air in triumph.*
▶ **punch** *noun* [C]: *a punch in the face* ◇ *Hill threw a punch at the police officer.*

slap (-pp-) [T] to hit sb/sth with your open hand: *I'll slap you if you do that again.* ◇ *She slapped him hard across the face.* ◇ *'Congratulations!' he said, slapping me on the back.*
▶ **slap** *noun* [C]: *She gave him a slap across the face.*

strike [T] (*formal*) to hit sb/sth with your hand or with sth that you are holding: *She struck him hard across the face.* ◇ *Did she ever strike you?* ◇ *He struck the table with his fist.* ◇ *Who struck the first blow* (= started the fight)?

smack [T] (*especially BrE*) to hit sb with your open hand, especially a child as a punishment: *I think it's wrong to smack children.*
▶ **smack** *noun* [C]: *You'll get a smack on your backside if you're not careful.*

spank [T] to hit sb, especially a child, several times on their bottom as a punishment: *She says she's never spanked her children.* ❶ In American English **spank** is generally used instead of **smack**; **spank** is also used in British English, but it is less frequent.

thump [T] to hit sb/sth hard with your hand: *She thumped the table angrily.* ◇ *She couldn't get her breath and had to be thumped on the back.*
▶ **thump** *noun* [C]: (*BrE, informal*) *She gave him a thump on the back.*

whack /wæk/ [T] (*informal, especially spoken*) to hit sb/sth hard: *She whacked him around the head.* ◇ *He whacked the ball back over the net.*
▶ **whack** *noun* [C]: *He gave the ball a good whack.*

swat /swɒt; AmE swɑːt/ (-tt-) [T] to hit sth, especially an insect, using your hand or a flat object: *She swatted the fly with a rolled-up newspaper.* ◇ *He swatted away the mosquitoes that were buzzing around his head.*

sock [T] (*informal, especially spoken*) to hit sb hard with your fist (= closed hand): *She got mad and socked him in the mouth.* ◇ *I had to stop myself from socking him one.*
▶ **sock** *noun* [C, usually sing.]: *He gave Mike a sock on the jaw.*

---

3 **hit · strike · attack · strike at sb/sth**

These words all mean to have a bad or harmful effect.

▶ a / an **earthquake / hurricane / storm** hits / strikes (sth)
▶ a **disease / virus** strikes / attacks sb / sth

hit [T, I] (*rather informal, especially journalism or spoken*) (of events or developments) to have a bad effect on sb/sth: *Rural areas have been worst hit by the strike.* ◇ *Spain was one of the hardest hit countries.* ◇ *Airlines were badly hit by the recession.* ◇ *His death didn't really hit me at first.* ◇ *A tornado hit on Saturday night.*

strike [I, T] (*written, especially journalism*) (of a disaster or disease) to happen suddenly and have a harmful effect on sb/sth: *Two days later tragedy struck.* ◇ *Disaster struck again when their best player was injured.* ◇ *The area was struck by an outbreak of cholera.*

attack [T] (especially of a disease) to have a harmful effect on sth that increases with time: *The vines had been attacked by mildew.* ◇ *The virus attacks different cells in the body.*

'strike at sb/sth *phrasal verb* (*written*) to have a damaging or serious effect on sb/sth, especially important principles or ways of doing things: *These proposals strike at the very fundamentals of a free press.* ◇ *The criticisms strike at the heart of the party's policies.*

---

hoarse *adj.*

hoarse · raucous · harsh · husky · thick · guttural · rough · strident · gruff

These words all describe people's voices when they sound as though they come from the speaker's throat.

▶ to be hoarse / husky / thick **with** sth
▶ a hoarse / raucous / harsh / guttural / rough **sound**
▶ a hoarse / raucous / harsh / husky / thick / guttural / rough / strident / gruff **voice**
▶ hoarse / harsh / husky / guttural / strident / gruff **tones**
▶ a hoarse / raucous / harsh / husky / guttural / gruff **laugh**
▶ hoarse / raucous / harsh **laughter**
▶ a hoarse / raucous / harsh / guttural **cry**
▶ a hoarse / harsh / husky / gruff **whisper**
▶ to **sound** hoarse / harsh / husky / thick / rough / gruff

hoarse /hɔːs/ (of a voice or person) sounding as if the voice is coming from the speaker's throat, especially because the throat is sore: *Her voice came out as a hoarse whisper.* ◇ *He shouted himself hoarse.*
▶ **hoarsely** *adv.*: *'You don't understand,' she whispered hoarsely.*

raucous /'rɔːkəs/ (*usually disapproving*) loud in an unpleasant way: *We could hear raucous laughter coming from the room next door.* ◇ *A group of raucous young men were standing on the corner of the street.*

harsh (*often disapproving*) (of sb's voice) loud in an unpleasant way: *'Stop it!' she said in a harsh voice.*
▶ **harshly** *adv.*: *Alec laughed harshly.*

> **NOTE** **HARSH OR RAUCOUS?** Harsh is usually used to talk about a single person's voice; **raucous** is more often used to talk about the unpleasant noise made by a group of people.

husky (of a voice or person) sounding deep, quiet and rough, sometimes in an attractive way: *She spoke in a husky whisper.* ◇ *Sorry, I'm a bit husky today – I've got a sore throat.*
▶ **huskily** *adv.*: *'You're beautiful,' he murmured huskily.*

thick (of sb's voice) deep and not as clear as normal, especially because of emotion or illness: *His voice was thick with emotion.*
▶ **thickly** *adv.*: *'Just leave me alone,' he said thickly.*

guttural /'ɡʌtərəl/ (*written*) (of a sound) made or seeming to be made at the back of the throat: *He spoke in a low guttural growl.*

rough (*often disapproving*) (of sb's voice) unpleasant to listen to; not kind or gentle: *'I suppose you expect me to apologize for this,' he said in a rough voice.*
▶ **roughly** *adv.*: *'What do you want?' she demanded roughly.*

> **NOTE** **HARSH** OR **ROUGH?** A **harsh** voice is likely to be higher in tone than a **rough** voice.

strident /ˈstraɪdnt/ (*disapproving*, *written*) loud, harsh and unpleasant: *She came behind him, shouting in her strident voice, 'Not there! Servants this way.'* ◇ *the strident ringing of the phone* ❶ **Strident** is often used to talk about loud and unpleasant voices with an upper-class accent.

gruff (*often disapproving*) (of a person or voice) deep and harsh, and often sounding unfriendly: *'Open up,' commanded a gruff voice.*

hold *verb*

hold · hold on · cling · clutch · grip · grasp · clasp · handle · hang on
These words all mean to have sb/sth in your hands or arms.

PATTERNS AND COLLOCATIONS
▸ to hold / clutch / grip / clasp sth **in your hand / hands / arms**
▸ to hold / clutch / clasp sb / sth **in your arms**
▸ to hold / hold on to / cling to / clutch / grip / grasp / clasp / hang on to sb / sth **by / with** sth
▸ to hold / clutch / grip / grasp / clasp / hang **on to** sth
▸ to hold / clutch / cling / hang **on**
▸ to hold / clutch / clasp sth **to you**
▸ to hold / hold on to / cling on to / clutch / grip / grasp / clasp sb's **hand**
▸ to hold / hold on to / cling to / clutch / grip / grasp / clasp / hang on to sb / sth **tightly**
▸ to hold / hold on to / cling to / clutch / grip / grasp / clasp sb / sth **firmly**
▸ to hold / hold on to / clutch / grip / clasp / hang on to sb / sth **tight**

hold [T] to have sb/sth in your hand or arms: *She was holding a large box.* ◇ *The captain held the trophy in the air.* ◇ *I held the baby gently in my arms.* ◇ *The girl held her father's hand tightly.* ◇ *They walked along the street, holding hands.* ◇ *He held her by the shoulders.* ◇ *The lovers held each other close.*
▶ **hold** *noun* [sing., U]: *His hold on her arm tightened.* ◇ *She tried to keep hold of the child's hand.*

hold 'on, **hold 'onto sb/sth** *phrasal verb* [no passive] to continue to hold sb/sth; to put your hand on sb/sth and not take your hand away: *Hold on and don't let go until I say so.* ◇ *It's very windy – you'd better hold on to your hat.* ◇ *He held onto the back of the chair to stop himself from falling.*

cling [I] to hold on to sb/sth tightly, especially with your whole body: *Survivors clung to pieces of floating debris.* ◇ *Leaves still cling to the branches.* ◇ *Cling on tight!* ◇ *They clung together, shivering with cold.*

clutch [T, I] to hold sb/sth tightly, especially in your hand; to take hold of sth suddenly: *She stood there, the flowers still clutched in her hand.* ◇ *He gasped, and clutched his stomach.* ◇ *He felt himself slipping and clutched at a branch.*

grip (-**pp**-) [T, I] to hold on to sth very tightly with your hand: *'Please don't go,' he said, gripping her arm.* ◇ *Grip the rope as tightly as you can.* ◇ *She gripped on to the railing with both hands.*
▶ **grip** *noun* [C, usually sing.]: *Keep a tight grip on the rope.* ◇ *The climber slipped and lost his grip.*

grasp /ɡrɑːsp; AmE ɡræsp/ [T] to take hold of sth firmly: *He grasped my hand and shook it warmly.* ◇ *Kay grasped him by the wrist.* ◇ *He grasped the pan by its handle.* ❶ The object of **grasp** is often sb's *hand* or *wrist*.
▶ **grasp** *noun* [C, usually sing.]: *I grabbed him, but he slipped from my grasp.*

clasp /klɑːsp; AmE klæsp/ [T] (*written*) to hold sb/sth tightly in your hand or in your arms: *He leaned forward, his hands clasped tightly together.* ◇ *They clasped hands (= held each other's hands).* ◇ *She clasped the children in her arms.* ◇ *He clasped her to him.* ❶ The object of **clasp** is often your *hands*, sb else's *hand* or another person.
▶ **clasp** *noun* [sing.]: *He took her hand in his firm clasp.*

handle [T] to touch, hold or move sth with your hands: *Our cat hates being handled.* ◇ *The label on the box said: 'Fragile. Handle with care.'*

hang 'on *phrasal verb* [no passive] to hold on to sth very tightly, especially in order to support yourself or stop yourself from falling: *Hang on tight. We're off!* ◇ *I hung on to him for support.*

hold sb/sth up *phrasal verb* See also the entry for
BLOCK 1

hold sb/sth up · delay · keep · stall · be/get bogged down · retard · set sb/sth back · stunt · detain
These words all mean to slow down the progress, movement or development of sb/sth.

PATTERNS AND COLLOCATIONS
▸ to be held up / delayed / stalled / set back **by / for hours / days / months, etc.**
▸ to hold up / delay / retard / stunt the **development / growth** of sth
▸ to delay / bog down / stall / retard a **process**
▸ to hold up / delay / retard the **progress** of sth
▸ to hold up / delay (a) **flight / traffic / work**
▸ to **seriously** hold up / delay / retard sth
▸ to be **unavoidably** delayed / detained

hold sb/sth 'up *phrasal verb* to slow down or prevent the movement or progress of sb/sth: *The launch was held up for several hours by environmental protesters.* ◇ *An accident is holding up traffic.* ◇ *I'm holding everybody up – you go ahead without me.*
▶ **'hold-up** *noun* [C]: *We should finish by tonight, barring hold-ups.* ◇ *What's the hold-up (= what is causing it)?*

delay [T, often passive] to make sb late or make them do sth more slowly; to make sth happen later than planned: *Thousands of commuters were delayed for over an hour.* ◇ *What could have delayed him?* ◇ *These arguments will inevitably delay the start of construction.* ◇ *The government is accused of using delaying tactics (= deliberately doing sth to delay a process, decision, etc).* See also **delay**
→ DELAY *verb*, **delay** → TAKE YOUR TIME
▶ **delay** *noun* [C]: *Commuters will face long delays on the roads today.* ◇ *We apologize for the delay in answering your letter.*

keep [T] (*especially spoken*) to make sb late when they are on their way somewhere, especially by making them stay in one place longer than they should: *You're an hour late – what kept you?* ◇ *I won't keep you long. I've just got a couple of quick questions.* ◇ *I must go now. I've kept you from your dinner too long.*

stall [T, I] to stop sth from happening until a later time; to stop making progress: *They could stall the process further by asking for a judicial review.* ◇ *There have been several attempts to revive the stalled peace plan.* ◇ *Discussions have once again stalled.*

be/get bogged down *phrase* to be prevented from making progress or getting sth done, often because there are so many difficult but unimportant problems to deal with: *We mustn't get bogged down in details.* ◇ *Try to avoid becoming bogged down with routine reporting procedures.*

retard /rɪˈtɑːd; AmE rɪˈtɑːrd/ [T] (*formal*) to slow down the development or progress of sth: *The progression of the disease can be retarded by early surgery.* ◇ *The lack of a rail link retarded the town's development.* **OPP accelerate**
→ ACCELERATE

,set sb/sth 'back *phrasal verb* to slow down the progress of sb/sth by a particular length of time: *The bad weather set back the building schedule by several weeks.* ◇ *Her recovery was going well, but this latest infection has really set her back.* See also **setback** → BLOW *noun*

stunt [T] to prevent sb/sth from growing or developing properly: *The constant winds had stunted the growth of plants and bushes.* ◇ *His illness had stunted his creativity.*

detain /dɪ'teɪn/ (*formal*) to delay sb or prevent them from going somewhere, usually by talking to them or keeping them busy: *I'm sorry — he'll be late; he's been detained at a meeting.*

hole *noun*

1 a hole in the wall
2 a hole in the ground

---

1 hole · space · gap · opening · slot · aperture
These words are all used for an open space in sth or between things, that sth can pass through or where sth is missing.

▸ a hole / space / gap / opening / slot / aperture **in** sth
▸ a space / gap **between** A and B
▸ a **small** / **narrow** hole / space / gap / opening / slot / aperture
▸ a **large** / **wide** hole / space / gap / opening / aperture
▸ to **leave** a hole / a space / a gap / an opening
▸ to **make** a hole / an opening / a slot

hole [C] an empty space that goes all the way through sth: *to drill/bore/punch/kick a hole in sth* ◇ *There were holes in the knees of his jeans.* ◇ *The children climbed through a hole in the fence.* ◇ *a bullet hole*

space [C] an area or place that is empty, especially between things or in the middle of sth: *a space two metres by three metres* ◇ *a parking space* ◇ *I'll clear a space for your books.* ◇ *Put it in the space between the table and the wall.*

gap [C] a space between two things or in the middle of sth, especially because there is a part missing: *a gap in a hedge/fence/wall* ◇ *Leave a gap between your car and the next.*

opening [C] a space or hole that sth can pass through: *The hall is lit by an opening in the roof.* ◇ *the dark opening of the tunnel* ◇ *The adult parasites have a simple mouth opening.*

slot [C] a long, narrow opening, into which you fit or put sth: *He slid a coin into the slot of the jukebox.* ◇ *a slot machine*

aperture /'æpətʃə(r); *AmE* -tʃʊr/ [C] (*formal or technical*) a small opening in sth; an opening that allows light to reach a lens (= a curved piece of glass or plastic, for example in a camera): *The bell ropes passed through apertures in the ceiling.* ◇ *Open up the lens aperture to maximize the brightness of the shot.*

---

2 hole · pit · hollow · crater · cavity
These are all words for an empty space in the ground or inside sth.

▸ a hole / pit / hollow / crater / cavity **in** sth
▸ a **deep** / **shallow** hole / pit / hollow / crater
▸ a **huge** hole / pit / crater
▸ to **dig** a hole / pit
▸ a bomb **blows** a hole / crater in sth

hole [C] an empty space in sth solid or in the surface of sth: *He managed to dig out a small snow hole.* ◇ *Water had collected in holes in the road.* ◇ *an operation for a hole in her heart*

pit [C] a large deep hole in the ground: *The body had been dumped in a pit.*

NOTE HOLE OR PIT? A **pit** is always large and in the ground; a **hole** can be any size and in anything. **Pit**, but not **hole**, is often used with a figurative meaning.: (*figurative*) *The human mind is a dark, bottomless pit.* ◇ *The human mind is a dark, bottomless hole.*

hollow [C] an area that is lower than the surface around it, especially on the ground; an empty space inside sth: *The village lay secluded in a hollow of the hills (= a small valley).* ◇ *She noticed the slight hollows under his cheekbones.* ◇ *The squirrel disappeared into a hollow at the base of the tree.*
▸ **hollow** *adj.*: *a hollow ball/centre/tube/tree* ◇ *hollow eyes/cheeks*

crater [C] a large hole in the top of a volcano; a large hole in the ground caused by the explosion of a bomb or by sth large hitting it: *volcanic peaks which tower above deep craters* ◇ *The bomb blew a crater 80 metres across.*

cavity (*formal or technical*) a hole or empty space inside sth solid, especially the body; a hole in a tooth: *the abdominal/nasal cavity* ◇ *Most dentists fill cavities right away.*

holiday *noun*

1 the school holidays
2 a camping holiday

---

1 See the Topic Map for SPORT AND LEISURE on p.892
holiday · vacation · break · leave · time off · day off · recess · sabbatical
These are all words for a period of time when you are not at work, school or college.

▸ **during** the holidays / the vacation / the break / the recess / a sabbatical
▸ to be **on** holiday / vacation / leave
▸ (the) **summer** / **Christmas** holiday / vacation / recess
▸ **annual** holiday / vacation / leave
▸ **paid** / **unpaid** holiday / vacation / leave / time off / sabbatical
▸ **three weeks'** / **two days'** / **a month's**, etc. holiday / vacation / leave / recess / sabbatical
▸ to **take** leave / time off / a day off / a sabbatical
▸ to **spend** your holiday / vacation / leave / time off / day off / sabbatical doing sth

holiday [U] (also **holidays** [pl.]) (*BrE*) a period of time when you do not have to go to work, school or college: *My assistant is on holiday this week.* ◇ *You are entitled to four weeks' annual holiday.* ◇ *Your **holiday entitlement** is 25 days a year.* ◇ *My sister's coming to stay in the holidays.* ❶ In both British and American English a **holiday** is also a day when most people do not go to work or school, especially because of a religious or national celebration: *The president's birthday was declared a national holiday.* ◇ *Today is a holiday in Scotland.* In American English **the holidays** means the time in late December and early January that includes Christmas, Hanukkah and New Year.

vacation [U, C] (*AmE*) a period of time when you do not have to go to work, school or college: *Their son is home on vacation.* ◇ *The schools were closed for summer vacation.* ◇ *Vacation time and other benefits were cut.* ❶ In Britain a **vacation** is one of the periods of time when universities or courts are closed: *the Christmas vacation* ◇ *the long (= university summer) vacation.* In the US, courts have a **recess**, like Congress or a committee (see below).

break ❶ In this meaning **break** is uncountable in American English but countable in British English. (*informal*) a period of time when school, college or university students do not have to go to classes: (*AmE*) *A lot of students go to Florida for Spring Break.* ◇ (*BrE*) *Have you got any plans for the Easter break?*

leave [U] a period of time when you do not have to be at work, either in order to take a holiday or for a special reason: *Sylvia's on* **maternity leave** (= after having a baby). ◇ *Fathers are allowed a week's* **paternity leave** (= after the birth of a baby). ◇ *There are new provisions for* **parental leave** (= for parents of young children). ◇ *He was on* **sick leave** *following a heart attack.* ◇ *She was given* **compassionate leave** *to attend the funeral.* ◇ *He applied for* **study leave** (= from teaching at a university) *to write the book.*

time 'off [U] time when you do not have to work: *Why not come with me if you can get the time off?* ◇ *Can you get some* **time off work**? ◇ *The children were given* **time off school** *to watch the ceremony.*

day 'off [C] a day when you do not have to work: *She's had only two days off in the past year.* ◇ *I've got the day off from school.* ◇ *Sunday is my only day off.*

recess /rɪˈses; ˈriːses/ [C, U] a period of time during the year when members of a parliament or committee do not meet: *Tomorrow MPs break for the Christmas recess.* ◇ *The peace talks resumed after a month-long recess.* ◇ *The report was published while Congress was* **in recess**. See also **recess** → REST *noun* 2

sabbatical /səˈbætɪkl/ [C, U] a period of time when sb, especially a teacher in a university, is allowed to stop their usual work in order to study, write or travel: *He's been given a year's sabbatical.* ◇ *She's on sabbatical until January.*

2 See also the entry for TRIP
holiday · vacation · break · getaway
These are all words for a period of time spent away from home relaxing or travelling around.

PATTERNS AND COLLOCATIONS
▸ a **great** / **relaxing** holiday / vacation / break / getaway
▸ a **dream** / **family** holiday / vacation
▸ a **summer** / **winter** holiday / vacation / break / getaway
▸ a holiday / vacation **abroad**
▸ a holiday / vacation **destination** / **home** / **resort** / **spot**
▸ to **go** / **be on** holiday / vacation
▸ to **take** a holiday / vacation
▸ to **cancel** a holiday / vacation / break
▸ a **week's** / **three-day, etc.** holiday / vacation / break

holiday [C] (*BrE*) a period of time spent travelling or relaxing away from home: *The neighbours are away on holiday.* ◇ *He's never had a holiday abroad.* ◇ *We're going on a skiing holiday in Austria.* ◇ **Package holidays** (= in which your flight, accommodation, etc. are all organized for you and included in the price) *are generally becoming less popular.* ◇ *Let's have a look at your holiday photos.*

vacation [C] (*AmE*) a period of time spent travelling or relaxing away from home: *The senator is on vacation in Maine.* ◇ *How was your vacation?* ◇ *They usually go on a* **ski vacation** *this time of year.* ◇ *The area is a popular vacation choice for families.*

break [C] a short holiday/vacation: *The prize is a three-night break in Paris.* ◇ *Choose from our range of city breaks.* ◇ *It's a great city for a* **weekend break**.

getaway /ˈɡetəweɪ/ [C, usually *sing.*] (*rather informal*) a short holiday/vacation; a place that is suitable for a holiday: *a romantic weekend getaway in New York* ◇ *the popular island getaway of Penang*
▸ **get a'way** *phrasal verb*: *We're hoping to get away* (= go away on holiday) *for a few days at Easter.*

holy *adj.*

holy · pure · saintly · blameless
These words all describe sb who is morally good.

PATTERNS AND COLLOCATIONS
▸ a holy / pure / saintly **man** / **woman** / **person**
▸ to live a holy / pure / saintly / blameless **life**

holy /ˈhəʊli; *AmE* ˈhoʊli/ (*often approving*) good in a religious and moral way: *He tries to live a holy life.* ◇ *They are good and holy people.* See also **holy** → RELIGIOUS

pure without any morally bad thought or actions, especially sexual ones; morally good: *The nuns here live a quiet and pure life.* ◇ *He insisted that his motives were pure.* See also **purity** → MORALITY

saintly (*sometimes disapproving*) very good or holy: *He was a saintly but somewhat ineffective archbishop.*

NOTE HOLY OR SAINTLY? The term **holy** is either approving, or simply descriptive, meaning that sb has devoted (= given) their life to religion: *He spent the rest of his life as a hermit and holy man, living in a mountain hut.* **Saintly** is not used in this descriptive way, and is either approving or disapproving: it can be used to suggest that sb is too good, in a way that is annoying, not practical or that does not seem real.

blameless /ˈbleɪmləs/ (*rather formal*) doing no wrong: *All three women had lived blameless lives.*

home *noun*

1 the family home
2 She made Spain her home.

1 See also the entry for HOUSE
home · address · place · dwelling · residence · abode
These words all mean a place where sb lives.

PATTERNS AND COLLOCATIONS
▸ **at** (a) home / an address / sb's place / a residence
▸ **in** a home / sb's place / a dwelling / a residence
▸ a **comfortable** home / place / dwelling / residence
▸ a **private** home / address / dwelling / residence
▸ a **family** home / dwelling / residence
▸ a **permanent** home / address / dwelling / residence / abode
▸ a **temporary** home / address / dwelling / residence / abode
▸ **no fixed** address / abode
▸ to **have** a home / an address / a place of your own

home [C, U] the house or flat that you live in, especially with your family: *We are not far from my home now.* ◇ *Old people prefer to stay in their own homes.* ◇ *She leaves home at 7 every day.* ◇ *She* **left home** (= left her parents) *and began an independent life at sixteen.* ◇ *Nowadays a lot of people* **work from home**.
▸ **home** *adv.*: *Come on, it's time to* **go home**. ◇ *What time did you* **get home** *last night?*

address [C] details of where sb lives or works and where letters can be sent: *What's your* **name and address**? ◇ *Is that your* **home address**? ◇ *Half the names in his* **address book** (= that you write addresses and phone numbers in) *are crossed out.* ◇ *an email address* ◇ *a web address* ◇ *Please note my* **change of address**. ◇ *Police found him at an address* (= a house or flat) *in West London.* See also **address** → SEND *verb* 1

place [*sing.*] (*informal*) a house or flat; a person's home: *What about dinner at* **my place**? ◇ *I'm fed up with living with my parents, so I'm looking for* **a place of my own**. ◇ *I thought I'd better clean the place up.*

dwelling [C] (*formal or literary*) a house, flat or other place where a person lives or is intended to live: *The development will consist of 66 dwellings and a number of offices.*

residence /ˈrezɪdəns/ [C] (*formal*) a house, especially a large or impressive one; the place where sb lives: *This desirable family residence is situated in the heart of the town* (= in an advertisement). ◇ *10 Downing Street is the British Prime Minister's official residence.* ❶ **Residence** [U] is the state of living in a particular place. See also **reside** → LIVE

abode /əˈbəʊd; AmE əˈboʊd/ [C, usually sing.] (*formal or humorous*) the building or place where sb lives: *His sole residence is in a hostel for people of* **no fixed abode** (= with no permanent home). ◇ *Welcome to my humble abode.* ❶ The **right of abode** is official permission that allows a person to live in a particular country: *The island's citizens will not be given the right of abode in Britain.*

---

2 home · homeland · hometown · birthplace
These words all mean the place where sb comes from.

PATTERNS AND COLLOCATIONS
▸ a **beloved / adopted** home / homeland / hometown
▸ a **tribal / traditional / spiritual** home / homeland
▸ to **return to** your home / homeland / hometown / birthplace
▸ to **leave** your home / homeland / hometown

home [C, U] the town, region or country that you come from, or where you are living and that you feel you belong to: *I often think about my friends* **back home**. ◇ *Juliet left England and made Spain her home.* ◇ *She made her home in Spain.* ◇ *Jamaica is* **home to** *over two million people.*

homeland /ˈhəʊmlænd; AmE ˈhoʊm-/ [C] the country where a person was born; a country or region that is closely identified with a particular race or group of people: *Many refugees have been forced to flee their homeland.* ◇ *After the war they wished to return to their traditional homelands.*

hometown /ˈhəʊmtaʊn; AmE ˈhoʊm-/ [C] the town or city where you were born or lived as a child: *He married a girl from his hometown and they went back there to live.* See also **town** → CITY

birthplace /ˈbɜːθpleɪs; AmE ˈbɜːrθ-/ [C] the house, district or town where a person was born, especially a famous person: *Shrewsbury is famous for being the birthplace of Charles Darwin.*

---

honest *adj.* See also the entry for PLAIN 2

---

honest · frank · direct · open · outspoken · straight · blunt · sincere · truthful · candid · straightforward · forthright
These words all describe people saying exactly what they mean without trying to hide feelings, opinions or facts.

PATTERNS AND COLLOCATIONS
▸ honest / frank / direct / open / outspoken / straight / sincere / truthful / candid / straightforward / forthright **about** sth
▸ honest / frank / direct / open / straight / blunt / truthful / candid / straightforward **with** sb
▸ honest / frank / outspoken / sincere / candid / forthright **in** your views / criticism, etc.
▸ an honest / an outspoken / a forthright **opinion / view**
▸ an honest / a direct / a straight / a blunt / a truthful **answer**
▸ an honest / a direct / an open / a sincere / a truthful **person**
▸ a frank / direct / blunt / forthright **manner**
▸ **quite / very** honest / frank / direct / open / outspoken / blunt / sincere / truthful / candid / straightforward / forthright
▸ **extremely** honest / frank / direct / open / outspoken
▸ **completely** honest / frank / open / straight / sincere / truthful
▸ **absolutely** honest / frank / open / straight / truthful
▸ **perfectly** honest / frank / sincere / candid
▸ **To be / Let's be** honest / frank / blunt…

honest (*often approving*) not hiding the truth about sth: *Give me your honest opinion.* ◇ *Are you being completely honest about your feelings?* ◇ *Thank you for being so honest with me.* ◇ (*spoken*) *To be honest, it was one of the worst books I've ever read.* ◇ *Let's be honest, she's only interested in Mike because of his money.* **OPP dishonest** → DISHONEST
▸ **honestly** *adv.*: *I didn't tell anyone, honestly!* ◇ *I honestly can't remember a thing about last night.*
▸ **honesty** *noun* [U]: *She answered all my questions with her usual honesty.* ◇ *The book isn't,* **in all honesty,** *as good as I expected.*

frank (*often approving*) honest in what you say, sometimes in a way that other people might not like: *a full and frank discussion* ◇ *a frank admission of guilt* ◇ *He was very frank about his relationship with the actress.*
▸ **frankly** *adv.*: *He spoke frankly about the ordeal.* ◇ *Quite frankly, I'm not surprised you failed.*
▸ **frankness** *noun* [U]: *They outlined their aims with disarming frankness.*

direct saying exactly what you mean in a way that nobody can pretend not to understand: *I need a direct answer to a direct question.* ❶ Being **direct** is sometimes considered positive (as opposed to being **indirect** and not saying clearly what you mean); but sometimes it is used as a 'polite' way of saying that sb is rude: *She has a very direct way of speaking* (= she does not bother to be polite to people when speaking to them). **OPP indirect** ❶ An **indirect** answer or way of speaking avoids saying sth in a clear and obvious way.
▸ **directness** *noun* [U]: *'What's that?' she asked with her usual directness.* ◇ *He presents his case with refreshing clarity and directness.*

open (*approving*) (of a person) not keeping thoughts and feelings hidden: *She was always open with her parents.* ◇ *He was quite open about his reasons for leaving.*
▸ **openly** *adv.*: *The men in prison would never cry openly* (= so that other people could see).

outspoken /aʊtˈspəʊkən; AmE ˈ-spoʊkən/ saying exactly what you think, even if this shocks or offends people: *He was known as an outspoken opponent of the leadership.* ◇ *She was outspoken in her criticism of the plan.*
▸ **outspokenly** *adv.*: *outspokenly critical*

straight (*usually approving*) honest and direct: *I don't think you're being straight with me.* ◇ *It's time for some* **straight talking.**

blunt saying exactly what you think without trying to be polite: *She has a reputation for blunt speaking.* ◇ *To be blunt, your work is appalling.*
▸ **bluntly** *adv.*: *To put it bluntly, I want a divorce.* ◇ *'Is she dead?' he asked bluntly.*

sincere (*approving*) saying only what you really think or feel: *He seemed sincere enough when he said he wanted to help.* ◇ *She is never completely sincere in what she says about people.* **OPP insincere** → FALSE. See also **sincerity** → TRUTH
▸ **sincerely** *adv.*: *I sincerely believe that this is the right decision.*

truthful (*approving*) saying only what is true; giving the true facts about sth: *Are you being completely truthful with me?* ◇ *She was unable to give a truthful answer.* See also **truth** → TRUTH
▸ **truthfully** *adv.*: *He answered all their questions truthfully.*

candid (*rather formal, often approving*) saying what you think openly and honestly: *The ex-minister gave a candid interview about his reasons for resigning.*
▸ **candidly** *adv.*: *She candidly admitted her mistakes.*
▸ **candour** (*BrE*) (*AmE* **candor**) /ˈkændə(r)/ *noun* [U]: *'I don't trust her,' he said, in a rare moment of candour.*

straightforward /ˌstreɪtˈfɔːwəd; AmE -ˈfɔːrwərd/ (*approving*) (of a person or their opinions) honest and open; not trying to deceive sb or hide sth: *She's nice: very straightforward and easy to get on with.* ❶ A **straightforward** person is generally liked. **Straightforward** is often used with positive words like *intelligent, honest,* and *fair*.

forthright /ˈfɔːθraɪt; AmE ˈfɔːrθ-/ saying clearly and strongly what you think, without being afraid of what other people might think: *a woman of forthright views* ◇ *He spoke in a forthright manner but without anger.*

> **NOTE WHICH WORD?** Honest, frank and candid all refer to *what* you say as much as *how* you say it: *a/an honest/ frank/candid admission of guilt.* They are all generally positive words, although it is possible to be *too* frank in a way that other people might not like. **Direct, outspoken, blunt** and **forthright** all describe sb's

manner of saying what they think. Of these, **forthright** is the most positive, suggesting that you are not afraid of what other people think. **Outspoken** suggests that you are willing to shock people by saying what you believe to be right. **Blunt** and **direct** often suggest that you think honesty is more important than being polite. **Open** and **straightforward** are both positive and both describe sb's character: *He's a very open/straightforward person.*

hooligan *noun* See also the entry for THUG

hooligan · vandal · lout
These are all words for a young person who behaves in a noisy and violent way in public, usually in a group.

PATTERNS AND COLLOCATIONS
▸ a **drunken** hooligan / lout
▸ a **gang of** hooligans / vandals

hooligan /ˈhuːlɪɡən/ [C] a young person who behaves in an extremely noisy and violent way in public, usually in a group: *Seven English football hooligans have been sent home from the Cup Final.*
vandal /ˈvændl/ [C] a person who destroys or damages sth, especially public property, deliberately and for no good reason: *The glass has been specially treated to stop vandals from smashing it.* See also **vandalize** → VANDALIZE
lout /laʊt/ [C] (*BrE*) a rude, noisy and sometimes aggressive or violent boy or young man: *He claimed that he had been abused by drunken teenage louts.*
▸ **loutish** *adj.*: *loutish behaviour*

hope *noun*

1 hope for the future
2 your hopes and fears

1 hope · optimism · expectancy · wishful thinking
These are all words for a feeling that good things will happen.

PATTERNS AND COLLOCATIONS
▸ hope / optimism **for** sth
▸ hope / optimism **that**...
▸ **great / considerable / false / renewed** hope / optimism
▸ to **express / share** your hope / optimism
▸ hope / optimism **grows / rises**

hope [U, C] a belief that sth you want to happen will happen: *There is now hope of a cure.* ◇ *They have given up hope of finding any more survivors.* ◇ *There is still a glimmer of hope.* ◇ *She has high hopes of winning* (= is very confident about it). ◇ *Don't raise your hopes too high, or you may be disappointed.* ❶ **Hope** is usually used to talk about a belief that sth particular will happen, not just that things in general will be good. **OPP** despair, hopelessness → DESPAIR, See also **give up hope**, **lose hope** → DESPAIR *verb*, **hopeful** → OPTIMISTIC, **hopeful** → PROMISING
optimism /ˈɒptɪmɪzəm; *AmE* ˈɑːp-/ [U] (*rather formal*) a feeling that good things will happen and that sth will be successful; the tendency to have this feeling: *He returned with renewed optimism about the future.* ◇ *Some people talked of a mood of cautious optimism.* ❶ **Optimism** is often used in business or political contexts, when business managers or politicians express a belief that their company or policies will be successful. **OPP** pessimism → NEGATIVE *adj.*, See also **optimistic** → OPTIMISTIC
expectancy /ɪkˈspektənsi/ [U] (*rather formal, especially written*) the state of expecting or hoping that sth, especially sth good or exciting, will happen: *There was an air of expectancy among the waiting crowd.* ❶ **Expectancy** is often used by people on television or radio to describe crowds waiting for an exciting event to happen. See also **expectant** → OPTIMISTIC

,wishful 'thinking [U] the belief that sth that you want to happen is happening or will happen, although this is actually not true or very unlikely: *I've got a feeling that Alex likes me, but that might just be wishful thinking.*

2 See also the entry for DESIRE
hope · dream · aspiration · ambition · fantasy · expectation
These are all words for a wish to have or do sth.

PATTERNS AND COLLOCATIONS
▸ hopes / aspirations / expectations **for** sth
▸ aspirations / an ambition **to do** sth
▸ **high** hopes / aspirations / ambitions / expectations
▸ **(a) personal** hope / dream / aspiration / ambition / fantasy / expectations
▸ **political** hopes / aspirations / ambitions
▸ to **have** hopes / a dream / aspirations / an ambition / a fantasy / expectations
▸ to **cherish / harbour / nurture** a hope / a dream / an ambition / a fantasy
▸ to **fulfil** your hopes / dreams / aspirations / ambitions / fantasies / expectations
▸ to **achieve** your dreams / aspirations / ambitions
▸ to **abandon / give up** a hope / a dream / an ambition
▸ to **shatter** a hope / dream / fantasy

hope [C] a wish to have or do sth: *She told me all her hopes, dreams and fears.* ◇ *They have high hopes for their children.* **OPP** fear → FEAR
dream [C] a wish to have or do sth, especially one that seems difficult to achieve: *Her lifelong dream was to be a famous writer.* ◇ *If I win it will be a dream come true.* ◇ *What would be your dream job?* ◇ *I've finally found the man of my dreams.* See also **dream** → TRANCE *noun*, **dreamer** → VISIONARY
▸ **dream** *verb* [I, T]: *It was the kind of trip most people only dream about.* ◇ *I never dreamed I'd actually get the job!*
aspiration /ˌæspəˈreɪʃn/ [C, usually pl.] (*rather formal*) a wish to have or do sth, especially sth that would be considered an achievement or an improvement on your current life and position: *He had never had any aspirations to enter politics.* ◇ *What changes are needed to meet women's aspirations for employment?*
ambition /æmˈbɪʃn/ [C] a strong wish to do or achieve sth: *She never achieved her ambition of becoming a famous writer.* ◇ *His burning ambition was to study medicine.* See also **ambition** → AMBITION

NOTE ASPIRATION OR AMBITION? **Aspirations** are usually more general than **ambitions**. They are all the things that you hope to achieve in life, considered especially in terms of material possessions and social and career success; they are often talked about in a general way in phrases with *and*: *your hopes/needs/dreams/interests/ fears and aspirations*. An **ambition** is usually a particular thing, often connected with success in your career. While people most frequently talk about just *having* **aspirations**, they try to *achieve, fulfil, realize* or *satisfy* their **ambitions**.

fantasy /ˈfæntəsi/ [C] a pleasant situation that you imagine but that is unlikely to happen: *He spoke of his childhood fantasies about becoming a famous football player.* See also **fantasy** → IMAGINATION
▸ **fantasize** (*BrE* also **-ise**) /ˈfæntəsaɪz/ *verb* [I]: *Many people fantasize about winning the lottery.*
expectation /ˌekspekˈteɪʃn/ [C, usually pl., U] (*rather formal*) a hope that sth good will happen: *The results exceeded our expectations.* ◇ *The event did not live up to expectations.* ◇ *There was an air of expectation and great curiosity.* ❶ People typically talk about *exceeding, surpassing, meeting* or *fulfilling* **expectations**. See also **expectation** → EXPECTATION

hope

hope *verb* See also the entry for EXPECT

hope · wait · wish · aspire · set your sights on sth · set your heart on sth
These words all mean to want sth to happen very much.

PATTERNS AND COLLOCATIONS
▸ to hope/ wait/ wish **for** sth
▸ to hope/ wish **that**...
▸ to hope/ wait/ aspire **to do sth**
▸ to **still** hope for/ wait for/ wish for/ aspire to sth
▸ to **really/ secretly/ always/ never** hope for/ wish for/ aspire to sth
▸ to **just/ only** hope/ wish

hope [I, T] to want sth to happen and think that it is possible: *We're hoping for good weather on Sunday.* ◇ *All we can do now is wait and hope.* ◇ *'Do you think it will rain?' 'I hope not.'* ◇ *'Will you be back before dark?' 'I hope so, yes.'* ◇ *Let's hope we can find a parking space.* ◇ *It is hoped that over £10 000 will be raised.* ◇ *She is hoping to win the gold medal.*

wait [I, T] to hope or watch for sth to happen, especially for a long time: *The team had waited for success for eighteen years.* ◇ *This is just the opportunity I've been waiting for.* ◇ *He's waiting for me to make a mistake.* ◇ *I waited my chance and slipped out when no one was looking.*

wish [I] to think very hard that you want sth, especially sth that can only be achieved by good luck or magic: *If you wish really hard, maybe you'll get what you want.* ◇ *It's no use wishing for the impossible.* ◇ *He has everything he could possibly wish for.* See also **wish** → WISH *noun*, **wish** → WANT *verb*, **wish** → WISH *verb*

aspire /ə'spaɪə(r)/ [I] (*rather formal*) to have a strong desire to achieve or become sth: *She aspired to a scientific career.* ◇ *He aspired to be their next leader.*

set your sights on sth *idiom* (*especially journalism*) to decide that you want sth and try very hard to get it: *I had set my sights on a career in journalism.* ❶ **Set your sights on sth** is usually used to talk about things that people want to achieve in sport or business.

set your 'heart on sth, **have your heart 'set on sth** *idiom* to want sth very much, and not let anyone or anything make you change your mind: *They've set their heart on a house in the country.*

hospital

hospital *noun* See the Topic Map for HEALTH on p.890, See also the entry for SURGERY

hospital · clinic · medical center · hospice · infirmary · sanatorium
These are all words for a place where people can get medical treatment.

PATTERNS AND COLLOCATIONS
▸ a **local** hospital/ clinic/ medical center/ hospice
▸ a **private** hospital/ clinic/ medical center/ hospice/ sanatorium
▸ a/ an **eye/ maternity/ psychiatric** hospital/ clinic
▸ to **go to** (the) hospital/ a clinic
▸ to **visit** the hospital/ a clinic

hospital [C] a large building or group of buildings where people who are ill or injured are given medical treatment and care ❶ In British English you say *to hospital* or *in hospital* when you are a patient: (*BrE*) *I had to go to hospital.* ◇ *He died in hospital.* If you are a visitor, you use *the*: *I'm going to the hospital to visit my brother.* In American English you need to use *the* whether you are a patient or a visitor: (*AmE*) *I had to go to the hospital.* ◇ (*BrE*) *He was admitted to hospital complaining of chest pains.* ◇ *She was discharged from hospital and allowed to go home.* ◇ (*AmE*) *The injured were rushed to the hospital in an ambulance.*

clinic /'klɪnɪk/ [C] a building or part of a hospital where people can go for special medical treatment or advice: *Your local family planning clinic can give you advice about birth control.* ❶ Especially in British English, a **clinic** can also be a small private hospital or one that treats health problems of a particular kind: *He is being treated at a clinic in Harley Street.* ◇ *She was ordered to attend a drug rehabilitation clinic.*

'medical center [C] (*AmE*) a large hospital or group of hospitals that provides medical care and training for a city or region: *The medical center, including the teaching hospital, now has 100 buildings on 290 acres.*

hospice /'hɒspɪs; *AmE* 'hɑːs-/ [C] a hospital for people who are dying: *She founded an AIDS hospice with the help of a local doctor.*

infirmary /ɪn'fɜːməri; *AmE* -'fɜːrm-/ [C] (often used in names) a hospital; part of an institution, like a school or prison, that is used for treating people who are ill: *Surgeons at the Radcliffe Infirmary successfully removed a blood clot from her brain.* ◇ *He had to remain in the college infirmary for about a fortnight.*

sanatorium /ˌsænə'tɔːriəm/ (*AmE* also **sanitarium** /ˌsænə'teəriəm; *AmE* -'ter-/) (pl. **sanatoriums** or **sanatoria**) [C] a place like a hospital where patients who have a lasting illness or who are getting better after an illness are treated: *In the early twentieth century, tuberculosis sanatoriums were common in the US.*

hostage

hostage *noun* See also the entry for PRISONER

hostage · prisoner · captive · detainee · prisoner of war · POW
These are all words for a person who has been captured and is being kept somewhere.

PATTERNS AND COLLOCATIONS
▸ a **political** hostage/ prisoner/ detainee
▸ to **hold/ keep** sb hostage/ prisoner/ captive
▸ to **free/ release** a hostage/ prisoner/ captive/ detainee/ prisoner of war/ POW
▸ to **take sb** hostage/ prisoner/ captive
▸ a hostage/ prisoner/ captive/ detainee/ prisoner of war/ POW **escapes**

hostage /'hɒstɪdʒ; *AmE* 'hɑːs-/ [C] a person who is captured and held prisoner by a person or group, and who may be injured or killed if people do not do what the person or group is asking: *Three children were taken hostage during the bank robbery.* ◇ *The government is negotiating the release of the hostages.*

prisoner [C] a person who has been captured, for example by an enemy, and is being kept somewhere: *He was taken prisoner by rebel soldiers.* ◇ *They are holding her prisoner and demanding a large ransom.* ❶ The more frequent meaning of **prisoner** is 'a person who is kept in prison'. See also **prisoner** → PRISONER

captive /'kæptɪv/ [C] (*literary*) a person who is kept as a prisoner: *Talks have persuaded the terrorists to set the captives free.*

> **NOTE** PRISONER OR CAPTIVE? **Captive** is often used in more historical contexts involving people such as kings, queens and princesses: *Their king was now a captive in Talleyrand's chateau.* It is also sometimes used when talking about political organizations holding people against their will. **Prisoner** is more often used to talk about people who have been captured in war: *He spent half the war as a prisoner.*

detainee /ˌdiːteɪ'niː/ [C] (*rather formal*) a person who is kept in prison, especially for political reasons and often without a trial: *The detainee can make a formal complaint after release.*

prisoner of 'war [C] a person, usually a member of the armed forces, who is captured by the enemy during a war and kept in a prison camp until the war has finished: *After several more months as a prisoner of war, he escaped again.*

POW /ˌpiː əʊ 'dʌbljuː; *AmE* oʊ-/ (pl. **POWs**) [C] the abbreviation for 'prisoner of war': *He remained a POW for the rest of the war.*

hot *adj.* See also the entry for HUMID

hot · warm · heated · burning · feverish · red-hot · boiling
These words all describe a place, person or thing that is not cold.

warm	hot	burning
heated	feverish	red-hot
		boiling

PATTERNS AND COLLOCATIONS
▸ hot / warm **weather / sunshine / water**
▸ a hot / warm **climate / sun**
▸ a hot / burning / feverish **forehead**
▸ hot / burning **cheeks**
▸ hot / burning / red-hot **coals**
▸ to **feel / look** hot / warm / feverish
▸ to **keep sth** hot / warm / heated
▸ **nice and** hot / warm

hot having a high temperature; (of a person) feeling heat in an unpleasant or uncomfortable way; making you feel hot: *It's hot today, isn't it?* ◇ *It was the hottest July on record.* ◇ *Be careful — the plates are hot.* ◇ *I'll feel better after a hot bath.* ◇ *The canteen provides hot meals as well as salads and snacks.* ◇ *Eat it while it's hot.* ◇ *Is anyone too hot?* ◇ *Her cheeks grew **hot with** embarrassment.* ◇ *It had been a long hot journey.* **OPP** cold → COLD 1

warm at a fairly high temperature in a way that is pleasant, rather than being hot or cold; (of clothes or buildings) keeping you warm or staying warm in cold weather: *It's nice and warm in here.* ◇ *Are you warm enough?* ◇ *They stood on the corner, stamping their feet to keep warm.* ◇ *The leaves swayed slowly in the soft, warm breeze.* ◇ *Wash the blouse in warm soapy water.* ◇ *Make sure you pack some warm clothes.* **OPP** cold, cool → COLD 1, See also **warm** → HEAT *verb*

heated (of a room, building or other place) made warmer using a heater: *The hotel has a heated swimming pool, spa and sauna.* **OPP** unheated ❶ An **unheated** room, building, etc. has no form of heating: *an unheated bathroom* See also **heat** → HEAT *verb*

burning very hot; looking and feeling very hot, because of illness or emotion: *They felt the burning heat of the sun on their backs.* ◇ *The skin of his forehead was burning.* ◇ *She was **burning hot** with embarrassment and guilt.* See also **burn** → HURT 2

feverish /ˈfiːvərɪʃ/ suffering from a fever; caused by a fever: *She was aching and feverish.* ◇ *He fell into a troubled, feverish sleep.* See also **delirious** → HYSTERICAL
▸ **feverishly** *adv.*: *Her mind raced feverishly.*

red-'hot (of metal or sth burning) so hot that it looks red: *Red-hot coals glowed in the fire.*

boiling (*rather informal*) very hot: *You must be boiling in that sweater!* **OPP** freezing → FREEZING
▸ **boiling** *adv.*: (*informal*) *It's boiling hot in here!*

hotel *noun*

hotel · motel · bed and breakfast · hostel · guest house
These are all words for a building that you pay to stay in when you are away from home.

PATTERNS AND COLLOCATIONS
▸ a **small** hotel / bed and breakfast / hostel / guest house
▸ a **cheap** hotel / bed and breakfast / hostel
▸ a **comfortable** hotel / guest house
▸ to **stay in / at** a hotel / motel / bed and breakfast / hostel / guest house
▸ to **check in at / check into / check out of** a hotel / motel / bed and breakfast / hostel
▸ to **run** a hotel / motel / bed and breakfast / hostel / guest house

hotel [C] a building where people stay, usually for a short time, paying for their rooms and meals: *The trip includes two nights in a luxury hotel.* ◇ *It's a five-star hotel* (= a luxury hotel). ◇ *Most of the jobs are in the hotel and catering industry.*

motel [C] a hotel for people who are travelling by car, with space for parking cars near the rooms: *There are plenty of cheap roadside motels just outside town.*

,**bed and 'breakfast** (also *informal* **B and B, B & B, b and b, b & b**) /ˌbiː ən ˈbiː/ [C] a house, often the owner's own home, that provides rooms to sleep in and breakfast in the morning: *There are several good bed and breakfasts in the town.* ◇ *All the B & Bs were fully booked.*

hostel [C] a building that provides cheap accommodation and sometimes meals to travellers, students or workers: *Hostels in the city cost about $10 a night.* ◇ *a youth/student hostel* ◇ *They were on a walking tour, staying in **youth hostels**.* ◇ *The building had been used as a **student hostel**.*

'**guest house** [C] (in Britain) a small hotel: *It is a comfortable family-run guest house near the beach.*

house *noun* See also the entries for FLAT and HOME 1

house · home · cottage · bungalow · townhouse · ranch house
These are all words for a building where sb lives.

PATTERNS AND COLLOCATIONS
▸ a **detached / semi-detached** house / home / cottage / bungalow
▸ a **terraced** house / home / cottage
▸ a **one- / two- / three-bedroom** house / home / cottage / bungalow / townhouse / ranch house
▸ to **live in** a house / cottage / bungalow / townhouse / ranch house
▸ to **stay in** a house / cottage / bungalow
▸ to **rent** a house / home / cottage / bungalow

house [C] a building for people to live in, usually for one family: *Let's have the party at my house.* ◇ *What time do you leave the house* (= to go to work) *in the morning?* ◇ *House prices in London are still falling.*

home [C] a house or flat where sb lives, especially when you think of it as property that can be bought and sold: *A lot of new homes are being built on the edge of town.* ◇ *Private home ownership is increasing faster than ever.*

cottage /ˈkɒtɪdʒ; AmE ˈkɑːt-/ [C] a small house, especially in the country: *James lived in a charming country cottage with honeysuckle around the door.* ◇ *(BrE) They rented a holiday cottage in the middle of nowhere.*

bungalow /ˈbʌŋɡələʊ; AmE -loʊ/ [C] (BrE) a house built all on one level, without stairs: *He retired at 70 and moved to a bungalow in Rosecroft Gardens.*

townhouse /ˈtaʊnhaʊs/ [C] (*especially AmE*) a house that is one of a row of houses that are joined together on each side: *Their home was a modern brick townhouse on the edge of the park.* ❶ The usual British English term for houses that are joined together in a row is *terraced houses*. **Townhouse** (or **town house**) is used in British English to describe houses of this type that are particularly large and fine or historic: *a row of elegant Georgian town houses*

'**ranch house** /rɑːntʃ; AmE ræntʃ/ [C] (AmE) a house built all on one level, that is very wide but not very deep from front to back and has a roof that is not very steep: *Their home was a spacious ranch house.*

housing *noun*

housing · accommodation · accommodations · quarters · lodging · a place to stay
These words all mean a place where you can live or stay.

PATTERNS AND COLLOCATIONS
▸ (a) **temporary** housing / accommodation / accommodations / quarters / place to stay
▸ **permanent / comfortable** housing / accommodation / accommodations / quarters

▸ **spacious** / **cramped** accommodation / accommodations / quarters
▸ to **provide** housing / accommodation / accommodations / lodging
▸ to **have** housing / accommodation / accommodations / quarters / lodging / a place to stay
▸ to **look for** housing / accommodation / accommodations / a place to stay

housing /ˈhaʊzɪŋ/ [U] houses or flats that people live in, especially when referring to their type, price or condition: *Public housing is limited to low-income families and individuals.* ◇ *The study linked poor housing conditions to a variety of health problems.* ◇ *The housing market* (= the activity of buying and selling houses) *has had a good year.* See also **house** → ACCOMMODATE

accommodation [U] (*BrE*) a place to live, work or stay in: *I live in rented accommodation.* ◇ *The prize includes flights plus seven nights' hotel accommodation.* ◇ *The building plans include much-needed new office accommodation.* See also **accommodate** → ACCOMMODATE

accommodations [pl.] (*AmE*) a place to live or stay, often also providing food or other services: *More and more travelers are looking for bed and breakfast accommodations in private homes.*

quarters [pl.] a room or house that has been provided for sb to live in, especially servants or soldiers and their families: *We were moved to more comfortable **living quarters**.* ◇ *The building served as **married quarters** and barracks during the First World War.* ◇ *The back staircase led to the **servants' quarters**.*

lodging [U] temporary accommodation, especially when you pay for it: *The total fee, which includes **full board and lodging** (= all meals provided and a room to stay in), is $1 000.*

a ˌplace to ˈstay *phrase* temporary accommodation, especially when you are looking for somewhere to live or spend the night: *We should try to find a place to stay before it gets dark.*

hug *verb*

hug · embrace · cuddle · cradle · snuggle
These words all mean to put your arms around sb, especially to show that you like or love them.

PATTERNS AND COLLOCATIONS
▸ to hug / embrace / cuddle / cradle a / your **child / son / daughter**
▸ to hug / cuddle / cradle a **baby / doll**
▸ to hug / embrace / cuddle your **wife / husband**
▸ to hug / cuddle your **girlfriend / boyfriend**
▸ to hug / cuddle a **teddy**
▸ to hug / embrace **each other**
▸ to hug / embrace / cradle sb **gently**
▸ to hug / embrace sb **tightly / warmly**

hug (**-gg-**) [T, I] to put your arms around sb and hold them tightly, especially to show love or friendship: *They hugged each other.* ◇ *She hugged him tightly.* ◇ *He **hugged** Anna **to** him.* ◇ *They put their arms around each other and hugged.*
▸ **hug** *noun* [C]: *She gave her mother a big hug.* ◇ *He stopped to receive **hugs and kisses** from the fans.*

embrace /ɪmˈbreɪs/ [I, T] (*formal*) to put your arms around sb to show love or friendship: *They embraced and wept and promised to keep in touch.* ◇ *She embraced her son warmly.*
▸ **embrace** *noun* [C, U]: *There were tears and embraces as they said goodbye.* ◇ *She tried to escape from his embrace.*

cuddle [I, T] to hold sb/sth close in your arms to show love or affection: *A couple of teenagers were kissing and cuddling on the doorstep.* ◇ *The little boy cuddled the teddy bear close.* See also **cuddly** → SWEET
▸ **cuddle** *noun* [C, sing.]: *She gave him a cuddle.*

cradle [T] to hold sb/sth gently in your arms or hands, in the way that you might hold a baby: *The old man cradled the tiny baby in his arms.*

snuggle [I, T] (always used with an adverb or preposition) to get into, or put sb/sth into, a warm comfortable position, especially close to sb: *The child **snuggled up to** her mother.* ◇ *He **snuggled down** under the bedclothes.* ◇ *She snuggled closer.* ◇ *He snuggled his head onto her shoulder.*

huge *adj.* See also the entry for LARGE

huge · massive · vast · enormous · giant · tremendous · gigantic · immense · monumental · colossal
These words all describe sth which is extremely large.

PATTERNS AND COLLOCATIONS
▸ a huge / a massive / a vast / an enormous / a tremendous / a colossal **amount of** sth
▸ a huge / a massive / a vast / an enormous / a tremendous **number of** things
▸ the huge / massive / vast / enormous / tremendous / colossal **cost**
▸ a huge / a massive / a vast / an enormous **crowd / area**
▸ a huge / a massive / an enormous / a tremendous / a monumental **task**
▸ a huge / a massive / an enormous / a giant / a tremendous / a gigantic **step**
▸ a huge / a massive / an enormous / a tremendous / a colossal **explosion**
▸ huge / massive / enormous / tremendous / immense **pressure**
▸ a huge / a massive / an enormous / a tremendous **problem / success**
▸ huge / vast / enormous / tremendous / immense / colossal **power**
▸ massive / enormous / tremendous / immense **strength**
▸ to be of huge / massive / enormous / gigantic / monumental **proportions**
▸ to **be of / have** huge / enormous / tremendous / immense / monumental **significance / importance**
▸ **on a** huge / massive / vast / enormous / monumental / colossal **scale**
▸ **absolutely** huge / massive / enormous / tremendous
▸ **really** huge / massive / enormous / tremendous / gigantic

huge extremely large in size or amount; great in degree: *A huge crowd had gathered in the square.* ◇ *He gazed up at her with huge brown eyes.* ◇ *The company ran up huge debts.* ◇ *The party was a huge success.* **OPP** **tiny** → SMALL

massive extremely large or serious: *The explosion made a massive hole in the ground.* ◇ *The Chancellor is to announce a massive increase in spending.* ◇ *He suffered a massive heart attack.* ❶ Although **massive** is usually neither formal nor informal, in spoken British English it can sometimes sound informal, especially when talking about the large physical size of sth: (*BrE, informal, spoken*) *They've got a **massive great** house.* See also **massive** → HEAVY

vast extremely large in area, amount, numbers or size: *To the south lay a vast area of wilderness.* ◇ *At dusk bats appear in vast numbers.* ◇ *His business empire was vast.* ◇ *In the vast majority of cases this should not be a problem.*
▸ **vastness** *noun* [U] (*written*): *the vastness of space*

enormous huge: *They've bought an enormous house in the country.* ◇ *The council has spent an enormous amount of money on this project.* ◇ *The implications of such a proposal are enormous.* **OPP** **tiny** → SMALL

NOTE HUGE OR ENORMOUS? There is no real difference in meaning between these words and you can usually use either word. However, **huge** is used slightly more to talk about the physical size of sth, especially a piece of sth: *a huge chunk / pile / boulder / slab / mound / expanse.* **Enormous** is used slightly more to talk about the degree of sth such as a feeling, importance or a possibility: *enormous fun / pleasure / importance / significance / flexibility / scope*

giant [only before noun] extremely large; much larger or more important than similar things usually are: *The market is controlled by giant corporations which function as monopolies.* ◇ *Giant clams may grow to be a metre long.*

tremendous /trəˈmendəs/ extremely great, especially in a way that makes you feel impressed, admiring or sympathetic: *The noise of bombs, guns and engines was tremendous.* ◇ *A tremendous amount of work has gone into the project.* ◇ *He has been under tremendous pressure recently.*

gigantic /dʒaɪˈɡæntɪk/ (*rather informal*) extremely large, especially in physical size: *At the top of the steps stood eight gigantic marble columns.* ◇ *The problem can assume gigantic proportions if left untreated.*

immense /ɪˈmens/ extremely great in degree: *To my immense relief, he didn't notice my mistake.* ◇ *The benefits are immense.* ❶ **Immense** is used especially to describe feelings or qualities, especially positive ones: *immense satisfaction/relief/pleasure/respect* ◇ *immense prestige/popularity/charm/importance/significance/value*
▸ **immensity** /ɪˈmensəti/ *noun* [U]: *We were overwhelmed by the sheer immensity of the task.*

monumental /ˌmɒnjuˈmentl; *AmE* ˌmɑːn-/ [only before noun] (*rather formal*) extremely great or serious: *This book is a work of monumental significance.* ◇ *She had made one monumental error of judgement.* ❶ **Monumental** is used especially to describe actions that are very stupid and have serious consequences: *an act of monumental folly* ◇ *monumental incompetence* ◇ *a monumental error/disaster/cock-up*

colossal /kəˈlɒsl; *AmE* kəˈlɑːsl/ extremely large: *Outside stands a colossal statue of Queen Victoria.* ◇ *They have spent a colossal amount of money on construction.*

humid *adj.* See also the entry for HOT

humid · sultry · stuffy · steamy · stifling · airless
These words all describe a place which is hot and/or without fresh air.

PATTERNS AND COLLOCATIONS
▸ a humid / sultry / stuffy / steamy / stifling **atmosphere**
▸ humid / sultry / steamy / stifling **heat**
▸ humid / sultry / stuffy **air**
▸ a stuffy / an airless **room**
▸ humid **weather** / the **weather** is sultry
▸ **hot and** humid / sultry / stuffy / steamy
▸ It's stuffy / stifling **in here**!

humid /ˈhjuːmɪd/ (of the air or climate) warm and damp: *These ferns will grow best in a humid atmosphere.* ◇ *The island is hot and humid in the summer.* See also **humidity** → MOISTURE

sultry /ˈsʌltri/ (of the weather or air) very hot, often in a way that is uncomfortable: *We went out into the still, sultry heat of the afternoon.*

stuffy (of a room or building) warm in an unpleasant way and without enough fresh air: *It gets really stuffy in here in summer.*

steamy full of steam; covered with steam: *It was cold in London compared with the steamy heat of Tokyo.*

stifling /ˈstaɪflɪŋ/ too hot and/or without fresh air, so that it is difficult to breathe: *'It's stifling in here – can we open a window?'*

airless (*written*) not having any fresh or moving air or wind, and therefore unpleasant: *The night was hot and airless.*

humour (*BrE*) (*AmE* **humor**) *noun*

humour · wit · banter · comedy · funny side
These are all words for things that people say or write that are funny or amusing, or the quality in sth that makes it funny or amusing.

PATTERNS AND COLLOCATIONS
▸ gentle / wry humour / wit / comedy
▸ caustic / sardonic humour / wit
▸ dry / deadpan / black humour / comedy
▸ to **see** / **appreciate** the humour / comedy / funny side of sth

humour (*BrE*) (*AmE* **humor**) [U] the quality in sth that makes it funny or amusing; the ability to laugh at things that are amusing: *She ignored his feeble attempt at humour.* ◇ *She has her very own brand of humour.* ◇ *He has a good sense of humour.* See also **humorous** → FUNNY

wit [U, sing.] the ability to say or write things that are both clever and amusing: *a woman of wit and intelligence* ◇ *a book full of the wit and wisdom of his 30 years in politics* ◇ *He was blessed with great charm and a quick wit.* See also **witty** → FUNNY

banter [U] friendly remarks and jokes: *She engages in friendly banter with her customers.*

comedy /ˈkɒmədi; *AmE* kɑːm-/ [U] the quality in sth that makes it funny or amusing: *He didn't appreciate the comedy of the situation.* See also **comic** → FUNNY

'funny side [sing.] (*rather informal, spoken*) the quality in a situation that makes it amusing: *Try and see the funny side of it.*

hungry *adj.*

hungry · starving · ravenous
These words all describe people or animals that want or need to eat food.

hungry   starving
                   ravenous

PATTERNS AND COLLOCATIONS
▸ hungry / starving **for** sth
▸ hungry / starving **children** / **people**
▸ **absolutely** starving / ravenous

hungry feeling that you want to eat sth; not having enough to eat; making you feel that you want to eat sth: *I'm really hungry.* ◇ *Is anyone getting hungry?* ◇ *All this talk of food is making me hungry.* ◇ *There were eight hungry mouths to feed at home.* ◇ *Thousands are going hungry because of the failure of this year's harvest.* ◇ *All this gardening is hungry work.* See also **hunger** → APPETITE 1
▸ **the hungry** *noun* [pl.]: *Shipments of flour were sent to feed the hungry.*
▸ **hungrily** *adv.*: *They gazed hungrily at the display of food.*

starving suffering or dying because you do not have enough food to eat: *These pictures of starving children are very upsetting.* ❶ In informal spoken English **starving** can just mean 'very hungry': *When's dinner? I'm starving!*
▸ **the starving** *noun* [pl.]: *Food was flown in to help the starving.*

ravenous /ˈrævənəs/ (of people) very hungry; (of animals) fierce and hungry; (of hunger) very great: *What's for lunch? I'm absolutely ravenous.* ◇ *Go back in your imagination to the days when huge, ravenous beasts ruled the planet.* ◇ *He has a ravenous appetite.* ❶ When used to describe people, **ravenous** is only used after a linking verb, not before a noun, and is mostly used in informal spoken English; when used to describe animals or sb's hunger it comes before the noun and is used in less informal and written English.

hurry *verb*

hurry · rush · dash · fly · run · hasten · get a move on
These words all mean to go somewhere or do sth quickly, especially because you do not have enough time.

PATTERNS AND COLLOCATIONS
▸ to hurry / rush / run / hasten **to do sth**
▸ to hurry / fly / run **along**
▸ to rush / dash **off**
▸ to hurry / rush a **meal**

hurry [I, T] to do sth more quickly than usual because there is not much time; to make sb do sth more quickly; to move quickly in a particular direction: *You'll have to* *hurry if you want to catch the train.* ◇ *I wish the bus would* **hurry up** *and come.* ◇ *Hurry up! We're going to be late.* ◇ *The kids hurried to open their presents.* ◇ *A good meal should never be hurried.* ◇ *I don't want to hurry you but we close in twenty minutes.* ◇ *He picked up his bags and hurried across the courtyard.* ❶ In spoken English **hurry** can be used with *and* plus another verb, instead of with *to* and the infinitive, especially to tell sb to do sth quickly: *Hurry and open your present – I want to see what it is.* See also **hurried** → QUICK

▶ **hurry** *noun* [sing.]: *Take your time – there's no hurry.* ◇ **What's the hurry?** *The train doesn't leave for an hour.* ◇ *Sorry, I haven't got time to do it now – I'm* **in a hurry**. ◇ *Why are you in such a hurry to sell?*

rush [I, T] to move or to do sth with great speed, often too fast; to do sth or make sb do sth without thinking about it carefully: *We've got plenty of time; there's no need to rush.* ◇ *I've been* **rushing around** *all day, trying to get everything done.* ◇ *People rushed to buy shares in the company.* ◇ *We don't want to* **rush into** *having a baby.* ◇ *Don't rush me. I need time to think about it.* ◇ *I'm not going to* **be rushed into** *anything.*

▶ **rush** *noun* [sing.]: *Shoppers made a* **rush for** *the exits.* ◇ *I can't stop – I'm* **in a rush**. ◇ **What's the rush?** ◇ *'I'll let you have the book back tomorrow.' 'There's no rush.'*

dash [I] (usually used with an adverb or preposition) to go somewhere very quickly: *She dashed off to keep an appointment.* ◇ (*informal*) *I must dash* (= leave quickly), *I'm late.*

▶ **dash** *noun* [sing.]: *When the doors opened, there was a* **mad dash** *for seats.* ◇ *We waited for the police to leave, then* **made a dash for it** (= left quickly in order to escape).

fly [I] (usually used with an adverb or preposition) to go or move very quickly: *The train was flying along.* ◇ *She gasped and her hand flew to her mouth.* ◇ (*informal*) *It's late – I must fly* (= leave quickly).

NOTE DASH OR FLY? **Dash** is always used to talk about people: *The train was dashing along.* **Fly** is more often used to talk about things. Both words can be used informally in the phrase *I must dash/fly*, meaning 'I have to leave.'

run [I] (always used with an adverb or preposition) to hurry from one place to another: *I've spent the whole day running around after the kids.*

hasten /ˈheɪsn/ [T] (*rather formal, especially written*) to say or do sth without delay: *She saw his frown and hastened to explain.* ◇ *He has been described as a 'charmless bore' – not by me, I hasten to add.* ❶ In literary language **hasten** can also mean 'to do or go somewhere quickly': [I] (*literary*) *We hastened back to Rome.* See also **haste** → SPEED *noun*

get a ˈmove on *idiom* (*informal, spoken*) used to tell sb to hurry: *Get a move on! We'll miss the bus.* ◇ *We'd better get a move on if we don't want to be late.*

hurt *verb*

1 hurt sb's feelings
2 your feet hurt

1 **hurt** · **upset** · **wound** · **distress** · **break sb's heart** · **sadden** · **sting** · **pain**
These words all mean to make sb feel unhappy or upset.

PATTERNS AND COLLOCATIONS
▶ It hurt/upset/distressed/saddened/pained **me to** see/think/ know...
▶ It breaks my heart **to** see/think/know...
▶ It hurt/upset/distressed/saddened/pained **me that**...
▶ to hurt/wound **sb's feelings**
▶ to upset/distress **yourself**
▶ to **not want/not mean** to hurt/upset/wound/distress sb
▶ to **really** hurt sb/upset sb/wound sb/distress sb/break sb's heart/sting sb/pain sb
▶ to hurt/upset/wound/distress/sting/pain sb **deeply**

hurt [T, I] to make sb feel unhappy or disappointed because of sth unpleasant that sb has done: *I didn't want to hurt his feelings.* ◇ *It hurt me to think that he would lie to me.* ◇ *What really hurt was that he never answered my letter.* See also **hurt** → DISTRESS *noun* 1, **hurt** → UPSET *adj.*, **hurtful** → MEAN *adj.* 1

upset [T] to make sb/yourself feel unhappy, worried or annoyed: *This decision is likely to upset a lot of people.* ◇ *Try not to let him upset you.* ◇ *Don't upset yourself about it.* ◇ *It upset him that nobody had bothered to tell him about it.* See also **upset** → UPSET *adj.*, **upsetting** → PAINFUL 2

NOTE HURT OR UPSET? **Hurt** is used especially to talk about sb you like or thought you could trust doing sth to make you unhappy. **Upset** can be used in some of these cases, but it is not used with *feelings* or without an object: ~~upset his feelings~~ ◇ ~~What really upset was...~~ **Upset**, but NOT **hurt**, can also be used to talk about an action or person that worries or annoys sb, especially when this causes them to express their worry or anger, for example by crying or shouting. Being **upset** can be sth that people partly do willingly: you can *upset yourself* or *let sb upset you*: ~~Don't hurt yourself about it.~~ ◇ ~~Try not to let him hurt you.~~

wound /wuːnd/ [T, often passive] (*literary*) to hurt sb's feelings: *She felt deeply wounded by his cruel remarks.*

▶ **wounded** *adj.*: *She didn't know how to soothe his wounded pride.*

distress /dɪˈstres/ [T] (*rather formal*) to make sb feel very unhappy or worried: *It was clear that the letter had deeply distressed her.* ◇ *Don't distress yourself.* ❶ **Distress** is stronger and more formal than **upset** and does not have the additional meaning of 'annoy'. See also **distress** → DISTRESS, **distressed** → UPSET, **distressing** → PAINFUL 2

break sb's ˈheart *idiom* to make sb feel extremely unhappy, especially when they feel that they can never be happy again: *She broke his heart when she called off the engagement.* ◇ *It breaks my heart to see you like this.*

sadden [T, often passive] (not used in the progressive tenses) (*formal*) to make sb sad: *We were deeply saddened by the news of her death.* ◇ *It saddened her that people could be so cruel.*

sting [T] (not used in the progressive tenses) (*written*) to make sb feel angry or upset: *He was stung by their criticism.* ◇ *Their cruel remarks* **stung her into** *action.*

pain [T] (not used in the progressive tenses) (*formal*) to make sb feel unhappy or upset: *She was deeply pained by the accusation.* ◇ *It pains me to see you like this.* See also **pain** → DISTRESS *noun*, **painful** → PAINFUL 2

▶ **pained** *adj.*: *She looked at him with a pained expression.*

2 See the Topic Map for HEALTH on p.890
hurt · **ache** · **burn** · **sting** · **tingle** · **itch** · **tickle** · **throb**
These are all words that can be used when part of your body feels painful.

tingle	hurt	burn
itch	ache	throb
tickle	sting	

PATTERNS AND COLLOCATIONS
▶ your **eyes** hurt/ache/burn/sting/itch
▶ your **skin** hurts/burns/stings/tingles/itches
▶ your **flesh** hurts/burns/stings/tingles
▶ your **head** hurts/aches/throbs
▶ your **stomach/tummy** hurts/aches
▶ to **really** hurt/ache/burn/sting/tingle/itch/tickle/throb
▶ to hurt/ache/sting/tingle/itch/tickle/throb **slightly/a bit**
▶ to hurt/ache/sting/itch **badly/a lot**
▶ It hurts/stings/tingles/itches/tickles.

hurt [I] (of part of your body) to feel painful; (of an action) to cause pain: *My feet hurt.* ◇ *Ouch! That hurt!* ◇ *It hurts when I bend my knee.* See also **hurt** → INJURE *verb*, **hurt** → INJURED *adj.*

ache /eɪk/ [I] to feel a continuous dull pain: *I'm aching all over.* ◇ *Her eyes ached from lack of sleep.* See also **ache** → PAIN *noun*

burn [I] (of part of your body) to feel very hot and painful: *Your forehead's burning. Have you got a fever?* ◇ *Her cheeks burned with embarrassment.* See also **burning** → HOT

sting [I, T] to make sb feel a sharp burning pain or uncomfortable feeling in part of their body; (of part of your body) to feel this pain: *I put some antiseptic on the cut and it stung for a moment.* ◇ *My eyes were stinging from the smoke.* ◇ *Tears stung her eyes.*

tingle [I] (of part of your body) to feel as if a lot of small sharp points are pushing into the skin there: *The cold air made her face tingle.* ◇ *You may get a tingling sensation in your fingers.*

itch [I] to have an uncomfortable feeling on your skin that makes you want to scratch; to make your skin feel like this: *I itch all over.* ◇ *Does the rash itch?* ◇ *This sweater really itches.*

▶ **itch** *noun* [C]: *to get/have an itch*

tickle [T, I] to produce a slightly uncomfortable feeling in a sensitive part of the body; to have a feeling like this: *His beard was tickling her cheek.* ◇ *My throat tickles.*

throb (-**bb**-) [I] (of part of your body) to feel pain as a series of regular beats: *His head throbbed painfully.*

hut *noun* See also the entry for SHED

hut · shelter · cabin · shack · hovel · shanty
These words all mean a small, simply built structure like a small house.

PATTERNS AND COLLOCATIONS
▶ a **wooden** hut / shelter / cabin / shack
▶ a **stone** hut / shelter
▶ a **tin** hut / shack
▶ a **makeshift** hut / shelter
▶ to **build** a hut / shelter / cabin / shack
▶ to **make** a hut / shelter
▶ to **live in** a hut / cabin / shack / hovel

hut [C] a small, simply built structure with walls and a roof: *You can rent a beach hut for about $10 a night.* ◇ *Traditional mud huts gave way to concrete houses.*

shelter [C] (often in compounds) a structure built to give protection, especially from the weather or from attack: *They built a rough shelter from old pieces of wood and cardboard.* ◇ *an air-raid shelter* ◇ *a bus shelter* See also **shelter** → SHELTER *noun*

cabin /'kæbɪn/ [C] a small house, usually made of wood: *He was born in a log cabin in rural Kentucky.*

shack [C] a small building, usually made of wood or metal, that has not been built well: *The settlement consists only of shacks; there are no roads and no water.*

hovel /'hɒvl; AmE 'hʌvl/ [C] (*disapproving*) a house or room that is not fit to live in because it is dirty, in very bad condition or badly built: *Your house is a miserable hovel compared with my palace.*

shanty [C] a small house, built of pieces of wood, metal or whatever material is available, where very poor people live, especially on the edge of a big city: *The whole family lives in a shanty made of wood, mud and tin.* ◇ *Nearly 20% of the city's inhabitants live in shanty towns.*

hysterical *adj.* See also the entry for RESTLESS

hysterical · frantic · worked up · delirious · panicky · panic-stricken · beside yourself · overwrought · incoherent
These words all describe sb who is unable to control themselves or think clearly because they are very anxious, frightened, excited or ill.

worked up   panicky   hysterical
overwrought   frantic
                                        panic-stricken
                                        beside yourself
                                        delirious
                                        incoherent

PATTERNS AND COLLOCATIONS
▶ hysterical / frantic / delirious / beside yourself / incoherent **with** anger, rage, joy, etc.
▶ hysterical / frantic / worked up / panicky **about** sth
▶ to **become** hysterical / frantic / worked up / delirious / incoherent
▶ to **get** hysterical / frantic / worked up
▶ **almost** hysterical / frantic / delirious / beside yourself / incoherent

hysterical /hɪ'sterɪkl/ in a state of extreme excitement, and crying or laughing in an uncontrolled way: *Calm down, you're getting hysterical.* ◇ *Her screams broke into hysterical laughter.* See also **hysteria** → FEAR

▶ **hysterically** *adv.*: *to laugh/cry/scream/sob hysterically*

frantic unable to control your emotions because you are extremely frightened or worried about sth: *I've been almost frantic with worry for the last half-hour.* ◇ *Let's go back. Your parents must be getting frantic by now.* ◇ *The children are driving me frantic* (= making me very annoyed).

worked 'up [not before noun] (*informal, spoken*) very excited or upset about sth: *There's no point in getting all worked up about it.* ◇ *He was silly to get himself so worked up.*

delirious /dɪ'lɪriəs; BrE also -'lɪəriəs/ in a state of extreme excitement and not able to think or speak clearly, especially because of fever; extremely excited and happy: *He became delirious and couldn't recognize people.* ◇ *The crowds were delirious with joy.* See also **feverish** → HOT

panicky /'pænɪki/ (*informal*) so anxious about sth that you cannot act sensibly or think clearly; showing this: *He was feeling a bit panicky about the presentation.* ◇ *I got a panicky phone call from Emma yesterday.* See also **panic** → FEAR *noun*, **panic** → PANIC *verb*

'panic-stricken very panicky, often so that you cannot move or do anything: *He sounded panic-stricken on the phone.* ◇ *Jack caught a glimpse of her panic-stricken face.*

NOTE PANICKY OR PANIC-STRICKEN? Panic-stricken is a stronger, more serious feeling. You can be *a bit/slightly/very* panicky but **panic-stricken** cannot be qualified in this way. **Panic-stricken** can also suggest sth more physical; **panicky** refers more to your inner feelings: *I was feeling quite panicky.* ◇ *I was so panic-stricken that I could hardly speak.*

be'side yourself *idiom* unable to control yourself because of the strength of emotion you are feeling, such as worry, fear, anger or excitement: *Bella drew her breath in sharply, almost beside herself with rage.*

overwrought /,əʊvə'rɔːt; AmE ,oʊvər'r-/ (*rather formal*) very worried and upset; excited in a nervous way: *She was still a little overwrought.*

incoherent /,ɪnkəʊ'hɪərənt; AmE ,ɪnkoʊ'hɪr-/ unable to express yourself clearly, especially because of emotion: *She broke off, incoherent with anger.* **OPP** coherent → ARTICULATE

I i

idea *noun*

1 That's a good idea.
2 I've an idea where it might be.

---

1 idea · thought · concept · notion · image · prospect · abstraction · picture

These are all words for sth that you think or sth that comes into your mind.

idea [C] a plan or suggestion that is created or experienced in your mind: *That's a brilliant idea!* ◇ *The party was Jane's idea.* ◇ *The idea never crossed my mind.* ◇ *It seemed like a good idea at the time.* ◇ *I like the idea of living in a boat.* ◇ *He already had an* **idea for** *his next novel.* ◇ *Her family wanted her to go to college, but she* **had other ideas.** ◇ *The latest* **big idea** *is to get more women into the construction industry.*

thought [C] something that you think of: *I don't like the thought of you walking home alone.* ◇ *I've just had a thought.* ◇ *What a horrible thought!* ◇ *All kinds of thoughts raced through her mind.* ◇ *I'd be interested to hear your thoughts on the matter.* ◇ *She tried to put the thought out of her mind.*

concept /'kɒnsept; *AmE* 'kɑːn-/ [C] (*rather formal*) an idea or principle that is related to sth abstract rather than physical things or actual events: *We discussed concepts such as 'democracy' and 'equality'.* ◇ *The concept of infinity is almost impossible for us to comprehend.* See also **conceptual** → INTELLECTUAL *adj.* 1

notion /'nəʊʃn; *AmE* 'noʊʃn/ [C] (*rather formal*) an idea, a belief or an understanding of sth: *Our political system is based on notions of justice and equality.* ◇ *I had only the vaguest notion of what he was like.* ❶ A **notion** is usually about sth abstract or factual, rather than sth imaginative. You can have a *clear notion* of sb/sth, but NOT: *a vivid/ imaginative notion*. See also **notional** → SUPPOSED

image [C] an idea of what sb/sth is like that appears as a picture in your mind: *I always had an image of her standing by that window gazing out.* ◇ *Do human beings think in words or in images?*

prospect [sing.] an idea of what might or will happen in the future: *Travelling alone around the world is a daunting prospect.* ◇ *The prospect of becoming a father filled him with alarm.*

abstraction [C, U] (*formal*) a general idea that is not based on any particular real person, thing or situation: *Ideological abstractions are never going to attract many*

voters. ◇ *The increasing abstraction of modern art has tended to make it increasingly difficult to interpret.* See also **abstract** → INTELLECTUAL *adj.* 1

picture [C, usually sing.] an idea of what sb/sth is like or how sth might happen, that appears as a picture in your mind: *She had formed a picture of what the place would look like and was very disappointed.*

> **NOTE** IMAGE OR PICTURE? In many cases you can use either word. However, **image** often suggests a mental picture of one person or thing at one moment in time; **picture** often suggests a more complete imagining of a whole scene, including a number of different details and/or events that take place over a short period of time.

---

2 idea · instinct · feeling · hunch · inkling · suspicion · intuition · premonition · foreboding

These are all words for a feeling that you have that sth is true or that sth is happening, even though you do not have any evidence.

idea [sing.] a feeling that you have about where sth is, who sb is, or what is happening, even though you are not completely sure: *I had an idea of where it might be.* ◇ *What gave you the idea that he'd be here?* ◇ *I have a pretty good idea who might have said that.* ◇ *He hadn't had* **the slightest idea** *about what had been going on.*

instinct [C] a feeling that makes you believe that sth is true, even though it is not based on facts or reason: *Her instincts about him had been right.* ◇ *Marshall's gut instinct* (= basic instinct) *was to turn and run.* See also **instinctive** → NATURAL

feeling [sing.] an idea that makes you believe that sth is true, especially sth unpleasant, based on what you feel rather than on facts or reason: *I had a nasty feeling that she was lying to me.* ◇ *He suddenly had the feeling of being followed.*

> **NOTE** INSTINCT OR FEELING? A **feeling** in this meaning is usually a feeling that one particular unpleasant thing is true; your **instincts** may be more general – all the feelings you have about a particular person or situation – and they may be positive or negative: *Her instincts had been right – he was someone who could be trusted.* ◇ *Her feelings about him had been right.*

hunch [C] (*rather informal*) a feeling that sth is true even though you do not have any evidence to prove it: *My hunch is that the burglars are still in the area.* ◇ *I didn't know for certain – I was just going on a hunch.* ❶ **Hunch** is used especially when you are talking about the solution to a crime or mystery.

inkling [C, usually sing.] a slight knowledge of sth that is happening or about to happen: *He didn't have the slightest inkling of what was going on.*

suspicion [C] a feeling or belief that sth is true, especially sth unpleasant, even though you do not know for certain: *I had a horrible suspicion that we'd come to the wrong station.* See also **suspect** → SUPPOSE

intuition /ˌɪntjuˈɪʃn; *AmE* -tu-/ [C] an idea or strong feeling that sth is true even though you cannot explain why: *I had an intuition that something awful was about to happen.* See also **intuitive** → NATURAL

premonition /ˌpriːməˈnɪʃn; ˌprem-/ [C] (*rather formal, especially written*) a feeling that sth is going to happen, especially sth unpleasant: *a premonition of disaster* ◇ *He had a premonition that he would never see her again.*

foreboding /fɔːˈbəʊdɪŋ; *AmE* fɔːrˈboʊ-/ [U, C] (*rather formal, especially written*) a strong feeling that sth unpleasant or dangerous is going to happen: *The letter filled him with foreboding.* ◇ *He knew from her face that his forebodings had been justified.*

> **NOTE** PREMONITION OR FOREBODING? A **premonition** is usually a feeling that a particular unpleasant thing is going to happen; **foreboding** is a general sense that sth bad is going to happen, although you do not know exactly what.

ideal *adj.* See also the entries for BEST and FAVOURITE

ideal · perfect · optimum · just right · tailor-made
These words all describe sb/sth that is the best or most suitable for a particular person or purpose.

PATTERNS AND COLLOCATIONS
> ideal / perfect / just right / tailor-made **for** sb / sth
> an ideal / a perfect **opportunity / solution / candidate**
> **absolutely** ideal / perfect

ideal /aɪˈdiːəl/ exactly right for sb/sth: *This beach is ideal for children.* ◇ *His apartment would be an ideal place to stay.* ◇ *As a solution to the problem it was far from ideal.*
> **ideally** *adv.*: *They're ideally suited to each other.* ◇ *Ideally, I'd like to live in New York, but that's not possible at the moment.*

perfect exactly right for sb/sth: *It was a perfect day for a picnic.* ◇ *The location of the cottage makes it perfect for touring.* ◇ 'Will 2.30 be OK for you?' 'Perfect, thanks.'

> **NOTE** IDEAL OR PERFECT? These words have the same meaning but they have some different collocations. *An ideal day for sth* is a very convenient day; *a perfect day for sth* is one with very good weather conditions. **Perfect** is also slightly more informal than **ideal**.

optimum /ˈɒptɪməm; *AmE* ˈɑːp-/ [only before noun] the best possible; producing the best possible results: *We aim for optimum efficiency in all our operations.*
> **the optimum** *noun* [sing.]: *For efficient fuel consumption a speed of 60 mph is about the optimum.*

just ˈright *phrase* (*spoken*) exactly right for sb/sth: *That coat should be just right for Jenny.* ◇ *She adjusted the seasoning until it was just right.*

tailor-ˈmade made for sb/sth in particular, and therefore very suitable: *We can offer you a tailor-made financial package to suit your needs.*

identify *verb*

identify · know · recognize · name · make sb/sth out · isolate · discern · pinpoint · place · pick sb/sth out
These words all mean to be able to see or hear sb/sth and/ or be able to say who or what they are.

PATTERNS AND COLLOCATIONS
> to identify / know / recognize sb / sth **by** sth
> to identify / recognize / name / pinpoint sb / sth **as** sb / sth
> to identify / know / recognize / make out / isolate / pinpoint / discern **who / what / how…**
> to **immediately** identify / know / recognize / pinpoint / place / pick out sb / sth
> to **easily** identify / recognize / make out / isolate / discern / pick out sb / sth
> to **clearly / barely / hardly / just** identify / recognize / make out / discern / pick out sb / sth
> to **dimly** know / recognize / make out / discern sb / sth

identify [T] (not used in the progressive tenses) to be able to say who or what sb/sth is: *She was able to positively identify her attacker.* ◇ *Many of those arrested refused to identify themselves* (= would not say who they were). ◇ *First of all we must identify the problem areas within the system.* See also **identify** → FIND 3
> **identification** *noun* [U, C]: *Each product has a number for easy identification.* ◇ *Only one witness could make a positive identification.*

know [T] (not used in the progressive tenses) to be able to say who or what sth is when you see or hear it, because you have seen or heard it before: *I couldn't see who was speaking, but I knew the voice.* ◇ *She knows a bargain when she sees one.*

recognize (*BrE also* **-ise**) [T] (not used in the progressive tenses) to know who sb is or what sth is when you see or hear them/it, because you have seen or heard them/it before: *Do you recognize this tune?* ◇ *We barely recognized her – she had changed so much in ten years.* ◇ *I recognized him by the way he walked.*
> **recognition** *noun* [U]: *He glanced briefly towards her but there was no sign of recognition.*

> **NOTE** KNOW OR RECOGNIZE? **Know** is used especially to talk about sounds that seem familiar and when sb recognizes the quality or opportunity that sb/sth represents, as in the phrase *sb knows a … when they see one*: *I know/recognize that voice/laugh/tune.* ◇ *He knows/recognizes a lady when he sees one.* **Recognize** can also be used in these examples, but it sounds slightly more formal. **Know** in this meaning is NOT usually used to talk about people: *I knew him as soon as he came in the room.*

name [T] to say the name of sb/sth in order to show that you know who/what they are: *The victim has not yet been named.* ◇ *The missing man has been named as James Kelly.* ◇ *Can you name all the American states?*

make sb/sth ˈout *phrasal verb* (not used in the progressive tenses) to manage to see or hear sb/sth that is not very clear: *I could just make out a figure in the darkness.* ◇ *The sign was too far away for me to make out what it said.*

isolate [T] (*formal or technical*) to separate a part of a situation, problem, idea, etc. so that you can see what it is and deal with it separately: *It is possible to isolate a number of factors that contributed to her downfall.*

discern /dɪˈsɜːn; *AmE* -ˈsɜːrn/ [T] (not used in the progressive tenses) (*formal*) to recognize or know sth, especially sth that is not obvious; to manage to see or hear sth that is not very clear: *It is possible to discern a number of different techniques in her work.* ◇ *It is often difficult to discern how widespread public support is.* See also **distinguish** → DISTINGUISH 1, **discernible** → VISIBLE

pinpoint /ˈpɪnpɔɪnt/ [T] to find and show the exact position of sb/sth or the exact time that sth happened; to be able to give the exact reason for sth or to describe sth exactly: *He was able to pinpoint on the map the site of the medieval village.* ◇ *The report pinpointed the areas most in need of help.*

place [T] (usually used in negative sentences) to recognize sb/sth and be able to identify them/it: *I've seen her before but I just can't place her.* ◇ *His accent was impossible to place.*

pick sb/sth ˈout *phrasal verb* (not used in the progressive tenses) to recognize sb/sth from among other people or things: *See if you can pick me out in this photo.*

identity

identity *noun* See the Topic Map for THE INDIVIDUAL AND SOCIETY on p.894

identity · self · individuality · uniqueness
These are all words for the qualities or characteristics that make sb/sth different from others or for the quality of being different from others.

PATTERNS AND COLLOCATIONS
▸ **human** identity / individuality / uniqueness
▸ to **lack** identity / individuality / uniqueness
▸ to **express / lose** your identity / individuality / uniqueness
▸ to **retain / maintain** your identity / individuality
▸ a **sense of** identity / self / individuality / uniqueness
▸ an **expression of** identity / the self / individuality

identity [C, U] the characteristics, feelings and beliefs that make a person or group of people seem or feel different from others: *a sense of national/cultural/personal/group identity* ◇ *The organization has no clear **corporate** identity.* ◇ *The company forged its own identity by producing specialist vehicles.*

self [U] (also **the self** [sing.]) (*formal*) the essential part of a person's character that makes them different from other people: *Many people living in institutions have lost their sense of self.* ◇ *the inner self* (= a person's emotional and spiritual character) ◇ *Such problems stem from deep insecurity and a lack of confidence in the self.* See also **self** → PERSONALITY, **ego** → MIND *noun*

individuality /ˌɪndɪˌvɪdʒuˈæləti/ [U] the qualities in a person or thing that make them clearly different from other people or things: *She expresses her individuality through her clothes.* ◇ *The plot is credible but the characters lack individuality.* See also **individual** → UNIQUE, **originality** → INSPIRATION

uniqueness [U] the quality in a person or thing of being the only one of their kind and different from anyone/ anything else: *The author stresses the uniqueness of the individual.* See also **unique** → UNIQUE

ignorance *noun*

ignorance · innocence · inexperience · naivety · incomprehension
These are all words for the state of not knowing or not understanding sth.

PATTERNS AND COLLOCATIONS
▸ ignorance / innocence / naivety **about** sth
▸ **in** your ignorance / innocence / inexperience / naivety
▸ **through** ignorance / inexperience
▸ **complete / total** ignorance / innocence / incomprehension
▸ **youthful** ignorance / innocence / inexperience / naivety
▸ to **betray / show** (your) ignorance / inexperience
▸ to **take advantage of** sb's ignorance/innocence/inexperience/ naivety

ignorance /ˈɪɡnərəns/ [U, sing.] (*sometimes disapproving*) a lack of knowledge or information about sth: *There is widespread ignorance about the disease.* ◇ *I remained in blissful ignorance of what was going on.* ◇ *Children often behave badly **out of ignorance**.* OPP **knowledge** → KNOWLEDGE, **knowledge** → AWARENESS

innocence /ˈɪnəsns/ [U, sing.] (*approving*) lack of knowledge and experience of the world, especially of evil or unpleasant things: *The story is about a child's **loss of innocence**.* ◇ *There was a touching innocence about the child's request.* See also **innocent** → NAIVE

inexperience [U] lack of experience or knowledge of sth: *I'm afraid that in this instance the player's inexperience showed.* OPP **experience** → KNOWLEDGE, See also **inexperienced** → NAIVE

naivety (also **naïvety**) /naɪˈiːvəti/ [U, sing.] (*often disapproving*) lack of experience of life, knowledge, or good judgement, especially when this involves a tendency to always believe what people tell you: *They*
laughed at the naivety of his suggestion. ◇ *She showed a certain naivety in going to the press about the matter.* See also **naive** → NAIVE

incomprehension /ˌɪnˌkɒmprɪˈhenʃn; AmE -ˌkɑːm-/ [U] lack of understanding of sth: *His attempts to warn them were met with incomprehension and sometimes ridicule.*

ignorant

ignorant *adj.* See the Topic Map for EDUCATION on p.888

ignorant · illiterate · untrained · uneducated · uninformed · clueless
These words all describe sb who lacks knowledge about sth or is not educated.

PATTERNS AND COLLOCATIONS
▸ ignorant / uninformed / clueless **about** sth
▸ ignorant / illiterate / untrained / uneducated / uninformed / clueless **people**
▸ an ignorant / uninformed **comment**
▸ **completely** ignorant / illiterate / untrained / uneducated / uninformed / clueless
▸ **totally** ignorant / illiterate / uneducated / uninformed / clueless
▸ **largely** ignorant / illiterate / untrained / uneducated / uninformed

ignorant /ˈɪɡnərənt/ (*disapproving*) lacking knowledge about sth: *At that time I was young and ignorant, with little experience of the world.* ◇ *You should never make your students feel ignorant.* ◇ *Too many politicians are ignorant about the issues involved.* ❶ In most cases it is not polite to call a person **ignorant**. OPP **knowledgeable** → INFORMED

illiterate /ɪˈlɪtərət/ (of a person) not knowing how to read or write; (of a document or letter) badly written, as if by sb without much education: *A large percentage of the rural population was illiterate.* ◇ *Many of the application forms we received were virtually illiterate.* ❶ Illiterate can also be used after a noun or adverb to mean 'not knowing much about a particular subject area': *Even if you're **computer illiterate** you should be able to follow these simple instructions.* OPP **literate** ❶ A **literate** person is able to read and write.

untrained not trained to perform a particular job or skill: *It's unreasonable to expect untrained workers to achieve spectacular results.* ◇ *The troops were **untrained in** guerrilla warfare.* OPP **trained**, See also **train** → TRAIN *verb* 1

uneducated having had little or no formal education: *We're trying to work with a largely uneducated workforce.* OPP **educated** → INFORMED

uninformed /ˌʌnɪnˈfɔːmd; AmE -ˈfɔːrmd/ having or showing a lack of knowledge or information about sth: *The public is largely uninformed about this disease.* ◇ *Uninformed criticism certainly will not help us solve the problem.* OPP **informed** → INFORMED

clueless /ˈkluːləs/ (*informal, disapproving*) not able to understand or do sth: *He's completely clueless about computers.* OPP **clued-up, clued-in** ❶ A person who is **clued-up** (*BrE*)/**clued-in** (*AmE*) knows a lot about sth and understands it well.

ignore *verb*

ignore · disregard · overlook · turn a blind eye · take no notice · neglect · gloss over sth
These words all mean to pay little or no attention to sth.

PATTERNS AND COLLOCATIONS
▸ to ignore / disregard / overlook / turn a blind eye to / neglect / gloss over **the fact that...**
▸ to ignore/disregard/overlook/neglect **the importance/need/ possibility** of sth
▸ to ignore / disregard sb's **advice / rules / wishes**
▸ to ignore / overlook sb / sth's **faults / shortcomings**
▸ to **often** ignore/disregard/overlook/neglect/gloss over sb/sth
▸ to **completely/entirely/totally/largely/generally/frequently/ deliberately** ignore / disregard / overlook / neglect sth

▶ to **conveniently** ignore / overlook / turn a blind eye to / gloss over sb / sth
▶ to **consistently** ignore / overlook / neglect sth

ignore /ɪɡˈnɔː(r)/ [T] to pay no attention to sth; to pretend that you have not seen sb or that sb is not there: *He ignored all the 'No Smoking' signs and lit up a cigarette.* ◇ *I made a suggestion but they chose to ignore it.* ◇ *We cannot afford to ignore their advice.* ◇ *She ignored him and carried on with her work.* **OPP pay attention to sth** → HEAR

disregard /ˌdɪsrɪˈɡɑːd; AmE -ˈɡɑːrd/ [T] (*formal*) to not consider sth; to treat sth as unimportant: *The board completely disregarded my recommendations.* ◇ *Safety rules were disregarded.*
▶ **disregard** noun [U]: *She shows a total disregard for other people's feelings.*

overlook /ˌəʊvəˈlʊk; AmE ˌoʊvərˈlʊk/ [T] (*rather formal*) to see sth wrong or bad but decide to ignore it: *We could not afford to overlook such a serious offence.* ◇ *He's so friendly people are prepared to overlook his faults.*

turn a blind 'eye idiom to pretend not to notice sth bad that is happening, so that you do not have to do anything about it: *The authorities were either unaware of the problem or turned a blind eye to it.*

take no 'notice phrase to pay no attention to sb/sth, as if they/it were not there or did not exist: *Take no notice of what he says.* ◇ *Don't take any notice of what you read in the papers.* ◇ *Take no notice and they'll just go away.*

neglect /nɪˈɡlekt/ [T] (*rather formal*) to not give enough attention to sth: *Dance has been neglected by television.* ◇ *She has neglected her studies.* See also **neglect** → NEGLECT noun, **neglect** → LEAVE verb 5

gloss 'over sth phrasal verb to avoid talking about sth unpleasant or embarrassing by not dealing with it in detail: *There is a strong temptation to gloss over potential problems.* ◇ *He glossed over any splits in the party.*

illegal adj. See also the entry for WRONG 4

illegal · criminal · unlawful · unconstitutional · illicit · punishable · illegitimate · delinquent · pirate
These words all describe people, things or activities that are not allowed, especially by law.

PATTERNS AND COLLOCATIONS
▶ an illegal / a criminal / an unlawful / an unconstitutional / an illicit / a delinquent **act**
▶ illegal / criminal / unlawful / illicit / delinquent **activity / conduct**
▶ illegal / criminal / unlawful / illicit **possession** of drugs / weapons
▶ an illegal / illicit **substance / drug**
▶ a criminal / a punishable **offence**
▶ criminal / unlawful **violence**

illegal not allowed by the law: *Most of these jobs are done by illegal immigrants.* ◇ *It's illegal to drive through a red light.* ❶ **Illegal** can be used either before a noun or after a linking verb. Common collocates are *dumping, gambling, possession, practices, trade, transactions, exports* and *payments.* It is most common for **illegal** to be used to describe an activity, but it can also be used to describe a thing or person, especially in the phrases *illegal drugs / substances / organizations / immigrants.* **OPP legal** → LEGAL
▶ **illegally** adv.: *an illegally parked car* ◇ *He entered the country illegally.*

criminal [usually before noun] (*rather formal or law*) connected with or involving crime: *It should be a criminal offence to inflict cruelty on any wild animal.* ◇ *He had three criminal convictions and a history of violence.* ❶ **Criminal** is used in legal contexts, mainly to talk about acts. Common collocates of **criminal** are *activity, acts, assault, behaviour, charges, conviction, damage, gang, negligence, offence, sexual conduct, violence* and *wrongdoing.* See also **crime** → CRIME 1
▶ **criminally** adv.: *The owners were very negligent but they were not criminally negligent* (= their negligence was not a crime).

unlawful (*formal or law*) not allowed by the law: *The jury returned a verdict of unlawful killing.* ❶ **Unlawful** is used in legal contexts, especially to talk about acts that would be allowed by law in a different situation. Common collocates are *acts, conduct, killing, means, possession, sex, violence* and *wounding.* **OPP lawful** → LEGAL

unconstitutional /ˌʌnˌkɒnstɪˈtjuːʃənl; AmE -kɑːnstəˈtuː-/ not allowed by the constitution of a country or organization: *The judges declared the decision unconstitutional.* ❶ A **constitution** is the system or laws and basic principles that a country or organization is governed by. **OPP constitutional** → LEGAL

illicit /ɪˈlɪsɪt/ not allowed by the law: *They do not support any behaviour that involves illicit drugs.* ❶ **Illicit** is usually used to talk about drugs, and activities connected with them. You can also talk about *illicit sex,* but while *illegal sex* is not allowed by law, *illicit sex* is legal, but not approved of by the normal rules of society.

punishable (of a crime) that can be punished, especially by law: *This is a crime **punishable by / with** imprisonment.* ◇ *Giving false information to the police is a punishable offence.*

illegitimate /ˌɪləˈdʒɪtəmət/ (*formal*) not allowed by a particular set of rules or by law: *He has been accused of illegitimate use of company property.* **OPP legitimate** → LEGAL

delinquent /dɪˈlɪŋkwənt/ (*rather formal*) (especially of young people or their behaviour) showing a tendency to commit crimes: *She spent a year in an institution for delinquent teenagers.* See also **delinquency** → CRIME 1

pirate /ˈpaɪrət/ [only before noun] (of copies of books, CDs, DVDs, etc.) made and sold illegally; (of a radio station) broadcasting illegally: *a pirate CD / video / DVD / cassette / edition / copy / recording* ◇ *a pirate radio station*

illness noun See the Topic Map for HEALTH on p.890, See also the entry for DISEASE

illness · sickness · ill health · trouble
These are all words for the state of being physically or mentally ill.

PATTERNS AND COLLOCATIONS
▶ **due to / owing to / through** illness / sickness / ill health
▶ **chronic** illness / sickness / ill health
▶ **to suffer from** illness / sickness / ill health / heart, etc. trouble

illness [U] the state of being physically or mentally ill: *She suffered from mental illness throughout her life.* ◇ *I missed a lot of school through illness last year.* See also **ill** → SICK 1

sickness [U] (*rather formal*) illness; bad health: *I recommend you get insurance against sickness and unemployment.* See also **sick** → SICK 1

NOTE ILLNESS OR SICKNESS? Sickness is used especially in contexts concerning work and insurance. **Illness** has a wider range of uses and is used in more general contexts.

ill 'health [U] (*rather formal*) the state of being physically ill or having lots of health problems: *She was forced to resign because of ill health.* ❶ **Ill health** often lasts a long period of time.

trouble [U] illness or pain in a particular part of the body: *He suffers from heart trouble.* ◇ *I've been having trouble with my knee.*

illusion noun

illusion · myth · misunderstanding · delusion · misconception · fallacy · misinterpretation · false impression · the wrong idea
These are all words for a mistaken or false idea about sb / sth.

▸ an illusion / a myth / a misunderstanding / a delusion / a misconception / a fallacy / the wrong idea **about** sb / sth
▸ the illusion / myth / misunderstanding / delusion / misconception / fallacy / false impression **that...**
▸ **under** an illusion / a delusion / a false impression
▸ a **dangerous** illusion / myth / delusion / misconception / fallacy
▸ a **common** myth / misunderstanding / delusion / misconception / fallacy
▸ a **popular** myth / misconception / fallacy
▸ (a) **widespread** misunderstanding / misconception / fallacy
▸ to **have** an illusion / a delusion / the wrong idea
▸ to **be based on** a myth / misunderstanding / misconception / fallacy / misinterpretation
▸ to **give rise to** a myth / (a) misunderstanding / a misconception
▸ to **give sb** a false impression / the wrong idea
▸ to **correct** a misconception / misconception / false impression

illusion /ɪˈluːʒn/ [C, U] a false idea or belief about sb / sth, especially an idea that sb / sth is good when it is not: *I* *have no illusions about her feelings for me* (= I know that she does not love me). ◇ *He's under the illusion that* (= wrongly thinks that) *he will get the job.* ◇ *They wanted to create the illusion of being a close, happy family.* ◇ *He could no longer tell the difference between illusion and reality.*
▸ **illusory** /ɪˈluːsəri/ *adj.*: (*formal*) *Our new situation gave us an illusory sense of freedom.* ◇ *Any power he may seem to have is purely illusory.*

myth /mɪθ/ [C, U] something that many people believe but that does not exist or is false: *It is time to dispel the myth of the classless society* (= to show that it does not exist). ◇ *It's a myth that cats only swish their tails when they are angry.* ◇ *Contrary to popular myth, women are not worse drivers than men.*

misunderstanding [C, U] a situation in which sth is not understood correctly, especially when this leads to problems: *The meeting is a final chance to clear up any misunderstandings.* ◇ *There must be some misunderstanding – I thought I ordered the smaller model.* **OPP** under-standing → UNDERSTANDING, See also **misunderstand** → MISUNDERSTAND

delusion /dɪˈluːʒn/ [C, U] a false belief or opinion about yourself or your situation; the act of making yourself believe sth that is not true: *Don't go getting delusions of* *grandeur* (= a belief that you are more important than you really are). ◇ *My mother had a tremendous capacity for delusion.* ❶ **Delusions** can sometimes be caused by a mental illness: *Many people with this condition suffer from delusions.* See also **delude** → MISLEAD

misconception /ˌmɪskənˈsepʃn/ [C, U] (*rather formal*) a mistaken belief about sth, especially one based on incorrect information: *It's a widespread misconception that only women get breast cancer.* ◇ *Their views are based on misconception and prejudice.*

fallacy /ˈfæləsi/ [C, U] (*rather formal*) a false idea that a lot of people think is true; a false way of thinking about sth: *It's a fallacy to say that the camera never lies.* ◇ *He detected the fallacy of her argument.*

misinterpretation /ˌmɪsɪntɜːprɪˈteɪʃn; *AmE* -tɜːrp-/ [U, C] (*rather formal*) a mistaken idea or belief caused by sb not fully understanding sth or understanding it in the wrong way: *What he said could easily be open to misinterpreta-* *tion.* ◇ *Their conclusions were a result of a misinterpreta-tion of the data.* See also **misinterpret** → MISUNDERSTAND

false im'pression [C] a mistaken idea about sb / sth, especially one based on too little information: *Their main headline gave a completely false impression.* See also **false** → WRONG *adj.* 1

the ˌwrong iˈdea *phrase* (*rather informal*) a mistaken idea about sb / sth, especially an idea that sb / sth is worse than it really is: *Be careful about meeting him alone – you don't* *want people to get the wrong idea* (= the idea that you are having a relationship with him). ❶ **The wrong idea** is nearly always used with the verbs *get, have (got)* or *give.* See also **wrong** → WRONG *adj.* 1

image *noun*

image · reflection · mirror image
These are all words for a picture of sb / sth seen in a mirror, through a camera, or on a television or computer screen.

▸ an image / a reflection **in / on** sth
▸ a **clear / faint / blurred / distorted** image / reflection
▸ to **see / look at / stare at / watch / study** an image / a reflection
▸ an image / a reflection **looks...**

image [C] a picture of sb / sth seen on a television or computer screen, through a camera, in a mirror, on a shiny surface or on water: *Slowly, an image began to appear on the screen.* ◇ (*literary*) *He stared at his own image reflected in the water.* See also **image** → PICTURE

reflection [C] an image in a mirror, on a shiny surface or on water: *He admired his reflection in the mirror.*
▸ **reflect** *verb* [T]: *His face was reflected in the mirror.*

NOTE IMAGE OR **REFLECTION?** A picture on a television or computer screen or seen through a camera is an **image**. An **image** can also be a picture in a mirror, etc. but this is quite a literary use of the word; the usual word is **reflection**.

ˌmirror 'image [C] a picture, thing or person that is like a reflection of sb / sth else, because the right side of the original object appears on the left and the left side appears on the right: *Draw the hands as mirror images of each other.*

imagination *noun*

imagination · vision · fantasy · make-believe
These are all words for the act of creating pictures in your mind, or the pictures created in this way.

▸ (a) **romantic** imagination / vision / fantasy
▸ (a) **private / personal** vision / fantasy
▸ a **world of** fantasy / make-believe

imagination [U, C] the ability to create pictures in your mind; the part of your mind that does this; something that you have imagined rather than sth that exists: *He's got no imagination.* ◇ *It doesn't take much imagination to guess what happened next.* ◇ *She has a vivid imagination.* ◇ *I won't tell you his reaction – I'll leave that to your imagination* ◇ *Nobody hates you – it's all in your imagination.* ◇ *Is it my imagination or have you lost a lot of weight?* See also **imaginative** → CREATIVE

vision [C] an idea or picture in your imagination: *He had a vision of a world in which there would be no wars.* ◇ *I had visions of us getting hopelessly lost.*

fantasy /ˈfæntəsi/ [U] (*sometimes disapproving*) the act of imagining things; a person's imagination: *This is a work of fantasy.* ◇ *She was no longer able to distinguish between fantasy and reality.* ◇ *Stop living in a fantasy world.* **OPP** reality → FACT, See also **fantasy** → HOPE *noun* 2

NOTE IMAGINATION OR FANTASY? **Imagination** is usually a more approving term than **fantasy**. Having a *vivid imagination* is often thought to be a good thing as it enables people to enjoy themselves and to sympathize more with other people by imagining what it is like to be them. **Fantasy** is usually used to contrast imagined things with the real world, often in a negative way, suggesting that sb is unwilling or unable to face reality.

'make-believe [U] (*sometimes disapproving*) imagining or pretending that things are different or more exciting than they really are; imagining that sth is real, or that you are sb else, for example in a child's game: *They live in a world of make-believe.* ◇ *'Let's play make-believe,' said Sam.*

imagine verb

imagine · think · see · envisage · envision · picture · visualize · conceptualize · pretend
These words all mean to form an idea in your mind of what sb/sth might be like.

PATTERNS AND COLLOCATIONS
▶ to imagine / see / envisage / envision / picture / visualize / conceptualize sb / sth **as** sth
▶ to imagine / see / envisage / envision / picture / visualize (sb) **doing sth**
▶ to imagine / think / see / envisage / envision / picture / visualize **who / what / how…**
▶ to imagine / think / envisage / envision / pretend **that…**
▶ **Just** imagine / think / pretend…

imagine [T, I] to form an idea in your mind of what sb/sth might be like: *The house was just as she had imagined it.* ◇ *I can't imagine life without the children now.* ◇ *Close your eyes and imagine (that) you are in a forest.* ◇ *I can just imagine him saying that!* ◇ *I had imagined her to be older than me.* ◇ *(spoken)* '*He was furious.*' '*I can imagine!*'

think [T, no passive, I] to imagine sth that might happen or might have happened: *We couldn't think where you'd gone.* ◇ *Just think how nice it would be to see them again.* ◇ *Try to* **think yourself into** *the role.* ◇ **Just think** *– this time tomorrow we'll be lying on a beach.*

see [T] (not used in the progressive tenses) to consider sth as a future possibility; to imagine sb/sth as sth: *I can't see her changing her mind.* ◇ *His colleagues see him as a future director.*

envisage /ɪnˈvɪzɪdʒ/ [T] (*especially BrE, rather formal*) to imagine what will happen in the future: *What level of profit do you envisage?* ◇ **It is envisaged that** *the talks will take place in the spring.* ❶ The usual word for this in American English is **envision.**

envision /ɪnˈvɪʒn/ [T] (*rather formal*) to imagine what a situation will be like in the future, especially a situation that you intend to work towards: *They envision an equal society, free from poverty and disease.* ❶ **Envision** is used especially in business and political contexts. In American English it is also used as another form of the word **envisage:** *What level of profit do you envision?*

picture [T] to form a picture of sb/sth in your mind: *I can still picture the house I grew up in.* See also **picture** → DESCRIPTION *noun*

visualize (*BrE also* **-ise**) /ˈvɪʒuəlaɪz/ [T] (*rather formal*) to picture sb/sth in your mind: *Try to visualize yourself walking into the interview calmly and confidently.*
▶ **visualization** (*BrE also* **-isation**) *noun* [U, C]: *Visualization can be a useful technique in building confidence.*

> **NOTE** IMAGINE, PICTURE OR VISUALIZE? **Imagine** is the most general of these words and is used for any idea that you form of how a person, place, thing or experience might look or feel. **Picture** and **visualize** are used particularly for imagining sth in a picture or series of pictures. They are very similar in meaning but **visualize** is slightly more formal and is often used to talk about a deliberate attempt to imagine sth for a particular purpose.

conceptualize (*BrE also* **-ise**) /kənˈseptʃuəlaɪz/ [T, I] (*formal*) to form an idea of sth in your mind, especially an idea of sth that is difficult to imagine accurately: *How can we conceptualize the way the international economy works?* ◇ *The ability to conceptualize is one of the most likely indicators of who will be a successful manager.*

pretend [T, I] (*especially of children*) to imagine that sth is true as part of a game: *Let's pretend (that) we're astronauts.* ◇ *They didn't have any real money so they had to pretend.*

immediate adj.

immediate · instant · prompt · instantaneous
These words all describe sth that happens or is done without delay.

prompt   immediate   instantaneous
               instant

PATTERNS AND COLLOCATIONS
▶ an immediate / an instant / a prompt / an instantaneous **reaction / response / return**
▶ immediate / instant / prompt **action / attention / payment / relief**
▶ an immediate / instant **appeal / answer / solution / result / effect / impact / improvement**
▶ an immediate / a prompt **start / step**
▶ **almost** immediate / instant / instantaneous

immediate happening or done without delay: *Carrie's immediate reaction to the news was to laugh in relief.* ◇ *Local police took immediate action when they received the bomb alert.* ◇ *The cream brings immediate relief to dry and rough skin.* **OPP delayed** ❶ A **delayed** reaction happens some time after the event that causes it: *She's suffering a delayed reaction to the shock.*
▶ **immediately** *adv.*: *She answered almost immediately.* ◇ *The point of my question may not be immediately apparent.*

instant [usually before noun] happening or done immediately: *She took an instant dislike to me, the first time we met.* ◇ *This account gives you instant access to your money.* ◇ *The show was an instant success in New York.*
▶ **instantly** *adv.*: *Her voice is instantly recognizable.* ◇ *The driver of the car was killed instantly.*

prompt done without delay: *Prompt action was required as the fire spread.* ◇ *Prompt payment of the invoice would be appreciated.*
▶ **promptly** *adv.*: (*especially written*) *She read the letter and promptly burst into tears.*

instantaneous /ˌɪnstənˈteɪniəs/ happening immediately: *Her instantaneous response was to blame her parents.* ◇ *With certain poisons, death is almost instantaneous.*

> **NOTE** IMMEDIATE, INSTANT, PROMPT OR INSTANTANEOUS? **Prompt** describes sth that you do; **instantaneous** describes sth that happens; **immediate** and **instant** can describe either, although **instant** is used more to describe sth that happens than sth that you do. **Prompt** action is not quite as fast as an action or reaction that is **immediate, instant** or **instantaneous**. Action can be *very/fairly prompt* but NOT: *very/fairly immediate/ instant/instantaneous.* A reaction can be *almost immediate/instant/instantaneous* but NOT: *almost prompt.*

impact noun

impact · force · shock
These are all words for the strength and effect of a blow, crash or explosion.

PATTERNS AND COLLOCATIONS
▶ the impact / force of the **blow / crash**
▶ the force / shock of the **impact / explosion**
▶ the **full** impact / force of sth
▶ to **feel** the impact / force / shock of sth
▶ to **take** the impact / force of sth
▶ to **absorb** the impact / shock

impact [C, usually sing., U] the act of one object hitting another; the strength with which this happens: *craters made by meteorite impacts* ◇ *The impact of the blow knocked Jack off balance.* ◇ *The bomb explodes* **on impact** (= when it hits sth).

force [U] the physical strength of sth that is shown as it hits sth else: *The force of the blast hurled bodies into the air.* ◊ *She hits the ball with amazing force for someone so small.*

shock [C, U] a violent shaking movement that is caused by an explosion, earthquake or impact: *The shock of the explosion could be felt up to six miles away.* ◊ *The bumper absorbs shock on impact.*

importance *noun*

importance · significance · urgency · seriousness · consequence · substance · gravity
These are all words for the quality of being important and having an effect on people or things.

PATTERNS AND COLLOCATIONS
▸ to be **of** importance / significance **to** sb
▸ **great** importance / significance / urgency / seriousness / consequence
▸ the **utmost** importance / significance / urgency / seriousness / gravity
▸ **real** importance / significance / urgency / consequence
▸ **new** / **added** importance / significance / urgency / substance
▸ to **have** / **gain** importance / significance / substance
▸ to **give** sth importance / significance / urgency / substance
▸ to **assume** / **take on** importance / significance / an urgency
▸ to **appreciate** / **realize** / **recognize** / **understand** the importance / significance / urgency / seriousness / gravity of sth
▸ to **reflect** / **show** / **underline** the importance / significance / urgency / seriousness of sth
▸ to **assess** / **exaggerate** / **underestimate** the importance / significance / seriousness of sth
▸ a **matter of** importance / significance / urgency / substance

importance [U] the quality of being important and having an effect on people or things: *She stressed the importance of careful preparation.* ◊ *They attach great importance to the project.* ◊ *State your reasons in order of importance.* ◊ *He was very aware of his own importance (= of his status).*

significance /sɪɡˈnɪfɪkəns/ [U, C] (*rather formal, especially written*) the importance of sth, especially when this has an effect on what happens in the future: *This is a decision of major political significance.* ◊ *The new drug has great significance for the treatment of the disease.* ◊◻ **insignificance** → MINOR

urgency /ˈɜːdʒənsi; AmE ˈɜːrdʒ-/ [U, sing.] (*rather formal*) the need to deal with sth immediately: *This is a matter of some urgency.* ◊ *There was a note of urgency in his voice.* ◊ *The attack added a new urgency to the peace talks.* See also **urgent** → URGENT

seriousness [U, sing.] the need to treat sth as important, especially because there is cause for worry: *He had not understood the seriousness of the matter.* ◊ *The problem was not treated with the seriousness it deserved.* See also **serious** → SERIOUS 1

consequence /ˈkɒnsɪkwəns; AmE ˈkɑːnsəkwens/ [U] (*formal*) importance: *Don't worry. It's of no consequence.* ◊ *His work made him a person of some consequence in the art world.* ❶ You can describe things that are not important or not very important as being *of some/little/no consequence* or as being *without consequence*. If nothing important happens, you can say that *nothing of any consequence* happens. You can describe an important person or thing as *sb/sth of consequence*.

substance [U] (often used in negative sentences) (*formal, especially written*) important information, evidence or work: *Nothing of any substance was achieved in the meeting.* ◊ *Their accusations were without substance.* ❶ A report or rumour is said to *have substance* if it contains important information, or if there is evidence to support it. If not, it is said to *lack substance*. You can describe an important point for discussion as sth *of substance* or as a *matter of substance*.

gravity /ˈɡrævəti/ [U] (*formal*) seriousness: *I don't think you realize the gravity of the situation.* ◊ *Punishment varies according to the gravity of the offence.* See also **grave** → SERIOUS 1

important *adj.* See also the entry for ESSENTIAL

important · significant · big · great · notable · momentous
These words all describe sth that has a great effect, is noticeable or is of great value.

PATTERNS AND COLLOCATIONS
▸ to be important / significant **for** / **to** sb / sth
▸ to be important / significant / notable **that**…
▸ important / significant / big / great / notable / momentous **events** / **changes** / **developments**
▸ an important / a significant / a big / a great / a notable **difference** / **feature** / **achievement** / **success**
▸ an important / a big / a momentous **decision**
▸ **especially** / **particularly** important / significant / notable / momentous
▸ **really** / **quite** / **equally** important / significant / momentous
▸ **very** / **highly** / **increasingly** / **extremely** / **enormously** / **hugely** / **immensely** important / significant

important having a great effect on people or things; of great value: *I have an important announcement to make.* ◊ *Listening is an important part of the job.* ◊ *It is important to follow the manufacturer's instructions.* ◊ *It's very important to me that you should be there.* ◊ *The important thing is to keep trying.* ◻ **unimportant** → MINOR

▸ **importantly** *adv.*: *Most importantly, can he be trusted?*

significant /sɪɡˈnɪfɪkənt/ large or important enough to have an effect or be noticed: *There are no significant differences between the two groups of students.* ◊ *The results of the experiment are not statistically significant.* ◊ *These views are held by a significant proportion of the population.* ◻ **insignificant** → MINOR

▸ **significantly** *adv.*: *The two sets of figures are not significantly different from each other.* ◊ *Profits have increased significantly over the past few years.*

> **NOTE** IMPORTANT OR SIGNIFICANT? **Important** is the more general of these words. Things that are **significant** are important within a particular context or from a particular point of view. **Significant** is often used when sb wants to suggest that the level of importance of sth has been measured in some way. Figures can be *statistically significant* but NOT : *statistically important*. **Significant** but NOT **important** can mean 'great in degree': *an important proportion of the population*

big [only before noun] (*rather informal, especially journalism or business*) important or serious: *It's a big decision to have to make.* ◊ *You are making a big mistake.* ◊ *She took the stage for her big moment.*

great [only before noun] important and impressive: *The wedding was a great occasion.* ◊ *The great thing is to get it done quickly.* ◊ *One great advantage of this metal is that it doesn't rust.*

notable /ˈnəʊtəbl; AmE ˈnoʊ-/ (*rather formal*) deserving to be noticed or to receive attention because it is unusual, important or interesting: *The town is notable for its ancient harbour.* ◊ *It is notable that only 15% of senior managers are women.* ◊ *With a few notable exceptions, everyone gave something.*

▸ **notably** *adv.*: *The house had many drawbacks, most notably its price.*

momentous /məˈmentəs; AmE moʊˈm-/ (*rather formal*) (especially of events and occasions) very important or serious, especially because there may be important results: *At the same time, momentous events were taking place in Russia.*

impossible adj.

impossible · out of the question · unthinkable · inconceivable · unattainable
These words all describe things that cannot happen, be done or be true.

PATTERNS AND COLLOCATIONS
▶ to be impossible / unthinkable / inconceivable **to** sb
▶ to be impossible / out of the question / unthinkable / inconceivable **for sb to do sth**
▶ to be impossible / out of the question / unthinkable / inconceivable **that...**
▶ an impossible / unattainable **goal / ideal**
▶ to **find** sth impossible / unthinkable / inconceivable
▶ **quite** impossible / out of the question / unthinkable / inconceivable
▶ **almost** impossible / unthinkable / inconceivable

impossible that cannot exist or be done: *That's impossible! ◇ It's impossible for me to be there before eight. ◇ I find it impossible to lie to her. ◇ I realized it was an impossible dream.* **OPP** **possible** → POSSIBLE 1, **possible** → POSSIBLE 2, **possible** → LIKELY
▶ **the impossible** noun [sing.]: *He decided to attempt the impossible and set up an airline from scratch in three months.*
▶ **impossibly** adv.: *an impossibly difficult problem* (= impossible to solve)

out of the 'question idiom impossible or not allowed and therefore not worth discussing: *Another trip abroad this year is out of the question.*

unthinkable (*especially written*) impossible to imagine or accept, especially because it is so shocking: *It was unthinkable that she could be dead.*
▶ **the unthinkable** noun [sing.]: *The time has come to think the unthinkable* (= consider possibilities that used to be unacceptable).

inconceivable /ˌɪnkənˈsiːvəbl/ (*rather formal, especially written*) impossible to imagine or believe: *It is inconceivable that the minister was not aware of the problem.* **OPP** **conceivable** → POSSIBLE 2
▶ **the inconceivable** noun [sing.]: *Then the inconceivable happened — I lost my job.*

unattainable (*rather formal, written*) impossible to achieve, get or reach: *Setting unattainable goals will only lead to frustration.*

impress verb

impress · move · touch · dazzle · take sb's breath away · affect
These words all mean to make sb feel sth such as admiration, sympathy or sadness.

| impress | move | dazzle |
| touch | affect | take sb's breath away |

PATTERNS AND COLLOCATIONS
▶ impress / move / dazzle sb **with** sth
▶ it impresses / moves / touches sb **to see / hear** sth
▶ impress / move / touch / affect sb **deeply**
▶ to be **profoundly** impressed / moved / affected by sth

impress [T, often passive, I] (of a person or thing) to make you feel admiration for them/it: *We interviewed a number of candidates, but none of them impressed us. ◇ I was enormously impressed by their professionalism. ◇ She was suitably impressed* (= as impressed as sb had hoped) *with the painting. ◇ It impressed me that she remembered my name. ◇ The Grand Canyon never fails to impress.* See also **impression** → EFFECT, **unimpressed** → INDIFFERENT

move [T] to make you feel strong feelings, especially of sympathy or sadness: *The woman's story had really moved her. ◇ We were deeply moved by her plight. ◇ Grown men were moved to tears at the horrific scenes.* See also **moving** → MOVING, **unmoved** → RUTHLESS

touch [T] to make you feel grateful or sympathetic: *I had been touched by his kindness to my aunts. ◇ What he said really touched my heart.* See also **touching** → MOVING

dazzle [T, often passive] to impress sb very much with your beauty, skill, knowledge or personality: *He was dazzled by the warmth of her smile. ◇ He dazzled the chess world as he took the title at his first attempt.*

take sb's 'breath away idiom (of a sight, action or performance) to surprise or impress sb very much, especially with its beauty or skill: *My first view of the island from the air took my breath away. ◇ The spectacular two-hour performance took their breath away.* See also **breathtaking** → AMAZING

affect [T, often passive] (*rather formal*) to make you feel strong feelings of sadness or pity, for yourself or sb else: *Mrs Davis and her husband were profoundly affected by their experiences. ◇ They were deeply affected by the news of her death.*

NOTE MOVE, TOUCH OR AFFECT? You can be **moved** by what happens to sb else, especially sth sad that happens to them; you can be **touched** by what sb else does, especially a small act of kindness that they do for you; you are **affected** by sth that happens to you, or to sb else, but the emphasis is on the effect it has on you.

impressive adj. See also the entry for GOOD 4

impressive · expert · spectacular · consummate · masterly · virtuoso
These words all describe sb/sth that shows a lot of skill.

PATTERNS AND COLLOCATIONS
▶ an impressive / an expert / a spectacular / a masterly / a virtuoso **performance / display**
▶ impressive / expert / consummate / masterly / virtuoso **skill**
▶ an impressive / a spectacular **achievement**
▶ **quite** impressive / expert / spectacular
▶ **really / truly** impressive / spectacular

impressive (especially of an achievement) making you feel admiration because it is extremely good or skilful: *It is one of the most impressive novels published in recent years. ◇ The team are 12 points ahead after an impressive victory last night. ◇ She was very impressive in the interview.* **OPP** **unimpressive** ❶ An unimpressive achievement is not special in any way: *His academic record was unimpressive.* See also **impressive** → MAGNIFICENT, **impression** → EFFECT
▶ **impressively** adv.: *Although very old, the maps are impressively accurate.*

expert /ˈekspɜːt; AmE -pɜːrt/ done with, having or involving a lot of knowledge or skill: *It's a good idea to seek expert advice. ◇ They're all expert in this field. ◇ She's expert at making cheap but stylish clothes.* See also **expert** → EXPERT noun, **expertise** → SKILL 2
▶ **expertly** adv.: *He tied up the boat and expertly folded down the sails.*

spectacular /spekˈtækjələ(r)/ (of an achievement or skill) very impressive: *Rooney scored a spectacular goal. ◇ They were absolutely delighted with the show's spectacular success.* **OPP** **unspectacular** ❶ An achievement or skill that is **unspectacular** is not exciting or special: *He had a steady but unspectacular career.* See also **spectacular** → MAGNIFICENT, **spectacle** → PERFORMANCE
▶ **spectacularly** adv.: *It had been a spectacularly successful season.*

consummate /kənˈsʌmət; ˈkɒnsəmət; AmE ˈkɑːn-/ [usually before noun] (*formal*) (of a person) extremely skilled at sth; (of a skill or quality) very great: *a consummate performer/actor/politician ◇ He weaved his way past the England defenders with consummate ease.*

masterly /ˈmɑːstəli; *AmE* ˈmæstərli/ showing great skill or understanding: *Her handling of the situation was masterly.* ◇ *As a performer he shows a masterly sense of timing.*

virtuoso /ˌvɜːtʃuˈəʊsəʊ; -ˈəʊzəʊ; *AmE* ˌvɜːrtʃuˈoʊsoʊ; -ˈoʊzoʊ/ [only before noun] showing very great skill in performance: *a virtuoso pianist/player* ◇ *They gave a virtuoso display of Spanish dancing.*

improper *adj.*

improper · indecent · unseemly · undignified · indiscreet
These words all describe behaviour that is not appropriate or acceptable in a particular person or situation.

PATTERNS AND COLLOCATIONS
▸ unseemly / undignified **in** sb
▸ improper / indecent / unseemly **for** sb to do sth
▸ improper / indecent / unseemly / undignified **to do sth**
▸ improper / unseemly / undignified **behaviour**
▸ improper / unseemly **conduct**
▸ indecent / unseemly **haste**
▸ an unseemly / undignified **scramble**
▸ **very** improper / unseemly / undignified / indiscreet
▸ **rather / somewhat** indecent / unseemly / undignified

improper (*rather formal*) dishonest or morally wrong, especially in financial or sexual matters; not appropriate to the situation: *He had been indulging in improper business practices.* ◇ *There was nothing improper about our relationship* (= it did not involve sex). ◇ *It would be improper to comment at this stage.* **OPP proper** → RIGHT 2
▸ **improperly** *adv.*: *There was no suggestion that he had behaved improperly.*
▸ **impropriety** /ˌɪmprəˈpraɪəti/ *noun* [U]: *There was no evidence of impropriety.*
indecent /ɪnˈdiːsnt/ (*rather formal*) not showing enough respect for the dead or for other people's privacy, especially by paying them too little or too much attention (*especially BrE*) *They left the funeral with almost indecent haste* (= too quickly). ◇ *It is considered indecent for couples to be seen to be intimate in public.* ❶ In this meaning **indecent** is nearly always used in the phrases *indecent haste* and *indecent (for sb) to do sth.* **OPP decent** → RIGHT 2
unseemly (*formal*) not polite or suitable for a particular situation: *He had become embroiled in an unseemly dispute with the club president.* ◇ *There followed an unseemly rush for the exits.* ❶ **Unseemly** collocates with words for behaviour, arguments or a sudden movement forward by a lot of people, including *behaviour, conduct, dispute, squabble, row, haste, scramble* and *rush.*
undignified /ʌnˈdɪɡnɪfaɪd/ causing you to look silly and to lose the respect of other people: *There was an undignified scramble for the best seats.* ◇ *Public outrage at the proposals forced the government to beat an undignified retreat.* ❶ **Undignified** often describes an attempt by a lot of people to get sth, or an argument about who should have sth. Collocates include *scramble, struggle, squabble, fight,* and *tussle.* **OPP dignified** → PROUD 1
indiscreet /ˌɪndɪˈskriːt/ not careful about what you say or do; likely to embarrass or offend sb: *It would be indiscreet of me to say any more.* **OPP discreet** → TACT *noun*
▸ **indiscretion** /ˌɪndɪˈskreʃn/ *noun* [U]: *He talked to the press in a moment of indiscretion.* **OPP discretion** → TACT

improve *verb*

1 improve your knowledge/chances
2 your quality of life improves

1 improve · enhance · reform · refine · enrich
These words all mean to make sth better.

PATTERNS AND COLLOCATIONS
▸ to improve / enhance / refine / enrich your **understanding**
▸ to improve / enhance / refine your **knowledge**
▸ to improve / enhance / enrich your **life**
▸ to **further** improve / enhance / refine / enrich sth
▸ to **greatly** improve / enhance / enrich sth
▸ to **slightly** improve / enhance / refine sth

improve [T] to make sb/sth better than before: *You can significantly improve your chances of getting a job by compiling a good CV.* ◇ *We now offer a much improved service to our customers.* ◇ *I need to improve my French.* **OPP impair** → DAMAGE
▸ **improvement** *noun* [U, C]: *There is still room for improvement in your work.* ◇ *This is a great improvement on your previous work.* ◇ *improvements to the bus service*
enhance /ɪnˈhɑːns; *AmE* ˈhæns/ [T, often passive] (*rather formal*) to further improve the good quality, status or value of sth/sth: *The images can be enhanced using digital technology.* ◇ *Most people seek to enhance their status at work in whatever ways they can.* **OPP diminish** → FALL 1
reform [T, I] to improve a system, organization, law, etc. by making changes to it; to improve your behaviour; to make sb do this: *There are proposals to reform the welfare system.* ◇ *He has promised to reform.* ◇ *She thought she could reform him.* ◇ *a reformed character/alcoholic* See also **reformer** → ACTIVIST
▸ **reform** *noun* [U, C]: *a government committed to reform* ◇ *reforms in education*
refine /rɪˈfaɪn/ [T, often passive] to improve sth by making small changes to it: *Our methods have been gradually refined over the years.* ◇ *They would constantly refine their designs until they were almost perfect.*
enrich /ɪnˈrɪtʃ/ [T] (*written*) to improve the quality of sth, usually by adding sth to it: *Reading good literature can enrich all our lives.* ◇ *Most breakfast cereals are enriched with vitamins.*

2 See also the entry for DEVELOP 1
improve · get better · pick up · look up
These words all mean to become better than before.

PATTERNS AND COLLOCATIONS
▸ to **start / begin / continue to** improve / get better / pick up / look up
▸ to **fail to** improve / get better
▸ to improve / get better / pick up **slowly / gradually / slightly / dramatically**

improve [I] to become better: *His quality of life has improved dramatically since the operation.* ◇ *The doctor says she should continue to improve* (= after an illness). **OPP worsen, deteriorate** → WORSEN
▸ **improvement** *noun* [U, C]: *Sales figures continue to show signs of improvement.* ◇ *an improvement in Anglo-German relations*
get 'better *phrase* (often used in the progressive tenses) (*rather informal*) to improve: **Things got better** after my husband found a job. ◇ *It's not an ideal situation, but things can only get better.* ◇ *Our sales seem to be getting better and better.* ◇ *Computers are getting better all the time.* **OPP get worse** → WORSEN, See also **get better** → RECOVER 1
pick 'up *phrasal verb* (especially of business or the economy) to get better or stronger: *Exports are gradually picking up.* ◇ *Trade usually picks up in the spring.* ◇ *Sales have picked up 14% this year.*
look 'up *phrasal verb* (usually used in the progressive tenses or the infinitive) (*rather informal*) (of business or a situation) to improve after not being very good: *It had been a bad year, but things were looking up at last.*

inadequate *adj.*

inadequate · insufficient · lacking · meagre · scant · sparse · paltry · deficient
These words all describe an amount or level that is not as much or as many as sb needs or wants.

▸ lacking/ deficient **in** sth
▸ inadequate/ insufficient **for** sth
▸ inadequate/ insufficient **to do** sth
▸ an inadequate/ an insufficient/ a meagre/ a paltry **amount/ level/ number**
▸ an inadequate/ an insufficient/ a meagre/ scant **supply**
▸ inadequate/ insufficient/ meagre/ scant/ sparse **resources/ information**
▸ an inadequate/ a meagre/ a paltry **sum**
▸ inadequate/ insufficient/ scant **evidence/ knowledge**
▸ **rather** inadequate/ lacking/ meagre/ scant/ sparse/ paltry
▸ **very** inadequate/ meagre/ scant/ sparse/ deficient
▸ **totally/ seriously/ sadly** inadequate/ lacking/ deficient
▸ **quite/ wholly** inadequate/ insufficient/ lacking
▸ **woefully** inadequate/ insufficient/ lacking/ deficient

inadequate /ɪnˈædɪkwət/ not enough; not good enough: *They are blaming their failure on inadequate preparation.* ◇ *The system is inadequate for the tasks it has to perform.* ◇ *The food supplies are inadequate to meet the needs of the hungry.* **OPP** adequate → ADEQUATE, See also **inadequate** → INCOMPETENT, **unsatisfactory** → DISAPPOINTING
▸ **inadequately** *adv.*: *to be inadequately prepared/insured/funded*

insufficient /ˌɪnsəˈfɪʃnt/ (*rather formal*) not large, strong or important enough for a particular purpose: *I'm afraid we have insufficient evidence.* ◇ *His salary is insufficient to meet his needs.* ◇ *There are fears that the existing flood barrier may prove to be insufficient.* **OPP** sufficient ❶ The opposite is **sufficient**: *Make sure you allow sufficient time to get there.* ◇ *One dose should be sufficient.*
▸ **insufficiently** *adv.*: *insufficiently researched*

NOTE INADEQUATE OR INSUFFICIENT? Insufficient emphasizes the quantity or strength of sth: *There are insufficient funds in your account.* ◇ *to pay insufficient attention to sth.* Inadequate often emphasizes the quality as well as the quantity: *an inadequate understanding of how language works* ◇ *low pay and inadequate training*

lacking [not before noun] having none or not enough of sth: *She's not usually lacking in confidence.* ◇ *The book is completely lacking in originality.* See also **lack** → LACK *noun*

meagre (*BrE*) (*AmE* **meager**) /ˈmiːɡə(r)/ small in quantity and poor in quality: *They had to exist on a meagre diet of bread and water.* ◇ *She supplements her meagre income by cleaning offices at night.*

scant [only before noun] (*rather formal*) not very much and not as much as there should be: *I paid scant attention to what she was saying.* ◇ *The firefighters went back into the house with scant regard for their own safety.*

sparse only present in small amounts or numbers and often spread over a large area: *One characteristic of the islands is their sparse population.* ◇ *Vegetation becomes sparse higher up the mountains.*
▸ **sparsely** *adv.*: *a sparsely populated area* ◇ *a sparsely furnished room*

paltry /ˈpɔːltri/ [usually before noun] (of an amount or number) too small to be considered as important or useful: *This account offers a paltry 1% return on your investment.* ◇ *They worked long hours for paltry wages.*

deficient /dɪˈfɪʃnt/ not having enough of sth, especially sth that is essential: *Your diet is deficient in iron.* ◇ *An educational system which fails to teach basic arithmetic is seriously deficient.* See also **deficiency** → LACK *noun*

incentive *noun* See also the entry for BRIBE

incentive · motivation · stimulus · impetus · inspiration · inducement
These are all words for sth that encourages sb to do sth or to develop more quickly, or is the reason why sb does sth.

▸ the incentive/ motivation/ stimulus/ impetus/ inspiration **for** sth
▸ the incentive/ stimulus/ impetus/ inducement **to** sth
▸ the motivation/ impetus/ inspiration **behind** sth
▸ the incentive/ stimulus/ impetus/ inducement **to do** sth
▸ a **strong** incentive/ motivation/ impetus/ inducement
▸ a **powerful** incentive/ stimulus/ impetus/ inducement
▸ the **main** incentive/ motivation/ stimulus/ impetus/ inspiration
▸ a **new** incentive/ motivation/ stimulus/ impetus
▸ an **extra** incentive/ motivation/ stimulus/ impetus/ inducement
▸ the **necessary** motivation/ stimulus/ impetus/ inducement
▸ **sufficient** incentive/ motivation/ inducement
▸ to **provide/ give (sb/ sth)** the incentive/ motivation/ stimulus/ impetus/ inspiration/ inducement
▸ to **offer** an incentive/ an inducement

incentive /ɪnˈsentɪv/ [C, U] something that encourages you to do sth, especially because you will get sth in return: *There are no incentives for people to save fuel.* ◇ *The government has created* **tax incentives** *to encourage investment.* ◇ *There is little incentive for firms to increase the skills of their workers.* **OPP** disincentive ❶ A disincentive is sth that makes you less willing to do sth, especially because you will not gain much if you do: *A sudden fall in profits provided a further disincentive to investors.*

motivation /ˌməʊtɪˈveɪʃn; *AmE* ˌmoʊ-/ [C, U] the reason why sb does sth or behaves in a particular way; sth that makes sb want to be successful: *What is the motivation behind this sudden change?* ◇ *I soon understood his motivation in inviting me.* ◇ *He's intelligent enough but he lacks motivation.* See also **motivate** → INSPIRE, **motivate** → MAKE 4, **motive** → REASON
▸ **motivational** *adj.*: (*formal*) *an important motivational factor*

stimulus /ˈstɪmjələs/ (pl. **stimuli** /-laɪ/) [C, usually sing.] (*rather formal*) something that helps or encourages sb/sth to start or to develop better or more quickly: *Books provide children with ideas and a stimulus for play.* ◇ *He stressed the value of public investment as a stimulus to growth.* See also **stimulate** → INSPIRE

impetus /ˈɪmpɪtəs/ [U, sing.] something that encourages a process or activity to develop more quickly: *The debate seems to have lost much of its initial impetus.* ◇ *Each new rumour added a* **fresh impetus** *to the smear campaign.*

NOTE STIMULUS OR IMPETUS? Stimulus is often used to talk about starting things off; impetus is used to talk about how things develop: processes or activities can *gain/maintain/lose impetus*, or they can gain *added/ new/further/fresh impetus*. Stimulus is a more formal word, often used in academic or business contexts; impetus is often used in journalism or broadcasting when discussing trends and developments.

inspiration [C, usually sing.] a person or thing that is the reason why sb creates or does sth: *He says my sister was the inspiration for his heroine.* ◇ *Clark was the inspiration behind Saturday's victory.* See also **inspire** → INSPIRE

inducement /ɪnˈdjuːsmənt; *AmE* ɪnˈduːsmənt/ [C, U] something, especially money, that is given to sb to persuade them to do sth, especially sth that they would not normally do: *The higher payments were offered as an inducement.* ◇ *There is little inducement for them to work harder.* See also **induce** → MAKE 4

include *verb*
1 Does the price include tax?
2 Some people, and I include myself...

1 include · contain · cover · incorporate · encompass · involve · build sth in(to sth) · embrace · take sth in
These words all mean to have sb/sth as a part of sth or make sb/sth a part of sth.

PATTERNS AND COLLOCATIONS
▸ to include / contain / incorporate / involve sth **in** sth
▸ to incorporate / build sth **into** sth
▸ to be included / covered / incorporated / encompassed **as** sth
▸ to contain / cover / incorporate / encompass / involve / embrace particular **aspects** of sth
▸ to include / contain / cover / incorporate / encompass particular **material**
▸ to include / contain / incorporate particular **features**
▸ to cover / encompass / embrace particular **subjects** / **issues**
▸ to contain / cover / incorporate / encompass / involve / embrace a (wide) **range** of things
▸ to include / contain / cover / incorporate / encompass / involve / embrace the **whole** of sth
▸ to **directly** cover / encompass / involve sth
▸ to cover / incorporate / encompass / involve sb / sth **fully**

include [T] (not usually used in the progressive tenses) to have sb/sth as a part of sth; to make sb/sth part of sth: *The tour included a visit to the Science Museum.* ◇ *Does the price include tax?* ◇ *Your duties will include typing letters and answering the phone.* ◇ *You should include some examples in your essay.* ◇ *We all went,* **me included**. ◇ *Representatives from the country were included as observers at the conference.* ❶ When **include** means 'to have sb/sth as a part of sth', it is not used in the progressive tenses: ~~Is the price including tax?~~ **OPP** **exclude** → EXCLUDE 1, See also **inclusive** → OVERALL
▸ **including** *prep.* (*abbr.* **incl.**): *It's £7.50, including tax.* **OPP** **excluding** → EXCLUDE *verb* 1
▸ **inclusion** /ɪnˈkluːʒn/ *noun* [U, C]: *His inclusion in the team is in doubt.* ◇ *There were some surprising inclusions in the list.* **OPP** **exclusion** → EXCLUDE *verb* 1

contain [T] (not used in the progressive tenses) to have sth inside or as part of sth: *This drink doesn't contain any alcohol.* ◇ *The bottle contains* (= can hold) *two litres.* ◇ *He handed over a brown envelope containing a hundred dollar bills.* ◇ *Her statement contained one or two inaccuracies.*

cover [T] to include sth; to deal with sth: *The survey covers all aspects of the business.* ◇ *The lectures covered a lot of ground* (= a lot of material or subjects). ◇ *He manages the sales team covering the northern part of the country* (= selling to people in that area). ◇ *Do the rules cover* (= do they apply to) *a case like this?* ❶ When **cover** means 'to include sth' it is not used in the progressive tenses: ~~The survey is covering all aspects of the business.~~ See also **be about sth** → APPLY 2
▸ **coverage** /ˈkʌvərɪdʒ/ *noun* [U]: *magazines with extensive coverage of diet and health topics*

incorporate /ɪnˈkɔːpəreɪt; AmE -ˈkɔːrp-/ [T] (*rather formal*) to include sth so that it forms a part of sth: *Many of your suggestions have been incorporated into the plan.* ◇ *The new car design incorporates all the latest safety features.*

encompass /ɪnˈkʌmpəs/ [T] (not used in the progressive tenses) (*formal*) to include a large number or range of things: *The job encompasses a wide range of responsibilities.* ◇ *The group encompasses all ages.*

involve [T] (not used in the progressive tenses) to make sb take part in sth: *We want to involve as many people as possible in the celebrations.* ◇ *Parents should involve themselves in their children's education.* **OPP** **exclude** → EXCLUDE 2, See also **involvement** → INVOLVEMENT

build sth 'in, build sth 'into sth *phrasal verb* [often passive] to make sth a permanent part of a structure, plan or system: *We're having new closets built in.* ◇ *The pipes were built into the concrete.* ◇ *A certain amount of flexibility needs to be built into the system.*
▸ **built-'in** *adj.* [only before noun]: *built-in wardrobes/ closets/cupboards/units*

embrace /ɪmˈbreɪs/ [T, no passive] (not used in the progressive tenses) (*formal*) to cover or include sth; to unite different things: *The talks embraced a wide range of issues.* ◇ *The word 'mankind' embraces men, women and children.*

take sth 'in *phrasal verb* [no passive] (not used in the progressive tenses) to include sth, especially a place on a trip: *The tour takes in six European capitals.*

2 include · count · number
These words all mean to consider sb/sth as part of a larger group.

PATTERNS AND COLLOCATIONS
▸ to include sb / count (sb) / number (sb) **as** / **among** sb / sth
▸ to include / count / number **yourself** as / among sb / sth

include [T] to consider sb/sth to be part of a larger group: *Quite a few members are worried and I include myself among them.* ◇ *Helpers at the event included students from a local school, as well as their parents.*
▸ **including** *prep.* (*abbr.* **incl.**): *Six people were killed in the riot, including a policeman.* **OPP** **excluding**

count [T] to include sb/sth when you calculate a total; to include sb/sth in a particular group: *We have invited 50 people, not counting the children.* ◇ *I count him among my closest friends.*

number [T, I] (*formal*) to include sb/sth in a particular group; to be included in a particular group: *I number her among my closest friends.* ◇ *He numbers among the best classical actors in Britain.*

income *noun* See also the entry for REVENUE

income · wage/wages · pay · salary · earnings
These are all words for money that a person earns or receives for their work.

PATTERNS AND COLLOCATIONS
▸ (a) **high** / **low** / **basic** income / wage / wages / pay / salary / earnings
▸ (a) **good** income / wage / wages / pay / salary / earnings
▸ (an) **inadequate** income / wage / wages / pay / salary
▸ (a / an) **meagre** / **average** income / wage / wages / pay / salary / earnings
▸ to **receive** an income / a wage / wages / pay / a salary / earnings
▸ to **get** an income / a wage / wages / a salary
▸ to **earn** an income / a wage / wages / your pay / a salary
▸ to **pay** / **give sb** an income / a wage / wages / a salary
▸ to **have** / **live off** an income / a wage / wages / a salary / earnings
▸ to **be on** an income / a wage / wages / a salary

income [C, U] money that a person receives for their work, or from investments or business: *Organic food is simply not affordable for people on low incomes.* ◇ *They have a weekly* **disposable income** (= the money that is left to spend after tax) *of £200.* ◇ *She is definitely in the higher income bracket.* ❶ **Income** is also money received by a company or country from their business or investments. See also **income** → REVENUE, **money** → MONEY 1

wage [C] (also **wages** [pl.]) money that employees get for doing their job, usually paid every week: *There are extra benefits for people on low wages.* ◇ *He gets a weekly wage of £300.* ◇ *She earns £120 a week, which is nothing like a* **living wage** (= a wage that is high enough for sb to buy the things they need in order to live). ◇ *a* **minimum wage** (= the lowest wage that an employer is allowed to pay by law)

pay [U] money that employees get for doing their job: *Her job is hard work, but the pay is good.* ◇ *The job offers good rates of pay and excellent conditions.* ◇ (*BrE*) *a 3% pay rise* ◇ (*AmE*) *a 3% pay raise* See also **pay** → PAY *verb*

salary [C] money that employees get for doing their job, usually paid every month or twice a month: *He gets a basic salary plus commission.* ◇ *What salary band will I be on after two years in the company?*

NOTE WAGE, PAY OR SALARY? **Pay** is the most general of these three words. Employees who work in factories, shops, etc. get their **wages** each week. Employees who work in offices or professional people such as teachers or doctors receive a **salary** that is paid monthly (in Britain) or twice a month (in Canada and the US), but is usually expressed as an annual figure: *She's on a(n) annual salary of over $80 000.*

earnings [pl.] money that a person earns from their work: *There has been a definite rise in average earnings for factory workers.* ◊ *She received compensation for loss of earnings caused by the accident.* See also **earnings** → PROFIT, **earn** → MAKE 3

> **NOTE** INCOME OR EARNINGS? A person's **earnings** are money that they have earned for doing a job. They do not include *unearned income* which the person did nothing to earn, such as interest on a savings account at a bank. An **income** is typically about a regular amount that you can rely on. **Earnings** are whatever sb manages to earn and may vary from month to month or year to year.

incompetent *adj.*

incompetent · bad · rotten · poor · inept · useless · inadequate
These words all describe sb who does not have the skill or ability to do a task as it should be done.

PATTERNS AND COLLOCATIONS
▶ bad / rotten / poor / inept / useless **at** sth
▶ an incompetent / a bad / a rotten / a poor / a useless **teacher / driver**
▶ a bad / a rotten / a useless / an inadequate **mother / father / parent**
▶ **hopelessly** incompetent / inept / inadequate
▶ **completely / totally** incompetent / useless / inadequate
▶ **very** bad / poor / inept / inadequate

incompetent /ɪnˈkɒmpɪtənt; *AmE* -ˈkɑːm-/ (*rather formal*) not having the skill or ability to do your job or a task as it should be done: *She worked for years under an incompetent manager.* ◊ *They criticized his incompetent handling of the affair.* **OPP** **competent** → GOOD 4, See also **incompetent** → LOSER *noun 2*
▶ **incompetence** *noun* [U]: *government/police incompetence*
bad (*especially spoken*) not good or skilled at sth: *I would be a really bad teacher — I've no patience.* ◊ *He's a bad loser* (= he complains when he loses a game). ◊ *She is so bad at keeping secrets.* **OPP** **good** → GOOD 4
▶ **badly** *adv.*: *He plays really badly.*
rotten [usually before noun] (*informal*) very bad at sth: *She's a rotten singer.* ◊ *I've always been rotten at maths.* **OPP** **great** → GOOD 4
poor (*rather formal*) not good or skilled at sth: *Such a poor swimmer would not survive in that water for long.* ◊ *She's a good teacher but a poor manager.* **OPP** **good** → GOOD 4

> **NOTE** BAD OR POOR? **Poor** is more formal than **bad** and is used more in written English. **Bad** is used more in spoken English.

inept (*rather formal*) acting or done with no skill or judgement: *She was left feeling inept and inadequate.* ◊ *He made some particularly inept remarks.* ❶ **Inept** is usually used to talk about sb's lack of social skills.
▶ **ineptitude** /ɪˈneptɪtjuːd; *AmE* -tuːd/ *noun* [U]: *the ineptitude of the police in handling the situation*
useless (*informal*) very bad at sth; not able to do things well: *I'm useless at French.* ◊ *Don't ask her to help. She's useless.*

> **NOTE** ROTTEN OR USELESS? **Rotten** is used most often before a noun such as *businessman, cook, driver, husband* or *wife*; **useless** is more often used in the phrase *useless at* sth: *useless at football/your job/ remembering names.* Someone who is not able to do things well in general can be described as **useless**, but NOT 'rotten': ~~Don't ask her to help. She's rotten.~~

inadequate /ɪnˈædɪkwət/ not able, or not confident enough, to deal with a situation: *I felt totally inadequate as a parent.* ❶ In this meaning, **inadequate** is usually

used in the phrase *to feel inadequate.* When it comes before a noun, it usually describes a *mother, father* or *parent.* See also **inadequate** → INADEQUATE

inconsistent *adj.*

inconsistent · incompatible · contradictory · at odds · mutually exclusive · irreconcilable
These words all describe things being of different types that cannot be mixed or put together.

PATTERNS AND COLLOCATIONS
▶ inconsistent / incompatible / at odds / irreconcilable **with** sth
▶ **totally** inconsistent / incompatible / contradictory / at odds / irreconcilable
▶ **somewhat** inconsistent / incompatible / contradictory / at odds
▶ **apparently** inconsistent / incompatible / contradictory / irreconcilable
▶ **clearly** inconsistent / incompatible / at odds
▶ **mutually** inconsistent / incompatible / contradictory / exclusive

inconsistent /ˌɪnkənˈsɪstənt/ [not usually before noun] (*rather formal*) if two statements, etc. are **inconsistent**, or one is **inconsistent with** the other, they cannot both be true because they give the facts in a different way: *The report is inconsistent with the financial statements.* ◊ *The witnesses' statements were inconsistent.* ❶ Actions can also be *inconsistent with* a set of standards or ideas: *Her behaviour was clearly inconsistent with her beliefs.* **OPP** **consistent** ❶ Statements, etc. that are **consistent** agree with each other: *The results are entirely consistent with our earlier research.*
▶ **inconsistency** *noun* [U, C]: *There is some inconsistency between the witnesses' evidence and their earlier statements.* ◊ *I noticed a few inconsistencies in her argument.*
incompatible /ˌɪnkəmˈpætəbl/ (*rather formal, especially written*) (of two actions or ideas) not acceptable or possible together because of basic differences; (of two things) of different types so that they cannot be used or mixed together: *The hours of the job are incompatible with family life.* ◊ *New computer software is often incompatible with older computers.* ◊ *Those two blood groups are incompatible.* **OPP** **compatible** ❶ Actions, ideas or things that are **compatible** can exist or be used together: *compatible software* ◊ *Are measures to protect the environment compatible with economic growth?*
contradictory /ˌkɒntrəˈdɪktəri; *AmE* ˌkɑːn-/ (*rather formal, especially written*) containing or showing a lack of agreement between facts or opinions: *We are faced with two apparently contradictory statements.* ◊ *The advice I received was often contradictory.* See also **contradict** → CONFLICT *verb*, **contradiction** → CONFLICT *noun*
at 'odds *idiom* different from sth, when the two things should be the same: *These findings are at odds with what is going on in the rest of the country.* See also **be at odds** → CONFLICT *verb*
ˌmutually ex'clusive *phrase* (often used in negative statements) (*rather formal, especially written*) not able to exist or be true at the same time as sth else: *The two options are not mutually exclusive* (= you can have them both). ❶ *Not mutually exclusive* is used to talk about things that people might think are different or unable to exist together, but in fact are the same, or quite able to exist together. Typical collocates include *approaches, alternatives, options, assumptions, categories* and *possibilities.*
irreconcilable /ɪˈrekənsaɪləbl; ɪˌrekənˈsaɪləbl/ (*formal*) (of disagreements) so great that it is not possible to settle them; (of two different ideas or opinions) so different that it is impossible for sb to believe them both: *The break-up was due to 'irreconcilable differences'.* ◊ *This view is irreconcilable with common sense.*

increase noun

increase · growth · inflation · rise · gain · surge · hike · spiral · raise · upturn
These words all refer to a situation when the amount, level or number of sth goes up.

PATTERNS AND COLLOCATIONS
▸ an increase/growth/inflation/a rise/a gain/a surge/a hike/a spiral/an upturn **in** sth
▸ an increase/growth/inflation/a rise/a gain/a surge/a hike **of** 20%
▸ (a) **significant/ sharp** increase/ growth/ inflation/ rise/ gain/ surge/ hike/ upturn
▸ (a) **large/ considerable/ huge/ massive** increase/ growth/ inflation/ rise/ gain/ surge/ hike
▸ (a) **sudden** increase/ growth/ inflation/ rise/ gain/ surge/ hike/ upturn
▸ (a) **moderate** increase/ growth/ inflation/ rise/ hike
▸ (a) **slow/ gradual/ steady** increase/ growth/ inflation/ rise/ spiral
▸ (a) **tax/ price/ wage** increase/ growth/ inflation/ rise/ hike/ raise
▸ to **see** an increase/ growth/ inflation/ a rise/ a gain/ a surge/ a hike/ an upturn
▸ to **lead to/ mean/ report** an increase/ growth/ inflation/ a rise/ a gain/ a surge/ a hike
▸ to **cause/ represent** an increase/ growth/ inflation/ a rise/ a gain/ a surge
▸ to **show** an increase/ growth/ a rise/ a gain/ a surge

increase [C, U] a rise in the amount, number or level of sth: *There has been a steady increase in demand for the service. ◇ This year saw an increase of nearly 20% in the number of visitors. ◇ The figures show a significant **increase on** last year's turnover. ◇ Homelessness is **on the increase** (= increasing).* **OPP cut, decrease, reduction** → REDUCTION, See also **increase in sth** → GAIN *verb* 2, **increase** → RISE *verb*

growth [U, sing.] an increase in the size, amount or degree of sth: *The report links population growth with rural poverty. ◇ The growth in average earnings has remained constant. ◇ Recent years have seen a huge growth of interest in alternative medicine* See also **grow** → RISE *verb*

inflation /ɪnˈfleɪʃn/ [U] a rise in the prices of services and goods in a country, resulting in a fall in the value of money; the rate at which this happens: *The bank is introducing new measures to curb inflation ◇ Wage increases must be **in line with inflation** ◇ Inflation is currently **running at** 3%.*

rise [C] an increase in the number, amount or level of sth: *The industry is feeling the effects of recent price rises. ◇ There has been a sharp rise in the number of people out of work.* **OPP fall, decline, drop** → REDUCTION, See also **rise** → RISE *verb*

NOTE INCREASE, GROWTH OR RISE? In many cases you can use any of these words: *a rapid increase/growth/rise in the number of private cars.* **Growth** is often uncountable and is used especially to talk about size: *population growth* is much more typical than 'population increase/rise'. It is also more often used to talk about sth positive: *the growth in earnings/employment/demand.* **Increase** and **rise** are often used to talk about more negative things: *an alarming increase/rise in violent crime.* **Increase** is more general than **rise**, used for things that *increase* by themselves or that *are increased* deliberately by sb. **Rise** is used more for things that *happen to rise*, rather than for deliberate increases. *Price rises* are seen from the point of view of the people buying things, not selling them. Businesses *announce price increases*; customers *feel the effects of price increases/rises.*

gain [C, U] an increase in the amount of sth, especially in wealth or weight: *a £3 000 gain from our investment ◇ Regular exercise is the best way of preventing weight gain.* **OPP loss ❶ Loss** [U, C] is the state of no longer having sth or as much of sth, or the process that leads to this: *weight loss ◇ loss of blood ◇ The closure of the factory will lead to a number of job losses.* See also **loss** → DEBT, **gain** → GAIN *verb* 2

surge /sɜːdʒ; *AmE* sɜːrdʒ/ [C] a sudden increase that happens in the amount or number of sth; a large amount of sth: *Economists have reported a surge in consumer spending. ◇ After an initial surge of interest, there has been little call for our services.* See also **surge** → SOAR *verb*, **surge** → WAVE *noun* 2

hike [C] (*informal, especially journalism*) a large or sudden increase that sb makes in prices or taxes: *Higher crude oil prices mean price hikes for consumers too. ◇ Borrowers will be hit hard by the latest hike in interest rates.*

spiral /ˈspaɪrəl/ [U] a continuous harmful increase in sth, that gradually gets faster and faster: *How can we halt the destructive spiral of violence in the inner cities? ◇ The country is caught in a vicious spiral of rising wages and prices.* **❶ Spiral** can also be used to talk about a similar harmful decrease in sth: *The book gives a harrowing account of a **downward spiral** of drink, drugs and despair.*

raise [C] (*AmE*) an increase in the money you are paid for the work you do: *If I asked my boss for a raise he'd fire me.* **❶** In British English this is called a **rise**.

upturn /ˈʌptɜːn; *AmE* -tɜːrn/ [C, usually sing.] an increase in the amount of business that is done; a time when the economy becomes stronger: *The restaurant trade is on the upturn. ◇ an upturn in the economy* **OPP downturn** → REDUCTION

increase verb

increase · raise · boost · intensify · maximize · heighten · inflate · step sth up · turn sth up
These words all mean to make the amount, number or level of sth bigger or greater.

PATTERNS AND COLLOCATIONS
▸ to increase/ raise/ boost/ inflate/ step up sth **by** 15%, 250, £100, a third, etc.
▸ to increase/ raise/ boost/ inflate/ step up sth **from** 150, $500, etc
▸ to increase/ raise/ boost/ inflate/ step up sth **to** 150, $500, etc
▸ to increase/ raise/ boost/ maximize/ inflate **prices**
▸ to increase/ raise/ boost/ maximize your **income**
▸ to increase/ raise/ boost/ heighten **awareness/ interest**
▸ to increase/ raise/ boost/ maximize **support**
▸ to increase/ raise/ boost **confidence**
▸ to increase/ raise/ intensify/ step up the **pressure**
▸ to increase/ intensify/ maximize/ heighten/ step up **security**
▸ to increase/ raise/ boost/ intensify/ heighten/ inflate sth **greatly/ further**

increase [T] to make sth greater in amount, number, level, degree or value: *We need to increase productivity. ◇ They've increased the price by 50%. ◇ Last month the reward was increased from £20 000 to £40 000.* **OPP decrease, reduce** → REDUCE, See also **increase** → RISE *verb*
▸ **increased** *adj.* [only before noun]: *increased demand/ pressure/ spending*

raise [T] to increase the amount or level of sth: *The government has promised not to raise taxes. ◇ They raised their offer to $500. ◇ How can we raise standards in schools? ◇ Don't tell her about the job until you know for sure – we don't want to **raise her hopes** (= make her hope too much). ◇ I've never heard him even **raise his voice** (= speak louder because he was angry).* **OPP lower** → REDUCE

NOTE INCREASE OR RAISE? In many cases you can use either word. **Increase** is slightly more frequent when talking about numbers, prices and figures; **raise** is more useful for abstract nouns such as feelings and qualities: *to raise interest/awareness.* **Raise** is also used in idiomatic expressions such as *raise sb's hopes* and *raise your voice.*

boost /buːst/ [T] (*often approving, especially journalism*) to make sth increase, or become better or more successful: *The new service helped to boost pre-tax profits by 10%.* ◇ *A last-minute rush by Christmas shoppers boosted sales.* ◇ *Getting that job did a lot to boost his ego* (= make him feel more confident). ❶ **Boost** is always used to talk about a positive increase: *to boost productivity/sales/spending* ◇ *to boost sb's morale/career/confidence* ◇ ~~to boost taxes/pressure/tension~~

intensify /ɪnˈtensɪfaɪ/ [T, I] to increase an activity or feeling in degree or strength; (of an activity or feeling) to increase in degree or strength: *The opposition leader has intensified his attacks on the government.* ◇ *The reforms served only to intensify the misery of the poorer peasants.* ◇ *Violence intensified during the night.*

maximize (*BrE* also **-ise**) [T] (*rather formal, especially business*) to increase sth as much as possible; to make the best use of sth: *They drew up a six-point plan to maximize safety and efficiency in the use of the equipment.* ◇ (*computing*) *Maximize the window to full screen.* ◇ *The purpose of the restructuring is to maximize opportunities in the global market.* **OPP minimize** → REDUCE

heighten /ˈhaɪtn/ [T, I] to increase an effect or feeling or make it stronger; (of an effect or feeling) to increase or become stronger: *Fears of further racial conflict were heightened by news of the riots.* ◇ *Tension heightened after the recent bomb attack.*

NOTE INTENSIFY OR **HEIGHTEN?** Although both verbs can be used with or without an object, **heighten** is more often used with an object. **Heighten** is used especially to talk about feelings and attitudes; **intensify** can apply to actions too: *a heightened sense of loneliness/well-being* ◇ *to intensify the campaign/battle*

inflate /ɪnˈfleɪt/ [T] (*often disapproving, especially journalism*) to increase the price of sth: *The principal effect of the demand for new houses was to inflate prices.* ◇ *The profit margin had been artificially inflated.* ❶ **Inflate** can also be used without an object, but this is less frequent: [I] *House prices are no longer inflating at the same rate as last year.*

step sth 'up *phrasal verb* (-**pp**-) to increase the level of an activity: *He has stepped up his training to prepare for the race.* ◇ *Security has been stepped up in response to the recent terrorist threat.*

turn sth 'up *phrasal verb* to increase the noise, heat or light produced by a piece of equipment by moving its controls: *Could you turn the TV up?* ◇ *The music was turned up loud.* **OPP turn sth down** → REDUCE, See also **turn sth on** → TURN STH ON

incredible *adj.* See also the entry for UNLIKELY 2

incredible · unbelievable · beyond belief
These words all describe things that are very difficult to believe.

PATTERNS AND COLLOCATIONS
▸ incredible / unbelievable **to** sb
▸ to be incredible / unbelievable / beyond belief **that**...
▸ incredible / unbelievable **as it may seem**...
▸ to **find** sth incredible / unbelievable
▸ almost incredible / unbelievable / beyond belief
▸ completely / totally / just / quite / simply incredible / unbelievable

incredible /ɪnˈkredəbl/ impossible or very difficult to believe: *The speed of her recovery seems almost incredible.* ◇ *It's just incredible to me that only one person was hurt.* *It's incredible to think that the affair had been going on for years.* **OPP credible** → POSSIBLE 2
▸ **incredibly** *adv.*: *Incredibly, a year later the same thing happened again.*

unbelievable /ˌʌnbɪˈliːvəbl/ very difficult to believe and unlikely to be true: *It's all so unbelievable!* ◇ *It seemed unbelievable, but it was true.* ◇ *I found the ending of the novel a bit unbelievable.* **OPP believable** → POSSIBLE 2

▸ **unbelievably** *adv.*: *It was published, unbelievably, almost fifty years ago.*

NOTE INCREDIBLE OR **UNBELIEVABLE?** If you describe sth as **incredible** you usually have accepted that it is true, even though you still find it very difficult to believe. (There are exceptions to this when the context makes it clear that you do not believe sth: *You surely don't believe this incredible accusation against him?*) If you describe sth as **unbelievable**, you probably don't quite believe that it is true or possible.

beyond be'lief *idiom* (in a way that is) too great, difficult or shocking to be believed: *It is beyond belief that anyone could commit such a crime.* ◇ *Dissatisfaction with the government has grown beyond belief.* ❶ **Beyond belief** is used especially to express or describe negative feelings or opinions.

independence *noun*

independence · autonomy · sovereignty · self-determination · self-government
These are all words for the freedom a country or region has to govern itself without political control from other countries.

PATTERNS AND COLLOCATIONS
▸ independence / autonomy / sovereignty / self-determination / self-government **for** sb
▸ **complete** / **full** independence / autonomy / sovereignty
▸ **national** independence / autonomy / sovereignty / self-determination
▸ **local** / **regional** autonomy / self-determination / self-government
▸ **political** independence / autonomy / sovereignty / self-determination
▸ to **achieve** independence / autonomy / sovereignty / self-determination / self-government
▸ to **have** / **enjoy** / **give sb** / **grant sb** / **recognize sth's** independence / autonomy / sovereignty
▸ the **principle** / **right of** autonomy / sovereignty / self-determination / self-government

independence [U] a country's freedom from political control by other countries, especially after a period of outside control; the time when a country becomes politically independent: *Cuba gained* **independence from** *Spain in 1898.* ◇ *There has been international recognition for the island's* **declaration of independence.** ◇ *Namibia became a full member of the UN* **at independence** (= when it became independent). ◇ *Malaysia celebrates its* **independence day** *on 31st August.* See also **independence** → FREEDOM
▸ **independent** *adj.*: *Mozambique became independent in 1975.*

autonomy /ɔːˈtɒnəmi; *AmE* ɔːˈtɑːn-/ [U] (*rather formal, written*) freedom for a country or region to govern itself independently: *There has been a campaign for greater autonomy for the region.* See also **autonomy** → FREEDOM
▸ **autonomous** /ɔːˈtɒnəməs; *AmE* ɔːˈtɑːn-/ *adj.: an autonomous republic/state/province*

NOTE INDEPENDENCE OR **AUTONOMY?** In this meaning **independence** usually means the complete freedom for a whole country from outside political control, and a country either has **independence** or it has not. **Autonomy** is usually a degree of freedom that is less than complete independence.

sovereignty /ˈsɒvrənti; *AmE* ˈsɑːv-/ [U] (*written*) the state of being a country with freedom to govern itself: *The declaration proclaimed the full sovereignty of the republic.* ◇ *She has strong views on preserving national sovereignty.*
▸ **sovereign** *adj.: a sovereign state*

self-de termi'nation [U] (*rather formal, written*) the right of a country and its people to govern themselves and choose their own political system: *All nations have the right to self-determination.*

self-'government [U] the government or control of a country or organization by its own people or members, not by others: *There have been demands for a wider measure of regional self-government.*

independent *adj.*

independent · unrelated · unconnected · self-contained · free-standing · divorced from sth
These words all describe things which are not connected to each other, or to sth else.

PATTERNS AND COLLOCATIONS
▶ unrelated / unconnected **to** sth
▶ an independent / a self-contained / a free-standing **unit**
▶ independent / unrelated **data**
▶ unrelated / unconnected **events**
▶ **reasons** unrelated / unconnected to sth
▶ **wholly** unrelated / unconnected / self-contained / divorced

independent (especially of groups and organizations) not connected with or influenced by sth; not connected with each other: *The police force should be independent of direct government control.* ◇ *Two independent research bodies reached the same conclusions.*

unrelated (of facts, activities and events) not connected to sth; not connected with each other: *In my free time I like to do things that are unrelated to my work.* ◇ *The two events were totally unrelated.* **OPP** **related** → RELATED

unconnected (of facts and events) not connected to sth; not connected to each other: *The two crimes are apparently unconnected.* ◇ *Her employers insisted she had been dismissed for reasons unconnected with her pregnancy.* **OPP** **connected** → RELATED

NOTE UNRELATED OR UNCONNECTED? In many cases you can use either word. However, when you are talking about people, **unrelated** means 'not in the same family': *The judge was unrelated to the company representatives* (= he was not their father, brother, cousin, etc.). ◇ *The judge was unconnected with the company representatives* (= he did not have any link with them).

self-con'tained able to operate or exist without outside help or influence: *The village was an isolated and self-contained community.* ◇ *Each chapter is self-contained and can be studied in isolation.*

free-'standing [usually before noun] not supported by or attached to anything; not a part of anything else: *We can supply both free-standing and wall-mounted gas boilers.* ◇ *Modules may be offered as free-standing units or in integrated programmes of study.*

divorced from sth *phrase* (*formal*) appearing not to be affected by sth; separate from sth: *He seems completely divorced from reality.* ◇ *Studying history at school was about learning facts completely divorced from their meaning.*

indifferent *adj.* See also the entry for CASUAL

indifferent · lukewarm · unimpressed · half-hearted · uninterested · detached · apathetic · tepid
These words all describe a person or their behaviour when they show no interest or enthusiasm.

PATTERNS AND COLLOCATIONS
▶ indifferent / lukewarm / half-hearted / apathetic **about** sth
▶ indifferent / lukewarm / apathetic **towards** sb / sth
▶ lukewarm / half-hearted / uninterested **in** sth
▶ an indifferent / a lukewarm / a detached / an apathetic **attitude**

indifferent /ɪnˈdɪfrənt/ [not usually before noun] having or showing no interest in sb/sth: *Public opinion remained largely indifferent to the issue.*
▶ **indifference** *noun* [U, sing.]: *What she said is a matter of complete indifference to me.*

lukewarm /ˌluːkˈwɔːm; *AmE* -ˈwɔːrm/ not interested or enthusiastic: *Union leaders were at best lukewarm in their response.* ◇ *He was disappointed by the lukewarm support from Washington.* **OPP** **enthusiastic** → EAGER

unimpressed [not usually before noun] not thinking or that sb/sth is particularly good or interesting: *The city remained unimpressed by the chancellor's speech.* ◇ *Voters are unimpressed with his performance so far.* ◇ *She looked distinctly unimpressed.* **OPP** **impressed** ❶ If you are **impressed** you feel admiration for sb/sth because you think they are particularly good or interesting: *I must admit I am impressed.* See also **impress** → IMPRESS

half-'hearted done without enthusiasm or effort: *He made a half-hearted attempt to justify the decision.*

uninterested [not usually before noun] not interested; not wanting to know about sb/sth: *They were totally uninterested in politics.* **OPP** **interested** → INTERESTED, See also **uninteresting** → BORING

detached /dɪˈtætʃt/ (*especially written*) showing a lack of feeling: *He was able to talk about it in a cold, detached manner.* ◇ *She spoke in a normal, detached tone.*
▶ **detachment** *noun* [U]: *He answered with an air of detachment.*

apathetic /ˌæpəˈθetɪk/ (*rather formal, especially written*) showing no interest or enthusiasm: *She became apathetic and withdrawn.*
▶ **apathy** /ˈæpəθi/ *noun* [U]: *There is widespread apathy among the electorate.*

tepid /ˈtepɪd/ (*especially business*) not enthusiastic: *The play was greeted with tepid applause.* ◇ *The deal drew a tepid response from shareholders.*

industry *noun* See also the entry for BUSINESS 2

industry · trade · business · service
These are all words for a type of activity that involves producing goods or providing services.

PATTERNS AND COLLOCATIONS
▶ to be **in** a particular industry / trade / business / service
▶ the **book** / **tourist** / **car** / **catering** / **hotel** / **construction** industry / trade / business
▶ the **timber** / **fur** / **wool** / **wine** / **motor** / **building** industry / trade
▶ the **energy** / **oil** / **food** / **computer** / **advertising** / **insurance** / **entertainment** / **music** / **film** / **hospitality** industry / business
▶ **computer** / **insurance** / **catering** services
▶ to **work in** a particular industry / trade / business / service
▶ to **enter** / **dominate** the industry / trade / business

industry [C] the people and activities involved in producing a particular thing, or in providing a particular service: *Thousands of jobs were lost in the steel industry.* ◇ *We need to develop local industries.* ◇ *Weaving and knitting were traditional cottage industries* (= small businesses in which the work is done by people in their homes). ❶ **Industry** is mainly used to talk about the production of goods, especially in factories. When it is used to talk about a service, this is usually one that has become very successful: *the film / entertainment / tourist / advertising / insurance industry* See also **industry** → PRODUCTION

trade [C] a particular type of industry or business: *Employment in the building trade is notoriously irregular.* ◇ *He works in the retail trade* (= selling goods in shops). ❶ **Trade** is used more to talk about activities that do not require a high level of formal education, such as *the building / motor / construction trade*, or the buying and selling aspect of a particular activity: *the book / retail / car trade.* **The trade** [sing.+ sing./pl. *v.*] is a particular area of industry or business and the people or companies that are connected with it: *They offer discounts to the trade* (= to people who are working in the same business). ◇ *You should advertise in newspapers and trade magazines.* See also **trade** → TRADE *noun*, **trade** → WORK *noun* 2

business [C] a particular type of activity that involves producing, buying, selling or providing goods or services for money: *She works in the computer business.* ◇ *Falling prices are wreaking havoc in the oil business.* ❶ **Business**

places the emphasis more on the management activities involved in an industry or service, than on the physical work involved. It is used especially to talk about service industries: *the catering/hotel/entertainment/advertising/ insurance business.* It is also used to talk about very large industries that produce or trade in very basic products or raw materials, where it is a slightly more informal choice than **industry**, used especially in journalism: *the energy/ oil/food business.* See also **business** → COMPANY, **business** → TRADE

service [C, usually pl.] a business whose work involves doing sth for customers but not producing goods: *They are offering special incentives to the financial services sector.* ◇ *The service industries were most affected by the recession.* ❶ **Services** is often used in the plural after an adjective or noun: *computer/catering/financial/insur-ance/marketing/freight/accommodation services.* **Service** is not usually used alone; when it does not follow an adjective or noun in this way, it is generally followed by a word like *company, industry* or *sector.*

ineffective *adj.*

ineffective · inefficient · unproductive · counterproductive · ineffectual · self-defeating
These words all describe sth that does not achieve what is wanted or intended, or sb/sth that does not achieve very much.

PATTERNS AND COLLOCATIONS
▸ ineffective / inefficient / counterproductive **for** sb / sth
▸ ineffective / ineffectual **as** sth
▸ ineffective / inefficient **in / at** doing sth
▸ to be ineffective / inefficient / counterproductive / self-defeating **to do** sth
▸ largely ineffective / unproductive / ineffectual / self-defeating
▸ rather ineffective / inefficient / ineffectual
▸ relatively ineffective / inefficient / unproductive
▸ entirely ineffective / unproductive / counterproductive

ineffective not achieving what you want it to achieve; not having any effect: *It has been criticized as an unfair and ineffective system.* ◇ *The missiles are totally ineffective against tanks.* ◇ *High interest rates proved to be ineffective in reducing inflation.* **OPP** **effective** → SUCCESSFUL 1
▸ **ineffectively** *adv.*: *Why is this crime dealt with so ineffectively?* **OPP** **effectively** → SUCCESSFUL 1
inefficient /ˌɪnɪˈfɪʃnt/ not doing a job well and not making the best use of time, money, energy, etc: *The regime was both inefficient and corrupt.* ◇ *The boss thinks the new secretary is inefficient.* ◇ *This method of data storage is an inefficient use of memory.* **OPP** **efficient** → EFFICIENT
▸ **inefficiency** *noun* [U, pl.]: *The measures encouraged inefficiency and waste.* ◇ *inefficiencies in the system* **OPP** **efficiency** → EFFICIENCY
▸ **inefficiently** *adv.*: *The firm was inefficiently run.* **OPP** **efficiently** → EFFICIENT
unproductive not producing or achieving very much; not producing good results: *I've spent yet another unproduc-tive day.* ◇ *We had a series of unproductive meetings.* **OPP** **productive** → PRODUCTIVE
counterproductive [not usually before noun] having the opposite effect to the one intended: *Increases in taxation would be counterproductive.* ◇ *It would be counterproduc-tive to act hastily at this stage.*
ineffectual /ˌɪnɪˈfektʃuəl/ (*formal*) (of a person) not achieving much; weak; (of an action) not achieving what you want it to achieve: *The president is seen as weak and ineffectual.* ◇ *She made an ineffectual grab at the book.* ❶ **Ineffectual** is used especially when sb/sth does not achieve much because of weakness or lack of the necessary ability and is used especially about people and their attempts to do sth.
▸ **ineffectually** *adv.*: *He struggled ineffectually to get out from behind the wheel.*

self-de'feating causing more problems and difficulties instead of solving them; having the opposite effect to the one intended: *Paying children too much attention when they misbehave can be self-defeating.*

inequality *noun* See the Topic Map for THE INDIVIDUAL AND SOCIETY on p.894

inequality · injustice · unfairness · inequity
These are all words for an unfair difference between groups of people in society, by which some people have more money, power or opportunities than others.

PATTERNS AND COLLOCATIONS
▸ inequality / injustice / unfairness / inequity **in** sth
▸ inequality / inequity **between** sb / sth
▸ injustice / unfairness **to** sb / sth
▸ social / economic / racial inequality / injustice / inequity
▸ great / gross inequality / injustice / inequity
▸ to fight / tackle / struggle against inequality / injustice
▸ to redress / rectify / remedy inequality / injustice / inequity

inequality /ˌɪnɪˈkwɒləti; *AmE* -ˈkwɑːl-/ [U, C] the unfair difference between groups of people in society, by which some have more money, power or opportunities than others: *There is generally some inequality between men and women within the family.* ◇ *Inequalities in health tend to reflect inequalities in income.* **OPP** **equality** → JUSTICE, See also **unequal** → WRONG 4
injustice /ɪnˈdʒʌstɪs/ [U, C] the fact of a situation being unfair, when people do not get what they deserve; an unfair act or an example of unfair treatment: *I did not really see myself as a victim of injustice.* ◇ *Perhaps I'm doing you an injustice* (= being unfair to you). ◇ *The report exposes the injustices of the system.* **OPP** **justice** → JUSTICE, See also **unjust** → WRONG 4
unfairness [U] the fact of a situation being unfair, when people do not get what they deserve, especially when some people are treated better than others for no good reason: *There are several examples of unfairness in the recruitment system.* ◇ *She was still raging about the unfairness of it all.* **OPP** **fairness** → JUSTICE, See also **unfair** → WRONG 4
inequity /ɪnˈekwəti/ [C, U] (*formal*) something that is unfair because it treats different people or groups differently; the state of being unfair in this way: *There are huge inequities in funding for schools.* ◇ *The new government sought to justify social inequity by promoting ideals of self-help.* **OPP** **equity** → JUSTICE

inevitable *adj.*

inevitable · necessary · unavoidable · inescapable · inexorable
These words all describe sth that is impossible to avoid or prevent.

PATTERNS AND COLLOCATIONS
▸ an inevitable / a necessary / an unavoidable **consequence**
▸ an inevitable / a necessary / an inescapable **conclusion / fact**
▸ an inevitable / unavoidable **delay / problem**
▸ an inevitable / inescapable **fact**
▸ the inevitable / inexorable **slide** into / towards war, fascism, mediocrity, etc.
▸ the inevitable / inexorable **decline / rise** (of sth)
▸ seemingly inevitable / unavoidable / inescapable / inexorable
▸ almost inevitable / unavoidable / inescapable

inevitable /ɪnˈevɪtəbl/ (especially of sth unpleasant) that you cannot avoid or prevent: *It was an inevitable consequence of the decision.* ◇ *It was inevitable that there would be job losses.* ◇ *A rise in interest rates seems inevitable.* See also **inevitability** → CERTAINTY
▸ **the inevitable** *noun* [sing.]: *You have to accept the inevitable.*
▸ **inevitably** *adv.*: *Inevitably, the press exaggerated the story.*

necessary [only before noun] (*rather formal, written*) that must exist or happen and cannot be avoided: *A necessary condition for a steep fall in demand is a widespread collapse in confidence.* ◇ *This is a necessary consequence of progress.*
ⓘ In this meaning **necessary** is used especially to describe the *conditions* or *prerequisites* that must exist before a particular thing can happen; or the *results*, *outcome* or *consequence* that must happen in a particular situation or after a particular event. See also **necessary** → NECESSARY
▶ **necessarily** *adv.*: *The number of places available is necessarily limited.*

unavoidable /ˌʌnəˈvɔɪdəbl/ (of sth unpleasant) that you cannot avoid or prevent: *All dates are approximate and are subject to unavoidable delays.* **OPP** **avoidable** → UNNECESSARY
▶ **unavoidably** *adv.*: *I was unavoidably delayed.*

NOTE **INEVITABLE** OR **UNAVOIDABLE?** Inevitable is much more frequent than **unavoidable** and has a much wider range of collocates. **Unavoidable** always describes sth unpleasant, especially *delays* and *consequences*. Things that are **inevitable** are often unpleasant, but do not have to be; collocates include *change, comparison, conclusion, development, effect, outcome, part, product, question, response, result, tendency, conflict, tension* and *disappointment*.

inescapable /ˌɪnɪˈskeɪpəbl/ (of a fact or situation) that you cannot avoid or ignore: *It is an inescapable fact that how we eat affects how we feel.*
▶ **inescapably** *adv.*: *Despite its remodelling, the building remains inescapably linked to the past.*

inexorable /ɪnˈeksərəbl/ (*formal*) (of a process) that cannot be stopped or changed; (of logic) that cannot be argued against: *What is the reason for the inexorable rise in crime?* ◇ *This is where the **inexorable logic** of the theory breaks down.*
▶ **inexorably** *adv.*: *Pressure of population is leading inexorably towards a crisis.*

(be) **in favour (of sb/sth)** (*BrE*) (*AmE* **(be) in favor (of sb/sth)**) *phrase* See also the entry for SUPPORT 1

(be) in favour (of sb/sth) · **approve** · **believe in sth** · **subscribe to sth** · **be all for sth**
These verbs and phrases all mean to think that sth is good, acceptable or suitable.

PATTERNS AND COLLOCATIONS
▶ to be in favour of / approve of / believe in / subscribe to / be all for a(n) **idea** / **view**
▶ to be in favour of / approve of / be all for a **plan** / **course of action** / **policy** / **strategy** / **suggestion**
▶ to approve / believe in sth / subscribe to sth **wholeheartedly**
▶ to **fully** approve / subscribe to sth
▶ to **strongly** approve / believe in sth
▶ to be **wholeheartedly** / **fully** / **strongly** / **very much** / **thoroughly** in favour (of sth / sth)
▶ to **wholeheartedly** / **fully** / **strongly** / **very much** / **thoroughly** approve (of sth)

(be) in favour (of sb/sth) (*BrE*) (*AmE* **(be) in favor (of sb/sth)**) *phrase* to support and agree with sb/sth, especially a policy or plan that will affect a lot of people: *He argued in favour of a strike.* ◇ *There were 247 votes in favour (of the motion) and 152 against.* ◇ *I'm **all in favour of** (= completely support) equal pay for equal work.* ◇ *Most of the 'don't knows' in the opinion polls came down in favour of (= eventually chose to support) the Democrats.* **OPP** **opposed** → AGAINST SB/STH

approve *verb* [I] (not used in the progressive tenses) to think that sb/sth is good, acceptable or suitable: *I told my mother I wanted to leave school but she didn't approve.* ◇ *Do you **approve of** my idea?* ◇ *She doesn't approve of me leaving school this year.* **OPP** **disapprove** → DISAPPROVE, See also **approval** → PRAISE *noun*, **approving** → GOOD 6

NOTE **(BE) IN FAVOUR (OF SB/STH)** OR **APPROVE?** In favour is often used about sth that people might vote on, for example a government policy or a business strategy: *All those in favour, please raise your hand.* ◇ ~~In the class vote, three approved of the idea, four didn't.~~ **Approve** is used to talk about more personal matters that affect the actions you take and the way you live your life. It can be used to describe what parents, teachers, bosses, etc. think of the actions, plans or ideas of their children, students, employees, etc.: *I don't think your mother would approve of this behaviour, do you?* ◇ ~~My mother wasn't in favour of my behaviour.~~

be'lieve in sth/in doing sth *phrasal verb* (not used in the progressive tenses) to think that a way of doing sth or a way of behaving is good, right or acceptable: *I don't believe in hitting children.* ◇ *Do you believe in capital punishment?* **ⓘ** Believe in sth is used to talk about sth that you agree/don't agree with because of the principles involved and the way you would like to live your life. See also **belief** → FAITH

sub'scribe to sth *phrasal verb* (*formal*) to agree with or support an opinion or theory: *The authorities no longer subscribe to the view that disabled people are unsuitable as teachers.* **ⓘ** The most frequent noun collocate of **subscribe to sth** is *view*. Other common collocates are *opinion, theory, idea* and *belief*.

be all for sth/for doing sth *phrase* (*informal*) to believe strongly that sth should be done: *They're all for saving money where they can.* ◇ *What's the matter? You were all for it yesterday!* **ⓘ** This expression is sometimes used when you do not approve of an idea, suggestion, etc. that is closely connected or follows on from the first: *I'm all for giving people a second chance, but I'm afraid he's messed up too many times. I can't take him back.*

influence *noun*

influence · **force** · **example** · **lead**
These are all words for a person or action that other people copy or that affects the way a person behaves or thinks.

PATTERNS AND COLLOCATIONS
▶ an influence / example **for** sb
▶ an influence / a force **for** sth
▶ a **great** influence / force / example
▶ a **bad** influence / example
▶ a **decisive** / **positive** / **strong** influence / force / lead
▶ a **moral** influence / force / lead
▶ to **follow** sb's example / lead

influence [C] a person or thing that affects the way sb behaves or thinks: *She was by far the biggest **influence on** my writing.* ◇ *Those friends are a bad influence on her.* ◇ *Who were your early influences?* ◇ *There seem to be several influences at work in his paintings.*

force [C] a person or thing that has a lot of power to affect what happens or the way people behave or think: *The expansion of higher education was a powerful force for change.* ◇ *Many social and economic forces contributed to this trend.* ◇ *They see the world as a battleground between the forces of good and evil.* ◇ *Ron is the **driving force** (= the person who has the most influence) behind the project.*

example [C, usually sing.] a person's behaviour, either good or bad, that other people copy: *You're **setting a bad example to** the children.* ◇ *It would be a mistake to follow his example.* See also **example** → EXAMPLE 2

lead /liːd/ [sing.] an example or action for people to copy: *If one bank raises interest rates, others will follow their lead.* ◇ *Intellectuals **took the lead** in criticism of the government.* ◇ *You go first, I'll **take my lead from** you.*

influence *verb* See also the entry for AFFECT

influence · sway · prejudice · sour · poison · bias
These words all mean to affect the way that sb thinks or behaves, or to change sb's opinion about sb/sth, especially in a negative or unfair way.

PATTERNS AND COLLOCATIONS
▸ to influence / sway / prejudice / poison / bias sb / sth **against** sb / sth
▸ to influence / sway / bias sb / sth **in favour of** sb / sth
▸ to influence / bias sb / sth **towards / toward** sb / sth
▸ to influence / sway / bias the **result** of sth
▸ to influence / prejudice the **outcome** of sth
▸ to influence / sway a **decision**
▸ to sour / poison **relations / the atmosphere**
▸ to be **easily** influenced / swayed (by sth)

influence [T] to have an effect on the way that sb behaves or thinks, especially by giving them an example to follow: *His writings have influenced the lives of millions.* ◇ *Her parents tried to* **influence her** *in her choice of career.* ◇ *The wording of the question can* **influence how** *people answer.* See also **influence** → AFFECT *verb*

sway [T, often passive] to persuade or influence sb to believe sth or do sth, especially when they are forming an opinion or making a decision: *The panel was not swayed by his arguments.* ◇ *Don't allow yourself to be swayed by emotion.* ◇ *The speech was important in swaying public opinion.*

prejudice [T] to persuade or influence sb so that they have an unfair or unreasonable opinion about sb/sth: *Some argued that the media attention had prejudiced the jury.* ◇ *Poor handwriting might prejudice people against the applicant.* See also **prejudiced** → BIASED *adj.*

sour [I, T] (*written*) (of relationships, attitudes, situations or people) to change so that they become less pleasant or friendly than before; to make sth do this: *The atmosphere in the house had soured.* ◇ *The disagreement over trade tariffs soured relations between the two countries.* See also **sour** → BITTER *adj.* 2

poison [T] (*written*) to change a relationship, situation or opinion so that it becomes unpleasant or unfriendly: *She succeeded in* **poisoning their minds** *against me.* ◇ *His comment served only to poison the atmosphere still further.*

NOTE SOUR OR POISON? **Poison** is usually stronger than **sour**. If sth **sours** a relationship or situation it becomes less pleasant or friendly than before. If sth **poisons** it, it becomes very unpleasant or unfriendly, often involving strong feelings of anger or dislike.

bias /'baɪəs/ [T] to have an unfair effect on sb's decisions or opinions; to change the result of sth so that it is not correct: *The newspapers have biased people against her.* ◇ *The use of faulty equipment may have biased the result.* See also **biased** → BIASED *adj.*

informal *adj.*

informal · relaxed · casual
These words all describe occasions or places where you do not have to follow strict rules of how to behave, or the clothes that are suitable for these occasions.

PATTERNS AND COLLOCATIONS
▸ an informal / a relaxed **atmosphere**
▸ informal / casual **dress**

informal not following strict rules of how to behave or do sth, in a way that is pleasant and friendly; (of clothes) suitable for wearing at home or when relaxing rather than for a special or official occasion: *Discussions are held on an informal basis within the department.* ◇ *Dress is informal, and storage space often limited, so you'll be more comfortable travelling light.* **OPP** **formal** → FORMAL, **formal** → OFFICIAL
▸ **informally** *adv.*: *They told me informally* (= not officially) *that I had got the job.* ◇ *to dress informally*

relaxed (of a place) calm and informal: *It's a family-run hotel with a relaxed atmosphere.*

casual /'kæʒuəl/ (of clothes) informal: *She felt comfortable in casual clothes and wore them most of the time.* **OPP** **formal** → FORMAL

NOTE INFORMAL OR **CASUAL**? When you are talking about clothes, **casual** is more frequent than **informal**. You can talk about *informal/casual dress* when you mean informal/casual clothes in general, but to talk about particular items of clothing use **casual**: *a casual shirt/ jacket* ◇ *casual shoes* ◇ (*BrE*) *casual trousers* ◇ (*AmE*) *casual pants* ◇ ~~informal shirts/jackets/shoes/trousers/ pants~~.

information *noun* See the Topic Map for FACT AND OPINION on p.898, See also the entries for FIGURE, NEWS and SITUATION

information · data · detail · fact · point · material · intelligence · particular · info
These are all words for things about a situation, person, etc. that you know about, can find out about, or that are true.

PATTERNS AND COLLOCATIONS
▸ information / data / a detail / a fact / a point / material / intelligence / particulars / info **about / relating to** sb / sth
▸ information / data / material / intelligence / info **on** sb / sth
▸ information / intelligence / the fact / the point **that...**
▸ (an) **important** information / data / detail / fact / point / material / intelligence / particular / info
▸ **accurate / precise** information / data / details / facts / intelligence / info
▸ (a) **detailed** information / data / facts / point / material / intelligence / particulars
▸ **hard** information / data / facts / intelligence
▸ (a / an) **further / additional** information / data / details / fact / point / material / intelligence / particulars / info
▸ to **have** information / data / details / the facts / intelligence / particulars / info
▸ to **collect / gather** information / data / details / facts / material / intelligence / info
▸ to **get / receive** information / data / details / intelligence / info
▸ to **record** information / data / details / facts / info
▸ to **give (sb)** information / data / details / the facts / particulars / info
▸ to **provide** information / data / details / material / particulars / info
▸ a **piece** of information / data / intelligence

information [U] things that you know, are told, or can find out about sb/sth: *Do you have any information about local buses?* ◇ *He is accused of giving false information to the police.* ◇ *Information is stored on their computerized databases.* ◇ *For further information, contact us at the above address.* ◇ *You can go to the* **information desk** *for help.* ◇ *This letter is* **for information only**. See also **inform** → TELL 1

data [U] information that has been gathered about sth, especially when it is examined and used to find out things or to make decisions; information that is stored on a computer: *They are not allowed to hold data on people's private finances.* ◇ *What methods are you using to interpret the data?* ◇ *There is no hard data to support this theory.* ◇ *This is just* **raw data** (= data that has not been examined). ◇ *One vital item of data was missing.* ❶ **Data** is usually treated as an uncountable noun, but it is used as a plural noun in technical English, when the singular is **datum**: (*technical*) *These data were collected over a period of several months.*

detail [C] a small individual piece of information about what sth is like or what needs to be done; a less important piece of information: *The expedition was planned down to the last detail.* ◇ *He stood still, absorbing* every detail of his surroundings. ◊ Oh that's *just a detail* – we can deal with it later. ◊ Sharon *will fill you in on the details* (= tell you them). ❶ **Details** [pl.] are information, especially pieces of practical information about a person, event, service, etc. or the complete information about sth that happened: *Our personnel officer will take your details* (= take information about you). ◊ *'We had a terrible time.' 'Oh, spare me the details* (= I do not want to know all the details)*!'* See also **detail** → LIST *verb*, **detailed** → DETAILED

fact [C] a thing that is known to be true, especially sth that can be proved: *First, let's look at some basic facts about healthy eating.* ◊ *I've asked to see all the facts and figures before I make a decision.* ◊ *I wish you'd get your facts right!* ◊ *The judge ordered both lawyers to stick to the facts.* ◊ *It's time you learnt to face the facts* (= accept reality). ◊ *I know for a fact that he's involved in something illegal.* See also **fact** → FACT, **factual** → RELIABLE 2

point [C] a particular detail or fact: *Here are the main points of the news.* ◊ *Could you explain that point again?* ◊ *There are one or two points that aren't yet clear.*

material [U] information or ideas used in books, etc: *She's collecting material for her next novel.*

intelligence [U] secret information that is collected about enemies or criminals; the people that collect this information: *They had obtained secret intelligence about enemy plans.* ◊ *Intelligence sources* (= people who give this information) *report that a terrorist attack is highly probable.* ◊ *He's head of military intelligence.*

particular [C, usually pl.] (*formal*) a fact or detail, especially one that is officially written down: *The police officer took down all the particulars of the burglary.* ◊ *The new contract will be the same in every particular as the old one.* ❶ **Particulars** [pl.] are written information or details about a property, business, job, etc.: *We asked for the particulars of the house.*

info /ˈɪnfəʊ; AmE ˈɪnfoʊ/ [U] (*informal*) information: *Have you had any more info about the job yet?* ❶ **Info** is an informal word, often used to talk about details of sth such as a job, course or event, and often comes in printed form. **Info-** can also be used as a prefix in words such as *infosheet* and *infopack*: *We send all potential clients an infopack.*

informative *adj.*

informative · revealing · instructive · illuminating · telling · enlightening
These are all words describing sth that gives you information about sth.

PATTERNS AND COLLOCATIONS
▶ informative / revealing / instructive / illuminating / enlightening **about** sth
▶ to be instructive / illuminating / enlightening **to do sth**
▶ an informative / a revealing / an illuminating / a telling / an enlightening **insight / account**
▶ a revealing / an illuminating / a telling / an enlightening **comment**
▶ a revealing / an instructive / an illuminating / a telling **example**
▶ to **find sth** informative / instructive / illuminating / enlightening
▶ **very** informative / revealing / instructive / illuminating / telling / enlightening
▶ **highly / extremely / particularly / most** informative / revealing / instructive / illuminating / enlightening
▶ **not very** informative / revealing / instructive / illuminating / enlightening

informative /ɪnˈfɔːmətɪv; AmE -ˈfɔːrm-/ (of a written or spoken source of information) giving useful information: *The talk was both entertaining and informative.* ◊ *The book is not very informative about local customs.* **OPP** **uninformative** ❶ Something that is **uninformative** does not give enough information: *The reports of the explosion were brief and uninformative.* See also **inform** → TELL 1

revealing giving you interesting information that you did not know before: *The answers the students gave were extremely revealing.* ◊ *It was a most revealing remark.* ❶ A **revealing** remark or answer may actually tell you more about the speaker, their thoughts and attitudes, than they thought or knew they were telling you. See also **reveal** → REVEAL

instructive /ɪnˈstrʌktɪv/ (of an experience or activity) giving useful information: *It was a most instructive experience.* ◊ *He said he had found the meeting 'extremely instructive'.*

NOTE **INFORMATIVE** OR **INSTRUCTIVE**? Things that you read or hear may be **informative**; things that you do or experience may be **instructive**.

illuminating /ɪˈluːmɪneɪtɪŋ/ helping to make sth clear or easier to understand: *The examples he used weren't particularly illuminating.*

telling showing effectively what sb/sth is really like, but often without intending to: *The number of homeless people is a telling comment on the state of society.*

enlightening helping you to understand sth better, by giving you information that you did not know before: *A visit to her partner proved most enlightening.* See also **enlighten** → TELL 1

informed *adj.* See the Topic Maps for EDUCATION on p.888 and FACT AND OPINION on p.898

informed · educated · knowledgeable · thinking · well read
These words all describe sb/sth that has or shows a lot of knowledge or information about sth.

PATTERNS AND COLLOCATIONS
▶ informed / educated / knowledgeable **about** sth
▶ informed / educated / knowledgeable / thinking / well-read **people**
▶ **very / extremely** educated / knowledgeable / well read

informed [usually before noun] knowing a lot about sth; based on a lot of knowledge about a particular subject or situation: *The newspaper's readership is generally well informed and intelligent.* ◊ *They are not fully informed about the changes.* ◊ *Keep me informed of any developments.* ◊ *Informed sources say that the president may have received hospital treatment last year.* ◊ *It was a serious and informed debate.* ❶ **Informed** is often used to talk about the decisions that people make; common collocates include *decision, choice, discussion, debate, opinion, advice* and *consent.* **OPP** **uninformed** → IGNORANT

educated [usually before noun] having a high standard of education; based on or showing a high level of education or knowledge about sth: *She's an educated and articulate spokeswoman.* ◊ *He spoke in an educated voice.* ◊ *Let's make an educated guess* (= a guess that is based on some degree of knowledge, and is therefore likely to be correct). **OPP** **uneducated** → IGNORANT

knowledgeable /ˈnɒlɪdʒəbl; AmE ˈnɑːl-/ knowing a lot; knowing a lot about a particular subject: *Bill was nice enough and seemed extremely knowledgeable too.* ◊ *She's very knowledgeable about all kinds of music.* **OPP** **ignorant** → IGNORANT

thinking [only before noun] intelligent and able to think seriously about things: *Thinking people agreed on the need for radical reform.* ◊ (*rather informal*) *She is known as the thinking person's crime writer.* ❶ It is quite common in rather informal writing, especially journalism, to describe sb/sth that is popular but not stupid as *the thinking person/man/woman's…*

well ˈread /red/ having read a lot of books and therefore knowing a lot: *He became well read in French and German literature.* ◊ *She was better read than her husband.*

inherit *verb*

inherit · succeed · come into sth
These words all mean to receive money, property, a title or position from sb when they die.

PATTERNS AND COLLOCATIONS
▶ to inherit / succeed to the / sb's **throne / crown / title / estate**
▶ to inherit / come into a **fortune**
▶ to inherit / come into **money / property**

inherit [T, I] to receive money, property, a title or position from sb when they die: *He will inherit the title on the death of his uncle.* ◇ *Does he know that she stands to inherit* (= inherit a lot of money)? ❶ You can **inherit** things from people in two other ways: you can inherit physical features or personal qualities from your parents or grandparents; or you can inherit a situation from sb, by taking over responsibility for the situation from them, especially because you have replaced that person in their job: *She inherited a passion for music from her grand-father.* ◇ *I inherited a number of problems from my predecessor in the post.* See also **inheritance** → LEGACY, **disinherit** → REJECT

succeed [I] (*rather formal*) to gain the right to a title, position or property when sb dies: *She succeeded to the throne* (= became queen) *in 1558.*
▶ **succession** /sək'seʃn/ *noun* [U]: *He became chairman in succession to Bernard Allen.*

NOTE INHERIT OR SUCCEED? **Inherit** is used more to talk about receiving money or property; **succeed** is used more to talk about gaining a title or position, especially *the throne* (= the position of king or queen).

come 'into sth *phrasal verb* [no passive] to inherit money or property from sb when they die; to receive money or property that you inherited as a child and are now old enough to claim: *She came into a fortune when her uncle died.* ◇ *He comes into his money next year and will be able to spend it as he likes.*

injure *verb* See the Topic Map for HEALTH on p.890

injure · wound · hurt · bruise · maim · sprain · pull · tear · twist · strain
These words all mean to harm yourself or sb else physically, especially in an accident.

PATTERNS AND COLLOCATIONS
▶ to injure / hurt / strain **yourself**
▶ to injure / hurt / sprain / pull / tear / strain a **muscle**
▶ to injure / hurt / sprain / twist your **ankle / foot / knee**
▶ to injure / hurt / sprain your **wrist / hand**
▶ to injure / hurt / strain your **back / shoulder / eyes**
▶ to injure / hurt your **spine / neck**
▶ to be **badly** injured / wounded / hurt / bruised / maimed / sprained / torn
▶ to be **severely** injured / wounded / hurt / bruised / sprained
▶ to be **seriously** injured / wounded / hurt / bruised
▶ to be **slightly** injured / wounded / hurt / bruised / sprained
▶ to **accidentally** injure / wound / hurt sb / sth

injure [T] to harm yourself or sb else physically, especially in an accident: *He injured his knee playing hockey.* ◇ *Three people were killed and five injured in the crash.* ◇ *She injured herself during training.*

wound /wuːnd/ [T, often passive] (*rather formal*) to injure part of the body, especially by making a hole in the skin using a weapon: *He was wounded in the arm.* ◇ *About 50 people were seriously wounded in the attack.* ❶ **Wound** is often used to talk about people being hurt in war or in other attacks which affect a lot of people.

hurt [T, I] to cause physical pain to sb/yourself; to injure sb/yourself: *He hurt his back playing squash.* ◇ *Did you hurt yourself?* ◇ *Stop it. You're hurting me.* ◇ *My back is really hurting me today.* ◇ *Strong light hurts my eyes.* ◇ *My shoes hurt – they're too tight.* See also **hurt** → HURT *verb* 2

NOTE HURT OR INJURE? You can **hurt** or **injure** a part of the body in an accident. **Hurt** emphasizes the physical pain caused; **injure** emphasizes that the part of the body has been damaged in some way.

bruise /bruːz/ [T, I] to make a blue, brown or purple mark (a **bruise**) appear on the skin after sb has fallen or been hit; to develop a bruise: *She had slipped and badly bruised her face.* ◇ *Careful: I bruise easily.*
▶ **bruising** *noun* [U]: (*rather formal*) *She suffered severe bruising, but no bones were broken.*

maim [T] (*rather formal*) to injure sb seriously, causing permanent damage to their body: *Hundreds of people are killed or maimed in car accidents every week.*

sprain [T] to injure part of your body, especially your ankle, wrist or knee, by suddenly bending it in an awkward way, causing pain and swelling: *I stumbled and sprained my ankle.*
▶ **sprain** *noun* [C]: *a bad ankle sprain*

pull [T] to injure a muscle, etc., by stretching it too much: *She has pulled her Achilles tendon.*

tear /teə(r); AmE ter/ [T] to injure a muscle, etc., by stretching it too much: *She's torn a ligament in her right hand.*

NOTE PULL OR TEAR? To **pull** or **tear** a muscle is basically the same action, but *a torn muscle* is more badly injured than *a pulled muscle*: the injury or **tear** goes further across the muscle. You can talk about *a badly torn muscle* but NOT: *a badly pulled muscle.*

twist [T] to suddenly bend a part of your body, especially your ankle, wrist or knee, in an awkward way, causing an injury that involves pain and swelling: *She fell and twisted her ankle.*

NOTE SPRAIN OR TWIST? A **sprain** is an injury to your ankle, wrist or knee that causes pain and swelling; to **sprain** your *ankle/wrist/knee* is to injure it in this way. To **twist** your *ankle/wrist/knee* is to do the action (= to suddenly bend it in an awkward way) that causes the injury.

strain [T] to injure yourself or part of your body by making it work too hard: *Don't strain your eyes by reading in poor light.* ◇ *Are you sure you can carry all that? Don't strain yourself.*
▶ **strain** *noun* [C, U]: *a calf/groin/leg strain* ◇ *muscle strain*

injured *adj.* See the Topic Map for HEALTH on p.890

injured · wounded · hurt · bruised · bad
These words all describe a person or part of the body that has an injury or wound.

PATTERNS AND COLLOCATIONS
▶ an injured / a wounded / a bruised / a bad **arm / leg / shoulder / knee**
▶ an injured / a bruised **hand / wrist**
▶ an injured / a wounded **man / woman / person**
▶ **badly / slightly** injured / wounded / hurt / bruised
▶ **seriously** injured / wounded / hurt
▶ **severely** injured / wounded / bruised

injured having an injury: *Luckily, she isn't injured.* ◇ *His injured leg prevented him from walking.* **OPP** **uninjured** → SAFE 1
▶ **the injured** *noun* [pl.]: *Ambulances took the injured to a nearby hospital.*

wounded injured by a weapon, for example in a war: *The wounded soldiers were taken back to the camp.* ◇ *There were 79 killed and 230 wounded.*
▶ **the wounded** *noun* [pl.]: *Volunteers looked after the wounded in makeshift cabins.*

hurt [not usually before noun] injured, especially with only minor harm done: *None of the passengers was badly hurt.*
OPP **unhurt** → SAFE 1, See also **hurt** → INJURE *verb*, **hurt** → HURT *verb* 2

bruised /bruːzd/ having bruises (= blue, brown or purple marks on the skin after sb has fallen or been hit): *He suffered badly bruised ribs in the crash.*

bad [usually before noun] (of parts of the body) painful or injured: *I've got a bad back.* **OPP** **good** → WELL

injury *noun* See the Topic Map for HEALTH on p.890

injury · wound · cut · bruise · scratch · gash · graze
These are all words for harm to sb's body, usually when the skin is broken.

PATTERNS AND COLLOCATIONS
▸ an injury / a wound / cuts / a bruise / a gash **to** a part of the body
▸ (a) **severe** injuries / wound / bruise
▸ a **deep** wound / cut / scratch / gash
▸ **minor** injuries / wounds / cuts / bruises
▸ to **suffer** an injury / a wound / cuts / bruises / scratches / a gash
▸ to **sustain** an injury / a wound / cuts / bruises
▸ to **clean** a wound / cut
▸ a wound / cut / bruise **heals**
▸ **cuts and** bruises / scratches / grazes

injury [C, U] harm done to a person's or animal's body, for example in an accident: *As a result of the accident, several passengers sustained serious head injuries.* ◇ *She escaped with only minor injuries.* ◇ *Two players are out of the team because of injury.* ❶ The other words in this group generally refer to skin, but an **injury** can affect bones, muscles, or other parts of the body.

wound [C] an injury to part of the body, especially one in which a hole is made in the skin using a weapon: *She survived, despite receiving severe **stab wounds**.* ◇ *He proudly showed us his **war wounds**.* ❶ **Wound** often collocates with the name of the weapon that caused it: a *bullet / gunshot / knife / shrapnel wound*

cut [C] a place where a sharp object has made a hole in sb's skin: *He came home covered in cuts and bruises.* ◇ *Blood poured from the deep cut on his arm.* See also **cut** → CUT *verb* 4

bruise /bruːz/ [C] a blue, brown or purple mark on the skin after sb has fallen or been hit: *He had a huge bruise over his eye.* ◇ *(BrE) His legs were covered in bruises.* ◇ *(especially AmE) covered with bruises* ◇ *She was treated for minor **cuts and bruises**.*

scratch [C] a thin cut which produces very little or no blood: *Her hands were covered in scratches from the brambles.* See also **scratch** → SCRATCH *verb* 1

gash [C] a long, deep cut in the skin: *He had a nasty gash across his chest.* See also **gash** → CUT *verb* 4

graze [C] a small injury where the skin has been slightly broken by rubbing against sth: *Paul had a graze on his knee from where he had fallen over on the concrete.* See also **graze** → SCRATCH *verb* 1

in love *adj.*

in love · crazy about sb · smitten · besotted · infatuated
These words all describe sb who feels romantic love or attraction for sb.

PATTERNS AND COLLOCATIONS
▸ in love / smitten / besotted / infatuated **with** sb
▸ **completely / totally** in love / crazy about sb / smitten / besotted / infatuated

in love *phrase* loving sb in a romantic way: *We're in love!* ◇ *She was madly in love with him.* ◇ *They **fell in love** with each other.* See also **love** → LOVE *noun* 1

crazy about sb *phrase* (*informal*) liking sb very much; in love with sb: *I've been crazy about him since the first time I saw him.*

smitten [not usually before noun] (*often humorous*) suddenly feeling that you are in love with sb: *From the moment they met, he was completely **smitten by** her.*

besotted /bɪˈsɒtɪd; *AmE* -ˈsaːt-/ loving sb so much that you do not behave in a sensible way: *He was so besotted with her that he forgave her for everything.*

infatuated /ɪnˈfætʃueɪtɪd/ having a very strong feeling of love or attraction for sb so that you cannot think clearly or in a sensible way: *He's behaving like an infatuated teenager.* See also **infatuation** → LOVE *noun* 1

> **NOTE** **BESOTTED** OR **INFATUATED**? Both these words describe strong feelings that prevent you from thinking or behaving in a sensible way, but the feeling of being **infatuated** does not usually last long. It is often felt for sb that you do not know well. You are usually **besotted** **with** your boyfriend, girlfriend, partner, etc.: *She is still besotted with him after all these years.* ◇ *~~She is still infatuated with him after all these years.~~* ◇ *They've just got married, and are besotted with each other.* ◇ *~~They've just got married and are infatuated with each other.~~*

innocent *adj.*

innocent · not guilty · in the clear · blameless
These words all describe people who have not done anything wrong or illegal.

PATTERNS AND COLLOCATIONS
▸ to be innocent / not guilty **of** sth
▸ to **plead** innocent / not guilty
▸ to **find sb** innocent / not guilty

innocent not having done sth wrong or illegal: *They have imprisoned an innocent man.* ◇ *She was found innocent of any crime.* ◇ *He was the innocent party (= person) in the breakdown of the marriage.* ◇ *There must be an innocent explanation for her behaviour.* **OPP** **guilty** → GUILTY
▸ **innocence** *noun* [U]: *She protested her innocence (= said repeatedly that she was innocent).* **OPP** **guilt** → FAULT

not 'guilty *phrase* (*law*) not having done sth illegal: *The jury found the defendant not guilty of the offence.* ❶ People who have not done sth illegal **plead not guilty** to an offence. Someone may be **found not guilty** or a jury may **return a verdict of not guilty.** **OPP** **guilty** → GUILTY

in the 'clear *phrase* (*rather informal*) no longer thought to have done sth wrong or illegal: *It seems that the original suspect is in the clear.* See also **clear** → ACQUIT *verb*

blameless (*rather formal, written*) free from responsibility for doing sth bad: *None of us is entirely blameless in this matter.* See also **blame** → FAULT *noun*

insensitive *adj.*

insensitive · unsympathetic · uncaring · thoughtless · tactless · unthinking · inconsiderate
These words all describe sb who does not think or care about other people and their feelings, so often upsets or offends them.

PATTERNS AND COLLOCATIONS
▸ insensitive / unsympathetic **to** sb / sth
▸ thoughtless / tactless / inconsiderate **of** sb to do sth
▸ an unsympathetic / uncaring / inconsiderate **attitude**
▸ an insensitive / a thoughtless / a tactless **remark**
▸ thoughtless / unthinking **words**

insensitive /ɪnˈsensətɪv/ (*disapproving*) not realizing or caring how other people feel, and therefore likely to upset or offend them: *Many of the institutions were insensitive to the needs of their patients.* ◇ *It was a really insensitive thing to say.* **OPP** **sensitive** → SENSITIVE 1

unsympathetic (*disapproving*) not feeling or showing any sympathy: *I told him about the problem but he was totally unsympathetic.* **OPP** **sympathetic** → SENSITIVE 1

uncaring (*disapproving*) not sympathetic about the problems or suffering of other people: *He was so totally uncaring of anyone's feelings.* ◇ *We seem to be living in an increasingly uncaring society.* **OPP** **caring** → LOVING

thoughtless (*disapproving*) not thinking or caring about the possible effects of your words or actions on other people: *It was thoughtless of him to take the car without checking first.* **OPP** **thoughtful** → KIND

tactless (*disapproving*) saying or doing things that are likely to annoy or upset other people: *It had been tactless of her to mention it.* ◇ *It was so obviously a tactless question.* **OPP** **tactful** → TACT

unthinking (*written*) not thinking about the possible effects of your words or actions: *Unthinking, he started to cross the road.* ◇ *She blushed at being caught out in such unthinking prejudice.*

> **NOTE** THOUGHTLESS OR UNTHINKING A **thoughtless** action or comment is one that might have a negative effect on other people. It suggests that the person who made it should have thought more carefully about others. **Unthinking** is used more often when the bad effect of sth is only felt by the person doing the action. In this case, the action was just stupid and not thought about properly.

inconsiderate /ˌɪnkən'sɪdərət/ (*rather formal, disapproving*) not giving enough thought to other people's feelings or needs: *It was inconsiderate of you not to call.* **OPP** **considerate** → KIND

insert *verb*

insert · slip · slide · tuck · load · slot
These words all mean to put sth into sth else.

PATTERNS AND COLLOCATIONS
▶ to insert / slide / tuck / load / slot sth **in** / **into** sth
▶ to insert / slot sth **between** A and B
▶ to slip / slide / tuck sth **under** sth
▶ to insert / slip / slide / tuck / slot sth **quickly** into sth
▶ to insert / slide / tuck sth **carefully** / **gently** into sth

insert /ɪn'sɜːt; *AmE* ɪn'sɜːrt/ [T] (*rather formal*) to put sth into sth else or between two things: *Insert coins into the slot and press for a ticket.* ◇ *He winced as the doctor inserted the needle.* ◇ *She picked up a knife and inserted it between the top of the drawer and the desk.* ❶ **Insert** is used especially when there is a just a narrow space for sth to fit into.
▶ **insertion** /ɪn'sɜːʃn; *AmE* ɪn'sɜːrʃn/ *noun* [U, C]: *An examination is carried out before the insertion of the tube.*

slip (-**pp**-) [T] to give sth to sb or put sth somewhere quickly, quietly or secretly: *Anna slipped her hand into his.* ◇ *He slipped the letter back into its envelope.* ◇ *They'd slipped some money to the guards.*

slide [T] (always used with an adverb or preposition) to move sth quickly and quietly, for example in order not to be noticed: *The man slid the money quickly into his pocket.* ◇ (*figurative*) *He slid a shy look at Claire.*

> **NOTE** SLIP OR SLIDE? These words are very close in meaning and use. **Slip** emphasizes that sth is being done secretly. **Slide** emphasizes that sth is done with a smooth movement. Often either word can be used: *He slipped/slid the money into his pocket.* It is more usual to use **slip** to talk about giving sth to sb secretly: ~~They slid some money to the guards.~~

tuck [T] to put sth into a small space, especially in order to hide it or keep it safe or comfortable: *The letter had been tucked under a pile of papers.* ◇ *He sat with his legs tucked up under him.*

load [T] to put sth into a weapon, camera or other piece of equipment so that it can be used: *She loaded the camera with film.* ◇ *Is the gun loaded?*

slot (-**tt**-) [T, I] (always used with an adverb or preposition) to put sth into a space that is available or designed for it; to fit into such a space: *The bed comes in sections which can be quickly slotted together.* ◇ *The dishwasher slots neatly between the other units.*

inspection *noun*

inspection · observation · check · examination · audit · surveillance · survey · scan · check-up
These are all words for a careful look at sb/sth, especially to check that everything is satisfactory.

PATTERNS AND COLLOCATIONS
▶ (a) **detailed** inspection / observation / check / examination / audit / survey
▶ (a) **close** inspection / observation / check / examination / surveillance
▶ (a) **thorough** inspection / check / examination / audit / survey / check-up
▶ (a) **careful** inspection / observation / check / examination
▶ (a) **regular** inspection/observation/check/examination/audit/ surveillance / check-up
▶ (a / an) **routine** inspection / check / examination / surveillance / scan / check-up
▶ a **medical** inspection / check / examination / check-up
▶ to **carry out** / **do** an inspection / an observation / a check / an examination / an audit / surveillance / a survey / a scan
▶ to **conduct** an inspection / a check / an examination / an audit / surveillance / a survey
▶ to **give sb/sth** an inspection / a check / an examination / a scan / a check-up
▶ to **have** an inspection / a check / an examination / a scan / a check-up
▶ an inspection/observation/a check/an examination/an audit/ a survey / a scan / a check-up **reveals** / **shows** sth
▶ an inspection/observation/a check/an examination/a survey **confirms** sth

inspection [U, C] a careful look at sb/sth, especially to check that everything is satisfactory: *The documents are available for public inspection.* ◇ *On closer inspection, the notes proved to be forgeries.* ◇ *The principal went on a tour of inspection of all the classrooms.* ◇ *Council officials made one site inspection of the property.* See also **inspect** → CHECK *verb 1*

observation [U, C] the act of watching sb/sth carefully for a period of time, especially to find sth out: *Most of the information was collected by direct observation of the animals' behaviour.* ◇ *We managed to escape observation* (= we were not seen). ◇ *The report is based on scientific observations.* See also **observe** → LOOK *verb 1*

check [C] a close and careful look at sth to make sure that it is safe, correct or in good condition: *Could you give the tyres a quick check?* ◇ *Regular safety checks are conducted on the equipment used in the factory.* ◇ *In a series of spot checks* (= checks made without warning), *police searched buses crossing the border.* See also **check** → CHECK *verb 1*

examination [U, C] a close and careful look at sth, especially to find sth out or see if anything is wrong: *Careful examination of the ruins revealed an even earlier temple.* ◇ *Doctors gave him a thorough medical examination.* See also **examine** → CHECK *verb 1*

audit /'ɔːdɪt/ [C] (*especially business*) an official examination of business and financial records to see that they are true and correct; an official examination of the quality or standard of sth: *a tax audit* ◇ *Environmental audits are being carried out by many companies, showing the environmental impact of their activities.* See also **audit** → CHECK 1

surveillance /sɜː'veɪləns; *AmE* sɜːr'v-/ [U] the act of carefully watching a person suspected of a crime or a place where a crime may be committed: *The police are keeping the suspects under constant surveillance.*

survey [C] a careful look at an area of land in order to make a map or plan of it: *They carried out an aerial survey* (= made by taking photographs from an aircraft) *of the mountains.* ◇ *A geological survey revealed the presence of oil beneath the ground.* ❶ In British English a **survey** is also a careful look at the condition of a building, usually done for sb who is thinking of buying it: *We paid for a detailed structural survey, which identified two areas of dry rot in the attic.*

scan [C] a medical test in which a machine produces a picture of the inside of a person's body on a computer screen, using x-rays or ultrasound: *The brain scan revealed no signs of injury.*

'check-up [C] (*rather informal*) an examination of sth, especially a medical examination to make sure that you are healthy: *I went for my regular check-up.*

inspector *noun*

inspector · regulator · observer · watchdog · examiner · consumer group · monitor
These are all words for sb whose job is to check that rules are being obeyed.

PATTERNS AND COLLOCATIONS
▸ a **government** / **federal** inspector / regulator / observer / watchdog / examiner
▸ an **independent** inspector / regulator / observer / watchdog / examiner
▸ an **official** inspector / regulator / observer / watchdog
▸ a **local** inspector / regulator / observer / watchdog / consumer group
▸ a **safety** inspector / regulator / watchdog
▸ an **industry** regulator / observer / watchdog
▸ to **call** an inspector / a regulator / an examiner
▸ to **send** an inspector / an observer / an examiner / a monitor

inspector [C] a person whose job is to visit schools, factories, etc. to check that rules are being obeyed and that standards are acceptable: *a school inspector* ◊ *UN weapons inspectors have been called in to verify the government's claims.* See also **inspect** → CHECK 1

regulator /'regjuleɪtə(r)/ [C] a person or organization that officially controls an area of business or industry and makes sure that it is operating fairly: *Federal banking regulators have raised concerns about high levels of consumer debt.* See also **regulate** → REGULATE

observer /əb'zɜːvə(r); *AmE* -'zɜːrv-/ [C] a person who attends a meeting, lesson, etc. to listen and watch but not to take part: *A team of British officials were sent as observers to the conference.*

watchdog /'wɒtʃdɒɡ; 'wɔːtʃ-/ [C] (*rather informal, especially journalism*) a group of people whose job is to check that companies are not doing anything illegal or ignoring people's rights: *She is a member of the consumer watchdog for transport in London and Southern England.*

examiner [C] (*especially AmE*) a person who has the official duty to check that things are being done correctly and according to the rules of an organization; a person who officially examines sth: *He was the official examiner of electronic voting systems for Pennsylvania and Texas for 20 years.* See also **examine** → CHECK 1

con'sumer group [C] a group that represents people who use a particular service and tries to make sure that their rights are protected: *Consumer groups said lax safety measures and overcrowded trains were the underlying cause of the crash.*

NOTE REGULATOR, WATCHDOG OR CONSUMER GROUP? A **regulator** has official status and is usually appointed by the government to make sure that competition between companies is fair and that they are all operating within the law and respecting people's rights. A **regulator** can be a person or a group. **Watchdog** is often used in journalism as a more informal term for **regulator**, but a **watchdog** does not have to be an official organization (and cannot just be one person). It places the emphasis on protecting the rights of people who use a service, rather than the rights of individual companies within the industry. A **consumer group** is an unofficial **watchdog**.

monitor /'mɒnɪtə(r); *AmE* 'mɑːn-/ [C] a person whose job is to check that sth is done fairly and honestly, especially in a foreign country: *UN monitors declared the referendum fair.* See also **monitor** → MONITOR *verb*

inspiration *noun*

inspiration · creativity · vision · ingenuity · originality · imagination · inventiveness
These are all positive words for the ability to have exciting new ideas or to create new things.

PATTERNS AND COLLOCATIONS
▸ **great** inspiration / creativity / vision / ingenuity / originality / imagination / inventiveness
▸ to **have** inspiration / ingenuity / originality / imagination
▸ to **lack** / **be lacking in** inspiration / vision / ingenuity / originality / imagination
▸ to **show** creativity / ingenuity / originality / imagination / inventiveness
▸ to **use** your ingenuity / imagination

inspiration /ˌɪnspə'reɪʃn/ [U] the process that takes place when sb sees or hears sth that causes them to have exciting new ideas or makes them want to create sth new, especially in art, music or literature: *Looking for inspiration for a new dessert? Try this recipe.* ◊ *Both poets **drew their inspiration from** the countryside.* ◊ *Dreams can be a rich **source of inspiration** for an artist.*

creativity /ˌkriːeɪ'tɪvəti/ [U] the ability and imagination to create sth new or a work of art: *My job does not give me much scope for creativity.* See also **creative** → CREATIVE

vision [U] the ability to think about or plan the future with great imagination and intelligence: *a leader of great vision* ◊ *He's a competent politician but he lacks vision.* See also **visionary** → VISIONARY *noun*

ingenuity /ˌɪndʒə'njuːəti; *AmE* -'nuː-/ [U] the ability to invent things or solve problems in clever new ways: *There is always a solution, so long as you are prepared to use your ingenuity.* See also **ingenious** → CREATIVE

originality /əˌrɪdʒə'næləti/ [U] the ability to have interesting new ideas; the quality of being new and interesting in a way that is different from anything that has existed before: *His originality as a painter lies in his representation of light.* ◊ *Creativity and originality are more important than technical skill.* See also **original** → CREATIVE, **individuality** → IDENTITY

imagination [U] the ability to have exciting new ideas: *His writing lacks imagination.* ◊ *With a little imagination you can create a delicious meal from yesterday's leftovers.* See also **imaginative** → CREATIVE

inventiveness [U] the ability to create new things or have new ideas; the quality of being new and creative: *the inventiveness of modern advertising* See also **inventive** → CREATIVE

inspire *verb*

inspire · motivate · fire sb up · stimulate
These words all mean to make sb want to do sth or make sb excited about sth.

motivate   inspire   fire sb up
stimulate

PATTERNS AND COLLOCATIONS
▸ to be fired up / inspired **with** sth
▸ to inspire / motivate / stimulate sb **to** sth
▸ to inspire sb / motivate sb / fire sb up / stimulate sb **to do sth**
▸ to inspire sb / motivate sb / fire sb up **by doing sth**

inspire /ɪn'spaɪə(r)/ [T] to make sb want to do sth well or do sth new by giving them the necessary desire, confidence or enthusiasm: *The actors inspired the kids with their enthusiasm.* ◊ *His superb play inspired the team*

to a thrilling 5–0 win. ◇ *The actors visit schools and hope to inspire the children to put on their own productions.* See also **inspiration** → EXAMPLE 2, **inspiration** → INCENTIVE
▸ **inspired** *adj*.: *an inspired performance*
▸ **inspiring** *adj*.: *an inspiring teacher*

motivate /ˈməʊtɪveɪt; *AmE* ˈmoʊ-/ [T] to make sb want to do sth, especially sth that involves hard work or effort: *She's very good at motivating her students.* ◇ *The plan is designed to motivate employees to work more efficiently.* See also **motivation** → INCENTIVE
▸ **motivated** *adj*.: *a highly motivated student* (= one who is very interested and works hard)

,**fire sb ˈup** *phrasal verb* [often passive] to make sb excited or interested in sth, so they are very keen to do it well or to win a contest: *He's all fired up about his new job.*

stimulate /ˈstɪmjuleɪt/ [T] (*rather formal, especially written*) to make sb excited or interested in sth, so that they learn or do sth that is a bit difficult: *Parents should give children books that stimulate them* (= interest them and mentally challenge them). ◇ *Stimulate the patient to activity but don't push him too hard.* See also **stimulating** → INTERESTING, **stimulus** → INCENTIVE
▸ **stimulation** *noun* [U]: *Children need intellectual stimulation.*

instinct *noun*

instinct · intuition · sixth sense
These are all words for a natural ability to know or be able to do sth without being told, taught or trained.

PATTERNS AND COLLOCATIONS
▸ an instinct / an intuition / a sixth sense **for** sth
▸ an instinct / intuition **that...**
▸ to do sth **by** instinct / intuition
▸ to **have** an instinct / an intuition / a sixth sense
▸ to **rely on** your instinct / intuition
▸ your instinct / intuition / sixth sense **tells** you
▸ your instinct / intuition / sixth sense **warns** you

instinct [U, C] a natural tendency for people and animals to behave in a particular way or to know particular things, even though they have not been taught or trained in that way: *His first instinct was to run away.* ◇ *Children do not know the difference between right and wrong by instinct.* ◇ *I acted purely on instinct.* ◇ *Most people have a well-developed survival instinct* (= the instinct of trying to protect yourself from danger). See also **instinctive** → NATURAL

intuition /ˌɪntjuˈɪʃn; *AmE* -tu-/ [U] the ability to know sth by using your feelings rather than by considering the facts: *Intuition told her that he was telling the truth.* ◇ *Call it women's intuition if you like, but I knew he was up to something.* See also **intuitive** → NATURAL

,**sixth ˈsense** [sing.] a special ability to know sth without using any of the usual five senses of sight, hearing, touch, taste and smell: *Some kind of sixth sense warned me not to stay there.*

institution *noun*

institution · home · orphanage
These words all mean a place where people who cannot care for themselves live and are cared for by others.

PATTERNS AND COLLOCATIONS
▸ **in** an institution / a home / an orphanage
▸ to **live in** an institution / a home / an orphanage
▸ to **move to** an institution / a home

institution /ˌɪnstɪˈtjuːʃn; *AmE* -ˈtuːʃn/ [C] (*sometimes disapproving*) a building where people with special needs live and are taken care of, for example because they are old or mentally ill: *They had him committed to a mental institution.* ◇ *We want this to be like a home, not an institution.*

home [C] a place where people who cannot care for themselves live and are cared for by others: *She had to move to a residential care home when her health deteriorated.* ◇ *She has lived in a home since she was six.*
❶ This meaning of **home** is used in a number of compounds, including **children's home**, **retirement home**, **old people's home** (in British English only) and **nursing home** (= for people, especially older people, who need medical care as well as personal care).

orphanage /ˈɔːfənɪdʒ; *AmE* ˈɔːrf-/ [C] a home for children whose parents are dead or otherwise unable to care for them: *My sister and I were adopted from an orphanage.*
❶ **Orphanage** is usually used to talk about institutions in poorer countries or in the past. In richer countries these institutions are now usually called *children's homes* or *residential care homes*.

instructions *noun*

instructions · directions
These are both words for detailed information about how to do sth.

PATTERNS AND COLLOCATIONS
▸ instructions / directions **for** / **on** / **as to** sth
▸ **clear** / **precise** / **detailed** / **step-by-step** / **careful** instructions / directions
▸ to **give sb** / **follow** instructions / directions
▸ a **series** / **set of** instructions / directions

instructions [pl.] detailed information, often printed, on how to do or use sth: *He gave her instructions on the procedure to be followed.* ◇ *Follow the instructions on the packet carefully.* ◇ *The oven should be serviced according to the manufacturer's instructions.*

directions [pl.] detailed information about how to get somewhere or how to do sth: *Can you give me directions to the train station?* ◇ *Simple directions for assembling the model are printed on the box.* ◇ *Let's stop and ask for directions.*

insulting *adj*. See also the entry for OFFENSIVE

insulting · derogatory · disparaging · pejorative
These words all describe an expression of disapproval that may be offensive to sb.

PATTERNS AND COLLOCATIONS
▸ insulting / derogatory **to** sb
▸ an insulting / a derogatory / a disparaging **remark** / **comment**
▸ an insulting / a derogatory / a disparaging / a pejorative **term** / **word**

insulting causing or intending to cause sb to feel offended: *He denies charges of insulting behaviour to a police officer.* ◇ *She was really insulting to me.* See also **insult** → OFFEND
▸ **insultingly** *adv*.: *He behaved insultingly towards her and should apologize.*

derogatory /dɪˈrɒɡətri; *AmE* dɪˈrɑːɡətɔːri/ showing strong disapproval and a lack of respect towards sb: *He complained that the supervisor had made derogatory remarks about him.*

disparaging /dɪˈspærɪdʒɪŋ/ (*formal*) criticizing sb/sth in a way that suggests that they are not important or valuable: *She made some disparaging remarks about standards in education.*

NOTE DEROGATORY OR DISPARAGING? These words are very close in meaning. **Derogatory** remarks are usually about a person or group of people, and are usually unfair to them. **Disparaging** remarks may be fair or unfair, and may be about people or things.: *She made some derogatory remarks about standards in education.*

pejorative /pɪˈdʒɒrətɪv; AmE -ˈdʒɔːr-; -ˈdʒɑːr-/ (formal) (of a word or remark) expressing disapproval or criticism: *I'm using the word 'academic' here in a pejorative sense.*
▸ **pejoratively** adv.: *These days the term 'chauvinist' is always used pejoratively.*

integrity noun See also the entry for TRUTH

integrity · honesty · honour · probity
These are all words for sb's personal qualities of morality and goodness.

PATTERNS AND COLLOCATIONS
▸ a man / woman **of** integrity / honour
▸ **absolute / complete / total** integrity / honesty
▸ sb's **personal** integrity / honesty / honour / probity
▸ sb's **professional** integrity / honour / probity

integrity /ɪnˈtegrəti/ [U] the quality of knowing and doing what is morally right: *She behaved with absolute integrity.* ◇ *They preserved their integrity throughout the trial.*

honesty [U] the quality of always telling the truth and never stealing or cheating: *I always expect total honesty from my employees.* ◇ *At least he **had the honesty** to admit he was wrong.* **OPP** **dishonesty** → FRAUD 1
▸ **honest** adj.: *an honest man/woman*

honour (BrE) (AmE **honor**) [U] the quality of and/or reputation for knowing and doing what is morally right: *He would always fight to defend the **family honour**.* ◇ *Proving his innocence was a **matter of honour**.* ◇ *Many schoolchildren have a very strong **code of honour**.* ◇ *I give you my **word of honour** (= a solemn promise) that I will not forget what I owe you.* **OPP** **dishonour** → DISGRACE 2, See also **honourable** → RESPECTABLE

> **NOTE** **INTEGRITY** OR **HONOUR**? With **integrity** the emphasis is mainly on how you see yourself: being good and honest so that you can approve of your own character and actions. With **honour** the emphasis is more on how others see you: being good and honest in order to keep your reputation in a community. **Integrity** is mostly individual, although you can talk about the integrity of the *company/profession*. **Honour** can be individual or collective: *to defend the family integrity* ◇ *a strong code of integrity* ◇ *I give you my word of integrity.*

probity /ˈprəʊbəti; AmE ˈproʊ-/ [U] (formal) the quality of being completely honest, especially in business matters: *They have very high standards of **financial probity**.*

intellectual adj.

1 intellectual abilities/discussion
2 an intellectual audience/elite

1 intellectual · theoretical · psychological · mental · abstract · philosophical · academic · conceptual
These words all describe things that are connected with ideas or the mind rather than the physical world.

PATTERNS AND COLLOCATIONS
▸ an intellectual / a theoretical / a psychological / sb's mental / an abstract / a philosophical / an academic / a conceptual **approach**
▸ an intellectual / a theoretical / a philosophical / an academic / a conceptual **framework**
▸ intellectual / theoretical / psychological / abstract / philosophical / conceptual **terms**
▸ an intellectual / a theoretical / a psychological / a mental / an abstract / a philosophical **concept**
▸ intellectual / abstract / philosophical / academic / conceptual **thought / thinking**
▸ intellectual / theoretical / abstract / philosophical / academic **discussion / argument / debate**
▸ an intellectual / a theoretical / a psychological / a mental / a philosophical / a conceptual **problem**

▸ theoretical / psychological / philosophical / academic **study**
▸ **purely** intellectual / theoretical / psychological / mental / abstract / philosophical / academic / conceptual
▸ **highly / largely** intellectual / theoretical / abstract / academic

intellectual /ˌɪntəˈlektʃuəl/ [usually before noun] connected with or using sb's ability to think in a logical way and understand things: *It can be very difficult to measure intellectual ability.* ◇ *You can't really appreciate art from a purely intellectual standpoint.*
▸ **intellectually** adv.: *The party carries no weight intellectually.* ◇ *It's an intellectually demanding job.*

theoretical /ˌθɪəˈretɪkl; AmE ˌθiːə-/ [usually before noun] concerned with the ideas and principles on which a subject is based rather than with practice or experiments: *We aim to provide you with both theoretical and practical knowledge of your subject.* ◇ *The emphasis of his lectures is on theoretical physics.* **OPP** **practical**, **experimental** → PRACTICAL, See also **theory** → THEORY 1
▸ **theoretically** adv.: *Travelling faster than the speed of light is theoretically impossible.* ◇ *Theoretically, education is free in this country.*

psychological /ˌsaɪkəˈlɒdʒɪkl; AmE -ˈlɑːdʒ-/ [usually before noun] connected with the mind and how it works: *Victory in the previous game should give them a **psychological advantage** over their opponents.* ◇ *Her latest movie is a tense psychological drama.* ◇ *I think his illness is more psychological (= caused by the mind) than physical.*
▸ **psychologically** adv.: *Some of these so-called therapies can actually be psychologically harmful.*

mental [usually before noun] connected with or happening in the mind; involving the process of thinking: *The experience caused her huge amounts of mental suffering.* ◇ *Do you have a **mental picture** of the scene (= can you imagine what it looks like?)?* ◇ *I made a **mental note** to call her as soon as I got home.* ◇ *I have a complete **mental block** (= I cannot learn or remember) when it comes to physics.* ◇ *Are you any good at **mental arithmetic** (= mathematical calculations that you do in your mind rather than on paper)?*
▸ **mentally** adv.: *The team were outplayed, physically and mentally.* ◇ *You need to be mentally prepared for the race.*

abstract /ˈæbstrækt/ based on general ideas and not on any particular real person, thing or situation; existing in thought or as an idea but not having any physical reality: *Freedom is more than a purely abstract notion.* ◇ *We may talk of beautiful things but beauty itself is abstract.* **OPP** **concrete** → FINAL, See also **abstraction** → IDEA 1
▸ **the abstract** noun [sing.]: *Legal questions rarely exist **in the abstract**; they are based on real cases.*

philosophical /ˌfɪləˈsɒfɪkl; AmE -ˈsɑːf-/ [usually before noun] connected with philosophy; involving serious thinking about life, the universe and other important issues: *The level of philosophical debate is usually quite high.*
▸ **philosophically** adv.: *She is right-wing both politically and philosophically.*

academic [usually before noun] involving a lot of reading or studying rather than practical or technical skills: *I wasn't sure I could cope with the academic demands of the course.* ◇ *She had very few academic qualifications.*
▸ **academically** adv.: *They are all well qualified academically, but have little practical experience.*

conceptual /kənˈseptʃuəl/ (formal) connected with or based on ideas: *She presents a conceptual framework for the analysis of educational processes.* See also **concept** → IDEA 1
▸ **conceptually** adv.: *conceptually similar/distinct*

2 intellectual · cultured · literary · studious · learned · scholarly · highbrow · bookish
These are all words for sb who is interested in books, academic study, serious culture, etc.

intellectual → intelligent

PATTERNS AND COLLOCATIONS
▸ an intellectual / a cultured / a literary / a studious young / a learned / a scholarly / a bookish **man** / **woman**
▸ (a / an) intellectual / cultured / literary / learned / scholarly / highbrow **readers** / **readership**
▸ an intellectual / a cultured / a literary / a scholarly **elite**
▸ **highly** intellectual / cultured / literary

intellectual /ˌɪntəˈlektʃuəl/ well educated and enjoying activities that involve serious thought: *His works were popular among the intellectual elite of the time.* ◇ *Don't imagine that all college students are highly intellectual!* See also **intellectual** → SCHOLAR noun

cultured /ˈkʌltʃəd; AmE -tʃərd/ (*approving*) well educated and able to understand and enjoy art, literature, etc: *She was a deeply cultured woman who had travelled a great deal.* ◇ *He spoke with a cultured accent* (= the accent of a cultured person).

literary /ˈlɪtərəri; AmE -reri/ liking literature very much and knowing a lot about it; involved in studying or writing literature: *She was one of the great literary figures of her age.* ◇ *He was a literary man and had dreamed of becoming the Shakespeare of the movies.*

studious /ˈstjuːdiəs; AmE ˈstuː-/ spending a lot of time studying or reading: *She was a quiet, studious girl.* ◇ *He liked to wear glasses, which he thought made him look studious.*

learned /ˈlɜːnɪd; AmE ˈlɜːrnɪd/ [usually before noun] (*formal*) having a lot of knowledge based on serious study and reading: *The lecture was given by an elderly learned professor.* See also **learning** → KNOWLEDGE

scholarly /ˈskɒləli; AmE ˈskɑːlərli/ (*rather formal*) spending a lot of time studying and having a lot of knowledge about an academic subject: *He was a very scholarly young man.*

> **NOTE** STUDIOUS, LEARNED OR SCHOLARLY? **Studious** emphasizes a person's habits and how much time they spend studying; a **studious** person is usually young. **Learned** emphasizes how much a person knows, especially knowledge based on a lifetime of study; a **learned** person is usually old. **Scholarly** emphasizes both the habit of studying and the knowledge got from studying; a **scholarly** person can be young or old.

highbrow /ˈhaɪbraʊ/ (*sometimes disapproving*) concerned with or interested in serious artistic or cultural ideas: *The journal is aimed at a highbrow readership.* ❶ **Highbrow** usually describes newspapers and television programmes and the people who read or watch them; collocates include *readers, papers, press* and *television (programmes)*.

bookish (*sometimes disapproving*) interested in reading or studying rather than in more active or practical things: *Quiet and bookish, he was sometimes teased by the other boys.*

intelligence noun See the Topic Map for EDUCATION on p.888

intelligence · mind · genius · intellect · wits · brain · smarts
These are all words for sb's ability to think, learn and understand.

PATTERNS AND COLLOCATIONS
▸ (a) **great** intelligence / mind / genius / intellect / brain
▸ (a) **sharp** intelligence / mind / intellect / wits / brain
▸ (a) **keen** intelligence / mind / intellect / brain
▸ (a / an) **creative** / **artistic** / **musical** intelligence / mind / genius / intellect
▸ to **have** intelligence / a ...mind / genius / intellect / ... wits / a ... brain / smarts
▸ to **have** (the) intelligence / wits / smarts **to do sth**
▸ to **use** your intelligence / mind / wits / brain / smarts
▸ a **man** / **woman of** intelligence / genius / intellect

intelligence [U] the ability to learn, understand and think in a logical way about things; the ability to do this well: *Most people of average intelligence would find this task quite difficult.* ◇ *Each child had to do an **intelligence test**.* ◇ *Don't **insult my intelligence*** (= treat me as if I were stupid).

mind [C, usually sing.] your ability to think about things in a logical way; the particular way that sb thinks: *His mind is as sharp as ever.* ◇ *Did you know you have a nasty suspicious mind?* ◇ *I've no idea how her mind works.* ◇ *He has the body of a man but the mind of a child.* ◇ *Their evidence might give us some insight into the criminal mind.*

genius /ˈdʒiːniəs/ [U] unusually great intelligence, skill or artistic ability: *the genius of Shakespeare* ◇ *She was at the peak of her creative genius.* ◇ *It's undoubtedly a work of genius.* ◇ *That was a stroke of genius.*

intellect /ˈɪntəlekt/ [U, C] the ability to think in a logical way and understand things, especially at an advanced level: *A teacher recognized his outstanding intellect.* ◇ *She was a brilliant scholar with a formidable intellect.*

wits [pl.] a person's ability to think quickly and clearly and make good decisions: *He needed all his wits to get out of that situation.* ◇ *This will be your chance to **pit your wits against*** (= compete with, using your intelligence) *our reigning champion.* ◇ *The game was a long **battle of wits**.* ◇ ***Keep your wits about you.*** *This could be tricky.*

brain [U, C, usually pl.] (*rather informal*) intelligence: *It doesn't take much brain to work out that both stories can't be true.* ◇ *She must have inherited her mother's brains.*

smarts [U] (*AmE, informal*) intelligence: *She made it to the top on her smarts and hard work.* ◇ *You'll have to use all your smarts to figure this one out.*

intelligent adj. See the Topic Map for EDUCATION on p.888

intelligent · smart · clever · brilliant · bright
These words all describe people who are good at learning, understanding and thinking about things, and the actions that show this ability.

PATTERNS AND COLLOCATIONS
▸ clever / brilliant **at** sth
▸ an intelligent / a smart / a clever / a brilliant / a bright **child** / **boy** / **girl** / **man** / **woman**
▸ an intelligent / a smart / a clever / a brilliant **thing to do** / **move**
▸ **really** / **quite** intelligent / smart / clever / brilliant / bright
▸ **pretty** / **very** / **extremely** / **incredibly** intelligent / smart / clever / bright

intelligent good at learning, understanding and thinking in a logical way about things; showing this ability: *He's a **highly intelligent** man.* ◇ *She asked a lot of intelligent questions.* **OPP stupid** → STUPID

smart (*especially AmE*) quick at learning and understanding things; showing the ability to make good business or personal decisions: *She's smarter than her brother.* ◇ *If you're smart, you'll take my advice.* ◇ *That was a smart career move.* ◇ *OK, I admit it was not the smartest thing I ever did* (= it was a stupid thing to do). **OPP dumb, stupid** → STUPID

clever (*especially BrE, sometimes disapproving*) quick at learning and understanding things; showing this ability: *Clever girl!* ◇ *How clever of you to work it out!* ◇ *He's **too clever by half**, if you ask me.* ◇ *This book is clever, without being **merely clever**.* ◇ *That wasn't a very clever thing to do* (= that was a rather stupid thing to do). ❶ People use **clever** in the phrase: *Clever boy/girl!* to tell a young child that they have learnt or done sth well. When used to or about an adult **clever** can be disapproving (if sb/sth is *too clever* or *merely clever*), ironic (= meaning that you think sb/sth is not clever at all) or patronizing (= showing, in a way that can be insulting, that you find sb's cleverness surprising). **OPP stupid** → STUPID

brilliant very intelligent or skilful: *He's a brilliant young scientist.* ◇ *She has one of the most brilliant minds in the country.* ◇ *This is a brilliant and fascinating piece of writing.*

bright intelligent; quick to learn: *She's probably the brightest student in the class.* ◇ (*BrE, informal, ironic*) *Some* **bright spark** (= stupid person) *left the tap running all night.* **OPP** **dumb** → STUPID, See also **bright** → CHEERFUL

intend *verb*

intend · mean · plan · aim · have sb/sth in mind · propose
These words all mean to have a plan, result or purpose in your mind when you do sth.

PATTERNS AND COLLOCATIONS
▸ to intend / mean / plan / aim / have in mind / propose **to do sth**
▸ to intend / propose **doing sth**
▸ sb **originally** intended / meant / planned sth
▸ to **clearly** / **directly** intend / aim to do sth

intend [I, T] to have a plan, result or purpose in your mind when you do sth: *We finished later than intended.* ◇ *I* **fully** **intended** (= definitely intended) *to pay for the damage.* ◇ *The writer clearly intends his readers to identify with the main character.* ◇ (*BrE*) *I don't intend staying long.* ◇ *It is* **intended that** *production will start at the end of the month.* ◇ *The company intends a slow-down in expansion.* ❶ **Intend** is often used in the present to talk about future plans: *He intends to retire at the end of this year.* ◇ *What do you intend to do now?* When **intend** is used to talk about past events, it often describes sth which was planned or wanted but which did not happen: *They stayed much longer than they'd originally intended.* ◇ *She didn't intend to kill him* (= but she did). See also **intended** → DELIBERATE, **intention** → PURPOSE

mean [T] (*especially spoken*) to have sth as a purpose or intention in your mind when you do sth: *I've* **been** **meaning to** *call her, but I've been so busy lately.* ◇ *I'm sorry I hurt you.* *I* **didn't mean to**. ◇ (*especially BrE*) *You're* **meant to** (= you are supposed to) *pay before you go in.* ◇ *Don't be upset − I'm sure he* **meant it as** *a compliment.* ◇ *Don't laugh! I* **mean it** (= I am serious). ◇ *He* **means** **what he says** (= is not joking, exaggerating, etc.). ◇ *He* **means trouble** (= to cause trouble). ◇ *The chair was* clearly **meant for** *a child.* ❶ **Mean** is often used when sb does not in fact succeed in doing what they intended to do, or sth does not happen the way they intended.

plan (**-nn-**) [I, T] to have a clear idea in your mind about what you hope or expect to do, often when you have decided in detail how you will do it: *We hadn't* **planned on** *going anywhere this evening.* ◇ *They plan to arrive some time after three.* ◇ *We're planning a trip to France in the spring.* See also **plan** → PURPOSE

aim [I, T] to try or plan to achieve a particular goal: *The government is* **aiming at** *a 50% reduction in unemployment.* ◇ *We should* **aim for** *a bigger share of the market.* ◇ *We aim to be there around six.* See also **aim** → PURPOSE

have sb/sth in 'mind *idiom* to be thinking of sb/sth, especially for a particular purpose, job or activity: *Do you* **have** *anyone* **in mind** *for the job?* ◇ *Watching TV all evening wasn't exactly what I had in mind!* ◇ *I had (it) in mind to give you an overview first of all.*

propose [I] (*rather formal*) to intend to do sth in the future: *What do you* **propose** *to do now?* ◇ *How do you* **propose** *getting home?*

intense *adj.*

intense · passionate · fierce · heated · emotional · violent · fiery · ardent · fervent
These words all describe a person or action that shows very strong feelings.

PATTERNS AND COLLOCATIONS
▸ intense / passionate / fierce / heated / emotional **about** sth
▸ an intense / a passionate / a fierce / a heated / an emotional / a fiery **debate**
▸ a passionate / a fierce / a heated / an emotional / a violent **argument**
▸ an intense / a passionate / a fierce / a heated / a violent **controversy**
▸ a fierce / heated / fiery **exchange** / **dispute**
▸ intense / fierce / violent **opposition**
▸ a passionate / fierce / violent / fiery **temper**
▸ intense / passionate / fierce / fervent **devotion** / **conviction**
▸ a passionate / an ardent / a fervent **supporter**

intense having or showing very strong feelings, opinions or thoughts about sb/sth; serious and involving a lot of activity in a short period of time: *He's very intense about everything.* ◇ *She met his intense gaze.* ◇ *There was an intense relationship between mother and son.* ◇ *There has been intense speculation about divisions in the party.*
▸ **intensely** *adv.*: *She disliked him intensely.*
▸ **intensity** *noun* [U, sing.]: *intensity of feeling* ◇ *He was watching her with an intensity that was unnerving.*

passionate /ˈpæʃənət/ having or showing strong feelings of enthusiasm for sth or belief in sth: *She is passionate about her work.* ◇ *He has a* **passionate interest** *in music and opera.* ◇ *She was a passionate defender of civil liberties.* ❶ **Passionate** is used especially to talk about sb's beliefs and commitment as well as people themselves who strongly support sb/sth: *a passionate speech/sincerity/ attachment/belief/commitment/conviction* ◇ *a passionate supporter/defender of sth* See also **passion** → EMOTION, **passion** → TASTE *noun* 1
▸ **passionately** *adv.*: *She believes passionately in education and hard work.*

fierce (*especially of actions or emotions*) showing strong feelings or a lot of activity, often in a way that is violent: *He launched a fierce attack on the Democrats.* ◇ *His wife is his* **fiercest critic**. ◇ *Competition from abroad became fiercer in the 1990s.*
▸ **fiercely** *adv.*: *fiercely competitive/independent/proud*

heated (*of a person or discussion*) full of anger and excitement: *We all seem to be getting very heated about this.* ◇ *Their voices rose in heated argument.* See also **heat** → EMOTION
▸ **heatedly** *adv.*: *'You had no right!' she said heatedly.*

emotional (*sometimes disapproving*) showing strong emotions, sometimes in a way that other people think is unnecessary: *an emotional outburst/response/reaction* ◇ *They made an emotional appeal for help.* ◇ *He tends to get emotional on these occasions.* See also **emotion** → EMOTION

violent showing or caused by very strong emotion: *There was a violent reaction from the public.*
▸ **violence** *noun* [U]: *The violence of her feelings surprised him.*
▸ **violently** *adv.*: *They are violently opposed to the idea.*

fiery /ˈfaɪəri/ [*usually before noun*] quickly or easily becoming angry; showing strong emotions, especially anger: *He's a big strong lad with a fiery temper.* ◇ *John Wesley preached his fiery sermons to large crowds.*

ardent /ˈɑːdnt; *AmE* ˈɑːrdnt/ [*usually before noun*] (*rather formal, especially written*) having or showing strong feelings of admiration or enthusiasm for sb/sth: *He was one of the president's most ardent admirers.*
▸ **ardently** *adv.*: *They were ardently anti-Communist.*

fervent /ˈfɜːvənt; *AmE* ˈfɜːrv-/ [*usually before noun*] (*rather formal, especially written*) having or showing strong and sincere feelings or beliefs: *It is my fervent hope that she will find success in her chosen career.* ◇ *She was a fervent Catholic.* See also **fervour** → EMOTION
▸ **fervently** *adv.*: *She prayed fervently for his complete recovery.*

NOTE **PASSIONATE, ARDENT** OR **FERVENT**? In many cases you can use any of these words: *a passionate/ardent/ fervent supporter of sb/sth.* **Passionate** is used especially to talk about sb's *beliefs*; **fervent** is used especially to talk about sb's *hopes* or *prayers*; **ardent** is used especially to talk about sb who as an *admirer* or *fan* of sb/sth.

interest *noun*

1 places of interest
2 Her interests are music and gardening.

1 interest · attraction · appeal · glamour · magic · charm · spell · fascination

These are all words for a feature or quality that makes sth seem attractive, interesting or exciting to people.

PATTERNS AND COLLOCATIONS
▸ an interest/ an attraction/ an appeal/ a fascination **for** sb/ sth
▸ a **special** interest/ attraction/ appeal/ magic/ charm/ fascination
▸ **great/ considerable** interest/ attraction/ appeal/ charm/ fascination
▸ **obvious/ growing** interest/ attraction/ appeal/ fascination
▸ a **powerful** attraction/ appeal/ spell
▸ to **have** an interest/ an attraction/ an appeal/ glamour/ a magic/ charm/ a fascination
▸ to **hold** an interest/ an attraction/ an appeal/ a magic/ a charm/ a fascination
▸ to **exert** an attraction/ an appeal/ a spell/ a fascination
▸ the attraction/ appeal/ fascination (of sth) **lies in** sth
▸ to be **part of** the attraction/ appeal/ magic/ charm/ fascination

interest [U, sing.] the quality that sth has when it attracts sb's attention or makes them want to know more about it: *There are many places of interest around Oxford.* ◇ *The subject is **of no interest** to me at all.* ◇ *These plants will add interest to your garden.* ◇ *His books have a special interest for me.*
attraction [U, C] a feature, quality or person that makes sth seem interesting and enjoyable, and worth having or doing: *I can't **see the attraction of** sitting on the beach all day.* ◇ *And there's the **added attraction** of free champagne on all flights.* ◇ *She is the **star attraction** of the show.* See also **attractive** → POPULAR
appeal [U, sing.] a quality that makes sb/sth seem attractive or interesting to people: *We are trying to **broaden the appeal** of classical music.* ◇ *Her stories have a universal appeal.* See also **appealing** → POPULAR
glamour /ˈglæmə(r)/ [U] the attractive and exciting quality that makes a person, job or place seem special, often because of wealth or status: *Hopeful young actors are drawn by the glamour of Hollywood.* See also **glamorous** → FASHIONABLE
magic [U] a mysterious and wonderful quality or ability that sb/sth has that makes them/it seem very special: *The show is three hours of pure magic.* ◇ *Like all truly charismatic people, he can **work his magic** on both men and women.*
charm [U, C, usually pl.] the quality that a place or thing has of being pleasing or attractive, especially in a way that is slightly old-fashioned; a pleasing or attractive feature: *The hotel is full of charm and character.* ◇ *The route certainly had its charms.* See also **charming** → BEAU-TIFUL 2
spell [sing.] a quality that sb/sth has that makes them/it so attractive or interesting that they/it have a strong influence on you: *Since last century, the spell of the pyramids has drawn tourists to Egypt.* ◇ *I completely **fell under her spell**.*
fascination /ˌfæsɪˈneɪʃn/ [C, usually sing.] a very strong attraction that makes sth very interesting to people: *Water holds a fascination for most children.*

2 See the Topic Map for SPORT AND LEISURE on p.892
interest · hobby · game · pastime · entertainment · amusement

These are all words for activities that you do for pleasure in your spare time.

PATTERNS AND COLLOCATIONS
▸ a **popular** interest/ hobby/ pastime/ entertainment/ amusement
▸ to **have/ share** interests/ hobbies
▸ to **take up/ pursue** an interest/ a hobby

interest [C] an activity or subject that you do or study for pleasure in your spare time: *Her main interests are music and gardening.* ◇ *He was a man of wide interests outside his work.* See also **passion** → TASTE *noun* 1
hobby [C] an activity that you do for pleasure in your spare time: *Her hobbies include swimming and cooking.* ◇ *I only play jazz **as a hobby**.*
game [C] a children's activity when they play with toys, pretend to be sb else, etc.; an activity that you do to have fun: *The children invented a new game.* ◇ *He was playing games with the dog.* See also **game** → GAME 2
pastime /ˈpɑːstaɪm; *AmE* ˈpæs-/ [C] an activity that people do for pleasure in their spare time: *Eating out is the national pastime in France.*

> **NOTE** **INTEREST, HOBBY** OR **PASTIME?** A **hobby** is often more active than an **interest**: *His main hobby is football* (= he plays football). ◇ *His main interest is football* (= he watches and reads about football, and may or may not play it). **Pastime** is used when talking about people in general; when you are talking about yourself or an individual person it is more usual to use **interest** or **hobby**: *Eating out is the national interest/hobby in France.* ◇ *Do you have any pastimes?*

entertainment [C] a film, show or other event used to entertain people: *Local entertainments are listed in the newspaper.*
amusement [C, usually pl.] a game or activity that provides entertainment and pleasure: *traditional seaside amusements including boats, go-karts and a funfair*

interest *verb* See the Topic Map for SPORT AND LEISURE on p.892, See also the entry for DELIGHT

interest · appeal · attract · fascinate · intrigue · absorb · rivet · grip

These words all mean to catch and keep your attention.

interest	absorb	fascinate
appeal		rivet
attract		grip
intrigue		

PATTERNS AND COLLOCATIONS
▸ to attract/ rivet/ grip sb's **attention**
▸ a **question/ subject** interests/ fascinates/ intrigues sb
▸ to **really** interest sb/ appeal to sb/ attract/ fascinate/ intrigue sb

interest [T] to catch and keep your attention: *Politics just doesn't interest me.* ◇ *The museum has something to interest everyone.* ◇ *It **may interest you to know** that he didn't accept the offer.* ◇ *She has always **interested herself in*** (= given her attention to) *helping younger musicians.*
appeal [I] to be sth that you like: *The prospect of a long wait in the rain did not appeal.* ◇ *It's a book that **appeals to** people of all ages.*
attract [T, usually passive] (of a thing) to have qualities that you notice and like it; (of a person) to have qualities that make you like and admire them: *That was what first **attracted me to** the place.* ◇ *I had always been attracted by*

the idea of working abroad. ◇ *What first attracted me about her was her sense of humour.* **OPP** **repel** → SHOCK, See also **tempt** → TEMPT

fascinate /'fæsɪneɪt/ [T, I] to attract or interest sb very much, often because you feel that there is a lot you can learn or that sth is mysterious: *China has always fascinated me.* ◇ *The private lives of the rich and famous never fail to fascinate.*

intrigue /ɪn'triːɡ/ [T] to make sb very interested and want to know more about sth, usually because it seems unusual or mysterious: *There was something about him that intrigued her.*

absorb [T] to interest sb very much so that they pay no attention to anything else: *The work had absorbed him for several years.* ◇ *She was completely **absorbed in** the task.*

rivet /'rɪvɪt/ [T, usually passive] to hold sb's interest or attention so completely that they cannot look away or think of anything else: *I was absolutely riveted by her story.* ◇ *My eyes were **riveted on** the figure lying in the road.*

grip (-**pp**-) [T] to interest or excite sb very much; to hold sb's attention completely: *The book grips you from the first page to the last.* ◇ *The atmosphere of the World Cup gripped the nation.*

interested *adj.* See the Topic Map for SPORT AND LEIS-URE on p.892

interested · fascinated · absorbed · engrossed · attentive · rapt

These words all describe sb who is giving all their attention to sth.

interested	absorbed	fascinated
attentive	engrossed	rapt

PATTERNS AND COLLOCATIONS
▸ interested / absorbed / engrossed / rapt **in** sth
▸ interested / absorbed / engrossed **in doing** sth
▸ interested / fascinated **to do** sth
▸ an interested / a fascinated / an attentive / a rapt **expression**
▸ an interested / an attentive / a rapt **audience**
▸ **utterly** fascinated / absorbed / rapt
▸ **completely / totally** absorbed / engrossed

interested giving your attention to sth because you enjoy finding out about it or doing it; showing interest in sth and finding it exciting: *I'm very interested in history.* ◇ *Anyone interested in joining the club should contact us at the address below.* ◇ *We would be interested to hear your views on this subject.* ◇ *He's not the least bit interested in girls.* ◇ *She was watching with a politely interested expression on her face.* **OPP** **uninterested** → INDIFFERENT, **bored** → BORED

fascinated /'fæsɪneɪtɪd/ very interested in sth: *I've always been **fascinated by** his ideas.* ◇ *The children watched, fascinated, as the picture began to appear.*

absorbed [not usually before noun] so interested in reading, watching or doing sth that you are not paying attention to anything else: *She seemed totally absorbed in her book.* ◇ *He was too absorbed in watching the game to notice.*

engrossed /ɪn'ɡrəʊst; AmE ɪn'ɡroʊst/ [not usually before noun] so interested or involved in doing sth that you are not paying attention to anything else: *She was engrossed in conversation.* ◇ *Dawn was engrossed in stuffing clothes into a bag.*

attentive /ə'tentɪv/ listening or watching sb/sth carefully and with interest: *He listened, quiet and attentive.* ◇ *Never before had she had such an attentive audience.* **OPP** **inattentive** ❶ Someone who is **inattentive** is not paying attention to sb/sth: *an inattentive pupil* ◇ *inattentive to the needs of others*
▸ **attentively** *adv.*: *The children listened attentively to the story.*

rapt (*written*) so interested in sth that you give all your attention to it and do not notice anything else: *He watched her with a rapt expression.* ◇ *Jill stared at them blankly, rapt in thought.*

> **NOTE** ABSORBED, ENGROSSED OR RAPT? **Rapt** is the strongest of these three words, and is often used to describe sb's *expression* when they appear to look blank and not see what is in front of them. You can only be **absorbed** in sth that really interests you, especially in reading or watching sth; you can be **engrossed** in sth that you are doing that may not be particularly interesting but still takes all your attention: ~~Dawn was absorbed in stuffing clothes into a bag.~~

interesting *adj.* See the Topic Map for SPORT AND LEISURE on p.892

interesting · fascinating · compelling · stimulating · gripping · riveting · absorbing

These words all describe sb/sth that attracts or holds your attention because they are exciting, unusual or full of good ideas.

interesting	compelling	fascinating
stimulating	absorbing	gripping
		riveting

PATTERNS AND COLLOCATIONS
▸ interesting / fascinating / stimulating **for** sb
▸ interesting / fascinating **to** sb
▸ interesting / fascinating **that**...
▸ interesting / fascinating **to see / hear / find / learn / know**...
▸ an interesting / a fascinating / a compelling / a gripping **story / read / book**
▸ an interesting / a fascinating / a stimulating **experience / discussion / idea**
▸ an interesting / a fascinating **example**
▸ a compelling / riveting **performance**
▸ to **find sth** interesting / fascinating / compelling / stimulating / gripping / riveting / absorbing
▸ **very** interesting / fascinating / compelling / stimulating / gripping
▸ **really** interesting / fascinating / stimulating / gripping
▸ **especially / particularly** interesting / fascinating / compelling
▸ **absolutely** fascinating / gripping / riveting

interesting attracting your attention because it is exciting, unusual or full of good ideas: *That's an interesting question, Daniel.* ◇ *You seem to know a lot of very interesting people.* ◇ *It would be interesting to know what he really believed.* ◇ *I find it interesting that she claims not to know him.* ◇ *Can't we do something more interesting?* ◇ *Our survey produced some interesting results.* **OPP** **boring, dull, uninteresting** → BORING
▸ **interestingly** *adv.*: *Interestingly, there are very few recorded cases of such attacks.*

fascinating /'fæsɪneɪtɪŋ/ extremely interesting or attractive: *It's fascinating to see how different people approach the problem.* ◇ *The book provides a fascinating glimpse into Moroccan life.* ◇ *I fail to see what women find so fascinating about him.*

compelling (*written*) so interesting or exciting that it holds your attention and you cannot stop reading, watching or looking at it: *Her latest book makes compelling reading.* ◇ *His eyes were strangely compelling.*

stimulating /'stɪmjuleɪtɪŋ/ (*rather formal*) full of interesting or exciting ideas; making people feel enthusiastic: *Thank you for a most stimulating discussion.* ◇ *She was a very stimulating teacher who got the best out of her students.* See also **stimulate** → INSPIRE

gripping so exciting or interesting that it holds your attention completely: *The film is a gripping account of the early days of the revolution.*

riveting /ˈrɪvɪtɪŋ/ (*especially written*) so interesting or exciting that it holds your attention completely: *As usual, she gave a riveting performance.*

absorbing /əbˈsɔːbɪŋ; -ˈzɔːb-; *AmE* -ˈsɔːrb-; -ˈzɔːrb-/ so interesting or enjoyable that it holds your attention: *Chess can be an extremely absorbing game.*

> **NOTE** COMPELLING, GRIPPING, RIVETING OR ABSORBING?
> These words all describe sth that holds your attention. **Gripping** and **riveting** are stronger than **compelling** and **absorbing** and are used especially to talk about stories, films or performances that are exciting and dramatic. **Compelling** can also be used to describe books, but it usually describes factual books that hold your attention because they are true or because their arguments are so good. **Absorbing** describes books, subjects or activities that hold your attention in a quieter way.

interfere *verb*

interfere · impinge · intrude · meddle · invade · pry · encroach · muscle in
These words all mean to become involved in sth that does not concern you or to affect sb/sth in a negative way.

PATTERNS AND COLLOCATIONS
▸ to impinge / intrude / encroach **on** / **onto** / **upon** sb / sth
▸ to intrude / pry / encroach **into** sth
▸ to interfere / meddle **in** sth
▸ to interfere in / impinge on / intrude on / invade / encroach on sb's **privacy**
▸ to interfere in / intrude on / meddle in / pry into sb's **affairs**
▸ to interfere in / impinge on / intrude on / invade / pry into sb's **life**
▸ to interfere in / intrude on / pry into / encroach on sb's **private / personal life**
▸ to impinge on / intrude on / invade sb's **consciousness**
▸ to constantly interfere / impinge / invade / encroach

interfere /ˌɪntəˈfɪə(r); *AmE* ˌɪntərˈfɪr/ [I] (*disapproving*) to become involved in and try to influence a situation that does not concern you, in a way that annoys people: *I wish my mother would stop interfering and let me make my own decisions.* ◇ *The police are unwilling to interfere in family problems.* ◇ *Britain has no right to interfere in the internal affairs of other countries.*
▸ **interference** *noun* [U]: *They resent foreign interference in the internal affairs of their country.*

impinge /ɪmˈpɪndʒ/ [I] (*formal*) to have a noticeable effect on sb/sth, especially in a negative way: *He never allowed his work to impinge on his private life.* ◇ *The preparations for war were beginning to impinge.* See also **violate → BREAK 3**

intrude /ɪnˈtruːd/ [I] (*rather formal, disapproving*) to become involved in a situation where you are not wanted, especially sb's private affairs; to affect sb/sth in an unpleasant or annoying way: *We should not intrude upon their private grief.* ◇ *The sound of the telephone intruded into his dreams.*
▸ **intrusion** /ɪnˈtruːʒn/ *noun* [U, C]: *press intrusion into the affairs of the royals*
▸ **intrusive** *adj.*: *I don't like their intrusive sales methods.* ◇ *Some of the islanders found the presence of the film crew too intrusive.*

meddle [I] (*disapproving*) to become involved in sth that does not concern you, for example by offering advice or making changes, in a way that annoys people: *He had no right to meddle in her affairs.* ◇ *I'm not the sort of proprietor who meddles with editorial policy.*

invade [T] (*written, usually disapproving*) to have a noticeable effect on sth in an unpleasant or annoying way: *Does the press have the right to invade her privacy in this way?* ◇ *Consumerism now invades every aspect of our lives.*
▸ **invasion** /ɪnˈveɪʒn/ *noun* [C, U]: *The actress described the photographs as an invasion of privacy.*

pry /praɪ/ [I] (*disapproving*) to try to find out information about other people's private lives in a way that is annoying or rude: *I'm sick of you prying into my personal life!* ◇ *I'm sorry, I didn't mean to pry.*

encroach /ɪnˈkrəʊtʃ; *AmE* ɪnˈkroʊtʃ/ [I] (*formal, disapproving*) to gradually have a strong effect on sth, especially in a negative way, or to use up too much of sth: *He never allows work to encroach upon his family life.*

muscle ˈin *phrasal verb* (*informal, disapproving*) to force your way into a situation that does not concern you, in order to get sth for yourself: *A small-time Dutch gangster was trying to muscle in on the deal.* ◇ *Banks, too, are now muscling in on the insurance market.*

international *adj.*

international · global · worldwide · multinational · cosmopolitan · intercontinental · multiracial
These words all describe things that are connected with two or more countries or parts of the world.

PATTERNS AND COLLOCATIONS
▸ international / global / worldwide **attention / campaigns / influence / issues / markets**
▸ an international / a global / a worldwide **campaign / reputation**
▸ an international / a global / a multinational **company / corporation**
▸ an international / a cosmopolitan / a multiracial **society / community**
▸ an international / a global / a cosmopolitan **outlook**
▸ **truly** international / global / cosmopolitan

international [usually before noun] connected with or involving two or more countries: *the importance of preserving international peace and security* ◇ *In crucial areas of international relations the nation state still dominates.* ◇ *She is a professor of international law.* ◇ *He plays international rugby.* ◇ *The island now has an international airport* (= one with flights to and from foreign countries). **OPP** national → NATIONAL
▸ **internationally** *adv.*: *He was internationally famous.*

global /ˈɡləʊbl; *AmE* ˈɡloʊbl/ [usually before noun] covering or affecting the whole world: *The commission is calling for a global ban on whaling.* ◇ *the company's domestic and global markets* ◇ *a conference on global warming* (= the increase in temperature of the earth's atmosphere that is caused by the increase of particular gases, especially carbon dioxide) **OPP** local ❶ Local describes things that belong to or are connected with one particular place: *a local newspaper/radio station* ◇ *decisions made at a local rather than national level* See also **global → OVERALL**
▸ **globally** *adv.*: *globally accepted standards*

worldwide /ˈwɜːldwaɪd; *AmE* ˈwɜːrld-/ [usually before noun] covering or affecting all parts of the world: *The company has a worldwide sales force.* ◇ *She soon gained worldwide fame as a dancer.* ◇ *There was a danger of a worldwide recession.* ◇ *a worldwide flu epidemic*
▸ **worldwide** /ˌwɜːldˈwaɪd; *AmE* ˌwɜːrld-/ *adv.*: *We have 2 000 members worldwide.*

> **NOTE** GLOBAL OR WORLDWIDE? In many cases you can use either word: *global/worldwide attention/campaigns/ influence/issues/markets.* **Global** is used slightly more in political contexts; it places emphasis on the world as a single large community with a shared set of interests and problems. **Worldwide** is used slightly more in business contexts; it often places more emphasis on the great range of different communities in the world, with their own different interests and problems.

multinational [usually before noun] (*especially business or journalism*) (especially of a business) existing in or involving many countries: *the huge profits made by multinational drug manufacturers* ◇ *A multinational task force is being sent to the trouble spot.*
▸ **multinational** *noun* [C]: *one of the world's leading multinationals* (= multinational companies)

cosmopolitan /ˌkɒzmə'pɒlɪtən; *AmE* ˌkɑːzmə'pɑːl-/ (*approving*) (of a place) containing people of different types or from different countries, and influenced by their culture; (of a person) having or showing a wide experience of people and things from many different countries: *She liked the cosmopolitan atmosphere of the city.* ◇ *people with a truly cosmopolitan outlook*
▸ **cosmopolitan** *noun* [C]: *She's a real cosmopolitan.*

intercontinental /ˌɪntəˌkɒntɪ'nentl; *AmE* ˌɪntərˌkɑːn-/ [usually before noun] between continents: *intercontinental flights/missiles/travel/trade*

multiracial /ˌmʌlti'reɪʃl/ including or involving several different races of people: *We live in a multiracial society.*

interrupt *verb*

interrupt · disturb · bother · intrude · cut in · chip in · trouble · barge in
These words all mean to say or do sth that stops sb else from continuing to say or do sth.

PATTERNS AND COLLOCATIONS
▸ to interrupt / disturb sb / bother sb / cut in / chip in / trouble sb **with** sth
▸ intrude / cut in / chip in / barge in **on** sth
▸ to be **sorry to** interrupt sb / disturb sb / bother sb / intrude / cut in / trouble sb
▸ to **suddenly** interrupt / intrude / barge in

interrupt [I, T] to say or do sth that makes sb else stop what they are saying or doing, for example by starting to talk when they are speaking: *Please stop interrupting all the time!* ◇ *They were interrupted by a knock on the door.* ◇ *'What's his name?' John interrupted.* ◇ *I hope I'm not interrupting you.*
▸ **interruption** *noun* [C, U]: *He ignored her interruptions.* ◇ *She spoke for 20 minutes without interruption.*

disturb [T] to interrupt sb when they are trying to work, sleep, etc., especially by talking to them or making a noise: *If you're up early, try not to disturb the others.* ◇ *Don't disturb her when she's working.* See also **disturbance** → DISRUPTION

bother /'bɒðə(r); *AmE* 'bɑːð-/ [T] (*rather informal, especially spoken*) to interrupt sb, especially by talking to them or asking them questions when they are trying to do sth else: *Sorry to bother you, but there's a call for you on line two.* ◇ *Please stop bothering me with all these questions!* ◇ *Let me know if he bothers you again.*

> **NOTE** INTERRUPT, DISTURB OR BOTHER? You usually **interrupt** sb who is speaking by speaking yourself. You can **disturb** or **bother** sb who is trying to do sth on their own, by talking to them or asking questions. You can also **disturb** (but NOT **bother** or **interrupt**) sb who is trying to rest, by making a lot of noise: *Don't disturb/ bother me when I'm speaking.* ◇ *Stop interrupting me when I'm working.* ◇ *If you're up early, try not to interrupt/bother the others.*

intrude /ɪn'truːd/ (*rather informal*) to go or be somewhere where you are not wanted or are not supposed to be: *He didn't wish to intrude at such a sensitive time.* ◇ *They must be prevented from intruding into the family's private grief.*
▸ **intrusion** /ɪn'truːʒn/ *noun* [U, C]: *She apologized for the intrusion but said she had an urgent message.* ◇ *They claim the noise from the airport is an intrusion on their lives.* ◇ *This was another example of press intrusion into the affairs of the royals.*

,**cut 'in** *phrasal verb* to interrupt sb when they are speaking by saying sth: *She kept cutting in on our conversation.* ◇ *'What on earth are you talking about?' Maria cut in.*

,**chip 'in** *phrasal verb* (**-pp-**) (*informal*) to add a remark, suggestion or question to a conversation that is taking place among other people: *Pete and Ann chipped in with a few suggestions.*

trouble [T] (*rather formal*) to interrupt sb because you want to ask them sth: *Sorry to trouble you, but could you read this document through for me?* ◇ *I didn't want to trouble the doctor with such a small problem.* ❶ **Trouble** in this meaning is often used in polite requests and is more formal than **bother**.

barge in *phrasal verb* (*rather informal*) to enter a place or join a group, rudely interrupting what sb else is saying or doing: *I hope you don't mind me barging in like this.* ◇ *He just barged in on us while we were having a meeting.*

intervene *verb*

intervene · mediate · intercede · arbitrate
These words all mean to try to end a disagreement or to reach an agreement, especially on behalf of sb else.

PATTERNS AND COLLOCATIONS
▸ to intervene / mediate / intercede **on behalf of** sb
▸ to intervene / intercede **with** sb
▸ to intervene / mediate / arbitrate **between** A and B
▸ to intervene / mediate / arbitrate **in** sth
▸ to **ask sb to** intervene / mediate / intercede

intervene /ˌɪntə'viːn; *AmE* -tər'v-/ [I] (*rather formal*) to become involved in a situation in order to try and improve or help it: *He intervened with the authorities on the prisoners' behalf.* ◇ *The EU refuses to intervene to control the trade.* ◇ *She might have been killed if the neighbours hadn't intervened.*
▸ **intervention** *noun* [U, C]: *There have been calls for government intervention to save the steel industry.* ◇ *People resented his repeated interventions in the debate.*

mediate /'miːdieɪt/ [I, T] (*rather formal*) to try to end a disagreement between two or more people or groups by talking to them and trying to find things that everyone can agree on: *An independent body was brought in to mediate between workers and management.* ◇ *The UN attempted to mediate a solution to the conflict.* See also **mediator** → NEGOTIATOR

intercede /ˌɪntə'siːd; *AmE* -tər's-/ [I] (*formal*) to speak to sb in order to persuade them to show pity on sb else or to help end a disagreement: *I prayed that she would intercede for us.* ◇ *Their father made no attempt to intercede.*

> **NOTE** INTERVENE OR INTERCEDE? Intervene is a more general word which can refer to actions as well as discussions. You can **intervene** in any situation where you think you can help in some way. **Intercede** is often used in a situation where one person or group has power over another and you speak to the person with power to try to persuade them to treat the other person kindly or with pity.

arbitrate /'ɑːbɪtreɪt; *AmE* 'ɑːrb-/ [I, T] (*rather formal*) to officially settle an argument or disagreement between two people or groups: *A committee was created to arbitrate between management and the unions.* ◇ *He is the official responsible for arbitrating the case of disputed trades.* See also the entry for JUDGE *verb* 2
▸ **arbitration** *noun* [U]: *Both sides in the dispute have agreed to go to arbitration.*

interview *noun*

1 a TV interview
2 a job interview

1 interview · interrogation · audience · consultation
These are all words for a meeting at which sb is asked for their opinions or advice, or asked questions.

PATTERNS AND COLLOCATIONS
▸ an interview / an audience / a consultation **with** sb
▸ an **in-depth** interview / consultation
▸ a **police** interview / interrogation

▶ to **have / request** an interview / an audience / a consultation
▶ to **give / grant sb** an interview / an audience / a consultation
▶ to **carry out / conduct** an interview / interrogation
▶ interview / interrogation **procedures / techniques**

interview /ˈɪntəvjuː; AmE -tərv-/ [C] a meeting (often a public one) at which a journalist asks sb questions in order to find out their opinions; a private meeting between people when questions are asked and answered: *He's a very private man and rarely gives interviews* (= agrees to answer questions). ◇ *The survey team carried out over 200 interviews with retired people.* See also **interview** → QUESTION *verb*

interrogation [U, C] the process of asking sb a lot of questions, especially in an aggressive way, in order to get information; an occasion on which this is done: *He confessed after four days **under interrogation**.* ◇ *She hated her parents' endless interrogations about where she'd been.* See also **interrogate** → QUESTION *verb*

audience [C] a formal meeting with an important person: *The Pope granted her a private audience.*

consultation [C] a meeting with an expert, especially a doctor, to get advice or treatment: *A 30-minute consultation will cost £50.* See also **consult** → ASK *verb* 1

2 interview · audition · trial · tryout · screen test
These are all words for an occasion when sb tries to show that they are suitable for a particular job, a role in a play, film, etc. or a place in a team.

PATTERNS AND COLLOCATIONS
▶ an interview / an audition / trials / tryouts / a screen test **for** sth
▶ an interview / an audition / a trial / a tryout / a screen test **with** sb
▶ **in** an interview / an audition / trials / tryouts
▶ **at** an interview / audition
▶ **Olympic / international / national / club** trials / tryouts
▶ to **have** an interview / an audition / a trial / a tryout / a screen test
▶ to **go for** an interview / an audition / a screen test
▶ to **hold** interviews / auditions / trials / tryouts
▶ to **do / pass / fail** an audition / a screen test

interview [C] a formal meeting at which sb is asked questions to see if they are suitable for a particular job, or for a course of study at a college, university, etc: *I've got a **job interview** tomorrow.* ◇ *She's been called for (an) interview.*
▶ **interview** *verb* [T, I]: *We interviewed ten people for the job.* ◇ *The deadline for applications is 15 October and we will be interviewing early in November.*

audition /ɔːˈdɪʃn/ [C] a short performance given by an actor, singer, etc. so that sb can decide whether they are suitable to act in a play, sing in a concert, etc: *He went for an audition with the Royal Ballet.*
▶ **audition** *verb* [I, T]: *I auditioned and was given the part.* ◇ *We auditioned over 200 children for the role.*

trial [C, usually pl.] (*BrE*) a competition or series of tests to find the best players or athletes for a sports team or an important event: *She just missed selection when she came third in the trials.*

tryout /ˈtraɪaʊt/ [C, usually pl.] (*AmE*) a trial for a sports team or event: *He's now focusing on next week's Olympic tryouts.*

'screen test [C] a short performance by an actor which is filmed to see if they are suitable to appear in a film: *He asked Redford to read the script and **take a screen test**.*

introduce *verb*

1 introduce the latest technology
2 Can I introduce myself?

1 See also the entry for BEGIN
introduce · launch · initiate · institute · instigate · set/ put sth in motion · bring sth in · phase sth in
These words all mean to make people start using a new system or law or to start a process.

PATTERNS AND COLLOCATIONS
▶ to introduce / launch / initiate / institute / instigate / set in motion / bring in / phase in a **scheme / reform**
▶ to introduce / launch / initiate / institute / instigate / bring in / phase in a **system**
▶ to introduce / launch / initiate / institute / instigate / bring in a **policy**
▶ to introduce / launch / initiate / institute / instigate a **programme**
▶ to introduce / initiate / institute / instigate / set in motion / bring in / phase in **changes**
▶ to introduce / initiate / bring in (a) **legislation / law**
▶ to introduce / initiate / institute a **practice**
▶ to launch / initiate / institute / instigate (a / an) **campaign / enquiry / investigation / proceedings**
▶ to launch / initiate / set in motion a **plan**
▶ to introduce / launch / initiate / institute sth **formally**

introduce [T] to make sth such as a product, law, system or idea available for use or discussion for the first time: *The company is introducing a new range of products this year.* ◇ *We want to **introduce** the latest technology **into** schools.* ◇ *We are going to introduce a few changes to the system.*

launch [T] (*especially business or journalism*) to formally start an activity, especially an organized one: *The Duchess of Cornwall, president of the charity, will launch the appeal in London.* ◇ *Police have launched a murder enquiry.* ◇ *A massive attack was launched in the spring of 1918.* ❶ People in business typically **launch** an *appeal*, a *bid*, a *campaign*, an *enquiry*, an *initiative*, an *investigation*, an *operation*, a *plan*, a *project* or a *programme*. In military contexts, an army might **launch** an *attack*, an *assault*, a *raid* or an *invasion*. You can also **launch** a new product. See also **launch** → LAUNCH *noun*

initiate /ɪˈnɪʃieɪt/ [T] (*formal*) to introduce a system or policy or start a process: *The government has initiated a programme of economic reform.* ◇ *He initiated a national debate on reform.* ◇ *The organization may initiate legal action against you.*

institute [T] (*formal*) to introduce a system or policy or start a process: *The new management intends to institute a number of changes.* ◇ *They could institute criminal proceedings against you.*

NOTE INITIATE OR **INSTITUTE**? There is very little difference in meaning between these words. **Initiate** has a wider range of collocates than **institute**: it can be used to talk about starting either a formal process, such as legal action, or a more informal process, such as a *debate* or *discussion*. **Institute** is only used to talk about more formal processes: *He instituted a national debate on reform.*

instigate [T] (*especially BrE, formal*) to start a process or action, often sth official: *We will instigate a comprehensive review of defence policy.* ◇ *It was Rufus who instigated the whole thing.* ❶ **Instigate** is often used when there is some discussion about who made sth happen, or when the action taken is not popular with everyone involved.
▶ **instigation** *noun* [U]: *An appeal fund was launched **at the instigation of** the President.* ◇ *It was done **at his instigation**.*

set/put sth in 'motion *idiom* (*especially written*) to make a process start or happen: *The wheels of change have been set in motion.* ❶ **Set/put sth in motion** is usually used to talk about starting a process that consists of several steps: *to set in motion preparations / a process / a chain of actions / steps / a procedure / measures*

,bring sth 'in *phrasal verb* to introduce a new law: *They want to bring in a bill to limit arms exports.* ❶ **Bring sth in** is mainly used to talk about an *act*, a *bill*, a *law*, a *regulation* or *legislation*.

,phase sth 'in *phrasal verb* (*especially business*) to introduce or start using sth gradually in stages over a period of time: *The new tax will be phased in over two years.* **OPP phase sth out** ❶ To **phase sth out** is to stop using sth gradually in stages over a period of time.

2 introduce · present
These words both mean to tell two or more people who have not met before what each other's names are.

PATTERNS AND COLLOCATIONS
▸ to introduce / present sb **to** sb

introduce [T] to tell two or more people who have not met before what each other's names are; to tell sb what your name is: *Can I introduce my wife?* ◇ *He introduced me to a Greek girl at the party.* ◇ *Can I **introduce myself**? I'm Helen Robins.* See also **introduction** → MEETING 2

present [T] (*formal*) to introduce sb formally, especially to sb of higher rank or status: *May I present my fiancé?*

introduction *noun*
1 the introduction of modern farming methods
2 the introduction to a book

1 introduction · formation · establishment · foundation
These are all words for the act of bringing sth into use or existence for the first time.

PATTERNS AND COLLOCATIONS
▸ the **early / gradual / rapid / recent** introduction / formation / establishment of sth
▸ the **formal** introduction / establishment of sth
▸ to **lead to / result in / see** the introduction / formation / establishment / foundation of sth
▸ to **call for/support/allow (for)/enable/provide for/announce** the introduction / formation / establishment of sth

introduction [U] the act of bringing sth into use or existence for the first time, or of bringing sth to a place for the first time: *The need for a large army resulted in the introduction of compulsory military service.* ◇ *the gradual **introduction** of modern farming methods **into** traditional societies* ◇ *They celebrated the 1000th anniversary of the **introduction** of Christianity **to** Russia.*

formation /fɔːˈmeɪʃn; AmE fɔːrˈm-/ [U] the act of creating sth; the process of being created: *An agreement on the formation of a new government was reached on June 6.* ◇ *They've found evidence of recent star formation in the galaxy.* See also **form** → ESTABLISH *verb*

establishment [U] (*rather formal*) the act of starting or creating sth that is meant to last for a long time: *The speaker announced the establishment of a new college.* ◇ *His visit facilitated the establishment of diplomatic relations between the countries.* ❶ **Establishment** can be used to talk about a service, a belief or a project, as well as an organization. See also **establish** → ESTABLISH

foundation [U] (*rather formal*) the act of creating a new institution or organization: *The organization has grown enormously since its foundation in 1955.* ◇ *She used the money to go towards the foundation of a special research group.* See also **found** → ESTABLISH

2 introduction · preface · preamble · prologue · foreword
These are all words for the first part of a book or speech that gives a general idea of what is to follow.

PATTERNS AND COLLOCATIONS
▸ the introduction / preface / preamble / prologue / foreword **to** a book, etc.
▸ **in** the introduction / preface / preamble / prologue / foreword
▸ to **read / write** the introduction / a preface / a preamble / a prologue / a foreword

introduction [C, U] the first part of a book or speech that gives a general idea of what is to follow: *This book has an excellent introduction and notes.* ◇ *By way of introduction, let me give you the background to the story.* See also **introductory** → FIRST

preface /ˈprefəs/ [C] a piece of writing at the beginning of a book, especially one that explains the author's aims: *In his preface he claimed that he had created a new kind of*

music. ❶ A **preface** deals with the aims, range of subjects and limitations of the book. It is usually written by the author, and is found before the introduction in a book.
▸ **preface** *verb* [T]: *He prefaced the diaries with a short account of how they were discovered.*

preamble /priˈæmbl; ˈpriːæmbl/ [C, U] (*formal*) a piece of writing at the beginning of a book or written document; an introduction to sth you say: *the Preamble to the US Constitution* ◇ *She gave him the bad news **without preamble**.* ❶ A written **preamble** is usually found in an official document or factual book, rather than a novel or other literary work.

prologue /ˈprəʊlɒg; AmE ˈproʊlɔːg; -lɑːg/ [C] a speech or piece of writing at the beginning of a play, novel, etc. that introduces it: *the Prologue to Chaucer's 'Canterbury Tales'* ❶ A **prologue** usually forms part of the story, rather than being a separate piece of writing that the reader can choose to read or not.

foreword /ˈfɔːwɜːd; AmE ˈfɔːrwɜːrd/ [C] a short piece of writing at the beginning of a book: *He was asked if he would consider writing a foreword for her book.* ❶ The **foreword** to a book is usually written by sb other than the author. The writer of the **foreword** will sometimes give an account of a link he or she has with the author or contents of the book. The **foreword** is found before the introduction in a book.

invade *verb* See the Topic Map for CONFLICT on p.896, See also the entry for ATTACK 2

invade · occupy · seize · capture · annex · take · conquer
These words all mean to take control of a place using military force.

PATTERNS AND COLLOCATIONS
▸ to invade / occupy / seize / annex / conquer a **country / region**
▸ to invade / occupy / seize / capture / take / conquer a **town / city**
▸ to occupy / seize / capture / take a **building**
▸ to seize / take **control** of a place
▸ **troops / soldiers** invade / occupy / seize / capture / take a place
▸ a **country** invades / occupies / annexes / conquers a place

invade [I, T] to use military force to enter a place, especially a country: *Troops invaded on August 9th that year.* ◇ *When did the Romans invade Britain?* See also **invasion** → ATTACK *noun* 1

occupy [T] to enter a place in a large group, stay there and take control of it: *The capital has been occupied by the rebel army.* ◇ *Protesting students occupied the TV station.*
▸ **occupation** *noun* [U]: *The military occupation has created anger and resentment.*

seize /siːz/ [T] to take control of a place or situation, often suddenly and violently: *They seized the airport in a surprise attack.* ◇ *The army has seized control of the country.* ◇ *He **seized power** in a military coup.*
▸ **seizure** /ˈsiːʒə(r)/ *noun* [U]: *The invasion began with the seizure of the country's largest southern city.*

capture [T] to take control of sth from the enemy in a war by using military force: *The city was captured in 1941.* ◇ *He led the party that captured the enemy's flag.*
▸ **capture** *noun* [U]: *The capture of enemy territory followed the defeat of their air force.*

annex /əˈneks/ [T] to take possession of a country or part of a country, especially one that is next to your own, and claim it as part of your own country: *Germany annexed Austria in 1938.*
▸ **annexation** /ˌænekˈseɪʃn/ *noun* [U, C]: *The annexation of Texas was one of the causes of the Mexican War.*

take [T] to capture a place in war; to get control of sth: *The rebels succeeded in taking the town.* ◇ *The state has taken control of the company.*

conquer /ˈkɒŋkə(r); AmE ˈkɑːŋ-/ [T] (especially in the past) to take possession of a country or city and its people using military force: *In 330 BC Persia was conquered by Alexander the Great.*
▸ **conquest** *noun*: *The Norman Conquest of England in 1066 led to changes in the system of government.*

invent *verb* See also the entry for COME UP WITH STH

invent · make sth up · coin · fabricate · trump sth up
These words all mean to say or describe sth that is not true or to use a new word, phrase or name.

PATTERNS AND COLLOCATIONS
▸ to invent / make up / fabricate a **story**
▸ to invent / make up a / an **excuse** / **name**
▸ to invent / make up / coin a **word**
▸ to make up / fabricate **evidence**
▸ to fabricate / trump up **charges**

invent [T] to say or describe sth that is not true, especially in order to deceive people; to think of and use a new word, phrase or name: *I did not have to invent any tales about my past.* ◇ *He considered inventing some pretext for calling her.* ◇ *Many children invent an imaginary friend.* ◇ *The term 'sociology' was invented by Auguste Comte.*
▸ **invention** *noun* [C, U]: *The story is apparently a complete invention.* ◇ *What would he tell his parents? Some invention and quick thinking – that's what was needed.*

make sth 'up *phrasal verb* (*rather informal*) to invent a story, name, etc., especially in order to deceive or entertain sb: *He made up some excuse about his daughter being sick.* ◇ *You made that up!* ◇ *I told the kids a story, making it up as I went along.* ❶ **Make sth up** is more informal than **invent**. It is often used where the object of the verb is not clearly stated: *You're making it up.* ◇ *It turned out she had made the whole thing up.*
▸ **'made-up** *adj.*: *a made-up story/word/name*

coin [T] to invent a new word or phrase that other people then begin to use: *He was the first to coin the motto 'Make Love, Not War'.*

fabricate /'fæbrɪkeɪt/ [T, often passive] (*rather formal*) to invent false information in order to deceive people: *The prisoners claimed their confessions had been fabricated by police.* ◇ *She was found to have fabricated research data.* See also **fabrication** → LIE *noun*

trump sth 'up *phrasal verb* to make up a false story about sb/sth, especially accusing them of doing sth wrong: *Since her arrest, they've trumped up charges against her.*
▸ **'trumped-up** *adj.*: *She was arrested on trumped-up charges.*

investigate *verb*

investigate · explore · look into sth · research · probe · enquire into sth · delve into sth
These words all mean to examine sth in order to find out more about it.

PATTERNS AND COLLOCATIONS
▸ to look / research / probe / enquire / delve **into** sth
▸ to investigate / explore / look into / research / enquire into **what/ why / how / whether...**
▸ to investigate / explore / look into / research / enquire into a **problem / matter**
▸ to investigate / explore / look into / research / delve into a **subject**
▸ to investigate / look into / probe / enquire into an **allegation**
▸ to investigate / explore / probe **further**
▸ to look / enquire / delve **further** into sth
▸ to **carefully** investigate / explore / research sth
▸ to enquire **carefully** into sth
▸ to look / probe / enquire / delve **deep / deeper / deeply** into sth
▸ to investigate / explore / probe sth **in detail**

investigate [I, T] to carefully examine the facts of a situation, event or crime to find out the truth about it or how it happened; to try to find out information about sb's character or activities; to find out information about a subject or problem by study or research: *The FBI has been called in to investigate.* ◇ (*informal*) *'What was that noise?' 'I'll go and investigate.'* ◇ *Police are investigating possible links between the two murders.* ◇ *This is not the first time*

he has been investigated by the police for fraud. ◇ *The research investigates how foreign speakers gain fluency.* See also **investigation** → REPORT *noun* 1

explore [T] to examine or discuss an idea, issue or possibility completely or carefully in order to find out more about it: *These ideas will be explored in more detail in chapter 7.* ◇ *The study explores the differences between the way girls and boys talk.* ◇ *We need to **explore** every possible **avenue** (= every possibility).* See also **exploration** → RESEARCH *noun*

look 'into sth *phrasal verb* to examine sth to find out more about it or to see whether it is possible: *A working party has been set up to look into the problem.* ◇ *He was asked to look into the feasibility of a trial.*

research [T, I] to study sth carefully and in detail to try to discover new facts about it: *She's in New Zealand researching her new book.* ◇ *The book has been **poorly researched**.* ◇ *They're researching into new ways of improving people's diets.* ❶ People **research** things especially in order to write a book, develop a new product or method of doing sth or start a new line of business. See also **research** → RESEARCH *noun*

probe [I, T] (*especially journalism*) to ask questions in order to find out secret or hidden information about sb/sth: *Jim changed the subject before she could probe any further.* ◇ *He didn't like the media probing into his past.* ◇ *Scotland Yard to probe fraud allegations* (= in a news headline)

en'quire into sth (also **inquire into sth** especially in *AmE*) *phrasal verb*
to find out more information about sth, especially by asking questions: *He was instructed to enquire into where responsibility for the conflict lay.* ◇ *Jack knew not to enquire too closely into the affairs of his uncle.* See also **enquiry** → RESEARCH *noun*

delve into sth *phrasal verb* (*rather informal*) to try hard to find out more information about sth, especially sth complicated or difficult to find out about: *She had started to delve into her father's distant past.*

investigation *noun*

investigation · survey · poll · enquiry · case · probe · inquest · check
These are all words for a process to find out about sth, especially to find all the facts or the cause of sth.

PATTERNS AND COLLOCATIONS
▸ an investigation / a survey / an enquiry / a probe / an inquest **into** sth
▸ a survey / an inquest / a check **on** sth / sb
▸ **in** a survey / a poll / an enquiry
▸ a **full** investigation / survey / enquiry / inquest / check
▸ an **independent** investigation / survey / poll / enquiry / probe / inquest / check
▸ an **official** investigation / survey / enquiry / probe
▸ a **public** investigation / survey / enquiry / inquest
▸ a **murder** investigation / enquiry / case / probe
▸ a **police** investigation / enquiry / probe / check
▸ to **carry out** an investigation / a survey / a poll / an enquiry / a check
▸ to **conduct** an investigation / a survey / a poll / an enquiry / an inquest / a check
▸ to **order** an investigation / an enquiry / a probe / an inquest
▸ to **launch** an investigation / a survey / an enquiry / a probe
▸ an investigation / a survey / a poll / an enquiry / an inquest / a check **reveals / shows** sth
▸ an investigation / a survey / a poll / an enquiry / an inquest **finds** sth
▸ the **results / findings of** an investigation / a survey / a poll / an enquiry / an inquest

investigation [C, U] an official examination of the facts about a crime, accident or other situation: *The police have completed their investigations into the accident.* ◇ *These are the same methods used in **criminal investigations**.* ◇ *She is currently **under investigation** for possessing illegal drugs.*

survey [C] a process to find out the opinions or behaviour of a particular group of people, which is usually done by asking them questions: *According to the survey, many young adults have experimented with drugs.* ◇ *The charity did a survey of people's attitudes to the disabled.* See also **survey → SURVEY** *verb*

poll /pəʊl; *AmE* poʊl/ [C] a process of questioning people who are representative of a larger group to get information about general opinions: *Nelson has a clear lead in the opinion polls.* ◇ *A nationwide poll revealed differences in food preferences between the North and South.* See also **exit poll, straw poll → ELECTION, poll → SURVEY** *verb*

enquiry (also **inquiry** especially in *AmE*) [C] an official process to find out the cause of sth or to find out information about sth: *There will be a public enquiry into the impact of the proposed new road.* ◇ (*formal*) *The director has been suspended on full pay pending an internal enquiry.*

case [C] a matter that is being officially investigated, especially by the police: *A detective is on the case at the moment.* ◇ *Four police officers are investigating the case.* ◇ *They never solved the Jones murder case.*

probe [C] (*journalism*) a thorough and careful investigation into sth, especially sth that might be illegal: *There is to be a police probe into the financial affairs of the company.* ◇ *Arson probe after three die in blaze* (= in a news headline)

inquest /'ɪŋkwest/ [C] an official process to find out the cause of sb's death, especially when it has not happened naturally; a discussion about sth that has failed: *There will be a coroner's inquest into his death.* ◇ *There will inevitably be an inquest into the team's poor performance.*

check [C] (*rather informal*) an investigation to find out more information about sth: *Was any check made on Mr Morris when he applied for the job?* ◇ *The police ran a check on the registration number of the car.*

investment *noun*

investment · grant · funding · subsidy · backing · sponsorship · endowment
These are all words for money that a government or company pays to a person, company or organization, often in order to support them.

PATTERNS AND COLLOCATIONS
▸ investment/a grant/funding/a subsidy/backing/sponsorship/ an endowment **from** sb/ sth
▸ investment/a grant/funding/a subsidy/backing/sponsorship/ an endowment **for** sth
▸ a grant/ a subsidy **to** sb/ sth
▸ a grant/ funding **to do** sth
▸ (a) **substantial** investment/ grant/ funding/ subsidy/ backing/ sponsorship
▸ (a) **generous** grant/funding/subsidy/sponsorship/endowment
▸ (a) **government** investment/grant/funding/subsidy/backing/ sponsorship
▸ (a) **public** investment/ funding/ subsidy/ backing
▸ (a) **business/ commercial/ corporate** investment/ funding/ backing/ sponsorship
▸ (an) **annual** investment/ grant/ funding/ subsidy
▸ to **get** investment/ a grant/ funding/ a subsidy/ backing/ sponsorship
▸ to **receive/ increase** investment/ a grant/ funding/ a subsidy/ sponsorship/ an endowment
▸ to **cut** investment/ funding/ a subsidy
▸ to **attract** investment/ funding/ sponsorship
▸ to **apply for/ be eligible for/ qualify for** a grant/ funding/ a subsidy

investment [C, U] money that a company, government or person spends on property, a business or service, in order to make a profit or to make the organization or service work better: *We made an initial investment of $10 000.* ◇ *I'm hoping for a good return on my investment.* ◇ *We bought the house as an investment* (= to make money). ◇ *The country needs massive government investment in education.* See also **invest → SPEND** 1

grant [C] an amount of money that is given by a government or organization to be used for a particular purpose: *She has been awarded a research grant by Liverpool University.* ◇ *The hospital has applied for a government grant to buy a new scanner.*

funding [U] money that is given by a government or organization to be used for a particular purpose; the act of providing this money: *There have been large cuts in government funding for scientific research.* ◇ *the current debate on the funding of higher education* See also **fund → FUND** *verb*, **funds → MONEY** 1

NOTE **GRANT OR FUNDING?** A **grant** is an individual amount of money given to a particular person or organization, often for a particular project. **Funding** can also be used to talk about individual amounts or projects, but it is often a larger, less definite amount of money, given for a more general purpose to people or organizations of the same general type: *public funding for the arts* ◇ *public grants for the arts*

subsidy /'sʌbsədi/ [C, U] money that is paid by a government or organization to reduce the costs of services or of producing goods, so that their prices can be kept low: *The EU spends billions on subsidies to farmers every year.* ◇ *They want to reduce the level of government subsidy.* See also **subsidize → FUND** *verb*

backing [U] support, often including money, given to a person, organization or plan: *The museum has always received limited financial backing from the local authority.* ◇ *The police gave the proposals their full backing.* See also **back → SUPPORT** *verb* 1

sponsorship [U] money that is given by a company or person to pay for a concert, sporting event, etc. or for sb's training or education, usually in return for advertising: *The race organizers are trying to attract sponsorship from local firms.* See also **sponsor → SPONSOR** *noun*, **sponsor → FUND** *verb*

endowment [C, U] (*formal*) money that is given to a school, college or other institution to provide it with an income; the act of giving this money: *The purpose of the fund was to provide endowments for houses of historic interest that were threatened with sale.* See also **endow → FUND** *verb*

invisible *adj.*

invisible · out of sight · inconspicuous · imperceptible
These words all describe sb/sth that cannot be seen.

PATTERNS AND COLLOCATIONS
▸ invisible/ imperceptible **to** sb/ sth
▸ to **remain** invisible/ out of sight/ inconspicuous
▸ **almost** invisible/ out of sight/ imperceptible

invisible that cannot be seen: *The tanks were camouflaged so that they were invisible from the air.* ◇ *There are countless stars that are invisible to the naked eye.* OPP **visible → VISIBLE**

out of 'sight *phrase* in a place where you/it cannot be seen: *If you leave the camera in the car, put it out of sight under the seat.* ◇ *Keep out of sight* (= Stay where you cannot be seen). ◇ *She never lets her daughter out of her sight* (= always keeps her where she can see her). ◇ *Get out of my sight!* (= Go away!) OPP **in view → VISIBLE**

inconspicuous /ˌɪnkən'spɪkjuəs/ not attracting attention; not easy to notice: *She tried to look as inconspicuous as possible.* OPP **conspicuous → MARKED**

imperceptible /ˌɪmpəˈseptəbl; AmE -pərˈs-/ (rather formal) that cannot be felt, seen or noticed because it is very slight: *There are imperceptible changes in temperature occurring all the time.* ◊ *The differences were imperceptible to all but the most trained eye.*
▸ **imperceptibly** adv.: *The daylight faded almost imperceptibly into night.*

invite verb

invite · ask
These words both mean to ask sb to come to a social event.

PATTERNS AND COLLOCATIONS
▸ to invite / ask sb **to / for** sth
▸ to invite / ask sb **in / round / along / over / out**
▸ to invite / ask sb **to do sth**

invite [T] to ask sb to come to a social event: *Have you been invited to their party?* ◊ *They have invited me to go to Paris with them.* ◊ *They've invited us over for a drink.* ◊ *I'd have liked to have gone but I wasn't invited.*
▸ **invitation** noun [C, U]: *an invitation to the party* ◊ *A concert was held **at the invitation of** the mayor.* ◊ *Admission is **by invitation only**.*
ask [T] (usually used with an adverb or preposition) to ask sb to come to a social meeting or event: *Shall we ask Jon and Alison to dinner at the weekend?* ◊ *I didn't ask them in* (= to come into the house).

NOTE INVITE OR ASK? Ask is used especially to talk about arranging informal social meetings, usually where the invitation is spoken. Invite is also used to talk about an invitation to a more organized or formal social event, such as a party or wedding. You can invite sb to sth with a spoken or written invitation.

involvement noun See the Topic Map for SPORT AND LEISURE on p.892

involvement · role · part · contribution · participation · interest · input · stake · engagement · hand
These are all words for the fact of being active in an event or situation.

PATTERNS AND COLLOCATIONS
▸ involvement / a role / a part / an interest / a stake / engagement / a hand **in** sth
▸ involvement / a contribution / participation / input **from** sb
▸ a contribution / input **to** sth
▸ (a) **direct** involvement / role / part / contribution / participation / interest / input / stake / engagement
▸ (a) **greater** involvement / role / part / contribution / participation / interest / input / stake
▸ (a) **full** involvement / contribution / participation
▸ (a / an) **major / considerable / substantial / significant** involvement / role / part / contribution / interest / input / stake
▸ (a) **positive** involvement / role / part / contribution / participation / interest
▸ (an) **active** involvement / role / part / participation / interest / engagement
▸ (an) **alleged** involvement / role / part / participation
▸ (a) **valuable / useful / crucial / essential / important / key / constructive** role / part / contribution / input
▸ (a) **personal** involvement / role / contribution / participation / interest / input / stake / engagement
▸ (a) **public / limited** involvement / role / contribution / participation
▸ (a) **parental / political / military** involvement / role / participation / input
▸ to **encourage / increase** involvement / participation
▸ to **need / get / receive** a contribution / input
▸ to **have** a role / a part / an interest / an input / a stake / a hand in sth
▸ to **play** a role / part in sth
▸ to **have** a role / part **to play**

involvement [U, C, usually sing.] the fact of being active in an event or situation; the act of giving a lot of time and attention to sth you care about: *The success of the venture may lead to **involvement by** other foreign companies.* ◊ *The new album came out of her growing **involvement with** contemporary music.* ◊ *Nurses usually try to avoid **emotional involvement** with patients.* ◊ *He was found to have a deep involvement in drug dealing.* See also **involve** → INCLUDE 1, **involved** → BUSY 1, **be/get involved** → JOIN
role [C] the degree to which sb/sth is involved in a situation or activity and the effect that they have on it: *He stressed the role of diet in preventing disease.* ◊ *The media play a major role in influencing people's opinions.* ◊ *Regional managers have a crucial role in developing a strategic framework.*
part [C] sb/sth's role in sth: *She plays an active part in local politics.* ◊ *He **had no part in** the decision.* ◊ *How many countries **took part in** the last Olympic Games?*

NOTE ROLE OR PART? In this meaning **part** is used mainly in phrases: *have a part to play* ◊ *have/play a part in sth* ◊ *have/play/take no part in/of sth* ◊ *take part (in sth).* **Role** is slightly more formal, and common in business and economic contexts. It is used especially with adjectives like *key, important, essential, crucial, central, fundamental, major, pivotal, prominent* and *primary.*

contribution /ˌkɒntrɪˈbjuːʃn; AmE ˌkɑːn-/ [C, usually sing.] an action or service that helps to cause or increase sth, especially sth good or positive: *She has **made** a significant **contribution** to scientific knowledge.* ◊ *These measures would make a valuable **contribution towards** reducing industrial accidents.*
participation /pɑːˌtɪsɪˈpeɪʃn; AmE pɑːrˌt-/ [U] the act of taking part in an activity or event: *It's a show with lots of audience participation.* ◊ *A back injury prevented active participation in any sports for a while.* See also **participate** → JOIN

NOTE INVOLVEMENT OR PARTICIPATION? It is possible to have some **involvement** in a situation without actively choosing to do so; **participation** requires a greater level of choice from the person who is acting in a situation.

interest [C, U] a connection with sth that affects your attitude to it, especially because you may benefit from it in some way: *Organizations **have an interest in** ensuring that employee motivation is high.* ◊ *I should, at this point, **declare my interest.***
input [U, C] time, knowledge, ideas or effort that you put into work or a project in order to make it succeed: *I'd appreciate your input on this.* ◊ *There has been a big **input** of resources **into** the project from industry.*
stake [sing.] (always followed by *in*) an important part or share in a business, plan, etc. that is important to you and that you want to be successful: *She has a personal stake in the success of the play.* ◊ *Many young people no longer feel they have a stake in society.*
engagement [U] (formal) being involved with sb/sth in an attempt to understand them/it: *Her views are based on years of engagement with the problems of the inner city.*
hand [sing.] (always followed by *in*) (especially journalism) the part that sb/sth plays in a particular situation; sb's influence in a situation: *Several of his colleagues had a hand in his downfall.* ◊ *This appointment was an attempt to **strengthen her hand** in policy discussions.*

ironic adj.

ironic · sarcastic · wry · sardonic · satirical · dry
These words all describe sth that is humorous or makes fun of sb/sth in a way that is not obvious or direct, especially by using words that are the opposite of what you mean.

wry	ironic	sarcastic
dry	satirical	sardonic

PATTERNS AND COLLOCATIONS
▸ an ironic/ a sarcastic/ a wry/ a sardonic/ a satirical/ a dry **comment**
▸ ironic/ wry/ sardonic/ satirical/ dry **humour**
▸ a sarcastic/ wry/ satirical/ dry **wit**
▸ an ironic/ a sarcastic/ a wry/ a sardonic/ a dry **tone** / **smile**
▸ a sarcastic/ wry/ sardonic/ dry **look**
▸ an ironic/ a sarcastic/ a sardonic/ a dry **voice**
▸ ironic/ wry/ sardonic **amusement**

ironic /aɪˈrɒnɪk; *AmE* ˈrɑːn-/ apparently expressing the opposite of what you really mean, especially as a joke; (of a situation) strange or amusing because it is very different from what you expect: *He was greeted with ironic cheers from opposition MPs.* ◇ *It's ironic that she became a teacher – she used to hate school.*
▸ **ironically** *adv.*: *He smiled ironically.* ◇ *Ironically, the book she felt was her worst sold more copies than any of her others.*
▸ **irony** /ˈaɪrəni/ *noun* [U, C]: *His writing is rich in irony.* ◇ *The irony is that when he finally got the job, he found he didn't like it.* ◇ *It was one of life's little ironies.*

sarcastic /sɑːˈkæstɪk; *AmE* sɑːrˈk-/ (*usually disapproving*) using words that are the opposite of what you mean in order to be unpleasant to sb or to make fun of them: *Her tone was faintly sarcastic.* ◇ *There's no need to be sarcastic.*
▸ **sarcasm** /ˈsɑːkæzəm; *AmE* ˈsɑːrk-/ *noun* [U]: *Her voice was heavy with sarcasm.*

wry /raɪ/ [usually before noun] (*written, usually approving*) showing that you are both amused and disappointed or annoyed; amusing in an ironic way: *'At least we got one vote,' he said with a wry smile.* ◇ *The film takes a wry look at the British class system.*
▸ **wryly** *adv.*: *to grin/smile wryly*

sardonic /sɑːˈdɒnɪk; *AmE* sɑːrˈdɑːnɪk/ (*written, disapproving*) humorous in a way that shows that you think you are better than other people and do not take them seriously: *He looked at her with sardonic amusement.*

satirical /səˈtɪrɪkl/ criticizing sb/sth by using humour to show their faults or weaknesses: *The cartoon appeared in a popular satirical magazine.* ◇ *He is a sharp, satirical observer of the London social scene.*
▸ **satire** /ˈsætaɪə(r)/ *noun* [U, C]: *There is a strong tradition of political satire in this country.* ◇ *The novel is a stinging satire on American politics.*
▸ **satirize** (*BrE* also **-ise**) /ˈsætəraɪz/ *verb* [T]: (*rather formal*) *The cartoon satirizes middle-aged, middle-class liberals.*

dry (*approving*) very clever and often amusing, expressed in a quiet way that is not obvious, often using irony: *He was a man of few words with a delightful dry sense of humour.*

irrational *adj.* See also the entries for UNJUSTIFIED and UNOFFICIAL

irrational · illogical · unfounded · groundless · unconfirmed · unsubstantiated · unsupported · unscientific
These words all describe things that are not based on any good reason or evidence.

PATTERNS AND COLLOCATIONS
▸ an irrational/ illogical **fear**
▸ an unfounded/ a groundless/ an unsubstantiated/ an unsupported **claim** / **allegation** / **assertion**
▸ an unfounded/ a groundless/ an unsubstantiated **accusation**/ **charge**
▸ an unfounded/ an unconfirmed/ an unsubstantiated **rumour**
▸ an unfounded/ unconfirmed/ unsubstantiated **story** / **report**
▸ **totally** irrational/ illogical/ unfounded/ groundless/ unsubstantiated/ unsupported/ unscientific
▸ **completely** irrational/ unfounded/ groundless/ unsubstantiated/ unsupported
▸ **largely** unfounded/ groundless/ unsupported

irrational /ɪˈræʃənl/ not based on, or not using, clear logical thought: *These are just irrational fears.* ◇ *You're being irrational.* **OPP** **rational** → RATIONAL
▸ **irrationally** *adv.*: *to behave irrationally*

illogical /ɪˈlɒdʒɪkl; *AmE* -ˈlɑːdʒ-/ not sensible or thought out in a logical way: *From all this evidence he drew a strange and illogical conclusion.* **OPP** **logical** → RATIONAL
▸ **illogically** *adv.*: *He felt illogically that somehow he was responsible for the disaster.*

NOTE **IRRATIONAL** OR **ILLOGICAL?** In some cases you can use either word: *an irrational/illogical fear of insects.* **Irrational** emphasizes that there is no good reason for sth; **illogical** suggests that sb has used a false line of reasoning from facts that do not in fact support their reasoning. A person can *be irrational* but not '*be illogical*': ~~You're being illogical.~~

unfounded not based on fact or any good reason: *I was pleased to discover that my fears were unfounded.* ◇ *I dismissed the story as unfounded speculation.*

groundless not based on any good reason: *Most of his worries proved to be groundless.* ◇ *They denied what they called completely groundless allegations.*

NOTE **UNFOUNDED** OR **GROUNDLESS?** In many cases you can use either word: *unfounded/groundless claims/allegations/accusations/fears/worries.* However, **groundless** is NOT used to talk about things that ought to be based on fact rather than reasons: ~~groundless stories/reports/rumours/speculation~~

unconfirmed that has not yet been proved to be true: *Unconfirmed reports stated that at least six people had died.*

unsubstantiated /ˌʌnsəbˈstænʃieɪtɪd/ (*formal*) not proved to be true by evidence: *There were unsubstantiated rumours of abuse at the prison.*

unsupported not proved to be true by evidence: *Their claims are unsupported by any research findings.*

NOTE **UNSUBSTANTIATED** OR **UNSUPPORTED?** There is no real difference in meaning between these words. **Unsubstantiated** is more formal and is more often used before a noun; **unsupported** is more often used after a linking verb in the phrase *sth is unsupported by the evidence/findings, etc.*.

unscientific (*often disapproving*) not done in a careful, logical way, according to scientific principles: *Their approach to the problem was very unscientific.* **OPP** **scientific** → RATIONAL

irrelevant *adj.*

irrelevant · immaterial · extraneous · beside the point · inapplicable
These words all describe sth that is not important to or not connected with a situation.

PATTERNS AND COLLOCATIONS
▸ irrelevant/ immaterial/ extraneous/ inapplicable **to** sth
▸ to be irrelevant/ immaterial/ beside the point **whether...**
▸ to be irrelevant/ immaterial **that...**
▸ **quite** irrelevant/ immaterial/ beside the point

irrelevant /ɪˈreləvənt/ not important to or not connected with a situation or subject: *It's totally irrelevant whether I'm married or not.* ◇ *Many people consider politics to be irrelevant to their lives.* ◇ *Please keep all irrelevant remarks to yourself.* **OPP** **relevant** → RELEVANT
▸ **irrelevance** *noun* [U, C, usually sing.]: *the irrelevance of the curriculum to children's daily life* ◇ *His idea was rejected as an irrelevance.*

immaterial /ˌɪməˈtɪəriəl; *AmE* -ˈtɪr-/ [not usually before noun] (*rather formal*) not important in a particular situation: *The cost is immaterial.* ◇ *It is immaterial to me whether he stays or goes.* **OPP** **material** → RELEVANT

extraneous /ɪkˈstreɪniəs/ (*formal*) not important to or not connected with a situation or subject: *We do not want any extraneous information on the page.* ◇ *We shall ignore factors extraneous to the problem.*

NOTE IRRELEVANT, IMMATERIAL OR EXTRANEOUS? In a few cases you can use any of these words: *factors irrelevant/immaterial/extraneous to the case.* However, **extraneous** is not usually used after a linking verb, unless it is followed by *to*: *The cost is irrelevant/immaterial.* ◇ ~~The cost is extraneous.~~ It is used especially to talk about *factors, variables, considerations, information, material* or *matter* which are/is not important or wanted in a particular context. **Irrelevant** and **immaterial** are both often used in the structure *It is irrelevant/immaterial whether/that…* **Immaterial** is slightly stronger and can suggest a greater degree of impatience. **Immaterial** is not usually used before a noun: ~~immaterial remarks/thoughts~~

be,side the ˈpoint *phrase* (*especially spoken*) irrelevant: *'He's been married before.' 'That's beside the point.'* **OPP to the point** → RELEVANT
inapplicable /ˌɪnəˈplɪkəbl; ɪnˈæplɪkəbl/ [not before noun] (*rather formal, especially in written*) that cannot be used, or that does not apply, in a particular situation: *These regulations are inapplicable to international students.* **OPP applicable** → RELEVANT

irritable *adj.* See also the entry for MOODY

irritable · sullen · bad-tempered · grumpy · morose · sulky · petulant
These words all describe people who are in a bad, angry and/or silent mood.

PATTERNS AND COLLOCATIONS
▸ an irritable / a sullen / a bad-tempered / a grumpy / a morose **man**
▸ a sulky / petulant **child**
▸ to **look** sullen / grumpy / morose / sulky / petulant

irritable /ˈɪrɪtəbl/ getting annoyed easily; showing your anger: *He was tired and irritable.* ◇ *She waved him away with an irritable gesture.* See also **irritate** → ANNOY, **irritated** → ANNOYED, **irritating** → ANNOYING, **irritation** → FRUSTRATION
sullen (*disapproving*) silent and angry, especially in a way that other people think is unreasonable: *sullen teenagers* ◇ *He lapsed into a sullen silence.*
bad-ˈtempered often angry; in an angry mood: *Her husband was a bad-tempered man.* ◇ *What's making her so bad-tempered?*
grumpy (*informal, often disapproving*) not happy with things and complaining a lot, especially in a way that annoys other people: *Pay no attention to his moods – he's just a grumpy old man.*
morose /məˈrəʊs; AmE məˈroʊs/ (*written*) angry and unhappy and not talking very much: *She just sat there looking morose.*
sulky (*disapproving*) silent because you are angry about sth, especially in a way that other people think is unreasonable: *Sarah had looked sulky all morning.* See also **sulk** → TEMPER *noun*, **sulk** → BROOD *verb*

NOTE SULLEN OR SULKY? Typically, children are **sulky**: if you describe an adult as **sulky** it suggests that they are behaving like a child. **Sullen** is an even more disapproving word: people can be **sullen** on a particular occasion or it can describe their whole character because they behave like that all the time.

petulant /ˈpetjulənt; AmE ˈpetʃə-/ (*written, disapproving*) bad-tempered and unreasonable, especially because you cannot do or have what you want: *He behaved like a petulant child and refused to cooperate.*

isolate *verb*

isolate · cut sb/sth off · part · quarantine · divide · segregate
These words all mean to separate sb/sth from sb/sth else and keep them apart.

PATTERNS AND COLLOCATIONS
▸ to isolate / cut off / part / divide / segregate sb / sth **from** sb / sth else
▸ to isolate **yourself** / cut **yourself** off
▸ to isolate / quarantine / segregate a **patient**
▸ a **community** is isolated / cut off / segregated
▸ **completely / totally** isolated / cut off
▸ **socially** isolated / divided / segregated

isolate /ˈaɪsəleɪt/ [T, often passive] to separate sb/sth physically or socially from other people or things: *Patients with the disease should be isolated.* ◇ *He was immediately isolated from the other prisoners.* See also **isolation** → DIVISION 1, **separate** → DISPERSE
cut sb/sth ˈoff *phrasal verb* [often passive] to prevent sb/sth from leaving or reaching a place or communicating with people outside a place: *The army was cut off from its base.* ◇ *She feels very cut off living in the country.* ◇ *He cut himself off from all human contact.*
part [T, often passive] (*formal*) to prevent sb from being with sb else: *I hate being parted from the children.* ◇ *The puppies were parted from their mother at birth.*
quarantine /ˈkwɒrəntiːn; AmE ˈkwɔːr-; ˈkwɑːr-/ [T] to keep an animal or person who may have a disease away from others for a period of time, in order to prevent the disease from spreading: *Animals brought into the country are automatically quarantined.* ❶ It is more common to use **quarantine** as a noun. See also **quarantine** → DIVISION 1
divide [T] (*formal*) to separate two people or things: *Can it ever be right to divide a mother from her child?* **OPP unite** → COMBINE
segregate /ˈsegrɪgeɪt/ [T, often passive] (*formal*) to separate people of different races, religions or sexes and treat them differently: *It is a culture in which women are segregated from men.* ◇ *This is perhaps the most racially segregated city in the United States.* **OPP integrate** → COMBINE, See also **segregation** → DIVISION 1

issue *noun* See the Topic Map for FACT AND OPINION on p.898, See also the entry for SUBJECT

issue · matter · question · concern · item
These are all words for sth that people are discussing or need to deal with.

PATTERNS AND COLLOCATIONS
▸ an issue / a matter / a question / an item **relating to / concerning** sth
▸ **on** an issue / a matter / a question
▸ an **important** issue / matter / question / concern / item
▸ a **vital / key / major / serious / general / complex** issue / matter / question / concern
▸ a **controversial / contentious / sensitive** issue / matter / question / item
▸ a **difficult / delicate** issue / matter / question
▸ the **basic / fundamental / underlying** issue / question / concern
▸ a/an **political / moral / technical / economic / ethical / practical** issue / matter / question / concern
▸ to **discuss / consider / deal with / tackle / raise** an issue / a matter / a question / a concern / an item
▸ to **examine / explore / focus on / address** an issue / a matter / a question / a concern
▸ to **debate** an issue / a matter / a question / an item
▸ to **look at / touch on / bring up / broach / debate / clarify / decide / settle** an issue / a matter / a question
▸ an issue / a matter / a question **arises**

issue [C] something important that people are discussing or arguing about: *The union plans to raise the issue of overtime.* ◇ *This is a big issue; we need more time to think about it.* ◇ *She usually writes about environmental issues.* ◇ *You're just avoiding the issue.* ◇ *Don't confuse the issue.* ◇ *What you say is interesting, but it does not affect the point at issue here.*

matter [C] something that you must discuss or deal with: *It's a private matter.* ◇ *I always consulted him on matters of policy.* ◇ *The incident is definitely a matter for the police.* ◇ *That's a matter for you to take up with your boss.* ◇ *I don't have much experience in these matters.* ◇ *I wasn't prepared to let the matter drop* (= stop discussing it). ❶ **A matter** [sing.] is a situation that involves sth or depends on sth: *That's not a problem. It's simply a matter of letting people know in time.* ◇ *She resigned over a matter of principle.* ◇ *Just as a matter of interest* (= because it is interesting, not because it is important), *how much did you pay for it?* ◇ *'I think this is the best so far.' 'Well, that's a matter of opinion* (= other people may think differently).

question [C] something that you need or want to consider or deal with: *Let's look at the question of security.* ◇ *This raises fundamental questions about the nature of our society.* ◇ *Which route is better remains an open question* (= it is not decided).

NOTE MATTER OR QUESTION? In many cases you can use either word. A **matter** is often sth practical that needs to be dealt with: people typically *talk about, look at, discuss, debate, refer, pursue, deal with, handle, investigate, resolve* or *settle* a **matter**. A **question** may also be practical, but is often sth more philosophical that is interesting to think about without actually coming to any conclusions: people typically *think about, focus on, raise, address* or *ponder* a **question**. However, all these collocates can be used with either word.

concern [C] something that is important to a person, an organization or society: *What are your main concerns as a writer?* ◇ *The overriding concern of the organizers is the safety of the participants.* ◇ *Environmental concerns have been thrust to the head of the party agenda.* See also **consideration** → FACTOR

item [C] one thing on a list of things to buy, do or talk about: *What's the next item on the agenda?* ◇ *Check the list carefully, item by item.*

J j

jab verb

jab · prod · poke · nudge
These words all mean to push a pointed object into sth with a sudden strong movement.

jab (-**bb**-) [T, I] to push a pointed object, especially a finger, into or at sb/sth with a sudden strong movement: *She jabbed him in the ribs with her finger.* ◊ *He jabbed a finger in her direction.* ◊ *She started jabbing at the calculator.*
   ▶ **jab** *noun* [sing.]: *As a response he got a sharp jab in the stomach with a rifle.*
prod (-**dd**-) [T, I] to push sb/sth with your finger or a pointed object, usually fairly gently: *She prodded the dry ground with a stick.* ◊ *Martha prodded him awake.* ◊ *Dan prodded at his breakfast with a fork.*
   ▶ **prod** *noun* [sing.]: *She gave the pile of clothes another prod.*
poke [T, I] to push your finger or another pointed object hard into sb/sth: *I'm sick of being poked and prodded by doctors.* ◊ *He poked at the spaghetti with a fork* (= pushed at it repeatedly with small quick movements).
   ▶ **poke** *noun* [sing.]: *Carrie gave him a poke in the side.*
nudge [T] to push sb gently, especially with your elbow, in order to get their attention: *He nudged me and whispered 'Look who's just come in.'* ◊ *The kids were giggling and nudging each other.*
   ▶ **nudge** *noun* [sing.]: *She gave me a gentle nudge in the ribs.*

jail verb

jail · detain · hold · imprison · lock sb up/away · intern · send sb to prison · incarcerate
These words all mean to keep sb in a place and prevent them from leaving.

jail [T, usually passive] (*especially journalism*) to put sb in a prison for committing a crime: *He was jailed for life for murder.* See also **jail** → PRISON
detain /dɪ'teɪn/ [T] (*rather formal*) to keep sb in an official place, such as a police station, prison or hospital, and prevent them from leaving: *One man has been detained for questioning.*
   ▶ **detention** *noun* [U]: *police powers of arrest and detention*
hold [T] to keep sb and not allow them to leave: *Police are holding two men in connection with last Thursday's bank raid.* ◊ *He was held prisoner for two years.*
imprison /ɪm'prɪzn/ [T, often passive] (*rather formal*) to put sb in a prison for committing a crime; to keep sb in a place from which they cannot escape: *They were imprisoned for possession of drugs.* ◊ (*figurative*) *Some young mothers feel imprisoned in their own homes.* See also **prison** → PRISON

   ▶ **imprisonment** *noun* [U]: *He was sentenced to life imprisonment for murder.*
lock sb 'up/a'way *phrasal verb* (*informal*) to put sb in prison or a mental hospital, often because they are dangerous: *You ought to be locked up!* ◊ *After what he did, they should lock him up and throw away the key.*
intern /ɪn'tɜːn; AmE ɪn'tɜːrn/ [T, often passive] to put sb in prison during a war or for political reasons, although they have not been charged with a crime: *They were interned by the government for the duration of the war.*
   ▶ **internment** *noun* [U]: *the internment of suspected terrorists* ◊ *an internment camp*
send sb to 'prison *phrasal verb* to cause sb to be put in prison for committing a crime, especially when this is done by a court: *The judge sent her to prison for seven years.* See also **prison** → PRISON
incarcerate /ɪn'kɑːsəreɪt; AmE -'kɑːrs-/ [T, usually passive] (*formal*) to imprison sb, especially when this is felt to be wrong in some way, because it is unfair or because conditions are too harsh: *Thousands were incarcerated in labour camps.*

jealousy noun

jealousy · envy
These are both words for the feeling of wanting sth that sb else has.

jealousy [U, C] a feeling of being angry or unhappy because sb you like or love is showing interest in sb else, or because you wish you had sth that sb else has; an action or remark that shows that sb feels this way: *He felt a sudden stab of pure sexual jealousy.* ◊ *Her promotion aroused intense jealousy among her colleagues.* ◊ *I'm tired of her petty jealousies.*
   ▶ **jealous** *adj.*: *She's jealous of my success.* ◊ *Children often feel jealous when a new baby arrives.*
   ▶ **jealously** *adv.*: *She eyed Natalia jealously.*
envy [U] the feeling of wanting to be in the same situation as sb else; the feeling of wanting sth that sb else has: *She felt a pang of envy at the thought of his success.* ◊ *Her colleagues were green with envy* (= they had very strong feelings of envy).
   ▶ **envious** *adj.*: *Everyone is so envious of her having the chance to study abroad.*
   ▶ **enviously** *adv.*: *They look enviously at the success of their European counterparts.*
   ▶ **envy** *verb* [T]: *He envied her − she seemed to have everything she could possibly want.* ◊ *I don't envy Ed that job* (= I am pleased I do not have it).

NOTE JEALOUSY OR ENVY? Jealousy is often a nastier feeling than **envy** and can cause people to behave in an unkind or stupid way. People will admit to being **envious** but will rarely admit to being **jealous**. People sometimes enjoy *inspiring* or *arousing* **envy** in other people, but they do not generally like to *cause* or *provoke* **jealousy**.

job *noun* See also WORK 2

job · position · post · vacancy · opening · appointment · posting

These are all words for a position doing work for which you receive regular payment.

PATTERNS AND COLLOCATIONS
▸ a vacancy / an opening **for** sb
▸ a **temporary** job / position / post / vacancy / appointment / posting
▸ a **permanent** / **full-time** / **part-time** job / position / post / vacancy / appointment
▸ a **good** / **top** job / position / post / appointment
▸ a **well-paid** / **highly-paid** job / position / post
▸ to **have** / **have got** a job / a position / a post / a vacancy / an opening / an appointment / a posting
▸ to **apply for** a job / a position / a post / a vacancy / a posting
▸ to **hold** / **seek** a job / a position / a post / an appointment
▸ to **look for** / **give** sb a job / position / post / posting
▸ to **find** a job / position / post
▸ to **get** a job / a position / a post / an appointment / a posting
▸ to **offer** sb / **take** a job / a position / a post / an appointment / a posting
▸ to **fill** a job / position / post / vacancy
▸ to **land** / **resign from** / **leave** / **quit** / **keep** / **lose** a job / position / post
▸ to **create** / **provide** jobs / positions / posts / vacancies / openings

job [C] a position doing work for which you receive regular payment: *He's trying to get a **job in** teaching.* ◇ *I'm only **doing my job** (= I'm doing what I'm paid to do).* ◇ *He certainly **knows his job** (= is very good at his job).* ◇ *We provide training **on the job** (= while sb is actually doing the job).* ◇ *She's been **out of a job** (= unemployed) for six months now.* ◇ *She's never had a **steady job** (= a job that is not going to end suddenly).* ◇ *Her **job title** is Senior Advisor.* ◇ *__Job satisfaction__ (= being happy with the job you do) is very important to me.*

position [C] (*rather formal*) a job: *She holds a senior position in a large corporation.* ◇ *I would like to apply for the position of sales director.* ❶ **Position** usually refers to a particular job within an organization, especially at a high level, and is not usually used about jobs generally. It is also often used in job applications, descriptions and advertisements. See also **office** → ROLE

post [C] (*especially BrE*) a job, especially an important one in a large organization: *Ideally I'm looking for an academic post.* ◇ *She was offered a key post in the new government.* ❶ In American English **post** is only really used for an appointed government job; in other cases where British English uses **post**, American English uses **position**: *a Cabinet post* ◇ *an academic position*

vacancy /'veɪkənsi/ [C] a job that is available for sb to do: *We have several vacancies for casual workers.* ◇ *We'll let you know if any more vacancies come up.*

opening [C] a job that is available for sb to do: *There are several openings in the sales departments.*

NOTE VACANCY OR OPENING? These words have the same meaning and there is very little difference in their use. **Vacancy** is more frequent, especially in British English. **Opening** is slightly more informal and is used more in American English and in financial journalism.

appointment [C] (*especially BrE, rather formal*) a job or position of responsibility: *This is a permanent appointment, requiring commitment and hard work.* See also **appoint** → APPOINT

posting [C] (*especially BrE*) an act of sending sb to a particular place to do their job, especially for a limited period of time; the job that sb is sent to do: *He asked for a **posting** to the Middle East.* ◇ *Staff will work abroad on 2–5 year postings.* ❶ **Posting** is also used in American English, but usually only to refer to limited-term government jobs. See also **post** → SEND 2

join *verb* See the Topic Map for SPORT AND LEISURE on p.892

join · be/get involved · participate · take part · engage in sth · enter · join in (sth) · have/play a part · share · enter into sth

These words all mean to take part in sth or to do sth with sb else.

PATTERNS AND COLLOCATIONS
▸ to join sb / get involved / participate / take part / engage / play a part / share **in** sth
▸ to **get involved** / join in / share sth / enter into sth **with** sb / sth
▸ to **fully** participate / take part / engage in sth / enter into sth
▸ to **actively** / **directly** participate / take part / engage in sth
▸ to be **fully** / **actively** / **directly** involved in sth

join [T, I] to become a member of an organization, company or club; to do sth that sb else is also doing or go somewhere with them: *She joined the company three months ago.* ◇ *I've joined an aerobics class.* ◇ *It costs £20 to join.* ◇ *Will you join us for lunch?* ◇ *Members of the public joined the search for the missing boy.*

be/get involved *phrase* to do a particular type of activity; to be part of or connected with a group, club or society: *I got involved in politics when I was at college.* ◇ *She is very much involved with several local charitable groups.* See also **involvement** → INVOLVEMENT

participate /pɑː'tɪsɪpeɪt; *AmE* pɑːr't-/ [I] (*rather formal*) to be involved in an activity or event: *She didn't participate in the discussion.* ◇ *We want to encourage students to participate fully in the running of the college.* See also **participation** → INVOLVEMENT, **participant** → PARTICIPANT

take 'part *phrase* to be involved in an activity or event: *He had taken part in a demonstration several years earlier.* ◇ *How many countries took part in the last Olympic Games?* See also **part** → INVOLVEMENT

en'gage in sth *phrasal verb* (*rather formal*) to be involved in a particular type of activity: *Even in prison, he continued to engage in criminal activities.* See also **engagement** → INVOLVEMENT

NOTE BE/GET INVOLVED, PARTICIPATE, TAKE PART OR ENGAGE IN STH? You **participate** or **take part** in a particular activity or event: **participate** is more formal than **take part**. **Be/get involved** is a more general expression to talk about the kind of activity or area of interest that sb gives their time to: you might *be involved in politics* but would *participate/take part in a political debate*. **Engage in sth** is also used for more general types of activity, especially (but not only) activities that are bad in some way or cause disapproval.

enter [T, no passive] (*rather formal*) to become a member of an institution; to start working in an organization or profession; to begin or become involved in an activity or situation: *I entered politics late in life.* ◇ *She entered Parliament* (= became an MP) *in 1998.* ◇ *It was his aim to enter the church* (= become a priest). ◇ *When did the US enter the conflict?* ◇ *Several new firms have now entered the market.*
▸ **entry** *noun* [U]: *countries seeking entry into the European Union* ◇ *the American entry into the war*

NOTE JOIN OR ENTER? **Join** is the usual term for talking about becoming a member of an organization or club. **Enter** is used to talk about politics, professions such as law and medicine, and institutions such as universities, Parliament and the Church.

join 'in, join 'in sth *phrasal verb* to take part in sth with other people: *She listens but she never joins in.* ◇ *I wish he would join in with the other children.* ◇ *He didn't dare to join in the singing.*

have/play a 'part *phrase* to be involved in an activity or situation and influence its development: *She plays an active part in local politics.* ◇ *We all have a part in the making of this decision.* See also **part** → INVOLVEMENT

share [I, T] to work together with other people in an equal way to make work or responsibilities easier: *I try to get the kids to share in the housework.* ◊ *Don't try to do everything yourself: you will need to **share the load** with your partner.* ❶ Collocates of **share** in this meaning include *work, load, burden* and *responsibilities.* See also **share** → SHARE *noun*

'**enter into sth** *phrasal verb* (*rather formal*) to become involved in a formal or business relationship with sb; to take an active part in sth: *Read the small print before you enter into any agreement.* ◊ *I refuse to enter into correspondence with such people.*

joke *noun*

joke · quip · prank · pun · gag · one-liner · wisecrack
These are all words for sth you say or do for fun or in order to make people laugh.

PATTERNS AND COLLOCATIONS
▸ a joke / quip / gag / wisecrack **about** sb / sth
▸ to do sth **as** a joke / prank
▸ to **make** a joke / quip / pun / wisecrack
▸ to **tell (sb)** / **crack** a joke / gag
▸ to **laugh at** a joke / pun / gag

joke [C] something that you say or do to make people laugh, for example a funny story that you tell: *I can't tell jokes.* ◊ *I didn't **get the joke** (= understand it). ◊ I wish he wouldn't tell **dirty jokes** (= about sex). ◊ He's always playing **practical jokes** on people (= tricks that are played on people to make them look stupid and to make other people laugh). ◊ The trouble with Ruby is she can't **take a joke** (= she isn't able to laugh at a joke against herself).* ❶ A **joke** is often a story with a funny ending. The characters, events and even the words of the story are quite fixed, and it is passed around between people with few or no changes. The same is true of **gag** and sometimes **one-liner** below. The other words in this group describe more original remarks that you make as a reaction to a particular situation or what sb else has said.

quip [C] a clever and funny remark, especially one that is made quickly and without preparation: *The senator made several quips during the interview, which got the audience laughing.*

prank [C] a trick that is played on sb as a joke: *It was just a childish prank – don't take it so seriously.* ◊ *a silly/stupid prank* ◊ *a prank call/phone call* See also **trick** → TRICK

pun [C] the clever or humorous use of a word that has more than one meaning, or of words that have different meanings but sound the same: *We're banking on them lending us the money – no pun intended!* ❶ Instead of laughing, people often groan when they hear a **pun**. The phrases *forgive the pun, excuse the pun* and *pardon the pun* are used as a way of apologizing for making one (either by accident or on purpose): *So you collect pins? But what's the point in that, if you'll forgive the pun?*

gag [C] (*informal*) a joke or a funny story, especially one told by a professional comedian: *He was a non-stop comedian, cracking gags by the dozen.* ◊ *a **running gag** (= one that is regularly repeated during a performance)*

,**one-'liner** [C] (*informal*) a joke or a funny remark that consists of a single sentence: *He came out with some good one-liners.*

wisecrack [C] (*informal*) a clever remark or joke, especially one which could upset or offend people: *He promised not to make any wisecracks during the dinner.*

joke *verb*

joke · kid · jest · have sb on · quip · wisecrack
These verbs all mean to say sth to make people laugh, or to say sth that isn't true because you think it is funny.

PATTERNS AND COLLOCATIONS
▸ to joke / kid / jest / have sb on **about** sth
▸ I'm, she's, they were, etc. **only** / **just** joking / kidding / having you on

▸ You must be joking / kidding!
▸ You're joking / kidding / having me on!

joke [I] to say sth to make people laugh; to tell a funny story; to say sth that is not true because you think it is funny: *She was laughing and **joking with** the children.* ◊ *'I cooked it myself, so be careful!' he joked.* ◊ *I didn't mean that – I was only joking.* ◊ *She **joked that** she only loved him for his money.* ◊ *No way am I doing that. You must be joking (= I can't believe you are serious)!*

kid (-**dd**-) [I, T] (usually used in the progressive tenses) (*informal*) to tell sb sth that is not true, especially as a joke: *I thought he was kidding when he said he was going out with a rock star.* ◊ *I'm not kidding you. It does work.* See also **kid** → MISLEAD

NOTE JOKE OR KID? Both words can mean to say sth that is not true, as a joke. Both are usually used in the progressive tenses in this meaning: *Of course you don't have to work at weekends – I was only joking/kidding!* ◊ *Were you joking/kidding when you told him to leave? ◊ Did you joke/kid when you told him….* If you *laugh and joke* with sb about sth, you are having fun and not being serious. **Kid** cannot be used in this way, but the phrasal verb *kid around* can: *They were laughing and kidding around.* In general, **kid** is used more in spoken than in written English, and more in American than in British English.

jest [I] (*formal or humorous*) to say things that are not serious or true, especially in order to make sb laugh: *Would I jest about such a thing?*

,**have sb 'on** *phrasal verb* (usually used in progressive tenses) (*especially BrE, informal*) to try to make sb believe sth that is not true, usually as a joke: *You didn't really, did you? You're not having me on, are you?*

quip (-**pp**-) [I] to make a quick and clever remark that makes people laugh: *'Don't bank on it!' he quipped, when I asked him to be careful with the money.*

wisecrack [I, T] (*informal*) to make clever remarks or jokes, especially ones that could upset or offend people: *In this movie, he plays a wisecracking detective.*

joy *noun* See also the entry for SATISFACTION

joy · delight · ecstasy · bliss · euphoria
These are all words for a feeling of great happiness.

PATTERNS AND COLLOCATIONS
▸ sb's joy / delight / euphoria **at** sth
▸ **sheer** / **pure** joy / delight / ecstasy / bliss
▸ to **feel** / **be filled with** joy / delight / ecstasy

joy [U] a feeling of great happiness: *the pure joy I felt at being free again* ◊ *I literally **jumped for joy** (= was very happy and showed it) when I heard the news.* **OPP** grief → GRIEF. See also **joyful** → HAPPY

delight [U] a feeling of great pleasure: *Alex squealed with delight when he saw the monkeys.* ◊ *She takes great delight in proving others wrong.* See also **delight** → DELIGHT *verb*, **delight in sth** → ENJOY

ecstasy /'ekstəsi/ [U, C] a feeling or state of very great happiness: *Kate closed her eyes **in ecstasy** at the thought of a cold drink.* See also **ecstatic** → EXCITED

bliss [C] a feeling of great happiness: *The first six months of marriage were sheer bliss.* See also **blissful** → HAPPY

NOTE JOY, DELIGHT OR BLISS? Joy and delight are livelier feelings than bliss: you can *dance/jump/sing/weep for joy* or *scream/squeal/whoop with delight*. Bliss is more peaceful: *married/wedded/domestic bliss*

euphoria /ju:'fɔːriə/ [U] a feeling of great happiness and excitement that usually lasts only a short time: *I was in a state of euphoria all day.* ◊ *Euphoria soon gave way to despair.* See also **euphoric** → EXCITED

judge noun

1 a High Court judge
2 the competition judges

---

1 judge · magistrate · the bench · Justice of the Peace · JP

These are all words for a person in a court who has the authority to make legal decisions and decide how criminals should be punished.

PATTERNS AND COLLOCATIONS

▸ **before** a judge / a magistrate / the bench / a Justice of the Peace / a JP
▸ the **local** judge / magistrate / bench / Justice of the Peace / JP
▸ the **senior** / **presiding** / **district** / **investigating** / **chief** judge / magistrate
▸ to **appoint** sb as a judge / as a magistrate / to the bench / as a Justice of the Peace / as a JP
▸ to **address** the judge / bench
▸ the judge / magistrate / bench **hears** / **grants** sth
▸ a judge / magistrate **orders** / **awards** / **adjourns** / **upholds** / **considers** / **dismisses** / **decides** / **finds** sth
▸ a judge / magistrate **sentences** sb

judge [C] a person in a court who has the authority to decide how criminals should be punished or to make legal decisions: *The trial judge dismissed her compensation claim.* ◇ *By next year you could be sitting as a High Court judge.* ◇ *The case comes before Judge Cooper next week.*

magistrate /ˈmædʒɪstreɪt/ [C] an official who has the authority to make legal decisions and decide how people should be punished in the lowest courts of law: *Ten people are due to appear before magistrates today accused of drugs offences.* ◇ *a magistrate's court*

the bench [sing.] (*law*) a judge in court or the seat where he/she sits; the position of being a judge or magistrate; the group of judges or magistrates who work in a particular court, type of court or area: *His lawyer turned to address the bench.* ◇ *She has recently been appointed to the bench.*

Justice of the 'Peace (pl. **Justices of the Peace**) [C] (*formal*) a magistrate: *In 1579 he was appointed Justice of the Peace for Kent.*

> **NOTE** **MAGISTRATE, JUSTICE OF THE PEACE** OR **JP?** The exact use of these terms differs in the legal systems of different countries. In England and Wales **Justice of the Peace** is just the official title for a **magistrate**, used especially in historical contexts. In the US a **Justice of the Peace** is a judge of the lowest level in some state court systems.

JP /ˌdʒeɪ ˈpiː/ [C] the abbreviation for 'Justice of the Peace': *Helen Alvey JP* ◇ *She became a JP in 1939.*

---

2 judge · referee · examiner · umpire · arbiter · moderator · ref

These are all words for a person whose job or role is to make decisions or give their opinion about sth.

PATTERNS AND COLLOCATIONS

▸ an **independent** judge / examiner
▸ a **neutral** referee / umpire / arbiter
▸ the **ultimate** / **sole** / **final** judge / arbiter
▸ to **act as** (a) judge / (a) referee / (an) arbiter / (a) moderator
▸ a judge / a referee / an umpire **decides** / **awards** sth
▸ the judge's / referee's / umpire's / ref's **decision**

judge [C] a person who decides who has won a competition; a person who has the necessary knowledge or skills to give their opinion about the value or quality of sb/sth: *The judges' decision is final.* ◇ *The winner was chosen by a **panel of judges**.* ◇ *She's a good judge of character.* ◇ *You are the best judge of what your body needs.* ◇ *The last singer was the best – not that I'm any judge* (= I do not know much about the subject).

referee /ˌrefəˈriː/ [C] (in sports such as football, basketball and boxing) the official who controls the game and makes sure that the rules are not broken: *He was sent off for arguing with the referee.* ◇ *Graham is a qualified football referee.* ❶ A **referee** is also a person who reads and checks the quality of a technical article before it is published: *All papers are sent out to external referees.*

▸ **referee** *verb* [I, T]: *a refereeing decision* ◇ *Who refereed the final / this paper?*

examiner [C] (*BrE*) a person who writes the questions for, or marks, an exam: *She was a member of the **board of examiners** of the college.* ◇ *He is a former senior driving examiner.* See also **examine** → TEST *verb* 2

umpire /ˈʌmpaɪə(r)/ [C] (in sports such as tennis, cricket and baseball) an official who watches a game and makes sure that rules are not broken: *He received an official warning from the umpire for his conduct.*

▸ **umpire** *verb* [I, T]: *We need someone to umpire.* ◇ *to umpire a baseball game / a cricket match*

arbiter /ˈɑːbɪtə(r)/; *AmE* ˈɑːrb- [C] (*formal*) a person with the power or influence to make judgements and decide what will be done or accepted: *The law is the final arbiter of what is considered obscene.* ◇ *This style would be dismissed as too ornate by contemporary **arbiters of taste**.*

moderator /ˈmɒdəreɪtə(r)/; *AmE* ˈmɑːd- [C] (*especially AmE*) a person whose job is to make sure that a discussion or debate is fair: *The moderator of this week's quiz is Professor Edmund James.*

ref [C] (*informal*) (in sports such as football and basketball) a referee: *The game isn't over until the ref blows his whistle.*

---

judge verb

1 judge by appearances
2 judge a competition / judge sb guilty

---

1 See the Topic Map for FACT AND OPINION on p.898

judge · assess · evaluate · rate · gauge · size sb/sth up

These words all mean to form an opinion about sb/sth based on the information you have.

PATTERNS AND COLLOCATIONS

▸ to judge / assess / evaluate / rate sb / sth **as** sth
▸ to judge / assess / evaluate / rate sb / sth **on** / **according to** sth
▸ to judge / assess / evaluate / gauge sb / sth **by** sth
▸ to judge / assess / evaluate / gauge sb / sth **from** sth
▸ to judge / assess / evaluate / rate / gauge **how...**
▸ to judge / assess / evaluate / gauge **what** / **whether...**
▸ to judge / assess / evaluate / gauge the **extent** / **significance** / **success** / **effectiveness** / **effect** / **impact** of sth
▸ to judge / assess / evaluate / gauge sth's **progress** / **performance** / **quality** / **merits** / **potential**
▸ to judge / assess / evaluate / size up the **situation**
▸ to judge / assess / gauge the **mood** / **reaction**
▸ to judge / assess / evaluate / gauge sb / sth **accurately** / **correctly**
▸ to judge / assess / evaluate / rate sb / sth **fairly** / **accordingly**
▸ to judge / assess / evaluate sb / sth **properly** / **objectively**

judge [I, T] to form an opinion about sb/sth, based on the information you have: *As far as I can judge, they are all to blame.* ◇ *Judging from what he said, he was very disappointed.* ◇ *I don't really think that you're **in a position to judge**.* ◇ *You shouldn't judge by appearances* (= form an opinion about sb/sth from the way they look). ◇ *You shouldn't judge her too harshly.* ◇ *They judged it wise to say nothing.* See also **judgement** → VIEW 1, **judgemental** → CRITICAL

assess /əˈses/ [T] to make a judgement about the nature, ability or quality of sb/sth, after watching or testing them and using your expert knowledge: *The new patient is assessed by the nursing staff.* ◇ *I'd assess your chances of winning as pretty low.* ◇ *The committee assesses whether a building is worth preserving.* See also **assess** → TEST *verb* 2, **assessment** → ASSESSMENT

evaluate /ɪ'væljueɪt/ [T] to form an opinion of the amount, value or quality of sth after studying it carefully: *Our research attempts to evaluate the effectiveness of the different drugs.* ◇ *We need to evaluate how well the system is working.* See also **evaluation** → ASSESSMENT

> **NOTE** ASSESS OR **EVALUATE?** You usually assess sb/sth in order to make a judgement, often against a particular standard, to see if sb/sth is satisfactory. You usually **evaluate** sb/sth in order to understand it better so that more informed decisions can be made. Sometimes either word can be used: *Candidates are assessed/ evaluated on their ability to think independently.* In this example, a judgement is being made, but **evaluate** is often used in the context of people's performance in their jobs because it sounds more positive. In the context of students' performance in exams or class, however, the usual word is **assess**. See also **assess** → TEST *verb* 2

rate [T] (not used in the progressive tenses) to judge that sb/sth has a particular level of quality or value: *How did you rate her speech?* ◇ *The university is highly **rated** for its research.* ◇ *Voters continue to rate education high on their list of priorities.* See also **rate** → RANK *verb*, **rating** → CLASS 4

gauge (*AmE* also **gage**) /geɪdʒ/ [T] to form a judgement about sth, especially about people's feelings or attitudes: *He tried to gauge her mood.* ◇ *It was difficult to gauge whether she was angry or not.* See also **gauge** → CRITERION *noun*

size sb/sth 'up *phrasal verb* (*rather informal*) to form a judgement or opinion about sb/sth: *He sized up the situation very quickly.* ◇ *The children looked at each other warily, as if sizing each other up.*

2 judge · decide · adjudicate

These words all mean to make an official decision about sb/sth, for example in a competition or in court.

PATTERNS AND COLLOCATIONS
▸ to decide / adjudicate **on** / **in** sth
▸ to judge / decide / adjudicate a **case**
▸ to decide / adjudicate a **dispute**
▸ to decide / adjudicate (**in** / **on**) a **matter**

judge [T, I] to make an official decision about the result of a competition or about whether sb is guilty or innocent in court; to give your opinion about sb, especially when you disapprove of them: *She was asked to judge the essay competition.* ◇ *There will be judging in three age groups.* ◇ *They could dismiss workers participating in strikes **judged to be** illegal.* ◇ *What gives you the right to judge other people?* See also **judgment** → CONCLUSION

decide [T, I] (*law*) to make an official or legal judgement: *The case will be decided by a jury.* ◇ *He challenged her right as governor to decide on the matter.* ◇ *The Appeal Court **decided in their favour**.* ◇ *It is always possible that the judge may **decide against** you.*

adjudicate /ə'dʒuːdɪkeɪt/ [I, T] (*rather formal*) to make an official decision about who is right in a disagreement between two groups or organizations; to be a judge in a competition: *A special subcommittee adjudicates on planning applications.* ◇ *Their purpose is to **adjudicate** disputes **between** employers and employees.* ◇ *Who is adjudicating at this year's contest?* See also **arbitrate** → INTERVENE

▸ **adjudication** *noun* [U, C]: *The case was referred to a higher court for adjudication.* ◇ *The adjudication will be published tomorrow.*

jumble *verb*

jumble · shuffle · mix sth up · muddle
These words all mean to put things together in the wrong order or a different order.

PATTERNS AND COLLOCATIONS
▸ to jumble / mix / muddle things **up**
▸ to **be** jumbled / mixed / muddled **up**
▸ to be jumbled / muddled up **together**
▸ to jumble / mix up the **letters in a word** / **words in a sentence**
▸ to mix up / muddle sb's **papers**

jumble [T, usually passive] to mix things together without any order and in an untidy way: *The letters in these words have been jumbled up.* ◇ *Books, shoes and clothes were jumbled together on the floor.* See also **jumble** → MESS *noun* 1, **jumbled** → UNTIDY

shuffle [T] to move paper or things into different positions or a different order; to completely change the order of all the playing cards in a pack (= set) before playing a game: *He nervously shuffled the papers on his desk.* ◇ ***Shuffle the cards** and deal out seven to each player.*

mix sth 'up *phrasal verb* to change the order or arrangement of a group of things, often by mistake or in a way that you do not want: *Someone has mixed up all the application forms.* ◇ *The words in this proverb have been mixed up.*

muddle [T, often passive] (*especially BrE*) to accidentally change the order or arrangement of a group of things, usually in a way that you do not want: *Don't do that – you're muddling my papers.*

> **NOTE** JUMBLE, MIX STH UP OR **MUDDLE?** You can **jumble** or **mix** things **up** by mistake or deliberately; things are always **muddled** by mistake: ~~The words in this proverb have been muddled up.~~ You can **mix up** or **muddle** papers or forms by getting them in the wrong order; things that **are jumbled** are usually objects that are not in any order at all.

jump *verb*

1 jump over the wall
2 jump to your feet
3 The loud bang made me jump.

1 jump · leap · hop · vault · bounce · hurdle

These words all mean to make your body leave the ground by pushing with your legs and feet.

PATTERNS AND COLLOCATIONS
▸ to jump / leap / hop / vault / hurdle **over** (sth)
▸ to jump / leap / hop / bounce **up and down**
▸ to jump / leap / hop **about** / **around**
▸ to jump / leap / vault / hurdle a **fence** / **hedge** / **wall**
▸ to jump / leap / hop **3 feet** / **2 metres**, etc.

jump [I, T] to move quickly off the ground by pushing yourself with your legs and feet; to pass over or across sth by doing this: *I held my nose and jumped into the water.* ◇ *Can you jump over that fence?* ◇ *The dog kept jumping up at me.* ◇ *'Quick! Jump!' she shouted.* ◇ *He can jump over two metres.* ◇ *Her horse fell as it jumped the last fence.*

▸ **jump** *noun* [C]: *She managed a jump of 1.6 metres.*

leap [I, T] (always used with an adverb or preposition) (*written*) to jump high or a long way: *A dolphin suddenly leapt out of the water.* ◇ *The horse galloped on, leaping fences and hedges as it came to them.*

▸ **leap** *noun* [C]: *She took a flying leap and landed on the other side of the stream.*

hop (-**pp**-) [I] (of a person) to jump on one foot; to move by jumping on one foot; (of an animal or bird) to move by jumping with all or both feet together: *I couldn't put any weight on my ankle and had to hop everywhere.* ◇ *A robin was hopping around on the path.*

▸ **hop** *noun* [C]: *He crossed the hall with a hop, a skip and a jump.*

vault /vɔːlt/ [I, T] (*rather formal*) to jump over an object in a single movement, using your hands or a pole to push you: *She vaulted over the gate and ran up the path.* ◇ *There's no way he could have vaulted the fence with that injury.*

bounce [I, T] to jump up and down on sth; to move a child up and down while they are sitting on your knee: *She bounced up and down excitedly on the bed.* ◇ *I bounced the baby on my knee while Pat did the dishes.*

hurdle /ˈhɜːdl/; *AmE* ˈhɜːrdl/ [T, I] to jump over sth while you are running: *He hurdled two steel barriers in an attempt to escape from the police.* ◇ *She had to hurdle over three fences to reach the finishing line.* See also **hurdle** → BARRIER

2 jump · leap · spring · hop

These words all mean to move quickly and suddenly.

PATTERNS AND COLLOCATIONS
▸ to jump / leap / spring / hop **up** / **down** / **out**
▸ to jump / leap / spring / hop **out of bed**
▸ to jump / leap / spring **to your feet**
▸ to jump / leap / spring **into action** / **the air**
▸ to jump / leap / hop **into bed** / **your car**
▸ to jump / leap / hop **onto your bike**
▸ to jump / hop **on a bus** / **plane** / **train**
▸ to jump / hop **in a taxi** / **cab**
▸ Do you want a ride? Jump / Hop **in**.

jump [I] (always used with an adverb or preposition) to move quickly and suddenly: *He jumped to his feet when they called his name.* ◇ *Jump in and I'll give you a lift.*

leap [I] (always used with an adverb or preposition) to move or do sth quickly and suddenly: *She leapt out of bed.* ◇ *He leapt across the room to answer the door.* ◇ *They leapt into action immediately.*

spring [I] (usually used with an adverb or preposition) to move suddenly and with one quick movement into the air or in a particular direction: *The cat crouched ready to spring.* ◇ *The attacker sprang out at him from a doorway.*

hop (-**pp**-) [I] (always used with an adverb or preposition) (*informal*) to move or go somewhere quickly and suddenly, especially in, into or out of a vehicle, or to another town, city, etc. that is a relatively short distance away: *Hop in. I'll drive you home.* ◇ *We hopped over to Paris for the weekend.* ❶ In American English **hop** can also be used with an object: [T] (*AmE*) *I hopped a plane for New York.*

NOTE **WHICH WORD?** Jump is used most frequently when you are talking about sb changing their body position quickly, especially getting to their feet very quickly (*jump up/to your feet*). **Leap** is used typically for slightly longer distances (*leap across the room*) and more figurative actions (*leap into action/to sb's defence*). **Spring** is used especially about animals; you can *spring out of bed/your chair/your car*, but you can only *spring into action* (or *life*), in a more figurative sense: ~~Spring in and I'll give you a lift.~~ **Hop** is nearly always used about getting into or out of vehicles or travelling in a vehicle; it is the only one of these words that can be used about making a whole journey in a vehicle: ~~We jumped/leapt/sprang over to Paris for the weekend.~~

3 jump · flinch · cower · cringe · recoil · shrink

These words all mean to make a sudden movement or move back because you are surprised or afraid.

PATTERNS AND COLLOCATIONS
▸ to jump / flinch / cringe / recoil **at** sth
▸ to flinch / recoil / shrink **from** sth
▸ to flinch / cower / cringe / recoil **in fear**
▸ to **make sb** jump / flinch / cower / cringe / recoil

jump [I] to make a sudden movement because of surprise, fear or excitement: *A loud bang made me jump.* ◇ *She nearly **jumped out of her skin** when she saw me.*

flinch [I] to make a sudden movement with your face or body because of pain, fear or surprise: *She flinched away from the dog.* ◇ *He met my gaze without flinching.*

NOTE **JUMP** OR **FLINCH?** You **jump** with your whole body, especially because you are surprised. **Flinching** may be a smaller movement of the face or part of the body, caused by pain or fear.

cower /ˈkaʊə(r)/ [I] to bend low and/or backwards because you are frightened: *A gun went off and people cowered behind walls and under tables.*

cringe /krɪndʒ/ [I] to move back and/or away from sb because you are frightened: *She cringed back from him, pressing herself against the stove.* ❶ **Cringing** can also be an inner feeling of embarrassment or fear: *The very idea made him cringe inside.*

recoil /rɪˈkɔɪl/ (*written*) to move your body quickly away from sb/sth because you find them/it frightening or unpleasant: *He recoiled in horror at the sight of the corpse.*

shrink (*written*) to move back or away from sb/sth because you are frightened or shocked: *He shrank back against the wall as he heard them approaching.*

NOTE **COWER, CRINGE** OR **SHRINK?** You **cringe** when you are afraid of a person, especially one who has power over you. You may **cower** or **shrink** when you are afraid of sth happening.

junction

 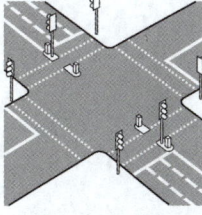

junction (*esp BrE*) **intersection** (*esp AmE*)   **crossroads**

junction noun

junction · intersection · crossroads · turning · turn · roundabout · exit

These are all words for a place where two or more roads meet.

PATTERNS AND COLLOCATIONS
▸ the junction / intersection **with…**
▸ the turning / turn / exit **for…**
▸ the **next** junction / intersection / crossroads / turning / turn / roundabout / exit
▸ a **busy** junction / intersection / crossroads / roundabout
▸ a **dangerous** junction / intersection / crossroads
▸ to **come to** a junction / an intersection / a crossroads / a roundabout / an exit
▸ to **take** the turning / turn / exit

junction /ˈdʒʌŋkʃn/ [C] (*especially BrE*) the place where two or more roads or railway lines meet: *Come off the motorway at the next junction.* ◇ *It was near the junction of City Road and Old Street.*

intersection /ˌɪntəˈsekʃn; *AmE* -tərˈs-/ [C] (*AmE or formal, BrE*) a junction: *It is a busy intersection, almost invariably clogged with traffic.*

crossroads /ˈkrɒsrəʊdz; *AmE* ˈkrɔːsroʊdz/ (pl. **crossroads**) [C] a place where two roads meet and cross each other: *At the next crossroads, turn right.*

turning [C] (*BrE*) a place where a road leads away from the one you are travelling on: *I think we must have taken a **wrong turning** somewhere.*

turn [C] (*especially AmE*) a turning: *Take the next turn on the left.*

roundabout /'raʊndəbaʊt/ [C] (*BrE*) a road junction in the shape of a circle with all the roads leading off it. All vehicles travel around the circle in the same direction until they reach the turning that they want: *At the roundabout, take the second exit.* ❶ In American English a roundabout is called a **traffic circle** or a **rotary**, but they are not at all common in the United States.

exit /'eksɪt; 'egzɪt/ [C] a place where vehicles can leave a road to join another road: *Take the exit for Trento.*

justice *noun*

justice · equality · fairness · fair play · equity
These are all words for a situation in which all people are treated fairly.

PATTERNS AND COLLOCATIONS
▸ justice / equality / fairness / fair play / equity **for** sb
▸ justice / equality / fairness / fair play **in** sth
▸ **strict** justice / equality / fairness
▸ **social** / **economic** justice / equality / fairness / equity
▸ to **ensure** justice / equality / fairness / fair play / equity
▸ to **guarantee** justice / equality / fairness / equity
▸ a **sense of** justice / equality / fairness / fair play

justice [U] the fair treatment of people, especially in society generally: *Our laws must be based on the principles of justice.* ◇ *Sometimes I feel that there's no justice in the world.* **OPP** **injustice** → INEQUALITY, See also **just** → REASONABLE

equality /i'kwɒləti; *AmE* i'kwɑː-/ [U] the fact of being equal in rights, status and advantages in society: *Sexual equality is an ideal that we have not yet achieved.* ◇ *The people were demanding full **equality with** their former masters.* ◇ ***Equality of opportunity** is our priority.* ◇ *We need to ensure **equality of opportunity** in all areas of work.* **OPP** **inequality** → INEQUALITY, See also **equal** → REASONABLE

fairness [U] the quality of treating people equally or in a way that is reasonable: *The system needs to be changed in the interests of **fairness** to genuine refugees.* ❶ In (all) **fairness (to sb)** is used to introduce a statement that defends sb who has just been criticized, or that explains another statement that may seem unreasonable: *In all fairness to him, he did try to stop her leaving.* **OPP** **unfairness** → INEQUALITY, See also **fair** → REASONABLE

fair 'play [U] the fact of playing a game or doing things honestly, fairly, and according to the rules: *As a player, he was always admired for his sense of fair play.* See also **fair** → REASONABLE

equity /'ekwəti/ [U] (*formal*) a situation in which everyone is treated fairly and equally: *They envisaged a society in which justice and equity prevailed.* **OPP** **inequity** → INEQUALITY

K k

keep verb

1 Where do you keep the sugar?
2 I've kept all her letters.
3 keep a diary
4 keep chickens/bees
5 keep a promise/an appointment

---

1 keep · store · hoard · stock up · stash · stockpile

These words all mean to put sth somewhere or get sth so that it can be used later.

keep [T] to put sth in a particular place so that you can use it later, especially if you use it regularly: *Keep your passport in a safe place.* ◇ *Where do you keep the sugar?* ◇ *The documents are all **kept under lock and key** (= locked up safely somewhere).*

store [T] to put sth somewhere and keep it there, especially for a long time, to use later: *The squirrels are **storing up** food for the winter.* ◇ *You can store coffee beans in the freezer to keep them fresh.* ◇ *He hoped the electronic equipment was safely stored away.* See also **store** → SUPPLY *noun*

> **storage** *noun* [U]: *tables that fold flat for storage* ◇ *There's lots of storage space in the attic.*

hoard [T] to collect and keep large amounts of sth such as food or money, especially secretly: *The prisoners used to hoard scraps of food in secret places.* See also **hoard** → SUPPLY *noun*

stock 'up *phrasal verb* to buy a lot of sth so that you can use it later: *We ought to **stock up on** film before our trip.* ◇ *I go shopping once a week to **stock up with** essentials.* ◇ *The store was full of families **stocking up for** Christmas.* See also **stock** → SUPPLY *noun*

stash [T] (*rather informal*) to store sth in a safe or secret place: *She's probably got loads of cash stashed away.* See also **stash** → FUND *noun*

stockpile /ˈstɒkpaɪl; AmE ˈstɑːk-/ [T] to collect and keep a large supply of sth, especially arms, food or fuel: *Consumers began to stockpile fuel amid fears of a shortage.* See also **stockpile** → SUPPLY *noun*

---

2 keep · retain · hold on to sth · save

These words all mean to continue to have sth.

keep [T] to continue to have sth and not give it back or throw it away: *She handed me a ten dollar bill. 'Here — **keep the change.'** ◇ I've kept all her letters.*

retain /rɪˈteɪn/ [T] (*formal*) to keep sth: *Please retain your ticket stub during the event.* ◇ *The house retains much of its original charm.* ◇ *She has **retained** her **title** (= won the competition again) for the third year.*

> **NOTE** KEEP OR RETAIN? Retain is formal and is used especially in official writing. It is not often used in spoken English. It sometimes suggests that the thing you keep will be necessary or useful in the future. **Keep** is a more general word and can be used in almost all situations.

hold 'on to sth, hold 'onto sth *phrasal verb* [no passive] to keep sth that is an advantage for you; to not give or sell sth to sb else: *You should hold on to your oil shares.* ◇ *She took an early lead in the race and held onto it for nine laps.*

save [T] to keep sth to use or enjoy in the future: *He's **saving** his strength **for** the last part of the race.* ◇ *We'll eat some now and save some for tomorrow.*

---

3 keep · hold · store · retain

These words all mean to continue to have or contain sth, especially information.

keep [T] to write sth down as a record: *She **kept a diary** for over twenty years.* ◇ *Keep **a note** of where each item can be found.* ◇ *Separate **accounts** must be **kept** for each different business activity.*

hold [T] to keep sth, especially documents or information, so that it can be used later: *Employees do not have access to personal records held on computer.* ◇ *Our solicitor holds our wills.*

store [T] to keep information or facts in a computer or in your brain: *Each department has a different system for storing and retrieving data.* ◇ *We are conducting research into how information is stored in the brain.*

retain /rɪˈteɪn/ [T] (*formal*) to continue to hold or contain sth: *These plants will need a soil that retains moisture during the summer months.* ◇ *This information is no longer retained within the computer's main memory.*

---

4 keep · breed · rear · raise

These words all mean to own and care for animals.

keep [T] to own and care for animals, especially at home or on a small scale: *Residents are not allowed to keep pets.* ◇ *to keep bees/goats*

breed [T] to keep animals or plants in order to produce new young animals or plants in a controlled way: *Greyhounds were originally bred as hunting dogs.* See also **breed** → PRODUCE

rear /rɪə(r); AmE rɪr/ [T] to breed or keep animals or birds, for example on a farm: *The young crocodiles were reared indoors at a constant temperature of 32°C.* See also **rear** → BRING SB UP

raise [T] to keep particular farm animals or grow particular crops in order to sell or make other use of them: *Farmers cleared the land in order to raise cattle.* See also **raise** → BRING SB UP

> **NOTE** REAR OR RAISE? Raise is more frequent than **rear** in American English. There is also a slight difference in emphasis: **rear** is often used when emphasizing

information about the animals' treatment and living conditions; **raise** is often used when talking about an animal or crop as a product, for example in farming.

---

5 keep · deliver · honour · carry sth out · follow through · stand by sth
These words all mean to do what you have promised to do.

PATTERNS AND COLLOCATIONS
▸ to deliver / follow through / carry through **on** sth
▸ to keep / deliver on / honour / carry out / follow through on / stand by a **promise**
▸ to keep / honour / follow through on / stand by **your word**
▸ to keep / honour / follow through on / stand by an **agreement**
▸ to keep to / carry out / follow through on / stand by a **plan**
▸ to carry out / follow through on a **threat**
▸ to honour / carry out / stand by a **commitment**

keep [T] to do what you have promised or agreed to do: *She kept her promise to visit them.* ◇ *He failed to keep his appointment at the clinic.* ◇ *If we all keep to the agreement there won't be any problems.* **OPP break** → BREAK 4

deliver [I, T] (*rather informal, especially journalism or business*) to do what you promised to do or what you are expected to do; to produce or provide what people expect you to: *He has promised to finish the job by June and I am sure he will deliver.* ◇ *She always delivers on her promises.* ◇ *If you can't deliver improved sales figures, you're fired.* ◇ *The team delivered a stunning victory last night.* ❶ **Deliver** is usually used to talk about producing what is expected in business or sport: *to deliver a (high-quality) service/product/range of benefits/left hook/victory*

honour (*BrE*) (*AmE* **honor**) [T] (*formal*) to do what you have promised or agreed to do: *I have every intention of honouring our contract.* ◇ *She is determined to honour her husband's dying wish.* ◇ *The bank refused to honour the cheque* (= to pay it).

NOTE KEEP OR HONOUR? You can **keep** or **honour** a *promise, agreement* or *your word*: in these collocations **honour** is much more formal than **keep**. You can also **keep** an *appointment* or *engagement* or **honour** sb's *wishes*: ~~He failed to honour his appointment.~~ ◇ ~~She is determined to keep her husband's dying wish.~~

,**carry sth 'out** *phrasal verb* to do what you have said you will do or what you have decided to do: *He carried out his threat after being released from prison.*

,**follow 'through** *phrasal verb* (*AmE, rather informal*) to do what you have said you will do or what you have decided to do: *It's up to you to follow through with the plan.* ◇ *You've vowed to stay in shape during your pregnancy – but will you follow through?*

NOTE CARRY STH OUT OR FOLLOW THROUGH? You can **carry out** or **follow through on** a *promise* or *threat*. **Follow through** is more informal, but is used mostly in American English. **Carry sth out** is used with a wider range of collocates, including *plan, resolution, commitment, responsibility* and *engagement*. You can also **carry out** what sb else has asked you to do: See also **carry sth out** → FOLLOW 3

'**stand by sth** *phrasal verb* to still believe or agree with sth you said, decided or agreed earlier: *She still stands by every word she said.* ❶ Other typical collocates of **stand by sth** are *findings, opinion, decision* and *story*.

kidnap *verb*

kidnap · seize · abduct
These words all mean to take sb away and keep them as a prisoner.

PATTERNS AND COLLOCATIONS
▸ to kidnap / seize / abduct sb's / your **son / daughter / child**

kidnap (-**pp**-, *AmE* also -**p**-) [T] to take sb away illegally and keep them as a prisoner, especially in order to get money or sth else for returning them: *Two businessmen have been kidnapped by terrorists.*
▸ **kidnapping** (also **kidnap**) *noun* [C, U]: *No group has yet claimed responsibility for the kidnappings.* ◇ *He admitted the charge of kidnap.*

seize /siːz/ [T] (*especially journalism*) to arrest or capture sb, either legally or illegally: *A Briton has been seized by border guards and jailed for eight years.* ◇ *Terrorists have seized his wife and children.*

abduct /æbˈdʌkt/ [T] to take sb away illegally, especially using force: *He had attempted to abduct the two children.* ❶ **Abduct** is the term used in law for this act. **Abduct** is usually used to talk about taking away women and children by force, especially when the motive (= reason) is sexual, not political or for money.
▸ **abduction** *noun* [U, C]: *child abduction*

kill *verb* See also the entry for SHOOT

kill · murder · execute · assassinate · slay · bump sb off · take sb/sth out · eliminate · finish sb/sth off
These words all mean to make sb/sth die.

PATTERNS AND COLLOCATIONS
▸ to kill / murder / assassinate sb **in cold blood**
▸ to **brutally** kill / murder / slay sb

kill [T, I] to make sb/sth die: *Cancer kills thousands of people every year.* ◇ *Three people were killed in the crash.* ◇ *He tried to kill himself with sleeping pills.* ◇ *I bought a spray to kill the weeds.* ◇ *Excessive tiredness while driving can kill.* See also **killing** → MURDER *noun*

murder [T] to kill sb deliberately and illegally: *He denies murdering his wife's lover.* See also **murder** → MURDER *noun*, **murderous** → VIOLENT

execute /ˈeksɪkjuːt/ [T, usually passive] to kill sb, especially as a legal punishment: *He was executed for treason.* ◇ *The prisoners were executed by firing squad.* See also **execution** → EXECUTION

assassinate /əˈsæsɪneɪt; *AmE* -sən-/ [T, often passive] to murder an important or famous person, especially for political reasons: *The prime minister was assassinated by extremists.* See also **assassination** → MURDER *noun*

slay [T] (*especially AmE, especially journalism*) to murder sb: *Two passengers were slain by the hijackers.* ❶ In old-fashioned or literary English, both British and American, **slay** means 'to kill sb/sth in a war or fight': *St George slew the dragon.* See also **slaying** → MURDER *noun*

,**bump sb 'off** *phrasal verb* (*informal, humorous*) to murder sb: *She'd had three husbands and bumped them all off for the insurance money.*

,**take sb/sth 'out** *phrasal verb* (*informal*) to kill sb or destroy sth, especially an enemy or sb/sth that causes problems for you: *They took out two enemy bombers.*

eliminate /ɪˈlɪmɪneɪt/ [T] (*rather formal, written*) to kill sb, especially an enemy or opponent: *Most of the regime's left-wing opponents were eliminated.* See also **eliminate** → REMOVE 1

,**finish sb/sth 'off** *phrasal verb* (*rather informal*) to kill or destroy sb/sth, especially sb/sth that is already badly injured or damaged: *The hunter moved in to finish the animal off.*

killer *noun*

killer · murderer · gunman · serial killer · assassin · sniper · hit man
These are all words for a person who kills or attempts to kill sb.

PATTERNS AND COLLOCATIONS
▸ a **notorious** killer / murderer / gunman
▸ a / an **would-be / alleged** killer / murderer / assassin
▸ a **vicious** killer / murderer / hit man
▸ a **professional / hired / contract** killer / assassin / hit man

▸ to **hunt** / **track down** / **catch** / **find** a killer / murderer
▸ to **hire** an assassin / a hit man
▸ a killer / murderer / gunman / serial killer / sniper **strikes**
▸ a murderer / an assassin / a sniper / a hit man **kills**

killer [C] a person, animal or thing that kills: *Police are hunting his killer.* ◇ *Heart disease is the biggest killer in Scotland.*

murderer [C] a person who has killed sb deliberately and illegally: *How do we know he's not a **mass murderer** (= one who has killed a lot of people)?*

gunman [C] a man who uses a gun to rob or kill people: *Two gunmen opened fire on the car.*

serial killer /ˌsɪəriəl ˈkɪlə(r); AmE ˌsɪr-/ [C] a person who murders several people one after the other in a similar way: *Police say that they have no proof that a serial killer is responsible for the four murders.* ❶ Another word for **serial killer** is **mass murderer**. **Mass murderer** is used more often than **serial killer** in less serious remarks about whether sb is dangerous or not: *I hardly think he's a mass murderer.*

assassin /əˈsæsɪn; AmE -sn/ [C] a person who murders sb important or famous, for money or for political reasons: *They hired a professional assassin to do the job for them.*

sniper [C] a person who shoots at sb from a hidden position: *Two soldiers were shot by snipers.*

'hit man [C] (*informal*) a criminal who is paid to kill sb: *Maybe somebody hired a hit man.*

kind *noun* See also the entry for CATEGORY

kind · sort · type · form · version · variety · style · genre · nature · brand
These are all words for a group of people or things that are the same in some way.

PATTERNS AND COLLOCATIONS
▸ a kind / sort / type / form / version / variety / style / genre / brand **of** sth
▸ **of a** / **the …** kind / sort / type / form / variety / style / nature
▸ **in** kind / type / form / style / nature
▸ **different** kinds / sorts / types / forms / versions / varieties / styles / genres
▸ **various** kinds / sorts / types / forms / versions / styles / genres
▸ a **different** kind / sort / type / form / version / style / nature / brand
▸ **another** kind / sort / type / form / version / variety / style / brand
▸ the **same** kind / sort / type / form / version / variety / style / genre / nature / brand
▸ **all** kinds / sorts / types / forms / varieties / styles / brands (of sth)
▸ **every** / **any** kind / sort / type / form / variety / style / nature
▸ **some** kind / sort / type / form / variety / nature (of sth)
▸ a **particular** kind / sort / type / form / version / variety / style / genre / nature / brand
▸ the **best** / **worst** kind / sort / type / form
▸ a / the / that kind / sort / type **of thing**
▸ **of this** / **that** kind / sort / type
▸ **of every** kind / sort / type / form / variety / style / nature

kind [C, U] a group of people or things that are similar in a particular way: *They play music of all kinds.* ◇ *The school is the first of its kind in the UK.* ◇ *She does the same kind of work as me.* ◇ *She isn't that kind of person.* ◇ *I miss him, in a funny kind of way.* ◇ *They sell all kinds of things.* ◇ *You're going to need some kind of cover to protect it from the rain.* ◇ *'I was terrible!' 'You were **nothing of the kind!'***

sort [C] (*especially BrE*) a group of people or things that are similar in a particular way: *'What sort of music do you like?' 'Oh, all sorts.'* ◇ *This sort of problem is quite common.* ◇ *He's the sort of person who only cares about money.* ◇ *Most people went on training courses of one sort or another.* ◇ (*spoken*) *What sort of price are you willing to pay* (= approximately what price)? See also **sort** → CLASSIFY *verb*

type [C] a class or group of people or things that share particular qualities or features or are part of a larger group: *He mixes with all types of people.* ◇ *What type of car do you drive?* ◇ *How much do you charge for this type of*

work? ◇ *This is the oldest existing shrine of its type.* ◇ *You can divide his novels into three main types.* ◇ *She has a very rare **blood type**.* ◇ *This is a new formula for all skin types.*

> **NOTE** **KIND, SORT OR TYPE?** **Kind** is the most frequent of these words in this meaning. **Sort** is also frequent but is slightly more informal than **kind** and is used more in spoken English than in written English, and more in British English than in American English. **Type** is slightly more formal than the other two words and tends to be used more to talk about things that can be divided into classes or groups in a fairly objective way, for example in official, scientific or academic contexts.

form [C] one type of a thing that exists in a number of different types, especially when these have different physical characteristics: *We need to look for an alternative form of energy.* ◇ *This is one of the most common forms of cancer.* ◇ *Will we ever discover intelligent **life forms** on other planets?* ◇ *Music is not like other **art forms**.* ❶ Different **forms** of a thing are usually different in their physical characteristics, in a way that different **types** of a thing need not be: ~~He mixes with all forms of people.~~ ◇ ~~Are there intelligent life types on other planets?~~ See also **form** → FORM 1

version [C] a copy of sth, especially a product, that is slightly different from the original thing: *the latest version of the Volkswagen Golf* ◇ *the de luxe / luxury version* ◇ *The English version of the novel is due for publication next year.*

variety [C] a type of a thing, for example a plant or language, that is different from the others in the same general group: *Apples come in a great many varieties.* ◇ *The variety of English that they speak is closer to American than British.* ◇ *They stock over 200 varieties of cheese.*

style [C, U] the features of a book, painting, building, etc. that make it typical of a particular author, artist, historical period, etc: *This is a fine example of the Gothic style.* ◇ *The city contains many different styles of architecture.* ◇ *They were told to write the passage in the style of Hemingway.*

genre /ˈʒɒrə; ˈʒɒnrə; AmE ˈʒɑ:nrə/ [C, U] (*formal*) a particular style or type of literature, art, music or film that can be recognized because of its special features: *Crime fiction is a genre which seems likely to stay with us for many years.* ◇ *His essay discusses theories of style and genre.*

nature /ˈneɪtʃə(r)/ [sing.] (*rather formal*) a particular type of sth: *His books were mainly of a scientific nature.* ◇ *Don't worry about things of that nature.* ◇ *Decisions of this nature often take a long time.* ❶ In this meaning **nature** is usually used in the phrase *of a …nature.*

brand [C] a particular type of sth, especially sb's particular way of doing or thinking about sth: *She has her own unique brand of humour.*

kind *adj.* See also the entry for NICE 2

kind · good · generous · benign · benevolent · considerate · sweet · thoughtful
These words all describe a person who cares about other people, is willing to help them, and considers their needs and feelings.

PATTERNS AND COLLOCATIONS
▸ kind / good / generous / benevolent / considerate **to** / **towards** / **toward** sb
▸ to be kind / good / generous / considerate / sweet / thoughtful **of** sb (to do sth)
▸ a kind / generous / benevolent / considerate / sweet / thoughtful **man** / **woman** / **person**
▸ a kind / generous / considerate / thoughtful **gesture**
▸ **very** kind / good / generous / considerate / sweet / thoughtful
▸ **extremely** kind / good / generous / considerate

kind (of a person) caring about others and willing to help them; gentle and friendly; (of an action or expression) showing these feelings: *They were taught to be kind to animals.* ◇ *It was really kind of you to help me.* ◇ *She may*

seem quite stern at times, but she has a kind heart. ◇ Thanks for your card – it was a very kind thought. **OPP** cruel → CRUEL, **unkind** → MEAN 1, See also **caring** → LOVING
▸ **kindly** adv.: She kindly agreed to give me a ride home.
▸ **kindness** noun [U]: She wanted to thank him for his kindness.

good [not usually before noun] (rather informal, especially spoken) willing to help; showing kindness to other people: He was very good to me when I was ill. ◇ It was good of you to come. ◇ I had a lot of time off work, but my boss was very good about it. ❶ **Good** is the most frequent of these words in spoken English. In this meaning it is not usually used before a noun: a good man/woman is a slightly more formal expression and has the more general meaning of sb who has good principles and lives a good, moral life; being kind to people is only part of the meaning. See also **good** → GOOD 5

generous kind in the way you treat people; willing to see what is good about sb/sth: Her generous spirit shone through in everything she did. ◇ He wrote a very generous assessment of my work. **OPP** mean → MEAN 1

benign /bɪˈnaɪn/ (formal) kind and gentle; not causing any harm: Her face was gentle and benign. ◇ The presence of women and children had a benign influence on the soldiers.
▸ **benignly** adv.: She smiled benignly as the students entered the room.

benevolent /bəˈnevələnt/ (formal) (especially of sb in authority) kind, helpful and generous: The colonel was benevolent, but not stupid. ◇ She took a benevolent interest in her nieces' education.

considerate /kənˈsɪdərət/ thinking of other people's feelings and wishes; careful not to hurt or upset others: Try to be a bit more considerate. ◇ Louis was a kind, caring and considerate young man. **OPP** inconsiderate → INSENSITIVE
▸ **consideration** noun [U]: You should show a little more consideration towards other people.

sweet (rather informal, especially spoken) having or showing a kind character: It was sweet of them to offer to help. ◇ She gave him her sweetest smile.

thoughtful showing that you are thinking about and care about other people: It was very thoughtful of you to send the flowers. **OPP** thoughtless → INSENSITIVE

NOTE CONSIDERATE OR THOUGHTFUL? **Thoughtful** is more often used when sb does a particular thing for sb else without being asked to. **Considerate** is used more about sb's general character and their attitude towards people.

king noun

king · queen · ruler · emperor · monarch · the crown · sovereign · regent
These are all words for sb who rules a country or area who is not elected but is usually a member of a royal family.

PATTERNS AND COLLOCATIONS
▸ **under** a king/ a queen/ a ruler/ an emperor/ a monarch
▸ a **great/ strong** king/ queen/ ruler/ emperor/ monarch
▸ the **rightful** king/ queen/ ruler/ sovereign
▸ the **former** king/ queen/ ruler/ emperor/ monarch
▸ the **reigning** king/ queen/ emperor/ monarch
▸ a/ an **deposed/ exiled** king/ queen/ emperor/ monarch
▸ a **hereditary/ absolute** ruler/ monarch/ sovereign
▸ to **become** king/ queen/ ruler/ emperor/ monarch/ regent
▸ to **crown sb (as)/ proclaim sb** king/ queen/ emperor
▸ a king/ a queen/ an emperor/ a monarch **reigns/ rules**
▸ a king/ a queen/ an emperor **abdicates**

king (also **King**) [C] the male ruler of an independent state that has a royal family; used as a title: The ceremony was attended by the King of Spain. ◇ His daughter, Anne, married King Richard III. ◇ He was crowned king at the age of fifteen. See also **kingdom** → REPUBLIC

queen (also **Queen**) [C] the female ruler of an independent state that has a royal family; the wife of a king; used as a title: The banquet will be hosted by the Queen (= the current Queen of England, Elizabeth II) at Buckingham Palace. ◇ She became queen after the sudden death of her brother. ◇ The King and Queen of Denmark attended the wedding. ❶ The wife of a **king** may be called a **queen** or **queen consort**, but the husband of a **queen** is not called a **king**; he usually has the title prince.

ruler [C] a person who rules a country or area: He established himself as **ruler over** both tribes. ◇ There was a successful coup against the country's **military rulers**. ❶ **Ruler** is a general word for sb who rules a country or area, usually one who is not elected. It can refer to the head of a royal family such as a king or queen or to an individual who has complete power and has usually come to power by force such as a military ruler or dictator. It can also refer to a more powerful country that rules over another country or area: Vietnam still had strong links with France, the former **colonial ruler**. See also **rule** → RULE verb 1

emperor (also **Emperor**) /ˈempərə(r)/ [C] the ruler of an empire (= a group of countries or states that are ruled or governed by one ruler or government); used as a title: It is the tomb of the first real emperor of China, Emperor Qin Shi Huang. ❶ A female ruler of an empire can be called an **empress**. See also **empire** → REPUBLIC

monarch /ˈmɒnək; AmE ˈmɑːnərk; -ɑːrk/ [C] a king, queen or emperor: The **constitutional monarch** (= a king or queen whose power is controlled by a set of laws), as head of state, has limited powers.

the crown (also **the Crown**) [sing.] the government of a country thought of as being represented by a king or queen; the position or power of a king or queen: Knights swore an oath of allegiance to the Crown. ◇ He had a claim to the crown of France. ❶ In the UK, **the Crown** is used to refer to the government or the state, especially in legal contexts. For example, in criminal trials, it is **the Crown** that brings a criminal charge against sb on behalf of the state: Who's appearing for the Crown in this case?

sovereign /ˈsɒvrɪn; AmE ˈsɑːvrən/ [C] (formal) the ruler of a country, especially a monarch: The islands are ruled by a governor, representing the British sovereign.

NOTE MONARCHS AND SOVEREIGNS **Monarch** and **sovereign** are both used to refer to any king or queen of a country rather than as a title for a particular king or queen, especially when describing the system of government in general. **Sovereign** is more formal than **monarch**.

regent (also **Regent**) /ˈriːdʒənt/ [C] a person who rules a country because the king or queen is too young, old or ill: She acted as regent until her son was old enough to be crowned king.

knife noun

knife · blade · dagger · scalpel · machete · cleaver · switchblade · penknife
These are all words for tools that have a sharp edge or edges for cutting.

PATTERNS AND COLLOCATIONS
▸ **with** a knife/ blade/ dagger/ scalpel/ machete/ cleaver/ switchblade/ penknife
▸ a **sharp** knife/ blade/ dagger/ penknife
▸ a **blunt** knife/ penknife
▸ a **long/ short** knife/ blade/ dagger
▸ to **hold/ use/ pick up/ put down** a knife/blade/dagger/scalpel/ machete/ cleaver/ switchblade/ penknife
▸ to **cut sth with** a knife/ blade/ scalpel/ machete/ penknife
▸ to **stab sb/ sth with** a knife/ blade/ dagger
▸ to **chop sth with** a knife/ machete/ cleaver
▸ to **slash sb/ sth with** a knife/ blade/ machete
▸ a knife/ blade/ dagger/ scalpel/ machete/ penknife **cuts** sth

knife (pl. **knives**) [C] a sharp blade with a handle, used for cutting or as a weapon: *Sara placed her **knife and fork** neatly on the plate.* ◇ *a kitchen/carving/hunting knife* ◇ *She was murdered in a frenzied knife attack.*

blade [C] the flat part of a knife, tool or machine, which has a sharp edge or edges for cutting: *Knife blades are generally made of stainless steel.* ◇ ***Razor blades** should always be sharp.* ❶ **Blade** is also used to mean 'knife' or (more frequently) 'sword': *The swordsmen weaved and dodged as their blades clashed over and over again.*

dagger [C] a short pointed knife that is used as a weapon: *Each man was armed with both sword and dagger.*

scalpel /ˈskælpəl/ [C] a small sharp knife used by doctors in medical operations: *The surgeon made the first incision with a wide-bladed scalpel.*

machete /məˈʃeti/ [C] a broad heavy knife used as a cutting tool or as a weapon: *She used her machete to clear a way through the jungle.*

cleaver [C] a heavy knife with a broad blade, often used for cutting large pieces of meat: *With a meat cleaver or heavy chef's knife, cut the chicken into large pieces.*

switchblade /ˈswɪtʃbleɪd/ [C] a knife with a blade inside the handle that jumps out quickly when a button is pressed: *Owning or carrying a switchblade is illegal in the United Kingdom.*

penknife /ˈpennaɪf/ [C] a small knife with one or more blades that fold down into the handle: *He pulled the penknife out of his pocket and opened it.*

knife

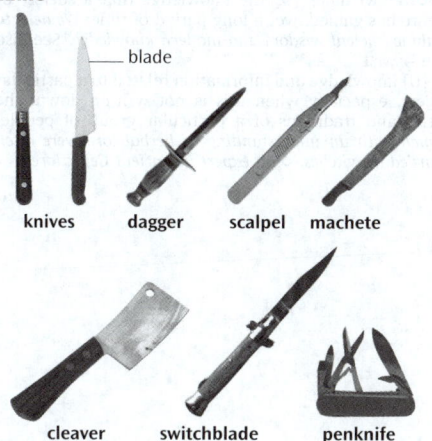

knives   dagger   scalpel   machete

cleaver   switchblade   penknife

knock *verb*

knock · tap · drum · rap
These words all mean to make a noise by hitting sth quite firmly.

PATTERNS AND COLLOCATIONS
▸ to knock/tap/rap **at** sth
▸ to knock/tap/drum/rap **on** sth
▸ to knock/tap/drum/rap **with** sth
▸ to knock/rap **loudly**
▸ to knock/tap **hard/gently**

knock [I] to hit a door, etc. firmly in order to make a noise that will attract sb's attention: *He knocked three times and waited.* ◇ *Somebody was knocking on the window.* See also **knock** → HIT 1

tap (-pp-) [I, T] to hit sth quickly and lightly with your fingers, feet, etc, making a noise: *He was busy tapping away at his computer.* ◇ *The music set everyone's feet tapping.* ◇ *He kept tapping his fingers on the table.* See also **tap** → PAT
▸ **tap** *noun* [C]: *a tap at/on the door*

drum (-mm-) [T, I] to hit a surface again and again, making a continuous low noise: *Impatiently, he drummed his fingers on the table.* ◇ *His fingers drummed on the door frame.*

rap (-pp-) [I, T] to hit sth several times quickly, making a sudden noise: *She rapped angrily on the door.* ◇ *He rapped the table with his pen.*

know *verb*
1 If only we'd known…
2 I know it's here somewhere!

1 know · realize · appreciate
These words all mean to understand or be aware of sth.

PATTERNS AND COLLOCATIONS
▸ **without** knowing/realizing/appreciating sth
▸ to know/realize/appreciate **that**…
▸ to know/realize/appreciate **what/how/why**…
▸ to know/realize **where**…
▸ to **begin/come to** know/realize/appreciate sth
▸ **hope** sb knows/realizes/appreciates sth
▸ **should have** known/realized/appreciated sth

know [T] (not used in the progressive tenses) to understand or be aware of a particular fact or situation: *He knew he was dying.* ◇ *I know exactly how you feel.* ◇ *You know perfectly well what she meant.* ◇ (spoken)'He's feeling really down.' 'I know.' ◇ ***If only we'd known** you were having so many problems!* ◇ *This case is hopeless **and he knows it** (= although he will not admit it).* See also **knowledge** → AWARENESS

realize (*BrE* also **-ise**) [T] (not used in the progressive tenses) to understand or become aware of a particular fact or situation: *I didn't realize (that) you were so unhappy.* ◇ *I don't think you realize how important this is to her.* ◇ *She soon realized her mistake.* ◇ *We make assumptions all the time without realizing it.* ◇ *They managed to leave without any of us realizing.* See also **realization** → AWARENESS

NOTE KNOW OR REALIZE? In this meaning **know** is NOT usually used with a noun object: ~~She soon knew her mistake.~~ To **realize** sth can mean to become aware of it, as well as to be aware of it; **know** can mean 'become aware' if it happens in a single moment: *As soon as/The moment I walked in the room I knew/realized something was wrong.* ◇ *Suddenly/All of a sudden/At once I knew/realized what he meant.* However, if the process of becoming aware takes any time, even a short time, use **realize**: *I soon/quickly/gradually/slowly realized what he meant.* ◇ ~~I soon/quickly/gradually/slowly knew what he meant.~~

appreciate /əˈpriːʃieɪt/ [T] (not used in the progressive tenses) (*rather formal*) to understand or realize that sth is true, especially that a situation is difficult for sb else: *You have to appreciate the difficulties we are facing.* ◇ *I don't think you appreciate how expensive it will be.* ◇ *As you'll appreciate, the task has not always been easy.* See also **appreciation** → UNDERSTANDING

2 know · bet · guarantee
These words all mean to say that you are certain about sth.

PATTERNS AND COLLOCATIONS
▸ to know/bet/guarantee **that**…
▸ you **can** bet/guarantee (that…)

know [T, I] to feel certain about sth: *I know it's here somewhere!* ◇ *I just knew that it was something I wanted to do.* ◇ (spoken)'You were right – someone's been spreading rumours about you.' 'I knew it!' ◇ 'She's the worst player in the team.' 'Oh, I don't know (= I am not sure that I agree) – she played well yesterday.'

bet [T] (*rather informal, spoken*) used to say that you are almost certain that sth is true or that sth will happen: *I bet we're too late.* ◇ *You can bet that the moment I sit down, the phone will ring.*

guarantee /ˌɡærənˈtiː/ [T] to be certain that sth will happen: *The film is virtually guaranteed to do well at the box office.*

knowledge *noun* See the Topic Map for EDUCATION on p.888

knowledge · experience · literacy · scholarship · learning · enlightenment · wisdom · lore
These are all words for the information, understanding and skills that you learn through education or experience.

PATTERNS AND COLLOCATIONS
▸ knowledge / learning / enlightenment / wisdom **about** sth
▸ **great** knowledge / experience / scholarship / learning / enlightenment / wisdom
▸ **ancient** / **traditional** / **folk** knowledge / wisdom / lore
▸ **human** knowledge / experience / enlightenment / wisdom
▸ **academic** knowledge / scholarship / learning
▸ **practical** knowledge / experience / wisdom
▸ to **acquire** knowledge / experience / literacy / learning / wisdom
▸ to **gain** knowledge / experience / enlightenment / wisdom
▸ to **increase** your knowledge / experience / learning

knowledge [U, sing.] the information, understanding and skills that you gain through studying sth or doing sth: *You do not need to have specialist knowledge to express an opinion about language.* ◇ *There will be a test of your* **general knowledge** (= your knowledge about things generally). ◇ *He has a wide knowledge of music and painting.* **OPP** **ignorance** → IGNORANCE, See also **know** → LEARN

experience [U] the knowledge and ability that you have gained through doing sth for a period of time; the process of gaining this: *I have over ten years' teaching experience.* ◇

Do you have any **previous experience** *of this type of work?* ◇ *She didn't get paid much but it was all* **good experience**. ◇ *We all* **learn by experience**. ❶ In this meaning **experience** is used especially in the context of work and careers. Your **work experience** is the work or jobs that you have done in your life so far: *The opportunities available will depend on your previous* **work experience** *and qualifications.* **OPP** **inexperience** → IGNORANCE See also **experience** → EVENT 1, **experience** → LIFE 3, **experienced** → EXPERIENCED, **experienced** → SOPHISTICATED, See also the entry for SKILL 1

literacy /ˈlɪtərəsi/ [U] the ability to read and write: *The government is running a campaign to promote* **adult literacy** (= the ability of adults to read and write). **OPP** **illiteracy**

scholarship /ˈskɒləʃɪp; *AmE* ˈskɑːlərʃɪp/ [U] the serious study of an academic subject and the knowledge and methods involved: *Oxford became one of the great centres of medieval scholarship.* See also **scholar** → SCHOLAR, **scholarly** → EDUCATIONAL

learning [U] knowledge that you get from reading and studying: *He is a teacher of great intellect and learning.* See also **learned** → INTELLECTUAL 2

enlightenment /ɪnˈlaɪtnmənt/ [U] (*formal*) knowledge about and understanding of sth; the process of understanding sth or making other people understand it: *Seeking enlightenment, I asked one of my professors about the matter.* ◇ *Mankind has long been on a quest for spiritual enlightenment.* See also **enlighten** → TELL 1

wisdom /ˈwɪzdəm/ [U] the knowledge that a society or culture has gained over a long period of time: *We need to combine ancient wisdom and modern knowledge.* See also **wise** → WISE

lore [U] knowledge and information related to a particular subject, especially when this is not written down; the stories and traditions of a particular group of people: *Women with an understanding of herbal lore were often regarded as witches.* ◇ *an expert in ancient Celtic lore*

label noun

label · tag · sticker
These are all words for a piece of paper, fabric or plastic that is attached to sth and gives information about it.

PATTERNS AND COLLOCATIONS
- a **price** label / tag / sticker
- a **name** label / tag
- to **have** a label / tag / sticker
- to **attach** / **put on** / **stick on** a label / tag / sticker
- The label / tag / sticker **says...**

label [C] a small piece of paper, fabric or plastic that is attached to sth in order to show what it is or give information about it: *The washing instructions are on the label.* ◇ *This program produces address labels from your database.* ◇ *He'll only wear clothes with a* **designer label***.* See also **label** → MARK *verb* 1

tag [C] (often used in compounds) a label: *Everyone at the conference had to wear a name tag.* ◇ *I attached a gift tag* (= tied it to a present). ◇ *The police use electronic tags to monitor the whereabouts of young offenders on probation.* See also **tag** → MARK *verb* 1

> **NOTE** **LABEL** OR **TAG?** Labels in clothes are usually made of fabric and sewn in. **Tags** on clothes are usually made of cardboard and cut off before you wear the clothes. A *name label/tag* is sewn into a piece of clothing to show who it belongs to. A *name tag* can also be stuck or tied onto sb to show who they are: *I had to sew name labels/ tags into all my son's clothes for school.* ◇ *All babies in the hospital have name tags tied around their ankles. Price tag* is much more frequent than *price label* and is used for both literal and figurative meanings: *What does the price tag say?* ◇ (*figurative*) *This wine is well worth its £8.95 price tag.* A **label** can also be a **sticker** that you put on an envelope.

sticker [C] a sticky label with a picture or message on it, that you stick on to sth: *The pack will contain a membership card, car stickers and a newsletter.*

label

| labels | price tag | sticker |

lack noun

lack · absence · deficit · shortage · shortfall · deficiency · scarcity
These are all words for talking about not having enough of sth or sth not being there.

PATTERNS AND COLLOCATIONS
- a shortage / shortfall / deficiency **in** sth
- a **serious** lack / deficit / shortage / shortfall / deficiency
- a **major** / **severe** lack / deficit / shortage / deficiency
- to **have** / **suffer from** a lack / absence / deficit / shortage / deficiency
- to **face** a lack / deficit / shortage / shortfall
- **There is no** lack / shortage / deficiency / scarcity **of** sth.

lack [U, sing.] the state of not having sth or not having enough of sth: *a lack of food/money/skills* ◇ *There was no lack of volunteers.* ◇ *They haven't won a game yet, but it isn't* **for lack** *of trying.* ◇ *The trip was cancelled* **through lack of** (= because there was not enough) *interest.* See also **lacking** → INADEQUATE
▸ **lack** *verb* [T, no passive]: *Some houses still lack basic amenities such as bathrooms.* ◇ *He lacks confidence.*

absence [U] the fact of sb/sth not existing or not being available: *The case was dismissed* **in the absence of** *any definite proof.* ◇ *I was surprised by the absence of any women on the board of directors.* **OPP** **presence** ❶ **Presence** is the fact of sb/sth being in a particular place or thing: *The test can identify the presence of abnormalities in the unborn child.*

deficit /ˈdefɪsɪt/ [C] the amount by which sth, especially an amount of money, is too small or smaller than sth else: *There's a deficit of $3 million in the total needed to complete the project.* ◇ *The team has come back from a 2–0 deficit in the first half.* ❶ In economics a **deficit** is the amount by which money spent or owed is greater than money earned in a particular period of time: *You cannot cut a budget deficit simply by raising taxes.* ◇ *The trade balance has been* **in deficit** *for the past five years.* **OPP** **surplus** → EXCESS *adj.*

shortage /ˈʃɔːtɪdʒ; AmE ˈʃɔːrt-/ [C, U] a situation in which there is not enough of the people or things that are needed: *The government must address the current acute shortage of teachers.* ◇ *The recent heavy rains have helped to ease the water shortage.* ◇ *There is no shortage of* (= there are plenty of) *things to do in the town.* **OPP** **surplus** → EXCESS *adj.*, See also **short** → SCARCE

shortfall /ˈʃɔːtfɔːl; AmE ˈʃɔːrt-/ [C] a situation in which there is not enough of sth, especially money or supplies of sth: *Last year there was a shortfall of over 500 000 tonnes in the grain supply.* ◇ *The estimated shortfall for this financial year is $1.2 million.*

> **NOTE** **SHORTAGE** OR **SHORTFALL?** Shortfall is used especially to talk about sth that is expected, for example the money that a company expects to make in a period of time. There can be a **shortage** of people as well as most things, but NOT: *a shortfall of people.*

deficiency /dɪˈfɪʃnsi/ [U, C] the state of not having or not having enough of, sth that is essential, especially sth that is important for your health: *Vitamin deficiency in the diet can cause illness.* ◇ *The condition is caused by a deficiency of calcium.* See also **deficient** → INADEQUATE

scarcity /ˈskeəsəti; AmE ˈskers-/ [U, C] a situation in which there is not enough of sth, especially food or other resources, and it is difficult to obtain it: *We must ensure that the animals are given food in times of scarcity.* ◇ *The job was made more difficult because of a scarcity of data.* See also **scarce** → SCARCE

lacklustre (BrE) (AmE lackluster) adj. See also the entry for TIRED 2

lacklustre · bland · banal · unimaginative · pedestrian · wooden
These words all describe things or people that are not interesting or exciting.

PATTERNS AND COLLOCATIONS
- a lacklustre / wooden **performance**
- a pedestrian / wooden **manner**
- banal / pedestrian **stuff**

▸ a bland / pedestrian **affair**
▸ **rather** lacklustre / bland / banal / unimaginative / pedestrian / wooden
▸ **somewhat** bland / unimaginative / pedestrian
▸ **very** bland / pedestrian / wooden

lacklustre (*BrE*) (*AmE* **lackluster**) /ˈlæklʌstə(r)/ (of a performance or performer) not of a high quality; lacking interest or excitement: *There were signs of discontent at the party's lacklustre performance.* ◇ *The vocal soloists were generally lacklustre.*

bland with little colour, interest or excitement; without anything to attract attention: *He was criticized for his bland image.* ◇ *The old town hall was replaced with a bland, glass-and-steel office building.*

banal /bəˈnɑːl; *AmE* also ˈbeɪnl/ very ordinary and containing nothing that is interesting or important: *They were having a banal conversation about the weather.* ❶ **Banal** is used especially to describe *conversation, remarks, questions* or any written or spoken *material*.

unimaginative without any original or new ideas: *He knew she thought him to be a stiff and unimaginative person.* ◇ *The food was adequate but unimaginative.* **OPP** imaginative → CREATIVE

pedestrian /pəˈdestriən/ (*rather formal, especially written*) without any imagination or excitement: *It is a factual and somewhat pedestrian programme.* ◇ *The curriculum is narrow and pedestrian.* ❶ **Pedestrian** is used especially to describe a way of considering or presenting a subject.

wooden not showing enough natural expression, emotion or movement: *The film has wooden acting and an appalling script.* ◇ *Her voice sounded wooden and lifeless.*

lake *noun*

lake · pond · waters · pool · reservoir · loch · lagoon
These are all words for a mass of water, especially one that is smaller than a sea.

PATTERNS AND COLLOCATIONS
▸ (a) **deep** lake / pond / waters / pool / reservoir / loch / lagoon
▸ the **edge** / **surface** / **bottom** / **middle** of the lake / pond / pool / reservoir / loch / lagoon

lake [C] a large area of water that is surrounded by land: *Do you want to go for a swim in the lake?* ◇ *We stayed in a hotel on the edge of Lake Ontario.*

pond [C] a small area of still water, especially one that is artificial: *a fish/duck/garden pond* ◇ *Never throw litter into ponds or streams.*

waters [pl.] the water in a particular lake, river, sea or ocean; lakes, rivers, etc. of a particular type: *the grey waters of the river Clyde* ◇ *These birds are rarely seen on inland waters.*

pool [C] a small area of still water, especially one that has formed naturally: *The waterfall cascades into the pool below.* ◇ *They went looking for crabs in rock pools.* ❶ **Pool** also means **swimming pool**. Note the difference between these sentences: *They have a pond in their garden* (= with plants and fish). ◇ *They have a pool in their garden* (= a swimming pool). ◇ *There was a pool of water at the bottom of the garden* (= formed by the rain or flooding).

reservoir /ˈrezəvwɑː(r); *AmE* ˈrezərv-/ [C] a natural or artificial lake where water is stored before it is taken by pipes to homes and businesses: *The water content of the country's reservoirs had fallen to less than 50% of their capacity.* ◇ *They got up early and went for a swim in the reservoir.*

loch /lɒk; lɒx; *AmE* lɑːk; lɑːx/ [C] (in Scotland) a lake or a narrow strip of sea almost surrounded by land: *The loch contains salmon and trout.* ◇ *Loch Ness*

lagoon /ləˈɡuːn/ [C] a lake of salt water that is separated from the sea by a long line of rocks or sand near the surface of the sea (= a reef): *This species is found in lakes and coastal lagoons.* ❶ In American English a **lagoon** may also be a small area of fresh water near a lake or river: *We loved to go swimming in the lagoon.*

land *noun*

1 the price of land
2 open/agricultural land

1 land · estate · real estate · farmland
These words all mean an area of ground that sb owns.

PATTERNS AND COLLOCATIONS
▸ **on** land / an estate / real estate / farmland
▸ (a) **private** land / estate / real estate / farmland
▸ **prime** land / real estate / farmland
▸ to **own** / **buy** / **sell** land / an estate / real estate / farmland
▸ a **piece of** land / real estate / farmland

land [U] (also *formal* **lands** [pl.]) the area of ground that sb owns, especially when you think of it as property that can be bought or sold: *The price of land is rising rapidly.* ◇ *During the war their lands were occupied by the enemy.* See also **land** → COUNTRY 2, **land** → FLOOR 1, **land** → SOIL

estate /ɪˈsteɪt/ [C] a large area of land, usually in the country, that is owned by one person or family: *The house is set on a 200-acre estate near the Black Mountains.*

ˈreal estate [U] (*especially AmE*) property in the form of land or buildings: *My father sold real estate.* ◇ *He bought a piece of real estate several years ago for $50 000.*

farmland /ˈfɑːrm-/ [U, pl.] land that is used for farming: *The United States loses over 4 000 acres of farmland every day.*

2 See also the entry for SOIL
land · lot · ground · space · plot
These words all mean an area of land that is used for a particular purpose.

PATTERNS AND COLLOCATIONS
▸ (an) **open** land / ground / space
▸ (a / an) **empty** / **vacant** land / lot / ground / plot
▸ **waste** / **derelict** land / ground
▸ a **burial** ground / plot

land [U] (also **lands** [pl.]) an area of ground, especially one that is used for a particular purpose: *The valley provides some rich grazing land for farmers.* ◇ *It's an attractive village in the heart of the county's agricultural lands.* See also **land** → FLOOR 1, **land** → SOIL

lot [C] (*AmE*) a piece of land that is used or intended for a particular purpose: *Some kids were playing ball in a vacant lot.* ◇ *Building lots will cost between $100 000 and $500 000.* ◇ *He backed the car into the parking lot.* ❶ The British English word for *parking lot* is **car park**.

ground [U, C] an area of land that is used for a particular purpose: *The kids were playing on waste ground near the school.* ◇ (*BrE*) *They're building a new football ground in the town.* ◇ *We visited the site of an ancient burial ground.*

NOTE LAND, LOT OR GROUND? **Land** is used for large areas of open land in the country, especially when it is used for farming. A **lot** is often a smaller piece of land in a town or city, especially one intended for building or parking on. **Ground** [U] is any area of open land; a **ground** [C] is an area of land designed or used for a particular purpose or activity.

space [U, C] a large area of land that has no buildings on it: *The city has fine buildings and plenty of open space.* ◇ *the wide open spaces of the Canadian prairies*

plot [C] a small piece of land used or intended for a particular purpose: *She bought a small plot of land to build a house.* ◇ *He was buried in the family plot at the cemetery.* ◇ *At the back of the house was a small vegetable plot.* See also **patch** → GARDEN 2

NOTE LOT OR PLOT? Either a **lot** or a **plot** can be used for building on. Only a **plot** can also be used for burying people or growing vegetables.

land verb

land · come to rest · come down · settle · touch down · alight · perch · bring sth down
These are all words that can be used when sth comes down through the air and onto the ground or another surface.

PATTERNS AND COLLOCATIONS
▶ to land/come to rest/come down/settle/touch down/alight/ perch/bring sth down **on** sth
▶ to land/come to rest/come down/touch down/bring sth down **at/in** sth
▶ to land/come to rest/come down/touch down/bring sth down **safely**

land [I, T] to come down through the air onto the ground or another surface; to make a plane come down to the ground in a controlled way: *Both aircraft landed safely.* ◇ *A fly landed on the tip of his nose.* ◇ *A single snowflake drifted down and landed on the windowsill.* ◇ *He landed the damaged aircraft in a field.* **OPP** take off → SET OFF
▶ **landing** noun [C, U]: *a perfect/smooth/safe landing* ◇ *The pilot was forced to make an **emergency landing**.* ◇ *a landing site*
come to ˈrest phrase (*written*) to stop moving, especially after flying or travelling in an uncontrolled way: *The car crashed through the barrier and came to rest in a field.* ◇ *His eyes came to rest on Clara's face.*
ˌcome ˈdown phrasal verb (of an aircraft) to come down to the ground, especially in an uncontrolled way because there is a problem: *Forty-two people died when a military aircraft came down in a remote area.*
settle [I] to fall or fly down onto sth and stay there for some time: *Dust had settled on everything.* ◇ *Two birds settled on the fence.* ◇ *Some snow fell but it didn't settle (= stay on the ground).*
ˌtouch ˈdown phrasal verb (of a plane or spacecraft) to land, especially under control or as planned: *The space capsule will touch down tomorrow.*
alight /əˈlaɪt/ [I] (always used with an adverb or preposition) (*formal or literary*) (of a bird or insect) to land on or in sth after flying to it: *A butterfly fluttered by and alighted on a rose.*
perch [I] (always used with an adverb or preposition) (of a bird) to land and stay on a branch, etc: *A robin flew down and perched on the fence.* ◇ *They found the parrot perched in a tree.*
ˌbring sth ˈdown phrasal verb to land an aircraft, usually in a situation where there is sth wrong: *The pilot brought the plane down safely before the passengers even realized there was a problem.*

language noun

1 Italian is my first language.
2 everyday language

1 language · dialect · tongue · idiom
These are all words for the different forms of words and speech used by people of a particular country, area or social group.

PATTERNS AND COLLOCATIONS
▶ to speak **in** a language/a dialect/a tongue/an idiom
▶ sb's **native** language/dialect/tongue
▶ a **local** language/dialect
▶ a **strange** language/dialect/tongue
▶ a **foreign** language/tongue
▶ to **speak/understand/use/learn/study** a language/dialect

language [C, U] the system of communication in speech and writing that is used by people of a particular country; the use by humans of such a system to communicate: *Italian is my **first language** (= the language I learned to speak first as a child).* ◇ *They fell in love in spite of the **language barrier** (= the difficulty of communicating when people speak different languages).* ◇ *Why study Latin? It's a **dead language** (= no longer spoken by anyone).* ◇ (*especially BrE*) *She's got a degree in **modern languages** (= languages that are spoken or written now, especially European languages).*
dialect /ˈdaɪəlekt/ [C, U] the form of a language that is spoken in one area, with grammar, words and pronunciation that may be different from other forms of the same language: *All languages and dialects change over time.* ◇ *She spoke in broad Yorkshire dialect.*
tongue [C] (*formal, literary or old-fashioned*) a language: *The market place was full of people speaking many strange tongues.* ◇ *I tried speaking to her in her **mother tongue**.* ❶ The term **mother tongue** is often used to talk about a person's first language, and is not as formal, and not at all as old-fashioned as the word **tongue** used by itself or in other combinations.
idiom [C, U] (*formal*) the kind of language and grammar used by particular people at a particular time or place: *He has produced a classical play in a modern idiom.* ◇ *The friends would sometimes revert to playground idiom (= the language that children use together at school).*

2 language · vocabulary · terms · wording · terminology · usage
These are all terms for the words and expressions people use when they speak or write, or for a particular style of speaking or writing.

PATTERNS AND COLLOCATIONS
▶ **in**... language/vocabulary/terms/terminology/usage
▶ **formal/informal/everyday** language/vocabulary/terms/ usage
▶ **simple** language/vocabulary/terms
▶ **sophisticated/business/scientific/technical/specialized** language/vocabulary/terminology
▶ to **use** ... language/vocabulary/terms/wording/terminology
▶ to **be couched in** ... language/vocabulary/terms
▶ A word **enters** the language/the vocabulary/...usage...

language [U] a particular style of speaking or writing: *Give your instructions in everyday language.* ◇ *the language of the legal profession* ◇ *They were shouting and using **bad/ foul language**.*
vocabulary [C, U] all the words that a person knows or uses; all the words in a particular language; the words that people use when they are talking about a particular subject: *to have a wide/limited vocabulary* ◇ *your **active vocabulary** (= the words that you use)* ◇ *your **passive vocabulary** (= the words that you understand but don't use)* ◇ *Reading will increase your vocabulary.* ◇ *When did the word 'bungalow' first enter the vocabulary?* ◇ *The word has become part of advertising vocabulary.*
terms [pl.] a way of expressing yourself or of saying sth: *I'll try to explain in simple terms.* ◇ *She spoke of you in **glowing terms** (= expressing her admiration of you).* ◇ (*rather formal*) *We wish to protest **in the strongest possible terms** (= to say that we are very angry).* See also **term** → WORD
wording [U, C, usually sing.] the words that are used in a piece of writing or speech, especially when they have been carefully chosen: *It was the standard form of wording for a consent letter.* ◇ *What was the exact wording of the message?* See also **word** → WORD
terminology /ˌtɜːmɪˈnɒlədʒi; AmE ˌtɜːrməˈnɑːl-/ [U, C] (*rather formal*) the set of technical words or expressions used in a particular subject; words used with particular meanings: *The article avoids using too much medical terminology.* ◇ *Scientists are constantly developing new terminologies.* ❶ *Literary/poetic terminology* is used for talking about literature or poetry. *Literary/poetic language* is used for writing in a literary or poetic style.
usage /ˈjuːsɪdʒ; juːz-/ [U, C] the way in which words are used in a language, and the meanings they have when people use them: *It's not a word in common usage.* ◇ *The dictionary focuses on the more usual words of the language and avoids rare usages of these words.*

large *adj.* See also the entries for HUGE and MAXIMUM

**large · big · great · substantial · considerable ·
extensive · hefty · sizeable · bumper · handsome**
These words all describe things that are much more than
average in size, degree or amount.

PATTERNS AND COLLOCATIONS
▶ a large/ a big/ a great/ a substantial/ a considerable/ an
extensive/ a sizeable/ a handsome **amount**
▶ a large/ big/ great/ substantial/ considerable/ hefty/ sizeable/
handsome **sum/ profit**
▶ a large/ a big/ a great/ a substantial/ a considerable/ an
extensive/ a sizeable **area**
▶ a large/ big/ great/ substantial/ considerable/ sizeable/
handsome **majority**
▶ a large/ big/ great/ substantial/ considerable/ hefty/ sizeable
increase
▶ a large/ big/ great/ substantial/ a considerable/ an
extensive/ a bumper/ a handsome **collection**
▶ a large/ big/ great/ substantial/ sizeable **crowd/ army**
▶ a large/ big/ substantial **meal/ breakfast**
▶ a large/ big/ bumper **crop/ harvest**
▶ a large/ great/ substantial/ considerable **size**
▶ a big/ a great/ a substantial/ a considerable/ an extensive
change/ improvement/ gain/ loss/ influence
▶ **very** large/ big/ great/ substantial/ considerable/ extensive/
hefty/ sizeable
▶ **really** large/ big/ substantial/ extensive/ hefty
▶ **quite/ fairly** large/ big/ substantial/ considerable/ extensive/
hefty/ sizeable
▶ **rather** large/ big/ substantial/ extensive/ hefty

large more than average in size, degree or amount: *Some
of the clothes looked very large.* ◇ *I grew up in a large
family.* ◇ *There were some very large sums of money
involved.* ◇ *Brazil is the world's largest producer of coffee.* ◇
Who is the rather large (= fat) *lady in the hat?* ❶ **Large**
(*abbreviation* **L**) *is also used to describe one size in a
range of sizes of clothes, food, products used in the
house, etc.: Would you like small, medium or large?*
OPP small, little → SMALL

big large in size, degree or amount: *This house is too big for
us now.* ◇ *This shirt isn't big enough.* ◇ *He was a big man —
tall and broad-shouldered.* ◇ *There's been a big increase in
prices.* ◇ *It's the world's biggest computer company.* ◇
(*informal*) *He had this **great big** grin on his face.* ◇ *They
were earning big money.* **OPP little, small** → SMALL

great [usually before noun] much larger or more than
average in size, amount or degree: *A great crowd had
gathered.* ◇ *He must have fallen from a great height.* ◇ *She
lived to a great age.* ◇ *The concert had been a great success.*
◇ *Her death was a great shock to us all.* ◇ *It gives me great
pleasure to welcome you here today.* ◇ *Take great care of it.*
◇ *You've been a great help.* ❶ *In informal English* **great** *can
be used to emphasize another adjective of size or
amount: There was a **great big** pile of books on the table.*

NOTE LARGE, BIG OR **GREAT?** These adjectives are
frequently used with the following nouns: *a **big** man/
house/car/boy/dog/smile/problem/surprise/question/
difference* ◇ (*a*) **large** *numbers/part/area/room/com-
pany/eyes/family/volume/population/problem* ◇ (*a*)
great *success/majority/interest/importance/difficulty/
problem/pleasure/beauty/surprise.* **Large** *is more formal
than* **big** *and should normally be used in writing unless
the writing is in an informal style. It is not usually used
to describe people, except to avoid saying 'fat'.* **Great**
*often suggests quality and not just size; however, it does
not usually describe the physical size of objects or
people:* a great house/boy/dog*. A* **great** *man means a
good, wise man that you admire, not a tall or large
man. Note also the phrases: a **large** amount of sth ◇ a
large number of sth ◇ a **large** quantity of sth ◇ a **great**
deal of sth ◇ in **great** detail ◇ a person of **great** age*

substantial /səb'stænʃl/ (*rather formal*) large in amount,
size or importance: *There were substantial sums of money
involved.* ◇ *We were able to see a substantial improvement.*
◇ *He ate a substantial breakfast.* ◇ *Their share of the
software market is substantial.*

considerable (*rather formal*) large in amount, degree or
importance: *The project wasted a considerable amount of
time and money.* ◇ *Damage to the building was considerable.* ◇ *Considerable progress has been made in finding a
cure for the disease.* ◇ *Caring for elderly relatives requires
considerable moral courage.*

NOTE SUBSTANTIAL OR **CONSIDERABLE? Considerable** is
NOT used to talk about solid things such as meals or
buildings. **Substantial** is NOT used to talk about
emotions or personal qualities, such as anger, concern,
courage or efficiency.

extensive covering a large area; great in amount: *The
house has extensive grounds.* ◇ *The fire caused extensive
damage.* ◇ *Extensive repair work is being carried out.* ◇
They have an extensive range of wines.

hefty (of an amount of money) large or larger than usual
or expected: *They sold it easily and made a hefty profit.* ◇
Interest rates have gone up to a hefty 12%.

sizeable (also **sizable**) /'saɪzəbl/ (*rather formal*) fairly
large: *The town has a sizeable Sikh population.* ◇ *Income
from tourism accounts for a sizeable proportion of the
area's total income.*

bumper [only before noun] (*approving*) unusually large;
producing an unusually large amount: *Don't miss next
month's bumper Christmas issue* (= of a magazine, etc.). ◇
Farmers have been celebrating bumper crops this year.

handsome /'hænsəm/ [only before noun] (*approving*) (of
an amount of sth, especially money) large: *They sold the
house two years later at a handsome profit.* ◇ *I enjoyed the
job, and was paid a handsome salary too.*
▶ **handsomely** *adv.*: *to be paid/rewarded handsomely*

last *det., adj.*
1 the last bus home
2 last night

**1 last · final · closing · later · eventual · ultimate ·
latter**
These words all describe sth that happens or comes after
all other similar things or people.

PATTERNS AND COLLOCATIONS
▶ the last/ final/ closing/ later/ ultimate/ latter **stage/ phase**
▶ the last/ final/ later/ eventual/ ultimate **aim/ goal/ outcome**
▶ eventual/ ultimate **success/ failure/ victory/ defeat**
▶ sb/ sth's last/ final/ closing/ later/ latter **years**
▶ sb's last/ final/ closing **speech/ address**
▶ the last/ final/ closing **remark/ chapter/ minutes**

last *det., adj.* happening or coming after all other similar
things or people; the only remaining thing or person: *We
caught the last bus home.* ◇ *It's the last house on the left.* ◇
She was last to arrive. ◇ *I wouldn't marry you if you were
the last person on earth!* ◇ *He knew this was his last hope
of winning.* **OPP first** → FIRST
▶ **lastly** *adv.*: *Lastly, I'd like to ask you about your plans.*
▶ **at 'last** *phrase*: *We're home at last!* ◇ *At long last the
cheque arrived.*

final *adj.* [only before noun] being or happening at the end
of a series of events, actions or statements; being the
result of a particular process: *His final act as president was
to pardon his predecessor.* ◇ *The referee blew the final
whistle.* ◇ *I'd like to return to the final point you made.* ◇
No one could have predicted the final outcome. **OPP initial**
→ FIRST
▶ **finally** *adv.*: *Finally, stir in the fruit and walnuts.* ◇ *The
performance finally started half an hour late.*

closing *adj.* [only before noun] coming at the end of a speech, a period of time or an activity, especially as a sign that sth is about to finish: *The closing ceremony proved to be a spectacular and memorable affair.* **OPP** **opening** → FIRST

later *adj.* happening or being near the end of a period of time: *the later part of the seventeenth century* ◇ *She found happiness in her later years.* **OPP** **earlier**
▸ **later** *adv.*: *His father died later that year.* ◇ *We're going to Rome later in the year.*

eventual /ɪˈventʃuəl/ *adj.* [only before noun] happening at the end of a period of time or of a process: *The school may face eventual closure.* ◇ *the eventual winner of the tournament*
▸ **eventually** *adv.*: *She hopes eventually to attend medical school and become a doctor.* ◇ *I'll get round to mending it eventually.*

ultimate /ˈʌltɪmət/ *adj.* [only before noun] (especially of sth that is planned or intended) happening at the end of a long process: *our ultimate goal/aim/objective/target* ◇ *The ultimate decision lies with the parents.* ◇ *We will accept ultimate responsibility for whatever happens.*
▸ **ultimately** *adv.*: *The campaign was ultimately successful.* ◇ *Ultimately, you'll have to make the decision yourself.*

latter *adj.* nearer to the end of a period of time than the beginning: *The latter half of the twentieth century saw huge growth in air travel.*
▸ **latterly** *adv.*: (*formal*) *Her health declined rapidly and latterly she never left the house.*

---

2 last · past · previous · preceding
These words all describe sth that happened or existed only a short time ago, or before a particular time, event or object.

PATTERNS AND COLLOCATIONS
▸ the last / past / previous / preceding **few days / week / month / year / decade / century**
▸ the last / past / previous **weekend / season / hundred years**
▸ the last / past **hour**
▸ last / the previous **night / Friday / July / summer**
▸ the last / previous / preceding **paragraph / section**
▸ the last / previous **page / chapter / time / visit / meeting / war**
▸ sb's last / previous **album / appearance**
▸ the previous / preceding **discussion / argument / analysis / example**

last *det.* most recent: *He got home late last night.* ◇ *Last summer we went to Greece for a month.* ◇ *The critics all hated her last book.* ◇ *This last point, that Hamish has mentioned, is crucial.* **OPP** **first** → FIRST, **next** → NEXT

past *adj.* [only before noun] (of a period of time) gone by recently; just ended: *I haven't seen much of her in the past few weeks.* **OPP** **next** → NEXT

> **NOTE** LAST OR PAST? You can only use **past** to talk about a period of time that has just gone by, especially a long or approximate period of time: *These past months have been terribly stressful for everyone.* **Past** is an adjective and must be used with *the* or a determiner such as *this* or *these*: it cannot be used on its own: *Last week was very busy.* ◇ *The past week has been very busy.* **Past** is not used to talk about particular dates or points in time, or about things: ~~He got home late past night.~~ ◇ ~~The critics hated her past book.~~

previous [only before noun] happening or coming immediately before the time or thing you are talking about: *He went jogging on Friday, despite the doctor's warnings the previous day* (= the day before the time mentioned). ◇ *We dealt with this in the previous chapter.* **OPP** **the following** → NEXT

preceding /prɪˈsiːdɪŋ/ [only before noun] (*formal*) previous: *This policy was pursued less vigorously in the 1880s than in the preceding decade* (= the 1870s). ◇ *The reasoning in the preceding paragraph applies equally to a number of other cases.* **OPP** **the following** → NEXT

---

late *adj.*

late · slow · overdue · belated
These words all describe sb/sth that arrives, happens or is done after the expected, arranged or usual time.

PATTERNS AND COLLOCATIONS
▸ late / overdue **for** sth
▸ late / slow **in doing** sth
▸ late / overdue **payment**
▸ overdue / belated **recognition**
▸ **two weeks / a year** late / overdue
▸ **very / extremely / rather / slightly** late / slow / belated

late [not usually before noun] arriving, happening or done after the expected, arranged or usual time: *I'm sorry I'm late.* ◇ *She's late for work every day.* ◇ *My flight was an hour late.* ◇ *Some children are very late developers.* ◇ *Because of the cold weather the crops are later this year.* **OPP** **early, on time, punctual** → EARLY
▸ **late** *adv.*: *Can I stay up late tonight?* ◇ *The big stores are open later on Thursdays.* ◇ *She married late.* ◇ *The birthday card arrived three days late.*

slow hesitating to do sth; not doing sth immediately: *She wasn't slow to realize what was going on.* ◇ *His poetry was slow in achieving recognition.* ◇ *They were very slow paying me.* **OPP** **quick** → QUICK, See also **slow** → SLOW

overdue /ˌəʊvəˈdjuː; *AmE* ˌoʊvərˈduː/ not paid, done or returned by the required or expected time; that should have happened or been done before now: *2% interest will be charged on overdue payments.* ◇ *My library books were overdue.* ◇ *Her baby is two weeks overdue.* ◇ *This car is overdue for a service* (= has needed a service for a long time). ◇ *A book like this is long overdue.*

belated /bɪˈleɪtɪd/ (*written*) (especially of an action or response) coming or happening late: *Many apologies for sending you such a belated birthday present.* ◇ *The government has been criticized for its belated response to the report.*
▸ **belatedly** *adv.*: *He apologized belatedly.*

---

laugh *verb*

laugh · giggle · chuckle · crack up · snigger · snicker · roar · be/have sb in stitches · titter
These words all mean to make the sounds and movements of your face that show that you think sth is funny.

PATTERNS AND COLLOCATIONS
▸ to laugh / giggle / chuckle / snigger / snicker / roar / titter **at** sth
▸ to laugh / giggle / chuckle / snigger / snicker / titter **about / over** sth
▸ to laugh / giggle / chuckle / snigger / snicker / roar **with** pleasure / amusement, etc.
▸ to **make sb** laugh / giggle / chuckle / crack up / snigger / snicker / roar / titter
▸ to giggle / chuckle **to yourself**
▸ to giggle / chuckle **softly / quietly**
▸ to giggle / titter **nervously**

laugh [I] to make the sounds and movements of your face that show you are happy or think sth is funny: *It was so funny I laughed out loud.* ◇ *You never laugh at my jokes!* ◇ *He burst out laughing* (= suddenly started laughing).
▸ **laugh** *noun*: *to give a short/harsh/bitter/nervous laugh* ◇ *His first joke got the biggest laugh of the night.*
▸ **laughter** *noun* [U]: *He threw back his head and roared with laughter.*

giggle /ˈɡɪɡl/ [I] to laugh in a silly way because you are amused, embarrassed or nervous: *The girls giggled at the joke.* ◇ *She giggled with delight.*
▸ **giggle** *noun* [C]: *She gave a nervous giggle.*

chuckle /ˈtʃʌkl/ [I] (especially *written*) to laugh quietly: *George chuckled at the memory.*
▸ **chuckle** *noun* [C]: *She gave a chuckle of delight.*

ˌcrack ˈup *phrasal verb* (*informal*) to start laughing a lot: *He walked in and everyone just cracked up.*

snigger [I] (*especially BrE, rather informal*) to laugh in a quiet unpleasant way, especially at sth rude or at sb's problems or mistakes: *What are you sniggering at?*

snicker [I] (*AmE, rather informal*) to snigger: *Although his friends snickered, they were still impressed.*

roar /rɔː(r)/ [I] (*rather informal*) to laugh very loudly: *It made them roar with laughter.* ◇ *He looked so funny, we all roared.* ❶ **Roar** is often used to talk about groups of people laughing together. It is more informal on its own than when it is used in the phrase *roar with laughter.*

▶ **roar** *noun* [C]: *The crowd burst into roars of laughter.*

be/have sb in ˈstitches *idiom* (*rather informal*) to laugh a lot; to make sb laugh a lot: *We were all in stitches from the beginning to the end of the play.* ◇ *The play had us in stitches.*

titter [I] to laugh quietly, especially because you are embarrassed or nervous: *There was an embarrassing pause on stage and the audience began to titter.*

laugh at sb/sth *phrasal verb*

laugh at sb/sth · mock · tease · ridicule · sneer · make fun of sb/sth · poke fun at sb/sth
These words all mean to make sb/sth look silly or not serious by making jokes about them/it.

PATTERNS AND COLLOCATIONS
▸ to laugh / mock / sneer / poke fun **at** sb / sth
▸ to laugh at / mock / tease / ridicule / sneer at sb / sth **for** sth
▸ to laugh at / poke fun at **yourself**
▸ to mock / tease / ridicule sb / sth **mercilessly**
▸ to mock / tease sb / sth **gently** / **a little**

ˈ**laugh at sb/sth** *phrasal verb* to make sb/sth look silly or not serious by making jokes about them/it: *Everybody laughs at my accent.* ◇ *She is not afraid to laugh at herself* (= not be too serious about herself). ❶ **Laugh at sb/sth** is often used when sb accuses or suspects sb of laughing at them, or predicts that people will do so: *Are you laughing at me?* ◇ *I'm not wearing that hat; everyone will laugh at me!*

mock [T, I] (*especially written*) to laugh at sb/sth in an unkind way, especially by copying what they say or do: *He's always mocking my French accent.* ◇ *The other children mocked her, laughing behind their hands.* ◇ *You can mock, but at least I'm willing to have a try!* See also **mockery** → CONTEMPT, **mocking** → CONTEMPTUOUS

tease /tiːz/ [I, T] to laugh at sb and make jokes about them, either in a friendly way or in order to annoy or embarrass them: *Don't get upset − I was only teasing.* ◇ *I used to get teased about my name.*

ridicule /ˈrɪdɪkjuːl/ [T] (*rather formal, especially written*) to make sb/sth look silly by making jokes about them/it and laughing at them in an unkind way: *At first, his theory was ridiculed and dismissed.* ◇ *She suspected him of trying to ridicule her.* See also **ridicule** → CONTEMPT *noun*

sneer [I] (*especially written*) to show that you have no respect for sb by the expression on your face or by the way you speak: *He sneered at people who liked pop music.* ◇ *'You? A writer?' she sneered.* ❶ A **sneer** is an unpleasant type of smile, look or comment.

make ˈfun of sb/sth *idiom* to make sb/sth look silly by making jokes about them/it, especially in an unkind way: *It's cruel to make fun of people who stammer.*

poke ˈfun at sb/sth *idiom* to make sb/sth look silly or not serious by making jokes about them/it, especially in a gentle, friendly way: *Her novels poke fun at the upper class.* ❶ **Poke fun at sb/sth** is used especially to talk about making jokes about groups of people, organizations or customs, rather than about individual people.

launch *noun*

launch · opening · premiere · first night
These are all words for an event at which an activity is officially started, or a product is made available to the public for the first time.

PATTERNS AND COLLOCATIONS
▸ **at** the launch / opening / premiere / first night
▸ a **successful** / **public** launch / opening / premiere
▸ a / an **formal** / **official** launch / opening
▸ to **go to** / **attend** the launch / opening / premiere / first night
▸ to **get ready for** / **prepare for** / **announce** / **coincide with** / **speak at** / **delay** / **postpone** the launch / opening
▸ a launch / an opening **party**

launch [C, usually sing.] (*especially business*) an event at which an activity is officially started, or a product is made available to the public for the first time: *Speaking at a recent product launch, he said that the company would continue to diversify.* ◇ *The official launch date is in May.* ❶ The sort of activity for which people hold a **launch** are a *campaign*, a *competition*, a *scheme*, a *programme*, an *exhibition*, and an *appeal*. See also **launch** → INTRODUCE *verb* 1, **launch** → PRESENT *verb* 1

opening [C, usually sing.] a ceremony to celebrate the start of a public event or the first time a new building, road, etc. is used: *Tickets are now available for the opening of the Olympic Games.* ◇ *I've been asked to attend the official opening of the new hospital.* See also **open** → BEGIN

premiere /ˈpremieə(r); *AmE* prɪˈmɪr; -ˈmjɪr/ [C] the first public performance of a film or play: *He was unable to attend the world premiere of his new play.* ◇ *The movie will have its premiere in July.*

▶ **premiere** *verb* [T, I]: *The play was premiered at the Birmingham Rep in 2006.* ◇ *His new movie premieres in New York this week.*

ˌ**first ˈnight** [C, usually sing.] the first public performance of a play: *I got tickets for the first night of 'Romeo and Juliet'.*

> **NOTE** PREMIERE OR FIRST NIGHT? The **premiere** of a film or play is a very special occasion to which famous people, journalists, actors, etc. are invited. **First night** is used to talk about plays much more than films; it does not have to be a new play, but is often a new production of a play that has been performed before; it can be a large, important production or a small, unknown one: *The first night of the school play is just days away and the cast still don't know their lines.*

law *noun*

law · legislation · constitution · code · charter
These are all words for a system or set of rules or principles which govern a country or organization.

PATTERNS AND COLLOCATIONS
▸ legislation / a charter **on** sth
▸ **under** / **in** the legislation / constitution / code / charter
▸ (a) **draft** legislation / constitution / code / charter
▸ (the) **civil** / **criminal** law / legislation / code
▸ (the) **state** / **federal** law / legislation / constitution
▸ to **draw up** / **draft** / **adopt** / **approve** / **amend** legislation / a constitution / a code / a charter
▸ to **break** the law / a code
▸ to **contravene** legislation / a constitution / a code
▸ to **be enshrined in** law / legislation / the constitution / a charter
▸ the law / legislation / the constitution **forbids** sth
▸ legislation / the constitution / a charter **guarantees** sth

law (also **the law**) [U] the system of rules that everyone in a country or society must obey; a particular branch of this system: *In Sweden it is against the law to hit a child.* ◇ *Defence attorneys can use any means within the law to get their client off.* ◇ *British schools are now required by law to publish their exam results.* ◇ *The reforms have recently become law.* ◇ *He specializes in international law.* See also **law** → RULE *noun*

legislation /ˌledʒɪsˈleɪʃn/ [U] a law or set of laws passed by a parliament: *The civil rights campaign resulted in legislation against segregation.* ◇ *There were calls for legislation to ban smoking in public places.* ◇ *The government is trying to push through a controversial piece of legislation.* See also **legislate** → RULE *verb* 2

constitution /ˌkɒnstrˈtjuːʃn; AmE ˌkɑːnstəˈtuːʃn/ [C] the system of laws and basic principles that a state, country or organization is governed by: *These rights are established in the federal constitution.* ◇ *A two-thirds majority is needed to amend the club's constitution.*

code [C] a system of laws or written rules that state how people in an organization or country should behave: *The company has drawn up a new disciplinary code.* ◇ *The law includes amendments to the **penal code**.*

charter [C] a written statement describing the rights that a particular group of people should have; a written statement of the principles and aims of an organization: *He fought for a social charter of workers' rights.* ◇ *Minority rights are protected by the UN charter.*

lawyer *noun*

lawyer · attorney · solicitor · counsel · barrister · the Bar · advocate
These are all words for a person who is qualified to advise people about the law or to represent them in court.

PATTERNS AND COLLOCATIONS
▸ a lawyer / an attorney / a solicitor / counsel / a barrister / an advocate **for** sb
▸ a **good** / **practising** lawyer / attorney / solicitor / barrister / advocate
▸ (an) **experienced** lawyer / attorney / solicitor / counsel / barrister / advocate
▸ the **chief** lawyer / attorney / counsel / advocate
▸ a **defence** lawyer / attorney / solicitor / counsel / barrister / advocate
▸ (a) **prosecuting** / **prosecution** lawyer / attorney / solicitor / counsel / barrister
▸ to **appoint** / **hire** / **instruct** / **consult** a lawyer / an attorney / a solicitor / counsel / a barrister
▸ a lawyer / an attorney / a solicitor / counsel / a barrister / an advocate **represents** sb
▸ a lawyer / an attorney / a solicitor / an advocate **acts for** sb
▸ a lawyer / an attorney / a solicitor / counsel **advises** sb
▸ a lawyer / an attorney / a solicitor / counsel **argues** / **claims** / **submits** sth
▸ a lawyer / an attorney / a solicitor / counsel / a barrister **cross-examines** sb

lawyer [C] a person who is trained and qualified to advise people about the law and to represent them in court, and to write legal documents: *Lawyers for the families said they were pleased with the decision.* ◇ *You'll be hearing from my lawyer.* ◇ *You would be wise to consult a lawyer.*

attorney /əˈtɜːni; AmE əˈtɜːrni/ [C] (*especially AmE*) a lawyer, especially one who can represent sb in court: *Acting on the advice of his attorney, he remained silent.*

solicitor /səˈlɪsɪtə(r)/ [C] (in Britain) a lawyer who prepares legal documents, for example the sale of land or buildings, advises people on legal matters, and can represent them in some courts: *Her first step was to contact a solicitor for advice.*

counsel /ˈkaʊnsl/ [U] (*law*) a lawyer or group of lawyers representing sb in court: *The court then heard counsel for the dead woman's father.* ◇ (*BrE*) *Williams is the **leading counsel** for the victims' groups* (= the main lawyer in the group representing them). ◇ (*AmE*) *the **lead counsel***

barrister /ˈbærɪstə(r)/ [C] (in England and Wales) a lawyer who has the right to argue cases in the higher courts: *The solicitor must instruct a barrister to appear before the court.*

the Bar [sing.] the profession of barrister or lawyer: *She studied law and **was called to the Bar*** (= was allowed to work as a qualified barrister) *in 2004.* ◇ *The changes were met with opposition from **members of the Bar**.* ❶ In Britain, **the Bar** refers only to the profession of barrister. In the US, **the Bar** refers to the profession of any kind of lawyer.

advocate /ˈædvəkət/ [C] a person who defends sb in court; (in Scotland) a lawyer who has the right to argue cases in higher courts: *Those charged should be represented by trained, qualified legal advocates.*

> **NOTE** LAWYER, ATTORNEY, SOLICITOR, COUNSEL, BARRISTER OR ADVOCATE? **Lawyer** is a general term for a person who is qualified to advise people about the law, to prepare legal documents or represent people in court. In American English, **attorney** can be used in the same way as **lawyer**. In England and Wales, a lawyer who is qualified to speak in the higher courts is called a **barrister**. In Scotland, this is called an **advocate**. **Counsel** is the formal legal word for a lawyer who is representing sb in court. **Solicitor** is the British term for a lawyer who gives legal advice and prepares documents, and sometimes has the right to speak in court, especially a lower court.

lax *adj.*

lax · sloppy · shoddy · careless
These words all describe work or standards of behaviour that show a lack of care, thought or effort.

PATTERNS AND COLLOCATIONS
▸ sloppy / shoddy **work**

lax (*disapproving*) not strict or careful enough about work, rules or standards of behaviour: *The incident has exposed the extremely lax security of the country's banks.* ◇ *The inspectors reported a lax attitude to health and safety regulations.* ❶ Typical collocates of **lax** are *attitude, control, discipline, controls, enforcement, security* and *standards.*
> **laxity** *noun* [U] (*formal*): *the moral laxity of today's society*

sloppy (*rather informal, usually disapproving*) showing a lack of care, thought or effort: *I'm usually a bit of a sloppy dresser at weekends.* ◇ *Regional accents are great; sloppy speech is not.* ◇ *Your work is sloppy.* ❶ **Sloppy** is used to talk about people's clothes or the way they dress: *sloppy clothes; a sloppy shirt/sweater/dresser*; the way people think and work: *sloppy work/thinking*; and the way people express themselves: *sloppy language/terminology.* *Sloppy habits* might involve leaving clothes lying on the floor, or not putting the top back on a toothpaste tube.

shoddy (*disapproving*) (of goods or work) made or done badly and showing a lack of care: *I always complain about bad service or shoddy goods.* ◇ *He was accused of shoddy workmanship.* ❶ **Shoddy** typically describes *goods, workmanship, work* and *service.*

careless (*disapproving*) resulting from a lack of attention, care and thought: *You've made rather a lot of careless mistakes in your work.* **OPP careful → DETAILED**

lead /liːd/ *noun*

1 take the lead in a race
2 have a narrow lead over sb

1 the lead · the foreground · the forefront · the fore · the cutting edge · the front
These are all words for a position ahead of everyone else in a race, a competition, an area of activity, the development of sth or a line of people.

PATTERNS AND COLLOCATIONS
▸ the foreground / forefront / cutting edge / front **of** sth
▸ **in** the lead / foreground / forefront
▸ **at** the forefront / fore / cutting edge / front
▸ to **come** / **bring** sth **to** the forefront / fore

the lead [sing.] the position ahead of everyone else in a race, game or competition: *The Democrats now appear to be in the lead.* ◇ *She **took the lead** in the second lap.* ◇ *As expected, Kicking King **went** straight **into the lead**.* ◇ *Redkal's penalty **gave** Norway **the lead**.*

the foreground [sing.] (*rather formal*) the part of a view or picture that is nearest to you when you look at it; an important position that is noticed by people: *The figure in the foreground is the artist's mother.* ◇ *Interest rates will be very much in the foreground of their election campaign.* **OPP** the background → ENVIRONMENT

the forefront [sing.] an important or leading position in a particular group or activity: *Women have always been at the forefront of the Green movement.* ◇ *The latest protest has brought prison conditions to the forefront of public attention.* ◇ *The court case was constantly in the forefront of my mind* (= I thought about it all the time). ❶ *The forefront is always used in the phrase at/in/to the forefront of sth.*

the fore [sing.] (*rather formal*) a position in which sb/sth is noticed by people or considered important: (*BrE*) *She has always been to the fore at moments of crisis.* ◇ (*AmE*) *She has always been at the fore...* ◇ *The problem has come very much to the fore again in recent months.* ❶ *People or things are to the fore in British English, but at the fore in American English;* **the fore** *is always used in the phrase be to/at the fore or come/bring sth to the fore.*

NOTE FOREFRONT OR FORE? The forefront is usually followed by *of*; **the fore** is not. If you need to say which group or activity sb/sth is important in, use **the forefront of sth**; if you do not need to say which group or activity, because sb/sth has just become important generally in the public mind, use **the fore**.

the cutting edge [sing.] the newest, most advanced stage in the development of sth, especially in science, technology or art: *We are working at the cutting edge of computer technology.* ◇ *At the time it was on the cutting edge of modern style.*

the front [sing.] the position which is furthest forward in a line or group of people: *He was always at the front of the line at dinner time.* ◇ *The kids pushed straight to the front.* **OPP** the back ❶ The back is the position furthest from the front: *We could only get seats at the back* (= of the room). ◇ *I found some old photos at the back of the drawer.* ◇ (*BrE*) *There's room for three people in the back* (= of a car). ◇ (*AmE*) *There's room for three people in back.*

2 lead · advantage · edge · the upper hand · head start

These are all words for a situation in which you are in a better position than sb/sth that you are competing against.

PATTERNS AND COLLOCATIONS
▶ a lead / an advantage / an edge / the upper hand / a head start **over** sb
▶ an edge / a head start **on** sb
▶ a lead / an advantage / an edge / the upper hand / a head start **in** sth
▶ a **slight / significant** lead / advantage / edge
▶ a **big / clear** lead / advantage
▶ a **decided / competitive** advantage / edge
▶ to **have** a lead / an advantage / an edge / the upper hand / a head start
▶ to **hold (onto) / maintain** a lead / an advantage / an edge
▶ to **give sb** a lead / an advantage / an edge / the upper hand / a head start
▶ to **gain** a lead / an advantage / an edge / the upper hand

lead [sing.] the amount or distance that sb/sth is in front of sb/sth else, in a competition or race in sport or politics: *She has a narrow lead over the other runners.* ◇ *They took a 3–0 lead in the first leg of the semi-final.* ◇ *The polls have given Labour a five-point lead.*

advantage [sing.] something that helps you to be better or more successful than sb else, especially sb you are competing against: *Being tall gave him an advantage over the other players.* ◇ *The company has an unfair advantage over its competitors.* **OPP** disadvantage → DISADVANTAGE

edge [sing.] (*rather informal*) a slight advantage over sb/sth, especially in sport or business: *They have the edge on us.* ◇ *He believes Marseilles have a slight edge as they face Rangers at home.* ◇ *The company needs to improve its competitive edge.*

the upper hand idiom an advantage over sb/sth else which means that you are in control of a particular situation: *Maggie felt she had the upper hand.* ◇ *Gradually their forward players began to get the upper hand.* ❶ The upper hand is used especially with the verbs *have, hold, gain* and *get*.

head start [sing.] an advantage that sb already has before they start doing sth: *Being able to speak French gave her a head start over the other candidates.* ◇ *We've got a real head start on the rest of the industry.*

lead *verb*

1 lead a race/the world in cancer research
2 lead an expedition
3 The path leads up the hill.

1 lead · be ahead of sb · overtake · pass · leave sb/sth behind · outpace · get ahead

These words all mean to be in or move into a position which is further forward, better or more advanced than sb/sth else.

PATTERNS AND COLLOCATIONS
▶ to lead / be ahead of sb / overtake sb / leave sb behind / get ahead **in** sth
▶ to lead / be ahead of / overtake a **rival**
▶ to **easily** overtake / outpace sb

lead [I, T] to be in first place, for example in a race or competition; to be the most advanced in a particular area or activity: *The champion is leading by 18 seconds.* ◇ *He led the race for eight laps until his engine blew.* ◇ *The department led the world in cancer research.* ◇ *The firm's solid construction standards still lead the field.* **OPP** trail → LOSE

be ahead of sb phrasal verb to be further forward in space or time than sb/sth; to be in front of sb/sth, for example in a race or competition; to be better or further advanced than sb/sth: *Three boys were ahead of us.* ◇ *He was already some way ahead of her.* ◇ *He's still ahead of his nearest rival.* ◇ *He was always well ahead of the rest of the class.* ◇ *His ideas were way ahead of his time.* **OPP** be behind sb

overtake [I, T] to go past a moving vehicle or person ahead of you because you are going faster than they are; to become greater in number, amount or importance than sth else: (*BrE*) *It's dangerous to overtake on a bend.* ◇ (*BrE*) *He pulled out to overtake a lorry.* ◇ *Later this century, nuclear energy could overtake oil as the main fuel.* ◇ *We mustn't let ourselves be overtaken by our competitors.*

pass [T, I] to overtake a vehicle or person ahead of you: *He pulled out to pass a truck.* ◇ *It's difficult to pass on this circuit.*

NOTE OVERTAKE OR PASS? In British English, both **overtake** and **pass** can be used to talk about going past sb/sth that is moving, for example, on the road or a track, although **overtake** is more frequent. In American English, **pass** is the normal word used.

leave sb/sth behind phrasal verb [usually passive] to make much better progress than sb, especially in business: *Britain is being left behind in the race for new markets.* ◇ *European manufacturers are afraid of getting left behind.*

outpace /ˌaʊtˈpeɪs/ [T] (*written, especially business*) to go, rise or improve faster than sb/sth: *He easily outpaced the other runners.* ◇ *Demand is outpacing production.* ◇ *Market growth has continued to outpace expectations.*

get a'head *phrasal verb* to make progress; to make progress faster or further than sb/sth else: *She wants to get ahead in her career.* ◇ *He soon got ahead of the others in the class.* ❶ **Get ahead** is used especially to talk about the progress of individual people in their work or studies.

---

2 lead · head · preside · chair · spearhead · captain
These words all mean to be in charge of sth or to be the leader of sth.

PATTERNS AND COLLOCATIONS
▸ to lead / head / captain a **team**
▸ to lead / captain a (sports) **side**
▸ to lead / head a (political) **party / the government**
▸ to lead / head / preside over / chair a / an **commission / committee / enquiry**
▸ to lead / preside over / chair a **meeting / debate**
▸ to lead / spearhead a **campaign / fight**
▸ to head / preside over a (legal) **case**
▸ to **jointly** lead / head / chair sth

lead [T, I] to be the leader of sth; to be in charge of sth: *Who will lead the party into the next election?* ◇ *He led the first **expedition** to the North Pole.* ◇ *Top management should be seen to **lead by example** (= to set a good example for others to copy).* See also **leadership** → GOVERNMENT 2

head [T] to be the head of sth; to be in charge of sth: *She has been appointed to head the research team.* ◇ *The committee will be jointly headed by two men.*

> **NOTE** LEAD OR HEAD? These two verbs can be used in very similar ways. However, a person who **heads** sth is the person who has the official position of being the head of it: for example, a government is headed by a prime minister, an enquiry might be headed by a judge, etc. It is usually an individual who **heads** sth. Sb who **leads** sth may also have an official position as the leader, but the verb **lead** emphasizes their leadership qualities. Sb who **leads** is the person who makes the important plans and decisions, and who other people follow. A group of people, such as an organization or a country can also **lead** sth.

preside /prɪˈzaɪd/ [I] (*formal*) to be in charge of a meeting, ceremony or official process such as a trial: *A tribunal, presided over by Lord Haskin, was established to investigate the allegations.* ◇ *The Archbishop presided at a special mass in the city's cathedral.*

chair [T] to be in charge of a meeting, discussion, or committee, telling people when they can speak: *Who's chairing the meeting?* ◇ *Lord Stansfield will chair the committee.*

spearhead /ˈspɪəhed; AmE ˈspɪrhed/ [T] (*especially journalism*) to begin or lead a campaign for sth or an attack on sb/sth: *He is spearheading a campaign for a new stadium in the town.* ◇ *Gardener spearheaded Britain's challenge at this year's World Championships.*

captain [T] to be the captain of a sports team or a ship: *He played in the West Indies team captained by Clive Lloyd.* ◇ *He told us about the ship he had captained during the war.*

---

3 lead · stretch · continue · go · extend · reach · span
These words all mean to cover the distance between two points or places.

PATTERNS AND COLLOCATIONS
▸ to lead / stretch / continue / go / extend / reach / span **beyond / across** sth
▸ to lead / stretch / continue / go / extend / reach **from** sth **to** sth
▸ to stretch / continue / extend **for** sth

lead [I, T] (always used with an adverb or preposition) to connect one object or place to another; (of a road, path or door) to go in a particular direction or to a particular place: *Disconnect the pipe leading from the top of the water tank.* ◇ *The wire led to a speaker.* ◇ *Which door leads to the yard?* ◇ *The track led us through a wood.*

stretch [I] (always used with an adverb or preposition) (of a road or area of land) to spread over a large area: *Beyond the mountains stretches a vast desert.* ◇ *Fields and hills **stretched out** as far as we could see.* See also **stretch** → STRETCH *noun*

continue [I] (usually used with an adverb or preposition) to go or move further in the same direction: *The path continued over rocky ground.* ◇ *He continued on his way.*
▸ **continuation** *noun* [C]: *There are plans to build a continuation of the bypass next year.*

go [I] (always used with an adverb or preposition) (of a road, path, line, rope, etc.) to lead or stretch from one place to another: *I want a rope that will go from the top window to the ground.* ◇ *Where does this road go?*

extend /ɪkˈstend/ [I, T] (always used with an adverb or preposition) (*rather formal*) to cover a particular area or distance; to make sth reach as far as sth: *Our land extends as far as the river.* ◇ *We extended a rope between the two posts.* See also **extent** → SIZE

reach [I, T] to be big or long enough to go from one point to another point: *The carpet only reached halfway across the room.* ◇ *Is the cable long enough to reach the power supply?*

span (**-nn-**) [T] to stretch right across sth, from one side to the other: *A series of bridges span the river.* ◇ *The roof was spanned by curved ribs of steel.*
▸ **span** *noun* [C]: *The bridge crosses the river in a single span.*

---

leader *noun*

1 political leaders
2 The company is a world leader in electrical goods.

---

1 See also the entry for MANAGER
leader · chairman · head · president · chief executive · chief · managing director · boss · governor · chair
These are all words for a person who is in charge of a company, organization, committee, etc.

PATTERNS AND COLLOCATIONS
▸ a **deputy** leader / chairman / head / president / chief executive / chief / managing director / boss / governor / chair
▸ a **vice** chairman / president / chair
▸ an **acting** chairman / head / president / chief executive / governor / chair
▸ the **honorary** chairman / president / chair
▸ a **joint** leader / head / president / managing director
▸ a **party** leader / chairman / president / chief / boss / chair
▸ a **union** leader / chairman / president / chief / boss
▸ a **company / club** chairman / president / chief executive / chief / managing director / boss
▸ a **council** leader / chairman / chief / boss / chair
▸ an **industry** leader / chairman / chief / boss
▸ to be **appointed (as)** leader / chairman / head / president / chief executive / chief / managing director / governor / chair
▸ to be **elected (as)** leader / chairman / head / president / chair
▸ to **nominate sb as** leader / chairman / president
▸ to **take over as** leader / chairman / head / president / chief executive / managing director / chair
▸ to **serve as** chairman / head / president / governor / chair
▸ to **resign / stand down / step down as** leader / chairman / head / president / chief executive / chief / managing director / governor / chair

leader [C] a person who leads a group of people, especially a country or organization: *He resigned as leader of the Democratic Party.* ◇ *Discuss any problems with your **team leader**.* ◇ *A **strong leader** is one who is not afraid of listening to people.* ◇ *She's a **born leader** (= she has the skills needed to be a good leader).* ◇ *He was not a **natural leader**.* See also **leadership** → GOVERNMENT 2

chairman [C] the person in charge of a committee or company; the person in charge of a meeting, who tells people when they can speak: *The chairman of the company presented the annual report.* ◇ *Sir Herbert took it upon himself to **act as chairman**.* ❶ A **chairman** is nearly always a man. A woman who holds this position can be called a **chairwoman**, but this is much less frequent. The term **chair** (see below) can be used for a man or a woman, but usually refers to sb in charge of a committee or meeting but NOT a company: *the committee/council/party chair* ◇ ~~the company/industry/union/club chair~~

head [C] the person in charge of a group of people or an organization: *The Bishop is head of the Church in Kenya.* ◇ *She resigned as head of department.* ◇ *It is a parliamentary democracy with a president as head of state.* See also **headship** → MANAGEMENT

president (also **President**) [C] the person in charge of some organizations, businesses, clubs or colleges: *She was elected president of the student's union.* ◇ (*especially AmE*) *He was appointed as vice president of business development the following year.* ❶ The title of **president** for heads and senior managers in commercial organizations is more frequent in American English than in British English.

chief e'xecutive /ɪɡ'zekjətɪv/ [C] the person with the highest position in a company or organization, who makes decisions about how the business is run: *The chief executive addressed the board.*

chief [C] a person in a high position or the highest position in a company or organization: *We spoke to a former CIA chief of European operations.* ◇ *Virgin chief, Richard Branson, may take legal action against the newspaper.* ❶ **Chief** is used as part of some official job titles, especially in American English: (*especially AmE*) *police/fire chief* ◇ *the chief of staff.* It is common in job titles for heads of government departments and other public organizations, such as the police and security services. In British English, especially in journalism, it is often rather informal: (*BrE, rather informal, journalism*) *Health chiefs say waiting times are down.*

managing di'rector [C] (*BrE*) the person in charge of a company, or a division of a company, who has responsibility for the daily running of the business: *The firm's managing director is now under investigation for corruption.* See also **manager, director** → MANAGER

> **NOTE** CHAIRMAN, PRESIDENT, CHIEF EXECUTIVE OR MANAGING DIRECTOR? The **chairman** of a company is usually the most senior member of its board (= group of directors). **President** is a title given to the most senior position in some companies. The **chief executive** or **managing director** is the person in charge of making decisions about how a business, or part of a business, is run. The **chief executive** or **managing director** is often also the **chairman**.

boss [C] (*informal, journalism*) a person in charge of a company or organization: *There's been criticism of bonuses paid to top oil company bosses.*

> **NOTE** CHIEF OR BOSS? Both of these words are used especially in journalism to refer to the people in charge of organizations or public services: *industry chiefs/bosses.* **Chief** is used especially for the people in charge of government or public services: *Health Service chiefs.* **Boss** is often used for the people in charge of particular companies and sports clubs: *a record label boss/the Sheffield United boss.* **Boss** is more informal.

governor [C] (*BrE*) a person in charge of an institution, such as a prison or bank: *He is a former governor of the Bank of England.* ◇ *A copy of the report was sent to the prison governor.* See also **governor** → MANAGER

chair [sing.] the position of being in charge of a meeting or committee; the person who holds this position: *She takes the chair in all our meetings.* ◇ *Who is in the chair today?* ◇ *All remarks should be addressed to the chair.* ◇ *He was elected chair of the city council.* ❶ See note at **chairman** (above).

---

2 leader · pioneer · market leader · innovator · front runner

These are all words for sb who is the best or most important in their area of activity or in a competition, or who is the first to do sth which others follow.

▸ a leader / a pioneer / a market leader / an innovator / a front runner **in** sth
▸ **among** the leaders / pioneers / front runners
▸ an **early** leader / pioneer / front runner
▸ a **great** pioneer / innovator
▸ a **clear / world** leader / market leader

leader [C] a person or thing that is the best, or in first place, in a race, a competition or an area of business: *She was among the leaders of the race from the start.* ◇ *The company is a world leader in electrical goods.* ◇ *They are the brand leader* (= most successful brand) *for herbs and spices in the UK.*

pioneer /ˌpaɪə'nɪə(r)/; *AmE* -'nɪr/ [C] a person who is the first to do sth or to study and develop a particular area of knowledge or culture that other people then continue to develop: *He is known as a pioneer in veterinary surgery.* ◇ *She later became a pioneer of education for women.* See also **pioneer** → DEVELOP *verb* 2

market 'leader [C] the company that sells the largest quantity of a particular kind of product; a product that is the most successful of its kind: *We are the market leader in hi-fi.* ◇ *The system is the market leader in the home PC market.*

innovator /'ɪnəveɪtə(r)/ [C] a person or organization that introduces new things, ideas or ways of doing things: *The company is a global innovator in science and technology.* ◇ *She is one of the great innovators of contemporary dance.* See also **innovation** → DEVELOPMENT, **innovative** → CREATIVE

front 'runner [C] a person, animal or organization that seems most likely to win sth such as a race, a competition, a contract, etc: *France and England are front runners for semi-final places.* ◇ *Auckland is still the front runner in the bid to host the event.*

leaflet *noun*

leaflet · brochure · booklet · pamphlet · circular · handout · flyer

These are all words for a sheet of paper or thin book containing information about sth.

▸ **in** a / the leaflet / brochure / booklet / pamphlet / circular / handout / flyer
▸ a **free** leaflet / brochure / booklet / pamphlet / handout
▸ a **promotional / publicity** leaflet / brochure / pamphlet
▸ to **produce** a leaflet / brochure / booklet / pamphlet / circular / handout / flyer
▸ to **issue / publish** a leaflet / brochure / booklet / pamphlet / circular
▸ to **distribute** a leaflet / brochure / booklet / pamphlet / circular / handout / flyer
▸ to **give out** leaflets / brochures / handouts / flyers
▸ to **hand out** leaflets / brochures / flyers
▸ a leaflet / brochure / booklet / pamphlet / circular **explains** sth
▸ a leaflet / brochure / flyer **advertises** sth

leaflet /'liːflət/ [C] a printed sheet of paper or a few printed pages that are given free of charge to advertise or give information about sth: *We picked up a few leaflets on local places of interest.* See also **notice** → POSTER

brochure /'brəʊʃə(r); *AmE* broʊ'ʃʊr/ [C] a small magazine or book containing pictures and information advertising goods or services that you can buy: *a travel brochure* ◇ *Send for your free colour brochure today!*

booklet [C] a thin book with a paper cover that contains information about sth or a set of tickets or vouchers for sth: *I had to refer to the instruction booklet.* ◇ *a booklet of tickets/vouchers/coupons*

pamphlet /'pæmflət/ [C] a very thin book with a paper cover, containing information about sth: *The government provides a pamphlet for all immigrants, outlining their rights.*

NOTE BOOKLET OR PAMPHLET? Booklets can be thicker than **pamphlets**. **Pamphlet** is not used for a small book of tickets. Historically, a **pamphlet** could also contain opinions and arguments about sth, especially politics: *He dismissed claims published in pamphlets that the King's powers had been usurped.*

circular [C] a printed letter, notice or advertisement that is sent to a large number of people at the same time: *The company will dispatch a circular to its shareholders giving details of the takeover.*

handout /'hændaʊt/ [C] a free document that gives information about an event or a matter of public interest, or that states the views of a political party, etc: *The party's press handout was largely ignored by journalists.* See also **hand sth out** → DISTRIBUTE

flyer (also **flier**) [C] a small sheet of paper that advertises a product or an event and is given to people, especially in the street: *We were asked to hand out flyers for the new club.*

NOTE HANDOUT OR FLYER? A **handout** is usually produced by a large organization and given to journalists or to shops and businesses to give to customers. A **flyer** may be produced by a smaller business and is given to people in the street.

leak *verb*

leak · seep · drip · discharge · ooze · leach · escape · secrete
These words are all used to talk about a liquid or gas moving into or out of sth.

PATTERNS AND COLLOCATIONS
▸ to leak / seep / drip / ooze / leach / escape **from** sth
▸ to leak / seep / drip / ooze **out of / through** sth
▸ to leak / seep / discharge / leach / escape **into** sth
▸ to drip / ooze **with** sth
▸ **water** leaks / seeps / drips / escapes
▸ **blood** leaks / seeps / drips / oozes
▸ **gas** leaks / seeps / escapes
▸ **chemicals** leak / seep / leach
▸ **radiation** leaks / escapes
▸ to discharge / leach / secrete **chemicals**
▸ to drip / ooze **blood**
▸ to **slowly** seep / drip / ooze

leak [I, T] to allow liquid or gas to get in or out through a small hole or crack; (of a liquid or gas) to get in or out through a small hole or crack in sth: *A pipe was leaking in her hotel room.* ◇ *The tank had leaked a small amount of water.* ◇ *A small stream of water leaked from the rock.*
▸ **leak** *noun* [C]: *a leak in the roof* ◇ *a gas leak*

seep [I] (always used with an adverb or preposition) (of a liquid or gas) to flow slowly and in small quantities through, out of or into sth: *Blood was beginning to seep through the bandages.*

drip (-pp-) [I, T] to produce drops of liquid: *The tap was dripping.* ◇ *Her hair dripped down her back.* ◇ *Be careful, you're dripping paint everywhere!* ❶ Water can also **drip** somewhere. See also **drip** → TRICKLE *verb*, **drip** → DROP *noun*

discharge /dɪs'tʃɑːdʒ; *AmE* -'tʃɑːrdʒ/ [I, T] (*formal*) (of a gas or liquid) to flow somewhere; to make a gas or liquid flow somewhere: *The river is diverted through the power station before discharging into the sea.* ◇ *The factory was fined for discharging chemicals into the river.*
▸ **discharge** /'dɪstʃɑːdʒ; *AmE* -tʃɑːrdʒ/ *noun* [U, C]: *a ban on the discharge of toxic waste*

ooze [I, T] (of a thick liquid) to flow from a place slowly; to make a thick liquid flow from a place slowly: *Blood oozed out of the wound.* ◇ *On his back there was an ugly swelling oozing with pus.* ◇ *There was a plate of toasted muffins oozing butter.* ❶ **Ooze** is often used in descriptive language to make sth seem particularly attractive or unattractive.

leach [I, T] (*technical*) (of chemicals or minerals) to be removed from soil by water passing through it; (of a liquid) to remove chemicals or minerals from soil: *Nitrates leach from the soil into rivers.* ◇ *Nutrients are quickly leached away from light and sandy soils.*

escape [I] (especially of a liquid or gas) to get out of a container, especially through a hole or crack: *Put a lid on to prevent heat escaping.* ◇ *As he twisted the pipe a trickle of water escaped.*

secrete /sɪ'kriːt/ [T] (*formal or technical*) (of part of the body or a plant) to produce a liquid substance: *Insulin is secreted by the pancreas.*
▸ **secretion** /sɪ'kriːʃn/ *noun* [U, C]: *the secretion of bile by the liver* ◇ *bodily secretions*

lean *verb*

1 lean back in your chair
2 lean sth against the wall

1 lean · tilt · tip · angle · slant · slope · bank
These are all words that can be used when sb/sth moves or is moved so that they are/it is not straight or upright.

PATTERNS AND COLLOCATIONS
▸ to lean / tilt / tip / angle / slant / slope (sth) **towards / away from** sth
▸ to lean / angle / slant (sth) **across** sth
▸ to tilt / tip / angle / slant / slope (sth) **up / down**
▸ to lean / tilt / tip (sth) **forwards / back / backwards / to one side**
▸ to lean / tilt / tip / angle / slant / slope / bank (sth) **slightly**
▸ to tilt / tip / angle your **head**

lean [I] (usually used with an adverb or preposition) (of a person) to bend from an upright position, especially with the upper half of the body; (of sth that usually stands upright) to be in a position that is not vertical: *I leaned back in my chair.* ◇ *A man was leaning out of the window.* ◇ *He leaned closer, lowering his voice.* ◇ *The tower is leaning dangerously.*

tilt [I, T] (usually used with an adverb or preposition) to move so that one end or side is higher than the other; to move sth into this position: *The seat tilts forward, when you press this lever.* ◇ *His hat was tilted slightly at an angle.* ◇ *She tilted her head back and looked up at me.*

tip (-pp-) [I, T] (usually used with an adverb or preposition) to move so that one end or side is higher than the other; to move sth into this position: *Suddenly the boat tipped to one side.* ◇ *She tipped her head back and laughed loudly.* ◇ *He tipped the wheelbarrow on its side.*

NOTE TILT OR TIP? Tilt is usually used for movements that are smaller, gentler or more controlled than **tip**: *The train tilts to one side when it goes round bends.* ◇ ~~The train tips to one side when it goes round bends.~~ ◇ *While trying to sit down, I tipped the tray and my entire dinner went onto the rug.* ◇ ~~While trying to sit down, I tilted the tray and my entire dinner went onto the rug.~~

angle [T] to move or place sth so that it is not straight or not directly facing sb/sth: *He angled his chair so that he could sit and watch her.* See also **angle** → ANGLE *noun*

slant /slɑːnt; *AmE* slænt/ [T, I] (used with an adverb or preposition) to place sth at an angle; to move in a direction that is not horizontal or vertical: *Slant your skis a little more to the left.* ◇ (*literary*) *The sun slanted through the window.*

slope [T] (usually used with an adverb or preposition) (of sth that usually stands upright) to be at an angle rather than being straight or vertical: *His handwriting slopes backwards.* ◇ *It was a very old house with sloping walls.* See also **slope** → ANGLE *noun*, **slope** → SLOPE *verb*

bank [I, T] (of a plane) to travel with one side higher than the other when turning; to make a plane do this: *The plane banked steeply to the left.* ◇ *The pilot banked the plane to give passengers a better look at the mountain.*

2 lean · rest · stand · balance · prop · steady · poise
These words all mean to put sth in a position where it is supported or does not fall.

PATTERNS AND COLLOCATIONS

▸ to lean / rest / stand / balance / prop (sth) **on** sth
▸ to lean / rest / stand / prop / steady (sth) **against** sth
▸ to prop / steady / poise **yourself** somewhere

lean [I, T] (always used with *on* or *against*) (of a person or thing) to put your/its weight against sth for support; to put sth against sth else in a sloping position, so that its weight is supported: *She walked slowly, leaning on her son's arm.* ◇ *A shovel was leaning against the fence.* ◇ *Can I lean my bike against the wall?*

rest [T, I] (always used with an adverb or preposition) to put sth on or against sth else so that its weight is supported; to be supported in this way: *He rested his chin in his hands.* ◇ *Their bikes were resting against the wall.*

stand [T, I] (usually used with an adverb or preposition) to put sb/sth in an upright position somewhere; (of a thing) to be in an upright position: *Stand the ladder up against the wall.* ◇ *I stood the little girl on a chair so that she could see.* ◇ *Books stood in piles in the corner.*

balance [I, T] to put your body or sth else into a position where it will stand without falling to either side, even though there is danger of this happening: *How long can you balance on one leg?* ◇ *She balanced the cup on her knee.*
▸ **balance** *noun* [U]: *He lost his balance and fell over.*

prop (-pp-) [T] (always used with an adverb or preposition) to support an object, especially by leaning it against sth or putting sth under it; to support a person in the same way: *She propped herself up on one elbow.* ◇ *He lay propped against the pillows.* ◇ *The door was propped open.*

steady [T, I] to stop yourself/sb/sth from moving, shaking or falling; to stop moving, shaking or falling: *She steadied herself against the wall.* ◇ *The elevator rocked slightly, steadied, and the doors opened.* See also **steady → FIRM** *adj.*

poise /pɔɪz/ [I, T] to be or hold sth steady in a particular position, especially above sth else: *The hawk poised in mid-air ready to swoop.* ◇ *She poised the javelin in her hand before the throw.*

learn *verb* See the Topic Map for EDUCATION on p.888

learn · study · know · acquire · do · memorize · pick sth up · master · get the hang of sth · revise · learn/ know sth by heart · review
These words all mean to gain knowledge or skill by studying, from experience or from being taught.

PATTERNS AND COLLOCATIONS

▸ to learn / know / pick up sth **from** sb / sth
▸ to study / revise / review (sth) **for** sth
▸ to learn / know / memorize / pick up / master / get the hang of **what...**
▸ to learn / know / master / get the hang of **how...**
▸ to learn / study to **be sth**
▸ to learn / study / know / do / pick up / master a **language**
▸ to learn / study / know / do / pick up / master **French / Arabic, etc.**
▸ to learn / study / know / do / master / revise / review a **subject**
▸ to learn / study / do / revise / review **geography / biology, etc.**
▸ to learn / acquire / pick up / master a **skill**
▸ to learn / do / memorize a **poem / speech**
▸ to memorize a **number**
▸ to learn / know a **poem / speech / number** (off) **by heart**
▸ to **quickly** learn / pick up / master sth
▸ to **thoroughly** learn / study / master / revise / review sth
▸ to study / revise **hard**

learn [T, I] to gain knowledge or skill by studying, from experience or from being taught; to read and repeat sth in order to be able to remember it: *I've forgotten most of what I learned at school.* ◇ *She's still quite young and she's got a lot to learn.* ◇ *She's very interested in* **learning** *more* **about** *Japanese culture.* ◇ *I'll need to learn how to use the new software.* ◇ *He* **learned to** *ride when he was about three years old.* ◇ *You'll have to learn your lines* (= for an acting part) *by next week.* ◇ *Most of the kids here are eager to learn.* ◇ *All children learn through play* (= by playing). ◇ *We have to learn one of Hamlet's speeches for school tomorrow.* See also **learning →** EDUCATION *noun*

study [I, T] to spend time learning about a subject by reading, doing research or going to school or college: *Michael studied at Sussex University.* ◇ *He sat up very late that night, studying.* ◇ *As a young composer he* **studied under** *Nadia Boulanger* (= Nadia Boulanger taught him to be a composer). ◇ *Did you ever study any sciences?* ◇ *She's studying to be an architect.* ❶ In American English **study** is the usual word for talking about preparing for a test or exam: *I have two tests tomorrow, and I've barely had time to study.* ◇ *I was up late studying for my biology final.* In British English the usual word for this is **revise**. See also **study →** EDUCATION *noun*

know [T] to have learned a skill or language; to have gained knowledge of sth: *Do you know how to use spreadsheets?* ◇ *Do you know any Japanese?* ◇ *He knows this city better than anyone.* See also **knowledge →** KNOWLEDGE

acquire /əˈkwaɪə(r)/ [T] (*formal*) to gain knowledge or a skill: *She has acquired a good knowledge of English.* ◇ *He decided to put his newly acquired skills to the test.* See also **acquire →** GET 1
▸ **acquisition** /ˌækwɪˈzɪʃn/ *noun* [U]: *theories of child language acquisition*

do [T] to study a subject, topic, book, etc., especially as a class at school or college: *I'm doing physics, chemistry and biology.* ◇ *Have you done any* (= studied anything by) *Keats?*

memorize (also *BrE* **-ise**) /ˈmeməraɪz/ [T] to learn sth carefully so that you can remember it exactly: *She had memorized his phone number.* ◇ *Each night I tried to memorize long lists of verbs.* See also **memory →** MEMORY

pick sth 'up *phrasal verb* (*rather informal*) to get information or gain a skill by chance, without making a deliberate effort: *I picked up one or two words of Thai while I was on vacation.* ◇ *This is a tip I picked up from my mother.*

master [T] to learn or understand sth thoroughly: *Once you've mastered the basics, you can begin to experiment a little.*

get the 'hang of sth *idiom* (*informal*) to learn how to do or use sth: *It seems tricky at first but you'll soon get the hang of it.* ◇ *I never quite got the hang of riding a bike.*

revise [I, T] (*BrE*) to prepare for an exam by looking again at sth you have studied and reminding yourself of what you have learned: *I can't come out tonight — I'm revising.* ◇ *She's revising for her exams at the moment.* ◇ *Have you revised geography yet?*
▸ **revision** *noun* [U]: *Have you started your revision yet?*

learn/know sth by 'heart *idiom* to learn and be able to remember sth such as a poem or set of facts exactly: *He was told to learn the passage by heart.* ◇ (*BrE*) *I had dialled the number so often that I knew it* **off by heart**.

review [T, I] (*especially AmE*) to look again at sth you have learned or studied, especially in order to prepare for a test: *Take a little time to review your notes the evening before.* ❶ If you are talking about an individual student, **review** must take an object: ~~I need to review for my math final.~~ Use **study** instead: *I need to study for my math final.* However, if you are talking about a teacher leading the class in a review, **review** can be used with or without an object: *I think it would be a good idea to review the material in chapter 10.* ◇ *Next week we're going to be reviewing for the final.*
▸ **review** *noun* [C, U]: *I should have time for a quick review of my notes before the test.* ◇ *We'll have time at the end of class for review.*

learner *noun* See the Topic Map for EDUCATION on p.888, See also the entry for STUDENT

learner · student
These are both words for sb who is interested in or is finding out about sth.

learner [C] a person who is finding out about a subject or how to do sth: *On windsurfers, children are particularly* **quick learners**. ◇ *I was a* **slow learner** − *I couldn't read until I was 14.* ◇ *(BrE) The* **learner driver** *often grips the wheel too tightly.*

student *(formal)* [C] a person who is interested in a particular subject: *She's a keen* **student of** *human nature.* ◇ *He was a deeply observant man, a close* **student of** *the natural world.* ◇ *(AmE)* **Student drivers** *often grip the wheel too tightly.*

leave *verb*

1 It's time we left.
2 leave home/school
3 leave your job
4 leave sb/sth behind
5 leave your husband/wife
6 leave sb in charge

1 See also the entry for SET OFF
leave · go · exit · depart · be off · part
These words all mean to go away from a person or place.

> **NOTE** LEAVE OR GO AWAY? The words in the **leave** entry emphasize the act or time of leaving sb/sth; the words in the **go away** entry emphasize the need or desire of the speaker to be somewhere else or for sb else to be somewhere else. See also the entry for GO AWAY

PATTERNS AND COLLOCATIONS
▶ to leave / go / exit / depart / part **from** sb / sth
▶ to leave / depart **for** sth
▶ to leave / go / depart **at** 9 a.m., midnight, etc.
▶ to **be ready / about / going to** leave / go / depart
▶ to **be forced to** leave / go / depart / part
▶ let's go / be off
▶ to leave / go / depart / be off **now / soon / at once**
▶ to leave / go / depart **quickly / immediately**
▶ to leave / go / be off **in a hurry**

leave [I, T] to go away from a place: *Come on − it's time we left.* ◇ *The plane leaves for Dallas at 12.35.* ◇ *They got into an argument and were asked to leave.* ◇ *John says he left the restaurant at around midnight.* ◇ *I hate leaving home.* **OPP arrive** → ARRIVE, **enter** → ENTER

go [I] to leave a place: *I must be going now.* ◇ *Has she gone yet?* ◇ *Don't go − I want to talk to you.* ◇ *He's been gone an hour* (= he left an hour ago). ◇ *The train goes in a few minutes' time.* **❶ Go** is often used with *on* to talk about sb leaving a place in order to travel, have a holiday or do sth different: *to go on a journey/tour/trip/cruise* ◇ *to go on holiday/vacation* **OPP stay** → STAY 1, See also **go** → GO 1, **go** → GO 2, **going** → DEPARTURE 1

exit [I, T] *(formal)* to leave a building, room, stage, vehicle or other place: *The bullet entered his chest and exited through his back.* ◇ *We exited via a fire door.* ◇ *Exit Hamlet* (= used in the text of a play to say who should come off the stage). ◇ *Passengers exited the aircraft through the rear door.* **OPP enter** → ENTER, See also **exit** → DEPARTURE noun 1

depart /dɪˈpɑːt; AmE dɪˈpɑːrt/ [I, T] *(rather formal)* to leave a place, especially to start a trip: *Flights for Amsterdam depart from Terminal 3.* ◇ *You must depart for England immediately.* ◇ *(AmE) The train departs Amritsar at 4.20 p.m.* ◇ *She waited until the last of the guests had departed.* **❶** In ordinary speech, **depart** is formal, but it is the usual official word used about planes, trains, etc. that are leaving. **OPP arrive** → ARRIVE, See also **departure** → DEPARTURE 1

be 'off *phrase (especially BrE, informal, spoken)* to leave a place: *It's time we were off.* ◇ **He's off to** *Rome in the morning.* ◇ *And they're off!* (= used by sb describing the start of a race)

part [I] *(formal)* (of people) to move apart in different directions; to leave another person: *We parted at the airport.* ◇ *He has recently parted from his wife* (= they have started to live apart). ◇ *I never forgot his* **parting words** (= what he said as he left).

2 leave · move · move out · emigrate · relocate · migrate · quit
These words all mean to stop living in a place, belonging to a group, studying at a place, etc.

PATTERNS AND COLLOCATIONS
▶ to move / move out / emigrate / relocate / migrate **from**...
▶ to move / move out / emigrate / relocate / migrate **to**...
▶ to leave / quit your **home / school / college / job**
▶ to leave / quit **town**
▶ to **threaten to** leave / move out / quit
▶ to **decide / plan / want to** leave / move / move out / emigrate / relocate / quit

leave [T, I] to stop living in a place, belonging to a group, studying at a place, etc: *She left school at 14 with no qualifications.* ◇ *He had left the organization some years before.* ◇ *Too many teachers are leaving the profession for higher-paid jobs.* ◇ *Hundreds of villagers have already left to seek work in the towns.* **OPP stay on ❶** To **stay on** is to continue studying, working, etc. somewhere for longer than expected or after other people have left: *How can we encourage more 16-year-olds to stay on at school?*

move [I, T] to change the place where you live, work or do business: *Moving* (= moving home) *can be an extremely stressful experience.* ◇ *All her family have* **moved away** *so she's on her own.* ◇ *The company is moving to Scotland.* ◇ *He worked as a sales rep before moving to the marketing department.* ◇ *They've* **moved house** *three times in the past year.* ◇ *I'm being moved to the New York office.*

move 'out *phrasal verb* to leave your old home: *They're moving out next week.* ◇ *Local people were forced to move out when the new settlers arrived.* **OPP move in** → MOVE IN

emigrate /ˈemɪɡreɪt/ [I] to leave your own country and go to live permanently in another country: *My grandparents emigrated from Vietnam to the US in the 1980s.* **OPP immigrate** → REFUGEE, See also **emigrant** → REFUGEE
▶ **emigration** *noun* [U, C]: *the mass emigration of Jews from eastern Europe*

relocate /ˌriːləʊˈkeɪt; AmE ˌriːˈloʊkeɪt/ [I, T] *(especially of a company or its workers)* to move or move sb/sth to a new place to work or operate: *A lot of people were unwilling to relocate.* ◇ *The company relocated its head office to Sacramento.* See also **locate** → BASE
▶ **relocation** *noun* [U]: *Most workers will get pay rises if they agree to relocation.* ◇ *We will pay all your* **relocation costs/expenses**.

migrate /maɪˈɡreɪt; AmE ˈmaɪɡreɪt/ [I] (of birds, animals, etc.) to move from one part of the world to another according to the season; (of a lot of people) to move from one town or country and go and live and/or work in another: *Swallows migrate south in winter.* ◇ *Thousands were forced to migrate from rural to urban areas in search of work.* See also **migrant** → REFUGEE
▶ **migration** *noun* [U, C]: *seasonal migration* ◇ *mass migrations*

quit [T, I] *(informal)* to leave the place where you live or study: *He was forced to quit college and find work.* ◇ *I decide to quit town and lie low for a while.* ◇ *The family has been given* **notice to quit** (= told to leave their home). **❶ Quit** can also mean to leave your job.

3 leave · retire · resign · quit · step down · give in/ hand in your notice · depart · stand down
These words all mean to stop working for an employer or to stop taking part in an activity in which you have been successful.

PATTERNS AND COLLOCATIONS

▸ to retire / resign / quit / step down / depart / stand down **as** director, chief executive, etc.
▸ to leave / resign / quit **over** pay, conditions, etc.
▸ to leave / retire from / resign from / quit / step down from / depart / stand down from a **post / position**
▸ to leave / retire from / resign from / quit / depart a **job**
▸ to **decide to** leave/retire/resign/quit/step down/hand in your notice / stand down
▸ to **have / be forced to** leave / retire / resign / quit / step down / depart / stand down
▸ to **be ready/ going to** leave / retire / resign / quit / step down / stand down
▸ to **ask sb to** leave / resign / quit / step down / stand down
▸ to **refuse to** leave / resign / quit / step down
▸ to **threaten to** leave / resign / quit

leave [I, T] to stop working for an employer: *My assistant is threatening to leave.* ◇ *She claims she was forced to leave her job after she became pregnant.* **OPP** **stay on** ❶ To **stay on** is to continue studying, working, etc. somewhere for longer than expected or after other people have left: *Fewer than half of the employees chose to stay on when the company was taken over.*

retire [I] to stop doing your job, especially because you have reached a particular age or because you are ill; to stop taking part in a professional sport: *He is retiring next year after 30 years with the company.* ◇ *My dream is to retire to a villa in France.* ◇ *The company's official retiring age is 65.* ◇ *She has decided to retire from international tennis.*
▸ **retirement** *noun* [U, C]: *to take early retirement* ◇ *This year we have seen the retirements of several senior personnel.*

resign /rɪ'zaɪn/ [I, T] (*rather formal*) to officially tell sb that you are leaving your job or an organization: *Two members resigned from the board in protest.* ◇ *My father resigned his directorship last year.*
▸ **resignation** /ˌrezɪg'neɪʃn/ *noun* [U, C]: *a letter of resignation* ◇ *Further resignations are expected.*

quit [I, T] (*informal*) to leave your job: *If I don't get more money I'll quit.* ◇ *He quit the show last year because of bad health.*

step 'down *phrasal verb* (**-pp-**) to leave an important job or position and let sb else take your place: *He stepped down as party leader a week ago.*

give in/ hand in your 'notice *idiom* to tell sb officially in writing that you are leaving your job: *She decided that she would hand in her notice and go travelling.*

depart /dɪ'pɑːt; *AmE* dɪ'pɑːrt/ [I, T] (*AmE or business*) to leave your job: *Giving a large pay-off to a departing executive may be seen as rewarding failure.* ◇ *He departed the troubled firm after less than a year in the post.*
▸ **departure** /dɪ'pɑːtʃə(r); *AmE* -'pɑːrt-/ *noun* [C]: *His departure leaves the board without a leader.*

stand 'down *phrasal verb* to leave an important job or position and let sb else take your place: *He stood down to make way for someone younger.*

NOTE STEP DOWN OR STAND DOWN? Stand down is often used with words like *have to, be obliged to, be asked to* and *refuse to,* suggesting that people do not always choose to **stand down** from an important position. **Stepping down**, is more likely to be an action motivated by a calm personal decision.

4 leave · lose · forget · mislay

These words all mean to not have sth because you forgot to take it with you or you do not know where it is.

PATTERNS AND COLLOCATIONS

▸ to leave / lose / forget / mislay your **keys / wallet / bag**

leave [T] to go away from a place without taking sb/sth with you: *I left my bag on the bus.* ◇ *I've left my phone somewhere but I can't remember where.* ◇ *He wasn't well, so we had to leave him behind.*

lose [T] to be unable to find sb/sth: *I've lost my keys.* ◇ *The tickets seem to have got lost.* ◇ *We've lost Alfie — is he with you?*

forget [T] to not remember or bring or buy sb/sth that you ought to bring or buy: *I forgot my purse.* ◇ *Hey, don't forget me* (= don't leave without me). ❶ If you want to mention the place where you left sth, use **leave**, NOT **forget**: *I forgot my bag on the bus.* **OPP** **remember** → REMEMBER, See also **forget** → FAIL 1

mislay /ˌmɪs'leɪ/ [T] (*especially BrE, rather formal*) to put sth somewhere and then be unable to find it again, especially for only a short time: *I seem to have mislaid my keys.* ◇ *Don't worry — I'm sure it's not lost, just mislaid.*

5 leave · abandon · dump · desert · strand · turn your back on sb/sth · neglect · walk out

These words all mean to reject sb or to leave them without help or support.

PATTERNS AND COLLOCATIONS

▸ to leave / dump / desert sb **for** sb else
▸ to leave / abandon / dump / desert / neglect / walk out on a **husband / wife**
▸ to leave / abandon / dump / desert a **lover**
▸ to abandon / desert / neglect a **child**
▸ sb's **husband / wife** leaves / abandons / dumps / deserts / neglects / walks out on them
▸ sb's **lover** leaves / abandons / dumps / deserts them
▸ sb's **boyfriend / girlfriend** leaves / dumps them
▸ sb's **mother / father** abandons / deserts / neglects them

leave [T] to leave your wife, husband or partner permanently: *She's leaving him for another man.*

abandon [T, often passive] to leave sb, especially sb you are responsible for, with no intention of returning: *People often simply abandon their pets when they go abroad.* ◇ *The study showed a deep fear among the elderly of being abandoned to the care of strangers.* See also **abandon** → ABANDON

dump [T] (*informal*) to end a romantic relationship with sb in a sudden and unkind way: *Did you hear he's dumped his girlfriend?*

desert /dɪ'zɜːt; *AmE* dɪ'zɜːrt/ [T] to leave sb without help or support: *She was deserted by her husband.* ◇ *Don't worry — I won't desert you.*

NOTE ABANDON OR DESERT? Abandon is more often used to talk about leaving people who are unable to support themselves; **desert** is used more to describe disloyal acts, including leaving friends without help.

strand [T, usually passive] to leave sb in a place which they have no way of leaving: *The strike left hundreds of tourists stranded at the airport.* ❶ **Strand** is most often used to talk about people who are travelling, for example at an airport waiting for a plane, or in a car or train that has broken down.

turn your back on sb/sth *idiom* to reject sb/sth that you have previously been connected with: *She turned her back on them when they needed her.* ◇ *Some newspapers have turned their backs on discussion and argument.* See also the entry for REJECT

neglect /nɪ'glekt/ [T] (*rather formal*) to fail to take care of sb: *She denies neglecting her baby.* See also **neglect** → IGNORE
▸ **neglect** *noun* [U]: *The law imposed penalties for the neglect of children.* See also **neglect** → NEGLECT *noun*

walk 'out *phrasal verb* (*informal*) to suddenly leave sb, especially sb that you have a responsibility for: *How could she walk out on her kids?* ◇ *I was just seven when my dad walked out.*

6 leave · refer sb/sth to sb/sth · hand sth over · delegate · turn sth over to sb · entrust

These words all mean to give sb else the responsibility for sth.

PATTERNS AND COLLOCATIONS
▸ to leave/refer/hand over/delegate/turn over/entrust sth **to** sb
▸ to leave/entrust sth **with** sth
▸ to leave/hand over/delegate/turn over the **task**/**job**/**responsibility**/**management** of sth to sb
▸ to leave/entrust sb with the **task**/**responsibility** of sth
▸ to leave/hand over/turn over a **project**/**business** to sb
▸ to hand over/delegate **authority**/**power** to sb
▸ to leave/refer/hand over/delegate sth to a **committee**

leave [T] to give sb else the responsibility for sth: *You can leave the cooking to me.* ◇ *Leave it with me — I'm sure I can sort it out.* ◇ *I leave it to you to decide what order to do things in.* ◇ *She left her assistant in charge.* ◇ *I was left to cope on my own.*

re'fer sb/sth to sb/sth *phrasal verb* (-**rr**-) (*rather formal*) to send sb/sth to sb/sth for help, advice or a decision: *My doctor referred me to a specialist.* ◇ *The case was referred to the Court of Appeal.*
▸ **referral** *noun* [U, C]: *illnesses requiring referral to hospitals*

,**hand sth 'over** *phrasal verb* to give sb else your position of power or the responsibility for sth: *He finally handed over his responsibility for the company last year.* ❶ **Hand sth over** is typically used with work-related words such as *job, project, business* and *responsibility.* In British English **hand over to sb** can also be used without an object: (*BrE*) *She resigned and handed over to one of her younger colleagues.*
▸ **handover** /'hændəʊvə(r)/; *AmE* -oʊvər/ *noun* [C, U]: *the smooth handover of power from a military to a civilian government*

delegate /'delɪɡeɪt/ [I, T] (*rather formal*) to give part of your work, power or authority to sb in a lower position than you: *Some managers find it difficult to delegate.* ◇ *The job had to be delegated to an assistant.* ❶ People typically **delegate** *powers, responsibilities, authority, decisions* and *work.*
▸ **delegation** /ˌdelɪ'ɡeɪʃn/ *noun* [U]: *the delegation of decision-making*

turn sth over to sb *phrasal verb* (*especially AmE*) to give the control of sth to sb: *He turned the business over to his daughter.*

entrust [T] (*formal*) to make sb responsible for doing sth or taking care of sb: *He entrusted the task to his nephew.* ◇ *He entrusted his nephew with the task.* ◇ *His mother entrusted him to doctors at Charing Cross hospital.* ❶ Note the three possible patterns used with **entrust**: *to entrust sth to sb* ◇ *to entrust sb with sth* ◇ *to entrust sb to sb.*

leave sb/sth out *phrasal verb*

leave sb/sth out · omit · miss sb/sth out · leave sb/sth off (sth)
These words all mean to fail to include sb/sth.

PATTERNS AND COLLOCATIONS
▸ to leave out/omit sth **from** sth
▸ to leave/miss sth out **of** sth
▸ to leave out/omit the **details**
▸ to leave out/omit a **reference**

,**leave sb/sth 'out** *phrasal verb* (*especially spoken*) to not include sb/sth either deliberately or because you have forgotten it/them: *Leave me out of this quarrel, please.* ◇ *He hadn't been asked to the party and was feeling very left out.* ◇ *She left out an 'm' in 'accommodation'.*

omit /ə'mɪt/ (-**tt**-) [T] (*formal*) to leave sb/sth out: *If you are a student, you can omit questions 16–18.* ◇ *People were surprised that Smith was omitted from the team.* See also **omission** → MISTAKE *noun* 1

> **NOTE** LEAVE SB/STH OUT OR OMIT? Use **leave sb out** when you are talking about not including sb in an argument or social situation; **omit** is only used in formal contexts, whether written or spoken.

,**miss sb/sth 'out** *phrasal verb* (*BrE*) to not include sb/sth, usually because you have forgotten it/them: *I'll just read through the form again to make sure I haven't missed anything out.*

,**leave sb/sth 'off**, ,**leave sb/sth 'off sth** *phrasal verb* (*rather informal, especially spoken*) to not include sb/sth on a list or in a series: *You've left off a zero.* ◇ *We left him off the list.*

lecturer *noun* See the Topic Map for EDUCATION on p.888, See also the entries for PROFESSOR and TEACHER

lecturer · professor · fellow · don
These are all words for a person who teaches at a university or college.

PATTERNS AND COLLOCATIONS
▸ lecturer/professor/fellow/don **at** sth
▸ lecturer/professor **in** sth
▸ a **university** lecturer/professor/fellow/don
▸ a **college** lecturer/professor/fellow
▸ a/an **Cambridge**/**Harvard**/**Oxford, etc.** professor/fellow/don
▸ a **chemistry**/**history etc.** lecturer/professor/fellow/don
▸ a **senior** lecturer/professor/fellow
▸ a **distinguished** lecturer/professor/fellow
▸ an **honorary** lecturer/professor/fellow
▸ to be **made**/**appointed** lecturer/professor/fellow

lecturer /'lektʃərə(r)/ [C] (*especially in Britain*) a person who teaches at a university or college: *He's a lecturer in French at London University.* See also **lecturer** → SPEAKER 2

professor [C] (*in the US*) a teacher at a university or college: *She was my professor when I was a grad student.* ❶ In Britain, **professor** is only used to refer to university teachers of the highest rank. See also **professor** → PROFESSOR

fellow [C] a member of an academic or professional organization: *He's a fellow of the Royal College of Surgeons.* ❶ In Britain a **fellow** is also a senior member of some colleges or universities: *She's a fellow of New College, Oxford.* In the US a **fellow** is also a graduate student who holds a fellowship (= an award of money to allow them to continue their studies or do research), which sometimes involves some teaching duties: *He became a teaching fellow at the University of Texas.*

don [C] (*BrE*) a teacher at a university, especially Oxford or Cambridge: *an Oxford don* See also **academic** → SCHOLAR

legacy *noun*

legacy · heritage · inheritance · estate · bequest · birthright
These are all words for money, property or traditions that are passed on to people over the generations.

PATTERNS AND COLLOCATIONS
▸ a legacy/an inheritance/a bequest **from** sb
▸ a **large**/**small** legacy/inheritance/estate/bequest
▸ a **shared** legacy/heritage/inheritance
▸ a **personal** legacy/estate/bequest
▸ a **rich** legacy/heritage/inheritance
▸ a/an **cultural**/**artistic** legacy/heritage/inheritance
▸ to **have**/**preserve** a legacy/a heritage/an inheritance/an estate
▸ to **leave (sb)** a legacy/an inheritance/your estate/a bequest
▸ to **receive** a legacy/an inheritance/a bequest
▸ to **bequeath (sb)**/**inherit** a legacy/an estate
▸ to **claim**/**divide** a legacy/an inheritance/an estate

legacy /'leɡəsi/ [C] (*rather formal, especially written*) money or property that you receive from sb when they die; a situation that exists now because of events that took place in the past: *They each received a legacy of £5 000.* ◇ *Future generations will be left with a legacy of pollution and destruction.*

heritage /ˈherɪtɪdʒ/ [C, usually sing.] the history, traditions and qualities that a country or society has had for many years and that are considered an important part of its character: *Spain's rich cultural heritage* ◊ *The building is part of our national heritage.*

inheritance /ɪnˈherɪtəns/ [C, usually sing., U] money or property that you receive from sb when they die; the fact of receiving sth when sb dies; something from the past or from your family that affects the way you look, think or behave: *She came into her inheritance* (= received it) *at eighteen.* ◊ *The title passes by inheritance to the eldest son.* ◊ *Physical characteristics are determined by genetic inheritance.* See also **inherit** → INHERIT

estate [C, U] (*law*) all the money and property that a person owns, especially everything that is left when they die: *Her estate was left to her daughter.* ◊ *He left estate valued at a million dollars.*

bequest /bɪˈkwest/ [C] (*formal*) money or property that you ask to be given to a particular person or organization when you die: *He left a bequest to each of his grandchildren.* ◊ *The picture was acquired by bequest in 1921.* ❶ **Bequest** is often used to talk about a sum of money or a thing such as a painting or a book collection given by a rich person for public enjoyment after their death. See also **bequeath** → PASS STH ON

birthright /ˈbɜːθraɪt/ [C, usually sing.] (*formal*) a thing that sb has a right to because of the family or country they were born in, or because it is a basic right of all human beings: *The property is the birthright of the eldest child.* ◊ *Education is every child's birthright.* ❶ **Birthright** is nearly always used after *his, her, their,* etc. or a noun in the possessive form. See also the entry for RIGHT *noun*

legal *adj.*

legal · statutory · legitimate · valid · lawful · constitutional

These words all describe sth that is allowed or required by law or connected with the law.

PATTERNS AND COLLOCATIONS
▸ a legal / statutory / legitimate / valid / lawful / constitutional **claim**
▸ legal / statutory / legitimate / valid / lawful / constitutional **means**
▸ a legal / statutory / legitimate / lawful **owner**
▸ a legal / legitimate / lawful **heir**
▸ perfectly legal / legitimate / lawful

legal connected with the law; allowed or required by law: *We were advised to take legal advice.* ◊ *They are facing a long legal battle in the US courts.* ◊ *Should euthanasia be made legal?* **OPP** illegal → ILLEGAL
▸ **legally** *adv.*: *a legally binding agreement* ◊ *It's an important case both legally and politically.*

statutory /ˈstætʃətri; *AmE* -tɔːri/ [usually before noun] fixed by law; required by law: *When you buy foods you have certain statutory rights.* ◊ *The authority failed to carry out its statutory duties.*

legitimate /lɪˈdʒɪtɪmət/ allowed and acceptable according to the law: *The legitimate government was reinstated after the uprising.* ◊ *Is his business strictly legitimate?* **OPP** illegitimate → ILLEGAL

valid /ˈvælɪd/ allowed by law or officially acceptable: *Do you have a valid passport?* ◊ *He bought a bus pass valid for one month.* ◊ *They have a valid claim to compensation.* **OPP** invalid ❶ Things that are **invalid** are not legally or officially acceptable: *The treaty was declared invalid because it had not been ratified.*
▸ **validity** /vəˈlɪdəti/ *noun* [U]: *The period of validity of the agreement has expired.*

lawful (*formal*) allowed or recognized by law: *Can an act that causes death ever be lawful?* ◊ *She is his lawful wife, and so is entitled to inherit the money.* **OPP** unlawful → ILLEGAL
▸ **lawfully** *adv.*: *The jury agreed that the doctor had acted lawfully.*

NOTE **LEGAL** OR **LAWFUL?** Legal and lawful can both mean 'allowed by law': *by legal / lawful means.* **Lawful** tends to be used in technical or literary contexts. The same is true of the opposites, **unlawful** and **illegal**, but **illegal** is used especially about criminal activities. **Legal** also means 'connected with the law': *the US legal system*

constitutional /ˌkɒnstɪˈtjuːʃənl; *AmE* ˌkɑːnstəˈtuː-/ connected with, allowed or limited by the constitution of a country or organization ❶ The **constitution** is the system of laws and basic principles that a state, country or organization is governed by: *She had long advocated constitutional reform.* ◊ *They can't pass this law. It's not constitutional.* ◊ *a constitutional monarchy* (= a country with a king or queen, whose power is controlled by a set of laws and basic principles) **OPP** unconstitutional → ILLEGAL

legend *noun*

1 the legend of Robin Hood
2 heroes of Greek legend

1 legend · story · fairy tale · fable · myth · epic

These are all words for a story that has been passed from person to person, especially over a long period of time.

PATTERNS AND COLLOCATIONS
▸ a legend / the story / a fairy tale / a fable / a myth / an epic **about** sth
▸ an **ancient** legend / story / fable / epic
▸ a **Greek / Roman** legend / myth / epic
▸ to **tell (sb)** a legend / the story / a fairy tale / a fable
▸ a legend / the story **begins**

legend /ˈledʒənd/ [C] a description of people and events from ancient times, which may or may not be true: *The film is based on the legend of Robin Hood.*

story (often **the story**) [C, usually sing.] a description of people and events that people tell each other, although it may not be correct: *She never saw him again – or so the story goes.* ◊ *The story goes that this castle was founded by Emperor Frederick Barbarossa.*

ˈfairy tale [C] a story about magic or fairies, usually for children: *He felt like the prince in a fairy tale.*

fable [C] a traditional short story that teaches a moral lesson, especially one with animals as characters: *Is there a copy of Aesop's Fables in the library?*

myth [C] a story from ancient times, especially one that was told to explain natural events or to describe the early history of a people: *The story parallels the creation myth* (= that explains how the world began) *of the ancient Babylonians.*

epic /ˈepɪk/ [C] a long poem about the actions of great men and women or about a nation's history: *He told us one of the great Hindu epics.*

2 legend · folklore · myth · mythology

These are all words for the ancient stories and traditions of a particular culture or community.

PATTERNS AND COLLOCATIONS
▸ **in** legend / folklore / myth / mythology
▸ **according to** legend / folklore
▸ **ancient / popular** legend / folklore / myth / mythology
▸ **local** legend / folklore / myth
▸ **classical / Greek / Roman** legend / myth / mythology
▸ to **be part of** legend / folklore / myth / mythology
▸ to **pass into** legend / folklore / mythology
▸ to **enter (into)** folklore / mythology
▸ legend / folklore / myth / mythology **has it that...**

legend /ˈledʒənd/ [U] stories from ancient times about people and events, that may or may not be true: *According to ancient legend, the river is a goddess.* ◊ *Legend has it that the lake was formed by the tears of a god.*

folklore /'fəʊklɔː(r); *AmE* 'foʊk-/ [U] the traditions and stories of a country or community: *stories from Irish folklore* ◇ *The story rapidly became part of family folklore.*

myth [U] ancient stories, especially those that were told to explain natural events or to describe the early history of a people: *the heroes of myth and legend* ◇ *The battle became part of national myth.*
- **mythical** *adj.*: *mythical beasts*

mythology /mɪ'θɒlədʒi; *AmE* -'θɑːl-/ [U, C] ancient stories in general; the ancient stories of a particular culture or society: *Narcissus was a character from Greek mythology.* ◇ *a study of the religions and mythologies of ancient Rome*
- **mythological** *adj.*: *historical and mythological subjects*

> **NOTE** WHICH WORD? **Folklore** usually belongs to a particular country, place or community: *local/popular/ family/Scottish/Chinese folklore.* It suggests traditions, beliefs and stories that have been passed down through generations of people until the present time. **Myth** and **mythology** often come from cultures that no longer exist, especially ancient Greece and Rome. **Mythology** is used especially to talk about the ancient stories of a particular culture: *a character/hero from Greek/Roman/ Norse/Hindu/Indian mythology.* **Myth** is used in a more general way in phrases such as *myth and fable/legend.* **Legend** is the most general of these words, used to talk about stories from ancient myth or local folklore.

leisure *noun* See the Topic Map for SPORT AND LEISURE on p.892

leisure · spare time · free time
These are all words for time when you are not working or studying.

PATTERNS AND COLLOCATIONS
- **in** your spare / free time
- to **have (more / no)** leisure / spare time / free time
- to **spend** your spare time / free time doing sth
- to **give up** your spare time / free time

leisure /'leʒə(r); *AmE* 'liːʒər/ [U] (*rather formal*) time that is spent doing what you enjoy when you are not working or studying: *These days we have more money and more leisure to enjoy it.* ◇ *leisure activities/interests/pursuits* ◇ *the growth of the leisure industry*

spare 'time [U] time when you are not doing your usual job or studies: *In her spare time she managed to complete her Master of Education degree.* ◇ *He spent most of his spare time watching television.* See also **spare** → FREE *adj.* 3

free 'time [U] spare time: *It's wonderful the way the students give up their free time to help these children.* See also **free** → FREE *adj.* 3

> **NOTE** LEISURE, SPARE TIME OR FREE TIME? **Leisure** is used when talking about people and society in general, especially in a business context; when talking about yourself or an individual person, use **spare time** or **free time**: ~~What do you do in your leisure?~~ ◇ ~~the spare/free time industry.~~ **Spare time** is used much more than **free time** with possessive pronouns such as *my, your, his, her, their,* etc.: *What do you do in your spare time?* ◇ *In my spare time I write stories.* **Free time** is used more to talk about how much time people have when they are not working or studying: *I don't have much free time.*

lend *verb*

lend · loan · advance
These words all mean to allow sb to use sth that belongs to you, which they have to return to you later, or to give sb money, which they have to pay back later.

PATTERNS AND COLLOCATIONS
- to lend / loan / advance sth **to** sb
- to lend / loan / advance **money**
- a **bank / building society** lends money
- to **kindly** lend / loan sth

lend [T, I] to give sth to sb or allow them to use sth that belongs to you, which they have to return to you later; to give money to sb on condition that they pay it back later: *I've lent the car to a friend.* ◇ *They refused to lend us the money.* ◇ *Banks are less willing to lend in these uncertain times.* **OPP** **borrow** → BORROW

loan [T] (*especially AmE*) to lend sth to sb, especially money: *The bank is happy to loan money to small businesses.* ◇ *A friend loaned me $1000.* ❶ Especially in British English, **loan** also means to lend a valuable object to a museum or art gallery: *This exhibit was kindly loaned by the artist's family.*
- **loan** *noun* [sing.]: *an exhibition of paintings* **on loan** (= borrowed) *from private collections* ◇ *I even gave her the loan of my car.* See also **loan** → LOAN *noun*

advance [T] (*rather formal*) to give sb money before the time it would usually be paid: *We are willing to advance the money to you.* ◇ *We will advance you the money.* See also **advance** → LOAN *noun*

measurements

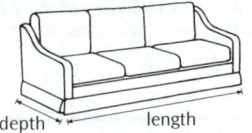
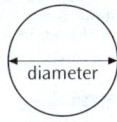

diameter

depth   length

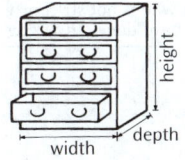

height

thickness

width   depth

length *noun*

length · height · depth · width · diameter · thickness
These are all words for a measurement of distance between two ends or sides of sth.

PATTERNS AND COLLOCATIONS
- sth **has a** length / height / depth / width / diameter / thickness **of** 20 cm / 30 m, etc.
- sth **is / measures** 20 cm / 30 m, etc. **in** length / height / depth / width / diameter / thickness
- sth is **of** a particular length / height / depth / width / diameter / thickness
- a **great** length / height / depth / width / thickness
- an **average** length / height / depth / width / diameter / thickness
- a **standard** length / height / width
- a **maximum / minimum** length / height / depth / width / diameter / thickness
- the **full** length / height / width / thickness of sth
- the **total** length / height / depth / width / thickness of sth
- to **measure** the length / height / depth / width / diameter / thickness of sth
- to **calculate** the length / height / depth / diameter / thickness of sth

length [U, C] the distance or measurement along sth from one end to the other: *This room is twice the length of the kitchen.* ◇ *The river is 300 miles in length.* ◇ *The snake usually reaches a length of 100 cm.* ◇ *He ran the entire length of the beach* (= from one end to the other).
- **long** *adj.*: *long hair* ◇ *a long corridor/bridge* ◇ *The table is six feet long.* **OPP** **short** → SHORT 2

height [U, C] the measurement of how tall a person or thing is: *Please state your height and weight.* ◇ *He is of medium height and slim build.* ◇ *You can adjust the height of the chair.* ◇ *The table is available in several different heights.* See also **high** → HIGH 2

depth [U, C] the distance or measurement from the top or surface to the bottom of sth: *What's the depth of the water here?* ◇ *Water was found at a depth of 30 metres.* ◇ *They dug down to a depth of two metres.* ❶ Depth can also be the distance from the front to the back of sth: *The depth of the shelves is 30 centimetres.*

▶ **deep** *adj.*: *a deep hole/well/river* ◇ *deep water/snow* ◇ *a deep cut/wound/space* ◇ *The water is only a few inches deep.* **OPP shallow** ❶ The opposite is **shallow**: *They were playing in the shallow end* (= of the swimming pool). ◇ *These fish are found in shallow waters around the coast.*

width [U, C] the distance or measurement across sth from one side to the other: *It's about 10 metres in width.* ◇ *The terrace runs the full width of the house.* ◇ *The carpet is available in different widths.* See also **wide** → WIDE 2

diameter /daɪˈæmɪtə(r)/ [U] the length of a straight line going from one side of a circle or any other round object to the other side, passing through the centre: *The radius of a circle is half its diameter.* ◇ *The dome is 42.3 metres in diameter.*

thickness [U, C] the distance through sth between its closest opposite surfaces or sides: *Use wood of at least 12 mm thickness.* ◇ *Roll the pastry to a thickness of about 5 mm.* ◇ *The board is available in four thicknesses.* See also **thick** → WIDE 2

lenient *adj.*

lenient · soft · forgiving · merciful
These words all describe a person who is not strict or who forgives sb, especially when they have done sth wrong.

PATTERNS AND COLLOCATIONS
▶ lenient/ soft **with** sb
▶ lenient/ merciful **to** sb
▶ a lenient/ soft **sentence / approach**
▶ lenient/ soft **treatment**
▶ a lenient/ forgiving **mood**
▶ **too** lenient/ soft

lenient /ˈliːniənt/ not as strict as expected when punishing sb or when making sure that rules are obeyed: *The police and courts may be more lenient with female offenders.* ◇ *The judge agreed that the sentence was unduly lenient.* **OPP strict, harsh** → STRICT

soft (*rather informal, usually disapproving*) not strict or severe; not strict or severe enough, especially in dealing with bad behaviour or crime: *The government is not becoming soft on crime.* ◇ *If you're too soft with these kids they'll never respect you.* **OPP tough** → STRICT

forgiving (*usually approving*) willing to forgive: *The public was more forgiving of the president's difficulties than the press.* ◇ *She had not inherited her mother's forgiving nature.* **OPP unforgiving** → STERN, See also **forgive** → FORGIVE, **forgiveness** → MERCY

merciful /ˈmɜːsɪfl/ AmE ˈmɜːrs- /- (*rather formal, especially written*) willing to forgive people and show them kindness: *They believe in a merciful God.* ◇ *They asked her to be merciful to the prisoners.* **OPP merciless** → RUTHLESS, See also **mercy** → MERCY

let sb in *phrasal verb*

let sb in/into sth · accept · admit · welcome · enrol · receive
These words all mean to allow sb to enter a place or join an organization.

PATTERNS AND COLLOCATIONS
▶ to let/ accept/ admit/ welcome/ enrol/ receive sb **into** sth
▶ to accept/ admit/ enrol sb **as** sth
▶ to let in/ admit/ welcome/ receive a **visitor**

▶ to let in/ welcome/ receive a **guest**
▶ to let in/ accept/ admit/ welcome **immigrants**
▶ to accept/ admit/ welcome/ enrol a **candidate / member / student**
▶ to accept/ admit/ welcome **applicants**
▶ to accept/ admit/ welcome/ receive sb **formally / officially**
▶ to accept/ welcome/ receive sb **with open arms**

let sb 'in, let sb into sth *phrasal verb* (*especially spoken*) to allow sb/sth to enter a place: *He let her into the house.* ◇ *I'll give you a key so that you can let yourself in.* **OPP keep sb/sth out** → EXCLUDE 2

accept [T] to make a decision to allow sb to join an organization, attend an institution or use a service, especially after they have applied to do so: *The college he applied to has accepted him.* ◇ *She was disappointed not to be accepted into the club.* ◇ *The landlord was willing to accept us as tenants.* ◇ *She was accepted to study music.* ❶ Accept is used especially to talk about whether a person is allowed to start a programme of study at a college or university, or to join an organization. **OPP reject** → REFUSE, See also **accept** → GREET

admit (-tt-) [T] (*formal*) to allow sb to enter a place; to allow sb to become a member of a club, school or organization: *Each ticket admits one adult and one child.* ◇ *You will not be admitted to the theatre after the performance has started.* ◇ *The society admits all US citizens over 21.* ❶ Admit is used especially to talk about whether a person is allowed to enter a public place. **OPP exclude** → EXCLUDE 2

▶ **admittance** /ədˈmɪtns/ *noun* [U]: *Hundreds of people were unable to gain admittance to the hall.* See also **admission** → ACCESS

welcome [T] to be pleased that sb has come or has joined an organization or activity: *They welcomed the new volunteers with open arms* (= with enthusiasm). See also **welcome** → GREET

enrol (*especially BrE*) (*AmE usually* **enroll**) /ɪnˈrəʊl; AmE ɪnˈroʊl/ (-ll-) [T] to arrange for yourself or for sb else to officially join a school, college or programme of study: *The centre will soon be ready to enrol candidates for the new-style programme.*

receive [T] (*formal*) to officially recognize and accept sb as a member of a group: *Three young people were received into the Church at Easter.* ❶ In this meaning, **receive** is mostly used to talk about sb becoming a member of a church. See also **receive** → GREET

letter *noun*

letter · message · email · mail · note · memo · fax · text · post · communication · correspondence
These words all mean sth that you write and send to sb in order to communicate with them.

PATTERNS AND COLLOCATIONS
▶ a letter/ a message/ an email/ mail/ a note/ a memo/ a fax/ a text/ post/ a communication/ correspondence **from / to** sb
▶ (a) **personal / private** letter/ message/ email/ mail/ note/ communication/ correspondence
▶ a **brief** letter/ message/ email/ note/ memo/ communication
▶ (a) **business** letter/ email/ mail/ memo/ correspondence
▶ a **thank-you** letter/ message/ email/ note
▶ to **send/ receive** a letter/ a message/ an email/ mail/ a note/ a memo/ a fax/ a text/ post/ a communication/ correspondence
▶ to **write** a letter/ a message/ an email/ a note/ a memo
▶ to **open** a letter/ a message/ an email/ the mail/ the post
▶ a letter/ a message/ an email/ the mail/ a fax/ the post **arrives**

letter [C] a piece of text that you write on paper and send to sb, usually in an addressed envelope, in order to tell them sth: *You should include a covering letter with your CV.* ◇ *They wrote a letter of complaint to the television network.* ◇ *You will be notified by letter.* ◇ (*BrE*) *to post a letter* ◇ (*AmE*) *to mail a letter*

message [C] a short piece of written or spoken information that you give to sb when you cannot speak to them directly: *I left a message on her answering machine.* ◇

Victoria's not here at the moment. Can I take a message? ◇ *The computer displays an error message when I try to run the program.*

email (also **e-mail**) [C, U] a written message that you send from your computer to another person's computer over a network such as the Internet: *I got an email from Andrew last week.* ◇ *I have to check my email.*
▸ **email** (also **e-mail**) *verb* [T]: *David emailed me yesterday.* ◇ *I'll email the documents to her.*

mail [U] the letters and packages which are sent and delivered by the postal system; messages that are sent or received on a computer: *There isn't much mail today.* ◇ *Is there a letter from them in the mail?* ◇ *You've got mail.*
❶ In British English **post** is often used instead of **mail** to mean the letters and packages that sb sends and receives. See also **mail** → SEND *verb* 1

note [C] a short informal letter: *Just a quick note to say thank you for a wonderful evening.* ◇ *I left a note for Judith on her desk.* ◇ *It is suspicious that he did not leave a suicide note.*

memo /ˈmeməʊ; *AmE* -moʊ/ (also *formal* **memorandum** /ˌmeməˈrændəm/) (pl. **memoranda** /ˌmeməˈrændə/) [C] an official note from one person to another in the same organization: *The confidential memo was leaked to the press.*

fax [U, C] a system for sending documents in electronic form along telephone wires, using a special machine that sends, receives and prints the documents; a document sent by fax: *a fax machine* ◇ *Can you send it to me by fax?* ◇ *What is your fax number?* ◇ *Did you get my fax?*
▸ **fax** *verb* [T]: *Can you fax me the latest version?* ◇ *Can you fax it to me?*

text (also ˈ**text message**) [C] a written message that you send using a mobile phone: *Send a text to this number to vote.*
▸ **text** (also ˈ**text-message**) *verb* [T]: *I texted him to say we were waiting at the hotel.*

post [U] (*BrE*) mail: *The book arrived in the morning post.* See also **post** → SEND *verb* 1

communication [C] (*formal*) a message, letter or telephone call: *If you no longer wish to receive communications from us, follow the instructions at the bottom of the email.* See also **communication** → COMMUNICATION, **communicate** → CONVEY, **communicate** → TALK

correspondence [U] (*rather formal*) the letters a person sends and receives: *The editor welcomes correspondence from readers on any subject.* ◇ *the correspondence column/page* (= in a newspaper) See also **correspondence** → COMMUNICATION

level *noun*

level · degree · scale · extent · size · proportions · magnitude
These are all words for the amount or importance of sth, especially if it is very large.

PATTERNS AND COLLOCATIONS
▸ the **true** level / extent / size of sth
▸ the **full** scale / extent / size of sth
▸ the **sheer** scale / extent / size / magnitude of sth
▸ (a) **manageable** level / scale / size / proportions
▸ (a) **global** level / scale / proportions
▸ to **assess / judge** the level / degree / scale / extent / size / magnitude of sth
▸ to **realize** the level / degree / scale / extent / size of sth
▸ to **calculate** the level / extent / size of sth
▸ the scale / extent / size / magnitude **of the problem**
▸ the scale / extent **of the damage**

level [C] the amount of sth that exists in a particular situation at a particular time: *These cities have relatively low levels of unemployment.* ◇ *a test to check the level of alcohol in the blood* ◇ *High stress levels will affect employees' productivity.* ◇ *The aim is to reduce pollution levels in the city.*

degree [C] how far sth is true; the level of a quality that sb/sth has or needs: *I agree with you to a certain degree.*

◇ *To what degree can parents be held responsible for a child's behaviour?* ◇ *Most pop music is influenced, to a greater or lesser degree, by the blues.* ◇ *Her job demands a high degree of skill.*

scale [U, sing.] how large or important sth is, especially when compared with sth else: *It was impossible to comprehend the full scale of the disaster.* ◇ *We are striving to achieve economies of scale in production* (= to produce many items so the cost of producing each one is reduced). ◇ *They entertain on a large scale* (= they hold expensive parties with a lot of guests). ◇ *Here was corruption on a grand scale.* See also **full-scale** → DETAILED, **large-scale** → WIDE 1

extent [U, sing.] how large or important sth is; how far sth is true; how great an effect sth has: *She was exaggerating the true extent of the problem.* ◇ *I was amazed at the extent of his knowledge.* ◇ *To some extent what she argues is true.* ◇ *To what extent is this true of all schools?*

> **NOTE** **SCALE** OR **EXTENT**? The **scale** of sth is how large it is; its **extent** is how far it goes. In many cases there is no real difference between the two: *the scale/extent of the problem/damage.* However, you are more likely to try to *assess/measure/calculate the extent of sth*, while you simply try to *comprehend/grasp the scale of sth*. Some qualities, such as *knowledge*, are considered as being wide rather than large, and so have **extent** rather than **scale**: ~~I was amazed at the scale of his knowledge.~~

size [U] the large amount or extent of sth: *You should have seen the size of their house!* ◇ *We were shocked at the size of his debts.*

proportions /prəˈpɔːʃnz; *AmE* -ˈpɔːrʃnz/ [pl.] the size and shape of an area; the scale of a task or problem: *The apartment is of generous proportions, with a large kitchen and dining area.* ❶ When describing a task or problem, **proportions** is often used in order to say whether the task/problem can be managed easily or not: *This method divides the task into more manageable proportions.* ◇ *The food shortage could soon reach crisis proportions.* ◇ *The virus has not yet reached epidemic proportions.*

magnitude /ˈmægnɪtjuːd; *AmE* -tuːd/ [U] (*formal*) how large or important sth is, especially when it is very large or important: *We did not realize the magnitude of the problem.* ◇ *This is a discovery of the first magnitude* (= it is very important). ◇ *We are talking about something of a different order of magnitude* (= so much larger or more important that it cannot easily be compared with other examples).

licence *noun* (*BrE*) (*AmE* **license**) See also the entries for CERTIFICATE and PERMISSION

licence · franchise · warrant · permit · charter · authorization · pass
These are all words for an official document that gives you permission to do sth.

PATTERNS AND COLLOCATIONS
▸ **under** (a) licence / franchise / charter
▸ a licence / franchise / warrant / permit / charter **to do sth**
▸ the **necessary** licence / permit / authorization
▸ to **have** a licence / a franchise / a warrant / a permit / a charter / an authorization / a pass
▸ to **get / obtain** a licence / a franchise / a warrant / a permit / a charter / an authorization / a pass
▸ to **give** (sb) a licence / franchise / permit / charter / pass
▸ to **grant** (sb) a licence / a franchise / a warrant / a permit / a charter
▸ to **issue** (sb) a licence / warrant / permit / charter / pass
▸ to **apply for** a licence / franchise / warrant / permit / charter / pass
▸ to **renew** a licence / franchise / permit / charter / pass
▸ to **revoke** sb's licence / permit / charter
▸ to **see / check** sb's licence / permit / authorization / pass
▸ a licence / franchise / permit / charter / pass **expires**
▸ a licence / franchise / permit / pass **holder**

licence (*BrE*) (*AmE* **license**) /'laɪsns/ [C] an official document that shows that permission has been given for you to do, own or use sth: *You need a licence to fish in this river.* ◇ *The beer is brewed under licence in the UK.* ◇ (*BrE*) *Do you have a valid* **driving licence**? ◇ (*AmE*) *a* **driver's license** ◇ *She* **lost** *her* **licence** (= had her driving licence taken away) *for six months.* ◇ *a* **marriage licence** ◇ *a* **liquor licence** (= giving permission to sell alcoholic drinks) ◇ *an* **export licence** (= a licence to export goods) ◇ *Is there a* **licence fee**? See also **license → ALLOW**

franchise /'fræntʃaɪz/ [C] formal permission given by a company to sb who wants to sell its goods or services in a particular area; formal permission given by a government to sb who wants to operate a public service as a business: *a catering franchise in the fast-food industry* ◇ *In the reorganization, Southern Television lost their franchise.* ◇ *They operate the business under franchise.*
▸ **franchise** *verb* [T, usually passive]: *The catering has been* **franchised (out) to** *a private company.*

warrant /'wɒrənt; *AmE* 'wɔːr-; 'wɑːr-/ [C] a legal document that is signed by a judge and gives the police authority to do sth: *They issued a* **warrant for** *her arrest.* ◇ *Police arrived with a* **search warrant**. ◇ *Federal agents tried to serve* **arrest warrants** *on him for firearms offences.*

permit /'pɜːmɪt; *AmE* 'pɜːrmɪt/ [C] an official document that gives sb the right to sth, especially for a limited period of time: *I asked to see his permit.* ◇ *His 30-day permit expires on Tuesday.* ◇ *a* **work permit** (= giving you permission to work in a foreign country) ◇ *a residence permit* See also **permit → ALLOW**

charter [C] an official document stating that a ruler or government allows a new organization, town or university to be established and gives it particular rights and privileges: *The BBC's charter was due to be renewed.* ◇ *The university received its* **Royal Charter** *in 1946.* ❶ In British English **charter** is sometimes used in an ironic way to describe a law or policy that seems likely to help criminals by giving them extra rights: *The new law will be a* **charter for** *unscrupulous financial advisers.*

authorization (*BrE* also **-isation**) /ˌɔːθəraɪ'zeɪʃn; *AmE* ˌɔːθərə'zeɪʃn/ [C] a document that gives sb official permission to do sth: *Can I see your authorization please?* See also **authorize → ALLOW**

pass [C] an official document or ticket that shows that you have the right to enter or leave a place, to travel on a bus, train, etc: *You can buy a three-day pass that gives you entry to all the major sights.* ◇ *a bus pass* ◇ *You will need a boarding pass to get onto the plane.*

lid *noun*

lid · top · cork · cap · plug
These are all words for a cover for a container.

PATTERNS AND COLLOCATIONS
▸ a **close-fitting / tight-fitting** lid / top / cap
▸ a **screw** top / cap
▸ a **pen** lid / top
▸ to **remove** the lid / top / cork / cap / plug
▸ to **put on / screw on / take off / unscrew** the lid / top / cap
▸ to **pull out** the cork / plug

lid [C] a cover over a container that can be removed or opened by turning or lifting it: *You'll need a jar with a tight-fitting lid.* ◇ *He cautiously lifted the lid of the box.* ◇ *Replace the saucepan lid and simmer for 10 minutes.*

top [C] a thing that you put over the end of sth such as a pen or bottle in order to close it: *Where's the top of my pen gone?* ◇ *The jar has a tight-fitting screw top.*

cork [C] a small round object made of cork or plastic that is used for closing bottles, especially wine bottles: *She pulled out the cork and poured a glass of wine.*

cap [C] (often in compounds) a top for a pen or a protective cover for sth such as the lens of a camera: *The safety cap should be completely waterproof.* ◇ *a lens cap*

plug [C] a piece of material that you put into a hole in order to block it; a flat round rubber or plastic thing that you put into the hole of a sink in order to stop the water from flowing out: *We fixed the leak with a plug made from an old cloth.* ◇ *She pulled out the plug and let the water drain away.*

lid

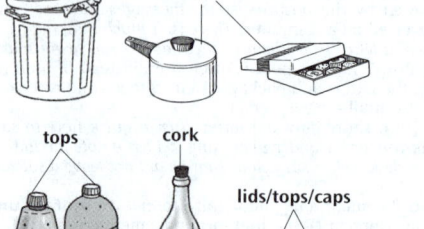

lids / tops / caps

lie 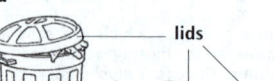 *noun* See also the entry for NONSENSE

lie · story · fiction · perjury · fabrication · falsehood · fib
These are all words for a statement made by sb knowing that it is not true.

PATTERNS AND COLLOCATIONS
▸ (a) **complete** lie / fiction / fabrication / falsehood
▸ **pure** fiction / fabrication
▸ a **little** lie / story / fiction
▸ a **plausible / convincing** lie / story
▸ a **malicious** lie / story / fabrication / falsehood
▸ to **tell (sb)** a lie / a story / a falsehood / a fib
▸ to **spread** lies / stories
▸ to **believe** a lie / a story / a fiction

lie [C] a statement made by sb knowing that it is not true: *I couldn't tell her a lie.* ◇ *The whole story is nothing but a* **pack of lies**. ◇ *What's the harm in telling a little* **white lie** (= a harmless or small lie)?
▸ **lie** *verb* [I]: *Don't lie to me!* ◇ *She lies about her age.* ◇ *You could see from his face that he was lying.*

story [C, usually pl.] (*rather informal*) a statement about sb/sth that is not true, especially one that sb makes in order to impress sb, or to make other people believe unpleasant things about sb: *She knew the child had been telling stories again.* ◇ *He's been spreading malicious stories about you.* ❶ A **tall story** (*BrE*) (or **tall tale** (*AmE*)) is a story that is difficult to believe because what it describes seems exaggerated and not likely to be true: *Sounds like another one of his tall stories to me.*

fiction [C, U] (*rather formal*) a thing that is invented or imagined and is not true; invented false information intended to deceive people: *For years he managed to keep up the fiction that he was not married.* ◇ *Fact and fiction became all jumbled up in his report of the robbery.* **OPP** fact → FACT

perjury /'pɜːdʒəri; *AmE* 'pɜːrdʒ-/ [U] (*law*) the crime of telling a lie in court: *She was found guilty of perjury.*
▸ **perjure yourself** [T]: *She admitted that she had perjured herself.*

fabrication /ˌfæbrɪ'keɪʃn/ [C, U] (*rather formal*) invented false information intended to deceive people; the act of inventing such information; a thing that is invented and is not true: *Her story was a complete fabrication from beginning to end.* ◇ *Much of the 'evidence' is rumour and conjecture; some of it is pure fabrication.* See also **fabricate → INVENT**

NOTE FICTION OR FABRICATION? A **fiction** is usually a single thing, presented as a fact, that is not true; a **fabrication** is usually a series of lies built up into a complete story: ~~For years he managed to keep up the fabrication that he was not married.~~ ◇ ~~Her story was complete fiction from beginning to end.~~

falsehood /'fɔːlshʊd/ [U, C] (*formal*) the state of not being true; the act of telling a lie; a lie: *He needed to test the truth or falsehood of her claims.* ◇ *It is an offence to deliberately publish a serious falsehood.* **OPP truth** → TRUTH

fib [C] (*informal*) a lie about sth that is not important: *Stop telling fibs.*
▸ **fib** *verb* [I]: *Come on, don't fib! Where were you really last night?*

lie *verb* See also the entries for SIT and STAND 1

lie · lie down · sprawl · lounge · bask · recline
These words all mean to be in a relaxed position, especially with your body stretched out flat or leaning back.

PATTERNS AND COLLOCATIONS
▸ to lie / lie down / sprawl **on your back / side / front**

lie [I] (usually used with an adverb or preposition) to be or get into a flat position so that you are not standing or sitting: *She lay on her back and looked up at the sky.* ◇ *The cat was lying fast asleep by the fire.*
lie 'down *phrasal verb* to be or get into a flat position, especially in bed, in order to sleep or rest: *Go and lie down for a while.* ◇ *He lay down on the sofa and soon fell asleep.*
sprawl [I] (usually used with an adverb or preposition) to sit or lie with your arms and legs spread out in a relaxed or awkward way: *He was sprawling in an armchair in front of the TV.* ◇ *Something hit her and sent her sprawling to the ground.* ◇ *I tripped and went sprawling.*
lounge /laʊndʒ/ [I] (usually used with an adverb or preposition) to stand, sit or lie in a lazy way: *Several students were lounging around, reading newspapers.*
bask /bɑːsk; AmE bæsk/ [I] (usually used with an adverb or preposition) to enjoy sitting or lying in the heat or light of sth, especially the sun: *We sat basking in the warm sunshine.* ◇ *A cat was basking on the window sill.*
recline /rɪ'klaɪn/ [I] (*formal*) to sit or lie in a relaxed way, with your body leaning backwards: *She was reclining on a sofa.* ◇ *a reclining figure* (for example in a painting)

life *noun*

1 no signs of life
2 all your life
3 make life easier

1 See the Topic Map for THE INDIVIDUAL AND SOCIETY on p.894
life · existence · survival
These are all words for the state or fact of living or existing.

PATTERNS AND COLLOCATIONS
▸ sb / sth's **very / continued / day-to-day** existence / survival
▸ to **threaten** sb / sth's life / existence / survival
▸ to **fight for** your life / survival
▸ a **struggle for** existence / survival

life [U, C] the state or fact of being alive as a person, animal or plant, shown by activities such as breathing, growing and reproducing; the state of being alive as a human being; an individual person's existence: *The body was cold and showed no signs of life.* ◇ *In spring the countryside bursts into life.* ◇ *The floods caused a massive loss of life* (= many people were killed). ◇ *He risked his life to save his daughter from the fire.* ◇ *The operation saved her life.* ◇ *My grandfather lost his life* (= was killed) *in the Second World War.* ◇ *You mustn't let anyone know — it's a matter of life and death* (= sb's life depends on it). ❶ The **life** of a thing is the period of time

when it exists or functions: *The International Stock Exchange started life as a London coffee shop.* ◇ *The product has a guaranteed shelf life* (= the length of time that food or other items can be kept before it is too old to be sold) *of 60 days.* **OPP death** → DEAD, See also **live** → EXIST, **live** → SURVIVE

existence [U] the state or fact of being real or living: *I was unaware of his existence until today.* ◇ *This is the oldest Hebrew manuscript in existence.* ◇ *Pakistan came into existence as an independent country after the war.* ◇ *The crisis threatens the industry's continued existence.* See also **exist** → EXIST

survival [U] the state of continuing to live or exist, often in spite of difficulty or danger: *His only chance of survival was to make his own way down the mountainside.* ◇ *Rhino poaching is now threatening the survival of the species.* ◇ *Exporting is necessary for our economic survival.* **OPP extinction** ❶ **Extinction** is a situation in which a plant, animal, way of life, etc. stops existing: *The mountain gorilla is in danger of extinction.* See also **survive** → SURVIVE

2 life · career · lifetime · in sb's day
These are all words for the time during which sb is alive or is doing a particular thing.

PATTERNS AND COLLOCATIONS
▸ **in / of** sb's life / career / lifetime / day
▸ **during** sb's life / career / lifetime
▸ sb's **entire / whole** life / career / lifetime
▸ sb's **school** life / career
▸ a life / career / lifetime **of doing sth**

life [C, U] the period between sb's birth and their death; a part of this period: *He's lived here all his life.* ◇ *He will spend the rest of his life in a wheelchair.* ◇ *My mother took up tennis late in life.* ◇ *There's no such thing as a job for life any longer.* ◇ *She is a life member of the club.* ◇ *He spent his entire adult life in France.* See also **live** → EXIST

career [C] the period of time that you spend in your life working or doing a particular thing: *She started her career as an English teacher.* ◇ *He is playing the best tennis of his career.* ◇ *Her stage career spans sixty years.*

lifetime /'laɪftaɪm/ [C, usually sing.] the length of time that sb lives or that sth lasts: *Only two volumes of his poetry were published during his lifetime.* ◇ *He has nothing to look forward to but a lifetime of misery.* ◇ *These spending commitments are not achievable in the lifetime of the present government.* ◇ *For the chance of a lifetime* (= a wonderful opportunity that you are not likely to get again) *fill in the coupon below and send it to the following address.*

in sb's 'day *idiom* during the middle or most important part of sb's career; when sb was young: *In her day she was one of the most famous dancers in Britain.* ◇ *It was different in my day, there were plenty of jobs when you left school.* ❶ **Of sb's / the day** is used to talk about a particular period of time when sb lived or which has already been mentioned: *He was regarded as the greatest architect of his day.* ◇ *The event attracted all the great names and popular artists of the day.* See also **day** → PERIOD

3 life · experience · lifestyle · way of life · living · existence
These are all words for the way in which people live.

PATTERNS AND COLLOCATIONS
▸ (sb's) **day-to-day** life / experience / living / existence
▸ (sb's) **daily / everyday** life / experience / existence
▸ a **comfortable / busy** life / lifestyle / existence
▸ a **miserable / communal** life / existence
▸ a **traditional** lifestyle / way of life
▸ to **have / lead / enjoy** a ... life / lifestyle / existence

life [C] the activities and experiences of a person during their life; a particular period of sb's life; the activities and experiences that are typical of all people or a particular way of living: *He has had a hard life.* ◇ *She led a life of luxury.* ◇ *Many of these children have led very **sheltered lives*** (= they have not had many different experiences). ◇ *He doesn't like to talk about his **private life**.* ◇ *She has a full **social life**.* ◇ *They emigrated to **start a new life** in America.* ◇ *She has been an accountant all her **working life**.* ◇ *They were very happy throughout their **married life**.* ◇ *He is young and has little experience of life.* ◇ *We bought a dishwasher to **make life easier**.* ◇ *In **real life*** (= when she met him) *he wasn't how she had imagined him at all.* ◇ *She enjoyed political life.* ◇ *How do you find life in America?*

experience [U] the things that have happened to you that influence the way you think and behave: *Experience has taught me that life can be very unfair.* ◇ *It is important to try and **learn from experience**.* ◇ *In my experience, very few people really understand the problem.* ◇ *She knew **from past experience** that Ann would not give up easily.* ◇ *The book is based on **personal experience**.* ◇ *He has had **direct/first-hand experience** of poverty.* See also **experience** → EVENT *noun* 1, **experience** → KNOWLEDGE *noun*, **experience** → HAVE *verb* 3

lifestyle /ˈlaɪfstaɪl/ [C, U] the way in which a person or a group of people lives and works: *She has had to curb her lavish lifestyle after losing millions in legal fees.* ◇ *Many people are trying to adopt a healthy lifestyle these days.*

a/the/sb's way of 'life *phrase* the typical pattern of behaviour of a person or group: *Making small adjustments to your way of life can allow you to find more time.* ◇ *The expansion in tourism is seen as a threat to the islanders' traditional way of life.*

> **NOTE** **LIFESTYLE** OR **WAY OF LIFE?** Often you can use either word: *to change/make adjustments to your lifestyle/way of life.* However, a **lifestyle** is typically more modern and more individual than a **way of life**. An individual person might have a *busy/hectic* lifestyle or choose to adopt a *modern/healthy/alternative* lifestyle. A **way of life** is more likely to be *traditional, old* or *British, Western, etc.* and shared by a whole community.

living [U] (especially in compounds or fixed phrases) a way or style of life: *The classes are about helping children make informed choices about healthy living.* ◇ *The prisoners' **living conditions** were appalling.* ◇ *Their **standard of living** is very low.* ◇ *The **cost of living** has risen sharply.*

existence [C] a way of living, especially when this is difficult or boring: *The family endured a miserable existence in a cramped and noisy apartment.* ◇ *They eke out a precarious existence* (= they have hardly enough money to live on). ◇ *The peasants depend on a good harvest for their **very existence*** (= in order to continue to live).

light *noun*

1 He blinked in the bright light.
2 Turn on the light.

1 light · lighting · brightness
These are all words for the energy that allows us to see, or a particular type of this energy.

light [U, sing.] the energy from the sun, a lamp or other source that makes it possible to see things; a particular type of light with its own colour and qualities; light colours in a picture, which contrast with darker ones: *She could just see **by the light of** the candle.* ◇ *a beam/ray of light* ◇ *Bring it **into the light** so I can see it.* ◇ *We could only just make out the path in the dim light.* ◇ *A cold grey*

light crept under the curtains. ◇ *Examine the artist's use of light and shade.* **OPP** **darkness**, **the dark**, **shade** → DARKNESS. See also **daylight, natural light, sunlight** → SUN

▶ **light** *adj.*: *We'll leave in the morning as soon as **it's light**.* ◇ *It **gets light** at about 5 o'clock.* ◇ *It was a light spacious apartment at the top of the building.* **OPP** **dark** → DARK 1

lighting [U] the arrangement or type of light in a place: *Good lighting is essential in the window displays.* ◇ *The play had excellent sound and lighting effects.*

brightness [U, sing.] the quality of being full of light or shining strongly: *He turned on the lights and blinked at the sudden brightness.* ◇ *Turn down the brightness on the screen.* ◇ *There was colour in her cheeks and a brightness in her eyes.* **OPP** **gloom** → DARKNESS

2 light · lamp · candle · torch · flashlight · lantern
These are all words for things which produce energy and allow us to see.

light [C] a thing that produces light, especially an electric light: *Turn on the lights!* ◇ *Suddenly all the lights went out.* ◇ *The lights dimmed and the curtain rose.* ◇ *Check your car before you drive to make sure that your lights are working.* ◇ *Keep going — the lights* (= traffic lights) *are green.* ◇ *It was getting dark and the street lights had come on.*

lights

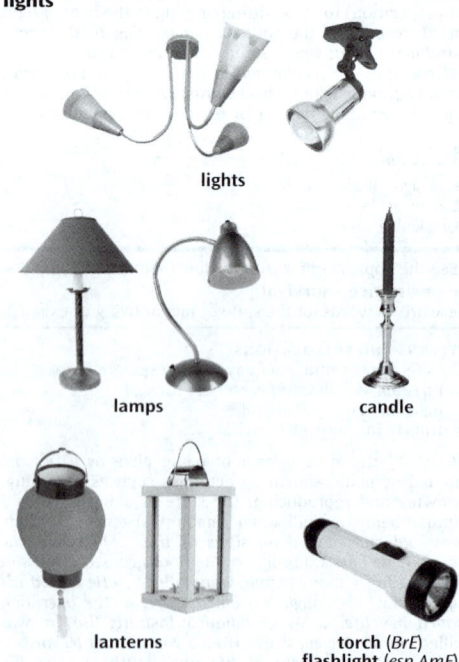

lights

lamps

candle

lanterns

torch (*BrE*)
flashlight (*esp AmE*)

lamp [C] a device that uses electricity, oil or gas to produce light; an electrical device that produces rays of heat and that is used for medical or scientific purposes: *He got into bed and switched off the bedside lamp.* ◇ *The specimen was viewed under an ultraviolet lamp.*

candle [C] a round stick of wax with a piece of string through the middle (= a wick) which is lit to give light as it burns: *The room was lit by candles.* ◇ *Aren't you going to blow out the candles (= on a birthday cake)?*

torch [C] (*BrE*) a small electric lamp that uses batteries and that you can hold in your hand: *Shine the torch on the lock while I try to get the key in.* ❶ In American English this is called a **flashlight**. In both British and American English a **torch** is also a long piece of wood that has material at one end that is set on fire and that people carry to give light: *Supporters carried flaming torches to welcome him.* ◇ *The Olympic torch will arrive next month.*

flashlight /ˈflæʃlaɪt/ [C] (*especially AmE*) an electric torch: *He shone a flashlight in the boy's face.*

lantern /ˈlæntən; *AmE* -tərn/ a lamp in a container, often a metal case with glass sides, that has a handle, so that you can carry it outside: *Coloured lanterns hung in the trees around the lawn.*

light *verb*

1 light a fire
2 well lit streets

---

1 light · set fire to sth/set sth on fire · ignite · torch

These words all mean to make sth start to burn.

PATTERNS AND COLLOCATIONS
▸ to light / ignite a **fire** / **flame**
▸ to set fire to / torch a **car** / **building**
▸ to set a **car** / **building** on fire
▸ to set fire to / torch **sb** / **yourself**
▸ to light / ignite the **gas**
▸ a **spark** lights sth / sets fire to sth / sets sth on fire / ignites sth

light [T] to make sth start to burn: *Come in, I'll light a fire and you can get warmed up.* ◇ *to light a match/cigarette/candle*

set 'fire to sth, set sth on 'fire *idiom* to make sth start to burn, especially sth big like a building: *Several youths had set fire to the police car.* ◇ *A candle had set the curtains on fire.* See also **be on fire** → BURN 1

ignite /ɪɡˈnaɪt/ [T] (*rather formal*) to make sth start to burn: *Flames melted a lead pipe and ignited leaking gas.*

NOTE LIGHT, SET FIRE TO STH OR IGNITE? **Light** is used especially when a person makes sth burn deliberately, often when it causes just one flame. It is used about sth that is supposed to burn, such as a *match*, a *cigarette* or a *fire*: *He lit a candle.* ◇ ~~He lit the curtains.~~ **Set fire to sth/set sth on fire** is used when lighting sth causes a big fire and not just one flame. It is used especially about sth that is not supposed to burn: *He set fire to the curtains.* ◇ ~~She set fire to a candle.~~ Sth is usually **ignited** not by a person but by a *spark* or *flame*: *He was badly injured when a spark ignited the gas.* ◇ ~~He ignited the gas.~~

torch [T] (*rather informal*) to set fire to a building or vehicle deliberately in order to destroy it; to set fire to sb/yourself: *Rioters threw bottles at police and torched a number of cars.*

---

2 light · light (sth) up · illuminate · flood · brighten

These words all mean to provide light to sth or to a place.

PATTERNS AND COLLOCATIONS
▸ to **be** lit / lit up / illuminated / flooded **with** sth
▸ to light / illuminate / flood / brighten a **room**
▸ to light / illuminate the **streets**
▸ the **sky** lights up / brightens
▸ the **sun** lights / lights up / illuminates / floods sth

▸ **sunlight** illuminates / floods sth
▸ to **suddenly** / **briefly** light / light up / illuminate (sth)
▸ to be **well** / **brightly** / **dimly** / **softly** lighted / illuminated

light [T, usually passive] to give light to sth or to a place: *The stage was lit by bright spotlights.* ◇ *Make sure you always park your car in busy, well lit streets.* ❶ In literary English **light** can also mean to guide sb with a light: *Our way was lit by a full moon.*

▸ **lighted** *adj.*: *scenes glimpsed through other people's lighted windows* **OPP** **unlit** → DARK 1

light 'up, light sth 'up *phrasal verb* to become bright with light or colour; to make sth bright with light or colour: *There was an explosion and the whole sky lit up.* ◇ *The night sky was lit up with fireworks.*

illuminate /ɪˈluːmɪneɪt/ [T] (*rather formal*) to shine light on sth: *Floodlights illuminated the stadium.* ◇ *The earth is illuminated by the sun.*

▸ **illuminated** *adj.*: *There is a large garden with an illuminated pond.* ◇ *The doctor examined his x-ray on an illuminated screen.*

flood [I, T] (of light or bright colours) to spread suddenly into sth: *She drew the curtains and the sunlight flooded in.* ◇ *She looked away as the colour flooded her cheeks.* ◇ *The room was flooded with evening light.*

brighten [I, T] to become or make sth lighter or brighter in colour: *The sky was beginning to brighten.* ◇ *This shampoo will brighten and condition your hair.*

---

like *verb* See also the entry for LOVE

like · love · be fond of sth · be keen on sth · adore · go for sb/sth

These words all mean to find sth pleasant, attractive or satisfactory, or to enjoy sth.

like	love	adore

be fond of sth
be keen on sth
go for sb/sth

PATTERNS AND COLLOCATIONS
▸ to like / love / be fond of / be keen on / adore **doing** sth
▸ to like / love **to do** sth
▸ to like / love **very much**
▸ I like / love / adore **it** here / there / when…
▸ to like / love / adore **the way** sb does sth
▸ to **really** like / love / adore / go for sb / sth
▸ to be **really** keen on / keen on sth
▸ to **just** / **simply** / **absolutely** / **clearly** / **obviously** love / adore sth

like [T] (not usually used in the progressive tenses) to find sth pleasant, attractive or satisfactory; to enjoy sth: *Which tie do you like best?* ◇ *How did you like Japan (= did you find it pleasant)?* ◇ *You've got to go to school, whether you like it or not.* ◇ *I didn't like him taking all the credit.* ◇ *I like to see them enjoying themselves.* ◇ *I like it in Spain (= I like the life there).* **OPP** **dislike** → HATE, See also **liking** → TASTE 1

love [T] (not usually used in the progressive tenses) to like or enjoy sth very much: *I just love it when you bring me presents!* ◇ *He loved the way she smiled.* ◇ *My dad loves going to football games.* ◇ (*especially AmE*) *I love to go out dancing.* ◇ (*informal*) *I'm loving every minute of this.* ◇ (*ironic*) *You're going to love this. They've changed their minds again.* **OPP** **hate** → HATE, See also **love** → TASTE 1, **lover** → FAN

be fond of sth *phrase* to like or enjoy sth, especially sth you have liked or enjoyed for a long time: *I'm particularly fond of music.* ◇ *We were fond of the house and didn't want to leave.* See also **fond** → LOVING

be keen on sth *phrase* (*BrE, informal, especially spoken*) (often used in negative statements) to like or enjoy sth: *I'm not keen on spicy food.* ◇ *She's not keen on being told what to do.* ◇ *He's very keen on golf.* See also **keen** → EAGER

adore /əˈdɔːr/ [T] (not used in the progressive tenses) (*informal*) to like or enjoy sth very much: *Don't you just adore that dress!* ◇ *She adores working with children.* **OPP** **loathe** → HATE

> **NOTE** **LOVE** OR **ADORE?** **Adore** is more informal than **love**, and expresses a stronger feeling.

'go for sb/sth *phrasal verb* (not used in the progressive tenses) (*informal*) to be attracted by sb/sth; to like or prefer sb/sth: *She goes for tall slim men.* ◇ *I don't really go for modern art.*

like *prep., adj.*

like · similar · close · alike
These words all describe sb/sth that is almost the same as sb/sth else.

PATTERNS AND COLLOCATIONS
▸ similar / close **to** sb / sth
▸ like sth / similar / close / alike **in** size, amount, etc.
▸ like / similar **age / circumstances / kind / manner**
▸ a like / similar **case / situation**
▸ to **look** like sth / similar / alike
▸ to **feel / sound / taste** like sth / similar
▸ **very / quite** like sth / similar / close / alike
▸ **rather / remarkably / basically** like sth / similar / alike
▸ **exactly** like sth / alike

like *prep.* almost the same as sb/sth else; in the same way as sb/sth: *She's wearing a dress like mine.* ◇ (*especially BrE*) *He's **very like** his father.* ◇ *She looks **nothing like** (= not at all like) her mother.* ◇ *Students were angry at being treated like children.* ◇ *You do it like this.* ◇ *Don't look at me like that.* ❶ In formal language **like** can also be used as an adjective before a noun, meaning 'having similar qualities to another person or thing': (*formal*) *You'll get a chance to meet people of **like mind** (= with similar interests and opinions).* ◇ *She responded in like manner.* **OPP** **unlike** → DIFFERENT, See also **likeness** → SIMILARITY
▸ **like** *noun* [sing.]: *I enjoy jazz, rock **and the like** (= similar types of music).* ◇ *I let the apartment to students, backpackers **and such like**.* ◇ *They experienced a period of expansion **the like of which** the world had rarely seen.* ◇ *You're not **comparing like with like**.*

similar *adj.* like sb/sth but not exactly the same: *We have very similar interests.* ◇ *My teaching style is similar to that of most other teachers.* ◇ *The two houses are similar in size.* ◇ *The brothers look very similar.* ◇ *Stir the paint with a piece of wood or something similar.* **OPP** **different, dissimilar** → DIFFERENT, See also **similarity** → SIMILARITY
▸ **similarly** *adv.*: *Husband and wife were similarly successful in their chosen careers.*

close /kləʊs; *AmE* kloʊs/ very similar to sth else or to an amount: *There's a close resemblance between them (= they look very similar).* ◇ *His feeling for her was close to hatred.* ◇ *We tried to match the colours, but this was the closest we could get.*
▸ **closely** *adv.*: *She closely resembled her mother at the same age.*

alike /əˈlaɪk/ [not before noun] very similar; almost the same: *My sister and I do not look alike.* ◇ *The two towns are very much alike in size and population.* ❶ **Alike** is often used in the phrases *pretty much alike, so (much) alike, very (much) alike* and *look alike*.
▸ **alike** *adv.*: *They tried to treat all their children alike.*

likely *adj.* See also the entry for PRONE TO STH

likely · possible · potential · prospective · probable
These words all describe things that are expected to exist, happen or be true.

| possible | prospective | likely |
| potential | | probable |

→ (arrow)

PATTERNS AND COLLOCATIONS
▸ to be likely / possible / probable **that...**
▸ a likely / possible / potential / prospective / probable **site**
▸ a likely / possible / potential / probable **cause / effect / consequence / outcome**
▸ a likely / possible / probable **explanation**
▸ the likely / possible / potential / probable **cost**
▸ a likely / possible / potential / prospective **candidate**
▸ a potential / prospective **husband / wife / parent**
▸ **quite** likely / possible / probable
▸ **hardly** likely / possible
▸ **very / extremely / highly** likely / probable

likely expected to exist, happen or be true: *What is the most likely cause of the infection?* ◇ *Tickets are **likely to** be expensive.* ◇ *It's **more than likely that** the thieves don't know how much it is worth.* ◇ *They might refuse to let us do it, but it's hardly likely.* **OPP** **unlikely** → UNLIKELY 1, See also **likelihood** → POSSIBILITY, **most likely** → PROBABLY

possible that might exist, happen or be true, but is not certain to: *They spoke of her as a possible future president.* ◇ *With the possible exception of the Beatles, no other band has become so successful so quickly.* ◇ *It's just possible that I gave them the wrong directions.* ◇ *'You might be wrong, of course!' 'It's possible, but I doubt it.'* **OPP** **impossible** → IMPOSSIBLE, See also **possibility** → POSSIBILITY

potential /pəˈtenʃl/ [only before noun] expected to develop into sth or to be developed in the future: *First we need to identify actual and potential problems.* ◇ *What are the potential benefits of these proposals?* ❶ **Potential** is used in several main ways: to talk about people who might buy a product or use a service: *a potential audience/buyer/client/consumer/customer*; to talk about things that might happen: *a potential complication/danger/disaster/drawback/embarrassment/hazard/pitfall/risk/threat*; and to talk about things that people might gain from: *a potential advantage/benefit/improvement/saving* **OPP** **actual** → REAL, See also **potential** → POTENTIAL *noun*
▸ **potentially** *adv.*: *a potentially dangerous situation*

prospective /prəˈspektɪv/ [only before noun] (*rather formal*) expected to do or become sth: *I had a phone call from a prospective client today.* ❶ **Prospective** is mainly used to talk about people: *a prospective buyer/client/customer/applicant/candidate/employee/employer/husband/wife/parent* See also **prospect** → POSSIBILITY, **prospects** → POTENTIAL

> **NOTE** **POTENTIAL** OR **PROSPECTIVE?** Both these words can be used to talk about people who are expected to become buyers, employees, etc. However, **prospective** is used more to talk about a person who has already shown some interest in a product or service; **potential** is used more to talk about people in general who could be targeted by a company's advertising, for example.

probable (*rather formal, especially written*) likely: *The probable cause of the fire was an electrical fault.* ◇ *It is quite probable that they will call an election next spring.* **OPP** **improbable** → UNLIKELY 1, See also **probability** → POSSIBILITY, **probably** → PROBABLY

> **NOTE** **LIKELY** OR **PROBABLE?** **Likely** can be used in a wider range of structures and registers than **probable**: *It is likely/probable that...* ◇ *sb/sth is likely to do sth* ◇ ~~sb/sth is probable to do sth~~. **Probable** is ten times more frequent in written English than in spoken English; **likely** is very frequent in both written and spoken English.

limit noun

1 a speed/time/age limit
2 a limit to what we can do

---

1 limit · restriction · control · constraint · restraint · limitation · ceiling · curb · check

These are all words for sth that limits what you can do or what can happen.

PATTERNS AND COLLOCATIONS

▶ limits/restrictions/controls/constraints/restraints/limitations/ a ceiling/ curbs/ checks **on** sth
▶ limits/ limitations/ checks **to** sth
▶ **without** limits/ restrictions/ controls/ constraints/ restraints/ limitations/ checks
▶ **severe** limits/ restrictions/ controls/ constraints/ restraints/ limitations/ checks
▶ **tight** limits/ restrictions/ controls/ constraints
▶ **effective** limits/ restrictions/ controls/ constraints/ restraints
▶ an **artificial** limit/ restriction/ constraint
▶ to **impose** limits/ restrictions/ controls/ constraints/ restraints/ limitations/ a ceiling/ curbs/ checks
▶ to **place** limits/ restrictions/ controls/ constraints/ restraints/ limitations/ a ceiling/ checks
▶ to **introduce** limits/ restrictions/ controls/ constraints/ limitations/ curbs/ checks
▶ to **remove/ accept** limits/ restrictions/ controls/ constraints/ restraints/ limitations
▶ to **lift** restrictions/ controls/ constraints/ restraints/ the ceiling
▶ to **tighten/ relax** restrictions/ controls/ constraints
▶ to **act as** a control/ constraint/ restraint/ limitation/ ceiling/ curb/ check

limit [C] the greatest or smallest amount of sth that is allowed: *The EU has set strict limits on pollution levels.* ◇ *He admitted that he had broken the speed limit.* ◇ *You can't drive – you're* **over the limit** (= you have drunk more alcohol than is legal when driving). ◇ *It is our job to keep government spending within acceptable limits.* See also **limit** → CONFINE SB/STH TO STH *phrasal verb*

restriction [C] (*rather formal*) a rule or law that limits what you can do: *Speed restrictions are in operation on the M4 due to poor visibility.* ◇ *The government has agreed to lift restrictions on press freedom.* ◇ *There are no restrictions on the amount of money you can withdraw.* See also **restrict** → CONFINE SB/STH TO STH *phrasal verb*

control [U, C] (often in compounds) the act of limiting or managing sth; a method of doing this: *traffic control* ◇ *talks on arms control* ◇ *A new advance has been made in the control of malaria.* ◇ *government controls on trade and industry* ◇ *Price controls on food were ended.* ◇ *A pest control officer was called in to deal with the rat problem.*

constraint [C] (*rather formal*) a fact or decision that limits what you can do: *We have to work within severe constraints of time and money.* ◇ *This decision will impose serious financial constraints on all schools.* See also **constrain** → CONFINE SB/STH TO STH *phrasal verb*

restraint [C, usually pl., U] (*rather formal*) a decision, rule, idea, etc. that limits what you can do; the act of limiting sth because it is necessary or sensible to do so: *The government has imposed export restraints on some products.* ◇ *There are certain social restraints on drinking alcohol.* ◇ *The unions are unlikely to accept any sort of wage restraint.* ◇ *They said that they would fight without restraint* (= completely freely) *for what they wanted.*

limitation [U, C] the act or process of limiting sth; a rule, fact or condition that limits sth: *They would resist any limitation of their powers.* ◇ *Disability is a physical limitation on your life.* ◇ *There should be no limitations to progress in the talks.*

> **NOTE** RESTRICTION, CONSTRAINT, RESTRAINT OR LIMITATION? These are all things that limit what you can do. A **restriction** is rule or law that is made by sb in authority. A **constraint** is sth that exists rather than sth that is made, although it may exist as a result of sb's decision. A **restraint** is also sth that exists: it can exist outside

yourself, as the result of sb else's decision; but it can also exist inside you, as a fear of what other people may think or as your own feeling about what is acceptable: *moral/social/cultural/conventional restraints.* A **limitation** is more general and can be a rule that sb makes or a fact or condition that exists.

ceiling [C] the highest limit on sth such as prices or wages: *They have put a ceiling on the price of fuel.* ◇ *The government has decided to lift price ceilings on bread and milk.*

curb /kɜːb; *AmE* kɜːrb/ [C] a rule or action that limits the level, amount or degree of sth: *We are in favour of strict curbs on government spending.* ◇ *Counselling acted as a curb on his violent behaviour.*

check [C] (*rather formal*) something that slows down the progress of sth else or stops it from getting worse: *A cold spring will provide a natural check on the number of insects.* ◇ *The House of Commons became the most fundamental check to the power of the British monarchy.*

---

2 limit · line · boundary · parameter · bounds · frontier · confines · borderline

These are all words for the edge of an area of thought, behaviour or possibility, or the division between one area of thought, etc. and another.

PATTERNS AND COLLOCATIONS

▶ the line/ boundary/ borderline **between** sth and sth else
▶ **beyond** the limits/ boundaries/ parameters/ bounds/ frontiers/ confines of sth
▶ **within** the limits/ boundaries/ parameters/ bounds/ confines of sth
▶ **outside** the limits/ parameters/ bounds/ confines of sth
▶ **at** the limits/ boundaries/ frontiers/ borderline of sth
▶ **on** the boundary/ borderline between/ of sth
▶ to **extend** the limits/ boundaries/ parameters/ bounds/ frontiers of sth
▶ to **set/ define/ establish** the limits/ boundaries/ parameters/ bounds of sth
▶ to **cross** the boundary/ borderline between/ of sth

limit [C] the point at which sth stops being possible or existing: *There is* **a limit to** *the amount of pain we can bear.* ◇ *There is* **no limit to** *what we can achieve.* ◇ *Our finances have been stretched* **to the limit.** ◇ *She pushed me* **to the limit of** *my abilities.* ◇ *She knew the limits of her power.*

line [C] the division between one area of thought or behaviour and another: *We want to cut across lines of race, sex and religion.* ◇ *There is a* **fine line** *between showing interest in what someone is doing and interfering in it.* ◇ *There is no clear* **dividing line** *between what is good and what is bad.*

boundary /ˈbaʊndri/ [C] something that marks the limits or edges of one area of thought or behaviour and/or separates it from another: *It is up to the teacher to set the boundary between acceptable and unacceptable behaviour.* ◇ *Scientists continue to push back the boundaries of human knowledge.*

> **NOTE** LINE OR BOUNDARY? A **line** between two areas of thought or behaviour is sth that exists and often needs to be judged carefully. A **boundary** does not just exist: it has to be decided by sb: *no clear dividing boundary* ◇ *a fine boundary between* ◇ *It is up to the teacher to set the line...* **Boundary** often directs your attention to what lies within the boundaries, which mark the edge of what you are considering: you can *push back/extend the boundaries of sth* but NOT: *push/back extend the lines*

parameter /pəˈræmɪtə(r)/ [C, usually pl.] (*formal*) something that marks the limits of what you are considering or how sth can be done: *We need to define the parameters of this debate.* ◇ *We had to work within the parameters that had already been established.*

bounds /baʊndz/ [pl.] (*rather formal*) the accepted or furthest limits of sth: *Public spending must be kept within reasonable bounds.* ◊ *It was not **beyond the bounds of possibility** that they would meet again one day.* ◊ *His enthusiasm **knew no bounds** (= was very great).*

frontier /ˈfrʌntɪə(r); AmE frʌnˈtɪr/ [C, usually pl.] the limits of what is known about sth or what sb/sth can do: *This research programme aims to push back the frontiers of science.*

confines /ˈkɒnfaɪnz; AmE ˈkɑːn-/ [pl.] (*formal*) a limited amount of space within walls or other barriers; the limits of what is known, allowed or possible in a situation: *He spent three years within the narrow confines of the prison.* ◊ *She wanted to experience things outside the close confines of family life.* See also **confine sb/sth to sth** → CONFINE SB/STH TO STH

> **NOTE** **FRONTIERS** OR **CONFINES**? Confines emphasizes how little space, knowledge etc. there is; **frontiers** emphasizes how much knowledge there is and how it is increasing.

borderline [C] the division between two qualities or conditions: *The biography sometimes crosses the borderline between fact and fiction.* See also **borderline** → VAGUE *adj.*

---

limit *verb* See also the entry for CONFINE SB/STH TO STH

---

limit · control · restrict · curb · contain · check · cap · rein sth in · suppress · hold/keep sth in check
These words all mean to stop sth increasing beyond a particular amount or level, from spreading or from getting worse.

PATTERNS AND COLLOCATIONS
▸ to be limited / restricted **to** sth
▸ to limit / control / restrict / curb / check / cap / rein in **spending**
▸ to limit / control / restrict / curb / check **growth**
▸ to limit / control / curb / contain / check **inflation**
▸ to keep **spending / inflation / growth** in check
▸ to limit / control / restrict / curb / cap **expenditure**
▸ to limit / control / curb / contain / check the **spread** of sth
▸ to limit / control / check the **expansion** of sth
▸ to limit / control / restrict the **size / number / extent / amount** of sth
▸ to limit / control / restrict / curb / check your **speed**
▸ to **drastically / greatly / severely** limit / restrict / curb sth

limit [T] to stop sth increasing beyond a particular amount or level: *Calorie intake is **strictly limited** to 1 000 a day.* ◊ *The amount of money you have to spend will limit your choice.* ◊ *They introduced measures to limit carbon dioxide emissions from cars.* ◊ *There is no evidence that the restrictions have limited the effectiveness of the advertising.*

control (-ll-) [T] to limit sth or make it happen in a particular way: *The government has announced new measures to control immigration.* ◊ *Many biological processes are controlled by hormones.* ◊ *Parents should control what their kids watch on television.*

restrict [T] to limit the size, amount or range of sth: *We restrict the number of students per class to ten.* ◊ *They tried to control traffic congestion by restricting entry to the city.* ◊ *Fog severely restricted visibility.* ◊ *There have been several attempts to restrict the sale of alcohol.*

> **NOTE** **LIMIT** OR **RESTRICT**? In many cases you can use either word; however, **restrict** is used more often to talk about limiting what people can do; **limit** is used both for limiting what people can do and for controlling the effects of sth: *to restrict carbon dioxide emissions from cars* ◊ *to restrict the effectiveness of advertising*

curb [T] to control or limit sth, especially sth bad: *A range of policies have been introduced aimed at curbing inflation.* ◊ *This legislation will greatly curb the power of local authorities.*

contain [T] (*written*) to stop sth harmful from spreading or getting worse: *Far more could have been done to contain the epidemic.* ◊ *He introduced repressive measures to contain the violence.*

check [T] to stop sth bad from continuing: *The government is determined to check the growth of public spending.* ◊ *She tied some strips of cloth around the wound to check the bleeding.*

> **NOTE** **CURB**, **CONTAIN** OR **CHECK**? To **contain** a problem is to stop it from getting worse or spreading over a larger area, but without actually getting rid of it from the areas where it already exists; to **curb** sth is to reduce it to a lower level; to **check** sth is to stop it altogether.

cap (-pp-) [T, usually passive] (*especially BrE*) to limit the amount of money that can be charged for sth or spent on sth: *We will continue to cap local government spending where necessary.* ◊ *The total annual fee is **capped at** 1.5 per cent.*

‚rein sth ˈin to start to control sth strictly, especially after it has been increasing too quickly: *This is part of a battle to rein in public spending on health.* ◊ *If the situation continues, she may not be able to rein in the military much longer.*

suppress /səˈpres/ [T] (*written*) to stop sth from growing, developing or continuing, especially a natural process or function: *Slimming drugs do help to suppress appetite.* ◊ *A 5 cm layer will suppress weed growth.* **OPP** stimulate → STIMULATE

hold/keep sth in ˈcheck *idiom* to control sth that could be a problem, so that it does not spread or get worse: *They want interest rates kept in check.* ◊ *We need to keep the rabbit population in check.*

---

limited *adj.*
1 limited resources
2 This offer is for a limited period only.

---

1 See also the entry for SCARCE

limited · narrow · restricted
These words all describe sth that is not very great in amount or extent.

PATTERNS AND COLLOCATIONS
▸ limited / narrow / restricted **in** scope
▸ a limited / narrow / restricted **range / scope / vocabulary**
▸ a limited / narrow **objective**
▸ limited / narrow **horizons**
▸ the limited / narrow **confines** of sth
▸ a limited / restricted **franchise**

limited not very great in amount or extent: *We are doing our best with the limited resources available.* ◊ *This animal's intelligence is very limited.* ◊ *These are issues that go beyond the limited confines of this book.* ❶ **Limited** is used especially to talk about how much of sth is available, or sb/sth's ability to do sth: *limited resources/funds/supplies* ◊ *a limited ability/capability/capacity/intelligence/intellect/knowledge/understanding* **OPP** unlimited ❶ Things are **unlimited** when you can have as much or as many of sth as you like: *The ticket gives you unlimited travel for seven days.* ◊ *You will be allowed unlimited access to the files.*

narrow (*usually disapproving*) limited in variety or numbers; limited in a way that ignores important issues or the opinions of other people: *She only has a narrow circle of friends.* ◊ *The exhibition is disappointingly narrow in scope.* ◊ *She has a very narrow view of the world.* **OPP** wide, broad → WIDE 1

restricted limited in amount or variety: *There is only a restricted range of goods available.* ◊ *He has a severely restricted diet.*

2 limited · restricted · controlled

These words all describe sth which is or must stay within a particular limit which has been set, often as part of a rule or law.

PATTERNS AND COLLOCATIONS
- to be limited / restricted **to** sth
- limited / restricted / controlled **access**
- **highly** / **tightly** restricted / controlled
- **strictly** limited / controlled

limited within, or only allowed within, a particular limit of numbers, time, etc., so that, for example only a particular number of people are able to do sth or it can only be done for a particular period of time: *The number of passengers is limited to fifteen.* ◇ *This offer is for a limited period only.* ◇ *Places are strictly limited, so you should apply as soon as possible.*

restricted only able to do sth within particular limits; controlled by rules or laws, especially ones that allow only a particular group to do or have sth: *In those days women led fairly restricted lives.* ◇ *They are closely guarded and severely restricted in their movements.* ◇ *The tournament is restricted to players under the age of 23.*

controlled managed by, or within the limits of, a law or rule: *In many countries the production of the drug is illegal or tightly controlled.* ◇ *He was charged with possessing a controlled drug.*

link *verb*

1 The two factors are directly linked.
2 The cameras are linked to a computer.

1 link · connect · couple sth with sth

These are all words that can be used when there is a connection between people or things.

PATTERNS AND COLLOCATIONS
- to be linked / connected / coupled **with** sb / sth
- to be **closely** / **intimately** / **directly** / **inextricably** / **obviously** / **necessarily** / **loosely** / **somehow** / **in some way** linked / connected

link [T, usually passive] if two things **are linked**, there is a relationship between them in which one causes the other, or each depends on the other: *Exposure to ultraviolet light is closely linked to skin cancer.* ◇ *The two factors are directly linked.* ◇ *The personal and social development of the child are inextricably linked.* See also **link** → RELATION *noun*

connect [T, usually passive] (*rather formal*) if two people or things **are connected**, there is a relationship between them, usually because they in the same family, group or subject area: *They are connected by marriage.* ◇ *The two subjects are closely connected.* ◇ *I've been applying for jobs connected with the environment.* See also **connection** → RELATION

> **NOTE** **LINK** OR **CONNECT**? In some cases you can use either word: *The two factors are directly linked/ connected.* However, **link** is often used when the connection between two things is stronger, because one causes the other, or the two depend on each other, in a way that makes it impossible to separate them: *to be indissolubly/inescapably/inevitably/inexorably/inextricably/inseparably linked.* **Connect** is often used when the connection is looser, and really means that the two things belong to the same general area. People can be **connected** with each other, but not linked: *~~They are linked by marriage.~~*

'couple sth with sth *phrasal verb* [usually passive] to combine sth with sth else, producing a particular result: *Overproduction, coupled with falling sales, has led to huge losses for the company.*

2 link · connect · join

These words all mean to make a physical or electronic connection between two or more things.

PATTERNS AND COLLOCATIONS
- to link / connect / join sth **to** sth
- to link / connect sth **with** sth
- to link / connect / join A **and** B
- to link / join A **and** B **together**
- to link / join (sth) **up**
- to connect / join **pieces**
- to link / connect **cities** / **rooms**
- to link / connect / join sth **to a computer**
- to be linked / connected / joined **by a line**
- **directly** linked / connected

link [T, often passive] to make a physical or electronic connection between one object, machine or place and another: *The computers are **linked into** the network.* ◇ *The tunnel links Britain with the rest of Europe.*

connect [T, I] to make a connection, usually a permanent one, between two or more places or things; to have a connection to sth: *The towns are connected by train and bus services.* ◇ *The canal was built to connect the city with the port.* ◇ *There is a **connecting door** between the two bedrooms.* ◇ *The two bedrooms connect.*

join [T, I] to fix or connect two or more things together, often things that have been specially made to fit together; to be fixed together or connected: *Join the two sections of pipe together.* ◇ *The island is joined to the mainland by a bridge.* ◇ *Draw a line joining (up) the dots.* ◇ *How do these two pieces join?* See also **join** → CONNECTION

list *noun*

list · index · table · catalogue · directory · register · inventory · roll · checklist · listing

These are all words for a series of names, items or figures, especially when they are written or printed one after the other.

PATTERNS AND COLLOCATIONS
- **in** a list / an index / a table / a catalogue / a directory / a register / an inventory / a listing
- **on** a list / a register / an inventory / a roll / a checklist
- a **comprehensive** / **complete** / **full** list / index / table / catalogue / register / inventory / listing
- a **detailed** list / index / catalogue / directory / register / inventory / listing
- an **alphabetical** list / index / catalogue / directory / listing
- to **compile** a list / an index / a table / a directory / a register / an inventory / a checklist
- to **draw up** a list / a table / a catalogue / a register / an inventory / a checklist
- to **create** a list / an index / a table / a directory / a register / an inventory
- to **produce** a list / a table / a catalogue / a directory / an inventory / a checklist / a listing
- to **keep** a list / an index / a register / an inventory
- to **list sth in** an index / a table / a catalogue / the directory / an inventory
- to **include sth in** a list / a table / a catalogue / an inventory / a checklist / a listing
- to **consult** / **look (sth up) in** an index / a table / a catalogue / a directory
- an index / a table / a catalogue / a directory / an inventory **lists** sth

list [C] a series of names, items or figures, especially when they are written or printed one after the other: *Is your name on the list?* ◇ *Make a list of all the places you've visited.* ◇ *This issue is pretty low on their list of priorities.* ◇ *What's on your shopping list?* ◇ *There's a long waiting list to get treatment.* ◇ *Do you want to be put on our mailing list?* ◇ *Over 200 people are on our guest list.* ◇ *Her name was at the top of the list.*

index [C] a list of names or topics that are referred to in a book, usually arranged at the end of the book in alphabetical order or listed in a separate file or book: *Look it up in the index.* ◇ *It's a general index to the whole work.*

▸ **index** verb [T, usually passive]: *The reports are indexed by subject and name.* ◇ *The article was indexed under 'Parliament' and 'Law'.*

table [C] a list of facts or numbers arranged in a special order, usually in rows and columns: *a table of contents* (= a list of the main points or information in a book, usually at the front of the book) ◇ *Table 2 shows how prices and earnings have increased over the last 20 years.* See also **chart** → DIAGRAM

catalogue (*AmE* also **catalog**) /ˈkætəlɒg; *AmE* -lɔːg; -lɑːg/ [C] a complete list of items, for example of things that you can look at or buy: *She consulted the museum catalogue.* ◇ *Please take a look at our online catalogue.* ◇ *a mail-order catalogue*

▸ **catalogue** (*AmE* also **catalog**) verb [T]: *She painstakingly catalogued all the photographs in the museum.* ◇ *The collection had never been properly catalogued.*

directory /dəˈrektəri; dɪ-; daɪ-/ [C] a book containing lists of information, usually in alphabetical order, for example people's phone numbers or the names and addresses of businesses in a particular area: *You can get some useful contacts from a trade directory.* ◇ (*formal*) *They are listed in the **telephone directory**.* ❶ In everyday spoken English this is usually called the **phone book**.

register /ˈredʒɪstə(r)/ [C] an official list or record of names or items; a book that contains such a list: *Could you sign the hotel register please?* ◇ (*BrE*) *The teacher called the register* (= checked that all the students on a class register were present by calling out their names). ❶ In American English this is called the **roll**. See also **register** → RECORD verb 1

inventory /ˈɪnvəntri; *AmE* -tɔːri/ [C] a written list of all the furniture and other items in a particular building: *She compiled an inventory of all the museum's contents.*

roll [C] an official list of names: *You can check that you are on the **electoral roll** by calling this number.* ◇ *Who would appear on your personal **roll of honour** (= a list of people who you think deserve special praise)?* ◇ (*AmE*) *The teacher **called the roll*** (= checked that all the students on a class register were present by calling out their names). ❶ In British English this is called the **register**. ❶ The **payroll** is a list of people employed by a company showing the amount of money to be paid to each of them: *We have 500 people on the payroll.*

checklist /ˈtʃeklɪst/ [C] a list of the things that you must remember to do, to take with you or to find out: *She ticked off the items on the checklist.* ◇ *I ran through my mental checklist of items.*

listing [C] a list, especially an official or published list of people or things, often arranged in alphabetical order: *The agency provides a comprehensive listing of all airlines.*

list verb

list · define · specify · detail · state · name · itemize
These words all mean to present things in a list or in a particular order.

PATTERNS AND COLLOCATIONS
▸ to list / define / specify / detail / state / name / itemize sth **as** sth
▸ to list / define / specify / detail / state / name / itemize sth **in** sth
▸ to list / define / specify / detail / itemize sth **under** sth
▸ to define / specify / detail / state **what / how / where / who…**
▸ to specify / state **that…**
▸ to list / define / specify / detail **tasks**
▸ to list / specify / state / itemize **details**
▸ to list / define / specify / detail / name / enumerate **items**
▸ to **fully / carefully** list / define / specify / detail / itemize sth
▸ to **clearly** define / specify / state sth
▸ to list / define / specify / itemize sth **separately**

list [T] to write the names of things in a particular order; to include sth in a list: *We were asked to list our ten*

favourite songs. ◇ *Towns in the guide are listed alphabetically.* ◇ *Articles may be listed under more than one heading.* ◇ *The names are **listed below**.*

define [T] to describe or show sth accurately: *We need to define the task ahead very clearly.* ◇ *The difficulty of a problem was **defined in terms of** how long it took to complete.* ◇ *It is difficult to define what makes him so popular.* See also **definition** → DEFINITION

specify /ˈspesɪfaɪ/ [T] (*rather formal*) to give exact details of sth such as a measurement, time or instructions: *Forms must be returned by the specified date.* ◇ *The contract clearly specifies who can operate the machinery.* ◇ *The regulations specify that calculators may not be used in the examination.*

▸ **specification** /ˌspesɪfɪˈkeɪʃn/ noun [C, U]: *the technical specifications of the new model* (= of car) ◇ *The house has been built exactly **to our specification**.*

detail [T] to give a list of facts or all the available information about sth: *The brochure details all the hotels in the area and their facilities.* See also **detail** → INFORMATION noun

state [T, usually passive] to fix or announce the details of sth, especially on a written document: *This is not one of their stated aims.* ◇ *You must arrive at the time stated.*

name [T] to specify sth exactly: *Name your price.* ◇ *They're engaged, but they haven't yet named the day* (= fixed a date for the wedding). ◇ *Activities available include squash, archery and swimming, **to name but a few**.* ◇ *Chairs, tables, cabinets — **you name it**, she makes it* (= she makes anything you can imagine). ❶ **Name** is less formal than **specify**, but it is mostly used in a few fixed phrases.

itemize (*BrE* also **-ise**) /ˈaɪtəmaɪz/ [T] to produce a detailed list of things: *The report itemized over 25 different faults.* ◇ *You can ask for an itemized phone bill* (= one which gives details of each call).

literature noun

literature · text · writing
These are all words for the written material that is contained in books.

PATTERNS AND COLLOCATIONS
▸ literature / writing **on** sth
▸ **publish** literature / text / writing
▸ **feminist / scientific / English** literature / writing
▸ to **read** literature / text
▸ a **piece of** literature / text / writing

literature [U] pieces of writing that are valued as works of art, especially novels, plays and poems (in contrast to technical books and newspapers, magazines, etc.); pieces of writing or printed information on a particular subject: *Milton's 'Paradise Lost' is one of the great **works of literature**.* ◇ *sales/promotional literature* ◇ *I've read all the available literature on keeping parrots.*

text [U] the main printed part of a book or magazine, not the notes, pictures, etc; any form of written material: *My job is to lay out the text and graphics on the page.* ◇ *Highlight the area of text on screen and press the 'delete' key.* See also **text** → BOOK, **text** → SCRIPT

writing [U] books, articles or sth that has been written or printed; words that have been written or painted on sth: *The class takes a student-centred approach to **creative writing**.* ◇ *There was writing all over the desk.* See also **writings** → WORK noun 4, **write** → WRITE 2

live verb

live · inhabit · occupy · reside · people
These words all mean to have your home in a particular place.

PATTERNS AND COLLOCATIONS

▶ to live / reside **in** / **among** / **near** sth
▶ to live in / inhabit / occupy / reside in a **house**
▶ to live in / inhabit / occupy a **building**
▶ to live in / inhabit / people the **world**
▶ to live in / inhabit in a **region**

live [I] (always used with an adverb or preposition) to have your home in a particular place: *I live in an old farmhouse.* ◇ *We used to live in London.* ◇ *Where do you live?* ◇ *She needs to find somewhere to live.*

inhabit /ɪnˈhæbɪt/ [T] to live in a particular place or type of place, especially an area or region: *Some of the rare species that inhabit the area are under threat.* ◇ *The island used to be inhabited* (= have people living there). See also **inhabitant** → RESIDENT

occupy /ˈɒkjupaɪ; AmE ˈɑːk-/ [T] (*formal*) to use a room or building for the purpose of living or working: *He occupies an office on the 51st floor.* See also **occupant** → TENANT

reside /rɪˈzaɪd/ [I] (always used with an adverb or preposition) (*formal*) to live in a particular place: *Do you still reside at 56 Elm Road?* ◇ *Their passports do not give them the right to reside in the United Kingdom.* See also **residence** → HOME 1, **resident** → RESIDENT

people [T, usually passive] (*written*) to live in a place or environment or fill it with people: *The town was peopled largely by workers from the car factory and their families.* ◇ *Her novels are peopled with interesting, complex characters.*

lively *adj.* See also the entry for ENERGETIC

lively · spirited · exuberant · hearty · ebullient · animated · vivacious · bubbly
These words all describe sb who is full of energy.

PATTERNS AND COLLOCATIONS

▶ a lively / an exuberant / an ebullient / a vivacious / a bubbly **personality**
▶ a lively / spirited / vivacious **young woman**
▶ a lively / vivacious / bubbly **girl**
▶ a lively / an exuberant / an ebullient **mood**
▶ a lively / a spirited / an exuberant **performance**

lively (*approving*) full of life and energy; active and enthusiastic: *She's an intelligent and lively young woman.* ◇ *He showed a lively interest in politics.* ◇ *Her eyes were bright and lively.* See also **life** → ENERGY 2
▶ **liveliness** *noun* [U]: *Her liveliness and wit impressed him.*

spirited [usually before noun] (*approving*) full of energy, determination or courage: *She was an attractive and spirited young woman.* ◇ *He put up a spirited defence in the final game.* See also **spirit** → DETERMINATION

exuberant /ɪɡˈzjuːbərənt; AmE -ˈzuː-/ (*especially written*) full of energy, excitement and happiness: *A noisy bunch of exuberant youngsters were gathered outside.* ◇ *She gave an exuberant performance.*
▶ **exuberance** *noun*: *Nothing will curb his natural exuberance.*

hearty (*sometimes disapproving*) loud, cheerful and full of energy: *'I'll do it!' he said in a hearty voice.* ◇ *Her laugh was far too hearty to be genuine.*

ebullient /ɪˈbʌliənt; -ˈbʊl-/ (*written*) full of confidence, energy and good humour: *The Prime Minister was in ebullient mood.* ◇ *The ebullient Mr Clarke was not to be discouraged.*
▶ **ebullience** *noun* [U]: *I put her remarks down to youthful ebullience.*

animated /ˈænɪmeɪtɪd/ (*especially of the way sb looks or speaks*) full of interest and energy: *Her face suddenly became animated.* ◇ *Sounds of animated conversation and laughter came from the next room.* **OPP impassive** → BLANK
▶ **animation** *noun* [U]: *His face was drained of all colour and animation.*

vivacious /vɪˈveɪʃəs; AmE vaɪˈv-/ (*approving*) (especially of a woman) having a lively, attractive personality: *He had three pretty, vivacious daughters.*
▶ **vivacity** /vɪˈvæsəti; AmE vaɪˈv-/ *noun* [U]: *He was charmed by her beauty and vivacity.*

bubbly (*rather informal, approving*) (especially of a girl or woman) having a cheerful, friendly and enthusiastic personality: *Anna has a bright, bubbly personality.*

loan *noun*

loan · credit · mortgage · advance · overdraft
These are all words for money that a person or an organization such as a bank lends sb.

PATTERNS AND COLLOCATIONS

▶ a loan / credit / a mortgage / an advance / an overdraft **from** sb / an organization
▶ a mortgage / an advance **on** sth
▶ a **large** / **huge** loan / mortgage / advance / overdraft
▶ (a) **low-interest** loan / credit / mortgage / overdraft
▶ (a) **cheap** loan / credit / mortgage
▶ (an) **interest-free** loan / credit / overdraft
▶ a **temporary** loan / mortgage / overdraft
▶ (a) **bank** loan / credit / mortgage / overdraft
▶ to **have** a loan / a mortgage / an advance / an overdraft
▶ to **get** a loan / credit / a mortgage / an advance
▶ to **obtain** / **arrange** / **apply for** / **refuse** sb / **deny** sb (a) loan / credit / a mortgage
▶ to **take out** / **request** / **pay off** / **repay** a loan / mortgage

loan [C] money that an organization such as a bank lends to sb: *I'm going to have to take out a bank loan* (= to borrow money from a bank) *to pay for the car.* ◇ *It took three years to repay my student loan* (= money lent to a student). ◇ *He ran up massive debts borrowing from loan sharks* (= people who lend money at very high rates of interest). See also **loan** → LEND *verb*

credit /ˈkredɪt/ [U] an arrangement that you make, for example with a shop, to pay later for sth you buy; money that a bank lends to you: *We bought the dishwasher on credit.* ◇ *We offer two months' interest-free credit.* ◇ *Your credit limit is now £2 000.* ◇ *The bank refused further credit to the company.* See also **debit** → DEBT

NOTE LOAN OR CREDIT? A **loan** is a particular official agreement to borrow an amount of money and pay it back later; **credit** is a general term for any money that a bank makes available to a customer, when that customer does not already have that amount in their own account.

mortgage /ˈmɔːɡɪdʒ; AmE ˈmɔːrɡ-/ [C] a legal agreement by which a bank or similar organization lends you money to buy a house or other property, and you pay the money back over a particular number of years; the sum of money that you borrow: *Do you have a mortage on this house?* ◇ *Fortunately we've already paid off our mortgage.* ◇ *Mortgage rates* (= of interest) *are up again this month.*
▶ **mortgage** *verb* [T]: *He had to mortgage his house to pay his legal costs.*

advance [C, usually sing.] money paid for work before it has been done or money paid earlier than expected: *They offered an advance of £5 000 after the signing of the contract.* ◇ *She asked for an advance on her salary.* See also **advance** → LEND

overdraft [C] /ˈəʊvədrɑːft; AmE ˈoʊvərdræft/ the amount of money that you owe to a bank when you have spent more money than is in your bank account; an arrangement that allows you to do this: *She had run up an overdraft of £3 000.* ◇ *I had to arrange an overdraft to pay for the car.*
▶ **overdraw** *verb* [T]: (*especially BrE*) *Customers who overdraw their accounts will be charged a fee.*
▶ **overdrawn** *adj.*: *I'm overdrawn by £100.* ◇ *Your account is £200 overdrawn.*

logic *noun* See also the entry for REASONING

logic · rationality · reason
These are all words for a way of thinking about or explaining sth that is based on logical thought rather than on emotions.

PATTERNS AND COLLOCATIONS
▸ the **logic** / rationality / reason **in** sth
▸ **strict** logic / rationality
▸ **commercial** / **economic** / **scientific** logic / rationality
▸ to **see** (the) logic / reason
▸ to **defy** logic / reason
▸ a **lack** of logic / rationality / reason

logic /'lɒdʒɪk; *AmE* 'lɑːdʒɪk/ [U, sing.] a way of thinking about or explaining sth; sensible reasons for doing sth: *I fail to see the* **logic behind** *his argument.* ◇ *There is a compelling* **logic to** *her main theory.* See also **logical** → RATIONAL

rationality /ˌræʃə'næləti/ [U] (*rather formal*) a way of thinking or behaving that is based on logical thought rather than on emotions and feelings: *The concept of scientific rationality is crucial to modern thinking.* See also **rational** → RATIONAL

reason [U] a way of thinking that is sensible and logical: *I can't get her to* **listen to reason**. ◇ *I'm willing to do anything –* **within reason** *– to get my case heard.* ◇ *It* **stands to reason** (= any sensible person would agree) *that people leave if you don't pay them enough.* See also **reasonable** → REASONABLE

logo *noun*

logo · trademark · arms · seal · emblem · stamp · colours · insignia · crest
These are all words for a name, design or symbol that an organization or other group uses as its special sign.

PATTERNS AND COLLOCATIONS
▸ the **royal** arms / seal / emblem / colours / insignia / crest
▸ an **official** seal / stamp
▸ to **bear** / **carry** a logo / the arms / a seal / an emblem / a stamp / the colours / an insignia / a crest
▸ to **display** a logo / the arms / an emblem / the colours / a crest
▸ to **feature** a logo / the arms / an emblem / a crest

logo /'ləʊgəʊ; *AmE* 'loʊgoʊ/ (pl. **-os**) [C] a printed design or symbol that a company or organization uses as its special sign: *All over the world there are red and white paper cups bearing the company logo.*

trademark /'treɪdmɑːk; *AmE* -mɑːrk/ (*abbr.* **TM**) [C] a name or design that a company uses for its products and that cannot be used by anyone else: '*Big Mac' is McDonalds' best-known trademark.*

arms [pl.] (also **coat of 'arms** [C]) (pl. **arms, coats of arms**) a design or shield that is a special symbol of a family, city or other organization: *The royal arms appear on the door of the Queen's carriage.*

seal [C] an official design or mark, stamped on a document to show that it is genuine and carries the authority of a particular person or organization: *The letter bore the president's seal.*

emblem /'embləm/ [C] a design or picture that represents a country or organization; sth that represents a perfect example or a principle: *America's national emblem, the bald eagle* ◇ *The dove is an emblem of peace.*

stamp [C] a design or words made by stamping sth onto a surface: *The passports, with the visa stamps, were waiting at the embassy.*

NOTE STAMP OR SEAL? **Stamp** is a more general word than **seal**. A **stamp** may show any kind of information, such as a date, a few words or a symbol. A **seal** is more official, and is likely to appear on legal documents. Both

words can be used figuratively to show that sth has been approved: (*figurative*) *The project has the government's seal/stamp of approval.*

colours (*BrE*) (*AmE* **colors**) [pl.] (*especially BrE*) a flag, badge, etc. that represents a team, country, ship, etc: *Most buildings had a flagpole with the national colours flying.*

insignia /ɪn'sɪgniə/ [U+sing./pl. *v.*] the symbol, badge or sign that shows sb's rank or that they are a member of a group or organization: *His uniform bore the insignia of a captain.*

crest [C] a design used as the symbol of a particular family or organization, especially one that has a long history: *The family crest consists of a crown and an eight-pointed star.*

NOTE ARMS, EMBLEM OR CREST? A **coat of arms** is found on a shield, and often displays particular designs such as standing lions or large feathers. A **crest** traditionally appeared above a coat of arms, but can now be used alone, and suggests that the owner has a high reputation and great respect. **Emblem** is a more general word: a coat of arms or a crest can be regarded as **emblems**, but **emblem** is usually used to describe sth smaller that represents an organization.

lonely *adj.*

lonely · alone · isolated · homesick · forlorn · bereft · desolate
These words all describe a person who is unhappy because they have no friends or little contact with other people.

lonely	alone	desolate
isolated	forlorn	
homesick	bereft	

PATTERNS AND COLLOCATIONS
▸ to **feel** lonely / alone / isolated / homesick / forlorn / bereft / desolate
▸ **utterly** alone / isolated / bereft / desolate
▸ **desperately** / **terribly** lonely / homesick

lonely unhappy because you have no friends or people to talk to: *She lives alone and often feels lonely.* ◇ *The support they give to lonely old people is invaluable.* See also **loneliness** → PRIVACY

alone [not before noun] (*rather informal*) unhappy because you have no friends or people to talk to or help you: *I've been so alone since you went away.* ◇ *Carol felt* **all alone** *in the world.*

NOTE LONELY OR ALONE? **Alone** is slightly more informal than **lonely** and cannot be used before a noun; it can also suggest that sb feels not only lonely but also vulnerable (= likely to be hurt) in some way.

isolated /'aɪsəleɪtɪd/ without much contact with other people and often unhappy because of this: *I felt very isolated in my new job.* ◇ *Elderly people easily become* **socially isolated**. See also **isolation** → PRIVACY

homesick /'həʊmsɪk; *AmE* 'hoʊm-/ unhappy because you are away from home and you miss your family and friends: *I felt* **homesick for** *Scotland.* ◇ *Seeing other families together made him terribly homesick.*
▸ **homesickness** *noun* [U]: *She soon got over her homesickness.*

forlorn /fə'lɔːn; *AmE* fər'lɔːrn/ (*written*) appearing lonely and unhappy: *She looked so forlorn, standing there in the pouring rain.*

bereft /bɪ'reft/ [not before noun] (*rather formal*) very unhappy and lonely because you have lost sb/sth: *He was utterly bereft when his wife died.*

desolate /'desələt/ [not usually before noun] very lonely and unhappy: *The thought that her husband did not want the baby made her feel utterly desolate.* See also **desolation** → DESPAIR *noun*

long verb

long · covet · crave · yearn · hanker · be dying for sth/ to do sth
These words all mean to want sth very much, especially when it is very difficult to get.

- to long/ yearn/ hanker/ be dying **for** sb/ sth
- to yearn/ hanker **after** sb/ sth
- to long/ yearn/ hanker/ be dying **to do sth**
- to **always/still** long for/ covet/ crave/ yearn for / hanker for sth
- to **desperately** long for/ crave/ yearn for sth
- to **secretly** long for/ yearn for / hanker for sth

long [I, T] (*especially written*) to want sth very much, especially when it does not seem likely to happen soon: *Lucy had always longed for a brother.* ◇ *He longed for Pat to phone.* ◇ *I'm longing to see you again.* See also **longing** → APPETITE 2
▸ **'longed-for** *adj.* [only before noun]: *the birth of a longed-for baby*

covet /ˈkʌvət/ [T] (*formal or written*) to want sth very much, especially sth that belongs to sb else: *He had long coveted the chance to work with a famous musician.* ◇ *They are this year's winners of the coveted trophy* (= that everyone would like to win).

crave [T] (*written*) to have a very strong desire for sth, especially when the desire is difficult to control: *She has always craved excitement.* ❶ **Crave** is used especially to talk about people having a very strong desire for pleasures that can be damaging if they take too much of them: *to crave alcohol/drugs/sweet food/carbohydrates/ cigarettes/coffee.* People who feel that sth is missing in their life may also *crave company/attention/affection/ power/success.* See also **craving** → APPETITE 2

yearn /jɜːn; AmE jɜːrn/ [I] (*literary*) to want sth very much, especially when it does not seem likely to happen soon: *The people yearned for peace.* ◇ *There was a yearning look in his eyes.* See also **yearning** → APPETITE 2

hanker [I] to want sth very much, especially a return to an old way of life: *She still hankered after her dancing days.*

be dying for sth/to do sth *idiom* (*informal*) to want sth very much: *I'm dying for a glass of water.* ◇ *I'm dying to know what happened.*

long adj.

long · prolonged · lengthy · protracted · long-lasting · extended
These words all describe things that last for a great amount of time.

- a long/ prolonged/ lengthy/ extended **period**
- a long/ prolonged/ lengthy/ protracted **delay/ dispute/ illness**
- a long/ lengthy/ protracted/ extended **process**
- long/ prolonged/ lengthy/ protracted/ extended **negotiations**
- **very/ relatively** long/ prolonged/ lengthy/ protracted/ long-lasting
- **quite** long/ prolonged/ lengthy/ long-lasting/ extended

long lasting or taking a great amount of time or more time than usual; seeming to last or take more time than it really does because, for example, you are very busy or not happy: *I haven't seen him for a long time.* ◇ *There was a long silence before she spoke.* ◇ *I like it now the days are getting longer* (= in spring). ◇ *a long book/film/list* (= taking a lot of time to read/watch/deal with) ◇ *Nurses have to work long hours* (= for more hours in the day than is usual). ◇ (*AmE*) *He stared at them for the longest time* (= for a very long time) *before answering.* ◇ *I'm tired. It's been a long day.* ◇ *We were married for ten long years.* ❶ **Long** is also used for asking or talking about

particular periods of time: *How long is the film?* ◇ *I think it's only about two hours long.* OPP **short**, **brief** → SHORT 1, **short** → SHORT 3

prolonged /prəˈlɒŋd; AmE -ˈlɔːŋd; -ˈlɑːŋd/ [only before noun] (*especially written*) continuing for a long time: *There were prolonged spells of dry weather.* ◇ *The drug becomes less effective after prolonged use.* See also **prolong** → MAINTAIN 1

lengthy (*rather formal, especially written*) taking a long time, often too long a time: *I had to go through the lengthy process of obtaining a visa.* ◇ *A court case will be expensive and lengthy.*

protracted /prəˈtræktɪd; AmE also proʊˈt-/ (*formal*) continuing for longer than expected or longer than usual: *There followed a protracted series of legal wrangles.* ◇ *A protracted strike carries a high risk of violence.*

long-'lasting (*especially of the effect of sth*) that can or does last for a long time: *The change brought about long-lasting improvements.* ◇ *The experience made an immediate and long-lasting impression on me.* OPP **short-lived** → SHORT 1, See also **lasting** → PERMANENT

extended [only before noun] (*rather formal, especially written*) long or longer than usual or expected; longer than before: *They are going to publish an extended version of the report.* ◇ *More staff will be needed when the extended opening hours are introduced.* See also **extend** → MAINTAIN 1

look noun

look · glance · sight · gaze · stare · glimpse · glare
These are all words for an act of looking, when you turn your eyes in a particular direction.

- a look/ glance **at** sb/ sth
- a **hard** look/ glance/ gaze/ stare/ glare
- a **cold/ penetrating/ piercing/ curious/ quizzical** look/ glance/ gaze/ stare
- an **angry** look/ glance/ gaze/ glare
- a **suspicious/ withering** look/ glance/ stare/ glare
- a **long/ disapproving** look/ glance/ stare
- a **brief/ fleeting/ momentary/ quick** look/ glance/ glimpse
- a **sharp/ questioning/ searching/ admiring/ anxious** look/ glance/ gaze
- to **have/ get/ take** a look/ glance/ glimpse
- to **fix sb with** a look/ stare/ glare
- to **send/ shoot/ throw sb** a look/ glance/ glare
- to **catch** sight/ a glimpse **of** sb/ sth
- to **draw** a/ sb's look/ glance/ gaze
- to **avoid** sb's glance/ gaze/ stare

look [C, usually sing.] an act of looking at sb/sth: *Here, have a look at this.* ◇ *It's an interesting place. Do you want to take **a look around**?* ◇ *I had a brief look through the report before the meeting.* ◇ *Make sure you get a **good look** at their faces.* ◇ *She threw him a **dirty look**.* ◇ *A look passed between them* (= they looked at each other). See also **look at sth** → CHECK *verb* 1

glance /glɑːns; AmE glæns/ [C] a quick look: *I had a glance at the newspaper headlines as I waited at the counter.* ◇ *She shot him a sideways glance.* ◇ *The sisters exchanged glances* (= looked at each other). ◇ *He could tell what was wrong **at a glance*** (= with only a quick look). See also **glance** → GLANCE *verb*

sight [U] the act of seeing sb/sth: *After ten days at sea, we had our first sight of land.* ◇ *She caught sight of a car in the distance.* ◇ *She kept sight of him in her mirror.* ◇ *I always faint **at the sight of** blood.* ◇ *He looked at first sight like an English tourist.* ◇ *The soldiers were given orders to **shoot on sight*** (= as soon as they saw sb). ◇ *I **know her by sight*** (= can recognize her but do not know her well). See also **sight** → SIGHT *noun*, **sight** → SEE *verb*

gaze [C, usually sing.] a long steady look at sb/sth: *She felt embarrassed **under his** steady **gaze**.* ◇ *He met her gaze* (= looked at her while she looked at him). ◇ *She dropped* her gaze (= stopped looking). ◇ *I followed her gaze and spotted a new arrival at the far side of the room.* See also **gaze → STARE** *verb*

stare [C] a long look at sb/sth, especially in a way that is unfriendly or that shows surprise: *She gave the officer a blank stare and shrugged her shoulders.* ◇ *He fixed the interviewer with a hard stare.* See also **stare → STARE** *verb*

glimpse [C] a look at sb/sth for a very short time, when you do not see the person or thing completely: *He caught a glimpse of her in the crowd.* ◇ *I came up on deck to get my first glimpse of the island.* See also **glimpse → SEE** *verb*

glare [C] a long angry look at sb/sth: *She fixed her questioner with a hostile glare.* See also **glare → STARE** *verb*

look *verb*

1 Look at that!
2 look for a job/your passport

1 See the Topic Map for THE MEDIA on p.900, See also the entries for GLANCE, NOTICE, SEE and STARE

look · watch · see · view · check sth out · observe · regard · catch · contemplate
These words all mean to to turn your eyes in a particular direction.

PATTERNS AND COLLOCATIONS
▸ to look/ watch/ view/ observe/ regard/ contemplate (sb/ sth) **from** somewhere
▸ to look/ watch **for** sb/ sth
▸ to watch/ observe **what/ who/ how...**
▸ to look/ watch/ view/ observe/ regard/ contemplate (sb/ sth) **with** amazement/ surprise/ disapproval, etc.
▸ to watch/ see/ view/ catch a **film/ movie/ show/ programme**
▸ to watch/ see/ catch a **match/ game/ fight**
▸ to look/ watch/ observe sb/ sth/ regard sb/ sth **closely**
▸ to look/ watch/ observe sb/ sth **carefully**
▸ to look/ watch/ regard sb/ sth **intently/ thoughtfully/ suspiciously/ expectantly/ warily/ impassively**

look [I] to turn your eyes in a particular direction: *If you look carefully you can just see our house from here.* ◇ *She looked at me and smiled.* ◇ '*Has the mail come yet?*' '*I'll look and see.*' ◇ *Look! I'm sure that's Brad Pitt!* ◇ *Don't look now, but there's someone staring at you!*

watch [T, I] to look at sb/sth for a time, paying attention to what happens: *I only let my kids watch television at the weekends.* ◇ *Watch what I do, then you try.* ◇ *She watched the kids playing in the yard.* ◇ *They watched the bus disappear into the distance.* ◇ '*Would you like to play?*' '*No thanks – I'll just watch.*' ◇ *She stood and watched as the taxi drove off.* ◇ *We watched to see what would happen next.*

see [T] (not usually used in the progressive tenses) to watch a game, television show, performance, etc: *Did you see that documentary about Brazil last night?* ◇ *Fifty thousand people saw the game.*

view [T] (*formal*) to look at sth, especially when you look carefully; to watch television, a film/movie, etc: *People came from all over the world to view her work.* ◇ *The eclipse should only be viewed through a special lens.* ◇ *The show has a viewing audience of six million* (= six million people watch it). See also **view → SIGHT** *noun*

> **NOTE** WATCH, SEE OR VIEW? You can *see/view a film/ movie/TV show* but you cannot: ~~see/view television~~. **View** is more formal than **see**, used especially in business contexts.

,check sth 'out *phrasal verb* (*informal, especially spoken*) to look at or examine sb/sth that seems interesting or attractive: *Check out the prices at our new store!* ◇ *Hey, check out that car!*

observe /əb'zɜːv; AmE əb'zɜːrv/ [T, I] (not usually used in the progressive tenses) (*formal*) to watch sb/sth carefully, especially to learn more about them: *The patients were observed over a period of several months.* ◇ *He observes keenly, but says little.* See also **observation → INSPECTION, observe → NOTICE** *verb*

regard /rɪ'ɡɑːd; AmE rɪ'ɡɑːrd/ [T] (*formal*) to look at sb/sth, especially in a particular way: *He regarded us suspiciously.*

catch [T] (*especially AmE, informal*) to see, hear or attend a film, game, event, etc: *Let's eat now and maybe we could catch a movie later.*

contemplate /'kɒntəmpleɪt; AmE 'kɑːn-/ [T] (*formal*) to look at sth carefully for a long time: *She contemplated him in silence.* ◇ *He sat there, contemplating his fingernails.*

2 **look · search · seek · hunt · forage · scout · cast about/around for sth**
These words all mean to try to find sth.

PATTERNS AND COLLOCATIONS
▸ to look/ search/ seek/ hunt/ forage/ scout **for** sth
▸ to look/ search/ hunt/ forage/ scout **around** (for sth)
▸ to look/ search/ hunt **through** sth
▸ to look/ search/ hunt/ forage **in** sth
▸ to look for/ search for/ seek/ cast around for a/ an **alternative/ way**
▸ to look/ search/ hunt **for clues**
▸ **police/ detectives** look for/ search for/ seek/ hunt sb/ sth
▸ to look/ search/ seek/ hunt/ cast around **desperately** (for sth)
▸ to look/ search/ seek/ cast around **in vain**
▸ to look/ search/ hunt **everywhere**

look [I] to try to find sth: *I can't find my book – I've looked everywhere.* ◇ *Are you still looking for a job?* ◇ *We're looking for someone with experience for this position.* ◇ *We're looking around for a house in this area.* ◇ *I was just about to* **come looking** *for you.* See also **look → SEARCH** *noun*

search [I, T] to look carefully to try to find sb/sth; to examine a particular place when trying to find sb/sth; (especially of the police) to examine sb's clothes, etc. in order to find sth that they may be hiding: *She searched in vain for her passport.* ◇ *The customs officers searched through her bag.* ◇ *I found out more about the company by searching online.* ◇ *Firefighters searched the building for survivors.* ◇ *Visitors are regularly searched as they enter the building.* See also **search → SEARCH** *noun*

seek [T, I] (*formal*) to try to find sb/sth: *Drivers are advised to seek alternative routes.* ◇ *Police are seeking witnesses to the accident.* ◇ *He admired her ability to* **seek out** *bargains* (= to look for and find them). ◇ (*BrE*) *They sought in vain for somewhere to shelter.* See also **seek → ASK 2, seek → TRY 1**

hunt [T, I] to try to find sth that is difficult to find; to try to find sb in order to catch them or harm them: *I've hunted everywhere, but I can't find it.* ◇ *She was hunting through her bag for her keys.* ◇ *Police are hunting an escaped criminal.* See also **hunt → SEARCH** *noun*

forage /'fɒrɪdʒ; AmE 'fɔː-; 'fɑː-/ [I] (*written*) (especially of animals) to try to find food; (of a person) to try to find sth, especially using your hands: *The female only leaves the young to* **forage for food**. ◇ *Her assistant was foraging in a drawer for some envelopes.*

scout /skaʊt/ [I, T] to search an area or various areas in order to find or discover sth: *The kids were scouting around for wood for the fire.* ◇ *They scouted the area for somewhere to stay the night.*

,cast a'bout/a'round for sth *phrasal verb* (*written*) to try hard to think of or find sth, especially when this is difficult: *She cast around desperately for a safe topic of conversation.* ◇ *The authorities are clearly casting about for someone to blame.*

look after sb *phrasal verb* See also the entry for
TREAT 1

look after sb · take care of sb · care for sb · tend · attend to sb/sth
These words all mean to be responsible for sb's health or safety, especially by giving them everything they need.

PATTERNS AND COLLOCATIONS
▶ to tend / attend **to** sb / sth
▶ to look after / take care of / care for / tend to **the sick**
▶ to look after / take care of / care for **the children / the elderly / an elderly relative**
▶ to look after / take care of **yourself**
▶ to care for / tend sb **lovingly**

look 'after sb *phrasal verb* (*especially BrE*) to be responsible for sb's general health and happiness, especially because they are ill, injured, very young or old: *My daughter was sick so I took the day off to look after her.* ◊ *Who's going to look after the children while you're away?* See also **look after yourself** → TAKE CARE OF YOURSELF

take 'care of sb *phrase* to look after sb: *Who's taking care of the kids while you're away?* ◊ *You should **take better care** of yourself.* ◊ *Don't you worry. I'll take care of you.* See also **take care of yourself** → TAKE CARE OF YOURSELF
▶ **care** *noun* [U]: *medical/patient care* ◊ *How much do men share housework and the care of the children?*

'care for sb *phrasal verb* (*rather formal, especially written*) to look after sb because they are seriously ill, injured or very old, and to make sure they have what they need: *She does some voluntary work, caring for the elderly.* ◊ *He gave up work to care for his wife.*

NOTE LOOK AFTER SB, TAKE CARE OF SB OR CARE FOR SB?
People often **look after sb** for a short time, while they are ill, or while the person who usually takes care of them is away. **Take care of sb** can be used in the same way, and in American English it is more frequent than **look after sb**. Both these expressions, but especially **take care of sb**, can suggest a feeling of love and care for the person, not just a position of responsibility. **Caring for sb** is more often a long-term, full-time occupation. To **care for sb** can also mean to love sb. See also **care for sb** → LOVE

tend [T, I] (*rather formal*) to look after animals, plants, or ill or injured people: *a shepherd tending his sheep* ◊ *We looked out of the window at the **well-tended** gardens.* ◊ *Ambulance crews were tending to the injured.*

at'tend to sb/sth *phrasal verb* (*rather formal*) to look after sb/sth and make sure they have everything they need: *A nurse attended to his needs constantly.*

look like sb/sth *verb*

look like sb/sth · resemble · take after sb
These words all mean to have a similar appearance, form or manner to sb/sth.

PATTERNS AND COLLOCATIONS
▶ to look like / resemble / take after your **mother / father / grandmother / grandfather / aunt / uncle**
▶ to look **superficially / remotely** like sb / sth
▶ to **superficially / remotely** resemble sb / sth

'look like sb/sth *phrase* (not used in the progressive tenses) to have a similar appearance to sb/sth: *That photograph doesn't look like her at all.*

resemble /rɪ'zembl/ [T, no passive] (not used in the progressive tenses) (*rather formal*) to look like or be similar to another person or thing: *She closely resembles her sister.* ◊ *The plant resembles grass in appearance.* See also **resemblance** → SIMILARITY

take 'after sb *phrasal verb* [no passive] (not used in the progressive tenses) to look or behave like an older member of your family, especially your mother or father: *She's small for her age; she obviously takes after her mother.*

lord *noun* See the Topic Map for THE INDIVIDUAL AND SOCIETY on p.894

lord · peer · noble · aristocrat · nobleman · lady
These are all words for a person of a high social class, especially sb with a special title.

PATTERNS AND COLLOCATIONS
▶ a **great / wealthy** lord / noble / aristocrat / nobleman / lady
▶ a **rich** lord / aristocrat / lady
▶ a **powerful** lord / noble
▶ a **local** lord / noble / aristocrat / nobleman
▶ a **hereditary** lord / peer / noble
▶ a / an **English / Scottish / Irish** lord / peer / noble / aristocrat / nobleman
▶ a **Hungarian / French / German, etc.** noble / aristocrat / nobleman
▶ to **become** a lord / peer

lord [C] (in Britain) a man of a high social rank, especially sb with a special title; a man who has been given the title of 'lord' and the right to sit and vote in the House of Lords (= the upper house of the British parliament): *She's married to a lord.* ◊ *He was made a peer and took the title Lord Northcliffe.*

peer [C] (in Britain) a person of a high social rank who has a special title; a person who has been given the title of 'lord' or 'lady,' and the right to sit and vote in the House of Lords: *Two-thirds of the Lords were hereditary peers who succeeded to their title automatically.* ◊ *The former athlete and MP Sebastian Coe was created a **life peer** (= a title which cannot be passed to a son) in 2000 as Baron Coe of Ranmore.*

NOTE LORD AND PEER **Lord** and **peer** can both be used to refer to a person in Britain who has a special title, including Duke, Marquess, Earl, Viscount or Baron. Some of these titles are inherited (= passed from father to son) and some are given to a person by the Queen for service to the country, for example in politics or business. A **peer** can use the title Lord or Lady before their name and, until recently, they could all sit in the *House of Lords* (= the upper house of the British parliament). Since 1999 most *hereditary peers* (= those who inherited their titles) have lost this right, but *life peers* (= who were given their titles by the Queen, but cannot pass them on) still have it. A **peer** can be either a man or a woman. When people talk about **lords** as a group, for example in the *House of Lords*, this often includes both men and women.

noble [C] (especially in some European countries in the past) a person who comes from a family of high social rank, especially sb who has a special title: *The regime was supported by a group of powerful nobles.* See also **nobility** → ELITE, **noble** → ARISTOCRATIC

aristocrat /'ærɪstəkræt; *AmE* ə'rɪst-/ [C] (especially in some European countries) a person who comes from a family of high social rank, especially sb who has a special title: *At that time, diplomatic posts were filled by aristocrats.* ◊ *He had the air of an aristocrat.* See also **aristocracy** → ELITE, **aristocratic** → ARISTOCRATIC

nobleman (especially in some European countries in the past) a man who comes from a family of high social rank, especially sb who has a special title: *He contemplated marrying his daughter to an English nobleman.* See also **noble** → ARISTOCRATIC

NOTE NOBLE, ARISTOCRAT OR NOBLEMAN? **Noble** and **nobleman** are often used when talking about the political power which these people used to have; **aristocrat** places slightly more emphasis on the social importance of these people. In modern contexts it is more usual to talk about **aristocrats**.

lady [C] (in Britain) a woman belonging to a high social class; a special title used by a woman of high social rank, or by a woman who has been made a peer and given the right to sit and vote in the House of Lords: *It is said that lords and ladies and royalty were entertained here.* ◊ *Lady Amos became a peer in 1997.*

lose verb

lose · trail · come off worse
These words all mean to fail to win sth such as a game or contest.

PATTERNS AND COLLOCATIONS
▸ to lose / trail / come off worse **in** sth
▸ to lose / trail **by** sth
▸ to lose / trail **badly**

lose [I, T] to fail to win a game, competition, contest, court case, argument, fight or war: *They deserved to lose.* ◇ *We lost **to** a stronger team.* ◇ *Newcastle lost 1–0 in the rematch.* ◇ *So far they haven't lost a game.* ◇ *He lost the seat by less than 100 votes.* ◇ *She resigned as party leader after they lost the election.* ◇ *He yesterday lost his appeal against a six-month ban.* ◇ *The South lost the war.* **OPP** **win** → WIN

trail [I, T] (usually used in the progressive tenses) to be losing a game or other contest; to be doing less well than others: *United were trailing 2–0 at half-time.* ◇ *We were trailing by five points.* ◇ *The party is trailing in the polls.* **OPP** **lead** → LEAD 1

come off 'worse (also **come off 'worst**) *idiom* (*rather informal*) to lose a fight or competition; to suffer more compared with others: *I **came off worse from** the encounter.* ◇ *He wasn't a quick thinker and always came off worse in an argument.* **OPP** **come off better/best**

lose out phrasal verb

lose out · miss · pass sth up
These words all mean to not get sth you wanted or could/ should have.

PATTERNS AND COLLOCATIONS
▸ to lose out on / miss / pass up a / an **chance / opportunity**
▸ to be **too good to** miss / pass up

lose 'out *phrasal verb* (*rather informal*) to not get sth you wanted or feel you should have: *While the stores make big profits, it's the customer who loses out.* ◇ *I just **lost out on** the first prize.*

miss [T] to not take the opportunity to do sth: *The sale prices were too good to miss.* ◇ *It was an opportunity **not to be missed**.*

pass sth 'up *phrasal verb* (*informal*) to choose not take the opportunity to do sth: *Imagine passing up an offer like that!*

loser noun

1 They were 16–3 losers to New Zealand.
2 a bunch of losers

1 loser · runner-up · also-ran
These are all words for sb who does not win or is not successful in a competition, race, game or election.

PATTERNS AND COLLOCATIONS
▸ a loser / runner-up / also-ran **in** sth
▸ a loser / runner-up **to** sb
▸ **winners and** losers / runners-up

loser [C] a person or team that is defeated in a competition: *Sweden will now play the losers of the other semi-final for the bronze medal.* ◇ *He's extremely competitive and a **bad loser** (= does not react well to losing).* **OPP** **winner** → WINNER

runner-'up (pl. **runners-up**) [C] a person or team that finishes second in a race or competition; sb who has not finished first but who wins a prize: *She was last year's runner-up to Sarah Jones.* ◇ *They finished **runners-up behind** Italy.* ◇ *Twenty runners-up will receive a $50 book voucher.* ◇ *There are three **runners-up prizes** of club shirts.*

'also-ran [C] (*often disapproving*) a person who is not successful, especially in a competition or election or when compared with other people: *The campaign transformed him from an also-ran in the polls to front-runner.*

2 loser · failure · incompetent · has-been · no-hoper · underachiever · disappointment · disaster
These are all words for a person who is unsuccessful or not as successful as they used to be or as they could be.

PATTERNS AND COLLOCATIONS
▸ to be a failure / disappointment / disaster **as** sth
▸ a **complete** failure / no-hoper / disaster
▸ a **group / bunch of** losers / incompetents / no-hopers

loser [C] (*often disapproving*) a person who is regularly unsuccessful, especially when you have a low opinion of them: *She's one of life's losers.* ◇ *He's a **born loser**.* **OPP** **winner** → SUCCESS

failure [C] a person who is not successful: *He was a failure as a teacher.* ◇ *I **felt** a complete **failure**.* **OPP** **success** → SUCCESS, See also **fail** → FAIL 2

incompetent /ɪnˈkɒmpɪtənt; *AmE* -ˈkɑːm-/ [C] (*disapproving*) a person who does not have the skill or ability to do their job or a task as it should be done: *The whole thing is being led by a bunch of incompetents.* See also **incompetent** → INCOMPETENT *adj.*

'has-been [C] (*informal, disapproving*) a person who is no longer as famous, successful or important as they used to be: *She's just an old has-been.* ◇ *He's very much a political has-been.*

no-'hoper [C] (*informal, disapproving*) a person, team or racehorse that is considered useless or very unlikely to be successful: *They were written off as a bunch of no-hopers.* ◇ *He backed an apparent no-hoper at odds of 100–1.*

underachiever /ˌʌndərəˈtʃiːvə(r)/ [C] a person who is less successful than they could be, especially in school work: *At school he was a **classic underachiever**.*

disappointment [C] a person who is disappointing to other people, because of their lack of achievement or bad behaviour: *I always felt I was a **disappointment to** my father.*

disaster [C] (*informal, disapproving*) a person who is a complete failure at sth, especially because of their lack of skill or ability: *He was a competent accountant, but as a manager he's a disaster.*

lose your temper idiom

lose your temper · get angry · get mad · go mad · lose patience · go berserk
These expressions all mean to become angry or very angry and show this in the way you talk or behave.

lose patience	lose your temper	go mad
	get angry	go berserk
	get mad	

PATTERNS AND COLLOCATIONS
▸ to lose your temper / get angry / get mad / lose patience **with** sb
▸ to lose your temper / get angry / get mad / go mad **at** sth
▸ to lose your temper / get angry **over** sth

lose your 'temper *idiom* to fail to control your anger: *She lost her temper with a customer and shouted at him.* ◇ *Try to ignore it. It's not worth losing your temper over.* **OPP** **keep your temper**, See also **temper** → TEMPER

get 'angry *idiom* to become angry: *Please don't get angry with me. I'm trying my best.*

NOTE **LOSE YOUR TEMPER** OR **GET ANGRY?** If you **lose your temper** you show it in your behaviour, for example by shouting at sb. If you **get angry**, you might shout but the emphasis is more on your feelings and less on your behaviour.

get 'mad *idiom* (*AmE*, *informal*) to become angry: *Please don't get mad at me.* ◇ *He got mad and walked out.*

go 'mad *idiom* (*BrE*, *informal*) to become very angry and fail to control your anger: *She went mad when I told her.*

> **NOTE** **GET MAD** OR **GO MAD?** **Get mad** is the usual expression for 'to become angry' in informal American English. **Go mad** is British English and is a stronger expression, used when sb becomes very angry and shows it, for example by shouting. **Go mad** can also mean 'go crazy' or 'get very excited'.

lose 'patience *idiom* to become annoyed or angry: *People have lost patience with the slow pace of reform.*

go berserk *idiom* to become very angry and fail to control your anger: *He went berserk when he found out where I'd been.*

loss-making *adj.*

loss-making · unprofitable · non-profit · uneconomic
These words all describe a business, organization or activity which is not making a profit.

PATTERNS AND COLLOCATIONS
▸ to be unprofitable / uneconomic **for** sb
▸ to be unprofitable / uneconomic **to do** sth
▸ a loss-making / an unprofitable / a non-profit **company**
▸ loss-making / unprofitable / uneconomic **industries**
▸ loss-making / unprofitable **routes / years**
▸ **increasingly** unprofitable / uneconomic

'**loss-making** (of a company or business activity) not making a profit; losing money: *The publisher sold its loss-making magazine business.* **OPP** **profit-making** → SUCCESSFUL 2, See also **loss** → DEBT

unprofitable (of a company, business activity or product) not making enough profit: *It became unprofitable to sell large electrical goods in high street stores.* **OPP** **profitable** → SUCCESSFUL 2

,**non-'profit** [usually before noun] (of an organization) not having the aim of making a profit: *The Arthritis Foundation is a non-profit organization which helps sufferers.* ❶ In British English **non-profit-making** is also used but is slightly old-fashioned. Especially in American English **not-for-profit** is also used, but often with a more specific meaning than **non-profit**, relating to the legal and tax status of the organization. **OPP** **commercial, profit-making** → SUCCESSFUL 2

uneconomic /ˌʌnˌiːkəˈnɒmɪk; ˌʌnˌek-; *AmE* -ˈnɑːm-/ (of a business or factory) not making a profit, especially because it is too small or old: *The plant had become uneconomic to run.* **OPP** **economic** → SUCCESSFUL 2

lot *noun* See also the entry for CARGO

lot · batch · shipment · load · consignment
These are all words for a group or quantity of people, things or goods.

PATTERNS AND COLLOCATIONS
▸ a **large / small** shipment / load / consignment
▸ to **order / receive / send / deliver** a batch / shipment / load / consignment

lot [C+sing./pl. v.] (*especially BrE, rather informal*) a group or set of people or things: *The first lot of visitors has/have arrived.* ◇ *I have several lots of essays to mark this weekend.* ◇ *Shall I put this lot* (= these things) *with the others?* ◇ (*informal, spoken*) *What do you lot* (= people) *want?* ❶ In this meaning, it is not possible to say 'a lot of sth'. *A lot of visitors* means 'many visitors', not 'a group of visitors'. Instead of *a*, use *this, that, the last, the other,* etc. before *lot.*

batch [C] a number of people or things that are dealt with as a group; an amount of food, medicine or goods produced at one time: *Each summer a new batch of students tries to find work.* ◇ *We deliver the goods in batches.* ◇ *Shall I make another batch of cookies?*

shipment [C] (*rather formal*) products or materials that are sent from one place to another, especially between different countries or over long distances: *They are trying hard to locate the missing arms shipment.* ◇ *There is to be a new EU directive on shipments of hazardous waste.* ❶ **Shipment** is often used to talk about an amount of weapons or drugs that are being sent somewhere. See also **ship** → TAKE *verb* 1

load [C] (often in compounds) the total quantity of things or people that can be carried in sth, especially a vehicle: *The plane took off with a full load.* ◇ *He put half a load of washing in the machine.* ◇ *They ordered three truckloads of sand.* ❶ When it is used with a plural noun, **load** can take a plural verb: *A busload of tourists has/have arrived.* See also **load** → FILL *verb*

consignment /kənˈsaɪnmənt/ [C] (*rather formal*) a quantity of goods that are to be delivered somewhere: *A consignment of medicines is on its way now.* ◇ *The consignment leaves tonight from Heathrow.*

> **NOTE** **SHIPMENT** OR **CONSIGNMENT**? **Shipment** is a slightly more general word than **consignment** and can be used to talk about goods or waste products. It emphasizes that the products have been sent (although not necessarily by sea), especially over a long distance or between countries; **consignment** is used to talk about goods, which may have been sent over a long or short distance, and emphasizes that they are intended for a particular person, company or place.

loud *adj.*

loud · noisy · deafening · roaring · ear-splitting
These words all describe a powerful noise made by sb/sth.

PATTERNS AND COLLOCATIONS
▸ a loud / a deafening / a roaring / an ear-splitting **noise**
▸ the loud / deafening **sound** of sth
▸ loud / deafening / roaring **applause**
▸ a loud / deafening **crash / roar**
▸ loud / deafening **music**
▸ a loud / deafening **cheer**
▸ a loud **voice**

loud (of a sound) making a lot of noise: *There was a loud bang and a big puff of smoke.* ◇ *That music's too loud – please turn it down.* **OPP** **quiet, soft** → QUIET 2
▸ **loud** *adv.*: (*rather informal*) *Do you have to play that music so loud?* ◇ *You'll have to speak louder – I can't hear you.*
▸ **loudly** *adv.*: *She screamed as loudly as she could.*

noisy (*often disapproving*) (of a person or thing) making a lot of noise; (of a place) full of noise: *The field was full of noisy children running around.* ◇ *The engine is very noisy at high speed.* ◇ *A noisy classroom is a poor learning environment.* **OPP** **quiet** → QUIET 1
▸ **noisily** *adv.*: *The children were playing noisily upstairs.*

deafening /ˈdefnɪŋ/ so loud that it makes you temporarily unable to hear anything else: *The team was greeted by deafening applause from the audience.* ◇ *The noise of the machine was deafening.*

roaring making a continuous loud deep noise: *All we could hear was the sound of roaring water.*

'**ear-splitting** (*rather informal*) so loud or high that it hurts your ears: *The ear-splitting noise made him feel quite lightheaded.*

love noun

1 fall madly in love with sb
2 a mother's love for her children

---

1 love · desire · passion · romance · lust · attraction · crush · infatuation

These are all words for a strong feeling of liking sb in a romantic or sexual way.

PATTERNS AND COLLOCATIONS

▸ love / desire / passion / lust / attraction / infatuation **for** sb
▸ love / passion / romance / attraction **between** A and B
▸ to kiss sb, look at sb, etc. **with** love / desire / passion
▸ **sexual** / **physical** / **mutual** love / desire / passion / lust / attraction
▸ **great** love / desire / passion / romance
▸ **overwhelming** love / desire / passion / attraction
▸ to **be consumed with** desire / passion / lust
▸ to **find** love / romance
▸ love / desire / passion / attraction **grows**
▸ love / desire / passion **dies**

love [U] a strong feeling of caring about sb and being sexually attracted to them: *We're in love!* ◇ *She was madly/deeply in love with him.* ◇ *They fell in love with each other.* ◇ *It was love at first sight* (= they were attracted to each other the first time they met). ◇ *At last she had found true love.* ◇ *a love song/story* See also in **love → IN LOVE**

desire [C, U] a strong wish to have sex with sb: *She felt a surge of love and desire for him.* ◇ *He felt he was nothing more to her than an object of desire.*

passion [U] a very strong feeling of sexual love: *His passion for her made him blind to everything else.* ◇ *They kissed with passion.*
▸ **passionate** adj.: *passionate love/feelings* ◇ *a passionate kiss/embrace/affair/lover*

NOTE LOVE, DESIRE OR PASSION? **Love** is a very general word and can be used in any context. It can sometimes refer to sex: *physical/sexual love* ◇ *to make love* (= to have sex), but it is more often to do with feelings and the way these make you behave: *romantic love.* **Desire** and **passion** are stronger words, and are much more to do with physical love and sex: *to burn with/be filled with desire/passion.* Both **desire** and **passion** can mean the feeling of wanting to have sex, but only **passion** can refer to the act of having sex: *a night of passion.*

romance [U] the feeling of being in love and the kind of behaviour that goes with this feeling: *How can you put the romance back into your marriage?* ◇ *People find romance in strange places.* See also **romance → RELATIONSHIP 2**
▸ **romantic** adj.: *a romantic candlelit dinner* ◇ *romantic stories/fiction/comedy*

lust [U] (*often disapproving*) very strong sexual desire, especially when love is not involved: *Their affair was driven by pure lust.*

attraction [U, sing.] a feeling of liking sb, especially in a sexual way: *Sexual attraction is a large part of falling in love.* ◇ *She felt an immediate attraction for him.* See also **be attracted to sb → ATTRACTED TO SB**

crush [C] a strong feeling of love, that usually does not last very long: *It's only a schoolgirl crush, it'll pass.* ◇ *I had a huge crush on her when I was younger.* ❶ A **crush** is usually a feeling that a young person has, often for sb older or for sb that they know they cannot have a relationship with. See also **have a crush on sb → ATTRACTED TO SB**

infatuation /ɪnˌfætʃuˈeɪʃn/ [C, U] a strong feeling of love or attraction for sb, especially when this is unreasonable or does not last long: *It isn't love, it's just a passing infatuation.* ◇ *My infatuation with her continued to grow.* ❶ You can also talk about **infatuation** with an activity or a thing: *the current infatuation with popular culture.* See also **infatuated → IN LOVE**

---

2 love · affection · tenderness · attachment · devotion · liking

These are all words for the feeling you have when you like and care about sb very much.

liking	love	devotion
	affection	
	tenderness	
	attachment	

PATTERNS AND COLLOCATIONS

▸ love / affection / tenderness / liking **for** sb
▸ attachment / devotion **to** sb
▸ affection / tenderness **towards** sb
▸ love / affection / tenderness / devotion **between** A and B
▸ to do sth **with** love / affection / tenderness / devotion
▸ **genuine** / **real** love / affection / tenderness / devotion
▸ **great** / **mutual** love / affection / tenderness / devotion / liking
▸ **deep** love / affection / attachment / devotion
▸ **undying** / **eternal** love / devotion
▸ to **show** love / affection / tenderness / devotion
▸ to **feel** love / affection / tenderness / an attachment
▸ to **have** love / affection / an attachment / a liking
▸ to **develop** an affection / an attachment / a liking for sb
▸ a **feeling of** love / affection / tenderness / attachment / devotion

love [U] the feeling of caring about sb very much, especially a family member or friend: *People say there is nothing greater than a mother's love for her children.* ◇ *He seems incapable of love.* ◇ *Bob sends his love.* **OPP** hatred, hate **→ HATRED**

affection [U, sing.] the feeling of caring about sb very much, often sb who depends on you: *Children need lots of love and affection.* ◇ *Open displays of affection always embarrassed her.* ◇ *He'll be remembered with genuine affection.*

NOTE LOVE OR AFFECTION? **Love** is the most general word in this group and can describe anything from quite a mild feeling to a very strong one. Compare: *Bob sends his love.* ◇ *Bob sends his best wishes/regards.* **Love** is slightly stronger here but not very much. Compare: *There is nothing greater than a mother's love for her children.* ◇ *There is nothing greater than a mother's affection for her children.* **Affection** is not as strong as **love** in this case. It is a gentle feeling, often shown in the way sb talks to, looks at or touches sb else: *She spoke/treated him/looked at him/hugged him with great affection.* **Affection** is typically felt by an adult for sb younger or much older than them, especially sb who depends on them in some way.

tenderness [U] the kind and gentle way in which you show your love or affection for sb: *She spoke with loving tenderness.* ◇ *There was tenderness in his face as he looked at her.*

attachment [C] a feeling of love for sb, especially one which makes you not want to leave them: *The children have a strong attachment to their parents.* ◇ *Prisoners can develop attachments to their warders.*

devotion /dɪˈvəʊʃn; AmE -ˈvoʊ-/ [U, sing.] great love, care and support for sb: *His devotion to his wife and family is touching.* ◇ *He cared for his mother with great devotion.* ❶ **Devotion** is the strongest word in this group. It suggests a feeling that is complete and does not change: *her total/undying/lifelong devotion to her husband* See also **devotion → DEVOTE**

liking [sing., U] the feeling that you like sb: *She had taken a liking to him on their first meeting.* ◇ *They have little liking for each other.* **OPP** dislike **→ HATRED**

love *verb* See also the entry for LIKE

love · like · be fond of sb · adore · be devoted to sb · care for sb · idolize · dote on/upon sb
These words all mean to to have feelings of love or affection for sb.

like	love	adore
be fond of	care for sb	be devoted to sb
		idolize
		dote on/upon sb

PATTERNS AND COLLOCATIONS
▸ to love/like/be fond of/adore/be devoted to/care for/dote on your **children**
▸ to love/like/be fond of/adore/be devoted to/care for your/sb's **husband** / **wife** / **mother** / **father**
▸ to **really** love/like/adore/care for/idolize/dote on sb
▸ to be **really** / **genuinely** fond of/devoted to sb
▸ to love/like/care for sb **very much**
▸ to love/care for sb **deeply**
▸ to **clearly** / **obviously** love/adore/idolize/dote on sb

love [T] (not used in the progressive tenses) to have strong feelings of affection for sb: *I love you.* ◊ *If you love each other, why not get married?* ◊ *He had become a well-loved and respected member of the team.* ◊ *Relatives need time to grieve over* **loved ones** *they have lost.* **OPP** hate, loathe, detest → HATE, See also **lovable** → SWEET
like [T] (not used in the progressive tenses) to find sb pleasant and enjoy being with them: *She's nice. I like her.* ◊ *He never did like me much, did he?* **OPP** dislike → HATE, See also **likeable** → NICE 2
be 'fond of sb *idiom* to feel affection for sb, especially sb you have known for a long time: *Over the years, I have* **grown** *quite* **fond** *of him.*
adore /ə'dɔːr/ [T] (not used in the progressive tenses) to love sb very much: *It's obvious that she adores him.* **OPP** loathe → HATE, See also **adorable** → SWEET
be de'voted to sb *idiom* to love sb very much and be loyal to them: *They are devoted to their children.*
'care for sb *phrasal verb* (not used in the progressive tenses) to love sb, especially in a way that is based on strong affection or a feeling of wanting to protect them, rather than sex: *He cared for her more than she realized.* ❶ **Care for** is often used when sb has not told anyone about their feelings or is just starting to be aware of them. It is also used when sb wishes that sb loved them, or doubts that sb does: *What if he realized she was beginning to care for him?* ◊ *If he really cared for you, he wouldn't behave like that.* See also **care for sb** → LOOK AFTER SB
idolize (*BrE* also **-ise**) /'aɪdəlaɪz/ [T] (not used in the progressive tenses) to admire or love sb very much and think that they are perfect: *He longed to be a pop star, idolized by millions of fans.* See also **idol** → HERO
'dote on/upon sb *phrasal verb* (not used in the progressive tenses) to feel and show great love for sb, ignoring their faults: *He dotes on his children.*

NOTE **IDOLIZE** OR **DOTE ON SB?** Young people often **idolize** a famous person such as a pop star or football player, or a person in authority, such as a teacher or parent. Parents, grandparents, uncles, aunts, etc. may **dote on** children in their family.

lover *noun* See also the entry for PARTNER 2

lover · mistress · concubine · gigolo
These are all words for a sexual partner in a relationship outside marriage.

PATTERNS AND COLLOCATIONS
▸ to **have** a lover/mistress/concubine
▸ to **be sb's** lover/mistress/concubine/gigolo

lover [C] a partner in a sexual relationship outside marriage: *He denied that he was her lover.* ◊ *We were lovers for several years.* ❶ If two people are **lovers**, this often, but not always, suggests that one or both of them are married to sb else: *He suspected his wife of having a lover.* ◊ *The park was full of young lovers holding hands.*
mistress [C] a woman who is having a sexual relationship with a married man: *The fact that he had a mistress didn't mean he didn't love his wife.* ❶ In the past, a **mistress** could also be the sexual partner of an unmarried man, but this is only used in more literary English today: *When do I cease to be your mistress and become your wife?*

NOTE **LOVER** OR **MISTRESS**? A **lover** can be male or female, but a **mistress** can only be a woman and there is no similar word to describe a man in the same position. **Mistress** is a more old-fashioned word, and is often used to describe the sexual partners of powerful men such as kings or politicians: *While he had no children with his wife, King Charles II fathered eight sons by his five mistresses.*

concubine /'kɒŋkjubaɪn; *AmE* 'kɑːŋ-/ [C] (especially in some societies in the past) a woman who lives with a man, often in addition to his wife or wives, but who is less important than they are: *The sultan's wives and concubines lived in the harem.*
gigolo /'ʒɪɡələʊ; 'dʒɪ-; *AmE* -loʊ/ (pl. **-os**) [C] a man who is paid to be the lover of an older woman, usually one who is rich: *It was a slick nightclub where the waiters flirted like gigolos.*

loving *adj.*

loving · caring · devoted · affectionate · romantic · tender · fond · adoring
These words all describe sb feeling or showing love for sb/sth.

PATTERNS AND COLLOCATIONS
▸ loving/affectionate/tender **towards** sb/sth
▸ a loving/a caring/a devoted/an affectionate/a fond/an adoring **mother** / **father** / **parent**
▸ a loving/a caring/a devoted/an affectionate/an adoring **husband** / **wife** / **family**
▸ a loving/a caring/a devoted/an affectionate **friend**
▸ a loving/a devoted/an affectionate **son** / **daughter** / **brother** / **sister**
▸ a loving/a caring/an affectionate/a romantic **man** / **woman** / **person**
▸ a loving/an affectionate **child** / **boy** / **girl**
▸ a loving/caring/affectionate/tender **relationship**
▸ a loving/caring **attitude**
▸ loving/romantic/tender/fond **feelings**
▸ a loving/an affectionate/a tender **kiss**
▸ a loving/a tender/a fond/an adoring **look**
▸ an affectionate/a tender **smile**

loving feeling or showing love and affection for sb/sth, especially a member of your family: *He came from a warm and loving family.* ◊ *She chose the present with loving care.*
▸ **lovingly** *adv.*: *He gazed lovingly at his children.*
caring [usually before noun] kind, helpful and showing that you care about other people and want to protect them: *She's a very caring person.* ◊ *Children need a caring environment.* **OPP** uncaring → INSENSITIVE, See also the entry for KIND *adj.*
devoted having great love for sb/sth and being loyal to them: *They are devoted to their children.* ◊ *She has left behind a devoted son and many good friends.* See also **faithful** → RELIABLE 1
affectionate /ə'fekʃənət/ showing caring feelings and love for sb, for example by hugging or kissing them: *He is very affectionate towards his children.* ◊ *She gave him an affectionate kiss.*
▸ **affectionately** *adv.*: *She kissed him affectionately on the cheek.*

romantic (of people) showing feelings of love: *Why don't you ever give me flowers? I wish you'd be more romantic.* ❶ **Romantic** describes a more sexual love than the other words in this group, for example the kind of love between husband and wife, boyfriend and girlfriend, etc. See also **romance** → RELATIONSHIP 2

tender kind, gentle and loving, especially because you want to look after sb: *I listened to his tender words, and started to feel better.* ◇ *What he needs now is a lot of **tender loving care*** (= sympathetic treatment).
▸ **tenderly** *adv.*: *He smiled tenderly down at her.*

fond [only before noun] showing love and affection for sb/sth: *She waved a **fond farewell** to her parents and sister.* ◇ *I have very **fond memories** of my time in Spain* (= I remember it with affection and pleasure). ❶ You can use **fond** to describe a person: *a fond father/mother*, but it is more often used to describe things or actions that result from a person's feelings: *a fond look/smile/memory*. See also **be fond of sth** → LIKE *verb*
▸ **fondly** *adv.*: *He looked at her fondly.* ◇ *She is still fondly remembered by her former students.*

adoring [usually before noun] showing a lot of love and admiration for sb: *She was looking at him with large, adoring eyes.* ◇ *He waved to the adoring crowds.*
▸ **adoringly** *adv.*: *She sat there, gazing adoringly at him across the table.*

luck *noun*

luck · chance · coincidence · accident · fortune · fate · destiny · providence
These are all words for things that happen or the force that causes them to happen.

PATTERNS AND COLLOCATIONS
▸ **by** ...luck / chance / coincidence / accident
▸ It's **no** coincidence / accident **that...**
▸ **pure / sheer** luck / chance / coincidence / accident
▸ **good / bad / ill** luck / fortune
▸ a / an **happy / unfortunate / strange** chance / coincidence / accident
▸ to **bring sb** good / bad luck / fortune
▸ to **have the ...** luck / fortune **to do sth**
▸ to **leave sth to** chance / fate / providence
▸ to **believe in** luck / coincidences / fate / destiny / providence
▸ to **tempt** fate / providence
▸ sb's luck / fortune **changes / turns**
▸ fate / providence **decides / decrees...**
▸ a **stroke of** luck / fortune / fate

luck [U] the force that causes good or bad things to happen to people: ***The best of luck with*** *your exams.* ◇ *Bad luck, Helen, you played very well.* ◇ *Never mind — **better luck next time**.* ◇ *It was his **hard luck** that he wasn't chosen.* ◇ (*BrE*) *It's **hard luck on** him that he wasn't chosen.* ◇ ***Just my luck** to arrive after they had left* (= used to show you are not surprised sth bad has happened to you, because you are not often lucky). See also **lucky** → TIMELY

chance [U, sing.] the way that some things happen without any cause that you can see or understand: *We met by chance at the airport.* ◇ *Chess is not a **game of chance**.* ◇ *We'll plan everything very carefully and **leave nothing to chance**.* ◇ *By a happy chance he bumped into an old friend on the plane.*

coincidence /kəʊˈɪnsɪdəns; *AmE* koʊ-/ [C, U] the fact of two things happening at the same time by chance, in a surprising way: *They met through a series of strange coincidences.* ◇ *It's not a coincidence that none of the directors is a woman.* ◇ *It was pure coincidence that they were both in Paris on the same day.*
▸ **coincidental** *adj.*: *I suppose your presence here today is not entirely coincidental.*
▸ **coincidentally** *adv.*: *Coincidentally, they had both studied in Paris.*

accident [C, U] something that happens unexpectedly and is not planned in advance: *It is no accident that men fill most of the top jobs in the profession.* ◇ *an **accident of** birth/fate/history* (= describing facts and events that are due to chance or circumstances) ◇ *It happened, whether **by accident or design*** (= by accident or on purpose), *that Steve and I were the last two people to leave.*
▸ **accidental** *adj.*: *I didn't think our meeting was accidental — he must have known I would be there.*

fortune [U] (*rather formal*) luck or chance, especially in the way it affects people's lives: *I have had the good fortune to work with some brilliant directors.* ◇ *The team had a dramatic **reversal of fortune** in the second half.* See also **fortunate** → TIMELY

fate [U, sing.] the power that is believed to control everything that happens and that cannot be stopped or changed: *Fate was kind to me that day.* ◇ *By a strange **twist of fate**, Andy and I were on the same plane.* ◇ *She felt it would be **tempting fate*** (= being too confident in a way that might bring her good luck to an end) *to try the difficult climb a second time.* ◇ *He believed that the universe was controlled by the whims of a cruel fate.*

destiny /ˈdestəni/ [U] the power that is believed to control future events: *I believe there's some force guiding us — call it God, destiny or fate.* ◇ *She was spurred on by a strong sense of destiny.* See also **destined** → CERTAIN

providence (also **Providence**) /ˈprɒvɪdəns; *AmE* ˈprɑːv-/ [U] (*formal*) God, or a force that some people believe controls our lives and the things that happen to us, usually in a way that protects us: *He trusted in divine providence.* ◇ *She believed her suffering was sent by providence.*

> NOTE **FATE, DESTINY** OR **PROVIDENCE? Providence** is usually seen as being kind: even when it sends suffering, this is accepted as being part of God's plan. **Fate** can be kind, but this is an unexpected gift; just as often, **fate** is cruel and makes people feel helpless. **Destiny** is more likely to give people a sense of power: people who have a *strong sense of destiny* usually believe that they are meant to be great or do great things.

lucky *adj.*

lucky · fortunate · in luck
These words all describe people who have good things happen to them by chance.

PATTERNS AND COLLOCATIONS
▸ to be lucky / fortunate **that...**
▸ to be lucky / fortunate **to do sth**
▸ to **feel / consider yourself / count yourself / think yourself** lucky / fortunate
▸ **very / really / extremely / quite** lucky / fortunate

lucky (*especially spoken*) having good things happen to you by chance: *His friend was killed and he knows he is lucky to be alive.* ◇ *You were lucky (that) you spotted the danger in time.* ◇ *Mark is **one of the lucky ones** — he at least has somewhere to sleep.* ❶ People often use **lucky** to describe sb who has escaped or avoided a dangerous or unpleasant situation. OPP **unlucky** → UNFORTUNATE 1
▸ **luckily** *adv.*: *Luckily for us the train was late.*

fortunate (*rather formal*) lucky: *I was **fortunate in** having a good teacher.* ◇ *Remember those less fortunate than yourselves.* ❶ *Less fortunate* is often used to talk about people who have less money or less comfortable lives than others. OPP **unfortunate** → UNFORTUNATE 1
▸ **fortunately** *adv.*: *I was late, but fortunately the meeting hadn't started.*

in 'luck *phrase* lucky: *You're in luck — there's one ticket left.* ❶ You can say that sb **is in luck** when they manage to get exactly what they want or need, especially when that thing is the last one available. OPP **out of luck** → UNFORTUNATE 1

luxury *noun*

luxury · splendour · glory · grandeur
These are all words for the quality of being impressive, beautiful and often expensive.

PATTERNS AND COLLOCATIONS
▸ **sheer** luxury / splendour / grandeur
▸ **faded / former / original** splendour / glory / grandeur
▸ **scenic / rugged** splendour / grandeur
▸ to **enjoy** the luxury / splendour / grandeur of sth
▸ to **admire** the splendour / grandeur of sth
▸ to **have** (a certain) splendour / grandeur
▸ to **restore sth to / recapture** its (former) splendour / glory
▸ see, etc. sth **in all its** splendour / glory

luxury [U] a situation in which you are very comfortable because you have special and expensive things to enjoy, especially food and drink, clothes and surroundings: *Now we'll be able to live in luxury for the rest of our lives.* ◇ *He was used to living a life of luxury.* ◇ *You've just won three weeks in a luxury hotel.* ◇ *They stock a wide range of luxury goods.*
▸ **luxurious** /lʌgˈʒʊəriəs; *AmE* -ˈʒʊr-/ *adj.*: *a luxurious hotel* ◇ *luxurious surroundings*

splendour (*BrE*) (*AmE* **splendor**) /ˈsplendə(r)/ [U] (*especially written*) grand and impressive beauty, especially of places and buildings: *The room has a view of Rheims Cathedral, in all its splendour.* ❶ The **splendours** of sth are the beautiful and impressive features or qualities of sth, especially a place: *the splendours of Rome* (= its fine buildings, etc.)

glory [U, C] great beauty; a special cause for pride, respect or pleasure: *The house has now been restored to its former glory.* ◇ *The temple is one of the glories of ancient Greece.* ❶ The uncountable use of **glory** is usually used in the phrases *in all its/his/her glory* and *its former/full glory*. See also **glorious** → MAGNIFICENT

grandeur /ˈɡrændʒə(r); -djə(r)/ [U] (*especially written*) the quality of being great and impressive in appearance: *The hotel had an air of faded grandeur.* ◇ *We admired the rugged grandeur of the mountain scenery.* ❶ **Grandeur** is used especially to talk about old buildings and wild, impressive landscapes. It is used more to talk about how impressive sth is, rather than its beauty. Typical collocates are *classical, faded, former, imperial* and *scenic, rugged* and *natural*. See also **grand** → MAGNIFICENT

M m

machine *noun*

machine · engine · motor · unit · appliance · contraption
These are all words for a piece of equipment with moving parts that is designed to do a particular job.

PATTERNS AND COLLOCATIONS
- a **powerful** machine / engine / motor
- a **modern** machine / engine / appliance
- a **reliable** / **defective** machine / engine / motor / unit
- an **electronic** / **electric** / **electrical** machine / motor / unit / appliance
- to **build** / **make** a machine / an engine / a motor / a unit / a contraption
- to **design** / **use** a machine / an engine / a motor / a unit / an appliance
- to **operate** / **run** / **install** / **service** / **switch on** / **switch off** / **turn on** / **turn off** a machine / an engine / a motor / a unit / an appliance
- to **start** / **stop** a machine / an engine / a motor
- a machine / an engine / a unit / an appliance **works** / **breaks down**
- a machine / an engine / a motor / a unit **runs** / **starts** / **stops** / **fails** / **dies**
- an engine / a motor / a unit **drives** sth

machine [C] (often in compounds) a piece of equipment with moving parts that is designed to do a particular job. The power used to work a machine may be electricity, steam, gas, etc. or human power: *Do you know how to operate this machine?* ◇ *How does this machine work?* ◇ *a sewing/washing machine* ◇ *It's a machine for making plastic toys.* ◇ *Machines replaced human labour in many industries.* ◇ *The potatoes are planted by machine.* ❶ In informal or spoken English **machine** can also be used to refer to a particular machine, for example in the home, when you do not refer to it by its full name: *Just put those clothes in the machine* (= the washing machine). ◇ *The new machines* (= computers) *will be shipped next month.* See also **machinery** → TECHNOLOGY

engine [C] the part of a vehicle that produces power to make the vehicle move: *Switch the engine off.* ◇ *Their helicopter had developed engine trouble.*

motor [C] a device that uses electricity or petrol to produce movement and makes a machine work or a vehicle move: *One of the wheels is fitted with an electric motor.* ◇ *He started the motor.* ◇ *motor vehicles*

> **NOTE** ENGINE OR MOTOR? Technically, **engines** use thermal (= heat) energy such as steam, petrol or diesel, and a **motor** turns electrical energy into movement, for example in an electrical machine such as a washing machine. In everyday language, **engine** is usually used when talking about vehicles, but people do also use the word **motor**, especially in the phrase *start/turn off the motor* or in the term *outboard motor* (= on a small boat). **Motor** is also the term used, especially in British English, to describe many things relating to vehicles: (*especially BrE*) *the motor industry/trade* ◇ (*AmE*) *the automobile industry/business*

unit [C] a small machine that has a particular purpose or is part of a larger machine: *a waste disposal unit* ◇ *the central processing unit of a computer* ◇ *an air-conditioning unit*

appliance /əˈplaɪəns/ [C] (*rather formal*) a machine that is designed to do a particular thing in the home, such as preparing food, heating or cleaning: *They sell household appliances.* ◇ *We repair modern heating appliances of all types.* ❶ **Appliances** are typically described as *electrical, domestic, household* or *kitchen appliances*.

contraption /kənˈtræpʃn/ [C] a machine or piece of equipment that looks strange: *She showed us a strange contraption that looked like a satellite dish.*

mad *adj.*

mad · crazy · nuts · batty · out of your mind · (not) in your right mind
These are all informal words that describe sb who has a mind that does not work normally.

batty	mad	out of your mind
	crazy	
	nuts	
	not in your right mind	

PATTERNS AND COLLOCATIONS
- to be mad / crazy / nuts / out of your mind / not in your right mind **to do** sth
- to **go** mad / crazy / nuts / batty
- to **drive** sb mad / crazy / nuts / batty / out of their mind
- to **think** sb (**must be**) mad / crazy / nuts / batty / out of their mind
- **completely** mad / crazy / nuts / batty / out of your mind

mad (not usually used in the comparative or superlative) (*especially BrE, informal, sometimes offensive*) having a mind that does not work normally: *The local people all thought he was mad.* ◇ *She seemed to have gone stark raving mad.* ❶ **Mad** is an informal word used to suggest that sb's behaviour is very strange, often because of extreme emotional pressure. It is offensive if used to describe sb suffering from a real mental illness; use **mentally ill** instead. **Mad** is not usually used in this meaning in American English; use **crazy** instead. See also the entries for MENTALLY ILL and ANGRY

crazy (*especially AmE, informal, sometimes offensive*) mad: *A crazy old woman rented the upstairs room.* ◇ *She was driven half-crazy by the thought of him in prison.* ◇ *Do you think I'm crazy?* ❶ Like **mad**, **crazy** is offensive if used to describe sb suffering from a real mental illness.

nuts [not before noun] (*informal, spoken*) mad: *That noise is driving me nuts!* ◇ *You guys are nuts!*

batty (*informal, especially BrE*) slightly mad, in a harmless way: *Her mum's completely batty.*

out of your ˈmind *idiom* (*informal*) unable to think or behave normally, especially because of extreme shock or anxiety: *He almost went out of his mind, waiting for news of his son.* ◇ *She was out of her mind with grief.*

(not) in your right ˈmind *idiom* (*informal*) (not) mentally normal: *No one in their right mind would choose to work there.*

magazine *noun* See the Topic Map for THE MEDIA on p.900, See also the entry for NEWSPAPER

---

magazine · journal · supplement · weekly · periodical · comic · mag · fanzine · monthly · quarterly

These are all words for a type of large thin book with a paper cover that is published regularly every week, every month or several times a year.

PATTERNS AND COLLOCATIONS
▶ **in** a magazine / journal / supplement / weekly / periodical / comic / mag / fanzine / monthly / quarterly
▶ a **weekly**/**monthly** magazine / journal / supplement / periodical / comic
▶ a **quarterly** magazine / journal / supplement / periodical
▶ a **fashion** magazine / mag / monthly
▶ a **scientific** / **trade** magazine / journal
▶ to **publish** a magazine / journal / supplement / weekly / periodical / comic / mag / monthly / quarterly
▶ to **read** a magazine / journal / weekly / comic / mag
▶ a magazine / journal **article**

magazine [C] a type of thin book with large pages and a paper cover, that contains articles and photographs and is published every week or month: *He was criticized for comments he made in a magazine interview.*

journal /ˈdʒɜːnl; *AmE* ˈdʒɜːrnl/ [C] a magazine or newspaper that is published regularly, usually about specialist or academic subjects: *Trade journals are excellent sources of information about industry trends.* ◇ *the British Medical Journal* ❶ **Journal** is also used in the title of some newspapers: *the Wall Street Journal*

supplement /ˈsʌplɪmənt/ [C] an extra separate section, often in the form of a magazine, that is sold with a newspaper: *It was the first paper in the UK to have a colour supplement.*

weekly [C] a newspaper or magazine that is published every week: *Men's weeklies are currently enjoying a growth in readership.*

periodical [C] /ˌpɪəriˈɒdɪkl; *AmE* ˌpɪriˈɑːd-/ (*rather formal*) a magazine that is published every week, every month or several times a year, especially one that is concerned with an academic subject: *The university library stocks some 5 000 current periodicals.*

comic /ˈkɒmɪk; *AmE* ˈkɑːmɪk/ [C] (also **'comic book**) a magazine, especially for children, that tells stories through pictures: *a comic book superhero* ❶ In American English **the comics** [pl.] means the section of a newspaper that contains **comic strips** (= series of drawings inside boxes that tell a story).

mag [C] (*informal*) a magazine: *She's always reading the fashion mags and spends loads of money on clothes.*

fanzine /ˈfænziːn/ [C] a magazine that is written and read by fans (= people who admire sb/sth very much) of a musician, sports team, television series, etc: *The first science fiction fanzine was published in 1930.*

monthly [C] a magazine published once a month: *The upmarket monthly covers topics such as fashion, food and lifestyle trends.*

quarterly [C] a magazine published four times a year: *It is an independent quarterly of literature, the arts and public affairs.*

---

magic *noun*

---

magic · witchcraft · sorcery · black magic · the supernatural · the occult · conjuring

These are all words for the secret power of making impossible things happen, or entertainment in which impossible things seem to happen.

PATTERNS AND COLLOCATIONS
▶ to do sth **by** magic / sorcery
▶ to **practise** magic / witchcraft / black magic
▶ to **use** magic / witchcraft / sorcery
▶ a magic / conjuring **trick**

magic [U] the secret power of making impossible things happen by saying special words or doing special things; the art of doing tricks that seem impossible in order to entertain people: *Do you believe in magic?* ◇ *This was a place of secret shadows and ancient magic.* ◇ *He suddenly appeared as if by magic.* ◇ *He earns extra money doing magic at children's parties.* See also **magician** → WITCH

witchcraft /ˈwɪtʃkrɑːft; *AmE* -kræft/ [U] the use of magic powers, especially evil ones: *She was accused of witchcraft.* ❶ Traditionally, people think of **witchcraft** as sth that is practised by women, although men have also been said to practise it. See also **witch** → WITCH

sorcery /ˈsɔːsəri; *AmE* ˈsɔːrs-/ [U] (*written*) magic that uses evil spirits: *She was said to have caused the king's illness by sorcery.* See also **sorcerer** → WITCH

black 'magic [U] magic that uses evil spirits: *People found guilty of practising black magic were hanged.*

> **NOTE** WITCHCRAFT, SORCERY OR BLACK MAGIC? Sorcery and **black magic** both involve the use of evil spirits or the power of the Devil in order to do evil. **Witchcraft** is wider in range: it typically means sorcery or black magic, but can also mean the practice of *white magic* or *natural magic* that involves using hidden forces within nature for good, not evil, purposes.

the supernatural /ˌsuːpəˈnætʃrəl; ˈsjuː-; *AmE* ˌsuːpərˈn-/ [sing.] (*rather formal*) events, forces or powers that cannot be explained by reason or science and that seem to involve gods or magic: *A strong belief in the supernatural characterizes many of these communities.*

the occult [sing.] the supernatural, especially when it is used for secret or evil purposes: *He's interested in witchcraft and the occult.*

conjuring /ˈkʌndʒərɪŋ/ [U] (*rather formal*) entertainment in the form of magic tricks, especially ones which seem to make things appear or disappear: *After dinner, Brian performed several conjuring tricks.*

---

magic *adj.*

---

magic · magical · mystical · supernatural · enchanted · occult · transcendental · other-worldly

These words all describe sb/sth that has or seems to have special powers or qualities that cannot be explained by science.

PATTERNS AND COLLOCATIONS
▶ magic / magical / mystical / supernatural / occult **powers**
▶ magical / mystical / supernatural / occult **forces**
▶ a magical / mystical **experience**

magic having or using special powers to make impossible things happen or seem to happen: *a magic spell / charm / potion* ◇ *Abu Ali and the princess escape by flying on a magic carpet.* ◇ *I wish I could wave a magic wand and make everything all right again.* ◇ *There is no magic formula for passing exams — only hard work.*

magical (*especially written*) containing magic; used in magic: *Her words had a magical effect on us.* ◇ *Mercury was believed to possess magical properties.* ❶ In this meaning **magical** often describes abstract things such as *powers, properties, forces* and *energy*, but it is not used to describe the things which have magical powers: *a magical spell / charm / potion / wand / carpet*

mystical (*especially written*) having spiritual powers or qualities that are difficult to understand or explain: *Wise men thought that mystical forces regulated the activities of the brain.* ◇ *Watching the sun rise over the mountain was an almost mystical experience.* ❶ **Mystical** is often used in religious contexts.

supernatural /ˌsuːpəˈnætʃrəl; ˈsjuː-; *AmE* ˌsuːpərˈn-/ that cannot be explained by reason or science and that seems to involve gods or magic: *Contestants wrestled with supernatural strength and powers of endurance.* ❶ Typical collocates of **supernatural** are *being, force, power* and *strength*.

enchanted /ɪnˈtʃɑːntɪd; AmE -ˈtʃæntɪd/ (written) placed under a spell (= magic words that have special powers): *The children made their way through the enchanted forest, their hearts beating fast.* ❶ **Enchanted** is often used in children's stories to talk about places where fairies and other magical creatures live.

occult /əˈkʌlt; ˈɒkʌlt; AmE ˈɑːk-/ [only before noun] (written) supernatural, especially when it is connected with evil and secrecy: *They assured us that their organization did not follow occult practices.*

transcendental /ˌtrænsenˈdentl/ [usually before noun] (written) going beyond the limits of human knowledge, experience or reason, especially in a religious or spiritual way: *He said that it was transcendental meditation that brought him inner peace.* ❶ **Transcendental** is most often used to talk about an *experience, meditation, reflection* or a *state*.

other-ˈworldly (written) concerned with spiritual thoughts and ideas rather than with ordinary life: *There was an other-worldly quality to her performance that night.* ❶ **Other-worldly** is usually used to talk about strange experiences, noises, states or qualities, which give the impression of being in a dream-world.

magnificent *adj.* See also the entries for BEAUTI-FUL 2 and WONDERFUL

---

magnificent · impressive · spectacular · grand · glorious · majestic · imposing
These words all describe things that are extremely attractive and make you feel admiration.

---

impressive	grand	magnificent
imposing	majestic	spectacular
		glorious

PATTERNS AND COLLOCATIONS
▸ a magnificent/ an impressive/ a spectacular/ a glorious/ a majestic **sight**
▸ a magnificent/an impressive/a spectacular/a glorious **display/ array**
▸ magnificent/impressive/spectacular/grand/glorious/majestic **scenery/ views**
▸ magnificent/ spectacular/ glorious **countryside**
▸ a magnificent/ an impressive/ a spectacular **waterfall**
▸ magnificent/ spectacular/ glorious **coastline/ sunset**
▸ magnificent/ spectacular/ majestic **mountains**
▸ a magnificent/an impressive/a grand/a majestic/an imposing **building**
▸ a magnificent/ a grand/ a majestic/ an imposing **castle**
▸ a magnificent/ a grand/ an imposing **palace/ staircase**
▸ glorious/ majestic **beauty**
▸ quite magnificent/ impressive/ spectacular/ grand
▸ **truly/ rather** magnificent/ impressive/ spectacular/ grand/ glorious
▸ **absolutely** magnificent/ spectacular/ glorious
▸ **very** impressive/ spectacular/ grand/ majestic/ imposing

magnificent /mægˈnɪfɪsnt/ extremely beautiful in a way that makes you feel wonder and admiration: *The Taj Mahal is a magnificent building.* ◊ *She looked magnificent in her wedding dress.* ◊ *It was an absolutely magnificent performance.*
▸ **magnificence** *noun* [U]: *the magnificence of the scenery*
▸ **magnificently** *adv.*: *The city boasts a wealth of magnificently preserved temples and palaces.*

impressive making you feel admiration, because it is very large, attractive or well or expensively made or built: *A large portico provides a suitably impressive entrance to the chapel.* ◊ *This is one of the most impressive novels of recent years.* ❶ **Impressive** is often used when you feel great admiration for a place or thing but do not necessarily find it beautiful. See also **impressive** → IMPRESSIVE

spectacular /spekˈtækjələ(r)/ (especially of scenery or a performance) extremely beautiful and impressive: *The coastal road has spectacular scenery.* ◊ *In the evening, there will be a spectacular display of fireworks.* See also **spectacular** → IMPRESSIVE, **breathtaking** → AMAZING

grand impressive and large or important: *It's not a very grand house.* ◊ *The wedding was a very grand occasion.* ❶ When **grand** is used to describe a thing, it is usually sth relating to a building or part of a building such as a *house, villa, hotel, castle, palace, staircase* or *entrance*. When **grand** is used to describe an occasion, it is usually one that involves rich people or the spending of a large amount of money. See also **grandeur** → LUXURY

glorious /ˈɡlɔːriəs/ extremely beautiful and impressive: *We sat on the beach and gazed at the glorious sunset.* ◊ *Both her daughters had glorious red hair.* ❶ **Glorious** is used especially to describe things that are bright and connected with summer or the colours of the sun − yellow, orange or red. See also **glory** → LUXURY

majestic /məˈdʒestɪk/ very impressive because of its size or beauty: *The college is close to Edinburgh's majestic castle.* ◊ *The Rockies are majestic in size.* ❶ **Majestic** is usually used to describe large and impressive buildings such as castles, mansions or hotels, or high natural features such as mountains or cliffs.
▸ **majestically** *adv.*: *The cliffs rise majestically from the ocean.*

imposing /ɪmˈpəʊzɪŋ; AmE -ˈpoʊz-/ impressive to look at; making a strong impression: *The Tower House is not a particularly grand or imposing building.* ◊ *She was a tall imposing woman.* ❶ **Imposing** people or things are likely to make you feel respectful, but also rather small or unimportant.

main *adj.* See also the entry for TOP

---

main · major · key · central · principal · chief · prime · primary · number one · predominant
These words all describe sb/sth that is the largest or most important of its kind.

PATTERNS AND COLLOCATIONS
▸ to be key/ central **to** sth
▸ a/ the main/ major/ key/ central/ principal/ chief/ prime/ primary/ number one/ predominant **concern**
▸ a/ the main/ major/ key/ central/ principal/ chief/ prime/ primary/ predominant **purpose/ source/ factor**
▸ a/ the main/ major/ key/ central/ principal/ chief/ prime/ primary **aim/ focus/ function/ objective/ task/ reason/ consideration**
▸ a/ the main/ major/ principal/ chief/ prime/ primary **object**
▸ a/ the main/ major/ key/ principal/ chief/ prime/ primary/ number one **cause**
▸ a/ the main/ major/ principal/ chief/ primary/ predominant **effect**
▸ a/ the main/ major/ key/ central/ principal/ chief/ prime **attraction**
▸ a/ the main/ major/ key/ central/ principal/ predominant **theme**
▸ a/ the main/ major/ key/ central/ principal/ prime/ predominant **role**
▸ a/ the main/ major/ principal/ prime/ number one **contender**
▸ the main/ chief/ prime/ number one **suspect**
▸ a/ the main/ major/ principal **road/ town/ city**
▸ the main/ key **thing** is to...
▸ to be **of** major/ key/ central/ prime/ primary **importance**

main [only before noun] largest or most important: *Be careful crossing the main road.* ◊ *We have our main meal at lunchtime.* ◊ *The main course was roast lamb.* ◊ *Reception is in the main building.* ◊ *Please use the main entrance.* ◊ *Poor housing and unemployment are the main problems.* ◊ (*spoken*) *The main thing is to remain calm.*
▸ **mainly** *adv.*: *They eat mainly fruit and nuts.* ◊ *The population almost doubles in August, mainly because of the film festival.*

major /'meɪdʒə(r)/ [usually before noun] very large or important: *A major road runs right through the centre of the town.* ◇ *He played a major role in setting up the system.* ◇ *We have encountered major problems.* ❶ **Major** is most often used after *a* with a singular noun or no article with a plural noun. When it is used with *the* or *my/your/his/her/our/their* it means 'the largest or most important': *Our major concern here is combatting poverty.* In this meaning it is only used to talk about ideas or worries that people have, NOT physical things, and it is also more formal than **main**: ~~Be careful crossing the major road.~~ ◇ ~~The major thing is to remain calm.~~ **OPP** **minor** → MINOR

key [usually before noun] most important; essential: *The key issue here is taxation.* ◇ *'Caution' is the key word in this situation.* ◇ *Attitude is a key concept in social psychology.* ❶ **Key** is used most frequently in business and political contexts. It can be used to talk about ideas, or the part that sb plays in a situation, but NOT physical things. It is slightly more informal than **major**, especially when used after a noun and linking verb: (*rather informal*) *Speed is key at this point.*

central (*rather formal*) most important; having power or control over other parts: *The central issue is that of widespread racism.* ◇ *She has been a central figure in the campaign.* ◇ *Reducing inflation is central to* (= is an important part of) *the government's economic policy.* ◇ *the central committee* (= of a political party) ◇ *The organization has a central office in New York.* ❶ **Central** is used in a similar way to **key**, but is more formal. It is most frequently used in the phrase *sth is central to sth else* and has a slightly smaller range of noun collocates than **key**. These mostly relate to the part sb/sth plays in sth (*character, component, feature, figure, motif, part, role, theme, topic*), what sb is trying to achieve (*aim, focus, issue, preoccupation, problem, recommendation*) or ideas that sb has about sth (*belief, concept, doctrine, truth*).

principal /'prɪnsəpl/ [only before noun] (*rather formal*) most important: *New roads will link the principal cities.* ◇ *Tourist revenue is now our principal source of wealth.* ◇ *My principal concern is to get the job done fast.* ❶ **Principal** is mostly used for statements of fact about which there can be no argument. To state an opinion, or to try to persuade sb of the facts as you see them, it is more usual to use **key** or **central**: *The key/central issue here is…*
▸ **principally** *adv.*: *The tax was very unpopular, principally because it hit the poor hardest.* ◇ *The farms are principally arable.*

chief [only before noun] (*especially written*) most important: *Unemployment was the chief cause of poverty.* ◇ *Her chief rival for the gold medal is Jones of the USA.* ❶ **Chief** also means 'highest in rank' when talking about the jobs that people have. In the meaning of 'most important' it is also often used to talk about people in various different roles: *sb's chief enemy/rival/opponent* ◇ *the chief architect/exponent of sth*
▸ **chiefly** *adv.*: *Defence spending was cut, chiefly by reducing national service by six months.* ◇ *The scientists cannot be held solely or even chiefly to blame.*

prime [only before noun] (*rather formal*) most important; to be considered first: *My prime concern is to protect my property.* ◇ *The care of the environment is of prime importance.* ◇ *He's the police's prime suspect in this case.*

primary [usually before noun] (*rather formal*) prime: *The primary aim of this class is to improve your spoken English.* ◇ *Our primary concern must be the children.*
▸ **primarily** *adv.*: *In the 1790s Britain was still primarily an agricultural country.* ◇ *History is after all primarily about people.*

NOTE PRIME OR PRIMARY? In many cases you can use either word: *your prime/primary concern/purpose/aim/object/objective/task* ◇ *to be of prime/primary importance.* However, **prime** is used in some fixed collocations where **primary** cannot be used: *the prime attraction/contender/suspect* ◇ ~~the primary attraction/contender/suspect~~ **Primary** also has the related meaning of 'earliest' or 'first'. See also **primary** → FIRST

number one [only before noun] (*informal*) most important or best: *Our number one priority is to find larger office space.* ◇ *I just love your work! I'm your number one fan.*

predominant /prɪ'dɒmɪnənt; AmE -'dɑːm-/ (*rather formal*) most obvious or noticeable: *A predominant feature of his work is the use of natural materials.* ◇ *Yellow is the predominant colour this spring in the fashion world.*
▸ **predominantly** *adv.*: *The firm has a predominantly female workforce.* ◇ *Ours is a predominantly Buddhist country.*

maintain *verb*

1 maintain law and order
2 a beautifully maintained house

---

1 maintain · preserve · sustain · extend · prolong · keep sth up · keep sth going · perpetuate · prop sth up
These words all mean to make sth continue at the same level or standard.

PATTERNS AND COLLOCATIONS
▸ to maintain / preserve / sustain / keep up **standards / a relationship**
▸ to maintain / sustain / keep up **levels / rates / morale / interest / growth / the momentum**
▸ to keep the **momentum** going
▸ to maintain / preserve / sustain / perpetuate a **system / myth**
▸ to maintain / preserve / sustain a / an **balance / illusion**
▸ to maintain / preserve / keep up a **tradition**
▸ to keep a **tradition** going
▸ to maintain / sustain / keep up a **pretence**
▸ to maintain / preserve **anonymity / confidentiality / order / the status quo / your heritage**
▸ to maintain / preserve / sustain / extend / prolong (sb's) **life**
▸ to extend / prolong a **visit / stay**
▸ to **still** maintain / preserve sth / sustain sth / keep sth up / keep sth going / perpetuate sth / prop sth up
▸ to maintain / preserve / sustain / prolong sth / keep sth going **indefinitely**
▸ to maintain / extend / prolong sth **deliberately**

maintain /meɪn'teɪn/ [T] (*rather formal*) to make sth continue at the same level or standard: *Our principal task is to maintain law and order.* ◇ *The two countries have always maintained close relations.* ◇ (*formal*) *She maintained a dignified silence.*

preserve [T] (*rather formal*) to keep a particular quality or feature; to make sure that a quality or feature is kept: *He was anxious to preserve his reputation.* ◇ *Efforts to preserve the peace have failed.* ◇ *She managed to preserve her sense of humour under very trying circumstances.*

sustain /sə'steɪn/ [T] (*rather formal*) to make sth continue for some time at the same level: *We are experiencing a period of sustained economic growth.* ◇ *She had been the victim of a sustained attack.* ◇ *She managed to sustain everyone's interest until the end of her speech.*
▸ **sustainable** *adj.*: *sustainable economic growth* **OPP** **unsustainable**

NOTE MAINTAIN OR SUSTAIN? In some cases you can use either word: *to maintain/sustain a balance/a pretence/people's interest/life.* **Maintain** is used especially to talk about keeping sth at its usual level for an unlimited period of time: *They believe that the role of the state is to maintain the status quo, rather than to promote major economic and social change.* **Sustain** is used more to talk about keeping sth at a higher than usual level for a long but not unlimited period: *How long can this level of growth be sustained?*

extend [T] (*rather formal*) to make sth last longer: *They've agreed to extend the deadline.* ◇ *The show has been extended for another six weeks.* ◇ *Careful maintenance can extend the life of your car by several years.* See also **extended** → LONG *adj.*
▸ **extension** *noun* [C]: *He's been granted an extension of the contract for another year.*

prolong /prə'lɒŋ; AmE -'lɔːŋ; -'lɑːŋ/ [T] (rather formal) to make sth last longer: *The operation could prolong his life by two or three years.* ◇ *Don't* **prolong the agony** (= of not knowing sth) − *just tell us who won!* See also **prolonged** → LONG adj.

NOTE EXTEND OR PROLONG? Extend is used especially in business contexts: *to extend a deadline/an overdraft/a trip/a visa/a right/a mandate.* Prolong is more often used to talk about making experiences last longer: *to prolong your stay/visit/life/survival/agony/misery*

,**keep sth 'up** phrasal verb to make sth stay at a high level; to continue to use or practise sth: *The high cost of raw materials is keeping prices up.* ◇ *They sang songs to keep their spirits up.* ◇ *We try to keep up the old customs.* ◇ *Do you still keep up your Spanish?*

,**keep sth 'going** phrase (rather informal, especially spoken) to make an effort to make a process, activity or tradition continue to happen or exist: *We have a chance of winning the championship as long as we can keep the momentum going* (= keep playing at the same high level).

perpetuate /pə'petʃueɪt; AmE pər'p-/ [T] (formal) to make sth such as a bad situation or a belief continue for a long time: *This new law just serves to perpetuate inequality.* ◇ *This system* **perpetuated itself** *for several centuries.* ◇ *Comics and books for children tend to perpetuate the myth that 'boys don't cry'.* ❶ Typical collocates of **perpetuate** are inequality, myth, stereotype and system.

,**prop sth 'up** phrasal verb (-pp-) (often disapproving, especially business) to help sth that is having difficulties, when it might be better to let it fail and use your resources for sth else: *The government was accused of propping up declining industries.* ❶ **Prop sth up** is used most often in financial contexts: *to prop up the economy/exchange value of sterling/pound/dollar/stockmarket*

2 **maintain · preserve · service · keep sth up**
These words all mean to keep sth in good condition.

PATTERNS AND COLLOCATIONS
▶ to maintain / preserve a **house**
▶ to maintain / service a / an **car / appliance**
▶ to **have / keep** sth maintained / preserved / serviced
▶ sth is **well / fully** maintained / preserved / serviced
▶ sth is **regularly** maintained / serviced
▶ sth is maintained / preserved **intact**

maintain /meɪn'teɪn/ [T] to keep sth such as a building or machine in good condition by checking or repairing it regularly: *The house is large and difficult to maintain.* ◇ *The grounds are beautifully maintained.* See also **maintenance** → REPAIR verb

preserve [T, often passive] to keep sth in its original state in good condition: *Three miles away is a perfectly preserved stretch of Roman road.* ◇ *(humorous) Is he really 60? He's remarkably well preserved.*
▶ **preservation** noun [U]: *building/environmental preservation*

service [T, usually passive] to examine a vehicle or machine and repair it if necessary so that it continues to work correctly: *We need to have the car serviced.* ◇ *Gas appliances should be regularly serviced.* See also **service**, **servicing** → REPAIR verb

,**keep sth 'up** phrasal verb to take care of a place, house or garden so that it stays in good condition: *We can't stay in this house − we simply don't have the money to keep it up.* See also **upkeep** → REPAIR

make verb
1 make your own clothes
2 make a profit
3 make a living
4 It made me think.

1 See also the entries for DEVELOP 2 and MANUFACTURE
make · do · create · produce · build · generate · form
These words all mean to make sth from parts or materials, or to cause sth to exist or happen.

PATTERNS AND COLLOCATIONS
▶ to make / create / produce / build / generate / form sth **from / out of** sth
▶ to make / form sth **into** sth
▶ to make / do / create / produce a **drawing / painting**
▶ to make / do / produce a **sketch**
▶ to make / create / produce **a meal**
▶ to make / produce **wine**
▶ Who made / created the **universe / world**?
▶ to create / produce / generate **income / profits / wealth**
▶ to produce / generate **electricity / heat / power**
▶ to make / create / produce a / an **noise / impression**
▶ to make / create a **fuss / mess**
▶ to create / build / form a **picture** of past societies

make [T] to create or prepare sth by combining materials or putting parts together; to cause sth to exist or happen: *She makes her own clothes.* ◇ *Wine is made from grapes.* ◇ *The grapes are made into wine.* ◇ *What's your shirt made of?* ◇ *She made us all coffee.* ◇ *He has made* (= directed or acted in) *several movies.* ◇ *She tried to* **make a good impression** *on the interviewer.* See also **making** → PRODUCTION

do [T] (rather informal, especially spoken) to make or prepare sth, especially sth artistic or sth to eat: *He did a beautiful drawing of a house.* ◇ *Who's doing the food for the party?* ◇ *Does this pub do* (= provide) *lunches?* ◇ *I'll do a copy for you.* ◇ *I'll do you a copy.*

create [T] to make sth exist or happen, especially sth new that did not exist before: *Scientists disagree about how the universe was created.* ◇ *The government plans to create more jobs for young people.* ◇ *Create a new directory and put all your files into it.* See also **creation** → DEVELOPMENT, **creative** → CREATIVE, **creator** → DESIGNER

NOTE MAKE OR CREATE? Make is a more general word and is more often used to talk about physical things: you would usually *make a table/dress/cake* but *create jobs/wealth.* You can use **create** to talk about sth physical in order to emphasize how original or unusual the object is: *Try this new dish, created by our head chef.* See also the entry for CAUSE

produce [T] to create sth using skill; to create power or money: *She produced a delicious meal out of a few leftovers.* ◇ *He argued that wealth is produced by the labour power of the workers.* See also **produce** → MANUFACTURE

build [T] to create sth, especially a way of life or an impression that you develop and improve over a period of time: *She's built a new career for herself.* ◇ *This information will help us build a picture of his attacker.*

generate [T] to produce or create sth, especially power, money or ideas: *The wind turbines are used to generate electricity.* ◇ *The lottery is expected to generate substantial funds for charity.* ◇ *Brainstorming is a good way of generating ideas.*

form [T, often passive] to make sth from sth else; to make sth into sth else: *Rearrange the letters to form a new word.* ◇ *Do you know how to form the past tense?* ◇ *The chain is formed from 136 links.* See also **form** → SHAPE verb

2 **make · raise · get · fetch · bring (sb) in sth · realize**
These words all mean to gain an amount of money, especially by selling sth.

PATTERNS AND COLLOCATIONS
▶ to make / raise / bring in **money**
▶ to make / raise / get / fetch / bring in / realize **$199 / £300 000**
▶ to make / realize £1 000 / $50 000 **on** a deal

make [T] to gain an amount of money by selling sth: *She sold her foreign investments last month and made $75 000.*

◇ *We need to think of new ways to make money from our existing products.* ◇ *The company is **making a loss** on its children's range.*

raise [T] to collect money for sth, by selling sth, borrowing money or asking people to give it: *The sale raised over £3 000 for charity.* ◇ *The hospital is trying to raise funds for a new kidney machine.* ◇ *He needed to raise a loan in order to set up in business.*

get [T, no passive] (*rather informal*) to gain an amount of money by selling sth: *We **got** £220 000 **for** the house.*

fetch [T] to be sold for a particular amount of money: *The painting is expected to fetch £10 000 at auction.*

,bring in 'sth, ,bring sb 'in sth *phrasal verb* to gain an amount of money by selling sth: *The garage sale brought in a lot more than we expected.* ◇ *Selling off the business would bring us in about £200 000.*

> **NOTE** MAKE, GET OR BRING IN STH? You can **make** money, a particular amount of money, or a profit or loss. You can **bring in** money or a particular amount of money. You can only **get** a particular amount of money: ~~The garage sale got a lot more than we expected.~~ ◇ ~~The company is getting/bringing in a loss.~~

realize (*BrE* also **-ise**) [T] (*formal*) to be sold for a particular amount of money: *The paintings realized $2 million at auction.*

---

3 make · earn · profit · net · bring (sb) in sth · gross · pocket · pull sth in · rake sth in

These words all mean to get money, especially by working or doing business.

PATTERNS AND COLLOCATIONS
▸ to make / earn / net / bring in / gross / pocket / pull in / rake in **$100 000 a year**
▸ to make / earn **money / a living / a fortune**

make [T] to get money as payment for work that you do, or as interest or profit on money that you lend or invest: *He makes a living as a stand-up comic.* ◇ *She made a fortune on the stock market.* ◇ *A movie with big name stars in it should make money.* ◇ *Did they **make any money out of** their invention?*

earn [T, I] to get money as payment for work that you do, or as interest or profit on money that you lend or invest: *She earns about £25 000 a year.* ◇ *His victory in the tournament earned him $50 000.* ◇ *Your money would earn more in a high-interest account.* ◇ *He was willing to **earn his keep** (= do useful things in return for being allowed to live somewhere).* ◇ *All her children are earning now (= working for their living).* See also **earnings** → INCOME

> **NOTE** MAKE OR EARN? You can **make** or **earn** money, a living or a fortune. **Earn** emphasizes the work you have to do to get the money. If the money comes as interest or profit, and the subject is a person use **make**: ~~She earned a fortune on the stock market.~~ If the subject is a business or factory, use either word: *The plant will make/earn £950 million for the UK.* If the subject is the money itself use **earn**: ~~Your money would make more in a high-interest account.~~

profit [I] (*rather formal*) to make money from an activity: *The private sector will **profit by** selling the surplus electricity abroad.* ◇ *Convicted criminals should not be allowed to **profit from** their crimes.* See also **profit** → PROFIT *noun*, **profit** → BENEFIT *verb*

net (**-tt-**) [T] to make an amount of money as profit after you have paid tax on it: *The sale of paintings netted £17 000.*

,bring sb 'in sth, ,bring 'in sth *phrasal verb* to earn or produce money: *His freelance work brings him in about £20 000 a year.* ◇ *New taxes are expected to bring in $12 billion in extra revenue.*

gross /grəʊs; *AmE* groʊs/ [T] to make an amount of money as profit before you have paid tax on it: *The tour grossed a massive £20 million at the box office.*

pocket [T] (*rather informal, sometimes disapproving*) to earn or win an amount of money: *Last year, she pocketed over $1 million in advertising contracts.* See also **pocket** → FUND *noun*, **bank** → SAVE 3

,pull sth 'in *phrasal verb* (*informal*) to earn or make a lot of money: *She must be pulling in over $100 000 a year.*

,rake sth 'in *phrasal verb* (*informal, often disapproving*) to earn or make a lot of money, especially when this is done easily: *The movie raked in more than $300 million.* ◇ *She's been **raking it in** since she started her new job.*

---

4 make · lead · prompt · motivate · induce · predispose

These words all refer to sth being the reason why sb does or thinks sth.

PATTERNS AND COLLOCATIONS
▸ to lead / predispose sb **to** sth
▸ to lead / prompt / motivate / induce / predispose **sb to do sth**
▸ to make **sb do sth**

make [T] (always followed by infinitive without *to*) to cause sb to think sth or decide to do sth: *Nothing will make me change my mind.* ◇ ***What makes you** say that (= why do you think so)?* ◇ *What he said certainly made us all think.* ◇ *Politeness made her go back to see him.*

lead /liːd/ [T] to be the reason why sb does or thinks sth, especially as part of a process of understanding sth: *What led you to this conclusion?* ◇ *What we found leads us to suspect that more people may be involved.* ◇ *The situation is far worse than we had been **led to believe**.*

prompt [T] (especially of an event or experience) to be the reason why sb decides to do sth: *What prompted you to choose this area?* ◇ *I understand your views and the reasons which prompted you to write.*

motivate /ˈməʊtɪveɪt; *AmE* ˈmoʊ-/ [T, often passive] to be the reason why sb decides to do sth or behave in a particular way: *He is motivated entirely by self-interest.* ◇ *What motivates people to carry out such attacks?* See also **motivation** → INCENTIVE

induce /ɪnˈdjuːs; *AmE* -duːs/ [T] (always followed by *to* + infinitive; used especially in negative statements) (*formal*) to persuade or influence sb to do sth: *Nothing would induce me to take the job.* ◇ *No amount of persuasion could induce her to stay longer.* See also **inducement** → INCENTIVE

predispose /ˌpriːdɪˈspəʊz; *AmE* -ˈspoʊz/ [T] (*formal*) (especially of sb's character, opinions, mood or experience) to influence sb so that they are likely to think or behave in a particular way: *One theory is that some people **are predisposed to** criminal behaviour because of their genetic make-up.* ◇ *Certain experiences can **predispose** a child **towards** a feeling of helplessness.*

maker *noun* See also the entry for DESIGNER

---

maker · manufacturer · producer · builder · craftsman

These are all words for people or companies that make or produce things.

PATTERNS AND COLLOCATIONS
▸ a **big / large / leading / major** manufacturer / producer
▸ a **local** manufacturer / producer / builder / craftsman
▸ a **car** maker / manufacturer / producer
▸ a **computer** maker / manufacturer
▸ a **steel / wine** producer
▸ a **chemical** manufacturer / producer

maker [C] (often in compounds) a person, company or piece of equipment that makes sth: *His father was a watchmaker and jeweller.* ◇ *a new movie from the makers of 'The Matrix'* ◇ *an electric coffee-maker* ◇ *a decision/law/policy maker*

manufacturer [C] a person or company that produces goods in large quantities: *the daughter of a rich textile manufacturer* ◇ *Always follow the manufacturer's instructions.* ◇ *Faulty goods should be returned to the manufacturers.* See also **manufacture** → MANUFACTURE

producer [C] a person, company or country that grows or makes food, materials or goods: *British milk producers* ◇ *The country is one of the world's largest oil producers.* See also **produce** → MANUFACTURE

NOTE **MAKER, MANUFACTURER** OR **PRODUCER?** All of these words can mean a company that produces sth or the person who runs that company. **Maker** and **manufacturer** are used especially when talking about goods such as cars and computers that are assembled (= made) from different parts. **Producer** is used more when talking about natural materials that are grown or obtained and processed, such as food and oil. For products for which quality and skill are seen to be important, such as steel and wine, **maker** is also frequent.

builder [C] (often in compounds) a person or company whose job is to build or repair houses or other buildings; a person or thing that builds, creates or develops sth: *We got a local builder to do the work for us.* ◇ *a shipbuilder* ◇ *Going on the course was a real confidence-builder for me.* See also **build** → BUILD

craftsman [C] (*often approving*) a person who does skilled work, making things with their hands: *rugs handmade by local craftsmen* ❶ The feminine form **craftswoman**, and the neutral form **craftsperson** are also possible, although neither is frequent. It is usual to use **craftsman** even if the gender is not known and it might be a woman.

man *noun*

1 a good-looking young man
2 the most poisonous substance known to man

1 man · guy · gentleman · male · bloke · dude
These are all words for an adult male person.

PATTERNS AND COLLOCATIONS
▸ a / an **young** / **old** man / guy / gentleman / male / bloke / dude
▸ a / an **middle-aged** / **older** man / guy / gentleman / male / bloke
▸ a / an **elderly** man / guy / gentleman / male
▸ a **big** / **little** man / guy / bloke / dude
▸ a **black** / **white** man / guy / male / dude
▸ an **ordinary** man / guy / bloke
▸ a **handsome** man / guy / gentleman / dude
▸ a **good-looking** man / guy / dude
▸ a **nice** man / guy / gentleman / bloke / dude
▸ a **good** / **great** / **funny** man / guy / bloke / dude
▸ a **decent** man / guy / bloke
▸ a **cool** guy / dude

man [C] an adult male person: *He's a good-looking young man.* ◇ *He's a family man who rarely goes out with his friends.* ◇ *Over 150 men, women and children were killed.* **OPP** **woman** → WOMAN

guy [C] (*informal*) a man: *He seemed like a nice guy.* ◇ *It was made by a guy called Alan Webster.* ◇ *At the end of the film, the bad guy gets shot.* **OPP** **girl** → GIRL

gentleman [C] (*formal*) a polite way of referring to a man, especially sb that you do not know: *There's a gentleman here to see you.* ❶ **Gentlemen** [pl.] is a polite way of addressing more than one man: *Ladies and gentlemen! Can I have your attention, please?* ◇ *Can I help you, gentlemen?* To address one man in this way, use **sir**: *Can I help you, sir?* In more informal speech, say: *Can I help you?* ◇ *There's someone to see you.* **OPP** **lady** → WOMAN

male [C] (*formal or technical*) a man: *The body is that of a white male aged about 40.* ◇ *Haemophilia is a condition that mostly affects males.* ❶ The noun **male** is mostly used in formal, official, scientific or medical contexts. It is used especially to refer to men as opposed to women. **OPP** **female** → WOMAN

bloke [C] (*BrE, informal*) a man: *I got chatting to a bloke in the pub.* ◇ *He was ever such a nice bloke.*

dude /duːd; djuːd/ [C] (*especially AmE, informal*) a man: *He's a real cool dude.* ◇ *Hey, dude, what's up?*

NOTE **GUY, BLOKE** OR **DUDE? Bloke** is only used in British English; **dude** is used especially in American English; **guy** is used in both. **Bloke** suggests that sb is a nice but ordinary person. **Dude** can suggest that sb is attractive and fashionable. A **guy** can be either.

2 man · humanity · mankind · the human race · humankind
These words all mean all people together considered as a group.

PATTERNS AND COLLOCATIONS
▸ to **save** humanity / mankind / the human race / humankind
▸ to **destroy** humanity / mankind / the human race
▸ to **belong to** mankind / the human race
▸ **all** (**of**) / **the whole of** humanity / mankind / humankind
▸ **the rest of** humanity / mankind / the human race / humankind

man [U] human beings as a group or from a particular period of history: *In man the brain is highly developed.* ◇ *This is the most poisonous substance known to man.* ◇ *They uncovered tools used by prehistoric man.*

humanity /hjuːˈmænəti/ [U] all people considered together as one group: *He was found guilty of crimes against humanity* (= very serious and cruel crimes against many people). ◇ *All the streets around the temple were just a mass of humanity* (= filled with people).

mankind [U] all people considered together as one group: *Some described it as 'the greatest disaster in the history of mankind'.* ◇ *These objects date back to the dawn of mankind.*

the ˌhuman ˈrace [sing.] all people considered together as one group: *Twenty-five percent of the entire human race could be affected by this disease.* ◇ *They are perhaps some of the most vulnerable members of the human race.* See also **race** → PEOPLE 2

humankind [U] all people considered together as one group: *This could provide new clues about the origins of humankind.*

NOTE **WHICH WORD? Man** is the most general of these words: it can be used to refer to people when compared with animals: *the relationship between man and nature*; to describe the development of people through history: *early/Stone Age/modern man*; or to talk about all the people, societies and cultures of the world: *all diseases known to man.* This last use is becoming old-fashioned, used mostly now in literary contexts. **Humanity, mankind** and **humankind** are used especially to talk about all people as part of human society and culture: **humanity** is often used when talking about general moral and ethical principles: *crimes against humanity.* **Mankind** or **humankind** is often used when talking about society and its development, as in the famous quotation of Neil Armstrong as he stepped onto the moon: *'That's one small step for a man, one giant leap for mankind.'* **The human race** is used especially to refer to people as a species when compared with animals or considered through history. **Man** and **mankind** have traditionally been used to mean 'all men and women', but some people now prefer gender neutral words which do not include the word 'man', such as **humanity** and **humankind**.

management *noun*

management · leadership · executive · administration · captaincy · directorate · directorship · headship
These are all words for a person or group of people who run a business, team, or other organization, or the period of time for which they run it.

PATTERNS AND COLLOCATIONS
▸ **under** the management / leadership / captaincy / directorship / headship **of** sb
▸ the **new** / **current** / **existing** management / leadership / executive / administration

▸ the **central** management / leadership / executive / administration / directorate
▸ the **local** management / leadership / executive / administration
▸ the **national** leadership / executive / administration / directorate
▸ the **college / hospital** management / administration
▸ the **party / union** leadership / executive

management [U+sing./pl. v., C] the people who run a business or other organization: *Union leaders are seeking talks with management over the proposed layoffs.* ◇ *It is a one-day workshop for* **senior** *and* **middle management**. ◇ *The store is now* **under new management**. ◇ *Most managements are keen to avoid strikes.* See also **management** → GOVERNMENT 2, **manage** → RUN 2

leadership [C+sing./pl. v.] the people who control or run an organization, political party or country: *The party leadership is divided.* ◇ *There have been disagreements within the leadership of the union.* ❶ When it is used to talk about the people who run a country, **leadership** usually refers to governments that are not elected or are not considered to be democratic: *the Communist/East German/military leadership* ◇ *the British/Australian/Indian leadership* See also **regime** → GOVERNMENT 1

executive /ɪgˈzekjətɪv/ [C+sing./pl. v.] a group of people who run a business or other organization: *She is a member of the party's national executive.* ◇ *She was* **on the executive** *of the Women's Social and Political Union.* ❶ In American English **executive** is mostly used before another noun: *There are still too few women in top executive positions.* ◇ *the executive board/committee* See also **executive** → EXECUTIVE

administration [C] the people who run a service, business or organization: *The prison administration is working hard to improve the service.* ◇ *He has been in dispute with the New Zealand cricket administration.* See also **administer** → RUN 2, **administrator** → ORGANIZER

NOTE MANAGEMENT, EXECUTIVE OR ADMINISTRATION? The **management** of a company can include a much larger group of people than the **executive**. There are different *levels of management* including *top, senior, middle* and *junior management*, although **management** used alone often refers just to top or senior management. The **executive** of a company is just the top management, especially members of the *executive board* who all meet together as a group to discuss the management of the company. **Executive** is also used to refer to the group of people who lead an organization such as a political party or trade union, especially when they are elected, not appointed. **Administration** is used especially to refer to the people who run an institution that provides a service or organizes an activity: *the school/college/university/prison/hospital administration*

captaincy /ˈkæptənsi/ [C, usually sing., U] the position of captain of a team; the period during which sb is captain: *The team won the league under the captaincy of Martin Jones.* ◇ *In 2006 he* **took over the captaincy** *from Vaughan.*

directorate /dəˈrektərət; dɪ-; daɪ-/ [C] (*rather formal*) the group of directors who run a company: *He is the longest-standing member of the bank's permanent directorate.*

directorship [C] the position of a company director; the period during which sb is a company director: *He was forced to resign his directorship of the company.* ◇ *Since leaving politics, he has* **held directorships** *of various financial companies.*

headship [C] (*BrE*) the position of being in charge of an organization, university department, school, etc.; the period during which sb is in charge: *He has just retired from the headship of the Diplomatic Service.* ◇ *She applied for the headship of a small, rural primary school.* ❶ **Headship** refers to positions with 'head' in the title such as *head teacher, head of department* or *Head of the Civil Service.* See also **head** → LEADER 1, **head** → PROFESSOR

manager *noun* See also the entry for LEADER 1

manager · director · employer · boss · supervisor · governor · superintendent · foreman
These are all words for a person who is in charge of running a business or part of one.

PATTERNS AND COLLOCATIONS
▸ to work **for** a manager / a director / an employer / a boss
▸ to work **under** a manager / supervisor / superintendent / foreman
▸ a **good** manager / director / employer / boss / supervisor / governor
▸ a **company** manager / director / boss
▸ to **have** a manager / a director / an employer / a boss / a supervisor / a governor / a foreman
▸ to **act as** manager / director / supervisor / governor
▸ to **work as** a manager / director / supervisor / foreman
▸ to **assist** the manager / director / supervisor / governor / superintendent
▸ to **appoint** a manager / director / supervisor / governor / superintendent
▸ to **become / make sb** a manager / director / supervisor / governor

manager [C] a person who is in charge of running a business, store or similar organization; a person who is in charge of a particular activity or department in a company: *a bank/hotel manager* ◇ *Sales manager Chris Jones says, 'We're thrilled with the results'.* ❶ There's a meeting of area managers next Tuesday. ❶ In British English, a person's **line manager** is the person in the company who is one rank above them and has direct responsibility for managing their work. **Line manager** or just **manager** can be a more formal way of saying **boss**: *I'll ask my manager if I can leave early.* See also **management** → GOVERNMENT 2, **managing director** → LEADER 1

director [C] one of a group of senior managers who run a company; a person who is in charge of a particular activity or department in a company, a college, etc: *She's on the board of directors.* ◇ *He was musical director at the National Theatre from 1976 to 1997.* See also **managing director** → LEADER 1, **direct** → RUN 2, **direction** → GOVERNMENT 2

NOTE MANAGER OR DIRECTOR? Both **manager** and **director** can be used to talk about a person who is in charge of a particular activity or department in a company: *a sales/marketing/finance/personnel/technical manager/director.* However, in a large company, a **director** is often in charge of several **managers**.

employer [C] a person or company that pays people to work for them: *They're very good employers* (= they treat the people that work for them well). ◇ *They're one of the largest employers in the area.* See also **employ** → EMPLOY

boss [C] (*rather informal, especially spoken or journalism*) a person who is in charge of other people at work and tells them what to do: *I'll ask my boss if I can have the day off.* ◇ *I like being* **my own boss** (= working for myself and making my own decisions). ◇ *Who's the boss* (= who's in control) *in this house?* ❶ **Boss** is usually used with a possessive pronoun, that is *his, her, my, your,* etc. People often use **the boss** in a fairly informal way to talk about the person who is in charge of them at work. *The boss* can also be used in a humorous way to talk about a person who is, or seems to be, in control in a particular situation or relationship.

supervisor /ˈsuːpəvaɪzə(r); ˈsjuː-; AmE ˈsuːpərv-/ [C] a person who is in charge of sb/sth and makes sure that everything is done correctly and safely: *I have a meeting with my supervisor about my research topic.* ◇ *All work is done under the guidance of a supervisor.* See also **supervise** → REGULATE, **supervision** → GOVERNMENT 2

governor [C] (*especially BrE*) a member of a group of people who are responsible for controlling an institution such as a school, college or hospital: *One way of getting* things changed is to become a school governor. ❶ In British English, a **governor** is also a single person who is in charge of a prison or bank. See also **governor** → LEADER 1

superintendent /ˌsuːpərɪnˈtendənt; *BrE* also ˌsjuː-/ [C] a person who has a lot of authority and manages and controls an activity, a place or a group of workers: *In 1945 he became superintendent of schools in Dallas.* ❶ Typically, **superintendents** are people in charge of hospitals, railways and schools. See also **superintend** → REGULATE

foreman /ˈfɔːmən; *AmE* ˈfɔːrmən/ [C] a worker who is in charge of a group of other factory or building workers: *He got a job as foreman of a building site.* ❶ A **foreman** can be either a man or a woman; there is a feminine form, **forewoman**, but this is not very frequent.

manipulate verb

manipulate · steer · engineer · manoeuvre · pull strings · turn sth to your advantage
These words all mean to control or influence sth in such a way that you get what you want.

PATTERNS AND COLLOCATIONS
▸ to manipulate / manoeuvre sb **into** sth
▸ to manipulate / engineer a **situation**
▸ to turn a **situation** to your advantage
▸ to manipulate / steer the **conversation**
▸ to **deliberately** manipulate / steer / engineer sth
▸ to **successfully** manipulate / manoeuvre sth

manipulate /məˈnɪpjuleɪt/ [T] (*disapproving*) to control or influence sb/sth, often in a dishonest way so that they do not realize it: *She uses her charm to manipulate people.* ◇ *He knows how to manipulate public opinion.* ◇ *They managed to **manipulate us into agreeing** to help.*
▸ **manipulation** /məˌnɪpjuˈleɪʃn/ noun [U, C]: *Advertising like this is a cynical manipulation of the elderly.*
▸ **manipulative** /məˈnɪpjələtɪv; *AmE* -leɪtɪv/ adj.: *manipulative behaviour*

steer [T] (always used with an adverb or preposition) to take control of a situation and influence the way in which it develops: *He managed to steer the conversation away from his divorce.* ◇ *She steered the team to victory.*

engineer [T] (*often disapproving*) to arrange for sth to happen or take place, especially when this is done secretly in order to give you an advantage: *She engineered a further meeting with him.*

manoeuvre (*BrE*) (*AmE* **maneuver**) /məˈnuːvə(r)/ [T, I] (*sometimes disapproving*) to control or influence a situation to give you an advantage in a skilful but possibly dishonest way: *The new laws have left us little **room for/to manoeuvre** (= not much opportunity to change or influence a situation).* ◇ *She manoeuvred her way to the top of the company.* See also **manoeuvre** → TACTIC noun

pull ˈstrings idiom (*rather informal*) to use your influence in order to get an advantage for sb: *By pulling strings he was able to get on a plane that night.*

turn sth to your adˈvantage idiom to use or change a bad situation so that you benefit from it: *She realized the whole situation could be turned to her advantage.*

mannerism noun

mannerism · idiosyncrasy · peculiarity · quirk · eccentricity
These are all words for characteristics or frequently repeated behaviour that are/is unusual or strange.

PATTERNS AND COLLOCATIONS
▸ an **individual** idiosyncrasy / peculiarity / quirk
▸ little / **peculiar** idiosyncrasies / quirks

mannerism [C] a habit, especially a particular way of speaking or moving that sb always has but usually is not aware of: *Ask a friend to tell you whether you have any irritating mannerisms.*

idiosyncrasy /ˌɪdiəˈsɪŋkrəsi/ [C] an aspect of a person's particular way of behaving or thinking, especially when it is unusual; an unusual aspect of the way in which a machine or system works: *We are all individuals, unique beings with our own special qualities and idiosyncrasies.* ◇ *By then she was familiar with the idiosyncrasies of the firm's accounting system.* See also **idiosyncratic** → UNIQUE

peculiarity /pɪˌkjuːliˈærəti/ [C] a strange or unusual feature or habit: *Many nicknames describe physical peculiarities.* ◇ *Despite its peculiarities the car was very reliable.* See also **peculiar** → STRANGE 1

quirk /kwɜːk; *AmE* kwɜːrk/ [C] an aspect of sb's personality or behaviour that is slightly strange: *They accepted it as one of her little quirks.*
▸ **quirky** adj.: *a quirky sense of humour*

eccentricity /ˌeksenˈtrɪsəti/ [C, usually pl.] an aspect of sb's personality or behaviour that is unusual and strange: *Her eccentricities were amusing rather than irritating.* See also **eccentric** → UNUSUAL adj.

> **NOTE** QUIRK OR ECCENTRICITY? **Eccentricities** are stranger than **quirks**. Even ordinary people may *have their little quirks*. **Eccentricities** tend to belong to more unusual people: *the eccentricities of genius* ◇ ~~the quirks of genius~~

manufacture verb See also the entry for MAKE 1

manufacture · produce · turn sb/sth out · churn sth out · mass-produce
These words all mean to make sth, especially in large quantities for sale.

PATTERNS AND COLLOCATIONS
▸ a **factory** that manufactures / produces **cars / mainframes / microchips**
▸ to manufacture / produce / turn out / churn out **900 cars a week**
▸ **manufactured** / mass-produced **goods**
▸ to produce / turn out / churn out **books / articles**

manufacture [T] to make goods in large quantities, using machinery: *This company manufactures the equipment used to make contact lenses.* ❶ **Manufacture** is the most frequent verb that specifically means to make goods in large quantities, but the verb **make**, which has a much more general meaning, is also often used in this context: *a factory that makes cars/mainframes/microchips* See also **manufacturer** → MAKER, **manufacturing, manufacture** → PRODUCTION

produce [T] to make things to be sold, especially in large quantities; to obtain and process raw materials for sale: *a factory that produces microchips* ◇ *the wine-producing regions of France* ◇ *The country produces more than two million barrels of oil per day.* See also **produce** → MAKE 1, **producer** → MAKER, **product** → PRODUCT, **production** → OUTPUT, **production** → PRODUCTION

> **NOTE** MANUFACTURE OR PRODUCE? **Produce** has a wider range of meanings than **manufacture** and can be used to talk about obtaining raw materials, growing things and writing things as well as making goods. **Manufacture** is more often used in business contexts and emphasizes the process of making goods, using machinery; **produce** places more emphasis on the result of that process, the finished product.

ˌturn sb/sth ˈout phrasal verb (*rather informal*) to produce goods, write books, prepare meals or train people, especially in large quantities: *If we can turn out plenty of work between us, we should manage.* ◇ *We turned the kitchen into a production line, turning out hot meals for the servicemen.* ◇ *The school has turned out some first-rate students.*

ˌchurn sth ˈout phrasal verb (*informal, disapproving*) to produce sth quickly and in large quantities, especially things of low quality: *She churns out novels at the rate of three a year.*

,mass-pro'duce [T, often passive] to produce goods in large quantities, using machinery: *Because the coins were mass-produced they can often be accurately dated.*

▶ **,mass-pro'duced** *adj.*: *He was wearing a cheap, mass-produced suit.*

map *noun*

map · plan · atlas · chart · globe
These are all words for a drawing of the earth's surface or a part of it, showing countries, towns, rivers, etc.

PATTERNS AND COLLOCATIONS
▶ **on** a map/ plan/ chart/ globe
▶ a/ an **detailed**/ **accurate** map/ plan/ chart
▶ a **simple**/ **rough** map/ plan
▶ a **large-scale**/ **small-scale** map/ plan/ atlas/ chart
▶ a **street**/ **route** map/ plan/ atlas
▶ a **road**/ **world** map/ atlas
▶ to **look at**/ **consult** a map/ a plan/ an atlas/ a chart
▶ to **read** a map/ chart
▶ to **find sth on** a map/ a plan/ a chart/ the globe
▶ to **draw** a map/ plan/ chart
▶ a map/ a plan/ an atlas/ a chart **shows** sth

map [C] a drawing of the earth's surface or part of it, showing countries, towns, rivers, etc: *a map of the world* ◊ *I'll draw you a map of how to get to my house.*

plan [C] a map of a building, town or city, especially a detailed one: *Do you have a plan of the museum?* ◊ *We asked for **street plan** of the city.*

atlas /'ætləs/ [C] a book of maps: *Do you have a road atlas of the UK?*

chart [C] a detailed map of the sea: *There are no charts available for this part of the ocean.*

globe [C] an object shaped like a ball with a map of the world on its surface, usually on a stand so that it can be turned: *Find Laos on the globe.*

march *verb*

march · storm · stomp · stalk · flounce
These words all mean to walk somewhere in an angry way.

PATTERNS AND COLLOCATIONS
▶ to march/ storm/ stomp/ stalk/ flounce **off**/ **away**
▶ to march/ storm/ stomp/ stalk/ flounce **in**/ **into**/ **out**/ **out of** (sth)

march [I] (always used with an adverb or preposition) to walk somewhere quickly in a determined or angry way: *She marched over to me and demanded an apology.* ◊ *He marched off, muttering something.* See also **march** → WALK *verb* 1

storm [I] (always used with an adverb or preposition) to go somewhere suddenly and quickly in an angry, noisy way: *Apparently she stormed out of the meeting after only 15 minutes.* ◊ *He thumped the table and then stormed off.*

stomp [I] (always used with an adverb or preposition) (*rather informal*) to walk somewhere with heavy steps, especially because you are annoyed: *She stomped angrily up the stairs.*

stalk /stɔːk/ [I] (always used with an adverb or preposition) to walk in an angry or proud way, especially away from sb/sth: *He stalked off without a word.*

flounce /flaʊns/ [I] (always used with an adverb or preposition) (*written*) to go somewhere in a way that draws attention to yourself, especially because you are angry or upset: *With that, she flounced out of the room.*
❶ **Flounce** is usually used about women or girls.

mark *noun*

mark · stain · fingerprint · streak · speck · blot · smear · blemish · smudge · spot
These are all words for a small area of dirt or another substance on a surface.

PATTERNS AND COLLOCATIONS
▶ a mark/ stain/ fingerprint/ streak/ speck/ blot/ smear/ blemish/ smudge/ spot **on** sth
▶ a streak/ speck/ blot/ smear/ smudge/ spot **of** sth
▶ a **greasy** mark/ stain/ smear
▶ an **ink** mark/ stain/ blot/ spot
▶ a **grease** mark/ stain/ spot
▶ to **leave** a mark/ stain/ fingerprint/ streak/ speck/ blot/ smear/ smudge
▶ to **remove** a mark/ stain/ fingerprint/ speck/ smear/ blemish/ smudge/ spot

mark [C] a small area of dirt or other substance on the surface of sth, especially one that spoils its appearance: *The kids left dirty marks all over the kitchen floor.* ◊ *There were **burn marks** on the carpet.* ◊ *A faint **pencil mark** showed where the house was on the map.*

stain [C] a dirty mark on sth that is difficult to remove, especially one made by a liquid: *I couldn't get the stains out of my jeans.* ◊ *A dark stain spread over the patterned carpet.* ◊ *blood/coffee/wine stains* See also **stained** → DIRTY

fingerprint /'fɪŋɡəprɪnt; *AmE* -ɡərp-/ [C] a mark on a surface made by the pattern of lines on the end of a person's finger, often used by the police to identify criminals: *His fingerprints were all over the gun.* ◊ *The police **took their fingerprints** (= made them leave the mark of their fingerprints as a record).*
▶ **fingerprint** *verb* [T]: *I was booked, fingerprinted (= my fingerprints were taken) and locked up for the night.*

streak /striːk/ [C] a long thin mark or line that is a different colour from the surface it is on: *There was a streak of blood on his face.* ◊ *She had streaks of grey in her hair.* ◊ *The sooty rain left dirty streaks on the window.*

speck [C] a very small mark, spot or piece of a substance on sth: *There isn't a **speck of dust** anywhere in the house.* ◊ *The bird has reddish specks on its breast.*

blot [C] a spot or dirty mark left on sth by a substance such as ink or paint being dropped on a surface: *There were ink blots all over the paper.*

smear /smɪə(r)/ [C] a mark made by sth such as oil or paint being spread or rubbed on a surface: *There was a smear of paint on his cheek.* See also **smear** → COVER *verb*

blemish /'blemɪʃ/ [C] (*especially written*) a mark on the skin or on an object that spoils its appearance and makes it less perfect: *Cover up unsightly blemishes with our new liquid make-up.* See also **imperfection** → DEFECT

smudge [C] a dirty mark with no clear shape made by sth such as paint or ink being rubbed onto a surface: *There was a smudge of lipstick on the cup.*

spot [C] a small dirty mark on sth: *His jacket was covered with spots of mud.* ◊ *There were grease spots all over the walls.*

mark *verb*

1 X marks the spot
2 mark exam papers; mark sth wrong

1 mark · label · tick · check · highlight · flag · tag
These words all mean to put sth such as a word, symbol or label on sth in order to give information about it.

PATTERNS AND COLLOCATIONS
▶ to mark/ label/ highlight/ flag/ tag sth **with** sth
▶ to mark/ highlight sth **in** red, yellow, etc.
▶ to tick/ check sth **off**
▶ to mark/ label **boxes**/ **bags**
▶ to mark/ tick/ check/ highlight/ flag an **item**
▶ to mark/ tick/ check a **box**
▶ to mark/ highlight/ flag a/ an **word**/ **paragraph**/ **passage**/ **section**/ **error**
▶ to mark/ label sth **clearly**/ **carefully**

mark [T] to write or draw a symbol, line, etc. on sth in order to give information about it; (of a symbol, line, etc) to show the position of sth: *Items marked with an asterisk* can be omitted. ◇ *Prices are marked on the goods.* ◇ *Do not open any mail marked 'Confidential'.* ◇ *The cross marks the spot where the body was found.*

label (-ll-, *AmE* -l-) [T, often passive] to fix a label on sth or write information on sth: *We carefully labelled each item with the contents and the date.* See also label → LABEL *noun*

> **NOTE** MARK OR LABEL? When you use **mark**, you usually have to say how sth is marked, for example with a cross, or particular words, or in a particular colour. When you say that sth is **labelled**, you mean that sb has written on it what it is, what is in it, or who it belongs to, and you do not need to give more details if the context is enough to give the meaning: *The path is marked in red.* ◇ *Make sure that all your luggage is clearly labelled* (= with your name and address).

tick [T] (*BrE*) to put a mark (✓) next to an answer or an item on a list to show that it is correct or has been dealt with: *Tick 'yes' or 'no' to each question.* ◇ *I've ticked off the names of the people who have paid.*

check [T] (*AmE*) to tick sth: *Check the box next to the right answer.* ◇ *Check the names off as the guests arrive.*

highlight [T] to mark part of a text with a special coloured pen, or to mark an area on a computer screen, to emphasize it or make it easier to see: *I've highlighted the important passages in yellow.* ◇ *Highlight the section that you want to delete.*

flag (-gg-) [T] to put a special mark next to information that you think is important: *I've flagged the paragraphs that we need to look at in more detail.*

> **NOTE** TICK, CHECK OR FLAG? When you **tick** or **check** sth, you put the particular mark (✓) next to it. When you **flag** sth you put any kind of mark next to it to show that it is important.

tag (-gg-) [T] to fasten a tag (= a small piece of paper, fabric or plastic) onto sb/sth to identify them or give information about them: *Each animal was tagged with a number for identification.* See also tag → LABEL *noun*

---

2 See the Topic Map for EDUCATION on p.888, See also the entry for TEST 2

mark · grade · correct
These words all mean to give a mark or grade to a student's work or to read it or listen to it and put right any mistakes.

> to mark / grade / correct a / an **paper / essay / assignment**
> to mark / grade / correct sb's **work / classwork / homework**
> to mark / grade a / an **test / exam / examination / project**
> to mark / grade a **student / pupil**
> to mark / grade sb / sth **A / B / C**, etc.
> to mark / grade sb / sth **fairly / unfairly**

mark [T, I] (*BrE*) to give a mark to a student's work: *If you don't hand your homework in on time I won't mark it.* ◇ *Most teachers spend at least two hours a day marking.* ❶ **Mark** is used in both British and American English when it means to write comments or symbols on a student's work to show whether it is right or wrong, good or bad: *Why have you **marked** this **wrong**?* ◇ *Sorry, I should have **marked** that **right**.* ◇ *She was **marked down** (= given a lower mark/grade) for bad spelling.* See also mark → SCORE *noun*

grade [T, I] (*especially AmE*) to give a grade to a student's work or a student: *She spent the weekend grading papers.* ◇ *Who grades the students?* ◇ *The best students are graded A.* ◇ *There is some concern that grading is not always fair.* See also grade → SCORE *noun*

correct [T] to put right the mistakes in a student's work, for example by writing the correct way of spelling sth: *When I've corrected your assignments, I want you to write them out again.* ◇ *It's simply not true that teachers no longer correct bad spellings.*

---

marked *adj.* See also the entries for CLEAR 1, OPEN and VISIBLE

marked · striking · distinct · conspicuous · unmistakable · sharp · pronounced · definite · decided
These words all describe sb/sth that is easy to see or notice, especially because they are unusual or different.

> a marked / striking / distinct / sharp / pronounced / definite **difference**
> a marked / striking / distinct / sharp **contrast**
> a marked / striking / distinct **resemblance**
> a marked / striking / distinct / sharp / definite / decided **improvement**
> a marked / striking / sharp / pronounced / definite **increase**
> a marked / striking / pronounced / definite **effect**
> a marked / striking / conspicuous **success**
> a marked / striking / distinct / conspicuous / pronounced **feature**
> a distinct / an unmistakable / a pronounced **flavour**
> **quite** marked / striking / distinct / unmistakable / sharp / pronounced / definite
> **very** marked / striking / distinct / conspicuous / sharp / pronounced / definite
> **fairly** distinct / sharp / pronounced / definite

marked (*especially written*) easy to see or notice: *The recent advertising campaign has had a marked effect on sales.* ◇ *She is quiet and studious, in marked contrast to her sister.*
> **markedly** *adv.*: *Her background is markedly different from her husband's.* ◇ *This year's sales have risen markedly.*

striking very likely to attract attention by being interesting and unusual: *She bears a striking resemblance to her older sister.* ◇ *What is immediately striking is how resourceful the children are.* See also **striking** → BEAUTIFUL 1
> **strikingly** *adv.*: *The two polls produced strikingly different results.*

distinct /dɪˈstɪŋkt/ easy to hear, see, feel, smell, taste or understand: *There was a distinct smell of gas.* ◇ *His voice was quiet but every word was distinct.* **OPP** indistinct → VAGUE
> **distinctly** *adv.*: *I distinctly heard someone calling my name.*

conspicuous /kənˈspɪkjuəs/ easy to see or notice; likely to attract attention by being unusual or different: *I felt very conspicuous in my new car.* ◇ *Bay windows are a conspicuous feature of his architecture.* **OPP** inconspicuous → INVISIBLE
> **conspicuously** *adv.*: *Women were conspicuously absent from the planning committee.*

unmistakable (also *less frequent* **unmistakeable**) that cannot be mistaken for sb/sth else: *Her accent was unmistakable.* ◇ *The main symptom is a scarlet rash that's quite unmistakable.* ◇ *the unmistakable sound of gunfire*
> **unmistakably**: *His accent was unmistakably British.*

sharp [usually before noun] clear and easy to see or understand: *The sky was dark, with only the outlines of dockside warehouses standing sharp on the skyline.* ◇ *She drew a sharp distinction between domestic and international politics.* ◇ *The issue must be brought into sharper focus.* ❶ In this meaning **sharp** is used to describe the contrast between different ideas or issues, or between different things in a view or picture. See also **stark** → PLAIN 2

pronounced (*especially written*) easy to see or notice: *He walked with a pronounced limp.* ◇ *She had a pronounced Scottish accent.*

definite [usually before noun] easy to see or notice: *The look on her face was a definite sign that something was wrong.* ◇ *There was a definite feeling that things were getting worse.*

> **NOTE** MARKED, PRONOUNCED OR DEFINITE? In many cases you can use any of these words, especially when talking about changes or differences. **Marked** is used most often for these, especially in a business context.

Pronounced is also more written than spoken, but is used more to talk about physical or personal characteristics. **Definite** is used to talk about things that you can see or feel.

decided [only before noun] easy to notice; that there can be no disagreement about: *Her recent work has shown a decided improvement.* ◇ *His height was a decided advantage in the game.*
▸ **decidedly** adv.: *Things were looking decidedly gloomy.*

market noun

1 the Japanese market
2 a street market

---

1 market · audience · public · clientele
These are all words for a particular area, country or section of the population that buy, or might buy, goods.

PATTERNS AND COLLOCATIONS
▸ a market / an audience **for** sth
▸ a **wide** market / audience / public / clientele
▸ a / an **large / small / international** market / audience / clientele
▸ to **serve** a market / an audience / the ... public / a clientele
▸ to **reach** a market / an audience / a wide public
▸ to **attract / build up** a market / an audience / clientele
▸ to **establish** a market / an audience

market [C] a particular area, country or section of the population that might buy goods: *The jacket is designed for the Japanese market.* ◇ *They supply beef to the domestic market.* ❶ **The market** [sing.] is also the economic system in which prices and the supply of goods are controlled by the way and how much people buy: *The market will decide if the TV station has any future.* ◇ *We now have an unprotected, market-led economy.* The **market** can also be the number of people who want to buy sth. See also **market → DEMAND**

audience [C] a number of people or a particular group of people who watch, read or listen to the same thing: *An audience of millions watched the wedding on TV.* ◇ *The target audience for this advertisement was mainly teenagers.* See also **audience → AUDIENCE**

public [sing.+ sing./pl. v.] a group of people who share a particular interest or who are involved in the same activity: *The show drew 12% of the viewing public.* ◇ *She knows how to keep her public* (= for example, the people who buy her books) *satisfied.* ❶ In this meaning **public** often follows an adjective describing a particular activity: *the book-buying / reading / sporting / theatre-going / travelling / viewing public*

clientele /ˌkliːənˈtel; AmE ˌklaɪənˈtel/ [sing.+ sing./pl. v.] all the customers or clients of a shop, restaurant or organization: *The facilities appeal to an international clientele.* See also **client → CUSTOMER**

---

2 market · mall · shopping centre · farmers' market · strip mall
These are all words for an area where people meet to buy and sell goods.

PATTERNS AND COLLOCATIONS
▸ **at** the market / mall / shopping centre
▸ a / an **covered / indoor** market / shopping centre
▸ to **go to** the market / mall / shopping centre

market [C] an open area or building where people meet to buy and sell goods; an occasion when people meet to buy and sell goods: *We buy our fruit and vegetables at the market.* ◇ *Thursday is* **market day** *in Poitiers.* ◇ *a fruit market* ◇ *a market stall* ◇ *It's a busy* **market town** (= a town in Britain where a regular market is or was held).

mall /mɔːl; BrE also mæl/ (also '**shopping mall**) [C] (*especially AmE*) a large group of shops built together under one roof and closed to traffic: *'Where'd you get those earrings?' 'At the mall.'* ◇ *Let's go to the mall.* ❶ **Mall**

is used increasingly frequently in British English. A **mall** often contains restaurants, a cinema and other public entertainment facilities.

'**shopping centre** (*BrE*) (*AmE* **shopping center**) [C] a group of shops built together, sometimes under one roof: *The two children were left unattended in the main shopping centre.* ❶ In American English a **shopping center** usually does NOT have one roof; if it does it is usually called a **mall**.

'**farmers' market** [C] (*especially AmE*) a market where you can buy fresh food directly from the grower: *I bought some delicious strawberries at the farmers' market.*

'**strip mall** [C] (*AmE, sometimes disapproving*) a small group of shops built in a line, with their own parking area: *It's just another of the many strip malls that are taking over the landscape.*

marriage noun

marriage · wedding
These are all words for the state of being married or the occasion of getting married.

PATTERNS AND COLLOCATIONS
▸ sb's **first, second, etc.** marriage / wedding
▸ a **forthcoming** marriage / wedding
▸ a **royal** marriage / wedding
▸ to **attend / go to / celebrate** a marriage / wedding
▸ a marriage / wedding **is held / takes place...**
▸ a marriage / wedding **ceremony**

marriage [C, U] the legal relationship between a husband and wife; the state of being married; the ceremony in which two people become married: *Theirs was a happy marriage.* ◇ *He was the child of a* **broken marriage** (= his parents divorced). ◇ *an* **arranged marriage** (= one in which the parents choose a husband or wife for their child) ◇ *My parents are celebrating 30 years of marriage.* ◇ *Their marriage took place in a local church.*
▸ **marital** /ˈmærɪtl/ adj. [only before noun]: *marital breakdown* ◇ *your* **marital status** (= whether you are single, married, divorced, etc.)

wedding [C] a marriage ceremony, and the meal or party that usually follows it: *Have you been invited to their wedding?* ◇ *Today is our* **wedding anniversary**.

NOTE MARRIAGE OR WEDDING? In most cases, **marriage** refers to the state of being married, and **wedding** refers to the occasion of getting married: *The marriage only lasted for two years* (= they were married for two years). ◇ *The wedding took place two years ago* (= they got married two years ago). ◇ *a marriage partner / certificate / licence / break-up* ◇ *a wedding dress / present / cake / reception / anniversary*. In some cases, **marriage** can also refer to the occasion, but this is less common and more formal than **wedding**: *Mr and Mrs Wall invite you to the marriage of their daughter Ann to Mr Thomas Lea* (= written on a formal invitation).

marry verb

marry · get married · wed · remarry
These words all mean to become a person's husband or wife.

PATTERNS AND COLLOCATIONS
▸ to **plan to / be going to** marry / get married / remarry
▸ to **hope / want to** marry / get married / remarry
▸ to marry **late / young**
▸ sb **never** married / got married / wed / remarried

marry [T, I] to become the husband or wife of sb: *He was 36 when he married Viv.* ◇ *I guess I'm* **not the marrying kind** (= the kind of person who wants to get married).
▸ **married** adj.: *a married man / woman / couple* ◇ *How long have you been married?* **OPP** **unmarried → SINGLE**

,get 'married *phrase* to become husband and wife: *Rachel and David are getting married on Sunday.*

> **NOTE MARRY OR GET MARRIED?** In spoken English or informal written English, it is more common to use **get married**, especially if there is no object: *We got married in December.* ◇ (*formal*) *We married in December.* If there is an object, **marry** is more common: *I should never have married him.* sounds more natural than: *I should never have got married to him.*

wed [I, T] (not used in the progressive tenses) (*old-fashioned or journalism*) to marry: *The couple plan to wed next summer.* ◇ *Rock star to wed top model.* (= in a newspaper headline)
▸ **wedded** *adj.* [usually before noun] (*old-fashioned or formal*): *your lawfully wedded husband/wife*

remarry /ˌriːˈmæri/ [I] to marry again after being divorced or after your husband or wife has died: *After his wife died, he swore he would never remarry.*

marsh *noun*

marsh · swamp · wetland · bog
These are all words for areas of land that are soft and wet.

PATTERNS AND COLLOCATIONS
▸ to **drain** a marsh / a swamp / wetlands / a bog
▸ to **sink into** the marsh / bog

marsh [C, U] an area of low land that is always soft and wet because there is nowhere for the water to flow away to: *Cows were grazing on the marshes.* ◇ *The land is colonized by various types of marsh vegetation.*
▸ **marshy** *adj.*: *The town is situated on what was once a marshy plain.*

swamp /swɒmp; *AmE* swɑːmp/ [C, U] an area of land that is very wet or covered with water and in which plants and trees are growing: *Most coal fields began life as swamps 300 million years ago.* ◇ *The country contains around 700 square km of swamp.*
▸ **swampy** *adv.*: *Swampy land is ideal for the cultivation of rice.*

> **NOTE MARSH OR SWAMP?** A **marsh** may have grass and other plants growing in it, but it does not have trees. A **swamp** has trees and other woody plants growing in it.

wetland /ˈwetlənd/ [U, C] an area of wet land, especially one that is protected or considered as a home for wildlife: *Measures are being taken to protect the country's dwindling areas of wetland.* ◇ *The wetlands are home to a large variety of wildlife.*

bog [C, U] an area of soft wet ground, formed from decaying plants: *We collected several interesting specimens from the bog.* ◇ *There was an area of bog behind the house.*
▸ **boggy** *adv.*: *The path through the moorland is boggy but still in use.*

massacre *noun* See also the entry for MURDER

massacre · bloodshed · carnage · genocide · slaughter · the Holocaust · extermination
These are all words for the killing of a large number of people.

PATTERNS AND COLLOCATIONS
▸ (a / an) **bloody / appalling / terrible** massacre / carnage / slaughter
▸ to **be killed** in the massacre / bloodshed / carnage / genocide / slaughter / Holocaust
▸ to **be responsible for** the massacre / bloodshed / carnage / genocide / slaughter / Holocaust
▸ to **escape/survive** the massacre / carnage / genocide / slaughter / Holocaust
▸ to **avoid** a massacre / bloodshed / carnage / slaughter / the Holocaust
▸ to **prevent** a massacre / bloodshed / genocide / the slaughter

▸ to **end in** a massacre / bloodshed / carnage
▸ to **stop / end** the bloodshed / genocide / slaughter

massacre /ˈmæsəkə(r)/ [C, U] the killing of a large number of people, especially in a cruel way: *The bloody massacre of innocent civilians took place in October of that year.* ◇ *Nobody survived the massacre.*
▸ **massacre** *verb* [T]: *Hundreds of innocent women and children were massacred.*

bloodshed /ˈblʌdʃed/ [U] (*rather formal*) the killing or wounding of people, usually during fighting or a war: *The two sides called a truce to avoid further bloodshed.*
❶ **Bloodshed** is often used in the phrase *to prevent/avoid (further) bloodshed.*

carnage /ˈkɑːnɪdʒ/ [U] the violent killing of a large number of people: *The scene of carnage was indescribable.* ◇ *How can we reduce the carnage on our roads?*

> **NOTE MASSACRE OR CARNAGE?** A **massacre** is an occasion on which a large number of people are deliberately and violently killed. **Carnage** is the result of a large number of people being killed in war or accidents, either on a particular occasion or over a period of time. It is often used to describe what the result of such violent killing looks like: common phrases include *scenes of carnage* and *to watch/see/survey/describe the carnage.*

genocide /ˈdʒenəsaɪd/ [U] (*rather formal*) the murder of a whole race or group of people: *He condemned the government's programme of 'genocide and torture against our people'.*

slaughter /ˈslɔːtə(r)/ [U] the act of cruelly killing large numbers of people at one time, especially in a war: *They told us of the wholesale slaughter of innocent people.* ❶ **Slaughter** is used most often in the phrase *the slaughter of...* It describes an act, rather than an event or situation.
▸ **slaughter** *verb* [T]: *Men, women and children were slaughtered and villages destroyed.*

the Holocaust [sing.] the killing of millions of Jews by the Nazis in the 1930s and 1940s: *He had produced a series of paintings based on the Holocaust.*

extermination /ɪkˌstɜːmɪˈneɪʃn; *AmE* -ˌstɜːrm-/ [U] (*rather formal*) the killing of all the members of a group of people or animals: *Millions died in the extermination camps.* ◇ *the extermination of rats and other vermin* ❶ When it is used to talk about people **extermination** usually refers to the killing of Jews by the Nazis in the 1930s and 1940s, or to the destruction of the whole human race in a future disaster: *The film foresees the extermination of the human race in a nuclear world war.* See also **exterminate** → DESTROY

match *verb*

1 The two sets of figures don't match.
2 a scarf with gloves to match

1 match · correspond · fit · correlate · tie in · coincide · agree
These words all mean to be the same or similar, or to be closely linked in some way.

PATTERNS AND COLLOCATIONS
▸ A corresponds / correlates / ties in / coincides / agrees **with** B
▸ **A and B** correspond / correlate / coincide / agree
▸ **figures** match / correspond / correlate / coincide / agree
▸ sb's **account / version** matches / corresponds / coincides / agrees with sb else's
▸ to match / fit / correlate / tie in **well**
▸ to **almost** match / correspond / correlate / coincide
▸ to **not quite** match / fit / correlate

match [I, T] (not used in the progressive tenses) if two things **match** or if one thing **matches** another, they are the same or very similar: *The two sets of figures don't match.* ◇ *Her fingerprints match those found at the scene of the crime.* ◇ *The dark clouds matched her mood.*
▸ **match** *noun* [C]: *I've found a vase that is an exact match of the one I broke.* ◇ *The paint is a close enough colour match to the original.*

correspond [I] (not used in the progressive tenses) (*rather formal*) to match or be closely connected with another set of figures or facts; to have a similar role or function to sb/sth else in a different place or situation: *Your account of events does not correspond with hers.* ◇ *Your account and hers do not correspond.* ◇ *The written record of the conversation doesn't **correspond to** (= is different from) what was actually said.* ◇ *The British job of Lecturer corresponds roughly to the US Associate Professor.* ❶ If you are talking about things which are not exactly the same, you can only use *to*. If you are talking about things which are exactly the same, you can use either *to* or *with*. See also **correspondence** → SIMILARITY, **corresponding** → EQUIVALENT *adj.*

fit (-tt-) [I, T] (not used in the progressive tenses) to match an explanation or way of thinking; to be suitable for a particular purpose; to make sth do this: *His pictures don't **fit into** any category.* ◇ *Something doesn't quite fit here.* ◇ *The facts certainly fit your theory.* ◇ *The punishment ought to fit the crime.* ◇ *We should **fit** the punishment **to** the crime.*
▸ **fit** *noun* [C]: *We need to work out the best **fit** between the people required and the people available.*

correlate /'kɒrəleɪt; *AmE* 'kɔːr-; 'kɑːr-/ [I] (*formal or technical*) if two or more facts or figures **correlate**, or if a fact or figure **correlates** with another, the facts or figures are closely connected and affect or depend on each other: *The figures do not seem to correlate.* ◇ *A high-fat diet correlates with a greater risk of heart disease.* See also **correlation** → RELATION

tie 'in *phrasal verb* (*rather informal*) to match another set of facts; to be linked to sth, by dealing with the same topics or ideas: *This evidence ties in closely with what we already know.* ◇ *The concert will tie in with the festival of dance taking place the same weekend.*

coincide /ˌkəʊɪn'saɪd; *AmE* ˌkoʊ-/ [I] (*rather formal, especially written*) (of ideas or opinions) to be the same or very similar: *The interests of employers and employees do not always coincide.* ◇ *Our views on this issue coincide closely with those of the Countryside Council.*

agree [I] (*rather formal, especially written*) to match another person's account of sth or another set of figures: *The figures do not agree.* ◇ *Your account of the accident does not agree with hers.*

---

2 match · blend · go · mix · coordinate
These words all mean to combine, or to cause things to combine, in an attractive or effective way.

PATTERNS AND COLLOCATIONS
▸ to blend / go / mix / coordinate **with** sth
▸ to blend / go **together**
▸ sth matches / goes with / coordinates with the **curtains / decor**
▸ sth matches / goes with sb's **dress**
▸ to match / coordinate **colours**
▸ **colours** match / blend / go with each other / coordinate
▸ to match / blend / go with sth / coordinate **perfectly / well**
▸ to **not quite** match / go with sth

match [T, I] if two things **match**, or if one thing **matches** another, they have the same colour, pattern or style and therefore look attractive together: *The doors were painted blue to match the walls.* ◇ *I've got her a scarf with gloves to match.* ◇ *None of these glasses match* (= they are all different). See also **matching** → EQUIVALENT *adj.*
▸ **match** *noun* [sing.]: *The curtains and carpet are a **good match**.* ◇ *Jo and Ian are a perfect **match for** each other.*

blend [I, T] (*especially written*) to combine with sth in an attractive or effective way; to combine sth in this way: *The old and new buildings blend together perfectly.* ◇ *The colour of the carpet doesn't **blend in**.* ◇ *Their music blends traditional and modern styles.* ❶ **Blend** is most often used to talk about how well colours, sounds (especially music), smells and building styles combine.

go (*rather informal, especially spoken*) (especially of clothes or colours) to combine with sth in an attractive or

effective way: *Does this jacket go with this skirt?* ◇ *Those colours don't really go (together).*

mix [I] (usually used in negative sentences) if two or more things, people or activities **do not mix**, they are likely to cause problems or danger if they are combined: *Children and fireworks don't mix.*

coordinate (*BrE* also **co-ordinate**) /kəʊ'ɔːdɪneɪt; *AmE* koʊ'ɔːrd-/ [I, T] (*rather formal*) (of colours, clothes or fabrics) to look nice together; to choose colours, clothes or fabrics that look nice together: *This shade coordinates with a wide range of other colours.* ◇ *The company has extended its coordinated clothing range.* ❶ **Coordinate** is often used in the clothing and textile industries, or by people whose job is to comment on or advertise these things.
▸ **coordination** (*BrE* also **co-ordination**) *noun* [U]: *advice on colour coordination*

material *noun*

---

material · substance · chemical · gas · liquid · fluid · stuff · matter · solid · element
These are all words for sth from which other things are made.

PATTERNS AND COLLOCATIONS
▸ a **natural** material / substance / chemical / gas
▸ a **chemical** substance / element
▸ **organic** material / substances / chemicals / liquid / matter / elements
▸ **radioactive** material / substances / chemicals / gas / liquid / matter / elements
▸ a **toxic** material / substance / chemical / gas / liquid / element
▸ a **flammable** material / substance / gas / liquid
▸ (a) **sticky** substance / stuff / liquid / fluid / solid
▸ **waste** material / chemicals / gas / matter

material [C, U] something that things can be made from: *Toxic chemicals and other materials have been found.* ◇ *There were bricks, sand and other **building materials** in the courtyard.* ◇ *Oil is the **raw material** for plastic.*

substance [C] a material that has particular qualities: *Psychoactive drugs are chemical substances that act on the brain.* ◇ *Substances can be divided into elements, compounds and mixtures.*

chemical [C] a substance obtained by or used in a chemical process (= a process that involves changes to molecules or atoms): *This chemical is often used to make cleaning products.* ◇ *Hormones are chemicals that are released in the body and control many important functions.*

gas [C, U] any substance like air that is neither a solid nor a liquid, for example hydrogen or oxygen: *Air is a mixture of gases.* ◇ *Producing methane gas from organic waste is another extremely practical use of resources.*

liquid [C, U] a substance that flows freely and is not a solid or a gas, for example water or oil: *She offered me a cup containing a dark brown liquid.* ◇ *As the air became warmer the droplets of liquid turned to invisible water vapour.*
▸ **liquid** *adj.*: *Water is liquid at room temperature.* ◇ *The samples were frozen in liquid nitrogen.* **OPP** **solid** → SOLID

fluid /'fluːɪd/ [C, U] (*formal or technical*) a liquid; a substance that can flow: *The doctor told him to drink plenty of fluids.* ◇ *The attacker's DNA pattern was identified from a sample of **body fluid**.*

NOTE Although a **fluid** is usually a **liquid**, it can be any substance which can flow, for example a gas or a liquid containing small solid pieces.

stuff [U] (*informal*) used to refer to a substance or material when you do not know the name, when the name is not important or when it is obvious what you are talking about: *What's all that sticky stuff on the carpet?* ◇ *The chairs were covered in some sort of plastic stuff.* ◇ *This wine is **good stuff**.* ◇ (*disapproving*) *I don't know how you can eat that stuff.* See also **stuff** → THING 3, **thing** → THING 2

matter [U] (*formal or physics*) a substance or things of a particular sort; physical substance in general that everything in the world consists of; not mind or spirit: *The soil is rich in organic matter.* ◇ *She didn't approve of their choice of reading matter.* ◇ *The behaviour of matter can be quantified by measures such as weight.*

solid [C] a substance or object that is hard or firm, not a liquid or gas: *Is calcium carbonate normally a solid or a liquid?* ◇ *The baby is not yet on solids* (= eating solid food). See also **solid** → SOLID *adj.*

element [C] (*chemistry*) a simple chemical substance that consists of atoms of only one type and cannot be split by chemical means into a simpler substance. Gold, oxygen and carbon are all elements: *All chemical substances, whether elements, compounds or mixtures, are made up of three types of particles.*

maximum *adj.* See also the entry for LARGE

maximum · intense · extreme · utmost · supreme
These words all describe sth that is very large in degree or amount.

PATTERNS AND COLLOCATIONS
▸ maximum / extreme / the utmost / supreme **importance**
▸ maximum / extreme / the utmost **care**
▸ maximum / extreme / the utmost **difficulty**
▸ maximum / intense / extreme **pleasure / enjoyment**
▸ intense / extreme / supreme **happiness**
▸ intense / extreme **discomfort / pain**

maximum [only before noun] as large, fast, etc. as is possible; the most that is possible or allowed: *Turn it right up to the maximum volume.* ◇ *For maximum effect do the exercises every day.* ◇ *The offence carries a maximum prison sentence of ten years.* **OPP minimum** ❶ **Minimum** describes the smallest or least of sth that is possible or allowed: *a minimum charge/price* ◇ *the minimum age for retirement* ◇ *The work was done with the minimum amount of effort.*

intense very great or strong: *We were all suffering in the intense heat.* ◇ *The President is under intense pressure to resign.* ◇ *He was startled by the intense blue of her eyes.*

extreme [usually before noun] very great in degree: *We are working under extreme pressure at the moment.* ◇ *There are still thousands of people living in extreme poverty.* ◇ *The heat in the desert was extreme.* See also **extreme** → SERIOUS 1, **extremely** → VERY *adv.*

NOTE INTENSE OR **EXTREME**? Intense describes a very strong or deep feeling or quality: *intense desire/interest/heat/blue eyes.* **Extreme** describes a feeling, quality, action or state that is at its limit: *extreme pain/heat/violence/danger.* **Extreme** very often describes negative things; **intense** describes both positive and negative things.

utmost [only before noun] the most that is possible: *This is a matter of the utmost importance.* ◇ *You should study this document with the utmost care.*

supreme /suːˈpriːm; BrE also sjuː-/ [usually before noun] very great or the greatest in degree: *She smiled with supreme confidence.* ◇ *It took a supreme effort to stay calm.* ◇ *During the war, many people made the supreme sacrifice* (= died for what they believed in).

NOTE UTMOST OR **SUPREME**? Supreme is often used with a positive meaning: *supreme effort/control/emphasis/courage.* **Utmost** can be used with a positive or a more negative meaning: *the utmost contempt/care/difficulty/importance/respect/severity*

meal *noun* See also the entries for DINNER and SNACK

meal · banquet · feast · feed
These are all words for occasions when people sit down to eat together.

PATTERNS AND COLLOCATIONS
▸ a **great / sumptuous** meal / banquet / feast
▸ a **lavish / formal** meal / banquet
▸ a **four-course / five-course, etc.** meal / banquet
▸ a **wedding** feast / banquet
▸ to **give / hold / attend** a feast / banquet

meal [C] an occasion when people sit down to eat food, especially breakfast, lunch or dinner: *Try not to eat between meals.* ◇ *Lunch is his main meal of the day.* ◇ *What time would you like your evening meal?* See also **meal** → FOOD

banquet /ˈbæŋkwɪt/ [C] a large or impressive meal, especially a formal meal for a large number of people, at which speeches are made: *A state banquet was held in honour of the visiting president.*

feast [C] (*formal*) a large or special meal, especially for a lot of people and to celebrate sth: *The wedding feast traditionally lasts three days.* See also **feast** → DINE *verb*

feed [C, usually sing.] a meal of milk for a young baby; a meal for an animal: *It's time for her morning feed.* ❶ **Feed** can also be used in informal language to mean a large meal: (*informal*) *They needed a bath and a good feed.*

mean *verb*

1 What does this sentence mean?
2 What do you mean by that remark?
3 This new order will mean working overtime.

1 See also the entry for SUGGEST

mean · mark · signal · signify · denote
These words all mean to be a sign that sth exists or is likely to happen.

PATTERNS AND COLLOCATIONS
▸ to **mean / signify** sth **to** sb
▸ to **mean / signify that...**
▸ to **mean / mark / signal / signify / denote** a **change** in sth
▸ to **mean / mark / signal / signify / denote** the **beginning / start / arrival / end** of sth
▸ to **clearly** mean / mark / signal / signify / denote sth

mean [T] (not used in the progressive tenses) to have sth as a meaning; to be a sign that sth has just happened or is going to happen: *What does this sentence mean?* ◇ *What is meant by 'batch processing'?* ◇ *Does the name 'David Berwick' mean anything to you* (= do you know who he is)? ◇ *The flashing light means (that) you must stop.* ◇ *Mr President, does this mean an end to the current conflict?*

mark [T] (not used in the progressive tenses) (*especially written, journalism*) to be a sign that sth has just happened or is going to happen: *The agreement marks a new phase in international relations.*

signal (-ll-, AmE -l-) [T] (not used in the progressive tenses) (*rather formal, especially written, journalism*) to be a sign that sth has just happened or is going to happen: *The scandal surely signals the end of his political career.*

NOTE MEAN, MARK OR **SIGNAL**? These words can all mean 'be a sign that sth has just happened or is going to happen': **mean** is used most frequently in spoken English, but **mark** and **signal** are used more frequently in this meaning in written English, especially in journalism.

signify /ˈsɪɡnɪfaɪ/ [T] (not used in the progressive tenses) (*rather formal*) to be a sign of sth; to have a particular meaning: *This decision signified a radical change in their policies.* ◇ *This mark signifies that the products conform to an approved standard.*

denote /dɪˈnəʊt; AmE dɪˈnoʊt/ [T] (not used in the progressive tenses) (*formal*) to be a sign of sth; to have a particular meaning: *A very high temperature often denotes a serious illness.*

NOTE SIGNAL, SIGNIFY OR **DENOTE**? Signal suggests that sth makes people realize sth; **signify** and **denote** usually suggest that one thing has a particular meaning, especially an official or accepted meaning: *The white belt signifies/denotes that he's an absolute beginner.* However, **signify** can suggest a more complicated meaning than **denote**, including the ideas suggested by a word or expression: *What does the term 'patrician' signify* (= what does it mean and what might it suggest)? ◊ *The Hebrew term used here simply denotes a young girl* (= it does not mean or suggest anything more than that).

2 mean · suggest · hint · imply · intend · what sb is getting/driving at · insinuate

These words all mean to intend to say sth, or to say sth in an indirect way.

▸ to mean / intend sth **by** / **as** sth
▸ to mean / suggest / hint / imply / insinuate **that**…
▸ to suggest / imply **agreement** / **acceptance**
▸ to suggest / imply an **intention**
▸ to **seem** / **appear** to mean / suggest / hint / imply sth
▸ to (not) **mean** / **intend** to suggest / imply sth
▸ to suggest / hint / imply sth **clearly** / **strongly**

mean [T] (not used in the progressive tenses) (*especially spoken*) to intend to say sth on a particular occasion: *What did he mean by that remark?* ◊ *'Perhaps we should try another approach.' 'What do you mean?* (= I don't understand what you are suggesting.)' ◊ *What do you mean, you thought I wouldn't mind?* (= of course I mind and I am very angry.) ◊ *I know what you mean* (= I understand and feel sympathy). *I hated learning to drive too.* ◊ *I see what you mean* (= I understand although I may not agree), *but I still think it's worth trying.* ◊ *'But Pete doesn't know we're here!' 'That's what I mean!* (= that's what I have been trying to tell you.)' ◊ *Did he mean (that) he was dissatisfied with our service?* ◊ *You mean* (= are you telling me) *we have to start all over again?*

suggest [T] (used especially in negative statements and questions) to state an opinion indirectly: *Are you suggesting (that) I'm lazy?* ◊ *I would never suggest such a thing.* See also **suggestion** → SUGGESTION

hint [I, T] to suggest that sth might be true without saying so directly: *What are you hinting at?* ◊ *They hinted (that) there might be more job losses.* See also **hint** → SUGGESTION *noun*

NOTE SUGGEST OR HINT? People use **suggest** especially in questions to ask sb if they feel or think sth, or in negative statements to deny that they do. **Hint** is used when people give facts or talk about possibilities in an indirect way.

imply /ɪmˈplaɪ/ [T] (*rather formal*) to suggest that sth is true or that you feel or think sth, without saying so directly: *His silence seemed to imply agreement.* ◊ *I disliked the implied criticism in his voice.*

intend [T] (not used in the progressive tenses) (*rather formal*) to plan that sth should have a particular meaning: *What exactly did you intend by that remark?* ◊ *He intended it as a joke.*

what sb is 'getting/'driving at idiom (*informal, spoken*) the thing that sb is trying to say or suggest: *I'm partly to blame? What exactly are you getting at?*

insinuate /ɪnˈsɪnjueɪt/ [T] (*rather formal, disapproving*) to suggest that sth unpleasant is true, without saying so directly: *The article insinuated that he was having an affair with his friend's wife.* ◊ *What are you trying to insinuate?*

3 mean · involve · entail · imply · necessitate · spell

These words all mean to have sth as a necessary or likely part or result.

▸ sth means / implies **that**…
▸ sth means / involves / entails / implies / necessitates a / an **increase** / **reduction**

▸ sth involves / entails / implies **risk**
▸ sth usually / inevitably / necessarily / actually means / involves / entails / implies sth
▸ sth ordinarily / typically means / involves sth

mean [T] (of an action or situation) to have sth as a result or a likely result: *Spending too much now will mean a shortage of cash next year.* ◊ *Do you have any idea what it means to be poor?* ◊ *We'll have to be careful with money but that doesn't mean (that) we can't enjoy ourselves.* ◊ *This new order will mean working overtime.*

involve [T] (*especially written*) (of an action or situation) to have sth as a necessary or important part: *Any investment involves an element of risk.* ◊ *Many of the crimes involved drugs.* ◊ *The test will involve answering questions about a photograph.*

entail /ɪnˈteɪl/ [T] (*rather formal, especially written*) to involve sth that cannot be avoided, especially in order to achieve sth: *The job entails a lot of hard work.* ◊ *The girls learn exactly what is entailed in caring for a newborn baby.* ◊ *It will entail driving a long distance every day.*

NOTE INVOLVE OR ENTAIL? In many cases you can use either word: *The job involves/entails a lot of hard work.* ◊ *to involve/entail answering questions/driving a long distance/loss/rejection/destruction/cost/risk.* However, a problem might **involve** an aspect, such as *drugs* or *violence*, that is not necessary to achieve sth, but defines the nature of the problem. **Entail** cannot be used in this way: ~~Many of the crimes entailed drugs/violence.~~

imply /ɪmˈplaɪ/ [T] (*rather formal, especially written*) (of an idea or action) to make sth necessary in order to be successful: *The project implies an enormous investment in training.* ◊ *Sustainable development implies a long-term perspective.*
▸ **implication** /ˌɪmplɪˈkeɪʃn/ *noun* [C, usually pl.]: *The development of the site will have implications for the surrounding countryside.* ◊ *They failed to consider the wider implications of their actions.*

necessitate /nəˈsesɪteɪt/ [T] (*formal*) (of an event or situation) to make sth necessary: *Recent financial scandals have necessitated changes in parliamentary procedures.* ◊ *Increased traffic necessitated widening the road.* See also **necessary** → NECESSARY, **necessity** → NEED *noun*

spell [T] (of an event) to have sth, usually sth bad, as a result: *The crop failure spelt disaster for many farmers.* ◊ *This defeat spelt the end of his hopes of winning the title again.*

mean adj.

1 a mean thing to do
2 mean with money

1 mean · nasty · unkind · obnoxious · objectionable · hurtful · unpleasant

These words all describe people not being kind.

unkind	mean	obnoxious
objectionable	nasty	
unpleasant	hurtful	

▸ to be mean / nasty / unkind / obnoxious / objectionable / hurtful / unpleasant **to** sb
▸ to be mean / nasty **about** sb
▸ to be mean / nasty / unkind **of** sb (to do sth)
▸ to be mean / nasty / unkind **to do sth**
▸ a mean / a nasty / an unkind / a hurtful **thing to say** / **do**
▸ a nasty / an unkind / a hurtful **remark**
▸ a nasty / an obnoxious / an unpleasant **little man**
▸ **very** mean / nasty / unkind / objectionable / hurtful / unpleasant
▸ **really** mean / nasty / obnoxious / objectionable / unpleasant
▸ **rather** mean / nasty / unkind / hurtful / unpleasant

mean (*rather informal, especially spoken*) not kind, for example by not letting sb have or do sth: *Don't be so mean to your little brother!* ◊ *I thought it was really mean of him*

not to let her use the car. ◊ *He has a **mean streak** in him* (= an unpleasant side to his character). **OPP** **generous**
→ KIND

nasty (*rather informal, especially spoken*) not kind, especially in what you say to or about sb else: *She's always making nasty remarks about people.* ◊ *She was nasty about* (= said nasty things about) *everyone.* ◊ *He has a nasty temper.* **OPP** **nice** → NICE 2

unkind not kind or friendly: *He was never actually unkind to them.* ◊ *It would be unkind to go without him.* ◊ *She never said anything unkind about anyone.* ❶ **Unkind** is often used as a softer way of saying **mean** or **nasty**. **OPP** **kind** → KIND, See also **cruel** → CRUEL
▸ **unkindly** adv.: *I'm sure it wasn't meant unkindly.*

obnoxious /əb'nɒkʃəs; AmE -'nɑːk-/ extremely unpleasant, especially in a way that is offensive or unkind: *What an obnoxious little man.*

objectionable /əb'dʒekʃənəbl/ (*rather formal*) (especially of people and their behaviour or attitudes) unpleasant or offensive: *His views on race are quite objectionable.*

hurtful (especially of things sb says or writes) unkind and making you feel upset and offended: *I cannot forget the hurtful things he said.* See also **hurt** → DISTRESS *noun*, **hurt** → HURT *verb* 1

unpleasant (*rather formal*) not kind, friendly or polite: *He was very unpleasant to me.* ◊ *She said some very unpleasant things about you.* ❶ **Unpleasant** suggests that sb is being rude or saying insulting things. **OPP** **pleasant** → FRIENDLY 1

2 mean · frugal · cheap · thrifty · stingy

These words all describe sb who is not willing to give or share things, especially money.

PATTERNS AND COLLOCATIONS
▸ mean / frugal / stingy **with** sth

mean (*BrE, disapproving*) not willing to give or share things, especially money; given unwillingly and in small quantities: *They were too mean to buy the kids proper beds.* ◊ *Don't be so mean with the chocolate sauce.* ◊ *It was difficult to manage the department on such a mean budget.* **OPP** **generous** → GENEROUS

frugal /'fruːgl/ using only as much money or food as is necessary: *The monks lead a frugal existence in their isolated monastery.*

cheap (*AmE, informal, disapproving*) not willing to spend money: *Don't be so cheap!* ◊ *She was just too cheap to buy a real present.*

thrifty (*approving*) careful about spending money; not wasting things: *He was brought up to be thrifty and never to get into debt.*

stingy /'stɪndʒi/ (*informal, disapproving*) mean: *Don't be so stingy with the cream!* ◊ *It was a stingy offer and he turned it down.*

NOTE **MEAN, CHEAP** OR **STINGY**? The main differences between these words are in geography and register. **Mean** is British, **stingy** is informal and **cheap** is American and informal. **Mean** and **stingy** can describe a person or an amount of money, but **cheap** can only describe a person.

meaning *noun*

meaning · sense · significance

These are all words for the thing or idea that a word, phrase or sign represents.

PATTERNS AND COLLOCATIONS
▸ the **original / exact / precise / general / true** meaning / sense / significance
▸ a **special / symbolic** meaning / sense / significance
▸ the **accepted / wide / narrow / literal / figurative / metaphorical / legal / technical** meaning / sense of sth
▸ the **real / hidden** meaning / significance
▸ to **have** a meaning / sense / significance

▸ to **grasp / understand** the meaning / significance of sth
▸ to **acquire / take on / gain** meaning / significance

meaning [C, U] the thing or idea that a word, phrase, sign, etc. represents; the things or ideas that sb wishes to communicate to you by what they say or do; the ideas that a writer, artist, etc. wishes to communicate through a book, painting, etc: *Words often have several meanings.* ◊ *I don't quite **get your meaning** (= understand what you mean to say).* ◊ *What's the meaning of this? I explicitly told you not to leave the room.* ◊ *The text manages to convey multiple layers of meaning.*

sense [C] the meaning that a word or phrase has; a way of understanding sth: *The word 'love' is used in different senses by different people.* ◊ *He was a true friend, **in every sense of the word** (= in every possible way).* ◊ *The medical care was excellent, **in a technical sense**.* ◊ ***In a sense** (= in one way) it doesn't matter any more.*

NOTE **MEANING** OR **SENSE**? You can say that a word has different **meanings** or different **senses**. **Sense**, however, is usually used in more technical or more formal contexts than **meaning**.

significance /sɪg'nɪfɪkəns/ [U, C] (*rather formal*) the meaning and importance of sb's words or actions; the meaning of a sign or symbol: *She couldn't grasp the full significance of what he had said.* ◊ *Do these symbols have any particular significance?* ❶ **Significance** is often used to talk about a special meaning that is not obvious.

meantime *noun*

meantime · interval · interim · interlude · lapse

These are all words for a period of time between two events.

PATTERNS AND COLLOCATIONS
▸ an interval / interlude **between** A and B
▸ **in the** meantime / interim
▸ a **brief** interval / interlude / lapse
▸ a **short** interval / interlude

meantime /'miːntaɪm/ [sing.] (always used in the phrase *in the meantime*) the period of time between two times or events: *My first novel was rejected by six publishers. In the meantime I had written a play.* ❶ **In the meantime** is used to talk about what sb did, or what they are going to do while waiting for sth particular to happen.

interval [C] (*especially written*) a period of time between two events: *The interval between major earthquakes might be 200 years.* ◊ *He knocked on the door and after a brief interval it was opened.* ❶ **Interval** is usually used when the amount of time between two events is important. Typical collocations are *a 15-minute / 3-month, etc. interval*, or *a brief / short interval*. It is also common to talk about *the interval between* two events.

interim /'ɪntərɪm/ [sing.] (always used in the phrase *in the interim*) (*rather formal, especially business*) the period of time between two events: *Her new job does not start until May and she will continue in the old job in the interim.* ❶ **In the interim** is used to talk about what sb did, or what they are going to do while waiting for sth particular to happen. It is more formal than **in the meantime** and used especially in business contexts.

interlude /'ɪntəluːd; AmE -tərl-/ [C] (*especially written*) a period of time between two events during which sth different happens: *She knew that their **romantic interlude** (= short romantic relationship) would soon be drawing to a close.* ◊ *Apart from a brief interlude of peace, the war lasted nine years.* ❶ **Interlude** is often used to talk about a calm or more peaceful time between two periods of war, or between two busier periods. Typical collocates of **interlude** are *brief, little, musical, peaceful* and *romantic*.

lapse /læps/ [C] a period of time between two events: *After a lapse of six months we met up again.* ◊ *He wrote to us after a considerable lapse of time.* ❶ In this meaning

lapse is almost always used in the pattern *a lapse of 3/5/ 10/20, etc. years*, or *a (considerable) lapse of time*. It is also possible to talk about a *time lapse*.

the media *noun* See the Topic Map for THE MEDIA on p.900

the media · the press · coverage · reporting · journalism · reportage
These are all words for sth that is used to communicate news stories and information from journalists to the public.

PATTERNS AND COLLOCATIONS
▸ **in** / **by** the media / press
▸ (the) **mainstream** media / press / coverage / reporting / journalism
▸ (a) **biased** media / press / coverage / reporting
▸ **media** / **press** / **newspaper** coverage / reporting / reportage
▸ **investigative** reporting / journalism
▸ **accurate** / **balanced** / **objective** coverage / reporting
▸ the **national** / **local** / **free** / **foreign** media / press
▸ media / press **reports** / **coverage**

the media [sing.+ sing./pl. *v.*] newspapers, magazines, radio and television considered as a group: *the news/ broadcasting media* ◊ *The media was accused of influencing the final decision.* ◊ *He became a media star for his part in the protests.* ◊ *the relationship between politics and the mass media*

the press (also **the Press**) [sing.+ sing./pl. *v.*] newspapers and magazines that report news; journalists and photographers who work for organizations that report news, especially newspapers or magazines: *The story was reported in the press and on television.* ◊ *Today's press briefing will be televised live.* ◊ *She has been harassed by the press, who desperately need a story.* ❶ **Press** [sing.] or [U] can also mean the type or amount of reports that newspapers write about sb/sth: *The airline has **had a bad press** recently* (= journalists have written unpleasant things about it). ◊ *The demonstration got very little press* (= there were few reports in the media).

coverage /ˈkʌvərɪdʒ/ [U] the attention given to a particular event or subject by the media: *There was blanket coverage* (= reports everywhere) *of the attacks.* ◊ *tonight's **live coverage** of the hockey game* See also **cover** → DESCRIBE *verb*

reporting [U] the communication of news stories to the public by journalists: *Reporting restrictions were not lifted at the trial yesterday.* See also **report** → DESCRIBE *verb*, **reporter** → REPORTER

journalism [U] the work of collecting and writing news stories by the media: *Was the article intentionally misleading, or just a piece of shoddy journalism?* See also **journalist** → REPORTER

reportage /ˈriːpɔːtɪdʒ; ˌrepɔːˈtɑːʒ; *AmE* rɪˈpɔːrt-/ [U] (*formal*) the activity of reporting news by journalists: *In addition to mere reportage, there was investigation and analysis.* ❶ **Reportage** is sometimes used to talk about the total amount of media coverage of a particular subject or event, especially when discussing the characteristics of the media in general: *There is increasing awareness of how biased media reportage can govern our perceptions.*

mediocre *adj.*

mediocre · not much of a... · indifferent · undistinguished · middling · so-so
These words all describe things or people that are not better than average.

PATTERNS AND COLLOCATIONS
▸ a mediocre / an indifferent / a so-so **performance** / **result** / **start**
▸ a mediocre / not much of a / a so-so **player**
▸ a mediocre / not much of a **writer**
▸ mediocre / indifferent / middling / so-so **quality**
▸ mediocre / middling **talent**

mediocre /ˌmiːdiˈəʊkə(r); *AmE* -ˈoʊkər/ (*disapproving*) not very good; of only average standard: *The player was under some pressure after some mediocre performances.* **OPP** **excellent** → EXCELLENT

'not much of a... *idiom* (*often disapproving*) not a good...: *I'm not much of a cook.* ◊ *It wasn't much of a party.* ◊ *He's not much of a drinker* (= He doesn't often drink alcohol).

indifferent /ɪnˈdɪfrənt/ (*often disapproving*) not very good: *He suffered from indifferent health.* ◊ *The festival has the usual mixture of films – good, bad and indifferent.*
▸ **indifferently** *adv.*: *The team played indifferently but they still won.*

undistinguished /ˌʌndɪˈstɪŋɡwɪʃt/ (*often disapproving*) not very interesting, successful or attractive: *A few interesting buildings have been replaced by typically undistinguished modern blocks.* ◊ *She had an undistinguished career as a university lecturer.* **OPP** **distinguished** → GREAT 2

middling [usually before noun] of average size, quality or status: *The tax affects 40 million people on middling incomes.* ◊ *The interviewer was a former golfer of middling talent.*

so-'so (*informal*) not particularly good or bad: *I've had a so-so sort of week.* ◊ *'She's really pretty, isn't she?' 'So-so,' he replied.*

medium *noun*

medium · vehicle · channel · catalyst · instrument
These are all words for a person, thing or system that makes sth happen or allows sth to happen.

PATTERNS AND COLLOCATIONS
▸ a medium / a vehicle / a channel / a catalyst / an instrument **of** / **for** sth
▸ the / a / an **main** / **important** / **major** / **effective** medium / vehicle / catalyst / instrument
▸ a **powerful** medium / vehicle / catalyst / instrument
▸ a **useful** medium / vehicle / channel / catalyst / instrument
▸ the **ideal** / **perfect** medium / vehicle / instrument
▸ a **key** / **great** catalyst / instrument
▸ (a / an / the) **appropriate** / **proper** / **right** medium / vehicle / channels
▸ (a) **political** vehicle / channels / catalyst / instrument
▸ a medium / a vehicle / channels / an instrument of **communication** / **expression**
▸ to **see** / **use sb** / **sth as** a medium / a vehicle / a catalyst / an instrument
▸ to **regard sb** / **sth as** a medium / a vehicle / an instrument

medium (pl. **media**) [C] (*rather formal*) a way of communicating information or ideas to people: *The internet is the modern medium of communication.* ◊ *The classes look at various electronic and audio-visual media.* ◊ *English is the **medium of instruction*** (= the language used to teach other subjects).

vehicle [C] (*rather formal*) something that can be used to express your ideas or feelings or as a way of achieving sth: *Art may be used as a vehicle for propaganda.* ◊ *The play is an ideal vehicle for her talents.*

channel [C] (also **channels** [pl.]) a method or system that people use to get information, to communicate, or to send sth somewhere; a way of expressing ideas and feelings: *Complaints must be made **through** the proper channels.* ◊ *The company has worldwide distribution channels.* ◊ *Music is a great channel for releasing your emotions.*

NOTE **VEHICLE** OR **CHANNEL**? **Channel** is used especially to talk about a method or system used to give information, or to direct feelings and ideas, that might otherwise become dangerous or difficult to deal with. **Vehicle** is used more to talk about a way of getting creative and political ideas or other beliefs across to the general public.

catalyst /'kætəlɪst/ [C] (*rather formal*) a person or thing that causes a change: *I see my role as being a catalyst for change.* ◇ *The riots were later seen as the catalyst for the new political developments.*

instrument [C] (*formal*) something that is used by sb in order to achieve sth; a person or thing that makes sth happen: *The law is not the best instrument for dealing with family matters.* ◇ *Financial aid can become an instrument of control rather than a support.*

meet verb

1 meet for a drink/talks
2 meet by chance
3 meet sb for the first time
4 meet sb's needs/conditions

---

1 meet · meet with sb · gather · get together · assemble · mass · rally · convene · meet up
These words all refer to people coming together in order to do sth.

PATTERNS AND COLLOCATIONS
▸ to meet/ meet with sb/ gather/ get together/ assemble/ mass/ rally/ convene/ meet up **for** sth
▸ to meet/ get together/ meet up **with** sb
▸ **crowds**/ **supporters** gather/ assemble/ rally
▸ **people** gather/ assemble/ mass
▸ to meet/ meet with sb/ gather/ get together/ convene **regularly**

meet [I, T, no passive] to come together formally in order to discuss sth; to come together socially after you have arranged it: *The committee meets on Fridays.* ◇ *Let's meet for a drink after work.* ◇ *The Prime Minister met other European leaders for talks.* ◇ *We're meeting them outside the theatre at 7.*

'meet with sb phrasal verb (*especially AmE*) to meet sb, especially for discussions: *The President met with senior White House aides.*

gather [I] to come together in one place to form a group: *A crowd soon gathered.* ◇ *Can you all gather round? I've got something to tell you.* ◇ *His supporters gathered in the main square.*

get to'gether phrasal verb (*rather informal*) to meet sb socially or in order to discuss sth: *We must get together for a drink sometime.* ◇ *We all get together every year at Christmas.* ◇ *Management should get together with the union.* ❶ **Get together** is slightly more informal than **meet** and is usually used for less definite arrangements: *The committee gets together on Fridays.* ◇ *We're getting together outside the theatre at 7.* See also **get-together** → EVENT 2

assemble /ə'sembl/ [I] (*rather formal*) to come together as a group: *The students were asked to assemble in the hall.*

mass [I] to come together in large numbers: *Demonstrators had massed outside the embassy.* ◇ *Dark clouds massed on the horizon.*

NOTE GATHER, ASSEMBLE, OR MASS? **Gather** is the most general of the three words, and can be used to talk about large or small groups of people coming together. **Assemble** is a more formal word and is used about more formal meetings, when a group of people has been told to meet in one place and it has not happened by accident. **Mass** emphasizes the large number of people involved.

rally [I] to come together in order to help or support sb/ sth: *The cabinet **rallied behind** the Prime Minister.* ◇ *Many national newspapers **rallied to** his support.* ❶ When people **rally** they don't always literally come together in one place, but they act together to give sb/sth their support.

convene /kən'viːn/ [I] (*formal*) to come together for a formal meeting: *The committee will convene at 11.30 next Thursday.*

,meet 'up phrasal verb (*rather informal*) to meet sb, especially by arrangement: *I met up with him later for a drink.*

---

2 meet · run into sb · encounter · bump into sb
These words all mean to be in the same place as sb by chance and talk to them.

PATTERNS AND COLLOCATIONS
▸ to meet/ run into/ bump into a **friend**

meet [I, T, no passive] to be in the same place as sb by chance and talk to them: *I hope we'll meet again soon.* ◇ *Did you meet anyone in town?*

,run 'into sb phrasal verb (*rather informal*) to meet sb by chance, especially sb you know: *Guess who I ran into today!*

encounter /ɪn'kaʊntə(r)/ [T] (*formal*) to meet sb, or discover sth, especially sb/sth new, unusual or unexpected: *She was the most remarkable woman he had ever encountered.* ◇ *Walruses were commonly encountered in the Shetland Islands until quite recently.* See also **come across sb/sth** → FIND 2

,bump 'into sb phrasal verb (*informal*) to meet sb by chance, especially sb you know: *I bumped into Tina this morning.*

NOTE RUN INTO SB OR BUMP INTO SB? There is very little difference in the meaning or range of these two verbs. **Bump into sb** is more informal and is used slightly less in American English.

---

3 meet · get to know sb · make sb's acquaintance
These words all mean to see and talk to sb for the first time.

PATTERNS AND COLLOCATIONS
▸ to **first** meet/ get to know/ make the acquaintance of sb

meet [T, no passive, I] to see and know sb for the first time; to be introduced to sb: *Where did you first meet your husband?* ◇ *There's someone I want you to meet.* ◇ *I don't think we've met.* ◇ (*especially BrE*) **Pleased to meet you.** ◇ (*especially AmE*) **Nice to meet you.** ❶ When you have just been formally introduced to sb it is usual to say *Pleased to meet you* (in British English) or *Nice to meet you* (in American English). You can say *Nice meeting you* (in British or American English) when you say goodbye to sb that you have met for the first time; in American English you can also say *Nice to meet you* when you say goodbye, but it is NOT usual to say *Pleased to meet you* at this point in either British or American English.

,get to 'know sb phrase to become familiar with sb over time: *She's very nice when you get to know her.* ❶ There are a few other expressions with **know** in this meaning: *Do you two know each other (= have you met before)?* ◇ *I've known David for 20 years.* ◇ *She was a secretary when I first knew her.*

make sb's acquaintance, make the acquaintance of sb phrase (*formal*) to meet sb for the first time: *I am delighted to make your acquaintance, Mrs Phillips.* ◇ *I made the acquaintance of several musicians around that time.* See also **acquaintance** → FRIEND, **acquaintance** → FRIENDSHIP

---

4 meet · suit · satisfy · fulfil · serve
These words all mean to be good enough for sb/sth or to provide what is needed for sb/sth.

PATTERNS AND COLLOCATIONS
▸ to meet/ suit/ satisfy/ fulfil/ serve a **requirement**/ **need**/ **purpose**
▸ to suit/ satisfy/ fulfil/ serve sb/ sth's **interests**
▸ to meet/ suit/ satisfy/ fulfil a **demand**/ **condition**
▸ to meet/ satisfy/ fulfil a/ an **standard**/ **obligation**
▸ to meet/ satisfy/ fulfil the **terms**/ **criteria**

meet [T] to do what is needed or asked for; to be enough for what sb/sth requires: *Until these conditions are met we can't proceed with the sale.* ◇ *50% of the candidates failed to meet the standard required.* ◇ *I can't possibly meet that deadline.*

suit [T, no passive] (not used in the progressive tenses) to be convenient or useful for sb: *Choose a computer to suit your particular needs.* ◇ *If you want to go by bus, that suits me fine.* ◇ *It suits me to start work at a later time.*

satisfy [T] (*rather formal*) to provide what is wanted, needed, or asked for; to be as good as what is wanted or needed: *It seemed that no amount of information would satisfy their curiosity.* ◇ *Our hunger satisfied, we continued our journey.* ◇ *She failed to satisfy all the requirements for entry to the college.*

fulfil (*BrE*) (*AmE* **fulfill**) /fʊlˈfɪl/ (**-ll-**) [T] (*formal, especially business*) to do or have what is required or what is necessary: *Failure to fulfil the terms of the agreements may result in legal action.* ◇ *He had fulfilled his promise to his father.*

serve [T] (*rather formal*) to be useful to sb in achieving sth or in providing what is needed or wanted: *These experiments serve no useful purpose.* ◇ *His linguistic ability served him well in his chosen profession.*

meeting *noun*

1 a business meeting
2 a chance meeting

1 meeting · conference · session · summit · gathering · assembly · convention · caucus

These are all words for an occasion when lots of people come together for a particular reason.

PATTERNS AND COLLOCATIONS

▸ an **annual** meeting/ conference/ session/ summit/ gathering/ assembly/ convention
▸ an **international** meeting/ conference/ summit/ gathering/ assembly/ convention
▸ a **public** meeting/ gathering/ assembly/ session
▸ a **two-day/three-day** conference/session/summit/convention
▸ a **bilateral/multilateral** meeting/summit/convention
▸ an **illegal** meeting/ gathering/ assembly
▸ to **hold** a meeting/ a conference/ a session/ a summit/ a gathering/ an assembly/ a convention/ a caucus
▸ to **host** a meeting/ a conference/ summit/ gathering/ convention
▸ to **call** a meeting/ a conference/ a session/ a summit/ an assembly/ a caucus
▸ to **attend** a meeting/ a conference/ a session/ a summit/ a gathering/ an assembly/ a convention
▸ to **chair** a meeting/ a conference/ a session/ a summit/ an assembly
▸ to **address** a meeting/a conference/a session/a gathering/an assembly/ a convention
▸ a meeting/conference/session/summit/gathering/convention **takes place**
▸ **delegates to** a conference/a session/a summit/an assembly/a convention

meeting [C] an occasion when people come together to discuss or decide sth: *a committee/staff meeting* ◇ *What time is the meeting?* ◇ *Helen will chair the meeting* (= be in charge of it). ◇ *I'll be in a meeting all morning – can you take my calls?* ◇ *A meeting of the United Nations Security Council was called.* ❶ **The meeting** [sing.] is the people at a meeting: *The meeting voted to accept the pay offer.*

conference [C, U] a large official meeting, usually lasting for a few days, at which people with the same work or interests come together to discuss their views; a meeting at which people have formal discussions: *She is attending a three-day conference on AIDS education.* ◇ *The AIDS conference will be held in Glasgow.* ◇ *He was in conference with his lawyers all day.* ❶ A **press conference** (*especially BrE*)/**news conference** (*AmE*) is a meeting at which sb talks to a group of journalists in order to answer their questions or to make an official statement.

session [C] a formal meeting or series of meetings of a court, parliament, etc.; a period of time when such meetings are held: *a session of the UN General Assembly* ◇ *The court is now in session.* ◇ *The committee met in closed session* (= with nobody else present).

summit [C] an official meeting or series of meetings between the leaders of two or more governments at which they discuss important matters: *The conference will form part of the European summit in Rome next month.* ◇ *The President of Costa Rica will chair the summit meeting.*

gathering [C] a meeting of people for a particular purpose: *a social/family gathering* ◇ *He was asked to speak at a gathering of religious leaders.*

assembly /əˈsembli/ [C, U] (*rather formal*) a meeting of people for a particular purpose: *He was to address a public assembly on the issue.* ◇ *Laws governing freedom of assembly were gradually being relaxed.* ❶ An **assembly** [C, U] is also a meeting of the teachers and students in a school, often at the start of the day, to give information, discuss school events or say prayers together: *There is a whole school assembly every Friday morning.* ◇ *I'm playing the flute in assembly tomorrow morning.*

> NOTE **GATHERING** OR **ASSEMBLY**? A **gathering** is often more informal than an **assembly**. A **gathering** may be a social event or an event at which people discuss matters of shared interest among themselves. An **assembly** is more often called to discuss a particular matter that people feel is very important, especially when they think it is not being properly addressed by the government or authorities.

convention [C] a conference, especially for the members of a profession, political party, fan club or other association: *The party's annual convention will be held on April 6.*

caucus /ˈkɔːkəs/ [C] (*especially AmE*) a meeting of the members or leaders of a political party to choose candidates or to decide policy; the members or leaders of a political party as a group: *20 states will hold precinct caucuses on Tuesday to choose delegates to the parties' national conventions.*

2 meeting · appointment · encounter · date · engagement · introduction

These are all words for an occasion when two or more people meet.

PATTERNS AND COLLOCATIONS

▸ a meeting/ an appointment/ an encounter/ a date/ an engagement **with** sb
▸ a meeting/ an encounter **between** people
▸ (a) **formal** meeting/ appointment/ encounter/ engagement/ introduction
▸ an **important** meeting/ appointment/ date/ engagement/ introduction
▸ a **casual** meeting/ encounter/ introduction
▸ a **dinner** appointment/ date/ engagement
▸ to **have** a meeting/ an appointment/ an encounter/ a date/ an engagement
▸ to **arrange** a meeting/ an appointment/ a date/ an introduction
▸ to **keep** an appointment/ a date/ an engagement
▸ to **make** an appointment/ a date/ introductions
▸ to **cancel** a meeting/ an appointment/ a date/ an engagement

meeting [C] a situation in which two or more people meet, because they have arranged it or by chance: *At our first meeting I was nervous.* ◇ *It was a chance meeting that would change my life.*

appointment [C] a formal arrangement to meet or visit sb at a particular time, especially for a reason connected with their work: *She made an appointment for her son to see the doctor.* ◇ *I've got a dental appointment at 3 o'clock.* ◇ *He had failed to keep the appointment.* ◇ *Viewing is by appointment only* (= only at a time that has been arranged in advance).

encounter [C] a meeting, especially one that is sudden, unexpected or violent: *Three of them were killed in the subsequent encounter with the police.* ◇ *I've had a number of* **close encounters** (= situations that could have been dangerous) *with bad drivers.* ◇ *It was his first sexual encounter* (= his first experience of sex).

date [C] a meeting that you have arranged with a boyfriend or girlfriend or with sb who might become a boyfriend or girlfriend: *I've got a date with Lucy tomorrow night.* ◇ *I can't believe you set me up on a* **blind date** (= a date with sb you have not met before). See also **date** → GO OUT *phrasal verb*

engagement [C] an arrangement to do sth at a particular time, especially sth official or sth connected with your job: *He has a number of social engagements next week.* ◇ *It was her first official engagement.* ◇ *I had to refuse because of a* **prior engagement**. See also **engaged** → BUSY 1

introduction [C, U] the act of making one person formally known to another, in which you tell each the other's name: *Introductions were made and the conversation started to flow.* ◇ *Our speaker today* **needs no introduction** (= he is already well known). See also **introduce** → INTRODUCE 2

melt *verb*

melt · dissolve · thaw · defrost
These words all mean to become or to make sth become liquid or soft and ready for cooking.

PATTERNS AND COLLOCATIONS
▸ to melt / dissolve **away**
▸ **ice** / **snow** melts / thaws
▸ to **completely** melt / dissolve / thaw
▸ to **gradually** melt / dissolve

melt [I, T] to become or make sth become liquid as a result of heating: *The snow showed no sign of melting.* ◇ *The sun had melted the ice.* ◇ *First, melt two ounces of butter.* OPP **freeze** → COOL

dissolve [I, T] (of a solid) to mix with a liquid and become part of it; to make a solid become part of a liquid: *Heat gently until the sugar dissolves.* ◇ *Dissolve the tablet in water.*

thaw [I, T] (of ice and snow) to turn back into water after being frozen; to become, or to let frozen food become, soft or liquid ready for cooking: *The snow started to thaw as the temperature kept up.* ◇ *Leave the meat to thaw completely before cooking.* ◇ *If a pipe has frozen, it can be* **thawed out** *with a hairdryer.* ❶ When **it thaws** or **it is thawing**, the weather becomes warm enough to melt snow and ice: *It's starting to thaw.* OPP **freeze** → COOL
▸ **thaw** *noun* [C, usually sing.]: *The river doubles in size during the spring thaw.*

defrost /ˌdiːˈfrɒst; AmE -ˈfrɔːst/ [I, T] to become, or to let frozen food become, soft or liquid ready for cooking: *A cheesecake was defrosting in the microwave.* ◇ *Make sure you defrost the chicken completely before cooking.* OPP **freeze** → COOL

memory *noun*

memory · mind · recollection · recall · reminiscence · remembrance
These are all words for the ability to remember things, the act of remembering or things that you remember.

PATTERNS AND COLLOCATIONS
▸ a memory / recollection / reminiscence **of** sb / sth
▸ **in** memory / remembrance **of** sb / sth
▸ a **vague** / **vivid** / **clear** memory / recollection
▸ to **have** a … memory / recollection / recall
▸ to **have no** memory / recollection of sb / sth

memory [C, U] your ability to remember things; the period of time that sb is able to remember events; a thought of sth that you remember from the past: *I have a*

bad **memory for** *names.* ◇ *People have* **short memories** (= they soon forget). ◇ *He had a* **long memory** *for people who had disappointed him.* ◇ *She can recite the whole poem* **from memory**. ◇ *There hasn't been peace in the country* **in/within my memory**. ◇ *This hasn't happened* **in living memory** (= nobody alive now can remember it happening). ◇ *childhood memories* ◇ *I have vivid memories of my grandparents.* ◇ *The photos* **bring back** *lots of good* **memories**. ◇ *He founded the charity in memory of his late wife.* See also **memorize** → LEARN

mind [C, usually sing.] your ability to remember things: *When I saw the exam questions my* **mind** *just went blank* (= I couldn't remember anything). ◇ *Sorry – your name has gone right out of my mind.* See also **bear sb/sth in mind** → REMEMBER

recollection /ˌrekəˈlekʃn/ [U, C] (*formal*) the act of remembering an event from the past; a memory from the past: *I have no recollection of meeting her before.* ◇ *My recollection of events differs from his.* ◇ **To the best of my recollection** (= if I remember correctly) *I was not present at that meeting.* ◇ *his early recollections of his father* See also **recollect** → REMEMBER

recall [U] the ability to remember facts or events: *She has amazing powers of recall.* ◇ *to have* **instant recall** (= to be able to remember sth immediately) ◇ *to have* **total recall** (= to be able to remember all the details of sth) See also **recall** → REMEMBER *verb*

reminiscence /ˌremɪˈnɪsns/ [C, usually pl., U] a spoken or written description of sth that sb remembers about their past life; the act of remembering events from the past: *The book is a collection of his* **reminiscences about** *the actress.* ◇ *The role of reminiscence in family history research should never be underestimated.* See also **reminisce** → REMEMBER

remembrance [U] (*rather formal*) the act or process of remembering an event in the past or a person who is dead: *A service was held in remembrance of local soldiers killed in the war.* ◇ *a remembrance service* ◇ *a chapel/ garden of remembrance* (= in memory of people who have died) ❶ In formal language a **remembrance** [C] is an object that causes you to remember sb/sth: *The cenotaph stands as a remembrance of those killed in the war.* See also **remember** → REMEMBER

mentally ill *adj.* See the Topic Map for HEALTH on p.890

mentally ill · insane · neurotic · psychotic · disturbed · crazed · deranged · unstable · psychopathic
These words all describe sb who is suffering from a mental illness.

neurotic	mentally ill	crazed
disturbed	insane	psychopathic
unstable	psychotic	
	deranged	

PATTERNS AND COLLOCATIONS
▸ insane / crazed / deranged **with** grief / sorrow / jealousy
▸ neurotic / psychotic / disturbed / unstable / psychopathic **behaviour**
▸ neurotic / psychotic / psychopathic **illnesses** / **disorders** / **symptoms** / **patients**
▸ a crazed / psychopathic **killer**
▸ **seriously** mentally ill / neurotic / psychotic / disturbed
▸ **emotionally** / **mentally** disturbed / unstable

mentally ˈill suffering from an illness of the mind, especially in a way that affects the way you think and behave: *She was unhappy and stressed, but I didn't think she was mentally ill.* ◇ *Services for mentally ill people have been cut yet again.* See also **ill** → SICK 1
▸ **the mentally ˈill** *noun* [pl.]: *the care of the mentally ill*

insane /ɪnˈseɪn/ [not usually before noun] (*especially written*) suffering from a serious mental illness and unable to live in normal society: *Doctors certified her as insane.* ◇ *The* question is, was the man insane when he committed the crime? ❶ In informal English **insane** can describe sb who is not suffering from a mental illness, but whose mind does not work normally, especially because they are under pressure. This meaning is used especially in the phrases go insane and drive sb insane: *She was driving me insane with her constant chatter.* **OPP** sane → SANE, See also the entry for MAD

▸ **the insane** noun [pl.]: *He's in a hospital for the criminally insane* (= people who are seriously mentally ill and are likely to commit dangerous crimes).

neurotic /njʊəˈrɒtɪk; *AmE* nʊˈrɑː-/ (*medical*) suffering from or connected with neurosis (= a mental illness in which a person suffers strong feelings of fear and worry): *the treatment of anxiety in neurotic patients* ❶ In informal English **neurotic** is also used to describe sb who is not suffering from a mental illness, but is not behaving in a calm way because they are worried about sth: *She became neurotic about keeping the house clean.* See also the entry for NERVOUS

psychotic /saɪˈkɒtɪk; *AmE* -ˈkɑːt-/ (*medical*) suffering from or connected with psychosis (= a serious mental illness in which thought and emotions lose connection with external reality): *a young mother with a psychotic illness* ◇ *He suffered a psychotic episode* (= an occasion on which he became psychotic) *two years ago.* ❶ In informal English **psychotic** is sometimes used to describe anyone suffering from a mental illness, but in correct medical usage it only describes people who have difficulty relating to external reality. It contrasts with **neurotic** which describes people who are less seriously mentally ill and are still able to distinguish what is real from what is not. **Psychotic** should not be confused with **psychopathic**: being **psychotic** does not make sb violent.

disturbed /dɪˈstɜːbd; *AmE* -ˈstɜːrbd/ mentally ill, especially because of very unhappy or shocking experiences: *He works with emotionally disturbed children.* ◇ *His behaviour is deeply disturbed.*

crazed /kreɪzd/ (*written, especially journalism*) not having any emotional or mental control: *A crazed killer stalked the streets.* ◇ *She was crazed with grief.*

deranged /dɪˈreɪndʒd/ (*especially written*) not able to behave and think normally, especially because of a mental illness: *The plan seemed to be the product of a deranged mind.* ◇ *At first I thought he was deranged.*

unstable /ʌnˈsteɪbl/ having emotions and behaviour that are likely to change suddenly and unexpectedly: *He's highly unstable, and liable to sudden fits of rage.* ◇ *emotionally unstable patients*

psychopathic /ˌsaɪkəˈpæθɪk/ suffering from or connected with a serious mental illness that causes the sufferer to behave in a violent way towards other people: *He was diagnosed as suffering from a psychopathic disorder.*

mention verb

mention · refer to sb/sth · speak · cite · quote · allude to sb/sth
These words all mean to write or speak about sb/sth, often in order to give an example or prove sth.

PATTERNS AND COLLOCATIONS
▸ to mention/refer to/speak of/cite/quote/allude to sb/sth **as** sb/sth
▸ to mention/refer to/cite/quote a/an **example/case/instance** of sth
▸ sth is **frequently/often** mentioned/referred to/spoken of/cited/quoted/alluded to
▸ to mention/refer to/speak of/quote/allude to sb/sth **briefly**
▸ the example mentioned/referred to/cited/quoted/alluded to **above/earlier/previously**

mention [T] to write or speak about sb/sth, especially without giving much information: *Nobody mentioned anything to me about it.* ◇ *Now that you mention it, she*

did seem to be in a strange mood. ◇ *Did she mention where she was going?* ◇ *He failed to mention that he was the one who started the fight.* See also **mention** → REFERENCE noun

re·fer to sb/sth phrasal verb (**-rr-**) (*rather formal*) to mention or speak about sb/sth: *I promised not to refer to the matter again.* ◇ *She always referred to Ben as 'that nice man'.* ◇ *The victims were not referred to by name.* See also **reference** → REFERENCE

speak [I] to mention or describe sb/sth: *She still speaks about him with great affection.* ◇ *Witnesses spoke of a great ball of flame.* ◇ *Speaking of travelling,* (= referring back to a subject just mentioned) *are you going anywhere exciting this year?*

cite /saɪt/ [T] (*formal*) to mention sth as a reason or example, or in order to support what you are saying: *He cited his heavy workload as the reason for his breakdown.* ◇ *She cited the case of Leigh v. Gladstone.* See also **cite** → QUOTE, **citation** → REFERENCE

quote [T] to mention an example of sth to support what you are saying: *He quoted one case in which a person had died in a fire.* See also **quote** → QUOTE, **quotation** → REFERENCE

NOTE CITE OR QUOTE? You can **cite** reasons or examples, but you can only **quote** examples.: ~~He quoted his heavy workload as the reason for his breakdown.~~ **Cite** is a more formal word than **quote** and is often used in more formal situations, for example in descriptions of legal cases.

al·lude to sb/sth phrasal verb (*formal*) to mention sth in an indirect way: *The problem had been alluded to briefly in earlier discussions.* See also **allusion** → REFERENCE

mercy noun

mercy · forgiveness · pardon · grace · clemency · charity
These are all words for a kind or forgiving attitude towards sb.

PATTERNS AND COLLOCATIONS
▸ forgiveness/pardon/clemency **for** sth
▸ **divine** mercy/forgiveness/grace
▸ to **ask (for)** mercy/forgiveness/pardon
▸ to **pray for** mercy/forgiveness/grace
▸ to **show (no)/receive** mercy/forgiveness/charity
▸ to **beg for/have** mercy/forgiveness
▸ to **plead for** mercy/clemency

mercy [U] a kind or forgiving attitude towards sb that you have the power to harm or the right to punish: *The terrorists are completely without mercy.* ◇ *God have mercy on us.* ◇ *I'm not going to put myself at the mercy of the bank.* See also **merciful** → LENIENT

forgiveness [U] the act of forgiving sb for sth bad that they have done; a forgiving attitude towards sb: *the forgiveness of sins* ◇ *He begged forgiveness for what he had done.* ◇ *There can be no progress without forgiveness.* See also **forgive** → FORGIVE, **forgiving** → LENIENT

pardon [U] (*formal or old-fashioned*) the act of forgiving sb for sth: *She begged his pardon for disturbing him.* See also **pardon** → FORGIVE

grace [U] the kindness that God shows towards the human race: *It was only by the grace of God that they survived.* ◇ *the power of divine grace*

clemency /ˈklemənsi/ [U] (*formal*) a kind attitude towards sb when they are being punished; willingness not to punish sb too severely: *His lawyers appealed for clemency on the grounds of ill health.*

charity [U] (*formal*) a kind and sympathetic attitude towards sb, especially when you are judging them: *Her article showed no charity towards her former friends.*

mess *noun*
1 The room was in a mess.
2 The economy is in a mess.

---

1 mess · clutter · jumble · disorder · muddle
These are all words you can use when a place or group of things is very untidy.

PATTERNS AND COLLOCATIONS
▸ a mess / clutter / jumble / muddle **of** sth
▸ to be **in** a mess / a jumble / disorder / a muddle
▸ (a) **complete** mess / jumble / disorder
▸ to **be a** mess / jumble / muddle
▸ a **bit of a** mess / jumble

mess [C, usually sing.] (*sometimes disapproving*) an untidy state in which things have been left in the wrong place or spread around: *The room was in a mess.* ◇ *Sorry, this place is a bit of a mess.* ◇ *The kids **made a mess** in the bathroom.* ◇ *'What a mess!' she said, surveying the scene after the party.* ◇ *My hair's a real mess!* See also **messy** → DIRTY, **messy** → UNTIDY
▸ ˌmess sth **'up** *phrasal verb*: *I don't want you messing up my nice clean kitchen.*
clutter [U, sing.] (*rather informal, disapproving*) a lot of things that make a place look untidy, especially when they are not needed or are not being used: *There's always so much clutter on your desk!* ◇ *There was a clutter of bottles, glasses and ashtrays on the table.* ❶ **Clutter** is sth that people often talk about trying to remove. Common collocates of **clutter** include *avoid, get rid of, shed, free sth from* and *clear sth of*. See also **cluttered** → UNTIDY
▸ **clutter** *verb* [T]: *Don't clutter the page with too many diagrams.* ◇ *I don't want all these boxes cluttering up the place.*
jumble [sing.] a lot of different things mixed together without any order and in an untidy way: *The room was a jumble of books, toys and sports equipment.* See also **jumble** → JUMBLE *verb*, **jumbled** → UNTIDY

NOTE CLUTTER OR JUMBLE? Clutter is a more disapproving term than **jumble**, which is more simply descriptive.

disorder [U] (*rather formal*) a situation in which a place is untidy because there is no order in the way things are arranged: *The room was in a state of disorder.* ◇ *He loves tidying up, making order out of disorder.* **OPP order** → EFFICIENCY, See also **disordered** → UNTIDY
muddle [C, usually sing., U] a state of confusion in which things are put together without any order and in an untidy way, so that it is difficult to find what you want: *My papers are all in a muddle.* ◇ *My desk was the usual muddle of books, files and papers.*

---

2 See also the entry for CHAOS
mess · dilemma · plight · predicament · vicious circle · corner · straits
These are all words for a difficult situation.

PATTERNS AND COLLOCATIONS
▸ **in** a mess / a dilemma / a plight / a predicament / a vicious circle / a corner / … straits
▸ a **real** / **terrible** mess / dilemma
▸ (a) **dire** predicament / straits
▸ (a) **financial** mess / dilemma / plight / predicament / straits
▸ a **moral** / **personal** dilemma / predicament
▸ to **find yourself in** a dilemma / a predicament / … straits
▸ to **put sb in** a dilemma / predicament
▸ to **be caught in** a dilemma / vicious circle

mess [C, usually sing.] (*rather informal*) a situation that is full of problems, usually caused by lack of organization or mistakes that sb has made: *The economy is in a mess.* ◇ *The whole situation is a mess.* ◇ *I feel I've **made a mess of** things.* ◇ *Let's try to **sort out** the mess.*
▸ **messy** *adj.*: *The divorce was painful and messy.*

dilemma /dɪˈlemə; daɪ-/ [C] a situation which causes problems, often one in which you have to make a very difficult choice between things of equal importance: *She faced a **dilemma about** whether to accept the offer or not.* ◇ *This poses a difficult **dilemma for** teachers.* ◇ *I could see no way of **resolving** this moral **dilemma**.*
plight /plaɪt/ [sing.] (*especially written*) a difficult or sad situation, especially one involving a person or group of people: *He has expressed deep concern about the plight of the flood victims.* ◇ *A neighbour heard of her plight and offered to help.*
predicament /prɪˈdɪkəmənt/ [C] (*rather formal*) a difficult or unpleasant situation, especially one where it is difficult to know what to do: *Other companies are in an even worse predicament than ourselves.*
ˌvicious ˈcircle [sing.] a situation in which one problem causes another problem which then makes the first problem worse: *He was trapped in a vicious circle of addiction and petty crime.*
corner [C, usually sing.] (*rather informal*) a difficult situation, especially one which it is difficult to find a way out of: *She was used to talking her way out of **tight corners**.* ◇ *He had her **backed into a corner** a couple of times with new facts she didn't know.*
straits [pl.] (*always used after an adjective*) a very difficult situation, especially caused by lack of money: *The factory is **in dire straits**.* ◇ *She found herself in desperate financial straits.*

---

message *noun* See the Topic Map for FACT AND OPINION on p.898

---

message · content · substance · subject matter · the thrust · thread · gist
These are all words for the main or general meaning of a piece of writing, a speech or a conversation.

PATTERNS AND COLLOCATIONS
▸ the **main** message / content / substance / subject matter / thrust / thread of sth
▸ the **general** message / content / thrust / gist of sth
▸ (a) **common** message / content / thread
▸ to **convey** a message / the gist
▸ to **get** / **understand** the message / gist of sth
▸ to **follow** the thread / gist of sth
▸ to **lack** content / substance

message [C, usually sing.] an important moral, social or political idea that a book, speech, campaign or work of art is trying to communicate: *This is a film with a strong religious message.* ◇ *The campaign is trying to **get the message across** to young people that drugs are dangerous.*
content /ˈkɒntent; AmE ˈkɑːn-/ [sing., U] (*rather formal, especially written*) the ideas or information contained in a book, speech or programme of study: *Your tone of voice is as important as the content of what you have to say.* ◇ *Her poetry has a good deal of political content.*
substance [U] (*rather formal*) the most important ideas in a book, speech, plan or political programme: *I agree with what he said **in substance**, though not with every detail.* ◇ *The party's manifesto is good on style but lacks real substance.*
ˈsubject matter [U] (*rather formal*) the main topic or idea discussed or represented in a book, speech or work of art: *She's searching for subject matter for her new book.* ◇ *The artist was revolutionary in both subject matter and technique.* See also **subject** → SUBJECT

NOTE CONTENT, SUBSTANCE OR SUBJECT MATTER? Content is all the ideas and information that are included in sth; it is used especially to talk about written texts, speeches and programmes of study. The **substance** of sth is the main ideas, without the details: it suggests sth important or worth considering; if sth contains nothing important or worth considering you can say that it *lacks substance*. The **subject matter** of sth is the main theme, before it has been given a particular treatment by a writer or artist; it is used especially to talk about books and works of art.

the thrust [sing.] (*rather formal*) the main point of an argument or policy: *The thrust of his argument was that change was needed.* ◇ *She explained the broad thrust of the party's policies.* ❶ **Thrust** is used to talk about the main points in sb's *argument* or *proposal*, or in a *strategy*, an *initiative*, a *plan* or a *policy* proposed by an organization such as the government.

thread [C] an idea or feature that is part of sth greater; an idea that connects the different parts of sth: *A common thread runs through these discussions.* ◇ *The author skilfully draws together the different threads of the plot.* ◇ *I lost the thread of the argument* (= I could no longer follow it). ❶ People talk about a *central/main/common/connecting thread* in an argument or story. You might try to *follow/keep the thread* of an argument or a writer might *draw together/pick up/pull together the threads* of a story.

gist /dʒɪst/ [sing., U] (*especially spoken*) the general meaning of what sb says or writes: *Just try to get* (= understand) *the gist of the argument.* ◇ *I'm afraid I don't quite follow your gist* (= what you really mean). ◇ *Students are taught the skill of reading for gist.*

metaphor *noun*

metaphor · imagery · image · allegory · simile · figure of speech
These are all words for a word or phrase used in an imaginative way to describe sb/sth else.

PATTERNS AND COLLOCATIONS
▸ (a) **striking** metaphor / imagery / image / simile
▸ (a) **powerful / vivid / poetic** metaphor / imagery / image
▸ an **appropriate / apt** metaphor / image
▸ to **use** a metaphor / imagery / an image / a simile / a figure of speech

metaphor /ˈmetəfə(r)/ [C, U] a word, phrase or idea used in an imaginative way to describe sb/sth else, in order to show that the two things have the same qualities and to make the description more powerful; the use of such words, phrases and ideas: *In the story, the game of football is used as a **metaphor for** the competitive struggle of life.* ◇ *The writer's use of metaphor is striking.* ❶ Examples of **metaphors** include: *She has a heart of stone.* ◇ *All the world's a stage.*
▸ **metaphorical** /ˌmetəˈfɒrɪkl; AmE -ˈfɔːr-; -ˈfɑːr-/ *adj.*: *metaphorical language* OPP **literal** ❶ The **literal** meaning of sth is the basic or original meaning, that does not rely on metaphor or imagination: *The literal meaning of 'petrify' is 'turn to stone'.*
▸ **metaphorically** *adv.*: *I'll leave you in Robin's capable hands — **metaphorically speaking**, of course!*

imagery /ˈɪmɪdʒəri/ [U] language that produces pictures in the minds of people reading or listening; the use of images: *The poem is full of religious imagery.*

image [C] a picture in the mind that is produced when you read sth: *Her writings are full of poetic images of the countryside.*

allegory /ˈæləɡəri; AmE -ɡɔːri/ [C, U] a story, play or picture in which each character or event is a symbol representing an idea or quality, such as truth, evil, death, etc.; the use of such symbols: *He gave the example of Orwell's political allegory 'Animal Farm'.* ◇ *We discussed the poet's use of allegory.*
▸ **allegorical** /ˌæləˈɡɒrɪkl; AmE -ˈɡɔːr-; -ˈɡɑːr-/ *adj.*: *an allegorical figure/novel*

simile /ˈsɪməli/ [C, U] (*technical*) a word or phrase that compares sth to sth else, using the words 'like' or 'as'; the use of such words and phrases: *The General liked to apply military similes to a very wide variety of matters.* ◇ *the writer's use of simile* ◇ Examples of **similes** include: *a face like a mask* ◇ *as white as snow*

figure of ˈspeech (pl. **figures of speech**) [C] (*technical*) a word or phrase used in a different way from its usual meaning in order to create a particular mental image or effect: *Children and foreign language learners sometimes take figures of speech literally.*
▸ **figurative** /ˈfɪɡərətɪv; AmE also ˈfɪɡjə-/ *adj.* [usually before noun]: *figurative language* OPP **literal**
▸ **figuratively** *adv.*: *She is, figuratively speaking, holding a gun to his head.*

NOTE **WHICH WORD? Metaphor, allegory** and **simile** are all types of **figure of speech**. These words all refer to the words, phrases, figures or ideas used to create an **image** in the mind of the reader.

the middle *noun*

the middle · centre
These are both words for the part of sth that is at an equal distance from all its edges or sides.

PATTERNS AND COLLOCATIONS
▸ the middle / centre **of** sth
▸ **in** the middle / centre

the middle [sing.] the part of sth that is at an equal distance from all its edges or sides; a point or a period of time between the beginning and the end of sth: *a lake with an island in the middle* ◇ *This chicken isn't cooked in the middle.* ◇ *His picture was **right/bang** (= exactly) **in the middle** of the front page.* ◇ *I should have finished **by the middle** of the week.* ◇ *I like a story with a beginning, a middle and an end.* ◇ *When they quarrel, I am often caught in the middle.* OPP **edge, end, side** → EDGE
▸ **middle** *adj.*: *Pens are kept in the middle drawer.* ◇ *She's the middle child of three.* ◇ *He was very successful in his middle forties.* ◇ *the middle-income groups in society*

centre (*BrE*) (*AmE* **center**) [C] the middle point or part of an area or thing: *the centre of a circle* ◇ *There was a long table in the centre of the room.* ◇ *chocolates with soft centres*
▸ **central** *adj.*: *Central London/America* ◇ *the central area of the brain* ◇ *The apartment is very central — just five minutes from Princes Street.* ◇ *The offices are in a central location.*

NOTE **THE MIDDLE** OR **THE CENTRE? Centre** usually describes the middle part of an area, although it can also describe the inside part of a thing. **The middle** can be used to talk about an area or thing, or a period of time or situation: ~~I should have finished by the centre of the week.~~ ◇ ~~When they quarrel, I am often caught in the centre.~~ The **centre** of an area may be a more precise point than **the middle**: *the centre of a circle* is the point in the exact middle; *the middle of a circle* is usually a larger area inside it. **Central** describes a place or area within a bigger place or object. **Middle** as an adjective is used more to describe objects or people than places, especially when there is an equal number of people or objects on either side: *the central shopping district* ◇ ~~the middle shopping district~~ ◇ *our middle son* (= we have three sons altogether) ◇ ~~our central son~~

the **middle class** *noun* See the Topic Map for THE INDIVIDUAL AND SOCIETY on p.894

the middle class · the bourgeoisie
These are both words for the social class whose members are neither very rich nor very poor and that includes business and professional people.

▸ **among** the middle class / bourgeoisie
▸ the **French / Russian / English, etc.** middle class / bourgeoisie
▸ the **new** middle class / bourgeoisie
▸ the **professional / urban / industrial** middle class / bourgeoisie

the ˌmiddle ˈclass [sing.+ sing./pl. v.] (also **the middle classes** [pl.]) the social class whose members are neither very rich, such as landowners and nobles, nor very poor working people, and that includes business and professional people: *The schools were originally created to educate the children of the middle classes.* ◇ *The move was bitterly resisted by sections of the professional middle class.* ◇ *the upper/lower middle classes* See also **the working class** → GENERAL PUBLIC, **the upper class** → ELITE, **class** → CLASS 4

the bourgeoisie /ˌbʊəʒwɑːˈziː; *AmE* ˌbʊrʒ-/ [sing.+ sing./ pl. v.] (*rather formal, politics*) the middle classes in society; (in politics) the capitalist class that owns or controls the means of production: *The rise of the industrial bourgeoisie in the nineteenth century brought new clashes.* OPP **the proletariat** → GENERAL PUBLIC

middle-class *adj.* See the Topic Map for THE INDIVIDUAL AND SOCIETY on p.894

middle-class · bourgeois
These words describe people belonging to the middle social class or ideas and attitudes typical of this class.

▸ a middle-class / bourgeois **family / institution**
▸ middle-class / bourgeois **culture / intellectuals / liberalism / values / tastes / attitudes**

ˌmiddle-ˈclass (*sometimes disapproving*) connected with or belonging to the middle social class; typical of people from the middle social class, for example interested mainly in social status and having traditional views: *They seemed like a fairly normal, well-adjusted, middle-class family.* ◇ *The school serves a predominantly middle-class area.* ◇ *The club has become very middle-class.* ❶ **Middle-class** is sometimes used to show disapproval of ideas or attitudes which you consider too traditional or put too much emphasis on possessions and social status. See also **upper-class** → ARISTOCRATIC, **working-class** → WORKING-CLASS

bourgeois /ˈbʊəʒwɑː; ˌbʊəˈʒwɑː; *AmE* ˌbʊrʒ-; ˈbʊrʒ-/ (*rather formal, often disapproving*) middle class: *The family has long been the basic unit of bourgeois society.* ◇ *They've become very bourgeois since they got married.* OPP **proletarian** → WORKING CLASS

NOTE MIDDLE CLASS OR BOURGEOIS? Both these words can be used to show disapproval of people and ideas which are too traditional or put too much emphasis on possessions and social status. **Bourgeois** is more frequently disapproving than **middle class** and can show stronger disapproval. However, in more formal writing about politics or history **bourgeois** is also used in a way which is not disapproving to describe a particular social class.

mild *adj.*

mild · bland · tasteless
These words all describe food which does not have a strong flavour.

▸ a mild / bland **taste / flavour**
▸ **food** is bland / tasteless
▸ **very** mild / bland

mild not strong, spicy or bitter in flavour: *a mild curry* ◇ *mild cheese* ◇ *If you like mild cheese, try pasteurised Stilton.* OPP **hot, strong** → STRONG 1 ❶ A **curry** that is not mild is *hot.* **Cheese** that is not *mild* is *strong.*

bland (*disapproving*) not having a strong or interesting taste: *They lived on a bland diet of soup and bread.*

tasteless (*disapproving*) having little or no flavour: *The food we get here is tasteless and monotonous.*

mind *noun*

mind · brain · head · soul · spirit · ego · the/your subconscious
These are all words for the part of sb which cannot be seen or touched, but which allows them to think, feel and be aware of things.

▸ the **human** mind / brain / soul / spirit
▸ a thought **enters** sb's mind / head
▸ **deep** in your mind / the brain / your subconscious

mind [C, U] the part of a person that makes them able to be aware of things, to think and to feel: *There were all kinds of thoughts running through my mind.* ◇ *There was no doubt in his mind that he'd get the job.* ◇ *She was in a disturbed state of mind before they returned.* ◇ *I could not have complete peace of mind before they returned.*

brain [C] the organ inside the head that controls movement, thought, memory and feeling: *The scan apparently showed no damage to the brain.* ◇ *brain cells* ◇ *She died of a brain tumour.* ◇ *Electrodes were used to measure brain activity during sleep.*

head [C] the mind: *I sometimes wonder what goes on in that head of yours.* ◇ *I wish you'd use your head* (= think carefully before doing or saying sth). ◇ *I can't work it out in my head – I need a calculator.* ◇ *I can't get that tune out of my head.* ◇ *When will you get it into your head* (= understand) *that I don't want to discuss this any more!* ◇ *For some reason she's got it into her head* (= believes) *that the others don't like her.*

NOTE MIND OR HEAD? **Head** is slightly more informal than **mind** in this meaning and is used especially to talk about thoughts and ideas that *get into* your head or that you *can't get out of* your head.

soul [C] the part of a person that includes their mind, feelings and character rather than their body; the spiritual part of a person, believed to exist after death; the spiritual and moral qualities of humans in general: *There was a feeling of restlessness deep in her soul.* ◇ *He believed his immortal soul was in peril.* ◇ *His poetry deals with the dark side of the human soul.*

spirit [C] a soul: *He felt a kind of lightness in his spirit as the sun came up.* ◇ *He is dead, but his spirit lives on.* ◇ *You are underestimating the power of the human spirit to overcome difficulties.* See also **spirit** → GHOST

NOTE SOUL OR SPIRIT? **Spirit** is often a more positive word than **soul**. People talk about *lost/tormented/ troubled souls* and *the dark side of the human soul*; and about sb's *indomitable spirit* and *the power of the human spirit.* When they are used to talk about the spiritual part of a person, a **spirit** is often considered to be separate from a living person, especially because the person has died. A **soul** is often considered as the spiritual part of a person who is still alive.

ego /ˈiːɡəʊ; ˈeɡəʊ; *AmE* ˈiːɡoʊ/ (pl. **-os**) [C] (*psychology*) the part of the mind that is responsible for your sense of who you are: *Freud introduced the idea that a part of the ego is unconscious.* See also **self** → IDENTITY

the/your subconscious [sing.] the part of your mind that contains feelings that you are not aware of: *She buried the guilt deep in her subconscious.* ◇ *Delving into the subconscious can be helpful in working through psychological problems.* See also **subconscious** → UNCONSCIOUS *adj.*

minor *adj.* See also the entry for SLIGHT

minor · trivial · petty · insignificant · peripheral · light · unimportant
These words all describe people or things that are not important or do not deserve serious attention.

PATTERNS AND COLLOCATIONS
▶ minor / trivial / petty / peripheral / unimportant **things**
▶ a minor / trivial / petty **problem**
▶ minor / trivial / insignificant / unimportant **details**
▶ a minor / a trivial / an insignificant **matter / incident**
▶ a minor / trivial / petty **offence**
▶ minor / petty **crime / theft / criminals**
▶ a minor / trivial **ailment**
▶ a trivial / an insignificant / an unimportant **fact**
▶ **very** minor / trivial / petty / insignificant / light / unimportant
▶ **apparently / seemingly** minor / trivial / insignificant / unimportant

minor [usually before noun] not very large, important or serious: *The new plan involves widening a minor road through the valley.* ◇ *There may be some minor changes to the schedule.* ◇ *Women played a relatively minor role in the organization.* ◇ *The CD contains a number of delightful short pieces by minor composers.* ◇ *Both the driver and the passenger suffered minor injuries.* ◇ *You may need to undergo minor surgery.* **OPP major** → MAIN, **serious**, **severe** → SERIOUS 1

trivial /ˈtrɪviəl/ (*often disapproving*) not important or serious; not worth worrying about: *I didn't want to bother you with such a trivial matter.* ◇ *I know it sounds trivial, but I'm worried about it.* ❶ **Trivial** is used especially to talk about an *incident*, a *matter* or a *detail*. People also often say that sth is *too trivial to bother about/worry about/mention/make a fuss about.*
▶ **triviality** /ˌtrɪviˈæləti/ *noun* [C, U]: (*disapproving*) *I don't want to waste time on trivialities.* ◇ *His speech was one of great triviality.*

petty [usually before noun] (*usually disapproving*) small and not important; not deserving serious attention: *I don't want to hear any more about your petty squabbles.* ◇ *There are plenty of petty bureaucrats* (= who do not have much power or authority) *who would report you for that.* ◇ *The removal of petty restrictions has made life easier.* ❶ **Petty** is used especially to talk about crimes and conflicts that are not very serious: *petty crime/theft/corruption/tyranny* ◇ *a petty criminal/thief/tyrant* ◇ *petty squabbles/jealousies/feuds*

insignificant (*rather formal, especially written*) not big or valuable enough to be considered important: *These results are statistically insignificant.* ◇ *The levels of chemicals in the river are not insignificant.* ◇ *He made her feel insignificant and stupid.* ❶ *Not insignificant* is a rather formal way of saying that sth is actually quite important, or more important than people might think. **Insignificant** can also be used to talk about a person who seems or feels as if they are not important or have no influence. **OPP significant** → IMPORTANT
▶ **insignificance** *noun* [U]: *Her own problems paled into insignificance beside this terrible news.* **OPP significance** → IMPORTANCE

peripheral /pəˈrɪfərəl/ (*formal, especially business*) not as important as the main aim or part of an activity: *The experiment looks at subjects' ability to take in peripheral information.* ◇ *Fund-raising is peripheral to their main activities.* ❶ **Peripheral** is used especially to talk about *information* or *details*, or *activities* and *developments*. See also **periphery** → EDGE *noun*

light entertaining rather than serious and not needing much mental effort: *Do you need some light reading for the beach?* ◇ *a concert of light classical music* ❶ **Light** is used especially to talk about leisure activities: *light reading/fiction/entertainment/comedy/music/opera*

unimportant (*especially written*) not important; not deserving serious attention: *Don't worry about these*

unimportant details. ◇ *They dismissed the problem as unimportant.* **OPP important** → IMPORTANT

minute *noun*

minute · moment · second · bit · instant · sec · split second
These are all words for a very short period of time.

instant	moment	minute	bit
split second	second		
	sec		

PATTERNS AND COLLOCATIONS
▶ **in** a minute / a moment / a second / a bit / an instant / a sec
▶ **for** a minute / a moment / a second / a bit / an instant / a sec / a split second
▶ **after** a minute / moment / second / bit
▶ **at / from that** minute / moment / second / instant
▶ **within** minutes / moments / seconds
▶ **just a** minute / moment / second / sec
▶ **this** minute / moment / second / instant
▶ a **brief / fleeting** moment / second / instant
▶ **one / a single** minute / moment / second / instant
▶ to **hang on / hold on / wait** a minute / moment / second / sec
▶ to **have / spare / give sb** a minute / moment / second
▶ to **last / take** a minute / moment / second
▶ a minute / a moment / a second / a bit / an instant / a split second **later**
▶ a minute / a moment / a second / a bit / an instant **longer**

minute [C] a unit for measuring time. There are 60 minutes in one hour: *It's four minutes to six.* ◇ *I'll be back in a few minutes.* ◇ *It's only a ten-minute bus ride into town.* ◇ *I enjoyed every minute of the party.* ❶ Especially in spoken English a **minute** [sing.] is a very short period of time: *Hang on* (= Wait) *a minute – I'll just get my coat.* ◇ *I just have to finish this – I won't be a minute.* ◇ *Could I see you for a minute?* ◇ *Don't leave everything till the last minute.*

moment [C] a very short period of time: *Could you wait a moment, please?* ◇ *One moment, please* (= Please wait a short time). ◇ *He thought for a moment before replying.* ◇ *I'll be back in a moment.* ◇ *Moments later, I heard a terrible crash.* ◇ *We arrived **not a moment too soon*** (= almost too late).

second [C] a unit for measuring time. There are 60 seconds in one minute: *She can run 100 metres in just over 11 seconds.* ◇ *The light flashes every 5 seconds.* ◇ *The water flows at about 1.5 metres per second.* ❶ Especially in spoken English a **second** is also just a very short period of time: *Hang on* (= Wait) *a second while I find my keys.* ◇ *I'll be finished with this in a couple of seconds.*

> **NOTE** MINUTE, MOMENT OR SECOND? In many cases you can use any of these words: *Wait/Hang on/Just a minute/moment/second.* **Minute** is the most frequent in spoken English, but it is more usual to use **moment** in written English, especially when telling a story: *He thought for a minute/second before replying.*

bit [sing.] (*especially BrE, informal*) a short period of time: *Wait a bit!* ◇ *Greg thought for a bit before answering.*

instant [C, usually sing.] (*especially written*) an extremely short period of time: *It was all over in an instant.* ◇ *Just for an instant I thought he was going to refuse.* ❶ An **instant** can be even shorter than a **minute**, **moment** or **second**. It is mostly used in written English, especially when telling a story.

sec [sing.] (*informal, spoken*) a very short period of time; a second: *Stay there. I'll be back in a sec.* ◇ *Hang on* (= Wait) *a sec.*

split ˈsecond [C] (*informal*) an extremely short period of time: *Their eyes met for a split second.*
▶ **ˈsplit-second** *adj.*: *She had to make a split-second decision.* ◇ *The success of the raid depended on **split-second timing**.*

miracle *noun*

miracle · wonder · phenomenon · marvel · fluke
These are all words for surprising things or events that you are pleased about or for people you admire.

PATTERNS AND COLLOCATIONS
▶ It's a miracle / wonder / fluke **(that)**...
▶ a miracle / wonder / phenomenon / marvel **of** sth
▶ a **natural** wonder / phenomenon / marvel
▶ to **do** wonders / marvels **(for** sb / sth)
▶ to **work / perform** a miracle / wonders
▶ a miracle / wonder **cure / drug**

miracle /ˈmɪrəkl/ [C] (*informal*) a good thing that happens that seemed unlikely or impossible; a very good example or product of sth: *It's a miracle that nobody was killed.* ◇ *It would take a miracle to make this business profitable.* ◇ *You shouldn't expect the treatment to work miracles.* ◇ *The car is a miracle of engineering.* See also **miraculous** → AMAZING

wonder [C] a thing or quality that fills you with surprise or admiration; a person or thing that is very good or effective: *The Canyon is one of the natural **wonders of the world**.* ◇ *It's all become possible, thanks to the wonders of modern technology.* ◇ *The news **did wonders for** (= had a very good effect on) our morale.* ◇ *It's a wonder* (= it's surprising) *more people weren't injured.* ◇ ***No wonder** you're tired! You didn't get any sleep last night.* ◇ *The club's new **boy wonder** scored two goals in the second half.* See also **wonderful** → WONDERFUL

phenomenon /fəˈnɒmɪnən; *AmE* fəˈnɑːm-/ (pl. (*BrE* **phenomena** or *AmE* **phenomenons**) [C] a very successful person or thing: *This young pianist is a phenomenon.* ◇ *Harry Potter was the greatest book publishing phenomenon ever.* See also **phenomenal** → REMARKABLE

marvel [C] a wonderful and surprising person or thing: *The design is a marvel of elegance and simplicity.* ❶ **Marvels** [pl.] are wonderful results or things that have been achieved: *The doctors have done marvels for her.* See also **marvellous** → WONDERFUL

fluke [C, usually sing.] (*informal*) a lucky or unusual thing that happens by accident, not because of planning or skill: *They are determined to show that their last win was no fluke.*

mislead *verb*

mislead · kid · delude · string sb along · lead sb on
These words all mean to deliberately make sb believe sth that is not true.

PATTERNS AND COLLOCATIONS
▶ to mislead / delude sb **about** sth
▶ to kid / delude sb **that**...
▶ to kid / delude **yourself**
▶ to **deliberately** mislead sb / lead sb on
▶ to **easily** mislead / kid / delude sb
▶ to **seriously / totally** mislead / delude sb

mislead /ˌmɪsˈliːd/ [T] (*rather formal*) to give sb the wrong idea or impression and make them believe sth that is not true: *He deliberately misled us about the nature of their relationship.* ◇ *The company **misled** hundreds of people **into** investing their money unwisely.*

kid (**-dd-**) [T] (*informal*) to allow sb/yourself to believe sth that is not true, especially that things are easier or better than they really are: *They're kidding themselves if they think it's going to be easy.* ❶ In this meaning **kid** is usually used in the phrase *kid myself/yourself/themselves, etc.* See also **kid** → JOKE *verb*

delude /dɪˈluːd/ [T] (*rather formal*) to make sb/yourself believe sth that is not true, especially that things are easier or better than they really are: *Don't be deluded into thinking that we are out of danger yet.* See also **delusion** → ILLUSION

string sb aˈlong *phrasal verb* (*informal*) to allow sb to believe sth that is not true, for example that you love them or intend to help them: *She has no intention of giving you a divorce – she's just stringing you along.*

lead sb ˈon *phrasal verb* (*informal*) to deceive sb and make them believe sth, especially that you love them or find them attractive: *He's used you and led you on; now find someone else who will make you happy.* See also **tease** → FLIRT

> **NOTE** STRING SB ALONG OR LEAD SB ON? **Lead sb on** is nearly always used to talk about making sb believe that you love them; **string sb along** has a wider range of uses relating to making people believe that you will do sth for them: *She suspected that they were just stringing her along with their promises of this and that.*

misleading *adj.*

misleading · ambiguous · deceptive · spurious
These words all describe things that give the wrong idea or impression and make you believe sth that is not true.

PATTERNS AND COLLOCATIONS
▶ a misleading / an ambiguous **statement**
▶ a misleading / spurious **argument / claim / impression**
▶ a misleading / deceptive **advertisement**
▶ **rather** misleading / ambiguous / deceptive / spurious
▶ **highly / very / dangerously** misleading / ambiguous / deceptive

misleading /ˌmɪsˈliːdɪŋ/ giving the wrong idea or impression and intended or likely to make you believe sth that is not true: *They face prosecution if they provide false or misleading information.* ◇ *It would be seriously misleading to suggest that television has no effect on children.*
▶ **misleadingly** *adv.*: *These bats are sometimes misleadingly referred to as 'flying foxes'.*

ambiguous /æmˈbɪgjuəs/ (*rather formal*) that can be understood in two or more different ways: *Her account was deliberately ambiguous.* ◇ *It is for the jury to decide what an ambiguous statement was intended to mean.* **OPP** **unambiguous** → CLEAR 2, See also the entry for VAGUE
▶ **ambiguously** *adv.*: *an ambiguously worded agreement*

deceptive /dɪˈseptɪv/ (*rather formal*) likely or intended to make you believe sth that is not true: *Appearances can be deceptive* (= things are not always as they seem).
▶ **deceptively** *adv.*: *a deceptively simple idea* (= an idea that seems simple but is not really)

> **NOTE** MISLEADING OR DECEPTIVE? Something that is **misleading** gives the wrong idea about sth, especially deliberately, but without actually lying. Something that is **deceptive** usually gives a false impression without meaning to: by far the most common collocate of **deceptive** is *appearances*. However, **deceptive** is sometimes used to talk about deliberate deceptions in more formal contexts.

spurious /ˈspjʊəriəs; *AmE* ˈspjʊr-/ (*rather formal*) seeming right or true but actually wrong or false; based on false ideas or ways of thinking: *He had managed to create the entirely spurious impression that the company was thriving.* ❶ Typical collocates of **spurious** are *argument, claim, grounds, impression* and *logic*.

miss *verb*

1 miss classes/meals
2 miss sb's name/the point

1 See the Topic Map for EDUCATION on p.888
miss · skip · shirk · skive · goof off
These words all mean to fail to be or go somewhere, or to fail to do sth.

PATTERNS AND COLLOCATIONS

▶ to skive / goof **off**
▶ to miss / skip a **class** / **meal**
▶ to miss / skip sth **altogether**

miss [T] to fail to be or go somewhere; to fail to do sth that you usually do or should do: *She hasn't missed a game all year.* ◇ *You missed a good party last night* (= because you did not go). ◇ *You can't afford to miss meals* (= not eat meals) *when you're in training.* ◇ *You have to* **miss a turn** (= to not play when it is your turn in a game). ◇ *You'd better hurry – you don't want to miss the bus.* **OPP catch** → GET 5 ❶ **Catch** is the opposite of **miss** only when you are talking about getting or not getting a bus, train, plane, etc.: *to catch a game/a party/the school play/meals/your turn*

skip (**-pp-**) [T, I] (*rather informal*) to fail to do sth that you usually do or should do; to leave out sth that would normally be the next thing that you would do, read, etc: *I often skip breakfast altogether.* ◇ *She decided to skip the afternoon's class.* ◇ *I skipped over the last part of the book.* ◇ *I suggest we* **skip to** *the last item on the agenda.* ❶ **Skip** is most often used to talk about deliberately missing meals (especially *breakfast* and *lunch*), *school*, a *meeting*, or part of a book such as a *paragraph* or *chapter*.

shirk /ʃɜːk; *AmE* ʃɜːrk/ [I, T] to avoid doing sth that you should do, especially because you are too lazy: *Discipline in the company was strict and no one shirked.* ◇ *She never shirked her responsibilities.* See also **get out of sth** → EVADE

skive [I, T] (*BrE, informal*) to avoid work or school by staying away or leaving early: *'Where's Tom?' 'Skiving as usual.'* ◇ *I always skived off school when I could.*

,goof 'off *phrasal verb* (*AmE, informal*) to spend time doing nothing, especially when you should be working: *He spends most of his time at the office goofing off.*

2 miss · overlook

These words both mean to fail to see or notice sth.

PATTERNS AND COLLOCATIONS

▶ to miss / overlook a / an **point** / **fact** / **detail** / **feature**
▶ to **be easy** / **hard** / **impossible to** miss / overlook sth
▶ to **completely** / **largely** / **often** / **frequently** miss / overlook sth
▶ to **be easily** missed / overlooked

miss [T] to fail to see, hear, notice or understand sth: *The hotel is the only white building on the road –* **you can't miss it.** ◇ *Don't miss next week's issue!* ◇ *Your mother will know who's moved in – she* **doesn't miss much.** ◇ *When you painted your bedroom you missed a bit* (= of the wall) *under the window.* ◇ *You're missing the point* (= failing to understand the main part) *of what I'm saying.*

overlook /ˌəʊvəˈlʊk; *AmE* ˌoʊvərˈlʊk/ [T] (*rather formal*) to fail to see, notice or consider sth: *He seems to have overlooked one important fact.* ◇ *That's a point which should not be overlooked.* ❶ **Overlook** is used especially to talk about people failing to consider a *point, fact, possibility* or *idea*, or particular *details* or *features* of sth.

mission noun

mission · purpose · vocation

These are all words for sth that you do, especially a job, that is important to you or that you feel is your duty.

PATTERNS AND COLLOCATIONS

▶ to **find** your mission / purpose / vocation
▶ a **sense of** mission / purpose / vocation
▶ sb's mission / purpose / vocation **in life**

mission /ˈmɪʃn/ [C] particular work that you feel it is your duty to do: *Her mission in life was to work with the homeless.* ◇ *We will continue our mission to close the gap between customers' expectations and the reality.*

purpose [C, U] the feeling that there is a definite aim in what you do and that it is important and valuable to you: *Teachers need to give a purpose to the activities and assignments they give to students.* ◇ *Volunteer work gives her life a sense of purpose.*

vocation /vəʊˈkeɪʃn; *AmE* voʊ-/ [C, U] a type of work or way of life that you strongly believe is especially suitable for you, especially one that involves helping other people; a belief in this; a belief that you have been chosen by God to be a priest or nun: *Nursing is not just a job – it's a vocation.* ◇ *She seems to have a* **vocation for** *healing.* ◇ *He spoke about his* **vocation to** *the priesthood.*

mistake noun

1 learn from your mistakes
2 a spelling mistake

1 mistake · error · omission · blunder · gaffe · oversight

These are all words for sth that you do, think or say that is not correct.

PATTERNS AND COLLOCATIONS

▶ sth happens **due to** a mistake / an error / an omission / a blunder / an oversight
▶ a **major** mistake / error / omission / blunder / gaffe
▶ a / an **serious** / **glaring** mistake / error / omission
▶ a / an **simple** / **stupid** / **dreadful** / **terrible** / **fatal** / **tragic** mistake / error / blunder
▶ an **unfortunate** mistake / error / oversight
▶ to **make** a mistake / an error / a blunder / a gaffe
▶ to **realize** / **admit** (**to**) a mistake / an error / a blunder
▶ to **correct** a mistake / an error / an omission / a blunder
▶ to **rectify** / **remedy** a mistake / an error / an omission

mistake [C] something that you do or think that is not correct, or that produces a result that you did not want: *Don't worry, we all make mistakes.* ◇ *I made the mistake of giving him my address.* ◇ *You must try to learn from your mistakes.* ◇ *Leaving school so young was the biggest mistake of my life.* ◇ *I took your bag instead of mine* **by mistake** (= accidentally; without meaning to). ◇ *Children may eat pills* **in mistake for** *sweets.* See also **mistaken** → WRONG 1

error [C, U] (*rather formal*) a mistake, especially one that causes problems or affects the result of sth: *No payments were made last week because of a computer error.* ◇ *I think you have made an error in calculating the total.* ◇ *He accused the prime minister of committing a serious* **error of judgement.** ◇ *The delay was due to* **human error** (= a mistake made by a person rather than a machine). ◇ *The computer system was switched off* **in error** (= by mistake). ◇ *Children learn to use computer programs by* **trial and error** (= by trying various methods until they find one that is successful).

omission /əˈmɪʃn/ [C] (*rather formal*) a thing that has not been included or done: *There were a number of errors and omissions in the article.* See also **omit** → LEAVE SB/STH OUT

blunder [C] a stupid or careless mistake: *After a series of political blunders he finally resigned.* ❶ **Blunder** is often used to talk about mistakes made by people who have important jobs serving the public. It is often used with adjectives such as *administrative, bureaucratic, economic* and *political.*

gaffe /gæf/ [C] a mistake that a person makes in public or in a social situation, especially sth embarrassing: *He made some real gaffes early in his career.* ◇ *Most people will politely look the other way if you commit some social gaffe.*

oversight /ˈəʊvəsaɪt/ [C, U] (*rather formal*) a mistake that you make because you forget to do sth or you do not notice sth: *I didn't mean to leave her name off the list; it was an oversight.* ◇ *You can never entirely eliminate human error and oversight.*

2 mistake · error · inaccuracy · slip · howler · misprint
These are all words for a word, figure or fact that is not said, written down or typed correctly.

PATTERNS AND COLLOCATIONS
▸ a mistake/an error/an inaccuracy/a slip/a howler/a misprint **in** sth
▸ a **simple** mistake/error/slip/misprint
▸ to **make** a mistake/an error/a slip/a howler
▸ to **contain/be full of** mistakes/errors/inaccuracies/howlers/misprints
▸ to **find / point out** a mistake/an error/an inaccuracy

mistake [C] a word or figure that is not said or written down correctly: *The waiter made a mistake in adding up the bill.* ◇ *Her essay is full of spelling mistakes.*
error [C] (*rather formal*) a mistake: *There are too many errors in your work.*
inaccuracy /ɪnˈækjərəsi/ [C, U] (*rather formal*) a piece of information that is not exactly correct: *The article is full of inaccuracies.* ◇ *The writer is guilty of bias and inaccuracy.* See also **inaccurate** → WRONG 1
slip [C] a small mistake, usually made by being careless or not paying attention: *He recited the whole poem without making a single slip.* ◇ *a **Freudian slip*** (= sth you say by mistake but which is believed to show your true thoughts)
howler [C] (*informal, especially BrE*) a stupid mistake, especially in what sb says or writes: *The report is full of howlers.* ❶ A **howler** is usually an embarrassing mistake which shows that the person who made it does not know sth that they really should know.
misprint /ˈmɪsprɪnt/ [C] a small mistake in a printed text: *The book was reprinted with a few misprints corrected.*

misunderstand *verb*

misunderstand · misinterpret · get sth wrong · get sb wrong · mistake · misread · misjudge
These words all mean to not understand sb/sth correctly.

PATTERNS AND COLLOCATIONS
▸ to misunderstand / misinterpret / mistake / misread sth **as** sth
▸ to misunderstand / misinterpret / mistake / misjudge **what…**
▸ to misunderstand / misinterpret / mistake sb's **meaning / intentions**
▸ to misunderstand/misinterpret/misread/misjudge a **situation**
▸ to get a **situation** wrong
▸ to **badly** misunderstand / mistake / misread / misjudge sb/sth
▸ to **seriously** misunderstand/mistake/misread/misjudge sb/sth
▸ to **completely** misunderstand/misinterpret/mistake/misread/misjudge sb/sth
▸ to **totally** misunderstand / mistake / misread sb/sth
▸ to get sb/sth **badly / seriously / totally / completely** wrong
▸ to **deliberately** misunderstand / misinterpret sb/sth
▸ to be **easily** misunderstood / misinterpreted / mistaken / misread / misjudged

misunderstand [I, T] to not understand sb/sth correctly: *I thought he was her husband – I must have misunderstood.* ◇ *Don't misunderstand me – I'm grateful for everything you've done.* ◇ *She must have misunderstood what I was trying to say.* **OPP understand** → UNDERSTAND 1, See also **misunderstanding** → ILLUSION
misinterpret /ˌmɪsɪnˈtɜːprɪt; *AmE* -ˈtɜːrp-/ [T, often passive] to understand sth/sb wrongly, by giving it/what they say a different meaning from the one intended: *His comments were misinterpreted as a criticism of the project.* See also **misinterpretation** → ILLUSION
get sth ˈwrong *idiom* (*rather informal, spoken*) to not understand a situation correctly: *No, you've got it all wrong. She's not his wife.* ◇ *Trust you to get it all wrong!*
get sb ˈwrong *idiom* (*rather informal, spoken*) to misunderstand what sb says or what their intentions are: *Don't get me wrong* (= don't be offended by what I am going to say), *I think he's doing a good job, but…*

mistake [T] to not understand or judge sb's behaviour or a situation correctly: *He mistook the other man's offer as a threat.* ◇ *There was no mistaking* (= it was impossible to mistake) *the bitterness in her voice.* See also **mistaken** → WRONG 1
misread [T] to judge a situation badly, especially by not realizing what is likely to happen: *She had seen the warning signs but she had misread them.*
misjudge [T] to form a wrong opinion about a person or situation, especially in a way that makes you deal with them/it unfairly: *She was beginning to realize that she had misjudged him.* ◇ *They had seriously misjudged the mood of the electorate.*

mix *verb* See also the entries for COMBINE and STIR

mix · mingle · blend
These words all refer to substances, qualities, ideas or feelings combining or being combined.

PATTERNS AND COLLOCATIONS
▸ to mix/ mingle/ blend (sth) **with** sth
▸ to mix/ mingle/ blend sth **into** sth
▸ to mix/ mingle/ blend sth **together**
▸ to mix/ blend sth **in**
▸ to mix/ mingle/ blend **flavours**
▸ to mix/ blend **colours / ingredients**
▸ **mixed / mingled feelings**
▸ to mix/ blend sth **thoroughly / well / gently**

mix [T, I] to combine two or more substances, qualities, ideas or feelings, usually in a way that means they cannot easily be separated; (of substances, qualities or feelings) to be combined in this way: *Mix all the ingredients together in a bowl.* ◇ *If you mix blue and yellow, you get green.* ◇ *Oil and water do not mix.* ◇ *Grief mixed with fear and rage as the people surveyed the ruins of their homes.* ◇ *I don't like to **mix business with pleasure*** (= combine social events with doing business). See also **mixture**, **mix** → COMBINATION
mingle [I, T] (*written*) to combine or be combined: *The sounds of laughter and singing mingled in the evening air.* ◇ *He felt a kind of happiness mingled with regret.* ❶ **Mingle** can be used to talk about sounds, colours, feelings, ideas, qualities or substances. It is used in written English to talk about how a scene or event appears to sb or how they experience it.
blend [T, I] to mix two or more substances or flavours together; (of substances or flavours) to be mixed together: *Blend the flour with the milk to make a smooth paste.* ◇ *Blend together the eggs, sugar and flour.* ◇ *This process allows the flavours to blend together.* See also **blend** → COMBINATION *noun*

NOTE **MIX** OR **BLEND**? If you **blend** things when you are cooking you usually combine them more completely than if you just **mix** them.

mixture *noun* See also the entry for COMBINATION

mixture · compound · solution · blend · alloy · concoction · suspension · mix · cocktail
These are all words for a substance which consists of two or more other substances combined.

PATTERNS AND COLLOCATIONS
▸ **in** solution / suspension
▸ a **special** mixture / blend / concoction / mix
▸ a **potent** compound / blend / cocktail
▸ **cake / spice** mixture / mix
▸ a **compound / a solution / an alloy / a suspension contains / containing** sth

mixture [C, U] a substance made by mixing two or more substances together: *Spread the cake mixture into a greased baking tin.* ◇ *Add the eggs to the mixture and beat well.* ❶ In chemistry a **mixture** is a combination of two or

mixture → modern

more substances that mix together without any chemical reaction taking place: *An alloy is a mixture of two types of metal.* See also **mixture** → COMBINATION

compound /'kɒm-/ [C] (*chemistry*) a substance formed by a chemical reaction of two or more elements in fixed amounts relative to each other: *Common salt is a compound of sodium and chlorine.* ❶ In non-technical language **compound** has the more general meaning of 'a thing consisting of two or more separate things combined together': *The air smelled like a compound of diesel and petrol fumes.*

solution [C, U] a liquid in which sth has been dissolved: *Stomach ache can often be eased with an alkaline solution such as bicarbonate of soda.*

blend [C] a mixture of different types of the same thing, especially drinks: *We offer several different blends of freshly ground coffee.*
▸ **blended** *adj.*: *blended whisky/tea*

alloy /'ælɔɪ/ [C, U] a metal that is formed by mixing two types of metal together, or by mixing metal with another substance: *Brass is an alloy of copper and zinc.* ◇ *alloy steel*

concoction /kən'kɒkʃn; *AmE* -'kɑːkʃn/ [C, U] a strange or unusual combination of things, especially drinks or medicines: *The pudding she made was a concoction of cream, egg white and rum.*

suspension /sə'spenʃn/ [C, U] (*technical*) a liquid with very small pieces of solid matter floating in it; the state of such a liquid: *The suspension was passed through a filter to separate out the solid particles.* ◇ *The material carried in suspension by the tide is deposited on the shore.*

mix [C, U] a combination of things that you need to make sth, often sold as a powder that you add water or other substances to: *I'll buy a packet of cake mix to save time.*

> **NOTE** MIXTURE OR MIX? A *cake mixture* is the substance you make after adding together all the ingredients, a *cake mix* is a powder that you buy and simply add water, milk, etc. to in order to produce the *mixture*.

cocktail /'kɒkteɪl; *AmE* 'kɑːk-/ [C] a mixture of different substances, usually ones that do not mix together well: *a lethal cocktail of drugs*

model *noun*

model · pattern · prototype · precedent · blueprint · template
These are all words for sth that can be copied by other people.

PATTERNS AND COLLOCATIONS
▸ a model / pattern / prototype / precedent / blueprint / template **for** sth
▸ to **provide / serve as / act as** a model / prototype / precedent / blueprint / template
▸ to **develop / create** a model / prototype / blueprint / template
▸ to **set** a pattern / precedent
▸ to **follow / copy** a model / pattern / precedent / blueprint / template

model [C] an example of sth such as a system that can be copied by other people: *The nation's constitution provided a model that other countries followed.* See also **model yourself/sth on sb/sth** → FOLLOW 4, **model** → EXAMPLE 2

pattern [C, usually sing.] an excellent example of sth such as a system that other people should copy: *This system sets the pattern for others to follow.*

> **NOTE** MODEL OR PATTERN? A system or organization *is/provides* a model but *sets* a pattern for people to follow. A **pattern** is always an excellent example and one that people should follow; a **model** is an example that people do follow, although this is usually because it works well.

prototype /'prəʊtətaɪp; *AmE* 'proʊ-/ [C] the first design of sth from which other forms are copied or developed: *He produced designs for the prototype of the modern bicycle.*

precedent /'presɪdənt/ [C, U] (*rather formal*) an official action or decision that has been taken in the past and that is seen as an example or rule to be followed in a similar situation later: *The ruling set a precedent for future libel cases.* ◇ *The decision of the local authority was based on historical precedent.*

blueprint /'bluːprɪnt/ [C] a plan which shows what can be achieved and how it can be achieved; a model showing how sth should be done or made: *The government has published a blueprint for an integrated transport system.* ◇ *They see the device as the blueprint for all future chip design.*

template [C] a thing that is used as a model for producing other similar examples: *If you need to write a lot of similar letters, set up a template on your computer.*

moderate *verb*

moderate · dampen · temper · blunt · tone sth down · modify
These words all mean to make sth less strong or extreme.

PATTERNS AND COLLOCATIONS
▸ to moderate / tone down / modify your **language**
▸ to moderate / modify your **behaviour / demands / views**

moderate /'mɒdəreɪt; *AmE* 'mɑːd-/ [T, I] (*rather formal*) to become or make sth become less extreme, severe or strong: *We agreed to moderate our original demands.* ◇ *She apologized immediately and moderated her voice.* ◇ *By evening the wind had moderated slightly.* ❶ **Moderate** is often used to talk about things that are done by people, for example *behaviour, criticism* or *language*, and usually has a person as the subject of the verb.

dampen [T] to make sth such as a feeling or reaction less strong: *None of the setbacks could dampen his enthusiasm.* ◇ *She wasn't going to let anything dampen her spirits today.*

temper [T, often passive] (*formal*) to make sth less severe by adding sth that has the opposite effect: *Justice must be tempered with mercy.* ◇ *The hot sunny days were tempered by a light breeze.*

blunt [T] to make a feeling or ability weaker or less effective: *Age hadn't blunted his passion for adventure.* ◇ *Living alone in the country had blunted her wits.*

tone sth 'down *phrasal verb* to make a speech or opinion less extreme or offensive: *The language of the article will have to be toned down for the mass market.*

modify /'mɒdɪfaɪ; *AmE* 'mɑːd-/ [T] (*formal*) to make your behaviour, attitude or language less extreme, especially in order to avoid offending sb: *The social worker at first aimed to get Mrs R to modify her behaviour, without success.*

modern *adj.* See also the entry for EXPERIMENTAL

modern · advanced · up to date · state of the art
These words all describe sth that uses the most recent technology or methods.

modern	up to date	state of the art
advanced		

PATTERNS AND COLLOCATIONS
▸ modern / advanced / up-to-date / state-of-the-art **design / technology / techniques**
▸ **very** modern / advanced / up to date
▸ **fairly / quite / relatively** modern / advanced / up to date

modern (*usually approving*) using the most recent technology, methods, designs or materials: *The company needs to invest in a modern computer system.* ◇ *It is the most modern, well-equipped hospital in the country.* ◇ *Modern methods of farming are destroying the countryside.*
OPP old-fashioned → OLD-FASHIONED

advanced using the most recent technology, methods or designs: *Even in advanced industrial societies, poverty persists.* ◇ *It is a technologically advanced society.* **OPP** **primitive** ❶ **Primitive** describes people and things belonging to a very simple society with no industry: *primitive societies/tribes/beliefs*

NOTE **MODERN** OR **ADVANCED**? In many cases you can use either word: *modern/advanced technology/techniques/ designs* ◇ *a modern/an advanced society/economy/ civilization/nation.* **Advanced** is used especially in the contexts of technology and economics: an *advanced society* is one with a complicated economic structure and that relies heavily on technology. The term *modern society* is used to discuss the way we live now in a more general way, including social relations and culture. **Modern** can also be used to describe art, fashion and ideas. See also **modern** → EXPERIMENTAL, **modern** → RECENT

up to 'date (of equipment, technology or methods) the most advanced: *We need to spend at least half a million on getting the most up-to-date equipment.* ◇ *This technology is* **bang up to date** (= completely modern). **OPP** **out of date** → OLD-FASHIONED

state of the 'art (*approving*) (of equipment, technology or methods) absolutely the most advanced; as good as it can be at the present time: *He spent thousands on a state-of-the-art sound system.*

modest *adj.*

modest · humble · unassuming · unpretentious
These words all describe a person who does not talk about or draw attention to themselves or their own abilities.

PATTERNS AND COLLOCATIONS
▶ a modest/a humble/an unassuming/an unpretentious **man/ person**
▶ in a modest / a humble / an unassuming **way**

modest /'mɒdɪst; *AmE* 'mɑːd-/ (*approving*) not talking much about your own abilities or status: *She's very* **modest about** *her success.* ◇ *Don't be so modest! You're a very talented player.* **OPP** **vain, boastful** → PROUD 2
▶ **modesty** /'mɒdəsti; *AmE* 'mɑːd-/ *noun* [U]: *He accepted the award with characteristic modesty.* ◇ *I hate false* (= pretended) *modesty.* **OPP** **pride, vanity** → PRIDE
humble (*especially written, approving*) showing that you do not think you are more important than other people: *Be humble enough to learn from your mistakes.* **OPP** **proud, self-important** → PROUD 2
▶ **humbly** *adv.*: *'Sorry,' she said humbly.*
▶ **humility** /hjuː'mɪləti/ *noun* [U]: *Her first defeat was an early lesson in humility.* **OPP** **arrogance** → PRIDE
unassuming /ˌʌnə'sjuːmɪŋ; *AmE* ˌʌnə'suː-/ (*approving*) not wanting to draw attention to yourself or to your abilities or status: *He did some wonderful work in a* **quiet and unassuming** *way.*
unpretentious /ˌʌnprɪ'tenʃəs/ (*approving*) not trying to appear more special, intelligent or important than you really are: *His family are unpretentious country folk.* **OPP** **pretentious** → FLASHY

moisture *noun*

moisture · damp · humidity · condensation · spray · dew
These are all words for water when it is in very small drops in the air or on a surface.

PATTERNS AND COLLOCATIONS
▶ condensation / dew **forms**
▶ drops of moisture / dew

moisture /'mɔɪstʃə(r)/ [U] very small drops of water that are present in the air, on a surface or in a substance: *Trees need moisture in order to maintain their growth.* ◇ *Beads of moisture were forming on his forehead.* See also **moist** → WET 1
damp [U] (*BrE*) the state of being slightly wet, often in a way that is unpleasant; areas that are like this on a wall or other surface: *The house smells of damp.* ◇ *One wall of my house is affected by* **rising damp**. See also **damp** → WET 1
humidity /hjuː'mɪdəti/ [U] the amount of water in the air; conditions in which the air is very warm and damp: *Instruments constantly monitor temperature and humidity.* ◇ *The humidity was becoming unbearable.* See also **humid** → HUMID
condensation /ˌkɒnden'seɪʃn; *AmE* ˌkɑːn-/ [U] drops of water that form on a cold surface when warm water vapour becomes cool: *The window was misty with condensation.*
spray [U, C] very small drops of a liquid that are sent through the air, for example by the wind: *A cloud of fine spray came up from the waterfall.*
dew /djuː; *AmE* duː/ [U] the very small drops of water that form on the ground and other surfaces during the night: *The grass was wet with early morning dew.*

money *noun*

1 make money
2 count the money
3 the family's money

1 money · cash · funds · capital · finance · means
These are all words for money that can be used to buy things.

PATTERNS AND COLLOCATIONS
▶ government / public money / cash / funds / capital / finance
▶ to **have / lack** (the) money / cash / funds / capital / finance / the means (**to do** sth)
▶ to **be short of** money / cash / funds / capital
▶ to **raise / provide / put up** money / cash / funds / capital / finance (**for** sth)
▶ to **get / obtain** money / cash / funds / finance (**for** sth)
▶ to **spend / borrow / invest** money / cash / funds / capital
▶ to **lend** money / cash / funds
▶ to **pay / save** money / cash

money [U] what you earn by working or by selling things, and use to buy things: *He hoped the project would* **make money**. ◇ *He returned the new TV to the store and got his* **money back**. ◇ *This desk is worth a lot of money.* ◇ *The money* (= the pay) *is great in my new job.* See also the entry for INCOME
cash [U] (*informal*) money that is available to be spent: *She refused to part with her* **hard-earned cash**. ◇ *The company is* **strapped for cash** (= without enough money).
funds [pl.] money that is available to be spent: *The hospital is trying to raise funds for a new kidney machine.* See also **fund** → FUND *noun*, **fund** → FUND *verb*, **funding** → INVESTMENT

NOTE **CASH** OR **FUNDS**? **Cash** is more informal than **funds** but both words can be used in both a personal and a business context: *I'm/The government is short of cash/ funds.* **Cash**, but not **funds**, can be used like an adjective before other nouns: *The company is having cash flow problems.* ◇ ~~The company is having funds flow problems.~~

capital [U, sing.] money or property that is owned by a business or person; money that is invested in a business: *We don't have enough capital to buy new premises.* ◇ *Our capital is all tied up in property.* ◇ *capital assets/goods/ stock* (= wealth in the form of buildings, equipment, etc.)
finance [U] (*rather formal*) money used to run a business, activity or project: *Finance for education comes from taxpayers.* ❶ **Finances** [pl.] are the money available to a person, organization or country or the way this money is

managed: *Moving house put a severe strain on our finances.* ◊ *The firm's finances are basically sound.* See also **finance** → FINANCE *noun*, **finance** → FUND *verb*

means [pl.] the money or income that a person has and can use to pay for things: *People should pay **according to their means*** (= according to what they can afford). ◊ *Private school fees are **beyond the means of** most people* (= more than they can afford). ◊ *Try to live **within your means*** (= not spend more money than you have).

2 money · cash · change

These are all words for money in the form of coins or paper notes.

PATTERNS AND COLLOCATIONS
▸ to **draw out / get out / take out / withdraw** money / cash
▸ **ready** money / cash (= money that you have available to spend immediately)

money [U] money in the form of coins or paper notes: *I counted the money carefully.* ◊ *Where can I change my money into dollars?* ◊ ***paper money*** (= money that is made of paper, not coins)

cash [U] money in the form of coins or paper notes: *How much cash do you have on you?* ◊ *Payments can be made by cheque or **in cash**.* ◊ *Customers are offered a 10% discount if they **pay cash**.* ◊ ***petty cash*** (= a small amount of money kept in an office for small payments) See also **cash** → CASH *verb*

> **NOTE** **MONEY** OR **CASH**? If it is important to contrast money in the form of coins and notes and money in other forms, use **cash**: *How much money/cash do you have on you?* ◊ ~~Payments can be made by cheque or in money.~~ ◊ ~~Customers are offered a discount if they pay money.~~

change [U] the money that you get back when you have paid for sth giving more money than the amount it costs; coins rather than paper money: *That's 40p change.* ◊ *The ticket machine doesn't give change.* ◊ *Do you have any change for the ticket machine?* ◊ *a dollar **in change*** (= coins that together are worth one dollar) ◊ *Can you give me **change for** a ten pound note* (= coins or notes that are worth this amount)? ◊ *I didn't have any **small change*** (= coins of low value) *to leave as a tip.* See also **change** → CASH *verb*

3 money · wealth · fortune · prosperity · riches · affluence

These are all words for the large amount of money and/or property that a rich person, organization or society has.

PATTERNS AND COLLOCATIONS
▸ (a) **great** wealth / fortune / prosperity / riches / affluence
▸ **growing / increasing / rising** wealth / prosperity / affluence
▸ (a) **personal / family** money / wealth / fortune / prosperity
▸ (a) **private** money / wealth / fortune / affluence
▸ **public** money / prosperity
▸ **national** wealth / prosperity
▸ to **have / possess / accumulate / acquire / inherit** money / wealth / a fortune / riches
▸ to **bring** money / wealth / prosperity / riches / affluence
▸ to **create** money / wealth / prosperity / affluence
▸ to **make** money / a fortune (on / out of sth)

money [U] all the money and property that sb owns: *He lost all his money in the 1929 stock market crash.* ◊ *The family made their money in the 18th century.*

wealth [U] a large amount of money and property that a person, organization or country owns; the state of being rich: *She called for a redistribution of wealth and power in society.* ◊ *The purpose of industry is to create wealth.* **OPP** **poverty** → POVERTY, See also **wealthy** → RICH

fortune [C, usually sing.] a large amount of money: *She inherited a share of the family fortune.* ◊ *You don't have to spend a fortune to give your family tasty, healthy meals.* ◊ *That ring must be worth a fortune.* ◊ *A car like that costs **a small fortune*** (= a lot of money).

prosperity /prɒˈsperəti; *AmE* prɑːˈs-/ [U] (*often approving*) the state of being financially successful and able to enjoy a good standard of living: *The future prosperity of the region depends on economic growth.* ◊ *The country is enjoying a period of **peace and prosperity**.* See also **prosper** → DO WELL, **prosperous** → RICH

riches [pl.] (*literary*) large amounts of money and valuable or beautiful possessions: *He embarked on a business career that eventually brought him fame and riches.* See also **rich** → RICH

affluence /ˈæfluəns/ [U] (*sometimes disapproving*) the state of being financially successful and able to enjoy a good standard of living: *The 1950s were an age of affluence in America.* See also **affluent** → RICH

> **NOTE** PROSPERITY OR AFFLUENCE? **Affluence** is often used to contrast rich people or societies with poor ones, in a way that suggests that it is not always a good thing: *the city's mixture of private affluence and public squalor.* **Prosperity** is not used in this way: it is always seen as a good thing and is sth that you can wish for other people: ~~the city's mixture of private prosperity and public squalor~~ ◊ *Please drink to the health and prosperity of the bride and groom.* It would be considered greedy to wish for money, wealth, fortune, riches or affluence, even for sb else: ~~Please drink to the health and money/wealth/ fortune/riches/affluence of the bride and groom.~~

monitor *verb*

monitor · track · keep an eye on sb/sth · watch · keep track of sb/sth · keep tabs on sb/sth
These words all mean to watch, listen to or check sth over a period of time.

PATTERNS AND COLLOCATIONS
▸ to monitor / track / keep an eye on / watch (sb / sth) **for** sth
▸ to monitor / track / keep an eye on / watch / keep track of / keep tabs on **what / who / where...**
▸ to monitor / track / watch **how...**
▸ to monitor / track / watch / keep track of / keep tabs on sb / sth's **movements**
▸ to monitor / keep an eye on / watch / keep tabs on a **situation**
▸ to **carefully / closely** monitor / track / watch sb / sth

monitor /ˈmɒnɪtə(r); *AmE* ˈmɑːn-/ [T, often passive] to watch and check sth over a period of time in order to see how it develops: *The animals' temperature and heartbeat are regularly monitored.* ◊ *Each student's progress is closely monitored over the term.* See also **monitor** → INSPECTOR *noun*

track [T] to watch the movements of sb/sth over a period of time, especially by using special electronic equipment; to watch and check sth over a period of time in order to see how it develops: *We continued tracking the plane on our radar.* ◊ *The research project involves tracking the careers of 400 law school graduates.*

> **NOTE** MONITOR OR TRACK? You **track** sth over a period of time because what you find out might be interesting. You **monitor** sth regularly or over a period of time because the information is necessary and you may need to take action.

keep an eye on sb/sth *idiom* (*rather informal, especially spoken*) to watch sb/sth over a period of time to make sure that they are not harmed or damaged, or in order to find out information about them, so that you are ready to take any necessary action: *We've asked the neighbours to keep an eye on the house for us while we are away.* ◊ *The police have been keeping a close eye on gang activity in the dock area.*

watch [T] to take care of sb/sth for a short time; to look at and follow the movements or development of sb/sth over a period of time: *Could you watch my bags for me while I buy a paper?* ◊ *This initiative is being closely watched by government regulators.* See also **watch** → WATCH *noun*

keep track of sb/sth *idiom* to watch the movements or development of sb/sth over a period of time in order to know where sb/sth is, what sb/sth is doing, or what is happening: *Satellites were used during the war to keep track of vehicle movements.* ◇ *Bank statements help you keep track of where your money is going.*

keep tabs on sb/sth *idiom* (*informal*) to watch the movements or development of sb/sth over a period of time in order to know what is happening so that you can control a particular situation: *It's not always possible to keep tabs on everyone's movements.* ◇ *It's my accountant's job to keep tabs on the financial situation at all times.*

> **NOTE** KEEP TRACK OF SB/STH OR KEEP TABS ON SB/STH?
> **Keeping track of sb/sth** is mostly about getting information; **keeping tabs on sb/sth** is more about being in control.

mood *noun*

mood · morale · spirits · frame of mind
These are all words for the way you are feeling at a particular time.

PATTERNS AND COLLOCATIONS
▸ **in** (a) (good / better, etc.) mood / spirits / frame of mind
▸ in the mood / frame of mind **for** sth
▸ in the mood / frame of mind **to do** sth
▸ (a) **good / better** mood / morale / spirits / frame of mind
▸ a **happy / confident / cheerful / calm / determined / positive / relaxed** mood / frame of mind
▸ the **right / wrong** mood / frame of mind
▸ sb's morale is / spirits are **high / low**
▸ to **get into / put sb in** a (good / positive, etc.) mood / frame of mind
▸ to **lift / raise** sb's morale / spirits
▸ sb's mood / morale / spirits **improve / improves**
▸ sb's mood / spirits **lift / lifts**

mood [C] the way you are feeling at a particular time: *She's in a good mood today.* ◇ *I'm just not in the mood for a party.* ◇ *The news had put Michelle in a foul mood.* ◇ *Some addicts suffer violent **mood swings** (= changes of mood) if deprived of the drug.* See also **mood** → TEMPER

morale /mə'rɑːl; *AmE* -'ræl/ [U] the amount of confidence and enthusiasm that a person or group has at a particular time: *Morale amongst the players is very high at the moment.* See also **demoralize** → DISCOURAGE 2, **demoralized** → DEPRESSED

spirits [pl.] the way you are feeling at a particular time, especially whether you are feeling good and positive or bad and negative: *She isn't in the best of spirits today.* ◇ *She was tired and her spirits were low.*

> **NOTE** MORALE AND SPIRITS **Morale** and **spirits** are usually described as either *high* or *low* and verbs used to describe sb's **morale** or **spirits** often involve movement up or down: *to lift/raise sb's morale/spirits* ◇ *sb's spirits lift/rise/soar* ◇ *The competition will **boost** children's morale and self-esteem.* ◇ *We sang songs to **keep our spirits up**.* ◇ *My **spirits sank** at the thought of starting all over again.*

frame of 'mind [sing.] the way you feel or think about sth at a particular time: *We'll discuss this when you're in a better frame of mind.*

moody *adj.* See also the entry for IRRITABLE

moody · unpredictable · volatile · excitable · temperamental
These words all describe sb whose mood or behaviour can change quickly.

PATTERNS AND COLLOCATIONS
▸ an unpredictable / a volatile **character / personality**
▸ unpredictable / volatile **behaviour**

▸ a moody / an unpredictable **man**
▸ **highly** unpredictable / volatile / excitable

moody (*disapproving*) (of a person) having moods that change quickly and often; bad-tempered or upset, often for no particular reason: *Moody people can be very difficult to deal with.* See also **mood** → TEMPER

unpredictable /ˌʌnprɪ'dɪktəbl/ if a person or their behaviour is **unpredictable**, you cannot predict how they will behave in a particular situation: *Her behaviour became so unpredictable when she had been drinking.* **OPP** **predictable** → PREDICTABLE 2

volatile /'vɒlətaɪl; *AmE* 'vɑːlətl/ (*sometimes disapproving*) (of a person or their moods) changing quickly from one mood to another, especially the opposite: *She was a more volatile personality than her sister.*

excitable /ɪk'saɪtəbl/ (of people or animals) likely to become easily excited: *She had trouble controlling the class of excitable ten-year-olds.* **OPP** **calm** → CALM

temperamental /ˌtemprə'mentl/ (*usually disapproving*) (of a person) having a tendency to become angry, excited or upset easily, and to behave in an unreasonable way: *You never know what to expect with her. She's so temperamental.*

moral *adj.*

moral · ethical
Both of these words describe sb/sth that is concerned with principles of what is right and wrong.

PATTERNS AND COLLOCATIONS
▸ a moral / an ethical **question / issue / problem / dilemma**
▸ moral / ethical **ideals / values / standards / principles / practices**

moral [only before noun] concerned with principles of what is right and wrong; based on your own sense of what is right and fair, not on legal rights or duties: *The basic moral philosophies of most world religions are remarkably similar.* ◇ *He's a deeply religious man with a highly developed moral sense.* ◇ *British newspapers were full of **moral outrage** at the weakness of other countries.* ◇ (*BrE*) *The job was to call upon all her skills of diplomacy and **moral courage** (= the courage to do what you think is right).* See also **moral** → GOOD 5, **morals**, **morality** → PRINCIPLE 1
▶ **morally** *adv.*: *Was the attack morally justified?*

ethical /'eθɪkl/ [only before noun] concerned with principles of what is right and wrong, especially in the context of business, politics or society: *There's an overwhelming ethical argument for the protection of the environment.* See also **ethical** → GOOD 5, **ethics** → PRINCIPLE 1, **ethic** → VALUES
▶ **ethically** *adv.*: *Paying workers less than a living wage is ethically unacceptable.*

> **NOTE** MORAL OR ETHICAL? **Moral** is used especially to talk about the behaviour and standards of individual people in their daily lives. It is particularly concerned with people's duties and feelings: collocates include *duty, obligation, imperative, sense, indignation, outrage, panic* and *courage*. **Ethical** is usually used to talk about the principles and practices of people in a particular profession or area of work, or of society generally. It can sound more formal and less forceful than **moral**, and is concerned with issues rather than duties or feelings: collocates include *guideline, criterion* and *proposition*.

morality *noun* See also the entry for PRINCIPLE 1

morality · right · good · goodness · purity · virtue · righteousness
These are all words for the principles about what is right and wrong or the quality of being morally good.

PATTERNS AND COLLOCATIONS
▸ to **do** right / good

morality /məˈræləti/ [U] principles about what is right and wrong, or good and bad behaviour: *He seems to have no **personal morality** at all.* ◇ *Do you think **standards of morality** are falling?* **OPP** immorality → EVIL

right [U, C, usually pl.] what is morally correct: *She doesn't understand the difference between **right and wrong**.* ◇ *You did right to tell me about it.* ◇ *They both knew he was in the right* (= had justice on his side). ◇ *It was difficult to establish **the rights and wrongs*** (= the true facts) *of the matter.* **OPP** wrong → EVIL

good [U] behaviour that is morally right or kind: *Do they know the difference between **good and evil**?* ◇ *Schools can definitely be seen as a **force for good** in this area.* ◇ *Look for an opportunity to do good whenever you can.* **OPP** evil → EVIL, See also **good** → GOOD *adj.* 5

NOTE RIGHT OR GOOD? Questions of **right** and wrong are questions of justice: they are about treating people in a fair way, not an unfair way. Matters of **good** and evil are about treating people in a kind way, not a cruel way.

goodness [U] the quality of being morally good: *We like to think that goodness exists in everyone.* See also **good** → GOOD *adj.* 5

purity /ˈpjʊərəti; AmE ˈpjʊr-/ [U] the quality of being morally good and pure, especially in sexual matters: *The veil was regarded as a symbol of the bride's purity.* See also **pure** → HOLY

virtue /ˈvɜːtʃuː; AmE ˈvɜːrtʃuː/ [U] *(rather formal)* behaviour or attitudes that show high moral standards: *a woman of **easy virtue*** (= a sexually immoral woman) ◇ *He was convinced of the inherent virtue of hard work.* **OPP** vice → EVIL, See also **virtuous** → GOOD 5

righteousness /ˈraɪtʃəsnəs/ [U] *(formal, especially religion)* the quality of being morally right and good: *the righteousness of God* ◇ *They had absolute faith in the righteousness of their cause.*

mother, father *nouns*

mother · father · parent · mum/mom · dad · daddy · mummy/mommy · guardian · stepfather/ stepmother · folks

These are all words for a man or woman who has a child or children.

PATTERNS AND COLLOCATIONS
▶ a **good / bad** mother / father / parent / mum / mom / dad
▶ a **caring / loving / doting / devoted / proud** mother / father / parent / mum / mom / dad
▶ a **stern / strict** mother / father / parent / guardian / stepfather / stepmother
▶ a / sb's **new** mother / father / parent / mum / mom / dad / stepfather / stepmother
▶ a **single** mother / father / parent / mum / mom
▶ (an) **unmarried** mother / father / parents / mum
▶ a **widowed** mother / father / parent
▶ sb's **birth / real / biological / natural** mother / father / parents
▶ a **foster** mother / father / parent / mum
▶ sb's **adoptive** mother / father / parents
▶ a **surrogate** mother / father / parent / mum / mom / dad
▶ (a) **working** mother / parents / mum / mom
▶ to **take after / inherit sth from** your mother / father / parents / mum / mom / dad / daddy / mummy / mommy
▶ to **become** a / sb's mother / father / parent / mum / mom / dad / guardian / stepfather / stepmother

mother [C] a woman who has a son or daughter, or a female animal who has produced young; a person who is acting as a mother to a child: *the relationship between mother and baby* ◇ *She's the mother of twins.* ◇ *She was a wonderful mother to both her natural and adopted children.* ◇ *an expectant* (= pregnant) *mother* ◇ *the mother chimpanzee caring for her young*
▶ **motherly** *adj.*: *motherly love/advice/instincts*

father a man who has a son or daughter, or a male animal who has young; a person who is acting as the father to a child: *Ben's a wonderful father.* ◇ *You've been like a father to me.* ◇ *Our new boss is a father of three* (= he has three children).
▶ **fatherly** *adj.*: *fatherly advice*

parent [C, usually pl.] a person's father or mother: *He's still living with his parents.* ◇ *There are many more **single parent families** than there used to be.*
▶ **parental** *adj.* [usually before noun]: *parental responsibility/rights*
▶ **parenting** *noun* [U]: *good/poor parenting* ◇ *parenting skills/classes*

mum *(BrE)* *(AmE* **mom***)* [C] *(informal, especially spoken)* (often used as a name) a mother: *My mum says I can't go.* ◇ *Mom can speak French and Spanish.* ◇ *Happy Birthday, Mom.* ◇ *A lot of **mums and dads** have the same worries.* ◇ *The group is aimed at new mums with young babies.*

dad [C] *(informal, especially spoken)* (often used as a name) a father: *That's my dad over there.* ◇ *Do you live with your mum or your dad?* ◇ *Is it OK if I borrow the car, Dad?*

NOTE MOTHER AND FATHER OR MUM AND DAD? In spoken language, **mum/mom** and **dad** are much more frequent. It sounds formal to say *my mother/father.*

daddy [C] *(informal, especially spoken)* (used especially by or to young children, often as a name) a father: *What does your daddy look like?* ◇ *Daddy, where are you?* ◇ *Come to Daddy.*

mummy *(BrE)* *(AmE* **mommy***)* [C] *(informal, especially spoken)* (used especially by or to young children, often as a name) a mother: '*I want my mummy!*' *he wailed.* ◇ *My knee hurts, Mommy!* ◇ *Mummy and Daddy will be back soon.*

guardian /ˈɡɑːdiən; AmE ˈɡɑːrd-/ [C] a person who is legally responsible for the care of another person, especially a child whose parents have died: *I was left alone to live with my aunt, who became my legal guardian.*

stepfather, stepmother [C] the man/woman who is married to your mother/father, but who is not your real father/mother: *He lives at home with his mother and stepfather.* ◇ *Is there a wicked stepmother in your story?* ❶ The word **step-parent** can be used, but it is not common.

folks /fəʊks; AmE foʊks/ [pl.] *(especially AmE, informal)* your parents: *I'm going to see my folks this weekend.* See also **folk** → PEOPLE 1

mourn *verb*

mourn · grieve · pine

These words all mean to feel very sad, especially because sb has died.

PATTERNS AND COLLOCATIONS
▶ to mourn / grieve **for** sb / sth
▶ to mourn / grieve the **death** of sb
▶ to mourn / grieve over a **loss**

mourn /mɔːn; AmE mɔːrn/ [T, I] to feel and show sadness because sb has died; to feel sad because sth no longer exists or is no longer the same: *He was still mourning his brother's death.* ◇ *Today we mourn for all those who died in two world wars.* ◇ *They mourn the passing of a simpler way of life.*
▶ **mourning** *noun* [U]: *She was still in mourning for her husband.* ◇ *The government has announced a day of national mourning for the victims.*

grieve /ɡriːv/ [I, T] to feel very sad because sb that you love has died: *The couple are **grieving over** the loss of their daughter.* ◇ *She had **grieved deeply** for her father.* ◇ *She grieved the death of her husband.* ◇ *He spoke on behalf of the grieving families.* See also **grief** → GRIEF

NOTE MOURN OR GRIEVE? When you say that sb is **grieving** you are describing just their feelings. When sb is **mourning**, they are often also showing their sadness, for example by their behaviour or, in many countries, by wearing black. Both words can be used directly before a noun (transitive) or can be followed by a preposition (intransitive), but it is more usual to say *mourn sb/sb's death* but *grieve for/over sb*.

pine [I] (*written*) to become very sad because sb has died or gone away, especially so that you behave in a different way from normal: *She pined for months after he'd gone.* ◇ *The Major's dog pined badly when her master died.*

move *verb*

move · shift · stir · dislodge · budge
These words all mean to change position or make sb/sth else change position.

PATTERNS AND COLLOCATIONS
▸ to move / shift / stir / dislodge / budge (sth) **from** sth
▸ to move / shift (sth) **from** sth **to** sth
▸ **won't / wouldn't / refuse to** move / shift / stir / budge
▸ to **hardly / barely** move / shift / stir / budge
▸ to move / shift / stir / budge **slightly / a little**

move [I, T] to change position; to make sb/sth else change position: *Don't move — stay perfectly still.* ◇ *The bus was already moving when I jumped onto it.* ◇ *He could hear someone moving around in the room above.* ◇ *I can't move my fingers.* ◇ *Move your chairs a little closer.*

shift [I, T] (*especially written*) to move your body or your eyes from one position or place to another: *She shifted uncomfortably in her chair.* ◇ *The little girl **shifted her weight** from one foot to another.* ◇ *He **shifted his gaze** from the child to her.* ❶ In informal British English **shift** can also mean 'to move sth by picking it up and carrying it': (*informal*) *Can you help me shift these boxes?*

stir (**-rr-**) [I, T] to move slightly or make sth move slightly: *She could hear the baby stirring in the next room.* ◇ *A slight breeze was stirring the branches.*

dislodge /dɪsˈlɒdʒ; *AmE* -ˈlɑːdʒ/ [T] (*rather formal*) to force sth from a position in which it was fixed or stuck: *The wind had dislodged one or two tiles from the roof.*

budge [I, T] (usually used in negative statements) (*rather informal*) to move slightly or make sth move slightly, especially from a fixed position: *I pushed hard at the door but it wouldn't budge.* ◇ *We all heaved on the rope, but still couldn't budge the car from the mud.*

move in, move into sth *phrasal verb*

move in/move into sth · settle · set up home
These words all mean to start living in a place that is your permanent home.

PATTERNS AND COLLOCATIONS
▸ to settle / set up home **in** a district, city, country, etc.
▸ to move in / set up home **together**

,**move 'in**, ,**move 'into sth** *phrasal verb* to start to live in your new home: *Our new neighbours moved in yesterday.* ◇ *So when do we move into our new home?* **OPP move out** → LEAVE 2

settle [I] (always used with an adverb or preposition) to make a place your permanent home: *She settled in Vienna after her father's death.*

set up 'home *idiom* (*BrE*) (used especially about a couple) to start living in a new place: *They got married and set up home together in Hull.*

movement *noun*

movement · motion · move · gesture · wave
These are all words for an act or the process of moving or moving sth.

PATTERNS AND COLLOCATIONS
▸ a **little / slight** movement / motion / gesture / wave
▸ a **hand** movement / gesture
▸ to **make** a movement / motion / move / gesture
▸ to **give** a gesture / wave
▸ a movement / motion / gesture **with your hand**
▸ a movement / motion / wave **of your hand**
▸ sb's **every** movement / move

movement [C, U] an act of moving or of moving sth, especially part of the body: *Don't make any sudden movements.* ◇ *She observed the gentle movement of his chest as he breathed.* ◇ *Choose loose clothes that give you greater freedom of movement.* ❶ Unlike the other words in this group, **movement** can be used after adjectives of direction, such as *downward, upward, forward, backward, horizontal, vertical* and *lateral*: *Power comes from the forward movement of the entire body.*

motion /ˈməʊʃn; *AmE* ˈmoʊʃn/ [U, C] (*rather formal*) the act or process of moving; the way sth moves; a particular movement you make, usually with your hand or arm: *The swaying motion of the ship was making me feel sick.* ◇ (*formal*) *He wound the key and set the toy in motion.* ◇ *Rub the cream in with a circular motion.*

move [C, usually sing.] a change of position or place: *He made a move towards the door.* ◇ *She felt that he was watching her every move.*

gesture /ˈdʒestʃə(r)/ [C, U] a movement that you make with your hands, head or face to show a particular meaning: *He made an obscene gesture with his hand.* ◇ *Expression and gesture are both forms of non-verbal communication.* See also **gesture** → NOD *verb*

wave [C, usually sing.] a movement of your hand and arm from side to side, for example to get sb's attention: *She sent him away with a wave of her hand.* See also **wave** → NOD *verb*

moving *adj.* See also the entry for EXCITING

moving · touching · poignant · haunting · uplifting
These words all describe sth which makes you feel strong emotions.

PATTERNS AND COLLOCATIONS
▸ a moving / a touching / a poignant / a haunting / an uplifting **story**
▸ a moving / touching / poignant **moment / tribute**
▸ a moving / a haunting / an uplifting **experience**
▸ **deeply** moving / poignant

moving causing you to have strong feelings, especially of sympathy or sadness: *His performance was very moving.* ◇ *He gave a moving account of his four years in captivity.* See also **move** → IMPRESS

touching causing you to have feelings of sympathy or gratitude; making you feel emotional: *I find his devotion to her rather touching.* ◇ *He wrote me a touching letter of thanks.* See also **touch** → IMPRESS

▸ **touchingly** *adv.*: *She remained touchingly faithful to the lover who had abandoned her.*

poignant /ˈpɔɪnjənt/ (*especially written*) having a strong effect on your feelings, especially in a way that makes you feel sad: *It was the city's street children who provided some of the most poignant images.* ◇ *Her face was a poignant reminder of the passing of time.*

▸ **poignantly** *adv.*: *The film poignantly captures the variety and conflict of feelings that followed the war.*

haunting /ˈhɔːntɪŋ/ beautiful, sad or frightening in a way that cannot be forgotten: *The area is celebrated for the haunting beauty of its landscape.* ◇ *The haunting melody played over and over in her mind.*

▸ **hauntingly** *adv.*: *a hauntingly beautiful landscape/ melody*

uplifting /ˌʌpˈlɪftɪŋ/ making you feel happier or more hopeful: *It's a gloriously funny, uplifting romantic comedy.* **OPP depressing** → NEGATIVE, See also **uplift** → ENCOURAGE 1

mundane *adj.* See also the entry for DAILY

mundane · routine · humdrum · prosaic
These words all describe things that are not considered interesting, because they happen every day in the same way.

PATTERNS AND COLLOCATIONS
▸ mundane / routine / humdrum **activities / affairs / jobs / work**
▸ a **mundane / routine / humdrum existence / task**
▸ mundane / routine **duties / questions / stuff / aspects / matters**
▸ a **mundane / humdrum life**
▸ the **mundane / prosaic level / world**
▸ **pretty / very** mundane / routine / humdrum

mundane /mʌnˈdeɪn/ (*disapproving*) not interesting or exciting; belonging to the world of ordinary things: *To return to more mundane matters – lunch is at half past twelve.*

routine /ruːˈtiːn/ [usually before noun] (*disapproving*) the same every day and therefore boring: *I have little patience with routine tasks such as washing up.* See also **routine** → USUAL

humdrum /ˈhʌmdrʌm/ (*disapproving*) without excitement because nothing unusual or interesting happens: *There is a lot of dull, humdrum work in local politics.*

prosaic /prəˈzeɪɪk/ (*written, disapproving*) not romantic or exciting: *Seafarers found it difficult to settle down to the more prosaic existence of life ashore.*

murder *noun* See also the entry for MASSACRE

murder · killing · suicide · assassination · homicide · slaying · manslaughter · euthanasia
These are all words for the act of killing sb.

PATTERNS AND COLLOCATIONS
▸ a **double / mass** murder / killing / suicide / slaying
▸ **(a) premeditated** murder / killing / homicide
▸ an **unsolved** murder / killing / slaying
▸ **(an) attempted** murder / suicide / assassination / homicide / manslaughter
▸ a **brutal** murder / killing / slaying
▸ to **commit** murder / suicide / homicide / manslaughter
▸ to **carry out** a murder / a killing / an assassination / euthanasia
▸ to **prevent** a murder / a killing / suicide / an assassination
▸ to **witness** a murder / a killing / a suicide / an assassination / a slaying
▸ a murder / a suicide / an assassination **attempt**

murder [U, C] the crime of killing sb deliberately: *He was found guilty of murder.* ◊ *She has been charged with the attempted murder of her husband.* ◊ *What was the **murder weapon**?* ◊ *The play is a **murder mystery***. See also **murder** → KILL *verb*, **murderous** → VIOLENT

killing [C, usually pl.] (*especially journalism*) an act of killing sb deliberately: *Refugees from the war-torn country brought accounts of mass killings, rape and torture.* See also **kill** → KILL

> **NOTE MURDER** OR **KILLING? Killing** is usually used in the plural about acts during a war, or by extreme political groups or organized groups of criminals. **Murder** more often refers to the killing of one person.

suicide /ˈsuːɪsaɪd; *BrE* also ˈsjuːɪ-/ [U, C] the act of killing yourself deliberately: *It was a case of attempted suicide (= one in which the person survives).* ◊ *He hadn't left a **suicide note** (= written before sb tries to commit suicide).* ◊ *The attack had been carried out by a **suicide bomber**.* See also **suicidal** → DESPERATE

assassination /əˌsæsɪˈneɪʃn; *AmE* -səˈn-/ [U, C] the murder of an important or famous person, especially for political reasons: *The president survived a number of assassination attempts.* See also **assassinate** → KILL

homicide /ˈhɒmɪsaɪd; *AmE* ˈhɑːm-/ [U, C] (*especially AmE, law*) the crime of killing sb: *He has been arrested on homicide and assault charges.* ❶ In legal English, the term

homicide can cover a wider range of meaning than **murder**, including **manslaughter** and *justifiable homicide*, in which the killing is judged not to be a crime at all. See also **homicidal** → VIOLENT

slaying [C] (*especially AmE, journalism*) a murder: *The papers told of the drug-related slayings of five people.* See also **slay** → KILL

manslaughter /ˈmænslɔːtə(r)/ [U] (*law*) the crime of killing sb illegally but not deliberately: *The charge has been reduced to manslaughter.*

euthanasia /ˌjuːθəˈneɪziə; *AmE* -ˈneɪʒə/ [U] the practice (illegal in most countries) of killing without pain a person who is suffering from a disease that cannot be cured: *They argued in favour of legalizing voluntary euthanasia (= people being able to ask for euthanasia for themselves).*

music *noun*

music · singing · song · harmony · melody
These are all words for musical sounds.

PATTERNS AND COLLOCATIONS
▸ **beautiful** music / singing / harmony
▸ **choral / folk** music / singing
▸ to **hear** music / singing of sth
▸ to **listen to** music / singing / the harmony / the melody

music [U] sounds that are arranged in a way that is pleasant or exciting to listen to, and that can be sung or played on musical instruments: *pop/dance/classical/church music* ◊ *It was a charming **piece of music**.* ◊ *He wrote the music but I don't know who wrote the words.* ◊ *The poem has been **set to music**.* ◊ *Every week they get together to **make music** (= to play music or sing).*
▸ **musical** *adj.*: *musical instruments* ◊ *She had a low, musical voice that thrilled him to hear.*

singing [U] the activity of making musical sounds with your voice: *There was singing and dancing all night.* ◊ *She has a beautiful singing voice.* See also **sing** → SING

song [U] the act of singing; singing when considered generally: *The story is told through song and dance.* ◊ *Suddenly he **burst into song** (= started to sing).*

harmony /ˈhɑːməni; *AmE* ˈhɑːrm-/ [U, C] the way in which different notes that are played or sung at the same time combine to make a pleasing sound: *They began to sing in perfect four-part harmony.* ◊ *With their tight vocal harmonies it is easy to understand the group's appeal.*

melody /ˈmelədi/ [U] the way in which different notes are played or sung one after another to make a tune: *A few bars of melody drifted towards us.*

mystery *noun*

mystery · problem · paradox · puzzle · enigma · secret
These are all words for sth that is difficult to understand or explain.

PATTERNS AND COLLOCATIONS
▸ a mystery / paradox / puzzle **about** sth
▸ a mystery / puzzle / enigma **to** sb
▸ a **great** mystery / problem / paradox / puzzle / enigma
▸ to **solve** a mystery / a problem / a puzzle / an enigma
▸ to **explain** a mystery / a problem / a paradox / the secrets of sth
▸ to **remain** a mystery / a problem / a puzzle / an enigma
▸ to **explore** the mysteries / problem / secrets of sth
▸ **something of** a mystery / a paradox / a puzzle / an enigma

mystery /ˈmɪstri/ [C] something that is difficult to understand or explain; a person or thing that is strange and interesting because you do not know much about them/it: *The police are close to solving the mystery of the missing murder weapon.* ◊ *It's a complete mystery to me why they chose him.* ◊ *He's a bit of a mystery.* ❶ **Mystery** is often used like an adjective before another noun to describe sb/sth that is unknown, strange or unexplained: *a mystery man/woman* ◇ *a mystery caller* ◇ *a mystery disease/illness/virus* See also **mysterious** → STRANGE 1

problem [C] a question that must be answered by using logical thought or mathematics: *a mathematical/philosophical problem* ◇ *This is one of the great problems of cosmology: where did the overall structure of the universe come from?*

paradox /'pærədɒks; *AmE* -dɑːks/ [C] a person, thing or situation that has two opposite features and seems strange or difficult to understand: *He was a paradox — a loner who loved to chat to strangers.* ◇ *It's a curious paradox that professional comedians often have unhappy personal lives.*

▶ **paradoxical** *adj.*: *It is paradoxical that some of the poorest people live in some of the richest areas of the country.*

puzzle [C, usually sing.] something that is difficult to understand or to explain: *There is a puzzle about how the plant first came to Britain.* ◇ *Another **piece of the puzzle** fell into place.* See also **puzzling** → CONFUSING

enigma /ɪ'nɪgmə/ [C] a person, thing or situation that seems strange and is difficult to understand: *The tower presents an enigma. How old is it? Who built it?*

▶ **enigmatic** /ˌenɪg'mætɪk/ *adj.*: *He gave an enigmatic smile.*

NOTE MYSTERY, PUZZLE OR ENIGMA? A **puzzle** always has a solution, if only you can work it out, usually by collecting evidence and thinking logically about it. A **mystery** may have a solution that can be found in this way, or it may be more puzzling than this and deal with wider and deeper issues: *the mysteries of life/death/science* ◇ *the puzzles of life/death/science.* An **enigma** is usually sth that can never be solved because the evidence does not exist and/or it is too complicated a matter for logical thought to solve on its own.

secret [C, usually pl.] something that is not yet fully understood or that is difficult to understand: *They hope to unlock the secrets of the universe.*

N n

naive (also naïve) *adj.*

naive · inexperienced · innocent · trusting · gullible · impressionable
These words all describe sb who has little experience of the world, and/or is too willing to believe or accept what other people tell them.

PATTERNS AND COLLOCATIONS
▸ an inexperienced / a trusting / a gullible / an impressionable **person**
▸ an innocent / impressionable **child**
▸ a naive / an innocent **belief**
▸ **very** naive / inexperienced / innocent / trusting / impressionable
▸ **politically** naive / inexperienced / innocent
▸ **sexually** inexperienced / innocent
▸ **young and** inexperienced / innocent / impressionable

naive (also **naïve**) /naɪˈiːv/ (*disapproving*) lacking experience of life, knowledge or good judgement, and too willing to believe what other people tell you: *He made some particularly naive remarks.* ◇ *It would be naive of us to think that football is only a game.* ❶ **Naive** is also, but less frequently, used in an approving way when describing people or their behaviour, to mean 'simple and having little knowledge of evil or unpleasant things': *Their approach to life is refreshingly naive.* **OPP** **sophisticated** → SOPHISTICATED, See also **naivety** → IGNORANCE
▸ **naively** *adv.*: *I naively assumed that I would be paid for the work.*

inexperienced (*especially written*) having little knowledge or experience of sth: *Inexperienced drivers can expect to pay higher insurance premiums.* ◇ *Some of the older teachers are inexperienced in modern methods.* ◇ *A child of his age is too young and inexperienced to recognize danger.* **OPP** **experienced** → SOPHISTICATED, See also **inexperience** → IGNORANCE

innocent having little experience of the world, especially of sexual matters, or of evil or unpleasant things: *He prefers to see his teenage daughter as an innocent young child.* See also **innocence** → IGNORANCE, **childlike** → CHILDISH

trusting (*often approving*) tending to believe that other people are good, sincere and honest: *There is a need for a trusting relationship between client and consultant.* ◇ *If you're too trusting, other people will take advantage of you.* See also **trust** → FAITH *noun*, **trust** → TRUST *verb*, **unsuspecting** → UNAWARE

gullible /ˈɡʌləbl/ (*disapproving*) too willing to believe what other people tell you and therefore easily tricked: *The advertisement is aimed at gullible young women worried about their weight.*

impressionable /ɪmˈpreʃənəbl/ (*especially written*) (of a person, especially a young one) easily influenced or affected by sb/sth: *He was a bad influence on the child, who was at an impressionable age.*

naked *adj.*

naked · bare · nude · undressed · in the nude
These words all describe sb who is not wearing any clothes.

PATTERNS AND COLLOCATIONS
▸ sb's naked / bare **skin / flesh / shoulder / thigh / torso**
▸ **completely / almost** naked / bare / nude

naked not wearing any clothes: *She was clutching the sheet around her naked body.* ◇ *The prisoners were stripped naked.* ◇ *They often wandered around the house stark naked* (= completely naked). ◇ (*AmE*) *buck naked* (= completely naked) ◇ *They found him half naked and bleeding to death.* ❶ **Naked** can describe either a person or a part of the body. When it describes a part of the body, this is often in a description of a sexual nature.

bare not covered by any clothes: *She likes to walk around in bare feet.* ◇ *When she stood up she was completely bare.* ❶ **Bare** is more often used to describe a part of the body than a person. When it describes a part of the body it is not usually a description of a sexual nature. When it is used to describe a person it usually comes after the noun, linking verb and adverb such as *completely* or *totally*.

nude /njuːd; *AmE* nuːd/ (especially of a human figure in art) not wearing any clothes; involving people who are naked: *He asked me to pose nude for him.* ◇ *Are there any nude scenes in the movie?* ◇ *Some of the resorts allow nude sunbathing on the beaches.*

undressed [not usually before noun] not wearing any clothes: *She began to get undressed* (= remove her clothes). ◇ *He said he felt undressed* (= felt that he wasn't completely dressed) *without a hat.* ◇ *He was half undressed when he answered the door.* ❶ **Undressed** is nearly always used after the verbs *get* or *feel*. When it is used with *be*, there is usually also an adverb such as *totally, completely* or *half*.

in the 'nude *phrase* not wearing any clothes: *She refuses to be photographed in the nude.* ◇ *He always slept in the nude.* ❶ **In the nude** is mainly used to talk about activities that people do while not wearing any clothes.

name *noun* See also the entry for NICKNAME

name · title · first name · surname · last name · full name · family name · label · middle name · maiden name · subtitle
These are all words for a word or words that a person, animal or object is known by.

PATTERNS AND COLLOCATIONS
▸ a name / title / first name / label / subtitle **for** sb / sth
▸ **under** the name / title (of) …
▸ **to use** a name / sb's title / sb's first name / sb's surname / your family name / your middle name / your maiden name
▸ **to change** sb / sth's name / title / surname
▸ **to adopt / take** a name / title / surname
▸ **to give sb / sth** a name / title / label / middle name / subtitle
▸ **to choose / decide on** a name / title / first name / middle name / subtitle
▸ **to address sb by** their title / first name / surname / last name / full name
▸ **to call sb by** their first name / surname / last name / full name
▸ **to have** a name / title / surname / family name / middle name / subtitle
▸ **to bear** a name / title / surname / family name

name [C] a word or words that a particular person, animal, place or thing is known by: *What's your name?* ◇ *What is/was the name, please?* (= a polite way of asking sb's name) ◇ *Please write your full name and address below.* ◇ *The tickets were booked in the name of McLean.* ◇ *Are you changing your name when you get married?* ◇ *Rubella is just another name for German measles.* ❶ Your **name** is either your whole name or one part of your name: *My name is Maria.* ◇ *His name is Tom Smith.* ◇ *The name's Bond.* **Name** is often used in compounds: *place name* ◇ *street name* ◇ *code name* ◇ *pet name* (= a name you use for sb instead of their real name, as a sign of affection) ◇ *pen-name* (= a name used by a writer instead of their real name) ◇ *brand name* (= the name given to a product by the company that produces it) See also **name** → CALL *verb* 1

title [C] the name of a book, poem, painting, piece of music, etc.; a word in front of a person's name to show their rank or profession, whether or not they are married, etc.; a name that describes sb's job: *His poems were published under the title of 'Love and Reason'.* ◇ *the title track from their latest CD* (= the song with the same title as the disc) ◇ *She has sung the title role in 'Carmen'* (= the role of Carmen in that opera). ◇ *The present duke inherited the title from his father.* ◇ *Give your name and title* (= Mr, Miss, Ms, Dr, etc.). ◇ *His **job title** is Special Projects Officer.* See also **entitle** → CALL *verb* 1

¹first name [C] a name that was given to you when you were born, that comes before your family name: *His first name is Tom and his surname is Green.* ◇ *Please call me by my first name.* ◇ *(BrE)* to be **on first-name terms** with sb (= to call them by their first name as a sign of a friendly informal relationship) ◇ *(AmE)* to be on **a first-name basis** ❶ Other words for sb's **first name** are **given name** (especially in American English), **forename** (in formal or official language) and **Christian name** (in British English, although this is now rather old-fashioned). These are all more formal and less frequent than **first name**.

surname [C] *(especially BrE)* a name shared by all the members of a family (written last in English names): *On marriage most women in this country still take their husband's surname.*

¹last name [C] your surname (written last in English names): *How do you spell your last name?*

¹full name [C] all your names, usually in the order first name + middle name(s) + last name: *His full name was William Augustus Grove.* See also **full** → WHOLE

¹family name [C] the part of your name that shows which family you belong to: *'Smith' is the most common family name in Britain.* ◇ *He wanted a son to carry on the family name.*

label [C] *(disapproving)* a word or phrase that is used to describe sb/sth in a way that seems too general, unfair or not correct: *I hated the label 'housewife'.* ◇ *He was cruelly given the label 'Mr Zero' by the Press.* See also **label** → CALL *verb* 1

¹middle name [C] a name that comes between your first name and your family name: *'What's your middle name?'* *'I don't have one/Well actually, I have two…'*

¹maiden name [C] a woman's family name before marriage: *Kate kept her maiden name when she got married* (= she did not change her surname to that of her husband). ❶ If a woman uses her husband's surname after they get married, the new name is her **married name**.

subtitle [C] a second title of a book or other written work that appears after the main title and gives more information: *This book's title is 'Oxford Learner's Thesaurus'. Its subtitle is 'A dictionary of synonyms'.*
▸ **subtitle** *verb* [T, usually passive]: *The article is subtitled 'New language for new times'.*

narrow *adj.*

narrow · thin · fine
These words all describe sth which measures a short distance from one side to the other.

PATTERNS AND COLLOCATIONS
▸ a narrow / thin / fine **crack / strip**
▸ narrow / thin **shoulders**
▸ (a) thin / fine **hair / thread / layer**
▸ very / extremely narrow / thin / fine
▸ quite narrow / thin

narrow measuring a short distance from one side to the other, especially in relation to its length: *I love walking down the narrow streets in the old city.* ◇ *I sat next to him on the narrow bed.* ◇ *The jacket looked very large across his narrow shoulders.* ◇ *There was only a narrow gap between the bed and the wall.* OPP **wide**, **broad** → WIDE 2, See also **narrow** → SHRINK *verb*

thin having a smaller distance between opposite sides or surfaces than other similar things or than normal: *Cut the vegetables into thin strips.* ◇ *A number of thin cracks appeared in the wall.* ◇ *The body was hidden beneath a thin layer of soil.* ◇ *The wind blew cold through his thin shirt.* OPP **thick** → WIDE 2

NOTE NARROW OR THIN? **Narrow** describes sth that is a short distance from side to side. **Thin** describes sth that has a short distance through it from one side to the other: *narrow/thin shoulders/strips/cracks* ◇ *thin streets* ◇ *a thin bed/gap* ◇ *a narrow layer/shirt*

fine very thin: *His fine blond hair came down almost to his shoulders.* ◇ *You could see the sweat in the fine hairs above his upper lip.* ◇ *Acupuncture uses fine needles inserted into the patient's skin.* ◇ *I need a brush with a fine tip.*

national *adj.*

national · domestic · civil · nationwide · internal · home
These all describe things connected with a particular country rather than foreign countries.

PATTERNS AND COLLOCATIONS
▸ national / domestic / home **news**
▸ domestic / internal / home **affairs**
▸ national / domestic **politics / law**
▸ the national / domestic / internal / home **market**
▸ national / domestic / internal **security**
▸ domestic / civil / internal **unrest / conflict**
▸ a domestic / an internal **flight / crisis**
▸ domestic / internal **trade**
▸ a national / civil **emergency**
▸ national / civil **defence**
▸ a national / nationwide **campaign / survey / strike**
▸ on the domestic / home **front**

national [usually before noun] connected with a particular country, rather than involving other countries; happening in or involving all parts of a particular country: *He has won medals in both national and international competitions.* ◇ *The country has a national debt of 80% of GNP.* ◇ *The state of our hospitals is a national disgrace.* ◇ *Decide whether it would be better to advertise in a national or a local newspaper.* OPP **international** → INTERNATIONAL, **local** ❶ Local describes things that belong to or are connected with the particular place or area that you are talking about or with the place where you live, not the whole country: *A local man was accused of the murder.* ◇ *decisions made at a local rather than national level* See also **nation** → COUNTRY 1
▸ **nationally** *adv.*: *He's a talented athlete who competes nationally and internationally.* ◇ *The programme was broadcast nationally.*

domestic [usually before noun] connected with or inside a particular country, rather than involving other countries: *The company has made losses in both its domestic and international operations.* ◇ *He was a chief White House adviser on domestic policy.* OPP **foreign**, **overseas** → FOREIGN
▸ **domestically** *adv.*: *domestically produced goods*

NOTE NATIONAL OR DOMESTIC? **National** contrasts both with *international* and *local*; **domestic** contrasts with *international* (or *foreign*) but NOT *local*. **Domestic** is mostly used in the contexts of business and politics; **national** has a wider range.

civil /ˈsɪvl/ [only before noun] connected with the people who live in a particular country: *Both are veterans of the country's long civil war* (= between groups of people in the same country). ◇ *Some groups have been calling for a non-violent civil disobedience campaign.* ❶ **Civil** is used especially to describe problems or violence involving the ordinary people within a country; collocates include *war, unrest, conflict, disorder, disturbance* and *disobedience.*

nationwide /ˌneɪʃnˈwaɪd/ [usually before noun] happening or existing in all parts of a particular country: *The study uses data from a nationwide survey of 5 000 people.* ◇ *The police conducted a nationwide hunt for the missing girl.*
▸ **nationwide** *adv.*: *The company has over 500 stores nationwide.*

> **NOTE** **NATIONAL** OR **NATIONWIDE?** Nationwide is used especially about activities or events in which people all over the country take part, or in which people travel all over the country; collocates include *campaign, drive, strike, survey, tour, hunt* and *search.* **National** is often used about organizations or institutions which serve the whole country, but **nationwide** is not used in this way: ~~a nationwide health service~~ ◇ ~~nationwide radio~~

internal /ɪnˈtɜːnl; *AmE* ɪnˈtɜːrnl/ [only before noun] connected with or inside a particular country, rather than involving other countries: *Nations should be left to resolve their own internal difficulties.* ◇ *The civil war led to considerable internal migration* (= people moving to different areas within a country). **OPP** **external** → FOREIGN

> **NOTE** **DOMESTIC** OR **INTERNAL?** There is very little difference in meaning or use between these words. **Domestic** is more frequent and is used especially in more ordinary situations in business and politics; collocates include *currency, demand, service, economy, policy, issue* and *law.* **Internal** is used slightly more in discussions of conflict situations; collocates include *conflict, strife, division, self-government* and *security.*

home [only before noun] (*especially BrE*) connected with your own country rather than involving other countries: *The newspaper has different sections for home news, international and foreign news.* ◇ (*BrE*) *The Home Secretary has drawn up national guidelines.* ❶ In Britain, **home** is used in the title of government departments and ministers who deal with issues inside the country, such as the *Home Office* and the *Home Secretary.* **OPP** **foreign, overseas** → FOREIGN

natural *adj.*

natural · genetic · intuitive · instinctive · innate · congenital · hereditary
These words all describe a characteristic, ability or disease that a person or animal has naturally or is born with.

PATTERNS AND COLLOCATIONS
▸ a natural / a genetic / an innate **characteristic**
▸ natural / intuitive / instinctive / innate **ability**
▸ natural / intuitive / instinctive / innate **understanding**
▸ natural / intuitive / innate **sense** (of sth)
▸ natural / intuitive / innate **intelligence**
▸ natural / instinctive / innate **knowledge**
▸ natural / instinctive / innate **desires / needs**
▸ natural / innate **instinct**
▸ a natural / an intuitive / an instinctive / an innate **response**
▸ a natural / an intuitive / an instinctive **reaction**
▸ a genetic / congenital / hereditary **disease / condition / disorder**
▸ **purely** natural / intuitive / instinctive

natural (of behaviour, qualities or feelings) part of the character that a person or animal was born with: *Hunting is one of a cat's natural instincts.* ◇ *His natural gifts as a preacher meant he was in great demand.* ◇ *It's only natural to worry about your children.* ❶ **Natural** can also

be used before a noun to describe a person who was born with a particular type of character or ability: *He's a natural rebel / leader.*
▸ **naturally** *adv.*: *She was naturally gifted when it came to music.*

genetic /dʒəˈnetɪk/ caused by genes ❶ Genes are the units of cells of a living thing that control its physical characteristics, and that are passed on from parents to children: *A person's intelligence is based on both genetic and environmental factors.* ◇ *There are about 4 000 inherited human genetic diseases.*
▸ **genetically** *adv.*: *genetically determined characteristics*

intuitive /ɪnˈtjuːɪtɪv; *AmE* -ˈtuː-/ (of ideas) obtained by using your feelings rather than by considering the facts; (of people) able to understand sth by using feelings rather than by considering the facts: *Our approach to the subject can be strictly rational or wholly intuitive.* ◇ *I don't think that women are necessarily more intuitive than men.* See also **intuition** → INSTINCT, **intuition** → IDEA 2
▸ **intuitively** *adv.*: *Intuitively, she knew that he was lying.*

instinctive /ɪnˈstɪŋktɪv/ based on a natural tendency to behave in a particular way, rather than on thought or training: *A bird's knowledge of its migratory route is partly learnt and partly instinctive.* ◇ *My instinctive reaction was to deny everything.* See also **instinct** → INSTINCT, **instinct** → IDEA 2
▸ **instinctively** *adv.*: *I knew instinctively that something was wrong.*

innate /ɪˈneɪt/ (*rather formal*) (of behaviour, qualities or feelings) part of the character that a person or animal was born with: *Many children seem to have an innate sense of justice.*
▸ **innately** *adv.*: *Some philosophers viewed human nature as innately good.*

> **NOTE** **NATURAL** OR **INNATE?** There is little difference in meaning or use betwen these words. **Natural** is more frequent and less formal. You might use **innate** in cases where there might be confusion with a different meaning of **natural**: for example *an innate response* is response that sb / sth makes because it is in their character; *a natural response* is more likely to be a response that sb else expects or understands: *Anxiety at a perceived threat is an innate response in any animal.* ◇ *It's a natural response to keep your troubles quiet.* See also **natural** → OBVIOUS

congenital /kənˈdʒenɪtl/ (of a disease or medical condition) existing since birth; existing as a basic part of sb's character that will never change: *Congenital abnormalities can occur in babies whose mothers drink heavily.* ◇ *He's a congenital liar!*

hereditary /həˈredɪtri; *AmE* -teri/ (especially of diseases) existing from birth as a result of being passed on by one or both parents: *It's a hereditary disorder that can cause abnormal growth.*

nature *noun*

1 the exact nature of the problem
2 the beauties of nature

1 nature · character · essence · stuff · spirit
These are all words for the basic or most important qualities of a thing.

PATTERNS AND COLLOCATIONS
▸ in nature / character / essence / spirit
▸ the **very** nature / character / essence / stuff / spirit of sth
▸ the **real / true** nature / character / essence / spirit of sth
▸ the **individual / fundamental** nature / character / essence of sth
▸ to **preserve / capture / convey / reflect** the nature / character / essence of sth
▸ to **consider / understand / reveal / define** the nature / character / essence of sth

nature [sing.] the basic qualities of a thing: *It's difficult to define the exact nature of the problem.* ◇ *My work is very specialized in nature.* ◇ *The future* **by its very nature** *is uncertain.* See also **nature** → PERSONALITY

character [C, usually sing., U] all the qualities and features that make a place or thing different from others; the way that sth is, or a particular quality or feature that a thing, event or place has: *The character of the neighbourhood hasn't changed at all.* ◇ *I love the delicate character of the light in the evening.* See also **character** → PERSONALITY

NOTE **NATURE OR CHARACTER? Nature** is used especially to talk about the basic qualities of abstract things, such as a *problem, work, society*, a *strategy, risks* or the *future*. **Character** is used more to talk about the qualities and features of places, buildings and other physical things, especially qualities and features that appeal to your senses and feelings and make a place or thing seem different or special in some way.

essence /'esns/ [U] the most important quality or feature of sth, that makes it what it is: *Like so many peasant foods, the essence of pasta is its simplicity.* ◇ *In essence* (= when you consider the most important points), *your situation isn't so different from mine.* See also **essential** → FUNDA-MENTAL

stuff [U] the most important feature of sth; sth that sth else is based on or is made from: *Parades and marches were the very stuff of politics in the region.* ◇ *Let's see what stuff you're made of* (= what sort of person you are).

spirit [sing., U] the real or intended meaning or purpose of sth: *The referee should try to obey the spirit as well as the letter* (= the narrow meaning of the words) *of the law.*

2 nature · the environment · wildlife · life · ecosystem · the wild · the natural world
These words all mean the world and the plants and animals that live in it.

PATTERNS AND COLLOCATIONS
▶ **in** nature / the environment / an ecosystem / the wild
▶ (a/an/the) **marine/terrestrial/aquatic** environment/wildlife/ life / ecosystem
▶ to **protect** the environment / wildlife / … life / the natural world
▶ to **damage** the environment / wildlife / … life
▶ to **benefit / preserve / save / affect / destroy** the environment / wildlife

nature (also **Nature**) [U] all the plants, animals and things that exist in the universe that are not made by people; the way that things happen in the physical world when it is not controlled by people: *Take time to appreciate the beauties of nature.* ◇ **The forces of nature** *are constantly reshaping our world.* ◇ *It seemed against* **the laws of nature** *that such a creature could even exist.* ◇ *Just let nature take its course.* ◇ *Her illness was Nature's way of telling her to do less.* ❶ You cannot use **the nature** to talk about plants, animals and the natural world: ~~the beauties of the nature.~~ When you are just talking about your immediate surroundings, it is usually better to use a different word: ~~They stopped to admire nature.~~ ◇ *They stopped to admire the scenery/countryside.* See also **countryside, scenery** → COUNTRY 2
▶ **natural** *adj.*: *a country's natural resources* (= its coal, oil, forests, etc.)
▶ **naturally** *adv.*: *naturally occurring chemicals*

the environment [sing.] the natural world in which people, animals and plants live, especially when it is threatened or has been damaged by human activity: *There is increasing public concern about pollution of the environment.*
▶ **environmental** *adj.*: *the environmental impact of pollution*
▶ **environmentally** *adv.*: *an environmentally sensitive area* (= one that is easily damaged or that contains rare animals, plants, etc.)

wildlife /'waɪldlaɪf/ [U] animals that are wild and live in a natural environment that is not controlled by people: *Development of the area would endanger wildlife.* ◇ *The area is an important wildlife habitat.*

life [U] living things: *pond life* ◇ *Yet more species of plant and animal life die out as their very specialized habitat is disturbed.* ◇ *Is there intelligent life on other planets?*

ecosystem /'iːkəʊsɪstəm; AmE 'iːkoʊ-/ [C] all the plants and living creatures in a particular area considered in relation to their physical environment: *Islands often support delicate ecosystems that evolved without any need for defence.*

the wild [C, sing.] a natural environment that is not controlled by people: *The bird is too tame now to survive in the wild.* ◇ *The animals were released back into the wild when they had recovered.*

the ˌnatural ˈworld [C, sing.] the earth's plants, animals and natural features that have not been created or changed by human actions: *Many medicines are made from ingredients found in the natural world.*

naughty *adj.*

naughty · defiant · bad · rebellious · disobedient
These words all describe people who are not willing to obey sb/sth.

PATTERNS AND COLLOCATIONS
▶ a naughty / defiant / bad / rebellious / disobedient **child**
▶ a naughty / bad / disobedient **boy / girl**
▶ a defiant / rebellious **teenager**
▶ naughty / defiant / bad / rebellious / disobedient **behaviour**
▶ a defiant / bad / rebellious **attitude**

naughty /'nɔːti/ (especially of children) behaving badly; not willing to obey: *You've been a very naughty boy!* ◇ *Come on now, that's naughty.* ❶ Adults sometimes use **naughty** in a humorous way to talk about things they do that they think they shouldn't do: (*humorous*) *I'm being very naughty — I've ordered champagne!* **OPP** **good** → GOOD 7

defiant /dɪ'faɪənt/ (*rather formal*) openly refusing to obey sb/sth, sometimes in an aggressive way: *The terrorists sent a defiant message to the government.* ◇ *He was in a defiant mood, unwilling to give way to anyone.* See also **defy** → OPPOSE

bad [usually before noun] (especially of children) not behaving well: *I will not tolerate this bad behaviour.* ◇ *I was always the 'bad boy' at school.* ❶ If you call a child *a bad boy/girl/child*, this is usually stricter or more unkind than calling them **naughty**, unless it is done in a slightly humorous way. **OPP** **good** → GOOD 7

rebellious /rɪ'beljəs/ (especially of teenagers) unwilling to obey rules or accept normal standards of behaviour or dress: *He has always had a rebellious streak.* See also **rebel** → OPPOSE, **rebel** → REBEL *verb*
▶ **rebelliously** *adv.*: *'I don't care!' she said rebelliously.*

disobedient /ˌdɪsə'biːdiənt/ (*formal*) failing or refusing to obey sb/sth: *I was very disobedient to my father.* **OPP** **obedient** → GOOD 7, See also **disobey** → OPPOSE
▶ **disobedience** *noun* [U]: *His behaviour was seen as another act of disobedience.* **OPP** **obedience** → GOOD 7

neat *adj.*

neat · tidy · ordered · orderly · uncluttered
These words all describe sth where everything is carefully arranged and things are in the place where they belong.

PATTERNS AND COLLOCATIONS
▶ neat / tidy / orderly **rows**
▶ a neat / a tidy / an orderly **arrangement**
▶ a neat / a tidy / an uncluttered **house / room**
▶ to **look / keep sth** neat / tidy
▶ to **leave sth** neat / tidy / uncluttered
▶ a **nice** neat / tidy…
▶ **clean / nice and** neat / tidy

neat (*approving*) carefully done or arranged with everything in the correct place or the correct order: *She was wearing a neat black suit.* ◇ *You've got very neat handwriting!* ◇ *He sorted his papers into a neat pile.* ◇ *This hairstyle is easy to keep* **neat and tidy.** See also **neat** → EFFICIENT

▸ **neatly** *adv.*: *The tools were neatly arranged on the bench.*

tidy (*especially BrE, approving*) (of a place) arranged neatly and with everything in order: *Someone needs to keep the place tidy.* ◇ *The house is much tidier now.* ◇ *The room was clean and tidy.* **OPP untidy** → UNTIDY, See also **tidy** → EFFICIENT *adj.*, **tidy** → TIDY *verb*

▸ **tidily** *adv.*: *Tubes of paint were set out tidily.*

ordered [usually before noun] carefully arranged or organized: *She tried not to think about the turmoil he had caused in her ordered existence.* ◇ *a well-ordered society* **❶** Unlike the other words in this group, **ordered** does not usually describe physical things or places, but the way sb's life or a society or system is organized. Collocates include *life, existence, society, universe* and *structure.* **OPP disordered** → UNTIDY, See also **order** → EFFICIENCY

orderly (*usually approving*) arranged in a neat and logical way: *The vegetables were planted in orderly rows.* See also **order** → EFFICIENCY

> **NOTE NEAT, TIDY** OR **ORDERLY? Neat** is the most general of these words and can describe sb's appearance, a place or an arrangement of things such as a *row* or *pile*; **tidy** usually desribes a place such as a *room* or *desk*; **orderly** usually describes the way things are arranged in rows or piles.

uncluttered (*approving*) not containing too many objects or any unnecessary items: *Keep the work area uncluttered and clean.* **OPP cluttered** → UNTIDY

necessary *adj.* See also the entry for ESSENTIAL

necessary · compulsory · mandatory · requisite · obligatory · forced · involuntary
These words all describe sth that sb has to do or have.

PATTERNS AND COLLOCATIONS
▸ it's necessary / compulsory / mandatory / obligatory **for** sb to do sth
▸ it's necessary / compulsory / mandatory / obligatory **to do sth**
▸ forced / involuntary **repatriation**
▸ almost / **legally** compulsory / obligatory

necessary that is needed for a purpose or a reason: *It may be necessary to buy a new one.* ◇ *Only use your car when absolutely necessary.* ◇ *If necessary, you can contact me at home.* ◇ *I'll make the necessary arrangements.* **OPP unnecessary** → UNNECESSARY, See also **necessary** → INEVITABLE, **necessitate** → MEAN *verb* 3

compulsory /kəmˈpʌlsəri/ (*rather formal*) that must be done because of a law or rule: *It is compulsory for all motorcyclists to wear helmets.* ◇ *English is a compulsory subject at this level.* **OPP voluntary, optional** → VOLUNTARY 1, See also **compulsion** → PRESSURE 2

mandatory /ˈmændətəri; *AmE* -tɔːri; *BrE* also mænˈdeɪtəri/ (*formal*) that must be done because of a law: *It is mandatory for blood banks to test all donated blood for the virus.* ◇ *The offence carries a mandatory life sentence.*

requisite /ˈrekwɪzɪt/ [only before noun] (*formal*) necessary for a particular purpose: *She lacks the requisite experience for the job.*

obligatory /əˈblɪgətri; *AmE* -tɔːri/ (*formal*) that must be done because of a law or rule: *It is obligatory for all employees to wear protective clothing.* **❶ Obligatory** is sometimes used humorously before a noun to talk about sth that often exists or is done, but that is not really necessary at all: *The hotel has a terrace with comfy chairs for that obligatory cocktail.* **OPP optional** → VOLUNTARY 1

> **NOTE COMPULSORY, MANDATORY** OR **OBLIGATORY? Compulsory** is used especially in the contexts of education, business and employment: *compulsory education/*

schooling / reading / subjects ◇ *compulsory insurance / liquidation / purchase / redundancy / retirement.* **Mandatory** is used especially in the context of the law: *a mandatory sentence / penalty / duty / requirement.* **Obligatory** is often used to talk about rules and laws relating to safety, for example in sport or the workplace: *Recently safety regulations have made it obligatory for all competitors to wear fist protectors.*

forced [usually before noun] happening or done without you wanting it to: *Many are unhappy about the forced repatriation of the refugees.* ◇ *I hope there will be no need for the forced sale of any property.*

involuntary /ɪnˈvɒləntri; *AmE* ɪnˈvɑːlənteri/ [usually before noun] (*rather formal, written*) happening or done without you wanting it to: *The distinction between voluntary and involuntary unemployment is often blurred.* **OPP voluntary** → VOLUNTARY 1

> **NOTE FORCED** OR **INVOLUNTARY? Forced** often suggests that sb is forcing sb to do sth; **involuntary** suggests that it is circumstances, not another person, that forces sb to do or be sth: ~~forced unemployment.~~ However, **involuntary** can also be used when it is in fact the actions or decision of another person that forces sb to do sth, as a more formal and less direct (or less honest) way of saying **forced**: *the forced / involuntary repatriation of the refugees*

need *noun*

need · requirement · necessity · essential · want
These words are all words for sth that you need, or a situation in which sth is necessary.

PATTERNS AND COLLOCATIONS
▸ a need / requirement / necessity **for** sth
▸ **basic** needs / requirements / necessities / essentials
▸ a / an **pressing / urgent / immediate / absolute / fundamental** need / requirement / necessity
▸ a **political / social / physical** need / requirement / necessity
▸ **human / bodily** needs / wants
▸ the **bare** necessities / essentials
▸ to **have** a need / a requirement / wants
▸ to **meet / satisfy** sb's needs / requirements / wants
▸ to **understand / be aware of / remove / reduce** the need / requirement / necessity for sth

need [sing., U] the fact that sth must happen or be done: *There is an urgent need for qualified teachers.* ◇ *There is* **no need** *for you to get up early tomorrow.* ◇ *I had no need to open the letter — I knew what it would say.* ◇ *The house is* **in need of** *a thorough clean.* **❶** Your **needs** [pl.] are the things that you must have in order to live in a comfortable way or achieve what you want: *First we will assess your financial needs.* ◇ *Your role will be to support children with special educational needs.* See also **need** → DESIRE *verb*

requirement [C] (*formal*) something that you need or want: *Our immediate requirement is extra staff.* ◇ *These goods are* **surplus to requirements** (= more than we need).

necessity /nəˈsesəti/ [C] (*rather formal*) the fact that sth must happen or be done; sth that you must have and cannot manage without: *There had never been any necessity for her to go out to work.* ◇ *Many people cannot even afford basic necessities such as food and clothing.* ◇ *Air-conditioning is an absolute necessity in this climate.* See also **necessitate** → MEAN *verb* 3

essential [C, usually pl.] something that you must have in a particular situation or in order to do a particular thing: *I only had time to pack the bare essentials* (= the most necessary things). ◇ *The studio had all the essentials like heating and running water.* **❶ Essentials** are often described as *bare* or *basic*. See also **essential** → ESSENTIAL *adj.*

want [C, usually pl.] something that you must have and cannot manage without, especially in order to live: *The snail does not need to travel far to satisfy all its bodily wants.* See also **want** → DESIRE *noun*

> **NOTE** NECESSITIES, ESSENTIALS OR WANTS? **Wants** are usually the most basic and physical of these: things that your body needs in order to go on living; the most common collocates are *human* and *bodily*. **Essentials** are usually more practical: the basic things that you need in order to do a particular thing or activity. **Necessities** is a more general word and can cover both physical and practical needs.

need *verb*

need · require · rely on/upon sb/sth · want · call for sth · demand
These words all mean to want to have sb/sth that is essential or very important.

PATTERNS AND COLLOCATIONS
▸ to **really** need / require / want / call for / demand sth
▸ to **just** need / require / want sth
▸ to **still** need / require / rely on / call for sth
▸ to **urgently** need / require / want sb / sth
▸ to **clearly / obviously** need / require / call for / demand sth

need [T] (not usually used in the progressive tenses) to want to have sb/sth because they are/it is essential or very important, not just because you would like to have them/it: *Do you need any help?* ◇ *Don't go – I might need you.* ◇ *They badly needed a change.* ◇ *Food aid is urgently needed.* ◇ *This shirt needs washing.* ◇ *I need to get some sleep.* See also **need** → DESIRE *noun*

require [T] (not usually used in the progressive tenses) (*formal*) to need sth; to depend on sb/sth: *This condition requires urgent treatment.* ◇ *These lentils do not require soaking before cooking.* ◇ *The situation required that he be present.*

re'ly on/upon sb/sth *phrasal verb* to need or depend on sb/sth, especially in order to be able to continue doing sth: *As babies, we rely entirely on others for food.* ◇ *These days we rely heavily on computers to organize our work.* ◇ *The industry relies on the price of raw materials remaining low.* ❶ **Rely upon sb/sth** is more formal than **rely on sb/sth**. See also **rely on/upon sb/sth** → TRUST

want [T] (not usually used in the progressive tenses) (*rather informal, especially spoken*) to need sth: *What this house wants is a good clean.* ◇ *The plants want watering daily.* ❶ If a person **is wanted** somewhere, they are needed to be present in the place or for the purpose mentioned: *She's wanted immediately in the director's office.* ◇ *Excuse me, you're wanted on the phone.*

'call for sth *phrasal verb* (not used in the progressive tenses) (of a situation) to need sth or cause sb to need sth: *The situation calls for prompt action.* ◇ *'I've been promoted.' 'This calls for a celebration!'* ❶ **Call for sth** is mainly used to talk about what is needed as a result of a particular situation, especially in the phrase *This calls for a celebration/a drink/patience/new ways of thinking.*

demand [T] (not usually used in the progressive tenses) (*rather formal*) to need sth in order to be done successfully: *This sport demands both speed and strength.* ❶ **Demand** is typically used to talk about situations which need qualities in people which relate to strength, hard work or high moral standards: *This demands commitment/skill/courage/mental effort/maturity/respect/honesty.*

negative *adj.*

negative · bleak · gloomy · depressing · dark · pessimistic · miserable · downbeat · black
These words all describe a person or attitude without hope or enthusiasm for the future and expecting bad things to happen.

downbeat	negative	miserable
	bleak	dark
	gloomy	black
	depressing	
	pessimistic	

PATTERNS AND COLLOCATIONS
▸ negative / pessimistic / miserable **about** sth
▸ a negative / bleak / gloomy / pessimistic **outlook**
▸ negative / gloomy / depressing / dark / black **thoughts**
▸ a negative / bleak / gloomy / pessimistic **view**
▸ a negative / gloomy / depressing / pessimistic **conclusion**
▸ a negative / gloomy / pessimistic **report**
▸ to **paint** a negative / bleak / gloomy / depressing / pessimistic **picture** (of sb / sth)
▸ to **sound** negative / gloomy / pessimistic / downbeat
▸ to **look** bleak / gloomy / pessimistic / black
▸ **very** negative / bleak / gloomy / depressing / dark / pessimistic / miserable / black
▸ **extremely** negative / bleak / depressing / dark / pessimistic
▸ **rather** negative / bleak / gloomy / depressing / pessimistic / miserable

negative thinking only about what is bad in a situation; without hope or enthusiasm: *He's been rather negative about the idea.* ◇ *Scientists have a fairly **negative attitude** to the theory.* ◇ *We try to pinpoint the cause of any negative feelings.* ◇ *'He probably won't show up.' 'Don't be so negative.'* **OPP** **positive** → OPTIMISTIC, **positive** → GOOD 6, See also **negative** → HARMFUL

bleak /bliːk/ (of a situation) without much hope of success or improvement in the future: *The future looks bleak for the fishing industry.* ◇ *The report paints an unnecessarily bleak picture of the town.*
▸ **bleakly** *adv.*: *'There seems no hope,' she said bleakly.*

gloomy (of an attitude or situation) without much hope of success or improvement in the future: *The committee's view was in fact far from gloomy.* ◇ *He's quietly confident despite the gloomy predictions.* See also **gloom** → GLOOM

> **NOTE** BLEAK OR GLOOMY? In many cases you can use either word: *Suddenly, the future didn't look so bleak/gloomy after all.* ◇ *to paint a bleak/gloomy picture of the situation.* However, **bleak** is used especially to describe a situation or the future: *The future/outlook is/looks bleak.* **Gloomy** can be used in this way too, but it is more often used to describe sb's *view* of the situation or future: *a gloomy forecast/prognosis* ◇ *gloomy predictions/prospects/thoughts*

depressing (of a situation) making you feel very sad and without enthusiasm: *Looking for a job these days can be very depressing.* ◇ *He found the whole visit a depressing experience.* **OPP** **uplifting** → MOVING, See also **depress** → DISCOURAGE 2, **depressed** → DEPRESSED, **depression** → GLOOM
▸ **depressingly** *adv.*: *a depressingly familiar experience*

dark (of an attitude or time) unpleasant and without offering any hope that sth good will happen: *The film is a dark vision of the future.* ◇ *The theatre stayed open even in the darkest days of the war.*

pessimistic /ˌpesɪˈmɪstɪk/ expecting bad things to happen or sth not to be successful: *They appeared surprisingly pessimistic about their chances of winning.* ◇ *He seems to take a rather pessimistic view of human nature.* **OPP** optimistic → OPTIMISTIC
▸ **pessimism** *noun* [U]: *a mood of pessimism* **OPP** optimism → HOPE *noun* 1

miserable /ˈmɪzrəbl/ (of a situation) making you feel very unhappy or uncomfortable: *I spent a miserable weekend alone at home.* ◇ *What a miserable day (= cold and wet)!* ◇ *The play was a miserable failure.* See also **misery** → DISTRESS
▸ **miserably** *adv.*: *He failed miserably as an actor.*

> **NOTE** DEPRESSING OR MISERABLE? **Depressing** is used especially to show feelings of sympathy for other people's problems or the bad state of the world in

general; **miserable** usually describes your unhappy feelings about your own situation: *The report on the state of water pollution paints a depressing picture.* ◇ ~~The report on the state of water pollution paints a miserable picture.~~ ◇ *My school days were thoroughly miserable.* ◇ ~~My school days were thoroughly depressing.~~

downbeat /ˈdaʊnbiːt/ (*rather informal*) (of an attitude) dull or depressing; not hopeful about the future: *The overall mood of the meeting was downbeat.* ◇ *Their assessment of the UK's economic prospects is downbeat.* **OPP** **upbeat** → OPTIMISTIC

black (*rather informal*) without hope; very depressing: *The future looks pretty black, I'm afraid.* ◇ *It's been another black day for the north-east with the announcement of further job losses.*

neglect *noun*

neglect · disrepair · disuse
These are all words for the state of not being used or in good condition.

PATTERNS AND COLLOCATIONS
▸ sth happens **through** neglect / disuse
▸ to **fall into** / **be in** disrepair / disuse
▸ a **period of** neglect / disuse

neglect /nɪˈglekt/ [U, sing.] the fact of not giving enough care or attention to a place or thing; the state of not receiving enough care or attention: *The buildings are crumbling from* **years of neglect**. ◇ *The place smelled of decay and neglect.* ◇ *The focus on extra-curricular activities has led to a neglect of academic work.*
▸ **neglect** *verb* [T]: *The buildings had been neglected for years.* See also **neglect** → IGNORE, **neglect** → LEAVE 5

disrepair [U] (especially of buildings) the state of being broken or in bad condition because of neglect: *The station quickly fell into disrepair after it was closed.* ◇ *The castle was in such a* **state of disrepair** *that they decided not to spend money on it.*

disuse /dɪsˈjuːs/ [U] (*especially BrE*) the state of no longer being used: *The factory fell into disuse twenty years ago.* ◇ *Muscles can become weak through disuse.*

negotiate *verb* See the Topic Map for CONFLICT on p.896

negotiate · deal with sb/sth · hold talks · bargain · do a deal · haggle
These words all mean to talk to sb in order to try and reach an agreement with them.

PATTERNS AND COLLOCATIONS
▸ to negotiate / deal / hold talks / bargain / do a deal / haggle **with** sb / sth
▸ to negotiate / hold talks / do a deal **on** sth
▸ to deal with sb / hold talks / bargain / do a deal / haggle **over** sth

negotiate /nɪˈgəʊʃieɪt; *AmE* -ˈgoʊ-/ [I] to try to reach an agreement or to settle a dispute by formal discussion: *The government will not negotiate with terrorists.* ◇ *We are* **negotiating for** *the release of the prisoners.* ◇ *They have refused to negotiate on this issue.* ◇ *Her financial adviser is* **negotiating on her behalf.** ◇ *Are the employers really willing to negotiate?*
▸ **negotiation** *noun* [C, usually pl., U]: *peace/trade/wage negotiations* ◇ *They begin another* **round of negotiations** *today.* ◇ *The rent is a* **matter for negotiation** *between the landlord and tenant.* ◇ *The issue is still* **under negotiation.**

'deal with sb/sth *phrasal verb* to do business, or try to reach an agreement, with a person, company or organization: *We deal with companies all over Europe.* ◇ *He had dealt with Mr Simpson on several occasions.* See also **dealings** → COMMUNICATION

,hold 'talks *phrase* (of governments, organizations or their leaders) to have formal discussions, especially in order to try and reach an agreement or solve a problem: *The two governments held secret talks on the nuclear threat.*
▸ **talks** *noun* [pl.]: *arms/pay/peace talks*

bargain [I] to discuss prices, conditions, etc. with sb in order to reach an agreement: *He said he wasn't prepared to bargain.* ◇ *In the market dealers were bargaining with growers over the price of coffee.* See also **bargain** → AGREEMENT *noun* 1

,do a 'deal *phrase* to make an agreement with sb, especially in business or politics, on particular conditions for buying or doing sth: *We did a deal with the management on overtime.* See also **deal** → AGREEMENT 1

haggle [I] to argue with sb in order to reach an agreement, especially about the price of sth: *I left him in the market haggling over the price of a shirt.*

negotiator *noun* See the Topic Map for CONFLICT on p.896

negotiator · mediator · intermediary · arbitrator · go-between · peacemaker · liaison officer
These are all words for a person who tries to help communication between people or groups, especially in order to settle a dispute.

PATTERNS AND COLLOCATIONS
▸ a mediator / an intermediary / a peacemaker **between** A and B
▸ **through** / **via** a mediator / an intermediary
▸ an **independent** mediator / intermediary / arbitrator
▸ to **act as** (a) mediator / (an) intermediary / (a) go-between / (a) peacemaker / (a) liaison officer

negotiator /nɪˈgəʊʃieɪtə(r); *AmE* -ˈgoʊʃi-/ [C] a person who is involved in formal political or financial discussions, especially as a job: *The chief union negotiator indicated that they would reject the pay award.* ◇ *She has an image as a tough negotiator.* ❶ **Negotiator** is a general word which can describe a person who tries to settle a dispute between people or groups, or who tries to agree, or *negotiate*, the terms of a deal, contract or agreement on behalf of a person or organization.

mediator /ˈmiːdieɪtə(r)/ [C] (*rather formal*) a person or organization that helps to get an agreement between people or groups who disagree with each other: *A Swedish diplomat acted as mediator between the government and the rebels.* See also **mediate** → INTERVENE

intermediary /ˌɪntəˈmiːdiəri; *AmE* ˌɪntərˈmiːdieri/ [C] (*rather formal*) a person or organization that helps to get an agreement between people or groups by acting as a means of communication between them: *All talks have so far been conducted through an intermediary.*

NOTE **MEDIATOR** OR **INTERMEDIARY?** A **mediator** or **intermediary** can play a similar role. Usually a **mediator** is involved in a discussion where the opposing people or groups meet to try to settle their dispute. The role of the **mediator** is to try to help the discussions. An **intermediary** is often involved in a situation where the two people or groups do not want to meet and the role of the **intermediary** is to act as a neutral person who can pass messages between them.

arbitrator /ˈɑːbɪtreɪtə(r); *AmE* ˈɑːrb-/ [C] (*rather formal*) a person who is chosen to settle a dispute: *Where no agreement can be reached, the matter will be referred to an independent arbitrator.*

'go-between [C] a person who takes messages between one person or group and another: *A number of local church leaders have acted as go-betweens with the paramilitaries.*

peacemaker /ˈpiːsmeɪkə(r)/ [C] a person who tries to persuade people or countries to stop arguing or fighting and to make peace: *She always acted as the peacemaker when family arguments boiled over.*

li'aison officer [C] a person whose job is to make sure that there is a good relationship between two groups of people or organizations: *The council has a number of community liaison officers.*

nervous *adj.*

nervous · neurotic · edgy · on edge · jittery
These words all describe people who are easily frightened or behaving in a frightened way.

PATTERNS AND COLLOCATIONS
▸ a nervous / neurotic **man / woman / girl**
▸ to **feel** nervous / edgy / on edge / jittery
▸ **a bit** nervous / edgy / on edge / jittery
▸ **very** nervous / edgy / jittery

nervous easily worried or frightened: *He's not the nervous type. ◇ She was of a nervous disposition.* OPP **relaxed** → CALM, See also **nervous** → WORRIED
▸ **nerves** *noun* [pl.]: *She was a bag/bundle of nerves. ◇ I need something to calm/soothe/steady my nerves.* See also **get on sb's nerves** → ANNOY

neurotic not behaving in a reasonable, calm way, because you are worried about sth: *She became neurotic about keeping the house clean. ◇ He's a brilliant but neurotic actor.* See also **neurotic** → MENTALLY ILL

edgy (*informal*) nervous or bad-tempered, especially because you are worried about what might happen: *He became edgy and defensive. ◇ After the recent unrest there is an edgy calm in the capital.*

on 'edge *idiom* edgy: *She was always on edge before an interview.*

> NOTE **EDGY** OR **ON EDGE**? These expressions have the same meaning but **edgy** can also describe a time or event: *It was an edgy match with both players making mistakes.* **On edge** can also describe sb's nerves: *His nerves had been on edge* (= he had been nervous or bad-tempered) *all day.*

jittery (*informal*) anxious and nervous, especially about what might happen: *All this talk of war was making him jittery.*
▸ **jitters** (*often* **the jitters**) *noun* [pl.]: *We all had the jitters — we were worried we'd lose our jobs.*

new *adj.*

1 a new book/idea/approach
2 a new dress/car
3 new to this job

1 new · fresh · novel
These words all describe sth that has not existed before and is therefore unfamiliar and interesting.

PATTERNS AND COLLOCATIONS
▸ a new / fresh / novel **idea / approach / way**
▸ a new / novel **concept / design / feature / form / method**
▸ **completely / entirely / totally / relatively** new / fresh / novel

new recently made, invented or introduced; that has not existed before: *Have you read her new book? ◇ This idea isn't new. ◇ The latest model has over 100 new features.* OPP **old** → OLD 1
▸ **the new** *noun* [U]: *The songs are a good mix of the old and the new* (= ones that are new).

fresh [usually before noun] new or different in a way that adds to or replaces sth; made or experienced recently: *The defence have found fresh evidence that could form the basis of an appeal. ◇ Fresh towels are provided every day. ◇ This is the opportunity he needs to make a fresh start* (= to try sth new after not being successful at sth else). *◇ There were fresh tracks through the snow. ◇ Let me write it down while it's still fresh in my mind* (= clearly remembered because recently experienced).
▸ **freshness** *noun* [U]: *I like the freshness of his approach to the problem.*

novel (*often approving*) different from anything known before; new, interesting and often seeming slightly strange: *It was an American who came up with the novel idea of drive-in restaurants.* See also **original** → CREATIVE
▸ **novelty** *noun* [U]: *It was fun working there at first but the novelty soon wore off* (= it became boring). *◇ There's a certain novelty value in this approach.*

2 new · brand new · untried
These words all describe sth that has been recently bought or that has not been used, tried or owned by anyone before.

PATTERNS AND COLLOCATIONS
▸ new / brand new / untried **technology**
▸ a new / brand new **product / computer / house**
▸ **relatively** new / untried

new recently bought; not used or owned by anyone before: *Let me show you my new dress. ◇ A second-hand car costs a lot less than a new one.* OPP **old** → OLD 1
brand 'new completely new: *We just spent a thousand pounds on a brand new computer. ◇ She bought her car brand new.*

untried /ˌʌnˈtraɪd/ (*written*) not yet tried or tested to discover if it works or is successful: *This is a new and relatively untried procedure.*

3 new · unfamiliar with sth · unused to sth · unaccustomed to sth
These words all describe sb who is not familiar with sth because they have not experienced it before.

PATTERNS AND COLLOCATIONS
▸ new / unused / unaccustomed **to** sth
▸ unused / unaccustomed **to doing** sth
▸ **totally / quite** new / unfamiliar / unused / unaccustomed to sth
▸ **completely / relatively** new / unfamiliar

new not yet familiar with a job, situation or place because you have only just started it, or arrived there: *I was fairly new to teaching at the time. ◇ You're new in this town, aren't you? ◇ We offer intensive training to all new recruits. ◇ New arrivals should have their passports ready for inspection.*

unfamiliar with sth [not before noun] not having any knowledge or experience of sth: *The crew were unfamiliar with the safety procedures. ◇ Those unfamiliar with the area should bring a good guide book with them.* OPP **familiar with sth** → USED TO STH

unused to sth [not before noun] (*rather formal, written*) not having much experience of sth and therefore not knowing how to deal with it; not used to sth: *If you are unused to exercise, start off gently. ◇ I was unused to speaking in public. ◇ He was so unused to people questioning his authority that he didn't know how to react.* OPP **used to sth** → USED TO STH

unaccustomed to sth [not before noun] (*formal, written*) unused to sth: *He was unaccustomed to hard work. ◇ I am unaccustomed to being told what to do.* OPP **accustomed to sth** → USED TO STH

> NOTE **UNUSED TO STH** OR **UNACCUSTOMED TO STH**?
> **Unaccustomed** is more formal than **unused**; however, it is even more usual, especially in spoken English, to use neither of these words and say *not used to sth* or *not used to doing sth*: *He was not used to hard work/exercise/ speaking in public/being told what to do/people questioning his authority.*

news *noun* See the Topic Map for THE MEDIA on p.900, See also the entry for INFORMATION

news · word · bulletin
These are all words for new facts or details about sth that has happened recently.

PATTERNS AND COLLOCATIONS
▸ news/ word/ a bulletin **about**/ **on** sb/ sth
▸ news/ word **of** sb/ sth
▸ to **have**/ **get**/ **receive**/ **hear** news/ word/ a bulletin

news [U] new facts or details about recent events; reports of recent events that appear in newspapers or on television or radio: *Have you heard the news? Pat's coming home!* ◇ *That's great news.* ◇ *Tell me all your news.* ◇ *Here's a **piece of news** that may interest you.* ◇ *Do you want the **good news** or the **bad news** first?* ◇ *It's **news to me** (= I haven't heard it before).* ◇ *News of a serious road accident is just coming in.* ◇ *Programmes were interrupted for a **newsflash**.* ◇ *She is always **in the news**.* ◇ *The wedding was front-page news.* ❶ **The news** [sing.] is a regular television or radio broadcast of the latest news: *to listen to/watch the news* ◇ *I saw it **on the news**.* See also **report** → REPORT 2

word [sing.] a piece of news or information, sometimes in the form of a message: *There's been no word from them since before Christmas.* ◇ *If word gets out about the affair, he will have to resign.*

bulletin /'bʊlətɪn/ [C] a short news report on the radio or television; an official statement about sth important; a printed report that gives news about an organization or group: *More details will be given in our next news bulletin.* ◇ *The government issued an official bulletin on the President's health.* ◇ *See the June bulletin for details of future events.*

newspaper *noun* See the Topic Map for THE MEDIA on p.900, See also MAGAZINE

newspaper · paper · newsletter · tabloid · daily · broadsheet
These words all mean a set of printed sheets of paper containing news, that is published every day.

PATTERNS AND COLLOCATIONS
▸ a **local** newspaper/ paper/ newsletter/ tabloid/ daily
▸ a **national** newspaper/ paper/ daily/ broadsheet
▸ a **popular** newspaper/ paper/ tabloid/ daily
▸ a **daily** newspaper/ paper
▸ a **weekly** newspaper/ paper/ newsletter
▸ a **Sunday** newspaper/ paper/ tabloid/ broadsheet
▸ to **publish** a newspaper/ paper/ newsletter/ daily
▸ to **read** a newspaper/ paper/ newsletter

newspaper [C] a set of printed sheets of paper loosely folded together that contains news stories and articles and is published every day or every week: *She works for the local newspaper (= the company that produces it).*

paper [C] a newspaper: *The papers (= newspapers in general) soon got hold of the story.* ◇ *Have you seen today's paper?*

NOTE NEWSPAPER OR PAPER? There is no real difference in meaning between these words. **Newspaper** is often shortened to **paper** when it is clear what is being talked about. In some situations using **paper** may not be clear because the word has many different meanings: *The archive includes a scrapbook of newspaper cuttings and photographs relating to his career.* ◇ *a scrapbook of paper cuttings*

newsletter /'njuːzletə(r)/; *AmE* 'nuːz-/ [C] a printed report containing news of the activities of a club or organization that is sent regularly to all its members: *Our sailing club produces a monthly newsletter.*

tabloid /'tæblɔɪd/ [C] (*sometimes disapproving*) a newspaper with small pages that are usually about half the size of those in larger papers: *The story made the front page in all the tabloids.* ❶ **Tabloids** usually have short articles and a lot of pictures and stories about famous people, and are thought of as less serious than other newspapers.

daily [C] a newspaper published every day except Sunday: *The story was in all the dailies.*

broadsheet /'brɔːdʃiːt/ [C] (*BrE*) a newspaper printed on a large size of paper, generally considered more serious than tabloid newspapers: *The 'Daily Telegraph' is a broadsheet newspaper.*

next *adj.*

next · the following · future · subsequent · coming · later · forthcoming · upcoming · prospective
These words all describe sth that happens, exists or is mentioned after sth else or at a time after the present.

PATTERNS AND COLLOCATIONS
▸ the next/ following **month**/ **decade**/ **generation**
▸ future/ subsequent/ coming/ later **months**/ **decades**/ **generations**
▸ the next **event**
▸ future/ subsequent/ coming/ later/ forthcoming/ upcoming **events**
▸ the next/ a future/ a subsequent/ a later/ the forthcoming/ the upcoming **meeting**/ **trial**
▸ sb's next/ future/ subsequent/ later/ forthcoming/ upcoming **book**/ **books**
▸ sb's next/ subsequent/ forthcoming/ upcoming **album**
▸ the next/ the following/ a future/ a subsequent/ a later **stage**/ **chapter**
▸ the next/ a future/ a subsequent/ a later **time**
▸ sb's next/ future/ subsequent/ forthcoming/ upcoming **marriage**

next [only before noun] happening or being straight after sb/sth in time, order or space: *The next train to Baltimore is at ten.* ◇ *The next six months will be the hardest.* ◇ *The next chapter deals with the post-war situation.* ◇ *Who's next?* ◇ *The woman in the next room was talking in a very loud voice.* ◇ *I fainted and **the next thing I knew** I was in the hospital.* ❶ **Next** usually comes after *the*, except in particular expressions of time for days of the week, months of the year, seasons or fixed time periods such as *week, month, year, etc.*: *I'm going away next month (= the month after this one).* ◇ *Next Thursday (= the Thursday after this one) is 12 April.* ◇ *Next time I'll bring a book.* **OPP** last, past → LAST 2
▸ **next** *adv.*: *What happened next?* ◇ *The next best thing to flying is gliding.*
▸ **next** *noun* [sing.]: *One moment he wasn't there, the next he was.* ◇ *the week **after next***

the following next in time; that is/are going to be mentioned next: *We set off on Monday evening and arrived in New Zealand the following afternoon.* ◇ *Answer the following questions.* **OPP** previous, preceding → LAST 2

future [only before noun] happening or existing at a time after the present: *Climate change will be a very serious issue for future generations.* ◇ *We try to predict future developments in computer software.* ◇ *He met his future wife at law school.* **OPP** ex-, former → FORMER, past, previous → PREVIOUS

subsequent /'sʌbsɪkwənt/ (*rather formal*) happening or coming after sth else: *Subsequent events confirmed our doubts.* ◇ *Developments on this issue will be dealt with in a subsequent report.*
▸ **subsequently** *adv.*: *The original interview notes were subsequently lost.*

coming [only before noun] (especially of a time period) happening soon; next: *The building work may cause some disruption in the coming months.* ◇ *This coming Sunday is her birthday.*

later [only before noun] happening after sth else or at a time in the future: *This is discussed in more detail in a later chapter.* ◇ *The game has been postponed to a later date.* **OPP** earlier
▸ **later** *adv.*: *See you later.* ◇ *I'm going out **later on**.*

NOTE FUTURE OR LATER? In some cases you can use either word: *The Committee will reconsider these proposals at a future/later date.* However, **future** is used especially to talk about situations or developments in the future: *future plans/prospects/prosperity/earnings/*

benefits/trends/growth/directions. **Later** is used especially to talk about a stage in an event, process or account: *a later stage/phase/chapter/section/addition/modification/alteration/age*

forthcoming /ˌfɔːˈθkʌmɪŋ; *AmE* ˌfɔːrθ-/ [only before noun] (*rather formal*) going to happen, be published, etc. soon: *Three main parties will contest the forthcoming elections.* ◇ *The band have added an extra date to their forthcoming UK tour.*

upcoming /ˈʌpkʌmɪŋ/ [only before noun] (*especially AmE*) forthcoming: *No one knows what the outcome of the upcoming presidential election will be.* ◇ *This is a single from the band's upcoming album.*

prospective /prəˈspektɪv/ [usually before noun] (*rather formal*) expected to happen soon: *They are worried about prospective changes in the law.*

> **NOTE** COMING, FORTHCOMING, UPCOMING OR PROSPECTIVE? These words are all used to talk about sth that will or may happen soon, in the future. Do not use them to talk about one thing happening after sth else: ~~Answer the coming/forthcoming/upcoming/prospective questions.~~ **Coming** is usually used to describe a period of time: *Media attention will be focused on the Prime Minister in the coming weeks.* Use **forthcoming** and **upcoming** to describe events that are planned to happen soon: *He is understandably nervous about his forthcoming/upcoming trial.* Use **prospective** to describe events that are expected or likely to happen soon: *On learning of a prospective sale, the lawyer should call the client as soon as possible.*

nice *adj.*

1 have a nice day
2 a really nice person

1 See also the entries for SATISFYING and WONDERFUL

nice · good · pleasant · enjoyable · pleasurable
These words all describe an experience, activity or event that gives you pleasure.

PATTERNS AND COLLOCATIONS
▸ a nice / a good / a pleasant / an enjoyable / a pleasurable **experience / thing (to do)**
▸ a nice / a good / a pleasant / an enjoyable **time / evening / party**
▸ a nice / a good / a pleasant / a pleasurable **feeling / sensation**
▸ nice / good / pleasant **weather**
▸ a pleasant / an enjoyable / a pleasurable **task**
▸ It's nice / good / pleasant **to be / feel / find / have / know / meet / see…**
▸ It would be nice / good / pleasant **if…**
▸ It's nice / good **that…**
▸ very nice / good / pleasant / enjoyable

nice (*rather informal*) that you enjoy; that gives you pleasure; attractive: *Have a nice day* (= enjoy yourself today)! ◇ *If it's a nice day tomorrow* (= if the weather is good), *shall we go out?* ◇ *The nicest thing about her is that she never criticizes us.* ◇ *'Do you want to come too?' 'Yes, that would be nice.'* ◇ *Nice to meet you!* ◇ *It's been nice meeting you.* ◇ *You look nice.* ❶ **Nice** can be used before adjectives or adverbs to emphasize how pleasant sth is: *a nice hot bath* ◇ *Everyone arrived nice and early.* **Nice and** with another adjective cannot be used before a noun: ~~a nice and quiet place~~ **OPP** nasty → BAD

good (*rather informal, especially spoken*) that you enjoy; that gives you pleasure: *Did you have a good time in America?* ◇ *This is very good news.* ◇ *It would be good if he moved to London.* ◇ *We are still friends though, which is good.* **OPP** bad → BAD, terrible → TERRIBLE 1

pleasant (*rather formal*) that gives you pleasure; attractive: *It was pleasant to be alone again.* ◇ *It's nice to live in pleasant surroundings.* **OPP** unpleasant → BAD

> ▸ **pleasantly** *adv.*: *a pleasantly cool room* ◇ *I was pleasantly surprised by my exam results.*

> **NOTE** NICE, GOOD OR PLEASANT? All these words can describe times, events, feelings and the weather. **Nice** and **pleasant** can also describe places, and **nice** can describe sb's appearance.

enjoyable that you enjoy: *I always try to make my lessons enjoyable.* ◇ *Swimming is a very enjoyable way of staying in shape.*

pleasurable /ˈpleʒərəbl/ (*formal*) that you enjoy: *She had the pleasurable sensation of being swept off her feet.*

> **NOTE** ENJOYABLE OR PLEASURABLE? **Pleasurable** is a more formal word than **enjoyable** and is used especially to describe physical pleasures and feelings.

2 See also the entries for FRIENDLY 1, KIND and SWEET

nice · wonderful · lovely · charming · charismatic · engaging · likeable · personable
These words all describe a person who has a friendly, pleasant personality and is easy to like.

nice	charming	wonderful
engaging	charismatic	lovely
likeable		
personable		

PATTERNS AND COLLOCATIONS
▸ a nice / a wonderful / a lovely / a charming / a charismatic / an engaging / a likeable / a personable **man**
▸ a nice / a wonderful / a lovely / a charming / an engaging / likeable **person**
▸ a nice / a wonderful / a lovely / a charming / an engaging **woman**
▸ a nice / a wonderful / a lovely / a charming / a charismatic / an engaging / a likeable **character / personality**
▸ very nice / charming / charismatic / engaging / likeable / personable
▸ extremely nice / charming / engaging / likeable / personable
▸ really nice / wonderful / lovely / charming / engaging / likeable
▸ rather nice / wonderful / lovely / charming / engaging
▸ quite (= rather) nice / likeable / personable
▸ quite (= very) wonderful / charming

nice (*rather informal, especially spoken, approving*) kind, friendly and pleasant to be with: *Our new neighbours are very nice.* ◇ *He's a really nice guy.* ◇ *Be nice to me. I'm not feeling well.* ◇ *It was nice of them to invite us.* ◇ *I complained to the manager and he was very nice about it.* ❶ **Nice** has a very general meaning and is extremely frequent in English, especially in informal and spoken language. In writing and in more formal contexts, it can be better to use a more precise or more interesting word such as one of the other words in this group. **OPP** nasty → MEAN 1

> ▸ **nicely** *adv.*: *If you ask her nicely she might say yes.*

wonderful (*rather informal, approving*) very kind, generous and friendly: *She's a truly wonderful person.* ◇ *You've all been absolutely wonderful!*

lovely (*especially BrE, rather informal, especially spoken, approving*) very kind, generous and friendly: *Her mother was a lovely woman.*

> **NOTE** WONDERFUL OR LOVELY? You can usually use either word. **Lovely** is more frequent in spoken British English; **wonderful** is more frequent in American English, both spoken and written.

charming (*usually approving*) very polite, friendly and attractive: *She's a charming person.* ❶ **Charming** emphasizes sb's pleasant manner and their good manners (= the polite and kind way they talk to and behave towards other people). These make people like them and do things for them. However, a person who is **charming** may also have negative qualities: *He was certainly charming, but he was also ruthless and ambitious.* ◇ *What is she really like behind that charming facade?* See also **charm** → CHARM *noun*, **charm** → DELIGHT *verb*

> ▸ **charmingly** *adv.*: *She smiled charmingly at me.*

charismatic /ˌkærɪz'mætɪk/ (*often approving*) (especially of a man) having a powerful personal quality that attracts and impresses other people: *the charismatic leader of a religious sect* See also **charisma** → CHARM

engaging interesting or pleasant in a way that attracts your attention: *She had an engaging smile, which charmed everyone.*

likeable (*especially BrE*) (also **likable** *AmE, BrE*) pleasant and easy to like: *He's a very likeable man.* See also **like** → LIKE *verb*

personable /'pɜːsənəbl; *AmE* 'pɜːrs-/ (*rather formal*) (especially of a man) pleasant in appearance, character or behaviour: *Her assistant seemed a very personable young man.* ❶ **Personable** is used especially to describe your impression of sb that you do not know well.

nickname *noun* See also the entry for NAME

nickname · pseudonym · alias
These are all words for a name for sb which is not their real name.

PATTERNS AND COLLOCATIONS
▸ a nickname / pseudonym / alias **for** sb
▸ to do sth **under the** pseudonym / alias **(of)** X
▸ to **use / adopt** a nickname / a pseudonym / an alias

nickname /'nɪkneɪm/ [C] an informal, often humorous, name for a person that is connected with their real name, their personality or appearance, or with sth they have done: *How did you get your nickname?* ◇ *We used to have nicknames for all our teachers.* See also **nickname** → CALL *verb* 1

pseudonym /'suːdənɪm; *BrE* also 'sjuː-/ [C] a name used by sb, especially a writer, instead of their real name: *She writes under a pseudonym.* ◇ *He adopted the pseudonym of George Banks.*

alias /'eɪliəs/ [C] a false or different name, especially one that is used by a criminal: *A conman used an alias to infiltrate the organization.* ◇ *He checked into the hotel under an alias.*
▸ **alias** *adv.*: *Mick Clark, alias Sid Brown*

night *noun*

1 I lay awake all night.
2 Let's go out tomorrow night.

1 night · midnight · the early hours · the middle of the night · night-time · the small hours
These are all words for the time of darkness between one day and the next, or a part of this time.

PATTERNS AND COLLOCATIONS
▸ **in** the night / early hours / middle of the night / night-time / small hours
▸ **at** night / midnight / night-time
▸ **until** midnight / the early hours / the small hours
▸ **(well) into** the night / early hours / small hours
▸ the early hours / small hours **of the morning**

night [U, C] the time of darkness between one day and the next, usually when people sleep: *They sleep by day and hunt **by night**.* ◇ *The accident happened on Friday night.* ◇ *Did you hear the storm **last night**?* ◇ *I lay awake **all night**.* ◇ *Where did you **spend the night**?* ◇ *You're welcome to **stay the night** here.* ◇ *What is he doing calling **at this time of night**?* ◇ *The hotel costs €65 per person **per night**.* **OPP** **day** → DAY
▸ **nights** *adv.*: *She works nights (= at night).*

midnight [U] 12 o'clock at night: *The ship set sail shortly after midnight.* ◇ *She heard the clock strike midnight.* ◇ *The law comes into effect **on the stroke of midnight** (= at midnight exactly) tomorrow.* **OPP** **midday** → DAY

the 'early hours *phrase* the period of time very early in the morning, soon after midnight: *The raid was carried out in the early hours of 25 May.*

the ˌmiddle of the 'night *phrase* the time during the night when most people are asleep: *He always calls me in the middle of the night.*

'night-time [U] the time when it is dark: *It was night-time, but no one was asleep.* ◇ *A night-time curfew will be imposed throughout the country.* **OPP** **daytime** → DAY

> **NOTE** NIGHT, THE MIDDLE OF THE NIGHT OR NIGHT-TIME? A **night** can either be seen as a completed whole, or as a period of time that is continuing; **night-time** is a period of time that is continuing, never a completed whole; **the middle of the night** is a point in time during the night: *during the night / night-time* ◇ *~~during the middle of the night~~* ◇ *I lay awake all night.* Use **the middle of the night** to emphasize that it is an unusual time for things to happen: *Go back to bed – it's the middle of the night!* **Night-time** is used especially in compounds: *a night-time curfew / raid / visit* ◇ *night-time entertainment*

the 'small hours *phrase* (*rather informal*) the early hours: *We worked well into the small hours.*

> **NOTE** THE EARLY HOURS OR THE SMALL HOURS? The early **hours** is often used before *of* and a date or day and may be used in official reports or journalism: *The robbery took place in the early hours of Monday morning.* The **small hours** is rather informal and is not used in these contexts. It is often used to talk about sth which started in the evening and continued after midnight.

2 night · evening · sunset · dusk · twilight · nightfall · sundown
These are all words for the time of day when it gets dark or after it has got dark.

PATTERNS AND COLLOCATIONS
▸ **at** night / sunset / dusk / twilight / nightfall / sundown
▸ **in** the evening / dusk / twilight
▸ **after / before / by / until / till** sunset / dusk / nightfall / sundown
▸ **tomorrow / yesterday / Monday** night / evening
▸ a **beautiful** night / evening / sunset
▸ night / evening / dusk **falls**

night [U, C] the part of the day from the end of the afternoon until the time you go to bed: *She doesn't like to walk home **late at night**.* ◇ *My mother-in-law came for dinner **last night**.* ◇ *I saw her in town **the other night** (= a few nights ago).* **OPP** **morning** → DAY

evening [U, C] the part of the day between the afternoon and the time you go to bed: *I'll come and see you **this evening**.* ◇ *The evening performance begins at 7.30.* ◇ *We spent the long winter evenings inside by the fire.* **OPP** **morning** → DAY
▸ **evenings** *adv.*: *He works evenings (= in the evenings).*

> **NOTE** NIGHT OR EVENING? In some cases you can use either word: *Let's go out on Saturday night / evening.* **Evening** emphasizes the earlier hours, from about six o'clock onwards; **night** emphasizes the later part of the evening and can include the early hours of the next day: *We were up late last night – I didn't get to bed until two o'clock.* **Night** can also mean the whole time until it gets light the next morning; only use it to mean 'evening' if the meaning is clear: *I'm going to my sister's for the evening (= and coming back later in the evening).* ◇ *I'm going to my sister's for the night (= and not coming back until the morning).*

sunset /'sʌnset/ [U, C] the time when the sun goes down and night begins; the colours in the part of the sky where the sun slowly goes down in the evening: *After sunset the temperature drops.* ◇ *We sat by the river and **watched the sunset**.* **OPP** **sunrise** → DAWN

dusk [U] the time of day when the light has almost gone, but it is not yet dark: *We arrived in town as dusk was falling.* ◇ *She works from **dawn to dusk** and sometimes at night.* **OPP** **dawn** → DAWN

twilight /'twaɪlaɪt/ [U] the faint light or period of time at the end of the day just after the sun has gone down: *It was hard to see him clearly in the thickening twilight.* ◇ *We went for a walk along the beach at twilight.*
▸ **twilit** /'twaɪlɪt/ *adj.*: (*literary*) *She hurried out into the twilit street.*

nightfall /'naɪtfɔːl/ [U] (*formal or literary*) the time in the evening when it becomes dark: *He wanted to be home before nightfall.* **OPP daybreak** → DAWN

sundown /'sʌndaʊn/ [U] (*especially AmE, especially written*) the time when the sun goes down and night begins: *The celebration begins at sundown.*

nightmare *noun*

nightmare · ordeal · horror · trauma · hell
These are all words for an unpleasant or frightening experience.

PATTERNS AND COLLOCATIONS
▸ a nightmare / ordeal / trauma **for** sb
▸ a **terrible** nightmare / ordeal / horror
▸ a / an **absolute** / **living** nightmare / hell
▸ a **terrifying** nightmare / ordeal
▸ to **suffer** a nightmare / an ordeal / a horror / a trauma
▸ to **experience** an ordeal / a horror / a trauma
▸ to **go through** an ordeal / a trauma / hell
▸ to **survive** a nightmare / an ordeal / a trauma

nightmare /'naɪtmeə(r); AmE -mer/ [C] (*rather informal*) an experience or situation that is very frightening and unpleasant, or very difficult to deal with: *The trip turned into a nightmare when they both got sick.* ◇ *Nobody knows what's going on — **it's a nightmare!** ◇ Losing a child is most people's **worst nightmare**. ◇ These new regulations will be an administrative nightmare.*

ordeal /ɔː'diːl; 'ɔːdiːl; AmE ɔːr'diːl/ [C, usually sing.] a difficult, painful or unpleasant experience, often one that lasts for some time: *They were spared the ordeal of giving evidence in court.* ◇ *The interview was less of an ordeal than she'd expected.*

horror [C, usually pl.] all the terrible things connected with a shocking or frightening situation or experience: *He witnessed the horrors of civil war.*

trauma /'trɔːmə; AmE 'traʊmə/ [C, U] an unpleasant or shocking experience that makes you feel upset and/or anxious, usually for a long time afterwards: *She felt exhausted after the traumas of recent weeks.* See also **traumatic** → PAINFUL 2, **traumatize** → FRIGHTEN

hell [U, sing.] (*rather informal*) a very unpleasant experience or situation in which sb suffers very much: *Her parents made her life hell.* ◇ *The last few weeks have been a living hell for the refugees.*

nod *verb*

nod · gesture · wave · signal · beckon · gesticulate
These words all mean to make a sign to sb by moving a part of your body, especially your head, hand or arm.

PATTERNS AND COLLOCATIONS
▸ to nod / gesture / wave / signal / beckon / gesticulate **to** sb
▸ to nod / gesture / wave / beckon **towards** sb / sth
▸ to nod / gesture / wave **in the direction of** sb / sth
▸ to gesture / wave / signal **for** sth
▸ to gesture / wave / signal / beckon sb **forward / over / to** (a place)
▸ to gesture / beckon **with** your head / hand, etc
▸ to nod at sb / gesture / wave / signal / beckon sb **to do sth**
▸ to nod / gesture / signal **for** sb **to do sth**
▸ to gesture / signal **that…** sb should do sth / it is time to do sth, etc.
▸ to gesture / wave / signal / gesticulate **wildly**

nod (**-dd-**) [I, T] to move your head up and down as a way of saying 'yes', to show understanding, approval or enthusiasm, to greet sb or as a sign to sb: *'Is this the right*

way?' she asked. The man nodded. ◇ *Her **head nodded** in agreement.* ◇ *He **nodded his head** sympathetically.* ◇ *She nodded her approval.* ◇ *The president nodded to the crowd as he passed.* ◇ *She nodded at him to begin speaking.* ◇ *Maria nodded towards the open door.* ◇ *Michael nodded a greeting to the other visitors.*
▸ **nod** *noun* [C]: *He gave a quick nod of recognition.*

gesture /'dʒestʃə(r)/ [I] (usually used with an adverb or preposition) (*written*) to make a movement, especially with your hand, as a way of telling sb what you mean or what you want: *'I see you read a lot,' he said, gesturing towards the wall of books.* ◇ *She gestured for them to follow her.* See also **gesture** → MOVEMENT *noun*

wave [I, T] (always used with an adverb or preposition) to show where sth is or show sb where to go by moving your hand in a particular direction: *She waved vaguely in the direction of the house.* ◇ *'He's over there' said Ali, waving a hand towards some trees.* ◇ *I showed my pass to the security guard and he waved me through.* See also **wave** → MOVEMENT *noun*

signal (**-ll-**, AmE **-l-**) [I, T] to make a movement or sound as a way of giving sb a message, order or instruction: *Don't fire until I signal.* ◇ *He signalled to the waiter for the bill.* ◇ *The referee seemed to be signalling a foul.* ❶ **Signal** has a wider range of meaning than the other words in this group. You can **signal** to sb not only by making a hand or arm movement, but also by using a light, waving sth in the air, or making a sound. See also **signal** → SIGNAL *noun*

beckon [I, T] to give sb a signal using your finger, hand or head, especially to tell sb to come towards you or follow you: *I saw someone beckoning from a doorway.* ◇ *Richard beckoned the man over.*

gesticulate /dʒe'stɪkjuleɪt/ [I] (*rather formal*) to move your hands and arms around quickly, usually in an excited way, in order to attract attention or to make sb understand what you are saying: *She gesticulated wildly at the clock.* ◇ *Both men were shouting and gesticulating.*

nonsense *noun* See also the entry for LIE

nonsense · (*taboo*) bullshit · rubbish · (*taboo*) crap · bull · garbage · (*taboo*) B.S. · gibberish
These are all words for sth that you think is ridiculous or obviously untrue.

PATTERNS AND COLLOCATIONS
▸ nonsense / bullshit / rubbish / crap / bull / garbage / B.S. **about** sth
▸ **pure** nonsense / rubbish / garbage
▸ **absolute** / **total** nonsense / rubbish / crap / garbage
▸ **complete** / **utter** nonsense / rubbish / garbage
▸ to **talk** nonsense / bullshit / rubbish / crap / gibberish
▸ to **believe** that nonsense / bullshit / rubbish / crap / bull / garbage / B.S.
▸ a **load / lot** of nonsense / bullshit / rubbish / crap / bull / garbage / B.S.
▸ **What** nonsense / bullshit / rubbish / bull / garbage

nonsense [U, sing.] (*often disapproving*) comments, ideas or beliefs that you think are stupid or obviously not true; words that have no sensible meaning: *'I heard he's resigning.' 'That's nonsense.'* ◇ *What's all this nonsense about you getting married?* ◇ *It's **nonsense to** say they don't care.* ◇ *The idea is an economic nonsense.* ◇ *a book of **nonsense poems** (= poems that seem not to make sense)* **OPP sense** → WISDOM

bullshit /'bʊlʃɪt/ [U] (*taboo, slang, spoken, disapproving*) comments or ideas that you think are stupid or not true ❶ **Bullshit** is very common in spoken English, used especially to say that you think that what sb has just said is nonsense. However, it should only be used in an informal situation to sb who is your equal in age and status. If said to sb who is older or who considers themselves more important than you, it could cause very great offence: *Don't give me that bullshit* (= stop talking nonsense)! ◇ *Don't listen to him — he's full of bullshit.*

rubbish [U] (*BrE, informal, especially spoken, disapproving*) comments or ideas that you think are stupid or obviously not true: *Rubbish! You're not fat!* ◇ *Then we were told a lot* of rubbish about 'leadership' and 'bonding'. ❶ **Rubbish** is more informal than **nonsense** and can show a greater lack of respect. It is only used in British English.

crap [U] (*taboo, slang, spoken, disapproving*) comments or ideas that you think are stupid or not true ❶ **Crap** should only be used in an informal situation to sb who is your equal in age and status. If said to sb who is older or who considers themselves more important than you, it could cause very great offence: *Let's just **cut the crap** (= stop talking nonsense) and get down to business.* ◇ (*BrE*) *You're talking a load of crap.* ◇ (*AmE*) *What a **bunch of crap**.*

bull [U] (*especially AmE, slang, spoken, disapproving*) comments or ideas that you think are stupid or not true ❶ **Bull** is a less offensive way of saying **bullshit**: *That's just bull and you know it.*

garbage [U] (*especially AmE, informal, disapproving*) rubbish: *That's complete garbage!* ◇ *Don't believe all that garbage the government tells you.*

B.S. /ˌbiː ˈes/ *abbr.* (*AmE, taboo, slang*) bullshit: *That guy's full of B.S.*

gibberish /ˈdʒɪbərɪʃ/ [U] words that have no meaning or are impossible to understand: *He speaks gibberish all the time. He's mad.*

normal *adj.*

normal · ordinary · average · common · typical
These words all describe people, things or events that are not special or different.

▸ to be normal / common **for sb to do sth / for sth to happen**
▸ the normal / ordinary / average / common **man**
▸ a normal / an ordinary / the average **person**
▸ the normal / ordinary / common **sort**
▸ a normal / an ordinary / an average / a typical **working day**
▸ **in the** normal / ordinary **course of events / business / things**
▸ **pretty / fairly** normal / ordinary / average / typical
▸ **quite** normal / ordinary / typical

normal what you would expect; happening in most cases: *Her temperature was normal.* ◇ *The help desk is available during normal office hours.* ◇ *He should be able to **lead a perfectly normal life**.* ◇ *It's normal to feel tired after such a long journey.* ◇ *Life continued **as normal**.* ◇ *The skin surface is resistant to infection **under normal circumstances**.* **OPP exceptional** → SPECIAL, **strange, odd, weird** → STRANGE 1
▸ **normality** /nɔːˈræm-/ *noun* [U]: *They are hoping for a **return to normality** now that the war is over.*
▸ **normally** *adv.*: *The exercise normally takes twenty minutes.* ◇ *His heart is beating normally.*

ordinary [usually before noun] not unusual or special in any way: *We were an ordinary family.* ◇ *The images can be printed on ordinary paper.* ◇ *It began as an ordinary sort of day.* ◇ *This was no ordinary meeting.* ◇ (*BrE*) *He was not a nervous person **in the ordinary way** (= usually).* **OPP extraordinary** → REMARKABLE, **special** → SPECIAL

NOTE NORMAL OR ORDINARY? Something that is **normal** is as it should be or as you would expect: ~~Her temperature was ordinary.~~ ◇ ~~It's ordinary to feel tired after such a long journey.~~ People or things that are **abnormal** are not as they should be. The word **ordinary** makes no comment about how things should be, only about how things are, whether you think this is good or bad. People or things that are **extraordinary** are special or unusual in some way and this also may be a good or a bad thing. See also **abnormal** → ABNORMAL, **ordinary** → AVERAGE

average approximately the same as most others: *An entrance fee of £5 is about average.* ◇ *The route is for walkers of average ability.* See also → AVERAGE

common [only before noun] not unusual or special in any way; ordinary: *I wanted a recording of the common cuckoo.* ◇ *Oats were the staple food of **the common people** (= the majority of the population, who are not rich).* ◇ *In*

most people's eyes she was nothing more than a **common criminal**. ◇ *Polite letters of rejection are a matter of **common courtesy**.* ❶ **Common** has the same meaning as **ordinary**, but is mostly used in a fixed number of different ways. It describes animals or plants that are of the most usual type and not rare or unusual in any way: *common gulls / frogs / ragwort*; it describes people who have no special rank or position: *common people / soldiers / criminals*; and it describes good qualities of a sort or level that you expect most people to have: *common courtesy / decency* See also **common sense** → WISDOM

typical happening in the usual way; showing what sth is usually like: *Each woman was asked to describe a typical working day.* ◇ *Typical interview questions are 'Why do you want to study law?' or 'Why did you choose this college?'* **OPP atypical** → UNUSUAL
▸ **typically** *adv.*: *The factory typically produces 500 cars a week.* ◇ *Typically, the contracts were for five years.*

note *noun*

note · sound · pitch · key · tone · timbre
These are all words for a characteristic of the sound made by the voice or a musical instrument.

▸ a **high / higher / low / lower** note / pitch
▸ a **deep / rich** tone / timbre
▸ a / the **wrong** note / key

note [C] a single musical sound made by the voice or a musical instrument; the written or printed sign for a musical note: *She played the first few notes of the tune on the piano.* ◇ *I played a lot of wrong notes because I was so nervous.*

sound [C, U] the effect that is produced by the music of a particular singer or group of musicians: *He has a sound unlike any other guitarist.* ◇ *I like their sound.*

pitch [sing., U] how high or low a sound is, especially a musical note: *The pitch of the drum can be raised by tightening the skin.*

key [C] a set of related notes, based on a particular note: *The sonata was written in the key of E flat major.* ◇ *This piece changes key many times.* ❶ Pieces of music are usually written using a particular **key**, from which the notes of the piece are taken.

tone [C] the quality of a sound, especially the sound of a musical instrument or one produced by electronic equipment: *The rich tone of the oboe is intended to give this piece a sad mood.* ◇ *The tone and volume controls allow you to adjust the sound of the radio.*

timbre /ˈtæmbə(r)/ [C, U] (*formal*) the quality of sound that is produced by a particular voice or musical instrument: *She thought she could listen forever to the warm, deep timbre of his voice.* ◇ *Timbre is what makes one instrument or voice sound different from another.*

NOTE TONE OR TIMBRE? These words are very close in meaning. **Tone** has a wider range, and is often used when the quality of sound can be adjusted, for example when playing or recording music electronically. **Timbre** is formal, and refers more to the essential quality of the sound that a voice or musical instrument has.

notice *verb* See also the entries for LOOK 1 and SEE

notice · note · detect · observe · witness · perceive · take sth in
These words all mean to see sth, especially when you pay careful attention to it.

▸ to notice / note / detect / observe / perceive **that...**
▸ to notice / note / detect / observe / perceive **how / what / where / who...**
▸ to notice / observe / witness **sth happen / sb do sth**
▸ to **quickly** notice / note / detect / take in sth

▸ to **immediately / suddenly / soon** notice / detect / perceive sth
▸ to **just** notice / note / observe sth

notice [T, I] (not usually used in the progressive tenses) to see, hear or become aware of sb/sth; to pay attention to sb/sth: *The first thing I noticed about the room was the smell.* ◇ *I couldn't help noticing that she was wearing a wig.* ◇ *I noticed them come into the room.* ◇ *I didn't notice him leaving.* ◇ *My husband hardly seems to notice me any more.* ◇ *She wears those strange clothes just to **get herself noticed**.* ◇ *People were making fun of him but he didn't seem to notice.* See also **notice** → ATTENTION *noun*, **noticeable** → VISIBLE

note [T] (not usually used in the progressive tenses) (*rather formal*) to notice or pay careful attention to sth: *Note the fine early Baroque altar inside the chapel.* ◇ *Note how these animals sometimes walk with their tails up in the air.* ◇ *It should be noted that dissertations submitted late will not be accepted.* ❶ **Note** is very common in business English: *We note your concerns regarding an increase in costs.* ◇ *Note that the prices are inclusive of VAT.*

detect /dɪ'tekt/ [T] (not usually used in the progressive tenses) (*rather formal*) to discover or notice sth, especially sth that is not easy to see, hear, etc: *The tests are designed to detect the disease early.* ◇ *This is an instrument that can detect very small amounts of radiation.* ◇ *Do I detect a note of criticism in your voice?*

observe /əb'zɜːv; *AmE* əb'zɜːrv/ [T] (not used in the progressive tenses) (*formal*) to see or notice sb/sth: *Have you observed any changes lately?* ◇ *He was observed to enter the bank.* ◇ *All the characters in the novel are closely observed* (= seem like people in real life). ❶ This pattern is only used in the passive. See also **observe** → LOOK *verb* 1, **observer** → WITNESS

witness [T] (*rather formal*) to see sth happen because you are there when it happens: *She was shocked by the violent scenes she had witnessed.* ◇ *Police have appealed for anyone who witnessed the incident to contact them.* ◇ (*formal*) *The last century witnessed an unprecedented increase in violent crime* (= It happened during that period). See also **witness** → WITNESS *noun*

perceive /pə'siːv; *AmE* pər's-/ [T] (not used in the progressive tenses) (*formal*) to notice or become aware of sth, especially sth that is not obvious: *I perceived a change in his behaviour over those months.* ◇ *The patient was perceived to have difficulty in breathing.* ❶ This pattern is usually used in the passive. See also **perception** → AWARENESS

,**take sth 'in** *phrasal verb* to notice sth with your eyes: *He took in every detail of her appearance.*

nuisance *noun*

nuisance · inconvenience · pain · headache
These are all words for things, people or situations that are annoying or make people angry.

▸ a **real** nuisance / pain / headache

nuisance /'njuːsns; *AmE* 'nuː-/ [C, usually sing.] (*disapproving*) a thing, person or situation that is annoying or causes trouble or problems: *I don't want to be a nuisance so tell me if you want to be alone.* ◇ *I hope you're not **making a nuisance of yourself**.* ◇ *It's a nuisance having to go back tomorrow.* ◇ *What a nuisance!*

inconvenience /ˌɪnkən'viːniəns/ [U, C] (*rather formal, sometimes disapproving*) trouble or problems, especially concerning what you need or would like yourself; a person or thing that causes problems or difficulties: *We apologize for the delay and regret any inconvenience it may have caused.* ◇ *I have already **been put to** considerable inconvenience.* ◇ *I can put up with minor inconveniences.* See also **inconvenience** → TAKE ADVANTAGE OF SB/STH *verb*, **inconvenient** → WRONG 3

pain [C, usually sing.] (*informal, disapproving*) a person, thing or situation that is very annoying: *She can be a real pain when she's in a bad mood.* ◇ *It's a pain having to go all that way for just one meeting.* ◇ *That man's **a pain in the neck**!*

headache [C] (*rather informal, disapproving*) a situation that causes worry or trouble: *The real headache will be getting the bank to lend you the money.*

number *noun*

1 a large number of people
2 He lives at number 12.

1 number · amount · volume · sum · quantity
These words are all used to refer to a group of people or things or a collection of sth, and to talk about how much/many there is/are.

▸ **the** number / amount / volume / quantity **of** sth
▸ **a / an** number / amount / quantity **of** sth
▸ a **number / quantity of people / things**
▸ an **amount / a volume / a quantity of information**
▸ an **amount / a sum of money**
▸ a **/ an reasonable / considerable / significant / large / substantial / great / huge / enormous / vast / small** number / amount / volume / sum / quantity
▸ **record / sufficient** numbers / amounts / volumes / sums / quantities
▸ a **limited** number / amount / volume / quantity
▸ a **tiny** number / amount / sum / quantity
▸ **growing / increasing** numbers / amounts / volumes / sums / quantities
▸ **the total / sheer** number / amount / volume / quantity

number [C] a group of people or things ❶ **Number** is often used to talk about how many of sb/sth there are: *The number of homeless people has increased dramatically.* ◇ *Huge numbers of* (= very many) *animals have died.* ◇ *A number of* (= some) *problems have arisen.* ◇ *I could give you **any number of** (= a lot of) reasons for not going.* ◇ *We were eight **in number** (= there were eight of us).* ◇ ***Sheer weight of numbers** (= the large number of soldiers) secured them the victory.* ❶ Because it is used with plural nouns, a plural verb is needed after *a (large, small etc.) number of...*: *A number of people were late for the meeting.*

amount [C, U] some money; a collection of sth: *You will receive a bill for the full amount.* ◇ *Small amounts will be paid in cash.* ◇ *The server is designed to store huge amounts of data.* ◇ *There's been **any amount of** (= a lot of) research into the subject.* ❶ **Amount** is usually used to talk about things that are uncountable nouns.

volume [U, C] (*rather formal*) the amount or number of sth: *We had to work hard to keep up with the sheer volume* (= large amount) *of business.* ◇ *New roads are being built to cope with the high volumes of traffic.* ◇ *Sales volumes fell 0.2% in June.* ❶ **Volume** is used to talk about how much/many there is/are of sth. In this meaning, it is not possible to say *a volume of sth* without qualifying it, either with an adjective or a clause: *He managed to get through a considerable volume of work.* ◇ *We were attracting a volume of business that, frankly, we could not handle.*

sum [C] an amount of money: *You will be fined the sum of £200.* ◇ *She inherited a large sum of money when her father died.* ◇ *He is now earning a six-figure sum.* ◇ *Huge sums have been invested in this project.* ◇ *She was given a **lump sum** (= an amount paid at once rather than on separate occasions).*

quantity [C, U] an amount or number of sth: *A substantial quantity of jewellery was taken during the burglary.* ◇ *It is a product that is cheap to produce **in large quantities**.* ◇ *There is a discount for goods bought **in quantity**.* ◇ *Is the medicine available in sufficient quantity?* ◇ *The data is limited in terms of both quality and quantity.*

NOTE NUMBER, AMOUNT OR QUANTITY? **Number** is used with plural countable nouns: *a number of books/dogs/people* ◇ *a number of money/rain/wood*. **Amount** is usually used with uncountable nouns: *a large amount of time/money/information* ◇ *a large amount of coins/dogs/girls*. **Quantity** can be used with both: *a large quantity of wine/food/books* but is slightly more formal and less frequent.

2 See also the entry for FIGURE

number · letter · figure · symbol · digit · character · mark · sign

These are all words for a single item that you write or print, that has a fixed meaning.

PATTERNS AND COLLOCATIONS
▸ to write sth **in** numbers / letters / figures / symbols
▸ the symbol / character / sign **for** sth
▸ a **single** letter / figure / symbol / digit / character
▸ **double** letters / figures / digits
▸ a **binary** / **decimal** number / figure / digit
▸ to **print** / **write** a number / letter / figure / digit / character / mark
▸ to **bear** / **be marked with** / **have** a number / letter / figure / symbol
▸ a symbol / character / sign **means** / **indicates** sth
▸ a **sequence** / **series** / **set** / **string** of numbers / letters / figures / symbols / digits / characters

number [C] used to show the position of sth in a series; a series of figures used to identify sth or to communicate by telephone or fax: *The song reached number 5 in the charts.* ◇ *What is your social security number, please?* ◇ *My phone number is 266998.* ◇ *I'm sorry, I think you have the **wrong** **number*** (= wrong telephone number). ◇ *He dialled the number, then changed his mind and hung up.*

letter [C] a written or printed symbol that represents a sound used in speech: *'B' is the second letter of the alphabet.* ◇ *Write your name in **capital letters**.*

figure [C] a written or printed symbol that represents one of the numbers between 0 and 9 ❶ **Figure** is usually used to talk about a series of symbols that represent an amount larger than 9. For a single symbol between 0 and 9, **number** is more often used: *She's earning a six-figure salary* (= over 100 000 pounds, dollars or euros). ◇ *His*

salary is now in six figures. ◇ (*BrE*) *Inflation is now in single/double figures.* ❶ In American English use *in single/double digits*.

symbol [C] a number, letter or shape that has a fixed meaning, especially in science, mathematics or music: *What is the chemical symbol for copper?* ◇ *A list of symbols used on the map is given in the index.*

digit /ˈdɪdʒɪt/ [C] any of the ten numbers from 0 to 9: *The number 57306 contains five digits.* ◇ (*AmE*) *Inflation is now in single/double digits.* ❶ In British English use *in single/double figures*.

NOTE FIGURE OR DIGIT? **Figure** is used to talk about amounts of money, but **digit** is usually used with 'number', when it means a series of figures to identify sth, not an amount: *The deal has been signed for a seven-figure sum.* ◇ *She dialled the four-digit extension number.* Either word can be used to talk about an increase, although **digit** is more common than **figure** in American English: *The company is currently experiencing double figure/digit growth.* **Digit** is used more often than **figure** in texts about the use of technology and numbers appearing on equipment such as radio alarm clocks, calculators, cash machines, etc.

character [C] (*rather formal or technical*) a letter, sign, mark or symbol used in writing, printing or on computers: *This size of type produces a line 30 characters long.* ◇ *These are the Chinese characters meaning 'wind' and 'water'.*

mark [C] (used in compounds) a written or printed sign that you use in order to write clearly, showing things such as where sentences end: *punctuation marks* ◇ *a question/exclamation mark*

sign [C] (used in compounds) a mark used to represent sth, especially in mathematics: *a pound/dollar sign* ◇ *a plus/minus sign*

NOTE SYMBOL OR SIGN? Apart from being used to talk about the letters representing chemical elements, **symbol** usually refers to a shape or small picture with a fixed meaning. A **sign** is likely to be more simple, consisting of one or two lines, such as a *dollar sign* or an *equals sign*. The meaning of a **symbol** may be less well-known than the meaning of a **sign**.

O o

objective *adj.*

objective · impartial · neutral · disinterested · non-partisan · unbiased

These words all describe sb/sth that is not influenced by personal opinions or feelings and can therefore be considered fair.

▸ objective/ neutral **about** sb/ sth
▸ an objective/ an impartial/ a neutral/ a disinterested/ an unbiased **observer**
▸ an objective/ an impartial/ a neutral/ an unbiased **opinion**/ **assessment**/ **analysis**
▸ objective/ impartial/ disinterested/ unbiased **advice**
▸ to **remain** objective/ impartial/ neutral
▸ **completely**/ **totally** objective/ impartial/ neutral/ disinterested/ non-partisan/ unbiased
▸ **quite** objective/ impartial/ neutral/ disinterested
▸ **fairly** objective/ impartial/ neutral
▸ **truly** objective/ impartial/ neutral/ unbiased
▸ **strictly** objective/ impartial/ neutral/ non-partisan

objective not influenced by personal opinions or feelings, but considering only the facts: *There's little objective evidence to suggest that he is guilty.* ◇ *It's hard for parents to be objective about their own children.* **OPP** **subjective**
→ OWN
▸ **objectively** *adv.*: *Try to weigh up the issues as objectively as you can.*
▸ **objectivity** /ˌɒbdʒek'tɪvəti; AmE ˌɑːb-/ *noun* [U]: *The survey's claims to scientific objectivity are highly dubious.*
impartial /ɪm'pɑːʃl; AmE ɪm'pɑːrʃl/ not supporting one person, group or idea more than another: *Teenagers need access to confidential and impartial advice.* ◇ *As chairman, I must remain impartial.*
▸ **impartiality** /ˌɪmˌpɑːʃi'æləti; AmE ˌpɑːrʃi-/ *noun* [U]: *The BBC is supposed to maintain strict impartiality in its broadcasts.*
▸ **impartially** *adv.*: *There are fears that the matter will not be investigated impartially.*
neutral /'njuːtrəl; AmE 'nuː-/ not supporting or helping either side in a disagreement, competition or debate: *Very few journalists are politically neutral.* ◇ *The UN are sending six neutral observers to the talks.*
▸ **neutrality** /nju:'træləti; AmE nu:-/ *noun* [U]: *I'm afraid we cannot guarantee the neutrality of the courts.*
disinterested not influenced by personal feelings, or by the chance of getting some advantage for yourself: *I was merely a disinterested spectator in the whole affair.* **OPP** **interested** ❶ An **interested** person is in a position to gain from a situation or be affected by it: *As an interested party, I was not allowed to vote.*
non-parti'san not supporting the ideas of any particular political party or set of political ideas: *Our work has always been non-violent and non-partisan.* **OPP** **partisan**
→ BIASED
unbiased (also **unbiassed**) /ʌn'baɪəst/ fair and not influenced by your own or sb else's opinions or wishes: *We'd like an unbiased opinion, if possible.* **OPP** **biased**
→ BIASED

obsession *noun*

obsession · preoccupation · mania · neurosis · hang-up · fixation · complex

These are all words for a state of mind in which sb thinks or worries about more than is normal.

▸ an obsession/ a preoccupation/ a neurosis/ a hang-up/ a fixation/ a complex **about** sb/ sth
▸ an obsession/ a preoccupation/ a mania/ a fixation **for** sb/ sth
▸ an obsession/ a preoccupation/ a fixation **with** sb/ sth
▸ sb's **current** obsession/ preoccupation/ fixation
▸ a **new** obsession/ preoccupation/ mania
▸ to **become** an obsession/ a preoccupation
▸ to **develop** an obsession/ a neurosis/ a complex

obsession /əb'seʃn/ [U, C] (*usually disapproving*) the state in which a person's mind is completely filled with thoughts about one particular thing or person so that they cannot think of anything else; a thing or person that sb thinks about too much: *Her devotion to him bordered on obsession.* ◇ *She has an unhealthy obsession with her diet.*
▸ **obsess** *verb* [T, usually passive, I]: *She's completely obsessed with him.* ◇ *I think you should try to stop obsessing about food.*
preoccupation /priˌɒkju'peɪʃn; AmE -ˌɑːk-/ [U, C] the state of thinking about sth continuously, especially when you ignore everything else, usually because you are worried about it; sth that you think or worry about frequently or for a long time: *She found his preoccupation with money irritating.* ◇ *Their chief preoccupation was how to feed their families.*
▸ **preoccupied** *adj.*: *He was too preoccupied with his own thoughts to notice anything wrong.*
mania /'meɪniə/ [C, usually sing., U] an extremely strong desire or enthusiasm for sth, often shared by a lot of people at the same time: *He had a mania for fast cars.* ◇ *Football mania is sweeping the country.*
neurosis /njʊə'rəʊsɪs; AmE nʊ'roʊ-/ (pl. **neuroses** /-əʊsiːz; AmE -oʊ-/) [C, U] (*medical*) a mental illness in which a person suffers strong feelings of fear and worry: *Those of anxious temperament are more likely to develop anxiety neurosis.* ❶ **Neurosis** is a serious medical condition; however, in non-medical usage **neurosis** is used to describe any strong fear or worry: *This obsession with time is a modern neurosis and one we all have to live with.*
'hang-up [C] (*informal, usually disapproving*) an emotional problem about sth that makes you particularly embarrassed or worried: *He's got a real hang-up about his height.*
▸ ˌhung 'up *adj.* [not before noun]: *You're not still hung up on that girl?*
fixation /fɪk'seɪʃn/ [C] (*usually disapproving*) a very strong interest in sb/sth, that is not normal or natural: *He's got this fixation with cleanliness.*
▸ **fixated** *adj.* [not before noun]: *He is fixated on things that remind him of his childhood.*
complex /'kɒmpleks; AmE 'kɑːm-/ [C] a mental state that is not normal; the state of being worried and confused about sth in a way that is not normal: *He suffers from a guilt complex.* ◇ *Don't mention her weight — she has a complex about it.*

obstacle *noun*

obstacle · barrier · hurdle · stumbling block · impediment · roadblock · handicap · hindrance
These are all words for sth that makes it difficult for sb to do or achieve sth.

PATTERNS AND COLLOCATIONS
▸ an obstacle / a barrier / a stumbling block / an impediment / a handicap / a hindrance **to** sb / sth
▸ **without** obstacles / impediment / hindrance
▸ **despite** the obstacles / barriers / handicap
▸ a **major** obstacle / barrier / hurdle / stumbling block / impediment / roadblock / handicap / hindrance
▸ a **big** obstacle / hurdle / stumbling block / roadblock / handicap
▸ a **real** obstacle / barrier / stumbling block / handicap / hindrance
▸ the **main** obstacle / barrier / hurdle / stumbling block / impediment / roadblock
▸ a **legal** obstacle / barrier / impediment / roadblock / handicap
▸ a **financial** obstacle / barrier / hurdle / roadblock
▸ to **face** an obstacle / a barrier / a hurdle / a roadblock
▸ to **remove** an obstacle / a barrier / a stumbling block / an impediment / a roadblock
▸ to **overcome** an obstacle / a barrier / a hurdle / a handicap

obstacle /ˈɒbstəkl; *AmE* ˈɑːb-/ [C] a situation or event that makes it difficult for sb to do or achieve sth: *The huge distances involved have proved to be an obstacle to communication.* ◇ *So far, we have managed to overcome all the obstacles placed in our path.*
barrier [C] a problem, situation or rule that prevents sb from doing sth or that makes sth impossible: *Cost should not be a barrier to the use of legal services.* ◇ *There has been a gradual reduction in subsidies and trade barriers.*

> **NOTE** OBSTACLE OR BARRIER? An **obstacle** makes it difficult to do sth, but it is usually still possible to do it by making a great effort; a **barrier** actually prevents sb from doing sth because it means that they do not or cannot attempt it.

hurdle [C] a problem or difficulty that must be solved or dealt with before sb can achieve sth: *Well, we've cleared the first hurdle; let's see what happens next.* ◇ *The next hurdle will be getting her parents' agreement.* ❶ **A hurdle** is often considered as one in a series of problems or difficulties.
'stumbling block [C] (*especially journalism*) a problem or disagreement that prevents sb from achieving sth, or sth from making progress: *The peace process encountered another stumbling block in mid-June.*
impediment /ɪmˈpedɪmənt/ *noun* [C] (*formal*) a fact or situation that makes it difficult for sb to do sth or for sth to make progress: *There are no legal impediments to their appealing against the decision.*
roadblock /ˈrəʊdblɒk; *AmE* ˈroʊdblɑːk/ [C] (*AmE, especially journalism*) something that prevents a plan from going ahead: *The project faces legal roadblocks.*
handicap [C] something, especially a lack of skill, knowledge or experience, that makes it more difficult for sb to do sth: *Not speaking the language proved to be a bigger handicap than I'd imagined.* See also **handicap** → DISABILITY, **handicap** → BLOCK *verb* 1
hindrance /ˈhɪndrəns/ [C, usually sing.] (*rather formal*) a person or thing that makes it more difficult for sb to do sth or for sth to happen: *To be honest, she was more of a hindrance than a help.* **OPP** help → GOOD THING, See also **hinder** → BLOCK 1

obvious *adj.*

obvious · natural · logical · understandable
These words all describe sth that is normal, usual and what you would expect.

PATTERNS AND COLLOCATIONS
▸ obvious / natural / logical / understandable **that...**
▸ natural / logical **to do sth**

▸ natural / logical **for** sb to do sth
▸ the obvious / natural / logical **thing to do / choice / conclusion / solution**
▸ the obvious / a natural / an understandable **temptation**
▸ a natural / a logical / an understandable **reaction / response**
▸ **perfectly / quite** obvious / natural / logical / understandable

obvious that most people would think of or agree to; normal and as you would expect: *There's an obvious question that no one has asked.* ◇ *The solution was obvious.* ◇ *'What should we do?' 'It's obvious, isn't it?'* ◇ *It's obvious that she'd be upset.*
> **obviously** *adv.*: *Obviously we don't want to spend too much money.*

natural normal; as you would expect: *It's natural that he would want to see his own son.* ◇ *It's perfectly natural for you to feel annoyed.* ◇ *Children have a natural desire for affection and security.* ◇ *The man died of **natural causes** (= not by violence).* ◇ *He thought inequality was all part of the **natural order** of things.* See also **natural** → NATURAL
> **naturally** *adv.*: *Naturally, I get upset when things go wrong.* ◇ *This leads naturally to my next point.*

> **NOTE** OBVIOUS OR NATURAL? **Obvious** is used especially to describe a decision, choice or course of action. **Natural** can be used in the same way, but is more frequently used to describe feelings: *a natural feeling / desire / fear / concern / anxiety / reluctance*. When **obvious** is used with these words, it does not mean 'as you would expect', but 'easy to notice': ~~Children have an obvious desire for affection.~~ ◇ *George ignored Lucy's obvious desire to be left alone.* Both **obvious** and **natural** can be used to describe behaviour in the phrase *It's obvious / natural that sb would...* but only **natural** can be used in the phrase *it's natural for sb to do sth*: ~~It's perfectly obvious for you to feel annoyed.~~

logical (of a course of action or line of reasoning) seeming natural, reasonable or sensible: *It was a logical thing to do in the circumstances.* ◇ *It seemed logical to try and contact the child's mother.* **OPP** illogical ❶ Something that is **illogical** is not sensible or not thought out in a logical way: *illogical behaviour / arguments*
> **logically** *adv.*: *The problem is that you can never trust them to act logically.*
understandable (of feelings, behaviour or reactions) seeming normal and reasonable in a particular situation: *Their attitude is perfectly understandable.* ◇ *It was an understandable mistake to make.*
> **understandably** *adv.*: *They were understandably disappointed by the result.*

occasional *adj.*

occasional · the odd... · sporadic · intermittent
These words all describe things that happen or appear sometimes but not very often or not at regular intervals.

PATTERNS AND COLLOCATIONS
▸ occasional / sporadic / intermittent **bursts** of sth
▸ on an occasional / a sporadic / an intermittent **basis**
▸ occasional / sporadic / intermittent **contact / attacks**
▸ the occasional / odd **bit / bout / spot** of sth

occasional [only before noun] happening or done sometimes but not very often: *He makes occasional references in the letters to the planned autobiography.* ◇ *She found occasional work on television.* ◇ *You have to expect a few difficulties and the occasional setback.* **OPP** regular, frequent → FREQUENT, See also **occasionally** → SOMETIMES
the odd... [only before noun] (*rather informal, especially spoken*) happening or appearing a few times, but not regular or frequent: *It doesn't matter on the odd occasion, but it's occurring regularly.* ◇ *I love the long bare hills with just the odd clump of trees.* ❶ When you use **the odd...** about things that are bad or wrong it suggests that you do not think they are very important: *You have to expect the odd mistake.* ◇ *He did take the odd afternoon off.*

sporadic /spə'rædɪk/ (*written*) happening at intervals that are not regular or very frequent; happening in only a few places without any pattern: *Sporadic gunfire was reported each night.* ◇ *Planning controls protect the countryside from sporadic development.* ❶ *Sporadic* usually describes sth unpleasant such as violence or disease.
▸ **sporadically** *adv.*: *Fighting continued sporadically for two months.*

intermittent /ˌɪntə'mɪtənt; *AmE* -ţər'm-/ stopping and starting often over a period of time, but not regularly: *A day of intermittent rainstorms followed.* ◇ *There had been twenty years of intermittent warfare.* **OPP** **continuous** → CONTINUOUS
▸ **intermittently** *adv.*: *The protests continued intermittently.*

occur to sb *phrasal verb*

occur to sb · come/spring to mind · cross your mind · dawn on sb · strike · hit · come to sb
These words are all used to talk about a thought or idea coming into sb's mind.

PATTERNS AND COLLOCATIONS
▸ It occurs to sb / crosses sb's mind / dawns on sb / strikes sb / hits sb / comes to sb **that**...
▸ It occurs to sb / crosses sb's mind **to do sth**
▸ a / an **thought** / **idea** occurs to sb / comes to mind / crosses your mind / strikes sb / hits sb / comes to sb
▸ to **suddenly** occur to / dawn on / strike / hit / come to sb

oc'cur to sb *phrasal verb* (**-rr-**) [no passive] (not used in the progressive tenses) (*rather formal*) (of an idea or thought) to come into sb's mind, so that they think of sth or suspect that sth is true: *The idea occurred to him in a dream.* ◇ *It didn't occur to him that his wife was having an affair.* ◇ *It never even occurred to her to ask for help.*

come/spring to 'mind *idiom* (not used in the progressive tenses) if sth **comes/springs to mind**, you suddenly remember or think of it: *When discussing influential modern artists, three names immediately come to mind.*

cross your 'mind *idiom* (not used in the progressive tenses) (of an idea or thought) to occur to sb: *It never crossed my mind that she might lose* (= I was sure that she would win).

NOTE **OCCUR TO SB** OR **CROSS YOUR MIND?** There is little difference in the meaning or range of these expressions. **Cross your mind** is often more casual, used when sb does not want it thought that sth is too important to them, or has a thought that they later reject: *'Were you hoping she'd offer you a job?' 'Well, the thought had crossed my mind* (= I was hoping, but not too much)'. ◇ *It crossed my mind to resist, but I thought better of it.* **Occur to sb** is often used when the thought is more important or sudden, or to express surprise (and sometimes to suggest criticism) that sb else has NOT thought of sth: *It suddenly occurred to me that no one had any idea where I was.* ◇ ~~It suddenly crossed my mind...~~ ◇ *It never even occurred to her to ask for help.* ◇ ~~It never even crossed her mind to ask for help.~~

'dawn on sb *phrasal verb* [no passive] if sth **dawns on you**, you begin to realize it for the first time: *Suddenly it dawned on me that they couldn't possibly have met before.* ◇ *The horrible truth was slowly dawning on me.*

strike [T] (not used in the progressive tenses) (of a thought or idea) to come suddenly into sb's mind with a powerful effect: *An awful thought has just struck me.* ◇ *I was struck by her resemblance to my aunt.*

hit [T, no passive] (not used in the progressive tenses) (*informal*) (of a thought or idea) to strike sb suddenly: *I couldn't remember where I'd seen him before, and then it suddenly hit me.*

NOTE **STRIKE** OR **HIT?** **Hit** is more informal and slightly stronger than **strike**. In this meaning **hit** is not usually followed by *by*: *I was struck by a thought.* ◇ ~~I was hit by a thought.~~

'come to sb *phrasal verb* [no passive] (not used in the progressive tenses) (of an idea) to come into your mind: *The idea came to me in the bath.*

odour (*BrE*) (*AmE* **odor**) *noun* See also the entry for
SMELL

odour · stench · smell · stink · reek
These are all words for an unpleasant smell.

| odour | stink | stench |
| smell | | reek |

PATTERNS AND COLLOCATIONS
▸ an odour / a stench / a smell / a stink / a reek **of** sth
▸ an **acrid** odour / stench / smell / stink
▸ a **foul** / **putrid** / **powerful** odour / stench / smell
▸ a **pungent** odour / smell / reek
▸ to **give off** an odour / a stench / a smell
▸ an odour / a stench / a smell / a stink / a reek **fills** sth
▸ an odour / a stench / a smell / a stink **comes from** sth

odour (*BrE*) (*AmE* **odor**) /'əʊdə(r); *AmE* 'oʊ-/ [C] (*rather formal, especially written*) a smell, especially a strong unpleasant one: *There was an odour of decay in the house.* ◇ *Use this spray to remove everyday household odours.* ◇ *He suffers badly from **body odour**.*

stench [sing.] (*especially written or literary*) a very strong unpleasant smell: *The stench of rotting fish filled the hut.* ◇ *The stench of death and decay hung in the air.* ❶ *A* **stench** is probably the strongest and most unpleasant of these smells. **Stench** is used especially in literary writing to describe smells connected with bodies and death; collocates include *blood, death, decay, fear, sweat, urine* and *rotting meat/flesh/fish/vegetables*.

smell [sing.] (*rather informal, especially spoken*) an unpleasant smell: *What's that smell?* ◇ *Yuk! What a smell!* ◇ *See if you can get rid of that smell.* See also **smelly** → SMELLY
▸ **smell** *verb* [I]: *It smells in here, can you open a window?*

stink [sing.] (*informal*) a strong unpleasant smell: *What a stink! Open the window!* ◇ *The room was filled with the stink of sweat and urine.* See also **stinking** → SMELLY
▸ **stink** *verb* [I]: (*informal*) *Her breath stank of garlic.* ◇ *It stinks of smoke in here.*

reek [sing.] a very strong unpleasant smell: *The reek of gunpowder and smoke grew stronger.* ❶ *A* **reek** is nearly as strong as a **stench** but it does not have such a strong connection with death.
▸ **reek** *verb* [I]: *His breath reeked of tobacco.*

offend *verb*

offend · insult · shock · abuse
These words all mean to upset sb because of sth that you say or do.

PATTERNS AND COLLOCATIONS
▸ to **feel** offended / insulted / shocked
▸ **deeply** offended / insulted / shocked

offend [T, often passive, I] to make sb feel upset because of sth that you say or do that is rude or embarrassing: *They'll be offended if you don't go to their wedding.* ◇ *Some people found his jokes funny but others were deeply offended.* ◇ *A TV interviewer must be careful not to offend.*
▸ **offence** *noun* [U]: *I'm sure he* **meant no offence** *when he said that.* ◇ *The photo on the cover of the book may* **cause offence** *to some people.* ◇ *No one will* **take offence** (= feel offended) *if you leave early.*

insult /ɪn'sʌlt/ [T, often passive] to say or do sth that is rude to sb and offends them: *I have never been so insulted in all my life!* ◇ *She felt insulted by the low offer.* ◇ *Do you really expect me to believe that? Don't* **insult my intelligence!** See also **insulting** → INSULTING
▸ **insult** /'ɪnsʌlt/ *noun* [C]: *The crowd was shouting insults*

at the police. ◇ *His comments were seen as an **insult to** the president.*

> **NOTE** **OFFEND** OR **INSULT?** To **insult** sb is to say or do sth that is rude to them, usually deliberately. To **offend** them is to make them feel upset, either because you have insulted them or because you have been rude or thoughtless about sb/sth else that is important to them.

shock [I, T] to make sb feel offended or disgusted by your bad language or behaviour, especially deliberately: *These movies deliberately set out to shock.* ◇ *She enjoys shocking people by saying outrageous things.* See also **shocking** → OUTRAGEOUS

abuse [T] to make rude or offensive remarks to or about sb: *Journalists covering the case have been threatened and abused.*

> ▸ **abuse** *noun* [U]: *to scream/hurl/shout abuse* ◇ *a* **stream/torrent of abuse**

offensive *adj.* See also the entry for INSULTING

offensive · abusive · bad · filthy · rude · foul · coarse
These words all describe unpleasant or shocking language or people.

PATTERNS AND COLLOCATIONS
▸ offensive / abusive **to** sb
▸ offensive / abusive / bad / filthy / rude / foul **language**
▸ an offensive / an abusive / a filthy / a rude / a coarse **word**
▸ an offensive / an abusive / a rude **gesture / remark / comment**
▸ an offensive / a filthy / a rude **joke**
▸ **very / quite** offensive / abusive / rude / foul / coarse
▸ **rather** offensive / rude / foul / coarse

offensive (*rather formal*) causing sb to feel upset, insulted or annoyed: *I've had enough of her offensive remarks.* ◇ *His comments were deeply offensive to a large number of single mothers.* ◇ *This job is stressful enough even without clients being offensive.* **OPP** **inoffensive** ❶ A person or thing that is **inoffensive** is not likely to offend or upset anyone: *a shy, inoffensive young man*

abusive /ə'bju:sɪv/ (*rather formal*) very offensive; criticizing sb in an unfair and offensive way: *He was fined for making abusive comments to the referee.* ◇ *He became abusive when he was drunk.*

bad [usually before noun] offensive: *Most of the complaints received were about bad language.* ❶ In this meaning, **bad** is always used in the phrase *bad language*.

filthy very offensive and usually connected with sex: *That's enough of your filthy language!* ◇ *He's got a filthy mind* (= is always thinking about sex).

rude (*especially BrE*) offensive or embarrassing and often connected with sex: *The joke is too rude to repeat.* ◇ *Someone made a rude noise.*

foul /faʊl/ [usually before noun] (of language) including rude words and swearing: *He called her the foulest names imaginable.* ◇ *I'm sick of her foul mouth* (= habit of swearing).

coarse /kɔ:s; AmE kɔ:rs/ (*rather formal*) rude and offensive, especially about sex: *He constantly made coarse jokes about his girlfriend.*

offer *noun*

1 an offer of help
2 an offer of £2 500 for the car

1 offer · approach · overture · advances · proposal
These are all words for an act of suggesting that you do sth for sb, or that sb does sth with you.

PATTERNS AND COLLOCATIONS
▸ an offer / an approach / overtures / advances / a proposal **to** sb
▸ an offer / overtures / a proposal **of** sth
▸ an offer / a proposal **of marriage**
▸ (a) **friendly** offer / approach / overtures
▸ to **make / receive** an offer / an approach / overtures / advances / a proposal

▸ to **reject** sb's offer / approach / overtures / advances / proposal
▸ to **respond to / spurn** sb's offer / overtures / advances / proposal
▸ to **accept / decline / refuse / turn down** an offer / a proposal

offer [C] an act of suggesting that you do sth for sb or that you give sth to sb: *Thank you for your kind offer of help.* ◇ *I accepted her offer to pay.* ◇ *I took him up on his offer of a loan.* ◇ *You can't just turn down offers of work like that.*

approach [C] (*rather formal*) an act of speaking to sb about sth, especially when making an offer or request: *The club has made an approach to a local company for sponsorship.* ◇ *She resented his persistent approaches.*

> ▸ **approach** *verb* [T]: *We have been approached by a number of companies that are interested in our product.*

overture /'əʊvətʃʊə(r); -tjʊə(r); AmE 'oʊvərtʃər; -tʃʊr/ [C, usually pl.] a suggestion or action by which sb tries to make friends, start a business relationship or have discussions with sb else: *He began making overtures to a number of merchant banks.* ◇ *Maggie was never one to reject a friendly overture.*

> **NOTE** **APPROACH** OR **OVERTURE? Approach** is often used to talk about a more businesslike way of speaking to sb; **overture** suggests more of an attempt to persuade sb to like you or want to do business with you.

advances [pl.] (*rather formal*) attempts to start a sexual relationship with sb: *He had made advances to one of his students.* ◇ *She rejected his sexual advances.* ❶ **Advances** are often described as *amorous* or *sexual*, but even when no adjective is used, the sexual meaning is understood.

proposal [C] an act of formally asking sb to marry you: *She had been hoping for a sweet old-fashioned proposal of marriage.* ❶ **Proposal** also has the much more frequent and general meaning of a formal suggestion or plan. See also **proposal** → PROPOSAL

> ▸ **propose** *verb* [I, T]: *He was afraid that if he proposed she might refuse.* ◇ *She **proposed to** me!* ◇ *to propose marriage*

2 offer · bid · tender
These are all words for the act of offering a particular amount of money to buy sth, or to do work or provide services for a particular amount of money.

PATTERNS AND COLLOCATIONS
▸ an offer / a bid / a tender **for** sth
▸ a **competitive** offer / bid / tender
▸ to **put in / receive / accept** an offer / a bid / a tender
▸ to **invite** offers / bids / tenders
▸ to **make / withdraw** an offer / a bid

offer [C] an amount of money that sb is willing to pay for sth: *I've had an offer of £2 500 for the car.* ◇ *They made me an offer I couldn't refuse.* ◇ *The original price was $3 000, but I'm **open to offers*** (= willing to consider offers that are less than that).

bid [C] (*especially business or journalism*) an offer by a person or company to pay a particular amount of money for sth; an offer to carry out work or provide goods or a service for a particular price, in competition with other companies: *The company mounted a hostile **takeover bid** for its rival.* ◇ *At the auction* (= a public sale where things are sold to the person who offers most), *the highest bid for the picture was £200 000.* ◇ *Any more bids?* ◇ *The company **submitted a bid** for the contract to clean the hospital.* ◇ (*AmE* also) *a **bid on** the contract*

> ▸ **bid** *verb* [I, T]: *They successfully bid for the contract.* ◇ (*AmE* also) *They successfully **bid on** the contract.* ◇ *Which other cities are bidding to host the 2016 Olympics?*

tender [C] (*especially BrE, rather formal, business*) a formal offer to carry out work or provide goods or a service for a particular price, in competition with other companies: *The local authority has invited tenders for the supply of school meals.* ◇ *Cleaning and laundry services have been **put out to tender*** (= companies have been asked to make offers to supply these services).

> ▸ **tender** *verb* [I]: *Local firms were invited to tender for the building contract.*

offer *verb*

1 offer good facilities/prospects
2 offer to help/offer sb a job

1 offer · extend · hold out sth · tender · volunteer
These words all mean to make sth available or to provide the opportunity for sth.

PATTERNS AND COLLOCATIONS
▶ to offer/ extend a / an **invitation** / **welcome**
▶ to offer/ extend **aid** / **credit** / **hospitality** / **sympathy** / **condolences** / **congratulations**
▶ to offer/ hold out the **hope** / **possibility** / **prospect** of sth
▶ to offer/ tender **advice**
▶ to offer/ volunteer a / an **suggestion** / **opinion**
▶ to offer/ volunteer **information**
▶ to offer/ tender your **apologies** / **resignation**

offer [T] to make sth available or to provide the opportunity for sth: *The hotel offers excellent facilities for families.* ◇ *The job didn't offer any prospects for promotion.* ◇ *He did not offer any explanation for his behaviour.*
extend [T] (*formal*) to offer or give sth to sb, especially as a way of welcoming sb or expressing kind feelings towards them: *We extend our sympathy to the families of the victims.* ◇ *The bank refused to extend credit to them* (= to lend them money). ❶ **Extend** is a more formal way of saying **offer** when you are talking about *aid, credit, hospitality*, a *welcome* or an *invitation*, or expressions of feelings including *greetings, congratulations, condolences* and *sympathy*.
hold 'out sth *phrasal verb* to offer a chance, hope or possibility of sth: *Doctors hold out little hope of her recovering.* ❶ **Hold out** is usually followed by *hope*, but other possible collocates are *possibility, promise* and *prospect*.
tender [T] (*formal*) to offer or give sth to sb: *He has tendered his resignation to the Prime Minister.* ❶ **Tender** is a more formal way of saying **offer** when you are talking about giving your *resignation* or *apologies*.
volunteer /ˌvɒlən'tɪə(r); *AmE* ˌvɑːlən'tɪr/ [T] (*written*) to suggest sth or tell sb without being asked: *Nobody asked her, and she didn't volunteer any information.* ❶ People typically **volunteer** a *statement*, a *suggestion*, *information*, a *comment* or an *opinion*.

2 offer · hold sth out · bid · volunteer
These words are all used for saying that sb is willing to do sth for sb or give sth to sb.

PATTERNS AND COLLOCATIONS
▶ to offer sth/ hold sth out **to** sb
▶ to offer sth/ bid / volunteer **for** sth
▶ to offer/ volunteer **to do sth**
▶ to offer/ volunteer **help** / **your services**
▶ to offer/ hold out your **hand**
▶ to offer/ hold out a **plate** / **glass**
▶ to offer/ bid **£2 000** / **a sum**

offer [T] to say that you are willing to do sth for sb or give sth to sb: *He offered £4 000 for the car.* ◇ *They are offering a reward for the return of their cat.* ◇ *They decided to offer the job to Jo.* ◇ *They decided to offer Jo the job.* ◇ *The kids offered to do the dishes.* ◇ *'I'll do it,' she offered.*
hold sth 'out *phrasal verb* to put your hand or arms, or sth in your hand, towards sb, especially to give or offer sth: *He held out the keys and I took them.* ◇ *I held out my hand to steady her.*
bid [T, I] to offer to pay a particular price for sth, especially at an auction ❶ An **auction** is a public event at which things are sold to the person who offers the most money for them: *I bid £2 000 for the painting.* ◇ *We wanted to buy the chairs but another couple were **bidding against** us.* ❶ **Bid** is usually used in a situation in which several people want to buy the same thing.

volunteer /ˌvɒlən'tɪə(r); *AmE* ˌvɑːlən'tɪr/ [I, T] to offer to do sth without being forced to do it or without getting paid for it: *Several staff members volunteered for early retirement.* ◇ *Jill volunteered to organize a petition.* ◇ *He volunteered his services **as** a driver.*
▶ **volunteer** *noun* [C]: *Are there any volunteers to help clear up?* ◇ *volunteer carers/helpers*

office *noun*

1 Are you going to the office today?
2 Come into my office.

1 office · headquarters · work · workplace · base
These are all words for a room, set of rooms or building where people work.

PATTERNS AND COLLOCATIONS
▶ (a / an) **permanent** / **temporary** / **main** / **local** / **regional** / **administrative** office / headquarters / base
▶ (a) **district** / **national** / **international** / **council** / **government** / **campaign** office / headquarters
▶ (a / an) **army** / **military** / **enemy** / **rebel** / **operational** / **business** headquarters / base
▶ to **go to** / **come to** / **arrive at** / **get to** / **leave** the office / headquarters / work
▶ to **have** / **establish** / **set up** an office / headquarters / a base

office [C] a room, set of rooms or building where people work, usually sitting at desks: *The company is moving to new offices on the other side of town.* ◇ *Are you going to the office today?* ◇ *We ought to inform **head office**.*
headquarters [C, U+sing./pl. v.] a place from which an organization or military operation is controlled; the people who work there: *Several companies have their headquarters in the area.* ◇ *I'm now based at headquarters.* ◇ *Headquarters in Dublin have agreed.* ❶ **Headquarters** is often abbreviated to **HQ**: *There's a general message to all staff from HQ.*
work [U] (used without *the*) the place where you do your job: *I go to work at 8 o'clock.* ◇ *The new legislation concerns health and safety **at work**.* ◇ *Her friends from work came to see her in the hospital.* See also **work** → WORK *noun* 2
workplace /'wɜːkpleɪs; *AmE* 'wɜːrk-/ [C] (*especially business or journalism*) the office, factory, etc. where people work: *The introduction of new technology into the workplace has affected everyone in some way.* ◇ *These safety standards apply to all workplaces.* ❶ **Workplace** is often used in the phrase *the workplace*. It is mostly used in broadcasting, journalism, and in fairly formal work contexts.
base [C] the main place where a business operates from: *The company has its base in New York, and branch offices all over the world.* ❶ **Base** is a fairly general term, and can also be used to talk about the main place where a person lives or stays.

2 office · study · studio · workroom
These are all words for a room in which a person works.

PATTERNS AND COLLOCATIONS
▶ a **large** / **small** office / study / studio / workroom

office [C] a room in which a particular person works, usually at a desk: *Some people have to share an office.* ◇ *Come into my office.* ❶ An **office** may be in a person's home or in a company building, but it is usually used for doing paid work rather than personal reading or writing.
study [C] a room, especially in sb's home, used for reading and writing: *She crossed the hallway and opened the door to her private study.*
studio /'stjuːdiəʊ; *AmE* 'stuːdioʊ/ [C] a room where an artist works: *He was hoping to convert the cellar into a photographic studio.*

workroom [C] a room in which work is done, especially work that involves making things: *The jeweller has a workroom at the back of his shop.* See also **workshop** → FACTORY

official *noun* See the Topic Map for THE INDIVIDUAL AND SOCIETY on p.894

official · officer · councillor · councilman/ councilwoman · mayor · commissioner · civil servant · secretary · bureaucrat
These are all words for sb who works in a government department or a large organization, especially in a position of authority.

PATTERNS AND COLLOCATIONS
▸ a **senior** official / officer / councillor / civil servant / bureaucrat
▸ a **chief** official / officer / commissioner / civil servant / secretary
▸ a **junior** official / officer / civil servant
▸ a **deputy** officer / mayor / commissioner / secretary
▸ a **local** official / officer / councillor / councilman / mayor / commissioner / civil servant / bureaucrat / secretary
▸ a **regional** / **district** official / officer / commissioner / secretary
▸ a **city** / **town** official / councillor / councilman / mayor
▸ a **public** official / officer
▸ a **government** official / officer / bureaucrat
▸ a **party** official / bureaucrat / secretary
▸ a **union** official / officer / secretary
▸ to **appoint** an official / an officer / a commissioner
▸ to **elect (sb as)** a councillor / mayor / councilman
▸ to **serve as** an officer / a councillor / a councilman / mayor / a commissioner / secretary

official [C] a person who is in a position of authority in a large organization or a government department: *A senior official in the State Department issued a statement.*

officer [C] (often in compounds) an official: *The charity has a full-time **press officer** working with the national newspapers.* ◇ *the company's Chief Executive/Financial Officer* (= CEO/CFO)

NOTE OFFICIAL OR OFFICER? Official is a general word which can refer to any person in a position of authority: *government/bank/Olympic officials.* Officer is often part of a job title for a particular position: *an environmental health officer* ◇ *the chief medical officer*

councillor (*AmE* also **councilor**) /ˈkaʊnsələ(r)/ [C] a member of a council (= a group of people who are elected to govern an area); used as a title: *Councillor Bob Harris.* ◇ *Talk to your **city councillor** about the problem.* ◇ (*BrE*) *She served as a Conservative **councillor for** Harwich for many years.*

'councilman, 'councilwoman (also **Councilman, Councilwoman**) [C] (*AmE*) a councillor: *'This is a first for the city,' said Councilman Wallis.*

mayor (also **Mayor**) /meə(r)/; *AmE* ˈmeɪər/ [C] the head of a town, borough or county council; the head of the government of a town or city: *He became the first directly elected mayor of London in 2000.*

commissioner (also **Commissioner**) /kəˈmɪʃənə(r)/ [C] a member of a commission (= an official group of people who are responsible for controlling sth or finding out sth): *a commissioner for the Central Collegiate Hockey Association* ◇ *The merger has been referred to the **European** Competition **Commissioner**.*

,civil 'servant /ˌsɪvl/ [C] a person who works in the civil service (= the government departments in a country), as a paid official, rather than as an elected politician: *The committee will question a number of ministers and high-ranking civil servants.*

secretary [C] an official of a club, society, political party or trade union, who deals with writing letters, keeping records and making business arrangements; (in Britain) an assistant of a government minister or an ambassador, either a senior civil servant or a junior minister: *She served as **club secretary** for 25 years.* ◇ *Anyone interested*

in joining the society should contact **membership secretary** Bob Barwood. ◇ *He had talks with the Chief **Secretary** to the Treasury.*

bureaucrat /ˈbjʊərəkræt; *AmE* ˈbjʊr-/ [C] (*often disapproving*) an official working in an organization or a government department, especially one who follows rules too strictly: *He was just another **faceless bureaucrat**.* See also **bureaucracy** → AUTHORITIES, **bureaucracy** → BUREAUCRACY

official *adj.* See the Topic Map for THE INDIVIDUAL AND SOCIETY on p.894

official · formal · authorized · licensed · accredited
These words all describe things that are connected with sb in a position of authority or done with their permission.

PATTERNS AND COLLOCATIONS
▸ to be authorized / licensed / accredited **by** sb / sth
▸ to be authorized / licensed **to do** sth
▸ official / formal / authorized / licensed **institutions**
▸ an official / a formal / an authorized **body**
▸ an official / a formal / an accredited **programme**
▸ an official / a formal **announcement** / **request** / **enquiry** / **complaint** / **protest** / **apology** / **agreement**
▸ an authorized / accredited **practitioner** / **representative** / **supplier**
▸ the official / authorized **biography** of sb

official [usually before noun] connected with the job of sb who is in a position of authority; agreed to, said or done by sb who is in a position of authority: *The minister was in Berlin on official business.* ◇ *She attended **in her official capacity** as mayor.* ◇ *The news is not yet official.* ◇ *The country's official language is Spanish.* ◇ *The report revealed official corruption* (= corrupt behaviour by officials) *in relation to road building.* ❶ *The* **official** *account of an event is the one that is told to the public by people in authority. It may or may not be true: That was the **official version** of events but nobody believed it.* ◇ *The **official line** is that the date for the election has not yet been decided.* **OPP unofficial** → UNOFFICIAL
▸ **officially** *adv.*: *The library will be officially opened by the local MP.* ◇ *Officially, he resigned because of ill health.*

formal following an agreed or official way of doing things: *Once the loan has been approved we'll send a formal agreement for you to sign.* ◇ *Formal diplomatic relations between the two countries were re-established in December.* ◇ *What this announcement does is put the arrangement on a formal basis.* **OPP informal** → INFORMAL
▸ **formally** *adv.*: *The accounts were formally approved by the board.*

authorized (*BrE* also **-ised**) /ˈɔːθəraɪzd/ done with or having the permission of sb in authority: *The family agreed to an authorized biography of the artist.* ◇ *There was a notice on the door: Authorized Personnel Only.* **OPP unauthorized** → UNOFFICIAL

licensed /ˈlaɪsnst/ done, owned or run with official permission; owning a licence to do sth: *There aren't enough licensed taxis in the city.* ◇ *The handgun had been bought from a licensed dealer.* ◇ *There are only two companies licensed to produce the vaccine.* **OPP unlicensed** → UNOFFICIAL

accredited /əˈkredɪtɪd/ [usually before noun] officially recognized or approved; working with official permission: *Only accredited golfing journalists were allowed near the players.* ◇ *The former business school is now a fully accredited British university.*
▸ **accreditation** /əˌkredɪˈteɪʃn/ *noun* [U]: *the accreditation of engineering qualifications*

offspring *noun*

offspring · baby · young · litter · brood
These are all words for baby animals.

PATTERNS AND COLLOCATIONS
▸ to **produce** / **rear** / **raise** offspring / babies / young / a litter / brood
▸ to **give birth to** offspring / a baby / young / a litter

offspring /ˈɒfsprɪŋ; AmE ˈɔːf-; ˈɑːf-/ (pl. **offspring**) [C, usually pl.] young animals that are born to parent animals: *Female badgers may give birth to as many as five offspring.*

baby [C] a very young animal: *What do you call a baby kangaroo? ◇ After some months, the baby learns to walk along branches by holding onto its mother's fur.*

young [pl.] young animals of a particular type or that belong to a particular mother: *It carries its young on its back.*

> **NOTE** OFFSPRING, BABY OR YOUNG? Offspring and young are more scientific, factual words. **Baby** is used in everyday language by people who are not experts, and can suggest that the speaker finds the animal attractive or lovable: *the lion's offspring/young ◇ a little baby lion.* The parent animal must be mentioned or understood when using **offspring** and **young**, but not with **baby**: *The females stay close to their offspring/young. ◇ Oh look! That one's just a baby! ◇ ~~That one's just an offspring/a young!~~.*

litter [C] a number of baby animals that a mother produces at one time: *a litter of puppies/kittens*

brood /bruːd/ [C+sing./pl. v.] all the young birds or creatures that a mother produces at one time: *A brood averages eight to ten ducklings.*

often *adv.*

often · frequently · a lot · routinely · habitually
These words all describe things that are done or happen many times.

PATTERNS AND COLLOCATIONS
▸ often / routinely **available**
▸ frequently / routinely / habitually **used**
▸ to **happen** often / frequently / a lot
▸ to **occur** often / frequently
▸ to **wear sth** often / frequently / a lot / habitually
▸ **how** often / frequently?
▸ **quite** often / frequently / a lot
▸ **fairly / very** often / frequently

often many times: *I've often wondered what he looked like. ◇ The dog often went missing for days. ◇ How often does it happen? ◇ You should come and see us more often. ◇ She likes to get out of the city as often as possible. ◇ It's not often that I receive fan letters.* **OPP** **rarely, seldom** → RARELY. See also **often** → USUALLY

frequently (*rather formal*) often: *It was a word he used frequently. ◇ Passengers complained that trains were frequently cancelled. ◇ It's the most frequently asked question these days.* **OPP** **infrequently** → RARELY See also **frequent** → FREQUENT

> **NOTE** OFTEN OR FREQUENTLY? In many cases you can use either word. **Frequently** is more formal than **often** and is used especially to talk about things that affect or are done by people in general; **often** is more often used to talk about things that you do or that affect you personally.

a lot (*informal, especially spoken*) often: *We used to go out quite a lot. ◇ They worry about it a lot.* **OPP** **not much** ❶ The opposite is **not much**: *We didn't go out much.*

routinely /ruːˈtiːnli/ as part of a routine; very often; (of doing sth bad) so often that it is considered normal: *A red blood cell count and blood pressure were routinely recorded. ◇ He is routinely cited as one of America's best businessmen. ◇ The regime was accused of routinely torturing prisoners.* See also **routine** → PROCESS *noun*, **routine** → USUAL *adj.*

habitually /həˈbɪtʃuəli/ as a habit; very often: *She was without the steel-framed glasses she habitually wore. ◇ The rules were habitually broken.* See also **habitual** → FREQUENT, **habitual** → USUAL

oil *noun*

oil · gas · fuel · coal · petrol · gasoline · petroleum · diesel · fossil fuel
These are all words for substances that provide heat or light energy when they are burnt.

PATTERNS AND COLLOCATIONS
▸ unleaded fuel / gas / petrol / gasoline
▸ sth **runs on** oil / gas / (a particular kind of) fuel / petrol / gasoline / diesel
▸ to **fill the car up with** gas / petrol / diesel
▸ to **run out of** oil / gas / fuel / petrol / diesel
▸ the oil / gas / fuel / coal / petroleum **industry**
▸ oil / gas / fuel / coal / petrol / gasoline / petroleum / diesel **prices**
▸ oil / gas / fuel / coal / petrol / gasoline / petroleum / diesel / fossil fuel **consumption**
▸ oil / gas / fuel / coal / petroleum / fossil fuel **reserves**
▸ an oil / a gas / a fuel / a petrol / a gasoline / a diesel **tank**
▸ an oil / a gas / a fuel **leak**
▸ an oil / a gas / a petrol / a gasoline / a diesel **engine**
▸ an oil / a gas / a fuel / a petrol / a gasoline **tanker**
▸ gas / petrol / gasoline / diesel **fumes**

oil [U] a thick liquid mineral that is found in rock under the ground or the sea and is used to produce several useful substances, especially ones that can be burnt to produce heat energy: *Several companies are **drilling for oil** in the region. ◇ oil wells ◇ At the time, oil was trading at around $18 per barrel.* ❶ **Crude oil** (also **crude**) is oil in its natural state, before it has been treated with chemicals. However, it is usually called simply **oil** unless you want to emphasize that it has not been treated.

gas [U] a particular type of gas or mixture of gases used as fuel for heating and cooking: *Much of Britain's energy is supplied by **natural gas** from the North Sea. ◇ All the apartments are fitted with gas central heating.* ❶ In American English **gas** is also the usual word for **petrol/gasoline** (see below): *He still had plenty of gas in the tank. ◇ We need to find a gas station.*

fuel [U, C] any material that produces heat or power, usually when it is burnt: *Most of the houses are heated with **solid fuel** (= wood or coal). ◇ Domestic fuel bills are set to rise again this winter.*

coal [U] a hard black solid mineral that is found below the ground and burnt to produce heat: *Put some more coal on the fire. ◇ a **lump of coal** ◇ a **coal mine***

petrol [U] (*BrE*) a liquid used as fuel, for example in car engines. **Petrol** is obtained from crude oil (= oil from under the ground/sea): *Does your car run on **unleaded petrol**?* ❶ In American English this is called **gas** or **gasoline**.

gasoline /ˈɡæsəliːn/ [U] (*AmE, rather formal*) petrol: *They bought a ten-gallon can of gasoline.* ❶ In most spoken and written American English, **gas** is used instead of **gasoline**.

petroleum /pəˈtrəʊliəm; AmE ˈtroʊ-/ [U] crude oil (= mineral oil that is found under the ground or the sea and is used to produce petrol, diesel, etc.): *The government suspended its supplies of petroleum to the country as a result of the crisis.*

diesel /ˈdiːzl/ a type of heavy oil used as a fuel instead of petrol, for example in buses and some cars: *The diesel engine burns its fuel much more efficiently.*

fossil fuel [C, U] a fuel such as coal, oil or natural gas, that was formed over millions of years from the remains of animals or plants: *Carbon dioxide is produced in huge amounts when fossil fuels are burnt.*

old *adj.*

1 old habits
2 an old man/woman

1 old · ancient · long-standing · antique
These words all describe sth that has existed for a long time.

PATTERNS AND COLLOCATIONS
▶ an old / an ancient / a long-standing **tradition / belief / method / problem**
▶ an old / ancient / antique **chair / clock / coin**
▶ an old / ancient **custom / way / ritual / city / civilization**

old that has existed or been used for a long time: *This carpet's getting pretty old now.* ◇ *It's not easy to break old habits.* ◇ *He always gives the same old excuses.* ◇ *It's one of the oldest remaining parts of the church.* **OPP new** → NEW 1, **new** → NEW 2

ancient /ˈeɪnʃənt/ that has existed for a very long time; that belongs to a period of history that is thousands of years in the past: *The area is still covered by huge ancient forests.* ◇ *This philosophy dates back to ancient Greece.* ◇ *(humorous) He's ancient — he must be at least fifty!* **OPP modern** → RECENT, See also **historic** → FAMOUS

long-'standing [usually before noun] *(rather formal)* that has existed for a long time: *The country's long-standing relationship with the US was finally under strain.* ◇ *Long-standing grievances were aired at the meeting.* ❶ **Long-standing** can describe relationships, customs and feelings but NOT objects, places or people. **OPP recent** → RECENT

antique /ænˈtiːk/ [usually before noun] *(of furniture, jewellery, etc.)* old and often valuable: *It's an antique mahogany desk that belonged to my great-grandfather.*

2 old · elderly · aged · long-lived · mature
These words all describe sb/sth that has lived for a long time or that usually lives for a long time.

PATTERNS AND COLLOCATIONS
▶ an old / an elderly / an aged / a long-lived / a mature **man / woman**
▶ an old / an elderly / an aged / a mature **gentleman / lady / couple**
▶ sb's old / elderly / aged **father / mother / aunt / uncle / relative**

old having lived for a long time; no longer young: *She's getting old — she's 75 next year.* ◇ *The old man lay propped up on cushions.* ◇ *These are some of the oldest trees in the world.* **OPP young** → YOUNG
▶ **the old** *noun* [pl.]: *The old (= old people) feel the cold more than the young.*

elderly *(rather formal)* *(of people)* used as a polite word for 'old': *She is very busy caring for two elderly relatives.* **OPP young** → YOUNG
▶ **the elderly** *noun* [pl.]: *caring for the elderly*

aged /ˈeɪdʒɪd/ *(formal)* *(usually of people)* very old: *Having aged relatives to stay in your house can be quite stressful.* ◇ *(informal, humorous) I'm not sure if my aged car can make it up that hill.* **OPP young** → YOUNG
▶ **the aged** *noun* [pl.]: *The authorities have a duty to provide services for the sick and the aged (= very old people).*

long-'lived having a long life; lasting for a long time: *Trout are a long-lived species.* ◇ *Everyone in my family is exceptionally long-lived.* ◇ *Good management was essential to the creation of a long-lived, successful business.*

mature /məˈtʃʊə(r); -ˈtjʊə(r); AmE -ˈtʃʊr; -ˈtʊr/ used as a polite or humorous way of saying that sb is no longer young: *The shop specializes in clothes for the mature woman.* ◇ *He's a man of mature years.* See also **mature** → ADULT

old-fashioned *adj.*

old-fashioned · obsolete · out of date · outdated · antiquated · dated
These words all describe sth which is not modern or fashionable, or sb who does not have modern or fashionable ideas.

PATTERNS AND COLLOCATIONS
▶ an old-fashioned / obsolete / outdated / antiquated **system**
▶ old-fashioned / outdated / antiquated / dated **attitudes / ideas / views**
▶ an old-fashioned / outdated **method / style**

▶ an old-fashioned / obsolete **word**
▶ old-fashioned / dated **clothes / furniture**
▶ to **become** old-fashioned / obsolete / out of date / outdated / dated
▶ to **look** old-fashioned / out of date / dated
▶ **rather** old-fashioned / out of date / outdated / antiquated / dated
▶ a **bit / little** old-fashioned / out of date / dated
▶ **very** old-fashioned / out of date / outdated / dated
▶ **now** obsolete / out of date / outdated / dated
▶ **already** obsolete / out of date / outdated / antiquated

old-'fashioned *(sometimes disapproving)* not modern; no longer fashionable; *(of a person)* believing in old or traditional ways; having traditional ideas: *The bedroom was full of heavy old-fashioned furniture.* ◇ *My parents are old-fashioned about marriage and relationships.* ❶ **Old-fashioned** is sometimes a slightly disapproving term, used by people who prefer modern things and attitudes. However, it can also be used in an approving way to show enthusiasm for the past: *(approving) It was a lovely little old-fashioned café.* **OPP modern** → EXPERIMENTAL, **modern** → MODERN

obsolete /ˈɒbsəliːt; AmE ˌɑːbsəˈliːt/ *(sometimes disapproving)* no longer used because sth new has been invented: *Factories cannot compete if they are using obsolete technology.* ◇ *With technological changes many traditional skills have become obsolete.*

out of 'date *(sometimes disapproving)* without the most recent information and therefore no longer useful: *These figures are several years out of date.* ◇ *an out-of-date map / dictionary* ◇ *(figurative) Suddenly she felt old and out of date.* **OPP up to date** → MODERN

outdated /ˌaʊtˈdeɪtɪd/ *(usually disapproving)* without the most recent information, ideas or technology and therefore no longer useful: *It is an outdated and inefficient system.* ◇ *The college was struggling with outdated equipment and facilities.*

NOTE OUT OF DATE OR OUTDATED? Sometimes you can use either word: *These figures are out of date / outdated.* **Out of date** is used especially to talk about information or sources of information; **outdated** is used especially to describe equipment, ideas or ways of doing things.

antiquated /ˈæntɪkweɪtɪd/ *(usually disapproving)* *(of things or ideas)* old-fashioned and no longer suitable for modern conditions: *The committee has recommended that all antiquated legal procedures should be simplified.* ◇ *The antiquated heating system barely heats the larger rooms.*

dated *(disapproving)* old-fashioned; belonging to a time in the past: *Those TV comedies were OK in their day but seem incredibly dated now.*

open *adj.* See also the entries for CLEAR 1 and MARKED

open · overt · blatant · under sb's nose · glaring
These words all describe sth that is done in a very obvious way without any attempt to keep it secret.

PATTERNS AND COLLOCATIONS
▶ an open / an overt / a blatant **attempt**
▶ open / overt / blatant **discrimination**
▶ overt / blatant **sexuality**
▶ a blatant / glaring **example**
▶ **quite** open / overt / blatant

open known to everyone; not kept hidden: *an open display of affection* ◇ *One more border skirmish could lead to open war.* ◇ *We need more open government, starting with a Freedom of Information Act.* **OPP secret** → SECRET 1
▶ **openly** *adv.*: *The men in prison would never cry openly (= so that other people could see).*

overt /əʊˈvɜːt; ˈəʊvɜːt; AmE oʊˈvɜːrt; ˈoʊvɜːrt/ [usually before noun] *(rather formal)* done in an open way and not secretly: *There was little overt support for the project.* ◇ *Her overt sexuality shocked cinema audiences.* **OPP covert** → SECRET 2 ❶ **Overt** is a less general word than **open**

and is only used to talk about actions and behaviour, not feelings, events or systems: *an overt display of affection* ◇ ~~overt admiration/war/government~~

▶ **overtly** *adv.*: *Charities are not allowed to be involved in overtly political activities.*

blatant /ˈbleɪtnt/ (*disapproving*) (of an action that is considered wrong) done in an obvious and open way without caring if people object or are shocked, or if laws are broken: *The opposition party made a blatant attempt to buy votes.* ◇ *It was a blatant lie.*

▶ **blatantly** *adv.*: *a blatantly unfair decision*

under sb's ˈnose *idiom* (*informal*) if sth happens **under sb's nose**, they do not notice it, even though it is not being done secretly: *The police didn't know the drugs ring was operating right under their noses.*

glaring /ˈgleərɪŋ/ [usually before noun] (*disapproving*) (of a mistake or sth bad) very easily seen: *The failure to mention the role of Italy was a glaring omission in the book.*

▶ **glaringly** *adv.*: *The mistakes were glaringly obvious.*

operate *verb* See also the entry for WORK 3

operate · run · control · work · manipulate
These words all mean to use a machine or device, or make it function.

PATTERNS AND COLLOCATIONS
▶ to operate / run / control / work a **machine**
▶ to operate / run / control a / an **engine / motor**
▶ to operate / run **machinery**
▶ to operate / run / manipulate the **controls / levers**

operate [T] (*rather formal*) to use a machine or make it work: *What skills are needed to operate this machinery?* See also **operate** → WORK *verb* 3

▶ **operation** *noun* [U]: *Operation of the device is extremely simple.*

run [T] to make a machine or device work, especially an engine or computer program: *Could you run the engine for a moment?* ◇ *What applications were you running when the problem occurred?* See also **run** → WORK *verb* 3

control (-ll-) [T] to make a machine or system work: *This knob controls the volume.* ◇ *The traffic lights are controlled by a central computer.* See also **control** → BUTTON *noun* 1

NOTE OPERATE, RUN OR CONTROL? A person **operates** or **runs** a machine; machines are often **controlled** by the controls, such as a *computer, knob, button, switch* or *lever.*

work [T] (*rather informal, spoken*) to make a machine or device function, especially a piece of household equipment: *Do you know how to work the coffee machine?* See also **work** → WORK *verb* 3

manipulate /məˈnɪpjuleɪt/ [T] (*rather formal*) to control or use sth in a skilful way: *I had to learn to manipulate the gears and levers of the machine.* ◇ *Computers are very efficient at manipulating information.*

▶ **manipulation** /məˌnɪpjuˈleɪʃn/ *noun* [U]: *data manipulation*

opportunity *noun*

opportunity · chance · turn · possibility · moment · occasion · break · start · window · go
These are all words for a time when a particular situation makes it possible to do or achieve sth.

PATTERNS AND COLLOCATIONS
▶ the opportunity / a chance / your turn **to do sth**
▶ an opportunity / possibilities / an occasion **for** sth
▶ a **suitable** opportunity / occasion / moment
▶ the **last** opportunity / chance / moment
▶ to **have** an opportunity / a chance / a turn / a break / a window / a moment / a go
▶ to **get / give sb** an opportunity / a chance / a turn / a break / a start / a window / a moment / a go

▶ to **wait for** an opportunity / a chance / your turn / the moment / an occasion
▶ to **take advantage of** an opportunity / a chance / the possibilities / a window
▶ to **take** the opportunity / your chance / turns
▶ to **seize** an opportunity / a chance / the moment
▶ to **miss** an opportunity / your chance / a turn / a go

opportunity [C, U] (*rather formal*) a time when a particular situation makes it possible to do or achieve sth: *I'd like to take this opportunity to thank my colleagues for their support.* ◇ *He is rude to me at every opportunity* (= whenever possible). ◇ *There are more job opportunities in the south.* ◇ *Our company promotes equal opportunities for women* (= women are given the same jobs, pay, etc. as men). ◇ *There'll be plenty of opportunity for relaxing once the work is done.*

chance [C] an opportunity: *Please give me a chance to explain.* ◇ (*BrE*) *We won't get another chance of a holiday this year.* ◇ (*AmE*) *We won't get another chance at a vacation this year.* ◇ *Jeff deceived me once already – I won't give him a second chance.* ◇ *This is your big chance* (= opportunity for success).

NOTE OPPORTUNITY OR CHANCE? In many cases you can use either word: *You'll have the opportunity/chance to ask questions at the end.* **Opportunity** tends to be used in more formal contexts than **chance**, and in some phrases only one of the words can be used: ~~job/equal chances~~ ◇ ~~I won't give him a second opportunity.~~

turn [C] (*especially spoken*) the time when sb in a group of people should do sth or is allowed to do sth: *Please wait your turn.* ◇ *Whose turn is it to cook?* ◇ *The male and female birds take turns sitting on the eggs.* ◇ (*BrE*) *We take it in turns to do the housework.*

possibility [C, usually pl.] something that gives you a chance to achieve sth: *The class offers a range of exciting possibilities for developing your skills.* ◇ *Career possibilities for women are much greater than they were fifty years ago.* ❶ In this meaning, **possibilities** is often used to talk about work-related situations: *career/employment/development/commercial/design possibilities.* It is also often used after positive-sounding adjectives: *excellent/interesting/exciting/creative possibilities.* Note that you cannot say 'a/the possibility to do sth': ~~I had the possibility to spend a year in Paris while I was a student.~~ In these cases use **opportunity** or **chance**: *I had the opportunity/chance to spend a year in Paris.* See also **possible** → POSSIBLE 1

moment [C] (*especially spoken*) a particular occasion; a time for doing sth: *I'm waiting for the right moment to tell him the bad news.* ◇ *Have I caught you at a bad moment?*

occasion [sing.] (*rather formal*) a suitable time for doing sth: *It should have been an occasion for rejoicing, but she could not feel any real joy.* ◇ *I'll speak to him about it if the occasion arises* (= if I get a chance). See also **occasion** → TIME 1

break [C] (*informal*) a chance to do sth, usually to get sth that you want or to achieve success: *I got my lucky break when I won a 'Young Journalist of the Year' competition.*

start [C, usually sing.] the opportunity that you are given to begin sth in a successful way: *They worked hard to give their children a good start in life.* ◇ *The job gave him his start in journalism.* See also **start** → START *noun*

window [C] (*especially business*) a time when there is an opportunity to do sth, although it may not last long: *We now have a small window of opportunity in which to make our views known.*

go (pl. **goes**) [C] (*BrE, spoken*) a person's turn to move or play in a game or activity: *Whose go is it?* ◇ *It's your go.* ◇ *'How much is it to play?' 'It's 50p a go.'* ◇ *Can I have a go on your new bike?* ❶ In American English use **turn**.

oppose *verb* See the Topic Map for CONFLICT on p.896

---

oppose · resist · fight · combat · defy · rebel · go against sb/sth · disobey · stand up to sb · flout
These words all mean to speak or act against things that you disagree with.

PATTERNS AND COLLOCATIONS
▶ to fight / rebel **against** sb / sth
▶ to oppose / resist / fight a **plan / proposal**
▶ to oppose / fight / defy / flout a **ban**
▶ to oppose / fight / defy / stand up to **the government**
▶ to defy / disobey your **parents**
▶ to oppose / defy / disobey / flout the **law**
▶ to defy / rebel against / disobey / flout **authority**
▶ to oppose / defy / go against / flout sb's **wishes**
▶ to fight / combat **crime / disease / pollution / inflation**
▶ to defy / disobey / flout a / an **rule / order**
▶ to **fiercely / bitterly / strongly** oppose / resist sth

oppose [T] to disagree strongly with a person, plan or policy, and to speak or act against them: *This party would bitterly oppose the re-introduction of the death penalty.* ◇ *He found himself opposed by his own deputy.* ◇ *I would oppose changing the law.* **OPP** **support** → SUPPORT 1, **propose** → PROPOSE, See also **opposition** → OPPOSITION, **opponent** → ENEMY

resist [T] to refuse to accept a change or what sb wants to do, and try to stop it from happening: *They are determined to resist pressure to change the law.* ◇ *The bank strongly resisted cutting interest rates.* See also **resistance** → OPPOSITION

fight [T, I] to use a lot of effort to oppose a decision or plan, or to stop or deal with sth bad: *Workers are fighting the decision to close the factory.* ◇ *We are committed to fighting poverty.* ◇ *We will fight for as long as it takes.* See also **battle** → COMPETE

combat /'kɒmbæt; *AmE* 'kɑːm-/ (-t- *or* -tt-) [T] (*rather formal*) to take action to stop or deal with sth bad: *He announced new measures to combat crime in the inner cities.* ◇ *The country has appealed for aid to combat serious shortages of foodstuffs.*

> **NOTE** **FIGHT** OR **COMBAT?** Fight has a wider range of collocates than **combat**, and is often used to talk about things that you oppose personally: *to fight a decision/ plan/ban* ◇ *to fight against sth* ◇ ~~to combat a decision/ plan/ban~~ ◇ ~~to combat against sth~~. Both **fight** and **combat** can be used to talk about official efforts to deal with economic and social conditions such as *poverty, crime, unemployment* and *inflation.* **Fight** is not normally used with *shortages*: ~~to fight serious shortages of foodstuffs~~

defy /dɪ'faɪ/ [T] to refuse to obey or show respect for sb/sth in authority, a law, rule or decision: *I wouldn't have dared to defy my teachers.* ◇ *Hundreds of people today defied the ban on political gatherings.* See also **defiant** → NAUGHTY
▶ **defiance** *noun* [U]: *Nuclear testing was resumed in defiance of an international ban.* ◇ *She held up a clenched fist in a gesture of defiance.*

rebel /rɪ'bel/ [I] to stop obeying sb/sth that has authority over you: *He later rebelled against his strict religious upbringing.* ◇ *Most teenagers find something to rebel against.* See also **rebellious** → NAUGHTY
▶ **rebellion** *noun* [U, C]: *Some members are in rebellion against proposed cuts in spending.* ◇ *Teenage rebellion often starts in the home.*

go a'gainst sb/sth *phrasal verb* to disagree with a rule or sb's wishes and do the opposite of what they say: *He would not go against his parents' wishes.*

disobey [T, I] to refuse to do what a law, order or sb in authority tells you to do: *He was punished for disobeying orders.* ◇ *How dare you disobey me!* **OPP** **obey** → FOLLOW 3, See also **disobedient** → NAUGHTY

,stand 'up to sb *phrasal verb* to refuse to accept bad treatment from a more powerful person or organization without complaining: *It was brave of her to stand up to those bullies.*

flout /flaʊt/ [T] to show that you have no respect for a law, rule or custom by openly not obeying it: *She likes flouting convention and doing her own thing.*

---

opposite *noun*

---

opposite · the contrary · the reverse · contrast · antonym
These are all words for a person or thing that is as different as possible from sb/sth else.

PATTERNS AND COLLOCATIONS
▶ a / the **complete** opposite / reverse / contrast
▶ the **exact / very** opposite / reverse
▶ to **be** the opposite / the reverse / a contrast
▶ to **represent** the opposite / a contrast
▶ to **do** the opposite / contrary / reverse
▶ **quite the** opposite / contrary / reverse
▶ **quite a** contrast

opposite [C] a person or thing that is as different as possible from sb/sth else: *Hot and cold are opposites.* ◇ *What is the opposite of heavy?* ◇ *I thought she would be small and blonde but she's the complete opposite.* ◇ *'Is it better now?' 'Quite the opposite, I'm afraid.'*

the contrary [sing.] (*rather formal*) used to emphasize that the opposite of what has been said or suggested is actually true: *In the end the contrary was proved true: he was innocent and she was guilty.* ◇ *'You're not rejecting them?' 'On the contrary, I plan to give them special status.'* ◇ *I don't find him funny at all. Quite the contrary.* ◇ *I will expect to see you on Sunday unless I hear anything to the contrary* (= showing or proving the opposite). ❶ **The contrary** is most often used in the phrases *on the contrary, quite the contrary* and *to the contrary.*

the reverse [sing.] (*rather formal, especially written*) the opposite fact, event or situation to the one just mentioned: *Although I expected to enjoy living in the country, in fact the reverse is true.* ◇ *This problem is the reverse of the previous one.* ❶ **The reverse** is most often used in these phrases: *The reverse is true/holds/is the case/happens.* ◇ *A is the reverse of B.* ◇ *Quite the reverse.*

contrast [C] a person or thing that is clearly different from sb/sth else: *The work you did today is quite a contrast to* (= very much better/worse than) *what you did last week.* See also **contrast** → COMPARE *verb* 1, **contrast** → CONFLICT *verb*, **contrasting** → DIFFERENT

antonym [C] (*technical*) a word that means the opposite of another word: *'Old' has two possible antonyms: 'young' and 'new'.*

---

opposite *adj.*

---

opposite · reverse · contrary · inverse · opposed
These words all describe sth that is as different as possible from sth else.

PATTERNS AND COLLOCATIONS
▶ the opposite / reverse **direction / side**
▶ the opposite / reverse **order / effect**
▶ an opposite / a contrary **view / opinion**
▶ Their **views / opinions** are opposed.
▶ **completely / directly / entirely / quite** contrary / opposed

opposite [usually before noun] completely different in nature or direction: *She tried calming him down but it seemed to be having the opposite effect.* ◇ *I'm trying to teach students at opposite ends of the ability range.* ◇ *Clothes are often used as a way of attracting the opposite sex.*

reverse [only before noun] (*rather formal*) completely different in direction: *The winners were announced in reverse order* (= the person in the lowest place was announced first). ◇ (*formal*) *Iron the garment on the reverse side* (= on the back or inside).

NOTE **OPPOSITE** OR **REVERSE?** **Reverse** is mostly used in more formal contexts than **opposite** and has a narrower range of collocates. **Opposite** can describe both the nature of sth or its direction, in either a physical or abstract sense. **Reverse** only describes the direction of sth, usually in a physical sense. When two people or things travel in *opposite directions* they can either start from the same place and move away from each other, or start from different places and travel towards each other. If you travel *in the reverse direction* you usually travel over the same ground, but start from the other end: *I watched them leave and then drove off in the opposite direction.* ◇ *He hit a truck travelling in the opposite direction.* ◇ *One year later she made the same journey in the reverse direction.* People or things on *opposite sides* of an area or object usually face each other; *reverse sides* of an object are back to back, facing away from each other: *He waved at me from the opposite side of the road.* ◇ *On the reverse side of the medal is a coat of arms.*

contrary /'kɒntrəri; *AmE* 'kɑːntreri/ [only before noun] (*rather formal*) completely different in nature: *Despite all the contrary evidence, they still believed that the Earth was flat.* ◇ *The contrary view is that prison provides an excellent education − in crime.*

NOTE **OPPOSITE** OR **CONTRARY?** **Contrary** is a more formal word than **opposite** and has a narrower range of collocates. **Opposite** can describe both physical things such as the sides of a object or area and abstract things such as opinions. Collocates of **opposite** include *direction, side, end, corner, extreme, effect* and *sex*. **Contrary** only describes abstract things and its collocates include *opinion, view, intention, argument* and *evidence*.

inverse /ˌɪn'vɜːs; *AmE* ˌɪn'vɜːrs/ [only before noun] (*rather formal*) opposite in amount or position to sth else ❶ **Inverse** usually describes a relationship between two things in which, as one element increases, the other decreases: *A person's wealth is often in inverse proportion to their happiness* (= the more money they have, the less happy they are). ◇ *There is often an inverse relationship between the power of the tool and how easy it is to use.*
▸ **inversely** *adv.*: *Can we assume that the demand for bank lending is inversely related to the rate of interest charged?*
opposed [not usually before noun] (*rather formal*) (of ideas or opinions) very different from sth: *Our views are diametrically opposed on this issue.*

opposition *noun* See the Topic Map for CONFLICT on p.896

opposition · protest · resistance · objection · hostility
These are all words for strong disagreement with sb/sth.

PATTERNS AND COLLOCATIONS
▸ opposition / resistance / objection / hostility **to** sth
▸ **in** opposition / protest / objection
▸ **without** opposition / resistance / hostility
▸ **widespread / strong / fierce** opposition / protests / resistance / objections / hostility
▸ **growing** opposition / resistance / hostility
▸ to **provoke / meet with / face** opposition / protests / resistance / objections / hostility
▸ to **arouse** opposition / resistance / hostility
▸ to **express** your opposition / protest / resistance / objections / hostility
▸ to **voice** your opposition / protest / resistance / objections

opposition [U] the act of strongly disagreeing with sb/sth, especially when you try to prevent sth from happening by arguing or fighting: *Delegates expressed strong opposition to the plans.* ◇ *The army met with fierce opposition in every town.* ◇ *Opposition forces have seized control of the airport.* See also **oppose** → OPPOSE, **opposed** → AGAINST
protest [U, C] the expression of strong disagreement with sth and the wish to prevent it from happening: *The director resigned in protest at the decision.* ◇ *The announcement raised a storm of protest.* ◇ *The building work will go ahead, despite protests from local residents.* ❶ A **protest** can also be an organized public meeting to protest about sth. See also **protest** → DEMONSTRATION See also **protest** → COMPLAIN *verb*
resistance [U, sing.] dislike of, opposition to, or refusal to obey an idea, plan or law; the act of using force to oppose sb/sth: *Resistance to change has nearly destroyed the industry.* ◇ *The demonstrators offered little or no resistance to the police.* ◇ *armed resistance* See also **resist** → OPPOSE, **resistant** → AGAINST
objection [U, C] a reason why you do not like or are opposed to sth; a statement about this: *I have no objection to him coming to stay.* ◇ *Because an objection was raised we decided to look at the matter again.* See also **object** → COMPLAIN *verb*
hostility /hɒ'stɪləti; *AmE* hɑː's-/ [U] strong and angry opposition towards an idea, plan or situation: *There is still considerable public hostility towards nuclear power.* See also **hostile** → AGAINST, **hostility** → TENSION

optimistic *adj.*

optimistic · hopeful · positive · bullish · upbeat · expectant
These words all describe sb feeling that sth will probably or certainly happen in the way that they want or expect.

PATTERNS AND COLLOCATIONS
▸ optimistic / hopeful / positive / bullish / upbeat **about** sth
▸ optimistic / hopeful **that...**
▸ an optimistic / a positive / a bullish / an upbeat / an expectant **mood**
▸ an optimistic / a positive / a bullish / an upbeat **note**
▸ an optimistic / a hopeful / a positive / a bullish **view**
▸ an optimistic / a positive / a bullish **attitude / outlook**
▸ an optimistic / a bullish **prediction / forecast**
▸ to **feel** optimistic / hopeful / positive / bullish
▸ to **remain** optimistic / hopeful / positive / bullish / upbeat

optimistic expecting good things to happen or sth to be successful: *She's not very optimistic about the outcome of the talks.* ◇ *They are cautiously optimistic that the reforms will take place.* ◇ *I think you are being a little over-optimistic.* **OPP** **pessimistic** → NEGATIVE, See also **optimism** → HOPE *noun* 1
▸ **optimistically** *adv.*: *He spoke optimistically about better relations between the two countries.*
hopeful [not usually before noun] believing that sth you want will probably happen: *I feel hopeful that we'll find a suitable house very soon.* ◇ *He is not very hopeful about the outcome of the interview.* **OPP** **hopeless** → DESPERATE, See also **hopeful** → PROMISING, **hope** → HOPE *noun* 1
positive thinking about what is good in a situation; confident and hopeful about the future: *She tried to be more positive about her new job.* ◇ *On the positive side, profits have increased.* **OPP** **negative** → NEGATIVE
bullish /'bʊlɪʃ/ (*especially business*) confident and hopeful about the future: *Fraser was in (a) bullish mood about the future of his company.*
upbeat /'ʌpbiːt/ (*rather informal, especially business*) positive and enthusiastic; making you feel that the future will be good: *The tone of the speech was upbeat.* ◇ *The presentation ended on an upbeat note.* **OPP** **downbeat** → NEGATIVE

expectant (*especially written*) hoping for sth, especially sth good and exciting: *A sudden roar came from the expectant crowd.* ◊ *An expectant hush came over the room.* ❶ **Expectant** is mainly used to talk about a *crowd*, people's *faces*, a *look* or the *hush* or *silence* of people waiting for sth exciting to happen. People are usually expectant about sth that they think is going to happen soon, rather than later in the future. See also **expectancy** → HOPE *noun* 1

▸ **expectantly** *adv.*: *She looked at him expectantly.*

option *noun*

option · choice · alternative · possibility · best/good/ safe bet

These are all words for sth that you choose to do in a particular situation.

PATTERNS AND COLLOCATIONS
▸ **with / without** the option / choice / possibility **of** sth
▸ (a / an) **real / realistic / viable / practical / obvious** option / choice / alternative / possibility
▸ (a / an) **good / acceptable / reasonable / healthy / available / possible / preferred / cheap / expensive** option / choice / alternative
▸ the **only** option / choice / alternative / possibility **open to** sb
▸ to **have / give sb / offer (sb)** several options / choices / alternatives / possibilities
▸ to **have** a / an / the option / choice **of doing sth**
▸ to **have no** option / choice / alternative (**but to** do sth)
▸ to **look at / limit** the options / choices / alternatives / possibilities
▸ a **number / range of** options / choices / alternatives / possibilities

option [C, U] something that you can choose to have or do; the freedom to choose what you do: *As I see it, we have two options…* ◊ *We are currently studying all the options available.* ◊ *Going to college was not an option for me.* ◊ *Students have the option of studying abroad in their second year.* ◊ *It is important at this stage to **leave your options open** (= avoid making a decision so that you still have a choice in the future).* ❶ **Option** is also the word used in computing for one of the choices you can make when using a computer program: *Choose the 'Cut' option from the Edit menu.* See also **opt** → CHOOSE, **optional** → VOLUNTARY 1

choice [U, C, usually sing.] the freedom to choose what you do; something that you can choose to have or do: *If I had the choice, I would stop working tomorrow.* ◊ *She's going to do it. She doesn't have much choice, really, does she?* ◊ *The choice is yours: a quiet drink in the bar, the late night disco or a stroll along the beach.* ◊ *There is a wide range of choices open to you.* See also **choice** → CHOICE 1, **choice** → CHOICE 2, **choose** → CHOOSE, **choose** → DECIDE

alternative /ɔːlˈtɜːnətɪv; *AmE* -ˈtɜːrn-/ [C] something that you can choose to have or do out of two or more possibilities: *You can be paid in cash weekly or by cheque monthly: those are the two alternatives.* ◊ *We had no alternative but to (= we had to) fire Gibson.* ◊ *There is a vegetarian alternative on the menu every day.*

NOTE OPTION, CHOICE OR ALTERNATIVE? Choice is slightly less formal than **option**, and **alternative** is slightly more formal. **Choice** is most often used for 'the freedom to choose', although you can sometimes also use **option** (but NOT usually **alternative**): *We had no choice/option/alternative but to…* ◊ *If I had the choice/option, I would…* ◊ *She doesn't have much choice/option.* ◊ ~~If I had the alternative, I would…~~ ◊ ~~She doesn't have much alternative.~~ ◊ *parental choice in education* ◊ *The choice is yours.* ◊ ~~parental option/alternative in education~~ ◊ ~~The option/alternative is yours.~~ Things that you can choose are **options**, **choices** or **alternatives**. However, **alternative** is more frequently used to talk about choosing between two things rather than several.

possibility [C] one of the different things that you can do in a particular situation: *I think we've exhausted all the possibilities.* ◊ *Selling the house is just one possibility that is open to us.* ◊ *The possibilities are endless.* ❶ **Possibility** can be used in a similar way to **option**, **choice** and **alternative**, but the emphasis here is less on the need to make a choice, and more on what is available. See also **possible** → POSSIBLE 1

the/your 'best bet, a 'good/'safe bet *idiom* (*informal*) the best action to take to get the result you want; something that is likely to succeed or be suitable: *If you want to get around London fast, the Underground is your best bet.* ◊ *Clothes are a safe bet as a present for a teenager.* **OPP** gamble → RISK 2

order *noun*

order · instruction · injunction · directive · decree · command

These are all words for sth that sb is told to do, especially by sb in authority.

PATTERNS AND COLLOCATIONS
▸ **under** sb's orders / sb's instructions / an injunction / a directive / a decree
▸ **in accordance with** an order / instructions / a directive / a decree
▸ **by** order / decree
▸ (a) **written** order / instructions / directive
▸ (a) **clear** order / instructions / directive / command
▸ (a) **direct / final** order / instructions / command
▸ to **issue** an order / instructions / an injunction / a directive / a decree / a command
▸ to **obey / ignore** an order / instructions / an injunction / a directive / a command
▸ to **sign** an order / an injunction / a directive / a decree
▸ to **implement / follow / comply with** an order / instructions / a directive
▸ to **give / receive / carry out** an order / instructions / a command

order [C] something that sb is told to do by sb in authority: *He gave **orders for** the work **to** be started.* ◊ *The general gave the **order to** advance.* ◊ *I'm **under orders** not to let anyone in.* ◊ *Interest rates can be controlled **by order of** the central bank.* ◊ *I don't **take orders** from you!* ◊ *Under the **court order**, she is allowed no contact with him.*

instruction [C, usually pl.] something that sb tells you to do: *She called you **on my instructions**.* ◊ *He left strict **instructions that** the box should only be opened after his death.* ◊ *She **carried out** his **instructions to the letter** (= followed them in every detail).*

injunction /ɪnˈdʒʌŋkʃn/ [C] (*law*) an official order given by a court which demands that sth must or must not be done: *The court granted an **injunction against** the defendants.* ◊ *She **took out an injunction** to prevent the press from publishing the information.* ◊ *It was agreed that the temporary **injunction** should be **lifted**.* ❶ In formal English, **injunction** can also have the more general meaning of 'a warning from sb in authority': *The rank and file members will follow the injunction of the party leadership.*

directive /dəˈrektɪv; dɪ-; daɪ-/ [C] an official instruction, especially about how sth should be done: *The EU has issued a new set of **directives on** pollution.* ◊ *Don't start anything without a clear directive from management.*

decree /dɪˈkriː/ [C, U] an official order from a ruler or government that becomes law: *In an emergency decree, the government banned all political gatherings.* ◊ *The general ruled by decree.* See also **decree** → RULE *verb* 2

command [C] an order given to a person, especially by a military officer, or to an animal: *He issued the command to retreat.* ◊ *Begin when I give the command.* ◊ *She has been teaching her dog simple commands.*

order *verb*

1 order sb to do sth
2 order goods/a taxi/a meal

---

1 See also the entry for RULE 2
order · tell · instruct · direct · command
These words all mean to use your position of authority to say to sb that they must do sth.

PATTERNS AND COLLOCATIONS
▸ to order / tell / instruct / direct / command sb **to do sth**
▸ to order / tell / instruct / direct / command **sb that...**
▸ to order / instruct / direct / command **that...**
▸ to **do** sth **as** ordered / told / instructed / directed / commanded
▸ to **specifically/expressly** order/tell/instruct/direct/command (sb to do sth)

order [T] to use your position of authority to tell sb to do sth: *The officer ordered them to fire.* ◇ *The government has ordered an investigation into the accident.* ◇ *They were ordered out of the class for fighting.* ◇ *'Come here at once!' she ordered.* ◇ *Stop trying to* **order** *me* **around***!*

tell [T] to say to sb that they must or should do sth: *He was told to sit down and wait.* ◇ *There was a sign telling motorists to slow down.* ◇ *I kept telling myself to keep calm.* ◇ *The doctor told me (that) I should lose some weight.* ◇ *Don't tell me what to do!* ◇ **Do as you're told***!*

instruct [T] (*rather formal*) to tell sb to do sth, especially in a formal or official way: *The letter instructed him to report to headquarters immediately.* ◇ *You will be instructed where to go as soon as the plane is ready.* ◇ *She arrived at ten o'clock as instructed.*

direct [T] (*formal*) to give an official order: *The judge directed the jury to return a verdict of not guilty.*

command /kə'mɑːnd; *AmE* kə'mænd/ [T] to use your position of authority to tell sb to do sth: *He commanded his men to retreat.* ◇ *She commanded the release of the prisoners.* See also **command → CONTROL noun**

NOTE ORDER OR COMMAND? **Order** is a more general word than **command** and can be used about anyone in a position of authority, such as a parent, teacher or government telling sb to do sth. **Command** is slightly stronger than **order.** It is the normal word to use about an army officer giving orders, or in any context where it is normal to give orders without any discussion about them. It is less likely to be used about a parent or teacher.

---

2 **order · book · hire · rent · charter · reserve**
These words all mean to ask for sth to be made available for you at a later time, or to pay to use sth temporarily.

PATTERNS AND COLLOCATIONS
▸ to order / book / hire / rent / charter / reserve sth **for sb**
▸ to book / reserve a **place / seat / table / ticket**
▸ to book / hire / rent / reserve a **room / hall**
▸ to book / rent a **DVD / video**
▸ to book / charter a **flight**
▸ to hire / rent **a bicycle / a boat / a car / equipment / a movie / a van / a vehicle**
▸ to hire / charter a **plane / vessel / yacht**
▸ to order / book / reserve sth **for eight o'clock / this evening / midday, etc.**

order [T, I] to ask for goods to be made or supplied or for sth to be provided; to ask to be served with sth to eat or drink: *The furniture can be ordered direct from the manufacturer.* ◇ *I'd like to order some books, please.* ◇ *I'll order you a taxi.* ◇ *I've ordered some sandwiches.* ◇ *The waiter asked if we were ready to order.* See also **order → REQUEST noun**

book [T, I] (*especially BrE*) to arrange with a hotel or theatre to have a room or seat on a particular date; to arrange for sb to have a seat on a plane, train or ship: *The hotel is* **fully booked** *that weekend.* ◇ *The seminars get*

quickly **booked up** (= have no more places available). ◇ *I've* **booked** *you* **on** *the 9.30 flight.* ◇ *Book early to avoid disappointment.* See also **book → SCHEDULE verb**

hire [T] (*BrE*) to pay money to borrow sth for a short time: *There's a place where you can hire bikes for the day.* ◇ *They hired a room above a pub for the wedding reception.*
▸ **hire** *noun* [U]: *bicycles* **for hire***, £4 an hour* ◇ *The costumes are* **on hire from** *the local theatre.*

rent [T] (*especially AmE*) to pay money to borrow sth for a short time: *She rented a car at the airport.* ◇ *He had a list of movies they had rented from the local video store.*

NOTE HIRE OR RENT? In British English you **hire** vehicles, rooms or tools, but you **rent** DVDs or videos. In American English **rent** is used for all these things. However, for larger vehicles that usually carry paying passengers, use **charter.**

charter [T] to hire a plane, boat, bus or train: *The club chartered a special flight from Manchester to Turin.*
▸ **charter** *noun* [U]: *a yacht available for charter*

reserve [T] (*rather formal*) to ask for a seat, table, room or place on a course to be available for you or sb else at a future time: *They had reserved seats on the train.* ◇ *Please reserve a place for me on the software training day.*

NOTE BOOK OR RESERVE? **Book** usually means to make a firm arrangement which often includes making a payment at the same time or being charged if you cancel. **Reserve** means to ask for sth to be kept for you and does not usually require payment in advance, except in the case of seats on a train. You can also say **make a reservation**, which is the most usual way to express this idea in American English: *I'd like to make a reservation for August 14.* See also **reserve → RESERVE, reservation → REQUEST**

---

organization (*BrE* also **-isation**) *noun* See the
Topic Map for THE INDIVIDUAL AND SOCIETY on p.894. See also the entry for UNION

---

organization · centre · institution · institute
These are all words for a group of people working together for a particular purpose, such as education, research or business, or a place used for such a purpose.

PATTERNS AND COLLOCATIONS
▸ an organization / a centre / an institution / an institute **for sth**
▸ a **private** organization / institution
▸ a **government** organization / institution / institute
▸ a **research / training** organization / centre / institution / institute

organization (*BrE* also **-isation**) [C] an organized group of people with a particular purpose, such as a business, club or government department: *There need to be changes throughout the* **organization***.* ◇ *Voluntary organizations working with the homeless are against the proposal.* ◇ *The World Health Organization has called for $10 million to purchase medical supplies.* ❶ **Organization** can be used as a general word for a business, club, society, government department, political party, trade union, pressure group or charity. It is not usually used to refer to a school, college or university. See also **foundation → CHARITY**

centre (*BrE*) (*AmE* **center**) [C] a building or place used for a particular purpose or activity; a place where a particular kind of work is done well: *They've set up a local centre for people with epilepsy.* ◇ *The classes are run by the Centre for Languages and Literature.* ◇ *The university is recognized as an international* **centre of excellence** *for training dentists.* ❶ **Centre** is often used in compounds: *a sports/leisure/community/shopping/conference/business centre*

institution /ˌɪnstɪ'tjuːʃn; *AmE* -'tuːʃn/ [C] a large, important organization that has a particular purpose, for example a university or bank: *The deal is backed by one of the country's largest* **financial institutions***.* ◇ *The system is targeted mainly at academic and research institutions.* See also **foundation → CHARITY**

institute /'ɪnstɪtjuːt; *AmE* -tuːt/ [C] an organization that has a particular purpose, especially one that is connected with education or a particular profession; the building used by this organization: *He is a member of the Institute of Chartered Accountants.*

> **NOTE** INSTITUTION OR INSTITUTE? **Institution** can refer to a range of organizations such as banks or government departments. Both **institution** and **institute** are words for academic and research organizations. **Institution** is usually used to describe a type of organization: *many research institutions.* **Institute** usually refers to a particular organization or its building, and is part of its name: *the Dundee Institute of Technology.*

organize (*BrE* also **-ise**) *verb*

organize · arrange · plan · operate · run · sort sth out · mount · orchestrate
These words all mean to do what is necessary for sth to happen.

PATTERNS AND COLLOCATIONS
▸ to arrange / plan **for** sth
▸ to arrange / plan **to do** sth
▸ to arrange / plan **that...**
▸ to arrange / plan / sort out **how / who / when / where...**
▸ **as** arranged / planned
▸ to organize / plan / operate / run / mount / orchestrate a **campaign**
▸ to organize / plan / run / mount an **operation**
▸ to organize / arrange / plan / mount an **exhibition**
▸ to organize / plan / run / mount an **event**
▸ to organize / plan / mount a **raid**
▸ to organize / arrange / operate / run / mount / orchestrate sth **successfully**
▸ to organize/plan/operate/run sth **efficiently/effectively/well**
▸ to organize / plan / run sth **badly**
▸ to **jointly** organize / arrange / plan / operate / run / mount sth

organize (*BrE* also **-ise**) [T] to be responsible for making sth happen or for sth being provided: *I've organized a lot of school trips.* ◇ *The committee will organize the food for the reception.* See also **organization** → PLANNING
arrange [T, I] to make arrangements for sth to happen; to agree with sb about when sth will happen: *A news conference was hastily arranged.* ◇ *I'll arrange for a car to meet you at the airport.* ◇ *We met at six, as arranged.* See also **arrangement** → AGREEMENT 1, **arrangement** → PLANNING
plan (-nn-) [T, I] to make detailed arrangements for sth to happen in the future; to decide what should happen in the future: *It took six months to plan the expedition.* ◇ *Everything went exactly as planned.* ◇ *I've been planning how I'm going to spend my last week here.* ◇ *It's always a good idea to plan ahead.* See also **plan** → PLAN *noun* 1, **planning** → PLANNING
operate [T] (*rather formal*) to organize a service; to use a system or process: *The airline operates flights to 25 countries.* ◇ *France operates a system of subsidized loans to dairy farmers.* See also **in operation** → ACTIVE
run [T] to organize a service or event and make it available to people: *The college runs several English classes for adults.* ◇ *Volunteer counsellors run a 24-hour helpline.*
sort sth 'out *phrasal verb* (*rather informal, especially spoken*) to organize sth successfully: *If you're going to the bus station, can you sort out the tickets for tomorrow?* ◇ *Paula sorted out all the travel arrangements for us.* See also **sort sb/sth out** → SOLVE 1
mount [T] (*written*) to organize and begin an event or series of planned activities: *The party successfully mounted a campaign to change the law.* ◇ *The National Gallery mounted a major exhibition of her work.*
orchestrate /'ɔːkɪstreɪt; *AmE* 'ɔːrk-/ [T] (*written*) to organize a complicated plan or event very carefully or secretly: *The party was accused of orchestrating violence at demonstrations.*

organizer (*BrE* also **-iser**) *noun*

organizer · administrator · planner
These are all words for sb who arranges, plans or manages things, or who is good at planning and making arrangements.

PATTERNS AND COLLOCATIONS
▸ an organizer / administrator **for** sth
▸ a **good** organizer / administrator / planner
▸ a / an **area / local / regional** organizer / administrator / planner

organizer (*BrE* also **-iser**) [C] a person who arranges for sth to happen or to be provided; sb who is good at organizing things: *Police had a number of meetings with the organizers of the race to discuss safety.* ◇ *She was an excellent organizer and fund-raiser for the club.* ❶ People often talk about *the organizers of an event* meaning the group or company that has planned it and arranged everything necessary for it to take place.
administrator /əd'mɪnɪstreɪtə(r)/ [C] a person whose job is to manage or organize the business affairs of a company or institution; a person who is good at organizing things: *Such organizational decisions are made by the hospital administrators.* ◇ *He is known as a good manager and an efficient administrator.* See also **administer** → RUN 2, **administration** → GOVERNMENT 2, **administration** → MANAGEMENT
planner [C] a person who makes plans for a particular area of activity, especially as a job: *Emergency planners are keeping a close eye on forecasts.* ◇ *The oil crisis gave economic planners a jolt.*

ornament *noun*

ornament · trinket · decoration
These are all words for an object that is used to make a person, place or thing look more attractive.

PATTERNS AND COLLOCATIONS
▸ a **little** ornament / trinket / decoration
▸ a **glass** ornament / decoration
▸ a **Christmas (tree)** ornament / decoration

ornament /'ɔːnəmənt; *AmE* 'ɔːrn-/ [C] (*rather formal*) an object that is used as decoration in a room or garden rather than for a particular purpose; an object that is worn as jewellery: *There were a few china ornaments on the shelf above the fireplace.* ◇ (*formal*) *Archaeologists have uncovered necklaces, pendants and other personal ornaments from the third century.* See also **ornament** → DECORATION *noun*, **ornament** → DECORATE *verb*, **ornamental** → DECORATIVE
trinket [C] (*rather formal, written*) a piece of jewellery or small ornament that is not worth much money: *On her dressing table there was a comb, a mirror and a few trinkets.*
decoration [C, usually pl.] a thing that makes sth look more attractive on special occasions: *It's a bit too soon to put up the Christmas decorations.* ◇ *We made our own table decorations.* See also **decoration** → DECORATION, **decorate** → DECORATE

outline *verb*

outline · set sth out · lay sth out · sketch
These words all mean to give a description of the main points or facts of sth in writing or speech.

PATTERNS AND COLLOCATIONS
▸ to outline / set out / lay out / sketch sth **for** sb
▸ to outline / set out / lay out / sketch a **plan / programme**
▸ to outline / set out / lay out / sketch the **details**
▸ to outline / set out / lay out sth **carefully / clearly**
▸ to outline / set out / lay out / sketch sth **briefly / simply**

outline [T] to give a description of the main facts or points involved in sth: *We **outlined** our proposals **to** the committee.* ◊ *Let me briefly **outline** what we are trying to achieve.* See also **outline** → SUMMARY *noun*

,set sth 'out *phrasal verb* to present ideas, facts, a plan or an argument in an organized way in speech or writing: *He set out his objections to the plan.*

,lay sth 'out *phrasal verb* (*especially AmE*) to set sth out: *All the terms and conditions are laid out in the contract.*

> **NOTE** SET STH OUT OR LAY STH OUT? These words have the same meaning: **set sth out** is used in both British and American English; **lay sth out** is used especially in American English and is slightly more informal than **set sth out**.

sketch [T] to give a general description of sth, giving only the basic facts: *She **sketched out** her plan for tackling the problem.* See also **sketch** → SUMMARY *noun*

> **NOTE** OUTLINE OR SKETCH? When you **outline** a plan or details, you give sb the main points involved. When you **sketch** a plan or details, you give a quick and basic description.

output *noun*

output · production · productivity · yield
These are all words for the amount of sth that is produced.

PATTERNS AND COLLOCATIONS
> a **high / low** output / productivity / yield
> **agricultural** output / production / productivity / yields
> **industrial / manufacturing** output / production / productivity
> to **boost / improve / increase / raise** output / production / productivity / yields
> to **reduce** output / production / productivity / yields

output [U, sing.] the amount of sth that a country, company, machine or person produces: *Manufacturing output has increased by 8%.*

production [U] the amount of sth that a country or company produces: *Production will drop by 60 000 next year.* See also **production** → PRODUCTION, **produce** → MANUFACTURE

> **NOTE** OUTPUT OR PRODUCTION? Output has a wider range of uses than **production** in this meaning: **output** can 'belong' to a country, company, machine or person: *the country's/company's total output* ◊ *her prodigious literary output.* **Production** is not used with the possessive in this way: *the country's/company's total production* ◊ *her prodigious literary production.*

productivity /ˌprɒdʌkˈtɪvəti; *AmE* ˌprɑːd-; ˌproʊd-/ [U] the rate at which a company, country or worker produces goods; the amount produced, compared with the amount of time, work and money that is needed to produce it: *Wage rates depend on levels of productivity.* ◊ *If you want to stay in this job you'll need to get your productivity up.*

yield [C, U] the amount of crops or milk that is produced: *This method of cultivation gives a higher yield.* ◊ *a reduction in milk yield* See also **yield** → PROVIDE *verb*

outrageous *adj.*

outrageous · shocking · disgraceful · shameful · criminal · scandalous · deplorable · unforgivable
These words all describe actions, behaviour and situations that shock you and are unacceptable.

PATTERNS AND COLLOCATIONS
> to be outrageous/shocking/disgraceful/shameful/scandalous/deplorable / unforgivable **that...**
> outrageous/ shocking / disgraceful / shameful / criminal / scandalous / deplorable **behaviour**
> an outrageous / a shocking / a disgraceful / a shameful / a criminal / a scandalous **waste**
> an outrageous / a shocking / a scandalous **story**
> a shocking / disgraceful / shameful / scandalous / deplorable **situation / condition**
> a shocking / disgraceful / shameful / criminal / deplorable **state**
> **quite** outrageous / shocking / disgraceful / deplorable / unforgivable
> **utterly** outrageous / disgraceful / scandalous / deplorable
> **absolutely** outrageous / shocking / disgraceful / scandalous

outrageous /aʊtˈreɪdʒəs/ that offends or upsets you because you think it is morally wrong: *'That's outrageous!' he protested.* ◊ *She thought it absolutely outrageous that he should be promoted over her.* See also **outrage** → ANGER *noun*, **outrage** → ANGER *verb*, **outraged** → FURIOUS

> **outrageously** *adv.*: *They behaved outrageously.* ◊ *The meal was outrageously expensive.*

shocking that offends or upsets you because it is morally wrong or very serious: *What a shocking waste of money!* ◊ *Today we reveal the shocking truth about heroin addiction among the young.* See also **shock** → OFFEND *verb*

> **shockingly** *adv.*: *a shockingly high mortality rate*

> **NOTE** OUTRAGEOUS OR SHOCKING? To talk about behaviour or actions that you think are morally wrong you can use either word: *outrageous/shocking behaviour* ◊ *a/an outrageous/shocking act/waste/story/suggestion.* If you are offended by sth because it seems unfair to you personally, use **outrageous**: *She thought it shocking that he should be promoted over her.* For situations that are very serious or dangerous, use **shocking**: *the outrageous truth about heroin addiction.*

disgraceful very bad or unacceptable; that people should feel ashamed about: *It's disgraceful that none of the family tried to help her.* See also **disgrace** → DISGRACE *noun* 1, **disgrace** → DISGRACE *noun* 2

> **disgracefully** *adv.*: *He considered that Liza was behaving disgracefully.*

shameful (*rather formal*) disgraceful: *It was shameful the way she was treated.* ◊ *We reveal one of the most shameful secrets of modern US history.* See also **shame** → DISGRACE *noun* 2

> **shamefully** *adv.*: *The buildings have been shamefully neglected.*

> **NOTE** SHAMEFUL OR DISGRACEFUL? Disgraceful is more frequent in spoken English than **shameful**, especially in British English. **Shameful**, but NOT **disgraceful**, is used to describe *secrets* and people's secret *thoughts*.

criminal that you think is morally wrong: *This is a criminal waste of resources.* See also **crime** → DISGRACE *noun* 1

scandalous that offends you because you think it is morally wrong: *It is scandalous that he has not been punished.* ◊ *The decision is nothing short of scandalous.* **ⓘ** Scandalous actions and situations are ones that you think are actually immoral, rather than ones that you think are unfair to you personally. They often involve people with power or money being treated much better than other people.

> **scandalously** *adv.*: *scandalously low pay*

deplorable /dɪˈplɔːrəbl/ (*formal*) very bad and unacceptable, often in a way that shocks people: *They were living in the most deplorable conditions.* ◊ *The acting was deplorable.* See also **deplore** → DISAPPROVE

> **deplorably** *adv.*: *They behaved deplorably.*

unforgivable /ˌʌnfəˈɡɪvəbl; *AmE* -fərˈɡ-/ (of sb's behaviour) so bad or unacceptable that you cannot forgive the person: *It was an unforgivable thing to say.* ◊ *He had committed the unforgivable sin — he had betrayed his friends.* **OPP** **forgivable** **ⓘ** Forgivable behaviour is behaviour that you can understand and forgive: *His rudeness was forgivable in the circumstances.*

> **unforgivably** *adv.*: *She was unforgivably rude.*

oven *noun*

oven · stove · microwave · cooker · furnace · kiln · hob
These are all words for a piece of equipment for cooking or baking things.

- **in** the oven / microwave / furnace / kiln
- **on** the stove / cooker / hob
- a / an **gas** / **electric** oven / stove / cooker / furnace / kiln / hob
- to **heat** sth in / on the oven / stove / microwave / cooker / furnace / hob
- to **cook** sth in / on the oven / stove / microwave / cooker / hob
- to **bake** sth in an oven / a kiln
- to **light** the oven / stove
- to **fire** a furnace / kiln

oven [C] a piece of equipment shaped like a box with a door on the front, in which food is cooked or heated. An oven is usually part of a **stove** or **cooker**: *Take the cake out of the oven.* ◇ *Pre-heat the oven to 180°C.* ◇ *Bake them in a warm oven until risen and golden brown.*

stove /stəʊv; *AmE* stoʊv/ [C] (*especially AmE*) a large piece of equipment for cooking food, containing an oven and gas or electric rings on top: *She put a pan of water on the stove.* ◇ (*AmE, BrE*) *Most people don't want to spend hours slaving over a hot stove* (= cooking). ❶ In British English a **stove** is usually called a **cooker**. In American English **stove** is also used to mean just the top part of the stove/cooker with the gas or electric rings (called **burners** in American English). The British English word for this is **hob**. See also **stove** → HEATING

microwave /ˈmaɪkrəweɪv/ (also *formal* ˌmicrowave ˈoven) [C] a type of oven that cooks or heats food very quickly using electromagnetic waves rather than heat: *You can always reheat the soup in the microwave.* ◇ *He lives on a diet of fast food and microwave meals.*

cooker [C] (*BrE*) a stove: *All the flats are fitted with gas cookers.*

furnace /ˈfɜːnɪs; *AmE* ˈfɜːrnɪs/ [C] an enclosed space or room for heating metal or glass to very high temperatures: *Iron ore is melted in a **blast furnace** to extract the metal.*

kiln [C] a large oven for baking clay and bricks or drying wood and grain: *The vases are then **fired in a kiln**.*

hob [C] (*BrE*) the top part of a cooker where food is cooked in pans on gas or electric rings; a similar surface that is built into a kitchen unit and is separate from the oven: *The wok can be used on both gas or electric hobs.* ❶ The American English word for this is **stove**.

oven

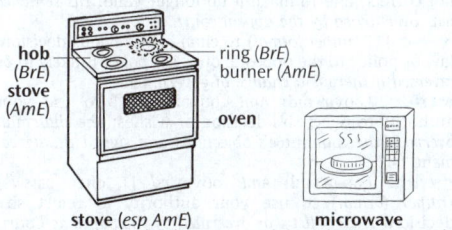

hob (BrE)
stove (AmE)

ring (BrE)
burner (AmE)

oven

stove (esp AmE)
cooker (BrE)

microwave
(also microwave oven)

overall *adj.* See also the entry for GENERAL 2

overall · gross · umbrella · global · across the board · blanket · all-round · inclusive
These words all describe sth which includes or covers all things or all of sth.

- an overall / umbrella **heading** / **title**
- an umbrella / a blanket / an inclusive **term**
- a global / blanket **ban**
- overall / gross **income**
- the overall / gross / inclusive **cost**
- overall / gross **profit** / **turnover**

overall /ˌəʊvərˈɔːl; *AmE* ˌoʊ-/ [only before noun] including all the people or things that are involved in a particular situation: *There will be winners in each of the three age groups, and one overall winner.* ◇ *The person with overall responsibility for the project will be Paul.* ◇ *The past century has seen an overall improvement in standards of living.*
▸ **overall** *adv.*: *The company will invest $1.6m overall in new equipment.* ◇ *Overall, this is a very useful book.*

gross /grəʊs; *AmE* groʊs/ [only before noun] (*finance*) being the total amount of sth before anything else is taken away: *The family have three children and a gross income of £50 000* (= before taxes, etc. are taken away). **OPP net**
❶ A **net** amount of money is the amount that remains when nothing more is to be taken away: *a **net profit** of £500* ◇ *net income/earnings* (= after tax has been paid)

umbrella [only before noun] containing many different parts or elements: *'Contact sports' is an umbrella term for a variety of different sports.* ◇ *Two separate political parties emerged from the **umbrella organization**.*
▸ **umbrella** *noun* [C]: *Many previously separate groups are now operating under the umbrella of the same authority.*

global [usually before noun] considering or including all the parts of sth: *We need to take a more global approach to the problem.* ◇ *We ran a global search on the database.* See also **global** → INTERNATIONAL
▸ **globally** *adv.*: *We need to start thinking globally.*

aˌcross the ˈboard *idiom* involving everyone or everything in an industry, a company or other organization: *The industry needs more investment across the board.* ◇ *The director is to announce an across-the-board wage increase.*
❶ When this idiom is used before a noun, it needs hyphens, but when it comes after a noun, it does not. It can also be used as an adverbial phrase: *The new plans will be implemented across the board.*

blanket [only before noun] including or affecting all possible cases, situations or people: *A blanket ban on tobacco advertising was introduced several years ago.*

ˌall-ˈround (*BrE*) (*AmE* ˌall-aˈround) [only before noun] including many different aspects, subjects or skills; (of a person) with a wide range of skills or abilities: *We are looking at the all-round development of the children and not merely their academic progress.* ◇ *She's a good all-around tennis player.*

inclusive /ɪnˈkluːsɪv/ (*rather formal*) having the total cost, or the cost of sth that is mentioned, contained in the price: *The **fully inclusive** fare for the trip is £320.* ◇ *These services offer inclusive insurance cover of up to $5 000.*
❶ Compare how **inclusive** and **included** are used after a noun: *Water and heating are included in the rent.* ◇ (*formal*) *The rent is inclusive of water and heating.* See also **include** → INCLUDE 1

overcome *verb*

overcome · get over sth · control · bring/get/keep sth under control · beat · conquer
These words all mean to gain control over sth or deal successfully with sth, especially a problem.

- to overcome / get over / control / beat / conquer a **problem**
- to bring a **problem** under control
- to overcome / get over / control / conquer a **fear**
- to overcome / get over a **difficulty** / **hurdle**
- to control a **fire** / bring a **fire** under control
- to **successfully** overcome sth / control sth / conquer sth
- to **finally** overcome sth / get over sth / control sth / conquer sth
- to **quickly** overcome sth / control sth / bring sth under control

overcome /ˌəʊvəˈkʌm; AmE ˌoʊvərˈkʌm/ [T] to succeed in dealing with a problem that could otherwise prevent you from doing sth: *She overcame injury to win the Olympic gold medal.* ◇ *Therapy helped her overcome her fear of flying.* ◇ *There are at least two major obstacles that must be overcome.*

get 'over sth *phrasal verb* (*rather informal*) to succeed in dealing with or gaining control of sth such as a problem or feeling: *She can't get over her shyness.* ◇ *This is going to be a big hurdle for Laura to get over.*

control (-ll-) [T] to stop sth bad from spreading or getting worse: *Firefighters are still trying to control the blaze.* ◇ *She was given drugs to control the pain.*

bring/get/keep sth under con'trol *idiom* to succeed in dealing with sth so that it does not cause any harm: *The police soon got the situation under control.* ◇ *Please keep your dog under control!* ◇ *He was obviously keeping his anger under tight control.*

beat [T] (*informal*) to succeed in gaining control of a problem so that it disappears: *He is struggling to beat his heroin addiction.* ◇ *Book a break in the sun to try to beat those winter blues* (= stop feeling sad).

conquer /ˈkɒŋkə(r); AmE ˈkɑːŋ-/ [T] (*written*) to succeed in dealing with or gaining control of sth such as a problem or feeling: *He was trying to conquer his alcoholism.* ◇ *The only way to conquer a fear is to face it.*

overhear verb

overhear · monitor · eavesdrop · tap · bug · listen in
These words all mean to listen to a conversation in which you are not involved.

▶ to eavesdrop / listen in **on** sth
▶ to **overhear** / monitor / eavesdrop on / bug / listen in to a **conversation**
▶ to monitor / eavesdrop on **communications**
▶ to tap / bug sb's **telephone**

overhear /ˌəʊvəˈhɪə(r); AmE ˌoʊvərˈhɪr/ [T] to hear, especially by accident, a conversation in which you are not involved: *We talked quietly so as not to be overheard.* ◇ *We overheard them arguing.* ◇ *I overheard him say he was going to France.*

monitor /ˈmɒnɪtə(r); AmE ˈmɑːn-/ [T] (especially of an official organization) to listen to telephone calls or foreign radio broadcasts or read emails, etc. in order to collect information, usually over a long period: *The company routinely monitors all its employees' emails.* ◇ *During the war his job was to monitor enemy radio broadcasts.*

eavesdrop /ˈiːvzdrɒp; AmE -drɑːp/ (-pp-) [I] to listen secretly to what other people are saying; to listen secretly to electronic communications in order to collect information: *We caught him eavesdropping outside the window.* ◇ *Hackers eavesdrop on phone networks to steal data* (= in a newspaper headline).

tap (-pp-) [T] to fit a device to a telephone or telephone line so that sb's calls can be listened to secretly: *He was convinced his phone was being tapped.*

bug (-gg-) [T] to put a special electronic listening device (= a bug) somewhere in order to listen secretly to sb's private conversations: *They bugged her hotel room.*

listen 'in *phrasal verb* to listen to a conversation that you are not supposed to hear, especially by means of electronics: *You shouldn't listen in on other people's conversations.* ◇ *They did not know that the police were secretly listening in.*

overthrow noun

overthrow · downfall · fall · nemesis · undoing
These are all words for sb's loss of power, money or social position, or the thing which causes this.

▶ to be sb's downfall / nemesis / undoing
▶ to **bring about** / lead to sb's overthrow / downfall / fall

overthrow /ˈəʊvəθrəʊ; AmE ˈoʊvərθroʊ/ [sing.] the act of taking power by force from a leader or government; a leader or government's loss of power: *A republic was declared following the overthrow of the monarchy.* ◇ *He was president from 1966 until his overthrow in 1970.* See also **overthrow** → REMOVE *verb* 2

downfall /ˈdaʊnfɔːl/ [sing.] the loss of sb's power, money or social position; the thing that causes this: *The sex scandal finally led to his downfall.* ◇ *Greed was her downfall.*

fall [sing.] a loss of political or economic power or success; the loss or defeat of a city or country in war: *The scandal undoubtedly contributed to his fall from power.* ◇ *His diary charts his dramatic fall from grace* (= loss of power and respect). ◇ *Napoleon's rise and fall* ◇ *the fall of Rome to the barbarians* **OPP** rise → PROGRESS

▶ **fall** *verb* [I]: *The coup failed but the government fell shortly afterwards.* ◇ *Troy finally fell to the Greeks.*

nemesis /ˈneməsɪs/ [U, sing.] (*formal*) punishment or defeat that is deserved and cannot be avoided; the thing that causes this: *This over-ambitious project eventually proved to be the company's nemesis.*

undoing /ʌnˈduːɪŋ/ [sing.] the reason why sb fails at sth or loses their power, money or social position: *That one mistake was his undoing.* **OPP** making ❶ If sth **is the making of** sb, it makes them become a better or more successful person: *College was the making of Joe.*

overturn verb

overturn · reverse · override · overrule · set sth aside · quash
These words all mean to officially decide that a legal decision is not correct, and to make it no longer valid.

▶ to overturn / reverse / override / overrule / set aside / quash a **decision**
▶ to overturn / reverse / override / quash a **ban**
▶ to overturn / reverse / set aside / quash a **conviction** / **verdict**
▶ to overturn / reverse / quash a **ruling**
▶ to overturn / override a / an **veto** / **injunction**
▶ to **finally** overturn / quash sth
▶ to **completely** overturn / reverse sth

overturn /ˌəʊvəˈtɜːn; AmE ˌoʊvərˈtɜːrn/ [T] (*especially journalism*) to officially decide that a legal decision is not correct, and to make it no longer valid: *His sentence was overturned by the appeal court.*

reverse [T] (*rather formal*) to change a previous decision, law or policy to the opposite one: *The policy is likely to be reversed if there is a change of government.*

override /ˌəʊvəˈraɪd; AmE ˌoʊvərˈr-/ [T] to use your authority to reject sb's decision or wishes: *The chairman overrode the committee's objections and signed the agreement.*

overrule /ˌəʊvəˈruːl; AmE ˌoʊvərˈr-/ [T, often passive] (*rather formal*) to use your authority to reject sb's decision: *The verdict was overruled by the Supreme Court.*

> **NOTE** OVERRIDE OR OVERRULE? **Override** suggests that there are more important factors to consider than the decision or wishes of one person or group; **overrule** places more emphasis on the use of sb's authority to reject sth.

set sth a'side *phrasal verb* to officially state that a decision made by a court is not legally valid: *The verdict was set aside by the Appeal Court.*

quash /kwɒʃ; AmE kwɑːʃ/ [T] (*written*) to officially state that a decision made by a court is not legally valid: *His conviction was later quashed by the Court of Appeal.*

overwhelm *verb*

overwhelm · swamp · bombard · flood · inundate
These words all refer to things or problems that are so many or so great that sb cannot deal with them.

PATTERNS AND COLLOCATIONS
▸ to overwhelm / swamp / bombard / flood / inundate sb / sth with sth
▸ to be swamped / bombarded / flooded / inundated with **complaints / requests**
▸ to be swamped / inundated with **offers / enquiries**
▸ to be bombarded / flooded / inundated with **calls / letters**
▸ to **suddenly** overwhelm / swamp sb

overwhelm /ˌəʊvəˈwelm; *AmE* ˌoʊvərˈw-/ [T] to be so bad or so great that sb cannot deal with it; to give sb more of sth than they want or can deal with: *The office was overwhelmed by the volume of work that was required.* ◊ *She thinks she knows all the answers and always overwhelms me with advice.* See also **overwhelming** → UNCONTROLLABLE

swamp /swɒmp; *AmE* swɑːmp/ [T, often passive] to be so great that sb cannot deal with it; to give sb more things than they can deal with: *This is a big task and I am finding myself swamped.* ◊ *Radio stations have been swamped with requests to play the song.*

NOTE OVERWHELM OR SWAMP? People are typically **overwhelmed** by the *amount, number* or *volume* of a thing; people are **swamped** by the things themselves – *complaints, requests, offers* or *enquiries.*

bombard /bɒmˈbɑːd; *AmE* bɑːmˈbɑːrd/ [T] to attack sb with a lot of questions or criticism, or by giving them too much information: *The interviewer bombarded her with intimate questions.* ◊ *We are bombarded daily with propaganda about what we should eat.*

flood [T, usually passive] to send sth somewhere in large numbers: *The office was flooded with applications for the job.* See also **flood** → FLOOD *noun* 2

inundate /ˈɪnʌndeɪt/ [T, often passive] to give or send sb so many things that they cannot deal with them all: *We have been inundated with offers of help.*

own *adj.* See the Topic Map for THE INDIVIDUAL AND SOCIETY on p.894

own · personal · individual · private · subjective · exclusive
These words are all used to talk about sth that belongs to or is connected with one particular person.

PATTERNS AND COLLOCATIONS
▸ sb's own / personal / individual / private / subjective **experience**
▸ sb's own / personal / private / subjective **opinion**
▸ sb's own / personal / private / exclusive **property**
▸ sb's own / personal / individual **needs / requirements / objectives / freedom**

own belonging to or connected with a particular person; done or produced by and for yourself: *It was her own idea.* ◊ *I saw it with my own eyes* (= I didn't hear about it from sb else). ◊ *Our children are grown up and have children of their own.* ◊ *For reasons of his own* (= special reasons that perhaps only he knew about) *he refused to join the club.* ◊ *The accident happened through no fault of her own.* ◊ *He wants to come into the business on his own terms.* ◊ *I need a room of my own.* ◊ *I have my very own room at last.* ◊ *She makes all her own clothes.*
❶ Own cannot be used after an article: *I need my own room.* ◊ *I need an own room.* ◊ *It's good to have your own room.* ◊ *It's good to have a room of the own.*

personal [only before noun] your own; not belonging to or connected with anyone else: *They packed up their personal belongings and left.* ◊ *The receptionist asked for my personal details* (= my name, age, etc.). ◊ *Of course, this is just a personal opinion.* ◊ *The novel is written from personal experience.* ◊ *All hire cars are for personal use* (= not business use) *only.* ◊ *Use stencils to add a few personal touches to walls and furniture.* ◊ *He has run a personal best of just under four minutes.*
▸ **personally** *adv.*: *Personally, I prefer the second option.*

individual [only before noun] connected with one person; designed for one person: *Respect for individual freedom is a cornerstone of our culture.* ◊ *Try to measure in individual portions how much people will eat.* OPP **communal** → COMMON, See also **individual** → PARTICULAR *adj.*, **individual** → PERSON *noun*
▸ **individually** *adv.*: *The manager spoke to them all individually.*

private [usually before noun] belonging to or for the use of a particular person or group; not for public use: *The sign said, 'Private property. Keep out.'* ◊ *Those are my father's private papers.* ◊ *The hotel has 110 bedrooms, all with private bathrooms.* OPP **public** → COMMON, See also **privacy** → PRIVACY

NOTE PERSONAL OR PRIVATE? **Personal** things, details, etc. actually belong to a particular individual person and not any other individual person. **Private** things belong to a particular person or group, or are for them to use; they are not for people in general. *Personal property* usually consists of small items that belong to a particular person; *private property* is land that belongs to a particular person or group of people.

subjective (*sometimes disapproving*) based on your own ideas and opinions rather than facts and therefore sometimes unfair: *a highly subjective point of view* ◊ *Everyone's opinion is bound to be subjective.* OPP **objective** → OBJECTIVE
▸ **subjectively** *adv.*: *People who are less subjectively involved are better judges.*

exclusive /ɪkˈskluːsɪv/ only to be used by one particular person or group; only given to one particular person or group: *The hotel has exclusive access to the beach.* ◊ *exclusive rights to televise the World Cup* ◊ *His mother has told 'The Times' about his death in an exclusive interview* (= not given to any other newspaper).

P p

pack
verb See also the entry for CROWD

---

pack · cram · stuff · squeeze · jam · wedge
These words all mean to push sb/sth into a small space.

PATTERNS AND COLLOCATIONS
- to pack/cram/stuff/squeeze/jam/wedge sb/sth **in**/**into** sth
- to pack/cram/stuff/squeeze/jam/wedge sb/sth **between** sth and sth else
- to pack/cram/stuff sth **with** sth
- to be packed/crammed/squeezed/jammed/wedged **together**
- to be packed/crammed/stuffed/squeezed/jammed/wedged **tightly**

pack [I, T] (usually used with an adverb or preposition) (of a group of people) to all get into a small space so that it is full, with everyone very close together; to fill a space or container tightly with sth: *We all packed together into one car.* ◇ *Fans packed the hall to see the band.* ◇ *Pack wet shoes with newspaper to help them dry.* See also **packed** → FULL *adj.*

cram (-**mm**-) [T, I] to push or force sb/sth into a small space; (of a group of people) to pack into a place: *I managed to cram down a few mouthfuls of food.* ◇ *Supporters crammed the streets.* ◇ *We all managed to cram into his car.* See also **crammed** → FULL *adj.*

NOTE PACK OR CRAM? In many cases you can use either word: *We all managed to pack/cram into the car.* However, **pack** can suggest that people or things are pushed or fitted in neatly in order to get as many/much in as possible; with **cram** there is often less order and more force: *I managed to pack down a few mouthfuls of food.*

stuff [T] to fill a space or container tightly with sth, especially in a careless or untidy way: *She had 500 leaflets to stuff into envelopes.* ◇ *The closet was stuffed to bursting.* ◇ *All the drawers were stuffed full of letters and papers.*

squeeze [T, I] (always used with an adverb or preposition) to force sb/sth/yourself into or through a small space: *We managed to squeeze six people into the car.* ◇ *They were able to squeeze through a gap in the fence.*

▸ **squeeze** *noun* [sing.]: *It was a tight squeeze but we finally got everything into the case.*

jam (-**mm**-) [T, usually passive] (always used with an adverb or preposition) to put sb/sth into a small space where there is very little room to move: *We were jammed together like sardines in a can.*

NOTE PACK, STUFF OR JAM? **Pack** emphasizes how tightly things are put into a space, often for a good reason: *Pack wet shoes with newspaper to help them dry.* You could also use **stuff** in this sentence, but NOT **jam**. **Stuff** often suggests that things have been put into a space in a quick, careless or untidy way: *All the drawers were stuffed full of letters and papers.* You could also use **jam** in this sentence, but NOT **pack**. **Jam** is often used in the passive, to suggest that people or things have been pushed into a space against their will, more as a result of circumstances than from anyone's considered action.

wedge [T] (always used with an adverb or preposition) to put or squeeze sth tightly into a narrow space, so that it cannot move easily: *The phone was wedged under his chin.*

---

packet
noun See also the entry for BOTTLE

---

packet · pack · package · can · jar · tin · carton · tube · pot · tub · sachet
These are all words for small containers that goods are put in so that they can be sold in shops.

PATTERNS AND COLLOCATIONS
- a packet/pack/package/can/jar/tin/carton/tube/pot/tub/sachet **of** sth
- **in** a packet/pack/package/can/jar/tin/carton/tube/pot/tub/sachet
- an **empty** packet/pack/package/can/jar/tin/carton/tube/pot/tub/sachet
- a **plastic** packet/pack/package/jar/carton/pot/tub
- to **open** a packet/pack/package/can/jar/tin/pot/tub
- to **empty** a packet/pack/can/jar/tin/carton
- a packet/pack/package/can/jar/tin/carton/tube/pot/tub/sachet **contains** sth

---

packaging

packet (*BrE*)
pack (*AmE*)

packet (*BrE*)
package (*AmE*)

can

tin/can (*BrE*)
can (*AmE*)

jar

carton

tube

pot

tub

sachet (*BrE*)
packet (*AmE*)

packet [C] (*BrE*) a small paper or cardboard container in which goods are packed or wrapped for selling: *a packet of biscuits/cigarettes/crisps* ❶ In American English this is called a **pack** or **package** (see below). In American English a **packet** is a closed paper or plastic container, like a small envelope, that contains a small amount of liquid or powder: *a packet of ketchup*. In British English this is called a **sachet** (see below).

pack [C] (*especially AmE*) a container, usually made of paper, that holds a number of the same thing or an amount of sth, ready to be sold: *a pack of cigarettes/gum* ◇ *You can buy the disks in packs of ten.*

package [C] (*AmE*) a box, bag or other kind of container in which things are wrapped or packed: *Check the list of ingredients on the side of the package.* ◇ *a package of cookies*

▶ **package** *verb* [T, often passive]: *We package our products in recyclable materials.*

can [C] a closed metal container for food and drink; a strong round metal container with straight sides and a lid in which liquids such as paint and glue are sold and stored: *a can of beans/beer/paint*

▶ **canned** *adj.*: *You can use fresh, canned or frozen fruit for this recipe.*

jar [C] a round glass or plastic container, like a bottle but with a very wide opening at the top and a lid: *She bought a set of storage jars for the kitchen.* ◇ *a jar of jam/coffee/honey* (= with jam/coffee/honey in it) ◇ *an empty jam jar*

tin [C] (*BrE*) a can for food, paint, glue, etc. (but not drink): *a tin of beans/soup/tomatoes/varnish* ◇ *The bedroom needed three tins of paint* (= in order to paint it).

▶ **tinned** *adj.*: (*BrE*) *tinned tomatoes*

> **NOTE** **CAN OR TIN?** In American English **can** is the usual word used for both food and drink. In British English **can** is used for drinks containers, but **tin** and **can** are both used for containers for food or paint, etc. **Tin can** usually means the container without anything in it: *We made a toy telephone out of two tin cans and a piece of string.*

carton [C] a light cardboard or plastic box that is used for holding liquids or soft food: *a carton of milk/fruit juice/ice cream* ◇ *an empty milk carton* See also **jug** → BOTTLE

tube [C] a long narrow container made of soft metal or plastic, with a lid, used for holding thick liquids that can be squeezed out of it: *a tube of toothpaste*

pot [C] (*especially BrE*) a small round container made of glass, clay or plastic, used for storing food in: *a pot of jam/honey/yogurt* ◇ *an empty yogurt pot*

tub [C] a small wide plastic or paper container with a lid, used for storing soft foods such as ice cream and margarine: *a tub of margarine/ice cream* ◇ *an empty margarine tub*

sachet /'sæʃeɪ; *AmE* sæ'ʃeɪ/ [C] (*BrE*) a closed paper or plastic container, like a small envelope, that contains a small amount of liquid or powder: *a sachet of sauce/sugar/shampoo* ❶ In American English this is called a **packet**.

page *noun*

page · sheet · slip · side
These are all words for a single piece of paper.

PATTERNS AND COLLOCATIONS
▶ a sheet / slip **of paper**
▶ **on** a / the page / sheet / slip / side
▶ **in the middle / at the top / at the bottom** of the page / sheet
▶ a / an **blank / loose / printed / separate / A4 / A5** page / sheet

page (*abbr.* **p**) [C] one side or both sides of a piece of paper, especially when there are several pieces of paper together, for example in a book, magazine or letter: *Turn to page 64.* ◇ *Someone has torn a page out of this book.* ◇ *The text refers to the photograph on the opposite/facing page.* ◇ *The article continues over the page.* ◇ *I never read the sports pages or the financial pages of the newspaper.*

sheet [C] a piece of paper for writing or printing on, usually in a standard size, but not one which is part of a book: *Take a clean sheet of paper* (= with no writing on it). ◇ *Start each answer on a fresh sheet.* ◇ *Pick up one of our free information sheets at reception.*

slip [C] a small piece of paper, especially one for writing on or with sth printed on it: *I wrote it down on a slip of paper.* ◇ *Please fill in the tear-off slip and return it to the office.*

side [C] the amount of writing needed to fill one side of a sheet of paper: *He told us to write no more than three sides.* ❶ **Side** is used instead of **page** to avoid confusion, as a **page** may be one or both sides of a piece of paper.

pain *noun* See the Topic Map for HEALTH on p.890

pain · ache · suffering · discomfort · agony
These are all words for the feelings that you have in your body when you have been hurt or when you are ill.

discomfort	pain	agony
	ache	
	suffering	

PATTERNS AND COLLOCATIONS
▶ **in** pain / discomfort / agony
▶ **(a) back / stomach** pain / ache
▶ **to cause** pain / suffering / discomfort
▶ **to inflict** pain / suffering
▶ **to suffer** pain / discomfort / agony
▶ **to relieve / ease** the pain / suffering / discomfort / agony

pain [U, C] the feelings that you have in your body when you have been hurt or when you are ill: *She was clearly in a lot of pain.* ◇ *He felt a sharp pain in his knee.* ◇ *He went to the doctor with chest pains.* ◇ *The booklet contains information on pain relief during labour.* ❶ **Pain** can also be a mental feeling. See also **pain** → DISTRESS *noun*, **pain** → HURT *verb* 1

ache /eɪk/ [C] a continuous feeling of pain in a part of the body: *You get more aches and pains as you get older.* ❶ **Ache** is often used in compounds: *Mummy, I've got a tummy ache.* ◇ *to have a stomach ache/headache/backache/toothache.* In British English, some of these compounds can be uncountable: [U] (*BrE*) *to have backache/toothache.* See also **ache** → HURT *verb* 2

suffering [U, pl.] physical pain, especially when it affects the whole body and continues for a long time: *Death finally brought an end to her suffering.* ◇ *The hospice aims to ease the sufferings of the dying.* ❶ **Suffering** can also be emotional pain. See also **suffering** → DISTRESS

▶ **suffer** *verb* [I]: *I hate to see animals suffering.*

discomfort /dɪs'kʌmfət; *AmE* -fərt/ [U] (*rather formal*) a feeling of slight pain or of being physically uncomfortable: *You will experience some minor discomfort during the treatment.*

agony /'æɡəni/ [U, C] extreme physical pain: *Jack collapsed in agony on the floor.* ◇ *The animal writhed in its death agonies.* ❶ **Agony** can also be emotional pain. See also **agony** → DISTRESS

painful *adj.*

1 a painful knee/injection/death
2 painful memories

1 See the Topic Map for HEALTH on p.890
painful · sore · raw · inflamed · excruciating · burning · itchy
These words all describe sth that causes you physical pain.

itchy	painful	excruciating
	sore	burning
	raw	
	inflamed	

PATTERNS AND COLLOCATIONS
▸ sore / inflamed / itchy **eyes**
▸ raw / inflamed / itchy **skin**
▸ a painful / an excruciating **death**
▸ a painful / a burning **sensation**
▸ excruciating / burning **pain**

painful causing you physical pain: *Is your knee still painful?* ◇ *Ulcers can be unbearably painful.* ◇ *I had to undergo a series of painful injections.* ◇ *It was a slow and painful death.* ❶ **Painful** can describe a part of the body, illness, injury, treatment or death. `OPP` **painless** ❶ Something that is **painless** causes no pain: *a painless death* ◇ *The treatment is painless.*
  ▸ **painfully** *adv.*: *He limped painfully to the door.*

sore (of a part of the body) painful and often red, especially because of infection or because a muscle has been used too much: *He had a high temperature and a sore throat.* ◇ *Their feet were sore after hours of walking.* See also **sore** → TUMOUR *noun*
  ▸ **soreness** *noun* [U]: *an ointment to reduce soreness and swelling*

raw (of a part of the body) red and painful, for example because of an infection or because the skin has been damaged: *His throat was raw and painful.* ◇ *The skin on her feet had been rubbed raw.*

inflamed /ɪnˈfleɪmd/ (of a part of the body) painful, red and hot because of an infection or injury: *Her finger was swollen and inflamed.* ◇ *The wound had become inflamed.* See also **inflammation** → TUMOUR *noun*

excruciating /ɪkˈskruːʃieɪtɪŋ/ extremely painful: *The pain in my back was excruciating.* ◇ *The process is painful, but not excruciating.* ◇ *She groaned at the memory, suffering all over again the excruciating embarrassment of those moments.* ❶ **Excruciating** can describe feelings, treatments or death but NOT parts of the body: *an excruciating throat/back/knee* It can describe mental as well as physical pain.
  ▸ **excruciatingly** *adv.*: *an excruciatingly painful death*

burning painful and giving a feeling of being very hot; feeling very hot: *She felt a burning sensation in her throat.* ◇ *The boy's forehead was burning.* ❶ **Burning** can describe a feeling or a part of the body.

itchy giving an uncomfortable feeling on your skin that makes you want to scratch; having this feeling: *The skin on my legs broke out in an itchy rash.* ◇ *I feel itchy all over.*

---

2 See also the entries for SAD, STRESSFUL and WORRYING
painful · traumatic · distressing · upsetting · harrowing · agonizing
These words all describe sth that makes you feel upset or anxious.

| painful | traumatic | harrowing |
| upsetting | distressing | agonizing |

PATTERNS AND COLLOCATIONS
▸ to be painful / traumatic / distressing / upsetting **for** sb
▸ to be painful / distressing / upsetting **to do sth**
▸ to be distressing / upsetting **that…**
▸ a painful / a traumatic / a distressing / an upsetting / a harrowing **experience**
▸ a painful / a traumatic / a distressing / a harrowing / an agonizing **time**
▸ a painful / distressing / harrowing **scene**
▸ a distressing / harrowing **sight**
▸ a painful / an agonizing **decision**
▸ **rather** painful / traumatic / distressing / pathetic / upsetting / harrowing
▸ **very / extremely / deeply / particularly** painful / distressing / upsetting

painful making you feel upset or embarrassed: *Seeing her again brought back painful memories.* ◇ *Their efforts were painful to watch.* See also **pain** → DISTRESS *noun*

---

traumatic /trɔːˈmætɪk; AmE traʊˈm-/ (especially of an experience) very unpleasant and making you feel very upset and/or anxious: *a traumatic childhood* ◇ *Divorce can be traumatic for everyone involved.* See also **trauma** → NIGHTMARE, **traumatize** → FRIGHTEN

distressing /dɪˈstresɪŋ/ making you feel very upset, especially because of sb's suffering: *The divorce was extremely distressing for the children.* ◇ *What could be more distressing than the death of their only child?* See also **distress** → DISTRESS *noun*, **distress** → HURT *verb* 1, **distressed** → UPSET

upsetting making you feel unhappy, anxious or annoyed: *I could see that it had been an upsetting experience for him.* ◇ *It's always upsetting to lose a patient.* See also **upset** → UPSET *adj.*, **upset** → HURT *verb* 1

harrowing /ˈhærəʊɪŋ; AmE -roʊ-/ very shocking or frightening and making you feel extremely upset: *There were harrowing scenes at the airport as relatives heard news of the crash.* ◇ *You've had a harrowing experience and a lucky escape.*

agonizing (BrE also -**ising**) /ˈæɡənaɪzɪŋ/ causing great pain, anxiety or difficulty: *his father's agonizing death* ◇ *It was the most agonizing decision of her young life.*

---

paint *verb*

paint · dye · colour · tint · stain
These words all mean to add colour to sth or change the colour of sth with a substance.

PATTERNS AND COLLOCATIONS
▸ to paint / dye / colour / tint / stain sth **with** sth
▸ to paint / dye / colour / tint / stain sth **red / yellow / green**, etc.
▸ to paint / stain **wood**
▸ to dye / colour your **hair**

paint [T] to cover a surface or object with paint: *We've decided to have the house painted.* ◇ *Paint the shed with weather-resistant paint.* ◇ *a brightly painted barge* ◇ *The walls were painted yellow.* See also **paint** → DRAW *verb*
  ▸ **paint** *noun* [U]: *The woodwork has recently been given a fresh coat of paint.* ◇ *The paint is starting to peel off.*

dye [T] to change the colour of hair or fabric by using a special liquid or substance: *to dye clothes/fabric/wool* ◇ *She dyed her hair blonde.* ◇ *dyed black hair*
  ▸ **dye** *noun* [U, C]: *hair dye* ◇ *natural/chemical/vegetable dyes*

colour (BrE) (AmE **color**) [T] to add colour to your hair by using a special liquid or substance: *How long have you been colouring your hair?* See also **colour** → DRAW
  ▸ **colour** (BrE) (AmE **color**) *noun* [C, U]: *a semi-permanent hair colour that lasts around six washes*

tint [T, usually passive] to add a small amount of colour to sth: *She's having her eyelashes tinted.* ◇ *tinted windows/ lenses* See also **tint** → COLOUR 1

stain [T] to change the colour of sth using a coloured liquid: *The floors had been stained dark brown.* ◇ *He stained the specimen before looking at it under the microscope.*
  ▸ **stain** *noun* [U, C]: *Apply two coats of white stain.* ◇ *a wood stain*

`NOTE` DYE OR STAIN? You **dye** hair or fabric; you **stain** wood.

---

palace *noun*

palace · mansion · country house · villa · manor · stately home · chateau
These words all mean a large house that belongs or used to belong to a rich or important family.

▸ a **magnificent** palace / mansion / country house / villa
▸ an **ancient** palace / mansion / manor
▸ a **medieval** palace / manor / chateau
▸ a **royal** palace / mansion / manor
▸ a **country** mansion / house / villa / manor

palace /'pæləs/ [C] the official home of sb such as a king, queen or president; any large impressive house, usually in a city: *Buckingham Palace is the official London residence of the Queen.* ◇ *The Old Town has a whole collection of churches, palaces and mosques.*

mansion /'mænʃn/ [C] a large impressive house in the country or the city: *It is a magnificent example of a 17th century country mansion.*

,**country 'house** [C] (*BrE*) a large house in the country, especially one that belongs or used to belong to a rich important family: *He used to entertain the politicians of the day at his country house.*

villa [C] a house in the country with a large garden, especially in southern Europe; (in Roman times) a country house or farm with land attached to it: *Once a private villa, the Stella d'Italia is now a hotel.* ◇ *They found the remains of an impressive Roman villa.*

manor /'mænə(r)/ (also '**manor house**) [C] a large country house surrounded by a large area of land that belongs to it: *He bought the old manor and set about turning himself into the local squire.*

,**stately 'home** [C] (*BrE*) a large, impressive house of historical interest, especially one that the public may visit: *There are many stately homes to visit in the area.*

chateau (also **château**) /'ʃætəʊ; *AmE* ʃæ'toʊ/ (pl. **chateaux** or **chateaus** /-təʊz; *AmE* -'toʊz/) [C] (from *French*) a castle or large country house in France: *The Loire Valley is home to more than 300 chateaux.*

pale *adj.*

1 a pale face
2 pale colours

---

1 See the Topic Map for HEALTH on p.890
pale · white · grey · sallow · ashen · wan
These words all describe skin that is whiter than other people's or whiter than usual.

▸ pale / white / grey / ashen **with** anger, fear, shock, pain, etc.
▸ a pale / a white / a grey / a sallow / an ashen / a wan **face**
▸ pale / white / sallow / ashen **cheeks**
▸ pale / white / grey / sallow **skin**
▸ a pale / white / sallow **complexion**
▸ to **look** pale / white / grey / sallow / ashen / wan
▸ to **turn** pale / white / grey
▸ to **go** pale / white / ashen
▸ **very** pale / white / grey

pale (*often disapproving*) (of a person or their face) having skin that is whiter than other people's, or whiter than usual because of illness or strong emotion: *She was deathly pale and very thin.* ◇ *His face went pale with anger.* ❶ Pale often has a negative meaning, but it does not have to: *She was tall, dark and pale, and very beautiful.*

white very pale, usually because of strong emotion: *She went as white as a sheet when she heard the news.*

grey (*especially BrE*) (*AmE* usually **gray**) (*disapproving*) pale and dull because of illness or tiredness: *The next morning she looked very grey and hollow-eyed.*

sallow pale with a slightly yellow colour that does not look healthy: *a sallow complexion / face* ◇ *The rosy bloom of her face had faded, leaving her sallow and drawn.*

ashen (*written*) very pale because of illness or fear: *His face was ashen and wet with sweat.*

wan (*written*) looking pale, weak and tired: *his grey, wan face* ◇ *She gave me a wan smile* (= showing no energy or enthusiasm).
▸ **wanly** *adv.*: *He smiled wanly.*

2 pale · light · soft · dull · pastel · subtle · dusky · neutral · cool
These words all describe light or a colour which is not bright or strong.

▸ a pale / light / soft / dull / pastel / subtle / neutral / cool **colour**
▸ a pale / light / soft / dull / pastel / subtle / neutral / cool **shade**
▸ pale / light / soft / pastel / subtle / neutral **tones**
▸ pale / light / soft / dull / pastel / subtle / dusky **pink**
▸ pale / light / soft / dull / pastel / subtle / cool **green**
▸ pale / light / soft / dull / dusky **red**
▸ pale / light / soft / dull / pastel / cool **blue**
▸ pale / light / soft / dull / cool **grey**
▸ pale / light / soft / dull **brown / yellow**
▸ pale / light / dull / dusky **orange**
▸ a pale / soft / dull / dusky **light**
▸ a pale / soft / dull **glow**
▸ a pale / dull **sky**
▸ pale / light / soft / cool **blue eyes**
▸ sth is pale / light / neutral **in colour**

pale (of a colour or light) containing a lot of white: *The bedroom walls are pale green.* ◇ *The rooftops and chimneys stood out against the pale sky.* ◇ *The flowers were pale and wilted.* **OPP** **dark, deep** → DARK 2

light pale in colour: *He's got light blue eyes.* ◇ *Lighter shades suit you best.* ◇ *People with pale complexions should avoid wearing light colours.* **OPP** **dark** → DARK 2

NOTE PALE OR LIGHT? When describing colours you can use either word: *pale/light blue/green/yellow/orange/ red/pink/purple/grey/brown* ◇ *pale/light colours/ shades/tones.* **Pale** is also used to describe a kind of light that contains a lot of white, especially when it is not very bright: *a pale light/glow/sky* ◇ ~~a light light/ glow/sky~~

soft [usually before noun] not too bright, in a way that is pleasant and relaxing to the eyes: *a colour scheme of soft pink and cream* ◇ *the soft glow of candlelight* **OPP** **harsh** → STRONG 2

dull not bright or shiny: *The blood stained the grass a dull red colour.* ◇ *The fire died down to a dull glow.* **OPP** **bright** → BRIGHT

pastel /'pæstl; *AmE* pæ'stel/ [only before noun] having a pale delicate colour: *The white walls were repainted in pastel shades.*
▸ **pastel** *noun* [C]: *The whole house was painted in soft pastels.*

subtle /'sʌtl/ [usually before noun] (*approving*) (of colours) not too bright or noticeable, in a way that is attractive: *Her paintings are characterized by sweeping brush strokes and subtle colours.*

dusky [usually before noun] (*literary*) dark or soft in colour: *The setting sun tinged the sky with a dusky orange.*

neutral /'nju:trəl; *AmE* 'nu:-/ (of colours) not very bright or strong, such as grey or light brown: *a neutral colour scheme* ◇ *Neutral tones will give the room a feeling of space.*

cool (*usually approving*) (of colours) making you feel pleasantly cool: *a room painted in cool greens and blues* **OPP** **warm** → DARK 2

pan *noun*

pan · pot · saucepan · frying pan · tin · cauldron · wok · casserole · skillet
These are all words for containers that are used for cooking or heating food.

▸ a pan / pot / saucepan **of** sth
▸ a **large** pan / pot / saucepan / frying pan / tin / cauldron / wok / casserole / skillet
▸ a **small** pan / pot / saucepan / frying pan / tin / casserole / skillet
▸ a **heavy** pan / pot / saucepan / frying pan / casserole / skillet
▸ a **non-stick** pan / frying pan / skillet

pan [C] a round metal container, usually with a handle or handles, used for cooking or heating food on top of a cooker: *Remove the pan from the heat and add the sugar.* ◇ *Bring a pan of water to the boil.* ❶ In American English **pan** can also mean a metal container without a lid that is used for cooking food in an oven: *Put your turkey on a rack in a shallow roasting pan.* In British English this is called a **tin**.

pot [C] (often used in compounds) (*especially AmE*) a deep round metal container, usually with two short handles, used for cooking or heating food on top of a cooker: *A large stock pot was simmering on the stove.* ◇ *a soup/fondue pot* ◇ *a pot of stew*

saucepan /ˈsɔːspən; AmE -pæn/ [C] a deep round metal pan with a lid and one long handle or two short handles, used for cooking or heating food on top of a cooker: *a saucepan of boiling water*

> **NOTE** PAN, POT OR SAUCEPAN? **Pan** is the most general of these words and can be any shape or size, with a lid or without. **Saucepan** can be used for a deep pan with a lid, especially if it has a long handle, although you can also just say **pan**. **Pot** is often preferred in American English for a deep pan, either with two short handles or no handles at all; however, it is usually used in compounds in the phrase *a pot of sth*. **Pots and pans** means several different containers that you use to cook food: *I washed all the pots and pans after dinner.*

'frying pan [C] a large shallow pan with a long handle, used for frying food in: *Heat the butter in a heavy-based frying pan.*

tin [C] (*BrE*) a metal container without a lid that is used for cooking food in an oven: *Line the cake tin with greaseproof paper.* ❶ In American English this is called a **pan**.

cauldron (*AmE also* **caldron**) /ˈkɔːldrən/ [C] (especially in the past or in stories) a large round metal container for cooking or heating liquids, usually supported or hung over a fire: *a witch's cauldron* ◇ *The emperor condemned him to be cast into a cauldron of boiling oil.*

wok [C] a large pan that is shaped like a bowl and used for frying food quickly in hot oil, especially Chinese food: *Heat a wok or large frying pan until hot and add the oil.*

casserole /ˈkæsərəʊl; AmE -roʊl/ (*also* **'casserole dish**) [C] a heavy, deep container with a lid, used for cooking meat, vegetables or other foods slowly in liquid, especially in an oven: *Place the chicken pieces in the bottom of a large casserole.*

skillet /ˈskɪlɪt/ [C] (*especially AmE*) a frying pan, especially one that is quite heavy: *Heat 1 inch of oil in a deep cast-iron skillet.*

pots and pans

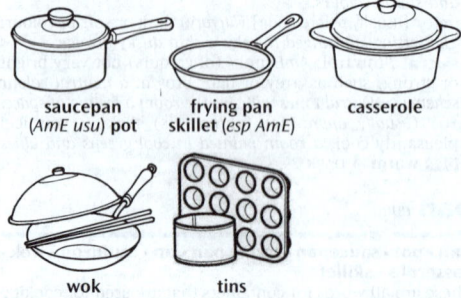

saucepan   frying pan   casserole
(AmE usu) pot   skillet (esp AmE)

wok   tins

panic *verb*

panic · freak out · lose your nerve · take fright · chicken out
These words all mean to feel frightened, usually so that you act in a stupid or dangerous way or so that you cannot do sth that you intended to do.

▸ to **just** panic / freak out / lose your nerve

panic (**-ck**) [I] to suddenly feel very frightened so that you cannot think clearly and you say or do sth stupid or dangerous: *I panicked when I saw smoke coming out of the engine.* ◇ *Don't panic! We need to try and stay calm.* See also **panic** → FEAR *noun*, **panicky**, **panic-stricken** → HYSTERICAL

,freak 'out *phrasal verb* (*informal*) to react very strongly to sth that makes you suddenly feel shocked, frightened or surprised: *I could hear her downstairs, and I was freaking out, hiding under the bed.*

,lose your 'nerve *idiom* to not do sth that you intended to do, because you are afraid: *I tried to go parachuting once, but I lost my nerve at the last minute and didn't jump.* **OPP** keep/hold your nerve

take 'fright *idiom* (*written*) to suddenly become frightened by sth so that you want to escape or get out of a situation: *The birds took fright and flew away.* ◇ *Investors took fright at the falling market.*

,chicken 'out (*informal, disapproving*) to decide not to do sth because you are afraid: *She chickened out of telling him what really happened.*

paper *noun* See also the entries for ARTICLE and ASSIGNMENT

paper · essay · thesis · dissertation · monograph · treatise · tract
These are all words for a piece of academic writing on a particular subject.

▸ a **paper** / an **essay** / a **thesis** / a **dissertation** / a **monograph** / a **treatise** / a **tract on** sth
▸ a **paper** / an **essay** / a **thesis** / a **dissertation** / a **monograph** / a **treatise about** sth
▸ a **short** paper / essay / thesis / monograph / treatise / tract
▸ a **long** paper / essay / dissertation / treatise / tract
▸ a **research** paper / essay / thesis / dissertation / monograph
▸ a **recent** paper / essay / dissertation / monograph
▸ a **scholarly** paper / essay / monograph / treatise
▸ to **write** / **read** a paper / an essay / a thesis / a dissertation / a monograph / a treatise / a tract
▸ to **publish** a paper / an essay / a thesis / a monograph / a treatise / a tract
▸ to **submit** a paper / an essay / a thesis / a dissertation

paper [C] an academic article about a particular subject that is written by and for specialists: *a recent paper in the Journal of Medicine* ◇ *She was invited to give a paper* (= a talk) *on the results of her research.* ❶ In American English **a paper** can also be a piece of written work done by a student: *Your grade will be based on four papers and a final exam.*

essay [C] a short piece of writing by a student as part of their studies; a short piece of writing on a particular subject, written in order to be published: *We have to write an essay on the causes of the First World War.* ◇ *The book contains a number of interesting essays on women in society.*

thesis /ˈθiːsɪs/ (pl. **theses** /ˈθiːsiːz/) [C] a long piece of writing completed by a student as part of a university degree, based on their own research: *Students must submit a thesis on an agreed subject within four years.* ◇ (*BrE*) *a doctoral/PhD thesis* ◇ (*AmE*) *a thesis for a master's degree* See also **thesis** → THEORY 2

dissertation /ˌdɪsəˈteɪʃn; AmE -sərˈt-/ [C] a long piece of writing on a particular subject, especially one written for a university degree: *She is writing her dissertation on the history of the Knights Templar.*

> **NOTE** THESIS OR DISSERTATION? These words are often used differently by different universities. For example, some universities use **thesis** in connection with a doctoral degree (= the highest level of degree), while others use **dissertation**. In general, **thesis** emphasizes

that the piece of writing contains original research that the writer has done in order to support a particular theory or idea.

monograph /'mɒnəgrɑːf; AmE 'mɑːnəgræf/ [C] (technical) a detailed written study of a single, often limited subject, usually in the form of a short book: He has published several books on Cubism and numerous monographs on individual artists.

treatise /'triːtɪs; -tɪz/ [C] (formal) a long and serious piece of writing that examines a particular subject: Any of these questions would deserve a lengthy treatise, perhaps even a small book.

tract [C] (sometimes disapproving) a short piece of writing, especially on a religious, moral or political subject, that is intended to influence people's ideas: He wrote several tracts on the dangers of alcohol. ◇ socialist/feminist tracts

parallel adj.

parallel · side by side · simultaneous · concurrent
These words all describe sth that happens or exists at the same time as sth else.

PATTERNS AND COLLOCATIONS
▸ side by side / simultaneous / concurrent **with** sth
▸ a parallel / simultaneous / concurrent **change**
▸ a parallel / simultaneous **increase / operation / process**
▸ parallel / concurrent **development**

parallel very similar; happening or existing at the same time: Two poisonings have been reported recently in London and now there has been a parallel case in the Netherlands. ◇ Though still a committed painter, in 1978 she launched a parallel career as a photographer.
▸ **parallel** adv.: The grammar classes **run parallel to** the literature class.
▸ **in 'parallel with sth** phrase: The city has grown in parallel with the growth of its industries.

side by 'side idiom together, without any difficulties: We have been using both systems, side by side, for two years. ◇ The two communities exist happily side by side.

simultaneous /ˌsɪmlˈteɪniəs; AmE ˌsaɪml-/ happening or done at the same time: There were several simultaneous attacks by the rebels. ◇ They will provide **simultaneous translation** of the President's speech into English.
▸ **simultaneously** adv.: The game will be broadcast simultaneously on TV and radio.

concurrent /kənˈkʌrənt; AmE -ˈkɜːr-/ (formal) happening or existing at the same time: He was imprisoned for two concurrent terms of 30 months and 18 months.
▸ **concurrently** adv.: The prison sentences will run concurrently.

park noun

park · gardens · playground
These are all words for an area of land where people can go to walk, play or relax.

PATTERNS AND COLLOCATIONS
▸ **at / in** the park / gardens / playground
▸ **to visit** the park / gardens

park [C] an area of public land in a town or city where people go to walk, play and relax: We went for a walk in the park. ◇ The Great Exhibition of 1851 was held in Hyde Park. ◇ a park bench See also **park** → GARDEN 1

gardens [pl.] (also **garden** [C] (especially in AmE) a public park with flowers, plants and places to sit: The **botanical gardens** (= a park where plants are grown for scientific study) are home to plants from all over the world. ◇ The public garden closes at 6 p.m. See also **garden** → GARDEN 1

playground /'pleɪɡraʊnd/ [C] an outdoor area where children can play, especially at a school or in a park: a school playground ◇ an **adventure playground** (= a playground with large structures, ropes, etc. for climbing on) See also **playing field** → PITCH

parody noun

parody · caricature · impersonation · spoof · impression · imitation
These are all words for a performance, film, piece of writing, etc. that deliberately copies sb/sth else.

PATTERNS AND COLLOCATIONS
▸ a parody / a caricature / an impersonation / a spoof / an impression / an imitation **of** sb / sth
▸ a **brilliant** parody / caricature
▸ a **grotesque** parody / caricature / imitation
▸ a **passable** impersonation / impression / imitation
▸ a **convincing** impersonation / impression
▸ a **poor** impersonation / imitation
▸ an **Elvis Presley / Marilyn Monroe, etc.** impersonation / impression / imitation
▸ to **do** a parody / an impersonation / a spoof / an impression / an imitation
▸ to **write** a parody / spoof

parody /'pærədi/ [C, U] a piece of writing, music, acting, etc. that deliberately copies the style of sb/sth in order to be amusing: He's currently working on a parody of a horror film. ◇ His personality made him an easy subject for parody.
▸ **parody** verb [T]: Her work parodies genres such as the thriller and the spy novel.

caricature /'kærɪkətʃʊə(r); AmE -tʃər; -tʃʊr/ [C] (sometimes disapproving) a description of a person or thing that makes them seem ridiculous by exaggerating some of their characteristics: He had unfairly presented a caricature of my views.
▸ **caricature** verb [T, often passive]: She was unfairly caricatured as a dumb blonde.

impersonation /ɪmˌpɜːsəˈneɪʃn; AmE -ˌpɜːrs-/ [C, U] a performance in which sb copies the way a person speaks or behaves in order to deceive people or to entertain them: He did an extremely convincing impersonation of the singer. See also **impersonate** → POSE

spoof /spuːf/ [C] (informal) a humorous copy of a film or television programme that exaggerates its main features: It's a **spoof on** horror movies. ◇ They did a very clever game show spoof.

impression [C] an amusing performance in which sb copies the way a person speaks or acts: She did her Marilyn Monroe impression.

imitation [C] an amusing performance in which sb copies the way a person speaks or acts: He does a hilarious imitation of George W Bush. See also **imitate** → POSE

> **NOTE** IMPERSONATION, IMPRESSION OR IMITATION? An **impersonation** of sb can be more serious than an **impression** or **imitation**. An **impression** or **imitation** (or a humorous **impersonation**) just copies the most obvious features of a person's voice, manner or behaviour, that people will instantly recognize, in order to be amusing. An **impersonation** can be a serious attempt to copy a person's whole appearance and character, either in order to deceive sb by really making them believe you are the person impersonated, or as part of a serious dramatic performance. An **impression** and an **imitation** are almost the same, but an **impression** may be more successful: a convincing impression ◇ a poor imitation

partial adj.

partial · incomplete · unfinished · fragmentary
These words all describe sth which is not whole.

PATTERNS AND COLLOCATIONS
▸ the incomplete / unfinished / fragmentary **nature** of sth
▸ partial / incomplete **information**
▸ an incomplete / unfinished **sentence**
▸ unfinished / fragmentary **works**

partial /'pɑːʃl; AmE 'pɑːrʃl/ not complete or whole: *It was only a partial solution to the problem.* ◇ *Our success was only partial.* ◇ *Astronomers are gathering in mid Wales to watch a **partial eclipse** of the sun.* ❶ **Partial** often describes the answer to sth: *a partial answer/explanation/indicator/solution,* or an action that stops or allows sth, but only partly: *a partial ban/blockade/closure/withdrawal* ◇ *partial compensation/exemption/fulfilment/relaxation.* The emphasis can either be on what has been achieved or what has not. See also **partially**
→ PARTLY

incomplete not having everything that sth should have; not complete or finished: *The statistics only provide an **incomplete picture**.* ◇ *The recorded data was incomplete and it was necessary to make approximate estimates.* ❶ **Incomplete** is used especially to describe information; the emphasis is on what is NOT known, rather than on what is known. **OPP** complete → WHOLE
▸ **incompletely** *adv.*: *The causes of the phenomenon are still incompletely understood.*

unfinished not finished: *We have some **unfinished business** to settle.* ◇ *Her last work was left unfinished.* ◇ *His unfinished lasagne was still on the table.* ❶ **Unfinished** is used especially to describe work, things that are being written, read or created, games, food or drink. See also **finish** → FINISH

fragmentary /'frægməntri; AmE -teri/ (*formal*) made of small parts that are not connected or complete: *There is only fragmentary evidence to support this theory.*

participant *noun* See also the entry for CANDIDATE

participant · contender · challenger · contestant · competitor
These are all words for sb who takes part in sth such as a sport, competition or election.

PATTERNS AND COLLOCATIONS
▸ a contender / challenger / contestant / competitor **for** sth
▸ a participant / contender / challenger / contestant / competitor **in** sth
▸ a **likely / possible** participant / contender
▸ a **main / major** participant / contender / challenger
▸ a **serious / strong** contender / challenger / competitor
▸ a **Democratic / Republican / presidential** contender / challenger
▸ to **take on** a contender / challenger
▸ a contestant / competitor **enters** sth

participant /pɑːˈtɪsɪpənt; AmE pɑːrˈt-/ [C] a person who is taking part in an activity or event: *Enrolment will be limited to 35 participants.* ◇ *She was an **unwilling participant** in his downfall.* See also **participate** → JOIN

contender [C] a person who is taking part in a competition or is trying to win sth, especially sb who has a good chance of winning: *She is a strong contender for the party leadership.* ◇ *Germany last night emerged as a contender to stage next year's event.*

challenger /'tʃælɪndʒə(r)/ [C] a person who competes with sb else in sport or politics for an important title or position that the other person already holds: *These two teams are the main challengers for the European title.* ◇ *He has been tipped as a potential **challenger to** the prime minister.* See also **challenge** → CHALLENGE

contestant /kənˈtestənt/ [C] a person who is taking part in a contest, such as a quiz: *Please welcome our next contestant.* See also **contest** → COMPETITION 1

competitor /kəmˈpetɪtə(r)/ [C] a person who is taking part in a competition, such as a sport or game: *Over 200 competitors entered the race.* ◇ *She is one of the sport's top competitors.* See also **compete** → PLAY *verb* 2, **competition** → COMPETITION 1, **competition** → COMPETITION 2

particular *adj.*

particular · certain · separate · specific · individual · single · respective · distinct
These words are all used to talk about one person or thing, not others.

PATTERNS AND COLLOCATIONS
▸ sth is separate / distinct **from** sth else
▸ a particular / certain / specific / individual **person**
▸ a particular / a certain / a separate / a specific / an individual / a single / a distinct **category / region**
▸ respective **categories / regions**
▸ a particular / certain / separate / specific / single **event / incident / occasion**
▸ a particular / certain / separate / specific **location**
▸ particular / certain / separate / individual / single / distinct **components**
▸ particular / certain / specific / individual / respective / distinct **needs / requirements**
▸ a particular / certain / specific / single / distinct **context**
▸ respective **contexts**
▸ a particular / certain / specific / single / distinct **objective / purpose**
▸ a particular / certain / specific **date**
▸ respective **dates**
▸ a particular / a separate / an individual / a single / a distinct **strand**
▸ a / an separate / individual / single / distinct **entity**
▸ a particular / a certain / a separate / a specific / an individual / a distinct **type** of sth
▸ a particular / certain / specific / distinct **kind** of sth
▸ **quite** separate / specific / distinct

particular [only before noun] used to emphasize that you are referring only to one person, thing or type of thing and not others: *There is one particular patient I'd like you to see.* ◇ *The policy seems to discriminate against particular groups of people.* ◇ *Here, **in no particular order** (= the order is not important and has not been deliberately chosen), is a selection of readers' comments.*
▸ **particularly** *adv.*: *Traffic is bad, particularly on the way into town.* ◇ *I enjoyed the play, particularly the second half.*

certain [only before noun] used to mention a particular thing, person or group without giving any more details about it / them: *Certain people might disagree with this.* ◇ *They refused to release their hostages unless certain conditions were met.* ❶ In formal English **certain** can be used when mentioning a person who has been named but who is not known: *It was a certain Dr Davis who performed the operation.*

separate forming a unit by itself; not with or joined to sth else; (of several things of the same type) different and not connected: *They sleep in separate bedrooms.* ◇ *Raw meat must be **kept separate** from cooked meat.* ◇ *Write a list of names on a separate piece of paper.* ◇ *It happened on three separate occasions.* ◇ *For the past three years they have been leading totally separate lives.* **OPP** joint, communal → COMMON
▸ **separately** *adv.*: *They were photographed separately and then as a group.* ◇ *That matter will be considered separately from the main agenda.*

specific /spəˈsɪfɪk/ [usually before noun] connected with one particular thing or type of thing, especially one that is well defined and different from others in important details: *Each debate will focus on a specific political issue.* ◇ *The money was collected for a specific purpose.*
▸ **specifically** *adv.*: *a magazine aimed specifically at working women*

NOTE PARTICULAR OR SPECIFIC? A **particular** person, group or thing is that one and not a different one: John, not Mary; the French, not the Germans; that book not this one. A **specific** group or thing is a particular one in all its details, not a general group or type of which this is one example: school children with learning difficulties, not school children in general; the issue of long-term unemployment in declining industrial centres, not the issue of unemployment in general.

individual [only before noun] considered separately rather than as part of a group: *We interviewed **each individual** member of the community.* ◇ *The minister refused to comment on individual cases.* **OPP** **collective** → COMMON, See also **individual** → OWN
▸ **individually** *adv.*: *individually wrapped chocolates*

single [only before noun] used to emphasize that you are referring to one particular person or thing on its own: *Unemployment is the **single most** important factor in the rising crime rates.* ◇ *We eat rice **every single day**.*
▸ **singly** *adv.*: *The stamps are available singly or in books of ten.*

respective /rɪ'spektɪv/ [only before noun] (usually used before a plural noun) (*rather formal*) belonging or relating separately to each of the people or things already mentioned: *They are each recognized as specialists in their respective fields.*
▸ **respectively** *adv.*: *Julie Wilson and Mark Thomas, aged 17 and 19 respectively*

distinct /dɪ'stɪŋkt/ clearly different or of a different kind: *The results of the survey fell into two distinct groups.* ◇ *Jamaican reggae music is quite distinct from North American jazz or blues.* ◇ *We are talking about rural areas, **as distinct from** major cities.*

partly *adv.* See also the entry for QUITE 1

partly · in part · partially · half · to some extent · somewhat · moderately · up to a point
These words all mean to some degree, but not completely.

NOTE WHICH WORD? Compare these words with the words in the entry for **quite 1** . Those words are generally more positive and emphasize the degree to which sth *is* good, successful, difficult, etc., even if it is not completely so. The words in this entry are slightly less positive: some tend to look at both how far sth *is* and *is not* true, successful, etc.; others tend to emphasize how far from being completely true, successful, etc. sth is.

PATTERNS AND COLLOCATIONS
▸ partly / partially / moderately **successful**
▸ partly / partially / half **true**
▸ to some extent / somewhat **arbitrary**
▸ partly / in part / partially / to some extent **because...**
▸ partly / in part / to some extent **due to** sth
▸ **only** partly / partially / half / to some extent / moderately / up to a point

partly to some degree; not completely: *The measure was popular, partly because it was a way of avoiding tax.* ◇ *The result is partly a matter of skill and partly of chance.* ◇ *He was only partly responsible for the accident.* ◇ *It was partly my fault.* **OPP** **completely** → QUITE 2

in 'part *idiom* (*rather formal, especially written*) partly; not completely: *Her success was due in part to luck.* ◇ *The money was at least in part provided by the families.*

partially /'pɑːʃəli; AmE 'pɑːrʃ-/ partly; not completely: *The road was partially blocked by a fallen tree.* ◇ *Machines replaced, at least partially, the skills of human workers.* ◇ *She teaches blind and **partially sighted** children.* See also **partial** → PARTIAL

NOTE PARTLY, IN PART OR PARTIALLY? These expressions all mean 'not completely': *The road is partly / partially finished.* **Partly** and **in part** are used especially to talk about the reason for sth and are often followed by *because of* or *due to*: *I didn't enjoy the trip very much, partly because of the weather.* ◇ *Health problems attributed to air pollution may in part be due to heavy smoking.* **In part** is more formal than **partly** and is used

---

mostly in writing. When you are talking about permanent physical conditions you should use **partially**: *The accident left her partially blind / deaf / disabled.*

half to the extent of half; partly: *The bottle was only half full.* ◇ *I was still half asleep.* ◇ *He felt half afraid, half excited.* ◇ *She is half Italian.* ◇ *I half expected them to follow us.* ◇ *The result was **not half** as (= not nearly as) bad as expected.*

to some extent *phrase* (*rather formal, especially written*) used to show that sth is partly true or valid, but not completely: *To some extent, this is still the case.* ◇ *By this time, animals were, to some extent at least, tamed if not domesticated.*

somewhat (*AmE or rather formal, BrE*) to some extent; rather: *Her version of what happened was somewhat different.* ◇ *He was somewhat taken aback by the girl's directness.*

moderately /'mɒdərətli; AmE 'mɑːd-/ (*rather formal*) to an average degree; fairly but not very: *The plan was only moderately successful.* ◇ *Cook in a moderately hot oven.*

up to a 'point *phrase* to some degree but not completely: *I agree with you up to a point.* ◇ *That is true only up to a point.* ◇ (*especially BrE*) *I was successful **up to a certain point**.* ❶ **Up to a point** is the least positive of the expressions in this entry; the emphasis is really on the extent to which sb does *not* agree or sth is *not* true.

partner *noun*

1 a business / dancing partner
2 Come to the party and bring your partner.

1 See also the entry for FRIEND

partner · colleague · associate · contact · ally · classmate · co-worker · collaborator · workmate · teammate
These are all words for sb you work, study or do an activity with.

PATTERNS AND COLLOCATIONS
▸ a **business** partner / colleague / associate / contact / ally
▸ a **political** colleague / associate / contact / ally
▸ a **junior / senior** partner / colleague / associate
▸ a **former** partner / colleague / associate / ally / classmate / co-worker / collaborator / workmate / teammate
▸ an **old** colleague / associate / ally / classmate
▸ a **new** partner / colleague / associate / contact / ally / classmate
▸ a **long-term** partner / associate / collaborator
▸ a **close** partner / colleague / associate / contact / ally / collaborator

partner [C] one of the people who owns a business and shares the profits; a person that you are doing an activity with, such as dancing or playing a game: *He has recently been made a junior partner in the family business.* ◇ *Choose a partner for the next activity.* ◇ *My regular dancing partner has broken her ankle.* See also **partnership** → GROUP 3, **partnership** → RELATIONSHIP 1
▸ **partner** *verb* [T]: *Gerry offered to partner me (= be my partner) at tennis.*

colleague /'kɒliːɡ; AmE 'kɑː-/ [C] a person that you work with, especially in a profession or business: *I'd like you to meet a colleague of mine from the office.* ◇ *the Prime Minister and his Cabinet colleagues*

associate /ə'səʊʃiət; AmE ə'soʊ-/ [C] (*rather formal*) a person that you work with, do business with or spend a lot of time with: *The company is called Landor Associates.* ◇ *He was known to be one of the convicted man's associates.* See also **association** → RELATIONSHIP 1

NOTE COLLEAGUE OR ASSOCIATE? **Colleague** is much more frequent than **associate** and is a general word for sb you work with, especially in an office, a school, in government, etc. An **associate** is used more to describe sb you have a business connection with, for example because you have done or are doing business with them.

contact [C] a person that you know, especially sb who can be helpful to you in your work: *I've made some useful contacts in journalism.* ◇ *It takes time to build up good contacts.*

ally /'ælaɪ/ [C] a person who helps and supports sb who is in a difficult situation, especially a politician: *He's a close friend and ally of the prime minister.* ◇ *His sister was his ally against their grandparents.* **OPP enemy** → ENEMY

classmate /'klɑːsmeɪt; AmE 'klæs-/ [C] a person who is or was in the same class as you at school or college: *Are you curious to know where your former classmates are now?*

'co-worker [C] a person that sb works with, doing the same kind of job: *He is worried about his job after seeing his co-workers laid off.*

collaborator /kə'læbəreɪtə(r)/ [C] a person who works with another person to create or produce sth, such as a book: *He is working on a new series with his long-time collaborator Michel Baudin.*

workmate /'wɜːkmeɪt; AmE 'wɜːrk-/ [C] (*especially BrE*) a person that you work with, often doing the same job, in an office, factory, etc: *Her workmates organized a leaving party for her last day in the office.*

NOTE CO-WORKER OR **WORKMATE**? **Workmate** is used more in British English; **co-worker** is used more in American English. **Workmate** is also slightly more informal, and suggests that you are quite friendly with the person you work with.

teammate /'tiːmmeɪt/ [C] a member of the same team or group as yourself: *He was determined not to let his teammates down.*

2 See also the entries for LOVER and WIFE
partner · girlfriend · boyfriend · man · date · fiancée · fiancé · sweetheart · suitor · admirer
These are all words for the man or woman that sb is having a romantic relationship with.

PATTERNS AND COLLOCATIONS
▸ a **steady** / **serious** girlfriend / boyfriend
▸ sb's **new** partner / girlfriend / boyfriend / man / admirer
▸ sb's **ex**-partner / girlfriend / boyfriend / fiancée / fiancé
▸ sb's **former** / **current** partner / girlfriend / boyfriend
▸ sb's **old** girlfriend / boyfriend
▸ to **have** a partner / a girlfriend / a boyfriend / a man / a date / a fiancée / a fiancé / an admirer
▸ to **get** a girlfriend / boyfriend / man
▸ to **find** a partner / girlfriend / boyfriend / man

partner [C] the person that you are having a serious romantic or sexual relationship with, especially sb that you live with: *This is my partner, Mark.* ❶ A **partner** is usually a person that sb lives with but is not married to, but it can also refer to a husband or wife, especially if you do not know, or it is not important, if a couple is married or not: *Come to the New Year disco and bring your partner.* **Partner** is also used when you do not know or are not interested in what sex sb's partner is.

girlfriend [C] a girl or woman that sb is having a romantic relationship with: *He's got a new girlfriend.*

boyfriend [C] a man or boy that sb is having a romantic relationship with: *I just ran into my ex-boyfriend.*

NOTE PARTNER OR **GIRLFRIEND/BOYFRIEND**? **Partner** can suggest a more serious and long-term relationship than **girlfriend** or **boyfriend**. A **partner** is usually sb that you live with; you may or may not live with a **girlfriend** or **boyfriend**. **Partner** can also suggest a more mature relationship, so teenagers and young people have **boyfriends/girlfriends** more than **partners**, although this does not mean that the relationship will not last a long time or develop into something more serious: *I've been going out with my girlfriend for seven years and she wants us to get married.*

man [C] a husband or boyfriend: *What's her new man like?* ◇ *I now pronounce you man and wife* (= you are now officially married).

date [C] (*especially AmE*) a person with whom you have arranged a romantic meeting, who might become a boyfriend or girlfriend: *My date is meeting me at seven.* See also **date** → GO OUT *phrasal verb*

fiancée /fi'ɒnseɪ; -'ɑːns-; AmE ˌfiːɑːn'seɪ/ [C] the woman that a man is engaged to (= has agreed to marry): *Paul and his fiancée were there.*

fiancé /fi'ɒnseɪ; -'ɑːns-; AmE ˌfiːɑːn'seɪ/ [C] the man that a woman is engaged to: *Linda and her fiancé were there.*

sweetheart /'swiːthɑːt; AmE -hɑːrt/ [C] (*becoming old-fashioned*) a person with whom sb is having a romantic relationship: *They were **childhood sweethearts**.* ❶ **Sweetheart** is now a rather old-fashioned word, except in the phrase *childhood sweethearts*. It suggests an innocent relationship, especially between very young people, involving romance and friendship but not usually sex.

suitor /'suːtə(r); BrE also 'sjuː-/ [C] (*formal or old-fashioned*) a man who wants to marry a particular woman: *In the play, the heroine has to choose between three suitors.* ❶ **Suitor** is used mainly to talk about people in the past, or in novels or plays set in the past.

admirer [C] a man who is attracted to a woman and admires her: *She never married but had many admirers.*

party *noun*

1 a political party
2 a birthday party
3 a coach party of tourists

1 party · faction · camp · lobby
These are all words for groups of people who have the same aims and ideas and oppose those with different aims and ideas, especially in politics.

PATTERNS AND COLLOCATIONS
▸ **rival** / **opposing** parties / factions / camps
▸ the **socialist** party / camp
▸ to **belong to** a party / faction / camp

party (also **Party**) [C+sing./pl. v.] a political organization that you can vote for in elections and whose members have the same aims and ideas: *the Democratic and Republican Parties in the United States* ◇ *the ruling/ opposition party* ◇ *the party leader/manifesto/policy*

faction [C+sing./pl. v.] a small group of people within a larger one whose members have some different aims and beliefs to those of the larger group: *There are rival factions within the administration.*

camp [C+sing./pl. v.] a group of people who have the same ideas about sth and oppose people with other ideas: *The scientists split into two camps over the validity of animal studies.*

lobby [C+sing./pl. v.] a group of people who try to influence politicians on a particular issue: *The gun lobby is against any change in the law.* See also **lobby** → CAMPAIGN *verb*

2 See also the entry for EVENT 2
party · dance · disco · ball · shower · rave · bash
These are all words for a social occasion when people come together to have fun.

PATTERNS AND COLLOCATIONS
▸ **at** a party / dance / disco / ball / shower / rave / bash
▸ a **charity** dance / ball / bash
▸ an **all-night** party / rave / bash
▸ a **birthday** party / bash
▸ a **dinner** party / dance
▸ a **school** dance / disco
▸ to **have/hold** a party / dance / disco / ball / shower / rave / bash
▸ to **host** a party / dance / ball / shower / bash
▸ to **throw** a party / shower / bash
▸ to **invite** sb to a party / dance / ball / shower
▸ to **go to/attend** a party / dance / disco / ball / shower / rave / bash
▸ party / dance / disco / rave **music**

party [C] a social occasion, often in a person's home, at which people eat, drink, talk, dance and enjoy themselves: *Did you go to their party?* ◊ *They threw a party to celebrate the end of term.* ◊ *He gave a dinner party for some old friends.* ◊ *There were fizzy drinks, cake and party games.* See also **party** → PLAY *verb* 1

dance [C] a social event at which people dance: *We hold a dance every year to raise money for charity.* ◊ *I took her to my first high school dance.* ❶ In British English a **dance** is usually an event at which people do formal dancing in couples or sets. If the 'dancing' consists of jumping around to pop music the event is usually called a **disco**. In American English **dance** is used to talk about both kinds of event.

disco (pl. **-os**) [C] (*BrE*) a party or club where people dance to recorded pop music: *That song always reminds me of school discos.* ❶ In American English this is just called a **dance**.

ball [C] a large formal party with dancing: *They've hired a 10-piece band for the summer ball.*

shower [C] (*AmE*) a party at which you give presents to a woman who is getting married or having a baby: *A bridal shower is usually organized by the bridesmaids.* ◊ *a baby shower*

rave [C] a large party, held outside or in an empty building, at which people dance to fast electronic music and often take illegal drugs: *Police were out in force last night to prevent an illegal rave from going ahead.*

bash [C] (*rather informal, especially journalism*) a large party or celebration: *Journalists were refused access to the actor's star-studded birthday bash at a Beverly Hills hotel.*

3 See also the entries for GROUP 2 and TEAM 1
party · gang · band · contingent · company · pack
These are all words for a group of people, usually together in one place, who are doing sth together or who have sth in common.

PATTERNS AND COLLOCATIONS
▸ a party / gang / band / contingent / pack **of** sth
▸ **in** a party / gang / band / company / pack
▸ a **small / large** party / gang / band / contingent
▸ a **10-strong / 20-strong,** etc. party / gang / band / contingent
▸ a **growing / strong** band / contingent
▸ to **join** a party / gang / band
▸ a party / gang / pack **leader**
▸ a **member of** a party / gang / band / contingent / pack

party [C+sing./pl. *v.*] a group of people who are doing sth together, such as travelling or visiting somewhere; a group of people given a job to do together: *The theatre gives a 10% discount to parties of more than 10.* ◊ *a coach party of German tourists* ◊ *It was decided to send out a search party to look for the missing climbers.*

gang [C+sing./pl. *v.*] an organized group of criminals; a group of young people who spend a lot of time together and often cause trouble or fight against other groups: *The robbery was carried out by an armed gang.* ◊ *a criminal gang* ◊ *We were in the same gang.* ◊ *Fights had ensued between rival gangs of football fans.* See also **ring, gang** → TEAM 1

band [C+sing./pl. *v.*] a group of people who do sth together or who share a common interest, feature or achievement: *She persuaded a small band of volunteers to help.* ◊ *They are members of a growing band of enthusiasts.*

contingent /kən'tɪndʒənt/ [C+sing./pl. *v.*] a group of people at a meeting or event who have sth in common, especially the place they come from, that is not shared by other people at the event: *The largest contingent was from the United States.* ◊ *A strong contingent of local residents were there to block the proposal.*

company [U] (*formal*) all the people who are together somewhere at a particular time, for example at a meeting or party: *Those children don't know how to behave in company* (= in a group of people). ◊ *It's not the type of*

joke you'd tell **in mixed company** (= with men and women present). ◊ *She told the assembled company what had happened.*

pack [C+sing./pl. *v.*] (*often disapproving*) a group of similar people or things, especially one that you do not like or approve of: *We avoided a pack of journalists waiting outside.*

passenger *noun* See also the entry for TOURIST

passenger · traveller · commuter
These are all words for a person who travels on or in a vehicle.

PATTERNS AND COLLOCATIONS
▸ a **regular** passenger / traveller / commuter
▸ **rail** passengers / travellers / commuters
▸ passenger / commuter **fares / services / traffic / trains**

passenger [C] a person who is travelling in a car, bus, train, plane or ship and who is not driving it or working on it: *The car can carry up to five passengers.* ◊ *None of the passengers or crew was injured.* ◊ *Airline passengers face steep rises in fares.*

traveller (*especially BrE*) (*AmE usually* **traveler**) [C] a person who is travelling or who often travels: *He passed the time chatting to his fellow travellers.* ◊ *Seasoned travellers* (= experienced travellers) *know which places to avoid.* See also **travel** → GO 1

commuter /kə'mjuːtə(r)/ [C] a person who travels into a city to work each day, usually from quite far away: *The train was packed with commuters.* ◊ *There has been an increase in the numbers of daily commuters into London.* ◊ *A commuter plane crashed in heavy fog.* ◊ *She lives in a small commuter town, 25 miles from San Francisco.*
▸ **commute** *verb* [I, T]: *She commutes from Cambridge to Boston every day.* ◊ *People are prepared to commute long distances if they are desperate for work.*

passive *adj.*

passive · docile · amenable · submissive · meek · compliant
These words all describe sb who is easy to control or to influence.

PATTERNS AND COLLOCATIONS
▸ amenable / submissive **to** sb / sth
▸ a passive / submissive / compliant **role**
▸ a docile / an amenable / a submissive / a compliant **child**
▸ passive / meek **obedience**

passive /'pæsɪv/ accepting what happens or what people do without trying to change anything or oppose them: *He played a passive role in the relationship.* ◊ *Throughout this time I was simply a passive observer of events.* **OPP active** → BUSY 1
▸ **passively** *adv.*: *He passively accepted everything that was decided for him.*

docile /'dəʊsaɪl; *AmE* 'dɑːsl/ (of people and animals) quiet and easy to control: *a docile child / horse / temperament* ◊ *It is a cheap and docile workforce.*

amenable /ə'miːnəbl/ (*rather formal, especially written, approving*) easy to control; willing to be influenced by sb / sth: *The manager was very amenable: nothing was too much trouble.* ◊ *He seemed most amenable to my idea.*

submissive /səb'mɪsɪv/ willing to obey sb, whatever they want you to do: *A woman was expected to be submissive to her husband.* ◊ *She followed him like a submissive child.* **OPP assertive** → AGGRESSIVE 2, See also **submit** → GIVE WAY

meek quiet, gentle, and always ready to do what other people want without expressing your own opinion: *They hung their heads in meek submission.* ◊ *They called her Miss Mouse because she was so meek and mild.* **OPP bold** → BOLD
▸ **meekly** *adv.*: *He meekly did as he was told.*

compliant /kəm'plaɪənt/ (*written, often disapproving*) willing (often too willing) to agree with other people or to obey rules: *We should not be producing compliant students who do not dare to criticize.* ◇ *Henry seemed less* **compliant with** *his wife's wishes than he had before.* See also **comply** → FOLLOW 3

pass sth on *phrasal verb*

pass sth on · spread · infect · leave · transmit · give · bequeath · hand sth down
These words all mean to give sth to sb else, especially after receiving, having or using it yourself.

PATTERNS AND COLLOCATIONS
▸ to pass sth on / spread sth / leave sth / transmit sth / give sth / bequeath sth / hand sth down **to** sb
▸ to pass on / spread / infect sb with / transmit / give sb a / an **disease / infection / virus**
▸ to pass on / spread / transmit **information / a message**
▸ to pass on / spread / hand down **knowledge**
▸ to pass on / hand down **skills**
▸ to pass on / leave / bequeath your **property / estate**
▸ to pass on / leave / bequeath a **legacy**
▸ to leave / bequeath (sb) your **money / art collection**
▸ to leave / bequeath (sb) **£50 000 / the sum of…**
▸ to pass sth on / transmit sth **genetically**

,pass sth 'on *phrasal verb* to give sth to sb else, especially after receiving it or using it yourself: *Pass the book on to me when you've finished with it.* ◇ *I passed your message on to my mother.* ◇ *Much of the discount is pocketed by retailers instead of being passed on to customers.* See also **pass sth on** → CONVEY
spread [I, T] to affect or make sth affect, be known by or used by, more and more people: *Use of computers spread rapidly during that period.* ◇ *I wish he would stop spreading lies about me.* ◇ *The disease is spread by mosquitoes.*
infect [T] to make a disease or illness spread to a person, animal or plant; to make sb share a particular feeling: *It is not possible to infect another person through kissing.* ◇ *people* **infected with** *HIV* ◇ *I became infected with the same enthusiasm which led Ransome to write the books.* See also **infection** → DISEASE
leave [T] to say in a will that you want sb to have your property or money after you die: *She left £1 million to her daughter.* ◇ *She left her daughter £1 million.*
transmit /træns'mɪt; trænz-/ (**-tt-**) [T] (*rather formal*) to pass sth from one person to another: *Young people need more information on sexually transmitted diseases.* ◇ *Parents can unwittingly transmit their own fears to their children.* ❶ **Transmit** is used especially to talk about passing on *diseases, infections* and *viruses,* as well as *information* or thoughts and feelings.
▸ **transmission** /træns'mɪʃn; trænz-/ *noun* [U]: (*formal*) *There are several ways of preventing transmission of the virus.* ◇ *Our classes are based on discussion rather than one-way transmission of knowledge.*
give [T] (*rather informal, especially spoken*) to infect sb with an illness: *You've given me your cold.*
bequeath /bɪ'kwiːð/ [T] (*formal*) to leave your money or property to sb in your will (= a legal document) after your death; to leave the results of your work, knowledge or ideas for other people to use or deal with: *He bequeathed his entire estate to his daughter.* ◇ *The previous government had bequeathed a legacy of problems.* See also **bequest** → LEGACY
,hand sth 'down *phrasal verb* [usually passive] to give or teach sth to your children or people younger than you: *Most of his clothes were handed down to him by his older brother.* ◇ *These skills used to be handed down from father to son.*

the past *noun*

the past · history · the old days
These are all words for the time before the present.

PATTERNS AND COLLOCATIONS
▸ **in** the past / (sth's) history / the old days
▸ sth's **colourful / rich / chequered / glorious** past / history
▸ sth's **cultural / political / imperial / industrial** past / history
▸ (the / sth's) **recent / ancient / medieval** past / history
▸ to **be lost in** (the) past / history
▸ to **distort / rewrite** (the) past / history

the past [sing.] the time before the present: *I used to go there often in the past.* ◇ *Don't worry about it – it's all in the past now.* ◇ *It all happened in the* **distant past**. ◇ *We have to stop* **living in the past** *and invest in new technology.* ◇ *Writing letters seems to be* **a thing of the past**. See also **past** → PREVIOUS *adj.*
history [U, sing.] all the events that happened in an earlier time, especially as part of the political or social development of a country; the set of facts that are known about the past existence of a place or group of people: *Many people* **throughout history** *have dreamt of a world without war.* ◇ *These events changed* **the course of history**. ◇ *He will* **go down in history** (= be remembered) *as a wise politician and a kind man.* ◇ *The country has suffered several invasions* **during its history**. ◇ *Venice has a rich and colourful history.*
▸ **historical** *adj.*: *the historical background to the war* ◇ *historical documents / records / research* ◇ *a historical novel / setting*
▸ **historically** *adv.*: *The book is historically inaccurate.*
the old days *phrase* (*rather informal*) a time in the past, or an earlier time in sb's life, when things were different from the way they are now: *Meeting up with school friends reminded her again of the* **good old days**. ◇ *That was in the* **bad old days** *of rampant inflation.* ◇ *Deciding what to watch on television was so much easier in the old days.*

pat *verb*

pat · tap · clap
These words all mean to hit a person or animal lightly, with your open hand or your fingers.

PATTERNS AND COLLOCATIONS
▸ to pat / tap / clap sb **on the back / shoulder**
▸ to pat / tap / clap sb **gently / lightly / affectionately**

pat (**-tt-**) [T] to hit a person or animal lightly several times with your open hand, especially as a sign of affection: *She patted the dog on the head.* ◇ *He patted his sister's hand consolingly and wiped away her tears.*
tap (**-pp-**) [T] to hit sb quickly and lightly several times with your fingers: *Ralph tapped me on the shoulder to get my attention.* See also **tap** → KNOCK
clap (**-pp-**) [T] to hit sb with your open hand in a friendly way: *'Cheer up Tony,' I said, and clapped him on the shoulder.*

patch *noun*

patch · dot · mark · spot
These are all words for a small part on sth that is a different colour from the rest.

PATTERNS AND COLLOCATIONS
▸ a patch / dot / mark / spot **on** sth
▸ **with** patches / dots / marks / spots
▸ a **blue / black / red**, etc. patch / dot / mark / spot

patch [C] an area of sth, especially one which is different from the area around it: *a white dog with a black patch on its back* ◇ *He had a bald patch on the top of his head.* ◇ *There were damp patches on the wall.* ◇ *patches of dense fog*

dot [C] a small round mark on sth, especially one that is printed: *The letters 'i' and 'j' have dots over them.* ◇ *The graphics are printed at 500 dots per inch.* ◇ *She was wearing a yellow skirt with red polka dots on it.* ◇ *The island is a small green dot on the map.* ◇ *Two helicopters appeared as black dots on the horizon.*

mark [C] a noticeable area of colour on the body of a person or animal: *The horse had a white mark on its head.* ◇ *Do you have any **distinguishing marks** (= marks on your body that help to prove your identity)?*

spot [C] a small round area that is a different colour or feels different from the surface it is on: *The male bird has a red spot on its beak.* ◇ *(BrE) She was wearing a white dress with red spots.*

path noun

path · trail · pavement · sidewalk · track · footpath
These are all words for a long narrow piece of land that forms a route for people to walk on.

PATTERNS AND COLLOCATIONS
▸ a path / trail / track / footpath **through** sth
▸ a path / trail / track / footpath **to** sth
▸ a **long** path / trail / track
▸ a **narrow** path / pavement / sidewalk / track
▸ a **dusty** pavement / trail / track
▸ a **muddy** path / trail / track / footpath
▸ to **follow** a path / trail / track / footpath
▸ to **keep to** the path / pavement / sidewalk
▸ to **leave** the path / track
▸ to **step off / mount** the pavement / sidewalk
▸ a path / track **forks / divides**
▸ a path / trail / track / footpath **leads to** sth

path [C] a long narrow piece of ground for people to walk along, either built or made by the action of people walking: *a garden path* ◇ *They took the cliff path as far as the lighthouse.* ◇ *They have cleared a path (= made one by cutting down plants) through the forest.* ◇ *He walked down the garden path to the front gate.*

trail [C] a path through the countryside, often a very long route or a path that has been made for a particular purpose: *We set off to walk the trail that winds along the Colorado River.* ◇ *They have made a new **nature trail** (= a path where you can see interesting plants and animals) through the woods.*

pavement [C] *(BrE)* a flat, raised part at the side of a road for people to walk on: *A parked car was blocking the pavement.* ◇ *A bus mounted the pavement and hit her.*

sidewalk [C] *(AmE)* a pavement: *The crowd filled the church and spilled onto the sidewalk outside.* ◇ *We stopped for coffee at a sidewalk cafe.*

track [C] *(especially BrE)* a rough path or road, usually one that has not been built but has been made by the action of people, animals or vehicles travelling along the same route many times: *The path joins a **farm track** (= one used by tractors) near a barn.* ❶ This meaning of **track** is mainly used in British English; in American English **tracks** is usually just used to mean the marks that sb/sth has left behind. See also **track** → TRAIL

footpath /'fʊtpɑːθ; *AmE* -pæθ/ [C] *(especially BrE)* a path for people to walk along, especially in the country: *Follow the marked footpath.* ◇ *A **public footpath** (= one that everyone has the right to use) crosses his land.*

patience noun

patience · tolerance · resignation
These are all words for the ability or willingness to accept sb/sth annoying or difficult without complaining.

PATTERNS AND COLLOCATIONS
▸ patience / tolerance **for** sb / sth
▸ **with** patience / tolerance / resignation
▸ **great / infinite / little** patience / tolerance

▸ to **have / lack / require / show / exercise / learn** patience / tolerance

patience [U] the ability to stay calm and accept a delay or sth annoying without complaining: *People have **lost patience with** the slow pace of reforms.* ◇ *I have **run out of patience** with her.* ◇ *The children were beginning to **try my patience** (= make it hard for me to remain patient).* **OPP** **impatience** → RESTLESS, See also **patient** → CALM *adj.*

tolerance /'tɒlərəns; *AmE* 'tɑːl-/ [U] the willingness to accept sb/sth or allow sb to do sth, especially opinions or behaviour that you may not agree with, or people who are not like you: *She had no **tolerance for** jokes of any kind.* ◇ *She showed greater **tolerance towards** her younger sister than before.* ◇ *He was a strong advocate of **religious tolerance**.* ◇ *Howard County has a **zero tolerance** policy on alcohol use by teenagers.* **OPP** **intolerance** → DISCRIMINATION, See also **tolerant** → TOLERANT, → **tolerate** → STAND 2

resignation /ˌrezɪɡ'neɪʃn/ [U] the willingness to accept without complaining a difficult or unpleasant situation that you cannot change or prevent: *They accepted their defeat with resignation.* See also **resign yourself to sth** → ACCEPT

patient noun

patient · case · victim · sufferer · the sick · invalid · the dying
These are all words for people who are not well and need medical help.

PATTERNS AND COLLOCATIONS
▸ a / the **long-term** patient / victim / sufferer / sick
▸ a **chronic** patient / case / sufferer / invalid
▸ a / an **cancer / AIDS** patient / case / victim / sufferer
▸ an **asthma** patient / sufferer
▸ a **stroke** patient / victim
▸ to **care for** a patient / a sufferer / the sick / an invalid / the dying
▸ to **treat** a patient / a case / a victim / a sufferer / the sick

patient [C] a person who is receiving medical treatment, especially in a hospital; a person who receives treatment from a particular doctor or dentist: *He made friends with another patient on the ward.* ◇ *She's one of Dr Shaw's patients.*

case [C] the fact of sb having a disease or injury; a person suffering from a disease or injury: *Over 500 000 cases of cholera were reported in 1991.* ◇ *The most serious cases were treated at the scene of the accident.*

victim [C] a person who is suffering from a disease or medical condition: *AIDS victims are prone to pick up infections.*

sufferer [C] a person who is suffering from a disease or medical condition: *Local services provide residential care for dementia sufferers.* ◇ *She received many letters of support from fellow sufferers.* See also **suffer from sth** → SUFFER FROM STH

NOTE **VICTIM** OR **SUFFERER**? Both these words are usually used after another noun for the name of a disease, and in many cases you can use either word: *cancer/AIDS/ leukaemia victims/sufferers.* **Victim** is more frequent in these cases and can make the disease sound worse, but **sufferer** is used with a wider range of medical conditions, especially long-term conditions: *dementia/ asthma/arthritis/sclerosis sufferers.* A **victim** can also be sb who has been hurt as the result of a crime or accident. See also **victim** → VICTIM 1

the sick [pl.] people who are seriously ill: *He healed the sick and comforted the broken-hearted.* See also **sick** → SICK 1

invalid /'ɪnvəlɪd; 'ɪnvəliːd/ [C] a person who needs other people to take care of them, because of illness that they have had for a long time: *She had been a delicate child and her parents had treated her as an invalid.*

the dying [pl.] people who are dying: *Volunteer nurses were tending to the sick and the dying.*

patronizing (*BrE* also -**ising**) *adj*. See also the entry for PROUD 2

patronizing · superior · condescending · snooty · snobbish
These words all describe a person whose behaviour or attitude shows that they think they are better than other people.

PATTERNS AND COLLOCATIONS
▶ patronizing / superior / snooty / snobbish **about** sth
▶ patronizing / condescending **to** / **towards** sb
▶ a patronizing / superior / condescending **attitude** / **tone** / **smile** / **manner** / **way**

patronizing (*BrE* also -**ising**) /'pætrənaizıŋ; *AmE* 'peitrənaizıŋ/ (*disapproving*) showing, especially by what you say, that you think you are better or more intelligent than sb else: *He adopted a rather patronizing attitude towards his younger colleagues.* ◇ *I didn't mean to sound patronizing.*
▶ **patronize** (*BrE* also -**ise**) *verb* [T]: *Some television programmes tend to patronize children.*
superior (*disapproving*) showing by your behaviour that you think you are better than other people: *Michael's superior air had begun to annoy her.*
condescending /ˌkɒndɪ'sendɪŋ; *AmE* ˌkɑːn-/ (*rather formal, especially written, disapproving*) showing by your behaviour that you think you are more important or more intelligent than sb else: *He looked around and made some condescending remark.*
▶ **condescend** *verb* [I]: *When giving a talk, be careful not to condescend to your audience.*
▶ **condescension** *noun* [U]: *Her smile was a mixture of pity and condescension.*

NOTE PATRONIZING, SUPERIOR OR CONDESCENDING?
Superior especially describes sb's *air* or *manner* and they may show their feelings of superiority by keeping apart from other people and not being too friendly. People who are **patronizing** or **condescending** often talk to people in a way that they may think is kind or helpful, but which actually shows that they do not consider the other person to be their equal.

snooty /'snuːti/ (*rather informal, disapproving*) treating people as if they are not as good or as important as you, and do not deserve your time or respect: *Reviewers are still a little snooty about self-published books.*
snobbish (*disapproving*) thinking that having a high social class is very important; feeling that you are better than other people because you are more intelligent or like things that not many people like: *He fell into the snobbish habit of connecting high social status with moral superiority.* ◇ *She was quite snobbish about pop culture.* See also **snobbery** → PRETENSION

pattern *noun*
1 an irregular sleeping pattern
2 a pattern of diamonds and squares

1 pattern · cycle · rhythm
These are all words for the regular way in which sth happens or is done.

PATTERNS AND COLLOCATIONS
▶ a / an **regular** / **irregular** pattern / cycle / rhythm
▶ a **natural** cycle / rhythm
▶ to **break** a pattern / cycle / rhythm
▶ the cycle / rhythm of the **seasons**

pattern [C] the regular way in which sth happens or is done: *changing patterns of behaviour/work/weather* ◇ *an irregular sleeping pattern* ◇ *The murders all seem to **follow** a (similar) pattern* (= happen in the same way). ◇ *There is no set pattern for these meetings.*

cycle [C] the fact of a series of events being repeated many times, always in the same order: *They could not break the cycle of harvest failure, food shortages, price increases and misery.* ◇ *This cycle of events continually repeats itself.* ◇ *the **life cycle** of the butterfly* (= the series of forms into which it changes as it develops)
▶ **cyclic** /'saıklık; 'sık-/ (also **cyclical**) *adj*. [usually before noun]: *the cyclic processes of nature* ◇ *Economic activity often follows a cyclical pattern.*
rhythm [C] a regular pattern of changes or events: *the rhythm of the tides* ◇ *Lack of sleep can upset your daily rhythm.* ◇ *My body rhythms had not yet adapted to the ten-hour time difference.* See also **rhythm** → RHYTHM

NOTE PATTERN, CYCLE OR RHYTHM? A **cycle** is the most regular of these and a **pattern** is the least regular and most likely to change over time: ~~changing cycles/rhythms of behaviour/work/weather~~. **Pattern** is used especially to talk about people's work and behaviour; **cycle** is used especially to talk about events in the natural world; **rhythm** is used especially to talk about how people's bodies adapt to changing conditions.

2 pattern · design · motif
These are all words for an arrangement of lines and shapes, or a simple picture, especially one that is used to decorate sth.

PATTERNS AND COLLOCATIONS
▶ a pattern / design / motif **on** sth
▶ **in** a pattern / design
▶ a **simple** / **floral** pattern / design / motif
▶ a / an **elaborate** / **intricate** / **abstract** / **geometric** / **symmetrical** pattern / design
▶ to **have** / **make** a pattern / design / motif
▶ to **print** / **produce** / **weave** a pattern / design
▶ to **design** a pattern / motif

pattern [C] a regular arrangement of lines, shapes and colours, either used to decorate sth or made or formed by chance: *a pattern of diamonds and squares* ◇ *He wore a shirt with a floral pattern.* ◇ *He had arranged the glasses in a pattern.* ◇ *The ice **formed patterns** on the windows.* See also **decoration** → DECORATION
design [C] an arrangement of lines and shapes, used as a decoration on an object or in a building: *The building has intricate geometric designs on several of the walls.* ◇ *The tiles come in a huge range of colours and designs.* See also **decoration** → DECORATION

NOTE PATTERN OR DESIGN? A **pattern** is a design that is repeated in a regular way. It is usually made up of lines, shapes and colours, rather than pictures of things, although simple pictures can form part of a pattern: *a leaf/flower/floral pattern*. A **pattern** can be deliberately created as a decoration or accidentally formed by the way things come together. A **design** is always deliberately created as a decoration. It can be a repeated pattern or a single decoration; it can be simple or complicated, made up of lines and shapes, or including pictures of things; but it is always deliberately created as a decoration.

motif /məʊ'tiːf; *AmE* moʊ-/ [C] a design used as a decoration: *The rug was decorated with a simple flower motif.* ◇ *The jacket has a rose motif on the collar.* ❶ A **motif** is often a small, simple picture of sth that is used once, or repeated in different places or parts of sth.

pause *noun*

pause · break · interruption · lull · gap
These are all words for a period of time when sth stops before starting again.

PATTERNS AND COLLOCATIONS
▶ a pause / a break / an interruption / a lull / a gap **in** sth
▶ **after** a pause / a break / an interruption / a lull / a gap

▶ **without** pause / a break / interruption
▶ a **short** pause / break / interruption / lull / gap
▶ a **long** pause / break / gap
▶ a **sudden** pause / break / lull
▶ to **fill** a pause / gap

pause [C] (*especially written*) a period of time during which sb stops talking or when sth stops before starting again: *There was a long pause before she answered.* ◇ *After a brief pause, they continued climbing.*

break [C] a period of time when sth stops before starting again; a pause for advertisements in the middle of a television or radio programme: *I need a break in my daily routine.* ◇ *She wanted to take a **career break** in order to have children.* ◇ *More news after the break.* ◇ *a **commercial break*** ❶ **Break** is often used to talk about people stopping work for a period of time. See also **break** → REST *noun* 2

interruption [C] something that temporarily stops an activity or situation; a period of time when an activity is stopped before starting again: *The birth of her son was a minor **interruption** to her career.* ◇ *There's been an interruption in the power supply.* ◇ *I managed to work for two hours without interruption.* ❶ An *interruption to/in sth* is often used in announcements or statements about *the power supply/normal service/sb's career/activities/output/production* being stopped for a period of time. See also **interrupt** → DISRUPT

lull [C, usually sing.] (*especially written*) a quiet period between times of activity: *There was a lull in the conversation.* ◇ *Just before an attack everything would go quiet, but we knew it was just **the lull before the storm*** (= before a time of noise or trouble). ❶ **Lull** is often used in business contexts to talk about a period of time when people are not buying many products or services: (*business*) *There will probably be a lull over the winter, followed by a resurgence of activity next spring.*

gap [C] (*especially spoken*) a period of time when sth stops before starting again, or between two events: *I waited for a gap in the conversation.* ◇ *They met again after a gap of twenty years.*

> **NOTE** BREAK, LULL OR GAP? A **break** is often planned: you need a **break** in your own activities in order to have a rest or do sth different. A **lull** in a conversation, in fighting or in business activity is sth that just happens without being planned. A **gap** also usually happens without being planned: it is usually either a *gap in the conversation* or a period of time between two events.

pause *verb*

pause · hesitate · break off · dither
These words all mean to stop speaking or doing sth, or to be slow to speak or act, because you feel uncertain about how to continue.

PATTERNS AND COLLOCATIONS
▶ to hesitate / dither **over** sth
▶ to hesitate / dither **between** two things
▶ to pause / hesitate / break off **(for) a moment**
▶ to pause / hesitate **briefly / momentarily / a little**
▶ to pause / break off **abruptly**

pause [I] to stop speaking or doing sth for a short time before continuing: *Anita paused for a moment, then said, 'All right.'* ◇ *The woman spoke almost without **pausing for breath*** (= very quickly). ◇ *Pausing only to pull on a sweater, he ran out of the house.* ❶ **Pause** is often used with the adverbs *briefly, (for) a moment, (for) an instant* and *momentarily.*

hesitate [I] to be slow to speak or act because you feel uncertain or nervous: *She hesitated before replying.* ◇ *I didn't **hesitate** for a moment **about** taking the job.* See also **hesitate** → HESITATE, **hesitant** → HESITANT
▶ **hesitation** *noun* [C, U]: *He spoke fluently and without unnecessary hesitations.*

break 'off *phrasal verb* (*especially written*) to suddenly stop speaking or doing sth in the middle of a sentence: *He broke off in the middle of a sentence.* ❶ People often **break off** *suddenly* or *abruptly*, often because of a sudden strong emotion: *She broke off and turned away to hide the tears.*

dither /'dɪðə(r)/ [I] (*especially BrE, rather informal, disapproving*) to hesitate about what to do because you are unable to decide: *She was dithering over what to wear.* ◇ *Stop dithering and get on with it.* ❶ **Dither** is usually used in a disapproving way. A person who **dithers** is generally seen as being rather weak and irritating.
▶ **dither** *noun* [sing.]: (*informal*) *She was in a total dither about the party.*

pay *verb* See also the entry for SPEND 1

pay · give · settle · meet · defray · clear
These words all mean to pay the money that you owe.

PATTERNS AND COLLOCATIONS
▶ to pay / settle / meet / clear your **debts**
▶ to pay / settle / meet a **bill**
▶ to pay / meet / defray the **cost** of sth
▶ to meet / defray the **expense** of sth

pay [I, T] to give sb money for work, goods, services, etc: *I'll pay for the tickets.* ◇ *My company pays well* (= pays high salaries). ◇ *There's a 5% discount if you **pay cash.*** ◇ *She pays £200 a week for this apartment.* ◇ *Would you mind paying the taxi driver?* ◇ *He still hasn't paid me the money he owes me.* ◇ *I'm paid $100 a day.* See also **pay** → INCOME *noun*

give [T] to pay in order to have or do sth: *How much will you **give me for** the car?* ◇ *I gave £50 for the lot.* ◇ *I'd give anything to see him again.*

settle [T, I] to pay a bill or pay back money that you owe: *The insurance company is refusing to **settle her claim.*** ◇ *Let me **settle with** you for the meal.* ◇ *I'll pay now — we can **settle up** later.*

meet [T] to pay all of a cost or debt: *The school had to sell off its playing fields to meet its debt repayments.*

defray /dɪ'freɪ/ [T] (*formal*) to pay part or all of a cost: *Proceeds from the raffle always help to defray the expenses of the annual dance.*

clear [T] to pay back all the money you owe: *We are economizing for a few months to try to clear our overdraft.*

> **NOTE** SETTLE, MEET, DEFRAY OR CLEAR? **Settle** and **clear** mean to pay all of an amount of money: **settle** is used for bills and debts, **clear** only for debts. **Defray** is a formal word usually used when sb/sth helps to pay part of a cost. **Meet** is used especially about payments that you make regularly.

payment *noun*

payment · premium · contribution · subscription · repayment · deposit · settlement · instalment
These are all words for an amount of money that you pay or are expected to pay, or for the act of paying.

PATTERNS AND COLLOCATIONS
▶ a payment / premium / subscription / repayment / deposit / settlement **for** sth
▶ a payment / a premium / a repayment / a deposit / an instalment **on** sth
▶ to pay sth **by** subscription / instalments
▶ (a / an) **monthly / annual** payment / premium / contributions / subscription / repayment / deposit / settlement / instalment
▶ (a) **regular** payment / premium / contributions / subscription / repayment / deposit / instalment
▶ (a) **cash** payment / premium / deposit / settlement / instalment
▶ (an) **immediate** payment / repayment / deposit / settlement
▶ (a) **final** payment / repayment / settlement / instalment
▶ (a) **full** payment / premium / subscription / repayment / deposit / settlement
▶ payment / repayment / settlement **in full**

▶ to **pay** a premium / contributions / a subscription / a deposit / a settlement / an instalment
▶ to **make** a payment / repayment / deposit / settlement
▶ to **meet/keep up (with)** the payments / premiums / repayments / instalments
▶ to **accept** payment / repayment / a deposit / settlement
▶ (a / an) payment / premium / subscription / repayment / settlement / instalment **is due**
▶ a payment / a subscription / a repayment / a settlement / an instalment **plan**

payment [C, U] an amount of money that you pay or are expected to pay; the act of paying: *They are finding it difficult to meet the payments on the new car.* ◇ *There will be a penalty for late payment of bills.*

premium /ˈpriːmiəm/ [C] an amount of money that you pay once or regularly for an insurance policy; an extra payment added to the basic rate; a higher amount of money than usual: *We pay a monthly premium of £6.25 for home contents insurance.* ◇ *You have to pay a high premium for express delivery.* ◇ *Daytime calls are charged at premium rate.*

contribution [C] a sum of money that you pay regularly to your employer or the government in order to pay for benefits such as health insurance, a pension, etc: *You can increase your monthly contributions to the pension plan.*

subscription /səbˈskrɪpʃn/ [C, U] an amount of money you pay in advance to receive regular copies of a newspaper or magazine, to receive a service or as a gift to a charity; the act of paying this money: *Do you think we should get a subscription to 'Newsweek'?* ◇ *to cancel/renew a subscription* ◇ *(BrE) A statue in his memory was erected by public subscription.* ❶ In British English a **subscription** is also money that you pay to be a member of a club: *Club subscriptions are due annually by the end of January.* In American English this is called **dues** or a **membership fee.** See also **fee, dues** → RATE 2

▶ **subscribe** /səbˈskraɪb/ *verb* [I]: *Which journals does the library subscribe to?*

repayment [C, usually pl., U] an amount of money that you pay regularly to a bank, etc. until you have returned all the money that you owe; the act of paying this money: *We were unable to keep up the repayments on the loan.* ◇ *The loan is due for repayment by the end of the year.* See also **repay** → REPAY

deposit /dɪˈpɒzɪt; *AmE* -ˈpɑːz-/ [C, usually sing.] an amount of money that you pay as the first part of a larger payment: *We've put down a 5% deposit on the house.* ❶ A **deposit** is also an amount of money that you pay when you rent sth and that is returned to you if you do not lose or damage the thing you are renting: *The car costs $50 per day in rental, plus a $200 deposit which you will get back at the end of the week.*

settlement [U] the act of paying back money that you owe: *She had to pay over $5 000 in settlement of her debts.* ◇ *Settlement is made monthly by direct debit.*

instalment (*especially BrE*) (*AmE* usually **installment**) /ɪnˈstɔːlmənt/ [C] one of a number of payments that you make regularly over a period of time until you have paid for sth: *We paid for the car by/in instalments.*

peace *noun* See the Topic Map for CONFLICT on p.896

peace · order · law and order · the rule of law · calm
These are all words for a situation or period of time in which there is no war or violence in a country or area and people obey the law.

PATTERNS AND COLLOCATIONS
▶ an **uneasy** peace / calm
▶ **relative / comparative** peace / calm
▶ to **maintain / establish / preserve** peace / order / law and order / the rule of law
▶ to **restore** peace / order / law and order / the rule of law
▶ to **enforce** peace / order / law and order / the rule of law
▶ peace / order / law and order / the rule of law / calm **prevails**
▶ order / law and order / the rule of law **breaks down**
▶ the **breakdown of** order / law and order / the rule of law

peace [U, sing.] a situation or period of time in which there is no war or violence in a country or area: *Any hopes of peace between the two nations seem to have faded.* ◇ *The two communities now live together in peace.* ◇ *England and France were once again at peace with each other.* ◇ *Peace finally returned to the city streets.* ◇ *The negotiators are trying to make peace between the warring factions.* ◇ *Troops were brought in to keep the peace.* ◇ *Obviously world peace is our ultimate goal.* ◇ *After years of war, the people longed for a lasting peace.* **OPP** **war** → WAR

order [U] the state that exists when people obey laws, rules or authority: *The army had been brought in to maintain order in the capital.* ◇ *Some teachers find it hard to keep order in their classes.* ◇ *Some teachers find it difficult to keep their classes in order.* ◇ *It is our duty to preserve public order.* **OPP** **disorder** → TROUBLE 1

ˌlaw and ˈorder *idiom* a situation in which people obey the law and behave in a peaceful way: *They regarded the forces of law and order* (= the police and the courts) *as their enemy.*

the rule of ˈlaw *idiom* (*rather formal*) the situation in which all members of society, including its leaders, accept the authority of the law: *It is our duty to uphold the rule of law.*

calm [U, sing.] a situation in which there is no violence, angry protests or arguments: *The police appealed for calm.* ◇ *An uneasy calm descended on the streets.* See also **calm** → QUIET *adj.* 1

peak *noun*

peak · top · height · highlight · climax · high · culmination · prime · heyday · high point
These are all words for the point when sb/sth is best, most successful, strongest, or at their highest level.

PATTERNS AND COLLOCATIONS
▶ the peak / top / height / highlight / climax / culmination / prime / heyday / high point **of** sth
▶ a peak / high / high point **of** $40 a barrel
▶ **at** its peak / the top / its height / its climax / a high / its culmination / a high point
▶ **in** your / its prime / heyday
▶ a **new** peak / height / high / high point
▶ to **reach** its peak / the top / its height / its climax / a high / its culmination / a high point
▶ to **represent** the peak / climax / culmination / high point of sth
▶ to **mark** the climax / culmination / high point of sth
▶ to **pass / be past** its peak / prime / heyday

peak [C, usually sing.] the point when sb/sth is at its best, most successful, strongest or highest level: *She's at the peak of her career.* ◇ *Membership of the club has fallen from a peak of 600 people in 2005.* ◇ *Economic life moves in cycles of peaks and troughs.* ◇ *Peak-rate phone calls cost more.* ◇ *You want your hair to look in peak condition.* **OPP** **trough** → RECESSION

▶ **peak** *verb* [I]: *North Sea oil production peaked in 1999.* ◇ *Unemployment peaked at 17%.*

top [sing.] the highest or most important rank or position: *He's at the top of his profession.* ◇ *She is determined to make it to the top* (= to achieve the highest level of fame or success). ◇ *This decision came from the top.* ◇ *They finished the season at the top of the league.* ◇ *We have a lot of things to do, but packing is at the top of the list.* ◇ *This printer is a top of the range model* (= the best it is possible to buy.) **OPP** **bottom** ❶ The **bottom** is the lowest position in a class, on a list, etc., or the person, team, etc. that is in this position: *a battle between the teams at the bottom of the league* ◇ *You have to be prepared to start at the bottom and work your way up.* ◇ *I was always bottom of the class in English.*

height [sing.] the point when sth is at its best, most successful, strongest or highest level: *She is still at the height of her powers.* ◇ *The fire reached its height at around 2 a.m.* ◇ *I wouldn't go there in the height of summer.*

❶ Heights [pl.] are a better or greater level of success or happiness: *Their success had reached new heights.* ◇ *She dreamed of reaching the **dizzy heights** of stardom.*

> **NOTE PEAK OR HEIGHT? Peak** is the more frequent and more general of these two words. A person can be *at the peak/height of their career/powers* but otherwise, **height** is NOT used to talk about a person: *She seems to be reaching her peak after a great three-set victory over Henin-Hardenne.* ◇ *She seems to be reaching her height...* You can talk about *the peak/height of sth* or sth being at *a peak* of a particular number or level but NOT *a height of* a number or level (although you can say *a high of* a number or level − see below). **Peak** is used in compounds or before other nouns (*peak hours/period/season/time/year/demand/rate/level/efficiency/performance/fitness/form/condition*) but **height** is not. However, you cannot say: *the peak of summer*.

highlight [C] the best, most interesting or most exciting part of sth: *One of the highlights of the trip was seeing the Taj Mahal.* ◇ *The highlights of the game will be shown later this evening.*

climax /ˈklaɪmæks/ [C] the most exciting or important event or point in time, that usually happens near the end of a period or after some time; the most exciting part of a story, film or piece of music, that usually happens near the end: *The team's 3–1 victory in the final provided a fitting climax to a great season.* ◇ *The story builds up to a powerful climax with the murder of Nancy by her lover Bill Sikes.* **OPP anticlimax →** DISAPPOINTMENT
  ▸ **climax** verb [I]: (*rather informal*) *The festival will climax on Sunday with a gala concert.* ❶ In American English **climax** can also be used with an object: [T] (*AmE*) *The sensational verdict climaxed a six-month trial.*

high [C] (*business or journalism*) the highest level or number, especially of prices, sales, etc.; the highest temperature reached during a particular day, week, etc: *Profits reached an all-time high last year.* ◇ *Oil prices hit a high of $70 a barrel yesterday.* ◇ *Highs today will be in the region of 25°C.* **OPP low** ❶ The opposite is **low**: *The dollar has fallen to an all-time **low against** the pound.* ◇ *The government's popularity has hit a new low.*

culmination /ˌkʌlmɪˈneɪʃn/ [sing.] (*rather formal, especially written*) the highest point or end of sth, usually happening after a long time: *The reforms marked the successful culmination of a long campaign.*
  ▸ **culminate** verb [I]: *Months of hard work culminated in success.*

prime [sing.] the time in your life when you are strongest, most active or most successful: *She was then a great artist in her prime.* ◇ *He was barely 30 and **in the prime of (his) life** when he had the accident.*

heyday /ˈheɪdeɪ/ [C, usually sing.] the time when sb/sth had most power or success, or was most popular: *In its heyday in the 1820s, 80 horse-drawn coaches passed through the town each day.* ◇ *This is a fine film from the heyday of Italian cinema.*

'high point [C] the point when sth is most interesting, enjoyable or successful or at its highest level: *It was the high point of the evening.* ◇ *From a high point of nearly 140 000 in the 1950s, the workforce had fallen to 74 000 by 1984.* ❶ **High point** usually has a positive meaning: *The violence reached its peak/height in the summer of that year.* ◇ *The violence reached a high point in the summer of that year.* **OPP low point**

peer *noun*

peer · equal · match
These are all words for a person or thing that is like another person or thing in some way.

PATTERNS AND COLLOCATIONS
  ▸ **among** your peers / equals
  ▸ to **be sb's equal** / match

peer [C, usually pl.] a person who is the same age or who has the same social status as you: *She enjoys the respect of her peers.* ◇ *Children are worried about failing in front of their peers.* ◇ ***Peer pressure** is strong among young people* (= they want to be like other people of the same age). See also **peer group →** AGE

equal [C] (*rather formal*) a person or thing of the same ability or quality, or with the same status or rights as another: *As a poet, he had few equals.* ◇ *Our cars are the equal of those produced anywhere in the world.* ◇ *She treats the people who work for her as her equals.* See also **equal →** COMPARE *verb 2*, **equal →** EQUAL *adj.*

match [sing.] a person who is equal to sb else in strength, skill, intelligence, etc: *I was **no match for** him at tennis.* ◇ *She knew she had **met her match** and tried to retreat.* See also **match →** COMPARE *verb 2*

people *noun*

1 young/working-class/disabled people
2 tribal peoples

1 See also the entry for PERSON
people · folk
These words are both used to refer to people in general.

PATTERNS AND COLLOCATIONS
  ▸ **young** / **elderly** / **old** / **rich** / **poor** / **black** / **white** people / folk
  ▸ **common** / **ordinary** / **working** / **working-class** / **everyday** people / folk
  ▸ **decent** / **good** / **honest** / **law-abiding** / **friendly** people / folk
  ▸ **city** / **country** / **local** people / folk

people [pl.] more than one person; persons in general; everyone: *At least ten people were killed in the crash.* ◇ *Many young people are out of work.* ◇ *He doesn't care what people think of him.* ◇ *She tends to annoy people.*

folk /fəʊk; *AmE* foʊk/ (also **folks** especially in *AmE*) [pl.] (*informal*) people in general: *It's the ordinary everyday folk who come to shop at the market.* ◇ *I'd like a job working with old folk or kids.* ◇ (*AmE*) *Folks say that he is a hard man.* See also **folks →** MOTHER

2 people · race · nationality · tribe · clan · ethnic group
These are all words for a group of people from the same place, or belonging to the same nation, race or culture.

PATTERNS AND COLLOCATIONS
  ▸ a race / tribe / clan **of** sth
  ▸ **from** a race / a tribe / a clan / an ethnic group
  ▸ **between** peoples / races / nationalities / tribes / clans / ethnic groups
  ▸ **among** peoples / races / ethnic groups
  ▸ **different** / **other** peoples / races / nationalities / tribes / clans / ethnic groups
  ▸ a **minority** people / nationality / tribe / ethnic group
  ▸ a **local** people / tribe / clan / ethnic group
  ▸ to **belong to** a race / a nationality / a tribe / a clan / an ethnic group

people [C] all the men, women and children who live in a particular place or belong to a particular nation, race or culture: *The organization campaigns for the rights of **tribal peoples**.* ◇ *The book contains translations of folk poetry of the Slav peoples.* ◇ *We should strive for peace among the **peoples of the world**.*

race [C, U] one of the main groups that humans can be divided into according to their physical differences, for example the colour of their skin: *This custom is found in people of all races throughout the world.* ◇ *Black and **mixed race** (= with parents of different races) employees complained of harassment.* ◇ *There is legislation against discrimination on the grounds of race or sex.* ◇ *Immigration and **race relations** were key political issues at the time.* See also **race →** CULTURE, **the human race →** MAN 2, **racial →** CULTURAL, **racism →** RACISM

nationality /ˌnæʃəˈnæləti/ [C] a group of people with the same language, culture and history, who form part of a political nation: *The city is home to more than a hundred nationalities.*

tribe [C] (*sometimes offensive*) (in developing countries or in the past) a group of people of the same race, and with the same language, customs and religion, living in a particular area and often led by a chief: *She went to live with a nomadic tribe in Mongolia.* ❶ The word **tribe** was used in the past to describe a group of people living together in a simple society with little or no industry. **Tribe** is still sometimes used to describe groups in developing countries, especially where they continue to live in a traditional way, often separate from other people. Some people find the term **tribe** offensive, because it suggests simple people who are not civilized. **Ethnic group** is now becoming more frequent. See also **tribal** → CULTURAL

clan [C+sing./pl. v.] (especially in Scotland in the past) a group of families who are related to each other and live together in a social group: *His grandfather was a descendant of the Guthrie clan in Scotland.*

ethnic 'group [C] a group of people from the same race, tribe or nation: *The school has a large number of students from different ethnic groups.* ❶ **Ethnic group** is often used as a general word to describe a person's race or nationality. When talking about a group of people living in a place where most people are from a different race and/or nationality, the terms *minority ethnic group* or *ethnic minority* are often used. See also **ethnic** → CULTURAL

perfect *adj.*

perfect · impeccable · exemplary · unspoiled · pristine · flawless · immaculate · faultless
These words all describe sth that has no faults or weaknesses.

PATTERNS AND COLLOCATIONS
▶ perfect / impeccable / exemplary **behaviour**
▶ a perfect / an impeccable / an exemplary / a flawless / an immaculate / a faultless **performance**
▶ a perfect / an impeccable / an exemplary / an immaculate **record**
▶ perfect / impeccable / pristine / immaculate **condition**
▶ perfect / impeccable / flawless / faultless **English / French**
▶ perfect / pristine / immaculate **hair / make-up**
▶ almost perfect / flawless / faultless

perfect without any faults or weaknesses; as good as it is possible to be: *He smiled, revealing a perfect set of teeth.* ◇ *Well, I'm sorry, but nobody's perfect* (= used when sb has criticized you). ◇ *In a perfect world no one would need to pay for health care.* **OPP** **imperfect** ❶ Something that is **imperfect** contains faults or mistakes: *an imperfect world* ◇ *an imperfect understanding of English* ◇ *All our sale items are slightly imperfect.*
▶ **perfection** /pəˈfekʃn; *AmE* pərˈf-/ *noun* [U]: *The fish was cooked to perfection* (= perfectly). ◇ *We were encouraged to strive for perfection* (= try to achieve perfection).
▶ **perfectly** *adv.*: *The dress fitted perfectly.*

impeccable /ɪmˈpekəbl/ (*rather formal*) without any faults or mistakes: *impeccable manners/taste* ◇ *She came to the company with impeccable credentials* (= a perfect record, perfect qualifications, very highly recommended by previous employers, etc.).
▶ **impeccably** *adv.*: *They behaved impeccably.* ◇ *She was always impeccably dressed.*

exemplary /ɪɡˈzempləri/ (*rather formal*) providing a good example of behaviour, that other people are recommended to copy: *He was known as a man of exemplary character.*

unspoiled (*BrE* also **unspoilt**) (of countryside) beautiful because it has not been changed or built on; (of a child) not made unpleasant or bad-tempered by being praised too much or given too many presents: *It's a country of stunning landscapes and unspoiled beaches.* ◇ *She was an affectionate child and remarkably unspoiled.* **OPP** **spoiled** ❶ A **spoiled** (*BrE* also **spoilt**) child is rude and badly behaved because they are given everything they ask for and not enough discipline: *a spoiled brat* ◇ (*BrE*) *He's spoilt rotten* (= very spoiled).

pristine /ˈprɪstiːn/ fresh and clean, as if new: *The car is in pristine condition.* ◇ *All the tables were covered with pristine white linen.*

flawless (*rather formal*) (of sb/sth's appearance or performance) without any faults, marks or bad features and therefore perfect: *She has a flawless complexion.* ◇ *It's a demanding piece to play and requires a flawless technique.*

immaculate /ɪˈmækjələt/ (*rather formal*) (of sb/sth's appearance or condition) so clean and neat that it is perfect; (of sb's record or performance) containing no mistakes: *She always looks immaculate.* ◇ *The incident ruined an otherwise immaculate safety record.*

faultless (of a performance or argument) perfect and without any mistakes: *He gave a faultless performance.* ◇ *Her logic was always faultless.*

performance *noun*

performance · show · production · display · act · spectacle
These are all words for an occasion on which a play, concert or some other form of entertainment is performed.

PATTERNS AND COLLOCATIONS
▶ **in** a performance / a show / a production / a display / an act / a spectacle
▶ **at** a performance / show / production / display / spectacle
▶ **during** a performance / a show / a display / an act
▶ a **great** performance / show / display / spectacle
▶ a **brilliant / superb** performance / show / production / display
▶ a **magnificent** performance / display / spectacle
▶ a **live** performance / show / production / act
▶ a **stage** performance / show / production
▶ a **public** performance / display / spectacle
▶ a/an **amateur / professional** performance / show / production
▶ a **musical** performance / show / production / act
▶ to **do** a performance / a show / a production / an act
▶ to **put on / stage** a performance / show / production / display
▶ to **perform** a show / an act
▶ to **see** a performance / a show / a production / a display / an act
▶ to **watch** a performance / show / production / display

performance [C] an occasion on which a play, concert or some other form of entertainment is performed: *They gave a magnificent performance of Ravel's String Quartet.* ◇ *Please refrain from talking during the performance.* See also **perform** → PLAY *verb* 3

show [C] a theatre performance, especially one that includes singing and dancing: *This one-man show had the audience falling about with laughter.* ◇ *She's the star of the show!* See also **show** → CONCERT

production [C] a film, play or broadcast that is prepared for the public: *She's currently performing in a new production of 'King Lear'.* ❶ **Production** is most often used to talk about plays and musicals. See also **produce** → PLAY *verb* 3

display [C] an act of performing a skill or of showing sth happening, in order to entertain people: *Most of the local people attended the firework display.* ◇ *We watched a breathtaking display of aerobatics.*

act [C] one of several short pieces of entertainment in a show: *The show includes clowns and other circus acts.*

spectacle /ˈspektəkl/ [C, U] a performance or event that is very impressive and exciting to look at: *The carnival parade was a magnificent spectacle.* See also **spectacular** → IMPRESSIVE

period noun

period · century · decade · day · time · era · age · generation · epoch
These are all words for a length of time, especially in the life of a particular person or the history of a particular country.

PATTERNS AND COLLOCATIONS
▸ **in** a period / the ... century / a decade / ...day(s) / the time of... / ...times / an era / the age of... / a generation / an epoch
▸ **during** the period / century / decade / days / era / age / epoch
▸ a **new** period / century / decade / era / generation / epoch
▸ (the) **present** period / century / decade / day / time / era / generation / epoch
▸ (the) **modern** period / day / time / era / age
▸ (the) **medieval/Victorian/post-war, etc.** period / days / time / era / age
▸ to **enter** a period / a century / a decade / an era / an age
▸ to **usher in** a period / an era / an age
▸ a period / a century / a decade / a time / an era / an age **begins/ ends**
▸ the **beginning/end of** a period / a century / a decade / an era / an age / an epoch

period [C] a length of time in the history of a particular country or in the life of a particular person: *Which period of history would you most like to have lived in?* ◇ *This textbook covers the post-war period.* ◇ *The picture was painted by Picasso during his blue period.* ◇ *Most teenagers go through a period of rebelling.* ❶ **Period** is often used to describe a time in a country's history that is studied as a historical subject. See also **period** → TIME 2
century [C] a period of 100 years; any of the periods of 100 years before or after the birth of Christ: *A century ago, weavers and bricklayers in this working class district won some of the earliest strikes for the ten-hour day.* ◇ *the 20th century* (= AD 1901–2000 or 1900–1999) ◇ *eighteenth-century writers*
decade [C] a period of ten years, especially a period such as 1910–1919 or 2000–2009: *The effects of climate change have been increasingly apparent over the last decade.* ◇ *The nineties were a decade of rapid advances.*
day [C, usually pl.] a period of time that is different from other periods because of particular characteristics or events: *Dickens gives us a vivid picture of poverty in Queen Victoria's day.* ◇ *Most women stayed at home in those days* (= in the past). ◇ *Kids grow up so quickly these days* (= in the present). ◇ *This book is a study of European drama, from Ibsen to the present day.* ◇ *Slavery continues to exist, even in this day and age* (= in the present). See also **in sb's day** → LIFE 2
time [U, pl.] a period of time that is connected with particular events or experiences in people's lives: *The movie is set at the time of the Russian revolution.* ◇ *The Industrial Revolution took place in Victorian times.* ◇ *The violence of our times* (= the present period of history) *is nothing new.* ◇ *Times are hard for the unemployed.* ◇ *Times have changed since Grandma was young.* See also **time** → TIME 2
era /'ɪərə; AmE 'ɪrə; 'erə/ [C] (*rather formal*) a long period of time that is thought of as having particular characteristics or events: *It is one of the most famous churches built in the Victorian era.* ◇ *When she left the firm, it was the end of an era* (= things were different after that). ◇ *This is the start of a new era of peace and prosperity.*
age [C] a period of time, usually in history, that is different from other periods, especially because it represents a stage in the development of technology or tools: *Are the laws of war still relevant in the nuclear age?* ◇ *This is the age of the computer.* ◇ *They dug up several examples of Bronze Age pottery.* ◇ *The golden age of cinema was in the 1950s.* ◇ *The museum is putting on an exhibition of spinning through the ages.*
generation [C] the average time in which children grow up, become adults and have children of their own, usually considered to be about 30 years: *Divorce is much*

more common now than it was a generation ago. ◇ *My family have lived in this house for generations.* See also **generation** → AGE
epoch /'iːpɒk; AmE 'epək/ [C] (*formal*) a long period of time in history during which important events or changes happen: *The death of the emperor marked the end of an epoch in the country's history.*

> **NOTE** DAY, TIME, ERA, AGE OR EPOCH? Era, age and epoch are used more often to mean a period in history. **Day** and **time** are often used, especially in the plural, to talk about the present: *these days* ◇ *modern times.* When **day** or **time** means a period in history, it is often used after a person's name: *The battle happened in King Alfred's day.* ◇ *The family was very poor in my great-grandmother's time.*

permanent adj.

permanent · eternal · lasting · enduring · immortal
These words all describe things that will last for a long time in the future or forever.

PATTERNS AND COLLOCATIONS
▸ permanent / eternal / lasting / enduring **value**
▸ a permanent / a lasting / an enduring **relationship / solution / legacy**
▸ eternal / lasting / enduring **love / friendship**

permanent lasting for a long time or for all time in the future; existing all the time: *No permanent damage was done.* ◇ *The sheds were replaced with a permanent brick building.* ◇ *She was unable to find a permanent job.* ◇ *I'm not planning to move in here on a permanent basis.* ◇ *The house is in a permanent state of chaos.* **OPP** temporary → SHORT 1
▸ **permanently** adv.: *She had decided to settle permanently in France.* ◇ *The stroke left his right side permanently damaged.* **OPP** temporarily → SHORT adj. 1
eternal /ɪ'tɜːnl; AmE ɪ'tɜːrnl/ without an end; existing or continuing forever: *The two heroes swore eternal friendship.* ◇ *She's the eternal optimist* (= she always expects that the best will happen). ◇ *The story is about a woman who is offered the elixir of eternal youth.*
▸ **eternally** adv.: *I would be eternally grateful if you could help me with this matter.* ◇ *He is eternally optimistic about the country's political future.*
lasting [usually before noun] continuing to exist or to have an effect for a long time: *Few of the songs made any lasting impact.* ◇ *It's a solution that could bring lasting peace.* **OPP** short-lived → SHORT 1, See also **long-lasting** → LONG adj.
enduring /ɪn'djʊərɪŋ; AmE -'dʊr-/ lasting for a long time, especially because of its high quality: *What is your most enduring memory of her?* ◇ *What is the reason for the game's enduring appeal?* **OPP** short-lived → SHORT 1
immortal that will never die: *He believed himself immortal.* ◇ *She believed that her immortal soul was in danger.* **OPP** mortal ❶ Mortal creatures cannot live for ever and must die: *We are all mortal.*

permission noun See the Topic Map for THE INDIVIDUAL AND SOCIETY on p.894, See also the entries for APPROVAL and LICENCE

permission · consent · authorization · authority · clearance · the go-ahead · leave
These are all words for allowing sth to happen or allowing sb to do sth.

PATTERNS AND COLLOCATIONS
▸ permission / consent / authorization / authority / clearance **for sth**
▸ **without** sb's permission / consent / authorization / authority / leave
▸ **with** sb's permission / consent / authorization / authority / leave

▶ permission / consent / authorization / authority / clearance / the go-ahead / leave **to do sth**
▶ **formal** permission / consent / authorization / authority / clearance
▶ **special** permission / consent / authorization / leave
▶ **official** permission / authorization / clearance
▶ **prior / written** permission / consent / authorization / authority
▶ to **give** (sb) permission / consent / authorization / authority / clearance / the go-ahead / leave
▶ to **get** permission / consent / authorization / authority / clearance / the go-ahead / leave
▶ to **receive** authorization / clearance / the go-ahead
▶ to **have** (sb's) permission / consent / authorization / authority / clearance / leave
▶ to **require** permission / consent / authorization / authority / leave
▶ to **refuse** (sb) permission / consent / authorization / clearance / leave

permission [U] the fact of being allowed to do sth, by sb who has the authority or right to decide: *I asked permission to photograph the house.* ◊ *Who gave permission for this?* ◊ *He had taken the car without his father's permission.* ◊ *The portrait is reproduced* **by kind permission** *of the artist.* ◊ *The council refused* **planning permission** (= official permission for new buildings or changes to existing ones). See also **permit** → ALLOW

consent /kən'sent/ [U] (*rather formal*) permission that you give for sth, especially sth that affects you personally, your family or your property: *He was accused of taking a vehicle without the owner's consent.* ◊ *The written consent of a parent is required.* ◊ *Children under sixteen cannot give* **consent to** *medical treatment.* ◊ *The girl was under the* **age of consent** (= the age at which sb is legally old enough to agree to have sex). **OPP** **refusal** → REFUSAL. See also **consent** → AGREE 2

NOTE **PERMISSION OR CONSENT?** **Permission** is often (though not always) official, given by sb in authority; the important thing is for the person who wants to do sth to *have* or *get* the permission: *Have you got permission to do that?* ◊ ~~Have you got consent to do that?~~ **Consent** is often more personal, concerning what is done with sb's private property or their body; it is often used in the context of medical treatment or sexual relations; the important thing is for the person that sth is being done to to *give* their consent: *Children under sixteen cannot give consent to medical treatment.* ◊ ~~Children under sixteen cannot give permission for medical treatment.~~ However, in less formal contexts, **permission** may be used instead of **consent**: *You need written permission from your parents.* In more formal contexts **consent** may be used instead of **permission**: *They had planning consent for a hotel and conference centre on the site.*

authorization (*BrE* also **-isation**) /ˌɔːθəraɪˈzeɪʃn; *AmE* ˌɔːθərəˈzeɪʃn/ [U, C] (*rather formal*) official permission to do sth; the act of giving permission: *You may not enter the security area without authorization.* ◊ *The order was, in effect, an authorization to plan a coup.* ◊ *The department is responsible for the authorization of spending.* See also **authorize** → ALLOW

authority [U] (*rather formal*) official permission or power to do sth: *The government was accused of selling the land without formal authority.* ◊ *The minister must answer to Parliament for anything his officials have done* **under his authority.**

NOTE **AUTHORIZATION OR AUTHORITY?** There is not much difference in meaning between these words. **Authorization** is nearly always permission for a particular action, or the act of giving this permission; **authority** can be more general, meaning 'the power to give permission': things can be done *under sb's authority* but NOT 'under sb's authorization'.

clearance /ˈklɪərəns; *AmE* ˈklɪr-/ [U, C] (*rather formal*) official permission that sb must get before they can work somewhere, have particular information, or do sth they

want to do; official permission for a person or vehicle to enter or leave an airport or country: *It is safest to seek advance clearance from the tax office.* ◊ *Allow a minimum of six weeks to obtain the necessary clearances.* ◊ *The aircraft received clearance to taxi out for take-off.* See also **clear** → ALLOW

the 'go-ahead [sing.] (*rather informal, especially journalism*) permission for sb to start doing sth: *The company hopes to get the go-ahead for the new service.* ◊ *Councils were given the go-ahead to spend more on housing.* ❶ **The go-ahead** is nearly always used with the verbs *get* or *give*.

leave [sing.] (*formal*) official permission to be or go somewhere; official permission to bring a case or make a request in court: *In May the officer went* **absent without leave.** ◊ *The school gave him* **leave of absence** (= permission to be away) *to play in the final.* ◊ *An application for* **leave to appeal** (= against a decision in court) *must be made within four weeks.*

persist *verb*

persist · keep going · hang on · persevere · keep at sth · struggle along/on
These words all mean to continue to do sth in spite of difficulties.

PATTERNS AND COLLOCATIONS
▶ to persist / persevere **with / in** sth

persist /pəˈsɪst; *AmE* pərˈs-/ [I, T] (*rather formal*) to continue trying to do or achieve sth in difficult circumstances, or in spite of opposition, in a way that can seem unreasonable: *Why do you persist in blaming yourself for what happened?* ◊ *He persisted with his questioning.* ◊ *'So, did you agree or not?' he persisted.* See also **persistence** → DETERMINATION, **persistent** → DETERMINED 2

,keep 'going *phrase* (*especially spoken*) to make an effort to live normally when you are in a difficult situation or when you have experienced great suffering; used to encourage sb to continue doing sth: *You just have to keep yourself busy and keep going.* ◊ *Keep going, Sarah, you're nearly there.*

,hang 'on *phrasal verb* (*rather informal, especially journalism*) to continue trying to do or achieve sth in difficult circumstances: *The team hung on for victory.*

persevere /ˌpɜːsɪˈvɪə(r); *AmE* ˌpɜːrsəˈvɪr/ [I] (*rather formal, approving*) to continue trying to do or achieve sth in difficult circumstances: *Despite a number of setbacks, they persevered in their attempts to fly around the world in a balloon.* ◊ *You have to persevere with difficult students.* See also **perseverance** → DETERMINATION

,keep 'at sth *phrasal verb* (*rather informal, especially spoken*) to continue trying to do or achieve sth; used to encourage sb to continue doing sth: *Encouraged by his confidence in us, we kept at it.* ◊ *Come on, keep at it, you've nearly finished!*

,struggle a'long/'on *phrasal verb* to continue in difficult circumstances: *The business struggled along for some time.* ◊ *Life is hard but we all have to struggle on.* ❶ **Struggle along/on** suggests a sense of tiredness and difficulty rather than great enthusiasm or a strong desire to achieve sth.

person *noun* See the Topic Map for THE INDIVIDUAL AND SOCIETY on p.894. See also the entry for PEOPLE 1

person · individual · figure · human · human being · mortal · type · character · soul · thing
These are all words for a man, woman or child.

PATTERNS AND COLLOCATIONS
▶ a / an **average / normal / ordinary** person / individual / human / human being / mortal
▶ a **rational** person / individual / human being
▶ an **intelligent** person / human / human being
▶ a **sad** person / individual / figure / character

▸ a **brave / kind** person / soul
▸ a **mere** human / mortal
▸ a / an **key / powerful / independent** person / individual / figure
▸ the person / individual **concerned / responsible**

person [C] a man, woman or child; sb who is not identified: *What sort of person would do a thing like that?* ◇ *He's a fascinating person.* ◇ *What is she like as a person?* ◇ *He's just the person we need for the job.* ◇ *I had a letter from the people who used to live next door.* ◇ *I'm not really a city person* (= I don't like cities)*.* ◇ *The price is $40 per person.* ❶ The plural of **person** is usually **people**, but in formal language **persons** is often used: *This vehicle is licensed to carry 4 persons.* ◇ *(law) The verdict was murder by a person or persons unknown.*

individual [C] a person considered separately rather than as part of a group: *The competition is open to both teams and individuals.* ◇ *The teacher should treat each student as an individual.* ◇ *Each course has to be tailored to the needs of the individual.* ◇ *The school's reputation is being ruined by the bad behaviour of a few individuals.* ❶ An **individual** can also be a person of a particular type, especially a strange or unpleasant one: *This scruffy-looking individual wandered into the office.* See also **individual** → OWN *adj.*

figure [C] a person of the kind mentioned: *He's a leading figure in the music industry.* ◇ *a cult/public/political figure* ◇ *a figure of authority* ◇ *When she last saw him he was a sad figure – old and tired.* See also **public figure** → STAR 1

human [C] a person rather than an animal, a machine or, in science fiction, a creature from another planet: *Dogs can hear much better than humans.* ◇ *More work is needed on the interface between humans and machines.*
▸ **human** *adj.*: *the human body/brain* ◇ *a terrible loss of human life* ◇ *Contact with other people is a basic human need.*

human 'being [C] a human: *That is no way to treat another human being.* ◇ *He was just a normal human being with faults like the rest of us.*

> **NOTE** HUMAN OR HUMAN BEING? **Human** often refers to the biological characteristics of people compared with animals, machines or, in science fiction, with creatures from other planets: *Pigs are biologically very similar to humans.* **Human** is also used to refer to different stages in the development of the human race: *early/primitive/modern humans.* **Human being** is often used when talking about a person's ability to think, feel and be social when compared with animals: *She was not behaving like a rational human being.*

mortal [C] (*humorous*) a person, especially an ordinary person with little power, influence or skill: *She can deal with complicated numbers in her head, but we lesser mortals need calculators!*

type [sing.] (*informal*) a person of a particular character, with qualities or features: *She hangs around with all those artistic types.* ◇ *He's not the type to be unfaithful.* ◇ *She's not my type* (= not the kind of person I am usually attracted to)*.*

character [C] (usually used with an adjective) (*rather informal*) a person, especially a strange or unpleasant one or sb with a strong personality: *There were some really strange characters hanging around the bar.* ◇ *She's a reformed character nowadays.* ◇ *She's quite a character!* ❶ **Character** can describe a person who seems strange or unpleasant: *a/an unsavoury/undesirable/suspicious/shady character,* or a person who did bad things in the past but who has changed: *a reformed character,* or simply a person with a strong personality: *a tough/determined/shrewd character*

soul [C] a person of a particular type; (especially in negative sentences) a person: *It means bad news for some poor soul* (= an unlucky person that you feel sympathy for)*.* ◇ *A few brave souls queued all night to get tickets for centre court.* ◇ *There wasn't another soul in sight* (= no one around)*.* ❶ **Soul** is mainly used in a few fixed phrases, especially in negative sentences: *There was not a*

soul about/in sight/to be seen. ◇ *I won't tell a soul.* ◇ *She's completely exhausted, poor soul!* Otherwise, it is becoming old-fashioned or is used only in literary contexts.

thing [C] (used with an adjective) (*spoken*) used to talk to or about a person or animal, to show how you feel about them: *You silly thing!* ◇ *You must be starving, you poor things.* ◇ *The cat's very ill, poor old thing!*

personality *noun*

personality · nature · character · temperament · self · persona · make-up · disposition
These are all words for the qualities and characteristics that make a person who they are and different from others.

PATTERNS AND COLLOCATIONS
▸ **by** nature / temperament
▸ **in** sb's nature / character
▸ a **violent** personality / nature / character / temperament
▸ a / an **outgoing / charming** personality / character / disposition
▸ a **sunny** personality / nature / disposition
▸ a **generous** nature / character / disposition
▸ sb's **real / true** nature / character / self
▸ sth **reflects** sb's personality / nature / character
▸ an **aspect of** sb's personality / nature / character / temperament / disposition
▸ a **side of** sb's personality / nature / character
▸ a **part of** sb's personality / character / make-up

personality [C, U] a person's qualities and features that combine to make them different from other people: *The children all have very different personalities.* ◇ *His wife has a strong personality.* ◇ *He maintained order by sheer force of personality.* ◇ *There are likely to be tensions and personality clashes in any social group.*

nature [C, U] the usual way that a person or animal behaves that is part of their personality: *He has an inquisitive nature.* ◇ *It's not in her nature to be unkind.* ◇ *It was against his nature to tell lies.* ◇ *She is very sensitive by nature.* ◇ *It's only human nature to want more money.* ◇ *People are always taking advantage of her good nature* (= her kindness)*.* See also **nature** → NATURE 1

character [C, usually sing.] all the qualities and features that make a person or group of people different from others: *She revealed her true character when anyone disagreed with her.* ◇ *The lawyer argued that his client's violent behaviour was out of character.* ◇ *Generosity is part of the American character.* See also **character** → NATURE 1

temperament /'temprəmənt/ [C, U] a person's or an animal's nature as shown in the way they tend to behave or react to situations or people: *To become a champion, you have to have the right temperament.* ◇ *She was fiery by temperament.*

> **NOTE** PERSONALITY, NATURE, CHARACTER OR TEMPERAMENT? **Personality** is used especially to talk about the way sb behaves in the company of other people, for example whether they are lively or quiet, confident or shy, cheerful or bad-tempered. **Nature** is used especially to talk about what sb would normally do, often when contrasting this with behaviour that seems to be different from what they would normally do. **Character** is similar to **nature**, but is more often used in connection with a person's moral behaviour or how honest or strong-minded they are. **Temperament** is mostly used to talk about a person's emotional state, whether they are likely to react to a particular situation by, for example, becoming angry or sad or by staying calm.

self (pl. **selves**) [C, usually sing.] the type of person you are, especially the way you normally behave, look or feel: *He's not his usual happy self this morning.* ◇ *Only with a few people could she be her real self.* ◇ *You'll soon be feeling your old self again* (= feeling well or happy again)*.* ◇ *Her private and public selves were vastly different.* See also **self** → IDENTITY

persona /pə'səʊnə; *AmE* pər'soʊnə/ (pl. **personae** /-niː; -naɪ/ or **personas**) [C] (*formal*) the aspects of a person's character that they show to other people, especially when their real character is different: *His public persona is quite different from the private family man described in the book.*

'make-up [sing.] (*rather informal*) the different qualities that combine to form a person's character: *Jealousy is not part of his make-up.* ◇ *The report studies the psychological make-up of a serial killer.*

disposition /ˌdɪspə'zɪʃn/ [C, usually sing.] (*formal*) the natural qualities of a person's character, as shown in the way they tend to behave or react to sth: *Tom was everybody's favourite with his bouncy, cheerful disposition.* ◇ *Some scenes aren't recommended for viewers of a nervous disposition.*

persuade *verb* See also the entry for CONVINCE

persuade · get · convince · win sb over · coax · talk sb into sth · cajole · get round/around sb · convert
These words all mean to make sb agree to do sth, usually by talking to them and giving them good reasons why they should do it.

PATTERNS AND COLLOCATIONS
▶ to persuade sb/ get sb/ convince sb/ be coaxed/ be cajoled **to do sth**
▶ to persuade/ coax/ talk/ cajole sb **into** (doing) sth
▶ to **try to** persuade sb/ get sb to do sth/ convince sb to do sth/ win sb over/ coax sb/ talk sb into sth
▶ to **manage to** persuade sb/ get sb to do sth/ convince sb to do sth/ win sb over/ coax sb
▶ to **finally** persuade sb/ convince sb to do sth/ win sb over

persuade [T, I] to make sb agree to do sth by giving them good reasons for doing it: *Can you persuade him to come?* ◇ *Please try and persuade her.* ◇ *He was fairly easily persuaded.* ◇ *I allowed myself to be persuaded into entering the competition.* **OPP** dissuade → DISCOURAGE 1
▶ **persuasion** /pə'sweɪʒn; *AmE* pər's-/ *noun* [U]: *After a little gentle persuasion, he agreed to come.* ◇ *She has great powers of persuasion.*

get [T] (*informal*) to persuade sb to do sth: *He got his sister to help him with his homework.* ◇ *We had trouble getting enough people to sign up.* ◇ *It's not hard to get him talking – the problem is stopping him!*

convince sb to do sth [T] to make sb do sth by giving them good reasons for doing it: *I've been trying to convince him to see a doctor.*

NOTE PERSUADE OR CONVINCE? When followed by an infinitive with *to*, **persuade** and **convince** both mean that a person does sth because of sth you have said or done. You can *persuade sb to do sth* in many different ways, for example by making them believe it is right, by showing them that they will gain sth from it, or by giving them sth in return: *Nothing would persuade them to go back again.* ◇ *Subsequently he was persuaded by bribes to reverse his judgement.* When you *convince sb to do sth*, you usually make them believe that it is the right or the best thing to do: *He convinced me to get legal advice.* The use of **convince** with this meaning is fairly recent and is more common in American English. Many speakers of British English prefer to use **persuade** and they use **convince** only with the meaning 'to make sb believe that sth is true': *He convinced me that he was right.* See also **convince** → CONVINCE

,win sb 'over *phrasal verb* to get sb's support or approval, especially by persuading them that you are right when they disagreed with you before: *She's against the idea but I'm sure I can win her over.* ◇ *They were immediately won over by his famous charm.*

coax /kəʊks; *AmE* koʊks/ [T] (usually used with an adverb or preposition) to persuade sb to do sth by talking to them in a kind and gentle way; to make an animal or machine do sth by treating it gently: *He was coaxed out of*

retirement to help the failing company. ◇ *Police managed to coax him down from the ledge.* ◇ *She coaxed the horse into coming a little closer.*

,talk sb 'into sth *phrasal verb* (*rather informal*) to persuade sb to do sth, especially sth they are not very enthusiastic about: *I didn't want to go, but Bill talked me into it.* ◇ *She tried to talk him into staying a bit longer.* **OPP** **talk sb out of sth** → DISCOURAGE 1

cajole /kə'dʒəʊl; *AmE* kə'dʒoʊl/ [T, I] to persuade sb to do sth by talking to them in a gentle way and being very nice to them: *He didn't like the microphone and had to be cajoled into using it.* ◇ *He pleaded, cajoled, even offered bribes, but it was too late.*

NOTE COAX OR CAJOLE? In many cases you can use either word: *He was coaxed/cajoled out of retirement.* However, **coax** can suggest a kinder, gentler action than **cajole**: you **coax** sb to do sth that is good for them as well as you: ~~*Police managed to cajole him down from the ledge.*~~ **Cajole** can suggest that sb is only pretending to be nice to sb else in order to get them to do what they want; cajoling is sometimes used along with other, less gentle methods, such as *bullying, threatening, menacing* and *bribing*.

,get 'round sb (*BrE*) (also **get a'round sb** especially in *AmE*) *phrasal verb* (*rather informal*) to persuade sb to agree to sth or to do what you want, usually by being very nice to them: *She knows how to get round her dad.*

convert /kən'vɜːt; *AmE* -'vɜːrt/ [T] (*rather informal*) to persuade sb to change their opinion about sth or a habit: *I've never liked opera but you might convert me!* ❶ **Convert** is also used when sb changes their religion or beliefs. When it is used to talk about persuading sb to change other ideas or habits, it is slightly informal and often humorous, and suggests that the change is quite dramatic and surprising, for example, changing from disliking sth to being enthusiastic about it.

perverse *adj.*

perverse · difficult · unhelpful · awkward · obstructive · uncooperative
These words all describe sb who behaves in a way that is not helpful, is unreasonable or causes problems.

PATTERNS AND COLLOCATIONS
▶ unhelpful/ obstructive **to** sth
▶ to **be** difficult/ awkward **about** sth
▶ a difficult/ an awkward/ an uncooperative **child**
▶ a difficult/ an awkward **customer**
▶ **deliberately** perverse/ awkward/ obstructive

perverse /pə'vɜːs; *AmE* pər'vɜːrs/ (of a person or their behaviour) showing determination to behave in a way that most people think is wrong, unacceptable or unreasonable: *Do you really mean that, or are you just being deliberately perverse?* ◇ *For some perverse reason he is refusing to see a doctor.* ◇ *It would be perverse to quit now that we're almost finished.*
▶ **perversely** *adv.*: *She seemed perversely proud of her criminal record.*
▶ **perversity** *noun* [U]: *He refused to attend out of sheer perversity.*

difficult (of a person) not easy to please; not helpful: *Don't pay any attention to her – she's just being difficult.* ◇ *We have training in how to deal with difficult customers.*

unhelpful (of a person) not willing to help sb; (of an action) not helpful or useful: *The taxi driver was being very unhelpful.* ◇ *We were disappointed by the rather unhelpful response from the insurance company.* **OPP** helpful → HELPFUL, helpful → VALUABLE 2
▶ **unhelpfully** *adv.*: *'Who was that?' 'No idea,' she replied unhelpfully.*

awkward (of a person) difficult to deal with: *Please don't be awkward about letting him come.* ◊ *He can be an* ***awkward customer*** (= a difficult person to deal with generally).

obstructive /əbˈstrʌktɪv/ (of a person or their behaviour) trying to prevent sb/sth from making progress: *Of course she can do it. She's just being deliberately obstructive.* **OPP** **constructive ❶ Constructive** describes behaviour or a course of action that has a useful and helpful effect rather than being negative and with no purpose: *constructive criticism/suggestions/advice*

uncooperative /ˌʌnkəʊˈɒpərətɪv; *AmE* -koʊˈɑːp-/ (of a person) not willing to be helpful to other people or do what they ask: *The witness was extremely uncooperative.* **OPP** **cooperative** → HELPFUL

photograph *noun* See also the entry for PICTURE

photograph · picture · photo · shot · slide · snapshot/ snap · print
These are all words for a picture that has been made using a camera.

PATTERNS AND COLLOCATIONS
▸ a **colour** photograph / picture / photo / slide / snap / print
▸ to **take** a photograph / picture / photo / shot / snapshot
▸ a photograph / picture / photo / shot / slide / snapshot **shows** sb/ sth

photograph [C] a picture that has been made using a camera: *aerial/satellite photographs* ◊ *Please enclose a recent passport-sized photograph of yourself.* ◊ *I spent the morning taking photographs of the city.* See also **photograph** → RECORD *verb* 2
picture [C] a photograph: *We had our picture taken in front of the hotel.* ◊ *His picture appeared in the local paper.*
▸ **picture** *verb* [T, usually passive]: *She is pictured here* (= shown in a picture) *with her parents.*
photo [C] (*rather informal*) a photograph: *a colour/black-and-white/passport photo* ◊ *a photo album* ◊ *Stand there and I'll take your photo.*

NOTE PHOTOGRAPH, PICTURE OR PHOTO? These words all have the same meaning. **Photograph** is slightly more formal and **photo** is slightly less formal. **Picture** is used especially in the context of photographs in newspapers, magazines and books. In American English it is more common to talk about *taking pictures*, although *take photographs/photos* is also used.

shot [C] a photograph: *I tried to get a shot of him in the water.* ◊ *publicity shots* ❶ **Shot** often places more emphasis on the process of taking the photograph, rather than the finished picture.
slide [C] a small piece of film held in a frame that can be shown on a screen when you shine a light through it: *a talk with colour slides* ◊ *a slide show/projector*
snapshot /ˈsnæpʃɒt; *AmE* -ʃɑːt/ (*BrE* also, *informal* **snap**) [C] an informal photograph that is taken quickly, usually with a small, hand-held camera and not by a professional photographer: *snapshots of the children* ◊ (*BrE*) *She showed us her holiday snaps.*
print [C] a copy of a photograph that is produced from film or from a digital camera: *How many prints would you like?* ◊ *a colour print* See also **print** → PICTURE
▸ **print** *verb* [T]: *I'm having the pictures developed and printed.*

pick sb/sth up *phrasal verb*

pick sb/sth up · lift · raise · hoist · scoop · heave
These words all mean to move sb/sth upwards, or to take hold of sb/sth and move them to a different position.

PATTERNS AND COLLOCATIONS
▸ to pick / lift / raise / hoist / scoop sb / sth **up**
▸ to pick up / lift / hoist / heave a **bag** / **basket**
▸ to pick up / lift / heave a **chest** / **suitcase**

▸ to pick up / lift / hoist / scoop a **child** / **girl** / **boy**
▸ to pick up / lift the **phone** / **telephone** / **receiver**
▸ to lift/raise your **hand** / **arm** / **head** / **chin** / **face** / **eyes** / **eyebrows**
▸ to pick up / lift / raise sb / sth **carefully** / **gently** / **gingerly**
▸ to pick sb up / lift sb / scoop sb **bodily**

ˌpick sb/sth ˈup *phrasal verb* to take hold of sb/sth and move them/it up: *She went over to the crying child and picked her up.* ◊ *He picked up the phone and dialled the number.* **OPP** **put sb/sth down ❶** If you **put sb/sth down** you stop holding them/it and place them/it on the ground, on a table, etc.: *Put that knife down before you hurt somebody!* ◊ *It's a great book. I couldn't put it down* (= couldn't stop reading it).
lift [T, I] (usually used with an adverb or preposition) to move sb/sth or be moved to a higher position or level; to take hold of sb/sth and move them/it to a different position: *I lifted the lid of the box and peered in.* ◊ *Her eyebrows lifted. 'Apologize? Why?'* ◊ *He lifted the suitcase down from the rack.*

NOTE PICK SB/STH UP OR LIFT? **Pick sb/sth up** is usually used to talk about things and people that are not very heavy. **Lift** suggests that the person or thing is quite heavy. **Lift** is also used to talk about moving heavy people or things in different directions: *to lift sth up/ down/into sth/from sth.* **Pick sb/sth up** can only be used to talk about moving a person or thing upwards.

raise [T] (usually used with an adverb or preposition) (*especially written*) to lift or move sth to a higher level; to move sb/sth/yourself to an upright position: *She raised the gun and fired.* ◊ *He raised a hand in greeting.* ◊ *She raised her eyes from her work.* ◊ *Somehow we managed to raise him to his feet.* ◊ *She raised herself up on one elbow.* **OPP** **lower ❶** To **lower** sb/sth is to let or make them/it go down: *She lowered her newspaper and looked around.* ◊ *They lowered him down the cliff on a rope.*

NOTE LIFT OR RAISE? If you are talking about moving an object or part of the body to a higher position or level, you can use either word. **Raise** is slightly more formal and is used more in writing. It is used more to talk about parts of the body; **lift** is used more to talk about objects. Only **lift** can be used without an object: ~~Her eyebrows raised.~~

hoist [T] (usually used with an adverb or preposition) to raise or pull sth up to a higher position, often using ropes or special equipment: *She hoisted herself onto a high stool.* ◊ *The cargo was hoisted aboard by crane.*
scoop [T] (always used with an adverb or preposition) to move or lift sb/sth with a quick continuous movement: *He scooped the child up in his arms.* ◊ *She quickly scooped her clothes from the chair.*
heave [T, I] (always used with an adverb or preposition) to lift, pull or throw sb/sth very heavy with one great effort: *I managed to heave the trunk down the stairs.* ◊ *They heaved the body overboard.* ◊ *He heaved himself out of his armchair.* ◊ *We all heaved on the rope.*

picture *noun* See also the entry for PHOTOGRAPH

picture · painting · drawing · portrait · graphics · print · sketch · image · artwork · cartoon
These are all words for a scene, person or thing that has been represented on paper by drawing, painting, etc.

PATTERNS AND COLLOCATIONS
▸ to **draw** a picture / portrait / sketch / cartoon
▸ to **paint** a picture / portrait
▸ to **make** a painting / a drawing / a portrait / a print / a sketch / an image
▸ to **do** a painting / drawing / portrait / sketch
▸ to **show** / **display** / **exhibit** a picture / painting / drawing / portrait / print
▸ to **frame** / **hang** a picture / painting / portrait / print
▸ a picture / painting / drawing / portrait / print / sketch / cartoon **shows** sb / sth

picture [C] a scene, person or thing that has been represented on paper using a pencil, a pen or paint: *The children were drawing pictures of their pets.* ◇ *She got a famous artist to paint her picture* (= a picture of herself). ◇ *He likes books with lots of pictures in them.* See also **illustration** → DIAGRAM

painting [C] a picture that has been made using paint: *a collection of paintings by American artists* ◇ *cave paintings* See also **paint** → DRAW *verb*

drawing [C] a picture that has been made using a pencil or pen, not paint: *a pencil/charcoal drawing* ◇ *a drawing by Paul Klee* ◇ *He did a drawing of a yacht.* See also **draw** → DRAW *verb*

portrait /'pɔːtreɪt; -trət; *AmE* 'pɔːrtrət/ [C] a painting, drawing or photograph of a person, especially of the head and shoulders: *Vermeer's 'Portrait of the artist in his studio'* ◇ *She had her portrait painted.* ◇ *a self-portrait* (= a painting that you do of yourself) *in pen and ink* ◇ *a portrait painter* See also **portrait** → DESCRIPTION

graphics [pl.] designs or pictures that are used in the production of books and magazines and on television and computer screens: *computer graphics* ◇ *Text and graphics are prepared separately and then combined.*

print [C] a picture that has been copied from a painting using photography: *a Renoir print* ◇ *a framed set of prints* See also **print** → PHOTOGRAPH

sketch [C] a simple picture that is drawn quickly and does not have many details: *I usually do a few very rough sketches before I start on a painting.* ◇ *He drew me a quick sketch.* See also **sketch** → DRAW *verb*

image [C] (*formal*) a copy of sb/sth in the form of a picture or statue: *Images of deer and hunters decorate the cave walls.* ◇ *a wooden image of the Hindu god Ganesh* ❶ An **image** can also be a picture of sb/sth seen on a television or computer screen. See also **image** → IMAGE

artwork [U] pictures that are prepared for books, advertisements and magazines: *Can you let me have the finished artwork by Friday?*

> **NOTE** GRAPHICS OR ARTWORK? **Artwork** places more emphasis on the process of producing the picture (for example by painting or drawing); **graphics** places more emphasis on the finished items. **Artwork** is pictures or photographs; **graphics** can also be designs, diagrams or tables.

cartoon /kɑːˈtuːn; *AmE* kɑːrˈt-/ [C] an amusing drawing in a newspaper or magazine, especially one about politics or events in the news: *a political cartoon* ❶ A **cartoon** is also a series of drawings that tell a story: *a strip cartoon* ◇ *a full-length Disney cartoon*

piece *noun* See also the entries for BIT and FRAGMENT

piece · lump · block · slice · loaf · slab · bar · chunk · length · cube · wedge · hunk · rasher
These are all words for an amount of sth, especially food or substances that things can be made from.

PATTERNS AND COLLOCATIONS
▸ a piece / lump / slice / chunk / wedge / hunk of **cheese**
▸ a piece / lump / slice / slab / chunk / hunk of **meat**
▸ a piece / slice / loaf / chunk / hunk of **bread**
▸ a piece / lump / block / slab of **ice**
▸ a piece / lump / block of **wood**
▸ a piece / block / slab of **stone / marble**
▸ a piece / lump / slab of **concrete**
▸ a piece / lump of **coal**
▸ a piece / slice of **cake / ham / pizza / pie**
▸ a piece / slab / bar of **chocolate**
▸ a piece / slice / wedge of **lemon**
▸ **lemon** slices / wedges
▸ a **big** piece / lump / slice / loaf / slab / chunk of sth
▸ a **thick** piece / slab / slice of sth
▸ a **great** lump / slab / chunk / wedge of sth
▸ to **cut** sth **into** pieces / slices / chunks / lengths / cubes / wedges

piece [C] (used especially with *of* and uncountable nouns) an amount of sth that has been cut or separated from the rest of it; a standard amount of sth: *She wrote something on a small piece of paper.* ◇ *He cut the pizza into bite-sized pieces.* ◇ *I've got a piece of grit in my eye.* ◇ *You should have at least two good portions of vegetables and two pieces of fruit a day.* ❶ If you want to talk about a small amount of a substance there is a range of words you can use: you must choose the right one to go with the substance you are talking about. **Piece** is the most frequent of all these words and can be used to talk about a lot of different substances or things, including *bread, cake, cardboard, cheese, chocolate, fabric, glass, land, meat, paper, plastic* and *string.* See also **piece** → BIT

lump [C] a piece of sth hard or solid, usually without a particular shape: *He put a few more lumps of coal on the fire.* ◇ *This sauce has lumps in it.* ◇ (*BrE*) *She gave the pony a sugar lump.* ❶ In American English a 'sugar lump' is called a **sugar cube**.

block [C] a large piece of a solid material that is square in shape and usually has flat sides: *The wall was made from massive blocks of stone.*

slice [C] a thin flat piece of food that has been cut off a larger piece: *Cut the meat into thin slices.* ◇ *Another slice of cake, anyone?* See also **slice** → CUT *verb 2*

loaf [C] an amount of bread that has been shaped and baked in one piece: *He cut several thick slices from a loaf of bread.* ◇ *Two white loaves, please.*

slab [C] a thick flat piece of stone, ice or food: *The road was paved with smooth stone slabs.* ◇ *paving slabs* ◇ *They were sitting at the table, tucking into great slabs of meat.*

bar [C] a piece of sth with straight sides, especially chocolate or soap: *a bar of soap* ◇ (*especially BrE*) *a chocolate bar* ◇ (*AmE*) *a candy bar*

chunk [C] a thick solid piece that has been cut or broken off sth: *Chunks of masonry lay in the grass around the ruined building.* ◇ *He bit a great chunk out of the apple.*

length [C] (always followed by *of*) a long thin piece of sth: *Carry a whistle and a spare length of rope.* ◇ *The timber is sold in lengths of 2, 5 or 10 metres.*

cube [C] a piece of sth, especially food, with six sides: *Cut the meat into cubes.* ◇ *She put some ice cubes into her lemonade.* ◇ (*AmE*) *She offered the pony a sugar cube.* ❶ In British English a 'sugar cube' is called a **sugar lump**.

wedge [C] a piece of food that has been cut into a shape with one thick end and one thin pointed end: *Serve the fish with salad and wedges of lemon.* ◇ *He cut a great wedge out of the cake and began to eat it.*

hunk [C] a large piece of sth, especially food, that has been cut or broken from a larger piece: *He offered me a hunk of bread with some cheese.*

rasher [C] (*BrE*) a thin slice of bacon (= meat from the back or sides of a pig): *I'd like a fried egg and two rashers of bacon, please.*

pile *noun*

pile · heap · stack · mass · mound
These are all words for an amount of a substance or a number of things that form a shape.

PATTERNS AND COLLOCATIONS
▸ a pile / heap / stack / mass / mound **of** sth
▸ **in / into** a pile / heap / stack / mound
▸ a **great / huge / large** pile / heap / stack / mass / mound
▸ a **little / neat** pile / heap / stack / mound
▸ a **small** pile / heap / mass / mound
▸ to **make** a pile / heap / mound
▸ to **put sth on** a pile / heap
▸ a pile / heap / stack of **books / magazines / newspapers**
▸ a pile / heap / mass / mound of **rubble**
▸ a pile / heap / mass of **snow**
▸ a pile / heap / mound of **earth / rubbish**
▸ a pile / stack / mass / mound of **papers**

pile [C] a number of things that have been placed on top of each other; an amount of sth in a shape that is high in the middle and wider at the bottom than at the top: *He arranged the documents into neat piles.* ◊ *The body was hidden under a pile of leaves.* ◊ *He was spreading a small pile of manure around the strawberry plants.*
▸ **pile** *verb* [T]: *She piled the boxes one on top of the other.* ◊ *Snow was piled up against the door.*

heap [C] an untidy pile of sth: *Her clothes were lying in a crumpled heap.* ◊ *The building was reduced to a heap of rubble.* ◊ *Worn-out car tyres were stacked in heaps.*
▸ **heap** *verb* [T]: *Rocks were heaped up on the side of the road.* ◊ *She heaped food on my plate.*

stack [C] a pile of things, usually one that is neatly arranged: *He was counting a stack of dollar bills.* ◊ *She added her tray to the stack.*
▸ **stack** *verb* [T, I]: *They were busy stacking the shelves with goods.* ◊ *Do these chairs stack?*

mass [C] a large amount of a substance that does not have a definite shape: *A mass of snow and rocks was falling down the mountain.* ◊ *The sky was full of dark masses of clouds.*

mound [C] a pile of sth, especially one in a shape that is high in the middle and wider at the bottom than at the top: *He covered the mound of rice on his plate with the sauce.*

pipe *noun*

pipe · tube · pipeline · hose · line · duct · main
These are all words for a long hollow object that is used for transporting liquid or gas from one place to another.

PATTERNS AND COLLOCATIONS
▸ **through** a pipe / tube / pipeline / hose / duct
▸ a **plastic** / **metal** pipe / tube / hose
▸ a **rubber** tube / hose
▸ an **underground** pipe / pipeline / duct
▸ a **gas** pipe / pipeline / duct / main
▸ an **oil** pipe / pipeline

pipe [C, U] a long round hollow object through which liquid or gas can be transported from one place to another: *Insulation may reduce the risk of water pipes bursting in winter.* ◊ *The car's **exhaust pipe** was blocked with snow.* ◊ *All the old lead pipes were replaced with plastic and copper.* ◊ *Copper pipe is sold in lengths.*
▸ **pipe** *verb* [T]: *Water is piped from the reservoir to the city.*

tube [C] a narrow pipe made of metal, plastic, rubber or glass; a hollow object in the shape of a pipe or tube: *He had to be fed through a feeding tube for several months.* ◊ *The documents were rolled up in a cardboard tube.* ◊ *The bike's **inner tube** was punctured in several places.*

NOTE PIPE OR TUBE? **Pipe** emphasizes the function: to transport liquid or gas. **Tube** emphasizes the shape: long, thin and hollow. **Pipes** are often longer, thicker and more rigid (= not able to bend) than **tubes**, although this is not always the case.

pipeline [C] /ˈpaɪplaɪn/ a series of pipes that are used for carrying large quantities of oil, water or gas over long distances, often underground: *There are plans to lay a gas pipeline through the region.*

hose /həʊz; AmE hoʊz/ [C, U] a long narrow tube, usually made of material such as rubber or plastic that bends easily, used for putting water onto fires or gardens: *The firefighters trained their hoses on the burning building.* ◊ *a fire/garden hose* ◊ *a length of hose*
▸ **hose** *verb* [T]: *Firefighters hosed the burning car.*

line [C] a narrow pipe that carries liquid or gas from one place or part of a machine to another; a thick cable that carries electricity to buildings, towns and cities: *Disconnect the fuel line from the top of the pump.* ◊ *Take care when working near overhead **power lines**.*

duct [C] a large pipe or enclosed channel for carrying liquid, gas, air or cables: *They managed to get out of the building by crawling through a ventilation duct.*

main [C] a large pipe that carries water or gas to a building; a large cable that carries electricity to a building; a large pipe that carries waste water and sewage (= human waste) away from a building: *The area was evacuated after the discovery of a leaking gas main.*

pitch *noun* See the Topic Map for SPORT AND LEISURE on p.892

pitch · court · stadium · arena · field · ground · playing field · park · ballpark
These words all mean an area of land that is used for playing and watching sports such as football, cricket and baseball.

PATTERNS AND COLLOCATIONS
▸ **in** the stadium / arena / ground / park / ballpark
▸ **on** / **off** the pitch / court / field / playing field
▸ a **sports** pitch / stadium / arena / field / ground
▸ a **football** / **cricket** / **rugby** pitch / stadium / field / ground
▸ a **baseball** stadium / field / park

pitch [C] (*BrE*) an area of land specially prepared and marked for playing a sport such as football, rugby or cricket: *The game ended in chaos with fans invading the pitch.* ◊ *The rugby tour was a disaster both on and off the pitch* (= they lost and there was trouble before/after the games).

court [C] a place where games such as tennis are played: *a tennis/squash/badminton court* ◊ *He won after only 52 minutes **on court**.*

stadium /ˈsteɪdiəm/ (pl. **stadiums** or **stadia**) [C] an enclosed area of land with rows of seats around the sides where people can watch sports and entertainment: *Thousands of football fans packed into the stadium to watch the game.* ◊ *They're planning to turn the football ground into an all-seater stadium.*

arena /əˈriːnə/ [C] a place or hall with a large flat open area in the middle and rows of seats around the sides where people can watch sports and entertainment: *The band is due to play Wembley arena on the 9th September.* See also **amphitheatre** → HALL 2

NOTE STADIUM OR ARENA? In many cases you can use either word. A **stadium** is usually open-air (= without a roof), but some modern stadiums have roofs that can extend over the playing area in bad weather. An **arena** may be open-air or inside a large building (for example for playing basketball or ice hockey).

field [C] (especially in compounds or fixed phrases) an area of land used for playing a sport such as football, rugby, cricket or baseball: *Today they **take the field** (= play) against county champions Essex.* ◊ *Players are only reselected if they retain their form **on the field** (= when playing).*

ground [C] (*BrE*) (often in compounds) an area of land that is used for a particular sport or activity: *The council is spending £30 000 on new equipment for the recreation ground.*

NOTE PITCH, FIELD OR GROUND? **Pitch** is the main word in British English but is not used in American English. Both words are used to talk about the area of land that a game is played on. **Ground** is used to talk about the area of land where a sport is played, including any buildings or areas where spectators (= people watching the game) sit or stand. In some sports **pitch** and **field** have different meanings. For example, in cricket the **pitch** is a small strip in the middle of the **field**, where most of the action takes place.

'playing field [C] a large area of grass, usually with lines marked on it, where people play sports and games: *The school's playing fields offer facilities for tennis, football, hockey and athletics.* See also **playground** → PARK

park [C] (*AmE*) a piece of land for playing sports, especially baseball: *With a mighty swing he hit the ball right out of the park.*

ballpark [C] (*especially AmE*) a place where baseball is played: *Boston's Fenway Park remains the oldest major-league ballpark in use.*

place noun

1 a good place for a picnic/I hate this place!
2 Come and sit here – I've saved you a place.

---

1 place · site · area · position · point · location · scene · spot · venue · whereabouts

These are all words for a particular area or part of an area, especially one used for a particular purpose or where sth is situated or happens.

PATTERNS AND COLLOCATIONS
▸ a (good, etc.) place/site/position/location/spot/venue **for** sth
▸ **at** a place/site/position/point/location/scene/spot/venue
▸ **in** a place/an area/a position/a location/a venue
▸ the place/site/point/location/spot/venue **where…**
▸ a/an **good/ideal/suitable** place/site/position/location/spot/venue
▸ a/an **interesting/beautiful/convenient/remote** place/site/position/location/spot
▸ the **right** place/site/position/location/spot/venue
▸ a **central** site/position/location/venue
▸ a **prime** site/position/location
▸ the/sb/sth's **exact/precise** place/site/position/point/location/spot/whereabouts
▸ the/sb/sth's **current/present** site/position/location/whereabouts

place [C] a particular point, area, town, building, etc., especially one used for a particular purpose or where a particular thing happens: *Is this the place where it happened?* ◇ *This would be a good place for a picnic.* ◇ *I can't be in two places at once.* ◇ *The police searched the place.* ◇ *These streets are* **no place for** *a child to be out alone at night.* ◇ *We're looking for a* **place to eat.** ◇ *There was no* **hiding place.** ◇ *Please write your full name, date and* **place of birth.**

site [C] the place where sth, especially a building, is or will be situated; a place where sth happened or that is used for a particular purpose: *We visited the site of a 16th century abbey.* ◇ *All the materials are* **on site** *so that work can start immediately.* ◇ (*BrE*) *a building site* ◇ (*AmE, BrE*) *a construction site* ◇ *This was the site of a great battle.* ◇ *They say it's an ancient* **burial site.** ◇ *a camp/camping/caravan site* ◇ *The kids used to play on an old* **bomb site** (= a place that had been bombed in the past). See also **site → BASE** *verb*

area [C] a part of a room, building or particular space that is used for a special purpose; a particular place on an object: *the hotel reception area* ◇ *a play/parking/dining area* ◇ *Move the cursor to a blank area on the screen.* ◇ *The tumour had not spread to other areas of the body.* See also **area → AREA 1**

position [C, U] the place where a person or thing is situated; the place where sb/sth is meant to be: *From his position at the top of the hill, he could see the harbour.* ◇ *Radars determine the aircraft's position.* ◇ *Is everybody in* **position**? ◇ *The dancers all got* **into position.** ◇ *She* **took up her position** *by the door.* ❶ The **position** of sb/sth is often temporary: the place where sb/sth is at a particular time. See also **position → POSITION** *noun*, **position → PUT** *verb* 1

point [C] a particular place within an area, where sth happens or is supposed to happen: *I'll wait for you at the meeting point in the arrivals hall.* ◇ *the point at which the river divides* ◇ *No parking beyond this point.*

location /ləʊˈkeɪʃn; *AmE* loʊ-/ [C] a place where sth happens or exists, especially a place that is not named or is not known: *Please tell us your exact location.* ◇ *The company is moving to a new location.* ◇ *They got married at a secret location in Scotland.* ❶ A **location** is also a

place outside a film studio where scenes of a film are made: *A mountain in the Rockies became the location for a film about Everest.* ◇ *The movie was shot entirely* **on location** *in Italy.* See also **locate → BASE, locate → FIND 4**

scene [C, usually sing.] a place where sth happens, especially sth unpleasant: *Several onlookers gathered at the* **scene of the accident.** ◇ *The* **scene of the crime** *is being investigated by the police.* ◇ *Firefighters were* **on the scene** *immediately.*

spot [C] a particular point or area, especially one that has a particular character or where sth particular happens: *She stood* **rooted to the spot** (= unable to move) *with fear.* ◇ *The lake is one of the local* **beauty spots.** ◇ *He has reported from several of the world's major* **trouble spots** (= places where trouble often happens, especially violence and war).

venue /ˈvenjuː/ [C] the place where people meet for an organized event such as a performance or sports event: *The band will be playing at several different venues in the UK.* ◇ *Please note the change of venue for this event.*

whereabouts /ˈweərəbaʊts; *AmE* ˈwer-/ [U+sing./pl. *v.*] the place where sb/sth is: *Her whereabouts is/are still unknown.* ◇ *They were forced to reveal the whereabouts of the ship.* ❶ **Whereabouts** is often used to talk or ask about sb/sth when you do not know where that person or thing is.

---

2 place · seat

These words both mean an empty space or position where sb can sit.

PATTERNS AND COLLOCATIONS
▸ a/an **good/empty** place/seat
▸ to **take/book/reserve** a place/seat
▸ to **save sb** a place/seat
▸ to **return to** your place/seat

place [C] a position, seat or empty space, especially one that is available for or being used by a person or vehicle: *Come and sit here – I've saved you a place.* ◇ *I don't want to* **lose my place** *in the line.* ◇ *Would you like to* **change places** *with me so you can see better?* ◇ *I've set a place for you at the table.* ◇ *I couldn't find a* **parking place** *anywhere.* ❶ You can also say **parking space.**

seat [C] a place where you pay to sit, for example in a plane, on a train or at the theatre: *I reserved seats for a performance of 'King Lear' at the New Theatre.* ◇ *There are no seats left on that flight.* ◇ *Would you like an* **aisle seat** *or a* **window seat**?

place verb

place · put · attach · lay

These words are all used to emphasize that sb/sth is important or responsible for sth.

PATTERNS AND COLLOCATIONS
▸ to place/put/lay sth **on** sth
▸ to place/put/attach/lay (the) **blame**
▸ to place/put/lay **responsibility/emphasis**
▸ to place/attach **importance**

place [T] to give a particular level of sth such as importance, trust or value to sth: *Great importance is placed on education.* ◇ *They place a high value on punctuality.*

put [T] to give a particular level of sth such as emphasis, trust or value to sth: *Our company puts the emphasis on quality.* ◇ *He put a limit on the amount we could spend.*

> **NOTE** **PLACE OR PUT?** These words are very close in meaning and range. **Put** does NOT collocate with *importance* and is not usually used in the passive in this meaning: ~~Great importance is put on education.~~ See also **place, put → RANK**

attach [T] to give a particular level of importance to sth: *I attach great importance to this research.* ◇ *I wouldn't* **attach** *too much* **weight** *to these findings* (= take them too seriously). ❶ In this meaning **attach** collocates especially with *importance, significance, value* and *weight*.

lay [T] to express sth such as a claim in a serious or official way: *She laid the blame for the crisis at the Prime Minister's door* (= she blamed the Prime Minister). ❶ Lay is used with a noun to form a phrase that has the same meaning as the verb related to the noun: *He laid stress on the importance of cooperation* (= He stressed the importance of cooperation).

plain *noun*

plain · plateau · grassland · prairie · lowland · savannah · steppe · pampas
These words all mean a large area of land.

▸ **on** the plains / the plateau / grassland / the prairie / the savannah / the steppes / the pampas
▸ **in** grassland / the lowlands / the savannah / the steppes / the pampas
▸ the **open** plain / plateau / grassland / prairie / savannah
▸ the **rolling** plain / plateau / grasslands / prairie
▸ the **high** plains / plateau

plain [C] (also **plains** [pl.]) a large area of flat land: *To the east lies the flat coastal plain of the Yucatan peninsula.* ◇ *Millions of buffalo used to roam freely across the Great Plains.*

plateau /'plætəʊ; *AmE* plæ'toʊ/ [C] (pl. **plateaus** or **plateaux** /-təʊz; *AmE* -'toʊz/) an area of flat land that is higher than the land around it: *From a narrow fringe of coastal plain, the main island rises to a central plateau.*

grassland /'grɑːslænd; *AmE* 'græs-/ [U] (also **grasslands** [pl.]) a large area of open land covered with wild grass: *The lion adapted itself to dry, open grassland where a yellow coat was most effective.*

prairie /'preəri; *AmE* 'preri/ [C, U] a flat wide area of land in North America, without many trees and originally covered with grass: *The North American prairie was once the world's largest grassland.*

lowland /'ləʊlənd; *AmE* 'loʊ-/ [C, usually pl.] an area of land that is fairly flat and not very high above sea level: *the lowlands of Scotland* ◇ *Much of the region is lowland.* ᴏᴘᴘ **highlands** → HILL
▸ **lowland** *adj.*: *lowland areas / farmers*

savannah (also **savanna**) /sə'vænə/ [C, U] a wide flat open area of land that is covered with grass and has few trees, especially in Africa: *Mount Kilimanjaro rises straight up out of the African savannah.*

steppe /step/ [C, usually pl., U] a large area of land that is covered with grass but has few trees, especially in SE Europe and Siberia: *The Cossacks are best known as the roving horsemen of the Russian steppes.*

pampas /'pæmpəs; *AmE* also -pəz/ (usually **the pampas**) [sing. + sing. / pl. *v.*] the large area of land in South America that is covered in grass and has few trees: *The novel depicts life on the Argentine pampas.*

plain *adj.*

1 a plain white shirt
2 the plain truth

1 plain · simple · bare · stark · severe · austere
These words all describe things that have no decoration or other unnecessary additions.

plain	stark
simple	severe
bare	austere

▸ a plain / a simple / an austere **design**
▸ a plain / simple / bare **interior**
▸ the simple / stark / austere **lines** of sth
▸ a plain / simple / bare / stark **white…**
▸ a plain / simple / stark / severe **black…**
▸ **very** plain / simple / bare / austere
▸ **rather** plain / stark / severe / austere
▸ **almost** bare / severe / austere

plain without decoration, a pattern, marks or other additions; not complicated: *Wear it with a plain white shirt.* ◇ *Patterned carpet shows the dirt less than a plain colour.* ◇ *Do you want plain or lined paper?* ◇ *plain food / cooking* ◇ *plain yogurt* (= without sugar or fruit) ᴏᴘᴘ **fancy** → DECORATIVE, See also **plain** → UGLY
▸ **plainly** *adv.*: *She was plainly dressed and wore no make-up.*

simple (*especially written, usually approving*) basic or plain, without anything extra or unnecessary; consisting of only a few parts; not complicated in structure: *The best gowns are simple and elegant.* ◇ *We had a simple meal of soup and bread.* ◇ *The accommodation is simple but spacious.* ◇ *It's quite a simple machine* (= one that is not complicated and has only a few parts). ◇ (*grammar*) *a* **simple sentence** (= one with only one verb) ᴏᴘᴘ **fancy** → DECORATIVE
▸ **simplicity** *noun* [U]: (*approving*) *the simplicity of the architecture*
▸ **simply** *adv.*: *The rooms were simply furnished.* ◇ *They live simply* (= they do not spend much money).

bare (*especially written*) (of surfaces) not covered with or protected by anything: *bare wooden floorboards* ◇ *The walls were bare except for a small mirror.* ◇ *They found themselves in a huge bare hall.*

stark (*especially written, often disapproving*) without any colour, decoration or comfort: *The corridors were stark and uncarpeted.* ◇ *The hills stood stark against the winter sky.*

severe (*usually disapproving*) extremely plain and without anything that makes it look soft or beautiful: *Her hair was cut in a very short, severe style.* ◇ *She was wearing a severe dark grey jacket.*
▸ **severely** *adv.*: *Her hair was tied severely in a bun.*

austere /ɒ'stɪə(r); ɔː'st-; *AmE* ɔː'stɪr/ (*especially written, usually approving*) simple and plain, with no decoration, usually because that is what sb prefers: *the austere simplicity of the building* ◇ *the lonely, austere beauty of his painting of a station in the snow*

---

2 See also the entry for HONEST
plain · simple · stark · bare · unequivocal · bald
These words are all used to describe facts and statements that are very clear and direct, especially when they are unpleasant in some way.

▸ the plain / simple / stark / bare / unequivocal / bald **truth**
▸ a plain / a simple / a stark / a bare / an unequivocal / a bald **fact / statement**
▸ a plain / a simple / an unequivocal **answer**

plain used to describe a fact that other people may not like to hear; honest and direct in way that other people may not like: *The plain fact is that nobody really knows.* ◇ *He's a politician with a reputation for* **plain speaking**. ◇ *Let's be plain about this: we will need to make some difficult choices.* ◇ (*especially AmE*) *He was a plain, straightforward sort of man.* See also **plain** → AVERAGE, **plain** → CLEAR *adj.* 2
▸ **plainly** *adv.*: *To put it plainly, he's a crook.*

simple [only before noun] used to describe a fact that other people may not like to hear; very obvious and not complicated by anything else: *The simple truth is that we just can't afford it.* ◇ *I had to do it* **for the simple reason** *that* (= because) *I couldn't trust anyone else.* ◇ *It's* **a simple matter** *of giving them enough to eat.*
▸ **simply** *adv.*: *I don't want to be rude,* **it's simply that** *we have to be careful who we give this information to.* ◇ *He*

was loud, vulgar and arrogant – quite simply the rudest man I've ever met!

NOTE **PLAIN** OR **SIMPLE?** When it is being used to emphasize facts that other people may not like to hear, **plain** is usually used in the expression *the plain fact/ truth is that...* **Simple** can be used in this way too, but it can also be used in a wider variety of structures and collocations (such as with *reason* and *matter*): *The problem was due to the simple fact that...* ◇ ~~The problem was due to the plain fact that...~~ ◇ ~~for the plain reason that...~~ ◇ ~~It's a plain matter of...~~ Expressions with **simple** often suggest impatience with other people's behaviour: *Nobody wanted to believe the simple truth* (= it was easy to see and understand the true facts; people just didn't want to believe them).

stark (*especially written, usually disapproving*) used to describe an unpleasant fact or difference that is very obvious: *The government faced a **stark choice** between civil war and martial law.* ◇ *Social divisions in the city are stark.* ◇ *The good weather was **in stark contrast to** the storms of previous weeks.* See also **sharp** → MARKED
▸ **starkly** *adv.*: *These theories contrast starkly with the reality of everyday life.*

bare [only before noun] the most basic or simple, with nothing extra: *She gave me only the **bare facts** of the case.* ◇ *The family was short of even the **bare necessities** of life.* ◇ *We only had the **bare essentials** in the way of equipment.* ◇ *He did the **bare minimum** of work but still passed the exam.*

unequivocal /ˌʌnɪˈkwɪvəkl/ (*formal*) expressing your opinion or intention very clearly and firmly: *She gave a typically unequivocal answer.* ◇ *The reply was an unequivocal 'no'.* **OPP** **equivocal** ❶ An **equivocal** statement does not have one clear or definite meaning and can be understood in more than one way.
▸ **unequivocally** *adv.*: *He stated unequivocally that he knew nothing about the document.*

bald describing a rather unpleasant fact or statement that is given without any extra explanation or detail to help you accept what is being said: *The **bald fact** is that we don't need you any longer.* ◇ *The letter was a **bald statement** of our legal position.* ❶ A **bald fact** is usually more unpleasant than a *plain/simple fact*, but not as unpleasant as a *stark fact*.

plan *noun*

1 an action plan
2 a seating plan

1 See also the entry for PROPOSAL
plan · programme · policy · scheme · strategy · initiative · platform · manifesto
These are all words for a set of things you do in order to achieve sth, that you consider in advance.

PATTERNS AND COLLOCATIONS
▸ a plan / a programme / a policy / a scheme / a strategy / an initiative / a platform / a manifesto **for** sth
▸ a policy / a strategy / an initiative **on** sth
▸ a plan / a programme / a policy / a scheme / a strategy / an initiative **to do sth**
▸ a **comprehensive** / **coherent** plan / programme / policy / scheme / strategy
▸ a **detailed** plan / programme / strategy / manifesto
▸ a **major** programme / scheme / strategy / initiative
▸ a **long-term** / **short-term** plan / programme / policy / strategy
▸ an **economic** plan / programme / policy / strategy / initiative
▸ a **political** programme/strategy/initiative/platform/manifesto
▸ a **government** programme/policy/scheme/strategy/initiative
▸ a **training** plan / programme / policy / scheme / strategy / initiative
▸ to **have** / **propose** / **adopt** a plan / policy / scheme / strategy
▸ to **develop** a plan / a programme / a policy / a strategy / an initiative
▸ to **draw up** a plan / programme / scheme / strategy / manifesto

▸ to **approve** / **announce** a plan / a policy / a scheme / an initiative
▸ to **implement** a plan / programme / policy / scheme / strategy / manifesto
▸ to **launch** a plan / a programme / a scheme / an initiative / a manifesto
▸ to **carry out** a plan / programme / policy / scheme / strategy

plan [C] a set of things to do in order to achieve sth, especially one that has been considered in detail in advance: *The government has announced plans to create 50 000 new training places.* ◇ *You will need a clear and realistic **business plan**.* ◇ *an **action plan*** ◇ *a plan of action/campaign* ◇ *We need to **make plans** for the future.* ◇ *Let's hope everything goes **according to plan**.* See also **plan** → PURPOSE *noun*, **plan** → ORGANIZE *verb*

programme (*BrE*) (*AmE* **program**) [C] a plan of things that will be done over a period of time or included in the development of sth: *We were asked to devise a training programme for new employees.* ◇ *The new programme is designed to encourage investment in the region.*

policy [C, U] a plan of action to deal with an issue, that is agreed or chosen by a government, a political party, a business, etc: *The party's new policy on education has yet to be revealed.* ◇ *We should not let such concerns influence our economic policies.* ◇ *We operate a strict no-smoking policy.* ◇ *What aspects of **foreign policy** would you like to see changed?*

scheme /skiːm/ [C] (*especially BrE*) a plan or system for doing or organizing sth, especially one providing a service for people: *Over 10 000 people joined the training scheme.* ◇ *Under the new scheme only successful schools will receive extra funding.* ❶ The use of the word **scheme** to talk about an official plan by a government or large organization is mainly British English. In American English, **scheme** often suggests a plan that is unlikely to work or is slightly dishonest: *Is this just another of your crazy schemes?*

strategy /ˈstrætədʒi/ [C, U] a plan that is intended to achieve a particular purpose, especially over a long period of time; the process of planning sth or carrying out a plan in a skilful way: *What strategies will you use to achieve this goal?* ◇ *Agreeing to meet the rebels is obviously a high-risk strategy.* ◇ *Poor marketing strategy was blamed for the failure of the service to catch on.* See also **tactic** → TACTIC

initiative /ɪˈnɪʃətɪv/ [C] a new plan for dealing with a particular problem or for achieving a particular purpose: *Government leaders are meeting to discuss the latest peace initiative.*

platform [C] the aims of a political party and the things they say they will do if they are elected to power: *She campaigned **on a platform of** zero tolerance towards racist behaviour.*

manifesto /ˌmænɪˈfestəʊ; *AmE* -ˈfestoʊ/ (pl. **manifestos**) [C] a written statement in which a group of people, especially a political party, explain their beliefs and say what they will do if they win an election: *You should stick to the promises in your party manifesto.*

2 **plan · draft · design · blueprint**
These are all words for a drawing or diagram that shows how sth will be when it is built, made or arranged.

PATTERNS AND COLLOCATIONS
▸ a plan / draft / design / blueprint **of** sth
▸ a plan / design / blueprint **for** sth
▸ a **detailed** / **rough** plan / draft / design
▸ the **final** plan / draft / design / blueprint
▸ the **original** / **first** plan / draft / design
▸ an **initial** draft / design
▸ an **early** draft / blueprint
▸ to **draw up** / **produce** a plan / draft / design

plan [C] a detailed drawing of sth such as a building or machine that shows its size, shape and measurements; a diagram that shows how sth will be arranged: *Enemy spies stole the plans for the new aircraft.* ◇ *Who was* responsible for the **seating plan** (= a plan of where people will sit)? ◇ *The **floor plan*** (= showing how furniture etc. is arranged in a room) *is very simple.*

draft [C] a rough written version or drawing of sth, showing how it will be written, built or made: *This is only the first draft of my speech.* ◇ *The original drafts for the new building are with the architects.* ❶ A **draft** is usually not yet in its final form and may have changes made to it. The word is especially used to describe an early version of a piece of writing such as a letter, speech or book. See also **draft** → PREPARE verb 1

design [C] a drawing or plan from which sth will be made: *The design for the new model is top secret.* ◇ *The original designs were stolen.*

blueprint /'blu:prɪnt/ [C] a photographic print of a plan for a building or machine: *The watch was designed according to a 19th century blueprint.*

plan verb

plan · make · design · formulate
These words all mean to prepare sth or make a design for sth.

PATTERNS AND COLLOCATIONS
▸ to plan / make / design / formulate sth **to do sth**
▸ to plan / design / formulate a **strategy**
▸ to make / formulate a **plan** / **hypothesis**

plan (-nn-) [T] to make a design or outline for a thing, piece of writing or plan of action: *This is the place to visit if you are planning a new garden.* ◇ *You should always plan your essay before you start writing it.* ◇ *A well planned advertising campaign is necessary to bring in visitors.*

make [T] to write, create or prepare sth such as a law, plan or system: *These regulations were made to protect children.* ◇ *My lawyer has been urging me to make a will.*

design [T] to think of and plan a system or way of doing sth: *We need to design a new programme for the third year.* ◇ *It is easy enough to design systems that work well when everything is going well.*

formulate /'fɔːmjuleɪt; AmE 'fɔːrm-/ [T] (rather formal) to create or prepare sth carefully, giving particular attention to the details: *to formulate a policy/theory/plan/proposal* ◇ *His ideas are always very carefully formulated.* ◇ *The compost is specially formulated for pot plants.*

planning noun

planning · arrangement · preparation · provision · organization · coordination · logistics
These are all words for the act or process of making plans for sth.

PATTERNS AND COLLOCATIONS
▸ planning / arrangements / preparations / provision / organization **for** sb / sth
▸ planning / arrangements / preparations / provision **to do sth**
▸ **careful** / **detailed** / **meticulous** planning / preparation / organization
▸ **adequate** / **proper** arrangements / preparation / provision / coordination
▸ the **essential** / **necessary** planning / arrangements / preparation / provision / coordination
▸ **final** planning / arrangements / preparations
▸ **financial** / **economic** planning / arrangements / provision
▸ to **make** arrangements / preparations / provision
▸ to **need** / **require** planning / preparation / provision / coordination
▸ to **do** the planning / preparation / organization / coordination
▸ to **complete** / **finalize** the planning / arrangements / preparations
▸ a **lack of** planning / preparation / provision / organization / coordination

planning [U] the act or process of making plans for sth: *Planning for the future makes some people nervous.* ◇ *Sensible planning will minimize disruption to the schedule.* ◇ *The project is still at the early planning stage.* See also **plan** → ORGANIZE

arrangement [C, usually pl.] a plan that you make so that sth can happen: *I made arrangements for him to be met at the airport.* ◇ *I'll leave the practical arrangements to you.* ◇ *Have you finalized your travel arrangements yet?* See also **arrange** → ORGANIZE

preparation [U, C, usually pl.] the act or process of getting ready for sth or making sth ready; things that you do to get ready for sth or make sth ready: *Preparation for the party started early.* ◇ *The third book in the series is currently **in preparation**.* ◇ *The team has been training hard **in preparation for** the big game.* ◇ *The gallery is making preparations to celebrate the artist's centenary.* See also **preparatory** → FIRST, **prepare** → PREPARE 1, **prepare** → PREPARE 2

provision [U, C] preparations that you make for sth that might or will happen in the future: *You need to make adequate provision for your retirement.* ◇ *The company had made **provisions against** falls in land prices.* See also **provide for sth** → PREPARE 2

organization (BrE also **-isation**) [U] the act of making arrangements or preparations for sth: *An event on this scale takes a lot of organization.* ◇ *They blamed the government for the poor organization of the election.* See also **organize** → ORGANIZE

coordination (BrE also **co-ordination**) /kəʊˌɔːdɪˈneɪʃn; AmE koʊˌɔːrd-/ [U] the act of making the parts of sth or groups of people work together in an efficient and organized way: *There's a need for greater **coordination between** departments.* ◇ *The job requires a lot of **coordination with** others.* ◇ *The pamphlet was produced **in coordination with** residents' groups.*

logistics /lə'dʒɪstɪks/ [U+sing./pl. v.] the practical organization that is needed to make a complicated plan successful: *We have the aid money, but the logistics of getting it to those in need are daunting.*

plate noun

plate · bowl · dish · platter
These are all words for a container that you serve food on or in.

PATTERNS AND COLLOCATIONS
▸ a plate / bowl / dish / platter **of** sth
▸ **on** a plate / dish / platter
▸ **in** a bowl / dish
▸ an **empty** plate / bowl / dish / platter
▸ a **glass** / **silver** plate / bowl / dish / platter
▸ a **china** / **serving** plate / bowl / dish / platter
▸ a **plastic** plate / bowl / dish
▸ to **fill** a plate / bowl / dish / platter

plate [C] a flat, usually round, object with a slightly raised edge that you can put food on: *He barely touched the food on his plate.* ◇ *The set includes four dinner plates, four side plates and four soup bowls.* ◇ *We used plastic cutlery and ate off paper plates.* ◇ *He came in carrying a plate of sandwiches.* See also the entry for PORTION

bowl [C] (often in compounds) a deep round container with a wide open top, used especially for holding food or liquid; the food or liquid in a bowl: *a salad/fruit/sugar bowl* ◇ *a washing-up bowl* ◇ *a bowl of soup*

dish [C] a flat shallow container for cooking food in or serving it from: *an ovenproof dish* ◇ *Arrange the chicken and salad in a serving dish.* ❶ The **dishes** are the plates, bowls, cups, etc. that have been used for a meal and need to be washed: *I'll **do the dishes*** (= wash them).

platter [C] a large plate that is used for serving food: *I'll have the fish platter* (= several types of fish and other food served on a large plate).

play noun

play · drama · comedy · tragedy · sketch · farce
These are all words for a piece of writing that is intended to be performed as entertainment.

PATTERNS AND COLLOCATIONS
▸ a play / drama / comedy / tragedy / sketch / farce **by** sb
▸ a play / drama / comedy / tragedy / sketch / farce **about** sth
▸ a **Shakespearean** play / drama / comedy / tragedy
▸ a **television / radio** play / drama / comedy
▸ a **historical** play / drama
▸ to **write** a play / drama / comedy / tragedy / sketch / farce
▸ to **perform** a play / drama / sketch
▸ to **do** a play / sketch
▸ to **see** a play / drama / comedy / sketch

play [C] a piece of writing that is intended to be performed by actors in a theatre or on television or radio: *Kate's class decided to put on* (= organize and perform) *a play for the school.* ◇ *The theatre was refused permission to stage the play.* See also **playwright** → WRITER
drama /'drɑːmə/ [C] a play, especially one that has a very exciting or emotional story: *The story easily fits into the standard mould of a courtroom drama.* ◇ *It is a lavish costume drama* (= a film, especially on television, about a period in the past) *set in the early twentieth century.* See also **drama** → DRAMA, **dramatist** → WRITER
comedy /'kɒmədi; *AmE* 'kɑːm-/ [C, U] a play or film that is intended to be funny, usually with a happy ending; plays and films of this type: *It's a romantic comedy starring Meg Ryan and Tom Hanks.* ◇ *They spent hours watching comedy on television.*
tragedy /'trædʒədi/ [C, U] a serious play with a sad ending, especially one in which the main character dies; plays of this type: *Revenge tragedies were very popular in Elizabethan England.* ◇ *In Greek tragedy the main character usually identifies himself upon entering the stage.*
sketch /sketʃ/ [C] a short funny scene that is part of a longer show in a theatre or on television or radio: *The drama group did a sketch about a couple buying a new car.*
farce /fɑːs; *AmE* fɑːrs/ [C, U] a funny play for the theatre based on ridiculous and unlikely situations and events; this type of writing or performance: *Feydeau's classic bedroom farce* (= a funny play about sex) *is set in turn-of-the-century Paris.* ◇ *Farce is often looked down upon by serious theatre goers.*

play verb

1 children playing
2 play football / for England / against France
3 play the piano / the role of Hamlet

1 See the Topic Map for SPORT AND LEISURE on p.892
play · celebrate · have fun · enjoy yourself · have a good/great time · party · live it up
These words all mean to do things for pleasure and/or get enjoyment from sth.

PATTERNS AND COLLOCATIONS
▸ Let's play / celebrate / have fun / enjoy ourselves / have a good time / party / live it up

play [I, T] to do things for pleasure, as children do, instead of working: *A group of kids were playing with a ball in the street.* ◇ *You'll have to play inside today.* ◇ *I haven't got anybody to play with!* ◇ *There's a time to work and a time to play.* ◇ *Let's play a different game.* See also **play** → ENTERTAINMENT *noun*
celebrate [I, T] to show that a day or event is important by doing sth special on it: *Jake's passed his exams. We're going out to celebrate.* ◇ *We celebrated our 25th wedding anniversary in Florence.* ◇ *How do people celebrate New Year in your country?*
▸ **celebration** *noun* [U]: *Her triumph was a cause for celebration.* See also **celebration** → EVENT 2

have 'fun *phrase* (*informal, especially spoken*) to get enjoyment from what you are doing: *Have fun!* ◇ *The kids were having fun in the water.* ◇ *You can have a lot of fun with a cheap digital camera.* See also **fun** → FUN, **fun** → ENTERTAINMENT
en'joy yourself *phrase* to get enjoyment from what you are doing: *Enjoy yourselves!* ◇ *They kids all seemed to enjoy themselves at the party.* See also **enjoyment** → FUN
have a good 'time, have a 'great time *phrase* (*informal, especially spoken*) to get (great) enjoyment from what you are doing: *Did you have a good time in Spain?* ◇ *Yes, we had a great time.* ❶ **Have a great time** is not used in questions: *Did you have a great time?*

> **NOTE** HAVE FUN, ENJOY YOURSELF OR HAVE A GOOD TIME?
> **Have fun** and **have a good time** are more informal than **enjoy yourself** and used especially in spoken English. **Have fun** can be used ironically as an instruction to sb who is going to do sth that they do not expect to enjoy.: (*ironic*) *Oh, is it your exam today? Have fun!*

party [I] (*informal*) to enjoy yourself, especially by eating, drinking alcohol and dancing: *They were out partying every night.* See also **party** → PARTY *noun* 2
live it 'up *phrase* (*informal*) to enjoy yourself in an exciting way, usually spending a lot of money: *They had this great win on the lottery and now they're living it up in Hawaii.*

2 See the Topic Map for SPORT AND LEISURE on p.892
play · go in for sth · compete · enter
These words all mean to be involved in an activity, especially a game, race or competition.

PATTERNS AND COLLOCATIONS
▸ to play / compete **in** a competition, etc.
▸ to play / compete **against** sb
▸ to go in for / compete in / enter a **competition / contest / race**
▸ to compete in / enter a **tournament**
▸ to play / compete **well**

play [T, I] to be involved in a game; to compete against sb in a game; to take a particular position in a sports team: *They play football on Saturday mornings.* ◇ *Do you want to play cards with me?* ◇ *Have you ever played her at chess?* ◇ *France are playing Wales tomorrow.* ◇ *France are playing against Wales on Saturday.* ◇ *He plays for Cleveland.* ◇ *Evans played very well.* ◇ *Who's playing on the wing?* ◇ *I've never played right back before.*
go 'in for sth *phrasal verb* (usually used in negative statements) to enjoy and take part in sth as an interest or hobby: *She doesn't go in for team games.* ❶ In British English **go in for sth** also means to put your name on the list for an exam or competition: *She's going in for the Cambridge First Certificate.*
compete [I] to take part in a contest or game: *He's hoping to compete in the London marathon.* ❶ **Compete** is often followed by *in* with names of sports events like *the marathon, the Olympic Games, the Grand Prix* and *the British Open.* See also **competitor** → PARTICIPANT
enter [T, I] to put your name on the list for an exam or competition; to do this for sb: *1000 children entered the competition.* ◇ (*BrE*) *Only four British players have entered for the championship.* ◇ (*BrE*) *How many students have been entered for the exam?* See also **entrant** → CANDIDATE

3 **play · perform · stage · do · produce · act · put sth on · present**
These words all mean to play a musical instrument, sing, act in a play, etc., especially to entertain an audience.

PATTERNS AND COLLOCATIONS
▸ to play / perform / do a **piece**
▸ to play / act a **role / part**
▸ to perform / stage / do / produce / act in / put on / present a **play / show**
▸ to perform / stage / do / act in / put on a **production**

▶ to **stage** / **do** / **put on** / **present** a / an **performance** / **concert** / **exhibition**

▶ a **band** / **musician** plays / performs / does sth

▶ a **company** stages / does / produces / puts on / presents a play / show

▶ to play / perform / stage / act / present sth **well**

▶ to play / perform / stage / present sth **brilliantly**

▶ to play / perform / act sth **together**

▶ to play / perform / do sth **live** / **in public**

play [T, I] to make music on a musical instrument; to take a part in a play or film: *I'm learning to play the piano.* ◇ *Play us that new piece.* ◇ *In the distance a band was playing.* ◇ *The part of the Queen was played by Helen Mirren.* ◇ *He had always wanted to play Othello.*

perform [T, I] to entertain an audience by playing a piece of music, acting in a play, etc: *The play was first performed in 1987.* ◇ *I'd like to hear it performed live.* ◇ *I'm looking forward to seeing you perform.* See also **performance** → PERFORMANCE, **performer** → ACTOR

stage [T] (*especially written*) to organize a play or event for people to see: *The local theatre group is staging a production of 'Hamlet'.* ◇ *They're staging an exhibition in the church hall.* ◇ *Birmingham has bid to stage the next national athletics championships.* See also **stage** → DRAMA

do [T] (*rather informal, especially spoken*) to perform or organize a performance of a play, opera, concert, etc: *The local dramatic society is doing 'Hamlet' next month.*

produce [T] to be in charge of preparing a play, film or television programme for the public to see: *She produced a TV series about adopted children.* See also **production** → PERFORMANCE

act [I, T] to perform a part in a play or film: *Most of the cast act well.* ◇ *He just can't act* (= acts very badly). ◇ *The play was well acted.* ◇ *She is acting the role of Juliet.* See also **acting** → DRAMA, **actor** → ACTOR

NOTE PLAY OR ACT? In this meaning, **act** can be used with an object (*act a part/role*) as well as without (*He just can't act.*); **play** can only be used with an object. It is more common to talk about a person **playing** rather than **acting** a role or part. People usually talk about **acting** a part when they are talking about sb pretending to be a particular type of person in everyday life: *I found myself acting the part of the happy newly-married wife.* A *play* or *film* as a whole is **acted**, not **played**. See also **act** → PRETEND

,put sth 'on *phrasal verb* to organize or produce a play or event for people to see: *The local drama club is putting on 'Macbeth' at the Playhouse.*

present [T] (*written*) to organize or produce a play or event for people to see: *Compass Theatre Company presents a new production of 'King Lear'.* ◇ *We plan to present the film uncensored and without commercial breaks.*

NOTE STAGE, PUT STH ON OR PRESENT? You can **stage**, **put on** or **present** a live *performance, show, play, concert* or *exhibition*. You can **present** a *film* or a programme that has been recorded, but you cannot **stage** or **put on** a film. **Put on** is used especially to talk about amateur (= not professional) performances.

player *noun* See the Topic Map for SPORT AND LEISURE on p.892

player · athlete · runner · sportsman/sportswoman/ sportsperson · jock
These are all words for a person who takes part in sport.

PATTERNS AND COLLOCATIONS

▶ a **top** / **great** / **keen** player / athlete / runner / sportsman / sportswoman / sportsperson

▶ a / an **gifted** / **talented** / **outstanding** / **famous** player / athlete / sportsman / sportswoman / sportsperson

▶ a / an **average** / **good** / **world-class** player / athlete / runner

▶ a / an **all-round** / **amateur** / **professional** player / athlete / sportsman / sportswoman / sportsperson

▶ a player / an athlete / a runner / a sportsman / a sportswoman / a sportsperson **trains** / **practises**

▶ a player / an athlete / a runner / a sportsman / a sportswoman / a sportsperson **competes** (in sth)

player [C] a person who takes part in a game or sport: *We've lost two key players through injury.* ◇ *She's one of the country's top tennis players.*

athlete /'æθli:t/ [C] a person who competes in sports; a person who is good at sports and physical exercise: *Several Olympic athletes were accused of taking performance-enhancing drugs.* ◇ *It's clear that he's a natural athlete.* ❶ In British English **athlete** is used mainly to talk about a person who competes in sports such as running, jumping and throwing (**athletics**); in American English **athlete** is used more generally to talk about sb who plays any kind of sport.

runner [C] a person or animal that runs, especially taking part in a race: *She was a good runner and soon caught up with Tom.* ◇ *a marathon/long-distance/1500-metre runner* ◇ *Here is the list of runners and riders for the first race* (= horse race). See also **run** *run* 1

sportsman, **sportswoman**, **sportsperson** [C] (*especially BrE*) a person who takes part in sport, especially sb who is very good at it: *He's one of the country's top professional sportsmen.* ◇ *She's a naturally gifted sportswoman.* ❶ **Sportsman** and **sportswoman** are much more frequent than **sportsperson**; however, in contexts where you could be talking about a man or a woman, or a mixed group of men and women, use language that includes both: *Lynsey has already achieved more than most sportsmen and sportswomen dream of.* ◇ *The scheme finances coaching sessions for young sportspeople.* The usual word in American English is **athlete**.

jock [C] (*AmE, informal, sometimes disapproving*) a man or boy who plays a lot of sport: *Her boyfriend's a handsome jock, all brawn, no brains − you know the type.*

please *verb* See also the entry for DELIGHT

please · satisfy · make sb's day · gratify
These words all mean to make sb feel pleased or happy.

satisfy   please   make sb's day
                 gratify

PATTERNS AND COLLOCATIONS

▶ It pleased / satisfied / gratified **sb that...**

▶ It pleased / gratified **sb to** find / hear / know / see / think...

▶ to **really** please sb / make sb's day / gratify sb

▶ You **can't** please / satisfy **everybody** / **everyone**.

▶ **Nothing** pleases / satisfies sb.

please [T, I] to make sb feel pleased: *I did it to please my parents.* ◇ *There's just no pleasing some people* (= some people are impossible to please). ◇ *She's always very eager to please.* **OPP** displease → ANNOY. See also **pleased** → GLAD, **pleasing** → SATISFYING

satisfy [T] (not used in the progressive tenses; often used in negative sentences) to please sb by doing or giving them what they want: *Nothing satisfies him − he's always complaining.* ◇ *The proposed plan will not satisfy everyone.* See also **satisfied** → HAPPY, **satisfying** → SATISFYING

NOTE PLEASE OR SATISFY? **Please** is often a stronger and more positive word than **satisfy**. Something that **satisfies** you is just good enough, but sth might **please** you very much: *The result pleased us enormously.* ◇ ~~The result satisfied us enormously.~~ Both words can be used in negative sentences to say that sth is not good enough: *The planning policy failed to please/satisfy anyone.*

make sb's 'day *idiom* (*rather informal, especially spoken*) to make sb feel very happy on a particular day: *The phone call from Mike really made my day.*

gratify [T] (*rather formal, written*) to please sb by making them feel that they are good at sth, liked or valued: *It gratified him to think that it was all his work.* ◇ *I was gratified by their invitation.* See also **gratifying** → SATISFYING

pleasure *noun*

pleasure · delight · joy · privilege · treat · honour · pride
These are all words for things that make you happy or bring you enjoyment.

pleasure	delight
privilege	joy
treat	honour
	pride

PATTERNS AND COLLOCATIONS
▸ the pleasures / delights / joys **of** sth
▸ It's **a** great pleasure / joy **to me that...**
▸ It's **a** pleasure / delight / joy / privilege / treat / honour **to do sth**
▸ It's **a** pleasure / delight / joy **to see / find...**
▸ a pleasure / delight / joy **to behold / watch**
▸ a **real** pleasure / delight / joy / privilege / treat
▸ a **great** pleasure / joy / privilege / honour
▸ a **rare** joy / privilege / treat / honour

pleasure [C] a thing that brings you enjoyment or satisfaction: *the pleasures and pains of everyday life* ◇ *Chocolate is one of life's little pleasures.* ◇ (*spoken*) *It's been a pleasure meeting you.* ◇ *'Thanks for doing that.' 'It's a pleasure./My pleasure.'* **OPP** **pain** → DISTRESS

delight [C] a thing or person that brings you great enjoyment or satisfaction: *the delights of living in the country* ◇ *Savour the culinary delights of Morocco.* ◇ *It was a delight to see him so fit and healthy.* See also **delight** → DELIGHT *verb*

joy [C] (*rather informal*) a thing or person that brings you great enjoyment or happiness: *the joys and sorrows of childhood* ◇ *a dancer who is a joy to watch.* **OPP** **grief**, **sorrow** → GRIEF

> **NOTE** PLEASURE, DELIGHT OR JOY? A **delight** or **joy** is greater than a **pleasure**; a person, especially a child, can be a **delight** or **joy**, but not a **pleasure**; **joys** are often contrasted with **sorrows**, but **delights** are not.

privilege /ˈprɪvəlɪdʒ/ [sing.] (*rather formal*) something that you are proud and lucky to have the opportunity to do: *I hope to have the privilege of working with them again.* ◇ *It was a great privilege to hear her sing.*
▸ **privileged** *adj.* [not before noun]: *We are privileged to welcome you as our speaker this evening.*

treat [C] (*informal, especially spoken*) a thing that sb enjoyed or is likely to enjoy very much: *You've never been to this area before? Then you're in for a real treat/you have a real treat in store.* ◇ (*especially BrE*) *If you have never seen one of these fish then you have missed a treat.*

honour (*BrE*) (*AmE* **honor**) [sing.] (*formal*) something that you are very pleased or proud to do because people are showing you great respect: *It was a great honour to be invited here today.*
▸ **honoured** (*BrE*) (*AmE* **honored**) *adj.* [not before noun]: *I felt honoured to have been mentioned in his speech.*

pride [sing.] a person or thing that gives people a feeling of pleasure or satisfaction: *The new sports stadium is the pride of the town.* ◇ *He loves that boat, it's his pride and joy.*

plot *verb*

plot · conspire · scheme · collude · connive
These words all mean to secretly plan to do sth illegal or harmful.

PATTERNS AND COLLOCATIONS
▸ to plot / conspire / scheme **against** sb
▸ to plot / conspire / collude / connive **with** sb
▸ to plot / conspire / collude **together**
▸ to plot / conspire / scheme / collude / connive **to do sth**
▸ to **secretly** plot / conspire / scheme / connive

plot [I, T] to make a secret plan to harm sb, especially a government or its leader: *They were accused of plotting against the state.* ◇ *She spends every waking hour plotting her revenge.* ◇ *They were plotting to overthrow the government.* See also **plot** → CONSPIRACY *noun*, **plotter** → ACCOMPLICE

conspire /kənˈspaɪə(r)/ [I] (*formal*) to secretly plan with other people to do sth illegal or harmful: *They were accused of conspiring against the king.* ◇ *She admitted conspiring with her lover to murder her husband.* See also **conspiracy** → CONSPIRACY, **conspirator** → ACCOMPLICE

scheme /skiːm/ [I, T] to make secret plans to do sth that will help yourself and possibly harm others: *She seemed to feel that we were all scheming against her.* ◇ *His colleagues, meanwhile, were busily scheming to get rid of him.* ❶ **Scheme** is usually used with a preposition or in the phrase *scheme to do sth*; it does not usually take a noun phrase as object: *to scheme a coup/your revenge.* It is often used to suggest the general nature of sb's activities, rather than to talk about a particular plot against sb. See also **scheme** → CONSPIRACY *noun*

collude /kəˈluːd/ [I] to work together secretly to do sth illegal or harmful: *Several people had colluded in the murder.* ◇ *The president accused his opponents of colluding with foreigners.* See also **collusion** → CONSPIRACY

connive /kəˈnaɪv/ [I] (*formal*) to work together with sb to do sth illegal or harmful: *The government was accused of having connived with the security forces to permit murder.*

> **NOTE** CONSPIRE, COLLUDE OR CONNIVE? People who **conspire** together usually belong to one group who all want the same things. People who **collude** or **connive** usually belong to different groups or have different aims, but all benefit in some way from the plot. **Conspire** suggests the greatest degree of active involvement, and **connive** the least: it usually means helping or allowing sb else to do sth wrong.

point *noun* See the Topic Map for FACT AND OPINION on p.898

point · core · heart · body · crux · nucleus
These are all words for the most important idea or part of sth.

PATTERNS AND COLLOCATIONS
▸ **at** the core / heart / crux of sth
▸ the **main** point / core / body of sth
▸ the **very** core / heart / crux of sth
▸ to **form** the core / heart / body / nucleus of sth
▸ to **make up** the core / body of sth
▸ to **get to** the point / core / heart / crux (of sth)
▸ to **lie at / go to** the core / heart of sth
▸ the heart / crux **of the matter**

point [sing.] the main or most important idea in sth that is said or done: *The point is you shouldn't have to wait so long to see a doctor.* ◇ *I'll come straight to the point: we need more money.* ◇ *Do you see my point* (= understand)? ◇ *I think I missed the point* (= did not understand). ◇ *You have a point* (= your idea is right) — *it would be better to wait till this evening.* ◇ *'There won't be anywhere to park.' 'Oh, that's a (good) point.'* (= I had not thought of that) ◇ *It just isn't true. That's the whole point* (= the only important fact). ◇ *I know it won't cost very much but that's not the point.* See also **to the point** → RELEVANT

core [sing.] the most important part of a problem, activity or set of ideas: *This report goes to the core of the argument.* ◇ *Maths, English and science are the **core subjects** (= subjects that all the students have to do).* ◇ *What are the core activities of the job?*

heart [sing.] the most important part of a problem: *Cost is at the heart of the matter for the Government.* ◇ *The committee's report went to the heart of the government's dilemma.* See also **heart** → FOCUS *noun*

> **NOTE** **CORE** OR **HEART**? Heart is used to talk about the most important part of a problem, especially when morality or emotions are involved; it is used especially in the phrase *the heart of the matter/problem*. **Core** is used when the problem is seen in more logical or intellectual terms; **core** is also used to talk about the most important subjects or activities in education or business, and can be used like an adjective before another noun: *the core subjects/curriculum/activities/business* ◇ *the heart subjects/curriculum/activities/business*

body [sing.] the main part of sth, especially a building, vehicle or book or article: *the body of the plane* (= the central part where the seats are) ◇ *There are some references in the main body of the text.*

crux [sing.] the most important point about a situation: *Now we come to the crux of the matter.*

nucleus /ˈnjuːkliəs; *AmE* ˈnuː-/ [sing.] the central part of sth around which other parts are situated or collected: *These paintings will form the nucleus of a new collection.* ◇ *It was this cluster of houses which formed the nucleus of the village.* ❶ **Nucleus** is most often used to talk about the most important part of a place or exhibition, or the most important people within a group.

point *verb*

point · show
These words both mean to help sb see where or what sb/sth is by stretching out your finger or hand.

point [I, T, no passive] to stretch out your finger or sth held in your hand towards sb/sth in order to help sb see where a person or thing is: *It's rude to point!* ◇ *He **pointed to** the spot where the house used to stand.* ◇ *'What's your name?' he asked, **pointing at** the child with his pen.* ◇ *She pointed in my direction.* ◇ *She pointed her finger in my direction.* ❶ **Point** can also be used with an adverb or preposition to mean 'to show sb which way to go': *Could you point me in the right direction for the bus station?* ◇ *A series of yellow arrows **pointed the way** to the reception desk.*

show [T] to point to sth so that sb can see where or what it is: *He showed me our location on the map.* ◇ *Show me which picture you drew.* See also **show** → TAKE 2

point sth out *phrasal verb* See also the entry for STRESS

point sth out · highlight · draw attention to sb/sth · point to sth · point sth up
These words all mean to make people notice sth by mentioning it or making it obvious.

PATTERNS AND COLLOCATIONS
- to point out/highlight/point to **how...**
- to point out/highlight/draw attention to/point to/point up **the fact that...**
- to point out/highlight/draw attention to/point to/point up the **importance/difference**
- to point out/highlight/draw attention to/point to a/an **need/aspect**
- to highlight/draw attention to/point up an **issue**
- to point out/highlight/draw attention to the **weaknesses/inadequacy** in/of sb/sth
- to **clearly** point out/highlight/point to/point up sth
- to **further** point out/highlight/point to sth

,point sth 'out *phrasal verb* to mention sth in order to give sb information about it or make them notice it: *She tried in vain to **point out to** him the unfairness of his actions.* ◇ *He pointed out the dangers of driving alone.* ◇ *I should **point out that** not one of these paintings is original.* ◇ *'It's not very far,' she pointed out.*

highlight /ˈhaɪlaɪt/ [T] (*especially journalism*) to emphasize sth, especially a problem, so that people give it more attention: *The report highlights the major problems facing society today.* ◇ *The earthquake highlighted the vulnerability of elevated highways.* ❶ *Reports, studies, surveys* and *figures* most often **highlight** a *problem, need, issue, danger* or *difficulty.* People might deliberately **highlight** a problem because they want more people to notice it; or an event might have the effect of highlighting a problem by making people notice it. See also **underline**, **underscore** → STRESS

,draw a'ttention to sb/sth *phrase* to make people listen to, look at or think about sb/sth: *We need to draw people's attention to the dangers of this approach.* ◇ *He took care to avoid **drawing attention to himself.*** ❶ In formal language you can also **call attention to sth**: (*formal*) *He called their attention to the fact that many files were missing.*

point to sth *phrasal verb* to mention sth that you think is important and/or the reason why a particular situation exists: *The board of directors pointed to falling productivity to justify their decision.*

,point sth 'up *phrasal verb* (*formal*) to have the effect of making people notice sth: *The conference merely pointed up divisions in the party.* ❶ **Point sth up** is often used to talk about making people notice differences or problems within an organization.

poison *noun*

poison · toxin · venom
These are all words for substances that cause death or harm if they are swallowed or absorbed into the body.

PATTERNS AND COLLOCATIONS
- a **powerful** poison/toxin
- to **contain** poison/toxins
- to **produce** poison/toxins/venom
- poison/venom **glands**

poison [C, U] a substance that causes death or harm if it is swallowed or absorbed into the body: *Some mushrooms contain a **deadly poison.*** ◇ *How did he die? Was it poison?* ◇ *The dog was killed by rat poison* (= poison intended to kill rats). ◇ *poison gas*
▶ **poisonous** *adj.*: *poisonous substances/chemicals/plants/snakes* ◇ *This gas is highly poisonous.*

toxin [C] (*formal or technical*) a poisonous substance, especially one that is produced by bacteria in plants and animals: *The algae kills off plant and animal life and, in some cases, produces dangerous toxins.*
▶ **toxic** *adj.*: *toxic chemicals/fumes/gases/substances* ◇ *Many pesticides are highly toxic.*

venom /ˈvenəm/ [U, C] the poisonous liquid that some snakes, spiders, insects, etc., produce when they bite or sting you: *Centipedes kill their prey by injecting venom into them with a large pair of fangs.* ◇ *Snake venoms work in several ways.*
▶ **venomous** *adj.*: *venomous snakes*

poison *verb*

poison · drug · lace · dope
These words all mean to give sb poison, drugs or alcohol, often without them knowing it and in order to harm them.

PATTERNS AND COLLOCATIONS
- to poison/drug/lace/dope sb/sth **with** sth
- to poison/lace sb's **drink**

poison [T] to harm or kill a person or animal by giving them poison; to put poison in or on sth: *He was accused of poisoning his wife.* ◇ *a poisoned arrow* ◇ *Someone had been poisoning his food.* ◇ *Large sections of the river have been poisoned by toxic waste from factories.*
▸ **poisoning** *noun* [U, C]: *The police suspected poisoning.* ◇ *food/blood poisoning* ◇ *At least 10 000 children are involved in accidental poisonings every year.*

drug (-**gg**-) [T] to give a person or animal a drug, especially in order to make them unconscious or to affect their performance in a race or sport; to add a drug to sb's food or drink to make them unconscious or sleepy: *He was drugged and bundled into the back of the car.* ◇ *It is illegal to drug horses before a race.* ◇ *Her drink must have been drugged.* See also **drug** → DRUG *noun* 1

lace [T] to add a small amount of alcohol, a drug or poison to drink or food: *He had laced her milk with rum.*

dope [T] (*rather informal*) to drug a person or animal in order to make them unconscious or to affect their performance in a race or sport: *Thieves doped a guard dog and stole $10 000 worth of goods.* See also **dope** → DRUG *noun* 1

policeman *noun*

policeman · officer · detective · police officer · cop · constable · PC/WPC · policewoman · trooper
These are all words for a member of the police.

▸ a **uniformed** policeman / officer / police officer / cop / policewoman
▸ a **plain-clothes** policeman / officer / detective / police officer / cop / policewoman
▸ an **undercover** policeman/officer/detective/police officer/cop
▸ an **off-duty** policeman / officer / detective / police officer / policewoman / cop
▸ a **senior** policeman / officer / detective / police officer / policewoman
▸ a policeman / an officer / a detective / a police officer / a cop / a constable **arrests sb / investigates sth**
▸ a policeman / an officer / a police officer / a cop / a constable **patrols** sth

policeman [C] a male member of the police: *A policeman was called to the house just after midnight.*

officer [C] a member of the police, often used as a form of address: *Yes, officer, I saw what happened.* ◇ *We spoke to the duty officer at the police station.* ◇ *I tried to find out who was the officer in charge of the case.* ❶ In the US, **officer** is also used as a title for a member of the police: *Officer Dibble.*

detective /dɪ'tektɪv/ [C] a person, especially a member of the police, whose job is to examine crimes and catch criminals: *Detective Sergeant John Nelson* ◇ *Detectives investigating the case are appealing for witnesses to the attack.* ❶ **Detective** is a rank of a police officer who investigates crimes. It is often part of a title such as *Detective Inspector* or *Detective Constable.*

po'lice officer [C] a member of the police: *The plans were drawn up at a meeting of senior police officers.*

NOTE POLICEMAN, OFFICER OR POLICE OFFICER? Police-man is the most frequent word used for a member of the police, especially by ordinary people in conversation. **Officer** and **police officer** are words used by the police, in more formal contexts such as news reports, and in order to avoid referring to the gender of the person. **Officer** is used instead of **police officer** when the context makes it clear that you are talking about a police officer, not any other kind of officer, especially when it forms part of another compound noun: ~~We spoke to the duty police officer at the police station.~~

cop [C] (*informal*) a police officer: *The film is based on the true story of a New York cop.* ◇ *Somebody call the cops!* ❶ **The cops** is often used to mean 'the police' in general.

constable /'kʌnstəbl; *AmE* 'kɑːn-/ [C] (in the UK and some other countries) a police officer of the lowest rank: *Have you finished your report yet, Constable?* ◇ *The children were taken out of the room by a woman police constable.* ◇ **Special constables** provide part-time assistance for the regular police force. ❶ **Constable** is a rank and is mainly used within the police when referring to or talking to particular police officers with this rank, including as a title: *Constable Quinn.* It is not used to refer to groups of police officers or the police in general. In the UK, a **chief constable** is a senior police officer who is in charge of the police force in a particular area.

PC, WPC [C] (*BrE*) the abbreviations for 'police constable' and 'woman police constable'; used as titles: *PC Jason Adams is a community policeman patrolling the estate.* ◇ *WPC Karen Mills was praised for her swift action.*

policewoman [C] a female police officer: *A plain-clothes policewoman waited at the entrance to her office.*

trooper [C] (*AmE*) a member of a State police force: *The teenager was shot by a state trooper during a drugs raid.*

polite *adj.*

polite · civil · gracious · respectful · courteous · gentlemanly · deferential
These words all describe sb who behaves in a way that shows good manners and respect.

▸ polite / civil / gracious / respectful / courteous / deferential **to** sb
▸ a polite / civil / respectful / courteous / gentlemanly **manner**
▸ a polite / gracious / respectful / gentlemanly **way**
▸ a polite / gracious / courteous / gentlemanly **man**
▸ a polite / gracious / courteous **smile**
▸ polite / courteous **behaviour**
▸ **extremely / perfectly** polite / civil / courteous

polite (*usually approving*) having or showing good manners and respect for the feelings of others; socially correct but not always sincere: *Please be polite to our guests.* ◇ *In Western culture, it is polite to maintain eye contact during conversation.* ◇ *We all stood around making polite conversation.* ◇ *The performance was greeted with polite applause.* **OPP rude, impolite** → RUDE, See also **politeness** → RESPECT *noun*
▸ **politely** *adv.*: *The receptionist smiled politely.*

civil polite in a formal way, but possibly not friendly: *The less time I have to spend being civil to him the better!* **OPP uncivil** ❶ The opposite of **civil** is **uncivil**, but this is not very frequent. See also **civility** → RESPECT *noun*
▸ **civilly** *adv.*: *She greeted him civilly but with no sign of affection.*

gracious /'ɡreɪʃəs/ (*rather formal, approving*) kind, polite and generous, especially to sb of a lower social position: *Lady Caroline was gracious enough to accept our invitation.* ◇ *He has not yet learned how to be gracious in defeat.* **OPP ungracious** ❶ The opposite of **gracious** is **ungracious**, but this is not very frequent. See also **grace** → RESPECT *noun*
▸ **graciously** *adv.*: *She graciously accepted our invitation.*

respectful (*rather formal, approving*) showing or feeling respect: *We were brought up to be respectful of authority.* ◇ *We all stood in respectful silence.* **OPP disrespectful** → RUDE, See also **respect** → RESPECT *noun*, **respect** → RESPECT *verb*
▸ **respectfully** *adv.*: *He listened respectfully.*

courteous /'kɜːtiəs; *AmE* 'kɜːrt-/ (*approving*) polite and showing respect, especially to people who you do not know: *The hotel staff were friendly and courteous.* ◇ *I wrote him a short letter and received a courteous reply.* **OPP discourteous** → RUDE, See also **courtesy** → RESPECT *noun*
▸ **courteously** *adv.*: *'I don't think we have met,' said the chairman courteously.*

gentlemanly (*approving*) (of a man) behaving very well and showing very good manners; like a gentleman: *So far, the election campaign has been a very gentlemanly affair.*

deferential /ˌdefəˈrenʃl/ (*rather formal, especially written*) behaving in a way that shows that you respect sb/sth, especially to sb you think is of a higher social position: *Older people tend to be more deferential to medical authorities.*
▸ **deference** /ˈdefərəns/ *noun* [U]: *The women wore veils in deference to the customs of the country.*

politician *noun*

politician · MP · senator · Congressman/ Congresswoman · Representative · lawmaker · legislator · Member of Parliament · statesman
These are all words for a person whose job is concerned with politics.

PATTERNS AND COLLOCATIONS
▸ the MP / Member of Parliament **for** an area
▸ the senator / Congressman / Representative **from** an area
▸ a **great** politician / senator / legislator / statesman
▸ a **leading** politician / senator / lawmaker / statesman
▸ an **influential** politician / senator / Congressman / lawmaker
▸ a **local** politician / MP / Congressman / lawmaker / Member of Parliament
▸ a **state** senator / Representative / lawmaker / legislator
▸ a **Conservative / Labour, etc.** politician / MP / Member of Parliament
▸ a **Republican / Democratic, etc.** senator / Congressman / Representative / lawmaker / legislator
▸ an **opposition** politician / MP / lawmaker / legislator / Member of Parliament
▸ to **elect** a politician / an MP / a senator / a Congressman / a Representative / a Member of Parliament

politician [C] a person whose job is concerned with politics, especially as an elected member of parliament, etc: *The affair led to the resignations of three leading politicians.*
MP [C] the abbreviation for 'Member of Parliament': *You should write to your MP about it.* ◇ *A number of back-bench MPs* (= MPs who do not have senior positions) *have expressed doubts about the bill.* ❶ **MP** is much more frequent than the full form, **Member of Parliament**, both in spoken and written English.
senator (also **Senator**) /ˈsenətə(r)/ [C] a member of a senate (= one of the two groups of elected politicians who make laws in some countries and most US states); used as a title: *He was elected senator for Pennsylvania in 2004.* ◇ *I would like to thank Senator Kelman for his warm welcome.*
ˈ**Congressman**, ˈ**Congresswoman** [C] a member of Congress in the US, especially of the House of Representatives; used as a title: *Congressmen from energy-producing states have opposed the deal.* ◇ *Congresswoman Barbara Lee*
Representative [C] a member of the House of Representatives, the Lower House of the US Congress; a member of the House of Representatives in the lower house of a US state parliament: *He was elected state Representative in 1989.* ◇ *Representative Harris*
lawmaker /ˈlɔːmeɪkə(r)/ (*especially AmE, especially journalism*) a person in government who makes the laws of a country or state: *State lawmakers have been arguing over the new healthcare reform bill for months.*
legislator /ˈledʒɪsleɪtə(r)/ [C] (*formal*) a lawmaker: *Seven of the state's 90 legislators have been indicted.*

NOTE LAWMAKER OR LEGISLATOR? Legislator is formal; lawmaker is mostly used in journalism, especially in American English, where it is often used instead of politician.

ˌ**Member of ˈParliament** [C] (*rather formal*) a person who has been elected to represent the people of a particular area in a parliament, especially in Britain and Canada: *Phil Wilson, Member of Parliament for Sedgefield*

statesman [C] a wise, experienced and respected political leader: *Power still resided with the party's* **elder states-man.** ◇ *He has a reputation as a* **world statesman.**

poor *adj.*

1 poor people/countries
2 poor quality

1 See the Topic Map for THE INDIVIDUAL AND SOCIETY on p.894, See also the entry for BANKRUPT
poor · disadvantaged · needy · impoverished · deprived · penniless · destitute · hard up
These words all describe sb/sth that has very little or no money and therefore cannot satisfy their basic needs.

disadvantaged	poor	penniless
	needy	destitute
	impoverished	
	deprived	
	hard up	

PATTERNS AND COLLOCATIONS
▸ poor / disadvantaged / needy / impoverished / deprived / destitute / hard-up **people / families**
▸ poor / disadvantaged / needy / impoverished / deprived / destitute **children**
▸ poor / disadvantaged / needy / impoverished / penniless / hard-up **students**
▸ poor / disadvantaged / needy / impoverished / deprived **groups**
▸ poor / disadvantaged / needy / impoverished / deprived **areas**
▸ poor / disadvantaged / impoverished / deprived **regions**
▸ poor / disadvantaged / impoverished **countries**
▸ a poor / a disadvantaged / an impoverished / a deprived **background**
▸ a poor / an impoverished / a deprived **childhood**
▸ **very** poor / disadvantaged / needy / impoverished / deprived / hard up
▸ **really** poor / needy / hard up
▸ **relatively** poor / disadvantaged / impoverished / deprived

poor having very little money; not having enough money for basic needs: *They were too poor to buy shoes for the kids.* ◇ *They always treated me like a poor relation.* ◇ *We aim to help the poorest families.* ◇ *It's among the poorer countries of the world.* ◇ (*AmE, rather informal*) *I may be* **dirt poor**, *but I have my pride.* OPP **rich, wealthy, affluent** → RICH, See also **poverty** → POVERTY
▸ **the poor** *noun* [pl.]: *They provided food and shelter for the poor* (= people who are poor).
disadvantaged [usually before noun] having less money and fewer opportunities than most people in society: *socially disadvantaged sections of the community* ◇ *the issues facing farmers in disadvantaged rural areas of Europe*
▸ **the disadvantaged** *noun* [pl.]: *helping the poor and the disadvantaged*
needy poor: *It's a charity that provides help and comfort for needy children.* OPP **wealthy** → RICH, See also **need** → POVERTY
▸ **the needy** *noun* [pl.]: *They provide shelter and a hot meal to the homeless and the needy.*
impoverished /ɪmˈpɒvərɪʃt; AmE -ˈpɑːv-/ (*journalism*) poor: *Thousands of impoverished peasants are desperate to move to the cities.* OPP **prosperous, affluent** → RICH

NOTE POOR, NEEDY OR IMPOVERISHED? Poor is the most general of these words and can be used to describe yourself, another individual person, people as a group or a country or area. Needy is mostly used to describe people considered as a group; it is not used to talk about yourself or individual people: *poor/needy children/families* ◇ ~~They were too needy to buy shoes for the kids.~~ Impoverished is used, especially in journalism, to talk about poor countries and the people who live there. (To talk about poor areas in rich countries, use **deprived**.)

deprived [usually before noun] without enough food, education, and all the things that are necessary for people to live a happy and comfortable life: *It's a very deprived area, with no amenities.* ◇ *We try to identify and provide support for emotionally deprived children.* **OPP** **privileged** → RICH, See also **deprivation** → POVERTY

NOTE DISADVANTAGED OR DEPRIVED? With **disadvantaged** the main emphasis is on the lack of opportunities to earn money, get an education and make a better life. With **deprived** the emphasis is more directly on the lack of adequate food, housing and other material comforts. People who are *emotionally deprived* do not get enough love or emotional comfort.

penniless (*literary*) having no money; very poor: *She arrived in 1978 as a virtually penniless refugee.* ◇ *He died penniless in Paris.*

destitute /'destɪtjuːt; AmE -tuːt/ [not usually before noun] (*rather formal*) without money, food and the other things necessary for life: *When he died, his family was left completely destitute.* See also **destitution** → POVERTY
▸ **the destitute** noun [pl.]: *homes and refuges for the destitute*

hard 'up (*informal*) having very little money, especially for a short period of time: *After he lost his job he was so hard up he couldn't afford the price of a beer.* ◇ *A couple of hard-up students came looking for part-time jobs.* **OPP** **well off** → RICH

2 poor · bad · cheap · low · dismal · (*taboo*) crap · inferior · (*taboo*) shit · hopeless · second-rate
These words all describe sth that is of a low standard or quality.

PATTERNS AND COLLOCATIONS
▸ a poor / a bad / a cheap / an inferior / a second-rate **copy** / **imitation**
▸ poor / bad / low / inferior / second-rate **quality**
▸ poor / bad / low **visibility**
▸ a poor / bad / low **opinion** of sb / sth
▸ a poor / a bad / a dismal / a crap / an inferior / a shit **performance**
▸ a poor / a bad / dismal **result** / **record**
▸ a poor / a bad / a crap / an inferior / a shit **design**
▸ poor / bad / inferior / second-rate **service**
▸ poor / bad / inferior **workmanship**
▸ a poor / a low / a dismal / an inferior **standard**
▸ a bad / a cheap / a crap / an inferior / a shit / a second-rate **product**
▸ **very** poor / bad / low / inferior / second-rate

poor below the standard or quality that is acceptable or expected: *We discussed the party's poor performance in the election.* ◇ *She's been in poor health for some time now.* ◇ *On the whole he had a poor opinion of human nature.* ◇ *It was raining heavily and visibility was poor.* **OPP** **fine** → GOOD 1
▸ **poorly** adv.: *The job is relatively poorly paid.* ◇ *Our candidate fared poorly in the election* (= did not get many votes).

bad (*rather informal*) of a poor quality or standard: *I thought it was a very bad article.* ◇ *That's not a bad idea.* ◇ *This isn't as bad as I thought.* **OPP** **good** → GOOD 1
▸ **badly** adv.: *She sang two songs, very badly.* ◇ *The whole thing was badly organized.*

NOTE POOR OR BAD? **Poor** is more frequent in written English in this meaning, but **bad** is used more in informal spoken English. Some words do not collocate with both **poor** and **bad**: *They have a poor standard of living.* ◇ ~~a bad standard of living~~ ◇ *I don't think it's a bad school.* ◇ ~~I don't think it's a poor school.~~

cheap low in price and quality: *The room was filled with the smell of cheap perfume.* ◇ *The market has been flooded with cheap imports.* See also **cheap** → CHEAP
▸ **cheaply** adv.: *The leaflet had been cheaply produced and photocopied.*

low below the usual or expected standard or quality: *Much of the work was of a very low standard.* ◇ *These measures will lead to a lower quality of life for many older people.* **OPP** **high** → HIGH 1

dismal /'dɪzməl/ (*informal*) not skilful or successful; of a very low standard: *The singer gave a dismal performance of some old songs.* ◇ *Their recent attempt to increase sales has been a dismal failure.* ❶ **Dismal** most often collocates with *failure, performance, result, record* and *weather.*
▸ **dismally** adv.: *I tried not to laugh but failed dismally* (= was completely unsuccessful).

crap (*BrE*) (*AmE* **crappy**) (*taboo, slang*) of a very poor quality or standard ❶ **Crap** should only be used in an informal situation to sb who is your equal in age and status. If said to sb who is older or who considers themselves more important than you, it could cause very great offence: *I used to be in this really crap band.* ◇ *a crappy movie/apartment* See also **crap** → RUBBISH *noun*
▸ **crap** adv.: (*BrE*) *The team played crap yesterday.*

inferior /ɪn'fɪəriə(r); AmE -'fɪr-/ (*rather formal*) not as good as sth else of the same kind: *The cracks in the structure were due to the poor-quality materials and inferior workmanship.* ◇ *Modern music is often considered inferior to that of the past.* **OPP** **superior** → BETTER, **superior** → GOOD 1

shit (*BrE*) (*AmE* **shitty**) (*taboo, slang*) of a very poor quality or standard ❶ **Shit** should only be used in an informal situation to sb who is your equal in age and status. If said to sb who is older or who considers themselves more important than you, it could cause very great offence. It is an even stronger and more offensive term than **crap**: *I was a shit player.* ◇ *They're a shitty team.*

hopeless (*BrE, informal*) of a very low quality or standard of service: *The buses are absolutely hopeless these days.*

second-'rate not as good as sth else of the same kind: *Why do we only produce second-rate films?* **OPP** **first-rate** → EXCELLENT

popular *adj.*

popular · attractive · desirable · hot · appealing · in demand · enviable
These words all describe people or things that are liked or wanted by a large number of people.

PATTERNS AND COLLOCATIONS
▸ attractive / appealing **to** sb
▸ an attractive / appealing **idea** / **prospect**
▸ **very** popular / attractive / desirable / appealing / enviable
▸ **highly** popular / attractive / desirable
▸ **immediately** / **enormously** popular / attractive / appealing

popular (of people, things or activities) liked or enjoyed by a large number of people: *He was a hugely popular singer.* ◇ *This is one of our most popular designs.* ◇ *These policies are unlikely to prove popular with middle-class voters.* ◇ *These designs are popular among young people.* **OPP** **unpopular** → UNWANTED
▸ **popularity** /ˌpɒpjuˈlærəti; AmE ˌpɑːp-/ noun [U]: *Their music still enjoys widespread popularity among teenagers.*

attractive (*rather formal*) having features or qualities that make sth seem interesting and worth having: *They are able to offer attractive career opportunities to graduates.* ❶ **Attractive** is often used to talk about an idea or possibility that you are considering: *an attractive idea/theory/proposition/option/prospect/package/offer* **OPP** **unattractive** → UNATTRACTIVE, See also **attraction** → INTEREST *noun* 1

desirable /dɪˈzaɪərəbl/ (*formal*) that you would like to have or do; worth having or doing: *It is desirable that interest rates be reduced.* ◇ *It is no longer desirable for* adult children to live with their parents. ◇ She chatted for a few minutes about the qualities she considered **desirable in** a secretary. **❶ Desirable** is often used in selling, especially property: *a desirable home/feature/residence/property/ area* **OPP undesirable** → UNWANTED

▶ **desirability** /dɪˌzaɪərə'bɪləti/ *noun* [U]: *No one questions the desirability of cheaper fares.*

hot (*informal*) new, exciting and very popular: *They are one of this year's* **hot new** *bands on the rock scene.* ◇ *The couple are Hollywood's* **hottest property**. **❶** Things which are typically described as **hot** are *talent,* a *fashion* or *trend,* a *band,* a *new product* and a *name* (= a famous person). People and things can also be described as *the hottest thing in America/Japan, etc.* **Hot** is often used in this meaning in advertising and journalism.

appealing attractive or interesting; that you would like to have or do: *Spending the holidays in Britain wasn't a prospect that I found particularly appealing.* ◇ *Brightly coloured packaging made the pens especially appealing to children.* **OPP unappealing** → UNATTRACTIVE, See also **appeal** → INTEREST *noun* 1

in demand *phrase* wanted by a lot of people: *Good secretaries are always in demand.* **❶ In demand** is mostly used to talk about a product that a lot of people want to buy, or a person who has skills that a lot of people or employers want to use. People and things are typically *always, constantly, greatly, increasingly* and *much* **in demand**.

enviable /'enviəbl/ (*rather formal*) (of sth that sb has) that other people would like to have too: *He is in the enviable position of having two job offers to choose from.* **❶ Enviable** is typically used to describe sb's *position, reputation* or *record* (= sb's past achievements). **OPP unenviable ❶** An **unenviable** task or thing is sth unpleasant or difficult that you would not want to do or have: *She was given the* **unenviable task** *of informing the losers.*

porch *noun*

porch · balcony · terrace · patio · deck
These words all mean a flat area next to a building where people can sit.

PATTERNS AND COLLOCATIONS
▶ a **covered** porch / balcony / terrace / patio / deck
▶ a **sunny** balcony / terrace / patio / deck
▶ a **shaded** terrace / patio
▶ to **sit on** a porch / balcony / terrace / patio / deck
▶ a porch / balcony / terrace / patio / deck **overlooking** sth

porch [C] (*AmE*) an open raised area at the entrance to a house with a separate roof, stairs to the ground and a low wall, fence or screen around the edge: *After dinner we sat on the* **front porch** *and talked for hours.* **❶** In British English **porch** usually means a small covered area around the entrance to a building, often with solid walls.

balcony /'bælkəni/ [C] a platform that is built on the upstairs outside wall of a building, with a wall or rail around it. You can get out onto a balcony from an upstairs room: *We had drinks on the hotel balcony.*

terrace /'terəs/ [C] a hard, flat area where people can sit, eat and enjoy the sun, especially a flat area built outside a house, restaurant or hotel: *Close to the villa is a big pool with a sun terrace around it.* ◇ *All rooms have a balcony or terrace.*

patio /'pætiəʊ; *AmE* -oʊ/ [C] a hard, flat area where people can sit that is built outside, and usually behind, a house: *Let's have lunch out on the patio.*

deck [C] (*especially AmE*) a wooden floor that is built onto the back of a house where you can sit and relax: *After dinner we sat out on the deck.*

port *noun*

port · harbour · dock · marina
These are all words for places where boats or ships can go when they are not at sea.

PATTERNS AND COLLOCATIONS
▶ **in** port / harbour / dock / the marina
▶ to **enter / leave** port / harbour / the dock

port [C] a city or town where ships load and unload goods, or passenger ships take on passengers; a place where ships load and unload goods or shelter from storms: *a fishing/naval/container/ferry port* ◇ *a port city/town* ◇ *The ship spent four days in port.* ◇ *They reached port at last.* ◇ *Our next* **port of call** *was Piraeus.*

harbour (*BrE*) (*AmE* **harbor**) /'hɑːbə(r); *AmE* 'hɑːrb-/ [C] an area of water on the coast, protected from the open sea by strong walls, where boats and ships can stay when they are not at sea: *Several boats lay at anchor in the harbour.* ◇ *the harbour front/mouth/wall*

dock [C] an enclosed area of water in a port where a ship can load and unload goods, take on passengers, or be repaired. It includes both the water in the dock and the walls and platforms surrounding it: *The ship was in dock.* ◇ *the cargo stacked on the dock* ◇ *dock workers* ◇ *a dock strike* **❶** The **docks** [pl.] are a group of docks in a port, together with the buildings around them, that are used for repairing ships, storing goods, etc.: *There are plans to redevelop the old docks for new housing.*

marina [C] a specially designed harbour for small boats and yachts, especially boats used for pleasure, not business: *a new £250 million marina and leisure development*

portion *noun*

portion · helping · serving
These are all words for an amount of food which is enough for one person.

PATTERNS AND COLLOCATIONS
▶ a portion / helping / serving **of** sth
▶ a **large / small / generous** portion / helping / serving
▶ to **have** a portion / helping / serving of sth

portion /'pɔːʃn; *AmE* 'pɔːrʃn/ [C] an amount of food that is large enough for one person, especially when it has been measured equally: *She cut the cake* **into** *six* **portions**. ◇ *You should eat several portions of fruit a day.* See also **plate** → PLATE

helping [C] an amount of food given to sb at a meal: *We all had a second helping of pie.*

serving [C] (*rather formal, especially written*) an amount of food for one person, not necessarily when it is ready to be eaten: *This recipe will be enough for four servings.* See also **serve** → SERVE 1

pose *verb*

pose · do · imitate · impersonate · mimic · pass sb/yourself off as sb/sth
These words all mean to copy the way sb speaks or behaves, either in order to deceive people or to entertain them.

PATTERNS AND COLLOCATIONS
▶ to pose / pass yourself off **as** sb / sth
▶ to pose as / imitate / impersonate / mimic / pass yourself off as **somebody**
▶ to pose as / impersonate / pass yourself off as a **journalist / reporter / customer / doctor / scientist / police officer**
▶ to do / imitate / mimic an / sb's **accent**
▶ to imitate / mimic sb's **speech**

pose [I] to pretend to be sb in order to deceive other people: *The gang entered the building posing as workmen.*

do [T] to copy the way a well-known performer speaks or sings, especially in order to entertain people; to speak in a particular accent: *He does a great Elvis Presley.* ◇ *Can you do a Welsh accent?*

imitate /ˈɪmɪteɪt/ [T] to copy the way sb speaks or behaves, in order to show your lack of respect for the person, and/or to make people laugh: *She knew that the girls used to imitate her and laugh at her behind her back.* ◇ *He tried to imitate my Scots accent and we both laughed.* See also **imitation** → PARODY

impersonate /ɪmˈpɜːsəneɪt; AmE -ˈpɜːrs-/ [T] to pretend to be sb in order to deceive people or to entertain them: *He was caught trying to impersonate a security guard.* ◇ *They do a pretty good job of impersonating Laurel and Hardy.* See also **impersonation** → PARODY

mimic /ˈmɪmɪk/ [T] to copy the way sb speaks or behaves, especially in order to show your lack of respect for the person, and make other people laugh: *She's always mimicking the teachers.* ◇ *He mimicked her accent.*

> **NOTE** IMITATE OR MIMIC? **Mimic** is usually used to talk about copying sb's speech or behaviour in an unkind way; **imitate** may or may not be unkind.

ˌpass sb/yourself ˈoff as sb/sth, *phrasal verb* to pretend, and make people believe, that sb is sth that they are not, or that you are sth that you are not: *He escaped by passing himself off as a guard.* ❶ When you use **pass sb/yourself off as sb/sth** you place emphasis on the fact that sb has successfully managed to deceive people.

position *noun*

position · stance · posture · pose
These are all words for the way in which sb is standing or sitting.

▸ a **sitting** position / posture
▸ an **upright** position / stance
▸ a **relaxed** position / stance / posture / pose
▸ a **comfortable** position / posture
▸ a **stiff** posture / pose
▸ a **good** stance / posture
▸ the **correct** stance / posture
▸ to **adopt / take up** a position / stance / posture / pose
▸ to **keep / maintain** a position / stance / posture
▸ to **change** your position / stance / posture / pose

position [C, U] the way in which sb is sitting or standing; the way in which sth is arranged: *Can you get into a kneeling position?* ◇ *My arms were aching so I shifted (my) position.* ◇ *The soldiers had to stand for hours without changing position.* ◇ *Keep the box in an upright position.* See also **position** → PLACE *noun* 1, **position** → PUT *verb* 1

stance /stæns; BrE also stɑːns/ [C] the way in which sb stands, especially when playing a sport: *Widen your stance* (= move your feet wider apart) *for greater stability when hitting the ball.*

posture /ˈpɒstʃə(r); AmE ˈpɑːs-/ [U, C] (*rather formal*) the position in which you hold your body when standing or sitting: *Try to maintain an upright posture and keep your voice low and clear.* ◇ *Back pains can be the result of bad posture.* ❶ **Posture** is used especially when you are considering whether a particular position is good or bad for your health, or what sb's position and body language tells you about how they are feeling.

pose [C] a particular position in which sb stands, sits, etc., especially in order to be painted, drawn or photographed: *He adopted a dramatic pose for the camera.* ◇ *I can't hold this pose much longer!*
▸ **pose** *verb* [I]: *The delegates posed for a group photograph.*

possibility *noun*

possibility · chance · probability · odds · prospect · likelihood
These are all words for how likely sth is to happen, or for a thing that is likely to happen.

possibility	prospect	probability
chance		likelihood
odds		

▸ a possibility / a chance / a probability / the odds / the prospect / the likelihood **of** sth
▸ a possibility / a chance / the probability / the odds / the prospect / the likelihood **that...**
▸ a **real / reasonable** possibility / chance / probability / prospect / likelihood
▸ a **strong** possibility / chance / probability / likelihood
▸ a **high** chance / probability / likelihood
▸ a **realistic / serious / remote** possibility / chance / prospect
▸ **every** possibility / chance / probability / prospect / likelihood
▸ **little** chance / prospect / likelihood
▸ **There is (no)** possibility / chance / prospect / likelihood of sth.
▸ **The** chances / probability / odds / likelihood **is / are that...**
▸ to **have** the possibility / a chance / a ... probability / the prospect / a ...likelihood
▸ to **increase / reduce** the possibility / chance / probability / odds / likelihood
▸ to **calculate** the probability / odds / likelihood

possibility [U, C] the fact that sth might exist or happen, but is not certain to: *He refused to rule out the possibility of a tax increase.* ◇ (*especially BrE*) *It is not **beyond the bounds of possibility** that we'll all meet again one day.* ◇ *What had seemed impossible now seemed a **distinct possibility**.* ◇ *There is a remote possibility that we might have got it wrong.* See also **possible** → LIKELY

chance [C, U] a possibility that sth might exist or happen, especially sth that you want: *Is there any chance of getting tickets for tonight?* ◇ *The operation has a **fifty-fifty chance** of success.* ◇ *As long as there is an **outside chance** (= slight chance) we'll go for it.* ◇ *She has only a **slim chance** of passing the exam.* ◇ *There is **no chance** that he will change his mind.*

probability /ˌprɒbəˈbɪləti; AmE ˌprɑːb-/ [U, C] how likely sth is to happen; a thing that is likely to happen: *The probability is that prices will rise rapidly.* ◇ *A fall in interest rates is a strong probability in the present economic climate.* ❶ In mathematics a **probability** is a ratio showing the chances that a particular thing will happen: *There is a 60% probability that the population will be infected with the disease.* See also **probable** → LIKELY

odds (usually **the odds**) [pl.] how likely sth is to happen; something that makes it seem impossible to do or achieve sth: *The **odds are** very much **in our favour** (= we are likely to succeed).* ◇ *The **odds are** heavily **against him** (= he is not likely to succeed).* ◇ *What are the odds (= how likely is it) he won't turn up?* ◇ *Against all (the) odds, he made a full recovery.* ❶ In betting **odds** are the connection between two numbers that shows how much money sb will receive if they win a bet: *I put £10 on Middlesbrough to beat Manchester at odds of three to one (= three times the amount of money that has been bet by sb will be paid to them if they win).* ◇ *They are offering **long/short odds** (= the winnings will be high/low because there is a high/low risk of losing) on the defending champion.*

prospect [U, sing.] (*rather formal*) the possibility that sth might happen, especially sth good: *There is no immediate prospect of peace.* ◇ *A place in the semi-finals is **in prospect** (= likely to happen).* See also **prospective** → LIKELY

likelihood /ˈlaɪklihʊd/ [U, sing.] the possibility that sth might happen; how likely sth is to happen: *There is very little likelihood of that happening.* ◇ *The likelihood is that (= it is likely that) unemployment figures will continue to fall.* ◇ *In all likelihood (= very probably) the meeting will be cancelled.* See also **likely** → LIKELY

> **NOTE** PROBABILITY OR LIKELIHOOD? **Probability** is used more in scientific and technical contexts; **likelihood** is used more in business contexts. However, in everyday speech you can usually use either word.

possible adj.

1 It is possible to get there by bus.
2 several possible explanations

1 possible · viable · practical · realistic · feasible · workable · achievable

These words all describe things that can be done or achieved, or are worth trying because they are likely to be successful.

PATTERNS AND COLLOCATIONS

▶ to be possible/ realistic/ feasible **to do sth**
▶ a viable/ practical/ realistic/ feasible/ workable **solution/ policy/ plan**
▶ a viable/ practical/ realistic/ feasible/ workable **means**
▶ a viable/ practical/ realistic/ workable **alternative**
▶ a realistic/ an achievable **goal/ objective/ target**
▶ **perfectly** possible/ viable/ practical/ feasible
▶ **quite** possible/ practical/ realistic/ feasible
▶ **very** practical/ realistic/ feasible/ achievable
▶ **reasonably** practical/ realistic/ achievable

possible [not usually before noun] that can be done or achieved: *It is possible to get there by bus.* ◇ *This would not have been possible without you.* ◇ *Try to avoid losing your temper if (at all) possible* (= if you can). ◇ *Travel by bus whenever possible* (= when you can). ◇ *Do everything possible to get it finished on time.* ◇ *New technology has made it possible to communicate more easily.* **OPP** **impossible** → IMPOSSIBLE, See also **possibility** → OPPORTUNITY, **possibility** → OPTION, **possibilities** → POTENTIAL

viable /ˈvaɪəbl/ (*rather formal, especially business*) that can be done; that is likely to be successful and is therefore worth considering or supporting: *There is no viable alternative.* ◇ *If there was any delay then the rescue plan would cease to be viable.* ❶ A company, plan or project that is *commercially/economically/financially viable* is capable of producing a profit.

practical sensible and appropriate; likely to be successful: *It wouldn't be practical for us to go all that way just for the weekend.* ◇ *It was difficult to find a practical solution to the problem.* ❶ In this meaning **practical** is used to describe ideas, courses of action and ways of doing things: *a practical alternative/approach/measure/method/option/ possibility/proposition* **OPP** **impractical** → UNREALISTIC

realistic sensible and appropriate; that can be achieved: *We must set realistic goals.* ◇ *If you want to retain good employees, you have to pay a realistic salary.* ❶ **Realistic** is often used to talk about what you can hope to achieve in business or at work: *a realistic alternative/demand/ estimate/goal/hope/option/plan/solution/target* **OPP** **unrealistic** → UNREALISTIC

▶ **realistically** *adv.*: *Realistically, there is little prospect of a ceasefire.* ◇ *How many can you realistically hope to sell?*

feasible /ˈfiːzəbl/ that can probably be achieved and is therefore worth trying: *It's just not feasible to manage the business on a part-time basis.*

workable that can be used successfully and effectively: *Gradually, through discussion, a workable plan emerged.* ◇ *I'm sure we can come to some workable arrangement.* ❶ **Workable** is often used in business-related contexts to describe things such as a system or idea: *a workable arrangement/framework/plan/programme/proposal/solution/system* **OPP** **unworkable** → UNREALISTIC

achievable (*rather formal*) that can be achieved: *Profits of $20m look achievable.* ◇ *Setting achievable goals will help to build confidence in your staff.* ❶ **Achievable** most often collocates with *goal, objective, target* and *standard*.

2 possible · plausible · credible · conceivable · imaginable · believable

These words all describe sth that seems reasonable or is likely to be true.

PATTERNS AND COLLOCATIONS

▶ possible/ plausible/ credible/ conceivable/ imaginable/ believable **that...**
▶ a possible/ plausible/ credible/ believable **explanation/ excuse**
▶ a possible/ plausible/ credible **solution/ answer**
▶ a plausible/ credible/ believable **story/ account**
▶ to **sound** possible/ plausible/ credible/ believable
▶ **entirely/ perfectly/ quite** possible/ plausible/ credible/ conceivable
▶ **barely/ hardly/ scarcely** possible/ credible/ conceivable/ imaginable/ believable
▶ **every** possible/ conceivable/ imaginable...

possible reasonable or acceptable in a particular situation: *There are several possible explanations.* ◇ *It's scarcely possible that he knew nothing about it.* **OPP** **impossible** → IMPOSSIBLE

plausible /ˈplɔːzəbl/ (*rather formal*) (of an excuse or explanation) reasonable and likely to be true: *Her story sounded perfectly plausible.* ◇ *The only plausible explanation is that he forgot.* **OPP** **implausible** → UNLIKELY 2, See also **reasonable** → REASONABLE

▶ **plausibly** *adv.*: *He argued, very plausibly, that the claims were untrue.*

credible /ˈkredəbl/ that can be believed or trusted: *It's just not credible that she would cheat.* ◇ *There's only one credible witness in the case.* **OPP** **incredible** → INCREDIBLE

▶ **credibility** *noun* [U]: *The prosecution did its best to undermine the credibility of the witness.*

conceivable /kənˈsiːvəbl/ possible to imagine or believe: *It's not conceivable that she didn't know what was going on.* ◇ *We've examined the problem from every conceivable angle.* **OPP** **inconceivable** → IMPOSSIBLE

▶ **conceivably** *adv.*: *He might conceivably go on to win the finals.*

imaginable /ɪˈmædʒɪnəbl/ possible to imagine: *What those prisoners went through is hardly imaginable.* ❶ **Imaginable** is often used with superlatives and with *all* and *every* to emphasize that sth is the best, worst etc. that you could imagine or that it includes every possible example: *The house has the most spectacular views imaginable.* ◇ *They stock every imaginable type of music.* **OPP** **unimaginable** ❶ Something that is **unimaginable** is impossible to think of or to believe exists: *unimaginable wealth/possibilities* ◇ *This level of success would have been unimaginable just last year.*

believable that can be believed: *The characters in the play are simply not believable* (= you cannot believe they represent real people). **OPP** **unbelievable** → INCREDIBLE

post noun

post · pillar · column · plank · beam · rafter · support · buttress · girder · joist

These are all words for long pieces of wood, metal or stone that are used for support, often as part of a structure.

PATTERNS AND COLLOCATIONS

▶ a **heavy** post/ column/ plank/ beam/ girder
▶ a **massive** pillar/ column/ beam/ buttress
▶ **tall** posts/ pillars/ columns/ buttresses
▶ a **wooden** post/ pillar/ column/ plank/ beam/ rafter/ support
▶ a **steel** post/ pillar/ column/ beam/ support/ girder/ joist
▶ an **iron** post/ pillar/ column/ beam/ support/ girder
▶ a **concrete** pillar/ column/ beam/ joist
▶ a **stone** pillar/ column/ buttress
▶ a post/ pillar/ column/ beam/ buttress/ girder/ joist **supports sth**

post [C] (often in compounds) a piece of wood or metal that is set in the ground in an upright position, especially to support sth or to mark a position: *She tied the dog to a post.* ◇ *corner posts* (= that mark the corners of a sports field) ◇ (*especially BrE*) *The car skidded and hit a lamp post.*

pillar /ˈpɪlə(r)/ [C] a large round stone, metal or wooden post that is used to support a bridge, the roof of a building, etc., especially when it is also decorative: *The roof is supported by massive stone pillars.* ◇ *He was hiding behind a pillar near the back of the church.*

column [C] a tall, solid, upright post, usually round and made of stone, which supports or decorates a building or stands alone as a monument, built to remind people of a famous person or event: *The churches have classical columns and decoration.* ◇ *Nelson's Column in Trafalgar Square is one of London's best-known landmarks.*

plank [C] a long narrow flat piece of wood that is used for making floors, boats, etc: *a plank of wood* ◇ *The bridge was made of planks held together with rope.*

beam [C] a long horizontal piece of wood, metal, etc. used to support weight, especially as part of the roof in a building: *The cottage had low ceilings with exposed dark oak beams.*

rafter /ˈrɑːftə(r); AmE ˈræf-/ [C, usually pl.] one of the sloping pieces of wood that support a roof: *Ropes of onions and garlic hung from the ancient rafters.*

support [C] a thing that holds sth and prevents it from falling: *The supports under the bridge were starting to bend.* See also **support → SUPPORT** *verb 2*

buttress /ˈbʌtrəs/ [C] a stone or brick structure that is attached to a wall to support it: *It was necessary to strengthen the building with large external buttresses.*

girder /ˈɡɜːdə(r); AmE ˈɡɜːrd-/ [C] a long strong iron or steel beam used for building bridges and forming the structure of large buildings: *The unfinished building with its blue girders was being used as a huge climbing frame.*

joist [C, usually pl.] a long thick piece of wood or metal that is used for support under a floor or above a ceiling in a building: *Lift any loose floorboards and inspect the joists.*

poster *noun*

poster · banner · notice · placard
These are all words for a sheet of paper, cardboard or fabric showing pictures or giving information or a message, usually put in a public place.

PATTERNS AND COLLOCATIONS
▸ sth is **on** a poster/ notice/ placard
▸ an **election** poster/ notice
▸ to **display** a poster/ notice/ placard
▸ to **put up/ stick up** a poster/ notice
▸ to **carry** a banner/ placard

poster [C] a large sheet of paper, often with a picture on it, that is put in a public place to advertise sth; a large picture that is printed on paper and put on a wall as decoration: *Election posters were on every street.* ◇ *The walls are covered with posters of her favourite pop stars.*

banner [C] a long piece of fabric with a message on it that is carried between two poles or hung in a public place to show support for sth: *Protesters carried a banner reading 'Save Our Wildlife'.*

notice [C] a sheet of paper giving written or printed information, usually put in a public place: *There was a notice on the board saying the class had been cancelled.* See also **notice → SIGN 2,** See also the entry for LEAFLET

placard /ˈplækɑːd; -kɑːrd/ [C] a large written or printed notice that is put in a public place or carried on a stick in a march: *They were carrying placards and banners demanding that he resign.*

potential *noun*

potential · prospects · promise · possibilities
These are all words for the possibility of sth happening or being developed or used successfully.

PATTERNS AND COLLOCATIONS
▸ potential/ prospects/ possibilities **for** sth
▸ sb/ sth **with** potential/ prospects/ promise/ possibilities
▸ **real/ great** potential/ prospects/ promise/ possibilities
▸ **exciting/ future** potential/ prospects/ possibilities
▸ **commercial/ development/ economic** potential/ prospects/ possibilities
▸ to **have** potential/ prospects/ promise/ possibilities
▸ to **offer** potential/ prospects/ possibilities

▸ to **show** potential/ promise
▸ to **fulfil** sb/ sth's potential/ promise
▸ to **assess/ examine/ consider/ discuss/ explore** sb/ sth's potential/ prospects/ possibilities

potential /pəˈtenʃl/ [U] the possibility of sth happening or being developed or used; qualities that exist in sb/sth and can be developed: *It is clear that the potential for change is there.* ◇ *She has great potential as an artist.* ◇ *All children should be encouraged to realize their full potential.* ❶ People and things generally *have/show potential* when they have qualities that can be developed. When they use these qualities successfully, they *fulfil, reach* or *realize* their **potential**. See also **potential → LIKELY** *adj.*

prospects [pl.] the chances of being successful, especially in your career: *They want a reasonable salary and good career prospects.* ◇ *At 25 he was an unemployed musician with no prospects.* ◇ *What are the prospects of promotion in this job?* See also **prospective → LIKELY** *adj.*

promise [U] a sign that sb/sth will be successful: *Her work shows great promise.* ◇ *Their future was full of promise.* See also **promising → PROMISING**

possibilities [pl.] qualities that exist in sth and can be developed: *The house is in a bad state of repair but it has possibilities.* See also **possible → POSSIBLE 1**

> **NOTE** **POTENTIAL** OR **POSSIBILITIES?** People or things can have **potential**, but especially people; things, but NOT usually people, can have **possibilities**.

pour *verb*

pour · spill · decant · slop
These words all mean to make a liquid come out of a container.

PATTERNS AND COLLOCATIONS
▸ to pour/ spill/ slop sth **onto/ out of/ over** sth
▸ to pour/ decant/ slop sth **into** sth
▸ to pour/ spill/ slop **water/ beer**
▸ to pour/ spill/ decant **wine**
▸ to pour/ spill **oil/ milk**
▸ **water** pours/ spills/ slops

pour [T, I] to let a liquid or other substance flow from a container in a continuous stream, especially by holding the container at an angle; to serve a drink in this way: *Pour the sauce over the pasta.* ◇ *Will you pour the coffee?* ◇ *I was in the kitchen, pouring out drinks.* ◇ *Shall I pour?*

spill [I, T] (especially of liquid) to accidentally flow over the edge of a container; to make liquid do this: *Water had spilled out of the bucket onto the floor.* ◇ *He startled her and made her spill her drink.* ◇ *Thousands of gallons of crude oil were spilled into the ocean.*
▸ **spill** *noun* [C]: *Many seabirds died as a result of the oil spill.* ◇ *I wiped up the coffee spills on the table.*

decant /dɪˈkænt/ [T] (*rather formal*) to pour liquid, especially wine, from one container into another: *They buy wine in bulk and decant it into smaller bottles to sell.* See also **decanter → BOTTLE**

slop (-pp-) [I, T] (always used with an adverb or preposition) (*rather informal*) (of a liquid) to move around in a container, making a lot of noise and/or coming out over the edge; to make liquid or food come out of a container in an untidy way: *As she put the glass down the beer slopped over onto the table.* ◇ *She slopped some of the egg mixture over the side of the bowl.*

poverty *noun* See the Topic Map for THE INDIVIDUAL AND SOCIETY on p.894

poverty · need · deprivation · privation · destitution
These are all words for the state of having very little money, especially when this is not enough for basic needs.

▶ **in** poverty / need / destitution
▶ poverty / need / deprivation **among...**
▶ **great** poverty / need / deprivation / privation
▶ **extreme / real** poverty / need / deprivation
▶ **rural / inner-city / urban** poverty / deprivation
▶ **economic** poverty / need / deprivation / privation
▶ **material** poverty / need / deprivation
▶ **to endure / suffer** poverty / deprivation / privation

poverty /'pɒvəti; *AmE* 'pɑːvərti/ [U] the state of being poor: *Thousands of families are living in* **abject/dire poverty** *in the shanty towns.* ◇ *There are millions living on incomes below* **the poverty line** (= who are too poor to afford necessary items). OPP wealth → MONEY 3, See also **poor** → POOR 1, **hardship** → TROUBLE 2

need [U] the state of not having enough food, money or support: *The charity aims to provide assistance to people in need.* ◇ *He helped me in my* **hour of need.** See also **needy** → POOR 1

deprivation /ˌdeprɪ'veɪʃn/ [U] (*rather formal*) a lack of the basic things that people need for living, such as enough money, food, clothes and care: *In the inner cities you will find neglected children suffering from social deprivation.* See also **deprived** → POOR 1

privation /praɪ'veɪʃn/ [C, usually pl., U] (*formal*) a lack of the basic things that people need for living, such as enough money, food or clothes: *They suffered all the privations of poverty.* ◇ *They endured years of suffering and privation.*

destitution /ˌdestɪ'tjuːʃn; *AmE* -'tuːʃn/ [U] the state of having no money, food, home, etc: *Help from local charities meant that the degree of deprivation stopped short of actual destitution.* See also **destitute** → POOR 1

NOTE DEPRIVATION, PRIVATION OR DESTITUTION? Priva-tion and **deprivation** mean the lack of basic things such as proper food, clothes, etc. **Deprivation** can also mean a lack of care, for example the care that adults should take of children. **Destitution** is what you experience when you have no job, no money and no home.

power *noun*

power · influence · weight · leverage · say
These are all words for the ability that sb has to influence what people do or the way sth happens.

▶ sb's influence / leverage **over** sb
▶ **great** power / influence / weight / leverage
▶ **considerable / political** power / influence / weight / leverage
▶ **economic / financial** power / weight / leverage
▶ **to have** power / influence / leverage / a say
▶ **to use / exercise** (your) power / influence / leverage
▶ **to exert** (your) power / influence / leverage (over sb)

power [U] (used in compounds) strength in a particular area of activity: *The country's dominance was assured by its technological and military power.* ◇ *Increased trade union* **bargaining power** *led to higher wage settlements.* ◇ *Those aged over 55 now have a purchasing power of more than £30 billion annually* (= they have that amount available to spend).

influence [U] the ability of sb/sth to make sb/sth behave in a particular way: *Her parents no longer have any real influence over her.* ◇ *She could probably exert her* **influence with** *the manager and get you a job.* ◇ *Drug cartels wielded enormous influence in the city.*

weight [U] the importance given to sb/sth and their ability to influence sb/sth: *Your opinion* **carries weight with** *the boss.* ◇ *Environmental considerations were given* **due weight** *in making the decision.* ◇ *The president now has to* **lend** *his* **weight to** *the project.*

leverage /'liːvərɪdʒ; *AmE* 'lev-/ [U] (*formal*) the ability of sb to influence sb/sth, especially because of their position: *Retailers can exert leverage over producers by threatening to take their business elsewhere.*

say [U, sing.] the right or opportunity to influence sth by giving your opinion before a decision is made: *We* **had no say in** *the decision to sell the company.* ◇ *The judge has the* **final say on** *the sentence.* ◇ *She won't be happy until she's* **had her say** (= had the opportunity to express herself fully about sth).

powerful *adj.*

powerful · dominant · strong · influential · important · great · instrumental · high-powered
These words all describe people who have power or influence over other people or events.

▶ dominant / influential / important / instrumental **in** (doing) sth
▶ a powerful / a dominant / a strong / an influential / a great / an important **figure / leader / position**
▶ a powerful / a dominant / an influential / an important **individual / group**
▶ a powerful / strong / influential **lobby**
▶ a powerful / a dominant / a strong / an influential / an important / an instrumental **role**
▶ a powerful / a dominant / a strong / an important / a great **influence**
▶ **very** powerful / dominant / strong / influential / important / high-powered
▶ **economically** powerful / dominant / strong / important

powerful (of people or groups) having a lot of power to control and influence people and events: *He is one of the most powerful directors in Hollywood.* ◇ *This extremist movement has become increasingly powerful in recent years.* ◇ *Why are there still so few women in politically powerful positions?*

dominant /'dɒmɪnənt; *AmE* 'dɑːm-/ (of people, groups or ideas) having more power or influence than other people or things: *The firm has achieved a dominant position in the world market.* ◇ *The state of the economy has been the dominant theme of the election.* See also **dominate** → TAKE OVER
▶ **dominance** *noun* [U]: *The firm soon achieved dominance in the marketplace.* ◇ *Ex-colonial countries began to challenge the cultural dominance of Europe.*

strong (*approving*) (of people or groups) having a lot of power or influence: *Will this damage his image as a strong leader?* ◇ *What the country needs right now is a* **strong government.** OPP **weak** ❶ A weak person or group does not have much power and is easy to influence: (*disapproving*) *a weak and cowardly man* ◇ *In a* **weak moment** (= when I was easily persuaded) *I said she could borrow the car.*

influential /ˌɪnflu'enʃl/ (of people, groups and ideas) having a lot of influence on sth, especially within a particular area of interest: *The committee was influential in formulating government policy on employment.* ◇ *This was a* **highly influential** *book.*

important (of people or groups) having a lot of power or influence: *He likes to* **feel important.** ◇ *Many disabled people do now hold important jobs in industry.*

NOTE POWERFUL, STRONG, INFLUENTIAL OR IMPORTANT? People or groups who are **powerful, strong, influen-tial** or **important** all have a lot of power or influence. **Powerful** is the most general word and describes sb who has power, especially because of their position, and is able to use it to control people and events. Leaders, politicians and top business people are often described as **powerful. Strong** especially describes sb who is in a position of power and also has the skills and qualities needed to use their power effectively. A leader might be **powerful** because of their position, but a **strong leader** is confident and has leadership qualities. **Influential** describes sb/sth that people respect, listen to or take notice of and that therefore influences their opinions or behaviour. **Important** often describes sb who has a lot of influence on other people or events because they are respected or because what they do has a greater effect than what others do.

great having high status and a lot of influence: *the great powers* (= important and powerful countries) ◇ *We can make this country great again.* ◇ *Alexander the Great*

instrumental /ˌɪnstrəˈmentl/ (*rather formal*) important in making sth happen: *He was instrumental in bringing about an end to the conflict.*

high-'powered (of politicians and business people) having a lot of power and influence; (of jobs and activities) important or with a lot of responsibility: *She's a high-powered executive with a salary to match.* ◇ *He has a very high-powered job and a hectic schedule.*

practical *adj.*

practical · experimental · empirical · applied · hands-on
These words all describe things that are connected with real situations rather than with ideas or theories.

PATTERNS AND COLLOCATIONS
▸ practical / experimental / empirical / applied **knowledge**
▸ practical / hands-on **experience**
▸ a practical / an experimental / an empirical **investigation**
▸ experimental / empirical **evidence / research**

practical connected with real situations rather than with ideas or theories: *practical advice/help/support* ◇ *practical problems/difficulties* ◇ *There are some obvious practical applications of the research.* ◇ *In practical terms, it means spending less.* ◇ *From a practical point of view, it isn't a good place to live.* **OPP** **theoretical** → INTELLECTUAL 1

experimental connected with scientific experiments: *experimental conditions/methods/data* ◇ *experimental physics* **OPP** **theoretical** → INTELLECTUAL 1

empirical /ɪmˈpɪrɪkl/ [usually before noun] (*formal*) based on experiments or experience rather than ideas or theories: *an empirical study of children's language*

applied [usually before noun] (especially of a subject of study) used in a practical way: *applied mathematics* (= used by engineers, etc.) **OPP** **pure** ❶ **Pure** describes subjects that people study to increase their knowledge of the subject, rather than in order to use that knowledge in a practical way: *technology as opposed to pure science subjects*

hands-'on [usually before noun] (*rather informal*) doing sth rather than just talking about it: *hands-on computer training* ◇ *You will need to gain hands-on experience of industry.*

practise (*BrE*) (*AmE* **practice**) *verb* See also the entry for TRAIN 2

practise · rehearse · go over sth · run through sth
These words all mean to improve a performance or skill, or to study sth, especially by repeating it.

PATTERNS AND COLLOCATIONS
▸ to practise / rehearse **for** sth
▸ to practise / rehearse / go over sth / run through sth **again**
▸ to practise / rehearse **regularly**

practise (*BrE*) (*AmE* **practice**) [I, T] to do an activity or train regularly so that you can improve your skill: *You need to practise every day.* ◇ *She's been practising hard for her piano exam.* ◇ *I've been practising my tennis serve for weeks.* ◇ *He usually wants to practise his English on me.* ◇ *Practise reversing the car into the garage.* See also **practice** → TRAINING, **practised** → EXPERIENCED

rehearse /rɪˈhɜːs; *AmE* rɪˈhɜːrs/ [I, T] to practise or make people practise a play, piece of music, etc. in preparation for a public performance; to prepare in your mind or

practise privately what you are going to do or say to sb: *We were given only two weeks to rehearse.* ◇ *Today, we'll just be rehearsing the final scene.* ◇ *The actors were poorly rehearsed.* ◇ *She mentally rehearsed what she would say to Jeff.* See also **rehearsal** → TRAINING

go 'over sth *phrasal verb* to study or explain sth carefully, especially by repeating it: *Let's not go over all this again.* ◇ *Can we just go over those instructions one more time?* ◇ *He went over the events of the day in his mind* (= thought about them carefully). See also the entry for REPEAT 1

run 'through sth *phrasal verb* to perform, practise or repeat sth quickly: *Can we run through Scene 3 again?* ◇ *Could we run through your proposals once again?*
▸ **'run-through** *noun* [C]: *Can we have just one more run-through?*

praise *noun*

praise · credit · approval · acclaim · flattery · adulation · a pat on the back
These are all words for feelings or words that express admiration for sb's actions, achievements or appearance.

PATTERNS AND COLLOCATIONS
▸ praise / credit / approval / acclaim / a pat on the back **for** sth / doing sth
▸ praise / approval / acclaim / adulation / a pat on the back **from** sb
▸ **great** praise / credit / acclaim
▸ **public** praise / approval / acclaim / adulation
▸ **universal / widespread** praise / approval / acclaim
▸ to **deserve** praise / credit / acclaim / a pat on the back
▸ to **earn / win** praise / approval / acclaim
▸ to **get** praise / credit / approval / a pat on the back
▸ to **receive** praise / credit / approval / acclaim
▸ to **give sb** praise / credit / approval / a pat on the back

praise [U] (also *less frequent* **praises** [pl.]) words that show that you admire sb/sth or are pleased with what they have done: *His teachers are full of praise for the progress he's making.* ◇ *She wrote poems in praise of freedom.* ◇ *His latest movie has won high praise from the critics.* ◇ *They always sing his praises* (= praise him very highly).

credit [U] praise for sb because they are responsible for sth good that has happened: *I can't take all the credit for the show's success — it was a team effort.* ◇ *We did all the work and she gets all the credit!* ◇ *At least give him credit for trying* (= praise him because he tried, even if he did not succeed). **OPP** **blame** → FAULT

NOTE **PRAISE** OR **CREDIT**? **Praise** describes what you actually say, for example: *Well done!* ◇ *You did a great job.* ◇ *I think he's a wonderful cook.* **Credit** more often refers to an opinion or a feeling of admiration, not the actual words you say: *We should give due credit to the organizers of this event* (= we think they did a good job). **Credit** can suggest that you are rewarded for the good thing you have done: *Credit will be given in the exam for good spelling and grammar* (= you will get extra marks).

approval [U] the feeling that sb/sth is good or acceptable; a positive opinion of sb/sth: *Do the plans meet with your approval?* ◇ *Several people nodded in approval.* **OPP** **disapproval** → CRITICISM, See also **approve** → IN FAVOUR

acclaim /əˈkleɪm/ [U] (*rather formal*) public praise for sb/sth, especially an artistic achievement: *Her latest novel has received widespread critical acclaim.* ◇ *The play opened last week to universal acclaim.*

flattery [U] praise that is not sincere, especially in order to get what you want from sb: *You're too intelligent to fall for his flattery.* ◇ *Flattery will get you nowhere* (= it will not get you what you want). See also **flatter** → FLATTER

adulation /ˌædjuˈleɪʃn; *AmE* ˌædʒəˈl-/ [U] (*formal*) great admiration and praise for sb, especially for sb famous: *The band enjoy the adulation of their fans wherever they* go. **❶ Adulation** often suggests too much admiration: *He found it difficult to cope with the adulation from those around him.*

a ˌpat on the ˈback *idiom* (*rather informal*) praise or approval for sth that you have done well: *He deserves a pat on the back for all his hard work.* ◇ *Give yourself a pat on the back!*

praise *verb* See also the entry for FLATTER

praise · congratulate · hail · applaud · celebrate · acclaim · commend · glorify · compliment · rave
These words all mean to express admiration or approval of sb/sth.

praise	hail	glorify
congratulate	applaud	rave
commend	celebrate	
compliment	acclaim	

PATTERNS AND COLLOCATIONS
▸ to praise / congratulate / applaud / commend sb **for** (doing) sth
▸ to congratulate / commend / compliment sb **on** sth
▸ to praise / hail / acclaim sb / sth **as** sth
▸ to praise / hail / applaud / commend a **decision / plan**
▸ to praise / applaud / commend sb's **effort / courage**
▸ to praise / congratulate / applaud / commend sb **warmly**
▸ to be **highly / widely / universally** praised / acclaimed / commended
▸ sb **is to be / should be** congratulated / applauded / commended

praise [T] to express your approval or admiration for sb/ sth: *He praised his team for their performance.* ◇ *They were praised by police for reporting the theft.* ◇ *Critics praised the work as highly original.* **OPP** criticize → BLAME
congratulate /kən'grætʃuleɪt/ [T] to tell sb that you are pleased about their success or achievements: *I congratulated them all on their results.* ◇ *The authors are to be congratulated on producing such a clear and authoritative work.*

▸ **congratulations** /kənˌgrætʃu'leɪʃnz/ *noun* [pl.]: *Congratulations on your exam results!*

NOTE **PRAISE** OR **CONGRATULATE?** The object of the verb **praise** can be a person, or their qualities, abilities or achievements, but the object of **congratulate** must be a person: *I praised/congratulated him.* ◇ *I praised his ability to stay calm under pressure.* ◇ *I congratulated his ability to stay calm.* You might **praise** a child, an employee or sb else that you are responsible for or have authority over. You would NOT usually praise your friend, partner, boss or sb who is older than you or has authority over you: *He praised/congratulated his son/ class/team.* ◇ *He congratulated his colleague.* ◇ *He praised his colleague.* You would **congratulate** sb on sth they have achieved on a particular occasion, especially when there is an obvious result: *She congratulated me on passing my driving test.* ◇ *She praised me for the way I deal with difficult customers.*

hail [T, usually passive] (*especially journalism*) to describe sb/ sth publicly as being very good or special: *The conference was hailed as a great success.* ◇ *Teenager Matt Brown is being hailed a hero for saving a young child from drowning.*
applaud /ə'plɔːd/ [T] (not usually used in the progressive tenses) (*formal*) to express praise for sb/sth because you approve of them/it: *We applaud her decision.* ◇ *I applaud her for having the courage to refuse.* **❶** Common collocates of **applaud** are *decision, effort, attitude, determination* and *courage.*
celebrate [T] (*formal*) to publicly express admiration of sb/sth, especially in a film, song or work of art: *songs that celebrate the joys of romantic love* ◇ *It was a movie celebrating the life and work of Martin Luther King.*

acclaim /ə'kleɪm/ [T, usually passive] (*rather formal*) to praise or welcome sb/sth publicly, especially a book, film, performance, etc. or a writer or performer: *Mario Vargas Llosa, the internationally acclaimed novelist* ◇ *The work was acclaimed as a masterpiece.*
commend /kə'mend/ [T] (*formal*) to praise sb/sth, especially publicly or officially: *She was commended on her handling of the situation.* ◇ *His designs were highly commended by the judges* (= they did not get a prize but they were especially praised).
glorify [T] (*often disapproving*) to describe or show sth in a way that makes it seem better or more important than it really is: *He denies that the movie glorifies violence.* **❶** If violence, crime, drug-taking, war, etc. is **glorified**, it is not exactly praised, but it is shown in a positive way that may encourage people to think it is good or acceptable. The word is most often used about the way violence, etc. is shown in films, on television or in books.
▸ **glorification** *noun* [U]: *the glorification of war*
compliment [T] to tell sb that you like or admire sth they have done, their behaviour or their appearance: *She complimented him on his excellent German.* **❶** **Compliment** is most often used to describe what individuals say to each other rather than a public or official expression of praise. See also **compliment** → TRIBUTE *noun*, **complimentary** → GOOD 6
rave [I] (*rather informal, especially journalism*) to talk or write about sth in a very enthusiastic way: *The critics raved about his performance in 'Hamlet'.* **❶** **Rave** is often used to talk about sb's reaction to a film, book, play, etc., especially in newspapers and magazines.

pray *verb*

pray · worship · praise · venerate
These words all mean to speak to God or show your respect for him.

PATTERNS AND COLLOCATIONS
▸ to pray to / worship / praise **God**

pray [I, T] to speak to God, especially to give thanks or ask for help: *They knelt down and prayed.* ◇ *I'll **pray for** you.* ◇ *to pray for peace/rain/forgiveness* ◇ *She prayed to God for an end to her sufferings.* ◇ *We **prayed (that)** he would recover from his illness.* ◇ *He prayed to be forgiven.*
▸ **prayer** *noun* [C, U]: *to say your prayers* ◇ *prayers for the sick* ◇ *It was a prayer she had learnt as a child.* ◇ *They knelt in prayer.*
worship (-pp-) [T, I] to show respect for God or a god, by saying prayers, singing, etc. with other people in a church, temple, etc.; to go to a religious service: *The Mayans built jungle pyramids to worship their gods.* ◇ *We worship at St Mary's.*
▸ **worship** *noun* [U]: *an act/a place of worship* ◇ *devil/ ancestor worship* ◇ *morning/evening worship* (= a church service in the morning/evening)
praise [T] to express your thanks to or your respect for God: *Praise the Lord.* ◇ *Allah be praised.*
▸ **praise** *noun* [U]: *hymns/songs of praise* ◇ *Praise be (to God)!* (= expressing belief or joy)
venerate /'venəreɪt/ [T] (*formal*) to have and show a lot of respect for sb/sth, especially sb/sth that is considered to be holy: *He was later venerated as a saint.*
▸ **veneration** *noun* [U]: *The relics were objects of veneration.*

precaution *noun*

precaution · defence · shield · safeguard · screen · buffer
These are all words for sth that protects sb/sth from harm or danger.

PATTERNS AND COLLOCATIONS
▸ a precaution / defence / shield / safeguard / buffer **against** sth
▸ **as** a precaution / defence / shield / safeguard / screen / buffer

▸ an **adequate** precaution / defence / safeguard
▸ to **provide** a defence / shield / safeguard / screen / buffer

precaution /prɪˈkɔːʃn/ [C] (*rather formal*) something that is done in advance in order to prevent problems or avoid danger: *Serious injury can occur if proper **safety precautions** are not followed.* ◇ *You must **take** all reasonable **precautions** to protect yourself.* See also **precautionary** → PROTECTIVE

defence (*BrE*) (*AmE* **defense**) [C, U] something that provides protection against attack from sth that is harmful such as enemies, the weather or illness: *The town walls were built as a defence against enemy attacks.* ◇ *The harbour's sea defences are in poor condition.* ◇ *The body has natural **defence mechanisms** to protect it from disease.* See also **defend** → PROTECT, **defensive** → PROTECTIVE

shield /ʃiːld/ [C] a person or thing used to protect sb/sth, especially by forming a barrier: *The gunman used the hostages as a **human shield**.* ◇ *She hid her true feelings behind a shield of cold indifference.* See also **shield** → PROTECT

safeguard /ˈseɪfɡɑːd/ *AmE* -ɡɑːrd/ [C] an action or law that is designed to protect people from harm, risk or danger: *The measures have been introduced as a safeguard against fraud.* ◇ *Stronger legal safeguards are needed to protect the consumer.* See also **safeguard** → PROTECT

screen [C] something that prevents sb from seeing or being aware of sth, or that protects sb/sth: *All the research was conducted behind a screen of secrecy.* ◇ *We planted a screen of tall trees.*

buffer [C] a thing or person that reduces a shock or protects sb/sth against difficulties: *Support from family and friends acts as a buffer against stress.* ◇ *Peacekeepers have been sent in to establish a **buffer zone** (= an area that keeps two other areas distant from one another) between the rival forces.*

predict verb

predict · forecast · say · foresee · project · prophesy
These words all mean to say what you think will happen in the future.

▸ to predict / forecast / foresee / prophesy **that...**
▸ to predict / forecast / say / foresee / prophesy **what / how / when / where / who / whether...**
▸ to be predicted / forecast / projected **to do sth**
▸ to predict / forecast / foresee / prophesy the **future**
▸ to predict / forecast / foresee **a trend / the outcome**
▸ to predict / foresee / prophesy **war / danger / sb's death**
▸ to be **difficult / impossible to** predict / forecast / say / foresee / project
▸ sth was **originally** predicted / forecast / foreseen / projected
▸ to predict / forecast / say sth in **advance**

predict [T] to say that sth will happen in the future: *a reliable method of predicting earthquakes* ◇ *It is impossible to predict with any certainty what effect this will have.* ◇ *She predicted (that) the election result would be close.* ◇ *The trial is predicted to last for months.* See also **prediction** → EXPECTATION

forecast /ˈfɔːkɑːst/ *AmE* ˈfɔːrkæst/ [T] to say what you think will happen in the future based on information you have now: *Experts are forecasting a recovery in the economy.* ◇ *Snow is forecast for tomorrow.* ◇ *The costs were higher than those originally forecast.* See also **forecast** → EXPECTATION

NOTE PREDICT OR FORECAST? Someone **predicts** what will happen based on information available, their knowledge, their opinions or using religious or magic powers. Someone usually **forecasts** sth based on information available and often using scientific methods.

say [T, I] (used especially in negative sentences and questions) (*rather informal, especially spoken*) to express your opinion about what you think will happen in the future: *Who can say what will happen between now and then?* ◇ *'When will it be finished?' 'I couldn't say.'*

foresee /fɔːˈsiː; *AmE* fɔːrˈsiː/ [T] to think sth is going to happen in the future; to know about sth before it happens: *No one could have foreseen that things would turn out this way.* ◇ *We do not foresee any problems.* See also **foresight** → EXPECTATION

project /prəˈdʒekt/ [T, usually passive] (*especially business*) to estimate what the size, cost or amount of sth will be in the future, based on what is happening now: *A growth rate of 4% is projected for next year.* ◇ *The unemployment rate has been projected to fall.* See also **projection** → EXPECTATION

prophesy /ˈprɒfəsaɪ; *AmE* ˈprɑːf-/ [T] to say what will happen in the future, especially using religious or magic powers: *He prophesied that a flood would cover the Earth's surface.* ◇ *He experienced visions and later prophesied his own death.* See also **prophecy** → EXPECTATION

predictable adj.

1 predictable results
2 You're so predictable!

1 predictable · foreseeable · unsurprising · to be expected
These words all describe sth that you can predict or that is likely to happen.

▸ predictable / foreseeable / unsurprising / to be expected **that...**
▸ a predictable / a foreseeable / an unsurprising **result**
▸ predictable / foreseeable **consequences**

predictable /prɪˈdɪktəbl/ if sth is **predictable**, you know or can guess in advance that it will happen or what it will be like: *He asked whether this was **predictable** from previous performances.* ◇ *The disease follows a highly predictable pattern.* ◇ *In March and April, the weather is much less predictable.* OPP **unpredictable** → SURPRISING
▸ **predictably** *adv*.: *Prices were predictably high.* ◇ *Predictably, the new regulations proved unpopular.*

foreseeable /fɔːˈsiːəbl; *AmE* fɔːrˈs-/ (*rather formal, especially written*) that you can predict will happen: *The statue will remain in the museum for **the foreseeable future** (= the period of time when you can predict what is going to happen, based on present circumstances).* ◇ *Some of these problems were not foreseeable or preventable.* OPP **unforeseeable** → SURPRISING

unsurprising as you would expect; not causing surprise: *Her failure to win the leadership race is unsurprising.* ◇ *It is unsurprising that people with dogs walk more than others.* OPP **surprising** → SURPRISING
▸ **unsurprisingly** *adv*.: *Perhaps unsurprisingly, she refused to talk to the press.*

to be ex'pected *phrase* likely to happen in a particular situation; quite normal: *A little tiredness after taking these drugs is to be expected.* ◇ *Of course, it's only to be expected that people will moan about paying tax.* See also **expect** → EXPECT

2 predictable · flat · tame · uneventful · uninspiring · unexciting
These words describe people and things that are dull and boring because there is nothing unexpected or new in them.

▸ an uneventful / uninspiring **game**
▸ an uneventful / unexciting **life**
▸ **rather** predictable / flat / tame / uneventful / uninspiring / unexciting

predictable /prɪˈdɪktəbl/ (*disapproving*) behaving or happening in a way that you would expect and therefore boring: *You're so predictable!* ◇ *Rock music has become so totally predictable.* **OPP** **unpredictable** → MOODY

flat (*disapproving*) lacking interest or enthusiasm: *Life may seem a bit flat without you.* ◇ *It was a curiously flat note on which to end the election campaign.*

tame (*rather informal, disapproving*) not interesting or exciting, often because no risks are taken: *You'll probably find life here pretty tame after New York.* **OPP** **wild** ❶ The opposite is **wild**: *We had a wild time in Las Vegas.*

uneventful /ˌʌnɪˈventfl/ in which nothing interesting, unusual, exciting or dangerous happens: *It's been a happy life, if uneventful by most people's standards.* ◇ *Thankfully the journey across the desert was uneventful.* ❶ **Uneventful** is often used to describe periods of time when you were afraid that sth bad would happen. **OPP** **eventful** → BUSY 2
▸ **uneventfully** *adv.*: *The first two nights passed uneventfully.*

uninspiring /ˌʌnɪnˈspaɪərɪŋ/ (*disapproving*) not making people feel interested or excited: *The new king was a dull, uninspiring figure.* **OPP** **inspiring** ❶ The opposite is **inspiring**: *an inspiring teacher*

unexciting /ˌʌnɪkˈsaɪtɪŋ/ (*disapproving*) dull and boring: *He is an earnest, unexciting politician.* **OPP** **exciting** → EXCITING

prefer *verb*

prefer · favour · would rather…
These words all mean to like one thing better than another.

prefer (**-rr-**) [T] (not used in the progressive tenses) to choose one thing rather than sth else because you like it better: *I prefer jazz to rock music.* ◇ *I would prefer it if you didn't tell anyone.* ◇ *A local firm is to be preferred.* ◇ *I prefer my coffee black.* ◇ *The donor prefers to remain anonymous.* ◇ *I prefer not to think about it.* ◇ *Would you prefer me to stay?* ◇ *I prefer playing in defence.* See also **preference** → CHOICE 2, **preference** → TASTE 1, **preferred** → FAVOURITE

favour (*BrE*) (*AmE* **favor**) [T] (*rather formal*) to prefer one system, plan, way of doing sth, etc. to another: *Many countries favour a presidential system of government.* ◇ *It's a resort favoured by families with young children.* See also **favourite, favoured** → FAVOURITE

would rather… *phrase* (*especially spoken*) (usually shortened to *'d rather*) would prefer to: *I'd rather die than give a speech.* ◇ *'Do you want to come with us?' 'No, I'd rather not.'* ◇ *Would you rather walk or take the bus?* ◇ *'Do you mind if I smoke?' 'Well, I'd rather you didn't.'*

prepare *verb*

1 prepare a report for the meeting
2 prepare for trouble/an exam

1 prepare · draw sth up · draft · put sth together · get sb/sth ready
These words all mean to make sth ready to be used or carried out, or to make sb ready to do sth.

PATTERNS AND COLLOCATIONS
▸ to prepare sth/draw sth up/draft sth/put sth together/get sth ready **for** sth
▸ to prepare/draw up/draft/put together a **list/report/paper/ plan/programme/strategy**
▸ to prepare/draw up/draft a/an **document/contract/agenda/ budget/constitution/treaty/petition/will**
▸ to prepare/put together a **show** ready/to get a **show** ready
▸ to prepare sth/draw sth up/draft sth/put sth together **carefully**

prepare [T] (*rather formal*) to make sb/sth ready to be used or to do sth: *I've asked her to prepare a report for the meeting.* ◇ *A hotel room is being prepared for them.* ◇ *The*

college prepares students for a career in business. See also **preparation** → PLANNING, **preparatory** → FIRST, **prepared** → READY

draw sth 'up *phrasal verb* to make or write sth that needs careful thought or planning: *Let's draw up a list of possible guests.* ❶ **Draw sth up** is often used to talk about preparing an official document: *to draw up a contract/ lease/document/treaty/charter/will.* It is also often used in other business contexts: *to draw up an agenda/a memorandum/a report/a shortlist/a strategy*

draft (also **draught** especially in *BrE*) /drɑːft; *AmE* dræft/ [T] to write the first rough version of sth such as a letter, speech or book: *I'll draft a letter for you.* ◇ *Some of the clauses in the contract had been very poorly drafted.* See also **draft** → PLAN *noun* 2

put sth to'gether *phrasal verb* to make or prepare sth by fitting or collecting parts together: *I think we can put together a very strong case for the defence.*

get sb/sth 'ready *idiom* (*rather informal*) to prepare sth to be used; to prepare sb to do sth: *Can you help me get everything ready for the party?* ◇ *I'm just getting the kids ready for school.*

2 prepare · get ready · provide for sth · gear (yourself) up
These words all mean to make yourself ready for sth that you are going to do or that you expect to happen.

PATTERNS AND COLLOCATIONS
▸ to prepare/get ready/provide/gear up **for** sth
▸ to prepare/get ready/gear up **to do sth**
▸ to prepare **yourself**/gear **yourself** up

prepare [I, T] (*rather formal*) to make yourself ready for sth that you are going to do or that you expect to happen: *I had no time to prepare.* ◇ *The whole class is preparing for the exams.* ◇ *I had been preparing myself for this moment.* ◇ *I was preparing to leave.* See also **preparation** → PLANNING, **preparatory** → FIRST, **prepared** → READY

get 'ready *phrase* (*rather informal, especially spoken*) to prepare for sth, especially sth that is part of your everyday life: *I have to get ready for work.* ❶ Other typical collocates include *school, dinner* and *supper*.

pro'vide for sth *phrasal verb* (*formal*) to make preparations to deal with sth that might happen in the future: *It is impossible to provide for every eventuality.* See also **provision** → PLANNING

gear 'up, gear yourself 'up *phrasal verb* (*rather informal, especially journalism*) to prepare for sth, especially a special event or challenge: *Cycle organizations are gearing up for National Bike Week.* ◇ *The supermarkets have been gearing themselves up to meet increased customer demand.*

present *verb*

1 present a new product
2 present sth as a victory
3 present a report
4 present a TV show

1 present · show · display · produce · unveil · launch
These words all mean to make sth available for other people to see.

PATTERNS AND COLLOCATIONS
▸ to present/show/display/unveil/launch a new **product/ model**
▸ to present/show/display **your wares**
▸ to present/show/unveil **plans**
▸ to show/display **a painting/your work/a collection/a trophy**
▸ to present/show/display sth **proudly**

present [T] to offer a new product or plan for other people to look at: *They are going to present the new model at the trade fair.*

show [I, T] to be or make sth available for the public to see: *The film is being shown now.* ◇ *She plans to show her paintings early next year.* See also **show** → EXHIBITION *noun*, **showing** → PROGRAMME

display [T] to put sth in a place where people can see it easily; to show sth to people: *The exhibition gives local artists an opportunity to display their work.* ◇ *She displayed her bruises for all to see.* See also **display** → EXHIBITION *noun*, **display** → SHOW *verb* 3, **put sth up** → HANG

NOTE SHOW OR DISPLAY? **Show** is the less formal and more general of these words. Artists themselves usually talk about **showing** their work. **Display** emphasizes that sth has been put where as many people as possible will see it, and usually also that it has been arranged in an attractive way.

produce [T] to show sth or make sth appear from somewhere: *He produced a letter from his pocket.* ◇ *At the meeting the finance director produced the figures for the previous year.*

unveil /ˌʌn'veɪl/ [T] (*journalism*) to show or introduce a new product or plan to the public for the first time: *They will be unveiling their new models at the Motor Show.* ◇ *The government has unveiled plans for new energy legislation.*

launch /lɔːntʃ/ [T] to introduce or show a new book or product to the public for the first time: *The book was launched amid a fanfare of publicity.* ◇ *The new model will be launched in July.* See also **launch** → LAUNCH *noun*

NOTE UNVEIL OR LAUNCH? You can *unveil/launch a product/model*, *unveil plans* or *launch a book*, but you cannot: ~~launch plans~~ or: ~~unveil a book~~.

2 See also the entry for DESCRIBE
present · show · portray · depict · represent
These words all mean to show what sb/sth is like or how you would like people to see sb/sth.

PATTERNS AND COLLOCATIONS
▸ to present / show / portray / depict / represent sb / sth **as** sth
▸ to present / show / portray / depict / represent sb / sth **accurately**
▸ to present / show / portray / depict sb / sth **clearly**
▸ to present / show / portray / depict sth **vividly**

present [T] (not usually used in the progressive tenses) to show or describe sb/sth from a particular point of view or in a particular way: *The decision had decided it must present a more modern image.* ◇ *You need to present yourself better.* ◇ *The article presents these proposals as misguided.*

show [T] (not usually used in the progressive tenses) (of a picture or photograph) to be of sb/sth: *She had objected to a photo showing her in a bikini.* ◇ *The picture shows St George slaying the dragon.*

portray /pɔː'treɪ; *AmE* pɔːr't-/ [T] (not usually used in the progressive tenses) (*rather formal*) to show sb/sth in a picture or describe sb/sth in a piece of writing; to present sb/sth in a particular way, especially when this does not give a complete or accurate impression of what they are like: *His war poetry vividly portrays life in the trenches.* ◇ *Throughout the trial, he portrayed himself as the victim.* See also **portrayal** → DESCRIPTION

depict /dɪ'pɪkt/ [T] (not usually used in the progressive tenses) (*rather formal*) to portray sb/sth in a particular way, especially in a work of art: *The panels depict scenes from the life of St Ursula.* ◇ *The advertisements depict smoking as glamorous and attractive.* See also **depiction** → DESCRIPTION

represent [T] (not usually used in the progressive tenses) (*formal*) to show sb/sth, especially in a picture; to present sb/sth in a particular way, especially when this may not be fair: *The results are represented in fig 3 below.* ◇ *The risks were represented as negligible.* See also **representation** → DESCRIPTION

NOTE PORTRAY OR DEPICT OR REPRESENT? **Represent** is the most formal but also the most general of these words and is used in texts such as reports and formal journalism. **Depict** is slightly more technical than **portray** and is used more often when talking about art, especially art that is not just pictures or paintings; typical subjects include *work, scene, panel, mosaic, tapestry* and *fresco*. **Portray** is used more often to talk about how things are presented in the media; typical objects include *character, image, idea, view* and *society*.

3 **present · submit · file · hand sth in · lodge · table · send sth in · register · put sth in**
These words all mean to offer sth for other people to consider or deal with.

PATTERNS AND COLLOCATIONS
▸ to present / submit / hand sth in / send in / put in sth **to** sb
▸ to present / submit / file / lodge / send in / register / put in an **application**
▸ to present / submit / file / lodge / register / put in a **claim / complaint**
▸ to present / submit / file / lodge an **appeal**
▸ to submit / file / lodge / register a / an **objection / protest**
▸ to present / submit / put in a **proposal / request**
▸ to present / submit / table a **bill / motion / resolution**
▸ to present / register / send in your **views**
▸ to present / submit / file / send in a **report**
▸ to **formally** present / submit / file / table / register sth

present [T] to offer sth for other people to consider: *Eight options were presented for consideration.* ◇ *Are you presenting a paper at the conference?* ◇ *He presents a convincing case.*
▸ **presentation** *noun* [U]: *The trial was adjourned following the presentation of new evidence to the court.*

submit /səb'mɪt/ (-**tt**-) [T] (*rather formal*) to give a document or proposal to sb in authority so that they can study or consider it: *They have submitted an application for planning permission to build an extension.* ◇ *Completed projects must be submitted by 10 March.*
▸ **submission** /səb'mɪʃn/ *noun* [U]: *When is the date for the submission of proposals?*

file [T, I] to submit a legal document, claim or charge so that it can be officially recorded and dealt with; (of a journalist) to send a report or story to a newspaper or news organization: *He filed a lawsuit against the company for $100 000 in damages.* ◇ *She decided to file for divorce.* ◇ *More than one correspondent filed a story describing the spectacle of a cruise missile travelling up the street.* ❶ You can also **file** *a suit*, a *claim*, a *petition*, an *appeal*, an *application*, *charges* or *for bankruptcy*.

hand sth 'in *phrasal verb* to give sth to a person in authority, especially a piece of work or sth that is lost: *You must hand in this homework by the end of the week.* ◇ *I handed the watch in to the police.* ◇ *I advise you to hand in your notice* (= formally tell your employer that you want to stop working for them).

lodge [T] (*formal*) to make a formal statement about sth to a public organization or authority: *They lodged a compensation claim against the factory.* ◇ *Portugal has lodged a complaint with the International Court of Justice.* ❶ You can also **lodge** an *appeal*, an *application*, an *objection* or a *protest*.

table [T] (*BrE*) to present sth formally for discussion: *They have tabled a motion for debate at the next Party Conference.* ❶ You can also **table** an *amendment*, a *motion*, a *question* or a *resolution*. See also the entry for PROPOSE

send sth 'in *phrasal verb* to send sth by post to a place where it will be dealt with: *Have you sent in your application yet?*

register [T] (*formal*) to make your opinion known officially or publicly: *China has registered a protest over foreign intervention.* ❶ You can also **register** your *view,* opinion, disapproval or a *complaint*. When you **register** your opinion, you are usually making your disapproval of sth known.

,**put sth 'in** *phrasal verb* to officially make a claim or request: *The company has put in a claim for damages.* ❶ You can also **put in** a *bid*, an *offer*, a *request* or a *proposal*.

4 present · host · introduce

These words all mean to appear in a television or radio programme and give details about the show and the people who are in it.

PATTERNS AND COLLOCATIONS
▸ to present / host / introduce a **programme / show**

present [T] (*BrE*) to be the main speaker in a television or radio show and introduce the different items in it: *She used to present a gardening show on TV.*

host [T] to present a television or radio show: *Charlie Rose will host tonight's show.* ❶ In American English **host** is the usual word for presenting a show; it is also used in British English, but mostly for shows that have invited guests and/or a studio audience.

introduce [T] (*especially spoken*) (in a television or radio show) to tell the audience the name of the person who is going to speak or perform: *May I introduce my first guest on the show tonight…*

presentation *noun*

presentation · demonstration · demo
These are all words for an occasion on which sth is explained or shown to a group of people, or the act of doing this.

PATTERNS AND COLLOCATIONS
▸ a **sales / product** presentation / demonstration / demo
▸ to **give / watch** a presentation / demonstration / demo

presentation /ˌprezn'teɪʃn; *AmE* ˌpriːzen-/ [C, U] a meeting at which sth, especially a new idea, product or piece of work, is shown to a group of people; the act of doing this: *The sales manager will give a **presentation on** the new products.* ◇ *The main emphasis of the training will be on presentation skills.*

demonstration /ˌdemən'streɪʃn/ [C] an occasion on which sb shows or explains how sth works or is done; the act of doing this: *We were given a brief demonstration of the computer's functions.*

NOTE **PRESENTATION** OR **DEMONSTRATION?** A **presentation** can be of a thing or an idea; a **demonstration** is always practical, either of a thing or a technique: *Candidates have to give a short presentation on a subject of their choice.* ◇ *Can you give me a practical demonstration?*

demo /'deməʊ; *AmE* -moʊ/ [C] (*informal*) a demonstration, especially an informal one: *Look, I'll give you a demo.*

presenter *noun* See the Topic Map for THE MEDIA on p.900, See also the entry for REPORTER

presenter · announcer · host · anchor/anchorman/ anchorwoman · broadcaster · commentator · newscaster · newsreader
These are all words for a person who presents or talks on television or radio shows.

PATTERNS AND COLLOCATIONS
▸ a **radio / television / TV** presenter / announcer / host / anchor / anchorman / anchorwoman / broadcaster / commentator / newscaster / newsreader
▸ a **news** anchor / anchorman / anchorwoman
▸ a **sports** presenter / announcer / anchor / anchorman / anchorwoman / broadcaster / commentator

presenter [C] (*BrE*) a person who introduces the different sections of a radio or television show: *Jenni Murray, presenter of 'Woman's Hour'* ❶ In American English, a person who does this job is called an **announcer**.

announcer [C] a person who introduces, or gives information about, shows on radio or television: *The continuity announcer advertised a few forthcoming programmes.*

host [C] (*especially AmE*) a person who introduces and talks to guests on a television or radio show: *a TV game show host*

anchor /'æŋkə(r)/ (*especially AmE*) (also **anchorman**, **anchorwoman** *BrE, AmE*) [C] a person who presents a radio or television news programme and introduces reports by other people: *ABC news anchor Peter Jennings* ❶ In American English a **news anchor** presents news items and a **sports anchor** presents sports items. In British English an **anchorman**, **anchorwoman** or **news anchor** presents news items, but **sports anchor** is not usually used.

broadcaster [C] (*rather formal*) a person whose job is presenting or talking on television or radio programmes: *She is a writer and broadcaster on environmental matters.*

NOTE **PRESENTER, ANNOUNCER, HOST, ANCHOR** OR **BROADCASTER?** An **anchor** presents news programmes; a **presenter** (*BrE*) or **announcer** (*AmE*) presents any type of television or radio show. In British English a **host** presents an entertainment show with invited guests and/or a studio audience; in American English **host** can also describe sb who presents more serious shows. A **broadcaster** may present or talk on a variety of different shows but is not in charge of a particular show: *Jenni Murray, anchor/broadcaster of 'Woman's Hour'*

commentator /'kɒmənteɪtə(r); *AmE* 'kɑːm-/ [C] (*especially BrE*) a person who describes an event while it is happening, especially on television or radio: *He's one of the great sports commentators of our time.*

newscaster [C] (*formal*) a person who reads the news on television or radio: *She was named newscaster of the year.*

newsreader [C] (*BrE*) newscaster: *The newsreader reported that the man had not yet been named.*

president *noun*

president · prime minister · governor · chancellor · premier · head of state
These are all words for leaders of countries or governments.

PATTERNS AND COLLOCATIONS
▸ a **strong** president / prime minister
▸ the **acting / deputy** president / prime minister / governor / premier / head of state
▸ the **interim / incoming / outgoing** president / prime minister / governor
▸ to **elect sb / serve / be sworn in as** president / prime minister / governor / chancellor / head of state
▸ sb's **term as** president / prime minister / governor / chancellor
▸ the president's / prime minister's / governor's / chancellor's **office**

president (also **President**) [C] the leader of a republic, such as the United States; often used as a title: *Several presidents attended the funeral.* ◇ *President Obama is due to visit the country next month.* ◇ *Do you have any comment, Mr President?*

,**prime 'minister** (also **Prime Minister**) [C] the main minister and leader of the government in some countries: *She soon emerged as a strong prime minister.* ◇ *The Prime Minister is coming under yet more pressure over the issue.* ❶ In British English, **Prime Minister** is not used as a title: *I had a meeting with the Prime Minister, David Cameron.* However, in American English it can be used as a title in the same way as **President**: (*AmE*) *I would like to welcome Prime Minister Cameron.*

governor (also **Governor**) [C] a person who is the official leader of a country or region that is politically controlled by another country; the leader of the government of a state in the US; used as a title: *The report was written by Chris Patten, the former governor of Hong Kong.* ◇ *a* **provincial/State governor** ◇ *Governor Jon Corzine of New Jersey*

chancellor (also **Chancellor**) /'tʃɑːnsələ(r); *AmE* 'tʃæns-/ [C] the leader of the government in Germany or Austria; used as a title: *Helmut Kohl was the first chancellor of a united Germany.* ◇ *The talks will be headed by Germany's Chancellor Merkel.*

premier /'premiə(r); *AmE* prɪ'mɪr; -'mjɪr/ [C] (*journalism*) the leader of the country, state or province, especially a prime minister: *He expressed his concerns in a letter to the Irish premier.*

,head of 'state (pl. **heads of state**) [C] the official leader of a country who is sometimes also the leader of the government: *The Queen was joined by the US President and other heads of state from around the world.*

press *verb*

1 press the button
2 press sb to make a decision

1 press · push · squeeze

These words all mean to put pressure on part of a device with your finger, hand or foot in order to make it work.

PATTERNS AND COLLOCATIONS
▶ to press/ push/ squeeze **on** sth
▶ to press/ push a **bell** / **button** / **key** / **bell** / **switch**
▶ to press/ push/ squeeze (sth) **hard** / **gently**

press [T, I] to put pressure on part of a device or machine in order to make it work: *Press any key to restart your computer.* ◇ *She pressed the gas pedal gently.* ◇ *Press here to open.*

push [T] to press a button, switch, etc. with your finger or hand, usually in order to make a machine start working: *Push the red button to open the doors.* ❶ In this meaning **push** is usually used with *button*, although other words, like *switch* and *bell*, can also be used.

squeeze [T, I] to press sth firmly with your fingers or hand, especially in order to make sth work or do sth: *He slowly* **squeezed the trigger** (= of a gun). ◇ *She squeezed on the reins and the cart came to a halt.*

NOTE WHICH WORD? Press is the most general word. You can **press** sth with your finger, your hand or your foot. **Push** is mostly used with the word *button*. You **squeeze** sth by bending a finger or all your fingers round it.

2 press · push · pressure · coerce · pressurize · twist sb's arm

These words all mean to try hard to persuade or force sb to do sth that they do not want to do.

push	press	pressure	coerce
		pressurize	
		twist sb's arm	

PATTERNS AND COLLOCATIONS
▶ to press/ push/ pressure/ coerce/ pressurize sb **into** (doing) sth
▶ to press sb/ push sb/ pressure sb/ coerce sb/ pressurize sb/ twist sb's arm **to do sth**
▶ to press/ push sb **for** sth

press [T] to try hard to persuade sb to do sth, especially sth they do not want to do: *The bank is pressing us for repayment of the loan.* ◇ *They are pressing us to make a quick decision.* ◇ *I did not press him further on the issue* (= ask him more questions about it). ❶ People often say that sb **presses** sb to say sth or to answer a question, for example a journalist trying hard to get an answer or some

information from a politician, by questioning them repeatedly: *When pressed by journalists, he refused to comment.* See also **press for sth** → DEMAND *verb*

push [T] to try to persuade or encourage sb to do sth, especially sth they do not want to do: *My teacher pushed me into entering the competition.* ◇ *No one pushed you to take the job, did they?*

NOTE PRESS OR PUSH? In many cases you can use either word: *They were pressing/pushing the minister for a decision.* However, **press** can be more forceful than **push**: you **press** people to do things that you want or need them to do; you might **push** sb to do sth that you think they would actually enjoy or benefit from: ~~My teacher pressed me into entering the competition.~~

pressure [T, often passive] (*especially AmE*) to try to persuade or force sb to do sth, especially by making them feel that they have to or should do it: *Don't let yourself be pressured into making a hasty decision.* ◇ *No one has the right to pressure you. You can always say no.* ❶ In British English the more usual word for this is **pressurize**; however, **pressure** is also used.

coerce /kəʊ'ɜːs; *AmE* koʊ'ɜːrs/ [T] (*rather formal*) to force sb to do sth by using threats: *They were coerced into negotiating a settlement.* ◇ *She hadn't coerced him in any way.*

pressurize (*BrE* also **-ise**) /'preʃəraɪz/ [T, often passive] (*BrE*) to pressure sb: *Stop trying to pressurize me!*

twist sb's 'arm *idiom* (*informal*) to try to persuade or force sb to do sth, often in a friendly way: *No one twisted my arm. I wanted to come.*

pressure *noun*

1 the pressures of work
2 the pressure to conform

1 pressure · stress · tension · strain · demands · heat

These are all words for the feelings of anxiety caused by the problems in sb's life.

PATTERNS AND COLLOCATIONS
▶ to be **under** pressure/ stress/ strain
▶ pressure/ stress/ demands/ heat **on** sb
▶ **considerable** pressure/ stress/ tension/ strain/ demands
▶ **social** / **economic** / **financial** pressure/ stress/ demands
▶ to **cause** stress/ tension/ strain
▶ to **cope with** the pressure/ stress/ tension/ strain/ demands
▶ to **deal with** / **handle** the pressure/ stress/ tension/ demands
▶ to **relieve** / **release** the pressure/ stress/ tension/ strain
▶ to **feel** the pressure/ tension/ strain/ heat
▶ to **take** the pressure/ strain/ heat
▶ to **suffer from** stress/ tension

pressure [U] (also **pressures** [pl.]) difficulties and feelings of anxiety that are caused by the need to achieve sth or to behave in a particular way: *She was unable to attend because of the pressure of work.* ◇ *How can anyone enjoy the pressures of city life?* See also **under pressure** → TENSE

stress [U, C, usually pl.] pressure or anxiety caused by the problems in sb's life: *emotional/mental stress* ◇ *stress-related illnesses* ◇ *Stress is often a factor in the development of long-term sickness.* ◇ *She failed to withstand the **stresses and strains** of public life.* See also **stressful** → STRESSFUL, **stressed** → TENSE

NOTE PRESSURE OR STRESS? It is common to say that sb *is suffering from stress*; **pressure** may be the thing that causes **stress**.

tension [U, C, usually pl.] a feeling of anxiety and stress that makes it impossible to relax: *She was suffering from nervous tension.* ◇ *Walking and swimming are excellent for releasing tensions.* See also **tense** → STRESSFUL, **tense** → TENSE

strain [U, C] pressure on sb/sth because they have too much to do or manage; the problems, worry or anxiety that this produces: *Their marriage is under great strain at* the moment. ◊ These repayments are **putting a strain on** our finances. ◊ Relax, and let us take the strain (= do things for you). See also **strained** → STRESSFUL, **strained** → TENSE

demands [pl.] things that sb/sth makes you do, especially things that are difficult or make you tired or worried: *the demands of children/work* ◊ *Flying* **makes** *enormous* **demands** *on pilots.*

heat [U] (*rather informal, especially journalism*) pressure on sb to do or achieve sth: *The* **heat is on** *now that the election is only a week away.* ◊ *Can she take the heat of this level of competition?*

---

2 pressure · force · coercion · compulsion
These are all words for the act of trying to make sb do sth, sometimes using threats or violence.

pressure	coercion	force
	compulsion	

PATTERNS AND COLLOCATIONS
▸ pressure / compulsion **on** sb
▸ **under** pressure / coercion / compulsion
▸ **by** force / coercion / compulsion
▸ pressure / compulsion **to do sth**
▸ **physical** pressure / force / coercion
▸ **legal** pressure / compulsion
▸ to **use** force / coercion

pressure [U] the act of trying to persuade or force sb to do sth: *The* **pressure for** *change continued to mount.* ◊ *My parents never* **put any pressure on** *me to work in the family business.* ◊ *Teenagers may find it difficult to resist* **peer pressure** (= pressure to behave in the same way as others of your age).

force [U] physical violence used to make sb do sth or to achieve sth: *We will achieve much more by persuasion than by* **brute force.** ◊ *There were plans to seize power by* **force of arms** (= by military action). See also **force** → FORCE *verb*

coercion /kəʊˈɜːʃn; *AmE* koʊˈɜːrʒn/ [U] (*formal*) the act of making sb do sth that they do not want to, using threats or force: *His defence was that he was* **acting under coercion.**

compulsion [U, C] (*rather formal*) strong pressure that makes sb do sth they do not want to do, especially sth they should do according to a law, rule or contract: *You are* **under no compulsion** *to pay.* ◊ *There are no compulsions on students to attend classes.* See also **compel** → FORCE *verb*, **compulsory** → NECESSARY

---

pretence(*BrE*) (*AmE* **pretense**) *noun*

pretence · cover · mask · front · façade · act
These are all words for the act of behaving in a particular way, in order to make other people believe sth that is not true.

PATTERNS AND COLLOCATIONS
▸ a cover / mask / front **for** sth
▸ to **put on** a pretence / a mask / a front / an act
▸ to **maintain** a pretence / cover / front / façade
▸ to **keep up** a pretence / a front / an act
▸ to **see through** a pretence / an act

pretence (*BrE*) (*AmE* **pretense**) [U, sing.] the act of behaving in a particular way, in order to make other people believe sth that is not true: *By the end of the evening she had abandoned all pretence of being interested.* ◊ *She was unable to keep up the* **pretence that** *she loved him.*

cover [C, usually sing.] activities or behaviour designed to hide sb's real identity or feelings, or to hide sth illegal: *His work as a banker was a cover for his activities as a spy.* ◊ *It*

would only take one phone call to **blow their cover** (= make known their true identities and what they were really doing).

mask [C, usually sing.] (*literary*) a manner or expression that hides your true character or feelings: *Behind the* **mask** *of indifference she was grinning.* ◊ *The* **mask** *of politeness* **slipped** *for a moment.*

front [sing.] behaviour that is not genuine, designed to hide your true feelings or opinions: *It's not always easy putting on a* **brave front** *for the family.*

> **NOTE COVER** OR **FRONT**? **Cover** is often used to talk about behaviour or actions which hide illegal activities. **Front** is used about situations where sb tries to hide real feelings, because their real feelings might cause embarrassment, either to themselves or others.

façade [C, usually sing.] (*rather formal, especially written*) the way that sb/sth appears to be, which is different from the way sb/sth really is: *She managed to maintain a façade of indifference.* ◊ *Squalor and poverty lay behind the city's glittering façade.*

act [sing.] a way of behaving that is not sincere but is intended to have a particular effect on others: *Don't take her seriously – it's all an act.*

---

pretend *verb*

pretend · act · feign · put sth on · adopt · fake · bluff · assume
These words all mean to behave in a particular way, in order to make other people believe sth that is not true.

PATTERNS AND COLLOCATIONS
▸ to pretend / feign / assume **interest / indifference**
▸ to feign / fake **illness / injury**
▸ to put on / adopt / assume **an accent**
▸ to put on / adopt / assume **an air of** concern / indifference, etc.

pretend [I, T] to behave in a particular way, in order to make other people believe sth that is not true: *I'm tired of having to pretend all the time.* ◊ *Of course it was wrong; it would be hypocritical to* **pretend otherwise.** ◊ *I pretended to be asleep.* ◊ *He pretended not to notice.* ◊ *She* **pretended (that)** *she was his niece.* ◊ *He* **pretended to** *his family that everything was fine.* ◊ (*formal*) *He hurt her by pretending an interest he did not feel?* ❶ **Pretend** is followed by a noun only in formal contexts.

act [I] (used with a noun or adjective complement) to pretend by your behaviour to be a particular type of person: *He's been acting the devoted husband all day.* ◊ *I decided to act dumb.* See also **act** → PLAY *verb* 3

feign /feɪn/ [T] (*rather formal, written*) to pretend that you have a particular emotion or that you are ill, injured, asleep or dead: *He survived the massacre by feigning death.* ◊ *'A present for me?' she asked with feigned surprise.*

put sth 'on *phrasal verb* (*rather informal*) to pretend to be thinking or feeling sth; to pretend to have a particular way of speaking: *I don't think she was hurt. She was just* **putting it on.** ◊ *He put on an American accent.*

adopt [T] (*formal*) to use a particular manner, expression or way of speaking: *She adopted an air of indifference.* ◊ *He smiled and adopted a more casual tone of voice.*

fake [T, I] (*rather informal*) to pretend that you are ill, injured or have a particular physical feeling: *She's not really sick – she's just faking it.* ◊ *He faked a yawn.* ◊ *Do you think she's faking?* ❶ When **fake** is used without an object, it is usually in a negative statement or a question, and in the form *faking*: *But what if he wasn't faking?*

bluff [I, T] to try to make sb believe that you will do sth that you do not really intend to do, or that you know sth that you do not really know: *I don't think he'll shoot – I think he's just bluffing.* ◊ *She successfully* **bluffed her way** *through the interview* (= by pretending to be sb she was not or know things that she did not know). See also **bluff** → TRICK *noun*

assume /əˈsjuːm; *AmE* əˈsuːm/ [T] (*formal, sometimes disapproving*) to pretend to be thinking or feeling sth; to pretend to have a particular way of speaking: *She assumed an air of concern.* ◇ *He had assumed a stage Southern accent.*

> **NOTE** PUT STH ON, ADOPT OR ASSUME? Put sth on is rather informal; **adopt** and **assume** are formal. **Assume** is more disapproving than **adopt** and suggests that sb's behaviour is false.

pretension *noun*

pretension · snobbery · airs · affectation
These are all words for behaviour that shows that sb thinks they are more important, intelligent, etc. than they actually are, especially to impress other people.

PATTERNS AND COLLOCATIONS
▸ **without** pretension / affectation
▸ **intellectual / social** pretensions / snobbery

pretension /prɪˈtenʃn/ [C, usually pl., U] (*disapproving*) the act of trying to appear more important, more intelligent or of higher social status than you really are in order to impress other people: *The play mocks the pretensions of the new middle class.* ◇ *She was charmed by his lack of pretension.* See also **pretentious** → FLASHY
snobbery /ˈsnɒbəri; *AmE* ˈsnɑːb-/ [U] (*disapproving*) the attitudes and behaviour of people who think they are better than other people (especially because they think they are more intelligent or have better taste), or have no respect for people from the lower social classes: *We have to overcome a degree of snobbery about diesel cars.* ◇ *She quickly ran up against snobbery and prejudice.* ❶ In British English **inverted snobbery** is the attitude that disapproves of everything connected with high social status and that is proud of low social status. See also **snobbish** → PATRONIZING
airs [pl.] (*disapproving*) behaviour that shows that sb thinks they are more important, better educated or of higher social status than they really are: *I hate the way she puts on airs.* ◇ (*BrE*) *Even when he became a star he didn't have any airs and graces.*
affectation /ˌæfekˈteɪʃn/ [C, U] (*usually disapproving*) behaviour or an action that is not natural or sincere and that is often intended to impress other people: *His little affectations irritated her.* ◇ *He speaks clearly and without affectation.*

prevent *verb* See also the entry for THWART

prevent · stop · avoid · keep sb from sth · avert · preclude · rule sb/sth out · restrain
These words all mean to cause sth not to happen or sb not to do sth.

PATTERNS AND COLLOCATIONS
▸ to prevent / stop / keep / preclude / restrain **sb from doing sth**
▸ to prevent sb / stop / avoid / preclude **doing sth**
▸ to prevent / stop / avoid / avert a / an **crisis / accident**
▸ to prevent / avoid / avert a **disaster / catastrophe / tragedy / conflict**
▸ to prevent / stop the **spread** of sth
▸ to prevent / avoid / preclude / rule out the **possibility** of sth
▸ to prevent / avoid / preclude the **need / necessity** for sth / to do sth
▸ to **forcibly / physically** prevent / stop / restrain sb / sth
▸ to **narrowly** avoid / avert sth
▸ to prevent / avoid sth **altogether / at all costs**

prevent [T] to cause sth not to happen or sb not to do sth, especially by taking action before it happens: *These strategies are aimed at preventing crime.* ◇ *He is prevented by law from holding a licence.* ◇ *Nothing would prevent him from speaking out against injustice.* See also **preventive** → PROTECTIVE

▸ **prevention** *noun* [U]: *accident / crime prevention* ◇ *the prevention of disease*
stop (-**pp**-) [T] to prevent sb from doing sth; to prevent sth from happening: *I want to go and you can't stop me.* ◇ *The activists failed to stop the tests from going ahead.* ◇ *There's nothing to stop you from accepting the offer.*

> **NOTE** PREVENT OR STOP? In many cases you can use either word, although **stop** is less formal. **Prevent** is more likely to suggest action that sb plans in advance so that sth does not even start to happen; **stop** is used more to talk about immediate action that sb takes to end sth that is already in progress.

avoid [T] to prevent sth bad from happening: *The accident could have been avoided.* ◇ *They narrowly avoided defeat in the semi-final.* ◇ *Getting involved in a court case is something to be avoided at all costs.*
keep sb from sth *phrasal verb* to prevent sb from doing sth that they want or need to do: *I hope I'm not keeping you from your work.* ◇ *The church bells keep me from sleeping.*
avert /əˈvɜːt; *AmE* əˈvɜːrt/ [T] (*written*) to prevent sth bad or dangerous from happening, especially sth that was likely to happen soon: *A disaster was narrowly averted.* ◇ *He did his best to avert suspicion.* ◇ *Talks are taking place in an attempt to avert a strike.*
preclude /prɪˈkluːd/ [T] (*formal*) to prevent sth from happening or sb from doing sth; to make sth impossible: *Lack of time precludes further discussion.* ◇ *His religious beliefs precluded him serving in the army.* ❶ Circumstances and events, NOT people, **preclude** things.
rule sb/sth 'out *phrasal verb* to prevent sb from doing sth or sth from happening, especially by making it impossible according to rules or practical considerations: *His age effectively ruled him out as a possible candidate.* ◇ *Common sense and logistics ruled out this option.*
restrain /rɪˈstreɪn/ [T] (*rather formal, written*) to prevent sb/sth from doing sth, especially by using physical force: *I had to restrain her from hitting out at passers-by.*

previous *adj.*

previous · old · former · past · prior · distant · remote · bygone
These words all describe sth belonging to to an earlier time.

PATTERNS AND COLLOCATIONS
▸ (a) previous / former / past / distant / remote / bygone **era / times**
▸ a previous / past / distant / remote / bygone **age**
▸ a previous / former / past / prior **existence**
▸ (a) previous / past **experience / history / life**
▸ a previous / former / past **owner / president / prime minister**
▸ a previous / prior **engagement**
▸ previous / prior **knowledge**
▸ former / past **glories**
▸ the distant / remote **past**
▸ a distant / remote **ancestor**
▸ very / fairly old / distant / remote

previous [only before noun] happening or existing before the event or object that you are talking about: *No previous experience is necessary for this job.* ◇ *The car has only had one previous owner.* ◇ *She is his daughter from a previous marriage.* ◇ *We had met on two previous occasions.* **OPP** RECENT, **future** → NEXT
▸ **previously** *adv.*: *The building had previously been used as a hotel.* **OPP** currently → RECENT
old [only before noun] belonging to an earlier time or to an earlier time in your life: *Things were different in the old days.* ◇ *I went back to visit my old school.*
former [only before noun] (*rather formal*) gone by in time; belonging to an earlier time: *This fine ruin was, in former times, a royal castle.* ◇ *The historic quarter of the city has been restored to its former glory.* ◇ *It is one of the countries of the former Soviet Union.*

▶ **formerly** *adv.*: *I learned that the house had formerly been an inn.*

past [usually before noun] gone by in time; belonging to an earlier time: *In past years the industry received large subsidies.* ◇ *The book is a celebration of working class life in times past.* ◇ *The time for discussion is past.* ◇ *From past experience I'd say he'd probably forgotten the time.* ◇ *The reunion is for past and present students of the college.* ◇ *Let's forget about who was more to blame – it's all past history.* **OPP** present → RECENT, **future** → NEXT, See also **the past** → PAST

NOTE OLD, FORMER OR PAST? **Old** is used especially to talk about things from your own life: *my old school/teacher/colleagues.* You can use **former** in these cases but it sounds rather formal; **past** cannot be used: *my past school/teacher/friends/colleagues* Your **old** friends are friends that you have known for a long time; your *former* friends are people who are no longer your friends. **Old** is NOT used to talk about times that have gone by, except in the phrase *the old days*: *an old age/era* ◇ *in old times/years/centuries*. You can use either **former** or **past** in these cases: **former** sounds more formal; **past** sounds more personal or more literary. You can talk about your own *past experience*: these are things that have happened to you in the past, or what you have learnt from them; your *previous experience* is usually experience of a particular type of work: *your old/former experience*. **Former** can describe a country or organization that no longer exists or has changed: *the former Yugoslav republic* ◇ *the old/past Yugoslav republic*

prior /ˈpraɪə(r)/ [only before noun] (*formal*) previous: *Visits are by prior arrangement.* ◇ *This information must not be disclosed without prior written consent.* ◇ *They have a prior claim* (= already existing and therefore more important) *to the property.* ❶ **Prior** is a more formal way of saying **previous**, especially when you are talking about making arrangements, giving permission, or deciding which of two people or things is more important; collocates include *arrangement, engagement, commitment, notice, notification, warning, consent, approval, authorization, permission* and *claim.*

distant [usually before noun] far away in time: *The time we spent together is now a distant memory.* ◇ *We will be moving house in the not too distant future* (= quite soon).

remote /rɪˈməʊt; *AmE* rɪˈmoʊt/ [only before noun] very far away in time: *a remote ancestor* (= one who lived a long time ago)

NOTE DISTANT OR REMOTE? The *distant past/future* is not always as far away in time as the *remote past/future.* You can talk about the *not too distant past/future*, meaning 'not very long ago/quite soon', but NOT: *the not too remote past/future*

bygone /ˈbaɪɡɒn; *AmE* -ɡɔːn; -ɡɑːn/ [only before noun] (*written*) belonging to an earlier time: *The horse and cart belongs to a bygone era.*

price *noun* See also the entry for RATE 2

price · cost · value · expense · worth
These are all words for the amount of money that you have to pay for sth.

price [C, U] the amount of money that you have to pay for an item or service: *house/retail/oil/share prices* ◇ *The price includes dinner, bed and breakfast.* ◇ *He was charging a very high price for it.* ◇ *How much are these? They don't have a price on them.* ◇ *I can't afford it at that price.* ◇ *It's amazing how much computers have come down in price over the past few years.* ◇ *to pay half/full price for sth*

cost [C, U] the amount of money that you need in order to buy, make or do sth: *A new computer system has been installed at a cost of £80 000.* ◇ *Allow $25 per day to cover the cost of meals.* ◇ *Consumers will have to bear the full cost of these pay increases.* ◇ *The total cost to you* (= the amount you have to pay) *is £3 000.* ◇ *The plan had to be abandoned on grounds of cost* (= it was too expensive). ◇ *sharp rises in the cost of living* (= the amount of money that people need to pay for food, clothing and somewhere to live) See also **cost** → COST *verb*

value [U, C] how much sth is worth in money or other goods for which it can be exchanged: *The winner will receive a prize to the value of £1 000.* ◇ *Sports cars tend to hold their value well.* ◇ *Tickets were changing hands at three times their face value* (= the value shown on the front). ◇ *London property values are rising fast.* See also **valuable** → VALUABLE 1

NOTE PRICE, COST OR VALUE? The **price** is what sb asks you to pay for an item or service: *to ask/charge a high price* ◇ *to ask/charge a high cost/value.* Obtaining or achieving sth may have a **cost**; the **value** of sth is how much other people would be willing to pay for it: *house prices* ◇ *the cost of moving house* ◇ *The house now has a market value of twice what we paid for it.*

expense [U, C, usually sing.] the money that you spend on sth; sth that makes you spend money: *The garden was transformed at great expense.* ◇ *We were taken out for a meal at the company's expense* (= the company paid). ◇ *He's arranged everything: no expense spared* (= he spent as much money as could possibly be needed). ◇ *They went to all the expense of redecorating the house and then they moved.* ◇ *Their visit put us to a lot of expense.* ◇ *Running a car is a big expense.* See also **expenses** → COSTS, **expensive** → EXPENSIVE

worth /wɜːθ; *AmE* wɜːrθ/ [U] the financial value of sb/sth: *He has a personal net worth of $10 million.* ❶ **Worth**, as a noun, is more often used to mean the practical or moral value of sth. See also **worth** → VALUE 1
▶ **worth** *adj.*: *Our house is worth about $300 000.* ◇ *How much is this painting worth?* ◇ *to be worth a bomb/packet/fortune* (= a lot of money) ◇ *It isn't worth much.*
▶ **worthless** *adj.*: *Shares in the company are now almost worthless.* **OPP** valuable → VALUABLE 1

price *verb*

price · value · assess · cost · put a price on sth
These words mean to fix the price of sth at a particular level or to make a judgement about the price, value or cost of sth.

price [T, usually passive, I] to fix the price of sth at a particular level: *These goods are priced too high.* ◇ *Some leading UK firms are pricing themselves out of the market* (= charging such high prices for their goods or services that nobody wants to buy them). ◇ (*business*) *A dominant firm will price aggressively in markets where it faces new competitors.*

value [T, usually passive] to make a judgement about how much money sth is worth: *The property has been valued at over $2 million.* ◇ (*BrE*) *I took my violin into the shop to get it valued.* ❶ In American English use **assess** here. See also **valuation** → VALUATION, **valuable** → VALUABLE 1

assess /əˈses/ [T] to estimate or calculate the total amount, value or cost of sth: *They have assessed the amount of compensation to be paid.* ◇ *Damage to the building was assessed at £40 000.*

cost [T, usually passive] to estimate or calculate how much money will be needed for sth or what price should be charged for sth: *The project has been costed at $8.1 million.* ◇ *All telephone calls are logged, costed and charged to your account.* See also **costing** → VALUATION

put a ˈprice on sth *phrase* to say how much money sth valuable is worth: *They haven't yet put a price on the business.* ◇ *You can't put a price on that sort of loyalty.*

pride *noun*

pride · arrogance · vanity · egoism · hubris · conceit
These are all words for a feeling that you are better or more important than other people.

pride [U] (*disapproving*) the feeling that you are better or more important than other people: *Male pride forced him to suffer in silence.* ◇ *You're going to have to **swallow your pride** and ask for your job back.* OPP **modesty** → MODEST, See also **proud** → PROUD 2

arrogance /ˈærəɡəns/ [U] (*disapproving*) the behaviour of a person when they feel that they are more important than other people, know more than they do, and are certain that they are right, so that they are rude to them or do not consider them: *He has a reputation for rudeness and intellectual arrogance.* OPP **humility** → MODEST, See also **arrogant** → PROUD 2

vanity /ˈvænəti/ [U] (*disapproving*) a feeling of too much pride in your own appearance, abilities or achievements: *She had no **personal vanity** (= about her appearance).* ◇ *The invitation to head the committee flattered his vanity and he agreed.* OPP **modesty** → MODEST, See also **vain** → PROUD 2

egoism /ˈeɡəʊɪzəm; ˈiːɡ-; AmE -ɡoʊ-/ (also **egotism** /ˈeɡətɪzəm; ˈiːɡ-/) [U] (*disapproving*) the feeling that you are better or more important than other people, which makes you think only about yourself and talk about yourself all the time: *His egoism prevented him from really loving anyone but himself.* See also **ego** → DIGNITY

hubris /ˈhjuːbrɪs/ [U] (*formal or literary, disapproving*) too much pride and too much confidence that you will succeed, especially when this seems to be punished later by failure, disaster or death: *He thought he was above the law and was ultimately punished for his hubris.*

conceit /kənˈsiːt/ [U] (*rather formal, especially written, disapproving*) too much pride in your abilities or achievements: *Can you believe the conceit of the man?* See also **conceited** → PROUD 2

prim *adj.*

prim · demure · prudish
These words all describe sb who behaves in a careful way and is easily shocked by anything connected with sex.

prim (*especially written, disapproving*) always behaving in a careful, formal way and easily shocked by anything that is rude: *He had rather prim ideas about what things were suitable for the children.* ◇ *You can't tell her that joke — she's much too **prim and proper**.*

▸ **primly** *adv.*: *'You're not supposed to say that,'* she said primly.

demure /dɪˈmjʊə(r); AmE dɪˈmjʊr/ (*especially written*) (of a woman or girl) behaving in a way that does not attract attention to herself or her body; quiet and serious; suggesting that a woman or girl is like this: *a demure young woman* ◇ *She wore the demure dresses approved of by her father.*

▸ **demurely** *adv.*: *She sat with her eyes demurely downwards.*

prudish /ˈpruːdɪʃ/ (*disapproving*) easily shocked by things connected with sex: *She can be quite prudish.* ◇ *He grew up in the prudish moral climate of the late nineteenth century.*

principle *noun*

1 a matter of principle
2 the principle that education should be available to all

1 See also the entries for MORALITY and VALUES
principle · ethics · ideal · standards · morals · morality
These are all words for a moral rule or strong belief that influences people's actions.

principle [C, usually pl., U] a moral rule or strong belief that influences your actions: *I refuse to lie about it — it's **against my principles**.* ◇ *Stick to your principles and tell him you won't do it.* ◇ *He doesn't invest in the arms industry **on principle**.* See also **unprincipled** → CORRUPT

ethics /ˈeθɪks/ [pl.] moral principles that control or influence sb's actions; the degree to which sth is right or wrong according to these principles: *Their professional body is drawing up a **code of ethics** (= a statement of acceptable principles for a particular group).* ◇ *He began to question the ethics of his position.* ❶ **Ethics** is used especially about the principles that control a particular area of activity, especially business or professional life. Collocates include *professional, business* and *medical.* See also **ethical** → GOOD 5, **ethical** → MORAL, **ethic** → VALUES

ideal [C] an idea or standard that seems perfect and worth trying to achieve or obtain: *His followers sometimes found it hard to live up to his high ideals.* ◇ *Is true love an unattainable ideal (= one that can never be achieved)?*

standards [pl.] a level of behaviour that sb considers to be morally acceptable: *Standards aren't what they used to be.* ◇ *We intend to uphold **standards of behaviour** throughout the college.*

morals [pl.] standards or principles of good behaviour, especially in sexual matters: *He thinks that young people these days have no morals.* ◇ *The play was considered an affront to public morals.* See also **amoral** → CORRUPT, **moral** → GOOD 5, **moral** → MORAL

morality /məˈræləti/ [U] a system of moral principles followed by a particular person or group of people; the degree to which sth is right or wrong according to these principles: *Whatever her personal morality, she has no right to judge others.* ◇ *There is a continuing debate on the morality of abortion.* See also **moral** → GOOD 5, **moral** → MORAL

2 **principle · rule · law · tenet**
These are all words for a belief about the way sb should behave and what actions they should take.

▸ to **accept** a principle / rule / tenet
▸ to **apply** a principle / rule

principle [C, U] a belief that is accepted as a reason for acting or thinking in a particular way: *Their policy is based on the principle that free education should be available for all children.* ◇ *The order to show no mercy was contrary to the most basic principles of their religion.* See also **principle** → THEORY 1

rule [C] a statement of what you do, or are advised to do, in a particular type of situation: *I've made it a rule not to talk to the press.* ◇ *There are no hard and fast rules for planning healthy meals.* ◇ *The golden rule (= most important rule) of teaching is to remember that all children learn at different rates.* See also **rule** → HABIT, **rule** → RULE *noun*, **rule** → THEORY 1, **as a rule** → USUALLY

law [C, U] a rule or set of rules for good behaviour or how you should behave in a particular situation: *He frequently behaved as though moral laws did not exist.* See also **law** → RULE *noun*, **law** → THEORY 1

tenet /ˈtenɪt/ [C] (*formal*) one of the principles or beliefs that a theory or larger set of beliefs is based on: *Underlying Leninism was the tenet that revolution was inevitable.*

priority *noun*

priority · emphasis · stress · precedence
These are all words for the fact of giving sth special importance.

PATTERNS AND COLLOCATIONS
▸ priority / precedence **over** sb / sth
▸ (a) **particular / special / equal** priority / emphasis / stress
▸ the **main** priority / emphasis
▸ **great / undue** emphasis / stress
▸ to **have** priority / a ... emphasis / precedence
▸ to **take** priority / precedence
▸ to **give** sb / sth priority / emphasis / precedence
▸ to **put** emphasis / stress on sb / sth
▸ to **lay / place** emphasis / stress on sb / sth
▸ **in order of** priority / precedence

priority /praɪˈɒrəti; AmE -ˈɔːr-; -ˈɑːr-/ [C, U] something that you think is more important than other things and should be dealt with first; the condition of being more important than sb else and therefore coming or being dealt with first: *a high/low priority* ◇ *Education is a top priority.* ◇ (*especially BrE*) *You need to get your priorities right* (= decide what is important to you). ◇ (*AmE*) *You need to get your priorities straight.* ◇ *Club members will be given priority.* ◇ *Her family takes priority over her work.* ◇ *List the tasks in order of priority.* ◇ *Priority cases, such as homeless families, get dealt with first.* See also **prioritize** → STRESS *verb*

emphasis /ˈemfəsɪs/ (pl. **emphases** /-siːz/) [U, C] special importance that is given to sth: *The emphasis is very much on learning the spoken language.* ◇ *There has been a shift of emphasis from manufacturing to service industries.* ◇ *The classes have a vocational emphasis.* See also **emphasize** → STRESS *verb*

stress [U] special importance that is given to sth: *She lays great stress on punctuality.* ◇ *I think the company places too much stress on cost and not enough on quality.* See also **stress** → STRESS *verb*

NOTE EMPHASIS OR STRESS? There is very little difference in meaning between these two words. **Emphasis** is much more frequent and slightly more formal; **stress** is often more personal, used to talk about what a particular person thinks is important, rather than the focus of a debate, campaign or service, for example.

precedence /ˈpresɪdəns/ [U] (*rather formal*) the condition of being more important than sb/sth else and therefore coming or being dealt with first: *She had to learn that her wishes did not take precedence over other people's needs.* ◇ *The speakers came on to the platform in order of precedence.*

NOTE PRIORITY OR PRECEDENCE? In some cases you can use either of these words: *Her wishes did not take priority/precedence over other people's needs.* However, people or things usually *take precedence* on the basis of rank: because they are older, have a higher social status or a more senior position. People or things are usually *given priority* on the basis of need: ~~The speakers came on to the platform in order of priority.~~ ◇ ~~Homeless families will be given precedence.~~

prison *noun*

prison · jail · camp · detention centre · penitentiary · jailhouse · correctional facility
These are all words for a building where people are kept and prevented from leaving.

PATTERNS AND COLLOCATIONS
▸ **in** prison / jail
▸ **in a** prison / jail / camp / detention centre / penitentiary / jailhouse / correctional facility
▸ a **local** prison / jail / correctional facility
▸ a **juvenile** prison / jail / detention centre / correctional facility
▸ a **women's** prison / jail / correctional facility
▸ to **go to / be sent to / be released from / get out of** prison / jail
▸ a prison / jail **sentence / term**

prison [C, U] a large building or group of buildings where people are kept and prevented from leaving, either as a punishment for a crime they have committed or while they are waiting for trial: *He was sent to prison for five years.* ◇ *Since 1990, the US prison population (= the total number of prisoners in a country) has almost doubled.* ◇ (*especially BrE*) *Ten prison officers and three inmates needed hospital treatment following the riot.* ◇ (*AmE*) *prison guards* See also **imprison**, **send sb to prison** → JAIL *verb*

jail (*BrE* also **gaol**) /dʒeɪl/ [U, C] a prison, especially a small or local prison: *He will be freed from jail automatically after serving half the term.* ◇ *Woman faces jail for animal cruelty* (= newspaper headline). See also **jail** → JAIL *verb*

NOTE PRISON OR JAIL? In British English there is very little difference between these words. **Prison** is also used to talk about the system of keeping people in prisons, as well as the building or institution itself: *the prison service/system* ◇ ~~the jail service/system~~. In the US a **prison** is usually a place where people are sent for a long time after they have been found guilty of a crime. A **jail** is usually a place where people are locked up for a short time, especially until it can be decided what should be done with them next: *He was held overnight at the county jail.* **Jails** are usually smaller than prisons and are usually operated by the local county; **prisons** are larger and are operated by the state or the US government. However, the terms *in prison* and *in jail* are used in exactly the same way.

camp [C] (used in compounds) a place where people are kept in huts or tents, especially by a government and often for long periods: *Nearly a year after the disaster, many people are still living in refugee camps.* ◇ *He spent the rest of the war in a prison camp.* ◇ *Concentration camps were first used during the Boer War.*

detention centre (*BrE*) (*AmE* **detention center**) [C] a prison for young people: *The Juvenile Detention Center is where juveniles are held while awaiting their Juvenile Court hearing.*

penitentiary /ˌpenɪˈtenʃəri/ [C] (*AmE*) a large prison in the US, especially one for people who have committed serious crimes: *The execution was carried out at the state penitentiary in Fort Madison.*

jailhouse /ˈdʒeɪlhaʊs/ [C] (*AmE*) a small local prison, especially in the past: *The jailhouse housed the sheriff and his family as well as the prisoners.* ❶ **Jailhouse** is sometimes used as a less formal word for *prison* in compounds, and in journalism: *He became something of a jailhouse lawyer* (= a prisoner who knows a lot about the law). ◊ *Two prisoners die in jailhouse fire* (= newspaper headline).

cor'rectional facility [C] (*especially AmE, rather formal*) a prison or other institution that is intended to improve people's behaviour, usually by punishing them: *The court must decide whether the child should be placed in a correctional facility.*

prisoner *noun* See also the entry for HOSTAGE

prisoner · inmate · convict
These are all words for a person who is kept in prison as a punishment.

PATTERNS AND COLLOCATIONS
- ▸ a **fellow** / **former** / **young** prisoner / inmate
- ▸ an **escaped** prisoner / convict
- ▸ to **release** a prisoner / an inmate / a convict
- ▸ a prisoner / an inmate / a convict **escapes**
- ▸ a prisoner / an inmate / a convict **serves** a sentence

prisoner [C] a person who is kept in prison as a punishment, or while they are waiting for trial: *The number of prisoners serving life sentences has fallen.* ◊ *They are demanding the release of all political prisoners.* See also **prisoner → HOSTAGE**

inmate /'ɪnmeɪt/ [C] one of the people living in an institution such as a prison or mental hospital: *The jail has 500 inmates.* ◊ *He was attacked by a fellow inmate.*

convict /'kɒnvɪkt; AmE 'kɑːn-/ [C] a person who has been found guilty of a crime and sent to prison: *The novel begins with Pip's meeting with an escaped convict from the prison ship.*

NOTE PRISONER OR CONVICT? **Prisoner** has a wide range of uses; it can be used to talk about any person who has been sent to prison. **Convict** is used mainly in historical contexts, especially to talk about the British prisoners who were sent to Australia in the 18th and 19th centuries. **Convict** is also commonly used in written or literary contexts to talk about looking or feeling like sb who has been sent to prison: *He held the door open and she walked through, feeling like a convict.*

privacy *noun* See the Topic Map for THE INDIVIDUAL AND SOCIETY on p.894

privacy · loneliness · solitude · seclusion · isolation
These are all words for the state of being alone or of having little contact with other people.

PATTERNS AND COLLOCATIONS
- ▸ privacy / isolation **from** sth
- ▸ **in** privacy / solitude / seclusion / isolation
- ▸ **in the** privacy / solitude / seclusion **of** sth
- ▸ **complete** / **total** privacy / seclusion
- ▸ to **experience** / **suffer** / **feel** loneliness / isolation
- ▸ to **need** / **enjoy** privacy / solitude
- ▸ a **feeling** / **sense** of loneliness / solitude / isolation

privacy /'prɪvəsi; AmE 'praɪv-/ [U] (*approving*) the state of being alone and not watched or disturbed by other people; the state of being free from the attention of the public: *I value my privacy.* ◊ *He read the letter later in the privacy of his own room.* ◊ *She complained that the photographs were an invasion of her privacy.* See also **private → OWN, private → SECRET 1**

loneliness [U] (*disapproving*) the state of being unhappy because you have no friends or little contact with other people: *He experienced terrible loneliness after the loss of his wife.* See also **lonely → LONELY**

solitude /'sɒlɪtjuːd; AmE 'sɑːlətuːd/ [U] (*approving*) the state of being alone, especially when you find this pleasant: *She longed for peace and solitude.* ◊ *He shut himself away to pray in solitude.* See also **solitary → ALONE, solitary → SOLITARY**

seclusion /sɪ'kluːʒn/ [U] (*written, approving*) the state of being private or of having little contact with other people, especially when you find this pleasant: *For the long summer vacation, I prefer the relative seclusion of the countryside.*
▸ **secluded** *adj.*: *a secluded beach/spot* ◊ *to lead a secluded life*

isolation /ˌaɪsə'leɪʃn/ [U] (*written, disapproving*) the state of feeling alone and without friends or help: *Isolation from family and friends also contributes to their problems.* ◊ *Her social isolation was made worse by her inability to drive.* See also **isolated → LONELY**

NOTE PRIVACY, LONELINESS, SOLITUDE, SECLUSION OR ISOLATION? **Privacy** is considered a good thing, when you can be in your home or some other place that allows you to do things without being watched or disturbed by other people. **Seclusion** has a similar meaning but there is a stronger sense of being far away from other people and so protected from being disturbed. **Solitude** is even more positive, often suggesting peace and quiet as well as being away from other people. **Loneliness** has a negative meaning, suggesting feelings of unhappiness because you are on your own and have no contact with others. The emphasis with **isolation** is on being in a situation where you have no one to talk to or ask for help.

probably *adv.*

probably · presumably · no doubt · doubtless · (the) chances are… · most likely · in all probability…
These words are all used to say that sth is likely to happen or be true.

probably	presumably	no doubt
the chances are…	most likely	doubtless
	in all probability…	

probably (*especially spoken*) used to say that sth is likely to happen or be true: *You're probably right.* ◊ *It'll probably be OK.* ◊ *'Is he going to be there?' 'Probably.'* ◊ *'Do we need the car?' 'Probably not.'* See also **probable → LIKELY**

presumably /prɪ'zjuːməbli; AmE -'zuː-/ (*especially spoken*) used to say that you think that sth is probably true, based on the evidence you have: *Presumably this is where the accident happened.* ◊ *I couldn't concentrate, presumably because I was so tired.* See also **presume → SUPPOSE**

NOTE PROBABLY OR PRESUMABLY? **Probably** suggests a conclusion based on what is generally likely to be true; **presumably** suggests a conclusion based on particular evidence, even though neither word suggests certainty. **Presumably** can be used to suggest that sth should be the case: *Presumably you'll be leaving the children at home.* ◊ ~~Probably you'll be leaving the children at home.~~ or to ask sb to confirm what you already believe: *You'll be taking the car, presumably?* ◊ ~~You'll be taking the car, probably?~~ **Probably** can be used to agree with sb: *You're probably right.* ◊ ~~You're presumably right.~~ or to comfort sb: *It'll probably be OK.* ◊ ~~It'll presumably be OK.~~

ˌno 'doubt (*rather formal*) used to say that you think that sth is probably true, because it is what you would normally expect: *No doubt she'll call us when she gets there.*

doubtless (*rather formal, written*) almost certainly: *He would doubtless disapprove of what Kelly was doing.*

(the) chances are… *idiom* (*rather informal*) it is likely that…: *(The) Chances are you won't have to pay.*

most likely very probably: *The illness was caused, most likely, by a virus.* See also **likely → LIKELY**

in ˌall probaˈbility… *phrase* (*written*) it is very likely that…: *In all probability he failed to understand the consequences of his actions.*

problem *noun*

problem · difficulty · issue · challenge · trouble · the matter · complication
These are all words for a thing or situation which is not easy to deal with or to understand.

PATTERNS AND COLLOCATIONS
▸ a problem / a difficulty / an issue / trouble / the matter / a complication **with** sth
▸ a problem / an issue / a challenge / trouble **for** sb
▸ **further** problems / difficulties / issues / challenges / trouble / complications
▸ the **main** problem / difficulty / issue / challenge / trouble
▸ (a) **serious / real** problem / difficulties / issue / challenge / trouble
▸ **basic** problems / difficulties / issues / trouble
▸ **endless / severe** problems / difficulties / trouble
▸ a **major / minor** problem / difficulty / issue / challenge / complication
▸ (a) **big** problem / issue / challenge / trouble
▸ to **have** problems / difficulties / issues / trouble
▸ to **cause / avoid** problems / difficulties / trouble / complications
▸ to **create / bring / run into** problems / difficulties / trouble
▸ to **make** difficulties / an issue of sth / trouble
▸ a problem / a difficulty / an issue / a complication **arises / exists**
▸ the problem / difficulty / trouble **lies in** sth

problem [C] a thing that is not easy to deal with or understand: *Most students face the problem of funding themselves while they study.* ◇ *Unemployment is a very real problem for graduates now.* ◇ *There's no history of heart problems* (= disease connected with the heart) *in our family.* ◇ *It's a nice table.* **The only problem is** *it's too big for the room.* ◇ (*informal, spoken*) *'But what am I supposed to do now?' 'Don't ask me —* **it's not my problem/that's your problem** (= I don't care and you must deal with it yourself). ◇ *'Can I pay by credit card?' 'Yes,* **no problem***.'* See also **problematic** → SENSITIVE 2

difficulty [C, usually pl., U] a thing or situation that is not easy to deal with: *We've run into difficulties with the new project.* ◇ *He* **got into difficulties** *while swimming and had to be rescued.* ◇ *She works with children with* **learning difficulties**. ◇ *The bank is* **in difficulty** *at the moment.* See also **difficulty** → DIFFICULTY, **difficult** → DIFFICULT 1, **difficult** → DIFFICULT 1

NOTE PROBLEM OR DIFFICULTY? To talk about one particular thing that is difficult to deal with use **problem**: *The problem first arose in 2003.* To talk about a number of things together that are difficult to deal with you can use **problems** or **difficulties**: *The project has been fraught with problems/difficulties from the start.* To talk about a situation that is full of problems, you can use **difficulties** or **difficulty**: *What should you do if you see someone in difficulties/difficulty in the water?*

issue [C] (*rather informal*) a problem or worry that sb has with sth: *Money is not an issue.* ◇ *I don't think my private life is the issue here.* ◇ *I'm not bothered about the cost — you're the one who's making an issue of it.* ◇ (*especially AmE*) *She's always on a diet — she* **has issues about/with** *food.*

challenge [C] (*usually approving*) a new or difficult task that tests sb's ability and skill: *The role will be the biggest challenge of his acting career.* ◇ *She has taken on some exciting new challenges with this job.* ❶ Unlike the other items in this group, a **challenge** is usually seen as a positive thing: *an exciting/interesting challenge.* However, it is also used to describe a serious problem that you are determined to deal with in a positive way: *Destruction of the environment is one of the most serious challenges we face.* See also **challenging** → DIFFICULT 1

trouble [U, C] (*disapproving*) a problem or worry, or a situation that causes this: *We've never had much trouble with vandals around here.* ◇ *He could make trouble for me if he wanted to.* ◇ *She was on the phone for an hour telling me all her troubles.* ◇ **The trouble with you is** *you don't really want to work.*

the matter [sing.] (*especially spoken*) used (to ask) if sb is upset or unhappy or if there is a problem: *What's the matter? Is there something wrong?* ◇ *Is* **anything the matter***?* ◇ *Is* **something the matter** *with Bob? He seems very down.* ◇ *'We've bought a new TV.' 'What was the matter with the old one?'* ◇ **What's the matter with you** *today* (= why are you behaving like this)*?*

complication /ˌkɒmplɪˈkeɪʃn; *AmE* ˌkɑːm-/ [C, U] a thing that makes a situation more complicated or difficult: *The bad weather added a further complication to our journey.* See also **complicated** → COMPLEX

process *noun* See also the entries for ACTION and PRO-JECT

process · procedure · routine
These are all words for ways of doing things, especially the usual or correct way.

PATTERNS AND COLLOCATIONS
▸ a process / procedure / routine **for** sth
▸ the **usual / normal** process / procedure / routine
▸ (the) **standard** process / procedure / routines
▸ a **set / regular** procedure / routine
▸ a **painful** process / procedure
▸ to **go through** a process / procedure / routine
▸ to **adopt / follow** a procedure / routine
▸ a **matter of** procedure / routine
▸ a **change in** procedure / routine

process [C] a series of things that are done in order to achieve a particular result; a series of things that happen, especially ones that result in natural changes: *I'm afraid getting things changed will be a slow process.* ◇ *the Middle East* **peace process** ◇ *There is the whole consultation process that must be gone through.* ◇ *Find which food you are allergic to by* **a process of elimination**. ◇ *We're* **in the process** *of selling our house.* ◇ *I was moving some furniture and I twisted my ankle* **in the process** (= while I was doing it). ◇ *the digestive/ageing process* ◇ *It's a normal part of the learning process.*

procedure /prəˈsiːdʒə(r)/ [C, U] a way of doing sth, especially the usual or correct way: *She explained the procedure for calling a Special General Meeting.* ◇ *This is standard procedure after a suicide attempt.*

routine /ruːˈtiːn/ [C, U] the normal order and way in which you regularly do things: *We are trying to get the baby into a routine for feeding and sleeping.* ◇ *Make exercise a part of your* **daily routine**. ◇ *We clean and repair the machines as a matter of routine.* ◇ *It was claimed that torture of detainees was routine.* See also **routine** → USUAL *adj.*, **routinely** → OFTEN

produce *verb*

produce · have · give birth · breed · clone · reproduce · bear
These words all mean to grow sth as part of a natural process, or to have a baby or young animal.

PATTERNS AND COLLOCATIONS
▸ to produce / breed / clone sth **from** sth
▸ to produce / have / give birth to / bear a / an **child / son / daughter / heir**
▸ to produce / have / give birth to a **baby / litter**
▸ to breed / clone **animals**
▸ to produce / bear **fruit**
▸ to produce sth / breed / clone sth / reproduce **successfully**

produce [T] (*rather formal*) to grow or make sth as part of a natural process; to have a baby or young animal: *The fruit and vegetables are all produced locally.* ◇ *These shrubs produce bright red berries.* ◇ *Our cat produced a litter of kittens last week.* ◇ *Her duty was to produce an heir to the throne.* ❶ When it is used to talk about having a baby, **produce** suggests a lack of emotion in the speaker. It is used especially when people are talking about having a son who will inherit an important position.

have [T] to produce a baby or young animal: *She's going to have a baby.* ◇ *Our cat has just had five kittens.*

give 'birth *phrase* (*rather formal*) to produce a baby or young animal: *She died shortly after giving birth.* ◇ *Mary has given birth to a healthy baby girl.*

> **NOTE** HAVE OR GIVE BIRTH? **Have** is the most usual verb to use when a woman or animal produces a baby or young animals; it can be used in a general way about the process of being pregnant and then giving birth. **Give birth** is used to talk about the actual act of making a baby come out of your body: *She's going to have a baby* (= she is pregnant). ◇ *She is about to give birth* (= the baby is in the process of being born). ◇ *She died shortly after giving birth* (= within a few hours of the baby being born). ◇ *She died shortly after having a baby* (= within a few days or weeks).

breed [I, T] (of animals) to have sex and produce young; to keep animals in order to produce young ones in a controlled way: *Many animals breed only at certain times of the year.* ◇ *The rabbits are bred for their long coats.* See also **breed** → KEEP 4

clone [T] (*technical*) to produce an exact copy of an animal or plant from its cells: *A team from the UK were the first to successfully clone an animal.* ◇ *They produced Dolly, the cloned sheep.*

reproduce /ˌriːprəˈdjuːs; AmE -ˈduːs/ [I, T] (*rather formal or technical*) (of animals, plants or cells) to produce new animals, plants or cells: *Most reptiles reproduce by laying eggs on land.* ◇ *These cells reproduce themselves every twenty minutes.*
> **reproduction** *noun* [U]: *sexual reproduction*

bear [T] (*formal or literary*) to give birth to a child; to produce flowers or fruit: *She was not able to bear children.* ◇ *She had borne him six sons.* ◇ *These trees take a long time to bear fruit.*

product *noun*

product · goods · commodity · merchandise · produce
These are all words for things that are produced to be sold.

PATTERNS AND COLLOCATIONS
▶ consumer / industrial products / goods / commodities
▶ household products / goods
▶ farm products / produce
▶ perishable products / goods / commodities / produce
▶ durable products / goods
▶ luxury products / goods / commodities
▶ to sell / market a product / goods / a commodity / merchandise / produce
▶ to export a product / goods / a commodity / merchandise
▶ to buy / purchase a product / goods / a commodity / merchandise / produce

product [C, U] a thing that is produced or grown, usually to be sold: *meat/pharmaceutical products* ◇ *to create/ develop/launch a new product* ◇ (*business*) *We need new product to sell* (= a range of new products). See also **produce** → MANUFACTURE

goods [pl.] things that are produced to be sold: *cotton/ leather/paper goods* ◇ *electrical/sports goods* ◇ *factories which produce luxury goods for the export market* ◇ *consumer goods* (= goods such as food and clothing that are bought by individual customers) ◇ *increased tax on goods and services*

commodity /kəˈmɒdəti; AmE -ˈmɑːd-/ [C] (*economics*) a product or raw material that can be bought and sold, especially between countries: *rice, flour and other basic commodities* ◇ *Crude oil is the world's most important commodity.*

merchandise /-daɪz; AmE ˈmɜːrtʃ-/ [U] goods that are bought or sold; things that you can buy that are connected with or advertise a particular event or organization: *These tokens can be exchanged for merchandise in any of our stores.* ◇ *official Olympic merchandise*

> **NOTE** GOODS OR **MERCHANDISE**? Use **goods** if the emphasis is on what the product is made of or what it is for: *leather/household goods.* Use **merchandise** if the emphasis is less on the product itself but on its brand or the fact of buying/selling it.

produce /ˈprɒdjuːs; AmE ˈprɑːduːs; ˈproʊ-/ [U] things that have been grown or made, especially things connected with farming: *We sell only fresh local produce.* ◇ *It says on the label 'Produce of France'.*

production *noun*

production · construction · industry · manufacturing · building · making · manufacture · assembly
These are all words for the process of making or building sth.

PATTERNS AND COLLOCATIONS
▶ commercial / industrial production / construction / manufacturing / building / manufacture
▶ local production / construction / industry / manufacturing / building / manufacture
▶ large-scale / small-scale production / industry / manufacturing / manufacture
▶ car / textile / food production / manufacture
▶ house / road construction / building
▶ production / construction / manufacturing / building / assembly methods / processes / systems / techniques
▶ construction / manufacturing / building companies / costs / firms / jobs / materials / work
▶ the construction / (a / the) manufacturing / the building industry
▶ a production / construction / manufacturing / building / assembly worker
▶ a production / an assembly line

production [U] the process of making or growing goods, materials or food, especially in large quantities: *Production of the new aircraft will start next year.* ◇ *The new model will be in production by the end of the year.* ◇ *to go into production* ◇ *The car went out of production in 2005.* ◇ *the mass production of consumer goods* (= production of goods in large quantities, using machinery) See also **production** → OUTPUT, **produce** → MANUFACTURE

construction [U] the process of building or making sth, especially roads, buildings, bridges, etc: *Work has begun on the construction of the new airport.* ◇ *Our new offices are still under construction.* **OPP** demolition → DEMOLISH, See also **construct** → BUILD, **construction** → STRUCTURE

industry [U] economic activity concerned with processing raw materials or producing goods, especially in factories: *Pollution from the country's heavy industry is probably the worst in Europe.* ◇ *It is the home of light industry, with several small businesses based in the town.* ◇ *On leaving college she got a job in industry.* See also **industry** → INDUSTRY
> **industrial** *adj.*: *industrial output* ◇ *industrial chemicals* ◇ *the world's leading industrial nations*

manufacturing [U] the industry of producing goods in large quantities in factories: *Many jobs in manufacturing were lost during the recession.* ◇ *The company has established its first manufacturing base in Europe.* See also **manufacture** → MANUFACTURE

building [U] the process and work of building: *the building of the new stadium* ◊ *There's building work going on next door.* **OPP** **demolition** → DEMOLISH. See also **build** → BUILD

NOTE CONSTRUCTION OR BUILDING? In many cases you can use either word. **Construction** is a more technical word and is used more in business and industrial contexts. **Building** is a more everyday word and is used more to talk about building work that is smaller in scale.

making [U] (often in compounds) the process of making sth: *film-making* ◊ *dressmaking* ◊ *tea and coffee making facilities* ◊ *the making of social policy* ◊ *This model was two years in the making* (= being made). ❶ **Making** is a very general word and can be used to talk about anything that you make, but not to talk about things that you build: *house-making* See also **make** → MAKE 1

manufacture [U] the process of making goods in large quantities: *cloth/vehicle manufacture* ◊ *What is the date of manufacture?* See also **manufacture** → MANUFACTURE

NOTE PRODUCTION, MANUFACTURING OR MANUFACTURE? **Production** and **manufacture** emphasize the process of actually making the goods: *car/steel production/manu-facture.* **Manufacturing** emphasizes the business of making goods in large quantities: *manufacturing industry* ◊ *production/manufacture industry.* **Production** can be used to talk about growing food and obtaining raw materials as well as making goods, but **manufacture** can only be used to talk about goods and food that is made, not grown: *oil/meat/wheat manu-facture*

assembly [U] the process of putting together the parts of sth such as a vehicle or piece of furniture: *the correct assembly of the parts* ◊ *a car assembly plant* ◊ *Some assembly of the equipment is required.* See also **assemble** → BUILD

productive *adj.*

productive · fertile · fruitful · prolific · rich
These words all describe sth that produces a lot of things or produces good results.

PATTERNS AND COLLOCATIONS
▸ productive / fertile / rich **land / soil**
▸ a productive / fruitful **collaboration / discussion / meeting**
▸ a fertile / fruitful **source** of sth
▸ **highly** productive / fertile

productive making goods or growing crops, especially in large quantities; achieving a lot: *highly productive farming land/manufacturing methods* ◊ *productive farmers/work-ers* ◊ *My time spent in the library was very productive.* **OPP** **unproductive** → INEFFECTIVE
▸ **productively** *adv.*: *We need to use the land more productively.* ◊ *It's important to spend your time product-ively.*
fertile /ˈfɜːtaɪl; *AmE* ˈfɜːrtl/ (of land or soil) that plants grow well in; that produces many good results or encourages activity: *a fertile region/valley* ◊ *a fertile source of argument/dispute* ◊ *(figurative) The region at the time was fertile ground for revolutionary movements* (= there were the necessary conditions for them to develop easily).
fruitful producing a lot of good or useful results: *The research has proved extremely fruitful.* **OPP** **fruitless** → USELESS. See also the entry for VALUABLE 2
prolific /prəˈlɪfɪk/ producing a lot of books, works of art, goals, fruit, wine, young, etc: *a prolific author/writer/composer* ◊ *He was noted for his prolific output — ten books a year was normal.* ◊ *a prolific scorer/striker* ◊ *The kiwi fruit is known for its prolific yield and good export price.*
rich (of soil) containing the substances that make it good for growing plants in: *rich farming land* ◊ *a rich well-drained soil* **OPP** **poor**

professor *noun* See the Topic Map for EDUCATION on p.888. See also the entries for LECTURER and TEACHER

professor · principal · head · head teacher · headmaster · dean · chancellor · headmistress
These are all words for sb who has a senior position in a university, college or school.

PATTERNS AND COLLOCATIONS
▸ a **school** principal / head / head teacher / headmaster / headmistress
▸ a **college** professor / principal / dean
▸ a **university** professor / principal / chancellor
▸ a **deputy** principal / head / head teacher / headmaster / headmistress
▸ an **associate / assistant** professor / dean
▸ an **acting** principal / head

professor [C] a university or college teacher of the highest rank: *He is a distinguished professor of law at the University of Illinois.* ◊ *She is a former history professor.* ◊ *Professor Smith* ❶ In Britain, most university teachers are known as **lecturers** and the title **professor** is only given to the most senior teachers. In the US, there are several levels of college teachers who have the position of **professor**. These include **assistant professors** and **associate professors** who are equivalent to senior lecturers in Britain. An American college teacher with the highest rank is a **full professor**. This describes their position, but is not used as a title. See also **professor** → LECTURER
principal [C] the person who is in charge of a college, university or school: *The college principal says he's pleased with this year's results.* ◊ *The regulations have been opposed by local high school principals.* ❶ In Britain, **principal** is usually only used to refer to the person in charge of a college or university, but not a school. In the US, a **principal** is the person in charge of a school, but not a college, and can be used as a title: *Principal Ray Smith.*
head (also **Head**) [C] (*BrE*, rather *informal*) the person in charge of a school or college: *I've been called to see the Head.* ◊ *She is deputy head of Greenlands Comprehensive, a struggling inner city school.* See also **headship** → MANAGE-MENT
head 'teacher [C] (*BrE*) a teacher who is in charge of a school: *We interviewed the head teacher of the local school.*
headmaster /ˌhedˈmɑːstə(r); *AmE* -ˈmæs-/ [C] (*BrE*, becoming *old-fashioned*) a male teacher who is in charge of a school, especially a private school: *He is a retired headmaster, living in Edinburgh.*
dean [C] a person who is in charge of a university or college department; (especially at Oxford and Cambridge Universities) a person who is responsible for the discipline of students: *He was appointed dean of the faculty of theology at London University.*
chancellor (also **Chancellor**) /ˈtʃɑːnsələ(r); *AmE* ˈtʃæns-/ [C] the official head of a university in Britain; the head of some American universities: *The prime minister was shown around by the chancellor of the university.* ❶ In Britain, **chancellor** is an honorary position (= given as an honour, without any real duties) and the person who is in charge of running a university is the **vice chancellor**.
headmistress /ˌhedˈmɪstrəs/ [C] (*BrE*, *old-fashioned*) a female teacher who is in charge of a school, especially a private school: *She wrote to her old headmistress at Kingswood School.*

NOTE HEAD, HEADMASTER, HEAD TEACHER OR HEADMIS-TRESS? Different schools in Britain choose different titles for the teacher in charge of the school. In general, **headmaster**, and especially **headmistress**, are becom-ing less frequent and rather old-fashioned. Most schools instead have a **head teacher**; in more informal contexts and journalism, this person is often called the **head**. These words are used to describe the position, but not as titles.

profit *noun*

profit · interest · earnings · dividend · return · surplus · gain

These are all words for money that a company or person makes from selling sth or from investments, after paying the costs involved.

PATTERNS AND COLLOCATIONS
▸ (a) profit/interest/earnings/dividend/return/surplus/gain **on** sth
▸ (a) profit/interest/earnings/dividend/return/surplus/gain **from** sth
▸ to do sth **for** profit/gain
▸ to be **in** profit/surplus
▸ (a) **good** profit/interest/earnings/dividend/return/gains
▸ (a) **record** profit/interest/earnings/dividend/return/surplus/gains
▸ (a) **high/low** profit/interest/earnings/dividend/return/gains
▸ (a) **large/huge/small** profit/dividend/return/surplus/gains
▸ (a) **net** profit/earnings/interest/dividend/return/surplus/gains
▸ (a) **gross/taxable** profit/earnings/interest/dividend/return/gains
▸ (an) **annual** profit/earnings/interest/dividend/return/surplus
▸ to **generate** a profit/earnings/interest/a return/a surplus
▸ to **make/produce** a profit/return/surplus/gain
▸ to **pay** interest/a dividend
▸ a **rate** of interest/return

profit [C, U] the money that you make in business or by selling things, especially after paying the costs involved: *The company made a healthy profit of $106m last year.* ◇ *We should be able to sell the house* **at a profit.** ◇ *The agency is voluntary and not run for profit.* **OPP** loss → DEBT, See also **profit** → MAKE *verb* 3, **proceeds** → REVENUE

interest [U] (*finance*) the extra money that you pay back when you borrow money or that you receive when you invest money: *They're paying 16% interest on the loan.* ◇ *The Gold Account pays monthly interest of 5.5%.* ◇ *The money was repaid* **with interest.** ◇ *Interest rates have risen by 1%.*

earnings [pl.] (*finance*) the profit that a company makes: *The company's earnings per share have fallen to 29p.* ◇ *Whisky accounts for a large percentage of Scotland's export earnings.* See also **earnings** → INCOME

dividend /'dɪvɪdend/ [C] (*finance*) a part of a company's profit that it pays to people who own shares in the company: *Shareholders will receive an interim dividend payment of 50 cents a share.*

return [U, C] (*finance*) the profit produced by an investment: *The bank offers a higher rate of return on investments over $10 000.* ◇ *The capital she invested failed to generate much of a return.*

surplus [C, U] (*finance*) the amount by which the amount of money received is greater than the amount of money spent: *Britain at that time enjoyed a trade surplus of £400 million.* ◇ *The balance of payments was in surplus last year* (= the value of exports was greater than the value of imports).

gain [U, C, usually pl.] (*often disapproving*) profit: *She only seems to be interested in personal gain.* ◇ *He spent his* **ill-gotten gains** *on fast cars and women.*

programme (*BrE*) (*AmE* **program**) *noun* See the
Topic Map for THE MEDIA on p.900

programme · show · broadcast · webcast · transmission · showing

These are all words for sth that you watch or listen to on television, the radio or the Internet.

PATTERNS AND COLLOCATIONS
▸ a programme/show/broadcast **about** sth
▸ a broadcast/webcast/transmission **from** somewhere
▸ to be **on** a programme/show

▸ **in** a programme/show/broadcast/webcast/transmission
▸ a **radio/television/TV** programme/show/broadcast/transmission
▸ a **live** programme/show/broadcast/webcast/transmission
▸ a **family/popular** programme/show/broadcast
▸ to **see/watch** a programme/show/broadcast/webcast/transmission/showing
▸ to **listen to/record** a programme/show/broadcast/transmission
▸ to **host/present** a programme/show
▸ a programme/show **features** sb/sth

programme (*BrE*) (*AmE* **program**) [C] something that people watch on television or listen to on the radio: *She presents a news programme on Channel 4.* ◇ *Did you see that* **programme on** *India last night?* ◇ *What time is that programme on?*

show [C] a programme on television or the radio: *He hosts a late-night radio show.* ◇ *Have you seen that new TV quiz show?* ◇ (*BrE*) *a chat show* ◇ (*AmE*) *a talk show* See also **show** → CONCERT

NOTE PROGRAMME OR SHOW? In British English **show** is usually used in compounds, and is generally used to talk about fairly informal and entertaining TV or radio programmes. **Programme** is a more general word and can be used to talk about anything, apart from advertising, that you watch or listen to on TV or radio. In American English the more general word is **show**; **program** is a more formal word and is used especially in compounds to describe more serious TV and radio shows: (*AmE*) *What time is that show on?* ◇ *She hosts a news program on TV.*

broadcast [C] (*rather formal*) a radio or television programme: *We watched a live broadcast of the speech* (= one shown at the same time as the speech was made). (*BrE*) ❶ **Broadcast** is often used to talk about a TV programme that is shown at the time of a special event, such as an election. It is commonly used in the phrase *live broadcast* or *special broadcast*. When it is used to talk about radio, **broadcast** is slightly less specialized: it is a slightly more formal way of saying **programme**.
▸ **broadcast** *verb* [T, I]: *The concert will be* **broadcast** *live* (= at the same time as it takes place) *tomorrow evening.* ◇ *They began broadcasting in 1922.*

webcast [C] a live broadcast that is sent out on the Internet: *We were able to watch a live webcast of the eclipse.*

transmission /træns'mɪʃn; trænz-/ [C] (*rather formal*) a radio or television message or broadcast: *We now go to a live transmission from Sydney.* ◇ *The first transmission of the programme was on October 2 1952.* ❶ **Transmission** is often used to talk about a broadcast that is made over a long distance or under difficult conditions, or about particular broadcasts from the past.
▸ **transmit** /træns'mɪt; trænz-/ *verb* (-tt-) [T, I]: *The ceremony was transmitted live by satellite to over 50 countries.* ◇ *a short-wave radio that can transmit as well as receive*

showing [C] an occasion on which a film or television programme is shown: *There are three showings a day.* ◇ *And now, by popular demand, a repeat showing of the powerful drama, 'The Lost Prince'.* See also **show** → PRESENT 1

progress *noun*

progress · development · advance · rise · promotion · progression · advancement

These are all words for how sth progresses, develops or grows.

PATTERNS AND COLLOCATIONS
▸ progress/development/an advance/advancement **in** sth
▸ sb's/sth's rise/promotion/progression/advancement **to** sth
▸ sth is **in** progress/development
▸ (a) **rapid** progress/development/advance/rise/promotion/progression/advancement
▸ (a) **steady** progress/development/advance/progression

▸ (a) **slow / gradual / smooth** progress / development / progression
▸ **further** progress / development / advances / promotion / advancement
▸ **scientific / technical / technological / economic / political / social** progress / development / advances / advancement
▸ **personal / individual** development / advancement
▸ **career** development / progression / advancement
▸ to **achieve** progress / development / advances / promotion / progression
▸ to **make** progress / advances
▸ to **chart / halt** the progress / development / rise / progression of sth
▸ to **assist** the progress / development / rise / advancement of sth

progress [U] (*often approving*) the process of improving or developing, or of getting nearer to achieving or completing sth: *We have made great progress in controlling inflation.* ◇ *Technological progress is changing the demand for labour.* ◇ *Work on the new offices is now in progress.* ◇ *I have one file for completed work and one for **work in progress**.* ◇ *They asked for a **progress report** on the project.* ❶ **Progress** is often used as a positive way of talking about technological changes, particularly when there are other people who feel that the changes are having a damaging effect on society. See also **progress** → DEVELOP *verb* 1, **progressive** → RADICAL

development [U] the gradual growth of sth so that it becomes more advanced or stronger: *a baby's development in the womb* ◇ *the development of basic skills such as literacy and numeracy* ◇ *The company can offer a number of opportunities for career development.* ❶ **Development** is used especially to talk about growing (as a child) and learning (throughout life). See also **develop** → DEVELOP *verb* 1

advance [C, U] progress or development in a particular activity or area of understanding: *recent advances in medical science* ◇ *This represents an **advance on** existing techniques.* ◇ *We live in an age of rapid technological advance.* ❶ **Advance** or **advances** is used especially to talk about scientific, technological and medical achievements. See also **advance** → DEVELOP *verb* 1

rise [sing.] the act of becoming more important, successful or powerful: *The film traces the rise of fascism in Europe.* ◇ *the **rise and fall** of the Roman Empire* ◇ *His eventual fall was as fast as his **meteoric rise** to power.* ❶ **Rise** is usually used to describe how a party, social class, state, religion or political system increases in importance, often suddenly, or how a person suddenly becomes powerful or famous, especially in the phrase *sb's rapid/swift/spectacular/meteoric rise to power/fame*. **OPP** **fall** → OVERTHROW

▸ **rise** *verb* [I]: *She **rose to power** in the 70s.* ◇ *He rose to the rank of general.*

promotion /prə'məʊʃn; AmE -'moʊʃn/ [U, C] a move to a more important job or rank in a company or organization; a move by a sports team from playing in one group of teams to playing in a better group: *Her promotion to Sales Manager took everyone by surprise.* ◇ *The new job is a promotion for him.* ◇ *The players were paid bonuses for winning promotion to the First Division.* **OPP** **demotion**, **relegation** ❶ **Demotion** is the opposite of being promoted to a better job, but it is not very frequently used. **Relegation** is when a sports team moves down to play in a worse group of teams.

▸ **promote** *verb* [T]: *She worked hard and was soon promoted.* ◇ *They were promoted to the First Division last season.*

progression /prə'greʃn/ [U, C] (*rather formal*) the process of developing gradually from one stage or state to another: *What are the opportunities for career progression?* ◇ *The medication halts the rapid progression of the disease.* ◇ *This is all part of the natural progression from childhood to adolescence.* See also **progress** → DEVELOP *verb* 1

advancement [U, C] (*formal*) the process of helping sth to make progress or succeed; the progress that is made; progress in a job or social class: *the advancement of*

knowledge/education/science ◇ *There are good opportunities for advancement if you have the right skills.* ❶ **Advancement** is often used to talk about achievements in people's own lives: *career/material/personal/individual/social advancement* See also **advance** → DEVELOP *verb* 1

project *noun* See also the entry for PROCESS

project · activity · operation · venture · exercise · enterprise · pursuit · undertaking · occupation
These are all words for sth that you give your time and energy to, especially in order to achieve a particular aim.

PATTERNS AND COLLOCATIONS
▸ a **major / successful / joint** project / activity / operation / venture / exercise / enterprise / undertaking
▸ a **big / difficult** project / operation / exercise / enterprise / undertaking
▸ an **ambitious** project / operation / venture / exercise / enterprise / undertaking
▸ an **expensive** project / activity / operation / venture / exercise / undertaking
▸ a **profitable** activity / venture / exercise / enterprise
▸ a **worthwhile** project / activity / venture / exercise / pursuit / undertaking / occupation
▸ a **dangerous** activity / operation / exercise / enterprise / undertaking
▸ a **risky** project / activity / operation / venture / enterprise / undertaking
▸ a / an **business / commercial / industrial** project / activity / operation / venture / enterprise / undertaking
▸ to **set up / run / support** a project / an activity / an operation / a venture / an enterprise
▸ to **launch** a project / an operation / a venture / an enterprise
▸ to **carry out / supervise** a project / an activity / an operation / an exercise
▸ to **be involved in** a project / an activity / an operation / a venture / an exercise / an enterprise
▸ a project / a venture / an enterprise **fails / succeeds**

project [C] a planned piece of work that is designed to find information about sth, to produce sth new or to improve sth: *He's working on a research project in the department of social sciences.* ◇ *We want to set up a **project** to computerize the library system.*

activity [C] something that you do for interest or pleasure, or in order to achieve a particular aim: *The club provides a wide variety of activities including tennis, swimming and squash.* ◇ *The book contains plenty of ideas for classroom activities.*

operation [C] (*rather formal*) an organized activity that involves several people doing different things: *A major rescue operation was launched after two divers were reported missing.* ◇ (*BrE*) *It was a **tricky operation** to get all the barrels safely down on to the road.*

venture /'ventʃə(r)/ [C] a business project, especially one that involves taking risks: *The project is a joint venture between the public and private sectors.*

exercise [C] an activity that is designed to achieve a particular result: *Staying calm was an **exercise in** self-control.* ◇ *In the end it proved a pointless exercise.* ◇ *As a **public relations exercise** the festival was clearly a success.* ❶ In this meaning **exercise** is often used to talk about controlling or finding out what people think of an organization or person; collocates include *marketing, publicity, public relations, propaganda, damage limitation, consultation, evaluation* and *research*.

enterprise /'entəpraɪz; AmE -tərp-/ [C] a large project, especially one that is difficult: *The music festival is a new enterprise which we hope will become an annual event.*

pursuit /pə'sjuːt; AmE pər'suːt/ [C, usually pl.] (*rather formal*) something that you do for interest or pleasure, especially when you are not working: *She has time now to follow her various artistic pursuits.*

undertaking /ˌʌndə'teɪkɪŋ; AmE -dər't-/ [C] (*rather formal*) a task or project, especially one that is important and/or difficult: *He is interested in buying the club as a* commercial undertaking. ◇ *In those days, the trip across country was a dangerous undertaking.* See also **undertake** → DO 1

NOTE ENTERPRISE OR UNDERTAKING? **Undertaking** gives the impression that the task in question is difficult or complicated. Typical collocates are *major, large* or *massive.* **Enterprise** is also used to talk about a large or important project, but it also gives the impression that the aim of the task is to produce sth new or different.

occupation [C] (*rather formal*) something that you do for interest or pleasure, especially when you are not working: *Her main occupation seems to be shopping.*

NOTE ACTIVITY, PURSUIT OR OCCUPATION? **Activity** is the most general of these words, with a wide range of collocates relating to business, government and the military, education and sport and leisure: *business/ commerical/trading/training activities ◇ government/ economic/political/military/guerrilla/terrorist activities ◇ classroom/cultural/extra-curricular/educational/ learning activities ◇ leisure/outdoor/recreational/social/ sporting activities.* **Occupation**, in this meaning, is often used with *favourite,* and is used to talk about gentle activities that people enjoy doing to pass the time such as *knitting, watching the sun set, walking in the countryside, sitting on a bench watching people* or *going to a gallery.* **Pursuit** is often used in writing, and is used to talk about more structured sporting, cultural or intellectual activities.

promise *noun*

promise · commitment · word · pledge · guarantee · oath · assurance · vow
These are all words for a statement that you will definitely do or not do sth or that you are sure that sth will happen.

PATTERNS AND COLLOCATIONS
▸ a promise/a commitment/your word/a pledge/a guarantee/ an oath/ a vow **to do sth**
▸ a promise/ your word/ a pledge/ a guarantee/ an oath/ an assurance/ a vow **that...**
▸ a/ your **solemn** promise/ word/ oath/ assurance/ vow
▸ a **firm** promise/ commitment/ pledge/ guarantee/ assurance
▸ a **formal** commitment/ guarantee/ oath/ assurance
▸ a **written** promise/ commitment/ guarantee/ assurance
▸ to **give** a promise/ a commitment/ your word/ a pledge/ a guarantee/ an assurance
▸ to **make** a promise/ commitment/ pledge/ guarantee/ vow
▸ to **take** a pledge/ an oath/ a vow
▸ to **have** sb's promise/ commitment/ word/ assurance
▸ to **honour** your promise/ commitment/ word/ pledge/ assurance
▸ to **keep** your promise/ commitment/ word/ vow
▸ to **break** a promise/ a commitment/ your word/ a pledge/ a vow

promise [C] a statement that tells sb that you will definitely do or not do sth: *I try not to make promises that I can't keep.* ◇ *He simply broke every single promise he ever made me.* ◇ *She had obviously forgotten her promise to call me.* ◇ *You haven't gone back on your* **promise to** *me, have you?* ◇ *I won't be late. That's a promise!*

commitment [C, U] (*rather formal*) a promise or determination to do sth or to behave in a particular way; a promise to support sb/sth; the fact of making a commitment: *She doesn't want to make a big emotional commitment to Steve at the moment.* ◇ *The company's commitment to providing quality at a reasonable price has been vital to its success.* ◇ *He questioned the government's commitment to public services.* See also **committed** → RELIABLE 1

word [sing.] a promise that you will do sth or that sth will happen or is true: *I give you my word that it won't happen again.* ◇ *I never* **doubted her word.** ◇ *They claimed that the minister had* **gone back on her word** (= broken her

promise). ◇ *We only have his word for it that he wasn't there that night.* ◇ *She won't go to the police. You can* **take my word for it** (= believe me).

pledge [C] (*especially journalism*) a serious promise: *The new leader demanded a pledge of loyalty from each of his allies.* ◇ *Will the government honour its election pledge not to raise taxes?*

guarantee /ˌgærənˈtiː/ [C] a firm promise that you will do sth or that sth will happen: *The union wants cast-iron guarantees that there will be no job losses.*

NOTE PROMISE, PLEDGE OR GUARANTEE? **Promise** is the most frequent and most general of these words, and the only one of these three to use in the context of personal relationships: ~~She had obviously forgotten her pledge/ guarantee to call me.~~ **Pledge** is used especially in the context of politics and the things that politicians promise in order to get elected: *election/campaign/ manifesto pledges ◇ spending pledges given by the government.* **Guarantee** is used especially in matters of business involving companies or organizations.

oath /əʊθ; AmE oʊθ/ [C] (*rather formal*) a formal promise to do sth; a formal statement that sth is true: *All the barons were called on to* **swear an oath** *of allegiance to the king.* ◇ *Before giving evidence, witnesses in court have to* **take the oath** (= promise to tell the truth). ❶ If you are or do sth **on/under oath,** you have made a formal promise to tell the truth in court: *The judge reminded the witness that he was still under oath.*

assurance /əˈʃʊərəns; -ˈʃɔːr-; AmE əˈʃʊr-/ [C] (*rather formal*) a statement that sth will certainly be true or will certainly happen, particularly when there has been doubt about it: *They asked for* **assurances on** *the safety of the system.* ◇ *Despite* **assurances to the contrary** *the birds are still being sold as pets.*

vow /vaʊ/ [C] a formal and serious promise, especially a religious one, to do sth: *The monks take a vow of silence.* ◇ *She would not be unfaithful to her* **marriage vows.**

promise *verb*

promise · guarantee · swear · pledge · commit · assure · vow · undertake
These words all mean to tell sb that you will definitely do sth or that sth will happen.

PATTERNS AND COLLOCATIONS
▸ to swear/ vow **to** sb (that...)
▸ to promise/ guarantee/ swear/ pledge/ vow/ undertake **to do sth**
▸ to promise/ guarantee/ swear/ pledge/ vow **that...**
▸ to promise/ guarantee/ pledge your **support**
▸ to swear/ pledge **allegiance/ loyalty**
▸ to swear/ vow **revenge/ eternal friendship/ undying love**
▸ to **solemnly** promise/ swear/ vow/ undertake sth

promise [T, I] to tell sb that you will definitely do or not do sth, or that sth will definitely happen: *'Promise not to tell anyone!' 'I promise.'* ◇ *I'll see what I can do but I* **can't promise anything.** ◇ *You promised me (that) you'd be home early tonight.* ◇ *'I'll be back soon,' she promised.* ◇ *He promised the money to his grandchildren.*

guarantee /ˌgærənˈtiː/ [T] to tell sb that sth definitely will or will not happen, or that you defintely will or will not do sth: *Basic human rights, including freedom of speech, are now guaranteed.* ◇ *The ticket will guarantee you free entry.* ◇ *We guarantee to deliver your goods within a week.*

NOTE PROMISE OR GUARANTEE? When you **promise** sth, you make a personal commitment to the person you are talking to, usually to do sth. **Guarantee** is less personal: when you **guarantee** sth, you mean that you will make sure that it happens. You have a moral duty to do what you have promised, but no one can legally force you to do it. You may have a legal duty to do what you have guaranteed, but people often use the word **guarantee** without actually accepting a legal duty: they mean it as a stronger form of **promise.**

swear [T, I, no passive] to make a serious or official promise to do sth or to tell the truth, for example in court: *She made him swear not to tell anyone.* ◊ *He swore revenge on the man who had killed his father.* ◊ *I swear to God I had nothing to do with it.* ◊ *Witnesses were required to swear on the Bible.* ◊ *(spoken) I think I put the keys back in the drawer, but I couldn't swear to it* (= I'm not completely sure).

pledge [T] to formally promise to give or do sth: *Japan pledged $100 million in humanitarian aid.* ◊ *Politicians of all parties pledged their support for the idea.* ◊ *The government has pledged that it will not raise taxes.*

commit (-tt-) [T] to promise sincerely that you will definitely do sth or keep to an agreement or arrangement, knowing that failure to do so may make things difficult for you; to give an opinion or make a decision openly so that it is then difficult to change it: *Several countries were reluctant to commit themselves to the treaty.* ◊ *The party was committed to reforming the electoral system.* ◊ *You don't have to commit yourself now, just think about it.* See also **committed** → RELIABLE 1

assure /ə'ʃʊə(r); -ʃɔː(r); AmE ə'ʃʊr/ [T] to tell sb that sth is definitely true or is definitely going to happen, especially when they have doubts about it: *We were assured that everything possible was being done.* ◊ *She's perfectly safe, I can assure you.* ◊ *We assured him of our loyal support.*

vow /vaʊ/ [T] *(rather formal, especially written)* to make a formal and serious promise to do sth: *She vowed never to speak to him again.* ◊ *They vowed eternal friendship.*

NOTE SWEAR OR VOW? People can **swear** that things are, have been or will be true, but **vow** is more often used to talk about things you are determined to do in the future.

undertake /ˌʌndə'teɪk; AmE -dər't-/ [T] *(formal or business)* to agree or promise that you will do sth: *They undertook to finish the job by Friday.*

promising *adj.* See also the entry for TIMELY

promising · encouraging · bright · rosy · heartening · auspicious · hopeful
These words all describe sth that is likely to be successful or to give you a good result.

PATTERNS AND COLLOCATIONS
▸ to be / look promising / encouraging / bright / rosy / auspicious / hopeful **for** sb / sth
▸ to be encouraging / heartening **to find / know / see…**
▸ a promising / an encouraging / a bright / an auspicious / a hopeful **start**
▸ a promising / an encouraging / a bright / a rosy / a hopeful **future / prospect / outlook / picture**
▸ a promising / an encouraging / an auspicious / a hopeful **sign**
▸ encouraging / heartening / hopeful **news**
▸ **very** promising / encouraging / bright / reassuring / rosy / heartening / auspicious / hopeful
▸ **extremely** promising / encouraging / bright / reassuring / hopeful
▸ **highly** promising / encouraging / auspicious / hopeful

promising showing signs of being good or successful: *At that time, I had a promising career in TV.* ◊ *The weather doesn't look very promising.* **OPP** **unpromising** ❶ Something that is **unpromising** does not look likely to be successful: *The first attempt was unpromising.* See also **promise** → POTENTIAL

encouraging giving you hope that sb/sth will be good or successful: *Last year's results were very encouraging.* ◊ *The response we got from our readers was extremely encouraging.* **OPP** **discouraging** → DISAPPOINTING

NOTE PROMISING OR ENCOURAGING? In many cases you can use either word: *a promising/an encouraging sign/result/start/prospect.* **Promising**, but NOT **encouraging**, is used to talk about people's careers: *a promising young player/newcomer/candidate/career* ◊ ~~an encouraging young player/newcomer/candidate/career~~ **Encouraging**,

but NOT **promising**, is used to talk about other people's reactions to things: ~~The response we got from readers was extremely promising.~~

bright *(especially journalism or business)* likely to be successful; giving you reason to hope: *This young musician has a bright future.* ◊ *Prospects for the coming year look bright.* ◊ *Look on the bright side* (= be cheerful about a bad situation by thinking only of the advantages and not the disadvantages). *You managed to do more than I did.*

rosy *(journalism or business, sometimes disapproving)* likely to be good or successful; making sth seem likely to be good or successful, even if it is not: *The future is looking rosy for our company.* ◊ *She painted a rosy picture of what her life in Italy would be like* (= made it appear to be very good, and perhaps better than it really would be).

heartening /'hɑːtnɪŋ; AmE 'hɑːrt-/ making you feel encouraged and more hopeful: *It is heartening to see the determination of these young people.*

auspicious /ɔː'spɪʃəs/ *(formal)* showing signs that sth is likely to be successful in the future: *It seemed an auspicious start to the new year.* ❶ **Auspicious** usually describes a time or occasion; collocates include *day, moment, time, occasion, start* and *beginning.*

hopeful giving you more hope that sb/sth will get better or be more successful: *This is the first hopeful sign that the hostages might be released soon.* ◊ *The future did not seem very hopeful.* **OPP** **hopeless** → USELESS, See also **hopeful** → OPTIMISTIC, **hope** → HOPE *noun* 1

promote *verb*

promote · foster · further · advance · spur
These words all mean to help sth to develop or succeed.

PATTERNS AND COLLOCATIONS
▸ to promote / foster / further / advance **understanding** (of sth)
▸ to promote / further / advance sb's **interests / career**
▸ to promote / further / advance a **cause**
▸ to promote / foster / spur **development / growth**
▸ to promote / foster **awareness** (of sth)
▸ to further / advance **knowledge**
▸ to **actively / directly / deliberately / intentionally / energetically** promote / foster sth

promote [T] *(rather formal)* to help sth to happen or develop: *These measures are designed to promote economic growth.* ◊ *Basketball stars from the US have helped promote the sport in Italy and Spain.* ◊ *The church tries to promote racial harmony.*
▸ **promotion** *noun* [U]: *(formal) a society for the promotion of religious tolerance*

foster [T] *(rather formal, written)* to encourage sth to grow and develop: *The club's aim is to foster better relations within the community.* ◊ *The school has carefully fostered its progressive image.*

further [T] *(rather formal)* to help sth to develop or succeed: *She took the new job to further her career.* ◊ *We are committed to furthering the interests of our members.*

advance [T] *(rather formal)* to help sth to develop or to succeed: *Will excavating this site advance our knowledge of history in a significant way?*

NOTE PROMOTE, FOSTER, FURTHER OR ADVANCE? **Foster** is usually used to talk about encouraging sth which does not yet exist or is new or just starting. **Further** and **advance** are used to talk about helping sth to develop more or be more successful than it already is. **Promote** is used in both contexts.

spur (-rr-) [T] *(written)* to make sth happen faster or sooner: *The agreement is essential to spurring economic growth.* ◊ *An increase in the country's arsenal could spur an arms race in the region.*

prompt *verb* See also the entry for CAUSE

prompt · provoke · trigger · spark · set sth off
These words all mean to make sth start happening.

PATTERNS AND COLLOCATIONS
▸ to trigger / spark / set sth **off**
▸ to prompt / provoke / trigger / spark / set off a **debate / reaction**
▸ to prompt / provoke / trigger / spark / set off **protests**
▸ to prompt / provoke / trigger / spark a / an **crisis / attack**
▸ to prompt / provoke / trigger / spark **discussions / controversy / demonstrations**
▸ to prompt / provoke / trigger a **response**
▸ to prompt / provoke / spark **anger / criticism**
▸ to provoke / trigger / spark **riots / disturbances**
▸ an **event** prompts / triggers / sparks / sets off sth

prompt [T] (*especially written*) to cause sth to start or happen, especially discussion, questioning or criticism of sth: *The news prompted speculation that prices will rise further.* ◇ *His speech prompted an angry outburst from a man in the crowd.* ◇ *The discovery of the bomb prompted an increase in security.* ❶ Things that can be **prompted** include *debate, speculation, allegations, criticism* and *worry*.

provoke /prəˈvəʊk; *AmE* -ˈvoʊk/ [T] to cause a particular feeling or reaction, especially a negative one, sometimes deliberately: *The announcement provoked a storm of protest.* ◇ *The article was intended to provoke discussion.*

trigger [T] to cause sth to start suddenly, especially sth bad: *Nuts can trigger off a violent allergic reaction.* ◇ *An influx of refugees has triggered disturbances.* ❶ Things that can be **triggered** include sudden physical illnesses such as a *fit*, an *attack*, a *reaction* or a *relapse*, and conflict or fighting between people.
▸ **trigger** *noun* [C]: *The trigger for the strike was the closure of yet another factory.*

spark [T] (*especially journalism*) to cause sth, especially a problem or emergency, to start or develop, especially suddenly: *The riots were sparked off by the arrest of a local leader.* ◇ *Winds brought down power lines, sparking a fire.*

NOTE **PROVOKE** OR **SPARK?** In many cases you can use either word: *to provoke/spark a reaction/discussion/ protest/storm* ◇ *to provoke/spark controversy/criticism/ anger/outrage*. In these cases, **spark** is slightly more informal than **provoke**, used especially in newspapers. However, **spark** is used especially to talk about causing serious events when a situation gets out of control. **Provoke** is often used when sth is caused deliberately, or the result is easy to predict: *The suggestion inevitably provoked outrage from student leaders.* **Provoke** is also used to talk about causing feelings as well as reactions: *to provoke hostility/jealousy/resentment.* **Spark** is only used to talk about stronger feelings such as *anger* and *outrage* that are openly expressed.

set sth ˈoff *phrasal verb* to start a process or series of events: *Panic on the stock market set off a wave of selling.*

prone to sth *adj.* See also the entry for LIKELY

prone to sth · susceptible · inclined to do sth · liable to sth · subject to sth
These words all describe people or things that are likely to do sth or be affected by sth.

PATTERNS AND COLLOCATIONS
▸ to be prone / susceptible / inclined / liable / subject **to** sth
▸ to be prone / inclined / liable to **do sth**
▸ **very / rather** prone / susceptible / inclined to (do) sth
▸ **especially / particularly** prone / susceptible / liable to sth
▸ **increasingly** prone / inclined / subject to (do) sth
▸ **still** prone / susceptible / liable / subject to sth

prone to sth/to do sth *phrase* likely to be affected by sth unpleasant or to do sth bad: *You will be more prone to infection after the operation.* ◇ *Tired drivers were found to be particularly prone to ignore warning signs.* ❶ People are

typically **prone** to *accidents, allergies, infection, spots, depression, doubt, errors* and *failure*. Things and places are typically prone to *damp, fog, rotting* and *vandalism*. -**prone** is used in compound adjectives meaning 'likely to do or suffer the thing mentioned': *She was the most accident-prone of the four children* (= the one who had accidents most often). ◇ *error-prone* ◇ *injury-prone* ◇ *a crisis-prone/strike-prone industry*

susceptible /səˈseptəbl/ [not usually before noun] (*rather formal*) likely to be influenced, harmed or affected by sb/sth: *He's highly susceptible to flattery.* ◇ *Some of these plants are more susceptible to frost damage than others.* ◇ *There are few known diseases which are not susceptible to medical treatment.* ❶ **Susceptible** is often used in scientific texts, where it is used to talk about places and things that are likely to be affected by *acid rain, contamination, disease, erosion, frost* and *attack*. People are typically said to be susceptible to *corruption, depression, infection, flattery* and *persuasion*.
▸ **susceptibility** *noun* [U, sing.]: *susceptibility to disease/ infection*

inclined to do sth *phrase* tending to do sth; likely to do sth: *He's inclined to be lazy.* ◇ *They'll be more inclined to listen if you don't shout.* See also **inclination** → DESIRE

liable to sth/to do sth *phrase* likely to be affected by sth, especially sth unpleasant; likely to do sth, especially as a result of a fault or weakness: *You are more liable to injury if you exercise infrequently.* ◇ *The bridge is liable to collapse at any moment.*

subject to sth *phrase* (*formal*) likely to be affected by sth, especially sth unpleasant: *Flights are subject to delay because of the fog.* ◇ *Smokers are more subject to heart attacks than non-smokers.* ❶ **Subject to...** is often used with words relating to changes: *to be subject to change/ delay/alteration/cancellation/amendment.* It is also often used to talk about places that are affected by environmental factors: *subject to drought/flooding/erosion/severe weather conditions*

propaganda *noun* See the Topic Map for FACT AND OPINION on p.898

propaganda · misinformation · disinformation · indoctrination · brainwashing
These are all words for ideas or statements that may be false or exaggerated and that are used to gain support for a political or religious leader, set of beliefs, etc.

PATTERNS AND COLLOCATIONS
▸ propaganda / misinformation / disinformation **about** sth
▸ **political / religious** propaganda / indoctrination
▸ **government / official** propaganda / disinformation
▸ to **spread** propaganda / misinformation / disinformation
▸ a propaganda / misinformation / disinformation **campaign**

propaganda /ˌprɒpəˈgændə; *AmE* ˌprɑːpə-/ [U] (*disapproving*) ideas or statements that may be false or exaggerated and that are used in order to gain support for a political leader or party: *This document is pure party propaganda.* ❶ **Propaganda** may consist of true information, but it often fails to give a complete and balanced picture. The term is usually used in political contexts.

misinformation [U] (*rather formal, usually disapproving*) incorrect information, especially when this is intended to deceive sb: *Most of these attitudes are based on misinformation.*
▸ **misinform** /ˌmɪsɪnˈfɔːm; *AmE* -ˈfɔːrm/ *verb* [T, often passive]: *They were deliberately misinformed about their rights.*

disinformation [U] (*rather formal, disapproving*) incorrect information that is given deliberately, especially by government organizations: *It was a very plausible piece of disinformation.*

NOTE **MISINFORMATION** OR **DISINFORMATION?** Misinformation is information that is incorrect, and that may or may not be intended to deceive people. It is often used in contexts describing how the general public have been given the wrong information about sth. **Disinformation** is false information that is spread deliberately in order to deceive people, especially in the contexts of governments and spying.

indoctrination /ɪnˌdɒktrɪˈneɪʃn; AmE -ˌdɑːk-/ [U] (*rather formal, disapproving*) the activity of forcing sb to accept a particular belief or set of beliefs and not allowing them to consider any others: *They were accused of political indoctrination.* ❶ **Indoctrination** is often used to talk about unbalanced religious or political teaching directed at children.
▸ **indoctrinate** verb [T]: *It is not a teacher's place to indoctrinate students.*

brainwashing /ˈbreɪnwɒʃɪŋ; AmE -wɑːʃ; -wɔːʃ/ [U] (*disapproving*) the activity of forcing sb to accept your ideas or beliefs, for example by repeating the same thing many times or by preventing the person from thinking clearly: *They refused to accept that they were victims of brainwashing.* ❶ **Brainwashing** is often used to talk about the techniques or methods of forcing people to accepts beliefs: *It's a classic method of brainwashing.*
▸ **brainwash** verb [T]: *The group has been accused of brainwashing its younger members.* ◇ *They were brainwashed into believing that their leader was all-powerful.*

proposal noun See also the entry for PLAN 1

proposal · recommendation · suggestion · proposition · motion
These are all words for an idea or plan which sb suggests for sb else to consider.

PATTERNS AND COLLOCATIONS
▸ a proposal / recommendation / suggestion / motion **for** / **on** sth
▸ a recommendation / suggestion **about** sth
▸ a proposal / recommendation / suggestion / proposition / motion **that**...
▸ a **practical** / **specific** proposal / recommendation / suggestion
▸ to **accept** / **support** / **reject** / **discuss** a proposal / recommendation / suggestion / proposition / motion
▸ to **make** / **consider** a proposal / recommendation / suggestion / proposition
▸ to **submit** / **put forward** / **oppose** a proposal / recommendation / suggestion / motion
▸ to **put** a proposal / motion **to** sb
▸ to **welcome** a proposal / recommendation / suggestion
▸ to **adopt** a recommendation / suggestion / motion
▸ to **approve** a proposal / recommendation / motion

proposal [C, U] an idea or plan that sb formally suggests should be considered; the act of doing this: *I welcome the proposal to reduce taxes for the low-paid.* ◇ *His proposal that the system be changed was rejected.* ◇ *They judged that the time was right for the proposal of new terms for the trade agreement.* See also **proposal** → OFFER *noun* 1

recommendation /ˌrekəmenˈdeɪʃn/ [C] an idea or plan that a person or group officially suggests concerning the best thing to do, especially one contained in a report: *The committee made recommendations to the board on teachers' pay and conditions.* ◇ *The major recommendation is for a change in the law.* ◇ *I had the operation on the recommendation of my doctor.* See also **recommend** → RECOMMEND 1

suggestion [C] an idea or plan that you mention for sb else to think about: *Can I make a suggestion?* ◇ *Do you have any suggestions?* ◇ *We need to get it there by four. Any suggestions?* ◇ *We are open to suggestions* (= willing to listen to ideas from other people). See also **suggest** → RECOMMEND 2

proposition /ˌprɒpəˈzɪʃn; AmE ˌprɑːp-/ [C] an idea or plan that is suggested, especially in business: *I'd like to put a business proposition to you.* ◇ *He was trying to make it look like an attractive proposition.* ◇ *Is that a viable proposition?*

motion [C] a formal proposal that is discussed and voted on at a meeting: *The motion was carried by six votes to one.* ◇ *He proposed a motion of no confidence in the government* (= to show that there is no longer any support for government).

propose verb See also the entry for RECOMMEND 1

propose · suggest · put sth forward · move · advance · moot
These words all mean to tell people about a plan, idea or theory for them to discuss or consider.

PATTERNS AND COLLOCATIONS
▸ to propose / suggest / put forward / advance / moot sth **as** sth
▸ to propose / suggest / be put forward / move / be mooted **that**...
▸ to propose / suggest / put forward / advance / moot an **idea**
▸ to propose / suggest / put forward / advance / moot a **plan**
▸ to propose / suggest / put forward / moot a **scheme**
▸ to propose / suggest / put forward / advance a **solution**
▸ to propose / put forward / advance a **theory**
▸ to put forward / advance / moot a **proposal**
▸ to propose / suggest / put forward a / an **change** / **measure** / **alternative**
▸ to propose / put forward / advance a **view**

propose [T] (*rather formal*) to tell people about a plan or idea for them to think about and decide on; to tell people about a plan or idea at a formal meeting and ask them to vote on it; to suggest an explanation of sth for people to consider: *The measures have been proposed as a way of improving standards.* ◇ *He proposed changing the name of the company.* ◇ *It was proposed that the president be elected for a period of two years.* ◇ *It was proposed to pay the money from public funds.* ◇ *He will propose a motion* (= be the main speaker in support of an idea) *in tomorrow's debate.* ◇ *She proposed a possible solution to the mystery.* See also **oppose** → OPPOSE, **second** → SUPPORT 1, **table** → PRESENT 3

suggest [T] to tell people about a plan or idea for them to think about: *I suggest (that) we go out to eat.* ◇ *I suggested going in my car.* ◇ *He suggested to the committee that they should delay making a decision.* ◇ *It has been suggested that bright children take their exams early.* ◇ *The report suggested a two-stage process.*

‚put sth 'forward phrasal verb (*rather formal*) to tell people about a plan or idea for them to discuss, usually so that sth can be decided: *Several suggestions were put forward for possible venues.* ◇ *He put forward some very convincing arguments.*

> **NOTE** PROPOSE, SUGGEST OR PUT FORWARD? Suggest is often used in less formal situations than **propose** or **put sth forward**, especially when making personal suggestions or arrangements: *I suggest that we go out to eat.* You can say 'I propose that we go out to eat.' but this sounds very formal. **Put sth forward** is NOT used with *I* in this way: *I put forward that we go out to eat.* **Suggest** is sometimes less certain than **propose** or **put sth forward**: you might **suggest** sth in order to be helpful, or in a gentle way because you are not sure how welcome your suggestion will be; you are more likely to **propose** or **put sth forward** in a confident way and when you definitely want your idea to be accepted. When sth is to be considered in a formal process it is more usual to use **propose** or **put sth forward**: *They are ready to discuss plans proposed/put forward by the UN.* ◇ *They are ready to discuss plans suggested by the UN.* You can **put forward** but NOT propose or suggest a *suggestion* or *argument.*

move [T] (*formal*) to suggest sth formally, for example in parliament or in a formal debate, so that it can be discussed and decided: *I move that a vote be taken on this.* ◇ *The Opposition moved an amendment to the Bill.*

advance [T] (*formal*) to suggest an idea, theory or plan for people to discuss: *The article advances a new theory to explain changes in the climate.* ❶ **Advance** is a more formal way of saying **put sth forward**; it is used especially in theoretical contexts, to talk about an *idea*, a *theory*, a *thesis*, an *explanation* or an *argument*, although it can also be used in practical contexts to talk about plans and solutions.

moot /muːt/ [T, usually passive] (*formal*) to suggest a plan for people to discuss: *The idea was first mooted at last week's meeting.* ◇ *It had been mooted that there should be a study period after school.* ❶ An idea is usually **mooted** at a fairly early stage of thinking, before all the details have been worked out into a definite proposal.

protect *verb* See also the entry for SAVE 1

protect · defend · guard · preserve · safeguard · shield · shelter · secure
These words all mean to make sure that sb/sth is not harmed, injured or damaged.

PATTERNS AND COLLOCATIONS
▸ to protect/defend/guard/preserve/safeguard/shield/shelter/ secure sb/sth **from** sth
▸ to protect/defend/guard/safeguard/secure sth **against** sth
▸ to protect/defend **yourself**
▸ to protect/preserve/safeguard **jobs**
▸ to protect/preserve a **species**
▸ **heavily** protected/defended/guarded

protect [T, I] to make sure that sb/sth is not harmed, injured or damaged: *They huddled together to protect themselves from the wind.* ◇ *Each company is fighting to protect its own commercial interests.* ◇ *The paint helps protect against rust.* **OPP expose** → EXPOSE, See also **protection** → SECURITY

defend [T, I] to protect sb/sth from attack: *All our officers are trained to defend themselves against knife attacks.* ◇ *Troops have been sent to defend the borders.* ◇ *It is impossible to defend against an all-out attack.* See also **defence** → PRECAUTION

guard [T] to protect property, places or people from attack or danger: *Delegates at the conference were guarded by the police.* ◇ *You can't get in; the whole place is guarded.* ◇ (*figurative*) *The recipe is a closely guarded secret.* → **guard** → GUARD *noun*, → **guard** → WATCH *noun*

preserve [T] (*rather formal*) to keep sb/sth alive or existing, or safe from harm or danger: *To preserve life should always be the goal.* ◇ *The society was set up to preserve endangered species from extinction.* ◇ *She was determined to preserve her independence and way of life.*
▸ **preservation** *noun* [U]: *The central issue in the strike was the preservation of jobs.*

safeguard /'seɪfɡɑːd; AmE -ɡɑːrd/ [T, I] (*formal*) to protect sth from loss, harm or damage: *It is hoped that the order will safeguard jobs at the plant.* ◇ *The leaflet explains how to safeguard against dangers in the home.* See also **safeguard** → PRECAUTION

shield /ʃiːld/ [T] to protect sb/sth from danger, harm or sth unpleasant, especially by putting sb/sth between them and the source of danger: *I shielded my eyes against the glare.* ◇ *Police believe that somebody is shielding the killer.* ◇ *You can't shield her from the truth forever.* See also **shield** → PRECAUTION

shelter [T] to give sb/sth a place where they are protected from the weather or from danger: *Trees shelter the house from the wind.* ◇ *Perhaps I sheltered my daughter too much* (= protected her too much from unpleasant or difficult experiences). See also **shelter** → SHELTER *noun*

secure /sɪ'kjʊərəti; AmE sə'kjʊr-/ [T] to protect sth so that it is safe and difficult for other people to attack or damage: *No home can be completely secured against intruders.* ◇ *The windows were secured with locks and bars.* ◇ *The government has deployed 35 000 troops in an effort to secure the border.* See also **security** → SECURITY

protective *adj.*

protective · defensive · preventive · precautionary · waterproof
These words all describe sth that is intended to protect sb/sth.

PATTERNS AND COLLOCATIONS
▸ a protective/defensive/preventive/precautionary **measure/ action**
▸ a defensive/preventive/precautionary **approach**
▸ protective/waterproof **clothing**

protective /prə'tektɪv/ [only before noun] intended to keep sb/sth safe from injury, damage or loss: *Workers should wear full protective clothing.* ◇ *The ozone layer forms a protective barrier against the sun's rays.* See also **protection** → SECURITY

defensive /dɪ'fensɪv/ intended to keep sb/sth safe from attack: *Troops are taking up a defensive position around the town.* See also **defence** → PRECAUTION

preventive /prɪ'ventɪv/ (also **preventative** /prɪ-'ventətɪv/) [only before noun] intended to stop sth before it happens, especially sth that causes problems: *She stressed the importance of basic health education and preventive medicine.* ◇ *The police were able to take preventive action and avoid a possible riot.* See also **prevent** → PREVENT

precautionary /prɪ'kɔː.ʃənəri; AmE -neri/ (*rather formal*) done in order to prevent possible problems or avoid danger: *He was kept in hospital overnight as a precautionary measure.* See also **precaution** → PRECAUTION

waterproof /'wɔːtəpruːf; AmE 'wɔːtərp-; 'wɑːt-/ that does not let water go through: *a waterproof jacket* ❶ There are a number of other compound adjectives formed with **-proof**, that describe things that can resist or protect against the thing mentioned. Examples include *rainproof, windproof, heatproof, fireproof* and *shatter-proof*: *The car has childproof locks on the rear doors.* ◇ *an inflation-proof pension plan*

protester *noun*

protester · opponent · demonstrator · dissident · rebel
These are all words for a person who expresses opposition to sb/sth.

PATTERNS AND COLLOCATIONS
▸ a protester/demonstrator/rebel **against** sth
▸ **angry/peaceful** protesters/demonstrators
▸ an **anti-government** protester/demonstrator/rebel
▸ a **political** opponent/demonstrator/dissident
▸ protesters/opponents/demonstrators/rebels **call for/demand** sth

protester [C] a person who makes a public protest: *Police arrested more than 200 anti-nuclear protesters at the military base.* See also **protest** → COMPLAIN

opponent [C] a person who is opposed to sth and tries to change or stop it: *He has emerged as a leading opponent of the reforms.* ◇ *The regime has been accused of torturing and killing its opponents.* **OPP supporter** → SUPPORTER, **proponent** → ADVOCATE, See also **oppose** → OPPOSE

demonstrator [C] a person who takes part in a public meeting or march in order to protest against sb/sth or to show support for sb/sth: *Troops opened fire on a crowd of pro-democracy demonstrators.*

NOTE PROTESTER OR DEMONSTRATOR? Demonstrator is used more frequently than **protester** to refer to a person who is marching (= walking in a group to show opposition to sth): *A procession of 30 000 demonstrators marched to the parliament building.* Protester often refers to a person who expresses opposition in other ways: *Two anti-war protesters climbed the clock tower at the Houses of Parliament.*

dissident /'dɪsɪdənt/ [C] a person who strongly disagrees with and criticizes their government, especially in a country where this kind of action is dangerous: *Dissidents were often imprisoned by the security police.*

rebel /'rebl/ [C] a person who opposes sb/sth in authority over them within an organization: *A number of Labour rebels are planning to vote against the government.* See also **rebel → REBEL** *verb*

proud *adj.*

1 Don't be too proud to ask for advice.
2 too proud to be seen with his former friends

---

1 proud · dignified · self-respecting
These words all describe a person who has respect for themselves and/or who deserves respect.

PATTERNS AND COLLOCATIONS
▸ a proud / dignified / self-respecting **man** / **woman**

proud (*often approving*) having respect for yourself and not wanting to lose the respect of others: *They were a proud and independent people.* ◇ *Don't be too proud to ask for advice.* See also **pride → DIGNITY**, **proud → GLAD**

dignified /'dɪgnɪfaɪd/ (*approving*) calm and serious and deserving respect: *They left quietly in an orderly and dignified manner.* ◇ *Throughout his trial he maintained a dignified silence.* **OPP undignified → IMPROPER**, See also **dignity → DIGNITY**

self-re'specting [only before noun] (used especially in negative sentences) having respect for yourself because you believe that what you do is right and good: *No self-respecting journalist would ever work for that newspaper.* See also **self-respect → DIGNITY**

---

2 See also the entry for PATRONIZING
proud · arrogant · pompous · vain · cocky · haughty · self-important · high-handed · conceited · boastful
These words all describe sb who feels or behaves as if they are better or more important than other people.

PATTERNS AND COLLOCATIONS
▸ arrogant / vain / cocky / conceited **about** sth
▸ a proud / an arrogant / a pompous / a vain / a haughty / a self-important / a conceited **man**
▸ a proud / an arrogant / a vain / a haughty / a conceited **woman**
▸ an arrogant / a pompous / a haughty / a high-handed **way** / **manner**
▸ an arrogant / a cocky / a haughty / a high-handed **attitude**
▸ arrogant / self-important / high-handed **behaviour**

proud (*disapproving*) feeling that you are better and more important than other people: *She was too proud to admit she could be wrong.* ◇ *He was too proud now to be seen with his former friends.* **OPP humble → MODEST**, See also **pride → PRIDE**, **proud → GLAD**

arrogant /'ærəgənt/ (*disapproving*) behaving in an unpleasant way as if you are better or more important than other people, showing little thought for their feelings or opinions: *He was a rude, arrogant young man.* ◇ *The chief inspector disliked his arrogant manner.* See also **arrogance → PRIDE**
▸ **arrogantly** *adv.*: *Luke was arrogantly confident.*

pompous /'pɒmpəs/ *AmE* 'pɑːm-/ (*disapproving*) showing that you think you are more important than other people, especially by using long and formal words: *a pompous official* ◇ *She made a long, pompous speech.*
▸ **pomposity** /pɒm'pɒsəti; *AmE* pɑːm'pɑːs-/ *noun* [U]: *The prince's manner was informal, without a trace of pomposity.*

vain (*disapproving*) too proud of your appearance, abilities or achievements: *She's too vain to wear glasses.* ◇ *I don't think it's vain to care about how you look.* **OPP modest → MODEST**, See also **vanity → PRIDE**

cocky (*informal, disapproving*) too confident about yourself in a way that annoys other people: *Don't get cocky with me!*

haughty /'hɔːti/ (*especially written, disapproving*) behaving in an unfriendly way towards other people because you think that you are better than them: *She threw him a look of haughty disdain.*
▸ **haughtily** *adv.*: *She looked haughtily at me, waiting for me to leave .*

self-im'portant (*disapproving*) thinking that you are more important than other people: *He was a self-important little man.* **OPP humble → MODEST**

high-'handed (*disapproving*) using authority in an unreasonable way, without considering the opinions of other people: *Customers are angry over the bank's high-handed attitude.*

conceited /kən'siːtɪd/ (*disapproving*) too proud of yourself and what you can do: *It's very conceited of you to assume that your work is always the best.* See also **conceit → PRIDE**

boastful (*disapproving*) talking about yourself in a very proud way: *I tried to emphasize my good points without sounding boastful.* **OPP modest → MODEST**, See also **boast → BOAST**

provide *verb*

---

provide · give · supply · yield · issue · lend · put sth up
These words all mean to make sth available for sb to use.

PATTERNS AND COLLOCATIONS
▸ to provide / supply / put up sth **for** sb
▸ to give / supply / issue / lend sth **to** sb
▸ to provide / supply / issue sb **with** sth
▸ to provide / give / supply / issue **equipment** / **details** / **information**
▸ to provide / give / supply / put up **funds**
▸ to provide / give / supply / lend **protection**
▸ to provide / give / supply a **service**
▸ to provide / give / supply **housing** / **assistance**
▸ to provide / give / lend **support** / **credibility** / **weight** / **credence**
▸ to provide / give / yield / issue a **dividend**
▸ to provide / give / yield a / an **improvement** / **profit** / **result** / **return** / **revenue**
▸ to provide / give / supply an **alibi** / **alternative** / **answer**
▸ to provide / give / supply / issue sth **free (of charge)**

provide [T] (*rather formal, especially written*) to make sth available for sb to use: *The hospital has a commitment to provide the best possible medical care.* ◇ *Please answer questions in the space provided.* ◇ *The report was not expected to provide any answers.*
▸ **provision** /prə'vɪʒn/ *noun* [U, C, usually sing.]: *educational/housing provision* ◇ *The provision of specialist teachers is being increased.*

give [T] to provide sb with sth: *They were all thirsty so I gave them a drink.* ◇ *Give me your name and address.* ◇ *I was hoping you would give me a job.* ◇ *She wants a job that gives her more responsibility.* ◇ *He was given a new heart in a five-hour operation.* ◇ *They couldn't give me any more information.* ◇ *I'll give you (= allow you to have) ten minutes to prepare your answer.* ◇ *He gives Italian lessons to his colleagues.*

NOTE PROVIDE OR GIVE? **Provide** is more formal than **give**, used especially in written English. **Provide** is often used when sth is being made available to people in general, or to sb who is not mentioned; **give** is more often used when sth is being made available to a particular person: *The hospital aims to provide the best possible medical care.* ◇ *We want to **give you** the best possible care.*

supply [T] (*rather formal*) to provide sb/sth with sth that they need or want, especially in large quantities: *Foreign governments supplied the rebels with arms.* ◇ *Here is a list of foods supplying our daily vitamin needs.* ◇ *She was jailed for supplying drugs.* ◇ *This one power station keeps half the country supplied with electricity.* See also **supply → SUPPLY** *noun*
▸ **supply** *noun* [U]: *the electricity supply* ◇ *The UN has agreed to allow the supply of emergency aid.*

yield /jiːld/ [T] (*rather formal, especially business*) to produce or provide sth, for example a profit or result: *Higher-rate deposit accounts yield good returns.* ◇ *The research has yielded useful information.* See also **yield** → OUTPUT *noun*

issue [T, often passive] (*rather formal*) to provide sb with sth, especially officially: *We can issue a passport within a day.* ◇ *New members will be issued with a temporary identity card.* ◇ *Work permits were issued to only 5% of those who applied for them.*

lend [T] to provide help or support to a person, theory or cause: *I was more than happy to lend my support to such a good cause.* ◇ *He came along to lend me moral support.*

‚put sth 'up *phrasal verb* (*rather informal, especially business*) to provide or lend money: *A local businessman has put up the £500 000 needed to save the club.*

---

provide for sb *phrasal verb* See also the entry for SERVE 2

---

provide for sb · support · keep · maintain
These words all mean to give sb/sth everything necessary to live or exist.

PATTERNS AND COLLOCATIONS
▸ to provide for / support / keep / maintain a / your **family** / **children** / **wife** / **husband**
▸ to provide for / support / keep / maintain **yourself**
▸ to support / maintain sb **financially**

pro'vide for sb *phrasal verb* to give sb the things that they need to live, such as food, money and clothing: *Local authorities must do more to provide for children in need.* ◇ *He provided for her in his will.*

support [T] to provide for sb financially over a period of time; to provide the money or conditions necessary for sth to exist or continue: *Mark has two children to support from his first marriage.* ◇ *He turned to crime to support his drug habit.* ◇ *The atmosphere of Mars could not support life.*
▸ **support** *noun* [U]: *She has no visible means of support* (= no work or income).

keep [T] (*BrE*) to provide for sb financially over a period of time: *He scarcely earns enough to keep himself and his family.* ◇ (*disapproving*) *I need to work — I can't go on being a kept man* (= supported financially by, for example, my wife). ❶ In American English **keep** is only used in this meaning in the phrase *a kept man/woman*.
▸ **keep** *noun* [U]: *It's about time you got a job to earn your keep.*

maintain [T] (*rather formal*) to provide for sb financially over a period of time: *Her income was barely enough to maintain one child, let alone three.*
▸ **maintenance** *noun* [U]: (*BrE, law*) *He has to pay maintenance to his ex-wife.*

> NOTE WHICH WORD? You can **provide for sb** on a continuous basis, or by making one large payment that will give them enough to live on in the future. If you **keep**, **support** or **maintain** sb you provide for them on a continuous basis over a period of time. **Support** emphasizes the help that you give to sb; **keep** sometimes puts more emphasis on the fact that sb is unable or unwilling to provide for themselves, and can be disapproving: *I don't want to be a kept woman.* **Maintain** is less frequent and more formal.

---

provoke *verb*

---

provoke · goad · prod · sting
These words all mean to make sb react or do sth by doing or saying sth that you know will annoy them or make them angry.

PATTERNS AND COLLOCATIONS
▸ to provoke / goad / prod / sting sb **into** sth

▸ to provoke / goad / prod / sting sb **into doing sth**
▸ to provoke / goad / prod sb **to do sth**
▸ to provoke / goad / prod sting sb **into action**
▸ to **deliberately** provoke / goad sb

provoke /prəˈvəʊk; *AmE* -ˈvoʊk/ [T] to say or do sth that you know will annoy sb so that they react in an angry way: *She had been trying to provoke her sister into an argument.* ◇ *She laughed aloud, which provoked him to fury.* ◇ *Be careful what you say — he's easily provoked.*
▸ **provocation** /ˌprɒvəˈkeɪʃn; *AmE* ˌprɑːv-/ *noun* [U, C]: *The crime was committed under provocation.*

goad /ɡəʊd; *AmE* ɡoʊd/ [T] (*especially written*) to deliberately keep annoying sb/sth until they react: *Goaded beyond endurance, she turned on him and hit out.* ◇ *He goaded her into saying more than she intended.*

prod (-**dd**-) [T] (*rather informal*) to try to make sb do sth, especially when they are unwilling, often by deliberately annoying them or asking them sth repeatedly: *She finally prodded him into action.* ◇ *He kept very quiet until she prodded him to say what he was looking for.*

sting [T] to make sb do sth that they are unwilling to do by making them feel so angry or upset that they react: *He was stung into making a cheap retort.* ◇ *Their cruel remarks stung her into action.*

---

proximity *noun*

---

proximity · vicinity · locality · neighbourhood
These words all mean the area that is close to a particular place.

PATTERNS AND COLLOCATIONS
▸ **in** the vicinity / locality / neighbourhood
▸ **in the** proximity / vicinity / neighbourhood **of** sth
▸ the **immediate** proximity / vicinity / locality / neighbourhood

proximity /prɒkˈsɪməti; *AmE* prɑːk-/ [U] (*rather formal*) the state of being near sb/sth in distance or time: *The proximity of the college to London makes it very popular.* ◇ *The area has a number of schools in close proximity to each other.*

vicinity /vəˈsɪnəti/ (*usually* **the vicinity**) [sing.] (*rather formal*) the area that is close to a particular place or person: *Crowds gathered in the vicinity of Trafalgar Square.* ◇ *He usually objected strongly to anyone smoking in his vicinity.*

locality /ləʊˈkæləti; *AmE* loʊ-/ [C] (*rather formal*) the area that is close to a particular place: *There is no airport in the locality.*

neighbourhood (*BrE*) (*AmE* **neighborhood**) /ˈneɪbəhʊd; *AmE* ˈneɪbər-/ [C] the area that is close to a particular place or person, especially an area where many people live: *We searched the surrounding neighbourhood for the missing boy.* ◇ *Houses in the neighbourhood of Paris are extremely expensive.* See also **neighbourhood** → AREA 1

---

public *adj.*

---

public · state · national · federal
These words all describe things connected with the government of a country, especially government spending and services.

PATTERNS AND COLLOCATIONS
▸ public / state / national / federal **authorities** / **funding** / **expenditure** / **investment**
▸ public / state / federal **power** / **control** / **regulation** / **institutions** / **officials** / **employees** / **funds** / **money** / **finance** / **spending**
▸ public / state **education** / **hospitals** / **enterprise** / **ownership**
▸ the public / state **sector**
▸ the national / federal **government**

public [only before noun] connected with the government and the services it provides: *Their tax plans would hit public services.* ◇ *There has been massive investment in public housing.* ◇ *He spent much of his career in public office* (= working for the government). ❶ In the US,

Australia, Scotland and some other countries a **public school** is a free local school paid for by the government; in England this is called a **state school**. In Britain, especially England, a **public school** is a private school for young people between the ages of 13 and 18, who often live at the school while they are studying, and whose parents pay for their education. A **public company** or **public limited company** (in British English) or **public corporation** (in American English) is also not owned by the government, but a company that sells shares in itself to the public. However, in British English a **public corporation** is an organization that *is* owned by the government and that provides a national service. **OPP private ❶** A *private* service or institution is owned or managed by an individual person or an independent company rather than by the government: *private companies/schools* ◇ *a programme to return many of the state companies to private ownership*
▸ **publicly** *adv.*: *a publicly owned company*

state [only before noun] provided or controlled by the government: *The law applies only to schools within the state system.* ◇ *There needs to be an increase in the basic state pension.* ◇ *Many local families are dependent on state benefits* (= in Britain, government money given to people who are poor). **OPP private**, See also **state** → COUNTRY 1

national [usually before noun] owned, controlled or financially supported by the government: *The collection is housed at the national museum.* ◇ *The Romanian national airline has ordered seven of the new aircraft.*

federal /'fedərəl/ connected with national government rather than the local government of an individual state: *On 15th February a federal judge ruled in their favour.* ◇ *We will continue federal funding for the arts.* ❶ *Federal* is used about countries, especially the US, which have a system of government in which the individual states of a country have control over their own affairs, but are controlled by a central government for national decisions.
▸ **federally** *adv.*: *federally funded health care*

publish *verb*

1 publish results
2 publish a novel

---

1 publish · issue · release · advertise · print · publicize · circulate
These words all mean to make information known to the public.

PATTERNS AND COLLOCATIONS
▸ to issue / release / circulate sth **to** sb
▸ to publish / issue / release / print / circulate a **report** / **details**
▸ to publish / issue / release / print a **document** / **statement** / **description**
▸ to publish / issue / print an **apology**
▸ to publish / print a / an **picture** / **photo** / **article**
▸ to publish / advertise / publicize / circulate sth **widely**
▸ to publish / issue / release / advertise sth **formally**
▸ to publish / issue / release sth **officially**

publish [T] to print a letter, article, photograph, etc. in a newspaper or magazine; to make sth available to the public on the Internet: *The editors published a full apology in the following edition.* ◇ *The report will be published on the Internet.* ❶ In formal language **publish** can also mean 'to make official information available to the public': *The findings of the committee will be published on Friday.*
▸ **publication** *noun* [U]: *The newspaper continues to defend its publication of the photographs.*

issue [T] (*rather formal*) to make information formally available to the public: *They issued a joint statement denying the charges.* ◇ *The police have issued an appeal for witnesses.*
▸ **issue** *noun* [U]: *the issue of a joint statement by the French and German governments*

release [T] (*rather formal*) to make information formally available to the public: *Police have released no further details about the accident.*

NOTE PUBLISH, ISSUE OR RELEASE? These words can all be used to talk about things such as descriptions, reports, documents and statements being formally made available to the public. However, **issue** has the widest range of collocates in this meaning and is often found with words relating to announcements, for example *declaration, proclamation, joint/public statement, notice* and *communiqué*, as well as legal notices, such as *summons, warrant* and *writ*. **Publish**, but NOT **issue** or **release**, is also used to talk about letters and articles.

advertise [I, T] to let people know that sth is going to happen, or that a job is available by giving details about it in a newspaper, on a notice in a public place, etc; to show or tell sth about yourself to other people: *We are currently advertising for a new sales manager.* ◇ *We should have advertised the concert much more widely.* ◇ *If I were you, I wouldn't advertise the fact that you don't have a work permit.* See also **advertise** → ADVERTISE
▸ **advertisement** *noun* [U]: *We are employing an assistant to help with the advertisement of the group's activities.*

print [T] to publish sth in printed form: *The photo was printed in all the national newspapers.* ◇ *The magazine was sued for printing a libellous article about her family.*

publicize (*BrE* also **-ise**) /'pʌblɪsaɪz/ [T] to make sth known to the public: *They flew to Europe to publicize the plight of the refugees.* ◇ *In a much publicized speech* (= that has received a lot of attention on television, in newspapers, etc.) *she condemned the government for its inactivity.*

NOTE ADVERTISE OR PUBLICIZE? People usually **advertise** jobs or events in print, in a newspaper, on public notices or on the Internet. People **publicize** events or information by talking about them a lot in public or holding special events, which then get reported on television, in newspapers and on the Internet.

circulate /'sɜːkjəleɪt; *AmE* 'sɜːrk-/ [T] (*rather formal*) to send information to all the people in a group: *The document will be circulated to all members.*

---

2 See the Topic Map for THE MEDIA on p.900
publish · issue · print · release
These words all mean to produce sth such as a book, magazine or CD, and sell it to the public.

PATTERNS AND COLLOCATIONS
▸ to publish / issue / print / release a **book**
▸ to publish / issue / print a **booklet** / **brochure** / **newsletter** / **leaflet** / **pamphlet**
▸ to publish / issue / release a new **title** / **edition**
▸ to issue / release a / an **CD** / **single** / **album**
▸ to issue / print **banknotes**
▸ to publish / release sth **on CD-ROM**
▸ to issue / release sth **on CD**
▸ to be **newly** / **recently** published / issued / released
▸ to be **privately** published / printed

publish [T, I] to produce a book, magazine, CD-ROM, etc. and sell it to the public; (of an author) to have your work printed and sold to the public: *He works for a company that publishes reference books.* ◇ *Most of our titles are also published on CD-ROM.* ◇ *She hasn't published anything for years.* ◇ *University teachers are under pressure to publish.*
▸ **publication** *noun* [U]: *the publication of his first novel*

issue [T] (*rather formal*) to produce sth such as a magazine, new book or CD and sell it to the public; to offer new stamps, coins or shares in a company for sale to the public: *We issue a monthly newsletter.* ◇ *The Royal Mail issued a special set of stamps to mark the occasion.*
▸ **issue** *noun* [U]: *I bought a set of the new stamps on the date of issue.*

NOTE PUBLISH OR ISSUE? Publish is the usual word for talking about producing books for sale to the public: *a company that publishes reference books* ◇ ~~a company that issues reference books~~. However, if you are talking about a particular book, especially a new one, you can use either word: *They have just published/issued a new edition*. **Issue** is used more frequently with words relating to smaller publications produced by organizations, such as *booklet, newsletter, leaflet* or *pamphlet*, although **publish** can also be used with these.

print [T] to produce books, newspapers, etc. by printing them in large quantities: *They printed 30 000 copies of the book.* ◇ *The firm specializes in printing calendars.*

release [T] to make a film, book, CD or other product available to the public: *When was the film first released?* ◇ *There have been a lot of new products released onto the market.*
▸ **release** *noun* [U]: *The movie goes on general release (= will be widely shown in cinemas) next week.*

pull *verb*

1 pull a cart
2 pull the plug out
3 pull sb's hair

1 pull · drag · draw · haul · tow · trail · tug
These words all mean to move sth in a particular direction, especially towards or behind you.

▸ to pull / drag / draw / haul / tow / trail / tug sb / sth **along / down / towards** sth
▸ to pull / drag / draw / haul / tow / trail sb / sth **behind you**
▸ to pull / drag / draw / haul a **cart / sledge / sled**
▸ to pull / drag / draw a **coach / carriage**
▸ to pull / haul / tow a **truck**
▸ **horses** pull / draw / haul sth
▸ **dogs** pull / drag / haul sth

pull [T] to hold sth and move it in a particular direction; to hold or be attached to a vehicle and move it along behind you: *Pull the chair nearer to the table.* ◇ *She took his arm and pulled him along roughly.* ◇ *I quickly pulled on my sweater.* ◇ *They use oxen to pull their carts.* **OPP** **push** → PUSH 1

drag (-**gg**-) [T] to pull sb/sth in a particular direction or behind you, usually along the ground, and especially with effort and difficulty: *I dragged the chair over to the window.* ◇ *Police dragged protesters away from the embassy entrance.* ◇ *The sack is too heavy to lift — you'll have to drag it.* ◇ *Dogs drag the sledges for hundreds of miles across the snow.*

draw [T] (*written*) to move sb/sth by pulling them/it gently; to pull a vehicle such as a carriage: *He drew the cork out of the bottle.* ◇ *I drew my chair closer to the fire.* ◇ *I tried to draw him aside (= for example in order to talk to him privately).* ◇ *a horse-drawn carriage*

haul /hɔːl/ [T] to pull sb/sth to a particular place with a lot of effort: *He reached down and hauled her up onto the ledge.* ◇ *Fishermen were hauling in their nets.* ◇ *The trucks were hauled by steam locomotives.*

NOTE DRAG OR HAUL? You usually **drag** sth behind you along the ground; you usually **haul** sth towards you, often upwards towards you: ~~He reached down and dragged her up onto the ledge.~~ **Dragging** sth often needs effort, but **hauling** sth always does. You can say 'I hauled the chair over to the window', but only if it is a very heavy chair that is hard to move.

tow /təʊ/; *AmE* toʊ/ [T] to pull a car, boat or light plane behind another vehicle, using a rope or chain: *Our car was towed away by the police.*

trail [T, I] to pull sb/sth along behind sb/sth, usually along the ground; to be pulled along in this way: *She trailed her hand in the cool water as the boat moved along.* ◇ *The bride's dress trailed behind her.*

tug /tʌɡ/ (-**gg**-) [T] to pull sb/sth hard in a particular direction: *He tugged his hat down over his head.* ◇ *Annie appeared, tugging her little sister by the arm.*

2 pull · tear · pluck · extract · wrench · prise · pry · lever
These words all mean to remove sth from a place or position by holding it firmly and using force or effort to move it.

▸ to pull / tear / pluck / extract / wrench / prise / pry sth **from** sb / sth
▸ to pull / tear / pluck / wrench / prise / pry / lever sb / sth **out / out of** sth
▸ to pull / tear / wrench / prise / pry / lever sth **off / open / apart**
▸ to pull / tear / wrench sb / sth **free**
▸ to pull / tear / pluck / wrench / prise / pry sth from sb's **grasp**

pull [T] (usually used with an adverb or preposition) to remove sth from a place or position by holding it firmly and using force to move it towards you: *Pull the plug out.* ◇ *She pulled off her boots.* ◇ *You'll pull the handle right off if you tug so hard.* ◇ *The man pulled a gun/knife on him (= took it out and aimed it towards him).*

tear /teə(r); *AmE* ter/ [T] (usually used with an adverb or preposition) to remove sth from sth else by pulling it roughly or violently: *The storm nearly tore the roof off.* ◇ *I tore another sheet from the pad.*

pluck [T] (usually used with an adverb or preposition) to remove sth from a place by pulling it, especially quickly or sharply; to remove sth from a place or situation, especially one that is unpleasant or dangerous: *She plucked out a grey hair.* ◇ *He plucked the wallet from the man's grasp.* ◇ *Survivors were plucked to safety by a helicopter.*

extract /ɪkˈstrækt/ [T] (*formal*) to take or pull sth out, especially using force or effort: *The dentist may decide that the wisdom teeth need to be extracted.* ◇ *He rifled through his briefcase and extracted a file.*

wrench /rentʃ/ [T] (usually used with an adverb or preposition) (*written*) to remove sb/sth from a place by pulling or twisting it/them suddenly and violently: *The bag was wrenched from her grasp.* ◇ *The child wrenched himself free.*

prise (also **prize**) /praɪz/ [T] (usually used with an adverb or preposition) (*especially BrE*) to use force to separate sth from sth else: *He prised her fingers from the bag.* ◇ *We used a screwdriver to prise open the lid.*

pry [T] (*AmE*) to prise sth from sth else: *See if you can pry the lid off.*

lever /ˈliːvə(r); *AmE* ˈlevər/ [T] (usually used with an adverb or preposition) to remove or separate sth from sth using a lever (= a long piece of wood, metal, etc. used for moving or lifting sth): *I levered the lid off the pot with a knife.* ◇ *They managed to lever the door open.*

3 pull · yank · tug · jerk
These words all mean to hold sth firmly and use force to move it towards yourself.

▸ pull / yank / tug **on / at** sth
▸ pull / yank / tug sb / sth **toward / towards / out of** sth
▸ pull / yank / tug / jerk sth **open**
▸ pull / tug (at) sb's **hair / elbow / arm**
▸ pull / yank / jerk sb **to their feet**
▸ pull / yank / tug / jerk (sth) **hard**

pull [I, T] to hold sth firmly and use force to move it or try to move it towards yourself: *You push and I'll pull.* ◇ *Don't pull so hard or you'll break it.* ◇ *I pulled on the rope to see if it was secure.* ◇ *He keeps pulling my hair!* ◇ *She pulled him gently towards her.* ◇ *Mary pulled the blanket up over her head.* ◇ *Pull the door shut.* **OPP** **push** → PUSH 2
▸ **pull** *noun* [C]: *I gave the door a sharp pull.* ◇ *One last pull on the rope should do it.*

yank [T, I] (usually used with an adverb or preposition) (*informal*) to pull sb/sth hard, quickly and suddenly: *The man grabbed her hair and yanked her head back.* ◇ *Liz yanked at my arm.*
▸ **yank** *noun* [C]: *She gave the rope a yank.*

tug (-gg-) [I, T] to pull sth hard, often several times: *She tugged at his sleeve to get his attention.* ◇ *The baby was tugging her hair.*
▶ **tug** *noun* [C]: *I felt a little tug on my arm.*

jerk [T] (usually used with an adverb or preposition) to pull sth with a sudden short sharp movement: *She grabbed his hand and jerked him back from the kerb.*

pump *verb*

pump · extract · drain · squeeze · siphon · draw
These words all mean to make a liquid or gas move from one place to another.

PATTERNS AND COLLOCATIONS
▶ to pump / extract / drain / squeeze / siphon / draw sth **from** sth
▶ to pump / drain / squeeze / siphon / draw sth **out of** sth
▶ to pump / drain / squeeze / siphon sth **into** sth
▶ to pump / drain / siphon sth **away**
▶ to drain / siphon sth **off**
▶ to pump / extract / drain / squeeze / siphon / draw **water** from sth
▶ to pump / extract / drain / squeeze / siphon **oil / a liquid** from sth
▶ to pump / extract / siphon **gas** from sth

pump [T, I] (usually used with an adverb or preposition) to make a liquid, air or gas flow in a particular direction by using a pump or sth that works like a pump: *The engine is used for pumping water out of the mine.* ◇ *The lungs pump oxygen into the bloodstream.* ◇ *His heart pumped harder as he held his breath.*

extract /ɪkˈstrækt/ [T] (*rather formal*) to remove or obtain a substance from sth, for example by using an industrial or chemical process: *They developed a machine that can extract harmful gases from the air.* ◇ *Animals take in food and extract nutrients from it.* See also **obtain** → GET 1
▶ **extraction** /ɪkˈstrækʃn/ *noun* [U]: *oil / mineral / coal extraction* ◇ *the extraction of salt from the sea*

drain [T, I] (usually used with an adverb or preposition) to make liquid flow away from sth; (of liquid) to flow away: *Drain off the excess fat from the meat.* ◇ *She pulled out the plug and the water drained away.* See also **drain** → DRAIN *noun*, **drain** → DRAIN *verb*

squeeze [T] (always used with an adverb or preposition) to get liquid out of sth by pressing or twisting it hard: *Squeeze the juice of half a lemon over each fish.* ◇ *He took off his wet clothes and squeezed the water out.* ❶ Note that you can **squeeze** an *orange* or *lemon*, or you can squeeze the *juice*, *water* or *liquid* out of sth.

siphon (also **syphon**) /ˈsaɪfn/ [T] (usually used with an adverb or preposition) to move a liquid from one container to another with a **siphon** (= a special tube which uses pressure from the atmosphere to do this): *I siphoned some petrol into a can.* ◇ *The waste liquid needs to be siphoned off.*

draw [T] (*written*) to take or pull liquid or gas from somewhere: *She drew water from the well, and splashed her hands and face.* ◇ *The device draws water along the pipe.* ❶ In this meaning **draw** is mostly used to talk about taking water from a place such as a *well*, a *stream*, a *river* or a *canal*.

punish *verb*

punish · sentence · penalize · discipline · come down on sb
These words all mean to make sb suffer because they have broken a rule or law or done sth wrong.

PATTERNS AND COLLOCATIONS
▶ to punish / sentence / penalize / discipline / come down on sb **for** doing sth
▶ to punish / penalize / discipline sb **by** sth
▶ to punish / sentence / penalize / come down on an **offender**
▶ to punish / discipline a **child**
▶ to punish / penalize (bad, unacceptable, etc.) **behaviour**
▶ to punish / penalize / come down on sb **heavily**
▶ to punish / penalize sb **unfairly**

punish [T] to make sb suffer because they have broken a rule or law, or done sth wrong; to set the punishment for a particular crime: *He was punished for refusing to answer their questions.* ◇ *My parents used to punish me by not letting me watch TV.* ◇ *In those days murder was always punished with the death penalty.*

sentence [T, often passive] to say officially in court that sb is to receive a particular punishment: *to be sentenced to death / life imprisonment / three years in prison*

penalize (*BrE* also **-ise**) /ˈpiːnəlaɪz/ [T, often passive] to punish sb for breaking a rule or law by making them suffer a disadvantage, such as paying a fine or losing marks in an exam; to punish sb for breaking a rule in a sport or game by giving an advantage to their opponent: *You will be penalized for poor spelling.* ◇ *The goalkeeper was penalized for time-wasting.* ❶ If sb is *unfairly penalized*, they suffer a disadvantage because of sth they cannot control. The word **penalize** is often used to describe an unfair disadvantage: *Will he be penalized for absence due to ill health?*

discipline /ˈdɪsəplɪn/ [T] (*rather formal*) to punish sb for sth they have done: *The officers were disciplined for using racist language.* ❶ A person can be **disciplined** by sb who has authority over them, for example, a child by a parent or teacher, a worker by an employer, or a soldier by an officer. See also **discipline** → CONTROL *noun*

come ˈdown on sb *phrasal verb* [no passive] (*informal*) to punish sb or severely criticize them for sth they have done wrong: *Don't come down too hard on her.* ◇ *The courts are coming down heavily on young offenders.*

punishment *noun*

punishment · sentence · penalty · retribution · reckoning
These are all words for a way of making sb suffer because they have done sth wrong or illegal.

PATTERNS AND COLLOCATIONS
▶ punishment / a sentence / a penalty / retribution **for** sth
▶ a / an **heavy / harsh / severe / appropriate** punishment / sentence / penalty
▶ a **light** punishment / sentence
▶ to **impose** a punishment / sentence / penalty
▶ to **suffer** a punishment / penalty

punishment [U, C] an act or way of making sb suffer because they have done sth wrong or illegal: *The punishment should fit the crime.* ◇ *He was sent to his room as a punishment.* ◇ *There is little evidence that harsher punishments deter people.* OPP **reward** → AWARD

sentence [C, U] the punishment given by a court: *a jail / prison sentence* ◇ *She was given a life sentence* (= sent to prison for life). ◇ *a death sentence* ◇ *to be under sentence of death* ◇ *The judge passed sentence* (= said what the punishment would be). ◇ *The prisoner has served* (= completed) *his sentence and will be released tomorrow.*

penalty /ˈpenəlti/ [C] (*rather formal*) an official punishment given to sb because they have broken a law, rule or contract: *Assault carries a maximum penalty of seven years' imprisonment.* ◇ *Contractors who fall behind schedule incur heavy financial penalties.* ◇ *You can withdraw money from the account at any time without penalty.* OPP **reward** → AWARD

retribution /ˌretrɪˈbjuːʃn/ [U] (*formal*) severe punishment for sth seriously wrong that sb has done: *He saw his suffering as retribution for the sins of his past life.* ◇ *The public demanded swift justice and retribution.* ❶ **Retribution** includes the idea that punishment should mean that sb suffers in return for the suffering they have caused. People talk about **retribution** as part of a formal or legal system, or as carried out by groups or individuals, or (in the phrase *divine retribution*) by God. See also the entry for REVENGE

reckoning [C, usually sing., U] (*written*) a time when sb's actions will be judged to be right or wrong and they may be punished: *In the **final reckoning** truth is rewarded.* ◇ *Officials concerned with environmental policy predict that a **day of reckoning** will come.*

pure *adj.*

1 100% pure cotton
2 pure chance

---

1 pure · solid · refined

These words all describe sth which is not mixed with anything else.

PATTERNS AND COLLOCATIONS
▸ pure / solid / refined **gold** / **silver**
▸ pure / refined **oil**

pure [usually before noun] not mixed with anything else; with nothing added: *These shirts are 100% pure cotton.* ◇ *Classical dance **in its purest form** requires symmetry and balance.*

solid [only before noun] made completely of the material mentioned (that is, the material is not only on the surface): *Each piece is individually made in solid gold.* See also **solid** → SOLID

refined /rɪˈfaɪnd/ [usually before noun] (of a substance) made pure by having other substances taken out of it: *Avoid foods rich in fat or refined sugar.*

---

2 See also the entry for COMPLETE

pure · unconditional · sheer · unqualified · unmitigated · undivided

These words are all used to emphasize that a quality, feeling or situation is complete and not mixed with anything else.

PATTERNS AND COLLOCATIONS
▸ pure / unconditional **love**
▸ the pure / sheer **love of sth**
▸ pure / sheer **luck** / **chance** / **coincidence** / **delight** / **joy** / **bliss**
▸ unconditional / unqualified **support** / **acceptance** / **approval**
▸ unconditional / undivided **loyalty**

pure [usually before noun] complete and not mixed with anything else: *They met by pure chance.* ◇ *She laughed with pure joy.* ◇ *It was a **pure accident**. I'm not blaming anybody.* ❶ **Pure** is also used after a noun in the collocation **pure and simple**: *The man wants revenge, pure and simple.*
▸ **purely** *adv.*: *I saw the letter purely by chance.* ◇ *She took the job **purely and simply** for the money.*

unconditional [usually before noun] without any conditions or limits: *The war would continue until the unconditional surrender of their enemies.* ◇ *Unconditional love can only be received if it is also given.* **OPP** **conditional** ❶ An action or feeling that is **conditional** on sth depends on sth: *conditional approval/acceptance* ◇ *Payment is **conditional upon** delivery of the goods (= if the goods are not delivered, the money will not be paid).*
▸ **unconditionally** *adv.*: *We urge that all prisoners of conscience be immediately and unconditionally released.*

sheer [only before noun] complete and not mixed with anything else: *The concert was sheer delight.* ◇ *I only agreed out of sheer desperation.*

NOTE **PURE** OR **SHEER**? In many cases you can use either word: *pure/sheer luck/chance/coincidence/delight/joy/bliss/determination.* Use **pure** when you are talking about sth that sb has made up or guessed: *That's pure fantasy/fiction/speculation.* Use **sheer** when you are talking about more negative feelings or experiences: *sheer terror/panic/desperation/exhaustion/hell*

---

unqualified [usually before noun] complete; not limited by any negative qualities: *The event was not an **unqualified** success.* **OPP** **qualified** ❶ A quality that is **qualified** is limited in some way: *The plan was given only qualified support.*

unmitigated /ʌnˈmɪtɪɡeɪtɪd/ [only before noun] (*rather formal*) (usually when describing sth bad) complete: *The evening was an **unmitigated disaster**.*

undivided [usually before noun] complete; not divided between different people or things: *You must be prepared to give the job your **undivided attention**.*

---

purpose *noun* See also the entry for TARGET

purpose · aim · intention · plan · point · idea · intent

These are all words for talking about what sb/sth intends to do or achieve.

PATTERNS AND COLLOCATIONS
▸ **with** the purpose / aim / intention / idea / intent **of doing sth**
▸ sb's **purpose** / aim / intention / plan / intent **that...**
▸ sb's **intention** / plan / intent **to do sth**
▸ sb / sth's **original** purpose / aim / intention / plan / idea / intent
▸ a **specific** purpose / aim / intention / plan / intent
▸ the **whole** point / idea
▸ to **have** a purpose / an aim / an intention / a plan / a point / an intent
▸ to **state** your purpose / aim / intention
▸ to **declare** your aim / intention / intent
▸ to **achieve** / **fulfil** a purpose / an aim

purpose [C] what sth is supposed to achieve; what sb is trying to achieve: *The main purpose of the campaign is to raise money.* ◇ *A meeting was called **for the purpose of** appointing a new treasurer.* ◇ (*rather formal*) *He did not want anything to distract him from his purpose.*

aim [C] what sb is trying to achieve; what sth is supposed to achieve: *She went to London with the aim of finding a job.* ◇ *Our main aim is to increase sales in Europe.* ◇ *She set out the company's aims and objectives in her speech.* See also **aim** → INTEND *verb*

NOTE **PURPOSE** OR **AIM**? Your **purpose** for doing something is your reason for doing it; your **aim** is what you want to achieve. **Aim** can suggest that you are only trying to achieve sth; **purpose** gives a stronger sense of achievement being certain. **Aim** can be *sb's aim* or the *aim of sth.* **Purpose** is more usually *the purpose of sth*: you can talk about *sb's purpose* but that is more formal.

intention [C] what you intend to do: *I have no intention of going to the wedding.* ◇ *He has announced his intention to retire.* ◇ *I have every intention of paying her back what I owe her.* ◇ *She's full of **good intentions** but they rarely work out.* See also **intend** → INTEND

plan [C] what you intend to do or achieve: *Do you have any plans for the summer?* ◇ *There are no plans to build new offices.* ◇ *There's been a **change of plan**.* ◇ *We can't change our plans now.* See also **plan** → PLAN *noun* 1, **plan** → INTEND *verb*

NOTE **INTENTION** OR **PLAN**? Your **intentions** are what you want to do, especially in the near future; your **plans** are what you have decided or arranged to do, often, but not always, in the longer term.

point [U, sing.] (*rather informal, usually disapproving*) the purpose or aim of sth: ***What's the point** of all this violence?* ◇ *There's **no point in** getting angry.* ◇ *I **don't see the point** of doing it all again.*

idea [sing.] (*rather informal*) the purpose of sth; sb's aim: *The whole idea of going was so that we could meet her new boyfriend.* ◇ *What's the idea of all this?* ◇ *My original idea was to use amateur actors.*

NOTE **POINT** OR **IDEA**? **Point** is a more negative word than **idea**. If you say *What's the point...?* you are suggesting that there is no point; if you say *What's the idea...?* you are genuinely asking a question. **Point**, but NOT **idea**, is used to talk about things you feel annoyed or unhappy about: ~~There's no idea in…~~ ◇ ~~I don't see the idea of…~~ You might *miss the point of sth* (= fail to understand) but *get the idea* (= understand). You can talk about *the point/idea of sth* or *sb's idea* but NOT *sb's point*: ~~My original point was to use amateur actors.~~

intent /ɪnˈtent/ [U] (*formal or law*) what you intend to do: *She denies possessing the drug with intent to supply.* ◇ *He was charged with wounding with intent.*

push *verb*

1 push sb away
2 push to the front

1 push · thrust · force · shove · stick · ram · drive · poke · press

These words all mean to use your hands, arms or body in order to make sb/sth move forwards or away from you.

PATTERNS AND COLLOCATIONS

▶ to push/thrust/force/shove/stick/ram/drive/poke/press sth **into** sth
▶ to push/thrust/force/shove/stick/drive/poke sth **through** sth
▶ to push/thrust/force/shove sb/sth **away**
▶ to thrust/force/shove/press sth **into sb's hands/arms**
▶ to push/thrust/force/shove sth **open/shut**
▶ to push/thrust/shove/ram/drive (sth) **hard** (into/down, etc. sth)
▶ to push/poke/press (sth) **gently**
▶ to push/thrust/drive sth **deep** (into sth)

push [T, I] (often used with an adverb or preposition) to use your hands, arms or body to move sb/sth away from you; to move part of your body into a particular position: *He walked slowly up the hill, pushing his bike.* ◇ *Marty tried to kiss her but she pushed him away.* ◇ *Stop pushing me! Push hard when I tell you to.* ◇ *You push and I'll pull.* **OPP** pull → PULL 1

thrust [T, I] (usually used with an adverb or preposition) (*written*) to push sb/sth suddenly or violently in a particular direction; to move quickly in a particular direction: *He thrust the baby into my arms and ran off.* ◇ *She thrust her hands deep into her pockets.* ◇ *Mike thrust her towards the staircase.* ◇ *She thrust past him angrily.*

force [T] (often used with an adverb or preposition) to use physical strength to move sb/sth into a particular position: *She forced her way through the crowds.* ◇ *He forced the lid of his suitcase shut.* ◇ *Someone had tried to force an entry* (= enter a building using force). ◇ *We had to force the lock* (= break it open using force). See also **force** → FORCE *noun*

shove /ʃʌv/ [T] (usually used with an adverb or preposition) (*informal*) to put sth somewhere roughly or carelessly: *She shoved the book into her bag and hurried off.* ◇ *Just shove your suitcase under the bed.*

stick [T, I] (always used with an adverb or preposition) to push sth, usually a sharp object, into sth; to be pushed into sth: *The nurse stuck a needle into my arm.* ◇ *The little boy had stuck his head through the railings.* ◇ *I found a nail sticking in the tyre.*

ram (-**mm**-) [T] (always used with an adverb or preposition) to push sth somewhere using force: *She rammed the key into the lock.* ◇ *He rammed his foot down hard on the brake.*

drive [T] (always used with an adverb or preposition) to force sth to go in a particular direction or into a particular position by pushing it or hitting it: *He took a wooden peg and drove it into the ground.*

poke [T] (always used with an adverb or preposition) to push sth somewhere or move it in a particular direction with a small quick movement: *He poked his head around the door.* ◇ *Someone had poked a message under the door.*

press [T] to put sth into or onto sth by pushing it firmly: *He pressed a coin into her hand.*

2 push · shove · jostle · barge · shoulder · elbow

These words all mean to use force to move past sb/sth using your hands, arms or body.

PATTERNS AND COLLOCATIONS

▶ to push/shove/barge/shoulder/elbow **past** sb
▶ to push/barge/elbow **through** sb/sth
▶ to push/shove/shoulder/elbow sb **aside/out of the way**
▶ to push/shove/jostle/barge/shoulder/elbow **your way through/into/past**, etc. (sb/sth)
▶ to push/shove/shoulder sb **roughly**

push [I, T] (usually used with an adverb or preposition) to use force using your hands or arms to move past sb/sth or make them/it move out of your way: *There's no need to push!* ◇ *Please don't push in front of other customers.* ◇ *A woman pushed her way through the crowd.* **OPP** pull → PULL 3

shove /ʃʌv/ [I, T] to push sb/sth in a rough way, especially in order to get past them: *The crowd was pushing and shoving to get a better view.* ◇ *They shoved the guard aside.* ❶ When it is used with an object **shove** is always used with an adverb or preposition.

jostle /ˈdʒɒsl; *AmE* ˈdʒɑːsl/ [T, I] to push roughly against sb in a crowd, especially because you are trying to move in front of them: *The Senator was jostled by angry demonstrators.* ◇ *Anxious refugees jostled for a place in the line.*

barge [I, T] (always used with an adverb or preposition) to move forward in a forceful and careless way, pushing people out of the way or crashing into them: *He barged past me to get to the bar.* ◇ *They barged their way through the crowds.*

shoulder [I, T] (always used with an adverb or preposition) to push forward with your shoulder in order to get somewhere; to push sb with your shoulder: *She shouldered past a woman with a screaming baby.* ◇ *He shouldered the younger man aside.*

elbow /ˈelbəʊ/ [T] (usually used with an adverb or preposition) to push sb with your elbow, usually in order to get past them: *She elbowed me out of the way.* ◇ *He elbowed his way past the other shoppers.*

put *verb*

1 Put the cases down there.
2 put sth into perspective

1 put · place · lay · set · position · stuff · pop · dump · stick · settle · plant

These words all mean to move sth into a particular place or position.

PATTERNS AND COLLOCATIONS

▶ to put/place/lay/set/position/pop/dump/stick sth **on** sth
▶ to put/place/set/stuff/pop/dump/stick sth **in/into** sth
▶ to put/lay/set sth **down**
▶ to put/place/lay sth **carefully**

put [T] (always used with an adverb or preposition) to move sth into a particular place or position: *Put the cases down there, please.* ◇ *Put that knife down* (= stop holding it) *before you hurt somebody!* ◇ *Put your hand up if you need more paper.* ◇ *Did you put sugar in my coffee?*

place [T] (always used with an adverb or preposition) to put sth in a particular place, especially when you do it carefully or deliberately: *He placed his hand on her shoulder.* ◇ *A bomb had been placed under the seat.*

lay [T] (usually used with an adverb or preposition) to put sb/sth in a particular position, especially when you do it gently or carefully: *She laid the baby down gently on the bed.* ◇ *He laid a hand on my arm.* ◇ *Relatives laid wreaths on the grave.*

NOTE **PLACE** OR **LAY?** In many cases you can use either word. However, **place** is usually more deliberate, and **lay** is usually more gentle. You **place** things but not people; you can **lay** things or people: *A bomb had been laid under the seat.* ◇ *She placed the baby on the bed.*

set [T] (always used with an adverb or preposition) to put sb/sth in a particular place or position, especially sth that you have carried from somewhere else: *She set a tray down on the table.* ◇ *They ate everything that was set in front of them.* ◇ *When she fell he picked her up and set her on her feet again.*

position [T] (usually used with an adverb or preposition) to put sb/sth in a particular place, especially in order to be ready for sb/sth: *Large television screens were positioned at either end of the stadium.* ◇ *She quickly positioned herself behind the desk.* See also **position** → PLACE *noun* 1, **position** → POSITION *noun*

stuff [T] (always used with an adverb or a preposition) to push sth quickly and carelessly into a small space: *She stuffed the money under the pillow.* ◇ *His hands were stuffed in his pockets.*

pop (-**pp**-) [T] (always used with an adverb or a preposition) (*especially BrE, informal*) to put sth somewhere quickly, suddenly or for a short time: *He popped his head around the door and said hello.* ◇ *I'll pop the books in (= deliver them) on my way home.*

dump [T] (usually used with an adverb or preposition) to put sth down in a careless or untidy way, especially on the floor or a surface such as a table: *Just dump your stuff over there — we'll sort it out later.*

stick [T] (always used with an adverb or preposition) (*informal*) to put sth in a place, especially quickly or carelessly: *Stick your bags down there.* ◇ *Can you stick this on the noticeboard?*

settle [T] (always used with an adverb or preposition) to put sth carefully in a position so that it does not move: *She settled the blanket around her knees.*

plant [T] (always used with an adverb or preposition) to place sth or yourself firmly in a particular place or position: *They planted a flag on the summit.* ◇ *He planted himself squarely in front of us.*

---

2 put · set · place
These words all mean to cause sb/sth to be in a particular state or condition.

PATTERNS AND COLLOCATIONS
▸ to put / place sb **in charge / in sb's care / under command / under arrest**
▸ to put / set sb / sth **at ease / in motion**

put [T] (always used with an adverb or preposition) to bring sb/sth into the state or condition mentioned: *The incident put her in a bad mood.* ◇ **Put yourself in my position.** *What would you have done?* ◇ *I tried to put the matter into perspective.* ◇ *Don't go putting yourself at risk.*

set [T] to cause sb/sth to be in a particular state; to start sth happening: *Her manner immediately set everyone at ease.* ◇ *The new leader has set the party on the road to success.* ◇ *The hijackers set the hostages free.* ◇ *Her remarks set me thinking.*

place [T] (always used with an adverb or preposition) (*rather formal*) to put sb/yourself in a particular situation: *She was placed in the care of an uncle.* ◇ *His resignation placed us in a difficult position.* ◇ *The job places great demands on me.* ◇ *He has placed himself above party politics.*

put sth out *phrasal verb*

put sth out · extinguish · blow sth out · douse · snuff
These words all mean to stop sth from burning or shining.

PATTERNS AND COLLOCATIONS
▸ to put / blow / snuff sth **out**
▸ to put out / extinguish / blow out / douse / snuff (out) **a flame / flames**
▸ to put out / extinguish / blow out / snuff (out) **a candle**
▸ to put out / extinguish / douse **a fire / blaze**
▸ to put out / extinguish / douse **a light**
▸ to put out / extinguish **a cigarette**

put sth 'out *phrasal verb* to stop a fire or flame from burning or a light from shining: *Firefighters soon put the fire out.* ◇ *She lay down in bed and put out her light.* See also **turn sth off** → TURN STH OFF

extinguish /ɪkˈstɪŋgwɪʃ/ [T] (*formal*) to put sth out: *Please extinguish all cigarettes and fasten your safety belts.* ◇ *All lights had been extinguished.*

blow sth 'out *phrasal verb* to put out a flame by blowing: *She lit her cigarette and blew out the match.*

douse /daʊs/ [T] to stop a fire from burning by pouring water over it: *He doused the flames with a fire extinguisher.* See also **douse** → SOAK

snuff [T] to stop a small flame from burning, especially by pressing it between your fingers or covering it with sth: *He got into bed and snuffed (out) the candle.*

Q q

quality *noun*

quality · standard · level · grade · calibre
These are all words for how good or bad sth is, especially when compared with other things.

PATTERNS AND COLLOCATIONS
▸ to **be of** (a / the) ...quality / standard / level / grade / calibre
▸ **high / highest / low** quality / standard / level / grade / calibre
▸ **poor** quality / standard / level / grade
▸ **top** quality / level / grade
▸ to **raise / improve** the quality / standard / level / calibre of sth
▸ to **maintain** the quality / standard / level of sth
▸ to **reach** a standard / level

quality [U, C] how good or bad sth is, especially when compared with sth similar: *Most of the goods on offer are of very poor quality.* ◇ *Use the highest quality ingredients you can find.* ◇ *There's been a serious decline in **air quality** recently.* ◇ *Their **quality of life** improved dramatically when they moved to the US.*
standard [C, U] a level of quality, especially one that people generally think is acceptable: *There are real concerns about falling standards in schools.* ◇ *A number of Britain's beaches fail to **meet** European **standards** on cleanliness.* ◇ *Who **sets the standard** for water quality?* ◇ *sb's **standard of living** ◇ living standards ◇ Her work is not **up to standard** (= of a good enough standard).*
level [C, U] a particular standard or quality, for example of achievement, progress or ability: *Most of these students have a high level of language ability.* ◇ *This computer game has fifteen levels.* ◇ *(BrE) She studied psychology at **degree level**.*
grade [C] the quality of a particular product or material: *All the materials used were of the highest grade.* ◇ *(BrE) a piece of **top grade** beef ◇ (AmE) **Grade A beef***
calibre (BrE) (AmE **caliber**) /'kælɪbə(r)/ [U] the quality of sth, especially a person's ability: *The company needs more people of your calibre.*

question *noun*

question · enquiry · query
These are all words for a request for information.

PATTERNS AND COLLOCATIONS
▸ a question / an enquiry / a query **about / as to / concerning / on** sth
▸ a question / an enquiry / a query **from** sb
▸ a **specific / further** question / enquiry / query
▸ **detailed / routine / preliminary** questions / enquiries
▸ a **customer / general** enquiry / query
▸ to **address / direct** a question / an enquiry / a query to sb
▸ to **have / deal with / handle / reply to / respond to / answer** a question / an enquiry / a query
▸ to **raise / send (in) / put** a question / query

question [C] a sentence, phrase or word that asks for information or expresses doubt about sth: *She refused to answer questions about her private life.* ◇ *In the exam there's sure to be a question on energy.* ◇ *Question 3 was quite difficult.* ◇ *I hope the police don't **ask** any awkward **questions**.* ◇ ***The question is**, how much are they going to pay you?*
enquiry (also **inquiry**, especially in AmE) [C] a request for information or more details about sb/sth: *We received over 300 enquiries about the job.* ◇ *I'll have to **make** a few*

enquiries (= try to find out about it) *and get back to you.* ◇ *After the disaster, the police had a **flood of enquiries** about missing relatives.* See also **enquire** → ASK 1
query /'kwɪəri; AmE 'kwɪri/ [C] a question asking for information or expressing doubt about whether sth is correct or not: *If you have a query about your policy, contact our helpline.* ◇ *Our assistants will be happy to answer your queries.* ❶ You might put a **query** to sb, especially an organization, when you are not sure if you have understood sth properly or you would like it to be explained more clearly.

question *verb*

question · interview · interrogate · quiz · cross-examine · grill · debrief
These words all mean to ask sb questions about sth.

PATTERNS AND COLLOCATIONS
▸ to question / interview / interrogate / quiz / cross-examine / grill / debrief sb **on** sth
▸ to question / interview / interrogate / quiz / cross-examine / grill sb **about** sth
▸ to question / interview / quiz sb **in connection with** sth
▸ to question / interview / interrogate / cross-examine a **witness**
▸ to question / interview / interrogate a **suspect**
▸ to be questioned / interviewed / interrogated / quizzed / grilled **by police / detectives**
▸ a **journalist** questions / interviews sb
▸ to question / interview sb **further / in depth**

question [T] to ask sb questions about sth, especially officially: *A man is being questioned in connection with the robbery.* ◇ *Over half of those questioned said they rarely took any exercise.*
interview [T] to ask sb questions about their life, opinions, etc. especially on the radio or television or for a newspaper or magazine; to ask sb questions at a private meeting, especially officially: *Next week, I will be interviewing Spielberg about his latest movie.* ◇ *The police are waiting to interview the injured man.* See also **interview** → INTERVIEW *noun* 1
interrogate /ɪn'terəgeɪt/ [T] to ask sb a lot of questions over a long period of time, especially in an aggressive way: *He was interrogated by police for over 12 hours.* ◇ *Soon after we arrived, I was interrogated about my parents and our home life.* See also **interrogation** → INTERVIEW *noun* 1
quiz (-zz-) [T] (*especially journalism*) to ask sb a lot of questions in order to get information from them or find out what they have been doing: *Two men **quizzed over** betting shop killings (= in a newspaper headline).* ◇ *More than half the people quizzed in a poll said they would not use the new service.*
cross-e'xamine [T] to ask sb careful questions and in a lot of detail about answers that they have already given, especially in court: *The witness was cross-examined for over two hours.*
▸ **cross-exami'nation** *noun* [U, C]: *He broke down **under cross-examination** (= while he was being cross-examined) and admitted his part in the assault.*
grill [T] (*rather informal*) to ask sb a lot of difficult questions about their ideas, actions, etc., often in an unpleasant way: *They grilled her about where she had been all night.* ◇ *He was grilled by detectives for several hours.*
▸ **grilling** *noun* [C, usually sing.]: *The minister faced a tough grilling at today's press conference.*

debrief /ˌdiːˈbriːf/ [T] to ask sb questions officially in order to get information about the task that they have just completed: *He was taken to a US airbase to be debriefed on the mission.*

quick *adj.* See also the entries for FAST and SHORT 1

quick · rapid · fast · speedy · hasty · swift · hurried
These words all describe things taking or lasting a short time, or happening very soon.

▶ a quick/ rapid/ fast/ hasty/ swift/ hurried **exit**
▶ a quick/ rapid/ speedy/ hasty/ hurried **departure**
▶ a quick/ rapid/ fast/ hasty/ swift **change**
▶ quick/ rapid/ fast/ speedy/ swift **service**
▶ a quick/ rapid/ speedy/ hasty/ swift **decision**
▶ a quick/ rapid/ speedy **result**
▶ a quick/ rapid/ fast/ speedy **rate**
▶ a quick/ rapid/ fast **pulse** / **heartbeat**
▶ a quick/ rapid/ swift **movement**
▶ a quick/ rapid/ swift **look** / **glance**
▶ a quick/ rapid/ swift **answer** / **reply** / **assessment** / **calculation** / **rise** / **descent**
▶ in quick/ rapid/ swift **succession**
▶ **very**/ **fairly** quick/ rapid/ fast/ speedy/ swift
▶ **really**/ **extremely**/ **quite**/ **pretty** quick/ rapid/ fast

quick taking or lasting a short time; done or happening without delay: *She gave him a quick glance.* ◇ *Would you like a quick drink?* ◇ *These cakes are very **quick** and easy to make.* ◇ *It's quicker by train.* ◇ *Are you sure this is the quickest way?* ◇ *Have you finished already? That was quick!* ◇ *His quick thinking saved her life.* ◇ *We need to make a quick decision.* ◇ *There isn't a quick answer to this problem.* ❶ When it means 'done or happening without delay' **quick** is only used before a noun: ~~Their decision was quick.~~ **OPP** slow → LATE
▶ **quickly** *adv.*: *How quickly can you get here?*
rapid [usually before noun] (*rather formal*) happening in a short period of time; done or happening very quickly: *There has been a rapid rise in sales.* ◇ *The patient made a rapid recovery.* ◇ *The disease is spreading at a rapid rate.* ◇ *The guard fired four shots in rapid succession.* ❶ **Rapid** is most often used to describe the speed with which sth changes. **OPP** slow → SLOW, See also **rapidity** → SPEED *noun*
▶ **rapidly** *adv.*: *a rapidly growing economy* ◇ *Crime figures are rising rapidly.*
fast happening in a short period of time or without delay: *We've recorded the fastest rate of increase for several years.* ◇ *We can guarantee a fast response time.* **OPP** slow → SLOW
▶ **fast** *adv.*: *Children grow up so fast these days.*

> **NOTE** QUICK OR FAST? **Quick** is the most frequent word for talking about sth that takes a short amount of time. **Fast** can be used as well as **quick** with words relating to change (*recovery, rate, rise*) and services (*delivery, response, repair*) but not with words relating to meals (*breakfast, snack, lunch*) and acts performed by people such as *hug, kiss, wash* and *bath*. However, **fast** is the most frequent word for talking about sb/sth moving at high speed. See also the entry for FAST

speedy [usually before noun] (*rather informal*) happening or done quickly or without delay: *We wish you a speedy recovery* (= from an illness or injury). ◇ *They wanted to bring the war to a speedy end.* ❶ **Speedy** is usually used in contexts in which people wish or hope for a particular result. See also **speed** → SPEED *noun*, **speed** → ACCELERATE *verb*
▶ **speedily** *adv.*: *All enquiries will be dealt with as speedily as possible.*
hasty /ˈheɪsti/ (*often disapproving*) said, made or done very quickly, especially when this has bad results: *Let's not make any hasty decisions.* ◇ *She regretted her hasty words the moment she'd spoken.* ◇ (*written*) *The army beat a hasty retreat.* See also **haste** → SPEED *noun*

▶ **hastily** *adv.*: *She hastily changed the subject.*
swift (*especially written, especially journalism*) happening or done quickly or without delay; doing sth quickly: *Swift action was taken to recover the money.* ◇ *The White House was **swift to** deny the rumours.*
▶ **swiftly** *adv.*: *Surprise was swiftly followed by outrage.*
hurried [usually before noun] done too quickly because you do not have enough time: *I ate a hurried breakfast and left.* ◇ *She wrote a few hurried lines to him on the back of an envelope.* **OPP** unhurried → EASY 2, See also **hurry** → HURRY
▶ **hurriedly** *adv.*: *I hurriedly got up and dressed.*

quiet *adj.*

1 a quiet place/life
2 a quiet voice
3 quiet and shy

---

1 quiet · peaceful · silent · tranquil · calm · sleepy
These words all describe a place or period of time without much noise or activity.

▶ a quiet/ peaceful/ silent/ tranquil/ sleepy **place** / **village** / **town**
▶ a quiet/ peaceful/ tranquil/ calm **day** / **night** / **morning** / **afternoon** / **evening**
▶ a quiet/ peaceful/ tranquil/ calm/ sleepy **atmosphere**
▶ a quiet/ peaceful/ tranquil **life** / **setting**
▶ quiet/ peaceful/ tranquil **countryside** / **surroundings**

quiet without many people or much noise or activity; not disturbed by anyone: *The house was quiet except for the sound of the television.* ◇ *They had a quiet wedding.* ◇ *Business is usually quieter at this time of year.* ◇ *I was looking forward to a quiet evening at home.* **OPP** busy → BUSY 2, **noisy** → LOUD
peaceful not worried or disturbed in any way; quiet and calm: *I fell into a deep, peaceful sleep.* ◇ *It's so peaceful out here in the country.* See also **peace** → SILENCE *noun*
▶ **peacefully** *adv.*: *He died peacefully in her arms.*
silent where there is little or no sound; making little or no sound: *The streets were silent and deserted.* ◇ *As darkness began to fall, the cannon fell silent.* See also **silence** → SILENCE *noun*
▶ **silently** *adv.*: *She crept silently out of the room.*
tranquil /ˈtræŋkwɪl/ (*rather formal, written*) quiet and peaceful in a way that makes you feel relaxed: *It is a tranquil place of quiet beauty.* See also **tranquillity** → SILENCE *noun*
calm (of the sea) without large waves; (of the weather) without wind; (of the atmosphere in a place) without noise or violent feeling: *a calm, cloudless day* ◇ *The city is calm again* (= free from trouble and fighting) *after yesterday's riots.* **OPP** rough → ROUGH 2 ❶ The opposite, **rough**, only describes the sea and the weather, NOT times or places. See also **calm** → PEACE *noun*, **calm** → SILENCE *noun*
sleepy (*especially of a town or village*) quiet and where nothing much happens: *It was a sleepy little town before it became popular with tourists.*

---

2 quiet · soft · faint · inaudible · silent · hushed · dull · muffled
These words all describe sounds or voices that are not easy to hear because they make little or no noise.

▶ a quiet/a soft/a faint/an inaudible/a hushed/a muffled **voice**
▶ quiet/ soft/ hushed **tones**
▶ a quiet/ hushed/ muffled **conversation**
▶ quiet/ soft/ silent/ muffled **laughter**
▶ a quiet/ a soft/ a faint/ an inaudible/ a hushed **whisper**
▶ a soft/ faint/ silent/ muffled **cry**
▶ a quiet/ soft/ faint/ dull/ muffled **sound**
▶ a quiet/ soft/ faint/ dull **click**
▶ a soft/ faint/ dull/ muffled **noise** / **thud** / **thump**

quiet making very little noise: *We could hear quiet footsteps in the corridor.* ◇ *How would you like a quieter, more efficient engine?* ◇ *Could you **keep** the kids **quiet** while I'm on the phone?* ◇ *'**Be quiet**,' said the teacher.* ◇ *He went very quiet* (= did not say much) *so I knew he was upset.* `OPP` **loud** → LOUD, See also **quiet**, **quieten** → SILENCE *verb*
▸ **quietly** *adv.*: *I can't hear you – you're speaking too quietly.*

soft (of a voice or sound) not loud, and usually pleasant and gentle: *He chose some soft background music and lit the candles.* `OPP` **loud** → LOUD, **sharp** → HIGH 3
▸ **softly** *adv.*: *She closed the door softly behind her.*

faint (of sounds) that you cannot hear clearly, especially because they come from things or people in the distance: *We could hear their voices growing fainter as they walked down the road.*
▸ **faintly** *adv.*: *'Does it matter?' she said faintly.*

inaudible /ɪnˈɔːdəbl/ (of sounds) that you cannot hear: *She spoke in an almost inaudible whisper.* ◇ *The whistle was **inaudible to** the human ear.* `OPP` **audible** ❶ A sound that is **audible** can be heard, although it may not be very loud: *Her voice was **barely audible** above the noise.* ◇ *The alarm must be clearly audible in all bedrooms* (= in fire safety regulations).

silent [only before noun] not expressed with words or sound: *She closed her eyes to say a silent prayer.* ◇ *They nodded in silent agreement.* See also **silence** → SILENCE *verb*
▸ **silently** *adv.*: *She prayed silently.*

hushed [usually before noun] (of voices) speaking very quietly: *They spoke in hushed tones.* ◇ *They were deep in hushed conversation.* ❶ A **hushed** conversation is often one which the speakers do not want other people to hear.

dull [only before noun] (*written*) (of sounds) not clear or loud: *The gates shut behind him with a dull thud.*
▸ **dully** *adv.*: *The gates clanged dully behind him.*

muffled /ˈmʌfld/ (of sounds) not heard clearly because sth is in the way that stops the sound from travelling easily: *Muffled voices could be heard coming from the next room.* See also **muffle** → SILENCE *verb*

---

3 See also the entries for SHY and SOLITARY
quiet · reserved · reticent · taciturn · silent
These words all describe people not talking very much.

PATTERNS AND COLLOCATIONS
▸ a quiet / reserved / reticent / silent **person / man**
▸ He's the quiet / silent **type**.
▸ **very** quiet / reserved / reticent / silent
▸ **strangely** quiet / reticent / silent

quiet (of a person) tending not to talk very much: *She was quiet and shy, and never spoke up in class.*
▸ **quietly** *adv.*: *She sat quietly in the corner.*

reserved slow or unwilling to show feelings or express opinions: *Neighbours described him as a reserved man who didn't mix much.* ◇ *I think in her day people were more reserved.*

reticent /ˈretɪsnt/ (*formal*) unwilling to tell people about things: *He was extremely reticent about his personal life.* `OPP` **forthcoming** → TALKATIVE

taciturn /ˈtæsɪtɜːn; *AmE* -tɜːrn/ (*formal*) tending not to say very much, in a way that seems unfriendly: *He was a taciturn and serious young man.*

silent [only before noun] (especially of a man) not talking very much: *He's the strong, silent type.*

> `NOTE` A QUIET MAN OR A SILENT MAN? A **quiet** man is seen as being rather gentle, and perhaps not very confident. A **silent** man does not speak very much either, but his silence is considered to be a sign of strength and an unwillingness to waste time saying unnecessary things.

---

quite *adv.*
1 quite difficult
2 quite sure

1 See also the entry for PARTLY
quite · rather · pretty · fairly · reasonably
These words all mean to some degree.

> `NOTE` WHICH WORD? Compare these words with the words in the entry for **partly**. These words are generally more positive and emphasize the degree to which sth *is* good, successful, difficult, etc., even if it is not completely so. The words in the **partly** entry are slightly less positive in tone.

reasonably   fairly   quite   rather
                      pretty

PATTERNS AND COLLOCATIONS
▸ quite / rather **a / an…**
▸ quite / rather / pretty / fairly / reasonably **good / successful / high / large / quiet / common / easy / pleased / confident**
▸ quite / rather / pretty / fairly / reasonably **well / soon / quickly / easily**
▸ quite / rather / pretty / fairly **bad / big / heavy / new / tired / dull / difficult / rare / expensive / dangerous**
▸ quite / rather / pretty / fairly **recently / frequently**
▸ quite / rather / pretty **annoyed / exciting / nice / ill**
▸ rather / pretty / fairly / reasonably **harmless**
▸ rather / pretty / fairly **narrow / obvious**
▸ pretty / fairly / reasonably **certain / accurate / happy / safe / sure**
▸ I quite / rather **like** sth

quite (*especially BrE*) (not used in negative sentences) to some degree: *I went to bed quite late last night.* ◇ *I see him quite often.* ◇ *I think it's quite likely we'll win.* ◇ *He plays quite well.* ◇ *He's quite a good player.* ◇ *Her children are still quite young.* ◇ *Even quite young children can manage it.* ◇ *I quite like opera.* ❶ When **quite** is used with an adjective before a noun, it comes before *a* or *an*: *It's quite a small room.* ◇ *The room is quite small.* ◇ ~~It's a quite small room.~~ See also **quite** → VERY *adv.*

rather (*especially BrE*) to some degree: *The rules are rather complicated.* ◇ *I didn't fail the exam; in fact I did rather well!* ◇ *He looks rather like his father.* ◇ *I'm sorry, I've got rather a lot on my mind.* ◇ *It's **rather a** difficult question.* ❶ **Rather** is often used to express slight criticism, disappointment or surprise.

pretty (*AmE or informal, BrE*) to some degree: *I was pretty sure I'd seen the coin before.* ◇ *I'm afraid we're going to have to go pretty soon.*

fairly to some degree but not very: *The software is fairly easy to use.* ◇ *That's a fairly typical reaction.*

reasonably to some degree but not very: *I was reasonably happy with the situation.* ◇ *The hostages had been reasonably well cared for.* See also **reasonable** → ADEQUATE

> `NOTE` FAIRLY OR REASONABLY? Both these words are less strong than **quite**, **rather** and **pretty**; **fairly** is more positive than **reasonably**, which often suggests that sth is of an acceptable standard, but not the best.

---

2 quite · completely · totally · absolutely · fully · entirely · perfectly · utterly
These words are all used to mean to the greatest possible degree or to emphasize the following word or phrase.

PATTERNS AND COLLOCATIONS
▸ quite / completely / totally / absolutely / fully / utterly **sure / convinced**
▸ quite / completely / totally / absolutely / entirely / perfectly **normal**
▸ quite / completely / not totally / not entirely / utterly **irrelevant**
▸ quite / completely / totally / absolutely / perfectly / utterly **absurd**
▸ quite / completely / totally / entirely / utterly **different**

▸ quite / completely / totally / absolutely **exhausted**
▸ quite / totally / absolutely / perfectly / utterly **miserable**
▸ quite / completely / totally / perfectly **honest**
▸ quite / completely / absolutely / perfectly **still**
▸ quite / absolutely / perfectly **awful**
▸ quite / completely / not totally / not entirely / perfectly / utterly **happy**
▸ to quite / completely / totally / absolutely / fully **agree**
▸ to quite / completely / totally / fully / perfectly **understand**
▸ to quite / completely / totally / entirely **forget**
▸ to completely / totally / entirely / utterly **destroy** sth
▸ **not** quite / completely / totally / fully / entirely

quite (*especially BrE*) to the greatest possible degree: *quite delicious/amazing/perfect* ◇ *This is quite a different problem.* ◇ *It wasn't quite as simple as I thought it would be.* ◇ *Quite frankly, I couldn't care less.* ◇ *By then I had done quite enough.* ◇ *The bottle is not quite* (= almost) *empty.* ◇ *It's like being in the Alps, but not quite.* ◇ *I don't quite know what to do next.* ◇ *'I'm sorry to be so difficult.'* *'That's quite all right.'* ◇ (*BrE*) *Flying is quite the best way to travel.* ◇ (*BrE*) *It's too risky, quite apart from the cost.* ◇ (*BrE*)*'I almost think she prefers animals to people,'* *'Quite right too,'* said Bill. See also **quite → VERY** *adv.*

completely (used to emphasize the following word or phrase) in every way possible; to the greatest possible degree: *The technique is completely new.* ◇ *We were completely and utterly broke.* **OPP** **partly → PARTLY**, See also **complete → COMPLETE**

totally completely: *His behaviour is totally unacceptable.* ◇ *I'm still not totally convinced that he's right.* ◇ (*especially AmE, informal, spoken*) *The flight was totally awesome!* ◇ (*especially AmE, informal, spoken*)*'She's so cute!' 'Totally* (= I agree)*!'* ❶ The informal examples of totally are typical of the speech of young people. See also **total → COMPLETE, full → WHOLE**

absolutely (*especially spoken*) used to emphasize that sth is completely true or that you completely agree; used to emphasize sth negative; used with adjectives or verbs that express strong feelings or extreme qualities to mean 'extremely': *You're absolutely right.* ◇ *'They should have told me earlier, shouldn't they?' 'Absolutely.'* ◇ *There's absolutely nothing more the doctors can do for him.* ◇ *That man does absolutely no work!* ◇ *'Are you happy with the decision?' 'No, absolutely not.'* ◇ *I was absolutely furious with him.* ◇ *She absolutely adores you!* See also **absolute → COMPLETE**

fully (*rather formal*) completely: *She had not yet fully recovered from the operation.* ◇ *We are fully aware of the dangers.* ❶ In formal language **fully** is also used to emphasize that the whole of an amount is meant: (*formal*) *The disease affects fully 30 per cent of the population.* See also **full → WHOLE**

entirely (*rather formal*) completely: *I'm not entirely happy about the decision.* ◇ *The audience was almost entirely made up of children.* See also **entire → WHOLE**

perfectly (*especially spoken*) completely: *To be perfectly honest I don't like the colour.* ◇ *It's perfectly OK as it is* (= it doesn't need changing). ◇ *You know perfectly well I can't help you.* ◇ *'Do you understand?' 'Perfectly.'* See also **perfect → COMPLETE**

utterly completely: *We're so utterly different from each other.* ◇ *She utterly failed to convince them.* See also **utter → COMPLETE**

NOTE **WHICH WORD?** The main differences between these words are in register, not meaning. **Quite** is by far the most frequent in spoken British English, but it is not used so frequently in this meaning in American English. **Totally** is the most frequent in spoken American English. In written English the most frequently used terms are **completely** and, in more formal contexts, **fully. Entirely** is also rather formal, used especially in negative sentences and in the phrase *almost entirely.* **Perfectly** is less formal, used especially in spoken English. **Utterly** is not usually used in negative sentences, but it is often used when the idea being expressed is one of failure or impossibility.

quote *verb*

quote · cite · repeat · say · recite · narrate · dictate
These words all mean to repeat words that another person has said or written.

PATTERNS AND COLLOCATIONS
▸ to quote / cite / repeat / recite / dictate a **passage**
▸ to quote / repeat / say / recite a **line**
▸ to quote / recite (a) **poem** / **speech** / **poetry**
▸ to narrate / dictate a **story**

quote [T, I] to say or write the exact words that another person has said or written: *He quoted a passage from the prime minister's speech.* ◇ *The figures quoted in this article refer only to Britain.* ◇ *Don't quote me on this* (= this is not an official statement), *but I think she is going to resign.* ◇ *Quote this reference number in all correspondence.* ◇ *They said they were quoting from a recent report.* See also **quote → MENTION** *verb*, **quotation → REFERENCE**

cite [T] (*formal*) to say or write the exact words from a book, piece of writing or author, especially in order to support a statement in a piece of academic writing or a report: *She cited a passage from the President's speech.* See also **cite → MENTION** *verb*, **citation → REFERENCE**

repeat [T] to say aloud sth that sb else has said, often in order to learn it: *Listen and repeat each sentence after me.* ◇ *Can you repeat what I've just said word for word?*

say [T] to repeat the words of sth such as a prayer or speech: *He said a quiet prayer to himself.* ◇ *Try to say that line with more conviction.*

recite /rɪˈsaɪt/ [T] to say aloud a poem, piece of literature, etc. that you have learned, especially to an audience: *Each child had to recite a poem to the class.*

narrate /nəˈreɪt; AmE ˈnæreɪt/ [T] to speak the words that form the text of a film or television programme, especially a documentary (= a factual programme): *The film was narrated by Andrew Sachs.*

dictate /dɪkˈteɪt; AmE ˈdɪkteɪt/ [T, I] to say words aloud for sb else to write down: *She dictated a letter to her secretary.* ◇ *OK, you write, I'll dictate.*

R r

race *noun* See the Topic Map for SPORT AND LEISURE on p.892, See also the entry for COMPETITION 1

---

race · event · championship · tournament · cup · series · circuit

These are all words for sports competitions between teams or players.

PATTERNS AND COLLOCATIONS
▸ a **major** race / event / championship / tournament
▸ an / the **international** race / event / championship / tournament
▸ the **world** championship / cup / series
▸ to **hold / organize** a race / an event / a championship / a tournament
▸ to **compete** in a race / in an event / in a championship / in a tournament / in a cup / on the circuit
▸ to **enter** a race / an event / a tournament
▸ to **play** in an event / in a tournament / in a cup / in a series / on the circuit
▸ to **win** a race / an event / a championship / a tournament / a cup / a series
▸ to **be out of** a race / championship / tournament / cup

race [C] a competition between people, animals or vehicles to see which one is the fastest: *I bet I'd win a* **race** *the two of us!* ◇ *He's already in training for the big* **race against** *Bailey.* ◇ *It's a desperately* **close race**, *but I think Martinez is just ahead.* ◇ *Shall we* **have a race** *to the end of the beach?* ◇ *Their horse came third in the race last year.* ❶ **The races** [pl.] is used to refer to a series of horse races that happen at one place on a particular day: *He loves* **going to the races**. ◇ *We had a great day* **at the races**.
▸ **race** *verb* [I, T]: *Who will he be* **racing against** *in the next round?* ◇ *We raced each other back to the car.*

event [C] one of the races or competitions in a sports programme; a sports competition that takes place in one place over a short period of time, for example the Olympic Games: *The raft race was one of the final events of the River Festival.* ◇ *We're expecting to get medals in both* **track and field events**. ◇ *Is the city ready to stage such a major* **sporting event**?

championship /ˈtʃæmpiənʃɪp/ [C] (also **championships** [pl.]) a competition to find the best player or team in a particular sport: *the World Sports Car Championship* ◇ *He won a silver medal* **at the European Championships**. See also **champion** → WINNER

tournament /ˈtʊənəmənt; ˈtɔːn-; ˈtɜːn-; AmE ˈtʊrn-; ˈtɜːrn-/ [C] a competition to find the best player or team in a particular sport, in which teams or players compete in a series of games and must leave the competition if they lose. The competition continues until there is only one winner left: *She starts out as favourite to win the opening table tennis tournament of the season.* ◇ *The loser will be out of the tournament.*

cup (also **Cup**) [C, usually sing.] a sports competition in which a cup is given as a prize; used especially in the names of competitions: *They lost to Portugal in the World Cup quarter finals.* ◇ *We were leading 1–0 in the cup final.*

series [C] a set of sports games played between the same two teams: *The Boston Red Sox have won baseball's* **World Series** *for the first time in 86 years.* ◇ *So far England are 2–0 up in the* **Test series** *against India.*

circuit /ˈsɜːkɪt; AmE ˈsɜːrkɪt/ [C, usually sing.] a series of sports games or competitions in which the same group of players regularly take part: *This is her biggest triumph in nine years* **on the** *women's tennis* **circuit**.

racism *noun* See also the entry for DISCRIMINATION

---

racism · nationalism · patriotism · sexism · bigotry · ageism · chauvinism · xenophobia · sectarianism

These are all words for beliefs that some groups of people are better or more important than others, based on their race, nationality, sex or age.

PATTERNS AND COLLOCATIONS
▸ **rampant** racism / nationalism / sexism
▸ **overt / blatant** racism / sexism
▸ to **combat** racism / sexism / ageism
▸ a **form** of racism / nationalism / patriotism / sexism / bigotry / ageism / chauvinism

racism /ˈreɪsɪzəm/ [U] (*disapproving*) the unfair treatment of people who belong to a different race; violent behaviour towards them; the belief that some races of people are better than others: *a victim of racism* ◇ *ugly outbreaks of racism* ◇ *irrational racism* See also **race** → PEOPLE 2
▸ **racist** *noun* [C]: *He's a racist.*
▸ **racist** *adj.*: *racist thugs* ◇ *racist attitudes / attacks / remarks*

nationalism [U] the desire by a group of people who share the same race, culture, language, etc. to form an independent country; a feeling of love for and pride in your country: *Scottish nationalism* ❶ **Nationalism** is not usually a disapproving term; it can, however, be used in a disapproving way when sb's pride in their country turns into a feeling that their country is better than any other: (*disapproving*) *The war was fuelled by aggressive nationalism and feelings of cultural superiority.*
▸ **nationalist** *noun* [C]: *Scottish nationalists*
▸ **nationalist** *adj.*: *nationalist sentiments*

patriotism /ˈpeɪtriətɪzəm; BrE also ˈpæt-/ [U] (*usually approving*) love of your country and willingness to defend it: *The early war poems promoted patriotism, justice and principle.*
▸ **patriot** *noun* [C]: *I wouldn't say I'm a great patriot, but I would never betray my country.*
▸ **patriotic** /ˌpeɪtriˈɒtɪk; ˌpæt-; AmE ˌpeɪtriˈɑːtɪk/ *adj.*: *a patriotic man who served his country well* ◇ *patriotic songs*

sexism [U] (*disapproving*) the unfair treatment of people, especially women, because of their sex; the attitude that causes this: *legislation designed to combat sexism in the workplace* ◇ *a study of sexism in language*
▸ **sexist** *adj.*: *a sexist attitude* ◇ *sexist language*

bigotry /ˈbɪɡətri/ [U] (*disapproving*) the state of feeling, or the act of expressing, strong, unreasonable beliefs or opinions, especially concerning religion or race: *When religious people show bigotry and intolerance, they are in fact betraying the religion they uphold.*
▸ **bigot** *noun* [C]: *a religious / racial bigot*
▸ **bigoted** *adj.*: *a bigoted man*

ageism (also **agism**) /ˈeɪdʒɪzəm/ [U] unfair treatment of people because they are considered too old: *This form of ageism deprives older people of social status and role.*

chauvinism /ˈʃəʊvɪnɪzəm; AmE ˈʃoʊ-/ [U] (*disapproving*) an aggressive and unreasonable belief that your own country is better than all others; the belief held by some men that men are more important, intelligent, etc. than women: *national / cultural chauvinism* ◇ **Male chauvinism** *was rife in the medical profession in those days.*
▸ **chauvinist** *noun* [C]: *She denounced him as a* **male chauvinist pig**.

xenophobia /ˌzenəˈfəʊbiə; AmE -ˈfoʊ-/ [U] (disapproving) a strong feeling of dislike or fear of people from other countries: *a campaign against racism and xenophobia*

sectarianism /sekˈteəriənɪzəm; AmE -ˈter-/ [U] (disapproving, especially journalism) strong support for one particular religious or political group, especially when this leads to violence between different groups: *reports of a rise in religious and ethnic sectarianism* ◇ *victims of sectarianism*
▸ **sectarian** adj. [usually before noun]: *sectarian attacks/violence* ◇ *attempts to break down the sectarian divide in Northern Ireland* See also **sect** → RELIGION

radical adj.

radical · revolutionary · progressive · extreme
These words all describe ideas and views that are very new and/or different, especially in politics.

progressive radical extreme revolutionary

PATTERNS AND COLLOCATIONS
▸ radical / revolutionary / progressive / extreme **ideas** / **views**
▸ radical / revolutionary **proposals** / **solutions**
▸ a radical / revolutionary **leader**

radical /ˈrædɪkl/ [usually before noun] (of ideas) new, different, and likely to have a great effect; (of people or their opinions) in favour of thorough and complete political or social change: *He proposed a radical solution to the problem.* ◇ *the radical wing of the party* ◇ *radical politicians/students/writers* OPP **conservative** → CONSERVATIVE, See also **radical** → FUNDAMENTAL

revolutionary /ˌrevəˈluːʃənəri; AmE -neri/ involving a great or complete change; connected with political revolution: *It was a time of rapid and revolutionary change.* ◇ *At the time this idea was revolutionary.* ◇ *revolutionary uprisings* See also **revolution** → REVOLUTION 1, **revolutionary** → GUERRILLA noun

progressive /prəˈɡresɪv/ (usually approving) in favour of new ideas, modern methods and change: *progressive schools* ◇ *Are you in favour of progressive teaching methods?* OPP **conservative** → CONSERVATIVE, See also **progress** → PROGRESS

extreme (usually disapproving) (of people, political organizations or opinions) far from what most people consider to be normal, reasonable or acceptable: *extreme left-wing/right-wing views* OPP **moderate** → DISCIPLINED
▸ **extremism** noun [U]: *political/religious extremism*

rain noun

rain · shower · rainfall · drizzle · monsoon · downpour
These are all words for the water which falls or has fallen from the sky.

PATTERNS AND COLLOCATIONS
▸ **in** the rain / the drizzle / the monsoon / a downpour
▸ (a) **heavy** rain / shower / rainfall / downpour
▸ (a) **light** rain / shower / rainfall / drizzle
▸ (a) **torrential** rain / rainfall / downpour
▸ a **sudden** shower / downpour
▸ (a) **steady** rain / drizzle / downpour
▸ (a) **fine** / **thin** / **patchy** rain / drizzle
▸ to be / get **caught in** the rain / a shower / a downpour
▸ rain / drizzle **falls**

rain [U, sing.] water that falls from the clouds in separate drops: *Rain is forecast for the weekend.* ◇ *Don't go out in the rain.* ◇ *The rain poured down.* ◇ **It looks like rain** (= as if it is going to rain). ◇ *I think I felt a drop of rain.* ◇ *A light rain began to fall.* ◇ (BrE) *It's pouring with rain.* ❶ **The rains** [pl.] are the season of heavy continuous rain in tropical countries: *The rains come in September.* See also **rainy** → WET 1

shower [C] a short period of rain or snow: *We got caught in a heavy shower.*

rainfall /ˈreɪnfɔːl/ [U, sing.] the total amount of rain that falls in a particular area in a particular amount of time: *There has been below average rainfall this month.* ◇ *We have an average annual rainfall of around 750 mm.*

drizzle [U, sing.] light, fine rain: *The forecast for tomorrow is mist and drizzle.* ◇ *A light drizzle was falling as they left the cottage.*

monsoon /ˌmɒnˈsuːn; AmE ˌmɑːn-/ [C, usually sing.] a period of heavy rain in summer in S Asia; the rain that falls in this period; a wind in S Asia that blows from the south-west in summer, bringing rain, and the north-east in winter: *By the end of September it seemed that the monsoon season was drawing to a close.* ◇ *The monsoon blew relentlessly into our faces.* ❶ **Monsoon** is usually used in the form **the monsoon**, or like an adjective before another noun: *monsoon rains/winds/weather*

downpour /ˈdaʊnpɔː(r)/ [C, usually sing.] a heavy fall of rain that often starts suddenly: *The suddenness of the downpour had caught the three of them by surprise.*

rain verb

rain · fall · pour · come down · drizzle
These words are all used when water drops down from the sky.

drizzle rain   pour
    fall
    come down

PATTERNS AND COLLOCATIONS
▸ to pour / come **down**
▸ it's raining / pouring / drizzling
▸ the **rain** falls / pours / comes down
▸ to rain / fall **heavily** / **lightly** / **steadily**

rain [I] when **it rains**, water drops down from the sky in drops: *Is it raining?* ◇ *It had been raining all night.* ◇ *It hardly rained at all last summer.* ◇ *It started to rain.*

fall [I] (usually used with an adverb or preposition) (of rain or snow) to drop down from the sky: *The snow was falling steadily.* ◇ *70 millimetres of rain fell in just a few hours.*

pour [I] (of rain) to fall heavily: *The rain continued to pour down.* ◇ *It's pouring outside.* ◇ (BrE) *It's pouring with rain.* ❶ In American English you can say *It's pouring rain*, but it is more usual just to say *It's pouring*.

come 'down phrasal verb (of rain or snow) to fall: *The rain came down in torrents.*

NOTE RAIN, FALL OR COME DOWN? **Rain** is the most frequent verb and is used with the subject *it*. **Fall** and **come down** are used with a subject such as *rain* or *snow*. **Fall** is used when giving precise measurements of rainfall: *70 millimetres of rain fell in just a few hours.* ◇ ~~70 millimetres of rain came down in just a few hours.~~ ◇ ~~It rained 70 millimetres of rain in just a few hours.~~ **Come down** is often used with a description of how the rain falls: *The rain was coming down in a solid curtain.*

drizzle [I] (usually used in the progressive tenses, with *it* as the subject) to rain lightly: *It was drizzling outside.*

raise verb

raise · collect
These words both mean to ask people to give you money for a particular purpose.

PATTERNS AND COLLOCATIONS
▸ to raise / collect money **for** sth
▸ to raise / collect **money** / **funds**

raise [T] to ask people or organizations to give you money for a particular purpose: *The main part of my job is to raise funds for the playgroup.* ◇ *We are raising money for charity.* ❶ Typical collocates of **raise** in this meaning are *capital, cash, funds, loan, money* and *sponsorship*.

collect [I, T] to ask people to give you money for a particular purpose: *We're collecting for local charities.* ◇ *We collected over £300 for the appeal.*
▸ **collection** *noun* [C]: *a house-to-house collection for Cancer Relief*

> **NOTE** RAISE OR COLLECT? When you *raise money*, you are likely to do it by organizing events, or by approaching organizations to ask for money; if you *collect money*, you are more likely to do it by approaching people in the street or by knocking on people's doors with a box for them to put coins in. You might also *collect money* from friends or colleagues to pay for a present from all of you. Notice that **collect** does not always need an object: *I'm collecting for Patrick's retirement present.*

random *adj.*

random · haphazard · indiscriminate · disorganized · untidy · unsystematic
These words all describe things that are not organized or planned.

PATTERNS AND COLLOCATIONS
▸ the random / indiscriminate / random **use of sth**
▸ a random / haphazard **approach**
▸ random / indiscriminate **attacks**
▸ a haphazard / an indiscriminate **method**
▸ in a random / haphazard **fashion / manner**
▸ in a random / a haphazard / an unsystematic **way**
▸ **totally** random / haphazard / disorganized
▸ **very** haphazard / disorganized / untidy / unsystematic
▸ **rather** haphazard / disorganized / untidy
▸ **seemingly / apparently** random / haphazard / indiscriminate

random [usually before noun] done or chosen without sb deciding anything in advance; left to chance: *The group to be studied was selected on a random basis.* ◇ *There's no motive for this kind of random killing.* ◇ *Random numbers are generated by the computer.* ◇ *The names are listed in random order.* ❶ **Random** is often used in connection with statistics and research. Collocates include *allocation, distribution, effects, fluctuations, numbers,* and *sample.*
OPP predetermined → SET
▸ **at 'random** *idiom*: *She opened the book at random (= not at any particular page) and started reading.*
▸ **randomly** *adv.*: *The winning numbers are randomly selected by computer.*
haphazard /ˈhæpˈhæzəd; *AmE* -zərd/ (*disapproving*) done with no particular order or plan; not organized well: *It was the result of rather haphazard planning.* ◇ *In the early years training was haphazard.*
▸ **haphazardly** *adv.*: *She started packing, throwing things haphazardly into the case.*
indiscriminate /ˌɪndɪˈskrɪmɪnət/ (*disapproving*) (of actions) done without thought about the results, especially when it causes people to be harmed; (of people) acting without careful judgement: *indiscriminate violence/killing/slaughter* ◇ *The newspaper denounced the indiscriminate firing by the police.* ◇ *She's always been **indiscriminate** in her choice of friends.*
▸ **indiscriminately** *adv.*: *The soldiers fired indiscriminately into the crowd.*
disorganized (*BrE* also **-ised**) (*disapproving*) (of people) not able to plan or organize well; (of events) badly planned: *They are lazy and disorganized.* ◇ *It was a dismal, disorganized weekend.* **OPP organized** → EFFICIENT
untidy /ʌnˈtaɪdi/ (of people) not keeping things neat or well organized: *Why do you have to be so untidy?* **OPP tidy** → EFFICIENT
▸ **untidiness** *noun* [U]: *Their arguments were usually about his untidiness.*

unsystematic /ˌʌnˌsɪstəˈmætɪk/ without a clear system: *Training for volunteers is patchy and unsystematic.* **OPP systematic** → EFFICIENT

range *noun*

1 a full range of activities for children
2 an age/price range

---

1 See also the entry for COMBINATION
range · variety · choice · diversity · array · selection · assortment
These are all words for several different types of a particular thing.

PATTERNS AND COLLOCATIONS
▸ a **wide** range / variety / choice / diversity / array / selection / assortment
▸ a **great / huge / vast** range / variety / choice / diversity / array / selection
▸ a **rich** range / variety / choice / diversity / array / selection / assortment
▸ a **wonderful** range / variety / diversity / array / selection
▸ a / an **good / interesting** range / variety / choice / selection
▸ a **limited** range / variety / choice / selection
▸ an **odd** range / array / selection / assortment
▸ to **have** a range / a variety / a choice / diversity / an array / a selection / an assortment (of sth)
▸ to **offer / provide** a range / a variety / choice / diversity / an array / a selection / an assortment (of sth)
▸ to **choose from** a range / a variety / an array / a selection / an assortment of sth
▸ to **stock** a range / variety / selection of sth
▸ the range / variety / choice / selection / assortment **includes**...

range [C, usually sing.] several different types of a particular thing: *The hotel offers a wide range of facilities and services.* ◇ *There is **a full range of** activities for children.* ◇ *This material is available in a huge range of colours.* ❶ **Range** is often used in business and marketing in phrases such as *offer a large/wide/full range of sth.* See also **range** → DIFFER *verb*
variety [sing.] several different types of a particular thing: *There is a wide variety of patterns to choose from.* ◇ *He resigned for a variety of reasons.* ◇ *This tool can be used in a variety of ways.* ◇ *I was impressed by the variety of dishes on offer.* See also **vary** → DIFFER, **varied** → DIVERSE

> **NOTE** VARIETY OR RANGE? **Variety** emphasizes the amount of difference between the types of a particular thing; **range** emphasizes the (often large) number of things available.

choice [sing., U] a number or range of different things to choose from: *The menu has a good choice of desserts.* ◇ *There **wasn't much choice** of colour.* See also **choose** → CHOOSE
diversity /daɪˈvɜːsəti; *AmE* -ˈvɜːrs-/ [C, usually sing., U] (*rather formal*) a group of many people or things that are very different from each other; the quality or fact of including many people or things that are very different from each other: *There was a great diversity of opinion.* ◇ *the biological diversity of the rainforests* ◇ *There is a need for greater diversity and choice in education.* See also **diverse** → DIVERSE
array /əˈreɪ/ [C, usually sing.] (*rather formal*) a group or collection of things or people, often one that is large or impressive: *On the shelf was a vast array of bottles of different shapes and sizes.* ◇ *I was amazed by the dazzling array of talent.* ❶ **Array** is usually used with an adjective that suggests that the large number of things makes a strong impression on sb: *a vast/huge/rich/impressive/fascinating/colourful/glittering/bewildering/confusing/dazzling/wonderful array of sth*
selection [C] (*rather formal*) the number or range of different things to choose from: *The showroom has a wide selection of kitchens.* ❶ **Selection** is more formal than **choice** and is used especially in marketing. See also **select** → CHOOSE

assortment /əˈsɔːtmənt; *AmE* əˈsɔːrt-/ [C, usually sing.] (*rather formal*) a collection of different things or of different types of the same thing: *He was dressed in an odd assortment of clothes.* ❶ **Assortment** is often used to talk about groups of things that are strange because they are not usually found together: *a/an odd/strange/mixed/ motley/random assortment of objects/people/clothes* See also **assorted** → DIVERSE

---

2 range · scope · spectrum · reach · breadth
These are all words for the amount of variation that sth has within set limits.

▶ **within / beyond / outside** the range / scope / reach of sb / sth
▶ a / the **entire / full / whole** range / scope / spectrum / breadth
▶ the **complete** range / scope / spectrum / breadth
▶ a **wide / good / limited** range / scope / spectrum / breadth
▶ the **broad / narrow** range / scope / spectrum of sth
▶ a / the **geographical / global / political / social** range / scope / spectrum / reach
▶ to **expand / extend / increase / widen / limit / narrow / reduce / restrict / define / determine** the range / scope / spectrum / reach / breadth
▶ to **broaden** the range / scope / spectrum / reach
▶ to **cover / include** a range / spectrum / breadth

range [C, usually sing., U] the limits between which sth varies; the distance over which sth can be seen or heard or over which a gun or other weapon can hit things: *Most of the students are in the 17–20 age range.* ◇ *The students in Class 4 have a very wide range of abilities.* ◇ *It's difficult to find a house in our price range* (= that we can afford). ◇ *This was outside the range of his experience.* ◇ *The child was now out of Penny's range of vision* (= not near enough for Penny to see). ◇ *These missiles have a range of 300 miles.*
scope [U] the range of things that a subject, organization or activity deals with: *Our powers are limited in scope.* ◇ *These issues were outside the scope of the article.* ◇ *The police are broadening the scope of their investigation.* See also **scope** → SCOPE
spectrum /ˈspektrəm/ [C, usually sing.] (*rather formal*) a complete or wide range of related ideas, opinions or qualities: *We shall hear views from across the political spectrum.* ◇ *The policy has the support of a broad spectrum of opinion.*
reach [U] the limit to which sb/sth has the power or influence to do sth: *Such matters are beyond the reach of the law.* ◇ *Victory is now out of her reach.* ◇ *The basic model is priced well within the reach of most people.*
breadth /bredθ/ [U, sing.] (*rather formal*) a wide range of knowledge or interests: *He was surprised at her breadth of reading.* ◇ *The party needs a new leader with a breadth of vision* (= willingness to accept new ideas) *that can persuade others to change.* See also **broad** → WIDE 1

---

rank *verb*

rank · rate · grade · place · put · order
These words all mean to put things into a particular order, especially according to their quality.

▶ to rank / rate / grade / order sb / sth **according to** sth
▶ to rank / grade (sb / sth) **as** sb / sth
▶ to rank / grade / order sb / sth **by** sth
▶ to rank / rate / place / put / order sb / sth **above / below** sb / sth
▶ to rank / rate / grade / place / put sb / sth **in order of** sth
▶ to rank / rate (sb / sth) **with** sb / sth
▶ to rank / rate / grade sb / sth **for** sth

rank [T, I] (not used in the progressive tenses) to give sb/ sth a particular position on a scale according to quality, size or performance; to have a position of this kind: *The criteria are ranked in order of importance.* ◇ *They both lost*

to *top-ranked American players.* ◇ *The collection ranks among the finest in the country.* ◇ *It now ranks as Japan's fourth largest market.* See also **ranking** → CLASS 4
rate [T, usually passive] (not used in the progressive tenses) to put sb/sth in a particular position on a scale in relation to similar people or things: *The schools are rated according to their exam results.* ◇ *She is currently rated number two in the world.* See also **rate** → JUDGE *verb* 1, **rating** → CLASS 4
grade [T, often passive] to arrange people or things into groups according to a quality they share: *Eggs are graded from small to extra large.* ◇ *Responses were graded from 1 (very satisfied) to 5 (not at all satisfied).* ◇ *The grammar exercises are graded for difficulty.*
place [T] (always used with an adverb or preposition) to consider that sb/sth has a particular position or rank compared with other people or things: *I would place him among the top five tennis players in the world.* ◇ *Nursing attracts people who place relationships high on their list of priorities.*
put [T] (always used with an adverb or preposition) to place sb/sth in a particular position or rank: *I'd put her in the top rank of modern novelists.*

> **NOTE** **PLACE** OR **PUT**? There is very little difference in meaning or use between these words; **place** can sometimes suggest a more carefully considered opinion than **put**. See also **place, put** → PLACE *verb*

order [T, usually passive] (*formal*) to arrange things in a particular order: *The books are ordered alphabetically by title.* ◇ *In the periodic table elements are ordered according to atomic number.* See also **order** → SERIES *noun*

---

rape *verb*

rape · abuse · assault · molest
These words all mean to attack sb sexually.

molest   assault   rape
                                               abuse

▶ to **brutally** rape / abuse / assault sb
▶ to **sexually** abuse / assault / molest sb

rape [T] to force sb to have sex with you when they do not want to by threatening them or using violence: *She had been raped in her own home at the age of fifteen.* See also **rape** → ATTACK *noun* 2
abuse [T, often passive] (*rather formal*) to treat sb in a cruel or violent way, especially sexually: *He had abused his own daughter.* ❶ **Abuse** is used especially when the attacks or cruel treatment are repeated over a period of time and when the abuser is a person in a position of trust or authority, such as a parent, teacher or priest. See also **abuse** → EXPLOIT *verb*
▶ **abuse** *noun* [U]: *child/sexual abuse*
assault /əˈsɔːlt/ [T, often passive] (*rather formal*) to attack sb sexually in a violent way: *Four women have been sexually assaulted in the area recently.* ❶ **Assault** is a less serious crime than **rape** and need not involve full sexual intercourse. See also **assault** → ATTACK *noun* 2
molest /məˈlest/ [T] to touch a child or woman sexually when they do not want you to; to attack sb sexually: *He faces charges of sexually molesting their adopted daughter.* ❶ Any form of unwanted sexual touching can be called **molesting** sb.

---

rare *adj.*

rare · uncommon · infrequent
These words describe things that are not found or do not happen often.

PATTERNS AND COLLOCATIONS
- rare / uncommon / infrequent **in** sth
- rare / uncommon **among** sb
- rare / (not) uncommon (**for** sb / sth) **to do** sth
- rare / uncommon / infrequent **words**
- a rare / an uncommon **experience / feature / occurrence**
- a rare / no uncommon **thing**
- rare / infrequent **occasions / use**
- a rare / an infrequent **visitor**
- **fairly / rather / relatively / very** rare / uncommon / infrequent
- **not** uncommon / infrequent

rare not done, seen or happening very often; existing only in small numbers and therefore valuable or interesting: *It is rare for a prison sentence to be imposed for a first offence.* ◇ *This is a rare sight: badgers are normally active only at night.* ◇ *He suffers from a rare bone disease.* ◇ *The library has a collection of rare books and manuscripts.* ◇ *The farm specializes in rare breeds.* **OPP** **common** → GENERAL 1
  - **rarity** /ˈreərəti; *AmE* ˈrer-/ *noun* [U]: *The value of antiques will depend on their condition and rarity.*

uncommon not existing in large numbers or in many places: *Side effects from the injection are uncommon.* ◇ *It is not uncommon to find 30 different species on one tree.* **OPP** **common** → GENERAL 1

infrequent /ɪnˈfriːkwənt/ not happening often: *Examinations need to be carried out only at infrequent intervals.* ◇ *American trains are infrequent and the network is patchy.* **OPP** **frequent** → FREQUENT

rarely *adv.*

rarely · seldom · hardly ever · infrequently
These words and expressions are all used when sth happens or is done not often or almost never.

PATTERNS AND COLLOCATIONS
- rarely / seldom / hardly ever / infrequently **used**
- rarely / seldom / hardly ever **available / the case**
- to rarely / seldom / hardly ever **happen / speak**
- **only / relatively / very** rarely / seldom / infrequently

rarely not often: *He rarely spoke.* ◇ *That's something I very rarely do.* ◇ *Finding a hotel is rarely a problem.* **OPP** **often** → OFTEN

seldom (*rather formal*) not often: *She seldom smiled.* ◇ *He had seldom been happier in his life.* ◇ *Revenge was seldom, if ever, the motive in these cases.* **OPP** **often** → OFTEN

NOTE RARELY OR SELDOM? **Rarely** is slightly more formal than *not often* and **seldom** is slightly more formal than **rarely**. The use of **rarely** and **seldom** at the beginning of a sentence followed directly by the verb is literary or very formal: (*formal*) *Rarely has a debate attracted so much media attention.* ◇ *Seldom have I come across such vindictive reviews.*

hardly ever almost never: *We hardly ever see him.* ◇ *The room was hardly ever used.*

infrequently (*rather formal*) not often: *The satellites are launched only infrequently.* ◇ *The charges made for the drugs are not infrequently* (= very often) *excessive.* ❶ **Infrequently** is about as formal as **seldom**, but used more in official writing and with passive verbs; **seldom** is used more in literary writing and to talk about personal feelings and habits. **OPP** **frequently** → OFTEN

rate *noun*

1 the rate of change
2 sb's rate of pay

1 rate · speed · pace · momentum · tempo
These are all words for a measurement of how quickly sth happens or is done.

PATTERNS AND COLLOCATIONS
- **at** a ... rate / speed / pace
- a **fast / slow / steady** rate / speed / pace
- a **high** rate / speed
- to **increase** the rate / speed / pace / momentum / tempo
- to **gather** speed / pace / momentum
- to **gain / lose / pick up** speed / momentum
- to **slow** the rate / speed / pace of sth
- to **reduce** the rate / speed of sth
- to **maintain** the rate / speed / pace / momentum
- to **measure** the rate / speed / momentum
- the rate / speed / pace / tempo **increases**
- the rate / speed / pace **slows**
- a **change of** speed / pace / tempo
- the rate / speed / pace / momentum of **change**

rate [C] a measurement of how quickly sth happens or of the number of times sth happens during a particular period: *At the rate you're working, you'll never finish!* ◇ *There has been a fall in the rate of inflation.* ◇ *The birth rate was falling during this period.* ◇ *The number of reported crimes is increasing at an alarming rate.* ◇ *Local businesses are closing at the rate of three a year.* ◇ *the annual crime/divorce rate* ◇ *a high success/failure rate*

speed [C, U] the rate at which sb/sth moves or travels or sth happens or is done: *We travelled at an average speed of about 80 kph.* ◇ *at full/top speed* ◇ *She reduced speed before turning the corner.* ◇ *The classes are designed to let students progress at their own speed.* ◇ *We aim to increase the speed of delivery* (= how quickly goods are sent). See also **speed** → SPEED

pace [sing., U] the speed at which sb/sth walks, runs or moves; the speed at which sth happens; the fact of sth happening or changing quickly: *We set off at a leisurely pace.* ◇ *Traffic was reduced to walking pace.* ◇ *I prefer the more relaxed pace of life in the country.* ◇ *He gave up his job in advertising because he couldn't stand the pace* (= things happened and changed too fast for him) ◇ *The novel lacks pace* (= it develops too slowly).

momentum /məˈmentəm; *AmE* moʊˈm-/ [U] the ability to keep increasing or developing; a force that is gained by movement: *This deal adds fresh momentum to plans for a new rail link.* ◇ *There was an unstoppable momentum towards German reunification.* ◇ *The vehicle gained momentum as the road dipped.*

tempo (pl. **-os**) [C, U] (*written*) the speed of any movement or activity: *They soon adapted to the slower tempo of life on the island.* See also **tempo** → RHYTHM

2 See also the entry for PRICE
rate · charge · fee · rent · fine · fare · terms · dues · toll · rental
These are all words for an amount of money that is charged or paid for sth.

PATTERNS AND COLLOCATIONS
- a rate / a charge / a fee / rent / a fine / the fare / the terms / the rental / dues / a toll **for** sth
- a rate / a charge / a fee / rent / a toll / the rental **on** sth
- **at** a rate / charge / fee / rent / fare / rental of...
- **for** a charge / fee
- (a / an) **annual / monthly** rate / charge / fee / rent / dues / rental
- (a) **daily** rate / charge / fee / rent / rental
- (a) **reasonable** rate / charge / fee / rent / fare / terms / toll / rental
- (a) **high / low** rate / charge / fee / rent / fare / toll / rental
- (a) **fixed** rate / charge / fee / rent / fare / terms / rental
- (a) **flat** rate / charge / fee / fare
- the **full** rate / charge / fee / rent / fare / toll / rental
- to **pay** a rate / a charge / a fee / rent / a fine / a fare / your dues / a toll / the rental
- to **charge** a rate / a fee / rent / a fare / dues / a toll / rental
- to **increase / reduce** the rate / charge / fee / rent / fine / fare / dues / toll

rate [C] a fixed amount of money that is asked or paid for sth: *The job has a very low hourly rate of pay.* ◇ *We offer special reduced rates for students.* ◇ *What is the going rate* (= the usual level of payment) *for bar work?* ◇ *We were forced to borrow the money at an extortionately high rate of interest.* ◇ *The bank has announced a cut in interest rates.* See also **rates** → TAX

charge [C] an amount of money that is asked for goods or services: *We have to make a small charge for refreshments.* ◇ *Delivery is **free of charge** (= costs nothing).* ◇ *(BrE) The museum has introduced a £3 admission charge.* See also **charge** → CHARGE *verb*

fee [C] (*rather formal*) an amount of money that you have to pay for professional advice or services, to go to a school or college, join an organization or visit a place: *The family spent over £20 000 in legal fees.* ◇ *Does the bank charge a fee for setting up the account?* ◇ *Club members pay an annual membership fee of £775.* ◇ *(especially BrE) There is no entrance fee to the gallery.* ◇ *(especially AmE) an admission fee* See also **subscription** → PAYMENT

> **NOTE** CHARGE OR FEE? **Fee** can represent a larger amount of money than **charge**, especially in the combinations *legal fees* and *school fees*. **Charge** is used for smaller services in less formal or professional contexts: ~~We have to charge a small fee for refreshments.~~ Money that you pay to visit a place such as a museum is called an *admission charge* or *entrance fee* in British English, an *admission fee* or (less frequently) *entrance fee* in American English, (but never an 'entrance charge').

rent [U, C] an amount of money that you regularly have to pay for use of a building or room: *The landlord charged them a month's rent in advance.* ◇ *(BrE) They began falling behind with their rent (= paying it late or not at all).* ◇ *(AmE) They began falling behind in their rent.* ◇ *Rents are rising in the business district.*

fine [C] a sum of money that must be paid as punishment for breaking a law or rule: *a parking fine* ◇ *Offenders will be liable to a **heavy fine** (= one that costs a lot of money).* ◇ *She has already paid over $2 000 in fines.* See also **fine** → CHARGE *verb*

fare [C] the money that you pay to travel by bus, plane, taxi, etc: *Fares have been increased by 10%.* ◇ *a bus/taxi/rail/air fare* ◇ *(BrE) How much is the **return/single fare**?* ◇ *(AmE) **Round-trip fare** from New York to Cincinnati is $229.* ◇ *(AmE) one-way fare*

terms [pl.] conditions that you agree when you buy, sell or pay for sth; a price or cost: *to buy sth **on easy terms** (= paying for it over a long period)* ◇ *My terms are £20 a lesson.* See also **terms** → CONDITION

dues [pl.] an amount of money that you have to pay so that you can be a member of an organization: *He had not paid his trade union dues for six months.* See also **subscription** → PAYMENT

toll /təʊl; AmE toʊl/ [C] an amount of money that you have to pay to use a particular road or bridge: *She took enough money to pay for motorway tolls and ferry tickets.* ◇ *a toll road/bridge* ❶ In American English, a **toll** is also a charge for a telephone call that is calculated at a higher rate than a local call: *(AmE) Is San Jose to San Mateo a **toll call**? (= Do I have to pay extra for this call? Is it not a local call?)*

rental [U, C, usually sing.] an amount of money that you have to pay to use sth for a particular period of time: *Telephone charges include line rental.* ◇ *(BrE) The weekly rental on the car was over £200.*

> **NOTE** RENT OR RENTAL? **Rent** is money paid to use a building or room; for other items use **rental** or **rate**. In American English **rent** *verb* is used in connection with cars, but the usual noun is **rate**: *It costs us $300 a week to rent a car.* ◇ *The rate on the car was $300 a week.*

ratio *noun*

ratio · proportion · scale
These are all words for the amount or size of sth compared with sth else.

PATTERNS AND COLLOCATIONS
▶ the ratio / proportion **of** A **to** B
▶ a ratio / scale **of 1:25,** etc.
▶ **out of** proportion / scale
▶ a **high / low** ratio / proportion

ratio /ˈreɪʃiəʊ; AmE -oʊ/ (pl. **-os**) [C] the relationship between two groups of people or things that is represented by two numbers showing how much larger one group is than the other: *What is the ratio of men to women in the department?* ◇ *The school has a low student-teacher ratio (= there are few students for each teacher).* ◇ *The ratio of applications to available places currently stands at 100:1.*

proportion /prəˈpɔːʃn; AmE -ˈpɔːrʃn/ [U, pl.] the relationship of one thing to another, for example in size or amount; the correct relationship between these things: *The room is very long **in proportion to** (= relative to) its width.* ◇ *You haven't drawn the figures in the foreground **in proportion**.* ◇ *The head is **out of proportion** with the body.* ◇ *Always try to keep a **sense of proportion** (= of the relative importance of different things).* ◇ *It is an impressive building with fine proportions.* See also **proportional, proportionate** → RELATIVE

scale [C, U] the relation between the actual size of sth and its size on a map, diagram or model that represents it: *The map is **drawn to a scale** of 1:25000.* ◇ *Engineers have built a **scale model** of part of the coast.* ◇ *Is this diagram **to scale** (= are all the parts the same size and shape in relation to each other as they are in the thing represented)?*

rational *adj.* See also the entry for GOOD 3

rational · coherent · logical · scientific · reasoned
These words all describe behaviour or a way of thinking that is based on reason, facts and clear, careful thought.

PATTERNS AND COLLOCATIONS
▶ to be rational / scientific **about** sth
▶ a rational / coherent / logical / scientific / reasoned **argument / explanation**
▶ rational / coherent / logical / scientific / reasoned **thought**
▶ a rational / coherent / logical / scientific **approach**
▶ a rational / logical / scientific / reasoned **choice / decision / conclusion**
▶ rational / logical / scientific / reasoned **thinking**
▶ **perfectly** rational / coherent / logical

rational /ˈræʃnəl/ (of behaviour or a way of thinking) based on reason and of facts rather than emotions: *There's no rational explanation for his actions.* ◇ *In some ways their behaviour is perfectly rational.* **OPP irrational** → IRRATIONAL, See also **rationality** → LOGIC
▶ **rationally** *adv.*: *Scientific training helps you to think rationally.*

coherent /kəʊˈhɪərənt; AmE koʊˈhɪr-/ (of an idea, system or explanation) rational and well-organized; clear and easy to understand: *She gave a clear, coherent account to the court.* ◇ *They have yet to come up with a coherent policy on this issue.* ❶ **Coherent** is used especially to talk about plans and organization; typical collocates include *approach, framework, pattern, picture, plan, policy, programme, scheme, strategy, structure, system, theory* and *whole*. **OPP incoherent** → CONFUSED 2, See also **coherence** → EFFICIENCY

logical based on the rules of logic; showing clear thinking based on facts and reason: *The problem can be solved using a process of logical reasoning.* ◇ *A contradiction is a logical impossibility.* **OPP illogical** → IRRATIONAL, See also **logic** → LOGIC
▶ **logically** *adv.*: *If you look at it logically his argument makes no sense.*

scientific (of a way of doing sth or thinking) careful and logical: *He took a very scientific approach to management.* ◇ *We need to be more scientific about this problem.* **OPP unscientific** → IRRATIONAL
▶ **scientifically** *adv.*: *We should try to approach this scientifically.*

reasoned [only before noun] (of an argument or opinion) presented in a logical way that shows careful thought: *They refused the appeal without offering any reasoned argument.* See also **reason** → REASON *noun*, **reason** → CONCLUDE *verb*, **reasoning** → REASONING

read *verb* See the Topic Map for THE MEDIA on p.900

read · flick through sth · look through sth · leaf through sth · dip into sth · scan · skim · plough through sth
These words all mean to look at and understand the meaning of printed or written words.

PATTERNS AND COLLOCATIONS
▸ to read / flick / look / leaf / scan / skim / plough **through** sth
▸ to read / flick through / look through / leaf through / dip into / plough through a **book**
▸ to read / flick through / look through / leaf through / scan / skim a **newspaper / paper**
▸ to read / flick through / look through / leaf through a **magazine**
▸ to read / look through / plough through a **report**
▸ to flick through / look through / leaf through / scan / skim the **pages of** sth
▸ to **quickly** read / flick through / look through / leaf through / scan / skim sth

read [I, T] to look at and understand the meaning of written or printed words or symbols, for example in a book; to say the words in a book, etc. either silently to yourself or aloud to others: *He learned to read when he was three.* ◇ *Just read through what you've written before you send it off.* ◇ *What are you reading at the moment?* (= what book?) ◇ *Can you read music?* ◇ *I'm trying to read the map.* ◇ *I used to **read to** my younger brothers at bedtime.* ◇ *Will you read me a story?* ◇ *I read the words out loud* (= spoke them). ❶ **Read** also means to find out about sb/sth by reading: *I **read about it** in today's paper.* ◇ *I **read that** he'd resigned.*

flick 'through sth *phrasal verb* [no passive] to quickly turn the pages of a book, magazine, etc. and look at them without reading everything: *She was flicking through the pages of a magazine.* ◇ *I've only had time to flick through your report but it seems to be fine.*

look 'through sth *phrasal verb* [no passive] to turn the pages of a book, magazine, etc., and look at them without reading everything: *I caught him looking through my confidential files.* ◇ *She looked through her notes before the exam.*

> **NOTE** FLICK THROUGH STH OR LOOK THROUGH STH? If you **flick through sth** you do it more quickly than if you **look through sth**, which is usually more deliberate. You might just *look through a report* if you felt that it did not need more atttention, but you would not apologize for this: *I've looked through your report and it's fine.* ◇ *I've only had time to look through your report.*

leaf 'through sth *phrasal verb* [no passive] to quickly turn the pages of a book, without reading them or looking at them closely, especially in order to find sth in particular: *She leafed through the guide book until she found the page she wanted.*

dip into sth *phrasal verb* (-pp-) [no passive] to read only parts of sth: *It's a good book to dip into now and again.*

scan (-nn-) [T, I] to read sth quickly but not very carefully and not reading every word, especially in order to find particular information: *I scanned the list quickly, looking for my name.* ◇ *She scanned through the newspaper over breakfast.* ◇ *You should teach students to scan for essential information.*

skim (-mm-) [T, I] to read sth quickly in order to find the main points or a particular point: *I always skim the financial section of the newspaper.* ◇ *He skimmed through the article trying to find his name.*

> **NOTE** SCAN OR SKIM? Sometimes you can use either word: *I scanned/skimmed the list until I found my name.* However, **scan** is usually used when you are looking for

particular information; **skim** is more often used when you want to get a general idea of what sth is about. You do not 'skim for sth': *Teach students to skim for essential information.*

plough 'through sth (*BrE*) (*AmE* **plow through sth**) *phrasal verb* [no passive] to make slow progress through a difficult or boring book or document, etc: *I had to plough through dozens of legal documents.*

ready *adj.*

ready · prepared · set · be waiting
These words all describe sb/sth that is able and available to do, receive or be used for sth.

PATTERNS AND COLLOCATIONS
▸ ready / prepared / set / be waiting **for** sb / sth
▸ ready / prepared / set / be waiting **to do** sth
▸ **fully** ready / prepared / set
▸ **perfectly** ready / prepared

ready [not before noun] (of a person) able and available to do or receive sth; (of a thing) completed and available to be used: *Are you nearly ready?* ◇ *I'm just **getting** the kids **ready** for school.* ◇ *Right, we're ready to go.* ◇ *Come on, dinner's ready!* ◇ *The new building should be ready for 2012.*

prepared ready to deal with sth successfully; done or made in advance: *I was not prepared for all the problems it caused.* ◇ *The police officer read out a prepared statement.* See also **prepare** → PREPARE 1, **prepare** → PREPARE 2

set [not before noun] (always followed by *for* or *to* + infinitive) likely to do sth; ready for sth or to do sth: *The team looks set for victory.* ◇ *Interest rates look set to rise again.*

be waiting *phrase* (of a thing) to be ready for sb to have or use: *There's a letter waiting for you at home.* ◇ *The hotel had a taxi waiting to collect us.*

real *adj.*

real · actual · true · genuine · authentic · proper
These words all describe sth that is real and not imagined, false or artificial.

PATTERNS AND COLLOCATIONS
▸ a real / the actual / the true / a genuine / a proper **reason**
▸ the real / actual / true **cost** of sth
▸ a real / a true / a genuine / an authentic **work of art**
▸ real / genuine **leather / silk / gold**
▸ real / genuine / authentic **enough**

real [usually before noun] existing in fact and not imagined, false or artificial; having all the important qualities that sth should have to deserve to be called what it is called: *It wasn't a ghost; it was a real person.* ◇ *pictures of animals, both real and mythological* ◇ *Marilyn Monroe's real name was Norma Jean Baker.* ◇ *See the real Africa on one of our walking safaris.* ◇ *I do my best to hide my real feelings from others.* ◇ *Are those real flowers?* ◇ *She never had any real friends at school.* **OPP imaginary, pretend** → FICTIONAL
▸ **really** *adv.*: *Tell me what really happened.*

actual [only before noun] used to emphasize what sth is really like, rather than how it appears to be or how you might expect it to be: *What were his actual words?* ◇ *The actual cost was much higher than we had expected.* ◇ *James looks younger than his wife but **in actual fact** (= really) he is several years older.* **OPP hypothetical, notional** → SUPPOSED, **potential** → LIKELY
▸ **actually** *adv.*: *Well, what did she actually say?*

true real or exact, especially when this is different from how sth seems; having all the important qualities that sth should have to deserve to be called what it is called: *the true face of socialism* (= what it is really like rather than what people think it is like) ◇ *He reveals his true character* to very few people. ◇ It was **true love** between them. ◇ He's a true gentleman. ◇ The painting is a masterpiece **in the truest sense** of the word.

▸ **truly** adv.: He started the first truly international ballet company.

NOTE **REAL OR TRUE?** In many cases you can use either word: You're a real/true friend. ◇ He's a real/true gentleman. However, **real** looks at the necessary qualities of sth in a more practical way; **true** looks at those qualities in a more romantic way. **Real** is used more often than **true** in negative sentences; **true** is used more often to emphasize how rare or unique sth is: ~~She never had any true friends at school.~~ ◇ ~~It was real love between them.~~

genuine exactly what it appears to be; not artificial: Is the painting a genuine Picasso? ◇ Fake designer watches are sold at a fraction of the price of **the genuine article**. ◇ Only genuine refugees can apply for asylum. **OPP** fake, imitation → ARTIFICIAL 1

authentic /ɔːˈθentɪk/ known to be real and genuine and not a copy: I don't know if the painting is authentic.

NOTE **GENUINE OR AUTHENTIC?** These words are very close in meaning and range. **Genuine** describes sth that really belongs to a group of things of the same type. **Authentic** describes sth that has really been produced or created by sb/sth. This means that sometimes either word can be used: a genuine/an authentic Picasso

proper /ˈprɒpə(r)/ [only before noun] (BrE, spoken) that you consider to be real and satisfactory: Eat some proper food, not just toast and jam! ◇ When are you going to get a proper job? ❶ In American English, use **real**.

realistic adj.

1 take a realistic view of the situation
2 a realistic drawing

---

1 **realistic · pragmatic · practical · no-nonsense · down-to-earth · level-headed · matter-of-fact**
These words all describe people dealing with situations in a calm and sensible way, without being affected by emotions.

PATTERNS AND COLLOCATIONS
▸ to be realistic/ pragmatic/ practical/ down-to-earth/ matter-of-fact **about** sth
▸ a realistic/ pragmatic/ practical/ no-nonsense/ down-to-earth/ level-headed / matter-of-fact **approach**
▸ a realistic/ pragmatic/ practical/ no-nonsense/ down-to-earth/ matter-of-fact **attitude**
▸ a realistic/ pragmatic/ practical **solution**
▸ a no-nonsense/ practical / matter-of-fact **manner**/ way
▸ a no-nonsense/ matter-of-fact **tone**/ voice
▸ a down-to-earth/ practical / level-headed **person**
▸ **very** realistic/ pragmatic/ practical/ down-to-earth/ level-headed / matter-of-fact
▸ **quite** realistic/ pragmatic/ practical/ matter-of-fact

realistic (usually approving) accepting in a sensible way what it is actually possible to do or achieve in a particular situation: This report takes a much more realistic view of the situation. ◇ We have to be realistic about our chances of winning. ◇ It is not realistic to expect people to spend so much money. **OPP** unrealistic → UNREALISTIC
▸ **realistically** adv.: How many can you realistically hope to sell?

pragmatic /præɡˈmætɪk/ (usually approving, especially written) solving problems in a sensible way rather than by having fixed ideas or theories: We take a pragmatic approach to management problems. ❶ Being **pragmatic** often means finding solutions which do not follow traditional practices. **Pragmatic** is usually used to describe a course of action: a pragmatic response/ solution/approach/attitude
▸ **pragmatically** adv.: The company responded pragmatically to local conditions.

practical (usually approving) solving problems in a sensible way: Let's be practical and work out the cost first. **OPP** impractical → UNREALISTIC, See also **practicalities** → BASICS

no-'nonsense [only before noun] (of a person or the way they deal with sth) simple and direct, paying attention to the important practical things but not worrying about people's feelings: We adopt a no-nonsense approach to unpaid bills. ◇ She was a tough, no-nonsense leader.

down-to-'earth (approving) sensible and practical in a way that is helpful and friendly: She was friendly and down-to-earth, and quickly put me at my ease. ❶ **Down-to-earth** is often used to talk about people who do not think that they are more important or educated than they really are, or than other people.

level-'headed (approving) calm and sensible; able to make good decisions even in difficult situations: This position requires a level-headed person with experience in managing risk.

matter-of-'fact said or done without showing any emotion, especially in a situation in which you would expect sb to express their feelings: She told us the news of his death in a very matter-of-fact way. ◇ He was very matter-of-fact about the breakdown of his marriage.

2 **realistic · authentic · lifelike**
These words all describe sth that is a very close copy of the way sb/sth is in real life.

PATTERNS AND COLLOCATIONS
▸ to **look** realistic/ authentic/ lifelike
▸ **very** realistic/ authentic/ lifelike
▸ **truly**/ **quite** realistic/ authentic

realistic representing things as they are in real life: She made a very realistic drawing of a horse. ◇ We try to make these training courses as realistic as possible.
▸ **realistically** adv.: There was a fireplace with realistically glowing coals.

authentic /ɔːˈθentɪk/ made to be exactly the same as the original: He constructed an authentic model of the ancient town.
▸ **authentically** adv.: They serve a selection of authentically flavoured Mexican dishes.

lifelike /ˈlaɪflaɪk/ exactly like a real person or object: There is a very lifelike statue of him in the town.

reason noun See also the entry for ARGUMENT 2

reason · explanation · grounds · basis · excuse · motive · need · justification · cause · pretext
These are all words for why sth has happened or sb has done it.

PATTERNS AND COLLOCATIONS
▸ a reason/ an explanation/ grounds/ a basis/ an excuse/ a motive/ a need / justification/ cause/ a pretext **for** sth
▸ the reason/ motive **behind** sth
▸ **on** the grounds/ basis/ pretext **of**/ that...
▸ the reason/grounds/basis/excuse/justification/pretext **that...**
▸ (an) **obvious** reason/ explanation/ grounds/ excuse/ motive/ need / justification / cause/ pretext
▸ (a) **clear**/ **legitimate** reason/ grounds/ excuse/ motive/ need / justification/ cause/ pretext
▸ (a) **logical**/ **personal**/ **no apparent** reason/ explanation/ grounds/ excuse/ motive/ need / justification/ cause
▸ (a) **good**/ **valid** reason/ explanation/ grounds/ excuse/ motive/ justification/ cause
▸ (a) **convincing** reason/ explanation/ grounds/ excuse/ motive/ justification / pretext
▸ (a) **reasonable** explanation/ grounds/ excuse/ motive/ need / justification / cause/ pretext
▸ the **real** reason/ explanation/ grounds/ motive/ justification/ cause
▸ to **have** a reason/ an explanation/ grounds/ an excuse/ a motive/ a justification/ cause/ a pretext

▶ to **give** / **offer** (sb) a reason / an explanation / an excuse / a justification / a pretext

▶ to **suggest** a reason / an explanation / grounds / a motive / a justification

▶ to **see** / **understand** / **explain** (the / sb's) reasons / grounds / motive / justification

reason [C, U] why sth has happened or sb has done sth; a fact that makes it right or fair to do sth: *I'd like to know* **the reason why** *you're so late.* ◇ *He said no but he didn't give a reason.* ◇ *We aren't going for the **simple reason** that we can't afford it.* ◇ *For some reason* (= one that I don't know or don't understand) *we all have to come in early tomorrow.* ◇ *For reasons of security the door is always kept locked.* ◇ *They have reason to believe that he is lying.* ◇ *She complained, **with reason** (= rightly), that she had been underpaid.* See also **reason** → CONCLUDE *verb*, **reasoned** → RATIONAL

explanation [C, U] a statement, fact or situation that tells you why sth has happened; a reason given for sth: *The most likely explanation is that his plane was delayed.* ◇ *I can't think of any possible explanation for his absence.* ◇ *The book opens with an explanation of why some drugs are banned.* ◇ *She left the room abruptly **without explanation**.* See also **explain** → EXPLAIN 2

grounds [pl.] (*rather formal*) a good or true reason for saying, doing or believing sth: *You have no grounds for complaint.* ◇ *He retired from the job on health grounds.* ◇ *Employers cannot discriminate on grounds of age.*

basis [sing.] (*rather formal*) the reason why people take a particular action: *She was chosen for the job on the basis of her qualifications and ideas.* ◇ *On what basis will this decision be made?* ❶ *Basis* is usually used in the phrases *on the basis of / that…* or *On what basis…?*

excuse /ɪkˈskjuːs/ [C] a reason, either true or invented, that you give to explain or defend your behaviour; a good reason that you give for doing sth that you want to do for other reasons: *Late again! What's your excuse this time?* ◇ *There's no excuse for such behaviour.* ◇ *You don't have to* **make excuses** *for her* (= try to think of reasons for her behaviour). ◇ *It gave me an excuse to take the car.* See also **excuse** → FORGIVE *verb*

motive /ˈməʊtɪv; *AmE* ˈmoʊ-/ [C] a reason that explains sb's behaviour: *There seemed to be no motive for the murder.* ◇ *I'm suspicious of his motives.* ◇ *I have an* **ulterior motive** *in offering to help you.* See also **motivation** → INCENTIVE

need [sing., U] (usually used in negative statements) a good reason to do sth: *There is no need for you to get up early tomorrow.* ◇ *I had no need to open the letter – I knew what it would say.* (*spoken*) ❶ In this meaning, **need** is almost always used in the phrases *There is / was no need (for sb) to do sth.* and *have no need to do sth.*

justification /ˌdʒʌstɪfɪˈkeɪʃn/ [U, C] (*rather formal*) a good reason why sth exists or is done: *I can see no possible justification for any further tax increases.* ◇ *The government is struggling to find a justification for this war.* See also **justify** → EXPLAIN 2

> **NOTE** **GROUNDS** OR **JUSTIFICATION?** Justification is used to talk about finding or understanding reasons for actions, or trying to explain why it is a good idea to do sth. It is often used with words like *little, no, some, every, without,* and *not any.* Grounds is used more for talking about reasons that already exist, or that have already been decided, for example by law: *moral / economic / constitutional / environmental / ethical / medical / legal grounds*

cause [U] (*rather formal*) a reason for having particular feelings or behaving in a particular way: *There is no* **cause** *for alarm / concern.* ◇ *If your child is absent without good cause* (= without a good reason), *you may receive a warning from the school board.*

pretext /ˈpriːtekst/ [C, usually sing.] (*rather formal*) a false reason that you give for doing sth, usually sth bad, in order to hide the real reason: *The incident was used as a pretext for intervention in the area.* ◇ *He left the party early on the pretext of having work to do.*

reasonable *adj.* See the Topic Map for FACT AND OPINION on p.898

reasonable · fair · equal · just · equitable · even-handed
These words all describe sb/sth that treats or affects people in a sensible, appropriate and equal way.

PATTERNS AND COLLOCATIONS
▶ to be reasonable / fair / just / equitable **that**…
▶ to be reasonable / fair / just **to do sth**
▶ a reasonable / a fair / an equal / a just / an equitable **division** / **distribution** / **share** of sth
▶ a reasonable / a fair / a just / an equitable **system** / **settlement** / **solution**
▶ a reasonable / fair / just **law** / **punishment** / **sentence** / **judgement** / **person** / **man** / **woman**
▶ **perfectly** reasonable / fair / just

reasonable practical, sensible and treating people in an appropriate and equal way: *It is reasonable to assume that she knew beforehand that this would happen.* ◇ *It seems a perfectly reasonable request to make.* ◇ *Any reasonable person would have done exactly as you did.* ◇ *Be reasonable! We can't work late every night.* **OPP unreasonable** → UNACCEPTABLE, See also **reasonable** → FINE, **reason** → LOGIC, **plausible** → POSSIBLE 2
▶ **reasonably** *adv.*: *He couldn't reasonably be expected to pay back the loan all at once.*

fair treating people in a reasonable and appropriate way; treating everyone equally and according to the rules or the law: *All we're asking for is a fair wage.* ◇ *It's not **fair to** the students to keep changing the schedule.* ◇ (*BrE* also) *It's not **fair on** the students…* ◇ *It's **fair to say that** they are pleased with the latest offer.* ◇ *To be fair, she behaved better than we expected.* ◇ (*spoken*) *It's **only fair** that they should give us something in return.* ◇ (*spoken*) *It's not fair! He always gets more than me!* **OPP unfair** → WRONG 4, See also **fair** → FINE, **fairness**, **fair play** → JUSTICE
▶ **fairly** *adv.*: *He's always treated me very fairly.* ◇ *Her attitude could fairly be described as hostile.*

equal having the same rights or being treated the same as other people, without differences such as race, religion or sex being considered: **equal rights / pay** ◇ *The company has an **equal opportunities** policy* (= gives the same chances of employment to everyone). ◇ *the desire for a more equal society* (= in which everyone has the same rights and chances) **OPP unequal** → WRONG 4, See also **equality** → JUSTICE

just [usually before noun] (*rather formal*) morally fair and reasonable: *I think it was a just decision.* ◇ *Of course we all strive for a just and humane society.* ◇ *He was known to be a just man.* ◇ *The law must be seen to be just.* ❶ *Just* is often used in the context of the law or the way things are done in a society. It is not usually used in informal or private contexts. **OPP unjust** → WRONG 4, See also **justice** → JUSTICE

equitable /ˈekwɪtəbl/ (*formal*) (of a system or society) fair and reasonable; treating everyone in an equal way: *We need to construct an equitable and efficient method of local taxation.* **OPP inequitable** → WRONG 4

even-handed treating everyone fairly and equally: *They took an even-handed approach to industrial relations.* ◇ *He is **even-handed in** his criticism of the various political parties.* ❶ *Even-handed* describes sb's way of dealing with an issue, but it is not used to describe a person: ~~an even-handed person / man / woman~~

reasoning noun See also the entry for LOGIC

reasoning · thinking · thought · reflection
These are all words for the process of thinking about sth in a logical way, or the ideas and opinions that are based on this.

PATTERNS AND COLLOCATIONS
▸ reasoning/ thinking/ thought/ reflections **on** sth
▸ thinking/ thought/ reflections **about** sth
▸ the reasoning/ thinking/ thought **behind** sth
▸ **current/ traditional** reasoning/ thinking/ thought
▸ **critical** reasoning/ thinking/ thought/ reflections
▸ **logical/ scientific/ political** reasoning/ thinking/ thought
▸ a **line** of reasoning/ thinking/ thought

reasoning [U] (*written*) the process of thinking about sth in a logical way; the ideas or opinions that are based on this process: *Could you please explain the reasoning behind this decision?* ◇ *It was difficult to follow his line of reasoning.* See also **reason** → CONCLUDE *verb*, **reasoned** → RATIONAL

thinking [U] a set of ideas or opinions about a subject or problem: *What is the current thinking on this question?*

thought [U] ideas about a subject such as politics or science, especially when these are connected with a particular person, group or period of history: *There isn't much real evidence relating to early Greek thought.* ❶ In this meaning **thought** is almost always used after an adjective.

reflection [C, usually pl.] (*rather formal*) your written or spoken thoughts about sth, especially sth you know about or have experienced: *She concludes by providing some reflections on the gains of the previous decade.* See also **reflect** → CONSIDER

reassure verb See also the entry for ENCOURAGE 1

reassure · comfort · console · put/set sb's mind at rest
These words all mean to say or do sth in order to make sb else feel better or less worried about sth.

PATTERNS AND COLLOCATIONS
▸ to reassure sb/ comfort sb/ console sb/ put/set sb's mind at rest **with** sth
▸ to reassure/ comfort/ console **yourself**
▸ to **try to** reassure sb/ comfort sb/ console sb/ put/set sb's mind at rest
▸ to **do little to/ do nothing to/ do much to** reassure sb/ put/set sb's mind at rest
▸ to be **greatly** reassured / comforted
▸ It reassures/ comforts/ consoles **sb to know (that)** …

reassure /ˌriːəˈʃʊə(r); -ˈʃɔː(r); AmE -ˈʃʊr/ [T] to say or do sth that makes sb less frightened or worried: *They tried to reassure her, but she still felt anxious.* ◇ *The doctor reassured him that there was nothing seriously wrong.* See also **reassurance** → RELIEF
▸ **reassuring** *adj.*: *He gave her a reassuring smile.* ◇ *It's reassuring (to know) that we've got the money if necessary.*
OPP **alarming** → FRIGHTENING
▸ **reassuringly** *adv.*: *reassuringly normal* ◇ *She smiled reassuringly.*

comfort [T] to make sb who is worried or unhappy feel better by being kind and sympathetic towards them: *The victim's widow was today being comforted by family and friends.* ◇ *It comforted her to feel his arms around her.* See also **comfort** → RELIEF *noun*
▸ **comforting** *adj.*: *her comforting words* ◇ *It's comforting to know that you'll be there.*
▸ **comfortingly** *adv.*: *comfortingly familiar*

console /kənˈsəʊl; AmE -ˈsoʊl/ [T] to make sb who is unhappy or disappointed feel better by being kind and sympathetic towards them: *Nothing could console him when his wife died.* ◇ *You can console yourself with the thought that you did your best.* See also **consolation** → RELIEF
▸ **inconsolable** /ˌɪnkənˈsəʊləbl; AmE -ˈsoʊl-/ *adj.*: *His*

widow, Jane, was inconsolable (= she was unable to be comforted).

NOTE **COMFORT** OR **CONSOLE?** Both verbs can be used when sb is unhappy or upset about sth: *Her kitten had just died and she was devastated. I didn't know how to comfort/console her.* You can also **comfort** sb who is worried or frightened, especially by putting your arm around them, giving them a hug, holding their hand, etc.: *Her child had a nightmare and she took him into her bed to comfort him.* You can **console** sb who is disappointed, especially by saying sth that might help them see that the situation is not as bad as they think: *'Never mind,' she said, in an attempt to console him, 'You can always enter the competition again next year.'*

put/set sb's 'mind at rest *idiom* to do or say sth to make sb stop worrying about sth: *I know you're worried about Steve, but let me put your mind at rest. He's absolutely fine.*

rebel verb

rebel · rise · mutiny · revolt
These are all words that can be used when a group of people fight against or refuse to obey those in authority.

PATTERNS AND COLLOCATIONS
▸ to rebel/ rise/ mutiny/ revolt **against** sb/ sth
▸ **the people** rebel/ rise/ revolt

rebel /rɪˈbel/ (-ll-) [I] to fight against or refuse to obey an authority, for example a government or system: *In 1215 the barons rebelled against the king.* ◇ *The colonies rebelled and declared their independence.* See also **rebel** → GUERRILLA *noun*, **rebel** → PROTESTER *noun*, **rebellion** → REVOLUTION 1, **rebellious** → NAUGHTY

rise [I] (*formal*) to begin to fight against your ruler or government or against a foreign army: *The peasants rose in revolt.* ◇ *He called on the people to rise up against the invaders.* See also **uprising** → REVOLUTION 1

mutiny /ˈmjuːtəni/ [I] (especially of soldiers or sailors) to refuse to obey the orders of sb in authority: *There was a real chance the crew would mutiny.* See also **mutiny** → REVOLUTION *noun* 1

revolt /rɪˈvəʊlt; AmE -ˈvoʊlt/ [I] to take violent action against the people in power: *Finally the people revolted against the military dictatorship.* See also **revolt** → REVOLUTION *noun* 1

NOTE **REBEL** OR **REVOLT?** To **rebel** against sth can involve fighting or simply opposition. When people **revolt** it nearly always involves violence. **Rebel** is more often used to describe fighting against a government or political system, especially by people who already have some power or are a part of the same political system: *A total of 139 MPs rebelled against the government.* **Revolt** is more often used to describe the actions of ordinary people rejecting the authority that controls them, for example because it is treating them badly: *The peasants revolted against high taxes and the losses of the war.*

rebuild verb

rebuild · refurbish · restore · renovate · revamp · remodel · reconstruct · redecorate · reassemble · redevelop
These words all mean to repair or develop sth to make it more attractive or more useful.

PATTERNS AND COLLOCATIONS
▸ to rebuild/ refurbish/ restore/ renovate/ remodel/ redecorate a **house**
▸ to refurbish / restore / renovate / remodel / reconstruct a **building**
▸ to renovate/ remodel/ redecorate a **room**
▸ to rebuild/ refurbish/ restore/ renovate/ revamp/ remodel/ reconstruct/ redecorate sth **completely**
▸ to rebuild/ restore/ reconstruct sth **painstakingly**

▸ to rebuild / refurbish / restore / renovate sth **extensively**
▸ **newly / recently** rebuilt / refurbished / restored / renovated / redecorated

rebuild /ˌriːˈbɪld/ [T, I] to build or put sth together again; to make sb/sth complete and strong again: *After the earthquake, the people set about rebuilding their homes.* ◇ *When she lost her job, she had to rebuild her life completely.* ◇ *It could take ten years for the area to completely rebuild after the hurricane.*
▸ **rebuilding** *noun* [U, sing.]: *the rebuilding of London's churches after the Great Fire of 1666*

refurbish /ˌriːˈfɜːbɪʃ; AmE -ˈfɜːrb-/ [T] (*rather formal*) to clean and decorate a room or building in order to make it more attractive or more useful: *The theatre has been extensively refurbished.* ❶ **Refurbish** is usually used to talk about cleaning and decorating a building that is used by the public, or that will be used as offices or flats.
▸ **refurbishment** *noun* [U, C]: *The hotel is closed for refurbishment.* ◇ *This is just one of several planned refurbishments.*

restore /rɪˈstɔː(r)/ [T] to repair a building, work of art or piece of furniture so that it looks as good as it did originally: *Her job is restoring old paintings.* ◇ *The house has been lovingly restored to the way it looked in 1900.*
▸ **restoration** /ˌrestəˈreɪʃn/ *noun* [U, C]: *The palace is closed for restoration.*

renovate /ˈrenəveɪt/ [T] to repair and paint a building or piece of furniture so that it is in good condition again: *They spent the summer renovating a farmhouse in Kent.*
▸ **renovation** *noun* [U, C, usually pl.]: *buildings in need of renovation* ◇ *There will be extensive renovations to the hospital.*

NOTE **RESTORE** OR **RENOVATE**? **Restore** is used especially to talk about furniture and works of art, although it can also be used to talk about buildings; **renovate** is used especially to talk about buildings, although it can also be used to talk about furniture. **Restore** is often used with adverbs like *beautifully, carefully, faithfully, immaculately, lovingly, painstakingly, sympathetically* and *tastefully*; **renovate** is more neutral, used either with no adverb or an adverb relating to time: *a recently/newly renovated farmhouse*

revamp /ˌriːˈvæmp/ [T] (*rather informal*) to make changes to the form of sth, usually to improve its appearance: *The company is attempting to revamp its image.* ❶ People typically **revamp** an area such as a *town centre*, a room such as a *kitchen*, their, or their company's, *image* or the style of a regular TV show such as the *news*.

remodel /ˌriːˈmɒdl; AmE -ˈmɑːdl/ (-ll-, AmE -l-) [T] to change the structure or shape of sth: *The interior of the building has been completely remodelled.* ◇ *They put forward plans to remodel the education system.*

reconstruct /ˌriːkənˈstrʌkt/ [T] (*rather formal*) to build or put sth together again; to produce a copy of sth that existed in the past: *Old London Bridge was bought by an American and reconstructed in the US.* ◇ *They plan to reconstruct the settlement as it would have been in Iron Age times.*
▸ **reconstruction** /ˌriːkənˈstrʌkʃn/ *noun* [U, C]: *the reconstruction of the sea walls* ◇ *The doorway is a 19th century reconstruction of Norman work.* See also **reconstruction** → COPY *noun* 2

redecorate /ˌriːˈdekəreɪt/ [I, T] to put new paint and/or paper on the walls of a room or house: *We've just redecorated.* ◇ *The house has been fully redecorated.*

reassemble /ˌriːəˈsembl/ [T] to fit the parts of sth together again after it has been taken apart: *We had to take the table apart and reassemble it upstairs.* ❶ You can **reassemble** the parts of a piece of furniture or machinery.

redevelop /ˌriːdɪˈveləp/ [T, I] to change an area by building new roads, houses, factories, etc: *The city has plans to redevelop the site.* ◇ *We either need to sell or redevelop.*
▸ **redevelopment** *noun* [U]: *inner-city redevelopment*

recent *adj.*

recent · current · latest · present · modern · new · contemporary · present-day · modern-day
These words all describe sth that belongs to the present time because it is happening now or happened only a short time ago.

PATTERNS AND COLLOCATIONS
▸ recent / modern **times** / the present **time**
▸ recent / current / present / contemporary / present-day **events**
▸ the current / latest / present / contemporary / present-day **situation**
▸ recent / current / the latest / present / modern / contemporary **trends**
▸ the recent / current / latest / present / modern / new / contemporary / modern-day **version**
▸ recent / current / the latest / modern / new / contemporary / present-day **forms / theories**
▸ the current / modern / contemporary **scene**
▸ current / modern / new / contemporary **politics**
▸ modern / a new / contemporary / present-day / modern-day **society**
▸ modern / contemporary / present-day **life**
▸ the modern / a new / the contemporary **world**
▸ (a) recent / modern / new / contemporary / present-day **literature / writer**
▸ (a) modern / new / contemporary / present-day **art / artist / music**

recent [usually before noun] that happened or began only a short time ago: *The next chapter summarizes recent developments in the field.* ◇ *The Prime Minister discussed the issue during his most recent visit to Poland.* ◇ *There have been many changes in recent years.* **OPP** **long-standing** → OLD 1
▸ **recently** *adv.*: *We received a letter from him recently.* ◇ *I haven't seen them recently (= It is some time since I saw them).*

current [only before noun] happening or existing now: *The necklace would be worth over $5 000 at current prices.* ◇ *Ask your current employer to give you a reference.* ◇ *Our current financial situation is not good.* **OPP** **former, then, ex-** → FORMER, **previous** → PREVIOUS
▸ **currently** *adv.*: *This matter is currently being discussed by the Board.* **OPP** **previously** → PREVIOUS

latest [only before noun] the most recent or newest: *She always wears the latest fashions.* ◇ *Her latest novel has been shortlisted for a literary prize.* ◇ *Have you heard the latest news?*
▸ **the latest** *noun* [sing.]: (*rather informal*) *This is the latest in robot technology.* ◇ *Have you heard the latest?*

present [usually before noun] current: *The present owner of the house is a Mr T. Grant.* ◇ *This is a list of all club members, past and present.* ◇ *We do not have any more information at the present time.* **OPP** **past** → PREVIOUS
▸ **at present** *phrase*: (*rather formal*) *The council has no plans at present to develop this site.*
▸ **presently** *adv.*: (*especially AmE*) *The crime is presently being investigated by the police.*

NOTE **CURRENT** OR **PRESENT**? In many cases you can use either word: *the current/present situation/state/position/climate/trend/practice/arrangement/value/level/generation/crisis.* **Current** is used especially in financial contexts: *current spending/expenditure* ◇ *the current surplus/deficit/yield* and in the phrase *current affairs*. **Present** is used more often with lengths of time: *the present day/century/moment/time*, except in financial contexts: *What's the budget for the current year?*

modern [only before noun] of the present time or recent times; (of styles in art, music, fashion, etc.) new and intended to be different from traditional styles: *Modern European history* ◇ *Stress is a major problem of modern life.* ◇ *Shakespeare's language can be a problem for modern readers.* ◇ *The gallery has regular exhibitions of modern art.* **OPP** **ancient** → OLD 1, See also **modern** → MODERN

new (often with *the*) modern; of the latest type: *He couldn't stand the new breed of career politicians.* ◇ *Comedy is the new rock and roll.* ◇ *They called themselves the New Romantics.*

contemporary /kən'temprəri; *AmE* -pəreri/ (*rather formal*) (of life, society or culture) modern: *The film paints a depressing picture of life in contemporary Britain.* ◇ *She is one of the great innovators of contemporary dance.*

NOTE MODERN OR **CONTEMPORARY?** In many cases you can use either word, especially when talking about art, culture or society: *modern/contemporary art/architecture/dance/fiction/literature/music/painting/culture/society/politics/history* ◇ *the modern/contemporary world/scene.* **Modern**, but NOT **contemporary**, is also used to talk about science and technology: *modern technology/physics/medicine/warfare/equipment/machinery/techniques* See also **modern** → MODERN

present-'day [only before noun] (*especially written*) of the present time: *His theories have no relevance to present-day society.* ◇ *Serbia at that time already included present-day Macedonia.* ❶ **Present-day** is used especially to refer to sth in the form that it has now, when this is different from the form it had in the past: *present-day society/English/Russia*

▸ **the ,present 'day** *noun* [sing.]: *a study of European drama, from Ibsen to the present day*

'modern-day [only before noun] of the present time: *modern-day America* ❶ **Modern-day** is often used to describe a modern form of sb/sth, usually sb/sth bad or unpleasant, that existed in the past: *It has been called modern-day slavery.*

recession *noun*

recession · depression · slump · slowdown · trough
These are all words for a difficult period of time for business or the economy.

slowdown   slump   recession   depression
                  trough

PATTERNS AND COLLOCATIONS
▸ **in** recession / a depression / a slump / a trough
▸ a **major** / **serious** / **severe** recession / depression / slump
▸ an **economic** recession / depression / slump / slowdown
▸ a **worldwide** recession / depression / slump / slowdown
▸ to **cause** a recession / slump / slowdown
▸ to **go into** recession / depression

recession /rɪ'seʃn/ [C, U] a difficult time for the economy of a country, when there is less trade and industrial activity than usual and more people are unemployed: *How do you assess the impact of the current recession on manufacturing?* ◇ *We need active policies to pull the country out of recession.* ◇ *These industries have been hit hard by the recession.*

depression /dɪ'preʃn/ [C, U] a difficult time for a country when there is little economic activity and many people are unemployed and poor: *The country was in the grip of (an) economic depression.* ◇ *He grew up during the Great Depression of the 1930s.*

▸ **depressed** *adj.*: *They have made little attempt to bring jobs to economically depressed areas.*

slump [C] (*especially journalism or business*) a period when a country's economy or a business is doing badly: *Housing sales are finally coming out of a three-month slump.* ◇ *The toy industry is in a slump.* **OPP boom** → DO WELL, See also **slump** → REDUCTION

slowdown /'sləʊdaʊn; *AmE* 'sloʊ-/ [C] (*especially business*) a reduction in speed or activity, especially in business or the economy: *There has been a slowdown in economic growth in recent months.*

trough /trɒf; *AmE* trɔːf/ [C] (*especially business*) a period of time when the level of sth is low, especially a time when a business or the economy is not growing: *There have been peaks and troughs in the long-term trend of unemployment.* **OPP peak** → PEAK

NOTE WHICH WORD? A **slowdown** is the least serious of these and a **depression** is the most serious. A **slowdown**, **slump** or **trough** might affect the economy of a country generally, or just one particular business or industry; it usually lasts a period of months and is sometimes regarded as part of the normal business cycle. A **recession** affects a whole industry or a country's whole economy, and it can last for years. It is not usually regarded as part of the normal business cycle. However, a **recession** is still considered chiefly in terms of its effects on business and the economy; **depression** is used especially when you are considering the effect of recession on the lives of ordinary people, especially the difficult situation caused by poverty and unemployment when this affects a very large number of people. The *Great Depression* was the worldwide economic depression that followed the American stock market crash in 1929.

reckless *adj.* See also the entry for CRAZY

reckless · irresponsible · premature · unwise · rash · hasty
These words all describe people showing a lack of care or thought for the possible results of their actions.

PATTERNS AND COLLOCATIONS
▸ It would be reckless / irresponsible / premature / unwise / rash **to do sth**
▸ You would be unwise **to do sth**
▸ a reckless / a premature / an unwise / a rash / a hasty **decision**
▸ **rather** / **somewhat** reckless / irresponsible / premature / rash / hasty
▸ **extremely** / **very** reckless / irresponsible / unwise / rash

reckless (*usually disapproving*) showing a lack of care about danger and the possible results of your actions: *He showed a reckless disregard for his own safety.* ◇ *She had always been reckless with money.* See also **impulsive** → SPONTANEOUS

▸ **recklessly** *adv.*: *She had fallen hopelessly and recklessly in love.*
▸ **recklessness** *noun* [U]: *an act of sheer recklessness* **OPP caution** → CARE

irresponsible /,ɪrɪ'spɒnsəbl; *AmE* -'spɑːn-/ (*disapproving*) not thinking enough about the effects of what you do; not showing a feeling of responsibility: *He's fun but totally irresponsible.* ◇ *This was highly irresponsible behaviour.* ❶ **Irresponsible** is used especially to talk about *behaviour*, an *action*, *conduct*, an *attitude* or a *way of doing things*. People also say that it *is/would be irresponsible to* take some sort of risk, for example by ignoring a problem: *It would be irresponsible to carry on if there really was a problem.* **OPP responsible** → RELIABLE 1

premature /'premətʃə(r); *AmE* ,priːmə'tʃʊr; -'tʊr/ (*rather formal, especially business, sometimes disapproving*) happening or done too soon: *The incident brought the game to a premature conclusion.* ◇ *It is premature to talk about success at this stage* (= because it may not happen).

unwise (*rather formal, especially written, usually disapproving*) showing a lack of good judgement in a way that may cause difficulties in the future: *It would be unwise to comment on the situation without knowing all the facts.* ◇ *He made some very unwise investments and lost a lot of money.* **OPP wise** → BEST, See also **foolish** → CRAZY

▸ **unwisely** *adv.*: *Perhaps unwisely, I agreed to help.*

rash (*usually disapproving*) doing sth that may not be sensible without first thinking about the possible results; done in this way: *This is what happens when you make rash promises.* ◇ *It would be rash to assume that everyone will agree with you on this.* ◇ *Think twice before doing* *anything rash.* ❶ People typically make **rash** *promises, decisions* and *statements.* The pattern *It is/would be rash to...* is often used with verbs about expressing opinons or drawing conclusions, such as *assume, expect, state, conclude* and *say.*

▸ **rashly** *adv.*: *She had rashly promised to lend him the money.* ◇ *I see now that I may have acted rashly.*

hasty /ˈheɪsti/ (*often disapproving*) acting or deciding too quickly, without enough thought; said or done too quickly, especially when this has bad results: *Perhaps I was too hasty in rejecting his offer.* ◇ *Let's not make any hasty decisions.*

▸ **hastily** *adv.*: *Perhaps I spoke too hastily.*

recognizable (*BrE also* -isable) *adj.*

recognizable · identifiable · distinguishable
These words all describe sb/sth that is easy to know and identify.

PATTERNS AND COLLOCATIONS
▸ to be recognizable / identifiable / distinguishable **as** sb / sth
▸ to be recognizable / identifiable / distinguishable **by** sth
▸ to be recognizable / identifiable **to** sb
▸ **clearly / easily / readily** recognizable / identifiable / distinguishable
▸ **immediately / instantly / quite** recognizable / identifiable
▸ **barely / hardly / scarcely** recognizable / identifiable / distinguishable

recognizable (*BrE also* -**isable**) /ˈrekəgnaɪzəbl; ˌrekəgˈnaɪzəbl/ (of a person, place or thing) that you know when you see or hear them/it, because you have seen or heard them/it, or sb/sth of the same kind, before: *After so many years she was still immediately recognizable.* ◇ *Her face is instantly recognizable to countless millions all over the world.* ◇ *The building was easily recognizable as a prison.* **OPP** **unrecognizable** ❶ A person or thing that is **unrecognizable** is so changed or damaged that you do not recognize them/it: *He was unrecognizable without his beard.*

▸ **recognizably** (*BrE also* -**isably**) *adv.*: *The town was still recognizably the place I had grown up in.*

identifiable /aɪˌdentɪˈfaɪəbl/ (*rather formal*) (especially of a place or thing) that you know and can find and/or name because you know which features they have/it has: *The house is easily identifiable by the large tree outside.* ◇ *There are several clearly identifiable ethnic groups within the community.* **OPP** **unidentifiable** ❶ A place or thing that is **unidentifiable** cannot be identified: *He had an unidentifiable accent.*

> **NOTE** **RECOGNIZABLE** OR **IDENTIFIABLE**? People, places and things are **recognizable** from experience: you recognize things that you have seen or heard before. Places and things are **identifiable** from knowledge: you identify things that you know about, either from experience or because you have studied them, read about them or been told about them. **Identifiable** is NOT usually used to talk about individual people: *After so many years she was still immediately identifiable.*

distinguishable /dɪˈstɪŋgwɪʃəbl/ that can be identified as different from sth else that is similar; that can be seen: *The male bird is easily distinguishable from the female.* ◇ *The coast was barely distinguishable in the mist.* **OPP** **indistinguishable** → EQUAL, See also the entry for VISIBLE

recommend *verb*

1 recommend that sb do sth
2 recommend a good hotel

1 See also the entry for PROPOSE
recommend · advise · advocate · urge
These words all mean to tell sb what you think they should do in a particular situation.

recommend   advise   urge
advocate

PATTERNS AND COLLOCATIONS
▸ to recommend / advise / advocate / urge **that...**
▸ **It is** recommended / advised / advocated / urged **that...**
▸ to recommend / advise / urge **sb to do sth**
▸ to recommend / advise / advocate **doing sth**
▸ to recommend / advise / advocate / urge **caution**
▸ to advise / advocate / urge **restraint**
▸ to **strongly** recommend / advise / advocate sb / sth

recommend [T] to tell sb what you think they should do in a particular situation; to say what you think the price or level of sth should be: *I recommend (that) he see a lawyer.* ◇ *It is strongly recommended that the machines be checked every year.* ◇ *He recommended reading the book before seeing the movie.* ◇ *It is dangerous to exceed the recommended dose.* ◇ *a recommended price of $50* See also **recommendation** → PROPOSAL

advise [T, I] to tell sb what you think they should do in a particular situation: *Her mother was away and couldn't advise her.* ◇ *I'd advise extreme caution.* ◇ *I'd advise you not to tell him.* ◇ *I would strongly advise against going out on your own.* See also **advice** → ADVICE

> **NOTE** **RECOMMEND** OR **ADVISE**? **Advise** is a stronger word than **recommend** and is often used when the person giving the advice is in a senior position or a position of authority: *Police are advising fans without tickets to stay away.* ◇ ~~*Police are recommending fans without tickets to stay away.*~~ *I advise you...* can suggest that you know better than the person you are advising: this may cause offence if they are your equal or senior to you. *I recommend...* mainly suggests that you are trying to be helpful and is less likely to cause offence. **Recommend** is often used with more positive advice to tell sb about possible benefits and **advise** with more negative advice to warn sb about possible dangers: *He advised reading the book before seeing the movie.* ◇ *I would recommend against going out on your own.* You have to *recommend sth (to sb)*, not just 'recommend sb': ~~*Her mother was away and couldn't recommend her.*~~

advocate /ˈædvəkeɪt/ [T] (*formal*) to support or recommend sth publicly: *The group does not advocate the use of violence.* See also the entry for SUPPORT 1

urge [T] to recommend sth strongly: *The situation is dangerous, but the UN is urging caution.* ◇ *The report urged that all children be taught to swim.*

2 **recommend · suggest · nominate · endorse**
These words all mean to tell sb that sth is good or to suggest that sb is suitable for a particular job, position, etc.

PATTERNS AND COLLOCATIONS
▸ to recommend / suggest / nominate sb / sth **for / as** sth
▸ to recommend / suggest sb / sth **to** sb
▸ to recommend / suggest / nominate **sb to do sth**
▸ to recommend / suggest / nominate a **candidate**
▸ to recommend / endorse a **product**

recommend [T] to tell sb that sth is good or useful, or that sb would be suitable for a particular job, etc.; to make sb/sth seem attractive or good: *Can you recommend a good hotel?* ◇ *I recommend the book to all my students.* ◇ *They were invited to recommend likely candidates for the two new positions.* ◇ *The hotel's new restaurant comes* **highly recommended**. ◇ (*rather formal, written*) *The system has* **much to recommend it**. ❶ If you **recommend** sb/sth, it usually means that you have personal experience of the person or thing you are recommending. For example, you would only be able to recommend a person for a job if you knew them personally, and you could only recommend a book to sb if you had actually read it yourself. See also **recommendation** → ENDORSEMENT

suggest [T] to tell sb about a person, thing, method, etc. that might be suitable for a particular job or purpose: *Who would you suggest for the job?* ◇ *She suggested Paris as a good place for the conference.* ◇ *Can you suggest how I might contact him?* ❶ **Suggest** is less certain than **recommend**: you do not necessarily have personal experience of the person or thing − you may have just heard about them/it from sb else, but think they/it might be worth trying. See also **suggestion** → PROPOSAL

nominate /'nɒmɪneɪt; AmE 'nɑːm-/ [T, I] to formally suggest that sb/sth should be chosen for an important role, prize or position: *He was nominated as best actor.* ◇ *Each office will nominate a representative to sit on the committee.* ◇ *Ten critics were asked to nominate their Book of the Year.* See also **nomination** → CHOICE 1, **nominee** → CANDIDATE

endorse /ɪn'dɔːs; AmE ɪn'dɔːrs/ [T] to say in an advertisement that you use and like a particular product so that other people will want to buy it: *I wonder how many celebrities actually use the products they endorse.* See also **endorsement** → ENDORSEMENT

record *noun*

record · diary · minutes · blog · journal · log
These are all words for a written account of sth that is kept and can be referred to in the future.

PATTERNS AND COLLOCATIONS
▸ **in** a / the record / diary / minutes / blog / journal / log
▸ a **daily** record / diary / blog / journal / log
▸ (a) **detailed** record / diary / minutes / journal / log
▸ a **private** record / diary / blog / journal
▸ to **keep** a record / diary / blog / journal / log
▸ to **record** sth **in** a diary / the minutes / a journal / a log
▸ to **read** sb's diary / the minutes / a blog / a journal

record [C] a written account of sth that is kept so that it can be looked at again and used in the future: *You should keep a record of your expenses.* ◇ *Their records date back to 1846.* ◇ *I asked them to check their records again.* ◇ *No record of the transaction existed.* ◇ *Who has your **medical records**?* ◇ *Last summer was the hottest **on record**.*

diary /'daɪəri/ [C] a book in which you can write down your experiences and private thoughts each day: *I used to keep a secret diary when I was a teenager.* ◇ *This was the very last entry in her diary.* See also **diary** → SCHEDULE *noun*

minutes (usually **the minutes**) [pl.] a summary or record of what is said at a formal meeting: *We read through the minutes of the last meeting.* ◇ *Who is going to **take the minutes** (= write them)?*

blog [C] a personal record that sb puts on their website, giving an account of their activities and opinions, and discussing places on the Internet they have visited: *Do you know who is reading your blog?* ◇ *You can **post** anything **on a blog** − a message, link, photo or video clip.* ❶ **Blog** is a shortened form of **weblog**, formed from **web** + **log**, but the term **blog** is now much more frequently used.

journal /'dʒɜːnl; AmE 'dʒɜːrnl/ [C] a written record of your experiences each day and what you think about them: *She kept a journal of her travels in Asia.* ◇ *He noted in his journal that his wife was looking pale and tired.*

NOTE DIARY OR JOURNAL? A **diary** is likely to be more personal than a **journal**, containing personal thoughts and comments on other people; diaries are not usually intended for other people to read. A **journal** may be slightly less personal, kept as a record of a particular period, for example when sb is travelling, or of sb's thoughts on a particular subject, such as gardening or books. A **journal** may be intended for other people to read. The term **journal** is now most often used in a historical context, to refer to written records of personal experience that have become historical documents.

log [C] an official record of events during a particular period of time, especially a journey on a ship or plane: *A senior officer made a note in the ship's log.* ◇ *They keep a log of any accidents that occur at work.*

record *verb*
1 the figures recorded for 2007
2 record a TV show/concert

1 record · register · enter · document · chart · log · minute
These words all mean to put information in a list or describe events, in writing or in other ways that are permanent.

PATTERNS AND COLLOCATIONS
▸ to record / register / enter / document / log / minute sth **as** sth
▸ to record / register / enter / document sth **in** sth
▸ to record / document / chart **how...**
▸ to record / document / minute **that...**
▸ to record / document / chart the **history / progress** of sth
▸ to record / register / enter / log the **details** of sth
▸ to record / register / enter **names**
▸ to record / enter / log **data**
▸ to **carefully** record / enter / document / log sth
▸ to **accurately** record / document / chart sth

record [T] to keep a permanent account of facts or events, for example by writing them down or filming them: *The discussion was recorded in detail in his diary.* ◇ *The figures recorded for 2007 show an increase of 23 per cent.* ◇ *As a war artist she recorded the work of female volunteers.* ◇ *Examples can be found in every era of **recorded history**.*

register [T, I] to put the name of sb/sth on an official list: *The company's logo has not yet been registered as a trademark.* ◇ *All students must be **registered with** a local doctor.* ◇ *You need to go to the Registry Office to register the death.* ◇ *Many older people have **registered for** a postal vote.* See also **register** → LIST *noun*

enter [T] to put information in a list, book or computer: *He **entered** the details of the case **into** a file.* ◇ *Enter your name and age in the boxes (= on a form).* ◇ *The notebook window is where you can enter and display data.*

document [T, usually passive] to record the details of sth in writing: *His exploits have been well documented by the national press.* ◇ *The 790s are one of the best documented decades in Anglo-Saxon history.*

chart [T] to record or follow the progress of sth: *The exhibition charts the development of modern Irish painting.*

log (-**gg**-) [T] to put information in an official record: *The crimes were logged but not investigated.* ◇ *The call was logged at 16.20.*

minute /'mɪnɪt/ [T] (*especially BrE, rather formal*) to write down sth that is said or decided in the official record of a meeting: *I'd like that remark to be minuted.* ◇ *Meetings must be minuted and the minutes approved at the following meeting.*

2 See the Topic Map for THE MEDIA on p.900
record · film · photograph · shoot · video
These words all mean to make a film or photograph of sb/sth or to make a copy of a film, TV or radio show or musical performance.

PATTERNS AND COLLOCATIONS
▸ **beautifully** recorded / filmed / photographed
▸ to **record** / film sb / sth **secretly**
▸ to **film** / shoot sth **on location**

record [T, I] to make a copy of music, a film, etc. by storing it on tape or a disc so that you can listen to or watch it again; to perform music so that it can be copied onto and kept on tape: *Did you remember to record 'House' for me?* ◇ *a recorded programme/concert* ◇ *He recorded the class rehearsing before the performance.* ◇ *Tell me when the tape starts recording.* ◇ *The band is back in the US recording their new album.* ❶ You can also *record sth on* *film/video*, by making a film or videotape of it: *These early experiments were all recorded on film, but this historic footage has sadly been lost.*

film [I, T] to make a film of a story or a real event: *They are filming in Moscow right now.* ◊ *The show was filmed on location in New York.* ◊ *Two young boys were filmed stealing DVDs on the security video.* See also **film** → FILM *noun* 1

photograph [T] to take a photograph of sb/sth: *He has photographed some of the world's most beautiful women.* ◊ *She refused to be photographed nude.* ◊ *They were photographed playing with their children.* See also **photograph** → PHOTOGRAPH *noun*

shoot [I, T] to make a film or photograph of sth: *Cameras ready? OK, shoot!* ◊ *Where was the movie shot?* ◊ *The movie was shot in black and white.*

video [T] (*especially BrE*) to record a television programme using a video recorder; to film sb/sth using a video camera: *Did you remember to video that programme?* ◊ *Videoing students can be a useful teaching exercise.* See also **video** → FILM *noun* 1

recover *verb*

1 recover from an illness
2 recover the money

1 See the Topic Map for HEALTH on p.890, See also the entry for SURVIVE

recover · get better · heal · recuperate · get well · convalesce · shake sth off · pull through
These words all mean to stop suffering from an illness or injury.

PATTERNS AND COLLOCATIONS
▸ to recover / recuperate **from** sth
▸ to **gradually** recover / get better / heal
▸ to **completely / partially** recover / heal

recover /rɪˈkʌvə(r)/ [I] (of a person) to become healthy again after being ill or hurt; to return to a normal state after an unpleasant or unusual experience or a period of difficulty: *He's still recovering from his operation.* ◊ *Mother and baby are recovering well.* ◊ *It can take many years to recover from the death of a loved one.* ◊ *The economy is at last beginning to recover.* **OPP** relapse → WORSEN
  ▸ **recovery** *noun* [C, usually sing., U]: *My father has made a full recovery from the operation.* ◊ *The economy is showing signs of recovery.*

get 'better *phrase* (of a person or a part of the body) to recover from an illness or injury: *I hope you're getting better. We'll need you at work tomorrow!* ◊ *My wrist is getting better — I'll be able to play tennis again soon.* See also **get better** → IMPROVE 2

heal [I, T] (of a wound or injury) to become healthy again; to make a wound or injury healthy again: *It took a long time for the wounds to heal.* ◊ (*BrE*) *The cut healed up without leaving a scar.*

recuperate /rɪˈkuːpəreɪt/ [I] (*formal*) (of a person) to spend time getting back your health, strength or energy after being ill, tired or injured: *He's still recuperating from his operation.* ◊ *After an exhausting few weeks I needed some time to recuperate.*

get 'well *phrase* (of a person) to recover from an illness: *Get well soon!* (= for example, on a card) ◊ *Now all she had to do was get well.* ❶ **Get well** is used especially to talk about the wish or need for sb to recover; it is not used much in the past tense.

convalesce /ˌkɒnvəˈles; AmE ˌkɑːn-/ [I] (*formal*) to spend time getting your health and strength back after an illness: *She is convalescing at home after her operation.*

shake sth 'off *phrasal verb* (*rather informal*) to stop suffering from a particular illness, especially sth small like a cold: *I can't seem to shake off this cold.*

pull 'through *phrasal verb* (*rather informal*) to get better after a serious illness or operation: *The doctors think she will pull through.*

---

2 recover · regain · get sth back · retrieve · reclaim · recoup
These words all mean to get back sth that you no longer have.

PATTERNS AND COLLOCATIONS
▸ to recover sth / get sth back / retrieve / reclaim / recoup sth **from** sth
▸ to recover / regain / get back / reclaim **the lead**
▸ to recover / regain / get back **control**
▸ to recover / regain **consciousness**
▸ to recover / get back / retrieve / reclaim / recoup your **money**
▸ to recover / get back / reclaim / recoup **tax**
▸ to recover / reclaim / recoup your **costs / expenses**
▸ to recover / get back / recoup your **investment**
▸ to recover / get back / retrieve the **stolen property**

recover /rɪˈkʌvə(r)/ [T] (*rather formal*) to get back an amount of money that you have spent or that is owed to you; to get back or find sth that was lost, stolen or missing; to win back a position that has been lost: *He is unlikely ever to recover his legal costs.* ◊ *The police eventually recovered the stolen paintings.* ◊ *The team recovered its lead in the second half.*
  ▸ **recovery** *noun* [U]: *There is a reward for information leading to the recovery of the missing diamonds.*

regain /rɪˈɡeɪn/ [T] (*rather formal*) to get back sth you no longer have, such as an ability, quality or position: *I struggled to regain some dignity.* ◊ *She paused on the edge, trying to regain her balance.* ◊ *The party has regained control of the region.*

get sth 'back *phrasal verb* to obtain sth again after having lost it or spent it: *She's got her old job back.* ◊ *I never lend books — you never get them back.* ◊ *At the higher rate of interest, investors would get their money back after 9 years.*

retrieve /rɪˈtriːv/ [T] (*formal*) to bring or get sth back, especially from a place where it should not be: *She bent to retrieve her comb from the floor.* ◊ *The police have managed to retrieve some of the stolen money.*

reclaim /rɪˈkleɪm/ [T] (*especially written*) to get sth back or to ask to have it back after it has been lost or taken away: *The team reclaimed the title from their rivals.* ◊ *Charities can reclaim tax paid on money that is covenanted to them.*

recoup /rɪˈkuːp/ [T] (*rather formal*) to get back an amount of money that you have invested, spent or lost: *We hope to recoup our initial investment in the first year.*

---

recruit *noun* See also the entry for BEGINNER

recruit · trainee · apprentice · cadet · intern
These are all words for a person who has just started a job or activity and has very little experience.

PATTERNS AND COLLOCATIONS
▸ a trainee / an apprentice / an intern **with** a company
▸ to join a company **as** a trainee / an apprentice
▸ a **young / 19-year-old** recruit / trainee / apprentice / cadet / intern
▸ a **management** recruit / trainee
▸ to **have / become** a recruit / a trainee / an apprentice / a cadet / an intern
▸ to **work** as a trainee / an apprentice
▸ to **train** a recruit / an apprentice

recruit /rɪˈkruːt/ [C] a person who has recently joined the armed forces or the police; a person who joins a company or organization: *Army recruits are all trained in first aid.* ◊ *They are stepping up attempts to attract recruits to the nursing profession.* ◊ *All members were urged to go out and try to gain new recruits for the party.* ◊ *He spoke of us scornfully as raw recruits* (= people without training or experience). See also **recruit** → EMPLOY *verb*

trainee /ˌtreɪˈniː/ [C] a person who is being taught how to do a particular job: *She joined the company as a management trainee.* ❶ **Trainee** is usually used to talk about sb who is learning to do a job which requires a higher level of education than that required for an **apprentice**. In British English it is frequently used before another noun: (*BrE*) *a trainee teacher/pilot/nurse/journalist*. In American English use **student**: (*AmE*) *a student teacher/pilot/nurse/journalist*

apprentice /əˈprentɪs/ [C] a young person who works for an employer for a fixed period of time in order to learn the particular skills needed in their job: *She joined us as an apprentice chef in 1990.* ❶ **Apprentice** is usually used to talk about sb who is learning to do a job which requires practical skills, rather than academic achievement. It is frequently used before another noun: *an apprentice electrician/plumber/bricklayer/jockey/chef*

cadet /kəˈdet/ [C] a young person who is training to become an officer in the police or armed forces: *army cadets*

intern /ˈɪntɜːn; *AmE* ˈɪntɜːrn/ [C] (*AmE*) an advanced student of medicine, whose training is nearly finished and who is working in a hospital to get further practical experience; a student or new graduate who is getting practical experience in a job, for example during the summer vacation: *Interns in hospitals learn how to act professionally in the most dire emergencies.* ◊ *a summer intern at a law firm*

reduce *verb* See also the entry for CUT 1

reduce · lower · minimize · decrease · bring sth down · turn sth down
These words all mean to make sth smaller or less in size, amount or degree.

PATTERNS AND COLLOCATIONS
▸ to reduce sth / lower sth / bring sth down **from** 10 **to** 5
▸ to reduce / lower / decrease sth **by** half, 50, etc.
▸ to reduce / lower / minimize / decrease / bring down the **number / amount / level / cost** of sth
▸ to reduce / lower / minimize / decrease the **risk / chance / rate** of sth
▸ to reduce / lower / decrease / bring down the **price** of sth
▸ to reduce / lower / turn down the **volume / sound**
▸ to reduce / lower / decrease sth **significantly / gradually**
▸ to reduce sth / turn sth down **slightly**

reduce [T] to make sth less or smaller in size, amount, number or level: *The number of employees was reduced from 40 to 25.* ◊ *Costs have been reduced by 20% over the past year.* ◊ *Giving up smoking reduces the risk of heart disease.* ◊ *Reduce speed now* (= on a sign). **OPP** **increase** → INCREASE

lower [T] to reduce the level of sth: *This drug is used to lower blood pressure.* ◊ *The company may be forced to lower prices in order to stay competitive.* ◊ *He lowered his voice to a whisper.* ❶ **Lower** is used especially in the contexts of health and finance: *to lower blood pressure/cholesterol levels* ◊ *to lower prices/interest rates.* **Reduce** can also be used in these cases; however, if you are talking about the level of sb's voice, only **lower** can be used: ~~He reduced his voice to a whisper.~~ **OPP** **raise** → INCREASE

minimize (*BrE* also **-ise**) /ˈmɪnɪmaɪz/ [T] to reduce sth, especially sth bad, to the lowest possible level: *Good hygiene helps to minimize the risk of infection.* ◊ *They worked at night in order to minimize the disruption.* **OPP** **maximize** → INCREASE

decrease [T] (*rather formal*) to reduce the amount or level of sth: *People should decrease the amount of fat they eat.* ◊ *The dose was gradually decreased after eight weeks.* **OPP** **increase** → INCREASE ❶ **Decrease** is more formal and less frequent than **increase**; it is used especially in the contexts of health and medicine. The more usual opposite of **increase** is **reduce**.

bring sth ˈdown *phrasal verb* to reduce the price, number or level of sth: *We aim to bring down prices on all our computers.* ◊ *The economic recovery will bring down unemployment.*

turn sth ˈdown *phrasal verb* to reduce the noise, heat or light produced by a piece of equipment by moving its controls: *Please turn the volume down.* ◊ *He turned the lights down low.* **OPP** **turn sth up** → INCREASE, See also **turn sth off** → TURN STH OFF

reduction *noun*

reduction · cut · decline · fall · drop · downturn · decrease · slump · cutback
These are all words for a situation when the amount, level, number or size of sth goes down.

PATTERNS AND COLLOCATIONS
▸ a reduction / cut / decline / fall / drop / downturn / decrease / slump / cutback **in** sth
▸ a reduction / cut / decline / fall / drop / decrease / cutback **of 20%**
▸ **a 20%** reduction / cut / decline / fall / drop / decrease in sth
▸ (a) **sharp** reduction / cuts / decline / fall / drop / downturn / decrease / slump / cutbacks
▸ (a) **large / significant** reduction / cuts / decline / fall / drop / downturn / decrease / cutbacks
▸ (a) **big / huge / massive / major** reduction / cuts / decline / fall / drop / downturn / slump / cutbacks
▸ (a) **dramatic** reduction / cuts / decline / fall / drop / downturn / slump
▸ (a) **drastic** reduction / cuts / decline / fall / drop / downturn / cutbacks
▸ a **sudden** reduction / decline / fall / drop / downturn / decrease / slump
▸ a **slight** reduction / decline / fall / drop / downturn / decrease
▸ to **lead to / result in / cause** a reduction / cut / decline / fall / drop / decrease
▸ to **see** a reduction / decline / fall / drop / downturn / decrease
▸ to **make** reductions / cuts / cutbacks

reduction [C, U] an act of making sth less or smaller; the state of being made less or smaller: *This year has seen a 33% reduction in the number of hospital beds available.* ◊ *The report recommends further reductions in air and noise emissions.* ◊ *There are reductions* (= in the price) *for children sharing a room with two adults.* ◊ *There has been some reduction in unemployment.* **OPP** **increase** → INCREASE

cut [C] a reduction that is made in the amount, size or supply of sth: *They had to take a 20% cut in pay.* ◊ *The company has announced a new round of job cuts.* ◊ *The proposed tax cuts will come into effect next May.* **OPP** **increase** → INCREASE, See also **cut** → CUT *verb* 1, **lay-off** → UNEMPLOYMENT

NOTE **REDUCTION** OR **CUT**? Reduction can be used for things that become less or smaller by themselves, or things that are reduced deliberately by sb. A cut can only happen by itself — it has to be made by sb. A **cut** is often (but not always) a negative thing: *job/salary/pay cuts* and it cannot happen over time. A **reduction** can: *a gradual reduction* ◊ ~~a gradual cut~~.

decline [C, usually sing., U] a continuous reduction that happens in the number, value or quality of sth; the process of a place, tradition or institution gradually becoming less important or coming to an end: *These measures have failed to reverse the country's economic decline.* ◊ *His book charts the decline and fall of a great civilization.* ◊ *The town fell into (a) decline* (= started to be less busy, important, etc.) *after the mine closed.* ◊ *Industry in Britain has been in decline since the 1970s.* **OPP** **rise** → INCREASE, See also **decline** → FALL *verb* 1, **decline** → WORSEN *verb*

fall [C] (*especially business*) a reduction that happens in the size, number, rate or level of sth: *Share prices suffered a slight fall yesterday.* ◊ *This figure represents a fall of 23% on the same period last year.* **OPP** **rise** → INCREASE, See also **fall** → FALL *verb* 1

drop [C, usually sing.] (*especially journalism*) a reduction that happens in the size, number, rate or level of sth: *If you want the job, you must be prepared to take a drop in salary.* ◇ *The restaurant has suffered a 10% drop in trade.* **OPP** rise → INCREASE, See also **drop** → FALL *verb* 1

> **NOTE** DECLINE, FALL OR DROP? These words all describe a process that happens, rather than a deliberate action by sb. **Decline** tends to emphasize the process, whether this is fast or slow: *a steady/sharp decline in profits* ◇ *a civilization in terminal decline.* **Fall** and **drop** tend to emphasize the result of the process: *a fall/drop of 30%* A **fall**, like a **decline**, can happen over time, but a **drop** cannot: *a gradual decline/fall* ◇ *a gradual drop.*

downturn /ˈdaʊntɜːn; *AmE* -tɜːrn/ [C, usually sing.] a fall in the amount of business that is done; a time when the economy becomes weaker: *The building industry is experiencing a severe downturn in its workload.* **OPP** upturn → INCREASE

decrease /ˈdiːkriːs/ [C, U] a reduction that happens in the amount, level or number of sth: *There has been a decrease of nearly 6% in the number of visitors to the museum.* ◇ *Marriage is still on the decrease.* **OPP** increase → INCREASE, See also **decrease** → FALL *verb* 1 ❶ **Decrease** looks like the most direct opposite of **increase**, but it is not nearly as frequent as **increase**. For deliberate reductions, use **reduction** or **cut**. For reductions that happen, **fall** or **drop** are often preferred, especially in business contexts.

slump [C] a sudden fall in sales, prices or the value of sth: *The recession led to a slump in consumer spending.* ◇ *The present slump has hit manufacturing hard.* See also **slump** → RECESSION *noun,* **slump** → SLUMP *verb*

> **NOTE** DOWNTURN OR SLUMP? Both words can be used in the context of business or the economy: *a downturn/slump in demand/trade/business/profits.* However, a **slump** is a bigger and more sudden fall, usually seen from the point of view of the business that is losing money.

cutback /ˈkʌtbæk/ [C, usually pl.] a reduction that is made in sth, especially money spent, people employed or benefits: *Many theatres are having to make major cutbacks.* See also **cut sth back** → CUT 1

reference *noun*

reference · mention · quote · quotation · citation · allusion
These are all words for sth that you say or write that mentions or repeats sb/sth else.

PATTERNS AND COLLOCATIONS
▶ a quote / quotation / citation **(taken) from** sb / sth
▶ **in** a reference / an allusion **to** sb / sth
▶ a **brief** reference / mention / allusion
▶ the **earliest** reference to / mention of sb / sth
▶ to **make no** reference to / mention of sb / sth
▶ to **be full of** references / allusions to sth
▶ This quote / quotation / citation **comes from**...

reference [C, U] something that you say or write that mentions sb/sth else; the act of mentioning sb/sth: *In an obvious reference to the president, she talked of corruption in high places.* ◇ *She made no reference to her illness, but only to her future plans.* ◇ (*formal, written*) **With reference to** *your letter of 22 July...* See also **refer to sb/sth** → MENTION *verb*

mention [U, C, usually sing.] the act of mentioning sb/sth; sth that you say or write that mentions sb/sth else: *He went white* **at the mention of** *her name.* ◇ *We have several other products* **worthy of mention.** ◇ *The concert didn't even* **get a mention** *in the newspapers.* See also **mention** → MENTION *verb*

> **NOTE** REFERENCE OR MENTION? Reference is usually countable; the uncountable form is mostly used in fixed expressions in formal writing. **Mention** is more often uncountable; the countable form can be slightly informal, as in the phrase *get a mention.*

quote [C] (*informal*) words or lines taken from a book or play or sth that sb has said, and repeated because they are interesting or useful: *This quote comes from a poem by Robert Browning.* ◇ *The article included quotes from detectives who worked on the case.*

quotation /kwəʊˈteɪʃn; *AmE* kwoʊ-/ [C, U] (*formal or written*) words or lines taken from a book, play, speech, etc. and repeated because they are interesting or useful; the act of repeating a **quotation**: *The book began with a quotation from Goethe.* ◇ *The writer illustrates his point by quotation from a number of sources.*

> **NOTE** QUOTE OR QUOTATION? Both these words can refer to words taken from writing or formal speeches: *a quote/quotation from Shakespeare* but only **quote** is used when repeating informal speech: *quotations from detectives who worked on the case* See also **quote** → MENTION *verb,* **quote** → QUOTE *verb*

citation /saɪˈteɪʃn/ [C, U] (*formal or written*) a quotation from or reference to a book, piece or writing or author, especially in academic writing; the act of repeating a **citation**: *The report contained several citations taken from her PhD thesis.* ◇ *Space does not permit the citation of examples.* See also **cite** → MENTION, QUOTE

allusion /əˈluːʒn/ [C, U] (*rather formal*) something that is said or written that refers to another person or subject in an indirect way: *His statement was seen as an allusion to the recent drug-related killings.* ◇ *Her poetry is full of obscure literary allusion.* See also **allude to sb/sth** → MENTION

refer to sth *phrasal verb*

refer to sth · consult · look sth up
These words all mean to look at or in sth for information.

PATTERNS AND COLLOCATIONS
▶ to refer to / consult a / an **dictionary / encyclopedia / guide / manual / map / timetable / schedule / website**
▶ to refer to / consult your **notes**

reˈfer to sth *phrasal verb* (-rr-) to look in or at sth for information: *You may refer to your notes if you want.* ◇ *Refer to the Food Guide for nutrition recommendations.*
▶ **reference** /ˈrefrəns/ *noun* [U]: *The library contains many popular works of reference.* ◇ *a reference book* (= a dictionary, an encyclopedia, an atlas, etc.)

consult [T] (*rather formal, especially written*) to look in or at sth for information: *If you're not sure which plug to buy, consult the manual.* ◇ *He spent quite some time consulting his notes before he answered.* See also **consult** → ASK 1
▶ **consultation** /ˌkɒnslˈteɪʃn; *AmE* ˌkɑːn-/ *noun* [U]: *There is a large collection of texts available for consultation on-screen.*

ˌlook sth ˈup *phrasal verb* to look for information in a dictionary or reference book, or by using a computer: *Can you look up the opening times on the website?* ◇ *I looked it up in the dictionary.*

> **NOTE** REFER TO STH, CONSULT OR LOOK STH UP? There is little difference between **refer to sth** and **consult**, although **consult** is more formal and is used more in written language. **Look sth up** is slightly more informal and is used more in everyday language. The object of **look sth up** is the information you want to find rather than the place where you look to find the information: *Please refer to/consult* **the Help file** *for further information.* ◇ *Try looking up* **this word** *in the index.* ◇ *Look* **it** *up on the Internet.*

refuge *noun*

refuge · shelter · sanctuary · haven · hiding place · retreat · hideout · safe house
These are all words for a place where sb/sth can be protected or hidden.

PATTERNS AND COLLOCATIONS
▶ a refuge / shelter / sanctuary / haven / hiding place / retreat / hideout / safe house **for** sb / sth
▶ a refuge / sanctuary / haven / hiding place / retreat **from** sth
▶ a **secret** refuge / hiding place / retreat / hideout
▶ an **animal** refuge / shelter / sanctuary
▶ a **wildlife** refuge / sanctuary
▶ a **mountain** refuge / retreat / hideout
▶ an **island** refuge / retreat
▶ a refuge / shelter for the **homeless**

refuge /'refjuːdʒ/ [C] a place that provides protection from harm or danger for sb/sth; a building that provides a place to stay for people in need of protection from sb/sth: *He regarded the room as a refuge from the outside world.* ◇ *The marshes are a wetland refuge for seabirds, waders and wildfowl.* ◇ (*especially BrE*) *The best option for a female victim of domestic abuse is to contact a women's refuge.* ❶ In American English this is usually called a **women's shelter**. See also **refuge** → SHELTER

shelter [C] a building, usually owned by a charity, that provides a place to stay for people without a home, or protection for people or animals who have been badly treated: *a night shelter for the homeless* ◇ *We adopted a rescue dog from an animal shelter.* See also **shelter** → SHELTER

sanctuary /'sæŋktʃuəri; *AmE* -ueri/ [C] an area where wild birds or animals are protected and encouraged to breed; a safe place, especially one where people who are being chased or attacked can stay and be protected: *The island was declared a wildlife sanctuary in 1969.* ◇ *The church became a sanctuary for the refugees.* See also **sanctuary** → SHELTER

haven /'heɪvn/ [C] (*rather formal*) a place that is safe and peaceful where people go to rest or to be protected from sth: *The hotel is a haven of peace and tranquillity* ◇ *We have a duty to offer a safe haven to all refugees.*

'hiding place [C] a place where sb/sth can be hidden: *They used the cave as a hiding place for their weapons.* ◇ *As darkness fell, she emerged from her hiding place.*

retreat /rɪ'triːt/ [C] (*rather formal*) a quiet, private place that you go to in order to get away from your usual life: *She bought the cottage as a weekend retreat.* ❶ To go on a retreat is to stop your usual activities for a period of time and go to a quiet place for prayer and thought: *He went on a Buddhist retreat.*

hideout /'haɪdaʊt/ [C] a place where sb goes when they do not want anyone to find them, especially if they are hiding from the police: *Several terrorist hideouts were discovered in the area.*

'safe house [C] a house that is used by an organization in order to hide or protect people: *He is under heavy police guard in a safe house after receiving death threats.*

refugee *noun* See the Topic Map for THE INDIVIDUAL AND SOCIETY on p.894

refugee · immigrant · migrant · expatriate · exile · emigrant · asylum seeker · evacuee
These are all words for sb who has left the place where they lived and is going or has gone to find a new place to live or stay.

PATTERNS AND COLLOCATIONS
▶ a **would-be** refugee / immigrant / migrant / emigrant / asylum seeker
▶ a **genuine / bogus** refugee / asylum seeker
▶ an **illegal** immigrant / migrant / emigrant
▶ a **political** refugee / exile / asylum seeker
▶ an **economic** refugee / migrant

▶ refugees / migrants / expatriates / exiles / emigrants / asylum seekers / evacuees **return**
▶ immigrant / migrant **workers**
▶ a **flow / flood of** refugees / immigrants / migrants / emigrants
▶ an **influx of** refugees / immigrants / migrants

refugee /ˌrefjuˈdʒiː/ [C] a person who has been forced to leave their country or home, because there is a war or for political, religious or social reasons: *There has been a steady flow of refugees from the war zone.* ◇ *a refugee camp* See also **refuge** → SHELTER

immigrant /'ɪmɪɡrənt/ [C] a person who has come to live permanently in a country that is not their own: *Illegal immigrants are to be sent back to their country of origin.* ◇ *immigrant communities/families/workers*
▶ **immigrate** *verb* [I]: (*especially AmE*) *About 6.6 million people immigrated to the United States in the 1970s.* OPP **emigrate** → LEAVE 2
▶ **immigration** *noun* [U]: *laws restricting immigration into the US* ◇ *an immigration officer*

migrant /'maɪɡrənt/ [C] a person who moves from one place to another, especially in order to find work: *They claimed they were political refugees and not economic migrants.* See also **migrate** → LEAVE 2

expatriate /ˌeksˈpætriət; *AmE* -ˈpeɪt-/ [C] a person living in a country that is not their own: *FUSAC is a magazine for American expatriates in Paris.* ❶ In informal language, **expatriate** is sometimes shortened to **expat**: *There are more than two million British expats down under* (= in Australia).
▶ **expatriate** *adj.* [only before noun]: *expatriate Britons in Spain* ◇ *expatriate workers*

NOTE IMMIGRANT OR EXPATRIATE? An **immigrant** has gone to live permanently in another country; an **expatriate** usually intends to return after a few months or years.

exile /'eksaɪl; 'eɡzaɪl/ [C] (*rather formal*) a person who chooses or is forced to live away from their own country: *A general amnesty was granted, allowing political exiles to return freely.* ◇ *a tax exile* (= a rich person who moves to another country where taxes are lower) See also **exile** → EXPEL *verb*

emigrant /'emɪɡrənt/ [C] (*rather formal*) a person who leaves their country to live permanently in another: *My grandparents were Italian emigrants who settled in New York in the 1920s.* See also **emigrate** → LEAVE 2

NOTE IMMIGRANT OR EMIGRANT? **Immigrant** is used to talk about people coming to a country, especially when this is being considered as a current political or social issue; **emigrant** is used to talk about people leaving a country, especially when this is being considered in a historical context.

aˈsylum seeker /əˈsaɪləm/ [C] a person who has left their own country, usually because they were in danger for political reasons, and who is asking for protection from the government of another country: *Genuine asylum seekers should not be denied entry to the country.* See also **asylum** → SHELTER

evacuee /ɪˌvækjuˈiː/ [C] a person who is sent away from a place because it is dangerous, especially during a war: *During 1942 evacuee families started to arrive in the town.* See also **evacuate** → EVACUATE

refusal *noun*

refusal · veto · rejection · denial · rebuff · no
These are all words for the act of saying or showing that you do not accept sth or will not allow sth.

PATTERNS AND COLLOCATIONS
▶ a refusal / rejection / rebuff / no **from** sb
▶ a refusal / veto / rejection / rebuff **by** sb
▶ a rebuff / no **to** sb / sth
▶ a / an **outright / firm / blanket** refusal / rejection / no
▶ a **complete** refusal / veto / rejection

▸ to **receive** / **be met with** a refusal / rejection / rebuff
▸ to **give (sb)** a refusal / rejection / no

refusal [U, C] an act of saying or showing that you will not do, give or accept sth, especially that you will not do what sb has asked you to do or not accept sth that has been offered to you: *There were a number of reasons given for the refusal of the application.* ◇ *His refusal to discuss the matter is very annoying.* ◇ *What do you do in the case of a refusal by a patient to accept treatment?* **OPP** **agreement**, **acceptance** → APPROVAL, **consent** → PERMISSION

veto /'vi:təʊ; *AmE* -toʊ/ (pl. **-oes**) [C, U] the right to refuse to allow sth to be done, especially the right to stop a law from being passed or a decision from being taken: *The president has a veto on/over all political appointments.* ◇ *The British government used its veto to block the proposal.* ◇ *The Ministry of Defence has the power of veto over all arms exports.* See also **veto** → BAN *noun*

rejection /rɪ'dʒekʃn/ [U, C] the act of saying or showing that you will not accept, use or consider sb/sth: *It takes a very buoyant personality to cope with constant rejection.* ◇ *Eventually, after months of rejections, she was offered a job.* ◇ *Another rejection letter arrived this morning.* **OPP** **acceptance** → APPROVAL

denial /dɪ'naɪəl/ [C, U] a refusal to allow sb to have sth that they have a right to expect: *This advertising ban is a denial of freedom of speech.* ◇ *Pressure groups have drawn attention to the denial of human rights in some areas.*

rebuff /rɪ'bʌf/ [C] (*rather formal*) an unkind refusal of a friendly offer, request or suggestion: *In a rebuff to the president, Congress voted against the bill.* ◇ *Her offer has met with a sharp rebuff.*

no (pl. **noes**) [C] (*rather informal*) an answer that shows that you do not agree with sth or do not accept sth: *I think that's a no to the first question.* ◇ *Can you give me a straight yes or no?* ◇ *When we took a vote there were nine yesses and 3 noes.* **OPP** **yes**

refuse *verb*

refuse · reject · deny · decline · turn sb/sth down · veto · throw sth out · rebuff · disallow
These words all mean to decide or say that you will not accept or consider sth, such as an offer, proposal or request.

PATTERNS AND COLLOCATIONS
▸ to reject / turn down sth **in favour of** sth else
▸ to refuse / reject / decline / turn down / veto / throw out a **proposal**
▸ to refuse / reject / decline / turn down / rebuff a / an **offer** / **request**
▸ to refuse / reject / decline / turn down a / an **chance** / **opportunity** / **invitation**
▸ to refuse / reject / turn down / throw out / disallow an **appeal**
▸ to refuse / reject / turn down / veto / throw out a **plan**
▸ to refuse / reject / decline / turn down / veto / disallow an **application**
▸ to refuse / reject / veto / rebuff a **suggestion**
▸ to reject / veto / throw out a **bill**
▸ to refuse / deny sb **access** to sth
▸ to **politely** refuse / reject / decline sth

refuse [I, T] to say that you will not do sth that sb has asked you to do, or that you do not want sth that has been offered to you; to decide not to accept or consider sth; to say that you will not give sb sth that they want or need: *Go on, ask her. She can hardly refuse.* ◇ *She refused to accept that there was a problem.* ◇ *He flatly refused to discuss the matter.* ◇ *We invited her to the wedding but she refused.* ◇ *The job offer was simply too good to refuse.* ◇ *The government has refused all demands for a public enquiry.* ◇ *They refused him a visa.* ◇ *She would never refuse her kids anything.* **OPP** **agree** → AGREE 2, **accept** → TAKE 5, See also **refusal** → REFUSAL

reject [T] to decide or say that you will not accept or consider sth; to decide not to accept sb for a job or position: *He urged the committee to reject the plans.* ◇ *The*

proposal was rejected as too costly. ◇ *I've been rejected by all the colleges I applied to.* **OPP** **approve** → AGREE 2, **accept** → LET SB IN

deny [T] (*formal*) to refuse to allow sb to have sth that they want or need: *They were denied access to the information.* ◇ *Access to the information was denied to them.*

decline [T, I] (*formal*) to say politely that you do not want to accept or do sth: *Their spokesman declined to comment on the allegations.* ◇ *We politely declined her invitation.* **OPP** **accept** → TAKE 5

,turn sb/sth 'down *phrasal verb* to reject an offer or proposal or the person who makes it: *His appeal against conviction was turned down.* ◇ *He has been turned down for ten jobs so far.* ◇ *He asked her to marry him but she turned him down.* **OPP** **take sth up** → TAKE 5

veto /'vi:təʊ; *AmE* -toʊ/ [T] (*written*, *often disapproving*) to stop sth from happening or being done by using your official authority; to say that you will not accept or do what sb has suggested: *Plans for the dam have been vetoed by the Environmental Protection Agency.* ◇ *I wanted to go camping but the others quickly vetoed that idea.* ❶ It is usually a person in a position of authority who **vetoes** sth; often the decision or plan has already been agreed by other people. See also **veto** → BAN *noun*

,throw sth 'out *phrasal verb* to decide not to accept or consider a proposal, idea or legal case, often after having a vote to decide this: *The case was thrown out for lack of evidence.* ◇ *The recommendation was thrown out by an overwhelming majority.*

rebuff /rɪ'bʌf/ [T] (*written, often disapproving*) to refuse a friendly offer, request or suggestion in an unkind way: *They rebuffed her request for help.* ◇ *The offer was immediately rebuffed by union leaders.*

disallow /,dɪsə'laʊ/ [T, often passive] to officially refuse to accept sth, often because it has not been done correctly or a rule has been broken: *The second goal was disallowed.* ◇ *Her claim for unfair dismissal was disallowed.*

regard *verb* See also the entry for THINK

regard · call · find · consider · describe · see · view · count · reckon · look at sth
These words all mean to think or talk about sb/sth in a particular way.

PATTERNS AND COLLOCATIONS
▸ to regard / consider / describe / see / view / count / look at sb/sth **as** sth
▸ to regard / consider / see / view / look at sb/sth **from** a particular point of view
▸ to regard / see / view / look at sb/sth **with** sth
▸ to find / consider / see / reckon sb/sth **to be** sth
▸ to consider / reckon **that…**
▸ to regard / consider / describe / see / view / count / reckon **yourself** (as) sth
▸ **generally** / **widely** / **usually** / **still** regarded / considered / seen / viewed / reckoned as sth
▸ **no longer** regarded / considered / seen / viewed as sth
▸ to regard / consider / describe / see / view / look at sb/sth **differently**
▸ to consider / describe / see / view / look at sb/sth **objectively**
▸ to regard / view sb/sth **favourably** / **positively**

regard [T] (*rather formal*) (not used in the progressive tenses) to think of sb/sth in a particular way: *Her work is very highly/well regarded.* ◇ *Capital punishment was regarded as inhuman and immoral.* ◇ *I had come to regard him as a close friend.* ◇ *They regarded people outside their own village with suspicion.*

call [T] to say that sb/sth has particular qualities or characteristics: *I wouldn't call German an easy language.* ◇ *Are you calling me a liar?* ◇ *He was in the front room, the lounge, or whatever you want to call it.* ◇ *Would you call it blue or green?* ◇ *I make it ten pounds forty-three you owe me. Let's call it ten pounds.*

find [T] to have a particular feeling or opinion about sth: *You may find your illness hard to accept.* ◇ *You may find it hard to accept your illness.* ◇ *I find it amazing that they're still together.* ◇ *She finds it a strain to meet new people.*

consider [T] (not used in the progressive tenses) (*rather formal*) to think of sb/sth in a particular way: *Who do you consider (to be) responsible for the accident?* ◇ *Consider yourself lucky you weren't fired.* ◇ *These workers are considered (as) a high-risk group.* See also **consider** → CONSIDER

> **NOTE** **REGARD** OR **CONSIDER?** These two words have the same meaning, but they are used in different patterns and structures. In this meaning **consider** must be used with a complement or clause: you can *consider sb/sth to be sth* or *consider sb/sth as sth*, although very often the *to be* or *as* is left out: *He considers himself an expert.* ◇ *They are considered a high-risk group.* You can also *consider that sb/sth is sth* and again, the *that* can be left out: *The Home Secretary will release prisoners only if he considers it is safe to do so.* **Regard** is used in a narrower range of structures. The most frequent structure is *regard sb/sth as sth*; the *as* cannot be left out.: ~~I regard him a close friend.~~ You cannot: ~~regard sb/sth to be sth~~ or: ~~regard that sb/sth is sth.~~ However, **regard** (but NOT **consider** in this meaning) can also be used without a noun or adjective complement but with just an object and adverb or adverbial phrase: *sb/sth is highly regarded* ◇ *regard sb/sth with suspicion/jealousy/admiration*

describe [T] (always used with *as*) to say that sb/sth has particular qualities or characteristics: *Jim was described by his colleagues as 'unusual'.* ◇ *The man was described as tall and dark, and aged about 20.* See also **describe** → DESCRIBE

> **NOTE** **CALL** OR **DESCRIBE?** These words have the same meaning but they are used in different patterns. **Call** is used with a noun or adjective complement, without *as*: ~~I wouldn't call German as an easy language.~~ Noun complements are much more frequent with **call** than adjective complements: you can say 'I wouldn't call German easy.', but it would be more usual to use the noun phrase 'an easy language'. **Describe** is used with *as* and an adjective or noun phrase: ~~Jim was described by his colleages unusual.~~ Adjectives are more frequent with **describe** than nouns: longer noun phrases are possible, but with simple nouns use **call**: *Jim was described by his colleagues as an unusual man.* ◇ ~~Are you describing me as a liar?~~

see [T] (not used in the progressive tenses) to have an opinion of sth: *I see things differently now.* ◇ *Try to see things from her point of view.* ◇ *Lack of money is the main problem, as I see it* (= in my opinion). ◇ *The way I see it, you have three main problems.*

view [T] (not used in the progressive tenses) to think of sb/sth in a particular way: *When the car was first built, the design was viewed as highly original.* ◇ *How do you view your position within the company?* ◇ *You should view their offer with a great deal of caution.* ❶ **View** has the same meaning as **regard** and **consider** but is slightly less frequent and slightly less formal. The main structures are *view sb/sth as sb/sth* (you cannot leave out the *as*) and *view sb/sth with sth*. **View** is the most natural choice for a general question: *How do you view…?*(You can also say 'How do you regard…?', although this is less frequent; it is not usual to say: ~~How do you consider…?~~ in this meaning.

count [T, I] (not used in the progressive tenses) to think of sb/sth in a particular way; to be thought of in this way: *I count him among my closest friends.* ◇ *I count myself lucky to have known him.* ◇ *For tax purposes that money counts/is counted as income.*

reckon [T, usually passive] (not used in the progressive tenses) (*especially BrE, rather informal*) to regard sb/sth as sb/sth: *Children are reckoned to be more sophisticated nowadays.* ◇ *It was generally reckoned a success.* See also **reckon** → THINK

'look at sth *phrasal verb* to consider or view sth in a particular way: *Looked at from that point of view, his decision is easier to understand.* ◇ *It all depends on how you look at it.* ◇ *Look at it this way:…* ❶ **Look at sth** is used especially when you are considering the different ways in which a situation can be considered. See also **look at sth** → CONSIDER

regular *adj.* See also the entry for ADDICTIVE

regular · compulsive · habitual
These words all describe people who do a particular thing very often.

▸ a regular / compulsive / habitual **drinker**
▸ a compulsive / habitual **liar / gambler**
▸ a regular / habitual **user** of sth
▸ regular / habitual **offenders**

regular [only before noun] (of people) doing the same thing or going to the same place often: *They have been regular customers for many years.* ◇ *Her views on the subject will be familiar to regular readers of the paper.* ◇ *Many of them were regular users of heroin.* ◇ *He was a regular visitor to her house.*
▸ **regularly** *adv.*: *He said he did not use drugs regularly.*

compulsive /kəm'pʌlsɪv/ (of people) not able to control their behaviour; doing sth often and not able to stop: *The book offers advice and help for compulsive eaters.* ◇ *Can you be successful without being compulsive about work?*

habitual /hə'bɪtʃuəl/ [only before noun] (of people) doing sth often, usually sth that has become a habit and is therefore difficult to stop: *He was a habitual cocaine user.* ◇ *a habitual criminal* See also **habit** → HABIT
▸ **habitually** *adv.*: *She claimed she didn't habitually drink so heavily.*

regulate *verb*

regulate · supervise · oversee · administer · police · superintend
These words all mean to control or be responsible for sth and make sure that it is done correctly or that rules are obeyed.

▸ to regulate/supervise/oversee/administer the **affairs** of sb/sth
▸ to supervise / oversee / superintend **work**
▸ to be **properly** regulated / supervised / administered / policed
▸ to be **well** regulated / supervised / policed
▸ to be **effectively** regulated / supervised / administered / policed

regulate /'regjuleɪt/ [T] to control sth, especially a business activity, by means of rules: *The activities of credit companies are regulated by law.* ◇ *The Council was set up to regulate the fishing industry.* ◇ *The trade in these animals is highly regulated.* See also **regulation** → GOVERNMENT 2, **regulator** → INSPECTOR

supervise /'suːpəvaɪz; 'sjuː-; *AmE* 'suːpərv-/ [T, I] to watch sb/sth and make sure that a job or activity is done correctly or safely: *I will supervise the work personally.* ◇ *She supervised the children playing near the pool.* ◇ *Jenny decided to stay and supervise.* See also **supervision** → GOVERNMENT 2, **supervisor** → MANAGER

oversee /ˌəʊvə'siː; *AmE* ˌoʊvər'siː/ [T] to watch sb/sth and make sure that a job or activity is done correctly: *The director made regular visits to personally oversee operations.*

> **NOTE** **SUPERVISE** OR **OVERSEE?** Both **supervise** and **oversee** can be used to talk about watching a job or activity to make sure it is done correctly: *to supervise/ oversee building work/an election.* **Oversee** is mostly used about sb acting in an official position. **Supervise** can also be used to talk about watching a person, such

as a child or an inexperienced worker, to make sure that they are safe, to give help and to deal with any problems.

administer [T, often passive] (*formal*) to be responsible for laws, rules or tests, making sure that they are applied fairly and in the correct way: *The team is responsible for administering the tests and marking the papers.* ◇ *It is the function of the courts to administer the laws which Parliament has enacted.*

police [T] to make sure that a particular set of rules is obeyed: *The government has called on newspapers to* **police themselves.** ◇ *These sorts of regulations are very difficult to police.*

superintend /ˌsuːpərɪnˈtend; *BrE* also ˌsjuː-/ [T] (*formal*) to be in charge of sth and make sure that a job or activity is done correctly: *He superintended the building work.* See also **superintendent** → MANAGER

rein *noun*

rein · leash · lead · bridle · harness · tether · halter
These are all words for a piece of leather, rope or chain used for controlling or holding an animal, such as a dog or horse.

PATTERNS AND COLLOCATIONS
▸ **on** / **off** a / the leash / lead
▸ (a) **leather** reins / harness
▸ to **attach** a leash / lead / harness / halter
▸ to **pull on** the reins / leash / lead
▸ to **keep** a dog **on** a leash / lead

rein /reɪn/ [C, usually pl.] (in horse riding) a long, narrow leather band that is fastened to the bit (= metal bar) in the horse's mouth and is held by the rider in order to control the horse: *She pulled gently on the reins.*

leash /liːʃ/ [C] (*especially AmE*) a long piece of leather, chain or rope attached to a dog's collar, used for holding and controlling the dog: *Once she was away from the road, she could let the dogs off the leash.*

lead /liːd/ [C] (*BrE*) a leash: *Dogs must be kept on a lead in the park.*

bridle /ˈbraɪdl/ [C] a set of leather bands, attached to reins, which is put around a horse's head and used for controlling it: *She held his stirrup for him while Adam took the bridle.*

harness /ˈhɑːnɪs; *AmE* ˈhɑːrnɪs/ [C] a set of leather bands and metal pieces which is put around a horse's head and body so that the horse can be controlled and fastened to a cart, carriage, etc: *The sight of horses* **in harness** *hauling timber was common a hundred years ago.*
▸ **harness** *verb* [T]: *We* **harnessed** *two ponies to the cart.*

tether /ˈteðə(r)/ [C] a rope or chain used to tie an animal to sth, allowing it to move around in a small area: *The goat had got loose from its tether.* See also **tether** → RESTRAIN *verb*

halter /ˈhɔːltə(r)/; *BrE* also ˈhɒlt-/ [C] a rope or leather band put around the head of a horse for leading it with: *He led the mare by the halter towards the gate.*

reject *verb*

reject · disown · disinherit · wash your hands of sb/sth
These words all mean to decide that you no longer want to be connected with or responsible for sb/sth.

PATTERNS AND COLLOCATIONS
▸ His **father** / **family** rejected / disowned / disinherited him.
▸ Her **friends** / **mother** rejected / disowned her.
▸ to **virtually** disown / disinherit sb

reject [T] to fail to give a person or animal enough care or affection: *The lioness rejected the smallest cub, which died.* ◇ *He was only three when his father left and I think he still feels rejected.* **OPP** accept → GREET, See also **turn your back on sb/sth** → LEAVE 5
▸ **rejection** *noun* [U]: *painful feelings of rejection*

disown /dɪsˈəʊn; *AmE* -ˈoʊn/ [T] to refuse to be connected with or responsible for sb/sth any longer, especially in order to show your anger or disapproval: *Her family disowned her for marrying a foreigner.* ◇ *Later he* **publicly disowned** *the rebellion.*

disinherit /ˌdɪsɪnˈherɪt/ [T] to decide that sb, especially your son or daughter, will no longer receive your money or property after your death, especially because of sth that they have done: *He threatened to disinherit his eldest son.* See also **inherit** → INHERIT

wash your ˈhands of sb/sth *idiom* to give up trying to help sb or being involved in sth, often because your help or advice has been ignored, rejected or useless: *When her son was arrested again she washed her hands of him.* ◇ *I've washed my hands of the whole sordid business.*

relate *verb*

relate · associate · link · match · connect
These words all mean to show or make a connection between two or more things.

PATTERNS AND COLLOCATIONS
▸ to relate / link / match / connect sth **to** sth
▸ to associate / link / match / connect sth **with** sth
▸ to relate / associate / link / match / connect (sth) **directly**
▸ to relate / associate / link / connect sth **specifically**
▸ to relate / associate / link sth **explicitly**
▸ to associate / link / connect sth **firmly**

relate [T] (*rather formal*) to show or make a connection between things: *I found it difficult to relate the two ideas in my mind.* ◇ *In future, pay increases will be related to productivity.* ❶ **Relate** is often used in business texts, describing how one thing will change according to how much sth else changes: *performance-related pay* ◇ *income-related benefits* ◇ *an earnings-related pension scheme*

associate /əˈsəʊʃieɪt; -sieɪt; *AmE* əˈsoʊ-/ [T] (*rather formal*) to make a connection between people or things in your mind: *I always associate the smell of baking with my childhood.* ◇ *He is closely associated in the public mind with horror movies.* See also **association** → ASSOCIATION

link [T] (*especially journalism*) to state that there is a connection between people or things: *Detectives have linked the break-in to a similar crime in the area last year.* ◇ *Newspapers have linked his name with the singer.* ❶ **Link** is often used in newspapers to talk about people possibly being involved in a particular crime, or knowing sb who has been involved in a crime.

match [T] to find sb/sth that goes together with or is connected with another person or thing: *The aim of the competition is to match the quote to the person who said it.* ◇ *The control group in the experiment was* **matched for** *age and sex.*

connect [T] (*rather formal*) to notice or make a connection between people or things: *There was nothing to connect him with the crime.* ◇ *I was surprised to hear them mentioned together: I had never connected them before.*

> **NOTE** RELATE, ASSOCIATE OR CONNECT? When you **associate** two things in your mind, it just happens, often because of experiences you have already had. When you **relate** or **connect** two things in your mind, it requires more of an effort because the connection is not so obvious or natural to you: *I always associate the smell of baking with my childhood.* ◇ *I always relate/connect the smell of baking with/to my childhood.* ◇ *I found it hard to relate/connect the two ideas in my mind.* ◇ *I found it hard to associate the two ideas in my mind.* **Relate** can also be used to talk about a deliberate decision to make two things dependent on each other: *Pay increases will be related to productivity.* ◇ *Pay increases will be associated with/connected with productivity.* **Connect** can also be used to talk about facts or evidence that provide a link between things: *There was nothing to connect him with the crime.* ◇ *There was nothing to relate/associate him to/with the crime.*

related *adj.*

related · associated · resulting · attendant · consequent · ensuing · resultant · connected
These words all describe two things that are connected in some way.

PATTERNS AND COLLOCATIONS
▶ associated / connected **with** sth
▶ attendant / consequent **on** / **upon** sth
▶ related/associated/resulting/attendant/consequent/ensuing/resultant **problems** / **changes**
▶ a related / an associated / a resulting / a consequent / a resultant **increase**
▶ related / associated / attendant / consequent / resultant **costs** / **effects**
▶ an associated / a resulting / a consequent / the ensuing / a resultant **loss**
▶ an associated / a resulting / a consequent **reduction**
▶ associated / attendant / consequent **risks**
▶ **closely** related / associated / connected

related connected with sb/sth in some way: *Much of the crime in this area is **related to** drug abuse.* ◇ *These two problems are closely related.* ◇ *He was suffering from a stress-related illness.* **OPP** unrelated → INDEPENDENT

associated (*rather formal, especially business*) connected with sb/sth because the two things often happen or exist together or because one thing causes the other: *Salaries and associated costs have risen substantially.* ◇ *Young people need to be made aware of the risks associated with taking drugs.*

NOTE **RELATED** OR **ASSOCIATED**? **Related** is a more general word than **associated** and often describes more general things: *a related issue/question/problem/field/area/subject/matter/theme.* **Associated** is used especially in business contexts and to talk about *risks*: ~~the risks related to taking drugs~~

resulting (*especially of a loss or change in sth*) happening as a result of sth: *The major problem here is soil erosion and the resulting loss in crop productivity.* ◇ *The benefits would include greater publicity and the resulting increase in funding.* See also **result** → RESULT *noun,* **result** → FOLLOW *verb* 2, **result in sth** → CAUSE *verb*

attendant /əˈtendənt/ [usually before noun] (*formal*) happening as an effect of sth even bigger or more important that is happening at the same time: *She wanted to avoid the awards ceremony and all its attendant publicity.* ◇ *We had all the usual problems attendant upon starting a new business.*

consequent /ˈkɒnsɪkwənt/ (also *less frequent* **consequential** /ˌkɒnsɪˈkwenʃl; *AmE* ˌkɑːnsəˈk-/) (*rather formal*) (*especially of a loss or change in sth that may cause problems*) happening as a result of sth: *the lowering of taxes and the consequent increase in spending* ◇ *the responsibilities consequent upon the arrival of a new child* See also **consequence** → RESULT *noun*
▶ **consequently** *adv.*: (*rather formal, written*) *She failed her exams and was consequently unable to start her studies at college.*

ensuing /ɪnˈsjuːɪŋ; *AmE* -ˈsuː-/ (*especially of a fight, struggle or confused situation*) caused by the thing that happened immediately before; (*of a period of time*) following sth that has just been mentioned: *He had become separated from his parents in the ensuing panic.* ◇ *He married in 1782, and in the ensuing years produced a wealth of new music.* **ⓘ Ensuing** often describes a measurement of time such as weeks, months or years. See also **ensue** → FOLLOW 2

resultant /rɪˈzʌltənt/ [only before noun] (*formal*) resulting: *We deplore the use of force and the resultant loss of life.* ◇ *the growing economic crisis and resultant unemployment* See also **result** → RESULT *noun,* **result** → FOLLOW *verb* 2, **result in sth** → CAUSE *verb*

NOTE **RESULTING**, **CONSEQUENT** OR **RESULTANT**? In many cases you can use any of these words, especially to describe a loss or change in sth: *the war and the resulting/consequent/resultant loss of life* ◇ *lower taxation and the resulting/consequent/resultant increase in spending.* **Resulting** and **resultant** can also be used to talk about the result of a process: *The resulting product will be marketed by IBM.* ◇ *The resultant chemical structure is flexible.* ◇ ~~the consequent product/structure~~ **Resulting** and **resultant** can be used to talk about good or bad results; **consequent** is usually used to talk about results that cause problems in some way. **Resultant** is more formal and less frequent than **resulting**.

connected (*of facts and events*) having a connection with sth; having a connection with each other: *Do these sentences describe a connected sequence of events?* **OPP** **unconnected** → INDEPENDENT

relation *noun*

relation · connection · relationship · correlation · link · association · interdependence
These are all words for sth that connects similar things, or the way in which they are connected.

PATTERNS AND COLLOCATIONS
▶ the relation / connection / relationship / correlation / link / association / interdependence **between** A and B
▶ a connection / a relationship / a correlation / a link / an association **with** sb / sth
▶ a connection / link **to** sth
▶ the relation / relationship **of** sth **to** sth
▶ **in** connection / association **with** sb / sth
▶ a **close** / **significant** relation / connection / relationship / correlation / link / association
▶ a **direct** / **clear** / **strong** / **definite** / **possible** relation / connection / relationship / correlation / link / association
▶ a **complex** relation / connection / relationship / association / interdependence
▶ a **simple** relation / connection / relationship / correlation
▶ a **causal** connection / relationship / link / association
▶ a **positive** relation / connection / relationship / correlation / link
▶ a **negative** relation / relationship / correlation / link
▶ to **have** a relation / a connection / a relationship / a correlation / a link / an association
▶ to **show** / **examine** the relation / connection / relationship / correlation / link / association
▶ to **find** a relation / a connection / a relationship / a correlation / a link / an association
▶ to **prove** the relation / connection / relationship / link / association
▶ to **see** the connection / relationship / correlation / link

relation [U, C] (*rather formal*) the way in which two or more things are connected: *The fee they are offering **bears no relation** to the amount of work involved.* ◇ *Its brain is small **in relation to** (= compared with) its body.* ◇ (*formal*) *I have some comments to make **in relation to** (= concerning) this matter.* ◇ *The study shows a close relation between poverty and ill health.*

connection [C] something that connects two or more people or things: *Scientists have established a connection between cholesterol levels and heart disease.* ◇ *The union did not have a direct connection with any political party.* ◇ *How did you **make the connection** (= realize that there was a connection between two facts that did not seem to be related)?* See also **connect** → LINK 1

relationship [C, U] the way in which two or more things are connected: *the relationship between mental and physical health* ◇ (*rather formal*) *People alter their voices in relationship to background noise.* ◇ (*rather formal*) *There is an **inverse relationship** between disability and social contact* (= the greater sb's disability, the less social contact they have).

NOTE RELATION OR RELATIONSHIP? **Relation** is most often used in expressions such as in relation to sth and to bear no/little relation to sth. When people talk about the relation/relationship between two or more things, they often use **relation** in more technical contexts.

correlation /ˌkɒrəˈleɪʃn; AmE ˌkɔːr-; ˌkɑːr-/ [C, U] (rather formal) a connection between two things in which one thing changes as the other does: There is a direct correlation between exposure to sun and skin cancer. ◇ the correlation of social power with wealth See also **correlate** → MATCH 1

link [C] a connection between two or more people or things: Police suspect there may be a link between the two murders. ◇ The report failed to prove a causal link between violence on screen and in real life. See also **link** → LINK verb 1

NOTE CONNECTION OR LINK? There is no real difference in meaning between these words. Only **connection** is used in the collocation make the connection: How did you make the link? **Link** can be slightly more informal than **connection** and is often used in newspapers.

association [C] (rather formal) a connection between things in which one is caused by the other: Is there a proven association between passive smoking and cancer?
interdependence /ˌɪntədɪˈpendəns; AmE -tərdɪ-/ [U, C] (formal) a state in which people or things depend on each other, or consist of parts that depend on each other: The report stresses the interdependence of teaching and research in universities.

relationship noun

1 The brothers had a close relationship.
2 a sexual relationship

1 See also the entry for BOND
relationship · relations · partnership · tie · link · association · contact · affiliation
These are all words for a connection between two people, groups or countries.

PATTERNS AND COLLOCATIONS
▸ a relationship/ relations/ a partnership/ ties/ a link/ an association/ contacts/ an affiliation **with** sb/ sth
▸ a relationship/ relations/ a partnership/ ties/ links/ an association/ an affiliation **between** A and B
▸ (a) **close** relationship/ relations/ partnership/ ties/ links/ association/ contacts
▸ (a) **strong** relationship/ partnership/ ties/ links
▸ **economic / diplomatic / family** relations/ ties/ links
▸ **trade** relations/ links/ contacts
▸ (a) **business/ professional** relationship/ relations/ partnership/ ties/ links/ association/ contacts
▸ (a) **political** relationship/ relations/ partnership/ ties/ links/ association/ contacts/ affiliation
▸ (a) **personal** relationship/ relations/ ties/ links/ association/ contacts/ affiliation
▸ **international** relations/ partnership/ ties/ links/ contacts
▸ to **have** a relationship/ relations/ a partnership/ ties/ a link/ an association/ contacts/ an affiliation
▸ to **build / establish / foster** a relationship/ relations/ a partnership/ ties/ links/ contacts
▸ to **develop** a relationship/ relations/ a partnership/ ties/ links/ an association/ contacts
▸ to **improve / strengthen** a relationship/ relations/ a partnership/ ties/ links
▸ to **sever / break off** relations/ ties/ links

relationship [C, U] the way in which two people, groups or countries behave towards each other or deal with each other; the way in which a person is related to sb else in a family: The relationship between the police and the local community has improved. ◇ I have established a good **working relationship** with my boss. ◇ She has a **love-hate relationship** with her job (= her feelings for her job are a mixture of love and hatred). ◇ a father-son/mother-daughter relationship ◇ I'm not sure of the exact relationship between them — I think they're cousins.

relations [pl.] the way in which two people, groups or countries behave towards each other or deal with each other: US-Chinese relations ◇ Relations with neighbouring countries are under strain at present. ◇ The change of government led to improved **industrial relations** (= relations between employers and employees).

NOTE RELATIONSHIP OR RELATIONS? The word **relations** is often used to talk about how good or bad the relationship between people, groups or countries is: strained/difficult relations ◇ cordial/harmonious/improved relations. **Relationships** are often more personal than **relations**: international/race/cultural relations ◇ interpersonal/one-to-one/parent-child relationships

partnership [C, U] a relationship between two people, organizations, etc. in which the two work together for a result that is good for both of them; the state of having this relationship: Marriage should be an equal partnership. ◇ the school's partnership with parents ◇ a partnership between the United States and Europe See also **partner** → PARTNER 1

tie [C, usually pl.] a strong relationship between people or organizations: The firm has close ties with an American corporation. ◇ The community was bound by **family ties** and a strong church. ◇ Although he was raised as a Roman Catholic, he has **cut his ties** with the Church. ◇ the ties of friendship/kinship

link [C] a connection or relationship between two or more people, countries or organizations: They were keen to establish trade links with Asia. ◇ Social customs provide a vital link between generations.

NOTE TIE OR LINK? **Ties** are stronger than **links** and suggest that people or groups are closely connected or are dependent on each other in some way. The word **ties** is more frequent than **links** to refer to connections that are more emotional: trade/business ties/links but: family ties ◇ the ties of friendship ◇ family links ◇ the links of friendship

association /əˌsəʊʃiˈeɪʃn; -siˈeɪ-; AmE əˌsoʊ-/ [C, U] (rather formal) a connection or relationship between people or organizations, especially a business one: He was questioned about his alleged association with terrorist groups. ◇ The book was published in association with (= together with) British Heritage. See also **associate** → PARTNER noun 1

contact [C, usually pl.] (especially business) an occasion on which you meet or communicate with sb; a relationship with sb: We have good contacts with the local community. ◇ The company has maintained trade contacts with India.

affiliation /əˌfɪliˈeɪʃn/ [U, C] (formal) one group or organization's official connection with another, especially a political or religious one: Trade unions have a long history of affiliation to the Labour Party. ◇ the diverse religious affiliations of Ghanaian Americans

2 **relationship · affair · romance · love affair · courtship · liaison**
These are all words for a romantic or sexual friendship between two people.

PATTERNS AND COLLOCATIONS
▸ a relationship/ an affair/ a romance/ a love affair/ a liaison **with** sb
▸ a relationship/ an affair/ a romance/ a love affair/ a liaison **between** A and B
▸ a **brief / long** relationship/ affair/ romance/ love affair/ courtship
▸ a **passionate** relationship/ affair/ romance/ love affair
▸ a **secret** relationship/ affair/ romance/ love affair/ liaison
▸ to **have** a relationship/ an affair/ a romance/ a love affair/ a liaison
▸ to **start / begin / embark on** a relationship/ an affair/ a love affair
▸ a relationship/ an affair/ a romance/ a love affair **is over**

relationship [C] a loving and/or sexual friendship between two people: *He was not married but he was in a stable relationship.* ◇ *She's had a series of miserable relationships.* ◇ *Money problems have put a strain on their relationship.*

affair [C] a sexual relationship between two people, usually when one or both of them is married to sb else: *She is having an affair with her boss.*

romance /rəʊˈmæns; ˈrəʊmæns; *AmE* ˈroʊ-/ [C] an exciting, usually short, relationship between two people who are in love with each other: *They married after a whirlwind romance.* ◇ (*BrE*) *a holiday romance* ◇ (*especially AmE*) *a summer romance* See also **romance** → LOVE noun 1, **romantic** → LOVING

'love affair [C] a romantic and/or sexual relationship between two people who are in love and not married to each other: *So you're not going to tell me when your love affair with Sam ended?*

> **NOTE AFFAIR OR LOVE AFFAIR?** A **love affair** is usually more romantic than an **affair**; it need not involve sex, and can be between two people of whom neither is married.

courtship [C, U] (*old-fashioned*) the time when two people have a romantic relationship before they get married; the process of developing this relationship: *They married after a short courtship.* ◇ *Mr Elton's courtship of Harriet* ❶ **Courtship** is now quite an old-fashioned term, but it is still used to talk about people in the past. See also **court** → GO OUT

liaison /liˈeɪzn; *AmE* liˈeɪzɑːn/ [C] (*formal*) a secret sexual relationship, especially if one or both partners are married: *He finally admitted to several sexual liaisons.*

relative adj. See also the entry for EQUIVALENT

relative · proportional · proportionate
These words all describe things that are considered according to their position or connection with sth else.

relative considered according to its position or connection with sth else; considered and judged by being compared with sth else; that exists or has a particular quality only when compared with sth else: *the position of the sun relative to the earth* ◇ *You must consider the **relative merits** of the two plans.* ◇ *They now live in relative comfort* (= compared with how they lived before). ◇ *It's all relative though, isn't it? We never had any money when I was a kid and $500 was a fortune to us.*
▸ **relatively** *adv.*: *At first glance the poem seems to be relatively straightforward.* ◇ *The colleges had become, relatively speaking, short of funds.*

proportional /prəˈpɔːʃənl; *AmE* -ˈpɔːrʃ-/ (*rather formal*) increasing or decreasing in size, amount or degree according to changes in sth else: *Salary is directly proportional to years of experience.* ◇ *The number of teachers appointed is proportional to the total number of students.* See also **proportion** → RATIO
▸ **proportionally** *adv.*: *Families with children spend proportionally less per person than families without children.*

proportionate /prəˈpɔːʃənət; *AmE* -ˈpɔːrʃ-/ (*formal*) proportional, especially when it is a question of what is fair or reasonable: *Inner cities have more than a proportionate share of social problems.* ◇ *Penalties should be proportionate to the gravity of the offence.* **OPP disproportionate** → EXCESSIVE
▸ **proportionately** *adv.*: *Prices have risen but wages have not risen proportionately.*

> **NOTE PROPORTIONAL OR PROPORTIONATE?** In many cases you can use either word: *Salary is proportional/proportionate to experience.* ◇ *proportional/proportionate increases in costs.* In these cases **proportionate** is

more formal and less frequent than **proportional**. However, **proportionate** is often used when the question is not simply one of comparing two amounts, but of judging two actions or decisions and deciding whether one is fair or reasonable after considering the other: *The police response should be proportionate to the level of risk posed.* The opposite, **disproportionate**, can be used when an action or judgement is NOT fair or reasonable in response to another action or situation. The opposite of **proportional** is **inversely proportional**: *The amount of force needed is **inversely proportional** to the rigidity of the material* (= the more rigid the material, the less force is needed).

relax verb

1 Relax! Everything will be OK.
2 relax your muscles/grip

1 relax · calm down · pull yourself together · cool
These words all mean to become calmer.

relax [I] to become calmer and less worried: *I'll only relax when I know you're safe.* ◇ *Relax! Everything will be OK.* See also **relax** → REST verb

,calm 'down *phrasal verb* to become calm: *Look, calm down! We'll find her.* ◇ *We waited until things calmed down.*

> **NOTE RELAX OR CALM DOWN?** People can **relax**; people or a situation can **calm down**. To **relax** is to stop feeling worried. **Calm down** is more about behaviour than feelings: you may still feel worried, but you manage to behave in a calm way in spite of your feelings.

,pull yourself to'gether *phrasal verb* to take control of your feelings and behave in a calm way: *Stop crying and pull yourself together.*

cool [I] to become calmer, less excited or less enthusiastic: *I think we should wait until tempers have cooled.* ◇ *Relations between them have definitely cooled* (= they are not friendly with each other as they were). ◇ *Let things cool off for a while.* ◇ *I think you should wait until she's cooled down a little.* ❶ *Tempers, passions* and *relations* can **cool**; *things* can **cool off**; *people* can **cool down**.

2 relax · loosen · release · slacken
These words all mean to remove sth from a fixed position, or make sth less tight.

relax [I, T] (of a part of the body) to become less tight or stiff; to make a part of the body less tight or stiff; to hold sb/sth less tightly: *Allow your muscles to relax completely.* ◇ *The massage relaxed my tense back muscles.* ◇ *He relaxed his grip on her arm.* **OPP tighten, tense** → TIGHTEN

loosen /ˈluːsn/ [I, T] to become or make sth less tight or firmly fixed; to make hair or a piece of clothing loose, when it has been tied or fastened; to hold sb/sth less tightly: *The rope holding the boat had loosened.* ◇ *First loosen the nuts, then take off the wheel.* ◇ *She loosened her hair so that it fell over her shoulders.* ◇ *He loosened his grip and let her go.* **OPP tighten** → TIGHTEN

release [T] (*rather formal*) to remove sth from a fixed position, allowing sth else to move or function; to make sth less tight: *Now release the clutch and move away from the kerb.* ◇ *You need to release the tension in these shoulder muscles.* ❶ **Release** is often used to talk about moving parts of a piece of machinery from a fixed position: *to release a catch/a screw/a nut/the clutch/the brakes.* When **release** is used to talk about making sth less tight or tense, it usually refers to *energy, aggression, emotion* or *tension* in the body, or your *grip* on sth.

slacken [I, T] (*especially written*) to become or make sth become less tight: *His grip slackened and she pulled away from him.* ◇ *He slackened the ropes slightly.* **OPP tighten** → TIGHTEN

release *verb*

release · let sb go · free · liberate · set sb/sth free · ransom · emancipate · let sb/sth loose
These words all mean to let sb/sth leave a place where they have been kept or trapped.

PATTERNS AND COLLOCATIONS
▸ to release / free / liberate / set free / emancipate sb **from** sth
▸ to release / let go / free / liberate / set free / ransom a **prisoner / hostage**
▸ to **finally** release sb / let sb go / free sb / liberate sb
▸ to release / free sb **on bail**
▸ to release / free an animal / a bird **into the wild**

release [T] to let sb/sth leave prison or a place where they have been kept: *The kidnappers have agreed to release the hostages by 12 noon.* ◇ *He was **released without charge** (= not charged with committing a crime) after questioning by police.* ◇ *She was released on bail (= after paying a sum of money to make sure she would return) by the New York police.* ◇ *The birds were cleaned and fed and released again into the wild.* See also **release** → FREE *verb* 1
▸ **release** *noun* [U, sing.]: *The government has been working to secure the release of the hostages.* ◇ *She can expect an early release from prison.*

,let sb 'go *phrase* (*rather informal*) to allow sb to be free after keeping them somewhere by force for a short time: *He was beaten up quite badly before they let him go.* ◇ *Let me go! You're hurting me!* ❶ **Let sb go** is not usually used to talk about releasing ordinary criminals from prison, but it is used about hostages who have been taken prisoner illegally. See also **let go** → FREE *verb* 1

free [T] to let sb leave prison or a place where they have been kept by force; to let sb stop being a slave (= a person who is legally owned by another person and is forced to work for them): *Over 2 000 political prisoners were freed as a gesture of good will.* ◇ *The starting point for emancipation was the freeing of children of slaves born after a certain date.* See also **free** → FREE *adj.* 1, **free** → FREE *verb* 1

liberate /'lɪbəreɪt/ [T] (*rather formal*) to free a country or person from the control of sb else: *The city was liberated by the advancing army.*
▸ **liberation** *noun* [U, sing.]: *He took part in the liberation of the occupied countries.*

,set sb/sth 'free *phrase* to let sb leave prison or a place where they have been kept by force; to let an animal or bird go free after it has been tied up or kept in a cage: *Police were forced to set him free because of a lack of evidence.* ◇ *Dozens of laboratory animals were set free by animal rights activists.*

NOTE RELEASE, FREE OR SET FREE? **Free** emphasizes the decision to let sb go; **release** emphasizes the physical act of letting sb go. A court or the government might **free** the prisoners; the police or prison service would **release** them. **Set free** also emphasizes the physical act of letting sb/sth go, especially in cases where this is done by force, not authority: *Rioters stormed the prison and set all the prisoners free.*

ransom /'rænsəm/ [T] to pay money to sb so that they will release the person that they are keeping as a prisoner: *The hostages were ransomed and returned home unharmed.*
▸ **ransom** *noun* [C, U]: *The kidnappers demanded a ransom of £50 000 from his family.* ◇ *They are refusing to pay ransom for her release.*

emancipate /ɪ'mænsɪpeɪt/ [T, often passive] to free sb, especially from legal, political or social restrictions: *Slaves were not emancipated until 1863 in the United States.*
▸ **emancipation** *noun* [U]: *the struggle for the emancipation of women*

let sb/sth 'loose *idiom* to let sb/sth go free, especially sb/sth that might be dangerous or cause problems: *Who let the dogs loose?* ◇ *How did such a violent criminal get to be let loose in the community?* See also **loose** → FREE *adj.* 1

relevant *adj.*

relevant · applicable · pertinent · to the point · material
These words all describe sth that relates directly to what you are discussing or thinking about, or sth that is directly appropriate to people's lives and work.

PATTERNS AND COLLOCATIONS
▸ relevant / applicable / pertinent / material **to** sb / sth
▸ relevant / applicable / pertinent / material **for** sb / sth
▸ relevant / pertinent **to do** sth
▸ a relevant / pertinent / material **point / fact / factor**
▸ **particularly / directly** relevant / applicable / pertinent
▸ **very** relevant / pertinent / material
▸ **highly / extremely** relevant / pertinent

relevant /'reləvənt/ closely connected to the subject or situation that you are discussing or thinking about; having ideas that are useful or valuable to people in their lives and work: *I don't think that question is really very relevant.* ◇ *They are looking for someone with relevant experience in childcare.* ◇ *These comments are not directly relevant to this enquiry.* ◇ *Her novel is still relevant today.* **OPP irrelevant** → IRRELEVANT
▸ **relevance** *noun* [U]: *I don't see the relevance of your question.* ◇ *It's a classic play of contemporary relevance.*
▸ **relevantly** *adv.*: *She has experience in teaching and, more relevantly, in industry.*

applicable /ə'plɪkəbl; 'æplɪkəbl/ [not usually before noun] (*rather formal*) directly connected with sb/sth; likely to be true of sb/sth: *Many of the questions on the form were not applicable (= did not apply) to me.* ◇ *Give details of children where applicable (= if you have any).* ◇ *His rules are not universally applicable (= they do not apply to everyone or everything).* **OPP inapplicable** → IRRELEVANT

pertinent /'pɜːtɪnənt; *AmE* 'pɜːrtnənt/ (*formal*) relevant to a particular situation: *I reminded him of a few pertinent facts.* ◇ *Please keep your comments pertinent to the topic under discussion.*

to the 'point *idiom* (*approving*) relevant and expressed in a clear, simple way: *Her speech was brief and to the point.* ◇ *That remark was not really to the point.* **OPP beside the point** → IRRELEVANT, See also **point** → POINT *noun*, **concise** → SHORT 3

material (*formal or law*) important to a particular situation and needing to be considered: *She omitted information that was material to the case.* **OPP immaterial** → IRRELEVANT
▸ **materially** *adv.*: *Their comments have not materially affected our plans (= in a noticeable or important way).*

reliable *adj.*

1 She is reliable and hard-working.
2 reliable evidence/witnesses

1 reliable · loyal · dedicated · faithful · committed · true · trusted · staunch · responsible · trustworthy
These words all describe sb/sth you can rely on to do sth, especially to give support or to work hard.

PATTERNS AND COLLOCATIONS
▸ loyal / dedicated / faithful / committed / true **to** sb / sth
▸ a reliable / loyal / faithful / true / trusted / staunch / trustworthy **friend**

▶ a reliable / loyal / faithful / trusted / staunch **ally**
▶ a reliable / loyal / faithful / committed / staunch **supporter**
▶ a loyal / dedicated / faithful / true **fan / follower**
▶ a loyal / dedicated / faithful / committed / trusted / staunch / responsible **member** (of sth)
▶ reliable / loyal / dedicated / committed / trustworthy **staff**
▶ a loyal / dedicated / faithful **following**
▶ reliable / loyal / faithful **service**
▶ totally reliable / loyal / dedicated / trustworthy

reliable /rɪˈlaɪəbl/ (*often approving*) (of a person or thing) that can be trusted to do sth well; that you can rely on: *We are looking for someone who is reliable and hard-working.* ◇ *My car's not as reliable as it used to be.* ◇ *There is no reliable supply of electricity or running water.* **OPP unreliable ❶** An **unreliable** person or thing cannot be trusted or depended on: *The trains are notoriously unreliable.* See also **rely on/upon sb/sth** → TRUST
▶ **reliability** noun [U]: *The incident cast doubt on her motives and reliability.*
▶ **reliably** adv.: *You need to show that you can work reliably and be trusted to handle responsibility.*

loyal (*approving*) (of a person) staying with or supporting a particular person, organization or belief, especially as a matter of principle: *She has always remained loyal to her political principles.* ◇ *He is one of the president's most loyal supporters.* **OPP disloyal** → TREACHEROUS
▶ **loyally** adv.: *He loyally supported the government through the crisis.*
▶ **loyalty** noun [U, C]: *They swore their loyalty to the king.* ◇ *a case of divided loyalties* (= with strong feelings of support for two different people or causes) **OPP disloyalty** → BETRAYAL

dedicated /ˈdedɪkeɪtɪd/ (*approving*) (of a person) working hard at sth because it is very important to you: *She is dedicated to her job.* ◇ *The workforce is small but highly dedicated.* ◇ *The ship was painstakingly rebuilt by a dedicated team of engineers.* See also **dedicate** → DEVOTE
▶ **dedication** noun [U]: *I really admire Gina for her dedication to her family.* ◇ *The job requires total dedication.*

faithful (*approving*) (of a person) staying with or supporting a particular person, organization or belief, especially from feelings of affection; (of a person or thing) that you can rely on: *He remained faithful to the ideals of the party until his death.* ◇ *His faithful old dog sat by his feet.* ◇ *a faithful worker/correspondent* ◇ *my faithful old car* See also **devoted** → LOVING, **faith** → FAITH
▶ **the faithful** noun [pl.]: *The president will keep the support of the party faithful.*
▶ **faithfully** adv.: *He had supported the local team faithfully for 30 years.* ◇ *She promised faithfully not to tell anyone the secret.*

NOTE LOYAL OR FAITHFUL? In many cases you can use either word: *a loyal/faithful friend/ally/supporter/fan/follower/servant*. However, there can be a slight difference of emphasis: a *loyal friend/servant* remains loyal as a matter of principle; a *faithful friend/servant* remains faithful from affection.

committed /kəˈmɪtɪd/ (*approving*) (of a person) willing to work hard and give your time and energy to sth; believing strongly in sth: *The government remains committed to protecting Green Belt areas.* ◇ *They are committed socialists.* ◇ *We have a highly-motivated, trained and committed staff.* See also **commit** → DEVOTE, **commit** → PROMISE verb, **commitment** → PROMISE noun

true (*approving*) (of a person) showing respect and support for a particular person or belief in a way that does not change, even in different situations: *Many were executed for remaining true to their principles.* ◇ *He was true to his word* (= did what he promised to do). ◇ *Through that difficult period he proved to be a true friend.*

trusted (*approving*) (of a person) that sb feels they can rely on: *As time went on he became a trusted adviser to the king.* See also **trust** → FAITH noun, **trust** → TRUST verb

staunch /stɔːntʃ/ (*often approving*) (of a person) strong and loyal in your opinions and attitude: *a staunch Catholic* ◇ *She is one of the president's staunchest allies.*
▶ **staunchly** adv.: *She staunchly defended the new policy.* ◇ *The family was staunchly Protestant.*

responsible (of people or their actions or behaviour) that you can trust and rely on: *Clare has a mature and responsible attitude to work.* **OPP irresponsible** → RECKLESS

trustworthy /ˈtrʌstwɜːði; AmE -wɜːrði/ (*approving*) (of a person) that you can rely on to be good, honest and sincere: *Women were seen as more trustworthy and harder working.* **OPP untrustworthy**

2 See the Topic Map for FACT AND OPINION on p.898, See also the entry for TRUE

reliable · factual · authoritative · real-life · verifiable · authentic
These words all describe information or a source of information that is true and accurate.

PATTERNS AND COLLOCATIONS
▶ a reliable / a factual / an authoritative / a real-life / an authentic **account** (of sth)
▶ reliable / factual / authoritative / verifiable **evidence / information**
▶ a reliable / an authoritative / a verifiable / an authentic **source** (of information)

reliable /rɪˈlaɪəbl/ (of information or a source of information) that is likely to be correct or true: *These tests are a reliable indicator of future performance.* ◇ *Prosecution lawyers tried to show that she was not a reliable witness.* **OPP unreliable ❶** An **unreliable** person or thing cannot be trusted or depended on: *He's totally unreliable as a source of information.* See also **accurate** → EXACT
▶ **reliability** noun [U]: *The reliability of these results has been questioned.*
▶ **reliably** adv.: (*rather formal*) *I am reliably informed* (= told by sb who knows the facts) *that the company is being sold.*

factual /ˈfæktʃuəl/ based on or containing facts: *He fails to distinguish factual information from opinion.* ◇ *The essay contains a number of factual errors.* **OPP fictitious** → FICTIONAL, See also **fact** → FACT, **fact** → INFORMATION
▶ **factually** adv.: *It was factually correct, but I don't think it was fair.*

authoritative /ɔːˈθɒrətətɪv; AmE əˈθɔːrəteɪtɪv; əˈθɑːr-/ that you can trust and respect as true and correct: *He is credited with writing the most authoritative and up-to-date book on the subject.* See also **authority** → EXPERT noun

,real-'life [only before noun] actually happening or existing in life, not in books, stories or films: *The novel is a political thriller based on real-life events.* ◇ *The local press has been referring to them as a real-life Romeo and Juliet.* **OPP fictional** → FICTIONAL

verifiable /ˈverɪfaɪəbl/ that can be proved: *That's just your opinion, not a verifiable fact.* See also **verify** → CHECK 2

authentic /ɔːˈθentɪk/ true and giving an accurate and realistic description of sth: *He is the authentic voice of the poor, white working class.*

relief noun See also the entry for SYMPATHY

relief · comfort · reassurance · consolation
These are all words for the feeling of being less unhappy, or the person or thing that makes you less unhappy.

PATTERNS AND COLLOCATIONS
▶ a relief / comfort / consolation **to sb**
▶ relief / comfort / reassurance / consolation **in sth**
▶ the comfort / reassurance / consolation **that...**
▶ (a) **great** relief / comfort / reassurance / consolation
▶ to **seek / find / bring / offer (sb)** relief / comfort / reassurance / consolation

▶ to **give sb** comfort / reassurance
▶ to **take** comfort / consolation
▶ **It's a relief / comfort / consolation to** know / have / be, etc....

relief [U, sing.] the feeling of happiness that you have when sth unpleasant stops or does not happen; the act of removing or reducing pain, worry or suffering: *We all breathed a sigh of relief when he came back safely.* ◇ *Much to my relief the car was not damaged.* ◇ *It was a relief to be able to talk to someone about it.* ◇ *What a relief!* ◇ *modern methods of pain relief* ◇ *the relief of poverty/misery/suffering* See also **relieve** → EASE, **relieved** → GLAD

comfort [U, sing.] a feeling of being less unhappy or not suffering or worrying so much; a person or thing that helps you when you are suffering, worried or unhappy: *I drew comfort from his words.* ◇ *I tried to offer a few words of comfort.* ◇ *The children have been a great comfort to me through all of this.* ◇ *It's a comfort to know that she is safe.* See also **comfort** → REASSURE *verb*

reassurance /ˌriːəˈʃʊərəns; -ˈʃɔːr-; AmE -ˈʃʊr-/ [U, C] the fact of giving advice or help that takes away a person's fears or doubts; something that is said or done to take away a person's fears or doubts: *Teenagers need love, encouragement and reassurance from their parents.* ◇ *We have been given reassurances that the water is safe to drink.* See also **reassure** → REASSURE

consolation /ˌkɒnsəˈleɪʃn; AmE ˌkaːn-/ [C, U] a person or thing that makes you feel better when you are unhappy or disappointed; a feeling of being less worried or unhappy: *If it's any consolation, she didn't get the job either.* ◇ *When things went wrong, she found consolation in her religious beliefs.* See also **console** → REASSURE

NOTE COMFORT OR CONSOLATION? These words can be used in many of the same patterns: *If it's any comfort/consolation to you...* ◇ *It's a great comfort/consolation that...* ◇ *to seek/find/take comfort/consolation.* However, there is a slight difference in meaning. You might find **consolation** after a disappointment, such as losing a competition or not getting a job; you might find **comfort** in a more serious situation when sth has really made you unhappy or worried: *Chocolate is a great comfort food* (= it makes you feel better). ◇ *Six runners-up will get a consolation prize of a disposable camera* (= a small prize, even though they did not win the competition).

religion *noun*

religion · Church · faith · theology · cult · sect · denomination
These are all words for belief in a god or gods, or a group of people who believe in a particular god or gods.

PATTERNS AND COLLOCATIONS
▶ (a) **religious** faith / cult / sect
▶ to **practise** your religion / faith
▶ to **belong to** the Church / a cult / a sect / a denomination
▶ to **join** the Church / a cult / a sect

religion [U, C] belief in the existence of a god or gods, and the activities that are connected with the worship of them; one of the systems of religion that are based on belief in the existence of a particular god or gods: *Is there always a conflict between science and religion?* ◇ *the Jewish religion* ◇ *Christianity, Islam and other world religions*

Church [C] a particular group of Christians: *the Catholic Church* ◇ *the Anglican Church* ◇ *the Free Churches* ❶ **(the) Church** [sing.] is also the ministers of the Christian religion, considered as a group, or the institution of the Christian religion: *The Church has a duty to condemn violence.* ◇ *the conflict between Church and State* ◇ *to go into the Church* (= to become a Christian minister) See also **church** → CHURCH

faith [U, C] strong religious belief; a particular religion: *Faith is stronger than reason.* ◇ *I lost my faith when my parents died.* ◇ *the Christian faith* ◇ *The children learn to understand people of different faiths.* See also **faith** → FAITH

theology /θiˈɒlədʒi; AmE -ˈɑːlə-/ [U, C] the study of religion and beliefs; a set of religious beliefs: *a degree in Theology* ◇ *the theologies of the East*

cult [C] (*often disapproving*) a small group of people who have extreme religious beliefs and who are not part of any established religion: *Their son ran away from home and joined a cult.* ❶ In formal language a **cult** can also be a system of religious beliefs and practices; this use is not disapproving: *the Chinese cult of ancestor worship*

sect [C] a small group of people who belong to a particular religion but who have some beliefs or practices which separate them from the rest of the group: *The Shakers are an American religious sect, founded in the 18th century.* See also **sectarianism** → RACISM

denomination /dɪˌnɒmɪˈneɪʃn; AmE -ˌnaːm-/ [C] (*formal*) a branch of a particular religion, especially Christianity: *Christians of all denominations attended the conference.*

religious *adj.*

religious · holy · sacred · theological
These words all describe things which are connected with God or religion.

PATTERNS AND COLLOCATIONS
▶ religious / sacred **music / art**
▶ a holy / sacred **shrine / temple / relic / river / book / thing**

religious [only before noun] connected with religion or with a particular religion: *religious beliefs/faith* ◇ *religious education* (= education about religion) ◇ *religious instruction* (= instruction in a particular religion) ◇ *religious groups/leaders* ◇ *objects which have a religious significance* **OPP** **secular** ❶ Secular means 'not connected with religious matters': *secular art/education/music*

holy [usually before noun] special to believers in a particular religion; connected with God: *the Holy Bible/ Scriptures* ◇ *holy ground* ◇ *the holy city of Mecca* ◇ *a holy war* (= one fought to defend the beliefs of a particular religion) See also **holy** → HOLY

sacred /ˈseɪkrɪd/ connected with God or a god; considered to be holy: *a sacred image/grove* ◇ *sacred music* ◇ *Cows are sacred to Hindus.*

NOTE HOLY OR SACRED? There is very little difference in meaning between these words. However, **holy** is used especially in connection with the world religions that recognize only one God, that is Christianity, Judaism and Islam. **Sacred** is used more in connection with religions that worship, or at least recognize the existence of, more than one God, including Hinduism and ancient pagan religions. (There are exceptions for particular collocations: *music* and *art* are always **sacred**, NOT **holy**.)

theological /ˌθiːəˈlɒdʒɪkl; AmE -ˈlaːdʒ-/ connected with the study of religion and beliefs: (*BrE*) *a theological college* ◇ (*AmE*) *a theological seminary*

reluctant *adj.*

reluctant · unwilling · grudging
These words all describe a person who does not want to do sth or a thing that sb does not want to do.

PATTERNS AND COLLOCATIONS
▶ reluctant / unwilling **to do sth**
▶ reluctant / unwilling / grudging **acceptance**
▶ a reluctant / grudging **admiration / admission**
▶ a reluctant / an unwilling **participant**

reluctant /rɪˈlʌktənt/ hesitating before doing sth because you do not want to do it or because you are not sure that it is the right thing to do: *She was reluctant to admit she was wrong.* ◇ *They nodded in reluctant agreement.* ◇ *He finally gave a reluctant smile.* **OPP** eager → EAGER

▸ **reluctance** noun [U, sing.]: *There is still some reluctance on the part of employers to become involved in this project.*

▸ **reluctantly** adv.: *We reluctantly agreed to go with her.*

unwilling not wanting to do sth and refusing to do it; not wanting to do or be sth but forced to by other people: *They are unwilling to invest any more money in the project.* ◇ *He became the unwilling object of her affection.* **OPP** willing → HELPFUL

▸ **unwillingly** adv.: *Unwillingly she raised her eyes to his.*

▸ **unwillingness** noun [U, sing.]: *the government's unwillingness to reform*

grudging [usually before noun] given or done unwillingly: *There was grudging admiration in his voice.* See also **begrudge** → RESENT

▸ **grudgingly** adv.: *She grudgingly admitted that I was right.*

remain verb

remain · keep · stay · last · continue · be left · linger · live · stand
These words all mean to still be in the same state or condition.

▸ to linger / live **on**
▸ to remain / keep / stay **awake / calm / cheerful / cool / dry / fine / healthy / quiet / silent**
▸ to remain / stay **alert / alive / asleep / loyal / safe / the same / a secret / shut / sober / upright**
▸ to keep / stay **close / still / warm**
▸ sb's **memory** remains / lingers / lives (on)

remain [I, T] (not usually used in the progressive tenses) (*formal*) to be still in the same state or condition; to still exist or be present, especially after other parts have been removed or used; to still need to be done, said, or dealt with: *For a long time he remained motionless.* ◇ *Train fares are likely to remain unchanged.* ◇ *It remains true that sport is about competing well, not winning.* ◇ *In spite of their quarrel, they remain the best of friends.* ◇ *Very little of the house remained after the fire.* ◇ *There were only ten minutes remaining.* ◇ *Much remains to be done.* ◇ *I feel sorry for her, but **the fact remains (that)** she lied to us.* ◇ *It **remains to be seen** (= it will only be known later) whether you are right.* ◇ *There remained one significant problem.* See also **remain** → STAY 1

keep [I, T] to remain in the same condition or position; to make sb/sth do this: *We huddled together to keep warm.* ◇ *The notice said 'Keep off* (= Do not walk on) *the grass'.* ◇ *She kept the children amused for hours.* ◇ *He kept his coat on.* ◇ *Don't **keep us in suspense** – what happened next?* ◇ *She had trouble **keeping her balance**.* ◇ *I'm very sorry to **keep you waiting**.*

stay [I, T] to remain in the same state or condition: *I can't stay awake any longer.* ◇ *Inflation stayed below 4% last month.* ◇ *The store stays open until late on Thursdays.* ◇ *I don't know why they stay together* (= remain married or in a relationship). ◇ *We promised to stay friends for ever.* ❶ **Stay** is less formal than **remain** in this meaning, and is the word used in everyday speech. It is often followed by adjectives with positive associations: *to stay awake / alive / afloat / cool / healthy / dry / sober / calm / sane / constant / faithful / alert* See also **stay** → STAY 1

last [I, T] (not used in the progressive tenses) to keep existing or functioning well: *This weather won't last.* ◇ *He's making a big effort now, and I hope it lasts.* ◇ *These shoes should last you till next year.*

continue [I] (*rather formal, especially written*) to remain in a particular job or position: *I want you to continue as project manager.* ◇ *She will continue in her present job until a replacement can be found.*

be left [T, passive] to remain to be used or sold: *Is there any coffee left?* ◇ *How many tickets do you have left?* ◇ (*figurative*) *They are fighting to save what is left of their business.* ◇ *The only course of action **left to** me was to notify her employer.*

linger /ˈlɪŋɡə(r)/ [I] (*written*) to continue to exist for longer than expected: *The faint smell of her perfume lingered in the room.* ◇ *The civil war lingered on well into the 1930s.*

live [I] (always used with an adverb or preposition) (*especially written*) to continue to exist or be remembered: *She died ten years ago but her memory lives on.* ◇ *Her words have **lived with** me all my life.* ❶ In this meaning **live** is often followed by an expression such as *in my / our / their heart(s) / mind(s) / memory* or an expression of time, especially one which refers to a very long period of time: *to live (on) for decades / many years / all my life / the rest of my life*

stand [I] if an offer, a decision, etc. made earlier **stands**, it is still valid: *My offer still stands.* ◇ *The world record stood for 20 years.*

remains noun

1 prehistoric remains
2 the remains of a sandwich

1 remains · ruin · debris · wreckage · rubble · wreck
These are all words for parts of sth that is left after it has been destroyed or severely damaged.

▸ the remains / ruins / wreckage / wreck **of** a building / vehicle, etc.
▸ the debris / rubble **from** a building, etc.
▸ **in / amid / among / amongst** the remains / ruins / debris / wreckage / rubble
▸ **ancient / Roman** remains / ruins
▸ to **reduce** sth **to** ruins / rubble
▸ to **clear (away)** the debris / wreckage / rubble
▸ to **be trapped in** the wreckage / the rubble / a wreck
▸ to **sift through** remains / debris / wreckage
▸ a **piece / pile of** debris / wreckage

remains [pl.] the parts of ancient objects and buildings that have survived and are discovered in the present day; parts of sth that are left after it has been destroyed or severely damaged: *The museum has an impressive collection of prehistoric remains.* ◇ *They have found the remains of a Roman settlement on the land.* ◇ *The mangled remains of a bicycle were sticking out of the windscreen.*

ruin [C] (also **ruins** [pl.]) the parts of a building that remain after it has been destroyed or severely damaged: *The old mill is now little more than a ruin.* ◇ *We visited the ruins of a Norman castle.* ◇ *Years of fighting have left the area **in ruins**.*

▸ **ruined** adj.: *a ruined castle*

debris /ˈdebriː; ˈdeɪ-; AmE dəˈbriː/ [U] pieces of wood, metal, brick or other material that are left after sth has been destroyed: *Emergency teams are still clearing the debris from the plane crash.* ◇ *A man of 76 was fatally injured by flying debris* (= a piece of material flying through the air after an explosion).

wreckage /ˈrekɪdʒ/ [U] the parts of a vehicle or building that remain after it has been destroyed or severely damaged: *An elderly man was cut from the wreckage by firefighters.* ◇ *Pieces of wreckage were found several miles away from the scene of the explosion.*

rubble [U] broken stones or bricks from a building or wall that has been destroyed or damaged: *A bomb had reduced the house next door to rubble.*

wreck /rek/ [C] a ship that has sunk or that has been very badly damaged; a car, plane or other vehicle that has been very badly damaged in an accident: *A new search of the wreck of the Titanic has been launched.* ◇ *She was pulled from the burning wreck by firefighters.* See also **wreck** → CRASH

2 remains · remnant · scraps · leftover

These are all words for what is left of sth after most of it has been eaten, used, removed or destroyed.

PATTERNS AND COLLOCATIONS
▸ remains / remnants / scraps / leftovers **from** / **of** sth
▸ the **last** remains / remnants / scraps
▸ **surviving** remains / remnants
▸ the remains / remnants **of a meal**
▸ a remnant / leftover **from the days when...**

remains [pl.] the parts of sth that are left after the other parts have been used, eaten, removed or destroyed: *She sat watching some birds pecking at the remains of a sandwich that someone had dropped.* ◇ *In the middle of the clearing were the charred remains of a small fire.*

remnant /ˈremnənt/ [C, usually pl.] (*rather formal*) a part of sth that is left after the other parts have been used, removed or destroyed: *The woods are remnants of a huge forest which once covered the whole area.* ◇ *The institution is a remnant from the past.*

NOTE REMAINS OR REMNANT? Remains is used especially to talk about what is left of sth that has mostly been eaten or burnt: *the remains of a meal/sandwich/break-fast/lunch* ◇ *the charred remnant of a small fire* Remnant is mostly used to talk about much larger things that have become much smaller, either in the course of history or because of some great event: *the remnants of a forest/an empire/an army*

scraps [pl.] small pieces of food left after a meal: *Give the scraps to the dog.*

leftover /ˈleftəʊvə(r)/; *AmE* -oʊv-/ [C] food that has not been eaten at the end of a meal; an object, custom or way of behaving that remains from an earlier time: *You've always got good ideas for using up leftovers.* ◇ *He's a leftover from the 1960s* (= he acts or dresses like people did in the 1960s). See also **leftover** → EXCESS *adj.*

remarkable *adj.* See also the entry for AMAZING

remarkable · unique · extraordinary · incredible · exceptional · unbelievable · phenomenal · unusual
These words all describe things that you notice because they are unusually great, good or bad.

unusual	remarkable	unique
	exceptional	extraordinary
		incredible
		unbelievable
		phenomenal

PATTERNS AND COLLOCATIONS
▸ a remarkable / an extraordinary / an incredible / an exceptional / an unbelievable / a phenomenal / an unusual **amount**
▸ a remarkable / a unique / an extraordinary / an incredible / an exceptional **achievement**
▸ a remarkable / a unique / an extraordinary / an incredible / an exceptional / an unbelievable / a phenomenal **performance**
▸ remarkable / extraordinary / incredible / exceptional / unbelievable / phenomenal / unusual **speed**
▸ remarkable / unique / extraordinary / incredible / exceptional / unbelievable **beauty**
▸ remarkable / extraordinary / incredible / exceptional / phenomenal / unusual **strength**
▸ a unique / an extraordinary / an incredible / an exceptional **opportunity**
▸ a remarkable / an extraordinary / an incredible / a phenomenal / an unusual **success**
▸ remarkable / unique / extraordinary / incredible / exceptional / unusual **talent** / **skill**
▸ a remarkable / an incredible / an exceptional **career**
▸ **of** remarkable / extraordinary / exceptional / unusual **quality**

▸ **quite** remarkable / unique / extraordinary / incredible / exceptional / unbelievable / phenomenal
▸ **really** remarkable / unique / extraordinary / incredible / exceptional / unbelievable / phenomenal
▸ **just** extraordinary / incredible / unbelievable / phenomenal

remarkable unusual or surprising in a way that causes people to take notice: *She was a truly remarkable woman.* ◇ *The interior of the house was remarkable for its beauty.* ◇ *It was remarkable that the body had not been found sooner.* ◇ *What is even more remarkable about the whole thing is...* **OPP** **unremarkable** → AVERAGE
▸ **remarkably** *adv.*: *She looked remarkably fit for an eighty-year-old.*

unique /juˈniːk/ very special in a way that makes sb/sth different from all other people or things of the same type: *The museum is of unique historical importance.* ◇ *I have had a unique opportunity to observe the problems faced by the police in this city.* ❶ Unique also has the meaning 'being the only one of its kind' and in that meaning you cannot talk about sth being 'very unique' or 'more unique'; in the meaning of 'very special', you *can* say 'very unique' or 'more unique', but this can sound quite informal and is not good style in formal written English. See also **unique** → UNIQUE
▸ **uniquely** *adv.*: *He was a uniquely gifted teacher.*

extraordinary /ɪkˈstrɔːdnri; *AmE* ɪkˈstrɔːrdəneri/ not normal or ordinary; greater or better than usual: *They went to extraordinary lengths to obtain a copy of the report.* ◇ *I found an extraordinary number of errors in the document.* ◇ *She is a truly extraordinary woman.* **OPP** **ordinary** → AVERAGE, **ordinary** → NORMAL, See also **extraordinary** → SURPRISING
▸ **extraordinarily** *adv.*: *She was an extraordinarily attractive girl.*

incredible /ɪnˈkredəbl/ (*informal*) extremely large or extremely good: *The prize money is an incredible $6 million.* ◇ *The demand for the new product has been quite incredible.* ◇ *I felt an incredible sense of relief.*
▸ **incredibly** *adv.*: *incredibly attractive/boring*

exceptional /ɪkˈsepʃənl/ unusually good or great: *Exceptional students are given free tuition.* ◇ *He was a man of exceptional personal warmth and charm.*
▸ **exceptionally** *adv.*: *an exceptionally gifted child*

unbelievable /ˌʌnbɪˈliːvəbl/ (*informal*) extreme; extremely bad or good: *The pain was unbelievable.* ◇ *I've had three unbelievable years with the team.* ◇ *It's unbelievable that* (= very shocking) *he was allowed to escape.*
▸ **unbelievably** *adv.*: *unbelievably beautiful/loud/painful*

phenomenal /fəˈnɒmɪnl; *AmE* -ˈnɑːm-/ very great or impressive: *There was a phenomenal response to the appeal.* ◇ *He has a phenomenal memory for facts and figures.* ◇ *Exports have been phenomenal this year.* See also **phenomenon** → MIRACLE
▸ **phenomenally** *adv.*: *phenomenally successful*

unusual [only before noun] (*written*) unusually great or good: *He's a man of unusual strength and courage.* ◇ *The conference has generated an unusual degree of interest.*
▸ **unusually** *adv.*: *an unusually talented designer*

NOTE EXCEPTIONAL OR UNUSUAL? Exceptional is stronger in degree than **unusual**; sb/sth that is **exceptional** is very unusual.

remember *verb*

remember · recall · bear sb/sth in mind · look back · recollect · think back · reminisce
These words all mean to keep in your mind or bring to your mind a fact or event.

PATTERNS AND COLLOCATIONS
▸ to remember / recall / bear in mind / recollect **that...**
▸ to remember / recall / bear in mind / recollect **how** / **what** / **where** / **when...**
▸ **It should be** remembered / borne in mind **that...**

▸ to remember / recall / bear in mind the **facts**
▸ to remember / recall sb's **name**
▸ to **vaguely** / **vividly** remember / recall sth
▸ **as far as I can** remember / recall / recollect

remember [T, I] (not usually used in the progressive tenses) to have or keep an image in your memory of an event, person or place from the past; to keep in your mind, or bring back to your mind, a fact or piece of information; to not forget to do sth: *This is Carla. Do you remember her?* ◇ *I don't remember my first day at school.* ◇ *Do you remember switching the lights off before we came out?* ◇ *As far as I can remember, this is the third time we've met.* ◇ *I'm sorry – I can't remember your name.* ◇ *Can you remember how much money we spent?* ◇ *You were going to help me with this. Remember?* ◇ *Remember that we're going out tonight.* ◇ *It should be remembered that the majority of accidents happen in the home.* ◇ **Remember to** *call me when you arrive!* ◇ *Did you remember your homework* (= to bring it)? ❶ Notice the difference between *remember doing sth* and *remember to do sth*: *I remember posting the letter* (= I have an image in my memory of doing it). ◇ *I remembered to post the letter* (= I didn't forget to do it). **OPP** forget → FORGET, forget → FAIL 1, forget → LEAVE 4, See also **remembrance** → MEMORY

recall [T, I] (not used in the progressive tenses) (*formal*) to remember a fact or event: *She could not recall his name.* ◇ *I can't recall meeting her before.* ◇ *If I recall correctly, he lives in Boston.* See also **recall** → MEMORY *noun*

bear sb/sth in 'mind, bear in 'mind that... *idiom* (not usually used in the progressive tenses) to remember an important fact when you are doing or considering sth: *Bear in mind that money is one of the main causes of marriage break-up.* ◇ *Bearing in mind the rapid population growth of recent years, these figures look optimistic.* See also **mind** → MEMORY

look 'back *phrasal verb* (not usually used in the progressive tenses) to think about a time in your past: *When I look back on my childhood, it seems as if it was always sunny.* ◇ *If there's one thing I've learnt it's this: never look back.*

recollect /ˌrekə'lekt/ [T, I] (not used in the progressive tenses) (*formal*) to remember an event or fact, especially by making an effort to remember it: *She could no longer recollect the details of the letter.* ◇ *I recollect him saying that it was dangerous.* ◇ *As far as I can recollect, she wasn't there on that occasion.* See also **recollection** → MEMORY

think 'back *phrasal verb* (not usually used in the progressive tenses) to think about sth that happened in the past: *I keep thinking back to the day I arrived here.* ◇ *Lying in bed, she thought back over the conversation.*

NOTE LOOK BACK OR THINK BACK? You might **look back on** a time in the past for the mixed pleasure and sadness of remembering happy/sad times that are now over, or just to consider how things have changed. You might **think back to/over** an event in the distant or recent past because sth about it still interests or bothers you and you cannot get it out of your mind.

reminisce /ˌremɪ'nɪs/ [I] (*rather formal*) to think, talk or write about a happy time in your past: *We spent a happy evening reminiscing about the past.* See also **reminiscence** → MEMORY

remind sb of sb/sth *phrasal verb*

remind sb of sb/sth · evoke · conjure sth up · recall · take sb back
These words all mean to to bring a feeling, memory or image into your mind.

PATTERNS AND COLLOCATIONS
▸ to remind sb of / evoke / conjure up / recall / take sb back to **the past** / **past times**
▸ to evoke / conjure up a / an **memory** / **picture** / **image** / **feeling**
▸ to **vividly** remind sb of sth / evoke sth / conjure sth up

re'mind sb of sb/sth *phrasal verb* (not used in the progressive tenses) (of a person, place, thing or event) to make you think of another person, place, etc. because they are similar in some way: *You remind me of your dad when you say that.* ◇ *That smell reminds me of France.*

evoke /ɪ'vəʊk; AmE ɪ'voʊk/ [T] (*written*) to bring a memory, feeling or image into your mind: *The music evoked memories of her youth.* ◇ *His case is unlikely to evoke public sympathy.* See also **evocation** → DESCRIPTION

conjure sth 'up *phrasal verb* to make sth appear as a picture in your mind: *He strained to conjure up her face and voice, but they had vanished.*

NOTE EVOKE OR CONJURE STH UP? **Conjure sth up** can be more visual than **evoke** and usually means to remember sth in pictures or images. **Evoke** is used more for talking about memories and feelings: *He strained to evoke her face.* ◇ *His case is unlikely to conjure up sympathy.*

recall [T] (not used in the progressive tenses) (*formal*) to remind you of sb/sth: *The poem recalls Eliot's 'The Waste Land'.*

take sb 'back *phrasal verb* to make sb remember a time in the past: *The smell of the sea took him back to his childhood.* ◇ *That song takes me back 30 years.*

remove *verb*

1 remove stains/obstacles
2 remove sb from power

1 See also the entries for ABOLISH and ERADICATE
remove · get rid of sb/sth · eliminate · dispose of sb/sth · discard · dump · throw sth away/out · shed · dispense with sb/sth · scrap
These words all mean to make yourself free of sb/sth that you do not want or need.

PATTERNS AND COLLOCATIONS
▸ to remove / get rid of / eliminate sth **from** sth
▸ to remove / get rid of / eliminate / dispose of / discard / dump **waste**
▸ to remove / discard / dump / dispose of / throw away **rubbish** / **garbage** / **trash**
▸ to remove / get rid of / dispose of / dump a (**dead**) **body**
▸ to remove / get rid of / eliminate / dispose of a **problem**
▸ to eliminate / shed / scrap **jobs**
▸ to remove / discard / shed your **jacket** / **clothes**, etc.
▸ to remove / eliminate / discard / dispense with / scrap sth **altogether**
▸ to **entirely** remove / eliminate / dispose of / discard / dispense with sth
▸ to **completely** remove / eliminate / discard / dispense with / scrap sth
▸ to **quickly** remove / get rid of / eliminate / dispose of / discard / shed / dispense with sth
▸ to **easily** remove / eliminate / dispose of / discard sth

remove [T] to take sth away or make it disappear, especially because it is unpleasant, dirty or a problem: *the best way to remove stains* ◇ *She has had the tumour removed.* ◇ *A subsequent agreement removed the major obstacles to negotiations.* ◇ *The news removed any doubts about the company's future.*
▸ **removal** *noun* [U]: *stain removal* ◇ *the removal of trade barriers*

get 'rid of sb/sth *phrase* (*rather informal*) to make yourself free of sb/sth that is annoying you or that you do not want: *Try and get rid of your visitors before I get there.* ◇ *Get rid of weed seedlings before they grow into plants.* ◇ *I can't get rid of this headache.* ◇ *We got rid of all the old furniture.*

eliminate /ɪ'lɪmɪneɪt/ [T] (*rather formal*) to get rid of sb/sth that is a problem for you: *Credit cards eliminate the need to carry a lot of cash.* ◇ *This diet claims to eliminate toxins from the body.* ◇ *They attempted to eliminate him as a political rival.*

NOTE ELIMINATE OR GET RID OF SB/STH? The main difference between these expressions is register. **Get rid of sb/sth** is usually used in more informal and/or personal contexts. **Eliminate** is rather formal; it is NOT used to talk about physically throwing sth away: ~~We eliminated the old furniture.~~ If you **get rid of** a person you make them go away; you **eliminate** a person *as sth* by forcing them to give up a particular role; if you just **eliminate** sb, you kill them. See also **eliminate** → KILL

▶ **elimination** *noun* [U]: *the elimination of disease/ poverty/crime*

dispose of sb/sth *phrasal verb* (*rather formal*) to get rid of sb/sth that you do not want or cannot keep, especially by putting it somewhere carefully so that it will not be a problem: *the difficulties of disposing of nuclear waste* ◇ *Markets such as these are often used by thieves to dispose of stolen property.*

▶ **disposal** *noun* [U]: *a bomb disposal squad* ◇ *sewage disposal systems*

discard /dɪsˈkɑːd; *AmE* -ˈkɑːrd/ [T] (*formal*) to get rid of sth that you no longer want or need, especially by just leaving it somewhere and/or not giving it any more attention: *The floor was littered with discarded newspapers.* ◇ *He had discarded his jacket because of the heat.* ◇ *Most of the data was discarded as unreliable.*

dump [T, I] (*rather informal, disapproving*) to get rid of sth that you do not want, especially in a place which is not suitable: *Too much toxic waste is being dumped at sea.* ◇ *The dead body was dumped by the roadside.* ◇ *Any vessel dumping at sea without a licence will be prosecuted.*

throw sth aˈway/ˈout *phrasal verb* to get rid of sth that you no longer want, especially by putting it in the bin: *I don't need that – you can throw it away.* ◇ *The fish was off – I had to throw it out.*

shed [T] (*rather informal, especially journalism*) to get rid of sth that is no longer wanted, especially if you do not care what happens to it: *The defence industry is in decline and shedding jobs.* ◇ *It's a quick way to shed pounds* (= lose extra weight or fat on your body) *but it won't make you healthier.* ◇ *Museums have been trying hard to shed their stuffy image.* ◇ *Her mother had shed ten years since her marriage to Douglas* (= looked ten years younger). ❶ In this meaning **shed** usually collocates with *weight, pounds, jobs, staff, workers, employees, image, responsibility, burden* or *years*.

diˈspense with sb/sth *phrasal verb* (*formal*) to stop using sb/sth because you no longer need them/it: *Debit cards dispense with the need for cash altogether.* ◇ *The company now has no choice but to dispense with his services* (= to fire him). ◇ *I think we can dispense with the formalities* (= speak openly and naturally with each other).

scrap (-pp-) [T, often passive] to get rid of a vehicle or machine that is no longer useful: *The oldest of the aircraft should be scrapped.* See also **scrap** → WASTE *noun*

---

2 See the Topic Map for CONFLICT on p.896

remove · oust · overthrow · topple · depose · bring sb/sth down · usurp
These words all mean to make sb such as a leader or government lose their position of power.

PATTERNS AND COLLOCATIONS
▶ to remove / oust / depose sb **as** leader, chairman, etc.
▶ to remove / oust sb **from power**
▶ to remove / depose sb **from** their position
▶ to remove / oust / overthrow / topple / depose / bring down a **president / regime / government**
▶ to remove / oust a **chairman / director**
▶ to oust / overthrow / topple / depose a **leader / dictator**
▶ to overthrow / depose a **ruler / king / queen**
▶ to overthrow / bring down **communism / capitalism**

remove [T] to dismiss sb from their job or position: *After his arrest on corruption charges, he was immediately removed as party president.* ◇ *The elections removed the government from power.* ◇ *The shareholders of a company have the power to remove the board.*

▶ **removal** *noun* [U]: *events leading to the removal of the president from office*

oust /aʊst/ [T] (*written*) to force sb out of a job or position of power, especially in order to take their place: *He was ousted as chairman.* ◇ *The rebels finally managed to oust the government from power.*

overthrow /ˌəʊvəˈθrəʊ; *AmE* ˌoʊvərˈθroʊ/ [T] to force a leader or government out of power: *The president was overthrown in a military coup.* ◇ *They succeeded in overthrowing the fascist dictatorship.* See also **overthrow** → OVERTHROW *noun*

topple [T] (*rather informal, especially journalism*) to force a leader or government out of power: *The armed forces toppled the elected government in a bloodless coup.*

NOTE OVERTHROW OR TOPPLE? **Topple** is slightly more informal than **overthrow**, used especially in journalism.

depose /dɪˈpəʊz; *AmE* dɪˈpoʊz/ [T] (*written*) to remove a leader, ruler or government from power: *He deposed his father in a coup in 1970.*

ˌbring sb/sth ˈdown *phrasal verb* (of a person, group or situation) to cause a leader or government to lose power: *A small group of rebel MPs brought the coalition government down.* ◇ *The scandal may bring down the government.* ❶ As with the other verbs in this group, a person or group of people, such as the army or rebels, can **bring down** a leader or government. A situation, such as a problem, dispute or scandal, can also **bring sb down** by causing them to become so unpopular that they are forced to resign or are not elected again.

usurp /juːˈzɜːp; *AmE* -ˈzɜːrp/ [T] (*formal*) to take sb's position and/or power without having the right to do this: *He attempted to usurp the principal's authority.* ◇ *She is scheming to take my place and usurp my power.*

reorganize (*BrE* also **-ise**) *verb*

reorganize · restructure · redesign · rearrange · reshape · shake sth up · reshuffle
These words all mean to change the way in which sth has been arranged or structured.

PATTERNS AND COLLOCATIONS
▶ to reorganize / restructure / redesign / reshape a **system**
▶ to reorganize / restructure / reshape / reshuffle the **government**
▶ to reorganize / restructure a **company**
▶ to reorganize / restructure / redesign sth **completely**

reorganize (*BrE* also **-ise**) /riˈɔːɡənaɪz; *AmE* -ˈɔːrɡ-/ [T, I] to organize sth in a new and different way: *The laboratory was reorganized as a separate establishment.* ◇ *By 1998, the company had reorganized into fewer key businesses.*

▶ **reorganization** (*BrE* also **-isation**) *noun* [U, C]: *the reorganization of the school system*

restructure /ˌriːˈstrʌktʃə(r)/ [T, I] (*especially business*) to organize sth such as a system or company in a new and different way: *The company has been restructured to strengthen its international position.* ◇ *The company has restructured by selling off businesses.*

▶ **restructuring** *noun* [U, C, usually sing.]: *The company is undergoing major restructuring.*

NOTE REORGANIZE OR RESTRUCTURE? In many cases you can use either word, but **restructure** is used especially in business contexts; **reorganize** is a more general word.

redesign /ˌriːdɪˈzaɪn/ [T] to design sth again, in a different way: *The old Empire Theatre is being completely redesigned and refurbished.* ❶ Things which might be **redesigned** include a *machine*, a *camera*, a *plane*, a *building*, a *book*, a *magazine* or a *newspaper*.

rearrange /ˌriːəˈreɪndʒ/ [T] to change the position or order of things: *We've rearranged the furniture in the bedroom.* ❶ Note that you can **rearrange** a room OR the things in it: *We've arranged the bedroom/the furniture in the bedroom.*

reshape /ˌriːˈʃeɪp/ [T] to change the shape or structure of sth: *Their policies set out to reshape the welfare system.* ◇ *Tides and storms inexorably reshaped the land.* ❶ Things that can be **reshaped** include *policies, practices, systems* and *procedures*, as well as concrete things such as a piece of land or a town or city.

ˌ**shake sth ˈup** *phrasal verb* (*rather informal, especially journalism*) to make important changes in an organization, profession, etc. in order to make it more efficient: *The Government plans to shake up the National Health Service.*
▶ ˈ**shake-up** [C, usually sing.]: *What the industry needs is a good shake-up.*

reshuffle /ˌriːˈʃʌfl/ [T] to change around the jobs that a group of people do, especially in a government or sports team: *The Prime Minister eventually decided against reshuffling the Cabinet.* ◇ *After a six-game losing streak the coach decided to reshuffle the starting line-up.*
▶ **reshuffle** /ˈriːʃʌfl/ *noun* [C]: *a Cabinet reshuffle*

repair *noun*

repair · maintenance · service · servicing · upkeep
These are all words for the process or cost of keeping sth in good condition or putting it in good condition after being broken or damaged.

PATTERNS AND COLLOCATIONS
▶ **essential** / **car** repairs / maintenance / servicing
▶ to **take sth in for** repair / a service
▶ sb is **responsible for** repairs / the maintenance / the upkeep of sth
▶ repair / maintenance / servicing **costs** / **work**

repair [C, usually pl., U] an act of mending sth: *They agreed to pay for the cost of any repairs.* ◇ *The building was in need of repair.* ◇ *The car was damaged* **beyond repair** (= it was too badly damaged to be repaired). ◇ *The hotel is currently* **under repair** (= being repaired). See also **repair → STATE** *noun*

maintenance /ˈmeɪntənəns/ [U] the act of keeping sth in good condition by checking or repairing it regularly: *The school pays for heating and the maintenance of the buildings.* ◇ *Several lines are closed due to essential maintenance work.* See also **maintain → MAINTAIN 2**

service [C, U] an examination of a vehicle or machine followed by any work that is necessary to keep it operating well: *I've taken the car in for a service.* ◇ *We offer excellent after-sales service on all our goods.* See also **service → MAINTAIN** *verb* 2

servicing [U] (*especially BrE*) the act of checking and repairing a vehicle or machine to keep it in good condition: *Like any other type of equipment it requires regular servicing.* See also **service → MAINTAIN 2**

NOTE MAINTENANCE, SERVICE OR SERVICING? Maintenance of a building or machine is a continuous process that involves checking it regularly and doing repairs as they are needed. A **service** is a single act of checking a vehicle or machine and doing any repairs that are needed. **Servicing** is the fact of giving sth a service on a regular basis.

upkeep /ˈʌpkiːp/ [U] the cost or process of keeping sth in good condition: *Tenants are responsible for the upkeep of the property.* See also **keep sth up → MAINTAIN 2**

repair *verb*

repair · fix · mend · overhaul · patch · darn
These words all mean to work on sth that is damaged, torn or broken so that it is in good condition or working correctly again.

PATTERNS AND COLLOCATIONS
▶ to repair / fix / mend a **road** / **fence** / **roof** / **bike** / **puncture**
▶ to repair / fix / overhaul an **engine**
▶ to repair / fix a **car** / **television** / **fault** / **defect** / **leak**
▶ to repair / fix the **heating** / **damage**
▶ to repair / mend / patch **shoes** / **clothes**
▶ to **have** / **get** sth repaired / fixed / mended / overhauled

repair [T] to work on sth that is broken, damaged or torn so that it is in good condition or works correctly again: *We'll need to get someone to repair the roof.* ◇ *The damage to the ship had been repaired.* ◇ *Are you going to get the television repaired?* ◇ *The human body has an amazing capacity to repair itself.* See also **repair → STATE** *noun*

fix [T] to repair sth: *I had to take the car into the garage to get it fixed.* ◇ *We're not moving in until the heating's fixed.* ◇ *Mommy, can you fix my toy?*

NOTE REPAIR OR FIX? In British English **repair** is the most general word; **fix** is slightly more informal and is used especially to talk about repairing machines or equipment. In American English **fix** is the most usual word, used to talk about repairing anything that is broken or damaged, and **repair** sounds rather formal.

mend [T] (*especially BrE*) to repair sth that is broken, damaged or torn so that it can be used again: *He mended shoes for a living.* ◇ (*BrE*) *Could you mend my bike?* ❶ In American English, **mend** is only used about clothes, etc. that need to be repaired.

overhaul /ˌəʊvəˈhɔːl; AmE ˌoʊvərˈh-/ [T] to examine every part of a machine or system and make any necessary changes or repairs: *The engine has been completely overhauled.* ◇ *The company was called in to overhaul the railroad system.*

patch [T] to cover a hole or worn place, especially in clothes, with a piece of fabric or other material: *He was wearing patched jeans.* ◇ *We need to patch that hole in the roof.* ❶ To **patch sth up** is to repair sth, especially in a temporary way by adding a new piece of material: *Just to patch the boat up will cost £10 000.* To **patch sb up** is to treat sb's injuries, especially quickly or temporarily: *The doctor will soon patch you up.*

darn [T, I] to repair a hole in a piece of clothing by sewing stitches across the hole: *He was sitting darning his socks.*

repay *verb* See also the entry for RETURN 2

repay · pay sb back · compensate · reimburse · refund
These words all mean to pay money to sb either because you owe it to them or because you have hurt them or caused them to lose or spend money.

PATTERNS AND COLLOCATIONS
▶ to repay / pay sb back / compensate / reimburse / refund sb **for** sth
▶ to repay / pay sth back / refund sth **to** sb
▶ to repay / pay back / reimburse / refund **money**
▶ to repay / compensate / reimburse / refund sb / sth **fully** / **in full**

repay /rɪˈpeɪ/ [T] to return money that you borrowed from sb: *He has lost his job and is unable to repay his debts.* ◇ *I'll repay you for the ticket next week.* See also **repayment → PAYMENT**
▶ **repayable** *adj.*: *The loan is repayable in monthly instalments.*

ˌ**pay sb ˈback (sth)**, ˌ**pay sth ˈback** *phrasal verb* to repay money that you borrowed from sb: *I'll pay you back next week.* ◇ *Did he ever pay you back that $100 he owes you?* ◇ *You can pay back the loan over a period of three years.*

NOTE REPAY OR PAY SB BACK? Repay often sounds more formal than **pay sb back**; **pay sb back** is used especially in spoken or informal English, or when talking about less formal arrangements, for example when you have borrowed a small amount of money from a friend, rather than a large amount from a bank.

compensate /ˈkɒmpenseɪt; AmE ˈkɑːm-/ [T] to pay sb money because you have hurt them, caused them to lose money or damaged sth that they own: *Her lawyers say she should be compensated both for her injuries and for the suffering she has been caused.* See also **compensation → COMPENSATION**

reimburse /ˌriːɪmˈbɜːs; AmE -ˈbɜːrs/ [T] (formal) to pay back money to sb which you have caused them to spend or lose: We will reimburse any expenses incurred while you are on company business. ◇ You will be reimbursed for any loss or damage caused by our company. See also **reimbursement** → COMPENSATION

refund /rɪˈfʌnd/ to pay back money to sb, especially because they have paid too much or because they are not satisfied with sth they bought: Tickets cannot be exchanged or money refunded. ◇ We will refund your money to you in full if you are not entirely satisfied. See also **refund** → COMPENSATION noun
▶ **refundable** adj.: Tickets are not refundable.

repeat verb

1 I'm sorry – could you repeat that?
2 Try not to repeat your mistakes.

1 repeat · echo · reiterate · restate
These words all mean to say or write sth again or more than once.

PATTERNS AND COLLOCATIONS
▶ to repeat / reiterate / restate **that...**
▶ to repeat / echo / reiterate a **warning / sentiment**
▶ to reiterate / restate your **commitment / support / opposition**
▶ to **merely / simply** repeat / echo / reiterate / restate sth

repeat [T] to say or write sth again or more than once: I'm sorry – could you repeat that? ◇ She kept repeating his name softly over and over again. ◇ The president's opponents have been repeating their calls for his resignation. ◇ Do say if I'm repeating myself (= if I have already said this). See also **repeat** → CONVEY, **go over sth** → PRACTISE, **recap** → SUMMARIZE
▶ **repetition** /ˌrepəˈtɪʃn/ noun [U, C]: learning by repetition

echo /ˈekəʊ; AmE ˈekoʊ/ [T] (especially written) to repeat an idea or opinion because you agree with it; to repeat what sb else has just said, especially because you find it surprising: This is a view echoed by many on the right of the party. ◇ 'He's gone!' Viv echoed incredulously. See also **echo** → ECHO
▶ **echo** noun [C]: The speech **found an echo** in the hearts of many of the audience (= they agreed with it).

reiterate /riˈɪtəreɪt/ [T] (formal) to repeat sth that you have already said, especially to emphasize it: The government has reiterated its commitment to economic reform. ◇ Let me reiterate that we are fully committed to this policy. ❶ People **reiterate** things such as their commitment, support, willingness, determination and opposition.
▶ **reiteration** noun [sing., U]: a reiteration of her previous statement

restate /ˌriːˈsteɪt/ [T] (formal) to say sth again or in a different way, especially so that it is more clearly or strongly expressed: They restated their belief in the existence of a 'hidden agenda'. ❶ **Restate** is typically used to talk about beliefs, commitment, intentions, opposition and support.

2 See also the entry for SIMULATE
repeat · replicate · duplicate · redo
These words all mean to do or produce sth again or more than once.

PATTERNS AND COLLOCATIONS
▶ to repeat / replicate the **results**
▶ to **merely / simply** repeat / replicate / duplicate sth
▶ to repeat / replicate / duplicate sth **exactly**

repeat [T, I] to do or produce sth again or more than once: Try not to repeat your mistakes. ◇ The programmes will be repeated next year. ◇ They are hoping to repeat last year's victory. ◇ There is no point in merely repeating what we've done before. ◇ Lift and lower the right leg 20 times. Repeat with the left leg.
▶ **repeat** noun [C]: (rather informal) A repeat of the 1906 earthquake could kill thousands of people. ◇ (business) a repeat order (= for a further supply of the same goods)
▶ **repetition** /ˌrepəˈtɪʃn/ noun [C]: We do not want to see a repetition of last year's tragic events.

replicate /ˈreplɪkeɪt/ [T] (formal) to copy an experiment or system exactly; to produce the same results as before: Subsequent experiments failed to replicate these findings.

duplicate /ˈdjuːplɪkeɪt; AmE ˈduː-/ [T] (rather formal) to do sth again, especially when it is unnecessary: There's no point in duplicating work already done.
▶ **duplication** noun [U, C]: We want to avoid unnecessary duplication.

redo /ˌriːˈduː/ [T] to do sth again or differently: A whole day's work had to be redone. ◇ We've just redone the bathroom (= decorated it again). ❶ **Redo** is used in two main ways: to talk about having to do sth again because you failed to do it well enough the first time: to redo your sums/exams/test/work, or to talk about improving the appearance of a room in a house by painting the walls, changing the carpets, etc.

replace verb

1 Teachers will never be replaced by computers.
2 replace the old carpets

1 replace · stand in for sb/sth · fill in for sb/sth · substitute for sb/sth · cover for sb · deputize · relieve
These words all mean to take the place of sb/sth else in a particular role or situation.

PATTERNS AND COLLOCATIONS
▶ to stand in / fill in / substitute / cover / deputize **for** sb
▶ to stand in / fill in / cover for a **colleague**

replace [T] to be used instead of sb/sth else; to do sth instead of sb/sth else: The new design will eventually replace all existing models. ◇ Teachers will never be replaced by computers in the classroom. ◇ She replaced her husband as the local doctor.

,stand ˈin for sb/sth phrasal verb to take the place of sb/ sth else, especially sb/sth more important or famous: My assistant will stand in for me while I'm away. ◇ The scenes were filmed in North Wales, which had to stand in for the North West Frontier.

,fill ˈin for sb/sth phrasal verb (especially AmE) to stand in for sb/sth: He called me one Saturday morning and asked me to fill in for him. ◇ Most of the locations filling in for Venezuela are really in the United States.

NOTE STAND IN FOR SB/STH OR FILL IN FOR SB/STH? These verbs are used in the same way, but **stand in for sb/sth** is used more in British English and **fill in for sb/sth** is used more in American English.

substitute for sb/sth phrasal verb (rather formal) to take the place of sb/sth else: Nothing can substitute for the advice your doctor is able to give you. ◇ One of her colleagues agreed to substitute for her at the last minute. See also **substitution** → EXCHANGE

cover for sb phrasal verb to do sb's work or duties while they are away: I'm covering for Jane while she's on leave. ◇ You may be asked to cover for employees who are off sick.

NOTE STAND IN, FILL IN OR COVER? You **cover for** your colleagues at work, especially people who do similar jobs to you and have the same status. You **stand/fill in for** a person who is more senior than you in your organization, or a performer who is more famous and popular than you. When you **cover for sb** you are often considered to be doing them a favour; sb who **stands/ fills in for sb** is often seen as second best.

deputize (BrE also **-ise**) /ˈdepjutaɪz/ [I] (formal) to do sth that sb in a higher position than you would usually do: Ms Green has asked me to deputize for her at the meeting.

relieve /rɪ'liːv/ [T] to replace sb who is on duty: *to relieve a driver/sentry* ◇ *You'll be relieved at 6 o'clock.*

2 replace · switch · change · exchange · substitute · swap · trade · reverse · barter
These words all mean to remove sb/sth and put another person or thing in their place.

PATTERNS AND COLLOCATIONS
▶ to switch/change/exchange/substitute/swap/trade/barter A **for** B
▶ to replace/substitute/switch B **with** A
▶ to switch/exchange/swap/reverse A **and** B
▶ to replace/change a **battery/bulb/fuse/tyre/wheel**
▶ to switch/exchange/swap/reverse **roles**
▶ to change/exchange/swap/trade **places**
▶ to change/swap **seats/clothes**
▶ to exchange/swap/trade **stories/jokes**
▶ to exchange/swap **experiences/news/phone numbers**
▶ to exchange/trade **insults**
▶ to **simply** replace/switch/change/exchange/substitute/reverse sth
▶ to **easily** replace/switch/change/substitute/swap sth

replace [T] (*rather formal*) to remove sb/sth and put a different or better person or thing in their place: *He will be difficult to replace when he leaves.* ◇ *All the old carpets need replacing.* ◇ *She had an operation to replace both hips.* See also **replacement** → EXCHANGE

switch [T] (*rather informal*) to put one thing in the place of another, and put the second thing in the place of the first: *The dates of the last two exams have been switched.* ◇ *Do you think she'll notice if I switch my glass with hers?* ◇ *I see you've **switched** the furniture **around** (= changed its position).*

change [T] to replace one thing, person or service with sth new or different; to take sb else's position or place while they take yours: *Marie changed her name when she got married.* ◇ *That back tyre needs changing.* ◇ *At half-time the teams change ends.* ◇ *Can I change seats with you?* ◇ *I want to change my doctor.* ❶ The usual word in American English used to talk about giving sth back for a better thing of the same kind, is **exchange**; this sounds rather formal in British English: (*BrE*) *We changed the car for a bigger one.* ◇ (*AmE*) *We exchanged the car for a bigger one.*

exchange [T] to give sth to sb and at the same time receive the same type of thing from them; to give or return sth that you have and get sth different or better instead: *We use the forum to exchange ideas.* ◇ *I shook hands and exchanged a few words with the manager.* ◇ *Juliet and David **exchanged glances** (= they looked at each other).* ◇ *The two men **exchanged blows** (= hit each other).* ◇ *You can exchange your currency for dollars in the hotel.* ◇ *If it doesn't fit, take it back and the store will exchange it.* See also **exchange** → EXCHANGE *noun*, **exchange** → DISCUSSION *noun*

substitute [T] to use sb/sth instead of sb/sth else: *Margarine can be substituted for butter in this recipe.* ◇ *Butter can be substituted with margarine in this recipe.* ◇ *Gerrard was substituted in the second half after a knee injury (= sb else played instead of Gerrard in the second half).* ❶ You can *substitute A for B* or *substitute B with A*: in both cases you use A instead of B. You can also just say that you *substitute sth*: in this case the context needs to make clear whether the 'sth' is being used instead of sth, or is replacing sth else. See also **substitution** → EXCHANGE

swap (also **swop**) /swɒp/ *AmE* swɑːp/ (**-pp-**) [I, T] to exchange sth with sb: *I've finished this magazine. Can I swap with you?* ◇ *I swapped my red scarf for her blue one.* ◇ *We spent the evening in the bar swapping stories (= telling each other stories) about our travels.* ◇ (*especially BrE*) *Can we swap places? I can't see the screen.* ❶ Especially in British English, **swap** can also mean to give or return sth that you have and get sth different or better instead: *I think I'll swap this sweater for one in another colour.* See also **swap** → EXCHANGE *noun*

trade [T] (*especially AmE or journalism*) to exchange sth with sb: *She traded her posters for his CD.* ◇ *I wouldn't mind trading places with her for a day.* ◇ *Cabinet colleagues traded insults over the future of the pound.*

> **NOTE** SWITCH, EXCHANGE, SWAP OR TRADE? **Switch** is often used when one thing is exchanged for another without sb else being asked or even knowing about it: *The two babies had been switched at birth.* ◇ ~~*The two babies had been exchanged/swapped/traded at birth.*~~ **Exchange** is more formal than **swap** or **trade** and is often used in fixed phrases when people look at or talk to each other: *to exchange glances/a few words* ◇ ~~*to swap/trade glances/a few words.*~~ You can also *exchange information/ideas.* **Swap** is used more for physical things, although you can *swap stories/jokes*; **trade** is used for things and *places, stories, jokes* and *insults* in American English; in British English it is mostly used just for *stories, jokes* and *insults*, not physical things. In British English you *change/swap places*.

reverse [T] to exchange the positions or functions of two people or things: *It felt as if we had reversed our roles of parent and child.* ◇ *She used to work for me, but our situations are now reversed.* ❶ In this meaning, **reverse** collocates with *roles, situations* and *positions.* See also **reversal** → EXCHANGE *noun*

barter [T, I] to exchange goods, property or services for other goods, etc. without using money: *The local people bartered wheat for farm machinery.* ◇ *The prisoners tried to barter with the guards for items like writing paper and books.* See also **barter** → EXCHANGE *noun*

replacement *noun*

replacement · substitute · reserve · surrogate · relief · understudy · stand-in · cover · proxy
These are all words for a person or thing that you use or have instead of the one you normally use or have.

PATTERNS AND COLLOCATIONS
▶ a replacement/a substitute/a surrogate/an understudy/a stand-in/cover/a proxy/a stopgap **for** sb/sth
▶ (an) **adequate** replacement/substitute/stand-in/cover
▶ a/an **good/satisfactory/appropriate/suitable/likely/possible/ideal/poor** replacement/substitute
▶ to **act as** a replacement/a substitute/surrogate/understudy/stand-in/proxy
▶ to **get** a replacement/a substitute/cover
▶ to **appoint** a replacement/substitute/proxy
▶ to **go on as/use sth as** a replacement/substitute

replacement [C] (often used as an adjective) a thing that replaces sth, especially because the first thing is old or broken; a person who replaces another person in an organization, especially in their job: *a hip replacement* ◇ *replacement windows* ◇ *If your passport is stolen you should apply for a replacement immediately.* ◇ *We need to find a replacement for Sue.* See also **replacement** → EXCHANGE

substitute [C] a person or thing that you use or have instead of the one you normally use or have; an extra player who plays in a sports team when one of the other players is injured or not available to play: *a meat/milk substitute* ◇ *The book will teach you the theory but **there's no substitute for** practical experience.* ◇ *The local bus service was a poor substitute for their car.* ◇ *I regarded them as a substitute family.* ◇ *He was brought on as a substitute after half-time.* ❶ In informal language a **substitute** in sports can be called a **sub**. See also **substitution** → EXCHANGE

reserve [C] (*especially BrE*) a substitute player in a sports team: *The team consists of three competitors plus one reserve.* ❶ **The reserves** (*especially BrE*) [pl.] are a sports team that plays when the usual one is not available. **The reserve** [sing.]/**the reserves** [pl.] (*BrE, AmE*) is an extra military or police force that is not part of a country's regular forces, but is available to be used when needed: *The missile landed on a US army reserve barracks.*

surrogate /'sʌrəgət; AmE 'sɜːr-/ [C] (often used as an adjective) (*rather formal*) a person or thing that takes the place of, or is used instead of, sb/sth else: *She saw him as a sort of surrogate father.* ◇ *For these people, television is a surrogate for real life.* ❶ In everyday English, **surrogate** is most often used to talk about people who take the place of real parents. However, a **surrogate mother** is usually a woman who actually gives birth to a baby for another woman who is unable to have babies herself. When **surrogate** is used to talk about things, it is a more formal way of saying *substitute*.

relief [C+sing./pl. v.] (often used as an adjective) a person or group of people that replaces another when they have finished working for the day or when they are sick: *The next crew relief comes on duty at 9 o'clock.* ◇ *We have a pool of relief drivers available to us.*

understudy /'ʌndəstʌdi; AmE -dərs-/ [C] an actor who learns the part of another actor in a play so that they can play that part if necessary: *She worked as an understudy to Elaine Page.*

'stand-in [C] (*rather informal*) a person who does sb's job for a short time when they are not available; a person who replaces an actor in some scenes in a film, especially dangerous ones: *I acted as Tom's stand-in when he was away.* ◇ *Most of the stunts are performed by stand-ins.*

cover [U] the fact of sb doing another person's job when they are away or when there are not enough staff: *It's the manager's job to organize cover for employees who are absent.*

proxy [C, U] (*formal or law*) a person who has been given the authority to represent sb else: *Your proxy will need to sign the form on your behalf.*

report noun

1 commission a report on the health service
2 newspaper reports
3 a progress/medical report
4 unconfirmed reports of a shooting

---

1 report · study · investigation · review · survey
These are all words for an official document written by a person or group that has examined a particular situation or problem.

PATTERNS AND COLLOCATIONS
▸ a report / an investigation / a survey **into** sth
▸ a report / a study / an investigation / a review / a survey **by** sb
▸ a/an **new / recent / important / major / comprehensive / wide-ranging / extensive** report / study / investigation / review / survey
▸ the **latest** report / study / investigation / review / survey
▸ a/ an **government / official / public / independent** report / study / investigation / review / survey
▸ to **do** a report / a study / an investigation / a review / a survey
▸ to **undertake** a study / an investigation / a review / a survey
▸ to **order** a report / a study / an investigation / a review
▸ to **commission** a report / study / review / survey
▸ to **call for** a report / an investigation / a review
▸ to **publish / release / read** a report / study / review / survey
▸ a report / study / investigation / review / survey **finds / shows / reveals / suggests** sth
▸ a report / study / review **calls for / proposes / recommends** sth

report [C] an official document written by a group of people who have examined a particular situation or problem: *The committee will publish their report on the health service in a few weeks.* ◇ *We will have to wait until they deliver their report before we can come to any conclusions.*

study [C] a piece of research that examines a subject or question in detail, especially in order to recommend what should be done: *A recent study revealed an unacceptable level of air pollution in the city.* ◇ *The company undertook an in-depth feasibility study* (= a study into whether sth is possible and how it could be done) *before adopting the*

new system. ◇ *A **comparative study*** (= a study comparing two things) *was carried out into the environmental costs of different energy sources.* ❶ A **case study** is a detailed study of the development of a person, group or situation over a period of time. See also **study** → RESEARCH *noun*, **study** → EXAMINE *verb*

investigation [C, U] a formal or academic examination of a situation, especially in order to discover the facts: *The government has ordered an official investigation into the matter.* ◇ *Closer investigation showed this idea to be untenable.* See also **investigate** → INVESTIGATE

review [C] a report on a subject or series of events: *The first chapter presents a critical review of the existing preschool education system.* ❶ **Review** is often used to talk about a report that considers all the research and writing about a subject or events over a period of time, and gives an opinion about the current situation or state of knowledge. See also **review** → EXAMINE *verb*

survey /'sɜːveɪ; AmE 'sɜːrveɪ/ [C] a general study or description of sth: *They are carrying out a survey of small businesses in London.* See also **survey** → EXAMINE *verb*

---

2 See the Topic Map for THE MEDIA on p.900, See also the entry for DESCRIPTION

report · story · account · version · commentary · item
These are all words for a written or spoken description of events.

PATTERNS AND COLLOCATIONS
▸ a report / a story / an item **about** sth
▸ a report / commentary **on** sth
▸ a report / a story / an account / a version / an item **is based on** sth
▸ a **brief / short** report / story / account / item
▸ a **full** report / story / account / version / commentary
▸ a **true / false / conflicting** report / story / account / version
▸ a **news** report / story / item
▸ the **lead** story / item in a newspaper
▸ to **give** a report / an account / your version / a commentary

report [C] a written or spoken description of an event, especially one that is published or broadcast: *Are these newspaper reports true?* ◇ *And now over to Jim Muir, for a report on the South African election.* ◇ *I've asked Jen for a full report of the meeting.* ◇ *Police received reports of drug dealing in the area.* See also **report** → DESCRIBE *verb*, See also the entry for NEWS

story [C] a description, often spoken, of what happened to sb or of how sth happened; a report of events in a newspaper, magazine or news broadcast: *The police didn't believe her story.* ◇ *We must stick to our story about the accident.* ◇ *I can't decide until I've heard both sides of the story* (= two different people's account of the same event). ◇ *the front-page/cover story* ◇ *Now for a summary of the day's main stories.* ◇ *He was covering the story* (= reporting on the events) *for the 'Glasgow Herald'.* See also **story** → STORY 1

account [C] a written or spoken description of sth that has happened: *The diaries contained detailed accounts of the writer's experiences in China.* ◇ *I've never been there, but it's a lovely place by all accounts* (= according to what people say).

NOTE REPORT OR ACCOUNT? A **report** is always of recent events, especially news. An **account** may be of recent or past events.

version [C] a description of an event from the point of view of a particular person or group of people: *She gave us her version of what had happened that day.* ◇ *Their versions of how the accident happened conflict.*

commentary /'kɒməntri; AmE 'kɑːmənteri/ [C, U] (*especially BrE*) a spoken description of an event that is given while it is happening, especially on the radio or television: *a sports commentary on the radio* ◇ *BBC1 will give a live commentary on the election results.* ◇ *He kept up a running commentary on everyone who came in.* ❶ In American English people usually use other ways of expressing this idea, without using the word **commentary**: *We'll be bringing you all the action live beginning at 8 o'clock.* ◇ *We'll have all the play-by-play from the Superbowl.* However, *running commentary* is a common collocation in both British and American English.

item [C] a single piece of news in a newspaper, on television, etc: *There was an item on the radio about women engineers.*

3 report · statement · return
These are all words for a spoken or written description of sth containing information that is needed by sb.

PATTERNS AND COLLOCATIONS
▸ in a / the report / statement / return
▸ a **detailed** / **full** report / statement
▸ an **annual** report / statement / return
▸ a **monthly** / **quarterly** / **financial** report / statement
▸ to **prepare** / **complete** / **do** / **submit** / **file** a report / return
▸ to **send** / **receive** a statement / return

report [C] a spoken or written description of sth giving information that sb needs to have: *I have to do a report for my boss by tomorrow.* ◇ *She made her **report to** her senior colleagues.* ◇ *The company was asked to submit its annual report.* ◇ *Can you give us a **progress report**?* ◇ *The lab report seems to be missing.* See also **report** → DESCRIBE *verb*, **report** → TELL *verb 1*

statement [C] a printed record of money paid and/or received, especially one sent out by a bank, credit card company or other financial institution: *Their job is to prepare the company's annual financial statement.* ◇ *a bank/credit card statement* ◇ *The finance minister will submit his **budget statement** next week.*

return [C] an official report or statement that gives particular information to the government or other organization: *Have you submitted your **tax return** yet?* ◇ *The 2001 **census returns** showed that there were more unemployed people than was previously thought.*

4 report · rumour · talk · scandal · gossip · hearsay · dirt
These are all words for a story or piece of information that sb tells you, that may or may not be true.

PATTERNS AND COLLOCATIONS
▸ the reports / rumours / talk / scandal / gossip / hearsay / dirt **about** sb / sth
▸ reports / rumours / talk **of** sth happening
▸ **amid** reports / rumours / talk of sth
▸ reports / rumours / talk / gossip **that**…
▸ a / an **false** / **baseless** / **unconfirmed** report / rumour
▸ to **spread** reports / rumours / gossip
▸ to **hear** / **believe** reports / rumours / talk / gossip
▸ to **deny** / **confirm** reports / rumours

report [C] a story or piece of news that may or may not be true: *I don't believe these reports of UFO sightings.* ◇ *There are unconfirmed reports of a shooting in the capital.*

rumour (*BrE*) (*AmE* **rumor**) /'ruːmə(r)/ [C, U] a piece of information, or a story, that people talk about, and sometimes try to spread deliberately, but that may not be true: *There are widespread rumours of job losses.* ◇ *Some malicious rumours are circulating about his past.* ◇ *Rumour has it* (= people say) *that he was murdered.*
▸ **be rumoured** (*BrE*) (*AmE* **be rumored**) *verb* [T, passive]: *It's **widely rumoured that** she's getting promoted.* ◇ *He was rumoured to be involved in the crime.*

talk [U] stories that suggest that a particular thing might happen in the future: *There was talk in Washington of sending in troops.*

scandal [U] (*disapproving*) talk or news reports about shocking or immoral things that people have done, that are usually unkind and may not be true: *The newspapers are full of scandal about her private life.* ❶ (A) **scandal** [C, U] is an event or behaviour that people think is morally or legally wrong and causes public feelings of shock or anger: *a series of sex scandals* ◇ *to cause/create a*

scandal ◇ *The scandal broke* (= became known to the public) *in 2006.* ◇ *There has been no hint of scandal during his time in office.*

gossip [U] (*sometimes disapproving*) informal talk or stories about other people's private lives, that may be unkind or not true: *Tell me all the latest gossip!* ◇ *office gossip* See also **gossip** → CHAT *verb*

> **NOTE** **SCANDAL OR GOSSIP?** Scandal is always unkind and is usually more shocking than **gossip**.

hearsay /'hɪəseɪ; *AmE* 'hɪrseɪ/ [U] (often used in legal contexts) (*rather formal*) things that you have heard from another person but do not definitely know to be true: *Her evidence was dismissed as hearsay.*

dirt [U] (*informal*) unpleasant or harmful information about sb that could be used to damage their reputation or career: *Do you have any **dirt** on the new guy?* ◇ *She just loves to **dish the dirt*** (= tell people unkind or unpleasant things about sb). ◇ *He'd been trying to **dig up** some **dirt** on his political rival.*

reporter
noun See the Topic Map for THE MEDIA on p.900, See also the entries for PRESENTER and WRITER

reporter · journalist · editor · correspondent · columnist · reviewer · contributor · hack
These are all words for a person whose job is to write articles for newspapers and magazines.

PATTERNS AND COLLOCATIONS
▸ a **newspaper** / **magazine** / **news** / **sports** / **financial** reporter / journalist / editor / correspondent / columnist
▸ an **investigative** reporter / journalist
▸ to **tell** reporters / journalists

reporter [C] a person who collects and reports news for newspapers, radio or television: *I spoke to a reporter from the 'New York Times'.* ◇ *He's chief reporter on the 'Daily Herald'.* See also **report** → DESCRIBE *verb*, **reporting** → MEDIA

journalist [C] a person who collects and writes news stories for newspapers, magazines, radio or television: *He's had more than three decades of experience as a broadcast journalist.* See also **journalism** → MEDIA

> **NOTE** **REPORTER OR JOURNALIST?** Reporter is used especially to talk about sb whose job involves visiting places in order to create news reports about what is happening there. **Journalist** can be used generally for sb who works in journalism, including editors, photographers, artists and designers.

editor [C] a person who is in charge of a newspaper or magazine, or part of one, and who decides what should be included: *She's the editor of a national magazine.* ◇ *the fashion/industrial/economics editor*
▸ **edit** *verb* [T]: *She used to edit a women's magazine.*

correspondent /ˌkɒrə'spɒndənt; *AmE* ˌkɔːrə'spɑːn-; ˌkɑː-/ [C] a person who is employed by a newspaper or a television or radio station to report regularly on a particular subject or send regular reports from a foreign country: *She's the BBC's political correspondent.* ◇ *Now, a report from our Hong Kong correspondent.* ◇ *a foreign/legal correspondent*

columnist /'kɒləmnɪst; *AmE* 'kɑːl-/ [C] a journalist who writes regular articles, usually on a particular topic, for a newspaper or magazine: *The gossip columnists ran the story as fact without checking the source.* See also **column** → ARTICLE

reviewer [C] a person who writes reviews of books, films or plays: *The movie was enthusiastically received by the reviewers.* ◇ *a book reviewer for The Guardian* See also **review** → ASSESSMENT

contributor /'ænkə(r)/ [C] a person who writes articles for a magazine or book, or who talks on a radio or television programme or at a meeting: *She continues to be a regular contributor to the journal.*
▸ **contribute** *verb* [T, I]: *She contributed a number of*

articles to the magazine. ◇ *He contributes regularly to the magazine 'New Scientist'.*

hack [C] (*rather informal, disapproving*) a writer, especially of newspaper articles, who does a lot of low quality work: *His comments triggered nervous laughter from the assembled tabloid hacks.*

represent *verb*

1 represent a major breakthrough in AIDS research
2 represent sb's views/good qualities/the idea of peace

---

1 represent · constitute · pose · amount to sth · come down to sth · add up to sth

These words all mean to be considered to be sth or to result in sth.

PATTERNS AND COLLOCATIONS
▸ to represent/ constitute/ pose/ amount to a **challenge**/ **threat**
▸ to represent/ constitute/ pose a **problem**/ **danger**/ **risk**
▸ to represent/ constitute/ amount to a/ an **failure**/ **increase**/ **breach**
▸ to represent/ constitute an **achievement**/ **improvement**
▸ a/ an **result**/ **activity**/ **action** represents/ constitutes sth
▸ It all amounts to/ comes down to/ adds up to sth.

represent *linking verb* (not used in the progressive tenses) (*rather formal, written*) to be sth; to be the result of sth: *This contract represents 20% of the company's annual revenue.* ◇ *These results represent a major breakthrough in AIDS research.* ◇ *The peace plan represents* (= is the result of) *weeks of negotiation.*

constitute /ˈkɒnstɪtjuːt; *AmE* ˈkɑːnstətuːt/ *linking verb* (not used in the progressive tenses) (*formal*) to be sth; to be considered to be sth: *Does such an activity constitute a criminal offence?* ◇ *The increase in racial tension constitutes a threat to our society.*

> **NOTE** REPRESENT OR CONSTITUTE? **Represent** is used especially with words relating to change: *This represents a change/a break/a shift/a departure/a turning point/an improvement/an increase/a reduction/a decline.* **Constitute** is used more to talk about dangerous or negative situations or acts: *This constitutes a threat/danger/ crime/breach/nuisance/weakness/refusal.*

pose [T] to be or create a problem or threat that has to be dealt with: *The task poses no special problems.* ◇ *Pollutants in the river pose a real risk to the fish.*

a'mount to sth *phrasal verb* [no passive] (not used in the progressive tenses) (*rather formal*) to be equal to or the same as sth: *Her answer amounted to a complete refusal.* ◇ *Their actions amount to a breach of contract.* ◇ *We were jailed for a week — well, confined to quarters, but it amounted to the same thing.* ❶ **Amount to** is often used in relation to offences in law: *This amounts to dismissal/contempt of court/abuse/discrimination/obstruction/assault.*

come 'down to sth *phrasal verb* [no passive] (not used in the progressive tenses) (*rather informal*) to be able to be explained by a single important point: *What it comes down to is, either I get more money or I leave.*

add 'up to sth *phrasal verb* [no passive] (not used in the progressive tenses) to lead to a particular result; to show sth: *These clues don't really add up to very much* (= give us very little information).

2 represent · embody · symbolize · exemplify · typify · epitomize

These words all mean to be an example or expression of sth.

PATTERNS AND COLLOCATIONS
▸ to be embodied/ exemplified/ typified/ epitomized **in** sth
▸ to represent/embody/symbolize/epitomize the **spirit**/**essence** of sth
▸ to represent/ embody/ exemplify/ an **idea**/ **ideal**
▸ to represent/ embody/ exemplify a **principle**

▸ to exemplify/ typify/ epitomize a/ an **problem**/ **approach**
▸ to **clearly** represent/ embody/ symbolize/ exemplify/ typify sth

represent [T, no passive] (*rather formal*) to be an example or expression of an idea, quality or opinion: *The project represents all that is good in the community.* ◇ *Those comments do not represent the views of us all.* ◇ *The artist uses doves to represent peace.* See also **representation** → DESCRIPTION

embody /ɪmˈbɒdi; *AmE* ɪmˈbɑːdi/ [T] (not usually used in the progressive tenses) (*rather formal*) (especially of a person) to give a visible form to an idea, quality or feeling: *a politician who embodied the hopes of black youth* ◇ *We want to build a national team that embodies competitive spirit and skill.* See also **embodiment** → EXAMPLE 2

symbolize (*BrE* also **-ise**) [T] (not usually used in the progressive tenses) (of a person, object, quality, event or action) to represent a more general quality or situation: *The use of light and dark symbolizes good and evil.* ◇ *He came to symbolize his country's struggle for independence.* See also **symbol** → SIGN 1

> **NOTE** REPRESENT, EMBODY OR SYMBOLIZE? Sometimes you can use any of these words, especially when you are talking about a person: *He came to represent/embody/ symbolize his country's struggle for independence.* **Embody** is the most physical and visual of these words and is used to talk about real people becoming the basis for other people's hopes: the qualities that sb **embodies** are always good qualities. **Symbolize** is often more abstract (= existing as an idea rather than as a physical reality), and can be used to talk about objects or things, such as a dove (= a type of bird) being used to give the idea of peace, but it is a picture or idea of a dove, not a particular dove that really exists. **Represent** is the most general of these words: it can be used to mean **embody** or **symbolize** or it can simply mean 'express': *The comments represent the views of the majority.*

exemplify /ɪgˈzemplɪfaɪ/ [T, often passive] (not usually used in the progressive tenses) (*formal*) to be a good example of sth: *Her early work is exemplified in her book, 'A Study of Children's Minds'.* ◇ *His food exemplifies Italian cooking at its best.* See also **example** → EXAMPLE 2

typify /ˈtɪpɪfaɪ/ [T] (not usually used in progressive tenses) (*rather formal*) to be a typical example of sth; to be a typical feature of sth: *These are clothes that typify the 1960s.* ◇ *There's a new style of politician, typified by the Prime Minister.*

epitomize (*BrE* also **-ise**) /ɪˈpɪtəmaɪz/ [T] (not usually used in the progressive tenses) (*rather formal*) to be a perfect example of sth: *The fighting qualities of the team are epitomized by the captain.* ◇ *These movies seem to epitomize the 1950s.* See also **epitome** → EXAMPLE 2

> **NOTE** EXEMPLIFY, TYPIFY OR EPITOMIZE? Something can **exemplify** an idea or sb's work. Something can **typify** or **epitomize** a mood, style or atmosphere, especially of a particular time or place. **Epitomize** suggests that you cannot imagine a more typical example of sth. **Typify** is more neutral, and suggests that the example you are giving has all the usual qualities or features of a particular time, place or type of person or thing.

repression *noun*

repression · dictatorship · oppression · persecution · tyranny · bullying

These are all words for the cruel or unfair treatment of a person or group by sb with more power.

PATTERNS AND COLLOCATIONS
▸ repression/ oppression/ persecution **against** sb
▸ to be/ live **under** a dictatorship/ tyranny
▸ **brutal** repression/ dictatorship/ persecution

▸ **political** / **religious** repression / dictatorship / oppression / persecution

▸ **state** / **police** repression / oppression / persecution

▸ to **suffer** repression / oppression / persecution / tyranny

▸ to **face** repression / oppression / persecution

▸ to **fight** / **protest against** repression / oppression / tyranny

▸ to **escape** persecution / tyranny

▸ to **overthrow** a dictatorship / tyranny

▸ a **form of** repression / dictatorship / oppression / tyranny / bullying

▸ a **victim of** repression / oppression / persecution / bullying

repression /rɪ'preʃn/ [U] (*rather formal*) the unfair use of force to control a group of people and restrict their freedom: *There was a campaign of repression against minorities in the north*. See also **repress** → SUPPRESS 1

dictatorship /ˌdɪk'teɪtəʃɪp; *AmE* -tərʃ-/ [C, U] government by a dictator (= a ruler who has complete power); a country ruled by a dictator: *They had lived for almost 50 years under a fascist dictatorship*. ◇ *a military dictatorship* ◇ *The commission will investigate the atrocities which took place during his dictatorship*. See also **dictator** → DICTATOR

oppression /ə'preʃn/ [U] (*rather formal*) cruel and unfair treatment of sb, especially by not giving them the same rights and freedoms as other people: *He spoke out against the oppression of women*. See also **oppress** → SUPPRESS 1

persecution /ˌpɜːsɪ'kjuːʃn; *AmE* ˌpɜːrs-/ [U] (*rather formal*) cruel and unfair treatment of sb, especially because of their race, religion or political beliefs: *The organization helps refugees fleeing from persecution*. See also **persecute** → SUPPRESS 1

NOTE **REPRESSION, OPPRESSION OR PERSECUTION?** Repression is the use of force by those in power to control people in an unfair way, especially by restricting their freedom so that they cannot express their opinions, act as they want to, challenge those in power, etc., for example trade unions and political opposition groups. **Oppression** is the unfair use of power to stop one group of people from having the same rights and freedoms as other people, for example women or people of a particular racial group. **Persecution** is the unfair treatment, including harm and even death, of a group of people because they are different in a way which is considered offensive by others or by those in power, especially because of their race, religion or political beliefs.

tyranny /'tɪrəni/ [U, C] unfair and cruel use of power; the rule of a tyrant (= sb with complete power in a country); a country under this rule: *The children had no protection against the tyranny of their father*. ◇ *Any political system refusing to allow dissent becomes a tyranny*. See also **tyrant** → DICTATOR

bullying /'bʊliɪŋ/ [U] the use of strength or power to make sb do sth; the act of frightening or hurting a weaker person: *He was suspended from his position when several members accused him of bullying*. ◇ *Teenagers talk about their experiences of playground bullying*.

repressive *adj.* See also the entry for AUTHORITARIAN

repressive · oppressive · totalitarian · undemocratic · dictatorial · autocratic · tyrannical
These words all describe people or governments who have complete power or who control people in an unfair way.

PATTERNS AND COLLOCATIONS

▸ a repressive / an oppressive / a totalitarian / an undemocratic / a dictatorial / an autocratic / a tyrannical **regime**

▸ a repressive / a totalitarian / a dictatorial / an autocratic / a tyrannical **government**

▸ a repressive / a totalitarian / an autocratic **state**

▸ repressive / oppressive / totalitarian / dictatorial / autocratic / tyrannical **power**

▸ repressive / oppressive / undemocratic / autocratic / tyrannical **rule**

▸ a repressive / an oppressive / a totalitarian / an autocratic **system** / **structure**

▸ a repressive / an oppressive / a totalitarian **society**

▸ the repressive / oppressive / undemocratic **nature of** sth

repressive /rɪ'presɪv/ (of a system of government) controlling people by force and restricting their freedom: *The government used the incident to justify more repressive measures against the unions*.

oppressive /ə'presɪv/ (of people in positions of power) treating some people in a cruel and unfair way and not giving them the same freedoms and rights as other people: *The refugees were fleeing from oppressive social and political conditions*.

totalitarian /təʊˌtælə'teəriən; *AmE* toʊˌtælə'ter-/ (of a country or system of government) in which there is only one political party that has complete power and control over the people: *The country was closed to outsiders for many years under a totalitarian dictatorship*.

▸ **totalitarianism** *noun* [U]: *to oppose dictatorship and totalitarianism*

undemocratic /ˌʌndemə'krætɪk/ (of a government or political action) against or not acting according to the principles of democracy ❶ **Democracy** is a system of government in which the people of a country can vote to elect their representatives: *The system is fundamentally undemocratic*. ◇ *It is undemocratic to govern an area without an electoral mandate*. **OPP** **democratic** ❶ A **democratic** country, government, organization, society or action is based on the principle that all people or members have an equal right to be involved in electing a government, running the organization, etc.: *a democratic country/government/system/society* ◇ *a democratic decision*

dictatorial /ˌdɪktə'tɔːriəl/ connected with or controlled by a dictator (= a ruler who has complete power): *The military leader gradually assumed more and more dictatorial powers*. See also **dictator** → DICTATOR

autocratic /ˌɔːtə'krætɪk/ (of a system of government) having a ruler who has complete power: *The measures were seen as evidence of a more autocratic style of government*. See also **autocrat** → DICTATOR

tyrannical /tɪ'rænɪkl/ (of a person, leader or government) using power or authority over people in an unfair and cruel way: *His reputation as a tyrannical captain made it hard to find a crew*. See also **tyrant** → DICTATOR

republic *noun*

republic · kingdom · empire · union · commonwealth · federation
These are all words for countries with different types of government, or groups of countries that are linked politically.

PATTERNS AND COLLOCATIONS

▸ an **independent** republic / kingdom

▸ a **democratic** republic / federation

▸ an **ancient** kingdom / empire

▸ to **rule (over)** a republic / a kingdom / an empire

▸ to **govern** a republic / kingdom / federation

▸ to **expand** a kingdom / an empire

▸ to **defend** the republic / kingdom / empire

▸ to **be part of** an empire / a union / a commonwealth / a federation

republic [C] a country that is governed by a president and politicians elected by the people and where there is no king or queen: *They have declared themselves an independent democratic republic*. ❶ **Republic** is often used in the names of countries: *There will be elections in the Czech Republic next month*.

kingdom [C] a country ruled by a king or queen, or with a king or queen as the official head of state: *The reforms will affect all parts of the United Kingdom*. ◇ *He ruled the ancient kingdom of Kaffa*. ◇ *He was one of the most powerful landowners in the kingdom*. See also **king** → KING

empire [C] a group of countries or states that are controlled by one ruler or government: *These invasions almost led to the collapse of the Roman Empire.* ◇ *The mighty empire finally crumbled.* See also **emperor** → KING

union [C] a group of states or countries that have the same central government or that agree to work together ❶ **Union** is often used in the names of countries or groups: *the former Soviet Union* ◇ *a European Union country*

commonwealth (also **Commonwealth**) /ˈkɒmənwelθ; AmE ˈkɑːm-/ [C, usually sing.] an organization of countries that are politically or historically connected: *We want to create a commonwealth of democratic, self-governing countries.* ❶ **The Commonwealth** is an organization consisting of the United Kingdom and most of the countries that used to be part of the British Empire: *There is an annual meeting of Commonwealth heads of government.* **Commonwealth** is also used in the official names of, and to refer to, some states of the US (Kentucky, Massachusetts, Pennsylvania and Virginia): *the Commonwealth of Virginia.* In American English, **commonwealth** can also refer to an independent country that is strongly connected to the US: *Puerto Rico remains a US commonwealth.*

federation /ˌfedəˈreɪʃn/ [C] a country consisting of a group of individual states that have control over their own affairs but are controlled by a central government for national decisions: *Australia is a federation of six states and several territories.* ◇ *the Russian Federation*

reputation *noun* See also STATUS

reputation · image · profile · name · honour · stature · character
These are all words for the opinion that people in general have of sb/sth.

PATTERNS AND COLLOCATIONS
▸ sb's reputation / image / name / stature **as** sth
▸ **of** considerable reputation / stature
▸ (an) **international** reputation / image / profile / stature
▸ sb's **professional** reputation / image / honour / stature
▸ to **gain** a reputation / an image / a name as / for sth
▸ to **damage** sb's reputation / image / character
▸ to **blacken** sb's reputation / name / character
▸ to **protect** sb's reputation / image / name
▸ to **defend** / **restore** sb's reputation / image / honour

reputation [C, U] the opinion that people have about what sb/sth is like, based on what has happened in the past and what they have been told: *The restaurant has an excellent reputation.* ◇ *He acquired a dubious reputation for dealing in stolen goods.* ◇ *He had **staked his reputation** on the success of the play.* ◇ *The weather in England is **living up to its reputation** (= is exactly as expected).* See also **reputable** → RESPECTABLE, **disreputable** → SORDID

image [C, U] the impression that a person, organization, product, etc. gives to the public: *His public image is very different from the real person.* ◇ *The advertisements are intended to improve the company's image.* ◇ *the stereotyped images of women in children's books* ◇ *Image is very important in the music world.*

profile [C] the general impression that sb/sth gives to the public and the amount of attention they receive: *The deal will certainly **raise** the company's international **profile**.* ◇ *This issue has had a **high profile** (= a lot of public attention) in recent months.* ◇ *I advised her to **keep a low profile** (= not to attract attention) for the next few days.* ❶ Sb/sth's **profile** is usually considered in terms of height: they can have a *high/low profile* or you *raise/lower the profile* of sb/sth.

name [C, usually sing.] the fame and reputation of a person, group or organization: *She **made her name** as a writer of children's books.* ◇ *These practices give the*

industry a bad name. ◇ *We must avoid anything that might damage the **good name** of the firm.* See also **make a name for yourself** → SUCCEED

honour (*BrE*) (*AmE* **honor**) [U] a good reputation, especially for showing high moral standards; respect from other people: *She felt that she had to defend the honour of her profession.* ◇ *The family honour is at stake.* ◇ *She **brought honour** to her country by winning an Olympic gold medal.* **OPP** **dishonour** → DISGRACE 2, See also **honourable** → RESPECTABLE, **honourable** → WORTHY

stature /ˈstætʃə(r)/ [U] (*rather formal*) the importance and respect that a person or group has because of their ability and achievements: *The orchestra has **grown in stature**.* ◇ *The election result enhanced the party's stature.*

character [C, U] (*rather formal*) the opinion that people have of you, especially of whether you can be trusted or relied on: *He had been discharged without a **stain on his character**.* ◇ *My teacher agreed to be a **character witness** (= sb who says that a person can be trusted) for me in court.*

request *noun*

request · order · application · claim · demand · call · petition · plea · appeal · reservation
These are all words for the action of asking for sth formally and/or politely.

PATTERNS AND COLLOCATIONS
▸ a request / an order / an application / a claim / a demand / a call / a petition / a plea / an appeal **for** sth
▸ **on** request / order / application / demand
▸ a request / demand **that**...
▸ **repeated** requests / demands / calls / pleas / appeals
▸ a **formal** request / application / claim / demand / petition / appeal
▸ a **personal** request / application / plea / appeal
▸ an **urgent** request / order / demand / plea / appeal
▸ a / an **successful** / **unsuccessful** application / claim / demand / petition / appeal
▸ to **make** a request / an application / a claim / a demand / a plea / an appeal / a reservation
▸ to **put in** a request / an order / an application / a claim / a demand
▸ to **file** / **lodge** an application / a claim / a petition
▸ to **withdraw** a request / an application / a claim / a demand / a petition
▸ to **receive** a request / an order / an application / a demand / a petition / a plea / an appeal
▸ to **meet** a request / an order / a claim / a demand
▸ to **grant** a request / an application / a claim / a petition
▸ to **refuse** / **reject** a request / an application / a claim / a demand / a petition

request [C] (*rather formal*) the action of asking for sth formally and politely: *They made a request for aid.* ◇ *He was there **at his manager's request** (= because his manager had asked him to go).* ◇ *Catalogues are available on request.* See also **request** → ASK *verb* 2, **request** → WISH *noun*

order [C] a request to make or supply goods; a request for food or drinks in a restaurant or bar; the food or drinks that you ask for: *I would like to place an order for ten copies of this book.* ◇ *The machine parts are still on order (= they have been ordered but have not yet been received).* ◇ *These items can be made **to order** (= produced especially for a particular customer).* ◇ *May I take your order?* ◇ *a **side order** of fries (= that you eat with your main dish)* See also **order** → ORDER *verb* 2

application [C] a formal, often written, request for sth, such as a job, permission to do sth or a place at a college or university: *We put in our planning application about six weeks ago.* ◇ *We received over 100 applications for the job.* ◇ *Where can I get an **application form** (= a piece of paper on which to apply for sth)?* See also **apply** → ASK *verb* 2

claim [C] a request for a sum of money that you believe you have a right to, especially from a company or the government: *You can make a **claim on** your insurance policy.* ◇ *Nurses have put in a three per cent **pay claim**.* See also **claim** → ASK *verb* 2

demand [C] a very firm request for sth; sth that sb needs: *Their demand for higher pay was ignored.* ◇ *Our firm is constantly striving to satisfy customers' demands* (= to give them what they are asking for). See also **demand** → DEMAND *verb*

call [C] (*especially journalism*) a demand or request for sb to do sth or go somewhere: *There have been calls for the minister to resign.* ◇ *This is the last call for passengers travelling on British Airways flight 199 to Rome.* See also **call for sth** → ASK *verb* 2

petition /pə'tɪʃn/ [C] a written document signed by a large number of people that asks sb in a position of authority to do or change sth: *Would you like to sign our **petition against** experiments on animals?* See also **petition** → ASK *verb* 2

plea /pliː/ [C] (*formal*) an urgent emotional request: *She made an impassioned plea for help.* See also **plead** → BEG

appeal [C] (*rather formal, especially written*) an urgent and deeply felt request for money, help or information, especially one made by a charity or by the police: *They've just launched a TV appeal for donations to the charity.* ◇ *The police made an appeal to the public to remain calm.* See also **appeal** → ASK *verb* 2

reservation [C] (*rather formal*) an arrangement for a seat on a plane or train, a room in a hotel, etc. to be kept for you: *I'll call the restaurant and make a reservation.* ◇ *We have a reservation in the name of Grant.* See also **reserve** → ORDER *verb* 2

research *noun*

research · analysis · exploration · scrutiny · examination · study · discussion · enquiry
These are all words for the process of examining and finding out more about sth, or the result of this process.

PATTERNS AND COLLOCATIONS
▸ research / enquiry **into** sth
▸ **detailed** research / analysis / exploration / scrutiny / examination / study / discussion / enquiry
▸ **close** analysis / scrutiny / examination / study
▸ **scientific** research / analysis / exploration / scrutiny / examination / study / enquiry
▸ **historical** research / analysis / exploration / examination / study / enquiry
▸ to **carry out / conduct / undertake** research / analysis / exploration / an examination / a study
▸ to **do** research / analysis / a study
▸ research / analysis / exploration / scrutiny / examination / the study **reveals** sth
▸ research / analysis / examination / the study **shows / suggests** sth

research [U] (also **researches** [pl.]) the process of studying a subject in detail, especially in order to discover new information about it: *He's done a lot of research into renewable energy sources.* ◇ *I've done some research to find out the cheapest way of travelling there.* ◇ *Recent **research on** deaf children has yielded some interesting results.* ◇ *We're trying to raise money for cancer research.* ◇ *This is a **piece of research** that should be taken very seriously.* ◇ *James is a 24-year-old **research student** from Iowa.* ◇ *They pour millions of dollars into **research and development** (= researching and creating new products).* ◇ *I work for a **market research** organization (= an organization that finds out what people buy and why).* ◇ *In the course of my researches, I came across some of my grandfather's old letters.* See also **research** → INVESTIGATE *verb*

analysis /ə'næləsɪs/ [U, C] the process of studying sth in detail in order to understand more about it; the result of this study: *Most of the information we have so far is based on statistical analysis.* ◇ *The book is an analysis of poverty and its causes.* See also **analyse** → EXAMINE

NOTE **RESEARCH** OR **ANALYSIS?** When you do **research** you try to find out new information; when you do **analysis** you look in more detail at the information you already have, in order to understand it better.

exploration /ˌeksplə'reɪʃn/ [U, C] the act of travelling through a place in order to find out about it or look for sth; the act of looking at sth or considering it in detail in order to find out more about it: *The film is a chronicle of man's exploration of space.* ◇ *Extensive **oil exploration** was carried out using the latest drilling technology.* ◇ *This was the time of Humboldt's explorations in South America.* See also **explore** → INVESTIGATE *verb*

scrutiny /'skruːtəni/ [U] (*formal*) the act of considering sth in great detail, especially in order to see or decide if it is good enough: *Her argument doesn't really stand up to scrutiny.* ◇ *The documents should be available for public scrutiny.* ◇ *Foreign policy has **come under** close **scrutiny** recently.* See also **scrutinize** → STUDY

examination [U, C] the act of considering sth in detail, in order to understand more about it or to make a decision or judgement about it: *Your proposals are still **under examination**.* ◇ *On closer **examination**, her story did not seem to stand up.* ◇ *The chapter concludes with a brief examination of what causes family break-up.* See also **examine** → EXAMINE

study [U, C] the process of considering sth in detail, in order to understand or find out more about it: *The scientific study of American dialects began in 1889.* ◇ *A detailed study of the area was carried out.* See also **study** → REPORT *noun* 1, **study** → EXAMINE *verb*

NOTE **EXAMINATION** OR **STUDY?** **Examination** has a broader range of meaning than **study** in this meaning. **Study** is usually more academic, in order to find out more about a subject; **examination** may be more practical, in order to make a decision about sth.

discussion [C, U] a speech or piece of writing that discusses many different aspects of a subject: *Her article is a discussion of the methods used in research.* ◇ *There will be further discussion of these issues in the next chapter.* See also **discuss** → EXAMINE

enquiry (also **inquiry**) [U] the act of asking questions or collecting information about sb/sth: *Some regimes have tried to stifle scientific enquiry.* ◇ *We are following several lines of enquiry.* See also **enquire into sth** → INVESTIGATE *verb*

resent *verb*

resent · begrudge · take exception to sth
These words all mean to feel angry or unhappy about sth because you feel it is unfair.

PATTERNS AND COLLOCATIONS
▸ to resent / begrudge **(sb) doing sth**
▸ to resent / begrudge / take exception to **the fact that…**

resent /rɪ'zent/ [T] to feel bitter or angry about sth, especially because you feel it is unfair: *He **bitterly** resented being treated like a child.* ◇ *She **deeply** resented the fact that her husband had been so successful.* ◇ *She resented him making all the decisions.* See also **resentful** → BITTER 2

begrudge /bɪ'ɡrʌdʒ/ [T] (*often used in negative statements*) to feel unhappy that sb has sth because you do not think that they deserve it; to feel unhappy about having to do, pay or give sth: *You surely don't begrudge him his happiness.* ◇ *I don't begrudge her being so successful.* ◇ *I begrudge every second I spent trying to help him.* ◇ *Many people begrudge paying so much money for a second-rate service.* See also **grudging** → RELUCTANT

take ex'ception to sth *idiom* (*rather formal*) to feel angry about sth and strongly object to it, especially sth that sb has said or done: *I **take great exception to** the fact that you told my wife before you told me.* ◇ *No one could possibly take exception to his comments.*

resentment *noun*

resentment · bitterness · grudge · bad feeling · acrimony
These are all words for an angry feeling that exists between people after a bad experience.

PATTERNS AND COLLOCATIONS
▶ the resentment / bitterness / bad feeling / acrimony **between** them
▶ resentment / a grudge **against** sb
▶ resentment / bitterness / a grudge / bad feeling **about** sth
▶ resentment / bitterness **over** sth
▶ to do sth **without** resentment / bitterness / acrimony
▶ to **harbour** resentment / bitterness / a grudge
▶ to **bear** resentment / a grudge
▶ a **feeling** / **sense of** resentment / bitterness

resentment /rɪˈzentmənt/ [U, C] a feeling of anger and unhappiness that you have because you feel that you have been treated unfairly: *She could not conceal the deep resentment she felt at the way she had been treated.* ◇ *He felt a flash of **resentment towards** Helen.* ◇ *Old grievances and resentments came to the surface.* See also **resentful** → BITTER 2

bitterness [U] a feeling of anger and unhappiness that you have after a bad experience or about sth that you think is unfair: *The pay cut caused great bitterness among the workers.* See also **bitter** → BITTER 2

> **NOTE** RESENTMENT OR BITTERNESS? **Resentment** may be a less obvious feeling than **bitterness**: people try or fail to hide it. It grows more slowly, but it may be shared by many people: *his growing/increasing/mounting/smouldering resentment* ◇ *popular/public/widespread resentment.* **Bitterness** can be sudden and can last a long or a short time: *She felt touched with a momentary/sudden bitterness.* ◇ *The long occupation of the island has left a legacy of bitterness.*

grudge [C] a feeling of anger or dislike towards sb because of sth bad they have done to you in the past: *I bear him no grudge.* ◇ *He **has a grudge** against the world.* ◇ *I don't **hold any grudges** now.*

bad 'feeling [U] (also **bad 'feelings** [pl.] especially in *AmE*) anger between people, especially after an argument or disagreement: *There was a lot of bad feeling between the two groups of students.*

acrimony /ˈækrɪməni; *AmE* -moʊni/ [U] (*formal*) angry bitter feelings or words between people: *The dispute was settled without acrimony.* See also **acrimonious** → BITTER 2

reserve *verb*

reserve · save · keep · hold
These words all mean to prevent sth from being used so that it can be used in the future by a particular person or for a particular reason.

PATTERNS AND COLLOCATIONS
▶ reserve / save / keep sth **for** sb / sth
▶ reserve / save / keep / hold a **seat** / **place** for sb
▶ save / keep some **food** for sb

reserve [T, usually passive] to prevent sth from being used so that it can be used in the future by a particular person: *These seats are reserved for special guests.* ◇ *She got all the media attention usually reserved for celebrities.* ◇ *I am pleased to inform you that a place has been reserved for you in this class.* ❶ You can also **reserve** a seat, table, room, etc. for yourself by asking for it to be kept for you. See also **reserve** → ORDER *verb* 2

save [T] to reserve sth for sb else to use: *I've saved some food for you.* ◇ *I won't save you a seat if you're late.*

keep [T] (*especially BrE*) to save sth for sb: *I've kept two seats for us near the front.* ◇ *The man in the shop said he'd keep it for me until Friday.*

> **NOTE** RESERVE, SAVE OR KEEP? **Reserve** is used especially when sth is officially saved for sb/sth: you might have a place reserved for you in a class, but you would not 'reserve some food for sb'. **Save** is more often used if sth is reserved for you unofficially, for example by a friend. **Keep** is similar to **save** and is used especially in British English.

hold [T] (*formal*) to keep a seat, place or room reserved for sb: *We can hold your reservation for three days.*

resident *noun* See the Topic Map for THE INDIVIDUAL AND SOCIETY on p.894, See also the entry for TENANT

resident · citizen · inhabitant · dweller · householder · local · native
These are all words for a person who lives in a particular place.

PATTERNS AND COLLOCATIONS
▶ local residents / citizens / inhabitants / householders
▶ rural residents / inhabitants / dwellers / householders
▶ city / **urban** residents / dwellers
▶ **permanent** residents / inhabitants
▶ **private** citizens / householders

resident /ˈrezɪdənt/ [C] a person who lives in a particular place or who has their home there: *There were confrontations between local residents and the police.* ◇ *Japan has more than 1.1 million registered **foreign** residents.* See also **reside** → LIVE

citizen /ˈsɪtɪzn/ [C] a person who lives in a particular place: *She is a **prominent citizen** of the town.* ◇ *The king was visiting France as a private citizen* (= not as a head of state). ❶ **Citizen** is used especially to make a comment about people's character or status as members of the community: *This terrible crime has shocked all **law-abiding citizens**.* ◇ *When you're old, people treat you like a **second-class citizen*** (= with fewer rights than other people). See also **citizen** → CITIZEN

inhabitant /ɪnˈhæbɪtənt/ [C] a person or animal that lives in a particular place: *It is a town **of** about 10 000 inhabitants.* ◇ *He is Brixham's oldest inhabitant.* ◇ *The island's earliest inhabitants came from India.* See also **inhabit** → LIVE

> **NOTE** RESIDENT OR INHABITANT? **Resident** is the most general word here and can refer simply to all the people who live in a town, area or country. It can also refer to people who have their home in a particular place for official purposes, for example for paying tax. A **resident** is usually part of a modern society, living in a house or flat in a village, town or city. **Inhabitant** can be used in a similar way, or it can refer to people (or animals) living a more basic life either in the past or in a wilder environment: *the inhabitants of the rainforest/tundra/remote islands*

dweller [C] (especially in compounds) (*rather formal, written*) a person or animal that lives in the particular place that is mentioned: *The disease spread quickly among the poor **slum dwellers** of the city.* ◇ *Almost all Asian hornbills are **forest dwellers**.*

householder /ˈhaʊshəʊldə(r); *AmE* -hoʊld-/ [C] (*formal*) a person who owns or rents the house that they live in: *Single householders receive a 20% discount on their council tax.*

local [C, usually pl.] a person who lives in a particular place or area, especially compared with people coming from outside: *The locals are very friendly.* ◇ *Tensions have been growing between students and locals in the area.*

native [C] a person who lives in a particular place, usually sb who has lived there a long time, and especially compared with tourists or foreigners: *You can always tell the difference between the tourists and the natives.* ◇ *She speaks Italian **like a native**.* ❶ In the past the word **native** was used by Europeans to describe a person who lived in a place originally, before white people arrived there. This use of the word is now considered offensive and should be avoided. When using **native** simply to mean sb who has lived in a place for a long time, make it clear that the contrast is with tourists or foreigners (especially those who speak a different language), NOT with white people or Westerners. In many cases it may be better to use **local** instead: *You can always tell the difference between the tourists and the locals.* However, in the context of language, use **native**: ~~She speaks Italian like a local.~~ See also **native** → CITIZEN *noun*, **native** → CULTURAL *adj.*

resist *verb*

resist · struggle · hold/keep sb/sth at bay · hold/stand your ground · hold out against sb/sth
These words all mean to fight against sb/sth who is attacking, threatening or opposing you.

PATTERNS AND COLLOCATIONS
▸ to struggle / hold your ground **against** sb / sth
▸ to resist / hold out against an **attack**
▸ to resist / hold out against **pressure**

resist [I, T] to fight back when attacked; to use force to stop sth from happening: *He tried to pin me down, but I resisted.* ◊ *She was charged with **resisting arrest**.* ◊ *He gathered forces to resist the invasion.* **OPP** **give in**, **submit** → GIVE WAY, See also **resistance** → OPPOSITION
struggle [I] to fight against sb/sth in order to prevent a bad situation or result: *He struggled against cancer for two years.* ◊ *We should all struggle against injustice.* ◊ *Lisa **struggled with** her conscience before talking to the police.* See also **struggle** → CAMPAIGN *noun*
hold/keep sb/sth at 'bay *idiom* to prevent an enemy from coming close or a problem from having a bad effect: *I'm trying to keep my creditors at bay.* ◊ *Charlotte bit her lip to hold the tears at bay.*
hold/stand your 'ground *idiom* to continue with your opinions or intentions when sb is opposing you and wants you to change; to face a situation and refuse to run away: *Don't let him persuade you – stand your ground.* ◊ *It is not easy to hold your ground in front of someone with a gun.*
hold 'out against sb/sth *phrasal verb* to continue to resist sb/sth, especially in a dangerous or difficult situation: *British troops held out against constant attacks.* ◊ *The Prime Minister held out against pressure to speed up the reforms.*

resolve *verb* See the Topic Map for CONFLICT on p.896,
See also the entry for SOLVE 1

resolve · settle · repair · mend · patch sth up
These words all mean to put an end to a disagreement, find a solution to a problem or improve a bad relationship.

PATTERNS AND COLLOCATIONS
▸ to settle / patch up sth **with** sb
▸ to resolve / settle / mend / patch up **your differences**
▸ to resolve/settle a/an **dispute/argument/crisis/matter/issue**
▸ to resolve / mend **matters**
▸ to repair / mend / patch up **a rift / the damage / relations**
▸ to mend / patch up a **relationship / marriage**

resolve /rɪˈzɒlv; *AmE* rɪˈzɑːlv/ [T] (*rather formal*) to find a satisfactory solution to a problem or argument: *Where can ordinary people get help with resolving family problems?* ◊ *The matter has never really been satisfactorily resolved.* See also **resolution** → SOLUTION
settle [T, I] to put an end to an argument or disagreement: *Talks will be held in an attempt to settle the dispute.* ◊ *I want this thing settled.* ◊ *The company agreed to **settle out of court** (= come to an agreement without going to court).* See also **settlement** → AGREEMENT 1
repair [T] to say or do sth in order to improve a bad situation or relationship: *They moved quickly to repair relations between themselves and the US.* ◊ *It was too late to repair the damage done to the relationship.*

mend [T] to find a solution to a disagreement or improve a bad situation or relationship: *They met in an attempt to mend their differences.* ◊ *Is it too late to **mend fences** with your ex-wife (=settle your disagreement with her)?*
patch sth 'up *phrasal verb* (*rather informal*) to stop quarrelling with sb and become friends again: *Have you managed to **patch things up** with him?*

respect *noun*

respect · manners · courtesy · formality · politeness · etiquette · grace · civility
These are all words for behaviour that is considered to be polite or correct.

PATTERNS AND COLLOCATIONS
▸ **with** respect / courtesy / politeness / grace / civility
▸ **out of** respect / courtesy / politeness
▸ **great** respect / courtesy / formality / politeness / civility
▸ **good** manners / grace
▸ **exaggerated** respect / courtesy / politeness / formality
▸ to **show** respect / manners / courtesy / politeness
▸ to **treat sb with** respect / courtesy / politeness / civility

respect [U, sing.] polite behaviour towards or care for sb/sth that you think is important: *They show a lack of **respect for** authority.* ◊ *He has no respect for her feelings.* ◊ *Everyone has a right to be treated with respect.* **OPP** **disrespect**, **contempt** → CONTEMPT, See also **respect** → ADMIRATION *noun*, **respect** → FOLLOW *verb* 3, **respectful** → POLITE
manners [pl.] behaviour that is considered to be polite and socially acceptable in a particular society or culture: *It is **bad manners** to talk with your mouth full.* ◊ *He has **no manners** (= behaves very badly).* ◊ *She could at least have the **good manners** to let me know she isn't coming.* ◊ *Those kids have no **table manners**.* ❶ People often talk about sb's **manners** in the context of how they behave when they eat a meal or how they treat other people.
courtesy /ˈkɜːtəsi; *AmE* ˈkɜːrt-/ [U, C, usually pl.] (*rather formal*) polite behaviour that shows respect for other people; a polite thing that you say or do when you meet people in formal situations: *It's only common courtesy to tell the neighbours we'll be having a party.* ◊ *We asked them as **a matter of courtesy**.* ◊ *The prime minister was welcomed with the usual courtesies.* See also **courteous** → POLITE
formality /fɔːˈmæləti; *AmE* fɔːrˈm-/ [U] correct and formal behaviour that deliberately avoids being too relaxed or friendly: *She greeted him with stiff formality.* ◊ *Different levels of formality are appropriate in different situations.* See also **formal** → FORMAL
politeness [U] polite behaviour that shows respect for other people: *He stood up out of politeness and offered her his seat.* **OPP** **rudeness** → RUDE, See also **polite** → POLITE
etiquette /ˈetɪket; -kət/ [U] the formal rules of correct or polite behaviour in society or among members of a particular profession: *What's the correct etiquette when addressing a judge?* ◊ *She is an expert on matters of etiquette.*
grace [U, sing.] a quality of behaviour that is polite and pleasant and deserves respect: *He conducted himself with grace and dignity throughout the trial.* ◊ *She didn't even **have the grace** to look embarrassed.* ◊ *We will simply have to accept the situation **with a good grace**.* See also **gracious** → POLITE
civility /səˈvɪləti/ [U] (*formal*) polite behaviour: *Staff members are trained to treat customers with civility at all times.* ❶ **Civilities** [pl.] are remarks that are said only to be polite and avoid being rude: *She didn't waste time on civilities.* See also **civil** → POLITE

respect *verb*

respect · admire · esteem · be/stand in awe of sb/sth · look up to sb
These words and expressions all mean to have a high opinion of sb/sth because of their good qualities or achievements.

| respect | admire | be/stand in awe of |
| esteem | look up to sb | sb/sth |

PATTERNS AND COLLOCATIONS
▶ to respect / admire / esteem / look up to sb **as** sth
▶ to respect / admire / esteem / look up to sb **for** sth
▶ to respect / admire **the way** sb does sth
▶ a respected / an esteemed **writer / teacher / scientist**
▶ **greatly / much** respected / admired / esteemed
▶ **highly** respected / esteemed
▶ to **really** respect / admire / look up to sb / sth

respect [T] (not used in the progressive tenses) to have a high opinion of sb/sth because of their good qualities or achievements: *She is always honest with me, and I respect her for that.* ◇ *She was a much loved and highly respected teacher.* ◇ *I respect Jack's opinion on most subjects.* See also **respect** → ADMIRATION, **respectful** → POLITE

admire [T] (not used in the progressive tenses) to have a very high opinion of sb/sth because of their good qualities or achievements: *I really admire your enthusiasm.* ◇ *The school is widely admired for its excellent teaching.* ◇ *You have to admire the way he handled the situation.* See also **admiration** → ADMIRATION, **admirer** → FAN, **admiring** → GOOD 6

NOTE **RESPECT** OR **ADMIRE?** **Admire** expresses a stronger feeling than **respect**: if you **admire** sb it usually means that you agree with them and/or would like to be like them. You can **admire** a person or their good qualities, but you do not usually admire sb's opinions: *I really admire her for her courage.* ◇ *I really admire her courage.* ◇ *I admire Jack's opinion on most subjects.* If you **respect** sb you might not agree with them or want to be like them, but you still recognize their good qualities: *These academics may be respected as experts in their field, but they can also be quite arrogant.* You can **respect** a person or their *opinions*; you can **respect** sb *for* their good qualities, but you do NOT usually respect the qualities themselves: *I respect him for his honesty.* ◇ *I respect his honesty.*

esteem [T, usually passive] (not used in the progressive tenses) (*formal*) to respect and admire sb/sth, especially because of their skills or qualities: *He was esteemed as a dedicated and imaginative scholar.* ◇ *Many of these qualities are esteemed by managers.* See also **esteem** → ADMIRATION

be/stand in 'awe of sb/sth *idiom* (not used in the progressive tenses) to admire sb/sth very much and be slightly frightened of them/it: *She was tall, confident and beautiful, and all the other girls were in awe of her.* See also **awe** → ADMIRATION

look 'up to sb *phrasal verb* (not used in the progressive tenses) to admire or respect sb, especially sb who is older than you or who is in a position of authority: *He's good with the kids, who really look up to him.* **OPP** **look down on sb** ❶ If you **look down on sb** you think that you are better than them: *She looks down on people who haven't been to college.*

respectable *adj.* See the Topic Map for THE INDIVIDUAL AND SOCIETY on p.894

respectable · decent · reputable · honourable · law-abiding
These words all describe sb/sth that is considered by society to be good and morally acceptable.

PATTERNS AND COLLOCATIONS
▶ a respectable / a decent / an honourable / a law-abiding **man / woman**
▶ respectable / decent / honourable / law-abiding **people**
▶ a respectable / decent / law-abiding **citizen / member of the community**
▶ respectable / decent / law-abiding **folk**
▶ a respectable / reputable **firm / organization**
▶ to **do the** decent / honourable **thing**
▶ **perfectly / very** respectable / decent / reputable / honourable

respectable considered by society to be socially or morally acceptable: *This is a respectable neighbourhood.* ◇ *I'm a respectable married woman.* ◇ *It's about time you got yourself a respectable job.* ◇ (*rather informal, spoken*) *Go and make yourself look respectable.* **OPP** **disreputable** → SORDID ❶ **Disreputable** is opposite in meaning to **respectable**, NOT **reputable**.
▶ **respectability** /rɪˌspektə'bɪləti/ *noun* [U]: *middle-class notions of respectability*
▶ **respectably** *adv.*: *Mrs Wilson dressed quietly and respectably in grey or black.*

decent /'di:snt/ [usually before noun] (of people or behaviour) honest and fair; treating people with respect and deserving the respect of others: *These are ordinary, decent, hard-working people.* ◇ *The chairman must now do the decent thing and resign.*
▶ **decency** *noun* [U]: *We need to restore values of decency, caring and understanding to our society.*
▶ **decently** *adv.*: *We always try to treat prisoners decently.*

reputable /'repjətəbl/ honest and known to provide a good service: *Buy your car from a reputable dealer.* ❶ **Reputable** is usually used about companies and people involved in business or trade. See also **reputation** → REPUTATION

honourable (*BrE*) (*AmE* **honorable**) /'ɒnərəbl; *AmE* 'ɑːnə-/ showing high moral standards; behaving in a way that means you keep the respect of other people: *He was an honourable man who could not lie.* ◇ *The only honourable thing to do is to resign.* **OPP** **dishonourable** → DESPICABLE, See also **honour** → INTEGRITY, **honour** → REPUTATION, **honourable** → WORTHY
▶ **honourably** (*BrE*) (*AmE* **honorably**) *adv.*: *He served honourably during his 44 years in office.*

NOTE **DECENT** OR **HONOURABLE?** Sometimes you can use either word: *It's time she did the decent/honourable thing and resigned.* However, being **honourable** often involves more serious moral choices than being **decent**. **Decent** people work hard and treat other people with respect in their ordinary, everyday lives. **Honourable** people tell the truth, are honest with money and loyal to other people and their country, even when this is very difficult or dangerous or when other people are lying or cheating. You can *live decently* and *die honourably* but NOT: *live honourably* and: *die decently.*

law-abiding /'lɔː əˌbaɪdɪŋ/ obeying and respecting the law: *The police have been preventing ordinary law-abiding citizens from going about their own business.* ❶ **Law-abiding** is usually used when sb who usually obeys the law is treated as if they have broken it, or in comparison with people who do break the law.

respond *verb*

respond · react · take · receive · greet · meet sth with sth
These words all mean to do sth or behave in a particular way as a reaction to sth that sb has said or done.

PATTERNS AND COLLOCATIONS
▶ to respond / react **by** doing sth
▶ to respond / react / meet sth **with** sth
▶ to respond / react / greet sth / meet sth with **anger**
▶ to react / receive sth / greet sth / meet sth with **dismay**
▶ to respond / react / take sth / receive sth **well / badly**
▶ to respond / react / receive sth **positively / favourably / sympathetically**

► to respond / react / receive sth / greet sth **coolly**
► to respond / react / greet sth **angrily**
► to respond / receive sth / greet sth **enthusiastically**

respond [I] (*rather formal*) to behave in a particular way because of sth that has happened or that sb has said or done; to act quickly or in the correct way as a result of sth: *Members of the public responded immediately to the charity's appeal for funds.* ◇ *The government responded by banning all future demonstrations.* ◇ *The car responds very well to the controls.* ◇ *You can rely on him to respond to a challenge.*

react [I] to change or behave in a particular way as a result of sth or in response to sth: *Local residents have reacted angrily to the news.* ◇ *I nudged her but she didn't react.* ◇ *You never know how he is going to react.* ◇ *The market reacted by falling a further two points.*

NOTE RESPOND OR REACT? **Respond** is generally used to talk about more detached, less emotional behaviour than **react**. **Respond** is used more frequently with adverbs like *immediately, instantly, promptly, quickly* and *rapidly*; **react** is used more frequently with adverbs like *angrily, violently* and *strongly*.

take [T] (always used with an adverb or preposition) to react to a statement, action or situation in a particular way: *He took the criticism surprisingly well.* ◇ *These threats are not to be taken lightly.* ◇ *I wish you'd take me seriously.* ◇ *She took it in the spirit in which it was intended.*

receive [T, usually passive] to react to sth new in a particular way: *The play was well received by the critics.* ◇ *The statistics were received with concern.*

greet [T, usually passive] (*especially written*) to react to sb/sth in a particular way: *The changes were greeted with suspicion.* ◇ *The team's win was greeted as a major triumph.* ◇ *Loud cheers greeted the athletes.*

NOTE RECEIVE OR GREET? New ideas, information, books and films can be **received** in a particular way; news, events and arrivals can be **greeted**. *Cheers, applause* or *silence* might **greet** sb/sth, but things can only be **received** by people.

'**meet sth with sth** *phrasal verb* [usually passive] to react to sth in a particular way: *His suggestion was met with howls of protest.* ❶ Things can be **met with** *approval, anger, dismay, etc.* or with actions that show how people feel: *to be met with shouts of joy/howls of protest/a glare of anger/a stony stare/protests and demonstrations*

response *noun*

response · reaction · feedback · reception · welcome
These are all words for what you do, say or think as a result of sth that has happened.

PATTERNS AND COLLOCATIONS
► a response / a reaction / feedback / a reception / a welcome **from** sb
► a response / reaction / reception / welcome **to** sb / sth
► **in** response / reaction **to** sth
► (a) **positive** / **favourable** response / reaction / feedback / reception
► the **initial** response / reaction / feedback / reception
► (an) **immediate** response / reaction / feedback / welcome
► (a / an) **negative** / **appropriate** / **instant** response / reaction / feedback
► an **enthusiastic** response / reaction / reception / welcome
► a **lukewarm** / **mixed** / **poor** / **hostile** response / reaction / reception
► the **critical** / **public** response / reaction / reception
► an **emotional** response / reaction / welcome
► a **friendly** / **warm** / **wonderful** response / reception / welcome
► to **give (sth)** / **get** / **have** / **receive** (a) ... response / reaction / feedback / reception / welcome
► to **meet with** a ... response / reaction / reception

response [C, U] what you do or say as a result of sth that has happened or been said: *The news provoked an angry response.* ◇ *I knocked on the door but there was no response.* ◇ *The product was developed in response to customer demand.* ◇ *There has been little response to our appeal for funds.*

reaction [C, U] what you do, say, think or feel as a result of sth that has happened: *What was his reaction to the news?* ◇ *My immediate reaction was one of shock.* ◇ *There has been a mixed reaction to her appointment as director.*

NOTE RESPONSE OR REACTION? Your **response** to sth is what you decide to do or say about it; a **reaction** is usually less carefully considered and may be what you feel about sth and not a matter of choice at all: ~~There has been little reaction to our appeal for funds.~~ ◇ ~~My immediate response was one of shock.~~

feedback /ˈfiːdbæk/ [U] advice, criticism or information about how good or useful sth or sb's work is: *I'd appreciate some feedback on my work.* ◇ *We need both positive and negative feedback from our customers.*

reception /rɪˈsepʃn/ [sing.] the way that people react to sth, which shows their opinion of it: *Her latest album has met with a mixed reception from fans.*

welcome [sing.] the way that people react to sth, which shows their opinion of it: *This new comedy deserves a warm welcome.* ◇ *The proposals were given a cautious welcome by the trade unions.* See also **welcome** → WELCOME *verb*

NOTE RECEPTION OR WELCOME? A **reception** is more likely than a **welcome** to be described using adjectives with negative associations: *a lukewarm/hostile/frosty/ critical/cool reception*. Both **welcome** and **reception** can be described using positive words like *warm* and *friendly*. A **welcome** can, however, also occasionally be *cautious* or *guarded*.

responsibility *noun* See the Topic Map for THE INDIVIDUAL AND SOCIETY on p.894

responsibility · duty · charge · obligation · burden · liability · job · commitment · accountability
These are all words for sth that you have to do, or the state of being responsible for sth.

PATTERNS AND COLLOCATIONS
► a duty / an obligation / a burden / a commitment / accountability **to** sb / sth
► a responsibility / duty **towards** sb
► responsibility / liability / accountability **for** sth
► (a) **heavy** responsibility / obligations / burden / commitments
► (a) **greater** responsibility / obligation / burden / liability / accountability
► (a) **personal** responsibility / duty / charge / obligation / commitment / accountability
► **collective** / **public** responsibility / duty / accountability
► (a) **professional** / **social** responsibility / duty / obligation / commitment / accountability
► (a) **financial** responsibility / duty / obligation / burden / commitment / accountability
► (a) **moral** responsibility / duty / obligation / accountability
► (a) **legal** responsibility / duty / obligation / liability / accountability
► (a) **family** responsibility / duty / obligations / commitments
► to **have** a responsibility / a duty / a charge / an obligation / liability / the job / a commitment
► to **accept** responsibility / a duty / an obligation / the burden / liability
► to **bear** / **shoulder** the responsibility / burden
► to **fulfil** / **meet** a responsibility / a duty / an obligation / a commitment
► a responsibility / a duty / the burden **falls on** sb

responsibility [U, C] (*rather formal*) a requirement to deal with sth, or help or take care of sb, because of your job or position: *It is their responsibility to ensure that the rules are* enforced. ◇ *I'm not ready to be in a **position of responsibility**.* ◇ *I don't feel ready to take on new responsibilities.* ◇ *I think we have a moral responsibility to help these countries.* ❶ If you have a **responsibility** for sb/sth, you are the person who should be blamed if sth goes wrong. See also **be responsible for sb/sth** → RUN 2

duty [C, U] something that you feel you have to do because it is your moral or legal responsibility: *It is my duty to report it to the police.* ◇ *I supposed we'd better **do our duty** and report the accident.* ◇ *I'll have to go I'm afraid – **duty calls**.* ◇ *The time he put in helping new recruits went **beyond the call of duty**.*

charge [U] the position of having control over sb/sth: *She **has charge of** the day-to-day running of the business.* ◇ *He **took charge of** the farm after his father's death.* ◇ *They left the nanny **in charge of** the children for a week.* ❶ You can *have/take charge of sb/sth* or you can *be in charge of sb/sth* or *leave/put sb in charge of sb/sth*. See also **be in charge** → RUN 2

obligation /ˌɒblɪˈɡeɪʃn; *AmE* ˌɑːb-/ [U, C] (*rather formal, especially written*) the state of being forced to do sth because it is your duty, or because of a law or rule; something which you must do because you have promised or because of a law or rule: *You are **under no obligation** to buy anything.* ◇ *She did not feel **under any obligation** to tell him the truth.* ◇ *We will send you an estimate for the work **without obligation** (= you do not have to accept it).* ◇ *You must fulfil your legal obligations.* See also **oblige** → FORCE verb

burden [C] (*rather formal*) a duty or responsibility that causes worry, difficulty or hard work: *The main burden of caring for old people falls on the state.* ◇ *I don't want to become a burden to my children when I'm old.* ◇ *How can we reduce the heavy **tax burden** on working people?*
▸ **burden** *verb* [T]: *They have **burdened themselves** with a large mortgage.* ◇ *I don't want to burden you with my worries.*

liability /ˌlaɪəˈbɪləti/ [U] (*rather formal, especially business or law*) the state of being legally responsible for sth: *The company cannot accept liability for any damage caused by natural disasters.*
▸ **liable** *adj.*: *You will be **liable for** any damage caused.*

job [C, usually sing.] (*rather informal, especially spoken*) a responsibility or duty: *It's not my job to lock up!* ◇ *It's the job of the press to expose wrongdoing.* ❶ In this meaning **job** is usually used in the phrase *It's my/your/his/her, etc. job to do sth* or *it's the job of sb/sth to do sth*.

commitment /kəˈmɪtmənt/ [C] (*especially business*) a thing that you have promised or agreed to do, or that you have to do, especially in connection with your work or family; the fact of having to pay an amount of money regularly: *He's busy for the next month with filming commitments.* ◇ *Women very often have to juggle work with their family commitments.* ◇ *Buying a house is a big financial commitment.*

accountability [U] (*formal*) the fact of being responsible for your decisions or actions and expected to explain them when you are asked: *There have been proposals for greater police accountability.* ◇ *the accountability of a company's directors to the shareholders*
▸ **accountable** *adj.* [not usually before noun]: *Politicians are ultimately **accountable to** the voters.* ◇ *Someone must be held **accountable for** the killings.*

rest *noun*

1 the rest of the world
2 take a rest

---

1 the rest · the remainder · balance · difference · excess

These are all words for the remaining people or things, or the remaining part of sth.

PATTERNS AND COLLOCATIONS
▸ the rest / remainder / balance **of** sth
▸ to **pay** the rest / remainder / balance / difference / excess

▸ to **find** / **make up** / **pocket** the rest / remainder / balance / difference
▸ to **split** the remainder / balance / difference

the rest [sing.+ sing./pl. v.] the remaining part of sth; the remaining people or things: *the rest of the world/my life/her money/the day/the people* ◇ *Take what you want and throw the rest away.* ◇ *Don't blame Alex. He's human, like the rest of us.* ◇ *The first question was difficult, but the rest were pretty easy.*

the remainder [sing.+ sing./pl. v.] (*rather formal*) the remaining part of sth; the remaining people, things or numbers: *She lived the remainder of her life in Denmark.* ◇ *I kept some of his books and gave the remainder away.*

> **NOTE** REST OR REMAINDER? **Remainder** is a more formal word than **rest**, which is much more general. **Remainder** is also used in mathematics to mean 'the numbers left after one number has been divided into another': *Divide 2 into 7, and the answer is 3, remainder 1.* Also note that when **the rest** or **the remainder** refers to a plural noun, the verb is plural: *Most of our employees work in Rome; the rest/remainder are in Milan.*

balance [C, usually sing.] the amount that is left after taking numbers or money away from a total; an amount of money still owed after some payment has been made: *I need to check my **bank balance** (= to find out how much money there is in my account).* ◇ *The balance of $500 must be paid within 90 days.*

difference [sing., U] the amount by which one number, amount or level is smaller or greater than sth else: *There's not much **difference in** price **between** the two computers.* ◇ *There's an age difference of six years between the two boys (= one is six years older than the other).* ◇ *I'll lend you £500 and you'll have to find the difference (= the rest of the money you need).*

excess /ɪkˈses/ [C, U] the amount by which one number or amount, especially a payment, is larger than another: *We cover costs up to €600 and then you pay the excess.*

---

2 See the Topic Maps for HEALTH on p.890 and SPORT AND LEISURE on p.892

rest · break · respite · time out · breathing space · breather · recess

These are all words for a short period of time spent relaxing.

PATTERNS AND COLLOCATIONS
▸ a rest / a break / respite / time out **from** sth
▸ to **have** / **take** a rest / a break / time out / a breather
▸ to **need** a rest / a break / respite / some time out
▸ to **give sb** a rest / a break / respite / a breathing space

rest [C, U] a period of relaxing, sleeping or doing nothing after a period of activity: *You need a rest from all your hard work.* ◇ *We stopped for a well-earned rest.* ◇ *Try to get some rest – you have a busy day tomorrow.*

break [C] a short period of time when you stop what you are doing and rest or eat: *Let's take a break.* ◇ *a coffee/lunch/tea break* ◇ *a break for lunch* ◇ *I need a break from mental activity.* ◇ *She worked all day without a break.* ❶ In British English **break** or **break time** [U] is a period of time between lessons at school: *Come and see me at break.* **Break** is also used in American English for a very short period of time between lessons to change classrooms; a longer period of free time between lessons is called **recess** in American English. See also **break** → PAUSE noun

respite /ˈrespaɪt; *AmE* ˈrespɪt/ [C, U] (*rather formal*) a short break from sth difficult or unpleasant; a short delay allowed before sth difficult or unpleasant must be done: *The drug brought a brief respite from the pain.* ◇ (*BrE*) *respite care* (= temporary care arranged for old, mentally ill, etc. people, so that the people who usually care for them can have a rest) ◇ *His creditors agreed to give him a temporary respite.*

time 'out [U] (*rather informal*) time for resting or relaxing away from your usual work or studies: *Take time out to relax by the pool.*

'breathing space [C] a short rest in the middle of a period of mental or physical effort: *This delay gives the party a breathing space in which to sort out its policies.*

breather /ˈbriːðə(r)/ [C] (*informal*) a short pause in an activity to rest or relax: *Can we take a five-minute breather?*

NOTE BREATHER OR BREATHING SPACE? You decide when to take a **breather**; a **breathing space** has to be given or won. A **breather** is for relaxing; a **breathing space** is for sorting things out.

recess /rɪˈses; ˈriːses/ [C] a short break in a trial in court: *The judge called a short recess.* ❶ In American English **recess** [U] is a period of time between lessons at school. The British English word for this is **break** or **break time**. See also **recess** → HOLIDAY 1

rest *verb* See the Topic Maps for HEALTH on p.890 and SPORT AND LEISURE on p.892

***
rest · relax · hang out · take it/things easy · sit back · unwind · chill out · potter · put your feet up
These words all mean to sleep, do very little or just enjoy yourself, especially after a period of activity or illness.
***

PATTERNS AND COLLOCATIONS
▸ to **try to** / **help sb (to)** rest / relax / unwind
▸ to **just** rest / relax / hang out / take it easy / sit back / unwind / potter
▸ to rest / relax / sit back **a little** / **bit**

rest [I, T] to relax, sleep or do nothing after a period of activity or illness; to not use a part of your body for some time: *The doctor told me to rest.* ◇ *Rest your eyes every half an hour.* ◇ *I awoke feeling rested and refreshed.*

relax [I] to rest by doing sth enjoyable, especially after work or effort: *When I get home from work I like to relax with a glass of wine.* ◇ *Just relax and enjoy the movie.* See also **relax** → RELAX 1, **relaxation** → ENTERTAINMENT

ˌhang ˈout *phrasal verb* (*especially AmE, informal*) to spend time relaxing; to spend a lot of time in a particular place or with a particular group of people: *Do we have to rush around today? I'd rather just hang out.* ◇ *The local kids hang out at the mall.*

ˌtake it/things ˈeasy *idiom* (*rather informal*) to relax and avoid working too hard or doing too much: *The doctor told me to take it easy for a few weeks.*

ˌsit ˈback *phrasal verb* (*rather informal*) to relax, especially by not getting too involved in or anxious about sth: *She's not the kind of person who can sit back and let others do all the work.* ❶ **Sit back** suggests that sb is resting and watching other people work.

unwind /ˌʌnˈwaɪnd/ [I] to stop worrying or thinking about problems and start to relax: *Listening to music helps me unwind after a busy day.*

ˌchill ˈout *phrasal verb* (also **chill**) (*informal*) to relax by being lazy after working hard, especially with other people: *They like to chill out and listen to music after work.*

potter [I] (always used with an adverb or preposition) (*BrE*) to do things or move without hurrying, especially when you are doing sth that you enjoy and that is not important: *I spent the day pottering around the house.*

put your ˈfeet up *idiom* (*rather informal*) to sit down and relax, especially with your feet raised and supported: *After a hard day's work, it's nice to get home and put your feet up.*

restless *adj.* See also the entries for WORRIED and HYS-TERICAL

***
restless · impatient · agitated · flustered · unsettled
These words all describe sb who is bored or nervous and not able to relax.
***

PATTERNS AND COLLOCATIONS
▸ to **become** restless / impatient / agitated / flustered / unsettled
▸ to **get** restless / impatient / agitated / flustered
▸ to **feel** / **look** restless / impatient / agitated / flustered ❶ unsettled

restless unable to stay still or be happy where you are, because you are bored and need a change: *The audience was becoming restless.* ◇ *After five years in the job, he was beginning to feel restless.*
▸ **restlessly** *adv.*: *He moved restlessly from one foot to the other.*

impatient annoyed or irritated by sb/sth, especially because you have to wait for a long time: *I'd been waiting for twenty minutes and I was getting impatient.* ◇ *Try not to be too impatient with her.* **OPP** **patient** → CALM
▸ **impatience** *noun* [U]: *She was bursting with impatience to tell me the news.* **OPP** **patience** → PATIENCE
▸ **impatiently** *adv.*: *We sat waiting impatiently for the movie to start.*

agitated /ˈædʒɪteɪtɪd/ showing in your behaviour that you are anxious or nervous: *She's agitated about getting there on time.* ◇ *Calm down! Don't get so agitated.* **OPP** **calm** → CALM, See also **agitate** → SHAKE 4, **agitation** → CONCERN
▸ **agitation** *noun* [U]: *Jen arrived in a state of great agitation.*

flustered nervous or confused because you have a lot to do or have to hurry: *She arrived late, looking hot and flustered.* **OPP** **composed** → CALM, See also **fluster** → SHAKE 4

unsettled [not usually before noun] not calm and not able to relax, especially because of changes or uncertainty: *They all felt restless and unsettled.* See also **unsettling** → WORRYING

restrain *verb*

***
restrain · bind · handcuff · chain · tie sb up · tether · hold sb down
These words all mean to stop a person, animal or thing from moving or escaping by using physical force or by fastening them with sth.
***

PATTERNS AND COLLOCATIONS
▸ to bind / handcuff / chain / tie up / tether sb / sth **to** sth
▸ to bind / handcuff / chain sb / sth **together**
▸ to bind / tie up sb **with** sth
▸ to handcuff / chain **yourself to** sth
▸ to bind / handcuff sb's **hands**
▸ to **firmly** bind / tie up / tether sb / sth

restrain /rɪˈstreɪn/ [T] to stop sb/sth from moving, especially by using physical force: *The prisoner had to be restrained by the police.*

bind /baɪnd/ [T, often passive] (*rather formal*) to tie sb/sth with rope, string, etc. so that they cannot move or are held together firmly: *She was bound to a chair.* ◇ *They bound his hands together.* ◇ *He was left bound and gagged* (= tied up and with a piece of fabric tied over his mouth).

handcuff /ˈhændkʌf/ [T, usually passive] to put handcuffs on sb; to fasten sb to sb/sth with handcuffs ❶ **Handcuffs** are a pair of metal rings joined by a chain, used for holding the wrists of a prisoner together: *Her hands were handcuffed behind her back.* ◇ *Protesters handcuffed themselves to the railings.*

chain [T, often passive] to fasten sb/sth to sb/sth with a chain, so that they cannot escape or be moved: *The dog was chained up for the night.* ◇ *She chained her bicycle to the gate.*

ˌtie sb ˈup *phrasal verb* to tie sb's arms and legs tightly so that they cannot move or escape: *The gang tied up a security guard.*

tether /ˈteðə(r)/ [T] (*rather formal, especially written*) to tie an animal to a post so that it cannot move very far: *She tethered her horse to a tree.* See also **tether** → REIN *noun*

,hold sb 'down *phrasal verb* to stop sb from moving using physical force, especially keeping them on the ground or on another surface: *It took three men to hold him down.*

restraint *noun* See also the entry for COMPOSURE

restraint · self-control · self-discipline
These are all words for the ability to behave calmly and with control.

PATTERNS AND COLLOCATIONS
▶ to have the self-control / self-discipline **to do sth**
▶ to **show** restraint / self-control / self-discipline
▶ to **exercise** restraint / self-control
▶ to **have** / **take** self-control / self-discipline
▶ a **lack of** restraint / self-control

restraint /rɪ'streɪnt/ [U] the quality of behaving calmly and with control, especially when you are feeling angry or excited: *He exercised considerable restraint in ignoring the insults.* ◇ *The police appealed to the crowd for restraint.* See also **restrain** → SUPPRESS 2, **restrained** → DISCIPLINED

,self-con'trol [U] the ability to remain calm and not show your emotions even though you are feeling angry or excited: *It took all his self-control not to shout at them.* ◇ *She struggled to keep her self-control.* ◇ *He suddenly lost all self-control and started shouting and swearing.* See also **control** → CONTROL *noun*, **control** → SUPPRESS *verb* 2

NOTE RESTRAINT OR SELF-CONTROL? Self-control is an ability that people have as part of their character. You can *have* self-control and you can *keep* or *lose* it on a particular occasion. **Restraint** is less a part of sb's character and more a matter of their behaviour: you can *exercise* or *show* restraint, but it is NOT sth that you have, keep or lose: *It took all his restraint not to shout.* ◇ *She struggled to keep her restraint.*

,self-'discipline [U] the ability to make yourself do sth, especially sth difficult or unpleasant: *It takes a lot of self-discipline to go jogging in winter.* See also **discipline** → CONTROL *noun*

result *noun* See also the entry for EFFECT

result · consequence · outcome · implication · product · the fruit/fruits of sth · repercussion · upshot
These are all words for a thing that is caused because of sth else.

PATTERNS AND COLLOCATIONS
▶ to have consequences / implications / repercussions **for** sb / sth
▶ **with** the result / consequence / outcome **that...**
▶ **as** a result / consequence...
▶ (a / an) **important** result / consequences / outcome / implications / repercussions
▶ the **possible** result / consequences / outcome / implications / repercussions
▶ the **likely** result / consequences / outcome / implications
▶ the **inevitable** result / consequences / outcome / product
▶ (a / an) **immediate** / **direct** / **negative** / **positive** result / consequences / outcome / implications / repercussions
▶ (a) **long-term** / **far-reaching** / **serious** results / consequences / implications / repercussions
▶ the **final** result / outcome / product
▶ (a / an) **unfortunate** results / consequences / outcome / implications
▶ (a / an) **disastrous** results / consequences / outcome
▶ to **have** a result / consequences / an outcome / implications / repercussions
▶ to **lead to** (a)... result / consequences / outcome / repercussions
▶ to **show** / **observe** / **assess** / **examine** / **measure** the results / consequences / outcome
▶ to **achieve** / **get** / **obtain** a result / an outcome

result [C, U] a thing that is caused or produced by sth else: *She died as a result of her injuries.* ◇ *The farm was flooded, with the result that most of the harvest was lost.* ◇ *This book is the result of 25 years of research.* See also **resulting**, **resultant** → RELATED, **result in sth** → CAUSE *verb*

consequence /'kɒnsɪkwəns; *AmE* 'kɑːnsəkwens/ [C] (*rather formal*) a result of sth that has happened, especially a bad result: *This decision could have serious consequences for the future of the industry.* ◇ *Two hundred people lost their jobs as a direct consequence of the merger.* ◇ *At some point you will have to face the consequences of your actions.* ❶ **Consequences** is used most frequently to talk about possible negative results of an action. It is commonly used with such words as *adverse, dire, disastrous, fatal, harmful, negative, serious, tragic* and *unfortunate*. Even when there is no adjective, **consequences** often suggests negative results: *Fearing the consequences, she left the company.* See also **consequent** → RELATED
▶ **consequently** *adv.*: *This poses a threat to agriculture and the food chain, and consequently to human health.*

outcome /'aʊtkʌm/ [C] the result of an action or process: *These costs are payable whatever the outcome of the case.* ◇ *We are confident of a successful outcome.* ◇ *Four possible outcomes have been identified.*

NOTE RESULT OR OUTCOME? **Result** is often used to talk about things that are caused directly by sth else: *Aggression is often the result of fear.* **Outcome** is more often used to talk about what happens at the end of a process when the exact relation of cause and effect is less clear: ~~Aggresssion is often the outcome of fear.~~ **Result** is often used after an event to talk about what happened. **Outcome** is often used before an action or process to talk about what is likely to happen.

implication /,ɪmplɪ'keɪʃn/ [C, usually pl.] a possible effect or result of an action or decision: *The development of the site will have implications for the surrounding countryside.* ◇ *They failed to consider the wider implications of their actions.*

product [C] (*rather formal*) a person or thing that is the result of sth: *The child is the product of a broken home.* ◇ *A complicated string of chemical reactions leads to the end product.*

the fruit/fruits of sth *idiom* (*rather formal*) the good results of an activity or situation: *Allow yourself to enjoy the fruits of your labour* (= the rewards for your hard work). ◇ *The book is the fruit of years of research.*

repercussion /riːpə'kʌʃn; *AmE* -pərk-/ [C, usually pl.] (*written*) an indirect and usually bad result of an action or event that may happen some time afterwards: *The collapse of the company will have repercussions for the whole industry.*

upshot (usually **the upshot**) [sing.] (*rather informal*) the final result of a particular series of events: *The upshot of it all was that he left college and got a job.* ❶ **The upshot** is common in spoken language. It is most frequently used at the beginning of a sentence, especially in the phrase *The upshot (of …) is/was that...*

return *verb*

1 return home
2 return books to the library

1 return · come back · go back · get back · turn back
These words all mean to come or go back from one place to another.

PATTERNS AND COLLOCATIONS
▶ to return / come back / go back / get back **to** / **from** / **with** sth
▶ to return / come back / go back / get back / turn back **again**
▶ to return / come back / go back / get back **home** / **to work**
▶ to return / come back / get back **safely**

return [I] (*rather formal*) to come or go back from one place to another: *I waited a long time for him to return.* ◇ *They were forced to return to their country of origin.* ◇ *He finally returned with the drinks.*
▸ **return** noun [sing.]: *He was met by his brother **on his return** from Italy.* ◇ *on the return flight/journey/trip*

,come 'back *phrasal verb* to return: *Come back and visit again soon!* ◇ *I asked her to come back to Japan with me.* ❶ **Come back** is usually used from the point of view of the person or place that sb returns to. **OPP** go away → GO AWAY

,go 'back *phrasal verb* to return to the place you recently or originally came from or that you have been to before: *Do you ever want to go back to China?* ◇ *John shrugged and went back downstairs.* ◇ *She's gone back to her husband* (= to live with him again). ◇ *This toaster will have to go back* (= to the shop) *– it doesn't work.* ❶ **Go back** is usually used from the point of view of the person who is returning.

,get 'back *phrasal verb* to arrive back somewhere, especially at your home or the place where you are staying: *What time did you get back last night?* ◇ *We only got back from our trip yesterday.* ◇ (*spoken*) *Oh, well. I must be getting back* (= going back home, back to work, etc.).

,turn 'back *phrasal verb* to return the way that you came, especially because sth stops you from continuing: *The weather got so bad that we had to turn back.*

---

2 See also the entry for REPAY

return · put sth back · give sth back · take sth back · replace · hand sth back · restore
These words all mean to give sth to the person who had it before or put sth in the place where it was before.

PATTERNS AND COLLOCATIONS
▸ to return sth/give sth back/take sth back/restore sth/hand sth back **to** sb/sth
▸ to put sth back/replace sth **on** sth
▸ to return/put back/give back/replace/hand back **money**
▸ to return/put back/give back/take back/replace a **book**
▸ to return/take back **faulty/unwanted goods**
▸ to put back/replace a **lid**
▸ to put back/replace the (**telephone**) **receiver**
▸ to return sth/put sth back/replace sth **quickly/soon**
▸ to put sth back/replace sth **firmly/gently/carefully**

return [T] (*rather formal*) to give, take or send sth to the person who had it, or place where it was before: *We had to return the hairdryer to the store because it was faulty.* ◇ *Completed questionnaires should be returned to this address.* ◇ *I returned the letter unopened.*
▸ **return** noun [U, sing.]: *We would appreciate the prompt return of books to the library.*

,put sth 'back *phrasal verb* to return sth to its usual place or the place where it was before it was moved: *If you use something, put it back!* ◇ *I put the book back on the shelf.*

,give sth 'back, ,give sb 'back sth *phrasal verb* to return sth to its owner; to allow sb to have sth again: *Give me back my pen!* ◇ *Give me my pen back!* ◇ *I picked it up and gave it back to him.* ◇ *The operation gave him back the use of his legs.*

,take sth 'back *phrasal verb* to return sth to the shop where you bought it, for example because it is the wrong size or does not work; (of a shop) to accept goods that have been taken back and repay the money or give sth else in exchange: *Don't worry. If you decide you don't like it, you can always take it back.* ◇ *The store refused to take the jacket back, claiming that it had already been worn several times.*

replace [T] (*rather formal*) to put sth back in the place where it was before: *I replaced the cup carefully in the saucer.*

,hand sth 'back *phrasal verb* to give or return sth to the person who owns it or to where it belongs, often by placing it in their hands: *She picked up the wallet and handed it back to him.* ◇ *Control of the territory was handed back to China.*

---

restore [T] (*formal*) to give sth that was lost or stolen back to sb: *The police have now restored the painting to its rightful owner.*

---

reveal *verb*

reveal · disclose · expose · uncover · leak · betray · divulge · give sb/sth away · bring sth to light
These words all mean to give information about sb/sth to sb, especially when that information is supposed to remain secret.

PATTERNS AND COLLOCATIONS
▸ to reveal/disclose/expose/leak/betray/divulge/give away sth **to** sb
▸ to reveal/disclose/expose/uncover sb/sth **as** sb/sth
▸ to reveal/disclose/betray/divulge/give away **that...**
▸ It was revealed/disclosed **that...**
▸ to reveal/disclose/betray/divulge **what/how/who/where/whether...**
▸ to reveal/disclose/uncover/leak/betray/divulge/give away a **secret**
▸ to reveal/disclose/expose/uncover/give away **the truth**
▸ to reveal/disclose/leak/divulge/give away **details** of sth
▸ to **fully/publicly** reveal/disclose/expose sth

reveal [T] to make sth known to sb, especially sth that was previously secret: *Her expression revealed nothing.* ◇ *The report reveals (that) the company made a loss of £20 million last year.* ◇ *Officers could not reveal how he died.* ◇ *Salted peanuts were recently revealed as the nation's favourite snack.* See also **reveal** → SHOW 2, **revealing** → INFORMATIVE
▸ **revelation** /ˌrevəˈleɪʃn/ *noun* [C, U]: *He was dismissed after revelations that confidential files were missing.* ◇ *The company's financial problems followed the revelation of a major fraud scandal.*

disclose /dɪsˈkləʊz; AmE -ˈkloʊz/ [T] (*rather formal*) to make sth known to sb, especially sth that was previously secret: *The spokesman refused to disclose details of the takeover to the press.* ◇ *It was disclosed that two women were being interviewed by the police.* See also **undisclosed** → SECRET 1
▸ **disclosure** /dɪsˈkləʊʒə(r); AmE -ˈkloʊ-/ *noun* [C, U]: (*formal*) *There were some startling disclosures about his private life.* ◇ *The bank will need full disclosure of your financial situation and assets.*

NOTE **REVEAL OR DISCLOSE?** There is no real difference in meaning between these words, but **disclose** is always rather formal; **reveal** can be used in formal or less formal contexts, including popular journalism: ~~Salted peanuts were recently disclosed as the nation's favourite snack.~~

expose [T] to tell the true facts about a person or situation, and show them/it to be bad or illegal: *She was exposed as a liar and a fraud.* ◇ *He threatened to expose the racism that existed within the police force.* See also **expose** → SHOW 2
▸ **exposé** /ek'spəʊzeɪ; AmE ˌekspoʊˈzeɪ/ *noun* [C]: (*journalism*) *The magazine contained a damning exposé of police corruption.*

uncover [T] to discover sth that was previously hidden or secret: *Police have uncovered a plot to kidnap the President's son.*

leak [T] (*journalism*) to give secret information to the public, for example by telling a newspaper: *The contents of the report were leaked to the press.* ◇ *He obtained a leaked document containing the views of some officials.* See also **leak out** → TURN OUT
▸ **leak** noun [C]: *There will be an enquiry into the alleged security leaks.*

betray [T] to tell sb or make them aware of a piece of information or a feeling, usually without meaning to: *His voice betrayed the worry he was trying to hide.* ◇ *She was terrified of saying something that would make her **betray herself*** (= show her feelings or who she was).

divulge /daɪˈvʌldʒ/ [T] (*formal*) to give sb information that is supposed to be secret: *Police refused to divulge the identity of the suspect.* ❶ **Divulge** is often used in the negative, or with a verb that has a negative meaning.

give sb/sth aˈway *phrasal verb* to make known sth that sb wants to keep secret: *She gave away state secrets to the enemy.* ◇ *His voice gave him away* (= showed who he really was). ◇ (*especially BrE*) *It was supposed to be a surprise but the children gave the game away.* See also **betray** → TELL 2

> **NOTE** **DIVULGE** OR **GIVE STH AWAY?** A person who **gives sth away** should really be keeping the information secret; a person who **divulges** information is more likely to have the authority to do so.

bring sth to ˈlight *idiom* to make new information known to people: *These facts have only just been brought to light.*

revenge *noun*

revenge · retaliation · vengeance · reprisal
These are all words for sth you do against sb because of sth they have done to you.

retaliation	revenge	vengeance
	reprisal	

PATTERNS AND COLLOCATIONS
▶ revenge / retaliation / vengeance / reprisals **for** sth
▶ retaliation / vengeance / reprisals **against** sb
▶ to take revenge / vengeance **on** sb
▶ **in** revenge / retaliation / vengeance / reprisal
▶ **in** revenge / retaliation / reprisal **for** sth
▶ to **take** / **seek** revenge / vengeance / reprisals
▶ to **fear** retaliation / vengeance / reprisals
▶ to **want** / **vow** / **swear** / **exact** / **wreak** revenge / vengeance

revenge /rɪˈvendʒ/ [U] something that you do in order to punish sb or make them suffer because they have harmed you or made you suffer: *The team wanted to get their revenge for their defeat earlier in the season.* ◇ *He swore to take revenge on his political enemies.* ◇ *His death set off a series of revenge killings.* See also **retribution** → PUNISHMENT

retaliation /rɪˌtæliˈeɪʃn/ [U] (*rather formal*) something that you do against sb in response to sth bad they have done to you: *The shooting may have been in retaliation for the arrest of the terrorist suspects.* See also **retaliate** → FIGHT BACK

vengeance /ˈvendʒəns/ [U] (*formal*) something violent that you do, such as killing or hurting sb, in order to make sb suffer because of sth harmful they have done to you: *Vengeance was swift and brutal.* ◇ *He swore vengeance on his child's killer.* See also **avenge** → FIGHT BACK

reprisal /rɪˈpraɪzl/ [C, U] (*written*) something violent or aggressive that a military force or political group does to punish the harm that one group of people did to it: *They were frightened to talk publicly for fear of reprisals.* ◇ *A dozen hostages were shot in reprisal for the killing of an army officer.*

> **NOTE** **WHICH WORD?** **Revenge** is the most general of these words and covers the whole range of actions from wanting to beat sb at a game after they have first beaten you, to killing sb because they have killed sb you love. It is often quite a personal, individual act that you do in response to sth that has been done to you personally. **Retaliation** and **reprisals** are often taken by a group such as a military force, against another group, who may not be the actual people responsible for the first crime, but are taken to represent them: *They fear retaliation against US troops and aid workers* (= for example, because of sth that the US government has done). **Vengeance** is the most extreme and violent of

these actions: it is often personal and can be much more extreme and violent than the original crime to which it is a response.

revenue *noun* See also the entry for INCOME

revenue · income · turnover · proceeds · receipts · takings · take
These are all words for money that is received from taxes or from selling goods or services.

PATTERNS AND COLLOCATIONS
▶ the revenue / income / turnover / proceeds / receipts / takings / take **from** sth
▶ the **gross** / **net** / **total** revenue / income / turnover / proceeds / receipts / takings / take
▶ the **expected** / **annual** revenue / income / turnover / proceeds / receipts
▶ the **potential** / **overall** revenue / income / turnover
▶ a **large** / **substantial** / **low** / **small** revenue / income / turnover
▶ to **increase** / **boost** / **reduce** (your) revenue / your income / turnover
▶ to **spend** / **use** your revenue / your income / the proceeds
▶ to **bring in** / **generate** / **produce** revenue / an income
▶ revenue / income / turnover / receipts **is** / **are up** / **down**

revenue /ˈrevənjuː; *AmE* -nuː/ [U, C] (*rather formal*) the money that a government receives from taxes or that a company or country receives from its business or investments: *The government is currently facing a shortfall in tax revenue.* ◇ *Advertising revenue finances the commercial television channels.* ◇ (*business*) *The company's annual revenues rose by 30% last year.*

income [C, U] the money that a company or country receives from its business or investments: *The company has an income of around $10 million a year.* ◇ *Tourism is the island's main source of income.*

> **NOTE** **REVENUE** OR **INCOME?** If you are talking about tax, use **revenue**. Otherwise, you can use either word, but **revenue** is more formal. **Income** is also used to talk about money that a person earns. See also the entry for INCOME

turnover /ˈtɜːnəʊvə(r); *AmE* ˈtɜːrnoʊ-/ [C, usually sing., U] (*business*) the money that a company receives for all the goods or services that it sells during a particular period of time: *The firm has an annual turnover of $75 million.* ◇ *A 10% rise in turnover would increase company profits by $3.3 million.*

proceeds /ˈprəʊsiːdz; *AmE* ˈproʊ-/ [pl.] the money that a person or company receives from selling goods or services, especially the amount available to be spent after paying the costs involved: *She sold her car and bought a piano with the proceeds.* ◇ *The proceeds of the concert will go to charity.* See also the entry for PROFIT

receipts /rɪˈsiːts/ [pl.] (*business*) the money that a company, bank or government receives during a particular period of time: *The accounts department is predicting net receipts of £750 000 for the summer season.*

takings [pl.] the money that a shop, restaurant, theatre, etc. receives from selling goods or tickets during a particular period of time: *Burglars forced open the safe containing the weekend takings.*

> **NOTE** **RECEIPTS** OR **TAKINGS?** **Receipts** is a more formal word and is often used for talking about bigger businesses, over a longer period of time. Both words are used for money made by a theatre or cinema, or by the film industry, especially in British English. In informal American English the word **take** is used: (*especially BrE*) *He estimated the film's box-office receipts/takings at £15 million.* ◇ (*AmE, rather informal*) *the movie's box-office take*

take [C, usually sing.] (*especially AmE, rather informal, business*) an amount of money that sb receives, especially money earned by a business from one particular source or piece of business: *Last year's take totaled $10.2 million.*

reverse *verb*

reverse · undo
These words both mean to change sth completely so that it is the opposite of what it was before.

PATTERNS AND COLLOCATIONS
▸ to reverse / undo the **effect / damage / reforms / years of hard work, neglect, etc.**
▸ to **completely** reverse / undo sth

reverse [T] (*rather formal, especially written*) to change sth completely so that it is the opposite of what it was before: *The government has failed to reverse the economic decline.* ◇ *It is sometimes possible to arrest or reverse the disease.* ❶ **Reverse** is most often used in texts relating to business and economics, especially when talking about changing the direction of a process or developement; collocates include *decline, trend, direction, process* and *situation*. See also **reversal** → REVOLUTION 2

undo /ʌnˈduː/ [T] to cancel the good or bad effect of sth: *He undid most of the good work of the previous manager.* ◇ *It's not too late to try and undo some of the damage.* ◇ *Just select 'Edit' and 'Undo' to cancel the previous action.* ❶ **Undo** is used equally often to talk about cancelling the effect of good and of bad things: *to undo the damage / harm / errors* ◇ *to undo the good work / years of endeavour / reforms*

revise *verb*

revise · edit · rewrite · rephrase
These words all mean to change a piece of writing in order to improve it.

PATTERNS AND COLLOCATIONS
▸ to revise / edit / rewrite a **text / report / book**
▸ to revise / edit a **document / manuscript**
▸ to revise / rewrite a **theory**
▸ to edit / rewrite / rephrase a **statement**
▸ to rewrite / rephrase a **sentence**
▸ to revise / rewrite / rephrase sth **slightly**

revise [T] to change sth, such as a book or estimate, in order to correct or improve it: *Have you got the revised edition of this textbook?* ◇ *We may have to revise this figure upwards.* See also **revise** → ADJUST, **revision** → CHANGE *noun* 2

edit /ˈedɪt/ [T] to prepare a book or piece of writing to be published by correcting the mistakes and making improvements to it: *He's editing a book of essays by Isaiah Berlin.* ◇ *This is the edited version of my speech* (= some parts have been taken out).

rewrite /ˌriːˈraɪt/ [T] to write sth again in a different way, usually in order to improve it or because there is some new information: *I intend to rewrite the story for younger children.* ◇ *This essay will have to be completely rewritten.*

rephrase /ˌriːˈfreɪz/ [T] to say or write sth again using different words in order to make it clearer or more acceptable: *Let me rephrase my question.* ◇ *I suggest you rephrase that remark* (= a polite way of telling sb that the way they have expressed sth is offensive or embarrassing).

revolution *noun*

1 the French Revolution
2 a technological revolution

1 See the Topic Map for CONFLICT on p.896
revolution · coup · riot · uprising · revolt · rebellion · rioting · insurgency · mutiny
These are all words for people acting together against authority.

PATTERNS AND COLLOCATIONS
▸ a revolution / a coup / an uprising / a revolt / a rebellion **against** sb / sth
▸ a **successful** revolution / coup / revolt
▸ a **major / full-scale** riot / revolt / rebellion
▸ a **military** coup / uprising / rebellion / mutiny
▸ a **popular** revolution / uprising / revolt / rebellion
▸ an **armed** coup / uprising / revolt / rebellion / insurgency
▸ (a) **violent** revolution / riot / uprising / rebellion / rioting
▸ to **plan** a revolution / coup / rebellion
▸ to **provoke** a riot / an uprising / a revolt / a rebellion
▸ to **stage / lead** a revolution / coup / revolt / rebellion / mutiny
▸ to **quell** a riot / an uprising / a revolt / a rebellion / rioting
▸ to **crush** an uprising / a revolt / a rebellion
▸ to **put down** a revolt / rebellion
▸ a revolution / a riot / a revolt / a rebellion / rioting **breaks out**

revolution [C, U] the use of force to replace a system of government with a very different system, carried out by the people of a country: *The French Revolution brought about great changes in the society and government of France.* ◇ *The country appears to be on the brink of revolution.* See also **revolutionary** → GUERRILLA *noun*, **revolutionary** → RADICAL *adj.*

coup /kuː/ [C] the illegal use of force to replace a particular leader or government, usually carried out by the military or a powerful group of people: *The regime was overthrown in a bloodless coup led by young army officers.* ◇ (*figurative*) *Months of unrest in the company led to a boardroom coup* (= a sudden change of power among senior managers in a company) *that saw four directors voted out.* ❶ **Coup** is a short form of **coup d'état** but **coup** is much more frequent.

riot /ˈraɪət/ [C] a situation in which a crowd of people behave in an uncontrolled and violent way in a public place, often as a protest: *Food riots resulted in two deaths and looting throughout the city.* ◇ *The demonstrators were held back by 6 000 riot police using tear gas and water cannon.*
▸ **riot** *verb* [I]: *The fans rioted after their team lost.*

uprising /ˈʌpraɪzɪŋ/ [C] a situation in which a lot of people act together to try to fight against the people who are in power in a country, region or city: *He used his troops to crush a popular uprising in the north.* ❶ **Uprising** is used in the names of particular uprisings that are remembered in history: *the 1956/Hungarian uprising.* An **uprising** is always defeated, often with great violence. If it is successful it is called a **revolution**. See also **rise** → REBEL *verb*

revolt [C, U] a protest against authority, especially that of a government, usually by a group of people, often involving violence; the action of protesting against authority: *27 members of the Bohemian nobility led the revolt against Ferdinand II.* ◇ *A shareholders' revolt against the chairman led to senior management changes.* ◇ *The people rose in revolt.* See also **revolt** → REBEL *verb*

rebellion [C, U] a situation in which part of a country or organization acts against the government or main authority, often using violence: *The army put down the rebellion.* ◇ *After years of protest, much of the country was now in open rebellion against the president.* See also **rebel** → REBEL *verb*, **rebel** → GUERRILLA *noun*

> **NOTE** **REVOLT OR REBELLION?** A **revolt** may be smaller or more limited than a **rebellion**: *The English Tudors faced six major rebellions and countless minor revolts.* A **rebellion** sometimes describes the opposition of a

group of people inside a bigger group or organization: *The prime minister faces a rebellion from junior members of his party.*

rioting /'raɪətɪŋ/ [U] the violent and uncontrolled activity of a group of people which takes place during a riot: *Serious rioting broke out in the capital.*

insurgency /ɪn'sɜːdʒənsi; AmE -'sɜːrdʒ-/ [U, C] (*formal*) a situation in which an armed group of people fight to try to take political control of their own country, often over a long period of time: *The government faces continuing insurgency in the north-east.* ◇ *The 23-year insurgency had cost an estimated 21 000 lives.* See also **insurgent** → GUERRILLA

mutiny /'mjuːtəni/ [U, C] the act of refusing to obey the orders of sb in authority, especially by soldiers or sailors: *Discontent among the ship's crew finally led to the outbreak of mutiny.* ◇ *The famous mutiny on the British Navy ship Bounty took place in 1789.* See also **mutiny** → REBEL verb

2 revolution · reversal · turnaround · U-turn · a change of heart · sea change
These are all words for a complete change of conditions, opinion, plan or behaviour.

PATTERNS AND COLLOCATIONS
▸ a revolution / reversal / turnaround / U-turn / sea change **in** sth
▸ a U-turn / a change of heart **on** / **over** sth
▸ a **complete** reversal / turnaround / U-turn / change of heart
▸ an **apparent** reversal / change of heart
▸ a **dramatic** reversal / turnaround / U-turn
▸ to **undergo** a revolution / change of heart / sea change
▸ to **represent** a revolution / reversal / turnaround / change of heart
▸ to **bring about** a revolution / reversal / change of heart

revolution [C] a great change in conditions, ways of working or beliefs that affects large numbers of people: *a cultural/social/scientific revolution* ◇ *A revolution in information technology is taking place.* ❶ The **Industrial Revolution** was the period in the 18th and 19th centuries in Europe and the US when machines began to be used to do work, and industry grew rapidly.

reversal [C] (*rather formal*) a change of sth so that it is the opposite of what it was: *The new figures suggest a reversal of the trend.* ◇ *The government suffered a total reversal of fortunes last week.* See also **reverse** → REVERSE

turnaround /'tɜːnəraʊnd; AmE 'tɜːrn-/ (*BrE also turnround*) [C, usually sing.] a situation in which sth changes from bad to good: *Is this the beginning of a turnaround in the economy?*

'U-turn [C] (*informal, especially journalism*) a complete change in policy or behaviour, usually one that is embarrassing: *The government may be forced into an embarrassing U-turn on education policy.* ❶ **U-turn** is used especially to talk about changes in policy by governments or politicians. See also **do a U-turn** → BREAK verb 4

a ‚change of ‘heart idiom if you have a **change of heart**, your attitude towards sth changes, usually making you feel more friendly, helpful, etc: *Dan did not want to get married but recently he's had a change of heart.*

'sea change [sing.] (*written*) a strong and noticeable change in a situation, especially in people's attitudes to sth: *It was one of those momentous events that cause a sea change in public attitudes.*

rhythm noun

rhythm · time · beat · tempo · metre
These are all words for a strong regular repeated pattern of sounds in music or poetry.

PATTERNS AND COLLOCATIONS
▸ **to** the rhythm / beat
▸ **in** rhythm / time
▸ a **slow** rhythm / beat / tempo
▸ a **fast** rhythm / tempo

▸ a **regular** / **strong** / **throbbing** rhythm / beat
▸ to **have** / **lack** a rhythm / beat / tempo
▸ to **clap** / **dance** / **sway to** the rhythm / beat

rhythm /'rɪðəm/ [U, C] a strong, regular repeated pattern of sounds or movements: *The dancers moved to the rhythm of the music.* ◇ *I listened to the steady rhythm of her breathing.* ◇ *She has a **natural sense of rhythm** (= ability to move/play in time to a beat).* ◇ *I love these jazz rhythms.* ◇ *Doctors discovered that he had an abnormal heart rhythm.* See also **rhythm** → PATTERN 1
▸ **rhythmic** adj.: *music with a fast, rhythmic beat*

time [U] the correct speed and rhythm of a piece of music; the number of beats in a bar of music: *Try and dance **in time to** the music (= with the same speed and rhythm).* ◇ *Clap your hands to **keep time** (= sing or play with the correct speed and rhythm).* ◇ *She always plays **in/out of** time.* ◇ *The conductor **beat time** with a baton.*

beat [C] the main rhythm, or unit of rhythm, in a piece of music or a poem: *This type of music has a strong beat to it.* ◇ *The piece has four beats to the bar.*

tempo /'tempəʊ; AmE -poʊ/ (**tempos** or **tempi** /'tempiː/) [C] (*music*) the speed or rhythm of a piece of music: *It's a difficult piece, with numerous changes of tempo.* See also **tempo** → RATE 1

metre (*BrE*) (*AmE* **meter**) [U, C] (*technical*) the arrangement of strong and weak stresses in lines of poetry that produces the rhythm; a particular example of this: *She knows a lot about verse metre.* ◇ *poems in a variety of metres*

rich adj.

rich · wealthy · prosperous · affluent · well off · privileged · comfortable · loaded
These words all describe sb/sth that has a lot of money, property or valuable possessions.

PATTERNS AND COLLOCATIONS
▸ a rich / a wealthy / a prosperous / an affluent / a well-off / a privileged **family**
▸ a rich / wealthy / prosperous / well-off **man** / **woman**
▸ a rich / a wealthy / a prosperous / an affluent **country** / **city** / **suburb**
▸ **very** rich / wealthy / prosperous / affluent / well off / comfortable
▸ **quite** / **fairly** / **reasonably** / **relatively** rich / wealthy / prosperous / affluent / well off / comfortable
▸ **newly** rich / wealthy / prosperous / affluent

rich (of a person) having a lot of money, property or valuable possessions; (of a country or city) producing a lot of wealth so that many of its people can live at a high standard: *She's one of the richest women in the world.* ◇ (*slang*) *He's **stinking/filthy** (= extremely) **rich**.* ◇ *Rich countries can afford to spend more on the environment.* **OPP** poor → POOR 1, See also **riches** → MONEY 3
▸ **the rich** noun [pl.]: *It's a favourite resort for **the rich and famous** (= people who are rich and famous).*

wealthy rich: *She comes from a very wealthy family.* ◇ *They live in a wealthy suburb of Chicago.* **OPP** poor, needy → POOR 1, See also **wealth** → MONEY 3
▸ **the wealthy** noun [pl.]: *He promised tax cuts for the wealthy (= people who are wealthy).*

NOTE RICH OR WEALTHY? There is no real difference in meaning between these two words. Both are very frequent, but **rich** is more frequent and can be used in some fixed phrases where **wealthy** cannot: *He's stinking/filthy wealthy.* ◇ *It's a favourite resort for the wealthy and famous.*

prosperous /'prɒspərəs; AmE 'prɑːs-/ (*rather formal*) rich and successful: *These countries became prosperous through trade, not aid.* ◇ *The 1960s were prosperous years for the company.* **OPP** impoverished → POOR 1, See also **prosper** → DO WELL, **prosperity** → MONEY 3

affluent /ˈæfluənt/ (*rather formal*) rich and with a good standard of living: *The affluent Western countries are better equipped to face the problems of global warming.* **OPP** **poor, impoverished** → POOR 1, See also **affluence** → MONEY 3

> **NOTE** PROSPEROUS OR AFFLUENT? Both **prosperous** and **affluent** are used to talk about people and places. **Prosperous** is used much more than **affluent** to talk about times and periods. **Affluent** is often used to contrast rich people or societies with poor ones, in a way that suggests that it is not always a good thing. Being **prosperous** is nearly always seen as a good thing: *It's good to see you looking so prosperous.* ◊ ~~It's good to see you looking so affluent.~~

‚well 'off (often used in negative sentences) rich: *His parents are not very well off.* ◊ *The less well-off families are finding it hard to survive on what they get.* **OPP** **hard up** → POOR 1

privileged /ˈprɪvəlɪdʒd/ (*sometimes disapproving*) having special rights or advantages because you come from a rich family: *She comes from a privileged background.* **OPP** **deprived** → POOR 1
> **privilege** *noun* [U]: (*disapproving*) *As a member of the nobility, his life had been one of wealth and privilege.*

comfortable having enough money to buy what you want without worrying about the cost: *They're not millionaires, but they're certainly very comfortable.* ◊ *He makes a comfortable living.*
> **comfortably** *adv.*: *You should be able to live comfortably on your allowance.*

loaded [not before noun] (*informal*) very rich: *Let her pay — she's loaded.*

ridiculous *adj.*

ridiculous · absurd · silly · ludicrous · foolish · laughable
These words all describe sth that has no sense or reason.

silly	ridiculous	ludicrous
foolish	absurd	
laughable		

PATTERNS AND COLLOCATIONS
▶ ridiculous/ absurd/ silly/ ludicrous **that...**
▶ It would be ridiculous/ absurd/ silly/ ludicrous/ foolish **to do sth**.
▶ a ridiculous/ an absurd/ a silly/ a ludicrous/ a foolish **idea/ notion**
▶ a ridiculous/ an absurd/ a silly/ a foolish **question**
▶ a ridiculous/ an absurd/ a ludicrous **suggestion/ situation**
▶ a silly/ a foolish **comment/ remark/ smile/ grin**
▶ **quite/ pretty** ridiculous/ absurd/ silly/ ludicrous/ foolish/ laughable
▶ **rather** ridiculous/ absurd/ silly/ ludicrous/ foolish
▶ **completely/ totally/ utterly/ downright** ridiculous/ absurd/ silly/ ludicrous
▶ **simply** ridiculous/ absurd/ ludicrous/ foolish

ridiculous without any sense or reason; deserving to be laughed at: *You look ridiculous in that hat!* ◊ *Don't be so ridiculous!* ◊ *It's ridiculous to suggest that she was involved in anything illegal.* ◊ *That's the most ridiculous thing I've ever heard.* ◊ *They ate and drank a ridiculous amount.* See also **ridicule** → CONTEMPT
> **ridiculously** *adv.*: *The food there is ridiculously expensive.*

absurd /əbˈsɜːd; *AmE* əbˈsɜːrd/ ridiculous; not at all logical or appropriate: *What an absurd idea!* ◊ *He has a good sense of the absurd* (= things that are absurd).
> **absurdity** *noun* [U]: *She failed to appreciate the absurdity of her position.*
> **absurdly** *adv.*: *I was offered an absurdly large amount of money.*

> **NOTE** RIDICULOUS OR ABSURD? There is very little difference in meaning between these words. Something that is **ridiculous** invites **ridicule** (= unkind laughter); something that is **absurd** is completely illogical or inappropriate, often in a way that causes laughter. **Absurd** is more frequent in British English than in American English, and is slightly more formal than **ridiculous**.

silly stupid or embarrassing, especially in a way that is more typical of a child than an adult: *I feel really silly in these clothes.* ◊ *She had a silly grin on her face.* ◊ *This is getting silly! I think we had all better calm down.*

ludicrous /ˈluːdɪkrəs/ completely ridiculous and unreasonable: *That's a ludicrous suggestion!* ◊ *This is ludicrous! Of course no one's going to murder you!*
> **ludicrously** *adv.*: *Everything here is ludicrously expensive.*

foolish (*rather formal*) feeling or seeming stupid and/or embarrassed at sth you have done; making you look stupid or feel embarrassed: *He didn't want to look foolish in front of his friends.* ◊ *She spoke as though to a child who had asked a foolish question.* See also **fool** → FOOL

laughable [not usually before noun] silly or ridiculous and not worth taking seriously: *The whole incident would be laughable if it wasn't so serious.* ◊ *He's so wrong it's almost laughable.*

right *noun* See the Topic Map for THE INDIVIDUAL AND SOCIETY on p.894

right · power · privilege · claim · authority · liberty · entitlement · title · due
These are all words for sth you are legally or morally allowed to have or do.

PATTERNS AND COLLOCATIONS
▶ sb's right/ power/ claim **over** sb/ sth
▶ a right/ a claim/ an entitlement/ a title **to** sth
▶ the right/ power/ authority/ entitlement **to do sth**
▶ a/ an **special/ exclusive** right/ power/ privilege/ claim
▶ a/ the **legal** right/ power/ claim/ authority/ entitlement/ title
▶ **personal** rights/ claims/ liberties
▶ **have** a/ the right/ the power/ the privilege/ a claim/ the authority/ an entitlement/ title
▶ **use/ exercise** your right/ powers/ privilege/ authority/ entitlement
▶ **give sb** a right/ the power/ a privilege/ title/ their due
▶ **grant sb** rights/ powers/ privileges/ liberties
▶ **revoke** a right/ the power/ a privilege/ the authority
▶ **lose** your right/ powers/ privilege/ entitlement
▶ **forfeit** your right/ privilege/ claim/ entitlement/ title
▶ **give up** your right/ powers/ privilege/ claim/ title
▶ **renounce** your right/ privilege/ claim/ title
▶ **waive** your right/ privilege/ claim
▶ **respect** sb's right/ claim/ liberties

right [C] something that you should definitely be allowed to do or have, either legally or morally: *Everyone has the right to a fair trial.* ◊ *What gives you the right to do that?* ◊ *You're* **quite within your rights** *to ask for your money back* (= you definitely have a right to do it). ◊ *She* **had every right** *to be angry.* ◊ **By rights** (= according to sb's rights) *half the money should be mine.* ◊ *This is a fundamental* **human right** (= a right that all people should have). ◊ *They have always fought hard for* **equal rights** (= the right of all people in society to be treated fairly and equally). See also **birthright** → LEGACY

power [U, C, usually pl.] the right of a person or group to do sth, especially sth that involves having control over sb else: *The Secretary of State has the power to approve the proposals.* ◊ *The president has the power of veto over all new legislation.* ◊ *The powers of the police must be clearly defined.*

privilege /ˈprɪvəlɪdʒ/ [C] a special right or advantage that a particular person or group has: *Education should be a universal right and not just a privilege.* ◊ *Club* members have special privileges, like being allowed to use the swimming pool. ❶ **Privilege** [U] is used in a disapproving way to mean 'the rights and advantages that only the rich or powerful people in a society have': (*disapproving*) *His life had always been one of wealth and privilege.*

claim [C, U] a right that sb believes they have to sth, for example property or land: *The court ruled that they had no* **claim on** *the land.* ◇ *The princess was forced to renounce her claim to the throne.* ◇ *He went back to* **lay claim to** *his inheritance.*
▶ **claim** *verb* [T]: *A lot of lost property is never claimed.* ◇ *The family arrived in the UK in the 1990s and claimed political asylum.*

authority [U] the right to do sth, especially because you hold a senior position in an organization: *Only the manager has the authority to sign cheques.*

> **NOTE** **POWER** OR **AUTHORITY?** In this meaning **authority** is usually used in the phrase *(have) the authority to do sth*. This authority usually comes from sb's position within a company or other organization and refers to what they are allowed to do within that organization. *The power to do sth* or *special powers* often come from the courts, the government or a country's constitution (= system of laws and political organization) and refer to what sb is allowed to do within the law or government of the country: ~~Only the manager has the power to sign cheques.~~ ◇ ~~The authority of the police must be clearly defined.~~

liberty /ˈlɪbəti; *AmE* -bərti/ [C] the legal freedom to do sth: *The right to vote should be a liberty enjoyed by all.* ◇ *This is a gross infringement of our* **civil liberties** (= the right of people to be free to say or do what they want while respecting others and staying within the law). ❶ In this meaning **liberty** is used especially in the phrases *personal/civil liberties*.

entitlement [U, C] (*especially BrE, formal*) the official right to have or do sth, especially to receive a payment or own property; something, especially an amount of money, that you have an official right to have or receive: *This may affect your entitlement to compensation.* ◇ *Your contributions will affect your pension entitlements.* ❶ This meaning of **entitlement** is not very frequent in American English. However, especially in American English the phrase *a sense of entitlement* is used in a disapproving way to talk about people who think they have a right to sth without actually working for it: (*especially AmE, disapproving*) *The only child of very wealthy parents, she embodies the spoiled brat with a sense of entitlement.* See also **entitle** → ALLOW

title [U, C] (*law*) the legal right to own sth, especially land or property; the document that shows you have this right: *He claims he has title to the land.* ◇ *Who holds the* **title deed** (= the legal document proving that sb is the owner of a particular property or piece of land)?

due /djuː; *AmE* duː/ [U] something, especially praise, that should be given to sb because they have earned it by their actions: *He received a large reward, which was no more than his due* (= what he deserved). ◇ *She's a slow worker, but to* **give her her due** (= be fair to her) *she is very thorough.* ❶ In this meaning **due** is always used in the phrase *my/your/his/her/our/their due*.

right *adj.*
1 the right decision
2 do the right thing

1 right · correct · proper
These words all describe a belief, opinion, decision or method that is suitable or the best one for a particular situation.

PATTERNS AND COLLOCATIONS
▶ right / correct **about** sb / sth
▶ right / correct **to do sth**
▶ right / correct **in thinking / believing / saying** sth

▶ the / a right / correct / proper **decision / judgement / conclusion**
▶ the right / correct / proper **way / method / approach**
▶ **absolutely / quite / undoubtedly** right / correct

right if sb is **right** to do or think sth, that is a good thing to do or think in that situation: *She was right about Tom having no money.* ◇ *You're right to be cautious.* ◇ *Am I right in thinking we've met before?* ◇ *He's made the right decision.* ◇ *'It's not easy.' 'Yeah, you're right.'* **OPP wrong** → WRONG 1
▶ **rightly** *adv.*: *She believed, quite rightly, that he had let her down.*

correct (*rather formal*) (of a method, belief, opinion or decision) right and suitable in a particular situation: *What's the correct way to shut the machine down?* ◇ *Am I correct in thinking that you know a lot about wine?* **OPP incorrect** ❶ The opposite is **incorrect**, but in this meaning it is very formal and not very frequent.
▶ **correctly** *adv.*: *Make sure the letter is correctly addressed.*

proper [only before noun] (*especially BrE*) (especially of a method or decision) right, appropriate or correct; according to the rules: *We should have had a proper discussion before voting.* ◇ *Please follow the proper procedures for dealing with complaints.* ◇ *Nothing is in its proper place.*
▶ **properly** *adv.*: *How much money do we need to do the job properly?*

> **NOTE** **RIGHT, CORRECT** OR **PROPER** Correct is more formal than **right** or **proper**; **proper** is not used so much in American English. People can be **right** or **correct** about sth, but NOT **proper**: ~~You're proper to be cautious.~~ ◇ ~~Am I proper in thinking...?~~ Correct and **proper** are more often used to talk about methods; **right** is more often used to talk about beliefs, opinions and decisions.

2 right · acceptable · proper · due · justified · decent · justifiable
These words all describe sth that is morally good or socially acceptable.

PATTERNS AND COLLOCATIONS
▶ right / acceptable / proper / justified / justifiable **to do sth**
▶ right / justified **in doing sth**
▶ right / acceptable / proper **that...**
▶ acceptable / proper / decent **behaviour**
▶ to **do** the right / proper / decent **thing**
▶ **scarcely / hardly / not really** right / acceptable / proper / justified
▶ **perfectly** right / acceptable / proper / justified / decent / justifiable
▶ **entirely** right / acceptable / proper / justified / justifiable
▶ **morally** right / acceptable / justified / justifiable
▶ **only** right / proper

right [not usually before noun] morally good; correct according to law or a person's duty: *You were quite right to tell me.* ◇ *It's right that he should be punished.* ◇ *Hunting may be legal, but that doesn't make it right.* ◇ *I hope we're doing the right thing.* **OPP wrong** → WRONG 4
▶ **rightly** *adv.*: *Rightly or wrongly, he was released early from prison.* ◇ *Politicians are asked to declare any business interests, and rightly so.*

acceptable (especially of behaviour or actions) thought to be right by most people in a society: *Children have to learn what is acceptable behaviour and what is not.* ◇ *Divorce is much more socially acceptable than it used to be.* **OPP unacceptable** → UNACCEPTABLE

proper /ˈprɒpə(r); *AmE* ˈprɑːp-/ (*rather formal*) socially and morally acceptable: *It is right and proper that parents take responsibility for their children's behaviour.* ◇ *I'll do whatever I think proper.* ◇ *The development was planned without proper regard for the feelings of the local residents.* **OPP improper** → IMPROPER
▶ **properly** *adv.*: *You acted perfectly properly in approaching me first.*

NOTE **ACCEPTABLE** OR **PROPER**? **Acceptable** has a wider general meaning than **proper**: things can be *socially/ morally acceptable* but NOT: *socially/morally proper* because the social/moral aspect is included in the meaning of **proper**. **Proper** is a more formal word than **acceptable**, and more frequent in British English than in American English. It can suggest a greater degree of approval: actions that are **proper** are actions that you approve of; actions that are **acceptable** are actions that you do not disapprove of.

due [only before noun] (*formal*) that is suitable or right in the circumstances: *After due consideration we have decided to appoint Mr Davis to the job.* ◊ *Your request will be dealt with in due course* (= at the right time and not before).

justified /'dʒʌstɪfaɪd/ [not usually before noun] having a good reason for doing sth; existing or done for a good reason: *She felt fully justified in asking for her money back.* ◊ *I don't think the death penalty is ever justified.* **OPP** un-justified → UNJUSTIFIED

decent /'diːsnt/ (*rather formal*) acceptable to people in a particular situation: *Local people made sure the soldiers were given a decent burial.* ◊ *I think he should do the decent thing and resign.* ◊ *She should have waited* **a decent interval** *before marrying again.* **OPP** indecent → IM-PROPER

justifiable /'dʒʌstɪfaɪəbl; ˌdʒʌstɪ'faɪəbl/ existing or done for a good reason and therefore acceptable: *She took a justifiable pride in her son's achievements.* ◊ *There were no justifiable grounds for sending him to prison.* **OPP** unjus-tifiable → UNJUSTIFIED

▸ **justifiably** *adv.*: *The college can be justifiably proud of its record.*

NOTE **JUSTIFIED** OR **JUSTIFIABLE**? A person or action can be **justified**; an action, feeling or reason can be **justifiable**: *She felt justifiable in asking for her money back.* ◊ *There were no justified grounds for sending him to prison.*

ring
verb See also the entry for CLINK

ring · sound · chime · clang · buzz · toll · clank · strike · jangle
These words all mean to make a sound like the sound made by clocks and bells.

PATTERNS AND COLLOCATIONS
▸ the **bell** rings / sounds / chimes / clangs / tolls / jangles
▸ the **doorbell** rings / sounds / chimes / buzzes / jangles
▸ the **clock** rings / sounds / chimes / strikes
▸ to ring / sound / chime / clang / buzz / clank / jangle **loudly**

ring [T, I] to make a sound with a bell; (of a bell) to make a sound: *Someone was ringing the doorbell.* ◊ *The church bells rang.* ◊ *Just ring for the nurse* (= attract the nurse's attention by ringing a bell) *if you need her.*
▸ **ring** *noun* [C]: *There was a ring at the door.* ◊ *He gave a couple of loud rings on the doorbell.*

sound [I] (of a bell, clock, etc.) to produce a sound: *An alarm sounded two minutes after midnight.* See also **sound** → BLOW *verb* 3

chime /tʃaɪm/ [I, T] (of a bell or clock) to make a musical ringing sound or play a short tune, especially in order to show the time: *I heard the clock chime.* ◊ *Eight o'clock had already chimed.* ◊ *The clock chimed midnight.*
▸ **chime** *noun* [C]: *The clock plays a little chime on the quarter hours.*

clang [I, T] to make a loud ringing noise like the noise of metal being hit; to make sth produce this sound: *Bells were clanging in the tower.* ◊ *The heavy iron gates clanged shut.* ◊ *The trams clanged their way along the streets.* See also **clang** → BANG *noun*

buzz [I] to make a low continuous sound like the sound made by a bee: *The doorbell buzzed loudly.* ◊ *A police helicopter was buzzing overhead.*
▸ **buzz** *noun* [C, usually sing.]: *The intercom on her desk gave a loud buzz.*

toll /təʊl; *AmE* toʊl/ [I, T] (*rather formal or literary*) (of a large bell) to ring slowly and for a long time, especially as a sign that sb has died; to ring a large bell in this way: *The Abbey bell tolled for those killed in the war.* ◊ *The bell tolled the hour.*

clank [I, T] to make a loud, dull sound like pieces of metal hitting each other; to make sth produce this sound: *The door clanked shut behind them.* ◊ *The guard clanked his heavy ring of keys.*
▸ **clank** *noun* [C, usually sing.]: *The lid hit the floor with a clank.*

strike [I, T] (*rather formal*) (of a clock) to show the time by making a ringing sound; to make a sound on a musical instrument by pressing a key or hitting sth: *Did you hear the clock strike?* ◊ *Four o'clock had just struck.* ◊ *The clock has just struck three.* ◊ *She struck a chord on the piano and the children began to sing.*

jangle [I, T] to make a harsh sound, like the sound of several small pieces of metal hitting each other; to make sth do this: *The shop bell jangled loudly.* ◊ *He jangled the keys in his pocket.*
▸ **jangle** *noun* [C, usually sing.]: *The shrill jangle of the doorbell made them both jump.*

rise
verb See also the entry for SOAR

rise · grow · increase · climb · go up · escalate
These are all words that can be used when the amount, level or number of sth gets bigger or higher.

PATTERNS AND COLLOCATIONS
▸ to rise / grow / increase / go up **in** price, number, etc.
▸ to rise / grow / increase / climb / go up **by** 10%; 2 000, etc.
▸ to rise / grow / increase / climb / go up / escalate **from** 2% **to** 5%
▸ the **price / number** rises / increases / climbs / goes up / escalates
▸ the **level / cost** rises / increases / goes up / escalates
▸ the **size / amount** grows / increases
▸ to rise / grow / increase / climb / go up / escalate **sharply**
▸ to rise / grow / increase / climb / go up **slightly / steadily / slowly / rapidly / dramatically**
▸ to rise / grow / increase / escalate **suddenly**
▸ to rise / increase / climb / go up **steeply**

rise [I] to become greater in number, level or amount: *rising fuel bills/divorce rates* ◊ *The price of gas has risen by 3%.* ◊ *Gas rose sharply in price.* ◊ *Interest rates are expected to rise from 4.5% to 5% in the next six months.* **OPP** fall, drop, sink → FALL 1, See also **rise** → INCREASE *noun*

grow [I] to become greater in size, number or strength: *The company profits are expected to grow by 5% next year.* ◊ *She is growing in confidence all the time.* ◊ *Their performance improved as their confidence grew.* ◊ *There is growing opposition to the latest proposals.* ◊ *The company is growing bigger all the time.* **OPP** shrink → SHRINK, See also **growth** → INCREASE *noun*, **expand** → EXPAND 1

increase [I] to become greater in amount, level, number, degree, value, size or strength: *The population has increased from 1.2 million to 1.8 million.* ◊ *Demand is expected to increase over the next decade.* ◊ *Disability increases with age* (= the older sb is, the more likely they are to have a disability). **OPP** decrease, decline → FALL 1, See also **increase** → INCREASE *noun*, **increase** → INCREASE *verb*

NOTE **RISE, GROW** OR **INCREASE**? Although it is the most frequent of these verbs, **rise** is most often used about the number or level of sth; **grow** and **increase** can also be used about size and strength: *Profits/Numbers have risen/grown/increased.* ◊ *Her confidence/fear grew/ increased.* ◊ *Her confidence/fear rose.* **Increase** is slightly more formal than **rise** or **grow**.

climb [I] (of a figure or temperature or a country's money) to become greater in level or value: *The dollar/ temperature has been climbing all week.* ◊ *The paper's circulation continues to climb.* ◊ *Membership is climbing steadily.* ❶ **Climb** is usually used to talk about a number rather than an amount: *Unemployment* (= the number of unemployed people) *is still climbing.* ~~The pollution/mess is climbing.~~ **OPP** **drop** → FALL 1

go 'up *phrasal verb* (*rather informal, especially spoken*) to become greater in level or value: *The price of cigarettes is going up.* ◇ *Do you think interest rates will go up again?* **OPP** **come down** → FALL 1

escalate /'eskəleɪt/ [I] (*rather formal*) to become greater, worse or more serious: *The fighting escalated into a full-scale war.* ◇ *the escalating costs of health care*

risk *noun*

1 the risk of heart disease
2 take a risk

1 risk · danger · threat · fear

These words all mean the possibility that sth bad or unpleasant will happen.

PATTERNS AND COLLOCATIONS
▸ the risk / danger / threat **of** sth happening
▸ the risk / danger / threat **that** sth will happen
▸ (a) **real / great / serious / grave** risk / danger / threat
▸ to **pose** a risk / danger / threat
▸ to **put** sth at risk / in danger / under threat

risk [C, U] the possibility that sth bad will happen, especially as a result of doing sth or trying to do sth: *There is still a risk that the whole deal will fall through.* ◇ *We don't want to run the risk of losing their business.* ◇ *We could probably trust her with the information but it's just not worth the risk.* ◇ *At the risk of showing my ignorance, how exactly does this system work?* ◇ *He dived in to save the dog at considerable risk to his own life.* See also **risk** → THREAT *noun*, **risk** → DARE *verb*, **risky** → DANGEROUS, **at risk** → VULNERABLE

danger [U, C] the possibility that sth bad will happen, especially sth that will injure, harm or kill sb or damage or destroy sth: *Danger! Keep Out!* (= written on a sign) ◇ *Children's lives are in danger every time they cross this road.* ◇ *The building is in danger of collapsing.* ◇ *Doctors said she is now out of danger* (= not likely to die). ◇ *There is a danger that the political disorder of the past will return.* See also **danger** → THREAT *noun*, **dangerous** → DANGEROUS

threat [U, C, usually sing.] the possibility that sth bad will happen because of the way that things are now: *These ancient woodlands are under threat from new road developments.* ◇ *There is a real threat of war.* See also **threat** → THREAT, **threaten** → THREATEN 2, **threaten** → THREATEN 3, **threatening** → THREATENING

fear [U] (*rather formal*) the danger of sth happening ❶ In this meaning **fear** is used only in the expressions *for fear of sth/of doing sth* and *for fear that...* to mean 'to avoid the danger of sth happening': *We spoke quietly for fear of waking the guards.* ◇ *I had to run away for fear that he might one day kill me.*

2 risk · gamble · chance · lottery

These are all words for sth you do that you know might have a bad result, but that you hope you will be a success.

PATTERNS AND COLLOCATIONS
▸ to take a risk / gamble / chance **on** sth
▸ to take a risk / chance **with** sth
▸ a **big** risk / gamble / chance
▸ a **huge / major / calculated** risk / gamble
▸ **something of / a bit of** a risk / gamble / lottery
▸ to **take** a risk / gamble / chance
▸ a risk / gamble **pays off**

risk [C] (usually used in the phrase *take a risk*) something that you do even though you know that sth bad could happen as a result: *That's a risk that I'm not prepared to take.* ◇ *You have no right to take risks with other people's lives.* ◇ *Thankfully the risk paid off* (= the action was successful). See also **risk** → DARE *verb*, **risky** → DANGEROUS

gamble [sing.] something that you do even though you know it could be unsuccessful or have a bad result, but when you hope the result will be a success: *It was the biggest gamble of his political career.* ◇ *She knew she was taking a gamble but decided it was worth it.* **OPP** **safe bet** → OPTION

▸ **gamble** *verb* [T, I]: *He gambled his reputation on this deal.* ◇ *It was wrong to gamble with our children's future.*

chance [C] (only used in the phrases *take a chance/take no chances*) something that you decide to do even though you know it might be the wrong choice or sth bad could happen as a result: *The manager took a chance on a young, inexperienced player.* ◇ *The police were taking no chances with the protesters.*

> **NOTE** RISK, GAMBLE OR CHANCE? Risk is used especially when you are putting your/sb's life or safety in danger; gamble is usually used when the danger is less serious, or you are risking money; *take a chance* or *take no chances* is often used when you decide to give/not to give sb the opportunity to do sth.

lottery /'lɒtəri; AmE 'lɑːt̮-/ [sing.] (*often disapproving*) a situation whose success or result is based on luck rather than on effort or careful organization: *Politicians have acknowledged that it is a bit of a lottery who gets funding.*

river *noun*

river · stream · canal · waterway · creek · tributary

These are all words for a flow of water in a channel in the ground.

PATTERNS AND COLLOCATIONS
▸ a **narrow** river / stream / canal / waterway
▸ an **underground** river / stream
▸ a river / stream / canal / creek / tributary **flows**
▸ a river / stream / canal / creek **runs**
▸ a river / stream / canal / tributary **feeds** a (larger) river, lake, etc.

river [C] a natural flow of water that continues in a long line across land to the sea or ocean: *They live in a houseboat on the river.* ◇ *They have a house on the river* (= beside it). ◇ *Eventually we came to the mouth of the River Thames* (= where it enters the sea).

stream [C] a small narrow river: *We waded across a little mountain stream.*

canal /kə'næl/ [C] a long straight passage dug in the ground and filled with water for boats and ships to travel along; a smaller passage used for carrying water, for example to crops in a field: *The barge moved slowly along the canal.* ◇ *It is important to keep the irrigation canals clear of vegetation.*

waterway /'wɔːtəweɪ; AmE 'wɔːt̮ərw-; 'wɑːt̮-/ [C] (*rather formal*) a river or canal along which boats can travel: *The Waterways Board controls over 3 600 km of inland waterways.*

creek [C] (*AmE, AustralE*) a small river or stream: *He stood on the steep bank above Ray's Creek.* ❶ In British English a **creek** is a narrow area of water where the sea flows into the land: *They drove to the little creek where they kept their fishing boat.*

tributary /'trɪbjətri; AmE -teri/ [C] a river or stream that flows into a larger river or lake: *We need to monitor the water quality of the tributaries that feed the lake.*

road *noun*

road · street · alley · lane · avenue · boulevard · row · terrace

These are all words for a hard surface built for vehicles to travel on, often with houses and other buildings on both sides.

PATTERNS AND COLLOCATIONS
▸ **in** the road / street / alley / lane / avenue
▸ **on** a road / street
▸ a **wide / broad** road / street / avenue / boulevard

▸ a **narrow** road / street / alley / lane / terrace
▸ a **main** road / street / avenue / boulevard
▸ a **back** / **side** road / street / alley
▸ a **straight** road / street / avenue / terrace
▸ a **tree-lined** road / street / avenue / boulevard
▸ to **cross** the road / street
▸ to **turn into** a road / a street / an alley / a lane / an avenue / a boulevard
▸ to **turn off** a road / a street / an avenue / a boulevard

road [C] a hard surface built for vehicles to travel on: *A man's body was lying in the road.* ◊ *She lives on a very busy road.* ◊ *My mother lives down the road.* ◊ *Take the first road on the left.* ◊ *It's a quiet residential road.* ◊ *It would be better to go by road.* ◊ *The aim is to reduce the number of* **road accidents**. ◊ *The children learn about* **road safety** (= ways to avoid road accidents).

NOTE All the words in this group are also used in street names, where they are written with a capital letter: *53 York Road* ◊ *Oxford Street* ◊ *Ocean Boulevard.* The abbreviations **Rd.**, **St.**, **Ave.** and **Blvd.** are often used in addresses. In British English these are usually written without a full point: *The letter was addressed to: Margaret Willis, 14 Hamilton Rd, London W3.*

street [C] a public road in a city or town that has houses and buildings on one or both sides: *I met him by chance in the street.* ◊ *I walked up the street as far as the post office.* ◊ *It's a medieval town, with narrow cobbled streets.* ◊ *(BrE) There are several banks in the* **high street** (= the main street in a town).

NOTE ROAD OR STREET? In a town or city **street** is the most usual word for a road with buildings on one or both sides: *a street map of London.* **Street** is not used to talk about roads between towns, but streets in towns are often called **Road**, especially in British English: *a road map of Britain* ◊ *Woodstock Road.* In American English **street** is more frequent than **road**.

alley /'æli/ [C] a narrow passage, too small for traffic, behind or between buildings, often between rows of old houses: *It is a medieval city of courtyards and twisting alleys.* ◊ *An alley ran along the side of the house.* ◊ *We walked up what turned out to be a* **blind alley** (= one that is blocked at the end). See also **passage** → CORRIDOR

lane [C] a narrow road in the country: *We walked down the quiet country lane towards the riverbank.* ❶ **Lane** is also used for names of streets in towns and cities, especially for the names of very old streets: *The address is 53 Chancery Lane.*

avenue /'ævənju:; *AmE* -nu:/ [C] a street in a town or city: *We stayed at a hotel on Lexington Avenue.* ❶ In British English **avenue** is also used to talk about a wide straight road with trees on both sides: *They drove along a broad, tree-lined avenue.*

boulevard /'bu:ləvɑ:d; *AmE* 'bʊləvɑːrd/ [C] *(AmE)* a wide main road: *A police car sped down the crowded boulevard.* ❶ In British English **boulevard** means a wide city street, often with trees on either side, and is usually used only when talking about foreign cities: *A number of little cafes lined the sunny boulevard.* In American English **boulevard** is also used in street names: *We visited the world-famous Hollywood Boulevard.*

row [C] *(AmE)* a continuous line of similar houses that are joined together in one block: *They live in a* **row house** *in Washington's Mount Pleasant neighborhood.* ❶ In British English, **Row** is used in the names of some roads, but the usual word for a continuous line of houses built together is **terrace**: *I live at 22 Western Row.*

terrace [C] *(BrE)* a continuous row of similar houses that are joined together in one block: *The houses were in long terraces, built in the nineteenth century.* ◊ *They sold their house in Brunswick Terrace.*

rob *verb* See also the entry for STEAL

rob · loot · break into sth · raid · plunder · ransack · burgle · burglarize · hold up sb/sth
These words all mean to steal money or property, especially from a place.

PATTERNS AND COLLOCATIONS
▸ to be robbed / plundered **of** sth
▸ to rob / loot / break into / raid / ransack / burgle / burglarize a **building** / **shop** / **store**
▸ to rob / break into / raid / ransack / burgle / burglarize a **house**
▸ to rob / hold up a **bank**
▸ to loot / plunder a **town** / **city**
▸ to rob / raid a **tomb**

rob (-**bb**-) [T] to steal money or property from a person or place: *An armed gang robbed a bank in Main Street last night.* ◊ *The gang had robbed and killed the drugstore owner.* ◊ *He was accused of robbing the company's pension funds.* ◊ *The tomb had been robbed of all its treasures.* See also **robber** → THIEF, **robbery** → THEFT

loot /luːt/ [T, often passive, I] to steal things from shops or buildings, especially after a place has been bombed, after a fire or during a riot (= a situation of violent disorder): *Most of the stores in the town had been looted.* ◊ *The invaders rampaged through the streets, looting and killing.* See also **looter** → THIEF

,**break 'into sth** *phrasal verb* to enter a building or open a vehicle by force, especially in order to steal things from it: *Thieves broke into the store and got away with $50 000.* ◊ *Our car got broken into last night.* See also **break-in** → THEFT

raid [T] to enter a place, usually using force, and steal things from it: *Many treasures were lost when the tombs were raided in the last century.* ◊ *(humorous) I caught him raiding the fridge again* (= taking food from it). See also **raid** → THEFT, **raider** → THIEF

plunder [I, T] *(formal)* to steal things from a place or region, especially during a war, using force: *The troops crossed the country, plundering and looting as they went.* ◊ *Delhi was captured and plundered in 1739.*

ransack /'rænsæk/ [T] to search a place, making it untidy and causing damage, because you are looking for sth, usually in order to steal it: *The house had been ransacked by burglars.* ◊ *Police completely ransacked the offices in their search for the missing files.*

burgle /'bɜːɡl; *AmE* 'bɜːrɡl/ [T] *(BrE)* to enter a building illegally, usually using force, and steal things from it: *Her house has been burgled five times.* ◊ *We were burgled while we were away* (= our house was burgled). See also **burglary** → THEFT

burglarize /'bɜːɡləraɪz; *AmE* 'bɜːrɡ-/ *(AmE)* to burgle sb/sth: *The doctor's office is frequently burglarized by drug addicts.*

NOTE RAID OR BURGLE/BURGLARIZE? Burgle/burglarize is only used to talk about buildings, especially people's homes; **raid** can be used to talk about any place, but is used especially about shops and businesses and with the word *tombs* (but NOT *graves* which can only be robbed).

,**hold up 'sb/sth** *phrasal verb* to rob a bank, shop or vehicle using a weapon: *Masked men held up a security van in South London yesterday.* ◊ *They were held up at gunpoint.*

role *noun*

role · place · office · capacity
These are all words for the function or position that sb has or is expected to have in an organization, in society or in a relationship.

PATTERNS AND COLLOCATIONS
▸ sb's role / office / sb's capacity **as** sth
▸ a role / place **in** sth

▸ (a / an) **important / prestigious / minor** role / place / office
▸ (a / an) **exalted / high** place / office
▸ a **subordinate** role / place / capacity
▸ (a) **public / judicial / ministerial** role / office / capacity
▸ to **take up** your role / your place / office
▸ to **take / assume** a role / office
▸ to **occupy / retain** a role / a place / office
▸ to **give up / leave / relinquish** a role / your place / office

role [C] the function or position that sb has or is expected to have in an organization, in society or in a relationship: *This report examines the role of the teacher in the classroom.* ◇ *She has a dual role as principal and French teacher.* ◇ *In many marriages there has been a complete* **role reversal** (= change of roles) *with the man staying at home and the woman going out to work.*

place [sing.] the role or importance of sb/sth in a particular situation, usually in relation to others: *He is assured of his* **place in history**. ◇ *Accurate reporting* **takes second place** *to lurid detail.* ◇ *It's* **not your place** *to give advice.* ◇ *At first she tried to take charge of the meeting but I soon* **put her in her place**. ◇ *Anecdotes* **have no place in** (= are not acceptable in) *an academic essay.*

office [U, C] an important position of authority, especially in government; the work and duties connected with this: *She* **held office** *as a cabinet minister for ten years.* ◇ *How long has he been* **in office**? ◇ *The party has been* **out of office** (= has not formed a government) *for many years.* ◇ (*especially AmE*) *Bush* **ran for office** *again in 2004.* ◇ (*BrE*) *He took over the office of treasurer last year.* See also **power** → CONTROL, See also the entry for JOB

capacity /kəˈpæsəti/ [C, usually sing.] (*rather formal*) the official position or function that sb has: *She was acting* **in her capacity as** *manager.* ◇ *We are simply involved in an advisory capacity on the project.* ❶ In this meaning, **capacity** is always used with *in: in his/her/your/their/my capacity as chairman/manager/President, etc.* ◇ *do sth in a business/judicial/professional/voluntary, etc. capacity* **Capacity** is usually used to explain why sb is behaving in a particular way. For example, if you say that sb is acting in *their capacity as manager,* you may be suggesting that they might not act in such a way in different circumstances. If you say that you are involved in a project *in an advisory capacity,* you mean that you are not expected to contribute in other ways.

roll *noun*

roll · bundle · reel · wad · spool
These are all words for sth that is rolled up or wrapped around sth in order to make it easier to use or carry.

PATTERNS AND COLLOCATIONS
▸ a roll / bundle / reel / wad / spool **of** sth
▸ **in** a roll / bundle / reel / wad / spool
▸ **on** a roll / reel / spool
▸ a **big / thick** roll / bundle / wad

roll [C] a long piece of a thin material such as paper, fabric or film, that has been wrapped around itself or a tube several times so that it forms the shape of a tube: *She put the new roll of film in the camera.* ◇ *Wallpaper is sold in rolls.* ◇ (*BrE*) *Around 600 million* **toilet rolls** (= rolls of toilet paper) *are sold each year in the UK.* ❶ Especially in American English, a **roll** is also a number of round objects such as coins or pieces of candy held together in a tube shape by paper wrapped around them: *a roll of dimes/mints* See also **roll** → WRAP SB/STH AROUND/ROUND SB/STH

bundle [C] a number of things tied or wrapped together; sth that is wrapped up: *I dropped the bundle of papers on his desk.* ◇ *He tied his belongings up in a bundle and left.*
▸ **bundle sth 'up/to'gether** *phrasal verb*: *He bundled up the dirty clothes and stuffed them into the bag.*

reel [C] a round object with top and bottom edges that stick out and around which you wind wire or film; the film or wire that is wound around a reel: *He wanted to buy a new* **fishing reel**. ◇ *She threaded a new reel of film*

into the projector. ◇ *The hero was killed in the final reel* (= in the final part of the film). ❶ In British English a **reel** can also be used for winding thread around: *The sewing basket and a box of* **cotton reels** *lay at her feet.* In American English a reel of thread is called a **spool**.

> **NOTE** **ROLL** OR **REEL**? A **roll** of film is what you use in a camera for taking still pictures (= photographs). A **reel** of film is used for making and playing back moving pictures (= films).

wad /wɒd; *AmE* wɑːd/ [C] a thick pile of sth, especially paper or paper money, that has been folded or rolled together: *He pulled a thick wad of notes out of his pocket.* ◇ *She came in with tears streaming down her face, clutching a wad of tissues.*

spool [C] (*especially AmE*) a reel for/of thread or thin wire: *Place a spool of thread on the sewing machine.*

roll *verb*

roll · turn (sth) over · flip · overturn · capsize · tip (sth) over
These words all mean to turn onto the other side or upside down.

PATTERNS AND COLLOCATIONS
▸ to roll / turn / flip / tip sth **over**
▸ to roll / overturn a **car**
▸ to overturn / capsize a **boat**
▸ to overturn / tip over a **chair**
▸ a **car** turns over / flips over / overturns
▸ a **boat** turns over / flips over / overturns / capsizes

roll [I, T] to turn onto the other side or upside down while moving across a surface; to make sb/sth do this: *She rolled over to let the sun brown her back.* ◇ *I rolled the baby over onto its stomach.* ◇ *Take it in turns to roll the dice* (= in a game). ◇ (*AmE*) *She rolled her car in a 100 mph crash.*

turn 'over, turn sth 'over *phrasal verb* to change position so that the other side is facing outwards or upwards; to make sb/sth do this: *She turned over and went to sleep.* ◇ *The car skidded and turned over.* ◇ *Brown the meat on one side and then turn it over.*

flip (-**pp**-) [I, T] to turn over with a sudden quick movement; to make sb/sth do this: *The plane flipped and crashed.* ◇ *It cannoned into the other car and flipped over onto its roof.* ◇ *He* **flipped** *the lid* **open** *and looked inside the case.*

overturn /ˌəʊvəˈtɜːn; *AmE* ˌoʊvərˈtɜːrn/ [I, T] to turn upside down or on its side; to make sth do this: *The car skidded and overturned.* ◇ *He stood up quickly, overturning his chair.*

capsize /kæpˈsaɪz; *AmE* ˈkæpsaɪz/ [I, T] (of a boat) to turn over in the water; to make a boat do this: *The boat capsized and sank.* ◇ *Wind pressure on the huge rotors could capsize the ship.*

tip 'over, tip sth 'over *phrasal verb* (-**pp**-) (of sth that stands upright) to turn over and fall; to make sth do this: *The mug tipped over, spilling hot coffee everywhere.* ◇ *The big man stood up, tipping his chair over.*

rope *noun*

rope · wire · string · thread · yarn · cord
These are all words for long thin materials used for tying, fastening, sewing or holding things in place.

PATTERNS AND COLLOCATIONS
▸ **thick** rope / wire / string / yarn / cord
▸ **thin** rope / wire / string / thread / yarn / cord
▸ **fine** wire / thread / yarn
▸ a **strong** rope / wire / thread
▸ to **tie sth with** rope / string / cord
▸ to **tighten / pull** the rope / wire / string / cord
▸ to **loosen** the rope / wire / string
▸ to **coil** the rope / wire
▸ to **wind** the string / thread / yarn / cord

▶ a rope / string / thread / cord **breaks**
▶ a **length / piece of** rope / wire / string / thread / cord
▶ a **coil of** rope / wire

rope [C, U] a very strong thick long material made by twisting threads, fibres or wires together: *The rope broke and she fell 50 metres onto the rocks.* ◇ *We tied his hands together with rope.*

wire [U, C] metal in the form of long thin pieces: *a coil of copper wire* ◇ *a wire rack/basket* ◇ *The box was fastened with a rusty wire.* See also **wire** → WIRE

string [U, C] material made of several threads twisted together, used for tying things together; a piece of string used to fasten or pull sth or keep sth in place: *He wrapped the package in brown paper and tied it with string.* ◇ *The key is hanging on a string by the door.*

thread [U] thin string made of cotton, wool, silk, etc., used for sewing or making fabric: *Have you got a* **needle and thread**? ◇ *a robe embroidered with gold thread*

yarn [U, C] thread that has been spun, used for knitting or weaving: *The yarn is woven into a coarse fabric.* ◇ *The sweaters are hand-knitted in cotton, linen or wool yarns.*

cord [U, C] a strong thick string or thin rope: *You need a piece of thick cord about two metres long.* ◇ *a silk bag tied with a gold cord*

rope

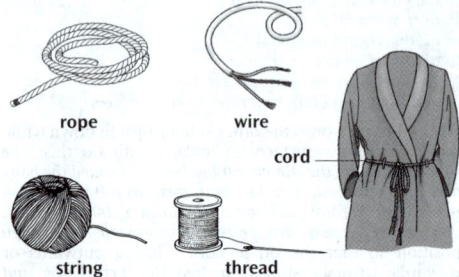

rope   wire
                    cord
string   thread

rotten *adj.* See also the entry for SMELLY

rotten · stale · sour · mouldy · bad · off
These words all describe food which is no longer fresh.

PATTERNS AND COLLOCATIONS
▶ rotten / stale / mouldy **food**
▶ rotten / bad **eggs**
▶ stale / mouldy **bread**
▶ to **go** rotten / stale / sour / mouldy / bad / off

rotten (of natural things such as food or wood) that has decayed and cannot be eaten or used: *The* **fruit** *is starting to go* **rotten**. ◇ *They pelted him with* **rotten eggs**. ◇ *He stepped on a rotten floorboard and felt it give way.*

stale (of food, especially bread and cake) no longer fresh and therefore unpleasant to eat: *There was one piece of* **stale** *chocolate* **cake** *left in the tin.* See also **stale** → SMELLY

sour (of milk or sb's breath) having an unpleasant taste or smell because it is not fresh: *The* **milk** *had turned* **sour**. ◇ *He smelled a sour whiff on the old man's breath.* See also **sour** → BITTER 1

mouldy (*BrE*) (*AmE* **moldy**) /ˈməʊldi; *AmE* ˈmoʊ-/ covered with or containing mould; old and not in good condition ❶ **Mould** is a fine soft green, grey or black substance like fur that grows on old food or on objects that are left in warm wet air: *The potatoes went mouldy before we'd had a chance to use them.* ◇ *We threw away all the mouldy old furniture.*

bad (of food) not safe to eat because it has decayed: *The meat had gone bad.* ◇ *There was a smell of bad eggs.*

off [not before noun] (*BrE*) (of food) no longer fresh enough to eat or drink: *The fish had gone off.* ◇ *The milk smells off.*

rough *adj.*

1 rough ground/edges
2 rough seas/weather

1 rough · rocky · rugged · uneven · bumpy · lumpy · rutted
These words all describe a surface or edge that is not level, smooth or flat.

PATTERNS AND COLLOCATIONS
▶ a rough / a rocky / an uneven / a bumpy **surface**
▶ a rough / an uneven / a bumpy / a rutted **road**
▶ rough / rocky / uneven / bumpy **ground / terrain**
▶ a rough / bumpy / rutted **lane / track**
▶ a rocky / rugged **landscape / hill / mountain / peak / cliff / coast / coastline**

rough having a surface or edge that is not even or regular: *The car is designed for travelling over rough ground.* ◇ *Trim any rough edges with a sharp knife.* **OPP** **smooth** → FLAT

rocky made of rock; full of rocks: *This plant grows in rocky soil on exposed hillsides.*

rugged /ˈrʌɡɪd/ (of landscape) not level or smooth and having rocks rather than plants or trees, especially in a way that is beautiful or romantic: *They admired the rugged beauty of the coastline.*

uneven /ʌnˈiːvn/ (of a surface) not level, smooth or flat: *She picked her way along the uneven path.* ◇ *The floor felt uneven under his feet.*

bumpy (of a surface) not even; with a lot of bumps: *She felt quite sick from the long drive over the bumpy road.* ❶ **Bumpy** is used especially to describe a piece of ground that you drive or cycle over.

lumpy full of lumps; covered in lumps: *I lay sleepless on my lumpy mattress.* ❶ **Lumpy** is most frequently used to talk about mattresses (= that you lie on) and pillows (= that you rest your head on).

rutted (of a road or path) with deep tracks that have been made by wheels: *The track was heavily rutted from the wheels of farm tractors.*

2 See also the entry for WET 2
rough · violent · stormy · turbulent · raging · choppy
These words all describe weather or the sea when there is a strong wind or large waves.

choppy   rough   violent
                stormy   raging
                turbulent

PATTERNS AND COLLOCATIONS
▶ a rough / violent / stormy / turbulent / raging / choppy **sea**
▶ rough / violent / stormy / turbulent / choppy **conditions**
▶ rough / stormy / turbulent / choppy **waters**
▶ rough / turbulent / choppy **water**
▶ rough / violent / stormy **weather**

rough (of the sea) having large and dangerous waves; (of the weather, especially at sea) with strong winds and rain: *It was too rough to sail that night.* ◇ *There's no way he could have swum ashore in such rough weather.* **OPP** **calm** → QUIET 1

violent (of the weather or the sea) very dangerous, with very strong winds and/or very large waves: *The islands were hit by a violent cyclone.* ◇ *Members of the lifeboat crew were presented with bravery awards for launching in violent seas.*

stormy with strong winds and heavy rain or snow: *She visited me one dark and stormy night in November.*

turbulent /'tɜːbjələnt; AmE 'tɜːrb-/ [usually before noun] (of air or water) changing direction suddenly and violently: *The aircraft is designed to withstand turbulent conditions.*

raging /'reɪdʒɪŋ/ [only before noun] (of natural forces such as wind, water and fire) very powerful: *The stream had become a **raging torrent**.* ◇ *The building was now a **raging inferno*** (= the fire was out of control).

choppy (of the sea or water) with a lot of small waves: *The choppy waters caused some of the boats to capsize.*

---

round *noun* See the Topic Map for SPORT AND LEISURE on p.892, See also the entry for STAGE 1

round · leg · lap · hole · game · set · heat · innings · inning · half · quarter
These are all words for a stage or section of a sports competition, match or race.

PATTERNS AND COLLOCATIONS
▸ **in** a round/a leg/a game/a set/a heat/an innings/an inning/ a half/a quarter
▸ the **first/second,** etc. round/leg/lap/hole/game/set/heat/ innings/inning/half/quarter
▸ the **opening** round/leg/lap/hole/game/set/heat/half/ quarter
▸ the **final** round/leg/lap/hole/game/set/heat/quarter
▸ to **play** a hole/a game/an innings/a set/a half/a quarter
▸ to **win** a round/leg/hole/game/set/heat

round [C] a stage in a sports competition; a part of a boxing or wrestling match: *Norwich City are **through to** the third **round** of the FA Cup.* ◇ *The fight only lasted five rounds.*
leg [C] one part of a race; one of a series of games played between the same opponents in a sports competition: *The Spanish team won the third leg.* ◇ *I really believe we can turn around that 4–2 first leg deficit and win this game.*
lap [C] one journey around a track during a race: *The 800m is two laps of the track.* ◇ *He was overtaken **on** the final **lap**.*
hole [C] (in golf) a hollow in the ground that you must get the ball into; one of the sections of a golf course with the tee at the beginning and the hole at the end: *The ball rolled into the hole and she had won.* ◇ *an eighteen-hole golf course* ◇ *She won by one hole.*
game [C] a section of a match in sports such as tennis, which forms a unit in scoring: *He's levelled the second set at two games all.*
set [C] one section of a match in sports such as tennis or volleyball, which consists of a number of games or points: *He's 3–1 up in the third set.* ◇ *The final went to five sets.* ◇ *She won **in straight sets*** (= without losing a set).
heat [C] one of a series of races or competitions, the winners of which compete against each other in the next part of the competition: *She won her heat.* ◇ *He did well in **the heats**; hopefully he'll do as well in the final.*

> **NOTE** ROUND OR HEAT? **Round** is a more general word to describe a stage of a competition. In some sports, a long competition over a whole year can be divided into events or races which are called **rounds**: *the third round of the championship in Japan.* A stage of a competition in which the winners in each part compete against each other in the next part of the competition, until only two teams or players are left in the final, can be called a **round** or a **heat**. **Heat** is used especially to describe a race between individuals, such as in running or swimming.

innings [C] (in cricket) a section of a match during which a team or individual player is batting (= hitting the ball): *Bangladesh are 90 for 5 in their second innings.*
inning [C] (in baseball) one of nine sections of a game in which each team has a turn at batting: *The Chicago Cubs scored two runs in the first inning.*
half [C] either of two periods of time into which a sports game is divided: *No goals were scored in the first half.*

---

quarter [C] one of the four periods of time into which a game of basketball or American football is divided: *Ford scored the winning touchdown early in the fourth quarter.*

row /rəʊ; AmE roʊ/ *noun*

row · line · queue · rank · cordon · file · column
These are all words for a number of people or things all standing next to each other or one behind the other.

PATTERNS AND COLLOCATIONS
▸ a row/line/queue/rank/file/column **of** sb/sth
▸ **in** a row/(a) line/a queue/file/a column
▸ a row/line/queue of **people**
▸ a line/queue of **traffic**
▸ (an) **orderly** row/line/queue/ranks
▸ to **form** a line/queue/cordon
▸ to **join** a line/queue
▸ a line/queue/cordon **forms**

row [C] a number of people standing or sitting next to each other in a line; a number of objects arranged in a line; a line of seats in a theatre, cinema, etc: *a row of children/houses/trees* ◇ *We sat in a row at the back of the room.* ◇ *The vegetables were planted in neat rows.* ◇ *Let's sit in the back row.* ◇ *Our seats are five rows from the front.*
line [C] a row of people or things next to each other or behind each other: *The children all stood in a line.* ◇ *They were stuck in a line of traffic.* ◇ *We had to **stand/wait in line** for hours to get tickets.* ◇ *A line formed at each teller window.*
> ▸ **ˌline ˈup, ˌline sb/sth ˈup** *phrasal verb*: *Line up, children!* ◇ *The suspects were lined up against the wall.*

> **NOTE** ROW OR LINE? People or things that are in a **row** are next to each other from side to side; people or things that are in a **line** can be next to each other from side to side, but are more often one behind the other from front to back. A **row** is often more permanent than a **line**: *a row of houses/shops/buildings.* People or vehicles in a **row** are not moving or waiting for anything; people or vehicles in a **line** usually are: *a row of parked cars* ◇ *There was a line of traffic waiting at the lights.*

queue /kjuː/ [C] (*BrE*) a line of people, cars, etc. waiting for sth or to do sth: *I had to join a queue for the toilets.* ◇ *There was a queue of traffic waiting to turn right.*
> ▸ **queue** *verb* [I]: (*BrE*) *We had to **queue up** for an hour for the tickets.* ◇ *Queue here for taxis.*

> **NOTE** LINE OR QUEUE? If you are waiting for sth, the usual word in British English is **queue**; in American English use **line**. To **line up** is to form a line; to be in a line, waiting for sth is to **stand/wait in line** in American English, or to **queue** or **queue up** in British English.

rank [C, usually pl.] a row of soldiers or police standing next to each other; a row of people or things: *They watched as ranks of marching infantry passed the window.* ◇ *They fired at random into the enemy ranks.* ◇ *massed ranks of spectators* ◇ *There were ranks of trestle tables piled high with food.*
cordon /'kɔːdn; AmE 'kɔːrdn/ [C] a line or ring of police officers, soldiers, etc. guarding sth or stopping people from entering or leaving a place: *Demonstrators tried to break through the police cordon.* See also **cordon sth off** → SEPARATE *verb* 2
file [C] a line of people or things, one behind the other: *They made their way **in single file** along the cliff path.* ❶ In this meaning **file** is most often used in the phrase *in single file.*
> ▸ **file** *verb* [I] (always used with an adverb or preposition): *The doors of the museum opened and the visitors began to file in.*
column [C] (*rather formal, especially written*) a long, moving line of people or vehicles: *a long column of troops and tanks*

rubbish *noun*

rubbish · (*taboo*) **crap** · **trash** · **garbage**
These are all words for sth that you think is of poor quality.

PATTERNS AND COLLOCATIONS
▶ **absolute** / **complete** / **total** rubbish / crap / trash / garbage
▶ to **read** / **watch** / **listen to** rubbish / trash / garbage
▶ to **eat** rubbish / crap
▶ a **load of** rubbish / crap / trash

rubbish [U] (*BrE, informal, especially spoken, disapproving*) something that sb has created such as a book, film or music, that you think is of poor quality; poor quality food: *I was told their new album's complete rubbish.* ◇ *Why are you eating such rubbish?* ❶ Rubbish can also be used before a noun like an adjective, when it can also be used to describe sb who does sth badly, especially their job: *Do we have to listen to this rubbish music?* ◇ *We had some rubbish teachers at school.*

crap [U] (*taboo, slang, spoken, disapproving*) rubbish ❶ Crap should only be used in informal situations among people of the same age and status. If spoken to sb who is older or considers themselves more important than you, it could cause great offence: *We eat a lot of crap and then wonder why we put on weight.* ◇ *'What did you think of their performance this afternoon?' 'Crap.'* ❶ Like **rubbish**, in British English **crap** can also be used before a noun like an adjective: *If I get any more of this crap work from you, you're fired.* ◇ *You're a crap singer.* In American English the adjective is **crappy**. See also **crap** → POOR *adj.* 2

trash [U] (*informal, disapproving*) an object, book, film or music, that you think is of poor quality: *You can buy lots of tacky trash in the souvenir shops, if that's what you want.* ◇ *What's this trash you're watching?* ❶ In British English **trash** can also be used before a noun like an adjective, but it only describes things, not people: *They listen to pop music and watch trash TV all day.* ◇ ~~*He's a trash teacher.*~~

garbage [U] (*AmE, informal, disapproving*) trash: *She just watches garbage on TV all day.*

rude *adj.*

rude · **cheeky** · **irreverent** · **insolent** · **disrespectful** · **impolite** · **impertinent** · **churlish** · **discourteous**
These are all words for people showing a lack of respect for other people.

cheeky	rude	insolent
irreverent	disrespectful	
	impolite	
	impertinent	
	churlish	
	discourteous	

PATTERNS AND COLLOCATIONS
▶ rude / cheeky / disrespectful / impolite / discourteous **to** sb
▶ rude / impolite / impertinent / churlish **to do sth**
▶ **very** rude / cheeky / impolite / impertinent / discourteous

rude (*disapproving*) having or showing a lack of respect for other people and their feelings: *He made a rude comment.* ◇ *She was very rude about my driving.* ◇ *Why are you so rude to your mother?* ◇ *It's rude to speak when you're eating.* **OPP** polite → POLITE
▶ **rudely** *adv.*: *They brushed rudely past us.* ◇ *'What do you want?' she asked rudely.*
▶ **rudeness** *noun* [U]: *She was critical to the point of rudeness.* ◇ *I want to apologize for my rudeness the other day.* **OPP** politeness → RESPECT

cheeky (*BrE, especially spoken, sometimes disapproving*) (especially of children) rude in an amusing or annoying way: *You cheeky monkey!* ◇ *He's got a cheeky grin.* ◇ *You're getting far too cheeky!*
▶ **cheek** *noun* [U, sing.]: (*BrE, informal, usually disapproving*) *He had the cheek to ask his ex-girlfriend to babysit for them.* ◇ *I think they've got a cheek making you pay to park the car.*
▶ **cheekily** *adv.*: *He grinned cheekily.*

irreverent /ɪˈrevərənt/ (*often approving*) not showing respect to sb/sth that other people usually respect: *He was famous for his irreverent wit.* ◇ *She has an irreverent attitude to tradition.* ❶ Irreverent is used especially to talk about public shows of disrespect by comedians, writers and broadcasters.

insolent /ˈɪnsələnt/ (*rather formal, disapproving*) very rude, especially to sb who is older or more important: *He was always an insolent child.* ❶ Insolent is used especially to talk about the behaviour of children towards adults.
▶ **insolence** *noun* [U]: *Her insolence cost her her job.*
▶ **insolently** *adv.*: *'Well?' he queried insolently.*

disrespectful (*rather formal, disapproving*) showing a lack of respect for sb/sth: *Some people said he had been disrespectful to the Queen in his last speech.* **OPP** respectful → POLITE. See also **disrespect** → CONTEMPT

impolite (*rather formal, disapproving*) not behaving in a pleasant way that follows the rules of society: *Some people think it is impolite to ask someone's age.* ❶ Impolite is often used in the phrase *It seems/would be impolite (to…)*: *Refusing to eat what was offered would be impolite.* **OPP** polite → POLITE

impertinent /ɪmˈpɜːtɪnənt; *AmE* -ˈpɜːrtn-/ (*rather formal, disapproving*) not showing respect for sb who is older or more important: *Don't ask such impertinent questions!* ❶ Impertinent is often used by people such as parents and teachers when they are telling children that they are angry with them for being rude: *Don't be impertinent!*
▶ **impertinence** *noun* [U, C, usually sing.]: *She had the impertinence to ask my age!*

churlish (*rather formal, disapproving*) rude, bad-tempered or unfriendly: *It would be churlish to refuse such a generous offer.* ❶ Churlish is most often used in the phrase *It would be/seems churlish to…*

discourteous /dɪsˈkɔːtiəs; *AmE* -ˈkɜːrt-/ (*formal, disapproving*) having bad manners and not showing respect: *He didn't wish to appear discourteous.* **OPP** courteous → POLITE

ruin *verb*

ruin · **spoil** · **mar** · **wreck**
These words all mean to make sth unsuccessful, unpleasant, or useless when it had been good.

spoil	ruin
mar	wreck

PATTERNS AND COLLOCATIONS
▶ to ruin / spoil / wreck sth **for** sb
▶ to ruin / spoil / mar / wreck sb's **career**
▶ to ruin / spoil / wreck **things** / **everything**
▶ to ruin / spoil / wreck sb's **plans** / **day** / **evening** / **life** / **chances** / **hopes**
▶ to ruin / mar / wreck sb's **happiness**
▶ to ruin / wreck **sb's health** / **sb's marriage** / **the economy**
▶ to **completely** / **totally** / **almost** / **nearly** ruin / spoil / mar / wreck sth
▶ to **effectively** ruin / spoil / wreck sth

ruin [T] to damage sth or have a completely negative effect on it so that it is no longer at all successful, enjoyable or useful: *The bad weather completely ruined our trip.* ◇ *You've ruined my whole life!* ◇ *Years of drinking had ruined his health.* ◇ *My shoes got totally ruined in the mud.* ◇ *The crop that year was ruined by drought.*

spoil [T] to change sth good into sth bad, unpleasant or useless: *Don't let him spoil your evening.* ◇ *Why do you always have to spoil everything?* ◇ *I don't want to spoil your fun, but it's nearly time to go home.* ◇ *I won't tell you what happens in the last chapter — I don't want to spoil it for you.*

NOTE RUIN OR SPOIL? Ruin is stronger than **spoil**: sth that is **ruined** is completely spoiled; sth that is **spoiled** may be ruined or just less good than it should be.

mar (-**rr**-) [T, often passive] (*rather formal*) to spoil sth good: *A few violent incidents marred the celebrations.* ◇ *A frown marred his handsome features.* ❶ **Mar** is often used to talk about the one thing that spoiled sth that was good in other ways. It is not often used in informal spoken English: *Why do you always have to mar everything?*

wreck /rek/ [T] to ruin sth completely: *A serious injury in 2006 threatened to wreck his career.* ◇ *His affair wrecked our marriage.* ❶ **Wreck** is used especially to talk about important things in people's lives. Important collocates are *life, career, marriage, health* and *happiness*.

rule *noun*

rule · law · regulation · act · statute · commandment
These are all words for an official statement of what may, must or must not be done in a particular situation.

PATTERNS AND COLLOCATIONS
▶ the rules / laws / regulations **on** sth
▶ a rule / law **against** sth
▶ **under** a rule / the regulations / an act / a statute
▶ **within** the rules / law / regulations / act / statute
▶ **against** the rules / law / regulations
▶ **strict** rules / laws / regulations
▶ to **pass** a law / a regulation / an act / a statute
▶ to **obey** a rule / a law / the regulations / a commandment
▶ to **comply with** a rule / a law / the regulations / a statute
▶ to **break** a rule / law / regulation / commandment
▶ to **contravene** / **be in breach of** a rule / a law / the regulations / an act / a statute
▶ to **repeal** a law / a regulation / an act / a statute
▶ to **tighten up** a rule / a law / the regulations
▶ a rule / a law / a regulation / an act / a statute **governs** / **prohibits** / **forbids** sth
▶ a rule / a law / a regulation / an act **allows (for)** sth
▶ a rule / a law / a regulation / an act **comes into force**

rule [C] a statement of what may, must or must not be done in a particular situation or when playing a game: *Tackling a player without the ball is against the rules.* ◇ *He was punished for breaking **school rules**.* ◇ *You and your room-mates should establish some **ground rules**.* ◇ *Without **unwritten rules** civilized life would be impossible.* ◇ *Couldn't they just **bend the rules** and let us in without a ticket?* See also **rule** → PRINCIPLE 1

law [C] a rule that everyone in a country or society must obey which deals with a particular crime or area of activity: *The government has introduced some tough new laws on food hygiene.* ◇ *There ought to be a law against it!* ◇ *The country has very strict gun laws.* See also **law** → LAW *noun*, **law** → PRINCIPLE 1

regulation [C, usually pl.] an official rule made by a government or some other authority: *It's against safety regulations to eat or drink in the laboratory.* ◇ *There are too many **rules and regulations**.* See also **regulation** → GOVERNMENT 2

act (*often* **Act**) [C] a law that has been passed by a parliament: *an Act of Parliament/Congress* ◇ *the Higher Education Act 1965* ◇ *The Act was passed by a majority of 175 votes to 143.*

statute /ˈstætʃuːt/ [C] a law that has been passed by a parliament, council, etc. and formally written down; a formal rule of an organization or institution: *Penalties are laid down **in the statute**.* ◇ *Corporal punishment was banned **by statute** in 1987.* ◇ *It is not yet **on the statute book** (= it has not yet become law).* ◇ *Under the statutes of the university they had no power to dismiss him.*

commandment [C] a law given by God, especially any of the Ten Commandments given to the Jews in the Bible: *You shall **keep the commandments** of the Lord your God.*

rule *verb*

1 rule a country
2 The court/judge ruled that...

1 rule · govern · be in power · reign
These words all mean to control a country or an area and its people.

PATTERNS AND COLLOCATIONS
▶ to rule / reign **over** sth
▶ to rule / govern a **country**
▶ a (political) **party** rules / governs / is in power
▶ a **king** / **queen** / **monarch** rules / reigns
▶ a **ruling** / governing **party** / **coalition** / **class** / **elite**

rule [T, I] to control and have authority over a country or area and its people: *The country was ruled by a brutal dictatorship.* ◇ *The family ruled London's gangland in the sixties.* ◇ *Charles I ruled for eleven years.* ◇ *She once ruled over a vast empire.* See also **rule** → CONTROL *noun*, **ruler** → KING

govern [T, I] to legally control a country or area and be responsible for introducing new laws organizing public services, managing the economy and directing foreign policy: *The PCP had governed the province for 23 years.* ◇ *He accused the opposition party of being **unfit to govern**.* See also **government** → GOVERNMENT 1, **government** → GOVERNMENT 2

NOTE RULE OR GOVERN? A government or party which **governs** a country or area has legal political control and has usually been elected. **Rule** is more often used to talk about an individual who has political power but has not been elected, such as a king or queen, an emperor, dictator or military ruler. It can also be used about a small group of people who exercise power over the rest of the country, sometimes in a less direct way: in this meaning it is often used like an adjective: *the ruling party/coalition/classes/elite*

be in power *phrase* to have political control of a country or area: *The present regime has been in power for two years.*

reign /reɪn/ [I] to rule a country as a king, queen or emperor: *Queen Victoria reigned from 1837 to 1901.* ◇ *It was the first visit by a British **reigning monarch** to Russia.* See also **reign** → RULE *verb* 1

2 See also the entry for ORDER 1
rule · prescribe · lay sth down · decree · order · legislate · dictate
These words all mean to give an official decision about sth or officially say that sth should happen.

PATTERNS AND COLLOCATIONS
▶ to rule / legislate **on** / **against** sth
▶ to rule / prescribe / lay down / decree / order / legislate / dictate **that...**
▶ to rule / prescribe / lay down / decree / order / dictate **how** / **what** / **who...**
▶ **It is** prescribed / laid down / decreed / ordered **that...**
▶ to **do** sth **as** prescribed / laid down / ordered / dictated
▶ to **officially** rule / prescribe / lay down / decree / order / legislate (that...)

rule [I, T] (especially of a judge or court) to give an official decision about sth: *The high court will rule on the legality of the action.* ◇ *The judge **ruled in favour of** the plaintiff.* ◇ *The court ruled that the women had been unfairly dismissed.* ◇ *The deal may be ruled illegal.* See also **ruling** → CONCLUSION

prescribe /prɪˈskraɪb/ [T] (*rather formal*) (especially of rules) to say what should be done or how sth should be done: *The syllabus prescribes precisely which books should be studied.*

lay sth ˈdown *phrasal verb* to state officially that people must obey a particular rule, law or principle: *You can't always lay down hard and fast rules.* ◇ *You should follow the regulations as laid down in the handbook.*

decree /dɪˈkriː/ [T] to decide sth officially, using your authority and without discussing it with other people: *The government decreed a state of emergency.* ◇ *It was decreed that the following day should be a holiday.* See also **decree** → ORDER *noun* 1

order [T] to use your position of authority to say that sth must happen: *They ordered that for every tree cut down two more be planted.* ◇ *The Justice Minister has ordered an investigation into the matter.*

legislate /ˈledʒɪsleɪt/ [I] (*formal*) to make a law affecting sth: *The government has been urged to legislate against discrimination in the workplace.* ◇ *The King restricted Parliament's power to legislate.* See also **legislation** → LAW

dictate /dɪkˈteɪt/ *AmE* ˈdɪkteɪt/ [T] to tell sb what to do or what should happen, especially in an annoying way: *What right do they have to dictate how we live our lives?* ◇ *I refuse to be dictated to.* ◇ *They are in no position to dictate terms.*

rumble *verb*

rumble · roar · thunder · roll · boom
These words all mean to make a deep sound.

PATTERNS AND COLLOCATIONS
▸ **thunder** rumbles / roars / rolls / booms
▸ **traffic** rumbles / roars / thunders
▸ to rumble / roar / thunder / roll / boom **loudly**

rumble [I] to make a long, deep sound or series of sounds: *They could hear thunder rumbling in the distance.* ◇ *I'm so hungry my stomach's rumbling.*
▸ **rumble** *noun* [C]: *He gave a low rumble of laughter.* ◇ *Inside, the noise of the traffic was reduced to a distant rumble.*

roar /rɔː(r)/ [I] to make a very loud, deep noise: *We heard a lion roar.* ◇ *The gun roared deafeningly.* ◇ *The engine roared to life* (= started roaring).
▸ **roar** *noun* [C, usually sing.]: *I could barely hear above / over the roar of the aircraft's engines.* ◇ *The car sped off with an almighty roar.*

thunder [I] to make a very loud deep noise that sounds like thunder (= the loud noise that you hear after a flash of lightning, during a storm): *A voice thundered in my ear.* ◇ *The horse raced across the pasture, its hooves thundering on the grass.*
▸ **thunder** *noun* [sing.]: *The thunder of hooves split the air as the horses burst through the mist.*

roll [I, T] to make a long continuous sound, especially the sound made by drums or thunder: *From the walls a trumpet sounded, a drum rolled and the gate swung open.*
▸ **roll** *noun* [C]: *Lightning flashed across the sky, immediately followed by a deep roll of thunder.*

boom /buːm/ [I] to make a loud deep noise that sounds like an explosion: *The ship's gun boomed and the shot fell only a hundred metres away.*
▸ **boom** *noun* [C, usually sing.]: *The deep boom of a foghorn echoed across the bay.*

run *verb*

1 run to catch a bus
2 run a business

1 See also the entry for FLY 2

run · race · jog · tear · sprint · charge · gallop · trot · bound · pound · stampede
These words all mean to move fast using your legs.

jog	run	race
trot	bound	tear
	pound	sprint
		charge
		gallop
		stampede

PATTERNS AND COLLOCATIONS
▸ to run / race / jog / sprint / charge / gallop / trot / bound / pound **towards** sb / sth
▸ to run / race / sprint / charge / gallop / trot / bound / pound **after** sb / sth
▸ to run / race / tear / sprint / gallop / trot / bound / pound **along** (sth)
▸ to run / race / tear / sprint / gallop / bound **off**
▸ to run / race / sprint / bound **away**
▸ to run / race / tear / sprint / bound **back**
▸ to run / race / tear / charge **around / round**
▸ to **come** running / racing / tearing / sprinting / charging / galloping / trotting / bounding

run [I, T] to move using your legs, going faster than when you walk; to travel a particular distance by running: *Can you run as fast as Mike?* ◇ *The boy went running off to get the ball.* ◇ *I had to run to catch the bus.* ◇ *Alan was running for a bus when he slipped on some ice.* ◇ *I like to go running* (= run as a form of exercise) *in the mornings before work.* ◇ *I ran four miles today.* ◇ *Terrified, he ran all the way home.* See also **runner** → PLAYER
▸ **run** *noun* [C]: *I go for a run every morning.* ◇ *He broke into a run* (= started running).
▸ **running** *noun* [U]: *to go running* ◇ *running shoes*

race [I] (always used with an adverb or preposition) (*written*) to run very fast, especially because it is important that you get somewhere quickly: *Peter raced ahead to be the first to tell his mother the news.* ◇ *We all raced back to the camp.*

jog (also **go jogging**) [I] to run slowly and steadily for a long time, especially for exercise: *I go jogging every evening.* ◇ *He jogged down the path and into the lane.*
▸ **jog** *noun* [sing.]: *I like to go for a jog after work.*
▸ **jogging** *noun* [U]: *He decided to take up jogging.*

tear /teə(r)/ *AmE* ter/ [I] (always used with an adverb or preposition) to run somewhere very quickly, especially in an excited way or because you are in a hurry: *The girls looked at each other and tore off towards the house.*

sprint [I, T] (usually used with an adverb or preposition) to run very fast for a short distance: *He sprinted towards the finishing line.* ◇ *I sprinted the last few metres.* ❶ When sb in a race starts **sprinting**, they start running as fast as they can, especially near the end of the race.
▸ **sprint** *noun* [C]: *a 100-metre sprint* ◇ *It was a sprint for the finishing line.*

charge [I] (always used with an adverb or preposition) to run or walk fast in a particular direction, especially making a noise or carelessly: *The kids were charging around outside.* ◇ *He came charging into my office and demanded an explanation.*

gallop /ˈɡæləp/ [I, T] (usually used with an adverb or preposition) (of a horse or similar animal) to move fast with an action that includes all four feet being off the ground at the same time; (of a person) to ride a horse when it is galloping; (of a person) to run very quickly, especially in an excited way and with noisy steps: *The horse neighed and galloped off across the field.* ◇ *The cavalry galloped past in a cloud of dust.* ◇ *She galloped her horse all the way home.* ◇ *The kids came galloping along the street.*
▸ **gallop** *noun* [sing.]: *Diane urged her horse into a gallop.*

trot (-tt-) [I, T] (of a horse) to move at a speed that is faster than walking, with each front leg being lifted at the same time as the opposite back leg; (of a person) to ride a horse when it is trotting; (of a person) to run slowly or walk fast, taking short quick steps: *I could hear the sound of several horses trotting along in the lane.* ◇ *Bob trotted his pony around the field.* ◇ *The dog trotted obediently at her heels.* ◇ *He trotted off to greet the other guests.*
▸ **trot** *noun* [sing.]: *She slowed her horse to a trot.* ◇ *She moved at a brisk trot.*

bound /baʊnd/ [I] (always used with an adverb or preposition) to run with long steps, especially in an enthusiastic way: *The dogs bounded ahead.*

pound /paʊnd/ [I] (usually used with an adverb or preposition) to run somewhere with heavy, noisy steps: *A group of men on horseback came pounding across the field.*

stampede /stæm'piːd/ [I] (of a group of large animals or people) to run fast, especially in a way that cannot be controlled: *The cattle started to stampede, as if they could sense the danger.* ◊ *A bunch of kids came stampeding down the corridor.*

---

2 run · manage · control · be responsible for sb/sth · be in charge · direct · administer · command

These words all mean to be in charge or in control of a business, organization, project or situation.

PATTERNS AND COLLOCATIONS

▶ to run / manage / control a / an **company** / **business** / **organization**
▶ to run / manage / be responsible for a **department**
▶ to run / manage a **hotel** / **store** / **club**
▶ to run / manage / control / be responsible for / direct / administer a **project**
▶ to run / manage / be responsible for / administer a **service**
▶ to run / manage / administer a **school**
▶ to manage / control / be responsible for / be in charge of / direct **operations**
▶ to manage / administer a **fund**
▶ to be **properly** / **efficiently** run / managed / administered
▶ to be **well** / **badly** run / managed
▶ to be **tightly** run / managed / controlled
▶ to be **centrally** run / managed / controlled / directed / administered
▶ to be **jointly** run / managed / controlled / administered by / with sb

run [T] to be in charge of a business, organization or project: *The shareholders want more say in how the company is run.* ◊ *The programme will be jointly run with NASA in the US.* ◊ *It is a small, privately run (= not owned or controlled by a large organization) hotel.* ◊ *Stop trying to run my life (= organize it) for me.*

manage [T, I] to be in charge of a business, organization, project or team: *Organizers are looking for someone to manage the project.* ◊ *We need a new approach to managing our hospitals.* ◊ *We need people who are good at managing.* See also **management** → GOVERNMENT 2, **management** → MANAGEMENT

> **NOTE** RUN OR MANAGE? These two verbs can often be used in the same way: *The hotel is run/managed by two brothers.* **Run** emphasizes the tasks involved in the operation of a business – planning, ordering stock, organizing transport of goods, etc. Someone can **run** a small business (without any employees), part of a business, a department or a larger organization. **Manage** often refers to organizing other workers. A **manager** makes decisions about how a business, department, etc. is **run**, but they usually tell other people what to do rather than doing it themselves.

control (-ll-) [T] to have power over a business, organization, project or country, so that you are able to decide how it is run: *The whole territory is now controlled by the army.* ◊ *By the age of 21 he controlled the company.*

be responsible for sb/sth *phrase* to have the job or duty of doing sth or taking care of sb/sth, so that you may be blamed if sth goes wrong: *Mike is responsible for designing the entire project.* ◊ *Even where parents no longer live together, they each continue to be responsible for their children.* See also **responsibility** → RESPONSIBILITY

be in charge *phrase* to be in the position of having control over sb/sth: *I've usually been the one in charge of the petty cash.* ◊ *Who's in charge here?* See also **charge** → RESPONSIBILITY

direct [T] to be in charge of a project or process: *He was asked to take command and direct operations.* See also **direction** → GOVERNMENT 2, **director** → MANAGER

administer [T, often passive] to manage and organize the affairs or a company, organization or country: *The country has to face up to the high cost of administering medical services.* ◊ *The pension funds are administered by*

commercial banks. See also **administration** → GOVERNMENT 2, **administration** → MANAGEMENT, **administrator** → ORGANIZER

command [T] to be in charge of a group of people in the army, navy or air force: *He was the officer commanding the troops in the Western region.* ◊ *The squadron was commanded by Major Frank Broad.* See also **command** → CONTROL *noun*

---

ruthless *adj.* See also the entries for CRUEL and STERN

---

ruthless · hard · callous · unmoved · heartless · merciless · cold-blooded · brutal

These words all describe sb who shows no kindness, pity or sympathy for other people.

---

unmoved	hard	ruthless
	callous	cold-blooded
	heartless	
	merciless	
	brutal	

PATTERNS AND COLLOCATIONS

▶ a ruthless / hard / callous / heartless **man** / **woman**
▶ a ruthless / merciless / cold-blooded **attack**
▶ a ruthless / hard / brutal **side**
▶ ruthless / brutal **honesty**
▶ a callous / cold-blooded **murder**
▶ **totally** ruthless / callous / unmoved

ruthless /'ruːθləs/ (*usually disapproving*) cruel and showing no sympathy; determined to get what you want and not caring if you hurt other people: *He's a violent, ruthless man who will stop at nothing.* ◊ *He has a ruthless determination to succeed.* ◊ *Like all great survivors, she has a ruthless streak.* ❶ Although being **ruthless** is generally considered very bad, the word is sometimes used with apparent approval of the determination that sb needs to get what they want: *We'll have to be ruthless if we want to make this company more efficient.*

▶ **ruthlessly** *adv.*: *The regime ruthlessly crushed all opposition.*

hard (*usually disapproving*) showing no sympathy or affection: *My father was a hard man.* ◊ *She gave me a hard stare.* ◊ *He said some very hard things to me.* **OPP** soft → SENSITIVE 1

callous /'kæləs/ (*disapproving*) acting as you like without caring about other people's feelings or suffering: *The troops showed a callous disregard for life and property.*

unmoved [not before noun] not feeling pity or sympathy in reaction to sth, especially in a situation where it would be normal to do so: *Alice seemed totally unmoved by the whole experience.* See also **move** → IMPRESS

heartless (*disapproving*) showing no pity or sympathy for other people in what you say or do: *How can you be so heartless!* ◊ *The decision does seem a little heartless.*

merciless /'mɜːsɪləs/; *AmE* 'mɜːrs-/ (*rather formal, especially written*) showing no kindness or pity: *He was left reeling after a merciless attack by the opposition.* ◊ *It brought relief from the merciless summer heat.* **OPP** merciful → LENIENT

cold-'blooded (*disapproving*) showing no feelings or pity for other people while doing terrible things: *a cold-blooded killer* ◊ *There was something very cold-blooded about the way he used his father's death.*

> **NOTE** WHICH WORD? **Unmoved** is the weakest of these words because it describes sb not reacting to sb else's distress or anger, not sb who actively causes sb else's distress. **Hard, callous** and **heartless** can describe sb reacting without sympathy to sb's distress, or sb actively doing things that hurt people without caring about the effects on those people. **Ruthless** and **cold-blooded** are stronger still: a **ruthless** person will do anything to get what they want; a **cold-blooded** person not only feels no sympathy, but feels no emotions at all (such as anger) that might explain their cruel behaviour.

brutal /ˈbruːtl/ (*usually disapproving*) direct and clear about sth unpleasant; not thinking of people's feelings: *With brutal honesty she told him she did not love him.* See also **brutal** → CRUEL

▶ **brutally** *adv.*: *Let me be brutally frank about this.*

S s

sad *adj.* See also the entries for UNHAPPY 1 and PAINFUL 2

sad · tragic · pathetic · heartbreaking
These words all describe sth that makes you feel unhappy or upset.

→

sad	tragic	heartbreaking
pathetic		

PATTERNS AND COLLOCATIONS
▶ to be sad / tragic / heartbreaking **for** sb
▶ to be sad / heartbreaking **to do sth**
▶ to be sad / tragic **that...**
▶ a sad / tragic / pathetic / heartbreaking **story**
▶ a sad / pathetic **sight**

sad making you feel unhappy, especially about sth that has happened to sb/sth else: *It was sad to see them go.* ◇ *It is sad that so many of his paintings have been lost.* ◇ *We had some sad news yesterday.* ◇ *The sad truth is, he never loved her.* See also **sadness** → GRIEF, **sad** → UNHAPPY 1
▶ **sadly** *adv.*: *Sadly, after eight years of marriage they had grown apart.*

tragic /ˈtrædʒɪk/ making you feel very sad, usually because sb has died or suffered a lot: *He was killed in a tragic accident at the age of 24.* ◇ *Cuts in the health service could have tragic consequences for patients.* ◇ *It would be tragic if her talent remained unrecognized.* See also **tragedy** → CRISIS
▶ **tragically** *adv.*: *Tragically, his wife was killed in a car accident.* ◇ *He died tragically young.*

pathetic /pəˈθetɪk/ making you feel pity or sadness: *The starving children were a pathetic sight.*

heartbreaking /ˈhɑːtbreɪkɪŋ; AmE ˈhɑːrt-/ making you feel extremely sad: *It's heartbreaking to see him wasting his life like this.* See also **heartbreak** → GRIEF, **heartbroken** → UNHAPPY 1

NOTE TRAGIC OR HEARTBREAKING? A **tragic** event is often more serious than an event that is **heartbreaking**: very often it will involve sb suffering or dying. However, **heartbreaking** usually expresses a greater degree of personal sadness. **Tragic** is used especially to describe terrible events that happen to other people: **heartbreaking** describes events that affect you personally.

safe *adj.*

1 safe and well
2 a safe distance

1 **safe · OK · all right · in one piece · unharmed · out of harm's way · unscathed · unhurt · alive and well · secure · uninjured**
These words all describe sb/sth that is protected from danger or harm or is not harmed, damaged or injured.

PATTERNS AND COLLOCATIONS
▶ safe / secure **from** sth
▶ unharmed / unscathed / unhurt **by** sth
▶ to **remain** safe / OK / all right / in one piece / unharmed / unscathed / alive and well / secure
▶ to **escape** unharmed / unscathed / unhurt / uninjured
▶ **apparently** / **completely** safe / unharmed / unscathed / secure
▶ **perfectly** safe / OK / all right / secure
▶ **otherwise** OK / all right / unharmed / unhurt / secure

safe [not usually before noun] protected from any danger or harm; not hurt, damaged or lost: *The children are quite safe here.* ◇ *Will the car be safe parked in the road?* ◇ *They aim to make the country safe from terrorist attacks.* ◇ *The girl was eventually found safe and well.* ◇ *They turned up safe and sound* (= with no harm done to them). See also **safety** → SHELTER
▶ **safely** *adv.*: *Let me know you've arrived safely.* ◇ *The money is safely locked in a drawer.*

OK (also **okay**) [not usually before noun] (*informal, spoken*) safe; not hurt or ill: *Are you OK?* ◇ *Write and let me know you're OK.* ◇ *She worries too much — I'll be perfectly OK.*
▶ **OK** (also **okay**) *adv.*: (*informal, spoken*) *Did they get there OK?*

all ˈright [not usually before noun] (*rather informal, spoken*) safe; not hurt or ill: *I hope the kids are all right.* ◇ *He'll be perfectly all right, you'll see.*
▶ **all ˈright** *adv.*: (*rather informal, spoken*) *Did they get there all right?*

NOTE OK OR ALL RIGHT? There is no real difference in meaning between these words. Both are rather informal but **OK** is slightly more informal than **all right**. See also the entry for WELL

in one ˈpiece *idiom* (*rather informal*) not injured or damaged, especially after a journey or dangerous experience: *She's had a bit of a shock, but she seems to be all in one piece.*

unharmed [not usually before noun] (not used in the comparative or superlative) not injured or damaged after a dangerous or frightening experience: *He was released unharmed after being held hostage for three weeks.*

out of harm's ˈway *idiom* in a safe place where sb/sth cannot be injured or damaged or cannot do any harm to sb/sth else: *They sent the children to stay with their grandmother, where they would be out of harm's way.* ◇ *She put the knife in a drawer, out of harm's way.*

unscathed /ʌnˈskeɪðd/ [not before noun] (not used in the comparative or superlative) (*rather formal, written*) not injured or damaged after a dangerous or frightening experience: *Not many European cities survived the war unscathed.*

unhurt [not before noun] (not used in the comparative or superlative) not hurt after an experience: *He was bruised but otherwise unhurt.* **OPP** **hurt** → INJURED

aˌlive and ˈwell *idiom* alive and not injured, especially after being in a situation in which sb was worried that you might be harmed or killed or when sb did not know what had happened to you: *He turned up alive and well on my doorstep, after an absence of ten years.* ◇ (*rather informal*) *She's alive and well and living in Detroit.*

secure /sɪˈkjʊə(r); AmE səˈkjʊr/ (*rather formal*) (of sth important or valuable) in a place or condition that means it cannot be affected or harmed by sth: *Information must be stored so that it is secure from accidental deletion.* ◇ *The roof was secure against the coming winter rains.*

uninjured [not usually before noun] not injured in any way, especially after being in danger: *They were shocked but otherwise uninjured.* ❶ **Uninjured** is not used before a noun, except before nouns like *arm, hand, leg, foot*, etc., when one arm, etc. is injured and the other is not: *He grasped the rope with his uninjured hand.* **OPP** **injured** → INJURED

NOTE UNHARMED, UNSCATHED, UNHURT OR UNINJURED? These words all mean 'not hurt after an experience'. **Unharmed** and **unscathed** both emphasize the dangerous, frightening or unpleasant nature of the experience; **unhurt** and **uninjured** are more factual in tone. **Unharmed** is often used when sb has been a prisoner and been released; either **unharmed** or **unscathed** is used when sb has managed to survive or escape.

2 safe · harmless · benign

These words all describe sth that is not able or not likely to harm sb/sth.

PATTERNS AND COLLOCATIONS

▸ a harmless / benign **substance**
▸ **relatively / pretty / fairly / quite / apparently / seemingly** safe / harmless / benign
▸ **totally / perfectly** safe / harmless
▸ **environmentally** safe / harmless / benign

safe not likely to lead to any physical harm or danger: *Is the water here* **safe** *to drink?* ◇ *The street is not* **safe** *for children to play in.* ◇ *It is one of the safest cars in the world.* ◇ *We watched the explosion* **from a safe distance**. **OPP** **dangerous, unsafe →** DANGEROUS

harmless unable or unlikely to cause damage or harm: *Most bacteria are* **harmless** *to humans.* ◇ *Safety glass will break into relatively* **harmless** *pieces when it is hit hard.* **OPP** **harmful →** HARMFUL, **dangerous →** DANGEROUS
▸ **harmlessly** *adv.*: *The missile fell* **harmlessly** *into the sea.*

benign /bɪˈnaɪn/ (*formal* or *medical*) not dangerous or likely to cause harm or death: *She is recovering after surgery to remove a* **benign tumour.** ❶ **Benign** can also describe a *substance*, an *effect* or *influence*, the *nature* of sth or a *disease* or *condition*.

safety *noun*

safety · security · welfare · well-being
These are all words for the protection of sb/sth from harm or danger.

PATTERNS AND COLLOCATIONS

▸ **for** safety / security
▸ **comparative / reasonable / relative** safety / security
▸ **economic / financial / material** security / welfare / well-being
▸ to **improve** safety / security / sb's welfare / sb's well-being
▸ to **promote** the safety / welfare / well-being of sb / sth

safety [U] the state of being protected from danger or harm; the state of not being dangerous: *Children need a place where they can play* **in safety.** ◇ *He was kept in custody* **for his own safety.** ◇ *I'm worried about the safety of the treatment.* ◇ *He is involved in local campaigns to improve* **road safety.** ◇ *The airline has an excellent* **safety record.**

security [U] protection against sth bad that might happen in the future; the state of feeling happy and safe from danger or worry: *The plan offers your family financial security in the event of your death.* ◇ *Job security* (the guarantee that you will keep your job) *is a thing of the past.* ◇ *She'd allowed herself to be lulled into* **a false sense of security** (= a feeling that she was safe when in fact she was in danger).

NOTE SAFETY OR SECURITY? **Safety** is used especially to talk about protection from physical harm or danger; in this meaning **security** is used more to talk about being or feeling financially or emotionally protected.

welfare /ˈwelfeə(r); *AmE* -fer/ [U] the general health, happiness, comfort or safety of a person, animal or group: *We are concerned about the child's welfare.*

'well-being [U] the general good health, happiness or comfort of a person or community: *Physical and emotional well-being are closely linked.* ◇ *This industry is vital to the economic well-being of the city.* ◇ *She was filled with a sense of well-being.*

NOTE WELFARE OR WELL-BEING? Sb's **welfare** is their level of health, happiness or safety, whether this is good or bad: ~~She was filled with a sense of welfare.~~ **Well-being** is a level of health, happiness or comfort that is good; it is not usually used to talk about sb's safety: ~~We are concerned about the child's well-being.~~

salesman *noun*

salesman/saleswoman/salesperson · rep · representative · auctioneer · assistant · clerk
These are all words for a person whose job is to sell goods.

PATTERNS AND COLLOCATIONS

▸ a **sales** rep / representative / assistant / clerk
▸ a **company** rep / representative
▸ a **car / computer** salesman / saleswoman / salesperson
▸ a salesman / a saleswoman / a salesperson / a rep / a representative / an auctioneer / an assistant / a clerk **sells** sth

salesman, saleswoman, salesperson [C] a person whose job is to sell goods, either in a shop or by travelling around visiting companies, organizations or people's houses: *He began his career as an insurance salesman.* ◇ *a travelling salesman* ◇ *A saleswoman came out from behind the counter and asked if she could help.* ◇ *The salesperson should adopt a question-and-listen procedure.* ❶ The term **salesperson** is used especially in training material for people whose job is to sell goods. Although a **salesperson** may be either a man or a woman, it is less often used to refer to a particular man or woman whose job is to sell things, for which the words **salesman** or (less frequently) **saleswoman** are still used: ~~He began his career as an insurance salesperson.~~ ◇ ~~A salesperson came out from behind the counter.~~

rep (also **'sales rep**) [C] (*rather informal*) a person who works for a company and travels around selling its products: *She's a sales rep for a recording company.*

representative /ˌreprɪˈzentətɪv/ [C] (*formal*) a sales rep: *He works as a sales representative for an insurance company.* ◇ *She's our representative in France.* See also **representative →** SPOKESMAN

auctioneer /ˌɔːkʃəˈnɪə(r); ˌɒk-; *AmE* ˌɔːkʃəˈnɪr/ [C] a person whose job is to direct an auction and sell the goods ❶ An **auction** is a public event at which things are sold to the person who offers the most money for them: *'Yours for £200,' said the auctioneer.*

assistant (also **'shop assistant, 'sales assistant**) [C] (*BrE*) a person whose job is to serve customers in a shop: *She's a sales assistant in a department store.* ◇ *Maybe one of our assistants can help you make your choice?*

NOTE SALESMAN/WOMAN/PERSON OR ASSISTANT? **Salesman/woman/person** is usually used to talk about a person who is more highly trained in the job, or has more specialized knowledge of the goods that they are selling than an **assistant** or **shop/sales assistant**.

clerk /klɑːk; *AmE* klɜːrk/ (also **'sales clerk**) [C] (*AmE*) a shop assistant: *The sales clerk answered all our questions.*

sane *adj.* See the Topic Map for HEALTH on p.890

sane · rational · normal · in your right mind
These words all describe sb who has a healthy mind and is able to think clearly and sensibly.

PATTERNS AND COLLOCATIONS

▸ a sane / rational / normal **person**
▸ **perfectly / quite / completely / otherwise** sane / rational / normal

sane having a healthy mind; not mentally ill: *No sane person would do a thing like that.* ◇ (*rather informal*) *Being able to get out of the city at weekends* **keeps me sane.** **OPP** **insane →** MENTALLY ILL
▸ **sanity** /ˈsænəti/ *noun* [U]: *His behaviour was so strange that I began to doubt his sanity.*

rational /ˈræʃnəl/ able to think clearly and make decisions based on reason rather than emotions: *Humans are essentially rational beings.* ◇ *She said that she had not been fully rational when she signed the form.* **OPP irrational** ❶ A person or thing that is **irrational** does not use, or is not based on, clear logical thought: *You're being irrational.*

normal having a healthy mind and body; not mentally ill: *He had been a completely normal, healthy little boy.* ◇ *People who commit these crimes can't be normal, can they?* **OPP abnormal** → ABNORMAL

> **NOTE** SANE OR NORMAL? Sometimes you can use either word: *No sane/normal person would do a thing like that.* **Sane** is often used in a rather informal, slightly humorous way, to talk about yourself: if you talk about the need to ~~stay sane~~ or say that sth *keeps you sane*, you are really talking about avoiding stress rather than serious mental illness. **Normal** is always used to talk about other people: ~~Having a laugh helps me stay normal.~~ In some contexts **normal**, but NOT **sane**, refers to both mental and physical health: *a completely sane, healthy little boy*

in your right 'mind *idiom* mentally normal: *No one in their right mind would agree to such an idea!*

satisfaction *noun* See also the entry for JOY

satisfaction · happiness · pride · contentment · fulfilment
These are all words for the good feeling that you have when you are happy or when you have achieved sth.

PATTERNS AND COLLOCATIONS
▶ satisfaction / happiness / pride / contentment / fulfilment **in** sth
▶ **with** satisfaction / pride / contentment
▶ **great** satisfaction / happiness / pride
▶ **real** satisfaction / happiness / pride / contentment / fulfilment
▶ **true** satisfaction / happiness / contentment / fulfilment
▶ **deep** satisfaction / happiness / contentment
▶ **quiet** satisfaction / pride / contentment
▶ to **feel** satisfaction / happiness / pride / contentment
▶ to **bring sb** satisfaction / happiness / pride / contentment / fulfilment
▶ to **give sb** satisfaction / happiness
▶ to **find** satisfaction / happiness / contentment / fulfilment
▶ to **take** satisfaction / pride in sth
▶ to **sigh with** satisfaction / happiness / contentment

satisfaction [U] the good feeling that you have when you have achieved sth or when sth that you wanted to happen does happen: *He derived great satisfaction from knowing that his son was happy.* ◇ *She had the satisfaction of seeing her book become a best-seller.* ◇ *The company is trying to improve* **customer satisfaction**. ◇ *How would you rate your level of* **job satisfaction**? **OPP regret** → GRIEF, **dissatisfaction** → UNHAPPY 2 ❶ You feel **regret** when you have not achieved all that you wanted; you feel **dissatisfaction** when other people do things, or things do not happen, as you want. **Dissatisfaction** is rather formal: *Many people have expressed their dissatisfaction with the arrangement.* See also **satisfied** → HAPPY

happiness [U] the good feeling that you have when you are happy: *Her eyes shone with happiness.* ◇ *Money can't buy you happiness.* **OPP sadness, unhappiness** → GRIEF, See also **happy** → HAPPY

pride [U, sing.] a feeling of pleasure or satisfaction that you get when you or people who are connected with you have done sth well or own sth that other people admire: *The sight of her son graduating filled her with pride.* ◇ *Success in sport is a source of national pride.* ◇ *I take (a) pride in my work.* **OPP shame** → GUILT, See also **proud** → GLAD, **pride yourself on sth** → BOAST

contentment [U] (*rather formal*) a feeling of happiness or satisfaction with what you have: *They found contentment in living a simple life.* See also **content, contented** → HAPPY

fulfilment (*BrE*) (*AmE* **fulfillment**) [U] a feeling of happiness or satisfaction with what you do or have done: *her search for personal fulfilment*

> **NOTE** SATISFACTION, HAPPINESS, CONTENTMENT OR FULFILMENT? You can feel **satisfaction** at achieving almost anything, small or large; you feel **fulfilment** when you do sth useful and enjoyable with your life. **Happiness** is the feeling you have when things give you pleasure and can be quite a lively feeling; **contentment** is a quieter feeling that you get when you have learned to find pleasure in things.

satisfying *adj.* See also the entries for NICE 1 and WONDERFUL

satisfying · rewarding · pleasing · gratifying · fulfilling
These words all describe an experience, activity or fact that gives you pleasure because it provides sth you need or want.

PATTERNS AND COLLOCATIONS
▶ to be satisfying / rewarding / pleasing / gratifying **to do sth**
▶ a satisfying / rewarding / gratifying / fulfilling **experience**
▶ (a) satisfying / rewarding / fulfilling **job / career / work**
▶ to **find** sth satisfying / rewarding / pleasing / gratifying
▶ **very / extremely / particularly** satisfying / rewarding / pleasing / gratifying
▶ **immensely** satisfying / rewarding / gratifying

satisfying that gives you pleasure because it provides sth that you need or want: *a satisfying meal* ◇ *It's satisfying to play a game really well.* ◇ *It's hard work, but very satisfying.* See also **satisfy** → PLEASE

rewarding /rɪˈwɔːdɪŋ; *AmE* -ˈwɔːrd-/ (of an experience or activity) that makes you happy because you think it is useful or important; worth doing: *Nursing can be a very rewarding career.* ◇ *Teaching is not very financially rewarding* (= is not very well paid). **OPP unrewarding** ❶ An **unrewarding** activity or task does not bring feelings of satisfaction or achievement.

pleasing (*rather formal*) that gives you pleasure, especially to look at, hear or think about: *It was a simple but pleasing design.* ◇ *You can create a very pleasing effect with pale colours on a dark background.* See also **please** → PLEASE

gratifying /ˈɡrætɪfaɪɪŋ/ (*formal*) that gives you pleasure, especially because it makes you feel that you have done well: *It is gratifying to see such good results.* See also **gratify** → PLEASE

fulfilling (of an experience or activity) that makes you happy, because it makes you feel your skills and talents are being used: *I'm finding the work much more fulfilling now.*

> **NOTE** SATISFYING, REWARDING OR FULFILLING? Almost any experience, important or very brief, can be **satisfying**. **Rewarding** and **fulfilling** are used more for longer, more serious activities, such as jobs or careers: *What is the most satisfying moment in your career so far?* ◇ *All in all, it's been an extremely rewarding/fulfilling career.* **Satisfying** and **fulfilling** are used more to talk about your personal satisfaction or happiness; **rewarding** is used more to talk about your feeling of doing sth important and being useful to others.

save
1 save sb's life
2 save up for a new bike
3 save a little each week
4 save time/energy

---

1 See also the entry for PROTECT
save · rescue · bail sb out · redeem
These words all mean to prevent sb/sth from dying, losing sth or being harmed or embarrassed.

▸ to save / rescue / redeem sb / sth **from** sth
▸ to save / rescue / redeem a **situation**
▸ to save / redeem **sinners / mankind**
▸ to rescue sb / bail sb out **financially**

save [T] to prevent sb/sth from dying, being harmed or destroyed or losing sth: *Doctors were unable to save him.* ◊ *Money from local businesses helped save the school from closure.* ◊ *We made one last attempt to save our marriage.* ◊ *There's no doubt that the firefighters* **saved** *my daughter's* **life** (= prevented her from dying).

rescue [T] to save sb/sth from a dangerous or harmful situation: *He was drowned in an attempt to rescue the child.* ◊ *They were rescued by a passing cruise ship.* ◊ *You rescued me from a very embarrassing situation.*
▸ **rescue** *noun* [U, C]: *A wealthy benefactor* **came to their rescue** *with a generous donation.* ◊ *Ten fishermen were saved in a daring sea rescue.*

bail sb 'out *phrasal verb* to rescue sb/sth from a difficult situation, especially by providing money: *Don't expect me to bail you out if it all goes wrong.* ◊ *The government had to* **bail** *the company* **out of** *financial difficulty.*

redeem /rɪˈdiːm/ [T] (*formal, religion*) (in Christianity) to save sb from the power of evil: *He was a sinner, redeemed by the grace of God.* ❶ **Redeem** is also used in non-religious language in the phrase *redeem a situation,* which means to prevent a situation from being as bad as it might be: *In an attempt to redeem the situation, Jed offered to help sell tickets.*
▸ **redemption** /rɪˈdempʃn/ *noun* [U]: *the redemption of the world from sin*

2 See also the entry for CUT 1
save · budget · economize · tighten your belt · skimp
These words all mean to spend less money.

▸ to save up / budget **for** sth
▸ to economize / skimp **on** sth

save [I] to keep money instead of spending it, often in order to buy a particular thing: *I'm not very good at saving.* ◊ *I'm saving for a new bike.* ◊ *We've been* **saving up** *to go to Australia.* See also **savings** → FUND *noun*
budget [I, T] to be careful about the amount of money you spend; to plan to spend an amount of money for a particular purpose: *If we budget carefully we'll be able to afford the trip.* ◊ *I've budgeted for two new assistants.* ◊ *Ten million euros has been budgeted for the project.* ◊ *The project has been budgeted at ten million euros.* See also **budget** → FUND *noun*
economize (*BrE* also **-ise**) [I] to use less money, time, etc. than you normally use: *Old people often try to economize on heating, thus endangering their health.* ◊ *Managers have been ordered to economize.*
tighten your 'belt *idiom* (*rather informal*) to spend less money because there is less available: *After price increases on most goods, we are all having to tighten our belts.*
skimp [I] to try to spend less money or time on sth than is really needed: *Older people should not skimp on food or heating.*

3 **save · deposit · put/set sth aside · bank**
These words all mean to keep money instead of spending it.

▸ to save / deposit / put aside / bank **money / £100, etc.**
▸ to save / deposit **cash**
▸ to deposit / bank a **cheque**

save [T] to keep money instead of spending it: *You should save a little each week.* ◊ *I've saved almost £100 so far.* See also **savings** → FUND *noun*

deposit /dɪˈpɒzɪt; *AmE* -ˈpɑːz-/ [T] to put money into a bank account: *Millions were deposited in Swiss bank accounts.* ◊ *You can withdraw and deposit money in any of our branches.*

put/set sth a'side *phrasal verb* (*especially spoken*) to save money for a particular purpose: *How much have you got put aside?* ◊ *We ought to set some money aside for emergencies.* ❶ **Put sth aside** is used slightly more in British English; **set sth aside** is used slightly more in American English.

bank [T] to put money, especially a lot of money, into a bank account, especially because you have been paid: *She is believed to have banked* (= been paid) *$10 million in two years.* See also the entry for MAKE 3

4 **save · conserve**
These words both mean to use no more of sth than necessary.

▸ to save / conserve **energy / water / fuel**

save [T, I] to avoid wasting sth such as time, money or resources, or using more than necessary: *We'll take a cab to* **save time**. ◊ *Book early and save £50!* ◊ *Factory and farm managers were told to* **save electricity** *during peak hours.* ◊ *This new system could* **save us** *a lot of* **money**. ◊ *I* **save on** *fares by walking to work.*
conserve /kənˈsɜːv; *AmE* -ˈsɜːrv/ [T] (*rather formal*) to use as little of sth as possible so that it lasts a long time, especially natural resources such as water or fuel: *You can conserve heat by insulating your home.* ◊ *Desert rats conserve water by remaining underground by day.*
▸ **conservation** *noun* [U]: *to encourage the conservation of water/fuel* ◊ *energy conservation*

say *verb*
1 'Hello!' she said.
2 I can't say I blame her.
3 We'll finish in, let's say, three months.

1 **say · speak · talk**
These words all mean to use your voice to express sth, especially in words.

▸ to say sth / speak / talk **to** sb
▸ to say sth / speak / talk **about** sth
▸ They were speaking / talking **(in) French**.

say [T] to tell sb sth, using words: *She said nothing to me about it.* ◊ *That's a terrible* **thing to say**. ◊ *I didn't believe a word she said.* ◊ *He said (that) his name was Sam.* ◊ *She finds it hard to* **say what** *she feels.* ◊ *'Why can't I go out now?' 'Because I* **say so**.' ◊ *He said to meet him here.* ❶ In stories, the subject often comes after **said, says** or **say** when it follows the actual words spoken, unless it is a pronoun: *'Hello!' she said.* ◊ *'That was marvellous,' said Daniel.*
speak [I] to use your voice to say sth: *He can't speak because of a throat infection.* ◊ *Please speak more slowly.* ◊ *Without speaking, she stood up and went out.* ◊ *What language are they speaking in?* ◊ *He speaks with a strange accent.* ❶ **Speak** also means 'to be able to use a particular language'. In this meaning it is not used in the progressive tenses: [T] *She speaks several languages/a little Urdu/an unusual dialect.* ◊ *Do you speak English?* See also **speak** → TALK, **speaker** → SPEAKER 1
talk [I, T] to say words in a language: *Alex can't talk yet — he's only just one year old.* ◊ *Are they talking Swedish or Danish?* See also **talk** → TALK, **talker** → SPEAKER 1

NOTE SPEAK OR TALK? **Talk** is much more frequent than **speak** in spoken English. If sb *can't speak* they are physically unable to speak because of illness, disability or emotion. If you are talking about a baby who has not learned to talk yet, use **talk**.

2 See also the entries for DECLARE and SHOW 2

say · talk · express · put · voice · air · phrase

These words all mean to let people know how you feel or what you think by speaking.

PATTERNS AND COLLOCATIONS

▶ to express / voice / air your **thoughts** / **opinions** / **views** / **concerns**

▶ to express / put / phrase sth **clearly**

▶ to talk / express yourself / air sth **openly**

▶ to talk / express yourself **freely**

say [T, I] to give an opinion on sth: *Say what you like* (= although you disagree) *about her, she's a fine singer.* ◇ *I'll say this for them, they're a very efficient company.* ◇ *Anna thinks I'm lazy – what do you say* (= what is your opinion)*? ◇ It's hard to say what caused the accident.* ◇ *I can't say I blame her for resigning* (= I think she was right). ◇ *I wouldn't say they were rich* (= in my opinion they are not rich). ◇ *'When will it be finished?' 'I couldn't say* (= I don't know).'

talk [I, T] to say things, especially in order to express feelings or ideas; to say things that are / are not sensible: *Stop talking and listen!* ◇ *He talked excitedly of his plans.* ◇ *She talks a lot of sense.* ◇ *You're talking nonsense!* See also the entry for TALK

express [T] (*rather formal*) to show or make known a feeling, opinion or idea by words, looks or actions: *Teachers have expressed concern about the emphasis on testing.* ◇ *Perhaps I have not expressed myself very well.* ◇ *She expresses herself most fully in her paintings.* ❶ **Express** is often followed by a noun describing a feeling or emotion: *to express (your, my, etc.) dissatisfaction / fear / horror / gratitude / desire.* **Say** and **talk** cannot be used in this way. Use **express yourself** to talk about saying what you think or feel so that people understand, or with *by*, *through* or *in* to talk about showing your feelings in a particular way, such as through art or poetry. See also **expression** → EXPRESSION 1

put [T] (always used with an adverb or preposition) to express or state sth in a particular way: *She put it very tactfully.* ◇ *Put simply, we accept their offer or go bankrupt.* ◇ *I was, to put it mildly, annoyed* (= I was extremely angry). ◇ *He was too trusting – or, to put it another way, he had no head for business.* ◇ *She had never tried to put this feeling into words.*

voice [T] (*rather formal*) to tell people your feelings or opinions about sth: *A number of parents have voiced concern about their children's safety.*

air [T] (*rather formal*) to express your opinions publicly: *The weekly meeting enables employees to air their grievances.*

> **NOTE** VOICE OR AIR? You can **voice** an opinion to one person, but if you **air** an opinion, you are usually sharing it with many people, at a meeting for example.

phrase [T] to say or write sth, arranging the words in a particular way: *I agree with what he says, but I'd have phrased it differently.*

3 say · suppose · speculate · presume · postulate · presuppose

These words all mean to suggest or give sth as a possibility, or act as if sth were true even though you have no definite proof.

PATTERNS AND COLLOCATIONS

▶ to say / suppose / speculate / presume / postulate / presuppose that...

▶ to suppose / presume / postulate / presuppose the **existence** of sth

▶ let's (just) / let us say / suppose (that...)

say [T, no passive] (*especially spoken*) used to give or suggest sth as an example or possibility: *You could learn the basics in, let's say, three months.* ◇ *Take any writer, say* (= for example) *Dickens...* ◇ *Say you lose your job. What then?*

suppose [T] to pretend that sth is true; to imagine what would happen if sth were true: *Suppose all the flights are booked on that day. Which other day could we go?* ◇ *Let us suppose, for example, that you are married with two children.* ◇ *Suppose him dead – what then?*

speculate /ˈspekjuleɪt/ [T] to form an opinion about sth without knowing all the details or facts: *Everyone speculated wildly about the reasons for her resignation.* ◇ *It's useless to speculate why he did it.* See also **speculation** → SPECULATION, **speculative** → SUPPOSED

presume /prɪˈzjuːm; *AmE* -ˈzuːm/ [T] (*rather formal*) to accept that sth is true until it is shown not to be true, for example in court; to accept sth as true or real and take action on that basis: *Twelve passengers are missing, presumed dead.* ◇ *In English law, a person is presumed innocent until proven guilty.* See also **presumption** → SPECULATION, **presume** → SUPPOSE

postulate /ˈpɒstjuleɪt; *AmE* ˈpɑːstʃəl-/ [T] (*formal*) to suggest or accept that sth is true so that it can be used as the basis of a theory or argument: *Some linguists have postulated a change in English pronunciation from around 1600.*

presuppose /ˌpriːsəˈpəʊz; *AmE* -ˈpoʊz/ [T] (*formal*) (of a person) to accept sth as true or real and base your actions on that before it has been proved; (of an argument or reason) to depend on sth else being true in order to exist or be valid: *Teachers sometimes presuppose a fairly high level of knowledge on the part of the students.* ◇ *This argument presupposes that all children start off life with equal advantages.* See also **presupposition** → SPECULATION

saying noun

saying · maxim · proverb · platitude

These are all words for a well-known statement that says sth that is generally true or gives advice.

PATTERNS AND COLLOCATIONS

▶ the saying / maxim / platitude **that**...

▶ a / an **well-known** / **old** saying / maxim / proverb

saying [C] a well-known statement that gives advice or says sth that is generally true about life: *'Accidents will happen,' as the saying goes.* ◇ *the sayings of Jesus / the Prophet / Chairman Mao*

maxim [C] a statement that says sth that is generally true or gives a rule for sensible behaviour: *There is some truth in the old maxim, 'You get what you pay for.'*

proverb /ˈprɒvɜːb; *AmE* ˈprɑːvɜːrb/ [C] a traditional saying that gives advice or says sth that is generally true about life: *a dictionary of proverbs* ◇ *As a Chinese proverb has it: 'The fish will be the last to discover the water.'*

> **NOTE** SAYING OR PROVERB? A **saying** is any kind of phrase, old or new, used to express an idea that people believe to be wise or true. A **proverb** is a traditional saying that is usually expressed as a metaphor (= in terms of sth else): *Don't count your chickens before they are hatched* (= Don't depend on money or success that you think you are going to get before you have actually got it). Especially in British English, proverbs are often used in a short form, sometimes with the phrase *it's a case of* or *and all that*: *Well, I suppose it's a case of not counting your chickens.* ◇ *Better the devil you know, and all that.*

platitude /ˈplætɪtjuːd; *AmE* -tuːd/ [C] (*rather formal, disapproving*) a comment or statement that has been made very often before and is therefore not interesting: *The prime minister's speech was full of platitudes and empty promises.*

scale noun

scale · hierarchy · ladder · line · the rankings · pecking order

These are all words for a range of levels that increase in size, importance, price, etc.

PATTERNS AND COLLOCATIONS

▶ **in** the hierarchy / rankings / pecking order
▶ **on a / the** scale / ladder
▶ **up / down** the ladder / line / pecking order
▶ the **social** scale / hierachy / ladder
▶ to **move up** the scale / hierarchy / ladder / rankings / pecking order
▶ to be **at the top / bottom of** the scale / hierarchy / ladder / rankings / pecking order
▶ **high / higher / low / lower in** the hierarchy / rankings / pecking order
▶ sb's / sth's **position / place in** the hierarchy / rankings / pecking order

scale [C] a range of levels or numbers used for measuring sth; the set of all the different levels of sth, from the lowest to the highest: *a salary/pay scale ◇ Please see the attached sheet for our scale of fees. ◇ Benefits are paid on a* **sliding scale** (= the amount you get might change), *according to your income. ◇ How would you judge our service* **on a scale of one to ten** (= one being the lowest mark and ten being the highest)? *◇ Farm workers were always considered to be low down on the social scale.*

hierarchy /ˈhaɪərɑːki; *AmE* -rɑːrki/ [C, U] a system, especially in a society or organization, in which people are organized into different levels of importance from the highest to the lowest: *She's fairly high up in the management hierarchy. ◇ At the bottom of the corporate hierarchy are part-time low-paid workers.*

ladder [C, usually sing.] a series of stages by which you can make progress, especially in a career or organization: *How quickly you move up the* **career ladder** *depends largely on your level of commitment. ◇ She was not interested in* **climbing the** *corporate* **ladder.**

line [C, usually sing.] a series of people in order of importance: *Who do you think is* **next in line** *for promotion? ◇ He is second* **in line** *to the throne. ◇ Orders are usually passed down through* **the line of command.**

the rankings [pl.] an official list showing the best players in a particular sport in order of how successful they are: *He is currently 16th in* **the world rankings**. *◇ The team has worked its way slowly up the rankings.*

ˈpecking order [C, usually sing.] (*informal*) the order of importance of sb/sth in relation to the others in a group: *Dogs high up in the pecking order are often the most aggressive. ◇ They insist there is no pecking order within the team.*

scarce *adj.* See also the entry for LIMITED 1

scarce · low · in short supply · short · few and far between
These words all describe sth that does not exist in many places or in large numbers.

PATTERNS AND COLLOCATIONS

▶ **resources** are scarce / low / in short supply / short
▶ **food** is scarce / low / in short supply / short
▶ **time / money** is scarce / short

scarce /skeəs; *AmE* skers/ not easily available; not available in the amounts that you need: *Land suitable for building on is scarce. ◇ This is a criminal waste of* **scarce resources**. ❶ Scarce can also describe animals, birds or plants that only exist in small numbers in a particular area. It is used especially in the phrases *getting/becoming scarce/scarcer*, usually to suggest how bad this change is, rather than to say how interesting the animal, etc. is: *Butterflies are getting scarcer and scarcer in industrialized areas. ◇ ~~This species is extremely scarce.~~* **OPP** **plentiful** ❶ If sth is **plentiful** it is available or exists in large amounts or numbers: *There was always a plentiful supply of food. ◇ In those days jobs were plentiful.* See also **scarcity** → LACK

low [not before noun] having a reduced amount or not enough of sth: *The reservoir was low after the long drought. ◇ Our supplies are* **running low** (= we have only a little left). *◇ They were* **low on** *fuel.*

in ˌshort supˈply *idiom* scarce: *Basic foodstuffs were in short supply. ◇ Shelter and warm clothing are in very short supply.*

short [not before noun] scarce: *When food was short they used to pick berries in the woods. ◇ He felt his time was* **running short** (= becoming short). See also **shortage** → LACK

> **NOTE** **WHICH WORD?** **Short** is used especially to talk about *time* and *money*. **Low** is used especially to talk about your own supplies of sth when you have not much left. **Scarce** and **in short supply** are used to talk about resources that are not generally available. **Scarce** is the only word that can be used before a noun: *~~a waste of low/short resources~~*

ˌfew and ˌfar beˈtween *idiom* not existing in large numbers; not happening often: *Well-paid acting jobs are few and far between. ◇ There were some inspired moments in the performance, but these were few and far between.* ❶ **Few and far between** is usually used to talk about sth that you wish there were more of, or happened more often, although it can also be used when you are glad that sth is rare: *Disappointments were few and far between.*

scatter *verb*

scatter · spread · strew · spray · shower · rain · sprinkle
These words all mean to make lots of small pieces of sth cover an area.

PATTERNS AND COLLOCATIONS

▶ to strew / shower / sprinkle sth **with** sth
▶ to scatter / spread / strew / spray / shower / rain / sprinkle sth **on / onto / over** sth
▶ to scatter / spread / strew / spray sth **across** sth
▶ to scatter / spread / sprinkle **seeds**
▶ to scatter / spray **crumbs**
▶ to scatter / shower / rain **ash**
▶ to scatter / shower **debris**
▶ to scatter / spread / sprinkle sth **evenly**

scatter [T] to throw or drop things in different directions so that they cover an area of ground: *Scatter the grass seed over the lawn. ◇ They scattered his ashes at sea.*

spread [T] to arrange objects so that that they cover a large area and can be seen easily: *Papers had been* **spread out** *on the desk.*

strew /struː/ [T, usually passive] to cover a surface with things: *Clothes were strewn across the floor. ◇ The streets were strewn with corpses.*

spray [T, I] to cover sb/sth with a lot of small things with a lot of force: *The gunman sprayed the building with bullets. ◇ Pieces of glass sprayed all over the room.*

shower [T] to drop a lot of small things onto sb: *The bride and groom were showered with rice as they left the church. ◇ The roof collapsed, showering us with dust and debris.* See also **shower** → FLOOD *noun* 2

rain [T] to make sth fall on sb/sth in large quantities: *The volcano erupted, raining hot ash over a wide area.*

sprinkle [T] to throw small pieces of sth or drops of a liquid on sth: *She sprinkled sugar over the strawberries.*

scene *noun*

scene · passage · line · extract · excerpt · clip · snatch · reading
These are all words for a short section of a work, such as a book, film or piece of music.

> **NOTE** Compare the words in this entry with the words in the entry for **section**. These words generally refer to literature, films and music. The words in the **section** entry generally refer to factual, legal or technical documents.

PATTERNS AND COLLOCATIONS

▶ a scene / a passage / a line / an extract / an excerpt / a clip / snatches / a reading **from** sth
▶ a line / an extract / a clip / snatches **of** sth
▶ a **long** scene / passage / extract
▶ a **short** scene / passage / extract / excerpt / clip
▶ (a) **brief** scene / passage / extract / clip / snatches
▶ the **opening** scene / passage / line
▶ a **famous** scene / passage / line
▶ to **read** / **quote** a passage / a line / an extract
▶ to **publish** a passage / an extract / an excerpt
▶ a passage / an extract / an excerpt / a reading **is taken from** sth (e.g. a book)
▶ sth **includes** passages / extracts / excerpts / clips

scene [C] a part of a film, play or book in which the action happens in one place or is of one particular type: *The movie opens with a scene in a New York apartment.* ◊ *I got nervous before my big scene* (= the one where I have a very important part). ◊ *The film contains some minor **sex scenes.***

passage [C] a short section from a piece of writing or music, sometimes separated from the whole: *Read the following passage and answer the questions below.* ◊ *His fifteenth symphony quotes a famous passage from the William Tell Overture.*

line [C] a row of words written on a page or the empty space where they can be written; a row of words in a poem or song: *Look at line 5 of the text.* ◊ *Write the title of your essay on the top line.* ◊ *I can only remember the first two lines of that song.*

extract /'ekstrækt/ [C] a short section from a piece of writing or music, especially one that gives you an idea of what the whole thing is like: *The following extract is taken from her new novel.*

excerpt /'eksɜːpt; AmE -sɜːrpt/ [C] an extract: *The show features excerpts from classic jazz recordings.*

> **NOTE** **EXTRACT** OR **EXCERPT?** Extract is used more often when talking about a piece of writing; **excerpt** is used more often when talking about a piece of music. An **excerpt** from a piece of writing is often shorter than an **extract.** In a report or academic text, where passages of text are included and given numbers, **extract** is used: *Extract 15 illustrates the importance of careful planning.* ◊ *Excerpt 15 illustrates the importance of careful planning.*

clip [C] a short part of a film that is shown separately: *Here is a clip from her latest movie.*

snatch [C] (*informal*) a very small part of a conversation or piece of music that you hear, especially by chance: *I only caught snatches of the conversation.* ◊ *I heard a snatch of music coming from the bar.*

reading [C] a short section from a book that is read aloud, especially a section from the Bible as part of a religious service: *The reading today is from the Book of Daniel.* ◊ *He was invited to give a poetry reading as part of the literary festival.*

scepticism (*BrE*) (*AmE* skepticism) *noun*

scepticism · disbelief · suspicion · distrust · cynicism
These are all words for an attitude or feeling that you cannot believe or trust sb/sth.

PATTERNS AND COLLOCATIONS

▶ scepticism / suspicion / distrust / cynicism **towards** sth
▶ scepticism / suspicion / cynicism **about** sth
▶ scepticism / suspicion **over** sth
▶ **with** scepticism / disbelief / suspicion / cynicism
▶ scepticism / disbelief **that...**
▶ **deep** / **growing** scepticism / suspicion / distrust
▶ **healthy** / **widespread** scepticism / suspicion / distrust / cynicism
▶ to **express** scepticism / disbelief / suspicion / distrust
▶ to **greet** sb / sth with scepticism / disbelief / suspicion / cynicism
▶ to **regard** sb / sth with scepticism / suspicion / distrust

scepticism (*BrE*) (*AmE* **skepticism**) /'skeptɪsɪzəm/ [U] an attitude of doubting that claims or statements are true or that sth will happen: *Other scientists have expressed scepticism about these results.* See also **sceptical** → SUSPICIOUS 1

> ▶ **sceptic** (*BrE*) (*AmE* **skeptic**) *noun* [C]: *He was unable to convince the sceptics in the audience.*

disbelief /ˌdɪsbɪ'liːf/ [U] the feeling of not being able to believe sth: *He stared at me* **in disbelief.** ◊ *Disbelief in God was her way of rebelling against her strict religious upbringing.* ◊ *To enjoy the movie you have to* **suspend your disbelief** (= pretend to believe sth, even if it seems very unlikely). See also **disbelieve** → SUSPECT *verb*, **disbelieving** → SUSPICIOUS 1

suspicion [U] the feeling that you cannot trust sb/sth to be honest or good: *Their offer was greeted with some suspicion.* See also **suspicion** → DOUBT *noun* 2, **suspect** → SUSPECT *verb*, **suspicious** → SUSPICIOUS 1

distrust /dɪs'trʌst/ [U, sing.] a feeling that you cannot trust sb/sth: *They looked at each other with distrust.* ◊ *He has a deep distrust of all modern technology.* See also **distrust** → SUSPECT *verb*

cynicism /'sɪnɪsɪzəm/ [U] (*often disapproving*) the belief that people only do things to benefit themselves, rather than for good or sincere reasons: *In a world full of cynicism she was the one person I felt I could trust.* See also **cynical** → SUSPICIOUS 1

> ▶ **cynic** *noun* [C]: *Don't be such a cynic!*

schedule *noun*

schedule · agenda · timetable · calendar · programme · diary · itinerary
These are all words for a plan of particular activities or events that will be done or will happen in the future.

PATTERNS AND COLLOCATIONS

▶ the schedule / agenda / timetable / calendar / programme / diary / itinerary **for** tomorrow / next week
▶ to be / put sth **in** the schedule / the timetable / the programme / your calendar / your diary / the itinerary
▶ to be / put sth **on** the schedule / agenda / timetable / programme / calendar / itinerary
▶ a **busy** / **full** / **packed** schedule / agenda / timetable / calendar / programme / diary / itinerary
▶ a **detailed** schedule / agenda / timetable / programme / itinerary
▶ a / an **realistic** / **ambitious** schedule / agenda / timetable / programme
▶ a **hectic** / **demanding** schedule / timetable / programme
▶ a **daily** / **weekly** schedule / timetable / programme / itinerary
▶ to **look at** the schedule / the agenda / the timetable / the calendar / the programme / your diary
▶ to **check** / **consult** the schedule / the timetable / the calendar / your diary
▶ to **agree (on)** / **draw up** a schedule / an agenda / a timetable / a programme / an itinerary
▶ to **follow** / **change** the schedule / agenda / timetable / programme / itinerary
▶ to **keep** / **stick** / **adhere to** the schedule / agenda / timetable / programme

schedule /'ʃedjuːl; AmE 'skedʒuːl/ [C, U] a plan that lists all the work that you have to do and when you must do each thing; a list of the television and radio shows that are on a particular channel and the times that they start: *We're working to a* **tight schedule** (= we have a lot of things to do in a short time). ◊ *Filming began* **on schedule** (= at the planned time). ◊ *The new bridge has been finished two years* **ahead of schedule.** ◊ *The tunnel project has already fallen* **behind schedule.** ◊ *The show trebled ratings for the channel's afternoon schedule.* ❶ In American English, a **schedule** is also a list showing the times when buses or trains leave or arrive at a place or showing which classes a student is taking in school: *a bus/flight/train schedule* ◊ *What's your schedule like next semester?* The British English word for this is **timetable.**

agenda /əˈdʒendə/ [C] a list of items to be discussed at a meeting; the issues that sb/sth considers important: *The next item on the agenda is the publicity budget.* ◇ *For the government, education is now at the top of the agenda* (= most important). ◇ *Newspapers have been accused of trying to set the agenda for the government* (= decide what is important). ❶ Do NOT use **agenda** to mean **diary** or **calendar**: ~~Let me just check my agenda.~~

timetable [C] a plan of when you expect or hope particular events to happen: *I have a busy timetable this week* (= I have planned to do many things). ◇ *The government has set out its timetable for the peace talks.* ❶ In British English a **timetable** is also a list showing the times when buses or trains leave or arrive at a place or showing which classes a student is taking in school: *a bus/flight/train timetable* ◇ *We have a new timetable each term.* The American English word for this is **schedule**.

> **NOTE** **SCHEDULE** OR **TIMETABLE?** Often you can use either word: *I have a busy schedule/timetable this week.* However, a **schedule** is usually a plan of what must happen and is often used about work. You can talk about *work/production schedules* and work can be on/ ahead of/behind schedule: ~~work/production timetables~~ ◇ ~~on/ahead of/behind timetable.~~ **Timetable** is often used about a plan of what you hope will happen if things go according to plan, but this may partly depend on things outside your control: *the government's timetable for the peace talks* ◇ ~~the government's schedule for the peace talks~~

calendar /ˈkælɪndə(r)/ [C] a page or series of pages showing the days, weeks and months of a particular year, especially one that you hang on a wall; an electronic record of the days, weeks and months of a particular year, where you can make a note of your appointments; a list of important events or dates of a particular type during the year: *Did you get a calendar for 2008/a 2008 calendar?* ◇ *I think I'm free on that day — let me check my calendar.* ◇ *This is one of the biggest weeks in the racing calendar.* ◇ *It is a major festival in the church's calendar.*

programme (*BrE*) (*AmE* **program**) [C] an organized order of performances or events: *We have an exciting musical programme lined up for you.* ◇ (*spoken*) *What's the programme for* (= what are we going to do) *tomorrow?*

diary /ˈdaɪəri/ [C] (*BrE*) a book with a space for each day of the year in which you can write down things you have to do in the future: *I'll just make a note of that date in my diary.* ◇ *I'm afraid my diary is full* (= I have no available time) *for this week, but I could see you next Monday.* ❶ In American English use **calendar** or **schedule**; also use **calendar** in both American and British English for a diary in electronic form, for example on your computer. A **diary** is also a book for recording thoughts or events after they happen. See also **diary** → RECORD *noun*

itinerary /aɪˈtɪnərəri; *AmE* aɪˈtɪnəreri/ [C] a plan of a journey, including the route and places that you will visit: *He drew up a detailed itinerary.* ◇ *Visits to four different countries are included in your itinerary.*

schedule *verb*

schedule · set · fix · time · line sb/sth up · set sth up · timetable · book
These words all mean to arrange a particular time for sth to happen or for sb to do sth.

PATTERNS AND COLLOCATIONS
▶ to schedule/set/fix/time/line up/set up/timetable/book sth **for** sth
▶ to schedule/set/fix/time/line up/set up/timetable/book sb/sth **to do sth**
▶ to schedule/set/time sth **to begin/start/take place**
▶ to schedule/set/fix/time/set up/timetable a **meeting**
▶ to schedule/fix/set up/book an **appointment**
▶ to schedule/set up/timetable an **event**
▶ to schedule/set/fix/book a **time/date/day**

▶ to **provisionally** schedule/set/fix/book sth

schedule /ˈʃedjuːl; *AmE* ˈskedʒuːl/ [T, usually passive] to arrange for sth to happen at a particular time: *The meeting is scheduled for Friday afternoon.* ◇ *Filming is scheduled to begin in May.* ◇ *The movie is scheduled for release next month.* ◇ *I'll try to schedule you in* (= arrange a time to see you) *next week.* ❶ Especially in American English, to **schedule** is also to arrange the times when classes take place in school: *No regular classes were scheduled on Wednesdays.* In British English the usual word for this is **timetable**.

set [T] to arrange a time for sth to happen; to decide on a date or limit: *The first students are set to arrive in September.* ◇ *Have they set a date for their wedding?* ◇ *Set a time limit for your studying each night.*

fix [T] to decide on a date or time for sth: *Their departure was fixed for 14 August.* ◇ *The dates have to be fixed well in advance.* ❶ **Fix** can also mean to arrange to do sth, especially at a particular time; this meaning is more informal, used especially in spoken English: *How are you fixed* (= do you have any plans) *for Thursday?* ◇ *I've fixed up for you to see the doctor tomorrow.*

time [T, often passive] to choose a particular time to do sth or for sth to happen: *She timed her arrival for shortly after 3.* ◇ *Publication of the book was timed to coincide with his 70th birthday celebrations.* ◇ *The request was badly timed* (= it was not a good time to make it).

line sb/sth ˈup *phrasal verb* to arrange for sth to happen or be done in the future; to arrange for sb to be available to do sth: *I already had a job lined up when I left college.* ◇ *I have a busy month lined up.* ◇ *She had lined up some interesting guest speakers.*

set sth ˈup *phrasal verb* to make the necessary arrangements for sth to happen: *The meeting of foreign ministers had taken months to set up.*

timetable /ˈtaɪmteɪbl/ [T, usually passive] (*especially BrE*) to arrange for sth to take place at a particular time or to be regularly repeated at the same time: *There were several timetabled events in the evenings.* ◇ *The lessons were timetabled on Wednesday from 10 to 12.* ❶ In American English the usual word for this is **schedule**.

book [T] to make a firm arrangement for a singer, etc. to perform on a particular date: *Have you booked the band for the party yet?* ◇ *He's booked to appear on 3 November at Central Hall.* See also **book** → ORDER *verb* 2

scholar *noun* See the Topic Map for EDUCATION on p.888

scholar · philosopher · intellectual · academic · theorist · thinker
These are all words for a person who is very intelligent or who thinks a lot about important matters.

PATTERNS AND COLLOCATIONS
▶ a **great/leading** scholar/philosopher/intellectual/academic/ theorist/thinker
▶ an **eminent** scholar/philosopher/intellectual/academic
▶ a **distinguished** scholar/philosopher/academic
▶ a **true** scholar/philosopher/intellectual
▶ a **religious** scholar/philosopher/intellectual/thinker
▶ a **classical** scholar/philosopher/theorist
▶ a **political/social** philosopher/theorist/thinker

scholar /ˈskɒlə(r); *AmE* ˈskɑːl-/ [C] a person who knows a lot about a particular subject because they have studied it in detail: *an eminent German scholar* ◇ *a scholar of the Enlightenment* See also **scholarly** → EDUCATIONAL, **scholarship** → KNOWLEDGE

philosopher [C] a person who studies or writes about philosophy; a person who thinks deeply about things: *We studied the writings of the Greek philosopher Aristotle.* ◇ *She seems to be a bit of a philosopher.*

intellectual /ˌɪntəˈlektʃuəl/ [C] a person who is interested in subjects, ideas and activities that involve serious thought, especially sb who is well educated: *He was a leading intellectual of his day.* See also **intellectual** → INTELLECTUAL *adj.* 2

academic /ˌækəˈdemɪk/ [C] a person who teaches and/or does research at a university or college: *Many senior academics are taking up positions overseas.* See also **academic** → EDUCATIONAL *adj.*, **don** → LECTURER, See also the entry for PROFESSOR

theorist /ˈθɪərɪst; *AmE* ˈθiːə-; ˈθɪr-/ [C] a person who develops new ideas and principles about a particular subject: *Feminist theorists have long talked about the way women are represented in the media.* ◇ *There are plenty of* **conspiracy theorists** (= people who think sth is the result of secret activities by sb in power) *with some wacky ideas.*

thinker [C] a person who thinks seriously, and often writes, about important things such as society, science or philosophy; a person who thinks in a particular way: *He's a radical social thinker and historian.* ◇ *She was not a deep thinker.* ◇ *The company needs more* **original thinkers**. ◇ *I'm not really a* **creative thinker**.

school *noun* See the Topic Map for EDUCATION on p.888

school · college · university · academy · seminary
These are all words for a place where people are taught or are trained in a skill.

PATTERNS AND COLLOCATIONS
▸ **at / in** school / college / university
▸ **at / a / the** school / college / university / academy / seminary
▸ to **go to / attend** school / college / university / an academy / a seminary
▸ to **study at** a college / a university / an academy / a seminary
▸ to **graduate from** high school / a college / a university / an academy / a seminary
▸ to **leave** school / college / university / an academy / a seminary
▸ to **finish / quit** school / college / university

school [C, U] a place where children are taught; the process of learning in a school; the time during your life when you go to a school; the time during the day when children are learning in a school: *My sister and I went to the same school.* ◇ *More money is needed for roads, hospitals and schools.* ◇ (*BrE*) *an infant/a junior/a primary/a secondary school* ◇ (*AmE*) *an elementary/a junior high/a high school* ◇ *In Britain children start school when they are five.* ◇ (*BrE*) *My younger son is still at* **school**. ◇ (*AmE*) *My younger son is still* **in school**. ◇ (*AmE*) *to* **teach school** (= teach in a school) ◇ *I'll meet you after school today.* ◇ *An announcement was made to the whole school* (= all the children and teachers in a school). ❶ When **school** is being referred to as an institution it is used without *the*: *to go to school*. When you are talking about a particular building, *the* is used: *His parents went to the school to talk to his teacher.* ❶ **School** is also used in compounds to mean a place where people (not necessarily children) go to learn a particular subject or skill: *a language/riding school* ◇ *The university has a school of dentistry.* ◇ *She wants to go to* **drama school**. In informal American English **school** can also refer to a college or university or the time that you spend there: (*AmE*, *informal*) *famous schools like Yale and Harvard* ◇ *Where did you go to school?*

college [C, U] a place where students go to study or receive training after they have left school: *a college of further education* ◇ *When I left school I went to secretarial college.* ◇ (*AmE*) *He got interested in politics when he was* **in college**. ◇ *He's hoping to go to college next year.*

university [C, U] an institution at the highest level of education where you can study for a degree or do research: *How many universities are there in Britain?* ◇ *the University of York/York University* ◇ *Ohio State University* ◇ (*BrE*) *Both their children are* **at university**. ◇ (*BrE*) *He's hoping to go to university next year.*

> **NOTE** COLLEGE OR UNIVERSITY? In British English the usual word for an institution where you can study for a degree is **university**. In American English **university** is used in the names of particular institutions, but the usual word to talk about studying at a university in

general is **college**: (*BrE*) *She's* **at university**. ◇ *to go to university* ◇ (*AmE*) *She's* **in college**. ◇ *to go to college* **College** is used in both British and American English to talk about a place where you can do further studies after leaving school, especially in technical subjects, that do not lead to a degree: *a technical/secretarial college* A **college** can also be one of the separate institutions that some British universities, such as Oxford and Cambridge, are divided into: *King's College, Cambridge*

academy /əˈkædəmi/ [C] a school or college for special training; (in Scotland) a secondary school; (in the US) a private school: *She trained at the Royal Academy of Music.* ◇ *He went to Ayr Academy.*

seminary /ˈsemɪnəri; *AmE* -neri/ [C] a college where priests, religious ministers and rabbis are trained: *They spend six years in a seminary.* ◇ *He went to the Northern Catholic Seminary to train for the ministry.*

scold *verb* See also the entry for BLAME

scold · lecture · tell sb off · rebuke · reprimand · chide · castigate · berate · reproach
These words all mean to tell sb that you disapprove of sth they have done.

PATTERNS AND COLLOCATIONS
▸ to scold / tell sb off / rebuke / reprimand / chide / castigate / berate / reproach sb **for** sth
▸ to scold / rebuke / chide / castigate / berate / reproach **yourself**
▸ to scold / tell sb off / rebuke / reprimand / castigate / berate sb **severely**
▸ to scold / rebuke / reprimand / chide sb **gently**
▸ to **publicly** rebuke / reprimand / castigate / berate sb

scold [T] (*written*) to tell sb, especially a child, that you disapprove of sth that they have done: *Rose scolded the child gently for her behaviour.* ◇ *'Don't be such a baby!' he scolded.*
▸ **scolding** *noun* [C, usually sing.]: *She got a scolding from her mother.*

lecture /ˈlektʃə(r)/ [T] (*disapproving*) to criticize sb or tell them how you think they should behave, especially when it is done in an annoying way: *Don't start lecturing me!* ◇ *He's always* **lecturing her about** *the way she dresses.*
▸ **lecture** *noun* [C]: *I know I should stop smoking – don't give me a lecture about it.*

tell sb 'off *phrasal verb* (*especially BrE*, *spoken*) to speak angrily to sb for doing sth wrong: *I told the boys off for making so much noise.* ◇ *Did you* **get told off**?
▸ **telling-'off** *noun* [C, usually sing.]: (*BrE*, *informal*) *The nurse gave him a telling-off for smoking in the hospital.*

> **NOTE** SCOLD OR TELL SB OFF? There is no verb for telling sb that you disapprove of their actions that is neither formal nor informal. **Scold** is the most frequent of these verbs in written English, particularly in stories, but it is not used much in spoken English. **Tell sb off** is by far the most frequent in spoken British English but it is not used much in written English or American English.

rebuke /rɪˈbjuːk/ [T, often passive] (*formal*) to tell sb, publicly or privately, that you blame them for doing sth wrong: *The company was publicly rebuked for having neglected safety procedures.* ◇ *She rebuked herself for her stupidity.*
▸ **rebuke** *noun* [C, usually sing., U]: *He was silenced by her stinging rebuke.*

reprimand /ˈreprɪmɑːnd; *AmE* -mænd/ [T] (*formal*) to tell sb officially that you disapprove of their actions, especially if they have broken a rule or law: *The judge reprimanded him for using such language in court.*
▸ **reprimand** *noun* [C, U]: *He received a severe reprimand for his behaviour.*

NOTE REBUKE OR REPRIMAND? Rebuke has a wider range of meaning, and can usually be used instead of reprimand. Reprimand cannot always be used instead of rebuke: ~~She reprimanded herself for her stupidity.~~

chide /tʃaɪd/ [T] (*formal*) to tell sb gently that you disapprove of sth that they have done: *She chided herself for being so impatient with the children.*

castigate /ˈkæstɪgeɪt/ [T] (*formal*) to criticize sb/sth severely because you think they have failed or done sth wrong: *The minister castigated schools for falling standards in education.* ❶ **Castigate** can be used when you talk *to* sb to tell them their faults, or talk *about* them publicly, for example in a speech.

berate /bɪˈreɪt/ [T] (*formal*) to speak angrily to sb because you do not approve of sth that they have done: *The minister was berated by angry demonstrators as he left the meeting.* ❶ **Berate** is often used when the criticism is both public and spoken directly to the person (not written): ~~The minister was scolded/told off/rebuked/reprimanded/chided/castigated/reproached by angry demonstrators.~~

reproach /rɪˈprəʊtʃ; AmE -ˈproʊtʃ/ [T] (*formal*) to tell sb that you blame them or are disappointed in them because you think they have done sth wrong; to feel guilty about sth that you think you should have done differently: *She was reproached by colleagues for leaking the story to the press.* ◇ *He reproached himself for not telling her the truth.* ❶ Several of the words in this group can be used with *yourself/himself/herself*, etc. to show that sb feels guilty or is angry with themselves, but **reproach** is the most frequent in this pattern.

▸ **reproach** *noun* [U, C, usually sing.]: (*formal*) *His voice was full of reproach.* ◇ *He listened to his wife's bitter reproaches.*

scope *noun*

scope · room · margin
These are all words for the opportunity to do sth, the possibility of sth happening, or the extra time, space, money, etc. needed for this.

PATTERNS AND COLLOCATIONS
▸ scope / room / margin **for** sth
▸ to **have** scope / room for sth
▸ to **give** / **allow** sb scope / room for sth

scope [U] the opportunity or ability to do or achieve sth: *Her job offers very little scope for creativity.* ◇ *The extra money will give us the scope to improve our facilities.* ◇ *First try to do something that is within your scope.* See also **scope** → RANGE 2

room [U] (always used with *for* or *to* + infinitive) the possibility of sth existing or happening; the opportunity to do sth: *He had to be certain. There could be no room for doubt.* ◇ *There's some room for improvement in your work* (= it is not as good as it could be). ◇ *It is important to give children room to think for themselves.*

margin /ˈmɑːdʒɪn; AmE ˈmɑːrdʒən/ [C, usually sing., U] an extra amount of sth such as time, space, money, etc. that you include in order to make sure that sth is successful: *The equipment has been designed to give an increased safety margin.* ◇ *The narrow gateway left me little margin for error as I reversed the car.*

score *noun* See the Topic Map for EDUCATION on p.888

score · result · point · mark · grade
These are all words for the number of points or goals scored by a player or team in a competition, or given to a student in a test.

PATTERNS AND COLLOCATIONS
▸ a **high** / **low** / **good** / **poor** score / mark / grade
▸ the **final** score / result / mark / grade
▸ to **get** a score / your results / a point / a mark / a grade

score [C] the number of points, goals, etc. scored by each player or team in a game or competition: *What's the score now?* ◇ *The final score was 4–3.* ◇ *I'll keep (the) score* (= keep a record of the score). ◇ (*BrE*) *A penalty in the last minute of the game levelled the score 2–2.* ❶ Especially in American English, sb's **score** on a test is the number of points they get for correct answers on the test: *college entrance test scores* ◇ *an IQ score of 120* ◇ *to get a perfect score* (= no incorrect answers)

▸ **score** *verb* [T, I]: *to score a goal/try/touchdown/victory* ◇ *Fraser scored again in the second half.*

result [C] the final score or the name of the winner in a sports event, competition or election: *They will announce the result of the vote tonight.* ◇ *the election results* ◇ *the football results* ❶ In British English your **results** are the score you get in an exam or in a number of exams: *Have you had your results yet?*

point [C] an individual unit that adds to a score in a game or sports competition: *to win/lose a point* ◇ *Australia finished 20 points ahead.* ◇ *They won on points* (= by scoring more points rather than by completely defeating their opponents).

mark [C] (*especially BrE*) a number or letter that is given to show the standard of sb's work or performance or is given to sb for answering sth correctly: *What's the pass mark* (= the mark you need in order to pass)? ◇ *I got full marks* (= the highest mark possible) *in the spelling test.* See also **mark** → MARK *verb* 2

grade [C] a mark given in an exam or for a piece of school work: (*BrE*) *She got good grades in her exams.* ◇ (*AmE*) *She got good grades on her exams.* See also **grade** → MARK *verb*

NOTE MARK OR GRADE? In British schools **marks** can be given for any piece of school work, test or performance; a **grade** is usually given only for an important exam or a whole year's work in a subject. A **mark** is often more precise than a **grade**, expressed as a particular number out of 10 or 100, for example; a **grade** is usually a letter such as A, B, C, D or E, with each grade covering a range of marks. In American schools, a **grade** can be a letter or a number and can be given for any piece of school work, test or performance, or for a whole year's work in a subject. You can also talk about sb's **score** in a test, but **mark** is NOT usually used in American English.

scratch *verb*

1 scratch yourself on a nail
2 scratch at an insect bite/a cat scratches

1 scratch · scrape · rub · scuff · graze
These words all mean to damage a surface or to remove sth from it by moving sth sharp and hard across it.

PATTERNS AND COLLOCATIONS
▸ to scratch sth / scrape sth / rub / scuff sth / graze sth **on** sth
▸ to scrape / graze your **knee** / **knuckles** / **elbow** / **shin**
▸ to scratch / scrape / graze a **surface**
▸ to scratch / scuff / graze sth **badly**

scratch [T] to damage the surface of sth, especially accidentally, by making thin shallow marks on it; to cut or damage your skin slightly with sth sharp: *Be careful not to scratch the furniture.* ◇ *The car's paintwork is badly scratched.* ◇ *I'd scratched my leg and it was bleeding.* ◇ *She scratched herself on a nail.* See also **scratch** → INJURY *noun*

scrape [T] to rub sth accidentally against sth rough, so that it gets damaged or hurt: *I scraped the side of my car on the wall.* ◇ *Sorry, I've scraped some paint off the car.* ◇ *She fell and scraped her knee.* ◇ *The wire had scraped the skin from her fingers.*

NOTE SCRATCH OR SCRAPE? If you **scratch** a surface you make a long thin line on it; if you **scrape** it, you usually make a wider mark. If you **scratch** a part of your body, the damage is not very bad; if you **scrape** it, the damage is usually a little greater.

rub (-**bb**-) [I] (of a surface) to move backwards and forwards many times against sth while pressing it, especially causing pain or damage: *The back of my shoe is rubbing.* ◇ *The wheel is rubbing on the mudguard.* ◇ *The horse's neck was rubbed raw* (= until the skin came off) *where the rope had been.*

scuff [T] to make a mark on the smooth surface of sth when you rub it against sth rough: *I scuffed the heel of my shoe on the stonework.*

graze [T] to break the surface of your skin by rubbing it against sth rough: *I fell and grazed my knee.* ◇ *He grazed his elbow on a sharp piece of rock.* See also **graze** → INJURY noun

> **NOTE** SCRAPE OR GRAZE? **Graze** is only used to talk about parts of the body; **scrape** can be used to talk about damaging many types of surface. **Scrape** places more emphasis on the action; **graze** places more emphasis on the injury.

2 scratch · claw
These words both mean to rub or tear sth with claws or nails.

PATTERNS AND COLLOCATIONS
▸ to scratch / claw **at** sth
▸ to scratch / claw sth **with** sth
▸ to scratch / claw sb **frantically**

scratch [T, I] to rub your skin with your nails, usually because it is itching (= making you feel uncomfortable); to cut sb's skin slightly with your nails: *John yawned and scratched his chin.* ◇ *Try not to scratch.* ◇ *She scratched at the insect bites on her arm.* ◇ *She had obviously tried to scratch her attacker.* ◇ *Does the cat scratch?*

claw [I, T] to scratch or tear sb/sth with claws (= one of the sharp curved nails on an animal's or bird's foot) or with your fingernails: *The cat was clawing at the leg of the chair.* ◇ *She had clawed Stephen across the face.* ❶ When it is used to describe people's actions, **claw** is mostly used in literary writing, and may be used to talk about particularly desperate or violent acts: *She flew at him, clawing blindly with her nails.*

scream *verb* See also the entry for SHOUT

scream · cry out · screech · wail · squeal · shriek · howl · yelp
These words all mean to give a loud high cry, or to make a loud high noise.

PATTERNS AND COLLOCATIONS
▸ to scream / cry out / screech / wail / squeal / shriek / howl / yelp **at** sb
▸ to scream / cry out / screech / wail / squeal / shriek / howl / yelp **in** / **with** pain / terror, etc.
▸ **brakes** / **tyres** scream / screech / squeal / shriek
▸ a **dog** howls / yelps
▸ to **almost** scream / cry out / wail / shriek
▸ to screech / squeal / shriek **to a halt**

scream [I] (of a person) to give a loud, high cry, because you are hurt, frightened, excited, etc; (of things) to make a loud, high noise or to move fast, making this noise: *He covered her mouth to stop her from screaming.* ◇ *The kids were screaming with excitement.* ◇ *Lights flashed and sirens screamed.* ❶ **Scream** is usually used without an object, but it can take an object in the phrase *scream yourself hoarse/silly/to death*: [T] *The baby was screaming itself hoarse.* **Scream** is most often used to talk about women and girls. When men **scream**, there is often a suggestion of a particularly extreme pain or fear. **Scream** can also be used as a speech verb. See also **scream** → SHOUT
▸ **scream** noun [C]: *She let out a scream of pain.* ◇ *He drove off with a scream of tyres.*

cry 'out *phrasal verb* to make a loud sound without words because you are hurt, afraid, surprised, etc: *He cried out in fear.* ◇ *She cried out loud with the pain.* ❶ **Cry out** can also be used as a speech verb: See also **cry out** → CALL 3
▸ **cry** noun [C]: *He gave a loud cry of despair.*

screech [I] (especially of a person or animal) to make a loud high unpleasant sound; (of a vehicle) to make a loud high unpleasant sound as it moves: *He screeched with pain.* ◇ *Monkeys were screeching in the trees.* ◇ *The car screeched to a halt outside the hospital.* ❶ **Screech** can also be used as a speech verb: [T] *'No, don't!' she screeched.* ◇ *He screeched something at me.*
▸ **screech** noun [C]: *She suddenly let out a screech.* ◇ *The car came to a halt with a screech of brakes.*

wail [I] (of a person or animal) to make a long loud cry, especially because they are sad or in pain; (of things) to make a long high sound: *The little girl was wailing miserably.* ◇ *The cat was wailing to be let out.* ◇ *Ambulances raced by with sirens wailing.* ❶ **Wail** can also be used as a speech verb: [T] *'It's broken!' she wailed.*
▸ **wail** noun [C]: *He let out a wail of anguish.* ◇ *She could hear the distant wail of sirens.*

> **NOTE** SCREAM OR WAIL? A **wail** is longer than a **scream**, but less strong and extreme; it can be high or low in pitch, but a **scream** is always high.

squeal [I] (especially of pigs, excited children and vehicles) to make a long high sound: *The pigs were squealing.* ◇ *Children were running around squealing with excitement.* ◇ *The car squealed to a halt.* ❶ **Squeal** can also be used as a speech verb: [T] *'Don't!' she squealed.*
▸ **squeal** noun [C]: *a squeal of pain/delight* ◇ *The car stopped with a squeal of brakes.*

shriek /ʃriːk/ [I] to give a loud high cry, for example when you are excited, frightened or in pain: *She shrieked in fright.* ◇ *The audience was shrieking with laughter.* ❶ **Shriek** can also be used as a speech verb: [T] *'Look out!' she shrieked.*
▸ **shriek** noun [C]: *She let out a piercing shriek.*

howl /haʊl/ [I] to make a loud cry when you are in pain, angry, amused, etc: *The child howled in pain.* ◇ *We howled with laughter.* ◇ *The baby was howling* (= crying loudly) *all the time I was there.* ❶ **Howl** is used to describe the long, loud, high, almost sad, cry made by wolves, and sometimes dogs. It can also be used as a speech verb: [T] *'Ouch!' howled Ricky.*
▸ **howl** noun [C]: *The suggestion was greeted with howls of laughter.*

yelp [I] to give a sudden short cry, usually of pain: *The dog yelped with pain and surprise.*

script *noun*

script · text · manuscript · line · lyrics · score · screenplay · libretto
These words all mean the written form of sth such as a speech, a play or a piece of music.

PATTERNS AND COLLOCATIONS
▸ **in** the script / text / manuscript / line / lyrics / score / screenplay / libretto
▸ the **original** / **full** script / text / manuscript / score
▸ a **film** script / score / screenplay
▸ to **write** a script / the text / a manuscript / the line / the lyrics / the score / a screenplay / a libretto
▸ to **read** the script / text / manuscript / line / lyrics / score / screenplay
▸ the script / text / lyrics / screenplay is / are **based on** sth

script /skrɪp/ [C] the written form of a film, play, broadcast or speech: *That line isn't in the original script.*
▸ **script** verb [T, often passive]: *The series was scripted to appeal to an international audience.*

text [C] the exact written form of a speech, a play or an article: *The newspaper had printed the full text of the president's speech.* ◇ *Can you act out this scene without referring to the text?* See also **text → BOOK, text → LITERATURE**

manuscript /ˈmænjuskrɪpt/ [C] the original copy of a book, a play, an article or a piece of music before it is printed: *I read her plays **in manuscript**.* ◇ *an unpublished manuscript*

line [C] the words spoken by an actor in a play or film: *a line from the film 'Casablanca'* ◇ *to study/learn your lines*

lyrics /ˈlɪrɪks/ [C, pl.] the words of a song: *music and lyrics by Rodgers and Hart*

score [C] the written or printed form of a piece of music showing what each instrument is to play or what each voice is to sing: *an orchestral score*
▸ **score** *verb* [T, usually passive]: *The piece is scored for violin, viola and cello.*

screenplay /ˈskriːnpleɪ/ [C] the words that are written for a film, together with instructions for how it is to be acted and filmed: *She won an Oscar for the movie's screenplay.*

libretto /lɪˈbretəʊ; *AmE* -toʊ/ (pl. **librettos** or **libretti**) [C] (*music*) the words that are sung or spoken in an opera or musical (= a play or film in which the story is told using songs): *The collection contains hundreds of Italian opera librettos.*

scruffy *adj.*

scruffy · messy · dishevelled · unkempt · tangled · tousled · matted · straggly
These words all describe sb/sth's appearance when it is untidy.

PATTERNS AND COLLOCATIONS
▸ a scruffy / a messy / a dishevelled / an unkempt **appearance**
▸ a scruffy / a dishevelled / an unkempt **man / woman / child**
▸ messy / dishevelled / unkempt / tangled / tousled / matted / straggly **hair**
▸ unkempt / tangled / straggly **trees / bushes / hedges, etc.**
▸ slightly scruffy / messy / unkempt

scruffy (*especially BrE, rather informal, disapproving*) (of a person, their clothes or general appearance) untidy: *He looked a bit scruffy.* ◇ *She was wearing her scruffy old jeans.* **OPP smart → ELEGANT**

messy (*AmE, disapproving*) (of sb's hair, clothes or general appearance) untidy: *Her long black hair was messy and dirty.*

dishevelled (*BrE*) (*AmE* usually **disheveled**) (*literary, disapproving*) (of a person, their hair or general appearance) untidy: *She returned at 1 a.m. in a dishevelled state.*

NOTE SCRUFFY, MESSY OR DISHEVELLED? Scruffy is much more frequent in British English than American English. **Messy**, meaning 'untidy', is only used to describe sb's appearance in American English; in British English it can only describe a place. You can talk about *a scruffy/ dishevelled man/woman/child*, but *a messy man/woman/child* is sb who makes a mess, NOT sb who looks untidy. A **scruffy** person, or sb with a **messy** appearance, is untidy because they have not taken care of their appearance. A **dishevelled** person has become untidy as a result of sth, for example being out in wind and rain. **Scruffy** clothes are old and often dirty or with holes, etc.; **messy** clothes are untidy (in American English) or dirty (in British English). See also **messy → DIRTY, messy → UNTIDY**

unkempt (*formal, disapproving*) (especially of sb's hair or general appearance) untidy because it is not well cared for: *He had greasy, unkempt hair.* ◇ *Behind the house was a wild and unkempt garden.*

tangled twisted together in an untidy way or with knots in: *They had to fight their way through the tangled undergrowth.* ◇ *Her hair was a tangled mass of damp curls.* ◇ *Three people were cut from the tangled wreckage of the*

train. ❶ **Tangled** can describe quite a lot of different things. Typical collocates include *hair, curls, mass, mess* and words for plants such as *trees, creepers* and *undergrowth.*

tousled /ˈtaʊzld/ (*written, often approving*) (of sb's hair) untidy, especially in an attractive way: *She was an adorable child, with a tousled mass of dark curls.*

matted (of hair or fur) stuck together in a thick mass, especially after getting wet or dirty: *The dog's coat easily becomes matted.* ◇ *The back of her head was **matted with** blood.*

straggly (*disapproving*) (of hair or plants) growing or hanging in separate long thin bits that need cutting, in a way that is not tidy or attractive: *She was a thin woman with straggly grey hair.* ◇ *Cut the hedge regularly to prevent it becoming straggly.*

sea *noun*

sea · ocean · waters
These are all words for the salt water that covers the earth's surface.

PATTERNS AND COLLOCATIONS
▸ by / on / across / beneath / under the sea / ocean
▸ in the sea / the ocean / … waters
▸ to **cross / sail** the sea / ocean

sea [U, C] (*often* **the sea**) the mass of salt water that covers most of the earth's surface and surrounds its continents and islands; a large area of this salt water: *The waste is dumped in the sea.* ◇ *The goods were sent **by sea**.* ◇ *Her husband was in the navy and spent a lot of time away **at sea**.* ◇ *She stood on the cliff, **looking out to sea**.* ◇ *I asked for a room with a sea view.* ◇ (*BrE*) *They live in a cottage by the sea.* ◇ *the North Sea* ❶ **Seas** [pl.] may also be used in a literary context: *the cold seas of the Antarctic* ◇ *They sailed the **seven seas** in search of adventure.* **OPP land → FLOOR 1**, See also **sea → WAVE 1**

ocean [C] (*often* **the ocean**) the mass of salt water that covers most of the earth's surface and surrounds its continents and islands; one of the five large areas that this is divided into: *Ocean levels are rising.* ◇ (*AmE*) *The plane hit the ocean several miles offshore.* ◇ (*AmE*) *Our beach house is just a few miles from the ocean.* ◇ *the Antarctic/Arctic/Atlantic/Indian/Pacific Ocean*

NOTE SEA OR OCEAN? In British English the usual word for the mass of salt water that covers most of the earth's surface is the **sea**. In American English the usual word is **ocean**: (*BrE*) *a cottage by the sea* ◇ (*AmE*) *a house on the ocean.* It is also common to say *a week at the seaside* in British English or *a week at the beach* in American English. When talking about one of the five large areas that this is divided into, **ocean** is used (or **Ocean**, when it is part of a name): *the Pacific Ocean.* When talking about a particular area in an ocean or between areas of land, **sea** is used (or **Sea**, when it is part of a name): *the Mediterranean Sea.* See also the entry for **COAST**

waters [pl.] an area of sea or ocean that belongs to a particular country: *British/international waters* ◇ *The treaty prohibited the use of the country's navy outside its own **territorial waters**.*

search *noun*

search · pursuit · quest · hunt · look
These are all words for an act of looking for or trying to find sb/sth.

PATTERNS AND COLLOCATIONS
▸ a search / quest / hunt / look **for** sb / sth
▸ **in** search / pursuit / quest **of** sth
▸ the search / hunt **is on** (for sb / sth)
▸ a / an / the **successful / relentless / endless** search / pursuit / quest
▸ a **major / massive / nationwide / police** search / hunt

▶ to **begin** / **launch** / **help in** a search / quest / hunt
▶ to **abandon** / **be involved in** the search / quest / hunt
▶ to **be engaged in** the search / pursuit / quest
▶ to **mount** / **lead** / **join (in)** / **call off** a search / hunt

search [C] an act of trying to find sb/sth, especially by looking carefully for them/it: *After a long search for the murder weapon, the police found a knife.* ◇ *Detectives carried out a thorough search of the building.* ◇ *She went into the kitchen in search of* (= looking for) *a drink.* See also **search** → LOOK *verb* 1

pursuit /pəˈsjuːt; *AmE* pərˈsuːt/ [U] (*written*) the act of trying to find or achieve sth, especially a goal, an achievement or a quality such as happiness: *She travelled the world in pursuit of her dreams.* ◇ *The purpose of the award is to encourage the pursuit of excellence.* See also **pursue** → SEEK

quest [C] (*written*) the pursuit of sth, especially over a long period of time, and especially sth that is valuable for spiritual reasons or reasons of honour, not for material gain: *The team will continue its quest for Olympic gold this afternoon.* ◇ *This is an important stage in their quest for the truth.* ◇ *The initiative aims to foster the province's quest to reinforce its distinct cultural identity.*

NOTE PURSUIT OR QUEST? In some cases you can use either word: *He set off in pursuit/quest of adventure.* However, **pursuit** is the word used when sb is trying to achieve a particular goal or objective, especially when this is connected with making money or personal fulfilment: *the pursuit of wealth/profit/self-interest/a career/love/happiness.* A **quest** is usually more spiritual, often for some universal quality that can never be completely grasped: *to be on an endless/a spiritual quest* ◇ *the quest for truth/knowledge/perfection.* Note that **pursuit** is uncountable and you talk about *the pursuit of sth*; **quest** is countable and you talk about *a quest for sth.* Both words can be used in the pattern *in pursuit/quest of sth.*

hunt [C, usually sing.] (*rather informal, especially journalism*) an act of looking for sb/sth that is difficult to find: *The hunt is on for a suitable candidate.* ◇ *Police forces in five counties are now involved in the murder hunt.* See also **hunt** → LOOK *verb* 2

look [C, usually sing.] (*rather informal*) an act of trying to find sb/sth: *I had a look for websites on Egyptian music.* ◇ *We've had a good look around downstairs, but can't find your keys.* See also **look** → LOOK *verb* 2

secret *adj.*

1 secret information/a secret passage
2 a secret drinker/your secret fears

---

1 secret · private · confidential · personal · undisclosed · intimate · classified
These words all describe information which is not known about by other people or not meant to be known about.

PATTERNS AND COLLOCATIONS
▶ secret / private / confidential / personal / undisclosed / classified **information**
▶ secret / private / confidential / personal / classified **documents**
▶ a secret / confidential / personal **file**
▶ a private / confidential / personal **letter**
▶ secret / confidential / classified **material**
▶ (a) secret / private **talks** / **meeting**
▶ a secret / an undisclosed **location**
▶ sb's private / personal **life**
▶ to **remain** secret / private / confidential / undisclosed / classified
▶ to **keep sth** secret / private / confidential
▶ **highly** secret / confidential / personal / classified
▶ **entirely** secret / private / confidential

secret known about by only a few people; kept hidden from others: *The ceasefire was agreed following secret talks between the two leaders.* ◇ *There's a secret passage leading to the beach.* ◇ *He tried to keep it secret from his family.* ◇

This information has been classified **top secret** (= completely secret, especially from other governments).
OPP open → OPEN

▶ **secrecy** /ˈsiːkrəsi/ *noun* [U]: *the need for absolute secrecy in this matter* ◇ *Everyone involved was* **sworn to secrecy**.
▶ **secret** *noun* [C]: *Can you* **keep a secret**? ◇ *trade/official/State secrets*
▶ **secretly** *adv.*: *The police had secretly recorded the conversations.*

private intended for or involving a particular person or group of people, not for people in general; that you do not want other people to know about; not connected with your work or official position: *You shouldn't listen in on other people's private conversations.* ◇ *They were sharing a private joke.* ◇ *She was scared of revealing her private thoughts and feelings.* ◇ *The media are obsessed with the star's private life.* **OPP** public → FAMOUS. See also **privacy** → PRIVACY
▶ **privately** *adv.*: *Can we speak privately?*

confidential /ˌkɒnfɪˈdenʃl; *AmE* ˌkɑːn-/ meant to be kept secret and not told or shared with other people: *Your medical records are* **strictly confidential** (= completely secret). ◇ *The envelope says it is private and confidential.*
▶ **confidentiality** /ˌkɒnfɪˌdenʃiˈæləti; *AmE* ˌkɑːn-/ *noun* [U]: *They signed a confidentiality agreement.*
▶ **confidentially** *adv.*: *She told me confidentially that she is going to retire early.*

personal not connected with your work or official position: *The letter was marked 'Personal'.* ◇ *I'd like to talk to you about a personal matter.* ◇ *I try not to let work interfere with my personal life.* ◇ *She's a personal friend of mine* (= not just sb I know because of my job).

NOTE PRIVATE OR PERSONAL? You can usually use either word to describe sth that is not connected with your work or official position: *your private/personal life* ◇ *a private/personal matter* ◇ *a letter marked 'Private/Personal'* but: *a private friend of mine.* It is more usual to talk about the *private lives* of famous or important people, but use either word to talk about yourself or ordinary people.

undisclosed /ˌʌndɪsˈkləʊzd; *AmE* -ˈkloʊzd/ [usually before noun] (*rather formal*) not made known or told to anyone: *The painting was sold for an undisclosed sum to a private collector.* ◇ *Several inmates were moved to an undisclosed location in the south.* See also **disclose** → REVEAL

intimate /ˈɪntɪmət/ private and personal, often in a sexual way: *The article revealed intimate details about his private life.* ◇ *the most intimate parts of her body*

classified /ˈklæsɪfaɪd/ [usually before noun] (*rather formal*) (of information) officially secret and available only to particular people: *The magazine printed a controversial article based on classified material.* ◇ *We are not in a position to divulge that information: it is classified.* **OPP** **unclassified** ❶ Unclassified information is not secret and is available to everyone.

2 secret · covert · undercover · clandestine · underground
These words all describe actions or behaviour which other people do not know about.

PATTERNS AND COLLOCATIONS
▶ secret / covert / undercover / clandestine / underground **activity**
▶ a secret / a covert / an undercover / a clandestine **operation**
▶ a secret / an undercover / a clandestine / an underground **organization**
▶ a clandestine / an underground **movement**
▶ a secret / clandestine **meeting** / **relationsip** / **affair**
▶ a secret / an undercover **agent**
▶ covert / undercover **surveillance**

secret [only before noun] used to talk about actions, behaviour and feelings that you do not tell other people about and do not want them to know: *He's a secret drinker.* ◇ *I didn't know you were a secret football fan.* ◇ *She could not tell him her secret hopes and fears.*
▶ **secret** *noun* [C]: *He made no secret of his ambition* (= he didn't try to hide it).
▶ **secretly** *adv.*: *She was secretly pleased to see him.*

covert /ˈkʌvət; ˈkəʊvɜːt; *AmE* ˈkoʊvɜːrt/ [usually before noun] (*formal*) (of actions or behaviour) secret or hidden, making it difficult to notice: *There were widespread allegations of the use of covert surveillance.* ◇ *He stole a covert glance at her across the table.* **OPP** overt → OPEN
▶ **covertly** *adv.*: *He watched her covertly in the mirror.*

undercover /ˌʌndəˈkʌvə(r); *AmE* -dərˈk-/ [usually before noun] working or done secretly in order to find out information, especially for the police or a government: *Police made twelve arrests yesterday following a three-week undercover operation.*
▶ **undercover** *adv.*: *The illegal payments were discovered by a journalist working undercover.*

clandestine /klænˈdestɪn; ˈklændəstaɪn/ [usually before noun] (*formal, usually disapproving*) (of actions, behaviour or a relationship) secret, especially because you would be ashamed if people knew: *A clandestine meeting was held between leaders of the two parties.* ◇ *She could see no future in her clandestine relationship.*

underground /ˈʌndəgraʊnd; *AmE* -dərg-/ [usually before noun] (especially of an organization) operating secretly and often illegally, especially against a government: *Slowly, an underground resistance movement grew.*
▶ **underground** /ˌʌndəˈgraʊnd; *AmE* -dərˈg-/ *adv.*: *If the group is outlawed they will go underground.*

secretive *adj.*

secretive · secret · furtive · surreptitious · conspiratorial · stealthy
These all describe sb or the actions or behaviour of sb who does not want to attract attention.

PATTERNS AND COLLOCATIONS
▶ to be secretive / secret **about** sth
▶ a secret / conspiratorial **smile**
▶ a furtive / surreptitious **glance**
▶ a surreptitious / conspiratorial **manner**

secretive /ˈsiːkrətɪv/ (*often disapproving*) (of a person) tending or liking to hide your thoughts, feelings and ideas from other people: *He's very secretive about his work.* ◇ *The child became secretive and withdrawn.*
▶ **secretively** *adv.*: *They acted so secretively about the whole thing.*

secret [not usually before noun] (*sometimes disapproving*) (of a person or their behaviour) liking to have secrets that other people do not know about; showing this: *They were so secret about everything.* ◇ *Jessica caught a secret smile flitting between the two of them.*

furtive /ˈfɜːtɪv; *AmE* ˈfɜːrtɪv/ (*especially written, disapproving*) (of a person or their behaviour) showing that you want to keep sth secret and do not want to be noticed: *She cast a furtive glance over her shoulder.*
▶ **furtively** *adv.*: *He peered furtively around the corner.*

surreptitious /ˌsʌrəpˈtɪʃəs; *AmE* ˌsɜːr-/ [only before noun] (*written*) (of sb's behaviour) done secretly or quickly, in the hope that other people will not notice: *She sneaked a surreptitious glance at her watch.*
▶ **surreptitiously** *adv.*: *She crept surreptitiously around the fence.*

conspiratorial /kənˌspɪrəˈtɔːriəl/ (of sb's behaviour) suggesting that a secret is being shared: *'I know you understand,' he said and gave a conspiratorial wink.*

stealthy /ˈstelθi/ (of a person or the way they move) doing things quietly or secretly; quiet or secret: *She was stealthy as a cat in her movements.* ◇ *There was a stealthy movement at the edge of the wood.*
▶ **stealth** *noun* [U]: *Lions rely on stealth when hunting.* ◇

The government was accused of trying to introduce the tax by stealth.
▶ **stealthily** *adv.*: *They moved forward swiftly and stealthily.*

section *noun*

section · paragraph · clause · article
These are all words for a part of a written text.

NOTE Compare the words in this entry with the words in the entry for **scene**. These words generally refer to factual, legal or technical documents. The words in the **scene** entry generally refer to literature, films and music.

PATTERNS AND COLLOCATIONS
▶ in / under (a particular) section / paragraph / clause / article
▶ a **key** section / paragraph / clause / article
▶ to **include** / **add** / **amend** / **contravene** / **be in breach of** a section / a paragraph / a clause / an article
▶ the **terms of** a section / a paragraph / a clause / an article

section [C] a separate part of a book, document or other piece of writing: *These issues will be discussed more fully in the next section.* ◇ *Can you pass me the sports section* (= of a newspaper)? ◇ *Section 3 applies to clauses which restrict liability.*

paragraph /ˈpærəgrɑːf; *AmE* -ɡræf/ [C] a section of a piece of writing, usually consisting of several sentences dealing with a single subject: *The opening paragraph sets the scene very well.* ◇ *Write a paragraph on each of the topics given below.* ◇ *See paragraph 15 of the handbook.*
❶ The first sentence of a paragraph starts on a new line, usually after an indentation (= a space left at the beginning of a line). In official and legal texts, paragraphs are often numbered: *Debt restructuring is permitted by virtue of paragraph 1.4.(iii).*

clause [C] an item in a legal document that says that a particular thing must or must not be done: *There is a clause in the contract forbidding tenants to sublet.* ◇ *Clause 2.7.3 should be studied carefully.*

article [C] (*law*) a separate item in an agreement or contract, especially an important or international one: *The proposal breaches article 10 of the European Convention, which guarantees free speech.*

security *noun*

security · protection · defence · cover
These are all words for a situation where sb/sth is protected by sb/sth.

PATTERNS AND COLLOCATIONS
▶ protection / defence **from** / **of** / **against** sth
▶ **adequate** security / protection / defence
▶ **effective** protection / defence
▶ to **provide** security / protection / defence / cover

security /sɪˈkjʊərəti; *AmE* səˈkjʊr-/ [U] the activities involved in protecting a country, building or person against attack or danger: *The incident has provoked calls to tighten airport security.* ◇ *The government claimed that the organization posed a threat to national security* (= the defence of a country). ◇ *The visit took place amidst tight security* (= the use of many police officers). ◇ *The demonstrations were brutally broken up by the security forces* (= the police, army, etc.). ◇ *Investigations are continuing into a security alert in the city yesterday.* See also **secure** → PROTECT

protection [U] (*rather formal*) the act of protecting sb/sth against injury, damage, attack, danger or being used in the wrong way; the state of being protected in this way: *Remember to bring clothes that provide adequate protection against the wind and rain.* ◇ *He asked to be put under* police **protection**. ◇ *She acknowledged that much work needs to be done to improve data protection laws.* See also **protect** → PROTECT, **protective** → PROTECTIVE

defence (*BrE*) (*AmE* **defense**) [U] the act of protecting sb/sth against attack or criticism: *He paid tribute to all those who had died* **in defence of** *their country.* ◇ *What points can be raised in defence of this argument?* ◇ *When her brother was criticized she* **leapt to his defence.** ◇ *He has shown courage in* **coming to the defence of** *the embattled president.* ❶ **Self-defence** is the act of doing or saying sth to protect yourself when you are being attacked or criticized: *The man later told police that he was acting in self-defence.* See also **defend** → EXPLAIN 2

cover [U] support and protection that is provided when sb is attacking or in danger of being attacked: *The ships needed air cover* (= protection by military planes) *once they reached enemy waters.*

---

see *verb* See also the entries for LOOK 1 and NOTICE

---

see · spot · catch · glimpse · sight
These words all mean to become aware of sb/sth by using your eyes, especially suddenly or when they are not easy to see.

PATTERNS AND COLLOCATIONS
▸ to see / spot **that / how / what / where / who...**
▸ to **just** see / spot / catch / glimpse sb / sth
▸ to **suddenly** see / spot / catch / glimpse sb / sth

see [T] (not used in the progressive tenses) to become aware of sb/sth by using your eyes: *She looked for him but couldn't see him in the crowd.* ◇ *He could see (that) she had been crying.* ◇ *Did you see what happened?* ◇ *I hate to see you unhappy.* ◇ *She was seen running away from the scene of the crime.* ◇ *I saw you put the key in your pocket.*

spot (-tt-) [T] (not used in the progressive tenses) to see or notice sb/sth, especially suddenly or when they are not easy to see or notice: *I've just spotted a mistake on the front cover.* ◇ *Can you spot the difference between these two pictures?* ◇ *Her modelling career began when she was spotted by an agent at the age of 14.*

catch [T] to see or notice sth for a moment, but not clearly or completely: *She* **caught sight** *of a car in the distance.* ◇ *He caught a glimpse of himself in the mirror.* ◇ *I caught a look of surprise on her face.*

glimpse [T] (*written*) to see sb/sth for a moment, but not clearly or completely: *He'd glimpsed her through the window as he passed.* See also **glimpse** → LOOK *noun*

sight [T] (*written*) to suddenly see sth, especially sth that you have been looking for: *After twelve days at sea, they sighted land.* See also **sight** → LOOK *noun*

---

seek *verb*

---

seek · pursue · go after sth
These words all mean to try to achieve sth.

PATTERNS AND COLLOCATIONS
▸ to seek / go after a **job**
▸ to **actively / successfully** seek / pursue sth
▸ to be **currently** seeking / pursuing sth

seek [T, I] (*formal*) to try to obtain or achieve sth: *We are currently seeking new ways of expanding our membership.* ◇ *She fled the country and is now* **seeking asylum** *in Sweden.* ◇ (*especially BrE*) *To receive the benefit, you have to be actively* **seeking work.**

pursue /pəˈsjuː; *AmE* pərˈsuː/ [T] (*formal*) to do sth or try to achieve sth over a period of time: *She wishes to pursue a medical career.* ◇ *I decided the matter was not worth pursuing.* ◇ *How can we most effectively pursue these aims?* See also **pursuit** → SEARCH

ˌgo ˈafter sth *phrasal verb* (*rather informal*) to try to get sth: *We're both going after the same job.* ◇ *These days I only go after a story I think is really worthwhile.*

---

seem *linking verb*

---

seem · look · appear · sound · feel · come across · strike · come over
These words all mean to give the impression of being or doing sth.

PATTERNS AND COLLOCATIONS
▸ to seem / look / appear / sound / feel **odd / OK / nice, etc.**
▸ to come across / strike sb / come over **as** (being) odd, etc.
▸ to seem / look / appear **to be** sth
▸ to seem / look / sound / feel **like** sth
▸ to seem / look / sound / feel **as if / as though...**
▸ It seems / appears / strikes sb **that...**
▸ It would seem / appear **that...**

seem *linking verb* (not used in the progressive tenses) to give the impression of being or doing sth: *Do whatever seems best to you.* ◇ *He seems a nice man.* ◇ *It seemed like a good idea at the time.* ◇ *It always seemed as though they would get married.* ◇ *They seem to know what they're doing.* ◇ *'He'll be there, then?' 'So it seems* (= people say so).*' ❶ **Seem** is often used to make what you say about your thoughts, feelings or actions less forceful or to suggest that sth is true when you are not certain or when you want to be polite: *I seem to have left my book at home.* ◇ *I can't seem to* (= I've tried, but I can't) *get started today.* ◇ *It seems only reasonable to ask students to buy a dictionary.* ◇ (*rather formal*) *It would seem that we all agree.* See also **seeming** → APPARENT

look *linking verb* (not usually used in the progressive tenses) to seem, especially from what people can see; to have a similar appearance to sb/sth; to have an appearance that suggests that sth is true or will happen; to seem likely: *You look tired.* ◇ *That photograph doesn't look like her at all.* ◇ *It looks like rain* (= it looks as if it's going to rain). ◇ (*especially BrE*) *That looks an interesting book.* ❶ In American English it is more usual to use **look** like with a noun phrase: (*AmE, BrE*) *That looks like an interesting book.* ❶ In spoken English people often use **like** instead of *as if* or *as though*, especially in American English: *You look as though you slept badly.* ◇ *It doesn't look as if we'll be moving after all.* ◇ (*spoken, especially AmE*) *You look like you slept badly.* ◇ *It doesn't look like we'll be moving after all.* This is considered incorrect in written British English. ❶ Unlike **seem**, **look** can sometimes be used in the progressive tenses, if you are talking about how sb/sth looked at a particular time, especially if this is different from how they usually look: *I thought she was looking rather tired last night.* See also **look** → APPEARANCE

appear *linking verb* (not used in the progressive tenses) (*rather formal*) to seem, especially from what people can see: *She didn't appear at all surprised at the news.* ◇ *They appeared not to know what was happening.* ❶ **Appear** is more formal than **look**; it can also suggest that you, or the person you are speaking to, does not quite believe that sb/sth really is as they seem: *He appears to be a perfectly normal person* (= but there is still some reason to suppose that he might not be). ◇ *It would appear that this was a major problem* (= although I don't really understand why it should be). It can also be used, like **seem**, when you are not certain about sth or don't want to accuse sb too directly of doing sth wrong: *There appears to have been a mistake.* In British English you can use *appear* + noun phrase; in American English you need to use *appear to be* + noun phrase (which is also acceptable in British English): (*BrE*) *He appears a perfectly normal person.* See also **apparent** → APPARENT, **appearance** → APPEARANCE

sound *linking verb* (not used in the progressive tenses) to give a particular impression when heard or read about: *His voice sounded strange on the phone.* ◇ *Her explanation sounds reasonable to me.* ◇ *Leo* **made it sound** *so easy. But it wasn't.* ◇ *She sounds like just the person we need for the job.* ◇ *You sounded just like your father when you said that.* ◇ *I hope I don't sound as if I'm criticizing you.*

feel *linking verb* (not used in the progressive tenses) to give you a particular feeling or impression; to have a particular physical quality which you become aware of by touching: *It felt strange to be back in my old school.* ◇ *The interview only took ten minutes, but it felt like hours.* ◇ *It feels like rain* (= seems likely to rain). ◇ *Her head felt as if it would burst.* ◇ *It felt as though he had run a marathon.* ◇ *How does it feel to be alone all day?* ◇ *The water feels warm.* ◇ *This wallet feels like leather.* See also **feeling, feel** → ATMOSPHERE, **feeling** → SENSE, **the feel** → TEXTURE

> **NOTE SOUND OR FEEL?** Use **sound** to talk about an impression you get from hearing sb/sth, and **feel** to talk about your own or another people's real feelings: *He sounded happy, but I don't think he felt it.* With both these verbs, in spoken English people often use *like* instead of *as if* or *as though*, especially in American English, but this is not considered correct in written British English: *You sound like you're ready to give up.* ◇ *He felt like he'd run a marathon.*

,come a'cross *phrasal verb* to make a particular impression: *She comes across well in interviews.*

strike [T] to give sb a particular impression: *His reaction struck me as odd.* ◇ *She strikes me as a very efficient person.* ◇ *How does the idea strike you?*

,come 'over *phrasal verb* to make a particular impression: *He came over as a sympathetic person.*

> **NOTE COME ACROSS OR COME OVER Come across** is more usually followed by an adverb; **come over** is more usually followed by *as a/an....*

seize *verb*

seize · confiscate · commandeer · appropriate · requisition · impound
These words all mean to officially take sth away from sb, especially as a punishment.

PATTERNS AND COLLOCATIONS
▸ to seize / confiscate / appropriate / requisition **land**
▸ to seize / confiscate / appropriate **assets / funds / property**
▸ to seize / commandeer / requisition a **building**
▸ to seize / confiscate / commandeer / impound a **vehicle / car**
▸ the **government** seizes / confiscates / commandeers / requisitions sth
▸ the **authorities** seize / commandeer / requisition / impound sth
▸ the **police** seize / confiscate / impound sth
▸ the **army** seizes / commandeers / requisitions sth

seize /siːz/ [T, often passive] (*especially journalism*) to use legal authority to take sth away from sb, especially illegal or stolen goods: *A large quantity of drugs was seized during the raid.*
▸ **seizure** /'siːʒə(r)/ *noun* [U, C]: *The court ordered the seizure of his assets.*
confiscate /'kɒnfɪskeɪt; *AmE* 'kɑːn-/ [T] (*rather formal*) to officially take sth away from sb, especially as a punishment: *Their land was confiscated after the war.* ◇ *The teacher threatened to confiscate their yo-yos if they kept playing in class.*
▸ **confiscation** /,kɒnfɪ'skeɪʃn; *AmE* ,kɑːn-/ *noun* [U, C]: *If found guilty of this crime they face heavy fines, confiscation of goods and even imprisonment.*
commandeer /,kɒmən'dɪə(r); *AmE* ,kɑːmən'dɪr/ [T] (*rather formal*) to take control of a building, vehicle or other equipment for military purposes during a war, or by force for your own use: *The soldiers had commandeered the farm and the villa five months ago.* ◇ *A group of young men had commandeered a truck, and were driving around the town in it.*
appropriate /ə'prəʊprieɪt; *AmE* ə'proʊ-/ [T] (*formal*) to take or give sth, especially money for a particular purpose: *Five million dollars has been appropriated for research into the disease.*

requisition /,rekwɪ'zɪʃn/ [T] (*formal*) to officially demand the use of a building, vehicle or other equipment or supplies, especially for military purposes during a war or in an emergency: *The school was requisitioned as a military hospital.*
▸ **requisition** *noun* [U, C]: *the requisition of ships by the government*

> **NOTE COMMANDEER OR REQUISITION?** A group of soldiers might **commandeer** a building or vehicle by quickly taking control of it and using it. The military or national authorities might **requisition** sth by ordering that it be used for the purpose of war.

impound /ɪm'paʊnd/ [T] (*rather formal*) (of the police or a court) to take sth away from sb, so that they cannot use it: *The car was impounded by the police after the accident.* **❶ Impound** is usually used to talk about a vehicle, or the goods that a ship or lorry is carrying.

selfish *adj.*

selfish · self-centred · self-serving · egotistical · egocentric
These words all describe sb who thinks only about themselves.

PATTERNS AND COLLOCATIONS
▸ a selfish / a self-centred / an egotistical **person**
▸ a selfish / a self-centred / an egotistical / an egocentric **man**
▸ a selfish / a self-centred / egocentric **nature**
▸ a selfish / a self-serving / an egotistical **way**

selfish (*disapproving*) caring only about yourself rather than about other people: *It was selfish of him to leave all the work to you.* ◇ *Do you think I'm being selfish by not letting her go?* ◇ *What a selfish thing to do!* ◇ *He did it for purely selfish reasons.* **OPP unselfish, selfless ❶** An **unselfish** or **selfless** person thinks more about the needs and happiness of other people than about their own needs, etc. **Selfless** is a more literary word than **unselfish**: *His motives were completely unselfish.* ◇ *a life of selfless service to the community*
▸ **selfishly** *adv.*: *She looked forward, a little selfishly, to a weekend away from her family.*
▸ **selfishness** *noun* [U]: *He was the victim of his own greed and selfishness.*
,self-'centred (*BrE*) (*AmE* ,self-'centered) (*disapproving*) tending to think only about yourself and not thinking about the needs or feelings of other people: *Your father's too self-centred to care what you do.*
,self-'serving (*disapproving*) interested only in gaining an advantage for yourself: *He was portrayed as a self-serving careerist.*
egotistical /,egə'tɪstɪkl; ,iːgə-/ (*especially written, disapproving*) thinking that you are better or more important than anyone else: *For all his charm, he was arrogant and egotistical.*
egocentric /,egəʊ'sentrɪk; ,iːg-; *AmE* ,iːgoʊ-/ (*especially written, disapproving*) thinking only about yourself and not thinking about the needs or feelings of other people: *In the film he appears egocentric and opinionated.*

sell *verb*

1 sell your car/house
2 sell a range of products

1 sell · sell sth off · auction · sell up · liquidate · auction sth off
These words all mean to give sth to sb in exchange for money.

PATTERNS AND COLLOCATIONS
▸ to sell sth / sell sth off / auction sth / auction sth off **to** sb/a place
▸ to sell sth / sell sth off / auction sth off **for** £100, $47 000, etc.
▸ to sell / sell off / auction / liquidate **property / assets**
▸ to sell / sell off / liquidate **shares / a company**
▸ to sell / sell off / auction / auction off a **collection**

▸ to sell / sell off / auction **land**
▸ to sell / auction a **house**

sell [T, I] to give sth to sb in exchange for money: *I sold my car to James for £800.* ◇ *I sold James my car for £800.* ◇ *They sold the business at a profit/loss* (= they gained/lost money when they sold it). ◇ *We offered them a good price but they wouldn't sell.*

,sell sth 'off *phrasal verb* to sell things cheaply because you want to get rid of them or because you need the money; to sell all or part of an industry, a company or land: *The Church sold off the land for housing.* ◇ *In the nineties most state-owned industries were sold off.*

auction /'ɔ:kʃn; 'ɒk-; *AmE* 'ɔ:k-/ [T, usually passive] (*especially BrE*) to sell sth at an auction (= a public event at which things are sold to the person who offers the most money for them): *The costumes from the movie are to be auctioned for charity.* ❶ In American English it is more usual to say **auction sth off**.

,sell 'up *phrasal verb* to sell your home, possessions, business, etc., usually because you are leaving the country or retiring (= giving up work because you have reached a particular age): *They sold up and moved to France.*

liquidate /'lɪkwɪdeɪt/ [T] (*finance*) to sell sth in order to get money: *The shares are easy to sell, should you wish to liquidate your assets.* ❶ Typical collocates of **liquidate** are *assets, endowment, share portfolio, company, firm* and *debts*.

,auction sth 'off *phrasal verb* to sell sth at an auction, especially sth that is no longer needed or wanted: *The Army is auctioning off a lot of surplus equipment.*

2 sell · trade · export · import · do business · deal in sth · stock · carry · handle · deal · retail
These words all mean to offer sth for people to buy.

PATTERNS AND COLLOCATIONS
▸ to trade / do business **with** sb
▸ to sell / trade / export / import / deal in / stock / handle / retail **goods**
▸ to sell / trade / deal in **shares/futures/stocks/bonds/securities**
▸ to sell / deal in **furniture / antiques / property**
▸ to sell / import / deal in / deal **drugs**
▸ to sell / stock / carry / retail a **range / line** of goods

sell [T] to offer sth for people to buy: *Most grocery stores sell a range of organic products.* ◇ *Do you sell stamps?* ◇ *He works for a company that sells insurance.*

trade [I, T] to buy and sell things; to exist and operate as a business or company: *After settling in Madeira they began trading in flour, sugar and leather.* ◇ *Early explorers traded directly with the Indians.* ◇ *Our products are now traded worldwide.* ◇ *The firm has now ceased trading.* See also **trade, trading** → TRADE *noun*

export [T] to sell and send goods to another country: *The islands export sugar and fruit.* ◇ *90% of the engines are exported to Europe.* **OPP** **import**
▸ **export** *noun* [U, C, usually pl.]: *Then the fruit is packaged for export.* ◇ *the country's major exports* **OPP** **import**

import [T] to bring a product, service or idea into one country from another: *The country has to import most of its raw materials.* ◇ *goods imported from Japan into the US* ◇ *customs imported from the West* **OPP** **export**
▸ **import** *noun* [U, C, usually pl.]: *The report calls for a ban on the import of hazardous waste.* ◇ *food imports from abroad* **OPP** **export**

,do 'business *phrase* to take part in the activity of buying or selling goods or services: *It's been a pleasure to do business with you.* ◇ *I don't like his way of doing business.* See also **business** → TRADE *noun*, See also the entry for BUSINESS 2

'deal in sth *phrasal verb* to buy and sell a particular product: *The company deals in computer software.* See also **dealing** → TRADE

NOTE TRADE IN STH OR **DEAL IN STH?** **Trade in sth** is most often used to talk about buying and selling raw materials such as *animals, coal, sugar, leather, fur* and

ivory, as well as textiles such as *cloth* and *silk*. **Deal in sth** is used more to talk about manufactured products such as *cars, antiques, furniture* and *electronics*. **Deal in sth** is also frequently used to talk about criminal buying and selling; typical collocates are *drugs, guns* and *stolen goods*. Both **trade in sth** and **deal in sth** are used to talk about buying and selling items in financial markets, for example *shares, futures, stocks, bonds* and *securities*.

stock [T] (*rather formal, especially business*) (of a shop) to keep a supply of a particular type of goods to sell: *We stock a wide range of camping equipment.* See also **stock** → SUPPLY *noun*

carry [T] (*AmE or formal*) (of a shop) to stock sth: *We carry a range of educational software.*

NOTE STOCK OR **CARRY?** These words vary in register in British and American English. In British English they are both used especially by people who work in shops and in advertisements for shops. **Carry** is more formal than **stock**. In everyday spoken British English most people would say **sell**: *Do you sell green tea?* (*BrE*): *Do you stock/carry green tea?* However, in American English, **carry** is less formal than **stock** and might be used in everyday speech: (*AmE*) *We do carry green tea, but we don't have any (in stock) right now.*

handle [T] to buy and sell sth, especially illegally: *They were arrested for handling stolen goods.* ❶ In this meaning **handle** is usually used with *stolen goods*.

deal [I, T] to buy and sell illegal drugs: *You can often see people dealing openly on the streets.* ◇ *He was sent to jail for dealing drugs to his friends.* ❶ In British English you can talk about sb who *deals drugs* or *deals in drugs*; in American English, it is more usual to say **deal** (without *in*). With the more informal **dope** and with the names of drugs such as *cocaine* or *heroin*, it is also more usual to say **deal** (without *in*), in both British and American English.

retail /'ri:teɪl/ [T] (*business*) to sell goods to the public, usually through shops: *The firm manufactures and retails its own range of sportswear.*

send *verb*
1 send a letter
2 send sb to bed

1 send · mail · post · address · forward · dispatch · send sth on
These words all mean to make sth go or be taken to a place, especially by mail.

PATTERNS AND COLLOCATIONS
▸ to send / mail / post / address / forward / dispatch / send on sth **to** sb
▸ to send / mail / post / address / forward / dispatch / send on a **letter**
▸ to send / mail / post / address / forward a **message**
▸ to send / mail / post / forward / dispatch a **document**
▸ to send / mail / post / address a/an **invitation / package / parcel / postcard / reply**
▸ to send / post / address / forward **mail**
▸ to send / address / forward **correspondence**
▸ to send / forward an **email**
▸ to send / dispatch **goods**

send [T] to make sth go or be taken to a place, especially by mail, email, fax or radio: *Have you sent a postcard to your mother yet?* ◇ *Have you sent your mother a postcard yet?* ◇ *A radio signal was sent to the spacecraft.* ◇ *The CD player was faulty so we sent it back to the manufacturers.*

mail [T] (*especially AmE*) to send sth to sb using the postal system; to put a letter, etc. into a mailbox: *The company intends to mail 50 000 households in the area.* ◇ *Don't forget to mail that letter.* See also **mail** → LETTER *noun*

post [T] (*BrE*) to mail sth: *Is it OK if I post you the cheque next week?* ◇ *Could you post this letter for me?* See also **post** → LETTER *noun*

address [T, usually passive] to write on an envelope or package the name and address of the person or company that you are sending it to by mail: *The letter was correctly addressed, but delivered to the wrong house.* ◇ *Address your application to the Personnel Manager.* See also **address** → HOME 1

forward [T] to send a letter that has been sent to sb's old address to their new address; to send an email that you have received to sb else: *Could you forward any mail to us in New York?* ◇ *I'm forwarding you this email that I had from Jeff.* ❶ In formal language **forward** can just mean to send or pass goods or information to sb: *We will be forwarding our new catalogue to you next week.*

dispatch (*BrE* also **despatch**) /dɪˈspætʃ/ [T] (*formal, especially business*) to send a letter, message, goods or information to sb: *Goods are dispatched within 24 hours of your order reaching us.*

,send sth ˈon *phrasal verb* to send sth to a place so that it arrives before you get there; to send a letter that has been sent to sb's old address to their new address; to send sth from one place or person to another: *We sent our furniture on by ship.* ◇ *They promised to send on our mail when we moved.* ◇ *They arranged for the information to be sent on to us.*

---

2 send · put · place · station · assign · dispatch · post
These words all mean to arrange for, or tell sb, to go somewhere, especially for a special purpose.

PATTERNS AND COLLOCATIONS
▸ to send / assign / dispatch / post sb **to** a place
▸ to send / assign / dispatch sb **to do** sth
▸ to send / assign / dispatch / station a **force**
▸ to send / station / dispatch **troops**
▸ to send / dispatch **reinforcements**
▸ to station / post a **guard**
▸ to send / dispatch a / an **delegation / envoy**
▸ to send / station / post sb **abroad / overseas**

send [T] to tell sb to go somewhere or do sth; to arrange for sb to go somewhere: *Ed couldn't make it so they sent me instead.* ◇ *She sent the kids to bed early.* ◇ *The judge sent her to prison for two years.* ◇ *We are being **sent on** a training course next month.* ◇ *I've sent Tom to buy some milk.*

put [T] (always used with an adverb or preposition) to cause sb to go or be taken to a particular place: *He put Ray on guard with a gun.* ◇ *Her family put her into a nursing home.*

place [T] to find a suitable home, job, etc. for sb: *The children were placed with foster parents.* ◇ *The agency placed about 2 000 secretaries last year.*

station [T, often passive] (always used with an adverb or preposition) to send sb, especially from one of the armed forces, to work in a place for a period of time: *The country has over 5 000 troops currently stationed abroad.*

assign /əˈsaɪn/ [T, often passive] to provide a person for a particular task or position, especially in police or social work; to send a person to work under the authority of sb or in a particular group, especially in the armed forces: *Two senior officers have been assigned to the case.* ◇ *He was assigned to the Royal Canadian Navy in 1975.*

dispatch (*BrE* also **despatch**) /dɪˈspætʃ/ [T, often passive] (*formal*) to send sb/sth somewhere, especially for a special purpose: *Troops have been dispatched to the area.* ◇ *A courier was dispatched to collect the documents.* ❶ In this meaning, **dispatch** is often used to talk about sending a military or police force somewhere.

post [T, often passive] (always used with an adverb or preposition) to send sb to a place for a period of time as part of their job; to put sb, especially a soldier, in a particular place so that they can guard a building or area: *Most employees get posted abroad at some stage.* ◇ *Guards have been posted along the border.* See also **posting** → JOB

---

sense *noun*

sense · feeling · impression · idea · sensation
These are all words for sth that you feel or think through the mind or the senses.

PATTERNS AND COLLOCATIONS
▸ a **strong** sense / feeling / impression / idea / sensation
▸ an **overwhelming** sense / feeling / impression / sensation
▸ a **good / definite / distinct / vague** sense / feeling / impression / idea
▸ a **strange** sense / feeling / impression / idea / sensation
▸ a / an **wonderful / warm / uncomfortable** sense / feeling / sensation
▸ to **have** a sense / a feeling / an impression / an idea / a sensation
▸ to **have the** sense / feeling / impression / sensation **that...**
▸ to **get / give sb / leave sb with / convey** a sense / a feeling / an impression / an idea

sense [C] (often followed by *of*) something that you feel, especially in your mind, about sth important: *He felt an overwhelming sense of loss.* ◇ *Doesn't she have any sense of guilt about what she did?* ◇ *Helmets can give cyclists a **false sense of security**.* ◇ *I had the sense that he was worried about something.* See also **sense** → FEEL *verb*

feeling [C] something that you feel through the mind or the senses: *There was a feeling of sadness in the room.* ◇ *You need to stop having these guilty feelings.* ◇ *I've got a tight feeling in my stomach.* ◇ (*spoken*)*'I really resent the way he treated me.' 'I know the feeling.'* (= I know how you feel.) ❶ Your **feelings** [pl.] are also your emotions. See also **feeling** → EMOTION, **feel** → FEEL, **feel** → SEEM

impression [C] a feeling or opinion that you get about sb/sth, or that sb/sth gives you: *My **first impression** of him was favourable.* ◇ *I **get the impression** there are still a lot of problems.* ◇ *She **gives the impression** of being very busy.* ◇ *Try and smile. You don't want to give people the **wrong impression*** (= that you are not friendly). ❶ **Impression** is used especially to talk about what you think when you first meet sb or experience sth.

idea [sing., U] a picture or impression in your mind of what sb/sth is like: *The brochure should give you a good idea of the hotel.* ◇ *If this is your idea of a joke, then I don't find it very funny.* ◇ *I had **some idea of** what the job would be like.*

sensation /senˈseɪʃn/ [C] (*rather formal*) a feeling that you get when sth affects your body: *You may get a tingling sensation in your fingers.* ◇ *I had a sensation of falling, as if in a dream.*

NOTE FEELING OR SENSATION A **feeling** may be physical or mental; a **sensation** is a physical feeling. **Sensation** is used especially to talk about a feeling that you do not immediately recognize or understand: *a sensation of falling/floating/movement/nausea/sinking*

---

sensitive *adj.*

1 a sensitive and caring man
2 a sensitive topic
3 sensitive to criticism

---

1 sensitive · sympathetic · gentle · humane · compassionate · understanding · soft
These words all describe a person who shows kindness and understanding towards others.

PATTERNS AND COLLOCATIONS
▸ sensitive / sympathetic / gentle / compassionate / understanding **towards** sb
▸ sensitive / sympathetic **to** sb / sth
▸ a sensitive / sympathetic / gentle / humane / compassionate **manner / man**
▸ (in) a sensitive / sympathetic / gentle / humane / compassionate **way**
▸ (a) sensitive / sympathetic / gentle **handling / approach**

▶ sensitive / sympathetic / humane **treatment**
▶ a humane / compassionate **society**

sensitive (*approving*) aware of and able to understand other people and their feelings: *a sensitive and caring man* ◇ *She is very sensitive to other people's feelings.* ◇ *This type of situation requires a sensitive approach by doctors.* **OPP** insensitive → INSENSITIVE, See also **sensitivity** → TACT
▶ **sensitively** *adv.*: *She handled the matter sensitively and effectively.*

sympathetic (*approving*) kind to sb who is hurt or upset; showing that you understand and care about their problems: *a sympathetic friend/listener/employer* ◇ *I did not feel at all sympathetic towards Kate.* ◇ *I'm here if you need a **sympathetic ear** (= sb to talk to about your problems).* **OPP** unsympathetic → INSENSITIVE, See also **sympathy** → SYMPATHY, **sympathize** → SORRY FOR SB, **sorry** → UPSET
▶ **sympathetically** *adv.*: *to nod/look/smile at sb sympathetically*

gentle (*approving*) calm and kind; doing things in a quiet and careful way: *Be gentle with her!* ◇ *She agreed to come, after a little gentle persuasion.* ◇ *He looks scary, but he's really a **gentle giant**.* **OPP** rough → VIOLENT
▶ **gently** *adv.*: *She held the baby gently.* ◇ *'You miss them, don't you?' he asked gently.*

humane /hju:'meɪn/ (*rather formal, approving*) showing kindness towards people and animals by making sure that they do not suffer more than is necessary: *a caring and humane society* ◇ *The animals must be reared in humane conditions.* **OPP** inhumane, cruel → CRUEL, See also **humanity** → SYMPATHY
▶ **humanely** *adv.*: *The dog was humanely destroyed.*

compassionate /kəm'pæʃənət/ (*rather formal, approving*) feeling or showing sympathy for people who are suffering: *Are these the actions of a compassionate and caring society?* ◇ *He was granted compassionate leave to visit his mother in hospital.* See also **compassion** → SYMPATHY

understanding (*approving*) showing sympathy for other people's problems and being willing to forgive them when they do sth wrong: *She has very understanding parents.* See also **understand** → UNDERSTAND 2, **understanding** → SYMPATHY *noun*

soft (*usually approving*) kind and sympathetic; easily affected by other people's suffering: *Julia's **soft heart** was touched by his grief.* **OPP** hard → RUTHLESS

2 sensitive · tricky · problematic · awkward · delicate · emotive
These words all describe sth that is difficult to deal with or needs to be dealt with carefully.

PATTERNS AND COLLOCATIONS
▶ a sensitive / a tricky / a problematic / an awkward / a delicate **matter / situation**
▶ a sensitive / a tricky / an awkward / a delicate / an emotive **question / subject**
▶ a sensitive / a tricky / an awkward / a delicate **problem**
▶ a sensitive / a tricky / a problematic / an emotive **issue**
▶ a sensitive / tricky / problematic / delicate **business**
▶ a sensitive / a problematic / an awkward / a delicate **relationship**
▶ the sensitive / problematic / delicate / emotive **nature** of sth
▶ **very / rather** sensitive / tricky / problematic / awkward / delicate / emotive
▶ **extremely / somewhat** sensitive / tricky / problematic / awkward / delicate
▶ **highly** sensitive / problematic / emotive

sensitive that you have to treat with great care because it may offend people or make them angry: *It might be better to avoid such a sensitive topic.* ◇ *She is currently involved in highly sensitive negotiations.* ◇ *Health care is a **politically sensitive** issue.* ◇ *The exact figure has not been released because it is judged to be **commercially sensitive** information.*

tricky (*rather informal*) difficult to do or to deal with, especially when it needs special care or skill: *The incident has raised some tricky questions about the future of the project.* ◇ *Getting it to fit exactly is a tricky business.* ◇ *The equipment can be tricky to install.*

problematic /ˌprɒblə'mætɪk; AmE ˌprɑːb-/ difficult to deal with or to understand; full of problems; not certain to be successful: *The situation is more problematic than we first thought.* ◇ *Providing the necessary care for elderly people can be problematic.* **OPP** unproblematic, See also **problem** → PROBLEM

awkward (of a situation or sb's behaviour) difficult to deal with, especially because it could cause embarrassment to sb: *Don't ask awkward questions.* ◇ *You've put me in an **awkward position**.* ◇ *It makes things awkward for everyone when you behave like that.*

delicate needing skilful, careful or sensitive treatment: *The delicate surgical operation took five hours.* ◇ *I wasn't sure how to approach the delicate matter of pay.*

emotive /ɪ'məʊtɪv; AmE ɪ'moʊ-/ (of an issue or sb's language) causing people to feel strong emotions: *Capital punishment is a highly emotive issue.* ◇ *Try to keep your report factual and avoid using **emotive language**.*

3 sensitive · touchy · prickly
These words all describe a person who is easily upset or offended.

PATTERNS AND COLLOCATIONS
▶ to be sensitive / touchy / prickly **about** sth
▶ **very** sensitive / touchy / prickly

sensitive (*sometimes disapproving*) easily offended or upset: *You're far too sensitive.* ◇ *She's acutely **sensitive to** criticism.* ◇ *He's depicted as an insecure and **sensitive soul**.*

touchy [not usually before noun] (*rather informal, often disapproving*) easily offended or upset, especially in a way that is not reasonable: *He's a little touchy about his weight.* ◇ *She gets very touchy if you mention the divorce.*

prickly (*BrE, informal, often disapproving*) easily offended or annoyed: *She's still a bit prickly about the whole incident.* ◇ *He could be very prickly with journalists.*

NOTE WHICH WORD? People who are **sensitive** or **touchy** are likely to get upset or cry; both words can be slightly disapproving but **touchy** usually suggests greater disapproval than **sensitive**. People who are **prickly** are more likely to get slightly aggressive than to cry.

separate *verb*
1 separate the white from the yolk/belief from emotion
2 separated by a wall/a thousand miles

1 separate · divorce · disentangle · filter sth out · sort sth out
These words all mean to divide two or more things which are mixed together into different parts or groups.

PATTERNS AND COLLOCATIONS
▶ to separate / divorce / disentangle / sort out sth **from** sth else
▶ to separate / disentangle the **strands** of sth
▶ to separate sth **completely** / be **completely** divorced from sth
▶ to be **totally** / **easily** separated / divorced from sth

separate /'sepəreɪt/ [I, T] to divide into different parts or groups; to divide things into different parts or groups: *Stir the sauce constantly so that it does not separate.* ◇ *First, separate the eggs* (= separate the yolk from the white). ◇ *It is impossible to separate belief from emotion.* ◇ *Make a list of points and **separate them into** 'desirable' and 'essential'.* See also **separation** → DIVISION 1, **separate** → DISPERSE

divorce [T, often passive] (*formal*) to separate sb/sth, especially an idea, subject or person, from sth else: *They believed that art should be divorced from politics.* ◇ *When he was depressed, he felt utterly divorced from reality.*

disentangle /ˌdɪsɪnˈtæŋgl/ [T] to separate different things, especially arguments or ideas, that have become confused: *It's not easy to disentangle the truth from the official statistics.* ◇ *It is important to disentangle all the factors that may be causing your stress.*

ˌfilter sth ˈout *phrasal verb* to remove sth that you do not want from a liquid, gas, light or sound, sometimes by using a special device or substance: *Wear a mask to filter out the smoke in the air.* ◇ *We learn to filter out background noise when we are listening to something in particular.*

ˌsort sth ˈout *phrasal verb* to separate sth from a larger group: *Could you sort out the toys that can be thrown away?* ◇ *It was difficult to sort out the lies from the truth.*

2 separate · seal sth off · divide · partition · cordon sth off · mark sth off · fence sth off
These words all mean to split an area into more than one section, especially in order to prevent people from entering one section.

PATTERNS AND COLLOCATIONS
▸ to seal / divide / partition / cordon / mark / fence sth **off**
▸ to separate / divide / partition sth **into** different areas
▸ to separate / divide / partition sth into different **sections / areas**
▸ to separate / seal off / divide / partition / cordon off / mark off / fence off an **area**
▸ to seal off / cordon off a **street / road / city centre**
▸ to divide / partition / fence off **land**
▸ to divide / partition a **country**
▸ the **army / police** seal / cordon sth off
▸ a **wall** separates / divides sth from sth else
▸ to be **clearly** separated / divided

separate /ˈsepəreɪt/ [T] to be between two people, areas, countries or things, so that they are not touching or connected: *A thousand kilometres separate the two cities.* ◇ *A high wall separated our block from the playing field.* See also **separation** → DIVISION 1

ˌseal sth ˈoff *phrasal verb* (of the police or army) to prevent people from entering a particular area: *Police sealed off the building following a security alert.*

divide [T] to be the real or imaginary line or barrier that separates two people or things: *A fence divides off the western side of the grounds.* ◇ *The city was divided into four sectors.*

partition /pɑːˈtɪʃn/ *AmE* pɑːrˈt-/ [T, often passive] to divide sth, especially a country or city, into two or more parts; to separate one part of a room or area from another with a wall or screen: *The country was partitioned a year after the elections.* ◇ *The room is partitioned into three sections.* See also **partition** → DIVISION *noun* 1, **partition** → WALL *noun*

ˌcordon sth ˈoff *phrasal verb* (of the police or army) to prevent people from entering a particular area by surrounding it with police or other guards: *Police cordoned off the area until the bomb was made safe.* See also **cordon** → ROW *noun*

ˌmark sth ˈoff *phrasal verb* to separate sth by marking a line between it and sth else: *The playing area was marked off with a white line.*

ˌfence sth ˈoff *phrasal verb* [often passive] to separate one area from another with a fence: *One end of the yard had been fenced off for the chickens.* See also **fence** → WALL

series *noun*

series · sequence · order · chain · string · succession · catalogue · chronology · line
These are all words for a number of events, things or people of a similar kind that come one after the other.

PATTERNS AND COLLOCATIONS
▸ a series / sequence / chain / string / succession / catalogue / chronology / line **of** sth
▸ **in** a / an (...) series / sequence / order / string
▸ **in** sequence / order (of sth) / succession
▸ **out of** sequence / order

▸ a **whole** series / sequence / string / succession / catalogue
▸ a / an **long / endless / continuous / unbroken** series / sequence / chain / string / succession / line
▸ a **random** series / sequence / order / string
▸ a series / sequence / chain / string / succession / chronology **of** events
▸ a series / string / catalogue **of errors**
▸ a series / sequence / string **of numbers / letters**
▸ the **first / last / latest in** a series / sequence / string / succession / line

series (*pl.* **series**) [C] (always followed by *of*) several events or things of a similar kind that happen one after the other: *This is the first in a series of articles about rock 'n' roll legends.* ◇ *The shooting was the latest in a series of violent attacks in the city.*

sequence /ˈsiːkwəns/ [C, U] a set of events, actions or numbers that follow one another in a particular order and which lead to a particular result; the order that events, actions, etc. happen in or should happen in: *The novel contains a long **dream sequence** (= describing a dream).* ◇ *Put these numbers into the correct sequence.* ◇ *The computer generates a random sequence of numbers.* ◇ *The papers were all out of sequence.*

NOTE **SERIES** OR **SEQUENCE**? A **series** of things is usually a set of individual items; although similar in some way, each one is a distinct example of sth, different from the others. A **series** of things does not have to be in any logical order, but a **sequence** of things probably will be. **Sequence** usually suggests that each event, action or number is connected in some way to the previous one.

order [U, C] the way in which a number of people or things are placed or arranged in relation to each other, that decides what comes first, what comes second, etc: *The names are listed in alphabetical order.* ◇ *We will deal with cases in order of importance.* ◇ *Winners are announced in reverse order.* ◇ *The information is given in no particular order.* ❶ The emphasis with **order** is on the system used to arrange things, rather than the set of things themselves. See also **order** → RANK *verb*

chain [C] a series of connected things or people, especially when they lead to a particular result: *I was next in the **chain of command** (= a system by which instructions are passed from one person to another).* ◇ *Middlemen are important **links in the chain**.* ◇ *Volunteers formed a **human chain** to pass buckets of water to each other.* ❶ The collocates of **chain** in this meaning bring to mind the literal meaning of the word. Collocates include *link*, *break* and *unbroken*.

string [C] a series of similar things or people that come closely one after the other or are found close together: *He retired after a string of chart hits in the 1980s.* ◇ *The company owns a string of casinos in Nevada.* ❶ You talk about a **string** of things to emphasize the fact that there are a lot of them.

succession /səkˈseʃn/ [C, usually sing., U] a series of people or things that follow each other in time or order; the regular pattern of one thing following another: *She was cared for by a succession of nannies.* ◇ *The team lost the final six years in succession.* ◇ *They won several games **in quick succession**.* ❶ You talk about a **succession** of things to emphasize the fact that one thing follows after another, without a break or interruption.

catalogue (*AmE* also **catalog**) /ˈkætəlɒg; *AmE* -lɔːg; -lɑːg/ [C, usually sing.] (always followed by *of*) (*especially BrE*) a long series of things that happen, especially bad things: *What followed was a whole catalogue of disasters.* ◇ *Child protection officers uncovered a catalogue of cruelty and abuse.*

chronology /krəˈnɒlədʒi; *AmE* -ˈnɑːl-/ [U, C] the order in which a series of events happened; a list of these events in order: *Historians seem to have confused the chronology of these events.* ◇ *At the front of the book is a chronology of the artist's life.* ❶ The emphasis with **chronology** is on *when* each event happened in relation to the other events.

line [C, usually sing.] a series of people, things or events that follow one another in time: *She came from a long line of doctors* (= there were many doctors in her family in the past). ◇ *Property was passed down through the male line* (= through the males in the family). ◇ *The novel is the latest in a long line of thrillers that he has written.* See also **lineage** → FAMILY 3

serious *adj.*

1 a serious problem/illness
2 a serious person/mood/expression
3 a serious debate/newspaper

---

1 See the Topic Map for HEALTH on p.890
serious · severe · extreme · critical · grave · acute · drastic · desperate · dire · bad · life-threatening
These words all describe things and situations that involve or cause harm or damage to sb/sth.

---

serious	severe	extreme
critical	grave	drastic
bad	acute	desperate
		dire
		life-threatening

PATTERNS AND COLLOCATIONS
▸ a serious/ a severe/ a critical/ a grave/ an acute/ a desperate/ a bad/ a life-threatening **problem**
▸ a serious/ a severe/ an extreme/ a critical/ an acute/ a desperate/ a dire **shortage**
▸ serious/ severe/ extreme/ grave/ acute **danger**
▸ a serious/ a severe/ a grave/ a dire **threat**
▸ serious/ severe/ extreme/ acute/ desperate/ dire **poverty**
▸ a serious/ an extreme/ a critical/ an acute/ a desperate/ a dire **need**
▸ serious/ grave/ drastic/ dire/ bad **consequences**
▸ a serious/ a severe/ a critical/ a grave/ an acute/ a life-threatening **illness**
▸ a serious/ a severe/ an acute/ a life-threatening **disease**
▸ a serious/ a severe/ a grave/ an acute/ a bad/ a life-threatening **injury**
▸ a serious/ a severe/ an acute/ a life-threatening **infection**
▸ a serious/ a severe/ an acute/ a bad **attack/ bout**
▸ **particularly** serious/ severe/ extreme/ grave/ acute/ dire/ bad
▸ **very / extremely** serious/ severe/ grave/ acute/ bad

serious unpleasant or dangerous; that involves or might cause harm or damage to sb/sth: *The storm caused serious damage to farm buildings.* ◇ *They pose a serious threat to security.* ◇ *The consequences could be serious.* **OPP minor** → MINOR, See also **seriousness** → IMPORTANCE
▸ **seriously** *adv.*: *Smoking can seriously damage your health.*
severe very serious: *The victim suffered severe brain damage.* ◇ *The bridge has been closed due to severe weather conditions.* ◇ *Strikes are causing severe disruption to all train services.* **OPP minor** → MINOR, **mild** → GENTLE
▸ **severely** *adv.*: *Anyone breaking the law will be severely punished.*
▸ **severity** /sɪˈverəti/ *noun* [U]: *The chances of a full recovery will depend on the severity of her injuries.*

> **NOTE SERIOUS OR SEVERE?** Severe is most often used to describe medical conditions and weather conditions. **Serious** is NOT used to describe weather conditions: ~~serious weather~~ ◇ ~~a serious winter~~. **Serious** is used to describe medical conditions in everyday English, but in medical English **severe** is used: *a serious illness* ◇ *severe learning difficulties*

extreme (of a situation or action) not ordinary or usual; serious or severe: *Children will be removed from their parents only in extreme circumstances.* ◇ *Don't go doing anything extreme like leaving the country.* ◇ *It was the most extreme example of cruelty to animals I had ever seen.* ◇ *extreme weather conditions* See also **extreme** → MAXIMUM

critical (*rather formal*) serious, uncertain and possibly dangerous: *The first 24 hours after the operation are the most critical.* ◇ (*BrE*) *One of the victims of the fire remains* **in a critical condition**. ◇ (*AmE*) *One of the victims remains* **in critical condition**. ◇ *This is a critical moment in our country's history.* ❶ **Critical** is often used with *illness* and *condition* to describe medical situations in which there is a possibility that the patient may not survive. **Critical** is also often used with words relating to time such as *moment, period, phase, point, stage, time* and *years* to talk about a time during which an important situation could end in failure or success.
▸ **critically** *adv.*: *He is critically ill in hospital.*
grave (*formal*) very serious and important; giving you a reason to feel worried: *I fear you are making a very grave mistake.* ◇ *The police have expressed grave concern about the missing child's safety.* ◇ *We were in grave danger.* ❶ **Grave** is used with such words as *error, mistake, offence* and *violation* to talk about things that people do wrong. **Grave** is also used with words like *concern, doubt, misgivings, reservations, suspicions* and *worries* to talk about strong feelings that people have when they are worrying about sth. When **grave** is used to talk about situations, it is often used with such words as *consequences, danger, implications, problems, risk* and *threat.* See also **gravity** → IMPORTANCE
▸ **gravely** *adv.*: *Local people are gravely concerned.*
acute /əˈkjuːt/ (*rather formal*) very serious or severe: *The scandal was an acute embarrassment for the President.* ◇ *Competition for jobs is acute.* ❶ An **acute** illness is one that has quickly become severe and dangerous: *He was suffering from acute chest pains.* **OPP chronic** A **chronic** illness or problem is one that lasts for a long time and is difficult to cure or get rid of: *chronic bronchitis/arthritis/ asthma* ◇ *the country's chronic unemployment problem*
▸ **acutely** *adv.*: *She suddenly felt acutely embarrassed.*
drastic (especially of an action) extreme in a way that has a sudden, serious or violent effect on sth: *The government is threatening to* **take drastic action**. ◇ *Talk to me before you do anything drastic.*
▸ **drastically** *adv.*: *Output has been drastically reduced.* ◇ *Things have started to go drastically wrong.*
desperate /ˈdespərət/ extremely serious or dangerous: *The children are in desperate need of love and attention.* ◇ *They face a desperate shortage of clean water.* ❶ **Desperate** is used to talk about situations in which people need sth.
▸ **desperately** *adv.*: *She felt desperately in need of human company.*
dire /ˈdaɪə(r)/ [usually before noun] (*especially BrE, formal*) extremely serious: *They were living in dire poverty.* ◇ *The firm is* **in dire straits** (= in a very difficult situation) *and may go bankrupt.* ❶ **Dire** is not used to talk about medical conditions. In American English it is only used in the phrase *in dire straits.*
bad (*rather informal, especially spoken*) serious; severe: *The engagement was a bad mistake.* ◇ *It was a very bad winter that year.* ◇ *My headache is getting worse.* ❶ **Bad** can be used to describe many unpleasant situations, but it is not used to describe danger or an emergency. It is rather informal and used especially in spoken English; in formal or written English it is often better to choose one of the other words in this group.
▸ **badly** *adv.*: *The building is badly in need of repair.*
¹life-threatening that is likely to kill sb: *His heart condition is not life-threatening.* ◇ *Aid workers are having to deal with very difficult, sometimes life-threatening situations.* ❶ **Life-threatening** is used to talk about medical conditions, and dangerous situations in which accidents might happen.

---

2 **serious · grave · earnest · sombre · solemn · sober · humourless**
These words all describe sb who thinks and behaves carefully and sensibly, but often without much joy or laughter.

▶ a serious / a grave / an earnest / a sombre / a solemn / a sober **expression**
▶ a serious / a grave / an earnest / a solemn / a sober **face**
▶ a serious / sombre / solemn / sober **mood** / **atmosphere**
▶ **on a** serious / sombre / sober **note**
▶ **very** serious / grave / earnest / sombre / solemn / sober

serious thinking about things in a careful and sensible way; not laughing about sth: *He's not really a very serious person.* ◇ *Suddenly the conversation turned serious.* ◇ *Be serious for a moment; this is important.* **OPP** light-hearted → FUNNY
▶ **seriously** adv.: *You need to think seriously about your next career move.* ◇ *They're no help at all – they're refusing to take the problem seriously.*

grave (*rather formal, written*) (of a person) serious in manner, as if sth sad, important or worrying has just happened: *He looked very grave as he entered the room.*
▶ **gravely** adv.: *He nodded gravely as I poured out my troubles.*

earnest /'ɜːnɪst; AmE 'ɜːrn-/ (*rather formal*) serious and sincere: *The earnest young doctor answered all our questions.* ◇ *I could tell that she spoke in earnest* (= seriously and sincerely).

sombre (*BrE*) (*AmE* **somber**) /'sɒmbə(r); AmE 'sɑːm-/ (*written*) sad and serious: *The year had ended on a sombre note* (= in a sombre way). ◇ *Her expression grew sombre.*

solemn /'sɒləm; AmE 'sɑːləm/ (*rather formal*) looking or sounding very serious, without smiling; done or said in a very serious and sincere way: *She looked at the solemn faces of the children.* ◇ *You have all taken a solemn oath of loyalty to your country.* ◇ *I made a solemn promise that I would return.*
▶ **solemnly** adv.: *He nodded solemnly.*

sober /'səʊbə(r); AmE 'soʊ-/ (*rather formal, written*) serious and sensible: *On sober reflection* (= after thinking about it seriously) *I have decided to drop the case.*

humourless (*BrE*) (*AmE* **humorless**) (*disapproving*) too serious and seeming unable to make jokes or to recognize when sth is amusing: *He gave a short, humourless laugh* (= a laugh that does not express any amusement).

3 serious · deep · profound
These are all words that describe sth that needs or shows careful thought and attention.

▶ a serious / deep / profound **question** / **issue** / **analysis**
▶ a serious / deep **conversation** / **discussion**
▶ a deep / profound **understanding** / **insight**

serious needing or showing careful thought and attention; not only for pleasure: *This book is the first serious study of the subject.* ◇ *Please give this matter some serious thought.* ◇ *Why do you waste your time reading that? It's hardly a serious newspaper, is it?*
▶ **seriously** adv.: *The research group's findings need to be considered seriously.*

deep showing a lot of knowledge or understanding; difficult to understand: *None of the insights contained in the book were particularly deep.* ◇ (*humorous or ironic*) *This discussion is getting too deep for me.* See also **depth** → UNDERSTANDING
▶ **deeply** adv.: *I was young then and had never thought very deeply about anything.*

profound /prə'faʊnd/ (*rather formal*) showing a lot of knowledge or understanding; needing a lot of study or thought: *Her book offers some profound insights into the nature of suffering.*

NOTE DEEP OR PROFOUND? Profound is more formal than **deep**. **Deep** is sometimes used in a slightly humorous or ironic way to suggest that a comment or discussion may not in fact be as serious and important as it seems.

servant noun

servant · maid · housekeeper · butler · cleaner · footman · valet
These are all words for a person who works in another person's house, and cooks and cleans for them or serves them in some other way.

▶ a **personal** servant / maid
▶ a **live-in** maid / housekeeper
▶ to **have** a servant / maid / housekeeper / butler / cleaner / footman / valet

servant [C] a person who works in another person's house, and cooks, cleans, etc. for them: *She got a job as a domestic servant.* ◇ *They treat their mother like a servant.* **ℹ** Servant is usually only used to talk about people who did this work in the past, or people who work for extremely rich or noble families in modern times. It would be considered offensive to call sb who cooks or cleans for an ordinary family a **servant**.

maid [C] a female servant in a house or hotel: *She was a lady's maid to Lady Fleetham.* ◇ *There is a maid to do the housework.* ◇ *The maid was changing the sheets when we got back to our room.* **ℹ** Like **servant**, **maid** is used to talk about a person who did this work in the past, or sb who works for a rich or noble family in modern times. However, **maid** or **chambermaid** is also used to talk about a girl or woman who cleans rooms in a hotel or holiday home.

housekeeper /'haʊskiːpə(r)/ [C] a person, usually a woman, whose job is to manage the shopping, cooking, cleaning, etc. in a house or institution: *Miss Mack had been housekeeper at the Hall for many years.*

butler [C] the main male servant in a large house: *The butler announced that dinner was served.*

cleaner [C] a person whose job is to clean other people's houses or offices, etc: *I met him while I was working as a cleaner in a hospital.*

footman /'fʊtmən/ [C] a male servant in a house in the past, who opened the door to visitors, served food at table, etc: *She summoned a footman, who duly arrived.*

NOTE BUTLER OR FOOTMAN? The **butler** is the chief male servant of a household who is in charge of other employees, receives guests, directs the serving of meals, and performs various personal services; a **footman** is a person, especially in the past, who wore a uniform and opened doors for people. A **footman** sometimes served at the table as well.

valet /'væleɪ; 'vælɪt; AmE also væ'leɪ/ [C] a man's personal servant who takes care of his clothes, serves his meals, etc: *His valet brought him his letters.* **ℹ** In modern American English a **valet** is a person who parks your car for you at a hotel or restaurant: *Do they have valet parking?*

serve verb

1 Breakfast is served between 7 and 10 a.m.
2 The centre serves the whole community.

1 serve · feed · nourish · dish (sth) up · cater
These words all mean to provide food for sb.

▶ to serve / feed / nourish sb / sth **with** sth
▶ to feed / nourish sb / sth **on** sth
▶ to serve / dish up a **meal**
▶ to be **well** / **properly** fed / nourished

serve [T, I] to give sb food or drink, for example at a restaurant or during a meal, especially a formal meal; (of an amount of food) to be enough for sb / sth: *Breakfast is served between 7 and 10 a.m.* ◇ *Serve the lamb with new potatoes and green beans.* ◇ *This dish will serve four hungry people.* **ℹ** Although **serve** usually has an object,

the object is often left out, especially in recipes or instructions for serving food: *Pour the sauce over the pasta and serve immediately.* ◇ *Serve chilled* (= used about wine or drinks). ◇ *Shall I serve?* See also **serving** → PORTION
▸ **service** noun [U]: *The food was good but the service was very slow.*

feed [T] to give food to sb; to provide food for sb: *The baby can't feed herself yet* (= can't put food into her own mouth). ◇ *They've got a large family to feed.* ◇ (*rather informal*) *There's enough here to feed an army.*

nourish /ˈnʌrɪʃ; AmE ˈnɜːrɪʃ/ [T] to keep a person, animal or plant alive and healthy with food: *All the children were well nourished and in good physical condition.* ◇ *Most plants are nourished by water drawn up through their roots.* See also **nourishment** → FOOD

dish 'up, dish sth 'up phrasal verb (*rather informal*) to serve food onto plates for a meal, especially a meal at home. *Should I dish up?* ◇ *He gave me a glass of wine and dished up the dinner.*

cater /ˈkeɪtə(r)/ [I, T] to provide food and drinks for a social event: (BrE) *Most of our work now involves* **catering for** *weddings.* ◇ (AmE) *Who will be catering the wedding?*
▸ **catering** noun [U]: *Who did the catering for the wedding?*

2 See also the entry for PROVIDE FOR SB

serve · cater for sb/sth · cater to sb/sth
These words all mean to give a group of people the things that they need or want.

PATTERNS AND COLLOCATIONS
▸ sb/sth is **well** served/catered for
▸ to serve/cater for sb/sth **adequately**

serve [T] (*rather formal*) to offer a product or service to an area or group of people: *The town is well* **served with** *buses and major road links.* ◇ *The centre will serve the whole community.*

'cater for sb/sth phrasal verb to give or offer the things that a particular person or situation needs or wants: *The class caters for all ability ranges.* ❶ **Cater for sb/sth** is used to talk about either the wide range of things that is offered or particular things that are offered: *to cater for all/a wide range of ages/tastes/abilities/interests* ◇ *to cater for individual preferences/children with special needs*

'cater to sb/sth phrasal verb (*sometimes disapproving*) to give or offer the things that a particular type of person wants: *They only publish novels which cater to the mass market.* ❶ *Organizations typically* **cater to** *the mass market, tourists, an elite or local tastes.*

> **NOTE** CATER FOR SB/STH OR CATER TO SB/STH? If you **cater for** sb/sth, you provide the things that they need; if you **cater to** sb/sth you give them what they want.

service noun

service · agency · office · bureau · ministry
These are all words for an organization or company that provides sth for the public or does sth for the government.

PATTERNS AND COLLOCATIONS
▸ to do sth **through** a service/an agency/an office/a bureau
▸ a **government/federal/public/state** service/agency/office/bureau/ministry
▸ a/an **local/employment/press/information/intelligence/security/advisory** service/agency/office/bureau
▸ a/an **private/international/counselling/police/recruitment/travel** service/agency/office
▸ a/an **independent/outside/commercial/news** service/agency/bureau

service [C] an organization, company or department that provides sth for the public or does sth for the government: *She works for the prison service.* ◇ *The news was reported on the BBC World Service last night.* ❶ **Service** is often used in the names of government departments: (BrE) *the Diplomatic Service* ◇ (AmE) *the Foreign Service*

agency /ˈeɪdʒənsi/ [C] a business or organization that provides a particular service, especially on behalf of other businesses or organizations; (especially in the US) a government department that provides a particular service: *He works for an advertising agency.* ◇ *International aid agencies are caring for many of the refugees.* ◇ *the Central Intelligence Agency*

office [C] (usually in compounds) a room or building used for a particular purpose, especially to provide information or a service: *You should be able to get a map at the local tourist office.* ◇ *There was a long wait at the ticket office.* ❶ **Office** is used in the names of some British government departments: *the Foreign Office* ◇ *the Home Office* ◇ *the Office of Fair Trading*

bureau /ˈbjʊərəʊ; AmE ˈbjʊroʊ/ [C] an office or organization that provides information on a particular subject, (in the US) a government department or part of a government department: *She works for an employment bureau.* ◇ *the Federal Bureau of Investigation*

ministry [C] (in the UK) a government department that has a particular area of responsibility: *The Ministry of Defence has issued the following statement.* ◇ *A ministry spokesperson defended the measures.*

servile adj.

servile · smooth · slick · smarmy · ingratiating
These words all describe people who want too much to please sb or are too polite in an unpleasant or insincere way.

PATTERNS AND COLLOCATIONS
▸ a smooth/slick **talker**
▸ a servile/a smarmy/an ingratiating **manner**
▸ a smarmy/an ingratiating **tone**

servile /ˈsɜːvaɪl; AmE ˈsɜːrvl; -vaɪl/ (*rather formal, disapproving*) wanting too much to please sb and obey them: *Parents have no right to demand servile obedience from their children.*

smooth (*often disapproving*) (of people, especially men, and their behaviour) very polite and pleasant, but in a way that is often not very sincere: *I don't like him. He's far too smooth for me.* ◇ *He's something of a* **smooth operator.**

slick (*especially AmE, often disapproving*) smooth: *a slick, fast-talking car salesman* ◇ *I don't like him. He's way too slick for me.*

smarmy (*informal, disapproving*) too polite in a way that is not sincere: *To be honest I found the hotel staff rather smarmy.*

> **NOTE** SMOOTH, SLICK OR SMARMY? A person who is **smarmy** has an unpleasant manner which will make you react in a negative way towards them. A person who is **smooth** or **slick** has a confident and pleasant manner which may get them what they want, but actually should not be trusted: *He was a smooth/slick talker who seemed to be able to convince anyone to buy his rip-off radios.* **Smooth** is used more in British English; **slick** is used more in American English.

ingratiating /ɪnˈɡreɪʃieɪtɪŋ/ (*rather formal, disapproving*) trying too hard to please sb: *They weren't just helpful, they were positively ingratiating.* See also **ingratiate yourself** → FLATTER

set adj.

set · fixed · predetermined · prearranged
These words all describe sth that is planned or arranged in advance.

PATTERNS AND COLLOCATIONS
▸ set/fixed/predetermined **rules**
▸ a set/fixed/predetermined **number/level/quantity/pattern**
▸ a set/fixed **price**

set [usually before noun] planned or not changing; (of a meal in a restaurant) having a fixed price and a limited choice of dishes: *Each person was given set jobs to do.* ◇ *New vehicles must comply with set safety standards.* ◇ *There are restaurants nearby that offer a set meal for just a few dollars.* ◇ *the set menu*

fixed staying the same; not changing or that cannot be changed: *These accounts offer a fixed rate of interest over a defined period.* ◇ *The money has been invested for a fixed period.*

predetermined /ˌpriːdɪˈtɜːmɪnd; *AmE* -ˈtɜːrm-/ (*rather formal*) decided or chosen in advance, so that it does not happen by chance: *An alarm sounds when the temperature reaches a predetermined level.* **OPP** **random** → RANDOM

prearranged /ˌpriːəˈreɪndʒd/ (*rather formal*) planned or arranged in advance, especially between two or more people: *He gave the prearranged signal to attack.*

set off *phrasal verb* See also the entry for LEAVE 1

set off · take off · start · set out · set sail
These words all mean to begin a journey.

PATTERNS AND COLLOCATIONS
▶ to set off / take off / start / set out / set sail **for** / **from** sth
▶ to set off / take off / start (out) / set out / set sail **on** a journey, voyage, etc.
▶ to set off / take off / start / set out **early**

ˌset ˈoff *phrasal verb* to leave at the start of a journey: *We set off at dawn.* ◇ *They set off to explore the island.*

ˌtake ˈoff *phrasal verb* (of an aircraft) to leave the ground and begin to fly; (of a person) to set off in an aircraft: *The plane took off an hour late.* ◇ *What time do we take off?* ❶ In informal American English **take off** can be used when sb leaves a place to go somewhere else: *We took off for the beach.* **OPP** **land** → LAND

start [I] to begin a journey: *What time do we start?* ◇ *They had started out from Saigon the previous day.*

ˌset ˈout *phrasal verb* (*especially written*) to leave at the start of a journey: *He set out along the path the old man had shown him.*

> **NOTE** **SET OFF, START OUT** OR **SET OUT?** There is no real difference in meaning between these words. **Set off** is the most frequent and least formal. **Start (out)** and **set out** are used more in written English than in spoken English; **set out** especially can sound slightly literary.

set ˈsail *idiom* (*rather formal*) to begin a journey in a ship or boat: *The family set sail for a new life in Australia.*

shake *verb*

1 shake your head/shake hands
2 The ground shook./Shake the bottle.
3 shaking with fear
4 badly shaken by the news

1 See also the entry for WRIGGLE

shake · wave · wag · swish · flap · beat
These words all mean to move a part of your body from side to side or up and down.

PATTERNS AND COLLOCATIONS
▶ to shake your head / shake your fist / wave / wag sth **at** sb
▶ sth waves / wags / swishes its **tail**
▶ sth flaps / beats its **wings**
▶ to shake your head / shake sb's hand / wave / wag sth **vigorously**

shake [T] to turn your head from side to side; to take sb's hand and move it up and down; to hold up your fist (= closed hand) and move it up and down ❶ You **shake your head** as a way of saying 'no' or to show sadness, disapproval or doubt: *'Drink?' he offered. She shook her head.* ◇ *She shook her head in disbelief.* ❶ You **shake hands** with sb or **shake sb's hand** as a greeting or to show that you have agreed sth with sb: *The captains*

shook hands before the game commenced. ◇ *He shook my hand warmly.* ◇ *She refused to shake hands with him.* ◇ *They shook hands on the deal* (= to show that they had reached an agreement). You can also **shake sb by the hand**, especially to show enthusiasm or admiration: *If I met him I'd shake him by the hand and congratulate him.* ❶ You **shake your fist** at sb in order to show that you are angry with them or in order to threaten them: *The man shook his fist at the court after he was sentenced.*
▶ **shake** *noun* [C, usually sing.]: *He dismissed the idea with a firm shake of his head.*

wave [I, T] to move your hand or arm in the air in order to attract attention, as a greeting or to say goodbye: *The people on the bus waved and we waved back.* ◇ *The man in the water was waving his arms around frantically.* ◇ *Wave goodbye to Daddy.* ◇ *My mother was crying as I waved her goodbye.*
▶ **wave** *noun* [C, usually sing.]: *He gave us a wave as the bus drove off.*

wag (**-gg-**) [T, I] if a dog **wags** its tail or its tail **wags**, its tail moves repeatedly from side to side; if a person **wags** their finger or their head, they move it from side to side or up and down, often as a sign of disapproval: *The dog bounded forwards, wagging its tail excitedly.* ◇ *The dog bounded forwards, its tail wagging.* ◇ *'Just remember what I said,' she repeated, wagging her finger at him.*
▶ **wag** *noun* [C, usually sing.]: *Flossie managed a feeble wag of her tail.*

swish [I, T] (especially of an animal's tail) to move quickly through the air in a way that makes a soft sound; to make sth do this: *The pony's tail swished from side to side.* ◇ *The cows were swishing their tails lazily.* ◇ *She swished her racket aggressively through the air.*
▶ **swish** *noun* [C, usually sing.]: *She turned away with a swish of her skirt.*

flap (**-pp-**) [T, I] if a bird **flaps** its wings or its wings **flap**, they move up and down; if a person **flaps** their arms, they move them up and down: *The bird flapped its wings and flew away.* ◇ *The gulls flew off, wings flapping.* ◇ *She walked up and down, flapping her arms to keep warm.* See also **flap** → BLOW 1
▶ **flap** *noun* [C, usually sing.]: *With a flap of its wings the bird was gone.*

beat [T, I] if a bird **beats** its wings or its wings **beat**, they move quickly up and down, especially making a noise: *The bird was frantically beating its wings.* ◇ *Its wings beat feebly against the window.*

2 shake · rattle · vibrate · clatter · wobble · shudder · jolt · rock · jiggle · jar · bump
These words all mean to move or to make sth move with very short quick movements from side to side or up and down.

PATTERNS AND COLLOCATIONS
▶ to shake / rattle / vibrate / shudder / rock / jar **with** sth
▶ to rattle / clatter / shudder / jolt / bump **along**
▶ to rattle / clatter / wobble / jiggle / bump **around** / **about**
▶ to shake / rattle / vibrate / shudder / rock (sth) **violently**
▶ to shake / vibrate / rock / bump (sth) **gently**
▶ to shake / shudder / rock (sth) **suddenly**

shake [I, T] to move or to make sb/sth move with short quick movements from side to side or up and down; to move sth in a particular direction by shaking: *The whole house shakes whenever a train goes past.* ◇ *Shake the bottle well before use.* ◇ *He shook her violently by the shoulders.* ◇ *Tom bent down to shake a pebble out of his shoe.*
▶ **shake** *noun* [C, usually sing.]: *Give the bottle a good shake.*

rattle [I, T] to make a series of short loud sounds when hitting against sth hard; to make sth do this; (of a vehicle) to make a series of short loud sounds as it moves somewhere: *Every time a bus went past, the windows rattled.* ◇ *She stood there, rattling the collecting tin.* ◇ *A convoy of trucks rattled past.*

▶ **rattle** (also **rattling**) *noun* [C, usually sing.]: *the rattle of gunfire* ◊ *From the kitchen came a rattling of cups and saucers.*

vibrate /vaɪˈbreɪt; *AmE* usually ˈvaɪbreɪt/ [I, T] to move or make sth move from side to side with extremely small movements and extremely quickly: *The ground beneath their feet began to vibrate.* ◊ *The male spider will vibrate one of the threads of the female spider's web.*

▶ **vibration** *noun* [C, U]: *We could feel the vibrations from the trucks passing outside.* ◊ *Is it possible to reduce the level of vibration in the engine?*

clatter [I] (of hard objects) to knock together and make a loud noise; to move making a loud noise like hard objects knocking together: *He dropped the knife and it clattered on the stone floor.* ◊ *The cart clattered over the cobbles.*

▶ **clatter** (also **clattering**) *noun* [sing.]: *the clatter of horses' hooves*

wobble [I, T] to move or make sth move from side to side in an unsteady way: *This chair wobbles.* ◊ *The vase wobbled and then crashed to the ground.* ◊ *Don't wobble the table — I'm trying to work.*

shudder [I] (especially of a vehicle or machine) to shake very hard: *The boat's engines shuddered, and it began to leave the shore.* ◊ *The bus shuddered to a halt.*

▶ **shudder** *noun* [C, usually sing.]: *The elevator rose with a shudder.*

jolt /dʒəʊlt; *AmE* dʒoʊlt/ [I, T] to move or to make sb/sth move suddenly and roughly: *The truck jolted and rattled over the rough ground.* ◊ *He was jolted forward as the train moved off.*

▶ **jolt** *noun* [C, usually sing.]: *The plane landed with a jolt.*

rock [I, T] (*rather informal, especially journalism*) to shake or make sth shake violently: *The whole house rocked when the bomb exploded.* ◊ *The town was rocked by an earthquake.* ◊ *The raft was rocked by a huge wave.*

jiggle [I, T] (*informal*) to move up and down or from side to side with short quick movements; to make sth small and light do this: *Stop jiggling around!* ◊ *She jiggled with the lock.* ◊ *He stood jiggling his car keys in his hand.*

jar (-rr-) [T, I] to give or receive a sudden painful knock: *The jolt seemed to jar every bone in her body.* ◊ *The spade jarred on something metal.*

bump [I, T] to move across a rough surface in a particular direction, in a way that is not smooth; to make sth move in this way: *The jeep bumped along the dirt track.* ◊ *She entered the subway, bumping her bags down the step.*

---

3 shake · tremble · shudder · twitch · shiver · convulse
These words all mean to make short quick movements that you cannot control, especially because you are frightened or cold.

PATTERNS AND COLLOCATIONS
▶ to shake / tremble / shiver / be convulsed **with fear**
▶ to shake / tremble / shiver **with cold**
▶ to tremble / shudder / shiver **at** a thought / memory, etc.
▶ sb's **whole body** shakes/trembles/shudders/twitches/shivers/ convulses
▶ sb's **hands** shake / tremble / twitch
▶ sb's **legs** shake / tremble
▶ sb's **mouth / lip** trembles / twitches
▶ to shake / tremble / shudder / twitch / shiver **slightly**
▶ to shake / tremble / shudder / twitch / shiver / convulse **violently**
▶ to shake / shudder / shiver **suddenly**

shake [I] to make short quick movements that you cannot control, for example because you are frightened or cold: *I was shaking like a leaf.* ◊ *Her hands started to shake.* See also **shaking** → SHIVER *noun*

tremble [I] to shake in a way that you cannot control, especially because you are very nervous, excited or frightened: *He opened the letter with trembling hands.* ◊ *I trembled at the thought of making a speech.* See also **tremble** → SHIVER *noun*

shudder [I] (not usually used in the progressive tenses) to shake suddenly because you are frightened or cold, or because of a strong emotion: *Alone in the car, she shuddered with fear.* ◊ *I shudder to think what might have happened.* See also **shudder** → SHIVER *noun*

NOTE TREMBLE OR SHUDDER? Tremble describes a repeated shaking movement; **shudder** is usually only a single shake: *He trembled* (= he was shaking). ◊ *He shuddered* (= he shook once).

twitch [I, T] (of part of the body) to make a sudden quick movement, sometimes one that you cannot control; to make a part of your body do this: *Her lips twitched with amusement.* ◊ *The dog twitched its ears and looked very intently.* See also **twitch** → SHIVER *noun*

shiver [I] to shake slightly because you are cold, ill, frightened or excited: *Don't stand outside shivering — come in and get warm.* ❶ Shiver is more often used to describe shaking from cold or illness than from fear. See also **shiver** → SHIVER *noun*

convulse /kənˈvʌls/ [T, I] to cause a sudden strong shaking movement in sb's body; to make this movement: *She was convulsed by a bout of sneezing.* ◊ *His whole body convulsed.* See also **convulsion** → SHIVER *noun*

---

4 shake · unnerve · agitate · fluster · disconcert
These words all mean to make sb feel anxious, uncomfortable or not calm.

PATTERNS AND COLLOCATIONS
▶ to be shaken / unnerved / agitated / flustered / disconcerted **by** sth

shake [T] (not used in the progressive tenses) (of an event) to shock or upset sb, so that they cannot relax or feel calm for a long time: *He was badly shaken by the news of her death.* ◊ *The accident really shook her up.*

unnerve [T] (not used in the progressive tenses) to make sb feel nervous or frightened or lose confidence: *I was completely unnerved by the way she kept staring at me.* ◊ *He's just trying to unnerve you.* See also **unnerving** → WORRYING

agitate /ˈædʒɪteɪt/ [T] (*written*) (not used in the progressive tenses) (of a feeling or action) to make sb show that they are angry, anxious or nervous: *Richard felt agitated by a mixture of anger, fear and pleasure.* ◊ *This remark seemed to agitate her guest.* See also **agitated** → RESTLESS, **agitation** → CONCERN

fluster [T, often passive] (not used in the progressive tenses) (*written*) to make sb nervous and/or confused, especially by giving them a lot to do or by making them hurry: *She was clearly flustered by Marshall's unexpected arrival.* See also **flustered** → RESTLESS

disconcert [T] (*rather formal, written*) (not used in the progressive tenses) to make sb feel anxious, confused or embarrassed: *The abrupt change of subject disconcerted her.* See also **disconcerting** → WORRYING

▶ **disconcerted** *adj.*: *I was very disconcerted to find that everyone else already knew it.*

shape *noun*

shape · figure · form · shadow · outline · profile · silhouette · line · contour
These are all words for the physical form or appearance of sb/sth, especially the shape of the outer edges of sb/sth.

PATTERNS AND COLLOCATIONS
▶ **in** shape / form / outline / profile / silhouette
▶ a **tall** shape / figure / form / shadow / silhouette
▶ a **slender** shape / figure / form
▶ a **black/dark** shape/figure/shadow/outline/profile/silhouette
▶ a **shadowy** shape / figure / form / outline
▶ a **ghostly** shape / figure / form / shadow
▶ (a) **sleek** shape / outline / profile / lines
▶ (a) **sharp** outline / lines / contours

▶ to **make out/ see** a shape/ a figure/ a form/ an outline/ a silhouette
▶ to **trace** a shape/ an outline/ the line/ the contours

shape [C, U] the form of the outer edges or surfaces of sth; an example of sth that has a particular form; a person or thing that is difficult to see clearly: *The building has a rectangular shape.* ◇ *The pool was* **in the shape of** *a heart.* ◇ *The island was originally circular in shape.* ◇ *Candles come in* **all shapes and sizes**. ◇ *You can recognize the fish by the shape of their fins.* ◇ *This old T-shirt has completely lost its shape.*

figure [C] the shape of a person seen from a distance or not clearly: *There before him stood a tall figure in black.* See also **figure** → BODY 1

form [C] the shape of sb/sth; a person or thing of which only the shape can be seen: *Her slender form and graceful movements entranced him.* ◇ *The human form has changed little over the last 30 000 years.* ◇ *They made out a shadowy form in front of them.* See also **form** → FORM *noun* 1

shadow [C] a dark shape that sb/sth's form makes on a surface, for example on the ground, when they are between the light and the surface: *The children were having fun, chasing each other's shadows.* ◇ *The ship's sail* **cast a shadow** *on the water.* ◇ *The shadows lengthened as the sun went down.* See also **shadow** → DARKNESS

outline /'aʊtlaɪn/ [C] the line that goes around the edge of sth, showing its main shape but not the details: *At last we could see the dim outline of an island.* See also **outline** → SUMMARY

profile /'prəʊfaɪl; *AmE* 'proʊ-/ [C] the outline of a person's face when you look from the side, not the front: *He turned his head so his strong profile was facing the camera.* ◇ *The portrait shows her in profile.*

silhouette /ˌsɪlu'et/ [C, U] the dark outline or shape of a person or object that you see against a light background; the shape of a person's body or an object: *The trees were black silhouettes against the pale sky.* ◇ *The mountains stood out in silhouette.* ◇ *The dress is fitted to give you a flattering silhouette.*

line [C] the edge, outline or shape of sth, especially sth that has been designed or created: *With its sleek lines and powerful engine, the XK8 is the definition of a luxury sports car.* ◇ *He traced the line of her jaw with his finger.*

contour /'kɒntʊə(r); *AmE* 'kɑːntʊr/ [C] (*written*) the outer edges of sth; the outline of its shape or form: *The road follows the natural contours of the coastline.*

shape *verb*

shape · form · carve · fashion · mould · sculpt · cast
These words all mean to make sth into a particular shape or from a particular substance.

▶ to shape/ form/ carve/ fashion/ mould/ sculpt sth **into** sth
▶ to shape/ form/ carve/ fashion/ mould/ sculpt/ cast sth **from/ out of** sth
▶ to carve/ fashion/ mould/ sculpt/ cast sth **in** sth
▶ to shape/ carve/ fashion/ sculpt **wood**
▶ to shape/ fashion/ mould/ sculpt **clay**
▶ to carve/ sculpt **stone/ marble**

shape [T] to make sth into a particular shape: *Shape the dough into balls.* ◇ *This tool is used for shaping wood.*

form [T, often passive] to produce a particular shape; to make sth into a particular shape: *Bend the wire so that it forms a 'V'.* ◇ *Games can help children learn to form letters.* See also **form** → MAKE 1

carve [T, I] to make objects or patterns, etc. by cutting away material from wood or stone: *The beads were carved from solid ivory.* ◇ *She carves in both stone and wood.*

fashion [T] (*rather formal, written*) to make or shape sth, especially with your hands: *She fashioned a pot from the clay.* ◇ *She fashioned the clay into a pot.*

mould (*BrE*) (*AmE* **mold**) [T] to shape a soft substance into a particular form or object by pressing it or putting it into a shaped container (= a mould): *First, mould the clay into the desired shape.* ◇ *The figure had been moulded in clay.*

sculpt [T, usually passive] to make figures or objects by carving or shaping wood, stone, clay, metal, etc: *a display of animals sculpted in ice* ◇ *The figures were sculpted from single blocks of marble.* See also **sculptor** → ARTIST

cast [T] to shape hot liquid metal or a similar substance by pouring it into a shaped container (= a mould) and letting it cool: *a statue cast in bronze*

share *noun*

share · quota · allocation · commission · allowance · ration · cut · percentage
These are all words for an amount of sth which is given to sb/sth.

▶ a share/ quota/ allocation/ allowance/ ration/ cut/ percentage **of** sth
▶ a **full** share/ quota/ allocation/ commission/ allowance/ ration
▶ a **large** share/ quota/ allocation/ commission
▶ a **small** share/ quota/ allocation/ commission/ percentage
▶ an **annual** quota/ allocation/ allowance
▶ a **fixed** share/ quota/ commission/ percentage
▶ to **get** your share/ your quota/ an allocation/ a commission/ a cut/ a percentage
▶ to **receive** a share/ an allocation/ a commission/ a percentage
▶ to **take** a share/ commission/ cut/ percentage
▶ to **have** your share/ quota/ ration
▶ to **be entitled to** a share/ an allocation/ a commission

share [C, usually sing.] one part of sth that is divided between two or more people; a part that sb has in a particular activity that involves several people; an amount of sth that is thought to be normal or acceptable for one person: *How much was your share of the winnings?* ◇ *Next year we hope to have a bigger share of the market.* ◇ *I'm hoping for a* **share in** *the profits.* ◇ *We all* **did our share** *of the work.* ◇ *Everyone must accept their share of the blame.* See also **share** → JOIN

quota /'kwəʊtə; *AmE* 'kwoʊtə/ [C] the limited number of people or things that is officially allowed; an amount of sth that sb expects or needs to have or achieve: *They are bringing in a quota system for accepting refugees.* ◇ *The show is good fun and yields its full quota of laughs.*

allocation /ˌæləˈkeɪʃn/ [C] an amount of sth, especially money, that is given to sb for a particular purpose: *We have spent our entire allocation for the year.* See also **allocate** → ALLOCATE

commission /kəˈmɪʃn/ [U, C] an amount of money that is paid to sb for selling goods, which increases with the value of goods that are sold; an amount of money that is charged, for example by a bank, for providing a particular service: *In this job you work* **on commission** (= are paid according to the amount you sell). ◇ *You get a 10%* **commission on** *everything you sell.* ◇ *One per cent commission is charged for cashing traveller's cheques.*

allowance /əˈlaʊəns/ [C] the amount of sth that is allowed in a particular situation: *There is a maximum* **baggage allowance** *of 20 kilos.*

ration /'ræʃn/ [C] a fixed amount of sth, especially food, that you are officially allowed to have when there is not enough for everyone to have as much as they want, for example during a war: *I gave him my butter ration at breakfast one morning.* ◇ *a ration book/card/coupon* (= allowing you to claim a ration of sth) ❶ A **ration** [sing.] is also an amount of sth that is thought to be normal or acceptable for one person: *As part of the diet, allow yourself a small daily ration of sugar.* See also **rations** → SUPPLIES

▶ **ration** *verb* [T, often passive]: *Eggs were rationed during the war.* ◇ *The villagers are* **rationed to** *two litres of water a day.*

NOTE SHARE, QUOTA OR RATION? These words can all be used to mean 'an amount of sth that is thought to be normal or acceptable for one person'. **Share** and **quota** can both be used to talk about pleasant or unpleasant things such as *luck, laughs, work* or *blame*. **Share** is much more frequent; **quota** is only used in this meaning in more formal or written language. **Ration** is used to talk about food, or about sth nice that you must not have or expect too much of.

cut [C, usually sing.] (*rather informal*) a share in sth, especially the profits of sth: *They were rewarded with a cut of 5% from the profits.* ◇ *There wasn't much left after his agents took their cut.*

percentage /pə'sentɪdʒ; AmE pər's-/ [C, usually sing.] a share of the profits of sth: *He gets a percentage for every car sold.*

NOTE CUT OR PERCENTAGE? **Percentage** is used especially in a situation where money is paid to sb for doing a job, for example to an employee. **Cut** is used more often if people divide a total sum of money among themselves. If the percentage figure is given, the word **cut** is used: *Our manager gets a cut of 10%.* ◇ *Our manager gets a percentage of 10%.*

share verb

share · divide · split · pool · carve sth up
These words all mean to separate sth into parts or to collect things together so that different people can have a part of it or can use it.

PATTERNS AND COLLOCATIONS
▸ to share sth / divide sth / split sth / carve sth up **between** / **among** different people
▸ to share / split / pool sth **with** sb
▸ to share / divide / split the **money** / **work**
▸ to share / divide the **spoils** / **booty**
▸ to divide / split your **time**
▸ to share / divide / split sth **equally** / **evenly**

share [T, I] to have or use sth at the same time as sb else; to give some of what you have to sb else or let sb use sth that is yours; to separate sth into parts so that two or more people can have a part of it: *She shares a house with three other students.* ◇ *There isn't an empty table. Would you mind sharing?* ◇ *Tom shared his chocolate with the other kids.* ◇ *The conference is a good place to share information and exchange ideas.* ◇ *The old man* **shared** *his money* **out** *among his six grandchildren.*

divide [T] to separate and share sth; to use different parts of sth for different activities or purposes: *The story is about a father who divides his property among his sons.* ◇ *Jen* **divided up** *the rest of the cash.* ◇ *He divides his energies between politics and business.* See also **division** → DIVISION 1

split [T] (*rather informal*) to separate and share sth between different people, things or places: *She split the money she won with her brother.* ◇ *Four of us live here and we* **split** *all the bills* **four ways***.* ◇ *His time is split between the London and Paris offices.* See also **split** → DIVISION 1

NOTE SHARE, DIVIDE OR SPLIT? Things can be **shared** between people; things can be **divided** between people, uses or places or **split** between people, things or places. **Divide** is often used to talk about things that are considered very important, such as land and large amounts of money. Use **share** to talk about things that are not so important: *He shared his sweets out among his four friends.* ◇ *He divided his sweets among his four friends.* **Split** is used in less formal contexts to talk about money, time or work.

pool [T] to collect money, information, etc. from different people so that it can be used by all of them: *The students work individually, then pool their ideas in groups of six.* ◇ *Police forces across the country are pooling resources in*

order to solve this crime. ❶ People **pool** things in order to increase their chance of success in a particular shared aim. Common collocates are connected with money (for example *funds*), information (*knowledge, ideas, results*) and other useful or desirable things (*talent, efforts, resources*, etc.). See also **pool** → SUPPLY noun

carve sth 'up phrasal verb (*disapproving*) to divide sth such as a company or an area of land into smaller parts in order to share it among a small group of people, companies or countries, and not let those outside the group have any: *They have been accused of carving up the industry for their own benefit.* ◇ *The territory was carved up by the colonizing powers.*

sharp

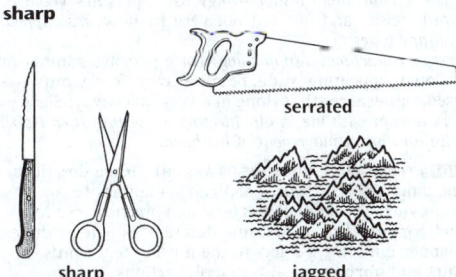

serrated

sharp   jagged

sharp adj.

1 a sharp knife
2 a sharp tongue

1 **sharp · jagged · serrated**
These words all describe sth that has a very fine edge or point that cuts well, or that can make holes.

PATTERNS AND COLLOCATIONS
▸ a sharp / jagged / serrated **edge**
▸ a sharp / serrated **blade** / **knife**
▸ a sharp / jagged **rock**
▸ sharp / jagged **teeth**

sharp having a fine edge or point, especially of sth that can cut or make a hole in sth: *You'll need a really sharp knife for this job.* ◇ *Careful — the kittens have* **razor-sharp** *teeth.* **OPP** **blunt** ❶ A **blunt** knife or object does not have a sharp edge or point: *This pencil's blunt!* ◇ *The police said he had been hit with a* **blunt instrument***.*

jagged /'dʒægɪd/ with rough, pointed, often sharp edges: *It is a stark landscape of black, jagged peaks.* ◇ *The floor was covered with jagged pieces of glass from smashed bottles.* ❶ Typical collocates of **jagged** are *edge, glass, knife, mountain, peak, rocks* and *teeth*.

serrated /sə'reɪtɪd/ having a series of sharp points on the edge like a saw (= a tool used for cutting wood or metal): *Use a knife with a serrated edge for cutting bread.*

2 See also the entry for SHORT 3
sharp · terse · curt · brusque · clipped · abrupt
These words all describe speaking in an unfriendly way and/or using few words.

PATTERNS AND COLLOCATIONS
▸ sharp / curt / brusque / abrupt **with** sb
▸ a sharp / terse / curt / brusque / clipped **voice**
▸ a sharp / curt / brusque / clipped **tone**
▸ a sharp / terse / curt **reply**
▸ a curt / a brusque / an abrupt **manner**
▸ **rather** sharp / curt / brusque / abrupt

sharp (*usually disapproving*) (of a person or what they say) critical or harsh: *sharp criticism* ◇ *He was very sharp with me when I was late.* ◇ *Emma has a* **sharp tongue** (she often speaks in a harsh or unkind way).
▸ **sharply** adv.: *'Is there a problem?' he asked sharply.*

terse (*sometimes disapproving*) (of sb's speech or writing) using few words and often not seeming polite or friendly: *The President issued a terse statement denying the charges.*

curt (*usually disapproving*) (of a person's manner, actions or writing) appearing rude because very few words are used, or because sth is done in a very quick way: *She dismissed him with a curt nod of the head.* ◇ *She ignored the curt order.* ◇ *A curt note of rejection arrived from the company director.*

brusque /bruːsk; brʊsk; *AmE* brʌsk/ (*usually disapproving*) (of a person or what they say) using very few words and sounding rude: *I'm sorry if I was a bit brusque with you.*

clipped (*sometimes disapproving*) (of a person's voice or words) clear and fast but not very friendly: *his clipped, military tones*

abrupt (*sometimes disapproving*) (of a person's manner or actions) appearing rude because very few words are used, or because sth is done in a very quick way: *She was very abrupt with me in our meeting.* ◇ *He indicated Isabel with an abrupt movement of his head.*

NOTE TERSE, CURT, BRUSQUE OR ABRUPT? **Terse** describes the language sb/sth uses and can sometimes be approving: *The manual was terse and practical.* ◇ *a terse and gripping thriller.* **Brusque** describes people or their manner but always refers to them using few words. **Curt** and **abrupt** can also describe actions: *a curt/abrupt nod/gesture.* **Terse** and **curt** can be used for written words as well as speech: *a terse/curt letter of dismissal*

---

shed *noun* See also the entries for HUT and WAREHOUSE

shed · barn · stable · outbuilding
These are all words for a building used for keeping tools, equipment or animals in.

shed [C] a small simple building, usually built of wood or metal, used for keeping things in: *a tool shed* ◇ (*BrE*) *a garden shed.* ❶ In British English **shed** can also mean a large industrial building that is used for working in or keeping equipment in: *The engine shed is used for storing and servicing the locomotives.*

barn [C] a large farm building for storing grain or keeping animals in: *The bales were stacked up high in the hay barn.* ◇ *They live in a converted barn* (= a barn that has been turned into a house).

stable [C] a building in which horses are kept: *The horse was led back to its stable.*

outbuilding /ˈaʊtbɪldɪŋ/ [C, usually pl.] a building such as a shed or stable that is built near to, but separate from, a main building: *It's a large farmhouse with several outbuildings.*

---

shelter *noun*

shelter · asylum · safety · cover · refuge · sanctuary
These words all mean a place where sb/sth can find protection from sb/sth.

PATTERNS AND COLLOCATIONS
▶ shelter / asylum / refuge / sanctuary **from** sth
▶ **temporary** shelter / asylum / refuge / sanctuary
▶ to **seek / find** shelter / asylum / refuge / sanctuary
▶ to **take** cover / refuge / sanctuary
▶ to **run for** shelter / cover
▶ a **place of** safety / refuge / sanctuary

shelter [U] the fact of having a place to live or stay, considered as a basic human need; protection from the weather, danger or attack: *They were anxious to find shelter for the night.* ◇ *He took shelter from the rain under a bridge.* ◇ *The fox ran for the shelter of the trees.* See also **shelter** → HUT *noun*, **shelter** → REFUGE *noun*, **shelter** → PROTECT *verb*

asylum /əˈsaɪləm/ [U] protection that a government gives to people who have left their own country, usually because they were in danger for political reasons: *She was granted **political asylum** by Canada in 2003.* See also **asylum seeker** → REFUGEE

safety [U] a place where you are not in danger: *I managed to swim **to safety**.* ◇ *We watched the lions **from the safety** of the car.* See also **safe** → SAFE 1

cover [U] a place that provides shelter from bad weather or protection from an attack: *After the explosion the street was full of people running for cover.*

refuge /ˈrefjuːdʒ/ [U] shelter or protection from danger, trouble or problems: *A further 300 people have taken refuge in the embassy.* ◇ *As the situation at home got worse she increasingly **took refuge in** her work.* See also **refuge** → REFUGEE, **refugee** → REFUGEE

sanctuary /ˈsæŋktʃuəri; *AmE* -ueri/ [U] (*formal*) safety and protection, especially for people who are being chased or attacked: *During the uprising the royal family took sanctuary in an abbey.* See also **sanctuary** → REFUGE

---

shine *verb*

shine · gleam · glow · sparkle · glisten · shimmer · glitter · twinkle · glint
These words all mean to produce or reflect light.

PATTERNS AND COLLOCATIONS
▶ to shine / gleam / sparkle / glisten / shimmer / glitter / glint **on** sth
▶ to shine / gleam / glow / sparkle / glisten / shimmer / glitter / twinkle / glint **with** sth
▶ to shine / gleam / sparkle / glisten / shimmer / glitter / glint **in the sunlight**
▶ to shine / gleam / glisten / shimmer / glitter / glint **in the moonlight**
▶ to shine / gleam / glow / glitter / twinkle **in the dark**
▶ a **light** shines / gleams / glows
▶ the **stars** shine / glitter / twinkle
▶ sb's **eyes** shine / gleam / glow / sparkle / glisten / glitter / twinkle / glint
▶ the **water / river / sea** gleams / sparkles / glistens / shimmers / glitters
▶ to shine / gleam / glow / glitter **brightly**
▶ to shine / gleam / glow / shimmer **softly**
▶ to shine / gleam / glow **faintly**

shine [I] to produce or reflect light, especially brightly: *The sun was shining and the sky was blue.* ◇ *They could see a faint light shining in the distance.* ◇ *The polished wood shone like glass.* ◇ *Their faces shone white in the moonlight.*
▶ **shine** *noun* [sing., U]: *Use a buffer to bring a natural shine to your nails.* ◇ *the shine of the polished wood*
▶ **shiny** *adj.*: *A shiny red car was parked in the drive.* ◇ *His face was red and shiny.*

gleam [I] to shine with a clear bright or pale light, especially a reflected light: *Moonlight gleamed on the water.* ◇ *The house was gleaming with fresh white paint.* ◇ *Laughter gleamed in his eyes.*
▶ **gleam** *noun* [C, usually sing.]: *We could see the gleam of moonlight on the water.*

glow [I] (often of sth hot or warm) to produce a dull steady light: *The embers still glowed in the hearth.* ◇ *He has a watch that glows in the dark.*
▶ **glow** *noun* [sing.]: *Now the city was just a red glow on the horizon.*

sparkle [I] to shine brightly with small flashes of light: *Her necklace sparkled in the candlelight.* ◇ *Her eyes sparkled with excitement.*
▶ **sparkle** *noun* [C, U]: *the sparkle of light on the water*

glisten /ˈɡlɪsn/ [I] (of sth wet) to shine: *Her eyes were glistening with tears.* ◇ *Sweat glistened on his forehead.*

shimmer [I] (*written*) to shine with a soft light that seems to shake slightly: *Everything seemed to shimmer in the heat.*
▶ **shimmer** *noun* [sing., U]: *the shimmer of silk in the candlelight*

glitter [I] to shine brightly with a lot of small flashes of reflected light: *The water glittered in the sunlight.*
▸ **glitter** *noun* [sing.]: *the glitter of diamonds*

> **NOTE** SPARKLE OR GLITTER? There is very little difference in meaning between these two words. **Glitter** is nearly always used to talk about light reflected off a surface, that is always moving and changing, and can sometimes suggest a lack of depth, especially when it is used figuratively as a noun: (*figurative*) *the superficial glitter of show business*. **Sparkle** is also often used to talk about light reflected off a surface, but things that produce light can also sparkle: *Stars sparkled in the sky.*

twinkle [I] to shine with a light that changes rapidly from bright to faint to bright again: *Stars twinkled in the sky.* ◇ *His eyes twinkled with laughter.*

glint [I] to give small bright flashes of reflected light: *A flash of a blade glinted in the darkness.* ◇ *Amusement glinted in his eyes.*
▸ **glint** *noun* [sing.]: *He saw the glint of a knife and froze.* ◇ *There was a glint of admiration in her eyes.*

shiver *noun* See the Topic Map for HEALTH on p.890

shiver · tremor · twitch · tremble · shudder · spasm · convulsion · tic · shaking · quiver
These are all words for a continuous or sudden shaking movement or feeling, especially one that you cannot control.

PATTERNS AND COLLOCATIONS
▸ a **slight** shiver / tremor / twitch / tremble / shudder / spasm / convulsion / quiver
▸ a **little** shiver / tremor / shudder / spasm / quiver
▸ a **small** shiver / tremor / shudder / spasm
▸ a **faint** tremor / tremble / shudder / quiver
▸ a **violent** tremor / shudder / spasm / convulsion
▸ a **nervous** tremor / twitch / tic
▸ to **cause** a shiver / tremor / shudder / spasm / convulsion
▸ to **feel** a shiver / tremor / twitch / tremble / shudder / spasm / quiver
▸ to **send** a shiver / tremor / shudder / spasm / quiver down, through, etc. sth
▸ to **have** a tremor / a twitch / convulsions / a tic
▸ a shiver / tremor / shudder / quiver **goes** / **runs through** sb / sth

shiver /ˈʃɪvə(r)/ [C] a sudden shaking movement of your body because you are cold, ill, frightened or excited: *She gave a little shiver as she walked into the cold room.* ◇ *He felt a cold shiver of fear run through him.* ◇ *The sound sent shivers down her spine* (= was very frightening). See also **shiver** → SHAKE *verb* 3

tremor /ˈtremə(r)/ [C, U] a slight shaking movement in a part of your body, caused by sth such as cold or fear: *An uncontrollable tremor shook his mouth.* ◇ *She could hear the tremor in his voice* (= his voice was shaking with emotion). ◇ (*technical*) *Large doses of the drug produce tremor and rigidity.*

twitch [C] a sudden quick movement in one of your muscles that you cannot control; a sudden quick movement or feeling: *He has a nervous twitch in his cheek.* ◇ *I felt a twitch of anxiety.* ❶ A person usually has a **twitch** in part of the face such as the eye or lips. See also **twitch** → SHAKE *verb* 3

tremble /ˈtrembl/ [C, usually sing.] a slight shaking movement or feeling that you cannot control, especially caused by being very nervous, excited or frightened: *The only sign of fear was a slight tremble in his legs.* See also **tremble** → SHAKE *verb* 3

shudder [C, usually sing.] a sudden shaking movement that you make because you are cold, frightened or disgusted: *a shudder of fear* ◇ *She gave an involuntary shudder.* See also **shudder** → SHAKE 3

spasm /ˈspæzəm/ [C, U] (*rather formal*) a sudden and often painful tightening of a muscle, that you cannot control: *Cholera reduces heartbeat and causes muscle spasms.* ◇ *The injection sent his leg into spasm.*

convulsion /kənˈvʌlʃn/ [C, usually pl.] (*formal*) a sudden strong shaking movement of the body that you cannot control: *The child went into convulsions.* ◇ *She started to have convulsions again.* See also **convulse** → SHAKE *verb* 3

tic /tɪk/ [C] a sudden small quick movement of a muscle, especially in the face or head, that you cannot control: *He has a nervous tic around his left eye.*

shaking [U] short quick movements of your body that you cannot control, for example because you are frightened or cold: *The shaking got less as the boy calmed down.* See also **shake** → SHAKE *verb* 3

quiver /ˈkwɪvə(r)/ [C] (*especially written*) a slight shaking movement in your body or voice, often caused by a strong emotion: *He felt a quiver of anticipation run through him.* ◇ *She couldn't help the quiver in her voice.*

shock *noun*

1 a feeling of shock
2 It came as a shock.

1 shock · horror · dismay
These are all words for the feeling you have when you receive an unpleasant surprise.

| dismay | shock | horror |

PATTERNS AND COLLOCATIONS
▸ shock / horror / dismay **at** sth
▸ **in** / **with** shock / horror / dismay
▸ **to sb's** horror / dismay
▸ **to fill sb with** horror / dismay

shock [U] a sudden feeling that you have as a result of sth unexpected happening: *He's still in shock.* ◇ *The team suffered a shock defeat in the first round.* ❶ **Shock** is usually unpleasant, but it does not have to be: *Since winning the competition, we've all been a state of shock.*

horror [U] a feeling of great shock, fear or disgust: *She recoiled in horror at the sight.* ◇ *His eyes were wide with horror.* ◇ *There was a terrible look of horror on his face.*

dismay /dɪsˈmeɪ/ [U] a worried, disappointed feeling you get when you receive an unpleasant surprise: *She could not hide her dismay at the result.* ◇ *I felt a jolt of dismay.* See also **dismayed** → UPSET

2 shock · scare · fright
These are all words for a thing or event that causes a sudden feeling of fear.

PATTERNS AND COLLOCATIONS
▸ to **get** / **have** a shock / scare / fright
▸ to **give sb** a shock / scare / fright

shock [C] an unexpected event that causes a sudden feeling, especially an unpleasant one: *The news of his death came as a shock to us all.* ◇ (*informal*) *If you think it'll be easy, you're in for a shock!*

scare [C] a situation in which a lot of people are anxious or frightened about sth; something that causes you to be suddenly worried or frightened about sth: *There was a bomb scare at the airport.* ◇ *recent scares about pesticides in food* ◇ *Les had a health scare two years ago and was ordered to cut down on drinking.*

fright [usually sing., C] an experience that makes you feel afraid: *Did I give you a fright? Sorry.* ❶ In this meaning **fright** is usually used in the patterns *to give sb a fright* and *to have a fright*. See also **fright** → FEAR *noun*

shock *verb*

shock · appal · horrify · disgust · rock · scandalize · sicken · repel · dismay
These words all mean to surprise and upset sb very much.

shock   disgust   appal
rock   horrify
scandalize   sicken
repel
dismay

▸ shocked/appalled/horrified/disgusted/scandalized/dismayed at sb/sth
▸ to shock/appal/horrify/disgust/scandalize sb that...
▸ to shock/appal/horrify/disgust/scandalize/sicken/dismay sb to think/see/hear/find/learn...
▸ It shocks/appals/horrifies/disgusts/sickens me that...
▸ a **thought** shocks/appals/horrifies/sickens sb
▸ an **idea** shocks/appals/horrifies/disgusts sb
▸ sb's **behaviour** shocks/appals/scandalizes sb
▸ **violence** shocks/appals/horrifies/disgusts sb
▸ **deeply** shocked/disgusted/dismayed

shock [T, often passive] (not used in the progressive tenses) to surprise sb, usually in a way that upsets them: *It shocks you when something like that happens.* ◇ *We were all shocked at the news of his death.* ◇ *I was shocked to hear that he had resigned.* See also **shock** → OFFEND
▸ **shocked** adj.: *I was deeply shocked when she told me what had happened.*

appal (*BrE*) (*AmE* **appall**) /əˈpɔːl/ (-ll-) [T] (not used in the progressive tenses) to shock and upset sb very much: *The brutality of the crime has appalled the public.* ◇ *It appalled me that they could simply ignore the problem.*
▸ **appalled** adj.: *We watched appalled as the child ran in front of the car.*

horrify /ˈhɒrɪfaɪ; *AmE* ˈhɔːr-; ˈhɑːr-/ [T] (not used in the progressive tenses) to make sb feel extremely shocked, upset or frightened: *The whole country was horrified by the killings.*
▸ **horrified** adj.: *She stared at him in horrified disbelief.*

disgust [T] (not used in the progressive tenses) to make sb feel shocked and almost ill because sth is so unpleasant: *The level of violence in the film really disgusted me.* ◇ *The feel of it, all cold and slimy, disgusted him.* See also **disgusting** → DISGUSTING 1, **disgusting** → DISGUSTING 2

rock [T, often passive] (*rather informal*) to shock sb, especially a country or community, especially in a way that makes sb/sth's position in the country or community less strong or certain: *The country was rocked by a series of political scandals.* ◇ *The news rocked the world.*

scandalize (*BrE* also **-ise**) /ˈskændəlaɪz/ [T] to do sth that people find very shocking: *She scandalized her family with her extravagant lifestyle.*

sicken [T] (not used in the progressive tenses) (*BrE*) to disgust sb very much: *The public is becoming sickened by these continual images of violence and death.*

repel /rɪˈpel/ (-ll-) [T, often passive] (not used in the progressive tenses) (*rather formal*) to make sb feel rather disgusted: *I was repelled by the smell of drink on his breath.* ◇ *Her heartlessness repelled him.* **OPP attract** → INTEREST, See also **repulsive** → DISGUSTING 1

dismay /dɪsˈmeɪ/ [T, often passive] to make sb feel shocked and disappointed: *Their reaction dismayed him.* ◇ *He was dismayed at the change in his old friend.* ◇ *They were dismayed to find that the ferry had already left.* ❶ Dismay is used to talk about a reaction to a situation or to sb's behaviour or actions: *I was dismayed to find that he was still there when I arrived home.* ◇ *He dismayed me.* See also **dismayed** → UPSET

shoot *verb* See also the entry for KILL

shoot · fire · open fire · launch
These words all mean to use a gun or to send a weapon from somewhere, for example a ship.

▸ to shoot/fire **at** sb/sth
▸ to fire/open fire **on** sb/sth
▸ to shoot/fire **wide/back**

▸ to shoot/fire **blanks/bullets/arrows**
▸ to fire/launch a **missile/torpedo**
▸ a **gun** shoots/fires

shoot [I, T] to use a gun or bow and arrow; (of a gun, etc.) to shoot bullets or arrows; to kill or wound a person or animal by shooting at them: *Don't shoot – I surrender.* ◇ *The police rarely shoot to kill* (= try to kill the people they shoot at). ◇ *Does this gun actually shoot?* ◇ *This is just a toy gun – it doesn't shoot real bullets.* ◇ *A man was shot in the leg.* ◇ *He shot himself during a fit of depression.* ◇ *Three people were shot dead during the robbery.* ❶ In British English you can *shoot bullets/arrows* but you cannot 'shoot a gun' or larger weapons such as missiles: *He shot his gun into the air.* ◇ *Missiles were shot at the enemy.* It is possible to use shoot in this way in American English: (*AmE*) *Have you ever shot a gun before?*

fire [I, T] to shoot bullets from a gun; to shoot an arrow or missile into the sky or through water; (of a gun) to shoot bullets: *The officer ordered his men to fire.* ◇ *Soldiers fired on the crowd, killing several people.* ◇ *He fired the gun into the air.* ◇ *They ran away as soon as the first shot was fired.* ◇ *We heard the sound of guns firing.*

open 'fire idiom to start firing shots from a gun: *The gunmen opened fire on the police.*

launch /lɔːntʃ/ [T] to send a weapon such as a missile into the sky or through water: *The ship was hit by three torpedoes launched from the enemy submarine.*

shop *noun*

shop · store · supermarket · grocery store · outlet · boutique · salon
These are all words for a place where goods or services are sold.

▸ a **large** shop/store/supermarket/grocery store/outlet/salon
▸ a **small** shop/store/supermarket/grocery store/outlet/boutique/salon
▸ a **big/local** shop/store/supermarket/grocery store/outlet/salon
▸ a **specialist** shop/store/outlet/boutique
▸ an **expensive/exclusive** shop/store/boutique/salon
▸ a shop/a store/a supermarket/a grocery store/an outlet/a boutique **sells** sth
▸ a shop/a store/a supermarket/a grocery store/an outlet/a salon **offers** sth
▸ to **open** a shop/a store/a supermarket/a grocery store/an outlet/a boutique/a salon
▸ to **own/have** a shop/a store/a supermarket/a grocery store/an outlet/a boutique/a salon
▸ to **manage** a shop/a store/a supermarket/a grocery store/an outlet/a salon

shop [C] (*especially BrE*) a building or part of a building where you can buy goods or services: *a pet/gift shop* ◇ (*BrE*) *The local corner shop stays open until midnight.*

store [C] a shop: *a health food/liquor store* ◇ *a department store* ◇ *a general store* (= a shop that sells a wide variety of goods). ◇ *These small towns are dominated by chain stores* (= that belong to a series of similar stores owned by the same company).

NOTE SHOP OR STORE? The usual word in British English is **shop**; in American English it is **store**: (*BrE*) *I'm just going down to the shops.* ◇ (*AmE*) *I'm going to the store.* **Store** is used in British English to talk about a large shop, especially one that sells many different types of goods: *a department store*; it is also used in business English, journalism and advertising: *The chain has endured another terrible month at its high-street stores.* ◇ *Ask at your local hardware store.* In American English, **shop** is only used to talk about small, specialist shops, especially ones that sell expensive or luxury goods: *a/an gift/flower/antique shop*

supermarket [C] a large shop that sells food, drinks and goods used in the home. People choose what they want from the shelves and pay for it as they leave: *More and more of us are doing all our shopping in supermarkets.* ◇ *An increasing amount of organic produce is to be found on supermarket shelves.*

'grocery store /ˈɡrəʊsəri; *AmE* ˈɡroʊ-/ (*AmE*) [C] a shop that sells food and other things used in the home: *Do you know where I could find a grocery store?* ◇ *Sales at grocery stores fell 0.3% in April.*

NOTE SUPERMARKET OR GROCERY STORE? In American English a **supermarket** is often called a **grocery store**; however, a **grocery store** does not have to be a **supermarket**, because it may be a small or local shop that is not owned by a large company. In British English a **grocer's** or **grocer's shop** is an old-fashioned type of food shop where customers do not just choose what they want from the shelves, but have to ask for it, but this type of shop hardly exists any more.

outlet /ˈaʊtlet/ [C] (*business*) a shop or organization that sells goods made by a particular company or of a particular type: *The business has 34 retail outlets in this state alone.* ◇ *a fast-food/pizza outlet* ❶ In American English an **outlet** is also a store that sells goods of a particular make at reduced prices: *the Nike store in the outlet mall*

boutique /buːˈtiːk/ [C] a small shop that sells fashionable clothes or expensive gifts: *The city has a lot of smart restaurants and chic boutiques.*

salon /ˈsælɒn; *AmE* səˈlɑːn/ [C] (especially in compounds) a shop that gives customers hair or beauty treatment: *a beauty/hairdressing salon*

short *adj.*

1 a short time/book/memory
2 short people/legs
3 the short answer to your query

1 See also the entry for QUICK

short · temporary · brief · short-lived · fleeting · momentary · passing

These words all describe sth that lasts for a small amount of time.

PATTERNS AND COLLOCATIONS
▸ a short/ brief/ fleeting/ passing **moment**
▸ a short/ temporary/ brief **stay**
▸ a short/ brief/ fleeting **visit**
▸ a short/ brief/ momentary **silence/ pause**
▸ a temporary/ short-lived/ momentary/ passing **interest**
▸ a temporary/ brief/ short-lived **success**
▸ a brief/ fleeting/ momentary/ passing **glance/ glimpse**
▸ a brief/ fleeting/ momentary **look/ smile**
▸ a brief/ fleeting/ passing **reference**
▸ **very/ relatively** short/ temporary/ brief/ short-lived
▸ **only** temporary/ brief/ fleeting/ momentary

short lasting or taking a small amount of time or less time than usual: *I'm going to France next week for a short break.* ◇ *Which is the shortest day of the year?* ◇ *It's quite a short book* (= that takes a short time to read). ◇ *She has a very short memory* (= remembers only things that have happened recently). ❶ **Short** is also used before a noun to describe a period of time that seems to have passed very quickly: *Just two short years ago he was the best player in the country.* **OPP long** → LONG, See also **shorten** → SHRINK

temporary lasting or intended to last for only a short time: *25 000 households are living in temporary accommodation.* ◇ *The job's only temporary, while their secretary's on maternity leave.* ◇ *More than half the employees are temporary.* **OPP permanent** → PERMANENT
▸ **temporarily** /ˈtemprərəli; *AmE* ˌtempəˈrerəli/ *adv.*: *We regret that this service is temporarily unavailable.* **OPP permanently** → PERMANENT adj.

brief /briːf/ (*especially written*) lasting for only a short time: *The prime minister is due to make a brief visit to South Korea.* ◇ *Sean gave a brief glance at the screen.* ◇ *There was a brief silence after I made my announcement.* ◇ *Mozart's life was brief.* **OPP long** → LONG
▸ **briefly** *adv.*: *He had spoken to Emma only briefly.*

NOTE SHORT OR BRIEF? **Short** is used more often than **brief** in informal and spoken English: ~~I'm going to France for a brief break.~~ ◇ *The Dutch prime minister is making a short/brief visit.* **Short**, but NOT **brief** is used to describe books, lists, projects, etc. that take only a short time to read/deal with/complete. **Brief** is used more frequently than **short** to describe a *look, glance, glimpse, smile* or *sigh*.

short-'lived (especially of sth good or pleasant) lasting for only a short time: *The benefits are likely to be short-lived.* ◇ *It was a very short-lived government.* ◇ *The stars enjoyed an intense but short-lived romance.* **OPP long-lasting** → LONG, **lasting, enduring** → PERMANENT

fleeting [usually before noun] (*written*) (especially of sth good or pleasant) lasting for only a very short time: *A fleeting smile touched his lips.* ◇ *Alone on deck, I experienced a fleeting moment of happiness.*
▸ **fleetingly** *adv.*: *She smiled fleetingly.*

NOTE SHORT-LIVED OR FLEETING? Both **short-lived** and **fleeting** are used especially to talk about good or pleasant things that last only a short time. **Fleeting** is a more literary word than **short-lived** and usually describes even shorter actions or experiences; although it describes pleasant things it can create a feeling of sadness because the thing lasts such a short time.

momentary /ˈməʊməntri; *AmE* ˈmoʊmənteri/ (*especially written*) lasting for only a very short time: *There was a momentary flicker of pain in his face.* ◇ *The accident was the result of a momentary lapse of concentration.* ❶ **Momentary** is used especially to describe moments of doubt or failure and collocates include *doubt, hesitation, pause, silence, confusion, unease, panic, lapse* and *aberration*.

passing [only before noun] lasting for only a short time: *My son is very jealous at the moment, but I think it's just a passing phase.* ◇ *He makes only a passing reference to the theory in his book.* ❶ **Passing** is used especially to describe periods of time, references to sth and periods of being interested in sth. Collocates include *phase, fashion, fad, craze, interest, mention* and *reference*.

2 **short · diminutive · petite · stubby · stunted · dumpy**

These words all describe sb who is not as tall as an average person or a part of the body that is smaller than usual.

PATTERNS AND COLLOCATIONS
▸ a short/ diminutive/ petite/ dumpy **woman**
▸ a short/ diminutive **man**
▸ a short/ petite/ dumpy **girl**
▸ a short/ diminutive/ petite/ dumpy **figure**

short (of a person) small in height; (of a part of the body) not as long as normal: *He was a short, fat little man.* ◇ *I'm slightly shorter than you.* ◇ *The little boy ran as fast as his short legs could carry him.* **OPP tall** → TALL, **long** → LENGTH

diminutive /dɪˈmɪnjətɪv/ (*formal*) (especially of a person) very small: *She was a diminutive figure beside her husband.*

petite /pəˈtiːt/ (*approving*) (of a girl, a woman, or her figure) small and thin in an attractive way: *She was fair-haired and petite.* ◇ *With her slim, petite figure, she could have been any age from 13 to 30.*

stubby (often of a part of the body, for example sb's fingers) short and thick: *He pointed with his stubby finger to the page.*

stunted that has not been able to grow or develop as much as it should: *Instead of grass, there was a strip of thin scrub and stunted trees.* ◇ *Lack of adequate nutrition often leads to stunted growth in children.*

dumpy (*disapproving*) (especially of a person) short and fat: *That skirt makes you look dumpy.*

3 See also the entry for SHARP 2
short · brief · concise · abbreviated · succinct · economical · pithy
These words all describe sth that uses few words or letters, or fewer words than sth else.

PATTERNS AND COLLOCATIONS
▶ a short / a brief / a concise / an abbreviated / a succinct **account**
▶ a short / a brief / a concise / an abbreviated **version**
▶ a short / brief / concise / succinct **summary / answer / statement**
▶ a brief / pithy **comment**
▶ a concise / a succinct / an economical / a pithy **style**
▶ **very** short / brief / concise / succinct / economical
▶ **relatively** short / brief / succinct

short using few words; being a shorter form of a name or word: *The short answer to your query is that he has acted completely illegally.* ◇ *Try to keep your sentences short.* ◇ *I've only read the shorter version of the report.* ◇ *Call me Jo – it's short for Joanna.* ◇ *file transfer protocol or FTP for short* OPP **long** → LONG, See also **shorten** → SHRINK
brief using few words: *The author makes only a brief mention of the role of Japan in this period.* ◇ *Please be brief* (= say what you want to say quickly). ◇ *Now the rest of the news in brief.*
▶ **briefly** adv.: *Briefly, the argument is as follows...*

NOTE **SHORT** OR **BRIEF?** In many cases you can use either word: *a short/brief account/version/description/summary/statement/answer.* **Brief** is often used when you are talking about speech rather than writing: ~~Please be short...~~ However, although a *mention* is usually **brief** whether in speech or writing, an *answer* is more likely to be **short**, even if it is spoken.

concise /kən'saɪs/ (*rather formal*) giving only the information that is necessary and important, using few words: *She gave us clear and concise instructions.* ❶ **Concise** can also be used to describe a book that is shorter than the original book, on which it is based. In this meaning it is only used before a noun, not after a linking verb: *This is just a concise dictionary – you should get yourself something bigger.* See also **to the point** → RELEVANT
▶ **concisely** adv.: *He spoke clearly and concisely.*
abbreviated /ə'briːvieɪtɪd/ (of a word, phrase or name) shorter than usual because some letters have been left out, or only the first letters in each word are used: *On the map, abbreviated forms such as USA and UK are consistently used.*
▶ **abbreviate** verb [T]: *Et cetera is usually abbreviated to etc.*
succinct /sək'sɪŋkt/ (*approving*) (of a comment or piece of writing) expressed clearly and using few words: *Keep your answers as succinct as possible.* OPP **long-winded** ❶ Speech or writing that is **long-winded** continues for too long and is boring and may be hard to understand.
▶ **succinctly** adv.: *You put that very succinctly.*
economical (*rather formal*) using no more words, space or energy than is necessary: *He uses an economical prose style.* ◇ *an economical use of land/space*
▶ **economically** adv.: *She writes elegantly and economically.*

NOTE **CONCISE, SUCCINCT** OR **ECONOMICAL?** **Concise** and **succinct** are used more to talk about how facts are presented; **economical** is used more often to talk about sb's style of speaking or writing. **Succinct** suggests that you approve of the way sth is expressed because it is clear and wastes no words; **concise** is a more factual term, neither approving nor disapproving.

pithy /'pɪθi/ (*approving*) (of a comment or piece of writing) short but expressed well and full of meaning: *a pithy advertising slogan*

shout verb See also the entries for CALL 3 and SCREAM

shout · yell · cry · scream · cheer · bellow · raise your voice · roar · holler · bawl
These words all mean to say sth in a very loud voice.

PATTERNS AND COLLOCATIONS
▶ to shout / yell / cry / raise your voice / holler **to** sb
▶ to shout / yell / scream / bellow / roar / holler / bawl **at** sb
▶ to shout / yell / cry out / scream / bellow / roar / holler **in** pain / anguish / rage, etc.
▶ to shout / cry out / scream **for** joy / excitement / delight etc.
▶ to shout / yell / cry out / scream / roar **with** excitement / triumph, etc.
▶ to shout / yell / scream / bellow / roar / holler / bawl at sb **to do sth**
▶ to shout / yell / scream / bellow / holler **that...**
▶ to shout / yell / cry / scream / roar / bawl **out**
▶ to shout / yell / bellow / bawl **orders / instructions**
▶ to shout / yell / scream **abuse**
▶ to shout / yell / cry / scream **for help**
▶ to shout / cry / scream / holler **out loud**
▶ to shout / yell / scream **at the top of your voice / lungs**

shout [I, T] to say sth in a loud voice; to speak loudly and often angrily to sb: *Stop shouting and listen!* ◇ *He started shouting and swearing at her.* ◇ *Protesters threw stones and shouted abuse at the Senator.* ◇ *'Run' he shouted.* OPP **whisper** → WHISPER
▶ **shout** noun [C]: *We heard angry shouts coming from the apartment below.*
yell [I, T] to shout loudly, for example because you are angry, excited, frightened or in pain: *She yelled at the boy to get down from the wall.* ◇ (*especially BrE*) *I had to yell at the top of my voice to make myself heard.* ◇ (*especially AmE*) *I had to yell at the top of my lungs.* ◇ *The crowd yelled encouragement to the team.* ◇ *'Watch out!' he yelled.*
▶ **yell** noun [C]: *He let out a yell of delight.*
cry [I, T] (*written*) to shout loudly: *She ran over to the window and cried for help.* ◇ *'You're safe!' Tom cried with delight.* ◇ *He bit his lip, trying not to cry out in pain.*
▶ **cry** noun [C]: *Her answer was greeted with cries of outrage.*
scream [I, T] to shout sth in a loud, high voice because you are afraid, angry or excited: *He screamed at me to stop.* ◇ *'Help!' he screamed.* See also **scream** → SCREAM
cheer [I, T] (especially of a crowd of people) to shout loudly to show support or praise for sb, or to give them encouragement: *We all cheered as the team came onto the field.* ◇ *The spectators cheered the runners on.* ◇ *The crowd cheered the president as he drove slowly by.*
▶ **cheer** noun [C]: *A great cheer went up from the crowd.* ◇ *Three cheers for the winners!* (= used when you are asking a group of people to cheer three times, in order to congratulate sb, etc.)
bellow /'beləʊ; AmE -loʊ/ [I, T] to shout in a loud deep voice, especially because you are angry: *He fell to the floor, bellowing with pain and rage.* ◇ *'Quiet!' the teacher bellowed.*
▶ **bellow** noun [C]: *He let out a bellow of rage.*
raise your 'voice idiom to speak loudly to sb, especially because you are angry: *She never once raised her voice to us.* ◇ *'Just you get in here,' he said, raising his voice.*
roar /rɔː(r)/ [I, T] (*written*) to shout sth very loudly, for example because you are angry, in pain, or very excited: *The crowd roared with excitement.* ◇ *Fans roared their approval.* ◇ *'Stand back,' he roared.*
holler [I, T] (*AmE, informal*) to shout loudly: *Don't holler at me like that!* ◇ *'Look out,' I hollered.*
bawl /bɔːl/ [I, T] (*disapproving*) to shout loudly, especially in an unpleasant or angry way: *She bawled at him in front of everyone.* ◇ *He sat in his office bawling orders at his secretary.*

show verb

1 opinion polls show...
2 Show me that letter.
3 show courage/respect

---

1 show · prove · indicate · demonstrate · illustrate

These words all mean to make sth clear or show that sth is true.

indicate   show   prove
               demonstrate
               illustrate

PATTERNS AND COLLOCATIONS

► to show / prove / indicate / demonstrate sth **to** sb
► to show / prove / indicate / demonstrate / illustrate **that / what / how...**
► **figures / studies** show / prove / indicate / demonstrate / illustrate sth
► **research** shows / proves / indicates / demonstrates / illustrates sth
► to show / prove / indicate / demonstrate / illustrate sth **clearly**
► to show / prove / demonstrate sth **conclusively / beyond doubt**

show [T] to use facts or evidence to make sth clear; to make clear what sb/sth is or what they can do: *The government's popularity is declining rapidly, as the opinion polls show.* ◇ *Let me show you exactly what this will mean.* ◇ *They have published a report showing the company's current situation.* ◇ *He has shown himself to be a caring father.* ◇ *(informal) They think I can't do it, but I'll show them!*

prove [T] to use facts or evidence to show that sth is true: *This proves (that) I was right.* ◇ *She was determined to prove everyone wrong.* ◇ *They hope this new evidence will prove her innocence.* ◇ *'I know you're lying.' 'Prove it!'* ◇ *He felt he needed to* **prove his point** (= show other people that he was right). ◇ *Are you just doing this to* **prove a point?** OPP **disprove** → DISPROVE. See also **proof** → EVIDENCE, **proven** → FINAL *adj.*

> **NOTE** SHOW OR PROVE? **Prove** is often preferred to **show** to give a stronger sense of justice being done.

indicate [T] (*rather formal*) to show or suggest that sth is true or exists: *Record profits in the retail market indicate a boom in the economy.* ◇ *Kingston-upon-Thames, as the name indicates, is situated on the banks of the Thames.* See also **indication, indicator** → SIGN 1, **indicate** → DECLARE, **indicate** → SUGGEST

demonstrate /'demənstreɪt/ [T] (*rather formal*) show that sth is true: *These results demonstrate convincingly that our campaign is working.* ◇ *The theories were demonstrated to be false.* See also **demonstration** → EVIDENCE

illustrate [T] (*rather formal*) to show that sth is true or exists: *The incident illustrates the need for better security measures.* See also **illustrate** → EXPLAIN 1, **illustration** → EXAMPLE 1

> **NOTE** INDICATE, DEMONSTRATE OR ILLUSTRATE? **Demonstrate** is the strongest of these words and **indicate** is the weakest. In this meaning one thing **indicates** or **illustrates** another: these words cannot take a person as subject, although **demonstrate** can: *Let me demonstrate to you some of the difficulties we are facing.* ◇ *Let me indicate/illustrate to you the difficulties we are facing.*

---

2 show · reveal · expose

These words all mean to let or enable sb to see sth.

PATTERNS AND COLLOCATIONS

► to show / reveal sth **to** sb

show [T] to let sb see sth: *If there's a letter from France please show it to me.* ◇ *You have to show your ticket as you go in.* ◇ *Have you shown your work to anyone?* ◇ *Have you shown anyone your work?*

reveal [T] (*rather formal*) to show sth that previously could not be seen: *He laughed, revealing a line of white teeth.* ◇ *X-rays revealed a fracture.* ◇ *She crouched in the dark, too frightened to reveal herself.* See also **reveal** → REVEAL

expose [T] (*rather formal*) to show sth that is usually hidden: *Miles of sand are exposed at low tide.* ◇ *He did not want to expose his fears and insecurity to anyone.* See also **expose** → REVEAL

> **NOTE** REVEAL OR EXPOSE? In some cases you can use either word: *He laughed, revealing/exposing a line of white teeth.* **Reveal** can suggest that people did not even know sth existed before it was revealed; **expose** merely suggests that sth could not be seen before it was exposed: *X-rays exposed a fracture.* ◇ *Miles of sand are revealed at low tide.*

---

3 See also the entry for SAY 2

show · reflect · display · demonstrate

These words all mean to make known sth such as a feeling, opinion or quality, especially through your behaviour or actions.

PATTERNS AND COLLOCATIONS

► to show / demonstrate **that...**
► to show / reflect / display / demonstrate **interest**
► to show / reflect / demonstrate **concern**
► to show / reflect / display (your) **feelings / emotions**
► to show / display / demonstrate **commitment / courage**
► to show / display / demonstrate good, anti-social, etc. **behaviour**
► to show / reflect / display / demonstrate sth **clearly**

show [T, I] to make it clear that you have a particular quality or feeling; (of a quality or feeling) to be clear to people: *She showed great courage in the face of danger.* ◇ *He has shown himself to be ready to make compromises.* ◇ *Her expression showed her disappointment.* ◇ *She tried not to let her disappointment show.* See also **show** → EXPRESSION *noun* 1

reflect [T] (*rather formal*) to show or be a sign of the nature of sth or of sb's attitude or feeling: *Our newspaper aims to reflect the views of the local community.* ◇ *His music reflects his interest in African culture.* ◇ *Her face reflected the power of her feelings.* ❶ One thing **reflects** another; **reflect** cannot take a person as subject: *She showed great interest in his research.* ◇ *She reflected great interest in his research.*

display [T] (*rather formal*) to show that you have a particular feeling, quality or ability: *I have rarely seen her display any sign of emotion.* ◇ *He dearly loved to display his knowledge.* See also **display** → EXPRESSION *noun* 1, **display** → PRESENT *verb* 1

demonstrate /'demənstreɪt/ [T] (*rather formal*) to show by your actions that you have a particular quality, ability or feeling: *You need to demonstrate more self-control.* ◇ *We want to demonstrate our commitment to human rights.* See also **demonstration** → EXPRESSION *noun* 1

> **NOTE** DISPLAY OR DEMONSTRATE? When you **demonstrate** a quality, ability or feeling this is always deliberate, because you want people to see your good qualities such as *commitment, understanding* and *willingness*. People can **display** feelings without meaning to: *to display/exhibit signs of emotion/fatigue* ◇ *to demonstrate signs of emotion/fatigue.* People can also deliberately **display** abilities that they are proud of, but these often show how clever they are rather than how good they are.

---

shrewd adj.

shrewd · perceptive · astute · incisive · canny · discriminating · discerning

These words all describe sb who can judge people and situations intelligently and accurately, or the judgements that they make.

PATTERNS AND COLLOCATIONS
▸ a shrewd / an astute / a canny **businessman / politician**
▸ a shrewd / a perceptive / an astute **observer**
▸ a perceptive / an astute / an incisive **analysis**
▸ a shrewd / a perceptive / an astute **observation**
▸ a shrewd / a perceptive / an incisive **comment**
▸ a shrewd / astute / canny **move**

shrewd /ʃruːd/ (*often approving*) clever and good at making judgements about a situation; showing good judgement and likely to be right: *My mother was a shrewd judge of character.* ◇ *I could take a pretty **shrewd guess** at who had sent the letter.* ◇ *She had a **shrewd idea** of what their motives were.*

perceptive /pəˈseptɪv; AmE pərˈs-/ (*approving*) having or showing the ability to notice or understand things quickly, especially things that are not obvious: *It was very perceptive of you to notice that.* ◇ *The article gives a perceptive analysis of the way bureaucracies work.*

astute /əˈstjuːt; AmE əˈstuːt/ (*approving*) intelligent and good at judging what to do in a particular situation, especially how to get an advantage: *An astute politician, he understood the need to get them on his side.*

incisive /ɪnˈsaɪsɪv/ (*approving*) showing clear thought, a good understanding of what is important, and the ability to express this: *He had a clear, incisive mind.* ◇ *She is an incisive critic of the current education system.*

canny intelligent, careful and showing good judgement, especially in business or politics: *It was a canny move, which brought Palmer in on their side.* ❶ **Canny** is less completely approving than most of the words in this group: it can sometimes suggest that sb is too clever for you: *Her opponent proved to be more canny than she'd thought.*

discriminating /dɪˈskrɪmɪneɪtɪŋ/ (*approving*) able to show good judgement about the relative quality of different things: *They are very **discriminating about** what restaurants they go to.*
▸ **discrimination** *noun* [U]: *The president has been criticized for his lack of discrimination in his choice of political allies.*

discerning /dɪˈsɜːnɪŋ; AmE -ˈsɜːrn-/ [usually before noun] (*approving*) able to show good judgement about the quality of sth: *There is growing demand for the product from discerning customers.* ◇ *To the **discerning eye** (= to sb who is discerning), the quality may seem quite poor.*
▸ **discernment** *noun* [U]: *She saw herself as a woman of taste and discernment.*

NOTE DISCRIMINATING OR DISCERNING? **Discriminating** people choose one thing rather than another because they can see that it is better quality; **discerning** people are able to judge the quality of any individual thing. **Discerning** is used especially in the phrase *discerning eye* and before nouns for people who buy things: *discerning clients/customers/collectors/travellers.*

shrink *verb*

shrink · narrow · contract · shorten
These words all mean to become smaller or to be narrower at one end.

PATTERNS AND COLLOCATIONS
▸ to shrink / narrow / contract / shorten (sth) **to** a particular size
▸ to shrink / narrow / contract / shorten (sth) **by** a particular amount
▸ **a market / the economy** shrinks / contracts
▸ shrink / narrow / contract (sth) **slightly**
▸ to shrink / narrow / contract / shorten (sth) **considerably**
▸ to narrow / contract **sharply**

shrink [I, T] to become or make sth smaller in size or amount: *The tumour had shrunk to the size of a pea.* ◇ *The market for their products is shrinking.* ◇ *Households have been shrinking in size but increasing in number.* ◇ *In some ways, the Internet has shrunk the world.* ❶ **Shrink** is the word to use when clothes or fabrics become smaller when they are washed in water that is too hot: *My sweater shrank in the wash.* **OPP** **grow** → RISE
▸ **shrinkage** /ˈʃrɪŋkɪdʒ/ *noun* [U]: *the shrinkage of heavy industry* ◇ *She bought a slightly larger size to allow for shrinkage.*

narrow [I, T] to become or make sth narrower: *This is where the road narrows.* ◇ *Her **eyes narrowed** (= almost closed) to slits.* ◇ *The gap between the two teams has **narrowed** to three points.* ◇ *We need to narrow the health divide between rich and poor.* **OPP** **widen, broaden** → EXPAND 1, See also **narrow** → NARROW *adj.*

contract /kənˈtrækt/ [I, T] (*rather formal*) to become or make sth smaller in size or amount: *Glass contracts as it cools.* ◇ *The electrical market is forecast to contract by 2% this year.* ◇ *The heart muscles contract to expel the blood.* ◇ *'I will' and 'I shall' are usually contracted to 'I'll' (= made shorter).* **OPP** **expand** → EXPAND 1
▸ **contraction** *noun* [U]: *the expansion and contraction of the metal* ◇ *The sudden contraction of the markets left them with a lot of unwanted stock.*

NOTE SHRINK OR CONTRACT? Clothes and fabric **shrink**; other materials, such as glass and metal **contract**, especially as they become cooler. A *market* or the *economy* can **shrink** or **contract**, but **contract** is more formal. Muscles **contract**, and words can **be contracted** to their shorter forms. Most other things **shrink**. The opposite of **shrink** is **grow**; the opposite of **contract** is **expand**.

shorten [T, I] to make sth shorter; to become shorter: *Injury problems could shorten his career.* ◇ *They performed a shortened version of the play in just 40 minutes.* ◇ *Katherine generally shortens her name to Kay.* ◇ *In November the temperature drops and the days shorten.* **OPP** **lengthen** → EXPAND 1, See also **short** → SHORT 1, **short** → SHORT 3

shy *adj.* See also the entries for QUIET 3 and SOLITARY

shy · insecure · timid · coy · diffident · inhibited
These words all describe a person who is not confident or is nervous or embarrassed about meeting and speaking to other people.

PATTERNS AND COLLOCATIONS
▸ shy / insecure / timid / coy / diffident / inhibited **about** sth
▸ a shy / an insecure / a timid **(young) man / woman / child**
▸ a shy / timid **girl / boy / creature / animal**
▸ a shy / coy / diffident **smile / manner**

shy (of a person) nervous or embarrassed about meeting or speaking to other people; showing this; (of animals) easily frightened and not willing to come near people: *Don't be shy — come and say hello.* ◇ *He gave a shy little smile.* ◇ *The panda is a shy creature.*
▸ **shyly** *adv.*: *She smiled shyly.*
▸ **shyness** *noun* [U]: *He tried to overcome his shyness.*

insecure /ˌɪnsɪˈkjʊə(r); AmE -ˈkjʊr/ not confident about yourself or your relationships with other people: *He's very insecure about his appearance.* **OPP** **confident** → CONFIDENT
▸ **insecurity** /ˌɪnsɪˈkjʊərəti; AmE -ˈkjʊr-/ *noun* [U, C, usually pl.]: *feelings of insecurity* ◇ *We all have our fears and insecurities.*

timid /ˈtɪmɪd/ (*especially written*) (of people or animals) shy and nervous: *I was too timid to ask anyone.* ◇ *They're pretty timid creatures who will run away at the slightest noise.* **OPP** **bold** → BOLD

coy shy or pretending to be shy and innocent, especially about love and sex, sometimes in order to make people more interested in you: *She gave him a coy smile.*

diffident /ˈdɪfɪdənt/ (*especially written*) not having much confidence in yourself; not wanting to talk about yourself: *He was modest and diffident about his own success.* ◇ *Greg was the quiet, diffident type.*

▸ **diffidence** *noun* [U]: *She overcame her natural diffidence and spoke with great frankness.*

inhibited /ɪnˈhɪbɪtɪd/ unable to relax or express your feelings in a natural way: *Boys are often more inhibited than girls about discussing their problems.* **OPP** **uninhibited** → SOCIABLE

▸ **inhibition** /ˌɪnhɪˈbɪʃn; ˌɪnɪˈb-/ *noun* [C, U]: *The children were shy at first, but soon lost their inhibitions.*

sick *adj.*

1 a sick child
2 a sick feeling in your stomach

1 See the Topic Map for HEALTH on p.890
sick · ill · not (very) well · bad · ailing · unwell · unfit · sickly · unhealthy
These words all describe sb who is suffering from an illness or not in good health.

PATTERNS AND COLLOCATIONS
▸ sick / ill / unwell **with** flu, a fever, etc.
▸ a sick / an ailing **mother / father / parent / husband / wife**
▸ sick / seriously ill / sickly / unhealthy **children**
▸ to **look** sick / ill / not (very) well / bad / unwell / sickly / unhealthy
▸ to **feel** ill / not (very) well / bad / unwell
▸ to **become / get / fall** sick / ill
▸ **very** sick / ill / unwell

sick suffering from an illness; not feeling in good health: *Her mother's very sick.* ◇ *Don't ask a babysitter to look after a sick child.* ◇ *Peter has been off sick* (= away from work because he is sick). ◇ *Emma has just called in sick* (= phoned to say she will not be coming to work because she is sick). **OPP** **well** → WELL, See also **sickness** → ILLNESS, **the sick** → PATIENCE

ill [not usually before noun] (*especially BrE*) sick: *Her father is* **seriously ill** *in St Luke's hospital.* ◇ *Uncle Harry is* **terminally ill** *with cancer.* ◇ *(BrE) We both started to feel ill shortly after the meal.* **OPP** **well** → WELL, See also **mentally ill** → MENTALLY ILL, **illness** → DISEASE, **illness** → ILLNESS

NOTE SICK OR ILL? In British English the more usual word is **ill**, especially when talking about serious illnesses: *He is seriously sick in hospital.* However, if you are talking about taking time off work because of illness, use **sick**: *Peter has been off ill.* ◇ *Emma has just called in ill.* Also, **ill** is not usually used before a noun, unless it follows an adverb; in those cases, the noun is usually plural: *an ill child* ◇ *terminally ill children.* In American English the usual word is **sick**; **ill** is more formal and is only used to talk about very serious illnesses. In British English the more usual meaning of **sick** is 'feeling that you want to vomit'. See also **sick** → SICK 2

not (very) well sick/ill: *I wasn't feeling very well so I decided not to go to the concert.* ◇ *(especially BrE) I'm a bit worried – she's not well.* **❶** **Not (very) well** is mostly used when talking about less serious illnesses, especially when you don't know exactly what the problem is. In American English it is usually used with the verb **feel**.

bad (*rather informal, especially spoken*) sick/ill: *I'm afraid I'm feeling pretty bad.* **❶** In this meaning **bad** is always used after *feel* or *look*. **OPP** **good** → WELL

ailing (*formal*) ill and not improving: *She cares for her ailing father.*

unwell /ʌnˈwel/ [not before noun] (*rather formal*) sick/ill: *She said she was feeling unwell and went home.* **OPP** **well** → WELL

unfit /ʌnˈfɪt/ [not usually before noun] (*BrE*) not in good physical condition; not fit, because you have not taken exercise: *The captain is still unfit and will miss tonight's game.* ◇ *I'm so unfit – I'm out of breath just from walking up the steps!* **❶** In both British and American English **unfit** can be used in the phrases *unfit for sth* and *unfit to do sth* meaning 'not capable of doing sth because of illness or

injury': *He's still unfit for work.* ◇ *The company's doctor found that she was unfit to carry out her normal work.* **OPP** **fit** → WELL

sickly often ill; looking ill: *He was a sickly child.* ◇ *She looked* **pale and sickly.** **OPP** **healthy** → WELL

unhealthy [not usually before noun] not in good health; showing a lack of good health: *They looked poor and unhealthy.* **OPP** **healthy** → WELL, See also **unhealthy** → UNHEALTHY

2 See the Topic Map for HEALTH on p.890
sick · nauseous · queasy
These words all describe people who feel as if they may vomit (= bring food from the stomach back out through the mouth).

PATTERNS AND COLLOCATIONS
▸ sick / nauseous / queasy **with** fear
▸ to **feel** sick / nauseous / queasy
▸ to **make sb** sick / nauseous / queasy
▸ **a bit / a little / slightly / very** sick / nauseous / queasy

sick [not usually before noun] feeling as if you may vomit: *Whenever I think about my exams I feel* **physically sick.** ◇ *I had a sick feeling in my stomach.* **❶** The suffix *-sick* is often used in compounds which mean feeling sick as a result of travelling: *I was feeling seasick so I went up on deck for some fresh air.* ◇ *airsick* ◇ *carsick* ◇ *travel sick* See also **be sick** → VOMIT

▸ **sickness** *noun* [U]: (*especially BrE*) *After a few minutes the sickness subsided.*

nauseous /ˈnɔːziəs; ˈnɔːsiəs; AmE ˈnɔːʃəs/ [not usually before noun] (*formal*) feeling as if you may vomit: *She felt dizzy and nauseous.* See also **nauseating** → DISGUSTING 1

▸ **nausea** /ˈnɔːziə; ˈnɔːsiə/ *noun* [U]: *A wave of nausea swept over me.*

queasy /ˈkwiːzi/ [not usually before noun] feeling slightly sick: *Travelling by boat makes me queasy.*

sight *noun*

sight · view · vision
These are all words for the area or distance that you can see from a particular position.

PATTERNS AND COLLOCATIONS
▸ **in / out of** sight / view
▸ **in / within** sight / view **of** sth
▸ **in full / plain** sight / view
▸ to **come into / disappear from** sight / view / sb's vision
▸ to **come in** sight / view **of** sb / sth
▸ to **block** sb's view / vision
▸ sb's **line of** sight / vision
▸ sb's **field of** view / vision

sight [U] the area or distance that you can see from a particular position: *He looked up the street, but there was no one in sight.* ◇ *He strode by, in full sight of the guards.* ◇ *At last we came in sight of a few houses.* ◇ *A bicycle came into sight on the main road.* ◇ *Leave any valuables in your car out of sight.* ◇ *Don't let him out of your sight* (= Make sure that you can always see him, wherever he goes). See also **sight** → LOOK *noun*, **sight** → VIEW 2

view [U, sing.] (*especially written*) the area or distance that you can see from a particular position: *The sun disappeared from view.* ◇ *The carriage was put* **on view** *for the public to see.* ◇ *The knife was in plain view on the kitchen table.* ◇ *I didn't have a good view of the stage.* See also **view** → VIEW *noun* 2, **view** → LOOK *verb* 1

vision [U] the area that you can see from a particular position: *The couple moved outside her field of vision* (= total area you can see from a particular position). ◇ *He glimpsed something on the edge of his vision.*

NOTE SIGHT, VIEW OR VISION? **View** is more literary than **sight** or **vision**. It is the only word for talking about how well you can see: *I didn't have a good sight/vision of the stage.* **Vision** must always be used with a possessive pronoun: *my/his/her, etc. (field of) vision*. It is not used with the prepositions *in, into* and *out of* that are very frequent with **sight** and **view**: ~~There was nobody in vision.~~ ◇ ~~A tall figure came into vision.~~

sign *noun*

1 a sign of stress/trouble/sth wrong
2 a road/street/shop sign

1 See also the entry for SUGGESTION

sign · indication · symptom · symbol · indicator · signal · trace · mark · hallmark
These are all words for an event, action or fact that shows that sth exists, is happening or may happen in the future.

PATTERNS AND COLLOCATIONS
▶ a sign/ an indication/ a symptom/ a symbol/ an indicator/ a signal/ a trace/ a mark/ a hallmark **of** sth
▶ a sign/an indication/a symptom/an indicator/a signal **that**...
▶ a **clear** sign/ indication/ symptom/ symbol/ indicator/ signal/ trace
▶ an **obvious** sign/indication/symptom/symbol/indicator/trace
▶ a **good / reliable** sign/ indication/ indicator/ signal
▶ a **powerful** sign/ symbol/ indicator/ signal
▶ an **early** sign/ indication/ symptom/ indicator/ signal
▶ an **outward** sign/ indication/ symbol/ mark
▶ to **have** (the) signs/symptoms/traces/marks/hallmarks of sth
▶ to **bear** (the) signs/ traces/ marks/ hallmarks of sth
▶ to **give** a sign/ an indication/ a signal
▶ a sign/an indication/a symptom/an indicator **shows/suggests** sth
▶ **no / any** sign/ indication/ trace of sth

sign [C, U] an event, action or fact that shows that sth exists, is happening or may happen in the future: *Headaches may be a sign of stress.* ◇ *Call the police at the first sign of trouble.* ◇ *The fact that he didn't say 'no' immediately is a good sign.* ◇ *The gloomy weather shows no sign of improving.* ◇ *There was no sign of life in the house* (= there seemed to be nobody there).

indication [C, U] (*rather formal*) a remark or sign that shows that sth is happening or what sb is thinking or feeling: *They gave no indication as to how the work should be done.* ◇ *All the indications are that the deal will go ahead as planned.* ◇ *He shows every indication* (= clear signs) *of wanting to accept the post.* See also **indicate** → DECLARE, **indicate** → SHOW 1, **indicate** → SUGGEST

> **NOTE** SIGN OR INDICATION? An **indication** often comes in the form of sth that sb says; a **sign** is usually sth that happens or sth that sb does.

symptom /'sɪmptəm/ [C] a change in your body or mind that shows that you are not healthy; a sign that sth exists, especially sth bad: *cold/flu symptoms* ◇ *Symptoms include a headache and sore throat.* ◇ *The rise in inflation was just one symptom of the poor state of the economy.*

symbol [C] a person, object or event that represents a more general quality or situation: *The dove is a universal symbol of peace.* ◇ *The company car is an outward symbol of the employee's status.* ◇ *A stressful job can actually be a status symbol.* See also **symbolize** → REPRESENT 2

indicator [C] (*rather formal*) a sign that shows you what sth is like or how a situation is changing: *The economic indicators for the end of the year are better than expected.* See also **indicate** → SHOW 1, **indicate** → SUGGEST

signal [C] a sign of sth: *Chest pains can be a warning signal of heart problems.* ◇ *Reducing prison sentences would send the wrong signals to criminals.*

> **NOTE** SIGN OR SIGNAL? **Signal** is often used to talk about an event, action or fact that suggests to sb that they should do sth. **Sign** is not usually used in this way: ~~Reducing prison sentences would send the wrong signs to criminals.~~

trace [C, U] a sign or object that shows that sb/sth existed or was present: *It's exciting to discover traces of earlier civilizations.* ◇ *Police searched the area but found no trace of the escaped prisoners.* ◇ *The ship had vanished without (a) trace.* ❶ **Trace** is often used in the phrases *no trace of* and *disappear/vanish without (a) trace*. See also **trace** → FIND 4

mark [C] a sign that a quality or feeling exists: *On the day of the funeral businesses remained closed as a mark of respect.* ◇ *Such coolness under pressure is the mark of a champion.*

hallmark /'hɔːlmɑːk; *AmE* -mɑːrk/ [C] (*journalism*) a feature or quality that is typical of sb/sth: *Police said the explosion bore all the hallmarks of a terrorist attack.*

2 **sign · board · plaque · notice · plate · noticeboard · bulletin board**
These are all words for a piece or metal, wood or stone that has writing or a picture on it that gives you information, instructions or a warning.

PATTERNS AND COLLOCATIONS
▶ **on** a sign/ board/ plaque/ notice/ plate/ noticeboard/ bulletin board
▶ to **put up / see / read** a sign/ board/ plaque/ notice/ plate/ noticeboard/ bulletin board
▶ a sign/ board/ plaque/ notice **appears / goes up**
▶ a sign/ plaque/ notice **says / reads** sth

sign [C] a piece of metal, wood or paper that has writing or a picture on it that gives information, instructions or a warning: *All the road signs are in both languages.* ◇ *A sign on the wall said 'Now wash your hands'.* ◇ *Follow the signs for the Performing Arts Centre.*

board [C] (*often in compounds*) a large flat piece of wood or other strong material, that is used for displaying information or for teachers to write on in class: *The exam results went up on the board.* ◇ *I'll write it up on the blackboard/whiteboard.*

plaque /plæk; *BrE* also plɑːk/ [C] a flat piece of metal or stone, usually with a name and dates on, attached to a wall in memory of a person or event: *A bronze plaque marks the house where the poet was born.*

notice [C] a board or sign giving information, an instruction or a warning: *There was a notice saying 'Keep off the Grass'.*

> **NOTE** SIGN OR NOTICE? A **notice** always gives its information, instruction or warning in words. **Signs** often use pictures or symbols. In this meaning **sign** is a more frequent word, used in a wider range of contexts: *a road/traffic/street/shop/pub sign* ◇ ~~a road/traffic/shop/pub notice~~. However, **notice** also has the closely related meaning of 'a piece of paper giving written or printed information'. See also **notice** → POSTER

plate [C] a flat piece of metal or plastic with some information on it, for example sb's name or the registration number of a car: *A brass plate beside the door said 'Dr Alan Tate'.* ◇ *A nameplate was fitted to the side of the boat.* ◇ (*BrE*) *a vehicle's number plates* ◇ (*AmE*) *vehicle's license plates*

noticeboard /'nəʊtɪsbɔːd; *AmE* 'noʊtɪsbɔːrd/ [C] (*BrE*) a board for putting notices on: *Please check the noticeboard by the library for news of future events.*

'bulletin board [C] (*AmE*) a noticeboard: *Please keep an eye on the bulletin board for further details.*

signal *noun*

signal · sign · cue
These are all words for a movement, sound or event that gives sb information or tells sb to do sth.

PATTERNS AND COLLOCATIONS
▶ a signal/ sign/ cue **for** sb/ sth
▶ a signal/ sign/ cue (for sb) **to do sth**
▶ a **clear** signal/ sign/ cue

▶ a **warning** signal / sign
▶ to **wait for / miss** a / your signal / sign / cue
▶ to **understand / misunderstand** a / sb's signal / sign
▶ to **give sb** a signal / sign / cue
▶ to **make** a signal / sign

signal [C] a movement or sound that you make to give sb information, instructions, a warning, etc: *a danger/ distress signal* ◇ *At an agreed signal they left the room.* ◇ *The siren was a signal for everyone to leave the building.* ◇ *When I give the signal, run!* ◇ *(AmE) All I get is a **busy signal** when I dial his number* (= his phone is being used). See also **signal** → NOD *verb*

sign [C] a movement or sound that you make to tell sb sth: *He gave a thumbs-up sign.* ◇ *She nodded as a sign for us to sit down.*

NOTE SIGNAL OR SIGN? A **sign** is usually a hand movement, and is often fairly fixed and likely to be understood by people in general; **signal** has a wider range, and may have been invented by individuals in a particular situation: *sign language* (= a system of communicating with people by using hand movements rather than spoken words) ◇ *a V-sign* (= a sign that you make by holding up your hand and making a V-shape with your first and second fingers) ◇ *We agreed on a signal to mean 'stop'.*

cue [C] an action or event that is a signal for sb to do sth: *Jon's arrival was a cue for more champagne.* ◇ *I think that's my cue to explain why I'm here.* ◇ *(figurative)'Where is that boy?' As if **on cue**, Simon appeared in the doorway* (= as if sb had given him a signal). ◇ *(figurative) Investors are **taking their cue from** the big banks and selling dollars* (= taking what other people do as a sign for them to do the same).

silence *noun*

silence · peace · quiet · tranquillity · hush · calm
These are all words for a lack of noise.

PATTERNS AND COLLOCATIONS
▶ **in** silence / peace / tranquillity
▶ **absolute / total** silence / peace / quiet / tranquillity / calm
▶ **relative** silence / peace / quiet / tranquillity / calm
▶ a **sudden** silence / quiet / hush / calm
▶ to **break** the silence / peace / quiet / calm
▶ silence / quiet / a hush **falls** on sth

silence [U] a complete lack of noise or sound: *Their footsteps echoed in the silence.* ◇ *A scream broke the silence of the night.* See also **silent** → QUIET 1

peace [U] a lack of interruption from noise, problems, worry or unwanted actions: *She lay back and enjoyed the peace of the summer evening.* ◇ *He never felt really **at peace** with himself.* ◇ *He just wants to be **left in peace*** (= not to be disturbed). ◇ *I need to check that she is all right, just for my own **peace of mind*** (= so that I do not have to worry). See also **peaceful** → QUIET 1

quiet [U] the state of being without much noise: *He seemed to prefer the quiet of his own room.* ◇ *I go to the library for a little **peace and quiet**.*

tranquillity (*especially BrE*) (*AmE usually* **tranquility**) /træŋ'kwɪləti/ [U] (*rather formal, written*) the state of being without noise, violence or anxiety: *It is the perfect place to relax in an atmosphere of peace and tranquillity.* See also **tranquil** → QUIET 1

hush [sing.] a period of silence, especially following a lot of noise, or when people are expecting sth to happen: *There was a **deathly hush** in the theatre.* ◇ *A hush fell over the landscape.*

calm [U, C] a quiet and peaceful time or situation: *We sat together for a while in the calm of the evening.* See also **calm** → QUIET *adj.* 1

silence *verb*

silence · quiet · quieten · shush · muffle
These words all mean to become quieter or stop sb/sth from making so much noise.

PATTERNS AND COLLOCATIONS
▶ to **quiet** / quieten (sb) **down**
▶ to **quiet** / quieten a **crowd**

silence [T] (*written*) to make sb/sth stop speaking or making a noise: *She quickly silenced him with a glare.* ◇ *Our bombs silenced the enemy's guns* (= they destroyed them). See also **silent** → QUIET *adj.* 2

quiet [I, T] (*especially AmE*) to become calmer or less noisy; to make sb/sth calmer or less noisy: *The demonstrators quieted down when the police arrived.* ◇ *He's very good at quieting the kids.* See also **quiet** → QUIET *adj.* 2

quieten [I, T] (*BrE*) to become calmer or less noisy; to make sb/sth calmer or less noisy: *Things seem to have quietened down a bit this afternoon* (= we are not as busy as we were). ◇ *The police appealed for calm, but it failed to quieten the protesters.* See also **quiet** → QUIET *adj.* 2

shush [T] (*rather informal*) to tell sb to be quiet, especially by saying 'shush', or by putting your finger against your lips: *He rudely shushed the whole room and demanded silence.*

muffle [T] to make the sound produced by sb/sth quieter or less clear, especially by covering it with sth: *He tried to muffle the alarm clock by putting it under his pillow.* ◇ *He saw shadowy figures slip by him, their footsteps muffled by the fog.* See also **muffled** → QUIET *adj.* 2

silent *adj.*

silent · speechless · dumb · mute · inarticulate
These words all describe a person who does not or cannot speak, or an action that is not expressed in words.

PATTERNS AND COLLOCATIONS
▶ speechless / dumb / inarticulate **with** rage / anger

silent (of a person) not speaking: *They huddled together in silent groups.* ◇ *As the curtain rose, the audience **fell silent**.*
▶ **silently** *adv.*: *They marched silently through the streets.*

speechless unable to speak, especially because you are extremely angry or surprised: *Laura was speechless with rage.* ◇ *His words left her speechless.*

dumb /dʌm/ not speaking: *We were all struck dumb with amazement.* ◇ *We all sat there in dumb silence.* ❶ **Dumb** also means 'unable to speak': *She was born deaf and dumb.* However, this meaning of **dumb** is old-fashioned and can be offensive.
▶ **dumbly** *adv.*: *'Are you all right?' Lucy nodded dumbly.*

mute (*literary*) not speaking or making a sound; not expressed in words or sounds; unable to speak: *The child sat mute in the corner of the room.* ◇ *She gave him a look of mute appeal.* ◇ *The film concerns a mute Scottish widow and her passion for music.*
▶ **mutely** *adv.*: *He nodded mutely.*

NOTE DUMB OR MUTE? In the meaning 'unable to speak', both **dumb** and **mute** are rather old-fashioned, and **dumb** can be offensive. An acceptable alternative is **speech-impaired**, but this is not at all frequent, and the phrase 'unable to speak' is often used instead: *The 2nd Duke of Montrose was deaf and unable to speak.*

inarticulate /ˌɪnɑː'tɪkjələt; *AmE* -ɑːr'tɪk/ (*rather formal*) (of people) not able to express ideas or feelings clearly or easily; (of speech) not using clear words; not expressed clearly: *You can't expect an inarticulate young child to defend himself in court.* ◇ *She was inarticulate with rage.* ◇ *He gave a particularly inarticulate reply.* **OPP articulate** → ARTICULATE

similarity *noun* See also the entry for COMPARISON

similarity · resemblance · uniformity · equivalence · likeness · parallel · affinity · correspondence · there's no comparison
These are all words for the state of being similar or the same.

▶ a similarity / a resemblance / an equivalence / a likeness / a parallel / an affinity / a correspondence / no comparison **between** A and B
▶ a similarity / a resemblance / an equivalence / a likeness / a parallel **to** sth
▶ similarity / uniformity / equivalence / a parallel **in** sth
▶ a similarity / equivalence / a parallel / an affinity / a correspondence / no comparison **with** sth
▶ a **close** similarity / resemblance / likeness / parallel / affinity / correspondence
▶ a **strong** similarity / resemblance / likeness / parallel / affinity
▶ (a) **remarkable** similarity / resemblance / uniformity / parallel / affinity / correspondence
▶ (a) **great** similarity / resemblance / uniformity / affinity
▶ **broad** similarity / uniformity / equivalence
▶ a **direct** equivalence / parallel / correspondence
▶ a **superficial / physical** similarity / resemblance / likeness
▶ to **bear** a similarity / a resemblance / a likeness / an affinity / no comparison
▶ to **have** similarities / uniformity / a parallel / an affinity / a correspondence
▶ to **show** a similarity / a resemblance / uniformity / a likeness / an affinity / a correspondence
▶ to **see** a similarity / a resemblance / likeness / parallel

similarity /ˌsɪməˈlærəti/ [U, C] the state of being like sb/sth but not exactly the same; a feature that makes things or people have that makes them like each other: *There is some similarity in the way they sing.* ◇ *They are both doctors but that is where the similarity ends.* ◇ *We carried out a study of the similarities and differences between the two countries.* **OPP** **difference** → DIFFERENCE, See also **similar** → LIKE *prep., adj.*

resemblance /rɪˈzembləns/ [C, U] (*rather formal*) the fact of looking or being similar to sb/sth: *The resemblance between the two signatures was remarkable.* ◇ *She bears a striking resemblance to the Queen.* ◇ *The movie bears little resemblance to the original novel.* ❶ **Resemblance** is most often used to talk about appearance. See also **resemble** → LOOK LIKE SB/STH

uniformity /ˌjuːnɪˈfɔːməti/ [U, sing.] (*rather formal*) the state of everything being the same in all parts at all times: *They tried to ensure uniformity across the different departments.* ◇ *The drab uniformity of the houses depressed me.* See also **uniform** → EQUAL *adj.*

equivalence /ɪˈkwɪvələns/ [U, C] (*formal*) the quality of being equal in value, amount, meaning or importance: *There is no straightforward equivalence between economic progress and social well-being.* See also **equivalent** → EQUIVALENT *noun,* **equivalent** → EQUIVALENT *adj.*

likeness [C, U] the fact of looking similar to sb/sth: *There's a superficial likeness, but they're really very different.* ◇ *I can't see any likeness between her children.* See also **like** → LIKE *prep., adj.*

> **NOTE** RESEMBLANCE OR LIKENESS? **Resemblance** is a much more frequent and general word. **Likeness** is mostly used to talk about physical appearance, especially comparing members of the same family; typical collocates include *physical* and *family*. A **likeness** is also a painting or drawing of a person, especially one that looks very like them: *The drawing is said to be a **good likeness** of the girl's attacker.*

parallel [C, usually pl.] (*rather formal*) a similar feature: *There are interesting parallels between the 1960s and the first decade of this century.* ◇ *It is possible to **draw a parallel** between (= find similar features in) their experience and ours.* See also **parallel** → EQUIVALENT *noun*

affinity /əˈfɪnəti/ [U, C] (*formal*) a close relationship between two people or things that have similar qualities, structures or features: *There is a close affinity between Italian and Spanish.*

correspondence /ˌkɒrəˈspɒndəns; AmE ˌkɔːrəˈspɑːn-; ˌkɑː-/ [C, U] (*rather formal*) a connection between two things; the fact of two things being similar: *There is a close correspondence between the two extracts.* ❶ In this meaning, **correspondence** is used especially in the phrases a / an close/direct/exact/one-to-one correspondence between A and B. See also **correspond** → MATCH 1, **corresponding** → EQUIVALENT *adj.*

there's no com'parison *phrase* used to emphasize the difference between two people or things that are being compared: *In terms of price there's no comparison* (= one thing is much more expensive than the other). ◇ *The education system **bears no comparison** with that in many Eastern European countries* (= it is not as good).

simulate *verb* See also the entry for REPEAT 2

simulate · recreate · reconstruct · reproduce · model · remake
These words all mean to create a copy of a situation or event, usually for a particular purpose.

▶ to recreate / reconstruct / reproduce sth **from** sth
▶ to simulate / reproduce / model sth **closely**
▶ to recreate / reconstruct / reproduce / model sth **accurately**

simulate /ˈsɪmjuleɪt/ [T] (*rather formal*) to create particular conditions that exist in real life using computers or models, usually for study or training purposes: *Computer software can be used to simulate conditions on the sea bed.* ◇ *Role-play is a way of simulating real-life situations.*
▶ **simulation** *noun* [C, U]: *a computer simulation of how the planet functions* ◇ *An important part of training is role-play and the simulation of court cases.*

recreate /ˌriːkriˈeɪt/ [T] to make sth that existed in the past exist or seem to exist again: *The movie recreates the glamour of 1940s Hollywood.* ❶ **Recreate** is often used to talk about people trying to make sth that seems attractive or romantic exist again, for example through film or by building sth such as an old-fashioned street for a museum. People usually try to recreate an *atmosphere,* a *feeling,* a *mood,* a *spirit, excitement, glamour, the past* or a *'golden age'.*
▶ **recreation** *noun* [C, U]: *The writer attempts a recreation of the sights and sounds of childhood.*

reconstruct /ˌriːkənˈstrʌkt/ [T] (*rather formal*) to be able to describe or show exactly how sth looked or happened in the past, using the information you have gathered: *Investigators are trying to reconstruct the circumstances of the crash.* ❶ **Reconstruct** is used especially to talk about solving crimes or finding the cause of accidents, or finding out more about how events in history really happened.
▶ **reconstruction** *noun* [C]: *Last night police staged a reconstruction of the incident.*

reproduce /ˌriːprəˈdjuːs; AmE -ˈduːs/ [T] (*rather formal*) to produce sth again; to make sth happen again in the same way: *The computer program reproduces the effects of earthquakes on buildings.* ◇ *Unfortunately, he was never able to reproduce this level of performance in a competition.*

model [-ll-, AmE -l-] [T] (*computing or technical*) to create a copy of an activity or situation, especially using a computer, so that you can study it before dealing with the real thing: *The program can model a typical home page for you.*
▶ **model** *noun* [C]: *a mathematical model for determining the safe level of pesticides in food*

remake /ˌriːˈmeɪk/ [T] to make a new or different version of sth such as an old film or song: *'The Seven Samurai' was remade in Hollywood as 'The Magnificent Seven'.*
▶ **remake** *noun* [C]: *He plays the lead in a remake of the 1920s comedy classic.*

sing verb

sing · chant · whistle · hum
These words all mean to make musical sounds with your voice or mouth.

PATTERNS AND COLLOCATIONS
▸ to sing / chant / whistle / hum **at** sb / sth
▸ to sing / whistle **to** sb / sth
▸ to sing / whistle / hum a **song / tune**
▸ to sing / chant / whistle / hum **loudly / softly**

sing [I, T] to make musical sounds with your voice in the form of a song or tune: *I just can't sing in tune!* ◇ *Will you sing us a song?* ◇ *We all sang 'Happy Birthday' to her.* ◇ *She sang the baby to sleep* (= sang until the baby went to sleep). See also **singing** → MUSIC

chant /tʃɑːnt; *AmE* tʃænt/ [T, I] to sing or shout the same words or phrases many times; to sing or say a religious song or prayer using only a few notes that are repeated many times: *The crowd chanted their hero's name.* ◇ *A group of protesters, chanting and carrying placards, waited outside.* ◇ *In a nearby temple, our guide chanted a prayer and lit a stick of incense.*

whistle [T, I] to make a high sound or a musical tune by forcing your breath out when your lips are closed: *He started to whistle a tune.* ◇ *She whistled in amazement.* ◇ *The crowd booed and whistled as the player came onto the field.* See also **whistle** → WHISTLE *noun*

hum (-mm-) [I, T] to sing a tune with your lips closed: *She was humming softly to herself.* ◇ *He began to hum along with the music.* ◇ *What's that tune you're humming?*

single adj.

single · divorced · unmarried · lone · estranged · widowed · separated
These words all describe people who are not married or not having a romantic relationship with sb.

PATTERNS AND COLLOCATIONS
▸ to be divorced / estranged / separated **from** sb
▸ a single / a divorced / an unmarried / a lone / a widowed / a separated **man / woman / parent / mother / father**
▸ a divorced / an unmarried / a separated **couple**

single not married; not having a romantic relationship with sb: *The apartments are ideal for single people living alone.* ◇ *Are you still single?* ❶ A **single parent/mother/father** is a person who looks after their child or children without a husband, wife or partner: *Marriage breakdown is common and there are a large number of single-parent families.*

divorced no longer married because the marriage has been legally ended: *Many divorced people remarry and have second families.* ◇ *My parents are divorced.* ◇ *Are they going to get divorced?* See also **divorce**, **get divorced** → DIVORCE

unmarried not married: *He remained unmarried all his life.* ◇ *Unmarried couples do not have the same rights as married couples.* **OPP married** → MARRY

lone [only before noun] (*especially BrE, rather formal, especially written*) without a husband, wife or partner to share the care of children: *Nine out of ten lone parents are women.* ◇ *Lone fathers tend to be older than lone mothers.* ❶ **Lone** is not often used in normal spoken English, but it is common in journalism and in official reports.

estranged /ɪˈstreɪndʒd/ (*formal*) no longer living with your husband or wife: *He is being questioned in connection with the death of his estranged wife.* ◇ *She has been estranged from her husband since 1999.* See also **estrangement** → DIVISION 2

widowed /ˈwɪdəʊd; *AmE* ˈwɪdoʊd/ if sb is **widowed**, their husband or wife has died: *She was widowed by the time she was 35.* ◇ *She spent twenty years looking after her widowed father.*

separated [not usually before noun] no longer living with your husband, wife or partner: *Her parents are separated but not divorced.* ◇ *He's separated from his wife.* See also **separate** → DIVORCE

NOTE ESTRANGED OR SEPARATED? An **estranged** couple are married but no longer live together or have any sort of relationship or communication. A **separated** couple no longer live together but may still communicate, for example to organize the care of children. **Separated** can also refer to a couple who were not married but used to live together.

sip noun

sip · drop · drink · swig · gulp
These are all words for an act of taking in liquid when you drink.

PATTERNS AND COLLOCATIONS
▸ a sip / drop / drink / swig / gulp **of** sth
▸ to **have** a sip / drop / drink / swig / gulp
▸ to **take** a sip / drink / swig / gulp

sip [C] a very small amount of a drink that you take into your mouth: *She took another sip of her drink.* See also **sip** → DRINK *verb*

drop [C, usually sing.] (*especially spoken*) a small quantity of a liquid: *Can I have a drop more milk in my coffee, please?*

drink [C, usually sing.] an amount of liquid that you drink: *She took a drink from the glass and then put it down.* See also **drink** → DRINK *verb*

swig [C] (*informal*) a big sip, especially of alcohol: *They exchanged a few words in between swigs from the bottle.* See also **swig** → DRINK *verb*

gulp [C] an amount of a drink or air that you swallow or breathe quickly: *She emptied her glass in one gulp.* ◇ *He leaned out of the window and took a few gulps of sea air.*

sit verb See also the entries for LIE and STAND 1

sit · sit down · be seated · take a seat · perch
These words all mean to rest your weight on your bottom with your back upright, for example on a chair.

PATTERNS AND COLLOCATIONS
▸ to sit / sit down / be seated / take a seat / perch **on** sth
▸ to sit / sit down / be seated / take a seat **in** sth

sit [I] to rest your weight on your bottom with your back upright, for example on a chair: *May I sit here?* ◇ *I was sitting at my desk, gazing out of the window.* ◇ *Sit still, will you!* ◇ *Sit up straight — don't slouch.* ◇ *She sat back and stretched out her legs.* ❶ **Sit** is usually used with an adverb or prepositional phrase to show where or how sb sits, but sometimes another phrase or clause is used to show what sb does while they are sitting: *We sat talking for hours.* ◇ *He sat and stared at the letter in front of him.* You sit **on** a chair with a straight back and no arms and you also sit *on* a sofa; you sit *in* an armchair. **OPP stand**, **stand up** → STAND 1

sit ˈdown, sit yourself ˈdown *phrasal verb* to move from a standing position to a sitting position: *Please sit down.* ◇ *He sat down on the bed.* ◇ *Come in and sit yourselves down.* **OPP get up**, **stand up** → STAND 1

be seated [T] (*formal*) to be sitting: *She was seated at the head of the table.* ◇ *Wait until all the guests are seated.* ❶ **Be seated** is often used as a formal way of inviting sb to sit down: *Please be seated.*

take a ˈseat *phrase* to sit down: *Please take a seat. I'll be with you shortly.* ◇ *He took a seat at the opposite end of the table.* ❶ **Take a seat** is used especially as a polite way of inviting sb to sit down See also **seat** → CHAIR

perch [I, T] (always used with an adverb or preposition) (*rather informal*) to sit on sth, especially on the edge of sth: *We perched on a couple of high stools at the bar.* ◇ *She perched herself on the edge of the bed.*

situation *noun* See also the entry for INFORMATION

situation · circumstance · position · conditions · things · the case · state of affairs
These are all words for the conditions and facts that are connected with and affect the way things are.

PATTERNS AND COLLOCATIONS
▸ **in** (a) particular situation / circumstances / position / state of affairs
▸ the **general / current / present / real** situation / circumstances / position / conditions / state of affairs
▸ the / sb's **economic / financial / social** situation / circumstances / position / conditions
▸ (a / an) **normal / unusual / ideal** situation / circumstances / position / conditions / state of affairs
▸ (a / an) **favourable / difficult / exceptional / desperate** situation / circumstances / position / conditions
▸ (a) **healthy / satisfactory** situation / position / conditions / state of affairs
▸ (a / an) **happy / unhappy** situation / circumstances / position / state of affairs
▸ to **create** a situation / circumstances / conditions
▸ to **describe / explain** the situation / circumstances / position / things / state of affairs
▸ to **look at / review** the situation / circumstances / conditions / things

situation [C] all the things that are happening at a particular time and in a particular place: *You need to consider the present economic situation.* ◇ *In your situation, I would look for another job.* ◇ *He could see no way out of the situation.* ◇ *You could get into* **a situation where** *you have to decide immediately.*

circumstance [C, usually pl.] the facts that are connected with and affect a situation, event or action; the conditions of a person's life, especially the money they have: *Police said there were no* **suspicious circumstances** *surrounding the boy's death.* ◇ **Under the circumstances** (= considering the facts of the situation), *it seemed better not to tell him about the accident.* ◇ **Under no circumstances** *you lend Paul any money.* ◇ *Grants are awarded according to your financial circumstances.* ❶ **Circumstance** [U] is a formal word for 'situations and events that affect and influence your life and that are not in your control': *a* **victim of circumstance** (= a person who has suffered because of a situation that they cannot control) ◇ *He had to leave the country through* **force of circumstance** (= events or the situation made it necessary).

position [C, usually sing.] the situation that sb is in, especially when it affects what they can and cannot do: *This put him and his colleagues in a difficult position.* ◇ *The company's financial position is not certain.* ◇ *I'm afraid I am* **not in a position** *to help you.*

conditions [pl.] the circumstances in which people live, work or do things; the physical situation that affects how sth happens: *These neglected children are living* **under** *the most appalling* **conditions.** ◇ *They held a one-day strike to demand improvements in* **pay and conditions.** ◇ *Beware of treacherous* **driving conditions.**

> **NOTE** CIRCUMSTANCES OR CONDITIONS? **Circumstances** refers to sb's financial situation; **conditions** are things such as the quality and amount of food or shelter they have, or the things that they get from their employer, such as holiday and sickness pay and a pleasant working environment. The **circumstances** that affect an event are the facts surrounding it; the **conditions** that affect it are usually physical ones, such as the weather.

things [pl.] (*rather informal, especially spoken*) the general situation, as it affects sb: *Things haven't gone entirely to plan.* ◇ (*informal*) *Hi, Jane!* **How are things?** ◇ *Think*

things over before you decide. ◇ **As things stand** at present, *he seems certain to win.* ◇ **All things considered** (= considering all the difficulties or problems), *she's done very well.* ◇ *Why do you make things so difficult for yourself?* ❶ **Things** is used more in spoken than written English, and in slightly informal contexts, especially when talking about your personal life (rather than politics, business, etc.): *Things are rather difficult at home.* ◇ *the political situation* ◇ ~~political things~~

the case [sing.] the true situation: *If that is the case* (= if the situation described is true), *we need more people.* ◇ *It is simply not* **the case that** *prison conditions are improving.* See also the entry for FACT

state of af'fairs [sing.] a situation: *How did this unhappy state of affairs come about?* See also **state →** STATE

> **NOTE** SITUATION OR STATE OF AFFAIRS? **State of affairs** is mostly used with *this*. It is also used with adjectives describing how good or bad a situation is, such as *desirable, happy, sorry, shocking, sad* and *unhappy*, as well as those relating to time, such as *present* and *current*. **Situation** is much more frequent and is used in a wider variety of contexts.

size *noun*

size · measurement · area · capacity · dimension · volume · bulk · extent
These are all words for how large sth is or the amount of space it covers.

PATTERNS AND COLLOCATIONS
▸ an area / a capacity / a volume **of** 30 metres / litres, etc.
▸ **in** size / area / capacity / volume / bulk / extent
▸ the **exact** size / measurements / area / dimensions / extent
▸ a **large / small** size / area / capacity / volume
▸ **maximum** size / capacity / dimensions / volume / extent
▸ **total** size / area / capacity / volume
▸ (a) **limited** size / area / capacity / dimensions
▸ to **measure** the size / area / dimensions / volume of sth
▸ to **calculate** the size / area / volume of sth

size [U, C] how large a person or thing is: *It's an area* **the size of** (= the same size as) *New Jersey.* ◇ *It's similar in size to a tomato.* ◇ *The kitchen is a good size* (= not small). ◇ *Dogs come in* **all shapes and sizes.**

measurement [C, usually pl.] the size, length or amount of sth: *The exact measurements of the room are 3 metres 20 by 2 metres 84.* ◇ *I'll need to* **take** *your waist* **measurement.** ◇ *Do you know your measurements* (= the size of parts of your body)? ◇ *By* **making** *careful* **measurements** *of the eclipses, astronomers have made great progress in understanding them.*

> **measure** *verb* [I, T]: *The main bedroom measures 12ft by 15ft.* ◇ *A ship's speed is measured in knots.* ◇ *This is a special device that measures the level of radiation in the atmosphere.*

area [C, usually sing., U] the amount of space covered by a flat surface or piece of land, described as a measurement: *How do you work out the area of a right-angled triangle?* ◇ *The room is 12 square metres in area.* ◇ *The country has a total area of around a million square miles.*

capacity [C, usually sing., U] the number of people or things that a container or space can hold: *The theatre has a seating capacity of 2 000.* ◇ *The fuel tank has a capacity of 50 litres.* ◇ *a hard disk storage capacity of 500 megabytes* ◇ *The hall was filled* **to capacity** (= was completely full). ◇ *They played to a* **capacity crowd** (= one that filled all the space or seats).

dimension /daɪˈmenʃn; dɪ-/ [C, usually pl.] a measurement in space, for example the height, width or length of sth: *We measured the dimensions of the kitchen.* ◊ *The images can be viewed in three dimensions using these special glasses.*

volume [U, C] the amount of space that an object or substance fills; the amount of space that a container has: *How do you measure the volume of a gas?* ◊ *What volume of water would be needed to fill the aquarium?* ◊ *In the experiment, lighted candles were put under jars of different volumes.*

bulk [U] the large size or quantity of sth: *Despite its bulk and weight, the car is extremely fast.* ◊ *A charge of £2.50 per copy is made for **bulk orders** (= for a large number of similar items).* ◊ *It's cheaper to **buy in bulk**.*

extent [U] the physical size of an area: *You can't see the **full extent** of the beach from here.* ◊ *The island is 300 square kilometres in extent.* See also **extend** → LEAD *verb* 3

skill *noun*

1 practical skills
2 a high level of skill

---

1 skill · ability · talent · art · gift · flair · knack · aptitude
These are all words for sth that sb is able to do well.

PATTERNS AND COLLOCATIONS
▶ a talent / a gift / a flair / a knack / an aptitude **for** (doing) sth
▶ (a) **great** skill / ability / talent / gift / flair / aptitude
▶ a **useful** skill / talent / gift
▶ (a) **rare** skill / ability / talent / gift
▶ a **special** skill / ability / talent / gift / aptitude
▶ (a) **natural** skill / ability / talent / gift / flair / aptitude
▶ (an) **artistic** skill / ability / talent / gift / flair
▶ (a) **musical** skill / ability / talent / gift
▶ (an) **entrepreneurial / organizational** skill / ability / talent / flair
▶ to **have** a skill / an ability / a talent / the art / a gift / flair / the knack / the aptitude
▶ to **need / lack** a skill / an ability / a talent / a gift / flair
▶ to **show** a skill / an ability / a talent / a gift / flair / an aptitude
▶ to **demonstrate** a skill / an ability / a talent / flair / an aptitude
▶ to **acquire** a skill / an ability / the knack
▶ to **develop** a skill / an ability / a talent / the art / a gift / a flair / the knack / the aptitude
▶ to **master / perfect** a skill / the art
▶ to **lose** a skill / an ability / a talent / the art / the knack

skill [C] something that sb is able to do well, especially when this has been acquired through practice: *We need people with practical skills like carpentry.* ◊ *The course focuses on management skills and customer service.* ❶ **Skill** or **skills** often comes after an adjective or noun that describes a particular type of ability. Skills are usually a result of experience and training. See also **skilled, skilful** → GOOD 4, **experience** → KNOWLEDGE

ability [U, C] a level of skill or intelligence; something that sb is able to do well, especially because they are just naturally good at it: *Almost everyone has some musical ability.* ◊ *Are you used to teaching students of mixed abilities?* ◊ *This programme is about discovering the natural abilities of each child.* See also **able** → GOOD 4

talent /ˈtælənt/ [U, C] a natural ability to do sth well: *Hard work is important but it is no substitute for raw talent.* ◊ *She showed considerable talent for getting what she wanted.* ◊ *He's a man of many talents.* See also **talented** → GOOD 4

art [C, U] (*especially written*) a skill that you can develop with training and practice: *Painting is **the art of** reaching the soul through the eyes.* ◊ *Letter-writing is a lost art nowadays.* ◊ *Appearing confident at interviews is **quite an art** (= rather difficult).*

NOTE **SKILL** OR **ART?** **Skills** are usually practical or technical things, using your hands or managing or organizing people or things. An **art** is usually more about expressing yourself and/or relating to other people: *the art of fiction/poetry/painting/film* ◊ *the art of conversation/communication/persuasion/negotiation/compromise/healing/listening/love*

gift [C] (*especially written*) a natural ability to do sth very well: *She has a great gift for music.* ◊ *He has the gift of making friends easily.* See also **gifted** → GOOD 4

NOTE **TALENT** OR **GIFT**? **Gift** is often used in more literary contexts, especially to talk about people's ability in the arts, as well as in relationships and helping people: *a gift for drawing/painting/writing/drama/improvisation/languages/music* ◊ *a gift for friendship/teaching/humour/calming people down/bringing people together/healing.* **Talent** is used more often than **gift** in spoken English. It can also be used to talk about people's abilities in the arts, but it is commonly used to talk about business skills: *a talent for business/computing/diplomacy/leadership/figures/governing/management/organization*

flair [sing., U] (*especially written*) a natural ability to do sth well; the ability to do sth with style and imagination: *He has a flair for languages.* ◊ *She dresses with real flair.*

knack /næk/ (*rather informal*) a special skill that you have naturally or can learn: *It's easy, once you've got the knack.* ◊ *He had a knack for picking winners.*

aptitude /ˈæptɪtjuːd; AmE -tuːd/ [U, C] (*rather formal, especially written*) a natural ability to do sth well: *She showed a natural aptitude for the work.* ◊ *They may ask you to do an **aptitude test** (= one designed to show whether sb has the natural ability for a particular job or educational course).*

---

2 skill · expertise · competence · technique · know-how · prowess · proficiency · dexterity · artistry
These are all words for the ability to do sth well, especially through learning and practising it for a long time.

PATTERNS AND COLLOCATIONS
▶ skill / expertise / competence / know-how / prowess / proficiency **in** sth
▶ skill / prowess **as** sb / sth
▶ to do sth **with** skill / expertise / competence / dexterity / artistry
▶ **great** skill / expertise / competence / technique / proficiency / dexterity
▶ **remarkable** skill / expertise / prowess
▶ the **necessary** skill / expertise / competence
▶ **practical** skill / expertise / technique / know-how
▶ **technical** skill / expertise / competence / know-how / prowess / proficiency
▶ **scientific / technological** skill / expertise / competence / know-how / prowess
▶ to **have** the skill / expertise / competence / technique / know-how / dexterity
▶ to **need / lack** the skill / expertise / competence / technique / know-how
▶ to **demonstrate / show** your skill / expertise / competence / technique / prowess / proficiency
▶ to **use** your skill / expertise / know-how
▶ to **acquire** skill / expertise / competence / technique / the know-how / proficiency
▶ to **develop** your skill / expertise / competence / technique / proficiency

skill [U] the ability to do sth well, especially because of training and practice: *The job requires skill and an eye for detail.* ◊ *She is a negotiator of considerable skill.* See also **skilled, skilful** → GOOD 4

expertise /ˌekspɜːˈtiːz; AmE -pɜːrˈt-/ [U] expert knowledge or skill in a particular subject, activity or job: *They have considerable expertise in dealing with oil spills.* ◊ *We have the expertise to help you run your business.* ❶ **Expertise** is used especially in the context of work and business. See also **expert** → EXPERT *noun*, **expert** → IMPRESSIVE *adj.*

competence /ˈkɒmpɪtəns; AmE ˈkɑːm-/ [U] (*rather formal*) the ability to do sth well, especially to the level that is required for a particular purpose such as doing a particular job: *She gained a high level of competence in*

English. ◇ *The course is aimed at developing professional competence in language teachers.* See also **competent** → GOOD 4

technique /tekˈniːk/ [U, sing.] the skill with which sb is able to do sth practical: *Her technique has improved a lot over the past season.* ◇ *He needs to work on his interview technique if he's going to get a job.*

ˈknow-how [U] (*informal*) expertise: *We need skilled workers and technical know-how.*

prowess /ˈpraʊəs/ [U] (*formal*) great skill at doing sth: *academic/athletic/sporting prowess* ◇ *He was complimented on his prowess as an oarsman.* ❶ **Prowess** is mainly used to talk about physical and mental ability, especially in men.

proficiency /prəˈfɪʃnsi/ [U] (*rather formal*) the ability to do sth well because of training and practice: *The exercise is aimed at developing proficiency.* ◇ *A high level of oral proficiency in English is required for the job.* See also **proficient** → GOOD 4

dexterity /dekˈsterəti/ [U] (*rather formal*) skill in using your hands; the ability to do sth skilfully: *You need manual dexterity to be good at video games.* ◇ *Desirable qualities for this type of career include charm, verbal dexterity and charisma.*

artistry [U] (*especially written*) the skill of an artist: *He played the piece with effortless artistry.* ◇ *They showed an appreciation of the beauty and artistry of the painting.*

sleep *verb*

sleep · doze · nap · snooze
These words all mean to rest with your eyes closed and your mind and body not active.

PATTERNS AND COLLOCATIONS
▸ to sleep / doze **lightly** / **fitfully**
▸ to doze / snooze **gently**

sleep [I] to rest with your eyes closed and your mind and body not active: *Did you sleep well?* ◇ *No, I slept pretty badly.* ◇ *How did you sleep?* ◇ *I couldn't sleep last night.* ◇ *She hardly slept at all the following night.* ◇ *He slept soundly* (= very well) *that night.* ◇ *Let her sleep – it'll do her good.* ◇ *She slept at her sister's house last night* (=spend the night there). ◇ *I slept late* (= into the morning), *and didn't hear the news till midday.* ❶ It is more usual to say that sb is **asleep** than that they are **sleeping**; but if you use an adverb to say how they are sleeping, use **sleeping**: *'What's Ashley doing?' 'Sh! She's asleep.'* ◇ *The baby was sleeping peacefully.* ◇ ~~The baby was asleep peacefully.~~ **Sleep** can only be used in the passive when it is followed by a preposition such as *in* or *on*: *Her bed hadn't been slept in.*
   ▸ **sleep** *noun* [U, sing.]: *I need to get some sleep.* ◇ *I can't get to sleep.* ◇ *Go to sleep – it's late.* ◇ *He cried out in his sleep.* ◇ *Did you have a good sleep?* ◇ *I'll feel better after a good night's sleep.*

doze [I] to sleep lightly, waking up easily, often when you are not in bed: *I dozed fitfully until dawn.* ◇ *She would often doze off in the armchair after lunch.*
   ▸ **doze** *noun* [sing.]: *I had a doze on the train.*

nap (-pp-) [I] to sleep for a short time, especially during the day: *Try not to nap during the day.*
   ▸ **nap** *noun* [sing.]: *to have/take a nap*

snooze [I] (*informal*) to sleep lightly for a short time, especially during the day and usually not in bed: *My brother was snoozing on the sofa.*
   ▸ **snooze** *noun* [sing.]: *I often have a snooze after lunch.*

slide *verb*

slide · roll · glide · sail · cruise · skate · slither · sweep
These words all mean to move smoothly and easily.

PATTERNS AND COLLOCATIONS
▸ to slide / roll / glide / sail / slither / sweep **into** / **out of** sth
▸ to slide / roll / glide / cruise / skate / slither **along** (sth)

▸ to slide / roll / glide / sail / cruise / sweep **past** (sth)
▸ to slide / roll / glide / skate / slither **on** sth
▸ to slide / roll / glide / slither **to** the floor / bottom, etc.

slide [I, T] (usually used with an adverb or preposition) to move easily over a smooth or wet surface; to make sth move in this way: *Make sure the drawers can slide in and out easily.* ◇ *A tear slid slowly down his pale cheek.* ◇ *The automatic doors slid open as we approached.* ◇ *She slid her hand along the rail.*

roll [I, T] (usually used with an adverb or preposition) to move smoothly across a surface, especially on wheels; to make sth do this: *The car began to roll back down the hill.* ◇ *Tanks rolled triumphantly into the city.* ◇ *A tear rolled down her cheek.* ◇ *He rolled the trolley across the hall.*

glide [I] (usually used with an adverb or preposition) to move smoothly and quietly, especially as though it takes no effort: *Swans went gliding past.* ◇ *The dancers glided smoothly across the floor.*

sail [I] (always used with an adverb or preposition) to move quickly, easily and smoothly in a particular direction, especially in the air: *The ball sailed over the goalkeeper's head.* ◇ *White clouds sailed across the sky.*

cruise /kruːz/ [I] (usually used with an adverb or preposition) (of a car, plane or other vehicle) to travel smoothly at a steady speed: *The plane was cruising at 40 000 feet.* ◇ *I was cruising comfortably along the main highway.*

skate [I] to move across ice on skates (= boots with thin metal blades on the bottom): *That afternoon we went skating on the lake.*

slither /ˈslɪðə(r)/ [I] (always used with an adverb or preposition) to move across a surface smoothly, usually close to or on the ground and often twisting from side to side: *The snake slithered away as we approached.*

sweep [I] (always used with an adverb or preposition) to move somewhere quickly and smoothly, especially in a way that impresses or is intended to impress other people: *Without another word, she swept out of the room.*

slight *adj.* See also the entry for MINOR

slight · small · modest · little · marginal · minimal · negligible
These words all describe things that are not very important or serious in degree.

PATTERNS AND COLLOCATIONS
▸ a slight / small / modest / little / marginal / minimal **change** / **difference** / **improvement**
▸ a small / modest / minimal / negligible **amount**
▸ a slight / small / little **error** / **mistake** / **defect** / **accident** / **problem**
▸ a slight / small / minimal **chance**
▸ a modest / marginal / minimal / negligible **effect** / **impact**
▸ a small / modest / minimal **investment** / **outlay** / **sum** / **charge**

slight not very important or serious; small in degree: *I woke up with a slight headache.* ◇ *The picture was at a slight angle.* ◇ *A slight breeze was blowing.* ◇ *The damage was slight.* ◇ *She takes offence at the slightest thing* (= is very easily offended). ◇ *There was not the slightest hint of trouble.*
   ▸ **slightly** *adv.* to a small degree; not very or not very much: *This author takes a slightly different approach.* ◇ *It will make the cost slightly higher.* ◇ *The door was slightly ajar.*

small [usually before noun] not very important, serious or difficult: *I made only a few small changes to the report.* ◇ *Can I ask you a small favour?* ◇ *Everything had been planned down to the smallest detail.* ◇ *It was no small achievement getting her to agree to the deal.*

NOTE **SLIGHT OR SMALL?** You can use either word to talk about changes or problems: *a slight/small adjustment/ alteration/amendment/change/improvement/reduction/ rise/variation* ◇ *a slight/small mistake/error/defect/ flaw/blemish/discrepancy/problem/snag/accident.* Use

slight but NOT **small** to talk about medical problems, feelings or things that affect the senses: *a slight cold/ headache/movement/noise/touch* ◇ *slight discomfort/ embarrassment*. Use **small** but NOT **slight** to talk about amounts or numbers: *a small amount/number/quantity/degree/proportion/minority*. Both words are often used in the superlative, but especially **slightest**, often in negative sentences: *He is, without the slightest doubt, the greatest living novelist.* ◇ *I did not feel the slightest inclination to hurry.*

modest /'mɒdɪst; AmE 'mɑ:d-/ not very large, expensive or grand: *There has been a modest improvement in the situation.* ◇ *He charged a relatively modest fee.* ◇ *She grew up in a modest little house in the suburbs.* ◇ *The research was carried out on a modest scale.* ❶ **Modest** is used especially to talk about aims and achievements: *a modest aim/achievement/ambition/goal/success*; amounts of money that people spend or earn: *a modest contribution/expenditure/fee/gain/investment/outlay/profit/sum*; buildings that are not very expensive or grand: *a modest house/flat/villa* ◇ *modest premises*; and the size of sth: *a modest size/amount/quantity/scale/share/proportion*
▸ **modestly** *adv.*: *modestly priced goods*

little [usually before noun] (*rather informal, especially spoken*) not very important; not serious: *I can't remember every little detail.* ◇ *You'll soon get used to these little difficulties.* ◇ *We had a little adventure yesterday.* ❶ **Little** is often used to talk about problems, events or mysteries that are not very serious or important: *a little error/mistake/defect/ problem/argument/accident/incident/adventure/mystery/ quirk/secret*

marginal /'mɑ:dʒɪnl; AmE 'mɑ:rdʒ-/ (*rather formal*) only slight: *The story will only be of marginal interest to our readers.* ◇ *The difference between the two estimates is marginal.*
▸ **marginally** *adv.*: *He's in a new job but he's only marginally better off.*

minimal /'mɪnɪməl/ very small in size or amount; as small as possible: *The work was carried out at minimal cost.* ◇ *The damage to the car was minimal.*

negligible /'neglɪdʒəbl/ (*especially written*) so small or unimportant that it is not worth considering: *The cost was negligible.* ◇ *Tests found only a negligible amount of the chemical in the product.* ❶ When you use **negligible**, you mean that an amount of the thing described exists or is present, but that there is not enough of it to have an effect.

slip *verb*

1 slip away quietly
2 slip on the ice/slip out of your hand

1 slip · creep · sneak · slink · tiptoe · prowl · slide · pad
These words all mean to move somewhere quietly, especially in order not to be noticed.

PATTERNS AND COLLOCATIONS
▸ to slip/ creep/ sneak/ slink/ tiptoe/ slide/ pad **away**/ **in**/ **out**
▸ to creep/ sneak/ prowl/ pad **around**/ **about**
▸ to slip/ creep/ sneak/ tiptoe **up to** sb/ sth
▸ to creep/ sneak **up on** sb
▸ to creep/ tiptoe (somewhere) **quietly**
▸ to slip/ creep/ pad (somewhere) **silently**

slip (-**pp**-) [I] (always used with an adverb or preposition) to go somewhere quickly and quietly, especially without being noticed: *The ship slipped into the harbour at night.* ◇ *I slipped away before the end of the performance.*

creep [I] (always used with an adverb or preposition) to move slowly, quietly and carefully because you do not want to be seen or heard: *The cat was creeping stealthily through the long grass.* ◇ *Don't creep up on me like that!*

sneak [I] (always used with an adverb or preposition) (*usually disapproving*) to go somewhere secretly, trying to avoid being seen: *I caught him trying to sneak in without paying.*

NOTE **SLIP** OR **SNEAK**? You *sneak into/out of* a place because you do not want to be seen, often because you are doing sth wrong. You *slip into/out of* a place either because you do not want to be seen or because you do not want to disturb people, but it does not usually suggest that you are doing anything wrong.

slink [I] (always used with an adverb or preposition) to move somewhere very quietly and slowly, especially because you are ashamed, afraid or do not want to be seen: *She slunk out of the room, feeling like a criminal.*

tiptoe /'tɪptəʊ; AmE -toʊ/ [I] (always used with an adverb or preposition) to walk on your toes, so that you don't make any noise: *I tiptoed over to the window.*

prowl /praʊl/ [I, T] (usually used with an adverb or preposition) (of an animal) to move quietly and carefully around an area, especially when hunting; (of a person) to move quietly and carefully around an area, especially with the intention of committing a crime: *Wolves were prowling around outside.* ◇ *He prowled the streets, looking for likely victims.*

slide [I] (always used with an adverb or preposition) to move somewhere quickly, quietly and smoothly: *He slid into bed.* ◇ *She slid out while no one was looking.*

pad (-**dd**-) [I] (always used with an adverb or preposition) to walk with quiet regular steps, often without shoes or on a soft surface: *The girl padded barefoot over to the window.*

2 slip · skid
These words all mean to slide a short distance, usually accidentally.

PATTERNS AND COLLOCATIONS
▸ to slip/ skid **on** the ice/ the wet grass, etc.

slip (-**pp**-) [I] to slide a short distance accidentally so that you fall or nearly fall; to slide out of position or out of your hand: *She slipped on the ice and broke her leg.* ◇ *As I ran up the stairs my foot slipped.* ◇ *His hat had slipped over one eye.* ◇ *The child slipped from his grasp and ran off.*

skid (-**dd**-) [I] (usually of a vehicle) to slide sideways or forwards in an uncontrolled way: *The car skidded and crashed into a wall.* ◇ *The taxi skidded to a halt just in time.*
▸ **skid** *noun* [C]: *The motorbike went into a skid.*

slogan *noun*

slogan · formula · motto · mantra · catchphrase
These are all words for a word or short phrase that is easy to remember and is often repeated in order to suggest an idea to people.

PATTERNS AND COLLOCATIONS
▸ to **come up with** a slogan/ formula
▸ to **coin**/ **adopt** a slogan/ motto
▸ to **use** a slogan/ motto/ mantra/ catchphrase
▸ to **chant** a slogan/ mantra

slogan /'sləʊgən; AmE 'sloʊ-/ [C] a word or phrase that is easy to remember, used for example by a political party or in advertising to attract people's attention or to suggest an idea quickly: *The crowd began chanting anti-government slogans.* ◇ *They came up with a catchy new advertising slogan.*

formula /'fɔ:mjələ; AmE 'fɔ:rm-/ (pl. **formulas** or **formulae** /-li:/) [C] (*rather formal*) a fixed form of words used in a particular situation: *What are the correct legal formulae for this kind of letter?* ◇ *The prime minister keeps coming out with the same tired formulas.*
▸ **formulaic** /ˌfɔ:mju'leɪɪk; AmE ˌfɔ:rm-/ *adj.*: (*rather formal*) *Traditional stories make use of formulaic expressions like 'Once upon a time…'*

motto /'mɒtəʊ; AmE 'mɑ:toʊ/ (pl. **mottoes** or **mottos**) [C] a short sentence or phrase that expresses the aims and beliefs of a person, group or institution and is used as a rule of behaviour: *The school's motto is: 'Duty, Honour, Country'.* ◇ *'Live and let live.' That's my motto.*

mantra /ˈmæntrə/ [C] a word, phrase or sound that is repeated again and again, especially during prayer or meditation: *He was chanting a Buddhist mantra.*

catchphrase /ˈkætʃfreɪz/ [C] a popular phrase that is connected with the politician or entertainer who used it and made it famous: *It was PC Dixon who gave us the catchphrase 'Evening all!'.*

slope noun

slope · ramp · bank · drop · incline
These are all words for land or a surface that leads downwards or upwards.

PATTERNS AND COLLOCATIONS
▶ **on** / **upon** / **down** a slope / a ramp / a bank / an incline
▶ a **steep** slope / ramp / bank / drop / incline
▶ a **gentle** slope / incline
▶ a **long** / **short** slope / ramp / drop
▶ to **climb (up)** a slope / ramp / bank
▶ to **go down** a slope / ramp

slope [C] a surface or piece of land that is higher at one end than the other: *The house sits comfortably at the bottom of a grassy slope.* ◇ *The town is built on a slope.*

ramp [C] a slope that joins two parts of a road, path or other structure when one is higher than the other: *Ramps should be provided for wheelchair users.*

bank [C] a raised area of ground that slopes at the sides, often at the edge of sth or dividing sth; an artificial slope built at the side of a road, so that cars can drive fast around bends: *There were low banks of earth between the rice fields.* ◇ *The girls ran down the steep grassy bank.*

drop [C, usually sing.] a place where the land or a surface suddenly goes from a high level to a low level: *There was a twenty-foot **drop onto** the stones beneath.* ◇ *We were inches away from a sheer **drop to** the crashing waves below.*

incline /ˈɪnklaɪn/ [C] (*formal or technical*) a slope: *The vehicle was parked on a steep incline.*

slope verb

slope · dip · rise · descend · climb · drop
These are all words that can be used when land or a surface leads downwards or upwards.

PATTERNS AND COLLOCATIONS
▶ to slope / rise / descend / climb **towards** sth
▶ to slope / dip / drop **down**
▶ a **road** / **path** slopes / dips / descends / climbs / drops
▶ to slope / dip / rise / descend / climb / drop **steeply**
▶ to slope / dip / rise **gently** / **slightly**

slope [I] (usually used with an adverb or preposition) (of a horizontal surface) to be at an angle so that it is higher at one end than the other: *The path sloped gently down.* ◇ *The garage is rectangular with a sloping roof.* See also **slope** → ANGLE *noun*, **slope** → LEAN *verb* 1

dip (-pp-) [I, T] (usually used with an adverb or preposition) (of ground or a road or path) to lead downwards suddenly: *The road dipped suddenly as we approached the town.*
▶ **dip** *noun* [C]: *a dip in the road*

rise [I] (of land) to slope upwards: *Behind the house the ground rises steeply to the north.*

descend /dɪˈsend/ [I] (*rather formal*) (of a feature such as a hill, a road or stairs) to lead downwards: *At this point the path descends steeply.* **OPP** climb

climb [I] (of a road) to lead upwards: *From here the path climbs steeply to the summit.* **OPP** descend

drop (-pp-) [I] (of land or a road or path) to slope steeply downwards: *In front of them the valley **dropped** sharply **away from** the road.*

---

slow *adj.* See also the entry for EASY 2

slow · gradual · sluggish · measured
These words all describe people or things taking or lasting a long time.

PATTERNS AND COLLOCATIONS
▶ a slow / gradual **improvement** / **change** / **acceptance**
▶ slow / sluggish **progress**
▶ (a) slow / measured **pace** / **steps**

slow not moving, acting or done quickly; taking a long time; not going or allowing you to go at a fast speed: *a slow driver/walker/reader* ◇ *Oh you're so slow; come on, hurry up!* ◇ *Progress was slower than expected.* ◇ *Collecting data is a painfully slow process.* ◇ *She gave a slow smile.* ◇ *I missed the fast train and had to get the slow one* (= the one that stops at all the stations). **OPP** **fast**, **quick** → FAST, **rapid**, **fast** → QUICK, See also **slow** → LATE
▶ **slowly** *adv.*: *Please could you speak more slowly?* ◇ *Slowly things began to improve.*

gradual happening slowly over a long period: *a gradual change in the climate* ◇ *Recovery from the disease is very gradual.* **OPP** **sudden** → SUDDEN
▶ **gradually** *adv.*: *The weather gradually improved.* ◇ *Gradually, the children began to understand.*

sluggish (*written, often disapproving*) moving, reacting or working more slowly than normal and in a way that seems lazy: *sluggish traffic* ◇ *the sluggish black waters of the canal* ◇ *He felt very heavy and sluggish after the meal.* ❶ **Sluggish** can also describe a business, economy, etc. that is not very busy, active or successful: (*business*) *a sluggish economy* ◇ *Sales were sluggish.*
▶ **sluggishly** *adv.*: *Traffic moved sluggishly along the London Road.*

measured /ˈmeʒəd; AmE -ərd/ [only before noun] slow and controlled: *She replied in a measured tone to his threat.* ◇ *He walked down the corridor with measured steps.* ❶ **Measured** usually describes the way sb talks or walks.

---

slump verb See also the entry for FALL 1

slump · plunge · tumble · plummet
These are all words that can be used when the value or level of sth goes down suddenly.

PATTERNS AND COLLOCATIONS
▶ to slump / plunge / tumble / plummet **by** 100, 25%, a half, etc.
▶ to slump / plunge / tumble / plummet **from** 15 000 **to** 1 000
▶ to plunge / plummet **in** value
▶ **prices** / **profits** / **sales** slump / plunge / tumble / plummet
▶ **rates** plunge / tumble / plummet
▶ to slump / plunge **dramatically** / **suddenly**
▶ to plunge / tumble **sharply**

slump [I] (not usually used in the progressive tenses) (*business*) to fall in price, value or level, suddenly and by a large amount: *Profits slumped by over 50%.* **OPP** **jump**, **surge** → SOAR, See also **slump** → REDUCTION *noun*

plunge (*especially business*) to fall in price, value or level, suddenly and by a large amount: *Stock markets plunged at the news of the coup.* **OPP** **leap** → SOAR
▶ **plunge** *noun* [sing.]: *a dramatic plunge in profits*

tumble (*especially business*) to fall rapidly in price, value or level: *The price of oil is still tumbling.* **OPP** **soar** → SOAR
▶ **tumble** *noun* [sing.]: *Share prices **took a tumble** following news of the merger.*

plummet (*especially business*) to fall suddenly and quickly in price, value or level, from a high level or position: *Share prices plummeted to an all-time low.* ◇ *Her spirits plummeted at the thought of having to meet him again.* **OPP** **soar**, **rocket** → SOAR

> **NOTE** WHICH WORD? There is very little difference in meaning between these words in a business context. Prices **slump** because there is nothing to keep them up any more; they **plunge** because sth has pushed them down. When prices **tumble** they fall quickly several

times, rather than making one big fall all at once, as they do if they **slump** (which is not used in the progressive tenses): *The price of oil is still slumping.* **Plummet** often suggests the biggest fall, though not the fastest, from the highest level to the lowest.

small *adj.*

small · little · tiny · miniature · compact · minute · microscopic
These words all describe sth that is not large in size, number, degree or amount or not as large as sth else of the same type.

small	tiny	minute
little		microscopic
miniature		
compact		

PATTERNS AND COLLOCATIONS
▸ a small / little / tiny / miniature **house / town / room**
▸ a small / little / tiny / miniature / compact **car**
▸ a small / little / tiny / minute / microscopic **detail**
▸ a small / little / tiny **baby / child**
▸ a small / little **boy / girl / man / woman**
▸ small / little / tiny / minute / microscopic **particles / organisms / creatures**
▸ a small / little / tiny **bit** (of sth)
▸ **very / quite / relatively / comparatively** small / little / tiny / compact
▸ **extremely / really** small / little / tiny
▸ **rather** small / little / compact

small not large in size, number, degree or amount; not as large as other things of the same type: *Their apartment's pretty small. ◇ That dress is too small for you. ◇ They're having a relatively small wedding. ◇ These shoes are too big. Do you have some in a smaller size?* **OPP** **large, big → LARGE**
little [usually before noun] (not usually used in the comparative or superlative) small: *A little boy was standing on the doorstep. ◇ What a cute little baby! ◇ She gave a little laugh. ◇ I was a little bit afraid of him. ◇ Here's a little something (= a small present) for your birthday.* **OPP** **big, large → LARGE**

> **NOTE** SMALL OR LITTLE? **Small** is the most usual opposite of **big** or **large**. **Little** is often used to show how you feel about sb/sth, especially after other adjectives, such as *ugly, nice* or *cute*. It can also be used when you think sb/ sth is not important: *You'll feel a little sting. ◇ What a horrible little man!* The forms **littler** and **littlest** are rare; it is more common to use **smaller** and **smallest**.

tiny /'taɪni/ very small in size or amount: *His room is absolutely tiny. ◇ She held the tiny baby in her arms. ◇ Only a tiny minority hold such extreme views. ◇ We come from a tiny town in up-state New York. ◇ There's only one little tiny problem with the booking.* **OPP** **huge, enormous → HUGE**
miniature /'mɪnətʃə(r); AmE also -tʃʊr/ [only before noun] (no comparative or superlative) much smaller than the usual size of other things of the same type: *It belongs to a rare breed of miniature horses. ◇ In the centre of the table was a bowl filled with miniature roses. ◇ They expect their children to behave like miniature adults.* ❶ **Miniature** versions of plants or animals are usually deliberately bred to be small.
compact /kəm'pækt/ small and easy to carry; using or filling only a small amount of space: *a compact camera ◇ The kitchen was compact but well-equipped.*
minute /maɪ'njuːt; AmE also -'nuːt/ extremely small: *There were minute traces of the drug present in his blood. ◇ The kitchen on the boat is minute.*

microscopic /ˌmaɪkrə'skɒpɪk; AmE -'skɑːpɪk/ [usually before noun] extremely small and difficult or impossible to see without a microscope (= an instrument used in scientific study to make very small things look larger): *It is claimed that the fumes contain microscopic particles of carbon.*

smash *verb* See also the entry for BREAK 1

smash · shatter · break (sth) up · splinter
These are all words that can be used when sth breaks into lots of small pieces.

PATTERNS AND COLLOCATIONS
▸ to smash / shatter / break up **into** small / a thousand pieces
▸ to smash / shatter a **window / windscreen**
▸ **glass** smashes / shatters / splinters
▸ sb's smashed / shattered / splintered **bones / skull**

smash [T, I] to break sth or be broken, violently and noisily, into lots of small pieces: *She flew into one of her rages and started smashing crockery. ◇ His right hand was smashed and his shoulder dislocated. ◇ The glass bowl smashed into a thousand pieces.* ❶ If sb **smashes up** a place or room, they destroy it by breaking all the furniture, etc.: *Youths had broken into the bar and smashed the place up.*
shatter [I, T] to suddenly break into small pieces; to make sth do this: *He dropped the vase and it shattered into pieces on the floor. ◇ The explosion shattered all the windows in the building. ◇ Shattered homes were ablaze.*

> **NOTE** SMASH OR SHATTER ? People **smash** things deliberately; things get **shattered** as a result of explosions, flying bullets, stones, etc.: *The thief smashed a window to get into her car. ◇ ~~The thief shattered a window to get into her car.~~ ◇ Windows were shattered in the blast. ◇ ~~Windows were smashed in the blast.~~*

break 'up, break sth 'up *phrasal verb* to separate, or make sth separate, into smaller pieces, either violently or carefully: *The ship broke up on the rocks. ◇ The grey clouds had begun to break up. ◇ The ship was broken up for scrap metal. ◇ Break up the chocolate and place it in a bowl.*
splinter [I, T] (of wood, glass, stone or bone) to break into long, thin, sharp pieces; to make wood, glass, etc. break in this way: *The mirror cracked but did not splinter. ◇ She could hear the talons shredding and splintering the wood.*

smell *noun* See also the entry for ODOUR

smell · scent · aroma · fragrance · whiff
These are all words for the quality of sth that people and animals can sense through their noses, especially when this is pleasant.

PATTERNS AND COLLOCATIONS
▸ a smell / the scent / an aroma / the fragrance / a whiff **of** sth
▸ a **faint** smell / scent / aroma / fragrance / whiff
▸ a **strong** smell / scent / aroma / whiff
▸ a / an **pungent / heady** smell / scent / aroma
▸ a **fresh** smell / scent / fragrance
▸ to **have / give off** a smell / a scent / an aroma / a fragrance / a whiff
▸ to **be filled / fill sth** with a smell / a scent / an aroma / a fragrance
▸ to **catch** the smell / the scent / a whiff of sth
▸ a smell / a scent / an aroma **hangs / lingers / comes / wafts** somewhere

smell [C, U] the quality of sth that people and animals can sense through their noses: *There was a musty smell in the attic. ◇ What a terrible smell! ◇ Do you like the smell of coffee?*
▸ **smell** *verb* [T, no passive] (not used in the progressive tenses; often used with can or could): *Can you smell something burning? ◇ I bent down to smell the flowers.*
scent /sent/ [U, C] a light, pleasant smell: *The air was filled with the scent of wild herbs.*
▸ **scented** *adj.*: *scented soap*

aroma /əˈrəʊmə; *AmE* əˈroʊmə/ [C] a pleasant, fairly strong, smell, especially of food or drinks such as coffee: *The aroma of fresh coffee wafted towards them.*
▸ **aromatic** /ˌærəˈmætɪk/ *adj.*: *aromatic oils/herbs*

fragrance /ˈfreɪɡrəns/ [U, C] a pleasant smell, for example of flowers or fruit: *The flowers are chosen for their delicate fragrance.* ◊ *The bath oils come in various fragrances.*
▸ **fragrant** *adj.*: *fragrant herbs/flowers/oils*

whiff /wɪf/ [C] (usually followed by *of*) a smell, especially one that you only smell for a short time: *He caught a whiff of her perfume as she passed.* ◊ *She can't bear the slightest whiff of tobacco smoke.*

smelly *adj.* See also the entry for ROTTEN

smelly · stale · dank · musty · stinking
These words all describe sth that smells bad.

PATTERNS AND COLLOCATIONS
▸ a stale / dank / musty **smell**
▸ a stale / musty **odour**
▸ a smelly / dank / musty **room**
▸ stale / dank / musty **air**
▸ stale / stinking **breath**
▸ to **smell** stale / dank / musty

smelly (*rather informal, disapproving*) having an unpleasant smell: *My boyfriend's got smelly feet.* See also **smell** → ODOUR

stale (of air, smoke or sth that smells) no longer fresh; smelling unpleasant: *The room was thick with stale cigarette smoke.* ◊ *The room smelt of stale sweat.* See also **stale** → ROTTEN

dank (especially of a place) damp, cold and smelling unpleasant: *They found themselves in a large, dank cave.*

musty (especially of air or a place) smelling damp and unpleasant because of a lack of fresh air: *The hallway was musty and dark.*

stinking [usually before noun] (*disapproving*) having a very strong, unpleasant smell: *The black, stinking water was covered with scum.* See also **stink** → ODOUR

smile *verb*

smile · grin · beam · smirk · simper
These words all mean to have a happy expression on your face with the corners of your mouth turned upwards.

smirk   smile   grin
simper   beam

PATTERNS AND COLLOCATIONS
▸ to smile / grin / beam / smirk / simper **at** sb / sth
▸ to smile / grin / beam / smirk **with** sth
▸ to smile / grin / smirk **to yourself**
▸ to smile / grin / beam broadly / widely / happily / cheerfully / from ear to ear
▸ to smile / grin / smirk slightly / maliciously

smile [I, T, no passive] to have or make a happy expression appear on your face with the corners of your mouth turned upwards; to say or express sth with this expression: *She smiled at him and he smiled back.* ◊ *I had to smile at* (= was amused by) *his optimism.* ◊ *The memory still made her smile.* ◊ *She smiled a smile of dry amusement.* ◊ *'Perfect,' he smiled.* **OPP frown** → FROWN
▸ **smile** *noun* [C]: *He had a big smile on his face.*

grin (-nn-) [I, T, no passive] to smile widely; to say or express sth with a wide smile: *He was grinning from ear to ear.* ◊ *'Don't be daft,' he grinned.* **OPP scowl** → FROWN
▸ **grin** *noun* [C]: *Take that grin off your face!*

beam [I, T, no passive] to have a big happy smile on your face; to say or express sth with a big happy smile: *She was positively beaming with pleasure.* ◊ *'I'd love to come,' she beamed.*

NOTE GRIN OR BEAM? People always **beam** with happiness or pleasure; a **grin** can show happiness or pleasure, but it can also show stupidity, embarrassment or amusement, including slightly unkind amusement at sb else: *to grin inanely/sheepishly/apologetically/ruefully/wryly/cheekily/wickedly/maliciously*

smirk /smɜːk; *AmE* smɜːrk/ [I] (*disapproving*) to smile in a silly or unpleasant way that shows that you are pleased with yourself, are secretly laughing at sb or know sth that other people do not know: *What are you smirking at?* ◊ *He smirked unpleasantly when we told him the bad news.*
▸ **smirk** *noun* [C]: *She had a self-satisfied smirk on her face.*

simper [I, T] (*written, disapproving*) to smile in a silly and annoying way: *She was nothing like the silly, simpering village girls back home.* ◊ *'You're such a darling,' she simpered.*

smoke *noun*

smoke · fumes · exhaust · smog
These are all words for a type of gas which is poisonous and makes the air dirty.

PATTERNS AND COLLOCATIONS
▸ toxic / poisonous **smoke** / fumes
▸ car / petrol / diesel **fumes** / exhaust
▸ to **emit** / **produce** / **give off** smoke / fumes
▸ to **reduce** smoke / smog
▸ smoke / exhaust **emissions** / **pollution**
▸ a **cloud of** smoke / fumes

smoke [U] the grey, white or black gas that is produced by sth burning: *The room was thick with cigarette smoke.* ◊ *Clouds of thick black smoke billowed from the car's exhaust.*

fumes [pl.] smoke, gas or sth similar that smells strongly or is dangerous to breathe in: *Benzene is found in car exhaust fumes.* ◊ *She was overcome by smoke and fumes.*

exhaust /ɪɡˈzɔːst/ [U] waste gases that come out of a vehicle, engine or machine: *The proposals include new limits on car exhaust emissions.*

smog [U] a form of air pollution, especially in cities, that is or looks like a mixture of smoke and fog; a period of time when there is smog in the air: *The city has had only limited success in reducing smog levels.* ❶ In British English **smog** can also be countable: (*BrE*) *Nowadays, smogs are very common in major cities.* See also **fog** → CLOUD 1

smug *adj.*

smug · complacent · self-righteous · self-satisfied · sanctimonious
These words all describe sb who seems too pleased with themselves, their achievements or their behaviour.

PATTERNS AND COLLOCATIONS
▸ smug / complacent / self-righteous / sanctimonious **about** sth
▸ a smug / complacent / self-satisfied **smile**
▸ a self-righteous / sanctimonious **tone**
▸ a complacent / self-righteous **attitude**

smug (*disapproving*) looking or feeling too pleased about your own achievements: *What are you looking so smug about?* ◊ *There was an air of smug satisfaction in Luke's voice.*
▸ **smugly** *adv.*: *Virtue is its own reward, I thought smugly.*

complacent /kəmˈpleɪsnt/ (*disapproving*) too satisfied with yourself or with a situation, so that you do not feel that any change is necessary: *Nobody can afford to be complacent about security.* ◊ *Don't go getting too complacent before the exams.* ❶ A person or group, such as a government, can be described as **complacent** when they are not paying enough attention to sth because they think everything is all right, especially when there is actually a problem or could be a problem, or when sth goes wrong.
▸ **complacency** /kəmˈpleɪsnsi/ *noun* [U]: *Despite signs of*

an improvement in the economy, there is no room for complacency.

▸ **complacently** adv.: He smiled complacently.

self-'righteous /'raɪtʃəs/ (disapproving) feeling or behaving as if what you say or do is always morally right, and other people are wrong: He was in one of his self-righteous moods.

self-'satisfied (disapproving) looking or feeling too pleased with yourself or your own achievements: He had a self-satisfied smirk on his face.

sanctimonious /ˌsæŋktɪ'məʊniəs; AmE -'moʊ-/ (disapproving) behaving as if you are better or more moral than other people: I'm fed up with his sanctimonious attitude.

snack noun See also the entry for MEAL

snack · something to eat · refreshments
These are all words for an amount of sth to eat which is smaller than a meal.

PATTERNS AND COLLOCATIONS
▸ (a) **light** snack / refreshments
▸ to **have / grab** a snack / something to eat
▸ to **stop for** a snack / something to eat / refreshments

snack [C] a small meal or amount of food, often eaten in a hurry: I only have time for a **quick snack** at lunchtime. ◇ I think it's time for a mid-morning snack. See also **snack** → DINE verb

something to eat [sing.] a snack: We stopped for something to eat. ◇ Would you like something to eat?

NOTE SNACK OR SOMETHING TO EAT? A **snack** is less than a meal, but it may be eaten instead of a meal or at a particular time of day. **Something to eat** is less specific than a **snack**; it may be a light meal, or it may be much less than that, eaten, or offered to sb at any time that they may be hungry, but not at a regular time: a mid-morning snack ◇ a mid-morning something to eat

refreshments [pl.] (rather formal) drinks and snacks that are provided or sold to people in a public place or at a public event: Light refreshments will be sold during the interval. ◇ Tickets include the price of refreshments.

snow noun

snow · hail · snowfall · snowflake · sleet · slush · snowdrift · hailstone
These are all words for the frozen water which falls or has fallen from the sky.

PATTERNS AND COLLOCATIONS
▸ **in / through** the snow / hail / sleet / slush
▸ (a) **heavy / light** snow / snowfall
▸ **falling / swirling** snow / snowflakes
▸ **melting** snow / slush
▸ snow / hail / snowflakes / sleet / hailstones **falls / fall**
▸ snow / snowflakes / slush **melts / melt**

snow [U] small soft white pieces of frozen water that fall from the sky in cold weather; this substance when it is lying on the ground: Snow was falling heavily. ◇ Children were playing in the snow. ◇ The snow didn't settle (= stay on the ground). ❶ **Snows** [pl.] is used in a literary context to mean an amount of snow that falls in one particular place or at one particular time: the first snows of winter ◇ the snows of Everest See also **snowstorm** → STORM
▸ **snow** [I]: It's been **snowing** heavily all day.
▸ **snowy** adj.: snowy fields ◇ a snowy weekend

hail [U] small balls of ice that fall like rain: Rain and hail pounded on the tiled roof.
▸ **hail** [I]: It's **hailing**!

snowfall /'snəʊfɔːl; AmE 'snoʊ-/ [C, U] an occasion when snow falls; the amount of snow that falls in a particular place in a period of time: There had been a heavy snowfall and the cars were almost buried beneath the snow. ◇ What is the average annual snowfall for this state?

snowflake /'snəʊfleɪk; AmE 'snoʊ-/ [C] one separate small piece of snow that falls: A single snowflake landed on her nose.

sleet [U] a mixture of rain and snow: The rain was turning to sleet.
▸ **sleet** [I]: It's sleeting!

slush /slʌʃ/ [U] partly melted snow that is usually dirty: In the city the clean white snow had turned to grey slush.

snowdrift /'snəʊdrɪft; AmE 'snoʊ-/ [C] a deep pile of snow that has been blown together by the wind: The car got stuck in a snowdrift.

hailstone /'heɪlstəʊn; AmE -stoʊn/ [C, usually pl.] a small ball of ice that falls like rain; a single piece of hail: We struggled up the hill in a wind full of dust and hailstones.

soak verb

soak · dip · drench · wet · flood · moisten · dampen · douse · immerse
These words all mean to make sth wet.

dip	wet	soak	flood
moisten		drench	
dampen		douse	
		immerse	

PATTERNS AND COLLOCATIONS
▸ to soak / drench / wet / moisten / dampen / douse sth **with** sth
▸ to soak / dip / drench / douse / immerse sth **in** sth
▸ to soak / drench / douse / immerse **yourself** in sth
▸ to dip / wet / moisten / dampen a **brush** (in sth)
▸ to wet / moisten **your lips**
▸ **rain** soaks / drenches / floods sb / sth
▸ to be soaked / drenched sth with **blood / sweat**
▸ to soak / douse sth in / with **petrol**
▸ to be soaked / drenched **to the skin**
▸ to **completely / totally** soak / drench / immerse sth
▸ to **thoroughly** soak / drench / wet / moisten / dampen sth
▸ to **slightly** wet / moisten / dampen sth

soak [T, I] to make sb/sth completely wet; to put sth in liquid for a time so that it becomes completely wet; to become completely wet in this way: A sudden shower of rain soaked the spectators. ◇ His shirt was soaked with blood. ◇ If you soak the tablecloth before you wash it, the stains should come out. ◇ I'm going to go and **soak in the bath**. See also **soaked** → WET 1

dip (-pp-) [T] to put sth quickly into liquid and take it out again: He dipped the brush into the thick white paint. ◇ Dip your hand in to see how hot the water is.

drench [T, often passive] to make sb/sth completely wet: We were caught in the storm and got drenched to the skin. ◇ His face was drenched with sweat. ◇ (figurative) She drenched herself in perfume. See also **drenched** → WET 1

NOTE SOAK OR DRENCH? In some cases you can use either word. **Drench** is used especially when a lot of water falls on or pours down sb/sth; **soak** is used more often than **drench** when liquid comes up from underneath sth and makes it completely wet. **Soak**, but NOT **drench** is used when you deliberately put sth in water.

wet [T] to make sth wet: Wet the brush slightly before putting it in the paint. ◇ He wet his finger to test the wind. See also **wet** → WET adj. 1

flood [T] to fill or cover a place with water; (of a river) to become so full that it spreads out onto the land around it: If the pipe bursts it could flood the whole house. ◇ The river flooded the valley. See also **flood** → FLOOD noun 1, **flood** → FLOOD verb

moisten /'mɔɪsn/ [T] to make sth slightly wet: *He moistened his lips before he spoke.* ◇ *Wash the wound gently with a piece of moistened cotton wool.* See also **moist** → WET *adj.* 1

dampen [T] to make sth slightly wet: *He dampened his hair to make it lie flat.* ◇ *Perspiration dampened her face and neck.* See also **damp** → WET *adj.* 1

NOTE MOISTEN OR DAMPEN? Moisten is a slightly more positive word than **dampen**. You **moisten** things that you want to be wet or that are naturally wet, such as *lips* or *soil*. You **dampen** things that are naturally dry such as *paper, cloth* or *brushes*. Things can also be **dampened** by *water, rain* or *sweat*.

douse /daʊs/ [T] to pour a lot of liquid over sb/sth; to soak sb/sth in liquid, especially a liquid that can catch fire and burn easily: *The horses are doused with buckets of cold water.* ◇ *The car was doused in petrol and set alight.* See also **douse** → PUT STH OUT

immerse /ɪ'mɜːs; *AmE* ɪ'mɜːrs/ [T] (*formal*) to put sb/sth into a liquid so that they or it are completely covered: *The seeds will swell when immersed in water.*

▸ **immersion** /ɪ'mɜːʃn; *AmE* ɪ'mɜːrʃn; -ʒn/ *noun* [U]: *Immersion in cold water resulted in a rapid loss of heat.*

---

soar *verb* See also the entry for RISE

---

soar · jump · surge · spiral · rocket · leap · shoot up
These are all words that can be used when an amount, level or number increases quickly.

PATTERNS AND COLLOCATIONS
▸ to soar / jump / shoot up **in** price, number, etc.
▸ to soar / jump / surge / rocket / leap / shoot up **(by) 10%, 2 000,** etc.
▸ to soar / jump / rocket / leap / shoot up **from 2% to 5%**
▸ **the price** soars / jumps / surges / spirals / rockets / leaps / shoots up
▸ **the cost** soars / jumps / surges / spirals / rockets
▸ **profits** soar / jump / surge / leap
▸ **the number / level** soars / jumps / shoots up
▸ to soar / jump / surge / leap / shoot up **suddenly**
▸ to jump / surge / leap / shoot up **dramatically**

soar [I] (*written*) to increase very quickly in value, amount or level: *Soaring costs have made progress difficult.* ◇ *Air pollution is set to soar above safety levels.* **OPP** tumble, plummet → SLUMP

jump [I] (*especially journalism*) to increase suddenly and by a large amount: *Prices jumped by 60 % last year.* **OPP** slump → SLUMP

surge [I] (*especially business*) (of prices, profits or the rate of sth) to suddenly increase in value or level: *Profits from cigarettes surged to $225m last year.* **OPP** slump → SLUMP, See also **surge** → INCREASE *noun*

spiral /'spaɪrəl/ (-ll-, *AmE usually* -l-) [I] (*disapproving*) to increase quickly in level or amount: *Prices are spiralling out of control.* ❶ **Spiral** is nearly always used with a negative meaning: *spiralling debt / price / budget deficit.* To **spiral down/downwards** is to decrease rapidly: *Shares in the company continued to spiral downwards.*

rocket [I] (of an amount or rate) to increase very quickly and suddenly: *They were forced to move out because of the rocketing crime rate.* **OPP** plummet → SLUMP

leap [I] (*often approving*) to increase suddenly and by a large amount: *The company saw pre-tax profits leap to £14.5 million in 2004.* **OPP** plunge → SLUMP

shoot 'up *phrasal verb* (*rather informal, often disapproving*) to increase suddenly and by a large amount: *Ticket prices shot up last year.*

NOTE JUMP, LEAP OR SHOOT UP? Leap is usually used when the increase is seen as a positive thing: *profits, shares* and *prices* can **leap** or **jump** but costs can only **jump**. **Leap** usually suggests a more dramatic, surprising or significant increase: *Raw material costs jumped 1 per cent last month.* ◇ ~~Raw material costs leaped 1 per cent last month.~~ **Shoot up** is used in more informal

---

contexts, and especially when the increase is seen as a negative thing: *Prices/charges/interest rates have shot up.*

---

so-called *adj.*

so-called · fake · false · bogus · dummy · counterfeit · phoney · sham
These words all describe things and people that are not genuine, or not what they appear to be.

PATTERNS AND COLLOCATIONS
▸ a so-called / fake / bogus / phoney **doctor**
▸ a fake / false / bogus **identity**
▸ a fake / false / counterfeit / phoney **money / currency**
▸ a fake / false / counterfeit **coins**
▸ a fake / false / phony **document / passport / invoice**
▸ a fake / false **beard / moustache / nose / tan**
▸ a fake / bogus / sham **marriage**
▸ a fake / dummy / phony **bomb**
▸ a fake / dummy **gun**
▸ fake / counterfeit **goods**
▸ a fake / phoney **accent**
▸ a false / bogus **claim / application**
▸ obviously **fake / false / bogus / phoney**

,so-'called [only before noun] (*disapproving*) used to show that you do not think that the word or phrase that is being used to describe sb/sth is appropriate: *The court heard the opinion of a so-called 'expert'.* ◇ *How have these so-called improvements helped the local community?* ❶ **So-called** always expresses disapproval; **bogus, phoney** and **sham** also often suggest disapproval, but the other words in this group are more simply descriptive.

fake not genuine, but made to seem real to deceive people: *There were a few stalls selling fake designer clothing.* ◇ *The caller appeared to have a fake American accent.* See also **fake** → FAKE *noun*

false fake: *The case had a false bottom where documents or even a small radio could be hidden.* ◇ *She was accused of obtaining money under false pretences* (= by pretending to be sb/sth she was not).

NOTE FAKE OR FALSE? In many cases you can use either word; however, **false** is used more frequently to describe documents and parts of the body such as *eyelashes, teeth* or a *beard, moustache* or *nose* (although **fake** is preferred for *tan*). **Fake** is used more frequently to describe other objects: *fake goods/flowers/pearls/bombs.* See also **fake, false** → ARTIFICIAL 1

bogus /'bəʊgəs; *AmE* 'boʊ-/ (*usually disapproving*) pretending to be genuine: *The bogus doctor had been working from premises in Chelsea.* ◇ *Bogus claims of injury by workers are costing companies thousands of pounds.* ❶ **Bogus** is most often used with nouns for jobs such as *doctor, health worker, social worker, official* and *police officer* and nouns for people who need help such as *refugee* and *asylum seeker*. False *claims* and *applications* made by such people can also be described as **bogus**.

dummy [only before noun] made to look real, although it is actually a copy which does not work: *The soldiers train using dummy rifles.* See also **dummy** → FAKE *noun*

counterfeit /'kaʊntəfɪt; *AmE* -tərf-/ (*rather formal*) (of money and goods for sale) made to look exactly like sth in order to trick people into thinking that they are getting the real thing: *He was arrested for attempting to sell counterfeit watches.* ◇ *Are you aware these notes are counterfeit?* ❶ Typical collocates of **counterfeit** are *notes, currency, money, clothing, goods, software, tapes* and *videos*.

phoney (*BrE*) (also **phony,** especially in *AmE*) /'fəʊni; *AmE* 'foʊni/ (*informal, often disapproving*) not genuine, but made to seem real to deceive people: *She spoke with a phoney Russian accent.* ◇ (*AmE*) *He was arrested on charges of supplying illegal aliens with phony papers.* ❶ **Phony** has a much wider range of collocates in American English than **phoney** has in British English. In both British and American English it is frequently used to talk about people behaving in a way that does not seem natural, for example trying to be more interesting, funny or fashionable than they really are. A *phoney accent* is likely to be used in order to impress people; a *fake accent* is more likely to be used simply to deceive sb. In American English you can also talk about *phony documents/passports/papers/money*; in British English it is more usual to say **false** or **fake**.

sham [only before noun] (*disapproving*) not genuine but intended to seem real: *She soon realized she was trapped in a sham marriage.* ◇ *His relationship was all a sham.* ❶ A **sham** marriage or relationship is one in which the people involved try to give the impression that their relationship is normal, when in fact they do not really love or care for each other.

sociable *adj.* See the Topic Map for SPORT AND LEISURE on p.892

sociable · social · outgoing · uninhibited · extrovert · gregarious · demonstrative
These words all describe a person who enjoys spending time with other people or is confident about showing their feelings to others.

PATTERNS AND COLLOCATIONS
▸ a sociable / a social / an outgoing / an extrovert / a gregarious **person**
▸ a sociable / a social / an outgoing / a gregarious **nature**
▸ an outgoing / extrovert **personality / character**

sociable /ˈsəʊʃəbl; AmE ˈsoʊ-/ (*approving*) enjoying spending time with other people: *She's a sociable child who'll talk to anyone.* ◇ *I'm not feeling very sociable this evening.* ◇ *We had a very sociable weekend* (= we did a lot of things with other people). **OPP** unsociable, antisocial → SOLITARY

social (*especially AmE, approving*) sociable: *He's not very social tonight, he just got dumped.*

outgoing /ˈaʊtɡəʊɪŋ; AmE -ɡoʊ-/ liking to meet people, enjoying their company and being friendly towards them: *She was always cheerful and outgoing.* ◇ *I think the role needs a more outgoing personality.* **OPP** introverted → SOLITARY

uninhibited /ˌʌnɪnˈhæbɪtɪd/ behaving or expressing yourself freely without worrying about what other people think: *His friends were a lively, uninhibited crowd.* ◇ *It was an evening of uninhibited fun.* **OPP** inhibited → SHY

extrovert /ˈekstrəvɜːt; AmE -vɜːrt/ lively and confident and enjoying spending time with other people: *Ray was a much more extrovert character.* **OPP** introverted → SOLITARY

gregarious /ɡrɪˈɡeəriəs; AmE -ˈɡer-/ (*rather formal, especially written*) liking to be with other people: *Hugh was a popular and gregarious man.* **OPP** solitary → SOLITARY

NOTE SOCIABLE OR GREGARIOUS? **Sociable** is an approving term and can describe sb's character, behaviour or mood; its opposite is **unsociable** which is a disapproving term. **Gregarious** is a descriptive term, neither approving nor disapproving, and so is its opposite, **solitary**. These words can describe sb's character or general behaviour, but not their mood: *I'm not feeling very gregarious this evening.*

demonstrative /dɪˈmɒnstrətɪv; AmE -ˈmɑːn-/ showing feelings openly, especially feelings of affection: *We were a very physically demonstrative family, giving lots of hugs and kisses.*

social *adj.* See the Topic Map for THE INDIVIDUAL AND SOCIETY on p.894

social · public · popular · civic
These words all describe things connected with society and ordinary people.

PATTERNS AND COLLOCATIONS
▸ social / public / popular **awareness / pressure / support / unrest**
▸ social / public / civic **responsibility**
▸ social / public **issues / values / policy / welfare**
▸ public / popular **opinion**
▸ a public / popular **outcry**

social [only before noun] connected with society and the way it is organized; connected with your position in society: *social changes/problems* ◇ *Applicants should have a degree in the social sciences* (= the study of people in society). ◇ *The study found that health was strongly affected by social class.*
▸ **socially** *adv.*: *The reforms will bring benefits, socially and politically.* ◇ *a socially disadvantaged family* (= one that is poor and from a low social class)

public [only before noun] connected with ordinary people in society in general: *Levels of waste from the factory may be a danger to public health.* ◇ *Why would the closure of hospitals be in the public interest* (= useful to ordinary people)?

popular [only before noun] connected with ordinary people in society in general: *They won the largest share of the popular vote.* ◇ *The regime was overthrown by a popular uprising.*
▸ **popularly** *adv.*: *a popularly elected government*

NOTE PUBLIC OR POPULAR? In many cases you can use either word: *public/popular pressure/awareness/opinion.* **Popular** usually describes sth, such as an idea or action, which comes from ordinary people: *popular support* ◇ *a popular movement/uprising.* **Public** is more general and can also describe things which are for, about or involve everyone: *public health* ◇ *the public interest*

civic /ˈsɪvɪk/ [usually before noun] (*rather formal*) connected with the people who live in a town or city: *The competition would be an opportunity to foster civic pride* (= pride that people feel for their town or city). ◇ *Voting should be a matter of civic duty.*

soft *adj.* See also the entry for WET 1

soft · soggy · gooey · spongy · slimy · mushy · squishy
These words all describe a thing or substance which is not hard, especially because it is wet.

PATTERNS AND COLLOCATIONS
▸ a soft / soggy / gooey / spongy **mass**
▸ a soft / gooey / slimy **substance**
▸ a soggy / gooey / slimy **mess**
▸ a soft / spongy **texture**
▸ soft / soggy **ground / bread**
▸ soft / slimy **mud**
▸ to **go (all)** soft / soggy / gooey / mushy

soft changing shape easily when pressed; not stiff or firm; less hard than average: *Soft margarine is better for you than butter or hard margarine.* ◇ *He sank back gladly into the soft feather pillows.* ◇ *Soft rocks such as limestone are easily eroded.* ◇ *It is a soft cheese with a hard rind.* **OPP** firm, hard → SOLID

soggy (*rather informal, usually disapproving*) wet and soft, usually in a way that is unpleasant: *We squelched over the soggy ground.* ◇ *I hate it when cornflakes go all soggy.*

gooey /ˈɡuːi/ (*informal, usually disapproving or approving*) soft and sticky, in a way that is either considered very unpleasant, or considered very pleasant: *The chocolate had gone all gooey in the heat.* ◇ *He bought them a couple of lovely gooey Danish pastries.*

spongy /ˈspʌndʒi/ soft and able to absorb water like a sponge ❶ A **sponge** is a piece of artificial or natural material that is full of holes, used for washing and cleaning: *This bread has a spongy texture.*

slimy /ˈslaɪmi/ (*disapproving*) like or covered with slime (= any unpleasant thick liquid substance): *The walls were black, cold and slimy.*

mushy /ˈmʌʃi/ (*rather informal, often disapproving*) soft and thick, like mush (= a soft thick mass or mixture): *Cook until the fruit is soft but not mushy.*

squishy (*informal*) soft and a little bit wet: *The leaves were soft and squishy underfoot.*

soil *noun* See also the entry for LAND 2

soil · mud · dust · clay · land · earth · dirt · ground · peat
These are all words for the top layer of the earth in which plants grow.

▸ **dry** soil / mud / dust / clay / land / earth / dirt / ground / peat
▸ **wet / soft** soil / mud / clay / earth / dirt / ground / peat
▸ **damp / moist** soil / clay / earth / dirt / ground / peat
▸ **heavy** soil / mud / clay / land / dirt / ground
▸ **marshy** soil / land / ground
▸ **sandy** soil / earth / dirt / ground
▸ **good / rich** soil / land / earth / peat
▸ **fertile / infertile / poor** soil / land / ground
▸ to **dig** the soil / mud / clay / land / earth / ground / peat
▸ to **cultivate / till / fertilize / drain** the soil / land / ground

soil [U, C] the top layer of the earth in which plants grow: *Plant the seedlings in damp soil.* ◇ *Cutting down forest trees can lead to serious soil erosion.* ◇ *the study of rocks and soils* See also **soil** → FLOOR 1

mud [U] wet soil that is soft and sticky: *The car wheels got stuck in the mud.* ◇ *Your boots are covered in mud.* ◇ *They live in mud huts with grass roofs.* See also **muddy** → DIRTY

dust [U] a fine powder that consists of very small pieces of rock, earth, etc: *A cloud of dust rose as the truck set off.* ◇ *They rolled in the dust, fighting.* ◇ *The workers wear masks to stop them from inhaling the dust.*
▸ **dusty** *adj.*: *They plodded along the dusty road.*

clay [U] a type of heavy sticky soil that becomes hard when it is baked and is used to make things such as pots and bricks: *Not much can grow in the wet clay here.* ◇ *She moulded the clay into the shape of a head.*

land [U] an area of ground, especially of a particular type: *an area of rich, fertile land* ◇ *His family had worked the land for generations* (= grown crops or raised animals on it). ◇ *They own a small plot of land.* See also **land** → FLOOR 1, **land** → LAND *noun* 1, **land** → LAND *noun* 2

earth [U] the substance that plants grow in: *She put a couple of handfuls of earth into the pot.* ◇ *In the air was the smell of freshly dug earth.* ❶ **Earth** is often used to talk about the soil found in gardens or used for gardening. See also **earth** → FLOOR 1
▸ **earthy** *adj.*: *earthy colours/smells*

dirt [U] (*especially AmE*) soil, especially loose soil: *He picked up a handful of dry dirt.* ◇ *Pack the dirt firmly around the plants.* ◇ *They lived in a shack with a dirt floor.*

ground [U] an area of soil: *Dig a hole in the ground about ten inches across.* ◇ *There was a small patch of ground at the side of the cottage.* ❶ **Ground** is NOT used to talk about loose soil: *a handful of dry ground* See also **ground** → FLOOR 1

peat [U] a soft black or brown substance formed from decaying plants just under the surface of the ground, especially in cool wet areas. It can be used to improve garden soil or burned as a fuel: *Dig some peat into the soil before planting.* ◇ *a peat bog* (= the place where peat is naturally formed)
▸ **peaty** *adj.*: *peaty soils*

soldier *noun* See the Topic Map for CONFLICT on p.896, See also the entry for GUERRILLA

soldier · warrior · serviceman/servicewoman · mercenary · combatant · fighter
These are all words for a person who is a member of an armed force.

▸ a **wounded / dead** soldier / warrior
▸ a **good / great / trained** soldier / warrior / fighter
▸ an **experienced** soldier / warrior
▸ a **retired** soldier / warrior / servicewoman
▸ a **foreign** soldier / mercenary / fighter
▸ a soldier / warrior / serviceman / servicewoman / mercenary / combatant **fights / is killed**

soldier [C] a member of an army, especially one who is not an officer: *What was life like for the common soldier?*

warrior /ˈwɒriə(r)/; *AmE* ˈwɔːr-; ˈwɑːr-/ [C] (*formal*) a person who fights or fought in a battle or war, especially in the past: *A Viking warrior would be buried with his weapons: usually his sword, spear, shield and battleaxe.*

serviceman, servicewoman [C] (*rather formal, especially journalism*) a man or woman who is a member of the armed forces: *A servicewoman carried the state's flag and stood at attention throughout the ceremony.*

mercenary /ˈmɜːsənəri; *AmE* ˈmɜːrsəneri/ [C] a soldier who will fight for any country or group that offers payment: *Swiss pikemen fought as mercenaries in the armies of many European states.*

combatant /ˈkɒmbətənt; *AmE* ˈkɑːm-/ [C] (*formal*) a person or group involved in fighting a war or battle: *He was involved in the war, but not as a combatant.* **OPP** **non-combatant** ❶ A **non-combatant** is a member of the armed forces who does not actually fight, for example an army doctor. It is also another word for a **civilian**: a person involved in a war situation who is not a member of the armed forces.

fighter [C] a person who fights, especially sb who is not part of a regular army or force: *Rebel fighters still control most of the city.*

solid *adj.*

solid · stiff · rigid · firm · hard
These words all describe things that are not soft to touch or are difficult to bend, break or move.

▸ solid / stiff / rigid **material**
▸ a solid / firm / hard **surface**
▸ firm / hard **ground**
▸ to **go** stiff / hard

solid not in the form of a liquid or gas; not soft; difficult to bend, break or move: *It was so cold that the stream had frozen solid.* ◇ *The boiler uses solid fuel* (= not oil or gas). ◇ *She had refused all solid food* (= would not eat, only drink). ◇ *The door was solid as rock.* **OPP** **liquid** → MATERIAL, See also **solid** → PURE *adj.* 1, **solid** → MATERIAL *noun*

stiff not easy to fold or change in shape: *a sheet of stiff black cardboard* ◇ *Scrub away any residue with a stiff brush.* ❶ People or parts of the body can be **stiff** if their muscles hurt when they move them, often because of cold: *I felt stiff all over.* ◇ *I've got a stiff neck from sleeping in a draught.* ◇ *My fingers had gone stiff with cold.* See also **stiff** → TIGHT

rigid /ˈrɪdʒɪd/ difficult to bend or press out of shape: *Sandwiches are best packed in a rigid container.* ◇ *The material is rigid and brittle.* ◇ People can go **rigid** with fear, anger or some other emotion: *His body suddenly went rigid with fear.* **OPP** **flexible** → FLEXIBLE 2

firm (*approving*) not soft; not easy to press into another shape: *It was good to feel the firm ground underfoot.* ◇ *four large tomatoes, ripe but firm* ◇ *Bake the cakes until they are firm to the touch.* **OPP** **soft** → SOFT, See also **firm** → FIRM, **firm** → TIGHT

hard not soft; impossible to press into another shape: *Wait for the concrete to go hard.* ◇ *a hard bench/chair* ◇ *The ground is still rock-hard.* **OPP** **soft** → SOFT

> **NOTE** **FIRM** OR **HARD?** **Hard** things are harder than **firm** things. **Hard** can mean 'very hard': *Diamonds are the hardest known mineral.* or 'too hard': *a hard mattress* **Firm** is always a positive word: *a hard mattress* is a bad thing, but a *firm mattress* is good.

solitary *adj.* See also the entries for QUIET 3 and SHY

solitary · introverted · reclusive · withdrawn · antisocial · unsociable
These words all describe a person who prefers to spend time alone rather than with other people.

PATTERNS AND COLLOCATIONS
▸ a solitary / reclusive **figure / man**
▸ to **feel** antisocial / unsociable
▸ **rather** solitary / introverted / withdrawn / antisocial / unsociable

solitary /'sɒlətri; AmE 'sɑ:ləteri/ (of a person or animal) enjoying being alone; frequently spending time alone: *He was a solitary child.* ◇ *Tigers are solitary animals.* **OPP** gregarious → SOCIABLE, See also **solitude** → PRIVACY

introverted /'ɪntrəvɜːtɪd; AmE -vɜːrt-/ more interested in your own thoughts and feelings than in spending time with other people: *His teachers perceived him as shy and introverted.* **OPP** **outgoing, extrovert** → SOCIABLE

reclusive /rɪ'kluːsɪv/ living alone and avoiding other people: *They lived a reclusive life and were hardly ever seen.*
▸ **recluse** /rɪ'kluːs; AmE 'rekluːs/ *noun* [C]: *He led the life of a recluse* (= a reclusive person).

withdrawn /wɪð'drɔːn/ not wanting to talk to other people; extremely shy and quiet, often as a result of sth that has happened to you: *The doctor noticed how withdrawn she had become.*

> **NOTE** **SOLITARY, INTROVERTED, RECLUSIVE** OR **WITHDRAWN?** **Solitary** and **introverted** usually describe sb's character: that is the type of person they are. **Reclusive** and **withdrawn** describe sb's behaviour: they have chosen to behave in this way, or been driven to it by sth that has happened to them.

antisocial /ˌænti'səʊʃl; AmE -'soʊʃl/ (*usually disapproving*) not wanting to spend time with other people: *They'll think you're being antisocial if you don't go.* **OPP** **sociable** → SOCIABLE

unsociable /ʌn'səʊʃəbl; AmE -'soʊ-/ not enjoying the company of other people; not friendly: *I was feeling very unsociable, so I didn't go to the party.* **OPP** **sociable** → SOCIABLE

> **NOTE** **ANTISOCIAL** OR **UNSOCIABLE?** These words are very similar, and describe sb's behaviour rather than their character. It is often a temporary way of behaving, in contrast to what you would expect from a particular person or in a particular situation: *We've got guests. Why are you being so antisocial/unsociable?* ◇ *an antisocial/ unsociable man.* **Antisocial** can be a more negative word, suggesting that sb is behaving this way deliberately and that you are annoyed about it.

solution *noun*

solution · answer · key · resolution · remedy · way out · fix
These are all words for a way of solving a problem or dealing with a difficult situation.

PATTERNS AND COLLOCATIONS
▸ the solution / answer / key / resolution / remedy / fix **to** sth
▸ the solution / answer / remedy / fix **for** sb / sth
▸ a **simple** solution / answer / resolution / remedy / fix
▸ an **easy** solution / answer / remedy / way out
▸ a **quick** solution / answer / resolution / fix
▸ a **satisfactory** solution / answer / resolution / remedy
▸ to **look for** a solution / an answer / the key / a fix
▸ to **seek** a solution / an answer / a resolution / a remedy / a fix
▸ to **find / provide** a solution / an answer / the key / a resolution / a remedy
▸ to **offer** a solution / an answer / the key / a fix
▸ to **arrive at** a solution / an answer / a resolution

solution [C] a way of solving a problem or dealing with a difficult situation; the act of solving a problem; the correct reply to a puzzle: *Do you have a better solution?* ◇ *Will this lead to a peaceful solution of the conflict?* ◇ *The solution to last week's quiz is on page 81.*

answer [C] something that you write or say in reply to a question in a test, exercise or competition; the correct reply to a question in a test, etc.; a way of solving a problem: *Write your answers on the sheet provided.* ◇ *The sender of the first correct answer to be drawn will receive £100.* ◇ *Do you know the answer to question 12?* ◇ *The answers are at the back of the book.* ◇ *This could be the answer to all our problems.* ◇ *The obvious answer would be to cancel the party.*

key [C, usually sing.] something that makes you able to understand, achieve or deal with sth: *The key to success is preparation.* ◇ *The driver of the car probably holds the key to solving the crime.* ◇ (*especially AmE*) **The key is,** how long can the federal government control the inflation rate?

resolution /ˌrezə'luːʃn/ [sing., U] (*rather formal*) the act of solving or settling a problem or dispute: *The government is pressing for an early resolution of the hostage crisis.* ◇ *Hopes for a peaceful resolution to the conflict were fading.* See also **resolve** → RESOLVE

remedy /'remədi/ [C] (*rather formal*) a way of dealing with or improving an unpleasant or difficult situation: *There is no simple remedy for unemployment.* ◇ *They advised him to exhaust all other remedies before applying to court.* See also **remedy** → CORRECT *verb*

way out [C, usually sing.] (*rather informal*) a way of dealing with a difficult or unpleasant situation, especially one which avoids dealing with the cause of the problem: *A local agreement is the only way out of the current crisis.* ◇ *She had taken the easy way out by returning the keys without a message.*

fix [C] (*informal*) a way of dealing with a problem, especially an easy or temporary one: *There is no quick fix for the steel industry.* ◇ *This is nothing other than a short-term political fix.* See also **fix** → CORRECT *verb*

solve *verb*

1 solve a dispute
2 solve a mystery

1 See also the entry for RESOLVE

solve · sort sb/sth out · sort · straighten sb/sth out
These words all mean to find a satisfactory solution to a problem or difficult situation.

PATTERNS AND COLLOCATIONS
▸ to solve / sort out / straighten out a **problem / situation**
▸ to solve / sort out a **dispute / conflict / crisis**
▸ to solve **things**
▸ to sort / straighten **things** out
▸ to sort / straighten **yourself** out
▸ to get **a problem / things / yourself** sorted
▸ to get sth sorted / sorted out / straightened out
▸ to **finally / eventually** solve / sort out / straighten out sth

solve [T] to find a way of dealing with a problem or difficult situation: *You can't solve all your difficulties by running away.* ◇ *Unemployment will not be solved by offering low-paid jobs in call centres.*

,sort sb/sth 'out *phrasal verb* (*especially BrE, rather informal, especially spoken*) to deal with a problem in a satisfactory way: *Don't worry, I'll try and sort it out.* ◇ *You load up the car and I'll sort the kids out.* ◇ *She tried to sort things out between them.* ◇ *I'm sure the problem will sort itself out eventually* (= be solved without anyone having to take any action). See also **sort sth out →** ORGANIZE

sort [T, usually passive] (*especially BrE, informal, especially spoken*) to sort sb/sth out: *Don't worry. We'll soon have this sorted.* ◇ *It's all sorted.* ◇ *It's time you got yourself sorted.* ❶ In this meaning **sort** is more informal than **sort sb/sth out** and is usually used in the phrases *be sorted, get/have sth sorted* or *get yourself sorted.*

,straighten sb/sth 'out *phrasal verb* to make a complicated or unsatisfactory situation better, by dealing with the particular things that are causing problems: *I need some time to straighten out my finances.* ◇ *I used to eat a lot of junk food, but my husband soon straightened me out.*

2 solve · work sth out · figure sb/sth out · do · clear sth up · crack
These words all mean to find the correct answer or explanation for sth.

PATTERNS AND COLLOCATIONS
▶ to work out / figure out **how / what / where / who / why...**
▶ to solve / work out / do a / an **puzzle / equation**
▶ to solve / clear up / crack a **case / mystery**
▶ to solve / clear up a **crime / murder / question**

solve to find the solution to a problem or explanation for sth that is difficult to understand or explain: *We were given clues to help us solve the puzzle.* ◇ *The mystery has not yet been completely solved.*

,work sth 'out *phrasal verb* (*especially BrE, rather informal, especially spoken*) to think about sth until you understand it, especially how to do sth, what has happened or how or why it happened: *I'm trying to work out how I could possibly have spent $150 last night.* ◇ *'Where could she have got to?' 'You work it out for yourself.'*

,figure sb/sth 'out *phrasal verb* (*especially AmE, rather informal, especially spoken*) to think about sth until you understand it, especially how to do sth, what has happened, how or why it happened or why sb behaves as they do: *I can't figure out how to do this.* ◇ *I've never been able to figure her out.*

NOTE **WORK STH OUT** OR **FIGURE SB/STH OUT?** **Work sth out** is used more in British English and **figure sb/sth out** is used more in American English. However, if you are talking about understanding sb's character and behaviour **figure sb out** is used in both British and American English.

do [T] to find the answer to a puzzle or problem, especially a word puzzle or maths problem: *Are you good at doing crosswords?* ◇ *I can't do this sum.*

,clear sth 'up *phrasal verb* (*rather informal*) to solve or explain sth that is mysterious or confusing: *Police are desperate to have this murder cleared up.* ◇ *We need to clear this matter up before we can offer him the job.*

crack [T] (*rather informal*) to find the solution to sth such as a crime or puzzle (= a game designed to test mental problem-solving skills): *'How's the investigation going?' 'I think we've cracked it.'* ◇ *A team of experts finally cracked the code* (= found out what it meant).

sometimes *adv.*

sometimes · occasionally · at times · from time to time · now and again/then · on occasion(s) · once in a while · every so often · off and on/on and off
These words and expressions are all used when sth is done or happens more than once or twice but not very often.

PATTERNS AND COLLOCATIONS
▶ to **appear** sometimes/occasionally/at times/from time to time
▶ to **seem** sometimes / occasionally / at times / on occasion

▶ to **happen** sometimes / occasionally / at times / from time to time / now and again
▶ to **crop up** occasionally / from time to time
▶ to **wonder** sometimes / occasionally / at times / from time to time
▶ to **think** sometimes / at times / from time to time **that...**
▶ to **stop** sometimes/from time to time/now and again/every so often
▶ **only** sometimes / occasionally / from time to time / now and then / on occasion
▶ **every** now and again / once in a while / so often

sometimes more often than once or twice, but not very often; in some cases: *They played tennis and golf and sometimes went swimming.* ◇ *Sometimes I look at him and wonder what is going on in his mind.* ◇ *It is sometimes difficult to know where to begin.*

occasionally more often than once or twice but not regularly; in some but not many cases: *We occasionally meet for a drink after work.* ◇ *Only occasionally was there any doubt that they would succeed.* ◇ *This type of allergy can very occasionally be fatal.* See also **occasional →** OCCASIONAL

at 'times *phrase* some of the time; in some cases: *The work is difficult and at times dangerous.* ◇ *He could be quite maddening at times.* ◇ *At times* (= in places) *the road is little better than a forest track.*

from ,time to 'time *phrase* sometimes but not necessarily regularly: *The payment will be reviewed from time to time in the light of inflation.*

now and a'gain/'then *phrase* sometimes but not necessarily regularly: *He still rings me now and again.* ◇ *Every now and then things happen to you in life that put everything else into perspective.*

on oc'casion(s) *phrase* sometimes but not normally: *He has been known on occasion to lose his temper.* ◇ *On occasions hospital doctors have to manage with little or no sleep.*

,once in a 'while *phrase* occasionally: *I feel I need to get away every once in a while.*

,every so ,often *phrase* at fairly regular intervals: *He paced up and down, pausing every so often to look at his watch.*

,off and 'on, ,on and 'off *phrase* for some but not all of the time; stopping and starting: *It rained on and off all day.* ◇ *She'd been learning Italian for about ten years, off and on.*

son, daughter *nouns* See also the entry for CHILD

son · daughter · child · girl · boy · baby · kid · family · descendant
These are all words for a person's male or female child.

PATTERNS AND COLLOCATIONS
▶ (a) **newborn** son / daughter / child / girl / boy / baby
▶ a **baby** son / daughter / girl / boy
▶ a **young** son / daughter / child / girl / boy / baby / kid / family
▶ sb's **eldest/oldest/youngest** son/daughter/child/girl/boy/kid
▶ a **teenage** son / daughter / child / girl / boy / kid
▶ a **grown-up** son / daughter / child
▶ a **male / female** child / descendant
▶ a / an **illegitimate / legitimate** son / daughter / child
▶ to **have** a son / daughter / child / girl / boy / baby / kid / family
▶ to **give birth to** a son / daughter / child / girl / boy / baby / kid
▶ to **bring up / raise** a son / daughter / child / girl / boy / kid / family
▶ a son / daughter / child / girl / boy / baby **is born**

son [C] a person's male child: *We have two sons and a daughter.* ◇ *He's the son of an Oxford professor.* ◇ *Maine & Sons, Grocers* (= the name of a company on a sign)

daughter [C] a person's female child: *His wife recently gave birth to a daughter.*

child (pl. **children**) [C] a son or daughter of any age: *They have three grown-up children.* ◇ *I'm an only child* (= I have no brothers or sisters). ❶ **Children** is often used to refer to both or all the children of a particular person:

Will you put the (= *our/my*) *children to bed?* 'The child' is NOT used in this way: ~~I'm just taking the child to school.~~ See also **child** → CHILD

NOTE **SON, DAUGHTER AND CHILD** These words are often combined with others to make compounds: *grandson/ granddaughter/grandchild* (= the son/daughter/child of your son or daughter) ◊ *stepson/stepdaughter/step-child* (= the son/daughter/child that your husband or wife has from an earlier marriage to another person) ◊ *son-in-law/daughter-in-law* (= the husband/wife of your daughter/son).

girl [C] a daughter, especially a young daughter: *Our youngest girl wants to go to art college.* See also **girl** → CHILD, **girl** → GIRL

boy [C] a son, especially a young son: *They have two boys and a girl.* ◊ *Her eldest boy has just started high school.* See also **boy** → CHILD

baby [C] a very young son or daughter: *My sister's expecting a baby.* ◊ *She had a baby last year.* See also **baby** → CHILD

kid [C, usually pl.] (*informal, especially spoken*) a son or daughter: *How are the kids* (= *your children*)? ◊ *Do you have any kids?* ❶ **Kid** is used more in spoken than written language, and is most often used in the plural: *I have to take the/my kids to school* is more common than *I have to take my kid to school.* See also **kid** → CHILD

family [C+sing./pl. v., U] a couple's or a person's children, especially young children: *I always wanted to have a large family.* ◊ *I addressed it to Mr and Mrs Jones and family.* ◊ *They got married last year and plan to* **start a family** (= have children) *soon.*

descendant /dɪ'sendənt/ [C] a person who is related to sb who lived in the past: *He was an O'Conor and a direct descendant of the last High King of Ireland.* ❶ **Descendant** refers to adults as well as children. **OPP** **ancestor** → FAMILY 3

song *noun*

song · tune · melody · track · part · number · theme
These are all words for a short piece of music.

PATTERNS AND COLLOCATIONS
▸ a song / tune / melody / track / number / theme **by** sb
▸ a **beautiful** song / tune / melody / theme
▸ a **haunting** song / melody / theme
▸ a **little / catchy** song / tune / melody / number
▸ a **folk** song / tune / melody
▸ to **sing** a song / tune / part / number
▸ to **play** a song / tune / melody / track / part / number / theme
▸ to **perform** a song / number / theme
▸ to **hum** a song / tune / melody / part / theme
▸ to **write** a song / tune / melody / track / part / theme
▸ to **compose** a song / tune / melody / part / theme
▸ to **record** a song / track / theme

song [C] a short piece of music with words that you sing: *a love/pop/popular song* ◊ *We sang a song together.* See also **piece** → WORK 4

tune [C] a series of musical notes that are played or sung in a particular order to form a piece of music: *It was a catchy* (= easily remembered) *little tune.* ◊ *It's sung* **to the tune of** (= using the tune of) *'When the saints go marching in'.*

melody /'melədi/ [C] a tune, especially the main tune in a piece of music written for several instruments or voices; a piece of music or a song with a clear or simple tune: *The melody is then taken up by the flutes.* ◊ *The musicians were playing a selection of old Irish melodies.*

track [C] a piece of music or a song on a record, tape or CD: *There are thirteen tracks on the album.*

part [C] music for a particular voice or instrument in a group singing or playing together: *I can play the guitar part to that song.* ◊ *The first two verses of the song are set in four-part harmony.*

number [C] a song or dance, especially one of several in a performance: *They sang a slow romantic number.*

theme /θiːm/ [C] a short tune that is repeated or developed in a piece of music; (in a film or television programme)a piece of music that is played at the beginning and end, or is often repeated in connection with a person or idea: *The trumpets' theme is then taken up by the rest of orchestra.* ◊ *He wrote and sang the theme to the hit TV series, 'Minder'.*

sophisticated *adj.*

sophisticated · experienced · suave · urbane
These words all describe sb who has experience of the world and who knows how to behave in social situations.

PATTERNS AND COLLOCATIONS
▸ a sophisticated / an experienced / a suave / an urbane **man / manner**

sophisticated /sə'fɪstɪkeɪtɪd/ (*often approving*) having a lot of experience of the world and knowing about fashion, culture and other things that people think are socially important: *Ben did his best to look sophisticated.* ◊ *Students have more sophisticated tastes nowadays.* **OPP** **naive** → NAIVE

experienced /ɪk'spɪəriənst; *AmE* -'spɪr-/ having knowledge as a result of doing sth for a long time, or having had a lot of different experiences: *She's very young and not very experienced.* ◊ *an experienced traveller* (= sb who has travelled a lot) ❶ **Experienced** is more neutral than the other words in this group, which can all suggest a more approving attitude towards sb. **OPP** **inexperienced** → NAIVE, See also **experienced** → EXPERIENCED, **experience** → KNOWLEDGE

suave /swɑːv/ (*often approving*) (especially of a man) confident, elegant and polite, sometimes in a way that does not seem sincere: *He gave his usual suave performance.* ◊ *He plays a* **suave and sophisticated** *detective.*

urbane /ɜː'beɪn; *AmE* ɜːr'b-/ (*written, often approving*) (especially of a man) good at knowing what to say and how to behave in social situations; appearing relaxed and confident: *He was charming and urbane, full of witty conversation.*

sordid *adj.*

sordid · seedy · sleazy · unsavoury · squalid · disreputable
These words all describe people and places that are very immoral or dirty and unpleasant.

PATTERNS AND COLLOCATIONS
▸ a sordid / seedy / sleazy / squalid **affair**
▸ sb's sordid / unsavoury / squalid / disreputable **past**
▸ a sordid / an unsavoury **business / story**
▸ the sordid / squalid **details**
▸ a seedy / a sleazy / an unsavoury / disreputable **character**
▸ a seedy / sleazy / disreputable **man / hotel / nightclub / bar**
▸ **pretty** sordid / seedy / sleazy
▸ **rather** sordid / seedy / unsavoury / disreputable

sordid (*disapproving*) (of sb's life or activities) immoral or dishonest; (of a place) very dirty and unpleasant: *I didn't want to hear the sordid details of their relationship.* ◊ *These were the urban poor, living in the sordid back streets and alleys of prosperous Victorian cities.* ❶ **Sordid** more often means 'immoral or dishonest' than 'dirty and unpleasant'. It is used to describe people's lives, but not people themselves; common collocates include *affair, details, facts, life, past, story* and *secret.*

seedy (*rather informal, disapproving*) dirty and unpleasant, and possibly connected with immoral or illegal activities: *He got a job in a seedy bar.* ◊ *A seedy-looking man offered me a cigarette.*

sleazy /'sliːzi/ (*informal, disapproving*) connected with immoral or illegal activities; dirty and unpleasant: *There was some sleazy reporter here asking for you.* ◇ *We ended up in a sleazy bar on the outskirts of the town.*

> **NOTE SEEDY OR SLEAZY? Seedy** can be used to describe people, but it is most often used to describe bars, pubs, nightclubs and hotels. **Sleazy** is often used to describe people, especially politicians, news reporters, lawyers and salesmen. It can also describe dirty or unpleasant bars and hotels, where you might be likely to meet immoral or dishonest people: **sleazy** suggests more strongly that there is sth immoral or illegal happening.

unsavoury (*BrE*) *AmE* **unsavory** /ʌnˈseɪvəri/ (*rather formal, disapproving*) unpleasant or offensive; not considered morally acceptable: *He has a rather unsavoury reputation.* ❶ **Unsavoury** is most often used with *character, reputation, business* and *incident*.

squalid /'skwɒlɪd; *AmE* 'skwɑːlɪd/ (*disapproving*) (of places and living conditions) very dirty and unpleasant; (of sb's life or activities) immoral or dishonest: *There were several squalid, overcrowded refugee camps.* ◇ *It was a squalid affair involving prostitutes and drugs.* ❶ **Squalid** is used most frequently to describe the places in which people have to live; collocates include: *slums, housing conditions, refugee camps, neighbourhood* and *streets.*

disreputable /dɪsˈrepjətəbl/ (*disapproving*) (especially of a person or place) that people consider to be dishonest and bad: *She spent the evening with her disreputable brother Stefan.* ◇ *a disreputable area of the city* ❶ **Disreputable** refers to sb/sth's *reputation* (= what people think and say about sb/sth, based on past experience or what they have been told). If sb/sth is **disreputable**, they have a bad reputation. See **reputation** → REPUTATION **OPP respectable** → RESPECTABLE ❶ The opposite of **disreputable** is **respectable**, which describes people, places and activities, NOT **reputable**, which mainly describes business companies.

sorry *adj.*

sorry · I'm afraid · bad · guilty · apologetic · ashamed
These words all describe people who feel sad because of sth wrong they have done or because of sth unpleasant or disappointing that has happened.

| I'm afraid | sorry | guilty |
| apologetic | bad | ashamed |

PATTERNS AND COLLOCATIONS
▸ sorry / bad / guilty / apologetic / ashamed **about** sth
▸ to feel sorry / bad / guilty / ashamed **that**...
▸ I'm sorry / afraid **that**...
▸ to feel bad / guilty / apologetic / ashamed
▸ to look guilty / apologetic / ashamed
▸ very sorry / bad / guilty / apologetic / ashamed
▸ deeply sorry / apologetic / ashamed
▸ really / quite / rather sorry / bad / guilty / ashamed
▸ almost / slightly guilty / apologetic / ashamed

sorry [not before noun] (*especially spoken*) feeling sadness and shame about sth wrong that you have done: *We're very sorry about the damage to your car.* ◇ *She was sorry that she'd lost her temper.* ◇ *If you say you're sorry we'll forgive you.* ❶ If you say *I'm/We're sorry* you mean that you realize that you have done wrong and that you would like sb to forgive you. If you tell sb that they should *say sorry*, you mean that they should do this. If you say that sb *is sorry that* sth has happened, you mean that they regret it, and that they wish that it hadn't happened.

I'm afraid *phrase* (*spoken*) used as a polite way of telling sb sth that is unpleasant or disappointing, or that you are sorry about: *I can't help you, I'm afraid.* ◇ *I'm afraid we can't come.* ◇ 'Is there any left?' **'I'm afraid not.'** ◇ 'Will it hurt?' **'I'm afraid so.'**

bad (always used after the verb *feel*) (*rather informal, especially spoken*) feeling shame because you have done sth that you know is wrong or have not done sth that you should have done: *She felt bad about leaving him.* ◇ *Why should I want to make you feel bad?*

guilty feeling shame because you have done sth wrong or have not done sth that you should have done: *I felt guilty about not visiting my parents more often.* ◇ *I had a guilty conscience and could not sleep.* See also **guilt** → GUILT

apologetic /əˌpɒləˈdʒetɪk; *AmE* əˌpɑː-/ feeling or showing that you are sorry for having done sth wrong or for causing a problem: *'Sorry,' she said, with an apologetic smile.* ◇ *They were very apologetic about the trouble they'd caused.* See also **apologize** → APOLOGIZE
> ▸ **apologetically** *adv.*: *'I'm sorry I'm late,'* he murmured *apologetically.*

ashamed [not before noun] feeling shame or embarrassment about sb/sth or because of sth you have done: *She was deeply ashamed of her behaviour at the party.* ◇ *You should be ashamed of yourself for telling such lies.* **OPP shameless, unabashed, unashamed** → COOL. See also **shame** → GUILTY

be/feel **sorry for sb** *verb*

be/feel sorry for sb · pity · sympathize · commiserate · feel for sb
These words all mean to feel sad about sb else's problems.

PATTERNS AND COLLOCATIONS
▸ to sympathize / commiserate **with** sb
▸ to **really** feel sorry for / sympathize (with sb) / feel for sb
▸ **It's easy / difficult / hard (not) to** feel sorry for sb / sympathize (with sb).

be/feel 'sorry for sb *phrase* to feel sad for sb because they are in a bad situation or sth bad has happened to them: *I'm sorry for those poor boys, working in that horrible place.* ◇ *He decided to help Jan as he felt sorry for her.* ❶ **Be/feel sorry for sb** is much more frequent than the other verbs in this group, especially in everyday and spoken language. You can be/feel *very/extremely/so* sorry for sb, *quite/rather* sorry for sb or *a bit/slightly* sorry for sb. You can also *feel sorry for yourself*. This is an informal and disapproving expression: *Stop feeling sorry for yourself and think about other people for a change.*

pity [T] (not used in the progressive tenses) to feel sorry for sb because of their situation: *I pity her having to work such long hours.* ◇ *Compulsive gamblers are more to be pitied than condemned.* See also **pity** → SYMPATHY *noun*

sympathize (*BrE* also **-ise**) /'sɪmpəθaɪz/ [I] to feel sorry for sb because you understand how they feel; to show that you understand and feel sorry about sb's problems: *I find it very hard to sympathize with him.* ◇ *I think we can all sympathize with her dilemma.* See also **sympathy** → SYMPATHY, **sympathetic** → SENSITIVE 1, **empathize** → UNDERSTAND 2

> **NOTE PITY OR SYMPATHIZE? Pity** is a stronger word and is used in more serious situations: *'I've got a terrible headache.' 'I can sympathize. I had one yesterday.'* ◇ *I pity that poor child, left all alone without her parents.* If you **sympathize** with sb, you understand how they feel and can imagine yourself in the same situation. **Pity** does not suggest this understanding, and can suggest a lack of respect for sb or a feeling of being superior: *He pitied people who were stuck in dead-end jobs* (= and was pleased with himself because he was not stuck in a dead-end job). People will be grateful if you say *I sympathize with you*, but they may not be pleased if you say *I pity you*: *He lied to you again and you just kept on forgiving him. I pity you.* ◇ *She gave me a pitying look, which just made me feel even worse.* You **pity** a person, but you can **sympathize with** a person or their situation: *I can really sympathize.* ◇ *I can really sympathize with her.* ◇ *I can really sympathize with what she's going through.*

commiserate /kəˈmɪzəreɪt/ [I] to show sb sympathy when they are upset or disappointed about sth, for example not winning a competition or failing an exam: *She commiserated with the losers on their defeat.* ❶ If you *commiserate with sb* this usually means that you say sth kind and sympathetic to them, such as 'I'm sorry' or 'Bad luck!'.

▸ **commiseration** /kəˌmɪzəˈreɪʃn/ *noun* [U, C]: *I offered him my commiseration.* ◇ *Commiserations to the losing team!*

'**feel for sb** *phrasal verb* (*rather informal*) to have sincere sympathy for sb: *I really felt for her when her husband died.* ◇ *I do feel for you, honestly.*

sound *noun*

1 a buzzing sound
2 turn the sound down

1 sound · noise
These are both words for sth that you can hear.

PATTERNS AND COLLOCATIONS
▸ a **big / deafening / loud / high-pitched / low** sound / noise
▸ to **hear / listen to / make / produce** a sound / noise
▸ a sound / noise **comes from** sth / a place
▸ a sound / noise **becomes / gets** louder, closer, etc.

sound [C] something that you can hear: *A scratching sound came from the front door.* ◇ *I sat listening to the soft sound of rustling leaves.* ◇ *He crept into the house trying not to make a sound.* ❶ **Sound** [U] is vibrations (= continuous rapid movements) that travel through air or water and can be heard when they reach a person's or an animal's ear: *Sound travels at about 340 metres per second.*
noise [C, U] a sound, especially when it is loud, unpleasant or disturbing: *There was a rattling noise coming from the back of the car.* ◇ *What's that noise?* ◇ *Don't make so much noise.* ◇ *We had to shout above the noise of the traffic.*

NOTE **SOUND OR NOISE? Sound** is anything you hear. A **noise** is usually loud and unpleasant: *the soft noise of rustling leaves*. **Noise** [U] is continuous noises. **Sound** [U] is slightly more technical, used in scientific contexts. It is not used with words for amounts like *much* and *a lot of*: *Don't make so much sound.*

2 sound · volume
These are both words for talking about what you can hear in terms of how loud or soft it is.

PATTERNS AND COLLOCATIONS
▸ the sound / volume **on** sth
▸ to **turn up / turn down / increase / reduce** the sound / volume

sound [U] what you listen to when you use electronic equipment such as radios and televisions, see a film or go to a concert: *Could you turn the sound down?* ◇ *The sound quality of the tapes was excellent.*
volume [U] the amount of sound that is produced by sth, especially electronic equipment such as radios and televisions: *She turned down the volume on the car stereo.* ◇ *Make sure the volume control is in the middle between the 'low' and 'high' settings.*

source *noun*

source · cause · origin · root · starting point · beginnings
These are all words for the point that sth starts from.

PATTERNS AND COLLOCATIONS
▸ (a) **common** source / cause / origin / roots / starting point
▸ a **possible / natural** source / cause / origin / starting point
▸ the **real** source / cause / origin / roots / beginnings
▸ the **true / obscure** source / cause / origin / beginnings
▸ a / an **known / unknown** source / cause / origin

▸ to **have** a source / a cause / origins / roots / a starting point / beginnings
▸ to **identify** the source / cause / origin / starting point / beginnings of sth
▸ to **find** the source / cause / origin / root / starting point of sth
▸ to **locate / discover / investigate / trace** the source / cause / origin / roots of sth

source [C] a place, person or thing that you get sth from: *We need to obtain more energy from renewable sources.* ◇ *Your local library will be a useful source of information.* ◇ *The tiny window was the only source of light.*
cause [C] the thing or person that makes sth happen: *Unemployment is a major cause of poverty.* ◇ *There was discussion about the fire and its likely cause.* ◇ *He died of natural causes.* See also **cause** → CAUSE *verb*
origin [C, U] (also **origins** [pl.]) (*especially written*) the point from which sth starts; the first or early ideas, signs or stages of sth: *The origin of the word remains obscure.* ◇ *Most coughs are viral in origin* (= caused by a virus). ◇ *Bottles are labelled by country of origin.* ◇ *The TV series examines the origins of life on earth.* ◇ *This particular custom has its origins in Wales.*
root [C] (*especially written*) the main cause of sth, such as a problem or difficult situation; the origin or basis of sth: *We have to get to the root of the problem.* ◇ *What lies at the root of his troubles is a sense of insecurity.* ◇ *What would you say was the root cause of the problem?* ◇ *The two languages share a common root.* ◇ *Flamenco has its roots in Arabic music.*

NOTE **ORIGINS OR ROOT?** In some cases you can use either word: *The custom has its origins/roots in Wales.* Both words can mean 'cause' but in slightly different ways: use **root** to talk about the cause of a problem: *We have to get to the origin of the problem.*; use **origin** to talk about when, where and how sth started: *the origin of life/species/the universe* ◇ *the roots of life/species/the universe.* The word **roots** can often suggest an emotional or cultural attachment; the word **origins** is more scientific. It is usual to talk about sb's *social origins* (= the social class they came from and the jobs their parents did) but their *cultural roots* (= the beliefs and customs of people in the family or place that they came from). See also **origin, roots** → FAMILY 2

'**starting point** [C] a thing, idea or set of facts that can be used to begin a discussion or process: *The TV documentary served as a useful starting point for our discussion.* ◇ *They reached the same conclusion from different starting points.* ❶ **Starting point** is often used after positive adjectives such as *convenient, good, suitable* and *useful.*
beginnings [pl.] (*especially written*) the first or early ideas, signs or stages of sth: *Did democracy have its beginnings in ancient Greece?* ◇ *From these small beginnings it grew into the vast company we know today.* ❶ **Beginnings** is usually used in the phrase *sth had its beginnings in...* or to describe how sth has changed from beginnings that were *humble, modest, simple* or *small.*

space *noun*

1 floor/office space; a feeling of space
2 the first woman in space

1 space · room · headroom · legroom
These are all words for the amount of an area or place that is empty or that is available for you to use.

PATTERNS AND COLLOCATIONS
▸ space / room **for / between** sth
▸ space / room **to do sth**
▸ **enough / sufficient** space / room / headroom
▸ **limited / restricted** space / headroom
▸ to **leave / make / create / save / take up** space / room

space [U] an amount of an area or place that is empty or available for use; the quality of being large and empty and allowing you to move freely: *office/floor/shelf/disk* space ◇ *There's very little storage space in the department.* ◇ *That desk takes up too much space.* ◇ *Could you make space for another person?* ◇ *Light, bright colours help give a feeling of space.*

room [U] empty space that can be used for sth: *Is there enough room for the car?* ◇ *There's room for one more at the table.* ◇ *You'll have to make room for all those books.*

> **NOTE** SPACE OR ROOM? **Room** is usually space that you have or need for some practical purpose; it is more frequent than **space** in most of these 'practical' examples, but is NOT usually used after another noun: ~~office/floor/shelf/disk room~~. **Space** can be sth that you have or need for some practical purpose, or it may be the feeling of space, that you enjoy for its own sake: ~~Light, bright colours help give a feeling of room.~~

headroom /'hedru:m; -rʊm/ [U] the amount of space between the top of a vehicle and sth it drives under; the amount of space between the top of your head and the roof of a vehicle or a ceiling: *The sign on the bridge said 'Maximum Headroom 2.5 metres.'* ◇ *The new model gives generous headroom for front and rear passengers.*

legroom /'legru:m; 'legrʊm/ [U] the amount of space available for your legs when you are sitting in a vehicle, theatre, etc: *The seats are comfortable, but there's very little legroom.*

2 space · universe · outer space · the cosmos
These are all words for the area outside the earth's atmosphere.

PATTERNS AND COLLOCATIONS
▸ **through / in** space / the universe / outer space / the cosmos
▸ the **entire** universe / cosmos
▸ **to go into** space / outer space

space [U] the area outside the earth's atmosphere where all the other planets and stars are: *Valentina Tereshkova was the first woman in space.* ◇ *The company plays a major role in the European space programme.*

universe [C, usually sing.] the whole of space and everything that exists in it: *The Big Bang Theory is a widely accepted theory of how the universe began.*

ˌouter ˈspace [U] the area immediately outside the earth's atmosphere; the relatively empty area between stars and planets: *Radio astronomy works by gathering radio waves from outer space.*

> **NOTE** SPACE OR OUTER SPACE? There is very little difference in the range and meaning of these words. **Space** is used in many compounds such as *space station* and *space travel*. **Outer space** is sometimes used to emphasize that the person is talking about an area either just outside or far outside the earth's atmosphere.

the cosmos /'kɒzmɒs; AmE 'kɑ:zmoʊs; -məs/ [sing.] the universe, especially when it is thought of as an ordered system: *Galileo made possible a profound new understanding of the structure of the cosmos.*

spacious *adj.*

spacious · cavernous · airy · roomy
These words all describe a place where there is plenty of space to move around.

PATTERNS AND COLLOCATIONS
▸ a spacious / a cavernous / an airy **room**
▸ a spacious / cavernous / roomy **kitchen**
▸ a spacious / cavernous **hall**
▸ a spacious / an airy **bedroom**
▸ a spacious / roomy **house**
▸ **bright and** spacious / airy

spacious /'speɪʃəs/ (*approving*) (especially of a room or building) large and with plenty of space for people to move around in: *The rooms are spacious and comfortable.* ◇ *The boat provides spacious accommodation for five people.* **OPP** cramped → CRAMPED

cavernous /'kævənəs; AmE -vərn-/ [usually before noun] (*written*) (of a room or space) very large and often empty and/or dark; like a cave: *We stepped into the vast, cavernous space of the empty concert hall.*

airy (*usually approving*) with plenty of fresh air because there is a lot of space: *The office is **light and airy**.*

roomy /'ru:mi; 'rʊmi/ (*rather informal, approving*) with a lot of space inside: *The kitchen is roomy enough for five people to sit around the table comfortably.*

> **NOTE** SPACIOUS OR ROOMY? In some cases you can use either word: *a spacious/roomy house/kitchen* However, **roomy** does not usually describe a *room* or any compounds with -*room* such as *bedroom, bathroom, sitting room, etc.* **Roomy** only describes places inside a building or vehicle; **spacious** can also describe places outside: *a spacious garden/plot* ◇ *spacious grounds*

speaker *noun*

1 native speakers of English
2 a fine public speaker

1 speaker · communicator · gossip · talker
These are all words for a person who talks or who is talking, especially in a particular way.

PATTERNS AND COLLOCATIONS
▸ a **good / great** speaker / communicator / talker
▸ an **effective / excellent** speaker / communicator

speaker [C] a person who is or was speaking; a person who speaks a particular language: *I looked around to see who the speaker was.* ◇ *He's a fluent Arabic speaker.* ◇ *They are all native speakers of English.* See also **speak** → SAY 1

communicator /kə'mju:nɪkeɪtə(r)/ [C] (*rather formal*) a person who is able to describe their ideas and feelings clearly to others: *The ideal candidate will be an effective communicator.* See also **communicate** → CONVEY

gossip [C] (*disapproving*) a person who enjoys talking about other people's private lives: *Myra is a dear, but she's also a terrible gossip.* See also **gossip** → DISCUSSION *noun*, **gossip** → CHAT *verb*

talker [C] a person who talks in a particular way or who talks a lot: *He's a very persuasive talker.* ◇ *She's a (great) talker* (= she talks a lot). ◇ *He's not much of a talker* (= he doesn't talk much). See also **talk** → SAY 1

> **NOTE** SPEAKER OR TALKER? **Talker** is used when you are talking about how much sb talks or how well they talk. It is not used to mean the person who is or was talking: ~~I looked round to see who the talker was.~~ You can say that sb is *a good/persuasive speaker* but that means that they are good at making speeches. If you mean that they speak well in conversation, use **talker**.

2 speaker · lecturer · orator
These are all words for a person who gives a talk or makes a speech.

PATTERNS AND COLLOCATIONS
▸ a **good / brilliant** speaker / lecturer / orator
▸ a **public** speaker / orator
▸ the **principal** speaker / lecturer
▸ a **visiting / guest** speaker / lecturer

speaker [C] a person who gives a talk or makes a speech: *Marina Warner was the keynote speaker at the conference.* ◇ *He is a brilliant public speaker.*

lecturer /ˈlektʃərə(r)/ [C] a person who gives a lecture (= a talk to a group of people in order to teach them about a particular subject): *Dr David Crystal is our visiting lecturer today.* ❶ A **lecturer** is also sb whose job is to give lectures at a university or college. See also **lecturer** → LECTURER

orator /ˈɒrətə(r); *AmE* ˈɔːr-; ˈɑːr-/ [C] (*formal*) a person who makes formal speeches in public, or who is good at public speaking: *She's a fine political orator.*

special *adj.* See also the entry for UNIQUE

special · exceptional · particular · extraordinary
These words all describe things or events that are different from what is usual or normal.

PATTERNS AND COLLOCATIONS
▸ a special / an exceptional **case** / **situation**
▸ special / exceptional **circumstances**
▸ exceptional / extraordinary **costs** / **losses** / **profit** / **items**
▸ a special / an extraordinary **meeting**
▸ a special / particular **threat**
▸ of special / particular **concern** / **importance** / **interest**
▸ to **take** special / particular **notice** of sb / sth

special [usually before noun] not ordinary or usual; different from what is normal: *Journalists were given no special privileges.* ◇ *The oil industry was treated as a special case.* ◇ *There really is something special about the place.* **OPP** ordinary → NORMAL, See also **special** → UNIQUE

exceptional /ɪkˈsepʃənl/ very unusual; (of costs or income) that you pay or receive only once: *The deadline can be extended only in exceptional circumstances.* ◇ *Exceptional items in the last financial year increased profits by $25 million.* **OPP** normal → NORMAL, See also **exception** → EXCEPTION
▸ **exceptionally** *adv.*: *There was an exceptionally high tide.* ◇ *Exceptionally, the director may override the decision of the committee.*

particular [only before noun] greater than usual: *The high inflation rates were of particular concern.* ◇ *The chemicals pose a particular threat to water quality.*
▸ **particularly** *adv.*: *Traffic is bad, particularly in the downtown area.* ◇ *'Did you enjoy it?' 'No, not particularly (= not very much).'* ◇ *The lecture was not particularly interesting.*

extraordinary /ɪkˈstrɔːdnri; *AmE* ɪkˈstrɔːrdəneri/ [only before noun] (*formal*) in addition to what is usual, regular or normal: *The club convened an extraordinary general meeting.*

speculation *noun* See also the entry for CONCLUSION

speculation · assumption · guess · presumption · presupposition · conjecture · guesswork
These are all words for an idea about what is true, correct, etc. that is not necessarily based on all the facts.

PATTERNS AND COLLOCATIONS
▸ speculation / an assumption / a guess / a presumption / a presupposition / conjecture / guesswork **about** sth
▸ speculation / the assumption / a guess / the presumption / the presupposition / the conjecture **that...**
▸ (a) **general** speculation / assumption / presumption / conjecture
▸ (a) **mere** speculation / guess / presumption / conjecture / guesswork
▸ **pure** / **sheer** speculation / conjecture / guesswork
▸ a **basic** assumption / presumption / presupposition
▸ to **make** an assumption / a guess / a presumption / a conjecture
▸ to **base sth on** an assumption / a guess / a presumption / presupposition

speculation /ˌspekjuˈleɪʃn/ [U, C] the act of forming opinions about what has happened or what might happen without knowing all the facts: *There has been increasing speculation over the future of the monarchy.* ◇ *She dismissed the newspaper report as pure speculation.* ◇

Speculation was rife (= there was a lot of speculation) that he was having an affair. ◇ *Our speculations proved correct.* See also **speculate** → SAY 3

assumption /əˈsʌmpʃn/ [C] a belief or feeling that sth is true or that sth will happen, although there is no proof: *There is a general but false assumption that intelligent people do better in life.* ◇ *We are working on the assumption that about 50 people will turn up.* See also **assume** → SUPPOSE

guess [C] an attempt to give an answer or make a judgement about sth without being sure of all the facts: (*BrE*) *Go on! Have a guess!* ◇ (*AmE*) *Take a guess!* ◇ *Who do you think I saw yesterday? I'll give you three guesses.* ◇ *My guess is that not many people will turn out today.* ◇ *At a guess, there were about 40 people there.* ◇ *It's probably about 300 kilometres away, but that's just a rough guess.* See also **guess** → ESTIMATE *verb*, **guess** → GUESS *verb*

presumption /prɪˈzʌmpʃn/ [C] (*rather formal*) something that is thought to be true or probable: *The general presumption is that the doctor knows best.* ❶ In legal English (a) **presumption** [U, C] is the act of supposing that sth is true, although it has not yet been proved or is not certain: (*law*) *Everyone is entitled to the presumption of innocence until they are proved guilty.* See also **presume** → SAY 3, **presume** → SUPPOSE

presupposition /ˌpriːsʌpəˈzɪʃn/ [C, U] (*formal, often disapproving*) an idea that you suppose to be true and that you use as the basis of an argument even though it has not been proved; the act of supposing sth to be true: *Try to clear your mind of any presuppositions.* ◇ *These theories are based on presupposition and guesswork.* See also **presuppose** → SAY 3

conjecture /kənˈdʒektʃə(r)/ [C, U] (*rather formal*) an idea that is not based on definite knowledge and is formed by guessing; the process of forming an opinion or idea that is not based on definite knowledge: *The truth of this conjecture was confirmed the next day.* ◇ *What was going on in the killer's mind is a matter for conjecture.* See also **conjecture** → GUESS *verb*

guesswork /ˈgeswɜːk; *AmE* -wɜːrk/ [U] the process of trying to find an answer by guessing when you do not have enough information to be sure: *A combination of guesswork and luck led them to the right address.*

speech *noun*

speech · lecture · address · talk · sermon
These are all words for a talk given to an audience.

PATTERNS AND COLLOCATIONS
▸ a **long** / **short** speech / lecture / address / talk / sermon
▸ a **public** speech / lecture / address / talk
▸ a / an **inaugural** / **farewell** / **keynote** speech / lecture / address
▸ a **formal** speech / lecture / talk
▸ an **informal** lecture / talk
▸ to **give** / **deliver** a speech / a lecture / an address / a talk / a sermon
▸ to **hear** a speech / a lecture / an address / a talk / a sermon
▸ to **attend** / **go to** a lecture / talk
▸ to **write** / **prepare** a speech / a lecture / an address / a talk / a sermon

speech [C] a formal talk given to an audience: *Several people made speeches at the wedding.*

lecture [C] a talk given to a group of people to tell them about a particular subject, often as part of a course of study: *He gave a very interesting and informative lecture on the Roman army.* ◇ *a series of lectures* ◇ *a lecture room / hall* ◇ (*BrE*) *a lecture theatre* See also **lecture** → TEACH *verb*

address [C] a formal speech given to an audience: *a televised presidential address*

NOTE SPEECH OR ADDRESS? A **speech** can be given on a public or private occasion; an **address** is always public: *He gave an address at the wedding.*

talk [C] a fairly informal session in which sb tells a group of people about a subject: *She gave an interesting talk on her visit to China.*

sermon [C] a talk on a moral or religious subject, usually given by a religious leader during a service: *He preached a long sermon against the war.*

speed *noun*

speed · velocity · haste · rapidity
These are all words that can be used when sth happens, travels or is done very quickly.

PATTERNS AND COLLOCATIONS
▶ **increasing** speed / velocity / rapidity
▶ **great** speed / haste / rapidity
▶ **maximum / constant** speed / velocity
▶ **reckless** speed / haste
▶ **alarming / amazing / bewildering / remarkable** speed / rapidity
▶ to **measure** speed / velocity

speed [U] the quality of being quick or happening quickly: *The accident was due to excessive speed.* ◊ *She was overtaken by the **speed of events** (= things happened more quickly than she expected).* ◊ *(formal) The car flashed past them **at speed**.* See also **speed** → RATE 1, **speedy** → QUICK

velocity /vəˈlɒsəti; AmE -ˈlɑːs-/ [U, C] (*technical or formal*) the speed of sth in a particular direction; high speed: *to gain/lose velocity* ◊ *Light travels at a constant velocity.* ◊ *Jaguars can move with an astonishing velocity.*

haste [U] (*formal*) speed in doing sth, especially because you do not have enough time: *In her haste to finish on time she made a number of mistakes.* ◊ *The letter had clearly been written **in haste**.* See also **hasten** → HURRY, **hasty** → QUICK

rapidity /rəˈpɪdəti/ [U] the fact of happening or changing very quickly or in a short period of time: *These changes happen with extreme rapidity.* See also **rapid** → QUICK

spend *verb*

1 spend money
2 spend time

1 See also the entry for PAY
spend · invest
These words all mean to give money to pay for goods or services.

PATTERNS AND COLLOCATIONS
▶ to spend / invest (money) **on** sth
▶ to spend / invest **money / £1 000**
▶ to spend / invest **a lot**

spend [T, I] to give money to pay for goods or services: *I've spent all my money already.* ◊ *She spent £100 on a new dress.* ◊ *He had grown used to spending freely, without worrying about the consequences.* See also **spending** → COSTS, **expend** → USE 2

invest /ɪnˈvest/ [I, T] to buy property, shares in a company, etc. in the hope of making a profit; (of an organization or government) to spend money on sth in order to make it better or more successful: *Now is a good time to **invest in** the property market.* ◊ *When exchange controls were lifted Swedes rushed to invest abroad.* ◊ *The college has invested $2 million on a new gymnasium.* See also **investment** → INVESTMENT

2 spend · occupy · take up sth · devote sth to sth · pass · fill · while sth away
These words all mean to use time for a particular purpose.

PATTERNS AND COLLOCATIONS
▶ time is occupied / taken up **with** sth
▶ to spend / occupy / take up / devote / pass / fill / while away (the) time

▶ to spend / occupy / take up / devote / pass / fill / while away **an hour / a couple of hours**

spend [T] to use time for a particular purpose: *We spent the weekend in Paris.* ◊ *How do you spend your spare time?* ◊ *How long did you **spend on** your homework?* ◊ *Most of her life was **spent in** caring for others.*

occupy [T] (*rather formal*) (especially of an activity) to use an amount of time: *Administrative work occupies half of my time.* ❶ It is usually an activity that **occupies** sb's time, rather than a person, except in formal language: *(formal) How do you occupy your time?*

take 'up sth *phrasal verb* (*sometimes disapproving*) to use an amount of time: *Her time is fully taken up with writing.* ❶ **Take up sth** is sometimes used when the speaker disapproves or regrets that time is being used in this way: *I won't take up any more of your time.*

devote sth to sth *phrasal verb* to give an amount of time or attention completely to sb/sth: *I could only devote two hours a day to work on the project.* ◊ *Many women devote years of their lives to bringing up children.*

pass [T] to spend time, especially when you are bored or waiting for sth: *We sang songs to pass the time.*

fill [T] to use up a particular period of time doing sth: *How do you fill your day now that you've retired?*

while sth a'way *phrasal verb* to spend time in a pleasant lazy way, especially while you are waiting for sth else to happen: *We whiled away the time reading and chatting.*

spin *verb*

spin · turn · circle · rotate · revolve · roll · orbit · whirl · go around/round (sth) · swivel · twist · twirl
These words all mean to move around a central point or to make sth do this.

PATTERNS AND COLLOCATIONS
▶ to spin / turn / circle / rotate / revolve / roll / orbit / whirl **around / round** (sth)
▶ to spin / turn / rotate / revolve / swivel **on** sth
▶ to spin / turn / rotate / whirl **faster (and faster)**
▶ to spin / turn / rotate **rapidly / quickly**
▶ to spin / turn / circle / rotate / revolve / orbit / twist / twirl (sth) **slowly**

spin [I, T] to turn round and round quickly; to make sth do this: *The dancers spun round and round.* ◊ *The Earth spins around a central axis.* ◊ *My **head was spinning** (= it felt as if it was spinning round).* ◊ *She spun the roulette wheel one last time.* ◊ *Spin your partner around (= in dancing).* ❶ With **spin** and the other verbs in this group, *round* is used especially in British English, and *around* especially in American English.
▶ **spin** *noun* [C, U]: *The dance was full of twists and spins.* ◊ *He lost everything on the spin of a roulette wheel.*

turn [I, T] to move or make sth move around a central point: *The blades of the helicopter were turning slowly.* ◊ *He turned the key in the lock.* ◊ *She turned the steering wheel as far as it would go.*
▶ **turn** *noun* [C]: *Give the handle a few turns.* ◊ *Rotate the image through a quarter turn.*

circle [I, T] to move in a circle, especially in the air: *Seagulls circled around the boat.* ◊ *A small aircraft was circling overhead.* ◊ *The bell rang and the two boxers began circling each other.*

rotate /rəʊˈteɪt; AmE ˈroʊteɪt/ [I, T] to move in a circle around a fixed central point; to make sth do this: *Make sure that the propellor can rotate freely.* ◊ *The earth takes 24 hours to rotate on its axis.* ◊ *Rotate the wheel through 180 degrees.*
▶ **rotation** *noun* [U, C]: *The length of a day is based on the rotation of the earth on its axis.* ◊ *This switch controls the number of rotations per minute.*

revolve /rɪˈvɒlv; AmE rɪˈvɑːlv/ [I] (*rather formal*) to move in a circle around a central point: *People used to think that the sun revolved around the earth.* ◊ *She saw him heading towards the **revolving door**.* ◊ *(figurative) The world doesn't revolve around you, you know.*

▶ **revolution** *noun* [C, U]: *The disk rotates at up to 500 revolutions per minute.* ◇ *The revolution of the earth around the sun takes one year.*

> **NOTE** ROTATE OR REVOLVE? When sth **rotates** it usually moves around its own centre or axis (= the imaginary line through the centre of an object, around which the object turns); when sth **revolves** it usually moves around a point outside itself, although **revolve** is sometimes used in the same way as **rotate**: *The ceiling fan rotated/revolved slowly overhead.*

roll [I, T] to turn over and over or round and round while remaining in the same place; to make sth do this: *A dog was rolling in the mud.* ◇ *Her eyes rolled.* ◇ *He was rolling a pencil between his fingers.*

orbit [T, I] (*rather formal*) to move in an orbit (= a curved path) around a much larger object, especially a star or planet: *The earth takes a year to orbit the sun.* ◇ *Stars near the edge of the galaxy orbit more slowly.* See also **orbit** → WAY noun 3

whirl /wɜːl; AmE wɜːrl/ [I, T] (*written*) to move or make sb/sth move around very quickly in a circle: *Leaves whirled in the wind.* ◇ *He whirled her around the dance floor.*

go a'round/'round, **go around/round sth** *phrasal verb* (*especially spoken*) to spin or move around in a circle: *The wheel was going round and round.* ◇ *He didn't even know that the earth goes around the sun!*

swivel /'swɪvl/ (-ll-, AmE -l-) [I, T] to turn or make sth turn around a fixed central point: *The ball should be able to swivel freely in the socket.* ◇ *She swivelled her chair around to face them.*

> **NOTE** ROTATE, REVOLVE OR SWIVEL? When sth **rotates** or **revolves** it moves round and round in a circle, continuing in the same direction; when sth **swivels** it is able to move back and forth around a central point, changing direction often.

twist [T] to turn sth round in a circle with your hand: *Try twisting the handle to the right.* ◇ *She was nervously twisting the ring on her finger.*

twirl [T] (*written*) to make sth turn quickly and lightly round and round: *He twirled his hat in his hand.*

spokesman *noun*

spokesman/spokeswoman/spokesperson · representative · delegate · diplomat · ambassador · messenger · envoy · consul
These are all words for a person who speaks or acts on behalf of a group or organization.

PATTERNS AND COLLOCATIONS
▶ a spokesman, etc./ a representative / a delegate / an ambassador / a messenger / a consul **for** sb / sth
▶ a spokesman, etc./a representative/a delegate/a diplomat/an ambassador / a messenger / an envoy **from** sb / sth
▶ a delegate / an ambassador / a messenger / an envoy **to** sb / sth
▶ a/ an **government**/ **official** spokesman, etc./ representative / delegate / envoy
▶ a **party**/ **trade union**/ **UN** spokesman, etc./ representative / delegate
▶ a **special** representative / ambassador / messenger / envoy
▶ to **send** a spokesman, etc./ a representative / a delegate / an ambassador / a messenger / an envoy
▶ to **appoint** a spokesman, etc./ a representative / a delegate / an ambassador / an envoy / a consul
▶ to **elect** a spokesman, etc./ a representative / a delegate
▶ a representative / a delegate / a diplomat / an ambassador **attends** sth

spokesman, **spokeswoman**, **spokesperson** [C] a person who speaks on behalf of a group or organization: *A police spokesman delivered the news to the crowd outside the hospital.* ◇ *A spokeswoman for the government denied the rumours.* ❶ **Spokesman** is still the most frequent of these words. However, many people feel that it is

important to use language that includes both men and women, and some people may be offended if you do not. Use **spokesperson** if you do not know whether it is a man or a woman, or to show that it is not important if it is a man or a woman: *A spokesperson for the band confirmed that a national tour is planned for 2009.*

representative /ˌreprɪˈzentətɪv/ [C] a person who has been chosen to speak or vote for sb else or on behalf of a group; a person chosen to take the place of sb else: *I was voted student representative for my class.* ◇ *He was the Queen's representative at the ceremony.* See also **representative** → SALESMAN

delegate /'delɪɡət/ [C] a person who is chosen or elected to represent the views of a group of people and vote on their behalf at a meeting: *The conference was attended by delegates from 56 countries.*

> **NOTE** DELEGATE OR REPRESENTATIVE? Representative is a more general word than **delegate**. A **delegate** is always sb who represents their group or organization at a meeting.

diplomat /'dɪpləmæt/ a government official whose job is to represent his or her country in a foreign country, for example an ambassador: *He served as a diplomat in Russia before the war.*

ambassador /æmˈbæsədə(r)/ [C] a government official who lives in a foreign country as the senior representative of his or her own country: *The British Ambassador to Italy has been contacted.*

messenger [C] a person who gives a message to sb or who delivers messages to people as a job: *Don't blame me for the bad news – I'm just the messenger.* ◇ *A motorcycle messenger arrived with a large parcel.*

envoy /'envɔɪ/ [C] a person who represents a government or organization and is sent as a messenger to talk to other governments and organizations: *A UN peace envoy is to be sent to the region as the warring parties hold ceasefire talks.*

consul /'kɒnsl; AmE 'kɑːnsl/ a government official who is the representative of his or her country in a foreign city: *She's the British consul in Miami.*

sponsor *noun*

sponsor · donor · patron · promoter · backer · contributor · benefactor · philanthropist
These are all words for a person or organization that gives money or other support to another person or organization.

PATTERNS AND COLLOCATIONS
▶ a donor/ contributor/ benefactor **to** sth
▶ the **main**/**principal** sponsor/donor/patron/promoter/backer/ contributor/ benefactor
▶ a **major**/ **potential** sponsor/ donor/ patron / backer/ contributor/ benefactor
▶ a **generous** sponsor/ donor/ patron / contributor / benefactor
▶ a **wealthy** donor/ patron / backer/ benefactor / philanthropist
▶ a **great** patron/ promoter/ benefactor / philanthropist
▶ a **private** sponsor/ donor/ patron / benefactor
▶ an **anonymous** donor/ patron / benefactor
▶ to **look for**/ **seek**/ **find**/ **get** a sponsor/ donor/ patron / backer
▶ a sponsor/ donor/ benefactor/ philanthropist **gives** sth
▶ a sponsor/ benefactor/ philanthropist **donates** sth
▶ a sponsor/ donor/ promoter/ backer/ philanthropist **supports** sb / sth

sponsor [C] a person or company that pays for a radio or television programme, or for a concert or sports event, usually in return for advertising; a person who agrees to give sb money for a charity if that person succeeds in completing a particular activity; a person or company that supports sb by paying for their training or education: *The race organizers are trying to attract sponsors.* ◇ *I'm collecting sponsors for next week's charity run.* ◇ *Unless he can find a sponsor he'll be forced to retire from athletics.* See also **sponsor** → FUND verb, **sponsorship** → INVESTMENT

donor /'dəʊnə(r); *AmE* 'doʊ-/ [C] a person or organization that makes a gift of money, clothes, food or other items to a charity; a person who gives blood or a part of their body to be used by doctors to help sick people: *She is one of the charity's main donors.* ◇ *a blood/an organ donor* See also **donate** → GIVE 5

patron /'peɪtrən/ [C] a person who gives money and support to artists and writers; a famous person who supports an organization such as a charity and whose name is used in the advertisements for the organization: *He was a great **patron of the arts** and helped to establish the Baltimore Museum.* ◇ *The Duchess of Cornwall is to be patron of the new Unicorn Theatre for Children.*
▶ **patronage** /'pætrənɪdʒ; 'peɪt-/ *noun* [U]: *Patronage of the arts comes from businesses and private individuals.*

promoter /prə'məʊtə(r); *AmE* -'moʊ-/ [C] a person or company that organizes or provides money for an artistic performance or sporting event: *The boxing promoter expects a full house when the World Champion defends his title.* ❶ A **promoter** is more commercial than most of the other types of people in this group: a promoter's aim is usually to use sport or the arts to make money, rather than to use money to help sport or the arts.

backer [C] (*especially business*) a person or company that gives support to sb/sth, especially financial support: *The project receives its money from European backers.* See also **supporter** → SUPPORTER

contributor /kən'trɪbjətə(r)/ [C] (*rather formal, especially business*) a person or a thing that provides money to help pay for sth, or support for a project: *Older people are important contributors to the economy.* ◇ *Which country is the largest net contributor to EU funds?* ❶ **Contributor** is often used to talk about the number of people, countries or customers who give their money to an organization or economy by paying their taxes or buying things. See also **contribute** → GIVE 5

benefactor /'benɪfæktə(r)/ [C] (*formal*) a person who gives money or other help to a person or an organization such as a school or charity: *He was a generous benefactor, providing schools and churches throughout the region.* ❶ Typical collocates of **benefactor** are *generous, kind, great* and *wealthy.* It is also common for **benefactors** to be *mysterious, anonymous* or *unknown.*

philanthropist /fɪ'lænθrəpɪst/ [C] (*rather formal*) a rich person who helps the poor and those in need, especially by giving money: *He was a wealthy businessman and philanthropist.*

spontaneous *adj.*

spontaneous · impromptu · impulsive · off-the-cuff
These words all describe things that have not been prepared or planned, or people who do things without planning or thinking about them first.

▶ a spontaneous/ an impulsive **gesture/ reaction/ act**
▶ a spontaneous/ an off-the-cuff **remark**

spontaneous /spɒn'teɪniəs; *AmE* spɑːn-/ (of an action) not planned but done because you suddenly want to do it; done naturally, without being forced or practised: *The audience burst into spontaneous applause.* ◇ *It was a wonderfully spontaneous performance of the piece.*
▶ **spontaneously** *adv.*: *We spontaneously started to dance.*

impromptu /ɪm'prɒmptjuː; *AmE* -'prɑːmptuː/ not planned or prepared: *She gave an impromptu speech.* ◇ *They often held impromptu meetings in their house.* ❶ **Impromptu** is usually used to describe public information occasions such as a *lecture*, a *meeting*, a *press conference* or a *speech*, which happen without being previously arranged.

impulsive /ɪm'pʌlsɪv/ acting or done suddenly without thinking carefully about what might happen as a result: *He told me not to be impulsive but to think it over.* ◇ *She has a generous and impulsive nature.* ❶ You might advise sb not to be **impulsive** but if you describe sb as **impulsive** it is not usually very disapproving: it often suggests

affection for the person or understanding of their faults. A more disapproving way of describing this behaviour would be **rash** or **reckless**. See also the entry for RECKLESS, See also **impulse** → DESIRE
▶ **impulsively** *adv.*: *Impulsively he reached out and took her hand.*

off-the-'cuff (*rather informal*) said without thinking about it first: *He was embarrassed when a journalist's microphone picked up an off-the-cuff remark.*
▶ **off the 'cuff** *adv.*: *I'm just speaking off the cuff here – I haven't seen the results yet.*

sport *noun* See the Topic Map for SPORT AND LEISURE on p.892

sport · exercise · PE · workout · aerobics
These are all words for activity that you do in order to stay healthy or become stronger.

▶ to **do** sport / exercises / PE / a workout / aerobics

sport [U] (*BrE*) (*AmE* **sports** [pl.]) activity that you do for pleasure or to keep fit and that needs physical effort and skill, usually done in a special area and according to fixed rules: *I'm not interested in sport.* ◇ (*BrE*) *Do you do a lot of sport?* ◇ (*AmE*) *We played sports together when we were kids.* ❶ The plural form **sports** is used in both British and American English when it comes before another noun: *sports shoes* ◇ *a sports club* See also **sport** → GAME 2

exercise [U, C] physical or mental activity that you do to stay healthy or become stronger; a set of movements or activities that you do to stay healthy or develop a skill: *Swimming is good exercise.* ◇ *I don't **get** much **exercise** sitting in the office all day.* ◇ (*BrE*) *Remember to **take** regular **exercise**.* ◇ *The mind needs exercise as well as the body.* ◇ *vigorous/gentle exercise* ◇ *breathing/relaxation/ stretching exercises* ◇ *Repeat the exercise ten times on each leg.* See also **exercise** → TRAIN *verb* 2, **training** → TRAINING

PE (*BrE*) (*AmE* **P. E.**) /ˌpiː 'iː/ [U] the abbreviation for 'physical education' (sport and exercise that is taught in schools): *a PE lesson/class/teacher*

workout /'wɜːkaʊt; *AmE* 'wɜːrk-/ [C] a period of physical exercise that you do to keep fit: *She does a 20-minute workout every morning.* See also **work out** → TRAIN *verb* 2

aerobics /eə'rəʊbɪks; *AmE* e'roʊ-/ [U] physical exercises intended to strengthen the heart and lungs, often done in classes, with music: *I go to aerobics (= to an aerobics class) every Monday.*
▶ **aerobic** *adj.*: *aerobic exercise*

spray *verb*

spray · squirt · splash · spatter
These words all mean to make sth, especially a liquid, cover sb/sth in small drops or pieces.

▶ to spray / squirt / splash / spatter sth **on** / **over** sth
▶ sth splashes / spatters **against** / **on** / **over** sth
▶ to be sprayed / splashed / spattered **with** sth
▶ to spray / squirt / splash **water**
▶ to spray / splash **paint**
▶ **blood** squirts / splashes / spatters
▶ **rain** splashes / spatters
▶ **water** sprays / splashes

spray [T, I] to cover sb/sth with very small drops of a liquid that are forced out of a container or sent through the air: *The crops are regularly sprayed with pesticide.* ◇ *She's had the car sprayed blue.* ◇ *Champagne sprayed everywhere.*

squirt /skwɜːt; *AmE* skwɜːrt/ [T, I] to force a liquid or gas in a thin fast stream through a narrow opening; to be forced out of a narrow opening in this way; to hit sb with a stream of sth that has been squirted: *The snake can* *squirt poison from a distance of a metre.* ◇ *When I cut the lemon, juice squirted in my eye.* ◇ *The children were squirting each other with water from the hose.*

▸ **squirt** *noun* [C]: *She sprayed a squirt of perfume behind each ear.*

splash [T] to make sb/sth wet by making a liquid fall on them/it: *He splashed cold water on his face.* ◇ *My clothes were splashed with mud.* ◇ *Stop splashing me!* See also **splash** → DROP *noun*

spatter [T] to cover sb/sth with liquid in large drops, especially accidentally, making it/them wet and often dirty: *They went in and saw the blood-spattered walls.* ◇ *As the bus passed, it spattered us with mud.*

spread *verb*

spread · lay sth out · lay · unfold · open · unroll
These words all mean to open sth flat such as paper or fabric so that it covers a greater area.

PATTERNS AND COLLOCATIONS
▸ to spread / lay / lay out / open sth **on** sth
▸ to spread / lay sth **over** sth
▸ to spread / lay / open sth **out**
▸ to spread out / lay out / unfold / open a **map**
▸ to spread / lay / unfold a **cloth / tablecloth**
▸ to unfold / open your **arms**

spread [T] to open sth that has been folded or rolled so that it is flat and covers a larger area than before: *Tom spread the map out on the floor.* ◇ *The bird spread its wings and flew away.*

lay sth 'out *phrasal verb* to spread sth out on a flat surface so that it can be seen easily or is ready to use: *Lay the material out flat.*

lay [T] (usually used with an adverb or preposition) to spread sth flat on sth; to cover sth with a layer of sth: *Before they started they laid newspaper on the floor.* ◇ *The grapes were laid to dry on racks.*

unfold /ʌnˈfəʊld; *AmE* ʌnˈfoʊld/ [T, I] to spread open or flat sth that has previously been folded; (of sth that has been folded) to become open or flat: *She unfolded the letter and read it yet again.* ◇ *He unfolded his arms and stood up.* ◇ *The collapsible ladder unfolds quickly and locks into place for added safety.* **OPP** fold → FOLD

open [I, T] (of sth that is folded or closed up) to spread out or become unfolded; to spread out or unfold sth that has been folded or closed: *What if the parachute doesn't open?* ◇ *The flowers open in the morning and close again in the evening.* ◇ *He opened his arms wide to embrace her.*

unroll /ʌnˈrəʊl; *AmE* ʌnˈroʊl/ [T, I] to make sth that is rolled up become open and flat; (of sth that is rolled up) to become open and flat: *We unrolled our sleeping bags.* **OPP** roll → WRAP SB/STH AROUND/ROUND SB/STH

staff *noun* See also the entry for WORKER 1

staff · personnel · workforce · manpower · sales force · human resources
These are all words for the people who work for, or are available to work for, an organization, or the skills and abilities they offer.

PATTERNS AND COLLOCATIONS
▸ (a / an) **female / male / skilled / unskilled / qualified / trained / experienced** staff / personnel / workforce
▸ (a / an) **10-strong / 2000-strong, etc.** staff / workforce / sales force
▸ to **join** the staff / workforce / sales force
▸ to **train / reduce / increase** staff / personnel / the workforce

staff [C, usually sing.] all the people employed in a company or organization considered as a group: *All medical staff are tested for the virus.* ◇ (*BrE*) *We have 20 part-time* **members of staff.** ◇ (*AmE*) *Three* **staff members** *were suspended after the incident.* ◇ (*especially BrE*) *He's a lawyer* **on the staff** *of the Worldwide Fund for Nature.* ❶ In British English **staff** can be singular or plural: *a staff of ten* (= a

group of ten people) ◇ *I have ten staff working for me.* If it is the subject of a verb this verb is plural: *The staff in this shop are very helpful.* In American English **staff** can only be singular: *a staff of ten* ◇ ~~ten staff~~ ◇ *The staff in this store is very helpful.* The plural form **staffs** is less frequent but is used in both British and American English to refer to more than one group of people: *the senator and his staff* ◇ *senators and their staffs* See also **staff member, member of staff** → WORKER 1, **staff** → WORKER 2

personnel /ˌpɜːsəˈnel; *AmE* ˌpɜːrsˈ-/ [pl.] (*business*) all the people employed in a company or organization or one of the armed forces considered as a group: *There is a severe shortage of skilled personnel.* ◇ *The bomb killed 28 military personnel.* ❶ **Personnel** is used especially after words such as *administrative, civilian, computer, key, medical, military, security, technical, skilled* and *trained.* **Personnel** is also often used instead of **staff** in business contexts. **Personnel** [U+sing./pl. *v.*] is also the department in a company that deals with employing and training people: *the personnel department* ◇ *Personnel is currently reviewing pay scales.*

workforce /ˈwɜːkfɔːs; *AmE* ˈwɜːrkfɔːrs/ [C+sing./pl. *v.*] all the workers employed in a company or organization considered as a group; all the people in a country or area who are available for work: *The factory will have to lose half of its 1 000-strong workforce.* ◇ *A quarter of the local workforce is unemployed.* ❶ **Workforce** is used especially to talk about the number of people working for an organization, or an increase or reduction in this number.

manpower /ˈmænpaʊə(r)/ [U] the number of workers needed or available to do a particular job: *We need to ensure best use of the available manpower.*

'sales force [C+sing./pl. *v.*] the people who work for a company, whose job is to sell products, either in a shop or by visiting customers in order to get orders: *The company has a 500-strong nationwide sales force.*

human re'sources [pl.] (*business*) people's skills and abilities, seen as sth a company or organization can make use of: *She's responsible for making the best use of human resources.* ❶ **Human resources** or **HR** [U+sing./pl. *v.*] is also the department in a company that deals with employing and training people: *the human resources director* ◇ *She works in human resources.* See also **resource** → SUPPLY

stage *noun*

1 the early stages of a process.
2 The performers went on stage.

---

1 See also the entry for ROUND

stage · phase · step · round · leg
These are all words for a period of development or a part of a process.

PATTERNS AND COLLOCATIONS
▸ a stage / phase / step / round / leg **of** sth
▸ the **first / second / third / next / final / last** stage / phase / step / round / leg
▸ the **initial / preliminary / opening** stage / phase / step / round
▸ the **early** stages / phases / steps / rounds
▸ the **opening / current / latest** stage / phase / round
▸ **successive** stages / phases / steps / rounds
▸ a / an **important / critical / crucial / key / difficult** stage / phase / step
▸ to **begin / enter / reach / finish** a stage / phase / round / leg

stage [C] a state or period that sb/sth passes through while developing or making progress; a separate part that a process is divided into: *The product is* **at the design stage.** ◇ *The children are at different stages of development.* ◇ **At one stage** *it looked as though they would win.* ◇ *The pay increase will be introduced* **in stages** (= not all at once). ◇ *We can take the argument one stage further.*

phase /feɪz/ [C] a period in a process of change or development: *We are now entering a critical phase of the campaign.* ◇ *His anxiety about the work was just* **a passing phase.** ◇ *Most teenagers go through a difficult phase.*

NOTE STAGE OR PHASE? A **phase** is always a period of time with a beginning and an end; you can *enter, go through* or *finish* a phase and you can talk about what happens *during* a phase and how long it will *last*. **Phase** is used especially to talk about planned stages of a project, or the different emotional stages of a person's life. **Stage** can be used in the same way, but it can also be used to talk about a particular state or moment within a longer period of time: sth can be *at* a particular stage, but NOT *at* a phase: *The product is at the design phase.* ◇ *At one phase it looked as though they would win.*

step [C] one of a series of things that sb does or that happen, which forms part of a process: *Having completed the first stage, you can move on to step 2.* ◇ *I'd like to take this idea a step further.* ◇ *The promotion was a big **step up** (= move to a better position) in his career.* ◇ *I'll explain it to you **step by step**.*

round [C] a set of events which form part of a longer process: *The party did very well in the final round of voting.*

leg [C] one part of a journey: *At last we were on the homeward leg of our journey.*

2 stage · box · platform · pulpit · podium · dock · dais
These are all words for a raised flat area where a public speaker or performer can stand.

PATTERNS AND COLLOCATIONS
▸ **on** the stage / a platform / the podium / the dais
▸ **in** the box / pulpit / dock
▸ a **raised** stage / platform / podium / dais
▸ to **mount** the stage / platform / pulpit / podium / dais
▸ to **approach** the stage / platform / podium / dais

stage [C] a large raised area, usually in a theatre, where actors, dancers or entertainers perform: *The audience threw flowers onto the stage.* ◇ *When he was **on** stage he became another person.* ◇ *She came **off** stage to great applause.*

box [C] a small enclosed area in a theatre or court, usually with seats: *The painting depicts two elegantly dressed women in a box at the opera.* ◇ *the jury box* ◇ *(especially BrE) He showed no emotion as he walked into the **witness box**.* ❶ In American English it is more usual to talk about the **witness stand**. The phrase *take the stand* is used in both British and American English: *He took the stand as the first witness.* ◇ *He took the box as the first witness.*

platform [C] a raised area in a large room, used by public speakers or performers so that the audience can see them: *The concert platform was high and almost semi-circular at the front.* ◇ *Representatives of both parties shared a platform (= they spoke at the same meeting).*

pulpit /ˈpʊlpɪt/ [C] (in a church) a small enclosed area, usually high above the floor, where sb can stand in order to speak to the congregation (= the people attending a church): *(figurative) The policy has been widely condemned from the pulpit (= by priests and other church leaders).*

podium /ˈpəʊdiəm; AmE ˈpoʊ-/ [C] a small platform that a person stands on when giving a speech, conducting (= directing a group of musicians), or receiving a prize for a sports competition: *He dreamed of standing on the victory podium at the Brazilian Grand Prix.*

dock [C] the part of a court where the person who has been accused of a crime stands or sits during a trial: *He's been **in the dock** (= on trial for a crime) several times already.*

dais /ˈdeɪɪs/ [C] (rather formal, especially written) a raised area, especially at one end of a room, on which people stand or sit, especially in order to show that they are more important than the other people present: *He was seated atop a raised dais with a double set of stairs leading up to the throne.*

stall noun

stall · booth · stand · kiosk
These are all words for a table or small shop with an open front that people sell things from.

PATTERNS AND COLLOCATIONS
▸ a **hot-dog** stall / stand
▸ a **food / refreshment** stall / kiosk
▸ a / an **information / ticket** booth / kiosk
▸ a **newspaper** stand / kiosk
▸ to **have / run** a stall / booth / stand / kiosk
▸ to **set up / man** a stall / stand

stall [C] a table or small shop with an open front that people sell things from, especially at a market: *He works on a market stall in the square.*

booth /buːð; AmE buːθ/ [C] a small tent or temporary structure at a market, exhibition or fairground, where you can buy things, get information or watch sth: *The stalls and booths were doing a brisk trade.* ❶ Typically, **booths** are *fairground*, *seaside* or *roadside* booths, in which you might buy sth, try to win sth, or have your future told, for example. Other **booths** are the sort of places where there is just enough space for one person to sit, giving people information, selling tickets or taking people's money for sth: *an information / a ticket / a toll booth*

stand [C] a table or upright structure that goods are sold from, especially in the street: *A crowd lined up outside her newspaper stand.* ❶ Typical collocates of **stand** are *hot-dog*, *doughnut*, *hamburger* and *newspaper* or *news*. Especially in British English, a **stand** can also be a table or upright structure where things are displayed or advertised, for example at an exhibition: *People crowded round Oxford University Press's stand at the book fair.* In American English use **booth**.

kiosk /ˈkiːɒsk; AmE -ɑːsk/ [C] (especially BrE) a small shop, open at the front, where newspapers, drinks, etc. are sold: *She stopped at a newspaper kiosk to pick up a copy of 'Private Eye'.* ❶ A **kiosk** is usually a small building, rather than an upright structure like a **stand** that can easily be taken down or moved.

stand verb
1 stand by the window
2 I can't stand it when you do that.

1 See also the entries for LIE and SIT

stand · get up · stand up · rise · get to your feet · be on your feet · pick yourself up
These words all mean to to be in an upright position with your weight on your feet, or to put yourself in this position.

PATTERNS AND COLLOCATIONS
▸ to get up / stand up / rise / pick yourself up **from** sth

stand [I] to be in an upright position with your weight on your feet; to put yourself in this position: *She was too weak to stand.* ◇ *He was standing on a chair, trying to change a light bulb.* ◇ ***Stand still** when I'm talking to you!* ◇ *The kids were **standing around** chatting.* ◇ *Everyone stood when the president entered the room.* ❶ **Stand** is usually used with an adverb or prepositional phrase to show where or how sb stands, but sometimes another phrase or clause is used to show what sb does while they are standing: *We stood talking for a few minutes.* ◇ *He stood and looked out to sea.* **OPP** sit → SIT

get 'up phrasal verb to get into a standing position from a sitting, kneeling or lying position: *He got up and strolled over to the window.* ◇ *Please don't get up!* **OPP** sit down → SIT

stand 'up phrasal verb to be in a standing position; to stand after sitting: *Stand up straight!* ◇ *He stood up and put on his coat.* **OPP** sit, sit down → SIT

NOTE STAND, GET UP OR STAND UP? **Stand** usually means 'to be in a standing position' but can also mean 'to get into a standing position'. **Stand up** can be used with either of these meanings, but its use is more restricted: it is used especially when sb tells sb or a group of people to stand. **Get up** is the most frequent way of saying 'get into a standing position', and this can be from a sitting, kneeling or lying position; if you **stand up**, this is nearly always after sitting, especially on a chair. If you want to tell sb politely that they do not need to move from their chair use **get up**: *Please don't stand up!*

rise [I] (*formal*) to get into a standing position from a sitting, kneeling or lying position: *They rose from the table.* ◇ *She rose to her feet.*

,get to your 'feet *phrase* (*written*) to stand up after sitting, kneeling or lying: *I helped her to get to her feet.*

be on your' feet *phrase* to be standing up: *I've been on my feet all day.*

,pick yourself 'up *phrasal verb* to stand up again after you have fallen: *He just picked himself up and went on running.* ◇ *She picked herself up off the dusty ground.*

2 stand · endure · take · bear · put up with sb/sth · tolerate
These words all mean to accept or deal with sth unpleasant or annoying.

PATTERNS AND COLLOCATIONS
▸ (can't / not) stand / endure / bear **doing sth**
▸ (can't / not) stand / bear / put up with **sb** / **sth doing sth**
▸ to stand / endure / bear / put up with **pain**
▸ to not stand / take / tolerate any **nonsense**
▸ to take / tolerate **criticism**
▸ sb **can't** stand / bear sth
▸ sb **has to** endure / bear / put up with / tolerate sth
▸ sb can **no longer** stand / endure / bear / tolerate sth
▸ sb can **hardly** stand / bear sth

stand [T, no passive] (not used in the progressive tenses; used with *can/could* in negative sentences and questions) to be able to accept and deal with sth unpleasant: *I can't stand his brother.* ◇ *I **can't stand it** when you do that.* ◇ *She couldn't stand being kept waiting.* ◇ *I can't stand people interrupting all the time.* ◇ *How can you stand it here?*

endure /ɪn'djʊə(r); AmE -'dʊr/ [T] (*formal*) to experience and deal with sth that is painful or unpleasant, especially without complaining: *He had to endure the racist taunts of the crowd.* ◇ *She could not endure the thought of parting.* See also **endurance** → STRENGTH

take [T, no passive] (not used in the progressive tenses; used especially in negative sentences) to be able or willing to accept or deal with sth unpleasant: *She can't take criticism.* ◇ *I don't think I can take much more of this heat.* ◇ *I find his attitude a little hard to take.*

bear [I, T] (not used in the progressive tenses; used especially with *can/could* in negative sentences and questions) to be able to accept and deal with sth unpleasant: *The pain was almost more than he could bear.* ◇ *How can you bear to eat that stuff?* ◇ *She bore it all with her usual patience.*

NOTE STAND OR BEAR? In many cases you can use either word, but **bear** is slightly stronger and slightly more formal than **stand**. **Stand** is never used in positive statements: ~~She stood it all with her usual patience.~~ See also the entry for HATE

,put 'up with sb/sth *phrasal verb* (*rather informal, especially spoken*) to accept sb/sth that is annoying or unpleasant without complaining: *I don't know how she puts up with him.*

tolerate /'tɒləreɪt; AmE 'tɑːl-/ [T] (*rather formal, especially written*) to put up with sb/sth: *There is a limit to what one person can tolerate.* See also **tolerance** → PATIENCE

star *noun*
1 a pop star
2 the star role in the play

1 See the Topic Map for THE MEDIA on p.900, See also the entry for HERO

star · celebrity · name · personality · superstar · legend · public figure · great
These are all words for a famous and successful person, especially in the areas of entertainment and sport.

celebrity	star	superstar
name		legend
personality		great
public figure		

PATTERNS AND COLLOCATIONS
▸ a **famous** / **top** star / celebrity / name / personality
▸ a **leading** / **prominent** name / personality / public figure
▸ a **big** star / celebrity / name
▸ an **international** star / celebrity / name / superstar
▸ a **television** / **TV** / **media** star / celebrity / personality
▸ a **showbiz** star / celebrity / personality / legend
▸ a **film** / **movie** / **pop** / **rock** star / superstar / legend
▸ a **screen** star / legend / great
▸ a **Hollywood** star / superstar / legend
▸ a **sporting** / **sports** star / celebrity / personality / legend
▸ to **make sb** a star / celebrity / superstar / legend / public figure

star [C] a famous performer, for example an actor, singer or sports player: *I wanted to be a pop star when I was a teenager.* ◇ *She acts well but she hasn't got **star quality**.* See also **stardom** → FAME, **icon** → HERO

celebrity /sə'lebrəti/ [C] a famous person, especially one who often appears on television: *She was the first TV celebrity he had met in the flesh.* ◇ *The show's success made her an overnight celebrity.* See also **celebrity** → FAME

name [C] a famous person, especially in the fields of culture or sport: *Some of the biggest names in the art world were at the party.* ◇ *The event attracted many famous names from the past.* ❶ **Name** is often used when people are talking about famous people who have been invited to an event, or who are employed in order to attract the public's attention.

personality [C] (*especially written*) a famous person, especially one who works in entertainment or sport: *Various personalities from the world of music were invited.* ◇ *In a viewers' poll he was voted TV Personality of the Year.*

superstar /'suːpəstɑː(r); 'sjuː-; AmE 'suːpərs-/ [C] (*rather informal*) a very famous performer, for example an actor, singer or sports player: *The movie made her an international superstar.*

legend /'ledʒənd/ [C] a very famous person, especially in the fields of sport, music or acting, who is admired by other people: *She was **a legend in her own lifetime**.* ◇ *Many of golf's **living legends** were playing.* ❶ A **legend** has a higher level of fame and a higher status than other types of famous people. It suggests that sb has shown real talent over a long career, and that they are famous because of this rather than because of their appearance or personality. See also **legendary** → FAMOUS

,public 'figure [C] (*rather formal*) a famous person, especially one who has a lot of influence in politics or society: *He is an important public figure with a significant influence on public policy.* See also **public** → FAMOUS, **figure** → PERSON

great [C, usually pl.] (*informal*) a very famous and successful person: *He was one of boxing's **all-time greats**.* ❶ **Greats** is mainly used to talk about people who were very popular in the past. People are typically described as *movie/Hollywood/all-time greats* or as *one of the greats of British comedy/the game*, etc. See also **great** → GREAT *adj.* 2

2 star · lead · hero · heroine · protagonist
These are all words for the main part in a play, film or story, or the person who plays it.

PATTERNS AND COLLOCATIONS
▸ a **young** star / hero / heroine / protagonist
▸ a **male / female** star / lead / protagonist
▸ a **romantic** lead / hero / heroine
▸ a **mythical / fictional / tragic / great** hero / heroine
▸ to **play** the lead / hero / heroine
▸ the star / lead **role**

star [C] a person who has the main part, or one of the main parts, in a TV show, film or play: *She was the star of many popular television series.* ◇ *The star of the show was a young Italian singer.* ❶ **Star** is usually used when talking about fairly light entertainment such as a TV show or a musical. See also **star** → FEATURE *verb*

lead /liːd/ [C] the main part in a play or film; the person who plays this part: *Who is playing the lead?* ◇ *I always dreamed of becoming the lead singer in a band.* ❶ **Lead** is usually used in the phrases *play the lead, the male/female/romantic lead* and *the lead role/actor/singer.*

hero /ˈhɪərəʊ; AmE ˈhɪroʊ; ˈhiː-/ (pl. **-oes**) [C] the main male character in a story, novel, play or film: *The hero of the novel is a ten-year-old boy.* ◇ *Tired of playing boring old romantic heroes, he sought out more challenging roles.*
OPP villain → VILLAIN

heroine /ˈherəʊɪn; AmE -roʊ-/ [C] the main female character in a story, novel, play or film: *The story is narrated entirely by the heroine.* ◇ *She has played several of Shakespeare's heroines − Portia and Juliet among them.*

protagonist /prəˈtægənɪst/ (*formal or written*) the main character in a play, film or book: *At that time, films rarely had a woman as the main protagonist.* ◇ *Bohi Di, first person narrator and protagonist of the novel*

NOTE **HERO, HEROINE** OR **PROTAGONIST?** These words all refer to the main character in a story, rather than the actual person who plays the part: *Oliver Twist, the young protagonist/hero* ◇ ~~Marilyn Monroe, the beautiful protagonist/heroine~~. **Protagonist** is more formal and is often used in reviews of plays, films, books, etc. It can refer to a man or a woman. **Hero** and **heroine** usually suggest a positive role; **protagonist** can be positive or negative.

stare *verb* See also the entries for GLANCE and LOOK 1

stare · gaze · peer · glare · squint · gawk
These words all mean to look at sb/sth for a long time.

PATTERNS AND COLLOCATIONS
▸ to stare / gaze / peer / glare / squint / gawk **at** sb / sth
▸ to stare / gaze / gawk **in** surprise / amusement, etc.
▸ to stare / gaze / peer / glare / squint **for a moment**
▸ to stare / gaze / peer / glare **suspiciously**
▸ to stare / gaze / peer **anxiously / intently**
▸ to stare / gaze / glare **wildly / fiercely**

stare [I] to look at sb/sth for a long time, especially with surprise or fear, or because you are thinking: *I screamed and everyone stared.* ◇ *Peter stared in disbelief at the message on the screen.* ◇ *He sat for hours just staring into space* (= looking at nothing). See also **stare** → LOOK *noun*

gaze [I] (*especially written*) to look steadily at sb/sth for a long time, especially with surprise or love, or because you are thinking: *We all gazed at Marco in amazement.* ◇ *She gazed adoringly into his eyes.* See also **gaze** → LOOK *noun*

peer [I] to look closely or carefully at sth, especially when you cannot see it clearly: *We peered into the shadows.* ◇ *She kept peering over her shoulder.*

glare [I] to look angrily at sb/sth for a long time: *I looked at her and she glared stonily back.* See also **glare** → LOOK *noun*

squint [I, T] to look at sb/sth with your eyes partly shut in order to keep out bright light or to see better: *She was squinting through the keyhole.* ◇ *When he squinted his eyes, he could just make out a house in the distance.*

gawk [I] (*informal*) to stare at sb/sth in such an obvious way that it looks rude or stupid: *Stop gawking like that!*

start *noun*

start · beginning · opening · outset · onset · birth · dawn · kick-off
These are all words for the first part or early stages of sth.

PATTERNS AND COLLOCATIONS
▸ the start / opening **to** sth
▸ **at** the start / beginning / opening / outset / onset / birth / dawn (of sth)
▸ **from the (very)** start / beginning / outset
▸ a **new** start / beginning / opening / birth / dawn
▸ a **slow** start / beginning / onset
▸ a / an **early / late** start / onset / kick-off
▸ a **delayed** start / opening / onset
▸ a **promising** start / beginning / opening
▸ to **mark** the start / beginning / opening / onset / birth / dawn (of sth)
▸ to **herald** the start / beginning / opening / onset / dawn (of sth)
▸ to **see** the start / beginning / opening / birth / dawn (of sth)
▸ to **delay** the start / opening / onset / kick-off (of sth)

start [C, usually sing.] the point at which sth begins; the act or process of beginning sth: *What a perfect start to the day!* ◇ *If we don't hurry, we'll miss the start of the game.* ◇ *We've had problems (right) from the start.* ◇ *The meeting got off to a good/bad start* (= started well/badly). ◇ *The trip was a disaster from start to finish.* ◇ *I'll paint the ceiling if you make a start on the walls.* ◇ *She's moving abroad to make a fresh start* (= to begin a new life). **OPP** finish → END, See also **start** → BEGIN *verb*, **start** → OPPORTUNITY *noun*

beginning [C, usually sing.] the first part or early stages of sth; the point at which sth begins: *We're going to Japan at the beginning of July.* ◇ *We missed the beginning of the movie.* ◇ *Let's start again from the beginning.* ◇ *I've read the whole book from beginning to end.* ❶ *At the beginning (of)* is used for the time and place when sth begins. *In the beginning* means 'at first', and suggests a contrast with a later situation. **OPP** end, ending → END, See also **begin** → BEGIN *verb*

NOTE **START** OR **BEGINNING?** Although these words have almost the same meaning, they tend to be used in slightly different ways. An event, such as a *game* or *meeting* usually has a **start**; a *story, book* or *movie* usually has a **beginning**. In these cases, the **start** is usually shorter than the **beginning**: *We'll miss the start of the game* (= the moment when it starts; the kick-off). ◇ *We missed the beginning of the movie* (= the first few scenes). Note that you say *from start to finish* and *from beginning to end* and NOT: ~~from start to end~~ or: ~~from beginning to finish~~. You usually say *at the beginning of* a particular month, season or decade: ~~at the start of July/summer/the 90s~~. With other periods of time you can use either word, although **beginning** is usually more frequent: *the beginning/start of the day/week/year/century/a new era.* Only **start** can mean 'the act or process of beginning sth': ~~I want to make an early beginning.~~

opening [C, usually sing.] (*especially written*) the first part or early stages of sth such as a play, film, game or other event: *The movie has an exciting opening.* ◇ *The New Zealanders quickly lost control after a promising opening.* **OPP** ending → END, See also **open** → BEGIN *verb*, **opening** → FIRST *det. adj.*

outset /ˈaʊtset/ [sing.] (only used in the phrase *at/from the outset*) (*rather formal*) the beginning of sth: *I made it clear right from the outset that I disapproved.*

onset /ˈɒnset; AmE ˈɑːn-; ˈɔːn-/ [sing.] (*especially written*) the beginning of sth, especially sth unpleasant: *An active and healthy lifestyle can delay the onset of disease in later life.* ❶ **Onset** is often used to talk about the early stages of illness or some other physical experience: *the onset of illness/infection/disease/depression/AIDS/symptoms/shock/menstruation/puberty.* Other typical collocations relate to the weather: *the onset of winter/cold weather*

birth [sing.] (*especially written*) the beginning of a new situation, idea or place: *This declaration marked the birth of a new society in South Africa.*

dawn [sing.] (*literary*) the beginning of a new situation, idea or place: *That's been going on since the dawn of civilization.* ◇ *Peace marked a new dawn in the country's history.*

'kick-off [C, U] the start of a game of football: *Kick-off is at 3.*

start *verb* See also the entry for BEGIN

start · begin · start off · kick off · commence · open
These words are all used to talk about things happening from the beginning, or people doing the first part of sth.

PATTERNS AND COLLOCATIONS
▶ to start/ begin/ start off/ kick off/ commence/ open **with** sth
▶ to start/begin/start off/kick off/commence/open **by** doing sth
▶ to start/ begin/ start off/ commence **as** sth
▶ a **campaign**/ **season**/ **tour**/ **competition**/ **match**/ **festival**/ **meeting** starts/begins/starts off/ kicks off/commences/opens
▶ a **film**/ **book**/ **chapter** starts/ begins/ starts off/ opens
▶ an **enquiry**/ **investigation** starts/ begins/ commences/ opens
▶ **work**/ **production** starts/ begins/ starts off/ kicks off/ commences
▶ **proceedings** start/ begin/ kick off/ commence/ open
▶ a **period** starts/ begins/ commences/ opens
▶ to have **just** started/ begun/ started off/ kicked off/ commenced/ opened
▶ to start/ begin/ start off/ kick off/ commence/ open **immediately**

start [I] (of an event or thing) to happen or exist, when it was not happening or did not exist just before; to start in a particular way or from a particular point: *When does the class start?* ◇ *There are a lot of small businesses* **starting up** *in that area.* ◇ *She started as a secretary but ended up running the department.* ◇ *The company* **started out** *with 30 employees.* ◇ *The evening started badly when the speaker failed to turn up.* ◇ *The trail starts just outside the town.* ◇ *Hotel prices start at £65 a night for a double room.* **OPP finish** → END, See also **start** → BEGIN *verb*

begin [I] to start to happen or exist; to start in a particular way or from a particular point; to start speaking: *When does the concert begin?* ◇ *The evening began well.* ◇ *Use 'an' before words beginning with a vowel.* ◇ *'Ladies and gentlemen,' he began, 'welcome to the Town Hall.'* **OPP end** → END, See also **begin** → BEGIN *verb*

> **NOTE START OR BEGIN?** There is not much difference in meaning between these words. **Start** is more frequent in spoken English and in business contexts; **begin** is more frequent in written English and is often used when you are describing a series of events: *The story begins on the island of Corfu.* **Start** is NOT used to mean 'begin speaking': *'Ladies and gentlemen,' he started.*

start 'off *phrasal verb* (*rather informal*) to start happening or doing sth; to start by doing or being sth: *The discussion started off mildly enough.* ◇ *The leaves start off green but turn red later.* ◇ *I started off working quite hard, but it didn't last.* **OPP finish up ❶** In British English, to **finish up...** is to be in a particular state or at a particular place after a series of events: (*BrE*) *If you're not careful, you could finish up seriously ill.*

kick 'off *phrasal verb* (*informal*) to start an event or activity, especially in a particular way; (of an event, activity, film or book) to start, especially in a particular way: *Tom will kick off with a few comments.* ◇ *The festival kicks off on Monday, September 13.* **OPP wind up** → END

commence /kə'mens/ [I] (*formal*) to start happening: *The meeting is scheduled to commence at noon.* ◇ *I will be on leave during the week commencing 15 February.* See also **commence** → BEGIN

open [I] to start an event or activity in a particular way; (of an event, film or book) to start, especially in a particular way: *He opened with a version of Elvis's 'Can't*

Help Falling in Love.' ◇ *The story opens with a murder.* **❶ Open** is a less informal way of saying **kick off**; however, it is NOT usually used to talk about the time that people begin a shorter or more informal activity: *What time do we kick off?* ◇ *What time do we open?* You can use it for the dates and times of longer or more formal events: *The Annual General Meeting opens at 1pm on March 15th.* **OPP close** → END, See also **open** → BEGIN *verb*

state *noun*

state · condition · shape · repair
These are all words for the quality or qualities that sth has at a particular time, for example whether it is good, bad, new, broken, etc.

PATTERNS AND COLLOCATIONS
▶ **in** (a) ... state/ condition/ shape/ repair
▶ (a) **good** state/ condition/ shape/ (state of) repair
▶ (a) **fine** state/ condition/ shape
▶ **excellent** condition/ shape/ repair
▶ (a) **reasonable** condition/ shape/ (state of) repair
▶ (a) **poor**/ **bad** state/ condition/ shape/ (state of) repair
▶ sth's **general** state/ condition/ state of repair
▶ sth's **physical** state/ condition/ shape
▶ sb's/ sth's **financial**/ **economic** state/ condition/ shape
▶ to **keep** sth **in** (a) ... state/ condition/ shape/ repair
▶ to **get** (sth) **into** (a) ... state/ condition/ shape

state [C] the quality or qualities that sth has at a particular time, for example whether it is generally good, bad, etc.; the fact of having these qualities: *There are serious concerns about the current state of the economy.* ◇ *His teeth were in an appalling state.* ◇ *Look at the state of this room* (= look how messy, dirty, etc. it is)! ◇ *The government has declared a* **state of emergency** *in the flooded regions.* See also **state of affairs** → SITUATION

condition [U, sing.] the state sth is in, especially how good or bad its physical state is: *The car was in perfect condition.* ◇ *The poor condition of our schools should be of concern to all of us.*

> **NOTE STATE OR CONDITION?** **State** is a more general word and is used especially for the quality sth has at a particular time. You use **state** when you are saying that sth has not been well looked after or is in a mess. **Condition** is mainly used to talk about the appearance or working order of sth, often when you are saying how old and worn sth is.

shape [U] (*rather informal*) the condition of sth, especially after sth has happened which you would expect to have an effect on it: *What sort of shape was your car in after the accident?* ◇ *The economy is still in pretty good shape.*

repair [U] the condition of sth, especially when you are talking about whether or not sth has been repaired over a period of time: *Try to keep your vehicle in good repair.* ◇ (*especially BrE*) *The old clock tower is in a* **poor state of repair**. **❶** In this meaning **repair** is usually used in the phrases *in good repair* or *in a poor state of repair.* See also **repair** → REPAIR *noun*

statement *noun*

statement · comment · announcement · remark · declaration · observation
These are all words for sth that you say or write, especially sth that gives information or an opinion.

PATTERNS AND COLLOCATIONS
▶ a statement/ a comment/ an announcement/ a remark/ a declaration/ an observation **about** sth
▶ a statement/ a comment/ an observation **on** sth
▶ an announcement/ a declaration **of** sth
▶ a **brief** statement/ comment/ announcement/ remark/ observation
▶ a/ an **public**/ **official** statement/ comment/ announcement/ declaration

▸ a **formal** statement / announcement / declaration
▸ a **casual** comment / remark / observation
▸ to **make** a statement / a comment / an announcement / a remark / a declaration / an observation
▸ to **issue** a statement / an announcement / a declaration

statement [C] something that you say or write that gives information or an opinion, often in a formal way: *A government spokesperson made a brief statement to the press.* ◇ *She made one of her sweeping statements about young people.* ◇ *The police asked me to make a statement* (= a written account of facts about a crime, used in court if legal action follows). See also **state** → DECLARE

comment [C, U] something that you say or write that gives an opinion on sth or is a response to a question about a particular situation: *She made helpful comments on my work.* ◇ *He handed me the document* **without comment**. ◇ *When asked about the rumours, the chairman replied,* '*No comment.*' See also **comment** → COMMENT *verb*

announcement [C, U] a spoken or written statement that informs people about sth; the act of publicly informing people about sth: *Today's announcement of a peace agreement comes after weeks of discussion.* ◇ *I have a few announcements to make.* ◇ *The announcement of the verdict was accompanied by shouts and cheers.* See also **announce** → DECLARE

remark [C] something that you say or write that gives an opinion or thought about sb/sth: *He made a number of rude remarks about the food.* ◇ *What exactly did you mean by that last remark?* See also **remark** → COMMENT *verb*

declaration /ˌdeklə'reɪʃn/ [C, U] (*rather formal*) an official or formal statement, especially one that states an intention, belief or feeling, or that gives information: *a declaration of love/support* ◇ *We were asked to sign a declaration to the effect that we were UK citizens.* ◇ *The summit has been postponed due to the declaration of war.* ◇ *The Declaration of Independence was signed on 4 July 1776 by representatives of the US states.* See also **declare** → DECLARE

observation [C] (*rather formal*) a comment, especially one based on sth you have seen, heard or read: *He began by making a few general observations about the report.* See also **observe** → COMMENT *verb*

> **NOTE** COMMENT, REMARK OR OBSERVATION? A **comment** can be official or private. A **remark** can be made in public or private but is always unofficial and the speaker may not have considered it carefully. An **observation** is unofficial but is usually more considered than a remark.

station *noun*

station · destination · terminal · stop · bus stop · terminus · depot
These are all words for a place where a train or bus stops or where a journey ends.

PATTERNS AND COLLOCATIONS
▸ a **rail** / **railway** / **railroad** station / terminal / terminus
▸ a **train** station / terminus / depot
▸ a **bus** station / terminal / terminus / depot
▸ to **arrive at** the station / your destination / the terminal / the stop / the bus stop
▸ to **reach** the station / your destination / the bus stop / the terminus
▸ to **get to** the station / your destination
▸ to **get off** at a station / stop
▸ to **go to** the station / terminal / bus stop
▸ to **wait at** the station / bus stop

station [C] a place where trains or buses stop so that passengers can get on or off; the buildings connected with this: *I bought a newspaper at the bus station.* ◇ *The train left the station on time.* ❶ In British English the word **station** used on its own usually refers to the train station:

Is this the way to the station? but you can also say *railway/ train station*. In American English it is usual to say which station you are talking about: *the railroad/train/subway/ bus station*

destination /ˌdestɪ'neɪʃn/ [C] a place to which sb/sth is going or being sent: *The destination is shown on the front of the bus.* ◇ *The flight stops at Hong Kong before going on to its* **final destination**.

terminal [C] a place, building or set of buildings where journeys by plane, train, bus or boat begin and end: *Your flight leaves from terminal 2.* ◇ *a bus/ferry terminal*

stop [C] a place where a bus or train stops regularly for people to get on and off: *I'm getting off at the next stop.* ◇ *Is this your stop?* ◇ *It's only a few stops on the subway.* See also **stop** → STOP *noun*

'bus stop [C] a place at the side of a road that is marked with a sign, where buses stop regularly to let people get on and off: *I saw him standing at the bus stop*

terminus /'tɜːmɪnəs; *AmE* 'tɜːrm-/ (pl. **termini** /'tɜːmɪnaɪ; *AmE* 'tɜːrm-/) [C] the last station at the end of a railway line or the last stop on a bus route: *It's the terminus for trains from the north.*

depot /'depəʊ; *AmE* 'diːpoʊ/ [C] (*AmE*) a small station where trains or buses stop: *The bus depot is on Lincoln Avenue.*

status *noun* See also REPUTATION

status · honour · prestige · glory
These are all words for the state of being respected, admired or considered important, especially by many people.

PATTERNS AND COLLOCATIONS
▸ **personal** / **national** honour / prestige / glory
▸ **social** status / prestige
▸ to **gain** / **bring** / **lose** / **seek** status / honour / prestige / glory
▸ to **enjoy** status / prestige
▸ status / honour / prestige **is attached to** sth

status [U, C, usually sing.] high rank or social position; the level of importance or respect that is given to sth: *The job brings with it status and a high income.* ◇ *The Chanel suit was the number one fashion* **status symbol**. ◇ *This reflects the* **high status** *accorded to science in our culture.* ◇ *In the teaching of literature, Shakespeare is given a* **special status**.

honour (*BrE*) (*AmE* **honor**) [U] great respect and admiration for sb: *The arch was built* **in honour of** *the Emperor.* ◇ *They organized a party* **in his honour**. ◇ *The president was the* **guest of honour** *at the banquet.*

prestige /pre'stiːʒ/ [U] the respect and admiration that sb/sth has because of their social position or what they have done: *The post carried great prestige within the civil service.* ◇ *The jobs are accorded different levels of prestige.* See also **prestigious** → GREAT 2

glory [U] fame, praise, respect or admiration that is given to sb because they have achieved sth important: *I do all the work and he gets all the glory.* ◇ *She basked in the* **reflected glory** *of her daughter's success.* ◇ *She wanted to enjoy her* **moment of glory**. See also **glorious** → FAMOUS

stay *verb*

1 stay where you are
2 stay at a hotel

1 stay · remain · hang around · stop · stick around · stay put · linger · loiter
These words all mean to continue to be in a particular place for a period of time without moving away.

PATTERNS AND COLLOCATIONS
▸ to stay / remain / hang around / stop / stick around / linger **for** a few minutes / weeks / years, etc.
▸ to stay / stop **for** sth
▸ to stay / remain / hang around / stop / stick around / linger **here**

▶ to stay / remain / hang around / linger **there**
▶ to stay / remain / stop **at home**
▶ to stay / remain / stop **behind / indoors**
▶ to stay / hang / stick **around**

stay [I] to continue to be in a particular place for a period of time without moving away: *I just want to stay in bed today.* ◇ *Stay there and don't move!* ◇ *'Do you want a drink?' 'No thanks, I can't stay.'* ◇ *We ended up staying for lunch.* ◇ *I'm **staying late** at the office tonight.* ◇ *She stayed at home* (= did not go out to work) *while the children were young.* ◇ *My hat won't stay on!* ◇ *We **stayed to** see what would happen.* ❶ In spoken English, **stay** can be used with *and* plus another verb, instead of with *to* and the infinitive, to show purpose or to tell sb what to do: *I'll stay and help you.* **OPP** go → LEAVE 1, See also **stay** → REMAIN

remain [I] (usually used with an adverb or preposition) (*rather formal*) to stay in the same place; to not leave: *They remained in Mexico until June.* ◇ *The plane remained on the ground.* ◇ *She left, but I remained behind.* See also **remain** → REMAIN

,hang a'round phrasal verb (*informal*) to wait or stay near a place, not doing very much: *You hang around here in case he comes, and I'll go on ahead.*

stop (-**pp**-) [I] (*BrE, informal*) to stay somewhere for a short time, especially at sb's house: *I'm not stopping. I just came to give you this message.* ◇ *Can you stop for tea?* See also **stop by** → VISIT verb

,stick a'round phrasal verb (*informal*) to stay in a place, waiting for sth to happen or for sb to arrive: *Stick around – we'll need you to help us later.*

stay 'put idiom (*rather formal*) (of a person or thing) to continue to be in the place where they are or have been put: *He chose to stay put while the rest of us toured the area.* ❶ **Stay put** is usually used to talk about a decision that sb makes not to move or go somewhere.

linger /ˈlɪŋɡə(r)/ [I] (usually used with an adverb or preposition) (*especially written*) to stay somewhere for longer because you do not want to leave; to spend a long time doing sth: *She lingered for a few minutes to talk to Nick.* ◇ *We lingered over breakfast on the terrace.*

loiter /ˈlɔɪtə(r)/ [I] (*sometimes disapproving*) to stand or wait somewhere, especially with no obvious reason: *Teenagers were loitering in the street outside.*

> **NOTE** HANG AROUND OR LOITER? If you **hang around** somewhere, you stay there without doing much, but you may have a reason for waiting and there is no real suggestion of disapproval; if sb **loiters** somewhere, there is often a suggestion that they have no good reason for being there and should really go away.

2 stay · visit · stop over · do
These words all mean to go to or live in a place for a short time.

PATTERNS AND COLLOCATIONS
▶ stay / visit / stop over **for** two nights, a week, etc.
▶ stay / stop over **in / at** a place
▶ to **come / go to** stay / visit

stay [I] to live in a place temporarily as a guest or visitor: *I'm staying at a hotel near the beach.* ◇ *She's **staying with** her sister.* ◇ *He stayed for over a week.* ◇ *Come and stay any time!* See also **stay** → VISIT noun

visit [I, T] to stay somewhere for a short time: *We don't live here. We're just visiting.* ◇ *Next time you visit the States you'll have to come and see us.* See also **visit** → VISIT noun, **visitor** → TOURIST

,stop 'over phrasal verb (-**pp**-) to stay somewhere for a short time during a long journey: *We had to stop over in Kuala Lumpur for a night.* See also **stopover** → VISIT noun, **stop by** → VISIT verb

do [T] (*informal*) to visit a place as a tourist: *We did Tokyo in three days.*

steady adj.

steady · stable · regular · constant · consistent · static · even · unchanging
These words all describe things that follow a pattern and do not change.

PATTERNS AND COLLOCATIONS
▶ a steady / a stable / a constant / an even **temperature**
▶ a steady / constant / consistent **trend / rate**
▶ a steady / constant **speed / stream / trickle**
▶ a steady / a constant / an even **flow**
▶ a consistent / an unchanging **pattern**
▶ steady / stable / regular **employment**
▶ a steady / regular / constant **supply**
▶ steady / regular / even **breathing**
▶ a steady / stable / regular **relationship**
▶ to **remain** steady / stable / constant / consistent / static / even / unchanging
▶ **more or less** steady / stable / constant / consistent / static / even
▶ **fairly** steady / stable / constant / consistent / static / even
▶ **very** steady / stable / consistent / static / even

steady developing, growing or changing gradually and in an even and regular way; not changing and not interrupted: *We are making slow but steady progress.* ◇ *The castle receives a steady stream of visitors.* ◇ *She drove at a steady 50 mph.* ◇ *She's got a **steady boyfriend*** (= with whom she has a serious relationship or one that has lasted a long time). See also **steady** → FIRM

▶ **steadily** adv.: *The company's exports have been increasing steadily.* ◇ *The situation got steadily worse.*

stable (*usually approving*) not likely to change or fail: *He was not married, but he was in a stable relationship.* ◇ *The industry should do everything it can to keep prices stable.* ◇ *The patient's condition is stable* (= it is not getting worse). ❶ In this meaning **stable** is used especially to talk about people's personal and home life: *a stable mind/relationship/family/home,* the economic, political or social situation: *a stable situation/environment/government/population* ◇ *stable employment,* or the condition of a patient who has been very ill, but who is not getting worse. **OPP** unstable → UNCERTAIN, See also **stable** → FIRM

regular following a pattern, especially with the same time and space between each thing and the next; (of a job, supply of sth or relationship) that continues for a long time, stays the same and can be relied on: *a regular pulse/heartbeat* ◇ *There is a regular bus service to the airport.* ◇ *A light flashed **at regular intervals**.* ◇ *The equipment is checked **on a regular basis**.* ◇ *She couldn't find any regular employment.* ◇ *This breed of dog benefits from a regular supply of green vegetables in its diet.* **OPP** irregular → VARIABLE, See also **regular** → FREQUENT

> **NOTE** STEADY OR REGULAR? Both **steady** and **regular** can be used to talk about a *job,* *work,* *employment,* an *income,* the *supply* of sth or a *relationship* that continues for a long time and that you can rely on. There is often no difference in meaning, but a *regular job* is sometimes used in contrast to another job that is not regular: *I decided to give up the freelance work and concentrate on my regular job.* **Steady** is not used in this way.

constant (*rather formal or technical*) not changing at all in level or speed over a period of time: *The samples need to be stored at a constant temperature.* ❶ Typical collocates of **constant** are *flow,* *rate,* *rhythm,* *speed,* *state,* *improvement* and *temperature.*

consistent /kənˈsɪstənt/ (*rather formal*) happening in the same way and continuing for a period of time: *There has been a pattern of consistent growth in the economy.* ❶ Typical collocates of **consistent** are *evidence,* *findings,* *results,* *quality,* *standards,* *growth,* *performance,* *success* and *failure.* **OPP** inconsistent → VARIABLE

▶ **consistently** adv.: *Her work has been of a consistently high standard.*

static /'stætɪk/ (*sometimes disapproving, especially business*) not moving, changing or developing: *Sales were up 5% on last year, but pre-tax profits remained static.* ❶ Unlike the other words in this group, **static** is often used when a lack of change is seen as a bad thing rather than a good thing, especially in business contexts. The opposite, **dynamic**, is an approving term. **OPP dynamic** → VARIABLE

even not changing very much in level or speed over a period of time: *Children do not learn at an even pace.* **OPP uneven** → VARIABLE

unchanging (*written*) that does not change, especially in terms of sth's basic pattern or principles: *The days went by, unchanging.* ◇ *The party stood for certain unchanging principles.*

steal *verb* See also the entry for ROB

steal · take · shoplift · poach · embezzle · nick
These words all mean to take sth from a person, shop, etc. without permission and without intending to return it or pay for it.

PATTERNS AND COLLOCATIONS
▸ to steal / take / shoplift / poach / embezzle / nick (sth) **from** sb / a place
▸ to steal / take / embezzle / nick sb's **money**
▸ to steal / take / embezzle sb's **property / funds**
▸ to steal / take / nick sb's **bag / purse / passport**
▸ to steal / take **food / goods / items**
▸ to steal / take / poach / nick sb's **ideas**

steal [I, T] to take sth from a person, shop etc. without permission and without intending to return it or pay for it: *We found out he'd been stealing from us for years.* ◇ *I had my wallet stolen.* ◇ *Thieves stole jewellery worth over $10 000.*
▸ **stealing** *noun* [U]: *You can't just take one! That's stealing!*

take [T] to remove sth without permission or by mistake: *Someone has taken my scarf.* ◇ *Did the burglars take anything valuable?* ❶ **Take** is used instead of **steal** to suggest that there has been a mistake, or when the context of stealing is already clear, for example because you are talking about *burglars*.

shoplift /'ʃɒplɪft; AmE 'ʃɑːp-/ [I] to steal goods from a shop by deliberately leaving without paying for them: *What do you do if you suspect a customer may be shoplifting?* See also **shoplifter** → THIEF, **shoplifting** → THEFT

poach (*especially BrE*) to take and use a person, idea or thing that belongs to sb/sth else, especially in a secret, dishonest or unfair way: *She accused him of poaching her ideas.* ◇ *Several of our employees have been poached by a rival firm.* ❶ **Poach** is used mainly to talk about business situations concerning workers, ideas and responsibilities.

embezzle /ɪm'bezl/ [T, I] to steal money that you are responsible for or that belongs to your employer: *He was found guilty of embezzling $150 000 of public funds.* See also **embezzlement** → THEFT

nick [T] (*BrE, informal*) to steal sth, especially sth that can be moved easily: *Who nicked my pen?*

step *noun*

step · footstep · pace · stride
These are all words for the act of lifting your foot and putting it down again in order to walk or move somewhere.

PATTERNS AND COLLOCATIONS
▸ to take a (few) step(s) / pace(s) / stride(s) **back / forward / to / towards** (sth)
▸ to take a step / pace **backwards**
▸ **quick** steps / footsteps / strides
▸ **light / heavy** steps / footsteps
▸ to **take** a step / pace
▸ to **hear** (sb's) steps / footsteps

step [C] the movement you make when you lift your foot and put it down in order to walk or move somewhere; the distance that you cover when you do this: *the baby's first steps* ◇ *He took a step towards the door.* ◇ *I could hear his steps coming closer.* ◇ *He turned and retraced his steps* (= went back the way he had walked). ◇ (*BrE*) *The hotel is only a short step* (= a short way to walk) *from the beach.* ◇ (*AmE*) *The hotel is only steps away from the beach.* See also **step** → WALK *noun*, **step** → WALK *verb* 1

footstep /'fʊtstep/ [C, usually pl.] the sound your foot makes when you take a step, either walking or running: *I could hear her footsteps echoing in the hall.*

pace [C] one step that you take when walking or running; the distance that you cover when you do this: *She took two paces forward.* ◇ *Jean followed a few paces behind.* See also **pace** → WALK *verb* 1

stride [C] one long step; the distance covered by one long step: *He crossed the room in two strides.* ◇ *She lengthened her stride to try and keep up with him.* See also **stride** → WALK *noun*, **stride** → WALK *verb* 1

stern *adj.* See also the entry for RUTHLESS

stern · grim · severe · steely · unforgiving · dour
These words all describe sb who looks or sounds serious and unfriendly.

PATTERNS AND COLLOCATIONS
▸ a stern / grim / severe / steely **look / voice**
▸ a stern / grim / severe / dour **expression / face**
▸ a stern / grim / severe **warning**
▸ **rather** stern / grim / severe / dour

stern serious and often disapproving; expecting sb to obey you: *Her mother appeared, looking very stern.* ◇ *His voice was suddenly stern.* ◇ *She was one of the government's sternest critics.*
▸ **sternly** *adv.*: *'Don't be stupid,' Marie told herself sternly.*

grim looking or sounding very serious: *Archer's expression was grim.* ◇ *They clung on to the edge of the boat with grim determination.*
▸ **grimly** *adv.*: *'It won't be easy,' he said grimly.* ◇ *grimly determined*

severe (*especially written*) not kind or sympathetic and showing disapproval of sb/sth: *She fixed them with a very severe look.* ◇ *She was a severe woman who seldom smiled.*
▸ **severely** *adv.*: *a severely critical report*
▸ **severity** /sɪ'verəti/ *noun* [U]: *He frowned with mock severity.*

steely (*especially written*) looking or sounding strong, hard and unfriendly: *She saw the look of steely determination in his eyes.* ◇ *Her eyes narrowed into a steely glare.*

unforgiving (*disapproving*) not sympathetic and not willing to forgive other people when they have done sth wrong: *I wonder what makes a man so unforgiving and hard?* **OPP forgiving** → LENIENT

dour /'daʊə(r); BrE also dʊə(r); AmE also dʊr/ (*disapproving*) seeming to be unfriendly and severe: *They were barely acknowledged by a dour receptionist.*

still *adj.*

still · motionless · stationary · inert · immobile · at a standstill
These words all describe sb/sth that is not moving.

PATTERNS AND COLLOCATIONS
▸ a motionless / an inert **body / figure**
▸ to **remain** still / motionless / stationary / inert / immobile
▸ to **stay / lie** still / motionless / inert / immobile
▸ to **sit / stand** still / motionless / immobile
▸ to **hold sb / sth** still / motionless / immobile
▸ **perfectly / quite** still / motionless / immobile
▸ **almost** motionless / stationary / immobile / at a standstill

still not moving: *Stand still when I'm talking to you!* ◇ *I wish you'd keep still.* ◇ *Hold the ladder still while I try to get over the wall.* ◇ *Keep your head still.* ◇ *The surface of* the lake was calm and still. **❶ Still** is the most general of these words and is used to talk not only about individual people, animals or objects, but also about things such as water and air.

motionless /'məʊʃnləs; AmE 'moʊʃn-/ (rather formal, written) (especially of a person or animal) not moving: *She sat motionless as the verdict was announced.*

stationary /'steɪʃənri; AmE -neri/ (rather formal) (especially of a vehicle or machine) not moving; not intended to be moved: *The car collided with a **stationary vehicle**.* ◇ *a stationary exercise bike*

inert /ɪ'nɜːt; AmE ɪ'nɜːrt/ (formal) not moving or active; without power to move or act: *He lay inert with half-closed eyes.* ◇ *They dragged the inert body out of the river.*

immobile /ɪ'məʊbaɪl; AmE ɪ'moʊbl/ [not usually before noun] (rather formal, written) (especially of a person or part of their body) not moving; prevented from moving: *She stood immobile by the window.* ◇ *The cast is used to keep the leg immobile.*

at a ˈstandstill idiom (especially of traffic or trains) not moving: *Traffic was at a complete standstill for over two hours.* ◇ *Trains were at a standstill yesterday as drivers went on strike.* **❶ At a standstill** is used to talk about sth that should be moving but has been made to stop. See also **standstill** → STOP noun

stimulate verb See also the entries for CAUSE and ENCOURAGE 3

stimulate · arouse · stir · inspire · excite
These words all mean to cause sb to feel a particular emotion or to react in a particular way.

PATTERNS AND COLLOCATIONS
▶ to stir / inspire / excite sth **in** sb
▶ to stimulate / arouse / stir / excite (sb's) **interest**
▶ to stimulate / arouse / stir / inspire / excite **feelings** (of sth)
▶ to arouse / stir / inspire **emotions**
▶ to stimulate / arouse / excite **curiosity / speculation**

stimulate /'stɪmjuleɪt/ [T] (approving) to make sth develop or to encourage sth, such as growth, interest, discussion, feelings or ideas: *A newspaper article can be used to stimulate discussion among students.* ◇ *Any increase in industrial activity will stimulate demand for electricity.* ◇ *The first workshop is intended to stimulate ideas.* **OPP** sup- press → LIMIT

arouse /ə'raʊz/ [T] to make sb have a particular feeling, attitude or reaction: *Her strange behaviour aroused our suspicions.* ◇ *The book aroused a lot of adverse criticism.* ◇ *The issue succeeds in arousing a great deal of controversy.* **❶** The object of **arouse** in this meaning is a feeling, attitude or reaction; if a person is the object of **arouse**, it means 'to make sb feel sexually excited': *He began to feel aroused* (= sexually excited). **OPP** suppress → SUPPRESS 2

stir (-rr-) [T] (especially written) to make sb excited or make them feel a strong emotion: *It's a book that really stirs the imagination.* ◇ *This brutal killing has stirred the nation's conscience.* ◇ *He was stirred by the child's sad story.*

inspire /ɪn'spaɪə(r)/ [T] (especially of a person's actions or the way they behave) to make sb have a particular feeling: *As a general, he **inspired** great **loyalty** in his troops.* ◇ *Henry did not **inspire confidence** as a figure of authority.*

excite [T] (rather formal) to make sb feel interest or react in a particular way: *This story **excited** some **comment** (= made people talk about it).* ◇ *The move excited more criticism abroad than at home.*

stir verb See also the entry for MIX

stir · beat · whip · whisk
These words all mean to mix a liquid or substance using a spoon or other tool.

PATTERNS AND COLLOCATIONS
▶ to stir / beat / whisk sth **into** sth
▶ to stir / beat / whisk sth **in**

▶ to stir / beat / whisk A and B **together**
▶ to stir / beat / whisk **ingredients / a mixture**
▶ to beat / whip / whisk **cream / eggs / egg whites**
▶ to stir / beat / whisk sth **thoroughly**

stir (-rr-) [T] to move a liquid or substance around, using a spoon or sth similar, in order to mix it thoroughly: *She stirred her tea.* ◇ *Stir the paint before you use it.* ◇ *The vegetables are stirred into the rice while it is hot.*
▶ **stir** noun [C, usually sing.]: *Could you give the rice a stir?*

beat [T] to mix liquid food with short quick movements with a fork or similar tool: *Beat the eggs to a frothy consistency.*

whip /wɪp/ (-pp-) [T] to stir cream or egg white very quickly until it becomes stiff: *Serve the pie with **whipped cream**.*

whisk /wɪsk/ [T] to mix liquid food into a stiff light mass, using a fork or whisk: *Whisk the egg whites until stiff.*

> **NOTE** BEAT, WHIP OR WHISK? These are very similar actions. **Beat** emphasizes how quickly and hard you stir the food; **whip** is used especially about cream; **whisk** is used especially when you use a hand whisk or electric whisk (= a special tool for stirring eggs, etc. very fast).

stomach noun

stomach · gut · belly · intestine · tummy · abdomen · insides · paunch
These are all words for the front part of the body below the chest and/or the organs inside this part of the body.

PATTERNS AND COLLOCATIONS
▶ **in** the / your **stomach / gut / belly / intestine / tummy / abdomen / insides**
▶ **on** your **stomach / belly / tummy**
▶ a **fat / flat stomach / belly / tummy**
▶ a / an **empty / full stomach / belly / tummy**
▶ a **beer gut / belly**

stomach [C] the organ inside the body where food goes when you swallow it; the front part of the body below the chest: *stomach pains* ◇ *an upset stomach* ◇ (BrE also) *a stomach upset* ◇ *It's not a good idea to drink* (= alcohol) *on an empty stomach.* ◇ *You shouldn't exercise on a full stomach.* ◇ *The attacker kicked him in the stomach.* ◇ *Lie on your stomach with your arms by your side.*

gut [C] the tube in the body through which food passes when it leaves the stomach: *It can take up to 72 hours for food to pass through the gut.* **❶** The **guts** [pl.] are the organs in and around the stomach, especially in an animal: *I'll only cook fish if the guts have been removed.* In informal language **gut** is also another word for a person's stomach, especially when it is large: *Have you seen the gut on him!*

belly [C] (rather informal) the front part of the body below the chest; the organs inside this part of the body: *They crawled along on their bellies.* ◇ *She felt the child in her belly kick.* ◇ (informal) *an ugly man with a red face and a beer belly* (= a fat stomach, caused by drinking a lot of beer over a long time)

intestine /ɪn'testɪn/ [C] (rather formal or medical) a long tube in the body between the stomach and the anus. Food passes from the stomach to the **small intestine** and from there to the **large intestine**: *the activity of bacteria in the small intestine*

tummy [C] (informal) (used especially by children or when speaking to children) the stomach or area around the stomach: *Mum, my tummy hurts.* ◇ *to have (a) tummy ache* ◇ *a tummy bug/upset* (= an illness when you feel sick or vomit)

abdomen /'æbdəmən/ [C] (formal or medical) the part of the body below the chest that contains the stomach and intestines: *Patients reported pain in the lower chest or upper abdomen.*

insides [pl.] (informal) a person's stomach and intestines: *She was so nervous, her insides were like jelly.*

paunch /pɔːntʃ/ [C] a fat stomach on a man: *The driver had a paunch hanging over his belt.*

stone *noun*

stone · rock · boulder · pebble
These are all words for a hard solid mineral substance that is found in the ground.

PATTERNS AND COLLOCATIONS
▸ **solid** stone / rock
▸ to **throw** a stone / rock / boulder / pebble

stone [U, C] (often used before nouns or in compounds) a hard solid mineral substance that is found in the ground, often used for building; a piece of stone shaped for a particular purpose: *Most of the houses are built of stone.* ◇ *stone walls* ◇ *a stone bridge/floor/carving* ◇ *a flight of stone steps* ◇ *These words are carved on the stone beside his grave.* ❶ Especially in British English a **stone** can be a small piece of stone of any shape: *(especially BrE) Some children were throwing stones into the lake.*
▸ **stony** *adj.*: *a stony beach*

rock [U, C] the hard solid mineral substance that forms part of the surface of the earth and some other planets; a large piece of rock sticking up out of the ground or the sea; a large single piece of rock: *They drilled through several layers of rock to reach the oil.* ◇ *volcanic/igneous/sedimentary rocks* ◇ *The ship crashed into the infamous Sker Point Rocks and broke into three pieces.* ◇ *They clambered over the rocks at the foot of the cliff.* ◇ *The sign said 'Danger: falling rocks'.* ❶ In American English a **rock** can also be a small stone: *(AmE) Demonstrators threw rocks at the police.*
▸ **rocky** *adj.*: *a rocky coastline*

NOTE STONE OR ROCK? In British English people *throw* stones and a **rock** is sth too big to pick up and throw. In American English **rock** is the usual word for a small piece of rock that you can pick up, and **stone** is not usually used in this way. In both British and American English **stone** [U] is used especially to talk about sth that has been cut or dug up from the ground, for example in order to build sth. **Rock** [U] is used especially to talk about sth that is still a part of or attached to the ground: *Most of the houses are built of stone.* ◇ *Most of the houses are built of rock.* ◇ *The rock walls of the canyon are almost a mile high.* ◇ *The stone walls of the canyon are almost a mile high.*

boulder /'bəʊldə(r); AmE 'boʊl-/ [C] a very large rock, often with a round shape that has been made by water or the weather: *As the ice sheet rode over the land, huge boulders were ripped from the underlying rock.*

pebble [C] a small, smooth stone that is found in or near water: *The hotel is located beside a pebble beach in a quiet bay.*

stop *noun*

stop · halt · standstill
These are all words for a situation in which activity has stopped.

PATTERNS AND COLLOCATIONS
▸ a / an **abrupt / sudden / complete / total** stop / halt / standstill
▸ a / an **brief / unscheduled / immediate** stop / halt
▸ to **come / bring sth to** a stop / halt / standstill
▸ to **draw / jolt / screech / shudder / skid to** a stop / halt

stop [C] an act of stopping; an act of stopping the movement or progress of sth; the state of being stopped: *The trip included an overnight stop in Brussels.* ◇ *Work has temporarily come to a stop while the funding is reviewed.* ◇ *It is time to **put a stop to** the violence.* See also **stop** → STATION

halt /hɔːlt; BrE also hɒlt/ [sing.] (*rather formal, especially written, especially business*) a stop: *The car skidded to a halt.* ◇ *Strikes have led to a **halt in** production.* ◇ *The economy seems to be **grinding to a halt**.* ◇ *They decided it was time to **call a halt to** the project* (= stop it officially).

NOTE STOP OR HALT? A **stop** is likely to be gentler than a **halt** and is more likely to be planned: *a lunch stop* ◇ *a stop for refreshments* ◇ *a lunch halt* ◇ *a halt for refreshments*. You can have a *grinding/shuddering halt* when a vehicle or work stops suddenly; things can *grind to a halt* or a vehicle can *jolt/lurch/scream/skid to a halt*: *a grinding/shuddering stop* ◇ *grind to a stop* ◇ *jolt/lurch/scream/skid to a stop*. You can *bring* a vehicle or work *to a stop/halt* or it can *come to a stop/halt* by itself. You can *put a stop to* (= take action to stop) sth you think is wrong or *call a halt to* (= decide to stop) sth that you think is not worth doing: *It's time to put a stop to the violence.* ◇ *It's time to call a stop to the project.*

standstill /'stændstɪl/ [sing.] (*especially written, especially business*) a situation in which all activity or movement has stopped: *The security alert brought the airport to a standstill.* ◇ *Traffic in the northbound lane is at a complete standstill.* See also **at a standstill** → STILL *adj.*

stop *verb*

1 stop talking
2 a car stops/stop a car
3 stop the bleeding

1 stop · give sth up · cease · drop · abandon · quit · discontinue · leave off · knock off (sth) · pack sth in
These words all mean to no longer continue to do sth or to make sb/sth no longer do sth.

PATTERNS AND COLLOCATIONS
▸ to stop / give up / cease / quit / leave off **doing sth**
▸ to stop / give up / cease / drop / abandon / quit / leave off **what you are doing**
▸ to stop / give up / cease / abandon / quit / leave off / knock off **work**
▸ to give up / abandon / quit / pack in your **job**
▸ to give up / abandon **hope**
▸ to give up / quit **smoking**
▸ **work** stops / ceases
▸ to **soon / finally** stop / give up / cease / abandon / quit / discontinue
▸ to **suddenly / immediately / almost / simply / never** stop / give up / cease / abandon / quit
▸ to stop / cease / quit / leave off **for a moment**

stop (-pp-) [T, I] to no longer continue to do sth; to make sb/sth no longer do sth: *That phone never stops ringing!* ◇ *He couldn't stop thinking about her.* ◇ *Mike immediately stopped what he was doing.* ◇ *(spoken) Stop me* (= Make me stop talking) *if I'm boring you.* ◇ **Stop it!** *You're hurting me.* ◇ *Can't you just stop?* ❶ Notice the difference between *stop doing sth* and *stop to do sth*: *We stopped taking pictures.* means 'We were no longer taking pictures.': *We stopped to take pictures.* means 'We stopped what we were doing so that we could start taking pictures.'

give sth 'up *phrasal verb* [no passive] to stop doing or having sth: *She didn't give up work when she had the baby.* ◇ *We'd given up hope of ever having children.* ◇ *You ought to give up smoking.* ◇ *He gave up medicine for a career in show business.* OPP **take sth up** → BEGIN

cease /siːs/ [I, T] (*formal*) to stop happening or existing; to stop sth from happening or existing: *Welfare payments cease as soon as an individual starts a job.* ◇ *You never cease to amaze me!* ◇ *The company ceased trading in June.* ◇ *He ordered his men to **cease fire*** (= stop shooting).

drop (-pp-) [T] (*rather informal, especially spoken*) to stop doing or discussing sth; to not continue with sth: *I dropped German* (= stopped studying it) *when I was 14.* ◇ **Drop everything** *and come at once.* ◇ *Look, can we just* *drop it* (= stop talking about it)? ◇ *I think we'd better* **drop the subject.** ◇ *The police decided to drop the charges against her.*

abandon [T] (*rather formal*) to stop doing sth, especially before it is finished; to stop having sth: *They were forced to abandon the game because of rain.* ◇ *We had to abandon any further attempt at negotiation.*

quit [T, I] (*especially AmE, informal*) to stop doing sth: *I'm still trying to quit smoking.* ◇ *Just quit it!* ◇ *We only just started. We're not going to quit now.*

discontinue [T] (*formal*) to stop doing, using or providing sth, especially sth that you have been doing, using or providing regularly: *It was decided to discontinue the treatment after three months.*

,**leave** '**off** *phrasal verb* (*informal*) to stop doing sth, especially temporarily: *Start reading from where you left off last time.*

,**knock** '**off**, ,**knock** '**off sth** *phrasal verb* (*informal*) to stop doing sth, especially work: *Do you want to knock off early today?* ◇ *What time do you knock off work?*

,**pack sth** '**in** *phrasal verb* (*informal*) to stop doing sth: *She decided to pack in her job.* ◇ (*especially BrE*) **Pack it in** (= stop behaving badly or annoying me)*, you two!*

NOTE WHICH WORD? **Give up, quit, leave off, knock off** and **pack sth in** are all informal ways of saying 'stop doing sth'. **Knock off** is usually used about work, when you stop work at the end of the day or for a short time. **Leave off** is also usually used when you stop sth temporarily and expect to start again later. If you *give up/quit work* you leave your job and don't get another one. You can't: ~~pack in work~~ but you can *give up/quit/ pack in your job* which means you leave your job and either get another one or do sth else such as start your own business or travel around the world. *Work* can also **cease** or **be abandoned** if a whole group of people working on a project decides or is told to stop: *Work on redeveloping the site has ceased/been abandoned.* If work **ceases** it may start again later; if it **is abandoned** it probably will not. **Stop** can be used with *work* in any of these ways: *What time do you stop/knock off work today?* ◇ *She stopped/gave up/quit work when she had the baby.* ◇ *Work on the project has stopped/ceased/been abandoned.*

2 stop · park · halt · pull up · pull (sb/sth) over

These words all mean to no longer move or to make a vehicle no longer move.

PATTERNS AND COLLOCATIONS
▶ to stop / park / halt a **car**
▶ to stop / park a **bus** / **cab** / **vehicle**
▶ to stop / halt (a) **train** / **traffic**
▶ a **car** stops / parks / pulls up / pulls over
▶ a **bus** / **cab** / **vehicle** stops / pulls up
▶ a **driver** stops / parks / pulls up / pulls over
▶ a **train** stops / halts

stop (-**pp**-) [I, T] (of a vehicle or person) to no longer move; to make a vehicle or its driver no longer move or drive: *Ann stopped in front of the house.* ◇ *This train doesn't stop at Royston.* ◇ *We stopped for the night in Port Augusta.* ◇ *He was stopped by the police for speeding.*

park [I, T] to leave a vehicle that you are driving in a particular place for a period of time: *You can't park here.* ◇ *A red van was parked in front of the house.*

halt /hɔːlt; *BrE also* hɒlt/ [I, T] (*rather formal, especially written*) to stop moving; to make sb/sth stop moving, especially by ordering them to do so: '*Halt!' the Major ordered* (= used as a command to soldiers). ◇ *The police were halting traffic on the parade route.* ❶ **Halt** is used especially about people walking, *trains* and *traffic*, especially in contexts where sb/sth is forced or ordered to halt.

,**pull** '**up** *phrasal verb* (of a vehicle or its driver) to stop: *He pulled up at the traffic lights.*

,**pull** '**over**, ,**pull sb/sth** '**over** *phrasal verb* (of a vehicle or its driver) to move to the side of the road in order to stop or let sth pass; (of the police) to make a driver or vehicle move to the side of the road: *She saw the ambulance coming up behind her and pulled over.* ◇ *She was pulled over by police for bad driving.*

3 stop · suspend · halt · stem · put a stop to sth

These words all mean to make sth end or finish.

PATTERNS AND COLLOCATIONS
▶ to stop / suspend / halt / stem the **flow** (of sth)
▶ to stop / halt / stem the **progress** / **development** / **advance** / **expansion** / **spread** / **decline** / **slide** (of sth)
▶ to stop / suspend / halt / put a stop to **plans** / **an activity** / **a practice**
▶ to stop / suspend / halt **production**
▶ to **effectively** / **temporarily** stop / suspend / halt / stem sth
▶ to **abruptly** / **immediately** stop / suspend / halt sth

stop (-**pp**-) [T] to make sth end or finish: *Doctors couldn't stop the bleeding.* ◇ *The referee was forced to stop the game because of heavy snow.* ◇ *This violence has got to be stopped.* ◇ *Measures must be taken to stop the spread of the virus.* **OPP** start → BEGIN

suspend /sə'spend/ [T] (*rather formal*) to officially stop sth for a time; to prevent sth from being active or used for a time: *The company has decided to suspend production at the plant.* ◇ *The constitution was suspended as the fighting grew worse.* **OPP** continue → CONTINUE 1
▶ **suspension** *noun* [U, sing.]: *These events have led to the suspension of talks.*

halt /hɔːlt; *BrE also* hɒlt/ [T] to stop sth from continuing or developing: *The trial was halted after the first week.* ◇ *The strike effectively halted production at the factory.*

stem (-**mm**-) [T] to stop sth from spreading or increasing further, especially the flow of sth: *The cut was bandaged to stem the bleeding.* ◇ *The government had failed to* **stem the tide** *of factory closures.*

,**put a** '**stop to sth** *phrase* to take action to make sth end or finish, especially sth bad: *There are no simple measures that will put a stop to the violence overnight.*

storm *noun*

storm · thunderstorm · hurricane · tornado · gale · blizzard · snowstorm · cyclone · typhoon · twister
These are all words for extreme weather conditions involving strong winds.

PATTERNS AND COLLOCATIONS
▶ a **heavy** storm / thunderstorm / snowstorm
▶ a **violent** storm / thunderstorm / gale / cyclone
▶ a **fierce** storm / hurricane / gale / blizzard
▶ a **howling** storm / gale / blizzard
▶ a storm / hurricane / gale **blows**
▶ a storm / thunderstorm / hurricane / tornado / gale / blizzard / cyclone / typhoon / twister **strikes** (sth)
▶ a storm / thunderstorm / hurricane / tornado / blizzard / cyclone / typhoon / twister **hits** sth
▶ a storm / hurricane / tornado / typhoon **sweeps through** sth
▶ a storm / hurricane / tornado / cyclone / typhoon / twister **destroys** sth
▶ storm / hurricane / tornado / gale / blizzard **warnings**
▶ the **eye** of a / the storm / hurricane / cyclone

storm [C] very bad weather with strong winds and rain: *Rail services were suspended as fierce storms lashed the country.* ◇ *A few minutes later* **the storm broke** (= began). ◇ *I think we're* **in for a storm** (= I think there will be one). ◇ *Does the insurance policy provide for storm damage?* ❶ **Storm** is often used in compounds meaning a particular type of storm: *an electrical storm* (= with lightning) ◇ *a tropical storm* ◇ *a dust storm* ◇ *a rainstorm* ◇ *a sandstorm* ◇ *a hailstorm*

thunderstorm /ˈθʌndəstɔːm; AmE ˈθʌndərstɔːrm/ [C] a storm with thunder and lightning and usually very heavy rain: *The church was struck by lightning during a violent thunderstorm.*

hurricane /ˈhʌrɪkən; AmE ˈhɜːrəkən; -keɪn/ [C] a violent storm with very strong winds that move in a circle, especially in the North Atlantic Ocean: *Hurricane-force winds hit the islands.* ◇ *Hurricane Rita is now approaching the coast of Florida.* ❶ Hurricanes are usually given names of people, such as *Hurricane Ana* or *Hurricane Bill*.

tornado /tɔːˈneɪdəʊ; AmE tɔːrˈneɪdoʊ/ (pl. **tornadoes** or **tornados**) [C] a violent storm with very strong winds that move in a circle. There is often also a tall cloud which is narrower at the bottom than at the top: *Tornadoes ripped into the southern United States yesterday.* ❶ A **tornado** is much more local and smaller in size (but not necessarily strength) than a **hurricane**. It might *touch down* in one place for just a short time before moving on: *The tornado touched down north-west of Hobbs, New Mexico, damaging a barn and trailer home.*

gale [C] a very strong wind: *The gale blew down hundreds of trees.* ◇ (*BrE*) *It's blowing a gale outside.*

blizzard /ˈblɪzəd; AmE -zərd/ [C] a heavy storm with snow and very strong winds: *More than a million lambs died in the worst blizzards to hit New Zealand in 30 years.*

snowstorm /ˈsnəʊstɔːm; AmE ˈsnoʊstɔːrm/ [C] a heavy fall of snow, usually with a strong wind: *We fought our way through a raging snowstorm.* See also **snow** → SNOW

cyclone /ˈsaɪkləʊn; AmE -kloʊn/ [C] a violent storm with strong winds that move in a circle, especially in tropical regions: *The island was hit by a cyclone which caused considerable damage.*

typhoon /taɪˈfuːn/ [C] a violent tropical storm with very strong winds that move in a circle, especially in the western Pacific oceans: *Earthquakes, typhoons and other natural disasters are frequent in that part of the Pacific.*

> **NOTE** HURRICANE, CYCLONE OR TYPHOON? **Cyclone** is the most general word for a violent storm with strong winds that move in a circle. Tropical cyclones with wind speeds of over 17 metres per second are called **tropical storms** and given names; if the wind reaches 33 m/s they are called **hurricanes** (in the North Atlantic Ocean) or **typhoons** (in the western Pacific Ocean).

twister [C] (*AmE, rather informal*) a tornado: *The twister, reported to be about 100 yards wide, caused major damage to the high school.*

story noun

1 a bedtime story
2 the story of his life

1 story · tale · plot · narrative · anecdote · saga · storyline
These are all words for a description of real or imagined events intended to entertain people.

PATTERNS AND COLLOCATIONS
▸ a story / a tale / a plot / a narrative / an anecdote / a saga / a storyline **about** sb / sth
▸ a **long** story / tale / narrative / anecdote / saga
▸ a / an **good** / **amusing** story / tale / plot / anecdote / storyline
▸ a **simple** story / tale / plot / narrative
▸ a **dramatic** / **romantic** / **complicated** story / tale / plot / saga
▸ a **popular** / **traditional** / **fictional** story / tale / narrative
▸ a / an **interesting** / **entertaining** / **humorous** / **charming** / **wonderful** / **apocryphal** story / tale / anecdote
▸ a / an **epic** / **extraordinary** / **sad** / **sorry** / **terrible** story / tale / saga
▸ a **great** story / plot / narrative / saga
▸ a **historical** story / narrative / saga
▸ to **tell** (**sb**) a story / a tale / a plot / an anecdote
▸ to **recount** / **relate** a story / a tale / an anecdote
▸ to **read** (**sb**) / **write** a story / tale / narrative / saga
▸ a story / tale / narrative / saga **begins** / **unfolds** / **ends**

story [C] a description of events and people that the writer or speaker has invented in order to entertain people: *a / an adventure/detective/ghost/love story* ◇ *a book of short stories* ◇ *a story about time travel* ◇ *It's the epic story of a family's escape from war.* ◇ *Shall I tell you a story?* ◇ *I always read the children a bedtime story.* See also **story** → REPORT 2

tale [C] (*especially written*) an imaginative story, especially one that is full of action and adventure; an exciting spoken description of an event, which may not be completely true: *I love listening to his tales of life at sea.* ◇ *I've heard tales of people seeing ghosts in that house.* ◇ *Her experiences provide a cautionary tale* (= a warning) *for us all.* ❶ A *moral* or *cautionary tale* is one that makes people think about right and wrong.

plot [C, U] the series of events which form the story of a novel, play, film, etc: *a conventional plot about love and marriage* ◇ *The novel is well organized in terms of plot.*

narrative /ˈnærətɪv/ [C] (*formal*) a description of events, especially in a novel: *She has written a gripping narrative of their journey up the Amazon.* See also **narrate** → DESCRIBE

anecdote /ˈænɪkdəʊt; AmE -doʊt/ [C, U] a short, interesting or amusing story about a real person or event; a personal account of an event: *He has lots of amusing anecdotes about his brief career as an actor.* ◇ *This research is based on anecdote, not fact.*

saga /ˈsɑːɡə/ [C] a long story about events over a period of many years: *She has written a compelling family saga.*

storyline /ˈstɔːrilaɪn/ [C] the basic story in a novel, play, film, etc: *Her novels always have the same basic storyline.*

2 story · history · chronicle
These are all words for an account of past events.

PATTERNS AND COLLOCATIONS
▸ to **read** / **write** the story / a history / a chronicle of sth
▸ to **tell** (**sb**) / **recount** / **relate** the story / history of sth

story [C, usually sing.] (usually **the story of sth**) a written or spoken account of past events or of how sth has developed: *He told us the story of his life.* ◇ *Tune in to 'The Story of the Beatles' tonight on Radio 2.*

history [C, usually sing.] (usually **a history of sth**) a written or spoken account of past events: *She's writing a new history of Europe.* ◇ *She went on to catalogue a long history of disasters.*

> **NOTE** STORY OR HISTORY? If you tell **the story of sth**, you suggest that there is only one true version of events and this is what you are telling; if you write **a history of sth** you suggest that there are several possible versions of events, but this is the one that you believe. **The story of sth** is usually more popular and less academic than a **history**.

chronicle /ˈkrɒnɪkl; AmE ˈkrɑːn-/ [C] a written record of events in the order in which they happened: *the Anglo-Saxon Chronicle* ◇ *Her latest novel is a fictional chronicle of life in a Devon village.* ❶ A **chronicle** is usually a record of events, rather than an account: it states what happened without trying to explain it. See also **chronicle** → DESCRIBE verb

strange adj.

1 A strange thing happened this morning.
2 Never accept rides from strange men.

1 See also the entry for UNUSUAL

strange · odd · weird · curious · mysterious · funny · bizarre · peculiar · uncanny
These words all describe people or things that are unusual or surprising, especially in a way that is difficult to understand.

PATTERNS AND COLLOCATIONS
▸ strange / odd / weird / curious / funny / bizarre / peculiar / uncanny **that…**
▸ strange / odd / weird / curious / funny / peculiar / uncanny **how** / **what…**

▶ a strange / an odd / a weird / a curious / a mysterious / a funny / a bizarre / a peculiar / an uncanny **way**
▶ a strange / an odd / a weird / a curious / a mysterious / a funny / a bizarre / a peculiar **thing**
▶ a strange / an odd / a weird / a curious / a mysterious / a funny / a peculiar **place**
▶ a strange / an odd / a curious / a funny / a bizarre / a peculiar **situation**
▶ a strange / an odd / a curious / a funny / a bizarre / a peculiar / an uncanny **feeling**
▶ a strange / an odd / a curious / a funny / a peculiar **smell**
▶ strange / odd / curious / mysterious / bizarre / peculiar **behaviour**
▶ a strange / an odd / a mysterious / a peculiar **person / man / woman**
▶ **something** strange / odd / weird / curious / mysterious / funny / bizarre / peculiar / uncanny
▶ **very** strange / odd / weird / curious / mysterious / funny / peculiar
▶ **really** strange / odd / weird / funny / bizarre / uncanny
▶ **rather** strange / odd / weird / curious / mysterious / funny / bizarre / peculiar / uncanny
▶ **slightly** strange / odd / weird / curious / mysterious / bizarre

strange unusual or surprising, especially in a way that is difficult to understand: *A strange thing happened this morning.* ◇ *It's strange (that) we haven't heard from him.* ◇ *That's strange — the front door's open.* ◇ *There was something strange about her eyes.* **OPP** normal → NORMAL
▶ **strangely** *adv.*: *She's been acting very strangely lately.* ◇ *Strangely enough, I don't feel at all nervous.*

odd strange: *They're very odd people.* ◇ *The odd thing was that he didn't recognize me.* ◇ *She had the oddest feeling that he was avoiding her.* **OPP** normal → NORMAL, See also **oddity** → EXCEPTION
▶ **oddly** *adv.*: *She's been behaving very oddly lately.* ◇ *He looked at her in a way she found oddly disturbing.*

NOTE STRANGE OR ODD? Strange can sometimes suggest that sb/sth is mysterious or frightening in some way: *Strange things have been happening round here.* (Compare: *A strange/an odd thing happened this morning.* This would be an unusual thing, but not a frightening thing.) **Odd** can suggest that you feel that sb/sth is hard to understand or not right in some way, but *odd people* probably won't hurt you; *strange people* might.

weird /wɪəd; *AmE* wɪrd/ (*rather informal, especially spoken, sometimes disapproving*) unusual or different: *I had a really weird dream last night.* ◇ *She's a very weird girl.* ◇ *It's weird seeing yourself on television.* ❶ When **weird** is used to describe other people or their ideas, there is often an element of judgement and/or disapproval: *He's got some weird ideas* (= ideas that I do not agree with at all). **OPP** normal → NORMAL
▶ **weirdly** *adv.*: *The town was weirdly familiar.*

curious /ˈkjʊəriəs; *AmE* ˈkjʊr-/ (*rather formal*) strange: *It was a curious feeling, as though we were floating on air.* ◇ *It was curious that she didn't tell anyone.* ❶ In this meaning **curious** is NOT usually used to describe people: *a curious person/man/woman* is sb who feels curious (= wants to know) about sth, not one who seems strange to other people. See also **curious** → CURIOUS
▶ **curiously** *adv.*: *His clothes were curiously old-fashioned.* ◇ *Curiously enough, a year later exactly the same thing happened again.*

mysterious strange and difficult to understand or explain: *He died in mysterious circumstances.* ◇ *A mysterious illness is affecting all the animals.* See also **mystery** → MYSTERY
▶ **mysteriously** *adv.*: *My watch had mysteriously disappeared.*

funny (*rather informal, especially spoken*) strange and difficult to understand: *That's funny — he was here a moment ago and now he's gone.* ◇ *The engine's making a very funny noise.* ◇ *I'm pleased I didn't get that job, in a funny sort of way.* ❶ In this meaning **funny** is a more informal way of saying **strange**, but it does not suggest that sth is slightly frightening, as **strange** sometimes does.
▶ **funnily** *adv.*: *Funnily enough, I met her only yesterday.*

bizarre /bɪˈzɑː(r)/ very strange: *What a bizarre story!* ◇ *He was exhibiting some very bizarre behaviour.*
▶ **bizarrely** *adv.*: *She was bizarrely dressed, in a sort of tent thing.*

peculiar /pɪˈkjuːliə(r)/ (*BrE or rather formal*) strange, especially in a way that is unpleasant or worrying: *I had a peculiar feeling we'd met before.* ◇ *He died in very peculiar circumstances.* ❶ **Peculiar** is rather formal in American English, but not in British English. See also **peculiarity** → MANNERISM, **peculiar** → UNIQUE

uncanny /ʌnˈkæni/ strange and difficult to explain: *It was uncanny really, almost as if she knew what I was thinking.* ◇ *He has an uncanny knack of being able to see immediately where the problem lies.* ❶ **Uncanny** is used mainly to talk about situations and abilities, especially ones for which you cannot find a normal scientific explanation.

2 strange · unknown · unfamiliar · alien
These words all describe people, places or things that you do not know or recognize.

PATTERNS AND COLLOCATIONS
▶ strange / unknown / unfamiliar / alien **to** sb
▶ a strange / an unknown / an unfamiliar / an alien **place**
▶ a strange / an unfamiliar / an alien **environment**
▶ a strange / an unfamiliar **situation / feeling**

strange that you do not know or recognize because you have not been there before or met the person before: *Never accept rides from strange men.* ◇ *She woke up in a strange bed in a strange room.* ◇ *At first the place was strange to me.*

unknown not known or identified: *a species of insect previously* **unknown** *to science* ◇ *He was trying, for some* **unknown** *reason, to count the stars.* ◇ *The man's identity remains unknown.*

unfamiliar that you do not know or recognize: *An unfamiliar sound came from the hall.* ◇ *Please highlight any terms that are unfamiliar to you.* **OPP** familiar ❶ A person, place or thing that is **familiar** is well known to you because you have often seen, met, etc. them before: *to look/sound/taste familiar* ◇ *He's a familiar figure in the neighbourhood.*

NOTE STRANGE OR UNFAMILIAR? In this meaning **strange** is used especially to describe people and places. If **strange** is used to describe other things, such as a *word, term, name, face, voice, sound* or *feeling* it is more likely to mean 'unusual': if you mean 'not known' use **unfamiliar**.

alien /ˈeɪliən/ (*written*) strange and frightening; different from what you are used to: *In a world that had suddenly become alien and dangerous, he was her only security.*

strangle verb

strangle · suffocate · throttle · choke
These words all mean to kill sb by preventing them from breathing.

PATTERNS AND COLLOCATIONS
▶ to **almost / half / nearly** strangle / suffocate / throttle / choke sb
▶ to strangle / suffocate / throttle / choke sb **to death**

strangle [T] to kill sb by squeezing their throat in order to stop them from breathing: *He strangled her to death as she slept.* ◇ *He strangled her with her own scarf.*
▶ **strangulation** /ˌstræŋɡjuˈleɪʃn/ *noun* [U]: *to die from/ of slow strangulation*

suffocate /ˈsʌfəkeɪt/ [I, T] to die because there is no air to breathe; to kill sb by preventing them from breathing air: *Many dogs have suffocated in hot cars.* ◇ *The couple were suffocated by fumes from a faulty gas fire.* ◇ *He put the pillow over her face and suffocated her.*
▶ **suffocation** *noun* [U]: *to die from/of suffocation*

throttle [T] (*rather informal*) to kill sb by squeezing their throat to stop them from breathing: *He throttled the guard with his bare hands.*

NOTE STRANGLE OR THROTTLE? There is not much difference in meaning between these words. **Throttle** is slightly more informal and is used especially in humorous spoken expressions to show that sb is very annoying; **strangle** can also be used in these expressions: *I felt like strangling/throttling him!*

choke [T] to make sb unable to breathe by blocking or squeezing their throat: *Thick clouds of dust choked him.*

strength *noun*

strength · resilience · endurance · stamina · resistance
These are all words for sb's ability to continue in a difficult situation or not to be affected by sth.

PATTERNS AND COLLOCATIONS
▸ resilience / resistance **to** sth
▸ the strength / resilience / stamina **to do** sth
▸ **great** strength / resilience / endurance / stamina
▸ **remarkable** strength / resilience / endurance
▸ **mental** strength / endurance / stamina
▸ to **have** strength / resilience / endurance / stamina / resistance
▸ to **show** strength / resilience / endurance
▸ to **build up** endurance / stamina / resistance
▸ sb's **reserves of** strength / resilience / stamina

strength [U, sing.] (in people) the quality of being brave and determined in a difficult situation: *During his ordeal he was able to **draw strength from** his faith.* ◇ *You have shown great **strength of character**.* ◇ *She has a remarkable **inner strength**.* **OPP** weakness → WEAKNESS 2
▸ **strong** *adj.*: *It's difficult, I know, but be strong!*

resilience /rɪ'zɪliəns/ [U, sing.] (in people and things) the ability not to be affected or to continue quickly after sth unpleasant, such as a shock, injury or disadvantage: *This comeback says much for the resilience of the team.* ◇ *The industry has developed a resilience to the dips the national economy may take.*
▸ **resilient** *adj.*: *He'll get over it – young people are amazingly resilient.*

endurance /ɪn'djʊərəns; AmE -'dʊr-/ [U] (in people) the ability to continue doing sth painful, unpleasant or difficult for a long period of time without complaining: *They were humiliated **beyond endurance**.* ◇ *This event tests both physical and mental endurance.* ◇ *She was almost at the **limits of her endurance**.* See also **endure** → STAND 2

stamina /'stæmɪnə/ [U] (in people) the physical or mental ability to continue doing sth difficult or tiring for long periods of time: *She didn't have the stamina to complete the course.*

resistance [U, sing.] (in people, animals and plants) the power not to be affected by sth, especially a disease or drug: *AIDS lowers the body's resistance to infection.* ◇ *Many viruses develop resistance to drugs.* See also **resist** → WITHSTAND
▸ **resistant** *adj.*: *plants that are **resistant to** disease* ◇ *heat-resistant materials*

strengthen *noun*

strengthen · reinforce · bolster · cement · shore sth up
These words all mean to make sb/sth stronger.

PATTERNS AND COLLOCATIONS
▸ to strengthen / reinforce a **view**
▸ to strengthen / bolster / cement the **case** (for sth)
▸ to strengthen / bolster / shore up the **economy**
▸ to strengthen / bolster / shore sth **up**
▸ to strengthen / reinforce / bolster / cement sth **further**

strengthen [I, T] to become stronger; to make sb/sth stronger: *The wind had strengthened overnight.* ◇ *Her position in the party has strengthened in recent weeks.* ◇ *Repairs are necessary to strengthen the bridge.* ◇ *The exercises are designed to strengthen your stomach muscles.* ◇ *Their attitude only strengthened his resolve to fight on.* ◇ *The experience of bereavement can strengthen family ties.*
❶ Strengthen is the most general of these words and can mean to make sb/sth stronger in any way: physically, emotionally, morally, politically or financially. **OPP** weaken → WEAKEN, **weaken** → WORSEN, **weaken** → TIRE, See also **strength** → FORCE *noun*

reinforce /ˌriːɪn'fɔːs; AmE -'fɔːrs/ [T] to make sth such as a feeling or idea stronger; to make a structure or material stronger, especially by adding another material to it: *The experience reinforced my sense of loss.* ◇ *The buildings were reinforced to withstand earthquakes.* ◇ *reinforced plastic/ steel/concrete*

bolster /'bəʊlstə(r); AmE 'boʊl-/ [T] to support or improve sth or make it stronger: *to bolster sb's confidence/courage/ morale* ◇ *Falling interest rates may help to bolster up the economy.* ◇ *I needed to stress the bus driver's evidence in order to bolster my case.* **❶** Bolster is used especially to talk about making sb/sth stronger emotionally or financially, or to make the *argument* or *case* for sth stronger.

cement /sɪ'ment/ [T] to make sth such as an agreement or relationship stronger: *The President's visit was intended to cement the alliance between the two countries.*

shore sth 'up *phrasal verb* to support part of a building or other large structure by placing large pieces of wood or metal against or under it so that it does not fall down; to help to support sth that is weak or going to fail: *Timbers were used to shore up the tunnel.* ◇ *The measures were aimed at shoring up the economy.*

stress *verb* See also the entry for POINT STH OUT

stress · emphasize · underline · underscore · weight · prioritize
These words all mean to give particular importance to sb/sth so that people notice them/it.

PATTERNS AND COLLOCATIONS
▸ to stress / emphasize / underline **that / how...**
▸ to stress / emphasize / underline / underscore **the fact that...**
▸ to stress / emphasize / underline / underscore the **importance / extent / necessity** of sth
▸ to stress / emphasize / underline / underscore / prioritize a **need**
▸ to stress / emphasize / underline / underscore a **point**
▸ to stress / emphasize / underline the **difference**
▸ to stress / emphasize / underline an **aspect** of sth
▸ to stress / emphasize a **word / syllable / phrase**
▸ to **clearly** stress / emphasize / underline / underscore / weight sth
▸ to **heavily** stress / emphasize / weight sth
▸ to **further** stress / emphasize / underline / underscore sth
▸ to **just** stress / emphasize / underline sth

stress [T] to give particular importance or attention to sth; to say sth in a way that makes people notice it and think about it; to give extra force to a word or syllable when saying it: *She stressed the importance of a good education.* ◇ *I must stress that everything I've told you is strictly confidential.* ◇ *It must be stressed that this disease is very rare.* ◇ *I want to stress how important this work is.* ◇ *You stress the first syllable in 'happiness'.* See also **stress** → PRIORITY *noun*

emphasize (*BrE* -ise) [T] (*rather formal*) to stress the importance of sth; to give extra force to a word or phrase when saying it, especially to show that it is important: *The report emphasizes the need for economic stability.* ◇ *It should be emphasized that this is only one possible explanation.* ◇ *He emphasized how little was known about the disease.* ◇ *'Let nothing... nothing,' he emphasized the word, 'tempt you.'* See also **emphasis** → PRIORITY

NOTE STRESS OR EMPHASIZE? When you are talking about giving particular importance to a fact or issue, you can use either word. **Stress** is slightly more informal, used more in spoken English and journalism, especially when the subject is human (*I must stress...*). **Emphasize** is slightly more formal, used more in written and academic English, especially when the subject is not human (*The report emphasizes...*). When you are talking about giving extra force to a word, use **stress** when you are talking about normal speech patterns, especially syllable stress. You can use **stress** or **emphasize** to talk about giving particular importance to a word.

underline /ˌʌndəˈlaɪn; *AmE* -ˈdərˈl-/ [T] (*rather formal*) to emphasize or show that sth is important or true: *The report underlines the importance of pre-school education.* ◇ *Her question only underlined how little she understood him.* ❶ A *report* or *statement* most often **underlines** a *fact*, *need* or *point*. A person might **underline** their *determination* or *commitment* to do sth.

underscore /ˌʌndəˈskɔː(r); *AmE* -ˈdərˈs-/ [T] (*especially AmE, especially business*) to emphasize that sth is important: *His speech underscored the need for a clear policy.*

NOTE UNDERLINE OR UNDERSCORE? In British English **underline** has a wider range of use than **underscore**, which is only used when sb/sth deliberately emphasizes sth. Something can **underline** sth if it shows it to be important or true without meaning to; in American English **underscore** can also be used in this way, but not in British English: *Her question only underlined how little she understood him.* ◇ (*AmE* also) *Her question only underscored how little she understood him.* In both British and American English you can also use **highlight** when you want to draw particular attention to sth. See also **highlight** → POINT STH OUT

weight [T, usually passive] (*technical*) to give different values to things to show how important you think each of them is compared with the others: *Each of these factors should be weighted according to their relative importance.*

prioritize (*BrE* also **-ise**) /praɪˈɒrətaɪz; *AmE* -ˈɔːr-; -ˈɑːr-/ [T, I] (*rather formal*) to put tasks or problems in order of importance, so that you can deal with the most important first: *You should make a list of all the jobs you have to do and prioritize them.* ◇ *You have to learn to prioritize.* See also **priority** → PRIORITY

stressful *adj.* See also the entry for PAINFUL 2

stressful · tense · strained · fraught · anxious · nerve-racking
These words all describe situations, events or times that cause worry and anxiety.

PATTERNS AND COLLOCATIONS
▸ a stressful / tense / fraught / anxious **time**
▸ a stressful / tense / fraught **meeting / situation**
▸ a tense / strained / fraught **atmosphere / silence / relationship**
▸ a tense / an anxious **wait**
▸ emotionally stressful / tense / fraught

stressful causing worry and anxiety: *a stressful job/lifestyle* ◇ *It was a very stressful time for all of us.* See also **stress** → PRESSURE 1, **stressed** → TENSE

tense in which people have strong feelings of worry or anger that often cannot be expressed openly: *I spent a few tense weeks waiting for the results of the tests.* ◇ *The atmosphere in the meeting was getting more and more tense.* See also **tense** → TENSE, **tension** → PRESSURE 1, **tension** → TENSION

strained involving feelings of worry or anger; not relaxed or friendly: *Relations between the two countries remain strained.* ◇ *The game was played in an atmosphere of strained silence.* See also **strained** → TENSE, **strain** → PRESSURE 1

fraught (*especially BrE*) causing or feeling worry and anxiety: *His relationship with his mother had always been fraught.* ◇ *She looked fraught.*

NOTE TENSE, STRAINED OR FRAUGHT? These words can all describe an atmosphere or relationship. **Tense** and **strained** are both used, especially in journalism, to describe formal or official relations, especially when these are outwardly polite; **fraught** describes more personal and emotional relationships.

anxious (of a time) causing anxiety; (of an expression) showing anxiety: *There were a few anxious moments during the game.* ◇ *There was an anxious expression on her face.* See also **anxious** → WORRIED

'nerve-racking (also **'nerve-wracking**) (of an experience) making you feel very nervous and a little afraid: *My first visit was rather nerve-racking.* See also **nervous** → WORRIED

stretch *noun*

stretch · expanse · tract · field
These are all words for a large open area of land or water.

PATTERNS AND COLLOCATIONS
▸ a stretch / an expanse / a tract / a field **of** sth
▸ a **great / large / huge / vast** stretch / expanse / tract / field
▸ a **wide / broad / continuous / open / emptydeserted / barren** stretch / expanse

stretch [C] an area of land or water: *This is a largely unspoilt stretch of coastline.* ◇ *The car overturned on a particularly dangerous stretch of road.* ◇ *A narrow stretch of water separates the island from the mainland.* ◇ *You rarely see boats on this stretch of the river.* ❶ **Stretch** is the most general of these words: a **stretch** may be long or short, wide or narrow, but it usually has a particular character (*unspoilt, dangerous, long, narrow*) or you use **stretch** to refer to a particular part of a place (*this/that stretch of the river*). See also **stretch** → LEAD *verb* 3

expanse /ɪkˈspæns/ [C] a wide and open area of sth, especially land or water: *He gazed out over the huge expanses of open prairie.* ◇ *Above them was a vast expanse of blue sky.*

tract [C] an area of land, especially a large one: *We flew over vast tracts of forest.* ◇ *Whole tracts of the countryside have been turned into industrial wasteland.*

field [C] (usually in compounds) an area of land covered with a particular thing; an area from which a particular thing is obtained: *The territory is covered with snow, bare rock and ice fields.* ◇ *Prisoners were sent to work in the gas fields in the north.*

strict *adj.* See the Topic Map for THE INDIVIDUAL AND SOCIETY on p.894

strict · tough · harsh · rigid · stringent · punitive · firm · severe
These words all describe a person or a set of rules that must be obeyed.

firm	strict	harsh
	tough	punitive
	stringent	severe

PATTERNS AND COLLOCATIONS
▸ strict / tough / harsh / firm / severe **with** sb / sth
▸ strict / tough / harsh / severe **on** sb / sth
▸ strict / tough / harsh / rigid / firm / severe **discipline**
▸ a tough / harsh / severe **penalty / sentence**
▸ strict / tough / rigid / stringent / firm **controls**
▸ strict / tough / rigid / stringent / severe **restrictions**
▸ strict / rigid / stringent / severe **limits**
▸ strict / tough / rigid / stringent **rules / standards**
▸ strict / tough / harsh / stringent **conditions / legislation**
▸ a strict / harsh / punitive **regime**

▸ tough / harsh / stringent / punitive / firm **measures**
▸ tough / punitive / firm **action**
▸ harsh / stringent / severe **criticism**
▸ **increasingly** strict / tough / harsh / stringent / punitive / severe
▸ **extremely** strict / tough / harsh / rigid / severe
▸ **excessively / unnecessarily** strict / harsh / rigid

strict (of rules or instructions) that must be obeyed exactly; (of a person) demanding that rules, especially about behaviour, should be obeyed: *She left strict instructions that she must not be disturbed.* ◇ *She's on a very strict diet.* ◇ *They were always very strict with their children.* ◇ *She's very **strict about** things like homework.* ◇ *I had a very strict upbringing.* **OPP lenient → LENIENT**
▸ **strictly** *adv.*: *The industry is strictly regulated.* ◇ *She was brought up very strictly.*

tough /tʌf/ (*rather informal*) demanding that particular rules be obeyed and not showing sympathy for any problems or suffering that this may cause: *Don't be too tough on him – he was only trying to help.* ◇ *The government has promised to **get tough on** crime.* ◇ *The school **takes a tough line on** (= punishes severely) cheating.* ◇ *There will be tough new controls on car emissions.* ◇ *Courts are imposing tougher penalties for street crime.* ❶ **Tough** can describe the people who make or enforce the rules, the rules themselves, or the punishment for not obeying the rules. **OPP soft → LENIENT**

harsh (*usually disapproving*) (of a judgement, punishment or situation) extreme and cruel or unkind, especially more extreme than is appropriate for the situation: *It may seem a bit harsh to criticize him after his death.* ◇ *He later regretted his harsh words.* ◇ *He accused her of being unduly harsh.* ◇ *We had to face up to the **harsh realities** of life sooner or later.* **OPP lenient → LENIENT**
▸ **harshly** *adv.*: *Don't judge him too harshly.*

rigid /'rɪdʒɪd/ (*often disapproving*) (of rules or methods) that must be obeyed or followed exactly and are difficult to change: *His rigid adherence to the rules made him unpopular.* ◇ *The warriors were governed by a rigid code of ethics.*
▸ **rigidly** *adv.*: *The speed limit must be rigidly enforced.*

stringent /'strɪndʒənt/ (*formal*) (of rules or procedures) that must be obeyed or followed exactly: *There are stringent quality control procedures.* ◇ *Safety standards were less stringent in those days.*

punitive /'pju:nətɪv/ [usually before noun] (*formal*) intended as a punishment; (of taxes or charges) very high and that people find very difficult to pay: *Punitive action will be taken against the hooligans.* ◇ (*AmE*) *They could impose **punitive tariffs** of up to 100% on imports.* ❶ *Punitive taxes, tariffs, charges, damages* or *sanctions* are or seem to be designed to punish sb or to put them at a disadvantage. For example, a government might impose *punitive tariffs* on goods from a particular country as part of a trade dispute.

firm (*often approving*) (of sb's behaviour) strong and in control: *People are looking towards him for firm leadership.* ◇ *Parents must be firm with their children.*
▸ **firmly** *adv.*: *'I can manage,' she said firmly.*

severe punishing sb in an extreme way when they break a particular set of rules: *He received a **severe reprimand** for his behaviour.* ◇ *The courts are becoming more severe on young offenders.*
▸ **severely** *adv.*: *Anyone breaking the law will be severely punished.*

strip noun

strip · ribbon · band · stripe · sash
These are all words for a long narrow piece of sth, especially paper, fabric or other material.

PATTERNS AND COLLOCATIONS
▸ a strip / ribbon / band **of** sth
▸ a **broad** strip / ribbon / band / stripe
▸ a **wide** strip / ribbon / band / sash
▸ a **narrow** strip / ribbon / band / stripe

▸ a **thin** strip / ribbon / band
▸ a **red / blue / yellow, etc.** band / ribbon / stripe / sash
▸ a **horizontal / vertical** strip / band / stripe
▸ to **wear** a ribbon / band / sash

strip [C] a long narrow piece of sth, especially paper, fabric or metal: *Cut a strip of paper 12cm wide.* ◇ *Cut the meat **into strips**.*

ribbon [U, C] a narrow strip of fabric, used to tie things or for decoration: *Her present was tied with yellow ribbon.* ◇ *She was wearing two blue silk ribbons in her hair.* ❶ A *ribbon of sth* is something that is long and narrow in shape: *The road was a ribbon of moonlight.*

band [C] a thin flat strip or circle of any material that is put around things; a strip of colour or material on sth that is different from what is around it: *She always ties her hair back in a band.* ◇ *All babies in the hospital have name bands on their wrists.* ◇ *The bundle was held together with a **rubber band**.* ◇ *She wore a simple **band of gold** (= gold ring) on her finger.* ◇ *The plate was white with a blue band around the edge.*

stripe [C] a long narrow line of colour that is a different colour from the areas next to it: *He was wearing a grey shirt with white stripes.* ◇ *Why does the zebra have black and white stripes?*
▸ **striped** (*BrE* also, *informal* **stripy**) *adj.*: *a blue and white striped jacket*

sash [C] a long strip of fabric worn around the waist or over one shoulder, especially as part of a uniform: *He withdrew his sword from inside his sash.* ◇ *She wore a white dress with a blue sash.*

stroke verb

stroke · pet · caress · fondle · grope
These words all mean to move your hand gently and slowly over a surface, a person's hair, an animal's fur, etc.

PATTERNS AND COLLOCATIONS
▸ to stroke / pet a **dog / cat / horse**
▸ to stroke / caress / fondle sb's **hair / ears / face / neck**
▸ to stroke / caress sb / sth **gently / lightly / tenderly / absently**

stroke [T] to move your hand gently and slowly over an animal's fur or hair; to move your hand gently over a surface, or sb's hair or skin: *He stroked her hair tenderly.* ◇ (*BrE*) *He's a beautiful dog. Can I stroke him?* ❶ Use **stroke** to talk about touching animals in British English, but in American English use **pet**. Especially in American English, **stroke** is often used to talk about touching sb in a sexual way.
▸ **stroke** *noun* [C, usually sing.]: *He gave the cat a stroke.*

pet (-tt-) [T] (*especially AmE*) to touch or move your hand gently over an animal or child in a kind and loving way: *He petted the dog and ruffled its fur.*

caress /kə'res/ [T] (*written*) to stroke sb/sth, especially in a sexual way or in order to show love: *His fingers caressed the back of her neck.*
▸ **caress** *noun* [C]: *the kisses and caresses of lovers*

fondle [T] to touch and move your fingers gently over sb/sth, especially in a sexual way, or in order to show love: *He kissed and fondled her face and neck.* ◇ *She fondled the dog's ears affectionately.*

grope [T] (*informal*) to touch sb sexually, especially when they do not want you to: *She described how he had groped her whenever they were alone.*

strong adj.

1 strong arms
2 strong cheese/coffee
3 strong sunshine

1 strong · powerful · muscular
These words all describe a person or animal that has a lot of physical power.

▸ (a) strong / powerful / muscular **build** / **body** / **arms** / **legs**
▸ strong / powerful **muscles** / **jaws**

strong (of people or animals) having a lot of physical power so that they can lift heavy weights, do hard physical work, etc: *He's strong enough to lift a car!* ◊ *She wasn't a strong swimmer* (= she could not swim well). **OPP** weak → WEAK, See also **strength** → FORCE *noun*

powerful (*especially written, usually approving*) (of a person or animal) physically strong: *He was lithe and powerful as an athlete.* See also **power** → FORCE *noun*

NOTE STRONG OR POWERFUL? In this meaning, **strong** is the most usual, simply descriptive word; **powerful** is used especially in an approving way in more literary writing.

muscular /ˈmʌskjələ(r)/ having large strong muscles: *He was tall, lean and muscular.*

2 strong · spicy · savoury · hot
These words all describe food or drink which has a lot of flavour.

▸ a strong / spicy / savoury / hot **flavour**
▸ a strong / spicy / savoury **taste**
▸ (a) spicy / savoury **food** / **dish** / **sauce**
▸ strong / hot **mustard**
▸ a spicy / hot **curry**

strong (of food) having a lot of flavour; (of drink) containing a lot of a substance: *strong cheese* ◊ *a cup of strong black coffee* **OPP** mild → MILD, **weak ❶** Cheese or spices that are not strong are **mild**; tea, coffee or other drinks that are not strong are **weak**: *a cup of sweet, weak tea*

spicy /ˈspaɪsi/ (of food) having a strong flavour because spices have been used to flavour it: *a plate of spicy chicken wings*

savoury (*BrE*) (*AmE* **savory**) /ˈseɪvəri/ having a taste that is salty and not sweet: *a savoury snack* ◊ *What's in the pastry? Is it sweet or savoury?* **OPP** sweet ❶ Sweet foods contain or taste of sugar: *I had a craving for something sweet.* ◊ *This wine is too sweet for me.*

hot containing pepper and spices and producing a burning feeling in your mouth: *You can make a curry hotter simply by adding chillies.* **OPP** mild → MILD

3 See also the entry for BRIGHT
strong · dazzling · harsh · glaring
These words all describe light that is so powerful that it is unpleasant or difficult to see.

▸ strong / dazzling / harsh / glaring **light**
▸ strong / dazzling / harsh **colours**
▸ strong / dazzling / glaring **sunshine**

strong (of light or colour) bright and/or powerful: *Stay indoors in the middle of the day, when the sun is strongest.* **OPP** weak → DIM 1

dazzling (of light or colour) so bright that you cannot see for a short time: *The sunlight was dazzling after being in the gloom for so long.* ◊ *He arrived wearing a dazzling white suit.* **OPP** soft → DIM 1

harsh (*disapproving*) (especially of light or colour) too strong and bright, in a way that is ugly or unpleasant to look at: *She was caught in the harsh glare of the headlights.* ◊ *The view was spoiled by the harsh lines of concrete towers.* **OPP** soft → DIM 1, **soft** → PALE 1

glaring /ˈɡleərɪŋ; *AmE* ˈɡler-/ (of light) very bright and unpleasant: *The room was lit by the glaring white light from a naked bulb.*

structure *noun* See also the entry for SYSTEM

structure · framework · form · composition · construction · fabric · make-up
These are all words for the way the different parts of sth combine together or the way that sth has been made.

▸ the **basic** structure / framework / form / composition / construction / fabric of sth
▸ a **simple** / **complex** / **coherent** / **rigid** / **flexible** structure / framework / form
▸ the **economic** / **political** / **social** structure / framework / composition / fabric / make-up of sth
▸ the **chemical** / **genetic** structure / composition / make-up of sth
▸ to **create** / **devise** / **establish** / **provide** a structure / framework **for** sth

structure [C] the way in which the parts of sth are connected together, arranged or organized, especially when there are a number of different levels: *the structure of the building / human body* ◊ *a career / salary / tax structure* ◊ *the grammatical structures of a language* ◊ *Students study the structure of human societies throughout history.* See also **structure** → EFFICIENCY

framework /ˈfreɪmwɜːk; *AmE* -wɜːrk/ [C] a set of beliefs, ideas or rules that forms the basis of a system or society: *They established a basic framework of ground rules for discussions.* ◊ *The report provides a framework for further research.*

form [U] the arrangement of parts in a whole, especially in a work of art or piece of writing: *The photographer always said that shape and form were more important to him than colour.* ◊ *The form of the poem is of great significance.*

composition [C] (*rather formal*) the different parts or people that combine to form sth; the way in which they combine: *recent changes in the composition of the workforce* ◊ *The two drugs are nearly identical in composition.* See also **be composed of sb / sth** → CONSIST OF SB / STH

construction [U] the way that sth has been built or made: *ships of steel construction* ◊ *The earliest Greek temples were small buildings, simple in construction.* See also **construction** → PRODUCTION, **construct** → BUILD

fabric [sing.] (*rather formal*) the basic structure of a society or organization that enables it to function successfully: *This is a worrying trend which threatens the very fabric of society.*

'make-up [sing.] (*rather informal, especially spoken or journalism*) the different people or things that combine to form sth; the way in which they combine: *the genetic make-up of plants and animals* ◊ *Ireland did show up a number of flaws in the England team's make-up.* See also **make up sth** → CONSIST OF SB / STH

NOTE COMPOSITION OR MAKE-UP? **Composition** is used more in scientific and technical contexts; **make-up** is used more in speech and journalism.

stubborn *adj.*

stubborn · obstinate · wilful · headstrong · strong-willed
These words all describe a person who is determined not to change their opinion or behaviour and refuses to listen to advice.

▸ a stubborn / an obstinate / a wilful **child**
▸ a stubborn / an obstinate **man** / **woman**
▸ a stubborn / an obstinate / a wilful **refusal**

stubborn /ˈstʌbən; *AmE* -bərn/ (*often disapproving*) determined not to change your opinion or attitude: *He was too stubborn to admit that he was wrong.* ◊ *She has inherited her mother's stubborn streak.* ◊ (*approving*) *He started out with nothing but raw talent and stubborn determination.*

▸ **stubbornly** *adv.*: *She stubbornly refused to pay.*

obstinate /ˈɒbstɪnət; *AmE* ˈɑːb-/ (*usually disapproving*) refusing to change your opinions or behaviour when other people try to persuade you to: *He can be very obstinate when he wants to.* ◇ *Their position remains one of obstinate denial, even in face of the new evidence.*

▸ **obstinately** *adv.*: *She obstinately refused to consider the future.*

wilful (*especially BrE*) (*AmE* usually **willful**) (*disapproving*) determined to do what you want; not caring about what other people want: *He was an aggressive, often selfish and wilful child.*

headstrong /ˈhedstrɒŋ; *AmE* -strɔːŋ/ (*disapproving, especially written*) determined to do things your own way and refusing to listen to advice: *She is too wild and headstrong to be guided by me.*

strong-'willed (*often disapproving*) determined to do what you want, even if other people advise you not to: *She was a fiercely independent and strong-willed woman.*

NOTE WHICH WORD? **Wilful** and **headstrong** are always disapproving terms: a wilful or headstrong person is always wrong and the people trying to oppose or advise them are always right. A **strong-willed** person may be right or wrong but does not listen to advice. **Obstinate** often suggests that sb will not change their behaviour simply in order to be difficult and cause problems for other people. **Stubborn** can suggest this too, but it can also be admiring or approving, as in the phrase *stubborn determination.*

student *noun* See the Topic Map for EDUCATION on p.888, See also the entry for LEARNER

student · pupil · schoolboy/schoolgirl · schoolchild
These are all words for a child who attends school.

PATTERNS AND COLLOCATIONS
▸ a/an **good/bright/able/brilliant/star/outstanding** student/ pupil
▸ (a) **naughty** schoolboy / schoolgirl / schoolchildren
▸ a **disruptive** student / pupil
▸ **older/younger** students / pupils / schoolboys / schoolgirls / schoolchildren
▸ a/ an **ex-/former** student / pupil
▸ a **school** student / pupil
▸ a **primary school / junior school / secondary school** student / pupil
▸ to **teach** students / pupils / schoolboys / schoolgirls / schoolchildren

student [C] a person who is studying in a school, especially an older child: *The more able students should manage these exercises easily.* ◇ *He was an outstanding student.*

pupil /ˈpjuːpl/ [C] (*especially BrE, becoming old-fashioned*) a person who is being taught, especially a child in a school: *The school has over 850 pupils.* **❶ Pupil** is starting to become old-fashioned. **Student** is often preferred, especially by teachers and other people involved in education, and especially when talking about older children. **Student** emphasizes that the children actively study; **pupil** can suggest children sitting still and being taught.

schoolboy, schoolgirl [C] a boy or girl who attends school: *A 13-year-old schoolboy was being hailed as a hero last night.* ◇ *Since she was a schoolgirl she had dreamed of going on the stage.* **❶** These words emphasize the age of the children or this period in their lives; they are less often used to talk about teaching and learning.: *an able schoolboy/schoolgirl*

schoolchild [C, usually pl.] a schoolboy or schoolgirl: *Younger schoolchildren will receive free milk and fruit.*

study *verb* See the Topic Map for THE MEDIA on p.900

study · scrutinize · scan · survey
These words all mean to look at sb/sth carefully, especially in order to find out sth.

PATTERNS AND COLLOCATIONS
▸ to study / scrutinize / scan / survey sth **for** sth
▸ to study / scrutinize / scan sb's **face**
▸ to study / scrutinize / scan / survey sth **carefully**
▸ to study / scrutinize / scan sth **closely / intently**
▸ to study / scrutinize / survey sth **in detail / thoroughly**

study [T] to look at sb/sth carefully in order to find out sth: *Scientists are studying photographs of the planet for signs of life.* ◇ *Fran was studying the menu.*

scrutinize (*BrE* also **-ise**) [T] (*especially written*) to look at or examine sb/sth carefully: *The statement was carefully scrutinized* (= considered) *before publication.* See also **scrutiny** → RESEARCH

scan (**-nn-**) [T] to look at every part of sth carefully, especially because you are looking for sth particular: *He scanned the horizon for any sign of land.*

survey /səˈveɪ; *AmE* sərˈveɪ/ [T] to look at the whole of sb/sth in order to get a general impression of it: *The next morning we surveyed the damage caused by the fire.*

stumble *verb*

stumble · stagger · limp · shuffle · lurch · reel · hobble · lumber
These words all mean to walk or move in an unsteady way or with difficulty.

PATTERNS AND COLLOCATIONS
▸ to stumble / stagger / limp / shuffle / hobble / lumber **along**
▸ to stumble / stagger / limp / shuffle / hobble **a few steps**
▸ to stumble / stagger / lurch / lumber **to your feet**
▸ to stumble / stagger / limp **slightly / a little**
▸ to stagger / lurch / reel **drunkenly**

stumble [I] (*always used with an adverb or preposition*) to walk or move in an unsteady way, almost falling over, for example because you are tired or it is dark: *We stumbled around in the dark, looking for a light switch.*

stagger [I] (*usually used with an adverb or preposition*) to walk with weak, unsteady steps without much control and as if you are about to fall over, for example because you are injured or drunk or are carrying sth heavy: *The injured woman staggered to the side of the road.*

limp [I] to walk slowly or with difficulty because one of your legs or feet is injured: *He had a sprained ankle and was limping.* ◇ *Joe limped painfully off the field.*

shuffle [I, T] (*usually used with an adverb or preposition*) to walk slowly without lifting your feet completely off the ground; to move your feet in an awkward or embarrassed way: *The line shuffled forward a little.* ◇ *She **shuffled her feet** nervously.*

lurch /lɜːtʃ; *AmE* lɜːrtʃ/ [I] (*usually used with an adverb or preposition*) to make a sudden unsteady movement forward or sideways: *A man lurched drunkenly along the street.* ◇ *The car lurched forward.*

reel [I] (*usually used with an adverb or preposition*) to move or walk in a very unsteady way, for example because you are drunk or have been hit: *I hit him hard, sending him reeling backwards.*

hobble [I] (*usually used with an adverb or preposition*) to walk with difficulty, especially because your feet or legs hurt or are injured: *He used to hobble around the yard on crutches.* ◇ *She hobbled painfully back to the hut.*

lumber [I] (*always used with an adverb or preposition*) to move in a slow and awkward way because of being large and heavy: *A dozen elephants lumbered slowly past.*

stupid adj.

stupid · dumb · thick · obtuse
These words all describe sb who is not intelligent.

▸ to **look** stupid / dumb / thick
▸ **very / really / rather / pretty** stupid / dumb
▸ **a bit** stupid / dumb / thick / obtuse
▸ **totally / completely** stupid / dumb / thick
▸ **Don't be so / How can you be so** stupid / dumb / obtuse!

stupid (*rather informal, especially spoken*) slow to learn or understand things; not clever or intelligent ❶ It is not polite to call sb **stupid**: *He'll be OK — he's not stupid.* ◇ *I felt completely stupid.* ◇ *You stupid idiot! Put that gun down!* **OPP** intelligent, smart, clever → INTELLIGENT ❶ The direct opposite of **intelligent** is **unintelligent**, but this is not very frequent. **Stupid** is a rather informal word, used more in spoken English than in written English. In formal or written English, it is more usual and more polite to describe sb as *not very intelligent.*
▸ **stupidity** /stju:'pɪdəti; *AmE* stu:-/ noun [U]: *He faked stupidity to try to escape punishment for the crime.*
▸ **stupidly** adv.: *She stared stupidly at the screen.*

dumb /dʌm/ (*especially AmE, informal*) stupid ❶ It is not usually polite to call sb **dumb**, but it is not as offensive as **stupid**: *If the police question you, act dumb* (= pretend you do not know anything). ◇ *She's going out with some dumb jock from her high school.* ◇ (*offensive*) *His new girlfriend is a classic dumb blonde.* **OPP** smart, bright → INTELLIGENT

thick (*BrE, informal*) stupid ❶ It is not polite to call sb **thick**: *Are you thick or what?* ◇ *I'm not completely thick, you know.* Unlike with **stupid**, people do not usually use **thick** about themselves: ~~I felt completely thick.~~

obtuse /əb'tju:s; *AmE* -'tu:s/ (*formal*) slow or unwilling to understand sth: *Are you being deliberately obtuse?* ❶ If you say that sb is being **obtuse** it often suggests that you think they are deliberately pretending not to understand sth.

style noun See also the entry for FASHION

style · elegance · flair · class · grace · glamour
These are all words for the quality of being pleasing to look at and/or doing things in an attractive and imaginative way.

▸ to do sth **with** style / elegance / flair / grace
▸ **great** style / elegance / flair / class / grace
▸ **sheer** style / elegance / class / grace
▸ **real** style / elegance / flair / class
▸ **natural** style / elegance / flair / grace
▸ **a certain** style / elegance / flair / class / grace / glamour
▸ to **give sb / sth** style / elegance / class / grace / glamour
▸ to **lend sb / sth** style / elegance / grace / glamour
▸ to **have / lack** style / elegance / flair / class / grace / glamour
▸ to **add** style / elegance / flair / class / glamour
▸ **a touch of** style / elegance / class / glamour

style [U] (*approving*) the quality of doing sth well, with ease, control and good judgement, in a way that is pleasing to see; the quality of being attractive and made to a high standard of design: *She does everything with style and grace.* ◇ *The hotel has been redecorated but it's lost a lot of its style.* See also **stylish** → ELEGANT
elegance /'elɪgəns/ [U] (*approving*) (in people) the quality of being attractive because you show care and good judgement about your appearance, clothes and behaviour; (in places and things) the quality of being designed or arranged with care and good judgement, in a way that is pleasing to the eye or mind: *She dresses with casual elegance.* ◇ *His writing combines elegance and wit.* See also **elegant** → ELEGANT

flair [U] (*approving*) the quality of being able to do things in an interesting and imaginative way: *She dresses with real flair.* ◇ *His designs are all right, but he lacks artistic flair.*
class [U] (*approving*) an elegant quality or a high level of skill that is impressive: *She has class all right — she looks like a model.* ◇ *There's a real touch of class about this team.* ❶ **Class** is used especially in the phrase *a touch of class.* Things that have associations with impressive lasting quality are often used to *add a touch of class* to sth: *A real parquet floor will add a touch of class to the room.* See also **classy** → FASHIONABLE, **classic** → ELEGANT
grace [U] (*approving*) an attractive quality of movement that is smooth, elegant and controlled: *She moves with the natural grace of a ballerina.* See also **graceful** → ELEGANT
glamour /'glæmə(r)/ [U] (*approving*) physical beauty that also suggests wealth or success: *Add a cashmere scarf under your jacket for a touch of glamour.* ❶ **Glamour** is often used when people are talking about the fashion and elegance associated with famous people. See also **glamorous** → FASHIONABLE

subject noun See the Topic Map for FACT AND OPINION on p.898, See also the entry for ISSUE

subject · theme · topic · motif · keynote
These are all words for a thing, person or idea that is being discussed or described.

▸ **on** a subject / theme / topic
▸ **a / an important / key / major / serious / general** subject / theme / topic
▸ **a central** theme / topic / motif
▸ to **discuss / consider / deal with / examine / explore / look at / focus on / touch on / tackle** a subject / theme / topic

subject [C] a thing or person that is being discussed, described or dealt with: *I have nothing more to say on the subject.* ◇ *Nelson Mandela is the subject of a new biography.* ◇ *I wish you'd change the subject* (= talk about sth else). ◇ *How did we get onto the subject of marriage? We seem to have got off the subject we're meant to be discussing.* ◇ *The subject of gambling has come up several times lately.* See also **subject** → AREA 2, **subject matter** → MESSAGE
theme /θiːm/ [C] the main idea in a talk, piece of writing or work of art: *North American literature is the main theme of this year's festival.* ◇ *Several familiar themes emerged from the discussion.* ◇ *The stories are all variations on the theme of unhappy marriage.*
topic [C] a subject that you talk, write or learn about: *The topic for tonight's discussion is...* ◇ *It might be better to avoid such a controversial topic.* ◇ *The main topic of conversation was Tom's new girlfriend.*
motif /məʊ'tiːf; *AmE* moʊ-/ [C] a subject, idea or phrase that is repeated and developed in a work of literature or piece of music: *Alienation is a central motif in her novels.*
keynote /'kiːnəʊt; *AmE* -noʊt/ [C, usually sing.] (*especially journalism or politics*) the central idea of a book, speech, etc: *Choice is the keynote of the new education policy.* ◇ *a keynote speech/speaker* (= a very important one, introducing a meeting or its subject)

succeed verb

succeed · make it · make your/a mark · achieve · arrive · make a name for yourself · conquer · get on
These words all mean to be or become successful, especially in your career or in a particular area of activity.

▸ to succeed / make it / make your mark / make a name for yourself / get on **in** sth
▸ to succeed / make it / make your mark / arrive / make a name for yourself **as** sth
▸ to make your mark / make a name for yourself **by doing sth**

succeed [I] to be successful in your career, earning money, power and/or respect: *You will have to work hard if you are to succeed.* ◇ *She doesn't have the ruthlessness to succeed in business.* **OPP fail** → FAIL 2, See also **succeed** → ACHIEVE

'make it idiom (*rather informal*) to be successful in your career: *You can make it if you believe in yourself.* ◇ *He never really made it as an actor.*

,make your/a 'mark idiom (*rather informal*) to become famous and successful in a particular area: *She has already made her mark on the music industry.*

achieve [I] to be successful in a particular area, especially in your studies: *Their background gives them little chance of achieving at school.* See also **achieve** → ACHIEVE

arrive [I] (usually used in the phrase *sb has/had arrived*) (*informal*) to become successful in a particular area: *He knew he had arrived when he was shortlisted for the Booker Prize.*

make a name for yourself idiom (*rather informal*) to become famous and gain a reputation: *She's made quite a name for herself.* See also **name** → REPUTATION

conquer /'kɒŋkə(r); *AmE* 'kɑːŋ-/ [T] (*rather informal*) to become very popular or successful in a particular place: *The band is now setting out to conquer the world.* ◇ *This is a British film which could conquer the US market.*

,get 'on phrasal verb (*BrE, rather informal*) to be successful in your career: *Parents are always anxious for their children to get on.* ◇ *I don't know how he's going to get on in life.*

> **NOTE** MAKE IT OR GET ON? **Make it** often suggests that there is there is one critical moment or achievement in sb's career, at which point you can tell whether they have been successful or not; it also suggests that success depends on talent and self-belief. **Get on** suggests a more gradual process of becoming successful through hard work.

success noun

success · hit · winner · best-seller
These are all words for sb/sth that is successful or popular.

PATTERNS AND COLLOCATIONS
▸ a **big** success/ hit/ winner
▸ an **instant** success/ hit/ best-seller
▸ a **runaway** success/ winner/ best-seller
▸ to **have** a success/ hit
▸ to **become** a hit/ best-seller

success [C] a person or thing that has achieved a good result and been successful: *The party was a great success.* ◇ *We had one or two outstanding successes.* ◇ *She wasn't a success as a teacher.* ◇ *He was determined to make a success of the business.* **OPP failure** → DISASTER, **failure** → LOSER 2

hit [C] (*rather informal*) a person or thing that is very popular and successful, especially a song or film: *The series has been a big hit with children.* ◇ *They are about to release an album of their greatest hits.* ◇ *He's just about to star in the smash hit musical, 'Chicago'.* **OPP flop** → DISASTER

winner [C, usually sing.] (*rather informal*) a thing or person that is successful or likely to be successful: *I think your idea is a winner.* ◇ *The design is very good. We could be onto a winner* (= we may have sth that will be successful). **OPP loser** → LOSER 2

best-'seller (also **bestseller**) [C] a product, especially a book, which is bought by large numbers of people: *Her autobiography is an international best-seller.*
▸ **,best-'selling** adj.: *a best-selling novel/author*

successful adj.

1 the successful candidate
2 a successful business

1 successful · effective · winning · victorious · triumphant
These words all describe sb/sth that wins in a contest or achieves their aim.

PATTERNS AND COLLOCATIONS
▸ successful / effective / victorious / triumphant **in** sth
▸ successful / effective / victorious **in doing** sth
▸ a successful / an effective / a victorious / a triumphant **campaign / challenge**
▸ a successful / victorious / triumphant **conclusion / return**
▸ a successful / winning / victorious **team**
▸ the successful / winning **side**
▸ a successful / triumphant **outcome**
▸ a successful / victorious **opponent**
▸ to **emerge / return** victorious / triumphant
▸ **eventually / ultimately** successful / victorious / triumphant

successful achieving your aims or what was intended: *The successful candidate will be responsible for a large research project.* ◇ *He had a phenomenally successful period as manager.* ◇ *The experiment was entirely successful.* ◇ *He had been successful at every job he had done.* **OPP unsuccessful, failed** → UNSUCCESSFUL, See also **succeed** → ACHIEVE
▸ **successfully** adv.: *The operation was successfully completed.*

effective producing the result that is wanted or intended: *Aspirin is a simple but highly effective treatment.* ◇ *drugs that are effective against cancer* ◇ *I admire the effective use of colour in her paintings.* **OPP ineffective** → INEFFECTIVE
▸ **effectively** adv.: *The company must reduce costs to compete effectively.* **OPP ineffectively** → INEFFECTIVE

winning [only before noun] that wins or has won sth, for example a race or competition: *Next week we will publish the winning entry in the short story competition.* ◇ *He scored the winning goal in the final.* ◇ *They had fought on the winning side.* **OPP losing** → UNSUCCESSFUL

victorious /vɪk'tɔːriəs/ (*rather formal, especially written*) having won a victory, for example in a battle, election or sport; that ends in victory: *The victorious army entered the city.* ◇ *Canada was victorious over Australia at the start of the World Championships.*

triumphant /traɪ'ʌmfənt/ (*especially written*) very successful, for example in winning or achieving sth, in a way that causes great satisfaction: *He had steered the campaign through to its triumphant conclusion.* ◇ *She rose above all the problems and emerged triumphant.*

2 successful · profitable · commercial · lucrative · buoyant · thriving · economic · profit-making
These words all describe sb/sth that is making money.

PATTERNS AND COLLOCATIONS
▸ a successful / profitable / lucrative / thriving / profit-making **business**
▸ a successful / profitable / lucrative / profit-making **enterprise**
▸ a successful / profitable / lucrative **investment / career / year**
▸ a profitable / lucrative / buoyant / thriving **market**
▸ **very / particularly / extremely / fairly / quite** successful / profitable / lucrative / buoyant
▸ **highly / immensely** successful / profitable / lucrative
▸ **relatively** successful / profitable / buoyant

successful making a lot of money, especially by being popular: *The play was very successful on Broadway.* ◇ *She has had a long and successful career in television.*

profitable making a profit: *She runs a highly profitable business.* ◇ *It is usually more profitable to sell direct to the public.* **OPP unprofitable** → LOSS-MAKING
▸ **profitability** noun [U]: *Downsizing is one way to increase profitability.*
▸ **profitably** adv.: *This is no way to run a business profitably.*

commercial [only before noun] making or intended to make a profit: *The movie was not a commercial success* (= made no profit). ◊ *They are an educational charity, not a commercial publisher.* **OPP** **non-profit** → LOSS-MAKING
▸ **commercially** *adv.*: *His invention was not commercially successful.*

lucrative /'luːkrətɪv/ (of business or work) producing or paying a large amount of money; making a large profit: *The firm has a lucrative business contract with the Scottish Executive.* ◊ *Many of the engineers left the service for more lucrative jobs abroad.*

buoyant /'bɔɪənt/ *AmE* 'buːjənt/ (*business*) (of prices or business activity) tending to increase or stay at a high level, usually showing financial success: *Car sales have remained buoyant.* ❶ Common collocates of **buoyant** include *market, economy, trading, sales* and *demand.*

thriving /'θraɪvɪŋ/ (of a business or area) economically strong and successful: *Twenty years ago London Road was a thriving commercial centre thronged with shoppers.* ❶ Common collocates of **thriving** include *company, business, industry, trade, market, economy, centre, town* and *port.* See also **thrive** → DO WELL

economic (often used in negative sentences) (of a process, business or activity) producing enough profit to continue: *It's simply not economic for these small farmers to start buying large amounts of expensive fertilizer.* **OPP** **uneconomic** → LOSS-MAKING

'profit-making [usually before noun] (of a business or activity) that makes or will make a profit: *I believe that public transport should be run as a service, not as a profit-making enterprise.* **OPP** **loss-making, non-profit** → LOSS-MAKING

successive *adj.*

successive · in a row · consecutive · straight · serial
These words all describe things or people that follow one after the other without interruption.

PATTERNS AND COLLOCATIONS
▸ the **second** / **third** / **fourth** successive / consecutive / straight sth
▸ the **second** / **third** / **fourth** sth in a row
▸ sb's second, etc. successive / consecutive **win** / **victory** / **defeat**
▸ sb's second, etc. **win** / **victory** / **defeat** in a row
▸ two, etc. successive / consecutive / straight **days** / **weeks** / **months** / **years**
▸ two, etc. **days** / **weeks** / **months** / **years** in a row
▸ successive / consecutive / straight **defeats** / **games** / **wins**
▸ **defeats** / **games** / **wins** in a row

successive /sək'sesɪv/ [only before noun] (*rather formal*) following immediately one after the other: *Successive governments have tried to tackle the problem.* ◊ *The road remained closed for the third successive day.*
▸ **successively** *adv.*: *The novel presents successively three different views of the same events.*

in a 'row *idiom* happening several times in the same way with nothing different happening in between: *She had several wins in a row.* ◊ *Labour lost for the fourth time in a row.*

consecutive /kən'sekjətɪv/ [usually before noun] (especially of periods of time) following one after another in a series, without interruption: *She was absent for nine consecutive days.* ◊ *He is beginning his fourth consecutive term of office.*
▸ **consecutively** *adv.*: *The plays were performed consecutively on one day.*

straight [only before noun] following one after another in a series, without interruption: *The team has had six straight wins.* ◊ *She won in straight sets* (= without losing a set in a tennis match). ❶ In this meaning **straight** is used especially in the context of sport.

serial /'sɪəriəl/ *AmE* 'sɪr-/ [only before noun] arranged in a series; doing the same thing in the same way several times: *Individual engines differ only in their serial numbers.* ◊ *The novel was first published in serial form*

(= in several parts). ◊ *She was the ninth victim of a serial killer* (= sb who murders several people in a similar way).

sudden *adj.*

sudden · sharp · dramatic · abrupt
These words all describe sth happening quickly or unexpectedly.

PATTERNS AND COLLOCATIONS
▸ a sudden / a sharp / a dramatic / an abrupt **increase** / **rise** (in sth)
▸ a sudden / sharp / dramatic **drop** / **fall** (in sth)
▸ a sudden / sharp / dramatic **change** / **improvement** / **deterioration**
▸ a sudden / a dramatic / an abrupt **end**
▸ a sudden / dramatic **appearance** / **arrival**
▸ a sudden / an abrupt **disappearance** / **departure** / **movement** / **stop** / **halt**

sudden happening or done quickly and unexpectedly: *Don't make any sudden movements.* ◊ *His death was very sudden.* ◊ *It was only decided yesterday. It's all been very sudden.* **OPP** **gradual** → SLOW
▸ **suddenly** *adv.*: *I suddenly realized what I had to do.* ◊ *It all happened so suddenly.*

sharp [usually before noun] (especially of a change in sth) sudden and rapid: *There has been a sharp drop in prices.* ◊ *He heard a sharp intake of breath.* ❶ **Sharp** is usually used to talk about sudden, big changes in numbers, prices, levels, rates, etc. Typical collocates are *rise, increase, drop* and *fall.*
▸ **sharply** *adv.*: *The temperature drops sharply at night.* ◊ *Profits fell sharply following the takeover.* ◊ *The road fell sharply to the sea.*

dramatic (of a change, an event, etc.) sudden, very great and often surprising: *I need to see a dramatic improvement in your work.* ◊ *The announcement had a dramatic effect on house prices.*
▸ **dramatically** *adv.*: *Prices have increased dramatically in the last few years.*

abrupt /ə'brʌpt/ sudden and unexpected, often in an unpleasant way: *His abrupt departure made me think I had done something to upset him.* ◊ *The accident brought his career to an abrupt end.*
▸ **abruptly** *adv.*: *The interview ended abruptly when I refused to work weekends.*

suffer from sth *verb*

suffer from sth · have · get · develop · catch · contract · come down with sth
These words all mean to be or become ill with a disease or illness

PATTERNS AND COLLOCATIONS
▸ to suffer from / have / get / develop / catch / contract a / an **disease** / **illness**
▸ to suffer from / have / get / catch / come down with a **bug**
▸ to suffer from / have / get / develop / contract **cancer** / **AIDS**
▸ to suffer from / have / get / catch / contract **a virus** / **HIV** / **malaria**
▸ to suffer from / have / get / catch / contract / come down with the **flu**
▸ to suffer from / have / get / catch / come down with a **cold**
▸ to suffer from / have / get a **headache**
▸ to suffer from / have / get / develop **a condition** / **arthritis** / **diarrhoea**
▸ to suffer from / have / develop a / an **allergy** / **disorder**

suffer from sth *phrasal verb* [T, no passive] to be badly affected by a disease, an illness, pain, sadness or a lack of sth: *The driver was taken to hospital suffering from shock.* ◊ *Many companies are suffering from a shortage of skilled staff.* See also **sufferer** → PATIENT

have (also **have got**) [T, no passive] (not used in the progressive tenses) to suffer from an illness or pain: *I had a cold yesterday and I couldn't come to work.* ◊ *I've got a headache.* ◊ *He found out that he had HIV just last year.*

get [T, no passive] to begin to have an illness, to suffer from a pain: *I got this cold off* (= from) *you!* ◊ *I think I'm getting a cold.* ◊ *She gets* (= often suffers from) *really bad headaches.* See also **pick sth up → GET 1**

develop [T, no passive] to get a disease, illness or problem: *She developed lung cancer at the age of sixty.* ◊ *The car developed engine trouble and we had to stop.*

catch [T, no passive] to get an infectious illness (= one that can be passed easily from one person to another): *I think I must have caught this cold from you.*

contract /kənˈtrækt/ [T] (*rather formal*) to get a disease, especially a serious one: *He contracted malaria while abroad.*

,come 'down with sth *phrasal verb* [T, no passive] to get an illness that is not very serious: *I think I'm coming down with something.*

---

suggest *verb* See also the entry for MEAN 1

suggest · imply · indicate · point
These words all mean to put an idea into people's minds that sth is possible or likely.

PATTERNS AND COLLOCATIONS
▸ to suggest / imply / indicate sth **to** sb
▸ to suggest / imply / indicate **that**...
▸ to suggest / imply / indicate / point **to** a **meaning**
▸ to suggest / imply / indicate an **idea**
▸ to suggest / indicate / point **to** a **feeling**
▸ to suggest/imply/indicate/point **to** a **great deal/high degree/ lack** of sth
▸ the **results / facts** suggest / imply / indicate / point to sth
▸ sb / sth's **behaviour** suggests / implies / indicates sth
▸ the **evidence** suggests / indicates / points to sth
▸ the **signs / symptoms** suggest / indicate / point to sth
▸ to **strongly** suggest / imply / indicate / point to sth

suggest [T] to put an idea into sb's mind; to make sb think that sth is true: *All the evidence suggests (that) he stole the money.* ◊ *The symptoms suggest a minor heart attack.* ◊ *The stage lighting was used to suggest a beach scene.*

imply /ɪmˈplaɪ/ [T] (*rather formal*) to make it seem likely that sth is true or exists: *The survey implies (that) more people are moving house than was thought.* ◊ *The fact that she was here implies a degree of interest.*

NOTE SUGGEST OR IMPLY? Often you can use either word. However, **suggest** is often used to talk about how a piece of research, a report or evidence shows a link, a relationship or a similarity between things: *Research suggests a link between a person's outlook and the immune system.* **Imply** is more usually used to talk about how data or facts show things such as the need for sth or the existence or possibility of sth: *Campaigners said the data implies the existence of 'a pressing social need'.*

indicate [T] (*rather formal*) to be a sign of sth; to show that sth is possible or likely: *A red sky at night often indicates fine weather the next day.* ◊ *Early results indicate that the government will be returned to power.* See also **indication, indicator → SIGN 1, indicate → DECLARE, indicate → SHOW 1**

'point [I, T] (always used with an adverb or preposition) to show that sth is possible or likely; to lead to or suggest a particular development or logical argument: *All the signs point to a successful year ahead.* ◊ *The evidence seems to point in that direction.* ◊ *The fans are looking to the new players to point the way to victory.*

---

suggestion *noun* See also the entry for SIGN 1

suggestion · clue · hint · pointer
These are all words for a piece of information, often given indirectly, that helps you find sth out.

PATTERNS AND COLLOCATIONS
▸ a suggestion / clue / hint / pointer **as to** how / what / why, etc.
▸ a suggestion / hint **that**...
▸ a/an **useful/valuable/obvious** suggestion / clue / hint / pointer
▸ an **important** suggestion / clue / pointer
▸ to **give sb / provide** a clue / hint / pointer

suggestion [U, C, usually sing.] (*rather formal*) a reason to think that sth, especially sth bad, is true: *A spokesman dismissed any suggestion of a boardroom rift.* ◊ *There was no suggestion that he was doing anything illegal.* See also **suggest → MEAN verb 2**

clue /kluː/ [C] an object, piece of evidence or some information that helps the police solve a crime, or that helps you discover the answer to a problem: *The police think the videotape may hold some vital clues to the identity of the killer.* ◊ *Diet may hold the clue to the causes of migraine.*

hint [C] something that suggests what will happen in the future: *At the first hint of trouble, they left.* ◊ *That was the first hint we had that things were going wrong.* See also **hint → MEAN verb 2**

pointer [C] a sign that sth exists; a sign that shows how sth may develop in the future: *The surge in car sales is an encouraging pointer to an improvement in the economy.*

NOTE HINT OR POINTER? Pointer is usually found in more technical contexts than **hint**. **Hint** is followed by *of* or *that*. Pointer is usually followed by *to*.

---

suitcase *noun*

suitcase · luggage · baggage · case · handbag · purse · bag · backpack · rucksack · chest · trunk · knapsack
These are all words for a container or the containers that you carry your clothes or personal items in, especially when you are travelling.

PATTERNS AND COLLOCATIONS
▸ a **heavy** suitcase / luggage / baggage / case / bag / backpack / rucksack / chest / trunk / knapsack
▸ to **carry** a suitcase / luggage / baggage / a case / a handbag / a purse / a bag / a backpack / a rucksack / a knapsack
▸ to **open / shut** a suitcase / case / chest / trunk
▸ to **check (in)** your suitcase / luggage / baggage / bag
▸ to **lift** a suitcase / case / bag / chest / trunk
▸ to **put on / take off** a backpack / rucksack / knapsack
▸ to **put down** your suitcase / luggage / baggage / case / bag
▸ to **pack/unpack/stuff sth into** a suitcase / case / bag / backpack / rucksack / trunk / knapsack
▸ to **search** sb's suitcase / luggage / baggage / bag

suitcase [C] a container made of hard or soft material with flat sides and a handle, used for carrying clothes, etc. when you are travelling: *He was carrying a battered leather suitcase.* ◊ *She had been living out of a suitcase* (= staying at many different places and having to carry her clothes, etc. around with her) *for weeks.*

luggage [U] the bags and cases that contain sb's clothes and other things when they are travelling: *Can I leave my luggage here?* ◊ *Several items fell from the luggage rack.*

baggage [U] luggage ❶ Baggage is only used in contexts relating to air travel: *Please do not leave baggage unattended.* ◊ *Go to the baggage claim area* (= the place where you collect your baggage after a flight) *on the ground floor.* ◊ *There is an excess baggage* (= baggage that weighs more than the official weight limit on a plane) *charge of $50.*

case [C] (*BrE, rather informal*) a suitcase: *She wanted to pack her case and leave immediately.*

handbag [C] a small bag for money, keys and other personal items, carried especially by women: *I had my handbag stolen in Liverpool.*

purse /pɜːs; *AmE* pɜːrs/ [C] (*AmE*) a handbag: *She fumbled in her purse for her glasses.*

luggage/baggage

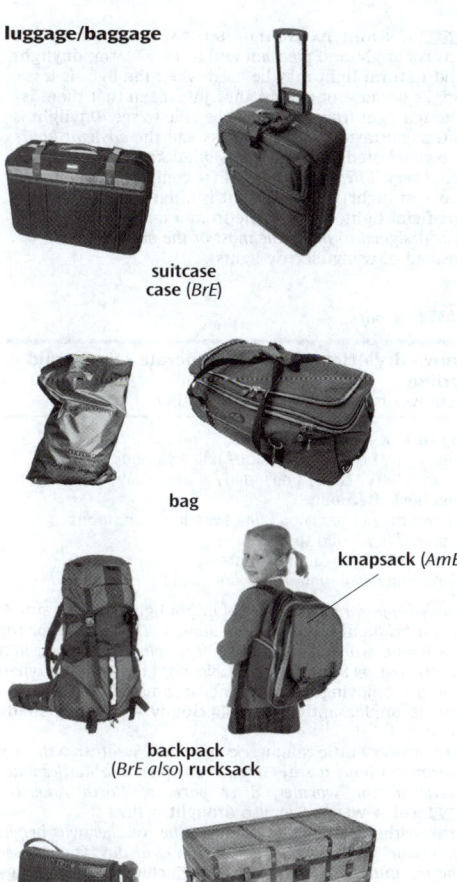

suitcase
case (BrE)

bag

knapsack (AmE)

backpack
(BrE also) rucksack

handbag
purse (AmE)

chest/trunk

bag [C] a container with a handle, made from fabric, plastic or leather that you carry clothes, etc. in while you are travelling: *I got my bag down from the rack.* **❶** A **bag** is a small piece of luggage but the plural is often used to mean all luggage including suitcases: *The porter will take your bags up to your room.*

backpack /'bækpæk/ [C] a bag carried on the back: *He was wearing a heavy backpack.* See also **backpack** → TOUR verb

rucksack /'rʌksæk/ [C] (BrE) a backpack: *She slung the little rucksack on her back.*

chest [C] a large strong box, often made of wood, used for storing things in and/or moving them from one place to another: *The documents were kept in an ancient oak chest with a brass lock.* ◇ *a pirate's treasure chest*

trunk [C] a large strong box with two handles, made of metal or wood with metal corners used for transporting or storing clothes, books, etc: *I found the documents at the bottom of an old tin trunk in the attic.*

> **NOTE** CHEST OR TRUNK? In some cases you can use either word. **Chest** is often used to describe sth larger, heavier and more old-fashioned than a **trunk** and can be more like a piece of furniture than a piece of luggage, used for storing things in rather than transporting them in.

knapsack /'næpsæk/ [C] (old-fashioned or AmE) a small backpack: *He had walked into the school yard that morning with his knapsack on his back and his lunchbox in his hand.*

> **NOTE** BACKPACK, RUCKSACK OR KNAPSACK? These are all bags that you carry on your back. **Backpack** is the most general word. It can be used for small bags carried by children or for large bags supported on a frame and used by people on climbing or walking trips. **Rucksack** is especially British, and can be a large bag with a frame or a small bag. **Knapsack** is always small and without a frame. It is old-fashioned in British English, but often used in American English.

summarize (BrE -ise) verb

summarize · sum (sth) up · condense · recap
These words all mean to repeat sth in less detail.

PATTERNS AND COLLOCATIONS
▸ to summarize sth / sum sth up **as**
▸ to summarize / sum up / recap **briefly**
▸ **Let me** summarize / sum up / recap.
▸ **To** summarize / sum up / recap...

summarize (BrE -**ise**) /'sʌməraɪz/ [T, I] to state the main points of sth in a short and clear form: *The results of the research are summarized at the end.*

sum 'up, ,sum sth 'up phrasal verb (-**mm**-) to summarize sth, especially when you give your own interpretation or opinion of sth: *Can I just sum up what we've agreed so far?* **❶** **Sum up** is also used when a judge gives a summary of the main facts and arguments in a legal case, near the end of a trial: *The judge will sum up the evidence tomorrow.*

condense /kən'dens/ [T] to put sth such as a piece of writing into fewer words; to put a lot of information into a small space: *The article was condensed into just two pages.* ◇ *The author has condensed a great deal of material into just 100 pages.*

recap /'ri:kæp/ (-**pp**-) [I, T] (not used in the perfect or past tenses) (rather informal, especially spoken) to repeat or give a summary of what has already been said or decided: *Let me just recap on what we've decided so far.* See also **repeat** → REPEAT 1

summary noun

summary · outline · overview · sketch · synopsis · abstract · rundown
These are all words for a short version of sth longer, especially a piece of writing or a discussion.

PATTERNS AND COLLOCATIONS
▸ a summary / an outline / an overview / a sketch / a synopsis / an abstract / a rundown **of** sth
▸ **in** summary / outline
▸ a **brief** summary / outline / overview / sketch / synopsis
▸ a **quick** / **short** / **general** summary / outline / overview
▸ a **full** summary / overview / rundown
▸ to **give sb** a summary / an outline / an overview / a sketch / a synopsis / an abstract
▸ to **provide** a summary / an outline / an overview / a sketch / a synopsis / an abstract

summary [C] a short statement that gives only the main points of sth, not the details: *The following is a summary of our conclusions.* ◇ *a news summary* ◇ *a two-page summary of a government report*

outline [C] a description of the main facts or points involved in sth: *This is a brief outline of the events.* ◇ *The article describes in outline the main findings of the research.* See also **outline** → OUTLINE verb, **outline** → SHAPE noun

overview /'əʊvəvju:; AmE 'oʊvərv-/ [C] a description or understanding of the main facts or points involved in sth: *The second chapter will provide an overview of the issues involved.* ◇ *My main concern is to get an overview of the main environmental problems facing the area.*

NOTE SUMMARY, OUTLINE OR OVERVIEW? A **summary** is always written or made after the full version of a text, discussion, etc. has been written or recorded; it may be read after, before or instead of reading the full text. An **outline** can be written or given before the full version is produced or worked out: *The first few pages give a biographical sketch of the author. See also* **sketch** → OUTLINE *verb*

The **outline agreement** about the country's transition to full democracy still has to be discussed at a multi-party forum. An **overview** is similar to an **outline**, but the emphasis is more on the fact that sb wants to look for general trends across a wide area, rather than that the details are still to be worked out. A **summary** or **outline** is *given* or *provided* by sb; an **overview** can be given, but a person may also *get*, *take* or *gain* an **overview** for themselves.

sketch [C] a short report or story that gives only basic details about sth: *The first few pages give a biographical sketch of the author.* See also **sketch** → OUTLINE *verb*

synopsis /sɪˈnɒpsɪs; *AmE* -ˈnɑːp-/ (*pl.* **synopses** /-siːz/) [C] (*rather formal*) a summary of a piece of writing, especially a book or play: *The programme gave a complete synopsis of the play.*

abstract /ˈæbstrækt/ [C] (*rather formal or technical*) a short piece of writing containing the main ideas in a document, especially an official or academic one: *Abstracts of about 300 words should be submitted to the conference committee who will decide which papers to accept.*

rundown /ˈrʌndaʊn/ [C, usually sing.] (*rather informal, especially spoken*) an explanation or description of sth: *Shall I give you a brief rundown of each of the job applicants?*

sun *noun*

sun · sunlight · sunshine · daylight · natural light
These are all words for the light and/or heat which allows you to see or makes you feel hot during the day.

PATTERNS AND COLLOCATIONS
▸ **in** sun / sunlight / sunshine / daylight / natural light
▸ **bright** sun / sunlight / sunshine / daylight
▸ **hot / direct / brilliant / morning / afternoon / spring / summer / autumn / winter** sun / sunlight / sunshine
▸ to **emerge into** the sun / sunlight / sunshine / daylight
▸ the sun / sunlight / sunshine / daylight **floods** (into) a place
▸ the sun / sunlight / daylight **filters through** sth
▸ a **ray / beam of** sunlight / sunshine

sun (usually **the sun**) [sing., U] the light and heat from the sun: *This room gets the sun in the mornings.* ◇ *We did our best to keep out of the sun.* ◇ *They're having a winter break in the sun* (= in a place that is warm and sunny). ◇ (*especially BrE*) *Her face had obviously caught the sun* (= become red or brown). **OPP** **shade** → DARKNESS

sunlight [U] the light from the sun: *The room was lit by a shaft of bright sunlight from the open shutter.* ◇ *The colour will fade if exposed to strong sunlight.* See also **light** → LIGHT *noun* 1

sunshine [U] (*approving*) the light and heat from the sun: *We had two weeks of glorious sunshine.* ◇ *The snow was melting in the warm spring sunshine.*

NOTE SUN OR SUNSHINE? **Sunshine** is always a good thing; it is possible to have too much **sun**: *It's too hot in the sun.* ◇ *It's too hot in the sunshine.*

daylight [U] the light that comes from the sun during the day: *The robbery occurred in broad daylight* (= in the clear light of day, when it is easy to see). ◇ *They left before daylight* (= before the sun had risen). See also **light** → LIGHT *noun* 1

natural light [U] the light that comes from the sun during the day: *High windows provide maximum natural light.* See also **light** → LIGHT *noun* 1

NOTE SUNLIGHT, DAYLIGHT OR NATURAL LIGHT? **Sunlight** is always bright and pleasant and usually warm; **daylight** and **natural light** may be used when the light is less bright because of clouds: they just mean that there is enough light from the sun to be able to see. **Daylight** is often contrasted with **darkness** and the *daylight hours* are contrasted with the *hours of darkness*: *The street looks very different in daylight* (= compared with how it looks at night). **Natural light** is often contrasted with **artificial light**, for example from a lamp: *The building was designed to make the most of the natural light* (= instead of using electric lights).

sunny *adj.*

sunny · dry · clear · good · temperate · fine · mild · glorious
These words all describe good weather.

PATTERNS AND COLLOCATIONS
▸ sunny / dry / clear / good / fine / mild / glorious **weather**
▸ a sunny / dry / clear / fine / mild / glorious **day / morning / evening / afternoon**
▸ sunny / dry / clear / good / fine (**weather**) **conditions**
▸ a sunny / dry / mild **spell**
▸ a dry / temperate / mild **climate**
▸ to **remain / stay** sunny / dry / fine / mild

sunny (*approving*) with a lot of bright light from the sun: *It was a brilliantly sunny day in June.* ◇ *The outlook for the weekend is warm and sunny.* ◇ *These plants grow best in a sunny spot.* ❶ **Sunny** is a positive word that you use when you are enjoying the sunshine. It is not used when the sun is unpleasantly hot. **OPP** **cloudy** → CLOUDY, **shady** → DARK 1

dry with very little rain: *weeks of hot dry weather* ◇ *the dry season* ◇ *I hope it stays dry for our picnic.* ◇ *Rattlesnakes occur in the warmer, drier parts of North America.* **OPP** **wet** → WET 2, See also **drought** → HEAT 2

clear without any cloud or mist: *The weather was bright and clear.* ◇ *a clear blue sky* ◇ *On a clear day, you can see the mountains in the distance.* **OPP** **cloudy, misty, foggy** → CLOUDY

good (*approving*) **good** weather is the type of weather that you want, for example because it is not cold or raining: *Let's hope we have good weather tomorrow.* **OPP** **bad** → WET 2

temperate /ˈtempərət/ [usually before noun] (*technical*) (of a climate or region) having a mild temperature, without extremes of heat or cold: *a country with a temperate climate* ◇ *In winter, the birds fly from the Arctic to more temperate zones.*

fine (*especially BrE, approving*) bright and without rain: *The next morning turned out fine again.* ◇ *That summer saw weeks of fine dry weather.*

mild not very cold, and therefore pleasant: *That winter was exceptionally mild.* ◇ *Most of the birds seek out milder climates during the winter months.* ❶ **Mild** is used especially to talk about weather that you might expect to be cold, for example winter weather, or when you are comparing an area with another area that is colder. **OPP** **cold** → COLD 1, **harsh** → HARSH, See also **mild** → GENTLE

glorious (*approving*) hot, with the sun shining: *They had three weeks of glorious sunshine.*

supplies *noun*

supplies · stores · rations · provisions
These are all words for essential items such as food and medicine.

PATTERNS AND COLLOCATIONS
▸ supplies / stores / rations **of** sth
▸ **food** supplies / stores / rations
▸ **emergency** supplies / rations / provisions

▶ **medical** / **military** supplies / stores
▶ to **buy** / **stock up on** supplies / provisions
▶ to **run out of** supplies / rations / provisions
▶ supplies / rations / provisions **run out**

supplies [pl.] the things such as food, medicines and fuel that are needed by a group of people, for example an army, especially when these things are not easily available: *We were running short of supplies.* ◇ *They didn't stop, except to pick up essential supplies.*

stores [pl.] goods of a particular kind or for a particular purpose: *The medical stores were kept in the cupboards in the back room.* ◇ *The car was packed with luggage and stores of food.*

rations /ˈræʃnz/ [pl.] a fixed amount of food given regularly to a soldier or to sb who is in a place where there is not much food available: *We're on short rations* (= allowed less than usual) *until fresh supplies arrive.* ◇ *Older people still remember what wartime rations were like.* See also **ration** → SHARE *noun*

provisions /prəˈvɪʒnz/ [pl.] supplies of food and drink, especially for a long journey: *We have enough provisions to last us two weeks.* See also **provision** → EQUIP *verb* 1

supply *noun*

supply · resource · stock · reserve · pool · hoard · bank · store · arsenal · stockpile
These are all words for an amount of sth which is available to be used when it is needed.

PATTERNS AND COLLOCATIONS
▶ a supply / a stock / a reserve / a pool / a hoard / a bank / a store / an arsenal / a stockpile **of** sth
▶ to be / have sth **in** supply / stock
▶ a supply / stocks / an arsenal / a stockpile **of weapons**
▶ a supply / bank / store **of information**
▶ a supply / a stock / stores **of food**
▶ a supply / reserves / a store **of water**
▶ supplies / stocks / reserves / stockpiles **of coal**
▶ (a) **vast** supply / resources / stock / reserve / hoard / bank / store / arsenal / stockpile
▶ (a) **large** supply / resources / stock / reserve / hoard / store / arsenal / stockpile
▶ (a) **dwindling** supplies / resources / stocks / reserves / pool / stockpiles
▶ a **secret** supply / stock / hoard / store
▶ (a) **food** supply / stocks / reserves / store / stockpile
▶ **weapons** supplies / stocks / stores
▶ **coal** supplies / stocks / reserves
▶ **oil** / **gas** supplies / reserves
▶ to **build up** a supply / resources / a stock / reserves / a bank / a store / an arsenal / a stockpile
▶ to **reduce** the supply / resources / stock / reserves / pool / stores
▶ to **use up** / **exhaust** the supply / resources / stock / reserves / store

supply [C] an amount of sth that is provided or available to be used: *The water supply is unsafe.* ◇ *Supplies of food are almost exhausted.* ◇ *We cannot guarantee adequate supplies of raw materials.* See also **supply** → PROVIDE *verb*

resource [C, usually pl.] a supply of sth that a country, organization or person has and can use, especially to increase their wealth: *the exploitation of minerals and other natural resources* ◇ *We do not have the resources* (= money) *to update our computer software.* ◇ *We agreed to pool our resources* (= so that everyone gives sth). See also **human resources** → STAFF

stock [U, C] a supply of goods that is available for sale in a shop; a supply of sth that is available to be used: *That particular model is not currently in stock.* ◇ *I'm afraid we're temporarily out of stock.* ◇ *We don't carry a large stock of pine furniture.* ◇ *I've built up a good stock of teaching materials over the years.* ◇ *Food stocks are running low.* See also **stock** → SELL *verb* 2, **stock** → EQUIP *verb* 1, **stock up** → KEEP *verb* 1

reserve [C, usually pl.] a supply of sth that is available to be used in the future or when it is needed: *The country is thought to have huge untapped oil and gas reserves.* ◇ *He discovered unexpected reserves of strength.* ◇ *The report calls for reserve funds to be established.*

pool [C] a supply of things or money that is shared by a group of people and can be used when needed: *There is a pool of cars used by the firm's salesmen.* ◇ *(BrE) a pool car* ◇ *The purpose of an insurance company is to provide a pool of funds from which to meet claims made by its customers.* See also **pool** → SHARE *verb*

hoard [C] a collection of sth valuable such as money or food, especially one that sb keeps in a secret place so that other people will not find or steal it: *They dug up a hoard of Roman coins.* ◇ *Police have uncovered a hoard of stolen goods which may help to trace the fugitives.* See also **hoard** → KEEP *verb*

bank [C] an amount of sth that is collected; a place where sth is stored ready for use: *They intend to establish a bank of information which will be accessible to the public.* ◇ *a blood / sperm bank*

store [C] an amount or supply of sth that you have and use: *her secret store of chocolate* ◇ *This is vital information to add to your store of knowledge.* See also **store** → KEEP *verb* 1

arsenal /ˈɑːsənl; *AmE* ˈɑːrs-/ [C] a collection of weapons such as guns and explosives: *The treaty requires them to reduce their nuclear arsenal by 30%.*

stockpile /ˈstɒkpaɪl; *AmE* ˈstɑːk-/ [C] a large supply of sth that is kept to be used in the future if necessary; a large supply of sth that cannot easily be used or destroyed: *Stockpiles of coal have reached a critically low level.* ◇ *The growing stockpile of used tyres is a worldwide problem.* See also **stockpile** → KEEP *verb* 1

support *verb*

1 support a party / policy
2 support the weight of sth

1 See also the entry for IN FAVOUR
support · vote · back · stand for sth · second · champion · side with sb
These words all mean to help or encourage a person, idea, policy, etc. by saying that you agree with them / it.

PATTERNS AND COLLOCATIONS
▶ to support / vote for / back / side with sb **in** sth
▶ to vote / side with sb **against** sb / sth
▶ to support / back / stand for / champion an **idea**
▶ to support / vote for / back / champion a **measure**
▶ to support / back / champion **reform**
▶ to support / vote for / back / second a **proposal** / **plan** / **motion** / **resolution**
▶ to support / vote for / back a **move** / **scheme**
▶ to support / back / champion a **cause**
▶ to support / back / stand for a **policy**
▶ to **openly** / **publicly** support / back / side with sb / sth
▶ to **overwhelmingly** / **unanimously** support / vote for / back sth

support [T] to help or encourage sb / sth by saying or showing that you agree with them / it: *If you raise it at the meeting, I'll support you.* ◇ *These measures are strongly supported by environmental groups.* **OPP oppose** → OPPOSE, See also **advocate** → RECOMMEND 1
▶ **support** *noun* [U]: *There is strong public support for the change.* ◇ *Only a few people spoke in support of the proposal.* ◇ *The idea has met with widespread support.*

vote [I, T] to show formally by marking a paper or raising your hand which person you want to win an election, or which plan or idea you agree with: *They all voted for the new tax.* ◇ *Over 60% of members voted in favour of the motion.* ◇ *We'll listen to the arguments on both sides and then vote on it.* ◇ *We voted Democrat in the last election.*

back [T] to give help or support to sb/sth: *Her parents backed her in her choice of career.* ◇ *Doctors have backed plans to raise tax on cigarettes.* ❶ **Back** is often used when it is sb in an influential, powerful or more senior position who is giving their support.
▸ **backing** *noun* [U]: *The police gave the proposals their full backing.* See also **backing** → INVESTMENT

'**stand for sth** *phrasal verb* (especially of an organization) to support a particular idea, belief or policy: *I hated the organization and all it stood for* (= the ideas that it supported).

second [T] to state officially at a meeting that you support another person's suggestion so that it can be discussed and/or voted on: *Any proposal must be seconded by two other members of the committee.* See also **propose** → PROPOSE

champion [T] to fight for or speak in support of a group of people or a belief: *He has always championed the cause of gay rights.*

'**side with sb** *phrasal verb* to support one person or group in an argument against sb else: *The kids always sided with their mother against me.*

---

2 support · hold sb/sth up · bear · hold · prop sth up · carry
These words all mean to hold sth in position so that it does not fall.

PATTERNS AND COLLOCATIONS
▸ to support / bear / hold / carry the **weight** of sb / sth

support [T] to hold sb/sth in position; to prevent sb/sth from falling: *The platform is supported by concrete pillars.* ◇ *Support the baby's head when you hold her.* ◇ *She walked carefully down the stairs, supported by her grandson.*
▸ **support** *noun* [U]: *She held on to his arm for support.* See also **support** → POST *noun*

hold sb/sth 'up *phrasal verb* [often passive] to support or raise sb/sth and stop them from falling: *His baggy grey trousers were held up with a piece of string.* ◇ *He held up his hands* (= raised his arms) *in a gesture of innocence.*

bear [T] (*rather formal*) to support the weight of sb/sth: *The ground was too soft to bear his weight.*

hold [T] to support the weight of sb/sth: *I don't think that branch will hold your weight.*

> **NOTE** BEAR OR HOLD? These words have the same meaning, but **bear** is slightly more formal. **Bear** can also be used figuratively, but **hold** is not used in this way: (*figurative*) *He seemed unable to bear the weight of his reponsibility.* ◇ ~~He seemed unable to hold the weight of his responsibility.~~

prop sth 'up *phrasal verb* (-**pp**-) to prevent sth from falling by putting sth under it to support it: *They had to prop up the tree with long poles under the branches.*

carry [T] to support the weight of sth, especially sth that is moving: *A road bridge has to carry a lot of traffic.*

---

supporter *noun* See also the entry for ADVOCATE

supporter · follower · voter · disciple
These are all words for a person who supports a person, political party or set of ideas.

PATTERNS AND COLLOCATIONS
▸ a **loyal** supporter / follower / voter / disciple
▸ a **leading** supporter / follower / disciple
▸ a/an **faithful** / **fervent** / **ardent** / **close** / **dedicated** supporter / follower / disciple
▸ to **attract** supporters / followers / voters / disciples
▸ to **persuade** / **convince** supporters / followers / voters
▸ a **band of** supporters / followers / disciples

supporter [C] a person who supports a political party, person or set of ideas: *She is an active supporter of democratic change.* ◇ *There has now been a backlash among government supporters.* **OPP** **opponent** → PROTESTER, See also **backer** → SPONSOR

follower [C] a person who supports and admires a particular person or set of ideas: *He is often referred to as a follower of Darwin.* ◇ *She still has many loyal followers.* See also **follow** → FOLLOW 4

voter [C] a person who regularly votes for a particular political party: *His parents were lifelong Conservative voters.*

disciple /dɪ'saɪpl/ [C] (*rather formal*) a person who believes in and follows the ideas or philosophy of a great teacher, especially a religious or political leader: *These ideas are central to the work of Freud and his disciples.*

---

suppose *verb*

suppose · assume · guess · suspect · imagine · expect · presume · take it · I dare say
These words all mean to say or think that sth is true or possible, based on the information you have.

PATTERNS AND COLLOCATIONS
▸ to suppose / assume / guess / suspect / imagine / expect / presume / take it / dare say **that...**
▸ to be supposed / assumed / suspected / imagined / presumed **to be** sth
▸ Let's / Let us suppose / assume / imagine / presume / take it...
▸ **can only** suppose / assume / imagine / presume / take it (that)...
▸ to **reasonably** suppose / assume / suspect / presume
▸ to **rightly** suppose / assume / suspect
▸ to be **widely** supposed / assumed / suspected / presumed
▸ to be **commonly** / **generally** supposed / assumed / imagined / presumed
▸ **always** supposing / assuming / presuming that...
▸ I suppose / assume / guess / suspect / imagine / expect / presume **so.**

suppose [T] (not used in the progressive tenses) to think or believe that sth is true or possible, based on the information you have: *Getting a visa isn't as easy as you might suppose.* ◇ *Prices will go up, I suppose.* ◇ *I suppose you think that's funny!* ◇ *Why do you suppose he resigned?* ◇ *I don't suppose for a minute that he'll agree* (= I'm sure that he won't). ❶ **Suppose** is also used to make a statement, request or suggestion less direct or less strong: *I could take you in the car, I suppose* (= but I don't really want to). ◇ *'Can I borrow the car?' 'I suppose so* (= Yes, but I'm not very happy about it).' ◇ *Suppose we take a later train?*

assume /ə'sjuːm; *AmE* ə'suːm/ [T] to think or accept that sth is true but without having any proof: *Let's assume for a moment that the plan succeeds.* ◇ *I think we can* **safely assume** *that this situation will continue.* ◇ *It's generally assumed that stress is caused by too much work.* ◇ *Don't always assume the worst* (= think that the worst thing will happen). See also **assumption** → SPECULATION

guess [T] (usually used in the form **I guess**) (*especially AmE, spoken*) to suppose that sth is true or likely: *I guess I'm just lucky.* ◇ *He didn't see me, I guess.* ❶ *I guess so* is used to agree to a statement, invitation or request, but in a way that shows you are hesitating about it: *'Can I have another cookie 'I guess so, but that's the last one.'*

suspect [T] (not used in the progressive tenses) to have an idea that sth is probably true or likely to happen, especially sth bad, but without having any definite proof: *If you suspect a gas leak, call the emergency services immediately.* ◇ *As I suspected all along, he was not a real policeman.* See also **suspicion** → DOUBT *noun* 2, **suspicion** → IDEA 2

imagine [T] to think that sth is probably true; to believe sth that is not true: *'Will we still be allowed in?' 'I imagine so.'* ◇ *I don't imagine he'll get here now, do you?* ◇ *He's always imagining that we're talking about him behind his back.*

expect [T] (not used in the progressive tenses) (*especially BrE, spoken*) to think that sth is probably true: *'Will Bill be there?' 'I expect so.'* ◇ *'Are you going out tonight?' 'I don't expect so.'* ◇ *I expect he'll be late, as usual.*

presume /prɪˈzjuːm; AmE -ˈzuːm/ [T] (*formal*) to suppose that sth is true, although you have no proof: *I presumed that he understood the rules.* ◇ *Little is known of the youngest son; it is presumed that he died young.* ❶ **Presume** is more formal than **assume**. It is often used when you are not interested enough in sth to find out if it is really true or not: *'Is he still abroad?' 'I presume so* (= but I don't actually know and I don't really care either).' See also **presume** → SAY 3, **presumably** → PROBABLY, **presumption** → SPECULATION

'take it *phrase* (*rather informal*) to suppose that sth is true: *I take it you won't be coming to the party.* ❶ **Take it** is always followed by a *that* clause, even if the word *that* is actually left out.

I dare say (also **I daresay**) *phrase* (*especially BrE, spoken*) used when you think that sth is probably true: *I dare say he'll cope.* ❶ **I dare say** is always followed by a *that* clause, even if the word *that* is actually left out.

supposed *adj.*

supposed · alleged · hypothetical · assumed · notional · speculative · theoretical
These words all describe people or things that are based on situations or ideas which are possible or imagined, not certainly true or real.

PATTERNS AND COLLOCATIONS
▸ **purely** hypothetical / speculative / theoretical
▸ **entirely** hypothetical / theoretical
▸ **highly / rather** speculative / theoretical

supposed [only before noun] (*usually disapproving*) used to show that you think that a claim, statement or way of describing sb/sth is not true or correct, although it is generally believed to be: *This is the opinion of the supposed experts.* ◇ *When did this supposed accident happen?*
▸ **supposedly** /səˈpəʊzɪdli; AmE -ˈpoʊ-/ *adv.*: *The novel is supposedly based on a true story.*

alleged /əˈledʒd/ [only before noun] (*formal*) used to describe sb/sth that is claimed to be a particular person or thing, when this has not actually been proved: *the alleged attacker/victim/killer* (= that sb says is one) ◇ *the alleged attack/offence/incident* (= that sb says has happened) ◇ *The girl gave evidence in court against her alleged attacker.* See also **allege** → CLAIM verb
▸ **allegedly** /əˈledʒɪdli/ *adv.*: *crimes allegedly committed during the war*

hypothetical /ˌhaɪpəˈθetɪkl/ (*rather formal*) based on situations or ideas which are possible and imagined rather than real and true: *Let us take the hypothetical case of Sheila, a mother of two...* ◇ *I wasn't asking about anybody in particular – it was a purely hypothetical question.* ❶ A **hypothetical** *example, question or situation* is used to illustrate a point or to help you work out a solution to a problem. **OPP** **actual** → REAL, See also **hypothesis** → THEORY 2

assumed /əˈsjuːmd; AmE əˈsuːmd/ [only before noun] (*rather formal, especially written*) that you believe to be true or to exist: *The report takes into account the assumed differences between the two states.*

notional /ˈnəʊʃənl; AmE ˈnoʊ-/ (*formal*) based on a guess, estimate or theory; not existing in reality: *My calculation is based on notional figures, since the actual figures are not yet available.* **OPP** **actual** → REAL, See also **notion** → IDEA 1

speculative /ˈspekjələtɪv; AmE also ˈspekjəleɪtɪv/ (*rather formal, especially written, often disapproving*) based on a guess, estimate or theory that has been formed without knowing all the facts: *The report is highly speculative and should be ignored.* See also **speculate** → SAY 3

NOTE **HYPOTHETICAL, NOTIONAL** OR **SPECULATIVE?** If you say that a figure, idea or story is **speculative**, you often mean that it is not reliable and you do not trust it. **Notional** is used in more technical contexts, in order to make the best estimate you can of an amount, number or time, when you do not have the actual figures.

Hypothetical is used to talk about an imagined person or thing that is used as an example to illustrate a point or work out a solution to a problem.

theoretical /ˌθɪəˈretɪkl; AmE ˌθiːə-/ [usually before noun] (*rather formal*) that could possibly exist, happen or be true, although this is unlikely: *It's a theoretical possibility.*
▸ **theoretically** *adv.*: *It is theoretically possible for him to overrule their decision, but highly unlikely.*

suppress *verb*

1 suppress a rebellion
2 suppress a feeling

1 suppress · persecute · quell · crush · put sth down · disenfranchise · subdue · oppress · repress
These words all mean to use political or military force to bring a group of people under control, to restrict their rights and freedoms, or to stop them from opposing the authorities.

disenfranchise	suppress	persecute
subdue	quell	crush
	put sth down	
	oppress	
	repress	

PATTERNS AND COLLOCATIONS
▸ to suppress / quell / crush / put down / repress a **rebellion**
▸ to suppress / quell / crush / put down a / an **uprising / revolt**
▸ to suppress / quell / crush **opposition**
▸ to suppress / quell / put down a **riot**
▸ to quell / crush / subdue **rebels**
▸ a persecuted / a disenfranchised / an oppressed **minority / people**
▸ the **army / troops / police** (are used / called in, etc. to) suppress / quell / crush / put down / subdue sb / sth
▸ a **government** suppresses / quells / crushes sb / sth
▸ to **brutally** suppress / crush / put down / repress sb / sth
▸ to **ruthlessly** suppress / crush / repress sb / sth

suppress /səˈpres/ [T] (*rather formal, written, disapproving*) (of a government or ruler) to stop a group or activity which is opposing or threatening authority, often by force: *The regime ruthlessly suppresses all dissent.* ◇ *Trade union rights were suppressed and casual work became the norm.*
▸ **suppression** *noun* [U]: *the suppression of a rebellion / free speech*

persecute /ˈpɜːsɪkjuːt; AmE ˈpɜːrs-/ [T, often passive] (*disapproving*) (especially of people in power) to treat sb in a cruel and unfair way, especially because of their race, religion or political beliefs: *Throughout history, people have been persecuted for their religious beliefs.* See also **persecution** → REPRESSION

quell [T] (*rather formal, written, disapproving*) (of a government or the authorities) to stop sth such as violent behaviour or protests, often by force: *Extra police were called in to quell the disturbances.*

crush [T] (*disapproving, journalism*) (of a government or ruler) to use violent methods to stop people who are opposing authority: *The army was sent in to crush the rebellion.*

‚put sth 'down *phrasal verb* (*disapproving*) (of a government or the authorities) to use force to stop sth, such as a group or activity which is opposing authority: *Troops loyal to the president put down an attempted coup.*

disenfranchise /ˌdɪsɪnˈfræntʃaɪz/ [T] (*formal*) to take away sb's rights, especially their right to vote: *Many disabled people were effectively disenfranchised because of lack of access.*

subdue /səbˈdjuː; AmE -ˈduː/ [T] (*formal, disapproving*) (of a government or the authorities) to bring sb/sth under control, such as a group or activity which is opposing authority, especially by using force: *Troops were called in to subdue the rebels.*

NOTE SUPPRESS, QUELL, CRUSH, PUT DOWN OR SUBDUE?
These words are all disapproving and suggest an unfair use of power. **Suppress** is the most general word. It can refer to stopping a range of different groups or activities, using different degrees of force from political pressure to physical violence. **Quell** usually refers to stopping violence, protests, riots, etc. This can be political protests or opposition, or other violence, such as football hooligans. **Crush** and **put down** both refer to using force to stop either opposition or protests and riots. **Crush** suggests the use of particularly violent methods and is used especially in journalism. **Subdue** is a more formal word to refer to bringing opposition under control, either with immediate action, for example by the police or army, or over a period of time.

oppress /ə'pres/ [T] (*rather formal, written, disapproving*) (especially of people in power) to treat sb in a cruel or unfair way, by not giving them the same rights and freedoms as other people: *The regime is accused of oppressing religious minorities.* See also **oppression** → RE-PRESSION

repress /rɪ'pres/ [T, often passive] (*rather formal, written, disapproving*) (of a government or the authorities) to control a group of people and restrict their freedom, especially a group who oppose or threaten authority, by using political or military force: *The government was quick to repress any opposition.* See also **repression** → REPRES-SION

NOTE PERSECUTE, DISENFRANCHISE, OPPRESS OR REPRESS?
Persecute is the most extreme of these verbs and refers to cruel treatment that can include harming and even killing a group of people because they are different in a way which is considered offensive by others or by those in power. People get persecuted especially because of their race, religion or political beliefs, for example the persecution of the Jews during World War II. **Disenfranchise** is the least emotional, most descriptive term, and means to take people's rights away, especially their right to vote. **Oppress** and **repress** lie between these two, meaning to restrict people's freedom so that they cannot express their opinions, act as they want to, challenge those in power, etc. In general people are **oppressed** and their activities are **repressed**.

---

2 suppress · control · stifle · contain · restrain · keep from sth · repress · hold sth back · check · curb
These words all mean to stop yourself from feeling or showing an emotion.

PATTERNS AND COLLOCATIONS
▸ to control / contain / restrain / check **yourself**
▸ to restrain / keep yourself **from doing sth**
▸ to suppress / control / contain / restrain / repress / hold back / check your **anger**
▸ to suppress / control / stifle / restrain / repress / check / curb an **impulse**
▸ to suppress / control / stifle / contain / restrain / repress an **urge**
▸ to suppress / control / stifle / contain / repress / check a / an **feeling / emotion**
▸ to suppress / control / check / curb an **instinct**
▸ to control / contain / restrain / curb your **impatience**
▸ to suppress / control / contain your **excitement**
▸ to control / contain / curb your **temper**
▸ to suppress / control / contain / restrain / hold back **tears**
▸ to suppress / control / stifle / restrain a **smile**
▸ to **barely** suppress / control / contain / restrain / repress / hold back sth
▸ to **hardly** suppress / control / contain / keep from sth

suppress /sə'pres/ [T] to stop yourself from feeling or showing an emotion or thinking about sth, even though you might want to: *She was unable to suppress a giggle.* ◇ *He had suppressed the painful memories of his childhood.* ◇ *Her face was charged with barely suppressed anger.*
OPP arouse → STIMULATE

▸ **suppression** *noun* [U]: *the suppression of emotion/ feelings*
control (-ll-) [T] to manage to make yourself remain calm, even though you are angry or upset: *I was so furious I couldn't control myself and I hit him.* ◇ *The clerk could scarcely control his excitement.* See also **self-control** → RESTRAINT
stifle /'staɪfl/ [T] to stop yourself from showing how you feel, especially through a physical action such as laughing, crying or yawning: *He stifled the urge to laugh.* ◇ *She managed to stifle a yawn.* ❶ You might **stifle** a laugh or a yawn because you don't want to seem rude.
contain [T] (*written*) to keep your emotions under control: *I was so furious I just couldn't contain myself.* ◇ *She could hardly contain her excitement.*
restrain /rɪ'streɪn/ [T] to stop yourself from feeling an emotion or doing sth that you would like to do, because you realize this might make a situation worse: *I restrained the urge to punch him.* ◇ *I was tempted to answer back, but I restrained myself.* See also **restraint** → RESTRAINT
'keep from sth, **'keep yourself from sth** *phrasal verb* to stop yourself from doing sth, especially showing an emotion: *She could hardly keep herself from laughing out loud.* ◇ *Caroline bit her lip to keep from telling him how wrong he was.*
repress /rɪ'pres/ [T] (*rather formal*) to try hard not to feel or show an emotion: *He burst in, making no effort to repress his fury.* ◇ *They tend to hide their emotions and repress their desires.*

▸ **repression** *noun* [U]: *sexual repression*

NOTE SUPPRESS OR REPRESS? Repress is less frequent and more formal than **suppress**. **Suppress** is used more often to describe a deliberate effort to prevent your feelings being seen by other people; **repress** is a slightly stronger word, often suggesting that you do not want your inner feelings to be expressed at all, even to yourself.

,hold sth 'back *phrasal verb* to stop yourself expressing how you really feel, especially through laughing or crying: *He bravely held back his tears.* ◇ *At times he could barely hold back his impatience.*
check [T] (*written*) to suddenly stop yourself from saying or doing sth or from showing an emotion: *She wanted to tell him the whole truth but she checked herself.* ◇ *She made no effort to check her tears and just let them run down her face.*
curb [T] to keep an aspect of your personality under control, especially a bad one or one that is considered bad: *He needs to learn to curb his temper.* ◇ *She has to curb her natural exuberance.*

sure *adj.*

sure · confident · convinced · certain · positive · clear · satisfied
These words all describe sb who knows without doubt that sth is true or will happen.

clear	sure	confident
satisfied	certain	convinced
		positive

PATTERNS AND COLLOCATIONS
▸ sure / confident / convinced / certain / positive / clear **about** sth
▸ sure / confident / convinced ❶ certain / satisfied **of** sth
▸ sure / confident / convinced ❶ certain / positive / clear / satisfied **that…**
▸ sure / certain / clear / satisfied **who / what / how**, etc.
▸ to **feel** sure / confident / convinced / certain / positive / satisfied
▸ **quite / absolutely / completely / fairly / pretty** sure / confident / convinced / certain / positive / clear / satisfied
▸ **fully** confident / convinced / satisfied
▸ **not altogether** sure / confident / convinced / certain / clear / satisfied
▸ **(not) very** sure / confident

sure [not before noun] without any doubt that you are right, that sth is true, that you will get sth or that sth will happen: *'Is that John over there?' 'I'm not sure.'* ◇ *You don't sound very sure.* ◇ *Are you sure about that?* ◇ *England must win this game to be sure of qualifying.* ◇ *Are you sure you don't mind?* ◇ *Ask me if you're not sure how to do it.* ❶ **Sure** is often used in negative statements and questions, because there is some doubt or anxiety over the matter. If there is no doubt, people often say quite sure: *I'm quite sure (that) I left my bag here* (= I have no doubt about it). ◇ *I'm pretty sure (that) he'll agree* (= but it is still just possible that he won't). **OPP** **unsure** → UNSURE

▸ **surely** *adv.*: *Surely you don't think I was responsible for this?* ◇ *'They're getting married.' 'Surely not!'*

confident completely sure that sth will happen in the way that you want or expect: *I'm quite confident that you'll get the job.* ◇ *The team feels confident of winning.* ❶ **Confident** is a stronger and more definite word than **sure** and is more often used in positive statements, when you feel no anxiety: *She was quietly confident that everything would go as planned.* ◇ ~~She was quietly sure that...~~ See also **confidence** → FAITH

▸ **confidently** *adv.*: *The report asserts confidently that the industry will grow.*

convinced /kən'vɪnst/ [not before noun] completely sure that sth is true or right, especially because the evidence seems to prove it or sb else has persuaded you to believe it: *I'm totally convinced of her innocence.* ◇ *I'm convinced that she's innocent.* ◇ *Sam nodded but he didn't look convinced.* **OPP** **unconvinced** ❶ If you are **unconvinced** of sth, you don't believe it or are not sure about it, despite what you have been told: *I remain unconvinced of the need for change.* ◇ *She seemed unconvinced by their promises.* See also **convince** → CONVINCE

certain [not usually before noun] sure that you are right or that sth is true: *Are you absolutely certain about this?* ◇ *She wasn't certain (that) he'd seen her.* **OPP** **uncertain** → UNSURE. See also **certainty** → FAITH

NOTE **SURE** OR **CERTAIN**? Like **sure**, **certain** is often used in negative statements and questions. It is slightly more formal than **sure**; **sure** is more frequent, especially in spoken English.

positive [not before noun] (*rather informal, especially spoken*) completely sure that sth is true: *She was positive that he'd been there.* ◇ *'Are you sure?' 'Positive.'*

clear (often used in negative statements and questions) having no doubt or confusion about sth: *My memory isn't really clear on that point.* ◇ *I'm still not clear what the job entails.* ◇ *We need a clear understanding of the problems involved.* **OPP** **vague** → VAGUE

satisfied [not before noun] believing or accepting that sth is true: *Police were satisfied that the death was accidental.* See also **satisfy** → CONVINCE

surge *verb*

surge · swarm · pour · flood · stream · pile
These words are all used when people or things move in a particular direction, especially in large numbers.

PATTERNS AND COLLOCATIONS
▸ to surge / swarm / pour / flood / stream / pile **into** sth
▸ to swarm / pour / flood / stream **out of** sth
▸ to surge / swarm / pour / stream **through / across** sth
▸ to pour / flood / stream / pile **in**
▸ **people** surge / swarm / pour / flood / stream / pile
▸ a **crowd** surges / swarms / pours / streams
▸ to **come** pouring / flooding / streaming in / out

surge /sɜːdʒ; *AmE* sɜːrdʒ/ [I] (always used with an adverb or preposition) to move quickly and forcefully in a particular direction: *The gates opened and the crowd surged forwards.* ◇ *A large wave sent water surging up towards them.*

swarm /swɔːm; *AmE* swɔːrm/ [I] (always used with an adverb or preposition) (*often disapproving*) (of people or animals) to move around in a large group; (of a place) to be full of people or animals: *There are tourists swarming all over the island at this time of year.* ◇ *The museum was swarming with schoolchildren.* See also **swarm** → HERD *noun*

pour [I] (always used with an adverb or preposition) to come or go somewhere continuously in large numbers: *Letters and cards poured in with offers of support for the victims.* ◇ *Commuters came pouring out of the station.*

flood [I] (always used with an adverb or preposition) to come or go somewhere in large numbers: *Refugees continue to flood into neighbouring countries.* See also **flood** → FLOOD *noun* 2

NOTE **POUR** OR **FLOOD**? In many cases you can use either word: *Telephone calls came pouring/flooding in from all over the country.* **Pour** emphasizes that the action continues over a period of time; **flood** places more emphasis on the large numbers of people or things involved, especially when the numbers are so large that they cause problems.

stream [I] (always used with an adverb or preposition) (of people or things) to move somewhere continuously in large numbers, one after the other in a line: *He stared out of the window at the cars streaming along the street.* See also **stream** → FLOW *noun*

pile [I] (always used with an adverb or preposition) (*informal*) (of a number of people) to go somewhere quickly without order or control: *The bus finally arrived and we all piled on.* ❶ **Pile** is used especially to talk about people getting into a vehicle.

surgery *noun* See the Topic Map for HEALTH on p.890, See also the entry for HOSPITAL

surgery · doctor's office · doctor's · clinic · health centre
These words all mean a place where you can see a doctor for advice and treatment.

PATTERNS AND COLLOCATIONS
▸ **at** the surgery / doctor's office / doctor's / clinic / health centre /
▸ a **local** surgery / clinic / health centre
▸ to **go** to the doctor's / a clinic

surgery /'sɜːdʒəri; *AmE* 'sɜːrdʒ-/ [C] (*BrE, rather formal*) a building or part of a building where a doctor, dentist or vet (= an animal doctor) sees their patients: *I phoned the dentist's surgery and made an appointment for 2.30.* See also **practice** → COMPANY

doctor's office [C] (*AmE*) a doctor's surgery: *I was sitting in the doctor's office, waiting to see her.*

doctor's [C, usually sing.] (*rather informal, especially spoken*) a doctor's surgery, especially when you are talking about the place where your own doctor works: *I have an appointment at the doctor's tomorrow morning.* See also **doctor** → DOCTOR

clinic /'klɪnɪk/ [C] (*AmE*) a building shared by a group of doctors or vets who work together: *Most of the crash victims were treated in a local clinic but a 13-year-old was hospitalized.* ❶ **Clinic** is often used to describe a doctor's office where people can go without an appointment, and/or one used especially by people on low incomes or without medical insurance.

'health centre (*BrE*) (*AmE* **health center**) [C] (*especially BrE*) a building where a group of doctors see their patients and where some local medical services have their offices: *There is a health centre on campus that provides medical care under the National Health Service.*

surprise verb

surprise · startle · amaze · stun · astonish · take sb aback · bowl sb over · astound · stagger
These words all mean to make to make sb feel surprised.

surprise	amaze
startle	stun
take sb aback	astonish
	bowl sb over
	astound
	stagger

PATTERNS AND COLLOCATIONS
▶ **It** surprises sb/startles sb/amazes sb/stuns sb/astonishes sb/ takes sb aback/ bowls sb over/ astounds sb/ staggers sb
▶ **What** surprises/startles/amazes/stuns/astonishes/astounds/ staggers sb **is…**
▶ to surprise/startle/amaze/stun/astonish/astound sb **that…**
▶ to surprise/amaze sb **what/how…**
▶ to surprise/startle/amaze/stun/astonish/astound sb **to know/find/learn/see/hear…**
▶ to be surprised/startled/stunned **into** (doing) sth
▶ to **really** surprise sb/startle sb/amaze sb/stun sb/astonish sb/ take sb aback/ bowl sb over/ astound/ stagger sb
▶ to **absolutely** amaze sb/ stun sb/ stagger sb

surprise [T] to give sb the feeling that you get when sth happens that you don't expect or don't understand, or sth that you do expect doesn't happen: *The outcome didn't surprise me at all.* ◇ *It's always surprised me how popular he is.* ◇ **It wouldn't surprise me** *if they got married soon.*
▶ **surprise** *noun* [C]: *What a nice surprise!* ◇ *a surprise attack/announcement/visit* ◇ *There are few surprises in this year's budget.* ◇ *Her letter* **came as a complete surprise.**
▶ **surprised** *adj.*: *a surprised look* ◇ *She looked surprised when I told her.* ◇ *I was surprised at how quickly she agreed.* ◇ *They were surprised to find (that) he'd already left.*

startle [T] to surprise sb suddenly in a way that slightly shocks or frightens them: *Sorry, I didn't mean to startle you.* ◇ *The explosion startled the horse.* See also **startled** → AFRAID, **alarm** → FRIGHTEN

amaze [T] to surprise sb very much: *Just the huge size of the place amazed her.* ◇ *What amazes me is how long she managed to hide it from us.* See also **amazing** → AMAZING
▶ **amazed** *adj.*: *an amazed silence* ◇ *I was amazed at her knowledge of French literature.* ◇ *She was amazed how little he had changed.*
▶ **amazement** *noun* [U]: **To my amazement,** *he was able to recite the whole poem from memory.* ◇ *She looked at him* **in amazement.**

stun (-nn-) [T] (*rather informal, especially journalism*) to surprise or shock sb so much that they cannot think clearly or speak: *Her words stunned me – I had no idea she felt that way.* ◇ *The company stunned investors with its third profits warning in five months.* See also **stunning** → AMAZING

astonish /əˈstɒnɪʃ; AmE əˈstɑːn-/ [T] to surprise sb very much: *You astonish me!* ◇ *The news astonished everyone.* See also **astonishing** → AMAZING
▶ **astonished** *adj.*: *He was astonished to learn (that) he'd won the competition.* ◇ *My parents looked astonished at my news.*
▶ **astonishment** *noun* [U]: **To my utter astonishment,** *she remembered my name.* ◇ *He stared* **in astonishment** *at the stranger.*

> **NOTE** AMAZE OR ASTONISH? In most cases you can use either word. If you are talking about sth that both surprises you and makes you feel ashamed, use **astonish**: *He was astonished by his own stupidity.*

take sb aˈback *phrasal verb* [usually passive] (*written*) (especially of sth negative) to surprise or shock sb: *We were rather taken aback by her hostile reaction.*

bowl sb ˈover *phrasal verb* [often passive] to surprise and impress sb a lot: *She was bowled over by his charm.*

astound /əˈstaʊnd/ [T] to surprise or shock sb very much: *His arrogance astounded her.*

stagger [T] (*rather informal*) (especially of sth negative) to surprise or shock sb very much: *The inspectors were staggered at the level of incompetence among senior staff.* See also **staggering** → AMAZING

surprising adj. See also the entry for AMAZING

surprising · unexpected · unpredictable · extraordinary · unforeseen · unforeseeable
These words all describe things that surprise you because you did not expect them.

PATTERNS AND COLLOCATIONS
▶ surprising/ unexpected/ unpredictable/ extraordinary/ unforeseen **events**
▶ surprising/ unexpected/ unpredictable/ extraordinary/ unforeseen **effects/ changes**
▶ surprising/ unexpected/ unpredictable/ extraordinary **results**
▶ a surprising/ an unexpected/ an extraordinary/ an unforeseen **development**
▶ unexpected/ unpredictable/ extraordinary/ unforeseen **demand/ problems**
▶ unexpected/ extraordinary/ unforeseen/ unforeseeable **circumstances**
▶ **quite** surprising/ unexpected/ unpredictable/ extraordinary/ unforeseen
▶ **totally** unexpected/ unpredictable/ unforeseen
▶ **very/ rather** surprising/ unexpected/ unpredictable/ extraordinary

surprising causing surprise: *It is not* **surprising (that)** *they lost.* ◇ *It is* **surprising how** *quickly rumours spread.* ◇ *It's* **surprising** *what people will do for money.* ◇ *The* **surprising thing** *is how little it costs.* ◇ *I find that rather surprising.* ◇ *Quite a surprising number of people turned up.* ❶ **Surprising** is by far the most frequent and most general of these words and can describe any fact or event that causes surprise. **OPP** **unsurprising** → PREDICTABLE 1
▶ **surprisingly** *adv.*: *The event was surprisingly popular.* ◇ *Not surprisingly, the request was refused.*

unexpected not expected and therefore surprising: *We had an unexpected visitor this morning.* ◇ *Although not unexpected, his death had still come as a shock.* ◇ *The following day something quite unexpected happened.* ❶ **Unexpected** can describe either an event that you did not expect to happen, or a person, when they do sth that you did not expect them to do.
▶ **the unexpected** *noun* [sing.]: *Police officers must be prepared for the unexpected.*
▶ **unexpectedly** *adv.*: *The plane was unexpectedly delayed.* ◇ *They encountered an unexpectedly high level of demand.*

unpredictable that cannot be predicted because it changes a lot or depends on too many different things: *The result is entirely unpredictable.* ◇ *The unpredictable weather in the mountains can make climbing extremely hazardous.* **OPP** **predictable** → PREDICTABLE 1

extraordinary unexpected, surprising or strange: *It's extraordinary that he managed to sleep through the party.* ◇ *What an extraordinary thing to say!* See also **extraordinary** → REMARKABLE

unforeseen /ˌʌnfɔːˈsiːn; AmE -fɔːrˈs-/ (*rather formal*) that you did not expect to happen: *We reserve the right to alter the timetable in the event of unforeseen circumstances.*

> **NOTE** UNEXPECTED OR UNFORESEEN? Unforeseen is more formal than **unexpected** and only describes events, NOT people: ~~an unforeseen visitor~~

unforeseeable /ˌʌnfɔːˈsiːəbl; AmE -fɔːrˈs-/ (*rather formal*) that you cannot predict: *You need to allow for any unforeseeable expenses.* **OPP** **foreseeable** → PREDICTABLE 1

surround *verb*

surround · enclose · line · flank · encircle · border
These words all mean to be in a position around sb/sth or on either side of sb/sth.

PATTERNS AND COLLOCATIONS
▶ to be surrounded/enclosed/lined/flanked/encircled/bordered **by/with** sth
▶ to be **completely** surrounded/enclosed/encircled
▶ to be **totally/entirely** surrounded/enclosed
▶ sth surrounds/encircles a **town/city**
▶ **walls/fences** surround/enclose/encircle sth

surround [T] to be all around sb/sth; to move into a position all around sb/sth, especially so that they cannot escape; to move sb/sth into a position in this way: *Tall trees surround the lake.* ◇ *The lake is surrounded with/by trees.* ◇ *the membranes surrounding the brain* ◇ *Police surrounded the building.* ◇ *He has now **surrounded** his house **with** barbed wire.*

enclose /ɪnˈkləʊz/; *AmE* ɪnˈkloʊz/ [T] to build a wall, fence or other structure around sth; (of a wall, fence, etc.) to surround sth: *The yard had been enclosed with iron railings.* ◇ *Low hedges enclosed the flower beds.* ◇ *I can't stand being shut in a small **enclosed space**.* ❶ When the wall, fence, etc. is the object of the verb **enclose**, the verb is nearly always passive: ~~They had enclosed the yard with iron railings.~~

line [T, often passive] (of people or things) to form lines or rows along sth: *Crowds of people lined the streets to watch the race.* ◇ *The walls were lined with books.*

flank [T] to be on one or both sides of sb/sth: *They drove through the flat cotton fields that flanked Highway 17.* ◇ *She left the courtroom flanked by armed guards.*

encircle /ɪnˈsɜːkl/; *AmE* ɪnˈsɜːrkl/ [T] (*written*) to surround sb/sth completely in a circular shape or movement: *The island is encircled by a coral reef.* ◇ *Jack's arms encircled her waist.*

border [T] (*written*) (especially of a natural feature) to form a line along or around the edge of sth: *Meadows bordered the path to the woods.*

survey *verb*

survey · poll · sample · canvass · ballot
These words all mean to find out about sth by asking a group of people questions.

PATTERNS AND COLLOCATIONS
▶ to poll/ballot sb **on** sth
▶ to canvass/ballot sb **for** sth
▶ to survey/canvass **opinion**
▶ to poll/ballot your **members**

survey [T] to find out about the opinions or behaviour of a group of people by asking them a series of questions: *We surveyed 500 smokers and found that over three quarters would like to give up.* ◇ *The aim of the project is to survey public attitudes to disability.* See also **survey** → INVESTIGATION *noun*

poll /pəʊl/; *AmE* poʊl/ [T, usually passive] to ask a large number of people, especially members of the public, what they think about sth: *Over 50% of those polled were against the proposed military action.* See also **poll** → INVESTIGATION *noun*

sample [T] (*technical*) to test part of sth or question part of a group of people in order to find out what the rest is like: *The survey was done using a group of 100 children randomly sampled from the school population.*
▶ **sample** *noun* [C]: *Samples of the water contained pesticide.* ◇ *The interviews were given to a **random sample** of students.*

canvass /ˈkænvəs/ [T] to ask people about sth in order to find out what they think about it: *I quickly canvassed opinion on the issue among my colleagues.* ◇ *People are being canvassed for their views on the proposed new road.*

ballot /ˈbælət/ [T] to ask sb to vote secretly in writing about sth, especially to find out the opinion of a group of people: *The union balloted its members on the proposed changes.* See also **ballot** → ELECTION *noun*

survive *verb* See also the entry for RECOVER 1

survive · live · live on sth · make it · weather · live through sth · come through (sth)
These words all mean to remain alive.

PATTERNS AND COLLOCATIONS
▶ to survive/live **on** (a diet of) sth
▶ to survive/live **for** a few days/many years, etc.
▶ to survive/make it / live/come **through** sth
▶ to survive/live **without** food/money, etc.
▶ to survive/weather a **storm/crisis/recession**
▶ to survive/come through an **operation**

survive [I, T] to remain alive or continue to exist; to remain alive or continue to exist in spite of a dangerous event or time: *She was the last surviving member of the family.* ◇ *Of the six people injured in the crash, only two survived.* ◇ *I can't survive on £40 a week (= it is not enough for my basic needs).* ◇ *The children had to **survive** by begging and stealing.* ◇ *Some strange customs have **survived from** earlier times.* ◇ *He **survived as** party leader until his second election defeat.* ◇ *Many birds didn't survive the severe winter.* ◇ *Few buildings survived the war intact.* See also **survival** → LIFE 1

live [I] to remain alive: *The doctors said he only had six months to live.* ◇ *Spiders can live for several days without food.* ◇ *She **lived to see** her first grandchild.* See also **life** → LIFE 1

live on sth *phrasal verb* to eat a particular type of food to exist; to have enough money for the basic things you need to live: *Small birds live mainly on insects.* ◇ *My salary isn't enough for us to live on.* ◇ *You don't want to end up **living on benefits** (= money from the state).* ❶ **Live on sth** can also be used in a disapproving way to mean 'to eat only or a lot of a particular type of food': *She seems to live on burgers.*

make it *idiom* (*rather informal*) to survive after a serious illness or accident; to deal successfully with a difficult experience: *The doctors think he's going to make it.* ◇ *I don't know how I made it through the week.*

weather [T] to manage to survive a difficult time or experience, especially in business or politics: *The company just managed to weather the recession.* ◇ (*figurative*) *She refuses to resign, intending to **weather the storm** (= wait until the situation improves again).*

live through sth *phrasal verb* to experience a disaster or other unpleasant situation and survive it: *He lived through two world wars.*

come through sth, come through *phrasal verb* to get better after a serious illness or an operation; to avoid injury or damage: *With such a weak heart she was lucky to come through the operation.* ◇ *If you've ever done something dangerous and come through unscathed, you'll know what I mean about this feeling.*

suspect *verb*

suspect · disbelieve · distrust · doubt
These words all mean to not believe or trust sb/sth.

PATTERNS AND COLLOCATIONS
▶ to suspect/distrust sb's **motives**
▶ to **still/never** suspect/disbelieve/distrust/doubt sb
▶ to **have (no) reason to** suspect/disbelieve/distrust/doubt sb

suspect [T] (not used in the progressive tenses) to feel that sb/sth is not good or honest; to have an idea that sb is guilty of sth, without having definite proof: *He resigned after being **suspected of** theft.* ◇ *The drug is suspected of* causing over 200 deaths. ◇ He dealt through a broker whose honesty he had no reason to suspect. See also **suspicion** → SCEPTICISM

disbelieve /ˌdɪsbɪˈliːv/ [T] (not used in the progressive tenses) (formal) to not believe that sth is true or that sb is telling the truth: Why should I disbelieve her story? **OPP** **believe** → FAITH, See also **disbelief** → SCEPTICISM

distrust /dɪsˈtrʌst/ [T] (rather formal, written) to feel that sb/sth is not good or honest; to not trust sb/sth: She distrusted his motives for wanting to see her again. **OPP** **trust** → TRUST, See also **distrust** → SCEPTICISM noun

NOTE **SUSPECT** OR **DISTRUST** You can suspect sb's motives or suspect sb of doing sth but you cannot just 'suspect sb'. **Distrust** is more general: you can distrust sb's motives or just distrust sb/sth – feel in a general way that sb/sth is not to be trusted – but you cannot distrust sb 'of' a particular action or crime.

doubt [T] to not believe what sb says: I had no reason to doubt him. See also **doubt** → DOUBT noun 2

suspicious adj.

1 be suspicious of sb/sth
2 suspicious circumstances

1 suspicious · sceptical · cynical · incredulous · disbelieving

These words all describe sb who feels or believes that sb is not telling the truth or that sth is not true.

▸ suspicious / sceptical / cynical / incredulous **about** sth
▸ suspicious / sceptical / incredulous **of** sb / sth
▸ suspicious / sceptical **as to** sth
▸ a suspicious / a sceptical / a cynical / an incredulous / a disbelieving **look**
▸ **very / deeply** suspicious / sceptical / cynical

suspicious feeling that sb has done sth wrong, illegal or dishonest, without having any proof; not willing or able to trust sb/sth: They became suspicious of his behaviour and contacted the police. ◇ She cast a suspicious glance at him. ◇ You have a very suspicious mind (= you always think that people are behaving in an illegal or dishonest way). ◇ Many were suspicious of reform. See also **suspicion** → SCEPTICISM, **suspicion** → DOUBT noun 2
▸ **suspiciously** adv.: The man looked at her suspiciously.

sceptical (BrE) (AmE **skeptical**) /ˈskeptɪkl/ having doubts that a claim or statement is true or that sth will happen: I am sceptical about his chances of winning. ◇ The public remain sceptical of these claims. ◇ She looked highly sceptical. See also **scepticism** → SCEPTICISM
▸ **sceptically** (BrE) (AmE **skeptically**) adv.: The announcement was greeted sceptically by the press.

cynical /ˈsɪnɪkl/ believing that people only do things to help themselves, rather than for good or honest reasons: Do you have to be so cynical about everything? ◇ Her lips curled into a cynical smile. See also **cynicism** → SCEPTICISM

incredulous /ɪnˈkredjələs; AmE -dʒəl-/ not able or not willing to believe sth; showing this: 'Here?' said Kate, incredulous. ◇ She shot him an incredulous look.
▸ **incredulously** adv.: He laughed incredulously.

disbelieving /ˌdɪsbɪˈliːvɪŋ/ not believing that sth is true or that sb is telling the truth: She gave him a disbelieving look. See also **disbelief** → SCEPTICISM
▸ **disbelievingly** adv.: She stared disbelievingly at the alarm clock.

NOTE **INCREDULOUS** OR **DISBELIEVING?** In many cases you can use either word. **Incredulous** often suggests that sth is too strange and surprising for sb to believe; **disbelieving** often suggests that sb will not believe sth because they do not trust the person telling them.

2 suspicious · suspect · questionable · dubious · dodgy · shifty · shady · fishy

These words all describe people or actions that make you feel that sth is wrong, illegal or dishonest.

▸ a suspicious / suspect / questionable / dubious / shifty / shady **character**
▸ a suspicious / questionable / dubious **circumstances**
▸ a suspicious / shifty **look / manner**
▸ a suspicious / suspect **package**
▸ a dodgy / shady **deal / past**
▸ a dodgy / fishy **business**
▸ There's **something** suspicious / suspect / shifty / shady / fishy **about** sb / sth.
▸ There's **something** suspicious / shady / fishy **going on**.
▸ **very** suspicious / suspect / questionable / dubious / dodgy / shifty / shady / fishy
▸ **a bit** suspicious / suspect / questionable / dubious / dodgy / shifty / fishy
▸ **rather / pretty** suspicious / suspect / questionable / dubious / dodgy / shifty
▸ **highly / slightly / somewhat** suspicious / suspect / questionable / dubious

suspicious making you feel that sth is wrong, illegal or dishonest: Didn't you notice anything suspicious in his behaviour? ◇ Police are not treating the death as suspicious. ◇ It might look suspicious if we arrived together. See also **suspicion** → DOUBT noun 2
▸ **suspiciously** adv.: Let me know if you see anyone acting suspiciously. ◇ Everything was suspiciously quiet.

suspect /ˈsʌspekt/ (especially journalism) that may be false and that cannot be relied on; that you suspect to be dangerous or illegal: Some of the evidence they produced was highly suspect. ◇ The police have been informed of the discovery of a suspect package (= that may contain drugs, a bomb, etc.).

questionable (rather formal) likely to be dishonest or morally wrong: Her motives for helping are questionable. **OPP** **unquestionable** → CONCLUSIVE

dubious /ˈdjuːbiəs; AmE ˈduː-/ (rather formal) likely to be dishonest or morally wrong: The man who sold it to him was known to be of dubious character.

NOTE **QUESTIONABLE** OR **DUBIOUS?** **Questionable** is used most often to talk about people's actions and motives (= the reasons for their actions). **Dubious** is more often used to talk about the value of things or people or their morals. A typical pattern is: sb/sth is of dubious character/nature/provenance/quality/reputation/value.

dodgy (BrE, informal) (especially of a business activity) likely to be dishonest: Travel websites that offer dodgy deals have been uncovered in a worldwide investigation.

shifty (informal) seeming to be dishonest; looking guilty about sth: I don't trust him – he's got shifty eyes. ◇ He was trying not to look shifty. ❶ **Shifty** is most often used to talk about people's eyes or the way they look.

shady /ˈʃeɪdi/ [usually before noun] (informal) seeming to be dishonest or illegal: He's a bit of a shady character. ◇ I don't want anything to do with your shady deals.

fishy (informal) that makes you suspicious because it seems dishonest: There's something fishy going on here. ◇ I don't know what they're up to. It sounds a distinctly fishy business. ❶ **Fishy** is mostly used in the phrases fishy business, something fishy and sth sounds fishy.

sweet adj. See also the entry for NICE 2

sweet · cute · adorable · lovable · dear old/little... · endearing · cuddly
These words all describe a person, child or animal who is attractive and easy to like.

PATTERNS AND COLLOCATIONS
▶ a sweet/a cute/an adorable/a lovable/a dear/an endearing little...
▶ a sweet/a cute/an adorable/a cuddly **baby**
▶ a sweet/a cute/an adorable **girl** / **boy** / **child** / **kid**
▶ an endearing/a cuddly **animal** / **creature**
▶ a sweet/cute/lovable **way**

sweet (*especially BrE, especially spoken, approving*) (especially of children, animals or small things) attractive in a way that makes you feel affection for sb/sth: *His sister's a sweet young thing.* ◊ *You look sweet in this photograph.* ◊ *What a sweet little dog!*
▶ **sweetly** *adv.*: *She smiled sweetly at him.*
cute (*especially spoken, approving*) sweet: *You were such a cute baby.* ◊ *She had a cute little nose.*

NOTE **SWEET** OR **CUTE?** You can usually use either word: *How sweet/cute!* ◊ *What a sweet/cute (little) baby, picture, dress, etc!* **Sweet** is more frequent in British English and **cute** is more frequent in American English.

adorable /ə'dɔːrəbl/ (*especially AmE, especially spoken, approving*) very attractive and easy to feel love for: *Isn't he just adorable?* ◊ *What an adorable child!* See also **adore** → LOVE *verb*
lovable (also **loveable**) (*approving*) having qualities that people find attractive and easy to love, often in spite of any faults: *People saw him as a lovable rogue.* See also **love** → LOVE *verb*
dear old/little... (*BrE, approving*) used to describe sb in a way that shows affection: *Dear old Sue! I knew she'd help.* ◊ *Their baby's a dear little thing.*
endearing (*approving*) causing people to feel affection: *I like his honesty. It's one of his most endearing qualities.*
▶ **endearingly** *adv.*: *an endearingly old-fashioned idea*
▶ **endear sb/yourself to sb** *phrasal verb*: *She was a talented teacher who endeared herself to* (= made herself popular with) *all who worked with her.*
cuddly (*informal, approving*) attractive in a way that makes people want to hold sb/sth close in their arms: *a tiny, cuddly kitten* ❶ **Cuddly** is often used to talk about animals, especially young ones with soft fur. A *cuddly person* is sb that you think looks soft and round. It is therefore used to describe babies more often than adults, who might feel that they are being described as fat. See also **cuddle** → HUG

swell *verb*

swell · inflate · blow sth up · bloat
These words all mean to become or make sth bigger, especially by filling it with sth.

PATTERNS AND COLLOCATIONS
▶ to swell/inflate sth **with** sth
▶ to inflate/blow up a **balloon** / **tyre**

swell [I, T] to become bigger or rounder; to curve or make sth curve outwards: *Her arm was beginning to swell up where the bee had stung her.* ◊ *Cook the lentils for 20 minutes until they swell and soften.* ◊ *If the rain continues the river could swell and burst its banks.* ◊ *The wind swelled the sails.* See also **swelling** → TUMOUR
inflate /ɪn'fleɪt/ [T, I] (*rather formal, especially written*) to fill sth or become filled with air or gas: *Inflate your life jacket by pulling sharply on the cord.* ◊ *The dinghy was in the water, fully inflated.* ◊ *The life jacket failed to inflate.*
▶ **inflatable** *adj.*: *an inflatable dinghy/mattress*
blow sth up *phrasal verb* (*rather informal, especially spoken*) to fill sth with air or gas so that it becomes firm: *Can you help me blow up these balloons?*

NOTE **INFLATE** OR **BLOW STH UP?** Inflate is more formal than **blow sth up**; it can also be used without an object: *The life jacket failed to blow up.*

bloat [T, often passive] to swell or make sth swell, especially in an unpleasant way: *Her features had been bloated by years of drinking and drug-taking.* ❶ **Bloat** is used especially about parts of the body.

swing *verb*

swing · rock · sway · oscillate
These words all mean to move backwards and forwards from a fixed point, or to make sth do this.

PATTERNS AND COLLOCATIONS
▶ to swing/sway/rock/oscillate **backwards and forwards**
▶ to swing/sway/rock **back and forth/to and fro/from side to side**
▶ to swing/sway/rock/oscillate **violently** / **wildly** / **slightly**
▶ to swing/sway/rock **gently**

swing [I, T] to move or make sb/sth move backwards and forwards or from side to side while hanging from a fixed point: *His arms swung as he walked.* ◊ *A set of keys swung from her belt.* ◊ *She sat on a stool swinging her legs.*
▶ **swing** [sing.]: *the swing of her hips*
rock [I, T] (usually used with an adverb or preposition) to move or make sb/sth move backwards and forwards or from side to side, especially gently: *The boat rocked from side to side on the water.* ◊ *He rocked the baby gently in his arms.*
sway [I, T] (usually used with an adverb or preposition) to move or make sth move slowly from side to side: *The branches of the trees were swaying in the wind.* ◊ *Vicky swayed and fell.* ◊ *She swayed her hips in time to the music.*
oscillate /'ɒsɪleɪt; AmE 'ɑːs-/ [I] (*physics*) to keep moving from one position to another and back again; (of an electric current, radio waves, etc.) to change in strength or direction at regular intervals: *The needle on the dial will oscillate when a magnetic field is present.* ◊ *The current oscillates between magnetic poles.*

switch *verb*

switch · change (sth) over · convert · swap
These words all mean to change or make sth change from one thing to another.

PATTERNS AND COLLOCATIONS
▶ to switch over/change over/convert **from** sth **to** sth
▶ to switch/change/swap **over**
▶ to switch/convert/swap **easily**

switch [I, T] (*rather informal*) to change or make sth change from one thing to another: *Press these two keys to switch between documents on screen.* ◊ *The meeting has been switched to next week.* ◊ *When did you switch jobs?* See also **switch** → CHANGE *noun* 2
change 'over, **change sth 'over** *phrasal verb* to change or make sth change from one system or position to another: *The farm has changed over to organic methods.* ◊ *We've changed the farm over to organic production.* See also **change** → CHANGE *noun* 2

NOTE **SWITCH** OR **CHANGE OVER?** Switch is more informal than **change over** and is often used in journalism. **Change over** is more often used with to than *from*: *to change over to nicotine gum/dairy farming/a nuclear policy.* **Switch** is often used to talk about moving between two opposite positions, or from an old-fashioned system to a new one: *to switch over from recovery to relapse* ◊ *to switch over to a metric standard/ electronic mail*

convert /kən'vɜːt; AmE -'vɜːrt/ [I] (*rather formal*) to change a habit or opinion: *I've converted to organic food.* See also **conversion** → CHANGE *noun* 2
swap (also **swop**) /swɒp; AmE swɑːp/ (**-pp-**) [I] to start doing sb else's job, etc. while yours do yours: *I'll drive there and then we'll swap over on the way back.* See also **swap** → EXCHANGE *noun*

sympathy *noun* See also the entry for RELIEF

sympathy · concern · compassion · pity · understanding · condolence · humanity
These are all words for the feeling you have when you are sorry for sb who is unhappy or suffering.

▸ sympathy / concern / compassion / pity **for** sb / sth
▸ to do sth **out of** sympathy / concern / compassion / pity
▸ to do sth **with** sympathy / concern / compassion / understanding / humanity
▸ **without** sympathy / compassion / pity
▸ **great** sympathy / concern / compassion / understanding / humanity
▸ **deep** sympathy / concern / compassion / understanding
▸ **real / genuine** sympathy / concern / compassion / pity / understanding / humanity
▸ to **feel / be full of** sympathy / concern / compassion / pity
▸ to **have** sympathy / compassion / pity (for sb / sth)
▸ to **express** (your) sympathy / concern / condolences
▸ to **show (sb)** sympathy / concern / compassion / pity / understanding / humanity
▸ to **offer (sb)** (your) sympathy / understanding / condolences
▸ to **give sb** (your) sympathy / compassion / pity / understanding / condolences

sympathy [U, C, usually pl.] the feeling of being sorry for sb; showing that you understand and care about sb's problems: *I have no sympathy for Jan; it's all her own fault.* ◊ *He didn't get much sympathy from anyone.* ◊ *Their plight aroused considerable public sympathy.* ◊ (*formal*) *May we offer our deepest sympathies on the death of your wife.* See also **empathy** → BOND, **sympathetic** → SENSITIVE 1, **sympathize** → SORRY FOR SB

concern [U] a feeling of wanting to protect and help sb/sth: *She forgot her own worries in her concern for her children.* ◊ *I appreciate everyone's concern and help at this difficult time.* ❶ People often feel **concern** for people they have or feel responsibility for, for example family members or friends.

compassion [U] (*rather formal*) a strong feeling of sympathy for people who are suffering and a desire to help them: *He was filled with overwhelming love and compassion for his wife.* ◊ *She was known as a hard woman with no compassion, no emotion.* See also **compassionate** → SENSITIVE 1

pity [U] a feeling of sympathy and sadness caused by the suffering and troubles of others: *I could only feel pity for what they were enduring.* ◊ *I took pity on her and lent her the money.* ◊ (*formal*) *I beg you to have pity on him.* See also **pity** → SORRY FOR SB *verb*

NOTE COMPASSION OR PITY? **Compassion** is a stronger feeling than **pity**. It is a warm, kind feeling that suggests that you understand what other people are feeling and that you share their suffering in some way. If you feel **pity**, you do not necessarily have this understanding, and you may not have or show as much respect for the person you feel pity for. For this reason, sb might say: *I don't want your pity!* but they are unlikely to say: *I don't want your compassion!.* **Pity** is often used in the phrases *have / take pity on sb.*

understanding [U, sing.] the ability to understand why people behave in a particular way and show them sympathy when things go wrong: *Please try to show a little more understanding.* ◊ *We are looking for a better understanding between the two nations.* See also **understanding** → SENSITIVE *adj.* 1

condolence /kən'dəʊləns; *AmE* -'doʊ-/ [C, usually pl., U] (*rather formal*) sympathy that you express for sb when a person in their family or that they know well has died:

Our heartfelt condolences go out to his wife and family. ◊ *a letter of condolence* ❶ *My/his/her/our, etc. condolences* is used in formal or official situations, for example in a speech or letter.

humanity /hjuː'mænəti/ [U] the quality of being kind to people and animals by making sure that they do not suffer more than is necessary: *The judge was praised for his courage and humanity.* **OPP** **inhumanity** → CRUEL, See also **humane** → SENSITIVE 1

system *noun* See also the entry for STRUCTURE

system · network · organization · web · apparatus · workings
These are all words for the way sth is organized or the way the different parts of sth connect with each other.

▸ a system / a network / an apparatus **for** sth
▸ **in / within** a system / a network / a web / the apparatus
▸ the **whole** system / network / web / apparatus
▸ a / the **complex** system / network / organization / web / apparatus / workings
▸ a **social** system / network / organization
▸ an **administrative** system / network / apparatus
▸ to **create** a system / network / web
▸ to **set up / establish** a system / network
▸ to **improve** a system / the organization of sth
▸ to **understand / explain** a system / the organization of sth / the workings of sth

system [C] the way in which sth is organized; a group of things or pieces of equipment that are connected or work together: *the educational/justice system* ◊ *a heating/ computer system* ◊ *Their existing system of government seems to work reasonably well.* ◊ *The **alarm system** had been switched off.*

network [C] a closely connected group of people or companies that exchange information and help each other: *She has a supportive network of close friends.* ◊ *The company has a network of regional offices.* ◊ *They have one of the most efficient distribution networks in Europe.*

organization (*BrE* also **-isation**) [U] the way in which the different parts of sth are arranged, especially in a society or institution: *The report studies the organization of labour within the civil service.* ◊ *They experimented with new forms of social organization.*

web [C] a complicated pattern of things that are closely connected, especially when they are difficult to deal with or understand: *An increasingly complex web of legislation has been considered.* ◊ *We were caught in a **tangled web** of relationships.* ◊ *She discovered a **web of intrigue** (= secret activities).* ◊ *a web of deceit/lies* ❶ Many of the collocates of the word **web** in this meaning make you think of the literal meaning of a spider's web. Collocates include *tangled, caught (up) in, entangled in, drawn into, spin, weave* and *centre of.*

apparatus /ˌæpə'reɪtəs; *AmE* -'rætəs/ [C, usually sing.] the structure of a system or organization, especially that of a government or political party, including all the people working at different levels with different degrees of power: *Under the new system there was to be no all-powerful central state apparatus.* ◊ *the apparatus of government*

workings [pl.] the way in which a system or organization works: *The classes give an introduction to the workings of Congress.* ◊ *In the book he tries to give a complete description of the workings of the human mind.* ❶ **Workings** is usually used in the phrases *the workings (of sth)* or *sth's workings.*

T t

tackle

tackle *verb* See also the entries for CONFRONT, DEAL WITH SB/STH and FACE

---

tackle · address · approach · grapple · get/come to grips with sth

These words all mean to make an effort to deal with a problem or difficult situation.

tackle [T] to make a determined effort to deal with a problem or difficult situation: *The government is determined to tackle inflation.* ◇ *Firefighters tackled a blaze in a garage last night.*

address [T] (*formal*) to think about a problem or situation and decide how you are going to deal with it: *Your essay does not address the real issues.* ◇ *We must address ourselves to the problem of traffic pollution.*

approach /ə'prəʊtʃ; *AmE* ə'proʊtʃ/ [T] to start dealing with a problem or task in a particular way: *What's the best way of approaching this problem?* See also **approach** → WAY *noun* 1

grapple [T] (*especially written*) to try hard to deal with a difficult problem or situation: *The new government has yet to grapple with the problem of air pollution.* ◇ *I was grappling to find an answer to his question.*

> **NOTE** **TACKLE** OR **GRAPPLE**? **Grapple** suggests that sb is having a lot of trouble solving a problem; **tackle** suggests that sb is approaching the problem with a lot of energy and determination and is more likely to succeed.

get/come to 'grips with sth *idiom* to begin to understand and deal with sth difficult: *I'm slowly getting to grips with the language.* ◇ *They have so far failed to come to grips with the ecological problems.*

tact *noun*

---

tact · sensitivity · discretion · diplomacy

These are all words for skill in dealing with people in difficult situations without upsetting or offending them.

tact [U] (*approving*) the ability to deal with people in difficult situations without upsetting or offending them: *Settling the dispute required great tact and diplomacy.* ◇ *She is not exactly known for her tact.* ❶ Using **tact** often involves NOT saying particular things that you know will upset or offend a particular person (because, for example, of sth that has happened to them). Sb who introduces subjects that will embarrass or offend a particular person can be considered *tactless*.

▶ **tactful** *adj.*: *That wasn't a very tactful thing to say!* **OPP** **tactless** → INSENSITIVE

sensitivity [U] (*approving*) the ability to understand other people's feelings: *Sensitivity to the needs of children is the main requirement for the job.* ◇ *She pointed out with tact and sensitivity exactly where he had gone wrong.* See also **sensitive** → SENSITIVE 1

discretion /dɪ'skreʃn/ [U] (*especially written, approving*) care in what you say or do, in order to keep sth secret or to avoid causing embarrassment or difficulty for sb: *This is confidential, but I know that I can rely on your discretion.* **OPP** **indiscretion** → IMPROPER

▶ **discreet** *adj.*: *He was always very discreet about his love affairs.* ◇ *You ought to make a few discreet enquiries before you sign anything.* **OPP** **indiscreet** → IMPROPER

diplomacy /dɪ'pləʊməsi; *AmE* -'ploʊ-/ [U] (*rather formal, especially written*) skill in dealing with people in difficult situations without upsetting or offending them: *She handled the situation with her usual quiet diplomacy.*

▶ **diplomatic** /ˌdɪplə'mætɪk/ *adj.*: *a diplomatic answer*

> **NOTE** **TACT** OR **DIPLOMACY**? **Tact** is a natural quality that some people have and that they use in order to avoid upsetting other people. **Diplomacy** is more of a skill that can be learned through practice and used to get an advantage for yourself as well as to help other people.

tactic *noun* See also the entry for TRICK

---

tactic · device · ploy · manoeuvre

These are all words for a particular, often clever, method you use to get what you want, especially to gain an advantage in a situation.

tactic [C, usually pl.] the particular method that you use to achieve sth: *The manager discussed tactics with his team.* ◇ *Confrontation is not always the best tactic.* ◇ *This was just the latest in a series of delaying tactics.* ◇ *They were desperate enough to try shock tactics.* See also **strategy** → PLAN 1

device [C] (*rather formal*) a method of doing sth that produces a particular result or effect: *We use a range of devices for testing children's numerical ability.* ❶ A **device** can be a neat and useful method of doing sth, as here, but it can also be a dishonest plan or trick. See also **device** → TRICK

ploy [C] (*often disapproving*) a clever method that you use in order to get an advantage over sb else or to make them do sth, sometimes by deceiving sb: *a clever marketing ploy* ◇ *It was all a ploy to distract attention away from his real aims.* See also **scheme** → CONSPIRACY

manoeuvre (*BrE*) (*AmE* **maneuver**) /mə'nuːvə(r)/ [C, U] a skilful plan or action, sometimes involving deceiving people, that is used to give sb an advantage: *It can be seen as a tactical manoeuvre to gain some time.* ◇ *The agreement was a result of weeks of diplomatic manoeuvre.* See also **manoeuvre** → MANIPULATE *verb*

take verb

1 take your things with you
2 take sb home
3 take your books off the table
4 I passed him the rope and he took it.
5 take a job/bribes/sb's advice
6 take an opportunity
7 take the blame
8 He took the painting for a genuine Van Gogh.
9 take drugs

---

1 See also the entry for GET 3
take · bring · deliver · ship · carry · transport · fly · ferry · leave
These words all mean to move sth from one place to another.

PATTERNS AND COLLOCATIONS
▶ to take/bring/deliver/ship/carry/transport/fly/ferry sb/sth **to/from** sb/sth
▶ to take/bring/ship/carry/transport/fly/ferry sb/sth **back/home**
▶ to take/bring sb/sth **with** you
▶ to take/bring/deliver/carry/transport/ferry sb/sth **by car/rail/truck**, etc.
▶ to take/bring/deliver/transport sb/sth **by air/sea/land**

take [T] to move or carry sth with you from one place to another: *Take this to the bank for me, would you?* ◇ *My things had already been taken to my room.* ◇ *Think about what you need to take for the trip.* ◇ *All she had taken was her passport and driving licence.* ◇ *Should I take him a gift?* ❶ You can also **take** a person somewhere. See also the entry for TAKE 2

bring [T] to have or carry sb/sth with you when you come to a place: *Remember to bring your books with you.* ◇ *The ferries brought tourists in their hundreds.* ◇ *I've brought something to show you.* ◇ *Bring a present for Helen.* ◇ *Bring Helen a present.*

> **NOTE** TAKE OR BRING? **Take** is used from the point of view of the person who is going somewhere with sth; **bring** is used from the point of view of sb who is already in the place the person is going to.

deliver [T, I] to take goods, letters, etc. to the person or people they have been sent to; to take sb somewhere: *Leaflets have been delivered to every household.* ◇ *to have groceries/flowers/packages delivered* ◇ *She delivered the kids on time at their father's house.* ◇ *We promise to deliver within 24 hours.* See also **delivery** → DELIVERY

ship (**-pp-**) [T] to send sb/sth by ship or by another means of transport: *The company ships its goods all over the world.* ◇ *He was arrested and shipped back to the UK for trial.* See also **shipment**, **shipping** → DELIVERY, **shipment** → LOT

carry [T] (often used in the progressive tenses) to take sb/sth from one place to another, especially in a vehicle: *The boat can carry up to five people.* ◇ *The truck was carrying illegal drugs worth up to $2 million.*

transport [T, often passive] to take sb/sth from one place to another in a vehicle: *Too many goods are currently being transported by road.* ◇ *The animals are transported in trucks, often without being fed or watered for days.* See also **transport** → DELIVERY *noun*

> **NOTE** CARRY OR TRANSPORT? **Carry** is used especially to talk about people; **transport** is used especially to talk about goods. When **transport** is used to talk about people or animals, it can suggest that they are being treated like goods.

fly [T] (always used with an adverb or preposition) to transport goods or passengers in a plane: *The stranded tourists were finally flown home.* ◇ *He had flowers specially flown in for the ceremony.*

ferry [T] (usually used with an adverb or preposition) to take people or goods from one place to another in a boat or other vehicle, especially for a short distance or as a regular service: *He offered to ferry us across the river in his boat.* ◇ *You really don't have to ferry us around while we're in town.*

leave [T] to deliver sth and then go away: *Someone left this note for you.* ◇ *Someone left you this note.* ❶ Common collocates of **leave** in this meaning are *letter, note, card,* etc., *parcel, package,* etc. and *present/gift.*

---

2 See also the entry for ACCOMPANY
take · lead · escort · drive · show · walk · guide · usher · direct
These words all mean to go with sb from one place to another.

PATTERNS AND COLLOCATIONS
▶ to take/lead/escort/drive/show/walk/guide/usher/direct sb **to/out of/into** sth
▶ to take/lead/escort/drive/walk/guide/usher/direct sb **there/somewhere**
▶ to take/lead/escort/drive/show/walk/guide sb **around/round**
▶ to take/lead/escort/drive/walk sb **home**
▶ to take/lead/escort/show/guide/usher sb **in/out**
▶ to take/lead/escort/guide sb **to safety**
▶ to lead/show **the way**

take [T] to go with sb from one place to another, for example in order to show them sth or to show them the way to a place: *It's too far to walk — I'll take you by car.* ◇ *The boy took us to our rooms.* ◇ *I asked them if they'd take me with them.* ◇ *I'm taking the kids swimming later.*

lead [T, I] to go with or go in front of sb in order to show them the way or to make them go in the right direction: *She led the horse back into the stable.* ◇ *Firefighters led the survivors to safety.* ◇ *If you lead, I'll follow.* **OPP follow** → FOLLOW 1

escort /ɪˈskɔːt; *AmE* ɪˈskɔːrt/ [T] to go with sb in order to protect or guard them or to show them the way: *The president arrived, escorted by twelve guards.* ◇ *The prisoners were escorted back to their cells.*

drive [T] to take sb somewhere in a car, taxi, etc: *My mother drove us to the airport.*

show [T] to take sb to a particular place, in the right direction, or along the correct route: *They'll need someone to show them the way.* ◇ *'There's a Mr Smith here to see you.' 'Show him in.'* See also **show** → POINT *verb*

walk [T] to go somewhere with sb on foot, especially in order to make sure that they get there safely; to take an animal, especially a dog, for a walk or make an animal walk somewhere: *He always walked her home.* ◇ *She walks the dog every day at about two o'clock.* ◇ *He walked the pony up and down the yard.*

guide [T] to show sb the way to a place, often by going with them; to show sb a place that you know well: *She guided us through the busy streets.* ◇ *We were guided around the museums.*

usher /ˈʌʃə(r)/ [T] (*rather formal, especially written*) to politely lead or show sb where they should go, especially within a building: *The secretary ushered me into her office.* ◇ *She ushered her guests to their seats.*

direct [T] (*rather formal*) to tell or show sb how to get somewhere or where to go: *A young woman directed them to the station.* ◇ *A police officer was directing the traffic.* ◇ *He was directed to a table beside the window.* See also **direction** → WAY 3

---

3 **take · remove · strip**
These words all mean to get sb/sth and move them away from a place or thing

PATTERNS AND COLLOCATIONS
▶ to take/remove/strip sb/sth **from** sb/sth
▶ to **simply/easily/quickly/carefully/forcibly/wrongfully/unlawfully/illegally** take/remove sth

take [T] (always used with an adverb or preposition) to get sb/sth and move them away from a place: *The sign must be taken down.* ◊ *He took some keys out of his pocket.* ◊ *My name had been taken off the list.*

remove [T] (*rather formal, especially written*) to take sb/sth away from a place: *He removed his hand from her shoulder.* ◊ *Illegally parked vehicles will be removed.* ◊ *Remove the pan from the heat and continue to stir the sauce.*

strip (-**pp**-) [T] to remove a layer from sth, especially so that it is completely bare: ***Strip off** all the existing paint.* ◊ *Deer had **stripped** the tree **of** its bark.* ◊ *After the guests had gone, I stripped all the beds* (= removed all the sheets in order to wash them).

---

4 take · grab · snatch · catch · seize

These words all mean to take or hold sb/sth with your hand suddenly, firmly or roughly.

PATTERNS AND COLLOCATIONS
▸ to take/ grab/ snatch/ seize sth **from** sb
▸ to grab/ snatch **at** sth
▸ to take/ grab/ catch/ seize **hold of** sb/ sth
▸ to take/ grab/ snatch/ catch/ seize sth **suddenly/ quickly**
▸ to take/ grab/ catch/ seize sth **immediately**

take [T] to put your hands or arms on or around sb/sth and hold them/it; to reach for sb/sth and hold them/it: *I passed him the rope and he took it.* ◊ *Free newspapers: please take one.* ◊ *Can you take* (= hold) *the baby for a moment?* ◊ *He took her hand/took her by the hand* (= held her hand, for example to lead her somewhere).

grab (-**bb**-) [T, I] to get your hands on and hold or pull sb/sth suddenly, firmly or roughly: *She grabbed the child's hand and ran.* ◊ *He grabbed hold of me and wouldn't let go.* ◊ *Someone grabbed me from behind.* ◊ *Don't grab — there's plenty for everyone.* ◊ *She grabbed at* (= tried to grab) *the branch, missed and fell.*

snatch [T, I] (usually used with an adverb or preposition) to take sth, usually from sb else, quickly and often rudely or roughly: *She managed to snatch the gun from his hand.* ◊ *He snatched at* (= tried to take hold of) *the steering wheel.*

> **NOTE** GRAB OR SNATCH? **Snatch** is most often used when sb takes sth directly from a person's hands; **grab** has a wider range of uses.

catch [T] to stop and hold a moving object, especially in your hands; to take hold of sb/sth: *She managed to catch the keys as they fell.* ◊ *'Throw me over that towel, will you?' 'OK. Catch!'* ◊ *The dog caught the stick in its mouth.* ◊ *He caught hold of her arm as she tried to push past him.* ❶ You can **catch** sth that is falling, or sth that has been thrown. Unlike with the other words in this group, you cannot 'catch sth from sb': *I threw the bag in the air and she caught it.* ◊ *She caught the bag from me and ran away.*

seize /siːz/ [T] (*rather formal, especially written*) to take sb/sth in your hand suddenly and using force: *She tried to seize the gun from him.* ◊ *He seized her by the arm.* ◊ *She seized hold of my hand.*

---

5 take · accept · take sb/sth on · take sth up

These words all mean to say 'yes' to an offer, invitation or request.

PATTERNS AND COLLOCATIONS
▸ to take/ accept/ take on a **job/ post/ position/ role/ responsibility**
▸ to take/ accept/ take on **new clients**
▸ to take/ accept/ take up an **offer**
▸ to accept/ take up a/ an **invitation/ suggestion**
▸ to take/ accept/ take on/ take up a **challenge**
▸ to take/ accept sth **gratefully/ reluctantly**
▸ to accept/ take sth on **gladly**

take [T] to say 'yes' to an offer or request; to agree to receive sth: *If they offer me the job, I'll take it.* ◊ *Does the hotel take credit cards?* ◊ *I'll take the call in my office.* ◊ *If you take my advice you'll have nothing more to do with him.* ◊ *Will you take $10 for the book* (= will you sell it for $10)? ◊ *The store took* (= sold goods worth)*$100 000 last week.* ❶ In this meaning, **take** is often used in business contexts: *take a job* ◊ *take a cheque/credit card/£50 note* ◊ *take a particular amount of money for sth*

accept [I, T] (*rather formal*) to say 'yes' to an offer, request or invitation; to take willingly sth that is offered: *He asked me to marry him and I accepted.* ◊ *Please accept our sincere apologies.* ◊ *She's decided not to accept the job.* ◊ *She said she'd accept $15 for it.* **OPP** **refuse, decline** → REFUSE
▸ **acceptance** /ək'septəns/ *noun* [U, C]: *Please confirm your acceptance of this offer in writing.* ◊ *So far we have had one refusal and three acceptances.*

take sb/sth 'on *phrasal verb* to decide to do sth; to agree to be responsible for sb/sth: *I can't take on any extra work.* ◊ *We're not taking on any new clients at present.* ❶ People typically **take on** *work, chores, tasks* or a particular *job, position, role, responsibility* or *challenge.* Companies may take on more *staff* or *clients.*

take sth 'up, take sb 'up on sth *phrasal verb* to say 'yes' to an offer or invitation: *He urged us to take up the challenge.* ◊ *She took him up on his offer of a drink.* ❶ **Take sth up** is most often used with *invitation, offer* or *challenge.* **OPP** **turn sb/sth down** → REFUSE

---

6 take · seize · seize on/upon sth · grab · jump at sth

These words all mean to be quick to make use of an opportunity to do or have sth.

PATTERNS AND COLLOCATIONS
▸ to take/ seize/ seize on/ grab/ jump at a/ an **chance/ opportunity**
▸ to take/ seize/ seize on/ grab the **initiative**
▸ to seize/ jump at an **idea**
▸ to take/ seize on sth **immediately/ eagerly**
▸ to seize/ grab sth **with both hands**

take [T] to make use of an opportunity to do or have sth: *Take the initiative and fill your life with exciting experiences.* ◊ *England failed to take their chances and had to settle for a draw.*

seize /siːz/ [T] (*especially journalism*) to be quick to make use of an opportunity to do or have sth: *The party seized the initiative with both hands* (= quickly and with enthusiasm).

> **NOTE** TAKE OR SEIZE? In this meaning both these words only collocate with *opportunity, chance* and *initiative.* **Seize** suggests greater eagerness than **take**. *Take a chance* has two possible meanings: it can mean 'take a risk' as well as 'take an opportunity'; *seize a chance* only means 'take an opportunity'.

seize on/upon sth *phrasal verb* to suddenly show a lot of interest in sth, especially because you can use it to your advantage: *Peter seized on her last comment.* ◊ *The rumours were eagerly seized upon by the local press.* ❶ People might **seize on/upon** anything that sb does or says if they want to criticize them or publish details of it.

grab (-**bb**-) [T, I] (*rather informal*) to be quick to make use of an opportunity to do or have sth: *This was my big chance and I grabbed it with both hands.* ◊ *He'll grab at any excuse to avoid hard work.*

jump at sth *phrasal verb* (*rather informal*) to enthusiastically accept an opportunity or offer: *I jumped at the chance of a new job.*

---

7 take · assume · carry · bear · accept · shoulder

These words all mean to begin to have responsibility for sth.

PATTERNS AND COLLOCATIONS
▸ to take/ assume/ carry/ bear/ accept/ shoulder sth **for** sb/ sth
▸ to take/ assume/ carry/ bear/ accept/ shoulder the **responsibility**

▶ to take / carry / bear / accept / shoulder the **blame**
▶ to take / bear / accept the **consequences**
▶ to assume / carry / bear / accept / shoulder the **burden**
▶ to carry / bear / accept / shoulder the **cost**
▶ to take / assume / accept sth **willingly / reluctantly**

take [T] to begin to have power or responsibility for sth; to suffer the results of sth, especially sth you have done wrong: *A military junta took control of the country.* ◇ *Why should I take the blame for somebody else's mistakes?* ❶ In this meaning **take** collocates with *responsibility, control, blame, brunt* and *consequences.*

assume /ə'sjuːm; AmE ə'suːm/ [T] (*formal*) to take or begin to have power or responsibility: *The court assumed responsibility for the girl's welfare.* ◇ *A military junta assumed power in 1988.*

carry [T] to take responsibility for sth; to suffer the results of sth bad, even when this is not your fault: *He is carrying the whole department (= it is only working because of his efforts).* ◇ *Their group was targeted to carry the burden of job losses.*

bear [T] (*rather formal, written*) to take responsibility for getting sth done; to suffer the results of sth bad, even when this is not your fault: *Do parents have to bear the whole cost of tuition fees?* ◇ *Schools will bear the brunt of cuts in government spending.* ❶ To **bear/take the brunt of sth** means to receive the main force of sth unpleasant.

accept [T] to admit that you are responsible or to blame for sth bad that has happened: *The company cannot accept liability for any damage caused by natural disasters.*

shoulder [T] to accept the responsibility for sth, especially for getting a job done or improving a bad situation: *These women shoulder the double burden of childcare and full-time work.*

8 take · mistake sb/sth for sb/sth · confuse · mix sb/sth up
These words all mean to think that sb/sth is sb/sth else.

PATTERNS AND COLLOCATIONS
▶ to take / mistake sb / sth **for** sb / sth
▶ to confuse sb / sth / mix sb / sth up **with** sb / sth
▶ to be **easily** mistaken for / confused with sb / sth

take [T] (not used in the progressive tenses) to consider sb/sth to be sb/sth, especially when you are wrong: *Even the experts took the painting to be a genuine Van Gogh.* ◇ *I mistakenly took her for the Senator's wife.* ◇ *He's not the fool you take him for.* ◇ (*spoken*) *Of course I didn't do it! What do you take me for (= what kind of person do you think I am)?*

mi'stake sb/sth for sb/sth *phrasal verb* to think wrongly that sb/sth is sb/sth else: *I think you must be mistaking me for someone else.* ◇ *She was annoyed when I mistook her for a waitress.*

confuse [T] to think wrongly that sb/sth is sb/sth else: *People often confuse me and my twin sister.* ◇ *Be careful not to confuse quantity with quality.* ◇ *The Tasmanian wolf is not to be confused with the dingo.*

mix sb/sth 'up *phrasal verb* (*rather informal, especially spoken*) to confuse sb/sth with sb/sth else: *She always gets her left and right mixed up.*

9 See the Topic Map for HEALTH on p.890
take · use · do
These words all mean to put drugs or medicine into your body.

PATTERNS AND COLLOCATIONS
▶ to take / use / do **drugs**
▶ to take / use **heroin**

take [T] to put medicine or drugs in your body: *The doctor has given me some medicine to take for my cough.* ◇ *He started taking drugs (= illegal drugs) at college.*

use [T, I] to take illegal drugs: *Most of the inmates here have used drugs at some point in their lives.* ◇ (*slang*) *She's been using since she was 13.*

do [T] (*informal*) to take illegal drugs: *He doesn't smoke, drink or do drugs.*

take advantage of sb/sth *verb*

take advantage of sb/sth · inconvenience · impose · put sb out
These words all mean to treat sb in a way that does not consider their needs or wishes, especially causing them trouble or extra work.

inconvenience   take advantage of sb/sth
impose
put sb out

PATTERNS AND COLLOCATIONS
▶ **I don't want to** inconvenience you / impose on you / put you out.

take ad'vantage of sb/sth *idiom* to make use of sb/sth in a way that is unfair or dishonest: *He took advantage of my generosity (= for example, by taking more than I had intended to give).* ◇ *You mustn't let them take advantage of you.*

inconvenience /ˌɪnkən'viːniəns/ [T] (*rather formal*) to cause trouble or difficulty for sb: *I hope that we haven't inconvenienced you.* See also **inconvenience → NUISANCE** *noun*

impose /ɪm'pəʊz; AmE ɪm'poʊz/ [I] to expect sb to do sth for you or spend time with you, when it may be inconvenient for them: *I feel imposed upon when I have to take work home.* ◇ *No, I won't come in – I don't want to impose.*

,put sb 'out *phrasal verb* (*rather informal*) to cause trouble or extra work for sb: *I hope our arriving late didn't put them out.*

take care of yourself *verb*

take care of yourself · look after yourself · fend for yourself · stand on your own (two) feet
These words all mean to be responsible for yourself, for your own care or safety, especially without help from anyone else.

PATTERNS AND COLLOCATIONS
▶ to **be able to** take care of yourself / look after yourself / fend for yourself / stand on your own feet
▶ to **be capable of** taking care of yourself / looking after yourself / fending for yourself
▶ to **learn to** fend for yourself / stand on your own feet

take care of yourself *phrase* to be responsible for yourself, your own care, safety, health and appearance: *He's old enough to take care of himself.* ◇ *You should take better care of yourself.* See also **take care of sb → LOOK AFTER SB**

,look 'after yourself *phrasal verb* (*especially BrE*) to be responsible for yourself, your own care, safety and health: *Don't worry about me – I can look after myself (= I don't need any help).* See also **look after sb → LOOK AFTER SB**

,fend for your'self *phrasal verb* to be responsible for yourself without help from anyone else, especially finding food and solving other practical problems: *His parents agreed to pay his rent but otherwise left him to fend for himself.* ◇ *The pups have been weaned and are now learning to fend for themselves.*

NOTE TAKE CARE OF YOURSELF, LOOK AFTER YOURSELF OR FEND FOR YOURSELF? **Take care of yourself** and **look after yourself** are often used in a similar way to talk about sb who is responsible for their own care, health and safety especially without help from anyone else.

Both are used as a way of expressing concern, especially for sb's health: *Take good care of yourself.* ◇ *You look after yourself and make sure you eat properly.* **Take care of yourself** can also be used to describe sb who takes care of their appearance and tries to look as young and attractive as possible: *It is natural for a woman to take good care of herself.* **Fend for yourself** is used to talk about dealing with more practical situations, such as finding food, money or shelter and is used about animals as well as people. It is often used to describe a person or animal that has to cope alone in a difficult situation or environment.

stand on your own (two) 'feet *idiom* to be independent and able to be responsible for yourself, especially financially: *When his parents died he had to learn to stand on his own two feet.*

take over, take sth over *phrasal verb*

take (sth) over · dominate · monopolize · reign · hog · corner
These words all mean to have or take control of sth, especially replacing sb/sth else or preventing sb/sth else from sharing it.

PATTERNS AND COLLOCATIONS
▶ to take over / dominate / monopolize / corner the **market**
▶ to take over / dominate / monopolize an **industry**
▶ to take over / dominate / monopolize the **conversation**
▶ a **company** takes over / dominates / monopolizes / corners a market, industry, etc.

,take 'over, ,take sth 'over *phrasal verb* to gain control of or responsibility for sth, especially in place of sb else; to gain control of a political party or country: *He took over as chairman last year.* ◇ *She took over the tenancy of the farm from her father.* ◇ *The army is threatening to take over if civil unrest continues.*
▶ **takeover** *noun* [C]: *a takeover bid for the company*
dominate /ˈdɒmɪneɪt; *AmE* ˈdɑːm-/ [T, I] (*often disapproving*) to control sb/sth or be the most important person, group or thing in a particular situation or area, especially in an unpleasant way: *As a child he was dominated by his father.* ◇ *United completely dominated the first half of the game.* ◇ *She always says a lot in meetings, but she doesn't dominate.* See also **dominant** → POWERFUL
▶ **domination** *noun* [U]: *The country is still under foreign domination.* ◇ *The film is about a mad professor set on world domination.*
monopolize (*BrE also* -ise) /məˈnɒpəlaɪz; *AmE* məˈnɑːp-/ [T] (*often disapproving*) to have or take control of the largest part of sth, so that other people are prevented from sharing it; to have or take a large part of sb's attention or time: *Men traditionally monopolized jobs in the printing industry.* ◇ *As usual, she completely monopolized the conversation.* ◇ *Don't let him monopolize you like he did at the last party.*
reign /reɪn/ [I] to be the best or most important person, group or thing in a particular situation or area of skill: *A handful of families have reigned over Bangkok's economy for many years.* ◇ *In the field of classical music, he still reigns supreme.* ◇ *She will face the reigning champion in her first round match.*
hog (-gg-) [T] (*rather informal, disapproving*) to use or keep most of sth yourself and prevent others from using or having it: *She preferred to keep in the background rather than hogging the limelight* (= trying to get lots of public attention). ◇ *Helen's always hogging the bathroom* (= spends a long time in it so that others cannot use it).
corner [T] to gain control of the trade in a particular type of goods or services: *The firm has cornered the UK computer market.* ◇ *They've cornered the market in silver.*
❶ **Market** is by far the most frequent collocate of **corner** in this meaning.

take sth off *phrasal verb*

take sth off · strip · remove · undress · get undressed
These words all mean to get clothes off your/sb's body.

PATTERNS AND COLLOCATIONS
▶ to take off / strip off / remove your **clothes / jacket / coat / shirt / sweater / jeans / gloves**
▶ to **quickly** take sth off / strip off / remove sth / undress / get undressed

,take sth 'off *phrasal verb* to get clothes, etc. off your/sb's body: *Please, take off your coat.* ◇ *He took off my wet boots and made me sit by the fire.* OPP **put sth on** → WEAR
strip (-pp-) [I, T] to take off all or most of your clothes: *I stripped and washed myself all over.* ◇ *We stripped off and ran down to the water.* ◇ *She stripped down to her underwear.* ◇ *He stood there stripped to the waist* (= the upper part of his body was bare). ◇ *He was stripped naked and left in a cell.*
remove [T] (*rather formal, written*) to take off clothes, etc. from your/sb's body: *She removed her glasses and rubbed her eyes.* ❶ **Remove** is usually used to talk about taking off things such as a *hat*, a *scarf*, *shoes*, *boots*, *glasses*, a *coat* or a *jacket*, rather than clothes that you wear next to your skin.
undress /ʌnˈdres/ [I, T] to take off all your clothes; to remove sb else's clothes: *She undressed and got into bed.* ◇ *to undress a child/doll* OPP **dress** → WEAR
get undressed *phrase* to take off all your clothes: *He got undressed and fell into bed.* OPP **get dressed** → WEAR

NOTE **STRIP, UNDRESS** OR **GET UNDRESSED**? People **strip** because they want to wash, because they will be more comfortable with fewer clothes on, or because sb has ordered them to (for example, in order to search them for weapons or drugs); when people are getting ready to go to bed they usually **undress** or **get undressed**. To **strip** is a quicker and less gentle action: a guard might order a prisoner to **strip**; a doctor would ask a patient to **undress** or **take off** their clothes.

take your time *verb*

take your time · stall · drag your feet · dawdle · buy time · procrastinate · delay
These words all mean to be deliberately slow in doing sth or making a decision.

PATTERNS AND COLLOCATIONS
▶ take your time / stall **over** sth

take your' time *idiom* to use as much time as you need without hurrying: *There's no rush — take your time.* ❶ **Take your time** is often used in an ironic way to say that you think sb is late or too slow in doing sth: *You certainly took your time getting here.*
stall [I] (*rather formal*) to avoid making a decision or giving a definite answer, in order to gain time: *They are still stalling on the deal.* ◇ *'What do you mean?' she asked, stalling for time.*
drag your 'feet *idiom* (-gg-) (*rather informal*) to be deliberately slow in doing sth or in making a decision: *They've been dragging their feet on settling the claim.*
dawdle [I] to take a long time to do sth or go somewhere, especially by walking slowly: *Stop dawdling! We're going to be late!* ◇ *They dawdled along by the river, laughing and talking.*
buy 'time *idiom* to do sth in order to delay an event or decision: *The negotiators kept the gunman talking to buy time for the hostages.* ❶ **Buying time** is often seen as a clever thing to do, rather than sth that is disapproved of.
procrastinate /prəˈkræstɪneɪt; *AmE* proʊ-/ (*disapproving*) to leave sth that you should do until a later time, usually because you do not want to do it: *People were dying of starvation while governments procrastinated.*

ℹ **Procrastinating** usually involves finding other, often unimportant, things to do, in order to avoid what you really should be doing.

delay [I] (often used in negative sentences) to not do sth until a later time: *Don't delay — call us today!* ◇ *We can't delay much longer.* See also **delay** → DELAY, **delay** → HOLD SB/STH UP

▸ **delay** *noun* [U]: *There's no time for delay.* ◇ *Report it to the police **without delay** (= immediately).*

talk *verb* See the Topic Map for FACT AND OPINION on p.898, See also the entry for CHAT

talk · discuss · speak · communicate · debate · consult · confer
These words all mean to share news, information, ideas or feelings with another person or other people, especially by talking with them.

PATTERNS AND COLLOCATIONS
▸ to talk/ discuss sth/ speak/ communicate/ debate/ consult/ confer **with** sb
▸ to talk/ speak **to** sb
▸ to talk/ speak to sb/ consult sb/ confer **about** sth
▸ to consult sb/ confer **on** sth
▸ to talk/ speak **of** sth
▸ to discuss/ debate **what/ how/ whether/ when/ who**...
▸ to talk/ discuss sth/ speak/ communicate/ debate sth **openly**
▸ to talk/ discuss sth/ speak/ debate sth **at length**
▸ to talk/ discuss sth/ speak/ confer **briefly**

talk [I] to speak in order to give information, express feelings or share ideas: *We talked on the phone for over an hour.* ◇ *Who were you talking to just now?* ◇ *When they get together, all they talk about is football.* ◇ *Mary is talking of looking for another job.* ℹ When **talk** is used meaning 'to share ideas' about sth, this is often sth serious or important: *This situation can't go on. We need to talk.* ◇ *Talk to your doctor if you're still worried.* In this meaning it can also be used with an object: [T] *They spent the whole evening talking business (= talking about business).* See also **talk** → DISCUSSION *noun*, **talk** → SAY *verb* 1, **talk** → SAY *verb* 2

discuss [T] (*rather formal*) to talk and share ideas on a subject or problem with other people, especially in order to decide sth: *Have you discussed the problem with anyone?* ◇ *I'm not prepared to discuss this on the phone.* ◇ *They briefly discussed buying a new car.* ℹ You cannot say 'discuss about sth': ~~I'm not prepared to discuss about this on the phone.~~ See also **discussion** → DISCUSSION

speak [I] to talk to sb about sth; to have a conversation with sb: *We spoke briefly on the phone.* ◇ *I've spoken to the manager about it.* ◇ (*especially AmE*) *Can I speak with you for a minute?* ◇ *'Can I speak to Susan?' 'Speaking.'* (= at the beginning of a telephone conversation) See also **speak** → SAY 1

NOTE **TALK** OR **SPEAK**? **Speak** can suggest a more formal level of communication than **talk**. You **talk** to sb in order to be friendly or to ask their advice. You **speak** to sb about sth to try to achieve a particular goal or to tell them to do sth: *'What were you two talking about?' 'Oh, this and that.'* ◇ *Have you talked to your parents about the problems you're having?* ◇ *I've spoken to Ed about it and he's promised not to let it happen again.*

communicate [I, T] (*rather formal*) to exchange information or ideas with sb: *We only communicate by email.* ◇ *Dolphins use sound to communicate with each other.* ◇ (*formal*) *Nobody had communicated the information to us.* ℹ **Communicate** is often used when the speaker wants to draw attention to the means of communication used. *Communicate sth to sb* is a formal way of saying *tell sb sth*. See also **communication** → COMMUNICATION, **communication** → LETTER

debate [T] to discuss sth, especially formally, before making a decision or finding a solution: *Politicians will be debating the bill later this week.* ◇ *The question of the*

origin of the universe is still **hotly debated** (= strongly argued about) *by scientists.* See also **debate** → DISCUSSION *noun*

consult [T, I] (*rather formal*) to discuss sth with sb in order to get their permission for sth, or to help you make a decision: *You shouldn't have done it without consulting me.* ◇ *I need to consult with my colleagues on the proposals.* ℹ When you **consult** sb, you ask their permission for sth. **Consult with** sb is a more formal way of saying **discuss** sth with sb. See also **consultation** → DISCUSSION *noun*

confer /kənˈfɜː(r)/ (-rr-) [I] (*rather formal*) to discuss sth with sb, especially in order to exchange opinions or get advice: *He wanted to confer with his colleagues before reaching a decision.*

talkative *adj.*

talkative · forthcoming · chatty
These words all describe people talking a lot.

PATTERNS AND COLLOCATIONS
▸ to be **in a** talkative/ chatty **mood**
▸ **very** talkative/ forthcoming/ chatty

talkative /ˈtɔːkətɪv/ tending to talk a lot: *He's not very talkative, except on the subject of his plants.* ◇ *She was in a talkative mood.*

forthcoming /ˌfɔːθˈkʌmɪŋ; AmE ˌfɔːrθ-/ [not before noun] (often used in negative sentences) (of a person) willing to give information about sth: *She's never very forthcoming about her plans.* **OPP** **reticent** → QUIET 3

chatty (*especially BrE, informal*) (of a person) talking a lot in a friendly way; (of writing) having a friendly informal style: *You're very chatty today, Alex.* ◇ *She received a long chatty letter from Ellen.*

tall *adj.*

tall · lanky · leggy · willowy
These words all describe a person who has a greater than average height or long legs.

PATTERNS AND COLLOCATIONS
▸ a tall/ lanky **man/ teenager/ youth/ figure**
▸ a tall/ leggy **woman**

tall (of a person) having a greater than average height: *She's tall and thin with light brown hair.* ◇ *He is quite tall for his age.* **OPP** **short** → SHORT 2

lanky (*often disapproving*) having long thin legs and arms and moving in an awkward way: *He was thin, lanky and pale-skinned.*

leggy (*informal, usually approving but sometimes offensive*) (especially of girls and women) having long legs; tall and sexually attractive: *She was a leggy redhead with a terrific figure.* ℹ Although **leggy** is often used in an approving way by men to describe women, some women might find it offensive because it describes them purely in terms of their sexual attractiveness.

willowy /ˈwɪləʊi; AmE ˈwɪloʊi/ (*approving*) (especially of women) tall, thin and graceful: *Dark and willowy, she has the natural grace of a ballerina.* ℹ **Willowy** is often a nicer way to describe a woman than **leggy**, because it suggests simple admiration, not sexual attraction.

target *noun* See also the entry for PURPOSE

target · objective · goal · object · end
These are all words for sth that you are trying to achieve.

PATTERNS AND COLLOCATIONS
▸ targets/ objectives/ goals **for** sth
▸ to work **towards** a target/ an objective/ a goal
▸ a **worthwhile** target/ objective/ goal/ object/ end
▸ the **main/ primary/ prime/ principal** target/ objective/ goal/ object
▸ the **ultimate** target/ objective/ goal/ object/ end
▸ a **common** target/ objective/ goal/ end

▸ a / an **ambitious** / **major** / **long-term** / **short-term** / **future** target / objective / goal
▸ **economic** / **financial** / **business** targets / objectives / goals
▸ to **define** a target / an objective / a goal / an object
▸ to **set** / **agree on** / **identify** / **reach** / **meet** / **exceed** a target / an objective / a goal
▸ to **achieve** a target / an objective / a goal / an end
▸ to **promote** / **pursue** / **accomplish** / **attain** an objective / a goal / an end

target [C] a result that you try to achieve: *Set yourself targets that you can reasonably hope to achieve.* ◇ *We're aiming to meet a target date of April 2009.* ◇ *Write a plan that sets out your business **goals and targets**.* ◇ *The new sports complex is **on target** to open in June.* ◇ *Our **target audience** (= the particular audience that the programme is aimed at) is men aged between 18 and 35.* ◇ *What's the **target market** for this product?*

objective [C] (*rather formal*) something that you are trying to achieve: *What is the main objective of this project?* ◇ *You must set realistic **aims and objectives** for yourself.*

goal [C] something that you hope to achieve: *He continued to pursue his goal of becoming a photographer.* ◇ *Their goal was to eradicate malaria.*

> **NOTE** TARGET, OBJECTIVE OR GOAL? A **target** is usually officially recorded in some way, for example by an employer or by a government committee. It is often specific, and in the form of figures, such as a number of sales or exam passes, or a date. People often set their own **objectives**: these are things that they wish to achieve, often as part of a project or a talk they are giving. **Goals** are often long-term, and relate to people's life and career plans or the long-term plans of a company or organization.

object [C] (*rather formal*) the purpose of sth; sth that you plan to achieve: *The object is to educate people about road safety.* ◇ *The whole **object of the exercise** is to get people to listen to each other.*

end [C] (*formal*) something that you plan to achieve: *She is exploiting the current situation for her own ends.* ◇ *He joined the society for political ends.* ◇ *With this end in view (= in order to achieve this) they employed 50 new sales reps.* ◇ *We are willing to make any concessions necessary **to this end** (= in order to achieve this).* ◇ *That's only OK if you believe that **the end justifies the means** (= bad methods of doing sth are acceptable if the final result is good).* ❶ **End** is usually used in the plural or in particular fixed expressions.

task noun See also the entry for ASSIGNMENT

task · work · duty · mission · job · business · housework · chore · errand · commission
These are all words for a piece of work that sb has to do.

PATTERNS AND COLLOCATIONS
▸ (a) **routine** task / work / duties / mission / job / business / chore
▸ (a) **daily** / **day-to-day** task / work / duties / job / business / chore
▸ (a / an) **easy** / **difficult** task / work / mission / job
▸ (a) **challenging** task / work / job
▸ (a) **dangerous** task / work / mission / job
▸ (a) **household** / **domestic** task / work / duties / job / chore
▸ to **do** a task / your work / a job / business / the housework / a chore / an errand
▸ to **have** a task / work / job / the housework / a chore / an errand **to do**
▸ to **get** the task / work / job / housework / chores **done**
▸ to **get on with** a task / your work / a job / the housework / a chore
▸ to **carry out** a task / the work / your duties / a mission / a job / a commission
▸ to **finish** a task / the work / a mission / a job / your business / the housework / the chores
▸ to **take on** / **undertake** a task / the work / your duties / a mission / a job
▸ to **tackle** / **approach** a task / the work / a job

▸ to **give sb** a task / some work / their duties / a mission / a job / a chore / a commission
▸ to **set (sb)** a task / their duties
▸ to **accept** a task / a mission / a commission
▸ to **be on** a mission / a job / business / an errand

task [C] a piece of work that sb has to do, especially a difficult or unpleasant one: *Our first task will be to set up a communications system.* ◇ *She had the unenviable task of talking to the missing girl's parents.* ◇ *The task eventually fell to me (= I had to do it).* ◇ *Getting hold of the information was **no easy task** (= it was difficult).*

work [U] the tasks and activities that are part of your job; tasks that need to be done: *Police work is mainly routine.* ◇ *I have some work for you to do.* ◇ *Stop talking and get on with your work.*

duty [U] (also **duties** [pl.]) the work that is your job; tasks that are part of your job: ***Report for duty** at 8 a.m.* ◇ *He was accused of neglecting his professional duties.* ◇ *Your duties will include setting up a new computer system.* ◇ *The suspect was charged with obstructing an officer **in the course of his duties** (= while doing what his job requires).*

> **NOTE** WORK OR DUTIES? Both these words refer to things that you do as part of your job, but **work** has a wider meaning than **duties**. Your **duties** are the list of tasks that you have to do because they are your responsibility and that you can be criticized or punished for not doing. Your **work** is all the activities that you do in the course of doing your job, and these activities may be seen as opportunities as much as responsibilities.

mission /ˈmɪʃn/ [C] an important official job that a person or group of people is given to do, especially when they are sent to another country: *a trade mission to China* ◇ *The mission ended in failure.* ◇ *They undertook a **fact-finding mission** in the region.*

job [C] a piece of work that sb has to do: *I've got various jobs around the house to do.* ◇ *Sorting these papers is going to be a long job.* ◇ *Bringing up kids is a full-time job.* ◇ *He spends his time doing **odd jobs** (= various jobs in the home).*

> **NOTE** TASK OR JOB? A **task** may be more difficult than a **job** and require you to think carefully about how you are going to do it. A **job** may be sth small that is one of several jobs that you have to do, especially in the home; or it can be sth that takes a long time and is boring and/or needs a lot of patience.

business [U] work that is part of your job, especially work that involves talking and doing deals with other people in business: *a business trip/lunch* ◇ *Is the trip to Rome **business or pleasure**?* ◇ *She's away **on business**.* **OPP** pleasure → ENTERTAINMENT, See also the entry for BUSINESS 2

housework /ˈhaʊswɜːk; AmE -wɜːrk/ [U] the work involved in taking care of a home and family, for example cleaning and cooking: *I spent all morning doing housework.*

chore [C] a task that you have to do regularly, especially one that you do in the home and find unpleasant or boring: *Of all the household chores, I hate ironing most.* ◇ *I find shopping a **real chore** (= a boring and unpleasant job).*

errand /ˈerənd/ [C] a job that you do for sb that involves going somewhere, for example in order to buy sth, deliver sth or take a message: *He often **runs errands** for his grandmother.*

commission /kəˈmɪʃn/ [C] a formal request to sb to do a piece of work for you, such as designing a building or doing a painting: *Who won the commission to design the new town hall?* ◇ *The work will be done **by commission** (= sb will be formally asked to do it).*

taste *noun*

1 a taste for foreign travel
2 a sweet taste

---

1 **taste · preference · love · passion · liking · weakness**
These are all words for the feeling of liking or preferring particular things or activities.

taste   love   passion
preference
liking
weakness

PATTERNS AND COLLOCATIONS
▶ a taste / preference / passion / liking / weakness **for** sth
▶ a **great** love / passion / liking for / of sth
▶ to **have** a taste / preference / love / passion / liking / weakness for / of sth
▶ to **develop** a taste / preference / love / passion / liking / weakness for / of sth
▶ to **share** a taste / preference / love / passion / liking for / of sth
▶ to **show** a preference / liking for sth
▶ sth is **to** sb's taste / liking
▶ **too** big, small, sweet, crowded, etc. **for** sb's taste / liking

taste [C, U] what a person likes or prefers: *That trip gave me a taste for foreign travel.* ◇ *She has a very expensive* **taste in** *clothes.* ◇ *Art is* **an acquired taste** *– no one is born knowing that Michelangelo is wonderful.* ◇ *The colour and style is a matter of personal taste.* ❶ *If you* have a taste *for sth, you like or enjoy it:* She has a real taste for adventure/designer clothes. *Your* taste in clothes, music, books, etc. *describes what type of clothes, music, etc. you prefer:* He has an unusual taste in music.

preference /'prefrəns/ [U, sing.] a greater interest in or desire for sb/sth than sb/sth else: *It's a matter of personal preference.* ◇ *Many people expressed a* **strong preference** *for the original plan.* ◇ *I can't say that I have any particular preference.* ◇ *Let's make a list of possible speakers,* **in order of preference***.*

NOTE TASTE OR PREFERENCE? A **preference** is always a choice between two or more things, places, people, etc.; **taste** does not include this idea of choice: *a taste for French bread* ◇ *a preference for brown bread* (= rather than white bread) See also **preference** → CHOICE 2, **prefer** → PREFER, **preferred** → FAVOURITE

love [U, sing.] (*approving*) the strong feeling of enjoyment that a thing or activity gives you: *I fell* **in love** *with the house.* ◇ *They share a love of classical music.* See also **love** → LIKE *verb*

passion [C] (*approving*) a very strong feeling of liking sth; a hobby, activity, etc. that you like very much: *The English have a passion for gardens.* ◇ *Music is a passion with him.* See also **passionate** → INTENSE, See also the entry for INTEREST 2

NOTE LOVE OR PASSION? **Passion** is stronger than **love**, and suggests that your interests may affect the way you live your life or the career you choose: *The royal family had a passion for art, it seems, for the palace was full of paintings and sculptures.* ◇ *He knew he was going to be a musician and eventually stopped attending high school. Music was the only thing he ever had a passion for.*

liking [sing.] the feeling that you like or enjoy sth: *The town was too crowded for my liking* (= I would prefer it less crowded). ◇ *Is the coffee to your liking, sir?* See also **like** → LIKE *verb*

weakness [C, usually sing.] difficulty in resisting sb/sth that you like very much, especially sth that is bad for you in some way: *He worries a lot about his weight, but can't overcome his weakness for fatty foods.*

---

2 **taste · flavour · tang**
These are all words for the quality that sth has which allows you to recognize it when you put it in your mouth.

PATTERNS AND COLLOCATIONS
▶ a **delicious / rich / spicy / bitter / sour / sweet** taste / flavour
▶ a **sharp / salty / distinctive** taste / flavour / tang
▶ to **have / give sth / add** taste / flavour
▶ to **enhance / spoil** the taste / flavour of sth

taste [C, U] the particular quality that different foods and drinks have that allows you to recognize them when you put them in your mouth: *The drink left a bitter taste in his mouth.* ◇ *The soup doesn't have much taste.* ◇ *Salt stimulates the* **taste buds** *on the tongue.*

flavour (*BrE*) (*AmE* **flavor**) [U, C] how food or drink tastes; a particular type of taste: *It is stronger in flavour than other traditional Dutch cheeses.* ◇ *This yogurt comes in ten different flavours.* ◇ *It is a wine with a delicate fruit flavour.*

NOTE TASTE OR FLAVOUR? In many cases you can use either word, especially when talking about how a meal tastes: *The tomatoes give extra taste/flavour to the sauce.* When talking about foods you can find in nature, it is more usual to use **taste**: *I don't like the taste of olives.* When talking about foods which have been designed by people to have a particular effect on the tongue, use **flavour**: *We have four different flavours of ice cream.*

tang [C, usually sing.] a strong sharp taste or smell: *The tea had a sharp, bitter tang.* ◇ *We could smell the salty tang of sea air from our bedroom window.*

tax *noun*

tax · duty · customs · tariff · rates
These are all words for money that you have to pay to the government.

PATTERNS AND COLLOCATIONS
▶ (a) tax / (a) duty / a tariff / rates **on** sth
▶ to pay an amount of money **in** tax / duty / customs / rates
▶ to **pay** tax / duty / customs / a tariff / rates
▶ to **collect** taxes / duties / rates
▶ to **increase / raise / reduce** taxes / duty / tariffs / rates
▶ to **cut** taxes / duties / rates
▶ to **impose** a tax / duty / a tariff
▶ to **levy** a tax / duty / rates
▶ to **put** a tax / duty **on** sth

tax [C, U] money that you have to pay to the government so that it can pay for public services: *The government had to raise taxes to pay for the war.* ◇ *The middle classes are demanding tax cuts.* ◇ *There's no tax on cigarettes in some countries.* ◇ *The business makes £750 000* **after tax***.* ❶ People pay tax according to their income and businesses pay tax according to their profits. Tax is also often paid on goods and services: *income/sales/road/property tax*
▶ **tax** *verb* [T]: *Any interest payments are taxed as part of your income.* ◇ *His declared aim was to tax the rich.*

duty [C, U] a tax that you pay on things that you buy, especially those that you bring into a country: *The company has to pay customs duties on all imports.* ◇ *Duty on wine and beer has been increased.* ❶ **Duty-free** goods are goods that you can bring into a country without paying tax on them: *duty-free cigarettes*

customs [pl.] tax that is paid when goods are brought in from other countries: *You must pay customs on all imports of alcohol.* ◇ *Imports from non-EU countries are subject to customs duty of 20 per cent.* ❶ **Customs** can also mean the government department that checks goods brought into a country and collects taxes on these goods; or the place at a port or airport where your bags are checked as you come into a country: *Customs have seized a large quantity of smuggled heroin.* ◇ *We had to go through customs before we could leave the airport.*

tariff /'tærɪf/ [C] a tax that is paid on goods coming into or going out of a country, often in order to protect industry from cheap imports: *A general tariff was imposed on foreign imports.*

rates [pl.] (in Britain) a tax paid by businesses to a local authority for land and buildings that they use, and in the past also paid by anyone who owned a house: *Business rates are very high in the city centre.* See also **rate** → RATE 2

teach *verb* See the Topic Map for EDUCATION on p.888, See also the entry for TRAIN 1

teach · educate · lecture · prepare · tutor
These words all mean to help sb learn sth.

PATTERNS AND COLLOCATIONS
▶ to teach / lecture (sb) **about** sth
▶ to teach / educate / lecture / prepare / tutor (sb) **effectively**

teach [I, T] to give lessons to students in a school, college, etc.; to help sb learn sth by giving information about it: *She teaches at our local school.* ◇ *He teaches English to advanced students.* ◇ *He teaches them English.* ◇ (*AmE*) *to* **teach school** (= teach in a school) See also **teach** → TRAIN 1, **teaching** → EDUCATION
educate [T, often passive] (*rather formal*) to teach sb over a period of time at a school, college, etc: *She was educated in the US.* ◇ *He was educated at his local comprehensive school and then at Oxford.* ❶ **Educate** in this meaning is usually used with the name of a country, town, school, college or university. See also **education** → EDUCATION
lecture /'lektʃə(r)/ [I] to give a talk or a series of talks to a group of people on a subject, especially as a way of teaching in a university or college: *She lectures in Russian literature.* See also **lecture** → SPEECH *noun*
prepare [T] (*rather formal*) to make students ready to do sth: *The college prepares students for a career in business.* ◇ *to prepare students for exams*
tutor /'tjuːtə(r); *AmE* 'tuː-/ [T, I] to teach an individual student or a small group; to work as a private teacher: *He tutors students in mathematics.* ◇ *Her work was divided between tutoring and research.* See also **tutoring** → EDUCATION

teacher *noun* See the Topic Map for EDUCATION on p.888, See also the entries for COACH, LECTURER and PROFESSOR

teacher · tutor · educator · schoolteacher · governess · educationalist
These are all words for a person whose job is teaching.

PATTERNS AND COLLOCATIONS
▶ a teacher / tutor / governess **to** sb
▶ a **former** teacher / tutor / schoolteacher / governess
▶ a / an **qualified** / **experienced** / **good** / **excellent** teacher / tutor
▶ a **private** teacher / tutor
▶ a **full-time** / **part-time** teacher / tutor
▶ a / an **history** / **music** / **English, etc.** teacher / tutor

teacher [C] a person whose job is teaching, especially in a school: *Who's your favourite teacher?* ◇ *We are looking for qualified and experienced English teachers.* See also **teaching** → EDUCATION
tutor /'tjuːtə(r); *AmE* 'tuː-/ [C] a private teacher, especially one who teaches an individual student or a very small group: *He worked as a tutor to the family's three young children.* ◇ *Children who miss a lot of schoolwork through illness are usually allowed a home tutor.* ❶ In British English a **tutor** is also a teacher who teaches adults, or a teacher who has a special role in a school or college: (*BrE*) *She's a part-time adult education tutor.* ◇ *Who's your form tutor?* See also **tutorial** → CLASS 2, **tutoring** → EDUCATION
educator [C] (*formal*) a person whose job is to teach or educate people: *The video is being used by health educators in remote areas.* ◇ *We have a wealth of resources for teacher educators* (= people who teach people to be teachers). ❶ **Educator** is also the usual American English word for

educationalist: *Modern educators prefer a different approach to the teaching of reading.* See also **education** → EDUCATION
schoolteacher /'skuːltiːtʃə(r)/ [C] (*becoming old-fashioned*) a person whose job is teaching in a school: *An elderly schoolteacher rented the apartment upstairs.*
governess /'gʌvənəs; *AmE* -vərn-/ [C] (especially in the past) a woman employed to teach the children of a rich family in their home and live with them: *She was educated at home by a series of governesses.*
educationalist (also **educationist**) [C] (*especially BrE*) a specialist in theories and methods of teaching: *Some leading educationalists have been cautious about this theory.* ❶ In American English this is usually called an **educator**.

team *noun*
1 work together as a team
2 a football team

1 See also the entries for PARTY 3 and GROUP 2
team · crew · squad · ring · detachment · corps · shift · gang
These are all words for a group of people working together.

PATTERNS AND COLLOCATIONS
▶ a team / crew / squad / detachment / corps / gang **of** sth
▶ **in** a team / crew / squad / gang
▶ a **5-strong** / **100-strong, etc.** team / crew / squad
▶ a **small** team / crew / squad / corps
▶ a **large** team / crew / squad / corps
▶ to **join** a team / crew / corps
▶ a team / squad / ring / gang **leader**
▶ a **member of** a team / crew / squad / ring / corps / gang
▶ **part of** a team / squad / ring / detachment

team [C+sing./pl. v.] a group of people who work together at a particular job: *A team of experts has been called in to investigate.* ◇ *He was part of a research team under Professor James.* ◇ *They need to learn to work together as a team.* ◇ *It took a team effort to finish the project on time.*
crew /kruː/ [C+sing./pl. v.] (especially in compounds) all the people working on a ship or plane; a group of people with special technical skills who work together: *None of the passengers or crew were injured.* ◇ *Two crews of six men carried out the work in shifts.* ❶ **Crew** is used especially in compounds in the contexts of filming, the emergency services, and technical support: *a TV/film/camera crew* ◇ *an ambulance/a fire crew* ◇ *a maintenance/support crew* In the context of aeroplanes, you can talk about the **aircrew**, **flight crew** or **cabin crew**, who work on the plane, or the **ground crew** who work at the airport and look after aircraft and passengers while they are on the ground.
squad /skwɒd; *AmE* skwɑːd/ [C+sing./pl. v.] a section of a police force that deals with a particular type of crime; a small group of soldiers working or being trained together; a group of people employed to kill sb's opponents, usually for political reasons: *He was deputy head of the force's serious crime squad.* ◇ *A squad of soldiers had arrived to arrest him.* ◇ *People lived in fear of the regime's notorious death squads.* ❶ Police squads deal with a variety of different types of crime: *the drugs/vice/anti-terrorist/bomb/riot/fraud squad* A death squad can also be called a *hit squad* or an *assassination squad.* See also **firing squad** → EXECUTION
ring [C] a group of people working together, especially in secret or illegally: *The four men are accused of running a drug smuggling ring.* ◇ *a spy ring* See also **gang** → PARTY 3
detachment /dɪ'tætʃmənt/ [C] a group of soldiers, sailors or ships sent away from a larger group, especially to do special duties: *A detachment of marines was left to guard the site.* ◇ *The attack wiped out the entire twelve-man detachment.* See also **unit** → ARMY

corps /kɔː(r)/ [C+sing./pl. v.] a group of people involved in a particular job or activity: *Local people worked alongside an international corps of volunteers.* ◇ *the press corps* ◇ *the diplomatic corps*

shift [C+sing./pl. v.] a group of workers working particular hours: *The drama began at 5.15 am as the **day shift** was going on duty.* ◇ *Most of the **night shift** had already left.* ◇ *As I left the next shift was settling in for the day.*

gang [C+sing./pl. v.] an organized group of workers or prisoners working together, especially doing physical work such as building work: *The work was done by convicts working in gangs.* ◇ *a prison/work gang* See also **gang → PARTY 3**

---

2 See the Topic Map for SPORT AND LEISURE on p.892
team · club · side · squad · line-up
These are all words for a group of people who play a sport together against other groups.

▸ a **successful** / **local** / **top** team / club / side
▸ the **junior** / **senior** / **youth** / **under-19** / **national** team / side / squad
▸ a / an **Irish** / **French**, etc. team / club / side / squad
▸ the **England** / **Ireland**, etc. team / club / squad / line-up
▸ a **football** / **rugby** / **cricket** team / club / side / squad
▸ to **join** a team / club / squad / line-up
▸ to **play for** / **sign for** a team / club / side
▸ to **name** a team / side / squad / line-up
▸ to **field** a team / side / line-up
▸ a team / club / side **plays** / **wins** / **loses** (a game / match)
▸ a **member of** a team / club / side / squad / line-up

team [C+sing./pl. v.] a group of people who play a particular game or sport against another group of people: *(BrE) Whose **team** are you **in**?* ◇ *(AmE) After two years out with injury, he's back **on the team**.* ◇ *You didn't **make the team** (= weren't chosen to play) I'm afraid.* ◇ *What team do you support?* ◇ *We want to encourage **team sports** in schools.*

club [C+sing./pl. v.] (BrE) a professional sports organization that includes players, managers, owners and members: *He is expected to sign for a Premier League club next season.* ◇ *Athletico Madrid Football Club* See also **club → UNION**

side [C+sing./pl. v.] (BrE) a sports team: *As captain, Pryce is confident of leading his side to victory.* ◇ *The French have a very strong side.*

> **NOTE TEAM, CLUB OR SIDE? Club** refers to the organization that includes players, managers and owners, throughout the club's history: players, managers and owners may change, but it remains the same club. **Team** and **side** usually refer more just to the players, and often (especially **side**) to the players at a particular point in the club's history, or in a particular game: *This team is arguably even better than the Welsh side of the seventies.*

squad /skwɒd; AmE skwɑːd/ [C+sing./pl. v.] the group of players or competitors from which a team is chosen for a particular game: *He has named a squad of 16 from which to pick the side for the two one-day games.*

line-up [usually sing.] the players who are going to take part in a particular game or stage of a competition: *The team returns this season with a new car and a new line-up of drivers.* ◇ *He was named in the **starting line-up** for the game against Chelsea.*

---

tear /teə(r); AmE ter/ verb

tear · rip · split · shred · pull sth apart
These words all mean to damage sth by pulling it in different directions or cutting it into pieces on sth sharp.

split   tear   rip   shred
                                          pull sth apart

▸ to tear / rip sth **from** / **out of** sth
▸ to tear / rip / pull sth **apart**
▸ to tear / rip sth **up** / **open**
▸ to tear / rip / shred **paper**
▸ to tear / rip your **clothes**
▸ to tear / rip / split your **trousers** / **pants** / **jeans**
▸ to tear / rip a **hole** in sth
▸ to tear / rip sth **in two** / **to shreds** / **to pieces**

tear [T, I] to damage sth by pulling it apart or by cutting it on sth sharp; to be damaged in this way; to make a hole in sth by force: *I tore my jeans on the fence.* ◇ *He tore the package open.* ◇ *She tore a page from her notebook.* ◇ *She tore up the letter (= tore it into small pieces).* ◇ *His jacket had been torn to shreds on the barbed wire.* ◇ *The dogs tore the fox apart.* ◇ *He **tore at** the meat with his bare hands.* ◇ *Careful — this fabric tears very easily.* ◇ *I tore a hole in my shirt.*
▸ **tear** noun [C]: *This sheet has a tear in it.*

rip (-pp-) [T, I] to tear sth or become torn, often suddenly or violently: *The flag had been ripped in two.* ◇ *I heard the tent rip.* ◇ *A bullet **ripped into** his shoulder.* ◇ *The nail ripped a hole in my jacket.*
▸ **rip** noun: *The jacket had a rip in the sleeve.*

> **NOTE Tear or rip? Ripping** is usually more violent than **tearing**. Both verbs, but especially **rip**, are often used with a preposition or adverb to show violent movement as the thing is ripped/torn.

split [I, T] (of fabric or wood) to tear or open along a straight line; to make sth tear or open in this way: *Her dress had split along the seam.* ◇ *The cushion split open and sent feathers everywhere.* ◇ *I was put to work splitting wood for the fire.*

shred (-dd-) [T] to cut or tear paper, fabric or vegetables into lots of small pieces: *Serve the fish on a bed of shredded lettuce.* ◇ *He was accused of shredding documents relating to the case.* ❶ **Shredding** paper is usually done in a machine called a **shredder** or **shredding machine**; if you do it with your hands you **tear/rip it up**. See also **shred → FRAGMENT** noun

pull sth a'part phrasal verb to separate sth into pieces by pulling different parts of it in different directions: *The wolves will pull the carcass apart.* ◇ *It is wise to pull the gearbox apart only when absolutely necessary.* ❶ **Pulling sth apart** may involve force or violence, but does not have to.

---

technology noun

technology · hardware · machinery · plant
These are all words for equipment designed using scientific knowledge.

▸ **existing** / **modern** / **new** technology / hardware / machinery / plant
▸ **current** / **the latest** / **basic** / **advanced** / **complex** / **sophisticated** technology / hardware / machinery
▸ **manufacturing** / **production** / **industrial** / **construction** / **agricultural** technology / machinery / plant
▸ to **have** / **use** / **invest in** technology / hardware / machinery / plant
▸ to **supply** / **install** / **update** technology / hardware / machinery
▸ technology / machinery / plant **breaks down**

technology [U] equipment designed using advanced scientific knowledge: *The company has invested in the latest technology.*

hardware /ˈhɑːdweə(r); AmE ˈhɑːrdwer/ [U] the machinery and electronic parts of a computer system: *It seems you've got a hardware problem; the disk drive is stuck.*

machinery /məˈʃiːnəri/ [U] machines as a group, especially large ones: *These workshops were built to house heavy machinery.* See also **machine → MACHINE**

plant [U] (technical) the large machinery that is used in industrial processes: *The company has been investing in new plant and equipment.*

tell verb

1 tell sb the news
2 Promise you won't tell.

---

1 See also the entry for CONVEY

tell · report · inform · notify · brief · alert sb to sth · fill sb in · enlighten

These words all mean to give information to sb by speaking or writing.

PATTERNS AND COLLOCATIONS
▶ to tell sb / report / inform sb / notify sb / brief sb that...
▶ to tell / inform / notify sb **of** sth
▶ to tell / inform / brief / enlighten sb **about** sth
▶ to report / brief sb / fill sb in / enlighten sb **on** sth
▶ to tell sb / report sth / inform sb / notify sb **officially**
▶ to tell sb / report sth / inform sb / notify sb **formally**
▶ to tell / inform sb / notify sb **in writing**
▶ to tell / inform / brief sb **personally**
▶ to tell sb / report sth / inform sb / notify sb **immediately**
▶ to report sth / inform sb / brief sb **regularly**
▶ to be **fully** informed / briefed

tell [T] (of a person) to give information to sb by speaking or writing; (of some writing, an instrument, a sign, etc.) to give information about sth: *Why wasn't I told about the accident?* ◇ *Did she tell you her name?* ◇ *Tell me where you live.* ◇ *'I'm ready to go now,' he told her.* ◇ *The advertisement told us very little about the product.* ◇ *This gauge tells you how much fuel you have left.* See also **tell** → DESCRIBE

report [I, T] to give people information about sth that you have heard, seen, done, etc: *The committee will report on its research next month.* ◇ *The crash happened seconds after the pilot reported engine trouble.* ◇ *The house was reported to be in excellent condition.* See also **report** → REPORT *noun* 3

inform [T] (*rather formal*) to tell sb about sth, often in a formal or official way: *Please inform us of any changes of address.* ◇ *The leaflet informs customers about healthy eating.* ◇ *Have the police been informed?* ◇ *I have been reliably informed* (= sb I trust has told me) *that the couple will marry next year.* See also **information** → INFORMATION, **informative** → INFORMATIVE

notify [T, often passive] (*formal*) to formally or officially tell sb about a fact or situation: *Competition winners will be notified by post.* ◇ *The police must be notified of the date of the demonstration.*

NOTE INFORM OR NOTIFY? **Notify** is often used for important facts that the authorities or public need to know. It is not used for more personal or general information: ~~I have been reliably notified that the couple will marry next year.~~ ◇ ~~The leaflet notifies customers about healthy eating.~~

brief /briːf/ [T] (*rather formal*) to give sb information about sth so that they are prepared to deal with it: *The officer briefed her on what to expect.* ◇ *I expect to be kept fully briefed at all times.*

alert sb to sth *phrasal verb* [often passive] (*rather formal*) to make sb aware of sth: *They had been alerted to the possibility of further price rises.* ❶ You can be **alerted to sth** either because sb tells you or because sth happens to make you notice it.

fill sb in *phrasal verb* (*rather informal*) to tell sb about sth that has happened: *Can you fill me in on what's been going on while I've been away?*

enlighten [T] (*especially written or humorous*) to give sb information so that they understand sth better: *She didn't enlighten him about her background.* See also **enlightening** → INFORMATIVE, **enlightenment** → KNOWLEDGE

---

2 **tell · betray · stab sb in the back · blow the whistle on sb/sth · turn King's/Queen's/State's evidence · grass · blab · inform on sb · finger**

These words all mean to let sb know a secret or give information about sb/sth to an enemy.

PATTERNS AND COLLOCATIONS
▶ to tell / blow the whistle / grass / inform **on** sb
▶ to betray sb / grass / blab **to** sb
▶ to tell on / betray / inform on a **friend**
▶ to betray / blow the whistle on / inform on a **colleague**
▶ to betray / blow the whistle on **your partner / husband / employer / wife / master**

tell [I] (*informal, especially spoken, often disapproving*) to let sb know a secret: *Promise you won't tell.* ◇ *'Who are you going out with tonight?' 'That would be telling!'* (= it's a secret) ◇ *Don't tell on me, will you?* (= Don't tell anyone in authority what I have done.)

betray [T] (*rather formal, disapproving*) to give information about sb/sth to an enemy: *For years they had been betraying state secrets to Russia.* ◇ *He was offered money to betray his colleagues.* See also **give sb/sth away** → REVEAL, **betray** → CHEAT, **betrayal** → BETRAYAL

stab sb in the 'back *idiom* (**-bb-**) (*informal*) to do or say sth that harms sb who trusts you: *It was very competitive and everyone was stabbing everyone else in the back.*

blow the 'whistle on sb/sth *idiom* (*informal, often approving, especially journalism*) to tell sb in authority about sth wrong or illegal that sb is doing: *It is getting more difficult for people to blow the whistle on their employers.*

turn King's/Queen's 'evidence (*BrE*) (*AmE* **turn State's 'evidence**) *idiom* to give information against other criminals in order to get a less severe punishment: *Two of the prisoners agreed to turn Queen's evidence.*

grass [I] (*BrE, slang, disapproving*) to tell the police about sb's criminal activities: *Who grassed on us?* ◇ *You wouldn't grass up your mates, would you?*

blab (**-bb-**) [I, T] (*informal, disapproving*) to tell sb sth that should be kept secret: *Someone must have blabbed to the police.* ◇ *Try not to blab the whole story.*

in'form on sb *phrasal verb* (*rather formal, often disapproving*) to tell the police or sb in authority about sb's criminal activities: *He informed on his own brother.*

finger [T] (*especially AmE, informal*) to accuse sb of doing sth illegal and tell the police about it: *Who fingered him for the burglaries?*

---

temper noun

temper · tantrum · rage · mood · sulk · huff

These are all words for a short period of angry behaviour or of feeling angry.

mood	temper	rage
sulk	tantrum	
huff		

PATTERNS AND COLLOCATIONS
▶ to be in a temper / rage / huff **at / about / over** sth
▶ **in** a temper / rage / mood / sulk / huff
▶ a **violent** temper / tantrum / rage
▶ to **have** a temper / a tantrum / the sulks
▶ to **get in** a temper / rage / huff
▶ to **fly into** a temper / rage

temper [C, usually sing., U] if sb has a **temper**, they get angry easily: *He has a short/quick temper* (= gets angry very easily). ◇ *You must learn to control your temper.* ◇ *After an hour of waiting tempers began to fray* (= people began to get angry). ◇ *She broke the plates in a fit of temper.* ❶ A **temper** is also a short period of feeling very angry: *She says awful things when she's in a temper.* See also **lose your temper** → LOSE YOUR TEMPER

tantrum /'tæntrəm/ [C] a sudden short period of angry, unreasonable behaviour, especially in a child: *They claimed she threw tantrums and was difficult to work with.* ◇ *Young children often have temper tantrums.*

rage [C] a period of violent anger that is difficult to control: *Sue stormed out in a rage.* ◇ *She attacked him in a jealous rage.* See also **rage** → ANGER *noun*

mood [C] a period of being angry or impatient: *I wonder why he's in such a mood today.* ◇ *She was **in one of her moods** (= one of her regular periods of being angry or impatient).* ◇ *to be in a bad/foul/filthy/terrible mood* See also **mood** → MOOD, **moody** → MOODY

sulk [C] (*BrE* also **the sulks** [pl.]) a period of being silent and bad-tempered because you are annoyed about sth: *Jo was in a sulk upstairs.* ◇ *Ed's got the sulks again.* See also **sulk** → BROOD *verb*, **sulky** → IRRITABLE

huff [C] (*informal*) a period of being bad-tempered, especially because sb has annoyed or upset you: *She went home in a huff.*

tempt *verb*

tempt · lure · entice · seduce
These words all mean to make sb do sth or want to do sth, even if they know it is wrong.

▸ to tempt / lure / entice / seduce sb **into** sth
▸ to be tempted / lured / enticed / seduced **by** sth
▸ to tempt / entice sb **to do** sth
▸ to be **easily** tempted / lured / enticed / seduced

tempt [T] to attract sb or make sb want to do or have sth, even if they know it is wrong: *I was tempted by the dessert menu.* ◇ *Don't tempt thieves by leaving valuables clearly visible.* ◇ *I was tempted to take the day off.* See also **temptation** → DESIRE *noun*, **attract** → INTEREST *verb*
▸ **tempting** *adj.*: *It was a tempting offer.* ◇ *That cake looks very tempting.*

lure /lʊə(r); ljʊə(r); *AmE* lʊr/ [T] (usually used with an adverb or preposition) (*usually disapproving*) to persuade or trick sb into going somewhere or doing sth by promising them a reward or making it seem very attractive: *The child was lured into a car but managed to escape.* ◇ *Young people are lured to the city by the prospect of a job and money.*
▸ **lure** *noun* [C, usually sing.]: *Few can resist the lure of adventure.*

entice /ɪn'taɪs/ [T] (usually used with an adverb or preposition) to persuade sb to go somewhere or do sth, usually by offering them sth: *The bargain prices are expected to entice customers away from other stores.* ◇ *Try to entice the child to eat by offering small portions of his or her favourite food.*

> **NOTE** LURE OR ENTICE? **Lure** is usually more disapproving than **entice**, and can involve tricking sb into a dangerous situation; if you **entice** sb you try to persuade them, often to do sth that is good for them. However, **lure** can also be used in a more informal, slightly humorous way, about a situation that is really not dangerous at all: *By careful management Jack had been lured away while the party preparations were made.*

seduce /sɪ'djuːs; *AmE* -'duːs/ [T] (*written*) to persuade sb to do sth that they would not usually agree to do by making it seem very attractive: *The promise of huge profits seduced him into parting with his money.*
▸ **seduction** *noun* [C, usually pl., U]: *Who could resist the seductions of a tropical island?* ◇ *the seduction of fame*

> **NOTE** LURE OR SEDUCE? You can lure sb *into a place* or seduce sb *into doing sth* but NOT the other way round: ~~The child was seduced into a car.~~ ◇ ~~He was lured into parting with his money.~~ Both of these words are frequently used in the passive in business journalism: *Operators are lured/seduced by the price of cheap oil.*

tenant *noun* See also the entry for RESIDENT

tenant · occupant · guest · resident · lodger
These are all words for a person who lives or stays in a particular house.

▸ a **new** tenant / occupant / lodger
▸ the **previous** / **current** / **sole** tenant / occupant

tenant /'tenənt/ [C] a person who pays rent for the use of sth such as a room, building or land to the person who owns it: *They had evicted their tenants for non-payment of rent.*

occupant /'ɒkjəpənt; *AmE* 'ɑːk-/ [C] (*rather formal, especially written*) a person who lives or works in a particular house, room or building; a person who is in sth at a particular time, such as a vehicle or seat: *All outstanding bills will be paid by the previous occupants.* ◇ *The car was badly damaged but the occupants were unhurt.* See also **occupy** → LIVE

guest [C] a person who is paying money to stay in a place such as a hotel: *Guests should vacate their rooms by 10.30 a.m.* ◇ *The accommodation secretary has a list of families who take **paying guests** (= people who are living in a private house, but paying as if they were in a hotel).* See also **guest** → VISITOR

resident /'rezɪdənt/ [C] (*formal*) a person who is staying in a hotel: *The hotel restaurant is open to non-residents.* See also **resident** → RESIDENT

lodger [C] (*especially BrE*) a person who pays for a room to live in, and usually for meals, in sb else's house: *Many people take in a lodger because they need the income.*

tendency *noun*

tendency · orientation · bias · propensity · bent
These are all words for the way a person or thing often behaves or is likely to behave.

▸ a tendency / an orientation / a bias **toward** / **towards** sth
▸ a tendency / a propensity **to do** sth
▸ a tendency / an orientation **to** sth
▸ a propensity / bent **for** sth
▸ a **natural** tendency / bias / propensity / bent
▸ an **innate** tendency / propensity
▸ to **have** a tendency / an orientation / a bias / a propensity / a bent

tendency /'tendənsi/ [C] a characteristic that makes sb/sth likely to behave in a particular way: *This material has a tendency to shrink when washed.* ◇ *There is a tendency for this disease to run in families.* ◇ *Several patients admitted to suicidal tendencies.* See also **tendency** → TREND
▸ **tend** *verb* [T]: *Women tend to live longer than men.* ◇ *When I'm tired, I tend to make mistakes.* ◇ *It tends to get very cold here in the winter.* ◇ *People **tend to think** that the problem will never affect them.*

orientation /ˌɔːriən'teɪʃn/ [U, C] (*rather formal*) the type of aims or interests that a person or organization has; a person's basic beliefs or feelings about a particular subject: *The classes are essentially theoretical **in orientation**.* ◇ *He belonged to a group with a specific religious and political orientation.* ◇ *legislation forbidding discrimination on the grounds of **sexual orientation** (= whether sb is attracted to men, women or both)*

bias /'baɪəs/ [C, usually sing.] an interest or ability in one thing more than others: *In British universities there was a bias towards pure science.* ◇ *These classes have a strong practical bias.*

propensity /prə'pensəti/ [C, usually sing.] (*formal*) a tendency to a particular kind of behaviour: *There is an increased propensity for people to live alone.* ◇ *They all knew about his propensity for violence.*

bent [C, usually sing.] a natural skill or interest in sth: *Some students have no natural bent for literature at all.*

tense *adj.*

tense · strained · stressed · under pressure · uptight
These words all describe people when they are too anxious to be able to relax.

PATTERNS AND COLLOCATIONS
▸ to **look** / **sound** / **seem** tense / strained / uptight
▸ to **get** tense / uptight
▸ sth **makes sb** tense / uptight

tense nervous or worried and unable to relax: *Try to relax. Are you always this tense?* ❶ You can be **tense** as a result of the situation you are in or because it is part of your personality and you are always that way: *She sounded tense and angry.* ◇ *He's a very tense person.* See also **tense** → STRESSFUL *adj.*, **tense** → TIGHTEN *verb*, **tension** → PRESSURE 1

strained showing the effects of worry or pressure: *Her face looked strained and weary.* ◇ *He spoke in a low, strained voice.* See also **strain** → PRESSURE 1, **strained** → STRESSFUL

stressed (also *informal* **stressed out**) too anxious and tired to be able to relax: *He was feeling very stressed and tired.* ◇ *Stressed out? Take a break in the sun.* ◇ *stressed business executives* See also **stress** → PRESSURE 1, **stressful** → STRESSFUL

under 'pressure *phrase* made to feel anxious about sth that you have to do: *The team performs well under pressure.* ◇ *I don't want to* **put** *you* **under pressure**, *but...* See also **pressure** → PRESSURE 1

uptight (*informal*) anxious and/or angry about sth: *She felt too uptight to do any work.* ❶ You can be **uptight** as a result of the situation you are in or because it is part of your personality and you are always that way: *Relax! You're getting too uptight about this.* ◇ *He's a very uptight person.* **OPP easy-going** → CALM

tension *noun* See the Topic Map for CONFLICT on p.896

tension · aggression · hostility · antagonism · animosity · antipathy · enmity
These are all words for an unfriendly situation or feelings between people.

PATTERNS AND COLLOCATIONS
▸ tension / hostility / antagonism / animosity / antipathy / enmity **between** A and B
▸ aggression / hostility / antagonism / animosity / antipathy / enmity **towards** sb / sth
▸ **mutual** / **personal** hostility / antagonism / animosity / antipathy / enmity
▸ **open** aggression / hostility
▸ **natural** antagonism / antipathy
▸ to **feel** the tension / hostility / antagonism / animosity / antipathy
▸ to **arouse** hostility / antagonism

tension [U, C, usually pl.] a situation in which people do not trust each other, or feel unfriendly towards each other, and which may cause them to attack each other: *There is mounting tension along the border.* ◇ *international / racial / political tensions* ◇ *Family tensions and conflicts may lead to violence.* See also **tense** → STRESSFUL

aggression /əˈɡreʃn/ [U] a willingness to threaten or attack sb / sth, often caused by feelings of anger or hatred: *Nowadays our aggression is channelled into sports.* See also **aggressive** → AGGRESSIVE 1

hostility /hɒˈstɪləti; AmE hɑːˈs-/ [U, sing.] unfriendly feelings or behaviour towards sb / sth: *There was open hostility between the two schools.* ◇ *The talk lasted well over an hour and he sensed a growing hostility from his audience.* See also **hostile** → AGGRESSIVE 1, **hostility** → OPPOSITION

antagonism /ænˈtæɡənɪzəm/ [U, C, usually pl.] (*written*) strong feelings of dislike between people or groups of people: *The gap between rich and poor is widening and class antagonism is growing.* ◇ *Natural antagonisms and rivalries between the communities became worse.* See also **antagonize** → ANGER *verb*

animosity /ˌænɪˈmɒsəti; AmE -ˈmɑːs-/ [U, C, usually pl.] strong feelings of personal dislike towards sb: *He felt no animosity towards his critics.* ◇ *Personal animosities between the leaders have made negotiations difficult.*

antipathy /ænˈtɪpəθi/ [U, C] (*formal*) strong feelings of dislike towards a thing, idea or person: *Growing antipathy to the government has led to a low voter turnout in local elections.* ◇ *His professional judgement was coloured by his personal antipathies.*

> **NOTE** ANTAGONISM, ANIMOSITY OR ANTIPATHY? Antagonism is often felt towards a whole group or class of people: *class / racial antagonism.* **Animosity** can suggest a very personal feeling, not based on principles or tradition but on a bad personal relationship with sb. **Antipathy** can suggest a feeling based on instinct (=natural tendencies), not thought or reason.

enmity /ˈenməti/ [U, C] strong, long-lasting feelings of hatred towards sb: *Her action earned her the enmity of two or three colleagues.* ◇ *Personal enmities and conflicts have soured relations within the department.*

terrible *adj.* See also the entry for BAD
1 a terrible thing to say
2 a terrible mess
3 a terrible accident
4 The acting was terrible.

1 See also the entries for BAD and DISGUSTING 1
terrible · awful · horrible · dreadful · vile · horrendous
These words all describe sth that is very unpleasant.

PATTERNS AND COLLOCATIONS
▸ terrible / awful / horrible / dreadful **for** sb
▸ a terrible / an awful / a horrible / a dreadful / a vile **thing**
▸ a terrible / an awful / a horrible / a vile **smell**
▸ a terrible / an awful / a horrible / a dreadful / a vile **business**
▸ a terrible / an awful / a horrible / a dreadful / a horrendous **time**
▸ a terrible / an awful / a horrible / a dreadful **noise** / **thought** / **feeling** / **shock**
▸ the terrible / awful / horrible / dreadful **truth**
▸ terrible / awful / dreadful / vile / horrendous **conditions**
▸ terrible / awful / dreadful / vile **weather**
▸ terrible / awful / dreadful **news**
▸ **really** / **pretty** terrible / awful / horrible / dreadful / vile / horrendous
▸ **rather** terrible / awful / horrible / dreadful / vile
▸ **absolutely** / **truly** terrible / awful / horrible / dreadful / horrendous

terrible very bad or unpleasant; making you feel unhappy, frightened, upset, ill, guilty or disapproving: *What terrible news!* ◇ *How terrible for you!* ◇ *It was a terrible thing to happen to someone so young.* ◇ *That's a terrible thing to say!* ◇ *I feel terrible – I think I'll go to bed.* ◇ *I feel terrible: it could so easily have ended in tragedy and I just didn't think.* **OPP good** → NICE 1

awful (*especially spoken*) very bad or unpleasant; used to describe sth that you do not like or that makes you feel depressed, ill, guilty or disapproving: *That's an awful colour.* ◇ *I feel awful – maybe it was something I ate.* ◇ *I feel awful about forgetting her birthday.* ◇ *The awful thing is, it was my fault.* ◇ *'They didn't even offer to pay.' 'Oh that's awful.'*

horrible (*especially spoken*) very unpleasant; used to describe sth that you do not like: *What a horrible child.* ◇ *The coffee tasted horrible.* ◇ *It was horrible sitting there all on my own.*

dreadful /ˈdredfl/ (*especially BrE, especially spoken*) very bad or unpleasant; used to describe sth that you do not like or that you disapprove of: *What dreadful weather!* ◇ *What a dreadful thing to say!* ◇ *It's dreadful the way they treat their employees.* ◇ *How dreadful!*

vile (*informal*) extremely bad or unpleasant: *There was a vile smell coming from the locked room.* ◇ *It was a vile business from beginning to end.*

horrendous /hɒˈrendəs; AmE hɔːˈr-; hɑːˈr-/ (*rather informal*) (of problems) extremely unpleasant and unacceptable: *The traffic around the city was horrendous.*

2 terrible · awful

These are both words that are used to emphasize how bad or extreme sb/sth is.

PATTERNS AND COLLOCATIONS
▸ a terrible/an awful **mistake/mess/nuisance/disappointment**
▸ a terrible/an awful **fool/snob**
▸ a/an **really/truly/absolutely/pretty/rather** terrible/awful…

terrible [only before noun] (*informal, especially spoken*) used to emphasize how bad or extreme sb/sth is: *The room was in a terrible mess.* ◇ *I had a terrible job* (= it was very difficult) *to persuade her to come.* ◇ *You'll be in terrible trouble if you're late again.*

awful [only before noun] (*informal, especially spoken*) used to emphasize sth such as an amount, a quality or how bad sth is: *It's going to cost **an awful lot of** money.* ◇ *The whole thing has been an awful nuisance.* ❶ When **awful** is used to emphasize an amount, it does not always refer to sth bad: *I feel an awful lot better than I did yesterday.*

3 terrible · awful · appalling · horrible · dreadful · horrific · horrifying · gruesome

These words all describe sth that is extremely shocking or frightening, or that causes great harm.

PATTERNS AND COLLOCATIONS
▸ a terrible/ an awful/ an appalling/ a horrible/ a dreadful/ a horrific/ a horrifying/ a gruesome **scene/sight**
▸ a terrible/ an awful/ an appalling/ a horrible/ a dreadful/ a horrific **crime**
▸ terrible/ appalling/ horrible/ dreadful/ horrific **injuries**
▸ terrible/ awful/ appalling/ horrible/ dreadful/ horrific **pain/ suffering**
▸ a terrible/ an awful/ an appalling/ a horrible/ a dreadful/ a horrific **nightmare**
▸ a terrible/ an awful/ an appalling/ a horrible/ a dreadful **tragedy**
▸ terrible/ awful/ appalling/ dreadful **consequences**
▸ a terrible/ an appalling/ a horrible/ a dreadful/ a horrific/ a horrifying **accident/ incident**
▸ a terrible/ an awful/ a horrible/ a dreadful/ a horrific/ a horrifying/ a gruesome **death**
▸ a terrible/ an awful/ a horrible/ a dreadful/ a gruesome **fate**
▸ a terrible/ an awful/ a horrible/ a dreadful **cry/ scream**
▸ a terrible/ an awful/ a dreadful/ a horrific/ a horrifying/ a gruesome **ordeal**
▸ a terrible/ dreadful/ horrific/ gruesome **attack**
▸ a terrible/ horrible/ dreadful/ horrific/ gruesome **murder**
▸ a terrible/ a horrible/ a horrific **slaughter/ massacre**
▸ to be in a terrible/ an awful/ an appalling/ a dreadful **state**
▸ **absolutely/quite** terrible/awful/appalling/horrible/dreadful/ horrific/ horrifying
▸ **truly** terrible/ awful/ appalling/ horrible/ dreadful/ horrific/ gruesome
▸ **really** terrible/ awful/ appalling/ horrible/ dreadful/ horrific
▸ **particularly** terrible/ awful/ horrible/ dreadful/ horrific/ horrifying/ gruesome
▸ **pretty** terrible/ awful/ horrible/ dreadful/ horrific/ gruesome
▸ **It's** terrible/ awful/ horrible/ dreadful/ horrific/ horrifying **to see/ think…**

terrible very bad or serious; involving great harm or injury: *He had suffered terrible injuries.* ◇ *It was the night of that terrible storm.* ◇ *I'll have to stay with her – she's in a terrible state.*
▸ **terribly** *adv.*: *They suffered terribly when their son was killed.* ◇ *The experiment went terribly wrong.*

awful very bad or shocking; involving great suffering: *He had never known the awful horrors of war.* ◇ *I woke from the most awful nightmare.* **OPP great** → GREAT 1

appalling /əˈpɔːlɪŋ/ (*BrE or formal, AmE*) very bad or shocking; involving great suffering or cruelty: *The prisoners were living in appalling conditions.* ◇ *The regime has an appalling record on human rights.*
▸ **appallingly** *adv.*: *They had to work under appallingly difficult circumstances.*

NOTE TERRIBLE, AWFUL OR APPALLING? **Awful** is used more often to describe events and experiences. Typical collocates are *dream, event, experience, happening* and *nightmare*. **Appalling** is most often used to describe accidents, crimes and the results of these as well as bad social conditions. Typical collocates are *accident, atrocity, tragedy, attack, crash, injuries, conditions, deprivation, hardship, human rights record* and *poverty*. **Appalling** is mostly used in British English. You can use **terrible** in all these examples in both British and American English, although it is slightly less strong than **appalling**.

horrible extremely shocking or frightening: *She woke from a horrible nightmare.* ❶ When **horrible** is used in this meaning, it is usually used with words such as *murder, mutilation, nightmare, injuries, slaughter* and *screaming*, or in the phrase *It was horrible.*
▸ **horribly** *adv.*: *The experiment went horribly wrong.*

dreadful /ˈdredfl/ [usually before noun] terrible: *There's been a dreadful accident.*
▸ **dreadfully** *adv.*: *They suffered dreadfully during the war.*

NOTE TERRIBLE OR DREADFUL? **Terrible** often suggests that you are personally upset by the experience; using **dreadful** can suggest that you are personally slightly less emotionally involved in the experience.

horrific /həˈrɪfɪk/ extremely shocking or frightening: *There's been a horrific murder.* ◇ *Her injuries were horrific.* ◇ *She's been through a horrific ordeal.*

horrifying extremely shocking or frightening: *It was a horrifying experience.* ◇ *It's horrifying to see such poverty.*

NOTE HORRIFIC OR HORRIFYING? **Horrific** is often used to talk about things which affect people directly, such as *injuries, wounds, burns* and *death*. **Horrifying** is more often used with words for events and experiences, such as *accident, dream, event, incident, ordeal, sight* and *story*. It is also used in the expression *it's horrifying to see/think sth*: ~~It's horrific to see such poverty.~~

gruesome /ˈɡruːsəm/ very unpleasant and filling you with horror, usually because it is connected with death or injury: *a particularly gruesome murder* ◇ *We were shown gruesome pictures of dead bodies.*

4 terrible · abysmal · atrocious

These words all describe sth that is very bad or of a very low standard.

PATTERNS AND COLLOCATIONS
▸ a terrible/ an abysmal/ an atrocious **record**
▸ a terrible/ an abysmal **lack**
▸ a terrible/ an atrocious **performance**
▸ terrible/ atrocious **weather/ behaviour**
▸ **absolutely** terrible/ abysmal
▸ **quite** terrible/ atrocious

terrible (*informal*) very bad; of a very low standard: *We had a terrible meal at that restaurant.* ◇ *I have a terrible memory for names.* ◇ *Your driving is terrible!* ❶ In this meaning **terrible** is less serious, less frequent and more informal than in some of its other meanings: *a terrible thing to say* and *a terrible accident* are more unpleasant or more serious than *a terrible meal*.

abysmal /əˈbɪzməl/ very bad; of a very low standard: *His manners are abysmal.* ◇ *The council has an abysmal record on education.*

atrocious /əˈtrəʊʃəs; AmE əˈtroʊ-/ very bad; of a very low standard: *Isn't the weather atrocious?* ◇ *She speaks French with an atrocious accent.*

NOTE TERRIBLE, ABYSMAL OR ATROCIOUS? These words are all very similar and in many cases you can use any of them; **terrible** is used especially when sth is very poor quality or is done badly; **abysmal** is used especially to talk about sth that you think is morally bad; **atrocious** is used especially to talk about sth that is unpleasant or done or performed badly.

territory *noun*

territory · colony · enclave · possession · dominion · satellite
These are all words for a country or area that is occupied or controlled by another country.

PATTERNS AND COLLOCATIONS
▸ (a) **British / Spanish, etc.** territory / colony / enclave / possession
▸ a **self-governing** territory / colony / dominion
▸ (a) **former** territory / colony / possession
▸ **overseas** territory / possessions

territory /'terətri; AmE -tɔːri/ [U, C] land that is under the control of a particular country or ruler: *They have refused to allow UN troops to be stationed in their territory.* ◇ *The killings had set off widespread rioting in the occupied territories.*
▸ **territorial** *adj.*: *territorial gains/disputes/claims*
colony /'kɒləni; AmE 'kɑːl-/ [C] a country or area that is governed by people from another, more powerful, country: *East Timor was a former Portuguese colony.*
▸ **colonial** /kə'ləʊniəl; AmE -'loʊ-/ *adj.*: *Western colonial attitudes*
enclave /'enkleɪv/ [C] (*rather formal*) an area of a country or city where the people have a different religion, culture or nationality from those who live in the country or city that surrounds it: *The northern part of the city is a Christian enclave.*
possession [C, usually pl.] (*formal*) a country that is owned and governed by another country: *The former colonial possessions are now independent states.*

> NOTE **COLONY** OR **POSSESSION**? **Colony** is used especially to talk about a country that many people moved to in order to make a new permanent home. A **colony** is usually far away from the country that controls it. **Possession** is often used in the plural to talk about all the countries and areas that make up a powerful country's empire.

dominion /də'mɪniən/ [C] (*formal*) an area controlled by one ruler: *He ruled over the vast dominions of the Holy Roman Empire.*
satellite /'sætəlaɪt/ [C] a town, country or organization that is controlled by and dependent on another larger or more powerful one: *Following the Second World War it became a satellite state of the Soviet Union.*

test *noun*

1 a blood test
2 a driving test

1 test · experiment · testing · trial · pilot study
These are all words for a procedure carried out in order to find sth out, or see if sth works.

PATTERNS AND COLLOCATIONS
▸ a test / an experiment / testing / a trial **on** sth
▸ an experiment / testing / a trial **with** sth
▸ **in / during** a test / an experiment / testing / a trial
▸ a test / an experiment / testing / a trial / a pilot study **to do sth**
▸ **successful** tests / experiments / testing / trials / pilot studies
▸ **extensive / rigorous** tests / experiments / testing / trials
▸ **scientific / practical / field / laboratory / pilot / clinical / medical** tests / experiments / testing / trials
▸ to **do** a test / an experiment
▸ to **carry out / conduct** a test / an experiment / testing / a trial / a pilot study
▸ to **set up / design** a test / an experiment / a trial / a pilot study
▸ to **undergo** tests / testing / trials
▸ tests / experiments / testing / trials / pilot studies **show** sth

▸ a test / an experiment / a trial / a pilot study **demonstrates / indicates** sth
▸ a test / an experiment / a trial **suggests / proves / finds** sth

test [C] a medical examination to discover what is wrong with sb or check the condition of their health; a procedure to discover whether or how well sth works, or to find out more information about it: *a/an eye/blood/pregnancy test* ◇ *He developed a simple test for diabetes.* ◇ *The hospital is doing some tests.* ◇ *Rigorous safety tests are being carried out on the new jet.* ◇ *Three athletes were sent home after failing drugs tests.* ◇ *Tests have shown high levels of pollutants in the water.*
experiment [C, U] a scientific test that is carried out in order to study what happens and to gain new knowledge; a new activity, idea or method that you try out to see what happens or what effect it has: *Many people do not like the idea of experiments on animals.* ◇ *Facts can be established by observation and experiment.* ◇ *The school decided to try an experiment in single-sex education.* ◇ *I've never cooked this before so it's a bit of an experiment.*
testing [U] the activity of testing sth/sb in order to find sth out or to see whether or how well it works: *All our cosmetics are produced without animal testing.* ◇ *He announced a moratorium on all nuclear testing.*
trial [C, U] the process of testing sth, such as a drug, in order to decide whether it is safe and effective enough to be used generally; a short period in which you use sth or employ sb to see how well they perform before you make a decision about them: *The new drug is undergoing clinical trials.* ◇ *She agreed to employ me for a trial period.* ◇ *The system was introduced on a trial basis.* ◇ *We had the machine on trial for a week.* ◇ *They are treating the trip as a trial run for their 500-mile sponsored ride later this month.*
'pilot study [C] a study done on a small scale in order to see if sth is successful enough to do on a large scale: *The Mayor's office has agreed to fund a pilot study into the plan.*

2 See the Topic Map for EDUCATION on p.888, See also the entry for ASSESSMENT
test · exam · examination · paper · quiz · oral · practical
These are all words for a set of questions for sb to answer or activities for them to carry out in order to see how much they know about a subject or what they can do.

PATTERNS AND COLLOCATIONS
▸ a test / an exam / an examination / a quiz **on** sth
▸ a test / an exam / an examination **in** sth
▸ a **written** test / exam / examination / paper / quiz
▸ a **practical** test / exam / examination / paper
▸ a/an **difficult/easy/important/final/end of year** test/exam/ examination
▸ a **chemistry/geography, etc.** test/exam/examination/paper/ quiz/practical
▸ to **pass/fail** a test / an exam / an examination / a paper / a quiz / an oral / a practical
▸ to **take** a test / an exam / an examination / a paper / a quiz / a practical
▸ to **do** a test / an exam / an examination / a paper / a quiz
▸ to **set / mark** a test / an exam / an examination / a paper
▸ to **grade** a test / an exam / an examination / a paper / a quiz
▸ test / exam / examination / quiz **questions**

test [C] a set of questions for sb to answer or activities for them to carry out to in order to see how much they know about a subject or what they can do: *There are end of year tests in English, maths and science.* ◇ *(BrE) a good mark in the test* ◇ *(AmE) a good grade on the test* ◇ *Is this a fair test of students' skills?* ◇ *(BrE) I took my driving test last week.* ◇ *(AmE) my driver's test*
exam [C] a formal written, spoken or practical test, especially at a school or college, to see how much you know about a subject or what you can do: *(BrE) She did well in her exams.* ◇ *(AmE) She did well on her exams.* ◇ *(BrE) to mark an exam* ◇ *(AmE) to grade an exam* ◇ *(BrE) I*

got my exam results today. ◊ (*AmE*) I got my exam grades/ scores today. ◊ (*BrE*) He's practising hard for his piano exam.

examination [C] (*formal*) an exam: *Students may* **enter** *for both* **examinations**. ◊ *There has been a fall in the number of* **examination candidates**.

NOTE TEST, EXAM OR EXAMINATION? An **exam** is a written, spoken or practical test at school or college, usually an important one at the end of a year, semester or course of study. In the US these are often called **final exams** or just **finals**. In Britain, **finals** is only used to mean the exams at the end of a degree programme. **Examination** is a much more formal word for an exam. A **test** is sth that students might be given in the middle of a year, semester or course of study, covering only part of the material. **Test** is also usually used when it is a practical skill or physical or mental ability, rather than academic knowledge, that is being tested: *an endurance test* ◊ *an IQ test* ◊ (*BrE*) *a driving test* ◊ (*AmE*) *a driver's test*

paper [C] (*BrE*) a set of exam questions on a particular subject; the answers that people write to the questions: *The geography paper was hard.* ◊ *She spent the evening marking* **exam papers**.

quiz (pl. **quizzes**) [C] (*especially AmE*) a short informal test given to students: *After reading a book, students take a short reading comprehension quiz.* ◊ *We had a* **pop quiz** (= one that we were not told about in advance) *in math class today.*

oral /ˈɔːrəl/ [C] a spoken exam: *I've got my French oral on Tuesday.* ◊ *He passed the written exam, but failed the oral.* ❶ In British English, an **oral** is usually an exam in a foreign language to test your speaking skills. In American English, an **oral** usually refers to a spoken exam in college in which the student answers questions in any subject.

practical [C] (*BrE, rather informal*) a lesson or exam in science or technology in which students have to do or make things, not just read and write about them: *The course involves lectures, demonstrations and practicals.* ◊ *The second part of the exam is a three-hour practical.*

test *verb*

1 test water for purity
2 test your English

1 See also the entry for TRY 2
test · experiment · try sb/sth out · pilot · put sb/sth to the test · screen
These words all mean to use or examine sth to find out how well it works or to check for problems.

PATTERNS AND COLLOCATIONS
▸ to test (sb/ sth)/ try sth out/ screen sb **for** sth
▸ to test sth/ experiment/ try sth out **on** sb/ sth
▸ to test/ screen **patients**
▸ to test a **theory**
▸ to put a **theory** to the test
▸ to **fully/ thoroughly** test/ pilot sth
▸ to test/ screen (sb/ sth) **regularly/ routinely**
▸ to **rigorously** test sth/ put sth to the test

test [T] to use or examine a machine, product or substance to find out how well it works or to find out more information about it; to examine the blood, a part of the body, etc. to find out what is wrong with sb or to check the condition of their health: *Our beauty products are not tested on animals.* ◊ *The water is regularly tested for purity.* ◊ *You should have your hearing tested.* ◊ *Two athletes* **tested positive** *for steroids.*

experiment [I] to carry out a scientific experiment or experiments; to try new things, ideas or methods to find out how successful they are or what effect they have: *Some people feel that experimenting on animals causes unnecessary suffering.* ◊ *He wanted to* **experiment** *more* **with** *different textures in his paintings.* ◊ *I experimented until I got the recipe just right.*

,**try sb/sth 'out** *phrasal verb* to use or test sb/sth in order to see how good or effective they are: *They're trying out a new presenter for the show.* ◊ *I've got an idea I'd like to try out.* See also **try** → TRY 2

pilot [T] to test a new product, system or idea with a few people or in a small area before it is introduced everywhere: *The recycling boxes have been successfully piloted in a number of areas.*

put sb/sth to the 'test *phrase* to put sb/sth in a situation which will show what their true qualities are or how good they are at sth: *His theories have never really been put to the test.* ◊ *He took her out on the ski slopes to put her skills to the test.*

screen [T, often passive] to examine or do tests on a lot of people in order to find out if they have a particular disease or illness: *Men over 55 should be regularly screened for prostate cancer.*

2 See the Topic Map for EDUCATION on p.888, See also the entry for MARK 2
test · examine · quiz · assess
These words all mean to check sb's knowledge or ability by asking them questions or giving them activities to carry out.

PATTERNS AND COLLOCATIONS
▸ to test/ examine/ quiz/ assess sb **on** sth
▸ to test/ examine sb **in** sth

test [T, I] to check sb's knowledge or ability by asking them questions or giving them activities to carry out: *All students are tested in English and mathematics.* ◊ *We test your English before deciding which class to put you in.* ◊ *Schools use various methods of testing.*

examine [T] (*formal*) to test sb's knowledge or ability, especially in a formal or official test: *The students will be examined in all subjects at the end of term.* ◊ *You are only being examined on this semester's work.* See also **examiner** → JUDGE *noun* 2

quiz (-zz-) [T] (*AmE*) to give students a short informal test: *You will be quizzed on chapter 6 tomorrow.*

assess [T] to find out a student's knowledge or ability while they are doing a programme of study, by giving them written work, tests, exams or practical exercises: *Students will be assessed on their use of these skills.* ◊ *The tests are used to assess individual students' ability and knowledge.* See also **assess** → JUDGE *verb* 1, **assessment** → ASSESSMENT

texture *noun*

texture · the feel · touch · consistency
These are all words for the way a surface, substance or fabric feels when you touch it.

PATTERNS AND COLLOCATIONS
▸ a/ the **smooth/ soft** texture/ feel/ consistency
▸ a/ the **silky/ firm** texture/ feel
▸ a **thick/ creamy** texture/ consistency
▸ to **have/ give** sth a … texture/ consistency

texture /ˈtekstʃə(r)/ [C, U] the way a surface, substance or fabric feels when you touch it, for example, how rough, smooth, hard or soft it is; the way food or drink tastes or feels in your mouth, for example, whether it is rough, smooth, light or heavy: *I love the soft texture of velvet.* ◊ *The two cheeses were very different in both taste and texture.* ❶ **Texture** is usually used to talk about the way soft, thick things such as *hair, skin, wool, cheese, textiles, soil* and *velvet* feel.

the feel [sing.] the way that sth feels when you put your hands or fingers on it or when it touches your body: *You can tell it's silk by the feel.* ◊ *She loved the feel of the sun on her skin.* See also **feel** → SEEM *verb*, **feel** → TOUCH *verb* 1

touch [sing.] the way that sth feels when you put your hand or fingers on it or when it touches your body: *The body was cold **to the touch**.* ◇ *He could not bear the touch of clothing on his sunburnt skin.* See also **touch** → TOUCH *verb* 1

NOTE FEEL OR TOUCH? When you talk about **the touch** of sth, you are suggesting you touch it, or it touches you, quickly. **Feel** suggests a longer experience, especially an enjoyable one: *the feel of the mild sea breeze/his strong hands/the sun on your skin*

consistency /kən'sɪstənsi/ [C, U] how thick or smooth a mixture or liquid substance is: *Beat the ingredients together to a creamy consistency.* ◇ *The cement should have the consistency of wet sand.*

thanks *noun*

thanks · gratitude · appreciation
These are all words for words, actions or feelings that show how grateful you are for sth.

PATTERNS AND COLLOCATIONS
▸ thanks / gratitude **for** sth
▸ **in / with** thanks / gratitude / appreciation
▸ **heartfelt / sincere** thanks / gratitude / appreciation
▸ **real / deep** gratitude / appreciation
▸ to **express / show / deserve** thanks / gratitude / appreciation
▸ to **get / accept / earn** sb's thanks / gratitude
▸ to **nod / smile** your thanks / appreciation
▸ a **word of** thanks / gratitude / appreciation
▸ a **token of** your thanks / gratitude / apreciation

thanks [pl.] words or actions that show that you are grateful to sb for sth: *Thanks are due to all those who worked so hard for so many months.* ◇ *She murmured her thanks.* ◇ *We **gave thanks** to God for all our blessings.* See also **thankful** → GRATEFUL

gratitude /'ɡrætɪtjuːd; *AmE* -tuːd/ [U] the feeling of being grateful and wanting to express your thanks: *She was presented with the gift **in gratitude for** her long service.* ◇ *I feel a deep sense of gratitude to her.* **OPP** **ingratitude** ❶ The opposite is **ingratitude**: *She accused him of ingratitude.* See also **grateful** → GRATEFUL

appreciation /ə,priːʃi'eɪʃn/ [U] (*rather formal*) the feeling of being grateful for sth and wanting to express your thanks: *Please accept this gift **in appreciation of** all you've done for us.* See also **appreciate** → WELCOME, **appreciative** → GRATEFUL

NOTE GRATITUDE OR APPRECIATION? **Gratitude** can be a more general feeling of being grateful. **Appreciation** is the act of reconginizing a particular thing that sb has done and being grateful for it: ~~I feel a deep sense of appreciation to her.~~

theft *noun*

theft · robbery · burglary · raid · break-in · embezzlement · shoplifting · larceny · heist
These are all words for the crime of stealing sth from a person or place.

PATTERNS AND COLLOCATIONS
▸ (an) **attempted** theft / robbery / burglary / break-in / larceny
▸ a **bank** robbery / raid / heist
▸ **grand / petty** theft / larceny
▸ to **commit** (a) theft / robbery / burglary / larceny
▸ to **carry out** a theft / robbery / burglary / raid
▸ to **take part in / foil** a robbery / burglary / raid
▸ to **report / investigate** a theft / robbery / burglary / raid / break-in
▸ a theft / robbery / burglary / raid / break-in **happens / takes place**

theft [U, C] the crime of stealing sth from a person or place: *Police are investigating the theft of computers from the company's offices.* ◇ *There has been a reduction in the number of car thefts.* See also **thief** → THIEF

robbery [U, C] the crime of stealing money or goods from a bank, shop, person, etc., especially using violence or threats: *He already had a conviction for **armed robbery** (= using a gun, knife, etc.).* ◇ *There has been a spate of robberies in the area recently.* See also **rob** → ROB, **robber** → THIEF

NOTE THEFT OR ROBBERY? **Theft** emphasizes the thing stolen: *car/computer theft* ◇ ~~car/computer robbery~~. **Robbery** emphasizes the place from which sth was stolen, especially a bank or other business, and often suggests that violence was used: *bank robbery* ◇ *armed robbery* ◇ ~~bank theft~~ ◇ ~~armed theft~~

burglary /'bɜːɡləri; *AmE* 'bɜːrɡ-/ [U, C] the crime of entering a building illegally and stealing things from it: *The youth was charged with three counts of burglary.* ◇ *There has been a rise in the number of burglaries committed in the area.* ❶ **Burglary** usually refers to the act of stealing things from people's homes. It usually takes place when the people are not there or asleep and does not usually involve threats or violence. See also **burgle**, **burglarize** → ROB, **burglar** → THIEF

raid [C] an attack on a building, place or vehicle in order to commit a crime, especially to steal sth: *He had once been involved in a bank raid.* ◇ *She was shot during an armed **raid on** a security van.* See also **raid** → ROB, **raider** → THIEF

'break-in [C] an act of entering a building using force, usually to steal sth: *Police were called to three break-ins in the same area last night.* See also **break into sth** → ROB

embezzlement [U] the crime of stealing money that you are responsible for or that belongs to your employer: *She was found guilty of embezzlement.* See also **embezzle** → STEAL

shoplifting /'ʃɒplɪftɪŋ; *AmE* 'ʃɑːp-/ [U] the crime of stealing goods from a shop by deliberately leaving without paying for them: *She was convicted of shoplifting.* See also **shoplift** → STEAL, **shoplifter** → THIEF

larceny /'lɑːsəni; *AmE* 'lɑːrs-/ [U, C] (*AmE or old-fashioned, BrE, law*) the crime of stealing sth from sb; an occasion when this takes place: *The couple were charged with grand/petty larceny* (= stealing things that are valuable/not very valuable).

heist /haɪst/ [C] (*especially AmE, informal*) an act of stealing sth valuable from a bank or shop: *It's a tense thriller about a diamond heist that goes badly wrong.* ◇ *a heist movie*

theory *noun*

1 the theory of relativity
2 I have this theory that...

1 theory · principle · law · rule · theorem
These are all words for an idea or set of ideas that explains why sth happens or why sth exists.

PATTERNS AND COLLOCATIONS
▸ a theory / law / rule / theorem **about** sth
▸ the theory / principle **behind** sth
▸ **in** theory / principle
▸ the theory / principle / law / rule / theorem **that...**
▸ a **basic / fundamental** theory / principle / law / rule / theorem
▸ a **mathematical** theory / principle / law / rule / theorem
▸ a **scientific** theory / principle / law / rule
▸ to **prove** a theory / principle / law / rule / theorem
▸ to **define** a law / rule
▸ to **apply** a theory / principle
▸ a theory / principle / law / rule / theorem **states that...**

theory [C, U] a formal set of ideas that is intended to explain why sth happens or exists; the ideas on which a particular subject is based: *There are conflicting theories as to the very early origins of mankind.* ◇ *According to Einstein's **theory of relativity**, nothing can travel faster than light.* ◇ *He wrote a number of books on political theory.* ◇ *In theory, all children get an equal chance at school.* See also **theoretical** → INTELLECTUAL 1

principle [C, U] an idea or theory that sth is based on; a general or scientific idea that explains how sth works or why sth happens: *The principle behind it is very simple.* ◇ *We must get back to* **first principles** (= the basic principles of sth). ◇ *It is based on the principle that heat rises.* ◇ *A tidal current turbine is similar in principle to a windmill.* See also **principle** → PRINCIPLE 2

law [C] the fact that sth always happens in the same way in an activity or in nature; a scientific statement made by sb that explains a natural process: *The usual laws of supply and demand do not seem to apply in this case.* ◇ *Do you remember anything about Ohm's Law?* See also **law** → PRINCIPLE 2

rule [C] a statement of what is possible according to a particular system, for example the grammar of a language: *He's a writer who doesn't seem to know the most basic rules of English grammar.* See also **rule** → PRINCIPLE 2

theorem /'θɪərəm; AmE 'θiːə-; 'θɪr-/ [C] (*technical*) a rule or principle, especially in mathematics, that can be proved to be true: *Work out the answer using Pythagoras's Theorem.*

2 theory · hypothesis · premise · thesis · proposition
These are all words for an idea that sb believes but that has not yet been proved, especially one used as the basis for another idea or proposal.

PATTERNS AND COLLOCATIONS
▸ a theory/ hypothesis/ thesis/ proposition **about** sth
▸ a theory/ hypothesis/ thesis **on** sth
▸ a theory/ hypothesis/ premise/ thesis/ proposition **that...**
▸ to **have** a theory/ hypothesis/ premise/ thesis
▸ to **formulate** a theory/ hypothesis/ thesis
▸ to **support** a theory/ hypothesis/ premise/ thesis/ proposition
▸ to **test** a theory/ hypothesis/ premise/ proposition
▸ to **prove** a theory/ hypothesis/ thesis/ proposition
▸ to be **based on** a theory/ hypothesis/ premise/ thesis/ proposition
▸ a theory/ hypothesis/ premise/ thesis/ proposition **is based on** sth

theory [C, U] an opinion or idea that sb believes is true but that has not been proved: *I have this theory that most people prefer being at work to being at home.* ◇ *This is all theory so far...you'll need to back it up with facts.*

hypothesis /haɪ'pɒθəsɪs; AmE -'pɑː.θ-/ (pl. **-theses** /-siːz/) [C] (*rather formal*) an idea or explanation of sth that is based on some known facts but has not yet been proved to be true or correct: *His hypothesis about what dreams mean provoked a lot of debate.* ◇ *This economic model is really a* **working hypothesis** (= sth that people are using as if it were true or correct but which may yet be proved wrong). See also **hypothetical** → SUPPOSED

premise /'premɪs/ [C] (*formal*) a statement or idea that forms the basis for a reasonable theory: *The basic premise of this argument is deeply flawed.* ◇ *The argument rests on a* **false premise**.

thesis /'θiːsɪs/ (pl. **theses** /'θiːsiːz/) [C] (*rather formal*) a statement or opinion that is discussed in a logical way and presented with evidence to prove that it is true: *The basic thesis of the book is fairly simple.* See also **thesis** → PAPER

proposition /ˌprɒpə'zɪʃn; AmE ˌprɑːp-/ [C] (*formal*) a statement that expresses an opinion, especially one used as the basis of an argument: *Her argument is based on the proposition that power corrupts.*

thief *noun*

thief · burglar · robber · pirate · raider · bandit · poacher · looter · pickpocket · highwayman · shoplifter
These are all words for a person who steals things from another person or a place.

PATTERNS AND COLLOCATIONS
▸ a **professional** thief/ burglar/ robber/ poacher/ pickpocket
▸ a **suspected** thief/ burglar/ robber/ poacher/ looter/ shoplifter
▸ a **would-be** thief/ burglar/ robber/ poacher/ looter/ pickpocket/ shoplifter
▸ **armed** robbers/ raiders/ bandits
▸ to **catch** a thief/ burglar/ robber/ poacher/ looter/ pickpocket/ shoplifter
▸ a thief/ burglar/ robber/ pirate/ raider/ looter/ pickpocket/ highwayman/ shoplifter **takes/ steals** sth
▸ a thief/ burglar/ robber/ looter **escapes/gets away/makes off** with sth
▸ a thief/ burglar/ robber **strikes** somewhere
▸ thieves/ burglars/ robbers/ pirates/ looters **raid** somewhere
▸ pirates/ raiders/ bandits **attack** sb
▸ a **gang** of thieves/ robbers/ raiders/ looters/ pickpockets/ shoplifters

thief [C] a person who steals sth from another person or place: *A car thief made off with a top director's BMW last night.* ❶ **Thief** is a general word that can be used to describe any of the people in this group. See also **theft** → THEFT

burglar /'bɜːglə(r); AmE 'bɜːrg-/ [C] a person who enters a building illegally in order to steal: *Burglars broke into the gallery and stole dozens of priceless paintings.* See also **burglary** → THEFT

robber [C] a person who steals from a person or place, especially using violence or threats: *The prison sentence ended his career as a bank robber.* ◇ *an armed robber* See also **rob** → ROB, **robbery** → THEFT

NOTE BURGLAR OR ROBBER? A **burglar** breaks into a building secretly in order to steal things; a **robber** usually enters a building such as a shop or bank, and uses violence or threats against the people there in order to steal sth.

pirate /'paɪrət/ [C] (in the past) a sailor who attacked and robbed other ships at sea: *There were reports that a pirate ship had come looking for treasure in the cove.*

raider [C] a person who makes a criminal raid (= attack) on a place: *A gang of armed raiders held up a bank in the city today.* See also **raid** → THEFT *noun*, **raid** → ROB *verb*

bandit [C] a member of an armed group of thieves who attack travellers: *Buses driving through the mountains have been attacked by bandits.* ❶ **Bandits** usually carry out their attacks in areas that are a long way away from towns or cities, especially in poorer countries.

poacher [C] a person who illegally hunts birds, animals or fish on sb else's property: *The measures are designed to protect the fish from poachers.*

looter /'luːtə(r)/ [C] a person who steals things from shops or buildings after a fire, a riot, etc: *Looters carried clothes and electrical equipment out of shop windows.* See also **loot** → ROB *verb*

pickpocket /'pɪkpɒkɪt; AmE -pɑːkɪt/ [C] a person who steals money, etc. from other people's pockets, especially in crowded places: *Watch out for pickpockets, especially at the train station.*

highwayman /'haɪweɪmən/ [C] (in the past) a man, usually on a horse and carrying a gun, who robbed travellers on public roads: *Lady Sybil's coach was held up by highwaymen on the Plymouth road.*

shoplifter /'ʃɒplɪftə(r)/ [C] a person who steals goods from a shop by deliberately leaving without paying for them: *Shoplifters will be prosecuted.* See also **shoplift** → ROB, **shoplifting** → THEFT

thin *adj.*

thin · slim · slender · lean · skinny · slight · underweight
These words all describe people who are not covered with much flesh.

PATTERNS AND COLLOCATIONS
- a thin / slim / slender / lean / skinny / slight **woman / man / boy**
- a thin / slim / slender / skinny / slight **girl**
- sb's thin / slim / slender / lean / skinny / slight **body / figure**
- sb's thin / slim / slender / slight **build**
- thin / slim / slender / lean / skinny **arms / legs / fingers**
- a slim / slender **waist**
- **very** thin / slim / slender / lean / skinny / underweight
- **quite** thin / slim / slender

thin (of a person or part of the body) not covered with much flesh: *He was tall and thin, with dark hair.* ◇ *She pinched her thin lips together.* ❶ In American English **thin** can be an approving term, used in the same way as **slim**; in British English it is either neutral or disapproving, suggesting that sb/sth is too thin. **OPP fat** → FAT

slim (*approving*) (of a person or part of the body) thin, in a way that is attractive: *He put his arms around her slim waist.* ◇ *How do you manage to stay so slim?* ❶ **Slim** is mostly used to describe women and girls, but can also describe men and boys. **OPP plump** → FAT

slender (*written, approving*) (of a person or part of the body) thin in an attractive or graceful way: *The dress flattered her slender figure.* ◇ *Her long slender fingers paused over the keyboard.* ❶ **Slender** is mostly used to describe women and girls. When it is used to talk about men, the writer or speaker is often suggesting that the man has feminine qualities.

lean (*written, usually approving*) (of a person or part of the body) without much flesh; thin and fit: *He had a lean, muscular body.* ◇ *He's tall, lean and handsome.* ❶ **Lean** is usually used to talk about men and their bodies, and some animals.

skinny (*informal, usually disapproving*) (of a person or part of the body) very thin, especially in a way that you find unpleasant or ugly: *She had wild hair and long skinny arms.* ◇ *He was such a skinny kid.* **OPP chubby** → FAT

slight (of a person) small and thin: *He was of slight build.* ◇ *She was smaller and slighter than I had imagined.* ❶ **Slight** is not usually used for describing parts of the body, but it is often used with words describing the general shape of sb's body such as *build*, *figure* and *physique*.

underweight /ˌʌndəˈweɪt; *AmE* -dərˈw-/ [not usually before noun] (*often disapproving*) (especially of a person) weighing less than the normal or expected weight: *She's dangerously underweight.* ◇ *She is a few pounds underweight for* (= in relation to) *her height.* **OPP overweight** → FAT

thing *noun*

1 a lot of things to do
2 Pass me that thing.
3 your swimming things/all things Japanese

1 thing · stuff

These words are both used to refer in general to facts, events, situations or actions, or to what sb does, says or thinks.

PATTERNS AND COLLOCATIONS
- (a) **good** thing / stuff
- a **lot / lots / loads of** things / stuff
- things / stuff **to do / say**

thing [C] a fact, event, situation or action; what sb says or thinks: *There are a lot of things you don't know about me.* ◇ *There's another thing I'd like to ask you.* ◇ *It's a good thing we got here early.* ◇ *A terrible thing happened last night.* ◇ *I've got loads of things to do today.* ◇ *The main thing to remember is to switch off the burglar alarm.* ◇ *I like camping, climbing and **that sort of thing**.* ◇ *She said the first thing that came into her head.* ◇ *'Why did you tell her our secret?' 'I did **no such thing**!'* ◇ *Let's forget the **whole thing*** (= everything).

stuff [U] (*informal*) used to refer in a general way to things that people do, say or think: *I've got loads of stuff to do today.* ◇ *I like reading **and stuff**.* ◇ *The band did some **great stuff** on their first album.* ◇ *I don't believe in **all that stuff** about ghosts.*

2 thing · object · whole · item · entity · artefact · commodity · thingy

These are all words for sth which can be seen and touched, but is not alive and which you do not name.

PATTERNS AND COLLOCATIONS
- a **precious / valuable** thing / object / item / artefact / commodity
- an **expensive** thing / item / artefact / commodity
- a **rare** thing / object / item / artefact / commodity
- a **single** thing / object / whole / item / entity
- a **physical** thing / object / item / entity
- a **basic** thing / object / item / entity / commodity
- a **separate** thing / object / item / entity
- **everyday / household** objects / items
- a **historical** object / item / artefact
- to **produce / manufacture** a thing / an object / an item / an artefact / a commodity

thing [C] something whose name you do not use because you do not need to or want to, or because you do not know it; something that is not alive in the way that people and plants are: *Can you pass me that thing over there?* ◇ *She's very fond of sweet things* (= sweet foods). *He's just bought one of those exercise things.* ◇ *Turn that thing off while I'm talking to you!* ◇ *Don't treat her like that — she's a person, not a thing!* ◇ *He's good at making things with his hands.* See also **stuff** → MATERIAL

object [C] a thing that can be seen and touched, but is not alive: *He uses everyday objects to teach basic scientific principles to the kids.* ◇ *Glass and plastic objects lined the shelves.*

NOTE THING OR OBJECT? Thing is a much more general word than **object**. An **object** is usually a fairly solid thing, in three dimensions (= it is not flat), that is not going to get used up quickly: food, drink and sheets of paper are not objects, although sth made out of paper might be. **Object** is used especially when you do not know exactly what sth is: *This looks a very unusual object. What is it exactly?* or when you are talking about a whole group of things that do not have enough in common to be called by a more particular word: *Furniture and other household objects were piled up outside the house.* In this example, the objects could include lamps, cushions, a vacuum cleaner and other things from around the house that do not come under the term 'furniture'.

whole [C] a thing that is complete in itself: *Four quarters make a whole.* ◇ *The subjects of the curriculum form a coherent whole.* ◇ *The festival will be great for our city and for the country **as a whole*** (= as one thing, not as separate parts or regions).

item [C] a single thing, considered separately from other similar things: *Can I pay for each item separately?* ◇ *The computer was my largest single **item of expenditure**.* ◇ *This clock is a **collector's item*** (= because it is rare and valuable).

entity /ˈentəti/ [C] (*formal*) something that exists separately from other things and has its own identity: *The unit has become part of a larger department and no longer exists as a separate entity.* ◇ *Each subsidiary of the company will be treated as a single entity.*

artefact (also **artifact** especially in *AmE*) /ˈɑːtɪfækt; *AmE* ˈɑːrt-/ [C] (*technical*) an object that is made by a person, especially sth of historical or cultural interest: *The museum has a superb collection of ancient artefacts from Nubia.*

commodity /kəˈmɒdəti; *AmE* -ˈmɑːd-/ [C] (*rather formal*) a thing that is useful or has a useful quality: *Water is a precious commodity that is often taken for granted in the West.*

thingy /ˈθɪŋi/ [C] (*informal, spoken*) used to refer to a person or thing whose name you do not know or have forgotten, or which you do not want to mention: *This new multimedia thingy means you can research things a lot more easily.*

3 See also the entry for EQUIPMENT

things · stuff · property · asset · possession · holding · junk · belongings · goods · valuables
These are all words for objects or items, especially ones that you own or have with you at a particular time.

▸ **personal** things/stuff/property/assets/possessions/holdings/ belongings
▸ **private** property/assets/possessions/holdings/belongings/ goods
▸ to **collect/gather/pack** your things/stuff/possessions/ belongings
▸ to **search** sb's/your/the things/stuff/property/belongings
▸ to **go through** sb's/your/the things/stuff/belongings
▸ to **buy** things/stuff/property/assets/a holding/goods
▸ to **acquire** things/stuff/property/assets/possessions/your holdings/goods
▸ to **sell** your things/stuff/property/assets/possessions/ holdings/belongings/goods/valuables

things [pl.] (*especially BrE, rather informal*) objects, clothing or tools that you own or that are used for a particular purpose: *Shall I help you pack your things?* ◇ *Bring your swimming things with you.* ◇ *I'll just clear away the breakfast things.* ◇ *Put your things (= coat, etc.) on and let's go.* ❶ In American English it is more usual to use **stuff**. However, in both British and American English **things** can be used, followed by an adjective, to mean 'all that can be described in a particular way'. This use is more formal: (*rather formal*) *She loves all things Japanese.*

stuff [U] (*informal*) used to refer to a group of objects when you do not know their names, when the names are not important or when it is obvious what you are talking about: *Where's all my stuff?* ◇ *They sell stationery and stuff (like that).* ◇ (*disapproving*) *Could you move all that stuff off the table?* ❶ **Stuff** can also refer to a substance or material. See also **stuff → MATERIAL**

property [U] (*rather formal*) a thing or things that are owned by sb: *This building is government property.* ◇ *Be careful not to damage other people's property.* ◇ *The youths were convicted of defacing public property.* ◇ (*BrE*) *I rang the lost property office at the station to see if my bag had been handed in.* ❶ In American English a lost property office is called the **lost and found**.

asset /ˈæset/ [C, usually pl.] (*especially business*) a thing of value, especially property, that a person or company owns, which can be used or sold to pay debts: *Her assets include shares in the company and a house in France.* ◇ *What is the net asset value of the company?* ◇ *financial/ capital assets* ◇ *income from fixed asset investments* **OPP** liability → DEBT

possession [C, usually pl.] something that you own, especially sth that can be moved: *The ring is one of her most treasured/prized possessions.* ◇ *Prisoners were allowed no personal possessions.* See also **possess → HAVE 1**

holding [C] (*formal or business*) an amount of property that is owned by a person, museum, library, etc.; a number of shares that sb has in a company: *one of the most important private holdings of Indian art* ◇ *She has a 40% holding in the company.*

junk [U] things that are considered useless or of little value: *I've cleared out all that old junk from the attic.* ◇ *This china came from a junk shop.* ◇ (*informal, disapproving*) *Is this all your junk (= are these all your things)?* See also the entry for WASTE

belongings [pl.] possessions that can be moved, especially ones that you have with you at a particular time: *She packed her few belongings in a bag and left.* ◇ *Please make sure you have all your belongings with you when leaving the plane.*

goods [pl.] (*especially written or law*) possessions that can be moved: *He was found guilty of handling stolen goods.* ◇ *The plastic bag contained all her worldly goods (= everything she owned).*

valuables [pl.] things that are worth a lot of money, especially small personal things such as jewellery or cameras: *Never leave cash or other valuables lying around.*

think *verb* See the Topic Map for FACT AND OPINION on p.898, See also the entry for REGARD

think · believe · feel · hold · reckon · make sth of sb/sth · be under the impression
These words all mean to have an idea that sth is true or possible or to have a particular opinion about sb/sth.

▸ to think/believe/feel/hold/reckon/be under the impression **that...**
▸ **It is** thought/believed/reckoned **that...**
▸ to be thought/believed/felt/held/reckoned **to be** sth
▸ to think/believe/feel/make sth **of** sb/sth
▸ to think/believe/feel sth **about** sb/sth
▸ to **sincerely/honestly** think/believe/feel/hold
▸ to **personally** think/believe/feel/reckon
▸ to **really/seriously/mistakenly** think/believe/feel
▸ to **firmly** believe/hold/be under the impression

think [T] (not used in the progressive tenses) to have an idea that sth is true or possible, although you are not completely certain; to have a particular opinion about sb/ sth: *Do you think (that) they'll come?* ◇ *I didn't think you liked sports.* ◇ *I think this is their house, but I'm not sure.* ◇ *We'll need about 20 chairs, I should think.* ◇ *It was once thought that the sun travelled around the earth.* ◇ *What did you think about the idea?* ◇ *Well, I like it. What do you think?* ◇ *'Will we make it in time?' 'I think so.'* ◇ *'Is he any good?' 'I don't think so.'*

believe [T] (not used in the progressive tenses) to think sth: *Police believe (that) the man may be armed.* ◇ *It is believed that the couple have left the country.* ◇ *The paintings are believed to be worth over $20 000 each.* ◇ *'Where does she come from?' 'Spain, I believe.'* ◇ *'Does he still work there?' 'I believe so/not.'* ◇ *She believes that killing animals for food or fur is completely immoral.* See also **belief → VIEW 1**

NOTE **THINK** OR **BELIEVE?** When you are expressing an idea that you have or that sb has of what is true or possible, **believe** is more formal than **think**. It is used especially to talk about ideas that other people have; **think** is used more often for talking about your own ideas: *Police believe... ◇ I think...* If you say 'I believe...', you can suggest that this is what you have been led to believe by sb else and so you are not responsible if the information is wrong. When you are expressing an opinion, **believe** is stronger than **think** and is used especially to talk about matters of principle; **think** is used more to talk about practical matters or matters of personal taste: *I believe that we have a responsibility towards the less fortunate in society.* ◇ *I think we should reserve seats in advance.* ◇ *I don't think he's funny at all.*

feel [T, I] (not used in the progressive tenses) to have a particular opinion about sth that has happened or about what you/sb ought to do: *We all felt (that) we were unlucky to lose.* ◇ *I felt (that) I had to apologize.* ◇ *She felt it to be her duty to tell the police.* ◇ *I felt it advisable to do nothing.* ◇ *This decision is, I feel, a huge mistake.* ◇ *This is something I feel strongly about.* See also **feeling → VIEW 1**

hold [T] (not used in the progressive tenses) (*rather formal*) to have an opinion or belief about sb/sth; to believe that sth is true: *He holds strange views on education.* ◇ *He has very firmly-held religious beliefs.* ◇ *She is held in high regard by her students (= they have a high opinion of her).* ◇ *Parents will be held responsible (= will be considered to be responsible) for their children's behaviour.*

reckon [T, I] (*especially BrE, informal, especially spoken*) to think that sth is true or possible: *I reckon (that) I'm going to get that job.* ◇ *He'll be famous one day.* **What do you reckon** (= Do you agree)? ◇ *It's worth a lot of money, I reckon.* ◇ *'They'll never find out.' 'You reckon?'* (= I think you may be wrong about that.) ❶ **Reckon** is also used in the passive in the phrase *It is reckoned that...*: *It is generally reckoned that about half of all job vacancies are never advertised publicly.* This passive use is not as informal as *I reckon...* and is used more in writing, but it is still slightly informal. See also **reckon** → REGARD

'**make sth of sb/sth** *phrasal verb* (usually used in negative statements and questions) to understand the meaning or character of sb/sth; to have an opinion about sb/sth: *I can't make anything of this note from Petra.* ◇ *I don't know what to make of the new manager.*

be ˌunder the imˈpression that... *idiom* to have an idea that sth is true especially when it later proves not to be true: *I was under the impression that the work had already been completed* (= but I have just learnt that it had not).

thoughtful *adj.*

thoughtful · reflective · pensive · introspective
These words all describe sb who is thinking about sth.

thoughtful quiet because you are thinking about sth; showing signs of careful thought: *You're looking very thoughtful.* ◇ *They sat in thoughtful silence.*
▸ **thoughtfully** *adv.*: *She rubbed her cheek thoughtfully.*

reflective /rɪˈflektɪv/ (*rather formal, written*) thinking deeply about things: *He's a quiet and reflective man.*

pensive /ˈpensɪv/ (*rather formal, written*) thinking deeply about sth, especially because you are sad or worried: *She sat with a pensive expression on her face.*

NOTE REFLECTIVE OR PENSIVE? **Reflective** can describe sb's character, or just a temporary mood; **pensive** describes a mood rather than a character: *Tom seemed to be in a reflective/pensive mood.* ◇ *a pensive man*

introspective /ˌɪntrəˈspektɪv/ (*rather formal*) tending to think a lot about your own thoughts and feelings; showing this: *There were a lot of family problems and Jim became increasingly introspective.* ◇ *This story is an almost painfully introspective piece of writing.*

threat *noun*

threat · risk · danger · hazard · menace
These are all words for sb/sth that may be dangerous or cause problems.

threat [C, usually sing.] a person or thing that is likely to cause damage, danger or trouble: *Drug abuse poses a major threat to the fabric of our society.* ◇ *He could be a real threat to the Spanish player in the final.* See also **threat** → RISK 1

risk [C] a person or thing that may cause problems or danger: *The group was considered to be a risk to national security.* ◇ *Tuberculosis threatens to become a major health risk worldwide.* See also **risk** → RISK 1

danger [C] a person or thing that may harm sb/sth: *Smoking is a serious danger to health.* ◇ *There are many hidden dangers for small children in the home.* See also **danger** → RISK 1, **dangerous** → DANGEROUS

hazard /ˈhæzəd; AmE -ərd/ a thing that can be dangerous or cause damage: *Avoid foam-filled sofas − they are a serious fire hazard.* ◇ *Getting injured is an occupational hazard for athletes* (= a hazard caused by their job). See also **hazardous** → DANGEROUS

NOTE THREAT, RISK, DANGER OR HAZARD? A **threat** is usually a probability; a **risk**, **danger** or **hazard** is a possibility. **Threat** is most often used in the phrase *a threat to sth*; the threat itself may be important (*a major threat to the fabric of society*) or less important (*a real threat to the Spanish player*). A **hazard** is the possibility of physical harm, especially to sb's health or safety; it is a thing, not a person. A **danger** is the possibility of physical or moral harm (*a danger to health/society*) and may be a thing or a person. **Risk** is often used in a similar way to **hazard**, especially in compounds: *a health/fire/safety risk*, but has a wider range that includes the *risk to national/personal security* or a *security risk*, which may be a person, group, thing or activity.

menace /ˈmenəs/ [C, usually sing.] a person or thing that people are afraid of because it causes or may cause harm or damage: *The government's new initiative is aimed at beating the menace of illegal drugs.* ◇ *The protesters remain a potential menace to the stability of the government.*

threaten *verb*

1 threaten sb with a gun
2 Pollution is threatening marine life.
3 a storm threatens

1 See also the entry for HARASS

threaten · intimidate · cow · steamroller · warn sb off (sth) · scare sb into (doing) sth
These words all mean to frighten sb or say that you will hurt them in order to make them do sth.

threaten [T] to say that you will cause trouble or hurt sb if you do not get what you want: *They broke my windows and threatened me.* ◇ *The attacker threatened them with a gun.* ◇ *The hijackers* **threatened to** *kill the passengers if their demands were not met.*
▸ **threat** *noun* [C, U]: *to make threats against sb* ◇ *She is prepared to* **carry out her threat** *to resign.* ◇ *He received death threats from right-wing groups.* ◇ *crimes involving violence or the threat of violence*

intimidate /ɪnˈtɪmɪdeɪt/ [T] (*rather formal*) to frighten or threaten sb so that they will do what you want: *They were accused of intimidating people into voting for them.* ◇ *She refused to be intimidated by their threats.* See also **intimidated** → AFRAID, See also the entry for FRIGHTEN
▸ **intimidation** /ɪnˌtɪmɪˈdeɪʃn/ *noun* [U]: *the intimidation of witnesses*

cow /kaʊ/ [T, usually passive] (*written*) to frighten sb in order to make them obey you: *He was easily cowed by people in authority.* ◇ *They were wrong if they thought she could be* **cowed into submission** *by threats.*

steamroller /'sti:mrəʊlə(r); *AmE* -roʊ-/ (*especially BrE*) (*AmE* usually **steamroll**) [T, I] to defeat sb or force them to do sth, using your power or authority and ignoring their wishes or opinions: *She had no intention of letting herself be steamrollered by him.* ◇ *The administration is trying to steamroll the bill through Congress.*

,**warn sb 'off**, ,**warn sb 'off sth** *phrasal verb* to tell sb to leave or stay away from a place or person, especially in a threatening way: *Some animals mark the territory to warn off rivals.* ◇ *The farmer warned us off his land when we tried to camp there.*

'**scare sb into sth/into doing sth** *phrasal verb* (*rather informal*) to frighten sb in order to make them do sth: *Local businesses were scared into paying protection money.* ◇ *It might be possible to scare him into silence.*

2 threaten · endanger · risk · jeopardize
These words all mean to be a danger to sb/sth.

PATTERNS AND COLLOCATIONS
▸ to threaten / endanger / risk sb's / your **life / health**
▸ to threaten / risk / jeopardize sb's / your **job / career**
▸ to threaten / endanger / jeopardize the **survival** of sth
▸ a threatened / endangered **species**
▸ to **seriously** threaten / endanger / jeopardize sth

threaten [T] to be likely to cause harm or damage to sb/sth: *She claimed that the conflict was threatening stability in the region.* ◇ *Many species are now* **threatened with** *extinction.* ◇ *Our marriage was constantly threatened by his other women.* See also **threat** → RISK 1

endanger /ɪn'deɪndʒə(r)/ [T] to put sb/sth in a situation in which they could be harmed, damaged or destroyed: *The health of our children is being endangered by exhaust fumes.* ◇ *That one mistake seriously endangered the future of the company.* ◇ *The sea turtle is an endangered species* (= it may soon no longer exist). See also **endangered** → VULNERABLE

risk [T] to put sth valuable or important in a dangerous situation, in which it could be damaged or lost: *He risked all his money on a game of cards.* ◇ *She has been willing to* **risk life and limb** (= risk being killed or injured) *to get a good close-up shot of the nesting birds.* ◇ *He had no desire to* **risk his neck** (= risk being killed, especially by being executed) *for the king and his favourites.* ❶ People usually choose to **risk** sth that is their own, such as their *life, health, money, job* or *career*, in the hope of gaining sth else, although sometimes the choice is not quite so deliberate: *In ignoring the warnings, she was risking her own and her children's health.* **Risk** is not used about things that are outside sb's control: ~~The health of our children is being risked by exhaust fumes.~~

jeopardize (*BrE* also -**ise**) /'dʒepədaɪz; *AmE* -pərd-/ [T] (*written*) to threaten the future development of sth such as sb's job, a plan or a system: *She would never do anything to jeopardize her career.* ◇ *This scandal could seriously jeopardize his chances of being re-elected.*

3 threaten · promise · herald · bode well/ill
These words all mean to seem likely to happen or to be a sign that sth will happen.

PATTERNS AND COLLOCATIONS
▸ to threaten / promise **to do sth**
▸ to threaten / promise / herald **rain**
▸ to promise / herald a (new) **beginning**

threaten [I, T] (of sth unpleasant) to seem likely to happen; to seem likely to cause sth unpleasant: *A storm was threatening.* ◇ *When war threatens, people act irrationally.* ◇ *This dispute threatens to split the party.* ◇ *The clouds threatened rain.* See also **threat** → RISK 1

promise [T] to make sth seem likely to happen, or show signs of sth happening, especially sth new or positive: *It* **promises to be** *an exciting few days.* ◇ *The new drug promises to bring relief to thousands of asthma sufferers.* ◇ *It was a disappointing end to a season which had promised so much for the team.*

▸ **promise** *noun* [U, sing.]: *The day dawned bright and clear, with the promise of warm sunny weather.*

herald /'herəld/ [T] (*written*) to be a sign that sth is going to happen, especially sth new and positive: *These talks could herald a new era of peace.* ◇ *Voices and footsteps outside heralded their return.*

▸ **herald** *noun* [C]: *The government claims that the fall in unemployment is the herald of economic recovery.*

bode 'well/'ill *idiom* (*written*) to be a sign that sth good/bad is going to happen: *These figures do not* **bode well for** *the company's future.*

threatening *adj.*

threatening · sinister · ominous · forbidding
These words all describe actions, people or things that seem likely to cause you harm or danger.

PATTERNS AND COLLOCATIONS
▸ a threatening / sinister / forbidding **look**
▸ a threatening / a sinister / an ominous **tone**
▸ threatening / ominous **black / dark clouds**
▸ **rather** threatening / sinister / ominous / forbidding
▸ **slightly / vaguely** sinister / forbidding

threatening expressing a threat of harm or violence; showing that bad weather is likely: *people who send threatening letters or make obscene phone calls* ◇ *The sky was dark and threatening.* See also **threat** → RISK 1

sinister /'sɪnɪstə(r)/ seeming evil or dangerous; making you think sth bad will happen: *There was something cold and sinister about him.* ◇ *There was a sinister undertone in his words.*

ominous /'ɒmɪnəs; *AmE* 'ɑːm-/ making you think that sth bad will happen; showing that bad weather is likely: *She picked up the phone but there was an ominous silence at the other end.* ◇ *There were ominous dark clouds gathering overhead.*

forbidding seeming unfriendly and frightening and likely to cause harm or danger: *a forbidding appearance/atmosphere/manner* ◇ *The house looked dark and forbidding.* **OPP** **welcoming** ❶ A **welcoming** place is attractive and looks comfortable to be in: *the welcoming atmosphere of the club* See also **welcoming** → FRIENDLY 1

throw *verb*

throw · toss · hurl · fling · chuck · lob · bowl · pitch
These words all mean to send sth from your hand through the air.

PATTERNS AND COLLOCATIONS
▸ to throw / toss / hurl / fling / chuck / lob / bowl / pitch sth **at / to** sb / sth
▸ to throw / toss / fling / chuck sth **aside / away**
▸ to throw / toss / hurl / fling / chuck / lob / bowl / pitch a **ball**
▸ to throw / toss / hurl / fling / chuck **stones / rocks / a brick**
▸ to throw / toss / fling / chuck sb a **towel**
▸ to throw / toss / hurl / fling sth **angrily**
▸ to throw / toss sth **casually / carelessly**

throw [T, I] to send sth from your hand or hands through the air: *Some kids were throwing things at the window.* ◇ *The body had been thrown into the river.* ◇ *Can you throw me that towel?* ◇ *They had a competition to see who could throw the furthest.*

▸ **throw** *noun* [C]: *a well-aimed throw* ◇ *It's your throw* (= it's your turn to throw the dice).

toss [T] to throw sth lightly or carelessly: *I got up, tossing aside my book.* ◇ *He tossed the ball to Anna.* ◇ *He tossed Anna the ball.*

hurl [T] to throw sth violently in a particular direction: *Rioters hurled a brick through the car's windscreen.*

fling [T] to throw sb/sth somewhere with a lot of force, especially because you are angry or in a hurry: *He flung her to the ground.* ◇ *I flung a few clothes into a bag.*

chuck [T] (*especially BrE, informal*) to throw sth carelessly: *Chuck me that newspaper, can you?*

lob (-**bb**-) [T] (*informal*) to throw sth so that it goes high through the air: *They were lobbing stones over the wall.*

bowl [I, T] (in cricket) to throw the ball to the batsman: *It was Peter's turn to bowl.* ◇ *He bowled him a gentle first ball.*

pitch [I, T] (in baseball) to throw the ball to the batter: *He pitched against UCLA last week.* ◇ *The pitcher pitched the ball right down the middle of the plate.*

thug *noun* See the Topic Map for CONFLICT on p.896, See also the entry for HOOLIGAN

---

thug · gangster · mobster · goon · heavy
These are all words for a violent person, especially a criminal.

PATTERNS AND COLLOCATIONS
▸ an **armed** thug / gangster / mobster
▸ to **set** your thugs / goons / heavies **on** sb
▸ to **call off** your thugs / goons / heavies
▸ a thug / goon **attacks** sb
▸ a **gang of** thugs / goons / heavies

thug [C] a violent person, especially a criminal: *A gang of thugs had attacked him with sticks.*

gangster [C] a member of a group of violent criminals who are involved in organized crime: *We watched a movie about Chicago gangsters.*

mobster [C] (*especially AmE*) a gangster: *De Niro plays the most menacing mobster of all.*

goon [C] (*informal, especially AmE*) a criminal who is paid to frighten or injure people: *Just call off your goons and no one will get hurt.*

heavy [C] (*informal*) a large strong man whose job is to protect a person or place, often using violence: *He lunged at the minister, but was soon pulled to the ground by a couple of heavies.*

thwart *verb* See also the entry for PREVENT

---

thwart · frustrate · derail · foil · dash sb's hopes · disappoint
These words all mean to prevent sth that sb wants to do or wants to happen.

PATTERNS AND COLLOCATIONS
▸ to be thwarted / frustrated / foiled / disappointed **in** sth
▸ to thwart / frustrate / dash / disappoint sb's **hopes**
▸ to thwart / frustrate / derail / foil sb's **plans**
▸ to thwart / frustrate sb's **efforts**
▸ to thwart / derail sb's **chances**
▸ to thwart / foil a **plot / raid / coup**
▸ to thwart / frustrate sb's **ambition**
▸ to be **easily / constantly** thwarted / frustrated / foiled
▸ to be thwarted / frustrated / foiled **in your attempt to** do sth

thwart /θwɔːt; AmE θwɔːrt/ [T, often passive] to prevent sb from doing what they want to do: *She was thwarted in her attempt to take control of the party.* ◇ *His ambition to be a painter was thwarted by poor eyesight.*

frustrate /frʌˈstreɪt; AmE ˈfrʌstreɪt/ [T] (*especially written*) to prevent sth from happening or succeeding as people had hoped; to prevent sb from doing sth, often deliberately: *The rescue attempt was frustrated by bad weather.* ◇ *He tried to frustrate his political opponents by denying them access to the media.*

derail /dɪˈreɪl/ [T] (*journalism*) to prevent a process from succeeding or continuing as planned or hoped, especially by creating a problem or disagreement: *This latest incident could derail the peace process.* **OPP** **get sth back on track** ❶ To get sth back on track (*informal*) is to get sth going in the right direction again after a mistake or failure: *I tried to get my life back on track after my divorce.*

foil [T] (*especially journalism*) to prevent sth that sb is planning to do, especially sth illegal: *Customs officials foiled an attempt to smuggle priceless paintings out of the country.*

dash sb's 'hopes idiom [usually passive] to destroy sb's hopes by making what they were hoping for impossible: *Hopes for a peaceful settlement have been dashed.*

disappoint [T] to prevent sth that sb hopes for from becoming a reality: *The new government had soon disappointed the hopes of many of its supporters.* See also **disappointment** → DISAPPOINTMENT

tidy *verb*

---

tidy · clean (sth) up · clear (sth) up · sort sth out
These words all mean to make sth look neat by putting things where they belong and removing rubbish or dirt.

PATTERNS AND COLLOCATIONS
▸ to tidy up / clean up / clear up **after** sb
▸ to tidy / clear up / sort out a **house / room**
▸ to tidy / sort out a **cupboard / your desk**
▸ to tidy / clean up / clear up the **mess**

tidy [T, I] (*especially BrE*) to make sth look neat by putting things in the place where they belong: *She wanted to tidy herself up before the appointment* (= comb her hair, etc.). ◇ *She was always cleaning and tidying.* ◇ *When you use the kitchen please **tidy up** after yourself.* See also **tidy** → NEAT *adj.*, **freshen up** → WASH

,**clean 'up**, ,**clean sth 'up** phrasal verb to make sth clean and neat by removing dirt and mess: *He always expected other people to clean up after him* (= when he had made the place dirty or untidy). ◇ *Who's going to clean up this mess?* ◇ *to clean up beaches after an oil spillage* See also **clean** → CLEAN *verb*
▸ **'clean-up** noun [usually sing.]: *a massive clean-up operation* ◇ *the clean-up of the river*

,**clear 'up**, ,**clear sth 'up** phrasal verb to make sth clean and neat, by removing rubbish or putting things in the place where they belong: *Start clearing up now.* ◇ *Let him clear up his own mess!* ◇ *They were still clearing up the debris after the accident.*

,**sort sth 'out**, ,**sort through sth** phrasal verb (*informal*) to organize the contents of sth: *We'll need to sort out the contents of the house.* ◇ *He was sorting through his desk and throwing away old papers.*

tie *verb*

---

tie · button · zip · fasten · do (sth) up
These words all mean to join two parts of sth so that it is closed.

PATTERNS AND COLLOCATIONS
▸ sth buttons / zips / fastens / does **up**
▸ to tie / button / zip / fasten / do **sth up**
▸ to tie / button / fasten / do up **at** the neck, waist, etc.
▸ to tie / do up your **laces / shoelaces**
▸ to button / fasten / do up your **coat**
▸ to fasten / do up **buttons**
▸ to tie / fasten sth **tight / firmly**

tie [T, I] to make a knot in a piece of string, rope, etc.; to be closed or fastened with a knot, etc: *She tied the ribbon in a bow.* ◇ *I tied a knot in the rope.* ◇ *Can you tie a bow tie?* ◇ *The robe ties at the waist.* **OPP** **untie** → UNDO

button [T, I] to close or join the two parts of sth with buttons; to be closed or joined in this way: *He buttoned up his shirt.* ◇ *The dress buttons at the back.* **OPP** **unbutton** → UNDO, See also **button** → BUTTON *noun 2*

zip (-**pp**-) [T, I] to close a bag or piece of clothing with a zip; (of a bag or piece of clothing) to be closed with a zip ❶ A **zip** (*BrE*) or **zipper** (*AmE*) is a type of fastener that consists of two rows of metal or plastic teeth that you can pull together to close sth or pull apart to open it: *She zipped the case shut.* ◇ *The children were safely zipped into* their sleeping bags. ◇ The sleeping bags can zip together. **OPP** unzip → UNDO, See also **zip, zipper** → BUTTON noun 2

fasten [T, I] to close or join together the two parts of sth; to become closed or joined together: Fasten your seat belts please! ◇ The dress fastens at the back. **OPP** unfasten → UNDO, See also **fastener** → BUTTON noun 2

,do sth 'up, ,do 'up phrasal verb (especially spoken) to fasten a piece of clothing; (of a piece of clothing) to be fastened: I can't do up this zip. ◇ The skirt does up at the back. ◇ Do up your coat – it's cold. **OPP** undo → UNDO

tight adj.

tight · firm · stiff · taut
These words all describe sth that is held or fixed strongly in position or stretched as far as it will go.

firm   tight   taut
              stiff

PATTERNS AND COLLOCATIONS
▸ a tight / firm **grip / hold**
▸ a **rope / wire** is tight / taut

tight held or fixed strongly in position; difficult to move or undo; stretched or pulled so that it cannot stretch much further: He kept a tight grip on her arm. ◇ She twisted her hair into a tight knot. ◇ The screw was so tight that it wouldn't move. ◇ The rope was stretched tight. **OPP** loose
ℹ Sth that is **loose** is not fixed where it should be: a loose button/tooth ◇ Check that the plug has not **come loose**.
▸ **tight** adv.: Hold tight! ◇ His fists were clenched tight.
▸ **tightly** adv.: Her eyes were tightly closed. ◇ He held on tightly to her arm.

firm (often approving) (of sb's hand movements) strong and steady: He handshake was cool and firm. ◇ Close the hatches with a firm push on the lever. See also **firm** → FIRM, **firm** → SOLID
▸ **firmly** adv.: He held her firmly but gently.

stiff (often disapproving) difficult to move: The windows were stiff and she couldn't get them open. **ℹ** In this meaning **stiff** is used to talk about things that are supposed to open or bend, such as windows, doors, lids or sb's knees, legs, etc. See also **stiff** → SOLID

taut /tɔ:t/ stretched tightly: Keep the rope taut. **OPP** slack
ℹ Sth that is **slack** is not stretched tightly: The rope suddenly went slack.

tighten verb

tighten · clench · tense · grit your teeth · screw your eyes/face up
These words all mean to make sth become tight or tighter.

PATTERNS AND COLLOCATIONS
▸ to tighten / clench / tense / grit your teeth / screw your eyes up **with / in** pain, irritation, etc.
▸ to tighten / clench your **hand / fist / jaw**
▸ to tighten / tense your **muscles**
▸ to clench / grit your **teeth**
▸ your **jaw / hand** tightens / clenches / tenses
▸ your **fist / stomach** tightens / clenches
▸ your **muscles** tighten / tense
▸ to tighten / clench / tense (sth) **involuntarily**
▸ to clench / grit your teeth / screw your eyes up **tight / tightly**

tighten [I, T] to become or make sth tight or tighter: His mouth tightened into a thin line. ◇ This tool is for tightening screws. ◇ She tightened her grip on his arm. ◇ The brake cable needs tightening up. **OPP** relax, loosen, slacken → RELAX 2

clench [T, I] to press your hands, teeth or stomach muscles together tightly, usually showing that you are angry, determined or upset; (of hands, teeth or stomach muscles) to be pressed together tightly in this way: He clenched his fists in anger. ◇ Through clenched teeth she told him to leave. ◇ His fists clenched slowly until his knuckles were white.

tense /tens/ [I, T] to make your muscles tight and stiff, especially because you are not relaxed: She tensed, hearing the strange noise again. ◇ He tensed himself, listening to see if anyone had followed him. ◇ Expecting a blow, she tensed every muscle in her body. **OPP** relax → RELAX 2, See also **tense** → TENSE adj.

grit your 'teeth idiom (-tt-) to bite your teeth tightly together; to be determined to continue to do sth in a difficult or unpleasant situation: She gritted her teeth against the pain. ◇ It started to rain harder, but we gritted our teeth and carried on.

NOTE GRIT YOUR TEETH OR CLENCH YOUR TEETH? Grit your teeth is used especially to talk about showing determination; clench your teeth is used more often to talk about keeping your mouth tightly shut in order to avoid making a noise such as shouting with anger or pain, or in order to stop your teeth from knocking together because you are cold or frightened.

,screw your 'eyes/'face up idiom to tighten the muscles of your eyes or face, for example because the light is too strong, you are in pain or you don't like the taste or look of sth: He took a sip of the medicine and screwed up his face.

time noun

1 It's time for lunch.
2 a long time ago

1 time · moment · point · occasion · hour · date · instant
These are all words for a particular point in time, especially a time when sth happens or when a stage of development is reached.

PATTERNS AND COLLOCATIONS
▸ a time / a moment / the point / sb's hour **of** sth
▸ **at** the time / the moment / that point / that instant
▸ **on** that occasion / date
▸ **from / until** that time / moment / point / date
▸ **for** the time / moment / occasion
▸ at/on **(any) given /one** time / moment / point / occasion / instant
▸ the **very / precise** time / moment / hour / instant
▸ a / an **memorable / emotional** time / moment / occasion
▸ **to choose / pick** a / your time / moment
▸ the time / moment / hour **comes / arrives**

time [U, C] a particular point in time, especially a time when sth happens or when sth should happen: What time do you finish work? ◇ It's **time for** lunch. ◇ I think it's **time to** go to bed. ◇ It's time the kids were in bed. ◇ **By the time** you get there the meeting will be over. ◇ You'll feel differently about it **when the time comes** (= when it happens). ◇ The train arrived right **on time** (= at exactly the correct time). ◇ A computer screen shows arrival and departure times. ◇ I want to fix a time for a meeting next month. ◇ Have I called at a bad time? ◇ **Every time** I hear that song I feel happy. ◇ **Next time** you're here let's have lunch together. ◇ He failed the test three times. ◇ He's determined to pass **this time**. ◇ When was the **last time** you saw her? ◇ (AmE) I remember **one time** (= once) we had to abandon our car in the snow.

moment [sing.] an exact point in time: We're busy **at the moment** (= now). ◇ **At that very** moment, the phone rang. ◇ I agreed **in a moment** of weakness. ◇ From that moment on, she never felt really well again. **ℹ** A **moment** [C] can also be a time when you have a particular feeling, or that is good or bad for doing a particular thing: That was one of the happiest moments of my life. ◇ Have I caught you at a bad moment?

point [C] a particular time or stage of development: The climber was **at the point of** death when they found him. ◇ We were **on the point** of giving up. ◇ Many people suffer from mental illness **at some point** in their lives. ◇ We had reached the point when there was no money left. ◇ **At this point in time** (= Now) *we just have to wait.* ❶ **Point** forms part of a lot of compounds that mean a particular time or stage in an event or process: *the high point/low point of the trip* ◇ *to reach boiling/freezing/melting/saturation point* ◇ *This could be the sticking point in the negotiations.* See also the entry for TURNING POINT

occasion [C] a particular time when sth happens: *They have been seen together on two separate occasions.* ◇ *He used the occasion to announce further tax cuts.* ◇ *He has even been known to go shopping himself* **on occasion** (= only a few times). See also **occasion →** OPPORTUNITY

hour [sing.] a particular point in time; the time when sth important happens: *You can't turn him away* **at this hour of the night.** ◇ *She thought her* **last hour** *had come.* ◇ *Don't desert me in my* **hour of need.**

date [sing., U] a point in time in the past or future that is not a particular day: *The details can be added at a later date.* ◇ *The coins are all of late Roman date.*

instant [sing.] an exact point in time: *At that (very) instant, the door opened.* ◇ *I recognized her* **the instant (that)** (= as soon as) *I saw her.* ◇ *Come here* **this instant** (= immediately)!

---

2 time · period · season · while · term · run · spell · interval · stint · span · patch
These are all words for a length of time during which sth lasts, happens or is done.

PATTERNS AND COLLOCATIONS
▸ a time/a period/a season/a term/a run/a spell/an interval/a stint/ a span/ a patch **of** sth
▸ a time/ period/ season/ term/ spell/ stint **as** sth
▸ **for** a time/ a period/ a season/ a while/ a term/ a spell/ an interval/ a stint/ a span
▸ **during** a time/ a period/ a season/ a term/ a run/ a spell/ an interval/ a stint/ a span/ a … patch
▸ **after** a time/ a period/ a season/ a while/ a term/ a run/ a spell/ an interval/ a stint/ a … patch
▸ a **long** time/ period/ season/ while/ term/ run/ spell/ interval/ stint/ span
▸ a **short** time/ period/ season/ while/ term/ spell/ interval/ stint/ span
▸ a **brief** time/ period/ season/ while/ spell/ interval/ stint/ span
▸ a **bad** time/ period/ season/ run/ spell/ patch
▸ a **difficult / lean** time/ period/ season/ spell/ patch
▸ a **successful** time/ period/ season/ term/ run/ stint
▸ to **have** a … time/ period/ season/ run/ spell/ patch
▸ to **enjoy** a time/ period/ season/ run/ spell
▸ to **go through** a … time/ period/ season/ spell/ patch
▸ to **do** a term/ spell/ stint

time [C] a period of time, either long or short, during which you do sth or sth happens: *I lived in Egypt for a time.* ◇ *His injuries will* **take a long time** *to heal.* ◇ *Her parents died* **a long time ago.** ◇ **At one time** (= at a period of time in the past) *Emily was my best friend.* ◇ *Mr Curtis was the manager* **in my time** (= when I was working there).* ◇ *The early morning is the best* **time of day.** ◇ *There were times – sometimes whole weeks – when I thought it wasn't worth trying to complete the project.* See also **time →** PERIOD

period [C] a length of time during which sth lasts, happens or is done: *There was a long period of uncertainty before we knew the final decision.* ◇ *The factory will be closed down over a period of two years.* ◇ *This compares with a 4% increase for the same period last year.* ◇ *The project will run for a six-month* **trial period.** See also **period →** PERIOD

NOTE **TIME** OR **PERIOD?** **Time** places more emphasis on the feeling of time passing and things happening during the period; **period** places more emphasis on the amount of time that passed or has passed, and the things that did happen or have happened: *I lived in Egypt for a period.* ◇ *The factory will be closed down over a time of two years.* When you are talking about things that happen

regularly, you can use either word, but **period** is slightly more formal: *There are extra buses at peak times/periods.*

season [C] a period during a year when a particular activity happens or is done, or when a particular style of clothes, hair, etc. is popular and fashionable: *the cricket/hunting/shooting season* ◇ *the breeding/mating/growing/planting season* ◇ *She scored her first goal of the season on Saturday.* ◇ *The hotels are always full during the peak season* (= the period when most people are on holiday). ◇ *(BrE) the holiday season* ◇ *(AmE) the tourist season* ◇ *(BrE) Best wishes for the festive season* (= Christmas). ◇ *(AmE) the holiday season* (= the time of Thanksgiving, Hanukkah, Christmas and New Year). ◇ *It's much cheaper to buy a* **season ticket** (= a single ticket that lasts a whole season). ◇ *This season's look is soft and romantic.* ❶ **Season** also means a period of time during which a play is shown in one place, or a series of plays, films or television programmes: *The play opens for a second season in London next week.* ◇ *a season of films by Alfred Hitchcock*

while [sing.] a period of time: *They chatted for a while.* ◇ *I'll be back in* **a little while** (= a short time). ◇ *I haven't seen him for* **quite a while** (= a fairly long time). (*written*) ❶ **While** is used especially to talk about the fairly long or fairly short time that sb spends doing sth or waiting for sth to happen, or how long sth takes.

term [C] a period during which sth lasts; a fixed or limited period of time: *during the president's first* **term of/in office** ◇ *He faces a maximum* **prison/jail term** *of 25 years.* ◇ *The term of agreement can be for either two or three years.*

run [C] a period during which sth good or bad lasts or is repeated; a series of performances of a play or film: *a run of good/bad luck* ◇ *Liverpool lost to Leeds, ending an unbeaten run of 18 games.* ◇ *The show is enjoying a record-breaking run at the Shaftesbury Theatre.*

spell [C] a short period during which sth lasts, especially weather; a short period that you spend working somewhere or doing sth: *We had a spell of warm weather in April.* ◇ *a cold/hot/wet/bright spell* ◇ *She went to the doctor complaining of* **dizzy spells.** ◇ *I spent a brief spell on the Washington Post.*

interval [C, usually pl.] a short period during which sth different happens from what is happening the rest of the time: *She's delirious most of the time, but has lucid intervals.* ◇ *She ruled for ten years, except for a brief interval.*

stint [C] a period that you spend working somewhere or doing a particular activity: *She did a stint abroad early in her career.* ◇ *He hated his two-year stint in the Navy.*

span [C] the length of time that sth lasts or is able to continue: *I worked with him several times over a span of six years.* ◇ *This textbook covers the entire span of Arab history.* ◇ *The project must be completed within a specific* **time span.** ◇ *Small children have a short* **attention span.**

patch [C] (*especially BrE, informal*) a period of the type mentioned, usually a difficult or unhappy one: *The team has been through a rough patch recently.*

---

timely *adj.* See also the entry for PROMISING

timely · lucky · happy · fortunate
These words all describe sth that happens at the right time.

PATTERNS AND COLLOCATIONS
▸ to be timely/ lucky/ fortunate **for** sb / sth
▸ to be timely/ lucky/ fortunate **that...**
▸ a lucky/ happy/ fortunate **coincidence / chance**
▸ in a happy/ fortunate **position**
▸ a lucky/ fortunate **escape**
▸ **very** timely/ lucky/ happy/ fortunate
▸ **extremely / particularly** timely/ lucky/ fortunate

timely /'taɪmli/ [usually before noun] happening at exactly the right time: *A nasty incident was prevented by the timely arrival of the police.* ◇ *This has been a **timely reminder** to us all.*

lucky happening as the result of good luck: *It was lucky for us that he didn't see us.* ◇ *That was the luckiest escape of my life.* ◇ *I didn't know he was there — it was just a **lucky guess**.* **OPP unlucky** → UNFORTUNATE 1, See also **luck** → LUCK
▸ **luckily** *adv.*: *We were late, but luckily for us that plane had been delayed.*

happy [only before noun] happening, usually by chance, at exactly the right time, or in the way that you want or like: *By a **happy coincidence**, John was in London at that time too.* ◇ *He is now in the happy position of never having to worry about money.*

fortunate /'fɔːtʃənət; *AmE* 'fɔːrtʃ-/ (*rather formal*) bringing an advantage, an opportunity or a piece of good luck: *It was fortunate for us that the guard was looking the other way.* ◇ *He was in a relatively fortunate position as far as work was concerned.* **OPP unfortunate** → UNFORTUNATE 2, See also **fortune** → LUCK
▸ **fortunately** *adv.*: *I was late, but fortunately the meeting hadn't started.*

tip *noun*

tip · point · spike · prong · nib
These are all words for the sharp end of an object.

PATTERNS AND COLLOCATIONS
▸ a **sharp** tip / point / spike
▸ the tip / point of a **knife**

tip [C] the end of sth, especially sth that is long and narrow; a small part that fits on or over the end of sth: *He ran the tips of his fingers over the bruise.* ◇ *The base is situated at the northern tip of the island.* ◇ *The walking stick was fitted with a rubber tip.*

point [C] the sharp thin end of sth: *She pressed so hard that the point of the pencil made a hole in the paper.*
▸ **pointed** *adj.*: *the pointed arches used in medieval buildings*

spike [C] a thin object with a sharp point, especially a pointed piece of metal or wood: *The wall had a row of iron spikes along the top.* ◇ *Her hair stood up in spikes.* See also **spiky** → COARSE

prong [C] each of the two or more long pointed parts of a fork: *One of the prongs of the garden fork went through his foot.*

nib [C] the metal point of a pen: *I dipped the nib into the ink and started to write.*

tire *verb*

tire · exhaust · wear sb/yourself out · weaken · tire sb/yourself out
These words all mean to make sb/yourself feel tired and want to sleep or rest.

PATTERNS AND COLLOCATIONS
▸ to tire / exhaust **yourself**
▸ to wear / tire **yourself** out

tire [I, T] (*rather formal*) to become tired and feel as if you want to sleep or rest; to make sb feel this way: *Her legs were beginning to tire.* ◇ *He has made a good recovery but he still tires easily.* ◇ *Long conversations tired her.*

exhaust /ɪg'zɔːst/ [T] to make sb feel very tired: *Even a short walk exhausted her.*

wear sb/yourself 'out *phrasal verb* to make sb/yourself feel very tired: *The kids have totally worn me out.* ◇ *You'll wear yourself out if you carry on like this.*

weaken [I, T] to become or to make sb/sth physically weaker: *He began to weaken as his opponent continued the onslaught.* ◇ *The explosion had weakened the building's foundations considerably.* **OPP strengthen** → STRENGTHEN

tire sb/yourself 'out *phrasal verb* (*rather informal, especially spoken*) to make sb/yourself feel very tired: *Working twelve hour shifts would really tire me out.*

> **NOTE EXHAUST, WEAR SB/YOURSELF OUT OR TIRE SB/YOURSELF OUT?** There is very little difference in meaning between these words. **Exhaust** is the most frequent, and the most suitable for use in formal writing, but it can be used in less formal contexts too. **Tire sb/yourself out** is the least formal, used mostly in spoken English.

tired *adj.*

1 feel tired
2 tired old jokes

1 See the Topic Map for HEALTH on p.890
tired · exhausted · drained · weary · sleepy · drowsy · worn out · shattered · pooped · fatigued
These words all describe sb who needs to sleep or rest.

tired	drained	exhausted
sleepy	weary	shattered
drowsy	worn out	pooped
	fatigued	

PATTERNS AND COLLOCATIONS
▸ tired / exhausted / weary / sleepy / drowsy / worn out / pooped **from** sth
▸ tired / worn / pooped **out**
▸ to **feel** tired / exhausted / drained / weary / sleepy / drowsy / worn out / shattered / fatigued
▸ to **look** tired / exhausted / drained / weary / sleepy / worn out / shattered / pooped / fatigued
▸ to **sound** tired / exhausted / weary / sleepy
▸ to **leave sb** tired / exhausted / drained
▸ to **make sb** sleepy / drowsy
▸ **very / a little** tired / weary / sleepy / drowsy
▸ **quite** tired / sleepy / drowsy / worn out
▸ **completely / totally / utterly** exhausted / drained
▸ **physically / mentally** tired / exhausted / drained

tired feeling that you would like to sleep or rest; needing rest: *I'm too tired even to think.* ◇ *They were cold, hungry and tired out (= very tired).* ◇ *The words danced on the page before his tired eyes.*

exhausted /ɪg'zɔːstɪd/ extremely tired: *I'm exhausted!* ◇ *The exhausted climbers were rescued by helicopter.*
▸ **exhaustion** /ɪg'zɔːstʃən/ *noun* [U]: *Her face was grey with exhaustion.*

drained [not usually before noun] very tired because you have used up all your physical, mental or emotional energy: *He suddenly felt totally drained.* ◇ *The experience left him physically and emotionally drained.*

weary /'wɪəri; *AmE* 'wɪri/ (*rather formal*) very tired, especially after you have been working hard or doing sth for a long time: *She suddenly felt old and weary.* ◇ *He gave a long, weary sigh.*
▸ **wearily** *adv.*: *He closed his eyes wearily.*

sleepy needing sleep; ready to go to sleep: *The heat and the wine made him sleepy.*
▸ **sleepily** *adv.*: *She yawned sleepily.*

drowsy /'draʊzi/ almost asleep; making you feel relaxed and sleepy: *The tablets may make you feel drowsy.* ◇ *She lay in the sun all through the long, drowsy afternoon.*
▸ **drowsiness** *noun* [U]: *The drugs tend to cause drowsiness.*

worn 'out [not usually before noun] (*rather informal*) very tired, especially as a result of hard work or physical exercise: *Can we sit down? I'm worn out.*

shattered [not usually before noun] (*BrE, informal*) extremely tired: *By the end of the day I was absolutely shattered.*

pooped /puːpt/ (also **pooped 'out**) [not usually before noun] (*AmE, informal*) extremely tired: *I'm pooped!*

fatigued /fə'tiːɡd/ [not usually before noun] (*formal*) very tired, both physically and mentally: *The troops were already fatigued from the long forced march.*
▸ **fatigue** *noun* [U]: *Driver fatigue was to blame for the accident.*

2 See also the entry for LACKLUSTRE

tired · corny · trite · stale · hackneyed · clichéd
These words all describe things, especially language, that are uninteresting because they have been used too much.

PATTERNS AND COLLOCATIONS
▸ a tired / trite / hackneyed / clichéd **phrase**
▸ tired / corny / stale **jokes**
▸ trite / clichéd **words**
▸ to **sound** corny / trite / clichéd
▸ a **bit** corny / stale / hackneyed / clichéd
▸ **rather** trite / clichéd

tired said or written so often that it has lost interest, meaning or humour: *He began with a few tired old jokes.* ◊ *It's the same tired advice that was given to my mother.*

corny /'kɔːni; AmE 'kɔːrni/ (*informal*) used too often to be interesting or to sound sincere: *I know it may sound corny but it happens to be true.* ◊ *You sound like someone out of a corny film!* ❶ **Corny** is used especially to describe jokes, stories, films and the situations and emotions shown in them.

trite /traɪt/ said or written so often that it has lost interest or meaning: *It is a trite observation that there is no such thing as a standard of international law.*

NOTE TIRED OR TRITE? **Tired** *phrases*, *jokes* and *advice* make the listener feel bored; **trite** *observations*, *questions* and *remarks* make the listener feel contemptuous (= lacking respect).

stale no longer interesting or exciting because it has been said or done too many times before: *What had seemed fresh and exciting at first was now stale and predictable.*

hackneyed /'hæknid/ (of a phrase or idea) used too often and therefore boring: *The artist should be careful to avoid hackneyed subjects.*

clichéd /'kliːʃeɪd; AmE kliːˈʃeɪd/ (of a phrase or idea) used so often that it no longer has any meaning: *The song is as clichéd as its title.*

toilet *noun*

toilet · bathroom · lavatory · loo · restroom · potty · latrine · ladies' room · men's room · urinal
These are all words for a room or building where you go to get rid of waste matter from your body.

PATTERNS AND COLLOCATIONS
▸ a **public** toilet / bathroom / lavatory / loo / restroom / latrine / urinal
▸ the **men's** toilet / bathroom / loo / restroom / urinal
▸ the **ladies'** toilet / bathroom / loo / restroom
▸ to **use** the toilet / bathroom / lavatory / loo / restroom / latrine / ladies' room / men's room / urinal
▸ to **go to** the toilet / bathroom / lavatory / loo / restroom / ladies' room / men's room
▸ to **need** the toilet / bathroom / lavatory / loo
▸ toilet / lavatory / loo **paper**

toilet [C] a large bowl attached to a pipe that you sit on or stand over when you get rid of waste matter from your body: *Have you flushed the toilet?* ◊ *a toilet seat* ◊ *Toilet facilities for the disabled are available.* ❶ In British English the **toilet** is also a room with a toilet in it: (*BrE*) *Every flat has its own bathroom and toilet.* ◊ *Who's in the toilet?* Also in British English a **toilet** or **the toilets** [pl.] are a room or small building containing several toilets, for example in a large building or a public place: *The toilets are located in the entrance area.*

bathroom [C] (*especially AmE*) a room with a toilet in it, and sometimes a bath or shower: *I have to go to the bathroom* (= use the toilet). ◊ *Where's the bathroom?* (= for example in a restaurant)

NOTE TOILET OR BATHROOM? In British English **bathroom** means a room with a bath or shower in it. It may also contain a toilet. In American English **bathroom** is often used to mean a room with a toilet in it, even if it does not also contain a bath or shower.

lavatory /'lævətri; AmE -tɔːri/ [C] (*BrE, formal*) a toilet, or a room with a toilet in it; a public building or part of a building, with toilets in it: *There's a bathroom and a lavatory upstairs.* ◊ *The nearest public lavatory is at the station.* ❶ In American English **lavatory** is only used to talk about the toilets on a plane.

loo [C] (*BrE, informal*) a toilet: *I just need to pop to the loo.*

restroom /'restruːm; -rʊm/ [C] (*AmE*) a room with a toilet in a public place, such as a theatre or restaurant: *The gas station restroom was locked.*

potty [C] (*rather informal*) a bowl that very young children use when they are too small to use a toilet: (*AmE*) *I have to go potty.* ❶ In British English a child would say: *I need a wee/poo.*

latrine /lə'triːn/ [C] a toilet in a camp or outside, especially one made by digging a hole in the ground: *We put up the tents and dug a latrine pit.*

'ladies' room [C] (*AmE*) a toilet for women in a public building or place: *Could you tell me where the ladies' room is?*

'men's room [C] (*AmE*) a toilet for men in a public building or place: *The men's room is located in the foyer.*

urinal /juə'raɪnl; 'juərɪnl; AmE 'jʊrənl/ [C] a type of toilet for men that is attached to the wall: *Modern waterless urinals can help to save the environment.*

tolerant *adj.* See the Topic Map for THE INDIVIDUAL AND SOCIETY on p.894

tolerant · liberal · enlightened · permissive · open-minded · indulgent
These words all describe people who accept that other people's opinions or behaviour are often different from their own.

PATTERNS AND COLLOCATIONS
▸ tolerant / liberal / permissive **in** sth
▸ tolerant / open-minded / indulgent **towards** sb / sth
▸ tolerant / indulgent **with** sb
▸ a tolerant / a liberal / an enlightened / a permissive / an open-minded **attitude**
▸ a tolerant / a liberal / an enlightened / a permissive **approach**
▸ tolerant / liberal / enlightened **views**
▸ a tolerant / a liberal / a permissive **atmosphere**
▸ a tolerant / a liberal / an enlightened / an open-minded **person** / **man** / **woman**
▸ liberal / permissive / indulgent **parents**
▸ a tolerant / a liberal / an enlightened / a permissive **society**
▸ **very** tolerant / liberal / enlightened / permissive / open-minded
▸ **remarkably** tolerant / liberal / enlightened

tolerant /'tɒlərənt; AmE 'tɑːl-/ (*approving*) able to accept what other people say or do even if you do not agree with it: *She was becoming less able to condemn and more tolerant of others.* ◊ *There is little chance of a tolerant democratic system emerging.* **OPP** intolerant → BIASED, See also **tolerance** → PATIENCE, **easy-going** → CALM *adj.*

liberal /'lɪbərəl/ (*usually approving*) willing to understand and respect other people's behaviour and opinions, especially when they are different from your own; believing people should be able to choose how they behave: *Her parents are very liberal and allow her a lot of freedom.* ◊ *His later films reflect the more liberal values of the 1960s.*

enlightened /ɪn'laɪtnd/ [usually before noun] (*approving*) having or based on an understanding of people's needs or a situation; not based on old-fashioned attitudes or prejudices: *More enlightened companies provided education for the workforce.* ◇ *My mother had more enlightened opinions than my father.*

permissive /pə'mɪsɪv; *AmE* pər'm-/ allowing or showing a freedom of behaviour that many people do not approve of, especially in sexual matters: *Even in the most permissive times fidelity in marriage is important to many.* ◇ *He grew up before* **the permissive society** (= the greater freedom in attitudes and behaviour that came in the 1960s and 1970s).

,open-'minded (*approving*) willing to listen to, think about or accept different ideas: *I encourage the children to be* **open-minded about** *new ideas and experiences.*

indulgent /ɪn'dʌldʒənt/ (*usually disapproving*) tending to allow sb to have or do whatever they want: *Mothers are sometimes less indulgent towards daughters.*

tool *noun*

tool · device · aid · instrument · gadget · implement · utensil

These are all words for a thing that helps you to do your job or to achieve sth.

PATTERNS AND COLLOCATIONS
- a **useful** tool / device / aid / gadget
- a **little** / **special** tool / device / instrument / gadget
- a **basic** tool / device / aid
- a **simple** / **crude** tool / device / instrument
- a **sharp** / **metal** tool / instrument / implement
- a **mechanical** / **hi-tech** device / aid / gadget
- an **electrical** / **electronic** device / gadget
- a **teaching** / **training** / **research** tool / device / aid
- a **measuring** / **navigation** / **navigational** tool / device / instrument
- a **drawing** / **writing** tool / aid / instrument / implement
- a **medical** / **surgical** device / instrument / implement
- a **kitchen** / **household** gadget / implement / utensil

tool [C] a thing such as a hammer, screwdriver, saw, etc. that you hold in your hand and use for making things or repairing things; a thing that helps you to do your job or to achieve sth: *First prize is this beautiful set of garden tools.* ◇ *You will need a good-quality, sharp* **cutting tool**. ◇ *Always select the right tool for the job.* ◇ *a tool kit* (= a set of tools in a box or bag) ◇ *We make use of various research tools such as questionnaires.*

device [C] (*rather formal*) an object or piece of equipment that has been designed to do a particular job: *This device enables pilots to navigate with pinpoint accuracy.* ◇ *The twentieth century saw the introduction of labour-saving devices around the home.* ❶ A **device** is usually a small piece of electrical equipment.

aid [C] (especially in compounds) an object, machine or tool that you use to help you do sth: *You may need a* **hearing aid**. ◇ *Photographs make useful teaching aids.* ❶ An **aid** can be a small piece of equipment such as a *hearing aid*, or any type of object used in teaching: *a classroom/teaching/visual aid*

instrument [C] a tool or device used for a particular task, especially for delicate or scientific work: *surgical instruments* ◇ *This pen is the ideal* **precision instrument** *for all your graphic needs.* ◇ *medieval instruments of torture*

gadget /'gædʒɪt/ [C] a small tool or device that does sth useful: *Modern gadgets like these make a huge difference to home life.* ❶ **Gadget** is usually used to talk about sth modern, especially sth electronic.

implement /'ɪmplɪmənt/ [C] (*rather formal*) a tool or instrument, often one that is quite simple and that is used outdoors: *Various local crafts and agricultural implements are represented in the exhibition.*

utensil /juː'tensl/ [C] (*rather formal*) a tool that is used in the house: *Wash your hands and all cooking utensils after preparing raw meat.* ❶ **Utensil** is generally used to talk about sth used in the kitchen, especially those that can be held in the hand.

top *adj.* See also the entry for MAIN

top · senior · chief · leading · high · first · high-ranking · premier · foremost · superior · elite

These words all describe sb/sth that is the highest in position, rank or degree.

PATTERNS AND COLLOCATIONS
- a top / senior / chief / leading / high-ranking / superior **officer**
- a top / senior / chief / leading **adviser** / **aide** / **economist** / **lawyer**
- a top / senior / chief / high-ranking **executive**
- a top / senior / leading / high-ranking **official**
- a senior / leading / high-ranking **figure** / **member**
- the chief / leading / foremost **exponent** of sth
- the leading / foremost **authority** / **expert** on sth
- a top / senior **grade** / **appointment** / **job**
- the top / first / premier **division** / **prize**
- top / high **grades** / **marks**

top [usually before noun] highest in position, rank or degree: *He lives on the top floor.* ◇ *She's one of the top players in the country.* ◇ *The car was travelling at top speed.* ◇ *This is top quality silk.* ❶ **Top** can be used after a linking verb, but only in British English: (*BrE*) *He finished top in the exam.* ◇ *They're top of the league.*
- ▶ **top** *noun* [C]: *She was standing* **at the top** *of the stairs.* ◇ *Write your name at the top.* ◇ *He's at the top of his profession.* ◇ *This decision came from the top* (= the most important person in an organization). **OPP** **bottom** → BOTTOM

senior high in rank or status; higher in rank or status than others: *She's a senior lecturer at the university.* ◇ *I'm looking for a more senior position.* ◇ *He is* **senior to** *me.* **OPP** **junior** ❶ A person in a **junior** position is low in rank or status, or lower than others: *junior employees* ◇ *She is junior to me.*

chief (*often* **Chief**) [only before noun] highest in rank: *Who is the new Chief Education Officer?* ◇ *The chief financial officer of the company paid us a visit.* ◇ *Detective Chief Inspector Williams* ❶ **Chief** is mainly used in names of positions.

leading [only before noun] most important or most successful: *She was offered the leading role in the new TV series.* ◇ *He's a leading business analyst.* ❶ **Leading** is often used in publicity for companies that produce products or provide services: *a leading brand/manufacturer/supplier* See also **prominent** → FAMOUS

high [usually before noun] near the top in rank or status: *She has held high office under three prime ministers.* ◇ *The case was referred to a higher court.* ◇ *He has friends* **in high places** (= among people of power and influence). ❶ In this meaning **high** is used in a fairly limited range of collocations: *high status/rank/position/office*; and in some more particular names of very important people and things: *a high court/magistrate/commissioner/priest*

first *det.* most important or best: *Your first duty is to your family.* ◇ *She won first prize in the competition.* ❶ When **first** means 'most important', typical collocates are *duty, importance* and *consideration.* When **first** means 'best in a competition', typical collocates are *prize* and *place.*

,high-'ranking [usually before noun] high in rank or status; important: *He's a high-ranking officer in the army.* ◇ *She's been offered a high-ranking post in the police force.* ❶ **High-ranking** is often used to talk about positions in the areas of politics and the military. Typical collocates are *(army/military) officer, bureaucrat, official,* and *(party) member.*

premier /'premiə(r); *AmE* prɪ'mɪr; 'mjɪr/ [only before noun] (*especially written or journalism*) most important, famous or successful: *The new Institute of Contemporary Art is one of Boston's premier attractions.* ◇ (*BrE, sport*) *They've just moved up to the Premier League* (= in football). ❶ **Premier** is often used in journalism and advertising to talk about popular and successful events or places, especially in relation to the country or place they can be found in: *Scotland's premier resort/hotel/exhibition/tourist attraction*

foremost /'fɔːməʊst; *AmE* 'fɔːrmoʊst/ (*rather formal, especially written*) most important, famous or successful; in a position at the front: *I'd like to introduce you to the world's foremost authority on the subject.* ◇ *The President was foremost among those who condemned the violence.* ◇ *This question has been foremost in our minds recently.*

NOTE PREMIER OR FOREMOST? Premier is used more to describe places and events; **foremost** is used more to describe people. **Foremost** is a more formal word and suggests greater seriousness; **premier** suggests greater popularity: *the world's foremost authority on/expert on/ exponent of sth* ◇ *Britain's premier chef*

superior /suː'pɪəriə(r); sjuː-; *AmE* suː'pɪr-/ higher in rank or status: *I'll need to check with my superior officer.* ❶ In this meaning, **superior** typically collocates with *officer, status, position* and *power.* **OPP inferior** ❶ An **inferior** officer or position is lower in rank or status.

NOTE SENIOR OR SUPERIOR? Superior is used more than **senior** when there is a strong sense of status in a system or organization, for example in the army. In an everyday office or work situation it is more usual to talk about a *senior colleague/manager/adviser/clerk/editor/ designer/teacher.*

elite /eɪ'liːt; ɪ'liːt/ [only before noun] powerful, and having a lot of influence, because of wealth, ability, family or business connections: *The secret was known only by an elite group of senior executives.* ◇ *He was trained at an elite military academy.* ❶ **Elite** is often used in texts relating to the army or education: *elite troops/force/corps* ◇ *an elite force/corps* ◇ *an elite education/private school.* **Elite** is also often used to describe a group of people who share special knowedge or secrets. See also **elite** → ELITE *noun*, **elitist** → EXCLUSIVE

touch *verb*

1 Can you touch your toes?
2 Her feet hardly touched the ground.

1 touch · feel · brush · graze

These words all mean to put your hands or fingers on sb/sth.

touch [T] to put your hands or fingers on sb/sth: *Don't touch that plate – it's hot!* ◇ *Can you touch your toes (= bend and reach them with your hands)?* ◇ *I touched him lightly on the arm.* See also **touch** → TEXTURE *noun*
▸ **touch** *noun* [C, usually sing., U]: *The gentle touch of his hand on her shoulder made her jump.* ◇ *She has learnt to recognize the raised patterns of Braille by touch.*
feel [T] to deliberately move your fingers over in order to find out what it is like: *Can you feel the bump on my head?* ◇ *Try to tell what this is just by feeling it.* ◇ *Feel how rough this is.* See also **feel** → TEXTURE *noun*
brush [I, T] to touch sb/sth lightly while moving close to them/it: *She brushed past him.* ◇ *His hand accidentally brushed against hers.* ◇ *The leaves brushed her cheek.*
graze [T] (*written*) to touch sth lightly while passing it: *The bullet grazed his cheek.*

NOTE BRUSH OR GRAZE? Brush is usually used to talk about sth soft that gently touches sth else; **graze** is usually used to talk about sth hard that gently touches sth else.

2 touch · meet · cross · join · merge

These are all words that can be used when two or more things come together so that there is no space between them or so that they form one thing.

touch [I, T] (of two or more things or surfaces) to be or come so close together that there is no space between: *Make sure the wires don't touch.* ◇ *Don't let your coat touch the wet paint.* ◇ *The dancer's feet hardly seemed to touch the ground.*
meet [I, T] (of two or more things) to come together so that there is no space between them or so that they form one thing: *The curtains don't meet in the middle.* ◇ *His hand met hers.* ◇ *That's where the river meets the sea.*
cross [I] to pass across each other: *The roads cross just outside the town.* ◇ *The straps cross over at the back and are tied at the waist.* ◇ *Our letters must have crossed in the mail (= each was sent before the other was received).* ◇ *Our paths were to cross again many years later (= we met by chance).*
join [I, T] (of two or more roads, rivers or lines) to come towards each other and meet at a point: *I'll meet you at the place where the two paths join.* ◇ *The path joins the road near the trees.*
merge [I] (of two or more things) to appear to form one thing, so that it is impossible to say where one ends and the other begins: *The hills merged into the dark sky behind them.* ◇ *They looked towards the point where the hills and sky merged.*

tour *verb*

tour · explore · backpack
These words all mean to spend time travelling around a place, for example for interest or pleasure.

tour [T, I] to travel around a place or area, for example to perform sth or for interest and enjoyment: *The band toured the UK last year.* ◇ *The town makes an ideal base for touring the Highlands.* ◇ *We spent six weeks touring in Australia.* See also **tour** → TRIP *noun*, **tour** → VISIT *noun*, **tourism** → TRAVEL
explore [T, I] to travel around an area or country in order to learn more about it: *The city is best explored on foot.* ◇ *They explored the land to the south of the Murray River.* ◇ *Bicycles can be hired if you want to explore further afield.* ◇ *Canadian companies are exploring for (= searching for) oil in the region.* See also **explorer** → EXPLORER
backpack (*usually* **go backpacking**) [I] to travel around an area, especially a large area, carrying your clothes and equipment with you in a backpack: *My son's backpacking in Thailand at the moment.* See also **backpack** → SUITCASE *noun*

tourist *noun* See also the entries for EXPLORER and PASSENGER

tourist · visitor · pilgrim · holidaymaker · vacationer · sightseer · backpacker
These are all words for a person who is travelling to or visiting another place, especially for pleasure or interest.

tourist [C] a person who is travelling or visiting a place for pleasure: *A busload of tourists arrived at the village.* ◇ *The temple is a major **tourist attraction**.* ◇ *Local people rely on the **tourist industry** for employment.* See also **tour → TRIP** *noun*, **tourism → TRAVEL**

visitor [C] a person who visits a place: *The palace is **open to visitors** from April to September.* ◇ *They publish a guide to Europe for overseas visitors.* See also **visit → VISIT** *noun*, **visit → STAY** *verb* 2

pilgrim /ˈpɪlgrɪm/ [C] a person who travels to a holy place for religious reasons: *Millions of pilgrims travel to Mecca.* ◇ *They were following one of the great medieval pilgrim routes.* See also **pilgrimage → TRIP**

holidaymaker /ˈhɒlədeɪmeɪkə(r); *AmE* ˈhɑːl- (*BrE* also -diməʳ/ [C] (*BrE*) a person who is visiting a place on holiday: *The resort attracts thousands of British holiday-makers.*

vacationer [C] (*AmE*) a person who is visiting a place on vacation: *Millions of vacationers come every year for the beaches and casinos.*

sightseer /ˈsaɪtsiːə(r)/ [C] a person who visits interesting buildings and places when they are on holiday: *Crowds of sightseers throng the streets in summer.* See also **sightseeing → TRAVEL**

backpacker /ˈbækpækə(r)/ [C] a person who travels for interest and enjoyment, usually carrying their clothes and equipment with them in a backpack: *A couple of backpackers were trying to hitch a ride to Chiang Mai.*

trade *noun* See also the entry for BUSINESS 2

trade · business · market · operation · trading · commerce · marketplace · trafficking · enterprise · dealing
These are all words for the activity of buying, selling or supplying goods or services for money, or the amount of goods and services sold.

PATTERNS AND COLLOCATIONS
▸ a trade / the market **in** sth
▸ trade / business / trading / commerce / trafficking / enterprise / dealing **between** people / countries
▸ trade / business / trading / commerce / dealing **with** sb / a country
▸ (the) **foreign** / **international** / **global** trade / business / market / operations / trading / commerce / marketplace
▸ (the) **domestic** / **internal** trade / business / market / operations / trading / commerce
▸ (a / the) **local** trade / business / market / operations / trading / marketplace / enterprise
▸ **illegal** trade / business / operations / trading / trafficking / enterprise / dealings
▸ (a) **profitable** trade / business / market / operations / trading
▸ (a) **free** trade / market / trading / enterprise
▸ to **engage in** trade / business / trading / commerce / enterprise
▸ to **encourage** / **promote** trade / business / commerce / enterprise
▸ trade / business / the market / an operation **expands** / **grows** / **increases**
▸ trade / business / the market **is booming** / **picks up** / **declines** / **falls**

trade [U, C] the activity of buying and selling or of exchanging goods or services between people or countries; the amount of goods or services that you sell: *Trade between the two countries has increased.* ◇ *The international trade in oil has been massively affected.* ◇ *Trade was very good last month.* ◇ (*especially BrE*) *Stores are doing a brisk trade in wizard accessories and vampire kits.* ❶ In American English it is more usual to say *doing brisk business in sth.* See also **trade → SELL** *verb* 2, **trader → DEALER**

business [U] the activity of producing, buying, selling or providing goods or services for money; the amount of work done by a company; the rate or quality of this work: *It's been a pleasure to **do business with** you.* ◇ *She has **set up in business** as a hairdresser.* ◇ *When he left school he **went into business** with his brother.* ◇ *What **line of business** are you in?* ◇ *There are strong links between*

politics and **big business** (= large companies that have a lot of power and influence). ◇ *How's business?* ◇ *If we close down for repairs, we'll lose business.* ◇ (*especially AmE*) *Stores are **doing brisk business in** wizard accessories and vampire kits.* ❶ In British English it is more usual to say *doing a brisk trade in sth.* See also **business → COMPANY**, **business → INDUSTRY**, **do business → SELL** *verb* 2

NOTE TRADE OR BUSINESS? **Trade** is used slightly more to talk about buying and selling goods rather than services. **Business** is often used when people are emphasizing the more personal aspects of these activities, such as making contacts, discussing and agreeing things and working together to provide goods or services.

market [sing.] the amount of trade in a particular type of goods: *They have 20% of the world market in coffee.* ◇ *We have increased our **share of the market** by 10%.* ◇ *There has been a downturn in the property market* (= the number and type of houses that are available). ◇ *They have **cornered the market** in sportswear* (= they sell the most).

operation [C, usually pl.] the activity or work done in an area of business or industry: *The firm's banking operations overseas have been affected by the disaster.*

trading [U] the activity of buying and selling things, especially in shops and on the stock market (= where shares in companies are bought and sold): *Stores everywhere reported excellent trading in the run-up to Christmas.* ◇ *Shares worth $8 million changed hands during a day of hectic trading.* See also **trade → SELL** 2, **trader → DEALER**

commerce /ˈkɒmɜːs; *AmE* ˈkɑːmɜːrs/ [U] (*rather formal*) trade, especially between countries: *Leaders of industry and commerce met at the summit in Paris.* See also **commercial → ECONOMIC**

marketplace /ˈmɑːkɪtpleɪs; *AmE* ˈmɑːrk-/ [sing.] the activity of competing with other companies to buy and sell goods and services: *They have successfully adapted to the demands of the global marketplace.*

trafficking [U] the activity of buying and selling sth illegally: *She was accused of drug trafficking.* ❶ *Drug* is by far the most frequent collocate of **trafficking**. Other collocates are *illegal, heroin* and *narcotic.*

enterprise /ˈentəpraɪz; *AmE* -tərp-/ [U] the development of businesses by the people of a country rather than by the government: *They provide grants to encourage enterprise in the region.* ◇ *The culture of dependency was replaced by an **enterprise culture*** (= in which people are encouraged to develop small businesses).

dealing [U, C] a way of doing business with sb; buying and selling: *We have a reputation for honest dealing.* ◇ *Drug dealing on our streets is becoming a growing problem.* ◇ (*especially BrE*) *Sales plummeted just after dealings in shares began.* See also **deal in sth → SELL** 2, **dealer → DEALER**

NOTE TRADING OR DEALING? **Trading** is used to talk about selling things in shops; **dealing** is used to talk about selling things illegally, especially drugs. Both words can be used to talk about buying and selling shares in companies, but in American English **trading** is more usual.

tradition *noun*

tradition · practice · custom · convention · norms
These are all words for behaviour that is accepted as usual by a group or society.

PATTERNS AND COLLOCATIONS
▸ **by** tradition / custom / convention
▸ a tradition / custom / convention **that…**
▸ (an) **established** tradition / practice / custom / convention / norms
▸ **accepted** practice / conventions / norms

▶ **social** practice / custom / convention / norms
▶ **cultural** tradition / practice / convention / norms
▶ a **local** / **British** tradition / practice / custom
▶ **traditional** practices / customs / norms
▶ to **follow** a tradition / a practice / a custom / convention /
  … norms
▶ to **break with** a tradition / practice / convention
▶ tradition / custom / convention **demands** sth

tradition [C, U] a belief or way of doing sth that has existed for a long time among a group of people; a set of these beliefs or ways of doing sth: *Germany has a tradition of good quality newspapers.* ◊ *There is a tradition in our family that one of our ancestors was a Cherokee Indian.* ◊ *The bride's parents are* ***by tradition*** *expected to pay for the wedding.* ◊ *He is* ***in the great tradition of*** *British travel writers.* ◊ *This year there will be* ***a break with tradition*** (= something different will be done). ◊ *Brittany has a lively and very distinctive sense of tradition.*

practice [U, C] a way of doing sth that is the usual or expected way in a particular organization or situation: *It is* ***standard practice*** *not to pay bills until the end of the month.* ◊ *They have produced a guide to* ***best practice*** *for employers.* ◊ *Members have to abide by the federation's* ***code of practice***. ◊ *They have been studying Japanese business practices.* ❶ ***Practices*** is often used to talk about the way in which businesses are run. Collocates include *business, corrupt, discriminatory, employment, management, recruitment, restrictive, trading* and *working*.

custom [C, U] a traditional and widely accepted way of doing things in a particular society, place or time: *They were unfamiliar with local customs and culture.* ◊ ***It is the custom*** *here to put flowers on the graves at Easter.* ◊ *They poured wine round the trees in accordance with local custom.*

convention [C, U] the way of doing sth that most people in a society consider to be polite or the right thing to do; a traditional method or style in literature, art or theatre: *The handshake is a social convention.* ◊ *She is a lively young woman who enjoys flouting convention.* ◊ *The novel conforms to the conventions of nineteenth-century realism.*

norms [pl.] standards of behaviour that are typical of or accepted in a particular group: *Norms of dress vary from society to society.* ◊ *She considered people to be products of the values and norms of the society they lived in.*

traditional *adj.* See also the entry for CONSERVATIVE

traditional · conventional · mainstream · classical · orthodox
These words all describe things or ideas that are based on what has happened or been accepted in the past.

PATTERNS AND COLLOCATIONS
▶ the **traditional** / **conventional** / **mainstream** / **classical** / **orthodox** **view**
▶ **traditional** / **conventional** / **mainstream** / **classical** / **orthodox** **theories** / **methods** / **approaches** / **economics**
▶ **traditional** / **conventional** / **mainstream** / **classical** **ideas** / **thinking** / **education**
▶ **traditional** / **conventional** / **mainstream** / **orthodox** **politics**
▶ **traditional** / **conventional** / **orthodox** **medicine**
▶ **traditional** / **mainstream** / **orthodox** **parties**
▶ **fairly** traditional / conventional / mainstream / orthodox
▶ **very** traditional / orthodox

traditional (*sometimes disapproving*) following older methods and ideas rather than modern or different ones: *Traditional attitudes to divorce were changing.* ◊ *I'm a very traditional guy.* **OPP** **modern** → EXPERIMENTAL
▶ **traditionally** *adv.*: *Housework has traditionally been regarded as women's work.*

conventional [usually before noun] (of an idea or method) following what is usually done and is not particularly new; (of a thing) of the kind that is usually used and is not particularly new: *It's not a hotel* ***in the conventional sense***, *rather a whole village turned into a hotel.* ◊ *You can use a microwave or cook it in a conventional oven.*

OPP **alternative** ❶ *Alternative* describes things that are different from the usual way in which sth is done: *alternative comedy/lifestyles/values* ◊ *alternative energy* (= electricity or power that is produced using the sun, wind, water, etc.)
▶ **conventionally** *adv.*: *Cooperatives perform at least as well as conventionally organized businesses.*

NOTE **TRADITIONAL** OR **CONVENTIONAL**? **Traditional** emphasizes how old a method or idea is; **conventional** emphasizes how usual it is now. For example, *conventional medicine* is the type of medicine now used by most people, using modern, scientific methods and drugs. *Traditional medicine* uses much older methods and medicines prepared from plants and other natural ingredients. This medicine may not have been scientifically tested but many people believe it to be effective: it is a form of *alternative medicine*, which is the opposite or complement of *conventional medicine*.

mainstream /'meɪnstriːm/ [usually before noun] following the ideas that are thought to be normal because they are shared by most people: *Many sports are not adequately covered in the mainstream media.* ◊ *She was an important figure in both avant-garde and mainstream cinema.*

classical [usually before noun] widely accepted and used for a long time; traditional in style or idea: *the classical economics of Smith and Ricardo* ◊ *the classical theory of unemployment* ◊ *classical and modern ballet/dance*

orthodox /'ɔːθədɒks; *AmE* 'ɔːrθədɑːks/ (*rather formal*) (of beliefs or behaviour) generally accepted or approved of; following generally accepted beliefs: *At that time the orthodox view was that secondary education should be selective.* ◊ *More orthodox scholars scoff at such theories.* **OPP** **unorthodox** → UNUSUAL

traffic *noun*

traffic · congestion · traffic jam · bottleneck · gridlock
These are all words for the vehicles that are on a road at a particular time.

PATTERNS AND COLLOCATIONS
▶ **severe** congestion / traffic jams
▶ **urban** traffic / congestion
▶ to **increase** / **reduce** traffic / congestion
▶ to **cause** congestion / traffic jams
▶ to **be stuck** / **caught** in traffic / a traffic jam

traffic [U] the vehicles that are on a road at a particular time: *I was stuck in* ***heavy traffic*** *for over an hour.* ◊ *The area is closed to* ***through traffic*** (= traffic that will not be stopping). ◊ *There will be an increase in the* ***volume of traffic***. ◊ *Flooding caused* ***traffic chaos***.

congestion /kən'dʒestʃən/ [U] (*rather formal*) a situation in which there is too much traffic in a particular area, with the result that it cannot move easily: *Better public transport would help ease traffic congestion.* See also **congested** → FULL

'traffic jam [C] a long line of vehicles on a road that cannot move or can only move very slowly: *Why sit in a traffic jam when it's quicker to walk?*

bottleneck /'bɒtlnek; *AmE* 'bɑːtl-/ [C] a narrow or particularly busy section of road where the traffic often gets slower and stops: *I came this way to avoid the bottleneck at the traffic lights.*

gridlock /'grɪdlɒk; *AmE* -lɑːk/ [U] a situation in which there are so many cars in the streets of a town that the traffic cannot move at all: *The protest march created gridlock.*

trail *noun*

trail · footprint · track · scent
These are all words for the marks or smell left by a person, animal or vehicle.

PATTERNS AND COLLOCATIONS
▸ **fresh** footprints / tracks / scent
▸ to **leave** a trail / footprints / tracks / your scent
▸ to **make** a trail / footprints / tracks
▸ to **follow** a trail / tracks / the scent
▸ to **be on** the trail / track / scent of sb / sth
▸ to **pick up / lose** sb / sth's trail / scent

trail [C] a long line or series of marks that is left by sth as it moves and that shows where it has been; a sign or smell that is left behind and can be followed, especially in hunting: *a trail of blood/footprints* ◇ *The hurricane left a* ***trail of destruction*** *behind it.* ◇ *The police are still on the trail of the escaped prisoner.* ◇ *Fortunately the trail was still warm* (= clear and easy to follow). ◇ *They had to find the kidnappers before the* ***trail went cold***. See also **trail** → FOLLOW *verb* 1

footprint /'fʊtprɪnt/ [C, usually pl.] a mark left on a surface by a person's foot or shoe or by an animal's foot: *footprints in the sand* ◇ *muddy footprints on the kitchen floor* ◇ *He could identify any animal from its footprints.*

track [C, usually pl.] marks left by a moving person, animal or vehicle: *We followed the bear's tracks in the snow.* ◇ *There were two sets of fresh tyre tracks outside.* See also **track** → PATH *noun*, **track** → FOLLOW *verb* 1

> **NOTE** **TRAIL OR TRACK?** A **trail** can consist of marks on the ground, a smell, objects that have been left behind by sb/sth or a series of clues. A **track** is always marks on the ground. **Trail** places the emphasis on where the marks are leading and that there is sb/sth to be found or caught at the end of the trail. **Track** places more emphasis on the marks themselves.

scent /sent/ [U, C, usually sing.] the smell that a person or animal leaves behind and that other animals such as dogs can follow: *The dogs must have lost her scent.* ◇ *The hounds were now on the scent of the fox.*

train *verb*

1 train as a teacher
2 train for the Olympics

1 See the Topic Map for EDUCATION on p.888, See also the entry for TEACH

train · teach · coach · show · educate · groom · instruct
These words all mean to teach sb/yourself or an animal the skills for a particular job or activity.

PATTERNS AND COLLOCATIONS
▸ to train / coach / educate / instruct sb **in** sth
▸ to train / coach / groom sb **for** sth
▸ to teach / educate sb **about** sth
▸ to train / groom sb **as** sth
▸ to train / teach / groom sb **to do sth**
▸ to teach / show sb **how to** do sth
▸ to teach / show sb **that…**
▸ to train / teach / educate / instruct a **pupil**
▸ to train / teach / educate a **teacher / doctor / nurse / student**
▸ to train / teach / educate **the workforce**
▸ to train / coach a **gymnast / athlete / footballer / player / team**
▸ to teach / coach **athletics / basketball / boxing / football / gymnastics / hockey / rugby / soccer**
▸ be **well** trained / taught / coached / instructed

train [T, I] to teach a person or animal the skills for a particular job or activity; to be taught these skills: *They train dogs to sniff out drugs.* ◇ *All members of the team have been trained in first aid.* ◇ *He trained as a teacher before becoming an actor.* See also **trainer** → COACH *noun*, **training** → EDUCATION, **untrained** → IGNORANT

teach [T] to show sb how to do sth so that they will be able to do it themselves; to make sb feel or think in a different way: *My father taught me how to ride a bike.* ◇ *Could you teach me to do that?* ◇ *She taught me to be less critical of other people.* ◇ *My parents taught me that*

honesty was always the best policy. ◇ *Our experience as refugees taught us many valuable lessons.* See also **teach** → TEACH

coach [T] to train sb to play a sport or improve a skill: *Her father coached her for the Olympics.* ◇ *She has coached hundreds of young singers.* ◇ *He coaches basketball and soccer.* See also **coach** → COACH *noun*, **coaching** → EDUCATION

> **NOTE** **TRAIN OR COACH?** Both these words are used to talk about preparing sportsmen and women for competition or preparing musicians, etc. for performance. You can **train** but NOT **coach** people in skills for their job: *All members of the team have been coached in first aid.* You can **train** but NOT **coach** animals: *They coach dogs to sniff out drugs.* You can **coach** a person or sport, but you can only **train** a person: *He trains basketball.*

show [T] to help sb to do sth by letting them watch you do it or by explaining it: *She showed her students the technique.* ◇ *Can you show me how to do it?*

educate [T] (*rather formal*) to teach sb about sth, especially in order to encourage them in responsible behaviour: *Children need to be* ***educated on*** *the dangers of drug-taking.* ◇ *Their task was to inform, educate and entertain the viewers.* See also **education** → EDUCATION

groom [T, often passive] (used especially in the progressive tenses) (*journalism*) to train or prepare sb for an important job or position: *She is already being groomed for the top job in the firm.*

instruct [T] (*formal*) to teach sb sth, especially a practical skill: *All our staff have been instructed in sign language.* See also **instruction** → EDUCATION, **instructor** → COACH *noun*

2 See the Topic Map for SPORT AND LEISURE on p.892, See also the entry for PRACTISE

train · exercise · work out · keep fit · warm up
These words all mean to do physical exercises in order to prepare your body for physical activity, or in order to improve your strength and health.

PATTERNS AND COLLOCATIONS
▸ to train / exercise / warm up **properly**
▸ to train / exercise / work out **regularly**
▸ to train / exercise a **horse / dog**

train [I, T] to prepare yourself for a particular activity, especially a sport, by doing a lot of exercise; to prepare a person or animal in this way: *We watched the athletes training for the Olympics.* ◇ *I train in the gym for two hours a day.* ◇ *She trains horses.* ◇ *He trains the Olympic team.*

exercise [I, T] to do sports or other physical activities in order to stay healthy or become stronger; to make an animal do this; to give a part of the body the movement and activity it needs to keep strong and healthy: *How often do you exercise?* ◇ *Horses need to be exercised regularly.* ◇ *These movements will exercise your arms and shoulders.* See also **exercise** → SPORT *noun*

work 'out *phrasal verb* to make your body stronger through physical exercise, especially using equipment in a gym: *I work out regularly to keep fit.* See also **workout** → SPORT *noun*

keep 'fit *idiom* (*especially BrE*) to stay healthy and strong, especially by doing regular physical exercise: *She tries to keep fit by jogging every day.*

warm 'up *phrasal verb* to prepare for physical exercise or a performance by doing gentle exercises or practice: *We arrived just as the players were warming up.* ❶ Performers such as dancers, as well as sportsmen and women, have to **warm up**.
▸ **'warm-up** *noun* [C, sing.]: *He swam ten lengths of the pool as a warm-up.* ◇ *warm-up exercises*

training *noun* See the Topic Map for SPORT AND LEISURE on p.892

---

training · rehearsal · practice · drill
These are all words for the process of preparing for an activity or an event which prepares for sth.

▸ training/ rehearsals **for** sth
▸ **in** training/ rehearsal
▸ **regular** training/ rehearsals/ practice/ drills
▸ **football/ hockey,** etc. training/ practice
▸ to **do** training/ rehearsals/ practice
▸ to **have** rehearsals/ practice
▸ a training/ rehearsal/ practice **session/ schedule**

training [U] the process of preparing to take part in a sport, especially a sports competition, by doing physical exercises: *Phillips is in serious training for the Olympics.* ◇ *She did six months' hard training before the marathon.* ❶ In American English **training** is serious preparation for a serious event; in British English it can be serious or less serious. For less serious training in American English use **practice**: (*BrE*) *I go to football training after school.* ◇ (*AmE, BrE*) *I go to soccer practice after school.* See also **exercise** → SPORT

rehearsal /rɪ'hɜːsl; *AmE* rɪ'hɜːrsl/ [U, C] time that a group of people spend practising together a play or piece of music in preparation for public performance; an experience or event that helps to prepare you for sth that is going to happen in the future: *Our new production of 'Hamlet' is currently in rehearsal.* ◇ *During the* **dress rehearsal** (= the final rehearsal in full costume) *she suddenly forgot her lines.* ◇ *These training exercises are designed to be a rehearsal for the invasion.* See also **rehearse** → PRACTISE *verb*

practice [U, C] doing an activity or training regularly so that you can improve your skill; the time you spend doing this: *The trainees need more* **practice in** *using the compass.* ◇ *His accent should improve* **with practice.** ◇ *If you don't play regularly you soon get* **out of practice.** ◇ *It* **takes** *a lot of* **practice** *to play the violin well.* ◇ *There's a basketball practice every Friday evening.* See also **practise** → PRACTISE *verb*

drill [C] a practice of what to do in an emergency, for example if there is a fire: *There'll be a* **fire drill** *sometime this morning.*

---

traitor *noun*

traitor · collaborator · defector · renegade · deserter
These are all words for a person who betrays their friends, their country or another group or organization to which they are supposed to be loyal.

▸ an **alleged** traitor/ collaborator

traitor /'treɪtə(r)/ [C] (*disapproving*) a person who betrays their friends, their country or another group or organization to which they are supposed to be loyal: *He was seen as a* **traitor to** *the socialist cause.* ◇ *She denied that she had* **turned traitor** (= become a traitor). ❶ **Traitor** is a fairly general word, and can be used to talk about any of the people described in this group of words.

collaborator /kə'læbəreɪtə(r)/ [C] (*disapproving*) a person who helps the enemy in a war, when they have taken control of the person's country: *Former collaborators are now facing public humiliation in the courts.*

defector /dɪ'fektə(r)/ [C] (*sometimes disapproving*) a person who leaves a country, political party or organization to join another that is considered to be an enemy: *He was one of the earliest Soviet* **defectors to** *the West.* ◇ *Many of the new members were* **defectors from** *the Labour party.*

renegade /'renɪɡeɪd/ [C] (often used as an adjective) (*formal, disapproving*) a person who leaves one religious or political group to join another that has very different views: *A renegade priest, he made no secret of his unorthodox ideas.*

deserter /dɪ'zɜːtə(r); *AmE* -'zɜːrt-/ [C] a person who leaves the army, navy, etc. without permission: *He was convicted of hiding deserters.* ❶ Although **deserter** can be used as a negative term, it is more often simply factual, without a judgement of the person being suggested.

---

tramp *noun* See also the entry for TRAVELLER

---

tramp · vagrant · beggar · drifter · bum · scrounger
These are all words for a person who travels from place to place and/or asks people for food or money.

> **NOTE** All the words in this group are disapproving or slightly disapproving. A frequent and more neutral way of talking about sb without a home is simply to say a *homeless person/man/woman*: *The number of young homeless people is on the rise.*

▸ an **old** tramp/ beggar/ bum

tramp [C] (*sometimes disapproving*) a person who has no home or job and who travels from place to place, usually asking people in the street for food or money: *An old tramp was sitting on a bench.*

vagrant /'veɪɡrənt/ [C] (*formal or law*) a tramp: *The accused was a vagrant who travelled around, sleeping in parks and bus shelters.*

beggar /'beɡə(r)/ [C] (*sometimes disapproving*) a person who lives by asking people for money or food: *There were a number of beggars sleeping in doorways.* See also **beg** → BORROW

drifter [C] (*especially AmE, often disapproving*) a person who moves from one job or place to another with no real purpose: *Several hundred drifters spend the night in the park.*

bum [C] (*informal, especially AmE, often disapproving*) a person who has no home or job and who asks other people for money or food; a person who does no work, but spends a lot of time in a place, doing very little: *The city at night intimidated me with the bums and dealers shouting out abuse.* ◇ *He left college to lead the life of a beach bum* (= sb who spends all their time on the beach, without having a job).

scrounger /'skraʊndʒə(r)/ [C] (*especially BrE, informal, disapproving*) a person who gets sth from sb by asking them for it rather than by paying for it; a person who gets money from the government without working for it: *He's such a scrounger. He tried to get me to pay his air fare home.* ◇ *The government has launched a campaign against welfare scroungers.* See also **scrounge** → BORROW

---

trance *noun*

trance · daze · reverie · daydream · stupor · dream
These are all words for a state in which sb seems to be asleep or not aware of what is happening around them.

▸ a reverie/ daydream **about** sth
▸ to be **in** a trance/ daze/ reverie/ daydream/ stupor/ dream
▸ to **go/ fall into** a trance/ stupor
▸ to be **lost in** a reverie/ daydream/ dream

trance /trɑːns; *AmE* træns/ [C, usually sing.] a state in which sb seems to be asleep but is aware of what is said to them, for example if they are hypnotized; a state in which sb is thinking so much about sth that they do not notice what is happening around them: *When the subject has gone into a deep trance, they are taken back to an earlier stage of their life.* ◇ *She drove, gripping the wheel in a trance, hardly aware of her surroundings.*

daze [sing.] a confused state, in which you do not know what is happening around you, often caused by a surprise or shock, especially a pleasant one: *I've been in a complete daze since hearing the news.* ❶ **Daze** is always used in the phrase *in a …daze.*

reverie /ˈrevəri/ [C, U] (*formal or literary*) a state of thinking about pleasant things, as if you were dreaming but in fact while you are awake: *As the train pulled away, he drifted into a reverie.*

daydream /ˈdeɪdriːm/ [C] pleasant thoughts that make you forget about your surroundings or about what is happening in the present: *In one of his daydreams, they were living in a little cottage in the country.*
▸ **daydream** *verb* [I]: *She would spend hours daydreaming about a house of her own.*

stupor /ˈstjuːpə(r); AmE ˈstuː-/ [sing., U] (*rather formal*) a state in which you are unable to think or hear clearly, especially because you have drunk too much alcohol, taken drugs or had a shock: *He drank himself into a stupor.* ◇ *They left him slumped in a drunken stupor.*

dream [C] a state of mind in which your thoughts do not seem to be connected to what is real or to what is actually happening around you: *She walked around in a dream all day.* ❶ In this meaning a **dream** is a state of mind and may not be a dream about anything in particular. *A dream about/of sth* is usually more definite, closer in meaning to a **hope**. See also **dream → HOPE noun 2**

transport *noun*

transport · transportation · traffic · shipping
These are all words for a system for carrying goods or people from one place to another using vehicles, roads, ships, etc.

▸ **international** transport / transportation / traffic / shipping
▸ **local / urban / city** transport / transportation / traffic
▸ **air / rail / river / road** transport / transportation / traffic
▸ **private / public** transport / transportation
▸ **passenger / freight / goods** transport / traffic
▸ transport / transportation / traffic / shipping **routes**
▸ the transport / transportation / shipping **industry**
▸ a **means / form / mode of** transport / transportation

transport [U] (*especially BrE*) a system for carrying people or goods from one place to another using vehicles, roads, etc.; a particular vehicle or method of travel: *Is it possible to get there by public transport* (= by train, bus, etc., not using your own vehicle)? ◇ *You need your own transport* (= a car or bicycle, etc.) *if you live there.* ◇ *Horses and carts were the only means of transport.*

transportation [U] (*especially AmE*) transport: *The storm disrupted transportation and wrecked homes.* ◇ *The city provided free transportation to the stadium.*

traffic [U] the movement of ships, trains or aircraft along a particular route; the movement of people or goods from one place to another: *The airline's transatlantic traffic fell by 8 per cent.* ◇ *He works as an air traffic controller* (= sb whose job is to guide planes in and out of airports). ◇ *Commuter traffic has increased again this year.*

shipping [U] the system of carrying goods from one place to another by ship; ships in general: *Merchant shipping has become increasingly specialized.* ◇ *These are some of the busiest shipping lanes* (= routes for ships sailing in a particular direction) *in the world.*

trap *verb*

trap · confine · lock sb/yourself in (sth) · cage · pen · shut sb/yourself in (sth) · coop sb/sth up
These words all mean to keep a person or animal in a small space.

▸ to be trapped / confined / locked / caged / penned / shut / cooped up **in** sth
▸ to be trapped / confined / locked in / caged / penned / shut in / cooped up **with** sb / sth
▸ to be caged / penned / cooped **up**

trap (**-pp-**) [T, usually passive] to keep sb in a dangerous place or bad situation that they want to get out of but cannot: *Help! I'm trapped!* ◇ *We became trapped by the rising flood water.* ◇ *I feel trapped in my job.*

confine /kənˈfaɪn/ [T, usually passive] (*rather formal*) to keep a person or animal in a small or closed space: *Keep the dog confined in a suitable travelling cage.* ◇ *The soldiers concerned were confined to barracks* (= had to stay in the barracks, as a punishment).

lock sb/yourself 'in (sth) *phrasal verb* to prevent sb from leaving a place by locking the door: *At 9 p.m. the prisoners are locked in for the night.* ◇ *She locked herself in her room.*

cage [T, usually passive] to put or keep an animal in a cage: *The dogs are caged up at night.* ◇ *He paced the room like a caged animal.*

pen (**-nn-**) [T] to shut an animal or person in a small space: *At clipping time sheep need to be penned.* ◇ *The whole family was penned up in one room for a month.*

shut sb/yourself 'in (sth) *phrasal verb* to put sb in a room and keep them there; to go to a room and stay there: *Her brothers used to shut her in the cellar and make her cry.* ◇ *Frank has shut himself in his room and won't come out.*

coop sb/sth 'up *phrasal verb* [usually passive] to keep a person or animal inside a building or in a small space: *I've been cooped up in that office all day.*

travel *noun*

travel · tourism · sightseeing · travelling
These are all words for the act or activity of going to places.

▸ travel / travelling **by** sth
▸ a **day's** travel / sightseeing / travelling
▸ to **go** sightseeing / travelling
▸ travel / travelling **costs / expenses / arrangements**

travel [U] the activity of going to different places for business or pleasure, especially over long distances: *Her interests include music and foreign travel.* ◇ *Continued fighting makes travel in the area dangerous.* ◇ *air/rail/space travel* ◇ *Expenditure on business travel was reduced.* ◇ *travel insurance/documents* ◇ *a travel guide/writer* ◇ *Do you suffer from travel sickness?* See also **travel → GO verb 2**

tourism [U] the business activity connected with providing accommodation, services and entertainment for people who are visiting a place for pleasure: *We hope that this investment will lead to increased tourism in the area.* See also **tour → TRIP noun, tour → TOUR verb, tourist → TOURIST**

sightseeing /ˈsaɪtsiːɪŋ/ [U] the activity of visiting interesting places and buildings as a tourist: *Did you have a chance to do any sightseeing?* ◇ *They were on a sightseeing trip to the Pyramids.* See also **sightseer → TOURIST**
▸ **see the 'sights** *phrase*: *In the afternoon there'll be a chance to see the sights of Brussels.*

travelling (*especially BrE*) (*AmE usually* **traveling**) [U] travel: *She enjoys skiing, travelling and music.* ◇ *She was joined in London by her travelling companions* (= the people who would make the journey with her).

NOTE TRAVEL OR TRAVELLING? **Travel** is used more to talk about journeys made by people in general; **travelling** is used more to talk about journeys made by a particular person: *The pass allows unlimited travel on all public transport.* ◇ *My job involves a lot of travelling.* **Travel** is often used after a noun or adjective to describe a particular kind of journey that people make: *air/rail/space/business/foreign travel* ◇ ~~air/rail/space/business/foreign travelling~~

traveller *noun* See also the entry for TRAMP

traveller · gypsy · nomad · Romany
These are all words for people who have no fixed or permanent home and who travel from place to place.

PATTERNS AND COLLOCATIONS
▸ a traveller / gypsy **site**
▸ traveller / gypsy **families**
▸ a gypsy / Romany **camp / caravan**
▸ the gypsy / nomad / Romany **population**

traveller [C] (*BrE*) a person who does not live in a building in one place but travels around living in a caravan, especially as part of a group: *There was a travellers' site* (= where travellers stay) *just outside the village.* ◇ *There is a programme to ensure access to education for traveller children.* ❶ In Britain **traveller** is used especially to talk about travelling people of Irish origin, but is also used as a word for all travelling people including from the **Gypsy/Romany** community.
Gypsy (also **Gipsy, gypsy, gipsy**) /ˈdʒɪpsi/ [C] (*sometimes offensive*) a member of a race of people, originally from Asia, who travel around and traditionally live in caravans: *An old gypsy woman offered to tell my fortune.* ❶ The name **Gypsy** is now often considered offensive and many people prefer to use the name **Romany**.
nomad /ˈnəʊmæd; *AmE* ˈnoʊ-/ [C] a member of a traditional community that moves with its animals from place to place: *The Tuareg are the largest tribe of nomads in the desert.*
Romany /ˈrɒməni; ˈrəʊm-; *AmE* ˈrɑːm-; ˈroʊm-/ [C] a member of a race of people, originally from Asia, who travel around and traditionally live in caravans: *They demanded protection for Romanies against attacks from racist groups.*

travelling (*especially BrE*) (*AmE usually* **traveling**) *adj.*

travelling · nomadic · migratory · itinerant
These are all words that describe sb/sth that travels from place to place.

PATTERNS AND COLLOCATIONS
▸ travelling / nomadic **people**
▸ a travelling / an itinerant **preacher**

travelling (*especially BrE*) (*AmE usually* **traveling**) [only before noun] going from place to place: *The travelling exhibition is currently in Moscow.* ◇ *He worked as a travelling salesman.*
nomadic /nəʊˈmædɪk; *AmE* noʊ-/ relating to a group of people who do not live in one place but travel from place to place with their animals; relating to a person who travels from place to place, for example for their work: *This is one of the oldest nomadic tribes in Central Asia.* ◇ *I was living the nomadic life of a foreign correspondent.*
migratory /ˈmaɪɡrətri; maɪˈɡreɪtəri; *AmE* ˈmaɪɡrətɔːri/ (*technical*) relating to animals or birds that regularly travel from one place to another according to the seasons: *The wetlands are home to migratory birds.* ◇ *They will soon start their spring migratory flight.*
itinerant /aɪˈtɪnərənt/ [usually before noun] (*formal*) travelling from place to place, especially to find work: *It was a hostel for itinerant workers.*

treacherous *adj.*

treacherous · unfaithful · disloyal · fickle
These words all describe people who betray their friends, partner, family or country.

PATTERNS AND COLLOCATIONS
▸ unfaithful / disloyal **to** sb
▸ a treacherous / unfaithful / disloyal **husband / wife**
▸ a treacherous / unfaithful / fickle **lover**
▸ a treacherous / fickle **friend**

treacherous /ˈtretʃərəs/ (*written*) (of a person or what they do or say) that cannot be trusted; intending or intended to harm you: *He was weak, cowardly and treacherous.* ◇ *She kept remembering his lying, treacherous words.*
unfaithful having sex with sb who is not your husband, wife or usual partner: *Have you ever been unfaithful to him?* ◇ *She remained loyal to her unfaithful husband.* **OPP faithful** ❶ Sb who is **faithful** to their partner does not have sex with anyone else.
disloyal /dɪsˈlɔɪəl/ failing to support or be loyal to your friends, family, country, etc: *He was accused of being disloyal to the government.* ◇ *It was very disloyal of you to repeat what I'd said to Peter.* **OPP loyal** → RELIABLE 1, See also **disloyalty** → BETRAYAL
fickle (of a person) often changing their mind in an unreasonable way so that you cannot rely on them; (of sb's behaviour) showing this: *She had been a fickle friend, even at the best of times.* ◇ *This was just another example of his fickle behaviour.*

treat *verb*
1 treat an illness
2 The crops are treated with insecticide.

1 See the Topic Map for HEALTH on p.890, See also the entry for LOOK AFTER SB
treat · nurse · dose
These words all mean to give medical care to sb.

PATTERNS AND COLLOCATIONS
▸ to treat / nurse **the sick**
▸ to treat / nurse a / an **cold / injury**

treat [T] to give medical care or attention to a person, illness or injury: *She was **treated for** sunstroke.* ◇ *The condition is usually **treated with** drugs and a strict diet.*
nurse [T] (*rather formal*) to look after sb who is ill or injured; to take care of an illness or injury: *He worked in a hospital for ten years, nursing cancer patients.* ◇ *He was **nursed back to health** by his wife.* ◇ *Several weeks after the match, he was still nursing a shoulder injury.*
dose /dəʊs; *AmE* doʊs/ [T] (*BrE*) to give sb/yourself a medicine or drug: *She **dosed** herself **up** with vitamin pills.* ◇ *He was heavily dosed with painkillers.* ❶ In American English the verb **dose** is not used, although you can *take a dose* or *give sb a dose* of sth.
▸ **dose** *noun* [C]: *to take/give sb a dose of medicine* ◇ *a high/low dose* ◇ *Repeat dose after 12 hours if necessary.*

2 treat · process
These words both mean to use a system, especially involving chemicals, to clean, protect, preserve or change sth.

PATTERNS AND COLLOCATIONS
▸ to treat / process **waste**
▸ to be **routinely / efficiently** treated / processed

treat [T, often passive] to use a chemical substance or process to clean, protect, preserve or change sth: *The crops are **treated with** insecticide.* ◇ *Water is discharged from the sewage works after being treated.*
▸ **treatment** *noun* [U, C]: *a sewage/water treatment plant* ◇ *an effective treatment for dry rot*
process [T, often passive] to treat sth, especially raw material or food, in order to change or preserve it: *When food is processed, many of the nutrients are stripped away.* ◇ *I sent three rolls of film away to be processed.* See also **process** → WAY *noun* 2

treatment *noun* See the Topic Map for HEALTH on p.890

treatment · surgery · medicine · therapy · operation · healing · medical care · cure · nursing
These are all words for the practice or study of making people well after illness or injury.

▸ treatment / surgery / therapy / an operation **for** sth
▸ surgery / an operation **on** sb / sth
▸ (an) **emergency** treatment / surgery / operation
▸ (a / an) **alternative / orthodox / conventional** treatment / medicine / therapy
▸ to **have** treatment / surgery / therapy / an operation / medical care
▸ to **undergo** treatment / surgery / therapy / an operation
▸ to **receive** treatment / surgery / therapy / medical care
▸ to **need / require** treatment / surgery / therapy / an operation / medical care
▸ to **give sb** treatment / therapy / medical care
▸ to **carry out** treatment / surgery / an operation
▸ to **perform** surgery / an operation

treatment [U, C] something that is done to cure an illness or injury, or to make sb look or feel good: *He is receiving treatment for shock.* ◇ *She is **responding well to treatment**.* ◇ *Guests at the health spa receive a range of beauty and fitness treatments.*

surgery /ˈsɜːdʒəri; *AmE* ˈsɜːrdʒ-/ [U] medical treatment of injuries or diseases that involves cutting open the body and often removing or replacing some parts; the branch of medicine connected with this treatment: *The doctor had to perform emergency **surgery to** the patient's head.* ◇ *She will require surgery on her left knee.* ◇ *My brother went on to study surgery.* ❶ **Plastic surgery** or **cosmetic surgery** is medical operations to repair injury to a person's skin, or to improve their appearance.

medicine [U] the study and treatment of diseases and injuries: *She went on to practise medicine after completing her studies.* ◇ *Which **branch of medicine** are you going to train in?* ◇ *He gave up general medicine to specialize in geriatric medicine.* See also **medicine** → DRUG 2

therapy /ˈθerəpi/ [U, C] the treatment of an illness or physical problem, especially using a particular method: *Most patients undergo some sort of drug therapy for leukaemia.* ◇ *She has trained in alternative therapies (=* therapies that do not use conventional drugs). ❶ **Therapy** is often used in compounds, meaning a particular kind of therapy: *physiotherapy, chemotherapy, radiotherapy, occupational therapy, speech therapy, psychotherapy.* **Therapy** can also be another word for **psychotherapy**, which is the treatment of mental illness by discussing sb's problems, rather than by giving them drugs.

operation [C] the process of cutting open a part of a person's body in order to remove or repair a damaged part: *Will I need to have an operation?* ◇ *an operation on her lung to remove a tumour* ◇ *He underwent a three-hour heart operation.*
▸ **operate** *verb* [I]: *The doctors operated last night.* ◇ *We will have to operate on his eyes.*

> **NOTE** SURGERY OR OPERATION? **Surgery** is uncountable; **operation** is countable: *The doctor recommended surgery.* ◇ *She's had three operations in the past two years.*

healing [U] the process of becoming or making sb / sth healthy again, usually through natural methods: *Homeopathy aims to reinforce the body's natural **healing powers**.* ◇ *Rest is an important part of the **healing process**.* ❶ **Faith healing** is a method of treating a sick person through the power of belief and prayer. See also **heal** → CURE

ˈmedical care [U] the practice of caring for sb when they are ill or injured: *Many people didn't receive **proper medical care** after the explosion.*

cure [C] the act of curing sb of an illness; the process of being cured: *Doctors cannot effect a cure if the illness has spread too far.* ◇ *The cure took six weeks.* See also **cure** → CURE *verb*, **cure** → DRUG *noun* 2

nursing [U] the job or skill of caring for people who are ill or injured: *He is planning to follow a career in nursing.* See also **nurse** → DOCTOR

trend *noun*

trend · tendency · movement · drift
These are all words for a change in a situation or in the way people think and behave that happens slowly.

▸ the trend / tendency / movement / drift **towards** sth
▸ the trend / movement / drift **away from** sth
▸ a trend / tendency **to do sth**
▸ a **general** trend / tendency / movement / drift
▸ a **downward / gradual** trend / movement / drift

trend [C] a general direction in which a situation is changing or developing: *a survey of social trends* ◇ *a downward/upward trend in sales* ◇ *There is a growing trend towards earlier retirement.* ◇ *The company managed to **buck the trend** (=* to be different from most others) *and increase profits this year.* See also **trend** → FASHION

tendency [C] a new custom that is starting to develop: *There is a growing tendency among employers to hire casual workers.* See also **tendency** → TENDENCY

movement [sing.] a gradual change in what people in society do or think: *A movement away from this idea can be seen in the second half of the century.* ◇ *The movement to greater liberalization was halted.*

drift [sing.] a gradual change or development from one situation to another, especially to sth bad that happens because nobody is aware of it or does anything to stop it: *Action is needed to prevent a drift into lawlessness.* ◇ *The polls show a drift back towards Labour.*

tribute *noun*

tribute · compliment · homage · toast · accolade · eulogy
These are all words for sth that you say, write or do to show your respect or admiration for sb.

▸ a tribute / compliment / homage / toast / eulogy **to** sb / sth
▸ to do sth **in** tribute / homage
▸ to do sth **as** a tribute / compliment
▸ a **great** tribute / compliment
▸ to **pay** tribute / a compliment / homage (to sb / sth)
▸ to **receive** a tribute / a compliment / homage / an accolade

tribute /ˈtrɪbjuːt/ [U, C] something that you say, do or offer to show your respect or admiration, especially for a dead person: *At her funeral her oldest friend paid tribute to her life and work.* ◇ *The crowd stood in silent tribute to those who had died in the war.* ◇ *This book is a fitting tribute to the bravery of the pioneers.*

compliment [C] something you say that expresses praise or admiration of sb: *She always paid me compliments on my hair and my clothes.* ◇ *'You understand the problem because you're so much older.' 'I'll **take that as a compliment**!'* ❶ **Compliment** is the only word in this group that does not suggest a public display of praise or respect. It is most often used to describe words spoken between individuals rather than a public announcement or event. See also **compliment** → PRAISE *verb*, **complimentary** → GOOD 6

homage /ˈhɒmɪdʒ; *AmE* ˈhɑːm-/ [U, C, usually sing.] (*formal*) something that is said or done to show respect for sb, especially in a formal or serious way: *The kings of France paid homage to no one.* ◇ *He describes his book as a 'homage to my father'.*

toast [C] the act of a group of people wishing sb happiness or success by drinking a glass of sth, especially alcohol, at the same time: *I'd like to **propose a toast** to the bride and groom.* ◇ *The committee **drank a toast** to the new project.* ▸ **toast** *verb* [T]: *We toasted the success of the new company.*

accolade /ˈækəleɪd/ [C] (*formal*) praise or an award for an achievement that people admire: *He was finally awarded **the ultimate accolade** — British Hairdresser of the Year — in 2007.*

eulogy /ˈjuːlədʒi/ [C, U] a speech or piece of writing praising sb/sth very much; a speech given at a funeral praising the person who has died: *The poem is a eulogy to marriage.* ◇ *He gave the eulogy at Aunt Louise's funeral.*

trick *noun* See also the entry for TACTIC

trick · trap · hoax · device · bluff · ruse · set-up
These are all words for sth that you do to deceive sb.

PATTERNS AND COLLOCATIONS
▸ a **clever** trick / trap / device / ruse
▸ a **simple** trick / device / ruse
▸ to **try** a trick / device / ruse
▸ to **use / resort to** a trick / device
▸ a trick / trap / device / bluff / ruse **works**

trick [C] something that you do to deceive sb or to annoy sb as a joke: *They had to think of a trick to get past the guards.* ◇ *The kids are always **playing tricks on** their teacher.* ◇ *She won't **fall for** such a stupid trick.* ◇ *It was a **trick question** (= one to which the answer seems easy but actually is not).* See also **trick** → CHEAT *verb*, **prank** → JOKE *noun*

trap [C] a clever plan designed to deceive sb, either by capturing them or by making them do or say sth that they did not mean to do or say: *She had **set a trap** for him and he had **walked** straight **into it**.*

hoax /həʊks; *AmE* hoʊks/ [C] (*especially journalism*) an act intended to make sb believe sth that is not true, especially sth unpleasant: *She described the deception as a cruel hoax.* ◇ *He was accused of using a **bomb hoax** to empty a rival restaurant.* ◇ *Detectives are still investigating the **hoax calls**.*

device [C] (*rather formal*) a plan or trick that sb uses to get what they want, without being honest about it: *The report was a device used to hide rather than reveal problems.* ❶ A **device** is not always dishonest: it can be just a neat and useful way of doing sth. See also **device** → TACTIC

bluff [C, U] an attempt to trick sb by making them believe that you will do sth when you really have no intention of doing it, or that you know sth when you do not, in fact, know it: *He said he would resign if he didn't get more money, but it was only a bluff.* ◇ *He threatened to resign but it was all bluff.* ❶ If you **call sb's bluff**, you tell them to do what they are threatening to do, because you believe that they will not be cruel or brave enough to do it: *She was tempted to call his bluff, hardly able to believe he'd carry out his threat.* See also **bluff** → PRETEND *verb*

ruse /ruːz/ [C] (*rather formal, written, sometimes disapproving*) a plan or trick that sb uses to get what they want, especially by cheating or deceiving sb: *She tried to think of a ruse to get him out of the house.*

> **NOTE DEVICE OR RUSE?** A **ruse** is often more dishonest than a **device**: it is deliberately designed to make sb believe sth that is not true. A **device** is more often a way of hiding your real intentions or reasons without actually lying about them.

'set-up [C, usually sing.] (*informal, usually disapproving*) a situation in which sb tricks you or makes it seem as if you have done sth wrong: *He didn't steal the goods. It was a set-up.*

trickle *verb* See also the entry for FLOW

trickle · drip · dribble
These words are all used when a small amount of a liquid flows or falls in a thin stream or small drops.

PATTERNS AND COLLOCATIONS
▸ to trickle / drip / dribble **down / from** sth
▸ to trickle / drip **into** sth
▸ **tears** trickle / drip
▸ **sweat / rain** trickles / drips
▸ **blood** trickles / drips / dribbles
▸ to trickle / drip / dribble **slowly**

trickle [I, T] (usually used with an adverb or preposition) (of liquid) to flow slowly in a thin stream; to make sth flow in this way: *Rainwater trickled through the cracks in the boards.* ◇ *Trickle some oil over the salad.* ▸ **trickle** *noun* [C]: *There was a trickle of blood at the corner of his mouth.*

drip (**-pp-**) [I] (usually used with an adverb or preposition) (of a liquid) to fall in small drops: *She was hot and sweat dripped into her eyes.* ◇ *Water dripped from the tap.* See also **drop** → DROP

dribble [I] (always used with an adverb or preposition) (of a liquid) to fall down the side of sth in small drops or in a thin stream: *Melted wax dribbled down the side of the candle.*

> **NOTE TRICKLE, DRIP OR DRIBBLE?** Something that **trickles** is flowing continuously, although in a very thin stream; sth that **drips** is not flowing continuously, but falling in drops; sth that **dribbles** may be in a very thin stream or in drops. Liquid can **drip** down the side or over the edge of sth, or just through the air; liquid can only **dribble** down the side or over the edge of sth, not through the air: *Water dribbled from the tap.*

trip *noun* See also the entry for HOLIDAY 2

trip · journey · tour · expedition · excursion · pilgrimage · outing · travels · day out
These are all words for an act of travelling to a place.

PATTERNS AND COLLOCATIONS
▸ a trip / a journey / a tour / an expedition / an excursion / a pilgrimage / an outing / a day out **to** sth / somewhere
▸ **on** a trip / a journey / a tour / an expedition / an excursion / (a) pilgrimage / an outing / your travels / a day out
▸ a **long** trip / journey / tour / expedition / day out
▸ a **short** trip / journey / tour / expedition / excursion
▸ a **pleasant** trip / journey / outing / day out
▸ a **successful** trip / journey / tour / expedition / outing
▸ a **foreign / overseas** trip / journey / tour / expedition
▸ a **bus / coach / train / rail** trip / journey / tour
▸ a **shopping** trip / expedition / excursion
▸ to **go on** a trip / a journey / a tour / an expedition / an excursion / a pilgrimage / an outing / your travels / a day out
▸ to **set out on / set off on** a trip / a journey / a tour / an expedition / an excursion / a pilgrimage / your travels
▸ to **come back from / return from** a trip / a journey / a tour / an expedition / an excursion / a pilgrimage / an outing / your travels / a day out
▸ to **make** a trip / a journey / a tour / an expedition / an excursion / a pilgrimage

trip [C] an act of travelling from one place to another, and usually back again: *a business trip* ◇ *a school trip to France* ◇ *Tomorrow there will be a **boat trip** to the island.* ◇ *We took a **day trip** to Siena.* ◇ *They had to make several trips to bring all the equipment over.* ◇ *From London to Oxford is a **round trip** of over 100 miles (= it is over 100 miles there and back again).*

journey [C] an act of travelling from one place to another, especially when they are a long way apart: *It was a long and difficult journey across the mountains.* ◇ *They continued their journey on foot.* ◇ *We **broke our journey** (= stopped for a short time) in Madrid.*

NOTE TRIP OR JOURNEY? Trip, NOT journey, is the most basic word in this group. It is more frequent than **journey** and used in a wider range of contexts. A **trip** is usually a journey to a place and back again; a **journey** is usually one-way. A **trip** is often shorter than a **journey**, although it does not have to be: *a trip to New York* ◊ *a round-the-world trip*. It is often short in time, even if it is long in distance. **Journey** is more often used when the travelling takes a long time and is difficult: *It was a long and difficult trip across the mountains.* In American English **journey** is NOT usually used for short trips: (*especially BrE*) *How far is your journey to work?* **Trip** is used especially when you travel for pleasure or for a particular purpose: *a day/school/business trip* ◊ *a day/school/business journey*

tour [C] a journey made for pleasure during which several different places are visited: *We're going on a* **tour** *of Bavaria.* ◊ *After a* **whirlwind tour** (= a very fast tour) *of the temples, it was time to find a hotel.* ◊ *If there are any problems, contact your* **tour operator** (= a company that arranges organized tours). See also **tour** → TOUR *verb*, **tourism** → TRAVEL, **tourist** → TOURIST

expedition /ˌekspəˈdɪʃn/ [C] an organized journey with a particular purpose, especially to find out about a place that is not well known; a short trip that you make when you want or need sth: *He* **led** *the first* **expedition** *to the South Pole.* ◊ *She made two expeditions to Brazil to study wild plants.* ◊ *Win a fantastic shopping expedition to New York!*

excursion /ɪkˈskɜːʃn; *AmE* ɪkˈskɜːrʒn/ [C] a short trip made for pleasure, especially one that has been organized for a group of people: *We decided to make an all-day excursion to the island.*

pilgrimage /ˈpɪlɡrɪmɪdʒ/ [C, U] a journey to a holy place for religious reasons; a journey to a place connected with sb that you admire or respect: *the annual pilgrimage to Mecca* ◊ *His grave has become a* **place of pilgrimage** (= a place that people go on pilgrimages to). See also **pilgrim** → TOURIST

outing [C] (*rather formal*) a short trip made for pleasure or education, usually with a group of people and lasting no more than a day: *a family outing to the seaside* ◊ *The children were on a day's outing from school.*

travels [pl.] time spent travelling from place to place, especially in foreign countries and for pleasure: *The novel is based on his travels in Asia.* ◊ *When are you* **off on your travels** (= going travelling)?

day ˈout (pl. **days out**) [C] (*especially BrE*) a trip to somewhere for a day, especially for pleasure: *We had a day out at the beach.*

trouble *noun*

1 A few drunks were causing trouble.
2 get/run into trouble

1 See the Topic Map for CONFLICT on p.896
trouble · unrest · disturbance · disorder · anarchy · agitation
These are all words for a situation involving violent behaviour and/or protests.

PATTERNS AND COLLOCATIONS
▸ trouble / unrest / disturbances / disorder / agitation **among** sb
▸ **serious** trouble / unrest / disturbances / disorder
▸ **public / political** unrest / disturbances / disorder / agitation
▸ **violent / civil / urban / social** unrest / disturbances / disorder
▸ to **cause** trouble / unrest / a disturbance
▸ to **lead to** unrest / a disturbance / disorder / anarchy
▸ to **quell** the unrest / disturbance / disorder
▸ trouble / unrest / a disturbance / disorder **occurs**

trouble [U] a situation in which people are violent and likely to fight: *As the bars closed the town was full of youths* **looking for trouble**. ◊ *The police were* **expecting trouble** *after the game.* ◊ *Troops were stationed nearby in case of crowd trouble.*

unrest /ʌnˈrest/ [U] (*rather formal*) a political situation in which people are angry and likely to protest or fight: *There was growing unrest among the city's ethnic minorities.*

disturbance [C, U] (*rather formal*) a situation in which people behave violently in a public place: *News of the arrests provoked serious disturbances in the streets.* ◊ *The army is trained to deal with riots and civil disturbance.*

disorder [U] (*rather formal*) a situation in which large groups of people behave violently in a public place: *The food crisis led to outbreaks of rioting and public disorder.* **OPP** order → PEACE, See also **disorderly** → WILD 1

anarchy /ˈænəki; *AmE* ˈænərki/ [U] a situation in a country or place in which there is no government, order or control: *Our nation is descending into anarchy.* ❶ A country can **descend into, slide into, fall into** or **plunge into** anarchy.

agitation /ˌædʒɪˈteɪʃn/ [U, C] (*rather formal*) public protest in order to achieve political change: *There has been widespread* **agitation for** *social reform.* ◊ *His political opponents have threatened to launch a mass* **agitation against** *the agreement.* See also **agitate** → CAMPAIGN *verb*

2 **trouble · hardship · misfortune · adversity**
These are all words for a difficult or dangerous situation that a person can be in.

PATTERNS AND COLLOCATIONS
▸ **great / real** trouble / hardship / misfortune / adversity
▸ **financial** trouble / hardship
▸ to **cause** trouble / hardship
▸ to **suffer / face / meet with** hardship / misfortune / adversity
▸ **in times of** trouble / hardship / adversity

trouble [U] (usually used after *in* or *into*) a situation that is difficult or dangerous; a situation in which you can be criticized or punished: *A yachtsman* **got into trouble** *off the coast and had to be rescued.* ◊ *The company* **ran into trouble** *early on, when a major order was cancelled.* ◊ *He's* **in trouble with** *the police.* ◊ *My brother was always* **getting me into trouble** *with my parents.*

hardship [U, C] (*rather formal*) a situation that is difficult and unpleasant, for example because you do not have enough money, food, clothes, etc: *The two men endured great hardship during their trek across Antarctica.* ◊ *People suffered many hardships during that long winter.* ◊ *It was* **no hardship** *to walk home on such a lovely evening.* See also **hard** → DIFFICULT 2, See also the entry for POVERTY

misfortune [U] (*formal*) bad luck; an unfortunate accident, condition or event: *He has known great misfortune in his life.* ◊ *We* **had the misfortune to** *run into a violent storm.* ◊ *She bore her misfortunes bravely.*

adversity /ədˈvɜːsəti; *AmE* -ˈvɜːrs-/ [U, C] (*formal*) a difficult or unpleasant situation: *She has shown great courage in the face of adversity.* ◊ *He overcame many personal adversities.*

trudge *verb*

trudge · plod · tramp · trail · traipse · troop · trek
These words all mean to walk slowly with heavy steps, for example because you are tired or the ground is difficult to walk on.

PATTERNS AND COLLOCATIONS
▸ to trudge / plod / tramp / trail / traipse / trek **through** the snow, etc.
▸ to trudge / plod / trail **slowly / wearily**
▸ to trudge / tramp **the streets**

trudge [I, T] (usually used with an adverb or preposition) to walk along slowly and with heavy steps, because you are tired or the ground is difficult to walk on: *They trudged wearily into the town.* ◊ *We trudged the last two miles across the wet sand.*

plod (-**dd**-) [I, T] (usually used with an adverb or preposition) to trudge: *We plodded on through the rain.* ◊ *I watched her* **plodding her way** *across the field.*

These words are very similar in meaning; **trudge** places slightly more emphasis on the difficulty of lifting your feet to walk; **plod** often gives a sense of sb making steady (if slow) progress.

tramp [I, T] (usually used with an adverb or preposition) to walk with heavy or noisy steps, especially for a long time: *I'm fed up with all these reporters tramping in and out.* ◇ *She's been tramping the streets looking for work.*

trail [I] (usually used with an adverb or preposition) to walk slowly because you are tired or bored, especially behind sb else: *We walked home in the rain, with the kids trailing along behind.*

traipse /treɪps/ [I] (always used with an adverb or preposition) (*rather informal*) to walk somewhere slowly and with heavy steps, especially because you are tired or unwilling to go somewhere: *We spent the afternoon traipsing around art galleries.*

troop [I] (always used with an adverb or preposition) (of a group of people) to walk somewhere together as a group: *After lunch we all trooped down to the beach.*

trek (-**kk**-) [I] (usually used with an adverb or preposition) (*rather informal*) to make a long or difficult journey, especially on foot: *I have to trek up that hill every day with the groceries.*

true *adj.* See the Topic Map for FACT AND OPINION on p.898, See also the entry for RELIABLE 2

---

true · right · correct
These words all describe sth that cannot be doubted as fact.

▸ right / correct **about** sb / sth
▸ the true / right / correct **answer**
▸ the right / correct **time**
▸ quite / absolutely / more or less true / right / correct

true connected with facts rather than things that have been invented or guessed: *That's not strictly true (= completely true).* ◇ *Indicate whether the following statements are true or false.* ◇ *Is it true (that) she's leaving?* ◇ *The novel is based on a true story.* ❶ **True** can be used to admit that a particular fact or statement is true, although you think that sth else is more important: *'We could get it cheaper.' 'True, but would it be as good?'* ❶ A **true** version or copy of sth is the same as the original in its details and/or its spirit: *The movie isn't really true to the book.* **OPP** untrue, false → WRONG 1, See also the truth → FACT

right that is true and cannot be doubted as a fact: *I got about half the answers right.* ◇ *What's the right time?* ◇ (*spoken*) *'David, isn't it?' 'Yes, that's right.'* ◇ *It was Monday you went to see Angie, right? (= is that right?)* **OPP** wrong → WRONG 1
▸ **right** *adv.*: *You guessed right.*

correct (*rather formal*) right according to the facts and without any mistakes: *Only one of the answers is correct.* ◇ *Check that all the details are correct.* ◇ *'Are you in charge here?' 'That's correct.'* **OPP** incorrect → WRONG 1
▸ **correctly** *adv.*: *Have you spelled it correctly?*

Correct is more formal than **right** and is more likely to be used in official or formal instructions or documents.

---

trust *verb*

---

trust · depend on/upon sb/sth · rely on/upon sth · take sb/sth for granted · count on sb/sth · believe in sb · pin your hopes on sb/sth · have confidence in sb/sth
These words all mean to believe that sb/sth will do what you hope or expect of them or that what they tell you is correct or true.

▸ to trust / depend on / rely on / count on sb **to do sth**
▸ to trust / believe / have confidence **in** sb / sth
▸ to trust / rely on / believe in / have confidence in **yourself**
▸ to trust / rely on / have confidence in **sb's judgement**
▸ to trust / rely on **sb's advice**
▸ to depend on / rely on / count on **sb's support**
▸ to trust / rely on **sb's figures / what sb tells you / what you read**
▸ to **completely** trust sb / depend on sb / rely on sb / take sb for granted / believe in sb
▸ to **really** trust / depend on / rely on / believe in sb / sth

trust [T] to believe that sb is good, honest, sincere, etc. and that they will do what you expect of them or do the right thing; to believe that sth is true or correct: *It seems you can't trust anyone these days.* ◇ *You can trust me not to tell anyone.* ◇ *I'd trust him with my life.* ◇ *I don't really trust his judgement.* ◇ *Don't trust what you read in the newspapers!* ◇ *Such figures are not to be trusted.* ❶ **Trust** always takes an object, but especially in British English it can also be used in the phrasal verbs **trust in sb/sth** and **trust to sth**: *She needs to trust more in her own abilities.* ◇ *I stumbled along in the dark, trusting to luck to find the right door (= hoping that I would be lucky enough to find the right door, as I had nothing to guide me).* **OPP** distrust → SUSPECT, See also **trust** → FAITH *noun*, **trusted** → RELIABLE 1, **trusting** → NAIVE

de'pend on/upon sb/sth *phrasal verb* (often used with *can/cannot/could/could not*) to trust sb/sth to do what you expect or want, to do the right thing, or to be true or correct; to be sure or expect that sth will happen: *He was the sort of person you could depend on.* ◇ *He knew he could depend on her to deal with the situation.* ◇ *Can you depend on her version of what happened?* ◇ (*ironic*) *You can depend on her to be (= she always is) late.* ❶ **Depend upon sb/sth** is more formal than **depend on sb/sth.**

re'ly on/upon sb/sth *phrasal verb* (used especially with *can/cannot/could/could not* and *should/should not*) to trust sb/sth to do what you expect or want, or to be honest, correct or good enough: *Can I rely on you to keep this secret?* ◇ *You can't rely on any figures you get from them.* ◇ *You can rely on our support.* ◇ *The local transport system can't be relied on.* ❶ **Rely upon sb/sth** is more formal than **rely on sb/sth.** See also **rely on/upon sb/sth** → NEED *verb*, **reliable** → RELIABLE 1

You can **trust** a person but NOT a thing or system: *The local transport system can't be trusted.* You can **trust** sb's *judgement* or *advice*, but NOT their support. You can **depend on** sb's *support*, but NOT their judgement or advice. **Rely on/upon sb/sth** is used especially with *you can/could* or *you should* to give advice or a promise: *I don't really rely on his judgement.* ◇ *You can't really rely on his judgement.*

take sb/sth for 'granted, take it for 'granted (that...) *phrase* (*sometimes disapproving*) to be so used to sb/sth that you do not recognize their true value any more and do not show you are grateful; to believe that sth is true without first making sure that it is: *Her husband was always there and she just took him for granted.* ◇ *We take having an endless supply of clean water for granted.* ◇ *I just took it for granted that he'd always be around.*

'count on sb/sth *phrasal verb* (often used with *can/cannot/could/could not*) to be sure that sb will do what you need them to do, or that sth will happen as you want it to happen: *I'm counting on you to help me.* ◇ *We can't count on the good weather lasting.* ◇ *Can we count on your support in the next election?* ◇ *'I'm sure he'll help.' 'Don't count on it.'* ❶ You **count on sb** to give you help when you need it, but NOT to give advice: *You can count on his judgement.* **Count on sb/sth** is often used with *can/could* to ask for help, to give a promise or to state sth that you think is true.

be'lieve in sb *phrasal verb* to feel that you can trust sb and/or that they will be successful: *They need a leader they can believe in.* ◇ *You've got to believe in yourself.* See also **belief** → FAITH

,pin your 'hopes on sb/sth *idiom* (**-nn-**) to rely on sb/sth completely for success or help: *The company is pinning all its hopes on the new project.*

have 'confidence in sb/sth *phrase* to feel that you can be sure of sb/sth's abilities or good qualities: *The players all have confidence in their manager.* ◇ *I have absolute confidence in her abilities.* See also **confidence** → FAITH

truth *noun* See also the entry for INTEGRITY

truth · good faith · sincerity
These are all words for the quality of being true, telling the truth or acting honestly.

PATTERNS AND COLLOCATIONS
▸ **in** truth / good faith / sincerity
▸ to **say** sth with truth / sincerity
▸ to **doubt** the truth / good faith / sincerity of sb / sth

truth [U] the quality of being based on fact: *There is no truth in the rumours.* ◇ *There is not a grain of truth in what she says.* **OPP falsehood** → LIE, See also **truthful** → HONEST

,good 'faith [U] (always used after *in*) the belief that what you are doing is right or that what you are saying is correct; the intention to do sth right or be helpful: *We printed the report in good faith but have now learnt that it was incorrect.* **OPP bad faith** → BETRAYAL

sincerity /sɪnˈserəti/ [U] (*approving*) the quality of being honest about what you think or feel and not lying or pretending; showing this quality: *I can say in all sincerity that I knew nothing of these plans.* ◇ *The sincerity of his beliefs is unquestionable.* See also **sincere** → DEEP 1, **sincere** → HONEST

try *verb*

1 try to do sth/try your hardest
2 try doing sth/try this new dish

1 **try · attempt · seek · struggle · strive · endeavour · have a go · go for sth**
These words all mean to make an effort to do or achieve sth.

PATTERNS AND COLLOCATIONS
▸ to try / attempt / seek / struggle / strive / endeavour **to do sth**
▸ to struggle / strive **for / against** sth
▸ to try / attempt / seek / struggle / strive **desperately / in vain**
▸ to be **constantly** trying / seeking / struggling / striving to do sth
▸ to **consciously** try / attempt / seek / strive to do sth
▸ to **deliberately** try / attempt / seek / endeavour to do sth
▸ to try / struggle / strive **hard**

try [I, T] to make an effort to do, achieve or get sth: *I don't know if I can come but I'll try.* ◇ *What are you trying to do?* ◇ *I tried hard not to laugh.* ◇ *She tried her best to solve the problem.* ◇ *Just try your hardest.* ❶ In spoken English **try** can be used with *and* plus another verb, instead of with *to* and the infinitive: *I'll try and get you a new one tomorrow.* ◇ *Try and finish quickly.* In this structure **try** can only be used in the infinitive, or to tell sb what to do. See also **try** → ATTEMPT *noun*

attempt [T] (*rather formal*) to try to do sth, especially sth difficult or dangerous: *The prisoner was shot while attempting to escape.* ◇ *The coastguard had advised them not to attempt a rescue.* ◇ *More than once, depression drove him to attempt suicide.* See also **attempt** → ATTEMPT *noun*

  ▸ **attempted** *adj.* [only before noun]: *attempted rape/ murder/robbery* (= that was attempted but was not successful)

NOTE TRY OR ATTEMPT? Try has a more general meaning and is used more often in informal conversation. **Attempt** is more formal and places the emphasis more on the act of starting to do sth rather than on the effort put into achieving it. When followed by a noun, **attempt** usually refers to an effort to do sth which was not successful or is unlikely to be successful: *The prisoners attempted an escape, but failed.*

seek [T] (always used in the phrase *seek to do sth*) (*formal*) to try to do sth, often sth that might take a long time: *The research project will seek to find an answer to this question.* See also **seek** → ASK *verb* 2, **seek** → LOOK *verb* 2

struggle [I, T] to try very hard to do sth when it is difficult or when there are a lot of problems: *Shona struggled for breath.* ◇ *The family struggled through the next few years.* ◇ *I'm really struggling with this essay.* ◇ *They struggled just to pay their bills.* See also **struggle** → EFFORT *noun*

strive [I] (*formal*) to try very hard, usually over a long period of time, to achieve sth or defeat sth: *We constantly strive for excellence in design.* ◇ *They were always striving towards perfection.*

endeavour (*BrE*) (*AmE* **endeavor**) /ɪnˈdevə(r)/ [T] (always followed by *to* + infinitive) (*formal*) to try very hard to do sth, especially sth that needs a lot of effort: *I will endeavour to do my best for my country.* See also **endeavour** → EFFORT *noun*

have a 'go *idiom* (*informal, especially spoken*) to make an attempt to do sth: *'I can't start the engine.' 'Let me have a go.'* ◇ *I've always wanted to have a go at windsurfing.*

'go for sth *phrasal verb* (*informal, spoken*) to put a lot of effort into sth in order to get or achieve sth: *Go for it, John! You know you can beat him.* ◇ *She'll be going for gold in the Olympics.*

2 See also the entry for TEST 1
try · taste · sample
These words all mean to use, do or experience sth in order to see what it is like.

PATTERNS AND COLLOCATIONS
▸ to try / sample a **new product**
▸ to try / taste / sample **food / wine**

try [T] to use sth, do sth or eat or drink a small amount of sth in order to see what it is like, or if it is good or successful: *Have you tried this new coffee? It's very good.* ◇ *Try these shoes for size — they should fit you.* ◇ *She tried the door, but it was locked.* ◇ *John isn't here. Try phoning his home number.* See also **try sb/sth out** → TEST *verb* 1

taste [T] to eat or drink a small amount of sth to see what it is like, especially to see if it tastes right: *Taste it and see if you think there's enough salt in it.*

sample /ˈsɑːmpl; *AmE* ˈsæmpl/ [T] (*written*) to eat a small amount of sth, or experience sth for a short time, to see what it is like: *I sampled the delights of Greek cooking for the first time.* ◇ *He put his head out of the window and sampled the morning air.*

tumour (*BrE*) (*AmE* **tumor**) *noun*

tumour · ulcer · sore · swelling · inflammation · blister · lump · bump · abscess · boil
These are all words for places on the skin or inside the body that are unhealthy and bigger than usual as a result of illness or injury.

PATTERNS AND COLLOCATIONS
▸ a tumour / an ulcer / sores / a swelling / a blister / a lump / an abscess / a boil **on** a part of the body
▸ a tumour / sores / a swelling / inflammation / a lump / an abscess **in** a part of the body
▸ (a) **painful** ulcers / sores / swelling / inflammation / blisters / lump / abscess / boil
▸ to **have** a tumour / an ulcer / a sore / a swelling / inflammation / a blister / a lump / a bump / an abscess / a boil

▶ to **develop** a tumour / an ulcer / a blister / an abscess
▶ to **get** an ulcer / sores / a blister / a bump / a boil
▶ to **treat** a tumour / an ulcer / a boil
▶ a tumour / an ulcer / a blister / an abscess **forms / develops**
▶ an ulcer / a blister / an abscess / a boil **bursts**

tumour (*BrE*) (*AmE* **tumor**) /'tjuːmə(r); *AmE* 'tuː-/ [C] a mass of cells growing in or on a part of the body where they should not, usually causing medical problems: *He has a* **malignant** (= harmful) **brain tumour.** ◇ *They were relieved to hear that the* **tumour** *was* **benign** (= not dangerous).

ulcer /'ʌlsə(r)/ [C] a painful area on the outside of the body or on the surface of an organ inside the body, which may bleed or produce a poisonous substance: *a stomach ulcer* ◇ (*BrE*) *a mouth ulcer* ❶ In American English a **mouth ulcer** is called a **canker sore.**

sore [C] a painful, often red, place on the body where there is a wound or infection: *The illness left them with* **open sores** *all over their backs.* ❶ A **cold sore** is a painful spot on the lips or inside the mouth that is caused by a virus. A **canker sore** is the American English word for a mouth ulcer, and is not caused by a virus. See also **sore** → PAINFUL *adj.* 1

swelling [U, C] the condition of being swollen (= larger or rounder than normal); a place on your body that has become swollen because of illness or injury: *Use ice to reduce the swelling.* ◇ *The fall left her with a painful swelling above her eye.* See also **swell** → SWELL

inflammation /ˌɪnflə'meɪʃn/ [U, C] a condition in which a part of the body becomes red, painful and swollen because of infection or injury: *The doctor's notes recorded inflammation of the ear.* See also **inflamed** → PAINFUL *adj.* 1

blister [C] a small, round, raised area of the skin that has become filled with liquid and is caused, for example, by rubbing or burning: *He'd got blisters on his feet from running.*

lump [C] a swelling under the skin, sometimes a sign of serious illness: *He was unhurt except for a lump on his head.* ◇ *Check your breasts for lumps every month.*

bump [C] (*rather informal*) a swelling on the body, often the head, where you have been hit by sth: *She was covered in bumps and bruises.*

abscess /'æbses/ [C] a swollen and infected area under the skin or in the body, full of a thick yellowish liquid (= pus): *He had a painful abscess on his gum.*

boil [C] a swollen and infected area under the skin which is full of a thick yellowish liquid (= pus): *The boil on his back was painful.*

> **NOTE** ABSCESS OR BOIL? A **boil** is always just under the skin on the surface of the body, and is usually less serious than an **abscess**, which can be deeper within the body and will usually need treatment by a doctor.

turn *verb*

1 turn away/turn your head away
2 turn sb into a frog

1 turn · turn (sb/sth) around/round · swing · twist · spin · wheel · whirl · swivel · pivot

These words all mean to move your body or part of your body in order to face another direction.

PATTERNS AND COLLOCATIONS

▶ to turn / swing / twist / spin / wheel / whirl / swivel / pivot **around / round**
▶ to turn / swing / spin / wheel / whirl / swivel **back / away**
▶ to turn / turn around / swing / spin / whirl / swivel / pivot **on** sth
▶ to turn / twist / swivel your **head**
▶ to turn / turn around / swing / twist / spin / wheel / whirl around / swivel **to face** sb / sth
▶ to turn / turn around / swing / spin / wheel / whirl **suddenly**
▶ to turn / turn around / swing / spin / wheel **sharply / quickly**
▶ to turn / turn around / twist **slowly**

turn [I, T] (usually used with an adverb or preposition) to move your body or part of your body in order to face or start moving in a different direction: *We* **turned and** *headed for home.* ◇ *He turned back to his work.* ◇ *Anne flushed and turned her head away.* ◇ *While his* **back was turned** *I sneaked a look at his notes.*

turn a'round/'round, **turn sb/sth a'round/'round** *phrasal verb* to change position or direction in order to face the other way; to make sb/sth do this: *Turn around and let me look at you.* ◇ *Turn your chair round.* ❶ In **turn around/round** and the other verbs in this group, *round* is used especially in British English, and *around* especially in American English.

swing [I, T] (always used with an adverb or preposition) to turn or change direction suddenly; to make sb/sth do this: *The bus swung sharply to the left.* ◇ *She swung around angrily, her eyes blazing.* ◇ *He swung the car round in a dangerous U-turn.*

twist [I, T] (usually used with an adverb or preposition) to turn part of your body around while the rest stays still: *She twisted in her chair to look.* ◇ *Hold your arms out to the sides and twist your upper body.*

spin [I, T] (always used with an adverb or preposition) to turn around quickly once; to make sb/sth do this: *She spun on her heel and walked out.* ◇ *He spun the child roughly around.*

wheel [I, T] (always used with an adverb or preposition) (*written*) to turn quickly or suddenly to face the opposite direction; to make sb/sth do this: *Jim wheeled back to face me.* ◇ *He wheeled his horse around.*

whirl /wɜːl; *AmE* wɜːrl/ [I, T] (usually used with an adverb or preposition) (*written*) to turn quickly or suddenly to face the opposite direction; to make sb do this: *She whirled on him, furious.* ◇ *He grasped her wrist and whirled her back to face him.* ❶ In this meaning **whirl** is only used about people; they are usually acting under a strong emotion, especially anger.

swivel /'swɪvl/ (-ll-, *AmE* -l-) [I, T] (*written*) to turn or move your body, eyes or head around quickly to face another direction: *He swivelled around to look at her.* ◇ *I swivelled my head to peer at him.*

pivot /'pɪvət/ [I] (usually used with an adverb or preposition) to turn or balance on a central point: *He pivoted on one foot and threw the ball to Gary.* ◇ *The mechanism pivots around a central point.*

2 turn · transform · convert · change · translate · evolve · mutate · metamorphose

These words all mean to change in appearance or character, or to make the appearance or character of sth change.

PATTERNS AND COLLOCATIONS

▶ to turn / transform sth / convert / change / translate / evolve / mutate / metamorphose **into** sth
▶ to turn / transform sth / convert / change / evolve / mutate / metamorphose **from** sth **into** sth
▶ to turn / transform sth / convert / change / evolve / mutate **rapidly** (into sth)
▶ to turn / transform sth / convert / change / evolve **quickly / slowly / gradually** (into sth)
▶ to turn / transform sth / change **suddenly / miraculously / overnight** (into sth)
▶ to transform / convert / change sth **completely**
▶ to **easily / automatically** turn / transform sth / convert / change / translate (into sth)

turn [I, T] (always used with *into* or *from* and *to*) to change into sb/sth different; to make sb/sth change into sth different: *The natural sugars turn into alcohol during brewing.* ◇ *The problem turned into an advantage.* ◇ *The leaves gradually turn from green to orange.* ◇ *There are plans to turn the old station into a hotel.* ❶ In fairy stories, a person who is able to do magic might **turn sb into sth**: *With a wave of her wand, she turned him into a frog.* In everyday English, sb might **turn into**, or circumstances might **turn sb into** *a criminal, a gambler, a tyrant, a hero* or a *film star*; or people might turn a *building* into a *hotel* or a *house* into a *home*. You can also use **turn into sth** or **turn sth into sth** when you are describing the way a situation changes, or people change a situation: *What began as a minor disagreement has turned into a major crisis.* ◇ *I managed to turn the whole thing into a joke.*

transform [T] to completely change the appearance or character of sth, especially so that it is better; to change the form of sth: *A new colour scheme will transform your bedroom.* ◇ *It was an event that would transform my life.* ◇ *The photochemical reactions transform the light into electrical impulses.* ❶ In everyday English, **transform** usually suggests that the change has been particularly dramatic; in scientific contexts **transform** does not necessarily refer to a dramatic change.

▸ **transformation** /ˌtrænsfəˈmeɪʃn; *AmE* -fərˈm-/ *noun* [C, U]: (*especially written*) *The country's transformation from dictatorship to democracy has been peaceful.* ◇ *What a transformation! You look great.*

convert /kənˈvɜːt; *AmE* -ˈvɜːrt/ [T, I] to change or make sth change from one form, purpose or system to another; to be able to be changed from one form, purpose, or system to another: *The hotel is going to be converted into a nursing home.* ◇ *Hot water is converted to electricity by a turbine.* ◇ *We've converted from coal to gas central heating.* ◇ *We need a sofa that converts into a bed.* ❶ **Convert** is often used to talk about changing old buildings to make them suitable for people to live in: *to convert a church/farm buildings/a barn/a house/stables/a mill (into sth)* ◇ *They live in a converted church/barn/mill.* **Convert** is often used without an object to talk about changing from one type of service to another: *All homes must convert to digital TV by 2012, when the analogue signal will be switched off.* It is also used to talk about changing money from one currency to another, or changing the way money is held: *to convert securities into shares* See also **conversion** → CHANGE *noun* 2, **convertible** → FLEXIBLE 1

change [I, T] (always used with *into* or *from* and *to*) to pass or make sb/sth pass from one state or form into another: *Caterpillars change into butterflies.* ◇ *The lights changed from red to green.* ◇ *With a wave of her wand, she changed the frog into a handsome prince.*

> **NOTE** TURN OR CHANGE? **Change** is only used in cases where sth changes naturally, automatically or by magic (although you can also use **turn** in these cases). **Change** is NOT usually used when people use their effort or skill to change one thing or situation into sth different, or when circumstances change a situation: ~~There are plans to change the old station into a hotel.~~ ◇ ~~I managed to change the whole thing into a joke.~~ ◇ ~~A minor disagreement has changed into a major crisis.~~

translate [T, I] (*rather formal*) to change sth, or to be changed, into a different form: *It's time to translate words into action.* ◇ *I hope all the hard work will translate into profits.* ◇ *Most attempts to translate Shakespeare to the small screen (= television) are not successful.* ❶ **Translate** is often used when people are talking about wanting to get good results: *You need to translate your ideas into practice/your enthusiasm into success.* It is also often used when people are talking about how easy or difficult it is to produce the same thing using a different medium, for example producing a play (which is meant for the theatre) on television, or about adopting a system in a different place: *I'm not sure how well the American system would translate to a European context.*

evolve /iˈvɒlv; *AmE* iˈvɑːlv/ [I] (*biology*) (of plants or animals) to develop gradually over many generations from a simple form to a more complicated one: *The three species evolved from a single ancestor.* ◇ *The dolphin has evolved a highly developed jaw.* See also **evolve** → DEVELOP 1

▸ **evolution** /ˌiːvəˈluːʃn; ˌev-/ *noun* [U]: *the evolution of the human species*

mutate /mjuˈteɪt; *AmE* ˈmjuːteɪt/ [I, T] (*biology or written*) to develop or make sth develop a new form or structure, because of a genetic change; to change into a new form:

We are studying the ability of the virus to mutate into new forms. ◇ *Scientists have been able to replace the mutated gene with a normal one.* ◇ *Rhythm and blues mutated into rock and roll.* ❶ A **genetic** change is one that is connected with the units in the cells of a living thing that control its physical characteristics. **Mutate** is used by writers, either to describe a gradual change into sth unpleasant: *to mutate into a monster/a writhing, biting snake/rotting vegetation*; or to describe a change that seems to take place gradually by itself, often in a strange or unexplained way: *Memories had mutated into bizarre myths.*

▸ **mutation** *noun* [U, C]: *These cells have been affected by mutation.* ◇ *The disease is caused by genetic mutations.*

metamorphose /ˌmetəˈmɔːfəʊz; *AmE* -ˈmɔːrfoʊz/ [I] (*formal*) to change into sth completely different, especially over a period of time: *The caterpillar will eventually metamorphose into a butterfly.* ◇ *She had metamorphosed from an awkward schoolgirl into a beautiful woman.*

▸ **metamorphosis** *noun* [C, U]: (*formal*) *We studied the metamorphosis of a caterpillar into a butterfly.*

turning point *noun*

turning point · head · landmark · watershed · crisis · crossroads
These are all words for a time or event when an important change takes place or you make an important decision.

PATTERNS AND COLLOCATIONS
▸ a turning point/landmark/watershed/crisis/crossroads **in** sth
▸ a turning point/landmark/watershed **for** sb/sth
▸ **at** a turning point/crossroads
▸ an **important** turning point/landmark/watershed/crossroads
▸ a **significant/major** turning point/landmark/watershed
▸ to **reach** a turning point/a watershed/a crisis/a crossroads
▸ to **come to** a head/a crisis/a crossroads
▸ to **see sth as/represent** a turning point/landmark/watershed

ˈturning point [C, usually sing.] a time or event when an important change takes place, usually with the result that a situation improves: *The promotion marked a turning point in her career.*

head [sing.] the time when you are forced to deal with a situation quickly because it suddenly becomes very bad: *The chairman's resignation finally brought matters to a head.* ◇ *Things came to a head when several of the nurses made a formal complaint.* ❶ In this meaning **head** is only used in the phrases *bring sth to a head* or *come to a head.*

landmark /ˈlændmɑːk; *AmE* -mɑːrk/ [C] an event, discovery or invention that is an important stage in a process or the development of sth: *The ceasefire was seen as a major landmark in the fight against terrorism.*

watershed /ˈwɔːtəʃed; *AmE* ˈwɔːtərʃed; ˈwɑːt-/ [C] (*rather formal, especially written*) an event or period of time when an important change takes place: *The granting of the vote represented a watershed for the rights of women.*

crisis /ˈkraɪsɪs/ (pl. **crises** /-siːz/) [C] a time when a problem, bad situation or illness reaches its worst point: *The fever has passed its crisis.* ◇ *Their marriage had reached crisis point.*

crossroads /ˈkrɒsrəʊdz; *AmE* ˈkrɔːsroʊdz/ [sing.] a time at which you must make an important decision, especially about what to do next: *He has reached a crossroads in his career.* ◇ *We are standing at an important crossroads in the history of Europe.*

turn out *phrasal verb*

turn out · emerge · come out · come to light · get out · transpire · leak out
These words are all used to talk about unknown information that becomes known.

PATTERNS AND COLLOCATIONS
▸ news/the truth emerges/comes out/gets out/leaks out
▸ It turns out/emerges/transpires that…
▸ it **now** turns out/emerges/transpires…
▸ to turn out/emerge/come out/come to light/transpire **later**

▶ to turn out / emerge / transpire / leak out **subsequently**
▶ to turn out / emerge / come out / come to light **finally**

,turn 'out *phrasal verb* to be finally discovered to be sth, especially when this is unexpected: *The job* **turned out to be** *harder than we thought.* ◇ *It turned out that she was a friend of my sister.*

emerge /iˈmɜːdʒ; *AmE* iˈmɜːrdʒ/ [I] (*rather formal*) (of facts, ideas or evidence) to become known: *No new evidence emerged during the investigation.* ◇ *It emerged that the company was going to be sold.* ◇ *One thing* **emerges** *very clearly* **from** *this study.*

,come 'out *phrasal verb* (of news, an account of sth or the truth) to become known to people: *The full story came out at the trial.* ◇ *It came out that he'd been telling lies.*

come to 'light *idiom* (of evidence or knowledge) to become known: *New evidence has recently come to light.*

,get 'out *phrasal verb* (not usually used in the progressive tenses) (*rather informal*) (of secret information) to become known: *If this gets out there'll be trouble.*

transpire /trænˈspaɪə(r)/ *verb* [I] (not usually used in the progressive tenses) (*formal*) (of secret or unknown information) to become known: *It transpired that the gang had had a contact inside the bank.* ◇ *This story, it later transpired, was untrue.*

,leak 'out *phrasal verb* (not usually used in the progressive tenses) (*rather informal*) (of secret information) to become known to the public: *Details of the plan soon leaked out.* See also **leak** → REVEAL

> **NOTE** **GET OUT** OR **LEAK OUT**? **Leak out** is used especially to talk about information that is only known by people inside a particular organization, for example a government. Information may **get out** either by accident or deliberately. If information **leaks out**, it is usually done deliberately, for example in order to influence or damage the organization.

turn sth off *phrasal verb*

turn sth off · switch sth off · shut sth off · disconnect · turn sth out · unplug
These words all mean to stop the flow of electricity, gas, water, etc. by moving a switch, button, etc.

PATTERNS AND COLLOCATIONS
▶ to turn off / switch off / disconnect / unplug a / the **machine / phone**
▶ to turn off / switch off / shut off / disconnect the **power / electricity supply**
▶ to turn off / shut off / disconnect the **gas / water**
▶ to turn off / switch off / turn out a **light / lamp**
▶ to turn off / switch off / unplug an / the **appliance / TV**
▶ to turn off / switch off the **motor / ignition / wipers / alarm / torch / computer**

,turn sth 'off *phrasal verb* (*especially spoken*) to stop a machine or light from working; to stop a supply of electricity, gas or water from flowing or reaching a place: *Please turn the television off before you go to bed.* ◇ *Turn that tap off!* ◇ *They've turned off the water while they repair a burst pipe.* ❶ **Turn sth off** can be used to talk about making electrical devices or machines stop working, as well as turning a tap to stop water or gas from flowing. **OPP** **turn sth on** → TURN STH ON, See also **put sth out** → PUT STH OUT, **turn sth down** → REDUCE

,switch sth 'off *phrasal verb* to turn a machine, light or electricity supply off by pressing a switch or button: *How do you switch this thing off?* ◇ *The electricity has been switched off.* ❶ **Switch sth off** is only used to talk about electrical devices, using a switch or button, not water, gas or taps. In British English **switch off** can also be used, without an object when you are talking about a television or radio: (*BrE*) *I switched off* (= the television/radio) *after five minutes – I thought the show was awful.* **OPP** **switch sth on** → TURN STH ON, See also **switch** → BUTTON *noun* 1

,shut sth 'off *phrasal verb* (*especially written or technical*) to turn off an engine or a supply of electricity, water or gas: *He shut off the engine and silence enfolded them.* ◇ *A valve shuts off the gas when the lid is closed.*

disconnect [T, often passive] (*especially written*) to remove a piece of equipment from a supply of gas, water or electricity; to officially stop the supply of telephone lines, water, electricity or gas to a building; to break the contact between two people who are talking on the telephone: *First, disconnect the boiler from the water mains.* ◇ *You may be disconnected if you do not pay the bill.* ◇ *We were suddenly disconnected.* **OPP** **connect** → CONNECTION

,turn sth 'out *phrasal verb* to switch a light off: *Remember to turn out the lights when you go to bed.* **OPP** **turn sth on** → TURN STH ON

unplug (**-gg-**) [T] to remove the plug of a piece of electrical equipment from the electricity supply: *If I'm very busy, I unplug the phone.* **OPP** **plug sth in** → TURN STH ON

turn sth on *phrasal verb*

turn sth on · switch sth on · start · plug sth in(to sth) · set sth off · start (sth) up · put sth on
These words all mean to make sth such as a machine or electrical device start working.

PATTERNS AND COLLOCATIONS
▶ to turn on / switch on / start / plug in / start up a **machine**
▶ to turn on / switch on / plug in / start up a **computer**
▶ to turn on / switch on / plug in an **appliance**
▶ to turn on / switch on / start / start up the **motor / engine**
▶ to turn on / switch on / start the **ignition**
▶ to turn on / switch on / plug in / put on the **lamp / light / television / radio / fire / heater**
▶ to turn on / switch on / put on the **gas / heating / oven / headlights / wipers**
▶ to switch on / plug in / put on the **kettle**

,turn sth 'on *phrasal verb* (*especially spoken*) to start the flow of electricity, gas, water, etc. by moving a switch, button, etc: *He turned on the taps and washed his hands.* ◇ *I'll turn the television on.* ❶ **Turn sth on** can be used to talk about making electrical devices or machines start to work, as well as turning a tap to make water or gas flow. **OPP** **turn sth off**, **turn sth out** → TURN STH OFF, See also **turn sth up** → INCREASE

,switch sth 'on *phrasal verb* to turn a light, machine, etc. on by pressing a button or switch: *How do you switch this thing on?* ❶ **Switch sth on** is only used to talk about making electrical devices start to work. In British English **switch on** can also be used without an object when you are talking about a television or radio: (*BrE*) *We only switched on* (= the television/radio) *halfway through the show.* **OPP** **switch off** → TURN STH OFF, See also **switch** → BUTTON *noun* 1

start [T, I] to make a vehicle or machine begin to operate; (of a vehicle or machine) to begin to operate: *Start the engines!* ◇ *I can't get the car started.* ◇ *The car won't start.*

,plug sth 'in, **,plug sth 'into sth** *phrasal verb* (**-gg-**) to connect a piece of electrical equipment to the main supply of electricity or to another piece of electrical equipment using a plug (= a small plastic object with two or three metal pins): *Is the printer plugged in?* ◇ *Simply plug the lamp into a 13-amp socket.* **OPP** **unplug** → TURN STH OFF

,set sth 'off *phrasal verb* to make a bomb, etc. explode; to make an alarm start ringing: *A gang of boys were setting off fireworks in the street.* ◇ *Opening this door will set off the alarm.*

,start sth 'up, **,start 'up** *phrasal verb* to start a vehicle or machine; (of a vehicle or machine) to start: *The first thing I do is start up my computer.* ◇ *I heard his car start up.* **OPP** **shut down** ❶ **Shut down** is the opposite of starting up a computer or other machine; you **stop** a vehicle (= make it stop moving) and then **turn off** the engine (but you do not 'turn off the car/vehicle').

NOTE START OR START UP? In some cases you can use either word: *Start/start up the engine!* Only **start** is used in the phrases *get sth started* and *sth won't start:* ~~I can't get the car started up.~~ ◇ ~~The car won't start up.~~ **Start sth up** is the usual word when talking about computers: ~~The first thing I do is start my computer.~~

put sth 'on *phrasal verb* (*especially spoken*) to switch on a piece of equipment; to make a tape, CD, etc. begin to play: *She put on the brakes suddenly.* ◇ (*BrE*) *I'll put the kettle on for tea.* ◇ *Do you mind if I put some music on?* ❶ **Put sth on** is often used to talk about making part of a car work: *to put on the brakes/headlights/indicator/turn signal/windscreen wipers/windshield wipers.* It is also often used to talk about listening to music: *to put on a CD/some music.* Finally, in the home, you would be most likely to *put on the kettle, the air conditioning, the heating* (in British English) or *the heat* (in American English).

twist *verb*

twist · bend · distort · deform · buckle · warp
These words all mean to force sth into a new shape that is not straight.

PATTERNS AND COLLOCATIONS
▸ to be **slightly** twisted / bent / distorted / deformed / warped
▸ to bend / buckle **under the weight of sth**
▸ to be twisted / bent **out of shape**

twist [T, I] to force sth into a particular shape, especially by turning each end in the opposite direction; to force sth into a shape or position that is not normal or natural; to be turned by force in this way: *Twist the wire to form a circle.* ◇ *He grabbed me and twisted my arm behind my back.* ◇ *Her face twisted in anger.* See also **twisted → BENT**

bend [T] to force sth that was straight into an angle or curve: *Mark the pipe where you want to bend it.* ◇ *The knives were bent out of shape.* See also **bent → BENT**

distort /dɪˈstɔːt; *AmE* dɪˈstɔːrt/ [T] to change the shape, appearance or sound of sth so that it is strange or not clear: *It was like one of those fairground mirrors that distort your shape.* ◇ *The loudspeaker seemed to distort his voice.*

deform /dɪˈfɔːm; *AmE* -ˈfɔːrm/ [T] to change or spoil the usual or natural shape of sth: *The disease had deformed his spine.* See also **deformed → BENT**

buckle [I, T] to become crushed or bent under a weight or force; to crush or bend sth in this way: *The steel frames began to buckle under the strain.* ◇ *The crash buckled the front of my car.* (*figurative*)

warp /wɔːp; *AmE* wɔːrp/ [I, T, usually passive] to become, or make sth become, twisted or bent out of its natural shape, for example because it has become too hot or too damp: *The window frames had begun to warp.* ◇ *The big double doors were warped with heat and humidity.*

typical *adj.*

typical · characteristic · symbolic · representative · classic · archetypal · stereotypical · quintessential
These words all describe things that have the usual qualities or features of a particular type of person, thing or group.

PATTERNS AND COLLOCATIONS
▸ typical / characteristic / symbolic / representative **of** sth
▸ a typical / a characteristic / a representative / a classic / an archetypal **example** of sth
▸ a typical / a characteristic / a symbolic / a representative / an archetypal **figure**
▸ a typical / characteristic / symbolic **gesture**

▸ typical / characteristic / stereotypical **behaviour**
▸ **very** typical / characteristic / symbolic / representative / stereotypical
▸ **highly** typical / characteristic / symbolic
▸ **fairly** typical / characteristic / representative / stereotypical

typical having the usual qualities or features of a particular type of person, thing or group: *It's a typical Italian café.* ◇ *This meal is typical of local cookery.* ◇ *The weather at the moment is not typical for July.* ❶ You can also use **typical** to talk about a person who behaves in the way that you expect, because you know their character so well. This use often shows disapproval: *It was typical of her to forget.* ◇ *He spoke with typical enthusiasm.* ◇ (*informal, spoken, disapproving*) *She's late again – typical!* **OPP** atypical → UNUSUAL
▸ **typically** *adv.*: *They treated us to some typically American hospitality.* ◇ *Typically, she couldn't find her keys.*

characteristic (*rather formal*) very typical of sth, or of sb's character or behaviour: *With characteristic modesty she insisted on sharing the credit with the whole team.* ◇ *They suffer from many of the environmental problems that are characteristic of inner-city areas.* **OPP** **uncharacteristic** ❶ Uncharacteristic describes sth that is not typical of sb/sth or the way sb usually behaves: *The remark was quite uncharacteristic of her.*
▸ **characteristically** *adv.*: *Characteristically, Helen paid for everyone.*

NOTE TYPICAL OR CHARACTERISTIC? When it is used to mean that sb behaves as you would expect, **typical** often shows disapproval (although it can show approval), but **characteristic** usually shows approval: *It was typical of her to forget.* ◇ *Such generosity was characteristic of Mike.*

symbolic /sɪmˈbɒlɪk; *AmE* -ˈbɑːlɪk/ containing symbols; being used as a symbol: *The dove is symbolic of peace.* ◇ *He shook his fist in a symbolic gesture of defiance.* ◇ *The new regulations are largely symbolic* (= they will not have any real effect).
▸ **symbolically** *adv.*: *a symbolically significant gesture*

representative (*rather formal*) typical of a particular group of people; containing or including examples of all the different types of people or things in a large group: *The paper-thin models in magazines are not representative of most women.* ◇ *We interviewed a representative sample of teachers.* **OPP** **unrepresentative** ❶ Sth that is unrepresentative of sb/sth is not typical of a group of people or things and therefore not useful as a source of information about them: *an unrepresentative sample*

classic very typical as an example of sth, with all the features you would expect to find: *It was a classic example of poor communication.* ◇ *She displayed the classic symptoms of depression.* ❶ Example is by far the most frequent collocate of **classic** in this meaning.

archetypal /ˌɑːkiˈtaɪpl; *AmE* ˌɑːrki-/ [usually before noun] (*rather formal, written*) having all the important qualities and characteristics that make sb/sth a typical example of a particular kind of person or thing: *The Beatles were the archetypal pop group.* ◇ *It was the archetypal British suburb, built in the 1930s.*

stereotypical /ˌsteriəˈtɪpɪkl/ (*often disapproving*) typical of the fixed idea or image that many people have of a particular type of person or thing, but which is often not true in reality: *She did not conform to his stereotypical image of feminine behaviour.*

quintessential /ˌkwɪntɪˈsenʃl/ [only before noun] (*formal*) perfect as an example of sth: *He was the quintessential tough guy.*
▸ **quintessentially** *adv.*: *a sense of humour that is quintessentially British*

U u

ugly adj.

ugly · hideous · unattractive · grotesque · plain · unsightly
These words all describe people or things that are not pleasant to look at.

unattractive	ugly	hideous
plain	unsightly	grotesque

PATTERNS AND COLLOCATIONS
- an ugly / a hideous / a grotesque / a plain **face**
- an ugly / an unattractive / a plain **girl / woman**
- an ugly / unattractive **man**
- to **look** ugly / hideous / unattractive / grotesque / unsightly
- **very** ugly / unattractive / plain / unsightly
- **pretty** ugly / hideous / unattractive
- **quite** ugly / hideous / grotesque
- **rather / extremely** ugly / unattractive / plain

ugly unpleasant to look at: *The room was full of heavy, ugly furniture.* ◇ *The screaming child in her arms was an ugly little thing.* **OPP beautiful** → BEAUTIFUL 1, **beautiful** → BEAUTIFUL 2

hideous /ˈhɪdiəs/ (*rather informal, especially spoken*) very ugly or unpleasant: *The curtains were a hideous brown colour.* ◇ *The whole experience had been like some hideous nightmare.*
- **hideously** adv.: *His face was hideously deformed.*

unattractive (*especially written*) not attractive or pleasant to look at: *His face creased into an unattractive smile.* ◇ *The women were young and not unattractive* (= they were attractive). **OPP attractive** → BEAUTIFUL 1, **attractive** → BEAUTIFUL 2

grotesque /ɡrəʊˈtesk; AmE ɡroʊ-/ very ugly in a strange way, often causing fear or laughter: *It was a grotesque figure with a snarling beast's head.*

plain (*especially written*) (especially of a woman or girl) not pretty or attractive: *As a child she was rather plain.* **OPP pretty** → BEAUTIFUL 1, See also **plain** → PLAIN adj. 1

unsightly (*rather formal*) not pleasant to look at: *There were unsightly marks on the walls caused by damp.* ◇ *an area of unsightly derelict buildings.* ❶ **Unsightly** describes things, not people; it is often used to describe marks, patches or things that spoil a thing or a scene that might otherwise be attractive.

unacceptable adj.

unacceptable · unreasonable · too much · intolerable · unbearable · out of line · out of order · insufferable
These words all describe sth that is so bad that you cannot accept or bear it.

PATTERNS AND COLLOCATIONS
- unacceptable / intolerable **to** sb
- too much / intolerable / unbearable **for** sb
- unacceptable / unreasonable / intolerable / unbearable **that...**
- unacceptable / unreasonable / too much / intolerable / unbearable / out of order **to do** sth
- unacceptable / unreasonable / intolerable **behaviour / demands / interference / levels**
- an unacceptable / unreasonable / intolerable **burden**
- an unacceptable / intolerable / unbearable **situation**
- **quite / completely / totally** unacceptable / unreasonable / intolerable / unbearable / out of order

- **absolutely / increasingly** unacceptable / intolerable / unbearable
- **a bit** unreasonable / too much / out of order
- **almost / nearly** too much / intolerable / unbearable

unacceptable (*rather formal*) that you cannot accept, allow or approve of: *Such behaviour is totally unacceptable in a civilized society.* ◇ *Such a solution would be quite unacceptable to the majority of people.* ◇ *Noise from the factory has reached an unacceptable level.* **OPP acceptable** → FINE, **acceptable** → RIGHT 2
- **unacceptably** adv.: *unacceptably high levels of unemployment*

unreasonable not fair; expecting too much: *It would be unreasonable to expect somebody to come at such short notice.* ◇ *The fees they charge are not unreasonable.* ◇ *He was being totally unreasonable about it.* **OPP reasonable** → REASONABLE

too much (*rather informal, spoken*) needing more skill or strength than you have; more difficult or annoying than you can bear: *What with the exams, and then his illness, things have become too much for him.* ◇ *This is too much! First she complains that I'm never in the office, then she wants to know why I'm not visiting so many clients.*

intolerable /ɪnˈtɒlərəbl; AmE -ˈtɑːl-/ (*rather formal*) (of a situation, a feeling or sb's behaviour) so difficult, unpleasant or wrong that you cannot bear it or accept it: *Keeping the secret put an intolerable burden on him.* ◇ *Her behaviour has become intolerable.* ◇ *It seems to me intolerable that children do not have the same legal protection as adults.* **OPP tolerable** ❶ The opposite **tolerable** is usually used as a way of saying that sth is *almost* intolerable: *At times, the heat was barely tolerable.*
- **intolerably** adv.: *It became intolerably hot by day.*

unbearable /ʌnˈbeərəbl; AmE -ˈber-/ (of a situation, feeling or person) so unpleasant, painful or annoying that you cannot bear it: *Some of the victims were suffering unbearable pain.* ◇ *The heat was becoming unbearable.* ◇ *He's been unbearable since he won that prize.* **OPP bearable** ❶ The opposite **bearable** is usually used as a way of saying that sth is *almost* unbearable: *She was the only thing that made life bearable.*
- **unbearably** adv.: *unbearably hot / painful / arrogant*

NOTE INTOLERABLE OR UNBEARABLE? In many cases you can use either word: *intolerable / unbearable heat / pain / suffering / tension / excitement*. However, **unbearable** is not usually used to talk about things that offend your sense of justice, rather than just your feelings: ~~It is unbearable that children do not have the same legal protection as adults.~~ It is used more for physical than mental suffering and is generally not used in situations where people have to do sth that is too difficult for them: ~~Keeping the secret was an unbearable burden.~~ People themselves can be **unbearable** but NOT **intolerable**: ~~He's been intolerable since he won that prize.~~

out of 'line idiom (*especially AmE, informal, spoken*) (of a person) behaving in a way that is not acceptable or right; (of their behaviour) not acceptable or right: *You'd better calm down — you're way out of line.* ◇ *If you step out of line one more time, you're fired.*

out of 'order idiom (*BrE, informal, spoken*) out of line: *What he did was right out of order.*

NOTE OUT OF LINE OR OUT OF ORDER? Out of order is more frequent in British English than out of line, but it is not used in American English. Someone can *get / step out of line* but NOT '*get / step out of order*'.

insufferable /ɪnˈsʌfrəbl/ (*rather formal*) (especially of a person or their personal qualities) so unpleasant or annoying that you cannot bear them: *She's totally insufferable!* ◇ *He bore a look of insufferable smugness.*

unattractive *adj.*

unattractive · off-putting · unappealing · unappetizing
These words all describe behaviour and things that are not good, interesting or pleasant.

PATTERNS AND COLLOCATIONS
▸ unattractive / off-putting / unappealing **to** sb
▸ an unattractive / unappealing **quality / prospect / character / personality**
▸ to **find sth** unattractive / off-putting
▸ to **look** unattractive / unappetizing
▸ **distinctly** unattractive / off-putting / unappealing / unappetizing
▸ **very / rather** unattractive / off-putting

unattractive (*rather formal*) having features or qualities that make you dislike or want to avoid it: *This is one of the more unattractive aspects of the free market economy.* ◇ *He was an unattractive character: selfish, moody and arrogant.* ❶ **Unattractive** is used to describe features, possibilities and people's characters. Collocates include *aspect, feature, alternative, proposition, prospect, personality* and *character.* **OPP** **attractive** → POPULAR

off-ˈputting (*especially BrE, informal*) not pleasant, in a way that prevents you from liking sb/sth: *I find his manner a bit off-putting.*

unappealing /ˌʌnəˈpiːlɪŋ/ (*rather formal*) unattractive: *The prospect of studying for another five years was distinctly unappealing.* ◇ *The book's main character is dull and unappealing.* **OPP** **appealing** → POPULAR

NOTE UNATTRACTIVE OR UNAPPEALING? There is not much difference in meaning or use between these words. **Unattractive** is more frequent, but it is also used to describe people who are not sexually attractive: you can say that sb has *an unattractive/unappealing personality* but *an unattractive man/woman* is usually sb who is not sexually attractive; *an unappealing man/woman* is more likely to have an unpleasant personality.

unappetizing (*BrE also* **-ising**) /ʌnˈæpɪtaɪzɪŋ/ (of food) unpleasant to eat; looking as if it will be unpleasant to eat: *She brought me an unappetizing meal of cold fried eggs on toast.* **OPP** **appetizing** → DELICIOUS

unaware *adj.*

unaware · oblivious · in the dark · unsuspecting · blind · ignorant · unwitting
These words all describe people who are not aware of sth or do not know about sth.

PATTERNS AND COLLOCATIONS
▸ unaware / oblivious / ignorant **of** sth
▸ oblivious / blind **to** sth
▸ an unsuspecting / unwitting **victim**
▸ **totally** unaware / oblivious / unsuspecting / blind / ignorant
▸ **completely / largely** unaware / oblivious / in the dark / ignorant
▸ **blissfully** unaware / ignorant

unaware /ˌʌnəˈweə(r); AmE -ˈwer/ [not before noun] not knowing or realizing that sth is happening or that sth exists: *He was completely unaware of the whole affair.* ◇ *They were apparently **unaware that** the girl was only 15.* **OPP** **aware** → AWARE

oblivious /əˈblɪviəs/ [not usually before noun] not aware of or concerned about sth, especially sth that you ought to be concerned about: *He drove off, oblivious to the damage he had caused.* ◇ *He was totally oblivious of her feelings.*

in the ˈdark *idiom* knowing nothing about sth: *Workers were **kept in the dark about** plans to sell off the factory.*

unsuspecting [usually before noun] (*especially written*) not aware of danger or of sth bad: *The attacker stood waiting in the alleyway for his unsuspecting victim.* ◇ *Illegal copies are widely on sale to an unsuspecting public.* See also **trusting** → NAIVE

blind [not before noun] not noticing or realizing sth: *She's totally blind to her husband's faults.* ◇ *I must have been blind not to realize the danger we were in.*

ignorant /ˈɪɡnərənt/ [not before noun] not knowing about or realizing sth, especially sth that might affect your actions or opinions if you did know about it: *At the time I was ignorant of events going on elsewhere.*

unwitting [only before noun] (*rather formal, written*) not aware of what you are doing or of the situation you are involved in: *He became an unwitting accomplice in the crime.* ◇ *She was the unwitting cause of the argument.*

uncertain *adj.* See also the entry for VARIABLE

uncertain · volatile · unstable · fickle · unsettled
These words all describe situations that are likely to change, especially in a negative or unpleasant way.

PATTERNS AND COLLOCATIONS
▸ the uncertain / volatile / fickle **nature** of sth
▸ an uncertain / a volatile / an unstable **situation**
▸ an uncertain / unstable **environment**
▸ uncertain / fickle / unsettled **weather**
▸ an uncertain / a volatile **temper / temperament**
▸ **very** uncertain / volatile / unstable / fickle / unsettled
▸ **rather / notoriously** uncertain / volatile / unstable / fickle

uncertain (*rather formal, usually disapproving*) likely to change, especially in a negative or unpleasant way: *Our future looks uncertain.* ◇ *He was a man of uncertain temper.* **OPP** **certain** → CERTAIN

volatile /ˈvɒlətaɪl; AmE ˈvɑːlətl/ (*disapproving, especially business or politics*) (of a situation) likely to change suddenly; easily becoming dangerous: *This is a highly volatile situation from which riots might develop.* ◇ *Exporting the product was difficult due to a volatile exchange rate.* ❶ **Volatile** is typically used to talk about the exchange rate, the economy, a political situation and markets or market conditions. It also collocates strongly with *character, nature* and *situation.*

unstable (*disapproving, especially business or politics*) likely to change suddenly, often causing serious problems: *The political situation remains highly unstable.* **OPP** **stable** → STEADY

fickle (*disapproving, especially journalism*) changing often and suddenly: *Such is life in the fickle world of fashion.* ◇ *The latest downturn in sales shows just what a fickle business this is.*

unsettled (*rather formal*) (of a situation) changing often; making people uncertain about what might happen next: *These were difficult and unsettled times.* ◇ *The weather has been very unsettled lately* (= it has changed a lot).

unclear *adj.*

unclear · uncertain · unresolved · in doubt · indefinite · in the balance · undecided
These words all describe sth that is not yet clear or decided.

PATTERNS AND COLLOCATIONS
▸ It is unclear / uncertain **what / whether…**
▸ to **remain** unclear / uncertain / unresolved / in doubt / in the balance / undecided
▸ to **leave sth** unclear / uncertain / unresolved / in doubt / undecided
▸ **still** unclear / uncertain / unresolved / in doubt / in the balance / undecided

unclear /ˌʌnˈklɪə(r); AmE -ˈklɪr/ not clear or definite; difficult to understand or be sure about: *His motives are unclear.* ◇ *Our plans are unclear at the moment.* ◇ *It is* unclear whether there is any damage. ◇ Some of your diagrams are unclear. **OPP** clear → CLEAR 1, **clear** → CLEAR 2

uncertain not definite or decided: *It is uncertain what his role in the company will be.* See also **uncertain** → UNSURE, **uncertainty** → DOUBT *noun 2*

unresolved /ˌʌnrɪˈzɒlvd; *AmE* -ˈzɑːlvd/ (*formal*) (of a problem or question) not yet solved, answered or decided: *These unresolved issues must be addressed.*

in ˈdoubt *phrase* (often used in negative statements) uncertain: *The success of the system is not in doubt.* **❶ In doubt** is used especially to talk about the result, future, success or nature of sth.

indefinite /ɪnˈdefɪnət/ lasting for a period of time that has no fixed end: *She will be away for the indefinite future.* ◇ *The workers have been on indefinite strike since July.*
▸ **indefinitely** *adv.*: *The trial was postponed indefinitely.*

in the ˈbalance *idiom* uncertain and waiting to be decided: *The long-term future of the space programme hangs in the balance.* ◇ *His life hung in the balance for two weeks as he lay in a coma.* **❶ In the balance** describes a situation in which the future of sb/sth, or the result of sth, is very uncertain for a time. It is often used when the future result is expected to be one of two very different things, such as success or failure, or life or death.

undecided /ˌʌndɪˈsaɪdɪd/ [not usually before noun] not having been decided yet: *The venue for the World Cup remains undecided.*

unconscious *adj.*

unconscious · unintended · unplanned · subconscious · unintentional
These words all describe sth that influences your behaviour and thoughts, even though you are not consciously aware of them.

PATTERNS AND COLLOCATIONS
▸ an unconscious / unplanned / unintentional **action**
▸ an unintended / unplanned **consequence**
▸ an unintended / unintentional **effect**
▸ at an unconscious / a subconscious **level**
▸ an unconscious / a subconscious **desire / feeling / fear / memory**
▸ the unconscious / subconscious **mind**
▸ largely unconscious / unintended / unintentional

unconscious (of feelings, thoughts or actions) that you are not consciously aware of, but that influence your behaviour; not deliberate or controlled: *Human beings are driven by many unconscious impulses.* ◇ *The brochure is full of unconscious humour.* ◇ *She researches into the depths of the unconscious mind.* **OPP** **conscious** → DELIBERATE
▸ **the unconscious** *noun* [sing.]: (*psychology*) the concept of the unconscious as first described by Freud
▸ **unconsciously** *adv.*: *She unconsciously began to relax in his company.* **OPP** **consciously** → DELIBERATE

unintended (of an effect, result or meaning) that you did not plan or intend to happen: *an unintended insult* ◇ *In law you are considered responsible for the unintended consequences of your actions.* **OPP** **intended** → DELIBERATE

unplanned not planned in advance: *The clinic provides advice on unplanned pregnancies.*

subconscious /ˌsʌbˈkɒnʃəs; *AmE* -ˈkɑːn-/ [usually before noun] connected with feelings that influence your behaviour but that you are not consciously aware of: *Some patients have a subconscious fear that they will die under anaesthetic.* ◇ *Early childhood events are stored in the subconscious memory.* **OPP** **conscious** → DELIBERATE, See also **the/your subconscious** → MIND
▸ **subconsciously** *adv.*: *Subconsciously, she was looking for the father she'd never known.*

NOTE **UNCONSCIOUS** OR **SUBCONSCIOUS?** Feelings may be **unconscious** or **subconscious** but actions can only be **unconscious**: *He pushed back his hair in an unconscious gesture of annoyance.* ◇ ~~*He pushed back his hair in a subconscious gesture.*~~ Both words can be used to describe the part of the mind that contains feelings that you are not aware of, but **the unconscious** is the more technical term in psychology.

unintentional /ˌʌnɪnˈtenʃənl/ happening by accident or without you intending it: *Perhaps I misled you, but it was quite unintentional.* **OPP** **intentional** → DELIBERATE
▸ **unintentionally** *adv.*: *They had unintentionally provided wrong information.* **OPP** **intentionally** → DELIBERATE

uncontrollable *adj.*

uncontrollable · overwhelming · intractable · irresistible · unmanageable
These words all describe sth that is difficult or impossible to control or deal with.

PATTERNS AND COLLOCATIONS
▸ an uncontrollable / overwhelming / irresistible **urge / impulse**
▸ an overwhelming / irresistible **force / influence / pressure / temptation / desire**
▸ **apparently** uncontrollable / overwhelming / intractable / irresistible / unmanageable
▸ **completely** uncontrollable / overwhelming / irresistible / unmanageable

uncontrollable /ˌʌnkənˈtrəʊləbl; *AmE* -ˈtroʊ-/ (of a feeling, thing or person) that you cannot control or prevent: *I had an uncontrollable urge to laugh.* ◇ *That child is uncontrollable* (= behaves very badly and cannot be controlled). See also **control** → CONTROL *verb*
▸ **uncontrollably** *adv.*: *She began shaking uncontrollably.*

overwhelming /ˌəʊvəˈwelmɪŋ; *AmE* ˌoʊvərˈw-/ (of a feeling or experience) so powerful that you cannot resist it or decide how to react: *She had an almost overwhelming desire to tell him the truth.* ◇ *You may find the whole experience somewhat overwhelming.* See also **overwhelm** → OVERWHELM

intractable /ɪnˈtræktəbl/ (*formal*) (of a problem or person) very difficult to deal with: *Unemployment was proving to be an intractable problem.* ◇ *There was no pleasing this intractable man.*

irresistible /ˌɪrɪˈzɪstəbl/ (of a feeling, event or argument) so powerful that it cannot be stopped or resisted: *The temptation to take a look proved to be irresistible.* ◇ *His arguments were irresistible.*
▸ **irresistibly** *adv.*: *They were irresistibly drawn to each other.*

unmanageable /ʌnˈmænɪdʒəbl/ (of a problem or person) difficult or impossible to control or deal with: *The costs involved had become unmanageable.* **OPP** **manageable** **❶** Something that is **manageable** is possible to control or deal with: *The debt has been reduced to a more manageable level.* See also **manage** → CONTROL *verb*

undermine *verb*

undermine · erode · weaken · sap · wear sb/sth down
These words all mean to gradually make sth weaker.

PATTERNS AND COLLOCATIONS
▸ to undermine / erode / weaken / sap sb's **confidence / morale**
▸ to undermine / erode / weaken sb's **position**
▸ to weaken / wear down sb's **resistance**

undermine [T] to make sth, especially sb's confidence or authority, gradually weaker or less effective: *The director saw this move as an attempt to undermine his authority.* ◇ *This crisis threatens to undermine the very foundations of social life.* **❶** Things that can be **undermined** include sb's *authority, credibility, faith, belief, confidence* or *morale* or the *foundations, security* or *stability* of sth.

erode /ɪˈrəʊd; *AmE* ɪˈroʊd/ [T, I] (*rather formal, especially business*) to gradually destroy the value of sth or people's confidence in sth: *Price rises have eroded profit margins.* ◇ *We live in a world whose moral base has been eroded.* ❶ Things that can be **eroded** include *profits, profitability, margins, revenues, the value of sth, sb's confidence* or *support*.

weaken [I, T] to become or make sb less determined or certain about sth; to make sb's position of authority weaker: *She felt herself beginning to weaken in the face of his persuasion.* ◇ *Nothing could weaken his resolve to continue.* ◇ *This new scandal has severely weakened the President's position.*

sap (-pp-) [T] to make sb/ sth less strong; to gradually destroy sb's energy, confidence or enthusiasm: *The hot sun sapped our energy.* ◇ *Years of failure have sapped him of his confidence.* ❶ Things that can be **sapped** include sb's *strength, energy, vitality, enthusiasm, will, confidence* and *morale*.

,wear sb/sth 'down *phrasal verb* To make sb/sth weaker or less determined, especially by continually attacking or putting pressure on them/it over a period of time: *Her persistence paid off and she eventually wore me down.* ◇ *This relentless pressure began to wear down their resistance.*

understand *verb*

1 understand French/how sth works
2 understand how sb feels

1 See the Topic Map for EDUCATION on p.888
understand · see · get · follow · grasp · comprehend · catch on · take sth in
These words all mean to know or realize sth, for example why sth happens, how sth works or what sth means.

PATTERNS AND COLLOCATIONS
▸ to understand/see/get/follow/grasp/comprehend/catch on to/take in **what/why/how**...
▸ to understand/see/grasp/comprehend/take in **that**...
▸ to understand/get/grasp/take in the **meaning** (of sth)
▸ to understand/see/get/grasp the **point/idea** (of sth)
▸ to understand/grasp a **concept/principle**
▸ to understand/follow the **instructions**
▸ **can/can't** understand/see/follow/grasp/comprehend/take in sth
▸ to **try to** understand/see/follow/grasp/comprehend/take in sth
▸ to **begin to** understand/see/grasp/comprehend/take in sth
▸ to be **easy/difficult/hard** to understand/see/follow/grasp/comprehend/take in
▸ to **easily** understand/see/grasp/comprehend
▸ to **(not) quite** understand/see/get/follow/grasp sth
▸ to **fully** understand/see/grasp/comprehend/take in sth

understand [T, I] (not used in the progressive tenses) to know or realize the meaning of words, a language, what sb says, etc.; to know or realize how or why sth happens, how it works or why it is important: *Do you understand French?* ◇ *He couldn't understand what she was saying.* ◇ *Doctors still don't understand much about the disease.* ◇ *The disease is still not fully understood.* ◇ *I could never understand why she was fired.* ◇ *I just don't understand! I don't want you doing that again. Do you understand?* **OPP** **misunderstand** → MISUNDERSTAND

see [I, T] (not used in the progressive tenses) (*especially spoken*) to understand what is happening, what sb is saying, how sth works or how important sth is: '*It opens like this.*' '*Oh, I see.*' ◇ *You see, she only heard about the plan yesterday.* ◇ *I don't think she saw the point of the story.* ◇ *Oh yes, I see what you mean.* ◇ *Can't you see that he's taking advantage of you?*

get [T, no passive] (not used in the progressive tenses) (*informal, especially spoken*) to understand a joke, what sb is trying to tell you, or a situation that they are trying to describe: *She didn't get the joke.* ◇ *I don't get you.* ◇ *I don't get it – why would she do a thing like that?* ◇ *I get the message – you don't want me to come.*

follow [I, T] (not used in the progressive tenses) to understand an explanation, a story or the meaning of sth: *Sorry – I don't quite follow.* ◇ *I don't follow you.* ◇ *The plot is almost impossible to follow.*

grasp /grɑːsp; *AmE* græsp/ [T] (not used in the progressive tenses) to come to understand a fact, an idea or how to do sth: *They failed to grasp the importance of his words.* ◇ *She was unable to grasp how to do it.*

NOTE UNDERSTAND OR GRASP? You can use **understand** or **grasp** for the action of realizing the meaning or importance of sth for the first time: *It's a difficult concept for children to understand/grasp.* For the state of knowing the meaning or importance of sth, use **understand** and **have grasped**: *By this time, engineers understood/had grasped the basic principles of aerodynamics.* ◇ *By this time, engineers grasped the basic principles...* Only **understand** can be used to talk about languages, words or writing: *I don't grasp French/the instructions.*

comprehend /ˌkɒmprɪˈhend; *AmE* ˌkɑːm-/ [T, I] (not used in the progressive tenses; often used in negative statements) (*formal*) to understand a fact, idea or reason: *The concept of infinity is almost impossible for the human mind to comprehend.* ◇ *He stood staring at the body, unable to comprehend.*

,catch 'on *phrasal verb* (not used in the progressive tenses) (*informal, especially spoken*) to come to understand a situation: *She still didn't catch on, even after all those hints.* ◇ *He finally caught on to what was going on.*

,take sth 'in *phrasal verb* (often used in negative statements) to understand and remember sth that you hear or read: *I realized I was reading without taking anything in.*

2 **understand · relate to sb/sth · identify with sb/sth · empathize**
These words all mean to know, realize or share what sb else feels or experiences.

PATTERNS AND COLLOCATIONS
▸ to **try to** understand/relate to/identify with/empathize (with) (sb/sth)
▸ to be **able/unable to** understand/relate to/identify with/empathize (with) (sb/sth)
▸ I, you, he, etc. **can/could** understand/relate to/identify with/empathize with sb/sth
▸ It's **easy/difficult/hard to** understand/relate to/identify with/empathize (with) (sb/sth)
▸ to **really/totally** understand/relate to/identify with/empathize (with) (sb/sth)
▸ to **easily** understand/relate to/identify with (sb/sth)

understand [T, I] to know sb's character, how they feel and why they behave in the way they do: *Nobody understands me.* ◇ *He doesn't understand women at all.* ◇ *They understand what I have been through.* ◇ *If you want to leave early, I'm sure he'll understand.* See also **understanding** → SENSITIVE 1

re'late to sb/sth *phrasal verb* to be able to understand and have sympathy with sb/sth: *Many adults can't relate to children.* ◇ *Our product needs an image that people can relate to.*

i'dentify with sb/sth *phrasal verb* to feel that you can understand and share the feelings of sb else, especially because you feel that you are similar to them or are in a similar situation: *I didn't enjoy the book because I couldn't identify with any of the main characters.*

NOTE RELATE TO SB/STH OR IDENTIFY WITH SB/STH? **Relate to sb/sth** is often used to talk about personal relationships. It can describe how successful a relationship is, for example between teacher and student, parent and child, boss and employee, etc.: *He's a successful and popular teacher because he really relates to the children.* If you **identify with sb**, you feel that you are similar to them in some way or that you have shared the same experiences. It often describes people's positive feelings towards characters in a book or film or famous people such as writers or actors: *Which character do you identify with most, the father or his son?*

empathize (*BrE* also **-ise**) /'empəθaɪz/ [I] to understand another person's feelings and experiences, especially because you can imagine yourself in a similar situation: *A glamorous 20-year-old stylist is unlikely to empathize with a working mother of three.* See also **empathy** → BOND, **sympathize** → SORRY FOR SB

understanding *noun* See the Topic Map for EDU-CATION on p.888

understanding · sense · insight · conception · comprehension · grasp · appreciation · depth
These are all words for sb's ability to understand situations, subjects, etc.

PATTERNS AND COLLOCATIONS
▸ sb's understanding/sense/conception/comprehension/grasp/ appreciation/depth **of** sth
▸ **beyond** (sb's) understanding/(sb's) conception/(sb's) comprehension/sb's grasp
▸ an understanding/a sense/an insight/the conception/an appreciation **that**...
▸ (a) **good** understanding/sense/insight/comprehension/grasp/ appreciation
▸ a **proper** understanding/sense/grasp/appreciation
▸ a **thorough** understanding/comprehension/grasp/ appreciation
▸ an **adequate** understanding/conception/comprehension/ grasp/appreciation
▸ (a) **historical** / **musical** understanding/sense/insight/ appreciation
▸ to **have** an understanding/a sense/(an) insight/a conception/a comprehension/a grasp/an appreciation/depth
▸ to **show** understanding/a sense/insight/a grasp/an appreciation
▸ to **increase**/**enhance** your understanding/your sense/insight/ comprehension/your appreciation
▸ to **improve** your understanding/your sense/insight/ comprehension/grasp
▸ to **develop**/**gain** an understanding/a sense/an insight/an appreciation
▸ a **level** of understanding/insight/comprehension/appreciation
▸ a **lack** of understanding/insight/comprehension/ appreciation/depth

understanding [U, sing.] the knowledge that sb has of a particular subject or situation: *The committee has little or no understanding of the problem.* ◇ *The vastness of the universe is beyond human understanding.* ◇ *His writings reflect a good understanding of the society he lived in.* **OPP misunderstanding** → ILLUSION
sense [sing.] an understanding of sth; an ability to make sensible judgements about sth: *She always had a strong sense of personal responsibility* (= an understanding that she is responsible for her own actions). ◇ *Babies seem to have an innate sense of rhythm* (= an ability to respond to the beat of music). ◇ *One of the most important things in a partner is a sense of humour* (= the ability to find things funny or make people laugh). ◇ *I've got a hopeless sense of direction* (= ability to know where I am and where I am going in relation to other places). ◇ *Always try to keep a sense of proportion* (= the ability to know what is important in relation to other things). ◇ *Ed doesn't have any dress sense* (= the ability to know what clothes look good) *at all!* ◇ *I developed a certain road sense* (= the ability to travel on roads safely) *during my years as a cyclist.* ❶ In this meaning **sense** is nearly always used in the phrases *a/sb's sense of sth* and *dress/road sense.*
insight /'ɪnsaɪt/ [U, C] (*often approving*) the ability to understand the truth about people or situations; an understanding of what sth is like: *She was a writer of*

great insight. ◇ *I hope you've gained some insight into the difficulties we face.* ◇ *The book gives us some fascinating insights into life in Mexico.*
conception /kən'sepʃn/ [U, C] (*rather formal*) an understanding or belief of what sth is or what sth should be: *He has no conception of what it's like to be unemployed.* ◇ *I had a rather romantic conception of life in the country.*
comprehension /ˌkɒmprɪ'henʃn; *AmE* ˌkɑːm-/ [U, sing.] (*rather formal, especially written*) the ability to understand sth: *His behaviour was beyond comprehension.* ◇ *The task requires a good comprehension of complex instructions.*
grasp /ɡrɑːsp; *AmE* ɡræsp/ [sing.] a person's understanding of a subject: *She has an excellent grasp of English grammar.* ◇ *Such complicated instructions are beyond the grasp of most of our students.*
appreciation /əˌpriːʃi'eɪʃn/ [U, sing.] (*rather formal*) a full or sympathetic understanding of a situation, problem or subject: *I had no appreciation of the problems they faced.* ◇ *Candidates should have a broad appreciation of contemporary issues.* See also **appreciate** → KNOW 1
depth [U] (*approving*) the quality of knowing or understanding a lot of details about sth; the ability to provide and explain these details: *a writer of great wisdom and depth* ◇ *a job that doesn't require any great depth of knowledge* ◇ *His ideas lack depth.* See also **deep** → SERIOUS 3

understate *verb*

understate · play sth down · make light of sth · minimize · trivialize
These words all mean to state that sth is smaller, less important or less serious than it really is.

PATTERNS AND COLLOCATIONS
▸ to understate/play down/minimize the **importance**/**extent** of sth
▸ to play down/minimize the **significance**/**role** of sb/sth
▸ to play down/make light of a **problem**
▸ to play down/trivialize an **issue**

understate /ˌʌndə'steɪt; *AmE* -dər's-/ [T] (*rather formal, especially written*) to state that sth is smaller, less important or less serious than it really is: *It would be a mistake to understate the seriousness of the problem.* ◇ *The figures probably understate the real unemployment rate.* **OPP overstate** → EXAGGERATE
▸ **understatement** *noun* [C, U]: *To say we were pleased is an understatement* (= we were extremely pleased). ◇ *He always goes for subtlety and understatement in his movies.*
play sth 'down *phrasal verb* (*rather informal, especially journalism*) to try to make sth seem less important or less serious than it really is: *The government has been playing down rumours of differences of opinion.* ❶ **Play sth down** is often used by journalists to report attempts by governments or other organizations to stop people from losing confidence in them.
make 'light of sth *idiom* to treat sth as not serious or important: *I didn't mean to make light of your injuries.* ◇ *Although he later made light of the experience, he had been in considerable danger.* ❶ When you **make light of** your own problems you try to have a positive attitude towards a difficult situation so that other people don't worry about it too much. If you **make light of** sb else's problems however, you may offend them, because they may think that you are suggesting that they are complaining about sth that is not really very serious.
minimize (*BrE* also **-ise**) /'mɪnɪmaɪz/ to try to make sth seem less important or less serious than it really is: *He always tried to minimize his own faults, while exaggerating those of others.* ❶ **Minimize** is most often used to talk about people trying to make personal strengths or weaknesses seem less important, or with *importance* or *significance* to talk about people trying to make any action or event seem less important than it really is.

trivialize (*BrE* also **-ise**) /'trɪvɪəlaɪz/ [T] (*rather formal, usually disapproving*) to make sth seem less important or less serious than it really is: *It is important not to trivialize children's worries.* ◇ *The magazine has been accused of trivializing serious issues.*

undo *verb*

undo · open · untie · unbutton · detach · unfasten · unzip · unwrap
These words all mean to open sth that is fastened, tied or wrapped, or to separate two things that are joined together.

PATTERNS AND COLLOCATIONS
▸ to undo / open / untie / unwrap a **parcel / package**
▸ to undo / untie a **knot / rope / string / ribbon / lace / shoelace**
▸ to open / unwrap a **present**
▸ to undo / unbutton / unfasten / unzip a **jacket / coat / fly**
▸ to undo / unbutton / detach / unfasten a **collar**
▸ to undo / unfasten a **belt / button / clip / strap / zip / buckle / catch / seat belt**
▸ to undo / unbutton a **blouse / shirt**

undo /ʌn'duː/ [T] to open sth that is fastened, tied or wrapped: *I can't undo this zip – it seems to be stuck.* ◇ *He undid his jacket and threw it over a chair.* ◇ *I undid the package and took out the books.* **OPP** **do (sth) up** → TIE
open [T] to remove the lid or undo the fastening of a container, etc. in order to see or get what is inside: *Shall I open another bottle?* ◇ *He opened the letter and read it.*
untie /ʌn'taɪ/ [T] to undo a knot in sth; to undo sth that is tied: *Can you untie this knot for me?* ◇ *He untied the rope and pushed the boat into the water.* ◇ *She untied his hands and let him go.* **OPP** **tie** → TIE, **tie** → ATTACH
unbutton [T] to undo the buttons on a piece of clothing: *He unbuttoned his shirt.* **OPP** **button** → TIE, See also **button** → BUTTON *noun* 2
detach /dɪ'tætʃ/ [T, I] (*rather formal*) to remove sth from sth larger; to become separated from sth: *Detach the coupon and return it as soon as possible.* ◇ *One of the panels had become **detached from** the main structure.* ◇ *The skis should detach from the boot if you fall.* **OPP** **attach** → ATTACH
unfasten [T] (*rather formal*) to open sth that is fastened: *Passengers are permitted to unfasten their seat belts.* **OPP** **fasten** → TIE, See also **fastener** → BUTTON *noun* 2
unzip /ʌn'zɪp/ (**-pp-**) [T] to undo a bag or piece of clothing by unfastening the zip; (of a bag or piece of clothing) to open with a zip **❶** A **zip** (*BrE*) or **zipper** (*AmE*) is a type of fastener that consists of two rows of metal or plastic teeth that you can pull together to close sth or pull apart to open it.: *She unzipped his jacket, as if he were a child.* ◇ *The bag unzips at the side.* **OPP** **zip** → TIE, See also **zip**, **zipper** → BUTTON *noun* 2
unwrap /ʌn'ræp/ (**-pp-**) [T] to take off the paper, etc. that covers or protects sth: *Don't unwrap your present until your birthday.* **OPP** **wrap** **❶** To **wrap sth (up)** is to cover it completely in paper or other material, for example when you are giving it as a present: *He spent the evening wrapping up the Christmas presents.* ◇ *individually wrapped chocolates*

undoubted *adj.* See also the entry for CONCLUSIVE

undoubted · unchallenged · undisputed · unquestioned · uncontested
These words all describe sth that you think everybody accepts as right or true.

PATTERNS AND COLLOCATIONS
▸ an undoubted / undisputed / uncontested **fact**
▸ unchallenged / undisputed / unquestioned **authority**
▸ the unchallenged / undisputed **leader**
▸ undisputed / uncontested **supremacy**
▸ to **go** unchallenged / unquestioned / uncontested

undoubted /ʌn'daʊtɪd/ [usually before noun] used to emphasize that sth definitely exists or is true: *She has an undoubted talent as an organizer.* ◇ *The event was an undoubted success.* See also **doubt** → DOUBT *verb*
▸ **undoubtedly** *adv.*: *There is undoubtedly a great deal of truth in what he says.*
unchallenged /ʌn'tʃælɪndʒd/ not doubted; accepted without question; (of a ruler or leader, or their position) not opposed by anyone: *She could not allow such a claim to go unchallenged.* ◇ *He is in a position of unchallenged authority.* See also **challenge** → DOUBT *verb*
undisputed /ˌʌndɪ'spjuːtɪd/ that cannot be questioned or proved to be false; that everyone accepts or recognizes to be true: *She began by laying out the undisputed facts of the case.* ◇ *The film is an undisputed masterpiece of the twentieth century.* See also **indisputable** → CONCLUSIVE, **dispute** → DOUBT *verb*
unquestioned /ʌn'kwestʃənd/ (*formal*) so obvious that it cannot be doubted; accepted as right or true without really being considered: *His courage remains unquestioned.* ◇ *There was an unquestioned assumption that the war would be short and relatively painless.* See also **unquestionable** → CONCLUSIVE, **question** → DOUBT *verb*
▸ **unquestioningly** *adv.*: *They accepted unquestioningly the rules he had laid down.*
uncontested /ˌʌnkən'testɪd/ without any opposition or argument: *He was officially elected mayor in an uncontested election.* ◇ *These claims have not gone uncontested* (= they have been contested). See also **contest** → DOUBT *verb*

unemployed *adj.*

unemployed · jobless · out of work · redundant · on the dole · on welfare
These words all describe people who do not have a job.

PATTERNS AND COLLOCATIONS
▸ unemployed / jobless **people**
▸ unemployed / redundant **workers**
▸ **currently / still** unemployed / out of work
▸ **newly** unemployed / redundant
▸ the **long-term** unemployed / jobless

unemployed without a job although able to work: *How long have you been unemployed?* ◇ *He's an unemployed builder.* See also **be employed** → WORK *verb* 2
▸ **the unemployed** *noun* [pl.]: *We're working on a programme to get the long-term unemployed back to work.*
jobless (*journalism*) unemployed: *The closure left 500 people jobless.* **❶** **Jobless** is used, especially in journalism, to talk about unemployed people as a group; it is not used to talk about individual unemployed people: *How long have you been jobless?*
,**out of 'work** unemployed: *She had been out of work for a year.* See also **be in work** → WORK *verb* 2

NOTE **UNEMPLOYED** OR **OUT OF WORK?** Out of work is used more in everyday conversation, especially when you are talking about a particular person. It can sound less permanent than unemployed, and is therefore a gentler term to use.

redundant /rɪ'dʌndənt/ (*BrE*) without a job because there is no more work available for you in a company: *I've been expecting to be **made redundant** for a year now.* See also **make sb redundant** → FIRE *verb*
,**on the 'dole** (*BrE, informal*) without a job and claiming money from the state: *He's been on the dole for a year.* **❶** A more formal way of saying **on the dole** is *claiming social security/unemployment benefit.*
,**on 'welfare** (*especially AmE*) without a job and claiming money from the state: *They would rather work than live on welfare.* See also **welfare** → AID

unemployment *noun*

unemployment · redundancy · dismissal · sacking · lay-off · discharge
These are all words for the state of not having a job, the fact of losing your job or the act of officially removing sb from their job.

PATTERNS AND COLLOCATIONS
▸ **mass** unemployment / redundancies / dismissals / lay-offs
▸ **large-scale** unemployment / redundancies / lay-offs
▸ to **face** unemployment / redundancy / dismissal
▸ to **lead to / avoid** unemployment / redundancies / dismissal

unemployment [U] the state of not having a job; the fact of a number of people not having a job; the number of people without a job: *Thousands of young people are facing long-term unemployment.* ◇ *It's an area of high unemployment.* ◇ *Last month saw a rise in both inflation and unemployment.* **OPP employment** → WORK 2

redundancy /rɪˈdʌndənsi/ [U, C, usually pl.] (*BrE, rather formal*) the situation when sb has to leave their job because there is no more work available for them: *Thousands of factory workers are facing redundancy in the New Year.* ◇ *She decided to take **voluntary redundancy** (=* to offer to leave her job). ◇ *The threat of **compulsory redundancies** still hangs over the firm.* ◇ *200 workers have been issued with **redundancy notices**.* See also **make sb redundant** → FIRE *verb*

dismissal [U, C] (*rather formal or law*) the act of officially removing sb from their job; an example of this: *He still hopes to win his claim against **unfair dismissal**.* ◇ *The dismissals followed the resignation of the chairman.* See also **dismiss** → FIRE *verb*

sacking [C] (*BrE, rather informal, especially journalism*) an act of dismissing sb from their job, especially because they have done sth wrong: *A council chief faced calls for his sacking yesterday over allegations that he had accepted bribes.* See also **sack** → FIRE *verb*

lay-off [C] (*rather informal, especially journalism*) an act of making sb unemployed because there is no more work available for them, especially temporarily: *We do not want to risk further lay-offs in the factory.* ❶ You can also talk about *job cuts* in this context. See also **cut** → REDUCTION, **lay sb off** → FIRE *verb*

discharge /ˈdɪstʃɑːdʒ; *AmE* -tʃɑːrdʒ/ [C, U] the act of officially allowing sb, or of telling sb, to leave their job, especially in the army: *The illness resulted in his discharge from the army.* See also **discharge** → FIRE *verb*

unfortunate *adj.*

1 an unfortunate person
2 an unfortunate situation

1 unfortunate · unlucky · ill-fated · out of luck
These words all describe sb/sth that has or causes bad luck.

PATTERNS AND COLLOCATIONS
▸ to be unfortunate / unlucky **for** sb
▸ to be unfortunate / unlucky **in** sth
▸ to be unfortunate / unlucky **that...**
▸ to be unfortunate / unlucky **(not) to do sth**
▸ **very / extremely / a bit / a little** unfortunate / unlucky

unfortunate (*rather formal*) having bad luck; caused by bad luck: *He was unfortunate to lose in the final round.* ◇ *It was an unfortunate accident.* ◇ *The unfortunate animal was locked inside the house for a week.* **OPP fortunate** → LUCKY

▸ **unfortunately** *adv.*: *Unfortunately for him, the police had been informed and were waiting outside.*

unlucky having bad luck; caused by or causing bad luck: *She has been **unlucky with** injuries this year.* ◇ *She was desperately unlucky not to win.* ◇ *By some unlucky chance, her name was left off the list.* ◇ *Some people think it's unlucky to walk under a ladder.* **OPP lucky** → LUCKY, **lucky** → TIMELY

▸ **unluckily** *adv.*: *He was injured in the first game and unluckily missed the final.*

ill-ˈfated (*written*) (of an event, journey or project) not lucky and ending sadly, especially in death or failure: *It is the story of their ill-fated 1970 expedition.* ◇ *She regretted ever meeting him at that ill-fated party.*

out of ˈluck *phrase* (*rather informal*) not lucky when trying to find or achieve sth: *If you're looking for Rachel, you're out of luck. She left 10 minutes ago.* **OPP in luck** → LUCKY

2 unfortunate · pity · a shame · pathetic · too bad · sad · sorry · feeble · regrettable
These words all describe things that are weak, useless or not successful, or that make you feel disappointed.

PATTERNS AND COLLOCATIONS
▸ **It's** a pity / a shame / too bad **about** sb / sth.
▸ unfortunate / a pity / a shame / pathetic / too bad / regrettable **that...**
▸ an unfortunate / a pathetic / a sad / a sorry **sight / story / state (of affairs)**
▸ an unfortunate / a sad / a sorry **affair / business / episode / saga / tale / plight**
▸ **rather** unfortunate / a pity / a shame / pathetic / feeble / regrettable
▸ **pretty / a bit / a little** unfortunate / pathetic / feeble
▸ **very** unfortunate / feeble / regrettable
▸ **a great / real / terrible** pity / shame
▸ **What** a pity / shame.

unfortunate that you wish had not happened or had happened differently; embarrassing and/or offensive: *It was unfortunate that he couldn't speak English.* ◇ *It was an unfortunate choice of words.* **OPP fortunate** → TIMELY

▸ **unfortunately** *adv.*: *Unfortunately I won't be able to attend the meeting.*

pity *noun* (*usually* **a pity**) [sing.] (*especially spoken*) used to say that sth is a cause for feeling sad or disappointed: *It's a pity that you can't stay longer.* ◇ *'I've lost it!' 'Oh, what a pity.'* ◇ *It seems a pity to waste this food.* ◇ *Oh, that's a pity.* ◇ *It would be a great pity if you gave up now.*

shame *noun* (*usually* **a shame**) [sing.] (*rather informal, especially spoken*) used to say that sth is a cause for feeling sad or disappointed: *What a shame they couldn't come.* ◇ *It would be a crying shame (= a great shame) to let all that talent go to waste.*

NOTE PITY OR SHAME? Both **pity** and **shame** are more frequent in spoken than written English, but **shame** is far more frequent in spoken English than **pity**.

pathetic /pəˈθetɪk/ (*informal, disapproving*) (of a person or their attempt to do sth) weak, useless or not successful, often in a way that makes other people not respect them: *That was an absolutely pathetic excuse.* ◇ *I know it sounds pathetic, but I can't ride a bike.* ◇ *You're pathetic!*

▸ **pathetically** *adv.*: *His attempt to fool the guard was pathetically unconvincing.*

too bad *phrase* (*informal, spoken*) a shame; a pity: *Too bad every day can't be as good as this.* ❶ **Too bad** is often used ironically to say 'bad luck' or 'it's a shame' when you do not really mean it: (*ironic*) *If sometimes they're the wrong decisions, too bad.*

sad [only before noun] (*often disapproving*) deserving or inviting criticism; making you feel pity: *This sad state of affairs does not have to continue.* ◇ *It's a sad fact that many of those killed were children.*

▸ **sadly** *adv.*: *If you think I'm going to help you again, you're sadly mistaken.*

sorry [only before noun] making you feel pity or disapproval: *The business is in a sorry state.* ◇ *They were a sorry sight when they eventually got off the boat.*

NOTE SAD OR SORRY? In many cases you can use either word: *a sad / sorry affair / business / episode / story / tale / saga / plight / sight.* However, **sorry** is used more often when you feel pity, and **sad** is used more often when you feel disapproval. **Sad**, but NOT **sorry**, is often used with words which refer to a sign that sth exists in a society or system: *truth*, *reality*, *fact*, *comment*, *example*, *indictment*, *reflection* and *reminder*.

feeble (of a person or their attempt to do sth) weak, useless or not successful: *He told a few feeble jokes.* ◇ *Don't be so feeble! Tell her you don't want to go.*

NOTE PATHETIC OR FEEBLE? Pathetic is more informal than **feeble** and can show stronger disapproval or contempt (= lack of respect).

regrettable (*formal*) that you are sorry about and wish had not happened: *It is regrettable that the police were not informed sooner.* ◇ *The loss of jobs is highly regrettable.*
▶ **regrettably** *adv.*: *Regrettably, crime has been increasing in this area.*

NOTE UNFORTUNATE OR REGRETTABLE? Both **unfortunate** and **regrettable** can be used to describe things that happen and collocates include *incident*, *occurrence*, *error*, *consequence* and *tendency*. However, sth that is **regrettable** is usually considered to have been at least partly within sb's control: the use of **regrettable** suggests that sb wishes to accept some blame, or blame sb else. Sth that is **unfortunate** is more often considered to be the result of bad luck.

unhappy *adj.*

1 an unhappy childhood
2 feel unhappy with their accommodation

1 See also the entries for SAD and DEPRESSED
unhappy · sad · miserable · melancholy · mournful · heartbroken
These words all describe a person who feels or shows that they are not happy.

unhappy	miserable	heartbroken
sad		
melancholy		
mournful		

PATTERNS AND COLLOCATIONS
▶ unhappy / sad / miserable / heartbroken **about** sth
▶ unhappy / sad / miserable / heartbroken **when** / **that...**
▶ an unhappy / a sad / a miserable / a melancholy / a mournful **face**
▶ an unhappy / a sad / a melancholy / a mournful **expression**
▶ sad / melancholy / mournful **eyes**
▶ to **feel** unhappy / sad / miserable
▶ to **look** unhappy / sad / miserable / mournful
▶ **very** unhappy / sad / miserable

unhappy not happy; showing that you are not happy: *He grew more unhappy as the years went by.* ◇ *She sounded so unhappy when I left her.* ◇ *He had an unhappy childhood.* **OPP happy → HAPPY, See also unhappiness → GRIEF**
▶ **unhappily** *adv.*: *He sighed unhappily.*

sad not happy; showing that you are not happy: *She was still feeling very sad about her father's death.* ◇ *We are sad to hear that you are leaving.* ◇ *He gave a slight, sad smile.* **OPP happy → HAPPY, See also sadness → GRIEF**
▶ **sadly** *adv.*: *She shook her head sadly.*

NOTE UNHAPPY OR SAD? You usually feel **unhappy** because of sth that has happened to you; you usually feel **sad** about sth that has happened to sb else: ~~He grew sadder as the years went by.~~ ◇ ~~She was very unhappy about her father's death.~~ A period or experience in your life can be **unhappy**; sth that you see or hear can be **sad**: *an unhappy childhood/marriage* ◇ ~~a sad childhood/marriage~~ ◇ *sad news* ◇ *a sad story* ◇ ~~unhappy news~~ ◇ ~~an unhappy story~~ See also **sad → SAD**

miserable /ˈmɪzrəbl/ very unhappy or uncomfortable: *We were cold, wet and thoroughly miserable.* ◇ *She knows how to make life miserable for her employees.* **OPP cheerful → CHEERFUL, See also misery → DISTRESS**
▶ **miserably** *adv.*: *They wandered around miserably in the rain.*

melancholy /ˈmelənkəli; -kɒli; *AmE* -kɑːli/ (*literary*) sad, especially over a long period of time and for no obvious reason: *He was a tall man with a long, melancholy face.* See also **melancholy → GRIEF** *noun*

mournful /ˈmɔːnfl; *AmE* ˈmɔːrnfl/ (*written*) (especially of how sb looks) sad: *I couldn't bear the mournful look on her face.*
▶ **mournfully** *adv.*: *The dog looked mournfully after its owner.*

heartbroken /ˈhɑːtbrəʊkən; *AmE* ˈhɑːrtbroʊkən/ extremely sad because of sth that has happened: *He was heartbroken when she left him.* See also **heartbreak → GRIEF, heartbreaking → SAD**

2 See also the entries for BORED and DISAPPOINTED
unhappy · dissatisfied · frustrated · disgruntled · aggrieved · displeased · discontented
These words all describe sb who feels annoyed or not satisfied because of a situation or sth that has happened.

PATTERNS AND COLLOCATIONS
▶ unhappy / dissatisfied / frustrated / disgruntled / displeased / discontented **with** sth
▶ unhappy / frustrated / disgruntled / aggrieved / displeased **at** sth
▶ unhappy / frustrated / disgruntled / aggrieved **about** sth
▶ unhappy / frustrated / disgruntled / displeased **that...**
▶ an unhappy / a dissatisfied **customer**
▶ to **feel** unhappy / dissatisfied / frustrated / disgruntled / aggrieved
▶ **deeply** unhappy / dissatisfied / frustrated / aggrieved
▶ **increasingly** unhappy / dissatisfied / frustrated

unhappy not pleased or satisfied with sth: *They were unhappy with their accommodation.* ◇ *He was unhappy at being left out of the team.* **OPP happy → HAPPY**

dissatisfied /dɪsˈsætɪsfaɪd; dɪˈsæt-/ (*rather formal*) not pleased or satisfied with sth: *If you are dissatisfied with our service, please write to the manager.* ◇ *The decision left us feeling deeply dissatisfied.* ◇ *He has to deal with complaints from dissatisfied guests.* **OPP satisfied → HAPPY**
▶ **dissatisfaction** *noun* [U]: *Many people have expressed their dissatisfaction with the arrangement.* **OPP satisfaction → SATISFACTION**

NOTE UNHAPPY OR DISSATISFIED? Dissatisfied is more formal than **unhappy** and is used especially in business or political contexts when people are not satisfied with a service they have received or goods they have bought, or with an official decision, policy or action. **Unhappy** can also be used in these cases, but is used especially in cases of more personal disappointment: *unhappy/ dissatisfied customers* ◇ ~~He was dissatisfied at being left out of the team.~~

frustrated /frʌˈstreɪtɪd; *AmE* ˈfrʌstreɪtɪd/ feeling annoyed and impatient because you cannot do or achieve what you want: *They felt frustrated at the lack of progress.* ◇ *Sometimes he gets really frustrated with his own violin playing.* See also **frustrate → ANNOY, frustrating → ANNOYING, frustration → FRUSTRATION**

disgruntled /dɪsˈɡrʌntld/ annoyed or disappointed because sth has happened to upset you: *I left feeling disgruntled at the way I'd been treated.* ◇ *Police believe it was probably sabotage by a disgruntled employee.*

aggrieved /əˈɡriːvd/ (*rather formal*, *written*) feeling that you have been treated unfairly: *He had every right to feel aggrieved at the decision.* ◇ *'What am I supposed to do about it?' he said in an aggrieved tone.* See also **grievance → COMPLAINT**

displeased [not before noun] (*formal*) upset, annoyed or not satisfied with sth: *Are you displeased with my work?* **OPP pleased → GLAD**

discontented /ˌdɪskən'tentɪd/ not happy because you are not satisfied with your situation: *He felt discontented with the way his life had turned out.* **OPP** contented → HAPPY

unhealthy *adj.*

unhealthy · bad · unhygienic · insanitary
These words all describe sth which is a risk to health, especially because it is not clean.

PATTERNS AND COLLOCATIONS
▸ an unhealthy / a bad **diet**
▸ unhealthy / unhygienic / insanitary **conditions**

unhealthy having a bad effect on your health; likely to make you ill: *Doctors say too many teenagers adopt an unhealthy lifestyle.* ◇ *The unhealthy climate made it an unattractive place in which to settle.* **OPP** healthy → HEALTHY, See also **unhealthy** → SICK 1

bad having a bad effect on your health: *Eating too much salt is **bad for** you.* ◇ *All those sugary drinks are bad for your teeth.* ◇ *Bad diet and lack of exercise can lead to serious health problems.* **OPP** good → HEALTHY

> **NOTE** UNHEALTHY OR BAD? Bad is used especially in the collocations *bad for you/your health, etc.* and *bad diet.* **Unhealthy** has a wider range of collocations, but is slightly more formal.

unhygienic /ˌʌnhaɪ'dʒiːnɪk; *AmE* usually -'dʒen-/ (*rather formal*) not clean and therefore likely to cause disease or infection: *The animals were kept in cramped and unhygienic conditions.* **OPP** hygienic → CLEAN

insanitary /ɪn'sænətri; *AmE* -teri/ (*especially BrE*) (*AmE* usually **unsanitary** /ʌn'sænətri; *AmE* -teri/) (*formal*) unhygienic: *The apartments where the workers are housed were overcrowded and insanitary.*

union *noun* See also the entries for GROUP 3 and ORGANIZATION

union · club · association · society · alliance · league · coalition · federation · guild
These are all words for groups of people, workers, political parties or other organizations who share an interest or purpose.

PATTERNS AND COLLOCATIONS
▸ a **national** union / club / association / society / league / coalition / federation
▸ a **local** union / club / association / society / coalition / federation
▸ an **international** union / club / association / league / coalition / federation
▸ a **strong** union / alliance / coalition / guild
▸ a **loose** association / alliance / coalition / federation
▸ a **trade** union / association / federation / guild
▸ a **political** club / association / society / alliance / coalition
▸ a **professional** union / club / association / society
▸ to **form** a union / a club / an association / a society / an alliance / a league / a coalition / a federation
▸ to **set up** a union / a club / an association / a society / a league / a federation
▸ to **join** a union / a club / an association / a society / an alliance / a league / a coalition / a federation
▸ to **belong to** a union / a club / an association / a society / an alliance / a federation
▸ a union / a club / an association / a society **meets**
▸ a **member of** a union / a club / an association / a society / an alliance / a league / a coalition / a federation / a guild

union [C] an organization of workers, especially from the same industry; a group of people or organizations with the same interests: *The union represents 40% of all hospital workers.* ◇ *He has been appointed head of the Welsh Rugby Union (= sports organization).* ❶ A workers' **union** is also called a **trade union** or **trades union** in British English, or a **labor union** in American English. **Trade unions** exist to protect the interests of workers and to improve their conditions of work.

club [C+sing./pl. v.] (especially in compounds) a group of people who meet together regularly for a particular activity or sport: *She plays at the local tennis club.* ◇ *She gives talks at local schools and **youth clubs**.* ◇ ***Fan club** members can get concert tickets at a discount.* ❶ In British English a **club** is also a professional sports organization that includes the players, managers, owners and members. See also **club** → TEAM 2

association [C+sing./pl. v.] an official group of people who have joined together for a particular purpose: *The Football Association has launched an investigation into the incident.* ◇ *Local councils have begun to work closely with **housing associations**.* ◇ *Do you belong to any professional or trade associations?*

society [C] (especially in names) a group of people who have joined together for a particular purpose: *the American Society of Newspaper Editors* ◇ *the Royal **Society** for the Protection of Birds* ◇ *He made few friends and joined few clubs or societies.*

> **NOTE** CLUB, ASSOCIATION OR SOCIETY? Groups of people who have a shared interest or purpose use all of these words as part of the name of their group, often for historical reasons. A **club** tends to be involved with a leisure interest, such as a sport or hobby and can be quite informal. A *drama club*, for example, might be more informal than a more traditional *dramatic society*. An **association** is usually an official group representing or concerned with a professional area or a social issue: *a trade/professional/residents'/housing association*. A **society** often has an academic interest. Most British universities have a number of **societies** which students with a particular interest, such as history, politics or music can join. **Society** is also often used in the names of charities.

alliance /ə'laɪəns/ [C] a group formed by several different people or groups, especially political parties, who work together for a particular purpose: *The Movement for Multiparty Democracy was a loose alliance of opposition parties.*

league /liːg/ [C] (often used in the names of organizations) a group of people or countries that have combined for a particular purpose: *the League of Nations* ◇ *a meeting of the Women's League for Peace*

coalition /ˌkəʊə'lɪʃn; *AmE* ˌkoʊə-/ [C] a group formed of several different groups, especially political parties, who agree to work together for a particular purpose: *The network is a global coalition of environmental and consumer groups.*

> **NOTE** ALLIANCE OR COALITION? An **alliance** can be formed by different people or groups coming together; a **coalition** can only be formed by two or more groups that already exist.

federation /ˌfedə'reɪʃn/ [C] a group of clubs, trade unions, etc. that have joined together to form a large organization: *He proposed a loose federation of small, local groups.* ◇ *the British Athletics Federation*

guild /gɪld/ [C+sing./pl. v.] an organization of people who do the same job or who have the same interests or aims; an association of skilled workers in the Middle Ages: *He is an active member of the Screen Actors' Guild.* ◇ *The building originally belonged to the guild of clockmakers.* ❶ Professional groups that have **guild** as part of their name often started as **guilds** of craftsmen in the past.

unique *adj.* See also the entry for SPECIAL

unique · special · distinctive · peculiar · individual · idiosyncratic
These words all describe things that are connected with one person, group or thing.

▸ sth unique / special / distinctive / individual **about** sth
▸ a species, etc. unique / peculiar **to …**
▸ sb's **own** unique / special / distinctive / peculiar / individual…
▸ a unique / a special / a distinctive / a peculiar / an individual / an idiosyncratic **style / character**
▸ the unique / special / distinctive / peculiar / individual / idiosyncratic **nature** of sth
▸ unique / special / distinctive / peculiar / individual / idiosyncratic **features**
▸ a unique / a special / a distinctive / a peculiar / an individual **flavour**
▸ a unique / a special / a distinctive / an individual / an idiosyncratic **personality**
▸ a unique / a special / a distinctive / an individual / an idiosyncratic **approach**
▸ sb / sth's unique / special / distinctive / peculiar **brand** of sth
▸ the unique / special / peculiar / individual **circumstances** of sth
▸ **quite** unique / distinctive
▸ **highly / very** distinctive / individual / idiosyncratic

unique being the only one of its kind; belonging to or connected with only one particular person, place or thing: *Every human being has a* **unique** *fingerprint that does not change over time.* ◇ *Each item has a* **unique** *6-digit code.* ◇ *Her lawyer said the case was* **unique in** *French law.* ◇ *There's nothing* **unique** *about the case.* ◇ *The pattern of stripes is* **unique** *to each individual animal.* See also **unique →** REMARKABLE, **uniqueness →** IDENTITY
▸ **uniquely** *adv.: Some of the regulations apply uniquely to the 16–19 age group.*

special used by or intended for one particular person or group of people: *She has a* **special** *way of smiling.* ◇ *The President ended with a* **special** *message for the people of Texas.* ◇ *The directors have their own* **special** *pension fund.* See also **special →** SPECIAL
▸ **specially** *adv.: She has to have her shoes specially made.*

distinctive /dɪˈstɪŋktɪv/ having a quality or characteristic that makes sth different and easily noticed: *The male bird has* **distinctive** *black and white markings on the head.* ◇ *There was nothing* **distinctive** *about the envelope in which the letter came.*
▸ **distinctively** *adv.: It's a blue cheese with a distinctively sharp taste.*

peculiar /pɪˈkjuːliə(r)/ belonging or connected with one particular place, situation, person or thing: *The species is* **peculiar** *to China.* ◇ *Each house had its own* **peculiar** *smell.*
▸ **peculiarity** /pɪˌkjuːliˈærəti/ *noun* [C]: *the cultural peculiarities of the English*
▸ **peculiarly** *adv.: It is a peculiarly English design.*

NOTE UNIQUE OR PECULIAR? In many cases you can use either word: *The problem is not* **unique/peculiar** *to this country.* **Peculiar** is used especially to talk about places; **unique** is used more to talk about individual people and animals. It is often a more positive word than **peculiar**, suggesting that sb/sth is special or rare; **peculiar** is sometimes (but NOT always) slightly more negative, suggesting that sb/sth is strange in some way. See also **peculiar →** STRANGE 1

individual (*usually approving*) typical of one particular person or thing in a way that is interesting and different from others: *A player's style is almost as* **individual** *as his DNA.* See also **individuality →** IDENTITY

idiosyncratic /ˌɪdiəsɪŋˈkrætɪk/ (*rather formal*) showing a person's particular way of behaving or thinking, especially when it is unusual or slightly strange: *She had an odd,* **idiosyncratic** *way of looking at things.* See also **idiosyncrasy →** MANNERISM

unjustified *adj.* See also the entry for IRRATIONAL

unjustified · unwarranted · untenable · gratuitous · unjustifiable · unnecessary · undeserved
These words all describe sth such as criticism, fears or unpleasant behaviour that there is no good reason for.

▸ an unjustified / unwarranted / untenable / unjustifiable **assumption**
▸ unjustified / unwarranted / gratuitous / undeserved **criticism**
▸ an unjustified / unwarranted / unnecessary **attack**
▸ (an) unjustified / unwarranted / unjustifiable / unnecessary **interference / intrusion / risk**
▸ an unjustified / a gratuitous / an unnecessary **comment**
▸ sb's **fears** are unjustified / unwarranted / unnecessary
▸ **quite / completely / totally** unjustified / unwarranted / untenable / gratuitous / unjustifiable / unnecessary / undeserved
▸ **somewhat** gratuitous / unnecessary / undeserved

unjustified /ʌnˈdʒʌstɪfaɪd/ (*sometimes disapproving*) not fair or necessary; not based on any good reason: *Her fear of failure is* **unjustified***.* ◇ *This is a wholly* **unjustified** *attack on individual freedoms.* **OPP** **justified →** RIGHT 2, See also **justify →** EXPLAIN 2

unwarranted /ʌnˈwɒrəntɪd; *AmE* -ˈwɔːr-; -ˈwɑːr-/ (*formal, sometimes disapproving*) unjustified: *The new law constitutes an* **unwarranted** *intrusion into people's privacy.*

NOTE UNJUSTIFIED OR UNWARRANTED? There is no real difference in meaning between these words. **Unwarranted** is more formal and is more often used before a noun; **unjustified** is more often used after a linking verb.

untenable /ʌnˈtenəbl/ (*formal*) (of sb's position, ideas or opinions) that cannot be defended against attack or criticism: *After such a scandal, the President's* **position** *became* **untenable** *(= he could not carry on being president).* **OPP** **tenable** ❶ The opposite, **tenable**, is used especially in negative sentences: *The old idea that this work was not suitable for women was no longer tenable.*

gratuitous /ɡrəˈtjuːɪtəs; *AmE* -ˈtuː-/ (*disapproving*) done without any good reason or purpose, especially in a way that offends people: *The public is getting fed up with scenes of* **gratuitous** *violence on TV.*
▸ **gratuitously** *adv.: The film was gratuitously offensive.*

unjustifiable /ʌnˈdʒʌstɪfaɪəbl/ (*rather formal, usually disapproving*) (of an action) impossible to excuse or accept because there is no good reason for it: *The court found there had been an* **unjustifiable** *delay in fulfilling the order.* **OPP** **justifiable →** RIGHT 2

unnecessary (*usually disapproving*) (of remarks or violence) not necessary in a particular situation and likely to be offensive: *That last comment was a bit* **unnecessary***, wasn't it?*

NOTE GRATUITOUS OR UNNECESSARY? **Gratuitous** is a slightly stronger word than **unnecessary** and is used especially when sth is said or done in order to offend or shock people. **Unnecessary** comments or violence may not be designed to offend people, but may have that effect because people have not thought carefully about the possible effects of their words or actions.

undeserved (*especially of criticism, praise or sb's reputation*) not deserved by sb and therefore unfair: *He has an* **undeserved reputation** *for being sexist.* See also **deserve →** DESERVE

unlikely *adj.*
1 unlikely to succeed
2 an unlikely explanation

1 unlikely · doubtful · improbable
These words all describe things that are not likely to happen or be true.

▸ to be unlikely / doubtful / improbable **that…**
▸ to **seem / look / make** sth unlikely / doubtful / improbable
▸ **very / highly / extremely / rather / somewhat** unlikely / doubtful / improbable

unlikely not likely to happen or be true: *The project seemed **unlikely to** succeed.* ◇ *It's most unlikely that she'll arrive before seven.* ◇ *In the **unlikely event of** a problem arising, please contact the hotel manager.* **OPP likely** → LIKELY

doubtful [not usually before noun] (*rather formal, especially written*) unlikely: *It is **doubtful if** this painting is a Picasso.* ◇ *It is **doubtful whether** the car will last another year.* ◇ *Terry is injured and is **doubtful for** the game tomorrow* (= unlikely to play). ◇ *In this meaning **doubtful** is nearly always followed by if, whether, for or that....* See also **doubt** → DOUBT *noun* 1, **doubt** → DOUBT *verb*

improbable (*rather formal, written*) unlikely: *The whole story sounded highly improbable.* ◇ *It seemed improbable that the fine weather would continue.* ❶ **Improbable** is more formal than **unlikely** and cannot be followed by to + infinitive: *The project seemed improbable to succeed.* **OPP probable** → LIKELY

2 See also the entry for INCREDIBLE
unlikely · weak · far-fetched · implausible · unconvincing · improbable
These words all describe things that are difficult to believe, or not what you would normally expect.

PATTERNS AND COLLOCATIONS
▸ an unlikely / a far-fetched / an implausible / an unconvincing **explanation**
▸ an unlikely / a far-fetched / an unconvincing / an improbable **story**
▸ an unlikely / improbable **situation**
▸ **rather** unlikely / weak / far-fetched / implausible / unconvincing / improbable
▸ **very** unlikely / weak / far-fetched / unconvincing / improbable
▸ **highly / inherently** unlikely / implausible / improbable
▸ **completely** unlikely / unconvincing / improbable

unlikely [only before noun] difficult to believe; not the person, thing or place that you would normally think of or expect: *She gave me a rather unlikely explanation for her behaviour.* ◇ *He seems a most unlikely candidate for the job.* ◇ *They have built hotels in the most unlikely places.* ❶ **Unlikely** is sometimes used to describe people who are successful when you would not expect them to be: *an unlikely hero/winner/rock star/celebrity*; or people who are trying to be chosen for sth, when they would not normally be considered suitable: *an unlikely candidate/applicant/contender*

weak that people are not likely to believe or be persuaded by: *weak arguments/evidence* ◇ *The case for the prosecution was rather weak.* ◇ *I enjoyed the movie but I thought the ending was very weak.* ❶ **Weak** is used especially to talk about a line of argument that sb hopes will persuade people to believe sth. **OPP strong** → CONVINCING

far-'fetched very difficult to believe: *The whole story sounds very far-fetched.* ❶ People typically say that sth is *a bit far-fetched*, or that sth *seems/sounds far-fetched*. It is also common to say that sth *may seem/sound far-fetched, but...* when you are about to say sth that is true, even though it is difficult to believe.

implausible /ɪm'plɔːzəbl/ (*rather formal*) difficult to believe because it does not seem reasonable: *This is a highly implausible claim.* ◇ *Her explanation is not implausible* (= it is plausible). **OPP plausible** → POSSIBLE 2

▸ **implausibly** *adv.*: *He argued, somewhat implausibly, that the accident could not have been prevented.*
unconvincing not seeming true or real; not making you believe that sth is true: *I find the characters in the book very unconvincing.* ◇ *His argument was unconvincing.* ◇ *She managed a weak, unconvincing smile.* ❶ **Unconvincing** is most often used to talk about sth that sb says, such as an *argument*, an *attempt*, an *explanation*, a *reason* or a *story*. But you can also talk about *an unconvincing smile*, when you do not believe that the person who is smiling is really happy, or *an unconvincing performance*, when you

do not think that an actor played a role very well, making it difficult for you to believe in the character being played. **OPP convincing** → CONVINCING
▸ **unconvincingly** *adv.*: *He laughed unconvincingly.*

improbable [usually before noun] (*written*) seeming strange because it is not what you would expect: *Her hair was an improbable shade of yellow.* ❶ **Improbable** is often used to talk about a successful *combination, match* or *friendship* that you would not expect, because the people involved do not seem to have much in common.

unnecessary *adj.*

unnecessary · redundant · needless · avoidable · preventable · expendable
These words all describe things that are not needed or can be avoided.

PATTERNS AND COLLOCATIONS
▸ an unnecessary / a needless / an avoidable / a preventable **death**
▸ unnecessary / needless / avoidable **risk / suffering / distress**
▸ unnecessary / needless **duplication / waste / anxiety**
▸ an unnecessary / an avoidable / a preventable **accident**
▸ an unnecessary / avoidable **cost / delay**
▸ **largely** unnecessary / redundant / preventable
▸ **entirely** unnecessary / avoidable / preventable
▸ **completely / totally** unnecessary / redundant
▸ **easily** avoidable / preventable

unnecessary /ʌn'nesəsəri; *AmE* -seri/ not needed; more than is needed: *Our first priority is to reduce unnecessary expense.* ◇ *They were found guilty of causing unnecessary suffering to animals.* ◇ *All this fuss is totally unnecessary.* ❶ **Unnecessary** is often used to talk about how much money people are spending when they don't actually need to: *(an) unnecessary expense/expenditure/cost/luxury*; or how much pain or inconvenience they suffer when they don't need to: *unnecessary pain/suffering/hardship/delay/complication/difficulty/fuss/anxiety/worry* **OPP necessary** → NECESSARY
▸ **unnecessarily** *adv.*: *There's no point worrying him unnecessarily.*

redundant /rɪ'dʌndənt/ (*rather formal, especially written*) not needed or useful: *There's a lot of redundant information that you could cut out here.*

needless (*rather formal, especially written*) that could or should have been avoided: *The report caused needless anxiety to hundreds of women.* ◇ *Banning smoking would prevent needless deaths.* ❶ **Needless** is used especially to describe *death, suffering, anxiety, fuss, risk* and *waste*. **Needless** often suggests a sense either of regret or of criticism.
▸ **needlessly** *adv.*: *Many soldiers died needlessly.*

avoidable (*rather formal*) that can be prevented: *Many deaths from heart disease are actually avoidable.* **OPP unavoidable** → INEVITABLE

preventable (*rather formal*) that can be prevented: *Each year some 14 million young children die of preventable diseases.*

NOTE AVOIDABLE OR PREVENTABLE? Preventable is mainly used to talk about medical conditions and accidents: *a preventable death/disease/illness/infection/accident.* **Avoidable** appears in a wider range of general collocations but is NOT used to talk about medical conditions: *(an) avoidable death/accident/risk/delay/cost/suffering/distress* ◇ *avoidable diseases/illnesses*

expendable (*rather formal, especially business*) if you consider people or things to be **expendable**, you think that you can get rid of them when they are no longer needed, or think it is acceptable if they are killed or destroyed: *It is a sad moment when you realize you are expendable in your job.*

unofficial *adj.* See also the entry for IRRATIONAL

unofficial · unauthorized · unlicensed · off the record
These words all describe things that are not approved by sb in authority.

PATTERNS AND COLLOCATIONS
▸ an unofficial / unauthorized **biography / copy**

unofficial that does not yet have permission or approval from sb in authority: *According to unofficial estimates about 200 died.* ◇ *There will be a review of the law on unofficial action and strikes in essential services.* ◇ *The result for the athlete was an unofficial world best of 2 minutes 27 seconds.* ◇ *It's one of numerous unofficial Harry Potter websites/fan clubs.* **OPP** official → OFFICIAL
▸ **unofficially** *adv.*: *The cost was unofficially estimated at £2 million.*

unauthorized (*BrE* also **-ised**) /ʌnˈɔːθəraɪzd/ (*formal*) without official permission: *There are special precautions to prevent unauthorized personnel from gaining access.* ◇ *Failure to complete the form will result in absences being regarded as unauthorized.* **OPP** authorized → OFFICIAL

> **NOTE UNOFFICIAL** OR **UNAUTHORIZED?** An action or statement that is **unofficial** has not yet been approved or confirmed by sb in authority, but may be approved or confirmed later. If an action is **unauthorized**, permission for it has not been given and may even have been refused: it is not simply a question of waiting for confirmation. Statements cannot usually be described as 'unauthorized'.

unlicensed /ʌnˈlaɪsnst/ (*rather formal*) without a licence (= an official document that gives you permission to do or own sth): *Tourists were warned never to use unlicensed taxis.* ◇ *The Act prohibits the unlicensed disposal of controlled waste.* **OPP** licensed → OFFICIAL

off the ˈrecord *idiom* told to sb, usually a journalist, although you do not want them to repeat it publicly, either because it is not yet official or because you do not want people to know that it was you who said it: *Stop the tape. This is off the record.* ◇ *Can I tell you something strictly off the record?*

unrealistic *adj.*

unrealistic · impractical · unworkable
These words all describe people who do not show or accept things as they are, or ideas or plans that are impossible or very difficult to achieve.

PATTERNS AND COLLOCATIONS
▸ **It is** unrealistic / impractical **to do sth**.
▸ an unrealistic / impractical / unworkable **plan**
▸ to **prove / become** unrealistic / impractical / unworkable
▸ to **make sth** unrealistic / impractical / unworkable
▸ to **consider sth** unrealistic / impractical
▸ **completely** unrealistic / impractical / unworkable
▸ **highly / quite / totally** unrealistic / impractical

unrealistic not showing or accepting things as they are; based on what sb hopes or wishes for, rather than on what is really possible: *Try not to have unrealistic expectations for your child.* ◇ *It is unrealistic to expect them to be able to solve the problem immediately.* ◇ *They were accused of being **unrealistic in** their demands.* **OPP** realistic → POSSIBLE 1, realistic → REALISTIC 1

impractical (*rather formal*) (of a plan or idea) not sensible; not likely to be true or successful: *It was totally impractical to think that we could finish the job in two months.* ❶ **Impractical** is usually used in the phrase *It is impractical to do sth* or to describe a *plan*, a *proposal*, a *suggestion*, an *idea*, a *design* or an *approach*. **OPP** practical → POSSIBLE 1, practical → REALISTIC 1

unworkable (of a plan or idea) impossible to do successfully: *They recognize the danger of introducing unworkable legislation.* ❶ **Unworkable** is mainly used to talk about a *policy*, a *plan*, a *proposal*, a *rule*, a *scheme* or *legislation.* **OPP** workable → POSSIBLE 1

unsuccessful *adj.*

unsuccessful · failed · losing
These words all describe actions or people that are not successful.

PATTERNS AND COLLOCATIONS
▸ an unsuccessful / a failed / a losing **bid**
▸ an unsuccessful / a failed **attempt / experiment / policy / venture / coup / candidate / company**
▸ the unsuccessful / losing **team**
▸ an unsuccessful / a losing **battle** against sth

unsuccessful (of an action or person) not successful; not achieving what you wanted to: *Unsuccessful applicants will be informed by post.* ◇ *We have been **unsuccessful in** finding a replacement for her.* ◇ *The secret service had been remarkably **unsuccessful at** catching spies.* **OPP** successful → SUCCESSFUL 1
▸ **unsuccessfully** *adv.*: *Burglars tried unsuccessfully to steal the safe.*

failed [only before noun] (of an action, person or relationship) not successful, especially after trying to achieve sth; (of a business) forced to close because it did not make a profit: *The rebel leader fled the country after the failed uprising.* ◇ *He still considered himself something of a failed journalist.* ◇ *She already had two failed marriages behind her.* ◇ *I paid off the debts left by our failed business.* **OPP** successful → SUCCESSFUL 1

losing [only before noun] (usually of a person, team or side) that did not win a game, contest or battle: *They had backed the losing side in the civil war.* ◇ *Last year she was a losing semi-finalist.* ◇ *The police were **fighting a losing battle** against the rising tide of crime.* **OPP** winning → SUCCESSFUL 1

unsure *adj.*

unsure · undecided · uncertain · hesitant · ambivalent · doubtful · dubious · in doubt
These words all describe sb who has feelings of doubt or uncertainty about sb/sth.

PATTERNS AND COLLOCATIONS
▸ unsure / undecided / uncertain / hesitant / ambivalent / doubtful / dubious / in doubt **about** sth
▸ unsure / undecided / uncertain / doubtful / dubious / in doubt **as to** sth
▸ unsure / uncertain / hesitant / doubtful / dubious **of** sth
▸ unsure / undecided / uncertain **what...**
▸ unsure / uncertain **how...**
▸ **a bit / rather / somewhat** unsure / hesitant / ambivalent / doubtful / dubious
▸ **somewhat** unsure / hesitant / ambivalent / doubtful / dubious
▸ **very** unsure / undecided / uncertain / hesitant / ambivalent / doubtful / dubious

unsure [not before noun] not certain or confident about sth; feeling doubt: *There were a lot of things I was unsure about.* ◇ *He was unsure of what to do next.* ◇ *I was unsure how to reply to this question.* **OPP** sure → SURE

undecided /ˌʌndɪˈsaɪdɪd/ [not usually before noun] not having made a decision about sb/sth: *I'm still undecided about who to vote for.* See also **decide** → DECIDE

uncertain [not usually before noun] not sure or confident about sth; feeling doubt: *They're both uncertain about what to do.* ◇ *I'm still uncertain of my feelings for him.* **OPP** certain → SURE, See also **uncertainty** → DOUBT *noun* 1

about people's feelings there is no real difference in meaning between these words, but **unsure** is about twice as frequent in both spoken and written English, and **uncertain** is slightly more formal. **Uncertain** (but NOT **unsure**) is more frequently used to talk about facts or situations that are not definite or decided. See also **uncertain** → UNCLEAR

hesitant /'hezɪtənt/ [not before noun] slow to speak or act because you feel uncertain, embarrassed or unwilling: *She's hesitant about signing the contract.* ◇ *Doctors are* **hesitant to** *comment on the new treatment.* See also **hesitant** → HESITANT

ambivalent /æm'bɪvələnt/ (*rather formal, especially written*) having or showing both good and bad feelings about sb/sth: *She is deeply ambivalent about her feelings for him.* ◇ *He has an ambivalent attitude towards her.*

doubtful thinking that sth is probably not possible or not a good idea; showing this: *He was doubtful about accepting extra work.* ◇ *A doubtful look crossed her face.* See also **doubt** → DOUBT *noun* 1
▸ **doubtfully** *adv.*: *He shook his head doubtfully.*

dubious /'dju:biəs/ *AmE* 'du:-/ [not usually before noun] doubtful: *I was rather dubious about the whole idea.* ◇ *Kate looked dubious, but did as she was asked.*
▸ **dubiously** *adv.*: *He looked dubiously at her.*

NOTE **DOUBTFUL** OR **DUBIOUS?** There is no real difference in meaning between these words; **dubious** is slightly more frequent in spoken English, but it is less often used before a noun.

in 'doubt *phrase* feeling unsure about sth, especially about what you should do: *If in doubt, wear black.*

untidy *adj.*

untidy · messy · cluttered · all over the place · disordered · out of place · jumbled
These words all describe places that are in a state of disorder, with things in the wrong places.

PATTERNS AND COLLOCATIONS
▸ an untidy / a messy / a cluttered **house**
▸ an untidy / a cluttered **room** / **desk**
▸ an untidy / a disordered **state**
▸ untidy / disordered **hair**
▸ an untidy / a messy / a jumbled **heap** / **pile** of sth
▸ an untidy / a jumbled **collection** of sth
▸ cluttered / jumbled **up**

untidy (*especially BrE, sometimes disapproving*) not neat or well arranged: *Try not to make the place untidy.* ◇ *The books were piled an untidy heap.* ◇ *Your hair is a little untidy.* **OPP** **tidy** → NEAT
▸ **untidily** *adv.*: *Her hair fell untidily about her shoulders.*
messy (*rather informal, sometimes disapproving*) in an untidy state with things left in the wrong place or spread around: *The house always looked messy.* ◇ *Sorry it's a bit messy in here.* ◇ *How did the place get so messy?* See also **messy** → SCRUFFY, **mess** → MESS *noun* 1

NOTE **UNTIDY** OR **MESSY?** In American English **messy** is the most frequent of these words and **untidy** is not used so much; in British English **untidy** is the most frequent in this meaning, and **messy** is used more in the sense of 'dirty'. See also **messy** → DIRTY

cluttered (*rather informal, disapproving*) (of a surface or place) filled with too many things, so that it looks untidy: *His apartment was small, cluttered and dirty.* ◇ *The study was* **cluttered with** *furniture.* **OPP** **uncluttered** → NEAT, See also **clutter** → MESS *noun* 1
all 'over the place *idiom* (*informal*) very untidy or completely disorganized: *She arrived out of breath and with her hair all over the place.*

disordered (*rather formal*) untidy because there is no order in the way things are arranged: *It is likely that the universe started out in a chaotic and disordered state.* **OPP** **ordered** → NEAT, See also **disorder** → MESS *noun* 1
out of 'place *idiom* (usually used in negative statements) not in the correct place: *He does not like things out of place.* ◇ *She never has a hair out of place.*
jumbled mixed together without any order and in an untidy way: *There was a jumbled collection of objects on the mantelpiece.* ◇ *The drawer was full of letters all* **jumbled together.** See also **jumble** → JUMBLE *verb*, **jumble** → MESS *noun* 1

unusual *adj.* See also the entry for STRANGE 1

unusual · eccentric · unorthodox · unconventional · atypical · different · offbeat · out of the ordinary
These words all describe things that are different from what is usual or normal.

PATTERNS AND COLLOCATIONS
▸ unusual / eccentric / unorthodox / unconventional / atypical **behaviour**
▸ unusual / eccentric / unorthodox / unconventional **ideas** / **views** / **ways**
▸ an unusual / an unorthodox / an unconventional / an offbeat **approach**
▸ unusual / unorthodox / unconventional **methods**
▸ sb's **approach** / **ideas** / **methods** / **views** is / are different
▸ **very** unusual / eccentric / unorthodox / unconventional
▸ **highly** / **rather** unusual / eccentric / unorthodox
▸ **pretty** unusual / eccentric / unconventional
▸ **somewhat** unusual / eccentric / unorthodox / atypical
▸ **a bit** unusual / eccentric / different / out of the ordinary

unusual different from what is usual or normal; different from other similar things and therefore interesting and attractive: *She has a very unusual name.* ◇ *It was unusual to see anyone out on the streets at this hour.* ◇ *It's* **not unusual** *for junior doctors to work 60 hours a week.* **OPP** **usual** → USUAL
▸ **unusually** *adv.*: *Unusually for him, he was dressed in a suit.* ◇ *She was unusually quiet that evening.*
eccentric /ɪk'sentrɪk/ (of a person or their behaviour) considered by other people to be strange or unusual, but usually in a way that is thought to be harmless rather than frightening: *She was the classic eccentric old lady, living with a houseful of cats.* ◇ *His behaviour grew increasingly eccentric as time went on.* See also **eccentricity** → MANNERISM
▸ **eccentric** *noun* [C]: *Most people considered him a harmless eccentric.*
unorthodox (often of methods, ideas or behaviour) different from what is usual or generally accepted, often in a way that leads to criticism: *His methods have been criticized as somewhat unorthodox.* ◇ *Their unorthodox beliefs often landed them in trouble with the authorities.* **OPP** **orthodox** → TRADITIONAL
unconventional (*often approving*) not following the way sth is usually done or what is considered normal or acceptable by most people, especially in an interesting way: *She's known for her unconventional approach to child-rearing.* ◇ *He thought of their lifestyle as daringly unconventional.* **OPP** **conventional** → CONSERVATIVE
▸ **unconventionally** *adv.*: *She dresses unconventionally.*
atypical /ˌeɪ'tɪpɪkl/ not having the usual qualities or features of a particular type of person, thing or group: *The so-called 'norm' of the nuclear family is in fact* **atypical** *of many families.* **OPP** **typical** → TYPICAL, **typical** → NORMAL
different [not usually before noun] (*especially spoken*) not like other people or things: *'Did you enjoy the play?' 'Well, it was certainly different.'* ❶ **Different** is often used as a way of avoiding criticizing sth: people say sth is **different** when they actually think it is strange and they are not really sure whether or not they like it or approve of it.

offbeat /ˌɒfˈbiːt; *AmE* ˌɑːf-/ [usually before noun] (*informal*) different from what most people expect: *He has a rather offbeat sense of humour.*

,out of the 'ordinary *idiom* unusual or different: *There seems to be nothing out of the ordinary about his application.*

unwanted *adj.*

unwanted · unpopular · unwelcome · unsolicited · undesirable · uninvited · unloved
These words all describe people and things that are not wanted, invited or asked for.

PATTERNS AND COLLOCATIONS
▸ an unwanted / an unpopular / an unloved **child**
▸ an unwanted / an unloved **baby**
▸ an unwanted / unwelcome / unsolicited **call**
▸ an unwanted / unwelcome / undesirable **change / effect**
▸ an unwanted / unwelcome / uninvited **guest / visitor**
▸ an unwanted / unwelcome **intruder / intrusion**
▸ unwanted / unwelcome **attention / publicity**
▸ unwanted / unsolicited **advice / goods / material**

unwanted not wanted by sb: *They aim to reduce unwanted pregnancies.* ◇ *It is very sad when children feel unwanted* (= feel that other people do not care about them).

unpopular not liked or enjoyed by a person, a group or people in general: *He made several unpopular decisions during his leadership.* ◇ *The proposed increase in income tax proved deeply* **unpopular with** *the electorate.* ◇ *The party is increasingly* **unpopular among** *young people.* **OPP** **popular** → POPULAR
▸ **unpopularity** /-ˌpɑːpˈ/ *noun* [U]: *the growing unpopularity of the military regime*

unwelcome not wanted by sb: *Security cameras around the building keep out unwelcome visitors.* ◇ *Jones's book revealed an unwelcome truth which no one really wanted to hear.* **OPP** **welcome ❶** A person or thing that is **welcome** is one that you are pleased to meet, invite, receive, have, etc.: *Children are always welcome at the hotel.* ◇ *The fine weather* **made a welcome change.**

NOTE UNWANTED OR UNWELCOME? *Guests, visitors, intruders, attention, publicity, changes or effects can be* either **unwanted** or **unwelcome**. *Children, babies, pregnancies, goods or advice can be* **unwanted**. *News, facts or the truth can be* **unwelcome**.

unsolicited /ˌʌnsəˈlɪsɪtɪd/ (*rather formal*) not asked for and sometimes not wanted: *I didn't appreciate his unsolicited advice.* ◇ *The record company receives dozens of unsolicited demo tapes each week.*

undesirable /ˌʌndɪˈzaɪərəbl/ (*rather formal*) not wanted or approved of; likely to cause trouble or problems: *What is the best way to deal with undesirable behaviour?* ◇ *It would be highly undesirable to increase class sizes further.* **OPP** **desirable** → POPULAR, **desirable** → BEST

uninvited (often used after the verb) doing sth or going somewhere when you have not been asked or invited, especially when sb does not want you to: *There were one or two uninvited guests at the party.* ◇ *He turned up uninvited.*

unloved (*rather formal*) not loved by anyone: *According to the theory, unloved children become bad parents.*

upright *adj.*

upright · vertical · erect · straight · on end
These words all describe the position that sth has when it goes straight up or down.

PATTERNS AND COLLOCATIONS
▸ an upright / a vertical **position**
▸ an upright / erect **posture**
▸ to **stand** upright / erect / straight / on end
▸ to **sit** upright / erect / straight
▸ to **hold** sth upright / vertical / erect / straight

upright (of a person) not lying down, and with the back straight rather than bent; (of an object) placed in a position that goes straight up or down: *Humans have evolved an upright stance.* ◇ *Gradually raise your body into an upright position.* ◇ *Keep the bottle upright.*
▸ **upright** *adv.*: *He managed to pull himself upright.* ◇ *She sat* **bolt upright** *in bed.*

vertical (of a line, surface or pole) going straight up or down from a level surface or from top to bottom in a picture: *The cliff was almost vertical.* ◇ *There was a vertical drop to the ocean.* ◇ *Temperature is shown on the vertical axis of the graph.* **OPP** **horizontal** → FLAT
▸ **vertically** *adv.*: *The cliffs rose up vertically out of the water.*

erect /ɪˈrekt/ (*formal*) (especially of a person or part of the body) in an upright position: *Stand with your arms by your side and your head erect.*

straight positioned in the correct way; level, upright or parallel to sth: *Is my tie straight?* ◇ *He stepped back to make sure that the picture was straight.*
▸ **straight** *adv.*: *Sit up straight!* ◇ *She pulled her hat straight.*
▸ **straighten** *verb* [T, I]: *He stood up and straightened his shoulders.*

on 'end *phrase* positioned so that the longest side of sth is in a vertical position: *It'll fit if you stand it on end.*

upset *adj.*

upset · sorry · distressed · devastated · hurt · distraught · dismayed · anguished
These words all describe sb who is unhappy, shocked or disappointed because sth unpleasant has happened.

upset	distressed	devastated
sorry	anguished	distraught
hurt		
dismayed		

PATTERNS AND COLLOCATIONS
▸ upset / distressed / devastated / hurt / dismayed **by** sth
▸ upset / distressed / devastated / dismayed **at** sth
▸ upset / sorry / distressed / devastated **about** sth
▸ upset / sorry / distressed / devastated / hurt / distraught / dismayed **that...**
▸ to be sorry / distressed / devastated / dismayed **to see / hear / find, etc....**
▸ a distressed / distraught **mother / relative**
▸ to **feel** upset / sorry / distressed / devastated / hurt / dismayed
▸ to **look** upset / distressed / devastated / hurt / distraught / dismayed / anguished
▸ **very** upset / sorry / distressed / hurt
▸ **deeply** upset / distressed / hurt
▸ **extremely** upset / sorry / distressed / distraught
▸ **absolutely / completely** devastated / distraught
▸ **too** upset / distressed / distraught **to do sth**

upset [not before noun] unhappy or disappointed because of sth unpleasant that has happened: *There's no point getting upset about it.* ◇ *I think she may be a bit* **upset with** *you.* ◇ *She was upset that he had left without saying goodbye.* See also **upset** → HURT 1, **upsetting** → PAINFUL 2

sorry [not before noun] feeling sad and sympathetic because of sth unpleasant that has happened to sb else: *I'm sorry that your husband lost his job.* ◇ *We're sorry to hear that your father's in hospital again.* ◇ *No one is sorrier than I am about what happened.* **OPP** **glad**, **happy** → GLAD, See also **sympathetic** → SENSITIVE 1

distressed /dɪˈstrest/ very upset: *He was too distressed and confused to answer their questions.* ◇ *She was in a somewhat* **distressed state** *when she came to see me.* See also **distress** → DISTRESS *noun*, **distress** → HURT *verb* 1, **distressing** → PAINFUL 2

devastated /ˈdevəsteɪtɪd/ (*rather informal*) extremely upset or shocked by sth: *I felt devastated at losing my job.* ◇ *His family is absolutely devastated.* See also **devastating** → DISASTROUS

hurt upset and offended by sth that sb has said or done: *a hurt look/expression* ◇ *She was deeply hurt that she had not been invited.* ◇ *Martha's hurt pride showed in her eyes.* See also **hurt** → DISTRESS *noun*, **hurt** → HURT *verb* 1

distraught /dɪˈstrɔːt/ extremely upset and anxious so that you cannot think clearly and cannot be calmed: *She's still too distraught to talk about the tragedy.* ◇ *The child's distraught parents pleaded for witnesses to contact the police.*

dismayed /dɪsˈmeɪd/ shocked and disappointed by sth: *He was dismayed at the change in his old friend.* ◇ *They were dismayed to find that the ferry had already left.* See also **dismay** → SHOCK *noun* 1, **dismay** → SHOCK *verb*

anguished /ˈæŋɡwɪʃt/ (*rather formal*) showing great pain or mental suffering: *She read the letter, gave an anguished cry and collapsed.* ◇ *He looked across at Kate's anguished face.* See also **anguish** → DISTRESS *noun*

urgent *adj.*

urgent · pressing · burning · compelling
These words all describe sth that needs to be dealt with immediately.

PATTERNS AND COLLOCATIONS
▸ an urgent / a pressing / a burning / a compelling **desire / need**
▸ an urgent / a pressing / a burning **issue / question**
▸ urgent / pressing **business / demands**
▸ an urgent / a pressing **problem / matter / task**

urgent needing to be dealt with immediately: *'Can I see you for a moment?' 'I'm very busy – is it urgent?'* ◇ *The situation calls for urgent action.* ◇ *The law is in urgent need of reform.* See also **urgency** → IMPORTANCE, **urge** → DESIRE
▸ **urgently** *adv.*: *New equipment is urgently needed.* ◇ *I need to speak to her urgently.*

pressing [usually before noun] (*rather formal, especially written*) urgent: *There is a pressing need for more specialist nurses.* ◇ *The government seems to think that international problems are more pressing than domestic ones.*

> **NOTE** URGENT OR PRESSING? Both these words can be used to describe needs, problems, requests and matters of business. **Urgent** has a wider range of collocates including *attention, consideration, action, measure, step, meeting, talks, letter, message* and *repair*. **Pressing** is more formal than **urgent** and used especially in written English.

burning [only before noun] (of a need or desire) so strong that you must do sth about it; (of an issue or question) very important and urgent: *He had a burning ambition to start his own business.* ◇ *Immigration was one of the burning issues of the day.*

compelling (*written*) (of a need or desire) so strong that you must do sth about it: *He was a sad man with a compelling need to talk about his unhappiness.* See also **compulsion** → DESIRE

use *noun*

use · application · practice · exercise
These are all words for the act of using sth or doing sth.

PATTERNS AND COLLOCATIONS
▸ effective / proper / continued / normal use / application / practice / exercise
▸ full / constant use / application / exercise
▸ free use / practice / exercise
▸ common / current / correct / safe / commercial / industrial / clinical use / application / practice
▸ sth has a use / an application
▸ to limit / regulate / justify the use / practice / exercise of sth

use [U, sing.] the act of using sth; the state of being used; the right or opportunity to use sth, for example sth that belongs to sb else; the ability to use your mind or body:

The software is designed for use in schools. ◇ *The chapel was built in the 12th century and is still in use today.* ◇ *The bar is for the use of members only.* ◇ *I have the use of the car this week.* ◇ *He lost the use of his legs (= became unable to walk) in an accident.* See also **use** → FUNCTION *noun*

application [U, C] (*rather formal*) the practical use of sth, especially a theory, discovery or invention: *This essay examines the application of new technology to teaching.* ◇ *The new invention would have a wide range of applications in industry.* See also **apply** → APPLY 1

practice [U] action rather than ideas: *The book is about the theory and practice of teaching.* ◇ *She's determined to put her new ideas into practice.* See also **put sth into practice** → APPLY 1, **practise** → DO 1

exercise [U] (always followed by *of*) (*rather formal*) the use of power, a skill, a quality or the right to make sth happen: *Sovereignty means more than just the exercise of power.* ◇ *One of these powers is the exercise of discretion by police officers.*

use *verb*

1 use a computer/the bus/force/your common sense
2 use electricity/all the milk

1 See also the entry for APPLY 1

use · exercise · employ · draw on/upon sth · exert · make use of sb/sth · utilize · resort to sth · fall back on sb/sth
These words all mean to do sth with a machine, method, object, skill or opportunity for a particular purpose.

PATTERNS AND COLLOCATIONS
▸ to use / employ / utilize sth **as** sth
▸ to use / employ / draw on / make use of / utilize / resort to / fall back on sth **to do sth**
▸ to use / exercise / employ / draw on / make use of / utilize / fall back on (a) **skill**
▸ to use / employ / make use of / utilize / resort to / fall back on a **method / technique**
▸ to use / exercise / employ / resort to **violence**
▸ to use / exercise / exert your **influence / power / authority**
▸ to use / employ / draw on / make use of / utilize **resources**
▸ to use / make use of / utilize **the facilities / a service / an opportunity**
▸ to **often / frequently** use / exercise / employ / draw on / make use of / utilize / resort to sb / sth
▸ to **usually** use / exercise / employ / resort to sb / sth
▸ to **commonly / occasionally** use / employ / resort to sb / sth
▸ to **rarely** use / exercise / employ / draw on / resort to sb / sth
▸ to use / exercise / employ sb / sth **widely**
▸ to use / employ / draw on / utilize sb / sth **extensively**
▸ to use / draw on / utilize sb / sth **heavily**

use [T] to do sth with a machine, method, object, skill or opportunity for a particular purpose: *Can I use your phone?* ◇ *Have you ever used this software before?* ◇ *How often do you use (= travel by) the bus?* ◇ *The blue files are used for storing old invoices.* ◇ *Police used tear gas to disperse the crowds.* ◇ *Don't keep asking me what to do – just use your common sense!* ❶ Of all the synonyms in this group, **use** is most frequently used to talk about doing things with objects: *to use a computer/comb/dictionary/fork/pen/pencil/phone/spoon/weapon, etc.*

exercise [T] (*formal*) to use your power, rights or personal qualities in order to achieve sth: *He was a man who exercised considerable influence over people.* ◇ *When she appeared in court she exercised her right to remain silent.*

employ [T] (*formal*) to use sth such as a skill or method for a particular purpose: *He criticized the repressive methods employed by the country's government.* ◇ *The police had to employ force to enter the building.*

'draw on/upon sth *phrasal verb* (*rather formal*) to use a supply of sth that is available to you: *I'll have to draw on my savings.* ◇ *The novelist draws heavily on her personal experiences.* ❶ **Draw on/upon sth** is most often used to talk about people using *experience, a range of styles, information, data, a theory, research findings* and *knowledge* in their work.

exert /ɪgˈzɜːt; *AmE* ɪgˈzɜːrt/ [T] (*rather formal*) to use your power or influence in order to achieve sth; to have a powerful effect on sb/sth: *He exerted all his authority to make them accept the plan.* ◇ *The moon exerts a force on the earth that causes the tides.*

> **NOTE** EXERCISE OR **EXERT**? A person or thing can **exert** *power, authority, influence, pressure* or *force* in a way that affects sb/sth. Only a person can use **exercise** sth, but as well as *power, authority* and *influence* they can also exercise a *right* or *privilege*, or personal qualities such as *care, caution, tact, discretion, diplomacy, judgement, discipline, restraint* and *self-control*.

make ˈuse of sb/sth *phrase* to use sb/sth, especially in order to get an advantage: *We could make better use of our resources.* ◇ *You should make use of your contacts.*

utilize (*BrE* also **-ise**) /ˈjuːtəlaɪz/ [T] (*formal*) to use sth, especially for a practical purpose: *The Romans were the first to utilize concrete as a building material.* ◇ *The resources at our disposal could have been better utilized.*

resort to sth *phrasal verb* to make use of sth, especially sth bad, as a means of achieving sth, often because there is no other possible solution: *They felt obliged to resort to violence.* ◇ *We may have to resort to using untrained workers.* ❶ Typical collocates of **resort to** are *bribery, force, terror* and *violence.*

fall ˈback on sb/sth *phrasal verb* [no passive] to have sth to use or go to sb for support when you are in difficulty: *I have a little money in the bank to fall back on.* ◇ *She fell back on her usual excuse of having no time.*

---

2 use · use sth up · consume · expend · deplete · drain · absorb · exhaust · get through sth
These words all mean to take sth for a particular purpose so that there is less or none of it left.

PATTERNS AND COLLOCATIONS
▸ to use/ use up/ consume/ expend/ deplete/ drain/ absorb/ exhaust **resources**
▸ to use/ use up/ deplete/ exhaust **a supply / supplies** of sth
▸ to use/ use up/ deplete/ drain/ exhaust **reserves** of sth
▸ to use/ use up/ consume/ expend **money**
▸ to use/ use up/ deplete/ drain/ exhaust **funds**
▸ to use/ consume/ expend/ absorb **time**
▸ to use/ use up/ consume/ expend/ drain/ absorb/ exhaust **energy**
▸ to use/ use up/ consume/ deplete/ absorb/ exhaust sth **quickly**
▸ to consume/ deplete/ absorb/ exhaust sth **rapidly**
▸ to use up/ consume/ drain/ absorb/ exhaust sth **completely**

use [T] to take a particular amount of time, money, energy or a substance in order to achieve or make sth: *This type of heater uses a lot of electricity.* ◇ *I hope you haven't used all the milk.* ◇ *You should learn to use your time more efficiently.*

use sth ˈup *phrasal verb* to use all of sth so that there is none left: *Making soup is a good way of using up leftover vegetables.* ◇ *I'm wondering how to arrange the furniture without using up too much space.*

consume /kənˈsjuːm; *AmE* ˈsuːm/ [T] (*rather formal, written*) to use sth, especially fuel, energy or time: *My new car consumes much less fuel.* ◇ *The production of new paper from wood pulp consumes vast amounts of energy.* ❶ People do not usually **consume** resources, but things and processes do: ~~The government has consumed large sums of public money.~~ ◇ *Bureaucracy consumes money that could have been spent on public services.* See also **consume** → EAT
▸ **consumption** /kənˈsʌmpʃn/ *noun* [U]: *Gas and oil consumption always increases in cold weather.*

expend /ɪkˈspend/ [T] (*formal*) to use sth, especially time, money, energy or effort: *The government has expended large sums of public money on a failing project.* ◇ *Unlike most animals, mussels do not expend energy looking for food.* See also **spend** → SPEND 1

▸ **expenditure** /ɪkˈspendɪtʃə(r)/ *noun* [U]: *This study represents a major expenditure of time and effort.*

deplete /dɪˈpliːt/ [T, usually passive] (*rather formal*) to reduce sth by a large amount so that there is not enough left: *Food supplies were severely depleted.* ◇ *Fossil fuel reserves are being depleted at an alarming rate.*
▸ **depletion** /dɪˈpliːʃn/ *noun* [U]: *ozone depletion* ◇ *the depletion of fish stocks*

drain [T] to make sb/sth poorer or weaker, by using up their/its money or strength: *My mother's hospital expenses were slowly **draining away** my income.* ◇ *I felt **drained of** energy.* ◇ *The experience left her **emotionally drained**.*
▸ **a drain on sth** *noun* [sing.]: *Military spending is a huge drain on the country's resources.*

absorb [T] to use up a large supply of sth, especially money or time: *The new proposals would absorb $80 million of the federal budget.*

exhaust /ɪgˈzɔːst/ [T] (*rather formal*) to use sth up: *Within three days they had exhausted their supply of food.* ◇ *Don't give up until you have **exhausted** all the possibilities.*

> **NOTE** USE STH UP OR **EXHAUST**? **Exhaust** is rather formal and is used especially when talking about using up things in large quantities or things which are very important. **Use sth up** is used especially to talk about smaller quantities of less important things: *They had exhausted their food supply.* ◇ ~~They had used up their food supply.~~ ◇ *Sorry — I've used up the milk.* ◇ ~~Sorry — I've exhausted the milk.~~

ˈget through sth *phrasal verb* to use a large amount of sth: *We got through a fortune while we were in New York!* ◇ *We get through a lot of paper in the office.*

---

used to sth *adj.*

used to sth · familiar with sth · accustomed to sth · up to date
These words all mean knowing sth very well or knowing about sth.

PATTERNS AND COLLOCATIONS
▸ used / accustomed **to** sth
▸ to be familiar/ up to date **with** sth
▸ to **get/ grow** used to/ accustomed to sth
▸ to **keep** (sb) familiar with sth/ up to date
▸ **already** used to sth/familiar with sth/accustomed to sth/up to date
▸ **fully** familiar with sth/ up to date

used to sth, used to doing sth *phrase* knowing sth very well because you do it or experience it often, so that you accept it as normal or usual: *I'm not used to eating so much at lunchtime.* ◇ *I found the job tiring at first but I soon got used to it.* **OPP** unused to sth → NEW 3

familiar with sth *phrase* knowing sth very well: *I wasn't familiar with the area.* ◇ *You will need to be thoroughly familiar with the software.* **OPP** unfamiliar with sth → NEW 2

accustomed to sth, accustomed to doing sth *phrase* (*rather formal*) familiar with sth and accepting it as normal or usual: *My eyes slowly grew accustomed to the dark.* ◇ *She was a person accustomed to having eight hours' sleep a night.* **OPP** unaccustomed to sth → NEW 2

ˌup to ˈdate [not before noun] having the most recent information: *I need to be kept up to date with any developments.* ◇ *She brought him up to date with what had happened.* ◇ *up-to-date information/records* **OPP** out of date → OLD-FASHIONED

---

useful *adj.*

useful · convenient · handy · practical · usable · great for sth · of use · functional
These words all describe sth which helps you do sth or is suitable for a particular purpose.

PATTERNS AND COLLOCATIONS
▶ to be useful / of use **to sb**
▶ to be useful / convenient / handy / great **for doing sth**
▶ useful / handy / practical **tips / hints**
▶ to **come in** useful / handy
▶ **very / quite** useful / convenient / handy / practical / usable / functional
▶ **highly** useful / convenient / practical / functional
▶ **extremely** useful / convenient / practical

useful that can help you to do or achieve what you want: *a useful book/gadget* ◊ *It can be useful to write a short summary of your argument first.* ◊ *He might be useful to us.* ◊ *Don't just sit watching TV – make yourself useful!* ◊ *Some products can be recycled at the end of their useful life.* **OPP** useless → USELESS

▶ **usefully** *adv.*: *The money could more usefully be spent on new equipment.*

convenient useful, easy or quick to use or do: *A bicycle is often more convenient than a car in towns.* ◊ *It is very convenient to pay by credit card.* ◊ *Fruit is a convenient source of vitamins and energy.* ◊ *(disapproving) He used his wife's birthday as a convenient excuse for not going to the meeting.*

▶ **conveniently** *adv.*: *The report can be conveniently divided into three main sections.*

handy *(informal)* convenient to use: *The introductory booklet contains some handy tips for getting started.* ◊ *Take your penknife – you never know when it might come in handy* (= be handy).

practical (of things) useful or suitable for a particular situation: *It's a practical little car – ideal for the city.* ◊ *Travel by boat was often faster and more practical than travel along the primitive roads.*

usable that can be used; in good enough condition to be used: *How can we display this data in a usable form?* ◊ *Take my bike – it's rusty, but it's perfectly usable.* **OPP** unusable → USELESS

great for sth *phrase (informal, especially spoken)* very suitable or useful for sth: *This gadget's great for opening jars.* ◊ *Try this cream – it's great for spots.*

of use *phrase (formal)* useful: *Can I be of any use* (= can I help)? ◊ *Your suggestion will be kept on file and may be of use should circumstances change.*

functional practical and useful; with little or no decoration: *Bathrooms don't have to be **purely functional**.* ◊ *The office is a functional working area, designed with efficiency in mind.*

useless *adj.*

useless · in vain · pointless · futile · hopeless · fruitless · vain · unusable
These words all describe sth which has no purpose or does not achieve what you want.

PATTERNS AND COLLOCATIONS
▶ to be useless / pointless / futile / hopeless / fruitless / vain **to do sth**
▶ to be useless / pointless **doing sth**
▶ a useless / pointless / futile / fruitless **exercise**
▶ a futile / hopeless / fruitless / vain **attempt**
▶ a futile / fruitless / vain **effort**
▶ a hopeless / fruitless / vain **task**
▶ a futile / hopeless / fruitless / vain **search**
▶ **largely** useless / in vain / pointless / futile / hopeless / fruitless / vain
▶ **seemingly** useless / in vain / pointless / futile / hopeless
▶ **completely** useless / pointless / futile / hopeless / unusable
▶ **utterly** useless / pointless / futile / hopeless

useless not useful; not doing or achieving what is needed or wanted: *This pen is useless.* ◊ *He knew it was useless to protest.* ◊ *It's useless worrying about it.* ◊ *The letter is **useless as** evidence.* ◊ *The land is **useless for** cattle.* ◊ *The drug is **useless in** the treatment of patients with AIDS.* ◊

*The information was **useless to** him.* ◊ *The quality ranged from acceptable to **worse than useless**.* **OPP** useful → USEFUL, **valuable** → VALUABLE 2

▶ **uselessly** *adv.*: *The sail flapped uselessly.*

in 'vain *idiom (written)* not achieving what is needed or wanted; without success: *All their efforts were in vain.* ◊ *They **tried in vain** to persuade her to go.* ◊ *She **waited in vain** for her son to return.*

pointless having no purpose; not worth doing because there is no hope of success: *Trying to foresee the future is a pointless exercise.* ◊ *It would be **pointless for** both of you to work on the same thing.* ◊ *I knew it was pointless expecting him to change his mind.* **OPP** worthwhile → VALUABLE 2

▶ **pointlessly** *adv.*: *He would argue pointlessly with his parents.*

futile /'fju:taɪl; *AmE* -tl/ *(rather formal)* ending in failure; having no effect or purpose: *It was a **futile gesture** as the real damage had already been done.* ◊ *Their efforts to revive him were futile.*

▶ **futility** /fju:'tɪləti/ *noun* [U]: *a sense of futility* ◊ *the futility of war*

hopeless with no hope of success, improvement or of producing useful results: *It's hopeless trying to convince her.* ◊ *Most students are making good progress, but Michael is **a hopeless case**.* **OPP** hopeful → PROMISING

fruitless *(rather formal)* producing no useful results: *He returned home after weeks of fruitless negotiations.* ◊ *The search proved fruitless.* **OPP** fruitful → PRODUCTIVE

vain [usually before noun] *(written)* not producing the result you want: *I knocked loudly **in the vain hope** that someone might answer.*

unusable /ˌʌn'ju:zəbl/ [not usually before noun] in such a bad condition or of such low quality that it cannot be used: *The damage rendered the building unusable.* ◊ *The plutonium is unusable for anything until it is reprocessed.* **OPP** usable → USEFUL

usual *adj.*

usual · traditional · standard · general · routine · regular · habitual
These words all describe things that happen in most cases, especially over a long period, or things that are considered typical of a person.

PATTERNS AND COLLOCATIONS
▶ to be usual / traditional / routine **to do sth**
▶ usual / traditional / routine **for sb / sth**
▶ the usual / traditional / standard / general / routine / regular **procedure / practice**
▶ the usual / traditional / standard / general / routine / regular / habitual **way**
▶ the usual / traditional / standard / general **approach**
▶ the usual / traditional / general **sense / style**
▶ sb's usual / traditional / habitual **role**
▶ usual / standard / general / routine / regular / habitual **behaviour**
▶ in the / sb's usual / traditional / standard / habitual **manner**
▶ **very** traditional / general / routine
▶ **fairly** usual / traditional / standard / general / routine

usual that happens or is done most of the time or in most cases: *It is usual to start a speech by thanking everybody for coming.* ◊ *It is usual for the employer to pay the costs.* ◊ *He came home later than usual.* ◊ *She arrived at the usual time.* ◊ *She made all the usual excuses.* ◊ *He didn't sound like his usual happy self.* ◊ *Despite the problems staff arrived for work **as usual**.* **OPP** unusual → UNUSUAL

traditional being part of the beliefs, customs or way of life of a group of people that have not changed for a long time: *The band plays traditional Celtic music.* ◊ *Most of the buildings are in the traditional style.* ◊ *It's traditional in America to eat turkey on Thanksgiving Day.*

▶ **traditionally** *adv.*: *Traditionally, markets are held in the open air.*

standard of the usual type, without special or unusual features: *Pizza dough is oilier than standard bread dough.* ◊ *Calls will be charged at the standard rate.* ◊ *The rifle was* standard issue for the British army before the First World War. ◇ *All vehicles come with a catalytic converter* **as standard**. **OPP** **non-standard** → ABNORMAL

general [usually before noun] that is true in most cases: *The machines all operate on the same general principle.* ◇ *As a* **general rule**, *the paler the roast the milder the coffee.* ◇ *In general, Japanese cars are very reliable.* See also **general** → GENERAL 1, **general** → GENERAL 2

routine /ruːˈtiːn/ [usually before noun] done or happening as a normal part of a job, situation or process; not unusual or different in any way: *The fault was discovered during a routine check.* ◇ *Don't worry — these are just routine enquiries.* ◇ *He died of heart failure during a routine operation.* See also **routine** → MUNDANE *adj.*, **routine** → PROCESS *noun*, **routinely** → OFTEN

regular [only before noun] (of an action or thing) that you usually do or use; (of a person) who usually does a job: *On Monday he would have to return to his regular duties.* ◇ *The other bag had my regular clothes in it.* ◇ *I couldn't see my regular doctor today.*
  ▸ **regularly**: *He regularly got up at four in the morning.*

habitual /həˈbɪtʃuəl/ [only before noun] (*rather formal*) typical of a particular person: *She reverted to her habitual frown.* ◇ *He sat smoking his habitual cigarette.* See also **habit** → HABIT, **habitually** → OFTEN

usually *adv.*

usually · often · normally · generally · commonly · mostly · most of the time · in general · as a rule · more often than not/as often as not
These words are all used when sth is done or happens in most cases.

PATTERNS AND COLLOCATIONS
  ▸ usually/ often/ generally/ commonly/ mostly **known as...**
  ▸ usually/often/normally/generally/commonly/mostly **called/ found...**
  ▸ usually/ often/ normally/ generally/ commonly/ mostly **used**
  ▸ usually/ normally/ generally/ commonly **accepted**
  ▸ to usually/ often/ normally/ generally/ commonly **happen**
  ▸ **not** usually/often/normally/generally/commonly/in general/ as a (general) rule
  ▸ **most** usually/ often/ generally/ commonly
  ▸ **quite** often/ generally/ commonly

usually in the way that is usual or normal; in most cases: *The journey usually takes an hour.* ◇ *Usually, there's no extra charge for delivery.* ◇ *Planning permission is not usually needed.* ◇ *Describe what usually happens.*

often in many cases: *Old houses are often damp.* ◇ *People often find it difficult to say goodbye.* ◇ *She's mean. Rich people very often are.* ◇ *Traffic has increased and the roads are* **all too often** *inadequate.* See also **often** → OFTEN

normally in normal circumstances: *The journey to work normally takes an hour.* ◇ *The Prime Minister would not normally be expected to attend the meeting.* ◇ *Normally it takes three or four years to complete the training.*

NOTE **USUALLY** OR **NORMALLY?** **Usually** gives general information about what happens in most cases; **normally** is used especially in the context of a particular case that is not normal: *It's normally much warmer than this in July* (= but this July is unusually cold). ◇ *He normally stayed in luxury hotels* (= but this time he could not afford to do so).

generally in most cases; usually: *Payments are generally made on an annual basis.* ◇ *Repairs are occasionally needed but generally the machine is quite reliable.* ❶ **Generally** is often slightly more formal than **usually**; it is used slightly more in written English, with passive structures, and when talking about general conditions rather than personal habits.

commonly very often; by most people: *To receive satellite TV you need an antenna (commonly known as a dish).* ◇ *These companies are commonly thought of as models of efficiency.* See also **common** → GENERAL 1

mostly in most cases; usually: *People mostly grew their own vegetables.* ◇ *She mostly calls me by my last name.* ◇ *Mostly he eats in a restaurant.* ❶ **Mostly** is often slightly more informal than **usually**, used especially in spoken English and more informal written contexts. It describes what people in general do, or what a particular person usually does; it does not usually describe what usually happens: *The journey mostly takes an hour.* ◇ *Describe what mostly happens.*

'most of the time *idiom* almost always: *Most of the time I quite liked being on my own.* ◇ *The weather was cold and it rained most of the time.*

in 'general *idiom* (*rather formal, especially written*) in most cases; usually: *In general the instruments are extremely reliable.* ◇ *The attacks were in general not reported in the media.* ❶ **In general** is a slightly more formal way of saying **generally**.

,as a 'rule *idiom* in most cases; usually: *As a rule students have one piano lesson a week.* ◇ *As a general rule the softer cheeses are less fattening.* ❶ **As a general rule** is used more often to mean 'as a guideline', to give advice about what you should do, rather than to say what usually happens: *As a general rule, mild mustards should be served with spicy food.* See also **rule** → HABIT, **rule** → PRINCIPLE 1

more ,often than 'not, as ,often as 'not *phrase* usually; in a way that is typical of sb/sth: *More often than not, the victims have serious medical problems.* ◇ *As a teenager he was in trouble at school as often as not.*

V v

vague *adj.*

vague · approximate · rough · indeterminate · indistinct · imprecise · ill-defined · borderline
These words all describe sth that is not clear or exact.

PATTERNS AND COLLOCATIONS
▸ vague/ imprecise **about** sth
▸ a vague/ an approximate/ a rough **idea**
▸ a vague/ an imprecise/ an ill-defined **term**
▸ a vague/ an ill-defined **concept**
▸ an approximate/a rough **calculation/figure/estimate/guide/translation**
▸ **very** vague/ approximate/ rough/ indistinct/ imprecise/ ill-defined/ borderline
▸ **somewhat** vague/ indeterminate/ indistinct/ imprecise/ ill-defined
▸ **rather** vague/ imprecise/ ill-defined

vague /veɪg/ not clear in a person's mind; not having or giving enough information or details about sth: *I have a vague recollection of meeting him when I was a child.* ◇ *She's a little vague about her plans for next year.* ◇ *He was accused of being deliberately vague.* **OPP** clear → SURE, **precise** → EXACT
▸ **vaguely** *adv.*: *I can vaguely remember my first day at school.* ◇ *a vaguely worded statement*
approximate /əˈprɒksɪmət; *AmE* əˈprɑːk-/ (*rather formal, especially written*) (especially of numbers and amounts) almost correct or accurate, but not completely so; not exact: *The cost given is only approximate.* ◇ *Use these figures as an approximate guide in your calculations.* **OPP** exact → EXACT
▸ **approximately** *adv.*: *The journey took approximately seven hours.* ◇ *The two buildings were approximately equal in size.*
rough not exact; not including all the details: *There were about 20 people there, at a rough guess.* ◇ *I made a rough sketch of the inside of the church.* **OPP** exact → EXACT
▸ **roughly** *adv.*: *We live roughly halfway between here and the coast.* ◇ *Roughly speaking, we receive about fifty letters a week on the subject.*

> **NOTE** APPROXIMATE OR ROUGH? **Approximate** most often describes the *number, amount, cost, etc.* of sth, although it can also describe an *estimate* or *idea* (but NOT a 'guess') of the number, amount, cost, etc. **Rough** can also describe the number, amount or cost of sth, but more often describes an *estimate, idea* or *guess* of sth. **Rough**, but NOT **approximate** can be used to describe a piece of writing or drawing: ~~an approximate draft/sketch of sth~~

indeterminate /ˌɪndɪˈtɜːmɪnət; *AmE* -ˈtɜːrm-/ (*rather formal, especially written*) that cannot be identified easily or exactly: *Her eyes were an indeterminate colour.* ◇ *She was a tall woman of indeterminate age.*
indistinct /ˌɪndɪˈstɪŋkt/ that cannot be seen, heard or remembered clearly: *an indistinct figure in the distance* ◇ *His memory of the incident was somewhat indistinct.* **OPP** distinct → MARKED
imprecise /ˌɪmprɪˈsaɪs/ not accurate; not giving exact details or not making sth clear: *The problems arise from an imprecise definition of terms.* ◇ *The witness's descriptions were too imprecise to be of any real value.* **OPP** precise → EXACT, See also **ambiguous** → MISLEADING
▸ **imprecisely** *adv.*: *These terms are often used imprecisely.*

ill-defined (*rather formal, disapproving*) not clearly described: *The precise aims of the committee remain ill-defined.*
borderline /ˈbɔːdəlaɪn; *AmE* ˈbɔːrdər-/ not clearly belonging to a particular condition or group; not clearly acceptable: *In doubtful and borderline cases teachers will take the final decision.* See also **borderline** → LIMIT *noun* 2

valley *noun*

valley · canyon · gorge · ravine · glen
These are all words for a long area of low land between hills or mountains.

PATTERNS AND COLLOCATIONS
▸ **in** a valley/ canyon/ gorge/ ravine/ glen
▸ to go, walk, travel, etc. **through** a valley/canyon/gorge/ravine/glen
▸ a **deep/ steep/ narrow** valley/ canyon/ gorge/ ravine
▸ a **rocky** valley/ canyon/ gorge/ ravine

valley [C] an area of low land between hills or mountains, often with a river flowing through it; the land that a river flows through: *a small town set in a valley* ◇ *the Shenandoah Valley* **OPP** hill → HILL
canyon /ˈkænjən/ [C] a deep valley with steep sides of rock: *the Grand Canyon, Arizona* ◇ *Massive rock formations, mountains and deep canyons present splendid views of nature's work.*
gorge [C] a deep narrow valley with steep sides: *the Rhine Gorge* ◇ *This is an area of spectacular gorges and jagged cliffs.*

> **NOTE** CANYON OR GORGE? There is no real difference in meaning between these words. Both are commonly used in place names. **Canyon** is the word most often used for places in North, Central and South America. In Europe, **gorge** is more frequent. In other parts of the world, either is used: *the Grand Canyon* (= in the US) ◇ *Cheddar Gorge* (= in the UK) ◇ *the Cataract Gorge* (= in Australia) ◇ *the Fish River Canyon* (= in Namibia).

ravine [C] a deep, very narrow valley with steep sides: *The track continued along the bottom of the ravine.* ◇ *She fell down a ravine.* ❶ A **ravine** is smaller and narrower than a **canyon** or **gorge**.
glen [C] a deep narrow valley, especially in Scotland or Ireland: *the Scottish glens* ◇ *A river ran through the wooded glen below the city.*

valuable *adj.*

1 valuable possessions
2 a valuable experience

1 **valuable · precious · priceless · irreplaceable**
These words all describe sth that is worth a lot of money or very important to sb.

PATTERNS AND COLLOCATIONS
▸ valuable/ precious/ priceless/ irreplaceable **to** sb
▸ valuable/ precious/ priceless/ irreplaceable **possessions**
▸ valuable/precious/priceless **antiques/jewels/jewellery/gems**

valuable worth a lot of money: *My home is my most valuable asset.* **OPP** worthless → PRICE *noun*, See also **value** → PRICE *noun*, **value** → PRICE *verb*

precious rare and worth a lot of money: *The crown was set with **precious stones** − diamonds, rubies and emeralds.* ◇ ***precious metals*** (= gold and silver)

priceless extremely valuable; loved or valued very much: *a priceless collection of antiques* ◇ *Our family photos are priceless.*

irreplaceable /ˌɪrɪˈpleɪsəbl/ too valuable or special to be replaced: *These paintings are irreplaceable.*

---

2 valuable · helpful · good · favourable · worthwhile · beneficial · constructive · positive · advantageous
These words all describe sth that is useful and important to sb/sth.

PATTERNS AND COLLOCATIONS

▸ valuable / helpful / good / favourable / beneficial / advantageous **for** sb / sth
▸ valuable / helpful / favourable / beneficial / advantageous **to** sb / sth
▸ to be valuable / helpful / good / worthwhile / beneficial / advantageous **to do sth**
▸ valuable / helpful / good / constructive / positive **suggestions / advice**
▸ a valuable / helpful / worthwhile / beneficial / constructive / positive **contribution**
▸ a valuable / good / worthwhile / beneficial / constructive / positive **experience**
▸ a valuable / good / positive **lesson**
▸ a good / a favourable / a beneficial / a constructive / a positive / an advantageous **effect**
▸ a good / favourable / beneficial / constructive / positive **influence**
▸ a good / favourable / beneficial / positive **result**
▸ a good / a favourable / an advantageous **position**
▸ **very** valuable / helpful / good / favourable / worthwhile / beneficial / constructive / positive / advantageous
▸ **highly** valuable / favourable / beneficial / constructive / positive / advantageous
▸ **extremely** valuable / helpful / good / favourable / worthwhile / beneficial / positive / advantageous
▸ **mutually** helpful / beneficial / advantageous

valuable (*approving*) very useful and important: *The Internet can be a very valuable learning tool.* ◇ *You should gain some valuable insights into the world of business.* ◇ *Spinach is a valuable source of iron.* **OPP useless** → USELESS, See also **fruitful** → PRODUCTIVE, **value** → APPRECIATE

helpful useful and able to improve a particular situation: *Here are some helpful hints for successful revision.* ◇ *Sorry I can't be more helpful.* ◇ *Role-play is **helpful in** developing communication skills.* ◇ *You might find it helpful to contact a self-help group.* **OPP unhelpful** → PERVERSE, See also **help** → HELP *noun*, **help** → HELP *verb* 2
▸ **helpfully** *adv.*: *She helpfully suggested that I try the local library.*

good having a helpful or useful effect on sb/sth: *Too much sun isn't good for you.* ◇ *My father once gave me some good advice.* ◇ *It's **no good** complaining − they never listen.* ◇ *This book is **no good to** me: I need the new edition.* **OPP bad** → HARMFUL

favourable (*BrE*) (*AmE* **favorable**) /ˈfeɪvərəbl/ (*rather formal*) good for sth and making it likely to be successful or have an advantage: *The terms of the agreement are favourable to both sides.* ◇ *An area with a favourable climate will inevitably be richer than one without.* ◇ *Winning the debate put him in a very favourable position.* **OPP unfavourable** → DIFFICULT 2

worthwhile /ˌwɜːθˈwaɪl; *AmE* ˌwɜːrθ-/ (*approving*) worth spending time, money or effort on because it is important, enjoyable, interesting, etc: *a worthwhile cause/discussion/job* ◇ *The smile on her face made it all worthwhile.* ◇ *High prices in the UK make it worthwhile for buyers to look abroad.* ◇ *It didn't seem worthwhile writing it all out again.* **OPP pointless** → USELESS

beneficial /ˌbenɪˈfɪʃl/ (*formal*) having a helpful or useful effect: *Relaxation classes can be beneficial to people of all ages.* ◇ *Lowering salt intake has a beneficial effect on blood pressure.* **OPP detrimental** → HARMFUL, See also **benefit** → BENEFIT *noun* 1, **benefit** → HELP *verb* 2

NOTE GOOD OR **BENEFICIAL**? **Beneficial** is a much more formal word than **good**. **Good** in this meaning is mostly used in the phrases *good for sb/sth, no good doing sth* and *no good to sb*.

constructive (*approving*) having a useful and helpful effect rather than being negative or with no purpose: *You should always welcome **constructive criticism** of your work.* ◇ *Can't you find something more constructive to do?*

positive [usually before noun] (*approving*) (of the effect of sb/sth on sb/sth) good or useful: *Local residents made a very positive contribution to the debate.* **OPP negative** → HARMFUL

advantageous /ˌædvənˈteɪdʒəs/ good or useful for a particular person or group: *An agreement would be advantageous to both sides.* **OPP disadvantageous** → DIFFICULT 2

---

valuation *noun*

---

valuation · estimate · quote · quotation · costing
These are all words for a judgement that is made about how much money sth is worth or will cost.

PATTERNS AND COLLOCATIONS

▸ an estimate / a quote / a quotation **for** a piece of work
▸ a **high / low** valuation / estimate / quote / quotation
▸ a **detailed** valuation / estimate / quote / quotation / costing
▸ a **stock / market / share** valuation / quote / quotation
▸ to **give / provide / get / obtain / accept** a valuation / an estimate / a quote / a quotation

valuation [C, U] a professional judgement about how much sth is worth; its estimated value: *Surveyors carried out a valuation of the property.* ◇ *methods of land valuation* ◇ *Experts set a high valuation on the painting.* See also **value** → PRICE *verb*

estimate [C] a statement of how much a piece of work will probably cost: *We got estimates for the repair work from three firms and accepted the lowest.* See also **estimate** → ESTIMATE *verb*

quote [C] (*informal, especially spoken*) a statement of exactly how much a piece of work will cost: *Theirs was the lowest quote, so we went with them* (= got them to do the work).
▸ **quote** *verb* [T]: *They quoted us £300 for installing a shower unit.*

quotation [C] (*rather formal*) a quote: *You should always get a written quotation from builders before they start work.*

NOTE QUOTE OR **QUOTATION**? These words have exactly the same meaning, but **quote** is more informal. In Business English both **quote** and **quotation** also mean 'a statement of the current value of goods or a company on the stock market': *It was the first football club to have a full stock market quotation.* ◇ (*informal*) *Check stock quotes and email messages on your mobile phone.* Business journalism often uses quite informal language; business letters are more formal.

costing [C] (*BrE*) an estimate of how much sth such as a new service or product will probably cost: *Here is a detailed costing of our proposals.* ◇ *You'd better do some costings.* See also **cost** → PRICE *verb*

NOTE ESTIMATE OR **COSTING**? An **estimate** is usually for a single piece of work. A **costing** or **costings** is/are for a service or product, including estimates of all the work involved. **Estimate** emphasizes the final figure; **costing** emphasizes the process of working out that figure.

value noun

1 the value of regular exercise
2 good value for money

1 value · quality · merit · worth · excellence · distinction · meaning

These are all words for the quality of being good or useful.

PATTERNS AND COLLOCATIONS
▸ sb/sth of value/quality/merit/worth/excellence/distinction
▸ value/merit/excellence/distinction in sth
▸ without value/merit/worth/distinction/meaning
▸ great/real value/quality/merit/worth/distinction/meaning
▸ true value/quality/worth/excellence/meaning
▸ considerable value/quality/merit/distinction
▸ dubious value/quality/merit/distinction
▸ artistic value/quality/merit/worth/excellence
▸ academic merit/excellence/distinction
▸ to have value/quality/merit/worth/distinction/meaning
▸ sb/sth proves their/its value/quality/merit/worth

value [U] the quality of being good, useful, or important: *The value of regular exercise should not be underestimated.* ◇ *The arrival of canals was of great value to many industries.* ◇ *This ring has great sentimental value for me* (= it is important because I associate it with people or places that are emotionally important to me). ◇ *I suppose it has a certain novelty value* (= it's interesting because it's new) *but you'll soon get bored of it.* See also **value** → APPRECIATE *verb*

quality [U] a high standard: *We aim to provide quality at reasonable prices.* ◇ *Get it right, even if it takes time; it's quality not quantity that matters.* See also **quality** → GOOD *adj.* 1

merit /'merɪt/ [U] (*rather formal*) the quality of being good and of deserving praise, reward or admiration: *It's a work of outstanding artistic merit.* ◇ *The plan is entirely without merit.* ◇ *I want to get the job on merit* (= because I deserve it, not as a favour). See also **merit** → DESERVE *verb*

worth [U] the practical or moral value of sb/sth: *The children here quickly gain a sense of their own worth.* ◇ *A good job interview should help candidates prove their worth.* ❶ **Worth** can also mean the financial value of sth. See also **worth** → PRICE *noun* See also **worthless** → DESPICABLE

excellence [U] the quality of being of an extremely high standard: *The college has a reputation for academic excellence.* ◇ *We want this hospital to be a centre of excellence.* See also **excellent** → EXCELLENT

distinction [U, sing.] (*rather formal*) the quality of being excellent, important or special: *a writer of great distinction* ◇ *She had the distinction of being the first woman to fly the Atlantic.*

meaning [U] the real importance of a feeling or experience; the quality or sense of purpose that makes you feel that your life is valuable: *With Anna he learned the meaning of love.* ◇ *Her life seemed to have lost all meaning.*

2 value · bargain · good buy · giveaway · a snip · a steal

These are all words for sth that is worth more than you pay for it.

PATTERNS AND COLLOCATIONS
▸ to be good value/a bargain/a good buy/a giveaway/a snip/a steal at a particular price
▸ bargain/giveaway prices

value [U] (*especially BrE*) how much sth is worth compared with its price: *This restaurant is excellent value* (= is worth the money it costs). ◇ *Charter flights give very good value for money.*

bargain [C] a thing bought for less than the usual price: *I picked up a few good bargains in the sale.* ◇ *The car was a bargain at that price.*

good 'buy [C] a thing that is worth the money that you pay for it: *That jacket was a really good buy.* **OPP** **bad buy** ❶ A **bad buy** is NOT worth the money that you pay for it.

giveaway /'ɡɪvəweɪ/ [C] (*informal*) something that a company gives free, usually with sth else that is for sale: *Comic books were first published in the US in 1933, for use as advertising giveaways.*

a snip [sing.] (*BrE, informal*) a thing that is cheap and good value: *It's a snip at only £25.*

a steal [sing.] (*especially AmE, informal*) a snip: *This suit is a steal at $80.*

values noun See also the entries for PRINCIPLE 1 and VIEW 1

values · teaching · belief · ideology · doctrine · philosophy · code · ethic · ethos

These are all words for an idea or set of ideas about what is morally or politically right and wrong.

PATTERNS AND COLLOCATIONS
▸ sb's **religious** values/teaching/beliefs/ideology/doctrine/philosophy/code/ethic/ethos
▸ sb's **moral** values/teaching/beliefs/doctrine/philosophy/code
▸ sb's **political** values/beliefs/ideology/doctrine/philosophy/ethic/ethos
▸ sb's **social** values/beliefs/ideology/philosophy/code/ethic/ethos
▸ sb's **cultural** values/beliefs/ideology/code/ethos
▸ **traditional** values/teaching/beliefs/ideology/doctrine/philosophy/code/ethic
▸ **conservative/liberal** values/beliefs/ideology/doctrine/philosophy
▸ to **have** values/beliefs/an ideology/a doctrine/a philosophy/a code/an ethic/an ethos
▸ to **subscribe to** values/teaching/an ideology/a doctrine/a philosophy/a code/an ethic
▸ to **hold** values/beliefs
▸ to **go/be against** sb's values/teaching/beliefs/doctrine/philosophy/code/ethos

values [pl.] ideas about what is right and wrong and what is important in life: *All major religions have certain values in common.* ◇ *Conservatives often talk about a return to family values without actually explaining what these are.*

teaching [U, C, usually pl.] the ideas of a particular person or group, especially about politics, religion or society, that are taught to other people: *These views go against traditional Christian teaching.* ◇ *The culture is based in the teachings of Confucius.*

belief [C, usually pl.] something that you believe, especially as part of your religion: *You need to examine your own attitudes and beliefs.*

ideology /ˌaɪdi'ɒlədʒi; *AmE* -'ɑːl-/ [U, C] (*sometimes disapproving*) a set of ideas that an economic or political system is based on; a set of beliefs, especially one held by a particular group, that influences the way people behave: *Individualism is central to capitalist ideology.* ◇ *It's difficult to stand outside the dominant ideology of your own society.*

doctrine /'dɒktrɪn; *AmE* 'dɑːk-/ [C, U] a belief or set of beliefs held and taught by a church or a political party: *She was deeply committed to political doctrines of social equality.* ◇ *He has written books on Catholic doctrine.*

philosophy [C] a particular set or system of beliefs resulting from a search for knowledge about life and the universe; a set of beliefs or an attitude to life that guides sb's behaviour: *He holds firmly to a Buddhist philosophy of life.* ◇ *My own philosophy is to take all the opportunities you can in life.*

code [C] a set of rules of behaviour that are generally accepted by or forced on a group or society: *The school enforces a strict code of conduct.* ◇ *There was a rigid code of honour associated with the cult.* ◇ *Young people unconsciously conform to a dress code but reject any kind of uniform.*

ethic /'eθɪk/ [sing.] a system of moral principles that guides people's behaviour: *They have a very strong* **work ethic** (= the principle that people should work hard). ❶ The term **ethic** is strongly associated with the Protestant Church which teaches the values of hard work and personal moral improvement. Its strongest collocates are *Protestant* and *work*. See also **ethics →** PRINCIPLE 1, **ethical →** MORAL

ethos /'i:θɒs; *AmE* 'i:θɑːs/ [sing.] (*formal*) the moral ideas and attitudes that belong to a particular group or society: *They tried to develop an ethos of public service.*

vandalize (*BrE* also -ise) *verb*

vandalize · wreck · trash · sabotage · smash sth up · deface
These words all mean to damage sth deliberately, usually for no good reason.

▸ to vandalize / wreck / trash / sabotage / smash up **equipment**
▸ to vandalize / wreck / trash / smash up **cars**
▸ to vandalize / wreck / deface a **building**
▸ to vandalize / deface **public property**
▸ to wreck / trash / smash up **a room / the place**

vandalize (*BrE* also -ise) /'vændəlaɪz/ [T, usually passive] to damage a place or equipment, especially public property, deliberately and for no good reason: *The pay phone had been vandalized and wasn't working.* See also **vandal →** HOOLIGAN
▸ **vandalism** *noun* [U]: *Police condemned the damage as an act of mindless vandalism.*
wreck /rek/ [T] to destroy a place or equipment, especially deliberately: *youths who steal and wreck fast cars* ◇ *The building had been wrecked by the explosion.* See also **wreck →** CRASH
trash [T] (*informal*) to deliberately destroy a place or equipment: *The band was famous for trashing hotel rooms.*
sabotage /'sæbətɑːʒ/ [T] to deliberately damage or destroy a place or equipment to prevent an enemy from using it: *The main electricity supply had been sabotaged by the rebels.*
▸ **sabotage** *noun* [U]: *The fire may have been an act of sabotage.*
smash sth 'up *phrasal verb* (*informal*) to deliberately destroy a place or equipment: *Youths had broken into the bar and smashed the place up.*

> **NOTE WRECK, TRASH** OR **SMASH STH UP?** People can **wreck, trash** or **smash up** a place when they destroy it deliberately; but places can also be **wrecked** but NOT **trashed** or **smashed up** by explosions, storms, floods, etc.: *Hurricane Gilbert wrecked tens of thousands of homes.* ◇ *Hurricane Gilbert trashed/smashed up tens of thousands of homes.*

deface [T] (*rather formal*) to deliberately damage the appearance of a book, painting, wall, etc., especially by drawing or writing on it: *a graffiti artist who defaced buildings and bridges*

variable *adj.* See also the entry for UNCERTAIN

variable · dynamic · irregular · inconsistent · fluid · uneven
These words all describe things that change often or are likely to change.

▸ variable / inconsistent / uneven **quality**
▸ a variable / dynamic / fluid **environment**
▸ a dynamic / fluid **situation**
▸ irregular / uneven **breathing / rhythms**
▸ **very** variable / irregular / inconsistent / fluid / uneven
▸ **highly** variable / dynamic / irregular / inconsistent / fluid
▸ **somewhat** variable / irregular / inconsistent / uneven

variable /'veəriəbl; *AmE* 'ver-; 'vær-/ often changing; likely to change: *The forecast is based on assumptions of variable temperature.* ◇ *The acting is of variable quality* (= some of it is good and some of it is bad). See also **variability →** CHANGE *noun* 1, **vary →** DIFFER
dynamic /daɪ'næmɪk/ (*usually approving, especially business*) (of a process or situation) always changing and making progress: *They want to promote a dynamic economy with a high level of employment.* ◇ *The business has managed to change and remain dynamic.* **OPP static →** STEADY
irregular /ɪ'reɡjələ(r)/ (*usually disapproving*) not happening at times that are at an equal distance from each other; not happening regularly: *an irregular heartbeat* ◇ *irregular attendance at school* ◇ *He visited his parents* **at irregular intervals.** **OPP regular →** STEADY, **regular →** FREQUENT
inconsistent /ˌɪnkən'sɪstənt/ (*disapproving*) tending to change too often; not staying the same: *The tests gave inconsistent results.* ◇ *Children find it difficult if a parent is inconsistent.* **OPP consistent →** STEADY
fluid /'fluːɪd/ (*formal*) (of a situation) likely to change; not fixed: *The fluid political situation made investment impossible.* ◇ *There is a fluid relationship between managers and workers.* ❶ **Fluid** is most often used to talk about a *state*, a *situation* or a *relationship*.
uneven /ʌn'iːvn/ not following a regular pattern: *Her breathing was quick and uneven.* ❶ Typical collocations of **uneven** are related to people's movements: *an uneven voice/laugh/pace/tread* **OPP even →** STEADY

very *adj.*

very · actual · exact · precise
These words are all used to emphasize that you are talking about a particular thing or moment.

▸ the very / actual / exact / precise **moment**
▸ sb's very / actual / exact **words**
▸ the actual / exact / precise **nature** of sth
▸ the very / exact **same** sth

very [only before noun] used to emphasize that you are talking about a particular thing or person and not about another: *Those were her very words.* ◇ *That's* **the very thing** *I need.*
actual /'æktʃuəl/ [only before noun] used to emphasize the most important part of sth: *The wedding preparations take weeks but the actual ceremony takes less than an hour.*
exact [only before noun] used to emphasize that sth happens at a particular time or in a particular way: *We need to know the exact time the incident occurred.* ◇ (*rather informal, especially spoken*) *I had the exact same problem as you when I first started.* See also **exact →** EXACT
▸ **exactly** *adv.*: *It happened almost exactly a year ago.*
precise /prɪ'saɪs/ [only before noun] (*rather formal*) used to emphasize that sth happens at a particular time or in a particular way: *Doctors found it hard to establish the precise nature of her illness.* See also **precise →** EXACT
▸ **precisely** *adv.*: *The meeting starts at 2 o'clock precisely.*

> **NOTE EXACT** OR **PRECISE?** In many cases you can use either word: *at that exact/precise moment* ◇ *the exact/ precise nature of sth.* However, **precise** is often more formal than **exact** and is not used in the more informal expressions: *I had the precise same problem.*

very *adv.*

very · well · so · really · quite · extremely · highly · most · desperately · truly · (*taboo*) **bloody**
These words are all used before adjectives, adverbs or verbs to mean 'to a high degree'.

PATTERNS AND COLLOCATIONS

▶ very / so / really / quite / extremely / highly **successful** / **intelligent** / **competitive** / **critical** / **sensitive**
▶ very / so / really / quite / extremely / most / desperately **anxious** / **concerned** / **disappointed** / **unhappy** / **important**
▶ very / so / really / quite / extremely / desperately / truly **sorry**
▶ very / so / really / quite / extremely / most / desperately **worried**
▶ very / so / really / quite / extremely / desperately **ill** / **sick** / **tired** / **poor** / **lonely** / **hard** / **close**
▶ very / so / really / quite / extremely / bloody **good** / **hot**
▶ so / really / truly / bloody **awful**
▶ very / so / really / quite / extremely / bloody **well**
▶ very / so / really / extremely **few**
▶ **not** very / so / really **happy** / **expensive**
▶ to really / desperately / truly **want** / **need** / **love** sb / sth

very used before adjectives, adverbs and determiners to mean 'to a high degree': *This room is very small/hot/ useful.* ◊ *They left very quickly/soon.* ◊ *Very few people know that.* ◊ *'Do you like it?' 'Yes, I do.* **Very much.'** ◊ *'Is it what you expected?' 'Oh yes,* **very much so.'** ◊ *'Are you busy?' 'Not very.'* ◊ *The new building has been very much admired.* ◊ *I'm* **not very** (= not at all) *impressed.*

well to a great extent or degree: *He was driving at well over the speed limit.* ◊ *It's a well-loved tale of love and romance.* ◊ *The castle is* **well worth** *a visit.* ◊ *He liked her* **well enough** (= to a reasonable degree) *but he wasn't going to make a close friend of her.* ❶ In informal spoken British English, **well** can be used in place of 'very': (*BrE, informal, spoken*) *I was well annoyed, I can tell you.*

so (*informal, especially spoken*) to a high degree; very: *The girls looked so pretty in their summer dresses.* ◊ *I'm so glad to see you.* ◊ *We have so much to do.* ◊ *Their attitude is so very English.* ◊ (*BrE*) *He sat there* **ever so** *quietly.*

really (*rather informal, especially spoken*) used before adjectives, adverbs and verbs to mean 'to a high degree': *This is a really nice place.* ◊ *I'm really sorry.* ◊ *We was driving really fast.* ◊ *I really hope we can meet up again soon.* See also **real** → COMPLETE

> **NOTE** **VERY, SO** OR **REALLY?** Very is the most frequent and most neutral of these words. **Really** is more informal and can be stronger in degree. **So** is also stronger in degree and is used more to emphasize a comment or your opinion. It is the most informal of these words and some people consider it incorrect in written English. **So** and **really** can be used with both weak and strong adjectives: *so/really good* (= weak) ◊ *so/really wonderful* (= strong); **very** is not used with strong adjectives: *very good* ◊ ~~very wonderful~~. **Very** and **really** can be used with adjectives both after a linking verb and before a noun phrase: *This place is very/really nice.* ◊ *This is a very/really nice place.* **So** can only be used after a linking verb; before a noun phrase use **such a...**: *This place is so nice.* ◊ *This is such a nice place.* **Really** can also be used with verbs: *I really love it here.* **Very** cannot be used in this way, although in some cases you can use *very much*: *I very much like the way they've arranged everything.*

quite (usually used with adjectives and adverbs) to a high degree; very: *You'll be quite comfortable here.* ◊ *I can see it quite clearly.* ❶ This is the most frequent meaning of **quite** in American English; in British English it is more often used to mean 'rather' or 'completely'. See also **quite** → QUITE 1, **quite** → QUITE 2

extremely (usually used with adjectives and adverbs) to a very high degree: *This issue is extremely complicated.* ◊ *I would be extremely grateful if you could have a word with her.* ◊ *Mark knew he had behaved extremely badly.* ❶ **Extremely** is stronger in degree than **very, so** or **really**; it is also slightly more formal. See also **extreme** → MAXIMUM

highly to a high degree; very: *a highly skilled workforce* ◊ *It is highly unlikely that she'll be late.* ❶ **Highly** collocates with a more limited range of adjectives than many of the words in this group. It is used especially with adjectives for qualities that can be measured and ranked on a scale,

and/or adjectives for personal qualities that people consider when they are judging sb: *highly successful/ intelligent/skilled/motivated/competitive* ◊ *highly critical/ sensitive*

most (*formal*) very; extremely; completely: *It was most kind of you to meet me.* ◊ *We shall most probably never meet again.* ◊ *This technique looks easy, but it most certainly is not.*

desperately to a very high degree, especially in a difficult or unhappy situation: *desperately ill/unhappy/lonely* ◊ *He took a deep breath, desperately trying to keep calm.* ◊ *They desperately wanted a child.*

truly (*rather formal*) used to emphasize a particular quality, especially a good or impressive quality: *It was a truly memorable occasion.* ◊ *They gave a truly magnificent performance.*

bloody (*BrE, taboo, spoken*) a swear word that many people find offensive that is used to emphasize a comment or angry statement: *What bloody awful weather!* ◊ *She did bloody well to win that race.* ◊ *'I'm not coming.' 'Yes you* **bloody well** *are.'* ◊ *'Will you apologize to him?' '* **Not bloody likely** (= Certainly not)*!'* ◊ *He doesn't bloody care about anybody.* ◊ *I can't get this bloody thing to work.*

vicious *adj.*

vicious · malicious · vindictive · spiteful · bitchy
These words all describe a person or their comments which show hatred and anger towards sb else.

PATTERNS AND COLLOCATIONS

▶ a vicious / malicious / vindictive / spiteful **attack**
▶ a vicious / malicious / spiteful / bitchy **remark**
▶ vicious / malicious **gossip** / **rumours**
▶ a vicious / malicious **campaign**

vicious /ˈvɪʃəs/ (*disapproving*) (of language or comments) full of hatred and anger: *She wrote me a vicious letter after the incident.* ◊ *The committee was particularly vicious in its criticism of the management.* See also **vicious** → CRUEL

malicious /məˈlɪʃəs/ (*disapproving*) having or showing hatred and a desire to harm or upset sb: *He took malicious pleasure in telling me what she had said.*
▶ **malice** /ˈmælɪs/ *noun* [U]: *He sent the letter out of malice.* ◊ *She is entirely without malice.*

vindictive /vɪnˈdɪktɪv/ (*disapproving*) trying to harm or upset sb, or showing that you want to, because you think that they have harmed you: *She's nothing but a jealous, vindictive, old woman.*
▶ **vindictively** *adv.*: *'It serves them right,' he thought vindictively.*

spiteful /ˈspaɪtfl/ (*disapproving*) behaving in an unkind way in order to hurt or upset sb: *Why had she made such a spiteful remark?*
▶ **spite** *noun* [U]: *I'm sure he only said it out of spite.* ◊ *She was angry and full of spite.*
▶ **spitefully** *adv.*: *'He doesn't want you there,' she said spitefully.*

bitchy (*informal, disapproving*) unpleasant and unkind about or towards other people: *Why is it that girls can be so bitchy towards each other?* See also **bitch** → VILLAIN

victim *noun*

1 victims of crime
2 victims of a cruel hoax

1 victim · casualty · fatality
These are all words for sb who has been hurt or killed in an attack or accident, or sth which is destroyed when sth else happens.

PATTERNS AND COLLOCATIONS

▶ a victim / casualty / fatality **of** sth
▶ **accident** victims / casualties
▶ a **war** victim / casualty
▶ a victim / casualty **of war**

victim [C] a person who has been attacked, injured or killed as the result of a crime or accident: *murder/rape victims* ◊ *accident/earthquake/famine victims* ◊ *victims of crime* ◊ *He shouldn't feel ashamed – he was an innocent victim.* See also **victim** → PATIENT

casualty /ˈkæʒuəlti/ [C] a person who is killed or injured in war or in an accident; a person who suffers or a thing that is destroyed when sth else takes place: *Our primary objective is reducing road casualties.* ◊ *Both sides had suffered heavy casualties* (= many people had been killed). ◊ *She became a casualty of the reduction in part-time work* (= she lost her job). ◊ *They say that truth is the first casualty of war.*

fatality /fəˈtæləti/ [C] a death that is caused in an accident or war or by some other act of violence: *Several people were injured, but there were no fatalities.* See also **fatal** → FATAL

---

2 victim · scapegoat · sucker · soft touch · patsy · fall guy · dupe
These are all words for a person who has been deceived, or who is easily deceived.

PATTERNS AND COLLOCATIONS
▸ a **poor** victim / scapegoat / sucker / dupe
▸ to **make sb** a victim / scapegoat / patsy / fall guy
▸ to **use sb as** a scapegoat / patsy / fall guy

victim [C] a person who has been tricked: *They were the victims of a cruel hoax.* ◊ *Tourists are easy victims for pickpockets.* ◊ *She fell victim to an unscrupulous landlord.*

scapegoat /ˈskeɪpɡəʊt; AmE -ɡoʊt/ [C] a person who is blamed for sth wrong that sb else has done or a mistake they have made, especially when this is done because it is convenient for other people: *She felt she had been made a scapegoat for her boss's incompetence.*

sucker [C] (*especially AmE, informal, disapproving*) a person who is easily tricked or persuaded to do sth: *I never did get that money back from him – what a sucker I am.*

soft 'touch [C] (*informal*) a person who is easily persuaded to do sth: *He saw her as a soft touch.*

patsy [C] (*especially AmE, informal, disapproving*) a weak person who is easily cheated or deceived, or who is forced to take the blame for sth that sb else has done wrong: *I thought you respected me – now I find out that I'm just another one of your patsies.*

fall guy /ˈfɔːl ɡaɪ/ [C] (*especially AmE, rather informal*) a scapegoat: *He realized he'd been set up as the fall guy.*

dupe /djuːp; AmE duːp/ [C] (*formal, written*) a person who is tricked or cheated: *These men were simply the dupes of their unscrupulous leaders.*

victory noun

victory · win · landslide · defeat · upset · result
These are all words for success in a game, competition, election or war.

PATTERNS AND COLLOCATIONS
▸ a victory / a win / a landslide / an upset / a result **for** sb
▸ a victory / a win / an upset / a result **against** sb
▸ a victory / win **over** sb
▸ a victory / a win / a landslide / an upset **in** sth
▸ a **stunning / surprise** victory / win / defeat / upset / result
▸ a **comprehensive / decisive / crushing / narrow** victory / win / defeat
▸ a **great** victory / win / upset / result
▸ a **Democrat / Labour, etc.** victory / win / landslide
▸ to **pull off / get** a victory / win / result
▸ to **clinch / secure / snatch / score / notch up / chalk up / gain / earn** a victory / win
▸ to **cruise to / sweep to / romp to / claim / deserve / celebrate** victory / a win
▸ to **win** a victory / by a landslide

victory [C, U] success in a game, competition, election, argument or war: *The team are celebrating a 3–2 victory over Poland.* ◊ *Labour swept to victory in the 1997 election.*
ℹ A **moral victory** is a situation in which your ideas or principles are proved to be right and fair, even though you may not have succeeded where practical results are concerned: *In spite of the result, we felt we had won a moral victory.* OPP **defeat** → DEFEAT *verb*, See also **victor** → WINNER

win [C] (*rather informal*) victory in a game, competition or election: *People still talk about the famous win against Brazil.* ◊ *Torino notched up a 2–1 win at Lazio.* ◊ *They have now gone 10 games without a win.* ◊ *After this year's election win, they have time on their side.* ℹ **Win** is a slightly informal word, used especially in sports journalism. It is not used to talk about victory in an argument or war. OPP **loss** ℹ A **loss** is a failure to win a game, competition or election: *Argentina's 2–1 loss to Brazil.* See also **win** → WIN *verb*, **winner** → WINNER

landslide [C, usually sing.] an election in which one person or party gets very many more votes than the other people or parties: *The National Party won by a landslide.* ◊ *No one expected a repeat of Labour's 1997 landslide victory.*

defeat [C, usually sing.] the act of winning a victory over sb in a game, competition, election or war: *They played a key role in Wellington's defeat of Napoleon at Waterloo.* ◊ *He almost pulled off a shock defeat of the reigning champion.* See also **defeat** → DEFEAT *verb*

upset [C] (*rather informal, especially journalism*) (in a competition) a situation in which a person or team beats the person or team that was expected to win: *The war veteran came close to pulling a stunning political upset in Ohio this summer* (= by nearly winning an election).

result [C, usually sing.] (*BrE, informal*) a victory, especially in a game of football: *We badly need to get a result from this match.* ◊ *This was a great result for us.*

view noun

1 sb's political views
2 a delightful sea view

---

1 See the Topic Map for FACT AND OPINION on p.898, See also the entries for ATTITUDE and VALUES

view · opinion · point · belief · idea · point of view · feeling · judgement · conviction · sentiment
These are all words for what you think about a particular issue.

PATTERNS AND COLLOCATIONS
▸ sb's view / opinion / point / beliefs / ideas / feelings / judgement / conviction / sentiments **about** sb / sth
▸ sb's view / opinion / ideas / point of view / feelings **on** sb / sth
▸ sb's view / opinion **of** sb / sth
▸ **in** sb's view / opinion / judgement
▸ the view / opinion / point / belief / idea / point of view / feeling / judgement / conviction **that...**
▸ **different** views / opinions / beliefs / ideas / points of view / convictions / sentiments
▸ a **general** view / opinion / belief / point of view / feeling / conviction / sentiment
▸ a **popular** view / opinion / belief / feeling / sentiment
▸ a **strong** view / opinion / belief / feelings / conviction / sentiment
▸ a **firm** view / opinion / belief / conviction
▸ a **personal / private** view / opinion / belief / point of view / feeling / judgement / conviction / sentiment
▸ a **political / religious** view / opinion / belief / idea / feelings / conviction / sentiment
▸ to **have / hold** a view / an opinion / a belief / a point of view / a conviction
▸ to **be of** the view / opinion / belief (that...)
▸ to **express** your view / opinion / beliefs / ideas / point of view / feelings / conviction / sentiments
▸ to **hear** sb's views / opinion / ideas / point of view
▸ to **change** your view / opinion / beliefs / idea / point of view / judgement
▸ to **support** a view / opinion / belief / an idea / a point of view / a conviction

view [C] what you think about sb/sth; your attitude towards sb/sth: *We have widely differing views on how to raise children.* ◇ *We take the view that it would be wrong to interfere.* ◇ *In my view it would be a complete waste of time.*

opinion [C, U] what you think about sb/sth; advice from a professional person about sth; the thoughts or feelings of a group of people about sb/sth: *I've recently changed my opinion of her.* ◇ *You can always ask for a **second opinion** (= the opinion of another professional person) if you're not sure.* ◇ *You need to be able to distinguish between fact and opinion.* ◇ ***Public opinion** (= what most people think) is shifting in favour of change.* ◇ ***Opinion is divided** about whether to join the new currency.* ◇ *'I think she's great.' 'Well, that's **a matter of opinion** (= other people may disagree)'.*

point [C] a thing that sb says or writes giving their opinion or argument for sth: *I **take your point** (= I understand and accept what you are saying).* ◇ *He's just saying that to **prove a point** (= to show his idea is right).* ◇ *OK, you've **made your point!*** ❶ Points can be facts as well as opinions or arguments. See also **point** → FACTOR

belief [C, U] sth that you believe to be true about sb/sth: *She acted in the belief that she was doing the right thing.* ◇ ***Contrary to popular belief** (= despite what most people think) he was not involved in the affair.* See also **believe** → THINK

idea [C, usually pl.] an opinion or belief about sth: *He has some very strange ideas about education.* ◇ *The idea that I was only interested in making money is ludicrous.*

point of 'view (pl. **points of view**) [C] the particular opinion that sb has about sth: *You have to try to see your opponent's point of view.* ◇ *He has always taken the opposite point of view.*

feeling [C, U] (*rather informal*) an opinion or attitude about sb/sth: *I don't have any strong feelings about it one way or another.* ◇ *My own feeling is that we should go for the cheaper option.* ◇ *She **had mixed feelings** about giving up her job.* ◇ *The general feeling of the meeting was against the decision.* See also **feel** → THINK

> **NOTE** IDEA OR FEELING? An **idea** is based more on principles or beliefs; a **feeling** is based slightly more on emotions.

judgement (also **judgment** especially in *AmE*) [C, U] an opinion that you form after thinking carefully about sth; the act of making this opinion known to other people: *It's not for me to make any judgements about the situation.* ◇ *He's always very ready to **pass judgement** on others.* ◇ *I'd like to **reserve judgement** until I see the report (= not form an opinion until I have seen it).* ◇ *I gave him the money **against my better judgement** (= even though I knew it was probably the wrong thing to do).* See also **judge** → JUDGE *verb* 1

conviction /kən'vɪkʃn/ [C, U] (*rather formal*) a strong opinion or belief: *We were sustained by the conviction that all would be well in the end.* ◇ *She was motivated by deep religious conviction.*

sentiment [C, U] (*formal*) a feeling or opinion, especially one based on emotions: *This is a sentiment that I totally agree with.* ◇ *Nationalist sentiment spread quickly, especially in the cities.*

2 view · sight · scene · panorama

These are all words for a thing that you can see, especially from a particular place.

PATTERNS AND COLLOCATIONS

▸ a view / panorama **of** sth
▸ a **beautiful / breathtaking** view / sight / scene / panorama
▸ a **magnificent / spectacular** view / sight / panorama
▸ a **picturesque** view / scene / panorama
▸ to **enjoy** the view / sight / scene / panorama
▸ to **take in** the view / sight / scene
▸ to **admire** the view / sight

view [C] what you can see from a particular place or position, especially beautiful natural scenery: *The **view from** the top of the tower was spectacular.* ◇ *The cottage had a delightful sea view.* ◇ *I'd like a room with a view, please.* See also **view** → SIGHT

sight [C] a thing that you see or can see, especially sth that is impressive or unusual: *He became a familiar sight on the streets of Oxford.* ◇ *He was a sorry sight, soaked to the skin and shivering.* ◇ *The museum attempts to recreate **the sights and sounds** of wartime Britain.* See also **sight** → SIGHT

scene [C] a view that you see, especially one with people and/or animals moving about and doing things: *It was a delightful rural scene.* ◇ (*especially BrE*) *They went abroad for **a change of scene** (= to see and experience new surroundings).* ❶ In American English it is more usual to say **a change of scenery**. See also **scenery** → COUNTRY 2

panorama /ˌpænə'rɑːmə; *AmE* -'ræmə/ [C] a view of a wide area of land: *There is a wonderful panorama of the mountains from the hotel.*

villain *noun*

villain · (*taboo*) **bastard** · (*taboo*) **bitch** · (*taboo*) **son of a bitch** · (*taboo*) **bugger** · **creep** · **pig** · **brute** · **monster**
These are all words for an unpleasant person who treats other people badly.

PATTERNS AND COLLOCATIONS

▸ an **evil** villain / bastard / bitch / son of a bitch / bugger / monster
▸ an **old** villain / bastard / bitch / son of a bitch / bugger / brute
▸ a / an **selfish / mean / arrogant** bastard / bitch / son of a bitch / bugger / pig / brute
▸ a **lazy** bastard / bitch / son of a bitch / bugger
▸ a **rotten** bastard / son of a bitch / bugger
▸ a **stupid** bastard / bitch / son of a bitch / bugger / pig
▸ an **ungrateful** bastard / bitch / bugger / creep / pig
▸ a **miserable** bastard / son of a bitch / bugger / creep
▸ You / The **little** bastard / bitch / son of a bitch / bugger / creep!

villain /'vɪlən/ [C] (*disapproving*) a wicked person; the main bad character in a story, play or film: *heroes and villains of the 20th century* ◇ *He often plays the part of the villain.* **OPP** hero → STAR 2

bastard [C] (*taboo, slang*) an offensive word for a man who is rude, unpleasant or cruel: *He's a real bastard.* ◇ *You bastard! You've made her cry.* ❶ Bastard is also used by some people to or about a person that they feel jealous of or sorry for: *What a lucky bastard!* ◇ *You poor bastard!* This use is not offensive when it is used between friends, but it is very informal.

bitch [C] (*taboo, slang*) an offensive way of referring to a woman, especially an unpleasant one: *You stupid little bitch!* ◇ *She can be a real bitch.* See also **bitchy** → VICIOUS

son of a 'bitch (pl. **sons of bitches**) [C] (*especially AmE, taboo, slang*) an offensive word for a man that you think is bad or very unpleasant: *I'll kill that son of a bitch when I get my hands on him!* ❶ In American English **son of a bitch** is often shortened to **SOB**. In American English slang it can also be used between friends to show that you like sb or feel sorry for them: *He's a tough old son of a bitch.* This use is not offensive but it is very informal.

bugger [C] (*BrE, taboo, slang*) an offensive word used to insult sb, and to show anger or dislike: *You stupid bugger! You could have run me over!* ◇ *Come here, you little bugger!* ❶ Bugger can also be used between friends to show that you like sb or feel sorry for them: *Poor bugger! His wife left him last week.* This use is not offensive but it is very informal.

creep [C] (*informal, disapproving*) a person that you dislike very much and find very unpleasant: *He's a nasty little creep!*

pig [C] (*informal, disapproving*) an unpleasant or offensive person: *Arrogant pig!* ◇ *He's a real **male chauvinist pig** (= a man who does not think women are equal to men).* ❶ Pig is usually used about a person who says rude or insulting things.

brute [C] (*disapproving*) a man who treats people in an unkind, cruel way: *His father was a drunken brute.*

monster [C] (*disapproving*) a person who is very cruel and evil: *The man is a monster; he terrifies me.*

violent *adj.* See the Topic Map for CONFLICT on p.896

violent · bloody · rough · murderous · homicidal · bloodthirsty
These words all describe people using physical force that is intended to hurt or kill sb.

rough	violent	murderous
	bloody	homicidal
		bloodthirsty

PATTERNS AND COLLOCATIONS
▸ violent / murderous / homicidal **towards** sb
▸ a violent / murderous / homicidal **attack**
▸ violent / murderous / homicidal **tendencies**

violent involving or caused by physical force that is intended to hurt or kill sb: *Violent crime has increased by 15 per cent.* ◇ *Her husband was a violent man.* ◇ *He later met a violent death on the battlefield.* ◇ *Children should not be allowed to watch violent movies* (= that show a lot of violence). ◇ *The crowd suddenly turned violent.*
▸ **violence** *noun* [U]: *crimes/acts/threats of violence* ◇ *He condemned the protesters' use of violence against the police.* ◇ *domestic violence* (= between family members)
▸ **violently** *adv.*: *The crowd reacted violently.*

bloody [usually before noun] (*especially journalism*) involving a lot of violence and killing: *A bloody battle has been fought in the region.* ◇ *The terrorists have halted their bloody campaign of violence.* ❶ **Bloody** can describe battle or fight, but NOT the people involved: *Her husband was a bloody man.*

rough (*rather informal*) not gentle or careful; violent: *They complained of rough handling by the guards.* ◇ *She doesn't like playing with the rough kids.* ◇ (*spoken*) *Don't try any rough stuff with me.* **OPP gentle** → SENSITIVE 1
▸ **roughly** *adv.*: *He pushed her roughly out of the way.*

murderous /'mɜːdərəs; *AmE* 'mɜːrd-/ (*written*) intending or likely to kill another person; making sb likely to kill another person: *The film turns a murderous villain into a hero.* ◇ *Some of the patients had suicidal or murderous tendencies.* ❶ **Murderous** is often used to describe people feeling anger or hatred: *a murderous look/glance/mood ◇ murderous intent/rage/jealousy.* See also **murder** → MURDER *noun*, **murder** → KILL *verb*

homicidal /,hɒmɪ'saɪdl; *AmE* ,hɑːm-/ (*rather formal*) murderous: *He's a homicidal maniac.* ◇ *She had clear homicidal tendencies.* See also **homicide** → MURDER

> **NOTE MURDEROUS** OR **HOMICIDAL?** **Murderous** expresses stronger feelings of fear or disgust than **homicidal**; it is often used to describe behaviour caused by strong emotions such as anger and hatred. **Homicidal** is a more technical and less emotive (= showing strong emotions) term; it is often used to describe behaviour caused by mental illness.

bloodthirsty /'blʌdθɜːsti; *AmE* -θɜːrsti/ wanting to kill or wound; enjoying seeing or hearing about killing and violence; describing or showing killing and violence: *We are not a bloodthirsty people.* ◇ *It's a bloodthirsty tale of murder and revenge.*

VIP *noun*

VIP · dignitary · heavyweight · someone · big shot
These are all words for a famous and important person with a lot of influence

PATTERNS AND COLLOCATIONS
▸ a **visiting** VIP / dignitary

VIP /,viː aɪ 'piː/ [C] a famous or important person who is treated in a special way: *The Priority Pass provides access to the VIP lounge.* ◇ *Two of our reps got the VIP treatment when they arrived at their hotel yesterday.* ❶ **VIP** is an abbreviation for 'Very Important Person'. It is often used before another noun, with the meaning 'intended or suitable for a VIP'.

dignitary /'dɪgnɪtəri; *AmE* -teri/ [C, usually pl.] (*rather formal*) a person who has an important official position: *The Prime Minister will be meeting local dignitaries and visiting places of work.* ❶ **Dignitary** is often used in the phrases *local/foreign/visiting dignitaries.* **Dignitaries** often represent their town or city, either as visitors to another town or city, or when other important people visit their town or city.

heavyweight /'heviweɪt/ [C] (*especially journalism*) an important person or organization that influences others: *His supporters say he's a political heavyweight who doesn't hesitate to get the job done.*

someone (also **somebody**) *pron.* a famous or important person: *He was a small-time lawyer keen to be someone.* ❶ **Somebody** (but NOT **someone**) can also be a countable noun: *'Let me tell you,' she yelled, 'Boyd and I are somebodies in this town.'* **OPP nobody** ❶ A **nobody** is a person who has no importance or influence: *She rose from being a nobody to become a superstar.*

big shot [C] (*informal*) a person who has an important position: *All of the town's big shots were there in their tuxedoes.*

visible *adj.* See also the entry for MARKED

visible · on display · noticeable · in evidence · discernible · in view
These words all describe sb/sth that can be seen or noticed.

PATTERNS AND COLLOCATIONS
▸ visible / noticeable / discernible **to** / **in** / **from** sb / sth
▸ a visible / a noticeable / a discernible **effect** / **feature** / **difference** / **change**
▸ **clearly** visible / in evidence / discernible / in view
▸ **still** visible / on display / noticeable / in evidence
▸ **particularly** visible / noticeable / in evidence
▸ **just** / **barely** visible / noticeable / discernible

visible that can be seen; that is obvious enough to be noticed: *The house is clearly visible from the beach.* ◇ *Most stars are not visible to the naked eye.* ◇ *He showed no visible sign of emotion.* **OPP invisible** → INVISIBLE, See also **distinguishable** → RECOGNIZABLE
▸ **visibly** *adv.*: *He was visibly shocked.*

on di'splay *phrase* put in a place where people can look at it: *Designs for the new sports hall are on display in the library.* ◇ *The old carriages were put on permanent display in the Museum of Transport.*

noticeable easy to see or notice; clear or definite: *Her scars are hardly noticeable now.* ◇ *It was noticeable that none of the family were present.* ◇ *The new filing system is a noticeable improvement on the old one.* See also **notice** → NOTICE
▸ **noticeably** *adv.*: *Her hand was shaking noticeably.* ◇ *Marks were noticeably higher for girls than for boys.*

in 'evidence *phrase* present and clearly seen: *The police were much in evidence at today's demonstration.*

discernible /dɪ'sɜːnəbl; *AmE* -'sɜːrn-/ (*formal*) that can be noticed, discovered or understood, especially when it is not easy to see, understand, etc: *There is often no discernible difference between rival brands.* ◇ *His face was barely discernible in the gloom.* See also **discern** → IDENTIFY

in 'view *phrase* that can be seen from where sb/sth is looking: *There was nobody in view.* ◇ *They cleared the fence and lay down in view of* (= where they could see) *the camp.* ◇ *He was shot in full view of* (= where he could be clearly seen by) *a large crowd.* **OPP out of sight** → INVISIBLE

visionary *noun*

visionary · dreamer · idealist · romantic
These are all words for a person who has grand ideas and plans for the future that may or may not be realistic.

▶ a **great** visionary / dreamer / romantic
▶ a **true** visionary / romantic

visionary /'vɪʒənri; AmE -ʒəneri/ [C] (*usually approving*) a person who has the ability to think about or plan the future in an intelligent, imaginative way: *The company needs visionaries to see opportunities.* See also **vision** → INSPIRATION
  ▶ **visionary** *adj.*: *a visionary leader*
dreamer [C] (*often disapproving*) a person who has ideas or plans that are not practical or realistic; a person who does not pay attention to what is happening around them, but thinks about other things instead: *My father was a romantic dreamer.* ◇ *He was a dreamer; I'd give him a job to do, come back, and find he hadn't started it.* See also **dream** → HOPE *noun* 2
idealist [C] a person who has a strong belief in perfect standards and tries to achieve them, even when this is not realistic: *He's too much of an idealist for this government.*
  ▶ **idealism** *noun* [U]: *She was full of youthful idealism.*
  ▶ **idealistic** *adj.*: *She's still young and idealistic.*
romantic [C] a person who is very imaginative and emotional, and who has ideas and hopes that may not be realistic: *She's an incurable romantic.* ◇ *He was a romantic at heart and longed for adventure.*

visit *noun*

visit · tour · stay · call · stopover
These are all words for an occasion or period of time when sb goes to see a person or place and spends time there.

▶ **on** a visit / tour / call
▶ **during** sb's visit / tour / stay
▶ an **overnight** stay / stopover
▶ to **go on** a visit / tour
▶ to **make** a visit / stay / call
▶ to **pay sb** a visit / call
▶ to **cut short** a visit / tour / stay
▶ to **cancel** a visit / tour

visit [C] an occasion or period of time when you go to see a person or place and spend time there: *Is this your first visit to New York?* ◇ *We had a visit from the police last night.* ◇ *Enjoy your visit!* ◇ *If you have time, pay a visit to the local museum.* ◇ *The prime minister is on an official visit to Jamaica.* See also **visit** → STAY *verb* 2, **visitor** → TOURIST
tour [C] an act of walking around, looking at and learning about a place, especially as a visitor or tourist: *In the afternoon we went on a tour of the ruins.* ◇ *We were given a guided tour of the palace.* ◇ *The minister continued with his tour of inspection* (= an official visit to examine a place) *of the prison.* See also **tour** → TOUR *verb*
stay [C] a period of staying somewhere on a visit: *I enjoyed my stay in Prague.* See also **stay** → STAY *verb* 2
call [C] a short visit to sb's home: *I'm afraid this isn't a social call.* ◇ *The doctor's out on a call at the moment.* ❶ **Call** is used especially about a short visit to sb's home made by a professional person, especially a doctor or nurse. It can also be used about friends visiting each other, but this now sounds rather old-fashioned: *He decided to pay a call on his old friend.*
stopover /'stɒpəʊvə(r); AmE 'stɑːpoʊ-/ [C] a short stay somewhere between two parts of a journey: *We had a two-day stopover in Fiji on the way to Australia.* See also **stop over** → STAY *verb* 2

visit *verb*

visit · go to sth · see · attend · call · drop in/round/by · pop in/round/over · stop by sth · look in on sb · look sb up
These words all mean to go to see a person or place for a period of time.

▶ to **call** / drop in / pop in / look in **on** sb
▶ to **visit** / see a / the **doctor** / **dentist**
▶ to **go to** the **doctor's** / **dentist's**
▶ to **come** / **go to** visit / see sb
▶ to **come** / **go and** visit / see sb
▶ to **call** / drop in / pop in / stop by **to see** sb
▶ to **often** visit / go to sth / see / drop in / pop in / stop by / look in
▶ to **regularly** visit / go to sth / see / attend / call / pop in
▶ to **occasionally** visit / go to sth / see / attend / call / drop in / look in

visit [T] (*rather formal*) to travel to a place to see it or to spend some time with a person: *The President will be visiting six European capitals.* ◇ *I visited her in hospital.*
'go to sth *phrasal verb* [no passive] to visit or spend time in a place for a particular purpose: *I have to go to the doctor's for a check-up.* ◇ *Do you go to church* (= regularly attend church services)*?* ◇ *I'm not prepared to go to prison for a crime I didn't commit.* ◇ *They sometimes go to the pub after work.*
see [T] to visit sb: *When was the last time you saw a dentist?* ◇ *Come and see us again soon!* ◇ *He said he'd been to see his sister.* ❶ In this meaning **see** is used especially in the expressions *come/go and see sb* and *come/go to see sb.*
attend [T] (*formal*) to go regularly to a place such as a church, school or hospital: *The children attended the local school.* ◇ *The patients all attend the clinic monthly.*
call [I] (*especially BrE, rather formal*) to visit sb at home for a short time: *We called but they were out.* ◇ *I called round at the house to check how things were.*
drop 'in/'round/'by, **drop 'into sth** *phrasal verb* (-**pp**-) [no passive] (*rather informal*) to visit a person or place for a short time, especially when you are not expected: *Don't forget to drop in on Harry.* ◇ *They dropped round for a drink.* ◇ *I'll drop by some time next week.* ◇ *I sometimes drop into the National Gallery for an hour or so.*
  ▶ **'drop-in** *adj.*: *a drop-in advice centre*
pop' in/'round/'over *phrasal verb* (-**pp**-) (*BrE, informal*) to visit a person or place for a short time, especially when you are not expected: *I was just passing and thought I'd pop in.*
stop 'by, **stop 'by sth** *phrasal verb* (-**pp**-) [no passive] (*rather informal*) to visit a place for a short time: *He used to stop by every day.* ◇ *She stopped by the store at about five o'clock.* See also **stop** → STAY 1, **stop over** → STAY 2
look 'in on sb *phrasal verb* (*rather informal*) to make a short visit to sb, especially sb who is old or ill: *Could you look in on Dad some time?*
look sb 'up *phrasal verb* [no passive] (*informal*) to visit or make contact with sb, especially when you normally live far away or have not seen them for a long time: *I promised to look her up next time I was in England.*

visitor *noun*

visitor · guest · caller · company
These are all words for a person who visits you, especially in your home.

▶ a visitor / guest / caller **at** / **from** sth
▶ **unexpected** visitors / guests / callers / company
▶ a / an **regular** / **unwelcome** visitor / guest / caller
▶ a / an **frequent** / **surprise** / **uninvited** visitor / guest
▶ to **have** visitors / guests / company
▶ to **have got** a visitor / company
▶ to **be expecting** / **entertain** / **invite** visitors / guests
▶ to **welcome** the visitors / guests

visitor [C] a person who visits you: *We've got visitors coming for the weekend.* ◇ *Do you get many visitors?* ◇ *He is still in hospital and is not well enough to receive visitors.*

guest [C] a person that you have invited to your house or to an event that you have organized: *Some of the wedding guests were staying in the hotel.* ◇ *Their names were not on the* **guest list**. ◇ *My father was the* **guest of honour** (= the most important guest) *at the dinner.* ◇ *Li was there* **as the guest of** (= had been invited by) *the President.* See also **guest** → TENANT

caller /'kɔːlə(r)/ [C] a person who goes to a house or other building: *Never open the front door to a caller unless you know the person.*

company [U] (usually used with the verb *have*) (*formal*) guests in your home: *I didn't realize you had company.*

voice *noun*

voice · accent · tone · pronunciation · speech · intonation
These are all words for the way in which people say words or the sounds produced when they speak.

PATTERNS AND COLLOCATIONS
▸ to speak **in** a / an... voice / accent / tone
▸ to speak **with** a / an ... accent / intonation
▸ to **have** (a / an) **excellent / good / poor** accent / pronunciation / intonation
▸ (a) **clear** voice / pronunciation / speech
▸ (a / an) **English / foreign** accent / pronunciation / intonation
▸ a **rising / falling** tone / intonation

voice [C, U] the sound or sounds produced through the mouth by a person speaking or singing: *I could hear voices in the next room.* ◇ *He recognized Sarah's voice.* ◇ *to speak in a deep/soft/loud/husky voice* ◇ *to* **raise/lower your voice** (= to speak louder/more quietly) ◇ **Keep your voice down** (= speak quietly). ◇ *Her voice shook with emotion.* ◇ *'There you are,' said a voice behind me.* ◇ *He was suffering from flu and had* **lost his voice** (= could not speak). ◇ *She has a good singing voice.*

accent /'æksent/ [C, U] a way of pronouncing the words of a language that can show which country, area or social class a person comes from: *He's got a strong/broad Scottish accent* (= one that is very noticeable). ◇ *She puts on a posh accent when she answers the phone.* ◇ *His French is excellent, without a trace of accent* (= without a trace of a foreign accent).

tone [C] the quality of sb's voice, especially expressing a particular emotion: *His tone was faintly mocking.* ◇ *She answered him in a brisk, businesslike tone.* ◇ *Don't speak to me in that* **tone of voice** (= in that unpleasant or critical way). ◇ *Don't you* **take that tone** *with me.*

pronunciation [U, C] the way in which a language or a particular word or sound is pronounced; the way in which a particular person pronounces the words of a language: *a guide to English pronunciation* ◇ *There is more than one pronunciation of 'garage'.* ◇ *She doesn't like having her pronunciation corrected.*

speech [U] the way in which a particular person speaks, especially how clearly they speak: *Her speech was slurred − she was clearly drunk.* ◇ *Clear speech with crisp consonant sounds is very important.*

intonation [U, C] (*phonetics*) the rise and fall of the voice in speaking, especially as this affects the meaning of what is being said: *She's studying intonation patterns in children's speech.* ◇ *In English, some questions have a rising intonation.*

voluntary *adj.*

1 Attendance at classes is purely voluntary.
2 voluntary work

1 voluntary · optional · discretionary
These words all describe sth which sb does, decides or has by choice, not because they have to.

PATTERNS AND COLLOCATIONS
▸ a voluntary / an optional **course / procedure / scheme**
▸ **entirely** voluntary / optional / discretionary
▸ **purely / largely** voluntary / optional

voluntary /'vɒləntri; *AmE* 'vɑːlənteri/ done willingly and by choice, not because you have to do it: *Many people pay voluntary contributions into a pension fund.* ◇ *Attendance at classes is purely voluntary.* ◇ (*BrE*) *He took* **voluntary redundancy**. **OPP** involuntary, compulsory → NECESSARY
▸ **voluntarily** *adv.*: *He was not asked to leave − he went voluntarily.*

optional that you can choose to do or have if you want to: *Certain classes are compulsory, others are optional.* ◇ (*BrE*) *This model comes with a number of* **optional extras** (= things you can choose to have but which you pay extra for). **OPP** compulsory, obligatory → NECESSARY, See also **option** → OPTION

NOTE VOLUNTARY OR OPTIONAL? Voluntary puts the emphasis on choosing to do or have sth without being forced to because of a rule or law; optional puts the emphasis on sth being available for you to choose if you want, when it is sth extra, not an essential part of sth.

discretionary /dɪ'skreʃənəri; *AmE* -neri/ [usually before noun] (*formal*) decided according to the judgement of a person in authority about what is necessary in each particular situation; not decided by rules: *Such awards are allocated on a discretionary basis.*
▸ **discretion** *noun* [U]: *Bail is granted* **at the discretion of** *the court.*

2 voluntary · unpaid · honorary
These words all describe work which people are not paid for or people who do a job without being paid.

PATTERNS AND COLLOCATIONS
▸ **on** a voluntary / an unpaid / an honorary **basis**
▸ voluntary / unpaid **work / service / overtime**
▸ a voluntary / an unpaid **worker / carer / helper**

voluntary /'vɒləntri; *AmE* 'vɑːlənteri/ [usually before noun] (of work) done by people who choose to do it without being paid; (of a person) doing a job without wanting to be paid for it: *I do some voluntary work at the local hospital.* ◇ *The day centre is operated by a* **voluntary organization**.

unpaid /ˌʌn'peɪd/ (of work or time off work) done or taken without being paid; (of a person) doing work without being paid for it: *Many of the children are used as unpaid labour.* ◇ *He chose to take 6 weeks of* **unpaid leave**. ◇ *The canteen is run by unpaid volunteers.*

honorary /'ɒnərəri; *AmE* 'ɑːnəreri/ (of an official position in an organization) held without the person being paid for doing it: *The post of treasurer is a purely honorary position.* ◇ *He became honorary president of the club.*

vomit *verb* See the Topic Map for HEALTH on p.890

vomit · throw (sth) up · be sick · puke · cough · barf · regurgitate
These words all mean to bring food back up from your stomach.

PATTERNS AND COLLOCATIONS
▸ to vomit / puke / cough **up** sth
▸ to vomit / throw up / regurgitate **your food**
▸ to vomit / cough up **blood**
▸ to **want to / make sb** vomit / throw up / puke / barf
▸ to vomit / throw up / be sick / puke / barf **all over sb / sth**
▸ to vomit / throw up **violently**
▸ to be **violently** sick

vomit /'vɒmɪt; *AmE* 'vɑːm-/ [I, T] to bring food from the stomach back out through the mouth: *The smell made her want to vomit.* ◇ *The injured man was vomiting blood.*

▶ **vomit** *noun* [U]: *You must ensure that an unconscious person does not choke on their own vomit.*

‚throw ˈup, **‚throw sth ˈup** *phrasal verb* [I, T] (*rather informal*) to vomit: *The smell made me want to throw up.* ◇ *He had thrown up his dinner.*

be ˈsick [I] (*especially BrE*) to vomit: *I was sick three times in the night.* ◇ *She had been violently sick.* ◇ *I think I'm going to be sick.* ❶ **Be sick** is the normal word for 'vomit' in British English, especially in spoken and more informal written contexts. It is less frequent in American English, where **vomit** is used in writing and more formal spoken contexts, and the more informal **throw up** is used in speech. However, **be sick** is sometimes used in American English as a gentler way of saying 'vomit' or 'throw up'. See also **sick** → SICK 2

▶ **sick** *noun* [U] (*BrE, informal*): *There was a pool of sick on the carpet.*

puke /pjuːk/ [I, T] (*informal*) to vomit: *The baby puked all over me this morning.* ❶ When it is used with an object, **puke** is followed by **up**: *I puked up my dinner.*

▶ **puke** *noun* [U]: *to be covered in puke*

cough [T] to force sth out of your throat or lungs by coughing: *Sometimes she coughed up blood.* ◇ *He coughed the dust out of his lungs.*

barf [I] (*AmE, informal*) to vomit: *Oh no! I think I'm going to barf!*

regurgitate /rɪˈɡɜːdʒɪteɪt; *AmE* -ˈɡɜːrdʒ-/ [T] (*formal*) to bring food that has been swallowed back up into the mouth: *The bird regurgitates half-digested fish to feed its young.*

vulnerable *adj.* See the Topic Map for THE INDIVIDUAL AND SOCIETY on p.894

vulnerable · at risk · helpless · endangered · open to sth · exposed · defenceless
These words all describe sb/sth that is not well protected.

PATTERNS AND COLLOCATIONS
▶ vulnerable / open / exposed **to** criticism, attack, etc.
▶ helpless / defenceless **against** sth
▶ vulnerable / helpless / defenceless **people / children**

▶ helpless / defenceless **civilians / victims**
▶ a vulnerable / an endangered **species**
▶ a vulnerable / a helpless / an exposed **position**
▶ to **feel** vulnerable / at risk / helpless / exposed / defenceless
▶ to **leave** sb / sth vulnerable / at risk / helpless / open to sth / exposed / defenceless
▶ **totally / completely** vulnerable / helpless / defenceless
▶ **highly** vulnerable / endangered / exposed
▶ **increasingly** vulnerable / at risk / exposed

vulnerable /ˈvʌlnərəbl/ weak and easily hurt physically or emotionally: *Exhaustion from their long and fruitless war had left them vulnerable to attack.* ◇ *We should protect the most vulnerable members of our society.*

‚at ˈrisk *phrase* in danger of sth unpleasant or harmful happening: *Butterflies are at risk from attack by birds.* ◇ *Lone parent families with young children are particularly at risk of becoming homeless.* ◇ *If we go to war, innocent lives will be put at risk.* See also **risk** → RISK 1

helpless unable to take care of yourself or do things without the help of other people: *Paul threw up his hands in a helpless gesture of surrender.* ◇ *He lay helpless on the floor.* ◇ *It's natural to feel helpless against such abuse.*

▶ **helplessly** *adv.*: *They watched helplessly as their home went up in flames.*

endangered /ɪnˈdeɪndʒəd; *AmE* -ərd/ at risk of disappearing or being destroyed: *The sea turtle is an endangered species* (= it may soon no longer exist). ◇ *The group has campaigned to save several endangered buildings in the area.* See also **endanger** → THREATEN 2

open to sth not well protected from sth such as attack, injury or criticism: *The system is open to abuse.* See also **lay sb open to sth** → EXPOSE

exposed /ɪkˈspəʊzd; *AmE* ɪkˈspoʊzd/ (of a person) not protected from danger, attack or criticism: *She was left feeling exposed and vulnerable.* ◇ *From the moment of birth, a baby is exposed to all the hazards in the external environment.* See also **expose** → EXPOSE, **exposed** → BARE

defenceless (*BrE*) (*AmE* **defenseless**) weak and not able to protect yourself; having no protection: *I can't believe that we persist in such cruelty to defenceless animals.* ◇ *The village is defenceless against attack.*

W w

wait *verb* See also the entry for EXPECT

---

wait · hang on · hold on · sit tight
These words all mean to stay where you are or delay doing sth until sb/sth comes or sth happens.

PATTERNS AND COLLOCATIONS
▶ to wait / hang on / hold on / sit tight **until** sth happens
▶ to wait / hang on / hold on a **minute / second**

wait [I, T] to stay where you are or delay doing sth until sb/sth comes or sth happens: *She rang the bell and waited.* ◇ *Have you been waiting long?* ◇ *I've been waiting (for) twenty minutes.* ◇ *Wait for me!* ◇ *We're waiting for the rain to stop before we go out.* ◇ *Hurry up! We're **waiting to** go.* ◇ *You'll just have to **wait your turn** (= wait until your turn comes).* See also **await** → EXPECT
  ▶ **wait** *noun* [C, usually sing.]: *We had a long wait for the bus.* ◇ *It took six months for the house to be finished, but it was **worth the wait**.*

hang 'on *phrasal verb (informal, spoken)* used to tell sb to wait for a short time or stop what they are doing: *Hang on – I'm not quite ready.* ◇ *Now hang on a minute – you can't really believe what you just said.*

hold 'on *phrasal verb (rather informal, spoken)* to hang on: *Hold on a minute while I get my breath back.* ◇ *Hold on! This isn't the right road.* ❶ **Hang on** is slightly more informal than **hold on.**

sit 'tight *idiom (written)* to stay in the same place, without moving away or changing position; to stay in the same situation, without changing your mind or taking any action: *We sat tight and waited to be rescued.* ◇ *Shareholders are being advised to sit tight until the crisis passes.*

wake up *phrasal verb*

---

wake up · get up · wake · come to · come round · come around · get out of bed
These words all mean to stop sleeping or to become conscious again.

PATTERNS AND COLLOCATIONS
▶ to wake up / wake / come to / come round / come around **from** sth
▶ to wake up / get up / wake / get out of bed **late / early / in the morning / at seven o'clock**
▶ to wake up / wake / come to **suddenly**
▶ to come to / come round / come around **slowly**

wake 'up *phrasal verb* to stop sleeping: *What time did you wake up this morning?* ◇ *He woke up to find himself alone in the house.* ◇ *Wake up! It's ten o'clock!* **OPP** **fall asleep, go to sleep** → FALL ASLEEP

get 'up *phrasal verb* to get out of bed after sleeping: *She always gets up early.*

wake [I] *(written)* to stop sleeping: *She woke from a deep sleep.* ◇ *They woke to a clear blue sky.* **OPP** **fall asleep, go to sleep** → FALL ASLEEP

NOTE WAKE UP OR WAKE? Wake is mostly used in written English, especially literary English. In everyday spoken English use **wake up.**

come 'to *phrasal verb* to become conscious after being unconscious: *When she came to, the room was in darkness.*

come 'round *phrasal verb (BrE)* to become conscious after being unconscious: *She hasn't come round from the anaesthetic yet.*

come a'round *phrasal verb (especially AmE)* to come round: *'Is she still unconscious?' 'She's just coming around.'*

NOTE COME TO, COME ROUND OR COME AROUND? With **come to** the emphasis is more on the moment of becoming conscious, less on the process; it is more likely to happen *suddenly* than *slowly* and more likely to describe the experience from the point of view of the person who has been unconscious. With **come round/ around** the emphasis is more on the process of becoming conscious, less on the moment; it is more likely to happen *slowly* than *suddenly* and more likely to describe the experience from the point of view of other people looking on, not the person who has been unconscious.

get out of 'bed *phrase* to get out of your bed, especially after sleeping: *I always find it hard to get out of bed in the morning.*

walk *noun*

---

walk · gait · step · stride · tread
These are all words for the way sb walks.

PATTERNS AND COLLOCATIONS
▶ with a / an ... walk / gait / stride / tread
▶ a **light / heavy** step / tread
▶ to have a / an ... walk / gait

walk [sing.] a way or style of walking; the act or speed of walking rather than running: *I recognized her by her walk.* ◇ *He did a funny walk and made the children laugh.* ◇ *The horse slowed to a walk.*

gait /geɪt/ [sing.] *(written)* the way that sb normally walks, especially when this is slightly unusual: *He walked with a rolling gait (= moving forward and from side to side).*

step [sing.] the way that sb walks, often when this shows how they are feeling: *I recognized her quick light step.* ◇ *I quickened my step.* ◇ *There was a new **spring in his step** (= he was walking in a cheerful and lively way).* See also **step** → STEP *noun*

stride [sing.] a way of walking or running with long steps, especially in a determined way: *He entered the clearing with his familiar, purposeful stride.* ◇ *Rooney scored from 20 metres without **breaking (his) stride** (= making it irregular).* See also **stride** → STEP *noun*

NOTE STEP OR STRIDE? Step is used more to describe the speed with which sb walks; **stride** is used more to describe the length of the steps sb takes. You *quicken your step*, but *lengthen your stride.* See also **step, stride** → STEP

tread /tred/ [sing.] *(written)* the way that sb walks, especially the sound that they make: *I could hear his heavy tread on the stairs.* ◇ *She moved with the light tread of a dancer.*

walk *verb*

1 He walked into the room.
2 go walking in the mountains

---

1 walk · step · stride · stroll · pace · march · tread · prowl
These words all mean to move or go somewhere by putting one foot in front of the other on the ground.

PATTERNS AND COLLOCATIONS
▸ to walk / step / stride / stroll / march **to** / **towards** sb / sth
▸ to walk / step / stroll / pace / march / prowl **around** / **round** (sth)
▸ to walk / stroll / pace / march / prowl **up and down**
▸ to walk / pace / prowl **to and fro** / **back and forth**
▸ to step / tread **in** / **on** sth
▸ to walk / step / stride / march **briskly**
▸ to walk / step / stride **quickly**
▸ to walk / step / tread **carefully** / **gingerly** / **lightly**
▸ to pace / prowl **nervously** / **restlessly**
▸ to walk / pace / prowl **the streets** / **corridors**

walk [I, T] (usually used with an adverb or preposition) to move or go somewhere by putting one foot in front of the other on the ground, but without running: *'How did you get here?' 'I walked'.* ◇ *The baby is just learning to walk.* ◇ *The door opened and Jo walked in.* ◇ *I had to walk all the way home.* ◇ *Women have to walk several miles each day to get water.*

step (-**pp**-) [I] (always used with an adverb or preposition) to lift your foot and move it in a particular direction or into a particular place; to move or walk a short distance: *Step forward when your name is called out.* ◇ *I accidentally stepped on her toe.* ◇ *We had to step carefully to avoid the broken glass.* ◇ *She stepped aside to let them pass.* ◇ *Could you step inside for a moment?* See also **step** → STEP *noun*

stride [I] (not used in the perfect tenses; usually used with an adverb or preposition) to walk with long steps in a particular direction, especially quickly or in a determined way: *He strode off in search of a taxi.* ◇ *She strode angrily into his office.* See also **stride** → STEP *noun*

stroll /strəʊl; AmE stroʊl/ [I] (usually used with an adverb or preposition) to walk somewhere in a slow relaxed way, often for pleasure: *People were strolling around in the grounds.* See also **amble**, **saunter** → WANDER

pace [I, T] (usually used with an adverb or preposition) to walk up and down in an area a lot of times, taking regular steps, especially because you are feeling nervous or angry: *She paced up and down outside the interview room.* ◇ *He was pacing the room like a caged animal.* See also **pace** → STEP *noun*

march [I] (usually used with an adverb or preposition) (of a group of people, especially soldiers) to walk with stiff regular steps at the same speed: *Guards were marching up and down outside the building.* ◇ *They marched 20 miles to reach the capital.* ◇ *Troops marched on the town.* ❶ **March** can also be used about an individual person, meaning 'to walk somewhere quickly in a determined way'. See also **march** → MARCH

tread /tred/ [I] (always used with an adverb or preposition) (*BrE*) to put your foot down while you are stepping or walking: *Ouch! You trod on my toe!* ◇ *Careful you don't tread in that puddle.*

> **NOTE** **STEP, STRIDE, PACE** OR **TREAD?** Each of these words has a different set of adverbs that tend to be used with it. You can **step** *briskly, quickly, carefully, lightly* or *gingerly*. You can **stride** *briskly, quickly, angrily, confidently* or *purposefully*. You can **pace** *nervously, restlessly* or *slowly*. You can **tread** *carefully, gingerly, softly, lightly, heavily* or *warily*. However, in American English use **step** instead of **tread**, unless the meaning is figurative: *(figurative) We must tread carefully* (= be careful about how we do this) — *we don't want to offend anyone.*

prowl /praʊl/ [T, I] (*written*) (usually used with an adverb or preposition) to walk around an area, especially because you are bored or anxious and cannot relax: *He prowled the empty rooms of the house at night.* ◇ *Her husband was prowling restlessly around the room.*

2 walk · hike · trek
These words all mean to spend time walking for pleasure.

PATTERNS AND COLLOCATIONS
▸ to **go** walking / hiking / trekking

walk (also **go walking**) [I, T] (*especially BrE*) to spend time walking for pleasure: *We're going walking in the mountains this summer.* ◇ *I walked across Scotland with a friend.* ◇ *Have you ever walked the Pennine Way?*
▸ **walk** *noun* [C]: *Let's go for a walk.* ◇ *She's taken the dog for a walk.* ◇ *It's only a short walk to the beach.* ◇ *There are some interesting walks* (= routes for walking) *around here.* ◇ *He set out on the long walk home.*
▸ **walking** *noun* [U]: *Activities on offer include walking and bird watching.* ◇ *This is superb walking country.*

hike (also **go hiking**) [I] to go for a long walk in the country; to spend time walking in the country for pleasure: *If the weather's fine, we'll go hiking this weekend.* ◇ *You'll need some strong boots for hiking over rough country.* ❶ In American English **hike** can also be used with an object: [T] (*AmE*) *I always wanted to hike the Rockies.*
▸ **hike** *noun* [C]: *They went on a ten-mile hike through the forest.*

trek (also **go trekking**) (-**kk**-) [I, T] to spend time walking for pleasure, especially in mountains and over long distances: *Last autumn we went trekking in Nepal.* ◇ *They trekked the 45 miles across the glacier.*
▸ **trek** *noun* [C]: *They reached the camp after an arduous two-day trek across the mountains.*

wall *noun*

wall · fence · railing · screen · partition
These are all words for structures that separate one space from another.

PATTERNS AND COLLOCATIONS
▸ a **high** / **low** wall / fence
▸ an **internal** wall / partition
▸ a **perimeter** wall / fence
▸ (a) **metal** / **wooden** fence / railings / screen / partition
▸ a **glass** screen / partition
▸ to **erect** a wall / a fence / railings / a screen / a partition
▸ to **put up** a wall / fence / screen / partition
▸ to **build** a wall / fence

wall [C] a long, upright solid structure, made of stone, brick or concrete, that surrounds, divides or protects an area of land; any of the upright sides of a building or room: *a stone/brick wall* ◇ *He sat on the wall and watched the others playing.* ◇ *Hang the picture on the wall* (= attach it to the wall) *opposite the window.*

fence [C] a structure made of wood or wire supported by posts that surrounds, divides or protects an area of land, for example to mark the limits of an area, to keep animals in or to keep people and animals out: *Security guards with dogs patrolled the perimeter fence.* See also **fence sth off** → SEPARATE 2

railing [C, usually pl.] a fence made of upright metal bars; one of these bars: *I chained my bike to the park railings.*

screen [C] an upright piece of furniture or equipment that is fixed or that can be moved to divide a room or to keep one area hidden or separate: *The nurse put a screen around the bed.*

partition /pɑːˈtɪʃn; AmE pɑːrˈt-/ [C] a wall or screen that separates one part of a room from another: *The family had to smash through a glass partition to escape the fire.* See also **partition** → SEPARATE *verb* 2

wallet *noun*

wallet · purse
These are both words for sth that you use to carry money around with you.

PATTERNS AND COLLOCATIONS
▸ **in** sb's wallet / purse
▸ a **leather** wallet / purse
▸ to **steal** / **open** sb's wallet / purse
▸ a wallet / purse **containing** $100, €250, etc.

wallet /'wɒlɪt; AmE 'wɑː-l-; 'wɔː-l-/ [C] a small flat folding case made of leather, plastic or fabric that can fit in your pocket and is used for carrying paper money and credit cards: *a wallet containing credit cards*

purse /pɜːs; AmE pɜːrs/ [C] a small bag made of leather, plastic or fabric for carrying coins and often also paper money and credit cards, used especially by women: *I took a coin out of my purse and gave it to the child.*

wallet

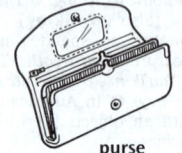

wallet   purse

wander *verb*

wander · roam · drift · amble · saunter
These words all mean to walk slowly around or to a place, often without having a clear purpose or direction.

PATTERNS AND COLLOCATIONS
▸ to wander / roam / drift / saunter **around / about** (sth)
▸ to wander / drift / amble / saunter **slowly**
▸ to wander / roam / drift **aimlessly**
▸ to wander / roam **freely**
▸ to wander / roam **the streets**

wander /'wɒndə(r); AmE 'wɑːn-/ [I, T] (usually used with an adverb or preposition) to walk slowly around or to a place, often without having any clear aim or direction: *The boy just wandered in one day and asked for a job.* ◇ *Visitors are free to wander throughout the grounds.* ◇ *During the day I would wander the streets, asking passers-by for a few cents.*
▸ **wander** *noun* [sing.]: *I went for a wander down by the river.*

roam /rəʊm; AmE roʊm/ [I, T] (usually used with an adverb or preposition) to walk or travel around an area without having any clear aim or direction, perhaps hoping to find sth: *Animals roam freely around the village.* ◇ *Gangs of barefoot children roam the city streets, begging for scraps.*

NOTE WANDER OR ROAM? Both **wander** and **roam** can suggest that sb (or an animal) is free to go wherever they want. **Wander** emphasizes that sb has no clear purpose. **Roam** can suggest that sb is searching for sth, often without knowing exactly what it is or where to find it.

drift [I] (always used with an adverb or preposition) to move or go somewhere slowly or without having any clear aim: *The crowd slowly drifted away from the scene.* ◇ *I spent the next decade drifting aimlessly from place to place.*

amble [I] (always used with an adverb or preposition) to walk in a slow relaxed way, taking your time to get somewhere: *We ambled down to the beach.*

saunter /'sɔːntə(r)/ [I] (always used with an adverb or preposition) to walk in a slow relaxed way: *Rod sauntered by, looking as if he had all the time in the world.*

NOTE AMBLE OR SAUNTER? **Amble** suggests that sb is enjoying taking their time walking somewhere, perhaps stopping from time to time, and not hurrying. **Saunter** can suggest that sb is walking in a casual way because they are feeling cheerful or confident, perhaps in a way that other people find annoying. See also **stroll** → WALK *verb* 1

want *verb*

want · would like sth · wish · like · feel like sth · desire · fancy
These words all mean to have a desire for sth.

PATTERNS AND COLLOCATIONS
▸ sb wants / would like / wishes / likes / desires **to do sth**
▸ to feel like / fancy **doing sth**
▸ **if you** want / wish / like
▸ **if you** feel like **it**
▸ sb **really** wants / would like / wishes / feels like / desires / fancies sth
▸ to **truly** want / wish / desire sth
▸ sb **just** wants / would like / feels like / fancies sth
▸ to **only** want / wish / desire sth
▸ to **always** want / wish / feel like / desire / fancy sth
▸ sb wants / would like / desires sth **very much**
▸ to want / wish **desperately** to do sth

want [T] (not usually used in the progressive tenses) (*rather informal, especially spoken*) to have a desire for sth: *Do you want some more tea?* ◇ *All I want is the truth.* ◇ *I can do whatever I want.* ◇ *What do you want to do tomorrow?* ◇ *'It's time you did your homework.' 'I don't want to!'* ◇ *Do you want me to help?* **❶** Note that you cannot say 'want that…': *I want that you do it quickly.* ◇ *I want it done quickly.* When you use the infinitive after **want**, it must have *to*: *I want study in America.* ◇ *I want to study in America.* See also **want** → DESIRE *noun*

would like sth *phrase* (*rather formal, especially spoken*) used as a polite way of saying what you want or to ask what sb wants: *Would you like a drink?* ◇ *I'd like to think it over.* ◇ *We'd like you to come and visit us.* ◇ (*formal*) *We would like to apologize for the delay.* **❶** In spoken English, *I would like* is nearly always shortened to *I'd like*.

wish [T] (not usually used in the progressive tenses) to want sth to happen or to be true even though it is unlikely or impossible: *I wish I were taller.* ◇ *I wish I hadn't eaten so much.* ◇ *I wish you wouldn't leave your clothes all over the floor.* ◇ *She wished herself a million miles away.* **❶** In formal language, especially in British English, **wish** can also mean to want to do sth: *I wish to speak to the manager.* See also **wish** → DESIRE *noun*, **wish** → HOPE *verb*

like [T, no passive] (not used in the progressive tenses) (*especially BrE, rather informal, especially spoken*) to want to do or have sth: *Do what you like – I don't care.* ◇ *You can dye your hair whatever colour you like.* ◇ *You can come too if you like.* **❶** In this meaning, **like** is only used in sentences with *what, whatever* and *if*. Sometimes people use *if you like* to agree to a suggestion, even though they would not have chosen to do that thing themselves: *'Let's go and see "The Last Samurai."' 'OK, if you like.'* This meaning of **like** is mostly used in British English; in American English it is more usual to use **want**: *Do what you want – I don't care.*

feel like sth *phrase* (not used in the progressive tenses) (*informal, spoken*) to want to have or do sth: *I feel like a drink.* ◇ *He felt like bursting into tears.* ◇ *We'll go for a walk if you feel like it.*

desire [T] (not used in the progressive tenses) (*formal*) to want to have or do sth: *The house had everything you could desire.* ◇ *The dessert can be topped with cream, if desired* (= if you like). ◇ *The medicine did not achieve the desired effect.* See also **desire** → DESIRE *noun*

fancy [T] (not used in the progressive tenses) (*BrE, informal, especially spoken*) to want to have or do sth: *Fancy a drink?* ◇ *I fancied a change of scene.*

war *noun* See the Topic Map for CONFLICT on p.896

war · battle · action · conflict · fighting · combat · warfare · campaign · hostilities · skirmish
These are all words for a situation in which two or more countries or groups of people fight against each other.

warehouse *noun* See also the entry for SHED

PATTERNS AND COLLOCATIONS
- a war/a battle/action/a conflict/fighting/combat/warfare/a campaign/hostilities/a skirmish **with/against/between** sb/sth
- **in** war/battle/action/conflict/fighting/combat/warfare/hostilities
- **in a** war/battle/conflict/campaign/skirmish
- (a) **civil/nuclear** war/conflict/warfare
- (a) **fierce/bloody** action/conflict/fighting/combat/warfare
- (a) **decisive** war/battle/action/conflict/campaign
- (a) **military** battle/action/conflict/combat/campaign
- to **win/lose** a war/battle/conflict/campaign/skirmish
- to **fight** a war/battle/campaign
- a war/a battle/action/a conflict/fighting/combat/a campaign/a skirmish **takes place**
- war/conflict/fighting/hostilities **breaks out/break out**
- a war/a battle/action/a conflict/fighting/combat/a campaign/hostilities **begins/begin**
- a war/a battle/a conflict/fighting/combat/a campaign/hostilities **ends/end**
- a war/a battle/action/a conflict/fighting/combat/warfare/a campaign **continues**
- a war/a battle/a conflict/fighting/combat/warfare/a campaign **goes on**
- the **outbreak of** war/conflict/fighting/combat/hostilities

war [U, C] a situation in which two or more countries or groups of people fight against each other over a period of time: *The two countries were **at war** for eight years.* ◊ *The USA **declared war** on Germany in 1917.* ◊ *The terrorists were charged with **waging war** against the state.* ◊ *My grandfather fought in two **world wars**.* ◊ *The country went to war in 1914.* **OPP** peace → PEACE

battle [C, U] a time when two or more armies meet and fight, especially during a war; a violent fight between two groups of people: *Napoleon was defeated at the Battle of Waterloo.* ◊ *His father had been killed in battle.* ◊ *Many young men were **sent into battle** without proper training.* ◊ *Scores of people have been hurt in running battles with police.*

action [U] (*especially journalism*) fighting in a battle or war: *He was killed during enemy action.* ◊ *He was reported missing in action.* ◊ *I never **saw action** during the war.*

conflict [C, U] a violent situation or period of fighting between two countries: *Peace talks have failed to end the 6-year-old conflict.* ◊ *Conflict between the two groups has left more than 8 000 dead.*

fighting [U] the violent activity that takes place when two or more countries or groups of people fight against each other: *Heavy fighting broke out in the east of the country.* ◊ *There were outbreaks of street fighting in three districts of the city last night.* See also **fight** → FIGHT *verb* 1

combat /'kɒmbæt; *AmE* 'kɑːm-/ [U] fighting, especially during a time of war: *The soldiers are in combat with rebel forces.* ◊ *The troops were locked in hand-to-hand combat.*

warfare /'wɔːfeə(r); *AmE* 'wɔːrfer/ [U] the activity of fighting a war, especially using particular weapons or methods: *He denied his country has developed the capability for chemical warfare.* ◊ *The fighting quickly turned into full-scale guerrilla warfare.*

campaign [C] a series of attacks or battles that are intended to achieve a particular military aim during a war: *The Russian campaign ended with the German defeat at Stalingrad.* ◊ *The terrorists responded with a bombing campaign directed at business and commerce.*

hostilities /hɒˈstɪlətiz; *AmE* hɑːˈs-/ [pl.] (*rather formal, especially journalism*) acts of fighting in a war: *Hostilities between the two countries ended in a ceasefire.* ❶ **Hostilities** is used especially to talk about when fighting begins, ends, stops for a short time or starts again. Collocating verbs include *begin, break out, cease, end, suspend* and *resume.* Phrases include *the outbreak/ cessation/suspension/resumption of hostilities.*

skirmish /'skɜːmɪʃ; *AmE* 'skɜːrmɪʃ/ [C] a short fight between small groups of soldiers, etc., especially one that is not planned: *Minor skirmishes broke out all along the border.* See also **skirmish** → FIGHT *verb* 1

warehouse *noun* See also the entry for SHED

warehouse · depot · repository · store · storehouse · armoury · arsenal · storeroom
These are all words for a place where things can be kept.

PATTERNS AND COLLOCATIONS
- a warehouse/depot/repository/store/storehouse **for** sth
- a repository/store/storehouse **of** sth
- a **food/fuel/goods** depot/store
- a **storage/distribution** warehouse/depot
- a **grain** warehouse/store
- an **underground** repository/store
- a repository/store/storehouse **of knowledge**
- a repository/storehouse **of information**
- sth is **stored in** a warehouse/depot/repository

warehouse /'weəhaʊs; *AmE* 'werh-/ [C] a building where large quantities of goods can be stored, especially before they are sent to shops to be sold: *Police are investigating a fire at a furniture warehouse.*

depot /'depəʊ; *AmE* 'diːpoʊ/ [C] a place where large quantities of sth, especially goods or equipment, can be stored: *Experts are attempting to establish the cause of an explosion at an **arms depot** last night.*

repository /rɪˈpɒzətri; *AmE* rɪˈpɑːzətɔːri/ [C] (*formal*) a place where large quantities of sth can be kept or stored: *The foundation is the largest repository of the artist's work.* ❶ **Repository** can also be used to mean 'a person, place or thing that is full of sth, especially information': *The database represents a huge repository of information.*

store [C] (*often* **stores** [pl.]) (especially in compounds) a place where goods of a particular kind are kept: *The mill ceased operations in 1940 and was used as a grain store.* ◊ *They had trouble keeping rats out of the food stores.*

> **NOTE** DEPOT, RESPOSITORY OR **STORE?** Depot is used more often than **repository** in the context of industry: *There is an inadequate network of freight depots.* **Repository** is often used in a figurative sense: *His grandfather was a repository of local knowledge.* **Store/stores** is used especially in compounds, following the word for the thing that is kept in the store: *grain/food/weapons stores*

storehouse /'stɔːhaʊs; *AmE* 'stɔːrh-/ [C] a building where things are stored; a place or thing that has a lot of sth: *A quantity of oats had been stolen from one of the storehouses during the night.* ◊ *This book is a storehouse of useful information.* ◊ *Italy is a storehouse of fine singers.*

armoury (*BrE*) (*AmE* **armory**) /'ɑːməri; *AmE* 'ɑːrm-/ [C] a place where weapons and armour are kept: *Several guns had been stolen from the palace armoury.*

arsenal /'ɑːsənl; *AmE* 'ɑːrs-/ [C] a building where military weapons and explosives are made or stored: *The building was used as an arsenal until the eighteenth century.*

storeroom /'stɔːruːm; -rʊm/ [C] a room used for storing things: *The room at the back was a storeroom for spare cables and lighting equipment.*

warn *verb*

warn · caution · alert · tip sb off
These words all mean to tell sb about sth bad that is going to happen so that they can do sth about it.

PATTERNS AND COLLOCATIONS
- to warn/caution (sb) **against** sth
- to warn sb/tip sb off **about** sth
- to warn/caution/alert sb/tip sb off **that...**
- to warn/alert/tip off the **police/authorities**

warn [T, I] to tell sb about sth dangerous or unpleasant, so that they can avoid it; to strongly advise sb to do or not to do sth in order to avoid danger or punishment: *I tried to warn him, but he wouldn't listen.* ◊ *He warned us against pickpockets.* ◊ *I had been warned what to expect.* ◊ *She **warned** Billy **to** keep away from her daughter.* ◊ *The* commander had been **warned of** the attack. ◇ 'I'm warning you!' said James, losing his patience. ◇ The guidebook warns against walking alone at night.

caution /'kɔːʃn/ [I, T] (formal) to tell sb about the possible dangers or problems of sth: I would caution against getting too involved. ◇ The government cautioned that pay increases could lead to job losses.

alert /ə'lɜːt; AmE ə'lɜːrt/ [T] to tell sb about a dangerous or urgent situation so that they can do sth about it: Neighbours quickly alerted the emergency services. ◇ Alerted by a noise downstairs, he sat up and turned on the light. See also **alert** → WATCH noun

‚tip sb 'off phrasal verb (**-pp-**) (rather informal) to tell sb secretly about sth that is going to happen, especially sth illegal or sth that will give them an advantage in business: Three men were arrested after police were tipped off about the raid. ◇ He allegedly tipped off his friends, who sold shares in advance of the news becoming public.

warning noun

warning · notice · alarm · alert · tip-off · caution
These are all words for a statement that tells sb that sth bad may happen.

PATTERNS AND COLLOCATIONS
▸ warning/ notice **of** sth
▸ warning/ notice **that**...
▸ **without** warning/ notice
▸ **adequate / advance / ample / prior / written** warning/ notice
▸ a **flood / bomb / health** warning/ alert
▸ to **give / receive** warning/ notice/ a tip-off
▸ to **sound** a warning/ an alarm/ an alert/ a note of caution

warning [C, U] a statement or event that tells sb that sth bad or unpleasant may happen in the future so that they can try to avoid it: Doctors issued **a warning against** eating any fish caught in the river. ◇ All tobacco products are required to carry a **government health warning**. ◇ Let me give you **a word of warning**. ◇ The bridge collapsed without any warning.

notice [U] information or a warning given in advance of sth that is going to happen, often as part of a plan; a formal letter saying that you will or must leave your job or house: You must give one month's notice of your intention to move out of the property. ◇ Prices may be altered without notice. ◇ The bar is closed **until further notice** (= until you are told that it is open again). ◇ He has **handed in his notice** (= his letter resigning from his job).

alarm [C, usually sing.] a loud noise or a signal that warns people of danger or a problem: I hammered on all the doors to **raise the alarm**. See also **alarm** → ALARM

alert /ə'lɜːt; AmE ə'lɜːrt/ [C] an official warning to people to be prepared to deal with sth dangerous or difficult: A flood alert has been issued in the city after last night's heavy rain. ◇ a bomb alert See also **alert** → WATCH noun

'tip-off [C] (informal) secret information that sb gives, for example to the police, to warn them about an illegal activity that is going to happen: The man was arrested after an anonymous tip-off.

caution /'kɔːʃn/ [U, C] (formal) a warning or a piece of advice about a possible danger or risk: Some companies have sounded a note of caution about the outlook for the second half of this year. ◇ Some cautions must be kept in mind when interpreting these results.

wash verb

wash · bath/bathe · shower · freshen (yourself) up · wash up · clean yourself up
These words all mean to make yourself or sb else clean using water and usually soap.

PATTERNS AND COLLOCATIONS
▸ to wash/ shower **quickly**
▸ to wash/ bath/ bathe/ shower **and change/ dress**

wash [I, T] (especially BrE) to make yourself clean using water and usually soap: I washed and changed before going out. ◇ She was no longer able to wash herself. ❶ In British English you can also say have a wash. In American English it is more usual to be more specific and say how you wash yourself: He washed his face. ◇ I took a shower. See also **wash** → BATH noun, **wash** → CLEAN verb

bath /bɑːθ; AmE bæθ/ (BrE) (AmE **bathe**) /beɪð/ [T] to give a bath to sb: He never bathed the kids when they were little. ❶ It is also possible to use **bath** or **bathe** without an object, meaning 'to have a bath', but this use is old-fashioned. It is much more common to say have a bath (BrE) or take a bath (AmE). See also **bath** → BATH noun

shower [I] to wash yourself under a shower: She showered and dressed and went downstairs. ❶ It is more common to say have a shower (BrE) or take a shower (AmE). See also **shower** → BATH noun

‚freshen 'up, **‚freshen yourself 'up** phrasal verb to wash and make yourself look clean and tidy, but usually without having a bath or shower: I'll just go and freshen up before supper. ◇ She kicked off her shoes and freshened herself up in the bathroom. See also **tidy** → TIDY

‚wash 'up phrasal verb (AmE) to wash your face and hands: Go get washed up — it's time to eat. ❶ In British English **wash up** means 'to wash plates, pans and other things after a meal': Since you made lunch, I'll wash up. See also **wash** → CLEAN verb

‚clean yourself 'up, **get (yourself) ‚cleaned 'up** phrasal verb (AmE) to wash yourself, for example by having a shower: You need to clean yourself up — you've been outside all day.

waste noun

waste · garbage · rubbish · trash · litter · debris · scrap · refuse
These are all words for things that are no longer needed and are thrown away or left somewhere.

PATTERNS AND COLLOCATIONS
▸ **organic** waste/ garbage/ rubbish/ debris
▸ **household / domestic** waste/ garbage/ rubbish/ trash/ refuse
▸ to **dump** waste/ garbage/ rubbish/ trash/ debris/ refuse
▸ to **produce** waste/ garbage/ rubbish/ trash/ debris
▸ to **take out** the garbage/ rubbish/ trash
▸ waste/ garbage/ rubbish/ trash/ refuse **disposal / collection**
▸ a waste/ garbage/ rubbish/ trash **dump**
▸ a garbage/ rubbish/ trash/ scrap **heap**
▸ a waste/ rubbish/ trash/ litter **bin**
▸ a garbage/ trash **can**

waste [U] (also (technical **wastes** [pl.]) materials that are no longer needed and are thrown away: Around four million tons of industrial waste are disposed of each year. ◇ the disposal of toxic/radioactive wastes ◇ Waste water is pumped from the factory into a nearby river.

garbage [U] (especially AmE) waste, especially food and other wet material: The garbage cans had just been emptied. ◇ The canal is full of garbage and bits of wood.

rubbish [U] (especially BrE) waste, especially paper, cardboard and other dry material that is thrown away by individual people and households: The streets were littered with rubbish. ◇ Over a third of British household rubbish is packaging. See also **junk** → THING 3

trash [U] (AmE) waste, especially paper, cardboard and other dry material: The subway entrance was blocked with trash. ◇ What are these letters doing in the trash? ◇ Don't forget to take out the trash.

litter [U] small pieces of rubbish/trash such as paper, cans and bottles, that people have left lying in a public place: There will be fines for people who **drop litter**.

debris /'debriː; 'deɪ-; AmE də'briː/ [U] (formal) pieces of material that are left somewhere where they are not wanted: Clear away leaves and other garden debris from the pond.

scrap [U] things that are not wanted or cannot be used for their original purpose, but which have some value for the material they are made of: *We sold the car **for scrap*** (= so that any good parts could be used again). ◊ *scrap metal/ iron* See also **scrap** → REMOVE 1

refuse /ˈrefjuːs/ [U] (*formal*) waste material that has been thrown away: *Domestic refuse can be burnt to produce electricity.*

> **NOTE** WASTE, GARBAGE, RUBBISH, TRASH OR REFUSE?
> **Rubbish** is the usual word in British English for the things that you throw away because you no longer want or need them. **Garbage** and **trash** are both used in American English. Inside the home, **garbage** tends to mean waste food and other wet material; **trash** more often refers to paper, cardboard and dry material, although you can in fact use either word for either type of waste. **Waste** is used especially when it is considered in very large amounts, and is not often used in the context of the home. It is a general word which can also refer to the solids and liquids that the human body no longer needs: *There were no toilet facilities and no way to dispose of human waste in a sanitary manner.* In British English you put your **rubbish** in a *dustbin* in the street to be collected by the *dustmen*. In American English your **garbage** and **trash** go in a *garbage/trash can* in the street and is collected by *garbage men/collectors*. **Refuse** is a formal word and is used in both British and American English. *Refuse collector* is the formal word for a dustman or garbage collector. See also **junk** → THING 3

waste *verb*

waste · lose · throw sth away · squander · blow · splurge
These words all mean to use or spend a lot of sth, especially on sth that is not necessary or useful.

PATTERNS AND COLLOCATIONS
▸ to waste/ lose/ throw away/ squander/ blow/ splurge sth **on** sth
▸ to waste/ lose/ throw away/ squander/ blow/ splurge **money**
▸ to waste/ lose/ throw away/ squander/ blow a **fortune**
▸ to waste/ lose/ throw away/ squander/ blow a/ an **chance/ opportunity**
▸ to waste/ throw away/ squander your **life**

waste [T] (*disapproving*) to use more money, time, food, energy, etc. than is necessary or useful; to not make good or full use of a person or opportunity; to offer or say sth good where it is not valued: *Why waste money on clothes you don't need?* ◊ *You're **wasting your time** trying to explain it to him* (= because he will not understand). ◊ *His talents are wasted in that job.* ◊ *You're wasted as a sales manager – you should have been an actor.* ◊ *Don't waste your sympathy on her – she got what she deserved.* See also **wasteful** → EXTRAVAGANT
▸ **waste** *noun* [U, sing.]: *I hate unnecessary waste.* ◊ *I hate to see good food **go to waste*** (= be thrown away). ◊ *These meetings are a complete waste of time.*

lose [T] to waste time, money or an opportunity: *We lost twenty minutes changing a tyre.* ◊ *Hurry – **there's no time to lose.*** ◊ *We lost a lot of money on that deal.* ❶ **Lose** in this meaning is less disapproving than **waste**: it often suggests that time or money has been wasted through an unfortunate accident rather than through sb's fault.

‚throw sth aˈway *phrasal verb* (*rather informal, disapproving*) to waste your life or an opportunity or money in a stupid or careless way: *You had everything you ever wanted and you threw it all away.* ◊ *The team threw away a three-goal lead.*

squander /ˈskwɒndə(r)/; *AmE* ˈskwɑːn-/ [T] (*disapproving*) to waste money, time, energy or an opportunity in a stupid or careless way: *The company squandered millions on two dead-end projects.* ◊ *The team squandered several good scoring chances.*

blow [T] (*informal, disapproving*) to waste money or an opportunity in a stupid or careless way: *He inherited over a million dollars and blew it all on drink and gambling.* ◊ *You had your chance and you **blew it**.*

> **NOTE** THROW STH AWAY, SQUANDER OR BLOW? **Blow** is the most informal of these and **squander** the least. **Throw away** is used less to talk about money and more to talk about other things. **Blow** is mostly used to talk about money and in the phrases *blow your chances* and *blow it*.

splurge [T, I] (*informal, sometimes disapproving*) to spend a lot of money at one time on sth that you do not really need: *He splurged his whole week's wages on a champagne dinner.*

watch *noun*

watch · guard · vigil · alert
These are all words for a situation when people are watching sb/sth in case sth bad happens.

PATTERNS AND COLLOCATIONS
▸ **on** watch/ guard/ alert
▸ a **close** watch/ guard
▸ a **round-the-clock** watch/ guard/ vigil
▸ to **keep** watch/ guard/ a vigil
▸ to **mount** a watch/ (a) guard

watch [sing., U] the act of watching sb/sth carefully in case of possible danger or problems: *The government is keeping a close watch on how the situation develops.* ◊ *Go in and see if you can find it in his study. I'll keep watch for you* (= watch and warn you if sb is coming). See also **watch** → MONITOR *verb*

guard [U] the act or duty of protecting property, places or people from attack or danger; the act or duty of preventing prisoners from escaping: *Two sentries stood on guard* (= at their post, on duty). ◊ *The escaped prisoner was brought back **under** armed **guard**.* See also **guard** → GUARD *noun*, **guard** → PROTECT *verb*

vigil /ˈvɪdʒɪl/ [U] the act of staying awake for a long time, especially at night, in order to watch a sick person, say prayers or protest against sth: *His parents kept a round-the-clock vigil at his bedside.* ◊ *Students held a candlelit vigil against the war.*

alert /əˈlɜːt; *AmE* əˈlɜːrt/ [U, sing.] a situation in which people are watching for danger or an emergency and ready to deal with it: *Police are warning the public to be **on the alert** for suspicious packages.* ◊ *More than 5 000 troops have been placed **on full alert**.* ◊ *Following the bomb blast, local hospitals have been put **on red alert**.* See also **alert** → WARNING *noun*, **alert** → WARN *verb*, **alert to sth** → AWARE

wave *noun*

1 Huge waves were breaking on the shore.
2 a wave of fear/desire
3 a wave of violence

1 **wave · sea · ripple · swell**
These are all words for a raised line that moves across the surface of liquid, especially the sea.

PATTERNS AND COLLOCATIONS
▸ a **small/ little** wave/ ripple
▸ a **big/ large** wave/ swell
▸ to **make** waves/ ripples
▸ to **send** waves/ ripples across sth
▸ a wave/ swell **breaks/ surges**

wave [C] a raised line of water that moves across the surface of the sea or other area of water: *Huge waves were breaking on the shore.* ◊ *The pool has a wave machine* (= for making waves). See also **tidal wave** → FLOOD 1

sea [C] (also **seas** [pl.]) the movement of the waves of the sea: *The sea was very calm.* ◇ *A boy drowned last night after being swept into* **rough seas** *by a large wave.* See also **sea** → SEA

ripple [C] a small wave on the surface of a liquid, especially water in a lake, river or pond: *The air was so still that there was hardly a ripple on the pond's surface.*

swell [C, usually sing.] the movement of the sea when it rises and falls without the waves breaking; a large wave before it breaks: *The boat was caught in a* **heavy swell***.*

---

2 wave · rush · surge · ripple · thrill

These are all words for a sudden increase in sth, especially a feeling.

wave [C] a sudden increase in a feeling: *Suddenly a wave of guilt washed over her.* ◇ *Guilt and horror flooded her* **in waves***.*

rush [sing.] a sudden strong feeling or sign of strong feeling: *She felt a rush of blood to her cheeks.* ◇ *You often get an* **adrenalin rush** *as the race begins.* ❶ In this meaning **rush** is usually followed by *of*, except in the phrase *adrenalin rush*.

surge /sɜːdʒ; *AmE* sɜːrdʒ/ [C] a sudden strong feeling: *She felt a sudden surge of anger.* ◇ *A huge surge of emotion swept through her.* ❶ In this meaning **surge** is usually followed by *of*, except in the phrase *adrenalin surge*. See also **surge** → INCREASE *noun*

NOTE WAVE, RUSH OR SURGE? **Wave** suggests a feeling that comes, grows stronger, and then grows weaker again. Feelings may come *in waves* if this experience is repeated several times. Both **rush** and **surge** suggest that a feeling comes more suddenly, faster and more strongly than with **wave**, but it usually comes only once: *Guilt and horror flooded her in rushes/surges.* A **rush** of feeling may be more sudden than a **surge**, but a **surge** may be stronger.

ripple [C] (usually followed by *of*) (*written*) a feeling that gradually spreads through a person or group of people: *A ripple of fear passed through him.* ◇ *The announcement sent a ripple of excitement through the crowd.*

thrill [C] (usually followed by *of*) a sudden feeling that you feel in your body, especially a mixture of excitement and pleasure: *A thrill of alarm ran through him.*

---

3 wave · outbreak · epidemic · spate · rash

These are all words for a sudden increase in a particular activity.

wave [C] (*especially journalism*) a sudden increase in a particular activity, often sth unpleasant: *A wave of violence swept the country.* ◇ *How are the police dealing*

with the latest **crime wave**? ◇ *The first wave of immigration came in the 1950s.* ❶ **Wave** is often used to describe activities that increase and decrease several times over a period of time; you can talk about a *new/fresh wave* of sth or *the first/second/next/latest wave* of sth.

outbreak /ˈaʊtbreɪk/ [C] the sudden start of sth unpleasant, especially violence or a disease: *the outbreak of war* ◇ *an outbreak of hostilities/typhoid* ◇ *Outbreaks of rain are expected in the afternoon.* See also **break out** → BREAK OUT

epidemic /ˌepɪˈdemɪk/ [C] a large number of cases of a particular disease happening at the same time in a particular community; a sudden rapid increase in how often sth bad happens: *An epidemic of measles broke out, and over 200 children died.* ◇ *Car theft is now reaching* **epidemic proportions***.* ❶ **Epidemic** can be used to talk about both the spread of an infectious disease and a large number of cases of diseases such as cancer and heart disease.

spate [C, usually sing.] (always followed by *of*) (*especially journalism*) a series of often unpleasant things that happen over a short period of time: *The bombing was the latest in a spate of terrorist attacks.*

rash [sing.] (always followed by *of*) (*especially journalism*) a series of often unpleasant things that happen over a short period of time: *Rising prices are the result of the recent rash of strikes in the steel industry.* ◇ *This is the latest in the recent rash of movies about life in prison.*

NOTE SPATE OR RASH? In many cases you can use either word. **Rash** is usually used to talk about *thefts, strikes, accidents* and *complaints*, but it is also often found in contexts relating to new *films, movies, books* and *newspaper headlines*. **Spate** is used more frequently than **rash** to talk about violence and other types of crime. Typical collocates of **spate** are *attacks, bombings, burglaries, incidents, muggings* and *thefts*.

---

way *noun*

1 in a friendly way
2 the easiest way to do it
3 the quickest way home

---

1 way · approach · style · manner

These are all words for the particular way in which sb does sth.

way [C] how sb does sth; how sth happens: *Try to approach this in a sensible way.* ◇ *He has a way of staring at you that is very unnerving.* ◇ *You won't impress the judges that way.* ◇ *I like* **the way (that)** *you did that.* ◇ *Infectious diseases can be passed on in several different ways.*

approach [C] a way of thinking about or dealing with a problem or subject: *The school has adopted a firmer* **approach to** *discipline.* ◇ *She favoured the direct approach.* See also **approach** → TACKLE *verb*

style [C] the particular way in which a person does sth or deals with other people: *His aggressive style of play sometimes got him into trouble.* ◇ *What's her teaching style like?* ◇ *I like your style!* ◇ *Caution was not her style* (= not the way she usually behaved)*.*

manner [sing.] (*formal*) a particular way in which sb does sth or sth happens, especially the way that sb behaves towards people: *She answered in a business-like manner.* ◇ *The manner in which the decision was taken is extremely regrettable.*

2 way · method · technique · means · process · mechanism · system · methodology

These are all words for a particular thing that you do in order to do or achieve sth.

PATTERNS AND COLLOCATIONS
▸ a method / technique / means / process / mechanism / system / methodology **for** (doing) sth
▸ a way / method / technique / means / system / methodology **of** (doing) sth
▸ an **effective** way / method / technique / means / mechanism / system
▸ a **good / practical** way / method / technique / means / system
▸ a **simple** way / method / technique / means / process / system
▸ a / the **traditional** way / method / technique / means / system / methodology
▸ a **new** way / method / technique / means / system / methodology
▸ an **alternative** way / method / technique / means / methodology
▸ to **use** a method / technique / means / process / system / methodology
▸ to **adopt** a method / technique / system / methodology
▸ to **devise / develop** a way / method / technique / means / process / system / methodology
▸ to **find** a way / method / means / system
▸ to **change** a way / method / system / methodology
▸ a method / technique / mechanism / system **works**

way [C] the things that you do in order to do or achieve sth: *There are several possible ways of dealing with this problem.* ◇ *That's not the way to hold a pair of scissors!* ◇ *I prefer to do things the easy way.* ◇ *We should have done it* **my way!** ◇ *I generally get what I want* **one way or another.**

method [C] one of the ways in which sth can be done, especially a way that is made up of several stages: *He's quite critical of modern teaching methods.* ◇ *This is a simpler method for making bread.* ◇ *There are various methods of dealing with this problem.*

technique /tek'niːk/ [C] a particular way of doing sth, especially one that involves a special skill or that you need to learn and practise: *The artist combines different techniques in the same painting.* ◇ *You will learn various techniques for dealing with difficult customers.* ◇ *He needs to improve his throwing technique.*

means [C] something that you use or do as a way of achieving sth: *TV is a highly effective means of communication.* ◇ *What* **means of transport** *did they use?* ◇ *We will use whatever means are necessary.* ◇ *The load was lifted* **by means of** (= using) *a crane.*

process [C] a method of doing or making sth, especially one used in industry: *They are made using the most advanced manufacturing processes.* See also **process** → TREAT *verb* 2

mechanism /'mekənɪzəm/ [C] (*rather formal*) a way of achieving sth: *Various mechanisms are in place for dealing with emergencies.* ◇ *Simple repetition was regarded as an effective learning mechanism.*

system [C] a particular way of doing sth, especially one that involves a planned and fixed series of actions that you follow each time: *This is a highly effective system for storing data.* ◇ *Once your systems are in place you can concentrate on the main focus of your business.* See also **systematic** → EFFICIENT

methodology /ˌmeθə'dɒlədʒi; AmE -'dɑːl-/ [U, C] (*formal*) a set of methods and principles used to perform a particular activity: *Please give a brief outline of your research methodology.* ◇ *Different people adopt different methodologies.*

3 way · route · direction · line · path · orbit · course · bearing

These are all words for the road, or piece of land, water or air that you travel on, across or through in order to get somewhere.

PATTERNS AND COLLOCATIONS
▸ a way / route / path / course **to** sth
▸ a / the way / route / line / path / course **from…to…**
▸ a / the way / route / line / path / course **through / along / across** sth
▸ **on** the way / route / path
▸ **in** sb / sth's way / line / path
▸ **in** the direction / line / path **of** sth
▸ the **right** way / route / direction / path / course
▸ the **shortest** way / route / line / path / course
▸ the **quickest** way / route
▸ a **straight** line / path / course
▸ the **opposite / other** way / direction
▸ a **direct** way / route / line / path / course
▸ to **follow** a way / a route / a line / a path / an orbit / a course
▸ to **take** a way / route / direction / path / course
▸ to **block** the / sb / sth's way / route / line / path
▸ to **know** the way / route
▸ to **change** direction / course

way [C, usually sing.] the route or road that you must take in order to reach a place; the route that sb / sth is moving along; the general position that sb / sth is moving towards: *I stopped to* **ask the way.** ◇ *They had to* **fight their way** *through the crowd.* ◇ **Get out of my way!** *I'm in a hurry!* ◇ *She was* **going my way,** *so we talked as we walked.* ◇ *They bought some supplies on the way.* ◇ *Which way did they go?* ◇ *He narrowly avoided a car coming the other way* (= towards him).

route [C] a way that you follow to get from one place to another, especially one that you plan in advance; a fixed way along which a bus, train, etc. regularly travels or goods are regularly sent: *It's the best route into the city from the south.* ◇ *Motorists are being advised to take an alternative route.* ◇ *We'll have to plan our route carefully.* ◇ *We took the* **scenic route** *through the hills.* ◇ *Is the hotel on a* **bus route?** ◇ *These were the ancient trade routes between Europe and Asia.*
▸ **route** *verb* [T] (usually used with an adverb or preposition): *Satellites route data all over the globe.*

direction [C, U] the general position that sb / sth moves or points towards; the general position that sb / sth comes or develops from: *He ran off in the direction of the river.* ◇ *The plane was flying in a northerly direction.* ◇ *The road was blocked in both directions.* ◇ *When the police arrived, the crowd scattered* **in all directions.** ◇ *I had lost all* **sense of direction** (= I did not know which way to go). ◇ *Support came from an unexpected direction.* See also **direct** → AIM *verb*, **direct** → TAKE 2

line [C, usually sing.] the direction that sb / sth is moving or situated in; a route from one place to another, especially when it is used for a particular purpose: *They followed the line of the river for three miles.* ◇ *Try to keep the boat sailing in a straight line.* ◇ *They were directly* **in the line of fire** (= the direction that sb is shooting in). ◇ *Their aim was to block the enemy's* **supply lines** (= the route that supplies come along).

path [C] a line along which sb / sth moves; the space in front of sb / sth as they move: *The diagram shows the path of the satellite between 10.20 and 10.34.* ◇ *The avalanche destroyed everything in its path.*

orbit /'ɔːbɪt; AmE 'ɔːrbɪt/ [C, U] a curved path followed by a planet or object as it moves around a star or planet: *There are slight changes in the Earth's* **orbit around** *the Sun.* ◇ *The satellite* **went into orbit** *last month.* ◇ *He spent eleven months* **in orbit** (= in space). See also **orbit** → SPIN *verb*

course [U, C, usually sing.] the direction or route followed by a ship or aircraft: *The plane was* **off course** (= was not following the correct route). ◇ *The ship* **set a course for** (= started to sail towards) *the Christmas Islands.*

bearing /'beərɪŋ; AmE 'ber-/ [C, usually pl.] (*technical*) a direction measured from a fixed point using a compass: *The log records the ship's bearings, wind direction and speed.* ◇ *You'll learn how to take your bearings with a compass.* ◇ *They took compass bearings on the tower.*

weak *adj.* See the Topic Map for HEALTH on p.890

weak · frail · infirm · feeble · delicate
These words all describe sb who is not physically strong.

▶ weak / frail / feeble / delicate **health**
▶ to **look** weak / frail / delicate
▶ **very** weak / frail / delicate

weak (of a person or part of the body) not physically strong: *She is still weak after her illness.* ◇ *She suffered from a weak heart.* **OPP strong** → STRONG 1, **strong** → WELL

frail (especially of an old person) weak and thin: *women caring for frail elderly relatives*

infirm /ɪn'fɜːm; AmE ɪn'fɜːrm/ (*rather formal*) ill and weak, especially over a long period of time or because of old age: *Father was becoming increasingly infirm.*

feeble very weak: *He's a bit feeble nowadays.* ◇ *The heartbeat was feeble and irregular.*

delicate (*rather formal*) weak and easily becoming ill: *She has a delicate constitution and has to be careful with what she eats.*

weaken *verb* See also the entry for WORSEN

weaken · make sth worse · add to sth · compound · exacerbate · aggravate
These words all mean to make sb/sth weaker or worse in some way.

▶ to add to / compound / exacerbate / aggravate a **problem**
▶ to add to / compound / exacerbate / aggravate **worries / concerns**
▶ to add to / exacerbate / aggravate **tensions**
▶ to compound / exacerbate / aggravate a **situation**
▶ to make **a situation / a problem** worse
▶ to **seriously** weaken / add to / compound / exacerbate / aggravate sth
▶ to **greatly** weaken / add to / exacerbate / aggravate sth
▶ to **only** add to / compound / exacerbate / aggravate sth
▶ to **only** make sth worse

weaken [T] (*rather formal*) to make sb/sth less strong or powerful: *The team has been weakened by injury.* ◇ *The new evidence weakens the case against her.* ◇ *This new story has severely weakened the President's position.* **OPP strengthen** → STRENGTHEN

make sth 'worse *phrase* (*rather informal*) to cause a problem or situation to be more difficult or less hopeful than it was before: *Don't tell her that – you'll only make things worse.* ◇ *To make matters worse, the value of homes has dropped dramatically.*

'add to sth *phrasal verb* to make a problem or bad feeling worse by introducing new difficulties to the situation: *The bad weather only added to our difficulties.*

compound /kəm'paʊnd/ [T, often passive] (*rather formal, written*) to make a problem, situation or feeling worse or more extreme by introducing new difficulties or facts: *The problems were compounded by severe food shortages.*

exacerbate /ɪg'zæsəbeɪt; AmE ɪg'zæsərb-/ [T] (*formal*) to make an illness, problem or difficult situation worse: *The symptoms may be exacerbated by certain drugs.* ◇ *His aggressive reaction only exacerbated the situation.* **OPP alleviate** → EASE

aggravate /'æɡrəveɪt/ [T] (*formal*) to make an illness, problem or difficult situation worse: *He aggravated an old shoulder injury during the win against Chelsea.* ◇ *Military intervention will only aggravate the conflict even further.* **OPP alleviate** → EASE

NOTE EXACERBATE OR AGGRAVATE? There is very little difference in meaning or use between these words. However, **aggravate** collocates much more strongly with *injury*: *He exacerbated an old shoulder injury.*

weakness *noun*

1 the weakness in this argument/approach/proposal
2 We all have our weaknesses.

1 weakness · limitation · shortcoming · failing
These are all words for sth that is wrong with a system, plan or argument.

▶ a weakness / a limitation / a shortcoming / a failing **in** sth
▶ **despite / in spite of** sth's weaknesses / limitations / shortcomings / failings
▶ a **great / serious / major** weakness / limitation / shortcoming / failing
▶ to **have / suffer from** weaknesses / limitations / shortcomings
▶ to **expose / reveal / identify / highlight** the weaknesses / limitations / shortcomings / failings of sth
▶ to **overcome** the weaknesses / limitations / shortcomings of sth

weakness [C] a weak point in a system, plan, argument or piece of work that makes it less successful than it could be: *Can you spot the weakness in that argument?* ◇ *Try to consider the relative strengths and weaknesses of your work.* **OPP strength** → BENEFIT 1

limitation [C, usually pl.] a limit on what sb/sth can do or how good they/it can be: *This technique is useful but it has its limitations.* ◇ *She has serious limitations as a poet.*

shortcoming /'ʃɔːtkʌmɪŋ; AmE 'ʃɔːrt-/ [C, usually pl.] a fault in a system, service, plan or piece of work that makes it fail in what it is supposed to do: *What are the real shortcomings in the inspection procedure?*

NOTE WEAKNESS OR SHORTCOMING? In many cases you can use either word. However, a **weakness** is usually sth that makes sth fail to be as good as it should be for its own sake: *We need to highlight any potential weaknesses in the proposal* (= or the proposal may not be accepted). A **shortcoming** is usually sth that makes sth fail in its duty to other people: *The report highlights the shortcomings of the prison service* (= where it is failing prisoners/society).

failing [C, usually pl.] a fault in a system, often a serious one: *The enquiry noted several failings in the current system.*

2 weakness · fault · inadequacy · frailty · vice · failing · flaw
These are all words for sth that is wrong with a person's character.

▶ a weakness / a fault / inadequacies / a vice / a failing / a flaw **in** sb / sth
▶ **despite / in spite of** sb's weaknesses / faults / inadequacies / failings / flaws
▶ sb's **own** weaknesses / faults / inadequacies / frailties / vices / failings
▶ sb's **only** weakness / fault / vice
▶ a **great** weakness / fault / vice / failing
▶ a **serious** weakness / fault / vice / flaw
▶ **moral** weakness / faults / inadequacy / failings
▶ **human** weakness / faults / frailty / failings
▶ **personal** weakness / inadequacy / failings
▶ to **have** weaknesses / faults / a vice / failings / a flaw

weakness [C, U] a weak point in sb's character: *She admits that her love of luxury is one of her greatest weaknesses.* ◇ *You need to be aware of your own strengths and weaknesses.* ◇ *He regarded asking for help as a sign of weakness.* **OPP strength** → STRENGTH, **strength** → BENEFIT 1

fault [C] something that is wrong or not perfect in sb's character: *We all have our faults.* ◇ *She was prepared to overlook his faults.* ◇ *I love her for all her faults* (= despite her faults). ◇ *She is blind to all her son's faults.*

> **NOTE** WEAKNESS OR FAULT? A **fault** is often more serious than a **weakness**. A **weakness** is often a weak point that people see in themselves; a **fault** is usually sth that they see in other people.

inadequacy /ɪnˈædɪkwəsi/ [C, usually pl., U] a weakness in sb's character that means they are not as good as they should or could be: *She had to face up to her own inadequacies as a mother.* ◇ *The prime minister's personal inadequacy contributed to the fall of the government.*

frailty /ˈfreɪlti/ [U, C, usually pl.] (*formal*) weakness in sb's character or morals, especially considered as a natural human characteristic: *He has shown enough evidence of human frailty.* ◇ *We are all subject to the frailties of human nature.*

vice [C] a bad or immoral quality in sb's character; sth bad or immoral that sb does: *Of his many vices, his cruelty was the worst.* ◇ (*humorous*) *The occasional cigar is my only vice.* **OPP virtue** ❶ A **virtue** is a particular good quality or habit: *Patience is not one of her virtues, I'm afraid.*

failing [C, usually pl.] a fault or weakness in sb's character, especially where they fail in the care or duty they owe other people: *She was well aware of her own failings.*

flaw [C] a weakness in sb's character: *The hero's fatal flaw is ambition.* ❶ **Flaw** is used especially to talk about the faults of characters in books and plays. A character's **fatal flaw** is a weakness that causes their own failure or destruction.

weapon *noun*

weapon · arms · weapons of mass destruction · WMD · armaments · munitions · the bomb
These are all words for equipment that is used for fighting or attacking sb.

PATTERNS AND COLLOCATIONS
▸ **nuclear** / **conventional** weapons / arms / armaments
▸ to **carry** weapons / arms
▸ to be **armed with** a weapon / weapons of mass destruction / WMD
▸ a weapons / arms / weapons of mass destruction / WMD / armaments **programme**
▸ a weapons / arms / armaments / munitions **factory**

weapon [C] an object such as a knife, gun or bomb that is used for fighting or attacking sb: *He was charged with carrying an offensive weapon.* ◇ *The police still haven't found the murder weapon.*

arms [pl.] (*rather formal*) weapons, especially as used by an army or the police: *Police officers in the UK do not usually carry arms.* ◇ *He encouraged his supporters to take up arms* (= prepare to fight) *against the state.* ◇ *The government called on the terrorists to lay down their arms* (= stop fighting). ❶ An **arms race** is a situation in which countries compete to get the most and best weapons: *The arms race between the superpowers escalated still more.* See also **arm** → EQUIP *verb* 1

weapons of mass deˈstruction [pl.] nuclear, chemical or biological weapons that are designed to kill large numbers of people: *Quite a few countries possess weapons of mass destruction, but few have ever used them.*

WMD /ˌdʌbljuː em ˈdiː/ (also **WMDs**) [pl.] (*especially journalism*) an abbreviation for **weapons of mass destruction**: *The likelihood of terrorists using WMD is low, but their successful use could cause massive casualties.*

armaments [C, usually pl.] weapons, especially large guns, bombs, tanks, etc: *Steel is the most important material in the armaments industry.*

munitions [pl.] ammunition (= the objects fired from weapons) and military weapons, especially those containing explosives: *The attack failed because of a shortage of munitions.*

the bomb [sing.] (*rather informal*) nuclear weapons: *None of the countries that have the bomb have actually used it since World War II.*

wear *verb*

wear · put sth on · dress · get dressed · have (got) sth on · change
These words all mean to have or put clothes on your body.

PATTERNS AND COLLOCATIONS
▸ to wear / put on / have on a **coat** / **jacket** / **suit** / **hat**
▸ to wear / put on / have on a **ring** / **badge** / **watch**
▸ to wear / put on / have on your **glasses**
▸ to wear / put on / have on **make-up** / **lipstick**

wear [T] to have sth on your body as a piece of clothing, ornament, etc: *Do I have to wear a tie?* ◇ *Was he wearing a seat belt?* ◇ *She always wears black* (= black clothes).

ˌput sth ˈon *phrasal verb* to start wearing a piece of clothing, ornament, etc: *Hurry up! Put your coat on.* ◇ *She's just putting on her make-up.* **OPP take sth off** → TAKE STH OFF

dress [I, T] to put clothes on yourself/sb; to wear a particular type or style of clothes; to put on formal clothes: *I dressed quickly.* ◇ *She dressed herself and the children in their best clothes.* ◇ *to dress well/badly/ fashionably/comfortably* ◇ *You should dress for cold weather today.* ◇ *She always dressed entirely in black.* ❶ To **dress up** is to wear clothes that are more formal than those you usually wear, or to put on special clothes, especially to pretend to be sb/sth different: *There's no need to dress up — come as you are.* ◇ *The kids love dressing up.* ◇ *The boys were all dressed up as pirates.* To **dress down** is to wear clothes that are more informal than those you usually wear, for example in an office: *Everyone dresses down on Fridays.* **OPP undress** → TAKE STH OFF

ˌget ˈdressed *phrase* to put all your clothes on: *Get up and get dressed!* ❶ You **get dressed** when you get up in the morning, or when you have not been wearing any clothes, for example because you have just taken a shower. If you are just taking off one set of clothes and putting on different clothes, use **change** or **get changed**. **OPP get undressed** → TAKE STH OFF

ˌhave sth ˈon (also **ˌhave got sth ˈon**) *phrasal verb* (not used in the progressive tenses) to be wearing sth: *She had a red jacket on.* ◇ *He had nothing* (= no clothes) *on.*

change [I, T] to put on different or clean clothes: *I went into the bedroom to change.* ◇ *She changed into her swimsuit.* ◇ *You need to change out of those wet things.* ◇ (*especially BrE*) *I didn't have time to get changed before the party.* ◇ (*especially AmE*) *I didn't have time to change clothes before the party.*

weather *noun*

weather · climate · the elements
These are all words for the conditions of the atmosphere.

PATTERNS AND COLLOCATIONS
▸ **in** (a) good, mild, etc. weather / climate
▸ (a) **hot** / **cold** / **warm** / **good** / **mild** / **harsh** / **severe** weather / climate
▸ to **have** (a) good, mild, etc. weather / climate
▸ to **brave** the weather / elements
▸ **open to** / **protected from** / **sheltered from** the weather / elements

weather [U] the condition of the atmosphere at a particular place and time, such as the temperature, and if there is wind, rain, sun, etc: *wet/fine/summer/windy weather* ◇ *The weather was awful.* ◇ *I'm not going out in this weather!* ◇ *We'll have lunch outside, weather permitting* (= if it doesn't rain). ◇ *a weather map/ chart/report*

climate [C, U] the regular pattern of weather conditions during the year in a particular region: *a temperate/ tropical climate* ◇ *the harsh climate of the Arctic regions* ◇ *the threat of global* **climate change** See also **climate** → AREA 1

the elements [pl.] the weather, especially bad weather with strong wind and rain that can cause damage: *The house was on the cliff, exposed to the elements.* ◇ *The ship had to battle against the elements.*

weight *noun*

weight · pressure · strain · stress · load · mass · density
These are all words for how heavy sth is or how much it presses on sth else.

PATTERNS AND COLLOCATIONS
▸ **under** the weight / pressure / strain / stress / load
▸ (a) **heavy** weight / pressure / strain / load
▸ (a / an) **considerable / enormous / great / immense** weight / pressure / strain / stress
▸ **high / low** pressure / stress / density
▸ to **put** weight / pressure / strain / stress on sth
▸ to **bear** the weight / strain / stress / load
▸ to **take** the weight / strain / stress

weight [U, C] how heavy sb/sth is; the fact of being heavy; an object that is heavy: *It is about 76 kilos* **in weight**. ◇ *Bananas are sold* **by weight**. ◇ *I just hoped the branch would take my weight.* ◇ *Don't put any weight on that ankle* (= don't stand on it) *for at least a week.* ◇ *The doctor said he should not lift heavy weights.* ❶ **Weight** is also used to talk about people becoming heavier/fatter or lighter/ thinner: *She is trying* **to lose weight** (= become less heavy and less fat). ◇ *He's* **put on/gained weight** (= become heavier and fatter) *since he gave up smoking.* ◇ *Sam has a* **weight problem** (= is too fat). ◇ *No more for me. I need to* **watch my weight**.
▸ **weigh** *verb* [T]: *How much do you weigh* (= how heavy are you)*?* ◇ *She weighs 60 kilos.* ◇ *These cases* **weigh a ton** (= are very heavy). ◇ *He* **weighed himself** *on the bathroom scales.*

pressure [U, C] the force or weight with which sth presses against sth else; the force produced by a particular amount of gas or liquid in an enclosed space: *The nurse applied pressure to his arm to stop the bleeding.* ◇ *The door swung open beneath the gentle pressure of Jill's hand.* ◇ *air/ water pressure* ◇ *Check the tyre pressure* (= the amount of air in a tyre) *regularly.* ◇ *She suffers from high* **blood pressure**.
▸ **press** *verb* [T, I] (always used with an adverb or preposition): *She pressed her lips together.* ◇ *He pressed up closer against the wall.*

strain [U, C] (*often disapproving*) the pressure that is put on sth when a physical force stretches, pushes or pulls it, especially when this pressure is too great: *The rope broke under the strain.* ◇ *You should try not to place too much strain on muscles and joints.*
▸ **strain** *verb* [I] (always used with an adverb or preposition): *The dogs were straining at the leash.*

stress [U, C] pressure put on sth that can damage it or make it lose its shape: *When you have an injury you start putting stress on other parts of your body.* ◇ *a stress fracture of the foot* (= one caused by such pressure) ◇ *Engineers calculated the stresses borne by each of the bridge supports.*

NOTE PRESSURE, STRAIN OR STRESS? Pressure can be *heavy, firm, gentle* or *light*. **Strain** and **stress** usually suggest that there is too much pressure. **Strain** is used especially when things are pulled or stretched. **Pressure** and **stress** are used more when things are pressed. **Stress** is often used to talk about pressure on parts of the body, or in buildings and other structures.

load [C, usually sing.] the amount of weight that is pressing down on sth: *Be careful not to demolish a load-bearing wall.* ◇ *Modern backpacks spread the load over a wider area.*

mass [U] (*physics*) the quantity of material that sth contains: *calculating the mass of a planet* ❶ In non-technical language **weight** is used for this meaning.

density [C, U] (*physics*) how heavy a solid, liquid or gas is in relation to its size or volume: *similar stars of the same mass and density* ◇ *Vitamin D deficiency causes a loss of bone density.* ❶ **Density** is measured by dividing the mass of sth by its volume.

welcome *verb*

welcome · appreciate
These words both mean to be pleased to receive or accept sth.

PATTERNS AND COLLOCATIONS
▸ to welcome / appreciate sb's **support / help / comments / view / suggestion**
▸ to welcome / appreciate the **chance / opportunity**
▸ **I'd** welcome / appreciate...

welcome [T] (not usually used in the progressive tenses) to be pleased to receive or accept sth: *I warmly welcome this decision.* ◇ *In general, the changes they had made were to be welcomed.* ◇ *I'd welcome any suggestions.* See also **welcome** → RESPONSE *noun*

appreciate /əˈpriːʃieɪt/ [T] (not usually used in the progressive tenses) to be grateful for sth that sb has done: *Thanks for coming. I appreciate it.* ◇ *Your support is greatly appreciated.* ◇ *I'd appreciate some help.* ◇ *I would appreciate it if you paid in cash.* See also **appreciation** → THANKS

NOTE WELCOME OR APPRECIATE? **Appreciate** is often used to say thank you to sb who has done sth to help you: *Thank you for your help. I do appreciate it.* **Welcome** is used to talk about being pleased that sth has happened: *I welcome this decision.* ◇ *The Party welcomed the Bill.* Both words are used with *I'd...* to ask for sth, but *I'd welcome...* is usually followed by *your/any comments/ enquiries/letters/views/suggestions* and sounds gentle and polite. *I'd appreciate...* is a polite but direct request: *I'd welcome any suggestions* (= I'd be happy to hear your suggestions if you have any to make). ◇ *I'd appreciate some help* (= I need help and I think you should help me, please).

well *adj.* See the Topic Map for HEALTH on p.890

well · all right · OK · fine · healthy · strong · fit · good · great
These words all describe sb who is not ill and is in good health.

all right	well	fine
OK	healthy	great
	strong	
	fit	
	good	

PATTERNS AND COLLOCATIONS
▸ all right / OK / fit **for** sth
▸ all right / OK / fit **to do** sth
▸ to **feel / look** well / all right / OK / fine / healthy / strong / fit / good / great
▸ to **keep (sb)** well / healthy / fit
▸ to **get** well / strong / fit
▸ **perfectly** well / all right / OK / fine / healthy / fit
▸ **very / extremely / apparently** well / healthy / fit
▸ **physically** well / healthy / strong / fit
▸ **fit and** well / healthy / strong

well [not usually before noun] (*especially spoken*) in good health: *I'm not feeling very well.* ◇ *You're looking well.* ◇ *Is he well enough to travel?* ◇ *Wait till you're better before you go back to work.* ◇ *I hope you're keeping well.* ◇ *'How are you?' 'Very well, thanks.'* ◇ **Get well soon** (= a message on a greetings card to sb who is ill). ◇ (*informal*) *He's not a well man.* ❶ **Well** is used especially to talk about your own health, to ask sb about their health or to make a comment on it. It is also used to talk about sb's health at a particular time, for example when they have just recovered from an illness. **OPP** **sick**, **ill**, **unwell** → SICK 1

all 'right [not before noun] (*rather informal, spoken*) not feeling ill; not injured: *Are you feeling all right?* ◇ *I'm all right now.*

OK (also **okay**) [not before noun] (*informal, spoken*) not feeling ill; not injured: *Are you OK?* ◇ *He should be OK for the game on Saturday.*

> **NOTE** ALL RIGHT OR OK? These words are slightly less positive than the other words in this group. They are both used in spoken English to talk about not actually being ill or injured, rather than being positively in good health. Both are rather informal but **OK** is slightly more informal than **all right**. Both words also mean 'safe'. See also the entry for SAFE 1

fine [not before noun] (not used in negative statements; not used in the comparative or superlative) (*especially spoken*) completely well: *'How are you?' 'Fine, thanks.'* ◇ *She was absolutely fine throughout the pregnancy.* ❶ **Fine** is used especially to talk about your own health, especially when sb asks you how you are. It is also used to talk about sb's health when you are talking to sb else. Unlike **well** it is NOT often used to ask sb about their health or make a comment on it: *Are you ~~keeping fine?~~* ◇ *~~You're looking fine!~~*

healthy in good health and not likely to become ill: *Keep healthy by eating well and exercising regularly.* ◇ *She gave birth to a healthy boy.* ◇ *Here are ten tips for a healthy heart.* **OPP** **sickly**, **unhealthy** → SICK 1, See also **health** → HEALTH

strong in good health and not suffering from an illness: *After a few weeks she was feeling stronger.* ❶ **Strong** is often used to talk about becoming healthy again after an illness. **OPP** **weak** → WEAK, See also **strength** → FORCE noun

fit (*especially BrE*) in good physical health, especially because you take regular physical exercise: *I used to go swimming every day in order to keep fit.* ◇ *A reasonably fit adult should have no difficulty with the climb.* ❶ **Fit** can be used in the phrases *fit for sth* and *fit to do sth*, to mean 'well enough to do sth'. It is often used in the context of sport to say that a sportsman or woman has recovered from an injury and is able to play or compete: *He's been ill and isn't fit enough for work yet.* ◇ *He should be fit to play in the match tomorrow.* ◇ *She won't compete unless she's fully fit.* **OPP** **unfit** → SICK 1, See also **fitness** → HEALTH

good (of a person or part of the body) healthy ❶ When used in this meaning about a person, **good** is usually used in negative statements: *I don't feel too good today.* However, in informal American English, it can also be used in positive statements, both as an adjective and an adverb: (*AmE, informal*) *'How are you?' 'I'm good, thanks!'* ◇ *I'm doing good.* ❶ **Good** can also be used to talk about a part of the body that is one of a pair, especially an eye or ear, when the other one of the pair is not healthy or does not work properly: *Can you speak into my good ear?* **OPP** **bad** → SICK 1, **bad** → INJURED

great (*rather informal, especially spoken*) in a very good state of physical or mental health: *I feel great today.* ◇ *Everyone's in great form.* ◇ *She seemed in great spirits* (= very cheerful).

wet *adj.*

1 wet clothes/grass/hair
2 wet weather/a wet day

1 See also the entry for SOFT

wet · moist · damp · soaked · sodden · drenched · saturated

These words all describe things that are covered with or full of liquid, especially water.

moist	wet	soaked
damp		sodden
		drenched
		saturated

PATTERNS AND COLLOCATIONS

▸ wet / moist / damp / soaked / drenched / saturated **with** sth
▸ soaked / drenched **in** sth
▸ sb's **clothes / hair** is/are wet/damp/soaked/sodden/drenched
▸ sb's **coat / shirt** is wet / damp / soaked / drenched
▸ sb's **shoes** are wet / damp / soaked / drenched
▸ wet / moist / damp / sodden / saturated **ground / earth**
▸ wet / moist / damp / saturated **soil**
▸ to **become** wet / moist / damp / soaked / drenched / saturated
▸ to **get** wet / moist / damp / soaked / sodden / drenched
▸ **very / slightly** wet / moist / damp
▸ **absolutely / thoroughly / completely** soaked / drenched / saturated

wet covered with or full of liquid, especially water: *The car had skidded on the wet road.* ◇ *You'll get wet* (= in the rain) *if you go out now.* ◇ *Try not to get your shoes wet.* ◇ *We were all soaking wet* (= extremely wet). ◇ (*BrE*) *My shirt was wet through* (= completely wet). **OPP** **dry** ❶ In this meaning **dry** has no synonyms of its own: *Is my shirt dry yet?* ◇ *Store onions in a cool dry place.* See also **wet** → SOAK *verb*

moist (*often approving*) slightly wet, often in a way that is pleasant or useful: *The warm moist air is perfect for growing fruit trees.* ◇ *a lovely rich moist cake* ◇ *Water the plants regularly to keep the soil moist.* See also **moisture** → MOISTURE, **moisten** → SOAK

damp (*sometimes disapproving*) slightly wet, often in a way that is unpleasant: *The cottage was cold and damp.* ◇ *Wipe the surface with a damp cloth.* See also **damp** → MOISTURE, **dampen** → SOAK

soaked /səʊkt/ *AmE* soʊkt/ (*rather informal*) very wet: *He woke up soaked with sweat.* ◇ *His soaked shirt stuck to his chest.* ◇ (*especially BrE*) *You're soaked to the skin* (= completely wet)! See also **soak** → SOAK

sodden very wet: *I had to get out of my sodden clothes.* ◇ *I preferred not to sit on the sodden grass.*

drenched /drentʃt/ [not usually before noun] very wet: *His face was drenched with sweat.* ◇ *Her clothes were drenched in blood.* See also **drench** → SOAK

> **NOTE** SOAKED, SODDEN OR DRENCHED? Soaked and **drenched**, but NOT **sodden** can be used with *with* or *in*: *soaked/drenched with/in sweat/blood/tears/perspiration* ◇ *~~sodden with/in sweat/blood/tears/perspiration~~.* **Soaked** and **sodden** but NOT usually **drenched** can also be used before a noun: *their soaked/sodden clothes/ sheets* ◇ *~~their drenched clothes/sheets~~.* Things that are **sodden** are usually wet with water, especially rain; it is often used to describe the ground: *the sodden earth/ ground/grass/turf/fields.* Things that are **soaked** or **drenched** can be wet with water, sweat or blood; these words are not used to describe the ground: *~~the soaked/ drenched earth/ground/grass/turf/fields~~*

saturated /ˈsætʃəreɪtɪd/ (*rather formal, written*) very wet: *Saturated soil lacks air, without which plant roots die.*

2 See also the entry for ROUGH 2

wet · bad · rainy

These words all describe the weather when it is not good.

▸ wet / bad / rainy **weather**
▸ a wet / rainy **day / morning / afternoon / evening / night / month / season**
▸ It's wet / rainy.
▸ **very** wet / bad / rainy

wet having or bringing rain: *What's the best thing to do with young children on a wet day?* ◇ *It's wet outside.* ◇ *It was the wettest October for many years.* **OPP** **dry** → SUNNY
bad (of the weather) unpleasant, cold, wet, etc: *On the last day the weather turned bad.* **OPP** **good** → SUNNY
rainy (*rather informal*) having or bringing rain: *We woke up to a rainy day.* ◇ *I went there during the rainy season.* ◇ *This valley is said to be the rainiest place in Britain.* See also **rain** → RAIN noun

> **NOTE** WET OR RAINY? **Wet** is used a little more frequently than **rainy**, especially in slightly more formal contexts such as the weather forecast. However, **rainy** is much more frequent than **wet** in the phrase *the rainy/wet season* (= the season during which it rains a lot in some parts of the world).

whisper *verb*

whisper · murmur · mutter · sigh · mumble · groan · mouth · moan
These words all mean to say sth in a quiet voice.

▸ to whisper / murmur / mutter / mumble / groan / mouth / moan (sth) **to** sb
▸ to whisper / murmur / mutter / mumble **about** sth
▸ to groan / moan **with** pain / pleasure etc.
▸ to whisper / murmur / mutter / mumble **that…**
▸ to whisper / murmur / mutter / mumble / mouth **something / an apology**
▸ to whisper / murmur / mutter / sigh / groan / moan **softly**
▸ to whisper / mutter / sigh / groan / moan **loudly**
▸ to whisper / murmur / mutter **thickly / incoherently**

whisper /'wɪspə(r)/ [I, T] to say sth quietly, using your breath, rather than your voice: *Don't you know it's rude to whisper?* ◇ *What are you two whispering about?* ◇ *'Can you meet me tonight?' he whispered.* ◇ *She leaned over and whispered something in his ear.* **OPP** **shout** → SHOUT
▸ **whisper** noun [C]: *They spoke in barely audible whispers.* ◇ *Her voice dropped to a whisper.*
murmur /'mɜːmə(r); AmE 'mɜːrm-/ [I, T] to say sth in a soft quiet voice that is difficult to hear: *She was murmuring in his ear.* ◇ *She murmured her agreement.*
▸ **murmur** noun [C]: *He took the mug of coffee with a murmur of thanks.*
mutter [I, T] to say sth in a quiet voice that is difficult to hear, especially because you are annoyed about sth: *She just sat there muttering to herself.* ◇ *I muttered something about needing to get back to work.*
▸ **mutter** noun [C]: *She gave a low mutter of apology.*
sigh [T] to say sth with a long deep breath that can be heard, rather than your voice, because you are disappointed, sad or tired: *'Oh well, better luck next time,' she sighed.*
▸ **sigh** noun [C]: *We all **breathed/heaved** a great **sigh of relief** when it was over.* ◇ *'I'll wait,' he said with a sigh.*
mumble [I, T] to say sth in a quiet voice in a way that is not clear, especially because you are shy, embarrassed or mad: *I could hear him mumbling to himself.* ◇ *'Sorry,' she mumbled.* ◇ *She mumbled an apology and left.*
▸ **mumble** noun [C, usually sing.]: *He spoke in a low mumble, as if to himself.*
groan [I] to make a long deep sound because you are disappointed, upset or in pain, or when you feel physical pleasure: *He lay on the floor groaning.* ◇ *We all **groaned** at his terrible jokes.* See also **groan** → CREAK
▸ **groan** noun [C]: *She let out a groan of dismay.*
mouth /maʊð/ [T] to move your lips as if you were saying sth, but without making a sound: *He mouthed a few obscenities at us and then moved off.*

moan [I] to make a long deep sound because you are unhappy or in pain, or when you feel physical pleasure: *He moaned with sheer pleasure.* ◇ *Most of the patients were moaning in pain.* See also **moan** → COMPLAIN
▸ **moan** noun [C]: *A low moan of despair escaped her.*

> **NOTE** GROAN OR MOAN? If you **moan** you may express a stronger feeling than if you **groan**: deep unhappiness or despair, not just disappointment, as well as stronger feelings of pain or pleasure.

whistle *noun*

whistle · boo · jeer · hiss · catcall
These are all words for a sound that people make when they want to show what they think of sb/sth, especially if they disapprove of it.

▸ whistles / jeers / hisses **of** sth
▸ whistles / boos / jeers / hisses / catcalls **from** the crowd / audience
▸ to **draw** boos / jeers
▸ to be **met / greeted** with whistles / boos / jeers / hisses / catcalls
▸ a **chorus** of whistles / boos / jeers / catcalls

whistle [C] the sound that you make by forcing your breath out when your lips are closed, often to show a feeling such as surprise, approval or disapproval: *He gave a low long whistle of surprise.* ◇ *From the audience came applause and whistles of appreciation.* ❶ Unlike most of the words in this group, a **whistle** more often shows approval than disapproval. When it is used to show disapproval it is often combined with another word from the group, such as **jeer**: *He attracted whistles and jeers and rotten tomatoes from the crowd.* See also **whistle** → SING verb
▸ **whistle** verb [I]: *The crowd booed and whistled as the player came onto the field.*
boo [C] a sound that people make to show disapproval of sb/sth, such as an actor, speaker or performance: *'Boo!' they shouted, 'Get off!'* ◇ *The speech drew loud boos from the audience.*
▸ **boo** verb [I, T]: *The audience booed as she started her speech.* ◇ *He was booed off the stage.*
jeer [C, usually pl.] a rude remark that sb shouts at sb else to show that they do not respect or like them: *He walked on to the stage to be greeted with jeers and whistles.*
▸ **jeer** verb [I, T]: *Disappointed fans jeered at the players.* ◇ *The police were jeered by the waiting crowd.*
hiss [C] a sound like a long 's' that is used to show disapproval of sb/sth, such as a speaker, politician or opinion that is expressed: *This comment was met with boos and hisses.* ❶ A **hiss** can seem more unpleasant than a **boo**, because it usually expresses moral disapproval, not just that you do not like a performance.
▸ **hiss** verb [T, I]: *He was booed and hissed off the stage.*
catcall /'kætkɔːl/ [C, usually pl.] a noise or shout expressing anger at or disapproval of sb who is speaking or performing in public: *A chorus of catcalls and boos erupted in the middle of the ballet.*

whole *adj.*

whole · full · total · entire · complete
These words all describe sth which is as big as it can or should be.

▸ a whole / a full / an entire / a complete **day / set**
▸ **the** whole / full / complete **truth / story**
▸ full / complete **details**
▸ full / a total **membership**
▸ your whole / a full / your entire **life**
▸ the whole / total / entire **population**
▸ **unusually / nearly / fairly / reasonably** full / complete
▸ **almost** full / total / complete

whole [only before noun] used to emphasize that all of sth is involved; used to emphasize how large or important sth is: *We drank a whole bottle each.* ◇ *The whole country* (= all the people in it) *mourned her death.* ◇ *She wasn't telling the whole truth.* ◇ *Let's forget* **the whole thing**. ◇ *We offer a whole variety of weekend breaks.* ◇ *I can't afford it — that's* **the whole point** (= that's exactly what I've been trying to explain).

full [usually before noun] including everyone, everything or every part; to the highest level or greatest amount possible: *A* **full refund** *will be given if the item is faulty.* ◇ *The address must be printed* **in full**. ◇ *Many people don't use their computers to their* **full potential**. ◇ *Students should* **take full advantage of** *the college's facilities.* ◇ *measures to achieve* **full employment** ◇ *I've always believed in living life* **to the full**. See also **fully** → QUITE 2, **full name** → NAME

total [usually before noun] being the amount or number after everyone or everything is counted or added together: *The total profit was more than £500.* ◇ *The club has a* **total membership** *of about 300.* See also **total** → COMPLETE *adj.*, **total** → BE *verb*, **total** → COUNT *verb*, **totally** → QUITE 2

▶ **total** *noun* [C]: *You got 47 points in the last game and 18 in this one, making a* **total** *of 65.* ◇ **Out of a total** *of 15 games, they only won 2.* ◇ *The repairs come to over £500* **in total** (= including everything).

entire /ɪnˈtaɪə(r)/ [only before noun] used to emphasize that all of sth is involved, especially when this is a bad thing: *I have never in my* **entire** *life heard such nonsense!* ◇ *The disease threatens to wipe out the* **entire** *population.* See also **entirely** → QUITE 2

> **NOTE** WHOLE OR ENTIRE? **Entire** emphasizes sth more strongly than **whole** and is used especially to emphasize how bad sth is: *I wasted a whole/an entire day on it.* ◇ *We spent the whole day on the beach.* ◇ ~~We spent the entire day on the beach.~~

complete including all the parts that are necessary: *A* **complete** *guide to events in Oxford is available from the office.* ◇ *the* **complete works** *of Tolstoy* OPP **incomplete** → PARTIAL

wide *adj.*

1 a wide range of goods
2 a wide road/river/smile

1 See also the entries for DIVERSE and GENERAL 1
wide · broad · extensive · large-scale · mass · sweeping · wide-ranging · far-reaching · wholesale
These words all describe sth which affects or involves a lot of people or things, or which covers a lot of different subjects.

PATTERNS AND COLLOCATIONS
▶ a wide/ a broad/ an extensive **range**
▶ a broad/ an extensive/ a large-scale/ a mass/ a sweeping/ a wide-ranging/ a far-reaching **programme**
▶ broad/ extensive/ large-scale/ sweeping/ wide-ranging/ far-reaching/ wholesale **changes**
▶ a broad/an extensive/a sweeping/a wide-ranging/a wholesale **review**
▶ a wide/ a broad/ an extensive/ a wide-ranging **debate**
▶ wide/ broad/ extensive/ large-scale/ mass **support**
▶ wide/ broad/ extensive/ sweeping/ wide-ranging **powers**
▶ a wide/ a broad/ an extensive/ a far-reaching **influence**
▶ a wide/ broad/ mass **appeal**
▶ wide/ broad/ extensive/ wide-ranging **interests**
▶ wide/ broad/ extensive **knowledge**
▶ extensive/ large-scale/ mass/ wholesale **destruction**

wide including a large number or variety of people or things; covering a large area: *We stock a* **wide range** *of goods.* ◇ *Jenny has a* **wide circle** *of friends.* ◇ *The museum is trying to attract a* **wider audience**. ◇ *The festival attracts people from a* **wide area**. OPP **narrow** → LIMITED 1

▶ **widely** *adv.*: *The idea is now* **widely** *accepted.* ◇ *He has travelled* **widely** *in Asia.*

broad including a large number or variety of people or things: *The course caters for a* **broad spectrum** *of interests.* ◇ *We have devised a* **broad** *and balanced curriculum.* ◇ *Having children gave her a* **broader outlook** *on life.* ◇ *The novel is about education in its* **broadest sense**. OPP **narrow** → LIMITED 1, See also **broad** → GENERAL 2, **breadth** → RANGE 2

> **NOTE** WIDE OR BROAD? In many cases you can use either word. However, **wide** is used more to talk about a *selection*, a *choice*, a *variety* or a *range* of things or people: ~~a broad audience~~ ◇ ~~a broad circle of friends~~. **Wide**, NOT broad, is used to talk about things affecting a large geographical area: ~~The festival attracts people from a broad area~~. **Broad** is used more to talk about the *affect* of sth on a large number of people: *to have a* **broad appeal** ◇ *to attract* **broad support**. **Broad** is also often used to talk about knowledge and education: *a* **broad curriculum** ◇ **broad experience/knowledge**; as well as in business-related contexts: *There is* **broad support** *amongst clients for the new initiative.*

extensive /ɪkˈstensɪv/ (*rather formal*) including or dealing with a wide range of information: **Extensive research** *has been done into this disease.* ◇ *His knowledge of music is* **extensive**. ◇ *She has* **extensive experience** *in computers.*

large-scale [usually before noun] involving a large number of people or things, especially over a wide area: *The proposals include* **large-scale investment** *in agriculture and industry.* ◇ *Large areas of the forest will be cleared for ranching as part of a* **large-scale development** *plan.* See also **scale** → LEVEL

mass [only before noun] affecting or involving a large number of people or things: *Their latest product is aimed at the* **mass market**. ◇ *The play was so awful that there was a* **mass exodus** *from the theatre at the interval.*

> **NOTE** LARGE-SCALE OR MASS? Both these words are used to talk about business and industry: **large-scale/mass** **production/unemployment**. **Large-scale** in particular is used to talk about business activities that need a lot of resources and affect a wide area: *a* **large-scale enterprise/project/operation**. **Mass** is more often used when a lot of people are affected or involved, especially all together in one place: *the* **mass media/market** ◇ *a* **mass movement/audience/protest/demonstration**. It also collocates with words relating to the killing of large numbers of people: *a* **mass murderer/grave** ◇ **weapons of mass destruction**

sweeping [usually before noun] having an important effect on a large number of people or things: *Shareholders have agreed to a series of* **sweeping changes** *in the organization of the company.* ◇ *Security forces were given* **sweeping powers** *to search homes.* ❶ Typical collocates of **sweeping** in this meaning are *changes*, *reforms* amd *powers*.

wide-ranging (*written*) including or dealing with a large number of different subjects or areas: *The commission has been given* **wide-ranging powers**. ◇ *The activities stimulated a* **wide-ranging discussion**. ❶ Typical collocations of **wide-ranging** are those relating to discussing things and those relating to change: *a* **wide-ranging debate/discussion/review** ◇ **wide-ranging talks** ◇ **wide-ranging reforms/changes/recommendations**

far-reaching [usually before noun] (*rather formal*) likely to have a lot of influence or many effects: *The decision by the European Court will have* **far-reaching consequences**.

wholesale /ˈhəʊlseɪl; AmE ˈhoʊl-/ [only before noun] (especially of sth bad) happening or done to a very large number of people or things: *Localized tensions had developed into* **wholesale slaughter**.

2 wide · thick · broad
These words all describe things that measure a lot from one side to the other; or they are used in measurements of the distance between opposite sides or surfaces.

PATTERNS AND COLLOCATIONS
▸ a wide/broad **road/street/river/stream/staircase/mouth/ smile/grin**
▸ **very/extremely/quite/fairly/rather/relatively** wide/thick/ broad

wide measuring a lot from one side to the other; used to ask about or state the distance between opposite sides of sth: *Her face broke into a wide grin.* ◇ *He wore a jacket with wide lapels.* ◇ *How wide is that stream?* ◇ *It's about 2 metres wide.* ◇ *The road was just wide enough for two vehicles to pass.* **OPP** **narrow** → NARROW, See also **width** → LENGTH

thick measuring a lot or more than normal between opposite surfaces; used to ask about or state the distance between opposite surfaces: *He cut two thick slices of bread.* ◇ *That's a very thick book* (= one that has a lot of pages). ◇ *She padded noiselessly across the thick carpet.* ◇ *Everything was covered in a thick layer of dust.* ◇ *How thick are the walls?* ◇ *They're two feet thick.* ❶ **Thick** is used to talk about solid things such as books, walls, doors and slices or pieces of food, and about layers of a substance or material. **OPP** **thin** → NARROW, See also **thickness** → LENGTH

NOTE WIDE OR THICK? Wide can also sometimes be used to talk about a solid object such as a door. A *wide door* is one that measures a lot from one side to other as you are facing it; a *thick door* is one that measures more than normal between its two main surfaces. A *thick door* is heavy and it is difficult to hear noises through it, as it is with *thick walls*.

broad /brɔːd/ (*often approving, especially written*) wide: *We drove down a broad avenue lined with trees.* ◇ *He's got broad shoulders.* **OPP** **narrow** → NARROW

NOTE WIDE OR BROAD? Broad is less frequent than **wide** and is used more in written English than in spoken English. It is often used to suggest that sth is wide in an attractive way: *a broad avenue lined with trees* ◇ *He was gorgeous — broad shoulders and twinkling eyes.* **Broad** is often used rather than **wide** to talk about parts of the body: *a broad back/chest/face/forehead.* However, both words can be used to talk about a *grin* or *smile*.

wife, husband nouns See also the entry for PART-NER 2

wife · husband · spouse · hubby · missus
These are all words for the man or woman a person is married to.

PATTERNS AND COLLOCATIONS
▸ a **good/loving/faithful** wife/husband
▸ sb's **darling/dear** wife/husband
▸ sb's. **first/second, etc.** wife/husband
▸ sb's **future** wife/husband/spouse
▸ sb's wife/husband-**to-be**
▸ sb's **former/ex-/late/estranged** wife/husband/spouse
▸ to **marry/divorce/leave/walk out on** your wife/husband

wife [C] the woman that a man is married to; a married woman: *This is my wife, Julie.* ◇ *At that time there was an increase in the number of working wives.*

husband [C] the man that a woman is married to; a married man: *He is her second husband.* ◇ *It had been a shock to find himself a husband and father.*

spouse /spaʊs/ [C] (*formal or law*) a husband or wife: *Fill in your spouse's name here.*
▸ **spousal** /'spaʊsl; 'spaʊsl/ adj. [only before noun]: (*AmE, formal*) *spousal consent/support* ◇ *spousal abuse*

NOTE WIFE/HUSBAND OR SPOUSE? Spouse is used in more formal contexts and especially in written English. **Spouse** is useful if you need one word to refer to both male and female partners: *All employees and their spouses or partners are invited to attend.* However, for

speaking in most contexts, it is more usual to say *husband and/or wife* or *husbands and/or wives*: *We are all married, and we all brought our husbands and wives to the party.* See also **partner** → PARTNER 2

hubby [C] (*informal, especially spoken*) a woman's husband: *She and her hubby are both doctors.* ❶ **Hubby** is used especially in spoken English, and is often used without an article or pronoun, such as *a, my, her, etc.*: *She went out, leaving hubby to put the kids to bed.*

missus (also **missis**) /'mɪsɪz/ [sing.] (used after *the, my, your* or *his*) (*informal, especially spoken*) a man's wife: *How's the missus* (= your wife)? ◇ *My missus won't let me smoke in the house.*

wild adj.
1 wild behaviour
2 wild with excitement

---

1 wild · disruptive · unruly · disorderly · rowdy
These words all describe people, behaviour or feelings that show a lack of control or are difficult to control.

PATTERNS AND COLLOCATIONS
▸ wild/disruptive/unruly/disorderly/rowdy **behaviour**
▸ an unruly/a disorderly/a rowdy **crowd**

wild behaving in a way that lacks discipline or control and is sometimes violent: *There is a wild side to him.* ◇ *He had a wild look in his eyes.* ◇ *Those girls have been allowed to* **run wild** (= behave as they like because nobody is controlling them).

disruptive /dɪs'rʌptɪv/ causing problems, noise, etc. so that sth is prevented from continuing or working in the normal way: *She was a disruptive influence on the rest of the class.* ◇ *Working such long hours can be extremely disruptive to home life.* See also **disrupt** → DISRUPT, **disruption** → DISRUPTION

unruly /ʌn'ruːli/ (*rather formal*) very difficult to control: *The police were attacked by an unruly mob.* ◇ *He struggled hard to control his unruly emotions.*

disorderly [usually before noun] (*formal*) behaving in a noisy or violent way in a public place: *He has been charged with disorderly conduct.* ◇ *They were arrested for being drunk and disorderly.* **OPP** **orderly** → EFFICIENT, See also **disorder** → TROUBLE 1

rowdy /'raʊdi/ (*of a group of people*) making a lot of noise and likely to cause trouble: *Some lads were getting a bit rowdy.* ◇ *The meeting had been quite rowdy.*

---

2 wild · frantic · furious · mad · frenzied
These words all describe sth which involves a lot of energy, activity or strong feeling, but in a way that is not organized or controlled.

PATTERNS AND COLLOCATIONS
▸ a wild/frantic/furious/mad **rush**
▸ a wild/frantic/frenzied **effort**
▸ a frantic/furious/frenzied **attempt/pace**
▸ frantic/frenzied **activity**
▸ to **go** wild/mad
▸ wild/mad **with excitement**

wild involving very strong feeling in a way that is not controlled: *Nothing could dull the sense of wild excitement that gripped them.* ◇ *His speech was greeted by wild applause.* ◇ *The crowd went wild.*
▸ **wildly** adv.: *She looked wildly around for an escape.* ◇ *His heart was beating wildly.*

frantic done quickly and with a lot of activity, but in a way that is not organized: *They began a frantic search for the missing child.* ◇ *Things are frantic in the office right now.*
▸ **frantically** adv.: *We worked frantically to finish on time.*

furious /'fjʊəriəs; AmE 'fjʊr-/ done with great energy, speed or anger: *A furious argument broke out.* ◇ *Play was fast and furious in the opening minutes of the game.*

▶ **furiously** *adv.*: *They worked furiously all weekend, trying to get it finished on time.*

mad (*rather informal*) done without thought or control; wild and excited: *Only a **mad dash** got them to the meeting on time.* ◇ (*especially BrE*) *The team won and the fans went mad.* ❶ In American English it would be more usual to say *the fans went wild*.

▶ **madly** *adv.* (only used after a verb): *She was rushing around madly trying to put out the fire.*

frenzied /ˈfrenzid/ [usually before noun] involving a lot of activity and/or strong feeling in a way that is not controlled and often violent or frightening: *He was the subject of a frenzied attack.*

win *verb* See also the entry for DEFEAT

win · prevail · win out · triumph · win the day · come out on top
These words all mean to be successful against sb or in spite of difficulties.

PATTERNS AND COLLOCATIONS
▶ to win / prevail / win the day **against** sb
▶ to prevail / win out / triumph **over** sb / sth
▶ to win / prevail / win out / triumph **in the end**
▶ to **eventually / ultimately** win / prevail / triumph / win the day / come out on top
▶ to **finally** win / prevail / win out / triumph / win the day

win [I, T] to be the most successful in a competition, race, election, argument, battle or war: *Which team won?* ◇ *France won by six goals to two against Denmark.* ◇ *He always won at cards.* ◇ *He narrowly won* (= by a small margin) *the seat for Labour.* ◇ *I think I won the argument.* ◇ *Historians still argue about who really won the war of 1812.* **OPP lose → LOSE**, See also **win → VICTORY** *noun*

prevail /prɪˈveɪl/ [I] (*formal*) (of ideas or opinions) to be accepted, especially after a struggle or argument: *Justice will prevail over tyranny.* ◇ *Fortunately, common sense prevailed.* ❶ **Prevail** can also mean to defeat an opponent in sport. See also **prevail → DEFEAT**

,win 'out *phrasal verb* (*rather informal*) to be successful in spite of difficulties: *It remains to be seen whether the archaeologists will win out over the planners in this dispute.* ◇ *Economic efficiency will always win out in the end.*

triumph /ˈtraɪʌmf/ [I] (*written*) to defeat sb/sth; to be successful, especially in spite of difficulties: *Italy triumphed 3–0 in the quarter-finals.* ◇ *As usual in this kind of movie, good triumphs over evil in the end.*

win the 'day *idiom* (*written, especially journalism*) to be successful against sb/sth, especially at the end of an argument or difficult situation: *Consumer pressure has finally won the day and forced a change in the law.*

come out on 'top *idiom* (*rather informal*) to be successful against sb in a contest or argument: *The older child, stronger and more experienced, is bound to come out on top.*

wind /wɪnd/ *noun*

wind · breeze · draught
These are all words for air when it moves.

PATTERNS AND COLLOCATIONS
▶ a **cold** wind / breeze / draught
▶ a **cool / warm / hot** wind / breeze
▶ a wind / breeze / draught **blows**
▶ to **sway in** the wind / breeze

wind (also **the wind**) [C, U] air that moves quickly as a result of natural forces: *Several trees were blown over in high winds.* ◇ *A chill north wind was blowing.* ◇ *A gust of wind blew my hat off.* ◇ *The weather was hot, without a breath of wind.*

▶ **windy** *adj.*: *a wet and windy day*

breeze [C] a light wind: *A light breeze was blowing.* ◇ *The pools are cooled by the sea breezes.* ◇ *The flowers were gently swaying in the breeze.*

draught /drɑːft/ (*BrE*) (*AmE* **draft** /dræft/) [C] a flow of cool air in a room or other enclosed space: *There's a draught in here.* ◇ *A cold draught of air blew in from the open window.* ◇ *I was sitting in a draught.*

▶ **draughty** (*BrE*) (*AmE* **drafty**) *adj.*: *a draughty room/ corridor*

winner *noun*

winner · champion · victor · medallist · conqueror · prizewinner
These are all words for sb who wins sth.

PATTERNS AND COLLOCATIONS
▶ a winner / victor **over** sb
▶ a **worthy** winner / champion / victor
▶ the **eventual** winner / champion / victor
▶ a **former** winner / champion / medallist
▶ the **overall** winner / champion
▶ a **clear / comfortable / runaway** winner / victor
▶ an **Olympic** champion / medallist
▶ to **emerge as** (the) winner / champion / victor

winner [C] a person, team, animal or thing that wins a game, competition, race, election or prize: *The winners of the competition will be announced next month.* ◇ *England were comfortable winners against Australia last night.* ◇ *Johnson rode his 48th winner of the year* (= in a horse race). ◇ *His first novel was an award winner and a bestseller.* ◇ *He's a three-time World Cup winner and Olympic champion.* ◇ *They were joint winners of the cup.* **OPP loser → LOSER 1**, See also **win → VICTORY** *noun*

champion [C] a person or team that has won a competition, especially in a sport: *He was the undisputed heavyweight champion of the world.* ◇ *The reigning champion will defend her title tonight.* ◇ *He was crowned champion after his fight in Atlanta.* See also **championship → AWARD, championship → RACE**

victor [C] (*written*) a person, team, etc. that wins a battle, competition or game: *The team emerged as worthy victors.* See also **victory → VICTORY**

medallist (*BrE*) (*AmE* **medalist**) /ˈmedəlɪst/ [C] a person who has received a medal, usually for winning a competition in a sport: *The event was opened by the double Olympic gold medallist, Seb Coe.* ◇ *a silver/bronze medallist* See also **medal → AWARD**

conqueror /ˈkɒŋkərə(r); *AmE* ˈkɑːŋ-/ [C] a person who defeats sb in a war or sports competition: *The disease was introduced by the Spanish conquerors in the sixteenth century.* ◇ (*rather informal*) *He is due to meet two of his conquerors at last year's European Championship.* ❶ In the context of sport **conqueror** is rather informal, used especially in newspapers.

prizewinner [C] a person who wins a prize: *The letter was signed by fifty-two Nobel prizewinners.* See also **prize → AWARD**

wipe *verb* See also the entry for BRUSH

wipe · mop · sponge
These words all mean to use sth damp to clean sth.

PATTERNS AND COLLOCATIONS
▶ to wipe / mop / sponge sth **down**
▶ to wipe / mop sth **up**
▶ to wipe / sponge sth **off**
▶ to wipe / mop **sweat** from sth
▶ to wipe / mop your **eyes / forehead / brow**
▶ to **gently** wipe / sponge sth

wipe [T] to rub a surface with sth such as a cloth in order to remove dirt or liquid from it; to rub sth against a surface in order to remove dirt or liquid from it; to remove dirt or liquid from a surface in this way: *She was* *sniffing and wiping her eyes with a tissue.* ◇ *He wiped his plate clean with a piece of bread.* ◇ *Please wipe your feet on the mat.* ◇ *She wiped off her make-up.*

▸ **wipe** *noun* [C, usually sing.]: *Can you give the table a quick wipe?*

mop (-**pp**-) [T] to wash the floor with a mop; to remove liquid from the surface of sth using a cloth: *She wiped all the surfaces and mopped the floor.* ◇ *Do you want some bread to mop up that sauce?* ❶ A **mop** is a tool for washing floors that has a long handle with a bunch of thick strings or soft material at the end.

sponge /spʌndʒ/ [T] to wash sb/yourself/sth with a wet sponge; to remove sth using a wet sponge: *She sponged his hot face.* ◇ *We tried to sponge the blood off my shirt.* ❶ A **sponge** is a piece of soft material which is full of holes and can hold water easily.

wire *noun*

wire · cable · cord · flex · lead
These are all words for a long piece of metal in the form of a thin thread that carries electricity or a signal.

PATTERNS AND COLLOCATIONS
▸ **along / down** a wire / cable / flex
▸ an **electric / electrical** wire / cable / cord / flex / lead
▸ **overhead / underground** wires / cables
▸ a **telephone** wire / cable / cord / lead
▸ a **trailing** wire / cable / cord / flex / lead
▸ to **connect / disconnect** a wire / cable / cord / flex / lead
▸ to **run** a wire / cable somewhere
▸ a wire / cable / cord / flex / lead **leads / goes / runs** somewhere
▸ a wire / cable / cord / lead **carries** sth
▸ a **length of** wire / cable / flex

wire [C, U] a long, thin piece of metal that is used to carry an electric current or signal: *The telephone wires had been cut.* ◇ *fuse wire* See also **wire** → ROPE

cable [C, U] a set of wires, covered in plastic or rubber, that carries electricity, telephone signals, etc: *Roads have to be dug up to lay underground cables.* ◇ *a 10 000 volt cable* ◇ *a length of electric cable*

cord [C, U] (*especially AmE*) a piece of wire that is covered in plastic, used for carrying electricity to a piece of equipment: *I followed the telephone cord and found the wall socket.* ❶ A telephone or electrical tool that is not connected to its power supply by wires is *cordless* in both British and American English: *a cordless phone/drill*

flex [C, U] (*BrE*) a cord: *Trailing flexes are a serious trip hazard.* ◇ *Side cutters are useful for cutting electrical flex to length.*

lead /liːd/ [C] (*BrE*) a cord: *We'll have to use an extension lead* (= an extra length of electric wire, because the existing wire is not long enough).

NOTE **CORD, FLEX OR LEAD?** Cord is used especially in American English, although it is also used in British English, especially in connection with telephones. **Flex** and **lead** are both used only in British English and usually you can use either. However, **flex** is used more to talk about a shorter cord on a smaller piece of equipment such as a kettle, iron or lamp. **Lead** is used more to talk about a longer cord, especially an *extension lead* that can be used on various different pieces of equipment.

wisdom *noun*

wisdom · common sense · sense · realism · pragmatism · sanity
These are all words for a person's ability to make sensible decisions and give good advice.

PATTERNS AND COLLOCATIONS
▸ wisdom / sense / realism / pragmatism **in** (doing) sth
▸ the wisdom / common sense / sense **to do** sth
▸ **great** wisdom / common sense / sense

▸ **political / economic** wisdom / common sense / sense / realism / pragmatism
▸ to **have** the wisdom / common sense / sense / realism / pragmatism
▸ to **show** (great) wisdom / common sense / sense
▸ to **question / doubt / have doubts about** the wisdom / common sense / sense / sanity of sth

wisdom /ˈwɪzdəm/ [U] (*rather formal or ironic*) the ability to make sensible decisions and give good advice because of the experience and knowledge that you have; how sensible sth is: *I was not quite so lacking in* **worldly wisdom** (= knowledge of the world) *as to accept this invitation from a complete stranger.* ◇ *Several people questioned the wisdom of building in that particular spot.* ◇ *Do you have any more* **words of wisdom** *for us?* ❶ **Conventional/received wisdom** is the view or belief that most people hold; the phrase is often used to show that the speaker disagrees with this view: *Conventional wisdom has it that all sense of community has gone, but that is not the case where I live.*

,**common 'sense** [U] the ability to think about things in a practical way and make sensible decisions: *If any problems arise, just* **use your common sense**. ◇ *We prefer to take a* **common sense approach** *to raising children.* See also **common** → NORMAL

sense [U] good understanding and judgement; the ability to know what is sensible or practical: *You should have the sense to take advice when it's offered.* ◇ **There's no sense in** *worrying about it now.* ◇ *He was respected for his humour and his* **good sense**. ◇ *I wish you'd* **talk sense** (= talk sensibly). OPP **nonsense** → NONSENSE

realism /ˈriːəlɪzəm; *BrE also* ˈrɪəl-/ [U] a way of accepting and dealing with situations as they really are without being influenced by your emotions or by false hopes: *There was a new mood of realism among the leaders at the peace talks.*

pragmatism /ˈprægmətɪzəm/ [U] (*formal*) a way of solving problems and dealing with situations that is based on what is practically possible rather than on ideas and theories: *The new government needs pragmatism, not some vague ideology.*

sanity /ˈsænəti/ [U] (*rather formal*) the state of being sensible and reasonable: *We need a return to economic sanity.* OPP **madness** ❶ **Madness** is crazy or stupid behaviour that could be dangerous: *It would be sheer madness to trust a man like that.* ◇ *In a* **moment of madness** *she had agreed to go out with him.*

wise *adj.*

wise · sensible · prudent
These words all describe sb who is able to make good decisions or give good advice because of the experience and knowledge that they have.

PATTERNS AND COLLOCATIONS
▸ a wise / sensible / prudent **person / man / woman**

wise able to make good decisions and give good advice because of the experience and knowledge that you have: *He was too wise and experienced to try to escape.* ◇ *I'm* **older and wiser** *after ten years in the business.* OPP **foolish** → CRAZY, See also **wisdom** → KNOWLEDGE
▸ **wisely** *adv.*: *She wisely turned down the offer.*

sensible able to make good decisions based on reason and experience rather than emotion: *I wish you'd be sensible for once!* ◇ *She was a pleasant, sensible woman.* OPP **stupid** → CRAZY, See also **mature** → ADULT
▸ **sensibly** *adv.*: *Sensibly they decided not to oppose the case.*

NOTE **WISE OR SENSIBLE?** Wise is often used to describe older people who are respected for the knowledge that they have gained through experience, and which they use to do good. **Sensible** can describe people of any age who make the right decisions in everyday, practical matters. Being **sensible** is a good quality but it is sometimes seen as rather boring.

prudent /'pru:dnt/ sensible and careful when making decisions, avoiding unnecessary risks: *She has always been a prudent businesswoman.* ❶ The opposite of **prudent** is **imprudent**, but this is used to describe actions and decisions much more than people. See also **prudence** → CARE

wish noun

wish · request · will
These are all words for sth that sb wants to have or happen.

PATTERNS AND COLLOCATIONS
▸ a wish / request **for** sth
▸ **against** sb's wish / will
▸ sb's **particular / personal / dying** wish / request
▸ sb's **conscious** wish / will
▸ to **have / express / consider / comply with / ignore** a wish / request
▸ to **obey / go against** sb's wishes / will

wish [C] (*rather formal*) a thing that you want to have or to happen: *He refused to carry out her wishes.* ◇ *I'm sure that you will get your wish.* ◇ *She married against her parents' wishes.* See also **wish** → DESIRE *noun*, **wish** → HOPE *verb*
request [C] (*rather formal*) a thing that you formally ask for: *My request was granted.* ◇ *a radio request programme* (= a programme of music that listeners have asked for) See also **request** → REQUEST *noun*, **request** → ASK *verb* 2
will [sing.] (*formal*) what sb wants to happen in a particular situation: *I don't want to go against your will.* ◇ *They governed according to the will of the people.* ❶ **Will** is often used in contexts relating to public life: *the collective / general / majority / national / popular / public will.* When people say that sth is *God's will*, they mean that we should accept that we do not have any control over what happens in life, even when bad things happen, because it is God who decides how things happen.

witch noun

witch · wizard · magician · sorcerer / sorceress
These are all words for a person who is believed to have magic powers.

PATTERNS AND COLLOCATIONS
▸ a **great / powerful** wizard / magician
▸ a witch / wizard / magician / sorcerer / sorceress **casts a spell**

witch [C] a woman who is believed to have magic powers, especially to do evil things. In stories, a witch usually wears a black pointed hat and flies on a broomstick: *Many people believed her to be a witch.* ◇ *He was turned into a rat by a wicked witch.* See also **witchcraft** → MAGIC *noun*
wizard /'wɪzəd; AmE -ərd/ [C] a man who is believed to have magic powers, often to do evil things: *There were rumours that Abbot was a wizard, practising magic and the black arts.*
magician /mə'dʒɪʃn/ [C] a person, especially a man, who can do magic tricks; (in stories) a person who has magic powers: *They had booked a magician for the children's party.* ◇ *'Fly through the air, little mouse!' cried the magician.* See also **magic** → MAGIC *noun*

NOTE **WITCH, WIZARD** OR **MAGICIAN?** In stories **witches** are usually evil and **wizards** often are too, but they are often seen in more a positive way than **witches**. **Witches** are typically ugly old women; **wizards** are often grand, wise old men, with long robes, pointed hats and long white beards. **Magicians** can be good or evil and can appear in many different ways; sometimes their appearance hides the truth about who they really are.

sorcerer /'sɔːsərə(r); AmE 'sɔːrs-/, **sorceress** /'sɔːsərəs; AmE 'sɔːrs-/ [C] (*especially written*) (in stories) a man / woman with magic powers, who is helped by evil spirits: *He was suspected of misusing his magical powers as a sorcerer.* ◇ *Circe was a powerful sorceress who hated men, and would poison and trick them.* ❶ Unlike a **witch**, a **sorceress** is often young and beautiful. See also **sorcery** → MAGIC *noun*

withdraw verb

1 withdraw troops
2 withdraw from a competition

1 **withdraw · retreat · pull sb / sth out · retire**
These words all mean to move back or away from a place or situation, or to make sb / sth do this.

PATTERNS AND COLLOCATIONS
▸ to withdraw / retreat / retire **to** a place
▸ to withdraw / pull out **troops / forces**
▸ to withdraw / retreat / retire to your **room / study**
▸ to withdraw / retreat **into your shell**

withdraw /wɪð'drɔː; wɪθ'd-/ [I, T] (*rather formal*) to move back or away from a place; to make sb / sth do this: *Government troops were forced to withdraw.* ◇ *He always withdrew to his study after dinner.* ◇ *Both powers withdrew their forces from the region.* ◇ *She withdrew her hand from his.* ❶ Troops, an army, forces or a country might **withdraw**; the *authorities* or a *government* might withdraw troops or forces. However, **withdraw** is not only used in military contexts. Anybody might withdraw from a place, or they might withdraw a part of their body which was stretched out.
▸ **withdrawal** /wɪð'drɔːəl; wɪθ'd-/ *noun* [U, C]: *the withdrawal of troops* ◇ *US withdrawal from Vietnam*
retreat /rɪ'triːt/ [I] (*rather formal*) to move away from a place or enemy because you are in danger or because you have been defeated; to escape to a place that is quieter or safer: *The army was forced to retreat after suffering heavy losses.* ◇ *Bored with the conversation, she retreated to her bedroom.* OPP **advance** → GO 1
▸ **retreat** *noun* [C, usually sing., U]: *The army was in full retreat* (= retreating very quickly).

NOTE **WITHDRAW** OR **RETREAT?** An army **withdraws** when a decision has been made for it to stop attacking or controlling an area. An army **retreats** when it is in danger or has been defeated.

‚pull sb / sth 'out *phrasal verb* to make sb / sth move away from a place, especially soldiers from a place where they have been fighting: *They are pulling their troops out of the war zone.*
▸ **'pull-out** *noun* [sing.]: *The general ordered a pull-out from the area.*
retire [I] (*formal*) to leave a place, especially to go somewhere quieter or more private: *The jury retired to consider the evidence.* ◇ *After dinner he likes to retire to his study.* See also **go off** → GO AWAY

2 **withdraw · pull out · back off · back out · retreat**
These words all mean to decide not to do sth that you were intending to do, or not to take part in sth that has been agreed.

PATTERNS AND COLLOCATIONS
▸ to withdraw / back off / retreat **from** sth
▸ to pull out / back out **of** sth
▸ to withdraw from / pull out of a **project / tournament / tour**
▸ to withdraw from / pull out of **talks**

withdraw /wɪð'drɔː; wɪθ'd-/ [I, T] (*rather formal*) to stop taking part in an activity or being a member of an organization; to stop sb / sth from doing these things: *There have been calls for Britain to withdraw from the EU.* ◇ *The horse had been withdrawn from the race.*
▸ **withdrawal** /wɪð'drɔːəl; wɪθ'd-/ *noun* [U, C]: *his withdrawal from the election*
‚pull 'out *phrasal verb* to stop being involved in a situation or taking part in an activity: *The project became so expensive that we had to pull out.*

back 'off *phrasal verb* to decide not to do sth that you were intending to do, especially in order to avoid dealing with the problems this might cause: *The government has backed off from a fundamental reform of the system.*

back 'out *phrasal verb* to decide that you are no longer going to take part in sth that has been agreed: *He lost confidence and backed out of the deal at the last minute.*

retreat /rɪ'triːt/ [I] (*rather formal, written*) to change your mind about sth because of criticism or because a situation has become too difficult: *The government had retreated from its pledge to reduce class sizes.* See also **back down** → GIVE WAY

withstand *verb*

withstand · tolerate · stand · resist · absorb · stand up to sth
These words all mean to be strong enough not to be harmed or damaged by sth.

PATTERNS AND COLLOCATIONS
▶ to withstand / tolerate / stand / resist **high temperatures / heat**
▶ to withstand / tolerate / stand (harsh, dry, etc.) **conditions**
▶ to withstand / resist / stand up to **stress / wear**
▶ to withstand / resist **attack / damage**
▶ to withstand / stand the **pressure / strain / weight**

withstand /wɪð'stænd; wɪθ's-/ [T] (*formal*) to be strong enough not to be harmed or damaged by extreme conditions or the use of force: *The boat was built to withstand just about every weather condition.* ◇ *They had withstood siege, hunger and deprivation.*

tolerate /'tɒləreɪt; AmE 'tɑːl-/ [T] (*rather formal*) (of people, animals and plants) to be able to be affected by a drug or difficult conditions without being harmed: *Young and elderly people cannot tolerate alcohol as well as other adults.* ◇ *Few plants will tolerate sudden changes in temperature.*

stand [T] (used especially with *can/could*) to be able to survive pressure or extreme conditions without being harmed or damaged: *His heart won't stand the strain much longer.* ◇ *Modern plastics can stand very high and very low temperatures.*

resist [T] to be strong enough not to be harmed or damaged by sth: *A healthy diet should help your body resist infection.* ◇ *This new paint is designed to resist heat.* **❶ Resist** is used to describe an object, material or structure which is strong enough not to be damaged by the force of an attack, extreme weather conditions, etc.: *The castle was built to resist attack.* ◇ *It is thick enough to resist breaking* (= it will not break), *even under impact.* It is also used to describe an object or material which will not allow sth, such as water, to enter through its surface and cause damage: *They are treated with silicone to enable them to resist damp.* If a person, plant or animal **resists** a disease or virus, they are strong enough to fight it and not become ill: *crops which resist disease and pest attack* See also **resistance** → STRENGTH

absorb /əb'sɔːb; -'zɔːb; AmE -'sɔːrb; -'zɔːrb/ [T] (of an object or material) to reduce the effect of a blow or hit: *This tennis racket absorbs shock on impact.*

stand 'up to sth *phrasal verb* (of materials or products) to remain in good condition in spite of rough treatment or extreme conditions: *The carpet is designed to stand up to a lot of wear and tear.*

witness *noun* See also the entry for AUDIENCE

witness · observer · onlooker · passer-by · bystander · eyewitness
These are all words for a person who sees sth happen.

PATTERNS AND COLLOCATIONS
▶ a witness / an observer / an onlooker / a passer-by / a bystander / an eyewitness **sees** sb / sth
▶ an observer / an onlooker / a passer-by / a bystander **witnesses** sth

witness [C] a person who sees sth happen and is able to describe it to other people; a person who gives evidence in court: *Police have appealed for **witnesses to** the accident.* ◇ *a prosecution/defence witness* ◇ *She appeared as a **witness for** the prosecution.* ◇ *Several witnesses testified that there had been two gunmen.* See also **witness** → NOTICE *verb*

observer /əb'zɜːvə(r); AmE -'zɜːrv-/ [C] a person who sees sth happen: *To the casual observer, it would have looked like any other domestic argument.* ◇ *According to observers, the plane exploded shortly after take-off.* See also **observe** → NOTICE *verb*

onlooker /'ɒnlʊkə(r); AmE 'ɑːn-; 'ɔːn-/ [C] a person who watches sth that is happening but is not involved in it: *A crowd of onlookers gathered at the scene of the crash.*

passer-'by (pl. **passers-by**) [C] a person who is going past sb/sth by chance, especially when sth unexpected happens: *Police asked passers-by if they had witnessed the accident.*

bystander /'baɪstændə(r)/ [C] a person who is near and can see what is happening when sth such as an accident or fight takes place: *Three **innocent bystanders** were killed in the crossfire.*

eyewitness /'aɪwɪtnəs/ [C] a person who has seen a crime or accident and can describe it afterwards: *One eyewitness saw the gunmen leave the building.* ◇ *He gave an **eyewitness account** of the suffering of the refugees.*

woman *noun*

woman · lady · female
These are all words for an adult female person.

PATTERNS AND COLLOCATIONS
▶ a / an **young / older** woman / lady / female
▶ a / an **middle-aged / old / elderly** woman / lady
▶ a **black / white** woman / lady / female
▶ a / an **married / single / unmarried** woman / lady
▶ a / an **beautiful / attractive** woman / lady / female
▶ a **nice / fine / charming** woman / lady

woman [C] an adult female person: *a 24-year-old woman* ◇ *Alcohol affects men and women differently.* ◇ *I prefer to see a woman doctor.* **OPP man** → MAN 1

lady [C] a polite way of referring to a woman, especially sb that you do not know: *There's a lady waiting to see you.* **❶ Ladies** [pl.] is a polite, formal way of addressing more than one woman: *Can I take your coats, ladies?* ◇ ***Ladies and gentlemen!** Can I have your attention, please?* To address one woman in this way, you can use **madam** or **ma'am**: *Can I take your coat, madam/ma'am?* However, some women do not like to be called **lady** or **madam**, so you can leave it out: *There's someone waiting to see you.* ◇ *Can I take your coats?* **OPP gentleman** → MAN 1

female [C] (*formal or technical*) a woman or girl: *The body is that of a white female aged about 30.* ◇ *More females than males are employed in the factory.* **❶** The noun **female** is mostly used in formal, official, scientific or medical contexts. **OPP male** → MAN 1

wonderful *adj.* See also the entries for EXCELLENT, GOOD 1, MAGNIFICENT, NICE 1 and SATISFYING

wonderful · lovely · marvellous · delightful · delicious
These words all describe an experience, feeling or sight that gives you great pleasure.

PATTERNS AND COLLOCATIONS
▶ a wonderful / lovely / marvellous / delightful / delicious **feeling / sensation**
▶ (a) wonderful / lovely / marvellous / delightful **experience / evening / time / party / place / views / scenery / weather**
▶ What a wonderful / lovely / marvellous / delightful / delicious **surprise!**
▶ It would be wonderful / lovely / delightful **if...**
▶ It's wonderful / lovely / marvellous **that...**

► It's wonderful / lovely / marvellous **to be** / **feel** / **find** / **have** / **know** / **see**…

► That **sounds** wonderful / lovely / marvellous / delightful.

► **really** / **quite** / **absolutely** wonderful / lovely / marvellous / delightful

wonderful that you enjoy very much; that gives you great pleasure; extremely good: *We had a wonderful time last night.* ◇ *It's wonderful to see you!* ◇ *The weather was absolutely wonderful.* ◇ *Note the wonderful skill in these sculpted hands and faces.* See also **wonder** → MIRACLE
► **wonderfully** *adv.*: *The hotel is wonderfully comfortable.* ◇ *Things have worked out wonderfully (well).*

lovely (*especially BrE, rather informal, especially spoken*) that you enjoy very much; that gives you great pleasure; very attractive: *We had a lovely day* (= we really enjoyed ourselves). ◇ *What a lovely day* (= the weather is very good)! ◇ *'Can I get you anything?' 'A cup of tea would be lovely.'* ◇ *It's been lovely having you here.* ◇ *It's a lovely old farmhouse.* ❶ In spoken British English **lovely** can be used before other adjectives to emphasize how pleasant sth is: *a lovely cool drink* ◇ *It's lovely and warm in here.* **Lovely and** with another adjective cannot be used before a noun: *a lovely and warm place*

marvellous (*BrE*) (*AmE* **marvelous**) /ˈmɑːvələs; *AmE* ˈmɑːrv-/ (*rather informal, especially spoken*) that gives you great pleasure; extremely good: *The food smells absolutely marvellous.* ◇ *This will be a marvellous opportunity for her.* ◇ *It's marvellous what modern technology can do.* See also **marvel** → MIRACLE
► **marvellously** *adv.* (*BrE*) (*AmE* **marvelously**): *This recipe is marvellously simple and quick.*

NOTE **WONDERFUL OR MARVELLOUS?** Marvellous is slightly more informal than **wonderful** and is used especially in spoken English.

delightful that gives you great pleasure; very attractive: *It has been a most delightful evening.* ◇ *It was a delightful little fishing village.*
► **delightfully** *adv.*: *The hotel is delightfully situated on the edge of the lake.*

NOTE **WONDERFUL, LOVELY OR DELIGHTFUL?** These words can all describe times, events, places, sights, feelings and the weather. **Wonderful** can also describe a chance or ability: *a lovely/delightful opportunity/skill.* **Lovely** is the most frequent in spoken British English, but in American English **wonderful** is the most frequent, both spoken and written. **Delightful** is used especially to talk about times, events and places.

delicious /dɪˈlɪʃəs/ (*literary*) that gives you great pleasure, especially physical pleasure: *the delicious coolness of the breeze* ◇ *A delicious shiver of excitement ran through his body.*
► **deliciously** *adv.*: *The water was deliciously cool.*

word *noun*

word • **term** • **phrase** • **expression** • **idiom**
These are all words for a unit of language used to express sth.

PATTERNS AND COLLOCATIONS
► a word / term **for** sth
► a / an **new** / **ambiguous** word / term / phrase / expression
► a **technical** / **colloquial** word / term / phrase / expression
► a **slang** word / term / phrase
► an **idiomatic** phrase / expression
► to **use** a word / a term / a phrase / an expression / an idiom
► to **coin** a word / a term / a phrase / an expression
► a word / a term / a phrase / an expression **means** sth
► a word / a term / a phrase / an expression **comes** / **derives** / **is derived from** sth

word [C] a single unit of language which means sth and can be spoken or written: *Do not write more than 200 words.* ◇ *He uses a lot of long words.* ◇ *What's the Spanish*

word for 'table'? ◇ *I could hear every word they were saying.* ◇ *I can't remember her exact words.* ◇ *Tell me what happened in your own words.* ◇ *He was a true friend in all senses of the word.* See also **wording** → LANGUAGE 2

term [C] (*rather formal*) a word or phrase used as the name of sth, especially one connected with a particular type of language: *technical/legal/scientific terms* ◇ *'Register' is the term commonly used to describe different levels of formality in language.* See also **term** → CALL *verb* 1, **terms** → LANGUAGE 2

phrase [C] a group of words that have a particular meaning when used together: *She was, in her own favourite phrase, 'a woman without a past'.* ❶ In grammar, a **phrase** is a group of words without a finite verb, especially one that forms part of a sentence: 'the green car' and 'on Friday morning' are phrases.

expression [C] a word or phrase: *He tends to use a lot of slang expressions that I've never heard before.*

idiom [C] a group of words whose meaning is different from the meanings of the individual words: *'Let the cat out of the bag' is an idiom meaning to tell a secret by mistake.*

work *noun*

1 hard work
2 find work
3 do pioneering work in microbiology
4 a work of fiction/art

---

1 work • labour • service • toil • drudgery • slog
These are all words for the use of physical strength or mental power in order to do or make sth.

PATTERNS AND COLLOCATIONS
► **hard** work / labour / toil / slog
► **daily** work / labour / toil / drudgery / slog
► **manual** / **physical** / **honest** / **unremitting** work / labour / toil
► **hours** / **a lifetime** of work / labour / service / toil / drudgery

work [U] the use of physical strength or mental power in order to do or make sth: *She earned her grades through sheer hard work.* ◇ We **started work** on the project in 2002. ◇ *Work continues on renovating the hotel.* ◇ *Let's* **get to work** (= start working). ◇ *She* **set them to work** *painting the fence.*

labour (*BrE*) (*AmE* **labor**) /ˈleɪbə(r)/ [U] work, especially physical work: *These women were generally accustomed to hard manual labour* (= work using their hands). ◇ *The price will include the labour and materials.* ◇ *The company wants to keep down* **labour costs**.

service [U] the work that sb does for an organization, especially when it continues for a long time or is admired very much: *She has just celebrated 25 years' service with the company.* ◇ *The employees have good conditions of service.*

toil [U] (*formal or literary*) hard unpleasant work that makes you very tired: *His hands bore the scars of a life of hardship and toil.*

drudgery /ˈdrʌdʒəri/ [U] (*disapproving*) hard boring work, especially housework or office work: *Once married, she was condemned to a life of domestic drudgery.*

slog [C, usually sing.] (*informal, disapproving*) sth that is difficult or boring, or that requires a lot of hard work, such as a long, tiring walk: *It was a long slog to the top of the mountain.* ❶ Especially in British English **slog** [U] can also be a period of hard work or effort: (*especially BrE*) *Writing the book took ten months of hard slog.*

---

2 See also the entry for JOB

work • employment • career • profession • occupation • practice • trade
These are all words for the work that sb does in return for payment, especially over a long period of time.

PATTERNS AND COLLOCATIONS
► sb's **chosen** work / employment / career / profession / occupation / trade
► (a) **professional** work / employment / career / occupation / practice

▸ (a) **skilled** / **manual** work / employment / occupation / trade
▸ (a) **full-time** / **part-time** / **permanent** work / employment / career / occupation
▸ (a) **regular** work / employment / occupation / trade
▸ (a) **casual** / **seasonal** work / employment / occupation
▸ (a) **well-paid** work / employment / profession / occupation
▸ (a) **low-paid** work / employment / occupation
▸ to **have** / **pursue** work / employment / a career / a profession / an occupation / a trade
▸ to **take up** work / employment / a career / a profession / an occupation / ...practice / a trade
▸ to **go back** / **return** to work / employment / a career / a profession / ...practice
▸ to **look for** / **seek** / **find** work / employment / a career / an occupation

work [U] the job that sb does, especially in order to earn money: *He's been **out of work** for over a year.* ◇ *(BrE) It is a country where most women with young children are **in** paid **work**.* ◇ *She's planning to return to work in September.* ◇ *Would you give up work if you won the lottery?* ◇ *Any kind of **work with** kids would suit him fine.* ◇ *'Where's John?' 'He's still **at work**.'* ◇ *She's been **off work** (= not at work) for three weeks.* ◇ *He **started work** as a security guard.* See also **work → OFFICE 1**

employment [U] *(rather formal)* work, especially when it is done to earn money; the situation in which people have work: *It's getting more and more difficult for young people to find regular employment.* ◇ *The government aims to have **full employment** (= a situation in which everyone who wants a job has one) within five years.* **OPP unemployment → UNEMPLOYMENT,** See also **employ → EMPLOY**

career [C] the job or series of jobs that sb has in a particular area of work, usually involving more responsibility as time passes: *I never wanted a military career.* ◇ *Kelly's career took off (= started to be successful) when she was spotted in a talent contest.* ◇ *His career spanned (= continued over) four decades.* ◇ *By 2001, she was at **the peak of her career** (= at the most successful point in her career).* ◇ *I didn't think it was a very good **career move**.* ◇ *It's time for a **career change**.*

profession [C] a type of job that needs special training or skill, especially one that needs a high level of education: *Alan's a teacher **by profession**.* ◇ *He hopes to **enter** the medical **profession**.* ◇ *I **joined** the profession when I was in my early twenties.* ◇ *She's at the **top of her profession**.* ❶ Especially in British English, **the professions** [pl.] are the traditional jobs that need a high level of education and training, such as being a doctor or lawyer: *employment in industry and the professions.* **The profession** [sing. + sing./pl. v.] is all the people who work in a particular profession.

▸ **professional** *adj.*: *Most of the people on the course were professional women.* ◇ *professional qualifications/skills*

occupation /ˌɒkjuˈpeɪʃn; *AmE* ˌɑːk-/ [C] *(rather formal)* a job or profession: *Please state your name, age, and occupation.* ◇ *Why is nursing still seen as a female occupation?*

practice [U] the work or business of some professional people such as doctors and lawyers: *Students should have prior experience of veterinary practice.* ◇ *My analyst is no longer in practice.* See also **practice → COMPANY**

trade [C] a job, especially one that involves working with your hands and requires special training and skills: *She's now a carpenter **by trade**.* ◇ *My parents always wanted me to leave school early and **learn a trade**.* See also **trade → INDUSTRY**

3 work · achievement · triumph · feat · accomplishment · coup · results
These are all words for sth that is produced as a result of work.

▸ a **great** / **remarkable** work / achievement / triumph / feat / accomplishment / coup
▸ a **major** / **spectacular** work / achievement / triumph / feat / coup
▸ a **significant** work / achievement / accomplishment / coup
▸ a / an **impressive** / **notable** work / achievement / feat / accomplishment
▸ a **brilliant** work / achievement / feat / coup
▸ a **real** achievement / triumph / feat / accomplishment / coup
▸ **your own** work / achievement / accomplishment
▸ a / an **literary** / **artistic** / **scientific** work / achievement / accomplishment
▸ to **constitute** / **represent** / **see sth as** an achievement / a triumph / a coup
▸ **quite a** / **an** achievement / feat / accomplishment / coup

work [U] a thing or things that are produced or achieved as a result of working: *She's an artist whose work I really admire.* ◇ *Is this **all your own work** (= did you do it without help from others)?* ◇ *The book is a detailed and thorough **piece of work**.* ◇ *Her written work is the best in the class.* ◇ *He did pioneering work on microbes.* ◇ *The art collection was **his life's work**.* ◇ *The showroom has been designed so that people can see **work in progress**.*

achievement [C] *(approving)* an impressive thing that sb has done, especially using their own effort and skill: *It was a remarkable achievement for such a young player.* ◇ *They were proud of their children's achievements.* ◇ *This is probably his greatest scientific achievement.* See also **achieve → ACHIEVE**

triumph /ˈtraɪʌmf/ [C] *(approving)* a great success, achievement or victory; an excellent example of how successful sth can be: *It was a personal **triumph over** her old rival.* ◇ *Her arrest was **a triumph of** international cooperation.*

feat [C] *(approving)* an action or a piece of work that needs skill, strength or courage: *The tunnel is a brilliant feat of engineering.* ◇ *Dragging the fully laden boat across the sand dunes was **no mean feat**.*

accomplishment /əˈkʌmplɪʃmənt; *AmE* əˈkɑːm-/ [C] *(rather formal, often approving)* an impressive thing that is done or achieved after a lot of work: *The administration's success in cutting the budget was an impressive accomplishment.* ◇ *the technical accomplishments of modern medicine* See also **accomplish → ACHIEVE**

NOTE ACHIEVEMENT OR ACCOMPLISHMENT? **Achievement** is usually used to talk about a person's academic, professional, artistic or sporting success. **Accomplishment** is often used to talk about a great success which has benefited others, especially in politics and in contexts in which important inventions are described.

coup /kuː/ [C, usually sing.] *(written, often approving)* an impressive and surprising success: *Getting this contract has been quite a coup for us.* ◇ *He **pulled off a** major diplomatic **coup** by winning agreement from all the warring factions on a permanent ceasefire.* ❶ **Coup** is often used with adjectives like *spectacular, significant, remarkable* and *greatest*. It is also used to describe successful information campaigns after nouns like *publicity, intelligence* and *propaganda*.

results [pl.] success achieved by actions or efforts: *The project is beginning to show results.* ◇ *He's a coach who knows how to get results from his players.*

4 work · writings · piece · masterpiece · composition · work of art · oeuvre
These are all words for sth that has been created by an artist, writer or musician.

▸ a work / piece / masterpiece / composition / work of art **by** sb
▸ a / an **great** / **original** work / piece / masterpiece / composition / work of art
▸ a / an **orchestral** / **choral** work / piece / masterpiece / composition
▸ a / an **classical** / **abstract** work / piece / composition
▸ sb's **collected** / **complete** works / writings
▸ to **perform** a work / piece / composition

work [C] a book, painting or piece of music that has been created by sb: *The film is based on an early work by Alan Moore.* ◇ *works of fiction/literature* ◇ *Chopin's piano works*

writings [pl.] a group of pieces of writing, especially by a particular person or on a particular subject: *His experiences in Morocco influenced his later writings.* ◇ *the writings of Sun Tzu* See also **writing** → LITERATURE, **write** → WRITE 2

piece [C] a single item of music, writing, poetry or art: *The orchestra performed pieces by Ravel and Prokofiev.* ❶ You can have *a piece of music/writing/poetry/art*, but **piece** on its own usually means a piece of music, except in formal language and where the context is clear: *Auditioning students are required to play a solo piece of their choice.* ◇ (*formal*) *They have some beautiful pieces* (= paintings, drawings, etc.) *in their home.* See also **piece** → ARTICLE, See also the entry for SONG

masterpiece /ˈmɑːstəpiːs; *AmE* ˈmæstərp-/ [C] a work of art, literature, film, etc. that is an excellent, or the best, example of the artist's work: *The work has been described as a literary masterpiece.* ◇ *This is an excellent production of Verdi's masterpiece.* ◇ *Her work is a masterpiece of simplicity* (= an excellent example of sth simple).

composition /ˌkɒmpəˈzɪʃn; *AmE* ˌkɑːm-/ [C] (*formal*) a piece of music, poetry or art: *one of Stravinsky's finest compositions* See also **compose** → WRITE 2

> **NOTE** WORK, PIECE OR COMPOSITION? **Work** emphasizes that sth has been created with effort by sb, and can be used to talk about any type of art, literature or music. **Piece** is often used to talk about shorter items of music. **Composition** is also mostly used to talk about music, but may also be used to talk about poetry and art.

work of ˈart (pl. **works of art**) [C] an object that has been created by an artist, especially a painting, drawing or statue: *A number of priceless works of art were stolen from the gallery.*

oeuvre /ˈɜːvrə/ [sing.] (from *French*, *formal*) all the works that have been created by a writer, artist or composer: *She created an oeuvre that is both refreshing and overwhelming.*

work *verb*

1 work on an assignment
2 work as a teacher/in education
3 The phone isn't working.

1 work · labour · toil · slave

These words all mean to do sth that involves physical or mental effort.

PATTERNS AND COLLOCATIONS
▶ to work / labour / toil **at** sth
▶ to labour / slave **over** sth
▶ to work / labour / toil / slave **away**
▶ to work / labour / toil **endlessly / long and hard / tirelessly**

work [I, T] to do sth that involves physical or mental effort, especially as part of a job: *I can't work if I'm cold.* ◇ *He is working on a new novel.* ◇ *She's outside, working on the car.* ◇ *Doctors often work very long hours.*

labour (*BrE*) (*AmE* **labor**) /ˈleɪbə(r)/ [I] (*rather formal, especially written*) to do hard physical work: *They laboured all day in the fields.*

toil [I] (*formal or literary*) to work very hard and/or for a long time: *Hundreds of men toiled for years at building the pyramid.*

slave [I] (*rather informal, especially spoken, usually disapproving*) to work very hard: *I've been slaving away all day trying to get this work finished.* ◇ *I haven't got time to spend hours slaving over a hot stove* (= doing a lot of cooking). ❶ **Slave** is usually used when you think that you have/sb has been working too hard.

2 work · be employed · have a job · earn a/your living · be in work · practise

These words all mean to earn money through work.

PATTERNS AND COLLOCATIONS
▶ to work / be employed / have a job / earn a living / practise **as** sth
▶ to work / be employed / have a job **at** a place

work [I] to do work for which you receive regular payment: *Both my parents work.* ◇ *She works for an engineering company.* ◇ *I've always worked in education.* ◇ *Do you enjoy working with children?*

be emˈployed [T, passive] (*rather formal*) to do work for which you receive regular payment: *For the past three years he has been employed as a firefighter.* ◇ *A number of people are employed to deal with the backlog of work.* See also **employ** → EMPLOY, **unemployed** → UNEMPLOYED

have a ˈjob *phrase* to do work for which you receive regular payment: *She had a job as a waitress.* ◇ *I've got a temporary job at the moment.* ◇ *She's never had a steady job* (= a job that is not going to end suddenly).

> **NOTE** WORK, BE EMPLOYED OR HAVE A JOB? **Work** is the most general of these words and can be used to talk about a particular job that sb has at a particular time, or the general type of work that they do, or just the fact that they work. **Be employed** is mostly used to talk about the particular job or type of work that sb does, often with *as* or *to: be employed as a teacher* ◇ *be employed to train users in the new system.* **Have a job** is often used to talk about the fact of not being unemployed: *Do you have a job?* It can also be used with *as* in a similar way to **work**: *She worked/had a job as a waitress in a cocktail bar.* In this use, **have a job** is most often used in the past tense, and also suggests that the period of employment is more temporary than **work**. **Have a job** can be a little more informal than **work**.

earn a/your ˈliving *phrase* to work for money to buy the things that you need in life: *She earns her living as a freelance journalist.*

be in ˈwork *phrase* (*BrE*) to have a job, as opposed to being unemployed (= not having a job): *Most of those who were in work had temporary jobs.* See also **out of work** → UNEMPLOYED

practise (*BrE*) (*AmE* **practice**) [I, T] to work as a doctor, lawyer, etc: *There are over 50 000 solicitors practising in England and Wales.* ◇ *He practised as a lawyer for many years.* ◇ *She was banned from practising medicine.*

3 See also the entry for OPERATE

work · function · run · operate · go

These are all words that can be used when a machine, system or device performs in the correct way.

PATTERNS AND COLLOCATIONS
▶ to **actually / still** work / function / go
▶ to work / function / run / operate **efficiently / satisfactorily / smoothly / independently / successfully / normally / reliably**
▶ to work / function / run **perfectly**
▶ to work / function / operate **effectively / properly / correctly**
▶ to work / function **well**
▶ to run / operate **continuously**
▶ **fully** functioning / operating

work [I] (of a machine or device) to perform in the correct way: *The phone isn't working.* ◇ *It works by electricity.* ◇ *Are they any closer to understanding how the brain works?* See also **work** → OPERATE

function [I] (usually used with an adverb or preposition) (*rather formal*) to work in the correct way: *Despite the power cuts, the hospital continued to function normally.* ◇ *Many children can't function effectively in large classes.* ◇ *We now have a functioning shower.*

run [I] to work in the correct way: *Stan had the chainsaw running.* ◇ *Our van runs on* (= uses) *diesel.* ◇ *Which operating system have you got running?* ❶ **Run** is usually used to talk about an engine or motor (or a machine that uses an engine or motor), or a computer program. See also **run** → OPERATE, **up and running** → ACTIVE *adj.*

operate [I] (usually used with an adverb or preposition) (*rather formal*) (especially of a machine) to work in a particular way; (of a service or system) to be working: *Solar panels can only operate in sunlight.* ◇ *Some people can only operate well under pressure.* ◇ *A new late-night service is now operating.* See also **operate** → OPERATE

▸ **operation** *noun* [U]: *Regular servicing guarantees the smooth operation of the engine.* See also **in operation**, **operational** → ACTIVE *adj.*

NOTE FUNCTION OR OPERATE? **Function** is used more to talk about whether sth works or how well or badly it works; **operate** is used more to talk about the conditions required for sth to work.

go [I] (*informal, especially spoken*) (of a machine) to work in the correct way: *What makes it go?*

worker *noun*

1 office workers
2 conflicts between employers and workers

1 See also the entry for STAFF
worker · employee · staff member · member of staff
These are all words for a person who works, especially in a company or other organization.

▸ a/ an **full-time/ part-time/ female/ male/ experienced/ key** worker/ employee/ staff member/ member of staff
▸ a **permanent/ junior/ senior** employee/ staff member/ member of staff
▸ to **have/ employ/ dismiss** a worker/ an employee/ a staff member/ a member of staff
▸ to **fire** a worker/ an employee/ a staff member
▸ to **sack** a worker/ an employee/ a staff member
▸ a worker/ an employee/ a staff member/ a member of staff **works**

worker [C] (often in compounds) a person who works, especially one who does a particular kind of work: *Aid workers quickly arrived at the scene of the disaster.* ◇ *There are few jobs available for manual workers.* ◇ *We will take on several casual workers over the summer months.* ❶ In this meaning **worker** is often used in compounds that show where sb works, the type of work they do or the type of employment contract they have: *office/farm/ factory workers* ◇ *rescue/aid/research workers* ◇ *skilled/ unskilled/manual/blue-collar/white-collar workers* ◇ *temporary/part-time/casual/seasonal/migrant workers*
employee /ɪmˈplɔɪiː/ [C] a person who is paid to work for sb: *The firm has over 500 employees.*
staff member [C] (*especially AmE*) a worker employed in an organization: *Three hospital staff members were suspended after the incident.*
member of 'staff [C] (*BrE*) a staff member: *All members of staff work as a team to achieve customer satisfaction.*

NOTE EMPLOYEE OR STAFF MEMBER/MEMBER OF STAFF? You can be an **employee** of a company with lots of other employees, or of just one person, who has no other employees. A **staff member** or **member of staff** works for a company or organization that employs several other people at least. However, **employee** is used most often for talking about employees in general, especially their terms and conditions of employment. When referring to individuals and the work that they do, it is more usual to use **staff member** or **member of staff**. See also **staff** → STAFF

2 **worker · labourer · staff · workman**
These are all words for a person who is below the level of manager in an organization, especially one who does physical work rather than organizing things or managing people.

▸ (a) **skilled** worker/ labourer/ workman
▸ (an) **unskilled** worker/ labourer
▸ (a) **female/ male** worker/ staff
▸ an **unemployed** worker/ labourer/ workman
▸ to **employ** a worker/ a labourer/ staff/ a workman
▸ workers/ labourers/ staff/ workmen **work**

worker [C] a person whose job involves physical work rather than organizing things or managing people: *Conflict between employers and workers intensified.* ◇ *Talks between workers and management have ended today.*
labourer (*BrE*) (*AmE* **laborer**) /ˈleɪbərə(r)/ [C] a person whose job involves hard physical work that is not skilled, especially work that is done outdoors: *He managed to get a job as an agricultural labourer.*
staff [sing.] (*AmE*) the people who work at a school, college or university, but who do not teach students: *Students, faculty and staff were all men in those days.* See also **staff** → STAFF
workman [C] a man who is employed to do physical work: *A gang of workmen were shovelling rubble into a truck.*

NOTE LABOURER OR WORKMAN? A **labourer** does hard, physical work, often on a farm or in the countryside. A **workman** usually does building or repair work. You can talk about both *skilled* and *unskilled labourers/workmen*, but in general a **workman** is more likely than a **labourer** to be skilled and to use machinery or technology. For example, a builder could be called a **workman**; a *builder's labourer* is sb who helps a builder, doing the less skilled jobs.

working-class *adj.* See the Topic Map for THE INDIVIDUAL AND SOCIETY on p.894

working-class · lowly · common · proletarian · humble
These words all describe people from a low social class or of low status, or things connected with low social class or low status.

▸ working-class/ common/ humble **people**
▸ working-class/ lowly/ humble **origins**
▸ (of) lowly/ humble **birth**
▸ a working-class/ proletarian/ humble **hero**

working-'class belonging to or typical of the social class whose members do not have much money or power and are usually employed to do work with their hands: *The group was set up and led largely by working-class women.* ◇ *She grew up in a working-class area.* See also **working class** → GENERAL PUBLIC, **upper-class** → ARISTOCRATIC, **middle-class** → MIDDLE-CLASS
lowly /ˈləʊli; *AmE* ˈloʊli/ (*often humorous*) (especially of a person or their job) low in status or importance: *His first job was as a lowly assistant gardener.*
common [not usually before noun] (*BrE, disapproving, often humorous*) typical of sb from a low social class and lacking good manners or culture: *She thought he was very common and uneducated.* ◇ *He's as common as muck, but he's a got a lot of posh friends.* ❶ To describe sb as **common** is now mostly considered to be snobbish (= showing that you think you are better than other people because of your high social class) and it is mostly used humorously. **OPP** **posh** → ARISTOCRATIC
proletarian /ˌprəʊləˈteəriən; *AmE* ˌproʊləˈter-/ (*rather formal, often disapproving*) (used especially when talking about the past) connected with ordinary people who earn money by working, especially those who do not own any property: *Marx hoped that the proletarian revolution would soon follow.* **OPP** **bourgeois** → MIDDLE-CLASS, See also **the proletariat** → GENERAL PUBLIC
humble (*literary or humorous*) (especially of a person or their job) low in status or social position: *He had worked his way up from humble beginnings.*

the **world** noun

the world · earth · the globe · the planet
These words all mean the planet that we live on.

PATTERNS AND COLLOCATIONS
▸ **around / across / all over** the world / earth / globe / planet
▸ **on** (the) earth / the globe / the planet
▸ to **save / destroy** the world / earth / planet
▸ the **world / earth** turns / revolves
▸ the **face / surface** of the earth / globe / planet
▸ the **(four) corners of** the world / earth / globe

the world [sing.] the planet that we live on; all the people or countries that exist: *He's always wanted to sail around the world.* ◇ *Which is the largest city **in the world**?* ◇ *French is spoken in many parts of the world.* ◇ *He's the world's highest paid entertainer.* ◇ *She spent much of her life campaigning for world peace.*

earth (also **the earth, Earth, the Earth**) [U, sing.] the planet that we live on: *The fossil record shows the history of life on earth.* ◇ *The earth revolves around the sun.* ◇ *In the story the aliens have a plan to destroy **planet earth**.*

NOTE **THE WORLD** OR **THE EARTH?** In some cases you can use either word: *I must be the happiest person in the world/on earth!* However, there is usually a difference of emphasis: use **the world** when you are only concerned with things that exist in the world, and not with anything that exists outside it. **Earth** is more often used when our planet is being considered in relation to other planets, its place in space, or heaven. Compare *world peace* (= peace between all the countries in the world) and *peace on earth* (= peace as a gift to people on earth from God in heaven).

the globe [sing.] the world, especially when emphasizing how big it is: *The resort attracts tourists from every corner of the globe.*

the planet [sing.] the world, especially when talking about the environment: *South East Asia has emerged as a key arena in the battle to save the planet.*

worried adj. See also the entries for AFRAID and RESTLESS

worried · concerned · nervous · anxious · uneasy · bothered · troubled · disturbed · apprehensive
These words all describe feeling unhappy and afraid because you are thinking about unpleasant things that might happen or might have happened.

PATTERNS AND COLLOCATIONS
▸ to be worried / concerned / nervous / anxious / uneasy / bothered / troubled / disturbed / apprehensive **about** sth
▸ to be worried / concerned / anxious **for** sb / sth
▸ to be worried / concerned / nervous / anxious / bothered / disturbed / apprehensive **that** …
▸ a worried / a concerned / a nervous / an anxious / an uneasy / a troubled / an apprehensive **expression / look / smile**
▸ a worried / a concerned / a nervous / an anxious / a troubled **voice**
▸ to **get** worried / nervous / anxious / apprehensive

worried thinking about unpleasant things that might happen or might have happened and therefore feeling unhappy and afraid: *Don't look so worried!* ◇ *I'm not worried about her — she can take care of herself.* ◇ *I was worried (that) I would fail the exam.* ◇ *Where have you been? I've been **worried sick** (= extremely worried).* See also **worry** → CONCERN *noun*
▸ **worriedly** *adv.*: *He glanced worriedly at his father.*

concerned worried and feeling concern about sth: *The President is deeply concerned about this issue.* ◇ *I was rather concerned at the severity of the punishment.* ◇ *Concerned parents held a meeting.* See also **concern** → CONCERN *noun*

NOTE **WORRIED** OR **CONCERNED?** **Concerned** is usually used when you are talking about a problem that affects another person, society, the world, etc.; **worried** can be used to talk about this or about more personal matters.

nervous feeling worried about sth or slightly afraid of sth: *Consumers are very nervous about the future.* ◇ *The horse may be nervous of cars.* ◇ *By the time the police arrived, I was a **nervous wreck**.* **OPP** relaxed → CALM, **confident** → CONFIDENT, See also **nervous** → NERVOUS, **nerve-racking** → STRESSFUL
▸ **nervously** *adv.*: *She smiled nervously.*

anxious feeling worried or nervous about sth: *He grew increasingly anxious as time went on.* See also **anxious** → STRESSFUL, **anxiety** → CONCERN *noun*
▸ **anxiously** *adv.*: *to ask/look/wait anxiously* ◇ *Residents are anxiously awaiting a decision.*

NOTE **WORRIED, NERVOUS** OR **ANXIOUS?** **Worried** is the most frequent word to describe how you feel when you are thinking about a problem or sth bad that might happen. **Anxious** can describe a stronger feeling and is more formal. **Nervous** is more often used to describe how you feel before you do sth very important such as an exam or interview, or sth unpleasant or difficult. **Nervous** can describe sb's personality: *a very nervous girl* is often or usually nervous; *a worried girl* is worried on a particular occasion or about a particular thing: **worried** describes her feelings, not her personality. **Anxious** can describe feelings or personality.

uneasy feeling worried or unhappy about a particular situation, especially because you think sth bad may happen or because you are not sure that what you are doing is right: *He had an uneasy feeling that something terrible was going to happen.* ◇ *She felt uneasy about leaving the children with him.* **OPP** easy → EASY 2, See also **unease** → CONCERN *noun*
▸ **uneasily** *adv.*: *I wondered uneasily what he was thinking.*

bothered (often used in negative sentences) (*rather informal*) worried, upset or annoyed about sth: *You don't sound too bothered about it. Don't you mind?*

troubled (*written*) worried or anxious: *She looked into his troubled face.* ❶ **Trouble** is used especially to describe people's expressions, faces or eyes.

disturbed (*rather formal, especially written*) anxious and unhappy about sth: *I was deeply disturbed and depressed by the news.*

apprehensive (*formal*) slightly afraid that sth bad might happen: *I was a little apprehensive about the effects of what I had said.* See also **apprehension** → CONCERN
▸ **apprehensively** *adv.*: *He was looking at me apprehensively.*

worry verb

1 You worry too much.
2 This did not worry me.

1 worry · fret · agonize · sweat
These words all mean to spend time thinking about a difficult situation or problem and feel worried or unhappy about it.

PATTERNS AND COLLOCATIONS
▸ to worry / fret / agonize **about** sth
▸ fret / agonize / sweat **over** sth
▸ **Don't** worry / fret.

worry [I] to keep thinking about unpleasant things that might happen or might have happened: *Don't worry about me. I'll be fine.* ◇ *I worry that I won't get into college.* ◇ *You worry too much.*

fret (**-tt-**) [I] (*especially BrE*) to be worried or unhappy and unable to relax: *Fretting about it won't help.*

agonize (*BrE* also **-ise**) [I] to spend a long time thinking and worrying about a difficult situation, problem or decision: *I spent days agonizing over whether to take the job or not.*

sweat /swet/ [I, T] (*informal*) to worry or feel anxious about sth: *They really made me sweat during the interview.* ◇ (*AmE*) *Don't sweat it* (= don't worry). *We'll be fine.*

2 worry · bother · concern · trouble · disturb · unsettle
These words all mean to make sb feel anxious or worried.

bother	concern	worry
	disturb	trouble
	unsettle	

PATTERNS AND COLLOCATIONS
▶ It worries/ bothers/ concerns/ troubles/ disturbs **sb that** ...
▶ **Is there something** worrying/ bothering/ troubling **you?**
▶ to worry/ bother/ concern/ trouble sb **with** sth
▶ to worry/ bother/ concern/ trouble **yourself about** sth
▶ sth **doesn't** worry/ bother/ concern sb **in the slightest/ least**
▶ **What** worries/ bothers/ concerns/ troubles/ disturbs **me is**...

worry [T] to make sb feel anxious about sth; to annoy sb: *What worries me is how I'm going to get another job.* ◇ *He's worried himself sick about his daughter.* ◇ *The noise never seems to worry her.*

bother [T] (*rather informal*) to annoy, worry or upset sb: *Does it bother you that she earns more than you?* ◇ *It bothers me to think of her alone in that big house.* ◇ *'I'm sorry he was so rude to you.' 'It doesn't bother me.'*

concern [T] (not usually used in the progressive tenses) to worry sb: *What concerns me is our lack of preparation for the change.* See also **concern** → CONCERN *noun*

trouble [T] to worry or upset sb: *What is it that's troubling you?*

disturb [T] to make sb worry: *The letter shocked and disturbed me.* ◇ *It disturbed her to realize that she was missing him already.*

> **NOTE** WORRY, BOTHER, CONCERN, TROUBLE OR DISTURB?
> These words all have very similar meanings. There are slight differences in strength, frequency and register. **Bother** is the most informal, especially in spoken phrases such as *It doesn't bother me* and *I'm not bothered.* **Concern** is the most formal and is not usually used in the progressive tenses: ~~What is it that's concerning you?~~

unsettle [T] to make sb feel upset or worried, especially because a situation has changed: *Changing schools might unsettle the kids.*

worrying *adj.* See also the entries for FRIGHTENING and PAINFUL 2

worrying · disturbing · unsettling · disconcerting · unnerving
These words all describe actions, events, situations, etc. that make you feel worried, nervous or uncomfortable.

PATTERNS AND COLLOCATIONS
▶ worrying/ disturbing/ unsettling/ disconcerting/ unnerving **for** sb
▶ a worrying/ disturbing **thought**
▶ a disturbing/ an unsettling/ an unnerving **effect/ experience**
▶ to **find sth** worrying/ disturbing/ unsettling/ disconcerting/ unnerving
▶ **very** worrying/ disturbing/ unsettling/ disconcerting/ unnerving

worrying making you worried: *a worrying development/ sign/trend* ◇ *It must be worrying not to know where he is.*

disturbing making you feel anxious and upset or shocked: *This is an extremely disturbing piece of news.*

unsettling making you feel upset, nervous or worried: *She found his questions deeply unsettling.* See also **unsettled** → RESTLESS

disconcerting making you feel worried, confused or embarrassed: *She had the disconcerting habit of saying exactly what she thought.* See also **disconcert** → SHAKE 4

unnerving making you feel nervous or not confident: *The whole experience was a little unnerving.* See also **unnerve** → SHAKE 4

> **NOTE** UNSETTLING, DISCONCERTING OR UNNERVING? These words all describe things, events, etc. that make you feel uncomfortable or not confident and calm. **Disconcerting** is used especially to talk about sb's actions, appearance or character, **unsettling** and **unnerving** often describe a situation, event or atmosphere.

worsen *verb* See also the entry for WEAKEN

worsen · get worse · weaken · deteriorate · decline · slip · degenerate · fail · relapse
These words all mean to get smaller, weaker or worse in some way.

PATTERNS AND COLLOCATIONS
▶ to deteriorate/ degenerate/ relapse **into** sth
▶ sb's **health** worsens/ gets worse/ deteriorates/ declines/ fails
▶ a **situation** worsens/ gets worse/ deteriorates/ degenerates
▶ **conditions** worsen/ get worse/ deteriorate
▶ the **weather** worsens/ gets worse/ deteriorates
▶ **sales** weaken/ deteriorate/ decline/ slip
▶ sb/ sth's **popularity** weakens/ declines/ slips
▶ **quality** deteriorates/ declines/ slips
▶ to worsen/ weaken/ deteriorate/ decline/ degenerate **rapidly**
▶ to worsen/ weaken/ deteriorate/ decline **significantly/ steadily**
▶ to worsen/ weaken/ decline/ slip **considerably**
▶ to worsen/ weaken/ decline **slightly**
▶ to worsen/ deteriorate/ decline **dramatically**
▶ to get **steadily/ considerably/ slightly** worse

worsen [I] (*rather formal*) to become worse: *The political situation is steadily worsening.* ◇ *Her symptoms have worsened considerably since we last saw her.* **OPP improve** → IMPROVE 2

get 'worse *phrase* (*rather informal, especially spoken*) to worsen; to become even more ill: *Things are just getting worse and worse.* ◇ *If he gets any worse we'll call the doctor.* **OPP get better** → IMPROVE 2

weaken [I] to become less strong or powerful: *His authority is steadily weakening.* **OPP strengthen** → STRENGTHEN

deteriorate /dɪˈtɪəriəreɪt; *AmE* -ˈtɪr-/ [I] (*rather formal*) to become worse: *The overall quality of rivers and canals has deteriorated.* ◇ *The discussion quickly deteriorated into an angry argument.* **OPP improve** → IMPROVE 2

> **NOTE** WORSEN OR DETERIORATE? In many cases you can use either word: *sb's health/a situation/conditions/ the weather/a relationship worsen(s)/deteriorate(s).* **Worsen** is often used to talk about particular problems, represented by countable nouns, including *problem, crisis, position* and *symptom:* ~~Her symptoms have deteriorated considerably.~~ **Deteriorate** is often used to talk about more general things, represented by un-countable nouns, including *life, work, behaviour, morale* and *quality*; it is also used in the phrase *sth deteriorates into sth:* ~~The overall quality of rivers and canals has worsened.~~ ◇ ~~The discussion worsened into an angry argument.~~

decline /dɪˈklaɪn/ [I] (*rather formal*) to become weaker: *Support for the party continues to decline.* ◇ *Her health was declining rapidly.* ❶ In this meaning **decline** is used to talk about sb's health, the economic strength of a country, area or industry, or support for sb/sth. Collocates include *health, economy, industry, fortunes, prosperity, support* and *popularity.* There is a closely related meaning of **decline**, 'to become lower in level or number'. See also **decline** → REDUCTION *noun*

slip (-pp-) [I] (*rather informal, especially business*) to fall to a slightly lower level; to become gradually worse: *His popularity has slipped recently.* ◇ *That's three times she's beaten me − I must be slipping!* ◇ *Pre-tax profits slipped to $3.7 million, from $3.9 million the previous year.*

degenerate /dɪˈdʒenəreɪt/ [I] (*rather formal*) to change into sth worse: *The march rapidly degenerated into a riot.* ❶ **Degenerate** is most often used in the phrase *degenerate into* sth. Typical collocations include *degenerate into a conflict/a riot/a battle/chaos/violence/a farce/a brawl.*

fail [I] (used especially in the progressive tenses) (of sb's health or sight) to become weak: *Her eyesight is failing.* ◇ *His last months in office were marred by failing health.*

relapse /rɪˈlæps/ [I] (*rather formal*) to go back into a worse state of health after making an improvement: *Two days after leaving the hospital she relapsed into a coma.* **OPP recover** → RECOVER 1
▸ **relapse** /rɪˈlæps; ˈriːlæps/ *noun* [C, U]: *to have/suffer a relapse*

worthy *adj.*

worthy · fine · noble · admirable · deserving · honourable · creditable
These words all describe sb/sth that deserves admiration and respect.

PATTERNS AND COLLOCATIONS
▸ to be worthy/ deserving **of** sth
▸ a worthy/ a fine/ a noble/ an admirable **man**/ **woman**
▸ a worthy/ a fine/ a noble/ a/ a creditable **effort**
▸ a worthy/ a fine/ a noble/ a deserving/ an honourable **cause**
▸ worthy/ fine/ noble **ideals**/ **principles**
▸ fine/ noble/ admirable **work**
▸ a fine/ an admirable/ a creditable **performance**

worthy /ˈwɜːði; *AmE* ˈwɜːrði/ (*formal, often approving*) deserving sth such as respect, attention or admiration: *A number of the report's findings are* **worthy of** *note.* ◇ *Several of our members are* **worthy of** *particular mention.* ◇ *He felt he was not worthy of her* (= that he did not deserve her love). ◇ *In Mason we have a worthy new champion* (= one who deserved to win). ◇ *The money we raise will be going to a very worthy cause.* ◇ *He's a very worthy man, I suppose, but he's very dull.* **OPP unworthy** ❶ A person or thing that is **unworthy** of sth does not have the necessary qualities to deserve sth, especially respect: *He considered himself* **unworthy of** *the honour they had bestowed on him.*

fine [only before noun] (*rather formal, approving*) having qualities that deserve respect and admiration, for example honesty and professionalism: *He was a fine man and a fine soldier* (= respected both as a man and as a soldier). ◇ *It was a fine example of leadership.*

noble /ˈnəʊbl; *AmE* ˈnoʊbl/ (*rather formal, approving*) having or involving qualities that people admire, for example courage, honesty and care for others: *She died in a noble cause.* ◇ *It was very noble of you to go so far to take him home.*
▸ **nobly** *adv.*: *They acted generously and nobly.*

admirable /ˈædmərəbl/ (*formal, approving*) having qualities that you admire and respect: *Her dedication to her work is admirable.* ◇ *He made his point with admirable clarity.*
▸ **admirably** *adv.*: *They cope admirably with the many demands put upon them.*

deserving /dɪˈzɜːvɪŋ; *AmE* -ˈzɜːrv-/ (*formal*) that deserves help, support or attention: *Only the most* **deserving cases** *ever get any state help.* ◇ *A distinction was made between the deserving and the undeserving poor.* **OPP undeserving** ❶ A person or thing that is **undeserving** does not deserve to have or receive sth: *He was* **undeserving of** *her affections.*

honourable (*BrE*) (*AmE* **honorable**) /ˈɒnərəbl; *AmE* ˈɑːnə-/ deserving respect; not bringing any shame: *She had a long and honourable career in government.* ◇ *The team managed an honourable 2–2 draw.* **OPP dishonourable** → DESPICABLE, See also **honour** → REPUTATION

NOTE FINE, NOBLE, ADMIRABLE OR HONOURABLE? Noble is the strongest of these words, used of actions like dying for your country. **Fine** suggests sb who does their duty honestly and well. **Admirable** often describes less personal qualities such as *balance* or *clarity*. **Honourable** in this meaning is a slightly less positive word: it is often used to say that sb has nothing to be ashamed of, especially when they have done sth fairly good in difficult circumstances. You would not talk about: ~~a fine/noble/admirable 2–2 draw~~: a *draw* is not good enough, and a sports result is not important enough to be **noble** or **admirable**, although you might talk about *a fine win.* You can talk about *a fine/noble/admirable man/woman* in this meaning; but *an honourable man/woman* means one who has high moral standards. See also **honourable** → RESPECTABLE

creditable /ˈkredɪtəbl/ (*formal*) of a fairly good standard, and deserving praise or approval: *The chairman welcomed the company's creditable performance in the previous year.* ◇ *Although they struggled, they ended up coming a creditable second* (= second in a race or competition). ❶ **Creditable** is used more about achievements than efforts. Typical collocates are *performance, result, achievement* and *showing.* It describes achievements of a standard that is fairly high but not excellent.
▸ **creditably** *adv.*: *All three players performed creditably.*

wrap sb/sth around/round sb/sth
phrasal verb

wrap · roll · coil · curl · wind · loop · twist
These words all refer to sth turning around itself or being put around sth else.

PATTERNS AND COLLOCATIONS
▸ to wrap sth/ coil/ curl/ wind sth/ loop sth/ twist sth **around**/ **round** sb/ sth
▸ to roll sth/ curl/ wind sth **into** a ball
▸ to roll/ coil/ curl **up**

wrap sb/sth a'round/'round sb/sth *phrasal verb* (-pp-) to put sth firmly around sb/sth: *The nurse wrapped a bandage tightly around my ankle.* ◇ *His arms were wrapped around her waist.* ❶ You usually **wrap** sth made of fabric or other material, or an arm or your arms **around/round** a person or part of the body.

roll [T, I] (usually used with an adverb or preposition) to make sth/yourself into the shape of a ball or tube: *I rolled the string into a ball.* ◇ *We rolled up the carpet.* ◇ *The hedgehog rolled up into a ball.* **OPP unroll** → SPREAD, See also **roll** → ROLL *noun*

coil [T, I] (usually used with an adverb or preposition) to turn sth around itself in a series of circles; (especially of a snake) to turn around itself in a series of circles: *He coiled the rope into a loop.* ◇ *Her hair was coiled on top of her head.* ◇ *The snake coiled up, ready to strike.*
▸ **coil** *noun* [C]: *The device consisted of a coil of copper wire, connected at either end to two electrodes.* ◇ *Shake the rope and let the coils unwind.*

curl [I, T] (usually used with an adverb or preposition) to form or make sth form into a curved shape: *The cat curled into a ball and went to sleep.* ◇ *The paper started to shrivel and curl up in the heat.* ◇ *She curled her legs up under her.*

wind /waɪnd/ [T] (usually used with an adverb or preposition) to wrap or turn sth long and thin around itself or sth else: *He wound the wool into a ball.* ◇ *Wind the bandage around your finger.*

loop /luːp/ [T] (always used with an adverb or preposition) to form or bend sth into a loop (= the shape of a curve or circle): *He looped the strap over his shoulder.* ◇ *The horse's reins were looped around its neck.*

▶ **loop** noun [C]: *Make a loop in the string.* ◊ *He attached the keys to a belt loop on his jeans.*

twist [T, I] (usually used with an adverb or preposition) to wind sth around or through an object; to move or grow by winding around sth: *She twisted a scarf around her head.* ◊ *The telephone cable has got twisted* (= wound around itself). ◊ *A snake was twisting around his arm.*

wriggle verb See also the entry for SHAKE 1

wriggle · writhe · fidget · squirm · wiggle · twist
These words all mean to turn or move your body or part of your body around with quick short movements.

PATTERNS AND COLLOCATIONS
▶ to wriggle / writhe / twist **about** / **around**
▶ to wriggle / squirm / twist **away** / **free**
▶ to wriggle / writhe / squirm **in** pain / discomfort / delight, etc.
▶ to wriggle / writhe / squirm **with** pain / embarrassment etc.
▶ to fidget / squirm / twist **in your chair** / **seat**
▶ to wriggle / wiggle **your toes**

wriggle /ˈrɪgl/ [I, T] to turn your body or part of your body with quick short movements; to move somewhere by turning your body in this way: *The children wriggled uncomfortably in their seats.* ◊ *They wriggled their way through the tunnel.* ◊ (*especially BrE*) *Can you wriggle your toes?* ❶ In American English it is more usual to say *wiggle your toes.*

writhe /raɪð/ [I] to twist and turn your body with big movements from side to side, often because you are in a lot of pain: *He was writhing around on the floor, clutching his side.* ◊ *She was writhing in agony.*

fidget /ˈfɪdʒɪt/ [I] to keep moving your body, your hands or your feet, because you are bored, nervous or excited: *Sit still and stop fidgeting!* ◊ *She fidgeted with her keys as she talked* (= kept moving them around with her fingers).

squirm /skwɜːm; *AmE* skwɜːrm/ [I] to move around a lot making small twisting movements, because you are uncomfortable, nervous or embarrassed.; to move somewhere making movements like this: *The little boy squirmed with embarrassment.*

wiggle [I, T] (*informal*) (of a part of the body) to move from side to side or up and down with short quick movements; to make a part of your body do this: *Her bottom wiggled as she walked past.* ◊ *Try to wiggle your hips.*

twist [I, T] to turn your body with quick sharp movements and change direction often: *She tried unsuccessfully to twist free.* ◊ *Rachel twisted and turned in her sleep.*

write verb

1 Write clearly in black ink.
2 write a book

1 write · sign · write sth down · put sth down · scribble · copy · scrawl · transcribe
These words all mean to form letters or numbers on a surface, especially using a pen or pencil.

PATTERNS AND COLLOCATIONS
▶ to write / sign / write sth down / put sth down / scribble / scrawl **on** sth
▶ to write / write sth down / put sth down / scribble / scrawl **in** sth
▶ to copy / transcribe sth **into** sth
▶ to write / sign / write sth down / put sth down / scribble / scrawl **with** sth
▶ to write / put / scribble / copy / scrawl sth **down**
▶ to write / copy sth **out**
▶ to write / write down / put down / scribble / copy / transcribe some **notes**
▶ to write / sign / write down / put down / scribble / scrawl your **name**
▶ to write / scribble / scrawl your **signature**

write [I, T] to form letters, words or numbers on a surface such as paper, especially using a pen or pencil; to give information in writing: *I haven't got anything to write with.* ◊ *Please write clearly in black ink.* ◊ *In some countries children don't start learning to read and write until they are six.* ◊ *Write your answer out again on a new sheet of paper.* ◊ *Ancient historians wrote of a lost continent beneath the ocean.* ◊ *In his latest book he writes that the theory has since been disproved.* ◊ *I'll write you a receipt.*

▶ **writing** noun [U]: *Our son's having problems with his reading and writing.* ◊ *There was writing all over the desk.* ◊ *Who's this from? I don't recognize the writing.*

sign [I, T] to write your name on a letter or document, to show that you have written it, that you agree with what it says, or that it is genuine: *Sign here, please.* ◊ *Sign your name here, please.* ◊ *You haven't signed the letter.* ◊ *The treaty was signed on 24 March.* ◊ *The player was signing autographs for a group of fans.* ◊ *He signed himself 'Jimmy'.*

▶ **signature** noun [C, U]: *Someone had forged her signature on the cheque.* ◊ (*formal*) *Two copies of the contract will be sent to you for signature.*

write sth ˈdown phrasal verb to write sth on paper, especially in order to remember or record it: *Write down the address before you forget it.* ◊ *Everything he said was written down.*

put sth ˈdown phrasal verb to write sth down: *The meeting's on the 23rd. Put it down in your diary.* ◊ *One day I'm going to put it all down on paper.*

NOTE WRITE STH DOWN OR PUT STH DOWN? There is no real difference in meaning between these two verbs. **Put sth down** is usually used with a prepositional phrase to show where or how sth is written: *Put it down in your diary/on paper/in writing.*

scribble [T, I] to write sth quickly and carelessly, especially because you do not have much time; to draw marks that do not mean anything: *He scribbled a note to his sister before leaving.* ◊ *Throughout the interview, the journalists scribbled away furiously.* ◊ *Someone had scribbled all over the table in crayon.*

▶ **scribble** noun [U, pl.]: *How do you expect me to read this scribble?* ◊ *The page was covered with a mass of scribbles.*

copy [T] to write sth exactly as it is written somewhere else: *She copied the phone number into her address book.* ◊ *I copied out several poems.*

scrawl [T, I] to write sth in a careless untidy way, making it difficult to read: *She had scrawled the directions on a piece of paper.* ◊ *Someone had scrawled all over my notes.*

▶ **scrawl** noun [C, U]: *Her signature was an illegible scrawl.* ◊ *I can't be expected to read this scrawl!*

NOTE SCRIBBLE OR SCRAWL? People **scrawl** when they are being careless, but not particularly because they do not have much time: ~~The journalists scrawled away furiously.~~

transcribe /trænˈskraɪb/ [T] to record thoughts, speech or data in a written form, or in a different form from the original: *Clerks transcribe everything that is said in court.* ◊ *The interview was recorded and then transcribed.* See also **transcript** → COPY noun 1

2 See the Topic Map for THE MEDIA on p.890
write · compose · dash sth off
These words all mean to produce sth in written form so that people can read, perform or use it.

PATTERNS AND COLLOCATIONS
▶ to write / compose / dash off a / an **letter** / **essay**
▶ to write / compose a / an **novel** / **poem** / **speech** / **song** / **opera** / **symphony**
▶ to write / compose **music**
▶ to write / dash off a **note**

write [T, I] to produce sth in written form so that people can read, perform or use it: *He hopes to write a book about his experiences one day.* ◇ *She had to write a report on the project.* ◇ *Students will be expected to write their own computer programs.* ◇ *I wanted to travel and then write about it.* ◇ *He writes for 'The New Yorker'* (= works as a writer). ◇ *She wrote him several poems.* See also **writing** → LITERATURE, **writings** → WORK *noun* 4

compose /kəmˈpəʊz; *AmE* -ˈpoʊz/ [T] (*rather formal*) to write music; to write a letter, speech, poem, etc. with a lot of care and thought: *Mozart composed his last opera shortly before he died.* ◇ *She composed a letter of protest.* See also **composition** → WORK *noun* 4

,dash sth 'off *phrasal verb* to write or draw sth very quickly: *I dashed off a note to my brother.*

writer *noun* See also the entry for REPORTER

writer · author · poet · novelist · playwright · biographer · scribe · scriptwriter · dramatist · screenwriter
These are all words for a person whose job is writing sth.

PATTERNS AND COLLOCATIONS
▸ an **award-winning** writer / author / poet / novelist / playwright / screenwriter
▸ a / an **famous** / **aspiring** writer / author / poet / novelist / playwright / screenwriter
▸ a **best-selling** / **romantic** writer / author / poet / novelist
▸ a **historical** / **science fiction** writer / author / novelist
▸ a writer / an author / a poet / a novelist / a playwright / a biographer / a scribe / a scriptwriter / a dramatist / a screenwriter **writes** sth

writer [C] a person whose job is writing; a person who has written a particular thing: *a travel/science/cookery writer* ◇ *the writer of this letter/article/computer program*

author [C] a person who has written sth such as a book, story or article: *She is a published author.* ◇ *Who's the author?*

poet /ˈpəʊɪt; *AmE* ˈpoʊət/ [C] a person who writes poems: *the Romantic poets*

novelist /ˈnɒvəlɪst; *AmE* ˈnɑːv-/ [C] a person who writes novels: *She is now a best-selling novelist.* See also **novel** → BOOK

playwright /ˈpleɪraɪt/ [C] a person who writes plays for the theatre, television or radio: *The famous playwright died in 1616 at the age of 52.* See also **play** → PLAY *noun*

biographer /baɪˈɒɡrəfə(r); *AmE* -ˈɑːɡ-/ [C] a person who writes a biography (= the story of another person's life): *As Dr Johnson's biographer, Boswell became quite famous in his own right.*

scribe /skraɪb/ [C] a person who made copies of written documents before printing was invented: *Before paper was common, medieval scribes used parchment or vellum.*

scriptwriter /ˈskrɪptraɪtə(r)/ [C] a person who writes the script (= a written text that is meant to be read or performed aloud) for plays, films or broadcasts: *Not even Hollywood scriptwriters had dreamt up such a horrific chain of events.*

dramatist /ˈdræmətɪst/ [C] (*rather formal*) a person who writes plays for the theatre, television or radio: *It is a powerful story written by a great dramatist.* See also **drama** → PLAY *noun*
▸ **dramatize** (*BrE* also **-ise**) /ˈdræmətaɪz/ *verb* [T]: *The book has been dramatized on television.*
▸ **dramatization** (*BrE* also **-isation**) /ˌdræmətaɪˈzeɪʃn; -təˈz-/ *noun* [C, U]: *a television dramatization of the trial*

> NOTE PLAYWRIGHT OR DRAMATIST? There is very little difference in meaning or use between these words. Both are used especially to talk about people who write plays for the theatre, although they can also refer to writers for television or radio. **Playwright** is used equally to talk about modern writers and writers in the past; **dramatist** is used slightly more to talk about writers in the past, although you can also talk about *modern dramatists*.

screenwriter /ˈskriːnraɪtə(r)/ [C] a person who writes screenplays (= scripts for films and television dramas): *an Oscar-winning screenwriter*

wrong *adj.*
1 the wrong answer
2 What's wrong?
3 the wrong thing to say
4 morally wrong

1 See the Topic Map for FACT AND OPINION on p.898
wrong · false · mistaken · incorrect · inaccurate · misguided · untrue
These words all describe sth that is not right or correct, or sb who is not right about sth.

PATTERNS AND COLLOCATIONS
▸ to be wrong / mistaken **about** sth
▸ a **prediction** is wrong / false / incorrect / inaccurate
▸ a **guess** is wrong / incorrect
▸ wrong / false / mistaken / incorrect / inaccurate / untrue **information**
▸ a wrong / a false / a mistaken / an incorrect / an inaccurate / a misguided **assumption**
▸ a false / a mistaken / an inaccurate / a misguided **belief**
▸ to **give** / **get** the wrong / a false / a mistaken / an inaccurate **impression**
▸ a wrong / an incorrect **answer**
▸ **totally** wrong / false / mistaken / incorrect / inaccurate / misguided / untrue
▸ **completely** wrong / false / mistaken / incorrect / misguided / untrue
▸ **quite** wrong / false / mistaken / inaccurate / misguided / untrue
▸ **clearly** wrong / false / incorrect / untrue
▸ **seriously** wrong / mistaken / incorrect / inaccurate
▸ **hopelessly** wrong / inaccurate / misguided
▸ **grossly** wrong / mistaken / incorrect / inaccurate / misguided
▸ **simply** wrong / incorrect / misguided / untrue
▸ **sadly** wrong / mistaken / misguided
▸ It is / would be wrong / false / incorrect / inaccurate / untrue **to say...**

wrong not right or correct; (of a person) not right about sb/sth: *I got all the answers wrong.* ◇ *He was driving on the wrong side of the road.* ◇ *Sorry, I must have dialled the wrong number.* ◇ *You're holding the camera the wrong way up.* ◇ (*BrE*) *That picture is the wrong way round.* ◇ (*AmE*) *the wrong way around* ◇ *I think she lives at number 40, but I could be wrong.* ◇ *She would prove him wrong whatever happened.* **OPP** **right** → RIGHT 1, **right** → TRUE, See also **the wrong idea** → ILLUSION
▸ **wrongly** *adv.*: *The sentence was wrongly translated.* ◇ *He assumed, wrongly, that she did not care.*

false not true or correct; wrong because it is based on sth that is not true or correct: *A whale is a fish.* **True or false?** ◇ *He used a false name to get the job.* ◇ *I don't want to raise any false hopes, but I think he's still alive.* ◇ *We had been lulled into a **false sense of security** (= wrongly made to feel safe).* ◇ *Buying a cheap computer is a **false economy** (= it will not save you money).* **OPP** **true** → TRUE, See also **false impression** → ILLUSION
▸ **falsely** *adv.*: *He had been falsely accused of murder.*

mistaken wrong in your opinion or judgement; based on a wrong opinion or bad judgement: *I thought I knew him, but I must have been mistaken.* ◇ *I told her my secret in the mistaken belief that I could trust her.* ◇ *It was a case of mistaken identity* (= when you think sb is a particular person but they are not). See also **mistake** → MISTAKE *noun* 1, **mistake** → MISUNDERSTAND *verb*
▸ **mistakenly** *adv.*: *He mistakenly believed that his family would stand by him.*

incorrect (*rather formal*) wrong according to the facts; containing mistakes: *Many of the figures were incorrect.* ◇ *Marks will be taken off for incorrect spellings.* ◇ *His version of what happened is incorrect.* ◇ *It's technically incorrect to talk about bats 'hearing' things.* **OPP** **correct** → TRUE
▸ **incorrectly** *adv.*: *A lot of people spell this incorrectly.*

inaccurate /ɪnˈækjərət/ wrong according to the facts; containing mistakes: *The movie is historically inaccurate, but well worth seeing.* ◇ *All the maps we had were wildly inaccurate.* **OPP** accurate → EXACT, See also **inaccuracy** → MISTAKE 2
▸ **inaccurately** *adv.*: *She has been inaccurately described as a soul singer.*

NOTE INCORRECT OR INACCURATE? A fact, figure or spelling that is wrong is **incorrect**; information, a belief or a description based on incorrect facts can be **incorrect** or **inaccurate**; something that is produced, such as a film, report or map, that contains incorrect facts is **inaccurate**.

misguided wrong because you have understood or judged a situation badly: *The new proposals are totally misguided.* ◇ *In her misguided attempts to help, she only made the situation worse.*

untrue [not usually before noun] not based on facts, but invented or guessed: *These accusations are totally untrue.* ◇ *It would be untrue to say that something like this could never happen again.* **OPP** true → TRUE

2 wrong · defective · faulty · up
These words all describe sth that causes problems or difficulties or is not as it should be.

PATTERNS AND COLLOCATIONS
▸ There is sth wrong/ up **with** sb/ sth.
▸ defective/ faulty **goods/ equipment/ parts/ workmanship**
▸ a defective/ faulty **memory**
▸ **seriously** wrong/ defective
▸ **Is anything** wrong/ up?
▸ **What's** wrong/ up?

wrong [not before noun] (*rather informal, especially spoken*) causing problems or difficulties; not as it should be: *Is anything wrong? You look worried.* ◇ *There's something wrong with the printer.* ◇ *The doctor could find nothing wrong with her.* **OPP** right → FINE
▸ **wrong** *adv.*: *Everything was going horribly wrong.*

defective (*rather formal*) /dɪˈfektɪv/ having sth wrong or not perfect; not working or made correctly: *The car was found to have defective brakes.* ◇ *She was born with defective hearing.* ❶ **Defective** can describe goods, equipment, parts in a machine, workmanship (= how sth is made), an organ in the body, or a function of the body such as sight, hearing or memory. See also **defect** → DEFECT

faulty having sth wrong or not perfect; not working or made correctly: *The retailers blamed faulty workmanship for the problem.* ◇ *I suppose her memory's a bit faulty.* ❶ **Faulty** can describe goods, equipment, parts in a machine or workmanship (= how sth is made). It can also describe sb's memory, but is NOT usually used for other functions or the body, or body organs. See also **fault** → DEFECT

up *adv.* [not before noun] (*informal, spoken*) used to say that sth is happening, especially sth unusual or unpleasant: *What's up with him? He looks furious.* ◇ *I could tell something was up by the looks on their faces.*

3 wrong · inappropriate · unsuitable · bad · inconvenient · unfit · awkward
These words all describe people or things that are not right for a particular situation.

PATTERNS AND COLLOCATIONS
▸ wrong/ inappropriate/ unsuitable/ inconvenient/ unfit/ awkward **for** sb/ sth
▸ wrong/ inappropriate/ unsuitable/ inconvenient/ unfit **to do sth**
▸ the wrong/ an inappropriate/ a bad/ an inconvenient/ an awkward **time**
▸ **most/ rather** inappropriate/ unsuitable/ inconvenient/ awkward
▸ **highly/ somewhat** inappropriate/ unsuitable/ inconvenient
▸ **quite/ completely/ totally** inappropriate/ unsuitable/ unfit
▸ **very/ extremely** unsuitable/ inconvenient/ awkward

wrong [usually before noun] not right for a particular situation or purpose: *He's the wrong person for the job.* ◇ *I realized that it was the wrong thing to say.* ◇ *We don't want this document falling into the wrong hands.* ❶ In this meaning, wrong usually comes after *the.* **OPP** right → GOOD 2

inappropriate (*rather formal*) not right or acceptable in a particular situation: *What's the best way for a teacher to deal with inappropriate behaviour?* ◇ *It would be inappropriate for me to comment on what your tutor said.* **OPP** appropriate → GOOD 2
▸ **inappropriately** *adv.*: *She was inappropriately dressed for a funeral.*

unsuitable not right or practical for a particular purpose, occasion or person: *He was wearing shoes that were totally unsuitable for climbing.* ◇ *They considered him quite unsuitable for their daughter.* **OPP** suitable → GOOD 2
▸ **unsuitably** *adv.*: *They were unsuitably dressed for the occasion.*

NOTE INAPPROPRIATE OR UNSUITABLE? Unsuitable clothes, equipment or facilities are usually wrong for a practical purpose. **Inappropriate** behaviour or clothes are usually wrong for social reasons.

bad [only before noun] causing problems for sb; not based on good judgement: *I know that this is a bad time to ask for help.* ◇ *He now realized that it had been a bad decision on his part.* ❶ In this meaning **bad** usually collocates with *time, timing, decision* or *reason.* **OPP** good → GOOD 2, **good** → GOOD 3

inconvenient (*rather formal*) causing trouble or problems, especially concerning what you need or would like yourself: *That's most inconvenient for me. I'm working that weekend.* **OPP** convenient → GOOD 2, See also **inconvenience** → NUISANCE

unfit not of an acceptable standard; not suitable: *They described him as unfit to govern.* ◇ *The meat was unfit for human consumption.* ◇ *The court claims she is an unfit mother.* ❶ **Unfit** is usually used in the phrases *unfit to do sth* or *unfit for sth*: *unfit to govern/rule/stand trial/drive* ◇ *unfit for human consumption/habitation.* When **unfit** comes before a noun, it is nearly always in the phrase *unfit mother.* **OPP** fit → GOOD 2

awkward not convenient: *Have I come at an awkward time?* ◇ *That's a bit awkward for me – could we make it earlier?*

NOTE INCONVENIENT OR AWKWARD? Inconvenient is more formal than **awkward** and can suggest a greater degree of inconvenience.

4 See also the entry for ILLEGAL
wrong · unfair · unjust · unequal · immoral · unethical · inequitable
These words all describe sb/sth that is not fair or morally right.

PATTERNS AND COLLOCATIONS
▸ wrong/ unfair/ unjust **of** sb
▸ wrong/ unfair/ unjust/ immoral/ unethical **to do sth**
▸ to be wrong/ unfair/ unjust **that...**
▸ an unfair/ unequal/ inequitable **share/ distribution** of sth
▸ immoral/ unethical **behaviour/ conduct**
▸ **very** wrong/ unfair/ unjust/ unequal
▸ **highly** unfair/ unjust/ unequal/ immoral/ unethical
▸ **quite/ totally** wrong/ unfair/ unjust/ immoral
▸ **patently** wrong/ unfair/ unjust

wrong [not usually before noun] not morally right: *Paying people such low wages is simply wrong.* ◇ *It's wrong to tell lies.* ◇ *It was wrong of me to lose my temper.* ◇ *This man has done nothing wrong.* ◇ *He knows that he's done wrong.* ◇ *There's nothing wrong with eating meat.* ◇ *What's wrong with leading a comfortable life?* **OPP** right → RIGHT 2, See also **wrong** → EVIL noun
▸ **wrongly** *adv.*: *She was wrongly accused of stealing.*

unfair not right or fair according to a set of rules or moral principles; not treating people equally or as they deserve: *Most of his criticisms were grossly unfair.* ◇ *It would be unfair not to let you have a choice.* ◇ *Life seems so unfair sometimes.* ◇ *The other team had definitely been given an unfair advantage.* ◇ *I don't want to be **unfair to** anyone, so you'll all get an equal chance.* ◇ (*BrE* also) *I don't want to be **unfair on** anyone …* **OPP** **fair** → REASONABLE, See also **unfairness** → INEQUALITY
▸ **unfairly** *adv.*: *He was beginning to wonder if he had treated her unfairly.*

unjust (*rather formal*) not deserved or fair: *Such unjust laws should be abolished.* ◇ *It's an unjust world that we live in.* ◇ *The system is corrupt and unjust.* ❶ **Unjust** is used especially to describe society and the legal system: collocates include *accusation, law, punishment, regime, society, system* and *world.* **OPP** **just** → REASONABLE, See also **injustice** → INEQUALITY
▸ **unjustly** *adv.*: *She felt that she had been unjustly punished.*

unequal /ʌnˈiːkwəl/ [usually before noun] in which people are treated in different ways or have different advantages in a way that seems unfair: *an unequal distribution of wealth* ◇ *They saw the war as an unequal contest between a massive superpower and a small and defenceless country.* **OPP** **equal** → REASONABLE, See also **inequality** → IN-EQUALITY

immoral (of people or their behaviour) not considered to be good or honest by most people: *There's nothing immoral about wanting to earn more money.* ◇ *I think this is an unjust and immoral war.* **OPP** **moral** → GOOD 5, See also **immoral** → EVIL *adj.*

unethical /ʌnˈeθɪkl/ not morally acceptable, especially by the standards of a particular profession or system: *Although it's not illegal, many people would consider it unethical.* **OPP** **ethical** → GOOD 5

inequitable /ɪnˈekwɪtəbl/ (*formal*) not fair; not treating people equally: *Distribution of wealth in the country is highly inequitable.* **OPP** **equitable** → REASONABLE

Y y

years noun

years · months · hours · ages · an eternity · aeon
These are all words for a long time.

PATTERNS AND COLLOCATIONS
▸ **for** years / months / hours / ages / an eternity / aeons
▸ years / months / hours / ages / an eternity / aeons **ago**
▸ to **spend** / **take** / **wait** years / months / hours / ages / an eternity
▸ years / months / hours **elapse** / **go by** / **pass**

years [pl.] (*informal*) a long time, especially a period of several years: *It's been years since we last met.* ◇ *They haven't seen each other for years.* ◇ *That's the best movie I've seen **in years**.*

months [pl.] a long time, especially a period of several months: *He had to wait for months for the visas to come through.* ◇ *It will be months before we get the results.*

hours [pl.] a long time, especially a period of several hours: *I've been waiting for hours.*

ages [pl.] (*especially BrE*) (*BrE* also **an age** [sing.]) (*informal*) a long time: *I waited for ages.* ◇ *'How long have you been here?' 'Ages.'* ◇ *It's been an age since we've seen them.*

an eternity [sing.] (*informal*) a period of time that seems to be very long or to never end: *After what **seemed like an eternity** the nurse returned with the results of the test.*

aeon (*BrE*) (also **eon** especially in *AmE*) /ˈiːən/ [C] (*formal*) an extremely long period of time; thousands of years: *These hills have been worn down over aeons of geological time.* ◇ *Only yesterday – and it seemed eons ago, not just a few hours – he had been a happily married man.*

young adj.

young · teenage · juvenile · junior · adolescent · teen
These words all describe sb/sth that has lived or existed for only a short time and is therefore not yet fully developed.

PATTERNS AND COLLOCATIONS
▸ a young / a teenage / an adolescent **boy** / **girl**
▸ a young / juvenile **offender**
▸ a young / teenage **fan**
▸ a teenage / teen **idol**

young having lived or existed for only a short time; not yet old; consisting of young people or young children: *young babies/children/animals* ◇ *Caterpillars eat the young leaves of this plant.* ◇ *Fruit Fresh is a young company that is growing fast.* ◇ *The team is full of talented young players.* ◇ *I am the youngest of four sisters.* ◇ *They **married young** (= at an early age).* ◇ *This cottage would be perfect for a couple with a young family (= a couple with young children).* OPP **old, elderly, aged** → OLD 2

teenage /ˈtiːneɪdʒ/ [usually before noun] between 13 and 19 years old; connected with people of this age: *The place was full of giggling teenage girls.* ◇ *He went through a brief period of teenage rebellion when he was 16.* See also **teenager** → GIRL

juvenile /ˈdʒuːvənaɪl; *AmE* -vənl/ [only before noun] (*formal or law*) connected with young people who are not yet adults: *What can be done to help these **juvenile delinquents** turn away from crime?* ◇ *The government has failed to deal with the problem of juvenile crime.* OPP **adult** → ADULT, See also **juvenile** → GIRL noun

junior [only before noun] connected with young people below a particular age, rather than with adults, especially in sports: *The world junior tennis championships will be held in Paris next month.* ❶ In Britain **junior** also describes a school or part of a school for children between the ages of 7 and 11 or 13: *My daughter goes into the junior school next year.* ◇ *the junior department*

adolescent /ˌædəˈlesnt/ of the age when a child develops into an adult, at some point between 12 and 18 years old: *the attitudes of adolescent girls* See also **adolescent** → GIRL

teen [usually before noun] (*especially AmE, informal*) teenage: *It was a teen magazine, full of glossy pictures of the latest pop idols.* See also **teenager** → GIRL

STUDY SECTION CONTENTS

Study Pages

Topic Maps and Exercises

Answer Key

A A Film Review

Read the following film review and do the exercise that follows.

★★★★ "I love this film"

Published in 2003 and directed by Sofia Coppola, **Lost in Translation** is a highly
applauded comedy drama that was _suggested_ for several Academy Awards, including
Best Picture.

The _narrative_ revolves around a chance meeting in Tokyo between a middle-aged
movie star (_performed_ by Bill Murray) and a young woman (Scarlett Johansson), and
the unlikely but intimate _acquaintance_ that develops between the two.

On one level, **Lost in Translation** is about the culture shock experienced by two
Americans in Japan. However, the film also _concerns_ the themes of loneliness and
companionship as the two _heroes_ find comfort in each other.

A stylish and intelligent film, **Lost in Translation**'s appeal lies in its moving portrayal
of a relationship between two lost and _alone_ souls. It benefits from a great _text_ and
superb performances from the two lead actors. It may only last for 105 minutes, but
this thought-provoking film will stay with you for days.

The <u>underlined</u> words in the text above are not used correctly. Can you find a better
word in each case? Look at the entries given in SMALL CAPS to help you.

1 published _____ (PUBLISH 2)

2 applauded _____ (PRAISE _verb_)

3 suggested _____ (RECOMMEND 2)

4 narrative _____ (STORY 1)

5 performed _____ (PLAY _verb_ 3)

6 acquaintance _____ (FRIENDSHIP)

7 concerns _____ (APPLY 2)

8 heroes _____ (STAR 2)

9 alone _____ (LONELY)

10 text _____ (SCRIPT)

Here are some more opinions about books or films. Are the underlined words used
correctly? If not, look at the entry given to find a better word.

11 I absolutely <u>liked</u> this book. (LIKE _verb_)

12 Apparently, he always does his own <u>stunts</u>. (ACTION)

13 This is one of my <u>preferred</u> films of all time. (FAVOURITE)

14 I was totally <u>gripped</u> from <u>start</u> to end. (INTEREST _verb_; START _noun_)

15 It's a <u>tragic</u> story, so don't expect a happy <u>conclusion</u>. (SAD; END _noun_)

B Find 10 pairs of synonyms in the box below. They are all <u>nouns</u>.

scriptwriter	lead /liːd/	sketch	episode
chapter	writing	clip	literature
score	author	work of art	drawing
masterpiece	entertainer	artist	sculptor
passage	lyrics	performer	star

Now use one of the nouns from each pair of synonyms to complete these sentences.

1 The show includes works by several renowned landscape _____.

2 He has been in a few films, but this is the first time he will be playing the _____.

3 I've nearly finished the book – I've only got two more _____ to read.

4 I think he writes the music for their songs and she writes the _____.

5 She's one of the country's most prolific _____ of children's fiction.

6 This majestic building is widely regarded as one of the country's architectural _____.

7 Welcome to the show. Let's begin by watching a _____ from your new movie.

8 The exhibition shows how the artist gets from his first rough _____ to the finished piece.

9 The course focuses on modern works of _____ rather than the classics.

10 They hired a children's _____ for their daughter's birthday party.

C Choose the best verb for each of these sentences, using the following <u>verb</u> entries to help you: DRAW, FEATURE, PLAY 3, RECORD 2.

1 She *drew*/*painted*/*sketched* a detailed map of the route for her guests.

2 The singer *featured*/*starred*/*appeared* on David Letterman's show last week to promote her latest album.

3 The London Ballet Company *played*/*staged*/*produced* an outdoor production of *Swan Lake* in the castle grounds.

4 It's a good story and the film is well *played*/*performed*/*acted*.

5 The movie was mostly *recorded*/*photographed*/*shot* on location in Brazil.

6 It's a great book – I highly *recommend*/*suggest*/*endorse* it.

D Look at the <u>adjectives</u> used in the descriptions below. Label each one very positive (++), positive (+), negative (–) or very negative (– –). Use the alphabetical index starting on p.921 to help you find the right entry.

1 a *lacklustre* performance _____
2 an *innovative* design _____
3 a *delightful* evening _____
4 an *abysmal* film _____
5 a *mediocre* writer _____
6 a *realistic* portrayal _____
7 a *classic* novel _____
8 an *eminent* poet _____
9 *wooden* acting _____
10 a *lifelike* statue _____

CUSTOMS AND TRADITIONS

A Thanksgiving Day

Read the following article and fill the gaps with the most suitable synonym from the entry given. Don't forget to use the right form of the synonym you choose.

In the US, we celebrate Thanksgiving Day on the fourth Thursday in November. Schools and most (1) _____ (COMPANY) close, and many people make the whole weekend a vacation.

The (2) _____ (SOURCE) of this holiday can be traced way back to 1621, when the Pilgrims celebrated the end of a bountiful harvest and gave (3) _____ (THANKS) to God for all the good things they had to eat, which meant they would not starve over the winter months.

Nowadays, it is a time when the whole family (4) _____ (MEET 1). The (5) _____ (USUAL) Thanksgiving Dinner (6) _____ (CONSIST OF SB/STH) a large roasted turkey, cranberry sauce, sweet potatoes, corn and other typically American vegetables. For dessert we have pumpkin pie.

On Thanksgiving there are special TV (7) _____ (PROGRAMME) and sporting (8) _____ (RACE). In New York there is a (9) _____ (FLEET) through the streets, and many people enjoy watching the football games on TV. The day after Thanksgiving is (10) _____ (REGARD) the beginning of the Christmas (11) _____ (TIME 2), so we can all start (12) _____ (EXPECT) to the next holiday!

....

B What are these sentences describing? Match each one with a synonym from the entry in SMALL CAPS.

BACKGROUND

1 My parents were quite strict, but I had a happy childhood.

2 I come from a middle-class family.

3 I was made Employee of the Year in 2006.

| record |
| upbringing |
| background |

TRADITION

4 Business letters to an unknown person begin 'Dear Sir/Madam'.

5 We keep our clients informed throughout the manufacturing process.

6 People send each other greetings cards at Christmas.

| tradition |
| practice |
| convention |

CULTURE

7 I'm British Asian. I love football but also traditional Punjabi music.

8 I've always been fascinated by the ancient Egyptians.

9 All the local farmers feel the same way about this issue.

| culture |
| community |
| civilization |

C Here are some descriptions of customs. Which word is best for each sentence? Look at the entries given to help you.

1 The children wore colourful **costumes/disguises** and performed a traditional dance. (COSTUME)

2 The whole village was invited to join in the evening's **function/festivities**. (EVENT 2)

3 Grandma, what special clothes did you use to wear in **history/the old days**? (THE PAST)

4 What is a traditional marriage **ceremony/ritual** like in your culture? (CEREMONY)

5 In a break with **tradition/custom**, no hot food was served. (TRADITION)

6 This national event **happens/takes place** every year in February. (HAPPEN)

7 You don't have to **wear/have on** a suit, but most men do. (WEAR)

8 It's an old family custom, **transmitted/handed down** through the generations. (PASS STH ON)

D Are these adjectives synonyms of words meaning normal or unusual? Write **N** or **U** next to each one, using these entries to help you: GENERAL, MUNDANE, NEW 3, STRANGE 2, TRADITIONAL, UNUSUAL

alien	unaccustomed to	mundane	eccentric
humdrum	mainstream	unknown	widespread
commonplace	unorthodox	conventional	unused to

Now choose a suitable word from the box above to complete these sentences, using the entries to help you. There may be more than one possible answer.

1 She has always been a popular teacher, despite her rather _____ teaching methods.

2 Free Internet access is becoming increasingly _____ in cafes, bars and restaurants.

3 For those of you who are _____ travelling alone, here are some general guidelines.

4 Bored with his _____ life, he left his job and set off on a round-the-world trip.

5 She had to learn to adjust to life in a culture that was completely _____ to her.

E Number the following sentences in order from the most frequent action (1) to the least frequent (6), using these entries to help you: OCCASIONAL, OFTEN, SOMETIMES, RARELY, USUALLY

1 On **the odd** occasion, when the weather has been really bad, we have held the event indoors. ___

2 **As a rule**, it is not considered polite to arrive more than five minutes late. ___

3 Young people **hardly ever** attend the event – it's really for adults. ___

4 I'm on my own a lot, which can get lonely **at times**. ___

5 Visitors' bags are **routinely** checked as they enter the building. ___

6 We **often** hold dances to celebrate special events. ___

GREEN ISSUES

A Recycling around the World

Read the following magazine article and do the exercise that follows.

We all know that we should recycle more and send less waste to our over-flowing landfill [1]sites, and some countries are better at doing this than others. In the second of our weekly reports on recycling in different countries around the world, Jurgen from Belgium explains why his country is at the [2]forefront of recycling in Europe.

"Recycling has become a way of life for us in Belgium. We recycle over 70% of household waste, which is more than most other countries in Europe. We have a 'pay-as-you-throw' [3]technique, which means that the more we [4]throw out, the more we pay.

All households pay a low, fixed, waste fee to the local council. We also pay each time our rubbish is [5]collected from our house. [6]Fines for this [7]vary according to what, and how much, we [8]eliminate. We separate all our rubbish into different bins, which are weighed before and after they are [9]drained.

We Belgians are very [10]aware of how much rubbish we produce. We buy food with less packaging and some of us even have chickens in the back garden to help [11]reduce our food waste!

I think this is a good system. It is an [12]effective way of [13]urging recycling and helping the [14]environment."

Look at the <u>underlined</u> words in the text. Some of them are not the best word to use; for each one, decide if the word given below would be a better choice. Look at the entry given to help you.

		✓/✗				✓/✗	
1	venues	✗	(PLACE *noun* 1)	8	throw away	___	(REMOVE 1)
2	fore	___	(LEAD *noun* 1)	9	emptied	___	(CLEAR *verb*)
3	system	___	(WAY 2)	10	conscious	___	(AWARE)
4	remove	___	(REMOVE 1)	11	decrease	___	(REDUCE)
5	picked up	___	(GET 3)	12	winning	___	(SUCCESSFUL 1)
6	charges	___	(RATE 2)	13	encouraging	___	(ENCOURAGE 2)
7	change	___	(CHANGE *verb* 2)	14	nature	___	(NATURE 2)

B Look at the entry for WASTE *noun*. Complete these sentences with a word from the entry, without using the same word more than once.

1 (*BrE*) Don't forget to take out the _____. The dustmen will be here early in the morning.

2 (*AmE*) Don't forget to take out the _____. The _____ men will be here early in the morning.

3 (*AmE/BrE*) New fines are being introduced for anyone caught dropping _____ in the street.

4 (*AmE/BrE*) _____ collectors in the city have been on strike for two weeks and the city's _____ is piling up on the streets.

C Are these synonyms used correctly? Correct any errors that you find, using these entries to help you: HABITAT, NATURE 2, THE WORLD. Remember some sentences are correct.

1 The first pictures of a giant squid in its natural **habitat** have been taken in deep water near Japan.

2 A male cat's natural instinct is to defend its **haunt** against other males.

3 Experience the indigenous **wildlife** of Borneo's rainforests at close quarters.

4 Moscow is one of the most expensive cities in the **planet** to live.

5 The average distance from the **world** to the sun is over 149.5 million kilometres.

D Choose the best verb to complete these sentences, using the entry in SMALL CAPS to help you.

1 Heavy use of pesticides can *harm*/*impair* the environment and people's health. (DAMAGE *verb*)

2 As the ice caps *melt*/*defrost*, sea levels will rise. (MELT)

3 Plastic bags washed into the ocean *endanger*/*risk* marine wildlife such as turtles. (THREATEN 2)

4 One third of the world's fish stocks are now *expended*/*depleted* or over-exploited. (USE *verb* 2)

5 In the wild, plant species *transform*/*evolve* with their environment. (TURN 2)

E What is being discussed in each sentence? Choose an item from the box, using these entries to help you: DIRT, OIL, SMOKE. In some cases two choices are possible.

air pollution	petroleum	exhaust fumes
crude oil	fossil fuels	smog

1 It has been identified as a cause of diseases such as asthma and bronchitis.

2 It is used to produce fuel oil and gasoline.

3 They occur when fuels such as natural gas and gasoline are burnt.

4 They take millions of years to form and reserves are rapidly being used up.

F Use these entries to find adjectives to describe the temperatures below: COLD 1, FREEZING, HOT, HUMID. Then arrange the adjectives in order from the coldest to the hottest.

1 a little too cold _____

2 cold and dry in a pleasant way _____

3 hot and damp _____

4 quite cold in a pleasant way _____

5 quite hot in a pleasant way _____

6 too hot and without fresh air _____

7 very cold, below 0°C _____

8 very hot and uncomfortable _____

DESCRIPTIONS

A Describing an Object

Read this description of an unusual object and do the exercises that follow.

> One of my favourite (1) _____ is a metal cast of a man's hand. It is very <u>heavy</u>, and is dark grey in colour. It is a very <u>large</u> hand, and (2) _____ on the wrist with the big, <u>thick</u> fingers pointing upwards and spread apart, as if they are reaching out to take hold of something.
>
> It is the hand of a man who has done physical work for many years, strong and <u>rough</u> and covered in lines and bumps. You can see every (3) _____ on the surface, from each tiny <u>crease</u> in the skin to every slight chip in the square, <u>flat</u> fingernails.
>
> The (4) _____ and shape of the hand <u>show</u> the man's strength and power, while the rough texture and physical (5) _____ give it great character.
>
> It is an <u>unusual</u> object. I <u>am very fond of</u> it because I think it is a beautiful (6) _____ of a man's strength and power. The artist who made it said it was the biggest, and one of the most interesting hands he had ever done. It is my husband's hand.

Choose the best word from each group of synonyms below to fill the numbered gaps in the text. Look at these entries to help you: THING 3, LEAN 2, INFORMATION, SIZE, DEFECT, SIGN 1

1	stuff	possessions	goods	valuables
2	leans	stands	props	steadies
3	information	detail	fact	particular
4	size	area	capacity	dimensions
5	faults	flaws	glitches	imperfections
6	indication	symptom	symbol	indicator

Look at the <u>underlined</u> words in the text. Can you replace them with the alternatives given here? Write YES (= can replace) or NO (= can't replace) for each one. Look at the entry given to help you.

7	heavy → bulky	_____	(HEAVY)
8	large → great	_____	(LARGE)
9	thick → wide	_____	(WIDE 2)
10	rough → rugged	_____	(ROUGH 1)
11	crease → line	_____	(FOLD *noun*)
12	flat → smooth	_____	(FLAT *adj.*)
13	show → reflect	_____	(SHOW 3)
14	unusual → different	_____	(UNUSUAL)
15	am very fond of → love	_____	(LIKE *verb*)

B Look up these adjectives in the alphabetical index starting on p.921 to find out if they are synonyms of words meaning **LARGE** or **SMALL**. Write **L** or **S** next to each one.

modest	vast	minor	compact	substantial
fine	narrow	tiny	broad	monumental

Now use each word once only to make common adjective-noun collocations. You will find the information in the PATTERNS AND COLLOCATIONS sections of the relevant entries.

LARGE   **SMALL**

a _____ breakfast   a _____ bit   a _____ fee

a _____ grin   a _____ camera   _____ hair

the _____ majority   a _____ detail   a _____ street

a _____ task

....

C Can you fill in one synonym for each of the following? Use these entries to check your ideas: SMALL, NORMAL, LARGE, HUGE

microscopic   → small   → normal   → big   → huge

_____   _____   _____   _____   _____

....

D When describing a person's size, some words are more positive than others. Label these comments as positive (+), negative (-) or neutral (N), using these entries to help you: SHORT 2, THIN, FAT *adj*.

1 'His wife is very *petite*.' _____

2 'All the women in my family are *short*.' _____

3 'She's tall and *slender*.' _____

4 'My doctor says I am *overweight* and need to take more exercise.' _____

5 'You were a happy, *chubby* baby.' _____

6 'He came home looking pale and *thin*.' _____

7 'You're looking rather *skinny*.' _____

....

E Which synonym fits best in each of the following? Use these entries to help you: SIZE, LEVEL, LENGTH

1 the _____ of the room (dimensions/volume)

2 the _____ of the jar (area/volume)

3 the _____ of the problem (level/scale)

4 the _____ of his knowledge (extent/size)

5 the _____ of the wood (depth/thickness)

6 the _____ of the swimming pool (height/depth)

7 the _____ of the ball (width/diameter)

A Read the text below and do the exercise that follows.

Enter our competition and you could WIN a fantastic treat for your WHOLE FAMILY!

Is there someone in your family who is extra ¹_____? Someone who is always there for you or other people? Perhaps someone who has ²_____ you through a difficult time in your life or has come through ³_____ times themselves?

We are ⁴_____ a competition to find a family member who is 'simply the best'. It could be anyone in your family – a parent, a grandparent, a cousin or a sibling. If you would like to ⁵_____ a ⁶_____ for this ⁷_____, write and tell us what makes them so special. What do you ⁸_____ about them and how have they ⁹_____ your life?

Send us your competition entry by the closing date, when our ¹⁰_____ of ¹¹_____ will choose one lucky winner and two ¹²_____. The ¹³_____ family will be treated to an all-¹⁴_____-paid outing for the whole family.

Choose the best word to fill each gap, using the entries given to help you.

1	special / exceptional / extraordinary	(SPECIAL)
2	assisted / supported / aided	(HELP *verb* 1)
3	tough / adverse / unfavourable	(DIFFICULT 2)
4	holding / hosting / giving	(HAVE 4)
5	recommend / suggest / nominate	(RECOMMEND 2)
6	family / relative / kin	(FAMILY 2)
7	award / reward / trophy	(AWARD)
8	respect / admire / esteem	(RESPECT *verb*)
9	influenced / impacted on / coloured	(AFFECT)
10	committee / board / panel	(COMMITTEE)
11	judges / referees / examiners	(JUDGE *noun* 2)
12	losers / runners-up / also-rans	(LOSER 1)
13	winning / victorious / triumphant	(SUCCESSFUL 1)
14	costs / spending / expenses	(COSTS)

B The nouns below all describe people. Decide which could be considered the odd one out in each group and for what reason. Use the meaning, usage and grammar information given in the entry in SMALL CAPS to help you.

#					
1	child	kid	youngster	brat	(CHILD)
2	youth	teenager	teen	adolescent	(GIRL)
3	friend	mate	buddy	acquaintance	(FRIEND)
4	parent	mom	daddy	mommy	(MOTHER)

Check the suggested answers in the key on page 916, then use the suggested 'odd ones out' to complete these sentences:

5   It can be hard bringing up a family as a single _____ .

6   He claimed that a gang of _____ had chased him out of the shop and down the street.

7   The funeral was attended by all his various friends and _____ .

8   Her family was very rich, but she never boasted about it or acted like a spoiled _____ .

....

C   Do these words refer to good or bad relationships? Use the following entries to help you label them **G** (good) or **B** (bad): ADMIRATION, ARGUMENT, BETRAYAL, BOND, DIVISION 2, LOVE *noun* 2.

affection	awe	bad faith	squabble
respect	bond	split	rapport
rift	quarrel	devotion	disloyalty

These sentences use some of the words from the box above. Are they used correctly? If not, replace them with another word from the list.

1   Because of her professional abilities she has earned the **awe** of her colleagues.

2   It is important for an effective interviewer to develop a **bond** with the interviewee.

3   She hoped that the meeting would be the first step towards healing the **rift** with her father.

4   People often look back with **devotion** on the teachers from their schooldays.

5   Her father had a terrible **squabble** with his brother two years ago, and they haven't spoken to each other since.

6   She heard her friend talking about her behind her back, and this **bad faith** hurt her.

....

D   Match each phrasal verb with a one-word equivalent, making a note of which entry you found them in.

bring sb up	tell sb off
fall out	take after sb
patch sth up	walk out (on sb)

resemble	resolve
raise	argue
abandon	reprimand

Phrasal verbs are often used in more informal contexts than one-word verbs. Decide which verb from the exercise above is suitable for the sentences below, using the entry given to help you. Don't forget to use the correct form of the verb.

1   Have you seen their son? He really _____ his grandad. (LOOK LIKE SB)

2   As a result of our enquiry, a significant number of employees have been _____ for their actions. (SCOLD)

3   My two brothers are always _____ , but they usually _____ again pretty quickly. (ARGUE; RESOLVE)

4   His Dad _____ his wife and kids, and left his wife to _____ the kids on her own. (LEAVE 5; BRING SB UP)

A A Job Advertisement

Read this job ad and do the exercises that follow.

> FEEL LIKE EARNING SOME EXTRA CASH DURING THE HOLIDAYS? Want to work in one of the hottest restaurants in town?
>
> We have two jobs available:
>
> We need a waiter or waitress, preferably with some experience. We need someone with a bubbly personality to join our team.
>
> We're also looking for someone who's great at cooking, to replace one of our assistant chefs, who's quitting next month. If you think you're cut out to work in a busy kitchen, and you're not scared of 'slaving over a hot stove', this could be the job for you!
>
> For either of these jobs, send in your CV/résumé and we'll sort out a time for you to drop by and chat about your suitability.

The ad has been written in *informal* English. Find a word or phrase in the ad to match with each of the less informal synonyms below, making a note of which entry you found the synonyms in.

1	require	_____	8	proficient	_____
2	leave	_____	9	suitable	_____
3	money	_____	10	lively	_____
4	position	_____	11	submit	_____
5	visit	_____	12	intimidated	_____
6	popular	_____	13	would like	_____
7	arrange	_____	14	discuss	_____

Here is the same job ad written in more formal English. Use some of the words above to fill in the gaps. Remember to use the correct form of the words you use.

> **15**_____ **earn some extra 16**_____ **during the holidays?**
>
> Waiter/waitress **17**_____ for **18**_____ town-centre restaurant. Experience preferred, but not essential. We need a **19**_____ person to join our waiting staff.
>
> **20**_____ cook also required for the post of Assistant Chef. The successful candidate will not mind working long hours in a busy kitchen.
>
> For either **21**_____, please **22**_____ a CV/résumé. We will contact applicants to **23**_____ an interview to **24**_____ suitability.

B Which of the following are NOT possible? Circle one 'odd one out' in each case, using these entries to help you: ASSISTANT, DEALER, EXECUTIVE, PARTNER 1, LEADER 1

1 He's just got a job as _____ to the Minister for Public Affairs.
    assistant   **aide**   **helper**   **right-hand man**

2 The road is lined with street _____ , selling everything from flowers to fish.
    traders   **sellers**   **vendors**   **shopkeepers**

3 Several local _____ were present at the event.
    businessmen   **businesswomen**   **entrepreneurs**   **tycoons**

4 Do you ever socialize with your _____ after work?
    colleagues   **allies**   **co-workers**   **workmates**

C Replace the bold word in each sentence with a more precise alternative from the same entry.

OFFICE 2

1 I have an **office** at the back of the shop, where I carry out all the repairs myself.
2 I'm looking for an empty apartment to use as an **office**, where I can create my pictures in peace.
3 My Dad often works at home in the evenings and at weekends, so he's converted the attic into an **office**.

LEAVE 3

4 Most people **leave** when they're 65.
5 After the negative press reports, I had no choice but to **leave** as chief executive.
6 If things carry on like this, I swear I'll **leave**!

TASK

7 My **tasks** range from answering the telephone to arranging transportation for visitors to our offices.
8 The boss gave me some extra **tasks** to do before I can go home.
9 I still have all the household **tasks** to do when I get home.

D Use a verb from the first box and a particle from the second to make a phrasal verb to replace the word or phrase in bold in the sentences below. Use the alphabetical index starting on p.921 to help you find the right entries.

bring	close	lay	take
churn	cover	set	turn

down	for	off	out
down	in	on	up

1 The business was doing so well that we had to **employ** extra staff.
2 He was offered a job in the shop, but he **refused** it.
3 The latest price increase will **raise** a further €10,000.
4 This new machine will enable us to **produce** hundreds of units every month.
5 The business was **established** by my grandfather over fifty years ago.
6 Apparently over 30 staff are going to be **made redundant**.
7 Unfortunately the company **ceased trading** last November.
8 Who is **replacing** Christine while she's away?

LANGUAGE AND COMMUNICATION

A Keeping in Touch the Modern Way

Read the following article and do the exercise that follows.

Is letter-writing a lost ¹art?

Nowadays we are more likely to ²discuss by phone or email. But amongst teenagers, it seems the most popular ³way of keeping in touch is by text message.

According to a recent ⁴enquiry, over 95% of 13-year-olds in the UK now own a mobile phone, and teenagers are texting far more than they talk. The ⁵common young person makes or receives 3.5 calls a day, but sends or receives an ⁶incredible 9.6 texts a day.*

Because text length is ⁷controlled to a maximum of 160 characters per message, young texters have developed a new way of writing words and phrases in a ⁸shrunk form, so as to use the smallest number of ⁹characters possible. For example, the message 'I hope to see you at the party later, love Jo' can be written *Hope 2CU @party L8R, luv Jo*.

Many people are ¹⁰nervous that the use of 'text speak' is eroding the English ¹¹dialect and damaging children's ability to write 'correct' English. However, a definite ¹²link between texting and a deterioration in children's writing has yet to be proved.

Source: The Mobile Life Youth Report 2006

Look at the underlined words in the text. Some of them are not the best word to use; for each one, decide if the word given below would be a better choice. Look at the entry given to help you.

		✓/✗				✓/✗	
1	skill	✗	(SKILL 1)	7	limited	___	(LIMIT *verb*)
2	communicate	___	(TALK)	8	shortened	___	(SHRINK)
3	process	___	(WAY 2)	9	digits	___	(NUMBER 2)
4	survey	___	(INVESTIGATION)	10	concerned	___	(WORRIED)
5	average	___	(NORMAL)	11	language	___	(LANGUAGE 1)
6	unbelievable	___	(INCREDIBLE)	12	relation	___	(RELATION)

Here is some more information about the language of texts. Looking at the entry given in each case, which word is most suitable for each gap?

13 Text language is a *combination/mix* of letters, numbers and symbols in order to *economize/skimp* on space. (COMBINATION; SAVE 2)

14 Some words can be *replaced/exchanged* by symbols or numbers, for example **@** (= at) and **4** (= for). (REPLACE 2)

15 Words can be spelt phonetically to make them *shorter/briefer*, for example *giv* (= give) and *sum* (= some). (SHORT 3)

16 Abbreviations and acronyms are very *general/common*, for example *thx* (= thanks) and *btw* (= by the way). (GENERAL 1)

17 These features can be *combined/merged* within a word or *term/phrase*, for example *2moro* (= tomorrow), *CUL8R* (= see you later) and NE1 (= anyone). (COMBINE; WORD)

B The verbs in this exercise all describe different ways of speaking. For each phrase, three verbs are possible and one is not. Circle the 'odd one out' in each case, using these entries to help you: CALL 3, CHAT, SCREAM, SHOUT, TALK, WHISPER

1 to _____ out loud   shout cry scream (raise your voice)

2 to _____ something to somebody   whisper mutter sigh mumble

3 to _____ for help   cry yell call bawl

4 to _____ in pain   murmur groan moan cry out

5 to spend hours on the phone _____.   talking speaking chatting gossiping

Now use one of the 'odd ones out' to complete each of these sentences. You may need to change the form of the verb.

6 He _____ something in her ear.

7 I've never known him _____ in anger.

8 I would like to _____ to the manager, please.

9 She _____ at him in front of the whole class.

10 Why are you _____? Are you bored?

....

C Do these adjectives describe successful or unsuccessful communication or communicators? Label each one **G** (good) or **P** (poor), using these entries to help you: ARTICULATE, CLEAR *adj.* 2, CONFUSING, MISLEADING

ambiguous	coherent	confused	eloquent
explicit	fluent	woolly	incomprehensible
intelligible	misleading	rambling	unambiguous

Now choose the best adjective to fill the gaps below.

    coherent   **eloquent**   **fluent**

1 He gave a terrific, passionate and _____ speech at the Annual Conference.

2 I became more _____ and was able to describe the horrifying experience I had just been through.

3 The ideal candidate will be a _____ Spanish speaker.

    incomprehensible   **misleading**   **rambling**

4 He gave a long, _____ reply that didn't really answer the question.

5 I found the technical jargon _____.

6 May I remind you that it is a criminal offence to make false or _____ statements on these forms?

    explicit   **unambiguous**   **intelligible**

7 A few words were _____, but most of the message was difficult to make out.

8 She left _____ instructions about how exactly the money should be spent.

9 The wording of the contract must be _____, so there can be no dispute about what it means.

A A Letter of Complaint

Read this formal letter and do the exercises below.

Dear Sir/Madam

I am writing to **1**_____ my dissatisfaction with the day **2**_____ you organized to Edinburgh last month. My wife and I were extremely disappointed with the day.

Firstly, I must **3**_____ about your so-called "luxury coach". It arrived 30 minutes late, and was certainly not luxurious. It was dirty and the air conditioning did not work. What is more, the driver was quite rude to my wife when she requested that he **4**_____ his music.

The roadworks meant that we were on the bus for nearly five hours, when the journey should have taken around two and a half. I am shocked that you did not check traffic **5**_____ in advance and plan an alternative **6**_____ . As a result, we had only two hours in Edinburgh when we should have had most of the day there. The driver would not **7**_____ us stay longer.

When I spoke to your customer services department about these matters, they were most **8**_____ . Frankly, I find this level of service **9**_____ and I am very unhappy about the whole experience.

I **10**_____ hearing from you with a response to my comments.

Yours faithfully

John Napier

John Napier

Choose the best word from each group of synonyms to fill the gaps in the text.
Look up the first word in each group to find the synonyms entries.

1	say	talk	express	put
2	trip	journey	tour	expedition
3	complain	grumble	moan	whine
4	reduce	decrease	bring down	turn down
5	situation	circumstance	conditions	things
6	way	route	path	course
7	allow	let	permit	authorize
8	perverse	unhelpful	awkward	obstructive
9	unacceptable	unreasonable	too much	out of line
10	expect	anticipate	await	look forward to

Here are some things that John Napier said to his friend about the trip. Choose an *informal* word or phrase to complete each sentence, using the entries in SMALL CAPS to help you.

11 The seats on the bus were really _____ .   (DIRTY)

12 The traffic on the way there was _____ .   (TERRIBLE 1)

13 I'm _____ with trying to speak to Customer Services about this.   (BORED)

14 If you ask me, the whole trip was a _____ .   (DISASTER)

15 We were _____ when we got home.   (TIRED 1)

B Find a one-word synonym for each of the following phrasal verbs, using these entries to help you: GET IN, GET OUT, SET OFF.

1 Could all passengers **get on** the bus now, please?   _____

2 He **got on** his horse and rode away.   _____

3 They **set off** at daybreak.   _____

4 The ship arrived at port and we all **got out**.   _____

Now find a phrasal verb synonym for each of the following one-word verbs, using these entries to help you: ARRIVE, LAND *verb*, RETURN.

5 What time does your train **arrive**?   _____

6 I waited for several hours, but she never **returned**.   _____

7 He finally **appeared**, nearly two hours late.   _____

8 I was relieved when our plane finally **landed**.   _____

C Find the best word from the entry given in SMALL CAPS to fit into each of the following sentences. There may be more than one possibility.

VISIT (*noun*)

1 It's a nine-hour flight, with a short _____ in Singapore.

2 If you have time, pay a _____ to the museum.

3 There's a guided _____ of the cathedral every day at 3.30pm.

TRIP

4 My son's gone off on a _____ of the Far East.

5 The day begins with a short boat _____ up the river.

6 Do you remember going on family _____ as a child?

HOLIDAY 2

7 This island is a popular _____ for city dwellers.

8 We're going on a weekend city _____ to Prague.

9 Do you usually go abroad on _____?

D Which synonym fits best in each of the following? Use these entries to help you: BEAUTIFUL 2, COUNTRY 2, MAGNIFICENT, VIEW 2

1 It was a ***charming*/*scenic*** little place in a tiny fishing village.

2 The furnishings in all the rooms were absolutely ***attractive*/*exquisite*!**

3 We stopped at the side of the road to admire the ***landscape*/*scenery*.**

4 We hiked for several hours over quite rough ***terrain*/*land*.**

5 We stood and gazed at Heidelberg's ***magnificent*/*glorious*** castle.

6 We sat and watched the ***impressive*/*glorious*** sunset.

7 The ***views*/*sights*** from the top of the hill were amazing.

8 We were lucky enough to be given a room with a sea ***view*/*scene*.**

education *noun*
full-time education

educational *adj.*
educational games

class 1 *noun*
take a biology class

class 2 *noun*
evening classes

class 3 *noun*
the oldest in the class

school *noun*
elementary school

school and college

teaching

teach *verb*
He teaches English.

teacher *noun*
a science teacher

train *verb* 1
train as a doctor

equip *verb* 2
equip sb for a
career in sth

professor *noun*
a professor of law

lecturer *noun*
a college lecturer

coach *noun*
a tennis coach

studying

assignment *noun*
a written assignment

focus *verb*
focus on an issue

student *noun*
school students

scholar *noun*
a classical scholar

learner *noun*
language learners

learn *verb*
learn a language

Education

testing

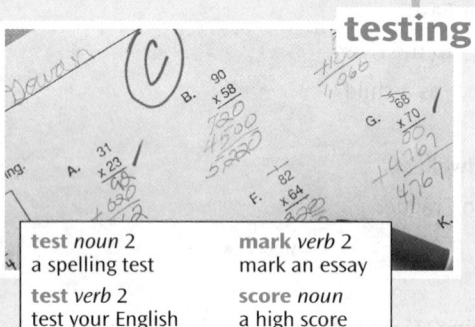

test *noun* 2
a spelling test

test *verb* 2
test your English

assessment *noun*
continuous assessment

mark *verb* 2
mark an essay

score *noun*
a high score

success

failure

ignorant *adj.*
ignorant about sth

miss *verb* 1
miss a class

fail *verb* 3
fail an exam

knowledge *noun*
specialist knowledge

graduate *verb*
graduate in history

informed *adj.*
well informed

understand *verb* 1
understand German

understanding *noun*
a good understanding

intelligent *adj.*
an intelligent person

intelligence *noun*
use your intelligence

Education

A Test your topic vocabulary

The words and phrases below can all be found somewhere in the entries shown in the Topic Map. Which parts of the Topic Map would you put them in? You can look up the underlined words in the alphabetical index to check which entry they belong to.

a stroke of <u>genius</u>
<u>homework</u>
to <u>skive</u> off school
a home <u>tutor</u>
to <u>review</u> your notes

teaching
school and college
studying
testing
success
failure

to <u>flunk</u> out of college
the <u>class</u> of 2008
a teacher <u>trainer</u>
the pass <u>mark</u>

B Matching synonyms

Add the words below to the table, so that each column contains words with a similar meaning. Use each word only once.

~~scholarly~~   pedagogic   illiterate   clever
grade   don   study   mark
clueless   bright   professor   get the hang of sth

educational adj.	lecturer noun	learn verb	score noun	intelligent adj.	ignorant adj.
scholarly					

C Collocation matching

Match the verbs on the left with the phrases on the right. You can look up the following entries to help you: EDUCATION, EQUIP 2, SCORE, LEARN, GRADUATE, MISS 1

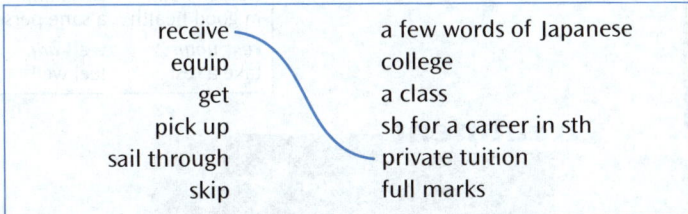

receive
equip
get
pick up
sail through
skip

a few words of Japanese
college
a class
sb for a career in sth
private tuition
full marks

D Which word?

Choose the best word in each case. Use the entries for the words in SMALL CAPS to help you.

1 Tom is in the seventh *class/grade* at school. CLASS 3
2 You will receive basic *training/teaching* in first aid. EDUCATION
3 The first part of the lesson *focused/targeted* on reading skills. FOCUS *verb*
4 Elizabeth studied hard every day and was *informed/well read* in the Classics. INFORMED
5 People who can't use a computer are said to be computer *ignorant/illiterate*. IGNORANT
6 This breed of dog needs to be trained gently, but they are quick *learners/students*.
   LEARNER

890

disease *noun*
a rare disease

illness *noun*
chronic illness

fatal *adj.*
a fatal heart condition

serious *adj.* 1
a serious illness

sick *adj.* 1
a sick child

mentally ill *adj.*
mentally ill people

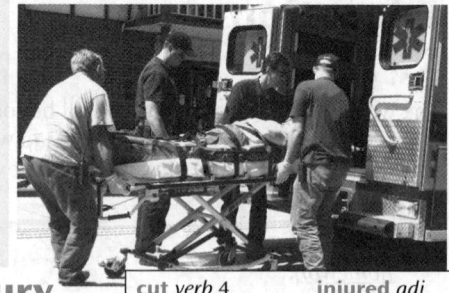

injury

cut *verb* 4
cut your finger

hurt *verb* 2
My head hurts.

injure *verb*
injure your wrist

injury *noun*
minor injuries

injured *adj.*
an injured hand

pain *noun*
back pain

painful *adj.* 1
a painful knee

illness

Health

symptoms

staying healthy

diet *noun*
a strict diet

health *noun*
in good health

rest *noun* 2
take a rest

rest *verb*
try to rest

sane *adj.*
a sane person

well *adj.*
feel well

cough *verb*
can't stop coughing

vomit *verb*
make sb vomit

attack *noun* 3
an asthma attack

shiver *noun*
feel a shiver

weak *adj.*
a weak heart

dizzy *adj.*
feeling dizzy

pale *adj.* 1
looking pale

sick *adj.* 2
feel sick

tired *adj.*1
cold, hungry and tired

treatment

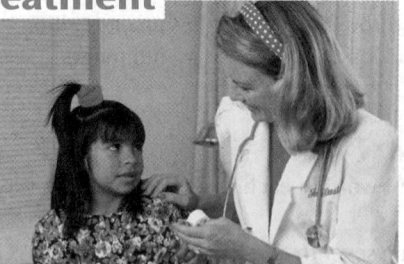

doctor *noun*
see a doctor

surgery *noun*
the doctor's
surgery

hospital *noun*
go to (the) hospital

drug *noun* 2
prescribe drugs

treatment *noun*
receive treatment
for shock

treat *verb* 1
treated with drugs

take *verb* 9
take medicine

cure *verb*
cure a disease

recover *verb* 1
recover from an
illness

Health

A Test your topic vocabulary

The words and phrases below can all be found somewhere in the entries shown in the Topic Map. Which parts of the Topic Map would you put them in? You can look up the underlined words in the alphabetical index to check which entry they belong to.

cuts and _bruises_

a _sallow_ complexion

heart _disease_

a strong _constitution_

a strict _regime_

illness

injury

symptoms

staying healthy

treatment

to _tear_ a muscle

on _prescription_

heavily _dosed_

a _terminal_ illness

B Matching synonyms

Add the words below to the table, so that each column contains words with a similar meaning. Use each word only once.

~~lethal~~   make sb better   sore   excruciating   terminal

exhausted   shape   condition   drowsy   heal

fatal _adj._	cure _verb_	tired _adj._	health _noun_	painful _adj._
lethal				

C Collocation matching

Match the verbs on the left with the phrases on the right. You can look up the following entries to help you: COUGH, DISEASE, INJURE, CUT 4, CURE

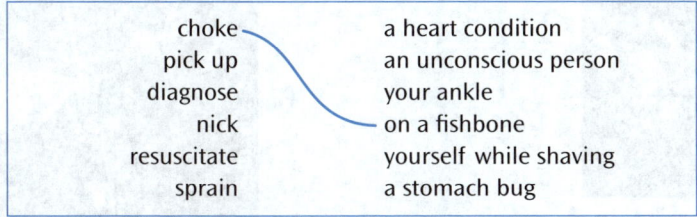

choke   a heart condition

pick up   an unconscious person

diagnose   your ankle

nick   on a fishbone

resuscitate   yourself while shaving

sprain   a stomach bug

D Which word?

Choose the best word in each case. Use the entries for the words in SMALL CAPS to help you.

1 She took a **fatal/lethal** dose of painkillers and had to be rushed to hospital. FATAL

2 I fell on the ice and **injured/wounded** my back. INJURE

3 Police and **surgeons/paramedics** were quick to arrive at the scene of the accident. DOCTOR

4 These tablets may make you feel **weary/drowsy**. TIRED

5 You may experience some minor **suffering/discomfort** during the treatment. PAIN

6 I can't seem to **shake off/pull through** this cold. RECOVER

sociable *adj.*
feeling sociable

exciting *adj.*
an exciting moment

event *noun* 2
a social event

excitement *noun*
cause excitement

enjoy *verb*
enjoy the moment

entertainment *noun*
live entertainment

entertain *verb*
keep sb entertained

play *verb* 1
kids playing

sport

having fun

play *verb* 2
play football

player *noun*
a tennis player

pitch *noun*
a rugby pitch

round *noun*
the final round

game *noun* 1
a game of football

game *noun* 2
ball games

train *verb* 2
train regularly

training *noun*
in training for
the Olympics

sport *noun*
play sports

team *noun* 2
a football team

race *noun*
win a race

join *verb*
join a club

eager *adj.*
eager to do sth

energetic *adj.*
energetic exercise

energy *noun* 2
full of energy

involvement *noun*
full involvement

Sport and Leisure

interests

getting involved

relaxing

interest *noun* 2
take up an interest

interest *verb*
the topic interests me

interesting *adj.*
an interesting subject

interested *adj.*
interested in architecture

fan *noun*
a music fan

creative *adj.*
creative talent

holiday *noun* 1
the summer holidays

leisure *noun*
leisure activities

easy *adj.* 2
an easy life

rest *verb*
try to rest

rest *noun* 2
a well-earned rest

Sport and Leisure

A Test your topic vocabulary

The words and phrases below can all be found somewhere in the entries shown in the Topic Map. Which parts of the Topic Map would you put them in? You can look up the <u>underlined</u> words in the alphabetical index to check which entry they belong to.

to take <u>part</u> in sth
the World Cup <u>finals</u>
<u>zest</u> for life
live <u>entertainment</u>
to do sth for <u>kicks</u>

having fun
sport
getting involved
interests
relaxing

an art-<u>lover</u>
Spring <u>Break</u>
a <u>leisurely</u> stroll
the national <u>pastime</u>

B Matching synonyms

Add the words below to the table, so that each column contains words with a similar meaning. Use each word only once.

~~recreation~~   dynamic   line-up   leave   sabbatical
squad   innovative   ingenious   vigorous   amusement

entertainment noun	team noun	energetic adj.	creative adj.	holiday noun
recreation				

C Collocation matching

Match the verbs on the left with the phrases on the right. You can look up the following entries to help you: PLAY *verb* 2, JOIN, TRAIN *verb* 2, ENJOY, REST *verb*

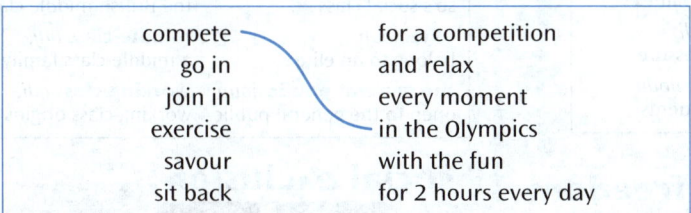

compete   for a competition
go in   and relax
join in   every moment
exercise   in the Olympics
savour   with the fun
sit back   for 2 hours every day

D Which word?

Choose the best word in each case. Use the entries for the words in SMALL CAPS to help you.

1 He's a devoted animal **fan/lover**, and has several pets. FAN
2 We're all very **eager/enthusiastic** about the idea. EAGER
3 I've always been **interested/fascinated** by the ancient Egyptians. INTERESTED
4 What do you do in your **leisure/spare time**? LEISURE
5 They challenged the other boys to a **game/match** of football. GAME 1
6 It was a big **excitement/thrill** to finally meet him in person. EXCITEMENT

894

person *noun*
a normal person

identity *noun*
a sense of identity

own *adj.*
my own opinion

privacy *noun*
need privacy

vulnerable *adj.*
vulnerable people

**take care of
yourself** *verb*
able to take care
of herself

right *noun*
human rights

life *noun* 1
fight for your life

the individual

the authorities

the authorities *noun*
the federal authorities

bureaucracy *noun*
government
bureaucracy

institution *noun*
a mental institution

control *noun*
assume control

official *noun*
a party official

official *adj,*
an official body

organization *noun*
a government
organization

strict *adj.*
strict controls

citizenship

The Individual and Society

the class system

citizen *noun*
a French citizen

community *noun*
the local community

cultural *adj.*
cultural identity

culture *noun*
Eastern culture

respectable *adj.*
respectable people

responsibility *noun*
accept your
responsibilities

social *adj.*
social pressure

resident *noun*
local residents

aristrocratic *adj.*
an aristocratic family

class *noun* 4
sb's social class

elite *noun*
belong to an elite

the general public *noun*
open to the general public

lord *noun*
a wealthy lord

the middle class *noun*
the British middle class

middle-class *adj.*
a middle-class family

working-class *adj.*
working-class origins

freedom

social exclusion

free *adj.* 1
a free man

freedom *noun*
personal freedom

authoritarian *adj.*
an authoritarian
attitude

permission *noun*
refused permission

allow *verb*
legally allowed

tolerant *adj.*
tolerant views

divide *verb* 2
a divided community

division *noun* 2
divisions within society

exclude *verb* 2
excluded from a club

exclusive *adj.*
an exclusive group

refugee *noun*
a political refugee

poor *adj.* 1
poor people

poverty *noun*
rural poverty

inequality *noun*
social inequality

The Individual and Society

A Test your topic vocabulary

The words and phrases below can all be found somewhere in the entries shown in the Topic Map. Which parts of the Topic Map would you put them in? You can look up the underlined words in the alphabetical index to check which entry they belong to.

freedom of choice
the needy
to fend for yourself
the landed gentry
humble origins

the individual
the authorities
citizenship
the class system
freedom
social exclusion

Australian nationals
alienation
the military top brass
a multicultural society

B Matching synonyms

Add the words below to the table, so that each column contains words with a similar meaning. Use each word only once.

~~individuality~~	destitution	ethnic	overbearing
autocratic	uniqueness	red tape	deprivation
paperwork	rank	status	folk

identity *noun*	bureaucracy *noun*	cultural *adj.*	class *noun*	authoritarian *adj.*	poverty *noun*
individuality					

C Collocation matching

Match the verbs on the left with the phrases on the right. You can look up the following entries to help you: ALLOW, DIVIDE 2, RESPONSIBILITY, BUREAUCRACY, ELITE, RIGHT *noun*

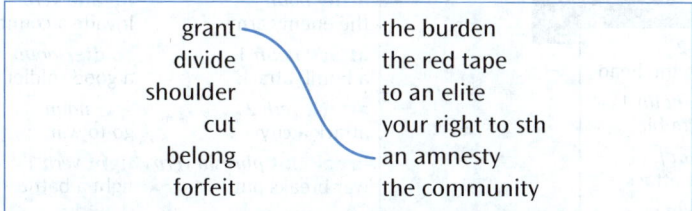

grant — the burden
divide — the red tape
shoulder — to an elite
cut — your right to sth
belong — an amnesty
forfeit — the community

D Which word?

Choose the best word in each case. Use the entries for the words in SMALL CAPS to help you.

1 People are looking towards him for *harsh/**firm*** leadership. STRICT
2 Finding *a reputable/**an honourable*** plumber can sometimes be difficult. RESPECTABLE
3 Despite her *common/**humble*** beginnings, she became very powerful. WORKING-CLASS
4 The government clearly recognizes that *social/**public*** opinion is against GM food. SOCIAL
5 By 1535, the original *residents/**inhabitants*** of the island were virtually extinct. RESIDENT
6 Throughout the drama, his *seclusion/**isolation*** and desperation increase. PRIVACY

Conflict

oppose

be against sb/sth *adj.*
I'm against the idea

challenge *verb*
challenge the leader

oppose *verb*
oppose a plan

opposition *noun*
opposition to the plans

enemy *noun*
know your enemy

tension *noun*
racial tensions

remove *verb* 2
remove sb from power

revolution *noun* 1
a popular revolution

disagree

argue *verb*
argue about sth

argument *noun* 1
a fierce argument

debate *noun*
a growing debate

conflict *verb*
conflicting opinions

controversial *adj.*
a controversial issue

disagree *verb*
disagree with sb/sth

fight

aggressive *adj.* 1
aggressive behaviour

attack *verb* 1
violently attacked

fight *noun*
get into a fight

fight *verb* 2
fight an attacker

hit *verb* 2
hit sb on the head

trouble *noun* 1
crowd trouble

violent *adj.*
a violent attack

thug *noun*
an armed thug

war

army *noun*
the enemy army

attack *noun* 1
a bomb attack

attack *verb* 2
attack a city

break out *phrasal verb*
war breaks out

guerrilla *noun*
a guerrilla war

invade *verb*
invade a country

soldier *noun*
a good soldier

war *noun*
go to war

fight *verb* 1
fight a battle

resolving conflict

negotiate *verb*
negotiate on sb's
behalf

negotiator *noun*
an independent
negotiator

resolve *verb*
resolve the crisis

peace *noun*
restore peace

contract *noun*
sign a contract

Conflict

A Test your topic vocabulary

The words and phrases below can all be found somewhere in the entries shown in the Topic Map. Which parts of the Topic Map would you put them in? You can look up the underlined words in the alphabetical index to check which entry they belong to.

to _mend_ fences
to _defy_ a ban
the armed _forces_
a _shouting_ match
to not see _eye to eye_

disagree
oppose
fight
war
resolving conflict

a street _brawl_
to _occupy_ a country
to hold _talks_
a storm of _protest_

B Matching synonyms

Add the words below to the table, so that each column contains words with a similar meaning. Use each word only once.

~~warrior~~   militant   mercenary   bicker   fall out
dare   throw down the gauntlet   mediator   intermediary   warlike

soldier noun	aggresive adj.	challenge verb	negotiator noun	argue verb
warrior				

C Collocation matching

Match the verbs on the left with the phrases on the right. You can look up the following entries to help you: WAR, HIT 2, ARGUMENT 1, REVOLUTION 1, NEGOTIATE, OPPOSE

declare
throw
pick
crush
negotiate
go against

sb's wishes
for the hostages' release
war
a quarrel
a punch
a rebellion

D Which word?

Choose the best word in each case. Use the entries for the words in SMALL CAPS to help you.

1 This is not the first time the two men have **conflicted/clashed** over this issue. CONFLICT _verb_
2 The violence threatened to **break out/erupt** into full-scale war. BREAK OUT
3 Insurgents managed to **invade/seize** the airport in a surprise attack. INVADE
4 There was open **tension/hostility** between the two teams. TENSION
5 Black bears are not the **bloody/bloodthirsty** killers many believe them to be. VIOLENT
6 The country has said it wants to **resolve/repair** the crisis diplomatically. RESOLVE

Fact and Opinion

claim

claim *verb*
rightly claim sth

claim *noun*
a false claim

controversial *adj.*
a controversial issue

balance and bias

distort *verb*
distort the truth

propaganda *noun*
government propaganda

biased *adj.*
a biased account

reasonable *adj.*
beyond reasonable doubt

subject matter

subject *noun*
a major subject

issue *noun*
debate an issue

message noun
convey a message

point *noun*
get to the point

focus *noun*
the focus of
attention

opinions

judge *verb* 1
judge sb's reaction

think *verb*
sincerely think

informed adj.
an informed opinion

attitude *noun*
a positive attitude

view *noun* 1
strong views

comment *verb*
refuse to comment

fact

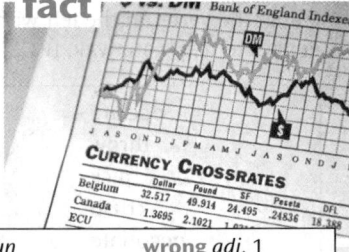

fact *noun*
face the facts

wrong *adj.* 1
the wrong answer

information *noun*
accurate information

reliable *adj.* 2
reliable evidence

true *adj.*
a true story

declare *verb*
declare sth publicly

discussion

discussion *noun*
under discussion

examine *verb*
examine a proposal

talk *verb*
talk openly

Fact and Opinion

A Test your topic vocabulary

The words and phrases below can all be found somewhere in the entries shown in the Topic Map. Which parts of the Topic Map would you put them in? You can look up the underlined words in the alphabetical index to check which entry they belong to.

a heated *exchange*
serious *allegations*
raw *data*
equal opportunities
an *authoritative* account

claim
balance and bias
subject matter
opinions
fact
discussion

a key *issue*
What do you *reckon*?
a *one-sided* debate
a *point of view*

B Matching synonyms

Add the words below to the table, so that each column contains words with a similar meaning. Use each word only once.

~~allege~~
substance
assert

partisan
feeling
prejudiced

dialogue
factual
consultation

point
authentic
the thrust

claim *verb*	message *noun*	view *noun*	biased *adj.*	reliable *adj.*	discussion *noun*
allege					

C Collocation matching

Match the verbs on the left with the phrases on the right. You can look up the following entries to help you: CLAIM *verb*, MESSAGE, COMMENT, DECLARE, EXAMINE, PROPAGANDA

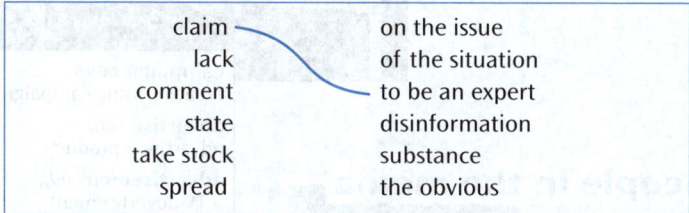

claim
lack
comment
state
take stock
spread

on the issue
of the situation
to be an expert
disinformation
substance
the obvious

D Which word?

Choose the best word in each case. Use the entries for the words in SMALL CAPS to help you.

1 Globalization is a highly *controversial/questionable* topic. CONTROVERSIAL
2 *Discussions/conversations* are still taking place between the two governments. DISCUSSION
3 They feel the situation was totally *misrepresented/misquoted* by the media. DISTORT
4 I lost the *thrust/thread* of the argument. MESSAGE
5 The couple refused to *comment/remark* to waiting journalists. COMMENT
6 Fans have complained that the film is *inaccurate/incorrect* in its portrayal of their hero. WRONG 1

900

the media *noun*
the mass media

newspaper *noun*
a daily newspaper

report *noun* 2
newspaper reports

magazine *noun*
a weekly magazine

news *noun*
a news flash

news

look *verb* 1
look carefully at sth

record *verb* 2
record an album

programme *noun*
a TV programme

film *noun* 1
a feature film

film *noun* 2
the film industry

audience *noun*
a live audience

TV, film and radio

the printed word

The Media

advertising

write *verb* 2
write an article

publish *verb* 2
publish a book

read *verb*
read a story

study *verb*
study the small print

campaign *noun*
an advertising campaign

advertise *verb*
advertise a product

advertisement *adj.*
a TV advertisement

people in the media

presenter *noun*
a TV presenter

analyst *noun*
a political analyst

fame *noun*
international fame

reporter *noun*
a news reporter

star *noun* 1
a pop star

famous *adj.*
a famous actor

The Media

A Test your topic vocabulary

The words and phrases below can all be found somewhere in the entries shown in the Topic Map. Which parts of the Topic Map would you put them in? You can look up the underlined words in the alphabetical index to check which entry they belong to.

to *flick through* sth
a *publicity* stunt
the *movie* industry
a *news* flash
a restaurant *critic*

— news
TV, film and radio
the printed word
advertising
people in the media

a live *broadcast*
a living *legend*
the mass *media*
to *plug* a product

B Matching synonyms

Add the words below to the table, so that each column contains words with a similar meaning. Use each word only once.

| ~~plug~~ | issue | the press | trailer | columnist |
| story | hack | print | journalism | item |

advertisement noun	the media noun	report noun	reporter noun	publish verb
plug				

C Collocation matching

Match the verbs on the left with the phrases on the right. You can look up the following entries to help you: LOOK *verb* 1, WRITE 2, ADVERTISE, PUBLISH 2, FAME

watch — a quick note
catch — TV all day
dash off — the idea of teamwork
push — stardom
release — new software on CD-ROM
shoot to — a show on the radio

D Which word?

Choose the best word in each case. Use the entries for the words in SMALL CAPS to help you.

1 The two witnesses each had a different *report/version* of events. REPORT 2
2 Did you remember to *record/film* that show for me? RECORD *verb* 2
3 We must get more *viewers/spectators* to watch the show. AUDIENCE
4 I *flicked through/scanned* a magazine while I was waiting. READ
5 She read the *trailer/blurb* on the back of the book and decided not to buy it after all. ADVERTISEMENT
6 Less *well known/prominent* brands may be better value for money. FAMOUS

This index lists entries under the following topics:

the arts

actor	entertainment	interview 2	photograph	song
appreciate	exhibition	introduction 2	picture	stage 2
artist	experimental	lacklustre	play noun	star 1
audience	fake noun	launch	play verb 3	star 2
award	feature verb	legend 1	poor 2	story 1
book	film 1	legend 2	present 2	subject
character	film 2	literature	record verb 2	success
concert	hall 1	mediocre	revise	terrible 4
creative	imagination	music	rubbish	wonderful
description	imagine	parody	scene	work noun 4
drama	inspiration	pattern 2	script	write 2
draw verb	intellectual 2	performance	sing	writer

conflict

accuse	challenge	explosion	murder	revolution 1
against	conflict noun	fight noun	negotiate	shoot
aggressive 1	conflict verb	fight verb 1	negotiator	soldier
anger verb	confront	fight verb 2	offend	solution
annoy	confrontation	fight back	oppose	solve 1
argue	controversial	force noun	opposition	suppress 1
argument 1	critical	fuss	overthrow	threaten 1
army	criticism	guard	peace	thug
attack noun 1	cruel	guerrilla	perverse	treacherous
attack noun 2	debate	gun	protect	trouble 1
attack verb 1	defeat	hit 2	protester	victory
attack verb 2	demonstration	invade	provoke	violent
blame	disagree	kill	rebel	war
bomb noun	divide 2	killer	remove 2	weapon
bomb verb	division 2	lose	resist	win
break out	enemy	lose your temper	resolve	winner
bullet	explode	massacre	revenge	withdraw 1
bully				

describing events

amazing	crash	endless	have 4	mean verb 3
artificial 2	crisis	event 1	hit 3	meet 1
attend	daily	event 2	hold sb/sth up	meet 2
bad	debut	exciting	impact	meet 3
begin	determine	face	important	meeting 2
blow noun	develop 1	fail 2	impressive	mess 2
boring	difficult 2	failure	improve 2	minor
busy 2	direction	finish	incredible	miracle
cause	disappointing	first	inevitable	mundane
certain	disaster	flood noun 2	informal	mystery
certainty	disastrous	follow 2	invite	next
chaos	disrupt	frequent	ironic	nice 1
compete	disruption	frightening	likely	nightmare
competition 1	do 2	fun	long adj.	normal
competition 2	early	future	luck	occasional
confusing	end noun	happen	make 4	often
context	end verb	have 3	meal	open

opportunity	rarely	slow	stressful	try 1
outrageous	recent	sometimes	successive	turn out
painful 2	respond	sordid	sudden	turning point
parallel	response	source	surprise	unfortunate 2
party 2	result	spend 2	surprising	unlikely 1
pattern 1	revolution 2	spontaneous	terrible 1	unlikely 2
peak	ruin	stage 1	terrible 2	unofficial
possibility	sad	start noun	terrible 3	unsuccessful
predictable 1	satisfying	start verb	threaten 3	usual
prevent	see	stay 1	thwart	usually
promising	series	stimulate	timely	valuable 2
promote	serious 1	stop noun	tradition	wave 3
prompt	shake 4	stop verb 1	traditional	witness
quick	short 1	stop verb 3	trend	worrying
rare	simulate	strange 1	trouble 2	

describing people

adult	dear	identity	people 1	sophisticated
age	despicable	ignorance	person	stern
aggressive 1	determination	ignorant	personality	strange 2
aggressive 2	determined 1	incompetent	perverse	strong 1
authoritarian	determined 2	insensitive	polite	stubborn
average	dignity	integrity	poor 1	stupid
background	disability	intellectual 2	powerful	style
beautiful 1	disabled	intelligence	pride	sweet
behave	dishonest	intelligent	prim	tact
black	eager	interested	prone to sth	talkative
body 1	efficient	irritable	proud 1	tall
bold	elegant	kind adj.	proud 2	tendency
brave	energy 2	lenient	quiet 3	tense
busy 1	experienced	life 2	realistic 1	thin
calm adj.	expert	life 3	reckless	thoughtful
careless	expression 2	like prep., adj.	reliable 1	tolerant
casual	fat adj.	lively	respect noun	tramp
charm	fold noun	look like sb/sth	respectable	traveller
cheat noun	fool	loser 2	restraint	travelling
cheerful	foreign	loving	rich	treacherous
child	formal	lucky	rude	typical
childish	former	mad	ruthless	ugly
cold 2	friendly 1	man 1	sane	unfortunate 1
colour 2	funny	mannerism	scruffy	vicious
composure	generous	mean adj.1	secretive	victim 2
confidence	genius	mean adj.2	seem	villain
confident	girl, youth	mentally ill	selfish	violent
confused 1	good 4	modest	sensitive 1	visionary
conscientious	good 7	naive	sensitive 3	visitor
cool adj.	greedy	naked	serious 2	vulnerable
courage	hairy	naughty	servile	way 1
coward	have 1	nervous	sharp 2	weak
crazy	have 2	new 3	short 2	weakness 2
creative	helpful	nice 2	shrewd	wild 1
cruel	honest	old 2	shy	wise
cunning	hostage	pale 1	smug	woman
dare	hungry	passive	sociable	worthy
darling	hysterical	peer	solitary	young
dead				

describing places

abandon	building	country 2	deserted	farm noun
angle	castle	courtyard	dim 2	field
area 1	chaos	cramped	ditch	flat noun
atmosphere	church	crowded	door	flat adj.
bar	city	dark 1	drab	floor 1
bare	coast	darkness	edge noun	floor 2
base	comfortable	decorate	environment	foreign
basement	corner	decoration	estate	forest
beautiful 2	corridor	desert	factory	full

describing things

education

friends and relationships

accomplice	equivalent *noun*	hate	love *noun* 1	relationship 1
adviser	exclude 2	hatred	love *noun* 2	relationship 2
age	family 1	help *noun*	love *verb*	reliable 1
alone	family 2	help *verb* 1	lover	respect *noun*
assistant	family 3	helpful	loving	respect *verb*
attracted to sb	flatter	hug	marriage	scold
betrayal	flirt	hurt 1	marry	selfish
bond	forgive	influence *verb*	meet 2	sensitive 1
bring sb up	friend	in love	meet 3	single
child	friendly 1	insensitive	meeting 2	sociable
cold 2	friendly 2	introduce 2	mother, father	solitary
darling	friendship	invite	offend	son, daughter
dear	go out	jealousy	partner 1	supporter
divide 2	grateful	leave 5	partner 2	trust
division 2	greet	lonely	peer	understand 2
divorce	greeting	look after sb	produce	visitor
encourage 2	group 2	look like sb/sth	reject	wife, husband
enemy	harass			

habits and customs

attend	family 3	mundane	polite	sometimes
background	famous	national	process	tradition
ceremony	frequent	new 3	rarely	traditional
conservative	general 1	occasional	recent	unusual
continuous	habit	often	regular	used to sth
costume	international	old 1	religion	usual
cultural	mannerism	the past	religious	usually
culture	meal	people 2	respect *verb*	wear
daily				

health

attack *noun* 3	disabled	hurt 2	rest *noun* 2	
bandage	disease	illness	rest *verb*	thin
blow *verb* 2	dizzy	injure	sane	threat
body 1	doctor	injured	scratch 1	threaten 2
breath	drug 1	injury	serious 1	tire
clean *adj.*	drug 2	life 1	shake 3	tired 1
collapse 2	drunk	look after sb	shiver	train 2
cough	ease	mentally ill	sick 1	treat 1
cure	energetic	obsession	sick 2	treatment
cut 4	energy 2	odour	sign 1	tumour
dangerous	fat *adj.*	pain	sleep	unhealthy
die	fatal	painful 1	sport	victim 1
diet	food	pale 1	strength	vomit
dirt	force *noun*	patient	suffer from sth	wave 3
dirty	health	poison *noun*	surgery	weak
disability	healthy	poison *verb*	survive	well
disable	hospital	recover 1	take 9	worsen

the individual and society

allow	common	exclude 2	home 2	join
alone	community	exclusive	hooligan	justice
aristocratic	conservative	expel	hope *noun* 2	legacy
authoritarian	control *noun*	family 1	hope *verb*	let sb in
authorities	country 1	follow 3	identity	licence
ban *noun*	crowd *noun*	follow 4	incentive	life 3
ban *verb*	crowd *verb*	forbidden	inequality	limit *noun* 1
bureaucracy	cultural	free *adj.* 1	influence *noun*	limit *verb*
certificate	culture	freedom	inspector	limited 2
charity	divide 2	gap	institution	live
choice 1	division 1	the general public	international	lonely
choose	division 2	greedy	intervene	lord
citizen	elite	group 2	involvement	man 2
class 4	example 2	habit	isolate	meet 1

language and communication

law and justice

peace	punish	rob	suspicious 2	trouble 1
plot	punishment	rule *noun*	tell 2	unjustified
policeman	rape	rule *verb* 2	theft	unofficial
principle 1	reason	secret 2	thief	values
principle 2	reasonable	seize	threaten 1	vandalize
prison	right *noun*	steal	thug	witness
prisoner	right *adj.* 2	strict	traitor	wrong 4

the media

advertise	describe	investigation	popular	report 4
advertisement	discredit	issue	power	reporter
analyst	fame	look *verb* 1	present 4	reputation
article	famous	magazine	presenter	show 3
audience	fashionable	market 1	programme	spokesman
biased	feature *verb*	the media	propaganda	star 1
book	film 1	medium	publish 1	study
campaign *noun*	film 2	news	read	survey
campaign *verb*	forum	newspaper	record *noun*	write 2
channel	fuss	objective	record *verb* 2	writer
chapter	investigate	parody	report 2	

money

bankrupt	estimate *noun*	increase *verb*	payment	rise
bill	estimate *verb*	investment	poor 1	save 2
borrow	expensive	lend	poverty	save 3
buy	fall 1	loan	price *noun*	sell 1
cash	figure	loss-making	price *verb*	sell 2
charge *verb*	finance	make 2	profit	soar
cheap	free *adj.* 2	make 3	raise	spend 1
compensation	fund *noun*	mean *adj.*2	rate 2	tax
cost	fund *verb*	money 1	reduce	valuable 1
costs	gift	money 2	reduction	valuation
count	give 5	money 3	repay	value 2
debt	high 1	number 1	revenue	wallet
discount	income	pay	rich	waste *verb*
economic	increase *noun*			

movement

beat 2	flow *verb*	move	shake 1	surge
blow *verb* 1	fly 1	movement	shake 2	swing
carry 1	fly 2	nod	shake 3	take 2
carry 2	fumble	pick sb/sth up	shiver	take 3
climb	go 1	place *verb*	signal	take 4
come 1	go away	pull 1	slide	throw
cross	hurry	pull 2	slip 1	touch 1
current	jab	pull 3	slip 2	trudge
curve *verb*	jump 1	push 1	spin	turn 1
direction	jump 2	push 2	spray	walk *noun*
disperse	jump 3	put 1	stand 1	walk *verb* 1
drag	land *verb*	put 2	step	walk *verb* 2
edge *verb*	lead *verb* 1	relax 2	still	wander
enter	lean 1	roll *verb*	stop *noun*	wrap sb/sth around/
flee	lean 2	run 1	stop *verb* 2	round sb/sth
float	lie *verb*	scatter	stroke	wriggle
flow *noun*	march	scratch 2	stumble	

the natural world

alive	forest	life 1	oil	soil
animal	habitat	live	plain *noun*	space 2
coast	harmful	man 2	poison *noun*	stone
country 2	harsh	marsh	produce	supply
desert	harvest	melt	productive	threaten 2
dirt	heat *noun* 2	natural	river	use *verb* 2
field	herd	nature 2	save 4	waste *noun*
fire *noun* 1	hill	night 2	sea	wave 1
flood *noun* 1	lake	offspring	smoke	the world
flood *verb*				

negative feelings

afraid	disappoint	grief	moody	shock *noun* 2
anger *noun*	disappointed	guilt	mourn	shock *verb*
anger *verb*	disappointment	hate	negative	sorry
angry	disapprove	hatred	nervous	stern
annoy	discourage 2	hesitant	nuisance	suppress 2
annoyed	distress	hesitate	offend	suspect
bitter 2	doubt *noun* 1	hurt 1	painful 2	suspicious 1
bored	doubt *noun* 2	hysterical	panic	tense
brood	embarrass	indifferent	pressure 1	tension
complain	embarrassed	influence *verb*	privacy	unhappy 1
complaint	emotion	insensitive	reluctant	unhappy 2
concern	encourage 3	intense	resent	unsure
confuse	false	irritable	resentment	upset
confused 1	fear	jealousy	restless	vicious
contempt	feel	jump 3	sad	wave 2
contemptuous	flush	laugh at sb/sth	scepticism	whistle
cry	frighten	lonely	scold	wild 2
depressed	frown	long *verb*	sense	worried
despair *noun*	frustration	lose your temper	shake 4	worry 1
despair *verb*	furious	march	sharp 2	worry 2
desperate	gloom	mood	shock *noun* 1	

politics

adviser	competition 2	government 2	politician	rule *verb* 1
advocate	compromise	independence	poverty	rule *verb* 2
agree 3	conservative	international	power	service
agreement 1	conspiracy	issue	powerful	slogan
agreement 2	contract	king	president	solution
aid	control *noun*	lead *verb* 2	propaganda	solve 1
approval	corrupt	leader 1	protester	support 1
ask 2	corruption	management	public	supporter
assembly	country 1	meeting 1	purpose	suppress 1
the authorities	county	official *noun*	radical	tackle
break 4	debate	oppose	relationship 1	tactic
campaign *noun*	demonstration	opposition	remove 2	territory
campaign *verb*	dictator	overthrow	repression	traitor
candidate	election	party 1	repressive	values
citizen	forum	plan *noun* 1	republic	visionary
committee	government 1	plot	revolution 1	

positive feelings

admiration	emotion	grateful	love *noun* 1	sense
calm *verb*	emotional	happy	love *noun* 2	smile
calm *adj.*	encourage 1	hope *noun* 1	love *verb*	sorry
cheerful	enjoy	hope *verb*	mood	sorry for sb
comfortable	excited	idea 2	moving	sure
confidence	excitement	impress	optimistic	surprise
confident	expression 1	in love	patience	sympathy
curious	expression 2	inspire	please	taste 1
deep 1	faith	intense	pleasure	thanks
delight	feel	joy	praise *noun*	trust
desire	forgive	laugh	praise *verb*	wave 2
dignity	fun	like *verb*	prefer	wild 2
eager	glad	long *verb*	satisfaction	

science and technology

area 2	design *verb* 1	equipment	material	technology
artificial 1	designer	expert	mixture	test *noun* 1
calculate	develop 2	factory	modern	test *verb* 1
classify	development	find 3	monitor	theory 1
complex	drug 2	lead *noun* 1	oil	theory 2
conclusion	electronic	logic	practical	tool
confirm 1	element 1	machine	progress	treat 2
cool *verb*	energy 1	manufacture	show 1	weight
current				

sound

bang *noun*	creak	hoarse	rumble	sing
bang *verb* 1	cry	loud	say 1	song
beat 2	deep 2	music	scream	sound 1
blow *verb* 3	echo	note	shout	sound 2
bubble	grunt	quiet 2	silence *noun*	voice
buzz	hear	rhythm	silence *verb*	whisper
call 3	high 3	ring	silent	whistle
crackle				

sport and leisure

audience	enjoy	garden 1	leisure	
award	entertain	garden 2	like *verb*	rest *verb*
bar	entertainment	holiday 1	lose	round
close *adj.*	event 2	holiday 2	loser 1	score
coach	excitement	interest *noun* 2	participant	sociable
compete	exciting	interest *verb*	party 2	sport
competition 1	exhibition	interested	pitch	team 2
concert	facilities	interesting	play *verb* 1	train 2
defeat	fan	interview 2	play *verb* 2	training
draw *noun*	film 1	invite	play *verb* 3	victory
easy 2	fun	involvement	player	walk *verb* 2
energetic	game 1	join	race	win
energy 2	game 2	judge *noun* 2	rest *noun* 2	winner

time and space

accelerate	end *verb*	lead *verb* 1	period	spacious
accommodate	endless	lead *verb* 3	permanent	spend 2
age	expand 1	length	previous	stage 1
air	expect	life 1	proximity	start *noun*
begin	fall 2	life 2	quick	start *verb*
border	fast	long *adj.*	rare	stop *verb* 1
childhood	fill	meantime	rarely	stop *verb* 3
come 1	finish	memory	rate 1	stretch
come 2	first	the middle	recent	successive
continue 1	former	minute	remain	sudden
continue 2	free *adj.* 3	next	remember	surround
continue 3	frequent	night 1	remind	take your time
continuous	full	night 2	rhythm	time 1
cramped	future	occasional	series	time 2
daily	go by	often	short 1	touch 2
dawn	hold sb/sth up	old 1	short 3	urgent
day	hole 1	pack	size	usual
delay	immediate	parallel	slow	usually
early	last 1	the past	sometimes	wait
edge *noun*	last 2	pattern 1	space 1	wide 2
empty	late	pause *noun*	space 2	years
end *noun*	lead *noun* 1	pause *verb*		

travel

accident	drive 1	go away	port	tour
accompany	driver	highway	quick	tourist
arrival 1	explorer	holiday 2	refugee	traffic
arrive	fast	hotel	return 1	tramp
boat	flight	housing	road	transport
border	fly 1	junction	schedule *noun*	travel
car	foreign	land *verb*	set off	traveller
cargo	get 3	leave 1	station	travelling
carriage 1	get 4	leave 2	stay 2	trip
carriage 2	get 5	map	stop *noun*	trudge
corner	get in	move in	stop *verb* 2	visit *noun*
cruise	get out	order *verb* 2	suitcase	visit *verb*
delivery	go 1	passenger	take 1	visitor
departure 1	go 2	path	tax	way 3

the weather

air	flood *noun* 1	hot	rough 2	sunny
cloud 1	flood *verb*	humid	snow	weather
cloudy	freezing	rain *noun*	storm	wet 2
cold 1	harsh	rain *verb*	sun	wind
darken	heat *noun* 2			

work and business

active	design *verb* 1	involvement	output	schedule *noun*
advertise	designer	job	partner 1	schedule *verb*
advertisement	develop 2	join	plan *noun* 1	sell 1
adviser	development	launch	plan *noun* 2	sell 2
aggressive 2	devote	lead *noun* 1	plan *verb*	send 2
agree 3	do 1	lead *verb* 2	planning	servant
agreement 1	do well	leader 1	predict	serve 2
ambition	drive 2	leader 2	present 1	service
appoint	economic	leave 3	pressure 1	shop
arrange	efficiency	logo	price *verb*	slump
assignment	efficient	loss-making	product	spokesman
assistant	effort	lot	production	sponsor
available	employ	make 1	productive	staff
bankrupt	endorsement	make 2	profit	successful 2
base	establish	make 3	progress	system
benefit 2	executive	maker	project	tackle
brand	expand 2	management	provide	take over
build	expectation	manager	provide for sb	target
bureaucracy	experienced	manufacture	publish 2	task
business 2	facilities	market 1	recession	team 1
candidate	factory	market 2	recover 2	top
charity	fire *verb*	meeting 1	recruit	trade
class 4	fund *noun*	money 1	reduction	unemployed
close *verb* 2	fund *verb*	mundane	regulate	unemployment
committee	government 2	negotiate	reorganize	union
company	group 3	negotiator	repair *noun*	urgent
competition 2	holiday 1	offer *noun* 2	repair *verb*	voluntary 2
compromise	income	office 1	replace 1	way 2
contract	industry	office 2	replacement	work *noun* 1
costs	ineffective	official *noun*	report 3	work *noun* 2
customer	inspection	official *adj.*	responsibility	work *noun* 3
cut 1	inspector	operate	revenue	work *verb* 1
dealer	interview 1	order *verb* 2	role	work *verb* 2
deal with sb/sth	interview 2	organization	run 2	work *verb* 3
delivery	introduce 1	organize	salesman	worker 1
demand *noun*	investment	organizer	scale	worker 2
department				

This key contains answers to the following exercises:

Thesaurus Trainer pages viii–xvi

Finding the Right Entry

A 1 become *verb*
2 schedule *noun*
3 courage *noun*
4 bold *adj.*

B 1 cook *verb*
2 schedule *verb*
3 attach *verb*
4 correct *verb*

C 1 bitter *adj.* 1
2 support *verb* 2
3 take *verb* 2
4 play *verb* 3

D 1 come up with sth *phrasal verb*
2 practise *verb*
3 refer to sth *phrasal verb*
4 scold *verb*

E 1 work *verb* 2
2 join *verb*
3 anger *verb*
4 lose your temper *idiom*

The Synonym Groups

A fabric *(= the most frequent)*
cloth
material
textile *(= the least frequent)*

B 1 intelligent
2 smart
3 clever
4 brilliant
5 bright

The General Definition

C 1 iii   2 i   3 ii

Synonym Scales

D *you like sth*: like, be fond of sth,
be keen on sth, go for sth
you like sth very much: love
you like sth very much indeed: adore

Patterns and Collocations

A 1 ✔ *(= correct)*
2 ✘ choose/select/pick/decide
3 ✔
4 ✘ chose/decided/opted

B 1 ✘ luck/chance/coincidence/accident
2 ✔
3 ✔
4 ✘ fate. *Providence* is also possible,
but is more formal.

C 1 schedule/~~agenda~~/programme
2 habits/ways/~~rules~~
3 got/~~obtained~~/acquired
4 ~~banned~~/prohibited/forbidden
5 satisfied/~~content~~/contented
6 hurts/~~aches~~/stings

The Individual Synonyms

Meaning

A discussion

B a *discussion* is more detailed and is about sth important; a *conversation* is more personal and more informal

C 1 conversation
2 conversation
3 discussion
4 discussions

Grammar

D reject *(= transitive only)*

E 1 rejected
2 refused
3 refuse
4 refuse

Register

F *slang:* –
informal: hot
rather informal: –
neither formal nor informal:
popular, appealing, in demand
rather formal: attractive, enviable
formal: desirable

G 1 a stink
2 receive
3 desirable
4 bad
5 ripped off

Use

H 1 pit
2 burglarize
3 messy
4 pack/package

I 1 journalism or business
2 law
3 medicine
4 physics

J 1 *cramped* is disapproving;
compact is approving
2 *innocence* is approving; *ignorance* is sometimes
disapproving, *naivety* is often disapproving
3 *cultured* is approving; *highbrow* and *bookish* are
sometimes disapproving
4 *solitude* is approving; *loneliness* and *isolation* are
disapproving

Examples

A 1 act
2 move
3 measure
4 step

B 1 ✔
2 ✘ route
3 ✔
4 ✘ embargo
5 ✘ deal
6 ✔
7 ✘ hazard
8 ✘ drop

Notes

A 1 countryside
2 terrain
3 countryside
4 terrain

B 1 gift
2 gift
3 gift
4 present (*Gift* is possible here, but *present* is better because it sounds more personal.)

C 1 ✘ fear
2 ✔
3 ✘ herd
4 ✔
5 ✔
6 ✘ inaccurate
7 ✘ comment
8 ✘ pond

Opposites

A accelerate — retard
condemn — condone
criticize — praise
hasten — delay
reject — approve
rough — exact
turn sb/sth down — take sth up
vague — clear

B 1 casual
2 juvenile
3 similar
4 accepted

Derivatives

1 Be careful not to disturb nesting birds.
2 Police made several arrests.
3 You have disgraced the whole school.
4 You owe her an apology for what you did.
5 The situation is constantly under review.
6 He ran onto the train with three police officers
in hot pursuit.

Study Pages page 871–887

Arts and Entertainment page 872

A 1 Released
2 acclaimed
3 nominated
4 plot
5 played
6 friendship
7 deals with (*or* is also about)
8 protagonists
9 lonely
10 script (*or* screenplay)
11 ✘ loved/adored
12 ✔
13 ✘ favourite
14 ✔; ✘ beginning
15 ✔; ✘ ending

B *Pairs of synonyms, with Thesaurus entries
given in* SMALL CAPS:
scriptwriter — author (WRITER)
chapter — episode (CHAPTER)
score — lyrics (SCRIPT)
masterpiece — work of art (WORK *noun* 4)
passage — clip (SCENE)
lead — star (STAR 2)
writing — literature (LITERATURE)
entertainer — performer (ACTOR)
sketch — drawing (PICTURE)
artist — sculptor (ARTIST)

1 artists
2 lead
3 chapters
4 lyrics
5 authors
6 masterpieces
7 clip
8 sketch
9 literature
10 entertainer

C 1 drew
  2 appeared
  3 staged
  4 acted
  5 shot
  6 recommend

D 1 –   6 +
  2 +   7 ++
  3 ++   8 ++
  4 – –   9 –
  5 –   10 +

Customs and Traditions page 874

A 1 businesses
  2 origins/origin
  3 thanks
  4 gets together (*or* gathers together)
  5 traditional
  6 consists of
  7 shows
  8 events
  9 parade
  10 considered
  11 season
  12 looking forward

B 1 upbringing
  2 background
  3 record
  4 convention
  5 practice
  6 tradition
  7 culture
  8 civilization
  9 community

C 1 costumes
  2 festivities
  3 the old days
  4 ceremony
  5 tradition
  6 takes place
  7 wear
  8 handed down

D *Synonyms of words meaning* **normal**:
  humdrum
  commonplace
  mainstream
  mundane
  conventional
  widespread

  Synonyms of words meaning **unusual**:
  alien
  unaccustomed to
  unorthodox
  unknown
  eccentric
  unused to

  1 unorthodox (*or* conventional, *although the meaning is the opposite*)
  2 commonplace (*or* widespread)
  3 unaccustomed to/unused to
  4 humdrum/mundane
  5 alien

E *Suggested order:*
  routinely (5) — as a rule (2) — often (6) — at times (4) — the odd (1) — hardly ever (3)

Green Issues page 876

A *This is the best choice of word in each case:*
  1 sites (✗ - do not replace)
  2 forefront (✗)
  3 system (✔ - replace)
  4 throw out (✗)
  5 collected (✗)
  6 Charges (✔)
  7 vary (✗)
  8 throw away (✔)
  9 emptied (✔)
  10 conscious (✔)
  11 reduce (✗)
  12 effective (✗)
  13 encouraging (✔)
  14 environment (✗)

B 1 rubbish
  2 trash; garbage
  3 litter
  4 Refuse; waste

C 1 ✔
  2 ✗ territory
  3 ✔
  4 ✗ world (or **on the planet**)
  5 ✗ earth

D 1 harm
  2 melt
  3 endanger
  4 depleted
  5 evolve

E 1 air pollution/smog
2 petroleum/crude oil
3 exhaust fumes
4 fossil fuels

F 1 chilly
2 crisp
3 humid
4 cool
5 warm
6 stuffy
7 freezing/icy
8 stifling

Suggested order:
freezing/icy — chilly — crisp — cool —
warm — humid — stuffy — stifling

Descriptions page 878

A 1 possessions
2 stands
3 detail
4 size
5 imperfections
6 symbol
7 no
8 no
9 no
10 no
11 yes
12 no
13 yes
14 no
15 yes

B *Synonyms of words meaning **large**:*
broad
monumental
substantial
vast

*Synonyms of words meaning **small**:*
compact
fine
minor
modest
narrow
tiny

Collocations:
a substantial breakfast
a broad grin
the vast majority
a monumental task
a tiny bit
a compact camera
a minor detail
a modest fee
fine hair
a narrow street

C *Suggested answers:*
microscopic: tiny/miniature/minute
small: little/compact
normal: ordinary/average
big: large/substantial/sizeable/bumper
huge: massive/vast/enormous/giant/gigantic/
immense/colossal

D 1 +
2 N
3 +
4 N
5 +
6 −
7 −

E 1 dimensions
2 volume
3 scale
4 extent
5 thickness
6 depth
7 diameter

Friends and Relationships page 880

A 1 special
2 supported
3 tough
4 holding
5 nominate
6 relative
7 award
8 admire
9 influenced
10 panel
11 judges
12 runners-up
13 winning
14 expenses

B *Suggested answers:*
1 brat (*brat* is disapproving)
2 youth (a *youth* is a young man; the others can
be male or female)
3 acquaintance (an *acquaintance* is not a close
friend)
4 parent (the others can all be used as names)
5 parent
6 youths
7 acquaintances
8 brat

C *Words that refer to **good** relationships:*
affection
respect
awe
bond
devotion
rapport

*Words that refer to **bad** relationships:*
rift
quarrel
bad faith
split
squabble
disloyalty

1 ✘ respect
2 ✘ rapport
3 ✔
4 ✘ affection
5 ✘ quarrel
6 ✘ disloyalty

D bring sb up — raise
fall out — argue
patch sth up — resolve
tell sb off — reprimand
take after sb — resemble
walk out (on sb) — abandon

1 takes after
2 reprimanded
3 falling out/arguing; patch things up
4 walked out on; bring up/raise

Work and Jobs page 882

A *Entries are given in* SMALL CAPS:
1 need (NEED *verb*)
2 quit (LEAVE 3)
3 cash (MONEY 1)
4 job (JOB)
5 drop by (VISIT *verb*)
6 hot (POPULAR)
7 sort out (ORGANIZE)
8 great (at sth) (GOOD 4)
9 cut out for sth (GOOD 2)
10 bubbly (LIVELY)
11 send in (PRESENT *verb* 3)
12 scared (AFRAID)
13 feel like/want (WANT)
14 chat (about sth) (CHAT; TALK)
15 Would you like to
16 money
17 required
18 popular
19 lively
20 Proficient
21 position
22 submit
23 arrange
24 discuss

B 1 helper
2 shopkeepers
3 tycoons
4 allies

C 1 a workroom
2 a studio
3 a study
4 retire
5 stand down (*or* step down)
6 quit
7 duties
8 work
9 chores

D 1 take on
2 turned it down
3 bring in
4 churn out
5 set up
6 laid off
7 closed down
8 covering for

Language and Communication page 884

A *This is the best choice of word in each case:*
1 art (✘ – do not replace)
2 communicate (✔ – replace)
3 way (✘)
4 survey (✔)
5 average (✔)
6 incredible (✘)
7 limited (✔)
8 shortened (✔)
9 characters (✘)
10 concerned (✔)
11 language (✔)
12 link (✘)
13 combination; economize
14 replaced
15 shorter
16 common
17 combined; phrase

B 1 raise your voice
2 sigh
3 bawl
4 murmur
5 speaking
6 murmured
7 raise his voice
8 speak
9 bawled
10 sighing

C *Successful communication:*
explicit
intelligible
coherent
fluent
eloquent
unambiguous

Unsuccessful communication:
ambiguous
misleading
confused
woolly
rambling
incomprehensible

1 eloquent
2 coherent
3 fluent
4 rambling
5 incomprehensible
6 misleading
7 intelligible
8 explicit
9 unambiguous

Travel and Tourism page 886

A 1 express
2 trip
3 complain
4 turn down
5 conditions
6 route
7 let
8 unhelpful
9 unacceptable
10 look forward to
11 grubby
12 horrendous (awful *and* dreadful would also be possible)
13 fed up
14 fiasco
15 worn out (*or* shattered *in BrE*/pooped *in AmE*)

B 1 board
2 mounted
3 started
4 disembarked
5 get in
6 came back
7 showed up/rolled in (*or* turned up, *although this does not fit the meaning so well*)
8 touched down

C 1 stopover
2 visit
3 tour
4 tour
5 trip
6 outings
7 getaway
8 break
9 holiday/vacation

D 1 charming
2 exquisite
3 scenery
4 terrain
5 magnificent
6 glorious
7 views
8 view

Topic Map Exercises pages 888–901

Education page 889

A *teaching:* a home tutor; a teacher trainer
school and college: the class of 2008
studying: homework; to review your notes
testing: the pass mark
success: a stroke of genius;
failure: to skive off school; to flunk out of college

B 1 educational; scholarly; pedagogic
2 lecturer; professor; don
3 learn; study; get the hang of sth
4 score; mark; grade
5 intelligent; clever; bright
6 ignorant; illiterate; clueless

C receive private tuition
equip sb for a career in sth
get full marks
pick up a few words of Japanese
sail through college
skip a class

D 1 grade
2 training
3 focused (*target* must take a direct object, without 'on')
4 well read
5 illiterate
6 learners

Health page 891

A *illness:* heart disease; a terminal illness
injury: cuts and bruises; to tear a muscle
symptoms: a sallow complexion
staying healthy: a strong constitution; a strict regime
treatment: on prescription; heavily dosed

B 1 fatal; lethal; terminal
2 cure; heal; make sb better
3 tired; exhausted; drowsy
4 health; condition; shape
5 painful; sore; excruciating

C choke on a fishbone
pick up a stomach bug
diagnose a heart condition
nick yourself while shaving
resuscitate an unconscious person
sprain your ankle

D 1 lethal
2 injured
3 paramedics
4 drowsy
5 discomfort
6 shake off

Sport and Leisure page 893

A *having fun:* live entertainment; to do sth for kicks
sport: the World Cup finals
getting involved: to take part in sth; zest for life
interests: an art-lover; the national pastime
relaxing: Spring Break; a leisurely stroll

B 1 entertainment; recreation; amusement
2 team; squad; line-up
3 energetic; vigorous; dynamic
4 creative; innovative; ingenious
5 holiday; leave; sabbatical

C compete in the Olympics
go in for a competition
join in with the fun
exercise for 2 hours every day
savour every moment
sit back and relax

D 1 lover
2 enthusiastic
3 fascinated
4 spare time
5 game
6 thrill

The Individual and Society page 895

A *the individual:* to fend for yourself
the authorities: the military top brass
citizenship: Australian nationals; a multicultural
society
the class system: the landed gentry; humble origins
freedom: freedom of choice
social exclusion: the needy; alienation

B 1 identity; individuality; uniqueness
2 bureaucracy; paperwork; red tape
3 cultural; ethnic; folk
4 class; rank; status
5 authoritarian; autocratic; overbearing
6 poverty; deprivation; destitution

C grant an amnesty
divide the community
shoulder the burden
cut the red tape
belong to an elite
forfeit your right to sth

D 1 firm
2 a reputable
3 humble
4 public
5 inhabitants
6 isolation

Conflict page 897

A *disagree:* to not see eye to eye; a shouting match
oppose: to defy a ban; a storm of protest
fight: a street brawl
war: the armed forces; to occupy a country
resolving conflict: to mend fences; to hold talks

B 1 soldier; warrior; mercenary
2 aggressive; militant; warlike
3 challenge; dare; throw down the gauntlet
4 negotiator; mediator; intermediary
5 argue; bicker; fall out

C declare war
throw a punch
pick a quarrel
crush a rebellion
negotiate for the hostages' release
go against sb's wishes

D 1 clashed   4 hostility
2 erupt   5 bloodthirsty
3 seize   6 resolve

Fact and Opinion page 889

A *claim:* serious allegations
balance and bias: equal opportunities;
a one-sided debate
subject matter: a key issue
opinions: What do you reckon?; a point of view
fact: raw data; an authoritative account
discussion: a heated exchange

B 1 claim; allege; assert
2 message; substance; the thrust
3 view; point; feeling
4 biased; prejudiced; partisan
5 reliable; factual; authentic
6 discussion; dialogue; consultation

C claim to be an expert
lack substance
comment on the issue
state the obvious
take stock of the situation
spread disinformation

D 1 controversial
2 Discussions
3 misrepresented
4 thread
5 comment
6 inaccurate

The Media page 991

A *news:* a news flash; the mass media
TV, film and radio: the movie industry;
a live broadcast
the printed word: to flick through sth
advertising: a publicity stunt; to plug a product
people in the media: a restaurant critic;
a living legend

B 1 advertisement; trailer; plug
2 the media; the press; journalism
3 report; story; item
4 reporter; columnist; hack
5 publish; issue; print

C watch TV all day
catch a show on the radio
dash off a quick note
push the idea of teamwork
release new software on CD-ROM
shoot to stardom

D 1 version
2 record
3 viewers
4 flicked through
5 blurb
6 well known

ALPHABETICAL INDEX

This index lists every synonym in the thesaurus in alphabetical order. For help with using this index see the Thesaurus Trainer on page viii at the front of this book.

A a

abandon verb
▸ ABANDON (abandon a vehicle)
▸ LEAVE 5 (abandon a baby)
▸ STOP 1 (abandon a match/an attempt/hope)

abandoned adj.
▸ DESERTED

abbey noun
▸ CHURCH

abbreviated adj.
▸ SHORT 3

abdicate verb
▸ GIVE STH UP

abdomen noun
▸ STOMACH

abduct verb
▸ KIDNAP

aberration noun
▸ EXCEPTION

abet verb
▸ **aid and abet** HELP 1

abhor verb
▸ HATE

abide by phrasal verb
▸ FOLLOW 3

ability noun
▸ ABILITY (have the ability to do sth)
▸ SKILL 1 (a child's natural abilities)

able adj.
▸ GOOD 4

abnormal adj.
▸ ABNORMAL

abode noun
▸ HOME 1

abolish verb
▸ ABOLISH

abominable adv.
▸ DISGUSTING 2

abomination noun
▸ DISGRACE 1

about adv.
▸ ALMOST

about prep.
▸ **be about sth** APPLY verb 2

abrupt adj.
▸ SHARP 2 (She was rather abrupt with me.)
▸ SUDDEN (an abrupt halt)

abscess noun
▸ TUMOUR

absence noun
▸ LACK

absent-minded adj.
▸ CARELESS

absolute adj.
▸ COMPLETE (an absolute fortune)
▸ FINAL (absolute proof)

absolutely adv.
▸ QUITE 2

absolve verb
▸ ACQUIT

absorb verb
▸ INTEREST (work absorbs sb)
▸ USE 2 (absorb money/time)
▸ WITHSTAND (absorb shock)

absorbed adj.
▸ INTERESTED

absorbing adj.
▸ INTERESTING

abstract noun
▸ SUMMARY

abstract adj.
▸ INTELLECTUAL 1

abstraction noun
▸ IDEA 1

absurd adj.
▸ RIDICULOUS

abuse verb
▸ EXPLOIT (abuse drugs/your position)
▸ OFFEND (verbally abused)
▸ RAPE (sexually abused)

abusive adj.
▸ OFFENSIVE

abysmal adj.
▸ TERRIBLE 4

academic noun
▸ SCHOLAR

academic adj.
▸ EDUCATIONAL (an academic career)
▸ INTELLECTUAL 1 (academic ability)

academy noun
▸ SCHOOL

accelerate verb
▸ ACCELERATE

accent noun
▸ VOICE

accept verb
▸ ACCEPT (accept the fact that…)
▸ AGREE 2 (accept a decision)
▸ GET 2 (accept a cheque)
▸ GREET (accept sb into your community)
▸ LET SB IN (accepted into the club)
▸ TAKE 5 (accept an offer)
▸ TAKE 7 (accept responsibility)

acceptable adj.
▸ ADEQUATE (The food was acceptable, but no more.)
▸ FINE (This solution is acceptable to everyone.)
▸ RIGHT 2 (acceptable behaviour)

acceptance noun
▸ APPROVAL

access noun
▸ ACCESS

accessible adj.
▸ CLEAR 2

accessory noun
▸ ACCOMPLICE (an accessory to murder)
▸ DECORATION (fashion accessories)

accident noun
▸ ACCIDENT (a road accident)
▸ LUCK (an accident of fate)

acclaim noun
▸ PRAISE

acclaim verb
▸ PRAISE

accolade noun
▸ TRIBUTE

accommodate verb
▸ ACCOMMODATE

accommodating adj.
▸ HELPFUL

accommodation noun
▸ HOUSING

accompany verb
▸ ACCOMPANY

accomplice noun
▸ ACCOMPLICE

accomplish verb
▸ ACHIEVE

accomplished adj.
▸ GOOD 4

accomplishment noun
▸ WORK 3

accord noun
▸ CONTRACT (a peace accord)
▸ **in accord** AGREEMENT 2

accord verb
▸ GIVE 1

account noun
▸ BILL (buy sth on account)
▸ FUND (a bank account)
▸ REPORT 2 (a full account of the incident)

accountability noun
▸ RESPONSIBILITY

account for phrasal verb
▸ EXPLAIN 2

accredited adj.
▸ OFFICIAL

accrue verb
▸ BUILD UP (interest can accrue)
▸ COLLECT (accrue interest/debts)

accumulate verb
▸ BUILD UP (debts began to accumulate)
▸ COLLECT (accumulate books/a fortune; dust accumulates)

accurate adj.
▸ EXACT

accusation noun
▸ CHARGE

accuse verb
▸ ACCUSE

accustomed to adj.
▸ USED TO STH

ache noun
▸ PAIN

ache verb
▸ HURT 2

achievable adj.
▸ POSSIBLE 1

achieve verb
▸ ACHIEVE (achieve your target)
▸ SUCCEED (achieve academically)

achievement noun
▸ WORK 3

acid adj.
▸ BITTER 1

acknowledge verb
▸ ADMIT 1 (acknowledge the facts)
▸ ANSWER (acknowledge a letter)

acknowledgement noun
▸ ANSWER

acquaintance noun
▸ FRIEND (friends and acquaintances)
▸ FRIENDSHIP (make sb's acquaintance)
▸ **make sb's acquaintance** MEET verb 3

acquiesce verb
▸ AGREE 2

acquiescence noun
▸ APPROVAL

acquire verb
▸ BUY (acquire new premises)
▸ GET 1 (acquire a taste for sth)
▸ LEARN (acquire new skills)

acquisitive adj.
▸ GREEDY

acquit adj.
▸ ACQUIT

acrid adj.
▸ BITTER 1

acrimonious adj.
▸ BITTER 2

acrimony noun
▸ RESENTMENT

act noun
▸ ACTION (an act of kindness)
▸ PERFORMANCE (a circus act)
▸ PRETENCE (put on an act)
▸ RULE (the Higher Education Act)

act verb
▸ ACT (act promptly)
▸ AFFECT (Alcohol acts on the brain.)
▸ BEHAVE (act strangely)
▸ PLAY 3 (act the role of Hamlet)
▸ PRETEND (act dumb)

acting noun
▸ DRAMA

action noun
▸ ACTION (take responsibility for your actions)
▸ ACTIVITY (films with plenty of action)
▸ CASE (a libel action)
▸ EFFECT (the action of sunlight on the skin)
▸ WAR (killed in action)
▸ **take action** ACT verb
▸ **in action** ACTIVE adj.
▸ **put sb/sth out of action** DISABLE verb

active adj.
▸ ACTIVE (the active ingredient in aspirin)
▸ BUSY 1 (active in politics)
▸ ENERGETIC (physically active)

activist noun
▸ ACTIVIST

activity noun
▸ ACTIVITY (physical/economic activity)
▸ PROJECT (classroom activities)

act on/upon phrasal verb
▸ FOLLOW 3

actor noun
▸ ACTOR

actress noun
▸ ACTOR

actual adj.
▸ REAL (in actual fact…)
▸ VERY (his actual words)

acute adj.
▸ SERIOUS 1

ad noun
▸ ADVERTISEMENT

adapt verb
▸ CHANGE 1

adaptable adj.
▸ FLEXIBLE 1

adaptation noun
▸ CHANGE 2

add verb
▸ COUNT (add 9 to the total)
▸ GIVE 4 (add a touch of class)

addict noun
▸ FAN

addictive adj.
▸ ADDICTIVE

address noun
▸ HOME 1 (your home address)
▸ SPEECH (a presidential address)

address verb
▸ CALL 1 (address him as 'Sir')
▸ FOCUS (address a remark to sb)
▸ SEND 1 (address a letter)
▸ TACKLE (address the issues)

add to phrasal verb
▸ WEAKEN

add up to phrasal verb
▸ BE (The numbers add up to 100.)
▸ REPRESENT 1 (These clues don't really add up to very much.)

adequate adj.
▸ ADEQUATE

adhere to phrasal verb
▸ FOLLOW 3

adjourn verb
▸ DELAY

adjudicate verb
▸ JUDGE 2

adjust verb
▸ ADJUST

adjustable adj.
▸ FLEXIBLE 1

adjustment noun
▸ CHANGE 2

administer verb
▸ GIVE 3 (administer first aid)

▶ REGULATE (administer tests)
▶ RUN 2 (administer a charity)

administration *noun*
▶ GOVERNMENT 1 (the Bush administration)
▶ GOVERNMENT 2 (administration costs)
▶ MANAGEMENT (hospital administration)

administrator *noun*
▶ ORGANIZER

admirable *adj.*
▶ WORTHY

admiration *noun*
▶ ADMIRATION

admire *verb*
▶ APPRECIATE (admire the view)
▶ RESPECT (I admire your determination.)

admirer *noun*
▶ FAN (an admirer of Picasso)
▶ PARTNER 2 (She had many admirers.)

admiring *adj.*
▶ GOOD 6

admission *noun*
▶ ACCESS

admit *verb*
▶ ADMIT 1 (Admit it! You were terrified!)
▶ ADMIT 2 (She admitted theft.)
▶ LET SB IN (Each ticket admits one adult.)

adolescence *noun*
▶ CHILDHOOD

adolescent *noun*
▶ GIRL

adolescent *adj.*
▶ YOUNG

adopt *verb*
▶ BRING SB UP (adopt a child)
▶ CHOOSE (adopt a name)
▶ PRETEND (adopt an air of indifference)

adorable *adj.*
▶ SWEET

adore *verb*
▶ LIKE (I adore those shoes.)
▶ LOVE (She adores him.)

adoring *adj.*
▶ LOVING

adorn *verb*
▶ DECORATE

adulation *noun*
▶ PRAISE

adult *adj.*
▶ ADULT

advance *noun*
▶ LOAN (an advance on your salary)
▶ OFFER 1 (make sexual advances)
▶ PROGRESS (technological advance)

advance *verb*
▶ DEVELOP 1 (technology advances)
▶ GO 1 (troops advance)
▶ LEND (advance sb money)
▶ PROMOTE (advance a cause)
▶ PROPOSE (advance a theory)

advanced *adj.*
▶ MODERN

advancement *noun*
▶ PROGRESS

advantage *noun*
▶ BENEFIT 1 (Is there any advantage in getting there early?)
▶ LEAD 2 (have an unfair advantage)
▶ turn sth to your advantage MANIPULATE *verb*
▶ take advantage of sb/sth TAKE ADVANTAGE OF SB/STH *verb*

advantageous *adj.*
▶ VALUABLE 2

advent *noun*
▶ ARRIVAL 1

adventurer *noun*
▶ EXPLORER

adventurous *adj.*
▶ BOLD

adversary *noun*
▶ ENEMY

adverse *adj.*
▶ DIFFICULT 2

adversity *noun*
▶ TROUBLE 2

advert *noun*
▶ ADVERTISEMENT

advertise *verb*
▶ ADVERTISE (advertise a product)
▶ PUBLISH 1 (advertise a job/fact)

advertisement *noun*
▶ ADVERTISEMENT

advice *noun*
▶ ADVICE

advisable *adj.*
▶ BEST

advise *verb*
▶ RECOMMEND 1

adviser *noun*
▶ ADVISER

advocate *noun*
▶ ADVOCATE (an advocate of free trade)
▶ LAWYER (a legal advocate)

advocate *verb*
▶ RECOMMEND 1

aeon *noun*
▶ YEARS

aerobics *noun*
▶ SPORT

affair *noun*
▶ BUSINESS 1 (That's my affair.)
▶ EVENT 1 (current affairs)
▶ RELATIONSHIP 2 (They had a passionate affair.)

affect *verb*
▶ AFFECT (It won't affect my decision.)
▶ IMPRESS (deeply affected by your experiences)

affectation *noun*
▶ PRETENSION

affection *noun*
▶ LOVE 2

affectionate *adj.*
▶ LOVING

affiliation *noun*
▶ RELATIONSHIP 1

affinity *noun*
▶ BOND (a deep affinity with nature)
▶ SIMILARITY (a close affinity between Italian and Spanish)

affirm *verb*
▶ CLAIM

affluence *noun*
▶ MONEY 3

affluent *adj.*
▶ RICH

affordable *adj.*
▶ CHEAP

aficionado *noun*
▶ EXPERT

afraid *adj.*
▶ AFRAID (afraid of the dark)
▶ I'm afraid SORRY

African American *adj.*
▶ BLACK

afternoon *noun*
▶ DAY

again *adv.*
▶ now and again SOMETIMES

against *prep.*
▶ AGAINST SB/STH

age *noun*
▶ AGE (at the age of 18)
▶ PERIOD (the nuclear age)
▶ YEARS (It's an age since I saw him.)

aged *adj.*
▶ OLD 2

age group *noun*
▶ AGE

ageism (also **agism**) *noun*
▶ RACISM

agency *noun*
▶ SERVICE

agenda *noun*
▶ SCHEDULE

agent *noun*
▶ AGENT

ages *noun*
▶ YEARS

aggravate *verb*
▶ WEAKEN

aggression *noun*
▶ ATTACK 1 (military aggression)
▶ TENSION (channel your aggression)

aggressive *adj.*
▶ AGGRESSIVE 1 (aggressive behaviour)
▶ AGGRESSIVE 2 (an aggressive marketing campaign)

aggrieved *adj.*
▶ UNHAPPY 2

agitate *verb*
▶ CAMPAIGN (agitate for reform)
▶ SHAKE 4 (agitated by a mixture of anger and fear)

agitated *adj.*
▶ RESTLESS

agitation *noun*
▶ CONCERN (in a state of agitation)
▶ TROUBLE 1 (agitation for reform)

agonize *verb*
▶ WORRY 1

agonizing *adj.*
▶ PAINFUL 2

agony *noun*
▶ DISTRESS (an agony of suspense)
▶ PAIN (collapse in agony)

agree *verb*
▶ AGREE 1 ('That's true,' she agreed.)
▶ AGREE 2 (agree to a proposal)
▶ AGREE 3 (agree a price)
▶ MATCH 1 (The figures do not agree.)

agreement *noun*
▶ AGREEMENT 1 (sign an agreement)
▶ AGREEMENT 2 (be in agreement)
▶ APPROVAL (secure the owners' agreement)

aid *noun*
▶ AID (£10 million in foreign aid)
▶ HELP (come to sb's aid)
▶ TOOL (a hearing/teaching aid)

aid *verb*
▶ HELP 1 (Each group is aided by a tutor or consultant.)
▶ aid and abet HELP 1

aide *noun*
▶ ASSISTANT

ailing *adj.*
▶ SICK 1

ailment *noun*
▶ DISEASE

aim *noun*
▶ PURPOSE

aim *verb*
▶ AIM (aim a gun at sb/sth)

▶ INTEND (We aim to be there around six.)
▶ be aimed at sth DESIGN 2 (measures aimed at preventing crime)
▶ be aimed at sb FOCUS (be aimed at a young audience)

air *noun*
▶ AIR (kick a ball into the air)
▶ APPEARANCE (an air of concern)
▶ PRETENSION (put on airs)

air *verb*
▶ SAY 2

airspace *noun*
▶ AIR

airy *adj.*
▶ SPACIOUS

aisle *noun*
▶ CORRIDOR

alarm *noun*
▶ ALARM (a burglar alarm)
▶ FEAR (a feeling of alarm)
▶ WARNING (raise the alarm)

alarm *verb*
▶ FRIGHTEN

alarmed *adj.*
▶ AFRAID

alarming *adj.*
▶ FRIGHTENING

alcohol *noun*
▶ DRINK 2

alert *noun*
▶ WARNING (a bomb/fire alert)
▶ on the alert WATCH *noun*

alert *verb*
▶ WARN

alert to *phrasal verb*
▶ TELL 1

alert to *adj.*
▶ AWARE

alias *noun*
▶ NICKNAME

alien *adj.*
▶ FOREIGN (alone in an alien land)
▶ STRANGE 2 (a world that is alien and dangerous)

alienate *verb*
▶ DIVIDE 2

alienation *noun*
▶ DIVISION 2

alight *verb*
▶ GET OUT (Alight here for the stadium.)
▶ LAND (The bird alighted on a branch.)

align *verb*
▶ ARRANGE

alike *adj.*
▶ LIKE *prep. adj.*

alive *adj.*
▶ ALIVE (dead or alive)
▶ alive and well SAFE 1

all *pron.*
▶ be all for sth IN FAVOUR (OF SB/STH)

all-around *adj.*
▶ OVERALL

allay *verb*
▶ EASE

allegation *noun*
▶ CLAIM

allege *verb*
▶ CLAIM

alleged *adj.*
▶ SUPPOSED

allegory *noun*
▶ METAPHOR

alleviate *verb*
▶ EASE

alley *noun*
▶ ROAD

alliance noun
▶ UNION

allocate verb
▶ ALLOCATE

allocation noun
▶ SHARE

allot verb
▶ ALLOCATE

allotment noun
▶ GARDEN 2

allow verb
▶ ALLOW (Smoking is not allowed.)
▶ ENABLE (clothing that allows easy movement)

allowance noun
▶ SHARE

alloy noun
▶ MIXTURE

all-purpose adj.
▶ FLEXIBLE 1

all right adj.
▶ ADEQUATE (Your work is just about all right.)
▶ FINE (Is it all right if…)
▶ SAFE 1 (I'll be all right.)
▶ WELL (Are you feeling all right?)

all-round adj.
▶ OVERALL

allude to phrasal verb
▶ MENTION

allusion noun
▶ REFERENCE

ally noun
▶ PARTNER 1

almost adv.
▶ ALMOST

alone adj., adv.
▶ ALONE (live alone)
▶ LONELY (Carol felt all alone.)

aloof adj.
▶ COLD 2

also-ran noun
▶ LOSER 1

alter verb
▶ CHANGE 1 (It doesn't alter the way I feel.)
▶ CHANGE 2 (He had not altered much in ten years.)

alteration noun
▶ CHANGE 2

alternate verb
▶ CHANGE 2

alternation noun
▶ CHANGE 1

alternative noun
▶ OPTION

amass verb
▶ COLLECT

amaze verb
▶ SURPRISE

amazing adj.
▶ AMAZING

ambassador noun
▶ SPOKESMAN

ambiguous adj.
▶ MISLEADING

ambition noun
▶ AMBITION (a woman of driving ambition)
▶ HOPE 2 (achieve your ambition)

ambitious adj.
▶ AGGRESSIVE 2

ambivalent adj.
▶ UNSURE

amble verb
▶ WANDER

amenable adj.
▶ PASSIVE

amend verb
▶ ADJUST

amendment noun
▶ CHANGE 2

amenity noun
▶ FACILITIES

amiable adj.
▶ FRIENDLY 1

amicable adj.
▶ FRIENDLY 2

ammunition noun
▶ BULLET

amoral adj.
▶ CORRUPT

amount noun
▶ NUMBER 1

amount to phrasal verb
▶ BE (His earnings amount to £300 000 per annum.)
▶ REPRESENT 1 (Her answer amounted to a complete refusal.)

amphitheatre (also **amphitheater**) noun
▶ HALL 1

amuse verb
▶ ENTERTAIN

amusement noun
▶ ENTERTAINMENT (What do you do for amusement?)
▶ INTEREST 2 (seaside amusements)

amusing adj.
▶ FUNNY

analogous adj.
▶ EQUIVALENT

analogy noun
▶ COMPARISON

analyse (also **analyze**) verb
▶ EXAMINE

analysis noun
▶ RESEARCH

analyst noun
▶ ANALYST

anarchy noun
▶ TROUBLE 1

anatomy noun
▶ BODY 1

ancestry noun
▶ FAMILY 3

anchor noun
▶ PRESENTER

anchorman noun
▶ PRESENTER

anchorwoman noun
▶ PRESENTER

ancient adj.
▶ OLD 1

anecdote noun
▶ STORY 1

anger noun
▶ ANGER

anger verb
▶ ANGER

angle noun
▶ ANGLE (sticking up at an angle)
▶ ATTITUDE (a fresh angle for the advertising campaign)

angle verb
▶ LEAN 1

angry adj.
▶ ANGRY (I was angry about the delay.)
▶ **get angry** LOSE YOUR TEMPER idiom

angst noun
▶ CONCERN

anguish noun
▶ DISTRESS

anguished adj.
▶ UPSET

animal noun
▶ ANIMAL

animate adj.
▶ ALIVE

animated adj.
▶ LIVELY

animosity noun
▶ TENSION

annex verb
▶ INVADE

annihilate verb
▶ DESTROY

anniversary noun
▶ BIRTHDAY

announce verb
▶ DECLARE

announcement noun
▶ STATEMENT

announcer noun
▶ PRESENTER

annoy verb
▶ ANNOY

annoyance noun
▶ FRUSTRATION

annoyed adj.
▶ ANNOYED

annoying adj.
▶ ANNOYING

annul verb
▶ CANCEL

anomalous adj.
▶ ABNORMAL

anomaly noun
▶ EXCEPTION

anorak noun
▶ COAT

answer noun
▶ ANSWER (an answer to sb's question/letter)
▶ SOLUTION (the answer to question 12)

answer verb
▶ ANSWER

antagonism noun
▶ TENSION

antagonistic adj.
▶ AGAINST SB/STH

antagonize verb
▶ ANGER

anticipate verb
▶ ANTICIPATE (anticipate and respond to changes)
▶ EXPECT (anticipate that sales will rise)

anticipation noun
▶ EXPECTATION

anticlimax noun
▶ DISAPPOINTMENT

antidote noun
▶ DRUG 2

antipathy noun
▶ TENSION

antiquated adj.
▶ OLD-FASHIONED

antique adj.
▶ OLD 1

antisocial adj.
▶ SOLITARY

antonym noun
▶ OPPOSITE

anxiety noun
▶ CONCERN

anxious adj.
▶ EAGER (anxious to finish)
▶ STRESSFUL (an anxious moment)
▶ WORRIED (feel anxious about sth)

anything pron.
▶ **not come to anything** FAIL verb 2

apartheid noun
▶ DISCRIMINATION

apartment noun
▶ FLAT

apathetic adj.
▶ INDIFFERENT

aperture noun
▶ HOLE 1

aplomb noun
▶ CONFIDENCE

apologetic adj.
▶ SORRY

apologize verb
▶ APOLOGIZE

appal (also **appall**) verb
▶ SHOCK

appalling adj.
▶ TERRIBLE 3

apparatus noun
▶ EQUIPMENT (breathing apparatus)
▶ SYSTEM (the apparatus of government)

apparel noun
▶ CLOTHES

apparent adj.
▶ APPARENT (an apparent lack of enthusiasm)
▶ CLEAR 1 (for no apparent reason)

apparition noun
▶ GHOST

appeal noun
▶ CASE (a legal appeal)
▶ INTEREST 1 (have universal appeal)
▶ REQUEST (an appeal for information)

appeal verb
▶ ASK 2 (appeal for help)
▶ INTEREST (appeal to all ages)

appeal court noun
▶ COURT

appealing adj.
▶ POPULAR

appear verb
▶ APPEAR (A rash appeared.)
▶ ARRIVE (By ten o'clock Lee still hadn't appeared.)
▶ FEATURE (appear on TV)
▶ SEEM (appear surprised)

appearance noun
▶ APPEARANCE (her general appearance)
▶ ARRIVAL 1 (his sudden appearance)

appease verb
▶ CALM

appetite noun
▶ APPETITE 1 (Don't spoil your appetite by eating between meals.)
▶ APPETITE 2 (an appetite for scandal)

appetizing adj.
▶ DELICIOUS

applaud verb
▶ PRAISE

appliance noun
▶ MACHINE

applicable adj.
▶ RELEVANT

applicant noun
▶ CANDIDATE

application noun
▶ REQUEST (an application for a job)
▶ USE (the application of a theory)

applied adj.
▶ PRACTICAL

apply verb
▶ APPLY 1 (apply sanctions)
▶ APPLY 2 (special conditions apply)
▶ ASK 2 (apply for a job)

appoint verb
▸ APPOINT

appointment noun
▸ JOB (a permanent appointment)
▸ MEETING 2 (a dental appointment)

appraisal noun
▸ ASSESSMENT

appreciate verb
▸ APPRECIATE (Her family doesn't appreciate her.)
▸ KNOW 1 (appreciate the difficulties involved)
▸ WELCOME (appreciate some help)

appreciation noun
▸ ADMIRATION (applaud in appreciation)
▸ THANKS (a token of our appreciation)
▸ UNDERSTANDING (a broad appreciation of sth)

appreciative adj.
▸ GOOD 6 (an appreciative smile)
▸ GRATEFUL (be appreciative of sb's efforts)

apprehend verb
▸ ARREST

apprehension noun
▸ CONCERN

apprehensive adj.
▸ WORRIED

apprentice noun
▸ RECRUIT

approach noun
▸ ARRIVAL 1 (the approach of winter)
▸ OFFER 1 (make an approach to a local company for sponsorship)
▸ WAY 1 (a different approach to the problem)

approach verb
▸ APPROACH (profits approaching $30 million)
▸ COME 1 (a train approaches)
▸ COME 2 (winter approaches)
▸ TACKLE (approach a problem)

approachable adj.
▸ FRIENDLY 1

appropriate verb
▸ SEIZE

appropriate adj.
▸ GOOD 2

approval noun
▸ APPROVAL (get official approval)
▸ PRAISE (win sb's approval)

approve verb
▸ APPROVE (approve the accounts)
▸ AGREE 2 (approve a plan)
▸ IN FAVOUR (OF SB/STH) (approve of an idea)

approving adj.
▸ GOOD 6

approximate verb
▸ APPROACH

approximate adj.
▸ VAGUE

apt adj.
▸ GOOD 2

aptitude noun
▸ SKILL 1

arbiter noun
▸ JUDGE 2

arbitrate verb
▸ INTERVENE

arbitrator noun
▸ NEGOTIATOR

arc noun
▸ CURVE

arc verb
▸ CURVE

arch noun
▸ CURVE

arched adj.
▸ CURVED

archetypal adj.
▸ TYPICAL

archetype noun
▸ EXAMPLE 2

architect noun
▸ DESIGNER

archive noun
▸ DOCUMENT

ardent adj.
▸ INTENSE

arduous adj.
▸ HARD

area noun
▸ AREA 1 (rural/urban areas)
▸ AREA 2 (areas of study)
▸ PLACE 1 (the hotel reception area)
▸ SIZE (the area of a triangle)

arena noun
▸ FORUM (the international arena)
▸ PITCH (Wembley Arena)

arguable adj.
▸ CONTROVERSIAL

argue verb
▸ ARGUE (always arguing)
▸ CLAIM (argue for the right to strike)

argument noun
▸ ARGUMENT 1 (get into an argument)
▸ ARGUMENT 2 (arguments for and against sth)

arise verb
▸ FOLLOW 2 (injuries arising from the accident)
▸ HAPPEN (a crisis arises)

the **aristocracy** noun
▸ ELITE

aristocrat noun
▸ LORD

aristocratic adj.
▸ ARISTOCRATIC

arm noun
▸ DEPARTMENT (the research arm of the Department of Transport)
▸ twist sb's arm PRESS verb 2

arm verb
▸ EQUIP 1

armaments noun
▸ WEAPON

armchair noun
▸ CHAIR

armoury (also **armory**) noun
▸ WAREHOUSE

arms noun
▸ LOGO (a coat of arms)
▸ WEAPON (arms and ammunition)
▸ take up arms FIGHT verb 1

army noun
▸ ARMY

aroma noun
▸ SMELL

around-the-clock adj.
▸ CONTINUOUS

arouse verb
▸ STIMULATE

arrange verb
▸ ARRANGE (arrange flowers/your books/your affairs)
▸ ORGANIZE (arrange a meeting)

arrangement noun
▸ AGREEMENT 1 (come to an arrangement over the price)
▸ DESIGN (a seating arrangement)
▸ PLANNING (travel arrangements)

array noun
▸ RANGE 1

arrears noun
▸ DEBT

arrest verb
▸ ARREST

arrival noun
▸ ARRIVAL 1 (the arrival of the train)
▸ ARRIVAL 2 (new arrivals)

arrive verb
▸ ARRIVE (arrive home safely)
▸ COME 2 (The day finally arrived.)
▸ SUCCEED (He knew he had arrived.)

arrive at phrasal verb
▸ ACHIEVE

arrogance noun
▸ PRIDE

arrogant adj.
▸ PROUD 2

arsenal noun
▸ SUPPLY (the country's nuclear arsenal)
▸ WAREHOUSE (The building was used as an arsenal.)

art noun
▸ SKILL 1

artefact (also **artifact**) noun
▸ THING 2

article noun
▸ ARTICLE (a newspaper article)
▸ SECTION (article 10 of the European Convention)

articulate adj.
▸ ARTICULATE

artificial adj.
▸ ARTIFICIAL 1 (artificial light)
▸ ARTIFICIAL 2 (an artificial situation)

artillery noun
▸ GUN

artist noun
▸ ARTIST (a graphic artist)
▸ ACTOR (a recording artist)

artiste noun
▸ ACTOR

artistic adj.
▸ CREATIVE

artistry noun
▸ SKILL 2

ascend verb
▸ CLIMB

ascertain verb
▸ FIND 3

ashamed adj.
▸ SORRY

ashen adj.
▸ PALE 1

ask verb
▸ ASK 1 (ask a question)
▸ ASK 2 (ask for sth)
▸ CHARGE (ask $50 for it)
▸ DEMAND (It's a lot to ask.)
▸ INVITE (ask sb in)

asleep adj.
▸ fall asleep FALL ASLEEP

aspect noun
▸ ASPECT

aspiration noun
▸ HOPE 2

aspire verb
▸ HOPE

assassin noun
▸ KILLER

assassinate verb
▸ KILL

assassination noun
▸ MURDER

assault noun
▸ ATTACK 1 (an assault by troops)
▸ ATTACK 2 (sexual assault)
▸ CRITICISM (a verbal assault)

assault verb
▸ ATTACK 1 (physically assaulted)
▸ RAPE (sexually assaulted)

assemble verb
▸ BUILD (easy to assemble)
▸ MEET 1 (assemble in the hall)

assembly noun
▸ ASSEMBLY (regional assemblies)
▸ MEETING 1 (a public assembly)
▸ PRODUCTION (a car assembly plant)

assent noun
▸ APPROVAL

assert verb
▸ CLAIM

assertion noun
▸ CLAIM

assertive adj.
▸ AGGRESSIVE 2

assertiveness noun
▸ CONFIDENCE

assess verb
▸ JUDGE 1 (assess sb/sth's performance)
▸ PRICE (assess the amount of compensation)
▸ TEST 2 (assess students' work)

assessment noun
▸ ASSESSMENT

asset noun
▸ BENEFIT 1 (She's an asset to the team.)
▸ THING 3 (financial assets)

assign verb
▸ ALLOCATE (assign a task to sb)
▸ SEND 2 (assign your best man to the job)

assignment noun
▸ ASSIGNMENT

assist verb
▸ HELP 1 (We'll do all we can to assist you.)
▸ HELP 2 (Two approaches might assist in tackling the problem.)

assistance noun
▸ HELP

assistant noun
▸ ASSISTANT (a personal assistant)
▸ SALESMAN (a sales assistant)

associate noun
▸ PARTNER 1

associate verb
▸ RELATE

associated adj.
▸ RELATED

association noun
▸ ASSOCIATION (historical associations)
▸ RELATION (an association between smoking and cancer)
▸ RELATIONSHIP 1 (in association with sb)
▸ UNION (trade associations)

assorted adj.
▸ DIVERSE

assortment noun
▸ RANGE 1

assume verb
▸ PRETEND (assume an air of concern)
▸ SUPPOSE (Let's assume…)
▸ TAKE 7 (assume control)

assumed adj.
▸ SUPPOSED

assumption noun
▸ SPECULATION

assurance noun
▸ CONFIDENCE (show assurance)
▸ PROMISE (despite assurances to the contrary…)

assure verb
▸ CHECK 2 (He assured himself of her safety.)
▸ ENSURE (assure sb a place in the finals)
▸ PROMISE (She's perfectly safe, I can assure you.)

assured verb
▸ CERTAIN

astonish verb
▸ SURPRISE

astonishing adj.
▸ AMAZING

astound verb
▸ SURPRISE

astronomical adj.
▸ HIGH 1

astute adj.
▸ SHREWD

asylum noun
▸ SHELTER

asylum seeker noun
▸ REFUGEE

athlete noun
▸ PLAYER

atlas noun
▸ MAP

atmosphere noun
▸ ATMOSPHERE (a friendly atmosphere)
▸ AIR (the earth's atmosphere)

atrocious adj.
▸ TERRIBLE 4

atrocity noun
▸ CRIME 2

attach verb
▸ ATTACH (attach the rope to sth)
▸ PLACE (attach importance to sth)

attachment noun
▸ LOVE 2

attack noun
▸ ATTACK 1 (a bomb attack)
▸ ATTACK 2 (a vicious knife attack)
▸ ATTACK 3 (an attack of flu/nerves)
▸ CRITICISM (a scathing attack on the government's policies)

attack verb
▸ ATTACK 1 (attack sb with a knife)
▸ ATTACK 2 (attack a city)
▸ BLAME (attack the government)
▸ HIT 3 (The disease attacks the central nervous system.)

attain verb
▸ ACHIEVE

attempt noun
▸ ATTEMPT (an attempt to do sth)
▸ ATTACK 2 (an attempt on sb's life)

attempt verb
▸ TRY 1

attend verb
▸ ATTEND (attend a conference)
▸ VISIT (attend church regularly)

attendant adj.
▸ RELATED

attend to phrasal verb
▸ LOOK AFTER SB

attention noun
▸ ATTENTION (get sb's attention)
▸ **pay attention** HEAR verb
▸ **draw attention to sb/sth** POINT STH OUT phrasal verb

attentive adj.
▸ INTERESTED

attitude noun
▸ ATTITUDE

attorney noun
▸ LAWYER

attract verb
▸ INTEREST (what first attracted me to the place)

be attracted to sb ATTRACTED TO SB

attraction noun
▸ INTEREST 1 (City life holds little attraction for me.)
▸ LOVE 1 (sexual attraction)

attractive adj.
▸ BEAUTIFUL 1 (an attractive man)
▸ BEAUTIFUL 2 (an attractive garden)
▸ POPULAR (an attractive offer)

attribute noun
▸ FEATURE

atypical adj.
▸ UNUSUAL

auction verb
▸ SELL 1

auctioneer noun
▸ SALESMAN

auction off phrasal verb
▸ SELL 1

audacity noun
▸ COURAGE

audience noun
▸ AUDIENCE (a live audience)
▸ INTERVIEW 1 (an audience with the Queen)
▸ MARKET 1 (the target audience)

audit noun
▸ INSPECTION

audit verb
▸ CHECK 1

audition noun
▸ INTERVIEW 2

auditorium noun
▸ HALL 1

aura noun
▸ ATMOSPHERE

auspicious adj.
▸ PROMISING

austere adj.
▸ PLAIN 1

authentic adj.
▸ REAL (an authentic signature)
▸ REALISTIC 2 (an authentic model)
▸ RELIABLE 2 (an authentic account)

authenticate verb
▸ CONFIRM 1

author noun
▸ WRITER

authoritarian adj.
▸ AUTHORITARIAN

authoritative adj.
▸ AUTHORITARIAN (his authoritative manner)
▸ RELIABLE 2 (an authoritative account)

authority noun
▸ AUTHORITIES (report sb to the authorities)
▸ CONTROL (have authority over sb)
▸ EXPERT (a leading authority on the subject)
▸ RIGHT (have the authority to sign company cheques)
▸ PERMISSION (You will need the written authority of the landlord.)

authorization noun
▸ LICENCE (sign an authorization)
▸ PERMISSION (give authorization for work to begin)

authorize verb
▸ ALLOW

authorized adj.
▸ OFFICIAL

autocrat noun
▸ DICTATOR

autocratic adj.
▸ AUTHORITARIAN (an autocratic approach to management)

▸ REPRESSIVE (an autocratic government)

automated adj.
▸ ELECTRONIC

automatic adj.
▸ ELECTRONIC

automobile noun
▸ CAR

autonomy noun
▸ FREEDOM (professional autonomy)
▸ INDEPENDENCE (political autonomy)

available adj.
▸ AVAILABLE (The information is freely available.)
▸ FREE 3 (Will she be available this afternoon?)

avant-garde adj.
▸ EXPERIMENTAL

avenge verb
▸ FIGHT BACK

avenue noun
▸ ROAD

average adj.
▸ AVERAGE (very average players)
▸ NORMAL (the average day)

aversion noun
▸ HATRED

avert verb
▸ PREVENT

avid adj.
▸ EAGER

avoid verb
▸ AVOID (He's been avoiding me.)
▸ PREVENT (avoid an accident)

avoidable adj.
▸ UNNECESSARY

await verb
▸ EXPECT

award noun
▸ AWARD (the best actor award)
▸ COMPENSATION (an award of £600 000 libel damages)

award verb
▸ GIVE 1

aware adj.
▸ AWARE

awareness noun
▸ AWARENESS

awe noun
▸ ADMIRATION (gaze in awe)
▸ **be/stand in awe of sb/sth** RESPECT verb

awesome adj.
▸ AMAZING (an awesome sight)
▸ GREAT 1 (The show was just awesome.)

awful adj.
▸ TERRIBLE 1 (awful weather)
▸ TERRIBLE 2 (an awful lot of money/an awful mess)
▸ TERRIBLE 3 (an awful nightmare)

awkward adj.
▸ EMBARRASSED (She is awkward with people she doesn't know.)
▸ PERVERSE (Please don't be awkward.)
▸ SENSITIVE 2 (put sb in an awkward position)
▸ WRONG 3 (an awkward time)

axe (also **ax**) verb
▸ ABOLISH (axe services)
▸ FIRE (axe jobs)

B b

babe noun
▸ DARLING

baby noun
▸ CHILD (Babies can't talk.)
▸ DARLING (Hi, baby!)

▸ OFFSPRING (a baby elephant)
▸ SON (She's had a baby boy.)

back noun
▸ **turn your back on sb** LEAVE 5 verb
▸ **a pat on the back** PRAISE
▸ **stab sb in the back** TELL verb 2

back verb
▸ SUPPORT 1

back down phrasal verb
▸ GIVE WAY idiom

backdrop noun
▸ CONTEXT (a backdrop of violence)
▸ ENVIRONMENT (a backdrop of hills)

backer noun
▸ SPONSOR

backfire verb
▸ FAIL 2

background noun
▸ BACKGROUND (sb's family background)
▸ CONTEXT (the historical background)
▸ ENVIRONMENT (the mountains in the background)

backing noun
▸ INVESTMENT

back off phrasal verb
▸ WITHDRAW 2

back out phrasal verb
▸ WITHDRAW 2

backpack noun
▸ SUITCASE

backpack verb
▸ TOUR

backpacker noun
▸ TOURIST

backtrack verb
▸ BREAK 4

back up phrasal verb
▸ CONFIRM 2

backup noun
▸ HELP

backyard noun
▸ GARDEN 1

bad adj.
▸ BAD (bad news)
▸ DIFFICULT 2 (a bad situation)
▸ EVIL (the bad guys)
▸ HARMFUL (bad for business)
▸ INCOMPETENT (bad at maths)
▸ INJURED (a bad back)
▸ NAUGHTY (bad behaviour)
▸ OFFENSIVE (bad language)
▸ POOR 2 (a bad idea/article)
▸ ROTTEN (bad eggs)
▸ SERIOUS 1 (a bad headache)
▸ SICK 1 (I'm afraid I'm feeling pretty bad.)
▸ SORRY (She felt bad about leaving him.)
▸ UNHEALTHY (bad for you)
▸ WET 2 (bad weather)
▸ WRONG 3 (bad timing)
▸ **not bad** ADEQUATE
▸ **too bad** UNFORTUNATE 2

bad faith noun
▸ BETRAYAL

bad feeling noun
▸ RESENTMENT

bad-tempered adj.
▸ IRRITABLE

baffle verb
▸ CONFUSE

baffling adj.
▸ CONFUSING

bag noun
▸ SUITCASE

baggage noun
▸ SUITCASE

bail out *phrasal verb*
► SAVE 1

bait *noun*
► BRIBE

bake *verb*
► BAKE

baking *noun*
► COOKING

balance *noun*
► REST 1 (a bank balance)
► **in the balance** UNCLEAR *adj.*

balance *verb*
► COMPENSATE (The good and bad effects will balance out.)
► LEAN 2 (balance on one leg)

balance against *phrasal verb*
► COMPARE 1

balcony *noun*
► PORCH

bald *adj.*
► PLAIN 2

balk *verb*
► HESITATE

ball *noun*
► PARTY 2

ballot *noun*
► ELECTION

ballot *verb*
► SURVEY

ballpark *noun*
► PITCH

ballroom *noun*
► HALL 1

ban *noun*
► BAN

ban *verb*
► BAN

banal *adj.*
► LACKLUSTRE

band *noun*
► PARTY 3 (a band of helpers)
► STRIP (a hair/name band)

bandage *noun*
► BANDAGE

Band-Aid™ *noun*
► BANDAGE

bandanna (also **bandana**) *noun*
► HAT

bandit *noun*
► THIEF

bang *noun*
► BANG

bang *verb*
► BANG 1 (The door banged shut.)
► BANG 2 (bang your head)
► HIT 1 (bang on the door)

bang into *phrasal verb*
► CRASH

banish *verb*
► DISMISS (banish all other thoughts from your mind)
► EXPEL (banished from the kingdom)

bank *noun*
► SLOPE (a bank of earth)
► SUPPLY (a blood bank)
► **burst its banks** FLOOD *verb*

bank *verb*
► LEAN 1 (a plane banks)
► SAVE 3 (bank money)

banking *noun*
► FINANCE

bankroll *verb*
► FUND

bankrupt *adj.*
► BANKRUPT (be made bankrupt)
► **go bankrupt** CLOSE *verb* 2

banned *adj.*
► FORBIDDEN

banner *noun*
► POSTER

banquet *noun*
► MEAL

banter *noun*
► HUMOUR

bar *noun*
► BAR (a wine/coffee bar)
► LAWYER (be called to the Bar)
► PIECE (a bar of chocolate/soap)

bar *verb*
► BAN (Certain activities are barred to women.)
► BLOCK 3 (bar sb's exit)

barbaric *adj.*
► CRUEL

barbecue *verb*
► BAKE

bar chart *noun*
► DIAGRAM

bare *adj.*
► BARE (a bare landscape)
► EMPTY (bare shelves)
► NAKED (bare feet)
► PLAIN 1 (bare walls/floorboards)
► PLAIN 2 (the bare facts)

barf *verb*
► VOMIT

bargain *noun*
► AGREEMENT 1 (make a bargain)
► VALUE 2 (pick up a bargain in the sales)

bargain *verb*
► NEGOTIATE

bargain for/on *phrasal verb*
► EXPECT

barge *noun*
► BOAT

barge *verb*
► PUSH 2

barge in *phrasal verb*
► INTERRUPT

barn *noun*
► SHED

barrage *noun*
► FLOOD 2

barrel *noun*
► BARREL

barricade *noun*
► BARRIER

barricade *verb*
► BLOCK 3

barrier *noun*
► BARRIER (Show your ticket at the barrier.)
► OBSTACLE (a psychological barrier to success)

barrister *noun*
► LAWYER

barter *noun*
► EXCHANGE

barter *verb*
► REPLACE 2

base *noun*
► BASIS (a philosophical base)
► BOTTOM (the base of a statue)
► OFFICE 1 (The company has its base in New York.)

base *verb*
► BASE

base *adj.*
► EVIL

basement *noun*
► BASEMENT

bash *noun*
► PARTY 2

bash *verb*
► HIT 1

basic *adj.*
► FUNDAMENTAL

basics *noun*
► BASICS

basis *noun*
► BASIS (the basis for a good marriage/our discussion)
► REASON (choose sth on the basis of…)

bask *verb*
► LIE

basket *noun*
► BOX

bask in *phrasal verb*
► ENJOY

bass *adj.*
► DEEP 2

bastard *noun* (taboo)
► VILLAIN

batch *noun*
► LOT

bath *noun*
► BATH

bath *verb*
► WASH

bathe *verb*
► CLEAN (bathe a wound)
► WASH (bathe the baby)

bathroom *noun*
► TOILET

batter *verb*
► BEAT 1

battery *noun*
► FLOOD 2

battle *noun*
► CAMPAIGN (a legal battle)
► WAR (killed in battle)

battle *verb*
► COMPETE

batty *adj.*
► MAD

baulk *verb*
► HESITATE

bawl *verb*
► SHOUT

bay *noun*
► **hold/keep sb/sth at bay** RESIST *verb*

be *verb*
► BE (Three and three is six.)
► COST (How much is that dress?)

beach *noun*
► COAST

bead *noun*
► DROP

be ahead of *phrasal verb*
► LEAD 1

beam *noun*
► POST

beam *verb*
► SMILE

bear *verb*
► CARRY 1 (arrive bearing gifts)
► HATE (can't bear sb/sth)
► PRODUCE (bear children/fruit)
► STAND 2 (bear the pain)
► SUPPORT 2 (bear sth's weight)
► TAKE 7 (bear the responsibility)
► **bear witness** CONFIRM 1
► **bear sb/sth in mind** REMEMBER

bearded *adj.*
► HAIRY

bearing *noun*
► WAY 3

bear out *phrasal verb*
► CONFIRM 2

beast *noun*
► ANIMAL

beat *noun*
► RHYTHM

beat *verb*
► BEAT 1 (beat a drum/child)
► BEAT 2 (a heart/drum beating)
► CONFUSE (It beats me why…)
► DEFEAT (beat sb at chess)
► OVERCOME (beat an addiction)
► SHAKE 1 (beating its wings)
► STIR (beat eggs)

beat to *phrasal verb*
► ANTICIPATE

beat up *phrasal verb*
► ATTACK 1

beautiful *adj.*
► BEAUTIFUL 1 (a beautiful woman)
► BEAUTIFUL 2 (a beautiful place)

beckon *verb*
► NOD

become *verb*
► BECOME

bed *noun*
► GARDEN 2 (flower beds)
► **get out of bed** WAKE UP *phrasal verb*

bed and breakfast *noun*
► HOTEL

beep *verb*
► CLINK

beg *verb*
► BEG (He begged me to stay.)
► BORROW (beg for food)
► **beg sb's pardon** APOLOGIZE

beggar *noun*
► TRAMP

begin *verb*
► BEGIN (begin work/to cry/talking)
► START (a concert begins)

beginner *noun*
► BEGINNER

beginning *noun*
► SOURCE (from small beginnings)
► START (the beginning of July)

begrudge *verb*
► RESENT

behave *verb*
► BEHAVE

being *noun*
► ANIMAL

belated *adj.*
► LATE

belief *noun*
► FAITH (belief in democracy)
► VALUES (religious beliefs)
► VIEW 1 (It's my belief that…)
► **beyond belief** INCREDIBLE *adj.*

believable *adj.*
► POSSIBLE 2

believe *verb*
► THINK

believe in *phrasal verb*
► IN FAVOUR (OF SB/STH) (I don't believe in hitting children.)
► TRUST (believe in yourself)

bellow *verb*
► SHOUT

belly *noun*
► STOMACH

belongings *noun*
► THING 3

beloved *noun*
► DARLING

beloved *adj.*
► DEAR

belt *noun*
► AREA 1 (the commuter belt)
► **tighten your belt** SAVE *verb* 2

beltway *noun*
► HIGHWAY

bemused *adj.*
▸ CONFUSED 1

bench *noun*
▸ CHAIR (a park bench)
▸ JUDGE 1 (address the bench)

benchmark *noun*
▸ CRITERION

bend *noun*
▸ CORNER

bend *verb*
▸ BEND (bend your head)
▸ CURVE (a road bends)
▸ TWIST (bend the wire)

benefactor *noun*
▸ SPONSOR

beneficial *adj.*
▸ VALUABLE 2

benefit *noun*
▸ BENEFIT 1 (the benefit of a good education)
▸ BENEFIT 2 (pay and benefits)

benefit *verb*
▸ BENEFIT (benefit from doing sth)
▸ HELP 2 (sth that will benefit everyone)

benevolent *adj.*
▸ KIND

benign *adj.*
▸ KIND (a benign expression)
▸ SAFE 2 (a benign tumour)

bent *noun*
▸ TENDENCY

bent *adj.*
▸ BENT

bent on *adj.*
▸ DETERMINED 1

bequeath *verb*
▸ PASS STH ON

bequest *noun*
▸ LEGACY

berate *verb*
▸ SCOLD

bereft *adj.*
▸ LONELY

beret *noun*
▸ HAT

berserk *adj.*
▸ go berserk LOSE YOUR TEMPER

beside *prep.*
▸ beside yourself HYSTERICAL *adj.*

besotted *adj.*
▸ IN LOVE

best *noun*
▸ make the best of sth ACCEPT *verb*

best *verb*
▸ DEFEAT

best *adj.*
▸ BEST (the best man for the job)
▸ the/your best bet OPTION *noun*

best-loved *adj.*
▸ FAVOURITE

bestow *verb*
▸ GIVE 1

best-seller *noun*
▸ SUCCESS

bet *noun*
▸ a/the best/good/safe bet OPTION

bet *verb*
▸ BET (bet money on sth)
▸ KNOW 2 (I bet we're too late.)

betray *verb*
▸ CHEAT (betray sb's trust)
▸ REVEAL (betray your emotion)
▸ TELL 2 (betray your country)

betrayal *noun*
▸ BETRAYAL

better *noun*
▸ get the better of sb DEFEAT *verb*

better *adj.*
▸ BETTER (there's nothing better)
▸ make sb better CURE *verb*
▸ get better IMPROVE *verb* 2 (things get better)
▸ get better RECOVER *verb* 1 (get better after an illness)

beverage *noun*
▸ DRINK 1

bewilder *verb*
▸ CONFUSE

bewildered *adj.*
▸ CONFUSED 1

bewildering *adj.*
▸ CONFUSING

bewitch *verb*
▸ DELIGHT

bias *noun*
▸ DISCRIMINATION (a bias in favour of employers against employees)
▸ TENDENCY (classes with a strong practical bias)

bias *verb*
▸ INFLUENCE

biased *adj.*
▸ BIASED

bicker *verb*
▸ ARGUE

bid *noun*
▸ OFFER 2

bid *verb*
▸ OFFER 2

big *adj.*
▸ IMPORTANT (a big decision)
▸ LARGE (a big house)

bigotry *noun*
▸ RACISM

big shot *noun*
▸ VIP

bilk *verb*
▸ DEFRAUD

bill *noun*
▸ BILL

bill *verb*
▸ CHARGE

billet *verb*
▸ ACCOMMODATE

bimbo *noun*
▸ FOOL

bind *verb*
▸ RESTRAIN

binder *noun*
▸ ENVELOPE

biographer *noun*
▸ WRITER

birth *noun*
▸ FAMILY 3 (French by birth)
▸ START (the birth of a new society)
▸ give birth PRODUCE

birthday *noun*
▸ BIRTHDAY

birthplace *noun*
▸ HOME 2

birthright *noun*
▸ LEGACY

bit *noun*
▸ BIT (a bit of paper/news)
▸ MINUTE (Wait a bit.)
▸ a bit much EXCESSIVE *adj.*

bitch *noun* (taboo)
▸ VILLAIN

bitchy *adj.*
▸ VICIOUS

bite *verb*
▸ BITE

bitter *adj.*
▸ BITTER 1 (a bitter taste)
▸ BITTER 2 (bitter feelings)
▸ FREEZING (a bitter wind)

bitterness *noun*
▸ RESENTMENT

bizarre *adj.*
▸ STRANGE 1

blab *verb*
▸ TELL 2

black *adj.*
▸ BLACK (black people)
▸ DARK 1 (It's pitch black outside.)
▸ NEGATIVE (The future looks black.)

blacklist *verb*
▸ EXCLUDE 2

black magic *noun*
▸ MAGIC

blackmail *noun*
▸ CORRUPTION

blackness *noun*
▸ DARKNESS

blade *noun*
▸ KNIFE

blame *noun*
▸ FAULT

blame *verb*
▸ BLAME (Don't blame me.)
▸ to blame GUILTY *adj.*

blameless *adj.*
▸ HOLY (live a blameless life)
▸ INNOCENT (not blameless in this matter)

bland *adj.*
▸ BLANK (a bland expression)
▸ LACKLUSTRE (a bland image)
▸ MILD (bland food)

blank *adj.*
▸ BLANK

blanket *adj.*
▸ OVERALL

blare *verb*
▸ BLOW 3

blasé *adj.*
▸ CASUAL

blaspheme *verb*
▸ CURSE

blast *noun*
▸ EXPLOSION (a bomb blast)
▸ FUN (The party was a blast.)

blast *verb*
▸ BLOW 3

blatant *adj.*
▸ OPEN

blaze *verb*
▸ BURN 1

blazer *noun*
▸ COAT

bleak *adj.*
▸ BARE (a bleak landscape)
▸ HARSH (a bleak November day)
▸ NEGATIVE (The future looks bleak.)

blemish *noun*
▸ MARK

blend *noun*
▸ COMBINATION (a blend of youth and experience)
▸ MIXTURE (a light blend of coffee)

blend *verb*
▸ MATCH 2 (a colour blends in)
▸ MIX (blend ingredients/flavours)

bless *verb*
▸ be blessed with sb/sth HAVE 2

blessing *noun*
▸ APPROVAL (official blessing)
▸ GOOD THING (count your blessings)

blind *noun*
▸ CURTAIN

blind *adj.*
▸ UNAWARE (blind to the dangers)
▸ turn a blind eye IGNORE *verb*

bliss *noun*
▸ JOY

blissful *adj.*
▸ HAPPY

blister *noun*
▸ TUMOUR

blizzard *noun*
▸ STORM

bloat *verb*
▸ SWELL

blob *noun*
▸ DROP

block *noun*
▸ BUILDING (a block of flats)
▸ PIECE (a block of ice)

block *verb*
▸ BLOCK 1 (block plans)
▸ BLOCK 2 (block the drain)
▸ BLOCK 3 (block sb's exit)
▸ FEND SB/STH OFF (Zola's shot was blocked by the goalie.)

block off *phrasal verb*
▸ BLOCK 3

block up *phrasal verb*
▸ BLOCK 2

blog *noun*
▸ RECORD

bloke *noun*
▸ MAN 1

blood *noun*
▸ FAMILY 3

bloodshed *noun*
▸ MASSACRE

bloodthirsty *adj.*
▸ VIOLENT

bloody *adj.*
▸ VIOLENT

bloody *adv.* (taboo)
▸ VERY

bloom *verb*
▸ DO WELL

blossom *verb*
▸ DO WELL

blot *noun*
▸ MARK

blot out *phrasal verb*
▸ FORGET

blow *noun*
▸ BLOW

blow *verb*
▸ BLOW 1 (The leaves were blown everywhere.)
▸ BLOW 2 (blow out smoke)
▸ BLOW 3 (blow a whistle)
▸ WASTE (blow your chance)
▸ blow the whistle on sb/sth TELL 2

blow out *phrasal verb*
▸ PUT STH OUT

blow up *phrasal verb*
▸ BOMB (blow up a building)
▸ BREAK OUT (a crisis blows up)
▸ EXPLODE (a car blows up)
▸ SWELL (blow up a balloon)

blubber *noun*
▸ FAT

blueprint *noun*
▸ MODEL (a blueprint for success)
▸ PLAN 2 (The blueprint showed plans for an underground shelter.)

the blues *noun*
▸ GLOOM

bluff *noun*
▸ TRICK

bluff *verb*
▸ PRETEND

blunder *noun*
▸ MISTAKE 1

blunt *verb*
▸ MODERATE

blunt *adj.*
▶ HONEST

blur *verb*
▶ COMPLICATE

blurb *noun*
▶ ADVERTISEMENT

blurt *verb*
▶ CALL 3

blush *verb*
▶ FLUSH

board *noun*
▶ COMMITTEE (the board of directors)
▶ SIGN 2 (The results were pinned on the board.)
▶ **take sth on board** AGREE 2
▶ **across the board** OVERALL *adj.*

board *verb*
▶ GET IN

boast *verb*
▶ BOAST (boast about your skill)
▶ HAVE 2 (The hotel boasts two swimming pools and a sauna.)

boastful *adj.*
▶ PROUD 2

boat *noun*
▶ BOAT

bode *verb*
▶ **bode well/ill** THREATEN 3

body *noun*
▶ BODY 1 (Her whole body trembled.)
▶ BODY 2 (a dead body)
▶ COMMITTEE (a governing body)
▶ FRAME (the body of the car)
▶ POINT (the body of the text)

bodyguard *noun*
▶ GUARD

bodywork *noun*
▶ FRAME

bog *noun*
▶ MARSH

bogged down *phrasal verb*
▶ **be/get bogged down** HOLD SB/ STH UP

bogus *adj.*
▶ SO-CALLED

boil *noun*
▶ TUMOUR

boiler *noun*
▶ HEATING

boiling *adj.*
▶ HOT

bold *adj.*
▶ BOLD (a bold move)
▶ BRIGHT (bold colours)

bolster *verb*
▶ STRENGTHEN

bolt *verb*
▶ CLOSE 1 (bolt the door)
▶ FLEE (a horse bolts)

bomb *noun*
▶ BOMB (drop bombs)
▶ WEAPON (countries that have the bomb)

bomb *verb*
▶ BOMB

bombard *verb*
▶ BOMB (bombard a city)
▶ OVERWHELM (bombard sb with questions)

bomber *noun*
▶ GUERRILLA

bond *noun*
▶ BOND

bonfire *noun*
▶ FIRE 2

bonnet *noun*
▶ HAT

bonus *noun*
▶ BENEFIT 2 (a Christmas bonus)
▶ GOOD THING (an added bonus)

boo *noun*
▶ WHISTLE

book *noun*
▶ BOOK

book *verb*
▶ ORDER 2 (book a table)
▶ SCHEDULE (book a band for a party)

bookish *adj.*
▶ INTELLECTUAL 2

booklet *noun*
▶ LEAFLET

boom *verb*
▶ DO WELL (Business is booming.)
▶ RUMBLE (thunder booms)

boon *noun*
▶ GOOD THING

boost *verb*
▶ INCREASE

booth *noun*
▶ STALL

booze *noun*
▶ DRINK 2

booze *verb*
▶ DRINK

border *noun*
▶ BORDER (on the northern border)
▶ GARDEN 2 (herbaceous borders)

border *verb*
▶ SURROUND

borderline *noun*
▶ LIMIT 2

borderline *adj.*
▶ VAGUE

border on *phrasal verb*
▶ APPROACH

bored *adj.*
▶ BORED

boring *adj.*
▶ BORING

born *adj.*
▶ **be born and bred** BRING SB UP *phrasal verb*

borough *noun*
▶ CITY

borrow *verb*
▶ BORROW

boss *noun*
▶ LEADER 1 (company bosses)
▶ MANAGER (I'll ask my boss.)

bossy *adj.*
▶ AUTHORITARIAN

bother *noun*
▶ DIFFICULTY

bother *verb*
▶ INTERRUPT (stop bothering me)
▶ WORRY 2 (It doesn't bother me.)

bothered *adj.*
▶ WORRIED (You don't sound very bothered about it.)
▶ **be bothered** CARE *verb* (I'm not bothered where we go.)

bottle *noun*
▶ BOTTLE

bottleneck *noun*
▶ TRAFFIC

bottom *noun*
▶ BOTTOM (the bottom of the page/ hill/door)
▶ **from the (bottom of your) heart** DEEP *adj.* 1

boulder *noun*
▶ STONE

boulevard *noun*
▶ ROAD

bounce *verb*
▶ JUMP 1

bouncer *noun*
▶ GUARD

bound *verb*
▶ RUN 1

bound *adj.*
▶ CERTAIN

boundary *noun*
▶ BORDER (a boundary wall)
▶ LIMIT 2 (the boundaries of knowledge)

bounds *noun*
▶ LIMIT 2

bourgeois *adj.*
▶ MIDDLE CLASS

the bourgeoisie *noun*
▶ MIDDLE CLASS *noun*

bout *noun*
▶ ATTACK 3 (a bout of flu)
▶ GAME 1 (a heavyweight bout)

boutique *noun*
▶ SHOP

bow *verb*
▶ BEND

bowl *noun*
▶ PLATE

bowl *verb*
▶ THROW

bowl over *phrasal verb*
▶ SURPRISE

bow to *phrasal verb*
▶ GIVE WAY

box *noun*
▶ BOX (a cardboard box)
▶ STAGE 2 (the witness box)

box *verb*
▶ FIGHT 2

boy *noun*
▶ CHILD (a bright little boy)
▶ FRIEND (a night out with the boys)
▶ SON (They have two boys.)

boycott *noun*
▶ BAN *noun*

boycott *verb*
▶ AVOID

boyfriend *noun*
▶ PARTNER 2

boyish *adj.*
▶ CHILDISH

bracket *noun*
▶ CATEGORY

bracket *verb*
▶ CLASSIFY

brag *verb*
▶ BOAST

brain *noun*
▶ GENIUS (the brains of the family)
▶ INTELLIGENCE (It doesn't take much brain to work that out.)
▶ MIND (brain cells)

brainwashing *noun*
▶ PROPAGANDA

branch *noun*
▶ AREA 2 (a branch of statistics)
▶ DEPARTMENT (Our New York branch is dealing with the matter.)

branch out *phrasal verb*
▶ EXPAND 2

brand *noun*
▶ BRAND (the leading brand)
▶ KIND (her unique brand of humour)

brand *verb*
▶ CALL 1

brand new *adj.*
▶ NEW 2

the brass *noun*
▶ AUTHORITIES

brat *noun*
▶ CHILD

brave *verb*
▶ FACE

brave *adj.*
▶ BRAVE

bravery *noun*
▶ COURAGE

brawl *noun*
▶ FIGHT

brawl *verb*
▶ FIGHT 2

brazen *adj.*
▶ COOL

breach *verb*
▶ BREAK 3

breadth *noun*
▶ RANGE 2

break *noun*
▶ HOLIDAY 1 (Spring Break)
▶ HOLIDAY 2 (a weekend break)
▶ OPPORTUNITY (a lucky break)
▶ PAUSE (a break in your routine)
▶ REST 2 (a lunch break)

break *verb*
▶ BREAK 1 (break a window/leg)
▶ BREAK 2 (a machine breaks)
▶ BREAK 3 (break the law)
▶ BREAK 4 (break a promise)
▶ CONVEY (break the news to sb)

break down *phrasal verb*
▶ BREAK 2 (a car breaks down)
▶ FAIL 2 (negotiations break down)

breakdown *noun*
▶ FAILURE

breakfast *noun*
▶ DINNER

breakfast *verb*
▶ DINE

break-in *noun*
▶ THEFT

break into *phrasal verb*
▶ ROB

break off *phrasal verb*
▶ PAUSE

break out *phrasal verb*
▶ BREAK OUT

break up *phrasal verb*
▶ DISPERSE (a meeting breaks up)
▶ DIVIDE 1 (clouds break up)
▶ DIVORCE (break up with your girlfriend/boyfriend)
▶ SMASH (The ships broke up on the rocks.)

breath *noun*
▶ BREATH (take a deep breath)
▶ **take sb's breath away** IMPRESS *verb*

breather *noun*
▶ REST 2

breathing space *noun*
▶ REST 2

breathtaking *adj.*
▶ AMAZING

bred *verb*
▶ **be born and bred** BRING SB UP *phrasal verb*

breed *verb*
▶ KEEP 4 (breed horses)
▶ PRODUCE (rabbits breed)

breeze *noun*
▶ WIND

brew *verb*
▶ COOK

bribe *noun*
▶ BRIBE

bribery *noun*
▶ CORRUPTION

bridle *noun*
▶ REIN

brief *verb*
▸ TELL 1

brief *adj.*
▸ SHORT 1 (a brief visit)
▸ SHORT 3 (Please be brief.)

bright *adj.*
▸ BRIGHT (bright light/colours)
▸ CHEERFUL (a bright smile)
▸ INTELLIGENT (a bright child)
▸ PROMISING (a bright future)

brighten *verb*
▸ LIGHT 2

brightness *noun*
▸ LIGHT 1

brilliant *adj.*
▸ BRIGHT (brilliant blue eyes)
▸ GREAT 1 (a brilliant goal)
▸ INTELLIGENT (a brilliant scientist)

bring *verb*
▸ TAKE 1

bring about *phrasal verb*
▸ CAUSE

bring down *phrasal verb*
▸ LAND (bring a plane down)
▸ REDUCE (bring down prices)
▸ REMOVE 2 (bring down the government)

bring in *phrasal verb*
▸ INTRODUCE 1 (bring in a bill to limit arms exports)
▸ MAKE 2 (The sale brought in a lot.)
▸ MAKE 3 (Her work brings her in about $2 million per year.)

bring up *phrasal verb*
▸ BRING SB UP

brisk *adj.*
▸ FAST

bristly *adj.*
▸ COARSE

brittle *adj.*
▸ FRAGILE

broad *adj.*
▸ GENERAL 2 (in broad terms)
▸ WIDE 1 (a broad range)
▸ WIDE 2 (a broad river/smile)

broadcast *noun*
▸ PROGRAMME

broadcaster *noun*
▸ PRESENTER

broaden *verb*
▸ EXPAND 1 (Her smile broadened.)
▸ EXPAND 2 (broaden your horizons)

broadsheet *noun*
▸ NEWSPAPER

brochure *noun*
▸ LEAFLET

broil *verb*
▸ BAKE

broke *adj.*
▸ BANKRUPT

broker *verb*
▸ AGREE 3

brood *noun*
▸ OFFSPRING

brood *verb*
▸ BROOD

bruise *noun*
▸ INJURY

bruise *verb*
▸ INJURE

bruised *adj.*
▸ INJURED

brush *verb*
▸ BRUSH (brush your hair)
▸ TOUCH 1 (brush past sb)

brush aside *phrasal verb*
▸ DISMISS

brusque *adj.*
▸ SHARP 2

brutal *adj.*
▸ CRUEL

brute *noun*
▸ VILLAIN

B.S. *noun (taboo)*
▸ NONSENSE

bubbly *adj.*
▸ LIVELY

buckle *noun*
▸ BUTTON 2

buckle *verb*
▸ TWIST

buddy *noun*
▸ FRIEND

budge *verb*
▸ MOVE

budget *noun*
▸ FUND

budget *verb*
▸ SAVE 2

budget *adj.*
▸ CHEAP

budgetary *adj.*
▸ ECONOMIC

buff *noun*
▸ EXPERT

buffer *noun*
▸ PRECAUTION

bug *noun*
▸ DEFECT (bugs in the software)
▸ DISEASE (a stomach bug)

bug *verb*
▸ ANNOY (Is there something bugging you?)
▸ OVERHEAR (bug sb's hotel room)

bugger *noun (taboo)*
▸ VILLAIN

build *noun*
▸ BODY 1

build *verb*
▸ BUILD (a house built of stone)
▸ MAKE 1 (build a new career)

builder *noun*
▸ MAKER

build in *phrasal verb*
▸ INCLUDE 1

building *noun*
▸ BUILDING (ten-storey building)
▸ PRODUCTION (building work)

build up *phrasal verb*
▸ BUILD UP

bulk *noun*
▸ SIZE

bulky *adj.*
▸ HEAVY

bull *noun*
▸ NONSENSE

bulldoze *verb*
▸ DEMOLISH

bullet *noun*
▸ BULLET

bulletin *noun*
▸ NEWS

bulletin board *noun*
▸ SIGN 2

bullish *adj.*
▸ OPTIMISTIC

bullshit *noun (taboo)*
▸ NONSENSE

bully *verb*
▸ BULLY

bullying *noun*
▸ REPRESSION

bum *noun*
▸ TRAMP

bump *noun*
▸ TUMOUR

bump *verb*
▸ BANG 2 (bump your head)
▸ HIT 1 (bump into sth)
▸ SHAKE 2 (The jeep bumped along.)

bumper *adj.*
▸ LARGE

bump into *verb*
▸ MEET 2

bump off *phrasal verb*
▸ KILL

bumpy *adj.*
▸ ROUGH 1

bunch *noun*
▸ GROUP 1 (a bunch of keys/grapes)
▸ GROUP 2 (a bunch of youngsters)

bundle *noun*
▸ ROLL

bundle *verb*
▸ DRAG

bungalow *noun*
▸ HOUSE

bunker *noun*
▸ BASEMENT

buoyant *adj.*
▸ SUCCESSFUL 2

burden *noun*
▸ CARGO (She shifted her burden from one arm to the other.)
▸ RESPONSIBILITY (the burden of caring for the elderly)

bureau *noun*
▸ CUPBOARD (a mahogany bureau)
▸ SERVICE (an employment bureau)

bureaucracy *noun*
▸ BUREAUCRACY (unnecessary bureaucracy)
▸ AUTHORITIES (the state bureaucracy)

bureaucrat *noun*
▸ OFFICIAL

burglar *noun*
▸ THIEF

burglarize *verb*
▸ ROB

burglary *noun*
▸ THEFT

burgle *verb*
▸ ROB

burn *verb*
▸ BURN 1 (a fire/house is burning)
▸ BURN 2 (burn paper/buildings)
▸ FLUSH (Her cheeks burned with shame.)
▸ HURT 2 (sb's forehead burns)

burning *adj.*
▸ HOT (the burning heat of the sun)
▸ PAINFUL 1 (a burning pain)
▸ URGENT (a burning desire/issue)

burst *noun*
▸ ATTACK 3

burst *verb*
▸ EXPLODE (a balloon/shell bursts)
▸ burst its banks FLOOD

burst out *phrasal verb*
▸ CALL 3

bury *verb*
▸ HIDE 1

bus *noun*
▸ CAR

bush *noun*
▸ DESERT

bushy *adj.*
▸ HAIRY

business *noun*
▸ BUSINESS 1 (none of your business)
▸ BUSINESS 2 (Thank you for your business.)
▸ COMPANY (a small business)
▸ EVENT 1 (a terrible business)
▸ INDUSTRY (the oil business)
▸ TASK (business or pleasure?)
▸ TRADE (set up in business)
▸ do business SELL *verb* 2

businesslike *adj.*
▸ EFFICIENT

businessman *noun*
▸ EXECUTIVE

businessperson *noun*
▸ EXECUTIVE

businesswoman *noun*
▸ EXECUTIVE

bus stop *noun*
▸ STATION

bust *verb*
▸ ARREST

bust *adj.*
▸ BANKRUPT (go bust)
▸ go bust CLOSE *verb* 2

bustle *noun*
▸ ACTIVITY

bustling *adj.*
▸ CROWDED

busy *adj.*
▸ BUSY 1 (a busy woman)
▸ BUSY 2 (a busy weekend)
▸ CROWDED (a busy airport)

butler *noun*
▸ SERVANT

butter *noun*
▸ FAT

button *noun*
▸ BUTTON 1 (press the red button)
▸ BUTTON 2 (a jacket with gold buttons)

button *verb*
▸ TIE

buttress *noun*
▸ POST

buy *verb*
▸ BUY (buy a new car)
▸ buy time TAKE YOUR TIME

buyer *noun*
▸ CUSTOMER

buzz *noun*
▸ EXCITEMENT

buzz *verb*
▸ BUZZ (Bees were buzzing.)
▸ RING (The doorbell buzzed.)

bygone *adj.*
▸ PREVIOUS

bypass *noun*
▸ HIGHWAY

bystander *noun*
▸ WITNESS

C c

cabin *noun*
▸ HUT

cabinet *noun*
▸ CUPBOARD (glass cabinets)
▸ GOVERNMENT 1 (cabinet ministers)

cable *noun*
▸ WIRE

cadet *noun*
▸ RECRUIT

cage *verb*
▸ TRAP

cajole *verb*
▸ PERSUADE

cake *verb*
▸ COVER

calamity *noun*
▸ CRISIS

calculate *verb*
▸ CALCULATE (calculate the volume of sth)

calculated (calculate that hundreds of species may be affected)
▸ ESTIMATE

calculated *adj.*
▸ DELIBERATE

calculating *adj.*
▸ CUNNING

calculation *noun*
▸ ESTIMATE

caldron *noun*
▸ PAN

calendar *noun*
▸ SCHEDULE

calibre (also **caliber**) *noun*
▸ QUALITY

call *noun*
▸ DEMAND (There's not much call for specialist shops.)
▸ REQUEST (calls for the president to resign)
▸ VISIT (a social call)

call *verb*
▸ CALL 1 (We called the baby Mia.)
▸ CALL 2 (call the police/a taxi)
▸ CALL 3 (hear a voice calling)
▸ HAVE 4 (call a meeting)
▸ REGARD (call sb a liar)
▸ VISIT (call on sb)

caller *noun*
▸ VISITOR

call for *verb*
▸ ASK 2

call off *phrasal verb*
▸ ABOLISH

callous *adj.*
▸ RUTHLESS

call up *phrasal verb*
▸ CALL 2

calm *noun*
▸ COMPOSURE (speak with studied calm)
▸ PEACE (appeal for calm)
▸ SILENCE (the calm of the evening)

calm *verb*
▸ CALM

calm *adj.*
▸ CALM (keep calm)
▸ QUIET 1 (a calm day/sea)

calm down *phrasal verb*
▸ CALM (try to calm sb down)
▸ RELAX 1 (Calm down! We'll find her.)

camaraderie *noun*
▸ FRIENDSHIP

camouflage *noun*
▸ COSTUME

camouflage *verb*
▸ HIDE 1

camp *noun*
▸ PARTY 1 (the anti-war camp)
▸ PRISON (a prison camp)

campaign *noun*
▸ CAMPAIGN (a/an leadership/advertising/anti-smoking campaign)
▸ WAR (a bombing campaign)

campaign *verb*
▸ CAMPAIGN

campaigner *noun*
▸ ACTIVIST

campfire *noun*
▸ FIRE 2

can *noun*
▸ PACKET

canal *noun*
▸ RIVER

cancel *verb*
▸ CANCEL (cancel an order)
▸ ABOLISH (cancel a flight)

cancel out *phrasal verb*
▸ COMPENSATE

candid *adj.*
▸ HONEST

candidate *noun*
▸ CANDIDATE

candle *noun*
▸ LIGHT 2

canister *noun*
▸ BARREL

cannon *noun*
▸ GUN

canny *adj.*
▸ SHREWD

canoe *noun*
▸ BOAT

canvass *verb*
▸ SURVEY

canyon *noun*
▸ VALLEY

cap *noun*
▸ HAT (a baseball cap)
▸ LID (a lens cap)

cap *verb*
▸ LIMIT

capability *noun*
▸ ABILITY

capable *adj.*
▸ GOOD 4

capacity *noun*
▸ ABILITY (an enormous capacity for hard work)
▸ ROLE (an advisory capacity)
▸ SIZE (a capacity of 50 litres)

cape *noun*
▸ COAT

capital *noun*
▸ MONEY 1

capital punishment *noun*
▸ EXECUTION

capsize *verb*
▸ ROLL

captain *verb*
▸ LEAD 2

captaincy *noun*
▸ MANAGEMENT

captivate *verb*
▸ DELIGHT

captive *noun*
▸ HOSTAGE

capture *verb*
▸ ARREST (capture a person)
▸ CATCH (capture an animal)
▸ INVADE (capture a city)

car *noun*
▸ CAR (go by car)
▸ CARRIAGE 1 (a buffet car)

caravan *noun*
▸ FLEET

carcass *noun*
▸ BODY 2

care *noun*
▸ CARE (take care when doing sth)
▸ **take care of sth** DEAL WITH SB/STH *phrasal verb*
▸ **take care of yourself** TAKE CARE OF YOURSELF *verb*
▸ **take care of sb** LOOK AFTER SB *phrasal verb*

care *verb*
▸ CARE

career *noun*
▸ LIFE 2 (sb's school career)
▸ WORK 2 (a career in journalism)

career *verb*
▸ FLY 2

care for *phrasal verb*
▸ LOOK AFTER SB (care for the elderly)
▸ LOVE (care for sb deeply)

careful *adj.*
▸ DETAILED

careless *adj.*
▸ CARELESS (a careless driver)
▸ LAX (careless mistakes)

caress *verb*
▸ STROKE

cargo *noun*
▸ CARGO

caricature *noun*
▸ PARODY

caring *adj.*
▸ LOVING

carnage *noun*
▸ MASSACRE

carp *verb*
▸ COMPLAIN

carriage *noun*
▸ CARRIAGE 1 (a railway carriage)
▸ CARRIAGE 2 (a horse-drawn carriage)

carry *verb*
▸ CARRY 1 (carry a bag/child)
▸ CARRY 2 (Pipes carry the water away.)
▸ SELL 2 (carry a range of goods)
▸ SUPPORT 1 (The bridge has to carry a lot of traffic.)
▸ TAKE 1 (a train carrying commuters)
▸ TAKE 7 (carry the burden of job losses)

carry on *phrasal verb*
▸ CONTINUE 1 (Carry on until you get to the junction.)
▸ CONTINUE 2 (carry on with your work)

carry out *phrasal verb*
▸ DO 1 (carry out tests)
▸ FOLLOW 3 (carry out orders)
▸ KEEP 5 (carry out a threat)

cart *noun*
▸ CARRIAGE 2

cart *verb*
▸ CARRY 1

carton *noun*
▸ BOX (a carton of cigarettes)
▸ PACKET (a carton of orange juice)

cartoon *noun*
▸ PICTURE

cartridge *noun*
▸ BULLET

carve *verb*
▸ CUT 2 (carve a joint of meat)
▸ SHAPE (carve a statue)

carve up *phrasal verb*
▸ SHARE

cascade *verb*
▸ FLOW

case *noun*
▸ CASE (a court case)
▸ ARGUMENT 2 (the case for/against sth)
▸ BOX (a pencil/packing case)
▸ EXAMPLE 1 (in this/sb's case)
▸ INVESTIGATION (a murder case)
▸ PATIENT (a case of pneumonia)
▸ SITUATION (It is not the case that…)
▸ SUITCASE (pack your case)

cash *noun*
▸ MONEY 1 (your hard-earned cash)
▸ MONEY 2 (pay in cash)

cash *verb*
▸ CASH

cash in *phrasal verb*
▸ BENEFIT (He was accused of cashing in on the singer's death.)
▸ CASH (cash in your bonds)

casing *noun*
▸ COVER

casserole *noun*
▸ PAN

cast *verb*
▸ SHAPE (a statue cast in bronze)
▸ **cast light on sth** EXPLAIN 1

cast about/around for *phrasal verb*
▸ LOOK 2

castigate *verb*
▸ SCOLD

castle *noun*
▸ CASTLE

casual *adj.*
▸ CASUAL (a casual attitude)
▸ INFORMAL (casual clothes)

casualty *noun*
▸ VICTIM 1

catalogue (also **catalog**) *noun*
▸ LIST (a mail-order catalogue)
▸ SERIES (a catalogue of disasters)

catalyst *noun*
▸ MEDIUM

catastrophe *noun*
▸ CRISIS (a global catastrophe)
▸ DISASTER (a catastrophe with the food for the party)

catastrophic *adj.*
▸ DISASTROUS

catcall *noun*
▸ WHISTLE

catch *noun*
▸ BUTTON 2 (a safety catch)
▸ DISADVANTAGE (What's the catch?)

catch *verb*
▸ CATCH (catch a fish)
▸ ARREST (catch the culprit)
▸ FIND 2 (catch sb doing sth)
▸ FLASH (catch the light)
▸ GET 5 (catch the train)
▸ HEAR (catch what sb said)
▸ LOOK 1 (catch a movie)
▸ SEE (catch sight of sth)
▸ SUFFER FROM STH (catch a cold)
▸ TAKE 4 (catch a ball)

catch on *phrasal verb*
▸ UNDERSTAND 1

catchphrase *noun*
▸ SLOGAN

catch up *phrasal verb*
▸ GET 4

categorical *adj.*
▸ FINAL

categorize *verb*
▸ CLASSIFY

category *noun*
▸ CATEGORY

cater *verb*
▸ SERVE 1

cater for *phrasal verb*
▸ SERVE 2

cater to *phrasal verb*
▸ SERVE 2

cathedral *noun*
▸ CHURCH

catwalk *noun*
▸ CORRIDOR

caucus *noun*
▸ MEETING 1

cauldron *noun*
▸ PAN

cause *noun*
▸ CHARITY (a good cause)
▸ REASON (no cause for alarm)
▸ SOURCE (the cause of poverty)

cause *verb*
▸ CAUSE

caution *noun*
▸ CARE (urge/exercise caution)
▸ WARNING (a word of caution)

caution *verb*
▸ WARN

cave in phrasal verb
▸ COLLAPSE 1

cavernous adj.
▸ SPACIOUS

cavity noun
▸ HOLE 2

cease verb
▸ STOP 1 (work has ceased)
▸ **cease trading** CLOSE 2

cede verb
▸ GIVE STH UP

ceiling noun
▸ LIMIT 1

celebrate verb
▸ PLAY 1 (Go out and celebrate.)
▸ PRAISE (a movie celebrating his life)

celebrated adj.
▸ FAMOUS

celebration noun
▸ EVENT 2

celebrity noun
▸ FAME (achieve celebrity)
▸ STAR 1 (a TV celebrity)

cellar noun
▸ BASEMENT

cement verb
▸ STRENGTHEN

censure noun
▸ CRITICISM

censure verb
▸ BLAME

central adj.
▸ MAIN

central heating noun
▸ HEATING

centre (also **center**) noun
▸ FOCUS (the centre of attention)
▸ MIDDLE (the centre of a circle)
▸ ORGANIZATION (a conference centre)

century noun
▸ PERIOD

ceremony noun
▸ CEREMONY

certain adj.
▸ CERTAIN (certain to agree/win)
▸ PARTICULAR (Certain people disagree.)
▸ SURE (Are you certain?)

certainty noun
▸ CERTAINTY (moral certainties)
▸ FAITH (say sth with certainty)

certificate noun
▸ CERTIFICATE

certify verb
▸ APPROVE (certify sb as a teacher)
▸ CONFIRM 2 (certify that sth is correct)

cessation noun
▸ END

chagrin noun
▸ FRUSTRATION

chain noun
▸ SERIES

chain verb
▸ RESTRAIN

chair noun
▸ CHAIR (sit on a chair)
▸ EXECUTION (see an innocent man get the chair)
▸ LEADER 1 (appoint a new chair)

chair verb
▸ LEAD 2

chairman noun
▸ LEADER 1

challenge noun
▸ PROBLEM

challenge verb
▸ CHALLENGE (challenge sb to a game of chess)
▸ CONFRONT (challenged by police)
▸ DOUBT (challenge an assumption)

challenger noun
▸ PARTICIPANT

challenging adj.
▸ DIFFICULT 1

chamber noun
▸ ASSEMBLY (the upper chamber of the legislature)
▸ HALL 1 (the debating chamber)

champion noun
▸ ADVOCATE (a champion of the poor)
▸ WINNER (an Olympic champion)

champion verb
▸ SUPPORT 1

championship noun
▸ AWARD (defend the championship)
▸ RACE (the World Championship)

chance noun
▸ LUCK (sth happens by chance)
▸ OPPORTUNITY (a chance to do sth)
▸ POSSIBILITY (have a good chance of doing sth)
▸ RISK 2 (take a chance on sb/sth)
▸ **the chances are...** PROBABLY adv.

chance verb
▸ DARE

chancellor noun
▸ PRESIDENT (Germany's chancellor)
▸ PROFESSOR (the chancellor of the university)

change noun
▸ CHANGE 1 (a change in the weather)
▸ CHANGE 2 (make changes to sth)
▸ MONEY 2 (change for the ticket machine)
▸ **a change of heart** REVOLUTION 2

change verb
▸ CHANGE 1 (change your habits)
▸ CHANGE 2 (changing attitudes towards education)
▸ CASH (Can you change a £20 note?)
▸ REPLACE 2 (change your doctor)
▸ TURN 2 (Caterpillars change into butterflies.)
▸ WEAR (change into your swimsuit)

change over phrasal verb
▸ SWITCH

channel noun
▸ CHANNEL (a TV channel)
▸ DITCH (drainage channels)
▸ MEDIUM (a channel of communication)

chant verb
▸ SING

chaos noun
▸ CHAOS

chapel noun
▸ CHURCH

chapter noun
▸ CHAPTER

char verb
▸ BURN 2

character noun
▸ CHARACTER (the main characters)
▸ CHARM (strength of character)
▸ NATURE 1 (buildings that are traditional in character)
▸ NUMBER 2 (the characters on the keyboard)
▸ PERSON (a strange character)
▸ PERSONALITY (your true character)

▸ REPUTATION (a man of good character)

characteristic noun
▸ FEATURE

characteristic adj.
▸ TYPICAL

charge noun
▸ CHARGE (face criminal charges)
▸ EXCITEMENT (get a real charge out of sth)
▸ RATE 2 (make a small charge for refreshments)
▸ RESPONSIBILITY (take charge of sth)
▸ **free of charge** FREE adj. 2
▸ **be in charge** RUN verb 2

charge verb
▸ CHARGE (charge sb half price)
▸ ACCUSE (charged with murder)
▸ ATTACK 2 (charge at the enemy)
▸ RUN 1 (The kids were charging around.)

charisma noun
▸ CHARM

charismatic adj.
▸ NICE 2

charity noun
▸ CHARITY (helping local charities)
▸ AID (give money to charity)
▸ MERCY (show no charity to sb)

charm noun
▸ CHARM (a man of great charm)
▸ INTEREST 1 (a hotel full of charm and character)

charm verb
▸ DELIGHT

charming adj.
▸ BEAUTIFUL 2 (a charming place)
▸ NICE 2 (a charming man)

chart noun
▸ DIAGRAM (The results are set out in the chart.)
▸ MAP (charts for a part of the ocean)

chart verb
▸ RECORD 1

charter noun
▸ LAW (a charter of rights)
▸ LICENCE (the BBC's charter)

charter verb
▸ ORDER 2

chase verb
▸ FOLLOW 1

chassis noun
▸ FRAME

chat noun
▸ DISCUSSION

chat verb
▸ CHAT

chateau noun
▸ PALACE

chatter noun
▸ DISCUSSION

chatter verb
▸ CHAT

chatty adj.
▸ TALKATIVE

chat up phrasal verb
▸ FLIRT

chauffeur noun
▸ DRIVER

chauvinism noun
▸ RACISM

cheap adj.
▸ CHEAP (cheap fares/shoes)
▸ DESPICABLE (a cheap joke/trick)
▸ MEAN 2 (She was too cheap to buy a present.)
▸ POOR 2 (cheap and nasty)

cheat noun
▸ CHEAT

cheat verb
▸ CHEAT

cheater noun
▸ CHEAT

check noun
▸ BILL (ask the waiter for the check)
▸ INSPECTION (do a routine check)
▸ INVESTIGATION (a police check)
▸ LIMIT 1 (provide a natural check)
▸ **hold/keep sth in check** LIMIT verb

check verb
▸ CHECK 1 (check for mistakes)
▸ CHECK 2 (Go and check that I've locked the windows.)
▸ LIMIT (check the growth of public spending)
▸ MARK 1 (check the box)
▸ SUPPRESS 2 (check your tears)

checklist noun
▸ LIST

check out verb
▸ LOOK 1

check over phrasal verb
▸ CHECK 1

check through phrasal verb
▸ CHECK 1

check-up noun
▸ INSPECTION

cheeky adj.
▸ RUDE

cheer verb
▸ ENCOURAGE 1 (be cheered by the news)
▸ SHOUT (a crowd cheers)

cheerful adj.
▸ CHEERFUL

cheer up phrasal verb
▸ ENCOURAGE 1

cheery adj.
▸ CHEERFUL

chemical noun
▸ MATERIAL

cherish verb
▸ APPRECIATE

cherished adj.
▸ DEAR

chest noun
▸ SUITCASE

chest of drawers noun
▸ CUPBOARD

chew verb
▸ BITE

chicken noun
▸ COWARD

chicken out phrasal verb
▸ PANIC

chide verb
▸ SCOLD

chief noun
▸ LEADER 1

chief adj.
▸ MAIN (sb's chief aim/rival)
▸ TOP (the Chief Education Officer)

chief executive noun
▸ LEADER 1

child noun
▸ CHILD (a three-year-old child)
▸ SON (She has three children.)

childhood noun
▸ CHILDHOOD

childish adj.
▸ CHILDISH

childlike adj.
▸ CHILDISH

chill verb
▸ COOL (best served chilled)
▸ REST (Chill, Mum! It's no big deal.)

chill adj.
▶ COLD 1

chilling adj.
▶ FRIGHTENING

chill out phrasal verb
▶ REST

chilly adj.
▶ COLD 1

chime verb
▶ RING

chink noun
▶ CRACK

chip noun
▶ FRAGMENT

chip in phrasal verb
▶ GIVE 5 (We each chipped in £5.)
▶ INTERRUPT (chip in with a remark)

choice noun
▶ CHOICE 1 (make a choice)
▶ CHOICE 2 (the first choice)
▶ OPTION (have no choice)
▶ RANGE 1 (not much choice)
▶ of choice FAVOURITE adj.

choke verb
▶ BLOCK 2 (The pond was choked with leaves.)
▶ COUGH (choke on sth)
▶ STRANGLE (choked by dust)

choose verb
▶ CHOOSE (choose from sth)
▶ DECIDE (choose not to marry)

chop verb
▶ CUT 2

choppy adj.
▶ ROUGH 2

chore noun
▶ TASK

christen verb
▶ CALL 1

chronicle noun
▶ STORY 2

chronicle verb
▶ DESCRIBE

chronology noun
▶ SERIES

chubby adj.
▶ FAT

chuck verb
▶ THROW

chuckle verb
▶ LAUGH

chuck out phrasal verb
▶ EVACUATE

chunk noun
▶ PIECE

church noun
▶ CHURCH (go to church)
▶ RELIGION (the Catholic Church)

churlish adj.
▶ RUDE

churn out phrasal verb
▶ MANUFACTURE

cinema noun
▶ FILM 2

circle noun
▶ CIRCLE (draw a circle)
▶ GROUP 2 (a circle of friends)

circle verb
▶ SPIN

circuit noun
▶ RACE

circulate verb
▶ FLOW (blood/air circulates)
▶ PUBLISH 1 (Copies will be circulated.)

circulation noun
▶ CURRENT

circumstance noun
▶ SITUATION

cissy noun
▶ COWARD

citation noun
▶ REFERENCE

cite verb
▶ ACCUSE (He was cited for contempt of court.)
▶ QUOTE (she cited a passage)
▶ MENTION (He cited the case of Bennett v Ashby.)

citizen noun
▶ CITIZEN (an Australian citizen)
▶ RESIDENT (law-abiding citizens)

city noun
▶ CITY

civic adj.
▶ SOCIAL

civil adj.
▶ NATIONAL (civil war)
▶ POLITE (behave in a civil manner)

civility noun
▶ RESPECT

civilization noun
▶ CULTURE

civil servant noun
▶ OFFICIAL

claim noun
▶ CLAIM (conflicting claims)
▶ REQUEST (a pay claim)
▶ RIGHT (sb's claim to the throne)

claim verb
▶ CLAIM (claim that sth is true)
▶ ASK 2 (claim compensation)

clamber verb
▶ CLIMB

clamour (also **clamor**) verb
▶ DEMAND

clan noun
▶ PEOPLE 2

clandestine adj.
▶ SECRET 2

clang noun
▶ BANG

clang verb
▶ RING

clank verb
▶ RING

clap verb
▶ PAT

clarify verb
▶ EXPLAIN 1

clash noun
▶ CONFLICT (a personality clash)
▶ CONFRONTATION (a clash between government ministers)
▶ FIGHT (a clash with police)

clash verb
▶ ARGUE (The two politicians clashed.)
▶ BANG 1 (Their swords clashed.)
▶ CONFLICT (clash over politics)
▶ FIGHT 2 (They clashed violently after the game.)

clasp noun
▶ BUTTON 2

clasp verb
▶ HOLD

class noun
▶ CLASS 1 (Which classes are you taking?)
▶ CLASS 2 (work hard in class)
▶ CLASS 3 (the youngest in the class)
▶ CLASS 4 (all classes of society)
▶ CATEGORY (different classes of drugs/hotel)
▶ STYLE (a touch of class)

class verb
▶ CLASSIFY

classic adj.
▶ ELEGANT (a classic design)

▶ EXCELLENT (a classic novel)
▶ TYPICAL (a classic example of sth)

classical adj.
▶ TRADITIONAL

classification noun
▶ CATEGORY

classified adj.
▶ SECRET 1

classify verb
▶ CLASSIFY

classmate noun
▶ PARTNER 1

classy adj.
▶ FASHIONABLE

clatter verb
▶ SHAKE 2

clause noun
▶ SECTION

claw adj.
▶ SCRATCH 2

clay noun
▶ SOIL

clean noun
▶ BATH

clean verb
▶ CLEAN

clean adj.
▶ CLEAN

cleaner noun
▶ SERVANT

cleaning noun
▶ BATH

cleanse verb
▶ CLEAN

clean up phrasal verb
▶ TIDY (clean up the mess)
▶ WASH (clean yourself up)

clear noun
▶ in the clear INNOCENT

clear verb
▶ CLEAR (clear the table)
▶ ACQUIT (be cleared of murder)
▶ ALLOW (The plane was cleared for take-off.)
▶ CASH (the cheque cleared)
▶ DISAPPEAR (rain/smoke clears)
▶ EVACUATE (clear the streets)
▶ PAY (clear your debts)
▶ clear your throat COUGH
▶ clear the way HELP 2

clear adj.
▶ CLEAR 1 (It's clear to me that…)
▶ CLEAR 2 (clear instructions)
▶ CLEAR 3 (clear blue water)
▶ SUNNY (a clear blue sky)
▶ SURE (Are you clear on that point?)

clear adv.
▶ steer clear AVOID

clearance noun
▶ PERMISSION

clear out phrasal verb
▶ GO AWAY

clear up phrasal verb
▶ SOLVE 2 (clear this matter up)
▶ TIDY (clear up a mess)

cleaver noun
▶ KNIFE

cleft noun
▶ CRACK

clemency noun
▶ MERCY

clench verb
▶ TIGHTEN

clerk noun
▶ SALESMAN

clever adj.
▶ INTELLIGENT

clichéd adj.
▶ TIRED 2

client noun
▶ CUSTOMER

clientele noun
▶ MARKET 1

climate noun
▶ AREA 1 (move to a warmer climate)
▶ ATMOSPHERE (a climate of fear)
▶ WEATHER (a tropical climate)

climax noun
▶ PEAK

climb verb
▶ CLIMB (climb a hill)
▶ RISE (The price of oil is climbing.)
▶ SLOPE (The path climbs steeply.)

clinch verb
▶ CONFIRM 3

cling verb
▶ HOLD

clinic noun
▶ HOSPITAL (a fertility clinic)
▶ SURGERY (a local health clinic)

clink verb
▶ CLINK

clip noun
▶ SCENE

clip verb
▶ CUT 3

clipboard noun
▶ ENVELOPE

clipped adj.
▶ SHARP 2

clique noun
▶ GROUP 2

cloak noun
▶ COAT

clog verb
▶ BLOCK 2

cloister noun
▶ COURTYARD

clone verb
▶ PRODUCE

close noun
▶ END

close verb
▶ CLOSE 1 (close a door/your eyes/a book)
▶ CLOSE 2 (a factory closes/close a factory)
▶ END (a meeting closes/close a meeting)

close adj.
▶ CLOSE 1 (a close finish)
▶ DETAILED (take a close look)
▶ LIKE prep. adj. (a close resemblance)

close down phrasal verb
▶ CLOSE 2

close in phrasal verb
▶ COME 1

closeness noun
▶ FRIENDSHIP

closet noun
▶ CUPBOARD

closing adj.
▶ LAST 1

cloth noun
▶ FABRIC

clothes noun
▶ CLOTHES

clothing noun
▶ CLOTHES

cloud noun
▶ CLOUD 1 (storm clouds)
▶ CLOUD 2 (a cloud of dust)

cloud verb
▶ DARKEN (the sky clouds over)

▸ COMPLICATE (cloud the issue)

cloudy adj.
▸ CLOUDY

club noun
▸ TEAM 2 (Real Madrid Football Club)
▸ UNION (the local drama club)

clue noun
▸ SUGGESTION

clueless adj.
▸ IGNORANT

clump noun
▸ GROUP 1

cluster noun
▸ GROUP 1

cluster verb
▸ CROWD

clutch verb
▸ HOLD

clutter noun
▸ MESS 1

cluttered adj.
▸ UNTIDY

coach noun
▸ COACH (an athletics coach)
▸ CAR (a coach driver)
▸ CARRIAGE 1 (a first-class coach)

coach verb
▸ TRAIN 1

coaching noun
▸ EDUCATION

coal noun
▸ OIL

coalition noun
▸ UNION

coarse adj.
▸ COARSE (coarse fabric/hair/sand)
▸ OFFENSIVE (coarse language)

coast noun
▸ COAST

coastline noun
▸ COAST

coat noun
▸ COAT

coat verb
▸ COVER

coax verb
▸ PERSUADE

cocktail noun
▸ MIXTURE

cocky adj.
▸ PROUD 2

code noun
▸ LAW (the penal code)
▸ VALUES (a code of conduct)

coerce verb
▸ PRESS 2

coercion noun
▸ PRESSURE 2

cogent adj.
▸ CONVINCING

coherence noun
▸ EFFICIENCY

coherent adj.
▸ ARTICULATE (coherent speech)
▸ RATIONAL (a coherent argument)

coil verb
▸ WRAP SB/STH AROUND/ROUND SB/STH

coin verb
▸ INVENT

coincide verb
▸ MATCH 1

coincidence noun
▸ LUCK

cold adj.
▸ COLD 1 (cold water/weather)
▸ COLD 2 (a cold look)

cold-blooded adj.
▸ RUTHLESS

collaborator noun
▸ PARTNER 1 (his collaborator on the project)
▸ TRAITOR (wartime collaborators)

collapse noun
▸ FAILURE

collapse verb
▸ COLLAPSE 1 (the roof collapses)
▸ COLLAPSE 2 (collapse from fatigue)
▸ CLOSE 2 (the market collapses)
▸ FAIL 2 (talks collapse)

colleague noun
▸ PARTNER 1

collect verb
▸ COLLECT (collect data/signatures)
▸ GET 2 (collect a prize)
▸ GET 3 (collect the children from school)
▸ RAISE (collect money)

collection noun
▸ GROUP 1

collective adj.
▸ COMMON

college noun
▸ SCHOOL

collide verb
▸ CRASH

collision noun
▸ ACCIDENT (a collision between two vehicles)
▸ CONFLICT (a collision of two different traditions)

collude verb
▸ PLOT

collusion noun
▸ CONSPIRACY

colony noun
▸ TERRITORY

coloration noun
▸ COLOUR 2

colossal adj.
▸ HUGE

colour (also **color**) noun
▸ COLOUR 1 (the colour of the sky)
▸ COLOUR 2 (people of colour)
▸ LOGO (the national colours)
▸ **of colour** BLACK adj.

colour (also **color**) verb
▸ AFFECT (colour your judgement)
▸ DRAW (colour sth in)
▸ FLUSH (sb's cheeks colour)
▸ PAINT (colour your hair)

coloured (also **colored**) adj.
▸ COLOURED (coloured lights)
▸ BLACK (coloured people)

colourful (also **colorful**) adj.
▸ COLOURED

colouring (also **coloring**) noun
▸ COLOUR 2

colourless (also **colorless**) adj.
▸ CLEAR 3 (a colourless liquid)
▸ DRAB (a colourless voice)

column noun
▸ ARTICLE (a newspaper column)
▸ POST (a stone column)
▸ ROW (a column of troops)

columnist noun
▸ REPORTER

comb verb
▸ BRUSH

combat noun
▸ WAR

combat verb
▸ OPPOSE

combatant noun
▸ SOLDIER

combination noun
▸ COMBINATION

combine verb
▸ COMBINE

combustion noun
▸ FIRE 1

come verb
▸ COME 1 (come here)
▸ COME 2 (when the time comes)
▸ ARRIVE (come early)
▸ ATTEND (come to a party)
▸ BECOME (come undone/loose)
▸ GO 2 (come by ship)

come about phrasal verb
▸ HAPPEN

come across phrasal verb
▸ FIND 2 (I came across some old photographs.)
▸ SEEM (He comes across well in interviews.)

come along phrasal verb
▸ ATTEND (Why don't you come along?)
▸ COME 1 (The bus came along.)

come around phrasal verb
▸ WAKE UP

come back phrasal verb
▸ RETURN 1

come between phrasal verb
▸ DIVIDE 2

comedian noun
▸ ACTOR

come down phrasal verb
▸ FALL 1 (prices come down)
▸ FALL 2 (come down the stairs)
▸ LAND (an aircraft comes down)
▸ RAIN (rain comes down)

come down on phrasal verb
▸ PUNISH

come down to phrasal verb
▸ REPRESENT 1

come down with phrasal verb
▸ SUFFER FROM STH

comedy noun
▸ HUMOUR (appreciate the comedy of the situation)
▸ PLAY (a romantic comedy)

come in phrasal verb
▸ ARRIVE (Our train came in.)
▸ ENTER (Tell her to come in.)

come into phrasal verb
▸ INHERIT

come on/along phrasal verb
▸ DEVELOP 1

come on to phrasal verb
▸ FLIRT

come out phrasal verb
▸ APPEAR (the sun comes out)
▸ TURN OUT (the truth comes out)

come over phrasal verb
▸ SEEM

come round phrasal verb
▸ WAKE UP

come through phrasal verb
▸ SURVIVE

come to phrasal verb
▸ OCCUR TO SB (The idea came to me in the bath.)
▸ WAKE UP (When she came to, the room was in darkness.)

come up phrasal verb
▸ EMERGE (a subject comes up)
▸ HAPPEN (Her birthday is coming up.)

come upon phrasal verb
▸ FIND 2

come up with phrasal verb
▸ COME UP WITH STH

comfort noun
▸ COMFORT (shoes designed for comfort)
▸ RELIEF (offer words of comfort)

comfort verb
▸ REASSURE

comfortable adj.
▸ COMFORTABLE (a comfortable chair/position)
▸ RICH (make a comfortable living)

comfy adj.
▸ COMFORTABLE

comic noun
▸ MAGAZINE

comic adj.
▸ FUNNY

coming noun
▸ ARRIVAL 1

coming adj.
▸ NEXT

command noun
▸ CONTROL (the chain of command)
▸ ORDER (the command to retreat)

command verb
▸ ORDER 1 (command sb to do sth)
▸ RUN 2 (command the troops)

commandeer verb
▸ SEIZE

commandment noun
▸ RULE

commemoration noun
▸ BIRTHDAY

commence verb
▸ BEGIN (commence work)
▸ START (the week commencing 15 May)

commend verb
▸ PRAISE

comment noun
▸ STATEMENT

comment verb
▸ COMMENT

commentary noun
▸ ASSESSMENT (social commentary)
▸ REPORT 2 (a sports commentary)

commentator noun
▸ ANALYST (a political commentator)
▸ PRESENTER (a sports commentator)

commerce noun
▸ TRADE

commercial noun
▸ ADVERTISEMENT

commercial adj.
▸ ECONOMIC (the commercial side of the organization)
▸ SUCCESSFUL 2 (a commercial success)

commiserate verb
▸ SORRY FOR SB

commission noun
▸ COMMITTEE (a commission of enquiry)
▸ SHARE (get a 10% commission)
▸ TASK (a commission for a painting)

commission verb
▸ APPOINT

commissioner noun
▸ OFFICIAL

commit verb
▸ DO 1 (commit a crime)
▸ PROMISE (commit yourself to reforming the system)
▸ DEVOTE (commit time to sth)

commitment noun
▸ PROMISE (make a commitment)
▸ RESPONSIBILITY (family/financial commitments)

committed adj.
▸ RELIABLE 1

committee noun
▸ COMMITTEE

commodity noun
▸ PRODUCT (basic commodities)
▸ THING 2 (Water is a precious commodity.)

common noun
▸ GRASS

common adj.
▸ COMMON (share a common interest)
▸ GENERAL 1 (a common sight)
▸ NORMAL (common frogs/decency)
▸ WORKING CLASS (She was very common and uneducated.)

commonly adv.
▸ USUALLY

commonplace adj.
▸ GENERAL 1

common sense noun
▸ WISDOM

commonwealth noun
▸ REPUBLIC

commotion noun
▸ CHAOS

communal adj.
▸ COMMON

communicate verb
▸ CONVEY (communicate your ideas)
▸ TALK (communicate by email)

communication noun
▸ COMMUNICATION (a method of communication)
▸ LETTER (an official communication)

communicator noun
▸ SPEAKER 1

community noun
▸ COMMUNITY (the local community)
▸ CULTURE (the city's Asian community)

commuter noun
▸ PASSENGER

compact adj.
▸ CRAMPED (The kitchen was compact but well equipped.)
▸ SMALL (a compact camera)

companion noun
▸ FRIEND

companionship noun
▸ FRIENDSHIP

company noun
▸ COMPANY (a computer company)
▸ PARTY 3 (get into bad company)
▸ VISITOR (I didn't realize you had company.)
▸ **keep sb company** ACCOMPANY verb

comparable adj.
▸ EQUIVALENT

compare verb
▸ COMPARE 1 (We compared the two reports carefully.)
▸ COMPARE 2 (Our results compare favourably with theirs.)

comparison noun
▸ COMPARISON (I enclose the two plans for comparison.)
▸ **there's no comparison** SIMILARITY

compartment noun
▸ CARRIAGE 1

compassion noun
▸ SYMPATHY

compassionate adj.
▸ SENSITIVE 1

compel verb
▸ FORCE

compelling adj.
▸ CONVINCING (a compelling reason to do sth)

▸ INTERESTING (sth makes compelling reading)
▸ URGENT (a compelling need)

compensate verb
▸ COMPENSATE (It compensated for her disappointment.)
▸ REPAY (compensate sb for the loss of sth)

compensation noun
▸ COMPENSATION

compete verb
▸ COMPETE (Smaller firms can't compete.)
▸ PLAY 2 (compete in the Olympics)

competence noun
▸ SKILL 2

competent adj.
▸ GOOD 4

competition noun
▸ COMPETITION 1 (a drawing/dancing competition)
▸ COMPETITION 2 (competition between businesses)
▸ ENEMY (She's gone to work for the competition.)

competitive adj.
▸ AGGRESSIVE 2 (a strong competitive streak)
▸ CHEAP (competitive prices)

competitiveness noun
▸ COMPETITION 2

competitor noun
▸ ENEMY (a business competitor)
▸ PARTICIPANT (one of the sport's top competitors)

complacent adj.
▸ SMUG

complain noun
▸ COMPLAIN

complaint noun
▸ COMPLAINT (make a complaint)
▸ DISEASE (a skin complaint)

complete verb
▸ FINISH

complete adj.
▸ COMPLETE (a complete surprise)
▸ WHOLE (collect the complete set)

completely adv.
▸ QUITE 2

complex noun
▸ BUILDING (a shopping complex)
▸ OBSESSION (a guilt complex)

complex adj.
▸ COMPLEX

complexion noun
▸ COLOUR 2

compliant adj.
▸ PASSIVE

complicate verb
▸ COMPLICATE

complicated adj.
▸ COMPLEX

complication noun
▸ PROBLEM

compliment noun
▸ TRIBUTE

compliment verb
▸ PRAISE

complimentary adj.
▸ FREE 2 (a complimentary breakfast)
▸ GOOD 6 (She was complimentary about his work.)

comply verb
▸ FOLLOW 3

component noun
▸ ELEMENT 1

compose verb
▸ WRITE 2 (compose an opera)
▸ **be composed of sb/sth** CONSIST OF SB/STH

composed adj.
▸ CALM

composite noun
▸ COMBINATION

composition noun
▸ STRUCTURE (the composition of the workforce)
▸ WORK 4 (an orchestral composition)

composure noun
▸ COMPOSURE

compound noun
▸ COURTYARD (the palace compound)
▸ MIXTURE (a chemical compound)

compound verb
▸ WEAKEN

comprehend verb
▸ UNDERSTAND 1

comprehensible adj.
▸ CLEAR 2

comprehension noun
▸ UNDERSTANDING

comprehensive adj.
▸ DETAILED

comprise verb
▸ CONSIST OF SB/STH

compromise noun
▸ COMPROMISE

compromise verb
▸ DAMAGE

compulsion noun
▸ DESIRE (feel a great compulsion to do sth)
▸ PRESSURE 2 (You are under no compulsion.)

compulsive adj.
▸ ADDICTIVE (a compulsive urge)
▸ REGULAR (compulsive gamblers)

compulsory adj.
▸ NECESSARY

compunction noun
▸ DOUBT 2

compute verb
▸ CALCULATE

computerized adj.
▸ ELECTRONIC

comradeship noun
▸ FRIENDSHIP

con noun
▸ FRAUD 2

con verb
▸ CHEAT

concave adj.
▸ CURVED

conceal verb
▸ HIDE 1

concede verb
▸ ADMIT 1 (concede there might be a problem)
▸ GIVE STH UP (concede power)

conceit noun
▸ PRIDE

conceited adj.
▸ PROUD 2

conceivable adj.
▸ POSSIBLE 2

conceive verb
▸ COME UP WITH STH

concentration noun
▸ ATTENTION

concept noun
▸ IDEA 1

conception noun
▸ UNDERSTANDING

conceptual adj.
▸ INTELLECTUAL 1

conceptualize verb
▸ IMAGINE

concern noun
▸ CONCERN (concern for her safety)
▸ BUSINESS 1 (none of your concern)
▸ ISSUE (social concerns)
▸ SYMPATHY (the parents' concern for their children)

concern verb
▸ AFFECT (It doesn't concern you.)
▸ APPLY 2 (This chapter is concerned with…)
▸ WORRY 2 (What concerns me is…)

concerned adj.
▸ WORRIED

concert noun
▸ CONCERT

concession noun
▸ COMPROMISE

concise adj.
▸ SHORT 3

conclude verb
▸ CONCLUDE (What do you conclude from that?)
▸ AGREE 3 (conclude a treaty)
▸ END (a speech concludes)

conclusion noun
▸ CONCLUSION (reach the conclusion that…)
▸ END (In conclusion…)
▸ **a foregone conclusion** CERTAINTY

conclusive adj.
▸ CONCLUSIVE

concoction noun
▸ MIXTURE

concrete adj.
▸ FINAL

concubine noun
▸ LOVER

concur verb
▸ AGREE 1

condemn verb
▸ BLAME

condemnation noun
▸ CRITICISM

condensation noun
▸ MOISTURE

condense verb
▸ SUMMARIZE

condescending adj.
▸ PATRONIZING

condition noun
▸ CONDITION (I agree, on one condition.)
▸ DISEASE (a medical condition)
▸ HEALTH (out of condition)
▸ SITUATION (working conditions)
▸ STATE (in perfect condition)

condo noun
▸ FLAT

condolence noun
▸ SYMPATHY

condominium noun
▸ FLAT

condone verb
▸ FORGIVE

conduct verb
▸ BEHAVE (conduct yourself well)
▸ CARRY 2 (conduct heat/electricity)
▸ DO 1 (conduct an experiment)

confer verb
▸ GIVE 1 (confer a degree on sb)
▸ TALK (confer with sb about sth)

conference noun
▸ MEETING 1

confess verb
▸ ADMIT 1 (confess your ignorance)
▸ ADMIT 2 (confess to murder)

confidant, confidante noun
▸ FRIEND

confidence noun
- ▶ CONFIDENCE (confidence in your own abilities)
- ▶ FAITH (confidence in the government)
- ▶ **have confidence in sb/sth** TRUST verb

confident adj.
- ▶ CONFIDENT (a confident person)
- ▶ SURE (feel confident of winning)

confidential adj.
- ▶ SECRET 1

configuration noun
- ▶ DESIGN

confined adj.
- ▶ CRAMPED

confines noun
- ▶ LIMIT 2

confine to phrasal verb
- ▶ CONFINE SB/STH TO STH

confirm verb
- ▶ CONFIRM 1 (His guilty expression confirmed my suspicions.)
- ▶ CONFIRM 2 (Can you confirm what happened?)
- ▶ CONFIRM 3 (The climb confirmed his fear of heights.)
- ▶ APPROVE (confirmed as captain)

confiscate verb
- ▶ SEIZE

conflict noun
- ▶ CONFLICT (a conflict of interests)
- ▶ DEBATE (the conflict over pay)
- ▶ WAR (a bloody conflict)

conflict verb
- ▶ CONFLICT

conformist adj.
- ▶ CONSERVATIVE

confound verb
- ▶ DISPROVE

confront verb
- ▶ CONFRONT (confront a robber)
- ▶ FACE (confront your fears)

confrontation noun
- ▶ CONFRONTATION

confuse verb
- ▶ CONFUSE (These instructions confused everyone.)
- ▶ COMPLICATE (confuse the issue)
- ▶ TAKE 8 (confuse sb with sb else)

confused adj.
- ▶ CONFUSED 1 (feel confused)
- ▶ CONFUSED 2 (a confused account)

confusing adj.
- ▶ CONFUSING

confusion noun
- ▶ CHAOS (The smoke bombs created confusion and panic.)
- ▶ DOUBT 1 (confusion about what to do next)

congenital adj.
- ▶ NATURAL

congested adj.
- ▶ FULL

congestion noun
- ▶ TRAFFIC

conglomerate noun
- ▶ GROUP 3

congratulate verb
- ▶ PRAISE (congratulate sb on sth)
- ▶ **congratulate yourself** BOAST

congress noun
- ▶ ASSEMBLY

Congressman noun
- ▶ POLITICIAN

Congresswoman noun
- ▶ POLITICIAN

conjecture noun
- ▶ SPECULATION

conjecture verb
- ▶ GUESS

conjure up phrasal verb
- ▶ REMIND SB OF SB/STH

conjuring noun
- ▶ MAGIC

con man noun
- ▶ CHEAT

connect verb
- ▶ LINK 1 (jobs connected with the environment)
- ▶ LINK 2 (The towns are connected by train services.)
- ▶ RELATE (There was nothing to connect him with the crime.)

connected adj.
- ▶ RELATED

connection noun
- ▶ CONNECTION (an electrical connection)
- ▶ FAMILY 2 (She's British but has German connections.)
- ▶ RELATION (a connection between smoking and cancer)

connive verb
- ▶ PLOT

connoisseur noun
- ▶ EXPERT

connotation noun
- ▶ ASSOCIATION

conquer verb
- ▶ INVADE (conquer a country)
- ▶ OVERCOME (conquer your fear)
- ▶ SUCCEED (conquer the US market)

conqueror noun
- ▶ WINNER

conscientious adj.
- ▶ CONSCIENTIOUS

conscious adj.
- ▶ AWARE (conscious of the problems)
- ▶ DELIBERATE (a conscious decision)

consciousness noun
- ▶ AWARENESS

consecutive adj.
- ▶ SUCCESSIVE

consensus noun
- ▶ AGREEMENT 2

consent noun
- ▶ AGREEMENT 2 (mutual consent)
- ▶ PERMISSION (give your consent)

consent verb
- ▶ AGREE 2

consequence noun
- ▶ IMPORTANCE (Don't worry. It's of no consequence.)
- ▶ RESULT (serious consequences)

consequent adj.
- ▶ RELATED

conservative adj.
- ▶ CONSERVATIVE

conserve verb
- ▶ SAVE 4

consider verb
- ▶ CONSIDER (consider your options)
- ▶ REGARD (consider yourself lucky)

considerable adj.
- ▶ LARGE

considerate adj.
- ▶ KIND

consideration noun
- ▶ CONSIDERATION (give the matter some consideration)
- ▶ FACTOR (Time is an important consideration.)

consignment noun
- ▶ LOT

consistency noun
- ▶ TEXTURE

consistent adj.
- ▶ STEADY

consist of phrasal verb
- ▶ CONSIST OF SB/STH

consolation noun
- ▶ RELIEF

console verb
- ▶ REASSURE

consolidate verb
- ▶ COMBINE

consortium noun
- ▶ GROUP 3

conspicuous adj.
- ▶ MARKED

conspiracy noun
- ▶ CONSPIRACY

conspirator noun
- ▶ ACCOMPLICE

conspiratorial adj.
- ▶ SECRETIVE

conspire verb
- ▶ PLOT

constable noun
- ▶ POLICEMAN

constant adj.
- ▶ FREQUENT (constant attention)
- ▶ STEADY (a constant speed)

constitute verb
- ▶ CONSIST OF SB/STH (constitute the majority of the labour force)
- ▶ REPRESENT 1 (constitute a criminal offence)

constitution noun
- ▶ HEALTH (a strong constitution)
- ▶ LAW (the country's constitution)

constitutional adj.
- ▶ LEGAL

constrain verb
- ▶ CONFINE SB/STH TO STH

constraint noun
- ▶ LIMIT 1

construct verb
- ▶ BUILD

construction noun
- ▶ PRODUCTION (the construction of the new airport)
- ▶ STRUCTURE (ships of steel construction)

constructive adj.
- ▶ VALUABLE 2

consul noun
- ▶ SPOKESMAN

consult verb
- ▶ ASK 1 (consult a doctor)
- ▶ REFER TO STH (consult the manual)
- ▶ TALK (consult your colleagues)

consultant noun
- ▶ ADVISER

consultation noun
- ▶ DISCUSSION (consultations between the two countries)
- ▶ INTERVIEW 1 (a 30-minute consultation)

consume verb
- ▶ EAT (consume red meat)
- ▶ USE 2 (consume fuel)

consumer noun
- ▶ CUSTOMER

consumer group noun
- ▶ INSPECTOR

consuming adj.
- ▶ ADDICTIVE

consummate adj.
- ▶ IMPRESSIVE

contact noun
- ▶ COMMUNICATION (lose contact)
- ▶ PARTNER 1 (business contacts)
- ▶ RELATIONSHIP 1 (trade contacts)

contain verb
- ▶ INCLUDE 1 (an envelope containing a hundred dollar bills)

contrary verb
- ▶ LIMIT (contain an epidemic)
- ▶ SUPPRESS 2 (contain your excitement)

container noun
- ▶ BOX

contemplate verb
- ▶ CONSIDER (too awful to contemplate)
- ▶ LOOK 1 (contemplate sb/sth in silence)

contemplation noun
- ▶ CONSIDERATION

contemporary adj.
- ▶ RECENT

contempt noun
- ▶ CONTEMPT

contemptible adj.
- ▶ DESPICABLE

contemptuous adj.
- ▶ CONTEMPTUOUS

contend verb
- ▶ CLAIM

contender noun
- ▶ PARTICIPANT

contend with phrasal verb
- ▶ DEAL WITH SB/STH

content adj.
- ▶ HAPPY

contented adj.
- ▶ HAPPY

contention noun
- ▶ CLAIM (It is my client's contention that…)
- ▶ DEBATE (a point of contention)

contentious adj.
- ▶ CONTROVERSIAL

contentment noun
- ▶ SATISFACTION

contents noun
- ▶ CHAPTER

contest noun
- ▶ COMPETITION 1 (a talent contest)
- ▶ COMPETITION 2 (the contest for the leadership of the party)

contest verb
- ▶ COMPETE (contest an election)
- ▶ DOUBT (contest a will)

contestant noun
- ▶ PARTICIPANT

context noun
- ▶ CONTEXT

contingent noun
- ▶ ARMY (the French contingent in the UN peacekeeping force)
- ▶ PARTY 3 (a contingent of local residents)

continual adj.
- ▶ FREQUENT (continual arguments)
- ▶ CONTINUOUS (in continual fear)

continue verb
- ▶ CONTINUE 1 (the rain continues)
- ▶ CONTINUE 2 (continue fighting)
- ▶ CONTINUE 3 (the story continues)
- ▶ LEAD 3 (a path continues)
- ▶ REMAIN (continue as project manager)

continuous adj.
- ▶ CONTINUOUS (a continuous process)
- ▶ FREQUENT (continuous attacks)

contour noun
- ▶ SHAPE

contract noun
- ▶ CONTRACT

contract verb
- ▶ EMPLOY (be contracted to work until August)
- ▶ SHRINK (glass contracts)
- ▶ SUFFER FROM STH (contract malaria)

contradict *verb*
► CONFLICT (two stories contradict each other)
► DENY (contradict yourself/sb else)

contradiction *noun*
► CONFLICT

contradictory *adj.*
► INCONSISTENT

contraption *noun*
► MACHINE

the contrary *noun*
► OPPOSITE

contrary *adj.*
► OPPOSITE

contrast *noun*
► DIFFERENCE (the contrast between East and West)
► OPPOSITE (quite a contrast to last week's work)

contrast *verb*
► COMPARE 1 (The poem contrasts youth and age.)
► CONFLICT (Her actions and promises contrasted sharply.)

contrasting *adj.*
► DIFFERENT

contribute *verb*
► GIVE 5

contribution *noun*
► GIFT (a contribution to charity)
► INVOLVEMENT (make a positive contribution to the success of sth)
► PAYMENT (monthly contributions to a pension plan)

contributor *noun*
► REPORTER (a frequent contributor to this magazine)
► SPONSOR (important contributors to the economy)

contrived *adj.*
► ARTIFICIAL 2

control *noun*
► CONTROL (under enemy control)
► BUTTON 1 (the controls of an aircraft)
► LIMIT 1 (traffic/arms control)
► **bring/get/keep sth under control** OVERCOME *verb*

control *verb*
► CONTROL (control a child)
► LIMIT (control inflation)
► OPERATE (This knob controls the volume.)
► OVERCOME (control the pain)
► RUN 2 (control a company)
► SUPPRESS 2 (control your temper)

controlled *adj.*
► CALM (a controlled, even voice)
► DISCIPLINED (controlled anger)
► LIMITED 2 (controlled drugs)

controversial *adj.*
► CONTROVERSIAL

controversy *noun*
► DEBATE

conurbation *noun*
► CITY

convalesce *verb*
► RECOVER 1

convene *verb*
► HAVE 4 (convene a committee)
► MEET 1 (a committee convenes)

convenient *adj.*
► GOOD 2 (a convenient time/place)
► USEFUL (It is convenient to pay by credit card.)

convention *noun*
► CONTRACT (the European Convention on Human Rights)
► MEETING 1 (the party's annual convention)
► TRADITION (social conventions)

conventional *adj.*
► CONSERVATIVE (the hypocrisy of conventional society)
► TRADITIONAL (conventional methods/ovens)

converge *verb*
► COME 1

conversation *noun*
► DISCUSSION

conversion *noun*
► CHANGE 2

convert *verb*
► PERSUADE (I've never liked opera but you might convert me!)
► SWITCH (I've converted to organic food.)
► TURN 2 (a sofa that converts into a bed)

convertible *adj.*
► FLEXIBLE 1

convex *adj.*
► CURVED

convey *verb*
► CONVEY (Colours like red convey a sense of energy.)
► CARRY 2 (Pipes convey hot water from the boiler.)

convict *noun*
► PRISONER

conviction *noun*
► FAITH (carry/lack conviction)
► VIEW 1 (religious convictions)

convince *verb*
► CONVINCE (Sceptics were not convinced.)
► PERSUADE (I convinced him to see a doctor.)

convinced *adj.*
► SURE

convincing *adj.*
► CONVINCING

convoluted *adj.*
► COMPLEX

convoy *noun*
► FLEET

convulse *verb*
► SHAKE 3

convulsion *noun*
► SHIVER

cook *verb*
► COOK

cookery *noun*
► COOKING

cooking *noun*
► COOKING

cool *noun*
► COMPOSURE

cool *verb*
► COOL (Glass contracts as it cools.)
► RELAX 1 (tempers cool)

cool *adj.*
► COOL (She took his keys and walked out, cool as you please.)
► CALM (cool, calm and collected)
► COLD 1 (in a cool dry place)
► COLD 2 (a cool reception)
► GREAT 1 (This song is really cool.)
► PALE 2 (cool colours)

cool down *phrasal verb*
► COOL

cooperate *verb*
► HELP 1

cooperation *noun*
► HELP

cooperative *noun*
► GROUP 3

cooperative *adj.*
► COMMON (a cooperative venture)
► HELPFUL (They weren't very co-operative.)

co-opt *verb*
► APPOINT

coop up *phrasal verb*
► TRAP

coordinate *verb*
► MATCH 2

coordination *noun*
► PLANNING

cop *noun*
► POLICEMAN

cope *verb*
► COPE

copy *noun*
► COPY 1 (a copy of a report)
► COPY 2 (a copy of a painting)

copy *verb*
► COPY (copy data/a document)
► FOLLOW 4 (copy what sb does)
► WRITE 1 (copy down a phone number)

cord *noun*
► ROPE (tied with a gold cord)
► WIRE (an electrical cord)

cordial *adj.*
► FRIENDLY 2

cordon *noun*
► ROW

cordon off *phrasal verb*
► SEPARATE 2

core *noun*
► POINT

cork *noun*
► LID

corner *noun*
► CORNER (a street corner)
► MESS 2 (in a tight corner)

corner *verb*
► TAKE OVER

corny *adj.*
► TIRED 2

corporation *noun*
► COMPANY

corps *noun*
► TEAM 1

corpse *noun*
► BODY 2

correct *verb*
► CORRECT (correct a fault)
► MARK 2 (correct spellings)

correct *adj.*
► RIGHT 1 (the correct method)
► TRUE (the correct answer)

correctional facility *noun*
► PRISON

correlate *verb*
► MATCH 1

correlation *noun*
► RELATION

correspond *verb*
► MATCH 1

correspondence *noun*
► COMMUNICATION (enter into correspondence with sb)
► LETTER (correspondence from readers)
► SIMILARITY (a close correspondence between the two extracts)

correspondent *noun*
► REPORTER

corresponding *adj.*
► EQUIVALENT

corridor *noun*
► CORRIDOR

corroborate *verb*
► CONFIRM 1

corrupt *adj.*
► CORRUPT

corruption *noun*
► CORRUPTION

cosmopolitan *adj.*
► INTERNATIONAL

the cosmos *noun*
► SPACE 2

cost *noun*
► COSTS (running costs)
► PRICE (the cost of living)

cost *verb*
► COST (How much does this cost?)
► PRICE (cost a project)

costing *noun*
► VALUATION

costly *adj.*
► EXPENSIVE

costume *noun*
► COSTUME (dressed in a giant chicken costume)
► CLOTHES (Welsh national costume)

cosy *adj.*
► COMFORTABLE

cottage *noun*
► HOUSE

couch *noun*
► CHAIR

cough *verb*
► COUGH (coughing and sneezing)
► VOMIT (cough up blood)

council *noun*
► ASSEMBLY (the local council)
► COMMITTEE (the General Medical Council)

councillor *noun*
► OFFICIAL

councilman *noun*
► OFFICIAL

councilwoman *noun*
► OFFICIAL

counsel *noun*
► LAWYER

counselling (also **counseling**) *noun*
► ADVICE

counsellor (also **counselor**) *noun*
► ADVISER

count *noun*
► ESTIMATE

count *verb*
► COUNT (count the votes)
► INCLUDE 2 (50 people, not counting the children)
► REGARD (count yourself lucky)

counter *verb*
► COMPENSATE

counteract *verb*
► COMPENSATE

counterfeit *adj.*
► SO-CALLED

counterpart *noun*
► EQUIVALENT

counterproductive *adj.*
► INEFFECTIVE

count on *verb*
► TRUST

country *noun*
► COUNTRY 1 (a foreign country)
► COUNTRY 2 (country life)
► COMMUNITY (The issue has divided the country.)

country house *noun*
► PALACE

countryside *noun*
► COUNTRY 2

county *noun*
► COUNTY

coup *noun*
► REVOLUTION 1 (a military coup)
► WORK 3 (pull off a major diplomatic coup)

couple with *phrasal verb*
- LINK 1

coupon *noun*
- FORM 2

courage *noun*
- COURAGE (show great courage)
- **pluck up (the) courage** DARE *verb*

courageous *adj.*
- BRAVE

course *noun*
- CLASS 1 (a course of study)
- DIRECTION (let things take their natural course)
- WAY 3 (The plane was off course.)

court *noun*
- COURT (a court case)
- PITCH (a tennis court)

court *verb*
- GO OUT

courteous *adj.*
- POLITE

courtesy *noun*
- RESPECT

courthouse *noun*
- COURT

court martial *noun*
- CASE

court of appeal *noun*
- COURT

court of law *noun*
- COURT

courtroom *noun*
- COURT

courtship *noun*
- RELATIONSHIP 2

courtyard *noun*
- COURTYARD

cover *noun*
- COVER (a waterproof cover)
- PRETENCE (a cover for illegal activities)
- REPLACEMENT (cover for absent staff)
- SECURITY (air cover)
- SHELTER (run for cover)

cover *verb*
- COVER (covered in mud)
- DESCRIBE (cover a story)
- GO 2 (cover many miles)
- HIDE 1 (cover your face)
- INCLUDE 1 (cover a subject)

coverage *noun*
- MEDIA

cover for *phrasal verb*
- REPLACE 1

covering *noun*
- COVER

covert *adj.*
- SECRET 2

covet *verb*
- LONG

cow *verb*
- THREATEN 1

coward *noun*
- COWARD

cower *verb*
- JUMP 3

co-worker *noun*
- PARTNER 1

coy *noun*
- SHY

cozy *adj.*
- COMFORTABLE

crack *noun*
- CRACK (cracks in the wall)
- BANG (the crack of a rifle shot)

crack *verb*
- BANG 1 (crack a whip)

- BANG 2 (crack your head on the ceiling)
- BREAK 1 (ice/leather/paint cracks)
- SOLVE 2 (crack a case/code)

crack up *phrasal verb*
- LAUGH

cradle *adj.*
- HUG

craft *noun*
- BOAT

craftsman *noun*
- MAKER

crafty *adj.*
- CUNNING

cram *verb*
- PACK

crammed *adj.*
- FULL

cramped *adj.*
- CRAMPED

crap *noun* (*taboo*)
- NONSENSE (Cut the crap!)
- RUBBISH (His work is crap.)

crap *adj.* (*taboo*)
- POOR 2

crash *noun*
- ACCIDENT (a car crash)
- BANG (a loud crash)

crash *verb*
- CRASH (crash a car)
- BANG 1 (thunder crashes)
- BREAK 2 (a computer crashes)
- CLOSE 2 (the market crashes)
- FALL 2 (A brick crashed through the window.)
- FALL ASLEEP (crash on sb's floor)

crate *noun*
- BOX

crater *noun*
- HOLE 2

crave *verb*
- LONG

craving *noun*
- APPETITE 2

crawl *verb*
- EDGE

craze *noun*
- FASHION

crazed *adj.*
- MENTALLY ILL

crazy *adj.*
- CRAZY (Are you crazy? You could have been killed!)
- MAD (a crazy old woman)
- **drive sb crazy** ANGER *verb*
- **crazy about sb** IN LOVE

creak *verb*
- CREAK

crease *noun*
- FOLD

crease *verb*
- CRUMPLE

create *verb*
- CAUSE (create confusion)
- MAKE 1 (create jobs)

creation *noun*
- DEVELOPMENT

creative *adj.*
- CREATIVE

creativity *noun*
- INSPIRATION

creator *noun*
- DESIGNER

creature *noun*
- ANIMAL

credentials *noun*
- CERTIFICATE

credible *adj.*
- POSSIBLE 2

credit *noun*
- LOAN (interest-free credit)
- PRAISE (give sb credit for sth)

creditable *adj.*
- WORTHY

creek *noun*
- RIVER

creep *noun*
- VILLAIN

creep *verb*
- EDGE (traffic creeps along)
- SLIP 1 (I crept into the house.)

creepy *adj.*
- FRIGHTENING

cremate *verb*
- BURN 2

crescent *noun*
- CURVE

crest *noun*
- LOGO

crevice *noun*
- CRACK

crew *noun*
- TEAM 1

crime *noun*
- CRIME 1 (the fight against crime)
- CRIME 2 (commit a crime)
- DISGRACE 1 (It's a crime to waste so much money.)

criminal *noun*
- CRIMINAL

criminal *adj.*
- ILLEGAL (a criminal offence)
- OUTRAGEOUS (a criminal waste)

cringe *verb*
- JUMP 3

cripple *verb*
- DISABLE

crisis *noun*
- CRISIS (a political crisis)
- TURNING POINT (The fever has passed its crisis.)

crisp *adj.*
- COLD 1

criterion *noun*
- CRITERION

critic *noun*
- ANALYST

critical *adj.*
- CRITICAL (critical of sb's efforts)
- ESSENTIAL (of critical importance)
- SERIOUS 1 (critical illness)

criticism *noun*
- CRITICISM (criticism of the management)
- ASSESSMENT (literary criticism)

criticize *verb*
- BLAME

critique *noun*
- ASSESSMENT

croak *verb*
- GRUNT

crony *noun*
- FRIEND

crook *noun*
- CRIMINAL

crooked *adj.*
- CORRUPT

crop *verb*
- CUT 3

crop up *phrasal verb*
- HAPPEN

cross *verb*
- CROSS (cross the border)
- TOUCH 2 (two roads cross)
- **cross your mind** OCCUR TO SB

cross *adj.*
- ANGRY

cross-examine *verb*
- QUESTION

crossing *noun*
- CRUISE

cross off *phrasal verb*
- DELETE

cross out *phrasal verb*
- DELETE

crossroads *noun*
- JUNCTION (Turn left at the crossroads.)
- TURNING POINT (a crossroads in his career)

crouch *verb*
- BEND

crowd *noun*
- CROWD (crowds of people)
- GENERAL PUBLIC (stand out from/follow the crowd)
- GROUP 2 (get in with the wrong crowd)

crowd *verb*
- CROWD

crowded *adj.*
- CROWDED

crown *noun*
- HAT (wear a crown)
- KING (allegiance to the Crown)

crucial *adj.*
- ESSENTIAL

cruel *adj.*
- CRUEL

cruise *noun*
- CRUISE

cruise *verb*
- SLIDE

cruiser *noun*
- BOAT

crumb *noun*
- FRAGMENT

crumble *verb*
- COLLAPSE 1

crumple *verb*
- CRUMPLE

crunch *verb*
- BITE

crusade *noun*
- CAMPAIGN

crusader *noun*
- ACTIVIST

crush *noun*
- CROWD (a big crush in the bar)
- LOVE 1 (a schoolgirl crush)
- **have a crush on sb** ATTRACTED TO

crush *verb*
- DISCOURAGE 2 (feel crushed)
- SUPPRESS 1 (crush a rebellion)

crux *noun*
- POINT

cry *verb*
- CRY (cry your eyes out)
- SHOUT (crying for help)

cry out *phrasal verb*
- CALL 3 (cry out sb's name)
- SCREAM (cry out in pain)

crypt *noun*
- BASEMENT

cube *noun*
- PIECE

cuddle *verb*
- HUG

cuddly *adj.*
- SWEET

cue *noun*
- SIGNAL

cuisine *noun*
- COOKING

culmination *noun*
- PEAK

culprit noun
▶ CRIMINAL

cult noun
▶ RELIGION

cultivate verb
▶ FARM

cultural adj.
▶ CULTURAL

culture noun
▶ CULTURE

cultured adj.
▶ INTELLECTUAL 2

cunning adj.
▶ CUNNING

cup noun
▶ AWARD (win cups for skating)
▶ RACE (play in the World Cup)

cupboard noun
▶ CUPBOARD

curb noun
▶ LIMIT 1

curb verb
▶ LIMIT (curb public spending)
▶ SUPPRESS 2 (curb your temper)

cure noun
▶ DRUG 2 (The only cure is rest.)
▶ TREATMENT (The cure took six weeks.)

cure verb
▶ CURE (cure an illness)
▶ CORRECT (cure inflation)

curious adj.
▶ CURIOUS (curious about sth)
▶ STRANGE 1 (a curious feeling)

curl verb
▶ WRAP STH/STH AROUND/ROUND SB/STH

current noun
▶ CURRENT

current adj.
▶ RECENT

curriculum noun
▶ CLASS 1

curse verb
▶ CURSE

curt adj.
▶ SHARP 2

curtain noun
▶ CURTAIN

curtsy verb
▶ BEND

curvature noun
▶ CURVE

curve noun
▶ CURVE

curve verb
▶ CURVE

curved adj.
▶ CURVED

cushion verb
▶ EASE

cushy adj.
▶ EASY 1

custom noun
▶ BUSINESS 2 (Thank you for your custom.)
▶ TAX (a customs officer)
▶ TRADITION (local customs)

customer noun
▶ CUSTOMER

cut noun
▶ INJURY (a deep cut on his arm)
▶ REDUCTION (a cut in salary)
▶ SHARE (a cut of 5%)

cut verb
▶ CUT 1 (cut taxes)
▶ CUT 2 (cut the bread)
▶ CUT 3 (have your hair cut)
▶ CUT 4 (cut your finger)

▶ DELETE (cut and paste)
▶ FREE 1 (cut the injured driver from the wreckage)

cut across phrasal verb
▶ CROSS

cut back phrasal verb
▶ CUT 1

cutback noun
▶ REDUCTION

cut down phrasal verb
▶ CUT 1 (cut the article down to 1 000 words)
▶ DEMOLISH (cut down a tree)

cute adj.
▶ BEAUTIFUL 1 (a cute guy)
▶ SWEET (a cute little puppy)

cut in phrasal verb
▶ INTERRUPT

cut off phrasal verb
▶ BLOCK 3 (cut off sb's escape)
▶ ISOLATE (cut off from all human contact)

cut out phrasal verb
▶ cut out for sth/cut out to be sth GOOD 2

cut through phrasal verb
▶ CROSS

the **cutting edge** noun
▶ LEAD 1

cut up phrasal verb
▶ DIVIDE 1

cycle noun
▶ PATTERN 1

cyclone noun
▶ STORM

cylinder noun
▶ BARREL

cynical adj.
▶ SUSPICIOUS 1

cynicism noun
▶ SCEPTICISM

D d

dad noun
▶ MOTHER

daddy noun
▶ MOTHER

dagger noun
▶ KNIFE

daily noun
▶ NEWSPAPER

daily adj.
▶ DAILY

dais noun
▶ STAGE 2

dam verb
▶ BLOCK 2

damage noun
▶ DAMAGE

damage verb
▶ DAMAGE

damaging adj.
▶ HARMFUL

damn verb
▶ CURSE

damning adj.
▶ CRITICAL

damp noun
▶ MOISTURE

damp adj.
▶ WET 1

dampen verb
▶ MODERATE (dampen your enthusiasm)
▶ SOAK (dampen your hair)

dance noun
▶ PARTY 2

danger noun
▶ RISK 1 (lives are in danger)

▶ THREAT (a danger to society)

dangerous adj.
▶ DANGEROUS

dank adj.
▶ SMELLY

dare verb
▶ DARE (He didn't dare to argue.)
▶ CHALLENGE (I dare you to do it.)
▶ I dare say SUPPOSE

daring noun
▶ COURAGE

daring adj.
▶ BOLD

dark noun
▶ DARKNESS (afraid of the dark)
▶ in the dark UNAWARE adj.

dark adj.
▶ DARK 1 (a dark night)
▶ DARK 2 (a dark colour)
▶ EVIL (dark forces)
▶ NEGATIVE (dark thoughts)

darken verb
▶ DARKEN

darkness noun
▶ DARKNESS

darling noun
▶ DARLING

darling adj.
▶ DEAR

darn noun
▶ REPAIR

dash noun
▶ ELEMENT 2

dash verb
▶ BEAT 1 (The boat was dashed against the rocks.)
▶ HURRY (I must dash.)
▶ dash sb's hopes THWART

dash off phrasal verb
▶ WRITE 2

data noun
▶ INFORMATION

date noun
▶ MEETING 2 (have a date with sb)
▶ PARTNER 2 (Who's your date for this evening?)
▶ TIME 1 (at a later date)
▶ up to date MODERN (up-to-date equipment)
▶ up to date USED TO STH (up to date with the issues)

date verb
▶ GO OUT

dated adj.
▶ OLD-FASHIONED

daub verb
▶ COVER

daughter noun
▶ SON

daunt verb
▶ DISCOURAGE 2

daunting adj.
▶ FRIGHTENING

dawdle verb
▶ TAKE YOUR TIME

dawn noun
▶ DAWN (wake at dawn)
▶ START (the dawn of civilization)

dawn on phrasal verb
▶ OCCUR TO SB

day noun
▶ DAY (Did you have a good day?)
▶ PERIOD (in Queen Victoria's day)
▶ in sb's day LIFE 2
▶ the old days PAST
▶ make sb's day PLEASE verb

daybreak noun
▶ DAWN

daydream noun
▶ TRANCE

daylight noun
▶ SUN

day off noun
▶ HOLIDAY 1

day out noun
▶ TRIP

daytime noun
▶ DAY

day-to-day adj.
▶ DAILY

daze noun
▶ TRANCE

dazed adj.
▶ CONFUSED 1

dazzle verb
▶ IMPRESS

dazzling adj.
▶ STRONG 3

dead adj.
▶ DEAD

dead heat noun
▶ DRAW

deadly adj.
▶ FATAL

deafening adj.
▶ LOUD

deal noun
▶ AGREEMENT 1 (cut a deal)
▶ do a deal NEGOTIATE

deal verb
▶ DISTRIBUTE (deal out the cards)
▶ SELL 2 (deal drugs)

dealer noun
▶ DEALER

deal in phrasal verb
▶ SELL 2

dealing noun
▶ COMMUNICATION (have dealings with sb)
▶ TRADE (honest/drug dealing)

deal with phrasal verb
▶ DEAL WITH SB/STH (deal with a problem)
▶ APPLY 2 (Her poems often deal with the subject of death.)
▶ NEGOTIATE (deal with companies all over Europe)

dean noun
▶ PROFESSOR

dear noun
▶ DARLING

dear adj.
▶ DEAR (my dear friend, Anna)
▶ dear old/little… SWEET (Dear old Sue!)

the **death penalty** noun
▶ EXECUTION

debacle noun
▶ DISASTER

debatable adj.
▶ CONTROVERSIAL

debate noun
▶ DEBATE (There has been much debate on the issue.)
▶ DISCUSSION (a debate in parliament)

debate verb
▶ TALK

debit noun
▶ DEBT

debit verb
▶ DISCOUNT

debrief verb
▶ QUESTION

debris noun
▶ REMAINS 1 (the debris from the plane crash)
▶ WASTE (clear away leaves and other garden debris)

debt noun
▶ DEBT

debunk verb
▶ DISPROVE

debut noun
▶ DEBUT

decade noun
▶ PERIOD

decamp verb
▶ GO AWAY

decant verb
▶ POUR

decanter noun
▶ BOTTLE

deceased verb
▶ DEAD

deceit noun
▶ FRAUD 1

deceitful adj.
▶ DISHONEST

deceive verb
▶ CHEAT

decent adj.
▶ DECENT (a decent meal)
▶ RESPECTABLE (decent people)
▶ RIGHT 2 (do the decent thing)

deception noun
▶ FRAUD 1

deceptive adj.
▶ MISLEADING

decide verb
▶ DECIDE (decide what to do)
▶ CHOOSE (decide between the two candidates)
▶ CONFIRM 3 (This news finally decided me.)
▶ DETERMINE (various factors decide sth)
▶ JUDGE 2 (The case will be decided by a jury.)

decided adj.
▶ MARKED

decimate verb
▶ DESTROY

decisive adj.
▶ ESSENTIAL

deck noun
▶ FLOOR 2 (the top deck of the ship)
▶ PORCH (sit out on the deck behind the house)

deck verb
▶ DECORATE

declaration noun
▶ STATEMENT

declare verb
▶ DECLARE

decline noun
▶ REDUCTION

decline verb
▶ FALL 1 (The number of tourists has declined.)
▶ REFUSE (decline an invitation)
▶ WORSEN (sb's health declines)

decorate verb
▶ DECORATE

decoration noun
▶ DECORATION (elaborate decoration on the carved wooden door)
▶ ORNAMENT (Christmas decorations)

decorative adj.
▶ DECORATIVE

decrease noun
▶ REDUCTION

decrease verb
▶ FALL 1 (Donations have decreased.)
▶ REDUCE (The dose was gradually decreased.)

decree noun
▶ ORDER

decree verb
▶ RULE 2

dedicate verb
▶ DEVOTE

dedicated adj.
▶ RELIABLE 1

deduce verb
▶ CONCLUDE

deduct verb
▶ DISCOUNT

deduction noun
▶ CONCLUSION

deed noun
▶ ACTION (good/evil deeds)
▶ DOCUMENT (title deeds)

deep adj.
▶ DEEP 1 (deep sympathy)
▶ DEEP 2 (a deep voice/sound)
▶ DARK 2 (a deep blue colour)
▶ SERIOUS 3 (a deep understanding)

deep-rooted adj.
▶ DEEP-SEATED

deep-seated adj.
▶ DEEP-SEATED

deface verb
▶ VANDALIZE

defame verb
▶ DISCREDIT

defeat noun
▶ VICTORY

defeat verb
▶ DEFEAT (defeat an army)
▶ CONFUSE (a question defeats sb)

defect noun
▶ DEFECT

defective adj.
▶ WRONG 2

defector noun
▶ TRAITOR

defence noun
▶ ARGUMENT 2 (conduct your own defence in court)
▶ PRECAUTION (sea defences)
▶ SECURITY (leap to sb's defence)

defenceless adj.
▶ VULNERABLE

defend verb
▶ EXPLAIN 2 (defend sb's behaviour)
▶ PROTECT (defend sth from attack)

defensive adj.
▶ PROTECTIVE

defer verb
▶ DELAY

deferential adj.
▶ POLITE

defiant adj.
▶ NAUGHTY

deficiency noun
▶ LACK

deficient adj.
▶ INADEQUATE

deficit noun
▶ LACK

define verb
▶ EXPLAIN 1 (define a term)
▶ LIST (define a task)

definite adj.
▶ CERTAIN (a definite answer)
▶ MARKED (a definite sign/feeling)

definition noun
▶ DEFINITION

definitive adj.
▶ FINAL

deflect verb
▶ FEND SB/STH OFF

deform verb
▶ TWIST

defraud verb
▶ DEFRAUD

defray verb
▶ PAY

defrost verb
▶ MELT

defy verb
▶ OPPOSE

degenerate verb
▶ WORSEN

degree noun
▶ LEVEL

dejected adj.
▶ DEPRESSED

delay verb
▶ DELAY (delay a decision)
▶ HOLD SB/STH UP (What could have delayed him?)
▶ TAKE YOUR TIME (Don't delay — call us today!)

delegate noun
▶ SPOKESMAN

delegate verb
▶ LEAVE 6

delegation noun
▶ COMMITTEE

delete verb
▶ DELETE

deliberate verb
▶ CONSIDER

deliberate adj.
▶ DELIBERATE

deliberation noun
▶ CONSIDERATION

delicate adj.
▶ FRAGILE (a delicate china cup)
▶ SENSITIVE 2 (the delicate matter of pay)
▶ WEAK (in delicate health)

delicious adj.
▶ DELICIOUS (delicious food)
▶ WONDERFUL (a delicious feeling)

delight noun
▶ JOY (squeal with delight)
▶ PLEASURE (culinary delights)

delight verb
▶ DELIGHT

delighted adj.
▶ GLAD

delightful adj.
▶ WONDERFUL

delight in phrasal verb
▶ ENJOY

delinquency noun
▶ CRIME 1

delinquent noun
▶ CRIMINAL

delinquent adj.
▶ ILLEGAL

delirious adj.
▶ HYSTERICAL

deliver verb
▶ KEEP 5 (deliver on your promises)
▶ TAKE 1 (deliver letters/goods)

delivery noun
▶ DELIVERY

delude verb
▶ MISLEAD

delusion noun
▶ ILLUSION

delve into phrasal verb
▶ INVESTIGATE

demand noun
▶ DEMAND (demand for a product)
▶ PRESSURE 1 (the demands of work)
▶ REQUEST (a demand for higher pay)
▶ **in demand** POPULAR adj.

demand verb
▶ DEMAND (demand an answer)
▶ ASK 1 ('Where were you?' he demanded.)

demanding adj.
▶ DIFFICULT 1

demo noun
▶ DEMONSTRATION (go on a demo)
▶ PRESENTATION (give sb a demo)

demolish verb
▶ DEMOLISH (demolish a building)
▶ DISPROVE (demolish a theory)

demonic adj.
▶ EVIL

demonstrate verb
▶ SHOW 1 (These results demonstrate...)
▶ SHOW 3 (demonstrate your commitment)

demonstration noun
▶ DEMONSTRATION (an anti-war demonstration)
▶ EVIDENCE (a clear demonstration of the truth of sth)
▶ EXPRESSION 1 (a demonstration of emotion/support/skill)
▶ PRESENTATION (a demonstration of the software)

demonstrative adj.
▶ SOCIABLE

demonstrator noun
▶ PROTESTER

demoralize verb
▶ DISCOURAGE 2

demoralized adj.
▶ DEPRESSED

demure adj.
▶ PRIM

denial noun
▶ DENIAL (a denial of responsibility)
▶ REFUSAL (a denial of human rights)

denomination noun
▶ RELIGION

denote verb
▶ MEAN 1

denounce verb
▶ BLAME

dense adj.
▶ HEAVY

density noun
▶ WEIGHT

denunciation noun
▶ CRITICISM

deny verb
▶ DENY (deny an accusation)
▶ REFUSE (deny sb access to sth)

depart verb
▶ LEAVE 1 (a train departs)
▶ LEAVE 3 (depart as chairman)

department noun
▶ DEPARTMENT

departure noun
▶ DEPARTURE 1 (his sudden departure)
▶ DEPARTURE 2 (a radical departure from tradition)

depend on/upon phrasal verb
▶ DEPEND ON/UPON STH (It depends on the circumstances.)
▶ TRUST (You can depend on him.)

depict verb
▶ PRESENT 2

depiction noun
▶ DESCRIPTION

deplete verb
▶ USE 2

deplorable adj.
▶ OUTRAGEOUS

deplore verb
▶ DISAPPROVE

deport *verb*
▸ EXPEL

depose *verb*
▸ REMOVE 2

deposit *noun*
▸ PAYMENT

deposit *verb*
▸ SAVE 3

depot *noun*
▸ STATION (a railroad depot)
▸ WAREHOUSE (an arms depot)

depress *verb*
▸ DISCOURAGE 2

depressed *adj.*
▸ DEPRESSED

depressing *adj.*
▸ NEGATIVE

depression *noun*
▸ GLOOM (a mood of depression)
▸ RECESSION (an economic depression)

deprivation *noun*
▸ POVERTY

deprived *adj.*
▸ POOR 1

depth *noun*
▸ LENGTH (the depth of the water)
▸ UNDERSTANDING (depth of knowledge)

deputize *verb*
▸ REPLACE 1

derail *verb*
▸ THWART

deranged *verb*
▸ MENTALLY ILL

derision *noun*
▸ CONTEMPT

derisive *adj.*
▸ CONTEMPTUOUS

derive from *phrasal verb*
▸ GET 2

derogatory *adj.*
▸ INSULTING

descend *verb*
▸ FALL 2 (a plane descends)
▸ SLOPE (a path descends)

descendant *noun*
▸ SON

descent *noun*
▸ FAMILY 3

describe *verb*
▸ DESCRIBE (describe what you saw)
▸ REGARD (describe sb as unusual)

description *noun*
▸ DESCRIPTION

descriptive *adj.*
▸ DESCRIPTIVE

desert *noun*
▸ DESERT

desert *verb*
▸ ABANDON (The villages had been deserted.)
▸ LEAVE 5 (Don't worry — I won't desert you.)

deserted *adj.*
▸ DESERTED

deserter *noun*
▸ TRAITOR

deserve *verb*
▸ DESERVE

deserving *adj.*
▸ WORTHY

design *noun*
▸ DESIGN (a design fault)
▸ DEVELOPMENT (the design of new products)
▸ PATTERN 2 (abstract designs)
▸ PLAN 2 (The designs were stolen.)

design *verb*
▸ DESIGN 1 (design a kitchen)

DESIGN 2 (instruments designed for use in cold conditions)
▸ PLAN (design a new course)

designate *verb*
▸ APPOINT (the man designated to succeed the president)
▸ CALL 1 (a designated nature reserve)

designer *noun*
▸ DESIGNER

desirable *adj.*
▸ BEST (a desirable objective)
▸ POPULAR (a desirable feature)

desire *noun*
▸ DESIRE (a desire to return)
▸ LOVE 1 (sexual desire)

desire *verb*
▸ WANT

desolate *adj.*
▸ BARE (wild and desolate terrain)
▸ LONELY (She felt utterly desolate.)

desolation *noun*
▸ DESPAIR

despair *noun*
▸ DESPAIR (close to despair)
▸ **in despair** DESPERATE

despair *verb*
▸ DESPAIR

despatch *verb*
▸ SEND 1 (despatch goods)
▸ SEND 2 (despatch troops)

desperate *adj.*
▸ DESPERATE (feel desperate)
▸ SERIOUS 1 (in desperate need)

desperately *adv.*
▸ VERY

desperation *noun*
▸ DESPAIR

despicable *adj.*
▸ DESPICABLE

despise *verb*
▸ HATE

despondency *noun*
▸ GLOOM

despondent *adj.*
▸ DEPRESSED

despot *noun*
▸ DICTATOR

destination *noun*
▸ STATION

destined *adj.*
▸ CERTAIN

destiny *noun*
▸ FUTURE (fulfil your destiny)
▸ LUCK (a sense of destiny)

destitute *adj.*
▸ POOR 1

destitution *noun*
▸ POVERTY

destroy *verb*
▸ DESTROY

destructive *adj.*
▸ HARMFUL

detach *verb*
▸ UNDO

detached *adj.*
▸ INDIFFERENT

detachment *noun*
▸ TEAM 1

detail *noun*
▸ INFORMATION

detail *verb*
▸ LIST

detailed *adj.*
▸ DETAILED

detain *verb*
▸ HOLD SB/STH UP (be detained at a meeting)
▸ JAIL (detain a suspect)

detainee *noun*
▸ HOSTAGE

detect *verb*
▸ NOTICE

detective *noun*
▸ POLICEMAN

detention centre *noun*
▸ PRISON

deteriorate *verb*
▸ WORSEN

determination *noun*
▸ DETERMINATION

determine *verb*
▸ DETERMINE (determined by social factors)
▸ DECIDE (A date has yet to be determined.)
▸ FIND 3 (determine the cause)

determined *adj.*
▸ DETERMINED 1 (determined to succeed)
▸ DETERMINED 2 (determined opposition)

detest *verb*
▸ HATE

detonate *verb*
▸ EXPLODE

detriment *noun*
▸ DAMAGE

detrimental *adj.*
▸ HARMFUL

devastate *verb*
▸ DESTROY

devastated *adj.*
▸ UPSET

devastating *adj.*
▸ DISASTROUS

develop *verb*
▸ DEVELOP 1 (develop from a small villlage into a thriving resort)
▸ DEVELOP 2 (develop products)
▸ BREAK OUT (a crisis was rapidly developing)
▸ SUFFER FROM STH (develop cancer)

developer *noun*
▸ DESIGNER

development *noun*
▸ DEVELOPMENT (product development)
▸ ESTATE (a housing development)
▸ EVENT 1 (the latest developments)
▸ PROGRESS (career development)

deviant *adj.*
▸ ABNORMAL

deviation *noun*
▸ DEPARTURE 2

device *noun*
▸ BOMB (a device explodes)
▸ TACTIC (a marketing device)
▸ TOOL (a labour-saving device)
▸ TRICK (a clever device)

devious *adj.*
▸ DISHONEST

devise *noun*
▸ COME UP WITH STH

devote *verb*
▸ DEVOTE

devoted *adj.*
▸ LOVING (devoted parents)
▸ **be devoted to sb** LOVE *verb*

devotee *noun*
▸ FAN

devote to *phrasal verb*
▸ SPEND 2

devotion *noun*
▸ LOVE 2

devour *verb*
▸ EAT

dew *noun*
▸ MOISTURE

dexterity *noun*
▸ SKILL 2

diagram *noun*
▸ DIAGRAM

dial *noun*
▸ BUTTON 1

dial *verb*
▸ CALL 2

dialect *noun*
▸ LANGUAGE 1

dialogue (also **dialog**) *noun*
▸ DISCUSSION

diameter *noun*
▸ LENGTH

diary *noun*
▸ RECORD (keep a secret diary)
▸ SCHEDULE (an appointments diary)

dice *verb*
▸ CUT 2

dictate *verb*
▸ DETERMINE (circumstances dictate that sth happens)
▸ QUOTE (dictate a letter)
▸ RULE 2 (dictate what sb should do)

dictate to *phrasal verb*
▸ DICTATE TO SB

dictator *noun*
▸ DICTATOR

dictatorial *adj.*
▸ REPRESSIVE

dictatorship *noun*
▸ REPRESSION

didactic *adj.*
▸ EDUCATIONAL

die *verb*
▸ DIE (die of cancer)
▸ **be dying for sth/to do sth** LONG

die out *phrasal verb*
▸ DISAPPEAR

diesel *noun*
▸ OIL

diet *noun*
▸ DIET (go on a diet)
▸ FOOD (a balanced diet)

differ *verb*
▸ DIFFER (The two languages differ in this respect.)
▸ DISAGREE (agree to differ)

difference *noun*
▸ DIFFERENCE (the differences between the two systems)
▸ DEBATE (a difference of opinion)
▸ REST 1 (a difference in price)

different *adj.*
▸ DIFFERENT (The room looks different without the furniture.)
▸ UNUSUAL (Her approach is certainly different.)

differentiate *verb*
▸ DISTINGUISH 1 (able to differentiate colours)
▸ DISTINGUISH 2 (What differentiates the two species?)

difficult *adj.*
▸ DIFFICULT 1 (a difficult task)
▸ DIFFICULT 2 (make life difficult for sb)
▸ PERVERSE (a difficult customer)

difficulty *noun*
▸ DIFFICULTY (have difficulty)
▸ PROBLEM (run into difficulties)

diffident *adj.*
▸ SHY

digit *noun*
▸ NUMBER 2

digital *adj.*
▸ ELECTRONIC

dignified *adj.*
▸ PROUD 1

dignitary *noun*
▸ VIP

dignity *noun*
▸ DIGNITY

digression *noun*
▸ DEPARTURE 2

dilemma *noun*
▸ MESS 2

diligent *adj.*
▸ CONSCIENTIOUS

dim *verb*
▸ DARKEN

dim *adj.*
▸ DIM 1 (a dim light/shape)
▸ DIM 2 (a dim room)

dimension *noun*
▸ ASPECT (the social dimension of unemployment)
▸ SIZE (the dimensions of the kitchen)

diminish *verb*
▸ FALL 1

diminutive *adj.*
▸ SHORT 2

dine *verb*
▸ DINE

dinghy *noun*
▸ BOAT

dingy *adj.*
▸ DIM 2

dinner *noun*
▸ DINNER

dip *verb*
▸ SLOPE (a road dips)
▸ SOAK (dip the brush in the paint)

dip into *phrasal verb*
▸ READ

diplomacy *noun*
▸ TACT

diplomat *noun*
▸ SPOKESMAN

dire *adj.*
▸ SERIOUS 1

direct *verb*
▸ AIM (direct a beam of light)
▸ FOCUS (direct a remark at sb)
▸ ORDER 1 (direct sb to do sth)
▸ RUN 2 (direct a project)
▸ TAKE 2 (direct sb somewhere)

direct *adj.*
▸ HONEST

direction *noun*
▸ DIRECTION (a new direction in party policy)
▸ GOVERNMENT 2 (the direction of a project)
▸ INSTRUCTIONS (give directions)
▸ WAY 3 (in the direction of the river)

directive *noun*
▸ ORDER

director *noun*
▸ MANAGER

directorate *noun*
▸ MANAGEMENT

directorship *noun*
▸ MANAGEMENT

directory *noun*
▸ LIST

dirt *noun*
▸ DIRT (covered in dirt)
▸ REPORT 4 (dish the dirt)
▸ SOIL (a dirt track)

dirty *adj.*
▸ DIRTY (dirty clothes/marks)
▸ CORRUPT (do the dirty work)

disability *noun*
▸ DISABILITY

disable *verb*
▸ DISABLE

disabled *adj.*
▸ DISABLED

disadvantage *noun*
▸ DISADVANTAGE

disadvantaged *adj.*
▸ POOR 1

disadvantageous *adj.*
▸ DIFFICULT 2

disagree *verb*
▸ DISAGREE

disagreement *noun*
▸ DEBATE

disallow *verb*
▸ REFUSE

disappear *verb*
▸ DISAPPEAR

disappoint *verb*
▸ DISAPPOINT (The movie disappointed us.)
▸ THWART (disappoint sb's hopes)

disappointed *adj.*
▸ DISAPPOINTED

disappointing *adj.*
▸ DISAPPOINTING

disappointment *noun*
▸ DISAPPOINTMENT (It was a great diappointment to us.)
▸ LOSER 2 (a disappointment as a singer)

disapproval *noun*
▸ CRITICISM

disapprove *verb*
▸ DISAPPROVE

disapproving *adj.*
▸ CRITICAL

disarray *noun*
▸ DISRUPTION

disaster *noun*
▸ DISASTER (Losing your job doesn't have to be a disaster.)
▸ CRISIS (a nuclear disaster)
▸ LOSER 2 (a disaster as a manager)

disastrous *adj.*
▸ DISASTROUS

disband *verb*
▸ DIVORCE

disbelief *noun*
▸ SCEPTICISM

disbelieve *verb*
▸ SUSPECT

disbelieving *adj.*
▸ SUSPICIOUS 1

disc *noun*
▸ CIRCLE

discard *verb*
▸ REMOVE 1

discern *verb*
▸ IDENTIFY

discernible *adj.*
▸ VISIBLE

discerning *adj.*
▸ SHREWD

discharge *noun*
▸ UNEMPLOYMENT

discharge *verb*
▸ FIRE (discharged from the army)
▸ LEAK (discharge chemicals into a river)

disciple *noun*
▸ SUPPORTER

discipline *noun*
▸ AREA 2 (scholars from various disciplines)
▸ CONTROL (strict discipline)

discipline *verb*
▸ PUNISH

disciplined *adj.*
▸ DISCIPLINED

disclaim *verb*
▸ DENY

disclaimer *noun*
▸ DENIAL

disclose *verb*
▸ REVEAL

disco *noun*
▸ PARTY 2

discomfort *noun*
▸ PAIN

disconcert *verb*
▸ SHAKE 4

disconcerting *adj.*
▸ WORRYING

disconnect *verb*
▸ TURN STH OFF

discontented *adj.*
▸ UNHAPPY 2

discontinue *verb*
▸ STOP 1

discount *verb*
▸ DISCOUNT (discounted prices)
▸ DISMISS (discount a possibility)

discourage *verb*
▸ DISCOURAGE 1 (discourage smoking)
▸ DISCOURAGE 2 (discouraged by failure)

discouraging *adj.*
▸ DISAPPOINTING

discourteous *adj.*
▸ RUDE

discover *verb*
▸ FIND 1 (He was discovered to be seriously ill.)
▸ FIND 2 (discover a leak)
▸ FIND 3 (discover a cure for cancer)

discoverer *noun*
▸ EXPLORER

discredit *noun*
▸ DISGRACE 2

discredit *verb*
▸ DISCREDIT (discredit the government)
▸ DISPROVE (discredit a theory)

discretion *noun*
▸ TACT

discretionary *adj.*
▸ VOLUNTARY 1

discriminating *adj.*
▸ SHREWD

discrimination *noun*
▸ DISCRIMINATION

discriminatory *adj.*
▸ BIASED

discursive *adj.*
▸ CONFUSED 2

discuss *verb*
▸ EXAMINE (This topic will be discussed in the next chapter.)
▸ TALK (discuss problems/plans)

discussion *noun*
▸ DISCUSSION (discussions between the two leaders)
▸ RESEARCH (further discussion of these issues in the next chapter)

disdain *noun*
▸ CONTEMPT

disdainful *adj.*
▸ CONTEMPTUOUS

disease *noun*
▸ DISEASE

disembark *verb*
▸ GET OUT

disenchanted *adj.*
▸ DISAPPOINTED

disenfranchise *verb*
▸ SUPPRESS 1

disengage *verb*
▸ FREE 1

disentangle *verb*
▸ FREE 1

disgrace *noun*
▸ DISGRACE 1 (a national disgrace)
▸ DISGRACE 2 (bring disgrace on your family)

disgraceful *adj.*
▸ OUTRAGEOUS

disgruntled *adj.*
▸ UNHAPPY 2

disguise *noun*
▸ COSTUME

disguise *verb*
▸ HIDE 1

disgust *verb*
▸ SHOCK

disgusting *adv.*
▸ DISGUSTING 1 (smell disgusting)
▸ DISGUSTING 2 (a disgusting thing to say)

dish *noun*
▸ PLATE

dishevelled (also **disheveled**) *adj.*
▸ SCRUFFY

dishonest *adj.*
▸ DISHONEST

dishonesty *noun*
▸ FRAUD 1

dishonour (also **dishonor**) *noun*
▸ DISGRACE 2

dishonourable (also **dishonorable**) *adj.*
▸ DESPICABLE

dish out *phrasal verb*
▸ DISTRIBUTE

dish up *phrasal verb*
▸ SERVE 1

disillusioned *adj.*
▸ DISAPPOINTED

disinformation *noun*
▸ PROPAGANDA

disinherit *verb*
▸ REJECT

disintegrate *verb*
▸ COLLAPSE 1

disinterested *adj.*
▸ OBJECTIVE

disjointed *adj.*
▸ CONFUSED 2

disk *noun*
▸ CIRCLE

dislike *noun*
▸ HATRED

dislike *verb*
▸ HATE

dislodge *verb*
▸ MOVE

disloyal *adj.*
▸ TREACHEROUS

disloyalty *noun*
▸ BETRAYAL

dismal *adj.*
▸ POOR 2

dismay *noun*
▸ SHOCK 1

dismay *verb*
▸ SHOCK

dismayed *adj.*
▸ UPSET

dismiss *verb*
▸ DISMISS (dismiss a suggestion)
▸ ABOLISH (Case dismissed!)
▸ FIRE (dismiss sb from their job)

dismissal *noun*
▸ UNEMPLOYMENT

dismount *verb*
▶ GET OUT

disobedient *adj.*
▶ NAUGHTY

disobey *verb*
▶ OPPOSE

disorder *noun*
▶ DISEASE (a blood disorder)
▶ MESS 1 (a state of disorder)
▶ TROUBLE 1 (public disorder)

disordered *adj.*
▶ UNTIDY

disorderly *adj.*
▶ WILD 1

disorganized *adj.*
▶ RANDOM

disorientated *adj.*
▶ CONFUSED 1

disoriented *adj.*
▶ CONFUSED 1

disown *verb*
▶ REJECT

disparaging *adj.*
▶ INSULTING

disparate *adj.*
▶ DIFFERENT

disparity *noun*
▶ DIFFERENCE

dispatch *verb*
▶ SEND 1 (dispatch goods)
▶ SEND 2 (dispatch troops)

dispense *verb*
▶ DISTRIBUTE (a machine dispenses drinks)
▶ GIVE 3 (dispense justice)

dispense with *phrasal verb*
▶ REMOVE 1

disperse *verb*
▶ DISPERSE

displace *verb*
▶ EXPEL

display *noun*
▶ EXHIBITION (a window display)
▶ EXPRESSION 1 (a display of affection/wealth/skill)
▶ PERFORMANCE (a firework display)
▶ on display VISIBLE *adj.*

display *verb*
▶ PRESENT 1 (display your work)
▶ SHOW 3 (display your knowledge)

displease *verb*
▶ ANNOY

displeased *adj.*
▶ UNHAPPY 2

displeasure *noun*
▶ FRUSTRATION

dispose of *phrasal verb*
▶ REMOVE 1

disposition *noun*
▶ PERSONALITY

disproportionate *adj.*
▶ EXCESSIVE

disprove *verb*
▶ DISPROVE

dispute *noun*
▶ DEBATE

dispute *verb*
▶ DISAGREE (disputed territory)
▶ DOUBT (dispute the figures)

disregard *verb*
▶ IGNORE

disrepair *noun*
▶ NEGLECT

disreputable *adj.*
▶ SORDID

disrepute *noun*
▶ DISGRACE 2

disrespect *noun*
▶ CONTEMPT

disrespectful *adj.*
▶ RUDE

disrupt *verb*
▶ DISRUPT

disruption *noun*
▶ DISRUPTION

disruptive *adj.*
▶ WILD 1

dissatisfied *adj.*
▶ UNHAPPY 2

dissent *noun*
▶ DEBATE

dissertation *noun*
▶ PAPER

dissident *noun*
▶ PROTESTER

dissimilar *adj.*
▶ DIFFERENT

dissolution *noun*
▶ DIVISION 1

dissolve *verb*
▶ DISAPPEAR (a crowd dissolves)
▶ MELT (dissolve in water)

dissuade *verb*
▶ DISCOURAGE 1

distance *noun*
▶ DIVISION 2 (the distance between his children and himself)
▶ **keep your distance** AVOID

distant *adj.*
▶ COLD 2 (He seemed distant.)
▶ PREVIOUS (the distant past)

distasteful *adj.*
▶ DISGUSTING 2

distinct *adj.*
▶ MARKED (a distinct smell of gas)
▶ PARTICULAR (two distinct groups)

distinction *noun*
▶ DIFFERENCE (draw a distinction)
▶ VALUE 1 (a writer of great distinction)

distinctive *adj.*
▶ UNIQUE

distinguish *verb*
▶ DISTINGUISH 1 (distinguish between right and wrong)
▶ DISTINGUISH 2 (what distinguishes humans from animals)

distinguishable *adj.*
▶ RECOGNIZABLE

distinguished *adj.*
▶ GREAT 2

distort *verb*
▶ DISTORT (distort the truth)
▶ TWIST (distort the shape of sth)

distraught *adj.*
▶ UPSET

distress *noun*
▶ DISTRESS

distress *verb*
▶ HURT 1

distressed *adj.*
▶ UPSET

distressing *adj.*
▶ PAINFUL 2

distribute *verb*
▶ DISTRIBUTE

distribution *noun*
▶ DELIVERY

distributor *noun*
▶ DEALER

district *noun*
▶ AREA 1 (a residential district)
▶ COUNTY (a postal district)

distrust *noun*
▶ SCEPTICISM

distrust *verb*
▶ SUSPECT

disturb *verb*
▶ INTERRUPT (Sorry to disturb you.)
▶ WORRY 2 (The letter disturbed me.)

disturbance *noun*
▶ DISRUPTION (try to avoid disturbance to local residents)
▶ TROUBLE 1 (serious disturbances in the streets)

disturbed *adj.*
▶ MENTALLY ILL (emotionally disturbed)
▶ WORRIED (disturbed by the news)

disturbing *adj.*
▶ WORRYING

disunity *noun*
▶ DIVISION 2

disuse *noun*
▶ NEGLECT

disused *adj.*
▶ DESERTED

ditch *noun*
▶ DITCH

dither *verb*
▶ PAUSE

diverge *verb*
▶ DIFFER

divergence *noun*
▶ DIFFERENCE

diverse *adj.*
▶ DIVERSE

diversify *verb*
▶ EXPAND 2

diversion *noun*
▶ DEPARTURE 2

diversity *noun*
▶ RANGE 1

divide *verb*
▶ DIVIDE 1 (cells divide)
▶ DIVIDE 2 (an issue divides people)
▶ ISOLATE (divide a mother from her child)
▶ SEPARATE 2 (A fence divides off the western side of the grounds.)
▶ SHARE (divide your money/time)

divided highway *noun*
▶ HIGHWAY

dividend *noun*
▶ PROFIT

division *noun*
▶ DIVISION 1 (a clear division between things)
▶ DIVISION 2 (a political division between people)
▶ DEPARTMENT (the sales division)

divorce *verb*
▶ DIVORCE (divorce your husband)
▶ SEPARATE 1 (Art should be divorced from politics.)
▶ **get divorced** DIVORCE

divorced *adj.*
▶ INDEPENDENT (divorced from reality)
▶ SINGLE (divorced people)

do *verb*
▶ DO 1 (do some research)
▶ DO 2 (do well at school)
▶ BEHAVE (Do as you're told.)
▶ GO 2 (do thousands of miles)
▶ LEARN (do biology/Shakespeare)
▶ MAKE 1 (do a drawing)
▶ PLAY 3 (do 'Hamlet')
▶ POSE (do an Irish accent)
▶ SOLVE 2 (do a puzzle/sum)
▶ STAY 2 (do Tokyo in three days)
▶ TAKE 9 (do drugs)
▶ **do something** ACT
▶ **have/be to do with sth** APPLY 2
▶ **be done** FINISH

do away with *phrasal verb*
▶ ABOLISH

docile *adj.*
▶ PASSIVE

dock *noun*
▶ PORT (The ship was in dock.)
▶ STAGE 2 (the prisoner in the dock)

dock *verb*
▶ DISCOUNT

doctor *noun*
▶ DOCTOR (call the doctor)
▶ SURGERY (go to the doctor's)

doctor's office *noun*
▶ SURGERY

doctrine *noun*
▶ VALUES

document *noun*
▶ DOCUMENT

document *verb*
▶ RECORD 1

documentation *noun*
▶ CERTIFICATE

dodge *verb*
▶ EVADE

dodgy *adj.*
▶ SUSPICIOUS 2

dogged *adj.*
▶ DETERMINED 2

doing *noun*
▶ ACTION

dole *noun*
▶ **on the dole** UNEMPLOYED *adj.*

dole out *phrasal verb*
▶ DISTRIBUTE

domain *noun*
▶ AREA 2

domed *adj.*
▶ CURVED

domestic *adj.*
▶ NATIONAL

dominant *adj.*
▶ POWERFUL

dominate *verb*
▶ TAKE OVER

dominion *noun*
▶ TERRITORY

don *noun*
▶ LECTURER

donate *verb*
▶ GIVE 5

donation *noun*
▶ GIFT

donor *noun*
▶ SPONSOR

doom *noun*
▶ FUTURE

door *noun*
▶ DOOR

doorway *noun*
▶ DOOR

dope *noun*
▶ DRUG 1

dope *verb*
▶ POISON

dork *noun*
▶ FOOL

dose *verb*
▶ TREAT 1

dossier *noun*
▶ DOCUMENT

dot *noun*
▶ PATCH (a red tie with blue dots)
▶ **on the dot** EARLY *adj.*

dote on/upon *phrasal verb*
▶ LOVE

double agent *noun*
▶ AGENT

doubt *noun*
▶ DOUBT 1 (a feeling of doubt)
▶ DOUBT 2 (express doubts)

▸ no doubt PROBABLY adv.
▸ in doubt UNCLEAR adj. (Its success is not in doubt.)
▸ in doubt UNSURE adj. (If in doubt, wear black.)
doubt verb
▸ DOUBT (I doubt it.)
▸ SUSPECT (I have no reason to doubt him.)
doubtful adj.
▸ UNLIKELY 1 (It is doubtful if he'll play tomorrow.)
▸ UNSURE (doubtful about sth)
doubtless adv.
▸ PROBABLY
do up phrasal verb
▸ TIE
dour adj.
▸ STERN
douse verb
▸ PUT STH OUT (douse the flames)
▸ SOAK (douse sth with petrol)
do well verb
▸ DO WELL
do without phrasal verb
▸ GO WITHOUT
down adj.
▸ DEPRESSED
downbeat adj.
▸ NEGATIVE
downfall noun
▸ OVERTHROW
downpour noun
▸ RAIN
downright adj.
▸ COMPLETE
downside noun
▸ DISADVANTAGE
downsize phrasal verb
▸ CUT 1
down-to-earth adj.
▸ REALISTIC 1
downturn noun
▸ REDUCTION
doze verb
▸ SLEEP
drab adj.
▸ DRAB
draft noun
▸ PLAN 2 (the original drafts for the building)
▸ WIND (sitting in a draft)
draft verb
▸ PREPARE 1
drag verb
▸ DRAG (I'm sorry to drag you all this way in the heat.)
▸ PULL 1 (Police dragged protesters away.)
▸ drag your feet TAKE YOUR TIME
drag on phrasal verb
▸ CONTINUE 1
drain noun
▸ DRAIN
drain verb
▸ DRAIN (leave the dishes to drain)
▸ CLEAR (drain and rinse the pasta)
▸ DRINK (drain your drink)
▸ PUMP (drain a tank)
▸ USE 2 (I felt drained of energy.)
drained adj.
▸ TIRED 1
drama noun
▸ DRAMA (a drama critic)
▸ PLAY (a costume drama)
dramatic adj.
▸ EXCITING (a dramatic event)
▸ SUDDEN (a dramatic change)
dramatist noun
▸ WRITER

dramatize verb
▸ EXAGGERATE
drape noun
▸ CURTAIN
drastic adj.
▸ SERIOUS 1
draught noun
▸ WIND
draught verb
▸ PREPARE 1
draw noun
▸ DRAW
draw verb
▸ DRAW (draw a picture)
▸ CLOSE 1 (draw the curtains)
▸ COME 1 (a car drew up)
▸ PULL 1 (draw up a chair)
▸ PUMP (draw water from a well)
▸ draw near COME 2
▸ draw attention to sb/sth POINT STH OUT
drawback noun
▸ DISADVANTAGE
drawing noun
▸ PICTURE
draw on/upon phrasal verb
▸ USE 1
drawstring noun
▸ BUTTON 2
draw up phrasal verb
▸ PREPARE 1
dread noun
▸ FEAR
dreadful adj.
▸ TERRIBLE 1 (dreadful weather)
▸ TERRIBLE 3 (a dreadful accident)
dream noun
▸ DREAM (Sweet dreams.)
▸ HOPE 2 (fulfil your dreams)
▸ TRANCE (walk around in a dream)
dreamer noun
▸ VISIONARY
dream up phrasal verb
▸ COME UP WITH STH
dreary adj.
▸ DIM 2
drench verb
▸ SOAK
drenched adj.
▸ WET 1
dress noun
▸ CLOTHES
dress verb
▸ WEAR (dressed in black)
▸ get dressed WEAR
dresser noun
▸ CUPBOARD
dressing noun
▸ BANDAGE
dribble verb
▸ TRICKLE
drift noun
▸ TREND
drift verb
▸ FLOAT (drift out to sea)
▸ WANDER (The crowd slowly drifted away.)
drifter noun
▸ TRAMP
drift off phrasal verb
▸ FALL ASLEEP
drill noun
▸ TRAINING
drink noun
▸ DRINK 1 (a drink of water)
▸ DRINK 2 (an alcoholic drink)
▸ SIP (take a drink from the glass)
drink verb
▸ DRINK

drip noun
▸ DROP
drip verb
▸ LEAK (a tap drips)
▸ TRICKLE (water drips)
drive noun
▸ AMBITION (He'll do very well — he has tremendous drive.)
▸ CAMPAIGN (an efficiency drive)
▸ FLIGHT (go for a drive)
drive verb
▸ DRIVE 1 (drive a car)
▸ DRIVE 2 (drive yourself too hard)
▸ FORCE (The urge to survive drove them on.)
▸ GO 2 (drive south)
▸ PUSH 1 (drive a peg into the ground)
▸ TAKE 2 (drive sb home)
▸ drive sb mad/crazy ANGER
▸ what sb is driving at MEAN 2
driver noun
▸ DRIVER
drizzle noun
▸ RAIN
drizzle verb
▸ RAIN
drone verb
▸ BUZZ
drop noun
▸ DROP (drops of water)
▸ REDUCTION (a drop in income)
▸ SIP (a drop of milk)
▸ SLOPE (a twenty-foot drop)
drop verb
▸ COLLAPSE 2 (work till you drop)
▸ EXCLUDE 2 (drop sb from a team)
▸ FALL 1 (the temperature drops)
▸ FALL 2 (drop to your death)
▸ SLOPE (The valley drops away.)
▸ STOP 1 (Let's drop the subject.)
drop in phrasal verb
▸ VISIT
drought noun
▸ HEAT 2
drove noun
▸ CROWD
drowsy adj.
▸ TIRED 1
drudgery noun
▸ WORK 1
drug noun
▸ DRUG 1 (take illegal drugs)
▸ DRUG 2 (prescribe drugs)
drug verb
▸ POISON
drum noun
▸ BARREL
drum verb
▸ KNOCK
drunk adj.
▸ DRUNK
drunken adj.
▸ DRUNK
dry adj.
▸ BORING (a dry debate)
▸ IRONIC (dry wit)
▸ SUNNY (hot, dry weather)
dry-clean verb
▸ CLEAN
dual carriageway noun
▸ HIGHWAY
dub verb
▸ CALL 1
dubious adj.
▸ CONTROVERSIAL (of dubious benefit)
▸ SUSPICIOUS 2 (dubious business practices)
▸ UNSURE (dubious about sth)

duck verb
▸ BEND (He has to duck to get through doors.)
▸ EVADE (duck out of sth)
duct noun
▸ PIPE
dude noun
▸ MAN 1
due noun
▸ RIGHT (give sb their due)
▸ RATE 2 (pay your dues)
due adj.
▸ RIGHT 2
dull adj.
▸ BORING (a dull life/place/game)
▸ CLOUDY (the dull afternoon light)
▸ PALE 2 (a dull red colour)
▸ QUIET 2 (a dull thud)
dumb adj.
▸ CRAZY (a dumb thing to do)
▸ SILENT (dumb amazement)
▸ STUPID (a dumb blonde)
dummy noun
▸ FAKE
dummy adj.
▸ SO-CALLED
dump verb
▸ LEAVE 5 (dump your girlfriend)
▸ PUT 1 (dump your bags)
▸ REMOVE 1 (dump toxic waste)
dumpy adj.
▸ SHORT 2
dupe noun
▸ VICTIM 2
dupe verb
▸ CHEAT
duplicate noun
▸ COPY 2
duplicate verb
▸ COPY (a duplicated letter)
▸ REPEAT 2 (duplicate work)
dusk noun
▸ NIGHT 2
dusky adj.
▸ PALE 2
dust noun
▸ DIRT (covered with dust)
▸ SOIL (a cloud of dust rises)
dust verb
▸ BRUSH
dust bowl noun
▸ DESERT
dusty adj.
▸ DIRTY
dutiful adj.
▸ GOOD 7
duty noun
▸ RESPONSIBILITY (It is my duty to report it to the police.)
▸ TASK (your professional duties)
▸ TAX (pay customs duties)
DVD noun
▸ FILM 1
dweller noun
▸ RESIDENT
dwelling noun
▸ HOME 1
dye verb
▸ PAINT
the dying noun
▸ PATIENT
dynamic adj.
▸ ENERGETIC (a dynamic personality)
▸ VARIABLE (a dynamic economy)
dynamism noun
▸ ENERGY 2
dynasty noun
▸ FAMILY 3

E e

eager *adj.*
► EAGER

earliest *adj.*
► FIRST

early *adj.*
► EARLY

earn *verb*
► DESERVE (a well-earned rest)
► GAIN 1 (earn respect)
► MAKE 3 (she is earning now)
► **earn a living** WORK 2

earnest *adj.*
► SERIOUS 2

earnings *noun*
► INCOME (average earnings)
► PROFIT (export earnings)

ear-splitting *adj.*
► LOUD

earth *noun*
► FLOOR 1 (under the earth)
► SOIL (freshly dug earth)
► WORLD (life on earth)

ease *noun*
► COMFORT

ease *verb*
► EASE (ease the pain)
► HELP 2 (ease access for the disabled)

easy *adj.*
► EASY 1 (Is it easy to make?)
► EASY 2 (anything for an easy life)
► FRIENDLY 2 (enjoy an easy relationship)

easy *adv.*
► **take it/things easy** REST *verb*

easy-going *adj.*
► CALM

eat *verb*
► EAT (eat your dinner)
► DINE (eat at a restaurant)
► **something to eat** SNACK *noun*

eavesdrop *verb*
► OVERHEAR

ebullient *adj.*
► LIVELY

eccentric *adj.*
► UNUSUAL

eccentricity *noun*
► MANNERISM

echo *verb*
► ECHO (Her footsteps echoed.)
► REPEAT 1 (echo sb else's views)

eclectic *adj.*
► DIVERSE

economic *adj.*
► ECONOMIC (economic growth)
► SUCCESSFUL 2 (it is not economic to do sth)

economical *adj.*
► CHEAP (These cars are economical to run.)
► SHORT 3 (an economical prose style)

economics *noun*
► FINANCE

ecosystem *noun*
► NATURE 2

ecstasy *noun*
► JOY

ecstatic *adj.*
► EXCITED

edge *noun*
► EDGE (the edge of the cliff)
► LEAD 2 (a slight edge over sb)
► **on edge** NERVOUS *adj.*

edge *verb*
► EDGE (She edged closer.)
► DECORATE (edged with lace)

edgy *adj.*
► NERVOUS

edit *verb*
► REVISE

edition *noun*
► CHAPTER

editor *noun*
► REPORTER

editorial *noun*
► ARTICLE

educate *verb*
► TEACH (be educated at Oxford)
► TRAIN 1 (be educated on healthy eating)

educated *adj.*
► INFORMED

education *noun*
► EDUCATION

educational *adj.*
► EDUCATIONAL

educationalist *noun*
► TEACHER

educator *noun*
► TEACHER

eerie *adj.*
► FRIGHTENING

effect *noun*
► EFFECT (have an effect on sth)
► **put sth into effect** APPLY *verb* 1

effect *verb*
► ACHIEVE

effective *adj.*
► SUCCESSFUL 1

efficiency *noun*
► EFFICIENCY

efficient *adj.*
► EFFICIENT

effort *noun*
► EFFORT (put effort into sth)
► ATTEMPT (make an effort)

effortless *adj.*
► EASY 1

egg on *phrasal verb*
► ENCOURAGE 2

ego *noun*
► DIGNITY (boost your ego)
► MIND (Part of the ego is unconscious.)

egocentric *adj.*
► SELFISH

egoism *noun*
► PRIDE

egotistical *adj.*
► SELFISH

eject *verb*
► EVACUATE

elaborate *adj.*
► COMPLEX

elapse *verb*
► GO BY

elastic *adj.*
► FLEXIBLE 2

elated *adj.*
► EXCITED

elbow *verb*
► PUSH 2

elderly *adj.*
► OLD 2

elect *verb*
► APPOINT (elect a government)
► DECIDE (elect to stay)

election *noun*
► ELECTION (a presidential election)
► CHOICE 1 (her election to the post)

the electric chair *noun*
► EXECUTION

electronic *adj.*
► ELECTRONIC

elegance *noun*
► STYLE

elegant *adj.*
► ELEGANT

element *noun*
► ELEMENT 1 (have all the elements of a soap opera)
► ELEMENT 2 (an element of risk)
► MATERIAL (a chemical element)
► WEATHER (brave the elements)

elementary *adj.*
► FUNDAMENTAL

eliminate *verb*
► EXCLUDE 1 (eliminate two suspects from the investigation)
► KILL (eliminate your opponents)
► REMOVE 1 (eliminate toxins from the body)

elite *noun*
► ELITE

elite *adj.*
► TOP

elitist *adj.*
► EXCLUSIVE

eloquent *adj.*
► ARTICULATE

elude *verb*
► ESCAPE

email *noun*
► LETTER

emancipate *verb*
► RELEASE

embargo *noun*
► BAN

embark *verb*
► GET IN

embark on/upon *phrasal verb*
► BEGIN

embarrass *verb*
► EMBARRASS

embarrassed *adj.*
► EMBARRASSED

embellish *verb*
► EXAGGERATE

embezzle *verb*
► STEAL

embezzlement *noun*
► THEFT

embittered *adj.*
► BITTER 2

emblem *noun*
► LOGO

embodiment *noun*
► EXAMPLE 2

embody *verb*
► REPRESENT 2

embrace *adj.*
► HUG (She embraced her son.)
► INCLUDE 1 (The talks embraced a wide range of issues.)

emerge *verb*
► EMERGE (emerging markets)
► APPEAR (emerge from the darkness)
► TURN OUT (new evidence emerges)

emergency *noun*
► CRISIS

emigrant *noun*
► REFUGEE

emigrate *verb*
► LEAVE 2

eminent *adj.*
► GREAT 2

emotion *noun*
► EMOTION

emotional *adj.*
► EMOTIONAL (emotional support)
► INTENSE (an emotional reaction)

empathize *verb*
► UNDERSTAND 2

empathy *noun*
► BOND

emperor *noun*
► KING

emphasis *noun*
► PRIORITY

emphasize *verb*
► STRESS

empire *noun*
► REPUBLIC

empirical *adj.*
► PRACTICAL

employ *verb*
► EMPLOY (How many people does the company employ?)
► USE 1 (employ tactics/force)
► **be employed** WORK 2

employee *noun*
► WORKER 1

employer *noun*
► MANAGER

employment *noun*
► WORK 2

empower *verb*
► ALLOW

empty *verb*
► CLEAR (empty out your pockets)
► DRAIN (The streets emptied.)

empty *adj.*
► EMPTY

emulate *verb*
► FOLLOW 4

enable *verb*
► ENABLE

enchant *verb*
► DELIGHT

enchanted *adj.*
► MAGIC

encircle *verb*
► SURROUND

enclave *noun*
► TERRITORY

enclose *verb*
► SURROUND

encompass *verb*
► INCLUDE 1

encounter *noun*
► MEETING 2

encounter *verb*
► HAVE 3 (encounter difficulties)
► MEET 2 (encounter sb)

encourage *verb*
► ENCOURAGE 1 (be encouraged by the news)
► ENCOURAGE 2 (encourage people to cycle)
► ENCOURAGE 3 (encourage violent behaviour/debate)

encouraging *adj.*
► PROMISING

encroach *verb*
► INTERFERE

end *noun*
► END (the end of the week)
► ASPECT (the marketing end of the business)
► EDGE (the end of the road/table)
► TARGET (for your own ends)
► **on end** UPRIGHT *adj.*

end *verb*
► END

endanger *verb*
► THREATEN 2

endangered *adj.*
► VULNERABLE

endearing *adj.*
► SWEET

endeavour (also **endeavor**) noun
▶ EFFORT

endeavour (also **endeavor**) verb
▶ TRY 1

ending noun
▶ END

endless adj.
▶ ENDLESS

endorse verb
▶ RECOMMEND 2

endorsement noun
▶ ENDORSEMENT

endow verb
▶ FUND (endow a scholarship)
▶ **be endowed with sth** HAVE 2

endowment noun
▶ INVESTMENT

endurance noun
▶ STRENGTH

endure verb
▶ STAND 2

enduring adj.
▶ PERMANENT

end-user noun
▶ CUSTOMER

enemy noun
▶ ENEMY

energetic adj.
▶ ENERGETIC

energy noun
▶ ENERGY 1 (nuclear/solar energy)
▶ ENERGY 2 (full of energy)
▶ EFFORT (your creative energies)

enforce verb
▶ APPLY 1

engage verb
▶ EMPLOY (engage sb's services)
▶ FIGHT 1 (engage the enemy)

engaged adj.
▶ BUSY 1

engage in phrasal verb
▶ JOIN

engagement noun
▶ INVOLVEMENT (engagement with the problems of the inner city)
▶ MEETING 2 (an official engagement)

engaging adj.
▶ NICE 2

engine noun
▶ MACHINE

engineer noun
▶ DESIGNER

engineer verb
▶ DESIGN 1 (The car is beautifully engineered.)
▶ MANIPULATE (engineer sb's downfall)

engrossed adj.
▶ INTERESTED

enhance verb
▶ IMPROVE 1

enigma noun
▶ MYSTERY

enjoy verb
▶ ENJOY (enjoy a party)
▶ HAVE 2 (enjoy good health)
▶ **enjoy yourself** PLAY 1

enjoyable adj.
▶ NICE 1

enjoyment noun
▶ FUN

enlarge verb
▶ EXPAND 1

enlighten verb
▶ TELL 1

enlightened adj.
▶ TOLERANT

enlightening adj.
▶ INFORMATIVE

enlightenment noun
▶ KNOWLEDGE

enmity noun
▶ TENSION

enormous adj.
▶ HUGE

enquire verb
▶ ASK 1

enquire into phrasal verb
▶ INVESTIGATE

enquiry noun
▶ INVESTIGATION (a murder enquiry)
▶ QUESTION (receive enquiries about a job)
▶ RESEARCH (a line of enquiry)

enrage verb
▶ ANGER

enraged adj.
▶ FURIOUS

enrich verb
▶ IMPROVE 1

enrol verb
▶ LET SB IN

ensue verb
▶ FOLLOW 2

ensuing adj.
▶ RELATED

ensure verb
▶ ENSURE

entail verb
▶ MEAN 3

enter verb
▶ ENTER (enter a room)
▶ JOIN (enter politics)
▶ PLAY 2 (enter a competition)
▶ RECORD 1 (enter the details in a file)

enter into phrasal verb
▶ JOIN

enterprise noun
▶ COMPANY (a state-owned enterprise)
▶ PROJECT (a new enterprise)
▶ TRADE (private enterprise)

entertain verb
▶ ENTERTAIN (entertain sb with amusing stories)
▶ GREET (entertain guests)

entertainer noun
▶ ACTOR

entertaining adj.
▶ FUNNY

entertainment noun
▶ ENTERTAINMENT (live entertainment)
▶ INTEREST 2 (local entertainments)

enthral (also **enthrall**) verb
▶ DELIGHT

enthusiast noun
▶ FAN

enthusiastic adj.
▶ EAGER

entice verb
▶ TEMPT

entire adj.
▶ WHOLE

entirely adv.
▶ QUITE 2

entitle verb
▶ ALLOW (entitled to a refund)
▶ CALL 1 (a song entitled 'Crazy')

entitlement noun
▶ RIGHT

entity noun
▶ THING 2

entrance noun
▶ ACCESS (an entrance fee)

▶ ARRIVAL 1 (his entrance on the scene)
▶ DOOR (the main entrance)

entrance verb
▶ DELIGHT

entrant noun
▶ ARRIVAL 2 (university entrants)
▶ CANDIDATE (the winning entrant)

entrenched adj.
▶ DEEP-SEATED

entrepreneur noun
▶ EXECUTIVE

entrust verb
▶ LEAVE 6

entry noun
▶ ACCESS (gain entry)
▶ HALL 2 (the entry to the house)

entryway noun
▶ HALL 2

envelope noun
▶ ENVELOPE

enviable adj.
▶ POPULAR

environment noun
▶ ENVIRONMENT (the home/working environment)
▶ NATURE 2 (protect the environment)

envisage verb
▶ IMAGINE

envision verb
▶ IMAGINE

envy noun
▶ JEALOUSY

eon noun
▶ YEARS

epic noun
▶ LEGEND 1

epidemic noun
▶ WAVE 3

episode noun
▶ CHAPTER (tonight's episode of 'Brothers and Sisters')
▶ EVENT 1 (episodes in the novel)

epitome noun
▶ EXAMPLE 2

epitomize verb
▶ REPRESENT 2

epoch noun
▶ PERIOD

equal noun
▶ PEER

equal verb
▶ BE (2x plus y equals 7)
▶ COMPARE 2 (unlikely to be equalled)

equal adj.
▶ EQUAL (equal parts)
▶ REASONABLE (equal rights)

equality noun
▶ JUSTICE

equip verb
▶ EQUIP 1 (equip yourself with a map)
▶ EQUIP 2 (equip students for a career in nursing)

equipment noun
▶ EQUIPMENT

equitable adj.
▶ REASONABLE

equity noun
▶ JUSTICE

equivalence noun
▶ SIMILARITY

equivalent noun
▶ EQUIVALENT

equivalent adj.
▶ EQUIVALENT

era noun
▶ PERIOD

eradicate verb
▶ ERADICATE

erase verb
▶ DELETE

erect verb
▶ BUILD

erect adj.
▶ UPRIGHT

erode verb
▶ UNDERMINE

errand noun
▶ TASK

error noun
▶ MISTAKE 1 (an error of judgement)
▶ MISTAKE 2 (a grammatical error)

erupt verb
▶ BREAK OUT (violence erupts)
▶ EXPLODE (a volcano erupts)

eruption noun
▶ EXPLOSION

escalate verb
▶ RISE

escape verb
▶ ESCAPE (escape death)
▶ LEAK (prevent heat escaping)

escort verb
▶ TAKE 2

essay noun
▶ PAPER

essence noun
▶ NATURE 1 (the essence of France)
▶ **of the essence** ESSENTIAL adj.

essential noun
▶ BASICS (the essentials of English grammar)
▶ NEED (the bare essentials)

essential adj.
▶ ESSENTIAL (Experience is essential for this job.)
▶ FUNDAMENTAL (the essential character of the town)

establish verb
▶ ESTABLISH (establish a company)
▶ FIND 3 (establish the facts)

establishment noun
▶ AUTHORITIES (kicking against the establishment)
▶ INTRODUCTION 1 (the establishment of a new college)

estate noun
▶ ESTATE (a housing estate)
▶ LAND 1 (a 300-acre estate)
▶ LEGACY (Her estate was left to her daughter.)

esteem noun
▶ ADMIRATION

esteem verb
▶ RESPECT

estimate noun
▶ ESTIMATE (a rough estimate of the size)
▶ VALUATION (get estimates for the repair work)

estimate verb
▶ ESTIMATE

estimation noun
▶ ASSESSMENT

estranged adj.
▶ SINGLE (his estranged wife)
▶ **be/become estranged** DIVIDE 2 verb

estrangement noun
▶ DIVISION 2

eternal adj.
▶ PERMANENT

an eternity noun
▶ YEARS

ethic noun
▶ PRINCIPLE 1 (a code of ethics)
▶ VALUES (a work ethic)

ethical *adj.*
▶ GOOD 5 (ethical practices)
▶ MORAL (ethical principles)

ethnic *adj.*
▶ CULTURAL

ethnic group *noun*
▶ PEOPLE 2

ethos *noun*
▶ VALUES

etiquette *noun*
▶ RESPECT

eulogy *noun*
▶ TRIBUTE

euphoria *noun*
▶ JOY

euphoric *adj.*
▶ EXCITED

euthanasia *noun*
▶ MURDER

evacuate *verb*
▶ EVACUATE (police evacuate people/a building)
▶ ABANDON (Locals were told to evacuate.)

evacuee *noun*
▶ REFUGEE

evade *verb*
▶ EVADE (evade taxes/the issue)
▶ ESCAPE (evade capture)

evaluate *verb*
▶ JUDGE 1

evaluation *noun*
▶ ASSESSMENT

even *adj.*
◀ CLOSE (The scores were even.)
▶ STEADY (an even pace)
▶ **get even** FIGHT BACK *phrasal verb*

even-handed *adj.*
▶ REASONABLE

evening *noun*
▶ NIGHT 2

event *noun*
▶ EVENT 1 (a sequence of events)
▶ EVENT 2 (a social event)
▶ RACE (sporting events)

eventful *adj.*
▶ BUSY 2

eventual *adj.*
▶ LAST 1

eventuality *noun*
▶ EVENT 1

everyday *adj.*
▶ DAILY

evict *verb*
▶ EVACUATE

evidence *noun*
▶ EVIDENCE (The evidence shows/suggests/indicates that…)
▶ **turn King's/Queen's/State's evidence** TELL *verb* 2

evidence *verb*
▶ CONFIRM 1

evident *adj.*
◀ CLEAR 1

evil *noun*
▶ EVIL (the forces of evil)
▶ DISGRACE 1 (the evils of drugs)

evil *adj.*
▶ EVIL

evocation *noun*
▶ DESCRIPTION

evoke *verb*
▶ REMIND SB OF SB/STH

evolve *verb*
▶ DEVELOP 1 (evolve into a major company)
▶ DEVELOP 2 (evolve your own way of working)
▶ TURN 2 (species evolve)

ex- *combining form*
▶ FORMER *adj.*

exacerbate *verb*
▶ WEAKEN

exact *verb*
▶ DEMAND

exact *adj.*
▶ EXACT (an exact copy)
▶ VERY (at that exact moment)

exaggerate *verb*
▶ EXAGGERATE

exalted *adj.*
▶ GREAT 2

exam *noun*
▶ TEST 2

examination *noun*
▶ INSPECTION (a medical examination)
▶ RESEARCH (careful examination of the evidence)
▶ TEST 2 (college examinations)

examine *verb*
▶ EXAMINE (examine an idea)
▶ CHECK 1 (a doctor examines sb)
▶ TEST 2 (examine students)

examiner *noun*
▶ INSPECTOR (the official examiner of electronic voting systems)
▶ JUDGE 2 (exam papers marked by an external examiner)

example *noun*
▶ EXAMPLE 1 (give an example)
▶ EXAMPLE 2 (Her courage is an example to us all.)
▶ INFLUENCE (follow sb's example)

exasperate *verb*
▶ ANNOY

exasperated *verb*
▶ ANNOYED

exasperation *noun*
▶ FRUSTRATION

excellence *noun*
▶ VALUE 1

excellent *adj.*
▶ EXCELLENT

exception *noun*
▶ EXCEPTION (Most families were poor and mine was no exception.)
▶ **take exception to sth** RESENT *verb*

exceptional *adj.*
▶ REMARKABLE (exceptional talent)
▶ SPECIAL (in exceptional circumstances)

excerpt *noun*
▶ SCENE

excess *noun*
▶ REST 1

excess *adj.*
▶ EXCESS

excessive *adj.*
▶ EXCESSIVE

exchange *noun*
▶ EXCHANGE (a fair exchange)
▶ DISCUSSION (a heated exchange)

exchange *verb*
▶ CASH (exchange currency)
▶ REPLACE 2 (exchange ideas)

excitable *adj.*
▶ MOODY

excite *verb*
▶ STIMULATE

excited *adj.*
▶ EXCITED

excitement *noun*
▶ EXCITEMENT

exciting *adj.*
▶ EXCITING

exclaim *verb*
▶ CALL 3

exclude *verb*
▶ EXCLUDE 1 (exclude sugar from your diet)
▶ EXCLUDE 2 (exclude sb from a club)

exclusive *adj.*
▶ EXCLUSIVE (an exclusive school)
▶ OWN (an exclusive interview)
▶ **mutually exclusive** INCONSISTENT

excommunicate *verb*
▶ EXCLUDE 2

excruciating *adj.*
▶ PAINFUL 1

excursion *noun*
▶ TRIP

excuse *noun*
▶ REASON

excuse *verb*
▶ EXEMPT (be excused from giving evidence)
▶ FORGIVE (excuse the mess)

execute *verb*
▶ KILL

execution *noun*
▶ EXECUTION

executive *noun*
▶ EXECUTIVE (a business executive)
▶ GOVERNMENT 1 (the powers of the executive)
▶ MANAGEMENT (the union's executive)

exemplary *adj.*
▶ PERFECT

exemplify *verb*
▶ REPRESENT 2

exempt *verb*
▶ EXEMPT

exercise *noun*
▶ ASSIGNMENT (grammar exercises)
▶ PROJECT (a public relations exercise)
▶ SPORT (get regular exercise)
▶ USE (the exercise of power)

exercise *verb*
▶ TRAIN 2 (exercise regularly)
▶ USE 1 (exercise care)

exert *verb*
▶ USE 1

exertion *noun*
▶ EFFORT

exhaust *noun*
▶ SMOKE

exhaust *verb*
▶ TIRE (The walk exhausted her.)
▶ USE 2 (exhaust a supply)

exhausted *adj.*
▶ TIRED 1

exhaustive *adj.*
▶ DETAILED

exhibit *noun*
▶ EXHIBITION

exhibition *noun*
▶ EXHIBITION (the Picasso exhibition)
▶ EXPRESSION 1 (an exhibition of skill/bad manners)

exhilarated *adj.*
▶ EXCITED

exhilarating *adj.*
▶ EXCITING

exhilaration *noun*
▶ EXCITEMENT

exhort *verb*
▶ ENCOURAGE 2

exile *noun*
▶ REFUGEE

exile *verb*
▶ EXPEL

exist *verb*
▶ EXIST

existence *noun*
▶ LIFE 1 (come into existence)
▶ LIFE 3 (a miserable existence)

exit *noun*
▶ DEPARTURE 1 (a quick exit)
▶ DOOR (a fire exit)
▶ JUNCTION (the exit for Trento)

exit *verb*
▶ LEAVE 1

exit poll *noun*
▶ ELECTION

exonerate *verb*
▶ ACQUIT

exorbitant *adj.*
▶ HIGH 1

expand *verb*
▶ EXPAND 1 (Student numbers are expanding.)
▶ EXPAND 2 (expand a business)

expanse *noun*
▶ STRETCH

expatriate *noun*
▶ REFUGEE

expect *verb*
▶ EXPECT (expect sth to happen)
▶ DEMAND (what is expected of you)
▶ SUPPOSE (I expect so.)
▶ **to be expected** PREDICTABLE 1

expectancy *noun*
▶ HOPE 1

expectant *adj.*
▶ OPTIMISTIC

expectation *noun*
▶ EXPECTATION (a general expectation that he would win)
▶ HOPE 2 (exceed your expectations)

expedition *noun*
▶ TRIP

expel *verb*
▶ EXPEL (expel illegal immigrants)
▶ EXCLUDE 2 (expel sb from school)

expend *verb*
▶ USE 2

expendable *adj.*
▶ UNNECESSARY

expenditure *noun*
▶ COSTS

expense *noun*
▶ COSTS (travel expenses)
▶ PRICE (do sth at great expense)

expensive *adj.*
▶ EXPENSIVE

experience *noun*
▶ EVENT 1 (a bad experience)
▶ KNOWLEDGE (previous experience of this type of work)

experience *verb*
▶ FEEL (experience pain)
▶ HAVE 3 (experience problems)

experienced *adj.*
▶ EXPERIENCED (an experienced teacher)
▶ SOPHISTICATED (She's young and not very experienced.)

experiment *noun*
▶ TEST 1

experiment *verb*
▶ TEST 1

experimental *adj.*
▶ EXPERIMENTAL (experimental theatre)
▶ PRACTICAL (experimental data)

expert *noun*
▶ EXPERT

expert *adj.*
▶ IMPRESSIVE

expertise noun
▶ SKILL 2

explain verb
▶ EXPLAIN 1 (explain how sth works)
▶ EXPLAIN 2 (explain your behaviour)

explanation noun
▶ REASON

explanatory adj.
▶ DESCRIPTIVE

explicit adj.
▶ CLEAR 2

explode verb
▶ EXPLODE (a bomb explodes)
▶ BANG 1 (thunder explodes)
▶ DISPROVE (explode a theory)

exploit verb
▶ EXPLOIT

exploration noun
▶ RESEARCH

explore verb
▶ INVESTIGATE (explore these ideas)
▶ TOUR (explore the city)

explorer noun
▶ EXPLORER

explosion noun
▶ EXPLOSION

explosive noun
▶ BOMB

exponent noun
▶ ADVOCATE

export verb
▶ SELL 2

expose verb
▶ EXPOSE (exposed to ridicule)
▶ REVEAL (expose sb as a liar)
▶ SHOW 2 (Miles of sand are exposed at low tide.)

exposed adj.
▶ BARE (an exposed position on the top of a hill)
▶ VULNERABLE (feeling exposed and vulnerable)

expound verb
▶ EXPLAIN 1

express verb
▶ SAY 2

express adj.
▶ CLEAR 2 (sb's express wish)
▶ FAST (an express train/service)

expression noun
▶ EXPRESSION 1 (expressions of sympathy)
▶ EXPRESSION 2 (a worried expression on her face)
▶ WORD (a slang expression)

expressionless adj.
▶ BLANK

exquisite adj.
▶ BEAUTIFUL 2

extend verb
▶ EXPAND 1 (extend a house)
▶ LEAD 3 (The garden extends to the river.)
▶ MAINTAIN 1 (extend the deadline)
▶ OFFER 1 (extend an invitation)

extended adj.
▶ LONG

extensive adj.
▶ LARGE (extensive grounds)
▶ WIDE 1 (extensive research)

extent noun
▶ LEVEL (the extent of his knowledge)
▶ SIZE (the full extent of the beach)
▶ **to some extent** PARTLY adv.

exterminate verb
▶ DESTROY

extermination noun
▶ MASSACRE

external adj.
▶ FOREIGN

extinguish verb
▶ PUT STH OUT

extortion noun
▶ CORRUPTION

extortionate adj.
▶ HIGH 1

extract noun
▶ SCENE

extract verb
▶ PULL 2 (extract a tooth)
▶ PUMP (extract oil/minerals)

extradite verb
▶ EXPEL

extraneous adj.
▶ IRRELEVANT

extraordinary adj.
▶ REMARKABLE (an extraordinary achievement)
▶ SPECIAL (an extraordinary general meeting)
▶ SURPRISING (What an extraordinary thing to say!)

extrapolate verb
▶ ESTIMATE

extravagant adj.
▶ EXTRAVAGANT

extreme adj.
▶ MAXIMUM (extreme pressure)
▶ RADICAL (extreme views)
▶ SERIOUS 1 (in extreme circumstances)

extremely adv.
▶ VERY

extrovert adj.
▶ SOCIABLE

exuberant adj.
▶ LIVELY

eye noun
▶ **not see eye to eye with sb** DISAGREE verb
▶ **turn a blind eye** IGNORE verb
▶ **keep an eye on sb/sth** MONITOR verb
▶ **screw your eyes up** TIGHTEN verb

eyewitness noun
▶ WITNESS

F f

fable noun
▶ LEGEND 1

fabric noun
▶ FABRIC (furnishing fabric)
▶ STRUCTURE (the fabric of society)

fabricate verb
▶ INVENT

fabrication noun
▶ LIE

fabulous adj.
▶ GREAT 1

façade noun
▶ PRETENCE

face noun
▶ EXPRESSION 2 (sb's face lights up)
▶ **screw your face up** TIGHTEN verb

face verb
▶ FACE (face a financial crisis)
▶ ACCEPT (face facts)

face up to phrasal verb
▶ ACCEPT

facilitate verb
▶ HELP 2

facilities noun
▶ FACILITIES

facsimile noun
▶ COPY 2

fact noun
▶ FACT (a story based on fact)

▶ INFORMATION (some basic facts about healthy eating)

faction noun
▶ PARTY 1

factor noun
▶ FACTOR

factory noun
▶ FACTORY

factual adj.
▶ RELIABLE 2

fad noun
▶ FASHION

fade verb
▶ DISAPPEAR

fail verb
▶ FAIL 1 (fail to attend)
▶ FAIL 2 (fail in your attempt)
▶ FAIL 3 (fail an exam)
▶ BREAK 2 (your brakes fail)
▶ CLOSE 2 (a business fails)
▶ DISAPPOINT (fail your family)
▶ WORSEN (sb's health is failing)

failed adj.
▶ UNSUCCESSFUL

failing noun
▶ WEAKNESS 1 (the failings of the economic system)
▶ WEAKNESS 2 (aware of their own failings)

failure noun
▶ FAILURE (the failure of a plan)
▶ DISASTER (a costly failure)
▶ LOSER 2 (I feel such a failure.)

faint verb
▶ COLLAPSE 2

faint adj.
▶ DIM 1 (a faint glimmer of light)
▶ DIZZY (feel faint)
▶ QUIET 2 (faint sounds)

fair noun
▶ EXHIBITION

fair adj.
▶ FINE (a fair achievement)
▶ REASONABLE (a fair wage/trial)

fairly adv.
▶ QUITE 1

fairness noun
▶ JUSTICE

fair play noun
▶ JUSTICE

fairy tale noun
▶ LEGEND 1

faith noun
▶ FAITH (show/lose faith in sb/sth)
▶ RELIGION (people of different faiths)

faithful adj.
▶ RELIABLE 1

fake noun
▶ FAKE

fake verb
▶ PRETEND

fake adj.
▶ ARTIFICIAL 1 (a fake fur jacket)
▶ SO-CALLED (a fake accent)

fall noun
▶ OVERTHROW (the rise and fall of the Roman Empire)
▶ REDUCTION (a fall in popularity)

fall verb
▶ FALL 1 (the temperature falls)
▶ FALL 2 (fall into the river)
▶ FALL 3 (slip and fall on the ice)
▶ RAIN (rain/snow falls)

fallacy noun
▶ ILLUSION

fall asleep verb
▶ FALL ASLEEP

fall back on phrasal verb
▶ USE 1

fall down phrasal verb
▶ FALL 3

fall guy noun
▶ VICTIM 2

fall out phrasal verb
▶ ARGUE

fall over phrasal verb
▶ FALL 3

fall through phrasal verb
▶ FAIL 2

false adj.
▶ FALSE (false modesty)
▶ ARTIFICIAL 1 (false teeth)
▶ SO-CALLED (a false passport)
▶ WRONG 1 (a false name)
▶ **false impression** ILLUSION noun

falsehood noun
▶ LIE

falsify verb
▶ DISTORT

faltering adj.
▶ HESITANT

fame noun
▶ FAME

famed adj.
▶ FAMOUS

familiar with adj.
▶ USED TO STH

family noun
▶ FAMILY 1 (a family of four)
▶ FAMILY 2 (the support of family and friends)
▶ FAMILY 3 (The painting has been in our family for generations.)
▶ SON (raise a family)

family name noun
▶ NAME

famous adj.
▶ FAMOUS

fan noun
▶ FAN

fanatic noun
▶ FAN

fancy verb
▶ ATTRACTED TO SB (I think she fancies him.)
▶ WANT (Fancy a drink?)

fancy adj.
▶ DECORATIVE

fancy dress noun
▶ COSTUME

fantastic verb
▶ GREAT 1

fantasy noun
▶ HOPE 2 (fantasies about fame)
▶ IMAGINATION (a work of fantasy)

fanzine noun
▶ MAGAZINE

far adj.
▶ **few and far between** SCARCE

far adv.
▶ **go so/as far as to…** DARE verb

farce noun
▶ PLAY

fare noun
▶ FOOD (traditional English fare)
▶ RATE 2 (a bus fare)

fare verb
▶ DO 2

far-fetched adj.
▶ UNLIKELY 2

farm noun
▶ FARM

farm verb
▶ FARM

farmers' market noun
▶ MARKET 2

farmland noun
▶ LAND 1

far-reaching adj.
► WIDE 1

fascinate verb
► INTEREST

fascinated adj.
► INTERESTED

fascinating adj.
► INTERESTING

fascination noun
► INTEREST 1

fashion noun
► FASHION

fashion verb
► SHAPE

fashionable adj.
► FASHIONABLE

fast noun
► DIET

fast adj.
► FAST (a fast car/pace/worker)
► QUICK (a fast response time)

fasten verb
► ATTACH (Fasten the papers together with a paper clip.)
► TIE (Fasten your seat belts.)

fastener (also **fastening**) noun
► BUTTON 2

fat noun
► FAT

fat adj.
► FAT

fatal noun
► FATAL

fatality noun
► VICTIM 1

fate noun
► FUTURE (The fate of the ship's captain is unknown.)
► LUCK (believe in fate)

father noun
► MOTHER

fatigued adj.
► TIRED 1

fault noun
► FAULT (It was your fault.)
► CRACK (a fault line)
► DEFECT (a technical fault)
► WEAKNESS 2 (in spite of his faults)
► **at fault** GUILTY adj.

faultless adj.
► PERFECT

faulty adj.
► WRONG 2

favour (also **favor**) noun
► APPROVAL (find favour with sb)
► **in favour (of sb/sth)** IN FAVOUR (OF SB/STH) phrase

favour (also **favor**) verb
► PREFER

favourable (also **favorable**) adj.
► GOOD 6 (a favourable impression/comment)
► VALUABLE 2 (favourable conditions)

favoured (also **favored**) adj.
► FAVOURITE

favourite (also **favorite**) noun
► CHOICE 2

favourite (also **favorite**) adj.
► FAVOURITE

favouritism (also **favoritism**) noun
► DISCRIMINATION

fawn verb
► FLATTER

fax noun
► LETTER

fear noun
► FEAR (a fear of flying)
► RISK 1 (for fear of sth/that...)

fearful adj.
► AFRAID

fearless adj.
► BRAVE

feasible adj.
► POSSIBLE 1

feast noun
► MEAL

feast verb
► DINE

feat noun
► WORK 3

feature noun
► FEATURE (an interesting feature of the city)
► ARTICLE (a magazine feature)

feature verb
► FEATURE

featureless adj.
► DRAB

feckless adj.
► DESPICABLE

federal adj.
► PUBLIC

federation noun
► REPUBLIC (the Russian Federation)
► UNION (the British Athletics Federation)

fed up adj.
► BORED

fee noun
► RATE 2

feeble adj.
► UNFORTUNATE 2 (a feeble excuse)
► WEAK (a feeble heartbeat)

feed noun
► MEAL

feed verb
► SERVE 1

feedback noun
► RESPONSE

feel noun
► ATMOSPHERE (the feel of a small town)
► TEXTURE (the feel of silk)

feel verb
► FEEL (feel happy/the sun on your back)
► FUMBLE (feel in your pockets for some money)
► HAVE 3 (feel the effects of sth)
► SEEM (It feels strange to be here.)
► THINK (I feel strongly that...)
► TOUCH 1 (feel a bump)
► **feel like sth** WANT

feel for phrasal verb
► SORRY FOR SB

feeling noun
► ATMOSPHERE (recreate the feeling of the original theatre)
► DIGNITY (hurt sb's feelings)
► EMOTION (arouse strong feelings)
► IDEA 2 (I had a nasty feeling he was lying.)
► SENSE (guilty feelings)
► VIEW 1 (My own feeling is...)

feign verb
► PRETEND

fell noun
► HILL

fell verb
► DEMOLISH

fellow noun
► LECTURER

fellowship noun
► FRIENDSHIP

felon noun
► CRIMINAL

felony noun
► CRIME 2

female noun
► WOMAN

fence noun
► WALL

fence off phrasal verb
► SEPARATE 2

fend for phrasal verb
► TAKE CARE OF YOURSELF

fend off phrasal verb
► FEND SB/STH OFF (She threw up an arm to fend him off.)
► EVADE (fend off questions)

ferry noun
► BOAT

ferry verb
► TAKE 1

fertile adj.
► PRODUCTIVE

fervent adj.
► INTENSE

fervour (also **fervor**) noun
► EMOTION

festivities noun
► EVENT 2

festoon verb
► DECORATE

fetch verb
► GET 3 (fetch a doctor)
► MAKE 2 (fetch a lot of money at auction)

feverish adj.
► HOT

few adj.
► **few and far between** SCARCE

fiancé noun
► PARTNER 2

fiancée noun
► PARTNER 2

fiasco noun
► DISASTER

fib noun
► LIE

fibre (also **fiber**) noun
► FIBRE

fickle adj.
► TREACHEROUS (a fickle friend)
► UNCERTAIN (the fickle world of fashion)

fiction noun
► LIE

fictional adj.
► FICTIONAL

fictitious adj.
► FICTIONAL

fiddle verb
► DISTORT

fidget verb
► WRIGGLE

field noun
► FIELD (a farmer's field)
► AREA 2 (a research field)
► PITCH (a sports field)
► STRETCH (gas/ice fields)

fierce adj.
► INTENSE

fiery adj.
► INTENSE

fight noun
► FIGHT (get into a fight)
► ARGUMENT 1 (a fight over money)
► CAMPAIGN (the fight against crime)
► GAME 1 (a world title fight)

fight verb
► FIGHT 1 (He fought in the war.)
► FIGHT 2 (My little brothers are always fighting.)
► ARGUE (It's not worth fighting about.)
► CAMPAIGN (Campaigners fought to save the hospital from closure.)
► COMPETE (fight an election)
► OPPOSE (fight poverty)

fight back phrasal verb
► FIGHT BACK

fighter noun
► ACTIVIST (She's a fighter – she never gives up.)
► SOLDIER (guerrilla fighters)

fighting noun
► WAR

figure noun
► FIGURE (unemployment figures)
► BODY 1 (She has a good figure.)
► DIAGRAM (This information is shown in figure 11.)
► NUMBER 2 (a six-figure sum)
► PERSON (a leading figure in the music industry)
► SHAPE (a tall figure in black)
► **put a figure on sth** CALCULATE verb

figure verb
► CALCULATE (The cost is figured at $15 000.)
► CONCLUDE (That's what I figured.)
► ESTIMATE (figure how much it would cost)
► FEATURE (figure in sb's plans)

figure of speech noun
► METAPHOR

figure out phrasal verb
► CALCULATE (figure out how much)
► SOLVE 2 (figure out why)

file noun
► DOCUMENT (confidential files)
► ENVELOPE (a box file)
► ROW (in single file)

file verb
► CLASSIFY (filed alphabetically)
► PRESENT 3 (file a lawsuit)

filings noun
► FRAGMENT

fill verb
► FILL (fill a glass)
► SPEND 2 (fill your day)

fill in phrasal verb
► TELL 1

fill in for phrasal verb
► REPLACE 1

fill up phrasal verb
► FILL

film noun
► FILM 1 (see a film)
► FILM 2 (the film industry)

film verb
► RECORD 2

film star noun
► ACTOR

filter verb
► FILTER

filter out phrasal verb
► SEPARATE 1

filthy verb
► DIRTY (filthy windows/streets)
► OFFENSIVE (filthy language)

final noun
► GAME 1

final adj.
► FINAL (have the final say)
► LAST 1 (the final outcome)

finale noun
► END

finalize verb
► FINISH

finance noun
► FINANCE (the Minister of Finance)

▶ MONEY 1 (finance for education)

finance *verb*
▶ FUND

financial *adj.*
▶ ECONOMIC

find *verb*
▶ FIND 1 (find that sth is true)
▶ FIND 2 (Look what I've found!)
▶ FIND 3 (find a cure for cancer)
▶ FIND 4 (I can't find my keys.)
▶ EXIST (insects found in tropical countries)
▶ REGARD (find sth hard to believe)

finding *noun*
▶ CONCLUSION

find out *phrasal verb*
▶ FIND 1

fine *noun*
▶ RATE 2

fine *verb*
▶ CHARGE

fine *adj.*
▶ FINE (That's fine by me.)
▶ GOOD 1 (fine wines)
▶ NARROW (a brush with a fine tip)
▶ SUNNY (fine dry weather)
▶ WELL ('How are you?' 'Fine, thanks.')
▶ WORTHY (a fine soldier)

the fine print *noun*
▶ CONDITION

finery *noun*
▶ DECORATION

finger *verb*
▶ TELL 2

fingerprint *noun*
▶ MARK

finish *noun*
▶ END

finish *verb*
▶ FINISH (finish your work)
▶ EAT (finish your dinner)
▶ END (a show finishes)

finish off *phrasal verb*
▶ KILL

fire *noun*
▶ FIRE 1 (destroyed by fire)
▶ FIRE 2 (Get warm by the fire.)
▶ ENERGY 2 (eyes full of fire)
▶ HEATING (a gas fire)
▶ **be on fire** BURN *verb* 1
▶ **set fire to sth/set sth on fire** LIGHT *verb* 1
▶ **open fire** SHOOT *verb*

fire *verb*
▶ FIRE (fire sb from their job)
▶ SHOOT (fire a gun)

firearm *noun*
▶ GUN

fire up *phrasal verb*
▶ INSPIRE

firing squad *noun*
▶ EXECUTION

firm *noun*
▶ COMPANY

firm *adj.*
▶ FIRM (a firm base)
▶ FINAL (firm beliefs)
▶ SOLID (firm ground)
▶ STRICT (firm discipline)
▶ TIGHT (a firm grip)

first *det., adj.*
▶ FIRST (first impressions)
▶ TOP (first prize)

first light *noun*
▶ DAWN

first name *noun*
▶ NAME

first night *noun*
▶ LAUNCH

first-rate *adj.*
▶ EXCELLENT

first thing *adv.*
▶ DAWN *noun*

fish *verb*
▶ FUMBLE

fishy *adj.*
▶ SUSPICIOUS 2

fissure *noun*
▶ CRACK

fit *noun*
▶ ATTACK 3

fit *verb*
▶ EQUIP 2 (be well fitted to a particular role)
▶ MATCH 1 (Do the facts fit the theory?)

fit *adj.*
▶ GOOD 2 (in no fit state)
▶ WELL (fit and healthy)
▶ **keep fit** TRAIN *verb* 2

fitness *noun*
▶ HEALTH

fit out *phrasal verb*
▶ EQUIP 1

fitting *adj.*
▶ GOOD 2

fix *noun*
▶ SOLUTION

fix *verb*
▶ ATTACH (fix the shelf to the wall)
▶ COOK (fix sb a drink)
▶ CORRECT (fix a problem)
▶ DISTORT (fix a match/race)
▶ REPAIR (fix the TV)
▶ SCHEDULE (fix a date)

fixation *noun*
▶ OBSESSION

fixed *adj.*
▶ DEEP-SEATED (fixed ideas)
▶ SET (a fixed period)

fixture *noun*
▶ GAME 1

flag *verb*
▶ MARK 1

flair *noun*
▶ SKILL 1 (a flair for languages)
▶ STYLE (She dresses with real flair.)

flak *noun*
▶ CRITICISM

flake *noun*
▶ FRAGMENT

flamboyant *adj.*
▶ COLOURED

flames *noun*
▶ FIRE 1

flank *verb*
▶ SURROUND

flap *verb*
▶ BLOW 1 (The curtains flapped in the breeze.)
▶ SHAKE 1 (flap its wings/your arms)

flash *verb*
▶ FLASH (a light flashes)
▶ FLY 2 (Out of the window the countryside flashed past.)

flash flood *noun*
▶ FLOOD 1

flashlight *noun*
▶ LIGHT 2

flashy *adj.*
▶ FLASHY

flask *noun*
▶ BOTTLE

flat *noun*
▶ FLAT

flat *adj.*
▶ FLAT (a flat surface)
▶ BLANK (a flat tone)
▶ PREDICTABLE 2 (Life seems flat.)

flatten *verb*
▶ DEMOLISH

flatter *verb*
▶ FLATTER

flattering *adj.*
▶ GOOD 6

flattery *noun*
▶ PRAISE

flavour (also **flavor**) *noun*
▶ ATMOSPHERE (the book's exotic flavour)
▶ TASTE 2 (a fruit flavour)

flaw *noun*
▶ DEFECT (flaws in security)
▶ WEAKNESS 2 (character flaws)

flawless *adj.*
▶ PERFECT

flee *verb*
▶ FLEE

fleet *noun*
▶ FLEET

fleeting *adj.*
▶ SHORT 1

flex *noun*
▶ WIRE

flexible *adj.*
▶ FLEXIBLE 1 (flexible working hours)
▶ FLEXIBLE 2 (flexible materials)

flicker *verb*
▶ FLASH

flick through *phrasal verb*
▶ READ

flier *noun*
▶ LEAFLET

flight *noun*
▶ FLIGHT

flinch *verb*
▶ JUMP 3

fling *verb*
▶ THROW

flip *verb*
▶ ROLL

flirt *verb*
▶ FLIRT

float *verb*
▶ FLOAT

flock *noun*
▶ HERD

flock *verb*
▶ CROWD

flood *noun*
▶ FLOOD 1 (The rain caused floods.)
▶ FLOOD 2 (a flood of calls/tears)

flood *verb*
▶ FLOOD (a cellar floods)
▶ LIGHT 2 (flooded with light)
▶ OVERWHELM (flooded with requests)
▶ SOAK (The river flooded the valley.)
▶ SURGE (Letters came flooding in.)

floor *noun*
▶ FLOOR 1 (sit on the floor)
▶ FLOOR 2 (the first floor)

flop *noun*
▶ DISASTER

flop *verb*
▶ CLOSE 2

flounce *verb*
▶ MARCH

flourish *verb*
▶ DO WELL

flout *verb*
▶ OPPOSE

flow *noun*
▶ FLOW (a continuous flow of refugees/traffic)
▶ CURRENT (the flow of blood from the wound)

flow *verb*
▶ FLOW

flow chart *noun*
▶ DIAGRAM

fluctuate *verb*
▶ CHANGE 2

fluctuation *noun*
▶ CHANGE 1

fluent *adj.*
▶ ARTICULATE

fluid *noun*
▶ MATERIAL

fluid *adj.*
▶ VARIABLE

fluke *noun*
▶ MIRACLE

flunk *verb*
▶ FAIL 3

flurry *noun*
▶ ATTACK 3

flush *verb*
▶ FLUSH

fluster *adj.*
▶ SHAKE 4

flustered *adj.*
▶ RESTLESS

flutter *verb*
▶ BEAT 2 (Her heart fluttered.)
▶ BLOW 1 (flutter in the breeze)
▶ FLY 1 (a butterfly flutters)

fly *verb*
▶ FLY 1 (a bird/plane flies)
▶ FLY 2 (A stone came flying through the window.)
▶ BLOW 1 (Flags were flying.)
▶ DRIVE 1 (fly a plane)
▶ GO 2 (fly business class)
▶ HURRY (flying along)
▶ TAKE 1 (The tourists were flown home.)

flyer *noun*
▶ LEAFLET

foam *noun*
▶ FOAM

focal point *noun*
▶ FOCUS

focus *noun*
▶ FOCUS

focus *verb*
▶ FOCUS (focus on an issue)
▶ AIM (focus your eyes/a camera)

foe *noun*
▶ ENEMY

fog *noun*
▶ CLOUD 1

foggy *adj.*
▶ CLOUDY

foil *verb*
▶ THWART

fold *noun*
▶ FOLD

fold *verb*
▶ FOLD (fold paper/a bed)
▶ CLOSE 2 (a business folds)

folder *noun*
▶ ENVELOPE

folk *noun*
▶ MOTHER (spend the weekend with your folks)
▶ PEOPLE 1 (ordinary everyday folk)

folk *adj.*
▶ CULTURAL

folklore *noun*
▶ LEGEND 2

follow *verb*
▶ FOLLOW 1 (You lead, I'll follow.)
▶ FOLLOW 2 (A news report will follow shortly.)
▶ FOLLOW 3 (follow instructions)
▶ FOLLOW 4 (follow the fashions)
▶ UNDERSTAND 1 (I don't follow.)
▶ **follow in sb's footsteps** FOLLOW 4

▶ **follow suit** FOLLOW 4
follower noun
▶ FAN (a follower of fashion)
▶ SUPPORTER (a loyal follower)
the **following** adj.
▶ NEXT
follow through phrasal verb
▶ FINISH (follow through with your ideas)
▶ KEEP 5 (follow through on your promises)
follow up phrasal verb
▶ GO ON TO STH
follow with noun
▶ GO ON TO STH
fond adj.
▶ LOVING (fond memories)
▶ **be fond of sth** LIKE verb
▶ **be fond of sb** LOVE verb
fondle verb
▶ STROKE
food noun
▶ FOOD
foodstuff noun
▶ FOOD
fool noun
▶ FOOL
fool verb
▶ CHEAT
foolish adj.
▶ CRAZY (How foolish of her!)
▶ RIDICULOUS (feel foolish)
foot noun
▶ BOTTOM (the foot of the stairs)
▶ **set foot in/on sth** ENTER verb
▶ **put your feet up** REST verb
▶ **be on your feet, get to your feet** STAND verb 1
▶ **stand on your own (two) feet** TAKE CARE OF YOURSELF verb
▶ **drag your feet** TAKE YOUR TIME verb
foothills noun
▶ HILL
footman noun
▶ SERVANT
footpath noun
▶ PATH
footprint noun
▶ TRAIL
footstep noun
▶ STEP (hear footsteps)
▶ **follow in sb's footsteps** FOLLOW verb 4
forage verb
▶ LOOK 2
forbid verb
▶ BAN
forbidden adj.
▶ FORBIDDEN
forbidding adj.
▶ THREATENING
force noun
▶ FORCE (use excessive force)
▶ ARMY (Allied forces)
▶ CONTROL (have the force of law)
▶ EFFECT (the force of her argument)
▶ IMPACT (the force of the blow)
▶ INFLUENCE (a force for change)
▶ PRESSURE 2 (the use of force)
▶ **in force** ACTIVE adj.
force verb
▶ FORCE (be forced to resign)
▶ PUSH 1 (force a door open)
forced adj.
▶ ARTIFICIAL 2 (forced smiles)
▶ NECESSARY (a forced sale)
forceful adj.
▶ AGGRESSIVE 2 (a forceful character)

▶ CONVINCING (a forceful argument)
the **fore** noun
▶ LEAD 1
foreboding noun
▶ IDEA 2
forecast noun
▶ EXPECTATION
forecast verb
▶ PREDICT
the **forefront** noun
▶ LEAD 1
forego verb
▶ GO WITHOUT
foregone adj.
▶ **a foregone conclusion** CERTAINTY noun
the **foreground** noun
▶ LEAD 1
foreign adj.
▶ FOREIGN
foreman noun
▶ MANAGER
foremost adj.
▶ TOP
foresee verb
▶ PREDICT
foreseeable adj.
▶ PREDICTABLE 1
foresight noun
▶ EXPECTATION
forest noun
▶ FOREST
forestall verb
▶ ANTICIPATE
foreword noun
▶ INTRODUCTION 2
forfeit verb
▶ GIVE STH UP
forgery noun
▶ FAKE
forget verb
▶ FORGET (Try and forget about it.)
▶ FAIL 1 (forget to do sth)
▶ LEAVE 4 (forget your purse)
forgetful adj.
▶ CARELESS
forgive verb
▶ FORGIVE
forgiveness noun
▶ MERCY
forgiving adj.
▶ LENIENT
forgo verb
▶ GO WITHOUT
forlorn adj.
▶ LONELY
form noun
▶ FORM 1 (The disease can take several different forms.)
▶ FORM 2 (an application form)
▶ KIND (a form of transport)
▶ SHAPE (the human form)
▶ STRUCTURE (the form of a poem)
form verb
▶ APPEAR (storm clouds form)
▶ DETERMINE (sth forms sb's character)
▶ ESTABLISH (form the new government)
▶ MAKE 1 (form a new word)
▶ SHAPE (bend the wire to form a 'V')
formal adj.
▶ FORMAL (a formal manner)
▶ OFFICIAL (a formal complaint)
formality noun
▶ RESPECT
format noun
▶ DESIGN

formation noun
▶ INTRODUCTION 1
former adj.
▶ FORMER (my former boss)
▶ PREVIOUS (former glory)
formula noun
▶ SLOGAN
formulate verb
▶ PLAN
fort noun
▶ CASTLE
forthcoming adj.
▶ NEXT (the forthcoming elections)
▶ TALKATIVE (She was not very forthcoming about her plans.)
forthright adj.
▶ HONEST
fortress noun
▶ CASTLE
fortunate adj.
▶ LUCKY (I was fortunate.)
▶ TIMELY (It was fortunate that…)
fortune noun
▶ FUTURE (tell sb's fortune)
▶ LUCK (have the good fortune to do sth)
▶ MONEY 3 (make a fortune)
forum noun
▶ FORUM
forward verb
▶ SEND 1
fossil fuel noun
▶ OIL
foster verb
▶ BRING SB UP (foster a child)
▶ PROMOTE (foster innovation)
foul adj.
▶ DISGUSTING 1 (a foul taste/smell)
▶ OFFENSIVE (foul language)
found verb
▶ ESTABLISH
foundation noun
▶ BASIS (a solid foundation for marriage)
▶ BOTTOM (the foundations of the houses)
▶ CHARITY (a charitable foundation)
▶ INTRODUCTION 1 (the foundation of a research group)
founder verb
▶ FAIL 2
foundry noun
▶ FACTORY
foyer noun
▶ HALL 2
fraction noun
▶ FIGURE
fracture verb
▶ BREAK 1
fragile adj.
▶ FRAGILE
fragment noun
▶ FRAGMENT
fragmentary adj.
▶ PARTIAL
fragrance noun
▶ SMELL
frail adj.
▶ WEAK
frailty noun
▶ WEAKNESS 2
frame noun
▶ FRAME
frame of mind noun
▶ MOOD
framework noun
▶ STRUCTURE
franchise noun
▶ LICENCE

frank adj.
▶ HONEST
frantic adj.
▶ HYSTERICAL (frantic with worry)
▶ WILD 2 (Things are frantic in the office.)
fraud noun
▶ FRAUD 1 (obtain sth by fraud)
▶ FRAUD 2 (a $1 million fraud)
fraudulent adj.
▶ CORRUPT
fraught adj.
▶ STRESSFUL
freak noun
▶ EXCEPTION (a freak of nature)
▶ FAN (a health freak)
freak out phrasal verb
▶ PANIC
free verb
▶ FREE 1 (free the passengers from the wreckage)
▶ FREE 2 (free the body of tension)
▶ RELEASE (free prisoners/slaves)
free adj.
▶ FREE 1 (a free man)
▶ FREE 2 (free tickets)
▶ FREE 3 (Are you free for lunch?)
▶ EMPTY (Is this seat free?)
▶ GENEROUS (free with your advice)
▶ **free of charge** FREE adj. 2
▶ **set sb/sth free** RELEASE verb
freedom noun
▶ FREEDOM
free-standing adj.
▶ INDEPENDENT
free time noun
▶ LEISURE
freeway noun
▶ HIGHWAY
freeze verb
▶ COOL
freezing adj.
▶ FREEZING
freight noun
▶ CARGO (the transport of freight)
▶ DELIVERY (freight charges)
freight car noun
▶ CARRIAGE 1
frenzied adj.
▶ WILD 2
frequency noun
▶ CHANNEL
frequent adj.
▶ FREQUENT
frequently adv.
▶ OFTEN
fresh adj.
▶ FRESH (fresh fruit)
▶ NEW 1 (make a fresh start)
freshen up phrasal verb
▶ WASH
fret verb
▶ WORRY 1
friend noun
▶ FRIEND
friendly adj.
▶ FRIENDLY 1 (a friendly person)
▶ FRIENDLY 2 (a friendly atmosphere)
friendship noun
▶ FRIENDSHIP
fright noun
▶ FEAR (shake with fright)
▶ SHOCK 2 (give sb a fright)
frighten verb
▶ FRIGHTEN
frightened adj.
▶ AFRAID

frightening adj.
▸ FRIGHTENING

frills noun
▸ DECORATION

fringe noun
▸ EDGE

front noun
▸ LEAD 1 (at the front of the line)
▸ PRETENCE (put on a brave front)

frontier noun
▸ BORDER (a frontier settlement)
▸ LIMIT 2 (the frontiers of science)

front runner noun
▸ LEADER 2

frosty adj.
▸ COLD 2 (a frosty reception)
▸ FREEZING (frosty weather)

froth noun
▸ FOAM

frown verb
▸ FROWN

frown on/upon phrasal verb
▸ DISAPPROVE

frozen adj.
▸ FREEZING

frugal adj.
▸ MEAN 2

fruit noun
▸ **the fruit/fruits of sth** RESULT

fruitful adj.
▸ PRODUCTIVE

fruitless adj.
▸ USELESS

frustrate verb
▸ ANNOY (What frustrates me is…)
▸ THWART (frustrate sb's plans)

frustrated adj.
▸ UNHAPPY 2

frustrating adj.
▸ ANNOYING

frustration noun
▸ FRUSTRATION

fry verb
▸ BAKE

frying pan noun
▸ PAN

fudge verb
▸ EVADE

fuel noun
▸ OIL

fuel verb
▸ ENCOURAGE 3

fulfil (also **fulfill**) verb
▸ ACHIEVE (fulfil your ambition)
▸ MEET 4 (fulfil a promise)

fulfilling adj.
▸ SATISFYING

fulfilment (also **fulfillment**) noun
▸ SATISFACTION

full adj.
▸ FULL (a full bottle of wine)
▸ BUSY 2 (lead a full life)
▸ DEEP 2 (a deep, full sound)
▸ WHOLE (your full potential)

full name noun
▸ NAME

full-scale adj.
▸ DETAILED

fully adv.
▸ QUITE 2

fumble verb
▸ FUMBLE

fumes noun
▸ SMOKE

fuming adj.
▸ FURIOUS

fun noun
▸ FUN (Sailing is great fun.)
▸ ENTERTAINMENT (fun and games)
▸ **make fun of sb/sth, poke fun at sb/sth** LAUGH AT SB/STH
▸ **have fun** PLAY verb 1

function noun
▸ FUNCTION (a useful function)
▸ EVENT 2 (weddings and other functions)

function verb
▸ WORK 3

functional adj.
▸ USEFUL

fund noun
▸ FUND (a pension fund)
▸ MONEY 1 (short of funds)

fund verb
▸ FUND

fundamental adj.
▸ FUNDAMENTAL

fundamentals noun
▸ BASICS

funding noun
▸ INVESTMENT

funny adj.
▸ FUNNY (a funny guy/story)
▸ STRANGE 1 (a funny noise/smell)

funny side noun
▸ HUMOUR

furious adj.
▸ FURIOUS (I was furious.)
▸ WILD 2 (a furious pace)

furnace noun
▸ HEATING (turn the furnace down)
▸ OVEN (a blast furnace)

furore noun
▸ FUSS

furrow noun
▸ DITCH

furry adj.
▸ HAIRY

further verb
▸ PROMOTE

furtive adj.
▸ SECRETIVE

fury noun
▸ ANGER

fuse verb
▸ COMBINE

fuselage noun
▸ FRAME

fuss noun
▸ FUSS

futile adj.
▸ USELESS

future noun
▸ FUTURE

future adj.
▸ NEXT

futuristic adj.
▸ EXPERIMENTAL

G g

gadget noun
▸ TOOL

gaffe noun
▸ MISTAKE 1

gag noun
▸ JOKE

gage noun
▸ CRITERION

gage verb
▸ ESTIMATE (gage the distance)
▸ JUDGE 1 (gage sb's mood)

gain noun
▸ INCREASE (weight gain)
▸ PROFIT (financial gain)

gain verb
▸ GAIN 1 (gain entry)
▸ GAIN 2 (gain confidence/weight)
▸ BENEFIT (Who stands to gain from these changes?)
▸ **gain ground** DEVELOP 1

gait noun
▸ WALK

gale noun
▸ STORM

gallant adj.
▸ BRAVE

galling adj.
▸ ANNOYING

gallop verb
▸ RUN 1

gallows noun
▸ EXECUTION

galvanize verb
▸ ENCOURAGE 2

gamble noun
▸ RISK 2

gamble verb
▸ BET

game noun
▸ GAME 1 (a game of football/chess)
▸ GAME 2 (ball/party games)
▸ FRAUD 2 (So that's his little game.)
▸ INTEREST 2 (playing games with the dog)
▸ ROUND (the opening game)

gang noun
▸ GROUP 2 (a gang of friends)
▸ PARTY 3 (an armed gang)
▸ TEAM 1 (a work gang)

gangster noun
▸ THUG

gaol noun
▸ PRISON

gap noun
▸ GAP (the gap between rich and poor)
▸ HOLE 1 (a gap in a fence)
▸ PAUSE (a gap of twenty years)

garbage noun
▸ NONSENSE (Don't believe all that garbage!)
▸ RUBBISH (watch garbage on TV)
▸ WASTE (a garbage dump)

garden noun
▸ GARDEN 1 (a back garden)
▸ GARDEN 2 (a rose garden)
▸ PARK (visit the botanical gardens)

garish adj.
▸ COLOURED

garment noun
▸ CLOTHES

garnish noun
▸ DECORATION

garnish verb
▸ DECORATE

garrison noun
▸ CASTLE (a fortified garrison)
▸ GUARD (a garrison of 5 000 soldiers)

gas noun
▸ MATERIAL (a mixture of gases)
▸ OIL (gas for heating)

gash noun
▸ INJURY

gash verb
▸ CUT 4

gasoline noun
▸ OIL

gasp noun
▸ BREATH

gasp verb
▸ BLOW 2

gate noun
▸ DOOR

gateway noun
▸ DOOR

gather verb
▸ COLLECT (gather your things)
▸ CONCLUDE (So I gather.)
▸ FOLD (He gathered his cloak around him.)
▸ HARVEST (gather the harvest)
▸ MEET 1 (a crowd gathers)

gathering noun
▸ MEETING 1

gaudy adj.
▸ COLOURED

gauge noun
▸ CRITERION

gauge verb
▸ ESTIMATE (gauge the distance)
▸ JUDGE 1 (gauge sb's mood)

gauntlet noun
▸ **throw down the gauntlet** CHALLENGE verb

gawk verb
▸ STARE

gaze noun
▸ LOOK

gaze verb
▸ STARE

gear noun
▸ CLOTHES (designer gear)
▸ EQUIPMENT (skiing gear)

gear up phrasal verb
▸ PREPARE 2

general adj.
▸ GENERAL 1 (a general problem)
▸ GENERAL 2 (in general terms)
▸ USUAL (as a general rule)
▸ **in general** USUALLY adv.

generally adv.
▸ USUALLY

the general public noun
▸ GENERAL PUBLIC

generate verb
▸ MAKE 1

generation noun
▸ AGE (people of my generation)
▸ PERIOD (a generation ago)

generous adj.
▸ GENEROUS (a generous man/gift)
▸ KIND (a generous spirit)

genetic adj.
▸ NATURAL

genial adj.
▸ FRIENDLY 1

genius noun
▸ GENIUS (a musical genius)
▸ INTELLIGENCE (a man of genius)

genocide noun
▸ MASSACRE

genre noun
▸ KIND

gentle adj.
▸ GENTLE (gentle rain/exercise)
▸ SENSITIVE 1 (a gentle man/voice)

gentleman noun
▸ MAN 1

gentlemanly adj.
▸ POLITE

the gentry noun
▸ ELITE

genuine adj.
▸ DEEP 1 (a very genuine person)
▸ REAL (Are the photos genuine?)

geography noun
▸ DESIGN

gesticulate verb
▸ NOD

gesture noun
▸ ACTION (a gesture of goodwill)
▸ MOVEMENT (a rude gesture)

gesture *verb*
▶ NOD

get *verb*
▶ GET 1 (get tickets/some sleep)
▶ GET 2 (get a letter/shock)
▶ GET 3 (Go and get help.)
▶ GET 4 (We got there at 9.)
▶ GET 5 (get the bus)
▶ BECOME (get angry/cold/fat)
▶ BUY (You can get the basic model for $100.)
▶ COOK (get sb sth to eat)
▶ GO 1 (get home/across the river)
▶ MAKE 2 (How much did you get for your car?)
▶ PERSUADE (get people to come)
▶ SUFFER FROM STH (get a cold)
▶ UNDERSTAND 1 (get a joke)
▶ **be getting on for sth** APPROACH
▶ **get out of here** GO AWAY

get across *phrasal verb*
▶ CONVEY

get ahead *phrasal verb*
▶ LEAD 1

get along *phrasal verb*
▶ DO 2

get around *phrasal verb*
▶ PERSUADE

get away *phrasal verb*
▶ ESCAPE (You'd better get away — the soldiers are coming.)
▶ GO AWAY (get away before 7)

getaway *noun*
▶ HOLIDAY 2

get back *verb*
▶ RECOVER 2 (get your old job back)
▶ RETURN 1 (get back home)

get back at *phrasal verb*
▶ FIGHT BACK

get back to *phrasal verb*
▶ ANSWER

get by *phrasal verb*
▶ COPE

get down *phrasal verb*
▶ DISCOURAGE 2

get in, get into *phrasal verb*
▶ GET IN (get into a car)
▶ ARRIVE (get in on time)

get off *phrasal verb*
▶ GET OUT

get on *phrasal verb*
▶ COPE (We can get on perfectly well without her.)
▶ DO 2 (get on well at school)
▶ GET IN (get on a bike)
▶ SUCCEED (get on in life)

get out *phrasal verb*
▶ GET OUT (get out of a taxi)
▶ TURN OUT (the truth gets out)

get out of *phrasal verb*
▶ EVADE (get out of doing sth)
▶ **get out of bed** WAKE UP

get over *phrasal verb*
▶ OVERCOME

get round *phrasal verb*
▶ PERSUADE

get through *phrasal verb*
▶ GRADUATE (get through an exam)
▶ USE 2 (get through the money)

get together *phrasal verb*
▶ MEET 1

get-together *noun*
▶ EVENT 2

get up *phrasal verb*
▶ STAND 1 (get up from your chair)
▶ WAKE UP (get up at 7a.m.)

ghastly *adj.*
▶ BAD

ghost *noun*
▶ GHOST

giant *adj.*
▶ HUGE

gibberish *noun*
▶ NONSENSE

gift *noun*
▶ GIFT (a birthday gift)
▶ SKILL 1 (have a gift for music)

gifted *adj.*
▶ GOOD 4

gig *noun*
▶ CONCERT

gigantic *adj.*
▶ HUGE

giggle *verb*
▶ LAUGH

gigolo *noun*
▶ LOVER

Gipsy *noun*
▶ TRAVELLER

girder *noun*
▶ POST

girl *noun*
▶ GIRL (the girl next door)
▶ CHILD (a bright little girl)
▶ FRIEND (a night out with the girls)
▶ SON (They have two girls.)

girlfriend *noun*
▶ PARTNER 2

girlish *adj.*
▶ CHILDISH

gist *noun*
▶ MESSAGE

give *noun*
▶ **give and take** COMPROMISE

give *verb*
▶ GIVE 1 (give sb a present)
▶ GIVE 2 (Give me the letter.)
▶ GIVE 3 (give sb drugs/advice)
▶ GIVE 4 (give sb a headache)
▶ GIVE 5 (give money to charity)
▶ HAVE 4 (give a party)
▶ PASS STH ON (give sb a cold)
▶ PAY (How much will you give me for the car?)
▶ PROVIDE (give sb a drink/job)

give away *phrasal verb*
▶ REVEAL

giveaway *noun*
▶ VALUE 2

give back *phrasal verb*
▶ RETURN 2

give in *phrasal verb*
▶ GIVE WAY (give in to pressure)
▶ **give in your notice** LEAVE 3

give out *phrasal verb*
▶ DISTRIBUTE

give over to *phrasal verb*
▶ DEVOTE

give up *phrasal verb*
▶ GIVE STH UP (give up your passport to the authorities)
▶ GO WITHOUT (give up your free time)
▶ STOP 1 (give up smoking/work)
▶ **give up hope** DESPAIR

give way *idiom*
▶ GIVE WAY (give way to sb's demands/your emotions)
▶ COLLAPSE 1 (The pillars gave way.)

glad *adj.*
▶ GLAD (Are you glad you came?)
▶ GRATEFUL (glad of sb's help)

glamorous *adj.*
▶ FASHIONABLE

glamour *noun*
▶ INTEREST 1 (add glamour to the occasion)
▶ STYLE (Her long dark hair lent her a certain glamour.)

glance *noun*
▶ LOOK

glance *verb*
▶ GLANCE

glare *verb*
▶ STARE

glaring *adj.*
▶ OPEN (a glaring omission)
▶ STRONG 3 (glaring sunshine)

glazed *adj.*
▶ BLANK

gleam *verb*
▶ SHINE

glen *noun*
▶ VALLEY

glide *verb*
▶ FLY 1 (a plane glides)
▶ SLIDE (swans glide)

glimpse *noun*
▶ LOOK

glimpse *verb*
▶ SEE

glint *verb*
▶ SHINE

glisten *noun*
▶ SHINE

glitch *noun*
▶ DEFECT

glitter *verb*
▶ SHINE

glitzy *adj.*
▶ FLASHY

gloat *verb*
▶ BOAST

global *adj.*
▶ INTERNATIONAL (global markets)
▶ OVERALL (a global search)

globe *noun*
▶ MAP (find Laos on the globe)
▶ WORLD (sail around the globe)

globule *noun*
▶ DROP

gloom *noun*
▶ GLOOM (filled sb with gloom)
▶ DARKNESS (the gloom of the hallway)

gloomy *adj.*
▶ DEPRESSED (Don't look so gloomy.)
▶ DIM 2 (gloomy weather)
▶ NEGATIVE (gloomy predictions)

glorify *verb*
▶ PRAISE

glorious *adj.*
▶ FAMOUS (a glorious victory)
▶ MAGNIFICENT (a glorious sunset)
▶ SUNNY (glorious weather)

glory *noun*
▶ LUXURY (sth's former glory)
▶ STATUS (your moment of glory)

glory in *phrasal verb*
▶ ENJOY

gloss over *phrasal verb*
▶ IGNORE

glow *verb*
▶ FLUSH (sb's cheeks glow)
▶ SHINE (a red light glows)

glowing *adj.*
▶ GOOD 6

glue *verb*
▶ ATTACH

glum *adj.*
▶ DEPRESSED

gnaw *verb*
▶ BITE

go *noun*
▶ ATTEMPT (It took three goes to get it right.)
▶ OPPORTUNITY (Can I have a go on your bike?)
▶ **have a go** TRY *verb* 1

go *verb*
▶ GO 1 (go into the kitchen)
▶ GO 2 (go to China)
▶ ATTEND (go to a party)
▶ BECOME (go blind/grey/wrong)
▶ COST (let the house go for £200 000)
▶ DO 2 (How did the interview go?)
▶ LEAD 3 (Where does this road go?)
▶ LEAVE 1 (Don't go — I need you.)
▶ MATCH 2 (Does this jacket go with this skirt?)
▶ WORK 3 (What makes this machine go?)
▶ **keep sth going** MAINTAIN 1
▶ **keep going** PERSIST

go about *phrasal verb*
▶ BEGIN

goad *verb*
▶ PROVOKE

go after *phrasal verb*
▶ SEEK

go against *phrasal verb*
▶ CONFLICT (go against your principles)
▶ OPPOSE (go against sb's wishes)

the go-ahead *noun*
▶ PERMISSION

goal *noun*
▶ TARGET

go along with *phrasal verb*
▶ AGREE 2

go around *phrasal verb*
▶ SPIN

go away *phrasal verb*
▶ GO AWAY

go back *phrasal verb*
▶ RETURN 1

go back on *phrasal verb*
▶ BREAK 4

go-between *noun*
▶ NEGOTIATOR

go by *phrasal verb*
▶ GO BY (time goes by)
▶ GET 5 (go by bus)

go down *phrasal verb*
▶ BREAK 2 (a computer goes down)
▶ FALL 2 (go down the stairs)

godsend *noun*
▶ GOOD THING

go for *phrasal verb*
▶ ATTRACTED TO SB (go for tall men)
▶ CHOOSE (go for the fruit salad)
▶ LIKE (I don't go for modern art.)
▶ TRY 1 (Go for it! You can do it.)

go in, go into *phrasal verb*
▶ ENTER

go in for
▶ PLAY 2

going *noun*
▶ DEPARTURE 1

go into *phrasal verb*
▶ ENTER (go into the kitchen)
▶ EXAMINE (go into a question)

good *noun*
▶ BENEFIT 1 (for your own good)
▶ MORALITY (good and evil)

good *adj.*
▶ GOOD 1 (in good condition)
▶ GOOD 2 (Now is a good time to…)
▶ GOOD 3 (a good idea/reason)
▶ GOOD 4 (a good actor)
▶ GOOD 5 (a good person/deed/life)
▶ GOOD 6 (a good impression)
▶ GOOD 7 (a good boy/girl/dog)
▶ HEALTHY (Fruit is good for you.)
▶ KIND (good of you to come)
▶ NICE 1 (good news)

- SUNNY (if the weather's good...)
- VALUABLE 2 (good advice)
- WELL (I don't feel too good.)
- ▶ **in a good mood** CHEERFUL
- ▶ **a good bet** OPTION *noun*
- ▶ **have a good time** PLAY *verb* 1

good buy *noun*
- VALUE 2

good faith *noun*
- TRUTH

good-looking *adj.*
- BEAUTIFUL 1

good-natured *adj.*
- FRIENDLY 1

goodness *noun*
- MORALITY

good point *noun*
- BENEFIT 1

goods *noun*
- CARGO (a goods train)
- PRODUCT (electrical goods)
- THING 3 (stolen goods)

good thing *noun*
- GOOD THING

good time *noun*
- FUN

gooey *adj.*
- SOFT

go off *phrasal verb*
- GO AWAY (He went off in search of a flashlight.)
- EXPLODE (a bomb/gun goes off)

goof off *phrasal verb*
- MISS 1

go on *phrasal verb*
- CONTINUE 1 (We can't go on like this.)
- CONTINUE 3 (She hesitated and then went on.)
- HARASS (go on at sb)

goon *noun*
- THUG

go on to *phrasal verb*
- GO ON TO STH

go on with *phrasal verb*
- CONTINUE 2

go out *phrasal verb*
- GO OUT

go over *phrasal verb*
- CHECK 1 (go over your work)
- PRACTISE (go over the instructions)

gorge *noun*
- VALLEY

gorgeous *adj.*
- BEAUTIFUL 1

go round *phrasal verb*
- SPIN

gossip *noun*
- DISCUSSION (have a gossip)
- REPORT 4 (the latest gossip)
- SPEAKER 1 (She's such a gossip!)

gossip *verb*
- CHAT

go through *phrasal verb*
- DO 1 (go through the formalities)
- HAVE 3 (go through a bad patch)

go to *phrasal verb*
- VISIT

go up *phrasal verb*
- BURN 1 (go up in flames)
- CLIMB (go up the stairs)
- RISE (a price goes up)

govern *verb*
- DETERMINE (sth governs prices)
- RULE 1 (govern a country)

governess *noun*
- TEACHER

government *noun*
- GOVERNMENT 1 (the British government)
- GOVERNMENT 2 (strong government)

governor *noun*
- LEADER 1 (the governor of the Bank of England)
- MANAGER (a school governor)
- PRESIDENT (the state governor)

go with *phrasal verb*
- ACCOMPANY

go without *phrasal verb*
- GO WITHOUT

GP *noun*
- DOCTOR

grab *verb*
- TAKE 4 (grab hold of sb/sth)
- TAKE 6 (grab an opportunity)

grace *noun*
- MERCY (by the grace of God)
- RESPECT (have the grace to look ashamed)
- STYLE (the natural grace of a ballerina)

graceful *adj.*
- ELEGANT

gracious *adj.*
- POLITE

grade *noun*
- CLASS 3 (students in seventh grade)
- CLASS 4 (the higher grades within an organization)
- QUALITY (low grade steel)
- SCORE (get a good grade)

grade *verb*
- MARK 2 (grade students/papers)
- RANK (graded for difficulty)

gradient *noun*
- ANGLE

gradual *adj.*
- SLOW

graduate *verb*
- GRADUATE

grain *noun*
- GRAIN (grains of wheat/rice)
- BIT (a grain of sand)

grand *adj.*
- MAGNIFICENT

grandeur *noun*
- LUXURY

grandiose *noun*
- FLASHY

grant *noun*
- INVESTMENT

grant *verb*
- ALLOW (Permission was granted.)
- ADMIT 1 (I'll grant you that.)
- ▶ **take sb/sth for granted** TRUST

graph *noun*
- DIAGRAM

graphics *noun*
- PICTURE

grapple *verb*
- FIGHT 2 (grapple sb to the ground)
- TACKLE (grapple with the problem)

grasp *noun*
- CONTROL (maintain your grasp of the situation)
- UNDERSTANDING (a good grasp of the facts)

grasp *verb*
- HOLD (grasp sb's hand)
- UNDERSTAND 1 (grasp a concept)

grasping *adj.*
- GREEDY

grass *noun*
- GRASS

grass *verb*
- TELL 2

grassland *noun*
- PLAIN

grateful *adj.*
- GRATEFUL

gratify *verb*
- PLEASE

gratifying *adj.*
- SATISFYING

gratitude *noun*
- THANKS

gratuitous *adj.*
- UNJUSTIFIED

gratuity *noun*
- GIFT

grave *adj.*
- SERIOUS 1 (a grave error)
- SERIOUS 2 (a grave manner)

gravity *noun*
- IMPORTANCE

graze *noun*
- INJURY

graze *verb*
- SCRATCH 1 (graze your knee)
- TOUCH 1 (The bullet grazed his cheek.)

grazing *noun*
- FIELD

grease *noun*
- FAT

great *noun*
- STAR 1

great *adj.*
- GREAT 1 (It's great to see you.)
- GREAT 2 (a great man)
- GOOD 4 (great at chess)
- IMPORTANT (a great occasion)
- LARGE (a great crowd/age)
- USEFUL (This gadget is great for opening jars.)
- WELL (I feel great.)
- ▶ **have a great time** PLAY *verb* 1

great time *noun*
- FUN

greedy *adj.*
- GREEDY

green *noun*
- GRASS

greet *verb*
- GREET (greet sb with a smile)
- RESPOND (greet sth with suspicion)

greeting *noun*
- GREETING

gregarious *adj.*
- SOCIABLE

grenade *noun*
- BOMB

grey *adj.*
- CLOUDY (grey skies)
- DRAB (grey men in suits)
- PALE 1 (grey with lack of sleep)

grid *noun*
- DIAGRAM

gridlock *noun*
- TRAFFIC

grief *noun*
- GRIEF

grievance *noun*
- COMPLAINT

grieve *verb*
- MOURN

grill *verb*
- BAKE (grilled fish)
- QUESTION (be grilled by detectives)

grim *adj.*
- BAD (a grim reminder)
- STERN (a grim expression)

grimace *verb*
- FROWN

grime *noun*
- DIRT

grimy *verb*
- DIRTY

grin *verb*
- SMILE

grip *noun*
- ▶ **get/come to grips with sth** TACKLE *verb*

grip *verb*
- HOLD (grip sb's arm)
- INTEREST (a story grips sb)

gripe *noun*
- COMPLAINT

gripping *verb*
- INTERESTING

grit *verb*
- ▶ **grit your teeth** TIGHTEN

groan *verb*
- CREAK (trees groan in the wind)
- WHISPER (groan with pain)

grocery store *noun*
- SHOP

groom *verb*
- BRUSH (groom a horse)
- TRAIN 1 (be groomed for the top job)

grope *verb*
- FUMBLE (grope around in the dark)
- STROKE (He tried to grope her.)

gross *verb*
- MAKE 3

gross *adj.*
- DISGUSTING 1 (gross habits)
- OVERALL (a gross profit of 26%)

grotesque *adj.*
- UGLY

ground *noun*
- FLOOR 1 (lying on the ground)
- GARDEN 1 (the castle grounds)
- LAND 2 (waste ground)
- PITCH (a sports ground)
- REASON (no grounds for complaint)
- SOIL (stony/muddy ground)
- ▶ **gain ground** DEVELOP *verb* 1
- ▶ **hold/stand your ground** RESIST *verb*

groundless *adj.*
- IRRATIONAL

group *noun*
- GROUP 1 (a group of people)
- GROUP 2 (a peer/drama group)
- GROUP 3 (a newspaper group)

group *verb*
- CLASSIFY

groupie *noun*
- FAN

grove *noun*
- FARM

grovel *verb*
- FLATTER

grow *verb*
- BECOME (grow old/bored)
- FARM (grow cabbages)
- RISE (grow in confidence)

grown *adj.*
- ADULT

grown-up *adj.*
- ADULT

growth *noun*
- INCREASE

grubby *adj.*
- DIRTY

grudge *noun*
- RESENTMENT

grudging adj.
▶ RELUCTANT

gruelling (also **grueling**) adj.
▶ HARD

gruesome adj.
▶ TERRIBLE 3

gruff adj.
▶ HOARSE

grumble verb
▶ COMPLAIN

grumpy adj.
▶ IRRITABLE

grunt verb
▶ GRUNT

guarantee noun
▶ PROMISE

guarantee verb
▶ ENSURE (guarantee you a job)
▶ FUND (guarantee a loan)
▶ KNOW 2 (You can guarantee she won't like it.)
▶ PROMISE (We guarantee to deliver within a week.)

guaranteed adj.
▶ CERTAIN

guard noun
▶ GUARD (a border/security guard)
▶ WATCH (under armed guard)

guard verb
▶ PROTECT

guardian noun
▶ MOTHER

guerrilla (also **guerilla**) noun
▶ GUERRILLA

guess noun
▶ SPECULATION

guess verb
▶ GUESS (You'll never guess.)
▶ ESTIMATE (guess his age)
▶ SUPPOSE (I guess so.)

guesswork noun
▶ SPECULATION

guest noun
▶ TENANT (hotel guests)
▶ VISITOR (dinner party guests)

guest house noun
▶ HOTEL

guidance noun
▶ ADVICE

guide noun
▶ ADVISER (his spiritual guide)
▶ BOOK (a TV/travel guide)
▶ CRITERION (as a rough guide)

guide verb
▶ TAKE 2

guideline noun
▶ CRITERION

guild noun
▶ UNION

guilt noun
▶ GUILT (feel a sense of guilt)
▶ FAULT (prove sb's guilt)

guilty adj.
▶ GUILTY (find sb guilty of a crime)
▶ SORRY (a guilty conscience)
▶ **not guity** INNOCENT

guise noun
▶ FORM 1

gulf noun
▶ GAP

gullible adj.
▶ NAIVE

gully noun
▶ DITCH

gulp noun
▶ BREATH (give a loud gulp)
▶ SIP (a gulp of sea air)

gun noun
▶ GUN

gunman noun
▶ KILLER

gunshot noun
▶ BULLET

guru noun
▶ EXPERT

gush verb
▶ FLOW

gusto noun
▶ ENERGY 2

gut noun
▶ COURAGE (guts and determination)
▶ STOMACH (food in the gut)

gutsy adj.
▶ BRAVE

gutter noun
▶ DRAIN

guttural adj.
▶ HOARSE

guy noun
▶ MAN 1

Gypsy noun
▶ TRAVELLER

H h

habit noun
▶ HABIT

habitat noun
▶ HABITAT

habitual adj.
▶ FREQUENT (habitual lateness)
▶ REGULAR (habitual criminals)
▶ USUAL (her habitual frown)

habitually adv.
▶ OFTEN

hack noun
▶ REPORTER

hackneyed adj.
▶ TIRED 2

haggle verb
▶ NEGOTIATE

hail noun
▶ FLOOD 2 (a hail of bullets)
▶ SNOW (hail and snow)

hail verb
▶ PRAISE

hailstone noun
▶ SNOW

hair noun
▶ FIBRE

hairpin bend noun
▶ CORNER

hair-raising adj.
▶ FRIGHTENING

hairy adj.
▶ HAIRY

half noun
▶ ROUND

half adv.
▶ PARTLY

half-hearted adj.
▶ INDIFFERENT

half-price adj.
▶ CHEAP

hall noun
▶ HALL 1 (a concert hall)
▶ HALL 2 (the entrance hall)
▶ CORRIDOR (walk down the hall)

hallmark noun
▶ SIGN 1

hallucination noun
▶ DREAM

hallway noun
▶ CORRIDOR (along the hallway)
▶ HALL 2 (the entrance hallway)

halt noun
▶ STOP

halt verb
▶ STOP 2 (halting traffic)
▶ STOP 3 (halt production)

halter noun
▶ REIN

halting adj.
▶ HESITANT

hammer verb
▶ BEAT 1

hammer out phrasal verb
▶ AGREE 3

hamper noun
▶ BOX

hamper verb
▶ BLOCK 1

hand noun
▶ INVOLVEMENT (have a hand in sth)
▶ **show of hands** ELECTION
▶ **lend (sb) a hand** HELP verb 1
▶ **the upper hand** LEAD 2
▶ **wash your hands of sb/sth** REJECT verb

hand verb
▶ GIVE 2

hand back phrasal verb
▶ RETURN 2

handbag noun
▶ SUITCASE

handcuff verb
▶ RESTRAIN

hand down phrasal verb
▶ PASS STH ON

handgun noun
▶ GUN

handicap noun
▶ DISABILITY (physical handicap)
▶ OBSTACLE (Lack of experience is a real handicap.)

handicap verb
▶ BLOCK 1

handicapped adj.
▶ DISABLED

hand in phrasal verb
▶ PRESENT 3 (hand in your homework)
▶ **hand in your notice** LEAVE 3

handle noun
▶ BUTTON 1

handle verb
▶ CONTROL (handle a horse)
▶ DEAL WITH SB/STH (handle the situation)
▶ DRIVE 1 (handle a car)
▶ HOLD (handle with care)
▶ SELL 2 (handle stolen goods)

handling noun
▶ DELIVERY

hand out phrasal verb
▶ DISTRIBUTE (hand out books)
▶ GIVE 3 (hand out advice)

handout noun
▶ AID (dependent on handouts)
▶ GIFT (a £70 000 government handout)
▶ LEAFLET (a publicity handout)

hand over phrasal verb
▶ GIVE 2 (hand over the money)
▶ LEAVE 6 (hand over responsibility)

handsome adj.
▶ BEAUTIFUL 1 (a handsome man)
▶ LARGE (a handsome salary)

hands-on adj.
▶ PRACTICAL

handy adj.
▶ USEFUL

hang noun
▶ **get the hang of sth** LEARN verb

hang verb
▶ HANG (hang your coat up)
▶ DECORATE (a room hung with tapestries)
▶ FLOAT (smoke hangs in the air)

hang around phrasal verb
▶ STAY 1

hanging noun
▶ CURTAIN (wall hangings)
▶ EXECUTION (a public hanging)

hang on phrasal verb
▶ DEPEND ON/UPON STH (A lot hangs on this decision.)
▶ HOLD (hang on to sth for support)
▶ PERSIST (hang on for victory)
▶ WAIT (Hang on a minute.)

hang out phrasal verb
▶ REST

hang-up noun
▶ OBSESSION

hanker verb
▶ LONG

haphazard adj.
▶ RANDOM

happen verb
▶ HAPPEN

happiness noun
▶ SATISFACTION

happy adj.
▶ HAPPY (a happy face/marriage)
▶ GLAD (I'm so happy for you.)
▶ TIMELY (a happy coincidence)

harass verb
▶ HARASS

harbour (also **harbor**) noun
▶ PORT

hard adj.
▶ HARD (hard work)
▶ DIFFICULT 1 (hard to believe)
▶ DIFFICULT 2 (a hard life)
▶ FINAL (hard evidence)
▶ HARSH (a hard winter)
▶ RUTHLESS (a hard man)
▶ SOLID (a hard chair)

hard copy noun
▶ COPY 1

hard-fought adj.
▶ CLOSE

hardly adv.
▶ **hardly ever** RARELY

hard-pressed adj.
▶ BUSY 1

hardship noun
▶ TROUBLE 2

hard up adj.
▶ POOR 1

hardware noun
▶ EQUIPMENT (a hardware store)
▶ TECHNOLOGY (computer hardware)

hard work noun
▶ EFFORT

hard-working adj.
▶ CONSCIENTIOUS

harm noun
▶ DAMAGE (No harm was done.)
▶ **out of harm's way** SAFE adj. 1

harm verb
▶ DAMAGE

harmful adj.
▶ HARMFUL

harmless adj.
▶ SAFE 2

harmony noun
▶ AGREEMENT 2 (live in harmony)
▶ MUSIC (four-part harmony)

harness noun
▶ REIN

harrowing adj.
▶ PAINFUL 2

harry verb
▶ HARASS

harsh adj.
▸ HARSH (a harsh winter)
▸ HOARSE (a harsh voice)
▸ STRICT (harsh criticism)
▸ STRONG 3 (harsh bright colours)

harvest verb
▸ HARVEST

has-been noun
▸ LOSER 2

hassle noun
▸ DIFFICULTY

haste noun
▸ SPEED

hasten verb
▸ ACCELERATE (hasten sb's death)
▸ HURRY (hasten to explain)

hasty adj.
▸ QUICK (a hasty departure)
▸ RECKLESS (Let's not be hasty.)

hat noun
▸ HAT

hatch noun
▸ DOOR

hatch verb
▸ COME UP WITH STH

hate noun
▸ HATRED

hate verb
▸ HATE

hateful adj.
▸ DISGUSTING 2

hatred noun
▸ HATRED

haughty adj.
▸ PROUD 2

haul verb
▸ DRAG (hauled off to jail)
▸ PULL 1 (haul sb/sth out of the water)

haulage noun
▸ DELIVERY

haunt noun
▸ HABITAT

haunting adj.
▸ MOVING

have verb
▸ HAVE 1 (have a car)
▸ HAVE 2 (have two children)
▸ HAVE 3 (have an accident)
▸ HAVE 4 (have a meeting/party)
▸ CONSIST OF SB/STH (have 900 members)
▸ EAT (have breakfast)
▸ PRODUCE (have a baby)
▸ SUFFER FROM STH (have a cold)
▸ **have to do with sth** APPLY 2

have got verb
▸ HAVE 1 (I haven't got a car/job.)
▸ HAVE 2 (She's got two children.)

haven noun
▸ REFUGE

have on phrasal verb
▸ JOKE (Are you having me on?)
▸ WEAR (She had a red jacket on.)

havoc noun
▸ CHAOS

hazard noun
▸ THREAT

hazard verb
▸ DARE

hazardous adj.
▸ DANGEROUS

haze noun
▸ CLOUD 1 (a heat haze)
▸ CLOUD 2 (a haze of cigarette smoke)

hazy adj.
▸ CLOUDY

head noun
▸ LEADER 1 (the head of department/state)
▸ MIND (use your head)
▸ PROFESSOR (the school's head)
▸ TURNING POINT (come to a head)

head verb
▸ GO 1 (head for home)
▸ LEAD 2 (head a team)

headache noun
▸ NUISANCE

headdress noun
▸ HAT

headgear noun
▸ HAT

heading noun
▸ CATEGORY

headmaster noun
▸ PROFESSOR

headmistress noun
▸ PROFESSOR

head of state noun
▸ PRESIDENT

headquarters noun
▸ OFFICE 1

headroom noun
▸ SPACE 1

headscarf noun
▸ HAT

headship noun
▸ MANAGEMENT

head start noun
▸ LEAD 2

headstrong adj.
▸ STUBBORN

head teacher noun
▸ PROFESSOR

heady adj.
▸ EXCITING

heal verb
▸ CURE (heal the sick)
▸ RECOVER 1 (a wound heals)

healing noun
▸ TREATMENT

health noun
▸ HEALTH

health centre noun
▸ SURGERY

healthy adj.
▸ HEALTHY (a healthy diet/lifestyle)
▸ WELL (a healthy child/heart)

heap noun
▸ PILE

hear verb
▸ HEAR (hear a noise)
▸ FIND 1 (Haven't you heard? She resigned.)

hearing noun
▸ CASE

hearsay noun
▸ REPORT 4

heart noun
▸ FOCUS (the heart of the city)
▸ POINT (the heart of the matter)
▸ **from the (bottom of your) heart** DEEP adj. 1
▸ **lose heart** DESPAIR verb
▸ **set your heart on sth** HOPE verb
▸ **break sb's heart** HURT verb 1
▸ **learn/know sth by heart** LEARN verb
▸ **a change of heart** REVOLUTION 2

heartache noun
▸ GRIEF

heartbreak noun
▸ GRIEF

heartbreaking adj.
▸ SAD

heartbroken adj.
▸ UNHAPPY 1

heartening adj.
▸ PROMISING

heartfelt adj.
▸ DEEP 1

heartless adj.
▸ RUTHLESS

hearty adj.
▸ LIVELY

heat noun
▸ HEAT 1 (the heat of the sun)
▸ HEAT 2 (the heat in the factory)
▸ EMOTION (in the heat of the argument)
▸ HEATING (turn on the heat)
▸ PRESSURE 1 (feel/take the heat)
▸ ROUND (a qualifying heat)

heat verb
▸ HEAT

heater noun
▸ HEATING

heating noun
▸ HEATING

heat up phrasal verb
▸ HEAT

heatwave noun
▸ HEAT 2

heave verb
▸ PICK SB/STH UP

the heavens noun
▸ AIR

heavy noun
▸ THUG

heavy adj.
▸ HEAVY

heavyweight noun
▸ VIP

hectic adj.
▸ BUSY 2

hector verb
▸ HARASS

heed verb
▸ HEAR

hefty adj.
▸ LARGE

height noun
▸ LENGTH (a man of medium height)
▸ PEAK (the height of summer)

heighten verb
▸ INCREASE

heist noun
▸ THEFT

hell noun
▸ NIGHTMARE

helmet noun
▸ HAT

help noun
▸ HELP (Run and get help.)
▸ AID (seek legal help)
▸ GOOD THING (a great help)

help verb
▸ HELP 1 (I was only trying to help.)
▸ HELP 2 (help reduce the pain)

helper noun
▸ ASSISTANT

helpful adj.
▸ HELPFUL (a helpful person)
▸ VALUABLE 2 (a helpful suggestion)

helping noun
▸ PORTION

helpless adj.
▸ VULNERABLE

help out phrasal verb
▸ HELP 1

henchman noun
▸ ASSISTANT

herald verb
▸ THREATEN 3

herd noun
▸ HERD

herd verb
▸ CROWD

here adv.
▸ **get here** ARRIVE verb
▸ **get out of here** GO AWAY verb

hereditary adj.
▸ NATURAL

heritage noun
▸ LEGACY

hero noun
▸ HERO (my childhood hero)
▸ STAR 2 (the hero of the novel)

heroic adj.
▸ BRAVE (a heroic figure)
▸ DETERMINED 2 (a heroic struggle)

heroine noun
▸ HERO (a national heroine)
▸ STAR 2 (the heroine of the novel)

heroism noun
▸ COURAGE

hesitant adj.
▸ HESITANT (a hesitant reply)
▸ UNSURE (hesitant about sth)

hesitate verb
▸ HESITATE (Don't hesitate to ask.)
▸ PAUSE (hesitate before replying)

heterogeneous adj.
▸ DIVERSE

heyday noun
▸ PEAK

hiccup (also **hiccough**) noun
▸ BLOW

hide verb
▸ HIDE 1 (hide your papers)
▸ HIDE 2 (Quick, hide!)

hideous adj.
▸ UGLY

hideout noun
▸ REFUGE

hiding place noun
▸ REFUGE

hierarchy noun
▸ SCALE

high noun
▸ EXCITEMENT (be on a high)
▸ PEAK (Profits are at a high.)

high adj.
▸ HIGH 1 (a high price/speed)
▸ HIGH 2 (a high mountain)
▸ HIGH 3 (a high voice/sound)
▸ TOP (high office)

highbrow adj.
▸ INTELLECTUAL 2

high-handed adj.
▸ PROUD 2

highlands noun
▸ HILL

highlight noun
▸ PEAK

highlight verb
▸ MARK 1 (highlight a passage)
▸ POINT STH OUT (highlight the major problems)

highly adv.
▸ VERY

high-pitched adj.
▸ HIGH 3

high point noun
▸ PEAK

high-powered adj.
▸ POWERFUL

high quality adj.
▸ GOOD 1

high-ranking adj.
▸ TOP

high-rise adj.
▸ HIGH 2

high-risk adj.
▸ DANGEROUS

high-speed *adj.*
▸ FAST

highway *noun*
▸ HIGHWAY

highwayman *noun*
▸ THIEF

hike *noun*
▸ INCREASE

hike *verb*
▸ WALK 2

hilarious *adj.*
▸ FUNNY

hill *noun*
▸ HILL

hinder *verb*
▸ BLOCK 1

hindrance *noun*
▸ OBSTACLE

hinge on/upon *phrasal verb*
▸ DEPEND ON/UPON STH

hint *noun*
▸ ELEMENT 2 (a hint of sadness)
▸ SUGGESTION (the first hint of trouble)

hint *verb*
▸ MEAN 2

hip *adj.*
▸ FASHIONABLE

hire *verb*
▸ EMPLOY (hire a lawyer)
▸ ORDER 2 (hire a car)

hiss *noun*
▸ WHISTLE

hiss *verb*
▸ BUZZ

historic *adj.*
▸ FAMOUS

history *noun*
▸ BACKGROUND (sb's medical history)
▸ PAST (the course of history)
▸ STORY 2 (write a new history of Europe)

hit *noun*
▸ SUCCESS

hit *verb*
▸ HIT 1 (hit by a car)
▸ HIT 2 (hit sb over the head)
▸ HIT 3 (hit by the recession)
▸ BANG 2 (hit your head on the ceiling)
▸ GET 4 (hit the main road)
▸ OCCUR TO SB (a thought hits sb)

hit back *phrasal verb*
▸ FIGHT BACK

hitch *noun*
▸ BLOW

hit man *noun*
▸ KILLER

hit on/upon *phrasal verb*
▸ COME UP WITH STH

hoard *noun*
▸ SUPPLY

hoard *verb*
▸ KEEP 1

hoarse *adj.*
▸ HOARSE

hoax *noun*
▸ TRICK

hob *noun*
▸ OVEN

hobble *verb*
▸ STUMBLE

hobby *noun*
▸ INTEREST 2

hog *verb*
▸ TAKE OVER

hoist *verb*
▸ PICK SB/STH UP

hold *noun*
▸ CONTROL (have a hold over sb)
▸ take (a) hold AFFECT *verb*
▸ get hold of sth GET 1

hold *verb*
▸ HOLD (hold a box/baby)
▸ HAVE 1 (Employees hold 30% of the shares.)
▸ HAVE 4 (hold a meeting)
▸ JAIL (hold sb prisoner)
▸ KEEP 3 (held on computer)
▸ RESERVE (hold a reservation)
▸ SUPPORT 2 (hold sb's weight)
▸ THINK (hold views)

hold back *phrasal verb*
▸ BLOCK 1 (hold back the negotiations)
▸ HESITATE (hold back from saying what you really think)
▸ SUPPRESS 2 (hold back your tears)

hold down *phrasal verb*
▸ RESTRAIN

holding *noun*
▸ THING 3

hold on *phrasal verb*
▸ HOLD (hold on to your hat)
▸ KEEP 2 (hold on to your oil shares)
▸ WAIT (Hold on a minute.)

hold out *phrasal verb*
▸ OFFER 1 (hold out little hope)
▸ OFFER 2 (He held out the keys.)

hold out against *phrasal verb*
▸ RESIST

hold out for *verb*
▸ DEMAND

hold up *phrasal verb*
▸ HOLD SB/STH UP (hold up the traffic)
▸ ROB (be held up at gunpoint)
▸ SUPPORT 2 (hold up your trousers/hands)

hole *noun*
▸ HOLE 1 (a hole in the wall)
▸ HOLE 2 (a hole in the ground)
▸ ROUND (play a few holes of golf)

hole up, be holed up *phrasal verb*
▸ HIDE 2

holiday *noun*
▸ HOLIDAY 1 (the school holidays)
▸ HOLIDAY 2 (a camping holiday)

holidaymaker *noun*
▸ TOURIST

holler *verb*
▸ SHOUT

hollow *noun*
▸ HOLE 2

hollow *adj.*
▸ FALSE

the Holocaust *noun*
▸ MASSACRE

holy *adj.*
▸ HOLY (a holy man/life)
▸ RELIGIOUS (a holy relic/war)

homage *noun*
▸ TRIBUTE

home *noun*
▸ HOME 1 (the family home)
▸ HOME 2 (make Spain your home)
▸ FAMILY 1 (a stable home life)
▸ HABITAT (a home to many species of bat)
▸ HOUSE (home ownership)
▸ INSTITUTION (a children's home)
▸ set up home MOVE IN *phrasal verb*

home *adj.*
▸ NATIONAL

homeland *noun*
▸ HOME 2

homely *adj.*
▸ COMFORTABLE

homesick *adj.*
▸ LONELY

homestead *noun*
▸ FARM

hometown *noun*
▸ HOME 2

homework *noun*
▸ ASSIGNMENT

homey *adj.*
▸ COMFORTABLE

homicidal *adj.*
▸ VIOLENT

homicide *noun*
▸ MURDER

homogeneous *adj.*
▸ EQUAL

homy *adj.*
▸ COMFORTABLE

honest *adj.*
▸ HONEST

honesty *noun*
▸ INTEGRITY

honey *noun*
▸ DARLING

honk *verb*
▸ BLOW 3

honorary *adj.*
▸ VOLUNTARY 2

honour (also **honor**) *noun*
▸ AWARD (the honours list)
▸ INTEGRITY (a matter of honour)
▸ PLEASURE (an honour to be invited)
▸ REPUTATION (the family honour)
▸ STATUS (the guest of honour)

honour (also **honor**) *verb*
▸ KEEP 5

honourable (also **honorable**) *adj.*
▸ RESPECTABLE (an honourable man/death)
▸ WORTHY (The team managed an honourable 2–2 draw.)

hood *noun*
▸ HAT

hook *noun*
▸ get (sb) off the hook, let sb off the hook EXEMPT *verb*

hooligan *noun*
▸ HOOLIGAN

hoop *noun*
▸ CIRCLE

hop *verb*
▸ JUMP 1 (hop from foot to foot)
▸ JUMP 2 (hop on a plane)

hope *noun*
▸ HOPE 1 (hope for the future)
▸ HOPE 2 (your hopes and fears)
▸ give up hope, lose hope DESPAIR *verb*
▸ dash sb's hopes THWART *verb*
▸ pin your hopes on sb/sth TRUST *verb*

hope *verb*
▸ HOPE

hopeful *adj.*
▸ OPTIMISTIC (feel hopeful)
▸ PROMISING (a hopeful sign)

hopeless *adj.*
▸ DESPERATE (feel hopeless)
▸ POOR 2 (These computers are hopeless.)
▸ USELESS (It's hopeless trying to convince her.)

hopelessness *noun*
▸ DESPAIR

horde *noun*
▸ CROWD

horizontal *adj.*
▸ FLAT

horn *noun*
▸ ALARM

horrendous *adj.*
▸ TERRIBLE 1

horrible *adj.*
▸ TERRIBLE 1 (horrible weather)
▸ TERRIBLE 3 (a horrible accident)

horrific *adj.*
▸ TERRIBLE 3

horrify *verb*
▸ SHOCK

horrifying *adj.*
▸ TERRIBLE 3

horror *noun*
▸ NIGHTMARE (the horrors of war)
▸ SHOCK 1 (recoil in horror)

hose *noun*
▸ PIPE

hose *verb*
▸ CLEAN

hospice *noun*
▸ HOSPITAL

hospitable *adj.*
▸ FRIENDLY 1

hospital *noun*
▸ HOSPITAL

hospitality *noun*
▸ GREETING

host *noun*
▸ PRESENTER

host *verb*
▸ HAVE 4 (host the World Cup finals)
▸ PRESENT 4 (host a TV show)

hostage *noun*
▸ HOSTAGE

hostel *noun*
▸ HOTEL

hostile *adj.*
▸ AGAINST SB/STH (hostile to an idea)
▸ AGGRESSIVE 1 (a hostile reception)

hostility *noun*
▸ OPPOSITION (public hostility)
▸ TENSION (sense hostility from sb)
▸ WAR (the outbreak of hostilities)

hot *adj.*
▸ HOT (hot weather/water)
▸ POPULAR (a hot new band)
▸ STRONG 2 (hot, spicy food)

hotel *noun*
▸ HOTEL

hound *verb*
▸ HARASS

hour *noun*
▸ TIME 1 (sb's hour of need)
▸ YEARS (wait for hours)
▸ the early hours, the small hours NIGHT 1

house *noun*
▸ HOUSE (a three-bedroom house)
▸ ASSEMBLY (the lower house of parliament)
▸ COMPANY (a publishing house)
▸ FAMILY 1 (wake the whole house)
▸ on the house FREE *adj.* 2

house *verb*
▸ ACCOMMODATE

household *noun*
▸ FAMILY 1

householder *noun*
▸ RESIDENT

housekeeper *noun*
▸ SERVANT

housework *noun*
▸ TASK

housing *noun*
▸ HOUSING

hovel *noun*
▶ HUT

hover *verb*
▶ FLOAT

howl *verb*
▶ SCREAM

howler *noun*
▶ MISTAKE 2

hub *noun*
▶ FOCUS

hubby *noun*
▶ WIFE

hubris *noun*
▶ PRIDE

huddle *verb*
▶ CROWD

hue *noun*
▶ COLOUR 1

huff *noun*
▶ TEMPER

hug *verb*
▶ HUG

huge *adj.*
▶ HUGE

hull *noun*
▶ FRAME

hum *verb*
▶ BUZZ (computers hum)
▶ SING (hum a tune)

human *noun*
▶ PERSON

human being *noun*
▶ PERSON

humane *adj.*
▶ SENSITIVE 1

humanity *noun*
▶ MAN 2 (crimes against humanity)
▶ SYMPATHY (show humanity)

humankind *noun*
▶ MAN 2

the human race *noun*
▶ MAN 2

human resources *noun*
▶ STAFF

humble *adj.*
▶ MODEST (feel humble)
▶ WORKING CLASS (sb's humble background/origins)

humdrum *adj.*
▶ MUNDANE

humid *adj.*
▶ HUMID

humidity *noun*
▶ MOISTURE

humiliate *verb*
▶ EMBARRASS

humorous *adj.*
▶ FUNNY

humour (also **humor**) *noun*
▶ HUMOUR

humourless (also **humorless**) *adj.*
▶ SERIOUS 2

hunch *noun*
▶ IDEA 2

hunch *verb*
▶ BEND

hunger *noun*
▶ APPETITE 1 (weak from hunger)
▶ APPETITE 2 (hunger for success)

hungry *adj.*
▶ HUNGRY (I'm really hungry.)
▶ EAGER (hungry for power)

hunk *noun*
▶ PIECE

hunker down *phrasal verb*
▶ BEND

hunt *noun*
▶ SEARCH

hunt *verb*
▶ FOLLOW 1 (hunt tigers)
▶ LOOK 2 (hunt an escaped criminal)

hurdle *noun*
▶ BARRIER (His horse fell at the final hurdle.)
▶ OBSTACLE (The next hurdle will be getting their agreement.)

hurdle *verb*
▶ JUMP 1

hurl *verb*
▶ THROW

hurricane *noun*
▶ STORM

hurried *adj.*
▶ QUICK

hurry *verb*
▶ HURRY

hurt *noun*
▶ DISTRESS

hurt *verb*
▶ HURT 1 (hurt sb's feelings)
▶ HURT 2 (sb's feet hurt)
▶ DAMAGE (hurt sb's chances)
▶ INJURE (hurt yourself/your back)

hurt *adj.*
▶ INJURED (sb's arm is hurt)
▶ UPSET (sb's feelings are hurt)

hurtful *adj.*
▶ MEAN 1

hurtle *verb*
▶ FLY 2

husband *noun*
▶ WIFE

hush *noun*
▶ SILENCE

hushed *adj.*
▶ QUIET 2

husky *adj.*
▶ HOARSE

hustle *verb*
▶ DRAG

hustler *noun*
▶ CHEAT

hut *noun*
▶ HUT

hygienic *adj.*
▶ CLEAN

hype *verb*
▶ ADVERTISE

hypocritical *adj.*
▶ DISHONEST

hypothesis *noun*
▶ THEORY 2

hypothetical *adj.*
▶ SUPPOSED

hysteria *noun*
▶ FEAR

hysterical *adj.*
▶ HYSTERICAL

I i

icon *noun*
▶ HERO

icy *adj.*
▶ FREEZING

ID *noun*
▶ CERTIFICATE

idea *noun*
▶ IDEA 1 (That's a good idea.)
▶ IDEA 2 (I've an idea where it might be.)
▶ PURPOSE (the whole idea of doing sth)
▶ SENSE (get an idea of what sth is like)

▶ VIEW 1 (He had some very strange ideas about education.)
▶ the wrong idea ILLUSION

ideal *noun*
▶ EXAMPLE 2 (sb's ideal of what sth should be)
▶ PRINCIPLE 1 (political ideals)

ideal *adj.*
▶ IDEAL

idealist *noun*
▶ VISIONARY

identical *adj.*
▶ EQUAL

identifiable *adj.*
▶ RECOGNIZABLE

identify *verb*
▶ IDENTIFY (identify the bodies)
▶ FIND 3 (identify the cause)

identify with *phrasal verb*
▶ UNDERSTAND 2

identity *noun*
▶ IDENTITY (national identity)
▶ AGREEMENT 2 (the identity between the fans and their team)

ideology *noun*
▶ VALUES

idiom *noun*
▶ LANGUAGE 1 (playground idiom)
▶ WORD (What does this idiom mean?)

idiosyncrasy *noun*
▶ MANNERISM

idiosyncratic *adj.*
▶ UNIQUE

idiot *noun*
▶ FOOL

idiotic *adj.*
▶ CRAZY

idol *noun*
▶ HERO

idolize *verb*
▶ LOVE

ignite *verb*
▶ LIGHT 1

ignorance *noun*
▶ IGNORANCE

ignorant *adj.*
▶ IGNORANT (an ignorant child)
▶ UNAWARE (ignorant of the facts)

ignore *verb*
▶ IGNORE

ill *adj.*
▶ HARMFUL (ill health/effects/will)
▶ SICK 1 (seriously ill)

ill-defined *adj.*
▶ VAGUE

illegal *adj.*
▶ ILLEGAL

illegitimate *adj.*
▶ ILLEGAL

ill-fated *adj.*
▶ UNFORTUNATE 1

ill health *noun*
▶ ILLNESS

illicit *adj.*
▶ ILLEGAL

illiterate *adj.*
▶ IGNORANT

illness *noun*
▶ ILLNESS (a period of illness)
▶ DISEASE (suffer from an illness)

illogical *adj.*
▶ IRRATIONAL

illuminate *verb*
▶ LIGHT 2

illuminating *adj.*
▶ INFORMATIVE

illusion *noun*
▶ ILLUSION (be under the illusion that...)
▶ DREAM (give an illusion of space)

illustrate *verb*
▶ DECORATE (an illustrated book)
▶ EXPLAIN 1 (illustrate a point)
▶ SHOW 1 (This incident illustrates...)

illustration *noun*
▶ DIAGRAM (colour illustrations)
▶ EXAMPLE 1 (an illustration of my point)

illustrative *adj.*
▶ DESCRIPTIVE

image *noun*
▶ IMAGE (an image on a screen)
▶ IDEA 1 (conjure up an image)
▶ METAPHOR (a poetic image)
▶ PICTURE (an image of a hunter)
▶ REPUTATION (sb's public image)

imagery *noun*
▶ METAPHOR

imaginable *adj.*
▶ POSSIBLE 2

imaginary *adj.*
▶ FICTIONAL

imagination *noun*
▶ IMAGINATION (a vivid imagination)
▶ INSPIRATION (lack imagination)

imaginative *adj.*
▶ CREATIVE

imagine *noun*
▶ IMAGINE (imagine what it would be like)
▶ SUPPOSE (I imagine so.)

imbalance *noun*
▶ DIFFERENCE

imitate *verb*
▶ FOLLOW 4 (provide a model for children to imitate)
▶ POSE (imitate sb's accent)

imitation *noun*
▶ FAKE (a poor imitation of the real thing)
▶ PARODY (imitations of celebrities)

imitation *adj.*
▶ ARTIFICIAL 1

immaculate *adj.*
▶ PERFECT

immaterial *adj.*
▶ IRRELEVANT

immature *adj.*
▶ CHILDISH

immediate *adj.*
▶ IMMEDIATE

immense *adj.*
▶ HUGE

immerse *verb*
▶ SOAK

immigrant *noun*
▶ REFUGEE

immobile *adj.*
▶ STILL

immobilize *verb*
▶ DISABLE

immoral *verb*
▶ WRONG 4

immorality *noun*
▶ EVIL

immortal *adj.*
▶ PERMANENT

impact *noun*
▶ IMPACT (the impact of the blow)
▶ EFFECT (the impact of tax changes on the economy)

impact *verb*
▶ AFFECT

impair verb
▸ DAMAGE

impairment noun
▸ DISABILITY

impart verb
▸ CONVEY (impart knowledge)
▸ GIVE 4 (impart a flavour to sth)

impartial noun
▸ OBJECTIVE

impassive adj.
▸ BLANK

impatient adj.
▸ EAGER (impatient to do sth)
▸ RESTLESS (Try not to be impatient with her.)

impeach verb
▸ ACCUSE

impeachment noun
▸ CHARGE

impeccable adj.
▸ PERFECT

impediment noun
▸ OBSTACLE

impel verb
▸ FORCE

imperative adj.
▸ ESSENTIAL

imperceptible adj.
▸ INVISIBLE

imperfection noun
▸ DEFECT

impersonal adj.
▸ COLD 2

impersonate verb
▸ POSE

impersonation noun
▸ PARODY

impertinent adj.
▸ RUDE

impetus noun
▸ INCENTIVE

impinge verb
▸ INTERFERE

implausible adj.
▸ UNLIKELY 2

implement noun
▸ TOOL

implement verb
▸ DO 1

implication noun
▸ RESULT

implore verb
▸ BEG

imply verb
▸ MEAN 2 (implied criticism)
▸ MEAN 3 (The project implies an enormous investment in training.)
▸ SUGGEST (The results imply…)

impolite adj.
▸ RUDE

import verb
▸ SELL 2

importance noun
▸ IMPORTANCE

important adj.
▸ IMPORTANT (important matters)
▸ POWERFUL (an important member of the team)

impose verb
▸ APPLY 1 (impose discipline)
▸ TAKE ADVANTAGE OF SB/STH (I don't want to impose.)

imposing adj.
▸ MAGNIFICENT

impossible adj.
▸ IMPOSSIBLE

impound verb
▸ SEIZE

impoverished adj.
▸ POOR 1

impractical adj.
▸ UNREALISTIC

imprecise adj.
▸ VAGUE

impress verb
▸ IMPRESS

impression noun
▸ EFFECT (a strong impression)
▸ PARODY (do impressions of celebrities)
▸ SENSE (get an impression of sb)
▸ **false impression** ILLUSION
▸ **be under the impression** THINK verb

impressionable adj.
▸ NAIVE

impressive adj.
▸ IMPRESSIVE (an impressive performance/victory)
▸ MAGNIFICENT (an impressive building)

imprison verb
▸ JAIL

improbable adj.
▸ UNLIKELY 1 (It seemed improbable that…)
▸ UNLIKELY 2 (an improbable shade of yellow)

impromptu adj.
▸ SPONTANEOUS

improper adj.
▸ IMPROPER

improve verb
▸ IMPROVE 1 (improve your knowledge/chances)
▸ IMPROVE 2 (your quality of life improves)

impulse noun
▸ DESIRE

impulsive adj.
▸ SPONTANEOUS

inaccuracy noun
▸ MISTAKE 2

inaccurate adj.
▸ WRONG 1

inadequacy noun
▸ WEAKNESS 2

inadequate adj.
▸ INADEQUATE (food supplies are inadequate)
▸ INCOMPETENT (feel inadequate)

inapplicable adj.
▸ IRRELEVANT

inappropriate adj.
▸ WRONG 3

inarticulate adj.
▸ SILENT

inaudible adj.
▸ QUIET 2

inauguration noun
▸ DEBUT

incapacitate verb
▸ DISABLE

incarcerate verb
▸ JAIL

incense verb
▸ ANGER

incensed adj.
▸ FURIOUS

incentive noun
▸ INCENTIVE

incessant adj.
▸ CONTINUOUS

inch verb
▸ EDGE

incident noun
▸ EVENT 1

incinerate verb
▸ BURN 2

incisive adj.
▸ SHREWD

incite verb
▸ ENCOURAGE 3

inclination noun
▸ DESIRE

incline noun
▸ SLOPE

inclined adj.
▸ PRONE TO STH

include verb
▸ INCLUDE 1 (The price includes tax.)
▸ INCLUDE 2 (Some people, and I include myself…)

inclusive adj.
▸ OVERALL

incoherent adj.
▸ CONFUSED 2 (incoherent thoughts)
▸ HYSTERICAL (incoherent with anger)

income noun
▸ INCOME (people on low incomes)
▸ REVENUE (a source of income)

incompatible adj.
▸ INCONSISTENT

incompetent noun
▸ LOSER 2

incompetent adj.
▸ INCOMPETENT

incomplete adj.
▸ PARTIAL

incomprehensible adj.
▸ CONFUSING

incomprehension noun
▸ IGNORANCE

inconceivable adj.
▸ IMPOSSIBLE

inconsiderate adj.
▸ INSENSITIVE

inconsistent adj.
▸ INCONSISTENT (The witnesses' statements were inconsistent.)
▸ VARIABLE (inconsistent results)

inconspicuous adj.
▸ INVISIBLE

inconvenience noun
▸ NUISANCE

inconvenience verb
▸ TAKE ADVANTAGE OF SB/STH

inconvenient adj.
▸ WRONG 3

incorporate verb
▸ INCLUDE 1

incorrect adj.
▸ WRONG 1

increase noun
▸ INCREASE

increase verb
▸ INCREASE (increase prices)
▸ RISE (a rate increases)

increase in phrasal verb
▸ GAIN 2

incredible adj.
▸ INCREDIBLE (The story seems incredible.)
▸ REMARKABLE (an incredible amount/feeling)

incredulous adj.
▸ SUSPICIOUS 1

incurable noun
▸ FATAL

incursion noun
▸ ATTACK 1

indebted adj.
▸ GRATEFUL

indecent adj.
▸ IMPROPER

indecision noun
▸ DOUBT 1

indefinite adj.
▸ UNCLEAR

independence noun
▸ INDEPENDENCE (a country gains independence)
▸ FREEDOM (financial independence)

independent adj.
▸ INDEPENDENT (an independent research body)
▸ CONFIDENT (make sb more independent)

in-depth adj.
▸ DETAILED

indeterminate adj.
▸ VAGUE

index noun
▸ LIST

indicate verb
▸ DECLARE (indicate your willingness)
▸ SHOW 1 (Profits indicate a boom in the economy.)
▸ SUGGEST (Early results indicate…)

indication noun
▸ SIGN 1

indicator noun
▸ SIGN 1

indict verb
▸ ACCUSE

indictment noun
▸ CHARGE

indifferent adj.
▸ INDIFFERENT (indifferent to the issue)
▸ MEDIOCRE (good, bad and indifferent)

indigenous adj.
▸ CULTURAL

indignant adj.
▸ ANGRY

indignation noun
▸ ANGER

indiscreet adj.
▸ IMPROPER

indiscriminate adj.
▸ RANDOM

indispensable adj.
▸ ESSENTIAL

indisputable adj.
▸ CONCLUSIVE

indistinct adj.
▸ VAGUE

indistinguishable adj.
▸ EQUAL

individual noun
▸ PERSON

individual adj.
▸ OWN (individual freedom/pizzas)
▸ PARTICULAR (each individual member)
▸ UNIQUE (two completely individual styles)

individuality noun
▸ IDENTITY

indoctrination noun
▸ PROPAGANDA

induce verb
▸ CAUSE (a drug-induced coma)
▸ MAKE 4 (Nothing would induce me to go.)

inducement noun
▸ INCENTIVE

induction noun
▸ DEBUT

indulgent adj.
▸ TOLERANT

industrialist noun
▸ EXECUTIVE

industrious adj.
▸ CONSCIENTIOUS

industry noun
▸ INDUSTRY (the steel industry)
▸ PRODUCTION (heavy industry)

ineffective adj.
▸ INEFFECTIVE

ineffectual adj.
▸ INEFFECTIVE

inefficient adj.
▸ INEFFECTIVE

inept adj.
▸ INCOMPETENT

inequality noun
▸ INEQUALITY

inequitable adj.
▸ WRONG 4

inequity noun
▸ INEQUALITY

inert adj.
▸ STILL

inescapable adj.
▸ INEVITABLE

inevitability noun
▸ CERTAINTY

inevitable adj.
▸ INEVITABLE

inexorable adj.
▸ INEVITABLE

inexpensive adj.
▸ CHEAP

inexperience noun
▸ IGNORANCE

inexperienced adj.
▸ NAIVE

inexplicable adj.
▸ CONFUSING

infancy noun
▸ CHILDHOOD

infant noun
▸ CHILD

infatuated adj.
▸ IN LOVE

infatuation noun
▸ LOVE 1

in favour (also in favor) phrase
▸ IN FAVOUR (OF SB/STH)

infect verb
▸ PASS STH ON

infection noun
▸ DISEASE

infer verb
▸ CONCLUDE

inference noun
▸ CONCLUSION

inferior adj.
▸ POOR 2

inferno noun
▸ FIRE 1

infidelity noun
▸ BETRAYAL

infirm adj.
▸ WEAK

infirmary noun
▸ HOSPITAL

inflamed adj.
▸ PAINFUL 1

inflammation noun
▸ TUMOUR

inflate verb
▸ EXAGGERATE (inflate the importance of sth)
▸ INCREASE (inflate prices)
▸ SWELL (inflate your life jacket)

inflated adj.
▸ HIGH 1

inflation noun
▸ INCREASE

inflexible adj.
▸ DEEP-SEATED

influence noun
▸ INFLUENCE (a bad influence)
▸ EFFECT (the influence of television on children)

influence verb
▸ INFLUENCE (influence your decision)
▸ AFFECT (influence the climate)

influential adj.
▸ POWERFUL

info noun
▸ INFORMATION

inform verb
▸ TELL 1

informal adj.
▸ INFORMAL

information noun
▸ INFORMATION

informational adj.
▸ EDUCATIONAL

informative adj.
▸ INFORMATIVE

informed adj.
▸ INFORMED

inform on phrasal verb
▸ TELL 2

infrequent adj.
▸ RARE

infrequently adv.
▸ RARELY

infringe verb
▸ BREAK 3

infuriate verb
▸ ANGER

infuriating adj.
▸ ANNOYING

ingenious adj.
▸ CREATIVE

ingenuity noun
▸ INSPIRATION

ingest verb
▸ EAT

ingrained adj.
▸ DEEP-SEATED

ingratiate yourself verb
▸ FLATTER

ingratiating adj.
▸ SERVILE

ingredient noun
▸ ELEMENT 1

inhabit verb
▸ LIVE

inhabitant noun
▸ RESIDENT

inherit verb
▸ INHERIT

inheritance noun
▸ LEGACY

inhibit verb
▸ BLOCK 1

inhibited adj.
▸ SHY

inhuman adj.
▸ CRUEL

inhumane adj.
▸ CRUEL

iniquity noun
▸ DISGRACE 1

initial adj.
▸ FIRST

initiation noun
▸ DEBUT

initiative noun
▸ PLAN 1

injunction noun
▸ ORDER

injure verb
▸ INJURE

injured adj.
▸ INJURED

injury noun
▸ INJURY

injustice noun
▸ INEQUALITY

inkling noun
▸ IDEA 2

in love adj.
▸ IN LOVE

inmate noun
▸ PRISONER

inn noun
▸ BAR

innate adj.
▸ NATURAL

inner adj.
▸ EMOTIONAL

inning noun
▸ ROUND

innings noun
▸ ROUND

innocence noun
▸ IGNORANCE

innocent adj.
▸ INNOCENT (an innocent man)
▸ NAIVE (an innocent young child)

innovation noun
▸ DEVELOPMENT

innovative adj.
▸ CREATIVE

innovator noun
▸ LEADER 2

inoperable adj.
▸ FATAL

inordinate adj.
▸ EXCESSIVE

input noun
▸ INVOLVEMENT

inquest adj.
▸ INVESTIGATION

inquire verb
▸ ASK 1

inquire into phrasal verb
▸ INVESTIGATE

inquiry noun
▸ INVESTIGATION (a murder inquiry)
▸ QUESTION (receive inquiries about a job)
▸ RESEARCH (a line of inquiry)

inquisitive adj.
▸ CURIOUS

insane adj.
▸ CRAZY (an insane risk)
▸ MENTALLY ILL (certified insane)

insanitary adj.
▸ UNHEALTHY

insatiable adj.
▸ GREEDY

inscrutable adj.
▸ BLANK

insecure adj.
▸ SHY

insensitive adj.
▸ INSENSITIVE

insert verb
▸ INSERT

insides noun
▸ STOMACH

insight noun
▸ UNDERSTANDING

insignia noun
▸ LOGO

insignificant adj.
▸ MINOR

insincere adj.
▸ FALSE

insinuate verb
▸ MEAN 2

insist verb
▸ CLAIM (insist on your innocence)
▸ DEMAND (insist on a refund)

insistent adj.
▸ DETERMINED 1

insolent adj.
▸ RUDE

insolvent adj.
▸ BANKRUPT

inspect verb
▸ CHECK 1

inspection noun
▸ INSPECTION

inspector noun
▸ INSPECTOR

inspiration noun
▸ INSPIRATION (draw your inspiration from sth)
▸ EXAMPLE 2 (an inspiration to us all)
▸ INCENTIVE (the inspiration behind Saturday's victory)

inspire verb
▸ INSPIRE (inspire sb with your enthusiasm)
▸ STIMULATE (inspire trust)

instalment (also **installment**) noun
▸ CHAPTER (the next instalment of the story)
▸ PAYMENT (pay in instalments)

instance noun
▸ EXAMPLE 1

instant noun
▸ MINUTE (pause for an instant)
▸ TIME 1 (at that very instant)

instant adj.
▸ IMMEDIATE

instantaneous adj.
▸ IMMEDIATE

instigate verb
▸ INTRODUCE 1

instinct noun
▸ INSTINCT (know sth by instinct)
▸ IDEA 2 (have a gut instinct)

instinctive adj.
▸ NATURAL

institute noun
▸ ORGANIZATION

institute verb
▸ INTRODUCE 1

institution noun
▸ INSTITUTION (a mental institution)
▸ ORGANIZATION (financial institutions)

instruct verb
▸ ORDER 1 (instruct sb to do sth)
▸ TRAIN 1 (instruct sb in sign language)

instruction noun
▸ INSTRUCTIONS (Follow the instructions on the box.)
▸ EDUCATION (religious instruction)
▸ ORDER (He called you on my instructions.)

instructional adj.
▸ EDUCATIONAL

instructive adj.
▸ INFORMATIVE

instructor noun
▸ COACH

instrument *noun*
- ▶ MEDIUM (an instrument of control)
- ▶ TOOL (a surgical instrument)

instrumental *adj.*
- ▶ POWERFUL

insufferable *adj.*
- ▶ UNACCEPTABLE

insufficient *adj.*
- ▶ INADEQUATE

insult *verb*
- ▶ OFFEND

insulting *adj.*
- ▶ INSULTING

insurgency *noun*
- ▶ REVOLUTION 1

insurgent *noun*
- ▶ GUERRILLA

integrate *verb*
- ▶ COMBINE

integrity *noun*
- ▶ INTEGRITY

intellect *noun*
- ▶ INTELLIGENCE

intellectual *noun*
- ▶ SCHOLAR

intellectual *adj.*
- ▶ INTELLECTUAL 1 (intellectual abilities/discussion)
- ▶ INTELLECTUAL 2 (an intellectual audience/elite)

intelligence *noun*
- ▶ INTELLIGENCE (use your intelligence)
- ▶ INFORMATION (secret intelligence)

intelligent *adj.*
- ▶ INTELLIGENT

intelligible *adj.*
- ▶ CLEAR 2

intend *verb*
- ▶ INTEND (What do you intend to do?)
- ▶ MEAN 2 (What do you intend by that remark?)
- ▶ be intended for/as/to be sth DESIGN 2

intended *adj.*
- ▶ DELIBERATE

intense *adj.*
- ▶ INTENSE (intense feeling/debate)
- ▶ MAXIMUM (intense heat)

intensify *verb*
- ▶ INCREASE

intent *noun*
- ▶ PURPOSE

intention *noun*
- ▶ PURPOSE

intentional *adj.*
- ▶ DELIBERATE

intent on/upon *adj.*
- ▶ DETERMINED 1

intercede *verb*
- ▶ INTERVENE

interchangeable *adj.*
- ▶ EQUAL

intercontinental *adj.*
- ▶ INTERNATIONAL

interdependence *noun*
- ▶ RELATION

interest *noun*
- ▶ INTEREST 1 (places of interest)
- ▶ INTEREST 2 (Her interests are music and gardening.)
- ▶ ATTENTION (lose interest in sth)
- ▶ INVOLVEMENT (declare your interest in sth)
- ▶ PROFIT (pay interest on a loan)

interest *verb*
- ▶ INTEREST

interested *adj.*
- ▶ INTERESTED

interesting *adj.*
- ▶ INTERESTING

interfere *verb*
- ▶ INTERFERE

interfere with *phrasal verb*
- ▶ BLOCK 1

interim *noun*
- ▶ MEANTIME

interlude *noun*
- ▶ MEANTIME

intermediary *noun*
- ▶ NEGOTIATOR

interminable *adj.*
- ▶ ENDLESS

intermittent *adj.*
- ▶ OCCASIONAL

intern *noun*
- ▶ RECRUIT

intern *verb*
- ▶ JAIL

internal *adj.*
- ▶ NATIONAL

international *adj.*
- ▶ INTERNATIONAL

internist *noun*
- ▶ DOCTOR

interpret *verb*
- ▶ EXPLAIN 1

interpretation *noun*
- ▶ DEFINITION

interpretative *adj.*
- ▶ DESCRIPTIVE

interrogate *verb*
- ▶ QUESTION

interrogation *noun*
- ▶ INTERVIEW 1

interrupt *verb*
- ▶ INTERRUPT (Stop interrupting!)
- ▶ DISRUPT (The game was interrupted by rain.)

interruption *noun*
- ▶ PAUSE

intersection *noun*
- ▶ JUNCTION

interstate *noun*
- ▶ HIGHWAY

interval *noun*
- ▶ MEANTIME (the interval between major earthquakes)
- ▶ TIME 2 (sunny intervals)

intervene *verb*
- ▶ INTERVENE

interview *noun*
- ▶ INTERVIEW 1 (a TV interview)
- ▶ INTERVIEW 2 (a job interview)

interview *verb*
- ▶ QUESTION

intestine *noun*
- ▶ STOMACH

intimacy *noun*
- ▶ FRIENDSHIP

intimate *adj.*
- ▶ SECRET 1

intimidate *verb*
- ▶ THREATEN 1

intimidated *adj.*
- ▶ AFRAID

intimidating *adj.*
- ▶ FRIGHTENING

into *prep.*
- ▶ be into sb ATTRACTED TO SB

intolerable *adj.*
- ▶ UNACCEPTABLE

intolerance *noun*
- ▶ DISCRIMINATION

intolerant *adj.*
- ▶ BIASED

intonation *noun*
- ▶ VOICE

intoxicated *adj.*
- ▶ DRUNK

intractable *adj.*
- ▶ UNCONTROLLABLE

intricate *adj.*
- ▶ COMPLEX

intrigue *noun*
- ▶ CONSPIRACY

intrigue *verb*
- ▶ INTEREST

intrigued *adj.*
- ▶ CURIOUS

introduce *verb*
- ▶ INTRODUCE 1 (introduce the latest technology)
- ▶ INTRODUCE 2 (Can I introduce myself?)
- ▶ PRESENT 4 (introduce a TV show)

introduction *noun*
- ▶ INTRODUCTION 1 (the introduction of modern farming methods)
- ▶ INTRODUCTION 2 (the introduction to a book)
- ▶ BASICS (An Introduction to Astronomy)
- ▶ DEBUT (my first introduction to modern jazz)
- ▶ MEETING 2 (sb needs no introduction)

introductory *adj.*
- ▶ FIRST

introspective *adj.*
- ▶ THOUGHTFUL

introverted *adj.*
- ▶ SOLITARY

intrude *verb*
- ▶ INTERFERE (intrude upon sb's private grief)
- ▶ INTERRUPT (Sorry to intrude.)

intuition *noun*
- ▶ IDEA 2 (have a sudden intuition)
- ▶ INSTINCT (women's intuition)

intuitive *adj.*
- ▶ NATURAL

inundate *verb*
- ▶ OVERWHELM

invade *verb*
- ▶ INVADE (invade a country)
- ▶ INTERFERE (invade sb's privacy)

invalid *noun*
- ▶ PATIENT

invalidate *verb*
- ▶ CANCEL (invalidate a guarantee)
- ▶ DISPROVE (Evidence invalidates his version of events.)

invasion *noun*
- ▶ ATTACK 1

invent *verb*
- ▶ INVENT (invent an excuse)
- ▶ DESIGN 1 (invent a machine)

invention *noun*
- ▶ DEVELOPMENT

inventive *adj.*
- ▶ CREATIVE

inventiveness *noun*
- ▶ INSPIRATION

inventor *noun*
- ▶ DESIGNER

inventory *noun*
- ▶ LIST

inverse *adj.*
- ▶ OPPOSITE

invest *verb*
- ▶ SPEND 1

investigate *verb*
- ▶ INVESTIGATE

investigation *noun*
- ▶ INVESTIGATION (a police investigation)
- ▶ REPORT 1 (awaiting the results of a formal investigation)

investment *noun*
- ▶ INVESTMENT

invisible *adj.*
- ▶ INVISIBLE

invite *verb*
- ▶ INVITE (invite sb to a party)
- ▶ ASK 2 (invite questions)

invoice *noun*
- ▶ BILL

involuntary *adj.*
- ▶ NECESSARY

involve *verb*
- ▶ INCLUDE 1 (involve as many people as possible in sth)
- ▶ AFFECT (an incident involving a gang of youths)
- ▶ MEAN 3 (Many of the crimes involved drugs.)

involved *adj.*
- ▶ BUSY 1 (deeply involved with the local hospital)
- ▶ COMPLEX (an involved process)
- ▶ be/get involved JOIN *verb*

involvement *noun*
- ▶ INVOLVEMENT

irate *adj.*
- ▶ ANGRY

ironic *adj.*
- ▶ IRONIC

irrational *adj.*
- ▶ IRRATIONAL

irreconcilable *adj.*
- ▶ INCONSISTENT

irregular *adj.*
- ▶ VARIABLE

irrelevant *adj.*
- ▶ IRRELEVANT

irreplaceable *adj.*
- ▶ VALUABLE 1

irresistible *adj.*
- ▶ UNCONTROLLABLE

irresponsible *adj.*
- ▶ RECKLESS

irreverent *adj.*
- ▶ RUDE

irritable *adj.*
- ▶ IRRITABLE

irritate *verb*
- ▶ ANNOY

irritated *adj.*
- ▶ ANNOYED

irritating *adj.*
- ▶ ANNOYING

irritation *noun*
- ▶ FRUSTRATION

isolate *verb*
- ▶ ISOLATE (isolate patients)
- ▶ IDENTIFY (isolate several factors)

isolated *adj.*
- ▶ LONELY

isolation *noun*
- ▶ DIVISION 1 (political isolation)
- ▶ PRIVACY (social isolation)

issue *noun*
- ▶ ISSUE (environmental issues)
- ▶ CHAPTER (the October issue)
- ▶ PROBLEM (Money is not an issue.)
- ▶ take issue with sb DISAGREE

issue *verb*
- ▶ PUBLISH 1 (issue a statement)
- ▶ PUBLISH 2 (issue a newsletter)
- ▶ PROVIDE (issue a passport)

itch *verb*
- ▶ HURT 2

itchy *adj.*
▸ PAINFUL 1

item *noun*
▸ ISSUE (an item on the agenda)
▸ REPORT 2 (a news item)
▸ THING 2 (pay for each item separately)

itemize *verb*
▸ LIST

itinerant *adj.*
▸ TRAVELLING

itinerary *noun*
▸ SCHEDULE

J j

jab *verb*
▸ JAB

jacket *noun*
▸ COAT

jagged *adj.*
▸ SHARP 1

jail *noun*
▸ PRISON

jail *verb*
▸ JAIL

jailhouse *noun*
▸ PRISON

jam *verb*
▸ PACK

jangle *verb*
▸ RING

jar *noun*
▸ PACKET

jar *verb*
▸ SHAKE 2

jealousy *noun*
▸ JEALOUSY

jeer *noun*
▸ WHISTLE

jeopardize *verb*
▸ THREATEN 2

jerk *noun*
▸ FOOL

jerk *verb*
▸ PULL 3

jest *verb*
▸ JOKE

jiggle *verb*
▸ SHAKE 2

jingle *verb*
▸ CLINK

jittery *adj.*
▸ NERVOUS

job *noun*
▸ JOB (apply for a job)
▸ DIFFICULTY (have a hard job to do sth in time)
▸ RESPONSIBILITY (It's not my job to lock up!)
▸ TASK (odd jobs)
▸ **have a job** WORK *verb* 2

jobless *adj.*
▸ UNEMPLOYED

jock *noun*
▸ PLAYER

jog *verb*
▸ RUN 1

join *noun*
▸ CONNECTION

join *verb*
▸ JOIN (join a club)
▸ LINK 2 (join the pipes together)
▸ TOUCH 2 (a path joins the road)

join in *phrasal verb*
▸ JOIN

joint *noun*
▸ CONNECTION

joint *adj.*
▸ COMMON

joist *noun*
▸ POST

joke *noun*
▸ JOKE

joke *verb*
▸ JOKE

jolly *adj.*
▸ CHEERFUL

jolt *verb*
▸ SHAKE 2

jostle *verb*
▸ PUSH 2

journal *noun*
▪ MAGAZINE (a scientific journal)
▪ RECORD (a journal of her travels)

journalism *noun*
▸ MEDIA

journalist *noun*
▸ REPORTER

journey *noun*
▸ TRIP

joy *noun*
▸ JOY (I felt pure joy.)
▸ PLEASURE (a joy to watch)

joyful *adj.*
▸ HAPPY

JP *noun*
▸ JUDGE 1

jubilee *noun*
▸ BIRTHDAY

judge *noun*
▸ JUDGE 1 (a High Court judge)
▸ JUDGE 2 (the competition judges)

judge *verb*
▸ JUDGE 1 (judge by appearances)
▸ JUDGE 2 (judge sb guilty)
▸ ESTIMATE (judge distances)

judgement (also **judgment**) *noun*
▸ CONCLUSION (a court judgment)
▸ VIEW 1 (In my judgement…)

judgemental (also **judgmental**) *adj.*
▸ CRITICAL

jug *noun*
▸ BOTTLE

jumble *noun*
▸ MESS 1

jumble *verb*
▸ JUMBLE

jumbled *adj.*
▸ CONFUSED 2 (jumbled sentences)
▸ UNTIDY (a jumbled collection of objects)

jump *verb*
▸ JUMP 1 (jump over the wall)
▸ JUMP 2 (jump to your feet)
▸ JUMP 3 (make sb jump)
▸ SOAR (Prices jumped by 60%.)

jump at *phrasal verb*
▸ TAKE 6

junction *noun*
▸ JUNCTION (a road junction)
▸ CONNECTION (a junction box)

jungle *noun*
▸ FOREST

junior *noun*
▸ CHILD

junior *adj.*
▸ YOUNG

junk *noun*
▸ THING 3

jurisdiction *noun*
▸ CONTROL

jury *noun*
▸ COMMITTEE

just *adj.*
▸ REASONABLE

just *adv.*
▸ **just right** IDEAL *adj.*

justice *noun*
▸ JUSTICE

Justice of the Peace *noun*
▸ JUDGE 1

justifiable *adj.*
▸ RIGHT 2

justification *noun*
▸ REASON

justified *adj.*
▸ RIGHT 2

justify *verb*
▸ EXPLAIN 2

juvenile *noun*
▸ GIRL

juvenile *adj.*
▸ YOUNG

juxtapose *verb*
▸ COMPARE 1

K k

keen *adj.*
▸ EAGER (a keen gardener)
▸ **be keen on sth** LIKE

keep *verb*
▸ KEEP 1 (Where do you keep the sugar?)
▸ KEEP 2 (I've kept all her letters.)
▸ KEEP 3 (keep a diary)
▸ KEEP 4 (keep chickens/bees)
▸ KEEP 5 (keep a promise)
▸ CONTINUE 2 (Keep smiling!)
▸ HOLD SB/STH UP (What kept you?)
▸ PROVIDE FOR SB (keep a family)
▸ REMAIN (keep warm)
▸ RESERVE (keep sb a seat)
▸ **keep sth going** MAINTAIN 1
▸ **keep going** PERSIST

keep at *phrasal verb*
▸ PERSIST

keep from *phrasal verb*
▸ PREVENT (keep sb from sleeping)
▸ SUPPRESS 2 (keep yourself from laughing)

keep on *phrasal verb*
▸ CONTINUE 1

keep out *phrasal verb*
▸ EXCLUDE 2

keep up *phrasal verb*
▸ CONTINUE 2 (Keep up the good work.)
▸ MAINTAIN 1 (keep up old customs)
▸ MAINTAIN 2 (keep up a house)

keep up with *phrasal verb*
▸ CONTINUE 2

kernel *noun*
▸ GRAIN

key *noun*
▸ BUTTON 1 (computer/piano keys)
▸ NOTE (the key of G)
▸ SOLUTION (the key to success)

key *adj.*
▸ MAIN

keynote *noun*
▸ SUBJECT

kick *noun*
▸ EXCITEMENT

kickback *noun*
▸ BRIBE

kick off *phrasal verb*
▸ START

kick-off *noun*
▸ START

kick out *phrasal verb*
▸ EVACUATE

kid *noun*
▸ CHILD (He's just a kid.)
▸ SON (Do you have any kids?)

kid *verb*
▸ JOKE (I'm just kidding.)
▸ MISLEAD (They're kidding themselves.)

kidnap *verb*
▸ KIDNAP

kill *verb*
▸ KILL

killer *noun*
▸ KILLER

killing *noun*
▸ MURDER

kin *noun*
▸ FAMILY 2

kind *noun*
▸ KIND

kind *adj.*
▸ KIND

king *noun*
▸ KING (the King of Spain)
▸ **turn King's evidence** TELL 2

kingdom *noun*
▸ REPUBLIC

kiosk *noun*
▸ STALL

kit *noun*
▸ EQUIPMENT

kitchen garden *noun*
▸ GARDEN 2

kit out *phrasal verb*
▸ EQUIP 1

knack *noun*
▸ SKILL 1

knapsack *noun*
▸ SUITCASE

kneel *verb*
▸ BEND

knife *noun*
▸ KNIFE

knob *noun*
▸ BUTTON 1

knock *noun*
▸ BLOW

knock *verb*
▸ KNOCK (knock on the door)
▸ BANG 2 (knock your head on the ceiling)
▸ HIT 1 (knock sth over/down)

knock down *phrasal verb*
▸ DEMOLISH

knock off *phrasal verb*
▸ DISCOUNT (knock off €10)
▸ STOP 1 (knock off work)

know *verb*
▸ KNOW 1 (If only we'd known…)
▸ KNOW 2 (I know it's here somewhere!)
▸ FEEL (know what it is like to be poor)
▸ LEARN (know how to use spreadsheets)
▸ **get to know sb** MEET 3

know-how *noun*
▸ SKILL 2

knowledge *noun*
▸ KNOWLEDGE (specialist knowledge)
▸ AWARENESS (without my knowledge)

knowledgeable *adj.*
▸ INFORMED

L l

label *noun*
▸ LABEL (price/address/name label)
▸ BRAND (a major record label)

▶ NAME (She hated the label 'housewife'.)

label *verb*
▶ CALL 1 (He was labelled a traitor.)
▶ MARK 1 (The file was labelled 'Private'.)

labour (also **labor**) *noun*
▶ WORK 1

labour (also **labor**) *verb*
▶ WORK 1

laboured (also **labored**) *adj.*
▶ ARTIFICIAL 2

labourer (also **laborer**) *noun*
▶ WORKER 2

lace *noun*
▶ BUTTON 2

lace *verb*
▶ POISON

lack *noun*
▶ LACK

lacking *adj.*
▶ INADEQUATE

lacklustre (also **lackluster**) *adj.*
▶ LACKLUSTRE

lad *noun*
▶ GIRL

ladder *noun*
▶ SCALE

ladies' room *noun*
▶ TOILET

lady *noun*
▶ LORD (lords and ladies)
▶ WOMAN (There's a lady waiting to see you.)

lagoon *noun*
▶ LAKE

laid-back *adj.*
▶ CALM

lake *noun*
▶ LAKE

lakeside *noun*
▶ COAST

lame *adj.*
▶ DISABLED

lamp *noun*
▶ LIGHT 2

land *noun*
▶ LAND 1 (the price of land)
▶ LAND 2 (open/agricultural land)
▶ COUNTRY 1 (sb's native land)
▶ COUNTRY 2 (live off the land)
▶ FLOOR 1 (travel by land)
▶ SOIL (fertile land)

land *verb*
▶ LAND (a plane/bird lands)
▶ ARRIVE (due to land at Heathrow)
▶ GAIN 1 (land a job)

landmark *noun*
▶ TURNING POINT

landscape *noun*
▶ COUNTRY 2

landslide *noun*
▶ VICTORY

lane *noun*
▶ ROAD

language *noun*
▶ LANGUAGE 1 (sb's first language)
▶ LANGUAGE 2 (everyday language)

languid *adj.*
▶ EASY 2

lanky *adj.*
▶ TALL

lantern *noun*
▶ LIGHT 2

lap *noun*
▶ ROUND

lapse *noun*
▶ MEANTIME

larceny *noun*
▶ THEFT

lard *noun*
▶ FAT

large *adj.*
▶ LARGE (a large number/family)
▶ **at large** FREE *adj.* 1

large-scale *adj.*
▶ WIDE 1

lash *verb*
▶ BEAT 1

last *verb*
▶ CONTINUE 1 (It lasted an hour.)
▶ REMAIN (This weather won't last.)

last *det., adj.*
▶ LAST 1 (the last bus home)
▶ LAST 2 (last night)

lasting *adj.*
▶ PERMANENT

last name *noun*
▶ NAME

late *adj.*
▶ LATE (late for work)
▶ DEAD (her late husband)

latecomer *noun*
▶ ARRIVAL 2

later *adj.*
▶ LAST 1 (the later part of the twentieth century)
▶ NEXT (at a later date)

latest *adj.*
▶ RECENT

lather *noun*
▶ FOAM

latrine *noun*
▶ TOILET

latter *adj.*
▶ LAST 1

laugh *verb*
▶ LAUGH

laughable *adj.*
▶ RIDICULOUS

laugh at *phrasal verb*
▶ LAUGH AT SB/STH

laugh off *phrasal verb*
▶ DISMISS

launch *noun*
▶ LAUNCH

launch *verb*
▶ INTRODUCE 1 (launch the appeal)
▶ PRESENT 1 (launch a book)
▶ SHOOT (launch a missile)

lavatory *noun*
▶ TOILET

lavish *adj.*
▶ EXTRAVAGANT

lavish on/upon *phrasal verb*
▶ GIVE 1

law *noun*
▶ LAW (against the law)
▶ PRINCIPLE 2 (moral laws)
▶ RULE (strict gun laws)
▶ THEORY 1 (Newton's laws)
▶ **lay down the law** DICTATE TO SB *phrasal verb*
▶ **law and order, the rule of law** PEACE

law-abiding *adj.*
▶ RESPECTABLE

law court *noun*
▶ COURT

lawful *adj.*
▶ LEGAL

lawmaker *noun*
▶ POLITICIAN

lawn *noun*
▶ GRASS

lawsuit *noun*
▶ CASE

lawyer *noun*
▶ LAWYER

lax *adj.*
▶ LAX

lay *verb*
▶ PLACE (lay the blame on sb/sth)
▶ PUT 1 (lay a hand on sb's arm)
▶ SPREAD (lay newspaper on the floor)

lay down *phrasal verb*
▶ RULE 2 (lay down rules)
▶ **lay down the law** DICTATE TO SB

lay off *phrasal verb*
▶ FIRE

lay-off *noun*
▶ UNEMPLOYMENT

lay out *phrasal verb*
▶ ARRANGE (a well laid out page)
▶ OUTLINE (lay out the terms)
▶ SPREAD (lay out a map)

layout *noun*
▶ DESIGN

lazy *adj.*
▶ EASY 2

leach *verb*
▶ LEAK

lead *noun*
▶ LEAD 1 (take the lead in a race)
▶ LEAD 2 (a narrow lead over sb)
▶ INFLUENCE (follow sb's lead)
▶ REIN (Dogs must be kept on a lead.)
▶ STAR 2 (Who is playing the lead?)
▶ WIRE (an extension lead)

lead *verb*
▶ LEAD 1 (lead a race)
▶ LEAD 2 (lead an expedition)
▶ LEAD 3 (Where does this path lead?)
▶ MAKE 4 (What led you to this conclusion?)
▶ TAKE 2 (You lead the way.)

leader *noun*
▶ LEADER 1 (political leaders)
▶ LEADER 2 (The company is a world leader in electrical goods.)

leadership *noun*
▶ GOVERNMENT 2 (show real leadership)
▶ MANAGEMENT (the party leadership)

leading *adj.*
▶ TOP

lead on *phrasal verb*
▶ MISLEAD

lead to *phrasal verb*
▶ CAUSE

leaflet *noun*
▶ LEAFLET

leaf through *phrasal verb*
▶ READ

league *noun*
▶ CATEGORY (in a league of your own)
▶ UNION (the League of Nations)

leak *verb*
▶ LEAK (gas/a pipe leaks)
▶ REVEAL (leak sth to the press)

leak out *phrasal verb*
▶ TURN OUT

lean *verb*
▶ LEAN 1 (lean back in your chair)
▶ LEAN 2 (lean sth against the wall)

lean *adj.*
▶ THIN

leap *verb*
▶ JUMP 1 (leap over a stream)
▶ JUMP 2 (leap out of bed)
▶ SOAR (shares leap in value)

learn *verb*
▶ LEARN (learn a language)

▶ FIND 1 (be surprised to learn sth)
▶ **learn sth by heart** LEARN

learned *adj.*
▶ INTELLECTUAL 2

learner *noun*
▶ LEARNER

learning *noun*
▶ EDUCATION (the learning process)
▶ KNOWLEDGE (a branch of learning)

leash *noun*
▶ REIN

leathery *adj.*
▶ COARSE

leave *noun*
▶ HOLIDAY 1 (annual leave)
▶ PERMISSION (absent without leave)

leave *verb*
▶ LEAVE 1 (It's time we left.)
▶ LEAVE 2 (leave home/school)
▶ LEAVE 3 (leave your job)
▶ LEAVE 4 (leave sb/sth behind)
▶ LEAVE 5 (leave your husband)
▶ LEAVE 6 (leave sb in charge)
▶ PASS STH ON (leave sb money in your will)
▶ REMAIN (Is there any coffee left?)
▶ TAKE 1 (He left this letter for you.)

leave behind *phrasal verb*
▶ LEAD 1

leave off *phrasal verb*
▶ LEAVE SB/STH OUT (leave sb off the list)
▶ STOP 1 (start from where you left off)

leave out *phrasal verb*
▶ LEAVE SB/STH OUT

lecture *noun*
▶ SPEECH

lecture *verb*
▶ SCOLD (Don't start lecturing me!)
▶ TEACH (lecture in philosophy)

lecturer *noun*
▶ LECTURER (a university lecturer)
▶ SPEAKER 2 (a visiting lecturer)

leeway *noun*
▶ FREEDOM

leftover *noun*
▶ REMAINS 2

leftover *adj.*
▶ EXCESS

leg *noun*
▶ ROUND (the first leg of the race)
▶ STAGE 1 (the homeward leg of the journey)

legacy *noun*
▶ LEGACY

legal *adj.*
▶ LEGAL

legend *noun*
▶ LEGEND 1 (the legend of Robin Hood)
▶ LEGEND 2 (the heroes of Greek legend)
▶ STAR 1 (a living legend)

legendary *adj.*
▶ FAMOUS

leggy *adj.*
▶ TALL

legion *noun*
▶ ARMY

legislate *verb*
▶ RULE 2

legislation *noun*
▶ LAW

legislator *noun*
▶ POLITICIAN

legislature *noun*
▶ ASSEMBLY

legitimate adj.
- ▸ GOOD 3 (a legitimate excuse)
- ▸ LEGAL (the legitimate heir)

legroom noun
- ▸ SPACE 1

leisure noun
- ▸ LEISURE (leisure activities)
- ▸ **at leisure** EASY 2 adj.

leisurely adj.
- ▸ EASY 2

lend verb
- ▸ LEND (lend money)
- ▸ GIVE 4 (lend an air of melancholy)
- ▸ PROVIDE (lend moral support)
- ▸ **lend (sb) a hand** HELP 1

length noun
- ▸ LENGTH (the length of the river)
- ▸ PIECE (a length of rope)

lengthen noun
- ▸ EXPAND 1

lengthy adj.
- ▸ LONG

lenient adj.
- ▸ LENIENT

less adv.
- ▸ **more or less** ALMOST

lesson noun
- ▸ CLASS 2

let verb
- ▸ ALLOW (Let me drive.)
- ▸ **let sb go** FIRE (let 100 employees go)
- ▸ **let (sb/sth) go** FREE 1
- ▸ **let sb go** RELEASE (Let me go! You're hurting me!)
- ▸ **let sb/sth loose** RELEASE

let down phrasal verb
- ▸ DISAPPOINT

let-down noun
- ▸ DISAPPOINTMENT

lethal noun
- ▸ FATAL

let in phrasal verb
- ▸ LET SB IN

let off phrasal verb
- ▸ EXEMPT

letter noun
- ▸ LETTER (send a letter)
- ▸ NUMBER 2 (the letters of the alphabet)

level noun
- ▸ LEVEL (the rising level of crime)
- ▸ ATTITUDE (On a personal level, I would like to thank…)
- ▸ FLOOR 2 (the lowest level of the site)
- ▸ CLASS 4 (the lower levels within a company)
- ▸ QUALITY (a high level of ability)

level verb
- ▸ DEMOLISH

level adj.
- ▸ CLOSE (The scores were level.)
- ▸ FLAT (level ground)

level-headed adj.
- ▸ REALISTIC 1

lever noun
- ▸ BUTTON 1

lever verb
- ▸ PULL 2

leverage noun
- ▸ POWER

levy verb
- ▸ CHARGE

liability noun
- ▸ DEBT (have liabilities of $90 000)
- ▸ RESPONSIBILITY (accept liability)

liable to adj.
- ▸ PRONE TO STH

liaison noun
- ▸ RELATIONSHIP 2

liaison officer noun
- ▸ NEGOTIATOR

libel verb
- ▸ DISCREDIT

liberal adj.
- ▸ GENEROUS (liberal with your money/criticism)
- ▸ TOLERANT (liberal attitudes)

liberate verb
- ▸ RELEASE

liberty noun
- ▸ FREEDOM (religious liberty)
- ▸ RIGHT (civil liberties)

libretto noun
- ▸ SCRIPT

licence (also **license**) noun
- ▸ LICENCE

license verb
- ▸ ALLOW

licensed adj.
- ▸ OFFICIAL

lid noun
- ▸ LID

lie noun
- ▸ LIE

lie verb
- ▸ LIE (lie on your back)
- ▸ **lie low** HIDE 2

lie down phrasal verb
- ▸ LIE

life noun
- ▸ LIFE 1 (no signs of life)
- ▸ LIFE 2 (all your life)
- ▸ LIFE 3 (make life easier)
- ▸ ENERGY 2 (inject some new life into the project)
- ▸ NATURE 2 (marine/pond life)
- ▸ **real life** FACT
- ▸ **a/the/sb's way of life** LIFE 3

life history noun
- ▸ BACKGROUND

lifeless verb
- ▸ DEAD

lifelike adj.
- ▸ REALISTIC 2

lifestyle noun
- ▸ LIFE 3

life-threatening adj.
- ▸ SERIOUS 1

lifetime noun
- ▸ LIFE 2

lift noun
- ▸ FLIGHT

lift verb
- ▸ CANCEL (lift a ban)
- ▸ PICK SB/STH UP (lift a suitcase)
- ▸ **lift/raise sb's spirits** ENCOURAGE 1

light noun
- ▸ LIGHT 1 (a beam of light)
- ▸ LIGHT 2 (Turn on the lights.)
- ▸ **shed/cast/throw light on sth** EXPLAIN verb 1
- ▸ **bring sth to light** REVEAL verb
- ▸ **come to light** TURN OUT phrasal verb

light verb
- ▸ LIGHT 1 (light a fire)
- ▸ LIGHT 2 (well lit streets)

light adj.
- ▸ GENTLE (light winds/exercise)
- ▸ MINOR (light reading)
- ▸ PALE 2 (light blue eyes)
- ▸ **make light of sth** UNDERSTATE verb

lighten verb
- ▸ EASE

light-headed adj.
- ▸ DIZZY

light-hearted adj.
- ▸ FUNNY

lighting noun
- ▸ LIGHT 1

light up phrasal verb
- ▸ LIGHT 2

like verb
- ▸ LIKE (I like your tie.)
- ▸ LOVE (I like her.)
- ▸ WANT (Do what you like.)
- ▸ **would like sth** WANT

like prep., adj.
- ▸ LIKE

likeable (also **likable**) adj.
- ▸ NICE 2

likelihood noun
- ▸ POSSIBILITY

likely adj.
- ▸ LIKELY

likely adv.
- ▸ **most likely** PROBABLY

likeness noun
- ▸ SIMILARITY

liking noun
- ▸ LOVE 2 (take a liking to sb)
- ▸ TASTE 1 (a liking for fast cars)

limit noun
- ▸ LIMIT 1 (a speed/time/age limit)
- ▸ LIMIT 2 (a limit to what we can do)
- ▸ EDGE (the city limits)

limit verb
- ▸ LIMIT (limit your calorie intake)
- ▸ CONFINE SB/STH TO STH (Families are limited to four tickets each.)

limitation noun
- ▸ LIMIT 1 (physical limitations)
- ▸ WEAKNESS 1 (the limitations of this approach)

limited adj.
- ▸ LIMITED 1 (limited resources)
- ▸ LIMITED 2 (This offer is for a limited period only.)

limp verb
- ▸ STUMBLE

line noun
- ▸ ATTITUDE (take a hard line on drugs)
- ▸ BORDER (state/county lines)
- ▸ FOLD (fine lines around his eyes)
- ▸ LIMIT 2 (the fine line between helping and interfering)
- ▸ PIPE (a fuel/power line)
- ▸ ROW (stand/wait in line)
- ▸ SCALE (the line of command)
- ▸ SCENE (the opening lines of the poem)
- ▸ SCRIPT (actors learn their lines)
- ▸ SERIES (She came from a long line of doctors.)
- ▸ SHAPE (the line of her jaw)
- ▸ WAY 3 (Go in a straight line.)
- ▸ **out of line** UNACCEPTABLE adj.

line verb
- ▸ SURROUND

lineage noun
- ▸ FAMILY 3

line up phrasal verb
- ▸ ARRANGE (lined up against the wall)
- ▸ SCHEDULE (have a job lined up)

line-up noun
- ▸ TEAM 2

linger verb
- ▸ REMAIN (a smell lingers)
- ▸ STAY 1 (linger over breakfast)

link noun
- ▸ CONNECTION (a link in a chain)
- ▸ RELATION (a link between the two murders)
- ▸ RELATIONSHIP 1 (trade links)

link verb
- ▸ LINK 1 (The two factors are directly linked.)
- ▸ LINK 2 (The cameras are linked to a computer.)
- ▸ RELATE (Newspapers have linked his name with the singer.)

liquid noun
- ▸ MATERIAL

liquidate verb
- ▸ SELL 1

liquor noun
- ▸ DRINK 2

list noun
- ▸ LIST

list verb
- ▸ LIST

listen verb
- ▸ HEAR

listener noun
- ▸ AUDIENCE

listen in verb
- ▸ OVERHEAR

listing noun
- ▸ LIST

literacy noun
- ▸ KNOWLEDGE

literary adj.
- ▸ INTELLECTUAL 2

literature noun
- ▸ LITERATURE

litigation noun
- ▸ CASE

litter noun
- ▸ OFFSPRING

little adj.
- ▸ SLIGHT (every little detail.)
- ▸ SMALL (a little girl)

liturgy noun
- ▸ CEREMONY

live verb
- ▸ LIVE (live in a house)
- ▸ EXIST (When did she live?)
- ▸ REMAIN (live in your memory)
- ▸ SURVIVE (only six months to live)

live adj.
- ▸ ALIVE

live it up phrasal verb
- ▸ PLAY 1

lively adj.
- ▸ LIVELY (a lively young woman)
- ▸ BUSY 2 (a lively trade)
- ▸ CROWDED (a lively bar/resort)

live on phrasal verb
- ▸ SURVIVE

live through phrasal verb
- ▸ SURVIVE

live with phrasal verb
- ▸ ACCEPT

living noun
- ▸ LIFE 3 (living arrangements)
- ▸ **earn a living** WORK verb 2

living adj.
- ▸ ALIVE

load noun
- ▸ CARGO (a truck sheds its load)
- ▸ LOT (three truckloads of sand)
- ▸ WEIGHT (a load-bearing wall)

load verb
- ▸ FILL (load a ship)
- ▸ INSERT (load a camera with film)

loaded adj.
- ▸ RICH

loaf noun
- ▸ PIECE

loan noun
- ▸ LOAN

loan verb
- ▸ LEND

loathe *verb*
▸ HATE

loathing *noun*
▸ HATRED

lob *verb*
▸ THROW

lobby *noun*
▸ HALL 2 (the hotel lobby)
▸ PARTY 1 (the gun lobby)

lobby *verb*
▸ CAMPAIGN

lobbyist *noun*
▸ ADVOCATE

local *noun*
▸ BAR (have a drink at your local)
▸ RESIDENT (friendly locals)

locality *noun*
▸ PROXIMITY

locate *verb*
▸ BASE (located in the town centre)
▸ FIND 4 (locate the missing sailors)

location *noun*
▸ PLACE 1

loch *noun*
▸ LAKE

lock *verb*
▸ CLOSE 1

lock away *phrasal verb*
▸ JAIL

lock in *verb*
▸ TRAP

lock up *phrasal verb*
▸ JAIL

lodge *verb*
▸ PRESENT 3

lodger *noun*
▸ TENANT

lodging *noun*
▸ HOUSING

lofty *adj.*
▸ HIGH 2

log *noun*
▸ RECORD

log *verb*
▸ RECORD 1

logic *noun*
▸ LOGIC

logical *adj.*
▸ OBVIOUS (the logical thing to do)
▸ RATIONAL (a logical argument)

logistics *noun*
▸ PLANNING

logo *noun*
▸ LOGO

loiter *verb*
▸ STAY 1

lone *adj.*
▸ SINGLE

loneliness *noun*
▸ PRIVACY

lonely *adj.*
▸ LONELY (feel lonely)
▸ ALONE (lonely nights at home)

long *verb*
▸ LONG

long *adj.*
▸ LONG

longing *noun*
▸ APPETITE 2

long-lasting *adj.*
▸ LONG

long-lived *adj.*
▸ OLD 2

long-serving *adj.*
▸ EXPERIENCED

long-standing *adj.*
▸ OLD 1

loo *noun*
▸ TOILET

look *noun*
▸ LOOK (have/take a look at sth)
▸ APPEARANCE (I don't like the look of that guy.)
▸ CONSIDERATION (take a look at the proposals)
▸ EXPRESSION 2 (the look in her eyes)
▸ FASHION (the punk look)
▸ SEARCH (have a look for sth)

look *verb*
▸ LOOK 1 (Look at that!)
▸ LOOK 2 (look for your passport)
▸ SEEM (You look tired.)
▸ **look like sb/sth** LOOK LIKE SB/STH

look after *phrasal verb*
▸ LOOK AFTER SB (look after a child)
▸ DEAL WITH SB/STH (look after sb's affairs)
▸ TAKE CARE OF YOURSELF (look after yourself)

look ahead *phrasal verb*
▸ EXPECT

look at *phrasal verb*
▸ CHECK 1 (get a doctor to look at your swollen ankle)
▸ CONSIDER (look at three different theories)
▸ REGARD (Look at it this way:...)

look back *phrasal verb*
▸ REMEMBER

look for *phrasal verb*
▸ EXPECT

look forward to *phrasal verb*
▸ EXPECT

look in on *phrasal verb*
▸ VISIT

look into *phrasal verb*
▸ INVESTIGATE

look like *phrase*
▸ LOOK LIKE SB/STH

lookout *noun*
▸ GUARD

look over *phrasal verb*
▸ CHECK 1

looks *noun*
▸ APPEARANCE

look through *phrasal verb*
▸ READ

look up *phrasal verb*
▸ IMPROVE 2 (Things are looking up.)
▸ REFER TO STH (Look it up in the dictionary.)
▸ VISIT (Look me up next time you're in the country.)

look up to *phrasal verb*
▸ RESPECT

loom *verb*
▸ APPEAR

loop *noun*
▸ CURVE

loop *verb*
▸ WRAP SB/STH AROUND/ROUND SB/STH

loose *adj.*
▸ FREE 1 (a horse breaks loose)
▸ **let sb/sth loose** RELEASE *verb*

loosen *verb*
▸ RELAX 2

loot *verb*
▸ ROB

looter *noun*
▸ THIEF

lop *verb*
▸ CUT 3

lord *noun*
▸ LORD

lore *noun*
▸ KNOWLEDGE

lorry *noun*
▸ CAR

lose *verb*
▸ LOSE (We lost 2–0.)
▸ ESCAPE (lose your pursuers)
▸ LEAVE 4 (lose your keys)
▸ WASTE (lose time)
▸ **lose heart, lose hope** DESPAIR
▸ **lose your temper** LOSE YOUR TEMPER

lose out *phrasal verb*
▸ LOSE OUT

loser *noun*
▸ LOSER 1 (They were 16–3 losers to New Zealand.)
▸ LOSER 2 (a bunch of losers)

losing *adj.*
▸ UNSUCCESSFUL

loss *noun*
▸ DEBT (operating at a loss)
▸ **at a loss** CONFUSED *adj.* 1

loss-making *adj.*
▸ LOSS-MAKING

lot *noun*
▸ LOT (the first lot of visitors)
▸ FUTURE (her lot in life)
▸ LAND 2 (a building lot)

lottery *noun*
▸ RISK 2

loud *adj.*
▸ LOUD (a loud noise)
▸ COLOURED (a loud jacket)

lounge *verb*
▸ LIE

lousy *adj.*
▸ BAD

lout *noun*
▸ HOOLIGAN

lovable *adj.*
▸ SWEET

love *noun*
▸ LOVE 1 (fall madly in love with sb)
▸ LOVE 2 (a mother's love for her children)
▸ DARLING (Goodbye, my love.)
▸ TASTE 1 (a love of nature)
▸ **in love** IN LOVE

love *verb*
▸ LOVE (I love you.)
▸ LIKE (I love the spring.)

love affair *noun*
▸ RELATIONSHIP 2

loved one *noun*
▸ DARLING

lovely *adj.*
▸ BEAUTIFUL 1 (a lovely face)
▸ BEAUTIFUL 2 (lovely countryside)
▸ NICE 2 (a lovely person)
▸ WONDERFUL (a lovely day)

lover *noun*
▸ LOVER (He suspected his wife of having a lover.)
▸ FAN (a lover of the arts)

loving *adj.*
▸ LOVING

low *adj.*
▸ DEEP 2 (low notes/voices)
▸ POOR 2 (low quality/standards)
▸ SCARCE (supplies run low)
▸ **lie low** HIDE 2

lower *verb*
▸ REDUCE

lowland *noun*
▸ PLAIN

lowly *adj.*
▸ WORKING CLASS

loyal *adj.*
▸ RELIABLE 1

lucid *adj.*
▸ CLEAR 2

luck *noun*
▸ LUCK (good/bad luck)
▸ **in luck** LUCKY *adj.*

lucky *adj.*
▸ LUCKY (lucky to be alive)
▸ TIMELY (It was lucky for me that...)

lucrative *adj.*
▸ SUCCESSFUL 2

ludicrous *adj.*
▸ RIDICULOUS

lug *verb*
▸ CARRY 1

luggage *noun*
▸ SUITCASE

lukewarm *adj.*
▸ COLD 1 (lukewarm water)
▸ INDIFFERENT (lukewarm support)

lull *noun*
▸ PAUSE

lumber *verb*
▸ STUMBLE

lump *noun*
▸ PIECE (a sugar lump)
▸ TUMOUR (a painful lump)

lumpy *adj.*
▸ ROUGH 1

lunch *noun*
▸ DINNER

lunch *verb*
▸ DINE

luncheon *noun*
▸ DINNER

lurch *noun*
▸ **leave sb in the lurch** DISAPPOINT *verb*

lurch *verb*
▸ STUMBLE

lurid *adj.*
▸ COLOURED

lurk *verb*
▸ HIDE 2

lust *noun*
▸ LOVE 1

luxury *noun*
▸ LUXURY

lying *adj.*
▸ DISHONEST

lyrics *noun*
▸ SCRIPT

M m

mac *noun*
▸ COAT

machete *noun*
▸ KNIFE

machine *noun*
▸ MACHINE

machine gun *noun*
▸ GUN

machinery *noun*
▸ TECHNOLOGY

mad *adj.*
▸ MAD (stark raving mad)
▸ ANGRY (She's mad at me.)
▸ CRAZY (a mad idea)
▸ EAGER (mad about football)
▸ WILD 2 (a mad rush for the exit)
▸ **drive sb mad** ANGER *verb*
▸ **get mad, go mad** LOSE YOUR TEMPER *idiom*

maddening *adj.*
▸ ANNOYING

mag *noun*
▸ MAGAZINE

magazine *noun*
▸ MAGAZINE

magic noun
▶ MAGIC (Do you believe in magic?)
▶ INTEREST 1 (the magic of India)

magic adj.
▶ MAGIC

magical adj.
▶ MAGIC

magician noun
▶ WITCH

magistrate noun
▶ JUDGE 1

magnate noun
▶ EXECUTIVE

magnificent adj.
▶ MAGNIFICENT

magnitude noun
▶ LEVEL

maid noun
▶ SERVANT

maiden name noun
▶ NAME

mail noun
▶ LETTER

mail verb
▶ SEND 1

maim verb
▶ INJURE

main noun
▶ PIPE

main adj.
▶ MAIN

mainstream adj.
▶ TRADITIONAL

maintain verb
▶ MAINTAIN 1 (maintain order)
▶ MAINTAIN 2 (a beautifully maintained house)
▶ CLAIM (maintain your innocence)
▶ PROVIDE FOR SB (maintain a family)

maintenance noun
▶ REPAIR

majestic adj.
▶ MAGNIFICENT

major adj.
▶ MAIN

make noun
▶ BRAND

make verb
▶ MAKE 1 (make your own clothes)
▶ MAKE 2 (make a profit)
▶ MAKE 3 (make a living)
▶ MAKE 4 (It made me think.)
▶ CAUSE (make a hole in sth)
▶ COOK (make a cake)
▶ FORCE (be made to work hard)
▶ GET 4 (The story made the papers.)
▶ PLAN (make a law/will)

make-believe noun
▶ IMAGINATION

make for phrasal verb
▶ GO 1

make it verb
▶ GET 4 (make it to the summit)
▶ SUCCEED (make it in show business)
▶ SURVIVE (She's very weak – I don't know if she'll make it.)

make of phrasal verb
▶ THINK

make off phrasal verb
▶ FLEE

make out phrasal verb
▶ IDENTIFY

maker noun
▶ MAKER

make up phrasal verb
▶ CONSIST OF SB/STH (Women make up 56% of the student numbers.)

INVENT (make up a story)

make-up noun
▶ PERSONALITY (Jealousy is not part of his make-up.)
▶ STRUCTURE (the genetic make-up of animals)

make up for phrasal verb
▶ COMPENSATE

making noun
▶ PRODUCTION

male noun
▶ MAN 1

malicious adj.
▶ VICIOUS

malign verb
▶ DISCREDIT

malignant noun
▶ FATAL

mall noun
▶ MARKET 2

man noun
▶ MAN 1 (a young man)
▶ MAN 2 (the most poisonous substance known to man)
▶ PARTNER 2 (her new man)

manage verb
▶ ACHIEVE (manage to do sth)
▶ ARRANGE (manage your time)
▶ CONTROL (manage an unruly child)
▶ COPE (How do you manage without a car?)
▶ RUN 2 (manage a project)

management noun
▶ MANAGEMENT (under new management)
▶ GOVERNMENT 2 (management techniques)

manager noun
▶ MANAGER

managing director noun
▶ LEADER 1

mandatory adj.
▶ NECESSARY

maneuver noun
▶ TACTIC

maneuver verb
▶ DRIVE 1 (maneuver a car)
▶ MANIPULATE (maneuver your way to the top of the company)

mania noun
▶ OBSESSION

manifest verb
▶ APPEAR

manifesto noun
▶ PLAN 1

manipulate verb
▶ MANIPULATE (manipulate public opinion)
▶ OPERATE (manipulate the gears and levers)

mankind noun
▶ MAN 2

man-made adj.
▶ ARTIFICIAL 1

manner noun
▶ APPEARANCE (She has a friendly, relaxed manner.)
▶ RESPECT (bad manners)
▶ WAY 1 (answer in a business-like manner)

mannerism noun
▶ MANNERISM

manoeuvre noun
▶ TACTIC

manoeuvre verb
▶ DRIVE 1 (manoeuvre a car)
▶ MANIPULATE (manoeuvre your way to the top of the company)

manor noun
▶ PALACE

manpower noun
▶ STAFF

mansion noun
▶ PALACE

manslaughter noun
▶ MURDER

mantra noun
▶ SLOGAN

manual noun
▶ BOOK

manufacture verb
▶ MANUFACTURE

manufacturer noun
▶ MAKER

manufacturing noun
▶ PRODUCTION

manuscript noun
▶ SCRIPT

map noun
▶ MAP

mar verb
▶ RUIN

march noun
▶ DEMONSTRATION

march verb
▶ MARCH (She marched straight past me.)
▶ WALK 1 (troops march)

margarine noun
▶ FAT

margin noun
▶ EDGE (the margins of society)
▶ GAP (win by a narrow margin)
▶ SCOPE (a safety margin)

marginal adj.
▶ CLOSE (marginal constituencies)
▶ SLIGHT (a marginal difference)

marina noun
▶ PORT

mark noun
▶ MARK (dirty marks on the walls)
▶ NUMBER 2 (a question mark)
▶ PATCH (a horse with a white mark on its head)
▶ SCORE (get full marks in the test)
▶ SIGN 1 (a mark of respect)
▶ leave your/its/a mark AFFECT verb
▶ make your/a mark SUCCEED verb

mark verb
▶ MARK 1 (X marks the spot.)
▶ MARK 2 (mark exam papers)
▶ MEAN 1 (mark a change in policy)

marked adj.
▶ MARKED

market noun
▶ MARKET 1 (the Japanese market)
▶ MARKET 2 (a street market)
▶ DEMAND (There's not much of a market for black and white TVs.)
▶ TRADE (corner the market)
▶ on the market AVAILABLE adj.

market verb
▶ ADVERTISE

market leader noun
▶ LEADER 2

marketplace noun
▶ TRADE

mark off phrasal verb
▶ SEPARATE 2

marriage noun
▶ MARRIAGE

marry verb
▶ MARRY (She married a German.)
▶ get married MARRY

marsh noun
▶ MARSH

marvel noun
▶ MIRACLE

marvellous (also **marvelous**) adj.
▶ WONDERFUL

mask noun
▶ PRETENCE

mask verb
▶ HIDE 1

mass noun
▶ GENERAL PUBLIC (cheap transport for the masses)
▶ PILE (a mass of snow and rocks)
▶ WEIGHT (the mass of a planet)

mass verb
▶ MEET 1

mass adj.
▶ WIDE 1

massacre noun
▶ MASSACRE

massive adj.
▶ HEAVY (massive rock formations)
▶ HUGE (a massive heart attack)

mass-produce verb
▶ MANUFACTURE

master verb
▶ LEARN

masterly adj.
▶ IMPRESSIVE

mastermind noun
▶ GENIUS

masterpiece noun
▶ WORK 4

match noun
▶ GAME 1 (a football/tennis match)
▶ PEER (I was no match for his superior strength.)

match verb
▶ MATCH 1 (The two sets of figures don't match.)
▶ MATCH 2 (a scarf with gloves to match)
▶ COMPARE 2 (match sb's performance)
▶ RELATE (match the quote to the person who said it)

match against phrasal verb
▶ COMPARE 1

matching adj.
▶ EQUIVALENT

mate noun
▶ FRIEND

material noun
▶ MATERIAL (building materials)
▶ EQUIPMENT (cleaning/teaching materials)
▶ FABRIC (a piece of material)
▶ INFORMATION (collect material for a novel)

material adj.
▶ RELEVANT

materialistic adj.
▶ GREEDY

materialize phrasal verb
▶ HAPPEN

matted adj.
▶ SCRUFFY

matter noun
▶ ISSUE (a matter for the police)
▶ MATERIAL (organic matter)
▶ PROBLEM (What's the matter?)

matter-of-fact adj.
▶ REALISTIC 1

mature verb
▶ DEVELOP 1

mature adj.
▶ ADULT (a mature attitude)
▶ OLD 2 (a cream for more mature skin)

maxim noun
▶ SAYING

maximize *verb*
► INCREASE

maximum *adj.*
► MAXIMUM

mayhem *noun*
► CHAOS

mayor *noun*
► OFFICIAL

meadow *noun*
► FIELD

meagre (also **meager**) *adj.*
► INADEQUATE

meal *noun*
► MEAL (a four-course meal)
► FOOD (Enjoy your meal.)

mean *verb*
► MEAN 1 (What does this sentence mean?)
► MEAN 2 (What do you mean by that remark?)
► MEAN 3 (This new order will mean working overtime.)
► DESIGN 2 (His father meant him to be an engineer.)
► INTEND (I didn't mean to hurt you.)

mean *adj.*
► MEAN 1 (a mean thing to do)
► MEAN 2 (mean with money)

meaning *noun*
► MEANING (the meaning of a word/text)
► VALUE 1 (the meaning of life)

means *noun*
► MONEY 1 (live within your means)
► WAY 2 (a means of communication)

meantime *noun*
► MEANTIME

measure *noun*
► ACTION (emergency measures)
► CRITERION (a measure of success)

measured *adj.*
► SLOW

measurement *noun*
► SIZE

mechanical *adj.*
► ELECTRONIC

mechanism *noun*
► WAY 2

medal *noun*
► AWARD

medallist (also **medalist**) *noun*
► WINNER

meddle *verb*
► INTERFERE

the media *noun*
► MEDIA

mediate *verb*
► INTERVENE

mediator *noun*
► NEGOTIATOR

medic *noun*
► DOCTOR

medical care *noun*
► TREATMENT

medical center *noun*
► HOSPITAL

medication *noun*
► DRUG 2

medicine *noun*
► DRUG 2 (cough medicine)
► TREATMENT (modern medicine)

mediocre *adj.*
► MEDIOCRE

meditate *verb*
► CONSIDER

meditation *noun*
► CONSIDERATION

medium *noun*
► MEDIUM

meek *adj.*
► PASSIVE

meet *verb*
► MEET 1 (meet for a drink/talks)
► MEET 2 (meet by chance)
► MEET 3 (meet sb for the first time)
► MEET 4 (meet sb's needs)
► GREET (meet sb at the airport)
► HAVE 3 (meet your death)
► PAY (meet the expense)
► TOUCH 2 (where the mountains meet the sea)

meeting *noun*
► MEETING 1 (a business meeting)
► MEETING 2 (a chance meeting)

meet up *phrasal verb*
► MEET 1

meet with *phrasal verb*
► MEET 1 (meet with officials)
► RESPOND (His suggestion was met with howls of protest.)

melancholy *noun*
► GRIEF

melancholy *adj.*
► UNHAPPY 1

melody *noun*
► MUSIC (melody and harmony)
► SONG (a haunting melody)

melt *verb*
► MELT (ice melts)
► DISAPPEAR (anger melts away)

Member of Parliament *noun*
► POLITICIAN

member of staff *noun*
► WORKER 1

memo *noun*
► LETTER

memorize *adj.*
► LEARN

memory *noun*
► MEMORY

menace *noun*
► THREAT

men's room *noun*
► TOILET

mend *verb*
► REPAIR (mend clothes/shoes)
► RESOLVE (mend your differences)

mental *adj.*
► INTELLECTUAL 1

mentally ill *adj.*
► MENTALLY ILL

mention *noun*
► REFERENCE

mention *verb*
► MENTION

mentor *noun*
► ADVISER

mentoring *noun*
► EDUCATION

mercenary *noun*
► SOLDIER

mercenary *adj.*
► GREEDY

merchandise *noun*
► PRODUCT

merchandise *verb*
► ADVERTISE

merchant *noun*
► DEALER

merciful *adj.*
► LENIENT

merciless *adj.*
► RUTHLESS

mercy *noun*
► MERCY

merge *verb*
► COMBINE (merge the two departments)
► TOUCH 2 (The hills merged into the sky.)

merit *noun*
► BENEFIT 1 (relative merits)
► VALUE 1 (artistic merit)

merit *verb*
► DESERVE

mess *noun*
► MESS 1 (The room was in a mess.)
► MESS 2 (The economy is in a mess.)

message *noun*
► MESSAGE (get a message across)
► LETTER (leave a message for sb)

messenger *noun*
► SPOKESMAN

messy *adj.*
► DIRTY (messy clothes/jobs)
► UNTIDY (The house looks messy.)

metamorphose *verb*
► TURN 2

metaphor *noun*
► METAPHOR

method *noun*
► EFFICIENCY (Apply some method to your research.)
► WAY 2 (teaching methods)

methodical *adj.*
► EFFICIENT

methodology *noun*
► WAY 2

meticulous *adj.*
► CONSCIENTIOUS

metre (also **meter**) *noun*
► RHYTHM

metropolis *noun*
► CITY

microscopic *adj.*
► SMALL

midday *noun*
► DAY

middle *noun*
► MIDDLE (the middle of the lake/week)
► **the middle of the night** NIGHT 1

the middle class *noun*
► MIDDLE CLASS

middle class *adj.*
► MIDDLE CLASS

middle ground *noun*
► COMPROMISE

middle name *noun*
► NAME

middling *adj.*
► MEDIOCRE

midnight *noun*
► NIGHT 1

might *noun*
► FORCE

migrant *noun*
► REFUGEE

migrate *verb*
► LEAVE 2

migratory *adj.*
► TRAVELLING

mild *adj.*
► MILD (a mild curry)
► GENTLE (a mild form of the disease)
► SUNNY (a mild winter)

milieu *noun*
► CONTEXT

militant *adj.*
► AGGRESSIVE 1

mill *noun*
► FACTORY

mimic *verb*
► FOLLOW 4 (robots that mimic human movements)
► POSE (mimic sb's voice)

mind *noun*
► MIND (thoughts run through your mind)
► INTELLIGENCE (a brilliant mind)
► MEMORY (My mind went blank.)
► **make up your mind** DECIDE *verb*
► **have sb/sth in mind** INTEND *verb*
► **out of your mind** MAD *adj.*
► **come/spring to mind, cross your mind** OCCUR TO SB *verb*
► **put/set your mind at rest** REASSURE *verb*
► **bear sb/sth in mind** REMEMBER *verb*
► **in your right mind** SANE *adj.*

mind *verb*
► CARE

minder *noun*
► GUARD

mindful *adj.*
► AWARE

mine *noun*
► BOMB

mingle *verb*
► MIX

miniature *adj.*
► SMALL

minimal *adj.*
► SLIGHT

minimize *verb*
► REDUCE (minimize the risk)
► UNDERSTATE (He always tried to minimize his own faults.)

ministry *noun*
► SERVICE

minor *noun*
► CHILD

minor *adj.*
► MINOR

minute *noun*
► MINUTE (It starts in ten minutes.)
► RECORD (the minutes of a meeting)

minute *verb*
► RECORD 1

minute *adj.*
► DETAILED (in minute detail)
► SMALL (minute traces of sth)

miracle *noun*
► MIRACLE

miraculous *adj.*
► AMAZING

mirror image *noun*
► IMAGE

miscellaneous *adj.*
► DIVERSE

misconception *noun*
► ILLUSION

misconduct *noun*
► CRIME 1

misdemeanour (also **misdemeanor**) *noun*
► CRIME 2

miserable *adj.*
► NEGATIVE (a miserable time)
► UNHAPPY 1 (feel miserable)

misery *noun*
► DISTRESS

misfortune *noun*
► TROUBLE 2

misgiving *noun*
► DOUBT 2

misguided *adj.*
► WRONG 1

mishap *noun*
► ACCIDENT

misinformation *noun*
► PROPAGANDA
misinterpret *verb*
► MISUNDERSTAND
misinterpretation *noun*
► ILLUSION
misjudge *verb*
► MISUNDERSTAND
mislay *verb*
► LEAVE 4
mislead *verb*
► MISLEAD
misleading *adj.*
► MISLEADING
misprint *noun*
► MISTAKE 2
misquote *verb*
► DISTORT
misread *verb*
► MISUNDERSTAND
misrepresent *verb*
► DISTORT
miss *verb*
► MISS 1 (miss classes/meals)
► MISS 2 (miss sb's name)
► LOSE OUT (miss your chance)
missile *noun*
► BOMB
mission *noun*
► MISSION (sb's mission in life)
► COMMITTEE (a fact-finding mission)
► TASK (mission accomplished)
miss out *phrasal verb*
► LEAVE SB/STH OUT
missus *noun*
► WIFE
mist *noun*
► CLOUD 1
mistake *noun*
► MISTAKE 1 (learn from your mistakes)
► MISTAKE 2 (a spelling mistake)
mistake *verb*
► MISUNDERSTAND
mistake for *phrasal verb*
► TAKE 8
mistaken *adj.*
► WRONG 1
mistress *noun*
► LOVER
misty *adj.*
► CLOUDY
misunderstand *verb*
► MISUNDERSTAND
misunderstanding *noun*
► ILLUSION
misuse *verb*
► EXPLOIT
mix *noun*
► COMBINATION (a good social mix)
► MIXTURE (a cake mix)
mix *verb*
► MIX (mix ingredients/colours)
► MATCH 2 (Children and fireworks don't mix.)
mixed *adj.*
► DIVERSE
mixed race *adj.*
► BLACK
mixture *noun*
► MIXTURE (cake mixture)
► COMBINATION (a mixture of old and new)
mix up *phrasal verb*
► JUMBLE (Someone has mixed up these forms.)
► TAKE 8 (You must be mixing me up with sb else.)

moan *verb*
► COMPLAIN (moan about your job)
► WHISPER (moan in pain)
moat *noun*
► DITCH
mob *noun*
► CROWD
mobile *adj.*
► ENERGETIC
mobster *noun*
► THUG
mock *verb*
► LAUGH AT SB/STH
mockery *noun*
► CONTEMPT
mocking *adj.*
► CONTEMPTUOUS
mock-up *noun*
► COPY 2
model *noun*
► MODEL (provide a model for sb to copy)
► BRAND (the latest model)
► COPY 2 (a model aeroplane)
► EXAMPLE 2 (a model student)
model *verb*
► SIMULATE
model on *phrasal verb*
► FOLLOW 4
moderate *verb*
► MODERATE
moderate *adj.*
► DISCIPLINED
moderately *adv.*
► PARTLY
moderator *noun*
► JUDGE 2
modern *adj.*
► MODERN (a modern computer system)
► EXPERIMENTAL (modern ideas)
► RECENT (modern times/art)
modern-day *adj.*
► RECENT
modernist *adj.*
► EXPERIMENTAL
modest *adj.*
► MODEST (modest about your success)
► SLIGHT (charge a modest fee)
modification *noun*
► CHANGE 2
modify *verb*
► ADJUST (modify equipment)
► MODERATE (modify your behaviour)
module *noun*
► ELEMENT 1
moist *adj.*
► WET 1
moisten *verb*
► SOAK
moisture *noun*
► MOISTURE
moldy *adj.*
► ROTTEN
mole *noun*
► AGENT
molest *verb*
► RAPE
mom *noun*
► MOTHER
moment *noun*
► MINUTE (Wait a moment.)
► OPPORTUNITY (wait for the right moment to do sth)
► TIME 1 (at that very moment)
momentary *adj.*
► SHORT 1

momentous *adj.*
► IMPORTANT
momentum *noun*
► RATE 1
mommy *noun*
► MOTHER
monarch *noun*
► KING
monetary *adj.*
► ECONOMIC
money *noun*
► MONEY 1 (make money)
► MONEY 2 (count the money)
► MONEY 3 (the family's money)
monitor *noun*
► INSPECTOR
monitor *verb*
► MONITOR (monitor a situation)
► OVERHEAR (monitor sb's phone calls)
monograph *noun*
► PAPER
monopolize *verb*
► TAKE OVER
monotonous *adj.*
► BORING
monsoon *noun*
► RAIN
monster *noun*
► VILLAIN
monthly *noun*
► MAGAZINE
months *noun*
► YEARS
monumental *adj.*
► HUGE
mood *noun*
► MOOD (in a bad mood)
► ATMOSPHERE (the mood of the meeting)
► TEMPER (in such a mood)
► **in a good mood** CHEERFUL
moody *adj.*
► MOODY
moor *noun*
► HILL
moorland *noun*
► HILL
moot *verb*
► PROPOSE
mop *verb*
► WIPE
mope *verb*
► BROOD
moral *adj.*
► MORAL (a moral issue/duty)
► GOOD 5 (lead a moral life)
morale *noun*
► MOOD
morality *noun*
► MORALITY (standards of morality)
► PRINCIPLE 1 (Christian morality)
morals *noun*
► PRINCIPLE 1
moratorium *noun*
► BAN
more *adv.*
► **more or less** ALMOST
morning *noun*
► DAY
moron *noun*
► FOOL
morose *adj.*
► IRRITABLE
morsel *noun*
► BIT
mortal *adj.*
► PERSON
mortar *noun*
► GUN

mortgage *noun*
► LOAN
mortify *verb*
► EMBARRASS
mosque *noun*
► CHURCH
most *adv.*
► VERY
mostly *adv.*
► USUALLY
mother *noun*
► MOTHER
motif *noun*
► PATTERN 2 (a flower motif)
► SUBJECT (a central motif in her novels)
motion *noun*
► MOVEMENT (a rocking motion)
► PROPOSAL (propose a motion)
► **set/put sth in motion** INTRODUCE *verb* 1
motionless *adj.*
► STILL
motivate *verb*
► INSPIRE (motivate the students)
► MAKE 4 (be motivated by self-interest)
motivation *noun*
► INCENTIVE
motive *noun*
► REASON
motley *adj.*
► DIVERSE
motor *noun*
► MACHINE
motorcade *noun*
► FLEET
motorist *noun*
► DRIVER
motorway *noun*
► HIGHWAY
motto *noun*
► SLOGAN
mould *verb*
► SHAPE
mouldy *adj.*
► ROTTEN
mound *noun*
► HILL (a grassy mound)
► PILE (the mound of rice on his plate)
mount *verb*
► CLIMB (mount a platform)
► GET IN (mount a horse)
► ORGANIZE (mount a campaign)
mountain *noun*
► HILL
mount up *phrasal verb*
► BUILD UP
mourn *noun*
► MOURN
mournful *adj.*
► UNHAPPY 1
mouth *noun*
► DOOR
mouth *verb*
► WHISPER
mouth-watering *adj.*
► DELICIOUS
move *noun*
► ACTION (this latest move by the government)
► MOVEMENT (Don't make any sudden moves.)
► **make a, your, etc. move** ACT *verb*
► **get a move on** HURRY *verb*
move *verb*
► MOVE (Don't move!)
► ACT (move quickly to do sth)

- ▶ DEVELOP 1 (Things are not moving as fast as we'd hoped.)
- ▶ GO 1 (traffic moves slowly)
- ▶ IMPRESS (moved by her plight)
- ▶ LEAVE 2 (move house)
- ▶ PROPOSE (I move that a vote be taken.)

move in, **move into** *phrasal verb*
- ▶ MOVE IN

movement *noun*
- ▶ MOVEMENT (a slight movement of your hand)
- ▶ TREND (a movement towards greater liberalization)

move on *phrasal verb*
- ▶ EVACUATE (a policeman moves sb on)
- ▶ EXPAND 2 (move on to the next item)

move out *phrasal verb*
- ▶ LEAVE 2

movie *noun*
- ▶ FILM 1 (a horror movie)
- ▶ FILM 2 (work in movies)

movie star *noun*
- ▶ ACTOR

moving *adj.*
- ▶ MOVING

mow *verb*
- ▶ CUT 3

MP *noun*
- ▶ POLITICIAN

much *pron.*
- ▶ not much of a... MEDIOCRE *adj.*
- ▶ too much UNACCEPTABLE *adj.*

much loved *adj.*
- ▶ DEAR

mud *noun*
- ▶ SOIL

muddle *noun*
- ▶ MESS 1

muddle *verb*
- ▶ JUMBLE

muddled *adj.*
- ▶ CONFUSED 1

muddle through *phrasal verb*
- ▶ COPE

muddy *adj.*
- ▶ DIRTY

muffle *verb*
- ▶ SILENCE

muffled *adj.*
- ▶ QUIET 2

mug *verb*
- ▶ ATTACK 1

mull over *phrasal verb*
- ▶ CONSIDER

multinational *adj.*
- ▶ INTERNATIONAL

multiply *verb*
- ▶ BUILD UP

multi-purpose *adj.*
- ▶ FLEXIBLE 1

multiracial *adj.*
- ▶ INTERNATIONAL

mum *noun*
- ▶ MOTHER

mumble *verb*
- ▶ WHISPER

mummy *noun*
- ▶ MOTHER

munch *verb*
- ▶ BITE

mundane *adj.*
- ▶ MUNDANE

municipality *noun*
- ▶ CITY

munitions *noun*
- ▶ WEAPON

murder *noun*
- ▶ MURDER

murder *verb*
- ▶ KILL

murderer *noun*
- ▶ KILLER

murderous *adj.*
- ▶ VIOLENT

murky *adj.*
- ▶ CLOUDY

murmur *verb*
- ▶ WHISPER

muscle in *phrasal verb*
- ▶ INTERFERE

muscular *adj.*
- ▶ STRONG 1

mushy *adj.*
- ▶ SOFT

music *noun*
- ▶ MUSIC

musty *adj.*
- ▶ SMELLY

mutate *verb*
- ▶ TURN 2

mute *adj.*
- ▶ SILENT

mutiny *noun*
- ▶ REVOLUTION 1

mutiny *verb*
- ▶ REBEL

mutter *verb*
- ▶ WHISPER

mutually *adv.*
- ▶ mutually exclusive INCONSIST-ENT *adj.*

mysterious *adj.*
- ▶ STRANGE 1

mystery *noun*
- ▶ MYSTERY

mystical *adj.*
- ▶ MAGIC

mystify *verb*
- ▶ CONFUSE

myth *noun*
- ▶ ILLUSION (Contrary to popular myth...)
- ▶ LEGEND 1 (a creation myth)
- ▶ LEGEND 2 (heroes of myth and legend)

mythology *noun*
- ▶ LEGEND 2

N n

nag *verb*
- ▶ HARASS

naive *adj.*
- ▶ NAIVE

naivety *noun*
- ▶ IGNORANCE

naked *adj.*
- ▶ NAKED

name *noun*
- ▶ NAME (What's your name?)
- ▶ REPUTATION (get a bad name)
- ▶ STAR 1 (famous names)
- ▶ make a name for yourself SUC-CEED *verb*

name *verb*
- ▶ APPOINT (name sb as captain)
- ▶ CALL 1 (name a baby)
- ▶ IDENTIFY (name the victims)
- ▶ LIST (name your price)

nap *verb*
- ▶ SLEEP

narcotic *noun*
- ▶ DRUG 1

narrate *verb*
- ▶ DESCRIBE (narrate a story)
- ▶ QUOTE (narrate a film)

narrative *noun*
- ▶ STORY 1

narrow *verb*
- ▶ SHRINK

narrow *adj.*
- ▶ NARROW (narrow streets)
- ▶ CLOSE (a narrow escape)
- ▶ LIMITED 1 (a narrow range)

nasty *adj.*
- ▶ BAD (a nasty accident/shock)
- ▶ MEAN 1 (be nasty about/to sb)

nation *noun*
- ▶ COMMUNITY (shock the nation)
- ▶ COUNTRY 1 (developing nations)

national *noun*
- ▶ CITIZEN

national *adj.*
- ▶ NATIONAL (national radio)
- ▶ CULTURAL (national heritage)
- ▶ PUBLIC (a national museum)

nationalism *noun*
- ▶ RACISM

nationality *noun*
- ▶ PEOPLE 2

nationwide *adj.*
- ▶ NATIONAL

native *noun*
- ▶ CITIZEN (a native of Austria)
- ▶ RESIDENT (speak like a native)

native *adj.*
- ▶ CULTURAL

natural *adj.*
- ▶ NATURAL (natural instincts)
- ▶ OBVIOUS (a natural desire for affection)

natural light *noun*
- ▶ SUN

the natural world *noun*
- ▶ NATURE 2

nature *noun*
- ▶ NATURE 1 (the nature of the problem)
- ▶ NATURE 2 (the beauties of nature)
- ▶ KIND (books of a scientific nature)
- ▶ PERSONALITY (She is very sensitive by nature.)

naughty *adj.*
- ▶ NAUGHTY

nauseating *adj.*
- ▶ DISGUSTING 1

nauseous *adj.*
- ▶ SICK 2

navigate *verb*
- ▶ DRIVE 1

near *verb*
- ▶ COME 1 (We neared the island.)
- ▶ COME 2 (be nearing completion)

near *adj.*
- ▶ CLOSE

near *adv.*
- ▶ draw near COME *verb* 2

nearly *adv.*
- ▶ ALMOST

neat *adj.*
- ▶ NEAT (neat handwriting)
- ▶ EFFICIENT (a neat person)

necessary *adj.*
- ▶ NECESSARY (necessary to do sth)
- ▶ INEVITABLE (a necessary condition/consequence)

necessitate *verb*
- ▶ MEAN 3

necessity *noun*
- ▶ CERTAINTY (Living in London was an unfortunate necessity.)
- ▶ NEED (basic necessities)

neck *noun*
- ▶ neck and neck CLOSE *adj.*
- ▶ stick your neck out DARE *verb*

need *noun*
- ▶ NEED (children with special needs)
- ▶ DESIRE (the need to talk)
- ▶ POVERTY (people in need)
- ▶ REASON (no need to do sth)

need *verb*
- ▶ NEED

needless *adj.*
- ▶ UNNECESSARY

needy *adj.*
- ▶ POOR 1

negative *adj.*
- ▶ NEGATIVE (a negative attitude)
- ▶ HARMFUL (a negative effect)

neglect *noun*
- ▶ NEGLECT

neglect *verb*
- ▶ FAIL 1 (neglect to mention sth)
- ▶ IGNORE (neglect your studies)
- ▶ LEAVE 5 (neglect a child)

negligent *adj.*
- ▶ CARELESS

negligible *adj.*
- ▶ SLIGHT

negotiate *verb*
- ▶ NEGOTIATE (We will not negotiate with terrorists.)
- ▶ AGREE 3 (negotiate a deal)
- ▶ CROSS (negotiate a sharp bend)

negotiator *noun*
- ▶ NEGOTIATOR

neighbourhood (also **neighborhood**) *noun*
- ▶ AREA 1 (We grew up in the same neighbourhood.)
- ▶ PROXIMITY (in the neighbourhood of Paris)

neighbourly (also **neighborly**) *adj.*
- ▶ HELPFUL

nemesis *noun*
- ▶ OVERTHROW

nerve-racking *adj.*
- ▶ STRESSFUL

nerves *noun*
- ▶ get on sb's nerves ANNOY *verb*

nervous *adj.*
- ▶ NERVOUS (a nervous disposition)
- ▶ WORRIED (nervous about sth)

nervous wreck *noun*
- ▶ COWARD

net *verb*
- ▶ GAIN 1 (net business)
- ▶ MAKE 3 (net money)

network *noun*
- ▶ CHANNEL (a TV network)
- ▶ SYSTEM (a network of offices)

neurosis *noun*
- ▶ OBSESSION

neurotic *adj.*
- ▶ MENTALLY ILL (neurotic patients)
- ▶ NERVOUS (neurotic about sth)

neutral *adj.*
- ▶ OBJECTIVE (politically neutral)
- ▶ PALE 2 (neutral colours)

never-ending *adj.*
- ▶ ENDLESS

new *adj.*
- ▶ NEW 1 (a new novel/idea)
- ▶ NEW 2 (a new dress/car)
- ▶ NEW 3 (new to this job)
- ▶ RECENT (the new breed of politician)

newcomer *noun*
- ▶ ARRIVAL 2

news noun
► NEWS

newscaster noun
► PRESENTER

newsletter noun
► NEWSPAPER

newspaper noun
► NEWSPAPER

newsreader noun
► PRESENTER

next adj.
► NEXT

nib noun
► TIP

nibble verb
► BITE

nice adj.
► NICE 1 (have a nice day)
► NICE 2 (a really nice person)

nick verb
► CUT 4 (nick your finger on sth)
► STEAL (nick sb's bag/pen)

nickname noun
► NICKNAME

nickname verb
► CALL 1

night noun
► NIGHT 1 (I lay awake all night.)
► NIGHT 2 (Let's go out tomorrow night.)
► **the middle of the night** NIGHT 1

nightfall noun
► NIGHT 2

nightmare noun
► NIGHTMARE (The trip turned into a nightmare.)
► DREAM (He still has nightmares about the accident.)

night-time noun
► NIGHT 1

no noun
► REFUSAL

the nobility noun
► ELITE

noble noun
► LORD

noble adj.
► ARISTOCRATIC (a noble family)
► WORTHY (a noble cause)

nobleman noun
► LORD

nod verb
► NOD

nod off phrasal verb
► FALL ASLEEP

no-hoper noun
► LOSER 2

noise noun
► SOUND 1

noisy adj.
► LOUD

nomad noun
► TRAVELLER

nomadic adj.
► TRAVELLING

no-man's land noun
► DESERT

nominate verb
► APPOINT (be nominated to the committee)
► RECOMMEND 2 (be nominated as best actor)

nomination noun
► CHOICE 1

nominee noun
► CANDIDATE

nondescript adj.
► DRAB

non-existent adj.
► FICTIONAL

no-nonsense adj.
► REALISTIC 1

non-partisan adj.
► OBJECTIVE

non-profit adj.
► LOSS-MAKING

nonsense noun
► NONSENSE

non-standard adj.
► ABNORMAL

non-stop adj.
► CONTINUOUS

non-white adj.
► BLACK

noon noun
► DAY

norm noun
► CRITERION (below international norms)
► TRADITION (the values and norms of society)

normal adj.
► NORMAL (normal office hours)
► SANE (normal people)

normally adv.
► USUALLY

nose noun
► **under sb's nose** OPEN adj.

nosy adj.
► CURIOUS

notable adj.
► IMPORTANT

not bad adj.
► ADEQUATE

note noun
► NOTE (play a note on the piano)
► LETTER (a quick note to say thank you)

note verb
► COMMENT (He noted in passing that...)
► NOTICE (Please note that...)

not guilty adj.
► INNOCENT

nothing pron.
► **come to nothing** FAIL verb 2
► **for nothing** FREE adj. 2

notice noun
► ATTENTION (bring sth to your notice)
► POSTER (a notice on the board)
► SIGN 2 (The notice read...)
► WARNING (until further notice)
► **take no notice** IGNORE verb
► **give in/hand in your notice** LEAVE verb 3

notice verb
► NOTICE

noticeable adj.
► VISIBLE

noticeboard noun
► SIGN 2

notify verb
► TELL 1

notion noun
► IDEA 1

notional adj.
► SUPPOSED

nourish verb
► SERVE 1

nourishing adj.
► HEALTHY

nourishment noun
► FOOD

novel noun
► BOOK

novel adj.
► NEW 1

novelist noun
► WRITER

novice noun
► BEGINNER

now adv.
► **now and again/then** SOMETIMES

nowhere adv.
► **get/go nowhere** FAIL verb 2

nuance noun
► ASSOCIATION

nucleus noun
► POINT

nude noun
► **in the nude** NAKED adj.

nude adj.
► NAKED

nudge verb
► JAB

nuisance noun
► NUISANCE

number noun
► NUMBER 1 (a large number of people)
► NUMBER 2 (He lives at number 12.)
► FIGURE (Think of a number and multilpy it by two.)
► SONG (a slow romantic number)
► **your opposite number** EQUIVALENT

number verb
► BE (The crowd numbered several thousand.)
► INCLUDE 2 (I number her among my closest friends.)

number one adj.
► MAIN

nurse noun
► DOCTOR

nurse verb
► TREAT 1

nursing noun
► TREATMENT

nut noun
► GRAIN

nutritional adj.
► HEALTHY

nutritious adj.
► HEALTHY

nuts adj.
► MAD

O o

oath noun
► PROMISE

obedient adj.
► GOOD 7

obese adj.
► FAT

obey verb
► FOLLOW 3

object noun
► TARGET (the object of the exercise)
► THING 2 (everyday objects)

object verb
► COMPLAIN

objection noun
► OPPOSITION

objectionable adj.
► MEAN 1

objective noun
► TARGET

objective adj.
► OBJECTIVE

obligation noun
► RESPONSIBILITY

obligatory adj.
► NECESSARY

oblige verb
► FORCE

obliging adj.
► HELPFUL

oblivious adj.
► UNAWARE

obnoxious adj.
► MEAN 1

observation noun
► INSPECTION (keep sb/sth under observation)
► STATEMENT (general observations about the report)

observe verb
► COMMENT (She observed to me that...)
► FOLLOW 3 (observe the ceasefire)
► LOOK 1 (The patients were observed.)
► NOTICE (observe a change)

observer noun
► ANALYST (political observers)
► INSPECTOR (observers at the conference)
► WITNESS (to the casual observer)

obsession noun
► OBSESSION

obsessional adj.
► ADDICTIVE

obsessive adj.
► ADDICTIVE

obsolete adj.
► OLD-FASHIONED

obstacle noun
► OBSTACLE (an obstacle to communication)
► BARRIER (an obstacle course)

obstinate adj.
► STUBBORN

obstruct verb
► BLOCK 1 (obstruct the peace process)
► BLOCK 3 (obstruct sb's view)

obstruction noun
► BARRIER

obstructive adj.
► PERVERSE

obtain verb
► GET 1

obtuse adj.
► STUPID

obvious adj.
► OBVIOUS (the obvious choice)
► CLEAR 1 (for obvious reasons)

occasion noun
► EVENT 2 (a special occasion)
► OPPORTUNITY (if the occasion arises)
► TIME 1 (on several occasions)
► **on occasion(s)** SOMETIMES adv.

occasional adj.
► OCCASIONAL

occasionally adv.
► SOMETIMES

the occult noun
► MAGIC

occult adj.
► MAGIC

occupant noun
► TENANT

occupation noun
► PROJECT (Shopping is her main occupation.)
► WORK 2 (a dangerous occupation)

occupied adj.
► BUSY 1

occupy verb
► INVADE (soldiers occupy sth)
► LIVE (occupy an office)
► SPEND 2 (occupy your time)

occur *verb*
▶ EXIST (minerals that occur in rocks)
▶ HAPPEN (an incident occurs)

occurrence *adj.*
▶ EVENT 1

occur to *phrasal verb*
▶ OCCUR TO SB

ocean *noun*
▶ SEA

odd *adj.*
▶ OCCASIONAL (the odd occasion)
▶ STRANGE 1 (an odd man/feeling)

oddity *noun*
▶ EXCEPTION

odds *noun*
▶ POSSIBILITY (The odds are that…)
▶ **be at odds** CONFLICT *verb* (Her story was at odds with his.)
▶ **be at odds** DISAGREE *verb* (They were at odds over how to do it.)
▶ **at odds** INCONSISTENT *adj.*

odour (also **odor**) *noun*
▶ ODOUR

oeuvre *noun*
▶ WORK 4

off *adj.*
▶ ROTTEN

off *adv.*
▶ **be off** LEAVE *verb* 1
▶ **off and on/on and off** SOMETIMES

offbeat *adj.*
▶ UNUSUAL

offence *noun*
▶ CRIME 2

offend *verb*
▶ OFFEND

offender *noun*
▶ CRIMINAL

offensive *noun*
▶ ATTACK 1

offensive *adj.*
▶ OFFENSIVE (offensive language)
▶ DISGUSTING 1 (an offensive smell)

offer *noun*
▶ OFFER 1 (an offer of help)
▶ OFFER 2 (an offer of £2 500)

offer *verb*
▶ OFFER 1 (offer good facilities)
▶ OFFER 2 (offer to help)

offhand *adj.*
▶ CASUAL

office *noun*
▶ OFFICE 1 (Are you going to the office today?)
▶ OFFICE 2 (Come into my office.)
▶ ROLE (hold office)
▶ SERVICE (the ticket office)

officer *noun*
▶ OFFICIAL (a press officer)
▶ POLICEMAN (uniformed officers)

official *noun*
▶ OFFICIAL

official *adj.*
▶ OFFICIAL

officialdom *noun*
▶ AUTHORITIES

off-putting *adj.*
▶ UNATTRACTIVE

offset *verb*
▶ COMPENSATE

offspring *noun*
▶ OFFSPRING

off-the-cuff *adj.*
▶ SPONTANEOUS

often *adv.*
▶ OFTEN (as often as possible)
▶ USUALLY (Old houses are often damp.)
▶ **every so often** SOMETIMES

▶ **more often that not/as often as not** USUALLY

oil *noun*
▶ OIL (the oil industry)
▶ FAT (olive/sunflower oil)

OK *verb*
▶ ALLOW

OK *adj.*
▶ FINE (Is it OK if…?)
▶ SAFE 1 (I'll be OK.)
▶ WELL (Are you feeling OK?)

old *adj.*
▶ OLD 1 (old habits)
▶ OLD 2 (an old man/woman)
▶ FORMER (my old house/school)
▶ **the old days** PAST

old-fashioned *adj.*
▶ OLD-FASHIONED

ominous *adj.*
▶ THREATENING

omission *noun*
▶ MISTAKE 1

omit *verb*
▶ FAIL 1 (omit to mention sth)
▶ LEAVE SB/STH OUT (omit question 4)

on *adv.*
▶ **off and on/on and off** SOMETIMES

once *adv.*
▶ **once in a while** SOMETIMES

one-liner *noun*
▶ JOKE

one-sided *adj.*
▶ BIASED

onlooker *noun*
▶ WITNESS

onset *noun*
▶ START

ooze *verb*
▶ LEAK

open *verb*
▶ BEGIN (open a meeting)
▶ SPREAD (a parachute opens)
▶ START (a shop opens)
▶ UNDO (open a letter/bottle)
▶ **open fire** SHOOT
▶ **open the way** HELP 2

open *adj.*
▶ OPEN (open admiration/war)
▶ HONEST (a very open person)
▶ VULNERABLE (open to abuse)
▶ **lay sb open to sth** EXPOSE *verb*

opening *noun*
▶ HOLE 1 (an opening in the roof)
▶ JOB (an opening in sales)
▶ LAUNCH (the opening of a new hospital)
▶ START (the movie's exciting opening)

opening *adj.*
▶ FIRST

open-minded *adj.*
▶ TOLERANT

operate *verb*
▶ OPERATE (operate a machine)
▶ ORGANIZE (operate flights)
▶ WORK 3 (solar panels operate)

operation *noun*
▶ COMPANY (a multinational operation)
▶ PROJECT (a rescue operation)
▶ TRADE (the firm's banking operations)
▶ TREATMENT (a medical operation)
▶ **in operation** ACTIVE *adj.*

operational *adj.*
▶ ACTIVE

opinion *noun*
▶ VIEW 1

opponent *noun*
▶ ENEMY (face your opponent)
▶ PROTESTER (opponents of the regime)

opportunity *noun*
▶ OPPORTUNITY

oppose *verb*
▶ OPPOSE

opposed *adj.*
▶ AGAINST SB/STH (opposed to sth)
▶ OPPOSITE (our views are opposed)

opposite *noun*
▶ OPPOSITE

opposite *adj.*
▶ OPPOSITE (the opposite direction/effect/sex)
▶ **your opposite number** EQUIVALENT *noun*

opposition *noun* >
▶ OPPOSITION (express strong opposition to sth)
▶ CONFLICT (the opposition of good and evil)
▶ ENEMY (He's got a job with the opposition.)

oppress *verb*
▶ DISCOURAGE 2 (The gloomy atmosphere oppressed her.)
▶ SUPPRESS 1 (oppressed people)

oppression *noun*
▶ REPRESSION

oppressive *adj.*
▶ REPRESSIVE

opt *verb*
▶ CHOOSE

optimism *noun*
▶ HOPE 1

optimistic *adj.*
▶ OPTIMISTIC

optimum *adj.*
▶ IDEAL

option *noun*
▶ OPTION

optional *adj.*
▶ VOLUNTARY 1

oral *noun*
▶ TEST 2

orator *noun*
▶ SPEAKER 2

orbit *noun*
▶ WAY 3

orbit *verb*
▶ SPIN

orchard *noun*
▶ FARM

orchestrate *verb*
▶ ORGANIZE

ordeal *noun*
▶ NIGHTMARE

order *noun*
▶ ORDER (obey orders)
▶ EFFICIENCY (create order out of chaos)
▶ PEACE (keep order)
▶ REQUEST (an order for ten copies)
▶ SERIES (in alphabetical order)
▶ **in order** FINE
▶ **law and order** PEACE
▶ **out of order** UNACCEPTABLE *adj.*

order *verb*
▶ ORDER 1 (order sb to do sth)
▶ ORDER 2 (order goods/a meal)
▶ RANK (ordered alphabetically)
▶ RULE 2 (order that sth must happen)

order around/about *phrasal verb*
▶ DICTATE TO SB

ordered *noun*
▶ NEAT

orderly *adj.*
▶ EFFICIENT (in an orderly way)
▶ NEAT (in orderly rows)

ordinary *adj.*
▶ AVERAGE (a very ordinary life)
▶ NORMAL (an ordinary family)
▶ **out of the ordinary** UNUSUAL

organism *noun*
▶ ANIMAL

organization *noun*
▶ ORGANIZATION (a political organization)
▶ EFFICIENCY (lack organization)
▶ PLANNING (the organization of a trip)
▶ SYSTEM (the organization of modern societies)

organize *verb*
▶ ORGANIZE (organize an event)
▶ ARRANGE (organize data)

organized *adj.*
▶ EFFICIENT

organizer *noun*
▶ ORGANIZER

orient (also **orientate**) *verb*
▶ FOCUS

orientation *noun*
▶ TENDENCY

origin *noun*
▶ FAMILY 3 (people of German origin)
▶ SOURCE (the origins of life)

original *adj.*
▶ CREATIVE (an original idea)
▶ FIRST (the original owner)

originality *noun*
▶ INSPIRATION

ornament *noun*
▶ ORNAMENT (china ornaments)
▶ DECORATION (simply for ornament)

ornament *verb*
▶ DECORATE

ornamental *adj.*
▶ DECORATIVE

orphanage *noun*
▶ INSTITUTION

orthodox *adj.*
▶ TRADITIONAL

oscillate *verb*
▶ SWING

ostensible *adj.*
▶ APPARENT

ostentatious *adj.*
▶ FLASHY

ostracize *verb*
▶ EXCLUDE 2

other-worldly *adj.*
▶ MAGIC

oust *verb*
▶ REMOVE 2

outback *noun*
▶ DESERT

outbreak *noun*
▶ WAVE 3

outbuilding *noun*
▶ SHED

outburst *noun*
▶ ATTACK 3

outcome *noun*
▶ RESULT

outcry *noun*
▶ FUSS

outdated *adj.*
▶ OLD-FASHIONED

outer space *noun*
▶ SPACE 3

outfit *noun*
▶ GROUP 3

outfit verb
‣ EQUIP 1

outgoing adj.
‣ SOCIABLE

outing noun
‣ TRIP

outlaw verb
‣ BAN

outlay noun
‣ COSTS

outlet noun
‣ SHOP

outline noun
‣ SHAPE (the outline of an island)
‣ SUMMARY (an outline of the events)

outline verb
‣ OUTLINE

outlook noun
‣ ATTITUDE

out of date adj.
‣ OLD-FASHIONED

outpace verb
‣ LEAD 1

outpouring noun
‣ FLOOD 2

output noun
‣ OUTPUT

outrage noun
‣ ANGER (public outrage)
‣ CRIME 2 (a terrorist outrage)

outrage verb
‣ ANGER

outraged adj.
‣ FURIOUS

outrageous adj.
‣ OUTRAGEOUS

outright adj.
‣ COMPLETE

outset noun
‣ START

outspoken adj.
‣ HONEST

outstanding adj.
‣ EXCELLENT

outward adj.
‣ APPARENT

oven noun
‣ OVEN

overall adj.
‣ OVERALL

overbearing adj.
‣ AUTHORITARIAN

overcast adj.
‣ CLOUDY

overcome verb
‣ OVERCOME (overcome a fear)
‣ DEFEAT (overcome opposition)

overcrowded adj.
‣ FULL

overdraft noun
‣ LOAN

overdue adj.
‣ LATE

overflow verb
‣ FLOOD

overhaul verb
‣ REPAIR

overhear verb
‣ OVERHEAR

overjoyed adj.
‣ GLAD

overlook verb
‣ IGNORE (overlook sb's faults)
‣ MISS 2 (overlook one key fact)

overpriced adj.
‣ EXPENSIVE

override verb
‣ OVERTURN

overrule verb
‣ OVERTURN

overseas adj.
‣ FOREIGN

oversee verb
‣ REGULATE

oversight noun
‣ MISTAKE 1

overstate verb
‣ EXAGGERATE

overt adj.
‣ OPEN

overtake verb
‣ LEAD 1

overthrow noun
‣ OVERTHROW

overthrow verb
‣ REMOVE 2

overtone noun
‣ ASSOCIATION

overture noun
‣ OFFER 1

overturn verb
‣ OVERTURN (overturn a decision)
‣ ROLL (overturn a chair)

overview noun
‣ SUMMARY

overweight adj.
‣ FAT

overwhelm verb
‣ OVERWHELM

overwhelming adj.
‣ UNCONTROLLABLE

overwork verb
‣ DRIVE 2

overwrought adj.
‣ HYSTERICAL

own verb
‣ HAVE 1

own adj.
‣ OWN

own pron.
‣ **on your own** ALONE adj. adv.

own up phrasal verb
‣ ADMIT 2

P p

pace noun
‣ RATE 1 (the pace of change)
‣ STEP (take two paces forward)

pace verb
‣ WALK 1

pacify verb
‣ CALM

pack noun
‣ HERD (a pack of dogs)
‣ PACKET (a pack of cigarettes)
‣ PARTY 3 (a pack of journalists)

pack verb
‣ PACK (Fans packed the stadium.)
‣ FILL (pack a suitcase)

package noun
‣ PACKET

packed adj.
‣ FULL

packet noun
‣ PACKET

pack in phrasal verb
‣ STOP 1

pack off phrasal verb
‣ DRAG

pact noun
‣ AGREEMENT 1

pad verb
‣ SLIP 1

paddock noun
‣ FIELD

page noun
‣ PAGE

pain noun
‣ PAIN (chest pains)
‣ DISTRESS (the pain of separation)
‣ NUISANCE (That man's a pain.)

pain verb
‣ HURT 1

painful adj.
‣ PAINFUL 1 (a painful knee)
‣ PAINFUL 2 (painful memories)

painless adj.
‣ EASY 1

painstaking adj.
‣ CONSCIENTIOUS

paint verb
‣ PAINT (paint the walls)
‣ DRAW (paint a picture)

painter noun
‣ ARTIST

pal noun
‣ FRIEND

palace noun
‣ PALACE

palate noun
‣ APPETITE 1

pale adj.
‣ PALE 1 (a pale face)
‣ PALE 2 (pale colours)

paltry adj.
‣ INADEQUATE

pampas noun
‣ PLAIN

pamphlet noun
‣ LEAFLET

pan noun
‣ PAN

pandemonium noun
‣ CHAOS

panel noun
‣ COMMITTEE

panic noun
‣ FEAR

panic verb
‣ PANIC

panicky adj.
‣ HYSTERICAL

panic-stricken adj.
‣ HYSTERICAL

panorama noun
‣ VIEW 2

pant verb
‣ BLOW 2

pantry noun
‣ CUPBOARD

paper noun
‣ PAPER (a research paper)
‣ CERTIFICATE (identification papers)
‣ DOCUMENT (sign the necessary papers)
‣ NEWSPAPER (the morning paper)
‣ TEST 2 (an exam paper)

paperwork noun
‣ BUREAUCRACY (a mound of paperwork)
‣ DOCUMENT (sign the necessary paperwork)

par noun
‣ **be on a par with sb/sth** COMPARE verb 2

parabola noun
‣ CURVE

parade noun
‣ FLEET

paradox noun
‣ MYSTERY

paragraph noun
‣ SECTION

parallel noun
‣ EQUIVALENT (This tradition has no parallel in our culture.)
‣ SIMILARITY (parallels between the 1960s and the late 1990s)

paralyse verb
‣ DISABLE

paramedic noun
‣ DOCTOR

parameter noun
‣ LIMIT 2

paramilitary noun
‣ GUERRILLA

paranoia noun
‣ FEAR

paranoid adj.
‣ AFRAID

pardon noun
‣ MERCY (ask sb's pardon)
‣ **beg sb's pardon** APOLOGIZE

pardon verb
‣ EXEMPT (pardon a criminal)
‣ FORGIVE (pardon my ignorance)

parent noun
‣ MOTHER

parentage noun
‣ FAMILY 3

parenthesis noun
‣ DEPARTURE 2

park noun
‣ PARK (a public park)
‣ GARDEN 1 (the park of a country house)
‣ PITCH (a baseball park)

park verb
‣ STOP 2

parkland noun
‣ GARDEN 1

parliament noun
‣ ASSEMBLY (the French parliament)
‣ GOVERNMENT 1 (a session of parliament)

parody noun
‣ PARODY

parry verb
‣ FEND SB/STH OFF

part noun
‣ AREA 1 (the northern part)
‣ CHAPTER (the final part)
‣ CHARACTER (the part of Hamlet)
‣ ELEMENT 1 (spare parts)
‣ INVOLVEMENT (an active part)
‣ SONG (the viola part)
‣ **have/play a part, take part** JOIN
‣ **in part** PARTLY adv.

part verb
‣ DISPERSE (the crowds part)
‣ ISOLATE (parted from her children)
‣ LEAVE 1 (part at the airport)

partial adj.
‣ PARTIAL

partially adv.
‣ PARTLY

participant noun
‣ PARTICIPANT

participate verb
‣ JOIN

participation noun
‣ INVOLVEMENT

particle noun
‣ BIT

particular noun
‣ INFORMATION

particular adj.
‣ PARTICULAR (a particular type)
‣ SPECIAL (particular importance)

partisan *noun*
▸ GUERRILLA

partisan *adj.*
▸ BIASED

partition *noun*
▸ DIVISION 1 (the partition of Germany)
▸ WALL (a glass partition)

partition *verb*
▸ SEPARATE 2

partly *adv.*
▸ PARTLY

partner *noun*
▸ PARTNER 1 (a business/dancing partner)
▸ PARTNER 2 (Come to the party and bring your partner.)

partnership *noun*
▸ GROUP 3 (a business partnership)
▸ RELATIONSHIP 1 (an equal partnership)

party *noun*
▸ PARTY 1 (a political party)
▸ PARTY 2 (a birthday party)
▸ PARTY 3 (a coach party of tourists)

party *verb*
▸ PLAY *verb* 1

pass *noun*
▸ LICENCE (a bus pass)
▸ **make a pass at sb** FLIRT *verb*

pass *verb*
▸ GIVE 2 (Pass the salt, please.)
▸ GO 1 (pass under the bridge)
▸ GO BY (time passes)
▸ GRADUATE (pass a test)
▸ LEAD 1 (pass a truck on a bend)
▸ SPEND 2 (pass the time)

passage *noun*
▸ CORRIDOR (a secret passage)
▸ CRUISE (the sea passage)
▸ CURRENT (the passage of light)
▸ SCENE (read a passage)

passageway *noun*
▸ CORRIDOR

pass away *phrasal verb*
▸ DIE

passenger *noun*
▸ PASSENGER

passer-by *noun*
▸ WITNESS

passing *adj.*
▸ SHORT 1

passion *noun*
▸ EMOTION (violent passions)
▸ LOVE 1 (sexual passion)
▸ TASTE 1 (a passion for painting)

passionate *adj.*
▸ INTENSE

passive *adj.*
▸ PASSIVE

pass off *phrasal verb*
▸ POSE

pass on *phrasal verb*
▸ PASS STH ON (Pass that book on to me when you've finished it.)
▸ CONVEY (pass on a message)

pass out *phrasal verb*
▸ COLLAPSE 2 (I must have passed out.)
▸ DISTRIBUTE (pass out the information sheets)

pass up *phrasal verb*
▸ LOSE OUT

past *noun*
▸ PAST (the recent past)
▸ BACKGROUND (sb's criminal past)

past *adj.*
▸ LAST 2 (the past few days)
▸ PREVIOUS (past events)

pastel *adj.*
▸ PALE 2

pastime *noun*
▸ INTEREST 2

pasture *noun*
▸ FIELD

pat *noun*
▸ **a pat on the back** PRAISE

pat *verb*
▸ PAT

patch *noun*
▸ PATCH (a white dog with black patches)
▸ GARDEN 2 (the vegetable patch)
▸ TIME 2 (go through a rough patch)

patch *verb*
▸ REPAIR

patch up *verb*
▸ RESOLVE

path *noun*
▸ PATH (a coastal path)
▸ DIRECTION (the path to success)
▸ WAY 3 (block sb's path)

pathetic *adj.*
▸ SAD (a pathetic sight)
▸ UNFORTUNATE 2 (a pathetic excuse)

patience *noun*
▸ PATIENCE (show great patience)
▸ **lose patience** LOSE YOUR TEMPER

patient *noun*
▸ PATIENT

patient *adj.*
▸ CALM

patio *noun*
▸ PORCH

patriotism *noun*
▸ RACISM

patron *noun*
▸ CUSTOMER (Patrons are requested not to smoke.)
▸ SPONSOR (the patron of many artists/a charity)

patronizing *adj.*
▸ PATRONIZING

patsy *noun*
▸ VICTIM 2

pattern *noun*
▸ PATTERN 1 (sleeping patterns)
▸ PATTERN 2 (a diamond pattern)
▸ MODEL (set a pattern)

paunch *noun*
▸ STOMACH

pause *noun*
▸ PAUSE

pause *verb*
▸ PAUSE

pavement *noun*
▸ PATH

pay *noun*
▸ INCOME

pay *verb*
▸ PAY (pay a bill)
▸ **pay attention** HEAR

pay back *phrasal verb*
▸ REPAY

payment *noun*
▸ PAYMENT

pay-off *noun*
▸ BRIBE

PC *noun*
▸ POLICEMAN

PE (also **P. E.**) *noun*
▸ SPORT

peace *noun*
▸ PEACE (world peace)
▸ SILENCE (peace and quiet)
▸ **at peace** DEAD *adj.*

peaceful *adj.*
▸ QUIET 1

peacemaker *noun*
▸ NEGOTIATOR

peak *noun*
▸ PEAK (the peak of her career)
▸ HILL (a mountain peak)

peat *noun*
▸ SOIL

pebble *noun*
▸ STONE

pecking order *noun*
▸ SCALE

peculiar *adj.*
▸ STRANGE 1 (peculiar circumstances)
▸ UNIQUE (peculiar to China)

peculiarity *noun*
▸ MANNERISM

pedagogic *adj.*
▸ EDUCATIONAL

pedestrian *adj.*
▸ LACKLUSTRE

pedigree *noun*
▸ FAMILY 3

peek *verb*
▸ GLANCE

peep *verb*
▸ GLANCE

peer *noun*
▸ PEER (peer pressure)
▸ LORD (a hereditary/life peer)

peer *verb*
▸ STARE

peer group *noun*
▸ AGE

pejorative *adj.*
▸ INSULTING

pen *verb*
▸ TRAP

penalize *verb*
▸ PUNISH

penalty *noun*
▸ PUNISHMENT

penitentiary *noun*
▸ PRISON

penknife *noun*
▸ KNIFE

penniless *adj.*
▸ POOR 1

pensive *adj.*
▸ THOUGHTFUL

penthouse *noun*
▸ FLAT

people *noun*
▸ PEOPLE 1 (young people)
▸ PEOPLE 2 (tribal peoples)

people *verb*
▸ LIVE

perceive *verb*
▸ NOTICE

percentage *noun*
▸ SHARE

perception *noun*
▸ AWARENESS

perceptive *adj.*
▸ SHREWD

perch *verb*
▸ LAND (a bird perches)
▸ SIT (perch on a stool)

perfect *adj.*
▸ PERFECT (perfect manners)
▸ COMPLETE (a perfect stranger)
▸ EXCELLENT (perfect weather)
▸ IDEAL (a perfect day for a picnic)

perfectly *adv.*
▸ QUITE 2

perform *verb*
▸ DO 1 (perform an experiment)

DO 2 (perform well in a test)
▸ PLAY 3 (perform a play)

performance *noun*
▸ PERFORMANCE

performer *noun*
▸ ACTOR

the performing arts *noun*
▸ DRAMA

perimeter *noun*
▸ EDGE

period *noun*
▸ PERIOD (the Victorian period)
▸ CLASS 2 (It's French next period.)
▸ TIME 2 (a period of time)

periodical *noun*
▸ MAGAZINE

peripheral *adj.*
▸ MINOR

periphery *noun*
▸ EDGE

perish *verb*
▸ DIE

perjury *noun*
▸ LIE

perk *noun*
▸ BENEFIT 2

permanent *adj.*
▸ PERMANENT

permission *noun*
▸ PERMISSION

permit *noun*
▸ LICENCE

permit *verb*
▸ ALLOW (what the rules permit)
▸ ENABLE (if time permits)

pernicious *adj.*
▸ HARMFUL

perpetual *adj.*
▸ ENDLESS (a perpetual state of chaos)
▸ FREQUENT (perpetual interruptions)

perpetuate *verb*
▸ MAINTAIN 1

perplex *verb*
▸ CONFUSE

perplexed *adj.*
▸ CONFUSED 1

persecute *verb*
▸ HARASS (The media persecuted him.)
▸ SUPPRESS 1 (a persecuted minority)

persecution *noun*
▸ REPRESSION

perseverance *noun*
▸ DETERMINATION

persevere *verb*
▸ PERSIST

persist *verb*
▸ PERSIST

persistence *noun*
▸ DETERMINATION

persistent *adj.*
▸ CONTINUOUS (persistent rain)
▸ DETERMINED 2 (a persistent salesman)
▸ FREQUENT (a persistent cough)

person *noun*
▸ PERSON

persona *noun*
▸ PERSONALITY

personable *adj.*
▸ NICE 2

personal *adj.*
▸ OWN (your personal belongings)
▸ SECRET 1 (a letter marked 'Personal')

personality noun
▸ PERSONALITY (have a strong personality)
▸ CHARM (sb with lots of personality)
▸ STAR 1 (a TV personality)

personnel noun
▸ STAFF

perspective noun
▸ ATTITUDE

persuade verb
▸ PERSUADE (Persuade her to come.)
▸ CONVINCE (No one was persuaded by his argument.)

persuasive adj.
▸ CONVINCING

pertinent verb
▸ RELEVANT

perverse adj.
▸ PERVERSE

pesky adj.
▸ ANNOYING

pessimistic adj.
▸ NEGATIVE

pester verb
▸ HARASS

pet verb
▸ STROKE

pet adj.
▸ FAVOURITE

petite adj.
▸ SHORT 2

petition noun
▸ REQUEST

petition verb
▸ ASK 2

petrified adj.
▸ AFRAID

petrol noun
▸ OIL

petroleum noun
▸ OIL

petty adj.
▸ MINOR

petulant adj.
▸ IRRITABLE

pew noun
▸ CHAIR

phase noun
▸ STAGE 1

phase in phrasal verb
▸ INTRODUCE 1

phenomenal adj.
▸ REMARKABLE

phenomenon noun
▸ EVENT 1 (natural phenomena)
▸ MIRACLE (This young pianist is a phenomenon.)

phial noun
▸ BOTTLE

philanthropist noun
▸ SPONSOR

philosopher noun
▸ SCHOLAR

philosophical adj.
▸ INTELLECTUAL 1

philosophy noun
▸ VALUES

phobia noun
▸ FEAR

phone verb
▸ CALL 2

phoney adj.
▸ SO-CALLED

photo noun
▸ PHOTOGRAPH

photocopy noun
▸ COPY 1

photocopy verb
▸ COPY

photograph noun
▸ PHOTOGRAPH

photograph verb
▸ RECORD 2

phrase noun
▸ WORD

phrase verb
▸ SAY 2

physician noun
▸ DOCTOR

physique noun
▸ BODY 1

pick noun
▸ CHOICE 1 (take your pick)
▸ CHOICE 2 (She was his pick for best actress.)

pick verb
▸ CHOOSE (pick a number)
▸ HARVEST (pick fruit)

pick on phrasal verb
▸ BULLY

pick out phrasal verb
▸ IDENTIFY

pickpocket noun
▸ THIEF

pick up phrasal verb
▸ PICK SB/STH UP (pick up the phone)
▸ BUY (pick up a few bargains)
▸ GET 1 (pick up a cold/£30 in tips)
▸ GET 3 (pick sb up from school)
▸ IMPROVE 2 (The economy is picking up.)
▸ LEARN (pick up a language)
▸ STAND 1 (pick yourself up)

picture noun
▸ PICTURE (draw a picture)
▸ DESCRIPTION (paint a gloomy picture of the economy)
▸ IDEA 1 (a sudden mental picture)
▸ PHOTOGRAPH (take a picture)

picture verb
▸ IMAGINE

picturesque adj.
▸ BEAUTIFUL 2

piece noun
▸ PIECE (a piece of apple pie)
▸ ARTICLE (a piece in today's paper)
▸ BIT (smash sth to pieces; a piece of research)
▸ ELEMENT 1 (One of the pieces is missing.)
▸ WORK 4 (a piece by Chopin)
▸ in one piece SAFE adj. 1

pie chart noun
▸ DIAGRAM

piercing adj.
▸ HIGH 3

pig noun
▸ VILLAIN

pigment noun
▸ COLOUR 2

pile noun
▸ PILE

pile verb
▸ SURGE

pile up phrasal verb
▸ BUILD UP

pile-up noun
▸ ACCIDENT

pilgrim noun
▸ TOURIST

pilgrimage noun
▸ TRIP

pillar noun
▸ POST

pilot verb
▸ DRIVE 1 (pilot a plane/boat)
▸ TEST 1 (pilot a new system)

pilot study noun
▸ TEST 1

pin noun
▸ BUTTON 2

pin verb
▸ pin your hopes on sb/sth TRUST

pinch noun
▸ ELEMENT 2

pine verb
▸ MOURN

ping verb
▸ CLINK

pinpoint verb
▸ IDENTIFY

pioneer noun
▸ EXPLORER (early pioneers in America)
▸ LEADER 2 (a pioneer of education for women)

pioneer verb
▸ DEVELOP 2

pip noun
▸ GRAIN

pipe noun
▸ PIPE

pipeline noun
▸ PIPE

pique noun
▸ FRUSTRATION

pirate noun
▸ THIEF

pirate adj.
▸ ILLEGAL

pissed adj. (taboo)
▸ ANGRY (get pissed with sb)
▸ DRUNK (get pissed on beer)

pissed off adj. (taboo)
▸ ANGRY

piss off phrasal verb (taboo)
▸ ANGER

pistol noun
▸ GUN

pit noun
▸ GRAIN (cherry/peach pits)
▸ HOLE 2 (dig a pit)

pit against phrasal verb
▸ COMPETE

pitch noun
▸ PITCH (a football pitch)
▸ NOTE (high in pitch)

pitch verb
▸ FOCUS (The new software is being pitched at banks.)
▸ THROW (pitch a fast ball)

pitcher noun
▸ BOTTLE

pitfall noun
▸ DISADVANTAGE

pithy adj.
▸ SHORT 3

pity noun
▸ SYMPATHY (full of pity)
▸ UNFORTUNATE adj. 2 (What a pity!)

pity verb
▸ SORRY FOR SB

pivot verb
▸ TURN 1

pivotal adj.
▸ ESSENTIAL

placard noun
▸ POSTER

placate verb
▸ CALM

place noun
▸ PLACE 1 (I love this place!)
▸ PLACE 2 (save sb a place)
▸ HOME 1 (a place of my own)
▸ ROLE (sb's place in history)
▸ be going places DO WELL verb
▸ take place HAPPEN verb
▸ a place to stay HOUSING
▸ all over the place, out of place UNTIDY adj.

place verb
▸ PLACE (place emphasis on sth)
▸ IDENTIFY (place sb's accent)
▸ PUT 1 (place a hand on sb's shoulder)
▸ PUT 2 (place sb under arrest)
▸ RANK (place sb among the top five players)
▸ SEND 2 (The children were placed with foster parents.)

placebo noun
▸ DRUG 2

place of worship noun
▸ CHURCH

placid adj.
▸ CALM

plain noun
▸ PLAIN

plain adj.
▸ PLAIN 1 (a plain white shirt)
▸ PLAIN 2 (the plain truth)
▸ AVERAGE (plain common sense)
▸ CLEAR 1 (plain to see)
▸ CLEAR 2 (plain English)
▸ UGLY (a plain girl)
▸ plain sailing EASY 1

plan noun
▸ PLAN 1 (an action plan)
▸ PLAN 2 (a seating plan)
▸ MAP (a street plan)
▸ PURPOSE (no plans to do sth)

plan verb
▸ PLAN (plan a garden/an essay)
▸ INTEND (They plan to arrive some time after three.)
▸ ORGANIZE (plan a campaign)

the planet noun
▸ WORLD

plank noun
▸ POST

planner noun
▸ DESIGNER (a town planner)
▸ ORGANIZER (an emergency/economic planner)

planning noun
▸ PLANNING

plant noun
▸ FACTORY (a nuclear power plant)
▸ TECHNOLOGY (a company invests in plant and equipment)

plant verb
▸ FARM (land planted with trees)
▸ PUT 1 (plant a flag)

plantation noun
▸ FARM (a banana plantation)
▸ FOREST (a conifer plantation)

plaque noun
▸ SIGN 2

plaster noun
▸ BANDAGE

plate noun
▸ PLATE (a dinner plate)
▸ SIGN 2 (the car's number plate)

plateau noun
▸ PLAIN

platform noun
▸ FORUM (a platform for their views)
▸ PLAN 1 (an election platform)
▸ STAGE 2 (the speaker's platform)

platitude noun
▸ SAYING

platter noun
▸ PLATE

plausible adj.
▸ POSSIBLE 2

play *noun*
- ▶ PLAY (a play by Shakespeare)
- ▶ ENTERTAINMENT (children at play)

play *verb*
- ▶ PLAY 1 (children playing)
- ▶ PLAY 2 (play football)
- ▶ PLAY 3 (play the piano)
- ▶ **play a part** JOIN

play down *phrasal verb*
- ▶ UNDERSTATE

player *noun*
- ▶ PLAYER

playground *noun*
- ▶ PARK

playing field *noun*
- ▶ PITCH

play-off *noun*
- ▶ GAME 1

playwright *noun*
- ▶ WRITER

plea *noun*
- ▶ ARGUMENT 2 (a plea of insanity)
- ▶ REQUEST (a plea for help)

plead *verb*
- ▶ BEG

pleasant *adj.*
- ▶ FRIENDLY 1 (a pleasant young man)
- ▶ NICE 1 (pleasant surroundings)

please *verb*
- ▶ PLEASE

pleased *adj.*
- ▶ GLAD

pleasing *adj.*
- ▶ SATISFYING

pleasurable *adj.*
- ▶ NICE 1

pleasure *noun*
- ▶ PLEASURE (a pleasure to meet you)
- ▶ ENTERTAINMENT (business or pleasure)
- ▶ FUN (take pleasure in sth)

pledge *noun*
- ▶ PROMISE

pledge *verb*
- ▶ PROMISE

plight *noun*
- ▶ MESS 2

plod *verb*
- ▶ TRUDGE

plot *noun*
- ▶ CONSPIRACY (a murder plot)
- ▶ LAND 2 (a plot of land)
- ▶ STORY 1 (the plot of the film)

plot *verb*
- ▶ PLOT

plotter *noun*
- ▶ ACCOMPLICE

plough (also **plow**) *verb*
- ▶ FARM

plough into (also **plow into**) *phrasal verb*
- ▶ CRASH

plough through (also **plow through**) *phrasal verb*
- ▶ READ

ploy *noun*
- ▶ TACTIC

pluck *verb*
- ▶ PULL 2 (pluck out a hair)
- ▶ **pluck up (the) courage** DARE

plug *noun*
- ▶ ADVERTISEMENT (a plug for his new book)
- ▶ LID (the bath plug)

plug *verb*
- ▶ ADVERTISE (plug his new book)
- ▶ BLOCK 2 (plug a hole)

plug in *phrasal verb*
- ▶ TURN STH ON

plume *noun*
- ▶ CLOUD 2

plummet *verb*
- ▶ SLUMP

plump *adj.*
- ▶ FAT

plunder *verb*
- ▶ ROB

plunge *verb*
- ▶ FALL 2 (plunge to your death)
- ▶ SLUMP (stock markets plunge)

plus *noun*
- ▶ BENEFIT 1

poach *verb*
- ▶ STEAL

poacher *noun*
- ▶ THIEF

pocket *noun*
- ▶ FUND

pocket *verb*
- ▶ MAKE 3

podium *noun*
- ▶ STAGE 2

poet *noun*
- ▶ WRITER

poignant *adj.*
- ▶ MOVING

point *noun*
- ▶ POINT (get to the point)
- ▶ FACTOR (an important point)
- ▶ FEATURE (It has its good points.)
- ▶ INFORMATION (the main points)
- ▶ PLACE 1 (a meeting point)
- ▶ PURPOSE (What is the point?)
- ▶ SCORE (win/lose points)
- ▶ TIME 1 (at some point in your life)
- ▶ TIP (the point of a knife/pencil)
- ▶ VIEW 1 (make your point)
- ▶ **beside the point** IRRELEVANT *adj.*
- ▶ **to the point** RELEVANT *adj.*
- ▶ **up to a point** PARTLY *adv.*

point *verb*
- ▶ POINT (Point to the one you want.)
- ▶ AIM (point a gun at sb)
- ▶ SUGGEST (The evidence points to…)

pointer *noun*
- ▶ SUGGESTION

pointless *adj.*
- ▶ USELESS

point of view *noun*
- ▶ ATTITUDE (a child's point of view)
- ▶ VIEW 1 (the opposite point of view)

point out *phrasal verb*
- ▶ POINT STH OUT

point to *phrasal verb*
- ▶ POINT STH OUT

point up *phrasal verb*
- ▶ POINT STH OUT

poise *noun*
- ▶ COMPOSURE

poise *verb*
- ▶ LEAN 2

poison *noun*
- ▶ POISON

poison *verb*
- ▶ POISON (poison sb's food)
- ▶ INFLUENCE (poison their minds)

poke *verb*
- ▶ JAB (poke sb in the ribs)
- ▶ PUSH 1 (poke your head around the door)
- ▶ **poke fun at sb/sth** LAUGH AT SB/STH

poke around/about *phrasal verb*
- ▶ FUMBLE

police *verb*
- ▶ REGULATE

policeman *noun*
- ▶ POLICEMAN

police officer *noun*
- ▶ POLICEMAN

policewoman *noun*
- ▶ POLICEMAN

policy *noun*
- ▶ HABIT (Honesty is the best policy.)
- ▶ PLAN 1 (economic policies)

polite *adj.*
- ▶ POLITE

politeness *noun*
- ▶ RESPECT

politician *noun*
- ▶ POLITICIAN

poll *noun*
- ▶ ELECTION (victory at the polls)
- ▶ INVESTIGATION (an opinion poll)

poll *verb*
- ▶ SURVEY

pollution *noun*
- ▶ DIRT

pompous *adj.*
- ▶ PROUD 2

pond *noun*
- ▶ LAKE

ponder *verb*
- ▶ CONSIDER

pool *noun*
- ▶ LAKE (rock pools)
- ▶ SUPPLY (a pool of cars)

pool *verb*
- ▶ SHARE

pooped *adj.*
- ▶ TIRED 1

poor *adj.*
- ▶ POOR 1 (poor people/countries)
- ▶ POOR 2 (poor quality)
- ▶ INCOMPETENT (a poor swimmer)

pop *verb*
- ▶ APPEAR (pop into view)
- ▶ BANG 1 (corks pop)
- ▶ PUT 1 (pop sth in the oven)

pop in/round/over *phrasal verb*
- ▶ VISIT

the populace *noun*
- ▶ GENERAL PUBLIC

popular *adj.*
- ▶ POPULAR (a popular singer)
- ▶ COMMON (Contrary to popular belief…)
- ▶ SOCIAL (popular support)

population *noun*
- ▶ COMMUNITY

porch *noun*
- ▶ PORCH

port *noun*
- ▶ PORT

portfolio *noun*
- ▶ ENVELOPE

portion *noun*
- ▶ PORTION

portrait *noun*
- ▶ DESCRIPTION (a portrait of life at the French court)
- ▶ PICTURE (a self-portrait)

portray *verb*
- ▶ PRESENT 2

portrayal *noun*
- ▶ DESCRIPTION

pose *noun*
- ▶ POSITION

pose *verb*
- ▶ POSE (pose as a doctor)
- ▶ ASK 1 (pose a question)
- ▶ REPRESENT 1 (pose a problem)

posh *adj.*
- ▶ ARISTOCRATIC

position *noun*
- ▶ POSITION (a sitting position)
- ▶ ATTITUDE (the party's position on education)
- ▶ CLASS 4 (sb's social position)
- ▶ JOB (a full-time position)
- ▶ PLACE 1 (be in position)
- ▶ SITUATION (a difficult position to be in)

position *verb*
- ▶ PUT 1

positive *adj.*
- ▶ COMPLETE (a positive miracle)
- ▶ FINAL (positive evidence)
- ▶ GOOD 6 (a positive response)
- ▶ OPTIMISTIC (a positive attitude)
- ▶ SURE ('Are you sure?' 'Positive.')
- ▶ VALUABLE 2 (a positive contribution)

possess *verb*
- ▶ HAVE 1 (possess a new car)
- ▶ HAVE 2 (possess a sense of humour)

possession *noun*
- ▶ TERRITORY (a country's colonial possessions)
- ▶ THING 3 (your treasured possessions)

possibility *noun*
- ▶ POSSIBILITY (the possibility of tax increases)
- ▶ OPPORTUNITY (career possibilities)
- ▶ OPTION (a range of possibilities)
- ▶ POTENTIAL (see the possibilities of the plan)

possible *adj.*
- ▶ POSSIBLE 1 (It is possible to get there by bus.)
- ▶ POSSIBLE 2 (several possible explanations)
- ▶ LIKELY (a possible future president)

post *noun*
- ▶ POST (a wooden post)
- ▶ JOB (resign from your post)
- ▶ LETTER (open the post)

post *verb*
- ▶ SEND 1 (post a letter)
- ▶ SEND 2 (post sb abroad)

poster *noun*
- ▶ POSTER

posting *noun*
- ▶ JOB

postmodernist *noun*
- ▶ EXPERIMENTAL

postpone *verb*
- ▶ DELAY

postulate *verb*
- ▶ SAY 3

posture *noun*
- ▶ POSITION

pot *noun*
- ▶ BOTTLE (a coffee pot)
- ▶ PACKET (a pot of jam)
- ▶ PAN (pots and pans)

potential *noun*
- ▶ POTENTIAL

potential *adj.*
- ▶ LIKELY

potter *verb*
- ▶ REST

potty *noun*
- ▶ TOILET

pound *verb*
- ▶ BEAT 1 (pound on the door)

▶ BEAT 2 (sb's head pounds)
▶ RUN 1 (pound along the corridor)

pour verb
▶ POUR (pour a drink)
▶ FLOW (tears pour down)
▶ RAIN (It's pouring with rain.)
▶ SURGE (Letters came pouring in.)

pout verb
▶ BROOD

poverty noun
▶ POVERTY

POW noun
▶ HOSTAGE

power noun
▶ POWER (air/bargaining power)
▶ ABILITY (the power of speech)
▶ CONTROL (seize power)
▶ COUNTRY 1 (a world power)
▶ EFFECT (the power of the media)
▶ ENERGY 1 (nuclear/solar power)
▶ FORCE (physical power)
▶ RIGHT (the power of veto)
▶ **be in power** RULE verb 1

powerful adj.
▶ POWERFUL (a powerful position)
▶ STRONG 1 (powerful muscles)

practical noun
▶ TEST 2

practical adj.
▶ PRACTICAL (practical experience)
▶ POSSIBLE 1 (a practical solution)
▶ REALISTIC 1 (Let's be practical.)
▶ USEFUL (practical shoes/clothing)

practicalities noun
▶ BASICS

practically adv.
▶ ALMOST

practice noun
▶ COMPANY (a law practice)
▶ HABIT (make it your practice to do sth)
▶ TRADITION (best practice)
▶ TRAINING (piano practice)
▶ USE (put an idea into practice)
▶ WORK 2 (medical practice)
▶ **put sth into practice** APPLY verb 1

practise (also **practice**) verb
▶ PRACTISE (practise the piano)
▶ DO 1 (practise your religion)
▶ WORK 2 (practise as a lawyer)

practised (also **practiced**) adj.
▶ EXPERIENCED

pragmatic adj.
▶ REALISTIC 1

pragmatism noun
▶ WISDOM

prairie noun
▶ PLAIN

praise noun
▶ PRAISE

praise verb
▶ PRAISE (praise sb's performance)
▶ PRAY (praise God)

prank noun
▶ JOKE

prat noun
▶ FOOL

pray verb
▶ PRAY

prayers noun
▶ CEREMONY

preamble noun
▶ INTRODUCTION 2

prearranged adj.
▶ SET

precaution noun
▶ PRECAUTION

precautionary adj.
▶ PROTECTIVE

precedence noun
▶ PRIORITY

precedent noun
▶ MODEL

preceding adj.
▶ LAST 2

precinct noun
▶ COURTYARD

precious adj.
▶ DEAR (precious possessions)
▶ VALUABLE 1 (precious stones)

precise adj.
▶ EXACT (precise instructions)
▶ VERY (at that precise moment)

preclude verb
▶ PREVENT

predetermined adj.
▶ SET

predicament noun
▶ MESS 2

predict verb
▶ PREDICT

predictable adj.
▶ PREDICTABLE 1 (predictable results)
▶ PREDICTABLE 2 (You're so predictable!)

prediction noun
▶ EXPECTATION

predispose verb
▶ MAKE 4

predominant adj.
▶ MAIN

pre-empt verb
▶ ANTICIPATE

preface noun
▶ INTRODUCTION 2

prefer verb
▶ PREFER

preferable adj.
▶ BETTER

preference noun
▶ CHOICE 2 (consumer preferences)
▶ TASTE 1 (personal preference)

preferred adj.
▶ FAVOURITE

prejudice noun
▶ DISCRIMINATION

prejudice verb
▶ INFLUENCE

prejudiced adj.
▶ BIASED

preliminary adj.
▶ FIRST

premature adj.
▶ RECKLESS

premeditated adj.
▶ DELIBERATE

premier noun
▶ PRESIDENT

premier adj.
▶ TOP

premiere noun
▶ LAUNCH

premise noun
▶ THEORY 2

premises noun
▶ BUILDING

premium noun
▶ PAYMENT

premonition noun
▶ IDEA 2

preoccupation noun
▶ OBSESSION

preparation noun
▶ PLANNING

preparatory adj.
▶ FIRST

prepare verb
▶ PREPARE 1 (prepare a report)
▶ PREPARE 2 (prepare for an exam)
▶ COOK (prepare a meal)
▶ TEACH (prepare students for exams)

prepared
▶ READY

prerequisite noun
▶ CONDITION

prescribe verb
▶ RULE 2

prescription noun
▶ DRUG 2

presence noun
▶ CHARM

present noun
▶ GIFT

present verb
▶ PRESENT 1 (present a new product)
▶ PRESENT 2 (present sth as a victory)
▶ PRESENT 3 (present a report)
▶ PRESENT 4 (present a TV show)
▶ EMERGE (an opportunity presents itself)
▶ GIVE 1 (present the prizes)
▶ INTRODUCE 2 (May I present my son?)
▶ PLAY 3 (present a play)

present adj.
▶ RECENT

presentation noun
▶ PRESENTATION

present-day adj.
▶ RECENT

presenter noun
▶ PRESENTER

preserve noun
▶ BUSINESS 1

preserve verb
▶ MAINTAIN 1 (preserve the peace)
▶ MAINTAIN 2 (This vase has been preserved intact.)
▶ PROTECT (preserve endangered species)

preside verb
▶ LEAD 2

president noun
▶ PRESIDENT (the French president)
▶ LEADER 1 (the president of the student's union)

the press noun
▶ MEDIA

press verb
▶ PRESS 1 (press the button)
▶ PRESS 2 (press sb to do sth)
▶ PUSH 1 (press a coin into sb's hand)

press ahead phrasal verb
▶ CONTINUE 2

press for phrasal verb
▶ DEMAND

pressing adj.
▶ URGENT

press on phrasal verb
▶ CONTINUE 2

pressure noun
▶ PRESSURE 1 (the pressures of work)
▶ PRESSURE 2 (the pressure to conform)
▶ WEIGHT (apply pressure to the wound)
▶ **under pressure** TENSE adj.

pressure verb
▶ PRESS 2

pressurize verb
▶ PRESS 2

prestige noun
▶ STATUS

prestigious verb
▶ GREAT 2

presumably adv.
▶ PROBABLY

presume verb
▶ DARE (I wouldn't presume to tell you what to do.)
▶ SAY 3 (missing, presumed dead)
▶ SUPPOSE (I presume so.)

presumption noun
▶ SPECULATION

presumptuous adj.
▶ COOL

presuppose verb
▶ SAY 3

presupposition noun
▶ SPECULATION

pretence noun
▶ PRETENCE

pretend verb
▶ PRETEND (pretend not to notice)
▶ IMAGINE (Let's pretend.)

pretend adj.
▶ FICTIONAL

pretension noun
▶ PRETENSION

pretentious adj.
▶ FLASHY

pretext noun
▶ REASON

pretty adj.
▶ BEAUTIFUL 1 (a pretty girl)
▶ BEAUTIFUL 2 (a pretty flower)

pretty adv.
▶ QUITE 1 (pretty good)
▶ **pretty much/well** ALMOST

prevail verb
▶ DEFEAT (Ultimately, Rome prevailed.)
▶ EXIST (the conditions prevailing in local prisons)
▶ WIN (Common sense prevailed.)

prevalent adj.
▶ GENERAL 1

prevent verb
▶ PREVENT

preventable adj.
▶ UNNECESSARY

preventive adj.
▶ PROTECTIVE

previous adj.
▶ PREVIOUS (previous experience)
▶ LAST 2 (the previous day)

price noun
▶ PRICE (the price of oil)
▶ **put a price on sth** PRICE verb

price verb
▶ PRICE

priceless adj.
▶ VALUABLE 1

pricey adj.
▶ EXPENSIVE

prickly adj.
▶ COARSE (a prickly bush)
▶ SENSITIVE 3 (He could be very prickly with journalists.)

pride noun
▶ PRIDE (Pride forced him to suffer in silence.)
▶ DIGNITY (Her pride was hurt.)
▶ PLEASURE (sb's pride and joy)
▶ SATISFACTION (national pride)

pride on phrasal verb
▶ BOAST

prim adj.
▶ PRIM

primary adj.
▶ FIRST (the primary stage)

▶ MAIN (the primary aim)

prime *noun*
▶ PEAK

prime *adj.*
▶ GOOD 1 (prime cuts/lamb)
▶ MAIN (my prime concern)

prime minister *noun*
▶ PRESIDENT

principal *noun*
▶ PROFESSOR

principal *adj.*
▶ MAIN

principle *noun*
▶ PRINCIPLE 1 (a matter of principle)
▶ PRINCIPLE 2 (the principle that…)
▶ THEORY 1 (It works on a very simple principle.)

principled *adj.*
▶ GOOD 5

print *noun*
▶ PHOTOGRAPH (a set of colour prints)
▶ PICTURE (a Renoir print)

print *verb*
▶ PUBLISH 1 (print sb's comments)
▶ PUBLISH 2 (print a book)

printout *noun*
▶ COPY 1

prior *adj.*
▶ PREVIOUS

prioritize *verb*
▶ STRESS

priority *noun*
▶ PRIORITY

prise *verb*
▶ PULL 2

prison *noun*
▶ PRISON (in prison)
▶ **send sb to prison** JAIL *verb*

prisoner *noun*
▶ PRISONER (prisoners serving life sentences)
▶ HOSTAGE (take/hold sb prisoner)

prisoner of war *noun*
▶ HOSTAGE

pristine *adj.*
▶ PERFECT

privacy *noun*
▶ PRIVACY

private *adj.*
▶ OWN (a private bathroom)
▶ SECRET 1 (a private conversation)

privation *noun*
▶ POVERTY

privilege *noun*
▶ PLEASURE (It was a great privilege to hear her sing.)
▶ RIGHT (Club members have special privileges.)

privileged *adj.*
▶ RICH

prize *noun*
▶ AWARD

prize *verb*
▶ APPRECIATE (prize sth highly)
▶ PULL 2 (prize the lid open)

prized *adj.*
▶ DEAR

prizewinner *noun*
▶ WINNER

probability *noun*
▶ POSSIBILITY (a high probability of success)
▶ **in all probability** PROBABLY *adv.*

probable *adj.*
▶ LIKELY

probably *adv.*
▶ PROBABLY

probe *noun*
▶ INVESTIGATION

probe *verb*
▶ INVESTIGATE

probity *noun*
▶ INTEGRITY

problem *noun*
▶ PROBLEM (financial problems)
▶ MYSTERY (a philosophical problem)

problematic *adj.*
▶ SENSITIVE 2

procedure *noun*
▶ PROCESS

proceed *verb*
▶ CONTINUE 2 (work proceeds)
▶ GO 1 (proceed to the exits)
▶ GO ON TO STH (proceed to do sth)

proceeding *noun*
▶ CASE (legal proceedings)
▶ EVENT 1 (watch the proceedings)

proceeds *noun*
▶ REVENUE

process *noun*
▶ PROCESS (in the process of doing sth)
▶ WAY 2 (industrial processes)

process *verb*
▶ TREAT 2

procession *noun*
▶ FLEET

proclaim *verb*
▶ DECLARE

procrastinate *verb*
▶ TAKE YOUR TIME

procure *verb*
▶ GAIN 1

prod *verb*
▶ JAB (prod sb in the ribs)
▶ PROVOKE (prod sb into action)

prodigy *noun*
▶ GENIUS

produce *noun*
▶ PRODUCT

produce *verb*
▶ PRODUCE (produce young/fruit)
▶ CAUSE (produce a result)
▶ MAKE 1 (produce a meal)
▶ MANUFACTURE (produce oil)
▶ PLAY 3 (produce a play)
▶ PRESENT 1 (produce sth from your pocket)

producer *noun*
▶ MAKER

product *noun*
▶ PRODUCT (create a new product)
▶ RESULT (the end product of sth)

production *noun*
▶ PRODUCTION (production of the new aircraft)
▶ OUTPUT (production increases)
▶ PERFORMANCE (a stage production)

productive *adj.*
▶ PRODUCTIVE

productivity *noun*
▶ OUTPUT

profession *noun*
▶ WORK 2

professional *adj.*
▶ GOOD 4

professor *noun*
▶ PROFESSOR (a distinguished professor at Cambridge)
▶ LECTURER (a college professor in the US)

proficiency *noun*
▶ SKILL 2

proficient *adj.*
▶ GOOD 4

profile *noun*
▶ DESCRIPTION (build up a customer profile)
▶ REPUTATION (raise the company's international profile)
▶ SHAPE (The portrait shows her in profile.)

profit *noun*
▶ PROFIT

profit *verb*
▶ BENEFIT (profit from the new legislation)
▶ MAKE 3 (profit from crimes)

profitable *adj.*
▶ SUCCESSFUL 2

profit-making *adj.*
▶ SUCCESSFUL 2

profound *adj.*
▶ SERIOUS 3

programme (also **program**) *noun*
▶ PROGRAMME (a TV programme)
▶ CLASS 1 (a training programme)
▶ PLAN 1 (a research programme)
▶ SCHEDULE (a programme of concerts/lectures)

progress *noun*
▶ PROGRESS

progress *verb*
▶ DEVELOP 1 (work progresses)
▶ GO BY (time progresses)

progression *noun*
▶ PROGRESS

progressive *adj.*
▶ RADICAL

prohibit *verb*
▶ BAN

prohibited *adj.*
▶ FORBIDDEN

prohibition *noun*
▶ BAN

prohibitive *adj.*
▶ HIGH 1

project *noun*
▶ PROJECT (a project to computerize the library)
▶ ASSIGNMENT (a school project)
▶ ESTATE (a housing project)

project *verb*
▶ PREDICT

projection *noun*
▶ EXPECTATION

proletarian *adj.*
▶ WORKING CLASS

the proletariat *noun*
▶ GENERAL PUBLIC

prolific *adj.*
▶ PRODUCTIVE

prologue *noun*
▶ INTRODUCTION 2

prolong *verb*
▶ MAINTAIN 1

prolonged *adj.*
▶ LONG

prominence *noun*
▶ FAME

prominent *adj.*
▶ FAMOUS

promise *noun*
▶ PROMISE (keep/break a promise)
▶ POTENTIAL (show great promise)

promise *verb*
▶ PROMISE (Promise not to tell!)
▶ THREATEN 3 (It promises to be an exciting few days.)

promising *adj.*
▶ PROMISING

promote *verb*
▶ PROMOTE (promote racial harmony)

ADVERTISE (promote a product)

promoter *noun*
▶ ADVOCATE (a leading promoter of European integration)
▶ SPONSOR (a boxing promoter)

promotion *noun*
▶ ADVERTISEMENT (sales and promotion)
▶ PROGRESS (promotion to Sales Manager)

prompt *verb*
▶ PROMPT (prompt an outburst)
▶ MAKE 4 (What prompted you to choose us?)

prompt *adj.*
▶ EARLY (Please be prompt.)
▶ IMMEDIATE (prompt action)

prone to *adj.*
▶ PRONE TO STH

prong *noun*
▶ TIP

pronounce *verb*
▶ DECLARE

pronounced *adj.*
▶ MARKED

pronunciation *noun*
▶ VOICE

proof *noun*
▶ EVIDENCE

prop *verb*
▶ LEAN 2

propaganda *noun*
▶ PROPAGANDA

propensity *noun*
▶ TENDENCY

proper *adj.*
▶ REAL (a proper job)
▶ RIGHT 1 (the proper procedures)
▶ RIGHT 2 (only right and proper)

property *noun*
▶ BUILDING (a property developer)
▶ FEATURE (physical properties)
▶ THING 3 (private property)

prophecy *noun*
▶ EXPECTATION

prophesy *verb*
▶ PREDICT

proponent *noun*
▶ ADVOCATE

proportion *noun*
▶ LEVEL (crisis proportions)
▶ RATIO (out of proportion)

proportional *adj.*
▶ RELATIVE

proportionate *adj.*
▶ RELATIVE

proposal *noun*
▶ PROPOSAL (a proposal to reduce taxes for the low-paid)
▶ OFFER 1 (a proposal of marriage)

propose *verb*
▶ PROPOSE (propose an idea)
▶ INTEND (What do you propose to do?)

proposition *noun*
▶ PROPOSAL (a business proposition)
▶ THEORY 2 (the proposition that power corrupts)

prop up *phrasal verb*
▶ MAINTAIN 1 (propping up declining industries)
▶ SUPPORT 2 (prop up a building)

prosaic *adj.*
▶ MUNDANE

prosecute *verb*
▶ ACCUSE

prosecution *noun*
▶ CASE

prospect *noun*
- ▶ IDEA 1 (an exciting prospect)
- ▶ POSSIBILITY (no prospect of peace)
- ▶ POTENTIAL (career prospects)

prospective *adj.*
- ▶ LIKELY (a prospective buyer)
- ▶ NEXT (prospective changes)

prosper *verb*
- ▶ DO WELL

prosperity *noun*
- ▶ MONEY 3

prosperous *adj.*
- ▶ RICH

protagonist *noun*
- ▶ STAR 2

protect *verb*
- ▶ PROTECT

protection *noun*
- ▶ SECURITY

protective *adj.*
- ▶ PROTECTIVE

protest *noun*
- ▶ DEMONSTRATION (an anti-war protest)
- ▶ OPPOSITION (a storm of protest)

protest *verb*
- ▶ COMPLAIN

protester *noun*
- ▶ PROTESTER

prototype *noun*
- ▶ MODEL

protracted *adj.*
- ▶ LONG

proud *adj.*
- ▶ PROUD 1 (Don't be too proud to ask for advice.)
- ▶ PROUD 2 (too proud to be seen with his former friends)
- ▶ GLAD (proud of your achievements)

prove *verb*
- ▶ SHOW 1

proven *adj.*
- ▶ FINAL

proverb *noun*
- ▶ SAYING

provide *verb*
- ▶ PROVIDE

provide for *phrasal verb*
- ▶ PROVIDE FOR SB (provide for children in need)
- ▶ PREPARE 2 (provide for every eventuality)

providence *noun*
- ▶ LUCK

province *noun*
- ▶ COUNTY

provision *noun*
- ▶ CONDITION (Under the provisions of the lease…)
- ▶ PLANNING (make adequate provision for your retirement)
- ▶ SUPPLIES (emergency provisions)

provision *verb*
- ▶ EQUIP 1

proviso *noun*
- ▶ CONDITION

provoke *verb*
- ▶ PROVOKE (He's easily provoked.)
- ▶ PROMPT (provoke a crisis)

prowess *noun*
- ▶ SKILL 2

prowl *verb*
- ▶ SLIP 1 (wolves prowl)
- ▶ WALK 1 (prowl around the room)

proximity *noun*
- ▶ PROXIMITY

proxy *noun*
- ▶ REPLACEMENT

prudence *noun*
- ▶ CARE

prudent *adj.*
- ▶ WISE

prudish *adj.*
- ▶ PRIM

pry *verb*
- ▶ INTERFERE (I didn't mean to pry.)
- ▶ PULL 2 (pry the lid open)

pseudonym *noun*
- ▶ NICKNAME

psychological *adj.*
- ▶ INTELLECTUAL 1

psychopathic *adj.*
- ▶ MENTALLY ILL

psychotic *adj.*
- ▶ MENTALLY ILL

pub *noun*
- ▶ BAR

puberty *noun*
- ▶ CHILDHOOD

public *noun*
- ▶ COMMUNITY (the general public)
- ▶ MARKET 1 (the viewing public)

public *adj.*
- ▶ PUBLIC (the public sector)
- ▶ COMMON (public transport)
- ▶ FAMOUS (a public figure)
- ▶ SOCIAL (public opinion)

publication *noun*
- ▶ BOOK

public figure *noun*
- ▶ STAR 1

public house *noun*
- ▶ BAR

publicity *noun*
- ▶ ADVERTISEMENT (work in publicity)
- ▶ FAME (attract publicity)

publicize *verb*
- ▶ PUBLISH 1

publish *verb*
- ▶ PUBLISH 1 (publish results)
- ▶ PUBLISH 2 (publish a novel)

puff *verb*
- ▶ BLOW 2

puke *verb*
- ▶ VOMIT

pull *verb*
- ▶ PULL 1 (pull a cart)
- ▶ PULL 2 (pull the plug out)
- ▶ PULL 3 (pull sb's hair)
- ▶ INJURE (pull a muscle)
- ▶ **pull strings** MANIPULATE

pull apart *phrasal verb*
- ▶ TEAR

pull in *phrasal verb*
- ▶ MAKE 3

pull off *phrasal verb*
- ▶ ACHIEVE

pull out *phrasal verb*
- ▶ WITHDRAW 1 (pull out troops)
- ▶ WITHDRAW 2 (pull out of a project)

pull over *verb*
- ▶ STOP 2

pull through *phrasal verb*
- ▶ RECOVER 1

pull together *phrasal verb*
- ▶ RELAX 1

pull up *verb*
- ▶ STOP 2

pulpit *noun*
- ▶ STAGE 2

pulse *verb*
- ▶ BEAT 2

pummel *verb*
- ▶ BEAT 1

pump *verb*
- ▶ PUMP

pun *noun*
- ▶ JOKE

punch *verb*
- ▶ HIT 2

punctual *adj.*
- ▶ EARLY

pundit *noun*
- ▶ EXPERT

pungent *adj.*
- ▶ BITTER 1

punish *verb*
- ▶ PUNISH

punishable *adj.*
- ▶ ILLEGAL

punishing *adj.*
- ▶ HARD

punishment *noun*
- ▶ PUNISHMENT

punitive *adj.*
- ▶ STRICT

punter *noun*
- ▶ CUSTOMER

pupil *noun*
- ▶ STUDENT

purchase *verb*
- ▶ BUY

purchaser *noun*
- ▶ CUSTOMER

pure *adj.*
- ▶ PURE 1 (100% pure cotton)
- ▶ PURE 2 (pure chance)
- ▶ CLEAN (pure drinking water)
- ▶ HOLY (a pure woman/life)

purge *verb*
- ▶ FREE 2

purify *verb*
- ▶ FILTER

purity *verb*
- ▶ MORALITY

purported *adj.*
- ▶ APPARENT

purpose *noun*
- ▶ PURPOSE (The purpose of this is to…)
- ▶ DETERMINATION (strength of purpose)
- ▶ FUNCTION (serve a purpose)
- ▶ MISSION (a sense of purpose)

purposeful *adj.*
- ▶ DELIBERATE

purse *noun*
- ▶ FUND (the public purse)
- ▶ SUITCASE (a shoulder purse)
- ▶ WALLET (a purse containing £22)

pursue *verb*
- ▶ CONTINUE 2 (pursue legal action)
- ▶ FOLLOW 1 (police pursue sb/sth)
- ▶ SEEK (pursue a medical career)

pursuit *noun*
- ▶ PROJECT (artistic pursuits)
- ▶ SEARCH (the pursuit of wealth)

push *verb*
- ▶ PUSH 1 (push sb away)
- ▶ PUSH 2 (push to the front)
- ▶ ADVERTISE (push a product)
- ▶ DRIVE 2 (push your students)
- ▶ PRESS 1 (push a button)
- ▶ PRESS 2 (push sb for an answer)

push around/about *phrasal verb*
- ▶ DICTATE TO SB

pushy *adj.*
- ▶ AGGRESSIVE 2

put *verb*
- ▶ PUT 1 (Put the cases down there.)
- ▶ PUT 2 (put sth into perspective)
- ▶ ATTACH (put posters on the walls)
- ▶ PLACE (put emphasis on sth)
- ▶ RANK (put sb in the top rank of novelists)

say 2 (put a feeling into words)

(continued)

- ▶ SAY 2 (put a feeling into words)
- ▶ SEND 2 (put sb in a nursing home)

put aside *phrasal verb*
- ▶ SAVE 3

put back *phrasal verb*
- ▶ RETURN 2

put down *phrasal verb*
- ▶ SUPPRESS 1 (put down a riot)
- ▶ WRITE 1 (put it down on paper)

put forward *phrasal verb*
- ▶ PROPOSE

put in *phrasal verb*
- ▶ PRESENT 3

put off *phrasal verb*
- ▶ DELAY

put on *phrasal verb*
- ▶ GAIN 2 (put on weight)
- ▶ PLAY 3 (put on a play)
- ▶ PRETEND (put on an American accent/a look of concern)
- ▶ TURN STH ON (put the kettle on)
- ▶ WEAR (put your coat on)

put out *phrasal verb*
- ▶ PUT STH OUT (put a fire out)
- ▶ TAKE ADVANTAGE OF SB/STH (I don't want to put you out.)

put out *adj.*
- ▶ ANNOYED

put through *phrasal verb*
- ▶ EXPOSE

put together *phrasal verb*
- ▶ PREPARE 1

put up *phrasal verb*
- ▶ ACCOMMODATE (put sb up for the night)
- ▶ BUILD (put up a tent)
- ▶ HANG (put up a poster)
- ▶ PROVIDE (put up the money)

put up to *phrasal verb*
- ▶ ENCOURAGE 2

put up with *phrasal verb*
- ▶ STAND 2

puzzle *noun*
- ▶ MYSTERY

puzzle *verb*
- ▶ CONFUSE

puzzled *adj.*
- ▶ CONFUSED 1

puzzling *adj.*
- ▶ CONFUSING

Q q

quad *noun*
- ▶ COURTYARD

quadrangle *noun*
- ▶ COURTYARD

qualification *noun*
- ▶ CONDITION

qualify *verb*
- ▶ ADJUST (qualify what you said)
- ▶ ALLOW (qualify for a pension)
- ▶ EQUIP 2 (qualify sb for a job)
- ▶ GRADUATE (qualify as a doctor)

quality *noun*
- ▶ QUALITY (poor quality goods)
- ▶ FEATURE (personal qualities)
- ▶ VALUE 1 (writers of quality)

quality *adj.*
- ▶ GOOD 1

qualm *noun*
- ▶ DOUBT 2

quantify *verb*
- ▶ CALCULATE

quantity *noun*
- ▶ NUMBER 1

quarantine *noun*
- ▶ DIVISION 1

quarantine *verb*
- ▶ ISOLATE

quarrel noun
- ARGUMENT 1

quarrel verb
- ARGUE

quarter noun
- AREA 1 (the Latin quarter of Paris)
- HOUSING (living quarters)
- ROUND (the fourth quarter of the game)

quarterly noun
- MAGAZINE

quash verb
- OVERTURN

queasy adj.
- SICK 2

queen noun
- KING (the Queen of Denmark)
- **turn Queen's evidence** TELL 2

quell verb
- SUPPRESS 1

query noun
- QUESTION

query verb
- DOUBT

quest noun
- SEARCH

question noun
- QUESTION (ask a question)
- DOUBT 1 (open to question)
- ISSUE (raise important questions)
- **out of the question** IMPOSSIBLE adj.

question verb
- QUESTION (be questioned by police)
- DOUBT (question sb's judgement)

questionable adj.
- CONTROVERSIAL (questionable conclusions)
- SUSPICIOUS 2 (questionable motives)

question mark noun
- **a question mark over/against sth** DOUBT 1

questionnaire noun
- FORM 2

queue noun
- ROW

quibble noun
- CRITICISM

quick adj.
- QUICK (a quick glance/drink)
- FAST (a quick learner)

quicken verb
- ACCELERATE

quiet noun
- SILENCE

quiet verb
- SILENCE

quiet adj.
- QUIET 1 (a quiet place/life)
- QUIET 2 (a quiet voice)
- QUIET 3 (quiet and shy)

quieten verb
- SILENCE

quintessential adj.
- TYPICAL

quip noun
- JOKE

quip verb
- JOKE

quirk noun
- MANNERISM

quit verb
- LEAVE 2 (quit town)
- LEAVE 3 (quit your job)
- STOP 1 (quit smoking)

quite adv.
- QUITE 1 (quite difficult)
- QUITE 2 (quite sure)

- VERY (quite sorry)
- **not quite** ALMOST

quiver noun
- SHIVER

quiz noun
- COMPETITION 1 (a general knowledge quiz)
- TEST 2 (a reading comprehension quiz)

quiz verb
- QUESTION (be quizzed by police)
- TEST 2 (You will be quizzed on chapter 6 tomorrow.)

quota noun
- SHARE

quotation noun
- REFERENCE (a quotation from Goethe)
- VALUATION (a free quotation)

quote noun
- REFERENCE (a quote from a poem)
- VALUATION (the lowest quote)

quote verb
- QUOTE (Don't quote me on this.)
- MENTION (Quote me an instance.)

R r

rabble noun
- CROWD

race noun
- RACE (a 10-mile race)
- COMPETITION 2 (the race for the presidency)
- CULTURE (a warlike race)
- PEOPLE 2 (people of different races)

race verb
- RUN 1

racial adj.
- CULTURAL

racism noun
- RACISM

racket noun
- FRAUD 2

rack up phrasal verb
- COLLECT

radiator noun
- HEATING

radical adj.
- RADICAL (radical politicians)
- FUNDAMENTAL (radical changes)

raft noun
- BOAT

rafter noun
- POST

rage noun
- ANGER (speechless with rage)
- TEMPER (storm out in a rage)

raging adj.
- ROUGH 2

raid noun
- ATTACK 1 (air raid)
- THEFT (a bank raid)

raid verb
- ROB

raider noun
- THIEF

railing noun
- WALL

rain noun
- RAIN

rain verb
- RAIN (Is it raining?)
- SCATTER (a volcano rains hot ash)

rainfall noun
- RAIN

rainforest noun
- FOREST

rainy adj.
- WET 2

raise noun
- INCREASE

raise verb
- RAISE (raise money for charity)
- BRING SB UP (raised a city boy)
- INCREASE (raise taxes)
- KEEP 4 (raise cattle)
- MAKE 2 (raise funds)
- PICK SB/STH UP (raise your hand)
- **raise sb's spirits** ENCOURAGE 1
- **raise your voice** SHOUT

rake in phrasal verb
- MAKE 3

rally verb
- MEET 1

ram verb
- PUSH 1

rambling adj.
- CONFUSED 2

ramp noun
- SLOPE

ranch noun
- FARM

ranch house noun
- HOUSE

random adj.
- RANDOM

range noun
- RANGE 1 (a range of activities)
- RANGE 2 (an age/a price range)

range verb
- DIFFER

rank noun
- CLASS 4 (officers of senior rank)
- ROW (ranks of marching soldiers)

rank verb
- RANK

ranking noun
- CLASS 4 (the No. 1 world ranking)
- SCALE (16th in the rankings)

rankle verb
- ANGER

ransack verb
- ROB

ransom verb
- RELEASE

rap noun
- CRITICISM

rap verb
- KNOCK

rape noun
- ATTACK 2

rape verb
- RAPE

rapid adj.
- QUICK

rapidity noun
- SPEED

rapport noun
- BOND

rapt adj.
- INTERESTED

rapturous adj.
- EXCITED

rare adj.
- RARE

rarely adv.
- RARELY

rash noun
- WAVE 3

rash adj.
- RECKLESS

rasher noun
- PIECE

rasp verb
- CREAK (a rasping cough)
- GRUNT ('Get out!' he rasped.)

rate noun
- RATE 1 (the rate of change)
- RATE 2 (sb's rate of pay)
- TAX (business rates)

rate verb
- JUDGE 1 (How did you rate it?)
- RANK (schools rated according to exam results)

rather adv.
- QUITE 1 (rather good)
- **would rather…** PREFER verb

ratify verb
- APPROVE

rating noun
- CLASS 4

ratio noun
- RATIO

ration noun
- SHARE (a ration of sugar/luck)
- SUPPLIES (wartime rations)

rational adj.
- RATIONAL (a rational argument)
- SANE (a rational man)

rationality noun
- LOGIC

rationalize verb
- CUT 1

rattle verb
- SHAKE 2

raucous adj.
- HOARSE

ravage verb
- DESTROY

rave noun
- PARTY 2

rave verb
- PRAISE

ravenous adj.
- HUNGRY

ravine noun
- VALLEY

raw adj.
- FRESH (raw eggs/meat)
- PAINFUL 1 (His skin was raw.)

raze verb
- DEMOLISH

reach noun
- RANGE 2

reach verb
- ACHIEVE (reach a target)
- CALL 2 (You can reach me on this number.)
- GET 4 (reach your destination)
- LEAD 3 (The cable won't reach the socket.)

react verb
- RESPOND

reaction noun
- RESPONSE

read verb
- READ

reading noun
- DEFINITION (my reading of events)
- SCENE (a reading from the Bible)

read into phrasal verb
- CONCLUDE

ready adj.
- READY (Dinner's ready!)
- **get sb/sth ready** PREPARE verb 1
- **get ready** PREPARE verb 2

real adj.
- REAL (the real reason/real leather)
- COMPLETE (He looks a real idiot.)
- DEEP 1 (real regret)
- **real life, the real world** FACT noun

real estate noun
- LAND 1

realism noun
▶ WISDOM

realistic adj.
▶ REALISTIC 1 (take a realistic view)
▶ REALISTIC 2 (a realistic drawing)
▶ POSSIBLE 1 (set realistic goals)

reality noun
▶ FACT

realization noun
▶ AWARENESS

realize verb
▶ KNOW 1 (realize sth is wrong)
▶ MAKE 2 (realize a lot of money)

real-life adj.
▶ RELIABLE 2

really adv.
▶ VERY

realm noun
▶ AREA 2

reap verb
▶ GET 2

rear verb
▶ BRING SB UP (rear a family)
▶ KEEP 4 (rear poultry)

rearrange verb
▶ REORGANIZE

reason noun
▶ REASON (the reason why…)
▶ LOGIC (listen to/see reason)

reason verb
▶ CONCLUDE

reasonable adj.
▶ REASONABLE (It is reasonable to assume that…)
▶ ADEQUATE (a reasonable standard of living)
▶ CHEAP (reasonable prices)
▶ FINE (make a reasonable offer)

reasonably adv.
▶ QUITE 1

reasoned adj.
▶ RATIONAL

reasoning noun
▶ REASONING

reassemble verb
▶ REBUILD

reassurance noun
▶ RELIEF

reassure verb
▶ REASSURE

rebate noun
▶ COMPENSATION

rebel noun
▶ GUERRILLA (armed rebels)
▶ PROTESTER (Labour rebels)

rebel verb
▶ REBEL (rebel against the king)
▶ OPPOSE (rebel against your upbringing)

rebellion noun
▶ REVOLUTION 1

rebellious adj.
▶ NAUGHTY

rebuff noun
▶ REFUSAL

rebuff verb
▶ REFUSE

rebuild verb
▶ REBUILD

rebuke verb
▶ SCOLD

rebut verb
▶ DISPROVE

rebuttal noun
▶ DENIAL

recall noun
▶ MEMORY

recall verb
▶ REMEMBER

recant verb
▶ BREAK 4

recap verb
▶ SUMMARIZE

receipts noun
▶ REVENUE

receive verb
▶ GET 2 (receive a letter)
▶ GREET (be received as an honoured guest)
▶ HAVE 3 (receive attention)
▶ LET SB IN (be received into the Church)
▶ RESPOND (well received by critics)

recent adj.
▶ RECENT

reception noun
▶ EVENT 2 (a wedding reception)
▶ GREETING (a warm reception)
▶ HALL 2 (hotel reception)
▶ RESPONSE (a mixed reception)

recess noun
▶ HOLIDAY 1 (the Christmas recess)
▶ REST 2 (The judge called a recess.)

recession noun
▶ RECESSION

recital noun
▶ CONCERT

recite verb
▶ QUOTE

reckless adj.
▶ RECKLESS

reckon verb
▶ ESTIMATE (They reckoned their profits were down 15%.)
▶ REGARD (It was reckoned a success.)
▶ THINK (I reckon it looks OK.)

reckoning noun
▶ ESTIMATE (By my reckoning…)
▶ PUNISHMENT (the day of reckoning)

reclaim verb
▶ RECOVER 2

recline verb
▶ LIE

reclusive adj.
▶ SOLITARY

recognition noun
▶ ADMIRATION

recognizable adj.
▶ RECOGNIZABLE

recognize verb
▶ ADMIT 1 (recognize that sth is a problem)
▶ APPROVE (recognized qualifications)
▶ IDENTIFY (recognize sb as an old friend)

recoil verb
▶ HESITATE (recoil from an idea)
▶ JUMP 3 (recoil in horror)

recollect verb
▶ REMEMBER

recollection noun
▶ MEMORY

recommend verb
▶ RECOMMEND 1 (recommend that sb do sth)
▶ RECOMMEND 2 (recommend a good hotel)

recommendation noun
▶ ENDORSEMENT (on sb's recommendation)
▶ PROPOSAL (make a recommendation)

reconcile verb
▶ ACCEPT

reconstruct verb
▶ REBUILD (reconstruct a building)

▶ SIMULATE (reconstruct the circumstances of the crash)

reconstruction noun
▶ COPY 2

record noun
▶ RECORD (financial records)
▶ BACKGROUND (sth's safety record)
▶ **off the record** UNOFFICIAL adj.

record verb
▶ RECORD 1 (the figures recorded for 2007)
▶ RECORD 2 (record a TV show)

recount verb
▶ DESCRIBE

recover verb
▶ RECOVER 1 (recover from an illness)
▶ RECOVER 2 (recover the money)

recreate verb
▶ SIMULATE

recreation noun
▶ ENTERTAINMENT

recrimination noun
▶ CHARGE

recruit noun
▶ RECRUIT

recruit verb
▶ EMPLOY

rectify noun
▶ CORRECT

recuperate verb
▶ RECOVER 1

redecorate verb
▶ REBUILD

redeem verb
▶ SAVE 1

redesign verb
▶ REORGANIZE

redevelop verb
▶ REBUILD

red-hot adj.
▶ HOT

redo verb
▶ REPEAT 2

redress verb
▶ CORRECT

red tape noun
▶ BUREAUCRACY

reduce verb
▶ REDUCE

reduction noun
▶ REDUCTION

redundancy noun
▶ UNEMPLOYMENT

redundant adj.
▶ UNEMPLOYED (redundant workers)
▶ UNNECESSARY (redundant information)
▶ **make sb redundant** FIRE verb

reek noun
▶ ODOUR

reel noun
▶ ROLL

reel verb
▶ STUMBLE

ref noun
▶ JUDGE 2

referee noun
▶ JUDGE 2

reference noun
▶ REFERENCE (with reference to your letter of 22 July)
▶ ENDORSEMENT (a reference from your last employer)

referendum noun
▶ ELECTION

refer to phrasal verb
▶ REFER TO STH (refer to your notes)

▶ APPLY 2 (This paragraph refers to the events of last year.)
▶ LEAVE 6 (refer sb to a specialist)
▶ MENTION (refer to the matter)

refill verb
▶ FILL

refine verb
▶ FILTER (refine oil/sugar)
▶ IMPROVE 1 (refine a theory)

refined adj.
▶ PURE 1

reflect verb
▶ CONSIDER (reflect on the situation)
▶ SHOW 3 (reflect local opinion)

reflection noun
▶ CONSIDERATION (a period of reflection)
▶ IMAGE (his reflection in the mirror)
▶ REASONING (reflections on childhood)

reflective adj.
▶ THOUGHTFUL

reform verb
▶ IMPROVE 1

reformer noun
▶ ACTIVIST

refreshment noun
▶ FOOD (take some refreshment)
▶ SNACK (light refreshments)

refrigerate verb
▶ COOL

refuge noun
▶ REFUGE (a women's refuge)
▶ SHELTER (take refuge)

refugee noun
▶ REFUGEE

refund noun
▶ COMPENSATION

refund verb
▶ REPAY

refurbish verb
▶ REBUILD

refusal noun
▶ REFUSAL

refuse noun
▶ WASTE

refuse verb
▶ REFUSE

refutation noun
▶ DENIAL

refute verb
▶ DENY (refute a suggestion)
▶ DISPROVE (refute an argument)

regain verb
▶ RECOVER 2

regard noun
▶ ATTENTION

regard verb
▶ REGARD (regard sb as a friend)
▶ LOOK 1 (regard sb suspiciously)

regent noun
▶ KING

regime noun
▶ DIET (a fitness regime)
▶ GOVERNMENT 1 (a military regime)

regimen noun
▶ DIET

region noun
▶ AREA 1 (tropical regions)
▶ COUNTY (an autonomous region)

register noun
▶ LIST

register verb
▶ PRESENT 3 (register a protest)
▶ RECORD 1 (be registered as unemployed)

regret noun
▸ GRIEF (have no regrets)
▸ GUILT (express your regret)

regret verb
▸ APOLOGIZE

regrettable adj.
▸ UNFORTUNATE 2

regular noun
▸ CUSTOMER

regular adj.
▸ REGULAR (regular customers)
▸ FREQUENT (regular exercise)
▸ STEADY (a regular job/boyfriend)
▸ USUAL (sb's regular duties)

regulate verb
▸ REGULATE

regulation noun
▸ GOVERNMENT 2 (regulation by the authorities)
▸ RULE (against the regulations)
▸ **rules and regulations** BUREAU-CRACY

regulator noun
▸ INSPECTOR

regurgitate verb
▸ VOMIT

rehabilitate verb
▸ CURE

rehearsal noun
▸ TRAINING

rehearse verb
▸ PRACTISE

reheat verb
▸ HEAT

reign noun
▸ GOVERNMENT 1

reign verb
▸ RULE 1 (reign over a country)
▸ TAKE OVER (reign supreme)

reimburse verb
▸ REPAY

reimbursement noun
▸ COMPENSATION

rein noun
▸ REIN

reinforce verb
▸ STRENGTHEN

rein in phrasal verb
▸ LIMIT

reiterate verb
▸ REPEAT 1

reject verb
▸ REJECT (rejected by your family)
▸ REFUSE (reject an offer)

rejection noun
▸ REFUSAL

relate verb
▸ RELATE (pay will be related to productivity)
▸ DESCRIBE (relate the facts)

related adj.
▸ RELATED

relate to phrasal verb
▸ APPLY 2 (information relating to national security)
▸ UNDERSTAND 2 (Many adults can't relate to children.)

relation noun
▸ RELATION (Its brain is small in relation to its body.)
▸ FAMILY 2 (Is he any relation to you?)
▸ RELATIONSHIP 1 (international relations)

relationship noun
▸ RELATIONSHIP 1 (The brothers had a close relationship.)
▸ RELATIONSHIP 2 (a sexual relationship)
▸ RELATION (the relationship between mental and physical health)

relative noun
▸ FAMILY 2

relative adj.
▸ RELATIVE

relax verb
▸ RELAX 1 (Relax! Everything is OK.)
▸ RELAX 2 (relax your muscles/grip)
▸ REST (Relax and enjoy the movie.)

relaxation noun
▸ ENTERTAINMENT

relaxed adj.
▸ CALM (relaxed and confident)
▸ CASUAL (a relaxed attitude)
▸ INFORMAL (a relaxed atmosphere)

relay verb
▸ CONVEY

release verb
▸ RELEASE (release prisoners)
▸ FREE 1 (release the driver from the wreckage)
▸ PUBLISH 1 (release details of sth)
▸ PUBLISH 2 (release a film/CD)
▸ RELAX 2 (release the tension)

relent verb
▸ GIVE WAY idiom

relentless adj.
▸ CONTINUOUS

relevant verb
▸ RELEVANT

reliable adj.
▸ RELIABLE 1 (reliable and hard-working)
▸ RELIABLE 2 (reliable evidence)

relief noun
▸ RELIEF (What a relief!)
▸ AID (famine relief)
▸ REPLACEMENT (a relief driver)

relieve verb
▸ EASE

relieved adj.
▸ GLAD

religion noun
▸ RELIGION

religious adj.
▸ RELIGIOUS

relinquish verb
▸ GIVE STH UP

relish verb
▸ ENJOY

relocate verb
▸ LEAVE 2

reluctant adj.
▸ RELUCTANT

rely on/upon phrasal verb
▸ NEED (rely on computers)
▸ TRUST (You can rely on me.)

remain verb
▸ REMAIN (remain unchanged)
▸ STAY 1 (remain in Mexico)

the remainder noun
▸ REST 1

remains noun
▸ REMAINS 1 (prehistoric remains)
▸ REMAINS 2 (the remains of a sandwich)
▸ BODY 2 (human remains)

remake verb
▸ SIMULATE

remark noun
▸ STATEMENT

remark verb
▸ COMMENT

remarkable adj.
▸ REMARKABLE

remarry verb
▸ MARRY

remedy noun
▸ DRUG 2 (herbal remedies)
▸ SOLUTION (no remedy for un-employment)

remedy verb
▸ CORRECT

remember verb
▸ REMEMBER

remembrance noun
▸ MEMORY

remind of phrasal verb
▸ REMIND SB OF SB/STH

reminisce verb
▸ REMEMBER

reminiscence noun
▸ MEMORY

remnant noun
▸ REMAINS 2

remodel verb
▸ REBUILD

remorse noun
▸ GUILT

remote adj.
▸ COLD 2 (cold and remote)
▸ PREVIOUS (the remote past)

remove verb
▸ REMOVE 1 (remove stains)
▸ REMOVE 2 (remove sb from power)
▸ TAKE 3 (Remove the pan from the heat.)
▸ TAKE STH OFF (remove your clothes)

renegade noun
▸ TRAITOR

renew verb
▸ CONTINUE 3

renounce verb
▸ GIVE STH UP

renovate verb
▸ REBUILD

renowned adj.
▸ FAMOUS

rent noun
▸ RATE 2

rent verb
▸ ORDER 2

rental noun
▸ RATE 2

reopen verb
▸ CONTINUE 3

reorganize verb
▸ REORGANIZE

rep noun
▸ SALESMAN

repair noun
▸ REPAIR (take sth in for repair)
▸ STATE (in a poor state of repair)

repair verb
▸ REPAIR (repair the roof)
▸ RESOLVE (repair relations)

repatriate verb
▸ EXPEL

repay verb
▸ REPAY

repayment noun
▸ PAYMENT

repeal verb
▸ CANCEL

repeat verb
▸ REPEAT 1 (Could you repeat that?)
▸ REPEAT 2 (repeat your mistakes)
▸ CONVEY (Don't repeat a word of this to anyone.)
▸ QUOTE (Repeat what I just said.)

repel verb
▸ FEND SB/STH OFF (repel invaders)
▸ SHOCK (repelled by the smell)

repentance noun
▸ GUILT

repercussion noun
▸ RESULT

repetitive adj.
▸ BORING

rephrase verb
▸ REVISE

replace verb
▸ REPLACE 1 (Teachers will never be replaced by computers.)
▸ REPLACE 2 (replace the old car-pets)
▸ RETURN 2 (replace the lid)

replacement noun
▸ REPLACEMENT (We need to find a replacement for Sue.)
▸ EXCHANGE (The furnishings are in need of replacement.)

replay noun
▸ GAME 1

replenish verb
▸ FILL

replica noun
▸ COPY 2

replicate verb
▸ REPEAT 2

reply noun
▸ ANSWER

reply verb
▸ ANSWER

report noun
▸ REPORT 1 (commission a report on the health service)
▸ REPORT 2 (newspaper reports)
▸ REPORT 3 (a progress report)
▸ REPORT 4 (unconfirmed reports of a shooting)

report verb
▸ DESCRIBE (report on royal stories for the BBC)
▸ TELL 1 (report engine trouble)

reportage noun
▸ MEDIA

reporter noun
▸ REPORTER

reporting noun
▸ MEDIA

repository noun
▸ WAREHOUSE

represent verb
▸ REPRESENT 1 (represent a major breakthrough in AIDS research)
▸ REPRESENT 2 (represent sb's views/the idea of peace)
▸ PRESENT 2 (a diagram represents sth)

representation noun
▸ DESCRIPTION

representative noun
▸ POLITICIAN (the Representative for Iowa)
▸ SALESMAN (a sales representative)
▸ SPOKESMAN (an elected represen-tative)

representative adj.
▸ TYPICAL

repress verb
▸ SUPPRESS 1 (repress the oppos-ition)
▸ SUPPRESS 2 (repress your fury)

repression noun
▸ REPRESSION

repressive adj.
▸ REPRESSIVE

reprimand verb
▸ SCOLD

reprisal noun
▸ REVENGE

reproach verb
▸ SCOLD

reproduce verb
▸ COPY (reproduce copyright mat-erial)
▸ PRODUCE (animals reproduce)

SIMULATE (reproduce the effects of earthquakes on buildings)

reproduction noun
▶ COPY 2

republic noun
▶ REPUBLIC

repudiate verb
▶ DENY

repugnant adj.
▶ DISGUSTING 2

repulsive adj.
▶ DISGUSTING 1

reputable adj.
▶ RESPECTABLE

reputation noun
▶ REPUTATION

request noun
▶ REQUEST (make a request for aid)
▶ WISH (grant sb's request)

request verb
▶ ASK 2

require verb
▶ DEMAND (required by law)
▶ NEED (require treatment)

requirement noun
▶ CONDITION (safety requirements)
▶ NEED (meet your requirements)

requisite adj.
▶ NECESSARY

requisition verb
▶ SEIZE

reschedule verb
▶ DELAY

rescue verb
▶ SAVE 1

research noun
▶ RESEARCH

research verb
▶ INVESTIGATE

resemblance noun
▶ SIMILARITY

resemble verb
▶ LOOK LIKE SB/STH

resent verb
▶ RESENT

resentful adj.
▶ BITTER 2

resentment noun
▶ RESENTMENT

reservation noun
▶ REQUEST

reserve noun
▶ FUND (reserves of capital)
▶ REPLACEMENT (play for the reserves)
▶ SUPPLY (oil reserves)

reserve verb
▶ RESERVE (A place has been reserved for you.)
▶ ORDER 2 (reserve a seat)

reserved adj.
▶ QUIET 3

reservoir noun
▶ LAKE

reshape verb
▶ REORGANIZE

reshuffle verb
▶ REORGANIZE

reside verb
▶ LIVE

residence noun
▶ HOME 1

resident noun
▶ RESIDENT (local residents)
▶ TENANT (hotel residents)

resign verb
▶ LEAVE 3

resignation noun
▶ PATIENCE

resign to phrasal verb
▶ ACCEPT

resilience noun
▶ STRENGTH

resist verb
▶ RESIST (resist arrest)
▶ OPPOSE (resist change)
▶ WITHSTAND (resist infection)

resistance noun
▶ OPPOSITION (resistance to change)
▶ STRENGTH (resistance to drugs)

resistant adj.
▶ AGAINST SB/STH

resolute adj.
▶ DETERMINED 2

resolution noun
▶ SOLUTION

resolve noun
▶ DETERMINATION

resolve verb
▶ RESOLVE (resolve a problem)
▶ DECIDE (resolve to do sth)

resolved adj.
▶ DETERMINED 1

resonate verb
▶ ECHO

resort to phrasal verb
▶ USE 1

resound verb
▶ ECHO

resounding adj.
▶ DEEP 2

resource noun
▶ FACILITIES (Time is a valuable resource.)
▶ SUPPLY (natural resources)

respect noun
▶ RESPECT (show a lack of respect)
▶ ADMIRATION (have great respect for sb)
▶ ASPECT (In this respect…)

respect verb
▶ RESPECT (a respected teacher)
▶ FOLLOW 3 (respect the law)

respectable adj.
▶ RESPECTABLE (a respectable woman/neighbourhood/job)
▶ DECENT (a respectable result)

respectful adj.
▶ POLITE

respective adj.
▶ PARTICULAR

respite noun
▶ REST 2

respond verb
▶ RESPOND (respond to an emergency)
▶ ANSWER (respond to an advertisement)

response noun
▶ RESPONSE (an angry response)
▶ ANSWER (a response to an advertisement)

responsibility noun
▶ RESPONSIBILITY (a position of responsibility)
▶ FAULT (accept responsibility for the mistake)

responsible adj.
▶ GUILTY (responsible for the mess)
▶ RELIABLE (a responsible attitude)
▶ **be responsible for sb/sth** RUN verb 2

rest noun
▶ REST 1 (the rest of the world)
▶ REST 2 (take a rest)
▶ **put/set your mind at rest** REASSURE verb

rest verb
▶ REST (The doctor told me to rest.)
▶ LEAN 2 (His chin rested on his hands.)
▶ **come to rest** LAND

restart verb
▶ CONTINUE 3

restate verb
▶ REPEAT 1

restitution noun
▶ COMPENSATION

restless adj.
▶ RESTLESS

restock verb
▶ FILL

rest on phrasal verb
▶ DEPEND ON/UPON STH

restore verb
▶ REBUILD (restore old paintings)
▶ RETURN 2 (restore sth to its owner)

restrain verb
▶ RESTRAIN (She had to be physically restrained.)
▶ PREVENT (restrain sb from doing sth)
▶ SUPPRESS 2 (restrain an urge)

restrained adj.
▶ DISCIPLINED

restraint noun
▶ RESTRAINT (appeal to the crowd for restraint)
▶ LIMIT 1 (export/social restraints)

restrict verb
▶ CONFINE SB/STH TO STH (I restrict myself to one cup of coffee a day.)
▶ LIMIT (restrict the number of students)

restricted adj.
▶ LIMITED 1 (a restricted range)
▶ LIMITED 2 (restricted access)

restriction noun
▶ LIMIT 1

restroom noun
▶ TOILET

restructure verb
▶ REORGANIZE

result noun
▶ RESULT (as a result of sth)
▶ SCORE (the election results)
▶ VICTORY (get a result from a game)
▶ WORK 3 (get results from sb)

result verb
▶ FOLLOW 2

resultant adj.
▶ RELATED

result in phrasal verb
▶ CAUSE

resulting adj.
▶ RELATED

resume verb
▶ CONTINUE 3

resuscitate verb
▶ CURE

retail verb
▶ COST (retail at £9.95)
▶ SELL 2 (retail a range of goods)

retailer noun
▶ DEALER

retain verb
▶ EMPLOY (retain sb's services)
▶ KEEP 2 (retain control/your ticket)
▶ KEEP 3 (retain facts)

retaliate verb
▶ FIGHT BACK

retaliation noun
▶ REVENGE

retard verb
▶ HOLD SB/STH UP

reticent adj.
▶ QUIET 3

retire verb
▶ LEAVE 3 (retire from teaching)
▶ WITHDRAW 1 (a jury retires)

retort noun
▶ ANSWER

retort verb
▶ ANSWER

retract verb
▶ BREAK 4

retraction noun
▶ DENIAL

retreat noun
▶ REFUGE

retreat verb
▶ WITHDRAW 1 (an army retreats)
▶ WITHDRAW 2 (retreat from a pledge)

retribution noun
▶ PUNISHMENT

retrieve verb
▶ RECOVER 2

return noun
▶ PROFIT (a return on an investment)
▶ REPORT 3 (submit your tax return)

return verb
▶ RETURN 1 (return home)
▶ RETURN 2 (return books to the library)

return to phrasal verb
▶ CONTINUE 3

reunion noun
▶ EVENT 2

revamp verb
▶ REBUILD

reveal verb
▶ REVEAL (reveal the truth)
▶ SHOW 2 (reveal a line of white teeth)

revealing adj.
▶ INFORMATIVE

revel in phrasal verb
▶ ENJOY

revenge noun
▶ REVENGE

revenue noun
▶ REVENUE

reverberate verb
▶ ECHO

reverie noun
▶ TRANCE

reversal noun
▶ EXCHANGE (a role reversal)
▶ REVOLUTION 2 (a reversal of fortunes)

the reverse noun
▶ OPPOSITE

reverse verb
▶ REVERSE (reverse a trend)
▶ OVERTURN (reverse a decision)
▶ REPLACE 2 (reverse roles with sb)

reverse adj.
▶ OPPOSITE

review noun
▶ ASSESSMENT (a book review)
▶ REPORT 1 (a critical review of the existing system)

review verb
▶ EXAMINE (review a decision)
▶ LEARN (review your notes)

reviewer noun
▶ REPORTER

revise verb
▶ REVISE (a revised edition)
▶ ADJUST (revise your opinion)
▶ LEARN (revise for exams)

revision noun
▶ CHANGE 2

revoke verb
▶ CANCEL

revolt noun
▶ REVOLUTION 1

revolt verb
▶ REBEL

revolution noun
▶ REVOLUTION 1 (the French Revolution)
▶ REVOLUTION 2 (a technological revolution)

revolutionary noun
▶ GUERRILLA

revolutionary adj.
▶ RADICAL

revolve verb
▶ SPIN

revolver noun
▶ GUN

reward noun
▶ AWARD

rewarding adj.
▶ SATISFYING

rewrite verb
▶ REVISE

ribbon noun
▶ STRIP

rich adj.
▶ RICH (rich people/countries)
▶ DARK 2 (a rich red colour)
▶ DEEP 2 (a rich singing voice)
▶ PRODUCTIVE (rich farming land)

riches noun
▶ MONEY 3

rid noun
▶ **get rid of sb/sth** REMOVE 1

rid verb
▶ FREE 2

ride noun
▶ FLIGHT

ride verb
▶ GO 2

ridge noun
▶ HILL

ridicule noun
▶ CONTEMPT

ridicule verb
▶ LAUGH AT SB/STH

ridiculous adj.
▶ RIDICULOUS

rife adj.
▶ GENERAL 1

riff-raff noun
▶ GENERAL PUBLIC

rifle noun
▶ GUN

rift noun
▶ DIVISION 2

rig verb
▶ DISTORT

right noun
▶ RIGHT (human rights)
▶ MORALITY (right and wrong)

right adj.
▶ RIGHT 1 (the right decision)
▶ RIGHT 2 (do the right thing)
▶ GOOD 2 (the right man for the job)
▶ TRUE (the right answer)
▶ **put sth right** CORRECT verb
▶ **just right** IDEAL
▶ **in your right mind** SANE

righteousness noun
▶ MORALITY

right-hand man noun
▶ ASSISTANT

rigid adj.
▶ DEEP-SEATED (rigid attitudes)
▶ SOLID (rigid and brittle)
▶ STRICT (a rigid code of ethics)

rigorous adj.
▶ DETAILED

rile verb
▶ ANGER

ring noun
▶ CIRCLE (onion rings)
▶ TEAM 1 (a drug smuggling ring)

ring verb
▶ RING (The doorbell rang.)
▶ CALL 2 (I'll ring you later.)
▶ ECHO (The house rang with laughter.)

ring out phrasal verb
▶ ECHO

ring road noun
▶ HIGHWAY

rinse noun
▶ BATH

rinse verb
▶ CLEAN

riot noun
▶ REVOLUTION 1

rioting noun
▶ REVOLUTION 1

rip verb
▶ TEAR

rip off phrasal verb
▶ DEFRAUD

ripple noun
▶ WAVE 1 (ripples on the water)
▶ WAVE 2 (a ripple of fear)

rise noun
▶ INCREASE (price rises)
▶ PROGRESS (the rise of fascism)
▶ **give rise to sth** CAUSE

rise verb
▶ RISE (interest rates rise)
▶ REBEL (rise up against an invader)
▶ SLOPE (the ground rises steeply)
▶ STAND 1 (rise to your feet)

risk noun
▶ RISK 1 (the risk of heart disease)
▶ RISK 2 (take a risk)
▶ THREAT (a security/fire risk)
▶ **at risk** VULNERABLE adj.

risk verb
▶ DARE (risk death/being caught)
▶ THREATEN 2 (risk your life)

risky adj.
▶ DANGEROUS

rite noun
▶ CEREMONY

ritual noun
▶ CEREMONY (a religious ritual)
▶ HABIT (follow a daily ritual)

rival noun
▶ ENEMY

rival verb
▶ COMPARE 2

rivalry noun
▶ COMPETITION 2

river noun
▶ RIVER

rivet verb
▶ INTEREST

riveting adj.
▶ INTERESTING

road noun
▶ ROAD (the main road)
▶ DIRECTION (on the road to recovery)

roadblock noun
▶ BARRIER (a police roadblock)
▶ OBSTACLE (a legal roadblock)

roam verb
▶ WANDER

roar verb
▶ LAUGH (roar with laughter)
▶ RUMBLE (an engine roars)

▶ SHOUT (a crowd roars)

roaring adj.
▶ LOUD

roast verb
▶ BAKE

rob verb
▶ ROB

robber noun
▶ THIEF

robbery noun
▶ THEFT

robotic adj.
▶ ELECTRONIC

rock noun
▶ STONE

rock verb
▶ SHAKE 2 (rocked by the earthquake)
▶ SHOCK (rocked by the scandal)
▶ SWING (rock back and forth)

rocket noun
▶ BOMB

rocket verb
▶ SOAR

rocky adj.
▶ ROUGH 1

rogue adj.
▶ ABNORMAL

role noun
▶ ROLE (the role of the teacher)
▶ CHARACTER (the role of Othello)
▶ INVOLVEMENT (have a role to play)

role model noun
▶ EXAMPLE 2

roll noun
▶ ROLL (a roll of paper/film/coins)
▶ LIST (the electoral roll)

roll verb
▶ ROLL (roll onto your back)
▶ FOLD (roll up your sleeves)
▶ RUMBLE (thunder rolls)
▶ SLIDE (a car rolls down a hill)
▶ SPIN (a dog rolls in the mud)
▶ WRAP SB/STH AROUND/ROUND SB/STH (roll up the carpet)

roll in phrasal verb
▶ ARRIVE

romance noun
▶ LOVE 1 (Romance is in the air.)
▶ RELATIONSHIP 2 (a summer romance)

romantic noun
▶ VISIONARY

romantic adj.
▶ LOVING

Romany noun
▶ TRAVELLER

rookie noun
▶ BEGINNER

room noun
▶ SCOPE (room for doubt)
▶ SPACE 1 (no room for the books)

roomy adj.
▶ SPACIOUS

root noun
▶ FAMILY 3 (my African roots)
▶ SOURCE (the root of the problem)

root out phrasal verb
▶ ERADICATE

rope noun
▶ ROPE

rosy adj.
▶ PROMISING

rotate verb
▶ SPIN

rotten adj.
▶ ROTTEN (rotten eggs)
▶ CORRUPT (The organization is rotten to the core.)
▶ INCOMPETENT (a rotten singer)

rough adj.
▶ ROUGH 1 (rough ground/edges)
▶ ROUGH 2 (rough seas/weather)
▶ COARSE (rough skin)
▶ DIFFICULT 2 (Life is rough.)
▶ HOARSE (a rough voice)
▶ VAGUE (a rough estimate/sketch)
▶ VIOLENT (rough kids/treatment)

round noun
▶ ROUND (the opening round)
▶ BULLET (rounds of ammunition)
▶ GAME 1 (a round of golf)
▶ STAGE 1 (the next round of talks)

round adj.
▶ CURVED

roundabout noun
▶ JUNCTION

rounded adj.
▶ CURVED

round off phrasal verb
▶ FINISH

round out phrasal verb
▶ FINISH

round-the-clock adj.
▶ CONTINUOUS

rout verb
▶ DEFEAT

route noun
▶ DIRECTION (sb's route to fame)
▶ WAY 3 (the best route into the city)

routine noun
▶ PROCESS

routine adj.
▶ MUNDANE (routine, boring and badly-paid jobs)
▶ USUAL (a routine operation)

routinely adv.
▶ OFTEN

row[1] /rəʊ; AmE roʊ/ noun
▶ ROW (planted in neat rows)
▶ ROAD (a row house)
▶ **in a row** SUCCESSIVE

row[2] /raʊ/ noun
▶ ARGUMENT 1 (have a row with sb)
▶ CONFRONTATION (a political row)

row[3] /raʊ/ verb
▶ ARGUE

rowdy adj.
▶ WILD 1

rub verb
▶ COVER (rub cream into your skin)
▶ SCRATCH 1 (My shoe is rubbing.)

rubbish noun
▶ RUBBISH (a rubbish film)
▶ NONSENSE (talk rubbish)
▶ WASTE (household rubbish)

rubble noun
▶ REMAINS 1

rub out phrasal verb
▶ DELETE

rucksack noun
▶ SUITCASE

rude adj.
▶ RUDE (rude to his mother)
▶ OFFENSIVE (a rude joke/noise)

rudimentary adj.
▶ FUNDAMENTAL

ruffle verb
▶ CRUMPLE

rugged adj.
▶ ROUGH 1

ruin noun
▶ REMAINS 1

ruin verb
▶ RUIN

rule noun
▶ RULE (school rules)
▶ CONTROL (majority rule)
▶ HABIT (make it a rule to do sth)

▸ PRINCIPLE 2 (a golden rule)
▸ THEORY 1 (rules of grammar)
▸ **rules and regulations** BUREAU-
   CRACY
▸ **the rule of law** PEACE
▸ **as a rule** USUALLY *adv.*
rule *verb*
▸ RULE 1 (rule a country)
▸ RULE 2 (The court ruled that…)
▸ DETERMINE (The pursuit of money
   ruled his life.)
rule out *phrasal verb*
▸ EXCLUDE 1 (rule out more taxes)
▸ PREVENT (Common sense ruled
   out this option.)
ruler *noun*
▸ KING
ruling *noun*
▸ CONCLUSION
rumble *verb*
▸ RUMBLE
rummage *verb*
▸ FUMBLE
rumour (also **rumor**) *noun*
▸ REPORT 4
rumple *verb*
▸ CRUMPLE
run *noun*
▸ DEMAND (a run on the dollar)
▸ TIME 2 (a run of good luck)
run *verb*
▸ RUN 1 (run to catch a bus)
▸ RUN 2 (run a business)
▸ FLOW (tears run down)
▸ GO 1 (a car runs off the road)
▸ GO 2 (Buses run hourly.)
▸ HURRY (running around after the
   kids all day)
▸ OPERATE (run the engine)
▸ WORK 3 (leave the engine run-
   ning)
▸ ORGANIZE (run evening classes)
▸ **up and running** ACTIVE *adj.*
▸ **run for it** FLEE
run away *phrasal verb*
▸ FLEE
rundown *noun*
▸ SUMMARY
run into *phrasal verb*
▸ HAVE 3 (run into trouble)
▸ MEET 2 (run into an old friend)
runner *noun*
▸ PLAYER
runner-up *noun*
▸ LOSER 1
run off *phrasal verb*
▸ FLEE
run through *phrasal verb*
▸ PRACTISE
run to *phrasal verb*
▸ BE
run up *phrasal verb*
▸ COLLECT
rupture *verb*
▸ EXPLODE
ruse *noun*
▸ TRICK
rush *noun*
▸ ACTIVITY (a last-minute rush)
▸ WAVE 2 (a rush of excitement)
rush *verb*
▸ DRAG (rush sb to hospital)
▸ HURRY (Don't rush off.)
ruthless *adj.*
▸ RUTHLESS
rutted *adj.*
▸ ROUGH 1

S s

sabbatical *noun*
▸ HOLIDAY 1
sabotage *verb*
▸ VANDALIZE
sachet *noun*
▸ PACKET
sack *noun*
▸ **give sb/get the sack** FIRE *verb*
sack *verb*
▸ FIRE
sacking *noun*
▸ UNEMPLOYMENT
sacrament *noun*
▸ CEREMONY
sacred *adj.*
▸ RELIGIOUS
sacrifice *verb*
▸ GIVE STH UP
sad *adj.*
▸ SAD (a sad story)
▸ UNFORTUNATE 2 (a sad state of affairs)
▸ UNHAPPY 1 (sad about his death)
sadden *verb*
▸ HURT 1
sadistic *adj.*
▸ CRUEL
sadness *noun*
▸ GRIEF
safe *adj.*
▸ SAFE 1 (safe and well)
▸ SAFE 2 (a safe distance)
▸ **a safe bet** OPTION *noun*
safeguard *noun*
▸ PRECAUTION
safeguard *verb*
▸ PROTECT
safe house *noun*
▸ REFUGE
safety *noun*
▸ SAFETY (road safety)
▸ SHELTER (swim to safety)
saga *noun*
▸ STORY 1
sail *noun*
▸ CRUISE (go for a sail)
▸ **set sail** SET OFF *phrasal verb*
sail *verb*
▸ DRIVE 1 (sail a boat)
▸ SLIDE (sail through the air)
sailing *noun*
▸ **plain sailing** EASY *adj.* 1
sail through *phrasal verb*
▸ GRADUATE
saintly *adj.*
▸ HOLY
salary *noun*
▸ INCOME
sale *noun*
▸ **for sale, on sale** AVAILABLE *adj.*
sales force *noun*
▸ STAFF
salesman *noun*
▸ SALESMAN
sallow *adj.*
▸ PALE 1
salon *noun*
▸ SHOP
saloon *noun*
▸ BAR
the same *adj.*
▸ EQUAL
sample *verb*
▸ SURVEY (12% of the children
   sampled said…)
▸ TRY 2 (sample his cooking)
sanatorium *noun*
▸ HOSPITAL

sanctimonious *adj.*
▸ SMUG
sanction *noun*
▸ BAN
sanction *verb*
▸ ALLOW
sanctuary *noun*
▸ CHURCH (the sanctuary where the
   priest stood at the altar)
▸ REFUGE (a wildlife sanctuary)
▸ SHELTER (take sanctuary)
sand *noun*
▸ COAST
sane *adj.*
▸ SANE
sanitarium *noun*
▸ HOSPITAL
sanity *noun*
▸ WISDOM
sap *verb*
▸ UNDERMINE
sarcastic *adj.*
▸ IRONIC
sardonic *adj.*
▸ IRONIC
sash *noun*
▸ STRIP
satanic *adj.*
▸ EVIL
satellite *noun*
▸ TERRITORY
satirical *adj.*
▸ IRONIC
satisfaction *noun*
▸ SATISFACTION
satisfactory *adj.*
▸ FINE
satisfied *adj.*
▸ HAPPY (a satisfied customer)
▸ SURE (I am satisfied that…)
satisfy *verb*
▸ CONVINCE (not satisfied by the
   answer)
▸ MEET 4 (satisfy demand)
▸ PLEASE (Nothing satisfies him.)
satisfying *adj.*
▸ SATISFYING
saturated *adj.*
▸ WET 1
saucepan *noun*
▸ PAN
saunter *verb*
▸ WANDER
savage *adj.*
▸ CRUEL
savannah *noun*
▸ PLAIN
save *verb*
▸ SAVE 1 (save sb's life)
▸ SAVE 2 (save up for a new bike)
▸ SAVE 3 (save a little each week)
▸ SAVE 4 (save time/energy)
▸ KEEP 2 (save some for tomorrow)
▸ RESERVE (save sb a seat)
savings *noun*
▸ FUND
savour *verb*
▸ ENJOY
savoury (also **savory**) *adj.*
▸ STRONG 2
say *noun*
▸ POWER
say *verb*
▸ SAY 1 ('Hello!' she said.)
▸ SAY 2 (I can't say I blame her.)
▸ SAY 3 (We'll finish in, let's say,
   three months.)
▸ PREDICT (Who can say where it
   will end?)
▸ QUOTE (say a quiet prayer)

▸ **I dare say** SUPPOSE
saying *noun*
▸ SAYING
scaffold *noun*
▸ EXECUTION
scald *verb*
▸ BURN 2
scale *noun*
▸ SCALE (on a scale of one to ten)
▸ LEVEL (the full scale of the disas-
   ter)
▸ RATIO (draw sth to scale)
scale *verb*
▸ CLIMB
scale back *phrasal verb*
▸ CUT 1
scale down *phrasal verb*
▸ CUT 1
scalpel *noun*
▸ KNIFE
scaly *adj.*
▸ COARSE
scam *noun*
▸ FRAUD 2
scan *noun*
▸ INSPECTION
scan *verb*
▸ READ (scan a list/an article)
▸ STUDY (scan sb's face)
scandal *noun*
▸ REPORT 4
scandalize *verb*
▸ SHOCK
scandalous *adj.*
▸ OUTRAGEOUS
scant *adj.*
▸ INADEQUATE
scapegoat *noun*
▸ VICTIM 2
scarce *adj.*
▸ SCARCE
scarcity *noun*
▸ LACK
scare *noun*
▸ SHOCK 2
scare *verb*
▸ FRIGHTEN
scared *adj.*
▸ AFRAID
scare into *phrasal verb*
▸ THREATEN 1
scary *adj.*
▸ FRIGHTENING
scathing *adj.*
▸ CONTEMPTUOUS
scatter *verb*
▸ SCATTER (scatter seeds)
▸ DISPERSE (a crowd scatters)
scene *noun*
▸ SCENE (the opening scene)
▸ FUSS (make a scene)
▸ PLACE 1 (the scene of the crime)
▸ VIEW 2 (a delightful scene)
scenery *noun*
▸ COUNTRY 2
scenic *adj.*
▸ BEAUTIFUL 2
scent *noun*
▸ SMELL (the scent of wild herbs)
▸ TRAIL (on the scent of the fox)
sceptical *adj.*
▸ SUSPICIOUS 1
scepticism *noun*
▸ SCEPTICISM
schedule *noun*
▸ SCHEDULE
schedule *verb*
▸ SCHEDULE

scheme *noun*
▸ CONSPIRACY (a scheme to avoid taxes)
▸ PLAN 1 (a training scheme)

scheme *verb*
▸ PLOT

scheming *adj.*
▸ CUNNING

schism *noun*
▸ DIVISION 2

scholar *noun*
▸ SCHOLAR

scholarly *adj.*
▸ EDUCATIONAL (a scholarly journal)
▸ INTELLECTUAL 2 (a scholarly young man)

scholarship *noun*
▸ KNOWLEDGE

school *noun*
▸ SCHOOL

schoolboy *noun*
▸ STUDENT

schoolchild *noun*
▸ STUDENT

schoolgirl *noun*
▸ STUDENT

schooling *noun*
▸ EDUCATION

schoolteacher *noun*
▸ TEACHER

scientific *noun*
▸ RATIONAL

scold *verb*
▸ SCOLD

scoop *verb*
▸ PICK SB/STH UP

scope *noun*
▸ SCOPE (scope for improvement)
▸ RANGE 2 (limited in scope)

scorch *verb*
▸ BURN 2

score *noun*
▸ SCORE (The final score was 4–3.)
▸ SCRIPT (a musical score)
▸ **settle a score** FIGHT BACK *verb*

scorn *noun*
▸ CONTEMPT

scornful *adj.*
▸ CONTEMPTUOUS

scout *verb*
▸ LOOK 2

scowl *verb*
▸ FROWN

scrabble *verb*
▸ FUMBLE

scramble *verb*
▸ CLIMB

scrap *noun*
▸ BIT (a scrap of paper/news)
▸ REMAINS 2 (food scraps)
▸ WASTE (scrap metal)

scrap *verb*
▸ ABOLISH (scrap plans)
▸ REMOVE 1 (scrap aircraft)

scrape *verb*
▸ CREAK (chairs scrape the floor)
▸ SCRATCH 1 (scrape your knee)

scratch *noun*
▸ INJURY

scratch *verb*
▸ SCRATCH 1 (scratch yourself on sth)
▸ SCRATCH 2 (a cat scratches)
▸ CREAK (mice scratch)

scratchy *adj.*
▸ COARSE

scrawl *verb*
▸ WRITE 1

scream *verb*
▸ SCREAM (scream in terror)
▸ SHOUT (scream at sb to stop)

screech *verb*
▸ SCREAM

screen *noun*
▸ CURTAIN (a screen door)
▸ PRECAUTION (a screen of secrecy)
▸ WALL (a wooden screen)

screen *verb*
▸ TEST 1

screenplay *noun*
▸ SCRIPT

screen test *noun*
▸ INTERVIEW 2

screenwriter *noun*
▸ WRITER

screw *verb*
▸ DEFRAUD (screw sb for $100)
▸ **screw your eyes/face up** TIGHTEN

scribble *verb*
▸ WRITE 1

scribe *noun*
▸ WRITER

script *noun*
▸ SCRIPT

scriptwriter *noun*
▸ WRITER

scrounge *verb*
▸ BORROW

scrounger *noun*
▸ TRAMP

scrub *verb*
▸ BRUSH

scruffy *adj.*
▸ SCRUFFY

scruple *noun*
▸ DOUBT 2

scrupulous *adj.*
▸ GOOD 5

scrutinize *verb*
▸ STUDY

scrutiny *noun*
▸ RESEARCH

scuff *verb*
▸ SCRATCH 1

scuffle *noun*
▸ FIGHT

scuffle *verb*
▸ FIGHT 2

sculpt *verb*
▸ SHAPE

sculptor *noun*
▸ ARTIST

sea *noun*
▸ SEA (I live by the sea.)
▸ WAVE 1 (swept into rough seas)

seaboard *noun*
▸ COAST

sea change *noun*
▸ REVOLUTION 2

seal *noun*
▸ LOGO

seal *verb*
▸ BLOCK 2 (a sealed plastic bag)
▸ BLOCK 3 (seal the border)

seal off *phrasal verb*
▸ SEPARATE 2

seam *noun*
▸ CONNECTION

sear *verb*
▸ BURN 2

search *noun*
▸ SEARCH

search *verb*
▸ LOOK 2

search out *phrasal verb*
▸ FIND 4

seashore *noun*
▸ COAST

seaside *noun*
▸ COAST

season *noun*
▸ TIME 2

seasoned *adj.*
▸ EXPERIENCED

seat *noun*
▸ CHAIR (the front passenger seat)
▸ PLACE 2 (book a seat on a flight)
▸ **take a seat** SIT *verb*

seat *verb*
▸ **be seated** SIT

sec *noun*
▸ MINUTE

seclusion *noun*
▸ PRIVACY

second *noun*
▸ MINUTE

second *verb*
▸ SUPPORT 1

second *adj.*
▸ **second thoughts** DOUBT *noun* 2

second-rate *adj.*
▸ POOR 2

secret *noun*
▸ MYSTERY

secret *adj.*
▸ SECRET 1 (secret information)
▸ SECRET 2 (a secret drinker)
▸ SECRETIVE (They were so secret about everything.)

secretary *noun*
▸ OFFICIAL

secrete *verb*
▸ LEAK

secretive *adj.*
▸ SECRETIVE

sect *noun*
▸ RELIGION

sectarianism *noun*
▸ RACISM

section *noun*
▸ SECTION (The report has a section on accidents at work.)
▸ ELEMENT 1 (It comes in sections that you assemble yourself.)

sector *noun*
▸ AREA 2

secure *verb*
▸ ATTACH (secure the rope)
▸ GAIN 1 (secure votes/a contract)
▸ PROTECT (secure a property against intruders)

secure *adj.*
▸ FIRM (a secure foothold)
▸ SAFE 1 (keep valuables secure)

security *noun*
▸ SECURITY (airport security)
▸ SAFETY (job security)

seduce *verb*
▸ TEMPT

see *verb*
▸ SEE (Did you see what happened?)
▸ GO OUT (Are you seeing anyone at the moment?)
▸ IMAGINE (I can't see her changing her mind.)
▸ LOOK 1 (see a movie)
▸ REGARD (see things differently)
▸ UNDERSTAND 1 (I see what you mean.)
▸ VISIT (see a dentist)
▸ **not see eye to eye with sb** DISAGREE
▸ **see to it that…** ENSURE

seed *noun*
▸ GRAIN

seedy *adj.*
▸ SORDID

seek *verb*
▸ SEEK (seek work)
▸ ASK 2 (seek advice/help)
▸ LOOK 2 (Police are seeking witnesses to the accident.)
▸ TRY 1 (seek to find an answer)

seem *verb*
▸ SEEM

seeming *adj.*
▸ APPARENT

seep *verb*
▸ LEAK

seething *adj.*
▸ FURIOUS

see-through *adj.*
▸ CLEAR 3

see to *phrasal verb*
▸ DEAL WITH SB/STH

segregate *verb*
▸ ISOLATE

segregation *noun*
▸ DIVISION 1

seize *verb*
▸ SEIZE (drugs seized by the police)
▸ INVADE (seize power/the airport)
▸ KIDNAP (Terrorists have seized his wife and children.)
▸ TAKE 4 (seize hold of sth)
▸ TAKE 6 (seize an opportunity)

seize on/upon *phrasal verb*
▸ TAKE 6

seldom *adv.*
▸ RARELY

select *verb*
▸ CHOOSE

select *adj.*
▸ EXCLUSIVE

selection *noun*
▸ CHOICE 1 (the selection process)
▸ CHOICE 2 (a selection of readers' comments)
▸ RANGE 1 (a wide selection of kitchens on offer)

self *noun*
▸ IDENTITY (your sense of self)
▸ PERSONALITY (not his usual self)

self-centred (also **self-centered**) *adj.*
▸ SELFISH

self-confidence *noun*
▸ CONFIDENCE

self-confident *adj.*
▸ CONFIDENT

self-conscious *adj.*
▸ EMBARRASSED

self-contained *adj.*
▸ INDEPENDENT

self-control *noun*
▸ RESTRAINT

self-defeating *adj.*
▸ INEFFECTIVE

self-determination *noun*
▸ INDEPENDENCE

self-discipline *noun*
▸ RESTRAINT

self-esteem *noun*
▸ DIGNITY

self-evident *adj.*
▸ CLEAR 1

self-government *noun*
▸ INDEPENDENCE

self-image *noun*
▸ DIGNITY

self-important *adj.*
▸ PROUD 2

selfish *adj.*
▸ SELFISH

self-respect *noun*
▸ DIGNITY

self-respecting *adj.*
▶ PROUD 1
self-righteous *adj.*
▶ SMUG
self-satisfied *adj.*
▶ SMUG
self-serving *adj.*
▶ SELFISH
sell *verb*
▶ SELL 1 (sell your car/house)
▶ SELL 2 (sell a range of products)
▶ COST (sell at/for £9.95)
seller *noun*
▶ DEALER
sell off *phrasal verb*
▶ SELL 1
sell up *phrasal verb*
▶ SELL 1
semicircle *noun*
▶ CURVE
seminar *noun*
▶ CLASS 2
seminary *noun*
▶ SCHOOL
senate *noun*
▶ ASSEMBLY
senator *noun*
▶ POLITICIAN
send *verb*
▶ SEND 1 (send a letter)
▶ SEND 2 (send sb to bed/prison)
▶ CONVEY (send a message)
▶ **send sb to prison** JAIL
send in *phrasal verb*
▶ PRESENT 3
send on *phrasal verb*
▶ SEND 1
senior *adj.*
▶ TOP
sensation *noun*
▶ SENSE
sensational *adj.*
▶ AMAZING
sense *noun*
▶ SENSE (a sense of loss/duty/guilt)
▶ MEANING (the different senses of a word)
▶ UNDERSTANDING (a sense of humour/direction/proportion)
▶ WISDOM (have the sense to ask for help)
sense *verb*
▶ FEEL
sensibility *noun*
▶ DIGNITY
sensible *adj.*
▶ BEST (a sensible idea)
▶ WISE (a sensible woman)
sensitive *adj.*
▶ SENSITIVE 1 (a sensitive and caring man)
▶ SENSITIVE 2 (a sensitive topic)
▶ SENSITIVE 3 (sensitive to criticism)
sensitivity *noun*
▶ TACT
sentence *noun*
▶ PUNISHMENT
sentence *verb*
▶ PUNISH
sentiment *noun*
▶ EMOTION (a display of sentiment)
▶ VIEW 1 (my sentiments exactly)
sentry *noun*
▶ GUARD
separate *verb*
▶ SEPARATE 1 (separate the white from the yolk)
▶ SEPARATE 2 (separated by a wall)
▶ DISPERSE (separate into search parties)

DIVIDE 2 (Politics is the only thing that separates us.)
▶ DIVORCE (separate from your wife/husband)
separate *adj.*
▶ PARTICULAR
separated *adj.*
▶ SINGLE
separate out *phrasal verb*
▶ DIVIDE 1
separation *noun*
▶ DIVISION 1
sequence *noun*
▶ SERIES
serial *adj.*
▶ SUCCESSIVE
serial killer *noun*
▶ KILLER
series *noun*
▶ SERIES (a series of events)
▶ RACE (baseball's World Series)
serious *adj.*
▶ SERIOUS 1 (a serious problem)
▶ SERIOUS 2 (a serious person)
▶ SERIOUS 3 (a serious newspaper)
seriousness *noun*
▶ IMPORTANCE
sermon *noun*
▶ SPEECH
serrated *adj.*
▶ SHARP 1
servant *noun*
▶ SERVANT
serve *verb*
▶ SERVE 1 (serve dinner)
▶ SERVE 2 (serve a community)
▶ MEET 4 (serve a purpose)
service *noun*
▶ SERVICE (the health service)
▶ CEREMONY (a religious service)
▶ FACILITIES (the bus service)
▶ HELP (the services of a lawyer)
▶ INDUSTRY (the financial services sector)
▶ REPAIR (take the car in for a service)
▶ WORK 1 (25 years' service with the company)
▶ **be of service** HELP *verb* 1
service *verb*
▶ MAINTAIN 2
serviceman *noun*
▶ SOLDIER
servicewoman *noun*
▶ SOLDIER
servicing *noun*
▶ REPAIR
servile *adj.*
▶ SERVILE
serving *noun*
▶ PORTION
session *noun*
▶ CLASS 2 (a training session)
▶ MEETING 1 (The court is in session.)
set *noun*
▶ CLASS 3 (in the top set for English)
▶ GROUP 1 (a set of chairs/novels)
▶ GROUP 2 (Berlin's smart set)
▶ ROUND (play a set of tennis)
set *verb*
▶ ALLOCATE (set sb a task)
▶ PUT 1 (set the tray down)
▶ PUT 2 (set sth in motion)
▶ SCHEDULE (set a date for sth)
set *adj.*
▶ SET (a set pattern/menu)
▶ DEEP-SEATED (set in your ways)
▶ READY (Inflation is set to rise.)

set about *phrasal verb*
▶ BEGIN
set apart *phrasal verb*
▶ DISTINGUISH 2
set aside *phrasal verb*
▶ DISMISS (set aside your feelings)
▶ OVERTURN (set aside a verdict)
▶ SAVE 3 (set some money aside)
set back *phrasal verb*
▶ COST (set you back over £200)
▶ HOLD SB/STH UP (Bad weather caused the project to be set back.)
setback *noun*
▶ BLOW
set off *phrasal verb*
▶ SET OFF (set off at dawn)
▶ PROMPT (set off a debate)
▶ TURN STH ON (set off the alarm)
set out *phrasal verb*
▶ ARRANGE (set out the tables)
▶ OUTLINE (set out your reasons)
▶ SET OFF (set out at dawn)
setting *noun*
▶ CONTEXT (the political setting)
▶ ENVIRONMENT (a perfect setting for a picnic)
settle *verb*
▶ AGREE 3 (settle your affairs)
▶ CONFIRM 3 (That settles it!)
▶ LAND (dust settles)
▶ MOVE IN (settle in Vienna)
▶ PAY (settle your debts)
▶ PUT 1 (settle the blanket around herself)
▶ RESOLVE (settle a dispute)
▶ **settle a score** FIGHT BACK
settlement *noun*
▶ AGREEMENT 1 (a peace settlement)
▶ PAYMENT (Settlement is made monthly.)
set up *phrasal verb*
▶ BUILD (set up roadblocks)
▶ ESTABLISH (set up a business)
▶ SCHEDULE (set up a meeting)
▶ **set up home** MOVE IN
set-up *noun*
▶ TRICK
severe *adj.*
▶ HARSH (severe weather)
▶ PLAIN 1 (a severe hairstyle)
▶ SERIOUS 1 (severe brain damage)
▶ STERN (a severe expression)
▶ STRICT (severe punishment)
sewer *noun*
▶ DRAIN
sexism *noun*
▶ RACISM
shack *noun*
▶ HUT
shade *noun*
▶ COLOUR 1 (a shade of blue)
▶ CURTAIN (a window shade)
▶ DARKNESS (in the shade of a tree)
shadow *noun*
▶ DARKNESS (standing in the shadows)
▶ SHAPE (cast a shadow on the wall)
shadowy *adj.*
▶ DARK 1
shady *adj.*
▶ DARK 1 (a shady spot for a picnic)
▶ SUSPICIOUS 2 (a shady character)
shaggy *adj.*
▶ HAIRY
shake *verb*
▶ SHAKE 1 (shake your head)
▶ SHAKE 2 (shake the bottle)
▶ SHAKE 3 (shake with fear)
▶ SHAKE 4 (badly shaken by the news)

shake off *phrasal verb*
▶ RECOVER 1
shake up *phrasal verb*
▶ REORGANIZE
shaking *noun*
▶ SHIVER
sham *adj.*
▶ SO-CALLED
shambles *noun*
▶ CHAOS
shame *noun*
▶ DISGRACE 2 (bring shame on your family)
▶ GUILT (hang your head in shame)
▶ UNFORTUNATE *adj.* 2 (What a shame!)
shame *verb*
▶ EMBARRASS
shameful *adj.*
▶ OUTRAGEOUS
shameless *adj.*
▶ COOL
shampoo *verb*
▶ CLEAN
shanty *noun*
▶ HUT
shape *noun*
▶ SHAPE (a triangular shape)
▶ FORM 1 (change the shape of broadcasting)
▶ HEALTH (stay in shape)
▶ STATE (The economy is still in pretty good shape.)
shape *verb*
▶ SHAPE (shape the dough)
▶ DETERMINE (shape policy)
shape up *phrasal verb*
▶ DEVELOP 1
shard *noun*
▶ FRAGMENT
share *noun*
▶ SHARE
share *verb*
▶ SHARE (share a house)
▶ JOIN (share in the work)
sharp *adj.*
▶ SHARP 1 (a sharp knife)
▶ SHARP 2 (a sharp tongue)
▶ BITTER 1 (a sharp taste)
▶ CUNNING (a sharp operator)
▶ HIGH 3 (a sharp voice/knock)
▶ MARKED (a sharp contrast)
▶ SUDDEN (a sharp rise/increase)
shatter *verb*
▶ SMASH
shattered *adj.*
▶ TIRED 1
shave *verb*
▶ CUT 3
shavings *noun*
▶ FRAGMENT
shawl *noun*
▶ COAT
shear *verb*
▶ CUT 3
sheath *noun*
▶ COVER
shed *noun*
▶ SHED
shed *verb*
▶ REMOVE 1 (shed pounds)
▶ **shed light on sth** EXPLAIN 1
sheepish *adj.*
▶ EMBARRASSED
sheer *adj.*
▶ PURE 2
sheet *noun*
▶ PAGE
shell *noun*
▶ BULLET (heavy shell fire)

▸ FRAME (the body shell of a car)

shell *verb*
▸ BOMB

shelter *noun*
▸ SHELTER (shelter for the night)
▸ HUT (an air-raid shelter)
▸ REFUGE (a shelter for the homeless)

shelter *verb*
▸ PROTECT

shelve *verb*
▸ DELAY

sherd *noun*
▸ FRAGMENT

shield *noun*
▸ PRECAUTION

shield *verb*
▸ PROTECT

shift *noun*
▸ CHANGE 1 (a shift in public opinion)
▸ TEAM 1 (the night/day shift)

shift *verb*
▸ CHANGE 1 (shift the focus of a debate)
▸ CHANGE 2 (your sympathies shift)
▸ MOVE (shift your weight/gaze)

shifty *adj.*
▸ SUSPICIOUS 2

shimmer *verb*
▸ SHINE

shine *verb*
▸ SHINE

ship *noun*
▸ BOAT

ship *verb*
▸ TAKE 1

shipment *noun*
▸ DELIVERY (ready for shipment)
▸ LOT (shipments of cars)

shipping *noun*
▸ DELIVERY (pack bananas for shipping)
▸ TRANSPORT (shipping lanes)

shirk *verb*
▸ MISS 1

shit *adj.* (taboo)
▸ POOR 2

shiver *noun*
▸ SHIVER

shiver *verb*
▸ SHAKE 3

shock *noun*
▸ SHOCK 1 (a feeling of shock)
▸ SHOCK 2 (It was rather a shock.)
▸ IMPACT (the shock of the earthquake)

shock *verb*
▸ SHOCK (shocked at the news)
▸ OFFEND (set out to shock)

shocking *adj.*
▸ OUTRAGEOUS

shoddy *adj.*
▸ LAX

shoelace *noun*
▸ BUTTON 2

shoot *verb*
▸ SHOOT (shoot sb dead)
▸ FLY 2 (a cat shoots out into the road)
▸ RECORD 2 (shoot a movie)

shoot up *verb*
▸ SOAR

shop *noun*
▸ SHOP

shop *verb*
▸ BUY

shopkeeper *noun*
▸ DEALER

shoplift *verb*
▸ STEAL

shoplifter *noun*
▸ THIEF

shoplifting *noun*
▸ THEFT

shopper *noun*
▸ CUSTOMER

shopping centre *noun*
▸ MARKET 2

shoreline *noun*
▸ COAST

shore up *phrasal verb*
▸ STRENGTHEN

short *adj.*
▸ SHORT 1 (a short time/book)
▸ SHORT 2 (short people/legs)
▸ SHORT 3 (the short answer)
▸ SCARCE (money is short)
▸ **in short supply** SCARCE

shortage *noun*
▸ LACK

short-change *verb*
▸ DEFRAUD

shortcoming *noun*
▸ WEAKNESS 1

shorten *verb*
▸ SHRINK

shortfall *noun*
▸ LACK

short-lived *adj.*
▸ SHORT 1

shot *noun*
▸ ATTEMPT (give sth a shot)
▸ BULLET (lead shot)
▸ PHOTOGRAPH (publicity shots)

shotgun *noun*
▸ GUN

shoulder *verb*
▸ PUSH 2 (shoulder sb aside)
▸ TAKE 7 (shoulder a burden)

shout *verb*
▸ SHOUT

shouting match *noun*
▸ ARGUMENT 1

shove *verb*
▸ PUSH 1 (shove the book in the bag)
▸ PUSH 2 (shove past sb)

show *noun*
▸ EXHIBITION (a fashion show)
▸ EXPRESSION 1 (a show of temper)
▸ CONCERT (a rock show)
▸ PERFORMANCE (a stage show)
▸ PROGRAMME (a TV show)
▸ **show of hands** ELECTION

show *verb*
▸ SHOW 1 (opinion polls show…)
▸ SHOW 2 (Show me that letter.)
▸ SHOW 3 (show courage/respect)
▸ APPEAR (The mark still shows.)
▸ ARRIVE (Nobody showed.)
▸ POINT (Show me on the map.)
▸ PRESENT 1 (show a film)
▸ PRESENT 2 (a photo shows sb/sth)
▸ TAKE 2 (show sb the way)
▸ TRAIN 1 (show sb how to do sth)

showbiz *noun*
▸ DRAMA

show business *noun*
▸ DRAMA

showdown *noun*
▸ CONFRONTATION

shower *noun*
▸ BATH (have/take a shower)
▸ FLOOD 2 (a shower of sparks)
▸ PARTY (a bridal/baby shower)
▸ RAIN (caught in a shower)

shower *verb*
▸ SCATTER (shower sth with dust)

▸ WASH (shower and dress)

showing *noun*
▸ PROGRAMME

show off *phrasal verb*
▸ BOAST

show up *phrasal verb*
▸ ARRIVE

showy *adj.*
▸ FLASHY

shred *noun*
▸ FRAGMENT

shred *verb*
▸ TEAR

shrewd *adj.*
▸ SHREWD

shriek *verb*
▸ SCREAM

shrill *adj.*
▸ HIGH 3

shrine *noun*
▸ CHURCH

shrink *verb*
▸ SHRINK (a market/sweater shrinks)
▸ JUMP 3 (shrink back in terror)

shrink from *phrasal verb*
▸ HESITATE

shrug off *phrasal verb*
▸ DISMISS

shudder *noun*
▸ SHIVER

shudder *verb*
▸ SHAKE 2 (shudder to a halt)
▸ SHAKE 3 (shudder with fear)

shuffle *verb*
▸ JUMBLE (shuffle papers)
▸ STUMBLE (shuffle your feet)

shun *verb*
▸ AVOID

shush *verb*
▸ SILENCE

shut *verb*
▸ CLOSE 1

shut in *phrasal verb*
▸ TRAP

shut off *phrasal verb*
▸ TURN STH OFF

shut out *phrasal verb*
▸ EXCLUDE 2 (shut sb out of the room)
▸ FORGET (shut out your fears)

shy *adj.*
▸ SHY

shy away from *phrasal verb*
▸ HESITATE

the sick *noun*
▸ PATIENT

sick *adj.*
▸ SICK 1 (a sick child)
▸ SICK 2 (a sick feeling)
▸ BORED (sick of waiting)
▸ **be sick** VOMIT *verb*

sicken *verb*
▸ SHOCK

sickening *adv.*
▸ DISGUSTING 2

sickly *adj.*
▸ SICK 1

sickness *noun*
▸ DISEASE (travel sickness)
▸ ILLNESS (sickness pay)

side *noun*
▸ ASPECT (see the funny side)
▸ ATTITUDE (both sides of the argument)
▸ EDGE (the side of the bed)
▸ PAGE (Write no more than three sides.)
▸ TEAM 2 (lead your side to victory)

sidekick *noun*
▸ ASSISTANT

sidestep *verb*
▸ EVADE

sidewalk *noun*
▸ PATH

side with *phrasal verb*
▸ SUPPORT 1

sieve *verb*
▸ FILTER

sift *verb*
▸ FILTER

sigh *verb*
▸ WHISPER

sight *noun*
▸ SIGHT (nobody in sight)
▸ LOOK (catch sight of sb/sth)
▸ VIEW 2 (a spectacular sight)
▸ **set your sights on sth** HOPE *verb*
▸ **out of sight** INVISIBLE *adj.*

sight *verb*
▸ SEE

sightseeing *noun*
▸ TRAVEL

sightseer *noun*
▸ TOURIST

sign *noun*
▸ SIGN 1 (a sign of stress)
▸ SIGN 2 (a road/street/shop sign)
▸ NUMBER 2 (a plus/minus sign)
▸ SIGNAL (a thumbs-up sign)

sign *verb*
▸ EMPLOY (sign a new player)
▸ WRITE 1 (sign your name)

signal *noun*
▸ SIGNAL (give sb a signal)
▸ SIGN 1 (a clear signal that sth is wrong)

signal *verb*
▸ MEAN 1 (signal a change in policy)
▸ NOD (Don't fire until I signal.)

significance *noun*
▸ IMPORTANCE (a decision of major political significance)
▸ MEANING (Do these symbols have any particular significance?)

significant *adj.*
▸ IMPORTANT

signify *verb*
▸ MEAN 1

silence *noun*
▸ SILENCE

silence *verb*
▸ SILENCE

silent *adj.*
▸ SILENT (fall silent)
▸ QUIET 1 (silent streets)
▸ QUIET 2 (a silent prayer)
▸ QUIET 3 (the strong, silent type)

silhouette *noun*
▸ SHAPE

silly *adj.*
▸ CRAZY (You silly boy!)
▸ RIDICULOUS (I feel really silly.)

similar *adj.*
▸ LIKE *prep. adj.*

similarity *noun*
▸ SIMILARITY

simile *noun*
▸ METAPHOR

simper *verb*
▸ SMILE

simple *adj.*
▸ AVERAGE (simple country people)
▸ EASY 1 (a simple method)
▸ PLAIN 1 (simple, elegant clothes)
▸ PLAIN 2 (the simple truth)

simulate *verb*
▸ SIMULATE

sin *noun*
▸ CRIME 2 (commit/forgive a sin)
▸ EVIL (turn away from sin)

sincere *adj.*
▸ DEEP 1 (sincere thanks)
▸ HONEST (seem sincere)

sincerity *noun*
▸ TRUTH

sinful *adj.*
▸ EVIL

sing *verb*
▸ SING

singe *verb*
▸ BURN 2

singing *noun*
▸ MUSIC

single *adj.*
▸ SINGLE (single people/parents)
▸ PARTICULAR (the single most important factor)

single-handed, **single-handedly** *adj., adv.*
▸ ALONE

single-minded *adj.*
▸ DETERMINED 2

single out *phrasal verb*
▸ CHOOSE

sinister *adj.*
▸ THREATENING

sink *verb*
▸ FALL 1 (The pound has sunk against the dollar.)
▸ FALL 2 (sink into a chair)

sinner *noun*
▸ CRIMINAL

sip *noun*
▸ SIP

sip *verb*
▸ DRINK

siphon *verb*
▸ PUMP

siren *noun*
▸ ALARM

sissy *noun*
▸ COWARD

sit *verb*
▸ SIT (sit at your desk)
▸ **sit tight** WAIT

sit back *phrasal verb*
▸ REST

sit down *phrasal verb*
▸ SIT

site *noun*
▸ PLACE 1

site *verb*
▸ BASE

situation *noun*
▸ SITUATION

sixth sense *noun*
▸ INSTINCT

size *noun*
▸ SIZE (an area the size of Wales)
▸ LEVEL (You should have seen the size of their house!)

sizeable *adj.*
▸ LARGE

size up *phrasal verb*
▸ JUDGE 1

skate *verb*
▸ SLIDE

skeleton *noun*
▸ BODY 1

skeptical *adj.*
▸ SUSPICIOUS 1

skepticism *noun*
▸ SCEPTICISM

sketch *noun*
▸ PICTURE (draw a sketch)
▸ PLAY (a comedy sketch)

▸ SUMMARY (a biographical sketch of the author)

sketch *verb*
▸ DRAW (sketch a view)
▸ OUTLINE (sketch out an idea)

skid *verb*
▸ SLIP 2

skilful *adj.*
▸ GOOD 4

skill *noun*
▸ SKILL 1 (practical skills)
▸ SKILL 2 (a high level of skill)

skilled *adj.*
▸ GOOD 4

skillet *noun*
▸ PAN

skim *verb*
▸ READ

skimp *verb*
▸ SAVE 2

skinny *adj.*
▸ THIN

skip *verb*
▸ MISS 1

skirmish *noun*
▸ WAR

skirmish *verb*
▸ FIGHT 1

skirt *verb*
▸ EVADE

skive *verb*
▸ MISS 1

sky *noun*
▸ AIR

slab *noun*
▸ PIECE

slacken *verb*
▸ RELAX 2

slam *verb*
▸ CLOSE 1 (slam the door)
▸ CRASH (slam into a tree)

slander *verb*
▸ DISCREDIT

slant *verb*
▸ LEAN 1

slap *verb*
▸ HIT 2

slash *verb*
▸ CUT 1 (slash prices)
▸ CUT 4 (slash a car's tyres)

slaughter *noun*
▸ MASSACRE

slave *noun*
▸ WORK 1

slay *verb*
▸ KILL

slaying *noun*
▸ MURDER

sleazy *adj.*
▸ SORDID

sleep *noun*
▸ **go to sleep**, **get to sleep** FALL ASLEEP

sleep *verb*
▸ SLEEP

sleepy *adj.*
▸ QUIET 1 (a sleepy village)
▸ TIRED 1 (a sleepy child)

sleet *noun*
▸ SNOW

slender *adj.*
▸ THIN

slice *noun*
▸ PIECE

slice *verb*
▸ CUT 2

slick *adj.*
▸ SERVILE

slide *noun*
▸ PHOTOGRAPH

slide *verb*
▸ SLIDE (slide down a slope)
▸ INSERT (slide sth into your pocket)
▸ SLIP 1 (slide out of bed)

slight *adj.*
▸ SLIGHT (The damage was slight.)
▸ THIN (her slight figure)

slim *adj.*
▸ THIN

slimy *adj.*
▸ SOFT

slink *verb*
▸ SLIP 1

slip *noun*
▸ MISTAKE 2 (make a slip)
▸ PAGE (a slip of paper)

slip *verb*
▸ SLIP 1 (slip away quietly)
▸ SLIP 2 (slip on the ice)
▸ INSERT (slip the letter into its envelope)
▸ WORSEN (sb's popularity slips)

slit *verb*
▸ CUT 4

slither *verb*
▸ SLIDE

sliver *noun*
▸ FRAGMENT

slog *noun*
▸ WORK 1

slogan *noun*
▸ SLOGAN

slop *verb*
▸ POUR

slope *noun*
▸ SLOPE (a grassy slope)
▸ ANGLE (the slope of the roof)

slope *verb*
▸ SLOPE (a path slopes)
▸ LEAN 1 (sloping walls)

sloppy *adj.*
▸ LAX

slot *noun*
▸ HOLE 1

slot *verb*
▸ INSERT

slow *adj.*
▸ SLOW (a slow driver)
▸ LATE (slow to realize sth)

slowdown *noun*
▸ RECESSION

sluggish *adj.*
▸ SLOW

slump *noun*
▸ RECESSION (The economy is in a slump.)
▸ REDUCTION (a slump in sales)

slump *verb*
▸ SLUMP

slush *noun*
▸ SNOW

sly *adj.*
▸ CUNNING

smack *verb*
▸ HIT 2

small *adj.*
▸ SMALL (a small house/number)
▸ SLIGHT (a small favour)
▸ **the small hours** NIGHT *noun* 1

the small print *noun*
▸ CONDITION

smarmy *adj.*
▸ SERVILE

smart *adj.*
▸ ELEGANT (a smart suit)
▸ FASHIONABLE (a smart new restaurant)

▸ INTELLIGENT (a smart girl)

smarts *noun*
▸ INTELLIGENCE

smash *verb*
▸ SMASH (a glass smashes)
▸ CRASH (a car smashes into a tree)

smash up *phrasal verb*
▸ VANDALIZE

smear *noun*
▸ MARK

smear *verb*
▸ COVER (smear mud on the walls)
▸ DISCREDIT (an attempt to smear the prime minister)

smell *noun*
▸ SMELL (a smell of burning/roses)
▸ ODOUR (Yuk! What a smell!)

smelly *adj.*
▸ SMELLY

smile *verb*
▸ SMILE

smirk *verb*
▸ SMILE

smitten *adj.*
▸ IN LOVE

smog *noun*
▸ SMOKE

smoke *noun*
▸ SMOKE

smolder *verb*
▸ BURN 1

smooth *adj.*
▸ FLAT (a smooth surface)
▸ SERVILE (a smooth manner)

smoulder *verb*
▸ BURN 1

smudge *noun*
▸ MARK

smug *adj.*
▸ SMUG

snack *noun*
▸ SNACK

snack *verb*
▸ DINE

snag *noun*
▸ DISADVANTAGE

snake *verb*
▸ CURVE

snap *noun*
▸ BANG (close with a snap)
▸ PHOTOGRAPH (holiday snaps)

snap *verb*
▸ BREAK 1

snapshot *noun*
▸ PHOTOGRAPH

snap up *phrasal verb*
▸ BUY

snatch *noun*
▸ SCENE

snatch *verb*
▸ TAKE 4

snazzy *adj.*
▸ FLASHY

sneak *verb*
▸ SLIP 1

sneaky *adj.*
▸ CUNNING

sneer *verb*
▸ LAUGH AT SB/STH

sneeze *verb*
▸ COUGH

snicker *verb*
▸ LAUGH

sniff *noun*
▸ BREATH

sniff *verb*
▸ BLOW 2

sniff out *phrasal verb*
▶ FIND 4

snigger *verb*
▶ LAUGH

a snip *noun*
▶ VALUE 2

snip *verb*
▶ CUT 3

sniper *noun*
▶ KILLER

snivel *verb*
▶ CRY

snobbery *noun*
▶ PRETENSION

snobbish *adj.*
▶ PATRONIZING

snooty *adj.*
▶ PATRONIZING

snooze *verb*
▶ SLEEP

snore *verb*
▶ BLOW 2

snort *verb*
▶ GRUNT

snow *noun*
▶ SNOW

snowdrift *noun*
▶ SNOW

snowfall *noun*
▶ SNOW

snowflake *noun*
▶ SNOW

snowstorm *noun*
▶ STORM

snowy *adj.*
▶ FREEZING

snuff *verb*
▶ PUT STH OUT

snug *adj.*
▶ COMFORTABLE

snuggle *verb*
▶ HUG

so *adv.*
▶ FACT *noun* (Is that so?)
▶ VERY (I was so glad)

soak *verb*
▶ SOAK

soaked *adj.*
▶ WET 1

soar *verb*
▶ SOAR (prices soar)
▶ FLY 1 (planes soar)

sob *verb*
▶ CRY

sober *adj.*
▶ DISCIPLINED (stay sober)
▶ SERIOUS 2 (on sober reflection)

so-called *adj.*
▶ SO-CALLED

sociable *adj.*
▶ SOCIABLE

social *adj.*
▶ SOCIAL (social changes/problems)
▶ SOCIABLE (not a very social person)

social security *noun*
▶ AID

society *noun*
▶ COMMUNITY (a wide cross-section of society)
▶ CULTURE (a multicultural society)
▶ ELITE (high society)
▶ UNION (a dramatic society)

sock *verb*
▶ HIT 2

sodden *adj.*
▶ WET 1

sofa *noun*
▶ CHAIR

soft *adj.*
▶ SOFT (soft margarine/pillows)
▶ DIM 1 (the soft evening light)
▶ LENIENT (soft on crime)
▶ PALE 2 (a soft pink colour)
▶ QUIET 2 (soft music)
▶ SENSITIVE 1 (a soft heart)
▶ **soft touch** VICTIM *noun* 2

soft drink *noun*
▶ DRINK 1

soften *verb*
▶ EASE

soggy *adj.*
▶ SOFT

soil *noun*
▶ SOIL (plant in damp soil)
▶ FLOOR 1 (on Canadian soil)

soiled *adj.*
▶ DIRTY

soldier *noun*
▶ SOLDIER

sole *adj.*
▶ ALONE

solemn *adj.*
▶ SERIOUS 2

solicitor *noun*
▶ LAWYER

solid *noun*
▶ MATERIAL

solid *adj.*
▶ SOLID (frozen solid)
▶ DECENT (a solid achievement)
▶ GOOD 3 (solid evidence/advice)
▶ PURE 1 (solid gold)

solidarity *noun*
▶ AGREEMENT 2

solitary *adj.*
▶ SOLITARY (a solitary child)
▶ ALONE (solitary walks)

solitude *noun*
▶ PRIVACY

solo *adj., adv.*
▶ ALONE

solution *noun*
▶ SOLUTION (a solution to a problem)
▶ MIXTURE (a saline solution)

solve *verb*
▶ SOLVE 1 (solve a dispute)
▶ SOLVE 2 (solve a mystery)

sombre (also **somber**) *adj.*
▶ SERIOUS 2

somebody *pron.*
▶ VIP *noun*

someone *pron.*
▶ VIP *noun*

something *pron.*
▶ **something to eat** SNACK *noun*

sometimes *adv.*
▶ SOMETIMES

somewhat *adv.*
▶ PARTLY

son *noun*
▶ SON

song *noun*
▶ SONG (sing a song)
▶ MUSIC (burst into song)

son of a bitch *noun* (taboo)
▶ VILLAIN

sonorous *adj.*
▶ DEEP 2

soot *noun*
▶ DIRT

soothe *verb*
▶ CALM (The music soothed her.)
▶ EASE (soothe the pain)

sop *noun*
▶ COMPROMISE

sophisticated *adj.*
▶ SOPHISTICATED

sorcerer *noun*
▶ WITCH

sorceress *noun*
▶ WITCH

sorcery *noun*
▶ MAGIC

sordid *adj.*
▶ SORDID

sore *noun*
▶ TUMOUR

sore *adj.*
▶ PAINFUL 1

sorrow *noun*
▶ GRIEF

sorry *adj.*
▶ SORRY (say sorry)
▶ UNFORTUNATE 2 (a sorry sight)
▶ UPSET (sorry to hear the news)
▶ **be/feel sorry for sb** SORRY FOR SB

sort *noun*
▶ KIND

sort *verb*
▶ CLASSIFY (sorted by age)
▶ SOLVE 1 (get this sorted)

sort out *phrasal verb*
▶ ARRANGE (sort out your things)
▶ ORGANIZE (sort out the details)
▶ SEPARATE 1 (sort out the lies from the truth)
▶ SOLVE 1 (sort out a problem)
▶ TIDY (sort out the drawers)

sort through *phrasal verb*
▶ TIDY

so-so *adj.*
▶ MEDIOCRE

soul *noun*
▶ MIND (the human soul)
▶ PERSON (a few brave souls)

sound *noun*
▶ SOUND 1 (a buzzing sound)
▶ SOUND 2 (turn the sound down)
▶ NOTE (a sound unlike any other guitarist)

sound *verb*
▶ BLOW 3 (sound your horn)
▶ RING (an alarm sounds)
▶ SEEM (sound reasonable)

sound *adj.*
▶ DECENT (a sound performance)
▶ GOOD 3 (sound advice)

sour *verb*
▶ INFLUENCE

sour *adj.*
▶ BITTER 1 (a sour taste)
▶ BITTER 2 (a sour old woman)
▶ ROTTEN (sour milk)

source *noun*
▶ SOURCE

sovereign *noun*
▶ KING

sovereignty *noun*
▶ INDEPENDENCE

space *noun*
▶ SPACE 1 (floor/office space)
▶ SPACE 2 (the first woman in space)
▶ HOLE 1 (a parking space)
▶ LAND 2 (wide open spaces)

spacious *adj.*
▶ SPACIOUS

span *noun*
▶ TIME 2

span *verb*
▶ LEAD 3

spank *verb*
▶ HIT 2

spare *verb*
▶ EXEMPT

spare *adj.*
▶ EXCESS (spare cash)
▶ FREE 3 (a spare moment)

spare time *noun*
▶ LEISURE

spark *noun*
▶ ENERGY 2

spark *verb*
▶ PROMPT

sparkle *verb*
▶ SHINE

sparse *adj.*
▶ INADEQUATE

spasm *noun*
▶ SHIVER

spate *noun*
▶ WAVE 3

spatter *verb*
▶ SPRAY

speak *verb*
▶ MENTION (speak highly of sb)
▶ SAY 1 (Please speak slowly.)
▶ TALK (speak to sb about sth)

speaker *noun*
▶ SPEAKER 1 (native speakers)
▶ SPEAKER 2 (a fine public speaker)

spearhead *verb*
▶ LEAD 2

special *adj.*
▶ SPECIAL (special circumstances)
▶ UNIQUE (his own special table)

specialism *noun*
▶ AREA 2

specialist *noun*
▶ EXPERT

specialty *noun*
▶ AREA 2

specific *adj.*
▶ EXACT (Please be more specific.)
▶ PARTICULAR (a specific purpose)

specify *verb*
▶ LIST

specimen *noun*
▶ EXAMPLE 1

speck *noun*
▶ BIT (specks of dust)
▶ MARK (The ship was now just a speck in the distance.)

spectacle *noun*
▶ PERFORMANCE

spectacular *adj.*
▶ IMPRESSIVE (a spectacular goal)
▶ MAGNIFICENT (spectacular scenery)

spectator *noun*
▶ AUDIENCE

spectrum *noun*
▶ RANGE 2

speculate *verb*
▶ SAY 3

speculation *noun*
▶ SPECULATION

speculative *adj.*
▶ SUPPOSED

speech *noun*
▶ SPEECH (an acceptance speech)
▶ VOICE (slurred speech)

speechless *adj.*
▶ SILENT

speed *noun*
▶ SPEED (excessive speed)
▶ RATE 1 (at top speed)

speed *verb*
▶ ACCELERATE (speed the development of sth)
▶ FLY 2 (He sped away on his bike.)

speed up *phrasal verb*
▶ ACCELERATE

speedy adj.
▸ QUICK

spell noun
▸ INTEREST 1 (fall under sb/sth's spell)
▸ TIME 2 (sunny spells)

spell verb
▸ MEAN 3

spell out phrasal verb
▸ EXPLAIN 1

spend verb
▸ SPEND 1 (spend money)
▸ SPEND 2 (spend time)

spending noun
▸ COSTS

spew verb
▸ FLOW

sphere noun
▸ AREA 2

spicy adj.
▸ STRONG 2

spike noun
▸ TIP

spiky adj.
▸ COARSE

spill verb
▸ POUR

spill over phrasal verb
▸ FLOOD

spin verb
▸ SPIN (dancers spin round)
▸ TURN 1 (spin around in terror)

spiny adj.
▸ COARSE

spiral noun
▸ INCREASE

spiral verb
▸ SOAR

spirit noun
▸ ATMOSPHERE (the spirit of the age)
▸ DETERMINATION (fighting spirit)
▸ DRINK 2 (a measure of spirits)
▸ GHOST (evil spirits)
▸ MIND (the power of the human spirit)
▸ MOOD (in the best of spirits)
▸ NATURE 1 (the spirit, as well as the letter, of the law)
▸ **lift/raise sb's spirits** ENCOURAGE 1

spirited adj.
▸ LIVELY

spiritual adj.
▸ EMOTIONAL

spiteful adj.
▸ VICIOUS

splash noun
▸ DROP

splash verb
▸ SPRAY

splendour (also **splendor**) noun
▸ LUXURY

splinter noun
▸ FRAGMENT

splinter verb
▸ SMASH

split noun
▸ DIVISION 1 (a split in the profits)
▸ DIVISION 2 (the split with his wife)

split verb
▸ CUT 4 (split your head open)
▸ DIVIDE 1 (split into groups)
▸ DIVIDE 2 (The debate has split the country.)
▸ DIVORCE (split with your wife)
▸ SHARE (split your money/time between people/places)
▸ TEAR (Her dress split.)

split second noun
▸ MINUTE

split up phrasal verb
▸ DIVIDE 1 (Let's split up and meet again later.)
▸ DIVORCE (split up with your boyfriend/girlfriend)

splurge verb
▸ WASTE

spoil verb
▸ RUIN

spokesman noun
▸ SPOKESMAN

spokesperson noun
▸ SPOKESMAN

spokeswoman noun
▸ SPOKESMAN

sponge verb
▸ WIPE

spongy adj.
▸ SOFT

sponsor noun
▸ SPONSOR

sponsor verb
▸ FUND

sponsorship noun
▸ INVESTMENT

spontaneous adj.
▸ SPONTANEOUS

spoof noun
▸ PARODY

spook verb
▸ FRIGHTEN

spooky adj.
▸ FRIGHTENING

spool noun
▸ ROLL

sporadic adj.
▸ OCCASIONAL

sport noun
▸ SPORT (do sport/play sports)
▸ GAME 2 (team/winter sports)

sportsman noun
▸ PLAYER

sportsperson noun
▸ PLAYER

sportswoman noun
▸ PLAYER

spot noun
▸ ELEMENT 2 (a spot of lunch/rain)
▸ MARK (grease/rust spots)
▸ PATCH (a leopard's spots)
▸ PLACE 1 (rooted to the spot)

spot verb
▸ SEE

spotless adj.
▸ CLEAN

spouse noun
▸ WIFE

sprain verb
▸ INJURE

sprawl verb
▸ LIE

spray noun
▸ MOISTURE

spray verb
▸ SPRAY (spray water on sth)
▸ SCATTER (spray a building with bullets)

spread noun
▸ FAT

spread verb
▸ SPREAD (a bird spreads its wings)
▸ COVER (spread butter on sth)
▸ PASS STH ON (spread disease)
▸ SCATTER (spread papers out)

spring verb
▸ JUMP 2 (spring out of bed)
▸ **spring to mind** OCCUR TO SB

springy adj.
▸ FLEXIBLE 2

sprinkle verb
▸ SCATTER

sprint verb
▸ RUN 1

spur verb
▸ ENCOURAGE 2 (be spurred into action)
▸ PROMOTE (spur economic growth)

spurious adj.
▸ MISLEADING

spurt noun
▸ ATTACK 3

spurt verb
▸ FLOW

spy noun
▸ AGENT

squabble noun
▸ ARGUMENT 1

squabble verb
▸ ARGUE

squad noun
▸ TEAM 1 (a crime/death squad)
▸ TEAM 2 (the Olympic squad)

squalid adj.
▸ SORDID

squander verb
▸ WASTE

square noun
▸ COURTYARD

squat verb
▸ BEND

squawk verb
▸ GRUNT

squeak verb
▸ CREAK

squeal verb
▸ SCREAM

squeeze verb
▸ PACK (squeeze through a gap)
▸ PRESS 1 (squeeze the trigger)
▸ PUMP (squeeze the juice from sth)

squint verb
▸ STARE

squirm verb
▸ WRIGGLE

squirt verb
▸ SPRAY

squishy adj.
▸ SOFT

stab noun
▸ ATTEMPT

stab verb
▸ **stab sb in the back** TELL 2

stable noun
▸ SHED

stable adj.
▸ FIRM (Is the ladder stable?)
▸ STEADY (a stable relationship)

stack noun
▸ PILE

stadium noun
▸ PITCH

staff noun
▸ STAFF (members of staff)
▸ WORKER 2 (students, faculty and staff)

staff member noun
▸ WORKER 1

stage noun
▸ STAGE 1 (the early stages)
▸ STAGE 2 (The performers went on stage.)
▸ DRAMA (a star of stage and screen)
▸ FORUM (the international stage)

stage verb
▸ PLAY 3

stagecoach noun
▸ CARRIAGE 2

stagger verb
▸ STUMBLE (stagger drunkenly)
▸ SURPRISE (It staggers me that…)

staggering adj.
▸ AMAZING

staid adj.
▸ FORMAL

stain noun
▸ MARK

stain verb
▸ PAINT

stained adj.
▸ DIRTY

stake noun
▸ INVOLVEMENT

stale adj.
▸ ROTTEN (stale bread)
▸ SMELLY (stale cigarette smoke)
▸ TIRED 2 (stale news)

stalk verb
▸ FOLLOW 1 (stalk deer/your victim)
▸ MARCH (stalk out of the room)

stall noun
▸ STALL

stall verb
▸ HOLD SB/STH UP (Discussions have stalled.)
▸ TAKE YOUR TIME (They are stalling on the deal.)

stamina noun
▸ STRENGTH

stamp noun
▸ LOGO

stampede verb
▸ RUN 1

stamp out phrasal verb
▸ ERADICATE

stance noun
▸ ATTITUDE (the newspaper's stance on the war)
▸ POSITION (Widen your stance when hitting the ball.)

stand noun
▸ ATTITUDE (take a tough stand on sth)
▸ STALL (a news stand)

stand verb
▸ STAND 1 (stand by the window)
▸ STAND 2 (I can't stand it when you do that.)
▸ HATE (I really can't stand him.)
▸ LEAN 2 (Stand the ladder against the wall.)
▸ REMAIN (an offer still stands)
▸ WITHSTAND (His heart won't stand the strain.)
▸ **stand your ground** RESIST
▸ **stand in awe of sb/sth** RESPECT
▸ **stand on your own (two) feet** TAKE CARE OF YOURSELF

standard noun
▸ CRITERION (by modern standards)
▸ PRINCIPLE 1 (moral standards)
▸ QUALITY (falling standards)

standard adj.
▸ USUAL

stand by phrasal verb
▸ KEEP 5

stand down phrasal verb
▸ LEAVE 3

stand for phrasal verb
▸ SUPPORT 1

stand-in noun
▸ REPLACEMENT

stand in for phrasal verb
▸ REPLACE 1

standing noun
▸ CLASS 4

standstill noun
▸ STOP (bring sth to a standstill)
▸ **at a standstill** STILL adj.

stand up *phrasal verb*
- STAND 1

stand up for *phrasal verb*
- EXPLAIN 2

stand up to *phrasal verb*
- OPPOSE (stand up to the bullies)
- WITHSTAND (stand up to wear and tear)

star *noun*
- STAR 1 (a pop star)
- STAR 2 (the star role in the play)

star *verb*
- FEATURE

stardom *noun*
- FAME

stare *verb*
- STARE

stark *adj.*
- PLAIN 1 (stark white walls)
- PLAIN 2 (the stark truth)

start *noun*
- START (make a start)
- OPPORTUNITY (a start in life)

start *verb*
- START (When does the class start?)
- BEGIN (start work)
- SET OFF (start out from Saigon)
- TURN STH ON (Start the engines!)

starting point *noun*
- SOURCE

startle *verb*
- SURPRISE

startled *adj.*
- AFRAID

start off *phrasal verb*
- START

start up *phrasal verb*
- TURN STH ON

starving *adj.*
- HUNGRY

stash *noun*
- FUND

stash *verb*
- KEEP 1

state *noun*
- STATE (the state of the economy)
- COUNTRY 1 (a one-party state)
- COUNTY (the State of Arkansas)
- **turn State's evidence** TELL 2

state *verb*
- DECLARE (state the facts)
- LIST (arrive at the time stated)

state *adj.*
- PUBLIC

stately home *noun*
- PALACE

statement *noun*
- STATEMENT (a government statement)
- REPORT 3 (a bank statement)

state of affairs *noun*
- SITUATION

state of the art *adj.*
- MODERN

statesman *noun*
- POLITICIAN

static *adj.*
- STEADY

station *noun*
- STATION (a train/bus station)
- CHANNEL (a TV station)

station *verb*
- SEND 2

stationary *adj.*
- STILL

statistics *noun*
- FIGURE

stats *noun*
- FIGURE

stature *noun*
- REPUTATION

status *noun*
- STATUS (The job brings status and respect.)
- CLASS 4 (the status of full-time mothers in society)

statute *noun*
- RULE

statutory *adj.*
- LEGAL

staunch *adj.*
- RELIABLE 1

stay *noun*
- VISIT

stay *verb*
- STAY 1 (stay where you are)
- STAY 2 (stay at a hotel)
- REMAIN (stay awake)
- **a place to stay** HOUSING *noun*
- **stay put** STAY 1

stay away *phrasal verb*
- AVOID

steady *verb*
- LEAN 2

steady *adj.*
- STEADY (steady progress)
- FIRM (a steady hand)

a steal *noun*
- VALUE 2

steal *verb*
- STEAL

stealthy *adj.*
- SECRETIVE

steamroller (also **steamroll**) *verb*
- THREATEN 1

steely *adj.*
- STERN

steep *adj.*
- HIGH 1

steer *verb*
- DRIVE 1 (steer a boat/car/plane)
- MANIPULATE (steer the conversation away from work)
- **steer clear** AVOID

stem *verb*
- STOP 3

stem from *phrasal verb*
- FOLLOW 2

stench *noun*
- ODOUR

step *noun*
- STEP (take a step forward)
- ACTION (a first step towards a united Europe)
- STAGE 1 (explain sth step by step)
- WALK (quicken your step)
- **take steps** ACT *verb*

step *verb*
- WALK 1

step down *phrasal verb*
- LEAVE 3

stepfather *noun*
- MOTHER

stepmother *noun*
- MOTHER

steppe *noun*
- PLAIN

step up *phrasal verb*
- INCREASE

stereotypical *adj.*
- TYPICAL

sterile *adj.*
- CLEAN

sterling *adj.*
- GOOD 1

stern *adj.*
- STERN

stick *verb*
- ATTACH (stick a stamp on the envelope)
- PUSH 1 (stick a pin in the balloon)
- PUT 1 (stick your hands up)
- **stick your neck out** DARE

stick around *phrasal verb*
- STAY 1

sticker *noun*
- LABEL

stick up for *phrasal verb*
- EXPLAIN 2

stick with *phrasal verb*
- CONTINUE 2

stiff *adj.*
- FORMAL (rather stiff and formal)
- SOLID (stiff black cardboard)
- TIGHT (The windows are stiff.)

stifle *verb*
- SUPPRESS 2

still *adj.*
- STILL

stimulant *noun*
- DRUG 1

stimulate *verb*
- STIMULATE (stimulate interest)
- INSPIRE (books that stimulate and challenge the children)

stimulating *adj.*
- INTERESTING

stimulus *noun*
- INCENTIVE

sting *noun*
- CONSPIRACY

sting *verb*
- HURT 1 (stung by criticism)
- HURT 2 (sb's eyes sting)
- PROVOKE (sting sb into action)

stingy *adj.*
- MEAN 2

stink *noun*
- ODOUR

stinking *adj.*
- SMELLY

stint *noun*
- TIME 2

stipulate *verb*
- DEMAND

stir *verb*
- STIR (stir tea/paint)
- MOVE (hear sb stirring)
- STIMULATE (stir the imagination)

stirring *adj.*
- EXCITING

stir up *phrasal verb*
- ENCOURAGE 3

stitch *noun*
- **be/have sb in stitches** LAUGH *verb*

stock *noun*
- SUPPLY (in/out of stock)
- **take stock** EXAMINE *verb*

stock *verb*
- EQUIP 1 (a well-stocked library)
- SELL 2 (stock a range of products)

stockpile *noun*
- SUPPLY

stockpile *verb*
- KEEP 1

stock up *phrasal verb*
- KEEP 1

stoke *verb*
- ENCOURAGE 3

stomach *noun*
- STOMACH

stomp *verb*
- MARCH

stone *noun*
- STONE (stone walls/throw stones)

- GRAIN (cherry/peach stones)

stool *noun*
- CHAIR

stoop *verb*
- BEND

stop *noun*
- STOP (come to a stop)
- STATION (get off at the next stop)
- **put a stop to sth** STOP *verb* 3

stop *verb*
- STOP 1 (stop talking)
- STOP 2 (a car stops/stop a car)
- STOP 3 (stop the bleeding)
- BLOCK 2 (stop the end of the hose)
- END (the rain stops)
- PREVENT (You can't stop me.)
- STAY 1 (Can you stop for tea?)

stop by *phrasal verb*
- VISIT

stop over *phrasal verb*
- STAY 2

stopover *noun*
- VISIT

store *noun*
- SHOP (a department store)
- SUPPLIES (stores of food)
- SUPPLY (a store of knowledge)
- WAREHOUSE (a grain store)

store *verb*
- KEEP 1 (store up food)
- KEEP 3 (store information)

storehouse *noun*
- WAREHOUSE

storeroom *noun*
- WAREHOUSE

storey *noun*
- FLOOR 2

storm *noun*
- STORM (storms lash the country)
- FUSS (a storm of protest)

storm *verb*
- ATTACK 2 (storm a building)
- MARCH (storm out of the room)

stormy *adj.*
- ROUGH 2

story *noun*
- STORY 1 (a bedtime story)
- STORY 2 (the story of his life)
- FLOOR 2 (a six-story building)
- LEGEND 1 (The story goes that…)
- LIE (spread malicious stories)
- REPORT 2 (The police didn't believe her story.)

storyline *noun*
- STORY 1

stout *adj.*
- FAT

stove *noun*
- HEATING (a wood-burning stove)
- OVEN (put a pan on the stove)

strafe *verb*
- BOMB

straggly *adj.*
- SCRUFFY

straight *adj.*
- HONEST (Be straight with me.)
- SUCCESSIVE (six straight wins)
- UPRIGHT (Is my tie straight?)
- **set sb/sth straight** CORRECT *verb*

straighten out *phrasal verb*
- SOLVE 1

straightforward *adj.*
- EASY 1 (a straightforward process)
- HONEST (straightforward and easy to get on with)

strain *noun*
- PRESSURE 1 (a strain on your finances)
- WEIGHT (break under the strain)

strain verb
▸ FILTER (strain off excess liquid)
▸ INJURE (Don't strain your eyes.)

straits noun
▸ MESS 2

strand noun
▸ ASPECT (every strand of opinion)
▸ FIBRE (a strand of hair/wool)

strand verb
▸ LEAVE 5

strange adj.
▸ STRANGE 1 (A strange thing happened this morning.)
▸ STRANGE 2 (Never accept rides from strange men.)

strangle verb
▸ STRANGLE

strap verb
▸ ATTACH

strategy noun
▸ PLAN 1

straw poll noun
▸ ELECTION

streak noun
▸ MARK

streak verb
▸ FLY 2

stream noun
▸ CLASS 3 (pupils in the top stream)
▸ FLOOD 2 (a stream of insults)
▸ FLOW (a stream of visitors/cars)
▸ RIVER (a mountain stream)

stream verb
▸ FLOW (Sunlight streamed in.)
▸ SURGE (People streamed across the bridge.)

street noun
▸ ROAD

strength noun
▸ STRENGTH (her inner strength)
▸ BENEFIT 1 (the strengths and weaknesses of the argument)
▸ FORCE (physical strength)

strengthen verb
▸ STRENGTHEN

strenuous adj.
▸ HARD

stress noun
▸ PRESSURE 1 (mental stress)
▸ PRIORITY (lay great stress on punctuality)
▸ WEIGHT (put stress on other parts of the body)

stress verb
▸ STRESS

stressed adj.
▸ TENSE

stressful adj.
▸ STRESSFUL

stretch noun
▸ STRETCH

stretch verb
▸ EXPAND 1 (This sweater has stretched.)
▸ LEAD 3 (The road stretches into the distance.)

strew verb
▸ SCATTER

strict adj.
▸ STRICT

stride noun
▸ STEP (cross the room in two strides)
▸ WALK (a purposeful stride)

stride verb
▸ WALK 1

strident adj.
▸ HOARSE

strike noun
▸ ATTACK 1

strike verb
▸ ATTACK 1 (The killer may strike again.)
▸ ATTACK 2 (strike enemy positions)
▸ HIT 1 (struck by a car)
▸ HIT 2 (strike sb in the face)
▸ HIT 3 (tragedy strikes)
▸ OCCUR TO SB (be struck by the thought that…)
▸ RING (The clock struck three.)
▸ SEEM (sth strikes you as odd)

strike at phrasal verb
▸ HIT 3

strike back phrasal verb
▸ FIGHT BACK

strike out phrasal verb
▸ DELETE

striking adj.
▸ BEAUTIFUL 1 (striking good looks)
▸ MARKED (a striking resemblance)

string noun
▸ ROPE (a piece of string)
▸ SERIES (a string of hit records)
▸ **pull strings** MANIPULATE

string along phrasal verb
▸ MISLEAD

stringent adj.
▸ STRICT

strip noun
▸ STRIP

strip verb
▸ TAKE 3 (strip off the paint)
▸ TAKE STH OFF (strip off your clothes)

stripe noun
▸ STRIP

strip mall noun
▸ MARKET 2

strive verb
▸ TRY 1

stroke verb
▸ STROKE

stroll verb
▸ WALK 1

strong adj.
▸ STRONG 1 (strong arms)
▸ STRONG 2 (strong cheese/coffee)
▸ STRONG 3 (strong light)
▸ CONVINCING (a strong case for doing sth)
▸ POWERFUL (a strong leader)
▸ WELL (feeling strong again)

stronghold noun
▸ CASTLE

strong-willed adj.
▸ STUBBORN

structure noun
▸ STRUCTURE (the structure of a building/society)
▸ BUILDING (a wooden structure)
▸ EFFICIENCY (Children need structure in their lives.)

struggle noun
▸ CAMPAIGN (the struggle between good and evil)
▸ EFFORT (It was a real struggle to be ready on time.)
▸ FIGHT (a violent struggle)

struggle verb
▸ COMPETE (struggle for control)
▸ FIGHT 2 (struggle with an intruder)
▸ RESIST (struggle against cancer)
▸ TRY 1 (struggle to pay the bills)

struggle along/on phrasal verb
▸ PERSIST

stubborn adj.
▸ STUBBORN

stubby adj.
▸ SHORT 2

student noun
▸ STUDENT (a school student)
▸ LEARNER (a student of human nature)

studio noun
▸ OFFICE 2

studious adj.
▸ INTELLECTUAL 2

study noun
▸ EDUCATION (good study skills)
▸ OFFICE 2 (sb's private study)
▸ REPORT 1 (a case study)
▸ RESEARCH (scientific study)

study verb
▸ STUDY (study a photograph)
▸ EXAMINE (study a proposal)
▸ LEARN (study English)

stuff noun
▸ MATERIAL (plastic/sticky stuff)
▸ NATURE 1 (the very stuff of politics in the region)
▸ THING 1 (loads of stuff to do)
▸ THING 3 (Move your stuff!)

stuff verb
▸ EAT (stuff your face with food)
▸ PACK (The drawers were stuffed full of papers.)
▸ PUT 1 (stuff sth in your pocket)

stuffed adj.
▸ FULL

stuffy adj.
▸ FORMAL

stumble verb
▸ STUMBLE (stumble around in the dark)
▸ FALL 3 (stumble and fall)

stumble on/upon/across phrasal verb
▸ FIND 2

stumbling block noun
▸ OBSTACLE

stump verb
▸ CONFUSE

stun verb
▸ SURPRISE

stunning adj.
▸ AMAZING (a stunning victory)
▸ BEAUTIFUL 1 (You look stunning.)

stunt noun
▸ ACTION

stunt verb
▸ HOLD SB/STH UP

stunted adj.
▸ SHORT 2

stupid adj.
▸ STUPID (a stupid person)
▸ CRAZY (a stupid thing to do)

stupor noun
▸ TRANCE

style noun
▸ STYLE (do everything with style and grace)
▸ FASHION (back in style)
▸ KIND (styles of architecture)
▸ WAY 1 (sb's teaching style)

stylish adj.
▸ ELEGANT

suave adj.
▸ SOPHISTICATED

sub noun
▸ BOAT

the/your subconscious noun
▸ MIND

subconscious adj.
▸ UNCONSCIOUS

subdivide verb
▸ DIVIDE 1

subdue verb
▸ SUPPRESS 1

subject noun
▸ SUBJECT (change the subject)
▸ AREA 2 (school subjects)
▸ CITIZEN (British subjects)

subjective adj.
▸ OWN

subject matter noun
▸ MESSAGE

subject to phrasal verb
▸ EXPOSE

subject to adj.
▸ PRONE TO STH

submarine noun
▸ BOAT

submissive adj.
▸ PASSIVE

submit verb
▸ GIVE WAY idiom (submit to threats)
▸ PRESENT 3 (submit a report)

subscribe to phrasal verb
▸ IN FAVOUR (OF SB/STH)

subscription noun
▸ PAYMENT

subsidize verb
▸ FUND

subsidy noun
▸ INVESTMENT

substance noun
▸ IMPORTANCE (No one raised any matters of substance.)
▸ MATERIAL (chemical substances)
▸ MESSAGE (Love and guilt form the substance of his new book.)

substantial adj.
▸ LARGE

substantiate verb
▸ CONFIRM 1

substitute noun
▸ REPLACEMENT

substitute verb
▸ REPLACE 2

substitute for phrasal verb
▸ REPLACE 1

substitution noun
▸ EXCHANGE

subtitle noun
▸ NAME

subtle adj.
▸ PALE 2

subtract verb
▸ DISCOUNT

succeed verb
▸ SUCCEED (succeed in business)
▸ ACHIEVE (a plan succeeds)
▸ INHERIT (succeed to the throne)

success noun
▸ SUCCESS

successful adj.
▸ SUCCESSFUL 1 (the successful candidate)
▸ SUCCESSFUL 2 (a successful business)

succession noun
▸ SERIES

successive adj.
▸ SUCCESSIVE

succinct adj.
▸ SHORT 3

suck verb
▸ DRINK

sucker noun
▸ VICTIM 2

sudden adj.
▸ SUDDEN

suds noun
▸ FOAM

suffer verb
▸ HAVE 3

sufferer *noun*
▶ PATIENT

suffer from *phrasal verb*
▶ SUFFER FROM STH

suffering *noun*
▶ DISTRESS (mental suffering)
▶ PAIN (the sufferings of the dying)

suffocate *verb*
▶ STRANGLE

suggest *verb*
▶ SUGGEST (The evidence suggests…)
▶ MEAN 2 (Are you suggesting I'm lazy?)
▶ PROPOSE (I suggested going in my car.)
▶ RECOMMEND 2 (suggest a good dictionary)

suggestion *noun*
▶ SUGGESTION (There was no suggestion of a rift.)
▶ PROPOSAL (Can I make a suggestion?)

suicidal *adj.*
▶ DESPERATE

suicide *noun*
▶ MURDER

suit *noun*
▶ CASE (file a suit against sb)
▶ **follow suit** FOLLOW *verb* 4

suit *verb*
▶ MEET 4

suitable *adj.*
▶ GOOD 2

suitcase *noun*
▶ SUITCASE

suite *noun*
▶ FLAT

suitor *noun*
▶ PARTNER 2

sulk *noun*
▶ TEMPER

sulk *verb*
▶ BROOD

sulky *adj.*
▶ IRRITABLE

sullen *adj.*
▶ IRRITABLE

sum *noun*
▶ NUMBER 1

summarize *verb*
▶ SUMMARIZE

summary *noun*
▶ SUMMARY

summit *noun*
▶ HILL (the summit of a mountain)
▶ MEETING 1 (a summit meeting)

sum up *phrasal verb*
▶ SUMMARIZE

sun *noun*
▶ SUN

sundown *noun*
▶ NIGHT 2

sunlight *noun*
▶ SUN

sunny *adj.*
▶ SUNNY

sunrise *noun*
▶ DAWN

sunset *noun*
▶ NIGHT 2

sunshine *noun*
▶ SUN

superb *adj.*
▶ EXCELLENT

superficial *adj.*
▶ APPARENT

superfluous *adj.*
▶ EXCESS

superintend *verb*
▶ REGULATE

superintendent *noun*
▶ MANAGER

superior *adj.*
▶ BETTER (be superior to sb/sth)
▶ GOOD 1 (of a superior quality)
▶ PATRONIZING (a superior manner)
▶ TOP (your superior officer)

supermarket *noun*
▶ SHOP

the supernatural *noun*
▶ MAGIC

supernatural *adj.*
▶ MAGIC

superpower *noun*
▶ COUNTRY 1

supersonic *adj.*
▶ FAST

superstar *noun*
▶ STAR 1

supervise *verb*
▶ REGULATE

supervision *noun*
▶ GOVERNMENT 2

supervisor *noun*
▶ MANAGER

supper *noun*
▶ DINNER

supple *adj.*
▶ FLEXIBLE 2

supplement *noun*
▶ MAGAZINE

supplier *noun*
▶ DEALER

supply *noun*
▶ SUPPLY (supplies of food)
▶ SUPPLIES (run short of supplies)
▶ **in short supply** SCARCE *adj.*

supply *verb*
▶ PROVIDE

support *noun*
▶ EVIDENCE (support for a theory)
▶ HELP (emotional/moral support)
▶ POST (the supports under the bridge)

support *verb*
▶ SUPPORT 1 (support a party)
▶ CONFIRM 1 (support a theory)
▶ FUND (support sth financially)
▶ HELP 1 (The organization supports people with AIDS.)
▶ PROVIDE FOR SB (support a family)

supporter *noun*
▶ SUPPORTER (an active supporter of democratic change)
▶ FAN (a football supporter)

suppose *verb*
▶ SUPPOSE (I suppose so)
▶ SAY 3 (Let's suppose you are married.)

supposed *adj.*
▶ SUPPOSED

suppress *verb*
▶ SUPPRESS 1 (suppress a rebellion)
▶ SUPPRESS 2 (suppress a feeling)
▶ LIMIT (suppress weed growth)

supreme *adj.*
▶ MAXIMUM

sure *adj.*
▶ SURE (Are you sure about that?)
▶ CERTAIN (sure to rain/a sure sign)
▶ **a sure thing** CERTAINTY *noun*
▶ **make sure** CHECK *verb* 2 (make sure the door is locked)
▶ **make sure** ENSURE *verb* (make sure no one finds out)

surf *noun*
▶ FOAM

surface *verb*
▶ EMERGE

surge *noun*
▶ INCREASE (a surge in demand)
▶ WAVE 2 (a surge of emotion)

surge *verb*
▶ SURGE (The crowd surged forwards.)
▶ SOAR (Profits surged to $225m.)

surgeon *noun*
▶ DOCTOR

surgery *noun*
▶ SURGERY (the doctor's surgery)
▶ TREATMENT (open heart surgery)

surmise *verb*
▶ GUESS

surname *noun*
▶ NAME

surplus *noun*
▶ PROFIT

surplus *adj.*
▶ EXCESS

surprise *verb*
▶ SURPRISE

surprising *adj.*
▶ SURPRISING

surrender *verb*
▶ GIVE STH UP

surreptitious *adj.*
▶ SECRETIVE

surrogate *noun*
▶ REPLACEMENT

surround *verb*
▶ SURROUND

surroundings *noun*
▶ ENVIRONMENT

surveillance *noun*
▶ INSPECTION

survey *noun*
▶ INSPECTION (an aerial survey)
▶ INVESTIGATION (a survey of people's attitudes)
▶ REPORT 1 (a survey of small businesses)

survey *verb*
▶ SURVEY (87% of the companies surveyed employ part-time staff.)
▶ EXAMINE (This chapter surveys…)
▶ STUDY (survey the damage)

survival *noun*
▶ LIFE 1

survive *verb*
▶ SURVIVE

susceptible *adj.*
▶ PRONE TO STH

suspect *verb*
▶ SUSPECT (suspect sb of doing sth)
▶ SUPPOSE (As I suspected…)

suspect *adj.*
▶ SUSPICIOUS 2

suspend *verb*
▶ DELAY (suspend plans)
▶ HANG (suspend sth from the ceiling)
▶ STOP 3 (suspend production at the factory)

suspension *noun*
▶ MIXTURE

suspicion *noun*
▶ DOUBT 2 (on suspicion of murder)
▶ IDEA 2 (I had a horrible suspicion I'd got it wrong.)
▶ SCEPTICISM (Their offer was greeted with suspicion.)

suspicious *adj.*
▶ SUSPICIOUS 1 (suspicious of sb/sth)
▶ SUSPICIOUS 2 (suspicious circumstances)

sustain *verb*
▶ APPROVE (Objection sustained!)
▶ MAINTAIN 1 (a sustained attack)

swallow *verb*
▶ EAT

swamp *noun*
▶ MARSH

swamp *verb*
▶ OVERWHELM

swap *noun*
▶ EXCHANGE

swap *verb*
▶ REPLACE 2 (swap places with sb)
▶ SWITCH (I'll drive there and then we'll swap over on the way back.)

swarm *noun*
▶ HERD

swarm *verb*
▶ SURGE

swat *verb*
▶ HIT 2

sway *verb*
▶ INFLUENCE (swayed by his arguments)
▶ SWING (sway in the breeze)

swear *verb*
▶ CURSE (swear loudly)
▶ PROMISE (She made him swear not to tell anyone.)

sweat *verb*
▶ WORRY 1

sweep *verb*
▶ BRUSH (sweep the floor)
▶ SLIDE (sweep out of the room)

sweeping *adj.*
▶ GENERAL 2 (a sweeping generalization)
▶ WIDE 1 (sweeping changes)

sweet *adj.*
▶ SWEET (a sweet little kitten)
▶ KIND (It's very sweet of you.)

sweetheart *noun*
▶ DARLING (Are you ok, sweetheart?)
▶ PARTNER 2 (his childhood sweetheart)

sweetie *noun*
▶ DARLING

swell *noun*
▶ WAVE 1

swell *verb*
▶ SWELL

swelling *noun*
▶ TUMOUR

swift *adj.*
▶ QUICK

swig *noun*
▶ SIP

swig *verb*
▶ DRINK

swindle *verb*
▶ DEFRAUD

swindler *noun*
▶ CHEAT

swing *noun*
▶ CHANGE 1

swing *verb*
▶ SWING (swing back and forth)
▶ CHANGE 2 (The state has swung from Republican to Democrat.)
▶ TURN 1 (swing around angrily)

swish *verb*
▶ SHAKE 1

switch *noun*
▶ BUTTON 1 (a light switch)
▶ CHANGE 2 (a policy switch)

switch *verb*
▶ REPLACE 2 (switch my glass with hers)
▶ SWITCH (switch over to a new system)

switchblade *noun*
► KNIFE

switch off *phrasal verb*
► TURN STH OFF

switch on *phrasal verb*
► TURN STH ON

swivel *verb*
► SPIN (swivel a chair)
► TURN 1 (swivel on your heel)

swop *noun*
► EXCHANGE

swop *verb*
► REPLACE 2 (swop places with sb)
► SWITCH (I'll drive there and then we'll swop over on the way back.)

syllabus *noun*
► CLASS 1

symbol *noun*
► NUMBER 2 (a chemical symbol)
► SIGN 1 (a symbol of peace)

symbolic *adj.*
► TYPICAL

symbolize *verb*
► REPRESENT 2

sympathetic *adj.*
► SENSITIVE 1

sympathize *verb*
► SORRY FOR SB

sympathy *noun*
► SYMPATHY

symptom *noun*
► SIGN 1

synagogue *noun*
► CHURCH

syndicate *noun*
► GROUP 3

synonymous *adj.*
► EQUAL

synopsis *noun*
► SUMMARY

synthetic *adj.*
► ARTIFICIAL 1

syphon *verb*
► PUMP

system *noun*
► SYSTEM (a political system)
► AUTHORITIES (fight the system)
► WAY 2 (an effective system for storing data)

systematic *adj.*
► EFFICIENT

T t

table *noun*
► LIST

table *verb*
► PRESENT 3

tabloid *noun*
► NEWSPAPER

taboo *noun*
► BAN

taboo *adj.*
► FORBIDDEN

tabs *noun*
► **keep tabs on sb/sth** MONITOR *verb*

taciturn *adj.*
► QUIET 3

tackle *noun*
► EQUIPMENT

tackle *verb*
► TACKLE (tackle inflation)
► CONFRONT (I tackled him about the money he owes me.)

tact *noun*
► TACT

tactic *noun*
► TACTIC

tactless *adj.*
► INSENSITIVE

tag *noun*
► LABEL

tag *verb*
► MARK 1

tag along *phrasal verb*
► ACCOMPANY

tail *verb*
► FOLLOW 1

tailor *verb*
► CHANGE 1

tailor-made *adj.*
► IDEAL

tails *noun*
► COAT

take *noun*
► REVENUE (the North Sea oil take)
► **give and take** COMPROMISE

take *verb*
► TAKE 1 (take your things with you)
► TAKE 2 (take sb home)
► TAKE 3 (take your books off the table)
► TAKE 4 (I passed him the rope and he took it.)
► TAKE 5 (take a job/sb's advice)
► TAKE 6 (take an opportunity)
► TAKE 7 (take the blame)
► TAKE 8 (He took the painting for a genuine Van Gogh.)
► TAKE 9 (take drugs)
► ARREST (take sb prisoner)
► BUY (I'll take the grey jacket.)
► CONSIDER (Take London, for example.)
► CONTINUE 1 (It takes an hour.)
► CROSS (take a corner very fast)
► DISCOUNT (take 5 from 12)
► GET 1 (take samples from the river)
► GET 5 (take the train)
► HAVE 3 (take a fall)
► INVADE (take a city)
► RESPOND (take sb/sth seriously)
► STAND 2 (sb can't take criticism)
► STEAL (What did the burglars take?)

take aback *phrasal verb*
► SURPRISE

take advantage of *idiom*
► TAKE ADVANTAGE OF SB/STH

take after *phrasal verb*
► LOOK LIKE SB/STH

take back *phrasal verb*
► BREAK 4 (OK, I take it all back!)
► REMIND SB OF SB/STH (That smell takes me back to my childhood.)
► RETURN 2 (take sth back to the store)

take care of *verb*
► **take care of yourself** TAKE CARE OF YOURSELF
► DEAL WITH SB/STH (take care of the travel arrangements)
► LOOK AFTER SB (take care of the kids)

take in *phrasal verb*
► ACCOMMODATE (take in lodgers)
► CHEAT (taken in by his stories)
► INCLUDE 1 (The tour takes in six European capitals.)
► NOTICE (take in every detail)
► UNDERSTAND 1 (read sth without taking much in)

take off *phrasal verb*
► TAKE STH OFF (take off your jacket)
► DISCOUNT (take $10 off the bill)
► FLEE (They took off in the opposite direction.)
► SET OFF (a plane takes off)

take on *phrasal verb*
► COMPETE (take sb on at chess)

► EMPLOY (take on new staff)
► TAKE 5 (take on more work)

take out *phrasal verb*
► GET 1 (take out a loan)
► KILL (take out enemy bombers)

take out of *phrasal verb*
► DISCOUNT

take over *phrasal verb*
► TAKE OVER

take up *phrasal verb*
► BEGIN (take up a post/hobby)
► CONTINUE 3 (take up the story)
► SPEND 2 (take up your time)
► TAKE 5 (take up a challenge)
► **take up arms** FIGHT 1

take your time *verb*
► TAKE YOUR TIME

takings *noun*
► REVENUE

tale *noun*
► STORY 1

talent *noun*
► SKILL 1

talented *adj.*
► GOOD 4

talk *noun*
► DISCUSSION (have a long talk)
► REPORT 4 (There was talk of sending in troops.)
► SPEECH (sales talk)
► **hold talks** NEGOTIATE

talk *verb*
► TALK (Who were you talking to?)
► SAY 1 (The baby can't talk yet.)
► SAY 2 (Stop talking!)

talkative *adj.*
► TALKATIVE

talker *noun*
► SPEAKER 1

talk into *phrasal verb*
► PERSUADE

talk out of *phrasal verb*
► DISCOURAGE 1

tall *adj.*
► TALL (a tall man)
► HIGH 2 (a tall building)

tally *noun*
► ESTIMATE

tally *verb*
► COUNT

tame *adj.*
► PREDICTABLE 2

tang *noun*
► TASTE 2

tangled *adj.*
► COMPLEX (tangled relationships)
► SCRUFFY (tangled hair)

tank *noun*
► BARREL

tantamount to *phrase*
► EQUAL *adj.*

tantrum *noun*
► TEMPER

tap *verb*
► KNOCK (tap your feet)
► OVERHEAR (tap a telephone)
► PAT (tap sb on the arm)

tape *verb*
► ATTACH

target *noun*
► TARGET

target *verb*
► FOCUS

tariff *noun*
► TAX

tarp *noun*
► COVER

tarpaulin *noun*
► COVER

task *noun*
► TASK

task force *noun*
► COMMITTEE

taste *noun*
► TASTE 1 (a taste for foreign travel)
► TASTE 2 (a sweet taste)

taste *verb*
► EAT (I've never tasted anything like it.)
► FEEL (taste freedom)
► TRY 2 (Taste it and see if there is enough salt.)

tasteless *adj.*
► MILD

tasty *adj.*
► DELICIOUS

taut *adj.*
► TIGHT

tavern *noun*
► BAR

tax *noun*
► TAX

taxing *adj.*
► DIFFICULT 1

taxpayer *noun*
► CITIZEN

tea *noun*
► DINNER

teach *verb*
► TEACH (teach history)
► TRAIN 1 (teach sb to swim)

teacher *noun*
► TEACHER

teaching *noun*
► EDUCATION (classroom teaching)
► VALUES (religious teaching)

team *noun*
► TEAM 1 (work together as a team)
► TEAM 2 (a football team)

teammate *noun*
► PARTNER 1

tear *verb*
► TEAR (tear paper)
► INJURE (tear a muscle)
► PULL 2 (tear down a poster)
► RUN 1 (tear off down the road)

tear down *phrasal verb*
► DEMOLISH

tears *noun*
► **be in tears** CRY *verb*

tease *phrasal verb*
► FLIRT (She teased him with a provocative smile.)
► LAUGH AT SB/STH (I used to get teased about my name.)

technique *noun*
► SKILL 2 (show great technique)
► WAY 2 (management techniques)

technology *noun*
► TECHNOLOGY

tedious *adj.*
► BORING

teen *noun*
► CHILDHOOD (in your teens)
► GIRL (awkward teens)

teen *adj.*
► YOUNG

teenage *adj.*
► YOUNG

teenager *noun*
► GIRL

telephone *verb*
► CALL 2

tell *verb*
► TELL 1 (tell sb the news)
► TELL 2 (Promise you won't tell.)
► DESCRIBE (tell lies)
► DISTINGUISH 1 (tell the difference)
► ORDER 1 (tell sb to do sth)

telling adj.
▶ INFORMATIVE

tell off phrasal verb
▶ SCOLD

temper noun
▶ TEMPER (have a short temper)
▶ **lose your temper** LOSE YOUR TEMPER

temper verb
▶ MODERATE

temperament noun
▶ PERSONALITY

temperamental adj.
▶ MOODY

temperate adj.
▶ SUNNY

template noun
▶ MODEL

temple noun
▶ CHURCH

tempo noun
▶ RATE 1 (the slow tempo of life on the island)
▶ RHYTHM (music with a fast tempo)

temporary adj.
▶ SHORT 1

tempt verb
▶ TEMPT

temptation noun
▶ DESIRE

tenacious adj.
▶ DETERMINED 2

tenacity noun
▶ DETERMINATION

tenant noun
▶ TENANT

tend verb
▶ LOOK AFTER SB

tendency noun
▶ TENDENCY (This material has a tendency to shrink.)
▶ TREND (a growing tendency among employers)

tender noun
▶ OFFER 2

tender verb
▶ OFFER 1

tender adj.
▶ LOVING

tenderness noun
▶ LOVE 2

tenet noun
▶ PRINCIPLE 2

tense verb
▶ TIGHTEN

tense adj.
▶ TENSE (make sb tense)
▶ STRESSFUL (a tense atmosphere)

tension noun
▶ TENSION (family tensions)
▶ PRESSURE 1 (nervous tension)

tentative adj.
▶ HESITANT

tepid adj.
▶ COLD 1 (tepid water)
▶ INDIFFERENT (a tepid response)

term noun
▶ CONDITION (your terms and conditions of employment)
▶ LANGUAGE 2 (explain in simple terms)
▶ RATE 2 (buy sth on easy terms)
▶ TIME 2 (a term of office)
▶ WORD (technical terms)
▶ **come to terms with sth** ACCEPT verb

term verb
▶ CALL 1

terminal noun
▶ STATION

terminal adj.
▶ FATAL

terminate verb
▶ END

termination noun
▶ END

terminology noun
▶ LANGUAGE 2

terminus noun
▶ STATION

terrace noun
▶ PORCH (the hotel terrace)
▶ ROAD (a terrace of cottages)

terrain noun
▶ COUNTRY 2

terrible adj.
▶ TERRIBLE 1 (terrible news)
▶ TERRIBLE 2 (a terrible mess)
▶ TERRIBLE 3 (a terrible accident)
▶ TERRIBLE 4 (terrible acting)

terrific adj.
▶ GREAT 1

terrified adj.
▶ AFRAID

terrify verb
▶ FRIGHTEN

terrifying adj.
▶ FRIGHTENING

territory noun
▶ TERRITORY (foreign territory)
▶ HABITAT (an animal defends its territory)

terror noun
▶ FEAR

terrorist noun
▶ GUERRILLA

terrorize verb
▶ BULLY

terse adj.
▶ SHARP 2

test noun
▶ TEST 1 (a blood test)
▶ TEST 2 (a driving test)
▶ CRITERION (a good test of the government's popularity)
▶ GAME 1 (a five-day test match)
▶ **put sb/sth to the test** TEST 1 verb

test verb
▶ TEST 1 (test water for purity)
▶ TEST 2 (test your English)

testify verb
▶ CONFIRM 2

testify to phrasal verb
▶ CONFIRM 1

testimonial noun
▶ ENDORSEMENT

testimony noun
▶ EVIDENCE

testing noun
▶ TEST 1

testing adj.
▶ DIFFICULT 1

tether noun
▶ REIN

tether verb
▶ RESTRAIN

text noun
▶ BOOK (a literary text)
▶ LETTER (send sb a text)
▶ LITERATURE (printed text)
▶ SCRIPT (the text of a speech)

textbook noun
▶ BOOK

textile noun
▶ FABRIC

texture noun
▶ TEXTURE

thankful adj.
▶ GRATEFUL

thanks noun
▶ THANKS

thaw verb
▶ MELT

theatre (also **theater**) noun
▶ DRAMA (an evening of music and theatre)
▶ HALL 1 (see a play at the theatre)

theft noun
▶ THEFT

theme noun
▶ SONG (the trumpets' theme)
▶ SUBJECT (the theme of this evening's lecture)

then adj.
▶ FORMER

then adv.
▶ **now and then** SOMETIMES

theological adj.
▶ RELIGIOUS

theology noun
▶ RELIGION

theorem noun
▶ THEORY 1

theoretical adj.
▶ INTELLECTUAL 1 (theoretical knowledge/physics)
▶ SUPPOSED (a theoretical possibility)

theorist noun
▶ SCHOLAR

theory noun
▶ THEORY 1 (the theory of relativity)
▶ THEORY 2 (I have this theory that…)

therapy noun
▶ TREATMENT

there adv.
▶ **get there** ARRIVE

thesis noun
▶ PAPER (a PhD thesis)
▶ THEORY 2 (research supports the thesis)

thick adj.
▶ HOARSE (a voice thick with emotion)
▶ STUPID (I'm not completely thick.)
▶ WIDE 2 (a thick book/carpet)

thickness noun
▶ LENGTH

thief noun
▶ THIEF

thin adj.
▶ THIN (He was tall and thin.)
▶ DIM 1 (the thin grey light of dawn)
▶ NARROW (a thin layer of soil)

thing noun
▶ THING 1 (lots of things to do)
▶ THING 2 (Pass me that thing.)
▶ THING 3 (your swimming things)
▶ ANIMAL (a living thing)
▶ PERSON (you poor things)
▶ SITUATION (How are things?)
▶ **a sure thing** CERTAINTY
▶ **take things easy** REST verb

thingy noun
▶ THING 2

think verb
▶ THINK (I think it looks good.)
▶ CONSIDER (I'll think about it.)
▶ EXPECT (It took longer than we thought.)
▶ IMAGINE (Just think how nice it would be.)
▶ **think twice** HESITATE

think back phrasal verb
▶ REMEMBER

thinker noun
▶ SCHOLAR

thinking noun
▶ REASONING

thinking adj.
▶ INFORMED

think up phrasal verb
▶ COME UP WITH STH

thorough adj.
▶ CONSCIENTIOUS (be thorough in your research)
▶ DETAILED (a thorough investigation)

thought noun
▶ CONSIDERATION (lost in thought)
▶ IDEA 1 (I've just had a thought.)
▶ REASONING (feminist thought)
▶ **second thoughts** DOUBT 2

thoughtful adj.
▶ THOUGHTFUL (a thoughtful expression/silence)
▶ KIND (How thoughtful of you!)

thoughtless adj.
▶ INSENSITIVE

thrash verb
▶ DEFEAT

thrash out phrasal verb
▶ AGREE 3

thread noun
▶ FIBRE (the threads of a spider's web)
▶ MESSAGE (thread of the argument)
▶ ROPE (embroidered with gold thread)

thread verb
▶ EDGE

threat noun
▶ THREAT (a threat to society)
▶ RISK 1 (the threat of war)

threaten verb
▶ THREATEN 1 (threaten sb with a gun)
▶ THREATEN 2 (Pollution is threatening marine life.)
▶ THREATEN 3 (a storm threatens)

threatening adj.
▶ THREATENING

thrifty adj.
▶ MEAN 2

thrill noun
▶ WAVE 2

thrilled adj.
▶ GLAD

thrilling adj.
▶ EXCITING

thrive verb
▶ DO WELL

thriving adj.
▶ SUCCESSFUL 2

throat noun
▶ **clear your throat** COUGH verb

throb verb
▶ BEAT 2 (the music throbs)
▶ HURT 2 (sb's head throbs)

throne noun
▶ CHAIR

throng noun
▶ CROWD

throng verb
▶ CROWD

throttle verb
▶ STRANGLE

throw verb
▶ THROW (throw a ball/stone)
▶ HAVE 4 (throw a party)
▶ **throw down the gauntlet** CHALLENGE
▶ **throw light on sth** EXPLAIN 1

throw away phrasal verb
▶ REMOVE 1 (throw away junk)
▶ WASTE (throw away all your chances in life)

throw out phrasal verb
▶ EVACUATE (throw sb out of the house)

► REFUSE (throw out a recommendation)
► REMOVE 1 (throw out junk)
throw up *phrasal verb*
► VOMIT
the thrust *noun*
► MESSAGE
thrust *verb*
► PUSH 1
thud *noun*
► BANG
thug *noun*
► THUG
thumb *noun*
► **thumbs up** APPROVAL
thump *noun*
► BANG
thump *verb*
► HIT 2
thunder *verb*
► RUMBLE
thunderstorm *noun*
► STORM
thwart *verb*
► THWART
tic *noun*
► SHIVER
tick *verb*
► MARK 1
tick away *phrasal verb*
► GO BY
tickle *verb*
► HURT 2
tidal wave *noun*
► FLOOD 1
tide *noun*
► FLOW
tidy *verb*
► TIDY
tidy *adj.*
► EFFICIENT (a tidy person)
► NEAT (a tidy desk)
tie *noun*
► DRAW (a tie for first place)
► GAME 1 (a cup tie)
► RELATIONSHIP 1 (family ties)
tie *verb*
► TIE (tie a knot)
► ATTACH (tie sth in a bundle)
tie in *phrasal verb*
► MATCH 1
tier *noun*
► FLOOR 2
tie up *phrasal verb*
► RESTRAIN
tiff *noun*
► ARGUMENT 1
tight *adj.*
► TIGHT (a tight hold)
► CRAMPED (a tight squeeze)
tight *adv.*
► **sit tight** WAIT *verb*
tighten *verb*
► TIGHTEN (tighten your grip)
► **tighten your belt** SAVE 2
tilt *verb*
► LEAN 1
timbre *noun*
► NOTE
time *noun*
► TIME 1 (It's time for lunch.)
► TIME 2 (a long time ago)
► PERIOD (times are hard)
► RHYTHM (in time to the music)
► **on time** EARLY *adj.*
► **have a good/great time** PLAY
verb 1
► **take your time, buy time** TAKE
YOUR TIME *verb*

► **most of the time** USUALLY *adv.*
► **at times, from time to time**
SOMETIMES *adv.*
time *verb*
► SCHEDULE
timely *adj.*
► TIMELY
time off *noun*
► HOLIDAY 1
time out *noun*
► REST 2
timetable *noun*
► SCHEDULE
timetable *verb*
► SCHEDULE
timid *adj.*
► SHY
tin *noun*
► BOX (a cake tin)
► PACKET (a tin of baked beans)
► PAN (a baking tin)
tinge *noun*
► COLOUR 1 (a reddish tinge)
► ELEMENT 2 (a tinge of regret)
tingle *verb*
► HURT 2
tinkle *verb*
► CLINK
tint *noun*
► COLOUR 1
tint *verb*
► PAINT
tiny *adj.*
► SMALL
tip *noun*
► TIP (the tip of her finger)
► ADVICE (useful tips)
► GIFT (leave the waiter a tip)
tip *verb*
► LEAN 1
tip off *phrasal verb*
► WARN
tip-off *noun*
► WARNING
tip over *phrasal verb*
► ROLL
tipsy *adj.*
► DRUNK
tiptoe *verb*
► SLIP 1
tire *verb*
► TIRE
tired *adj.*
► TIRED 1 (feel tired)
► TIRED 2 (tired old jokes)
tire out *phrasal verb*
► TIRE
tiresome *adj.*
► ANNOYING
title *noun*
► AWARD (an Olympic title)
► BOOK (publish several new titles)
► NAME (the title of the book)
► RIGHT (title deeds)
titter *verb*
► LAUGH
toast *noun*
► TRIBUTE
toast *verb*
► BAKE
toddler *noun*
► CHILD
together *adv.*
► **be together** GO OUT
togetherness *noun*
► FRIENDSHIP
toil *noun*
► WORK 1

toil *verb*
► WORK 1
toilet *noun*
► TOILET
tolerance *noun*
► PATIENCE
tolerant *adj.*
► TOLERANT
tolerate *verb*
► STAND 2 (I don't know how you
tolerate that noise!)
► WITHSTAND (tolerate high temperatures)
toll *noun*
► RATE 2
toll *verb*
► RING
tone *noun*
► ATMOSPHERE (the tone of the
book)
► NOTE (the rich tone of the trumpet)
► VOICE (sb's tone of voice)
tone down *phrasal verb*
► MODERATE
tongue *noun*
► LANGUAGE 1
tool *noun*
► TOOL
tooth *noun*
► **grit your teeth** TIGHTEN *verb*
top *noun*
► LID (the top of my pen)
► PEAK (the top of the range)
► **come out on top** WIN *verb*
top *adj.*
► TOP
the top brass *noun*
► AUTHORITIES
topic *noun*
► SUBJECT
topography *noun*
► COUNTRY 2
topple *verb*
► FALL 2 (a pile topples over)
► REMOVE 2 (topple the govern-
ment)
top up *phrasal verb*
► FILL
torch *noun*
► LIGHT 2
torch *verb* .
► LIGHT 1
tornado *noun*
► STORM
torrent *noun*
► FLOOD 1 (a raging torrent)
► FLOOD 2 (a torrent of abuse)
tortuous *adj.*
► COMPLEX
torture *noun*
► DISTRESS
toss *verb*
► THROW
total *verb*
► BE (Imports totalled $1.5 billion.)
► COUNT (points are totalled)
► CRASH (total a car)
total *adj.*
► COMPLETE (a total disaster)
► WHOLE (the total profit)
totalitarian *adj.*
► REPRESSIVE
totally *adv.*
► QUITE 2
tote *verb*
► CARRY 1
tot up *phrasal verb*
► COUNT

touch *noun*
► ELEMENT 2 (a touch of class)
► TEXTURE (cold to the touch)
► **soft touch** VICTIM 2
touch *verb*
► TOUCH 1 (touch your toes)
► TOUCH 2 (Her feet hardly touched
the ground.)
► APPROACH (The speedometer was
touching 90.)
► IMPRESS (Her story touched us.)
touch down *phrasal verb*
► LAND
touching *adj.*
► MOVING
touchy *adj.*
► SENSITIVE 3
tough *adj.*
► DIFFICULT 2 (a tough childhood)
► STRICT (get tough on crime)
tour *noun*
► TRIP (a coach/walking tour)
► VISIT (a tour of the castle)
tour *verb*
► TOUR
tourism *noun*
► TRAVEL
tourist *noun*
► TOURIST
tournament *noun*
► RACE
tousled *adj.*
► SCRUFFY
tow *verb*
► PULL 1
tower *noun*
► CASTLE
towering *adj.*
► HIGH 2
town *noun*
► CITY
townhouse *noun*
► HOUSE
toxin *noun*
► POISON
trace *noun*
► ELEMENT 2 (He spoke without a
trace of emotion.)
► SIGN 1 (They found no trace of the
boy.)
trace *verb*
► FIND 4
track *noun*
► CLASS 3 (pursue the literature
track at college)
► PATH (a woodland track)
► SONG (an album track)
► TRAIL (fresh tracks in the snow)
► **keep track of sb/sth** MONITOR
verb
track *verb*
► FOLLOW 1 (track and shoot bears)
► MONITOR (track sb/sth's move-
ments)
track down *phrasal verb*
► FIND 4
track record *noun*
► BACKGROUND
tract *noun*
► PAPER (publish a religious tract)
► STRETCH (vast tracts of land)
trade *noun*
► TRADE (international trade)
► INDUSTRY (the building trade)
► WORK 2 (learn a trade)
trade *verb*
► COST (Shares were trading at 95p.)
► REPLACE 2 (trade places with sb)
► SELL 2 (trade in silk/shares)
► **cease trading** CLOSE 2

trade fair noun
- ▶ EXHIBITION

trademark noun
- ▶ LOGO

trade-off noun
- ▶ COMPROMISE

trader noun
- ▶ DEALER

trade show noun
- ▶ EXHIBITION

trading noun
- ▶ TRADE (a day of hectic trading)
- ▶ **cease trading** CLOSE verb 2

tradition noun
- ▶ TRADITION

traditional adj.
- ▶ TRADITIONAL (traditional attitudes)
- ▶ USUAL (traditional Celtic music)

traditionalist adj.
- ▶ CONSERVATIVE

traffic noun
- ▶ TRAFFIC (road traffic)
- ▶ TRANSPORT (air traffic)

traffic jam noun
- ▶ TRAFFIC

trafficking noun
- ▶ TRADE

tragedy noun
- ▶ CRISIS (tragedy strikes)
- ▶ PLAY (a Greek tragedy)

tragic adj.
- ▶ SAD

trail noun
- ▶ TRAIL (a trail of blood)
- ▶ PATH (a nature trail)

trail verb
- ▶ FOLLOW 1 (police trail sb)
- ▶ LOSE (be trailing by five points)
- ▶ PULL 1 (trail your hand in the water)
- ▶ TRUDGE (trail around after sb)

trailer noun
- ▶ ADVERTISEMENT

train verb
- ▶ TRAIN 1 (train as a teacher)
- ▶ TRAIN 2 (train for the Olympics)

trainee noun
- ▶ RECRUIT

trainer noun
- ▶ COACH

training noun
- ▶ TRAINING (be in training for the Olympics)
- ▶ EDUCATION (a training course)

traipse verb
- ▶ TRUDGE

trait noun
- ▶ FEATURE

traitor noun
- ▶ TRAITOR

tramp noun
- ▶ TRAMP

tramp verb
- ▶ TRUDGE

trance noun
- ▶ TRANCE

tranquil adj.
- ▶ QUIET 1

tranquillity (also **tranquility**) noun
- ▶ SILENCE

transcendental adj.
- ▶ MAGIC

transcribe verb
- ▶ WRITE 1

transcript noun
- ▶ COPY 1

transfer verb
- ▶ GIVE 1

transform verb
- ▶ TURN 2

transit noun
- ▶ DELIVERY

transition noun
- ▶ CHANGE 2

translate verb
- ▶ TURN 2

translucent adj.
- ▶ CLEAR 3

transmission noun
- ▶ PROGRAMME

transmit verb
- ▶ CARRY 2 (transmit heat/radiation)
- ▶ PASS STH ON (transmit diseases)

transparent adj.
- ▶ CLEAR 3

transpire verb
- ▶ TURN OUT

transport noun
- ▶ TRANSPORT (public transport)
- ▶ DELIVERY (the transport of raw materials)

transport verb
- ▶ TAKE 1

transportation noun
- ▶ DELIVERY (transportation costs)
- ▶ TRANSPORT (transportation facilities)

trap noun
- ▶ TRICK

trap verb
- ▶ TRAP (Help! I'm trapped!)
- ▶ CATCH (trap an animal)

trash noun
- ▶ RUBBISH (watch trash on TV)
- ▶ WASTE (take out the trash)

trash verb
- ▶ VANDALIZE

trauma noun
- ▶ NIGHTMARE

traumatic adj.
- ▶ PAINFUL 2

traumatize verb
- ▶ FRIGHTEN

travel noun
- ▶ TRAVEL (foreign travel)
- ▶ TRIP (his travels in Asia)

travel verb
- ▶ GO 1 (The car was travelling north.)
- ▶ GO 2 (travel across the US)

traveller (also **traveler**) noun
- ▶ TRAVELLER (New Age travellers)
- ▶ PASSENGER (a regular traveller)

travelling (also **traveling**) noun
- ▶ TRAVEL

travelling (also **traveling**) adj.
- ▶ TRAVELLING

treacherous adj.
- ▶ TREACHEROUS (treacherous words)
- ▶ DANGEROUS (treacherous driving conditions)

tread noun
- ▶ WALK

tread verb
- ▶ WALK 1

treason noun
- ▶ BETRAYAL

treasure verb
- ▶ APPRECIATE

treasured adj.
- ▶ DEAR

treat noun
- ▶ PLEASURE

treat verb
- ▶ TREAT 1 (treat an illness)
- ▶ TREAT 2 (The crops are treated with insecticide.)
- ▶ APPLY 2 (The question is treated in more detail in the next chapter.)
- ▶ BEHAVE (treat people with respect)

treatise noun
- ▶ PAPER

treatment noun
- ▶ TREATMENT

treaty noun
- ▶ CONTRACT

treble adj.
- ▶ HIGH 3

trek verb
- ▶ TRUDGE (trek up four flights of stairs)
- ▶ WALK 2 (go trekking in Nepal)

tremble noun
- ▶ SHIVER

tremble verb
- ▶ SHAKE 3

tremendous adj.
- ▶ GREAT 1 (a tremendous experience)
- ▶ HUGE (tremendous pressure)

tremor noun
- ▶ SHIVER

trench noun
- ▶ DITCH

trend noun
- ▶ TREND (social trends)
- ▶ FASHION (fashion trends)

trendy adj.
- ▶ FASHIONABLE

trial noun
- ▶ CASE (trial by jury)
- ▶ INTERVIEW 2 (Olympic trials)
- ▶ TEST 1 (drug trials/a trial period)

tribal adj.
- ▶ CULTURAL

tribe noun
- ▶ PEOPLE 2

tribunal noun
- ▶ COURT

tributary noun
- ▶ RIVER

tribute noun
- ▶ TRIBUTE

trick noun
- ▶ TRICK

trick verb
- ▶ CHEAT

trickle noun
- ▶ FLOW

trickle verb
- ▶ TRICKLE

tricky adj.
- ▶ SENSITIVE 2

trigger verb
- ▶ PROMPT

trim verb
- ▶ CUT 3 (trim sb's beard)
- ▶ DECORATE (trimmed with fur)

trinket noun
- ▶ ORNAMENT

trip noun
- ▶ TRIP

trip verb
- ▶ FALL 3

trite adj.
- ▶ TIRED 2

triumph noun
- ▶ WORK 3

triumph verb
- ▶ WIN

triumphant adj.
- ▶ SUCCESSFUL 1

trivial adj.
- ▶ MINOR

trivialize verb
- ▶ UNDERSTATE

troop verb
- ▶ TRUDGE

trooper noun
- ▶ POLICEMAN

trophy noun
- ▶ AWARD

trot verb
- ▶ RUN 1

trouble noun
- ▶ TROUBLE 1 (A few drunks were causing trouble.)
- ▶ TROUBLE 2 (get/run into trouble)
- ▶ DIFFICULTY (go to the trouble of doing sth)
- ▶ ILLNESS (back trouble)
- ▶ PROBLEM (The only trouble is…)

trouble verb
- ▶ INTERRUPT (Sorry to trouble you.)
- ▶ WORRY 2 (Is something troubling you?)

troubled adj.
- ▶ WORRIED

trough noun
- ▶ RECESSION

trounce verb
- ▶ DEFEAT

truck noun
- ▶ CAR (a truck driver)
- ▶ CARRIAGE 1 (a railway truck)

trudge verb
- ▶ TRUDGE

true adj.
- ▶ TRUE (a true story)
- ▶ REAL (true love)
- ▶ RELIABLE 1 (true to his word)

truly adv.
- ▶ VERY

trump up phrasal verb
- ▶ INVENT

trunk noun
- ▶ SUITCASE

trust noun
- ▶ CHARITY (a charitable trust)
- ▶ FAITH (earn/betray sb's trust)

trust verb
- ▶ TRUST

trusted adj.
- ▶ RELIABLE 1

trusting adj.
- ▶ NAIVE

trustworthy adj.
- ▶ RELIABLE 1

truth noun
- ▶ TRUTH (no truth in the rumours)
- ▶ FACT (the truth of the matter)

truthful adj.
- ▶ HONEST

try noun
- ▶ ATTEMPT

try verb
- ▶ TRY 1 (try to do sth)
- ▶ TRY 2 (try doing sth)

trying adj.
- ▶ ANNOYING

try out phrasal verb
- ▶ TEST 1

tryout noun
- ▶ INTERVIEW 2

tsunami noun
- ▶ FLOOD 1

tub noun
- ▶ BARREL (tubs of flowers)
- ▶ PACKET (a tub of margarine)

tube *noun*
▸ PACKET (a tube of toothpaste)
▸ PIPE (a bike's inner tube)

tuck *verb*
▸ FOLD (tuck your shirt in)
▸ INSERT (The letter had been tucked under a pile of papers.)

tuck in *phrasal verb*
▸ EAT

tug *verb*
▸ PULL 1 (tug sb along)
▸ PULL 3 (tug at sb's sleeve)

tuition *noun*
▸ EDUCATION

tumble *verb*
▸ FALL 2 (The scaffolding came tumbling down.)
▸ SLUMP (prices tumble)

tummy *noun*
▸ STOMACH

tumour (also **tumor**) *noun*
▸ TUMOUR

tune *noun*
▸ SONG

tune in *phrasal verb*
▸ HEAR

turban *noun*
▸ HAT

turbulence *noun*
▸ DISRUPTION

turbulent *adj.*
▸ ROUGH 2

turf *noun*
▸ GRASS

turmoil *noun*
▸ DISRUPTION

turn *noun*
▸ CORNER (make a left turn)
▸ JUNCTION (take the next turn)
▸ OPPORTUNITY (Wait your turn.)

turn *verb*
▸ TURN 1 (turn your head away)
▸ TURN 2 (turn sb into a frog)
▸ AIM (turn a gun on sb)
▸ BECOME (turn brown/cold/sour)
▸ CURVE (The road turns east.)
▸ FOCUS (turn your attention to sth)
▸ SPIN (turn the wheel)

turn around *phrasal verb*
▸ TURN 1

turnaround *noun*
▸ REVOLUTION 2

turn back *phrasal verb*
▸ RETURN 1

turn down *phrasal verb*
▸ REDUCE (turn the volume down)
▸ REFUSE (turn down an invitation)

turning *noun*
▸ JUNCTION

turning point *noun*
▸ TURNING POINT

turn off *phrasal verb*
▸ TURN STH OFF

turn on *phrasal verb*
▸ TURN STH ON

turn out *phrasal verb*
▸ TURN OUT (turn out to be true)
▸ HAPPEN (turn out well)
▸ MANUFACTURE (The school turned out some fine students.)
▸ TURN STH OFF (turn out the lights)

turn over *phrasal verb*
▸ ROLL

turnover *noun*
▸ REVENUE

turn over to *phrasal verb*
▸ LEAVE 6

turnpike *noun*
▸ HIGHWAY

turn round *phrasal verb*
▸ TURN 1

turnstile *noun*
▸ DOOR

turn up *phrasal verb*
▸ ARRIVE (turn up for work)
▸ FIND 2 (If I turn anything up, I'll let you know.)
▸ INCREASE (turn the music up)

tussle *noun*
▸ FIGHT

tutor *noun*
▸ TEACHER

tutor *verb*
▸ TEACH

tutorial *noun*
▸ CLASS 2

tutoring *noun*
▸ EDUCATION

tuxedo (also **tux**) *noun*
▸ COAT

twice *adv.*
▸ **think twice** HESITATE

twilight *noun*
▸ NIGHT 2

twinkle *verb*
▸ SHINE

twirl *verb*
▸ SPIN

twist *noun*
▸ CORNER

twist *verb*
▸ TWIST (twist metal)
▸ CURVE (a road twists and turns)
▸ INJURE (twist your ankle)
▸ SPIN (twist the handle)
▸ TURN 1 (twist your head)
▸ WRAP SB/STH AROUND/ROUND SB/STH (The cable was twisted.)
▸ WRIGGLE (twist and turn in your sleep)
▸ **twist sb's arm** PRESS 2

twisted *adj.*
▸ BENT

twister *noun*
▸ STORM

twitch *noun*
▸ SHIVER

twitch *verb*
▸ SHAKE 3

two-faced *adj.*
▸ DISHONEST

tycoon *noun*
▸ EXECUTIVE

type *noun*
▸ KIND (a blood type)
▸ PERSON (He's not my type.)

typhoon *noun*
▸ STORM

typical *adj.*
▸ TYPICAL (a typical French cafe)
▸ NORMAL (the typical day)

typify *verb*
▸ REPRESENT 2

tyrannical *adj.*
▸ REPRESSIVE

tyrannize *verb*
▸ DICTATE TO SB

tyranny *noun*
▸ REPRESSION

tyrant *noun*
▸ DICTATOR

tzar *noun*
▸ KING

U u

ubiquitous *adj.*
▸ GENERAL 1

ugly *adj.*
▸ UGLY

ulcer *noun*
▸ TUMOUR

ultimate *adj.*
▸ FUNDAMENTAL (the ultimate truth)
▸ LAST 1 (the ultimate goal)

umbrella *adj.*
▸ OVERALL

umpire *noun*
▸ JUDGE 2

unabashed *adj.*
▸ COOL

unacceptable *adj.*
▸ UNACCEPTABLE

unaccompanied *adj.*
▸ ALONE

unaccustomed to *adj.*
▸ NEW 3

unaided *adj., adv.*
▸ ALONE

unambiguous *adj.*
▸ CLEAR 2

unanimity *noun*
▸ AGREEMENT 2

unappealing *adj.*
▸ UNATTRACTIVE

unappetizing *adj.*
▸ UNATTRACTIVE

unashamed *adj.*
▸ COOL

unassuming *adj.*
▸ MODEST

unattainable *adj.*
▸ IMPOSSIBLE

unattended *adj.*
▸ ALONE

unattractive *adj.*
▸ UNATTRACTIVE (an unattractive character)
▸ UGLY (an unattractive smile)

unauthorized *adj.*
▸ UNOFFICIAL

unavoidable *adj.*
▸ INEVITABLE

unaware *adj.*
▸ UNAWARE

unbalanced *adj.*
▸ BIASED

unbearable *adj.*
▸ UNACCEPTABLE

unbelievable *adj.*
▸ INCREDIBLE (seem unbelievable)
▸ REMARKABLE (an unbelievable feeling)

unbiased *adj.*
▸ OBJECTIVE

unbroken *adj.*
▸ CONTINUOUS

unbutton *verb*
▸ UNDO

uncanny *adj.*
▸ STRANGE 1

uncaring *adj.*
▸ INSENSITIVE

uncertain *adj.*
▸ UNCERTAIN (an uncertain future)
▸ HESITANT (uncertain steps)
▸ UNCLEAR (It is uncertain what…)
▸ UNSURE (uncertain about sth)

uncertainty *noun*
▸ DOUBT 1 (uncertainty about the future)
▸ DOUBT 2 (life's uncertainties)

unchallenged *adj.*
▸ UNDOUBTED

unchanging *adj.*
▸ STEADY

unclear *adj.*
▸ UNCLEAR

uncluttered *adj.*
▸ NEAT

uncomfortable *adj.*
▸ EMBARRASSED

uncommon *adj.*
▸ RARE

uncomplicated *adj.*
▸ EASY 1

unconditional *adj.*
▸ PURE 2

unconfirmed *adj.*
▸ IRRATIONAL

unconnected *adj.*
▸ INDEPENDENT

unconscious *adj.*
▸ UNCONSCIOUS

unconstitutional *adj.*
▸ ILLEGAL

uncontested *adj.*
▸ UNDOUBTED

uncontrollable *adj.*
▸ UNCONTROLLABLE

unconventional *adj.*
▸ UNUSUAL

unconvincing *adj.*
▸ UNLIKELY 2

uncooked *adj.*
▸ FRESH

uncooperative *adj.*
▸ PERVERSE

uncover *verb*
▸ REVEAL

undecided *adj.*
▸ UNCLEAR (The issue remains undecided.)
▸ UNSURE (I'm still undecided.)

undemanding *adj.*
▸ EASY 1

undemocratic *adj.*
▸ REPRESSIVE

undeniable *adj.*
▸ CONCLUSIVE

underachiever *noun*
▸ LOSER 2

undercover *adj.*
▸ SECRET 1

undercurrent *noun*
▸ ASSOCIATION

undergo *verb*
▸ HAVE 3

underground *adj.*
▸ SECRET 2

underhand *adj.*
▸ DISHONEST

underline *verb*
▸ STRESS

underlying *adj.*
▸ FUNDAMENTAL

undermine *verb*
▸ UNDERMINE

underscore *verb*
▸ STRESS

understand *verb*
▸ UNDERSTAND 1 (understand French/how sth works)
▸ UNDERSTAND 2 (understand how sb feels)
▸ AGREE 3 (I thought it was understood that I would be paid.)
▸ CONCLUDE (Am I to understand that you refuse?)

understandable *adj.*
▸ OBVIOUS

understanding *noun*
▸ UNDERSTANDING (show great understanding of sth)
▸ AGREEMENT 1 (come to an understanding with sb about sth)
▸ DEFINITION (sb's understanding of the situation)

▸ SYMPATHY (show understanding towards sb)

understanding adj.
▸ SENSITIVE 1

understate verb
▸ UNDERSTATE

understudy noun
▸ REPLACEMENT

undertake verb
▸ DO 1 (undertake an investigation)
▸ PROMISE (They undertook to finish the job by Friday.)

undertaking noun
▸ PROJECT

underweight adj.
▸ THIN

underwrite verb
▸ FUND

undeserved adj.
▸ UNJUSTIFIED

undesirable adj.
▸ UNWANTED

undignified adj.
▸ IMPROPER

undisclosed adj.
▸ SECRET 1

undisputed adj.
▸ UNDOUBTED

undistinguished adj.
▸ MEDIOCRE

undivided adj.
▸ PURE 2

undo verb
▸ UNDO (undo a button)
▸ REVERSE (undo the damage)

undoing noun
▸ OVERTHROW

undoubted adj.
▸ UNDOUBTED

undress verb
▸ TAKE STH OFF (She undressed and got into bed.)
▸ **get undressed** TAKE STH OFF

undressed adj.
▸ NAKED

undue adj.
▸ EXCESSIVE

unearth verb
▸ FIND 2

unease noun
▸ CONCERN

uneasy adj.
▸ WORRIED

uneconomic adj.
▸ LOSS-MAKING

uneducated adj.
▸ IGNORANT

unemotional adj.
▸ BLANK

unemployed adj.
▸ UNEMPLOYED

unemployment noun
▸ UNEMPLOYMENT

unequal adj.
▸ WRONG 4

unequivocal adj.
▸ PLAIN 4

unethical adj.
▸ WRONG 4

uneven adj.
▸ ROUGH 1 (an uneven floor)
▸ VARIABLE (uneven breathing)

uneventful adj.
▸ PREDICTABLE 2

unexciting adj.
▸ PREDICTABLE 2

unexpected adj.
▸ SURPRISING

unfair adj.
▸ WRONG 4

unfairness noun
▸ INEQUALITY

unfaithful adj.
▸ TREACHEROUS

unfamiliar adj.
▸ NEW 3 (sb is unfamiliar with sth)
▸ STRANGE 2 (an unfamiliar place)

unfasten verb
▸ UNDO

unfavourable (also **unfavorable**) adj.
▸ DIFFICULT 2

unfazed adj.
▸ CALM

unfinished adj.
▸ PARTIAL

unfit adj.
▸ WRONG 3 (unfit to rule)
▸ SICK 1 (feel unfit)

unfold verb
▸ DESCRIBE (a story unfolds)
▸ SPREAD (unfold a letter)

unforeseeable adj.
▸ SURPRISING

unforeseen adj.
▸ SURPRISING

unforgivable adj.
▸ OUTRAGEOUS

unforgiving adj.
▸ STERN

unfortunate adj.
▸ UNFORTUNATE 1 (an unfortunate person)
▸ UNFORTUNATE 2 (an unfortunate situation)

unfounded adj.
▸ IRRATIONAL

unfriendly adj.
▸ COLD 2

unhappiness noun
▸ GRIEF

unhappy adj.
▸ UNHAPPY 1 (an unhappy childhood)
▸ UNHAPPY 2 (unhappy with their accommodation)

unharmed adj.
▸ SAFE 1

unhealthy adj.
▸ UNHEALTHY (an unhealthy diet)
▸ SICK 1 (sb looks unhealthy)

unhelpful adj.
▸ PERVERSE

unhurried adj.
▸ EASY 2

unhurt adj.
▸ SAFE 1

unhygienic adj.
▸ UNHEALTHY

uniform adj.
▸ EQUAL

uniformity noun
▸ SIMILARITY

unify verb
▸ COMBINE

unimaginative adj.
▸ LACKLUSTRE

unimportant adj.
▸ MINOR

unimpressed adj.
▸ INDIFFERENT

uninformed adj.
▸ IGNORANT

uninhabited adj.
▸ DESERTED

uninhibited adj.
▸ SOCIABLE

uninjured adj.
▸ SAFE 1

uninspiring adj.
▸ PREDICTABLE 2

unintelligible adj.
▸ CONFUSING

unintended adj.
▸ UNCONSCIOUS

unintentional adj.
▸ UNCONSCIOUS

uninterested adj.
▸ INDIFFERENT

uninteresting adj.
▸ BORING

uninterrupted adj.
▸ CONTINUOUS

uninvited adj.
▸ UNWANTED

union noun
▸ UNION (a trade union)
▸ REPUBLIC (the former Soviet Union)

uniqeness noun
▸ IDENTITY

unique adj.
▸ UNIQUE (a unique 6-digit code)
▸ REMARKABLE (a unique opportunity)

unit noun
▸ ARMY (enemy units)
▸ CHAPTER (The present perfect is covered in Unit 8.)
▸ CUPBOARD (kitchen units)
▸ DEPARTMENT (the intensive care unit)
▸ ELEMENT 1 (the basic unit of society)
▸ MACHINE (a waste disposal unit)

unite verb
▸ COMBINE

unity noun
▸ AGREEMENT 2

universal adj.
▸ GENERAL 1

universe noun
▸ SPACE 2

university noun
▸ SCHOOL

unjust verb
▸ WRONG 4

unjustifiable adj.
▸ UNJUSTIFIED

unjustified adj.
▸ UNJUSTIFIED

unkempt adj.
▸ SCRUFFY

unkind adj.
▸ MEAN 1

unknown noun
▸ STRANGE 2

unlawful adj.
▸ ILLEGAL

unlicensed adj.
▸ UNOFFICIAL

unlike prep., adj.
▸ DIFFERENT

unlikely adj.
▸ UNLIKELY 1 (unlikely to succeed)
▸ UNLIKELY 2 (an unlikely explanation)

unlit adj.
▸ DARK 1

unload verb
▸ CLEAR

unloved adj.
▸ UNWANTED

unlucky adj.
▸ UNFORTUNATE 1

unmanageable adj.
▸ UNCONTROLLABLE

unmarried adj.
▸ SINGLE

unmistakable adj.
▸ MARKED

unmitigated adj.
▸ PURE 2

unmoved adj.
▸ RUTHLESS

unnecessary adj.
▸ UNNECESSARY (All this fuss is totally unnecessary.)
▸ UNJUSTIFIED (unnecessary comments)

unnerve verb
▸ SHAKE 4

unnerving adj.
▸ WORRYING

unoccupied adj.
▸ DESERTED

unofficial adj.
▸ UNOFFICIAL

unorthodox adj.
▸ UNUSUAL

unpack verb
▸ CLEAR

unpaid adj.
▸ VOLUNTARY 2

unperturbed adj.
▸ CALM

unplanned adj.
▸ UNCONSCIOUS

unpleasant adj.
▸ BAD (an unpleasant smell)
▸ MEAN 1 (be unpleasant to sb)

unplug verb
▸ TURN STH OFF

unpopular adj.
▸ UNWANTED

unpredictable adj.
▸ MOODY (an unpredictable personality)
▸ SURPRISING (unpredictable weather)

unpretentious adj.
▸ MODEST

unprincipled adj.
▸ CORRUPT

unproductive adj.
▸ INEFFECTIVE

unprofitable adj.
▸ LOSS-MAKING

unqualified adj.
▸ PURE 2

unquestionable adj.
▸ CONCLUSIVE

unquestioned adj.
▸ UNDOUBTED

unreadable adj.
▸ BLANK

unrealistic adj.
▸ UNREALISTIC

unreasonable adj.
▸ HIGH 1 (unreasonable prices)
▸ UNACCEPTABLE (unreasonable behaviour/demands)

unrelated noun
▸ INDEPENDENT

unremarkable adj.
▸ AVERAGE

unresolved adj.
▸ UNCLEAR

unrest noun
▸ TROUBLE 1

unroll verb
▸ SPREAD

unruly adj.
▸ WILD 1

unsafe *adj.*
▸ DANGEROUS
unsanitary *adj.*
▸ UNHEALTHY
unsatisfactory *adj.*
▸ DISAPPOINTING
unsavoury (also **unsavory**) *adj.*
▸ SORDID
unscathed *adj.*
▸ SAFE 1
unscientific *adj.*
▸ IRRATIONAL
unscrupulous *adj.*
▸ CORRUPT
unseemly *adj.*
▸ IMPROPER
unsettle *verb*
▸ WORRY 2
unsettled *adj.*
▸ RESTLESS (feel unsettled)
▸ UNCERTAIN (unsettled times)
unsettling *adj.*
▸ WORRYING
unshaven *adj.*
▸ HAIRY
unsightly *adj.*
▸ UGLY
unsociable *adj.*
▸ SOLITARY
unsolicited *adj.*
▸ UNWANTED
unspoiled *adj.*
▸ PERFECT
unstable *adj.*
▸ MENTALLY ILL (emotionally unstable)
▸ UNCERTAIN (an unstable situation)
unsubstantiated *adj.*
▸ IRRATIONAL
unsuccessful *adj.*
▸ UNSUCCESSFUL
unsuitable *adj.*
▸ WRONG 3
unsupported *adj.*
▸ IRRATIONAL
unsure *adj.*
▸ UNSURE
unsurprising *adj.*
▸ PREDICTABLE 1
unsuspecting *adj.*
▸ UNAWARE
unsympathetic *adj.*
▸ INSENSITIVE
unsystematic *adj.*
▸ RANDOM
untenable *adj.*
▸ UNJUSTIFIED
unthinkable *adj.*
▸ IMPOSSIBLE
unthinking *adj.*
▸ INSENSITIVE
untidy *adj.*
▸ UNTIDY (an untidy desk)
▸ RANDOM (He's so untidy.)
untie *verb*
▸ UNDO
untrained *adj.*
▸ IGNORANT
untried *adj.*
▸ NEW 2
untrue *adj.*
▸ WRONG 1
unusable *adj.*
▸ USELESS
unused to *adj.*
▸ NEW 3
unusual *adj.*
▸ UNUSUAL (an unusual name)
▸ REMARKABLE (an unusual degree of interest)
unveil *verb*
▸ PRESENT 1

unwanted *adj.*
▸ UNWANTED
unwarranted *adj.*
▸ UNJUSTIFIED
unwashed *adj.*
▸ DIRTY
unwelcome *adj.*
▸ UNWANTED
unwell *adj.*
▸ SICK 1
unwilling *adj.*
▸ RELUCTANT
unwind *verb*
▸ REST
unwise *adj.*
▸ RECKLESS
unwitting *adj.*
▸ UNAWARE
unworkable *adj.*
▸ UNREALISTIC
unwrap *verb*
▸ UNDO
unzip *verb*
▸ UNDO
up *adv.*
▸ WRONG *adj.* 2
upbeat *adj.*
▸ OPTIMISTIC
upbringing *noun*
▸ BACKGROUND
upcoming *adj.*
▸ NEXT
upheaval *noun*
▸ DISRUPTION
uphold *verb*
▸ APPROVE
upkeep *noun*
▸ REPAIR
uplift *verb*
▸ ENCOURAGE 1
uplifting *adj.*
▸ MOVING
upper *adj.*
▸ **the upper hand** LEAD *noun* 2
the upper class *noun*
▸ ELITE
upper class *adj.*
▸ ARISTOCRATIC
upright *adj.*
▸ UPRIGHT
uprising *noun*
▸ REVOLUTION 1
uproar *noun*
▸ CHAOS (The trial ended in uproar.)
▸ FUSS (provoke an uproar from environmentalists)
upset *noun*
▸ VICTORY
upset *verb*
▸ DISRUPT (upset sb's plans)
▸ HURT 1 (Don't upset yourself.)
upset *adj.*
▸ UPSET
upsetting *adj.*
▸ PAINFUL 2
upshot *noun*
▸ RESULT
uptight *adj.*
▸ TENSE
up to date *adj.*
▸ MODERN (up-to-date equipment)
▸ USED TO STH (up to date with the issues)
urbane *adj.*
▸ SOPHISTICATED
urge *noun*
▸ DESIRE
urge *verb*
▸ ENCOURAGE 2 (urge sb to do sth)
▸ RECOMMEND 1 (urge caution)
urgency *noun*
▸ IMPORTANCE
urgent *adj.*
▸ URGENT

urinal *noun*
▸ TOILET
usable *adj.*
▸ USEFUL
usage *noun*
▸ LANGUAGE 2
use *noun*
▸ USE (software for use in schools)
▸ FUNCTION (I'm sure you'll think of a use for it.)
▸ **make use of sb/sth** USE *verb* 1
▸ **of use** USEFUL *adj.*
use *verb*
▸ USE 1 (use a computer/the bus)
▸ USE 2 (use electricity/all the milk)
▸ EXPLOIT (I felt used.)
▸ TAKE 9 (use drugs)
used to *adj.*
▸ USED TO STH
useful *adj.*
▸ USEFUL
useless *adj.*
▸ USELESS (useless to protest)
▸ INCOMPETENT (useless at French)
use up *phrasal verb*
▸ USE 2
usher *verb*
▸ TAKE 2
usual *adj.*
▸ USUAL
usually *adv.*
▸ USUALLY
usurp *verb*
▸ REMOVE 2
utensil *noun*
▸ TOOL
utility *noun*
▸ FACILITIES
utilize *verb*
▸ USE 1
utmost *adj.*
▸ MAXIMUM
utter *adj.*
▸ COMPLETE
utterly *adv.*
▸ QUITE 2
U-turn *noun*
▸ REVOLUTION 2 (an embarrassing U-turn on education policy)
▸ **do a U-turn** BREAK *verb* 4

V v

vacancy *noun*
▸ JOB
vacant *adj.*
▸ EMPTY
vacate *verb*
▸ ABANDON
vacation *noun*
▸ HOLIDAY 1 (the summer vacation)
▸ HOLIDAY 2 (a ski vacation)
vacationer *noun*
▸ TOURIST
vagaries *noun*
▸ EXCEPTION
vagrant *noun*
▸ TRAMP
vague *adj.*
▸ VAGUE
vain *adj.*
▸ PROUD 2 (too vain to wear glasses)
▸ USELESS (a vain attempt)
▸ **in vain** USELESS
valet *noun*
▸ SERVANT
valid *adj.*
▸ GOOD 3 (a valid reason/argument)
▸ LEGAL (a valid passport/ticket)
validate *verb*
▸ APPROVE (officially validated courses)
▸ CONFIRM 1 (validate a claim)

valley *noun*
▸ VALLEY
valour (also **valor**) *noun*
▸ COURAGE
valuable *adj.*
▸ VALUABLE 1 (valuable possessions)
▸ VALUABLE 2 (a valuable experience)
valuables *noun*
▸ THING 3
valuation *noun*
▸ VALUATION
value *noun*
▸ VALUE 1 (the value of regular exercise)
▸ VALUE 2 (good value for money)
▸ VALUES (moral values)
▸ PRICE (property values)
value *verb*
▸ APPRECIATE (I value him as a friend.)
▸ PRICE (I got my violin valued.)
van *noun*
▸ CAR (a van driver)
▸ CARRIAGE 1 (the luggage van)
vandal *noun*
▸ HOOLIGAN
vandalize *verb*
▸ VANDALIZE
vanish *verb*
▸ DISAPPEAR
vanity *noun*
▸ PRIDE
vanquish *verb*
▸ DEFEAT
variability *noun*
▸ CHANGE 1
variable *adj.*
▸ VARIABLE
variance *noun*
▸ DIFFERENCE
variation *noun*
▸ CHANGE 1 (slight variations in pressure)
▸ DIFFERENCE (variation in tastes across the country)
varied *adj.*
▸ DIVERSE
variety *noun*
▸ KIND (a rare variety of orchid)
▸ RANGE 1 (a variety of patterns to choose from)
vary *verb*
▸ CHANGE 1 (vary your routine)
▸ CHANGE 2 (The menu varies with the season.)
▸ DIFFER (The students' work varies considerably in quality.)
vast *adj.*
▸ HUGE
vat *noun*
▸ BARREL
vault *verb*
▸ JUMP 1
vaulted *adj.*
▸ CURVED
vehicle *noun*
▸ CAR (motor vehicles)
▸ MEDIUM (a vehicle for sb's talents)
Velcro™ *noun*
▸ BUTTON 2
velocity *noun*
▸ SPEED
vendor *noun*
▸ DEALER
venerate *verb*
▸ PRAY
vengeance *noun*
▸ REVENGE
venom *noun*
▸ POISON
venture *noun*
▸ PROJECT

venture *verb*
▶ DARE

venue *noun*
▶ PLACE 1

verdict *noun*
▶ CONCLUSION

verge on *phrasal verb*
▶ APPROACH

verifiable *adj.*
▶ RELIABLE 2

verify *verb*
▶ CHECK 2 (We have no way of verifying his story.)
▶ CONFIRM 2 (Her version of events was verified by neighbours.)

versatile *adj.*
▶ FLEXIBLE 1

version *noun*
▶ KIND (the latest version of the operating system)
▶ REPORT 2 (her version of what happened)

vertical *adj.*
▶ UPRIGHT

very *adj.*
▶ VERY

very *adv.*
▶ VERY

vessel *noun*
▶ BOAT

vest *noun*
▶ COAT

veteran *adj.*
▶ EXPERIENCED

veto *noun*
▶ BAN (a veto on employing new staff)
▶ REFUSAL (have the right of veto)

veto *verb*
▶ REFUSE

viable *adj.*
▶ POSSIBLE 1

vial *noun*
▶ BOTTLE

vibrant *adj.*
▶ BRIGHT (vibrant colours)
▶ CROWDED (a vibrant city)

vibrate *verb*
▶ SHAKE 2

vice *noun*
▶ CRIME 1 (the vice squad)
▶ EVIL (a life of vice)
▶ WEAKNESS 2 (her only vice)

vicinity *noun*
▶ PROXIMITY

vicious *adj.*
▶ VICIOUS (vicious in its criticism)
▶ CRUEL (a vicious assault)

vicious circle *noun*
▶ MESS 2

victim *noun*
▶ VICTIM 1 (victims of crime)
▶ VICTIM 2 (victims of a cruel hoax)
▶ PATIENT (AIDS victims)

victimize *verb*
▶ BULLY

victor *noun*
▶ WINNER

victorious *adj.*
▶ SUCCESSFUL 1

victory *noun*
▶ VICTORY

video *noun*
▶ FILM 1

video *verb*
▶ RECORD 2

vie *verb*
▶ COMPETE

view *noun*
▶ VIEW 1 (sb's political views)
▶ VIEW 2 (a delightful sea view)
▶ ATTITUDE (an optimistic view)
▶ SIGHT (a good view of the stage)
▶ **in view** VISIBLE *adj.*

view *verb*
▶ CHECK 1 (view a property before buying)
▶ LOOK 1 (view an eclipse)
▶ REGARD (view sth with caution)

viewer *noun*
▶ AUDIENCE

vigil *noun*
▶ WATCH

vigorous *adj.*
▶ ENERGETIC

vigour (also **vigor**) *noun*
▶ ENERGY 2

vile *adj.*
▶ TERRIBLE 1

vilify *verb*
▶ DISCREDIT

villa *noun*
▶ PALACE

village *noun*
▶ CITY

villain *noun*
▶ VILLAIN

vindicate *verb*
▶ ACQUIT

vindictive *adj.*
▶ VICIOUS

vineyard *noun*
▶ FARM

violate *verb*
▶ BREAK 3

violent *adj.*
▶ VIOLENT (a violent man/crime)
▶ INTENSE (a violent reaction)
▶ ROUGH 2 (a violent storm)

VIP *noun*
▶ VIP

virtual *adj.*
▶ FICTIONAL

virtually *adv.*
▶ ALMOST

virtue *noun*
▶ BENEFIT 1 (the virtue of simplicity)
▶ MORALITY (a life of virtue)

virtuoso *adj.*
▶ IMPRESSIVE

virtuous *adj.*
▶ GOOD 5

virus *noun*
▶ DEFECT (a computer virus)
▶ DISEASE (pick up a virus)

visible *adj.*
▶ VISIBLE

vision *noun*
▶ DREAM (a prophetic vision)
▶ IMAGINATION (I had visions of us getting hopelessly lost.)
▶ INSPIRATION (a leader of great vision)
▶ SIGHT (sb's field of vision)

visionary *noun*
▶ VISIONARY

visit *noun*
▶ VISIT

visit *verb*
▶ VISIT (visit an old friend)
▶ CHECK 1 (inspectors visit a school)
▶ STAY 2 (visit the States)

visitor *noun*
▶ VISITOR (You've got a visitor.)
▶ TOURIST (overseas visitors)

visualize *verb*
▶ IMAGINE

vital *adj.*
▶ ESSENTIAL

vitality *noun*
▶ ENERGY 2

vivacious *adj.*
▶ LIVELY

vivid *adj.*
▶ BRIGHT

vocabulary *noun*
▶ LANGUAGE 2

vocation *noun*
▶ MISSION

vogue *noun*
▶ FASHION

voice *noun*
▶ VOICE (speak in a loud voice)
▶ **raise your voice** SHOUT *verb*

voice *verb*
▶ SAY 2

volatile *adj.*
▶ MOODY (volatile behaviour)
▶ UNCERTAIN (a volatile situation)

volley *noun*
▶ FLOOD 2

volume *noun*
▶ BOOK (a volume of poetry)
▶ CHAPTER (an encyclopedia in 20 volumes)
▶ NUMBER 1 (a huge volume of traffic)
▶ SIZE (the volume of a gas/jar)
▶ SOUND 2 (turn down the volume)

voluntary *adj.*
▶ VOLUNTARY 1 (Attendance at classes is purely voluntary.)
▶ VOLUNTARY 2 (voluntary work)

volunteer *verb*
▶ OFFER 1 (volunteer information)
▶ OFFER 2 (volunteer to do sth)

vomit *verb*
▶ VOMIT

voracious *adj.*
▶ GREEDY

vote *noun*
▶ ELECTION

vote *verb*
▶ SUPPORT 1

vote in, vote into/onto *phrasal verb*
▶ APPOINT

voter *noun*
▶ CITIZEN (60% of eligible voters)
▶ SUPPORTER (Conservative voters)

vouch for *phrasal verb*
▶ CONFIRM 2

vow *noun*
▶ PROMISE

vow *verb*
▶ PROMISE

voyage *noun*
▶ CRUISE

vulnerable *adj.*
▶ VULNERABLE

W w

wad *noun*
▶ ROLL

waft *verb*
▶ BLOW 1

wag *verb*
▶ SHAKE 1

wage *noun*
▶ INCOME

wage *verb*
▶ FIGHT 1

wagon *noun*
▶ CARRIAGE 1 (a railway wagon)
▶ CARRIAGE 2 (a hay wagon)

wail *verb*
▶ SCREAM

waistcoat *noun*
▶ COAT

wait *verb*
▶ WAIT (Wait for me!)
▶ DELAY (This letter isn't urgent so it can wait.)
▶ HOPE (the opportunity I've been waiting for)
▶ **be waiting** READY *adj.*

waive *verb*
▶ GIVE STH UP

wake *verb*
▶ WAKE UP

wake up *phrasal verb*
▶ WAKE UP

walk *noun*
▶ WALK

walk *verb*
▶ WALK 1 (walk into the room)
▶ WALK 2 (go walking in the mountains)
▶ TAKE 2 (walk sb home)

walk out *phrasal verb*
▶ LEAVE 5

walkway *noun*
▶ CORRIDOR

wall *noun*
▶ WALL

wallet *noun*
▶ WALLET

wallow in *phrasal verb*
▶ ENJOY

wan *adj.*
▶ PALE 1

wander *verb*
▶ WANDER

want *noun*
▶ DESIRE (the wants of her children)
▶ NEED (satisfy your bodily wants)

want *verb*
▶ WANT (Do you want some more?)
▶ ATTRACTED TO SB ('I want you so much,' he whispered.)
▶ NEED (The plants want watering.)

wanting *adj.*
▶ DISAPPOINTING

war *noun*
▶ WAR (countries at war)
▶ CAMPAIGN (the war on drugs)
▶ DEBATE (a trade war)

ward off *verb*
▶ FEND SB/STH OFF

wardrobe *noun*
▶ CLOTHES (your summer/winter wardrobe)
▶ CUPBOARD (a pine wardrobe)

warehouse *noun*
▶ WAREHOUSE

warfare *noun*
▶ WAR

warlike *adj.*
▶ AGGRESSIVE 1

warm *verb*
▶ HEAT

warm *adj.*
▶ DARK 2 (warm colours)
▶ FRIENDLY 1 (a warm welcome)
▶ HOT (warm water)

warmth *noun*
▶ HEAT 1

warm up *phrasal verb*
▶ HEAT (the weather warms up)
▶ TRAIN 2 (warm up before a match)

warn *verb*
▶ WARN

warning *noun*
▶ WARNING

warn off *phrasal verb*
▶ DISCOURAGE 1 (We were warned off buying the house.)
▶ THREATEN 1 (He warned us off his land.)

warp *verb*
▶ TWIST

warrant *noun*
▶ LICENCE

warrior *noun*
▶ SOLDIER

wash *noun*
▶ BATH

wash *verb*
▶ WASH (I washed and changed before going out.)
▶ CLEAN (wash the car/dishes)
▶ **wash your hands of sb/sth** REJECT

washout *noun*
▶ DISASTER

wash up *phrasal verb*
▸ WASH
waste *noun*
▸ WASTE (industrial waste)
▸ DESERT (the wastes of Siberia)
waste *verb*
▸ WASTE
wasted *adj.*
▸ DRUNK
wasteful *adj.*
▸ EXTRAVAGANT
wasteland *noun*
▸ DESERT
watch *noun*
▸ WATCH
watch *verb*
▸ LOOK 1 (watch television)
▸ MONITOR (watch sb's bags)
watchdog *noun*
▸ INSPECTOR
watcher *noun*
▸ ANALYST
watch for *phrasal verb*
▸ EXPECT
waterfront *noun*
▸ COAST
waterproof *adj.*
▸ PROTECTIVE
waters *noun*
▸ LAKE (the grey waters of the River Clyde)
▸ SEA (international waters)
watershed *noun*
▸ TURNING POINT
waterway *noun*
▸ RIVER
wave *noun*
▸ WAVE 1 (Huge waves were breaking on the shore.)
▸ WAVE 2 (a wave of fear/desire)
▸ WAVE 3 (a wave of violence)
▸ MOVEMENT (a wave of sb's hand)
wave *verb*
▸ NOD (wave the waiter over)
▸ SHAKE 1 (wave goodbye)
way *noun*
▸ WAY 1 (in a friendly way)
▸ WAY 2 (the easiest way to do it)
▸ WAY 3 (the quickest way home)
▸ DOOR (the way in/out)
▸ HABIT (change your ways)
▸ **be/get in sb's/the way** BLOCK 3
▸ **give way** COLLAPSE *verb* 1
▸ **make your way** GO *verb* 1
▸ **be/go on your way** GO AWAY *phrasal verb*
▸ **clear the way**, **open the way** HELP *verb* 2
▸ **a/the/sb's way of life** LIFE 3
▸ **out of harm's way** SAFE *adj.* 1
way out *noun*
▸ SOLUTION
weak *adj.*
▸ WEAK (a weak heart)
▸ DIM 1 (weak winter sunlight)
▸ UNLIKELY 2 (a weak argument)
weaken *verb*
▸ WEAKEN (weaken sb's position)
▸ TIRE (Her legs began to weaken.)
▸ UNDERMINE (weaken sb's resolve)
▸ WORSEN (sb's authority weakens)
weakness *noun*
▸ WEAKNESS 1 (the weakness in this argument/approach/proposal)
▸ WEAKNESS 2 (We all have our weaknesses.)
▸ TASTE 1 (a weakness for chocolate)
wealth *noun*
▸ MONEY 3
wealthy *adj.*
▸ RICH
weapon *noun*
▸ WEAPON

weapons of mass destruction *noun*
▸ WEAPON
wear *noun*
▸ CLOTHES
wear *verb*
▸ WEAR
wear down *phrasal verb*
▸ UNDERMINE
wear on *phrasal verb*
▸ GO BY
wear out *phrasal verb*
▸ TIRE
weary *adj.*
▸ TIRED 1
weather *noun*
▸ WEATHER
weather *verb*
▸ SURVIVE
weave *verb*
▸ DESCRIBE
web *noun*
▸ SYSTEM
webcast *noun*
▸ PROGRAMME
wed *verb*
▸ MARRY
wedding *noun*
▸ MARRIAGE
wedge *noun*
▸ PIECE
wedge *verb*
▸ PACK
weed out *phrasal verb*
▸ ERADICATE
weekly *noun*
▸ MAGAZINE
weep *verb*
▸ CRY
weight *noun*
▸ WEIGHT (a weight of 5 lbs)
▸ POWER (an opinion carries weight with sb)
weight *verb*
▸ STRESS
weird *adj.*
▸ STRANGE 1
welcome *noun*
▸ GREETING (give sb a warm welcome)
▸ RESPONSE (The proposals were given a cautious welcome.)
welcome *verb*
▸ WELCOME (I'd welcome your suggestions.)
▸ GREET (welcome sb home)
▸ LET SB IN (welcome the new volunteers)
welcoming *adj.*
▸ FRIENDLY 1
welfare *noun*
▸ AID (welfare provision for people with disabilities)
▸ SAFETY (the child's welfare)
▸ **on welfare** UNEMPLOYED *adj.*
well *adj.*
▸ WELL (feel/look well)
▸ **get well** RECOVER *verb* 1
▸ **alive and well** SAFE 1
▸ **not (very) well** SICK 1
well *adv.*
▸ VERY (well over the speed limit)
▸ **do well** DO WELL
well behaved *adj.*
▸ GOOD 7
well-being *noun*
▸ HEALTH (a sense of well-being)
▸ SAFETY (emotional well-being)
well dressed *adj.*
▸ ELEGANT
well founded *adj.*
▸ GOOD 3
well known *adj.*
▸ FAMOUS

well off *adj.*
▸ RICH
well read *adj.*
▸ INFORMED
wet *verb*
▸ SOAK
wet *adj.*
▸ WET 1 (wet clothes/grass/hair)
▸ WET 2 (wet weather/a wet day)
wetland *noun*
▸ MARSH
whack *verb*
▸ HIT 2
wheel *noun*
▸ BUTTON 1
wheel *verb*
▸ TURN 1
wheeze *verb*
▸ BLOW 2
whereabouts *noun*
▸ PLACE 1
whiff *noun*
▸ SMELL
while *noun*
▸ TIME 2 (a little while)
▸ **once in a while** SOMETIMES *adv.*
while away *phrasal verb*
▸ SPEND 2
whim *noun*
▸ DESIRE
whimper *verb*
▸ CRY
whine *verb*
▸ BUZZ (an engine whines)
▸ COMPLAIN (He's whining again.)
▸ CRY (a dog whines)
whip *verb*
▸ STIR
whip up *phrasal verb*
▸ ENCOURAGE 3
whirl *verb*
▸ SPIN (He whirled his arms around.)
▸ TURN 1 (She whirled around to face him.)
whirr *verb*
▸ BUZZ
whisk *verb*
▸ STIR
whisper *verb*
▸ WHISPER
whistle *noun*
▸ WHISTLE (a whistle of surprise)
▸ **blow the whistle on sb/sth** TELL *verb* 2
whistle *verb*
▸ BUZZ (the wind/a train whistles)
▸ SING (whistle a tune)
white *adj.*
▸ PALE 1
whizz *verb*
▸ FLY 2
whole *noun*
▸ THING 2
whole *adj.*
▸ WHOLE
wholehearted *adj.*
▸ DEEP 1
wholesale *adj.*
▸ WIDE 1
wholesaler *noun*
▸ DEALER
wicked *adj.*
▸ EVIL (wicked deeds)
▸ GREAT 1 (Those shoes are wicked.)
wickedness *noun*
▸ EVIL
wide *adj.*
▸ WIDE 1 (a wide range of goods)
▸ WIDE 2 (a wide road/river/smile)
widen *verb*
▸ EXPAND 1
wide-ranging *adj.*
▸ WIDE 1

widespread *adj.*
▸ GENERAL 1
widowed *adj.*
▸ SINGLE
width *noun*
▸ LENGTH
wife *noun*
▸ WIFE
wiggle *verb*
▸ WRIGGLE
the wild *noun*
▸ DESERT (the wilds of Scotland)
▸ NATURE 2 (released into the wild)
wild *adj.*
▸ WILD 1 (wild behaviour)
▸ WILD 2 (wild with excitement)
wilderness *noun*
▸ DESERT
wildlife *noun*
▸ NATURE 2
wilful *adj.*
▸ DELIBERATE (wilful damage)
▸ STUBBORN (a wilful child)
will *noun*
▸ WISH
willing *adj.*
▸ HELPFUL
willowy *adj.*
▸ TALL
wily *adj.*
▸ CUNNING
wimp *noun*
▸ COWARD
win *noun*
▸ VICTORY
win *verb*
▸ WIN (Which team won?)
▸ GAIN 1 (win support/a contract)
▸ **win the day** WIN *verb*
wind *noun*
▸ WIND
wind *verb*
▸ CURVE (The river winds through the valley.)
▸ WRAP SB/STH AROUND/ROUND SB/STH (wind the wool into a ball)
window *noun*
▸ OPPORTUNITY
windswept *adj.*
▸ BARE
wind up *phrasal verb*
▸ ANNOY (He's just winding you up.)
▸ END (wind up a discussion)
wing *noun*
▸ DEPARTMENT
winner *noun*
▸ WINNER (the winner of the competition)
▸ SUCCESS (I think your idea is a winner.)
winning *adj.*
▸ SUCCESSFUL 1
win out *phrasal verb*
▸ WIN
win over *phrasal verb*
▸ PERSUADE
wintry *adj.*
▸ FREEZING
wipe *verb*
▸ WIPE (wipe your eyes/feet)
▸ DELETE (wipe a tape/disk)
▸ FORGET (wipe sth from your memory)
wipe out *phrasal verb*
▸ DESTROY
wire *noun*
▸ WIRE (telephone wires)
▸ ROPE (a wire rack)
wisdom *noun*
▸ WISDOM (a man of great wisdom)
▸ KNOWLEDGE (ancient wisdom)
wise *adj.*
▸ WISE (a wise old woman)
▸ BEST (a wise precaution)

wisecrack noun
▶ JOKE
wisecrack verb
▶ JOKE
wish noun
▶ WISH (carry out sb's wishes)
▶ DESIRE (a wish for secrecy)
wish verb
▶ HOPE (everything you could wish for)
▶ WANT (I wish I were taller.)
wishful thinking noun
▶ HOPE 1
wit noun
▶ HUMOUR (a woman of charm and wit)
▶ INTELLIGENCE (pit your wits against sb)
witch noun
▶ WITCH
witchcraft noun
▶ MAGIC
withdraw verb
▶ WITHDRAW 1 (withdraw troops)
▶ WITHDRAW 2 (withdraw from a competition)
▶ BREAK 4 (withdraw your allegations)
withdrawn adj.
▶ SOLITARY
withering adj.
▶ CONTEMPTUOUS
withstand verb
▶ WITHSTAND
witness noun
▶ WITNESS (a witness to the accident)
▶ **bear witness** CONFIRM verb 1
witness verb
▶ NOTICE
wits noun
▶ INTELLIGENCE
witty adj.
▶ FUNNY
wizard noun
▶ WITCH
WMD noun
▶ WEAPON
wobble verb
▶ SHAKE 2
wok noun
▶ PAN
wolf verb
▶ EAT
woman noun
▶ WOMAN
wonder noun
▶ MIRACLE
wonder verb
▶ CONSIDER
wonderful adj.
▶ WONDERFUL (wonderful weather)
▶ NICE 2 (a wonderful person)
woo verb
▶ GO OUT
wood noun
▶ FOREST
wooden adj.
▶ LACKLUSTRE
woodland noun
▶ FOREST
woolly (also **wooly**) adj.
▶ CONFUSED 2
word noun
▶ WORD (long words)
▶ NEWS (spread the word)
▶ PROMISE (I give you my word.)
wording noun
▶ LANGUAGE 2
work noun
▶ WORK 1 (hard work)
▶ WORK 2 (find work)
▶ WORK 3 (do pioneering work in microbiology)

▶ WORK 4 (a work of fiction)
▶ FACTORY (a steelworks)
▶ OFFICE 1 (go to work)
▶ TASK (police work)
▶ **at work** BUSY adj. 1
▶ **out of work** UNEMPLOYED adj.
▶ **be in work** WORK verb 2
work verb
▶ WORK 1 (work on an assignment)
▶ WORK 2 (work as a teacher)
▶ WORK 3 (The phone isn't working.)
▶ AFFECT (work in your favour)
▶ CAMPAIGN (work for peace)
▶ DRIVE 2 (work sb too hard)
▶ FARM (work the land)
▶ OPERATE (How do you work the DVD player?)
workable adj.
▶ POSSIBLE 1
worked up adj.
▶ HYSTERICAL
worker noun
▶ WORKER 1 (office workers)
▶ WORKER 2 (conflicts between employers and workers)
workforce noun
▶ STAFF
the working class noun
▶ GENERAL PUBLIC
working class adj.
▶ WORKING CLASS
workings noun
▶ SYSTEM
workman noun
▶ WORKER 2
workmate noun
▶ PARTNER 1
work of art noun
▶ WORK 4
work out phrasal verb
▶ CALCULATE (work out the answer)
▶ COME UP WITH STH (work out a plan)
▶ SOLVE 2 (work out how to do sth)
▶ TRAIN 2 (I work out to keep fit.)
workout noun
▶ SPORT
workplace noun
▶ OFFICE 1
workroom noun
▶ OFFICE 2
works noun
▶ FACTORY
workshop noun
▶ CLASS 2 (a drama workshop)
▶ FACTORY (a car repair workshop)
world noun
▶ WORLD (sail around the world)
▶ CULTURE (the ancient world)
▶ **the real world** FACT
worldwide adj.
▶ INTERNATIONAL
worn out adj.
▶ TIRED 1
worried adj.
▶ WORRIED
worry noun
▶ CONCERN
worry verb
▶ WORRY 1 (You worry too much.)
▶ WORRY 2 (This did not worry me.)
worrying adj.
▶ WORRYING
worse adj.
▶ **come off worse** LOSE verb
▶ **get worse** WORSEN verb
▶ **make sth worse** WEAKEN verb
worsen verb
▶ WORSEN
worship verb
▶ PRAY
worth noun
▶ PRICE (your personal net worth)
▶ VALUE 1 (a sense of worth)

worthless adj.
▶ DESPICABLE
worthwhile adj.
▶ VALUABLE 2
worthy adj.
▶ WORTHY
wound noun
▶ INJURY
wound verb
▶ HURT 1 (wound sb's feelings)
▶ INJURE (wounded in the attack)
wounded adj.
▶ INJURED
WPC noun
▶ POLICEMAN
wrap noun
▶ COVER
wrap around phrasal verb
▶ WRAP SB/STH AROUND/ROUND SB/STH
wrapper noun
▶ COVER
wrapping noun
▶ COVER
wrap round phrasal verb
▶ WRAP SB/STH AROUND/ROUND SB/STH
wrap up phrasal verb
▶ FINISH
wreck noun
▶ ACCIDENT (a train wreck)
▶ REMAINS 1 (the wreck of the Titanic)
wreck verb
▶ CRASH (wreck a car)
▶ RUIN (wreck sb's life)
▶ VANDALIZE (wreck fast cars)
wreckage noun
▶ REMAINS 1
wrench verb
▶ PULL 2
wrestle verb
▶ FIGHT 2
wretched adj.
▶ BAD
wriggle verb
▶ WRIGGLE
wriggle out of phrasal verb
▶ EVADE
wrinkle noun
▶ FOLD
write verb
▶ WRITE 1 (write in black ink)
▶ WRITE 2 (write a book)
write back phrasal verb
▶ ANSWER
write down phrasal verb
▶ WRITE 1
write off phrasal verb
▶ CRASH
writer noun
▶ WRITER
writhe verb
▶ WRIGGLE
writing noun
▶ LITERATURE (a brilliant piece of writing)
▶ WORK 4 (the writings of Sun Tzu)
wrong noun
▶ CRIME 2 (forgive past wrongs)
▶ EVIL (sb can do no wrong)
▶ **in the wrong** GUILTY adj.
wrong adj.
▶ WRONG 1 (the wrong answer)
▶ WRONG 2 (What's wrong?)
▶ WRONG 3 (the wrong thing to say)
▶ WRONG 4 (morally wrong)
▶ **go wrong** FAIL verb 2
▶ **the wrong idea** ILLUSION noun
▶ **get sb wrong, get sth wrong** MISUNDERSTAND verb
wrongdoing noun
▶ CRIME 1
wry adj.
▶ IRONIC

wuss noun
▶ COWARD

X x
xenophobia noun
▶ RACISM

Y y
yacht noun
▶ BOAT
yank verb
▶ PULL 3
yard noun
▶ COURTYARD (the prison yard)
▶ FACTORY (a shipyard)
▶ GARDEN 1 (the front yard)
yardstick noun
▶ CRITERION
yarn noun
▶ ROPE
year noun
▶ YEARS (the best movie I've seen in years)
▶ CLASS 3 (students in their third year)
yearn verb
▶ LONG
yearning noun
▶ APPETITE 2
years noun
▶ YEARS
yell verb
▶ SHOUT
yelp verb
▶ SCREAM
yield noun
▶ OUTPUT
yield verb
▶ GIVE WAY idiom (yield to temptation/sb's demands)
▶ PROVIDE (yield good returns)
young noun
▶ OFFSPRING
young adj.
▶ YOUNG
youngster noun
▶ CHILD
yourself pron.
▶ **by yourself** ALONE adj., adv.
▶ **beside yourself** HYSTERICAL adj.
youth noun
▶ CHILDHOOD (throughout his youth)
▶ GIRL (a gang of youths)
youthful adj.
▶ CHILDISH
yummy adj.
▶ DELICIOUS

Z z
zap verb
▶ DESTROY
zealous adj.
▶ EAGER
zest noun
▶ ENERGY 2
zigzag noun
▶ CORNER
zigzag verb
▶ CURVE
zip noun
▶ BUTTON 2
zip verb
▶ TIE
zipper noun
▶ BUTTON 2
zone noun
▶ AREA 1 (a war zone)
▶ COUNTY (postal charges to countries in zone 2)
zoom verb
▶ FLY 2

This table lists all the verbs with irregular forms that are included in this thesaurus.

Infinitive	Past tense	Past participle	Infinitive	Past tense	Past participle
arise	arose	arisen	foresee	foresaw	foreseen
be	was/were	been	forget	forgot	forgotten
bear	bore	borne	forgive	forgave	forgiven
beat	beat	beaten	forgo	forwent	forgone
become	became	become	freeze	froze	frozen
begin	began	begun	get	got	got; (AmE, spoken) gotten
bend	bent	bent			
bet	bet	bet	give	gave	given
bid	bid	bid	go	went	gone, been
bind	bound	bound	grow	grew	grown
bite	bit	bitten	hang	hung	hung
blow	blew	blown	have	had	had
break	broke	broken	hear	heard	heard
breed	bred	bred	hide	hid	hidden
bring	brought	brought	hit	hit	hit
broadcast	broadcast	broadcast	hold	held	held
build	built	built	hurt	hurt	hurt
burn	burnt, burned	burnt, burned	keep	kept	kept
burst	burst	burst	kneel	knelt; (AmE also kneeled)	knelt; (AmE also kneeled)
buy	bought	bought			
cast	cast	cast	know	knew	known
catch	caught	caught	lay	laid	laid
choose	chose	chosen	lead	led	led
cling	clung	clung	lean	leaned; (BrE also leant)	leaned; (BrE also leant)
come	came	come			
cost	cost	cost	leap	leapt, leaped	leapt, leaped
creep	crept	crept	learn	learnt, learned	learnt, learned
cut	cut	cut	leave	left	left
deal	dealt	dealt	lend	lent	lent
do	did	done	let	let	let
draw	drew	drawn	lie	lay	lain
dream	dreamt, dreamed	dreamt, dreamed	light	lit	lit
drink	drank	drunk	lose	lost	lost
drive	drove	driven	make	made	made
eat	ate	eaten	mean	meant	meant
feed	fed	fed	meet	met	met
feel	felt	felt	mislay	mislaid	mislaid
fall	fell	fallen	mislead /ˌmɪsˈliːd/	misled /ˌmɪsˈled/	misled /ˌmɪsˈled/
fight	fought	fought			
find	found	found	misread /ˌmɪsˈriːd/	misread /ˌmɪsˈred/	misread /ˌmɪsˈred/
fit	fitted; (AmE usually fit)	fitted; (AmE usually fit)	mistake	mistook	mistaken
			misunderstand	misunderstood	misunderstood
flee	fled	fled	mow	mowed	mown, mowed
fling	flung	flung	offset	offset	offset
fly	flew	flown	overcome	overcame	overcome
forbid	forbade	forbidden	overhear	overheard	overheard
forecast	forecast, forecasted	forecast, forecasted	override	overrode	overridden

Infinitive	Past tense	Past participle	Infinitive	Past tense	Past participle
oversee	oversaw	overseen	spin	spun	spun
overtake	overtook	overtaken	split	split	split
overthrow	overthrew	overthrown	spoil	spoiled;	spoiled;
pay	paid	paid		(BrE also spoilt)	(BrE also spoilt)
plead	pleaded;	pleaded;	spread	spread	spread
	(AmE also pled)	(AmE also pled)	spring	sprang; (AmE	sprung
prove	proved	proved; (also proven		also sprung)	
		especially in AmE)	stand	stood	stood
put	put	put	steal	stole	stolen
quit	quit; (BrE also	quit; (BrE also	stick	stuck	stuck
	quitted)	quitted)	sting	stung	stung
read /ri:d/	read /red/	read /red/	stink	stank, stunk	stunk
rebuild	rebuilt	rebuilt	strew	strewed	strewed, strewn
redo	redid	redone	stride	strode	—
remake	remade	remade	strike	struck	struck; (AmE also
rewrite	rewrote	rewritten			stricken)
rid	rid	rid	string	strung	strung
ride	rode	ridden	strive	strove	striven
ring	rang	rung	swear	swore	sworn
rise	rose	risen	sweep	swept	swept
run	ran	run	swell	swelled	swollen, swelled
say	said	said	swing	swung	swung
see	saw	seen	take	took	taken
seek	sought	sought	teach	taught	taught
sell	sold	sold	tear	tore	torn
send	sent	sent	tell	told	told
set	set	set	think	thought	thought
shake	shook	shaken	throw	threw	thrown
shear	sheared	shorn, sheared	thrust	thrust	thrust
shed	shed	shed	tread	trod	trodden
shine	shone	shone	undergo	underwent	undergone
shoot	shot	shot	understand	understood	understood
show	showed	shown	undertake	undertook	undertaken
shrink	shrank, shrunk	shrunk	underwrite	underwrote	underwritten
shut	shut	shut	undo	undid	undone
sing	sang	sung	unwind	unwound	unwound
sink	sank	sunk	uphold	upheld	upheld
sit	sat	sat	upset	upset	upset
slay	slew	slain	wake	woke	woken
sleep	slept	slept	wear	wore	worn
slide	slid	slid	weave	wove	woven
slink	slunk	slunk	wed	wedded, wed	wedded, wed
slit	slit	slit	weep	wept	wept
smell	smelled;	smelled;	wet	wet, wetted	wet, wetted
	(BrE also smelt)	(BrE also smelt)	win	won	won
speak	spoke	spoken	wind /wamd/	wound /waʊnd/	wound /waʊnd/
speed	speeded, sped	speeded, sped	withdraw	withdrew	withdrawn
spell	spelt, spelled	spelt, spelled	withstand	withstood	withstood
spend	spent	spent	write	wrote	written
spill	spilled;	spilled;			
	(BrE also spilt)	(BrE also spilt)			

Abbreviations and symbols

adj.	adjective	**pl.**	plural
adv.	adverb	*prep.*	preposition
AmE	American English	**sb**	somebody
BrE	British English	**sing.**	singular
C	countable noun	**sth**	something
det.	determiner	**T**	transitive verb
etc.	et cetera (= and so on)	™	trademark
I	intransitive verb	**U**	uncountable noun
❶	information note	▶	introduces a derivative
OPP	opposite		

Usage labels

formal expressions are usually only used in serious or official language and would not be appropriate in normal everyday conversation, for example *impart, venerate*.

rather formal expressions are appropriate for serious or official contexts but may also be used in more ordinary situations, for example *modify, prosperous*.

rather informal expressions tend to be used in more relaxed and unofficial situations, for example *scared, show off*.

informal expressions are used between friends or in a relaxed or unofficial situation. They are not appropriate for formal situations, for example *comfy, rip sb off*.

slang is very informal language, for example *wasted (adj.)*

spoken expressions are used mainly in speech (usually informal conversation, but some spoken expressions are appropriate for formal situations), for example *I'm afraid, just right*.

written expressions are used mainly in writing, especially formal or imaginative writing, for example *hasten, shun*.

literary language is used mainly in literature and imaginative writing, for example *hue, valour*.

old-fashioned expressions are passing out of current use, for example *court (verb), pal*.

technical language is used by people who specialize in a particular subject area, for example *monograph, theorem*.

approving expressions show that you feel approval or admiration, for example *dynamic, snug*.

disapproving expressions show that you feel disapproval or contempt, for example *arrogance, squander*.

humorous expressions are intended to be funny, for example *jest, lowly*.

ironic language uses words to mean the opposite or something very different from the meaning they seem to have, for example *Oh great! They've left without us*.

figurative language is language that is used in a non-literal or metaphorical way, for example *He hammered the door with his fists*.

offensive expressions are used by some people to address or refer to people in a way that is insulting, especially in connection with their race, religion, sex or disabilities, for example *gypsy, jerk*. They should be avoided.

taboo words are likely to be thought by many people to be obscene or shocking, for example *bloody, shit*. You should generally avoid using them.

The following labels also show words from particular subject areas:

architecture	geometry	phonetics
biology	grammar	physics
business	journalism	politics
chemistry	law	psychology
computing	medical	religion
economics	music	sport
finance		

Grammar labels

Nouns

[C] Countable noun. A countable noun has a singular form and a plural form. When it is singular, it must always have a determiner (a word such as *a, the, both, each*) in front of it. In the plural it can be used with or without a determiner:

*I'm having **a** driving **lesson** this afternoon.*
*I've had **several lessons** already.*
***Lessons** cost £25 an hour.*

[U] Uncountable noun. An uncountable noun has only one form, not a separate singular and plural. It can be used with or without a determiner. If an uncountable noun is the subject of a verb, the verb is singular:

*Can we make **space** for an extra chair?*
*There isn't **much space** in this room.*
*Extra **money has been found** for this project.*

Some nouns can be countable or uncountable. These are labelled [C, U] or [U, C].

[pl.] Plural noun. Some nouns are always plural in form and take a plural verb:

*I'm going to buy **some** new **jeans**.*
***Police are searching** for a man who escaped from prison today.*

[sing.] Singular noun. Some nouns are always singular and have no plural.

*It seems **a pity** to waste this food.*

[sing. + sing./pl. v] [C + sing./pl. v] [U + sing./pl. v]

In British English some nouns for groups and organizations (such as *a team* or *the government*) can be used with a plural verb instead of a singular one, even when the noun is singular or uncountable:

*The **committee has/have** decided to dismiss him.*
***Personnel is/are** currently reviewing pay scales.*

In American English the singular form of these must take a singular verb:

*The government **says it is** committed to tax reform.*

The examples in this thesaurus generally show these nouns with a singular verb, since this is acceptable in both British and American English.

Verbs

[I] Intransitive verb. An intransitive verb takes no object:

*A large dog **appeared**.*

[T] Transitive verb. A transitive verb takes an object, which may be a noun phrase or a clause beginning with *that, which, what, whose, why, where, when, who, whom, how, if, whether,* or containing another verb in the infinitive or present participle (*-ing* form):

*Jill's behaviour **annoyed me**.*
*She **answered that** she would prefer to walk.*
*I **wonder what** the new job will be like.*
*He doesn't **care how** he looks.*
*She never **learned to** read.*
*He never **stops talking**!*

Some verbs can be transitive or intransitive. These are labelled [T, I] or [I, T].

linking verb

A linking verb is followed by an adjective or noun complement, which tells you more about the subject of the verb:

*His voice **sounds hoarse**.*
*Elena **became a doctor**.*

Adjectives

[only before noun] [usually before noun]

These adjectives are always or usually used before a noun and not after a linking verb:

*the **chief cause** of poverty*
~~This cause is chief.~~

[not before noun] [not usually before noun]

These adjectives are always or usually used after a linking verb and not before a noun:

***Rumours are rife** that the company is to be sold.*
~~rife rumours~~

PRONUNCIATION AND PHONETIC SYMBOLS

Pronunciation is given in the book for more difficult words, with separate British and American pronunciations where they are different. You can hear the British and American pronunciations of all single words on the CD-ROM.

Vowels

iː	see	/siː/	
i	happy	/ˈhæpi/	
ɪ	sit	/sɪt/	
e	ten	/ten/	
æ	cat	/kæt/	
ɑː	father	/ˈfɑːðə(r)/	
ɒ	got	/ɡɒt/	(British English)
ɔː	saw	/sɔː/	
ʊ	put	/pʊt/	
u	actual	/ˈæktʃuəl/	
uː	too	/tuː/	
ʌ	cup	/kʌp/	

ɜː	fur	/fɜː(r)/	
ə	about	/əˈbaʊt/	
eɪ	say	/seɪ/	
əʊ	go	/ɡəʊ/	(British English)
oʊ	go	/ɡoʊ/	(American English)
aɪ	my	/maɪ/	
ɔɪ	boy	/bɔɪ/	
aʊ	now	/naʊ/	
ɪə	near	/nɪə(r)/	(British English)
eə	hair	/heə(r)/	(British English)
ʊə	pure	/pjʊə(r)/	(British English)

Consonants

p	pen	/pen/
b	bad	/bæd/
t	tea	/tiː/
d	did	/dɪd/
k	cat	/kæt/
ɡ	get	/ɡet/
tʃ	chain	/tʃeɪn/
dʒ	jam	/dʒæm/
f	fall	/fɔːl/
v	van	/væn/
θ	thin	/θɪn/
ð	this	/ðɪs/

s	see	/siː/
z	zoo	/zuː/
ʃ	shoe	/ʃuː/
ʒ	vision	/ˈvɪʒn/
h	hat	/hæt/
m	man	/mæn/
n	now	/naʊ/
ŋ	sing	/sɪŋ/
l	leg	/leɡ/
r	red	/red/
j	yes	/jes/
w	wet	/wet/

The symbol (r) indicates that British pronunciation will have /r/ only if a vowel sound follows immediately, as in **far away**; otherwise the /r/ is omitted. In American English, all the /r/ sounds are pronounced.

The mark /~/ over a vowel shows that the vowel has a nasal quality. This sound may be kept in certain words that come from French, such as **avant-garde** /ˌævã ˈɡɑːd/.

/x/ represents a fricative sound as in /lɒx/ for Scottish **loch**.

Stress

The mark /ˈ/ shows the main stress in a word, for example **able** /ˈeɪbl/, **ability** /əˈbɪləti/. A stressed syllable is louder and longer than other syllables, and made noticeable by the pitch of the voice.

The mark /ˌ/ shows secondary stress, which can occur in longer words before the main stress, as in **probability** /ˌprɑbəˈbɪləti/, **coordination** /kəʊˌɔːdɪˈneɪʃn/. The secondary stress is weaker than the main stress.

Main stress and secondary stress are also given in compounds (ˈfrying pan), phrasal verbs (ˌgo aˈway) and idioms (lose your ˈtemper).